"Within the ultramodern secular cultural environment, with its emphasis on relativism, its lack of idealism, its reluctance to commitment, and its disrespect toward authority and the sacred, *Thy Word Is Still Truth* represents a major theological landmark. It reminds the church of the rich and significant heritage that we can draw on, going back not only to the Reformation but also to the early church fathers—a heritage that is deeply rooted in the apostolic faith. This book emphasizes the amazing theological unity, diversity, and coherence of the biblical doctrine of the Word of God. It underscores the relevance of Reformed faith as 'a living tradition engaging with the pressing questions of today.' Edited within a specific historical context, this anthology on the authority and interpretation of Scripture speaks eloquently and boldly to the whole of the contemporary church of Jesus Christ."

> —**Pierre Berthoud**, Professor Emeritus, Faculté Jean Calvin, Aix-en-Provence, France; President, Fellowship of European Evangelical Theologians

"Against those who think a 'high' view of Scripture was the creation of nineteenth-century Princetonians, and against those who think such a view of Scripture amounts to a defensive posture devoid of profound theological reflection, this excellent volume is a much-needed resource. It stands as a bulwark against every form of the question, 'Did God really say?' The excerpts and essays drawn from Martin Luther to the present represent an immense reservoir of diverse reflections—from Calvin's *Institutes* to Monod's *Farewell*, from Owen, Turretin, Gaussen, and Edwards to Spurgeon, Hengstenberg, and Machen, from Reformed confessions to the advent of contemporary biblical theology. Although this collection includes statements on recent controversies at Westminster Theological Seminary, its strength is not its coverage of the last half-century but its ample demonstration that today's Reformed Christians find themselves, on this subject, within a heritage rich in theological reflection and powerful synthesis. To lose sight of this heritage or to stand aloof from it is to impoverish our souls and to distance ourselves from the God who 'looks' to those who are contrite and humble in spirit and who tremble at his Word."

> —**D. A. Carson**, Research Professor of New Testament, Trinity Evangelical Divinity School, Deerfield, Illinois

"Lillback and Gaffin have assembled a trove of resources that will enable serious students of Scripture to mine the wealth of the church's testimony on one of the cardinal doctrines of the Christian faith—the doctrine of Scripture, which proclaims the abiding truthfulness and inerrancy of the Word of God. *Thy Word Is Still Truth* offers a scholarly exploration from a great cloud of witnesses that is historical, exegetical, and theological, yet eminently practical and hence immensely beneficial. This volume will serve the church for generations to come."

> —**J. V. Fesko**, Academic Dean and Professor of Systematic and Historical Theology, Westminster Seminary California

"Since its founding in 1929, Westminster Theological Seminary in Philadelphia has specialized in the doctrine of Scripture. Nearly everyone who has taught there over the years has made some contribution to the subject. The Westminster faculty published three collections of essays on Scripture: *The Infallible Word* (1946), *Scripture and Confession* (1973), and *Inerrancy and Hermeneutic* (1988). The present volume, however, is a contribution of a higher order. It not only republishes some of the best articles from the previous collections, but contains important writings on biblical authority from the Reformation and post-Reformation periods (including the churches' creedal statements) down to the present day. There are articles from the faculty of Old Princeton, from which Westminster takes its bearings, articles on controversial matters, and articles describing the rationale for Westminster's distinctive emphasis on biblical theology. And the volume is honest in facing up to the recent controversy over Scripture at Westminster itself and the seminary's forthright response reaffirming biblical inerrancy. Throughout the years, I have been moved again and again by Westminster's willingness to stand against the world and for the Word of God. The issue before the world today, as in the garden of Eden, is 'Has God said?' I know of no body of literature that can be of more help to people wrestling with this vital question."

— **John M. Frame**, J. D. Trimble Chair of Systematic Theology and Philosophy, Reformed Theological Seminary, Orlando

"Every generation of Christians must anew believe, confess, understand, and live out the Bible's teaching that it is the inerrant Word of God. This timely book brings together many invaluable historic and contemporary writings that will encourage us to defend and cherish the Scriptures. It will certainly be a great blessing to those who study it."

— **W. Robert Godfrey**, President and Professor of Church History, Westminster Seminary California

"In every generation it is required of the church (and its institutions) to defend and maintain its commitment to the Scriptures as God's Word written. Given the current climate in which pastors and scholars choose to ignore confessional boundaries and recast the faith to suit contemporary predilections, it is vital to establish that the trustworthiness of Scripture is an essential component of historic Christian orthodoxy and the foundational assumption of the Reformed tradition. No branch of the church has been as clearheaded and warmhearted in its defense and articulation of the riches and integrity of the Bible as the Reformed branch. And no seminary has been quite as clear or committed to the primacy of that Word in all its academic branches as Westminster Theological Seminary, following in the tradition of Old Princeton.

"This book invites us to review the rich legacy of the church, Westminster's place in that tradition, and the necessity of reasserting this conviction for the health of the church and the cure of souls. I cannot stress enough my gratitude to God that Westminster continues to assert this truth in the clearest and most unambiguous manner."

— **Liam Goligher**, Senior Minister, Tenth Presbyterian Church, Philadelphia

"Where do you go to learn what the Reformers and post-Reformation orthodoxy have to say about the Scriptures? Where do you procure a selection of relevant passages that span a few centuries and yet agree about the truth and the nature of scriptural revelation? Where can you find an anthology that shows the roots of Westminster Theological Seminary's core relationship to scriptural revelation, as well as the contours of a beautiful struggle to remain faithful to that tradition? Now here is a bird's-eye perspective in one volume. Kudos to Richard B. Gaffin and Peter A. Lillback for giving us something so good! This remarkable selection of key authors and passages shares the theme that for many of us is both a passion and an urgent necessity: the Word is still true and it is still truth. Please do not overlook this work."
  —**Davi Charles Gomes**, Chancellor, Mackenzie Presbyterian University, São Paulo, Brazil

"This is a unique anthology. It gathers material from the Reformation to the present day on the doctrine of Scripture, and does so in keeping with the historical position of Westminster Theological Seminary. The selection is far-reaching, and the addition of a section on biblical theology is an excellent decision. A superb resource has now been provided by this volume."
  —**Allan M. Harman**, Research Professor, Presbyterian Theological College, Melbourne, Australia

"The affirmation of the epistemological heart of the Christian faith in the Reformation watchcry of *sola Scriptura* necessarily entailed what the generations since the apostles had believed in, namely, the infallible nature of the Bible. Since the battles of the Reformation, this truth about God's Word has come under attack again and again—whether it be from Quaker enthusiasm, deistic rationalism, or liberal Protestantism—and only when this truth has been ardently defended have the fires of Christian piety continued to burn brightly. This tremendous collection of sources about the infallibility and inerrancy of the Scriptures is both a powerful reminder of these facts and a stirring impetus to be 'a people of the Book.' Wrought in recent conflict over this very issue, this volume is a welcome addition to the key reference works of all those who genuinely desire to be Christ-centered and gospel-focused."
  —**Michael A. G. Haykin**, Professor of Church History and Biblical Spirituality and Director of the Andrew Fuller Center for Baptist Studies at The Southern Baptist Theological Seminary

"This new anthology of the writings of Reformed thinkers on the infallibility and the inerrancy of Scripture, from the Reformation era to today, is timely and beneficial. Building on the title of E. J. Young's classic book *Thy Word Is Truth*, this collection is committed to the highest view of Scripture. And it affirms Scripture's truthfulness and trustworthiness, which are of crucial importance for the life of the church, her mission to the world, and the state of believers' souls. Reading this collection of contemporary texts, which reflects Westminster Theological Seminary's strong commitment to Scripture, one knows without a doubt that by the providence of God, Westminster has been faithful to and consistent with the historic Reformed theological and confessional tradition on the doctrine of Scripture. Through Peter Lillback and Richard Gaffin's masterful work, readers are equipped not only to profit from God's Word but also to defend and affirm its perfection."

—**Benyamin F. Intan**, President, International Reformed Evangelical Seminary, Jakarta, Indonesia

"Every one of the chapters in this book sounds a solid teaching note on how evangelical theology came to the positions it currently holds. Many among our younger scholars and church members will be richly rewarded as they trace the history of how the Spirit of God led his church in these essays and through these scholars, who fully trusted what God had said in his Word. It is a joy to commend this volume to a wide reading audience."

—**Walter C. Kaiser Jr.**, President Emeritus, Gordon-Conwell Theological Seminary, South Hamilton, Massachusetts

"The authority and inerrancy of the Bible should be objectively defended with as many historically authoritative sources as possible in order to counter evil powers today that attempt to destroy our faith in God and his Word. This book is a collection of the most authoritative literature on the Scriptures from the Reformation period up to the present day. It will prove to be an essential resource for those who want to apply and defend the Bible."

—**In Whan Kim**, Former President and Professor of Old Testament Studies, Emeritus, Chongshin University and Seminary, Seoul, South Korea

"*Thy Word Is Still Truth* is the definitive A-to-Z resource—historically rooted and biblically informed—on the doctrine of Scripture. It pulls together a wide array of writings into one convenient, comprehensive volume, and the result is a book that seems destined to become one of the best resources available for today's church, which finds herself in the midst of controversy on the view of Scripture."

—**Sam Ko**, Director of Global Ministries, SaRang Community Church, Seoul, South Korea; Chairman of the Board of Trustees, Wales Evangelical School of Theology, Bridgend, UK

"This magisterial anthology of important texts edited by Peter A. Lillback and Richard B. Gaffin Jr., respectively President and Professor of Biblical and Systematic Theology at Westminster Theological Seminary, stands in the grand tradition of biblical inerrancy espoused by Reformed theology for centuries and particularly for the past 85 years by Westminster. The title (without the *Still*) recalls the profoundly significant impact of the work by E. J. Young, one that shaped the thinking of many a budding theologian a half century ago, including this writer. Modernity, and especially Post-modernity, has generated the need for a reassessment and reaffirmation of the doctrine of biblical inerrancy because of its foundational underpinning to the whole corpus of biblical authority, reliability, and theology. Lillback and Gaffin have risen to the call and have led the way here to a renaissance of the views of the founders of the Seminary and their adherence to the sacred Scriptures that undergirded their potent and cherished Reformed faith."

—**Eugene H. Merrill**, Distinguished Professor of Old Testament Studies, Dallas Theological Seminary

"The first great lie of the deceiver was to question the Word of God (Gen. 3:1: 'Indeed, has God said?'). Since then, and mankind's tragic fall resulting from disobedience to the Word of the Lord, the attack on the inerrant and the infallible, self-attesting Word of the living God has continued unabated, and has, in fact, intensified. Seminaries—literally, the *seedbed* for pastors—have always been 'high-value' strategic fronts on which the enemy of God has launched his familiar, deadly assault. Each generation not only endures those insidious attacks, but also produces lost would-be soldiers of the cross, seducing and corrupting the minds of men to deny the mind of God. Such examples of treason have sad and regrettable consequences for those who surrender to the siren song of hell, 'Did God say?' Pastors have left seminaries and Bible colleges where this deadly chemical cloud of doubt in the Bible has drifted into their being, carried the hideous virus infecting their own souls into previously godly pulpits, and communicated its deadly effects to their poor parishioners. From that spreading disease of doubt in God's Word, once-faithful denominations rot from within, and once-flourishing cultures are infected and die.

"What is needed now, in Old Christendom, New Christendom, and the Next Christendom, and in every generation, is a strong and noble stand for the Word of God in the seminary. For this reason, I am thankful for *Thy Word Is Still Truth*, and I praise God for the incredible labors and dedicated scholarship of Westminster Theological Seminary, her Bible-loving board, her Scripture-saturated faculty and staff, her Word-loving students and supporters, and the trusted editors of this great anthology, Drs. Richard Gaffin and Peter Lillback. They have done what Westminster Theological Seminary has always done so well: leading the church (and stirring her sister seminaries) back to the confessional standards, to the timeless river of orthodoxy that flows from the testimonies of the Reformers' 'rediscovery of the written Word of God,' on through the tributaries of the great Reformed confessions that followed, eventually nourishing the faithful fields of stalwart theological timber—from the Old Princetonians to Edward J. Young and younger living branches such as John Frame, and, of course, Drs. Gaffin and Lillback themselves. This glorious river of confessional orthodoxy not only demolishes the idols of doubt concerning the very Word of God as it rushes down through the ages, but also ushers in soul-refreshment and living water for the people of God. The cleansing that this book brings comes, mercifully, at a time when we need it most.

"I thank almighty God for this magnificent volume. There are few books of which it can be said, 'This is a comprehensive presentation of the subject.' Yet I can say without reservation or hyperbole that this new anthology by P&R Publishing, edited by my esteemed colleagues at Westminster Seminary, is exactly that: a comprehensive presentation of the witness of the Reformed churches, with her finest pastor-scholars and her most radically biblical councils testifying in succeeding ages to the veracity and the life-and-death importance underscored in the title: *Thy Word Is Still Truth*."

—**Michael A. Milton**, Chancellor and Chief Executive Officer and James M. Baird Jr. Chair of Pastoral Theology, Reformed Theological Seminary, Orlando

"We have needed this book for a long time. In *Thy Word Is Still Truth*, Peter Lillback and Richard Gaffin have drawn together the comprehensive witness of the church on behalf of the total truthfulness and inerrancy of Scripture. No serious reader can doubt the case for inerrancy made so consistently and clearly in these pages, and no serious defender of Scripture can be without this vital volume that amounts to the most massive arsenal of documentation for the inerrancy of Scripture ever assembled in a single book."

—**R. Albert Mohler Jr.**, President, The Southern Baptist Theological Seminary, Louisville, Kentucky

"The embattled title casts this book as an apologia for Westminster Seminary's stand in a recent internal debate. Yes, it is all of that, but it is a great deal more. It is a massive array of extracts from major writers over five centuries, demonstrating both the breadth, strength, clarity, humility, and rootedness of international Reformed bibliology according to its historic confessional self-understanding, and also the insightful energy with which Westminster's own scholars have labored to vindicate the Reformed position as catholic Christian truth. The book excels as a resource for study and a witness to Westminster's integrity."

—**J. I. Packer**, Board of Governors' Professor of Theology, Regent College, Vancouver, British Columbia

"*Thy Word Is Still Truth* is an invaluable resource that upholds the inerrancy, inspiration, and final authority of Holy Scripture. Not only does it gather together the overwhelming testimony of the Reformed tradition for the Bible's inerrancy, it also brilliantly addresses matters of special concern today, such as canon formation and redemptive-historical interpretation. With this volume, Westminster Theological Seminary reassumes its position as the leading proponent of the historic Reformed doctrine of Scripture."

—**Richard D. Phillips**, Senior Minister, Second Presbyterian Church, Greenville, South Carolina

"Westminster Theological Seminary was established in no small part to faithfully uphold a robust doctrine of biblical inerrancy informed by the scriptural doctrine of inspiration. This doctrine, initially communicated to the public by the work of Dr. E. J. Young in *Thy*

Word Is Truth, has now been bolstered by a marvelous and needed volume, *Thy Word Is Still Truth*. Through the capable leadership and editorial work of Dr. Peter Lillback and Dr. Richard Gaffin, we now have a readable treasury of biblical expositions and sermons, as well as a thoughtful collection of articles and other works, that have effectively defended the reliability of God's Word as truth from the Reformation to the present. This volume is an indispensable resource both for research and for life-changing devotional reading in light of the renewed assault on the trustworthiness of God's Word in our day."
—**Harry L. Reeder III**, Senior Pastor/Teacher, Briarwood Presbyterian Church, Birmingham, Alabama

"This massive compendium is what it claims to be: a collection of essential writings on the doctrine of Scripture from the time of the Protestant Reformation right up to the present day. The evangelical theology of Scripture that emerged with particular clarity during the Reformation in Europe has enjoyed widespread international influence ever since. The creeds, confessions, sermons, essays, treatises, and personal testimonies in this anthology demonstrate astonishing consistency and remarkable progress across half a millennium of church history. Here, for the first time, a five-hundred-year library of thoughtful, faithful reflection on the nature of biblical truth has been gathered into a single indispensable volume."
—**Philip G. Ryken**, President, Wheaton College, Wheaton, Illinois

"The Reformation was spurred by Luther's return to the Bible as the highest authority in the church, the doctrine of the infallibility of Scripture has been taught in all evangelical confessions and denominations, and its development has been influenced by people from many confessions. Even so, it was the Reformed doctrine of Scripture, spreading from Switzerland, that became central to evangelicalism through the centuries, both in its terminology and in its manner of defense. For example, Calvin's application of the inner witness of the Holy Spirit to the doctrine of Scripture, declaring that the final evidence for Scripture as the Word of God comes from its Author, the Holy Spirit, directly to the believer's heart, has been central in the evangelical movement and has counteracted any impersonal approach to hermeneutics. No wonder, then, that Reformed seminaries have been at the forefront of formulating, developing, and defending the doctrine of Scripture. I am glad that Westminster Theological Seminary takes the lead again by gathering five hundred years of good tradition, proving how the old truth has been applied to ever-new ages again and again."
—**Thomas Schirrmacher**, Chairman, Theological Commission of World Evangelical Alliance; President, Martin Bucer Theological Seminary, Bonn, Zurich, Innsbruck, Prague, Istanbul, São Paulo

"This is a magnificent and unique sourcebook containing original texts and their fine translations. These testimonies on the divine character of Scripture demonstrate that despite the variety of Protestant Reformers, synods, and theologians, there was, is, and can be unity because of the common basis in the Word of God."

—**Herman Selderhuis**, Professor of Church History, Theological University Apeldoorn, The Netherlands; Director, Refo500

"When the Reformation reclaimed the historic apostolic tradition concerning Scripture as the inerrant and infallible Word of God, it became incumbent upon God's faithful people to build bridges of biblical continuity from generation to generation. This anthology of the Reformation heritage points to this faithfulness for our global Christianity. In our contemporary cosmic hostility to the gospel, *Thy Word Is Still Truth* is a timely reminder of the history of Christian faith as it stands on the abiding power of Scripture as the infallible Word of God that demands our total allegiance."

—**Philip Tachin**, Senior Lecturer in Systematic Theology, Theological College of Northern Nigeria, Jos, Nigeria

"In light of recent criticisms of the doctrine of biblical inerrancy, a reader containing some of the most important writings on the issue is very welcome. From Luther to familiar names of our own time (Murray, Gaffin, Ferguson), the editors have carefully assembled (with brief introductory comments) all the essential material. Reading this volume is a bit like discovering solid granite beneath our home. Reading through this volume, our confidence in Scripture's unassailable trustworthiness as the Word of God, infallible and inerrant, is greatly enhanced."

—**Derek W. H. Thomas**, Professor of Systematic and Historical Theology, Reformed Theological Seminary, Atlanta; Minister of Preaching and Teaching, First Presbyterian Church, Columbia, South Carolina

"The consistent spirit of Reformed tradition in holding the absolute and profound belief in Scripture as the true truth of the true revelation of the true God must be deeply and universally appreciated by all men in all times. To believe that God has unmistakably revealed his perfect will to men of all ages is an absolute necessity for those who truly understand and are totally obedient to the only true God. This kind of belief is sorely needed in our time of pluralism and uncertainty that is leading our society to nowhere. We thank God for the appearance of this monumental work in this crucial time."

—**Stephen Tong**, Evangelist at Large; Founder, International Reformed Evangelical Seminary, Jakarta, Indonesia

"The contemporary Christian is constantly told, 'Compromise or you'll have no place in today's world.' This compendium of historic Reformed theological and confessional traditions eloquently testifies that we don't have to yield to such urgings. It is heartwarming to be able to hold in one volume the Reformed faith's critical engagement with pressing questions through the ages. I sincerely hope that with the publication of this volume, the rediscovery of biblical authority in the Reformed traditions, which it encapsulates, will be made accessible to the world, thereby expanding the church's understanding of biblical authority. This will be one way of ensuring that the hold that the global south is taking of Christ will not be an ephemeral one. This volume could not have come at a more auspicious time; I recommend it wholeheartedly."

> —**Cephas T. A. Tushima**, Dean, Evangelical Churches of West Africa Theological Seminary, Jos, Nigeria; Secretary, Continuing Theological Engagement of the Lausanne Movement, Nigeria

"The title *Thy Word Is Still Truth* speaks for itself in a profound way. It expresses both the scriptural foundation and the Reformed position of Westminster Theological Seminary. The authority of the Scripture, the Holy Bible, is frequently questioned today by the liberal seminaries and technological and scientific institutions across the world. This book echoes the apologetic stand not only of the seminary but also of Christendom as a whole. 'Thy word is *still* truth' should be the position of every committed Christian at all times. The work is a massive collection of extracts from Christian scholars and godly men over five centuries who held the principle of *sola Scriptura*, the mandate of the Christian life. The undiluted position to vindicate the Reformed position of bibliology is repeatedly affirmed in this book, which was the attraction and the strong imprint placed on me by Westminster Seminary through my professors Richard B. Gaffin and Peter Lillback. The integrity of this seminary among other seminaries is its commitment to the Word of God. *Thy Word Is Still Truth* challenges the nonfoundational postmodernism of today. Every committed Christian and student of the Scripture must have this book, along with the Word of God."

> —**T. P. Varghese**, Principal, Bethel Bible College, Punalur, Kerala, India

"Books that are born in the cradle of controversy are usually books worth having on your shelf. *Thy Word Is Still Truth* proves this point beyond a shadow of a doubt. The genesis of this anthology can be traced back to Westminster Seminary's recent debates on the doctrine of Scripture. Now we can all benefit from what was learned through the process. The covers of this book hold together a veritable cornucopia of insights from top-notch theologians— both past and present—all united in one laudable aim: upholding the authority and clarity of the Holy Scriptures as God's inspired Word. Pick it up and read. You'll be simultaneously instructed and edified."

> —**Jason P. Van Vliet**, Professor of Dogmatics, Canadian Reformed Theological Seminary, Hamilton, Ontario

"Recent controversies on the doctrine of Scripture, both within and without Westminster Theological Seminary, have forced the seminary to define its position. This compendium is an attempt to put the present position of Westminster in the context of the historic Reformed position, both as originally formulated and as re-expressed in terms of later issues. Aside from its value to Westminster, this volume documents the continuity and the diversity of British and Continental thinking on Scripture as those streams have impacted the current Westminster position."

—**Noel Weeks**, Senior Lecturer in Ancient History and Associate of the Department of Classics and Ancient History, University of Sydney

"A magnificent compendium! It has drawn from the best, the truest, and the deepest works on, and affirmations about, the doctrine of Scripture. We need to hear these voices from our past. They are wise, discerning, and profound."

—**David F. Wells**, Distinguished Research Professor, Gordon-Conwell Theological Seminary, South Hamilton, Massachusetts

"This encyclopedic collection does remarkable service to the Reformed faith. In this fine bouquet, the hue and the scent of each flower contribute to the beauty of the ensemble. It will be valuable for those who want to admire the prime blooms, but even more it bears witness to the field where they were gathered. In a day of historical amnesia, we are reminded of the truth that cannot and must not be forgotten."

—**Paul Wells**, Adjunct Dean, Faculté Jean Calvin, Aix-en-Provence, France; Editor, *La Revue Réformée*; Director, Greenwich School of Theology, Clarborough, Retford, UK

"Can the church in the West find its bearings and return to God? Only if it finds the grace to dethrone the zeitgeist and re-enthrone the Lord and Holy Scripture, which reveals him. This volume is a manual for that enterprise. It is a sourcebook, history review, theology course, and exegesis guide all rolled into one. It should be required for seminary students, acquired by all pastors, and desired by anyone seeking to walk in the steps of the One who modeled and taught reverence for what we call the Bible as the foundation for valid knowledge as well as saving faith (John 17:17; 1 John 2:6)."

—**Robert W. Yarbrough**, Professor of New Testament, Covenant Theological Seminary, St. Louis, Missouri

THY WORD

IS STILL

TRUTH

THY WORD

IS STILL

TRUTH

Essential Writings on the
Doctrine of Scripture
from the Reformation to Today

EDITED BY

Peter A. Lillback and Richard B. Gaffin Jr.

PHILADELPHIA, PENNSYLVANIA

PUBLISHING

P.O. BOX 817 • PHILLIPSBURG • NEW JERSEY 08865-0817

Scripture references are from the translations in which they were quoted in the original publications of the texts found in this anthology.

Printed in the United States of America

Library of Congress Cataloging-in-Publication Data

Thy word is still truth : essential writings on the doctrine of scripture from the reformation to today / edited by Peter A. Lillback and Richard B. Gaffin, Jr.
       pages cm.
  Includes bibliographical references and index.
  ISBN 978-1-59638-447-7 (cloth)
  1. Bible--Evidences, authority, etc.--History of doctrines. 2. Reformed Church--Doctrines. 3. Westminster Theological Seminary (Philadelphia, Pa.) I. Lillback, Peter A. II. Gaffin, Richard B.
  BS480.T525 2013
  220.1--dc23
                        2013005310

This book is gratefully dedicated to all the students of
Westminster Theological Seminary past, present, and future.

Contents

Acknowledgments

THY WORD IS STILL TRUTH is a work that has come into being through the life and ministry of Westminster Theological Seminary. The title itself reminds us of the important impact of early faculty member E. J. Young, whose classic book on inerrancy was entitled *Thy Word Is Truth*. This anthology unapologetically borrows that title, emphasizing Westminster's abiding commitment to the entire truthfulness of the Holy Scriptures. Also with these pages, we recognize that our theological tradition is profoundly indebted to Reformed thinkers of bygone ages, as well as to the faculty members of Westminster Theological Seminary from its beginning to the present. So we gratefully acknowledge our dependence on all who have gone before.

We thank our families and the faculty, administration, and board of the seminary for their encouragement and support in many ways. We wish to say our special thanks to those who lent so much gracious help to enable this work to appear. In particular, we express our deep appreciation for the excellent labors of Dr. Bernard Aubert, who did much of the careful research for our bibliographies, our notes, and the accuracy of the selected passages. We also wish to thank the administrative support in the President's Office. We are especially grateful to Melinda Dugan, Patti Scherphorn, and Abbie Daise for their time and organized assistance in the production of our work. We also thank Westminster's library staff for their help. We wish to thank seminary counsel Jim Sweet for his numerous letters to secure permissions, and we also thank all those* who have granted them.

We thank our friends at P&R Publishing for their long and faithful partnership in this work as well as so many other projects, and we especially acknowledge Marvin Padgett, Bryce Craig, John J. Hughes, and Karen Magnuson for their guidance, suggestions, and editorial support.

Finally, we thank all of those too numerous to mention who have played other important roles in helping this multiyear and substantial project to become a reality.

With grateful hearts and sincere prayers we ask that God would bless this work for the strengthening of his church and the deepening of our commitments to the great prayer of our Lord Jesus Christ in John 17:17, "Sanctify them through thy truth: thy word is truth" (John 17:17 kjv). SOLI DEO GLORIA!

Your Brothers in Christ's Service,

Dr. Richard B. Gaffin Jr.,
Professor of Biblical and Systematic Theology, Emeritus,
Westminster Theological Seminary

Dr. Peter A. Lillback,
Professor of Historical Theology, President,
Westminster Theological Seminary

* Listed in the "Permissions" pages.

Permissions

THE PUBLISHER AND EDITORS are grateful for the permission to republish texts from the works cited below.

Baker

Pp. 389–448, 452–94 from Herman Bavinck, *Reformed Dogmatics*, vol. 1, *Prolegomena*, ed. John Bolt, trans. John Vriend. Copyright by the Dutch Reformed Translation Society. Published by Baker Book House Company.

Pp. 151–64 from Raymond B. Dillard, "Harmonization: A Help and a Hindrance," in *Inerrancy and Hermeneutic: A Tradition, A Challenge, A Debate*, ed. Harvie M. Conn. Copyright 1988 by Baker Book House Company.

Pp. 47–66 from Sinclair B. Ferguson, "How Does the Bible Look at Itself?" in *Inerrancy and Hermeneutic: A Tradition, A Challenge, A Debate*, ed. Harvie M. Conn. Copyright 1988 by Baker Book House Company.

Pp. 159–77, 178–200 from John M. Frame, "7. God and Biblical Language: Transcendence and Immanence," and "8. Scripture Speaks for Itself," in *God's Inerrant Word: An International Symposium on the Trustworthiness of Scripture*, ed. John Warwick Montgomery. Copyright 1974 by Bethany Fellowship, Inc., a division of Baker Publishing Group.

Pp. 165–83 from Richard B. Gaffin Jr., "The New Testament as Canon," in *Inerrancy and Hermeneutic: A Tradition, A Challenge, A Debate*, ed. Harvie M. Conn. Copyright 1988 by Baker Book House Company.

Pp. 188–225 from Ned B. Stonehouse, *The Witness of the Synoptic Gospels to Christ*. Copyright 1944 by Ned Bernard Stonehouse. Published by Baker Book House Company.

Banner of Truth

Pp. 9–26, 316–22 from *Collected Writings of John Murray*, vol. 1. Copyright 1976 by Valerie Murray. Published by the Banner of Truth Trust.

Christian Focus

Pp. 97–113 from John Calvin, "Christ the End of the Law," in *The Practical Calvinist: An Introduction to the Presbyterian & Reformed Heritage. In Honor of Dr. D. Clair Davis*, ed. Peter A. Lillback. Copyright 2002 by Peter A. Lillback. Published by Christian Focus Publications.

Eerdmans

Pp. 38–61 from Edward J. Young, *Thy Word Is Truth: Some Thoughts on the Biblical Doctrine of Inspiration*. Copyright 1957 by William B. Eerdmans Co.

Peter A. Lillback

Pp. 499–527 from Peter A. Lillback, "The Binding of God: Calvin's Role in the Development of Covenant Theology," Ph.D. diss, Westminster Theological Seminary, 1985.

Moody

Pp. 17–34 from Bruce K. Waltke, "Oral Tradition," in *A Tribute to Gleason Archer*, ed. Walter C. Kaiser Jr. and Ronald F. Youngblood. Copyright 1986 by Moody.

P&R Publishing Co.

Pp. 163–91 from Edmund P. Clowney, "6. Preaching Christ from All the Scriptures," in *The Preacher and Preaching: Reviving the Art in the Twentieth Century*, ed. Samuel T. Logan Jr. Copyright 1986 by P&R Publishing Co.

Pp. 283–339 from Peter A. Lillback, "'The Infallible Rule of Interpretation of Scripture': The Hermeneutical Crisis and the Westminster Standards," in *Resurrection and Eschatology: Theology in Service of the Church. Essays in Honor of Richard B. Gaffin Jr.*, ed. Lane G. Tipton and Jeffrey C. Waddington. Copyright 2008 by Lane G. Tipton and Jeffrey C. Waddington. Published by P&R Publishing Co.

Pp. 3–8, 26–35, 70–73, 139–44 from Adolphe Monod, *Living in the Hope of Glory*, ed. and trans. Constance K. Walker. Copyright 2002 by Constance K. Walker. Published by P&R Publishing Co.

Pp. 1–54 from John Murray, "The Attestation of Scripture," in *The Infallible Word*, ed. Paul Woolley, 3rd rev. printing. Copyright 1946 by Westminster Theological Seminary. Published by P&R Publishing Co., 1967.

Pp. 51–61 from Vern S. Poythress, *God-Centered Biblical Interpretation*. Copyright 1999 by Vern Sheridan Poythress. Published by P&R Publishing Co.

Pp. 92–140 from N. B. Stonehouse, "The Authority of the New Testament," in *The Infallible Word*, ed. Paul Woolley, 3rd rev. printing. Copyright 1946 by Westminster Theological Seminary. Published by P&R Publishing Co., 1967.

Pp. 55–167 from Francis Turretin, *Institutes of Elenctic Theology*, vol. 1, ed. James T. Dennison Jr., trans. George Musgrave Giger. Copyright 1992 by James T. Dennison Jr. Published by P&R Publishing Co.

Pp. 263–301 from Cornelius Van Til, "Nature and Scripture," in *The Infallible Word*, ed. Paul Woolley, 3rd rev. printing. Copyright 1946 by Westminster Theological Seminary. Published by P&R Publishing Co., 1967.

Pp. 55–91 from Edward J. Young, "The Authority of the Old Testament," in *The Infallible Word*, ed. Paul Woolley, 3rd rev. printing. Copyright 1946 by Westminster Theological Seminary. Published by P&R Publishing Co., 1967.

Reformed Academic Press

Pp. 100–107 from Richard B. Gaffin Jr., *God's Word in Servant-Form: Abraham Kuyper and Herman Bavinck on the Doctrine of Scripture*. Copyright 2008 by Richard B. Gaffin Jr. Published by Reformed Academic Press.

Pp. v–xvi from Peter A. Lillback, introduction to *God's Word in Servant-Form: Abraham Kuyper and Herman Bavinck on the Doctrine of Scripture*, by Richard B. Gaffin Jr. Copyright 2008 by Richard B. Gaffin Jr. Published by Reformed Academic Press.

Sprinkle Publications

Pp. 37–44 from *The Works of the Rev. John Witherspoon*, vol. 7. Copyright 2001 by Sprinkle Publications.

Westminster John Knox Press

Pp. 69–81 from John Calvin, *Institutes of the Christian Religion*, ed. John T. McNeill, trans. Ford Lewis Battles. LCC 20. Copyright 1960 by W. L. Jenkins. Originally published by Westminster Press, Philadelphia, and S. C. M. Press, Ltd., London.

Westminster Theological Journal

Pp. 129–44 from Richard B. Gaffin Jr., "Contemporary Hermeneutics and the Study of the New Testament," *WTJ* 31, 2 (May 1969).

Pp. 253–89 from Richard B. Gaffin Jr., "Old Amsterdam and Inerrancy?" *WTJ* 44, 2 (Fall 1982).

Pp. 241–79 from Vern S. Poythress, "Divine Meaning of Scripture," *WTJ* 48, 2 (Fall 1986).

Pp. 65–80 from Moisés Silva, "Old Princeton, Westminster, and Inerrancy," *WTJ* 50, 1 (Spring 1988).

Zondervan

Pp. 27–45, 77–97 from Moisés Silva, *Has the Church Misread the Bible? The History of Interpretation in the Light of Current Issues*, Foundations of Contemporary Interpretations 1. Copyright 1987 by Moisés Silva. Published by Zondervan Publishing House.

Introduction

We believe that these Holy Scriptures fully contain the will of God, and that whatsoever man ought to believe unto salvation, is sufficiently taught therein. For since the whole manner of worship which God requires of us is written in them at large, it is unlawful for any one, though an Apostle, to teach otherwise than we are now taught in the Holy Scriptures: *nay, though it were an angel from heaven*, as the Apostle Paul saith (Gal. 1:8–9). For since it is forbidden *to add unto or take away any thing from the Word of God* (Deut. 12:32; Prov. 30:6; Rev. 22:18; John 4:25), it doth thereby evidently appear that the doctrine thereof is most perfect and complete in all respects. Neither may we compare any writings of men, though ever so holy, with those divine Scriptures; nor ought we to compare custom, or the great multitude, or antiquity, or succession of times or persons, or councils, decrees, or statutes, with the truth of God, for the truth is above all: for all men are of themselves liars, and more vain than vanity itself. Therefore we reject with all our hearts whatsoever doth not agree with this infallible rule, which the Apostles have taught us, saying, *Try the spirits whether they are of God* (1 John 4:1); likewise, *If there come any unto you, and bring not this doctrine, receive him not into your house* (2 John 10). (Belgic Confession 7)

As light that passes through the colored glass of a cathedral window, we are told, is light from heaven, but is stained by the tints of the glass through which it passes; so any word of God which is passed through the mind and soul of a man must come out discolored by the personality through which it is given, and just to that degree ceases to be the pure word of God. But what if this personality has itself been formed by God into precisely the personality it is, for the express purpose of communicating to the word given through it just the coloring which it gives it? What if the colors of the stained-glass window have been designed by the architect for the express purpose of giving to the light that floods the cathedral precisely the tone and quality it receives from them? What if the word of God that comes to His people is framed by God into the word of God it is, precisely by means of the qualities of the men formed by Him for the purpose, through which it is given? When we think of God the Lord giving by His Spirit a body of authoritative Scriptures to His people, we must remember that He is the God of providence and of grace as well as of revelation and inspiration, and that He holds all the lines of preparation as fully under His direction as He does the specific operation which we call technically, in the narrow sense, by the name of "inspiration." (Warfield)

One of the hallmarks of Westminster Theological Seminary from its beginning in 1929 under the courageous leadership of Dr. J. Gresham Machen has been a high view of Scripture reflecting the historic Reformed theological and confessional tradition:

When we say that the Bible is the Word of God, we mean something very definite indeed. We mean that the Bible is true. We mean that the writers of the Bible, in addition to all their providential qualifications for their task, received an immediate and supernatural guidance and impulsion of the Spirit of God which kept them from the errors that are found in other books, and made the resulting book, the Bible, to be completely true in what it says regarding matters of fact, and completely authoritative in its commands. That is the great doctrine of the full or plenary inspiration of Holy Scripture. (Machen)

In recent years, this understanding of God's Word has been repeatedly challenged—not simply by those in the liberal Protestant tradition, but also by those in the broad evangelical perspective. In fact, in the past few years, Westminster addressed related issues in its own theological crisis, which was motivated by differing hermeneutical perspectives and broader understandings of confessional boundaries. Resolving the conflict required an extensive and often painful process of theological clarification, historical reappraisal, and financial risks, because the debate impacted friends of the seminary who took varying perspectives on the issues involved.

Having resolved this conflict and having begun to articulate once again a clear and historic witness to this core value, Westminster now gives to the world a theological testimony of the integrity of our views that we believe are grounded in the long and august Reformed tradition on the doctrine of Scripture.

In this context, *Thy Word Is Still Truth* offers a selection of texts on the doctrine of Scripture. The purpose of this book is to demonstrate that the conclusions reached in this controversy, whose focal point was at Westminster, are nothing less than the continuing flowering of the reformational views of Luther, Calvin, Bullinger, and the Reformed confessions on the doctrine of Scripture. Building on this foundation, the ongoing reflection and contributions of theologians from various traditions and confessions of the Reformed faith, we believe, led us ultimately to the Westminster Confession of Faith's conclusion as confirmed by this debate at Westminster Seminary.

The union of the many voices included in this volume that come together to support this conclusion is what makes the argument compelling. The selections included build a sweeping and elegant case for the conclusion that Westminster Seminary reached in this controversy. The climax of the debate was reached in a document entitled "Affirmations and Denials Regarding Recent Issues," which is one of the final pieces in this theological anthology:

> The Board wishes to reassure our constituencies and to assert to the watching world that it is still the core commitment of Westminster Theological Seminary to prepare pastors, leaders and scholars for the Church and the Kingdom of Christ. Such specialists in the Bible are discerning believers in Scripture who do not shirk the difficult questions, but who also address such questions from the vantage point of Westminster's historic heartfelt (ex animo) vow to the infallible Word of God. (Statement from the Board of Trustees, Westminster Theological Seminary [September 24, 2008])

Today, like Pilate at Jesus' trial, our world and even the church are confused about ultimate issues. Pilate's question to Jesus, "What is truth?" (John 18:38), is still as urgent today as it was back then. Earlier, in the High Priestly Prayer, Jesus had affirmed, "Thy word is truth" (John 17:17 KJV). When Edward J. Young looked for a title to his manifesto on the doctrine of inspiration, he turned to these words of Jesus. Jesus himself attested to the truth of God's Word; Young skillfully defended the truth of the Word. Today, we want to confess again in the presence of God, *Thy Word Is Still Truth*.

> That Word above all earthly pow'rs,
> No thanks to them, abideth;
> The Spirit and the gifts are ours,
> Through him who with us sideth.
> Let goods and kindred go,
> This mortal life also;
> The body they may kill;
> God's truth abideth still;
> His kingdom is forever.
> (Martin Luther, "A Mighty Fortress Is Our God")

> The Scriptures are perfect, inasmuch as they were uttered by the Word of God and His Spirit, though we want the knowledge of their mysteries. (Irenaeus)

> Therefore all Scripture is God-breathed, and in every way profitable so that one may best and most profitably to the soul search the Divine Scriptures. (John of Damascus)

Westminster Theological Seminary, in its commitment to the authority, sufficiency, self-attestation, and inerrant authority of Scripture, stands in continuity with the church universal and more specifically in line with the rediscovery and expansion of biblical authority in the Reformed traditions. This anthology presents chronologically and thematically major witnesses to this rich and varied understanding of God's Word. Two main strands of influence are clearly at work in the Westminster school: on the one hand, the Scots-Irish Presbyterian brand represented (e.g., John Murray); on the other, the Dutch heritage (e.g., Cornelius Van Til). The confessional sources of these two currents are the Westminster Standards and the Three Forms of Unity, respectively, which in turn are indebted to the Reformation in general and to Calvin in particular. Westminster Seminary's clear stance on Scripture is defined not in a vacuum, but with a great awareness of the difficult questions raised by the scholarship of its time. Indeed, Westminster, in the line of Old Princeton, has a long-standing tradition of interacting with the newest scholarship. This commitment is well illustrated by the training of several of its professors on European soil.

This anthology strives to document the diverse streams of influence that have shaped Westminster's strong commitment to Scripture, demonstrating not only how various themes have developed through the centuries, but also how the doctrine of Scripture was often shaped in the challenging furnaces of controversy. Our journey begins with the breakthrough of the Reformation in the sixteenth century. At the outset, several fronts were opened. On one side, Luther challenged the humanism of Erasmus by proclaiming the clarity of the Word even in thorny subjects such as the question of free will. On the other side, Zwingli, in debating Catholic traditions, unabashedly asserted the sole authority of Scripture in deciding controversial matters, thus making giant strides in defining the doctrine of *sola Scriptura*:

His will and true service we can learn and discover only from His true word in the Holy Scriptures and in the trustworthy writings of His twelve apostles, otherwise from no human laws and statutes. (Zwingli)

With Bullinger and Calvin, the doctrine of Scripture is further refined and defined. In particular, Calvin expounds the necessity of the Bible and the self-authenticating character of the Word of God in relation to the Holy Spirit:

Let this point therefore stand: that those whom the Holy Spirit has inwardly taught truly rest upon Scripture, and that Scripture indeed is self-authenticated; hence, it is not right to subject it to proof and reasoning. And the certainty it deserves with us, it attains by the testimony of the Spirit. (Calvin)

The pages that follow continue with a survey of what Reformed confessions profess about God's Word. From the morning light of the dawn of the Reformation to the more mature statements of such documents as Bullinger's Second Helvetic Confession and the Westminster Standards, we encounter a unified witness to the divine authority of Scripture shining throughout Europe. These documents express in succinct terms the authoritative teaching of the churches stemming out of the Reformation. By turning next to examples of biblical interpretation at the time of the Reformation, the anthology sheds light on another facet of the Reformed understanding of Scripture. Both Bullinger's *De Testamento* and Calvin's *Christ the End of the Law* were first published separately, and both were later inserted into larger volumes: Bullinger's text as an appendix to his commentary on the New Testament Epistles and Calvin's work as an introduction to the New Testament. Thus both works are essential representations of the Reformers' hermeneutics. The following selections in this section depict how Reformed interpretation unfolded in England, Scotland, and America.

In the next section, this book turns to the doctrine of Scripture at the time of Reformed orthodoxy. In the context of the more complex discussions of scholasticism and of the rise of rationalism, Reformed theologians took upon themselves the responsibility to defend the authority of Scripture. This anthology presents not only samples from the important Puritan theologians William Ames and John Owen, but also texts from Continental Europe by Francis Turretin and the Helvetic Consensus Formula, as well as Jonathan Edwards's defense of Scripture in light of rationalism. These theological writings have had a significant impact on Old Princeton and in turn the Westminster tradition.

The next three sections offer more proximate contexts for the affirmation of Scripture at Westminster.

First, as indicated above, the Scottish and Dutch legacies correspond to two main strands of theology at Westminster Seminary. The Scottish legacy itself is strongly influenced by the high view of Scripture presented in the Westminster Standards. The Dutch legacy is seen here from two angles: directly from Europe with Abraham Kuyper and Herman Bavinck and indirectly in the work of Louis Berkhof. Indeed, Berkhof was an important transmitter of Dutch theology in America.

Second, our window into the European contribution enables us to grasp early Reformed responses to the earlier rationalist attack on Scripture that is also characteristic of our time. The Swiss theologian Louis Gaussen offers a confessional stand on Scripture. Both

Adolphe Monod and Ernst Wilhelm Hengstenberg rejected their rationalist past to embrace a Reformed orthodox position on the Bible. A representative piece from Charles H. Spurgeon is also included.

Third, Old Princeton, the parent institution of Westminster, provides a natural background for better understanding Westminster's stance. This collection includes three representative theologians of Old Princeton: Charles Hodge, his natural child Archibald Alexander Hodge, and his spiritual heir B. B. Warfield. The father laid the groundwork, the son was known as an excellent communicator of the Princeton tradition, and Warfield brilliantly furthered the Princeton doctrine of Scripture. Moisés Silva's fine article offers a fitting summary and conclusion to this section.

Westminster was founded in the midst of raging controversies in the 1920s. The heart of the matter was the gulf between true supernatural Christianity and a watered-down, naturalistic version of Christianity. In this context, defending the supernatural character of Scripture was paramount. This defense was most clearly expressed by some of the founders of Westminster, specifically J. Gresham Machen, Robert Dick Wilson, and John Murray. Here Machen's address is most likely his last words on this issue; Wilson, the great Old Testament scholar, defends the Bible against the onslaught of modern scholarship; and Murray formulates the doctrine of Scripture in a characteristically precise and clear manner.

The doctrines of Scripture and of its interpretation were developed in different ways at Westminster as various challenges were being faced. In the footsteps of the pioneer efforts of Geerhardus Vos, Westminster advanced the discipline of biblical theology in a confessional framework:

> The line of revelation is like the stem of those trees that grow in rings. Each successive ring has grown out of the preceding one. But out of the sap and vigor that is in this stem there springs a crown with branches and leaves and flowers and fruit. Such is the true relation between Biblical and Systematic Theology. Dogmatics is the crown which grows out of all the work that Biblical Theology can accomplish. (Vos)

After presenting key texts by Vos himself, the collection shows how Ned B. Stonehouse applied this approach to his field of Gospel studies and how Edmund P. Clowney brought biblical theology with its Christological focus to the pulpit. The next three excerpts illustrate how a Reformed biblical-theological approach relates to specific concerns. Vern S. Poythress illustrates how a high view of inspiration harmoniously fits the endeavors of the human authors of Scripture. Moisés Silva, for his part, places the study of the Bible at Westminster squarely on the shoulders of Christian interpreters of all ages by considering central concerns in the history of interpretation.

> In clearly expressed passages of scripture one can find all the things that concern faith and the moral life (namely hope and love . . .). Then, after gaining familiarity with the language of the divine scriptures, one should proceed to explore and analyse the obscure passages, by taking examples from the more obvious parts to illuminate obscure expressions and by using the evidence of indisputable passages to remove the uncertainty of ambiguous ones.[1]

1. St. Augustine, *On Christian Teaching*, trans. R. P. H. Green (New York: Oxford University Press, 1997), 37.

Finally, Richard B. Gaffin Jr. examines how debates about hermeneutics raging in philosophical circles and among theologians relate to the interpretation of the New Testament.

One of the crucial questions of modern theological studies is that of the canon of Scripture. Westminster did not fail to address the problem as it relates to the inspiration, nature, and authority of the Bible. Early on in the life of the seminary, both Young and Stonehouse addressed the question from their respective fields of expertise. Later on, Gaffin revisited the question: while standing in continuation with Calvin and the Westminster Confession of Faith, he advances the debate by integrating the insights of a redemptive-historical approach. Besides the question of the canon, other challenges to the doctrine of Scripture arose; the articles in the next section respond to some of these.

A consideration of the history of the doctrine of Scripture in the Reformed tradition in general and during the life span of Westminster has brought to light two important aspects. On the one hand, the Reformed tradition has not failed to tackle the hard questions and to engage competing views, whether they be the traditionalism of Catholicism, the humanism of the Renaissance, or the rising of rationalism from the time of scholasticism to the emergence of modern theology and critical scholarship.

> The infallible rule of interpretation of Scripture is the Scripture itself; and therefore, when there is a question about the true and full sense of any Scripture (which is not manifold, but one), it may be searched and known by other places that speak more clearly. (WCF 1.9)

On the other hand, the Reformed faith also expressed a clear clarion sound in defense of the Scripture and its inspiration, authority, and inerrancy. May this anthology spur us forward in faithfulness to both Scripture and our calling to engage current issues. The texts of Sinclair B. Ferguson and Young assist us in defining and clarifying a biblical understanding of the inspiration of Scripture. Ferguson argues that not the shape of Scripture, but rather what Scripture asserts about itself, has priority in defining our doctrine of Scripture. Young's classic addresses thorny topics such as the comprehensive nature of inspiration and the role of human authorship. John M. Frame's two essays help us to refine our understanding of the self-witness of Scripture and assist us in responding to the philosophical and theological challenge that human language is inadequate to transmit revelation from God. While Raymond Dillard and Bruce Waltke address current issues in Old Testament studies, Peter Lillback presents controversies by relating our current hermeneutical crisis to the confessional standards of Westminster Seminary.

As our anthology comes to a close, we are now better equipped to observe how the conclusions reached during this time of crisis at Westminster build on the insights of previous generations. The section on the Westminster controversy presents two succinct documents summarizing the outcome of the theological reflection on Scripture that has taken place over these past few years. Finally, the anthology closes with Lillback's introduction to Gaffin's classic study on the doctrine of Scripture of Abraham Kuyper and Herman Bavinck and with Gaffin's concluding remarks to the same study.

In conclusion, a consideration of these many voices reveals that the Reformed faith is a living tradition engaging with the pressing questions of the day. While a careful reading of these texts unveils a certain diversity of views, there remains among all these theologians a broad consensus about the authority and inspiration of Scripture:

The hermeneutical flexibility that has characterized our tradition would probably come as a surprise to many observers who view Westminster as excessively rigid. Ironically, our confessional documents, the Westminster Confession and Catechisms, are far more extensive and detailed than those found in most evangelical institutions. Our theological parameters are indeed very clearly defined, and yet those parameters themselves have made possible a diversity of viewpoints that would not have been tolerated in some other institutions. (Silva)

This high view of Scripture is based on the testimony of Scripture itself about its nature. Thus, this foundation is sure and enables the church to rest secure as she faces the storms of controversy:

How firm a foundation, you saints of the Lord,
is laid for your faith in his excellent Word!
What more can he say than to you he has said,
to you who for refuge to Jesus have fled?
("How Firm a Foundation")

Our prayer is that God, by his grace, would use this anthology to further his kingdom. We hope this book will help our readers to discern that Westminster's theological position rightfully stands on the shoulders of many theological giants who have preceded it and prepared the way for its birth and development.

Son, all the books of Scripture, both Old Testament and New, are inspired by God and useful for instruction, as the Apostle says; but to those who really study it the Psalter yields especial treasure. Briefly, then, if indeed any more is needed to drive home the point, the whole divine Scripture is the teacher of virtue and true faith, but the Psalter gives a picture of spiritual life. And so you too, Marcellinus, pondering the Psalms and reading them intelligently, with the Spirit as your guide, will be able to grasp the meaning of each one, even as you desire. (Athanasius to Marcellinus)[2]

We must not suppose that the language proceeds from the men who are inspired, but from the Divine Word which moves them. (Justin Martyr)

We cannot say of the writings of the Holy Spirit that anything in them is useless or superfluous, even if they seem to some obscure. (Origen)

Dr. Richard B. Gaffin Jr.,
Professor of Biblical and Systematic Theology, Emeritus,
Westminster Theological Seminary

Dr. Peter A. Lillback,
Professor of Historical Theology, President,
Westminster Theological Seminary

---

2. St. Athanasius, "The Letter of St. Athanasius to Marcellinus on the Interpretation of the Psalms," in *On the Incarnation* (Crestwood, NY: St. Vladimir's Seminary, 2003), 97, 107, 119.

Abbreviations

ACW	Ancient Christian Writers. New York: Newman, 1946–.
ANF	Alexander Roberts and James Donaldson, eds. Ante-Nicene Fathers. Grand Rapids: Eerdmans, 1951–.
BDE	Timothy Larsen, ed. *Biographical Dictionary of Evangelicals*. Downers Grove, IL: InterVarsity, 2003.
Beeke & Ferguson. *Reformed Confessions*	Joel R. Beeke and Sinclair B. Ferguson, eds. *Reformed Confessions Harmonized*. Grand Rapids: Baker, 1999.
Bible Interpreters of the 20th Century	Walter A. Elwell and J. D. Weaver, eds. *Bible Interpreters of the 20th Century: A Selection of Evangelical Voices*. Grand Rapids: Baker, 1999.
BT	I. Epstein, ed. *The Babylonian Talmud*. London: Soncino Press, 1935–52.
The Cambridge Companion to Reformation Theology	David Bagchi and David C. Steinmetz, eds. *The Cambridge Companion to Reformation Theology*. New York: Cambridge University Press, 2004.
CCL	*Corpus Christianorum, Series Latina*. Turnhout: Brepols, 1953–.
CO	*Calvin opera quae supersunt omnia*. 1863–1900.
Cochrane. *Reformed Confessions*	Arthur C. Cochrane. *Reformed Confessions of the 16th Century*. Rev. ed. Louisville, KY: Westminster John Knox Press, 1966, 2003.
CR	*Corpus Reformatorum*. Berlin: C. A. Schwetschke, 1834–.
CSEL	*Corpus Scriptorum Ecclesiasticorum Latinorum*. Vienna: Tempsky, 1865–.
CTJ	*Calvin Theological Journal*.
Dennison. *Reformed Confessions*	James T. Dennison Jr. *Reformed Confessions of the 16th and 17th Centuries in English Translation*. Vol. 1, 1523–1552. Vol. 2, 1552–1566. Grand Rapids: Reformation Heritage Books, 2008, 2010.
DHT	Trevor A. Hart, ed. *The Dictionary of Historical Theology*. Grand Rapids: Eerdmans, 2000.

DMBI (2007)	Donald McKim, ed. *Dictionary of Major Biblical Interpreters.* Downers Grove, IL: InterVarsity, 2007.
DP&RTA	D. G. Hart and Mark A. Noll, eds. *Dictionary of the Presbyterian & Reformed Tradition in America.* Downers Grove, IL: InterVarsity, 1999.
DSCH&T	Nigel M. de S. Cameron, ed. *Dictionary of Scottish Church History & Theology.* Downers Grove, IL: InterVarsity, 1993.
EDT	Walter A. Elwell, ed. *Evangelical Dictionary of Theology.* Grand Rapids: Baker, 1984.
FC	Father of the Church. Washington, DC: Catholic University of America Press.
Hall. *Harmony*	Peter Hall, ed. *The Harmony of Protestant Confessions: Exhibiting the Faith of the Churches of Christ Reformed after the Pure and Holy Doctrine of the Gospel, throughout Europe.* London: John F. Shaw, 1844.
Inerrancy and Hermeneutic	Harvie M. Conn, ed. *Inerrancy and Hermeneutic: A Tradition, A Challenge, A Debate.* Grand Rapids: Baker, 1988.
Inerrancy and the Church	John D. Hannah, ed. *Inerrancy and the Church.* Chicago: Moody, 1984.
The Devoted Life	Kelly M. Kapic and Randall C. Gleason, eds. *The Devoted Life: An Invitation to the Puritan Classics.* Downers Grove, IL: InterVarsity, 2004.
LCC	John Baillie, John T. McNeill, and Henry P. Van Dusen, eds. Library of Christian Classics. Philadelphia: Westminster Press, 1953–66.
Leith. *Creeds of the Churches*	John H. Leith, ed. *Creeds of the Churches: A Reader in Christian Doctrine from the Bible to the Present.* Rev. ed. Richmond, VA: John Knox, 1963, 1973.
LF	A Library of the Fathers of the Holy Catholic Church. Oxford: John Henry Parker, 1838–81.
Loeb	The Loeb Classical Library. Cambridge, MA: Harvard University Press.
NDT	Sinclair B. Ferguson and David F. Wright, eds. *New Dictionary of Theology.* Downers Grove, IL: InterVarsity, 1988.
NIDCC	J. D. Douglas, ed. *The New International Dictionary of the Christian Church.* Grand Rapids: Zondervan, 1978.
NPNF1	Philip Schaff, ed. *Nicene and Post-Nicene Fathers, First Series.* Grand Rapids: Eerdmans, 1956.
NPNF2	Philip Schaff and Henry Wace, eds. *Nicene and Post-Nicene Fathers, Second Series.* Grand Rapids: Eerdmans, 1952.

NSHERK	*The New Schaff-Herzog Encyclopedia of Religious Knowledge.* Vols. 1–15. Grand Rapids: Baker, 1977.
PG	Jacques-Paul Migne, ed. *Patrologiae Cursus Completus, Series Graeca.* Paris: J.-P. Migne, 1857–66.
PL	Jacques-Paul Migne, ed. *Patrologiae Cursus Completus, Series Latina.* Paris: Garnieri Fratres, 1844–64.
PRE¹	*Realencyklopädie für protestantische Theologie und Kirche.* Edited by J. J. Herzog. 1st ed. 22 vols. Hamburg: R. Besser, 1854–68.
PRE²	*Realencyklopädie für protestantische Theologie und Kirche.* Edited by J. J. Herzog and G. L. Plitt. 2nd rev. ed. 18 vols. Leipzig: J. C. Hinrichs, 1877–88.
PRE³	*Realencyklopädie für protestantische Theologie und Kirche.* Edited by Albert Hauck. 3rd rev. ed. 24 vols. Leipzig: J. C. Hinrichs, 1896–1913.
Reformed Theology in America	David F. Wells, ed. *Reformed Theology in America: A History of Its Modern Development.* Grand Rapids: Eerdmans, 1985.
Reid, ed. *John Calvin: His Influence in the Western World.*	W. Stanford Reid, ed. *John Calvin: His Influence in the Western World.* Grand Rapids: Zondervan, 1982.
Schaff. *The Creeds of Christendom*	*The Creeds of Christendom.* Edited by Philip Schaff. Revised by David S. Schaff. 3 vols. Grand Rapids: Baker, 1931, 1983.
Schroeder. *Council of Trent*	H. J. Schroeder, ed. *Canons and Decrees of the Council of Trent.* St. Louis: Herder, 1941.
Scripture and Truth	D. A. Carson and John D. Woodbridge, eds. *Scripture and Truth.* Grand Rapids: Baker, 1992.
Str-B	H. L. Strack and P. Billerbeck. *Kommentar zum Neuen Testament aus Talmud und Midrasch.* 6 vols. Munich, 1922–61.
VD	Robert Bellarmine, "De Controversiis: Prima Controversia Generalis—De Verbo Dei." In *Opera Omnia.* Vol. 1. Neapoli: Josephum Giluiano, 1856.
WCF	Westminster Confession of Faith.
Werke WA	*Martin Luthers Werke.* Kritische Gesammtausgabe. Weimar.
WTJ	*Westminster Theological Journal.*

Notes on the Introductions
and Bibliographies

EACH SELECTION IS INTRODUCED by a short note that places the texts in their historical contexts and summarizes the main contributions of the documents. These introductions are followed by short bibliographies. These are meant to be suggestions for the readers who want to learn more; they are in no way comprehensive. A special place is given in these bibliographical notes to works written within the Princeton/ Westminster tradition.

Part One

SOLA SCRIPTURA:
THE REFORMERS' REDISCOVERY
OF THE WRITTEN WORD OF GOD

THE DOCTRINE OF SCRIPTURE defended at Westminster Theological Seminary has its roots in the Protestant Reformation of sixteenth-century Europe. The first part of this compendium reflects this period of crucial rediscovery of the authority of Scripture, the written Word of God, by presenting four key figures of the Reformation: Martin Luther, Ulrich Zwingli, Heinrich Bullinger, and John Calvin. Westminster Calvinism naturally appeals to the legacy of Calvin, and the Reformed faith also builds on a broader foundation. In many respects, the views of Calvin stand in continuity with those of Luther. Moreover, as it is commonly held, the Reformed tradition is not monolithic, stemming from only one source. Our anthology emphasizes this historical reality by integrating Zwingli, the founder of the Reformation in Zurich, and Bullinger, his successor.

The selections of texts show in addition that the Reformers defined their doctrine of Scripture in contrast to several opposing forces. All four writers had, of course, to assert the authority of Scripture alone over against that of the Catholic Church and her traditions. The text from Luther's *Bondage of the Will* depicts that he was also battling the humanism of Erasmus. In the context of the controversy over free will, he affirmed the clarity or perspicuity of Scripture. In other words, the Bible speaks clearly and authoritatively even on such thorny topics as free will and predestination. This angle on Scripture will be found later on in the Reformed tradition, especially in the struggle of the Synod of Dort and the Westminster Standards against Arminianism. In the first Zurich Disputation (1523), Zwingli responds to his Catholic critics. His reformation of practices in the church was based on his reading of Scripture, and thus he defends his work on the basis of the principle of *sola Scriptura*. This account reveals how, according to Zwingli and his colleagues, several traditional practices of the Catholic Church do not stand the test of Scripture. With his popular sermons, entitled *The Decades*, Bullinger strengthened not only the Reformation in Zurich, but also the one in England. Indeed, those were translated early on and spread widely. In the two sermons selected, he develops the doctrine of Scripture in contrast to Catholicism and to the early Anabaptists. Indeed, not only does Scripture teach salvation by faith alone, but also the message of the Bible unfolds progressively in its pages. The second sermon conveys that the Bible is to be heard and obeyed, thus leading to godliness. Selections by Bullinger are also found in the second part, where he conveys his view on Scripture and interpretation in the Second Helvetic Confession, and in the third part, where his treatise on the covenant is reproduced. Calvin's *Institutes of the Christian Religion* (1559) is the classic formulation of sixteenth-century Reformed theology. There the doctrine of Scripture is set in the context of God's general and special revelation. Calvin's first chapter here develops the necessity of Scripture for a right, saving knowledge of God. The second chapter develops the witness of the Spirit as the ultimate source of the authority of Scripture. This view contrasts with that of the Catholic Church, which sees the church as lending authority to the Bible.

While the four selections in this part present the doctrine of Scripture defended by the Reformers, the next part will consider the official statements of the Reformation of the sixteenth and seventeenth centuries. In addition, the third part will turn from the definition of the doctrine of Scripture to the implications of this doctrine for the interpretation of the Bible.

The Bondage of the Will

MARTIN LUTHER

Martin Luther, *The Bondage of the Will*, trans. Henry Cole with slight alteration from Edward Thomas Vaughan, corrected by Henry Atherton (Grand Rapids: Eerdmans, 1931), 18–29.

Martin Luther (1483–1546), the founder of Protestantism, was born in Eisleben, Germany, was educated at the University of Erfurt, and entered in 1505 the Augustinian monastery at Erfurt. He was a professor of the Bible at the University of Wittenberg and through his studies resolved his spiritual crisis by rediscovering the doctrine of justification by faith alone. It led him to reject the abuses of the Roman Catholic Church and to understand that "the righteous shall live by faith." The posting of his Ninety-five Theses at Wittenberg on October 31, 1517 marks the beginning of the Reformation. Further, he set forth the Reformation principle of *sola Scriptura* in his famous 1519 debate with John Eck at Leipzig. Luther's works fill up entire shelves; thus we can mention only a fraction of his writings. In 1520, he wrote several major reformational works, such as *On the Babylonian Captivity of the Church* and *The Freedom of a Christian Man*. He also wrote many biblical commentaries, for instance on Genesis, the Psalms, Romans, and Galatians. Though Luther clashed with Zwingli over the interpretation of the Lord's Supper, Luther's breakthrough impacted all branches of Protestantism; in particular, John Calvin was greatly indebted to his thought. Luther distanced himself not only from the Catholic Church, but also from Erasmus's humanism. While he could welcome Erasmus's scholarship, he challenged his doctrine of man. Our selection highlights this controversy with humanism.

In this selection taken from *The Bondage of the Will*, Luther debates with Erasmus over free will, and we see that his doctrine of Scripture alone is intimately coupled with the perspicuity of Scripture, or the clarity of God's Word in its central teachings. That Scripture speaks clearly even to such questions as free will and predestination was crucial to Luther, and after him to Calvin and the Synod of Dort.

Bibliography: J. Atkinson. "Luther, Martin (1483–1546)." Pp. 401–4 in *NDT*. Roland H. Bainton. *Here I Stand: A Life of Martin Luther*. Peabody, MA: Abingdon-Cokesbury, 1950. Martin Brecht. *Martin Luther: Shaping and Defining the Reformation*. 3 vols. Philadelphia: Fortress, 1985–93. T. George. "Luther, Martin (1493–1546)." Pp. 375–79 in *BDE*. R. W. Heinze. "Luther, Martin (1483–1546)." Pp. 665–67 in *EDT*. Scott Hendrix. "5. Luther." Pp. 39–56 in *The Cambridge Companion to Reformation Theology*. Bernhard Lohse. *Martin Luther's Theology: Its Historical and Systematic Development*. Ed. and trans. Roy A. Harrisville. Minneapolis: Fortress, 1999. "Luther, Martin." *NSHERK* 7:69–79. Martin Luther. *The Bondage of the Will*. Trans. J. I. Packer and O. R. Johnston. Grand Rapids: Fleming H. Revell, 1996. Carl S. Meyer. "Luther, Martin (1483–1546)." Pp. 609–11 in *NIDCC*. Robert D. Preus. "Luther and Biblical Infallibility." Pp. 99–142 in *Inerrancy and the Church*. David S. Yeago. "Luther, Martin (1483–1546)." Pp. 331–35 in *DHT*.

Erasmus's Preface Reviewed

Section I.—FIRST of all, I would just touch upon some of the heads of your PREFACE; in which, you somewhat disparage our cause and adorn your own. In the first place, I would notice your censuring in me, in all your former books, an obstinacy of assertion; and saying, in this book, "that you are so far from delighting in assertions, that you would rather at once go over to the sentiments of the sceptics, if the inviolable authority of the Holy Scriptures, and the decrees of the church, would permit you: to which authorities you willingly submit yourself in all things, whether you follow what they prescribe, or follow it not." These are the principles that please you.

I consider (as in courtesy bound) that these things are asserted by you from a benevolent mind, as being a lover of peace. But if any one else had asserted them, I should, perhaps, have attacked him in my accustomed manner. But, however, I must not even allow you, though so very good in your intentions, to err in this opinion. For not to delight in assertions, is not the character of the Christian mind: nay, he must delight in assertions, or he is not a Christian. But, that we may not be mistaken in terms, by *assertion*, I mean a constant adhering, affirming, confessing, defending, and invincibly persevering. Nor do I believe the term signifies any thing else, either among the Latins [or classical authors], or as it is used by us at this day.

And moreover, I speak concerning the asserting of those things, which are delivered to us from above in the Holy Scriptures. Were it not so, we should want neither Erasmus nor any other instructor to teach us, that, in things doubtful, useless, or unnecessary; assertions, contentions, and strivings, would be not only absurd, but impious: and Paul condemns such in more places than one. Nor do you, I believe, speak of these things, unless, as a ridiculous orator, you wish to take up one subject, and go on with another, as the Roman Emperor did with his Turbot; or, with the madness of a wicked writer, you wish to contend, that the article concerning "Free-will" is doubtful, or not necessary.

Be sceptics and academics far from us Christians; but be there with us assertors twofold more determined than the stoics themselves. How often does the apostle Paul require that assurance of faith; that is, that most certain, and most firm assertion of Conscience, calling it (Rom. 10:10) confession, "With the mouth confession is made unto salvation?" And Christ also saith, "Whosoever confesseth Me before men, him will I confess before My Father" (Matt. 10:32). Peter commands us to "give a reason of the hope" that is in us (1 Peter 3:15). But why should I dwell upon this; nothing is more known and more general among Christians than assertions. Take away assertions, and you take away Christianity. Nay, the Holy Spirit is given unto them from heaven, that He may glorify Christ, and confess Him even unto death; unless this be not to assert—to die for confession and assertion. In a word, the Spirit so asserts, that He comes upon the whole world and reproves them of sin (John 16:8); thus, as it were, provoking to battle. And Paul enjoins Timothy to reprove, and to be instant out of season (2 Tim. 4:2). But how ludicrous to me would be that reprover, who should neither really believe that himself, of which he reproved, nor constantly assert it! Why I would send him to Anticyra, to be cured.[1]

But I am the greatest fool, who thus lose words and time upon that, which is clearer than the sun. What Christian would bear that assertions should be contemned? This would be at once to deny all piety and religion together; or to assert, that religion, piety, and every doctrine, is nothing at all. Why therefore do you too say, that you do not delight in assertions, and that you prefer such a mind to any other?

But you would have it understood that you have said nothing here concerning confessing Christ, and His doctrines. I receive the admonition. And, in courtesy to you, I give up my right and custom, and refrain from judging of your heart, reserving that for another time, or for others. In the mean time, I admonish you to correct your tongue, and your pen, and to refrain henceforth from using such expressions. For, how upright and honest soever your heart may be, your words, which are the index of the heart, are not so. For, if you think the matter of "Free-will" is not necessary to be known, nor at all concerned with Christ, you speak honestly, but think wickedly: but, if you think it is necessary, you speak wickedly, and think rightly. And if so, then there is no room for you to complain and exaggerate so much concerning useless assertions and contentions: for what have they to do with the nature of the cause?

Erasmus's Scepticism

Section II.—BUT what will you say to these your declarations, when, be it remembered, they are not confined to "Free-will" only, but apply to all doctrines in general throughout the world—that, "if it were permitted you, by the inviolable authority of the sacred Writings and decrees of the church, you would go over to the sentiments of the Sceptics?"—

What an all-changeable Proteus[2] is there in these expressions, "inviolable authority" and "decrees of the church!" As though you could have so very great a reverence for the Scriptures and the church, when at the same time you signify, that you wish you had the liberty of being a Sceptic! What Christian would talk in this way? But if you say this in reference to useless and doubtful doctrines, what news is there in what you say? Who, in such things, would not wish for the liberty of the sceptical profession? Nay, what Christian is there who does not actually use this liberty freely, and condemn all those who are drawn away with, and captivated by every opinion? Unless you consider all Christians to be such (as the term

1. Ed. Note: Anticyra was a Greek port "known for hellebore (a medicinal plant)"; cf. *OCD* 104 [*Oxford Classical Dictionary*, ed. S. Hornblower and A. Spawforth; 3rd ed. (Oxford, 1996)].
2. Ed. Note: Proteus is "a minor sea-god" who "takes on various shapes . . . to escape"; cf. *OCD* 1265.

5

is generally understood) whose doctrines are useless, and for which they quarrel like fools, and contend by assertions. But if you speak of necessary things, what declaration more impious can any one make, than that he wishes for the liberty of asserting nothing in such matters? Whereas, the Christian will rather say this—I am so averse to the sentiments of the Sceptics, that wherever I am not hindered by the infirmity of the flesh, I will not only steadily adhere to the Sacred Writings every where, and in all parts of them, and assert them, but I wish also to be as certain as possible in things that are not necessary, and that lie without the Scripture: for what is more miserable than uncertainty.

What shall we say to these things also, where you add, "To which authorities I submit my opinion in all things; whether I follow what they enjoin, or follow it not."

What say you, Erasmus? Is it not enough that you submit your opinion to the Scriptures? Do you submit it to the decrees of the church also? What can the church decree, that is not decreed in the Scriptures? If it can, where then remains the liberty and power of judging those who make the decrees? As Paul teaches, "Let others judge" (1 Cor. 14:29). Are you not pleased that there should be any one to judge the decrees of the church, which, nevertheless, Paul enjoins? What new kind of religion and humility is this, that, by our own example, you would take away from us the power of judging the decrees of men, and give it unto men without judgment? Where does the Scripture of God command us to do this?

Moreover, what Christian would so commit the injunctions of the Scripture and of the church to the winds, as to say "whether I follow them, or follow them not?" You submit yourself, and yet care not at all whether you follow them or not. But let that Christian be anathema, who is not certain in, and does not follow, that which is enjoined him. For how will he believe that which he does not follow? Do you here, then, mean to say, that following is understanding a thing certainly, and not doubting of it at all in a sceptical manner? If you do, what is there in any creature which any one can follow, if following be understanding, and seeing and knowing perfectly? And if this be the case, then it is impossible that any one should, at the same time, follow some things, and not follow others: whereas, by following one certain thing, God, he follows all things; that is, in Him, whom whoso followeth not, never followeth any part of His creature.

In a word, these declarations of yours amount to this: that, with you, it matters not what is believed by any one, any where, if the peace of the world be but undisturbed; and if every one be but allowed, when his life, his reputation, or his interest is at stake, to do as he did, who said, "If they affirm, I affirm, if they deny, I deny" [Terence, *Eunuchus*, 2.252 (Loeb, 1.339)]: and to look upon the Christian doctrines as nothing better than the opinions of philosophers and men: and that it is the greatest of folly to quarrel about, contend for, and assert them, as nothing can arise therefrom but contention, and the disturbance of the public peace: "that what is above us, does not concern us." This, I say, is what your declarations amount to.—Thus, to put an end to our fightings, you come in as an intermediate peace-maker, that you may cause each side to suspend arms, and persuade us to cease from drawing swords about things so absurd and useless.

What I should cut at here, I believe, my friend Erasmus, you know very well. But, as I said before, I will not openly express myself. In the mean time, I excuse your very good intention of heart; but do you go no further; fear the Spirit of God, who searcheth the reins and the heart, and who is not deceived by artfully contrived expressions. I have, upon this occasion, expressed myself thus, that henceforth you may cease to accuse our cause of pertinacity or obstinacy. For, by so doing, you only evince that you hug in your heart a Lucian, or some other of the swinish tribe of the Epicureans; who, because he does not believe there is a God himself, secretly laughs at all those who do believe and confess it. Allow *us* to be assertors, and to study and delight in assertions: and do you favour your Sceptics and Academics until Christ shall have called you also. The Holy Spirit is not a Sceptic, nor are what He has written on our hearts doubts or opinions, but assertions more certain, and more firm, than life itself and all human experience.

[Of the perspicuity (clearness) of Scripture]

Section III.—Now I come to the next head, which is connected with this; where you make a "distinction between the Christian doctrines," and pretend that "some are necessary, and some not necessary." You say, that "some are abstruse, and some quite clear." Thus you merely sport the sayings of others, or else exercise yourself, as it were, in a rhetorical figure. And you bring forward, in support of this opinion, that passage of Paul, "O the depth of the riches both of the wisdom and goodness of God!" (Rom. 11:33). And also that of Isaiah 40:13, "Who hath holpen the Spirit of the Lord, or who hath been His counsellor?"

You could easily say these things, seeing that, you either knew not that you were writing to Luther, but for the world at large, or did not think that you were writing against Luther: whom, however, I hope you allow to have some acquaintance with, and judgment in, the Sacred Writings. But, if you do not allow it, then, behold, I will also twist things thus. This is the distinction which I make, that I also may act a little the rhetorician and logician— God, and the Scripture of God, are two things; no less so than God, and the Creature of God. That there are in God many hidden things which we know not, no one doubts: as He himself saith concerning the last day: "Of that day knoweth no man but the Father" (Matt. 24:36). And, "It is not yours to know the times and seasons" (Acts 1:7). And again, "I know whom I have chosen" (John 13:18). And Paul, "The Lord knoweth them that are His" (2 Tim. 2:19). And the like.

But, that there are in the Scriptures some things abstruse, and that all things are not quite plain, is a report spread abroad by the impious Sophists; by whose mouth you speak here, Erasmus. But they never have produced, nor ever can produce, one article whereby to prove this their madness. And it is with such scare-crows that Satan has frightened away men from reading the Sacred Writings, and has rendered the Holy Scripture contempt-ible, that he might cause his poisons of philosophy to prevail in the church. This indeed I confess, that there are many *places* in the Scriptures obscure and abstruse; not from the majesty of the things, but from our ignorance of certain terms and grammatical particulars; but which do not prevent a knowledge of all the *things* in the Scriptures. For what thing of more importance can remain hidden in the Scriptures, now that the seals are broken, the stone rolled from the door of the sepulchre, and that greatest of all mysteries brought to light, Christ made man: that God is Trinity and Unity: that Christ suffered for us, and will reign to all eternity? Are not these things known and proclaimed even in our streets? *Take Christ out of the Scriptures, and what will you find remaining in them?*

All the *things*, therefore, contained in the Scriptures, are made manifest, although some *places*, from the words not being understood, are yet obscure. But to know that all *things* in the Scriptures are set in the clearest light, and then, because a few words are obscure, to report that the things are obscure, is absurd and impious. *And, if the words are obscure in one place, yet they are clear in another.* But, however, the same *thing*, which has been most openly declared to the whole world, is both spoken of in the Scriptures in plain words, and also still lies hidden in obscure words. Now, therefore, it matters not if the *thing* be in the light, whether any certain representations of it be in obscurity or not, if, in the mean while, many other representations of the same thing be in the light. For who would say that the public fountain is not in the light, because those who are in some dark narrow lane do not see it, when all those who are in the open market place can see it plainly?

Section IV.—WHAT you adduce, therefore, about the darkness of the Corycian cavern,[3] amounts to nothing; matters are not so in the Scriptures. For those things which are of the greatest majesty, and the most abstruse mysteries, are no longer in the dark corner, but before the very doors, nay, brought forth and manifested openly. For Christ has opened our understanding to understand the Scriptures (Luke 24:45). And the Gospel is preached to every creature (Mark 16:15; Col. 1:23). "Their sound is gone out into all the earth" (Ps. 19:4). And "All things that are written, are written for our instruction" (Rom. 15:4). And again, "All Scripture is inspired from above, and is profitable for instruction" (2 Tim. 3:16).

Therefore come forward, you and all the Sophists together, and produce any one mystery which is still abstruse in the Scriptures. But, if many things still remain abstruse to many, this does not arise from obscurity in the Scriptures, but from their own blindness or want of understanding, who do not go the way to see the all-perfect clearness of the truth. As Paul saith concerning the Jews, "The veil still remains upon their heart" (2 Cor. 3:15). And again, "If our gospel be hid it is hid to them that are lost, whose heart the god of this world hath blinded" (2 Cor. 4:3–4). With the same rashness any one may cover his own eyes, or go from the light into the dark and hide himself, and then blame the day and the sun for being obscure. Let, therefore, wretched men cease to impute, with blasphemous perverseness, the darkness and obscurity of their own heart to the all-clear Scriptures of God.

You, therefore, when you adduce Paul, saying, "His judgments are incomprehensible," seem to make the pronoun *His* (*ejus*) refer to Scripture (*Scriptura*). Whereas Paul does not say, The judgments of the Scripture are incomprehensible, but the judgments of God. So also Isaiah 40:13, does not say, Who has known the mind of the Scripture, but, who has known "the mind of the Lord?" Although Paul asserts that the mind of the Lord is known to Christians: but it is in those things which are freely given unto us: as he saith also in the same place (1 Cor. 2:10, 16). You see, therefore, how sleepily you have looked over these places of the Scripture: and you cite them just as aptly as you cite nearly all the passages in defence of "Free-will."

In like manner, your examples which you subjoin, not without suspicion and bitterness, are nothing at all to the purpose. Such are those concerning the distinction of Persons: the union of the Divine and human natures: the unpardonable sin: the ambiguity attached to which, you say, has never been cleared up. If you mean the questions of Sophists that have been agitated upon those subjects, well. But what has the all-innocent Scripture done to you, that you impute the abuse of the most wicked of men to its purity? The Scripture simply confesses the Trinity of God, the humanity of Christ, and the unpardonable sin. There is

---

3. Ed. Note: The Corycian cavern was situated at Delphi; cf. *OCD,* 305. Luther contrasts here the clarity of Scripture and the mystery of the Delphic oracles.

nothing here of obscurity or ambiguity. But *how* these things are the Scripture does not say, nor is it necessary to be known. The Sophists employ their dreams here; attack and condemn them, and acquit the Scripture. But, if you mean the reality of the matter, I say again, attack not the Scriptures, but the Arians, and those to whom the Gospel is hid, that, through the working of Satan, they might not see the all-manifest testimonies concerning the Trinity of the Godhead, and the humanity of Christ.

But to be brief. The *clearnesss* [or perspicuity, *claritas*] of the Scripture is twofold; even as the *obscurity* is twofold also. The one is *external*, placed in the ministry of the word; the other *internal*, placed in the understanding of the heart. If you speak of the internal clearness, no man sees one iota in the Scriptures, but he that hath the Spirit of God. All have a darkened heart; so that, even if they know how to speak of, and set forth, all things in the Scripture, yet, they cannot feel them, nor know them: nor do they believe that they are the creatures of God, nor any thing else: according to that of Psalm 14:1, "The fool hath said in his heart, God is nothing." For the Spirit is required to understand the whole of the Scripture and every part of it. If you speak of the external clearness, nothing whatever is left obscure or ambiguous; but all things that are in the Scriptures, are by the Word brought forth into the clearest light, and proclaimed to the whole world.

The First Zurich Disputation

ULRICH ZWINGLI

The text and notes reproduced here are taken from Ulrich Zwingli, *Ulrich Zwingli (1484–1531): Selected Works*, trans. Lawrence A. McLouth (1901; repr., Philadelphia: University of Pennsylvania Press, 1972), 38–110.

Ulrich Zwingli (1484–1531), the leader of the Reformation in Zurich, was born shortly after Luther. Zwingli's education was more humanistic than Luther's. Zwingli, like Luther, began to work for reform within the church because of his growing conviction that Scripture is the church's sole authority. Zwingli came to Reformed convictions largely independently from Luther; his new understanding resulted in more radical reform. One of his early works, entitled *Of the Clarity and Certainty of God's Word* (1522), champions both *sola Scriptura* and the perspicuity of Scripture. Zwingli's insistence on *sola Scriptura* led him to return to the patristic practice of *lectio continua* preaching, or preaching verse by verse—a departure from church tradition in his day. Zwingli's theological insights established the beginnings of the Reformed tradition as it stands in distinction to Lutheranism.

In the first Zurich Disputation (1523), whose text we reproduce here, Zwingli applies the normative principle of *sola Scriptura* to the issues discussed in the debate over the new practices in the church in Zurich. Given that this document is somewhat difficult to access, we reproduce it in its entirety. This text is an early and important document showing the development of Reformed theology in the context of Roman Catholic traditional opposition. The text is in the form of a dialogue chiefly between Zwingli and the vicar of Constance. Zwingli's concern is to establish doctrine based on the Word, while the vicar is reluctant even to argue and wants a church's court to decide. The Sixty-seven Articles prepared by Zwingli for this debate are reproduced in chapter 5 of this volume.

Bibliography: G. W. Bromiley. "Zwingli, Ulrich (1484–1531)." Pp. 736–38 in *NDT*. Martin I. Klauber. "Zwingli, Ulrich (1484–1531)." Pp. 576–77 in *DHT*. A. N. S. Lane. "Zwingli, Ulrich (or Huldrych) (1484–1531)." Pp. 761–63 in *BDE*. M. A. Noll. "Zwingli, Ulrich." Pp. 1203–4 in *EDT*. Heiko A. Oberman. *Masters of the Reformation: The Emergence of a New Intellectual Climate in Europe*. New York: Cambridge University Press, 1981. Pp. 190–98, 210–39. Schaff. *The Creeds of Christendom* 1:360–84. W. Peter Stephens. *The Theology of Huldrych Zwingli*. Oxford: Clarendon Press, 1998. Idem. "8. The Theology of Zwingli."

Pp. 80–99 in *The Cambridge Companion to Reformation Theology*. Robert C. Walton. "Zwingli, Ulrich (Huldrych) (1484–1531)." Pp. 1073–74 in *NIDCC*. "Zwingli, Huldreich." *NSHERK* 12:538–46.

Acts of the Convention Held in the Praiseworthy City of Zurich on the 29th Day of January, On Account of the Holy Gospel—Being a Disputation Between the Dignified and Honorable Representative from Constance and Huldrych Zwingli, Preacher of the Gospel of Christ, Together with the Common Clergy of the Whole Territory of the Aforesaid City of Zurich, Held Before the Assembled Council in the Year 1523.[1]

To the worthy ecclesiastical Lord and Father Sir John Jacob Russinger,[2] Abbot at Pfäbers, to His gracious Lord Chamberlain Master Erhart Hegenwald[3] offers his willing service and wishes peace in Christ.

1. *Works*, 1:114–168. Translated from the Zurich German by Lawrence A. McLouth, Professor of German, New York University. The matter between brackets is that given in the *Works*, 1.158ff., as addenda, but here inserted in proper place.

The Protestant Reformation in German Switzerland, as for the most part in Germany and England, was largely dependent upon the good will of princes and other rulers, who joined it for political ends. No one can gainsay the great advantage of their support. So in Zurich Zwingli endeavored to win over to his side the members of the City Council, rightly arguing that if successful he would be able to preach the Reformation through the canton, no matter what might be the opposition. He made his appeal to the magistracy to be allowed to hold a public debate, at which they should sit as judges, and give the victory to that side which presented the stronger arguments. He looked forward with great confidence to such a public debate, for which he had prepared the way by his preaching and writing and talking ever since he came to Zurich in December, 1518. The City Council took up the idea, and were perhaps flattered by the position they would take in this debate. They issued the invitations to the people of the canton and city of Zurich and to the bishops of Constance and of the adjoining dioceses. Zwingli prepared and had printed 67 Articles as a programme for the debate, and looked forward with great eagerness to the time set, which was the 23rd of January, 1523.

On that eventful day six hundred persons—priests and laymen of the canton of Zurich, along with a few delegates from the bishop of Constance and some others—met in the Town Hall and held the debate, which is preserved to us by Erhart Hegenwald, a schoolmaster in Zurich, who informs us that he wrote it from memory immediately after hearing it. His account was edited by Zwingli and published in Zurich. John Faber (or Fabri), Vicar General of the diocese of Constance, one of the ablest disputants on the Roman Church side, bore the brunt of the attacks upon that church. Zwingli was the principal speaker on the other side. Fabri also published his account of the debate. "Ein warlich underrichtung wie es zie Zürich bey de Zwinglin uff den einen und zwentzigsten tag des monats Januarii rest verschine ergangen sey" (Leipzig? 1523). In it, naturally, he appeared to greater advantage than in Zwingli's account, but it seems to have given offence to an enthusiastic portion of the audience, and some of these young men thought they had a good opportunity to bring out a satire in the interests of the new faith, and so they concocted a book which was called "The Vulture Plucked." "Das gyren rupffen. Nalt inn wie Johann Schmidt Vicarge ze Costentz mit dem büchle darinn er verheiszt ein ware bericht wie es uff den 29 tag Jenner M.D.xxiii. ze Zürich gangen sye sich übersehe hat. Ist voll schimpff unud ernestes." This was a gross attack upon Fabri, and he was very indignant and appealed to the city authorities of Zurich to bring the offenders to book, but the city authorities regarded the whole affair as a kind of joke and took no action in the matter. The three accounts of this important debate supplemented one another; the one which may be said to be authentic is here translated, the second is somewhat colored in favor of the Roman Church, and the third, which contains a good deal of truth, along with more or less deliberate falsehood, have been properly drawn upon by the editors of Zwingli's works, and the corrections and additions they have made from the last two accounts are here incorporated.

The result of the debate was the enthusiastic approval of Zwingli's teachings, and an order from the authorities not only to continue their presentation, but enjoining such teaching upon all the priests of the canton. Thus this debate, which is known as the First Disputation, is of great historical interest as marking the official beginning of the Reformation in German Switzerland.

2. He was one of Zwingli's friends and correspondents, and active in the cause of the Reformation, but returned to the Roman Church after Zwingli's death.

3. He was a school teacher in Zurich.

Worthy ecclesiastical Lord and Father: I understand how your dignity and grace is inclined to read and further the Gospel doctrine and truth of God from Christian feeling, which fact I conclude among other things from the following: That Your Grace undertook to come to the meeting upon the day appointed by the burgomaster and the Council of the city of Zurich concerning the dissension and trouble which had arisen in the city on account of doctrines or sermons, but from business reasons and other accidental causes you were detained and hindered from attending. And although in addition to all the clergymen, preachers and priests that have livings in the city of Zurich and its territories there were invited and summoned to this praiseworthy meeting also many other foreign nobility and common people, prelates, doctors, masters, both secular and ecclesiastical lords, likewise the praiseworthy representative from Constance, when these had appeared at Zurich before the Council in session certain enemies of the Gospel truth (as I hear) ridiculed the matter, announcing and saying that a tinker's day was being held at Zurich, and that nothing but tinkers were attending. These things have influenced and caused me to describe all the actions, speeches either for or against, which took place in such praiseworthy assembly of learned, honest and pious men, both ecclesiastical and secular, so that every one might see and know whether such action taken and speeches made were by tinkers and pan-menders, also whether the opposing party (which has asserted that the matter is known abroad) tells the truth or lies. For I was there myself and sat with them, heard and understood and remembered all that was said there, and after that I wrote it down in my home, questioned and examined others who had been present at the meeting as to the cases in which I thought I might not have understood correctly. With the true knowledge and witness of all those who were there and took part, about six hundred or more, I may assert that I have written down not more nor less nor different words (as far as the content is concerned) than were spoken in the assembly. I write and send this to Your Grace, and beg Your Grace to accept it with good will and favor as a service. I also urge as a fellow brother in Christ Your Grace to remain in the future as in the past steadfastly by the Gospel truth, to practice and read industriously in the Gospel and Saint Paul and other Holy Scriptures as Your Grace has the reputation of doing, also to live in Christian conformity with the same according to your full power; to send such reports of action at Zurich to the others who are related to Your Grace in friendship or otherwise in Christian society, as for instance, the worthy and ecclesiastical Lord, etc., Abbot at Disentis,[4] to be read, so that the truth may be known, the Gospel advanced, Christian love increased, men fed with the word of God, our will and spirit may remain united with Christ through His word in peace, joy and harmony here for the time being and there forever. Amen.

Given in the praiseworthy city of Zurich the 3rd day of the month of March, in the year 1523.

In order that every one may understand the matter better I have prefixed and written down the mandate of those of Zurich, which mandate was sent out into all the territory and dependencies of the city beforehand as an argument as to the causes for the above-mentioned meeting:

We, the burgomaster, the Council and the Great Council, which they call the two hundred of the city of Zurich, announce to each and every priest, preacher, minister and clergyman

---

4. Andreas von Valara, who had been abbot since 1512.

who has a living and residence in our cities, counties, principalities, high and low courts and territories, our greeting, favorable and affectionate will, and would have you know that now for considerable time much dissension and trouble have arisen between those who preach from the pulpit the word of God to the common people, some believing that they have preached the Gospel faithfully and wholly, whereas others blame them as though they had not acted skillfully or properly. On the other hand the others call them sources of evil, deceivers and sometimes heretics; but to each one desiring it these offer to give account and reckoning about this everywhere with the aid of God's Scriptures to the best of their ability for the sake of the honor of God, peace and Christian unity. So this is our command, will and desire, that you preachers, priests, clergymen, all together and each one separately, if any especial priests desire to speak about this, having livings in our city of Zurich or outside in our territories, or if any desire to blame the opposing party or to instruct them otherwise, shall appear on the day after Emperor Charles' Day, the 29th day of the month of January, at the early time of the Council, in our city of Zurich, before us in our town hall, and shall announce in German, by the help of true divine Scripture, the matters which you oppose. When we, with the careful assistance of certain scholars, have paid careful attention to the matters, as seems best to us, and after investigations are made with the help of the Holy Scriptures and the truth, we will send each one home with a command either to continue or to desist. After this no one shall continue to preach from the pulpit whatever seems good to him without foundation in the divine Scriptures. We shall also report such matters to our gracious Lord of Constance, so that His Grace or His representative, if He so desire, may also be present. But if any one in the future opposes this, and does not base his opposition upon the true Holy Scriptures, with him we shall proceed further according to our knowledge in a way from which we would gladly be relieved. We also sincerely hope that God Almighty will give gracious light to those who earnestly seek the light of truth, and that we may in the future walk in that light as sons of the light.

Given and preserved under the imprinted seal of the city on Saturday after the Circumcision of Christ and after his birth in the twenty-third year of the lesser reckoning [Jan. 3, 1522].

Now when all of the priests, ministers and clergymen in the territories of Zurich obediently appeared at the hour and time announced there were in the Great Council room at Zurich more than six hundred assembled, counting the local and foreign representatives, together with the praiseworthy representation from Constance, to which an invitation to the same had been sent from Zurich, and when everybody had found a seat at the early time of the Council the burgomaster of Zurich began to speak as follows:

Very learned, noble, steadfast, honorable, wise, ecclesiastical Lords and Friends: For some time in my Lords' city of Zurich and her territories dissensions and quarrels have arisen on account of certain sermons and teachings delivered to the people from the pulpit by Master Ulrich Zwingli, our preacher here at Zurich, wherefore he has been attacked and blamed as a deceiver by some and by others as a heretic. Wherefore it has come about that not only in our city of Zurich, but also everywhere else in the land in my Lords' territories such dissensions have increased among the clergy, and also the laity, that daily complaints of the same come before my Lords, and the angry words and quarreling do not seem likely to come to an end. And so Master Ulrich Zwingli has frequently offered to give the causes and reasons for his sermons and doctrines preached here in the public pulpit so often in Zurich in case a public discussion before all the clergy and the laity were granted him. At this offer of Master Ulrich the honorable Council at Zurich, desiring to stop the disturbance and dissension, has granted

13

him permission to hold a public discussion in the German language before the Great Council at Zurich, which they call the two hundred, to which the honorable and wise Council has summoned all of you priests and ministers from her territories. It also requested the worthy Lord and Prince, etc., Bishop of Constance, to send his representative to this meeting, for which favor the honorable Council of Zurich expresses especial thanks to him. Therefore if there is any one here who may feel any displeasure or doubt in Master Ulrich's sermons or doctrines preached here at Zurich in the pulpit, or if any one desires to say anything or knows anything to say in the matter to the effect that such sermons and teachings are not true, but misleading or heretical, he can prove the truth of the same before my Lords, the often mentioned Master Ulrich, and show him at once his error by means of the Scriptures, and he shall be free and safe and with perfect immunity, so that my Lords may in the future be relieved of the daily complaints which arise from such dissension and quarrels. For my Lords have become weary of such complaints, which have been increasing gradually from both clergy and laity.

At these remarks and invitation Sir Fritz von Anwyl,[5] knight, and Chamberlain of the Bishop of Constance, made answer, and spoke as follows:

Very learned, worthy, noble, provident, wise, etc. The worthy Lord and Prince, Sir Hugo,[6] by grace of God Bishop of Constance, my gracious Lord, well knows and is for the most part well informed that now everywhere in his Grace's bishopric many quarrels and dissensions of many kinds with regard to doctrines or sermons have arisen in almost every place. And although his Grace has ever been of the desire and feeling, and always will be if God will, to show himself always gracious, kind and willing in all those things which can further peace and harmony, still his Grace at the especial request and petition of the wise and honorable Council of Zurich has ordered your accredited representatives here present, the worthy Lords, Sir Doctor Vergenhans, canon, his Grace's Vicar,[7] Sir Doctor Martin,[8] of Tübingen, together with myself, his Grace's servant, to listen to and to hear such causes of dissension. He has recommended us to act in such matters not otherwise than kindly, to say the best that we can in the matter, so that it result in the honor, peace and harmony for the honorable Council of Zurich, likewise the worthy clergy. Wherefore, learned, worthy, honorable, wise Lords and good friends, I say: If there is any one here present who desires to make any remonstrance or accusation on account of the doctrines or sermons that have been delivered here, we shall, according to the commands of my gracious Lord of Constance, as his Grace's representatives, listen gladly and willingly, and for the sake of peace and harmony, as far as in us lies, shall help to judge the dissension, if such has arisen or shall arise, in order that a worthy clergy may remain in peace and friendship until my gracious Lord and Prince, together with his Grace's scholars and prelates, shall further discuss and consider these matters. That was the sum of his whole discourse.

Then Master Ulrich Zwingli spoke in answer, and his remarks in the beginning were as follows:

Pious brothers in Christ, Almighty God has always shown His divine grace, will and favor to man from the beginning of the world, has been as kind as a true and almighty

---

5. He later went over to the Reformed Church.

6. Von Hohenlandenberg, died 1532.

7. Johannes Heigerlin, commonly called Faber or Fabri, because his father was a smith. He became successively pastor at Lindau, vicar-general of Constance (1516) and bishop of Vienna (1530). Born at Lentkirch, near Lake Constance, in 1478, he died at Baden, near Vienna, May 21, 1541.

8. Blansch. He wrote later at Constance against the Reformed preachers.

father, as we read and know from all the Scriptures, so that everlasting, merciful God has communicated His divine word and His will to man as a consolation. And although at some times He has kept away this same word, the light of truth, from the sinful and godless struggling against the truth, and although He has allowed to fall into error those men who followed their own will and the leadings of their wicked nature, as we are truly informed in all Bible histories, still He has always in turn consoled His own people with the light of His everlasting word, so that, whereas they had fallen into sin and error, they may again be lifted by His divine mercy, and He has never entirely forsaken them or let them depart from His divine recognition. This I say to you, dear brethren, for this purpose. You know that now in our time, as also many years heretofore, the pure, clear and bright light, the word of God, has been so dimmed and confused and paled with human ambitions and teachings that the majority who by word of mouth call themselves Christians know nothing less than the divine will. But by their own invented service of God, holiness, external spiritual exhibition, founded upon human customs and laws, they have gone astray, and have thus been persuaded by those whom people consider learned and leaders of others to the extent that the simple think that such invented external worship is spiritual, and that the worship of God, which they have put upon themselves, necessarily conduces to happiness, although all our true happiness, consolation and good consists, not in our merits, nor in such external works, rather alone in Jesus Christ our Saviour, to whom the heavenly Father Himself gave witness that we should hear Him as His beloved Son. His will and true service we can learn and discover only from His true word in the Holy Scriptures and in the trustworthy writings of His twelve apostles, otherwise from no human laws and statutes. Since now certain pious hearts have ventured to preach this by the grace and inspiration of God's Holy Spirit, and to bring it before the people, they call these preachers not Christians, but persecutors of the Christian Church, and even heretics. I am considered one of these by many of the clergy and the laity everywhere in the Confederation. And although I know that for the past five years I have preached in this city of Zurich nothing but the true, pure and clear word of God, the holy Gospel, the joyous message of Christ, the Holy Scripture, not by the aid of man, but by the aid of the Holy Ghost, still all this did not help me. But I am maligned by many as a heretic, a liar, a deceiver, and one disobedient to the Christian Church, which facts are well known to my Lords of Zurich, I made complaint of these things before them as my Lords; I have often entreated and begged of them in the public pulpit to grant me permission to give an account of my sermons and preachings (delivered in their city) before all men, learned or not, spiritual or secular, also before our gracious Lord, the Bishop of Constance, or his representative. This I also offered to do in the city of Constance, providing a safe permit was assured me, as has ever been done in the case of those from Constance. At such request of mine, my Lords, perhaps by divine will, you have granted me permission to hold a discussion in German before the assembled Council, for which privilege I thank you especially as my Lords. I have also brought together in outline the contents and import of all my speeches and sermons delivered at Zurich, have issued the same in German through the press, so that every one might see and know what my doctrine and sermons at Zurich have been, and shall be in the future, unless I am convinced of something else.[9] I hope and am confident, indeed I know, that my sermons and doctrine are nothing else than the holy,

9. This refers to the 67 Articles he issued preparatory to the Disputation.

true, pure Gospel, which God desired me to speak by the intuition and inspiration of His Spirit. But from what intent or desire God has wished such things to take place through me, His unworthy servant, I cannot know, for He alone knows and understands the secret of His counsels. Wherefore I offer here to any one who thinks that my sermons or teachings are unchristian or heretical to give the reasons and to answer kindly and without anger. Now let them speak in the name of God. Here I am.

At such remarks of Master Ulrich the Vicar[10] from Constance arose, and answered as follows:

Learned, worthy, noble, steadfast, favorable, wise, etc. My good fellow-brother and Lord, Master Ulrich, begins and complains that he has always preached the holy Gospel here publicly in Zurich, of which I have no doubt, for who would not truly and faithfully preach the holy Gospel and Saint Paul, providing God had ordained him as a preacher? For I am also a preacher, or priest, perhaps unworthy, but I have taught those entrusted to me for instruction in the word of God in nothing but the true Gospel, which I can also prove with true witness. And I shall for the future not in any way cease to preach this, providing God does not require me for other labors in the service of my gracious Lord of Constance. For the holy Gospel is a power of God, as Saint Paul writes to the Romans (Rom. 1:16), to each one who believes therein.

But now that Master Ulrich begins and complains that certain people blame him as not having spoken and preached the truth, but offers and has offered to answer for his speeches and sermons to any one, also (even) in Constance, I say, dear Lords, that if Master Ulrich, my good Lord and friend, should come to me in Constance I would show him as my good friend and Lord all friendship and honor as far as lay in my power, and if he so desires would also entertain him in my house, not only as a good friend, but also as a brother. Of this he is assured at my hands. Further, I say that I did not come here to oppose evangelical or apostolical doctrines, but to hear those who are said to speak or to have spoken against the doctrine of the holy Gospel, and if any dissension should arise or should have arisen to help to judge and to decide the matter in kindness, as far as may be, to the end of peace and harmony rather than disturbance (discord). For the Gospel and the divine Paul teach only what serves to grace and peace, not to disturbance and strife.[11] But if there is a desire to dispute and oppose good old customs, the ways and usages of the past, then in such case I say that I shall not undertake to dispute anything here at Zurich. For, as I think, such matters are to be settled by a general Christian assembly of all nations, or by a council of bishops and other scholars as are found at universities, just as occurred in times past among the holy apostles in Jerusalem, as we read in Acts 15. For if such matters touching the common customs and the praiseworthy usages of the past were discussed, and some decision reached against them, such changes would perhaps not please other Christians dwelling in other places, who would

10. That is the vicar-general.

11. ["You well understood how Zwingli spoke about peace and strife; and the words he spoke you refer to yourself. Zwingli spoke not about the strife of weapons or the discord of the faithful. For you know well that he said: 'God be thanked that the pious city of Zurich is so inclined to peace, and knows well that this comes from the word of God alone, which they hear and accept so faithfully.' But I say that the Gospel commands strife between the faithful and the Godless. Do you not know how Christ says in the Gospel of Matthew 10:34, 'I am not come,' etc.? How can it be preached in peace? Indeed, if the whole world were believers it might be; otherwise not. For Christ is the stumbling-block, at which many will be offended; these are of the world, and the devil is their Lord, who will undertake to maintain his empire without ceasing with his own?" (Hans Hager in "Gyrenrupfen.")]

16

doubtless assert that they had not consented to our views. For what would those in Spain, in Italy, in France and in the North say about it? Such things must surely, as I said, be ratified and maintained as formerly, by a general council, in order to be valid elsewhere. Therefore, dear lords, I speak now for myself. As a Christian member and brother in Christ I beg and urge you to consider these things well, lest hereafter further and greater strife and harm may result. Accordingly it would be my sincere advice to drop any difference or dissension that may have arisen concerning papal or other ecclesiastical ordinances (*constitutions*) of long standing, and without further disputing to lay aside and postpone them, to see if they could not be arranged meantime more peacefully and advantageously. For my gracious Lord of Constance is informed that it is decided at Nuremberg by the estates (*Ständen*) of the empire to hold a general council of the German nation within a year, in which I hear half the judges selected are secular and the other half ecclesiastical, and they are to judge and decide about the things which are now disturbing nearly all the world. If such takes place these matters should be referred to them as having the authority and power. And so it is the earnest desire of my Lord, as far as possible, to have such differences about the clergy settled without dispute for the good of yourselves and all (other) Christians. For though these old ordinances, laws and customs should be discussed *pro* and *con* upon scriptural basis, who would be judge of these matters? According to my opinion whatever such things one would discuss should be brought before the universities, as at Paris, Cologne or Louvain. (Here all laughed, for Zwingli interrupted by asking: "How about Erfurt? Would not Wittenberg do?" Then the legate said: "No; Luther was too near." He also said: "All bad things come from the North.") There one can find many taught in the Scriptures, who have ability to handle so great subjects. In this remark I do not wish to be taken as speaking to the discredit of any one's honor or knowledge, but as a Christian member, and with entire good nature I announce this. But as far as my office and commission are concerned, I have been sent here, as I said before, for no other purpose than to listen, and not to dispute.[12]

12. ["You have left out the right sense, namely, that everything should be written down. Now speak and give answer if we did not dispute fore and afternoon about a judge, when Master Ulrich Zwingli declared that he would not suffer any one as judge except all Christian believers. Have you not ears and heard that I have often referred to this opinion; always at times when heretics arose a council was held, and by its means the heretics had been thus subdued? Hereupon I named Arius, Sabellius, Nestorius, Manichee and many others; and what was thus recognized thereby it should remain. For if this were not done and held (have you not heard that I said?), there would be as many beliefs as there are many countries, yea as many as there are cities, villages, estates, houses and people, if one does come with matters pertaining to the interpretation of the Scriptures before the councils. I have further shown that in recent years in such matters as have arisen thus between scholars, and always in times of misunderstanding in regard to the Scripture, the universities have been chosen as judges. But when one of you spoke, his words were considered as flowing from the Spirit of God, as if into you alone the Spirit of God enters (as Saint Paul writes), and you alone were the wine-rooms of Jove, and all secrets of the empire of God were made known in them; but what the holy Fathers spoke, wrote and ordained, and also the speeches of us, the ambassadors, were to be considered as human nonsense, as I have related at length. Saint Paul himself awaited and received from the apostles a letter (Acts 15), in which they wrote: 'For it seemed good to the Holy Ghost and us,' etc., and yet he was ordained by God as magister, as 'magister gentium [teacher of the nations]' [2 Tim. 1:11]. Hence the worthy Master Ulrich Zwingli should justly also await and accept decision and judgment. This was said by me more than once before noon, but never before noon answered by the worthy Master Ulrich. To be sure, after noon he did say a little, but did not better the matter, but as far as he was concerned (as I understood it) made it worse (Faber).

"Hereupon Hans Hab, according to 'Gyrenrupfen,' answered: 'It may be that Zwingli forgot to answer in the forenoon; what does that matter? Who would have cared to answer your lengthy nonsense? But didn't he answer it after dinner? Hence let us sit in judgment upon the 15th chapter of the Acts, then we shall find it is against you, and not for you. You have spoken in this manner, we will now let it be, and as often as one wished to consider the books you have gotten out of it in another fashion.' Faber continues: 'In his little book about the choice of food Zwingli has permitted all food, and still it is found in the letter which Paul received at Jerusalem from the twelve apostles that the sacrifice of calves and other meat

Then Master Ulrich Zwingli spoke as follows: Pious brothers in Christ, the worthy Lord Vicar seeks so many evasions and subterfuges for the purpose of turning your simplicity from your understanding with artful, rhetorical, evasive words.[13] For he claims and says that he does not desire to discuss the good old customs or venerable usages concerning ecclesiastical ordinances, but I say that we do not want to ask here how long this or that custom or habit has been in use. But we desire to speak of the truth (to find out), whether a man is bound by divine ordinance to keep that which on account of long usage has been set up as law by men. For we of course think (as also the pope's own decree says) that custom should yield to truth. As to claiming that such matters should be settled by a Christian assembly of all nations, or by a council of bishops, etc., I say that here in this room is without doubt a Christian assembly.[14] For I hope that the majority of us here desire from divine will and love to hear, to further and to know the truth, which wish Almighty God will not deny us if we desire it to His honor with right belief and right hearts. For the Lord says: "Where two or three are gathered together in my name, I am there among them" [Matt. 18:20]. Also in times past did not bishops assemble in councils as secular princes? How then are we to claim and say that the pious fathers of past times assembled for Christian business? Were there not doubtless such powerful prelates and bishops as now, as they say there must be? This is truthfully proved by the testimony of trustworthy writings of old. And this is proved also by the word "Episcopus," which when properly turned into German means no more than a watchman or overseer who has the care and attention of his people, and who is also charged with instructing them in the divine belief and will; in good German this is a clergyman (Pfarrer). Since now here in this assembly there are so many honest, pious, Christian men, not alone living within the territories of my Lords of Zurich, but also coming from elsewhere, and also many learned, Godfearing bishops and clergymen, who sit here without doubt to further the truth of God and to hear and to know the divine truth, there is then, in spite of what the Vicar says, no reason why they should not discuss these matters, speak and decide the truth. To the remark that the other nations would not consent, I answer that this is just the complaint which is made every day concerning the "big moguls" (*grossen Hansen*, literally "big Jacks"), bishops and priests, that they undertake to keep the pure and clear Gospel, the Holy Scriptures, from the common people. For they say that it is not proper for any but themselves to expound the Scriptures, just as though other pious men were not Christians and had nothing to do with the spirit of God, and must be without knowl-

---

which was offered to the idols was forbidden. He thinks that this ordinance has expired if there is no more heathenism or idolatry, which I did not answer for good reason. But see whether there be not in Africa still idolatry, and Christians still live among them in the newly-discovered islands,' etc. Hereupon Hab (ibid.) again: 'Do you not remember that Zwingli said Paul himself did not keep it? Why don't you look at the Scriptures with him?' Faber continues: 'Not I, but Mr. Fritz von Anwyl, reported concerning this at the council of Nuremberg. For that I refer to him and your lords of Zurich. But if nevertheless I have said it, then see whether Master Ulrich or I had better information from Nuremberg—look at the decree of Nuremberg. But the new teachers and evangelists from the North do not wish any weight to be given to past or future decrees or councils unless they favor them. But they do rightly; they know that their doctrine would be condemned before even half of the fathers had gathered—they cannot endure the councils. Their song must not only be the song of the angels, but of God, and whatever the pious fathers say only human foolishness' (Faber, correction). How often have you heard from Zwingli that he did not wish to have only two judges, but to have all believers judge whether you or he is corrupting the Scriptures. But you were unable to come to this" ("Gyrenrupfen").]

13. ["Have you not heard that Zwingli said there was too much of my talk, and I thereupon offered to prove my statements if all things were noted down, for I do not care to speak into the air?" (Faber).]

14. ["In which there are many Godfearing curates; also many doctors and real friends of God" (Bullinger).]

edge of God's word. And there are also some of them who might say that it is improper to publish the secrets of the divine Scriptures.[15] For there is no doubt in my mind that if the pure truth of Christ alone, not adulterated with human ordinances, were preached to the above-mentioned peoples or nations, and not covered up with papal and imperial mandates and those of bishops, they would as pious Christian hearts accept the truth and let the customs or ordinances (*constitutions*) of men go, and enlightened by God's word, would be in harmony and agreement with the others. However, as to the council which is said to be announced at Nuremberg, it seems to me that the thing is proposed only to put off the common people desirous of God's word. For I tell you, dear Lords, that letters came to me about three days ago from Nuremberg,[16] which I could show if necessary, in which there was, to be sure, some mention made of a council, but I do not understand that anything has really been decided. For pope, bishops, prelates and the "big moguls" will allow no council in which the divine Scriptures were set forth in their clearness and purity. It is also plain that nothing will come of it this year, however much the common Christian earnestly did toward it, because sufficient supplies could not be collected in so short a time for so large an assembly. I concede also that a council will be announced in time. But meanwhile how are we to treat those whose consciences have gone astray so far as to desire eagerly to know the truth? Would you rob these thirsty souls of the truth, let them hang in doubt, frighten them by human ordinances, and let them live or die in uncertainty as to the truth? Really, my pious brethren, this is no small thing. God will not demand of us what pope, bishop and council establish and command, nor how long this or that has been in praiseworthy and ancient usage, but He will find out how His divine will, word and commandments have been kept.[17]

Now finally, since reference is made to the judges which my Lord Vicar thinks cannot be found outside the universities, I say that we have here infallible and unprejudiced judges, that is the Holy Writ, which can neither lie nor deceive. These we have present in Hebrew, Greek and Latin tongues; these let us take on both sides as fair and just judges.[18]

15. ["I did not write a book 'de non revelandis mysteriis,' but against the rash, against those who in an impious manner handle holy things or Scriptures" (Faber).]

16. These letters are no longer extant.

17. [Hager in "Gyrenrupfen" presents the dispute about the council thus: "After this Mr. Fritz, the majordomo, very cleverly presented the command of his master, saying that his master had been surely informed, that in a year there would be a council. Concerning this Zwingli did not wish to speak. Thereupon you immediately began to speak, and rose and said the same as Mr. Fritz had just said, and in a nice way referred to the future council and showed yourself a little more, just as if the matter had not also been commended to you. Thereupon Zwingli arose, and said we should not be led astray by the council; he also had had a letter in which he was informed how the German princes had demanded from the pope that he have a council within a year, but that the pope had formally assented had not yet happened, nor is it possible (he said) that within the space of a year a general council could be gathered together; furthermore the three mightiest lords, King of France, Emperor, and King of England, were at war with each other, who could not easily be conciliated; also that the fixing of the council would be left to the Germans. Hence one could see that the promise of a council was only a postponement, not a definite resolve; but it mattered little whether they had a council or not, for he believed that no man would live to see a council in which the word of God would be allowed to rule. Therefore, even if a council should be held at once, one would not care either, for we would depend upon and preach the word of God; may the councils determine herein what they please." After this he from Neftenbach arose and spoke.]

18. ["On the contrary I told how Paul did not boast of the languages when he went to the Corinthians, not 'in sublimitate sermonis (in loftiness of discourse)' or high wisdom. Thus one finds in the life of Hilary that the evil spirit often spoke in Greek and other tongues. And therefore I did not boast, rightly, about the languages, although I brought with me to you from Constance the Hebrew and Greek Bible; also had them both with you at the city hall. Do you think I have never heard or read Hebrew or Greek?" (Faber).]

Also we have here in our city, God be praised, many learned colleagues who are as sufficiently taught in these three languages as none at the universities just named and mentioned by the Lord Vicar. But I am speaking of those who conduct the above-mentioned universities as superiors and heads; I do not mean Erasmus of Rotterdam and others, who stay at times at the universities as strangers and guests. Here in this room are sitting also doctors of the Holy Writ, doctors of canonical law, many scholars from the universities. They should hear the Scriptures which are referred to, have them read, to see if that is so which they try and pretend to support by divine Scriptures. And as if all that was not sufficient there are in this assembly many Christian hearts, taught doubtless by the Holy Spirit, and possessing such upright understanding, that in accordance with God's spirit they can judge and decide which party produces Scripture on its side, right or wrong, or otherwise does violence to Scripture contrary to proper understanding. There is therefore no reason why excuse should here be made. Hence, dear friends, do not let the speeches here made frighten you. And especially you of Zurich should consider it a great blessing and power of God that such an undertaking should be made here in your city to the praise and honor of God, in order that the pious subjects of your territories and lands should no longer, as heretofore, be suspended in doubt and dissension. With humble hearts call upon God. He will not refuse you His divine recognition, as the epistle of James promises, if you ask in true faith, and do not let yourselves be dissuaded and deceived in any way by smooth and pleasant (well-appearing) words [cf. James 1:6].

At these words of Zwingli's every one remained silent for a time, and no one wanted to say anything upon the matter, till the burgomaster of Zurich arose and urged any there present who wished to say anything about the matter, or knew anything to say about the affair, to step forward. But no one spoke.

Since thus every one was silent, and no one was anxious to speak against Master Ulrich, who had before been called a heretic behind his back, Master Ulrich himself arose and spoke: For the sake of Christian love and truth I urge and beg all who have spoken earnestly to me on account of my sermons to step forward and to instruct me, for the sake of God, in the truth in the presence of so many pious and learned men. In case they do not do this I assure them that I shall summon publicly by name each of them, of whom I know many to be present. But on account of brotherly love I wish to inform them beforehand, so that they may arise of themselves unsummoned by me and prove me a heretic.[19] But no one desired to come forward or say anything against him.

Meantime Gutschenkel [a buffoon from Bern], standing in front by the door, cut a ridiculous caper, and cried out: "Where are now the 'big moguls' that boast so loudly and bravely on the streets? Now step forward! Here is the man. You can all boast over your wine, but here no one stirs." All laughed at that.

Then Master Ulrich arose again, urged and begged a second time all who had accused and attacked him about his sermons to step forth and prove him a heretic. In case they did not do that, and did not step forward unsummoned by name, he would for a third time publicly summon them, etc., as above. When every one remained silent as to the invitation and challenge of Master Ulrich a priest by the name of James Wagner arose, a clergyman

---

19. ["Am I not right? If you do not do that I shall name those who call me heretic, but I warn you in advance that it is more honest to step forward uncalled" (Bullinger). The word of the abbot of Cappel: "Where are they now who wish to burn us?" Bullinger places here.]

at Neftenbach,[20] and spoke as follows: Learned, wise, honorable, specially favorable, lords (gentlemen?) and princes: Since there is no one who wishes to speak of these matters after the repeated summons of Master Ulrich, I must, as the least skillful, say something. It is well known to you all, gentlemen, that our gracious Lord of Constance this year issued a mandate[21] ordering people to retain and keep the *traditiones humanas* [human traditions] until they were rescinded and changed by a general council. Now since no one will say anything against Master Ulrich's articles, which oppose the *constitutiones humanas* [human regulations], I say for my part, and hope and think, that we ought not to be bound to keep that mandate, but should preach the word of God, pure and unadulterated by human additions. You know also, dear Lords, how the clergyman of Fislisbach[22] was arrested according to the mandate, taken to Baden before the Diet, which afterwards gave him into the keeping of the bishop of Constance, who finally put him in prison. If we are to teach and preach according to the contents of the mandate, then Master Ulrich's words have no force. But since there is no one here present who dare (*darf*) say anything against them, to show them untrue, it is plain that proceedings with the gentleman from Fislisbach were too short. For this reason I speak, this good gentleman and clergyman said further, and I would like to have judgment as to how I should act in the future as to such mandate of the bishop.[23]

20. A village 12 miles northeast of Zurich.

21. In Füssli's *Beiträgen*, 4:125–29.

22. On the border of Switzerland, but in Baden. His name was Urban Weiss. He had announced from his pulpit on his return from the Zurich meeting of August 15, 1522, that he would no longer call upon the Virgin Mary or the saints. He also married. The bishop of Constance complained against him at the Diet of Baden, which wished him arrested, but some friends went surety for him. However, the Diet in November, 1522, ordered his arrest. He was examined in Constance, and apparently as the result of the use of torture recanted and then was liberated.

23. [Faber accuses Hegenwald of error in the order of his speeches.

"You note me down as if I had made the fourth speech, and bring forth a speech of which truly I would be ashamed, provided I could not erase it by means of the Scriptures better by the grace of God. You have noted me down as if I had immediately broken forth after the speech of Zwingli, which you know is not true. For I learnt long ago from Roman histories that an ambassador should not exceed his authority. This I have not forgotten, that one should not preach unless he be sent. Therefore since I have not been sent by my gracious lord as a combatant, but as a spectator, yea as a peaceful umpire, I did not wish to answer the many speeches and demands; also partly exhortation of Zwingli. And where there had been a long silence, you know that Mr. Ulrich having dared to name several, requested us from Constance urgently, still I maintained silence until the priest (whom you call), von Mittenbach (Neftenbach), referred to my gracious lord and myself so much and so clearly that I thought, and I also said it to the mighty lord Fritz Jacob von Anwyl, that I could not leave that unanswered. For although you closed the speech according to your wont, still you omit that the priest says among other things that the bishop of Constance had forbidden to preach the Gospel—write what the Vicar there said—then you will find that I said before, I am not here to suppress the Gospel and Saint Paul, for who would do that in view of the tale how the angel had brought and proclaimed to the shepherds upon the pasture when Christ was born the consoling message that in the Gospel was the salvation, yea the way and the truth, in comparing the New and Old Testament; also the four evangelists are the four rivers of Paradise, which make fruitful the whole world with the water of divine grace; it has been arranged with better order, as Saint Paul says, and I also have helped in it, since my 'scholastici doctores (scholastic doctors)' have been diligently read and underscored by me, so that they also have become dirty from my hands. Thus I have also seen that it would be better and more wholesome to leave sophistry and to bring forward the Gospel and the prophets and also other divine writings. Therefore I held to the first proposition, how this might happen and the Gospel be brought forth, which then is true even if Master Ulrich Zwingli had never come to Zurich. But I was not thus minded, and did not help to arrange the proposition so that the Gospel should be preached in a revolutionary manner, but according to the essential Christian and peaceful understanding. And furthermore I declared the Gospel does not consist in reading, but in the strength of God, yea in the correct interpretation and understanding, and I have proved by two places in the Gospel of Matthew, Matthew 4:6, where the tempter cites the saying Psalm 91:11–12. From this I have shown that also the evil spirit might, as an old scholar, use and know the Scriptures—and Matthew 2:6, where the scribes cite the saying of Micah of Bethlehem, but omitted the following correct point—thus by means of these two quotations I have well proven that it is not always sufficient to cite the Gospel or the Scriptures (although they have the first seat and the greatest honor), and that the Scriptures do not consist in the reading, but in the correct interpretation; thus and not otherwise it was done. Why didn't you note that down also for

At such complaint the Vicar from Constance again arose, and spoke as follows: These remarks are meant to refer partly to my gracious Lord of Constance and partly to me as his Grace's Vicar, therefore it is proper that I answer them. The good gentleman—I really do not know who he is—spoke first as follows, saying that this year our gracious Lord of Constance issued a mandate ordering people to keep the *constitutiones humanas*, that is the human ordinances and praiseworthy customs. To this I say, dear lords and gentlemen, there are truly many unfair, ungodly, unchristian opinions and errors at hand, which very often are preached and put before the people, not only here in the Confederation, but also elsewhere in my gracious Lord's (of Constance) bishopric by unskillful preachers, which opinions and errors, my dear lords and gentlemen, serve more to disobedience, disturbance and discord than the furthering of Christian unity. For they desire to estrange us from the good old inherited customs and usages descended upon us from our old pious Christian fathers many hundred years ago. Perhaps it was with this in mind that my gracious Lord issued the mandate for the sake of peace and unity in his Grace's bishopric. Of what the real contents of the mandate were I have no accurate knowledge, for at that time, as is known to many, I was absent from home. Therefore as far as concerns this mandate I do not desire to speak further. But since the good, pious gentleman (I don't know where he sits, because I cannot see him) has referred to the priest imprisoned at Constance my office requires me to make answer. You all know, dear sirs, how this priest was turned over to my gracious Lord of Constance by the common peers [lit. confederates: citizens of the Confederacy] in the diet at Baden as a guilty man. Accordingly my gracious Lord had the prisoner examined and questioned by appointees of his Grace, and the prisoner was found to be an ignorant and erring man in the divine Scriptures, and I myself have often pitied his unskillful remarks. For by my faith I can say that I questioned him myself, went to him in Christian love, set forth to him some of the Scriptures from Saint Paul, and he made—what shall I say?—very inaccurate answers. Ah, my dear sirs, what shall I say about this good, simple fellow? He is really untutored, and is not even a grammarian.[24] For in Christian brotherly love, kindly and without any anger, I mentioned to him some Scriptures, as for instance, that the noble Paul exhorted Timothy, saying: *Pietas ad omnia utilis* ["kindness and greatness are good in all things"], and his answer was so childish and unchristian as to be improper to mention and report in the Confederation. But that you may really know, my dear sirs, I spoke with him about praying to the dear saints and to the mother of God, also about their intercession, and I found him so ignorant and unchristian on these points that I pity his error. He insists on making living out of the dead, although the Scriptures show that also before the birth of Christ the dear saints were prayed to and called upon for others, as I finally convinced and persuaded him by means of Scriptures, that is, by Genesis, Exodus, Ezekiel and Baruch. I also brought matters so far that he recanted his error, and desires to recant all his errors about the mother of God and the dear saints. I also hope that he will be grateful to me and soon be released. Therefore, my dear sirs, with regard to the imprisoned priest there is truly no reason why

---

me? Why do you conceal that from me? And in still more unfair and wrongful fashion did you note down this and other of my speeches, how I so often cited the pope and the pope's affairs" (Faber, correction). "When you cited how also the devil had made use of the Scriptures, Zwingli had answered that is what he was there for, to give answer that he had used them correctly. But you do not wish to take hold of the Scriptures" (Hans Hager in "Gyrenrupfen").]

24. That is not a Latinist.

my gracious Lord of Constance, or his representative, should be blamed for this affair. For nothing has been done other than what was proper, fair and becoming.

To this Master Ulrich answered as follows: Dear brethren in Christ, it doubtlessly happened, not without especial destiny and will of God, that my Lord Vicar has just spoken about the praying to and the intercession of the saints and the mother of God. For that is not the least of the Articles issued by me, upon which I have preached somewhat, and at which so many simple folk are troubled as though they were frightened by a heretical [lit. unchristian] sermon. For I know, and truly find in the divine Scriptures, that Jesus Christ alone can bless us, who, as Paul says, alone is the justice of all men, who has expiated our sins, and He alone, our salvation and Saviour, is the means of intercession between His heavenly Father and us humans who believe, as Saint Paul clearly says to the Hebrews, and as you of Zurich have often heard from me when I preached to you from your favorite, the epistle to the Hebrews. Now since my Lord Vicar announces and publicly boasts of how he convinced the imprisoned priest at Constance, the clergyman of Fislisbach, by means of the divine Scriptures, of the fact that one should pray to the dear saints and the mother of God, therefore that they are our mediators with God, I beg of him for the sake of God and of Christian love to show me the place and location, also the words of the Scriptures, where it is written that one should pray to the saints as mediators, so that if I have erred, and err now, I may be better instructed, since there are here present Bibles in the Hebrew, Greek and Latin languages. These we will have examined by those present who are sufficiently well taught in the above-mentioned tongues, so I desire no more to be shown than the chapters in which such is written, as my Lord Vicar states, then we will have it found and read, so that we may see whether it is the meaning of Scripture that the saints are to be prayed to as mediators. In case that is so, and is really found to be in Scripture (as the Vicar also asserts to have convinced the imprisoned priest), I also will gladly, as an ignorant man, submit to instruction where I have erred.

Answer of the Vicar to the Words of Master Ulrich

DEAR SIRS: I see very well that the game is going beyond me. I said before that I was present not to dispute, but as the representative of my gracious Lord to speak kindly if any dissension arose on account of the disputation. Thus I very well see things are going with me as the wise man said, the foolish are easily caught in their words, but it is perhaps the fault of my folly that I undertook to speak not as a wise man. Since I have been summoned to answer by Master Ulrich, I will say that some hundreds of years ago it happened, my dear sirs, that heresy and dissension arose in the Church, the causes and beginners of which were Novatians, Montanists, Sabellians, Ebionites, Marcionites and others, under whose false teachings and error many articles like these of our times were planted in men, and by their teachings many believing folk went astray. Among these some asserted that praying to the dear saints and their intercession, as also of the mother of God, and that purgatory, too, did not exist, but were man's invention, and the like. In order to close up such misleading roads and ways of error many pious bishops and fathers met in many places, at one time in Asia, then in Africa, then somewhere in Greece, that they might hold synods and councils, and to avoid and stop heresy and such things. And afterward *constitutiones* (that is, ordinances and decisions) were made, prescribed and commanded about those matters by the holy fathers and the popes that such (heretical views) should not be held, having been rejected by the Christian Church. And although this was firmly and irrevocably ratified a long time ago by decrees of the popes and bishops, and considered wrong in Christian churches, still later schisms, dissenting parties and sects have sprung up in Europe, as, to mention their names, the Bohemians, Picards, who were led astray by such heretics as Wyclif and Hus, living contrary to the decrees and ordinances of the holy popes, acting contrary to the regulations of the Christian Church and not putting any faith in the intercession of the saints, or still less in purgatory. And although such heresy and error were later rejected by all men of Christian belief, and although those who live and remain in such error were considered, recognized and proclaimed by the holy councils as sundered members of the mother of Christian churches, still one now finds those who stir up these things anew, and undertake to bring into doubt that which many years ago was recognized and decided upon as untrue and erroneous by pope and bishop. They undertake to drive us from old customs, which have endured and stood in honor these seven hundred years, planning to overturn and upset all things. For first they went at the pope, cardinals and bishops, then they turned all cloisters topsy-turvy, after that they fell upon purgatory. And when they had left the earth they at last ascended to heaven and went at the saints and great servants of God. Saint Peter with his keys, indeed our dear Lady, the mother of God, could not escape their disgraceful attacks. And I know some places where they had gone so far as even to Christ Himself.

Shall it now go so far that not only the authorities and ecclesiastics on earth, but also God and the chosen in heaven, must be punished? If so, it is a pity. Shall not all that be nothing and count as nothing which the pious, holy fathers assembled in the Holy Spirit of God have made and unanimously decided? It cannot but have grown up to the great injury and disgrace of all Christendom. For the holy fathers and all our ancestors must have erred, and for now fourteen hundred years Christianity must have been misled and ruled in error, which it were unchristian to believe, I do not need to say. Now if the intercession of the dear saints has ever been ratified as necessary and useful by popes, bishops, fathers and councils, and if since the time of the holy pope Gregory II it has continued in use among all Christianity, it seems strange to me that now for the first time people desire to consider this wrong and erroneous, contrary to Christian ordinance, although there are few men who do not feel the aid of the mother of God and the dear saints, not alone among us Christians, but also among some unbelieving heathen. If we here at Zurich are now to speak and fight against such customs common to all the world, and especially those preserved so long by Christians, let each one think for himself how that would please those in the Orient, the Occident, from sunrise to sunset, also those in Hibernia, Mauritania, Syria, Cappadocia or in the Cyclades. I do not need to mention countries nearer our lands. Truly, dear sirs, it would be well to consider beforehand what dangers and dissensions might arise for Christianity if one were not in harmony and agreement with the whole community in these matters. For you see, as also a heathen called Sallust in *Jugurtha* testifies, that small things arise from unity, but from dissension great things decrease and fall away. Therefore my advice would be, not to consider anything of these affairs which pertain to the whole Church, but to save them for a general council. And although Master Ulrich refers to Bibles in Hebrew, Latin and Greek, and thereby consoles himself, which Scripture also those here present being taught sufficiently well in the three languages should examine, and such Scripture as is pertinent to the case they should judge and consider, still I say, in the first place, that is not a small gift of God to (be able to) expound the above-mentioned languages, and I do not boast that

I possess it. For these are especial gifts of God, as also Paul says to the Corinthians (1 Cor. 12:7–10): *Unique datur manifestatio spiritus ad utilitatem*, to each is given the manifestation of the spirit for use, to the one faith, to the other eloquence, to this one the interpretation of languages, etc. Of these graces or gifts I cannot boast of possessing any, as I know nothing of Hebrew, am not well taught in Greek, and understand Latin only tolerably. For I am no orator or poet, and do not pretend to be. Finally I say, the evangelical and apostolical Scripture is not found in the wise, brilliant or flowery, smooth words, but in the power of God, as Paul says (1 Cor. 2:4). Thus, as before, it seems to me not to be sufficient that one apply or bring forward Scripture, but it is also important that one understand Scripture correctly. With that in view perhaps one should attend to such matters at the universities (as at Paris, Cologne or Lyons, or elsewhere), as I said before.

Answer of Master Ulrich

Sir Vicar: There is no further need of such smooth and round-about words. I desire that you tell me only with what portion of Scripture you convinced the priest imprisoned at Constance, clergyman of Fislisbach, that he was not a Christian, and brought him to a revocation of his error. This is the point upon which we desire to hear in kindness your answer. Show us simply where in the books heretofore cited by you in the matter of praying to the saints and of their intercession it is stated that they are our mediators. This we desire to know from you. Therefore I beg you for the sake of Christian love, do this with plain, unadulterated, divine Scripture, as you boast to have done in the case of the priest imprisoned at Constance. Indicate the chapter and answer the question as asked in simple words, saying here or there it is written. Then we will see if it is so, and in case we are persuaded and convinced of it we will gladly submit to instruction. There is no need of long speeches.[25] For your long quoting and citing of many writings of the ancients looks more like seeking the praise and favor of the audience than the furthering of the truth. Probably I also could bring in many narratives and essays of the ancients, but it is not to the point. We well know that many things were decided upon in times past by the fathers in council assembled which were afterward repealed and revoked by others who thought they assembled in the Spirit of God, as is plainly found in the Nicene Council and that of Gangra,[26] in the first of which the clergy was allowed to marry, and all those who spoke against it were cursed, while the second decided upon the opposite.[27] It is also a fact that many times ordinances (*constitutiones*)

---

25. ["Upon Fathers and councils one no longer depends, unless they prove their case by the Scriptures" (Bullinger).]

26. [Held in the 4th century. Gangra was the capital of ten Asia Minor provinces of Paphlagonia.]

27. ["'Not a word is written concerning this in the canons of the council of Nicaea.' To be sure Zwingli said that Paphnutius in the council of Nicaea had been, by which Zwingli means that marriage at that time (although he partly errs) was permitted. Now in the council of Gangra you say in your report Zwingli had said it had been forbidden. How could you lose your memory in such fashion that you could write such? On the contrary he said that it had been permitted in the council of Gangra, and doubtlessly he based this upon another pamphlet, which he called 'Apologeticum,' and written in Latin quatering (see Latin version). *Rogo nunc ut concilio parendum*, etc. You do him wrong, now I must take his part. Furthermore beware, my pamphlet here will be read the sooner by those who are at Zurich and accepted as good. Zwingli also has referred to the Carthaginian council. In the first place I showed how there are two kinds of councils, namely, those of the general Christianity, which are called 'oecumenica' or 'universalia' in Greek and Latin; then the 'particularia.' Now it is never found that in the matter of faith the 'universalia' were ever opposed to each other. The Carthaginian council was only a special one. And to every bishop was left his free will and opinion; and only later the council of Nicaea was held by 318 Fathers, (thus) they may have had an honest excuse. Why have you omitted this report?" (Faber). Heinrich Wolf answered thereupon: "Zwingli simply said that in a council Paphnutius with difficulty had secured permission for the marriage of

25

have been issued and ordered by the fathers in council to which their successors paid no heed. For example, that the mother of God conceived without sin was decided in public council at Basel, and yet no preaching monk is so foolish as to speak against it. Also many ordinances or rules of the fathers are found which were changed afterwards, especially in our times, and otherwise not kept or given up by the influence of money, so that such things are allowed which were formerly forbidden by the fathers. From this we can see that councils have not always acted in the spirit of the Holy Ghost, but sometimes according to human will and judgment, which is of course forbidden by divine Scripture. For the Holy Ghost does not say this to-day and to-morrow that, but its ordinances and regulations must remain everlasting and changeless. The pious fathers whom we call holy are not for that reason to be dishonored and attacked as to their piety or holiness. For nothing is easier or from native weakness more natural than to err, especially when out of conceit or over-hasty judgment depended upon their own opinion instead of upon the rule of God's Word. This all shows us that the pillars and supports of many of the fathers, as Augustine and Jerome, are not in harmony in their writings; that often the one thinks not only something else, but by Scripture proves the contrary. But as to the fact that they say it would be too bad if we Christians, and especially our forefathers, had lived so long in error, since from the time of Gregory the intercession of the saints has been accepted and kept, I say that it is not a question of *when* a thing begun in the Church. We know well that the litany was established in the time of Gregory and kept down to the present. But all we desire is to hear the Scripture upon which my Lord Vicar bases his recommendation that we should pray to the saints. For if such a custom began at the time of Gregory then it did not exist before,[28] and if before that time men were Christians and were saved, though they did not hold to the intercession of the saints, and perhaps knew little of it, then it follows that they did not sin who believed in Christ alone and did not consider the intercession of the saints.

For we know really from the Scriptures that Jesus Christ alone is the mediator between us and God, his heavenly Father, as has been stated before. Furthermore, I say that many learned men have spoken and fought against the ordinances, and especially against the so-called holy ones, useless and superfluous customs, also against great power and tyrannical show; but the great moguls, popes, bishops, monks and prelates, do not wish to be touched on their sore spots, and tell the unlearned crowd that their rule has been erected by God, and that He has ordered them to govern thus, hence all those opposing, or only having such thoughts, are not alone heretics and shut out from the rest of Christianity, but as cursed and the property of the devil they have been exiled, outlawed, condemned, and some have been sentenced to the stake and burnt. Therefore, dear brethren, although one says to you—perhaps in order to frighten you the more—how our pious parents and ancestors have erred, and on account of such heresy have been deprived of salvation: I tell you (on the contrary) that the decisions and judgment of God are hidden from mankind and incomprehensible to us, and no one should

---

the priests, also spoke well against such statutes. Now you come forward and say that he placed Paphnutius in the Nicæan council, although he said to-day (as I asked him about it) that he had never read about a council which had forbidden marriage, but about popes 500 years after the birth of Christ. But since the papists speak so consistently about the Nicæan council he made his point, how he really had never read carefully the history of this council, and thus had believed you papists. And you have brought forth the Nicæan council, and not Zwingli; then you opposed the Gangrensian council by saying that it was not a general one" ("Gyrenrupfen").]

28. ["I said even more about the time further back, especially in the time of Cyprian, 1300 years ago, there was intercession of the saints; yes, I shall try it still further back" (Faber).]

impiously concern himself therewith. God knows that we all have faults and are sinners, yet through His mercy He makes up our deficiencies and enables us to accomplish something, yea even such deeds for which perhaps our strength alone is not sufficient. Consequently it is in no wise befitting that we desire to judge and pronounce upon the secrecy of God in such matters. He knows full well where He may overlook and pardon, and we must not interfere with His decision and compassion, in which manner He has treated and dealt with each one. We trust in Him as our eternally good Father, who can, as 2 Peter 2:9 says, well protect His own, and deliver the godless over to eternal suffering. Nor does it do any good to say that there are few people who will not feel comfort through the intercession of the saints. I say, where such help comes from God, we will not judge why God acts thus and helps man in such fashion as He desires. But where this occurs from infatuation by the devil as a judgment of God upon the unbelieving man, what shall we say then? Ye know well what work the devil has sometimes done in many places, which if it had not been obstructed would have resulted in great deception and injury of all Christendom. Furthermore, that is an evil teaching which proclaims that other nations will not consider us Christians if we do not obey the ordinances, i.e., the laws of former times, as this is ordered and demanded by the papal decrees. For indeed there are many ordinances in the canons of the Roman bishops and popes which the aforesaid nations do not obey and still they are none the less Christians. Concerning the above I shall make use of the following short comparison: Ecclesiastical property is (as they say) in the power of the Roman pope, and he may bestow and grant the estates to whomsoever he pleases. Now look ye how this ordinance is obeyed in Spain and France; there the ecclesiastical benefices or estates are not granted to any foreigner, let the pope say what he pleases. But we foolish Germans must permit the sending of stablemen and mule-drivers from the papal court to take possession of our benefices and curacies and be our spiritual guides, although they are ignorant of and know naught concerning the Scriptures, and if we do not tolerate this we are disobedient to the Christian Church. But the above-mentioned nations do not obey the ordinance and still are without question pious Christians. Hence, Sir Vicar, I desire that you do not make use of bombastic speeches, which do not even bear upon my question, but, as I have asked before, tell at once where is written in the Scriptures concerning the holy invocation and intercession of the Virgin Mary, as you pretended you could show in Exodus, Baruch, etc. That is what we desire to hear. Hence answer in regard to this obscure point. We do not ask what has been accomplished or decided in this or that council. This all does not bear upon the matters which we ask you, otherwise we will be speaking for a month concerning these matters.

Vicar

Gentlemen: I am accused of speaking very evasively and not to the point. I have excused myself before for not being able to speak eloquently, and I have also listened to you (Master Ulrich). [Here Master Ulrich interrupted: There is no need of so much teasing.] That you accuse me of seeking to add to my own fame rather than the advancement of truth I cannot prevent. I wished to assist in making peace and doing the best. But when Master Ulrich claims that I say much concerning things settled by councils of yore, and then changed by later ones, I say that there are two kinds of councils referred to. Some are known as "*concilia universalia*" (these are common or general gatherings), where many of the bishops and Christian leaders meet, as in the four foremost councils, Nicaea, Constantinople, Ephesus and Chalcedon, and some others. Whatever was accomplished and done in these has never been entirely changed by the others, but has been preserved like the Gospel. Some are known as "*concilia particularia*," of which there have been many, not consisting of all the fathers of the common parishes about, but of special ones, as was the council of Gangra, and many others. In these probably something has at times been settled which later, perhaps not without cause, has been decided otherwise. But it never has been that the priests were permitted to have wives. And although the Eastern Church, especially in Greece, wished to have this considered just, the pious fathers of other nations would not permit this and forbade it, considering from weighty reasons[29] that the marriage of priests is detrimental to the churches and not for the good of the service of God, as also Saint Paul says: "*Qui sine uxore*," etc. "He that is unmarried careth for the things that belong to the Lord" (1 Cor. 7:32) "*Solutus es ab*," etc. "Art thou loosed from a wife? seek not a wife!" (1 Cor. 7:27). There he speaks of those who serve the Gospel as priests. "Let every man abide in the same calling wherein he was called" (1 Cor. 7:20). Such and many other causes have induced the holy fathers not to allow and permit marriage to priests. Indeed it could not happen without partition of the property of the churches.

Zwingli

Marriage forbidden to priests is not found everywhere, as one pretends, but imposed by man contrary to a divine and just law. This is evident, first of all, in Saint Paul: "Nevertheless, to avoid fornication, let every man have his own wife, and let every woman have her own husband" (1 Cor. 7:2). Since he says "every" undoubtedly he does not wish the priests to be excluded. For he confirms and refers to the marriage of priests, especially in writing to Timothy: "A bishop (i.e., priest) then must be blameless, the husband of one wife, vigilant, sober, of good behavior, given to hospitality, apt to teach, etc. One that ruleth well his own house, having his children in subjection in all gravity" (1 Tim. 3:2, 4). In the same fashion he speaks concerning the deacon, whom we call evangelist (1 Tim. 3:8). And Paul also writes to Titus: "For this cause left I thee in Crete, that thou shouldest set in order the things that are wanting, and ordain elders (whom we call priests or deacons) in every city, as I had appointed thee: If any be blameless, the husband of one wife, having faithful children," etc. (Titus 1:5–6). Undoubtedly the holy Paul, inspired by the Holy Ghost, recognized our inability and incapacity to remain chaste by our own will except through the grace of God. Hence he says in the afore-mentioned place: "For I would that all men were even as I myself" (1 Cor. 7:7), and: "It would be good for man to be thus" (1 Cor. 7:1), but Paul adds and says: "But every man hath his proper gift of God, one after this manner and another after that" (1 Cor. 7:7). Therefore Paul places no restriction upon the marriage of priests, and indeed writes expressly: "A bishop (i.e., priest) and a deacon shall have a sober wife and well-bred children"; and furthermore he permits marriage to all people, and says: "But and if thou marry thou hast not sinned. But every man hath his proper gift of God," etc. (1 Cor. 7:28, 7). It is evident from this that marriage is not forbidden to priests by divine law, and that chastity is to be maintained, not by means of

29. ["Although I said that I wanted to defend it well against the destroyers of divine gifts and services. But I did not say it. You thought I would say it. Although I did not think of the pope, the ceremonies and many other things, it is no proof that such are useless" (Faber).]

our resolutions, but with the help of the grace of God. This real truth and wisdom of God Christ also proves to us: "His disciples say unto him, if the case of the man be so with his wife it is not good to marry. But he said unto them, all men cannot receive this saying save they to whom it is given. And there be eunuchs which have made themselves eunuchs for the kingdom of heaven's sake (that is, due to the evangelical doctrine). He that is able to receive it let him receive it!" (Matt. 19:10, 12). Do you hear that Christ says here that it is not possible for all people to keep chastity except such as have received it from God? Hence He does not forbid the twelve apostles to marry. Nor did God in vain give Adam a woman as helpmate; He could have given him a man as helpmate if He had wished to keep him chaste. But He said: "*Crescite et multiplicamini!* [increase and multiply]" (Gen. 1:22). And although this is known to every one, still the pope is able, by means of his ordinance, to demand from each priest or other ecclesiastic chastity and that he be unmarried contrary to divine law, and he can weigh down the poor consciences corrupted by sin and shame; and he permits public offense and sin contrary to the sunny and pure ordinance of God. I say that I know of no greater scandal in Christendom than that marriage is forbidden to priests (I am speaking about the pastors; the others let them lie, whatever they do), yet they are allowed to commit fornication publicly as long as they give money. They pretend that if the priests had wives the property of the churches would be divided and disappear. My God, what sort of a reason is this? Do we then never spend the property of the churches uselessly? We will our real and movable property to the illegitimate wives and children, if we have any, contrary to God's will. What would that harm the benefice if a priest had a dear wife and well-bred children brought up for the service of God out of the benefice? The benefice could retain its property and income, which it has, although the priests may at times have mismanaged. Priests have not always been forbidden to many. This is proved by Pelagius,[30] in which is found a decree of the pope (Diss. XXXI., cap. ante trienn.) that the subdeacons of Sicily shall forsake their wives, which they had taken in accordance with the divine ordinance, and shall not have intercourse with them; which statute Gregory I later on rescinded. Consequently if it was ordered in former times by Pelagius that priests shall have no wives, and this was rescinded by Gregory, then it could not always have been as at present, but the law must have been made by man, which God never required to be kept.

Vicarius

It has never happened since the time of Tertullian and the council of Nicaea, 1200 years ago, that priests had wives or were allowed to have them

Thereupon one of the council at Zurich said: But they are allowed to have mistresses.

The vicar was astonished for a while, but resumed: It is true that the subdeacons in Sicily who had taken wives previously contrary to the custom of the Roman churches were permitted by the aforesaid Gregory to keep them. But only on the condition that in future no one would be consecrated who would not pledge himself to remain unmarried and chaste. Thus also it was resolved in the council at Carthage that no bishop, priest or deacon should

---

30. Alvarus Pelagius, bishop of Silves, Portugal, died at Seville, 1352, whose *Summa de planctu Ecclesiae* ("The Chief Points of the Church's Complaint"), written in 1332, published, Ulm 1474, Venice 1560, is a frank statement of the disorders of his time and a plea for the exaltation of the Papal See.

have intercourse with women, but remain chaste without wife. Hence I say that it will be no easy matter to show that marriage was ever permitted to priests.[31]

Zwingli

And even if you say since the time of the apostles, still marriage is not forbidden to priests by divine ordinance, but allowed and permitted, as I have proved before. And that priests formerly had wives is sufficiently evident, since formerly many sons of priests have become popes and bishops, which could not have happened if they had not been born in wedlock. How is it that one always prefers human laws and human meddling, and always sets human traditions above the will of God? Although one finds that also the fathers have protested against many ordinances, and you know how vehemently the pious man Paphnutius[32] opposed such a statute and would not agree to marriage being forbidden to priests. Furthermore, Eusebius writes that some of the apostles had their wives with them, which facts are sufficient indications that the present custom was begun by people of later times, but that marriage was not forbidden by divine ordinance either to layman or priest. And although in the council of Nicaea, as you say, it was forbidden to priests to have wives, still what about that? In former times baptism by heretics was considered by many fathers as just and valid, as Cyprianus tells us, but later in the council at Carthage this was declared to be worthless and was set aside.

To such varied arguments of Master Ulrich the vicar had nothing more to oppose and say, except in regard to the baptism by heretics, and that on account of the following reasons: Master Ulrich has said that the baptism of heretics was considered valid by several, and thus referring to Cyprianus. But the vicar demanded that one should record the words

31. ["Don't you recollect that I said I do not like to speak concerning the marriage of priests? On account of this I have kept quiet and have omitted to state a better reason. But where have you hidden the fact that I said that from the time of the apostles one does not read that one who was consecrated as subdeacon, deacon, priest or bishop could marry again after his wife had died? Did I not say further that it is thus understood, not alone in the Western, but also in the Eastern Church—in Crete, Corcyra, etc., also in India, in the case of the Presbyter John, and among the Russians? so that any one who took a virgin as wife may be consecrated as priest, but that if she die that he can take no more; in the same manner if he has no wife before he is consecrated he can take none after the consecration; this I have shown. Why do you omit this? It was indeed necessary for you to include the subtile, honorable interruption of one who spoke about the prostitutes; and you also placed Gutschenkel † as a character in the comedy. Since the good Master Ulrich consoles himself much in his speeches and writings with a text which he found in XXVII. dist. c., 'Si quis discernit,' which is claimed to have been made in Gangrensian council, know then that there were not more than 16 bishops in that council; these made 19 canons against the majority that even desired to abolish holy marriage. But therein they did not reject the state of virginity and widowhood, hence also the marriage of priests was not, as you think, admitted by the pious Fathers. They spoke about the priests who had wives before the consecration—and bethink yourself what councils over 18 bishops would prefer, even although they should prefer it were so, as it is not, as Zwingli says. Now see how the supplication issued by your and our common gracious lord of Constance shall be answered. About the marriage of priests I do not like to speak (several times repeated). Accusations of two wrong quotations were made" (Faber).]

† The half-witted fellow mentioned above.

32. Bishop of a city in Upper Thebais; had his right eye gouged out and his left knee-cap injured in the Maximian persecution (305), and was banished to the mines. He appeared in the Nicene Council 325, and was honored as a confessor. When it was proposed to enact a law which forbade the married clergy to continue to live with their wives, Paphnutius declared very earnestly that so heavy a yoke ought not to be laid upon the clergy; that marriage itself is honorable and the bed undefiled; that the Church ought not to be injured by an undue severity. "For all men," said he, "cannot bear the practice of rigid continence; neither perhaps would the chastity of the wife be preserved." He favored dissuading clergymen from marrying after ordination, but allowing those who had married prior to ordination to retain their wives. His own known virginity and his sufferings for the cause gave so great weight to his words that he was unanimously sustained by the Council.

of Master Ulrich, because he believes he may catch him in small matters, for Master Ulrich may not have been very careful in the use of his words. Therefore he also demands that a copy of Cyprianus should be brought, so that the dispute may be decided. But the vicar said: Supposing the words of Cyprianus are as I think, and not as you? And thereupon a quarrel arose, which had naught to do with the questions which the vicar had been called upon so often to answer. Therefore I have not taken pains to remember and note this. But if I understood the matter both were right. For Zwingli referred to those who had been baptized by heretics, who should, according to Cyprianus, be baptized again in the churches, which several thought was needless. But the vicar was speaking of those who once baptized by Christians had gone over to heresy and later on wished to reenter the Christian Church; these did not need another baptism, but merely absolution by the imposition of hands, etc. Several were, however, also opposed to this, as Cyprianus writes in his letters to Pompeius and to Quintinus.

After there had been considerable talk concerning this matter, Dr. Sebastian Hofmann,[33] of Schaffhausen, a member of the order of the Barefoot Monks, spoke thus: Learned, spiritual, honorable, wise, favorable, gracious, dear gentlemen, it is necessary that I also speak in this matter. Last year I was lector at Lucerne, where, according to my best knowledge and belief, I preached, as I hope and know, nothing else except the word of God from the Scriptures, and in these sermons at Lucerne I have mentioned, like many others, the many useless customs of intercession and invoking of the saints and the mother of God, and I taught in accordance with the contents and teachings of the holy Scriptures. On account of such sermons, made, as stated above, at Lucerne, various accusations against me were sent to Constance, among which was the sermon about the invocation of the saints. I was accused of being a heretic, condemned, and therefore driven out of Lucerne. And now as my lord, the vicar, has pretended before and stated that the appeal and invocation of saints is founded upon the Scriptures and mentioned in the Old Testament, I pray for God's sake that the vicar, as he was wont to boast to have overcome the priest imprisoned at Constance, show the place, as formerly often had been asked of him, especially since on account of this I have been accused by my gracious lord at Constance of being a heretic, and I will accept it with many thanks and willingly allow myself to be taught in case I have perchance erred in my sermons, have not told the truth, or have misread or misunderstood the Scriptures.

Zwingli

We know from the Old and New Testaments of God that our only comforter, redeemer, savior and mediator with God is Jesus Christ, in whom and through whom alone we can obtain grace, help and salvation, and besides from no other being in heaven or on earth.

---

33. He was properly called Sebastian Hofmeister, or in the scholastic form Oikonomos. Because his father was a "wagner," i.e., wheelwright, he was himself erroneously called Wagner, or in Latinized form Carpentarius. He was born at Schaffhausen in 1476; entered the Barefoot (Franciscan) monks there; studied in Paris the classical tongues and Hebrew, and came home in 1520 as a Doctor of the Sacred Scriptures, and the same year he taught in the Franciscan monastery in Zurich and so came in contact with Zwingli. He embraced the Reformation, and introduced it into Lucerne and into Schaffhausen (both 1523), whither persecution drove him. It is indeed as the Reformer of Schaffhausen that he is best remembered, yet his career there was brief, for in 1525 he had to leave that city. He preached in Zurich (1526) and taught Hebrew in Bern (1528), but died September 26, 1533, as preacher at Zofingen, thirty miles sontheast of Basel. Two of his writings were commonly attributed to Zwingli.

The Vicar, Laughing

I well know that Jesus Christ alone is the comfort, redemption and salvation of all, and an intercessor and mediator between us and God, his heavenly Father, the highest round by which alone is an approach to the throne of divine grace and charity, according to Hebrews 4:16. Nevertheless one may perhaps attain the highest round by means of the lower.[34] It seems to me the dear saints and the Virgin Mary are not to be despised, since there are few who have not felt the intercession of the Virgin and the saints. I do not care what every one says or believes. I have placed a ladder against heaven; I believe firmly in the intercession of the much-praised queen of heaven, the mother of God, and another may believe or hold what he pleases.

Zwingli

That would indeed be a foolish piece of business if one could arrive at the highest round without the lower or without work, or if he were on it to begin at the lowest. Sir Vicar, we do not dispute here concerning how one should appeal to the saints or what your belief is. We desire only that you show us it in the Gospel, as has been formerly often demanded and begged of you.

Thereupon Master Leo Jud[35] arose and spoke thus: Gracious, careful, honorable, wise, favorable, dear gentlemen, I have been made by you, gentlemen, here at Zurich, a people's priest and pastor, perhaps unwisely, in order to proclaim to you the word of God, the Gospel of Christ, which I shall try to do according to my best capabilities, in as far as the grace of God will assist me and the Holy Ghost aid me. But surely now many ordinances of man have been retained from long habit in the churches, and have intermingled with the Gospel, so that the clergy frequently have preached and commanded their keeping equally with the Gospel: yet I now declare that I shall not obey such human ordinances, but shall present and teach from love the joyful and pure Gospel, and whatever I can really prove from the Scriptures, regardless of human ordinance or old traditions, since such human ordinances, decreed by pope or bishop, have been here recognized and proved to be by the Articles[36] emanating from Master Ulrich to be entirely opposed to the Gospel and truth, and still there is no one here who desires or is able to say anything truthful or fundamental against him. And so although my Sir Vicar has pretended to prove and show by means of the Gospel the invocation and intercession of the saints, such has not yet been done, although frequently requested. Therefore I also pray to hear and to know from him where it is written in the afore-mentioned biblical books concerning the invocation and intercession of the saints. For

34. ["I said, one may do that. 'Must' and 'can,' are they not two different things? The debate was not about 'must,' but about 'can.' Did you not hear from me about the ladder of Jacob fastened to heaven on which are many rounds? Did you not hear how quickly and speedily Zwingli wished to swing himself up to the cross of Christ? Do you not think if he wished to go to the Lord on the cross that then rightly he would also have found Mary, John and the other people of the Gospel?" (Faber).]

35. Born at Gemar, near Rappoltsweilen (or Ribeauville), Elsass, thirty miles southwest of Strassburg, the child of a clerical marriage, 1482; studied at Basel; inclined first to pharmacy, but took up theology, and had Zwingli as his fellow-student under Thomas Wyttenbach; M.A., 1506; became deacon of Saint Theodore's church, Basel; pastor of Saint Pilt, four miles east of his birthplace; people's priest at Einsiedeln in succession to Zwingli, and at his suggestion, 1518; the same, and by the same influence, at Saint Peter's, Zurich, 1522; coadjutor of Zwingli and Bullinger, particularly remembered as principal translator of the Zurich Bible; died in Zurich, June 19, 1542.

36. Referring to the *Sixty-seven Articles* issued by Zwingli for the basis of argument in the Disputation [cf. chap. 5 in this anthology].

perhaps also in my sermons, if God lends me grace, it will be declared and proclaimed that one should invoke to Jesus Christ alone, and only look to him for all compassion, all help, mercy and salvation, which shall be sought and demanded from no other being. Therefore, Sir Vicar, I desire that you teach me if I have erred, and report from the Gospel, showing place and location where it is written that the saints are to be invoked by us or that they are intercessors. Such I shall receive with many thanks, and will gladly allow myself to be taught by you.

Vicar

Ne Hercules quidem contra duos ["Not even Hercules (fights) against two"]. Shall I strive with two? That was considered even too difficult for the strong Hercules (according to a proverb of the ancients). Dear Sir, I have nothing to do with you.

Leo: But I have something to do with you.

Vicar: I do not know who you are.

Leo: I shall gladly be your good friend in so far as you desire.

Vicar: That I shall not refuse, for I am not here to become an enemy of any one. If you are then my good friend, as you say, it will happen to us as to Socrates and Solon,[37] who also through argumentation became good friends.

Leo: Then you have one friend more than formerly.

To prevent such and other gibes Master Ulrich began to speak: Would to God that the saying, *Ne Hercules quidem*, etc., would be understood and followed as readily by some as it ordinarily is the custom to quote it. Sir Vicar, we desire to hear the quotation concerning the invocation and intercession of the saints, not such useless talk and nonsense.

Vicar

It is the custom and usage of Christian churches, and is kept thus by all Christian folk confirmed by the litany and the canons missal, that we appeal to the Virgin to intercede for us; this the mother of God herself says in the gospel of Saint Luke. *Ex hoc beatam me dicent*: "All generations shall call me blessed," and her cousin Elizabeth addressed her in a friendly manner, saying: *Unde mihi hoc*, etc. "And whence is this to me, that the mother of my Lord should come to me?" Likewise, "blessed art thou among women," etc. This also the maiden in the Gospel proves to us, who cries: "Blessed is the body which has borne thee, and blessed the breasts which thou hast sucked." [Interruption by Zwingli: We are not asking concerning the holiness and dignity of Mary, but concerning invocation and intercession.] We also sing daily: *Sentiunt omnes tuum levamen*: "All feel thy aid who honor thy memory."[38] But since my talk is held to be useless and foolish I will rather keep still.

---

37. ["Look, how can you say that to excuse myself I quoted in the beginning the saying of Solon, how then it was written by the wise man Solon that when once he was sitting with scholars, who were debating, and Periander asked him whether he was silent from lack of words or because he was a fool, he answered no fool can keep quiet? Therefore I did not refer to Socrates (as you say), but to the saying of Xenocrates when he was one time asked why he alone kept still and allowed all the others to speak, he had answered that what I sometimes said I regretted, but that which I have not said that I have never regretted. Thus it happened, and not otherwise, and as a witness of the truth I cited the proverb: *Audiens sapiens sapientior erit* ["A wise listener will be wiser," cf. Prov. 1:5]. And as another witness Zwingli interrupted the speech by saying that there was no need of fawning and hypocritical style. Now look how you have hit it?" (Faber).]

38. ["Show us that in the Scriptures; the rest is human nonsense" (Bullinger).]

Thus the vicar kept still and sat down, and then Doctor Martin from Tübingen arose, and spoke thus concerning these matters:

Dear Sirs: Much has been said here against the usage and ordinance of the Christian churches which has been decreed and ordered by holy councils and fathers assembled in the name of the Holy Ghost, which, moreover, long has been held without fault as a praised custom and long usage. To oppose and to object to it is a sacrilegious deed, for what has been decreed and resolved by the holy councils and fathers, namely, by the four councils, should be obeyed in Christian churches like the Gospel, as we have written in Diss. XV. For the Church assembled in council in the name of the Holy Ghost cannot err. Therefore it behooves no one to speak against their decrees and ordinances, as Christ bears witness in the holy Gospel when he says: *Qui vos audit, me audit*: "He that heareth you heareth me, and he that despiseth you despiseth me." Thus Christ speaks to his disciples and those who in place of the twelve apostles (as bishop and pope) govern the Christian churches; as then the Roman Church is now since many centuries the mother of all others, which is confirmed by words of Christ (Matt. 16:18–19), as this is explained in Diss. X. and XII., cap. in nova et cap. quamvis. Concerning this there is here talked and quarreled against the invocation of the dear saints, just as if such honest and divine usage followed in Christendom many centuries were not founded upon the Scriptures, although Saint Jerome in *Ad Jovianum* writes much concerning the intercession of the saints, and that this is advantageous to us he proves from the hopeful Scriptures. That we also receive true report concerning this from the canon of the holy mass, introduced by the old popes and bishops, and composed by Gregory and sung in all Christendom, proves that the intercession and invocation of the dear saints and the Virgin Mary is not considered useless. We also see this in our daily experience of miracles which occur everywhere. Consequently it seems wrong to me to consider and value such as useless and contrary to the Scriptures, etc.

Zwingli

The good gentleman also intervenes and urges much in favor of the ordinances and usage of the Church, the fathers and councils gathered together and inspired by the Holy Ghost, and thinks one should not speak against them, etc. I say he will by no means prove that the councils have all been gathered in the name of the Holy Ghost for the purpose of all the ordinances which they made, since it has been proved before that they often have decreed contrarily, and have resolved upon, done and rescinded one thing to-day, to-morrow another, although the Holy Ghost is at all times alike, and does not oppose his decision once rendered. But when he says what has been decreed by councils and fathers is to be obeyed like the Gospels, I say what is as true as the Gospels and in accordance with the divine Spirit one is bound to obey, but not what is decreed in accordance with human reason. But as to what further than this is to be considered by pope or council as a mortal sin we do not think that we are in duty bound to treat that the same as the Gospels; we wish to be free, not to burden our consciences with that. E.g., if pope or council commands us, at risk of mortal sin, to fast, or to eat no egg, no butter, no meat, which God has not ordered us to do (Luke 10:7; Col. 2:16, 21), but is permitted and made voluntary, therefore we will not believe that such and other ordinances decreed by the councils are decreed by the Holy Ghost, and to be respected equally with the Gospel. How does it happen that they wish to order us to eat no cheese, no eggs, no milk, but stinking oil, with which they scarcely oil their shoes at Rome, and otherwise eat chickens and capons? But if one says it is thus written in the canons and decreed by the fathers, I say it is written otherwise in Paul, and Christ has given another and easier law. Now do we owe more obedience to God or the Holy Ghost, or to human beings? (Acts 5:32). But when he declares the Church has decreed such, she cannot err, I ask what is meant by "Church"? Does one mean the pope at Rome, with his tyrannical power and the pomp of cardinals and bishops greater than that of all emperors and princes? then I say that this Church has often gone wrong and erred, as every one knows, since it has destroyed the land and its inhabitants, burnt cities and ravaged the Christian people, butchering them for the sake of its earthly pomp, without doubt not on account of a command of Christ and his apostles. But there is another Church which the popes do not wish to recognize; this one is no other than all right Christians, collected in the name of the Holy Ghost and by the will of God, which have placed a firm belief and an unhesitating hope in God, her spouse. That Church does not reign according to the flesh powerfully upon earth, nor does it reign arbitrarily, but depends and rests only upon the word and will of God, does not seek temporal honor and to bring under its control much territory and many people and to rule other Christians. That Church cannot err. Cause: she does nothing according to her own will or what she thinks fit, but seeks only what the spirit of God demands, calls for and decrees. That is the right Church, the spotless bride of Jesus Christ [cf. Eph. 5:27] governed and refreshed by the Spirit of God. But the Church which is praised so highly by the Papists errs so much and severely that even the heathens, Turks and Tartars know it well. But when he refers here to the words of Christ, "He that heareth you heareth me, and he that despiseth you despiseth me" (Luke 10:16), and then refers this to pope, bishop, regents of the Roman churches, I say that such is not the meaning of Jesus Christ, that we should obey them in all things as they order. For Christ the Lord knew well that such great braggarts would sit upon the chair of Moses who would burden the necks of the poor with unbearable and heavy loads, which they themselves would not touch with a finger. Hence the saying, "He that heareth you heareth me," etc., will not serve for that for which the papists and sophists interpret it, but the right meaning is, as is also shown by what precedes and follows. When Christ sent his disciples to preach the Gospel in country and city he spake: "Go ye and preach," saying the kingdom of God is approaching, etc. And later Christ said: "He that receiveth you receiveth me," as Matthew 10:40 says. This means they should preach His word and bring it to the people, but not human foolishness and law. For one serves the Lord in vain if one prefers human doctrine and decree. And may the good gentleman furthermore remember what Jerome writes in *ad Jovinian* concerning the invocation or intercession of the saints that he has not read correctly. For it is written *Adversus Vigilantium*; but how Jerome twists the Gospel in regard to invocation or intercession of the saints, as he does often in other places, that all know who read Jerome with good judgment.[39] Finally, in regard to the canon which is read in the mass, and in which invocation and intercession of the saints are referred to, I say one sees readily that the canon has not been made by one alone, but composed by several. For there are many useless words therein, as *haec dona, haec munera* ["these gifts, these offerings"], etc., from which may be inferred that it has not been made by one scholar. The

---

39. ["Zwingli said that if he were only half a man, stood on one leg and closed one eye, he would nevertheless yield not to Jerome" (Faber). "Thereupon Heinrich Wolf said 'such words were never heard from his lips, yea never thought of during his lifetime.' To be sure, when you referred to Jerome in regard to the intercession of the saints, he said the argument which Jerome uses there has no basis in the Scriptures" ("Gyrenrupfen").]

apostles never celebrated mass thus; one also finds that in several instances the custom of the canon is different from ours, which I shall point out and shortly prove, if God wills it. Concerning the miracles which are done by the saints we have spoken before. Who knows through whom or why God decrees this?[40] We should not attribute this so readily on account of our unbelief to the saints when we hesitate concerning Christ and run to those creatures for help. This all is proof of a weak faith and small hope in Jesus Christ, whom we do not rightly and entirely trust. Why do we flee from Him and seek aid from the saints, especially as we do not recognize certainly from the Scriptures that they are our intercessors?

After this Dr. Sebastian,[41] from Schaffhausen, a member of the order of the Barefoot Monks, arose and began to admonish the assembled council that they should manage and protect the evangelical doctrine as until now, since there was no one there who could bring forward, upon frequent requests, anything more definite from the Scriptures. But he could not finish; the vicar interrupted and said:

Dr. Sebastian, you should keep still and not speak thus. You know well what you promised my gracious master; it does not behoove a man to be so vacillating, to be moved like a reed by the wind; you had not promised that before.

Answered the aforesaid Dr. Sebastian: Dear gentlemen, what I have promised the bishop that I have faithfully and honorably kept, but his people have not fulfilled and carried out what they promised to me; that you may testify what I have said here in public.

After this speech there arose another doctor, lector and preacher from Bern, of the order of the Barefoot Monks,[42] and admonished the wise council of Zurich, speaking as follows:

Honorable, careful, wise, gracious, favorable gentlemen of Zurich, your intention and opinion, published in all places by means of open letter for the aid of the Gospel, pleases me well, and praised be God that you are the people to further and not to obstruct the word of God, and pray God that He will not turn away and cause your wisdom to desert from such a godly undertaking, and that He will give and lend you power and might, strength and comfort, that you will be frightened by no temporal power, whether of pope, bishop or emperor, but so act in these matters that it will redound to God in the future and your eternal praise. And do not mind that you are a small body and few. I do not say this to scorn you, but I mean it thus, that you are not equal to a whole kingdom and are considered too few to struggle against so many nations. Remember that God has always by means of the

---

40. ["You have omitted that Zwingli even spoke against the public Gospel: 'when one says that the saints accomplished miracles then the devil has done it'" (Faber). "About the intercession of the saints he promises a separate book: 'the whole heavenly host will be with me, without suppressing Christ, but rather let him be mediator.' Luchsinger answers: He (Faber) thinks because Zwingli said something about the wrong craze for miracles, therefore no one should remember that any more, and each one think perhaps something has been said about it; it doubtlessly was as Hans Heyerli (Faber) said, The matter is this: Hans Heyerli and D. Martin Blansch, of Tübingen, wished to prove the intercession of the saints by means of the miracles (which has all occurred now in a roundabout manner, for as every one knows they have attacked no article). Yes, the saints have done miracles. Zwingli answered: Miracles are not a sign of divinity, as Christ himself declares (Matt. 7:22), but where real miracles do occur through the saints God does them himself, never the saints, as Saint Peter speaks in the Acts 3. But there occur many miracles by the aid of the devil, so Matthew 24:24: He also accomplishes miracles, and changes himself into the shape of an angel of light (cf. 2 Cor. 11:14). Thus Zwingli spoke, and that fool distorts it thus" ("Gyrenrupfen").]

41. Dr. Sebastian Hofmeister.

42. Sebastian Meyer, born at Neuenburg on the Rhine, in Elsass, twenty miles north of Basel, 1465; studied at Basel and in Germany; became D.D.; entered the Franciscan order; taught in monasteries in Strassburg and Bern; was a rather violent friend of the Reformation. He accepted Lutheran views on the Eucharist, and died in Strassburg, 1545, after preaching in Bern and Augsburg as well as there.

smallest and weakest caused His divine word and will to appear in the world, keeping the same hidden from the great sages of this world. Therefore fear not those who can injure the body; they cannot harm the soul [cf. Matt 10:28]. Do not mind that there are now opposed to the truth of the Gospel bishop, pope and sophists. Thus is it considered by God to make the wise of this world ignorant, and cause the truth to be made clear by the simple. Therefore I beg your wisdom to remain steadfast in the word of God, which I shall also faithfully report to my lords of Bern, whose preacher I am, not in the cathedral, but a lector of the order of Barefoot Monks, and I shall sing your honor and praise. Then he sat down again.

After this the mayor of Zurich again exhorts if any one wishes to say more in regard to these matters he should do it. My lords, he says, are tired of sitting. It will also soon be time to dine.

Then arose a canon of Zurich, by name Master Jacob Edlibach, and spoke thus:

Now listen, dear sirs: My good friend and brother, Master Ulrich, has before exhorted, in the name of Christian love, all those who have anything against him to speak. Now I have had a dispute with him concerning several matters and sayings, but the same was finally brought by both of us before the chapter, where it was settled, so that I thought it was over and should be referred to by no one any more. But now, since Master Ulrich has exhorted those who have spoken against him so frequently to step forth in the name of God, I have thought he may mean me also. Hence I say if Master Ulrich desires that that which was treated of between me and him remain in the knowledge of my lords of the chapter I am satisfied, and shall refer to it no more. For the matter is bad and worthless; also I know naught concerning Master Ulrich, except as a good friend and brother of the chapter. But in so far as he does not wish this, and urges me on, then I shall bring it before you gentlemen. For there are some behind there inciting and saying in scorn one dare not speak.

Zwingli

Dear sirs: I had earnestly resolved to call all those here three times by name who have accused me of being a heretic and the like, but I had really forgotten it now, and furthermore I would never have thought of the good gentleman, Master Jacob Edlibach. It is simply this, I did treat with him concerning a matter before the prior and chapter, which I did not think necessary to bring, indeed would never have thought of bringing forward here. But since he himself, uncalled for, arises and desires to refer to and settle the matter here, I am well satisfied.

Master Jacob

It is of no consequence. I came to Master Ulrich's house and he satisfied me, and although not entirely, still I am satisfied. I know nothing concerning him, except all good. I consider him a good gentleman and brother, hence if he wishes to leave matters as they have been settled before the prior and chapter, I am entirely content.

Zwingli

You may well refer to it here; I am well satisfied, and I had rather have it before these gentlemen, since you yourself reported it.

But there were several there, perhaps relatives of the aforesaid Master Jacob, who said and thought that Master Ulrich ought to act more politely, since one had scarcely incited Master Jacob to speak.

To this Master Ulrich answered that he had never thought of the said Master Jacob, nor would it have occurred to him that he should speak concerning this, etc.

Thus there arose a dispute; some of the councilors wanted the matter to be settled before the chapter, since it had been commenced there; the others thought that it should be tried in the presence of the scholars and gentlemen; but finally the matter was no more thought of and thus quieted, perhaps left to the chapter and thus remained unreferred to. This I report (although not serving much to the purpose) that I may not be accused of not understanding and refuting all speeches and opposition which occurred at that time.[43]

After this the mayor of Zurich permitted every one who did not belong to the council to go to his lodging and dine, until further request, for it was now approaching noon. But the councilors the aforesaid mayor ordered to remain, perhaps to consult further concerning this.[44] Thus they arose, and many of the strangers went to their lodging. This much was done in the forenoon.

After all had eaten they were told to appear again in the city hall to hear the decision made by the wise council of Zurich.[45]

After all had gathered, there was publicly read before the council as is written hereafter:

When in the name of the Lord and upon the request of the mayor, council and great council of the city of Zurich, and for the reasons contained in the letters sent to you, you had obediently appeared, etc., and when again a year having passed since the honorable embassy of our gracious Lord of Constance, on account of such matters as you have heard to-day, was here in the city of Zurich before the mayor, small and great councils, and when these matters having been discussed in various fashions it was reported that our gracious

---

43. ["How could you say truthfully that you have reported and understood all speeches and rebuttals, when I show to you that you have wronged not only me, but others, also Zwingli. You have omitted from my statements two quotations, with their additions: 'I am with you,' etc. (Matt. 28:20), and: 'I will pray the Father, and he shall give you another Comforter,' etc. (John 14:16). Do you know now what I said thereupon? Since the appealing to the saints has gone on, also the mass has been held as a sacrifice throughout the whole of Christendom, not only now for a thousand, but for thirteen and fourteen hundred years, and if it were not true or righteous, then Christ would have wickedly forgotten us and the eternal truth; yes, he would have badly kept his word. But he has said: Behold this is a mystery; nor has he also said: Only after 1000 or 1200 years shall I first come again to my bride the churches. He said: Every day unto the end of the world. And although we did not heed these words of Christ, regardless of the fact that his words are everlasting, according to Isaiah, and he alone is the truth, and furthermore cannot lie, according to Saint Paul, and he is the one whom Saint John calls the faithful and true, and sooner will heaven and earth perish rather than his words, still we would have the other promise of the Holy Ghost, who, it has been promised, will remain with us unto eternity. Hence I do not in great affairs carelessly leave or desert from the Church, but I entrust that rather to Christ. Now what I report has been kept by the Church for so many centuries, hence I would be very careful, since the two things in regard to the saints and the mass are not contrary to the Gospel, and I also can prove it with the Scriptures, and thus I feel like the honest old peasants: when one wishes to abolish their old traditions and praiseworthy usages, which are not contrary to God, they do not like to obey and allow it. And thus I feel in regard to the said sayings, I trust to Christ and God and the Holy Ghost that thus far they have not deserted us, and I say also agree with Saint Jerome, that in regard to these matters I shall rightly hold to the faith which I have received from the maternal breast. Although the doctrine of yourself and your brethren would be very acceptable to me, for I would not be allowed to pray, fast or do other good works, but if I did them I should commit a sin, therefore I would probably go to heaven. But since perchance I cannot ask much, therefore I do not wish to lose the intercession of the saints, and especially of the Virgin Mary" (Faber).]

44. ["Bullinger puts here the word of the mayor: And the sword with which he from Fislisbach was murdered does not wish to appear to fight."]

45. ["Which has been decided upon in accordance with the debate held" (Bullinger).]

Lord of Constance was about to call together the scholars in his bishopric, also the preachers of the neighboring bishoprics and parishes, to advise, help and treat with them, so that a unanimous decision might be reached and each one would know what to rely on, but since until now by our gracious Lord of Constance, perhaps from good reasons, not much has been done in this matter, and since more and more disputes are arising among ecclesiasts and laymen, therefore once more the mayor, council and great council of the city of Zurich, in the name of God, for the sake of peace and Christian unanimity, have fixed this day, and for the advantage of the praiseworthy embassy of our gracious Lord of Constance (for which they gave their gracious, high and careful thanks) have also for this purpose by means of open letter, as stated above, written, called and sent for all secular clergy, preachers and spiritual guides, together and individually, from all their counties into their city, in order that in the examination they might confront with each other those mutually accusing each other of being heretics. But since Master Ulrich Zwingli, canon and preacher of the Great Minster in the city of Zurich, has been formerly much talked against and blamed for his teachings, yet no one, upon his declaring and explaining his Articles, has arisen against him or attempted to overcome him by means of the Scriptures, and when he has several times also called upon those who have accused him of being a heretic to step forward, and no one showed in the least heresy in his doctrines, thereupon the aforesaid mayor, council and great council of this city of Zurich, in order to quell disturbance and dispute, upon due deliberation and consultation have decided, resolved, and it is their earnest opinion, that Master Ulrich Zwingli continue and keep on as before to proclaim the holy Gospel and the correct divine Scriptures with the Spirit of God in accordance with his capabilities so long and so frequently until something better is made known to him. Furthermore, all your secular clergy, spiritual guides and preachers in your cities and counties and estates shall undertake and preach nothing except what they can defend by the Gospels and other right divine Scriptures; furthermore, they shall in no wise in the future slander, call each other heretic or insult in such manner. Those which seem contrary and do not obey will be restrained in such manner that they must see and discover that they have committed wrong. Done the Thursday after Carolus, in the city of Zurich, on the 29th day of January, in the year 1523.

Thereupon Master Ulrich Zwingli arose and spoke thus:[46] God be praised and thanked whose divine word will reign in heaven and upon earth. And you, my lords of Zurich, the eternal God doubtlessly will also in other affairs lend strength and might, so that you may in future advance and preach the truth of God, the divine Gospel, in your country. Do not doubt that Almighty God will make it good and reward you in other matters. Amen.

Whether this decision having been read pleased the vicar of Constance or not I really don't know, for he spoke thus:[47] Dear gentlemen, much has been spoken to-day against the praiseworthy old traditions, usage and ordinance of the holy popes and fathers, whose ordinances and decrees have until now been held in all Christendom true, just and sinless.[48]

---

46. ["Zwingli spoke with great joy after the aforesaid decision had been read" (Bullinger).]

47. ["And first here the vicar became angry, saying: My dear gentlemen, I read to-day Master Ulrich's Articles for the first time, which before I had had no time to glance over" (Bullinger).]

48. ["'You know that it is true that before I or all priests had come to Zurich no one knew your word, whereon the dispute was based, and I tell you that I would have thought sooner of death than that there should be a debate at Zurich concerning the intercession of the saints. Hence you probably marked well that I said I thought I had come to Zurich, but I see I am in

To protect and maintain this I have offered myself to the high councils. But now when for the first time to-day I have looked and glanced through the Articles of Master Ulrich (for I have not read them before), it seems to me truly that these are wholly and entirely at variance with and opposing the ritual (i.e., opposed to the praiseworthy splendor and glory of the churches done and decreed for the praise and honor of God), to the loss of the divine teaching of Christ. This I shall prove.

Zwingli

Sir Vicar, do it. We would like to hear that very much.

Vicar

It is written: *Qui non est adversum vos*, etc. "He that is not against us is for us" (Luke 9:50). Now these praiseworthy services or splendor of the churches (like fasting, confession, having festival days, singing, reading, consecrating,[49] reading mass and other similar things) have always been decreed and ordered by the holy fathers, not against God, but only for the praise and honor of God Almighty, and it seems very strange and unjust to me to consider and refute them as though wrong.

Zwingli

When my Sir Vicar speaks and quotes from the Gospel, "He that is not against us is for us," I say that is true. "Now the customs and ordinances of the Church are ordered and decreed by men, not against God," etc. Sir Vicar, prove that. For Christ always despises human ordinance and decree, as we have in Matthew 15:1–9. When the Jews and Pharisees blamed and attacked the Lord because his disciples did not obey the doctrine and ordinance of the ancients Christ said to them: "Why do ye also transgress the commandment of God by your tradition?" etc. And the Lord spoke further: "Ye hypocrites, well did Esaias prophesy of you, saying, This people draweth nigh unto me with their mouth and knoweth me with their lips, but their heart is far from me. But in vain do they worship me, teaching for doctrines the commandments of men." One sees here that God does not desire our decree and doctrine when they do not originate with Him, despises them, and says we serve Him in vain, which also Saint Paul shows to us when he writes thus: Dear brethren, let no man beguile you by human wisdom and deceit, in accordance with the doctrine or decree of men, in accordance with the doctrines of this world, and not those of Christ. "Let no man therefore judge you in meat, or in drink, or in respect of a holiday, or of a new moon, or

---

Picardy, and this saying I explained to be from the heretic Picard.† Hence although I was not prepared nor thought about the matter, still I desired to argue concerning it, and show wherewith I had proved the imprisoned priest to be in error whom you wished to make a bishop, so that you also might fall into the Arian heresy' (Faber). And before he said: 'Master Ulrich had published the 67 articles only a day before this session, and before any one at Constance or any other city knew a word of it, and Master Ulrich also admitted it may perchance have been issued too late.' Werner Steiner remarks in writing: 'These (the Articles) were handed to him by the pastor of Frauenfeld ‡ on the journey hither, about 2 or 3 days ago.'"]

† Picard, the founder of an heretical sect of the Manichean order, the Picardists, in the 15th century. The customary charge of immorality was brought against them. It spread from its home in Picardy to France and Germany, finally to Bohemia, where it was ruthlessly suppressed by the great Hussite leader, Ziska, in 1421.

‡ Twenty-one miles northeast of Zurich.

49. [From the saying of Luke 9 not six words have been quoted ("Gyrnrupfen").]

of the Sabbath days. Which are a shadow of things to come," etc. (Col. 2:16ff.). God wants from us His decree, His will alone, not our opinion. God the Lord cares more for obedience to His word (although they use the word "obedience" for human obedience) than for all our sacrifices and self-created church usages, as we have it in all the divine writings of the prophets, twelve apostles and saints. The greatest and correct honor to show to God is to obey His word, to live according to His will, not according to our ordinances and best opinion.

Vicar

Christ said, according to John 16:12: "I have yet many things to say unto you, but ye cannot bear them now. Howbeit when he, the Spirit of truth, is come, he will guide you into all truth." Much has been inaugurated by the holy fathers inspired by the Holy Ghost, and especially the fasts and the Saturday by the twelve apostles, which also is not described in the Gospel, in which doubtlessly the Holy Ghost taught and instructed them.[50]

Zwingli

Sir Vicar, prove from the Scriptures that the twelve apostles have inaugurated Saturday and fasts. Christ said in the aforesaid place the Spirit of God will teach them all truth, without doubt not human weaknesses. For he spoke according to John 14:26: "The Holy Ghost, whom the Father will send in my name, he shall teach you (the twelve apostles are meant) all things, and bring all things to your remembrance (advise and recall) whatsoever I have said unto you." As if he said undoubtedly, not what you think fit, but what the Holy Ghost teaches you in my name in accordance with the truth, not with human thoughts. Now then the holy apostles have never taught, inaugurated, ordered and decreed otherwise than as Christ had told them in the Gospel. For Christ said to them, ye are my friends if ye do that which I have decreed and commanded [cf. John 15:14]. This the dear disciples diligently did, and did not teach otherwise than as the right Master had sent them to teach and instruct, which is proven by the epistles of Saint Paul and Saint Peter. Hence your arguments cannot avail anything. For that I can say truly that I could name more than sixty in this room from among my lords, laymen not learned in the Scriptures, who all could refute your argument as presented until now, and by means of the Gospel overcome and refute.

Vicar

Very well, Master Ulrich, do you admit that, that one should only keep what is writ in the Gospel, and nothing besides? Do you admit that?

Zwingli

Sir Vicar, I pity you that you present such sophistical, hairsplitting or useless arguments. Perhaps I could also indulge in such devices, perchance I have also read it formerly in the

---

50. ["Also the saying John 16:12 I did not refer to, for I knew the verse did not belong here; just as little did I say about fasting Saturdays" (Faber). Hereupon Heinrich Wolf maintains he referred to the quotation from John 16:12: Christ still had many things to say to the disciples, but they could not bear it now, and Zwingli answered him, and showed how he had distorted the word of Christ ("Gyrenrupfen").]

sophists, hence I do not wish to be entrapped by such subterfuges and tricks. I shall answer and argue with the pure Scriptures, saying there it is written. That is befitting a scholar, to defend his cause by the Scriptures.

Vicar

You have read in Saint Paul that he accepted and taught traditions which formerly were not written in the Gospel.[51] [Zwingli interrupts: That we wish to hear.] For when he inaugurated among the Corinthians the custom of the sacrament as he had received it from the Lord he said among other things: *Cetera, cum venero, disponam.* "And the rest will I set in order when I come" (1 Cor. 11:34). There Saint Paul announces that he will further teach them to honor and to use the sacrament. But that such was true, and that the twelve apostles gave instructions, presenting them as traditions which were not decreed by the Gospel, I shall prove from Saint Paul to the Thessalonians. Master Ulrich interrupts, asking: Where is it written? The vicar answers: You will find it in the second chapter. Zwingli says: We will look at it. But it is not there; we will look for it in the last epistle. But very well, continue. The vicar answers: Thus says Saint Paul: *Nos autem debemus gratias agere*, etc. "But we are bound to give thanks always to God of you, brethren beloved, etc., because God hath chosen you to salvation, etc., through belief of the truth, whereunto he called you by our gospel, etc. Therefore, brethren, stand fast and hold the traditions (i.e., teachings) which ye have been taught, whether by our word or our epistle" (2 Thess. 2:13–15). [Here Master Ulrich said: He is misusing the Scriptures; I shall prove it.] Saint Paul says here that one should stand fast and hold the traditions, whether emanating from his words or his epistle. This is proof that he taught and instructed that which formerly had not been written, but clearly and openly invented.

Zwingli

In the first place, when he says Saint Paul gave traditions to the people of Corinth which before had not been decreed, I say no, for he says in the same place: "For I have received of the Lord that which also I delivered unto you" (1 Cor. 11:23). But when he says: "And the rest will I set in order when I come" (1 Cor. 11:34), it does not mean what the vicar says; on the contrary he is punishing the Corinthians on account of misuse and mistake in the taking and use of the divine sacrament. For of the wealthy, who assembled in the churches for the sacrament, some overate themselves and became satiated, while the other poor people, at times hungry, had nothing to eat. This is what Saint Paul complains of when he writes [cf. 1 Cor. 11:22]: "What! have ye not houses to eat and to drink in?" as

---

51. ["That I said and say still, that we are bound to hold many things that are not openly written, but which the Church holds and we believe, and furthermore have been reported by the teachers of the first churches as having come to us by order of the 12 apostles; thus I wished to prove that the forty days' fast, also the Sunday which in the Apocalypse Saint John calls *diem dominicam* ['the Lord's day'] (Rev. 1:10), was decreed by the 12 disciples; if we do not wish to despise, depose or suppress them, then it is fitting that what so many centuries by Christendom generally, also by the heretics, has been held we should also keep, even if it be not openly printed in the Scriptures." Furthermore he remarks: "It is a harmful error not to admit anything unless it be expressly described in the Scriptures. The Sadduceans also denied the resurrection because it was not expressed in the Scriptures. I praise you all that you preach the Gospel and Saint Paul, for that is the right rock. But what we have also from the time of the 12 apostles you should not cast so carelessly aside. If your speech were true we would be obliged to leave the 'symbolo apostolorum,' the 'homoousio,' yes from the persons in the Godhead, from free will; we no more could believe that Anna was the mother of Mary," etc. (Faber).]

if he were saying the sacrament is not for the necessity of the body, but as a food for the souls. Therefore Saint Paul concludes: "And the rest will I set in order when I come." Not that he wishes to teach otherwise than as Christ has ordered him, but in order to stop and better their misuse does he say this, which the Word shows: *Tradidi vobis* ["I delivered unto you"], etc.

Secondly, since Sir Vicar pretends that human ordinance and teaching are to be held, this also is not written in the Gospel; he refers to Saint Paul to the Thessalonians, where he writes: "Therefore, brethren, stand fast and hold the traditions which ye have been taught, whether by word or our epistle." I say Paul did not speak, teach, write or instruct in anything except what the Lord had ordered him. For he testifies everywhere, and also proves it to be true, to have written or preached naught except the Gospel of Christ, which God had promised before in the Scriptures of His Son through the prophets.[52]

Vicar

Master Ulrich, you said in your Articles that the mass is no offering. Now I shall prove that for 1400 years *missal* has been considered a sacrifice and called an offering. For *missa* is a Hebrew word, known by us as sacrifice, and also the apostles were known as *missam sacrificium*.

Zwingli: Sir Vicar, prove that. Vicar: To-day I spoke as a Vicar; now I speak as a John. Zwingli: Yes indeed; had you long before to-day taken off your vicar's hat it would have suited you well at times to-day; then one could have spoken with you as with a John.[53] I say that you should prove from the Scriptures that the mass is a sacrifice, for, as Saint Paul says, Christ not more than once was sacrificed, not by other blood, but "by his own blood he entered once into the holy place," etc., nor yet that he should offer himself often, as the high priests in the Old Testament had to do for the sin of the people, for then must Christ often have suffered (Heb. 9:12, 25–26). Likewise, Saint Paul writes, "But this man after he had offered one sacrifice forever sat down on the right hand of God." Likewise, "For by one offering he hath perfected forever them that are sanctified" (Heb. 10:12, 14). Likewise, By so much does this sacrifice surpass the sacrifices in the Old Testament fulfilled by the high priest, by so much more powerful is this declared to be that it was sufficient once for the sins of all people (Heb. 7:22–27). Who is so unreasonable as not to note that Christ must never be sacrificed in the mass as a

---

52. ["And the traditions do not disagree with the Scriptures, so that when the apostles wrote one thing another was opposed to it" (Bullinger).]

53. [Hans Hab remarks: "Faber attacked the Articles severely, but could not prove that they are unchristian. It happened thus, when after dinner the decision was read: Just like the peasant boys, you first began in earnest after the matter was closed, and even then you did not wish to attack any Article, to make it unchristian by means of the Scriptures, as you attacked them, but you raised the Articles in your own hand and said: Now I do not wish to speak as a vicar, but as a John, and I say, Master Ulrich, that your Articles are not like unto the truth, and are not based upon the Gospel and the writings of the apostles." Zwingli answered: "Sir Vicar, if you had taken off your hat long ago one could have treated about something. But in answer to your speech I spoke thus: You shall prove your wicked speech with the deed, and do well and attack only one Article, so that we may not let this day pass by uselessly, for so well are these Articles founded that heaven and earth must break sooner than one of these Articles. Upon this you answered, as always before, this was not the place to debate, but you wished to debate in writing and have judges. Thereupon Zwingli answered he was indifferent whether one noted down everything that was spoken, but he wanted no judge over the word of God, for the word of God should judge the people, and not the people the word of God. About that you teased Zwingli, whether he would not take those of Zurich as judges? Zwingli replied, no—so much at this time, although much was still added thereto" ("Gyrenrupfen").]

sacrifice for us when he hears that the Holy Ghost speaks from the Scriptures, For not more than once (*semel*) by one offering he entered into the holy place; otherwise he must die often? Now matters have come to such a state that the papists have made out of the mass a sacrifice for the living and dead, contrary to the joyful Scriptures of God; they wish to protect this also, so that they may defend their name of scholar or their avarice. We also know well that "missa" does not come from Hebrew or Greek; but you present nothing from the Scriptures.

Vicar

I will do that and prove it before the universities, where learned judges sit. And choose a place, be it Paris, Cologne or Freiburg, whichever you please; then I shall overthrow the Articles presented by you and prove them to be wrong.

Zwingli

I am ready, wherever you wish, as also to-day I offered to give answer at Constance, if a safe conduct (as to you here) is promised to me and respected. But no judge I want, except the Scriptures, as they have been said and spoken by the Spirit of God; no human being, whichsoever it be; and before you overthrow one Article the earth must be overthrown, for they are the Word of God.

Vicar

This is a queer affair. When, e.g., two are quarreling about an acre or about a meadow, they are sent before a judge. Him they also accept, and you refuse to allow these matters to come before a judge. How would this be if I should propose that you take my lords of Zurich as judges? Would you not accept these and allow them to judge?

Zwingli

In worldly affairs and in quarrels I know well that one should go before the judges with the disputes, and I also would choose and have as judges my lords of Zurich, since they possess justice. But in these matters, which pertain to divine wisdom and truth, I will accept no one as judge and witness except the Scriptures, the Spirit of God speaking from the Scriptures.

Vicar

How would it be if you chose a judge and I also one, both impartial, be it here or somewhere else, would you not be satisfied what these two recognized and pronounced as true sentence?

Hereupon Sir Fritz von Anwyl, major-domo of the bishop of Constance, spoke:

Must we then all believe as those two, and not hold otherwise?

Hereupon there was a laugh, so that the vicar became silent and answered nothing. But when it had again become quiet the vicar spoke thus:

Christ in the Gospel[54] says, He will remain with us even unto the end of the world (Matt. 28:20). In another place, he says: "For ye have the poor always with you; but me ye have

---

54. ["I shall not be with you always, and then" (Bullinger).]

not always" (Matt. 26:11). Now if there were no one who decided concerning these sayings, who could know how one should grasp these two sayings thus opposed to each other? One must then have a judge.

Zwingli

The Spirit of God decided itself from the Scriptures that the Lord is speaking of two kinds of presences, of the corporal and the spiritual. The Scripture speaks evidently of the corporal presence or bodily attendance of Christ, and declares that Christ died, was buried, arose on the third day, and having ascended to the heavens sits on the right of his Father. Hence one notices readily from the Scriptures how one shall understand that when the Lord says: "Me ye have not always." In the same fashion, when He says He will remain with us even unto the end of the world, the Scriptures teach that Christ is the word of God, the wisdom, the will of his heavenly Father, the truth, the way, the light, the life of all believers. Therefore one evidently sees that spiritually he remains with us unto the end of the world. Hence one needs no other judge besides the divine Scriptures; the only trouble is that we do not search and read them with entire earnestness.[55]

Thereupon Dr. Martin of Tübingen speaks, saying:

You interpret the Scriptures thus according to your judgment, another interprets them another way; hence there must always be people who decide these things and declare the correct meaning of the Scriptures, as this is symbolized by the wheels of Ezekiel.

Zwingli

I do not understand the Scriptures differently than it is interpreted by means of the Spirit of God; there is no need of human judgment.[56] We know that the ordinance of God is spiritual (Rom. 7:14), and is not to be explained by the reasoning of man in the flesh. For the corporal man in the flesh does not understand the things which are of the Spirit of God (1 Cor. 2:14). Therefore I do not wish to have or accept a man as judge of the Scriptures.

Vicar

Arius and Sabelius would still walk on earth or rule if the matters had not been brought before judges.

Zwingli

I shall do as the fathers, who also conquered by means of the Scriptures, not by means of human understanding.[57] For when they were disputing with Arius they did not accept

55. ["In regard to the quotation from Matthew 28:20, Zwingli gave you (Faber) the following answer: It is true that Christ has promised to remain with us to the end of the world. That he also keeps his promise faithfully, ye pious brethren in Jesus Christ, you should have no doubt. God is with us probably as with no council. For we keep His word, and seek the truth from his word alone. Those who do that, God is with them" (Luchsinger in "Gyrenrupfen").]

56. ["The Scriptures decide themselves in the presence of men" (Bullinger).]

57. ["Did you not also hear that thereupon Zwingli answered: A council never overcame a heretic except with the Scriptures, for it would have been useless if one had tried to overcome Arius in another fashion except by the Scripture. Hence he also stood there, demanding that one listen to the Scriptures in regard to all the Articles; these should be judges over him, and according to that he would allow all Christians to recognize not only several, but all, whether he had used

men, but the Scriptures, as judges, as one finds. When Arius said it is also proven by the Scriptures, as he thought, that the Son of God is less than the Father (John 14:28), the dear fathers sought the Scriptures, allowing them to judge, and showed that it was written, "I and my Father are one" (John 10:30). Also, "He that hath seen me hath seen the Father. Believest thou not that I am in the Father and the Father in me?" Also, "The Father that dwelleth in me, he doeth the works" (John 14:9–10). Such declarations of the Scriptures the dear fathers considered, and showed that Christ had two natures, human and divine, and proved by the Scriptures, not by the judgment of men, that the saying which Arius quoted, The Father is more than I, referred to the humanity of Christ and the later sayings spoke of the Godhead, as was shown by the Scriptures themselves, and the Scriptures interpreted the Scriptures, not the fathers the Scriptures. Thus Saint Augustine overcame the Arians, Manicheans, etc.; Jerome the Jovians, Pelagians; Cyprian his opponents and heretics, at the same time with books referred to and Scriptures quoted, so that the Scriptures, and not they, were the judges. The Scriptures are so much the same everywhere, the Spirit of God flows so abundantly, walks in them so joyfully, that every diligent reader, in so far as he approaches with humble heart, will decide by means of the Scriptures, taught by the Spirit of God, until he attains the truth. For Christ whenever he argued with the learned Jews and Pharisees referred to the Scriptures, saying: "Search the Scriptures" (John 5:39). Also, "What is written in the law?" etc. (Luke 10:26). Therefore I say the matter needs no human judge. But that at various times such matters generally have been brought before human judges and universities is the reason that the priests no longer desired to study, and paid greater attention to wantonness, at times to chess, than reading the Bible. Hence it came about that one considered those scholars and chose them as judges who had attracted unto themselves only the appearance or diploma of wisdom, who knew naught concerning the right Spirit of God or the Scriptures. But now through the grace of God the divine Gospel and Scriptures have been born and brought to light by means of print (especially at Basel), so that they are in Latin and German, wherefrom every pious Christian who can read or knows Latin can easily inform himself and learn the will of God. This has been attained, God be praised, that now a priest who is diligent may learn and know as much in two or three years concerning the Scriptures as formerly many in ten or fifteen years. Therefore I wish all the priests who have benefices under my lords of Zurich or in their counties, and have them exhorted that each one is diligent and labors to read the Scriptures, and especially those who are preachers and caretakers of the soul, let each one buy a New Testament in Latin, or in German, if he does not understand the Latin or is unable to interpret it. For I also am not ashamed to read German at times, on account of easier presentation. Let one begin to read first the gospel of Saint Matthew, especially the fifth, sixth, and seventh chapters. After that let him read the other gospels, so that he may know what they write and say. After that he should take the Acts. After this the epistles of Paul, but first the one to the Galatians. Then the epistle of Saint Peter

---

the Scriptures rightly or not; and he asked who was judge between Hilary and Arians, between Jerome and Jovian, between Augustine and the Manicheans; with nothing besides the Scriptures they proved their cause, and thus allowed it to come before all people without a single judge. And what you attacked afterwards, just as if he had boasted of great abilities, that you invented. For Zwingli spoke of the rest who were there thus: There are in the hall probably men as learned in Hebrew, Greek and Latin as at Tübingen, Basel, Freiburg and elsewhere" (Hans Hab in "Gyrenrupfen"). He adds thereto: "Zurich has probably as many people learned in the three languages as he and his papists in a heap, and who understand the Scriptures better than those at Lyon and Paris."]

and other divine texts; thus he can readily form within himself a light Christian life, and become more skillful to teach this better to others also. After that let him work in the Old Testament, in the prophets and other books of the Bible, which, I understand, are soon to appear in print in Latin and German. Let one buy such books, and never mind the sophistical and other empty writings, also the decree and work of the papists, tell and preach to the people the holy Gospel, written by the four evangelists and apostles, then the people will become more willing and skillful in leading a peaceful Christian life. For matters have reached such a state that also the laymen and women know more of the Scriptures than some priests and clergymen.

Thereupon spoke a priest, decan of Glattfelden:

Shall one then not read Gregory or Ambrose, or cite their writings in the pulpit, but only the Gospel?

Zwingli

Yes, you may read them. And when you find something written therein which is like the Gospel or quoted from the Gospel, there is no need of using Gregory or Ambrose, but one first of all honors Christ and says, this the Gospel or Scriptures tell us. And this is not only my opinion, but Gregory or Ambrose is also of this opinion. For the dear fathers themselves confirm their writings with the Gospel and Scriptures, and where they depend upon their own thoughts they err readily and generally.

Another priest, by name Hans von Schlieren, asks:

But what shall he do who has a small benefice and not sufficient wherewith he could buy such books, the Testament? I have a poor little benefice; it is also necessary for me to speak.

Zwingli

There is, if God wills, no priest so poor but he cannot buy a Testament, if he likes to learn. Somewhere he will find a pious citizen and other people who will buy him a Bible, or otherwise advance the money so that he can pay for one.

After this the vicar began to speak roughly, saying:

Very well, Master Ulrich. I say that your Articles, as these are noted down, are opposed to the Gospel and Saint Paul, also not in harmony unto the truth. That I offer to prove in writing or orally, wherever you please. Choose for yourself judges for these matters, to render a decision therein, in whichever place suits you, then I shall prove to you in writing or orally that your Articles, which appeared in print, are untruthful and opposed to the Gospel.

Zwingli

Do that, when and wherever you please, and the quicker and sooner the more agreeable and satisfactory it is to me. Write against my Articles or opinions whenever you wish, or argue against them wherever you please. Why don't you do it here, right now? Attack one of my opinions, since you say they are opposed to the Gospel and Saint Paul; try to prove them wrong and false. I say, Vicar, if you can do that, and prove one of my Articles false by means of the Gospel, I will give you a rabbit cheese. Now let's hear it. I shall await it.

Vicar

A rabbit cheese, what is that?[58] I need no cheese. All is also not written in the Gospel that is unrighteous and opposed to Christ;[59] where do you find in the Gospel that one shall not have his daughter or his sister's daughter to wife?

Zwingli

It is also not written that a cardinal shall have thirty benefices.

Master Erasmus von Stein, canon at Zurich, said: It is written in Leviticus, and is forbidden. Answers the vicar, saying: Erasmus, you will not find it, although you search long for it. One could still live a friendly, peaceful and virtuous life even if there were no Gospel.[60]

Zwingli

You will find in Leviticus 18 that relationship of marriage with collateral lines, and even further than the sisters, is forbidden. And if the distant and further removed member of the house or blood relationship is forbidden, then much more is the nearest forbidden and not allowed, as you may read in Leviticus 18:17. I pity you that you come with such foolish or useless and thoughtless remarks, and thus cause offense among the people. That is to give real scandal and vexation to your neighbor. You could have kept that silent and opposed me with other writings; it would have been more worthy of you.

Now every one arose, and nothing more was said at that time; every one went to where he had something to attend to.[61]

58. "A rabbit cheese" is Swiss for a remarkably fine cheese. Glarus, where Zwingli was settled for ten years (1506–1516), was then and is still noted for its cheeses.

59. ["Where did I speak an unfit, immodest or worthless word, as Zwingli always did with his ridiculing and other things, which for the sake of peace I shall not repeat?" (Faber). Conrad Aescher answers: "Zwingli has treated the matter with such earnestness that he could not have been more in earnest; to be sure he had to laugh with the rest when you came with your old tales, which we tailors and shoemakers had also learned long ago. But you act like all bad women, blame other people for what they do themselves. Nobody began his speeches with more ridiculing than you; why you smiled so friendly that we were afraid that the stove of the room would become so attached to you that it would run after you. Zwingli has said nothing shameful or immodest, but you have, when you said, where is it forbidden in the Bible that a father may not marry his daughter? and when you said one could live righteously even without the Gospel," etc. ("Gyrenrupfen").]

60. ["At the end of your account you made the false statement that I said one might still live in a friendly, peaceful and virtuous way even if there were no Gospel. Do you think I am mad, and speak only in unchristian fashion thus? especially as before that I made such a speech in praise of the Gospel, and in my book against Martin Luther I praised so highly and emphasized the Gospel, etc.? And you dare to accuse me of these words which in my life I never thought of? Where were you sitting that you could hear what I said? While several were then speaking every one arose and went away, and no one sitting could have heard me. Do you wish to know what in the hum of voices, as the people were getting up and leaving, I said? Thus I spoke: One may preach the Gospel and still keep the peace. Zwingli thought it could not be, so I declared it could be. Thus you misquote me. Did not the Gospel come with the peace and the peace with the Gospel? But you say only: God has not sent peace upon earth" (Faber). Hans Hager answered him: "Why, how can you deny what one can witness and prove with so many true men, so that I offer to prove it before my lords of Zurich at whatever hour and moment you will? I do not say that it occurred at the end, because it did not occur at the end. It may also have happened to Erhard [Hegenwald] that he forgot it until the end. What does that matter? You said it, no matter when you said it. What does that matter, as long as you had to lie?" (Gyrenrupfen).]

61. ["And were very tired of the irrelevant quotations and speeches of the Vicar" (Bullinger).]

It was also said by the mayor of Zurich, as is afterwards written: The sword, with which the pastor of Fislisbach, captured at Constance, was stabbed, does not wish to appear. The aforesaid mayor remarks that the vicar had not yet shown any Scripture with which he boasted to have overcome the aforesaid lord of Fislisbach.

There also spoke the worthy Mr. R., abbot of Cappel,[62] saying: Where are they now who wish to burn us at the stake and bring wood; why do they not step forward now?

That is the sum and substance of all actions and speeches at the assembly of Zurich, etc., before the assembled council, where also other doctors and gentlemen were present on account of the praiseworthy message of the bishop of Constance and Master Ulrich Zwingli, canon and preacher at the great cathedral of Zurich, which (assembly) occurred at the time and on the day, as stated above, in the year 1523, on the 29th day of January.

---

62. Wolfgang Roupli (or Joner), son of the mayor of Frauenfeld; became abbot 1521; accepted the Reformation and reformed his monastery. He called there Bullinger, who was Zwingli's successor, as teacher of the cloister school, 1522.

The First Decade of Sermons

H ENRY B ULLINGER

The text and notes from Bullinger's two sermons are reprinted from Henry Bullinger, *The Decades of Henry Bullinger*, The First and Second Decades, ed. for The Parker Society by Thomas Harding, trans. H. I. (Cambridge: Cambridge University Press, 1849), 36–70; reprinted in *The Decades of Henry Bullinger*, ed. Thomas Harding, with new introductions by George Ella and Joel R. Beeke (Grand Rapids: Reformation Heritage Books, 2004).

    Johann Heinrich Bullinger (1504–75), a Swiss Reformer, continued the Reformation in Zurich after Zwingli's death. During his studies in Cologne, he was introduced to Luther's writings. Bullinger's influence on Reformed theology proved to be very great. In conflict with both Lutherans and Anabaptists, Bullinger developed an early form of covenant theology, building on Zwingli's theology. Zurich was a place of refuge for English Reformers while Queen Mary ("Bloody Mary") was on the throne. Through personal contact in Zurich and through Bullinger's *Decades*, the standard theological textbook in Elizabethan England, Bullinger influenced many of the independents and Presbyterians in England. He also played a key role in unifying the Reformed in Switzerland and supporting Protestants in France.

    The selection presented here is from Bullinger's *Decades*, which is a collection of his sermons. In these two sermons, Bullinger presents his conception of the Scriptures. In the first, he develops what can be called the progressive nature of God's revelation. He speaks of the Word from its inception to its fulfillment in Christ. Its chief content is to teach salvation. Scripture is authoritative, divine, sound, and uncorrupted. His views of salvation by faith and opposition to tradition contrast with Roman Catholicism. In the second, Bullinger continues to expound the doctrine of the Word: since it is written to us, we ought to hear and heed. Further, the Word is powerful to promote godliness. This exposition in the form of sermons will be complemented by his confession of faith (chap. 12) and his treatise on covenantal hermeneutic (chap. 19). Bullinger stands as an important player in the Reformation alongside John Calvin.

50

Bibliography: G. W. Bromiley. "Bullinger, Johann Heinrich (1504–75)." Pp. 114–14 in *NDT*. Idem, ed. *Zwingli and Bullinger*. LCC. Philadelphia: Westminster Press, 1953. Emil Egli. "Bullinger, Heinrich." *NSHERK* 2:294–302. A. N. S. Lane. "Bullinger, Johann Heinrich (1504–1575)." Pp. 94–96 in *BDE*. O. G. Oliver Jr. "Bullinger, Johann Heinrich (1504–1575)." Pp. 179–80 in *EDT*. Carl R. Trueman. "Bullinger, Heinrich (1504–75)." Pp. 90–91 in *DHT*. Robert C. Walton. "Bullinger, Johann Heinrich (1504–1575)." Pp. 165–66 in *NIDCC*.

THE FIRST SERMON: *OF THE WORD OF GOD; THE CAUSE OF IT; AND HOW, AND BY WHOM, IT WAS REVEALED TO THE WORLD*

All the decrees of Christian faith, with every way how to live rightly, well, and holily, and finally, all true and heavenly wisdom, have always been fetched out of the testimonies, or determinate judgments, of the word of God; neither[1] can they, by those which are wise men indeed, or by the faithful and those which are called by God to the ministry of the churches, be drawn, taught, or, last of all, soundly confirmed from elsewhere, than out of the word of God. Therefore, whosoever is ignorant what the word of God, and the meaning of the word of God is, he seemeth to be as one blind, deaf, and without wit, in the temple of the Lord, in the school of Christ, and lastly, in the reading of the very sacred scriptures. But whereas[2] some are nothing zealous, but very hardly drawn to the hearing of sermons in the church; that springeth out of no other fountain than this, which is, because they do neither rightly understand, nor diligently enough weigh, the virtue and true force of the word of God. That nothing therefore may cause the zealous desirers of the truth and the word of God to stay on this point;[3] but rather that that estimation of God's word, which is due unto it, may be laid up in all men's hearts; I will (by God's help) lay forth unto you, dearly beloved, those things which a godly man ought to think and hold, as concerning the word of God. And pray ye earnestly and continually to our bountiful God, that it may please him to give to me his holy and effectual power to speak, and to you the opening of your ears and minds, so that in all that I shall say the Lord's name may be praised, and your souls be profited abundantly.

Verbum, what it is. First, I have to declare what the word of God is. *Verbum* in the scriptures, and according to the very property of the Hebrew tongue, is diversely taken. For it signifieth what thing soever a man will; even as among the Germans the word *ding* **In English, a thing**. is most largely used. In Saint Luke, the angel of God saith to the blessed virgin: "With God shall no word[4] be unpossible"; which is all one as if he had said, all things are possible to God, or to God is nothing unpossible. *Verbum* also signifieth a word uttered by the mouth of man. Sometime it is used for a charge, sometime for a whole sentence, or speech, or prophecy: whereof in the scriptures there are many examples. But when *verbum*

1. Lat. *hodie*; at this time of day.
2. Lat. *imo quod*; Yea, and that.
3. Lat. *Ne quid remoretur*.
4. πᾶν ῥῆμα (Luke 1:37). Lat. and Vulg. *omne verbum*.

is joined with any thing else, as in this place we call it *verbum Dei*, then[5] is it not used in the same signification. **The word of God, what it is**. For *verbum Dei*, "the word of God," doth signify the virtue and power of God: it is also put for the Son of God, which is the second person in the most reverend Trinity. For that saying of the holy evangelist is evident to all men, "The word was made flesh."[6] But in this treatise of ours, the word of God doth properly signify the speech of God, and the revealing of God's will; first of all uttered in a lively-expressed voice by the mouth of Christ, the prophets and apostles; and after that again registered in writings, which are rightly called "holy and divine scriptures." The word doth shew the mind of him out of whom it cometh: therefore the word of God doth make declaration of God. But God of himself naturally speaketh truth; he is just, good, pure, immortal, eternal: therefore it followeth that the word of God also, which cometh out of the mouth of God, is true, just, without deceit and guile, without error or evil affection, holy, pure, good, immortal, and everlasting. For in the gospel saith the Lord, "Thy word is truth."[7] And the apostle Paul saith, "The word of God is not tied."[8] Again, the scripture everywhere crieth: "The word of the Lord endureth for ever."[9] And Salomon saith: "Every word of God is purely cleansed. Add thou nothing to his words, lest peradventure he reprove thee, and thou be found a liar."[10] David also saith: "The sayings of the Lord are pure sayings, even as it were silver cleansed in the fire, and seven times fined from the earth."[11]

Of the causes and beginnings of the word of God. This you shall more fully perceive, dearly beloved, if I speak somewhat more largely of the cause or beginning, and certainty, of the word of God. The word of God is truth: but God is the only well-spring of truth: therefore God is the beginning and cause of the word of God. And here indeed God, since he hath not members like to mortal men, wanteth also a bodily mouth: yet nevertheless, because the mouth is the instrument of the voice, to God is a mouth attributed. For he spake to men in the voice of a man, that is, in a voice easily understood of men, and fashioned according to the speech usually spoken among men. This is evidently to be seen in the things wherein he dealt with the holy fathers, with whom, as with our parents Adam and Eva, Noe, and the rest of the fathers, he is read to have talked many and oftentimes. In the mount Sina the Lord himself preached to the great congregation of Israel, rehearsing so plainly, that they might understand those ten commandments, wherein is contained every point of godliness. For in the fifth of Deuteronomy thus we read: "These words," meaning the ten commandments, "spake the Lord with a loud voice, from out of the midst of the fire, to the whole congregation."[12] And in the fourth chapter: "A voice of words you heard, but no similitude did you see beside the voice."[13] God verily used oftentimes the means of angels, by whose ministry he talked with mortal men. And it is very well known to all men, that the Son of God the Father, being incarnate, walked about in the earth; and,

5. Lat. *etiam sic.*
6. John 1:14.
7. John 17:17.
8. 2 Tim. 2:9.
9. Isa. 40:8; 1 Peter 1:25.
10. Prov. 30:5, 6.
11. Ps. 12:6.
12. Deut. 5:22.
13. Deut. 4:8.

being very God and man, taught the people of Israel almost for the space of three years.[14] But in times past, and before that the Son of God was born in the world, God, by little and little, made himself acquainted with the hearts[15] of the holy fathers, and after that with the minds of the holy prophets; and last of all, by their preaching and writings, he taught the whole world. So also Christ our Lord sent the Holy Ghost, which is of the Father and the Son, into the apostles, by whose mouths, words, and writings he was known to all the world. **The word of God revealed to the world by men**. And all these servants of God, as it were the elect vessels of God, having with sincere hearts received the revelation of God from God himself, first of all, in a lively expressed voice delivered to the world the oracles and word of God which they before had learned; and afterward, when the world drew more to an end, some of them did put them in writing for a memorial to the posterity. And it is good to know how, and by whom, all this was done: for by this narration the true cause, certainty, and dignity of the word of God doth plainly appear.

There are not extant to be seen the writings of any man, from the beginning of the world, until the time of Moses, which are come to our knowledge; although it be likely that that same ancient and first world was not altogether without all writings. For by Saint Jude, the apostle, and brother of Saint James, is cited the written prophecy of our holy father Enoch, which is read to have been the seventh from our father Adam.[16] Furthermore, the writing, or history, of Job seemeth to have been set forth a great while before. But howsoever it is, all the saints in the church of God give to Moses, the faithful servant of God, the first place among the holy writers.

How and by whom the word of God hath been revealed from the beginning of the world. From the beginning therefore of the world, God, by his Spirit and the ministry of angels, spake to the holy fathers; and they by word of mouth taught their children, and children's children, and all their posterity, that which they had learned at the mouth of God; when they verily had heard it, not to the intent to keep it close to themselves, but also to make their posterity partakers of the same. For God oftentimes witnesseth, that "he will be the God of the fathers and of their seed for evermore."[17] This is most plainly to be seen in the history of Adam, Noe, and Abraham, the first and great grandfathers.[18] **Abraham**. In the eighteenth of Genesis, verily, we read, that the angel of God, yea, and that more is, that even the Lord himself, did say to Abraham: "And shall I hide from Abraham what I mind to do? since of Abraham shall come a great and mighty people, and all the nations of the earth shall be blessed in him? And this I know, that he will command his children and his posterity after him, to keep the way of the Lord, and to do justice, judgment,"[19] and the rest. Abraham therefore, a faithful and zealous worshipper of God, did not (even as also those old fathers of the first world did not) wax negligent at all herein, but did diligently teach men the will and judgments of God: whereupon of Moses, yea, and of God himself,

---

14. The duration of our Lord's ministry is now usually admitted to have been three years and a half.—See Greswell, *Harmonia Evangelica*, and Dr. Robinson, *Harmony of the Gospels*.
15. Lat. *insinuavit se Deus animis*.
16. Jude 14–15.
17. Gen. 17:7.
18. Lat. *genearcharum*.
19. Gen. 18:17–19.

he is called a prophet.[20] That devout and lively tradition of the fathers, from hand to hand, was had in use continually, even from the beginning of the world until the time of Moses.

Moreover, God of his goodness did provide that no age at any time should be without most excellent lights, to be witnesses of the undoubted faith, and fathers of great authority. **The clearest lights of the first world**. For the world before the deluge had in it nine most excellent, most holy, and wise men; Adam, Seth, Enos, Kenam, Malaleel, Jared, Enoch, Methusalem, and Lamech. **Adam and Methusalem**. The chief of these, Adam and Methusalem, do begin and make an end of all the sixteen hundred and fifty-six years[21] of the world before the deluge. For Adam lived nine hundred and thirty years:[22] he dieth therefore the seven hundred and twenty-sixth year before the flood. And Methusalem lived nine hundred and sixty-nine years:[23] he dieth in the very same year that the flood did overflow; and he lived together with Adam two hundred and forty-three years, so that of Adam he might be abundantly enough instructed as concerning the beginning of things, as concerning God, the falling and restoring again of mankind, and all things else belonging to religion, even as he was taught of God himself. These two fathers, with the rest above named, were able sufficiently enough to instruct the whole age in the true salvation and right ways of the Lord.

After the deluge God gave to the world again excellent men, and very great lights. The names of them are Noe, Sem, Arphaxad, Sale, Heber, Palec, Reu, Saruch, Nachor, Thare, Abraham, Isaac, and Jacob. Here have we thirteen most excellent patriarchs, among whom the first two, Noe and Sem, are the chief; next to whom Abraham, Isaac, and Jacob, were more notable than the rest. **Noe**. Noe lived nine hundred and fifty years in all. He was six hundred years old when the flood drowned the world.[24] He therefore saw and heard all the holy fathers of the first world before the deluge, three only excepted, Adam, Seth, and Enos. And also he lived many years together with the other, which had both seen and heard them; so that he could be ignorant in no point of those things which Adam had taught. Noe dieth (which is marvel to be told, and yet very true) in the forty-ninth year of Abraham's age.[25] **Sem**. Sem, the son of Noah, lived many years with his father; for he lived in all six hundred years. He was born to Noah about ninety-six years before the deluge. He saw and heard, therefore, not only his father Noe and his grandfather Lamech, but also his great grandsire Methusalem, with whom he lived those ninety-six years before the deluge. Of him he might be informed of all those things which Methusalem had heard and learned of Adam and the other patriarchs. Sem dieth, after the death of Abraham, in the fifty-second year of Jacob, which was thirty-seven years after the death of Abraham, in the year one hundred and twelve of Isaac's age: so that Jacob, the patriarch, might very well learn all the true divinity of Sem himself, even as he had heard it of Methusalem, who was the third witness and teacher from Adam. **Jacob**. Furthermore, Jacob the patriarch delivered to his children that which he received of God[26] to teach to his posterity. In Mesopotamia there is born to Jacob his son

---

20. Gen. 20:7.

21. Cf. Bullinger's Treatise, "The Old Faith," translated in *Writings and Translations of Bishop Coverdale* (Cambridge: The Parker Society, 1844), 32, 36.

22. Gen. 5:5.

23. Gen. 5:27.

24. Gen. 7:6.

25. There is some great miscalculation here; for Abraham, if born at all before Noah's death, could only have been in his infancy. Yet Calvin also says, that "Abraham was nearly *fifty* years old, when his ancestor Noe died."—John Calvin, *Commentaries on the Book of Genesis* (Edinburgh: Calvin Translation Society, 1847), 310 on Gen. 9:28. But see note 29 below.

26. Lat. *a Deo per patres accepit*.

Levi, and to him again is born Kahad,[27] which both saw and heard Jacob. For Kahad lived no small number of years with his grandfather Jacob; for he is rehearsed in the roll of them which went with Jacob down into Egypt:[28] but Jacob lived seventeen years with his children in Egypt. **Kahad. Amram. Moses**. This Kahad is the grandfather of Moses, the father of Amram, from whom Moses did perfectly draw that full and certain tradition by hand, as concerning the will, commandments, and judgments of God, even as Amram his father had learned them of his father Kahad, Kahad of Jacob, Jacob of Sem, Sem of Methusalem and of Adam the first father of us all: so now that Moses is from Adam the seventh witness in the world. And from the beginning of the world to the birth of Moses are fully complete two thousand three hundred and sixty-eight years of the world. And whosoever shall diligently reckon the years, not in vain set down by Moses in Genesis and Exodus, he shall find this account to be true and right.[29]

The chief contents of the holy fathers' lively tradition. Now also it behoveth us to know those chief principles of that lively tradition, delivered by the holy fathers at the appointment of God, as it were from hand to hand, to all the posterity. The fathers taught their children that God, of his natural goodness, wishing well to mankind, would have all men to come to the knowledge of the truth, and to be like in nature to God himself, holy, happy, and absolutely blessed: and therefore that God, in the beginning, did create man to his own similitude and likeness, to the intent that he should be good, holy, immortal, blessed, and partaker of all the good gifts of God; but that man continued not in that dignity and happy state; but by the means of the devil, and his own proper fault, fell into sin, misery, and death, changing his likeness to God into the similitude of the devil. Moreover, that God here again, as it were, of fresh began the work of salvation, whereby mankind, being restored and set free from all evil, might once again be made like unto God; and that he meant to bring this mighty and divine work to pass by a certain middle mean, that is, by the Word incarnate. For as, by this taking of flesh, he joined man to God; so, by dying in the flesh, with sacrifice he cleansed, sanctified, and delivered mankind; and, by giving him his Holy Spirit, he made him like again in nature to God, that is, immortal, and absolutely blessed. And last of all, he worketh in us a willing endeavour aptly to resemble the property and conditions of him to whose likeness we are created, so that we may be holy both body and soul. They added moreover, that the Word should be incarnate in his due time and appointed age; and also, that there did remain a great day for judgment, wherein, though all men were gathered together, yet the righteous only should receive that reward of heavenly immortality.

So then, this is the brief sum of the holy fathers' tradition, which it is best to untwist more largely, and to speak of it more diligently, as it were by parts. **God**. First, therefore, the fathers taught, that the Father, the Son, and the Holy Ghost are one God in the most reverend Trinity, the maker and governor of heaven and earth and all things which are therein; **Creation of the world**. by whom man was made, and who for man did make all things, and put all things under mankind, to minister unto him things necessary, as a

27. *Kohath.*—Vulg., Caath.
28. Gen. 46:11.
29. It is scarcely necessary to observe that the system of chronology here used differs considerably from the received system according to Usher. Bullinger followed the vulgar Jewish chronology, upon which the arrangements of Scaliger, Petavius, and Usher were afterwards founded. See Hales, *Chronology*, vol. 1. The difference does not materially affect the argument.—The line of the patriarchal tradition may be seen traced in Robert Gray, *Key to the Old Testament* (London: Rivington, 1797), 80–81.

loving Father and most bountiful Lord. Then they taught, that man consisted of soul and body, and that he indeed was made good according to the image and likeness of God; **Sin and death**. but that by his own fault, and egging forward of the devil, falling into sin, he brought into the world death and damnation, together with a web of miseries, out of which it cannot rid itself: so that now all the children of Adam, even from Adam, are born the sons of wrath and wretchedness; but that God, whose mercy aboundeth, according to his incomprehensible goodness, **Grace, life, and redemption by Christ**. taking pity on the misery of mankind, did, even of his mere grace, grant[30] pardon for the offence, and did lay the weight of the punishment upon his only Son, to the intent that he, when his heel was crushed by the serpent, might himself break the serpent's head:[31] that is to say, God doth make a promise of seed, that is, of a Son, who, taking flesh of a peerless woman (I mean, that virgin most worthy of commendations) should by his death vanquish death and Satan, the author of death; and should bring the faithful sons of Adam out of bondage; yea, and that more is, should by adoption make them the sons of God, and heirs of life everlasting. **Faith**. The holy fathers, therefore, taught to believe in God, and in his Son, the redeemer of the whole world; when in their very sacrifices they did present his death, as it were an unspotted sacrifice, wherewith he meant to wipe away and cleanse the sins of all the world.

The lineal descent of Messias. And therefore had they a most diligent eye to the stock and lineal descent of the Messias. For it is brought down, as it were by a line, from Adam to Noe, and from Noe by Sem even to Abraham himself: and to him again it was said, "In thy seed shall all the nations of the earth be blessed":[32] in which words the promise once made to Adam, as touching Christ the redeemer and changer of God's curse into blessing, is renewed and repeated again. The same line is brought down from Abraham by Isaac unto Jacob;[33] and Jacob, being full of the Spirit of God, pointed out his son Juda to be the root[34] of the blessed Seed, as it is to be seen in the forty-ninth of Genesis. Lastly, in the tribe of Juda the house of David was noted, out of which that seed and branch of life should come.

The league of God. Moreover, the holy fathers taught, that God by a certain league hath joined himself to mankind, and that he hath most straitly bound himself to the faithful, and the faithful likewise to himself again. **The worship of God**. Whereupon they did teach to be faithful to God-ward, to honour God, to hate false gods, to call upon the only God, and to worship him devoutly. Furthermore, they taught, that the worship of God did consist in things spiritual, as faith, hope, charity, obedience, upright dealing, holiness, innocency, patience, truth, judgment, and godliness. And therefore did they reprehend naughtiness and sin, falsehood, lack of belief, desperation, disobedience, unpatientness, lying, hypocrisy, hatred, despiteful taunts, violence, wrong, unrighteous dealing, uncleanness, riotousness, surfeiting, whoredom, unrighteousness, and ungodliness. They taught, that God was a rewarder of good, but a punisher and revenger of evil. **Life eternal and the day of judgment**. They taught, that the souls of men were immortal, and that the bodies should rise again in

30. Lat. *promisisse*.
31. Gen. 3:15.
32. Gen. 22:18.
33. Lat. *per Isaacum* et *Jacobum*.
34. Lat. *genearcham*.

the day of judgment: therefore they exhorted us all so to live in this temporal life, that we do not leese[35] the life eternal.

The true historical narration delivered by the fathers to their children. This is the sum of the word of God revealed to the fathers, and by them delivered to their posterity. This is the tradition of the holy fathers, which comprehendeth all religion. Finally, this is the true, ancient, undoubted, authentical, and catholic[36] faith of the fathers.

Besides this, the holy fathers taught their children, and children's children, the account of the years from the beginning of the world, and also the true historical course, as well profitable as necessary, of things from the creation of the world even unto their own times; lest peradventure their children should be ignorant of the beginning and succession of worldly things, and also of the judgments of God, and examples of them which lived as well godly as ungodly.

I could declare unto you all this evidently, and in very good order, out of the first book of Moses, called Genesis, if it were not that thereby the sermon should be drawn out somewhat longer than the use is. But I suppose that there are few, or rather none at all, here present, which do not perceive that I have rehearsed this that I have said, touching the tradition of the ancient fathers, as it were word for word, out of the book of Genesis; so that now I may very well go forward in the narration which I have begun.

Moses in an history compileth the traditions of the fathers. So then, whatsoever hitherto was of the fathers delivered to the world by word of mouth, and as it were from hand to hand, that was first of all put into writing by the holy man Moses, together with those things which were done in all the time of Moses' life, by the space of one hundred and twenty years. And that his estimation might be the greater throughout all the world, among all men, and in all ages; and that none should but know, that the writings of Moses were the very word of God itself; Moses was furnished, and as it were consecrated by God, with signs and wonders to be marvelled at indeed, which the almighty by the hand, that is, by the ministry of Moses, did bring to pass: and verily, he wrought them not in any corner of the world, or place unknown, but in Egypt, the most flourishing and renowned kingdom of that age.

Those miracles were greater and far more by many, than that they can be here rehearsed in few words: neither is it needful to repeat them, because you, dearly beloved, are not unskilful or ignorant of them at all. After that also, God by other means procured authority to Moses. For many and oftentimes God had communication with Moses; and amongst the rest of his talk said he: "Behold, I will come to thee in a thick cloud, that the people may hear me talking with thee, and may believe thee for evermore."[37]

Neither was the Lord therewith content, but commanded Moses to call together all the people, six hundred thousand men, I say, with their wives and children. They are called out to the mount Sina, where God appeareth in a wonderful and terrible fashion; and he himself, preaching to the congregation, doth rehearse unto them the ten commandments. But the people, being terrified with the majesty of God, doth pray and beseech, that God himself would no more afterward preach to the congregation with his own mouth, saying, that it were enough, if he would use Moses as an interpreter to them, and by him speak to

---

35. leese: lose.
36. Lat. *authentica, orthodoxa, et catholica*.
37. Ex. 19:9.

the church.[38] The most high God did like the offer; and, after that, he spake to the people by Moses whatsoever he would have done. And for because that the people was a stiff-necked people, and by keeping company with idolaters in Egypt was not a little corrupted, Moses now began to set down in writing those things which the holy fathers by tradition had taught, and the things also which the Lord had revealed unto him. The cause why he wrote them was, lest peradventure by oblivion, by continuance of time, and obstinacy of a people so slow to believe, they might either perish, or else be corrupted. The Lord also set Moses an example to follow. For whatsoever God had spoken to the church in mount Sina, the same did he straightway after write with his own finger in two tables of stone, as he had with his finger from the beginning of the world written the same in the hearts of the fathers.[39] Afterward also, in plain words, he commanded Moses to write whatsoever the Lord had revealed. Moses obeyed the Lord's commandment, and wrote them. The Holy Ghost, which was wholly in the mind of Moses, directed his hand as he writ. There was no ability wanting in Moses, that was necessary for a most absolute writer. He was abundantly instructed by his ancestors: for he was born of the holiest progeny of those fathers, whom God appointed to be witnesses of his will, commandments, and judgments; suppose[40] Amram, Kahad, Jacob, Sem, Methusalem and Adam. He was able, therefore, to write a true and certain history, from the beginning of the world even until his own time. Whereunto he added those things which were done among the people of God in his own life-time, whereof he was a very true witness, as one that saw and heard them. Yea, and that more is, whatsoever he did set forth in his books, that did he read to his people, and amongst so many thousands was there not one found which gainsayed that which he rehearsed: so that the whole consent and witness-bearing of the great congregation did bring no small authority to the writings of Moses.

The authority of Moses very great. Moses therefore contained in the five books, called the five books of Moses, an history from the beginning of the world, even unto his own death, by the space of two thousand four hundred and eighty-eight years: in which he declared most largely the revelation of the word of God made unto men, and whatsoever the word of God doth contain and teach: in which, as we have the manifold oracles of God himself, so we have most lightsome[41] testimonies, sentences, examples, and decrees of the most excellent, ancient, holy, wise, and greatest men of the world, touching all things which seem to appertain to true godliness, and the way how to live well and holily. These books therefore found a ready prepared entrance of belief among all the posterity, as books which are authentical, and which of themselves have authority sufficient, and which, without gainsaying, ought to be believed of all the world. Yea, and that more is, our Lord Jesus Christ, the only-begotten Son of God, doth refer the faithful to the reading of Moses; yea, and that indeed in the chiefest points of our salvation: the places are to be seen (John 5; Luke 16). In the fifth of Matthew he saith: "Do not think that I am come to destroy the law and the prophets; for I am not come to destroy them, but to fulfil them. For, verily, I say unto you, though[42] heaven and earth do pass, one jot or tittle of

---

38. Ex. 20:19.
39. See Bullinger, "The Old Faith," 27, 40.
40. Lat. *puto autem.*
41. Lat. *clarissimorum.*
42. Lat. as in Eng. Ver. *donec prætereat.*

the law shall not pass, till all be fulfilled. Whosoever, therefore, shall undo one of the least of these commandments, and shall teach men so, he shall be called the least in the kingdom of heaven."[43]

There have verily some been found, that have spoken against Moses, the servant of God. But God hath imputed that gainsaying as done against his divine majesty, and punished it most sharply. The proofs hereof are to be seen in Exodus 16 and Numbers 12. And first, of the people murmuring against Moses; then of Mary, Moses's sister, speaking against her brother. But to the people it was said: "Not against the ministers, but against the Lord, are your complaints."[44] As for Mary, she was horribly stricken with a leprosy.[45] Theotectus was stricken blind, and Theopompus fell to be mad, because he had unreverently touched the word of God.[46] For, although the word of God be revealed, spoken, and written by men, yet doth it not therefore cease to be that which indeed it is; neither doth it therefore begin to be the word of men, because it is preached and heard of men: no more than the king's commandment, which is proclaimed by the crier, is said to be the commandment of the crier. He despiseth God, and with God all the holy patriarchs, whosoever doth contemn Moses, by whom God speaketh unto us, and at whose hand we have received those things which the patriarchs from the beginning of the world by tradition delivered to the posterity. There is no difference between the word of God, which is taught by the lively expressed voice of man, and that which is written by the pen of man, but so far forth as the lively voice and writing do differ between themselves: the matter undoubtedly, the sense, and meaning, in the one and the other is all one. By this, dearly beloved, you have perceived the certain history of the beginning of the word of God.

The proceeding of the word of God. Now let us go forward to the rest; that is, to add the history of the proceeding of the word of God, and by what means it shined ever and anon very clear and brightly unto the world. By and by, after the departure of the holy man Moses out of this world into heaven, the Lord of his bountifulness gave most excellent prophets unto his church, which he had chosen to the intent that by it he might reveal his word unto the whole world. **The prophets**. And the prophets were to them of the old time, as at this day amongst us are prophets, priests, wise men, preachers, pastors, bishops, doctors or divines, most skilful in heavenly things, and given by God to guide the people in the faith. And he, whosoever shall read the holy history, will confess that there flourished[47] of this sort no small number, and those not obscure, even till the captivity of Babylon. Amongst whom are reckoned these singular and excellent men, Phinees, Samuel, Helias, Heliseus, Esaias, and Jeremias. David and Salomon were both kings and prophets. In time of the captivity at Babylon, Daniel and Ezechiel were notably known. After the captivity flourished, among the rest, Zacharias the son of Barachias. Here have I reckoned up a few among many: who, although they flourished at sundry times, and

43. Matt. 5:17–19. Lat., *Quisquis autem fecerit et docuerit, hic magnus vocabitur in regno cœlorum*; omitted by the translator.

44. Ex. 16:8.

45. Num. 12:10. Miriam: Vulg. *Maria.*

46. Lat., *Theotectus tragœdiarum scriptor*. Theodectes, according to Suidas and Gellius, *Attic Nights* 10.18, was a tragedian, and contemporary with Theopompus, who was an orator and historian, a pupil of Isocrates. Josephus, *Jewish Antiquities* 12.2 and *The Letter of Aristeas* 312–16 relate the story referred to—namely, that each of these writers was preparing to put forth a part of the scriptures, as their own composition, when they were visited, the former with blindness, the latter with madness, which lasted thirty days.—Gerard Vossius. 1.7.

47. Lat. *in populo sive ecclesia Dei*; "in the people or church of God," omitted by the translator.

that the one a great while after the other, yet did they all, with one consent, acknowledge that God spake to the world by Moses, who (God so appointed it) left to the church in the world a breviary[48] of true divinity, and a most absolute sum of the word of God contained in writing. All these priests, divines, and prophets, in all that they did, had an especial eye to the doctrine of Moses. They did also refer all men, in cases of faith and religion, to the book[49] of Moses. **The law.** The law of Moses, which is indeed the law of God, and is most properly called *Thora*,[50] as it were the guide and rule of faith and life, they did diligently beat into the minds of all men. This did they, according to the time, persons, and place, expound to all men. For all the priests and prophets, before the incarnation of Christ, did by word of mouth teach the men of their time godliness and true religion. Neither did they teach any other thing than that which the fathers had received of God, and which Moses had received of God and the fathers; and straightways after committing it to writing, did set it out to all us which follow, even unto the end of the world: so that now in the prophets we have the doctrine of Moses and tradition of the fathers, and them in all and every point more fully and plainly expounded and polished, being moreover to the places, times, and persons very fitly applied.

The authority of the holy prophets was very great. Furthermore, the doctrine and writings of the prophets have always been of great authority among all wise men throughout the whole world. For it is well perceived by many arguments, that they took not their beginning of the prophets themselves, as chief authors; but were inspired from God out of heaven by the Holy Spirit of God: for it is God, which, dwelling by his Spirit in the minds of the prophets, speaketh to us by their mouths. And for that cause have they a most large testimony at the hands of Christ,[51] and his elect apostles. What say ye to this moreover, that God by their ministry hath wrought miracles and wonders to be marvelled at, and those not a few; that at the least by mighty signs we might learn that it is God, by whose inspiration the prophets do teach and write whatsoever they left for us to remember?

Furthermore, so many commonweals and congregations gathered together, and governed by the prophets according to the word of God, do shew most evident testimonies of God's truth in the prophets. Plato, Zeno, Aristotle, and other philosophers of the gentiles, are praised as excellent men. But which of them could ever yet gather a church to live according to their ordinances? And yet our prophets have had the most excellent and renowned commonweals or congregations, yea, and that more is, the most flourishing kingdoms in all the world under their authority. All the wise men in the whole world (I mean those which lived in his time) did reverence[52] Salomon, a king and so great a prophet, and came unto him from the very outmost ends of the world. Daniel also had the preeminence among the wise men at Babylon, being then the most renowned monarchy in all the world. He was moreover in great estimation with Darius Medus,

---

48. Lat. *compendium*.

49. Lat. *libros*.

50. תּוֹרָה, a verbo ירה, *instituere, docere.*—Foster, *Lex. Heb.*—תורה, *quam Legem vulgo vertimus, Hebræis ab indicando docendoque dicitur.*—Martin Bucer, *Psalmorum libri quinque* . . . (Geneva: Stephanus, 1554), 16 on Ps. 2. See also John Hooper, *Early Writings* (Cambridge: The Parker Society, 1843), 88.

51. Lat. *Dei Filio*; omitted.

52. Lat. *tantum non adorarunt*; almost worshipped.

the son of Astyages[53] or Assuerus, and also with Cyrus that most excellent king. And here it liketh me well to speak somewhat of that divine foreknowledge in our prophets, and most assured foreshewing of things which were to come after many years passed. And now, to say nothing of others, did not Esaias most truly foretell those things, which were afterward fulfilled by the Jews in our Lord Christ? Not in vain did he seem to them of old time to be rather an evangelist than a prophet[54] foretelling things to come. He did openly tell the name of king Cyrus one hundred and threescore years, at the least, before that Cyrus was born.[55] **Polyhistor**. Daniel also was called[56] of them in the old time by the name of one which knew much.[57] For he did foretell those things which are and have been done in all the kingdoms of the world almost, and among the people of God, from his own time until the time of Christ, and further until the last day of judgment, so plainly, that he may seem to have compiled a history of those things which then were already gone and past. All these things, I say, do very evidently prove, that the doctrine and writings of the prophets are the very word of God: with which name and title they are set forth in sundry places of the scriptures. Verily, Peter the apostle saith, "The prophecy came not in old time by the will of man: but holy men of God spake as they were moved by the Holy Ghost."

The word of God revealed by the Son of God. And although God did largely, clearly, plainly, and simply reveal his word to the world by the patriarchs, by Moses, by the priests and prophets; yet did he, in the last times of all, by his Son set it forth most clearly, simply, and abundantly to all the world. For the very and only-begotten Son of God the Father, as the prophets had foretold, descending from heaven, doth fulfil all whatsoever they foretold, and by the space almost of three years doth teach all points of godliness. For saith John: "No man at any time hath seen God; the only-begotten Son, which is in the bosom of the Father, he hath declared him."[58] The Lord himself, moreover, saith to his disciples: "All things which I have heard of my Father have I made known to you."[59] And again he saith: "I am the light of the world: whosoever doth follow me doth not walk in darkness, but shall have the light of life."[60] **The chief contents of Christ's doctrine**. Our Lord also did teach, that to him, which would enter into heaven and be saved, the heavenly regeneration was needful,[61] because in the first birth man is born to death, in the second to life; but that that regeneration is made perfect in us by the Spirit of God, which instructeth our hearts in faith, I say, in faith in Christ, who died for our sins, and rose again for our justification.[62] He taught that by that faith they which believe are justified; and that out of the same faith

---

53. That Astyages, son of Cyaxares the first, is the Ahasuerus, and Cyaxares the second, Astyages' son, the Darius the Mede, of scripture, see Humphrey Prideaux, *The Old and New Testament Connected*, ed. McCaul (London: Tegg, 1845), 1:72, 104, 120.

54. *Ita ut a quibusdam evangelista quam propheta potius diceretur (Esaias).*—Augustine, *The City of God* 18.29. Paris, 1531. Tom. v. *Deinde etiam hoc adjiciendum, quod non tam propheta, quam evangelista, dicendus sit (Isaias).*—Hieron. *Praef. in lib. Isai.*, ed. Paris, 1693–1706. Tom. I. col. 473. See also Bullinger's treatise, "The Old Faith," 66.

55. Isa. 44:28; 45:1.

56. Lat. *recte appellatus est*.

57. *Quartus vero (Daniel), qui et extremus inter quatuor prophetas, temporum conscius, et totius mundi philoïstoros,* etc.—Hieron. *Ep. L. Secund. ad Paulinum*, ed. Paris, 1706. Tom. IV. par. 2. col. 573.

58. John 1:18.

59. John 15:15.

60. John 8:12.

61. John 3:5.

62. Rom. 4:25.

do grow sundry fruits of charity and innocency, to the bringing forth whereof he did most earnestly exhort them. He taught furthermore, that he was the fulfilling, or fulness, of the law and the prophets; and did also approve and expound the doctrine of Moses and the prophets. To doctrine he joined divers miracles and benefits, whereby he declared, that he himself was that light of the world, and the mighty and bountiful Redeemer of the world. **The apostles of Christ**. And, to the intent that his doctrine and benefits might be known to all the world, he chose to himself witnesses, whom he called apostles, because he purposed to send them to preach throughout the world. Those witnesses were simple men, innocents, just, tellers of truth, without deceit or subtilties, and in all points holy and good; whose names it is very profitable often to repeat in the congregation. The names of the apostles are these: Peter and Andrew, James and John, Philip and Bartholomew, Thomas and Matthew, James the son of Alphe, and Judas his brother, whose surname was Thaddaeus, Simon and Judas Iscariot, into whose room (because he had betrayed the Lord) came Saint Matthias.[63] These had he, by the space almost of three years, hearers of his heavenly doctrine, and beholders of his divine works. These, after his ascension into the heavens, did he, by the Holy Ghost sent down from heaven, instruct with all kind of faculties. For, as they were in the scriptures passing skilful, so were they not unskilful, or wanting eloquence, in any tongue. And, being once after this manner instructed, they depart out of the city of Jerusalem, and pass through the compass of the earth, preaching to all people and nations that which they had received to preach of the Saviour of the world and the Lord Jesus Christ. And when for certain years they had preached by word of mouth, then did they also set down in writing that which they had preached. For some, verily, writ an history of the words and deeds of Christ, and some of the words and deeds of the apostles. Other some sent sundry epistles to divers nations. In all which, to confirm the truth, they use the scripture of the law and the prophets, even as we read that the Lord oftentimes did. **John Baptist and Paul**. Moreover, to the twelve apostles are joined two great lights of the world; John Baptist, than whom there was never any more holy born of women;[64] and the chosen vessel[65] Paul, the great teacher of the Gentiles.[66]

The authority of the apostles very great. Neither is it to be marvelled at, that the forerunner and apostles of Christ had always very great dignity and authority in the church. For, even as they were the ambassadors of the eternal King of all ages and of the whole world; so, being endued with the Spirit of God, they did nothing according to the judgment of their own minds. And the Lord by their ministry wrought great miracles, thereby to garnish the ministry of them, and to commend their doctrine unto us. And what may be thought of that, moreover, that by that word of God they did convert the whole world; gathering together, and laying the foundations of, notable churches throughout the compass of the world? Which verily by man's counsel and words they had never been able to have brought to pass. To this is further added, that they which once leaned to this doctrine, as a doctrine giving life, did not refuse to die: besides that, how many soever had their belief in the doctrine of the gospel, they were not afraid, through water, fire, and swords, to cut off this life, and to lay hand on the life to come.

63. Matt. 10:2–4; Acts 1:26.
64. Matt. 11:11.
65. Acts 9:15.
66. 1 Tim. 2:7; 2 Tim. 1:11.

The faithful saints could in no wise have done these things, unless the doctrine which they believed had been of God.

Although therefore that the apostles were men, yet their doctrine, first of all taught by a lively expressed voice, and after that set down in writing with pen and ink, is the doctrine of God and the very true word of God. **1 Thessalonians 2**. For therefore the apostle left this saying in writing: "When ye did receive the word of God which ye heard of us, ye received it not as the word of men, but, as it is indeed, the word of God, which effectually worketh in you that believe."[67]

The roll of the books of the divine scriptures. But now the matter itself and place require, that I gather also and plainly reckon up those books, wherein is contained the very word of God, first of all declared of the fathers, of Christ himself, and the apostles by word of mouth; and after that also written into books by the prophets and apostles. And in the first place verily are set the five books of Moses. Then follow the books of Josue, of Judges, of Ruth, two books of Samuel, two of Kings, two of Chronicles; of Esdras, Nehemias, and Hester one a-piece. After these come Job, David or the book of Psalms,[68] Proverbs, Ecclesiastes, and Cantica. With them are numbered the four greater prophets, Esaias, Jeremias, Ezechiel, and Daniel: then the twelve lesser prophets, whose names are very well known: with these books the Old Testament ended. The New Testament hath in the beginning the evangelical history of Christ the Lord, written by four authors, that is, by two apostles, Matthew and John; and by two disciples, Mark and Luke, who compiled a wonderful goodly and profitable book of the Acts of the Apostles. Paul to sundry churches and persons published fourteen epistles. The other apostles wrote seven which are called both canonical and catholic. And the books of the New Testament are ended with the Revelation of Jesus Christ, which he opened to the disciple whom he loved, John the evangelist and apostle; shewing unto him, and so to the whole church, the ordinance of God touching the church,[69] even until the day of judgment. Therefore in these few and mean,[70] not unmeasurable, in these plain and simple, not dark and unkemmed[71] books, is comprehended the full doctrine of godliness, which is the very word of the true, living, and eternal God.[72]

The scripture is sound and uncorrupted. Also the books of Moses and the prophets through so many ages, perils, and captivities, came sound and uncorrupted even until the time of Christ and his apostles. For the Lord Jesus and the apostles used those books as true copies and authentical; which undoubtedly they neither would, nor could, have done, if so be that either they had been corrupted, or altogether perished. The books also, which the apostles of Christ have added,[73] were throughout all persecutions kept in the church safe and uncorrupted, and are come sound and uncorrupted into our hands, upon whom the ends of the world are fallen. For by the vigilant care and unspeakable

---

67. 1 Thess. 2:13. Lat. *Sermonem,—quo Deum discebatis*; and Erasmus's rendering.
68. Lat. *Solomonis libelli tres*; omitted by the translator.
69. Lat. *fata ecclesiæ*.
70. Lat. *sobriis*.
71. unkemmed or unkempt: uncombed; Lat. *impexis*.
72. The canon of Scripture received by the church of Rome, containing most of those books which we call apocryphal, was first set forth by the council of Trent; and afterwards confirmed by the bull of pope Pius IV (A.D. 1564). On this subject see Burnet on the 6th Article, with the notes in Gilbert Burnet, *An Exposition of Thirty-nine Articles of the Church of England*, ed. James Robert Page (1839); and Bishop John Cosin, *A Scholastical History of the Canon of Scripture* (Oxford, 1849, 1672).
73. Lat. *una cum lege et prophetis*; omitted.

goodness of God, our Father, it is brought to pass, that no age at any time either hath or shall want so great a treasure.

Thus much hitherto have I declared unto you, dearly beloved, what the word of God is, what the beginning of it in the church was, and what proceeding, dignity, and certainty it had. The word of God is the speech of God, that is to say, the revealing of his good will to mankind, which from the beginning, one while by his own mouth, and another while by the speech of angels, he did open to those first, ancient, and most holy fathers; who again by tradition did faithfully deliver it to their posterity. Here are to be remembered those great lights of the world, Adam, Seth, Methusalem, Noe, Sem, Abraham, Isaac, Jacob, Amram, and his son Moses, who, at God's commandment, did in writing comprehend the history and traditions of the holy fathers, whereunto he joined the written law, and exposition of the law, together with a large and lightsome[74] history of his own lifetime. After Moses, God gave to his church most excellent men, prophets and priests; who also, by word of mouth and writings, did deliver to their posterity that which they had learned of the Lord. After them came the only-begotten Son of God himself down from heaven into the world, and fulfilled all, whatsoever was found to be written of himself in the law and the prophets. The same also taught a most absolute mean how to live well and holily: he made the apostles his witnesses: which witnesses did afterwards first of all with a lively expressed voice preach all things which the Lord had taught them; and then, to the intent that they should not be corrupted, or clean taken out of man's remembrance, they did commit it to writing: so that now we have from the fathers, the prophets, and apostles, the word of God as it was preached and written.

These things had their beginning of one and the same Spirit of God, and do tend to one end, that is, to teach us men how to live well and holily. He that believeth not these men, and namely[75] the only-begotten Son of God, whom, I pray you, will he believe? We have here the most holy, innocent, upright-living, most praiseworthy, most just, most ancient, most wise, and most divine men of the whole world and compass of the earth, and briefly, such men as are by all means without comparison. All the world cannot shew us the like again, although it should wholly a thousand times be assembled in councils. The holy emperor Constantine gathered a general council out of all the compass of the earth; thither came there together, out of all the world, three hundred and eighteen most excellent fathers: but they that are of the wisest sort will say, that these are not so much as shadows, to be compared to them, of whom we have received the word of God. Let us therefore in all things believe the word of God delivered to us by the scriptures. Let us think that the Lord himself, which is the very living and eternal God, doth speak to us by the scriptures. Let us for evermore praise the name and goodness of him, who hath vouchedsafe so faithfully, fully, and plainly to open to us, miserable mortal men, all the means how to live well and holily.

To him be praise, honour, and glory for evermore. Amen.

74. Lat. *luculenta*.
75. Namely: especially; *præsertim*.

THE SECOND SERMON: *OF THE WORD OF GOD; TO WHOM, AND TO WHAT END, IT WAS REVEALED; ALSO IN WHAT MANNER IT IS TO BE HEARD; AND THAT IT DOTH FULLY TEACH THE WHOLE DOCTRINE OF GODLINESS*

DEARLY beloved, in the last sermon you learned what the word of God is; from whence it came; by whom it was chiefly revealed; what proceedings[76] it had; and of what dignity and certainty it is.

Now am I come again, and, by God's favour and the help of your prayers, I will declare unto you, beloved, to whom, and to what end, the word of God is revealed; in what manner it is to be heard; and what the force thereof is, or the effect.

To whom the word of God is revealed. Our God is the God of all men and nations, who, according to the saying of the apostle, "would have all men to be saved, and to come to the knowledge of the truth":[77] and therefore hath he, for the benefit, life, and salvation of all men, revealed his word, that so indeed there might be a rule and certain way to lead men by the path of justice into life everlasting. God verily, in the old time, did shew himself to the Israelites, his holy and peculiar people, more familiarly than to other nations, as the prophet saith: "To Jacob hath he declared his statutes, and his judgments to Israel: he hath not dealt so with any nation, neither hath he shewed them his judgments":[78] and yet he hath not altogether been careless of the Gentiles. For as to the Ninivites he sent Jonas; so Esaias, Jeremias, Daniel, and the other prophets bestowed much labour in teaching and admonishing the Gentiles. And those most ancient fathers, Noe, Abraham, and the rest, did not only instruct the Jewish people which descended of them, but taught their other sons also the judgments of God. Our Lord Jesus Christ verily, laying open the whole world before his disciples, said: "Teach all nations: preach the gospel to all creatures."[79] And when as Saint Peter did not yet fully understand, that the Gentiles also did appertain to the fellowship of the church of Christ, and that to the Gentiles also did belong the preaching of the glad tidings of salvation, purchased by Christ for the faithful; the Lord doth instruct him by a heavenly vision, by speaking to him out of heaven, and by the message which came from Cornelius, as you know, dearly beloved, by the history of the Acts of the Apostles.[80] Let us therefore think, my brethren, that the word of God and the holy scriptures are revealed to all men, to all ages, kinds,[81] degrees and states, throughout the world. For the apostle Paul, also confirming the same, saith: "Whatsoever things are written, are written for our learning, that through patience, and comfort of the scriptures, we may have hope."[82]

Let none of us therefore hereafter say, "What need I to care what is written to the Jews in the Old Testament, or what the apostles have written to the Romans, to the Corinthians, and to other nations? I am a Christian. The prophets to the men of their time, and the apostles

---

76. Lat. *progressus*.
77. 1 Tim. 2:4.
78. Ps. 147:19–20.
79. Matt. 28:19; Mark 16:15.
80. Acts 10.
81. Lat. *Sexubus*.
82. Rom. 15:4.

to those that lived in the same age with them, did both preach and write." For if we think uprightly of the matter, we shall see that the scriptures of the Old and New Testaments ought therefore to be received of us, even because we are Christians. For Christ, our Saviour and Master, did refer us to the written books of Moses and the prophets. Saint Paul, the very elect instrument of Christ, doth apply to us the sacraments and examples of the old fathers, that is to say, circumcision in baptism (Col. 2:11–12); and the paschal lamb in the supper or sacrament (1 Cor. 5:7) In the tenth chapter of the same epistle he applieth sundry examples of the fathers to us. And in the fourth to the Romans, where he reasoneth of faith, which justifieth without the help of works and the law, he bringeth in the example of Abraham; and therewithal addeth: "Nevertheless it is not written for Abraham alone, that faith was reckoned unto him for righteousness, but also for us, to whom it shall be reckoned if we believe,"[83] etc.

The writings of the Old Testament are also given to Christians. "By that means," say some, "we shall again be wrapped in the law; we shall be enforced to be circumcised, to sacrifice flesh and blood of beasts, to admit again the priesthood of Aaron, together with the temple and the other ceremonies. There shall again be allowed the bill of divorcement, or putting away of a man's wife, together with sufferance to marry many wives." To these I answer: that in the Old Testament we must consider that some things there are which are for ever to be observed, and some things which are ceremonial and suffered only till time of amendment.[84] That time of amendment is the time of Christ, who fulfilled the law, and took away the curse of the law. The same Christ changed circumcision into baptism. He with his own only sacrifice made an end of all sacrifices; so that now, instead of all sacrifices, there is left to us that only sacrifice of Christ, wherein also we learn to offer our own very bodies and prayers, together with good deeds, as spiritual sacrifices unto God. Christ changed the priesthood of Aaron for his own and the priesthood of all Christians. The temple of God are we, in whom God by his Spirit doth dwell. All ceremonies did Christ make void, who also in the nineteenth of Matthew did abrogate the bill of divorcement, together with the marriage of many wives. But although these ceremonies and some external actions were abrogated and clean taken away by Christ, that we should not be bound unto them; yet notwithstanding, the scripture, which was published touching them, was not taken away, or else[85] made void, by Christ. For there must for ever be in the church of Christ a certain[86] testimonial, whereby we may learn what manner of worshippings and figures of Christ they of the old time had. Those worshippings and figures of Christ must we at this day interpret to the church specially;[87] and out of them we must, no less than out of the writings of the New Testament, preach Christ, forgiveness of sins, and repentance. So then, to all Christians are the writings of the Old Testament given by God; in like manner as the apostle[88] writ to all churches those things which bore the name or title of some particular congregations.

To what end the word of God is revealed. And to this end is the word of God revealed to men, that it may teach them[89] what, and what manner one God[90] is towards men; that he

---

83. Rom. 4:23–24.
84. Heb. 9:10. Lat., *tempus correctionis*. So Vulgate.
85. i.e., or; Lat. *vel*.
86. i.e., a sure; Lat. *certum*.
87. spiritually, ed. 1577; Lat. *spiritualiter*.
88. apostles, 1577; Lat. *apostoli*.
89. Lat. *De Deo et voluntate ejus*. Omitted by the translator: concerning God and his will.
90. What manner one; Lat. *qualis*.

would have them to be saved; and that, by faith in Christ: what Christ is, and by what means salvation cometh: what becometh the true worshippers of God, what they ought to fly, and what to ensue. Neither is it sufficient to know the will of God, unless we do the same and be saved.[91] And for that cause said Moses: "Hear, Israel, the statutes and judgments which I teach you, that ye may do them and live."[92] And the Lord in the gospel, confirming the same, crieth: "Blessed are they which hear the word of God and keep it."[93]

God's goodness to be praised for teaching us. And here is to be praised the exceeding great goodness of God, which would have nothing hid from us which maketh any whit to live rightly, well, and holily. The wise and learned of this world do for the most part bear envy or grudge, that other should attain unto the true wisdom: but our Lord doth gently, and of his own accord, offer to us the whole knowledge of heavenly things, and is desirous that we go forward therein; yea, and that more is, he doth further our labour and bring it to an end. For "whosoever hath," saith the Lord himself in the gospel, "to him shall be given, that he may have the more abundance."[94] "And every one that asketh receiveth, and he that seeketh findeth, and to him that knocketh it shall be opened."[95] Whereupon Saint James the apostle saith: "If any of you lack wisdom, let him ask of God, which giveth to all men liberally," that is, willingly, not with grudging, "neither casteth any man in the teeth, and it shall be given him."[96] Where, by the way, we see our duty; which is, in reading and hearing the word of God, to pray earnestly and zealously that we may come to that end, for the which the word of God was given and revealed unto us. But as touching that matter, we will say somewhat more, when we come to declare in what manner of sort the word of God ought to be heard.

All points of true godliness are taught us in the holy scriptures. Now, because I have said that the word of God is revealed, to the intent that it may fully instruct us in the ways of God and our salvation; I will in few words declare unto you, dearly beloved, that in the word of God, delivered to us by the prophets and apostles, is abundantly contained the whole effect of godliness,[97] and what things soever are available to the leading of our lives rightly, well, and holily. For, verily, it must needs be, that that doctrine is full, and in all points perfect, to which nothing ought either to be added, or else to be taken away. But such a doctrine is the doctrine taught in the word of God, as witnesseth Moses (Deut. 4 and 12) and Salomon (Prov. 30).[98] What is he, therefore, that doth not confess that all points of true piety are taught us in the sacred scriptures? Furthermore, no man can deny that to be a most absolute doctrine, by which a man is so fully made perfect, that in this world he may be taken for a just man, and in the world to come be called for ever to the company of God. But he that believeth the word of God uttered to the world by the prophets and apostles, and liveth thereafter, is called a just man, and heir of life everlasting. That doctrine therefore is an absolute doctrine. For Paul also, declaring more largely and fully the same matter, saith: "All scripture, given by inspiration of God, is profitable to doctrine, to reproof, to

---

91. Lat. *ut salvi fiamus*.
92. Deut. 5:1.
93. Luke 11:28.
94. Matt. 13:12.
95. Luke 11:10.
96. James 1:5.
97. Lat. *pietatis rationem*.
98. Deut. 4:2; 12:32; Prov. 30:6.

correction, to instruction which is in righteousness, that the man of God may be perfect, instructed to all good works."[99]

Ye have, brethren, an evident testimony of the fulness of the word of God. Ye have a doctrine absolutely perfect in all points.[100] Ye have a most perfect effect of the word of God, because by this doctrine the man of God, that is, the godly and devout worshipper of God, is perfect, being instructed, not to a certain few good works, but unto all and every good work. Wherein therefore canst thou find any want? I do not think that any one is such a sot, as to interpret these words of Paul to be spoken only touching the Old Testament; seeing it is more manifest than the day-light, that Paul applied them to his scholar Timothy, who preached the gospel, and was a minister of the New Testament. If so be then, that the doctrine of the Old Testament be of itself full; by how much more shall it be the fuller, if the volume of the New Testament be added thereunto! **The Lord both spake and did many things which are not written.** I am not so ignorant, but that I know that the Lord Jesus both did and spake many things which were not written by the apostles. But it followeth not therefore, that the doctrine of the word of God, taught by the apostles, is not absolutely perfect. For John, the apostle and evangelist, doth freely confess that the Lord did many other things also, "which were not written in his book"; but immediately he addeth this, and saith: "But these are written, that ye might believe that Jesus is Christ the Son of God and that in believing ye might have life through his name."[101] He affirmeth by this doctrine, which he contained in writing, that faith is fully taught, and that through faith there is granted by God everlasting life. But the end of absolute doctrine is to be happy and perfectly blessed. Since then that cometh to man by the written doctrine of the gospel; undoubtedly that doctrine of the gospel is most absolutely perfect.

I know, that the Lord in the gospel said, "I have many things to tell you; but at this time you cannot bear them": but therewithal I know too, that he immediately added this saying: "But when the Spirit of truth shall come, he shall lead you into all truth."[102] I know furthermore, that the Spirit of truth did come upon his disciples; and therefore I believe, that they, according to the true promise of Christ, were led into all truth, so that it is most assuredly certain, that nothing was wanting in them.

The apostles set down in writing the whole doctrine of godliness. But some there are, which, when they cannot deny this, do turn themselves and say, that "the apostles indeed knew all things, but yet taught them not but by word of mouth only, not setting down in writing all those things which do appertain to true godliness."[103] As though it were likely that Christ's most faithful apostles would, upon spite, have kept back any thing from their posterity. As though indeed he had lied which said, "These things are written, that in believing ye might have life everlasting" (cf. John 20:31). John therefore did let pass nothing which belongeth to our full instructing in the faith. Luke did omit nothing. Neither did the rest of

---

99. 2 Tim. 3:16–17.

100. Lat. *Habetis omnes partes absolutæ doctrinæ.*

101. John 20:30–31.

102. John 16:12–13. For this and the other texts, by which the Romanists maintain patristical and ecclesiastical tradition, see Archbishop Cranmer's treatise "Of Unwritten Verities," ch. IX in *The Works of Thomas Cranmer* (Cambridge: The Parker Society, 1846), 2:53–55.

103. *Ex quibus omnibus . . . evidens (est) . . . quod non omnia, quæ ad religionem nostram pertinent, auctore Christo apostolorum ministerio consignata ecclesiæ, . . . in scripturis explicata sint.*—Albertus Pighius, *Controversiarum præcipuarum . . . Explicatio . . .* Paris, 1549. fol. 95. b. Controversia 3. De Ecclesia.

the apostles and disciples of our Lord Jesus Christ suffer any thing to overslip them. Paul also wrote fourteen sundry epistles: but yet the most of them contained one and the self-same matter. Whereby we may very well conjecture, that in them is wholly comprehended the absolute doctrine of godliness. For he would not have repeated one and the selfsame thing so often, to so many sundry men, if there had yet been any thing else necessary more fully to be taught for the obtaining of salvation. Those things undoubtedly would he have taught, and not have rehearsed one and the same thing so many times. Verily, in the third chapter of his epistle to the Ephesians he doth affirm, that in the two first chapters of the same his epistle he did declare his knowledge in the gospel of Christ. "God," saith he, "by revelation shewed the mystery unto me, as I wrote before in few words; whereby when ye read ye may understand my knowledge in the mystery of Christ."[104] And this spake he touching that one and only epistle, yea, and that too touching the two first chapters of that one epistle. Whereunto when the most large and lightsome letters or epistles of Saint Paul himself, and also of the other apostles, are added, who, I pray you, unless he be altogether without sense, will once think, that the apostles have left in writing to us, their posterity, a doctrine not absolutely perfect?

Against the lively and unfeigned[105] traditions of the apostles. As for those which do earnestly affirm, that all points of godliness were taught by the apostles to the posterity by word of mouth, and not by writing, their purpose is to set to sale their own, that is, men's ordinances instead of the word of God.

But against this poison, my brethren, take this unto you for a medicine to expel it. Confer the things, which these fellows set to sale under the colour of the apostles' traditions, taught by word of mouth and not by writing, with the manifest writings of the apostles; and if in any place you shall perceive those traditions to disagree with the scriptures, then gather by and by, that it is the forged invention of men, and not the apostles' tradition. For they, which had one and the same Spirit of truth, left not unto us one thing in writing, and taught another thing by word of mouth. Furthermore, we must diligently search, whether those traditions do set forward the glory of God, rather than of men; or the safety of the faithful, rather than the private advantage of the priests. And we must take heed of men's traditions, especially since the Lord saith, "In vain do they worship me, teaching doctrines the precepts of men."[106] So that now the surest way is, to cleave to the word of the Lord left to us in the scriptures, which teacheth abundantly all things that belong to true godliness.

How the word of God is to be heard. It remaineth now for me to tell, in what manner of sort this perfect doctrine of godliness and salvation, I mean, the very word of God, ought to be heard of the faithful, to the intent it may be heard with some fruit to profit them abundantly. I will in few words contain[107] it. Let the word of God be heard with great reverence, which of right is due to God himself and godly things. Let it be heard very attentively; with continual prayers between, and earnest requests. Let it be heard soberly to our profit, that by it we may become the better, that God by us may be glorified, and not that we go curiously about to search out the hidden counsels of God, or desire to be counted skilful and expert in many matters. Let true faith, the glory of

104. Eph. 3:3–4.
105. fained, 1577; Lat. *confictas*.
106. Matt. 15:9; Mark 7:7.
107. Lat. *comprehendam*.

God, and our salvation be appointed as the measure and certain end of our hearing and reading. For in Exodus Moses, the holy servant of God, is commanded to sanctify the people, and make them in a readiness to hear the sacred sermon, which God himself did mind to make the next day after. Moses therefore cometh, and demandeth of the whole people due obedience to be shewed, as well to God, as to his ministers. Then commandeth he them to wash their garments, to abstain from their wives. After that he appointeth certain limits, beyond which it was not lawful upon pain of death for them to pass.[108] By this we plainly learn, that the Lord doth require such to be his disciples, to hear him, as do specially shew obedience and reverence to him in all things. For he, being God, speaketh to us men: all we men owe unto God honour and fear. A man, unless he become lowly, humble, and obedient to God, is altogether godless. Then is it required at the hands of those, which are meet hearers of the word of God, that they lay apart worldly affairs, which are signified by the garments; to tread under foot all filthiness and uncleanness of soul and body; to refrain for a season even from those pleasures which are lawful unto us. The Holy Ghost doth love the minds that are purely cleansed; which yet notwithstanding are not cleansed but by the Spirit of God. Needful it is to have a sincere belief in God, and a ready good-will and desire to live according to that which is commanded in the word of God. Moreover, we must be wise to sobriety.[109] Over curious questions must be set aside. Let things profitable to salvation only be learned. Last of all, let especial heed be taken in hearing and learning. For saith Salomon: "If thou wilt seek after wisdom as after gold, thou shalt obtain it."[110] Again he saith: "The searcher out of God's majesty shall be overwhelmed by his wonderful glory."[111] And again he saith: "Seek not things too high for thee, neither go about to search out things above thy strength; but what God hath commanded thee, that think thou always on: and be not over curious to know his infinite works; for it is not expedient for thee to see his hidden secrets with thine eyes."[112] Whereupon the apostle Paul saith: "Let no man think arrogantly of himself, but so think that he may be modest and sober, according as God to every one hath given the measure of faith."[113] And hereto belongeth that which the same apostle saith: "Knowledge puffeth up, and charity doth edify."[114]

The diseases and plagues of the hearers of God's word. But chiefly we must beware of those plagues, which choke the seed of the word of God, and quench it without any fruit at all in the hearts of the hearers. Those plagues and diseases hath the Lord rehearsed, or reckoned up, in the parable of the sower.[115] For first of all, wanton and vain cogitations, which always lie wide open to the inspirations of Satan and talk of naughty men, are plagues to the word of God. Also voluptuous and dainty lovers of this world, who cannot abide to suffer any affliction for Christ and his gospel, do without any fruit at all hear God's word, although they seem to give ear unto it very joyfully. Furthermore,

---

108. Ex. 19:10–15.

109. Rom. 12:3. *Sapere ad sobrietatem*: "to think soberly, to sobriety," marg. Author. Ver.

110. Prov. 2:4–5.

111. Prov. 25:27, according to the Vulgate version, which is: "Qui scrutator est majestatis, opprimetur a gloria." "He that is a searcher of majesty (viz. of God), shall be overwhelmed by glory."—Douay Version. Calvin uses the text in the same sense, *Institutes* 3.21.2.

112. Eccl. 3:21–23.

113. Rom. 12:3.

114. 1 Cor. 8:1.

115. Matt. 13:1–23.

"the care of this world, and the deceit of riches," are most pestilent diseases in the hearers of the word of God. For they do not only hinder the seed, that it cannot bring forth fruit in their hearts; but also they do stir up and egg men forward to gainsay the word of God, and to afflict the earnest desirers of God's word. Here therefore we must take heed diligently, lest, being infected with these diseases, we become vain and unthankful hearers of the word of God.

We must pray continually, that the bountiful and liberal Lord will vouchsafe to bestow on us his Spirit, that by it the seed of God's word may be quickened in our hearts, and that we, as holy and right hearers of his word, may bear fruit abundantly to the glory of God, and the everlasting salvation of our own souls. **What the power and effect of God's word is**. For what will it avail to hear the word of God without faith, and without the Holy Spirit of God to work or stir inwardly in our hearts? The apostle Paul saith: "He which watereth is nothing, nor he which planteth; but it is God which giveth increase."[116] We have need therefore of God's watering, that the word of God may grow to a perfect age, may receive increase, yea, and may come also to the bringing forth of ripe fruit within our minds. The same apostle Paul saith: "To us also is the word of God declared, even as unto our fathers. But it availed them nothing to hear the word, because it was not joined with faith in them that heard it: for they died in the desert." And immediately after he saith: "Let us therefore do our best to enter into that rest, so that no man die in the same example of unbelief."[117] If therefore that the word of God do sound in our ears, and therewithal the Spirit of God do shew forth his power in our hearts, and that we in faith do truly receive the word of God, then hath the word of God a mighty force and wonderful effect in us. For it driveth away the misty darkness of errors, it openeth our eyes, it converteth and enlighteneth our minds, and instructeth us most fully and absolutely in truth and godliness. For the prophet David in his Psalms beareth witness, and saith: "The law of the Lord is perfect, converting the soul; the testimony of God is true, and giveth wisdom unto the simple; the commandment of the Lord is pure, and giveth light unto the eyes."[118] Furthermore, the word of God doth feed, strengthen, confirm, and comfort our souls; it doth regenerate, cleanse, make joyful, and join us to God; yea, and obtaineth all things for us at God's hands, setting us in a most happy state: insomuch that no goods or treasure of the whole world are to be compared with the word of God.

And thus much do we attribute to the word of God, not without the testimony of God's word. For the Lord by the prophet Amos doth threaten hunger and thirst, "not to eat bread and to drink water, but to hear the word of God."[119] For in the Old and New Testaments it is said, "that man doth not live by bread only, but by every word that proceedeth out of the mouth of God."[120] And the apostle Paul saith, that "all things in the scriptures are written for our learning, that by patience and comfort of the scriptures we might have hope."[121] Also Peter saith: "Ye are born anew, not of corruptible seed, but of incorruptible, by the word of God which liveth and lasteth for ever. And this is the

---

116. 1 Cor. 3:7.
117. Heb. 3:17, and 4:2, 11.
118. Ps. 19:7–8.
119. Amos 8:11.
120. Deut. 8:3; Matt. 4:4.
121. Rom. 15:4.

word which by the gospel was preached unto you."[122] The Lord also in the gospel beareth witness to the same, and saith: "Now are ye clean by the word which I have spoken unto you."[123] Again in the gospel he crieth, saying: "If any man loveth me, he will keep my saying, and my Father will love him, and we will come into him, and make our dwelling-place in him."[124] Jeremy saith also: "Thy word became my comfort."[125] And the prophet David saith: "The statutes of the Lord are right, and rejoice the heart."[126] Whereunto add that saying of the Lord's in the gospel: "If ye remain in me, and my words remain in you, ask what ye will, and it shall be done for you."[127] In another place also the prophet crieth, saying: "If ye be willing and will hearken, ye shall eat the good of the land; but if ye will not hear my word, the sword shall devour you."[128] Moreover Moses doth very often and largely reckon up the good things that shall happen to them which obey the word of God (Lev. 26; Deut. 28). Wherefore David durst boldly prefer the word of God before all the pleasures and treasures of this world. "The fear of the Lord is clean, and endureth for ever; the judgments of the Lord are true, and righteous altogether: more to be desired are they than gold, yea, than much fine gold; sweeter also than honey, and the dropping honeycombs. For by them thy servant is plainly taught, and in keeping of them there is a great advantage. Therefore is the law of thy mouth more precious unto me than thousands of silver and gold. Unless my delight had been in thy law, I had perished in my misery."[129] To this now doth appertain that parable in the gospel, of him which bought the precious pearl; and of him also which sold all that he had, and bought the ground wherein he knew that treasure was hid.[130] For that precious pearl, and that treasure, are the gospel or word of God: which, for the excellency of it, is in the scriptures called a light, a fire, a sword, a maul which breaketh stones, a buckler,[131] and by many other names like unto these.

Dearly beloved, this hour ye have heard our bountiful Lord and God, "who would have all men saved and to come to the knowledge of the truth" [cf. 1 Tim 2:4], how he hath revealed his word to all men throughout the whole world, to the intent, that all men in all places, of what kind,[132] age, or degree soever they be, may know the truth, and be instructed in the true salvation; and may learn a perfect way how to live rightly, well, and holily, so that the man of God may be perfect, instructed to all good works. For the Lord in the word of truth hath delivered to his church all that is requisite to true godliness and salvation. Whatsoever things are necessary to be known touching God, the works, judgments, will and commandments of God, touching Christ, our faith in Christ, and the duties of an holy life; all those things, I say, are fully taught in the word of God. Neither needeth the church to crave of any other, or else with men's supplies to patch up that which seemeth to be wanting in the word of the Lord. For

122. 1 Peter 1:23, 25.
123. John 15:3.
124. John 14:23.
125. Jer. 15:16.
126. Ps. 19:8.
127. John 15:7.
128. Isa. 1:19–20.
129. Pss. 19:9–11 and 119:72, 92.
130. Matt. 13:44–46.
131. Ps. 119:105; Jer. 23:29; Eph. 6:17; Ps. 91:4.
132. Lat. *sexus*.

the Lord did not only, by the lively expressed voice of the apostles, teach our fathers the whole sum of godliness and salvation; but did provide also, that it, by the means of the same apostles, should be set down in writing. And that doth manifestly appear, that it was done for the posterity's sake, that is, for us and our successors, to the intent that none of us nor ours should be seduced, nor that false traditions should be popped into any of our mouths instead of the truth. We must all therefore beware, we must all watch, and stick fast unto the word of God, which is left to us in the scriptures by the prophets and apostles.

Finally, let our care be wholly bent, with faith and profit to hear whatsoever the Lord declareth unto us: let us cast out and tread under foot whatsoever, by our flesh, the world, or the devil, is objected to be a let to godliness. We know what the diseases and plagues of the seed of God's word, sowed in the hearts of the faithful, are. We know how great the power of God's word is in them which hear it devoutly. Let us therefore beseech our Lord God to pour into our minds his Holy Spirit, by whose virtue the seed of God's word may be quickened in our hearts, to the bringing forth of much fruit to the salvation of our souls, and the glory of God our Father. To whom be glory for ever.

4

Institutes of the Christian Religion (Book I)

JOHN CALVIN

The translation of these two chapters is taken from John Calvin, *Institutes of the Christian Religion*, ed. John T. McNeill, trans. Ford Lewis Battles, LCC 20 (Philadelphia: Westminster Press, 1960), 69–81. We have kept only some of the notes of this edition.

John Calvin (1509–64), French theologian and Reformer, was born in Noyon, France. Following Luther, he is the greatest of the Protestant Reformers. Initially, he studied theology for the priesthood in the Catholic Church, then law. He also developed a keen interest in the French humanist movement, and his first book, entitled *De Clementia* (1532), illustrates this pursuit. After his conversion to the Reformed faith, he went to Basel and there published the first edition of his *Institutes* in 1536. Besides a ministry to the French church in Strasbourg, Calvin's main achievement was spearheading the Reformation in the city of Geneva, which became a center of influence for the new Reformed faith. Calvin wrote many occasional treatises and commentaries on almost every book of the Bible; but his magnum opus is the *Institutes*, which he revised many times and became a crucial work for the Protestant Reformation.

Calvin begins his *Institutes* (1559) with a discussion of the Christian knowledge of God and the knowledge of self. He argues that these two types of knowledge are hard to separate, since all human beings are created in God's image and thus have knowledge of God. This knowledge, however, is suppressed and distorted by sin. So Calvin explains that the true knowledge of God as the Creator and Redeemer of mankind is found only in the Holy Scriptures. In this selection from the *Institutes*, Calvin explains these two kinds of knowledge. Further, he underscores that the Scriptures reveal to us knowledge of God that creation alone cannot, namely, the redemption found in Christ alone. Calvin asserts, too, the essential role of the Holy Spirit in convincing fallen men that the Scriptures are indeed the very Word of God.

Bibliography: R. Benedetto. "Calvin, John, Influence Of." Pp. 49–50 in *DP&RTA*. "Calvin, John." *NSHERK* 2:353–59. John Calvin. *Institutes of the Christian Religion* (1559). Trans. Henry Beveridge. 1845. Repr. with an introduction by John Murray, Grand Rapids: Eerdmans, 1989. David W. Hall and Peter A. Lillback, eds. *Theological Guide to Calvin's Institutes: Essays and Analysis*. The Calvin 500 Series. Phillipsburg, NJ: P&R Publishing, 2008. Anthony N. S. Lane. "Calvin, John (1509–64)." Pp. 100–103 in *DHT*. Richard A. Muller. *The Unaccommodated Calvin: Studies in the Foundation of a Theological Tradition*. Oxford Studies in Historical Theology. New York: Oxford University Press, 2000. John Murray. *Calvin on Scripture and Divine Sovereignty*. Grand Rapids: Eerdmans, 1960. James I. Packer. "John Calvin and the Inerrancy of Holy Scripture." Pp. 143–88 in *Inerrancy and the Church*. W. S. Reid. "Calvin, John (1509–1564)." Pp. 177–79 in *NIDCC*. Idem. "Calvin, John (1509–1564)." Pp. 185–86 in *EDT*. David C. Steinmetz. "10. The Theology of John Calvin." Pp. 113–29 in *The Cambridge Companion to Reformation Theology*. R. S. Wallace. "Calvin, John (1509–64)." Pp. 120–24 in *NDT*. B. B. Warfield. *Calvin and Augustine*. Ed. Samuel Craig. Philadelphia: Presbyterian and Reformed, 1956. François Wendel. *Calvin: Origins and Development of His Religious Thought*. Trans. Philip Mairet. New York: HarperCollins, 1963. Repr., Grand Rapids: Baker, 1997. D. F. Wright. "Calvin, John (1509–1564)." Pp. 109–12 in *BDE*.

Chapter VI: Scripture Is Needed as Guide and Teacher for Anyone Who Would Come to God the Creator

1. God bestows the actual knowledge of himself upon us only in the Scriptures

That brightness which is borne in upon the eyes of all men both in heaven and on earth is more than enough to withdraw all support from men's ingratitude—just as God, to involve the human race in the same guilt, sets forth to all without exception his presence portrayed in his creatures. Despite this, it is needful that another and better help be added to direct us aright to the very Creator of the universe. It was not in vain, then, that he added the light of his Word by which to become known unto salvation; and he regarded as worthy of this privilege those whom he pleased to gather more closely and intimately to himself. For because he saw the minds of all men tossed and agitated, after he chose the Jews as his very own flock, he fenced them about that they might not sink into oblivion as others had. With good reason he holds us by the same means in the pure knowledge of himself, since otherwise even those who seem to stand firm before all others would soon melt away. Just as old or bleary-eyed men and those with weak vision, if you thrust before them a most beautiful volume, even if they recognize it to be some sort of writing, yet can scarcely construe two words, but with the aid of spectacles[1] will begin to read distinctly; so Scripture, gathering up the otherwise confused knowledge of God in our minds, having dispersed our dullness, clearly shows us the true God. This, therefore, is a special gift, where God, to instruct the church, not merely uses mute teachers but also opens his own most hallowed lips. Not only does he teach the elect to look upon a god, but also shows himself as the God upon whom they are to look. He has from the beginning maintained this plan for his church, so that besides these common proofs he also put forth his Word, which is a more direct and more certain mark whereby he is to be recognized.[2]

1. Cf. 1.5.12, 15; 1.14.1.
2. Cf. 2.1–5.

(Two sorts of knowledge of God in Scripture)

There is no doubt that Adam, Noah, Abraham, and the rest of the patriarchs with this assistance penetrated to the intimate knowledge of him that in a way distinguished them from unbelievers. I am not yet speaking of the proper doctrine of faith whereby they had been illumined unto the hope of eternal life. For, that they might pass from death to life, it was necessary to recognize God not only as Creator but also as Redeemer, for undoubtedly they arrived at both from the Word. First in order came that kind of knowledge by which one is permitted to grasp who that God is who founded and governs the universe. Then that other inner knowledge was added, which alone quickens dead souls, whereby God is known not only as the Founder of the universe and the sole Author and Ruler of all that is made, but also in the person of the Mediator as the Redeemer. But because we have not yet come to the fall of the world and the corruption of nature, I shall now forego discussion of the remedy.[3] My readers therefore should remember that I am not yet going to discuss that covenant by which God adopted to himself the sons of Abraham, or that part of doctrine which has always separated believers from unbelieving folk, for it was founded in Christ. But here I shall discuss only how we should learn from Scripture that God, the Creator of the universe, can by sure marks be distinguished from all the throng of feigned gods. Then, in due order, that series will lead us to the redemption.[4] We shall derive many testimonies from the New Testament, and other testimonies also from the Law and the Prophets, where express mention is made of Christ. Nevertheless, all things will tend to this end, that God, the Artificer of the universe, is made manifest to us in Scripture, and that what we ought to think of him is set forth there, lest we seek some uncertain deity by devious paths.

2. The Word of God as Holy Scripture

But whether God became known to the patriarchs through oracles and visions or by the work and ministry of men, he put into their minds what they should then hand down to their posterity. At any rate, there is no doubt that firm certainty of doctrine was engraved in their hearts, so that they were convinced and understood that what they had learned proceeded from God. For by his Word, God rendered faith unambiguous forever, a faith that should be superior to all opinion. Finally, in order that truth might abide forever in the world with a continuing succession of teaching and survive through all ages, the same oracles he had given to the patriarchs it was his pleasure to have recorded, as it were, on public tablets. With this intent the law was published, and the prophets afterward added as its interpreters. For even though the use of the law was manifold, as will be seen more clearly in its place,[5] it was especially committed to Moses and all the prophets to teach the way of reconciliation between God and men, whence also Paul calls "Christ the end of the law" (Rom. 10:4). Yet I repeat once more: besides the specific doctrine of faith and repentance that sets forth Christ as Mediator, Scripture adorns with unmistakable marks and tokens the one true God, in that he has created and governs the universe, in order that he may not be mixed up with the throng of false gods. Therefore, however fitting it may be for man seriously to turn his eyes to contemplate God's works, since he has been placed

---

3. Cf. 2.6–7, and bk. 3, passim. On the covenant, see also 2.8.21; 2.10.1–5, 8; 2.11.4, 11; 3.17.6; 3.21.5–7; 4.14.6; 4.15.22; 4.16.5–6, 14; 4.17.20.

4. Cf. 2.5.7; 2.16.5–12.

5. Cf. 2.7 and 8.

in this most glorious theater to be a spectator of them, it is fitting that he prick up his ears to the Word, the better to profit. And it is therefore no wonder that those who were born in darkness become more and more hardened in their insensibility; for there are very few who, to contain themselves within bounds, apply themselves teachably to God's Word, but they rather exult in their own vanity. Now, in order that true religion may shine upon us, we ought to hold that it must take its beginning from heavenly doctrine and that no one can get even the slightest taste of right and sound doctrine unless he be a pupil of Scripture. Hence, there also emerges the beginning of true understanding when we reverently embrace what it pleases God there to witness of himself. But not only faith, perfect and in every way complete, but all right knowledge of God is born of obedience. And surely in this respect God has, by his singular providence, taken thought for mortals through all ages.

3. Without Scripture we fall into error

Suppose we ponder how slippery is the fall of the human mind into forgetfulness of God, how great the tendency to every kind of error, how great the lust to fashion constantly new and artificial religions. Then we may perceive how necessary was such written proof of the heavenly doctrine, that it should neither perish through forgetfulness nor vanish through error nor be corrupted by the audacity of men. It is therefore clear that God has provided the assistance of the Word for the sake of all those to whom he has been pleased to give useful instruction because he foresaw that his likeness imprinted upon the most beautiful form of the universe would be insufficiently effective. Hence, we must strive onward by this straight path if we seriously aspire to the pure contemplation of God. We must come, I say, to the Word, where God is truly and vividly described to us from his works, while these very works are appraised not by our depraved judgment but by the rule of eternal truth. If we turn aside from the Word, as I have just now said, though we may strive with strenuous haste, yet, since we have got off the track, we shall never reach the goal. For we should so reason that the splendor of the divine countenance, which even the apostle calls "unapproachable" (1 Tim. 6:16), is for us like an inexplicable labyrinth unless we are conducted into it by the thread of the Word; so that it is better to limp along this path than to dash with all speed outside it.[6] David very often, therefore, teaching that we ought to banish superstitions from the earth so that pure religion may flourish, represented God as regnant (Pss. 93:1; 96:10; 97:1; 99:1; and the like). Now he means by the word "regnant" not the power with which he is endowed, and which he exercises in governing the whole of nature, but the doctrine by which he asserts his lawful sovereignty. For errors can never be uprooted from human hearts until true knowledge of God is planted therein.

4. Scripture can communicate to us what the revelation in the creation cannot

Accordingly, the same prophet, after he states, "The heavens declare the glory of God, the firmament shows forth the works of his hands, the ordered succession of days and nights proclaims his majesty" (Ps. 19:1–2), then proceeds to mention his Word: "The law of the Lord is spotless, converting souls; the testimony of the Lord is faithful, giving wisdom to little ones; the righteous acts of the Lord are right, rejoicing hearts; the precept of the Lord

---

6. Augustine, *Enarrationes in Psalmos* 2.4 on Ps. 31 (PL 36.260; trans. LF *Psalms* I. 253); *Sermons* 141.4: "Melius est in via claudicare quam praeter viam fortiter ambulare" (PL 38.778; trans. LF *Sermons* 2.656f.). Cf. *Sermons* 169.15 (PL 38. 926; trans. LF *Sermons* 2.870–71).

is clear, enlightening eyes" (Ps. 19:7–8). For although he also includes other uses of the law,[7] he means in general that, since God in vain calls all peoples to himself by the contemplation of heaven and earth, this is the very school of God's children. Psalm 29 looks to this same end, where the prophet—speaking forth concerning God's awesome voice, which strikes the earth in thunder (v. 3), winds, rains, whirlwinds and tempests, causes mountains to tremble (v. 6), shatters the cedars (v. 5)—finally adds at the end that his praises are sung in the sanctuary because the unbelievers are deaf to all the voices of God that resound in the air (vv. 9–11). Similarly, he thus ends another psalm where he has described the awesome waves of the sea: "Thy testimonies have been verified, the beauty and holiness of thy temple shall endure forevermore" (Ps. 93:5). Hence, also, arises that which Christ said to the Samaritan woman, that her people and all other peoples worshiped they knew not what; that the Jews alone offered worship to the true God (John 4:22). For, since the human mind because of its feebleness can in no way attain to God unless it be aided and assisted by his Sacred Word, all mortals at that time—except for the Jews—because they were seeking God without the Word, had of necessity to stagger about in vanity and error.

Chapter VII: Scripture Must Be Confirmed by the Witness of the Spirit. Thus May Its Authority[8] Be Established as Certain; and It Is a Wicked Falsehood That Its Credibility Depends on the Judgment of the Church

1. Scripture has its authority from God, not from the church

Before I go any farther, it is worth-while to say something about the authority of Scripture,[9] not only to prepare our hearts to reverence it, but to banish all doubt. When that which is set forth is acknowledged to be the Word of God, there is no one so deplorably insolent—unless devoid also both of common sense and of humanity itself—as to dare impugn the credibility of Him who speaks. Now daily oracles are not sent from heaven, for it pleased the Lord to hallow his truth to everlasting remembrance in the Scriptures alone (cf. John 5:39). Hence the Scriptures obtain full authority among believers only when men regard them as having sprung from heaven, as if there the living words of God were heard. This matter is very well worth treating more fully and weighing more carefully. But my readers will pardon me if I regard more what the plan of the present work demands than what the greatness of this matter requires.

But a most pernicious error widely prevails that Scripture has only so much weight as is conceded to it by the consent of the church. As if the eternal and inviolable truth of God depended upon the decision of men! For they mock the Holy Spirit when they ask: Who can convince us that these writings came from God? Who can assure us that Scripture has come down whole and intact even to our very day? Who can persuade us to receive one book in reverence but to exclude another, unless the church prescribe a sure rule for all these matters? What reverence is due Scripture and what books ought to be reckoned within its canon

---

7. Cf. 2.7.6, 10, 12.

8. Cf. 4.8 for a related treatment of the authority and inspiration of Scripture.

9. Chapters 7–9 form an excursus on Biblical authority. The doctrine of the "inner testimony" is related to Calvin's view of the Spirit (cf. 1.13.14–15 and bk. 3, especially chs. 1–2).

depend, they say, upon the determination of the church.[10] Thus these sacrilegious men, wishing to impose an unbridled tyranny under the cover of the church, do not care with what absurdities they ensnare themselves and others, provided they can force this one idea upon the simple-minded: that the church has authority in all things. Yet, if this is so, what will happen to miserable consciences seeking firm assurance of eternal life if all promises of it consist in and depend solely upon the judgment of men? Will they cease to vacillate and tremble when they receive such an answer? Again, to what mockeries of the impious is our faith subjected, into what suspicion has it fallen among all men, if we believe that it has a precarious authority dependent solely upon the good pleasure of men!

2. The church is itself grounded upon Scripture

But such wranglers are neatly refuted by just one word of the apostle. He testifies that the church is "built upon the foundation of the prophets and apostles" (Eph. 2:20). If the teaching of the prophets and apostles is the foundation, this must have had authority before the church began to exist. Groundless, too, is their subtle objection that, although the church took its beginning here, the writings to be attributed to the prophets and apostles nevertheless remain in doubt until decided by the church. For if the Christian church was from the beginning founded upon the writings of the prophets and the preaching of the apostles, wherever this doctrine is found, the acceptance of it—without which the church itself would never have existed—must certainly have preceded the church.[11] It is utterly vain, then, to pretend that the power of judging Scripture so lies with the church that its certainty depends upon churchly assent. Thus, while the church receives and gives its seal of approval to the Scriptures, it does not thereby render authentic what is otherwise doubtful or controversial. But because the church recognizes Scripture to be the truth of its own God, as a pious duty it unhesitatingly venerates Scripture. As to their question—How can we be assured that this has sprung from God unless we have recourse to the decree of the church?—it is as if someone asked: Whence will we learn to distinguish light from darkness, white from black, sweet from bitter? Indeed, Scripture exhibits fully as clear evidence of its own truth[12] as white and black things do of their color, or sweet and bitter things do of their taste.

3. Augustine cannot be cited as counterevidence

Indeed, I know that statement of Augustine is commonly referred to, that he would not believe the gospel if the authority of the church did not move him to do so.[13] But it

---

10. Cf. Bullinger, *De scripturae sacrae authoritate* (1538), fo. 4a. The claim of church authority in the interpretation of Scripture is defended by Cochlaeus in *De authoritate ecclesiae et scripture* (1524), and in *De canonicae scripture et catholicae ecclesiae authoritate, ad Henricum Bullingerium* (1543). In the latter work (ch. 3), he states that no claim is made for the superior authority of the church over the Scripture, but holds (ch. 4) that the church has authority *circa scripturas*, and that such authority is most necessary. Cf. also John Eck, *Enchiridion* (1533), ch. 1, fo. 4a–6b.

11. This view of the antecedence of Scripture to the church was common to the Reformers. It appears in Luther's *Lectures on the Psalms* (*Werke* WA 3:454), where he says, "The Scripture is the womb from which are born the divine truth and the church."

12. Cf. 1.7.5.

13. Augustine, *Contra epistolam Manichaei quam vocant fundamenti*, ch. 5 (PL 42.176; trans. NPNF1, 4.131): "For my part, I should not believe the gospel except as moved by the authority of the catholic church." Luther, in his tract *That the Doctrines of Men Are to Be Rejected* (1522), had largely anticipated Calvin's interpretation of Augustine's meaning in this passage (*Werke* WA 10.2.89; trans. *Works of Martin Luther*, 2:451ff.).

is easy to grasp from the context how wrongly and deceptively they interpret this passage. Augustine was there concerned with the Manichees, who wished to be believed without controversy when they claimed, but did not demonstrate, that they themselves possessed the truth. Because in fact they used the gospel as a cloak to promote faith in their Mani, Augustine asks: "What would they do if they were to light upon a man who does not even believe in the gospel? By what kind of persuasion would they bring him around to their opinion?" Then he adds, "Indeed, I would not believe the gospel," etc., meaning that if he were alien to the faith, he could not be led to embrace the gospel as the certain truth of God unless constrained by the authority of the church. And what wonder if someone, not yet having known Christ, should have respect for men! Augustine is not, therefore, teaching that the faith of godly men is founded on the authority of the church; nor does he hold the view that the certainty of the gospel depends upon it. He is simply teaching that there would be no certainty of the gospel for unbelievers to win them to Christ if the consensus of the church did not impel them. And this he clearly confirms a little later, saying: "When I praise what I believe, and laugh at what you believe, how do you think we are to judge, or what are we to do? Should we not forsake those who invite us to a knowledge of things certain and then bid us believe things uncertain? Must we follow those who invite us first to believe what we are not yet strong enough to see, that, strengthened by this very faith, we may become worthy to comprehend what we believe (Col. 1:4–11, 23)—with God himself, not men, now inwardly strengthening and illumining our mind?"[14]

These are Augustine's very words. From them it is easy for anyone to infer that the holy man's intention was not to make the faith that we hold in the Scriptures depend upon the assent or judgment of the church. He only meant to indicate what we also confess as true: those who have not yet been illumined by the Spirit of God are rendered teachable by reverence for the church, so that they may persevere in learning faith in Christ from the gospel. Thus, he avers, the authority of the church is an introduction through which we are prepared for faith in the gospel. For, as we see, he wants the certainty of the godly to rest upon a far different foundation. I do not deny that elsewhere, when he wishes to defend Scripture, which they repudiate, he often presses the Manichees with the consensus of the whole church. Hence, he reproaches Faustus[15] for not submitting to the gospel truth—so firm, so stable, celebrated with such glory, and handed down from the time of the apostles through a sure succession. But it never occurs to him to teach that the authority which we ascribe to Scripture depends upon the definition or decree of men. He puts forward only the universal judgment of the church, in which he was superior to his adversaries, because of its very great value in this case. If anyone desires a fuller proof of this, let him read Augustine's little book *The Usefulness of Belief*.[16] There he will find that the author recommends no other inducement to believe except what may provide us with an approach and be a suitable beginning for inquiry, as he himself says; yet we should not acquiesce in mere opinion, but should rely on sure and firm truth.

14. Augustine, *Contra epistolam Manichaei quam vocant fundamenti*, ch. 14 (PL 42.183; trans. NPNF1, 4.136).

15. Augustine, *De ordine* 2.9.27–10.28 (PL 32.1007–8; trans. R. P. Russell, *Divine Providence and the Problem of Evil: A Translation of Augustine's De ordine*, 122–27); *Against Faustus the Manichaean* 32.19 (PL 42.509; trans. NPNF1, 4.339).

16. Augustine, *The Usefulness of Belief* 1.2–3 (PL 42.65ff.; trans. LCC 6.292ff.).

4. *The witness of the Holy Spirit: this is stronger than all proof*

We ought to remember what I said a bit ago:[17] credibility of doctrine is not established until we are persuaded beyond doubt that God is its Author.[18] Thus, the highest proof of Scripture derives in general from the fact that God in person speaks in it. The prophets and apostles do not boast either of their keenness or of anything that obtains credit for them as they speak; nor do they dwell upon rational proofs. Rather, they bring forward God's holy name, that by it the whole world may be brought into obedience to him. Now we ought to see how apparent it is not only by plausible opinion but by clear truth that they do not call upon God's name heedlessly or falsely. If we desire to provide in the best way for our consciences—that they may not be perpetually beset by the instability of doubt or vacillation, and that they may not also boggle at the smallest quibbles—we ought to seek our conviction in a higher place than human reasons, judgments, or conjectures, that is, in the secret testimony of the Spirit.[19] True, if we wished to proceed by arguments, we might advance many things that would easily prove—if there is any god in heaven—that the law, the prophets, and the gospel come from him. Indeed, ever so learned men, endowed with the highest judgment, rise up in opposition and bring to bear and display all their mental powers in this debate. Yet, unless they become hardened to the point of hopeless impudence, this confession will be wrested from them: that they see manifest signs of God speaking in Scripture. From this it is clear that the teaching of Scripture is from heaven. And a little later we shall see that all the books of Sacred Scripture far surpass all other writings. Yes, if we turn pure eyes and upright senses toward it, the majesty of God will immediately come to view, subdue our bold rejection, and compel us to obey.

Yet they who strive to build up firm faith in Scripture through disputation are doing things backwards.[20] For my part, although I do not excel either in great dexterity or eloquence, if I were struggling against the most crafty sort of despisers of God, who seek to appear shrewd and witty in disparaging Scripture, I am confident it would not be difficult for me to silence their clamorous voices. And if it were a useful labor to refute their cavils, I would with no great trouble shatter the boasts they mutter in their lurking places. But even if anyone clears God's Sacred Word from man's evil speaking, he will not at once imprint upon their hearts that certainty which piety requires. Since for unbelieving men religion seems to stand by opinion alone, they, in order not to believe anything foolishly or lightly, both wish and demand rational proof that Moses and the prophets spoke divinely.[21] But I reply: the testimony of the Spirit is more excellent than all reason. For as God alone is a fit witness of himself in his Word,[22] so also the Word will not find acceptance in men's hearts before it is sealed by the inward testimony of the Spirit. The same Spirit, therefore, who has spoken through the mouths of the prophets must penetrate into our hearts to persuade us that they faithfully proclaimed what had been divinely commanded. Isaiah very aptly

---

17. Cf. 1.7.1.

18. Cf. Aquinas, *Summa Theologica*, 1.1.10: "The author of Holy Scripture is God."

19. On Calvin's doctrine of the inner witness of the Holy Spirit to the truth of Scripture, see 1.7.4; 3.1.1; 3.1.3–4; 3.2.15, 33–36; *Geneva Catechism* (1545), questions 91 and 113; Commentary on 2 Timothy 3:16. Cf. also WCF 1.5.

20. Cf. Lactantius, *Divine Institutes* 3.1 (CSEL 19.178; trans. ANF 7.69).

21. This passage is associated with a letter sent by "Capnio" (Antoine Fumée) to Calvin from Paris, late 1542 or early 1543; cf. A. L. Herminjard, *Correspondance des Réformateurs dans les pays de langue française*, 8:228ff., and CR 11.490ff.

22. Cf. Hilary of Poitiers, *On the Trinity* 1.18: "For He whom we can know only through his own utterances is a fitting witness concerning himself" (PL 10.38; trans. NPNF2, 9.45).

expresses this connection in these words: "My Spirit which is in you, and the words that I have put in your mouth, and the mouths of your offspring, shall never fail" (Isa. 59:21). Some good folk are annoyed that a clear proof is not ready at hand when the impious, unpunished, murmur against God's Word. As if the Spirit were not called both "seal" and "guarantee" (cf. 2 Cor. 1:22) for confirming the faith of the godly; because until he illumines their minds, they ever waver among many doubts!

5. Scripture bears its own authentication

Let this point therefore stand: that those whom the Holy Spirit has inwardly taught truly rest upon Scripture, and that Scripture indeed is self-authenticated;[23] hence, it is not right to subject it to proof and reasoning. And the certainty it deserves with us, it attains by the testimony of the Spirit.[24] For even if it wins reverence for itself by its own majesty, it seriously affects us only when it is sealed upon our hearts through the Spirit. Therefore, illumined by his power, we believe neither by our own nor by anyone else's judgment that Scripture is from God; but above human judgment we affirm with utter certainty (just as if we were gazing upon the majesty of God himself) that it has flowed to us from the very mouth of God by the ministry of men. We seek no proofs, no marks of genuineness upon which our judgment may lean; but we subject our judgment and wit to it as to a thing far beyond any guesswork! This we do, not as persons accustomed to seize upon some unknown thing, which, under closer scrutiny, displeases them, but fully conscious that we hold the unassailable truth! Nor do we do this as those miserable men who habitually bind over their minds to the thralldom of superstition; but we feel that the undoubted power of his divine majesty lives and breathes there. By this power we are drawn and inflamed, knowingly and willingly, to obey him, yet also more vitally and more effectively than by mere human willing or knowing!

God, therefore, very rightly proclaims through Isaiah that the prophets together with the whole people are witnesses to him; for they, instructed by prophecies, unhesitatingly held that God has spoken without deceit or ambiguity (Isa. 43:10). Such, then, is a conviction that requires no reasons; such, a knowledge with which the best reason agrees—in which the mind truly reposes more securely and constantly than in any reasons; such, finally, a feeling that can be born only of heavenly revelation. I speak of nothing other than what each believer experiences within himself—though my words fall far beneath a just explanation of the matter.

I now refrain from saying more, since I shall have opportunity to discuss this matter elsewhere.[25] Let us, then, know that the only true faith is that which the Spirit of God seals in our hearts. Indeed, the modest and teachable reader will be content with this one reason: Isaiah promised all the children of the renewed church that "they would be God's disciples" (Isa. 54:13). God deems worthy of singular privilege only his elect, whom he distinguishes from the human race as a whole. Indeed, what is the beginning of true doctrine but a prompt eagerness to hearken to God's voice? But God asks to be heard through the mouth of Moses,

---

23. "αὐτόπιστον." Cf. 1.7.2 (end).

24. Cf. *Summary of Doctrine Concerning the Ministry of the Word and Sacraments*, doubtfully attributed to Calvin (CR 9.773–78; trans. LCC 22.171–77), esp. paragraphs 5–6.

25. The topic of the secret operation and testimony of the Spirit is resumed in 3.1.1, introducing the treatment of "the way in which we receive the grace of Christ," which is the subject of Book 3. See also note 19, above.

as it is written: "Say not in your heart, who will ascend into heaven, or who will descend into the abyss: behold, the word is in your mouth" [conflation of Deut. 30:12, 14 and Ps. 107:26). If God has willed this treasure of understanding to be hidden from his children, it is no wonder or absurdity that the multitude of men are so ignorant and stupid! Among the "multitude" I include even certain distinguished folk, until they become engrafted into the body of the church. Besides, Isaiah, warning that the prophetic teaching would be beyond belief, not only to foreigners but also to the Jews who wanted to be reckoned as members of the Lord's household, at the same time adds the reason: "The arm of God will not be revealed" to all (Isa. 53:1). Whenever, then, the fewness of believers disturbs us, let the converse come to mind, that only those to whom it is given can comprehend the mysteries of God (cf. Matt. 13:11).

Part Two

THE REFORMED CONFESSIONS

WESTMINSTER THEOLOGICAL SEMINARY appeals to the broad unified witness of the Reformed confessions of the sixteenth and seventeenth centuries concerning the doctrine of Scripture, and it appeals more specifically to the Presbyterian tradition embodied in the Westminster Standards (chap. 17 below) and the Dutch tradition with the Three Forms of Unity (chaps. 10, 11, and 16). The selection of texts also includes Swiss confessions that mark the early effort of Reformed Protestantism to distinguish itself from Roman Catholicism and the Anabaptists (cf. chaps. 5–7, 12). Other confessions from various geographical locations are also congenial with later Presbyterian creeds (cf. chaps. 8, 9, 13–15, 18).

This collection of Reformed confessional statements on Scripture witnesses to the development of key themes of the Reformation and post-Reformation. The first three short confessions bear testimony to the breakthrough of the Reformation in Switzerland. Crucial to this advance was the affirmation of the principle of *sola Scriptura*; an affirmation of the inspiration of Scripture and a concern for the centrality of salvation in Christ are also evident in these documents.

The anthology then presents confessions from other European countries to which the Reformed faith spread. The French Confession of Faith, mostly written by John Calvin, deals with general and special revelation, the witness of the Holy Spirit, and the authority of God's Word. The Scots Confession of Faith, associated with Calvin's disciple John Knox, insists on God's self-revealing activity in Christ in the context of polemic with Rome. The next part will give further excerpts from this confession to illustrate the redemptive-historical interpretation of the Reformation. The Belgic Confession, written by Guido de Brès, closely follows its French counterpart and was also written in the context of intense persecution. Noteworthy is its affirmation of inspiration, the witness of the Spirit, and the sufficiency of Scripture. The Heidelberg Catechism is the main text of the Reformed faith in Germany, but it has acquired an international appeal. Its statements on Scripture are more indirect, but they clearly convey that Scripture has ultimate authority in the church. The Second Helvetic Confession not only provides an elaborate statement of faith by Heinrich Bullinger, but also is an important unifying confession for the international Reformed community. This confession affirms *sola Scriptura* against tradition in the Catholic Church; it deals with both the nature and the interpretation of Scripture. In England, the Thirty-nine Articles convey a moderate Protestant and Reformed view of Scripture, speaking clearly on the sufficiency of Scripture, the canon, and the relation between the Word and the creeds. The Second Scots Confession offers a more polemic approach by sharply condemning Catholic abuses on the basis of *sola Scriptura*.

The remaining confessions belong to the seventeenth century and often provide a more mature expression of the Reformed faith. The Irish Articles of Religion, written by James Ussher, are, together with the Thirty-nine Articles, close ancestors of the Westminster Confession of Faith, including comments on the reading and translation of the Bible and an affirmation of the clarity of Scripture. The Canons of the Synod of Dort do not deal with the doctrine of Scripture per se, but respond to the challenge of the rising Arminian views of salvation. They are, however, an important witness to the clarity of Scripture concerning central doctrines such as predestination; in addition, they contain significant statements about the role of preaching. The Westminster Confession of Faith presents a remarkably full statement about Scripture, dealing with subjects such as the necessity, finality, sufficiency, and inspiration of Scripture. It also defines the canon of Scripture and, in line with Calvin, affirms the witness of the Holy Spirit and comments on the analogy of faith. This confession has a prominent place in discussions on Scripture in Presbyterian circles. As is the case with the Heidelberg Catechism, the witness of the Westminster Larger and Shorter Catechisms to the doctrine of Scripture is more indirect. In them, however, Scripture's authority is clearly affirmed. Notable also is their teaching on Christ's prophetic ministry, preaching, and the interpretation of the Decalogue. Finally, the Confession of the Waldenses from northern Italy communicates an expression of the Reformed faith close to that of the Reformation in Geneva in the face of intense persecution. It restates in particular the revelation of God in nature and Scripture and the witness of the Holy Spirit.

As secondary standards under the ultimate authority of Scripture, these confessions are crucial in the subsequent history of Reformed theology. Any consideration of the doctrine of Scripture in Reformed theology has to consider these texts. Even though some later developments occur in the formulation of the doctrine of Scripture, such as discussions about the incarnational analogy, Reformed confessions and catechisms have an enduring value and play a prominent role in later texts from Reformed theologians in this anthology. For instance, the Dutch tradition (Abraham Kuyper, Herman Bavinck, and Louis Berkhof) relied on the Three Forms of Unity. In addition, the Scottish theologians and Princetonians appealed directly to the Westminster Standards. French-speaking Continental theologians such as Louis Gaussen and Adolphe Monod naturally turned to the French Confession of Faith and the Second Helvetic Confession. At Westminster Theological Seminary, the faculty subscribes to the Westminster Standards; the seminary also acknowledges the Three Forms of Unity. The other confessions are part of the Reformed identity at Westminster as well.

5

The Sixty-seven Articles (1523)

ULRICH ZWINGLI

The Latin text is a reproduction of "Articuli sive conclusions LXVII. H. Zwinglii. A.D. 1523," in Schaff, *The Creeds of Christendom*, 3:197–207.

The English translation is taken from Ulrich Zwingli, "The Sixty-seven Articles of Zwingli," in *Selected Works*, ed. Samuel Macauley Jackson, introduction by Edward Peters (Philadelphia: University of Pennsylvania Press, 1972), 111–17. The introduction, conclusion, and titles in the English translation are from the German original.

The Sixty-seven Articles or Conclusions (1523) were presented by Zwingli as the guide for the theological debate that occurred at the first Zurich Disputation (see chap. 2 above). The members of the city council called for this debate so that they could evaluate Zwingli's theology that critiqued the Catholic Church's theology. At the end of the disputation, the city council decided to adopt Zwingli's agenda for the reformation of the church. Over six hundred people attended as Zwingli successfully made his case to reform the Roman Catholic Church according to the Word of God. These articles or theses articulate the scriptural and Christological principles of the Reformation over against Roman Catholic traditions. Zwingli's theses are similar to Luther's famous Ninety-five Theses (1517) and anticipate our next selection, the Ten Conclusions of Berne (chap. 6). Following the disputation, Zwingli worked on an exposition of the articles, which he published the same year as the disputation (1523).

Supplementary Bibliography (cf. chap. 2): Cochrane. *Reformed Confessions*. Pp. 33–44. Dennison. *Reformed Confessions* 1:1–8. Mark Noll. "Confessions of Faith." Pp. 262–66 in *EDT*. Schaff. *The Creeds of Christendom* 3:197–207. Ulrich Zwingli. "The Exposition of the Sixty-seven Articles." Pp. 7–373 in *Huldrych Zwingli Writings*. Vol. 1, *The Defense of the Reformed Faith*. Trans. E. J. Furcha. Pittsburgh Theological Monographs 12. Allison Park, PA: Pickwick Publications, 1984. Repr., Eugene, OR: Wipf & Stock, 2004. Idem. "Of the Clarity and Certainty of the Word of God." Pp. 49–95 in G. W. Bromiley, ed. *Zwingli and Bullinger*. LCC. Philadelphia: Westminster Press, 1953.

Elenchus Articulorum
in disputationem primam
promulgatorum
ab
Huldrico Zwinglio.

The articles and opinions below, I, Ulrich Zwingli, confess to have preached in the worthy city of Zurich as based upon the Scriptures which are called inspired by God [θεόπνευστος], and I offer to protect and conquer with the said articles, and where I have not now correctly understood [the] said Scriptures I shall allow myself to be taught better, but only from said Scriptures.

I. *Quicunque Evangelion nihil esse dicunt, nisi ecclesiae calculus et adprobatio accedat, errant, et Deum blasphemant.*

I. All who say that the Gospel is invalid without the confirmation of the Church err and slander God.

II. *Summa Evangelii est, quod Christus Filius Dei vivi notefecit nobis voluntatem Patris cœlestis, et quod innocentia sua nos de morte æterna redemit, et Deo reconciliavit.*

II. The sum and substance of the Gospel is that our Lord Jesus Christ, the true Son of God, has made known to us the will of his heavenly Father, and has with his innocence released us from death and reconciled God.

III. *Hinc sequitur Christum esse unicam viam ad salutem omnium, qui fuerunt, sunt et erunt.*

III. Hence Christ is the only way to salvation for all who ever were, are and shall be.

IV. *Quicunque aliud ostium vel quærit vel ostendit, errat; quin animarum latro est et fur.*

IV. Who seeks or points out another door errs, yea, he is a murderer of souls and a thief.

V. *Quicunque ergo alias doctrinas Evangelio vel æquant vel præferunt, errant, nec intelligunt quid sit Evangelion.*

V. Hence all who consider other teachings equal to or higher than the Gospel err, and do not know what the Gospel is.

VI. *Nam Christus Jesus dux est et imperator, a Deo toti generi humano et promissus et præstitus:*

VI. For Jesus Christ is the guide and leader, promised by God to all human beings, which promise was fulfilled.

VII. *Ut sit ipse salus et caput omnium credentium, qui corpus eius sunt, quod quidem absque ipso mortuum est, et nihil potest.*

VII. That he is an eternal salvation and head of all believers, who are his body, but which is dead and can do nothing without him.

VIII. *Ex his sequitur, quod omnes, qui in isto capite vivunt, sunt membra et Filii Dei. Et hæc est ecclesia seu communio sanctorum, sponsa Christi, ecclesia catholica.*

VIII. From this follows first that all who dwell in the head are members and children of God, and that is the church or communion of the saints, the bride of Christ, Ecclesia catholica [the church universal].

IX. *Quemadmodum membra corporis sine administratione capitis nihil possunt, sic in corpore Christi nemo quidquam potest sine capite eius, Christo.*

IX. Furthermore, that as the members of the body can do nothing without the control of the head, so no one in the body of Christ can do the least without his head, Christ.

X. *Quum membra absque capite aliquid operantur, ut, dum sese lacerant aut perdunt, demens est homo: sic, dum membra Christi sine capite Christo aliquid tentant, insana sunt, sese gravant et perdunt imprudentibus legibus.*

X. As that man is mad whose limbs (try to) do something without his head, tearing, wounding, injuring himself; thus when the members of Christ undertake something without their head, Christ, they are mad, and injure and burden themselves with unwise ordinances.

XI. *Colligimus hinc Ecclesiasticorum (quos vocant) traditiones et leges, quibus fastum, divitias, honores, titulos legesque suas fulciunt et defendunt, causam esse omnis insaniæ; nam capiti Christo non consonant.*

XI. Hence we see in the clerical (so-called) ordinances, concerning their splendor, riches, classes, titles, laws, a cause of all foolishness, for they do not also agree with the head.

XII. *Adhuc ergo insaniunt non pro capite, quod per gratiam Dei pii omnes summo studio conantur erigere, sed quod non permittuntur insanire et furere. Volunt enim pii soli capiti Christo auscultare.*

XII. Thus they still rage, not on account of the head (for that one is eager to bring forth in these times from the grace of God), but because one will not let them rage, but tries to compel them to listen to the head.

XIII. *Verbo Dei quum auscultant homines, pure et synceriter voluntatem Dei discunt. Deinde per Spiritum Dei in Deum trahuntur et veluti transformantur*

XIII. Where this (the head) is hearkened to one learns clearly and plainly the will of God, and man is attracted by his Spirit to him and changed into him.

XIV. *Summo igitur studio hoc unum in primis curent omnes Christiani ut Evangelium Christi unice et synceriter ubique prædicetur.*

XIV. Therefore all Christian people shall use their best diligence that the Gospel of Christ be preached alike everywhere.

XV. *Qui credit Evangelio, salvus erit; qui non credit, condemnabitur. Nam in Evangelio omnis veritas clarescit.*

XV. For in the faith rests our salvation, and in unbelief our damnation; for all truth is clear in him.

XVI. *In Evangelio discimus, hominum doctrinas et traditiones ad salutem nihil esse utiles:*

XVI. In the Gospel one learns that human doctrines and decrees do not aid in salvation.

ABOUT THE POPE

XVII. *Christus unicus æternus et summus est sacerdos. Qui ergo se pro summis sacerdotibus venditant, gloriæ et potentiæ Christi adversantur, et Christum rejiciunt.*

XVII. That Christ is the only eternal high priest, wherefrom it follows that those who have called themselves high priests have opposed the honor and power of Christ, yea, cast it out.

ABOUT THE MASS

XVIII. *Christus qui sese semel in cruce obtulit hostia est et victima satisfaciens in æternum pro peccatis omnium fidelium. Ex quo colligitur, missam non esse sacrificium, sed sacrificii in cruce semel oblati commemorationem et quasi sigillum redemptionis per Christum exhibitæ [effectæ].*

XVIII. That Christ, having sacrificed himself once, is to eternity a certain and valid sacrifice for the sins of all faithful, wherefrom it follows that the mass is not a sacrifice, but is a remembrance of the sacrifice and assurance of the salvation which Christ has given us.

XIX. *Christus unicus est Mediator inter Deum et nos.*

XIX. That Christ is the only mediator between God and us.

ABOUT THE INTERCESSION OF THE SAINTS

XX. *Omnia nobis per Christum et in nomine Christi præstat Deus. Hinc sequitur, nobis extra hanc vitam intercessore præter Christum nullo opus esse.*

XX. That God desires to give us all things in his name, whence it follows that outside of this life we need no mediator except himself.

XXI. *Quum mutuo pro nobis hic in terris oramus, in hoc [ita] facere debemus, quod per solum Christum omnia nobis dari confidamus.*

XXI. That when we pray for each other on earth, we do so in such fashion that we believe that all things are given to us through Christ alone.

ABOUT GOOD WORKS

XXII. *Christus est nostra institia. Hinc consequitur, opera nostra eatenus esse bona, quatenus sunt Christi; quatenus vero nostra, non esse vere bona.*

XXII. That Christ is our justice, from which follows that our works in so far as they are good, so far they are of Christ, but in so far as they are ours, they are neither right nor good.

CONCERNING CLERICAL PROPERTY

XXIII. *Quod Christus substantiam hujus mundi et fastum contemnit, docet, quod hi, qui sub Christi titulo divitias ad se rapiunt, ipsum magna infamia afficiunt, quum cupiditatis suæ et luxus eum patronum faciunt.*

XXIII. That Christ scorns the property and pomp of this world, whence from it follows that those who attract wealth to themselves in his name slander him terribly when they make him a pretext for their avarice and wilfullness.

CONCERNING THE FORBIDDING OF FOOD

XXIV. *Christianorum nullus ad ea opera, quæ Christus non præcepit, adstringitur; quolibet tempore, quolibet cibo vesci potest. Consequitur ergo literas, quas pro caseo et butyro dant pontificii, Romanas esse imposturas.*

XXIV. That no Christian is bound to do those things which God has not decreed, therefore one may eat at all times all food, wherefrom one learns that the decree about cheese and butter is a Roman swindle.

ABOUT HOLIDAY AND PILGRIMAGE

XXV. *Tempus et locus in potestate sunt hominis, non homo in illorum potestate. Qui ergo tempus et locum [tempore et loco] alligant, Christiana libertate pios fraudant et spoliant.*

XXV. That time and place is under the jurisdiction of Christian people, and man with them, wherefrom is learnt that those who fix time and place deprive the Christians of their liberty.

ABOUT HOODS, DRESS, INSIGNIA

XXVI. *Nihil magis displicet Deo quam hypocrisis. Hinc discimus hypocrisim esse gravem, et impudentem audaciam quidquid sanctum se simulat coram hominibus. Hic cadunt cuculli, signa, rasus vertex, etc.*

XXVI. That God is displeased with nothing so much as with hypocrisy; whence is learnt that all is gross hypocrisy and profligacy which is mere show before men. Under this condemnation fall hoods, insignia, plates, etc.

ABOUT ORDER AND SECTS

XXVII. *Omnes Christiani fratres sunt Christi, et fratres inter sese, patrem ergo super terram [in terris] vocare non debent. Hic cadunt factiones et sectæ.*

XXVII. That all Christian men are brethren of Christ and brethren of one another, and shall create no father (for themselves) on earth. Under this condemnation fall orders, sects, brotherhoods, etc.

ABOUT THE MARRIAGE OF ECCLESIASTS

XXVIII. *Quidquid Deus non vetat et permittit, juste fit. Ex quo discimus matrimonium omnibus ex æquo convenire.*

XXVIII. That all which God has allowed or not forbidden is righteous, hence marriage is permitted to all human beings.

XXIX. *Qui Ecclesiastici vulgo seu spirituales vocantur, peccant, dum, posteaquam senserint castitatem sibi a Deo negatam, non uxores ducunt aut nuhunt.*

XXIX. That all who are called clericals sin when they do not protect themselves by marriage after they have become conscious that God has not enabled them to remain chaste.

ABOUT THE VOW OF CHASTITY

XXX. *Qui vovent castitatem, stulta præsumptione et puerili arrogantia tenentur. Qui ergo ab eis vota hujusmodi vel exquirunt vel oblata recipiunt, injuriam eis faciunt et tyrannidem in simplices exercent.*

XXX. That those who promise chastity [outside of matrimony] take foolishly or childishly too much upon themselves, whence is learnt that those who make such vows do wrong to the pious being.

ABOUT THE BAN

XXXI. *Excommunicationem nemo privatus ferre potest, sed ecclesia in qua excommunicandus habitat una cum episcopo.*

XXXI. That no special person can impose the ban upon any one, but the Church, that is the congregation of those among whom the one to be banned dwells, together with their watchman, i.e., the pastor.

XXXII. *Nemo potest nec debet excommunicari, quam is, qui sceleribus suis publice offendit.*

XXXII. That one may ban only him who gives public offence.

ABOUT ILLEGAL PROPERTY

XXXIII. *Ablata injuste non templis, monasteriis, non monachis aut sacerdotibus, sed paupe ribus danda sunt, si iis quibus ablata sunt restitui commode non possunt.*

XXXIII. That property unrighteously acquired shall not be given to temples, monasteries, cathedrals, clergy or nuns, but to the needy, if it cannot be returned to the legal owner.

ABOUT MAGISTRY

XXXIV. *Potestas quam sibi Papa et Episcopi, aeterique quos spiritales vocant, arrogant, et fastus, quo turgent, ex sacris literis et doctrina Christi firmamentum non habet.*

XXXIV. The spiritual (so-called) power has no justification for its pomp in the teaching of Christ.

XXXV. *Magistratus publicus firmatur verbo et facto Christi.*

XXXV. But the lay has power and confirmation from the deed and doctrine of Christ.

XXXVI. *Jurisdictio aut juris administratio, quam sibi dicti spirituales arrogant, tota magistratus sæcularis est, si modo velit esse Christianus.*

XXXVI. All that the spiritual so-called state claims to have of power and protection belongs to the lay, if they wish to be Christians.

XXXVII. *Magistratibus publicis omnes Christiani obedire debent nemine excepto.*

XXXVII. To them, furthermore, all Christians owe obedience without exception.

XXXVIII. *Modo contra Deum nihil præcipiant!*

XXXVIII. In so far as they do not command that which is contrary to God.

XXXIX. *Leges magistratuum ad regulam divinæ voluntatis sunt conformandæ, ut oppressus et vim passos defendant et ab injuria asserant, etiam si nemo queratur.*

XXXIX. Therefore all their laws shall be in harmony with the divine will, so that they protect the oppressed, even if he does not complain.

XL. *Magistratus jure duntaxat occidere possunt, atque eos tantum qui publice offendunt, idque inoffenso Deo, nisi Deus aliud præcipiat.*

XL. They alone may put to death justly, also, only those who give public offence (if God is not offended let another thing be commanded).

XLI. *Quum illis, pro quibus rationem reddere coguntur, consilia et auxilia legitime administrant, debent et illi ipsi magistratibus subsidia corporalia.*

XLI. If they give good advice and help to those for whom they must account to God, then these owe to them bodily assistance.

XLII. *Quando vero perfide et extra regulam Christi egerint, possunt cum Deo deponi.*

XLII. But if they are unfaithful and transgress the laws of Christ they may be deposed in the name of God.

XLIII. *Hujus regnum optimum est et firmissimum qui ex Deo et cum Deo regnat; hujus vero pessimum et infirmissimum qui sua libidine.*

XLIII. In short, the realm of him is best and most stable who rules in the name of God alone, and his is worst and most unstable who rules in accordance with his own will.

ABOUT PRAYER

XLIV. *Veri adoratores invocant Deum in spiritu et veritate, corde orantes, non clamore coram hominibus.*

XLIV. Real petitioners call to God in spirit and truly, without great ado before men.

XLV. *Hypocritæ omnia opera sua faciunt ut videantur ab hominibus; propterea mercedem suam hic recipiunt.*

XLV. Hypocrites do their work so that they may be seen by men, also receive their reward in this life.

XLVI. *Cantiones ergo, seu verius boatus, qui in templis sine devotione pro mercede fiunt, aut laudem aut quæstum ab hominibus quærunt.*

XLVI. Hence it must always follow that church-song and outcry without devoutness, and only for reward, is seeking either fame before the men or gain.

ABOUT OFFENCE

XLVII. *Potius mortem eligere debet homo, quam Christianum offendere aut pudefacere.*

XLVII. Bodily death a man should suffer before he offend or scandalize a Christian.

XLVIII. *Qui ex infirmitate aut ignorantia absque causa vult offendi, non patiamur ut is infirmus et ignorans maneat; sed demus operam ut rite edoctus firmus tandem evadat, nec peccatum ducat quod peccatum non est.*

XLVIII. Who through stupidness or ignorance is offended without cause, he should not be left sick or weak, but he should be made strong, that he may not consider as a sin which is not a sin.

XLIX. *Maius et gravius scandalum non puto, quam quod sacerdotibus matrimonio legitimo interdicitur; concubinas et scorta habere accepta ab eis pecunia permittitur.*

XLIX. Greater offence I know not than that one does not allow priests to have wives, but permits them to hire prostitutes. Out upon the shame!

ABOUT REMITTANCE OF SIN

L. *Solus Deus peccata remittit, idque per solum Christum Jesum Dominum nostrum.*

L. God alone remits sin through Jesus Christ, his Son, and alone our Lord.

LI. *Qui remissionem peccatorum creaturæ tribuit, Deum gloria sua spoliat et idololatra est.*

LI. Who assigns this to creatures detracts from the honor of God and gives it to him who is not God; this is real idolatry.

LII. *Confessio ergo, quæ sacerdoti aut proximo fit, non pro remissione peccatorum, sed pro consultatione haberi debet.*

LII. Hence the confession which is made to the priest or neighbor shall not be declared to be a remittance of sin, but only a seeking for advice.

LIII. *Opera satisfactionis a sacerdote imposita humanæ sunt traditionis (excepta excommunicatione); peccatum non tollunt, sed aliis in terrorem imponuntur.*

LIII. Works of penance coming from the counsel of human beings (except the ban) do not cancel sin; they are imposed as a menace to others.

LIV. *Christus dolores nostros et omnes labores nostros tulit; qui vero operibus pœnitentialibus tribuit, quod Christi solius est, errat et Deum blasphemat.*

LIV. Christ has borne all our pains and labor. Hence whoever assigns to works of penance what belongs to Christ errs and slanders God.

LV. *Qui vel unicum peccatum pœnitenti remittere negat, is non Dei nec Petri, sed Diaboli vicem tenet.*

LV. Whoever pretends to remit to a penitent being any sin would not be a vicar of God or Saint Peter, but of the devil.

LVI. *Qui quædam tantum peccata idque pro mercede aut pecunia remittunt, Simonis et Balaami socii sunt, et veri Satanæ legati.*

LVI. Whoever remits any sin only for the sake of money is the companion of Simon and Balaam, and the real messenger of the devil personified.

ABOUT PURGATORY

LVII. *Scriptura sacra purgatorium post hanc vitam nullum novit.*

LVII. The true divine Scriptures know naught about purgatory after this life.

LVIII. *Defunctorum judicium soli Deo cognitum est.*

LVIII. The sentence of the dead is known to God only.

LIX. *Quo minus de hisce rebus nobis revelat Deus, hoc minus nobis pervestigandæ sunt.*

LIX. And the less God has let us know concerning it, the less we should undertake to know about it.

LX. *Si quis, pro mortuis sollicitus, apud Deum gratiam eis implorat aut precatur, non damno; sed tempus de hoc definire (septennium pro peccato mortali), et propter quæstum mentiri, non humanum est, sed diabolicum.*

LX. That man earnestly calls to God to show mercy to the dead I do not condemn, but to determine a period of time therefor (seven years for a mortal sin), and to lie for the sake of gain, is not human, but devilish.

ABOUT THE PRIESTHOOD

LXI. *De charactere, quem postremis hisce temporibus excogitarunt sacrifici, nihil novit divina Scriptura.*

LXI. About the consecration which the priests have received in late times the Scriptures know nothing.

LXII. *Scriptura alios presbyteros aut sacerdotes non novit quam eos qui verbum Dei annunciant.*

LXII. Furthermore, they know no priests except those who proclaim the word of God.

LXIII. *Illis vero presbyteris, de quibus diximus, qui Verbum Dei prædicant, Scriptura divina jubet, ut necessaria ministrentur.*

LXIII. They command honor should be shown, i.e., to furnish them with food for the body.

ABOUT THE CESSATION OF MISUSAGES

LXIV. *Qui errorem agnoscunt, illis nihil damni inferendum, ferantur autem donec in pace decedant, deinde sacerdotiorum bona juxta Christianam caritatem ordinentur.*

LXIV. All those who recognize their errors shall not be allowed to suffer, but to die in peace, and thereafter arrange in a Christian manner their bequests to the Church.

LXV. *Qui errorem non agnoscunt nec ponunt, Deo sunt relinquendi, nec vis corporibus illorum inferenda nisi tam enormiter ac tumultuose se gerant, ut parcere illis magistratui salva publica tranquillitate non liceat.*

LXV. Those who do not wish to confess, God will probably take care of. Hence no force shall be used against their body, unless it be that they behave so criminally that one cannot do without that.

LXVI. *Humilient se illico quicunque in Ecclesia sunt præfecti, crucemque Christi (non cistam) erigant; aut perditio eorum adest, nam securis radici arboris est admota.*

LXVI. All the clerical superiors shall at once settle down, and with unanimity set up the cross of Christ, not the money-chests, or they will perish, for I tell thee the ax is raised against the tree.

LXVII. *Si cui libet disserere mecum de decimis, reditibus, de infantibus non baptizatis, de confirmatione, non detrectabo colloquium.*

LXVII. If any one wishes conversation with me concerning interest, tithes, unbaptized children or confirmation, I am willing to answer.

Let no one undertake here to argue with sophistry or human foolishness, but come to the Scriptures to accept them as the judge (foras cares! the Scriptures breathe the Spirit of God), so that the truth either may be found, or if found, as I hope, retained. Amen.

Thus may God rule.

The basis and commentary of these articles will soon appear in print.

The Ten Conclusions of Berne (1528)

The German and Latin texts are a reproduction of "Theses Bernenses. A.D. 1528," in Schaff, *The Creeds of Christendom*, 3:208–10.

The English text, which follows the Latin text, apart from the first paragraph and the conclusion is a reproduction of "The Ten Theses of Berne," in Schaff, *The Creeds of Christendom*, 1:365–66.

The Ten Theses or Conclusions of Berne (1528) were written by Berthold Haller (1492–1536) and Francis (Franz) Kolb (1465–1535) and later revised by Zwingli. The Ten Theses were composed for a disputation in which Haller and Kolb expounded and defended the Theses. As a result of this disputation, held in 1528, most of the clergy in Bern subscribed to the Theses, thereby declaring their desire for church reform. The Ten Theses and the successful disputation were a major step forward in the establishment of the Reformation in Switzerland. The Ten Theses are remarkably succinct, focusing on the abuses of the Roman Catholic Church. Each thesis, except number 3, which is an affirmation that Christ is the only Savior, contains the term *Scripture* or *Word of God*. The Reformers' disagreement with the Roman Catholic Magisterium was motivated by a desire to reestablish the church as a community that was truly founded on the Word of God. We have added our own translation of the introduction and conclusion from the German text.

Bibliography: Irena Backus. *The Disputations of Baden, 1526 and Berne, 1528: Neutralizing the Early Church.* Studies in Reformed Theology and History 1.1. Princeton, NJ: Princeton Theological Seminary, 1993. "Bern, Disputation Of." *NSHERK* 2:61. Cochrane. *Reformed Confessions.* Pp. 45–50. Dennison. *Reformed Confessions* 1:40–42. "Haller, Berthold." *NSHERK* 5:126–27. "Kolb, Franz." *NSHERK* 6:370–71. Leith. *Creeds of the Churches.* Pp. 129–30. Richard Müller. "Reformed Confessions and Catechisms." Pp. 466–85 in *DHT*. Schaff. *The Creeds of Christendom* 1:364–66, 3:208–10.

Die zehen Schlußreden	**Theses Bernenses**	**The Ten Theses of Berne**
Ueber diese nachfolgenden Schlußreden wollen wir, Franciscus Kolb und Berchtoldus Haller, beide Prediger zu Bern, sammt andern, die das Evangelium bekennen, einem Jeden mit Gott Antwort und Bericht geben, aus heiliger biblischer Schrift, Neuen und Alten Testaments, auf angesetzten Tag zu Bern, Sonntag nach dem Feste der Beschneidung Christi, im Jahre 1528.	*De sequentibus Conclusionibus nos Franciscus Kolb et Berchtoldus Haller, ambo pastores Ecclesiæ Bernensis, simul cum aliis orthodoxiæ professoribus unicuique rationem reddemus, ex scriptis biblicis, Veteris nimirum et N. Testamenti libris, die designato, nimirum primo post dominicam primam circumcisionis, anno MDXXVIII.*	Concerning these following conclusions, we, Francis Kolb and Berthold Haller, both pastors of the Church of Berne, together with others who confess the gospel, want with God's help to give an answer and report to every one from the Holy Scripture, New and Old Testaments, on the appointed day at Berne, Sunday after the Feast of the Circumcision of Christ, in the year 1528.[1]
I. Die heilige christliche Kirche,[2] deren einiges Haupt Christus, ist aus dem Worte Gottes geboren; in demselben bleibt sie, und hört nicht die Stimme eines Fremden.	I. *Sancta Christiana Ecclesia, cujus unicum caput est Christus, nata est ex Dei Verbo, in eoque permanet, nec vocem audit alieni.*	1. The holy Christian Church, whose only Head is Christ, is born of the Word of God, and abides in the same, and listens not to the voice of a stranger.
II. Die Kirche Christi macht nicht Gesetze und Gebote ohne Gottes Wort; deshalb alle Menschensatzungen, die man Kirchengebote nennt, uns nicht weiter binden, als sie in Gottes Wort gegründet und geboten sind.	II. *Ecclesia Christi non condit leges et mandata extra Dei Verbum; ea propter omnes traditiones humanæ, quas Ecclesiasticas vocant, non ulterius nos obligant, quam quatenus in Dei Verbo sunt fundatæ et præceptæ.*	2. The Church of Christ makes no laws and commandments without the Word of God. Hence human traditions are no more binding on us than they are founded in the Word of God.
III. Christus ist unsre einige Weisheit, Gerechtigkeit, Erlösung und Bezahlung für aller Welt Sünde; deshalb ein anderes Verdienst der Seligkeit und Genugthuung für die Sünde bekennen, ist Christum verleugnen.	III. *Christus est unica sapientia, justitia, redemptio et satisfactio pro peccatis totius mundi; idcirco aliud salutis et satisfactionis meritum pro peccato confiteri, est Christum abnegare.*	3. Christ is the only wisdom, righteousness, redemption, and satisfaction for the sins of the whole world. Hence it is a denial of Christ when we confess another ground of salvation and satisfaction.

1. Our own translation of the German title given in Schaff, *The Creeds of Christendom*, 3:208.
2. Kilch.

IV. Daß der Leib und das Blut Christi wesentlich und leiblich in dem Brote der Danksagung empfangen wird, kann mit biblischer Schrift nicht bewiesen werden.

IV. Quod corpus et sanguis Christi essentialiter et corporaliter in pane Eucharistiæ percipiatur, ex Scriptura Sacra non potest demonstrari.

4. The essential and corporeal presence of the body and blood of Christ can not be demonstrated from the Holy Scripture.

V. Die Messe, wie sie jetzt im Gebrauche ist, darin man Christum Gott dem Vater für die Sünden der Lebenden [und] Todten aufopfere, ist der Schrift zuwider, dem allerheiligsten Opfer, Leiden und Sterben Christi eine Lästerung, und um der Mißbräuche willen ein Gräuel vor Gott.

V. Missa, ut hodie in usu est, in qua Christus Deo Patri offertur pro peccatis vivorum et mortuorum, Scripturæ est contraria, in sanctissimum sacrificium, passionem et mortem Christi blasphema et propter abusus coram Deo abominabilis.

5. The mass as now in use, in which Christ is offered to God the Father for the sins of the living and the dead, is contrary to the Scripture, a blasphemy against the most holy sacrifice, passion, and death of Christ, and on account of its abuses an abomination before God.

VI. Wie Christus allein für uns gestorben ist, so soll er, als alleiniger Mittler und Fürsprecher zwischen Gott dem Vater und uns Gläubigen, angerufen werden. Deßhalb ist das Anrufen aller andern Mittler und Fürsprecher außerhalb dieser Zeit ohne Grund der Schrift vorgeschrieben.

VI. Quemadmodum Christus solus pro nobis mortuus est, ita etiam solus ut mediator et advocatus inter Deum Patrem et nos fideles adorandus est. Idcirco alios mediatores extra hanc vitam existentes ad adorandum proponere cum fundamento Verbi Dei pugnat.

6. As Christ alone died for us, so he is also to be adored as the only Mediator and Advocate between God the Father and the believers. Therefore it is contrary to the Word of God to propose and invoke other mediators.

VII. Nach dieser Zeit wird kein Fegefeuer in der Schrift gefunden. Deshalb sind alle Todtendienste, als Vigilien, Seelenmessen, Septimen, Trigesimen,[3] Jahrzeiten,[4] Lampen,[5] Kerzen und vergleichen vergeblich.

VII. Esse locum post hanc vitam, in quo purgentur animæ, in Scriptura non reperitur; proin omnia officia pro mortuis instituta, ut vigiliæ, missæ pro defunctis, exequiæ, septimæ, trigesimæ, anniversariæ, lampades, cerei et id genus alia frustanea sunt.

7. Scripture knows nothing of a purgatory after this life. Hence all masses and other offices for the dead are useless.

3. Trußgost.
4. Jarzut.
5. Amplen.

VIII. Bilder machen zur Verehrung ist wider Gottes Wort des Neuen und Alten Testaments. Deßhalb sind sie abzuthun, wo sie mit Gefahr der Verehrung aufgestellt sind.

IX. Die heilige Ehe ist in der Schrift keinem Stande verboten, sondern, Hurerei und Unkeuschheit zu vermeiden, allen Ständen geboten.

X. Da ein öffentlicher Hurer nach der Schrift im wahren Banne ist, so folgt, daß Unkeuschheit und Hurerei des Aergernisses wegen seinem Stande schädlicher ist, als dem Priesterstande.

Alles Gott und seinem heiligen Worte zur Ehre.

VIII. *Imagines fabricare cultus gratia, Dei Verbo, Veteris et Novi Testamenti libris comprehenso repugnat. Idcirco si sub periculo adorationis proponantur, abolendæ.*

IX. *Matrimonium nulli ordini hominum in Scriptura interdictum est, sed scortationis et impuritatis vitandæ causa omnium ordinum hominibus præceptum et permissum.*

X. *Quia manifestus scortator juxta Scripturam excommunicandus; sequitur, scortationem aut impurum cœlibatum propter scandalum nulli ordini hominum magis quam sacerdotali damnosum esse.*

8. The worship of images is contrary to the Scripture. Therefore images should be abolished when they are set up as objects of adoration.

9. Matrimony is not forbidden in the Scripture to any class of men, but permitted to all.

10. Since, according to the Scripture, an open fornicator must be excommunicated, it follows that unchastity and impure celibacy are more pernicious to the clergy than any other class.

All honor to God and his holy Word.

The First Helvetic Confession (1536)

The German and Latin texts are a reproduction of "Confessio Helvetica Prior (sive Basileensis Posterior). The First Helvetic Confession. A.D. 1536," in Schaff, *The Creeds of Christendom*, 3:211–13.

The English text is reproduced from "II. From the Former Confession of Helvetia (Articles 1–5)," in Hall, *Harmony*, 4–5.

The First Helvetic Confession, or the Second Confession of Basel, was written in 1536 in Basel, Switzerland by Swiss Reformer Heinrich Bullinger (1504–75), along with Simon Grynaeus (1493–1541), Oswald Myconius (1488–1552), Leo Jud (1482–1542), and Kaspar Megander (1495–1545). The Strasbourg Reformers Martin Bucer (1491–1551) and Wolfgang Capito (1478–1541) also assisted in this endeavor. Luther originally welcomed the confession, but it ultimately failed to unify the Reformed and the Lutherans. It would, however, become the first common confession subscribed to by all of Switzerland (Helvetia).

The first five articles set forth a Reformed doctrine of Scripture including its inspiration by the Holy Spirit, *sola Scriptura*, and the principle of interpreting Scripture by Scripture. The explicit goal or drift of Scripture is to show forth the kindness of God revealed most clearly in Jesus Christ. Leo Jud translated the Latin text into German; an English version of this slightly augmented text can be found in Cochrane's collection of confessions.

Bibliography: Cochrane. *Reformed Confessions*. Pp. 97–111. Dennison. *Reformed Confessions* 1:342–52. Emil Egli. "Jud, Leo." *NSHERK* 6:242–43. Idem. "Megander (Grossmann), Kaspar." *NSHERK* 7:275–76. Idem. "Myconius, Oswald." *NSHERK* 8:64–65. Dirk Jellema. "Helvetic Confessions." P. 459 in *NIDCC*. E. F. Karl Müller. "Helvetic Confessions." *NSHERK* 5:216–17. Schaff. *The Creeds of Christendom* 1:385–89, 3:211–31. R. V. Schnucker. "Helvetic Confessions." Pp. 506–8 in *EDT*. R. Stähelin. "Grynaeus." *NSHERK* 5:90–91.

Ein gemeine bekantnus des helgen waren und uralten Christlichen gloubens und unsern mittburgern und Christlichn gloubgnossen, etc. Zurich. Bern. Basell. Straßburg. Costenz. Santgalln. Schaffhusn. Millhusen. Biel. Etc. zbazell uffgericht geordnet und gmacht uff untern bscheid, etc.
Im 1536. 1. 2. 3. et 4. Februarin.
Eine kurze und gemeine bekantnuß des gloubens der kelchen so in einer Eidtgnoschafft das Evangelium Christi angenomen habend, allen glöbigen und fromen zu erwegen, zu beschatzn und zu urteilen dargestelt.
1 Pet. 3; 1 Joh. 4.

I. Von der heiligen Schrift

Die heilige, göttliche, biblische Schrift, die da ist das Wort Gottes, von dem heiligen Geiste eingegeben, und durch die Propheten und Apostel der Welt vorgetragen, ist die allerälteste, vollkommenste und höchste Lehre, und begreift allein alles das, was zur wahren Erkenntniß, Liebe und Ehre Gottes, zu rechter, wahrer Frömmigkeit und Anrichtung eines frommen, ehrbaren und gottseligen Lebens dienet.

Helvet. Prior s. Basil. Posterior confessio fidei
Ecclesiarum per Helvetiam Confessio Fidei Summaria et Generalis, in hoc Aedita, Quod de ea Existimare Piis Omnibu Liceat

I. De Scriptura Sacra

Scriptura canonica Verbum Dei, Spiritu Sancto tradita, et per prophetas apostolosque mundo proposita, omnium perfectissima et antiquissima Philosophia, pietatem omnem, omnem vitæ rationem sola perfecte continet.

The First Helvetic Confession or the Second Confession of Basel

Article 1: Scripture

The Canonical Scripture, being the Word of God, and delivered by the Holy Ghost, and published to the world by the prophets and apostles, being of all others the most perfect and ancient philosophy, doth alone perfectly contain all piety and good ordering of life (2 Peter 1; 2 Tim. 3).

II. Von Auslegung der Schrift

Diese heilige, göttliche Schrift soll nicht anders, als aus ihr selbst ausgelegt und erklärt werden durch die Richtschnur des Glaubens und der Liebe.

II. De Interpretatione Scripturæ

Hujus interpretatio ex ipsa sola petenda est, ut ipsa interpres sit sui, caritatis fideique regula moderante.[1]

Article 2: Interpretation

The interpretation hereof is to be taken only from herself, that herself may be the interpreter of herself, the rule of charity and faith being her guide (John 5; Rom. 12; 1 Cor. 13).

III. Von den alten Lehrern

Wo nun die heiligen Väter und alten Lehrer, welche die Schrift erklärt und ausgelegt haben, von dieser Richtschnur nicht abgewichen sind,[2] wollen wir sie nicht allein für Ausleger der Schrift, sondern für auserwählte Werkzeuge, durch die Gott geredet und gewirft hat, erkennen und halten.

III. De Antiquis Patribus

A quo interpretationis genere, quatenus sancti patres non discessere, eos non solum ut interpretes Scripturæ recipimus, sed ut organa Dei electa veneramur.

Article 3: Fathers

Which kind of interpretation so far forth as the holy Fathers have followed, we do not only receive them as interpreters of the Scripture, but reverence them as the beloved instruments of God.

IV. Von Menschenlehren

Was sonst menschliche Lehren und Satzungen sind, sie seien so schön, hübsch, angesehen und lange gebraucht, als sie nur wollen, die uns von Gott und dem wahren Glauben abführen, halten wir für eitel und frastlos, wie es der heilige Matth. 15 selbst bezeugt, da er spricht: Sie ehren mich vergebens, wenn sie lehren die Lehren der Menschen.

IV. De Traditionibus Hominum

Per cætera de traditionibus hominum quantumvis speciosis et receptis, quæcumque nos abducunt, sic illud Domini respondemus, Frustra me colunt docentes doctrinas hominum.

Article 4: Human Traditions

But as for the Traditions of men, although never so glorious and received, how many soever of them do withdraw or hinder us [from the Scriptures], as of things unprofitable and hurtful, so we answer with that saying of the Lord, "They worship me in vain, teaching the doctrine of man" (Mark 7:7; Matt. 15; Isa. 29; Titus 1; 1 Tim. 4).

---

1. Sic *Christus facit* Matt. 4.
2. Über dise richtschnur nit gehowen habend.

V. Was der Zweck der heiligen Schrift sei, und worauf sie zuletzt hinweise.

V. Scopus Scripturæ

Article 5: The Drift [*Scopus*, lit. scope] of Scripture

Die ganze biblische Schrift sieht allein darauf, daß der Mensch verstehe, daß ihm Gott günstig sei und wohl-wolle, und daß er diese seine Gutwilligkeit durch Christum, seinen Sohn, dem ganzen menschlichen Geschlecht öffentlich dar-gestellt und bewiesen habe, die aber allein durch den Glauben zu uns komme, allein durch den Glauben empfangen, und durch die Liebe gegen den Näch-sten gezeigt und bewiesen werde.

Status hujus Scripturæ canonicæ totius is est, bene Deum hominum generi velle, et eam benevolentiam per Christum Filium suum declarasse. Quæ fide sola ad nos perveniat recipiaturque, caritate vero erga proximos exprimatur.

The Drift of the canonical Scripture is this: that God wisheth well to mankind; and by Christ the Lord his Son, hath declared this good-will; which is received by faith alone; and faith must be effectual through love, that it may be shewed forth by an innocent life (Gen. 3; John 3; Eph. 2).

The French Confession of Faith (1559)

"The French Confession of Faith. A.D. 1559," in Schaff, *The Creeds of Christendom*, 3:356–65.

Under the leadership of François Morel and in a time of persecution (1559), the young French Reformed Church secretly held its first national Synod in Paris. The French (Gallican) Confession of Faith along with a book of discipline was adopted as its official governing document. Yet the confession was not officially approved until 1571 at the national Synod in the town of La Rochelle; thus it is also known as the Confession of La Rochelle. Shortly before the Synod, Calvin was consulted for help in writing a confession. He promptly supplied one consisting of thirty-five articles, written with the help of his student Antoine de Chandieu (1534–91), and sent it to Paris. The Synod's main change to Calvin's text was to divide the first article into five. The consequence of this change was to begin with the doctrine of God rather than with Scripture, and to add statements about general revelation. Though these modifications are sometimes characterized as a betrayal of Calvin's original intention, the added themes are consonant with the rest of Calvin's corpus. The French Confession of Faith had a significant influence on the overall structure and content of the Belgic Confession.

We reproduce here a selection of the translation by Miss Emily O. Butler taken from Schaff's edition (vol. 3). We also include our own translation of the first original article by Calvin. Article I expounds God's unity and attributes. Article II teaches that God reveals himself through creation but more perfectly in his Word. While Article III lists the canonical books, Article IV insists on the inner witness of the Holy Spirit. In Article V, the confession affirms that the Scriptures come from God and are the Word of God; it "receives its authority from him alone." The rest of the selection sheds light on the historical context (the letter to the French king) and theological context (Articles VI–IX) of these statements.

Bibliography: Beeke & Ferguson. *Reformed Confessions*. P. ix. G. Bonet-Maury. "Gallican Confession." *NSHERK* 4:423–24. Cochrane. *Reformed Confessions*. Pp. 137–58. Pierre Courthial. "The Golden Age of Calvinism in France, 1533–1633." Pp. 79–81 in Reid, ed. *John Calvin: His Influence in the Western World*. Dennison. *Reformed Confessions* 2:140–54. Schaff. *The Creeds of Christendom* 1:490–98, 3:356–82. Theodor Schott. "Chandieu, Antoine de la Roche." *NSHERK* 3:1–2. Richard Stauffer. "Brève histoire de la Confession de La Rochelle." *Bulletin de la société de l'histoire du protestantisme français* 117 (1971): 356–66. Peter Toon. "Gallic Confession (1559)." P. 401 in *NIDCC*.

Les François Qui Desirent Vivre Selon la Pureté de l'Evangile de Nostre Seigneur Iésus Christ

Au Roy

Sire, nous rendons grâces à Dieu, de ce que n'ayans eu iusques icy aucun accés à vostre Maiesté, pour luy faire entendre la rigueur des persécutions que nous avons endurées, et endurons iournellement pour vouloir suyure la pureté de l'Evangile, et le repos de nostre conscience: maintenant il nous fait cet heur de veoir qu'avez la volonté de connoitre le mérite de nostre cause, suyvant l'Edit dernier donné à Amboise au moys de Mars, l'An présent 1559, qu'il a pleu à vostre Maiesté faire publier. Qui est la cause qu'à présent nous osons ouvrir la bouche: laquelle nous a esté parcidevant fermée par l'iniustice et violence de plusieurs voz officiers, estans plustost incitez de haine contre nous, que de bonne affection à vostre service. Et à fin, Sire, que nous puissions pleinement informer vostre Maiesté de ce qui concerne cette cause, nous vous supplions très-humblement de voir et entendre nostre Confession de Foy, laquelle nous vous présentons: espérans qu'elle nous sera défence suffisante contre tous les blasmes et opprobres, dont iusques icy avons esté chargez à grand tort par ceux qui ont tousiours fait mestier de nous condamner, premier que nostre cause leur fust connevë. En laquelle, Sire, nous pouvons protester qu'il n'y a aucune chose qui répugne à la parole de Dieu, ne qui contrevienne à l'hommage que nous vous devons.

The French Subjects Who Wish to Live in the Purity of the Gospel of Our Lord Jesus Christ

To the King

Sire, we thank God that hitherto having had no access to your Majesty to make known the rigor of the persecutions that we have suffered, and suffer daily, for wishing to live in the purity of the Gospel and in peace with our own consciences, he now permits us to see that you wish to know the worthiness of our cause, as is shown by the last Edict given at Amboise in the month of March of this present year, 1559, which it has pleased your Majesty to cause to be published. This emboldens us to speak, which we have been prevented from doing hitherto through the injustice and violence of some of your officers, incited rather by hatred of us than by love of your service. And to the end, Sire, that we may fully inform your Majesty of what concerns this cause, we humbly beseech that you will see and hear our Confession of Faith, which we present to you, hoping that it will prove a sufficient answer to the blame and opprobrium unjustly laid upon us by those who have always made a point of condemning us without having any knowledge of our cause. In the which, Sire, we can affirm that there is nothing contrary to the Word of God, or to the homage which we owe to you.

Car les articles de nostre Foy qui sont descrits assez au long en nostre Confession, reviennent tous à ce poinct, que puisque Dieu nous a suffisamment déclaré sa volonté par ses Prophètes et Apostres, et mesmes par la bouche de son fils nostre Seigneur Iésus Christ nous devons cet honneur et révérence à la parole de Dieu de n'y rien aioutter du nostre: mais de nous conformer entièrement à la reigle qui nous y est prescritte. Et pour ce que l'Eglise Romaine, laissant l'usage et coustume de la primitive Eglise, a introduit nouveaux commandemens et nouvelle forme du service de Dieu: nous estimons estre très-raisonnable de préférer les commandemens de Dieu, qui est la vérité mesme, aux commandemens des hommes: qui de leur nature sont enclins à mensonge et vanité. Et quoy que noz adversaires prétendent à l'encontre de nous, si pouvons nous dire devant Dieu et les hommes, que nous ne souffrons pour autre raison que pour maintenir nostre Seigneur Iésus Christ estre nostre Seul Sauveur et Rédempteur, et sa doctrine seule doctrine de vie et de salut.

Et cette est la seule cause, Sire, pour laquelle les bourreaux ont en tant de fois les mains souillées du sang de voz poures suiets, lesquels n'espargnent point leurs vies pour maintenir cette mesme confession de Foy, ont bien peu faire entendre à tous qu'ils estoyent poussez d'autre esprit que de celuy des hommes, qui naturellement ont plus de soucy de leurs repos et commoditez, que de l'honneur et gloire de Dieu.

For the articles of our faith, which are all declared at some length in our Confession, all come to this: that since God has sufficiently declared his will to us through his Prophets and Apostles, and even by the mouth of his Son, our Lord Jesus Christ, we owe such respect and reverence to the Word of God as shall prevent us from adding to it any thing of our own, but shall make us conform entirely to the rules it prescribes. And inasmuch as the Roman Church, forsaking the use and customs of the primitive Church, has introduced new commandments and a new form of worship of God, we esteem it but reasonable to prefer the commandments of God, who is himself truth, to the commandments of men, who by their nature are inclined to deceit and vanity. And whatever our enemies may say against us, we can declare this before God and men, that we suffer for no other reason than for maintaining our Lord Jesus Christ to be our only Saviour and Redeemer, and his doctrine to be the only doctrine of life and salvation.

And this is the only reason, Sire, why the executioners' hands have been stained so often with the blood of your poor subjects, who, sparing not their lives to maintain this same Confession of Faith, have shown to all that they were moved by some other spirit than that of men, who naturally care more for their own peace and comfort than for the honor and glory of God.

Et partant, Sire, suyvant, la bonté et douceur de laquelle promettez user envers voz poures suiets, nous supplions très-humblement vostre Maiesté nous faire cette miséricorde, que de prendre en main la connoissance de la cause, pour laquelle estans poursvyvis à toute heure ou de mort, ou de bannissement, nous perdons par ce moyen la puissance de vous faire le très-humble service que nous vous devons. Qu'il plaise donq à vostre Maiesté, Sire, à lieu des feus et glaives dont on a usé parcidevant, faire décider nostre confession de Foy par la parole de Dieu: donnant permission et sevreté pour ce faire. Et nous espérons que vous-mesmes serez iuge de nostre innocence, connoissant qu'il n'y a en nous ny hérésie, ny rébellion aucune: mais que nous tendons seulement à ce but, de pouvoir vivre en saine conscience, servans à Dieu selon ses commandemens, et honorans vostre Maiesté en toute obéissance et servitude.

Et par ce que nous avons nécessairement besoin d'estre, par la prédication de la parole de Dieu, retenus en nostre devoir et office tant envers luy: qu'envers vous: nous vous supplions très-humblement, Sire, qu'il nous soit permis d'estre quelquefois assemblez tant pour estre exhortez par la parole de Dieu à sa crainte, que pour estre conformez par l'administration des Sacremens que nostre Seigneur Iésus Christ a instituez en son Eglise. Et s'il plaist à vostre Maiesté nous donner lieu, auquel un chacun puisse voir ce qui se fait en noz assemblées, la seule veue nous absoudra de l'accusation de tant de crimes énormes, dont nosdittes assemblées ont esté diffamées parcidevant. Car on n'y pourra veoir que toute modestie et chasteté, et on n'y pourra ovyr que louanges de Dieu, exhortations à son service, et prières pour la conservation de vostre Maiesté et de vostre Royaume. Que s'il ne vous plaist nous faire tant de grâce, au moins qu'il nous soit permis de poursvyvre particulièrement entre nous avec repos l'ordre qui y est estably.

And therefore, Sire, in accordance with your promises of goodness and mercy toward your poor subjects, we humbly beseech your Majesty graciously to examine the cause for which, being threatened at all times with death or exile, we thus lose the power of rendering the humble service that we owe you. May it please your Majesty, then, instead of the fire and sword which have been used hitherto, to have our Confession of Faith decided by the Word of God: giving permission and security for this. And we hope that you yourself will be the judge of our innocence, knowing that there is in us no rebellion or heresy whatsoever, but that our only endeavor is to live in peace of conscience, serving God according to his commandments, and honoring your Majesty by all obedience and submission.

And because we have great need, by the preaching of the Word of God, to be kept in our duty to him, as well as to yourself, we humbly beg, Sire, that we may sometimes be permitted to gather together, to be exhorted to the fear of God by his Word, as well as to be confirmed by the administration of the Sacraments which the Lord Jesus Christ instituted in his Church. And if it should please your Majesty to give us a place where any one may see what passes in our assemblies, we shall thereby be absolved from the charge of the enormous crimes with which these same assemblies have been defamed. For nothing will be seen but what is decent and well-ordered, and nothing will be heard but the praise of God, exhortations to his service, and prayers for the preservation of your Majesty and of your kingdom. And if it do not please you to grant us this favor, at least let it be permitted us to follow the established order in private among ourselves.

Vous supplions très-humblement, Sire, de croyre, que oyant lire cette supplication qui vous est maintenant présentée, vous oyez les cris et gémissemens d'une infinité de voz poures suiets qui implorent vostre miséricorde: à ce qu'elle esteigne les feus que la cruanté de voz iuges a allumez en vostre Royaume. Et ainsi qu'il nous soit loisible, servans à vostre Maiesté de servir à celuy qui vous a élevé en vostre dignité et grandeur.

Et s'il ne vous plaist, Sire, d'ouyr nostre voix, qu'il vous plaise d'ouyr celle du Fils de Dieu, lequel vous ayant donné puissance sur noz biens, sur noz corps et sur nostre propre vie: vous demande que la puissance et domination sur noz ames et consciences (lesquelles il s'est acquises au pris de son sang) luy soyent réservées.

Nous le supplions, Sire, qu'il vous conduise tousiours par son Esprit, accroissant avec vostre aage, vostre grandeur et puissance, vous donnant victoire contre tous voz ennemis, establissant pour iamais en toute équité et iustice le throsne de vostre Maiesté: devant laquelle aussi il luy plaise nous faire trouver grâce, pour resentir quelque fruit de nostre présente supplication, à fin qu'ayons changé noz peines et afflictions à quelque repos et liberté, nous changeons aussi noz pleurs et larmes à une perpétuelle action de grâces à Dieu, et à vostre Maiesté, pour avoir fait chose à luy très-agréable, très-digne de vostre bonté et iustice, et très-nécessaire pour la conservation de voz plus humbles et plus obéissans suiets et serviteurs.

We beseech you most humbly, Sire, to believe that in listening to this supplication which is now presented to you, you listen to the cries and groans of an infinite number of your poor subjects, who implore of your mercy that you extinguish the fires which the cruelty of your judges has lighted in your kingdom. And that we may thus be permitted, in serving your Majesty, to serve him who has raised you to your power and dignity.

And if it should not please you, Sire, to listen to our voice, may it please you to listen to that of the Son of God, who, having given you power over our property, our bodies, and even our lives, demands that the control and dominion of our souls and consciences, which he purchased with his own blood, be reserved to him.

We beseech him, Sire, that he may lead you always by his Spirit, increasing with your age, your greatness and power, giving you victory over all your enemies, and establishing forever, in all equity and justice, the throne of your Majesty: before whom, may it please him that we find grace, and some fruit of this our present supplication, so that having exchanged our pains and afflictions for some peace and liberty, we may also change our tears and lamentations into a perpetual thanksgiving to God, and to your Majesty for having done that which is most agreeable to him, most worthy of your goodness and mercy, and most necessary for the preservation of your most humble and obedient subjects and servants.

CONFESSION DE FOI,

faite d'un commun accord par les François, qui desirent vivre selon la pureté de l'évangile de notre Seigneur Jésus-Christ. A.D. 1559.[1]

ART. I. *Nous croyons et confessons qu'il y a un seul Dieu, qui est une seule et simple essence, spirituelle, éternelle, invisible, immuable, infinie, incompréhensible, ineffable, qui peut toutes choses, qui est toute sage, toute bonne, toute juste, et toute miséricordieuse.*

II. *Ce Dieu se manifeste tel aux hommes, premièrement par ses œuvres, tant par la création que par la conservation et conduite d'icelles. Secondement et plus clairement, par sa Parole, laquelle au commencement révélée par oracles, a été puis après rédigée par écrit aux livres que nous appelons l'Ecriture sainte.*

CONFESSION OF FAITH,

made in one accord by the French people, who desire to live according to the purity of the Gospel of our Lord Jesus Christ. A.D. 1559.[2]

ART. I. We believe and confess that there is but one God, who is one sole and simple essence,[3] spiritual,[4] eternal,[5] invisible,[6] immutable,[7] infinite,[8] incomprehensible,[9] ineffable, omnipotent; who is all-wise,[10] all-good,[11] all-just,[12] and all-merciful.[13]

II. As such this God reveals himself to men;[14] firstly, in his works, in their creation, as well as in their preservation and control. Secondly, and more clearly, in his Word,[15] which was in the beginning revealed through oracles,[16] and which was afterward committed to writing[17] in the books which we call the Holy Scriptures.[18]

---

1. "*Pource que le fondement de croire, comme dit S. Paul, est par la parole de Dieu, nous croyons que le Dieu vivant est manifeste en sa Loy et par ses prophetes, et finalement en l'Evangile et y a rendu tesmoignage de sa volunté autant qu'il est expedient pour le salut des hommes. Ainsi, nous tenons les livres de la saincte Escripture du vieil et nouveau Testament comme la somme de la seule verité infaillible procedee de Dieu, à laquelle il n'est licite de contredire. Mesmes pource que là est contenue la regle parfaicte de toute sagesse, nous croyons qu'il n'est licite d'y rien adiouster ne diminuer mais qu'il y faut acquiescer en tout et par tout. Or comme ceste doctrine ne prend son autorité des hommes ne des anges, mais de Dieu seul, aussi nous croyons (d'autant que c'est chose surmontant tous sens humains, de discerner que c'est Dieu qui parle) que luy seul donne la certitude d'icelle à ses eleus, et la seelle en leurs coeurs par son Esprit.*" Original article in Calvin's version replaced by the first five articles in the French Confession of Faith; *Calvini opera,* 9:739–41.

2. The first five articles replaced the one following article, "Because the foundation of faith, as Saint Paul says, is the Word of God, we believe that the living God is manifested in his law and through his prophets, and finally in the gospel, and that there he has testified to his will as much as it is expedient for the salvation of men. Thus we hold the books of Holy Scripture of the Old and New Testament to be the sum of the only infallible truth proceeding from God, which it is not lawful to oppose. Especially because there is found the perfect rule of all wisdom, we believe that it is not lawful to add anything to it or to take away [from it], but that we must agree with it in all things and everywhere. Now since this doctrine does not derive its authority from men or angels, but from God alone, so we believe (as much as it is something beyond all human senses to discern that God himself speaks) that he himself grants certainty about it to the elect and seals it in their hearts by his Spirit" (translated from *OC* 9:739–41).

3. Deut. 4:35, 39; 1 Cor. 8:4, 6.
4. Gen. 1:3; John 4: 24; 2 Cor. 3:17.
5. Ex. 3:15–16, 18.
6. Rom. 1:20; 1 Tim. 1:47.
7. Mal. 3:6.
8. Rom. 11:33; Acts 7:48.
9. Jer. 10:7, 10; Luke 1:37.
10. Rom. 16:27.
11. Matt. 19:17.
12. Jer. 12:1.
13. Ex. 34:6–7.
14. Rom. 1:20.
15. Heb. 1:4.
16. Gen. 15:1.
17. Ex. 24:3–4.
18. Rom. 1:2.

III. *Toute cette Ecriture sainte est comprise aux livres canoniques du Vieux et du Nouveau Testament, desquels le nombre s'ensuit: les cinq livres de Moïse, savoir:* GENÈSE, EXODE, LÉVITIQUE, NOMBRES, DEUTÉRONOME. Item, JOSUÉ, JUGES, RUTH, *le premier et le second livres de* SAMUEL, *le premier et le second livres des* ROIS, *le premier et le second livres des* CHRONIQUES, *autrement dits Paralipomenon; le premier livre d'*ESDRAS. Item, NÉHÉMIE, *le livre d'*ESTHER, JOB, *les* PSAUMES *de David, les* PROVERBES *ou sentences de Salomon; le livre de l'*ECCLÉSIASTE, *dit le* PRÊCHEUR; *le* CANTIQUE *de Salomon*. Item, *le livre d'*ESAÏE, JÉRÉMIE, LAMENTATIONS *de Jérémie*, EZÉCHIEL, DANIEL, OSÉE, JOËL, AMOS, ABDIAS, JONAS, MICHÉE, NAHUM, ABAKUK, SOPHONIE, AGGÉE, ZACHARIE, MALACHIE. Item, *le saint Evangile selon saint* MATTHIEU, *selon saint* MARC, *selon saint* LUC, *et selon saint* JEAN. Item, *le second livre de saint Luc, autrement dit les* ACTES *des Apôtres*. Item, *les Epîtres de saint Paul, aux* ROMAINS *une, aux* CORINTHIENS *deux, aux* GALATES *une, aux* EPHÉSIENS *une, aux* PHILIPPIENS *une, aux* COLOSSIENS *une, aux* THESSALONICIENS *deux, à* TIMOTHÉE *deux, à* TITE *une, à* PHILÉMON *une*. Item, *l'Epître aux* HÉBREUX, *l'Epître de saint* JACQUES, *la première et la seconde Epîtres de saint* PIERRE, *la première, la deuxième, et la troisième Epîtres de saint* JEAN, *l'Epître de saint* JUDE. Item, *l'*APOCALYPSE *ou Révélation de saint Jean*.

III. These Holy Scriptures are comprised in the canonical books of the Old and New Testaments, as follows: the five books of Moses, namely: GENESIS, EXODUS, LEVITICUS, NUMBERS, DEUTERONOMY; then JOSHUA, JUDGES, RUTH, the first and second books of SAMUEL, the first and second books of the KINGS, the first and second books of the CHRONICLES, otherwise called Paralipomenon, the first book of EZRA; then NEHEMIAH, the book of ESTHER, JOB, the PSALMS of David, the PROVERBS or Maxims of Solomon; the book of ECCLESIASTES, called the Preacher, the SONG OF SOLOMON; then the book of ISAIAH, JEREMIAH, LAMENTATIONS of Jeremiah, EZEKIEL, DANIEL, HOSEA, JOEL, AMOS, OBADIAH, JONAH, MICAH, NAHUM, HABAKKUK, ZEPHANIAH, HAGGAI, ZECHARIAH, MALACHI; then the Holy Gospel according to St. MATTHEW, according to St. MARK, according to St. LUKE, and according to St. JOHN; then the second book of St. LUKE, otherwise called the ACTS of the Apostles; then the Epistles of St. PAUL: one to the ROMANS, two to the CORINTHIANS, one to the GALATIANS, one to the EPHESIANS, one to the PHILIPPIANS, one to the COLOSSIANS, two to the THESSALONIANS, two to TIMOTHY, one to TITUS, one to PHILEMON; then the Epistle to the HEBREWS, the Epistle of St. JAMES, the first and second Epistles of St. PETER, the first, second, and third Epistles of St. JOHN, the Epistle of St. JUDE; and then the APOCALYPSE, or Revelation of St. John.

IV. *Nous connaissons ces livres être canoniques, et la règle très-certaine de notre foi, non tant par le commun accord et consentement de l'Eglise, que par le temoignage et persuasion intérieure du Saint-Esprit, qui nous les fait discerner d'avec les autres livres ecclésiastiques, sur lesquels, encore qu'ils soient utiles, on ne peut fonder aucun article de foi.*

V. *Nous croyons que la Parole qui est contenue en ces livres, est procédée de Dieu, duquel seul elle prend son autorité, et non des hommes. Et d'autant qu'elle est la règle de toute vérité, contenant tout ce qui est nécessaire pour le service de Dieu et de notre salut, il n'est pas loisible aux hommes, ni même aux Anges, d'y ajouter, diminuer ou changer. D'où il s'ensuit que ni l'antiquité, ni les coutumes, ni la multitude, ni la sagesse humaine, ni les jugements, ni les arrêts, ni les édits, ni les décrets, ni les conciles, ni les visions, ni les miracles, ne doivent être opposés à cette Ecriture sainte, mais, au contraire, toutes choses doivent être examinées, réglées et réformées selon elle. Et suivant cela, nous avouons les trois symboles, savoir: des Apôtres, de Nicée, et d'Athanase, parce qu'ils sont conformes à la parole de Dieu.*

IV. We know these books to be canonical, and the sure rule of our faith,[19] not so much by the common accord and consent of the Church, as by the testimony and inward illumination of the Holy Spirit, which enables us to distinguish them from other ecclesiastical books upon which, however useful, we can not found any articles of faith.

V. We believe that the Word contained in these books has proceeded from God,[20] and receives its authority from him alone,[21] and not from men. And inasmuch as it is the rule of all truth,[22] containing all that is necessary for the service of God and for our salvation, it is not lawful for men, nor even for angels, to add to it, to take away from it, or to change it.[23] Whence it follows that no authority, whether of antiquity, or custom, or numbers, or human wisdom, or judgments, or proclamations, or edicts, or decrees, or councils, or visions, or miracles, should be opposed to these Holy Scriptures,[24] but, on the contrary, all things should be examined, regulated, and reformed according to them.[25] And therefore we confess the three creeds, to wit: the Apostles', the Nicene, and the Athanasian, because they are in accordance with the Word of God.

19. Pss. 19:9; 12:7.
20. 2 Tim. 3:15–16; 2 Peter 1:21.
21. John 3:31, 34; 1 Tim. 1:15.
22. John 15:11; Acts 20:27.
23. Deut. 12:32; 4:1; Gal. 1:8; Rev. 22:18–19.
24. Matt. 15:9; Acts 5:28–29.
25. 1 Cor. 11:1–2, 23.

VI. *Cette Ecriture sainte nous enseigne qu'en cette seule et simple essence divine, que nous avons confessée, il y a trois personnes, le Père, le Fils, et le Saint-Esprit. Le Père, première cause, principe et origine de toutes choses. Le Fils, sa parole et sapience éternelle. Le Saint-Esprit, sa vertu, puissance et efficace. Le Fils éternellement engendré du Père. Le Saint-Esprit procédant éternellement de tous deux, les trois personnes non confuses, mais distinctes, et toutefois non divisées, mais d'une même essence, éternité, puissance et égalité. Et en cela avouons ce qui a été déterminé par les conciles anciens, et détestons toutes sectes et hérésies qui ont été rejetées par les saints docteurs, comme saint Hilaire, saint Athanase, saint Ambroise, et saint Cyrille.*

VI. These Holy Scriptures teach us that in this one sole and simple divine essence, whom we have confessed, there are three persons: the Father, the Son, and the Holy Spirit.[26] The Father, first cause, principle, and origin of all things. The Son, his Word and eternal wisdom. The Holy Spirit, his virtue, power, and efficacy. The Son begotten from eternity by the Father. The Holy Spirit proceeding eternally from them both; the three persons not confused, but distinct, and yet not separate, but of the same essence, equal in eternity and power. And in this we confess that which hath been established by the ancient councils, and we detest all sects and heresies which were rejected by the holy doctors, such as St. Hilary, St. Athanasius, St. Ambrose, and St. Cyril.

VII. *Nous croyons que Dieu en trois personnes coopérantes, par sa vertu, sagesse et bonté incompréhensible, a créé toutes choses, non-seulement le ciel, la terre et tout ce qui y est contenu; mais aussi les esprits invisibles, desquels les uns sont déchus et trébuchés en perdition, les autres ont persisté en obeissance. Que les premiers s'étant corrompus en malice, sont ennemis de tout bien, par conséquent de toute l'Eglise. Les seconds ayant été préservés par la grâce de Dieu, sont ministres pour glorifier le nom de Dieu, et servir au salut de ses élus.*

VII. We believe that God, in three co-working persons, by his power, wisdom, and incomprehensible goodness, created all things, not only the heavens and the earth and all that in them is, but also invisible spirits,[27] some of whom have fallen away and gone into perdition,[28] while others have continued in obedience.[29] That the first, being corrupted by evil, are enemies of all good, consequently of the whole Church.[30] The second, having been preserved by the grace of God, are ministers to glorify God's name, and to promote the salvation of his elect.[31]

26. Deut. 4:12; Matt. 28:19; 2 Cor. 13:14; 1 John 5:7 [?]; John 1:1, 17, 32.
27. Gen. 1:1; John 1:3; Jude 6; Col. 1:16; Heb. 1:2.
28. 2 Peter 2:4.
29. Ps. 103:20–21.
30. John 8:44.
31. Heb. 1:7, 14.

VIII. *Nous croyons que non-seulement il a créé toutes choses, mais qu'il les gouverne et conduit, disposant, ordonnant selon sa volonté, de tout ce qui advient au monde; non pas qu'il soit auteur du mal, ou que la coulpe lui en puisse être imputée, vu que sa volonté est la règle souveraine et infaillible de toute droiture et équité; mais il a des moyens admirables de se servir tellement des diables et des méchants, qu'il sait convertir en bien le mal qu'ils font, et duquel ils sont coupables. Et ainsi en confessant que rien ne se fait sans la providence de Dieu, nous adorons en humilité les secrets qui nous sont cachés, sans nous enquérir par-dessus notre mesure; mais plutôt appliquons à notre usage ce qui nous est montré en l'Ecriture sainte pour être en repos et sûreté, d'autant que Dieu, qui a toutes choses sujettes à soi, veille sur nous d'un soin paternel, tellement qu'il ne tombera point un cheveu de notre tête sans sa volonté. Et cependant il tient les diables et tous nos ennemis bridés, en sorte qu'ils ne nous peuvent faire aucune nuisance sans son congé.*

VIII. We believe that he not only created all things, but that he governs and directs them,[32] disposing and ordaining by his sovereign will all that happens in the world;[33] not that he is the author of evil, or that the guilt of it can be imputed to him,[34] as his will is the sovereign and infallible rule of all right and justice;[35] but he hath wonderful means of so making use of devils and sinners that he can turn to good the evil which they do, and of which they are guilty.[36] And thus, confessing that the providence of God orders all things, we humbly bow before the secrets which are hidden to us, without questioning what is above our understanding; but rather making use of what is revealed to us in Holy Scripture for our peace and safety,[37] inasmuch as God, who has all things in subjection to him, watches over us with a Father's care, so that not a hair of our heads shall fall without his will.[38] And yet he restrains the devils and all our enemies, so that they can not harm us without his leave.[39]

32. Ps. 104.
33. Prov. 16:4; Matt. 10:29; Rom. 9:11; Acts 17:24, 26, 28.
34. 1 John 2:16; Hos. 13:9; 1 John 3:8.
35. Pss. 5:5; 119; Job 1:22.
36. Acts 2:23–24, 27.
37. Rom. 9:19–20; 11:33.
38. Matt. 10:30; Luke 21:18.
39. Job 1:12; Gen. 3:15.

IX. *Nous croyons que l'homme ayant été créé pur et entier, et conforme à l'image de Dieu, est, par sa propre faute, déchu de la grâce qu'il avait reçue, et ainsi s'est aliéné de Dieu, qui est la fontaine de justice et de tous biens, en sorte que sa nature est du tout corrompue. Et étant aveuglé en son esprit, et dépravé en son cœur, a perdu toute intégrité sans avoir rien de reste. Et bien qu'il ait encore quelque discrétion du bien et du mal, nonobstant nous disons, que ce qu'il a de clarté, se convertit en ténèbres quand il est question de chercher Dieu, tellement qu'il n'en peut nullement approcher par son intelligence et raison. Et bien qu'il ait une volonté par laquelle il est incité à faire ceci ou cela, toutefois elle est du tout captive sous péché, en sorte qu'il n'a nulle liberté à bien, que celle que Dieu lui donne.*

IX. We believe that man was created pure and perfect in the image of God, and that by his own guilt he fell from the grace which he received,[40] and is thus alienated from God, the fountain of justice and of all good, so that his nature is totally corrupt. And being blinded in mind, and depraved in heart, he has lost all integrity, and there is no good in him.[41] And although he can still discern good and evil,[42] we say, notwithstanding, that the light he has becomes darkness when he seeks for God, so that he can in nowise approach him by his intelligence and reason.[43] And although he has a will that incites him to do this or that, yet it is altogether captive to sin, so that he has no other liberty to do right than that which God gives him.[44]

40. Gen. 1:26; Eccl. 7:10; Rom. 5:12; Eph. 2:2–3.
41. Gen. 6:5; 8:21.
42. Rom. 1:21; 2:18–20.
43. 1 Cor. 2:14.
44. John 1:4–5, 7; 8:36; Rom. 8:6–7.

The Scots Confession of Faith (1560)

The Latin text is a reproduction of "Confessio Fidei Scoticana I," in Schaff, *The Creeds of Christendom*, 3:460–66.

The English text is reproduced from "VII. From the Confession of Scotland," in Hall, *Harmony*, 226–27, 9–10.

The roots of the Scottish Reformation in Scotland date to the early 1500s with Tyndale's Bible and the Reformers Patrick Hamilton (1504?–28) and George Wishart (1491–1546). These men sought to make the Bible accessible to every Christian. This early movement found its leader in John Knox (1514–72) when he returned to Scotland from Geneva in 1560. In August 1560, the Scottish Parliament in Edinburgh appointed John Knox, and five others each also named John, to draw up a Protestant statement of faith. The Scots Confession was composed in only four days. It was adopted on August 17, 1560. Later in the history of the Scottish church, the Westminster Standards would gain greater importance than the Scots Confession.

The confession is composed of twenty-five articles, the first ten of which are a positive exposition of faith and the last fifteen of which are polemic. One of the significant features of this confession is its covenantal, or redemptive-historical, approach to the Scriptures. It teaches that the essence of Scripture is God's self-revealing activity, seen most clearly in the person and work of Jesus Christ. This confession also displays a sharp Scottish polemical spirit. This spirit is seen in the two articles quoted here on the authority of Scripture, written in opposition to the Roman Catholic Church. In a subsequent section, we will excerpt additional articles to illustrate the confession's interpretation of Scripture. For this volume, we used the text provided in Hall's *Harmony*.

Bibliography: Cochrane. *Reformed Confessions*. Pp. 159–84. Dennison. *Reformed Confessions* 2:186–206. J. D. Douglas. "Calvinism's Contribution to Scotland." Pp. 220–21 in Reid, ed. *John Calvin: His Influence in the Western World*. W. Ian P. Hazlett. "Scots Confession." Pp. 751–52 in *DSCH&T*. Idem. "The Scots Confession 1560: Context, Complexion and Critique." *Archiv für Reformation Geschichte* 78 (1987): 287–320. R. Kyle. "Scots Confession (1560)." P. 990 in *EDT*. W. S. Reid. "Scots Confession." P. 891 in *NIDCC*. Schaff. *The Creeds of Christendom* 1:680–85. Philip Schaff and D. S. Schaff. "Scotch Confession of Faith." *NSHERK* 10:298. David F. Wright. "14. The Scottish Reformation: Theology and Theologians." Pp. 174–93 in *The Cambridge Companion to Reformation Theology*.

CONFESSIO FIDEI SCOTICANA I

CONFESSIO FIDEI & DOCTRINÆ
Per ECCLESIAM Reformatam Regni
SCOTIÆ professæ,
Exhibitæ ordinibus Regni ejusdem in publicis Parliamenti, ut vocant, Comitiis, & eorum communi consensu approbatæ, uti cerissimis fundamentis verbi Dei innixæ consentaneæ, 1560; deinde in conventu ordinum, lege confirmatæ & stabilitæ, 1567.

ART. XVIII: QUIBUS INDICIIS VERA
ECCLESIA DISTINGUATUR A FALSA, ET
QUIS IN ECCLESIASTICÆ DOCTRINÆ
CONTROVERSIIS SIT JUDEX

Quia Satan ab initio simper laboravit, ut pestilentem synagogam veræ Dei ecclesiæ titulo insigniret, animosque crudelium homicidarum accendit, ut veram ecclesiam ejusque membra premerent, turbarent, et infestarent (velut Cain Abel, Ismaal Isaac, Esau Jacob, totusque sacerdotum Judaicorum ordo, primum Christum ipsum, deinde Apostolos ejus capitali odio sunt persecuti) imprimis necessarium videtur, veram ecclesiam ab impura synagoga certis et manifestis distinguere indiciis; ne in eum incidamus errorem, ut alteram pro altera cum nostro amplectamur exitio. Notas autem et indicia, quibus intemerata Christi sponsa ab impura illa et abominanda meretrice (ecclesiam impiorum intellige) discerni possit, asseveramus, neque ab antiquitatis præerogativa repetendas, nec usurpatis falso titulis, nec a successione perpetua episcoporum, nec a certi loci designatione, nec a multitudine hominum in eundem errorem consentient-

THE SCOTS CONFESSION OF FAITH

THE CONFESSION OF THE FAITH
AND DOCTRINE,
Believed and professed by the
Protestants of Scotland,
Exhibited to the Estates of the same in Parliament, and by their public vote authorized, as a Doctrine grounded upon the infaillible Word of God, *August* 1560. And afterwards established and publicly confirmed by sundry Acts of Parliament, and of lawful General Assemblies.[1]

Article 18: *Of the Notes, by which the true Church is discerned from the false; and who shall be Judge of the Doctrine*

Because that Satan from the beginning hath laboured to deck his pestilent Synagogue with the title of the Church of God, and hath inflamed the hearts of cruel murderers, to persecute, trouble, and molest the true Church, and members thereof; as Cain did Abel (Gen. 4:8), Ishmael Isaac (Gen. 21:9), Esau Jacob (Gen. 27:41), and the whole priesthood of the Jews, Christ Jesus himself, and his Apostles after him (Matt. 23:34–36; John 11:47, 53; Acts 3:15; 5:17–18):[2] it is a thing most requisite, that the true Church be discerned from the filthy Synagogues by clear and perfect notes, lest we, being deceived, receive and embrace to our condemnation the one for the other. The notes, signs, and assured tokens, whereby the immaculate spouse of Christ Jesus is known from the horrible harlot, the Church malignant, we affirm are neither antiquity, title usurped, lineal descent, place appointed, nor multitude of

---

1. This introduction is taken, but with modernized spelling, from Schaff, *The Creeds of Christendom*, 3:437.
2. John 15:18–20, 24; Acts 4:1–3.

ium. Cain *enim ætate et primogenituræ prærogativa* Abel *et* Seth *anteibat; item* Hierosolyma, *cætera totius orbis oppida; huc accedebat in sacerdotibus, ab* Aarone *usque, perpetua familiæ et successionis series; majorque erat eorum numerus qui scribas et Pharisæos sectabantur, quam qui* Jesum Christum *ejusque doctrinam ex animo probabant: neque tamen arbitramur quemquam, cui purum et solidum sit judicium, commissurum ut ulli ex iis quas modo commemoravi ecclesiis Dei nomen attribuat. Igitur, quam nos veram Dei ecclesiam credimus et fatemur ejus primum est indicium, vera Verbi Divini prædicatio, per quod Verbum Deus ipse sese nobis revelavit, quemadmodum scripta Prophetarum et Apostolorum nobis indicant; proximum indicium est, legitima sacramentorum* Jesu Christi *administratio, quæ cum verbo et promissionibus divinis conjungi debent, ut ea in mentibus nostris obsignent et confirment. Postremum est, ecclesiasticæ disciplinæ severa, et ex Verbi Divini præscripto, observatio, per quam vitia reprimantur, et virtutes alantur. Ubicunque hæc indicia apparuerint, atque ad tempus perseveraverint, quantumvis exiguus fuerit numerus, procul dubio ibi est ecclesia* Christi, *qui, juxta suam promissionem, in medio eorum est. Non illam dicimus universalem ecclesiam, de qua superius facta est mentio, sed particularem; tales erant* Corinthia, Gallogræca, *et* Ephesina, *aliæque complures, in quibus verbi ministerium a* Paulo *fuerat*

men approving an error. For Cain in age and title was preferred to Abel and Seth;[3] Jerusalem had prerogative above all places of the earth,[4] where also were the Priests, lineally descended from Aaron; and greater number followed the Scribes, Pharisees, and Priests, than unfeignedly believed and approved Christ Jesus and his doctrine.[5] And yet, as we suppose, no man sound judgment will grant, that any of the forenamed were the Church of God. The notes, therefore, of the true Church of God, we believe, confess, and avow to be, first, the true preaching of the word of God, in the which God hath revealed himself unto us, as the writings of the Prophets and Apostles do declare (John 1:18; 10:15, 30):[6] secondly, the right administration of the Sacraments of Christ Jesus, which must be annexed unto the word and promise of God, to seal and confirm the same in our hearts (Rom. 4:11):[7] lastly, Ecclesiastical discipline, uprightly ministered, as God's word prescribeth, whereby vice is repressed, and virtue nourished (1 Cor. 5:4–5).[8] Wheresoever, then, these former notes are seen and of any time continue (be the number never so few, about two or three), there, without all doubt, is the true Church of Christ; who, according to his promise, is in the midst of them:[9] not in the universal, of which we have before spoken; but particular, such as was in Corinth,[10] Galatia,[11] Ephesus,[12] and other places, in which the ministry was planted by Paul (Acts 16:1–2; 18:1–2),

3. Gen. 4.
4. Ps. 98:2–3; Matt 5:35.
5. John 12:42.
6. John 3:34; 5:39; 16:15; 18:37; 1 Cor. 1:23–24; 3:10–11; Eph 2:20.
7. Acts 2:42; Matt. 28:19–20; Mark 16:15–16; 1 Cor. 11:23, 26.
8. Matt. 18:15–18.
9. Matt. 18:19–20.
10. 1 Cor. 1:2; 2 Cor. 1:1.
11. Gal. 1:2.
12. Acts 20:17.

plantatum, quasque ipse Dei ecclesias vocat. Hujusmodi ecclesias, qui in regno Scotorum nomen Christi profitemur, in oppidis, vicis, aliisque locis in quibus veræ pietatis cultus est restitutus, nos habere asseveramus: ea enim in iis doctrina traditur quæ Dei Verbo scripto continentur; novi et veteris Testamenti eos intelligimus libros, qui ab infantia usque ecclesiæ semper habiti sunt canonici. Quibus in libris omnia quæ ad humani generis salutem sunt necessaria, asserimus sufficienter esse expressa. Hujus Scripturæ interpretandi potestas penes nullum est hominem, sive is privatam, sive publicam gerat personam; nec penes ullam est ecclesiam, quacunque illa, sive loci seu personæ prærogativa sibi blandiatur: sed penes Spiritum Dei, cujus instinctu illa ipsa Scriptura confecta est. Igitur, cum de Scripturæ sensu et interpretatione, aut loci alicujus, aut sententiæ quæ in ea contineatur controversia oritur, aut cum de collapsæ disciplinæ emendatione agitur in ecclesia, spectare debemus non tam quid homines qui nos antecesserunt dixerint aut fecerint, quam quid perpetuo sibi consentiens Spiritus Sanctus in Scripturis loquatur; præterea, quid Christus ipse fecerit aut fieri jusserit: illud enim omnes uno fatentur ore, Spiritum Dei (qui et unitatis item est spiritus) nunquam secum pugnare. Itaque, si qua cujusvis doctoris, aut ecclesiæ, aut concilii interpretatio, decretum aut opinio, cum expresso Dei Verbo quod in alia Scripturæ parte continetur, pugnaverit, luce clarius est, eam nec esse veram explicationem, nec mentem Spiritus Sancti, quantumvis eam

and which were of himself named the Churches of God (1 Cor. 1:2; Acts 20:28): and such Churches we, the inhabitants of the realm of Scotland, professors of Christ Jesus, profess ourselves to have in our cities, towns, and places reformed. For the doctrine taught in our Churches is contained in the written word of God, to wit, in the books of the Old and New Testaments; in those books we mean, which of the ancients have been reputed Canonical. In the which we affirm that all things necessary to be believed for the salvation of mankind, are sufficiently expressed (John 21:24–25).[13] The interpretation whereof, we confess, neither appertaineth to private nor public person; neither yet to any Church, for any pre-eminence, or prerogative, personal or local, which one hath above another; but appertaineth to the Spirit of God, by whom also the Scripture was written.[14] When controversy, then, happeneth for the right understanding of any place or sentence of Scripture, or for the reformation of any abuse within the Church of God, we ought not so much to look what men before us have said or done, as unto that which the Holy Ghost uniformly speaketh within the body of the Scriptures, and unto that which Christ Jesus himself did, and commanded to be done (1 Cor. 11:23).[15] For this is one thing universally granted, that the Spirit of God, which is the Spirit of unity, is nothing contrary to himself.[16] If, then, the interpretation, determination, or sentence of any Doctor, Church, or Council, repugn to the plain word of God, written

13. John 20:31; 2 Tim. 3:16–17.
14. 2 Peter 1:20–21.
15. John 5:39.
16. 1 Cor. 2:10–11; 12:4–6; Eph. 4:3–4.

concilia, regna, et nationes probaverint ac receperint. Nos enim nullam interpretationem recipere aut admittere audemus, quæ pugnet aut cum aliquo ex præcipuis fidei nostræ capitibus, aut cum perspicua Scriptura, aut cum caritatis regula.

in any other place of the Scripture, it is a thing most certain that there is not the true understanding and meaning of the Holy Ghost; although that Councils, Realms, and Nations have approved and received the same. For we dare not receive or admit any interpretation, which repugneth to any principal point of our faith, or to any other plain text of Scripture, or yet unto the rule of charity.

ART. XIX. De Scripturæ Autoritate

Article 19: *Of the Authority of the Scriptures*

Quemadmodum credimus et confitemur, ex Scripturis divinis Dei cognitionem abunde hominibus tradi; ita affirmamus atque asseveramus, a nullo hominum aut angelorum, sed a Deo solo Scripturæ autoritatem pendere. Igitur qui tantam esse Scripturæ autoritatem volunt, quantam illi ecclesiæ concedunt suffragia, eos constanter asserimus adversus Deum blasphemos esse, adversus veram ecclesiam contumeliosos; quæ sui sponsi, suique pastoris vocem audit, eique obtemperat, neque tantum sibi assumit ut domina ejus videri velit.

As we believe and confess the Scriptures of God sufficient to instruct and make the man of God perfect (2 Tim. 3:16–17);[17] so do we affirm and avow the authority of the same to be of God, and neither to depend on men nor angels. We affirm, therefore, that such as allege the Scripture to have no other authority but that which it hath received from the Church, are blasphemous against God, and injurious to the true church; which always heareth and obeyeth the voice of her own Spouse and Pastor (John 10:27), but taketh not upon her to be mistress over the same.

ART. XX. De Conciliis Generalibus, Deque Eorum Potestate, Autoritate et Causis Cur Cogantur

Article 20: *Of General Councils, Of Their Power, Authority, and Cause of Their Convention*

Quemadmodum quæ ab hominibus piis, legitime ad generale concilium convocatis nobis proposita sunt, ea non temere aut præcipitanter damnamus; ita nec sine justa examinatione recipere audemus, quicquid generalis concilii nomine nobis obtruditur: quippe cum homines eos fuisse constet, qui in manifestos inciderint errores, idque in rebus non minimi momenti. Itaque sicubi concilium perspicuo verbi divini testimonio sua decreta confirmat, statim ea reveremur atque amplectimur: sed si homines

As we do not rashly condemn that which godly men, assembled together in General Council lawfully gathered, have proponed unto us; so without just examination we do not receive whatsoever is obtruded unto men under the name of a General Council: for plain it is, as they were men, so have some of them manifestly erred, and that in matters of great weight and importance.[18] So far then as the Council proveth the determination and commandment that it giveth by the plain word of God, so soon

17. 1 Tim. 2 [?].
18. Gal. 2:11–14.

nova fidei dogmata, constitutionesve cum Verbo Dei pugnantes edant, iisque interim nomen concilii prætendant, ea nos penitus rejicimus atque recusamus tanquam doctrinam diabolicam, quæ a Dei Verbo ad constitutiones et doctrinas hominum animas nostras avocent. Causa igitur cur generalia concilia cogerentur non ea fuit, ut leges quas Deus non jussisset velut perpetuo duraturas rogarent; neque ut nova de fide dogmata comminiscerentur, neque ut Verbum Dei autoritate sua confirmarent; multo etiam minus ut pro Verbo Dei, aut verbi divini interpretatione nobis obtruderent, quod neque Deus antea voluisset, nec per scripturas suas nobis indicasset: sed cogebantur concilia (de iis loquimur quæ hoc nomine censeri merentur) partim ut hæreses confutarent, partim, ut publicam fidei suæ confessionem ad posteros transmitterent: atque horum utrunque faciebant ex verbi divini scripti autoritate, non autem quod putarent, hujus conventionis causa hac se prærogativa donatum iri, ut errare non possent. Atque hanc præcipuam illis fuisse causam existimamus publicorum conventuum. Erat et altera illa ad disciplinam ordinandam, ut in ecclesia, quæ Dei familia est, omnia honeste atque ordine gererentur: *nec hoc tamen in eum sensum accipi volumus, ut credamur existimare unam aliquam legem, et ceremoniarum ritum præscribi posse, qui omnibus et locis et sæculis convenire possit; nam ut ceremoniæ omnes ab hominibus excogitatæ temporariæ sunt, ita cum temporum momentis mutari possunt, et mutari etiam debent, quoties earum usus superstitionem potius alat, quam ecclesiam ædificet.*

do we reverence and embrace the same. But if men, under the name of a Council, pretend to forge unto us new articles of our faith, or to make constitutions repugnant to the word of God, then utterly we must refuse the same, as the doctrine of devils, which draweth our souls from the voice of our only God, to follow the doctrine and constitutions of men (1 Tim. 4:1–3). The cause, then, why that General Councils came together, was neither to make any perpetual law which God before had not made, neither yet to forge new articles of our belief, neither to give the word of God authority; much less to make that to be his word, or yet the true interpretation of the same, which was not before his holy will expressed in his word.[19] But the cause of Councils (we mean, of such as merit the name of Councils) was partly for confutation of heresies,[20] for giving public confession of their faith to the posterity following; which both they did, by the authority of God's written word, and not by any opinion of prerogative, that they could not err, by reason of their general assembly. And this we judge to have been the chief cause of General Councils. The other was, for good policy and order to be constitute and observed in the church; wherein (as in the house of God[21]) it becometh "all things to be done decently, and in order" (1 Cor. 14:40). Not that we think that one policy and one order in ceremonies can be appointed for all ages, times, and places; for as ceremonies, such as men have devised, are but temporal, so may and ought they to be changed, when they rather suffer superstition, than edify the Church using the same.

19. Col. 2:16, 18–22.
20. Acts 15.
21. 1 Tim. 3:15; Heb. 3:2.

The Belgic Confession of Faith (1561)

"The Belgic Confession," in Schaff, *The Creeds of Christendom*, 3:383–89.

The Belgic Confession is the earliest doctrinal standard of the Reformed Churches of the Netherlands. It is believed to have been drafted in French by Guido de Brès (1522–67), an itinerant minister in 1561 in the United Netherlands, an area that included the territory of the modern countries of the Netherlands and Belgium. The confession was adopted at the Synod of Emden (1571) and officially endorsed by the Synod of Dort (1619). As one of the Three Forms of Unity, this confession is part of the standards of many Reformed churches, especially in the Netherlands and America.

As indicated earlier, this confession has many affinities with the French Confession. This is also true for our selected text on God and Scripture. After presenting the doctrine of God (Article I), de Brès, in a Calvinistic fashion, develops the two-fold knowledge of God—in creation and the Word (Article II)—and then defines the Reformed doctrine of Scripture, affirming its inspiration by the Holy Spirit (Article III), the contours of the canon, and the witness of the Spirit (Articles IV–VI). In Article VII, the sufficiency of Scripture is presented as well as its perfection, completeness, and infallibility. We use here the English translation found in Schaff's *Creeds of Christendom*.

Bibliography: Beeke & Ferguson. *Reformed Confessions*. P. ix. "Belgic Confession." *NSHERK* 2:32. Cochrane. *Reformed Confessions*. Pp. 185–219. Dennison. *Reformed Confessions* 2:424–49. W. Robert Godfrey. "Calvin and Calvinism in the Netherlands." Pp. 100–101 in Reid, ed. *John Calvin: His Influence in the Western World*. Nicolaas H. Gootjes. *The Belgic Confession: Its History and Sources*. Text & Studies in Reformation & Post-Reformation Thought. Grand Rapids: Baker Academic, 2007. I. J. Hesselink. "Belgic Confession." P. 30 in *DP&RTA*. Dirk Jellema. "Belgic Confession." P. 116 in *NIDCC*. Schaff. *The Creeds of Christendom* 1:502–8, 3:383–436. L. A. van Langeraad. "Brès, Guy de (Guido de Bray)." *NSHERK* 2:262.

La Confession de Foi des Églises Réformées Wallonnes et Flamandes

De l'ancien texte du manuscrit authentique de 1580, avec la révision de Dortrecht de 1619

Article I: De Natura Dei

Nous croyons tous de cœur et confessons de bouche, qu'il y a une seule et simple essence spirituelle, laquelle nous appelons Dieu éternel, incompréhensible, invisible, immuable, infini; lequel est tout puissant, tout sage, juste, et bon, et source très-abondante de tous biens.

Article II: De Cognitione Dei

Nous le connaissons par deux moyens. Premièrement: Par la création, conservation et gouvernement du monde universel, d'autant que c'est devant nos yeux comme un beau livre, auquel toutes créatures, petites et grandes, servent de lettres pour nous faire contempler les choses invisibles de Dieu, savoir sa puissance éternelle et sa divinité, comme dit l'Apôtre saint Paul (Rom. 1:20). Toutes lesquelles choses sont suffisantes pour convaincre les hommes, et les rendre inexcusables.

Secondement: Il se donne à connaître à nous plus manifestement et évidemment par sa sainte et divine Parole, tout autant pleinement qu'il nous est de besoin en cette vie pour sa gloire et le salut des siens.

The Confession of Faith of the Reformed Church

Revised in the National Synod, held at Dordrecht, in the Years 1618 and 1619

Article I: There Is One Only God

We all believe with the heart, and confess with the mouth, that there is one only simple[1] and spiritual[2] Being, which we call God; and that he is eternal,[3] incomprehensible,[4] invisible,[5] immutable,[6] infinite,[7] almighty, perfectly wise,[8] just,[9] good,[10] and the overflowing fountain of all good.[11]

Article II: By What Means God Is Made Known unto Us

We know him by two means: first, by the creation, preservation, and government of the universe;[12] which is before our eyes as a most elegant book, wherein all creatures, great and small, are as so many characters leading us to contemplate *the invisible things of God*, namely, *his eternal power and Godhead*, as the Apostle Paul saith (Rom. 1:20). All which things are sufficient to convince men, and leave them without excuse.

Secondly, he makes himself more clearly and fully known to us by his holy and divine Word;[13] that is to say, as far as is necessary for us to know in this life, to his glory and our salvation.

---

1. Eph. 4:6; Deut. 6:4; 1 Tim. 2:5; 1 Cor. 8:6.
2. John 4:24.
3. Isa. 40:28.
4. Rom. 11:33.
5. Rom. 1:20.
6. Mal. 3:6.
7. Isa. 44:6.
8. 1 Tim. 1:17.
9. Jer. 12:1.
10. Matt. 19:17.
11. Ed. note: Or "A most plentiful well-spring of all good things" (Hall, *Harmony*, 32). James 1:17; 1 Chron. 29:10–12.
12. Ps. 19:2; Eph. 4:6.
13. Ps. 19:8; 1 Cor. 12:6.

ARTICLE III: DE SACRA SCRIPTURA

Nous confessons que cette Parole de Dieu n'a point été envoyée ni apportée par volonté humaine: mais les saints hommes de Dieu ont parlé étant poussés du Saint-Esprit, comme dit saint Pierre. Puis après, par le soin singulier que notre Dieu a de nous et de notre salut, il a commandé à ses serviteurs les Prophètes et Apôtres de rédiger ses oracles par écrit: et lui-même a écrit de son doigt les deux Tables de la Loi. Pour cette cause, nous appelons tels écrits: Écritures saintes et divines.

ARTICLE IV: DE CANONICIS LIBRIS VETERIS ET NOVI TESTAMENTI

Nous comprenons l'Écriture Sainte aux deux volumes du Vieux et du Nouveau Testament, qui sont livres canoniques, auxquels il n'y a rien à répliquer. Le nombre en est tel en l'Église de Dieu.

Dans l'Ancien Testament: Les cinq livres de Moïse, le livre de Josué, des Juges, Ruth, les deux livres de Samuël, et deux des Rois, les deux livres des Chroniques dits Paralipomènes, le premier d'Esdras, Néhémie, Ester, Job, les Psaumes de David, les trois livres de Salomon, savoir: les Proverbes, l'Écclésiaste, et le Cantique; les quatre grands Prophètes: Esaïe, Jérémie, Ezéchiel, et Daniel. Puis les autres douze petits Prophètes: Osée, Joël, Amos, Abdias, Jonas, Michée, Nahum, Habacuc, Sophonie, Aggée, Zacharie, Malachie.

ARTICLE III: OF THE WRITTEN WORD OF GOD

We confess that this Word of God was not sent nor delivered by the will of man, but that *holy men of God spake as they were moved by the Holy Ghost*, as the Apostle Peter saith.[14] And that afterwards God, from a special care which he has for us and our salvation, commanded his servants, the Prophets[15] and Apostles,[16] to commit his revealed Word to writing; and he himself wrote with his own finger the two tables of the law.[17] Therefore we call such writings holy and divine Scriptures.

ARTICLE IV: CANONICAL BOOKS OF THE HOLY SCRIPTURES

We believe that the Holy Scriptures are contained in two books, namely, the Old and New Testaments, which are canonical, against which nothing can be alleged. These are thus named in the Church of God.

The books of the Old Testament are: the five books of Moses, viz., Genesis, Exodus, Leviticus, Numbers, Deuteronomy; the book of Joshua, Judges, Ruth, two books of Samuel, and two of the Kings, two books of the Chronicles, commonly called Paralipomenon, the first of Ezra, Nehemiah, Esther; Job, the Psalms of David, the three books of Solomon, namely, the Proverbs, Ecclesiastes, and the Song of Songs; the four great Prophets: Isaiah, Jeremiah, Ezekiel, and Daniel; and the twelve lesser Prophets, viz., Hosea, Joel, Amos, Obadiah, Jonah, Micah, Nahum, Habakkuk, Zephaniah, Haggai, Zechariah, and Malachi.

---

14. 2 Peter 1:21.
15. Ex. 24:4; Ps. 102:19; Hab. 2:2.
16. 2 Tim. 3:16; Rev. 1:11.
17. Ex. 31:18.

Dans le Nouveau Testament: *les quatre Évangélistes, saint Matthieu, saint Marc, saint Luc, saint Jean; les Actes des Apôtres, les quatorze Épîtres de saint Paul: aux Romains, deux aux Corinthiens, aux Galates, Éphésiens, Philippiens, Colossiens, deux aux Thessaloniciens, deux à Timothée, à Tite, Philémon, aux Hébreux; et les sept Épîtres des autres Apôtres, savoir une de saint Jacques, deux de saint Pierre, trois de saint Jean, et une de saint Jude; enfin l'Apocalypse de saint Jean Apôtre.*

Those of the New Testament are: the four Evangelists, viz., Matthew, Mark, Luke, and John; the Acts of the Apostles; the fourteen Epistles of the Apostle Paul, viz., one to the Romans, two to the Corinthians, one to the Galatians, one to the Ephesians, one to the Philippians, one to the Colossians, two to the Thessalonians, two to Timothy, one to Titus, one to Philemon, and one to the Hebrews; the seven Epistles of the other Apostles, viz., one of James, two of Peter, three of John, one of Jude; and the Revelation of the Apostle John.

ARTICLE V: DE AUCTORITATE SACRÆ SCRIPTURÆ

ARTICLE V: WHENCE DO THE HOLY SCRIPTURES DERIVE THEIR DIGNITY AND AUTHORITY

Nous recevons tous ces livres-là seulement, pour saints et canoniques, pour régler, fonder et établir notre foi, et croyons pleinement toutes les choses qui y sont contenues, non pas tant parce que l'Eglise les reçoit et approuve tels, mais principalement parce que le Saint-Esprit nous rend témoignage en notre cœur, qu'ils sont de Dieu, et aussi qu'ils sont approuvés tels par eux-mêmes; car les aveugles mêmes peuvent apercevoir que les choses adviennent qui y sont prédites.

We receive all these books, and these only, as holy and canonical, for the regulation, foundation, and confirmation of our faith; believing, without any doubt, all things contained in them, not so much because the Church receives and approves them as such, but more especially because the Holy Ghost witnesseth in our hearts that they are from God, whereof they carry the evidence in themselves. For the very blind are able to perceive that the things foretold in them are fulfilling.

126

Article VI: De Discrimine Librorum Canonicorum et Apocryphorum

Nous mettons différence entre ces saints livres et les livres apocryphes, qui sont le troisième et quatrième livre d'Esdras, le livre de Tobie, Judith, Sapience, Ecclésiastique, Baruc, ce qui a été ajouté à l'histoire d'Ester, le cantique des trois Enfants en la fournaise, l'histoire de Susanne, l'histoire de l'idole Bel et du Dragon, l'Oraison de Manassé, et les deux livres des Maccabées, lesquels l'Église peut bien lire et y prendre instruction dans les choses conformes aux livres canoniques; mais ils n'ont point telle force et vertu que par un témoignage qui en est tiré, on puisse arrêter quelque chose de la foi ou religion chrétienne, tant s'en faut qu'ils puissent ramoindrir l'autorité des autres saints livres.

Article VI: The Difference Between the Canonical and Apocryphal Books

We distinguish these sacred books from the apocryphal, viz., the third and fourth book of Esdras, the books of Tobias, Judith, Wisdom, Jesus Syrach, Baruch, the appendix to the book of Esther, the Song of the Three Children in the Furnace, the History of Susannah, of Bell and the Dragon, the Prayer of Manasses, and the two books of Maccabees. All which the Church may read and take instruction from, so far as they agree with the canonical books; but they are far from having such power and efficacy as that we may from their testimony confirm any point of faith or of the Christian religion; much less to detract from the authority of the other sacred books.

Article VII: De Perfectione Sacræ Scripturæ

Article VII: The Sufficiency of the Holy Scriptures to Be the Only Rule of Faith

Nous croyons que cette Écriture Sainte contient parfaitement la volonté divine, et que tout ce que l'homme doit croire pour être sauvé, y est suffisamment enseigné. Car puisque toute la manière du service que Dieu requiert de nous y est très au long décrite, les hommes, même fussent-ils Apôtres, ne doivent enseigner autrement que ce qui nous a été enseigné par les Saintes Écritures, encore même que ce fût un ange du Ciel, comme dit saint Paul: car puisqu'il est défendu d'ajouter ni diminuer à la Parole de Dieu, cela démontre bien que la doctrine est très-parfaite et accomplie en toutes sortes. Aussi ne faut-il pas comparer les écrits des hommes, quelque saints qu'ils aient été, aux écrits divins, ni la coutume à la vérité de Dieu (car la vérité est par-dessus tout), ni le grand nombre, ni l'ancienneté, ni la succession des temps ni des personnes, ni les conciles, décrets, ou arrêts: car tous hommes d'eux-mêmes sont menteurs, et plus vains que la vanité même. C'est pourquoi nous rejetons de tout notre cœur tout ce qui ne s'accorde à cette règle infaillible, comme nous sommes enseignés de faire par les Apôtres, disant: Éprouvez les ésprits s'ils sont de Dieu, et: Si quelqu'un vient à vous et n'apporte point cette doctrine, ne le recevez point en votre maison.

We believe that these Holy Scriptures fully contain the will of God, and that whatsoever man ought to believe unto salvation, is sufficiently taught therein.[18] For since the whole manner of worship which God requires of us is written in them at large, it is unlawful for any one, though an Apostle, to teach otherwise[19] than we are now taught in the Holy Scriptures: *nay, though it were an angel from heaven,* as the Apostle Paul saith.[20] For since it is forbidden *to add unto or take away any thing from the Word of God,*[21] it doth thereby evidently appear that the doctrine thereof is most perfect and complete in all respects. Neither may we compare any writings of men, though ever so holy, with those divine Scriptures;[22] nor ought we to compare custom, or the great multitude, or antiquity, or succession of times or persons, or councils, decrees, or statutes, with the truth of God,[23] for the truth is above all: for all men are of themselves liars,[24] and more vain than vanity itself. Therefore we reject with all our hearts whatsoever doth not agree with this infallible rule,[25] which the Apostles have taught us, saying, *Try the spirits whether they are of God;*[26] likewise, *If there come any unto you, and bring not this doctrine, receive him not into your house.*[27]

---

18. Rom. 15:4; John 4:25; 2 Tim. 3:15–17; 1 Peter 1:1; Prov. 30:5; Gal. 3:15; Rev. 22:18; John 15:15; Acts 2:27.
19. 1 Peter 4:11; 1 Cor. 15:2–3; 2 Tim. 3:14; 1 Tim. 1:3; 2 John 10.
20. Gal. 1:8–9; 1 Cor. 15:2; Acts 26:22; Rom. 15:4; 1 Peter 4:11; 2 Tim. 3:14.
21. Deut. 12:32; Prov. 30:6; Rev. 22:18; John 4:25.
22. Matt. 15:3; 17:5; Mark 7:7; Isa. 1:12; 1 Cor. 2:4.
23. Isa. 1:12; Rom. 3:4; 2 Tim. 4:3–4.
24. Ps. 62:10.
25. Gal. 6:16; 1 Cor. 3:11; 2 Thess. 2:2.
26. 1 John 4:1.
27. 2 John 10.

The Heidelberg Catechism

The Reformation appeared later in the history of the province of the Palatinate, Germany. Under the leadership of the Elector Frederick III (1515–76), his province moved from Lutheran convictions to Reformed ones. In this move, he commissioned the composing of the Heidelberg Catechism (1563) for the purpose of instructing and unifying the church. Scholars have now acknowledged that the catechism was written by a team of theologians, among whom were Caspar Olevianus (1536–87) and Zacharias Ursinus (1534–83). Originally published in German and Latin, the catechism was translated into many languages. It is one of the most popular Reformed catechisms. As one of the Three Forms of Unity, it belongs to the standards of many Reformed churches. Though it was born within controversies with Lutherans and Catholics, it is pastoral and irenic in character. It has a very characteristic threefold structure: man's misery, redemption in Christ (the creed and sacraments), and thankfulness to God (the law and prayer).

While the catechism does not contain a separate developed statement about Scripture, the entire work is undergirded by the authority of God's Word; thus we offer a sample of scattered questions and answers. It begins with the famous introduction (Questions 1–2); then it deals with how Christ's work and the creed are rooted in the gospel and the Word (Questions 16–25). Christ as Prophet communicates his Word, and as King he rules by his Word (Question 31); in the church, Spirit and Word have a conjoined effect (Question 54); and the sacraments and the Word go hand in hand (Question 67). The exposition of the commandments illustrates the authority of the Word (Questions 95–98, 101, 103). Finally, prayer is regulated by the Word (Questions 116–18, 122–23). To supplement our selection from the Heidelberg Catechism, we offer the exposition of Ursinus on the sections on faith (Question 21) and Christ's offices (Question 31).

Bibliography: Beeke & Ferguson. *Reformed Confessions*. Pp. ix–x. Lyle D. Bierma, ed. *An Introduction to the Heidelberg Catechism: Sources, History, and Theology; with a Translation of the Smaller and Larger Catechisms of Zacharias Ursinus*. Grand Rapids: Baker Academic, 2005. Colin Buchanan. "Catechism." Pp. 199–201 in *NIDCC*. M. J. Coalter. "Heidelberg Catechism." P. 119 in *DP&RTA*. Cochrane. *Reformed Confessions*. Pp. 305–31. D. Clair Davis. "The Reformed Church of Germany: Calvinists as an Influentential Minority." Pp. 129–34 in Reid, ed. *John Calvin: His Influence in the Western World*. Dennison. *Reformed Confessions* 2:769–99. M. Lauterburg. "Heidelberg Catechism." *NSHERK* 5:204–6. Schaff. *The Creeds of Christendom* 1:529–54, 3:307–55. R. V. Schnucker. "Heidelberg Catechism (1563)." P. 504 in *EDT*. Bard Thompson, Hendrikus Berkhof, Eduard Schweitzer, and Howard G. Hageman, eds. *Essays on the Heidelberg Catechism*. Philadelphia: United Church Press, 1963. Cornelius Van Til. *The Triumph of Grace: The Heidelberg Catechism*. Philadelphia: Westminster Theological Seminary, 1958. Willem Van't Spijker, ed. *The Church's Book of Comfort*. Trans. Gerrit Bilkes. Grand Rapids: Reformation Heritage Books, 2009.

THE HEIDELBERG CATECHISM (1563)[1]

"The Heidelberg Catechism. A.D. 1563," in Schaff, *The Creeds of Christendom*, 3:307–8, 312–15, 317–18, 324–25, 328–29, 342–43, 344, 345, 350–51, 352–53.

Catechismus
Oder
Christlicher Underricht
Wie der in Kirchen und Schulen der
Churfürstlichen
Pfaltz getrieben
wirdt

Gedruckt in der Churfürstlichen Stad
Heydelberg/durch
Johannem Mayer
1563

Catechism
or
CHRISTIAN INSTRUCTION
as conducted in the Churches and
Schools
of the
Electoral Palatinate

Printed in the Electoral City
of Heidelberg by
JOHN MAYER
1563

LORD'S DAY 1

Frage 1. Was ist dein einiger Trost im Leben und im Sterben?

Question 1: *What is thy only comfort in life and death?*

---

1. We have added the references to the Lord's Days and the title of the various parts to Schaff's text. In addition, the Scripture references in the English text are from early editions, and the references in the footnotes are from later editions.

Antwort. Daß ich mit Leib und Seele, beides im Leben und im Sterben, nicht mein, sondern meines getreuen Heilandes Jesus Christi eigen bin, der mit seinem theuren Blute für alle meine Sünden vollkommen bezahlet, und mich aus aller Gewalt des Teufels erlöset hat; und also bewahret, daß ohne den Willen meines Vaters im Himmel kein Haar von meinem Haupte kann fallen, ja auch mir alles zu meiner Seligkeit dienen muß. Darum er mich auch durch seinen heiligen Geist des ewigen Lebens versichert, und ihm forthin zu leben von Herzen und bereit macht.

Frage 2. Wie viele Stücke sind dir nöthig zu wissen, daß du in diesem Troste seliglich leben und sterben mögest?

Antwort. Drei Stücke: Erstlich, wie groß meine Sünde und Elend seien. Zum Andern, wie ich von allen meinen Sünden und Elend erlöset werde. Und zum Dritten, wie ich Gott für solche Erlösung soll dankbar sein.

Answer: That I, with body and soul, both in life and in death (Rom. 14:7–9; 1 Thess. 5:9–10), am not my own (1 Cor. 6:19–20), but belong to my faithful Saviour Jesus Christ (1 Cor. 3:22–23),[2] who with his precious blood (1 Peter 1:18–19) has fully satisfied for all my sins (1 John 1:7; 2:1–2), and redeemed me from all the power of the devil (1 John 3:8; Heb. 2:14–15);[3] and so preserves me (John 6:38–40; 10:27–30)[4] that without the will of my Father in heaven not a hair can fall from my head (Matt. 10:29–31; Luke 21:18–19); yea, that all things must work together for my salvation (Rom. 8:28). Wherefore, by his Holy Spirit, he also assures me of eternal life (Rom. 8:15–16; 2 Cor. 1:21–22; 5:5; Eph. 1:13–14), and makes me heartily willing and ready, henceforth to live unto him (Rom. 8:14).[5]

Q. 2: *How many things are necessary for thee to know, that thou in this comfort mayest live and die happily?*

A: Three things (Luke 24:46–47; 1 Cor. 6:11; Titus 3:3–7):[6] First, the greatness of my *sin* and *misery* (John 9:41).[7] Second, how I am *redeemed* from all my sins and misery (John 17:3).[8] Third, how I am to be *thankful* to God for such redemption (Eph. 5:8–11; Rom. 6:11–14; 2 Tim. 2:15–16; 1 Peter 2:9–12; Matt. 5:16; Pss. 50:14–15; 116:12–13).[9]

2. Titus 2:14.
3. John 8:34–36.
4. 2 Thess. 3:3; 1 Peter 1:5.
5. Rom. 7:22; Phil. 2:13; Heb. 13:20–21; 1 John 3:3; 4:13; Ezek. 36:27.
6. Matt. 11:28–30.
7. John 15:22; Rom. 3:10; 7:24; Matt. 9:12; 1 John 1:9, 10; Rom. 1:18–3:21.
8. Acts 4:12; 10:43; Rom. 7:25; Col. 1:13–14; 1 Peter 1:18–19; 1 John 1:7; Rev. 1:5; Rom. 3:21–11:36; Phil. 2:5–11.
9. Rom. 6:1–2; 12:1–16:27.

Der andere [zweite] Theil.
Von des Menschen Erlösung

THE SECOND PART:
OF MAN'S REDEMPTION

LORD'S DAY 6

Frage 16. Warum muß Er ein wahrer und gerechter Mensch sein?

Antwort. Darum, weil die Gerechtigkeit Gottes erfordert, daß die menschliche Natur, die gesündiget hat, für die Sünde bezahle, aber Einer, der selbst ein Sünder wäre, nicht könnte für Andere bezahlen.

Q. 16: *Why must he be a true and sinless man?*

A: Because the justice of God requires that the same human nature which has sinned should make satisfaction for sin (Rom. 5:12–15; 1 Peter 3:18; Isa. 53:3–5);[10] but no man, being himself a sinner, could satisfy for others (Jer. 33:15; 1 Peter 3:18).[11]

Frage 17. Warum muß Er zugleich wahrer Gott sein?

Antwort. Daß er aus Kraft seiner Gottheit die Last des Zornes Gottes an seiner Menschheit ertragen, und uns die Gerechtigkeit und das Leben erwerben und wieder geben möchte.

Q. 17: *Why must he be at the same time true God?*

A: That by the power of his Godhead[12] he might bear, in his manhood, the burden of God's wrath (Isa. 53:4–5, 11; Acts 2:24; 1 Peter 3:18),[13] and so obtain for and restore to us righteousness and life (John 3:16; Acts 20:28; 1 John 1:2; 4:9–10).[14]

Frage 18. Wer ist aber derselbe Mittler, der zugleich wahrer Gott und ein wahrer gerechter Mensch ist?

Antwort. Unser Herr Jesus Christus, der uns zur vollkommenen Erlösung und Gerechtigkeit geschenkt ist.

Q. 18: *But who, now, is that mediator, who is at the same time true God*[15] *and a true, sinless man*[16]?

A: Our Lord *Jesus Christ* (Matt. 1:21, 23; Isa. 7:14; 1 Tim. 3:16; Luke 2:11; John 14:6; 1 Tim. 2:5),[17] who is freely given unto us for complete redemption and righteousness (1 Cor. 1:30).

---

10. Ezek. 18:20; 1 Cor. 15:21; Heb. 2:14–16.
11. Heb. 7:26–27; Ps. 49:7–8.
12. Isa. 9:6; 63:3 [?].
13. Deut. 4:24; Nah. 1:6; Ps. 130:3.
14. 2 Cor. 5:21; Jer. 23:5–6; John 1:4; 6:51; 2 Tim. 1:9–10; Rev. 19:15–16.
15. 1 John 5:20; Rom. 8:3; Gal. 4:4; Isa. 9:6; Jer. 23:5–6; Mal. 3:1.
16. Rom. 9:5; Luke 1:42; 2:6–7; Rom. 1:3; Phil. 2:7; Heb. 2:14, 16–17; 4:15; Isa. 53:9, 11; Luke 1:35; John 8:46; Heb. 7:26; 1 Peter 1:19; 2:22; 3:18.
17. Heb. 2:9.

Frage 19. Woher weißt du das?

Antwort. Aus dem heiligen Evangelio, welches Gott selbst anfänglich im Paradies hat geoffenbaret, in der Folge durch die heiligen Erzväter und Propheten lassen verkündigen, und durch die Opfer und andere Ceremonien des Gesetzes vorgebildet, endlich aber durch seinen eingeliebten Sohn erfüllet.

Q. 19: *Whence knowest thou this?*

A: From the Holy Gospel, which God himself first revealed in Paradise (Gen. 3:15), afterwards proclaimed by the holy Patriarchs (Gen. 22:18; 26:4; 49:10–11)[18] and Prophets (Rom. 1:1–4; Heb. 1:1–2; Acts 3:22–24; Acts 10:43),[19] and foreshadowed by the sacrifices and other ceremonies of the law (John 5:46; Heb. 10:1, 7),[20] and finally fulfilled by his well-beloved Son (Rom. 10:4; Gal. 4:4–5; 3:24–25; Heb. 13:8).[21]

LORD'S DAY 7

Frage 20. Werden denn alle Menschen wiederum durch Christum selig, wie sie durch Adam sind verloren worden?

Antwort. Nein: sondern allein diejenigen, die durch wahren Glauben ihm werden einverleibt, und alle seine Wohlthaten annehmen.

Q. 20: *Are all men, then, saved by Christ, as they have perished by Adam?*

A: No; only such as by true faith are ingrafted into him, and receive all his benefits (Matt. 22:14; John 1:12, 13; 3:36; Isa. 53:11; Ps. 2:12; Rom. 11:19–20; Heb. 4:2–3; 10:39).[22]

18. Gen.12:3; 28:14.
19. Isa. 53; 42:1–4; 43:25; 49:5–6, 22–23; Jer. 23:6; 31:32–33; 32:39–41; Mic. 7:18–20.
20. Lev. 1–7; Heb. 9:13–15.
21. Col. 2:17.
22. Matt. 1:21; 7:13–14, 21; 7:24; Mark 16:16; John 17:9; Rom. 3:22; Heb. 5:9; 11:6.

Frage 21. Was ist wahrer Glaube?

Antwort. Es ist nicht allein eine gewisse Erkenntniß, dadurch ich Alles für wahr halte, was uns Gott in seinem Worte hat geoffenbaret, sondern auch ein herzliches Vertrauen, welches der heilige Geist durch's Evangelium in mir wirket, daß nicht allein Andern, sondern auch mir Vergebung der Sünden, ewige Gerechtigkeit und Seligkeit von Gott geschenket sei, aus lauter Gnaden, allein um des Verdienstes Christi willen.

Frage 22. Was ist aber einem Christen nöthig zu glauben?

Antwort. Alles, was uns im Evangelio verheißen wird, welches uns die Artikel unseres allgemeinen ungezweifelten christlichen Glaubens in einer Summa lehren.

Frage 23. Wie lauten dieselben?

Antwort. Ich glaube in Gott Vater, den Allmächtigen, Schöpfer Himmels und der Erden.

Q. 21: *What is true faith?*

A: It is not only a certain knowledge, whereby I hold for truth all that God has revealed to us in his Word (James 2:19–20; Heb. 11:1–4),[23] but also a hearty trust (Rom. 4:16–21; 5:1; 10:9–10; Luke 1:68; 2:14, 29–30)[24] which the Holy Ghost works in me (Matt. 16:17; John 3:5; Gal. 5:22; Phil. 1:19, 29)[25] by the Gospel (Rom. 1:16; 10:17; 1 Cor. 1:21; Mark 16:15–16; Acts 16:14),[26] that not only to others, but to me also, forgiveness of sins, everlasting righteousness and salvation, are freely given by God (Hab. 2:4; Rom. 1:17; Gal. 5:11),[27] merely of grace, only for the sake of Christ's merits (Eph. 2:7–9; Heb. 10:38–39; Gal. 2:16; Rom. 3:24–26; 5:19; Eph. 2:8; Luke 1:77–78; John 20:31).[28]

Q. 22: *What is it, then, necessary for a Christian to believe?*

A: All that is promised us in the Gospel (John 20:31; Matt. 28:20; Mark 1:15),[29] which the articles of our catholic, undoubted Christian faith teach us in sum.

Q. 23: *What are these Articles?*

A: *I believe in God the Father Almighty, Maker of heaven and earth.*

23. John 6:68–69; 17:3, 17; James 1:18; Rom. 2:18–20.
24. Eph. 3:12; James 1:6; Heb. 4:14–16.
25. 2 Cor. 1:21–22; 4:13; John 3:13 [?]; 6:29.
26. Eph. 1:13; Acts 10:44.
27. Heb. 11:7–10; Matt. 9:2; Gal. 3:11; Heb. 10:10.
28. Gal. 2:20.
29. Acts 10:34–43; 24:14.

Und in Jesum Christum, seinen einge-bornen Sohn, unsern Herrn; der empfan-gen ist von dem heiligen Geiste, geboren aus Maria der Jungfrau; gelitten unter Pontio Pilato, gekreuziget, gestorben und begraben; abgestiegen zu der Hölle; am dritten Tage wieder auferstanden von den Todten; auge-fahren gen Himmel; sitzet zu der Rechten Gottes, des allmächtigen Vaters; von dan-nen Er kommen wird zu richten die Leben-digen und die Todten.

Ich glaube in den heiligen Geist; eine hei-lige, allgemeine christliche Kirche; die Gemeinschaft der Heiligen; Vergebung der Sünden; Auferstehung des Fleisches, und ein ewiges Leben.

And in Jesus Christ, his only-begotten Son, our Lord: who was conceived by the Holy Ghost, born of the Virgin Mary; suffered under Pontius Pilate, was crucified, dead, and buried; he descended into Hades; the third day he rose from the dead; he ascended into Heaven, and sitteth at the right hand of God the Father Almighty; from thence he shall come to judge the quick and the dead.

I believe in the Holy Ghost; the holy Catho-lic Church; the communion of saints; the forgiveness of sins; the resurrection of the body, and the life everlasting.

LORD'S DAY 8

Frage 24. Wie werden diese Artikel abgetheilt?

Antwort. In drei Theile: Der erste ist von Gott dem Vater und unserer Erschaffung. Der andere von Gott dem Sohne und unserer Erlösung. Der dritte von Gott dem heiligen Geiste und unserer Heiligung.

Frage 25. Dieweil nur ein einig göttlich Wesen ist, warum nennest du drei, den Vater, Sohn und heiligen Geist?

Antwort. Darum, weil sich Gott also in sei-nem Wort geoffenbaret hat, daß diese drei unterschiedlichen Personen der einige wah-rhaftige ewige Gott sind.

Q. 24: *How are these Articles divided?*

A: Into three parts: The first is of *God the Father* and our *creation*;[30] the second, of *God the Son* and our *redemption*;[31] the third, of *God the Holy Ghost* and our *sanctification*.[32]

Q. 25: *Since there is but one Divine Being* (Deut. 6:4; Isa. 42:6; 45:5; 1 Cor. 8:4, 6; Eph. 4:5–6),[33] *why speakest thou of three, Father, Son, and Holy Ghost?*

A: Because God has so revealed himself in his Word (Matt. 3:16–17; 28:19; 2 Cor. 13:14; 1 John 5:7; Rom. 11:36; Titus 3:5–6; John 10:30; 14:16–17, 26)[34] that these three distinct Persons are the one, true, eternal God.

30. Gen. 1:26–27.
31. 1 Peter 1:18–20.
32. 1 Peter 1:2, 21–23.
33. Isa. 44:6; 6:3.
34. Gen. 1:1–3, 26; Num. 6:24–26; Ps. 33:6; Luke 4:18; Isa. 48:16; 61:1; 63:8–10; Ps. 110:1; John 1:18; Gal. 4:6; Eph. 2:18; John 15:26.

Von Gott dem Sohn

Frage 31. Warum ist Er Christus, das ist, ein Gesalbter, genannt?

Antwort. Weil Er von Gott dem Vater verordnet und mit dem heiligen Geiste gesalbet ist zu unserm obersten Propheten und Lehrer, der uns den heimlichen Rath und Willen Gottes von unserer Erlösung vollkommen offenbaret; und zu unserm einigen Hohenpriester, der uns mit dem einigen Opfer seines Leibes erlöset hat, und immerdar mit seiner Fürbitte vor dem Vater vertritt; und zu unserm ewigen König, der uns mit seinem Wort und Geist regieret, und bei der erworbenen Erlösung schützet und erhält.

Von Gott dem Heiligen Geiste

Frage 54. Was glaubest du von der heiligen allgemeinen Christlichen Kirche?

OF GOD THE SON

LORD's DAY 12

Q. 31: *Why is he called* Christ, *that is,* Anointed?

A: Because he is ordained of God the Father, and anointed with the Holy Ghost (Heb. 1:9; Ps. 45:7; Isa. 61:1; Luke 4:18),[35] to be our chief Prophet and Teacher (Deut. 18:15; Acts 3:22; 7:37; John 1:18; Matt. 11:27),[36] who fully reveals to us the secret counsel and will of God concerning our redemption (John 1:18; 15:15; Matt. 11:27); and our only High Priest (Ps. 110:4; Heb. 7:21), who by the one sacrifice of his body has redeemed us (Heb. 10:12, 14),[37] and ever liveth to make intercession for us with the Father (Rom. 8:34; 5:9–10);[38] and our eternal King (Ps. 2:6; Luke 1:33),[39] who governs us by his Word and Spirit, and defends and preserves us in the redemption obtained for us (Matt. 28:18; John 10:28).[40]

OF GOD THE HOLY GHOST

LORD's DAY 21

Q. 54: *What doth thou believe concerning the* Holy Catholic Church?

35. Luke 3:21–22; Acts 10:38.
36. Luke 7:16; Isa. 55:4.
37. Heb. 9:12.
38. Heb. 9:24; 1 John 2:1.
39. Mark 11:1–10; Matt. 21:5; Zech. 9:9.
40. Rev. 12:10–11.

Antwort. Daß der Sohn Gottes aus dem ganzen menschlichen Geschlechte sich eine auserwählte Gemeine zum ewigen Leben, durch seinen Geist und Wort, in Einigkeit des wahren Glaubens, von Anbeginn der Welt bis an's Ende versammle, schütze und erhalte; und daß ich derselben ein lebendiges Glied bin, und ewig bleiben werde.

A: That out of the whole human race (Gen. 26:4),[41] from the beginning to the end of the world (Ps. 71:18; Isa. 59:21),[42] the Son of God (John 10:11),[43] by his Spirit and Word (Isa. 59:21; Rom. 1:16; 10:14–17; Eph. 5:26), gathers, defends, and preserves (Matt. 16:18; John 10:28–29; Eph. 4:3–5)[44] for himself unto everlasting life, a chosen communion (Rom. 8:29; Eph. 1:10–13; 1 Peter 1:20–21)[45] in the unity of the true faith (Acts 2:42; Eph. 4:3–6);[46] and that I am, and forever shall remain, a living member of the same (Ps. 71:9, 18; Rom. 8:35–37; 1 Cor. 1:8–9; 2 Cor. 13:5; 1 John 2:19; 3:14, 21).[47]

Von den heiligen Sacramenten

OF THE HOLY SACRAMENTS

Lord's Day 25

Frage 67. Sind denn beide, das Wort und die Sacramente, dahin gerichtet, daß sie unsern Glauben auf das Opfer Jesu Christi am Kreuz, als auf den einigen Grund unserer Seligkeit, weisen?

Q. 67: *Are both these, then, the Word and the Sacraments, designed to direct our faith to the sacrifice of Jesus Christ on the cross as the only ground of our salvation?*

Antwort. Ja freilich: denn der Heilige Geist lehret im Evangelio, und bestätigt durch die heiligen Sacramente, daß unsere ganze Seligkeit stehe in dem einigen Opfer Christi, für uns am Kreuz geschehen.

A: Yes, truly; for the Holy Ghost teaches us in the Gospel, and by the holy Sacraments assures us, that our whole salvation stands in one sacrifice of Christ made for us on the cross (Rom. 6:3; Gal. 3:26–27).[48]

41. Deut. 10:14–15; Rev. 5:9.
42. 1 Cor. 11:26.
43. Acts 20:28; Eph. 4:11–13; 5:23, 25; Col. 1:18.
44. Ps. 129:1–5; Isa. 49:6; Acts 13:48.
45. Rom. 9:24; 1 Peter 2:9.
46. John 10:14–16.
47. Ps. 23:6; John 10:28; Rom. 8:10, 16; 1 Peter 1:5; 1 John 1.
48. 1 Cor. 2:2; 11:26.

Der dritte Theil. Von der Dankbarkeit

THE THIRD PART:
OF THANKFULNESS

LORD'S DAY 34

Frage 95. Was ist Abgötterei?

Q. 95: *What is idolatry?*

Antwort. An Statt des einigen wahren Gottes, der sich in seinem Wort hat offenbaret, oder neben demselben, etwas anderes dichten oder haben, darauf der Mensch sein Vertrauen setzt.

A: It is, instead of the one true God who has revealed himself in his Word, or along with the same, to conceive or have something else on which to place our trust (Gal. 4:8; Eph. 2:12; 5:5; 1 Peter 4:3; Phil. 3:19; 1 Chron. 16:26; 1 John 2:23; 5:21; 2 John 9).[49]

LORD'S DAY 35

Frage 96. Was will Gott im andern Gebot?

Q. 96: *What does God require in the second commandment?*

Antwort. Daß wir Gott in keinem Wege verbilden, noch auf irgend eine andere Weise, denn Er in seinem Wort befohlen hat, verehren sollen.

A: That we in nowise make any image of God (Deut. 4:15–19; Isa. 40:18–25; Rom. 1:23–25; Acts 17:29), nor worship him in any other way than he has commanded in his Word (1 Sam. 15:23; Deut. 12:30–32; Matt. 15:9 [quoting Isa. 29:13]).[50]

Frage 97. Soll man denn gar kein Bildniß machen?

Q. 97: *Must we, then, not make any image at all?*

Antwort. Gott kann und soll keineswegs abgebildet werden; die Creaturen aber, ob sie schon mögen abgebildet werden, so verbietet doch Gott derselben Bildniß zu machen und zu haben, daß man sie verehre, oder ihm damit diene.

A: God may not and can not be imaged in any way; as for creatures, though they may indeed be imaged, yet God forbids the making or keeping any likeness of them, either to worship them, or by them to serve himself (Ex. 23:24–25; 34:14, 17; Num. 33:51–52; Deut. 4:12, 15–18; 7:5; 12:3; 16:22; 2 Kings 18:4; Ex. 35:30–33).[51]

49. Eph. 1:12–13; 2 Chron. 16:12; Matt. 6:24; John 5:23.
50. Lev. 10:1–7; John 4:23–24.
51. Lev. 26:1; Ps. 97:7; Isa. 40:18, 25; 46:5; Rom. 1:23.

Frage 98. Mögen aber nicht die Bilder als der Laien Bücher in den Kirchen geduldet werden?

Antwort. Nein: denn wir sollen nicht weiser sein denn Gott, welcher sein Christenheit nicht durch stumme Götzen, sondern durch die lebendige Predigt seines Worts will unterwiesen haben.

Frage 101. Mag man aber auch gottselig bei dem Namen Gottes einen Eid schwören?

Antwort. Ja: wenn es die Obrigkeit von ihren Unterthanen oder sonst die Noth erfordert, Treue und Wahrheit zu Gottes Ehre und des Nächsten Heil dadurch zu erhalten und zu fördern. Denn solches Eidschwören ist in Gottes Wort gegründet, und derhalben von den Heiligen im alten und neuen Testament recht gebraucht worden.

Q. 98: *But may not pictures be tolerated in churches as books for the laity?*

A: No; for we should not be wiser than God, who will not have his people taught by dumb idols (Jer. 10:8–10; Hab. 2:18–19),[52] but by the lively preaching of his Word (2 Peter 1:19; 2 Tim. 3:16–17).[53]

LORD'S DAY 37

Q. 101: *But may we not swear by the name of God in a religious manner?*

A: Yes; when the magistrate requires it, or it may be needful otherwise[54] to maintain and promote fidelity and truth,[55] to the glory of God and our neighbor's good. For such swearing is grounded in God's Word (Deut. 6:13; 10:20; Isa. 48:1; Heb. 6:16),[56] and therefore was rightly used by the saints in the Old and New Testament (Gen. 21:23–24; 31:53–54; Josh. 9:15, 19; 1 Sam. 24:21–22; 2 Sam. 3:35; 1 Kings 1:29–30; Rom. 1:9; 2 Cor. 1:23).[57]

---

52. Deut. 27:15.
53. Rom. 10:14–15, 17; Heb. 4:12.
54. Cf. Matt. 5:33–37; 26:63.
55. Ex. 22:11; Neh. 13:25.
56. Jer. 4:1–2.
57. Rom. 9:1.

Frage 103. Was will Gott im vierten Gebot?

Q. 103: *What does God require in the fourth commandment?*

Antwort. Gott will erstlich, daß das Predigtamt und Schulen erhalten werden, und ich, sonderlich am Feiertag, zu der Gemeine Gottes fleißig komme, das Wort Gottes zu lernen, die heiligen Sacramente zu gebrauchen, den Herrn öffentlich anzurufen, und das christliche Almosen zu geben. Zum andern, daß ich alle Tage meines Lebens von meinen bösen Werken feiere, den Herrn durch seinen Geist in mir wirken lasse, und also den ewigen Sabbath in diesem Leben anfange.

A: In the first place, that the ministry of the Gospel and schools be maintained (Titus 1:5; 1 Tim. 3:14–15; 4:13–16; 5:17; 1 Cor. 9:11–14; 2 Tim. 2:2; 3:15);[58] and that I, especially on the day of rest, diligently attend [the] church [of God] (Ps. 40:9–10; 68:26; Acts 2:42, 46),[59] to learn the Word of God (1 Cor. 14:19, 29, 31),[60] to use the holy Sacraments (1 Cor. 11:33–34),[61] to call publicly upon the Lord (1 Tim. 2:1–3, 8–9; 1 Cor. 14:16),[62] and to give Christian alms (1 Cor. 16:2).[63] In the second place, that all the days of my life I rest from my evil works, allow the Lord to work in me by his Spirit, and thus begin in this life the everlasting Sabbath (Isa. 66:23).[64]

Vom Gebet

OF PRAYER

Frage 116. Warum ist den Christen das Gebet nöthig?

Q. 116: *Why is prayer necessary for Christians?*

Antwort. Darum, weil es das vornehmste Stück der Dankbarkeit ist, welche Gott von uns fordert, und weil Gott seine Gnade und Heiligen Geist allein denen will geben, die ihn mit herzlichem Seufzen ohne Unterlaß darume bitten, und ihm dafür danken.

A: Because it is the chief part of thankfulness which God requires of us (Ps. 50:14–15),[65] and because God will give his grace and Holy Spirit only to such as earnestly and without ceasing beg them from him and render thanks for them (Matt. 7:7; 13:12; Luke 11:9–13; Ps. 50:14–15).

58. Deut. 6:4–9, 20–25.
59. Lev. 23:3; Deut. 12:5–12; Heb. 10:23–25.
60. Rom. 10:14–17; 1 Tim. 4:13, 19 [?].
61. Acts 20:7.
62. Col. 3:16.
63. Ps. 50:14; 2 Cor. 8–9.
64. Heb. 4:9–11.
65. Ps. 116:12–19; 1 Thess. 5:16–18.

Frage 117. Was gehört zu einem solchen Gebet, das Gott gefalle, und von ihm erhört werde?

Antwort. Erstlich, daß wir allein den einigen wahren Gott, der sich uns in seinem Wort hat geoffenbaret, um alles, das er uns zu bitten befohlen hat, von Herzen anrufen. Zum andern, daß wir unsere Noth und Elend recht gründlich erkennen, uns vor dem Angesicht seiner Majestät zu demüthigen. Zum dritten, daß wir diesen festen Grund haben, daß Er unser Gebet, unangesehen, daß wir's unwürdig sind, doch um des Herrn Christi willen gewißlich wolle erhören, wie Er uns in seinem Wort verheißen hat.

Frage 118. Was hat uns Gott befohlen, von ihm zu bitten?

Antwort. Alle geistliche und leibliche Nothdurft, welche der Herr Christus begriffen hat in dem Gebet, das Er uns selbst gelehret.

Q. 117: *What belongs to such prayer as God is pleased with and will hear?*

A: First, that from the heart (John 4:23–24; Ps. 145:18–20) we call only upon the one true God (John 4:22, 24; Rev. 22:9),[66] who has revealed himself to us in his Word, for all that he has commanded us to ask of him (Rom. 8:26–27; 1 John 5:14–15);[67] secondly, that we thoroughly know our need and misery (2 Chron. 20:12),[68] so as to humble ourselves before the face of his divine majesty (Ps. 2:11; 34:18; Isa. 66:2)[69]; thirdly, that we be firmly assured (Rom. 10:14 [?]; 8:15–16; James 1:6–8) that, notwithstanding our unworthiness, he will, for the sake of Christ our Lord (John 14:13–16; 15:7, 16; Dan. 9:17–18),[70] certainly hear our prayer, as he has promised us in his Word (Matt. 7:8; Ps. 143:1; 27:8).

Q. 118: *What has God commanded us to ask of him?*

A: All things necessary for soul and body, which Christ our Lord has comprised in the prayer taught us by himself (James 1:17; Matt. 6:33).[71]

66. Matt. 4:10; Rev. 19:10.
67. James 1:5.
68. Luke 18:13.
69. 2 Chron. 7:14; Ps. 62:8; Rev. 4.
70. John 16:23.
71. Matt. 6:9–10; Luke 11:2.

Frage 122. Was ist die erste Bitte?

Q. 122: *What is the first petition?*

Antwort: Geheiliget werde dein Name; das ist: Gieb uns erstlich, daß wir dich recht erkennen, und dich in allen deinen Werken, in welchen leuchtet deine Allmächtigkeit, Weisheit, Güte, Gerechtigkeit, Barmherzigkeit und Wahrheit, heiligen, rühmen und preisen. Danach auch, daß wir unser ganzes Leben, Gedanken, Worte und Werke dahin richten, daß dein Name um unsertwillen nicht gelästert, sondern geehret und gepriesen werde.

A: *Hallowed be thy name.*[72] That is: Enable us rightly to know thee (John 17:3; Jer. 9:23–24; 31:33–34; Matt. 16:17; James 1:5; Ps. 119:105), and to hallow, magnify, and praise thee in all thy works,[73] in which shine forth thy power, wisdom, goodness, justice, mercy, and truth (Ps. 119:137–38; Luke 1:46–55; Ps. 145:8–9, 17; Ex. 34:6–7; Jer. 31:3; 32:18–19, 40–41; 33:11, 20–21; Rom. 3:4; 2 Tim. 2:19; Matt. 19:17; Rom. 11:22–23);[74] and likewise so to order our whole life, in thought, word, and work, that thy name may never be blasphemed, but honored and praised on our account (Ps. 71:8; 115:1; Rom. 11:33).[75]

Frage 123. Was ist die andere Bitte?

Q. 123: *What is the second petition?*

Antwort. Dein Reich komme; das ist: Regiere uns also durch dein Wort und Geist, daß wir uns dir je länger je mehr unterwerfen; erhalte und mehre deine Kirche, und zerstöre die Werke des Teufels und alle Gewalt, die sich wider dich erhebt, und alle bösen Rathschläge, die wider dein heiliges Wort erdacht werden, bis die Vollkommenheit deines Reichs herzukomme, darin du wirst Alles in Allen sein.

A: *Thy kingdom come.*[76] That is: So govern us by thy Word and Spirit that we may submit ourselves unto thee always more and more (Matt. 6:33; Ps. 119:5; 143:10);[77] preserve and increase thy Church (Ps. 51:18; 122:6–7);[78] destroy the works of the devil, every power that exalteth itself against thee, and all wicked devices formed against thy holy Word (1 John 3:8; Rom. 16:20), until the full coming of thy kingdom (Rev. 22:17, 20; Rom. 8:22–23), wherein thou shalt be all in all (1 Cor. 15:28).

72. Matt. 6:9.
73. Ps. 100:3–4.
74. Luke 1:68–75.
75. Matt. 5:16; 1 Cor. 10:31.
76. Matt. 6:10.
77. Pss. 86:11; 119:105.
78. Ps. 102:14–15; Matt. 16:18; Acts 2:42–47.

THE COMMENTARY ON THE HEIDELBERG CATECHISM

ZACHARIAS URSINUS

Zacharias Ursinus, *The Commentary on the Heidelberg Catechism*, trans. G. W. Williard (1852; repr., Phillipsburg, NJ: Presbyterian and Reformed, n.d.), 107–112, 169–76.

OF FAITH

Question 21. What is true faith?

Answer. True faith is not only a certain knowledge, whereby I hold for truth all that God has revealed to us in his word, but also an assured confidence, which the Holy Ghost works by the gospel in my heart; that not only to others, but to me also, remission of sin, everlasting righteousness, and salvation, are freely given by God, merely of grace, only for the sake of Christ's merits.

Exposition

The subject of faith is introduced next in order: 1. Because it is the means by which we are made partakers of the Mediator. 2. Because the preaching of the gospel profits nothing without faith. In speaking of faith, we must enquire:

I. *What is faith?*
II. *Of how many kinds of faith do the Scriptures speak?*
III. *In what does faith differ from hope?*
IV. *What are the efficient causes of justifying faith?*
V. *What are the effects of faith?*
VI. *To whom is it given?*[79]

I. WHAT IS FAITH?

The word *faith*, according to Cicero, is derived from *fiendo*, which signifies *doing*, because that which is declared is performed. It is, according to him, the assurance, and truth of contracts, and of whatever may be spoken, and is the foundation of justice. According to the common definition, faith is a certain knowledge of facts, or conclusions, to which we assent on the testimony of faithful witnesses, whom we may not disbelieve, whether it be God, or angels, or men, or experience. But since, according to the most general distinction, there

---

79. Ed. note: The last three points are not included in this selection.

is one kind of faith in divine, and another in human affairs, we must here enquire, what is faith in divine things, or what is theological faith? The definition of faith, therefore, taken generally, must be given somewhat more exactly, and yet it must be such as to comprise in it all the different forms of faith spoken of in the Scriptures.

Faith, in general, of whatever kind mention is made in the Holy Scriptures, is an assent to, or a certain knowledge of what is revealed concerning God, his will, works, and grace, in which we confide upon divine testimony. Or, it is to yield assent to every word of God delivered to the church, in the law and gospel, on account of the declaration of God himself.

Faith is, also, often taken for the doctrine of the church, or for those things of which the word of God informs us, and which are necessary to faith, as when it is called *the Christian faith, the Apostolic faith*. It is, likewise, often used for the fulfillment of ancient promises, or for the things themselves, which are believed; as "Before faith came, we were kept under the law, shut up unto the faith which should afterwards be revealed" (Gal. 3:23).

II. OF HOW MANY KINDS OF FAITH DO THE SCRIPTURES SPEAK?

There are four kinds of faith enumerated in the Holy Scriptures, viz.: historical, temporary, the faith of working miracles, and justifying or saving faith. The difference which exists between the different kinds of faith here specified, will appear by giving a proper definition of each.

Historical faith is to know and believe that every word of God is true which is divinely delivered and revealed, whether by the voice, or by oracles, or by visions, or by any other method of revelation by which the divine will is made known unto us, upon the authority and declaration of God himself. It is called historical because it is merely a knowledge of those things which God is said to have done, or now does, or will hereafter do. The Scriptures speak of this faith in these places: "If I have all faith so that I could remove mountains," which may also be understood of all the different kinds of faith, except justifying (1 Cor. 13:2). "The devils believe and tremble" (James 2:19). "Simon also believed," viz.: that the doctrine of Peter was true, yet he had no justifying faith (Acts 8:13).

Temporary faith is an assent to the doctrines of the church, accompanied with profession and joy, but not with a true and abiding joy, such as arises from a consciousness that we are the objects of the divine favor, but from some other cause, whatever it may be, so that it endures only for a time, and in seasons of affliction dies away. Or, it is to assent to the doctrine delivered by the prophets and apostles, to profess it, to glory in it, and to rejoice for a time in the knowledge of it; but not on account of an application of the promise to itself, or on account of a sense of the grace of God in the heart, but for other causes. This definition is drawn from what Christ says in the explanation of the parable of the sower: "He that received the seed into the stony places, the same is he that heareth the word, and anon with joy receiveth it; yet hath he not root in himself, but endureth for a while, for when tribulation or persecution ariseth because of the word, by and by he is offended" (Matt. 13:20–21). The causes of this joy are in a manner infinite, and different in different individuals; yet they are all temporary, and when they fade, the faith that is built upon them, vanishes away. Hypocrites rejoice in hearing the gospel, either because it is new to them, or because it seems to calm their minds, whilst it delivers them from the burdens which men, by their traditions, have imposed upon them, as does the doctrine of christian liberty, justification, etc.; or, because they seek, under its profession, a cloak for their sins, and hope to reap rewards and advantages, both public and private, such as riches, honors, glory, etc., which shows itself when they are called to bear the cross; for then, because they have no root in themselves, they fall away. But hypocrites do not rejoice as true believers, from a sense of the grace of God, and from an application to themselves of the benefits offered in the divine word, which may be regarded as the cause of true and substantial joy in the faithful—the removal of which single cause is sufficient to make their faith temporary.

This temporary faith differs from historical only in the joy which accompanies it. Historical faith includes nothing more than mere knowledge; whilst this has joy connected with this knowledge; for these time-serving men "receive the word with joy." The devils believe, historically, and tremble, but they do not rejoice in the knowledge which they have; but rather wish it were extinguished; yea, they do not even profess themselves to be followers of this doctrine, although they know it to be true; but hate and oppose it most bitterly. In men, however, historical faith is sometimes joined with profession, and sometimes not; for men often, whatever may be the causes, profess that truth and religion which they hate. Many also who know the doctrine to be true, still oppose it. *Sie wollten daß die Bibel im Rhein schwimme* ["They want that the Bible swims in the Rhine"]. These sin against the Holy Ghost.

Objection: But the devil has often professed Christ. Therefore he cannot be said to hate this doctrine. Answer: He did not, however, profess Christ from any desire of advancing and promoting his doctrine, but that he might mingle with it his own falsehoods, and thus cause it to be suspected. It is for this reason that Christ commands him to keep silent, as Paul also does in Acts 16:18.

The faith of miracles is a special gift of effecting some extraordinary work, or of foretelling some particular event by divine revelation. Or, it is a firm persuasion, produced by some divine revelation, or peculiar promise in regard to some future miraculous working, which the person desires to accomplish, and which he foretells. This faith cannot be drawn, simply, out of the general word of God, unless some special promise or revelation be connected with it. The Apostle speaks of this kind of faith, when he says, "If I had all faith so that I could remove mountains," etc. (1 Cor. 13:2). This declaration may, however, be understood of all the different kinds of faith, except justifying, yet it is spoken with special reference to the faith of miracles.

That this is a distinct kind of faith, is proven:

1. From the declaration of Christ. "If ye have faith as a grain of mustard seed, ye shall say unto this mountain, Remove hence to yonder place, and it shall remove," etc. (Matt. 17:20). Many holy men also have had strong faith, as Abraham, David, etc., and yet they did not remove mountains. Therefore, this species of faith is distinct from justifying faith, which all true christians possess.

2. Exorcists, as the sons of Sceva (Acts 19:14), have endeavored to cast out devils, when they had not the gift or power of accomplishing it, who were afterwards severely punished, when the evil spirit fell upon them, overcame and wounded them.

3. Simon Magus is said to have believed, and yet he was not able to work miracles; he, therefore, desired to purchase this gift.

4. The devil has a knowledge of what is historical, and yet he cannot work miracles; because no one, except the Creator, is able to change the nature of things.

5. Judas taught, and wrought miracles, as did the other Apostles; therefore, he had a historical faith (perhaps also temporary) and the faith of miracles; and yet he had not that faith which justifies; for Christ said of him, "he is a devil" (John 6:70).

6. Many shall say unto Christ, "Lord, Lord, have we not in thy name cast out devils?" to whom he will nevertheless reply, "I never knew you" (Matt. 7:22).

7. Lastly, the other kinds of faith extend to all things which the word of God reveals, and requires us to believe. The faith of miracles, however, refers merely to certain works and extraordinary events. It is, therefore, a distinct kind of faith.

Justifying faith is properly that which is defined in the catechism; according to which definition, the *general nature* of saving faith consists in knowledge and an assured confidence; for there can be no faith in a doctrine that is wholly unknown. It is proper for us, therefore, to obtain a knowledge of that in which we are to believe, before we exercise faith; from which we may see the absurdity of the implicit faith of the Papists. The *difference*, or formal character of saving faith, is the confidence and application which every one makes to himself, of the free remission of sins by and for the sake of Christ. The *property*, or peculiar character of this faith, is trust and delight in God, on account of this great benefit. The *efficient cause* of justifying faith is the Holy Ghost. The instrumental cause is the gospel, in which the use of the sacraments is also comprehended. The *subject* of this faith is the will and heart of man.

Justifying or saving faith differs, therefore, from the other kinds of faith, because it alone is that assured confidence by which we apply unto ourselves the merit of Christ, which is done when we firmly believe that the righteousness of Christ is granted and imputed unto us, so that we are accounted just in the sight of God. Confidence is an exercise or motion of the will and heart, following something good—resting and rejoicing in it. The German has it, *vertrauen, sich ganz und gar darauf verlassen* ["to have confidence, to rely completely on something"]. Πίστις and πιστεύειν the former of which means belief, and the latter to believe, are from πέπεισμαι, which means strongly persuaded; whence πιστεύειν, even among profane writers, signifies to wax confident, or to rest upon any thing; as we read in Phocilides, "Believe not the people, for the multitude is deceitful." And in Demosthenes, "Thou art confident in thyself," etc.

Justifying faith differs from historical, because it always includes that which is historical. Historical faith is not sufficient for our justification. The same thing may also be said of the other two kinds of faith. Justifying faith, again, differs from all other kinds of faith, in this, that it is by it alone that we obtain righteousness, and a title to the inheritance of the saints. For if, as the Apostle says, we are justified by faith, and faith is imputed for righteousness, and by faith is the inheritance, then this faith must be one of the four kinds of which we have spoken. But it is not historical faith; for then the devils would also be accounted just, and be heirs of the promise. Neither is it temporary faith; for Christ rejects this. Nor is it the faith of miracles; for in that case, Judas would also be an heir. Hence it is by justifying faith alone that we obtain righteousness, and an inheritance among the saints; which the Scriptures properly and simply call faith, and which is also peculiar to the elect.

No man, however, truly knows what justifying faith is, except he who believes, or possesses it; as he, who never saw or tasted honey, knows nothing of its quality or taste, although you may tell him many things of the sweetness of honey. But the man who truly believes, experience these things in himself, and is able, also, to explain them to others.

1. He believes that every thing which the Scriptures contain is true, and from God.

2. He feels himself constrained firmly to believe and embrace these things; for if we confess that they are true and from God, it is proper that we should assent to them.

3. He sees, embraces, and applies particularly, to himself, the promise of grace, or the free remission of sins, righteousness and eternal life, by and for the sake of Christ, as it is said: "He that believeth on the Son hath everlasting life" (John 3:36).

4. Having this confidence, he trusts and rejoices in the present grace of God, and from this he thus concludes in reference to future good: since God now loves me, and grants unto me such great blessings, he will also preserve me unto eternal life; because he is unchangeable, and his gifts are without repentance.

5. Joy arises in the heart, in view of such benefits, which joy is accompanied with a peace of conscience that passes all understanding.

6. Then he has a will and an earnest desire to obey all the commands of God, without a single exception, and is willing to endure patiently whatever God may send upon him. The man, therefore, who possesses a justifying faith, does that which is required of him, regardless of the opposition of the world, and the devil. He who truly believes, experiences all these things in himself; and he who experiences these things in himself, truly believes.

III. IN WHAT DOES FAITH DIFFER FROM HOPE?

We must not confound justifying faith with hope, although both have respect to the same blessing. Faith lays hold of present good, whilst hope has respect to that which is future. Objection: But we believe in everlasting life, which is, nevertheless, something that is future. Therefore, faith also has respect to future good. Answer: Eternal life is a future good as to its consummation; and, in this respect, we do not simply believe in it, but hope for it. "For we are saved by hope" (Rom. 8:24). "Now are we the sons of God, and it doth not yet appear what we shall be" (1 John 3:2). But life everlasting is also a present good, in respect to the will of God, who grants it unto us, and in respect to the beginning of it even in this life, in which respect it is not hoped for, but believed, as it is said: "He that believeth on the Son of God, hath everlasting life, and is passed from death unto life" (John 5:24). "This is life eternal, that they might know thee, the only true God," etc. (John 17:3). By faith, therefore, we are persuaded that those benefits are ours, which we have not as yet, on account of the promise of God; and by hope, we confidently look for the full consummation of these things. It is in this sense that Paul speaks of faith when he says, "Faith is the substance of things hoped for" (Heb. 11:1). That is, it is that which makes those things hoped for, present and real; and is the evidence of those things which do not appear as it respects their consummation.

There are some who make the following distinction between faith and hope: Faith embraces the promises contained in the creed concerning things to come; whilst hope comprehends the things themselves which are future. This distinction, however, is less popular, and not as easily understood as the former.

TWELFTH LORD'S DAY

Question 31. Why is he called Christ, that is, anointed?

Answer. Because he is ordained of God the Father, and anointed with the Holy Ghost, to be our chief Prophet and teacher; who has fully revealed to us the secret counsel and will of God concerning our redemption, and to be our only High Priest, who, by the one sacrifice of his body, has redeemed us, and makes continual intercession with the Father for us; and also to be our Eternal King, who governs us by his word and Spirit, and who defends and preserves us in the enjoyment of that salvation he has purchased for us.

Exposition

Jesus is the proper name of the mediator; Christ is, as it were, an additional appellation; for he is Jesus in such a manner that he is also the Christ, the promised Saviour and Messiah. Both titles designate his office, yet not with the same clearness; for whilst the name Jesus denotes the office of the mediator in a general way, that of Christ expresses it more fully and distinctly; for the name Christ expresses the three parts of his office, viz.: prophetical, sacerdotal, and regal. The name Christ signifies the anointed. Therefore, he is Jesus the Saviour, in such a manner that he is Christ, or the anointed, having the office of one that is anointed, which consists of three parts, as has just been remarked. The reason why these three things are comprehended in the name of Christ, is, because prophets, priests and kings were anciently anointed, by which was signified both an ordination to the office, and also a conferring of those gifts which were necessary for the proper discharge of the duties thereby imposed. *Therefore, we thus conclude*: He who is to be a prophet, priest, and king, and is called the anointed, he is so called on account of these three offices. Christ was to be a prophet, priest and king, and is called the anointed. Therefore, he is called the anointed, or Christ, on account of these three, so that these parts of the office of the mediator are expressed in the one title of the Messiah, the Christ, the Anointed. In discussing this question of the Catechism, we must enquire:

I. *What is meant by the anointing of Christ, seeing the Scriptures no where speak of his being anointed?*
II. *What is the prophetical office of Christ?*
III. *What is the priestly office of Christ?*
IV. *What is the regal office of Christ?*

I. WHAT IS THE UNCTION, OR ANOINTING OF CHRIST?

Anointing was a ceremony by which prophets, priests and kings were confirmed in their office by being anointed either with common, or with a particular kind of oil. This anointing signified, 1. An ordination, or calling to the office for which they were thus set apart. 2. It signified the promise and bestowment of the gifts necessary for the purpose of sustaining those upon whom the burden of either of these offices was imposed. There was also an analogy between the sign, or the external anointing, and the thing signified thereby: because as oil strengthens, invigorates, renovates, and makes firm the dry and feeble members of the body, and renders them active and fit for the discharge of their office; so the Holy Spirit enlivens and renews our nature, unfit of itself for the accomplishment of any thing that is good, and furnishes it with strength and power to do that which is agreeable to God, and to discharge properly the duties imposed upon us in the relations in which we are called to serve him.

Moreover, those who were anointed under the Old Testament were types of Christ, so that it may be said that their anointing was only a shadow, and so imperfect. But the anointing of Christ was perfect. For "in him dwelleth all the fullness of the Godhead bodily" (Col. 2:9). He alone received all the gifts of the Spirit in the highest number and degree. Another point of difference is seen in this, that none of those who were anointed under the Old Testament received all the gifts—some received more, others less; but no one received all, neither did all receive them in the same degree. Christ, however, had all these gifts in the fullest and highest sense. Therefore, although this anointing was proper to those of the Old Testament, as well as to Christ, yet it was real and perfect in no one excepting Christ.

Objection: But we no where read of the anointing of Christ in the holy Scriptures. Answer: It is true, indeed, that it is no where said that Christ was anointed ceremoniously; but he was anointed really and spiritually, that is, he received the thing signified thereby, which was the Holy Ghost. "Therefore God, thy God hath anointed thee with the oil of gladness above thy fellows" (Ps. 45:7; Heb. 1:9). "The Spirit of the Lord is upon me, because the Lord hath anointed me" (Isa. 61:1). The anointing of Christ is, therefore, spoken of both in the Old and New Testament. It behooved Christ to be, not a typical prophet, priest and king, but that one which was signified and true, of whom all the others were but shadows. Hence it behooved him to be anointed, not typically, but really; for it was necessary that there should be an analogy between the office and the anointing, and, as a matter of consequence, it became necessary that his anointing should not be sacramental, but spiritual; not typical, but real.

Christ was, then, anointed, 1. Because he was ordained to the office of mediator by the will of his Heavenly Father. "I am not come of myself, but the Father hath sent me" (John 7:28). "God hath spoken unto us by his Son, whom he hath appointed heir of all things" (Heb. 1:1). 2. Because his human nature was endowed with the gifts of the Holy Spirit without measure; so that he had all the gifts and graces necessary for restoring, ruling and preserving his church, and for administering the government of the whole world, and directing it to the glory of God, and the salvation of his people. "For he whom God hath sent speaketh the words of God; for God giveth not the Spirit by measure unto him" (John 3:34). These two parts of the anointing of Christ differ from each other in this manner, that the conferring of gifts has respect to the human nature only, whilst his ordination to the office of mediator has respect to both natures.

Hence, an answer is readily furnished to another objection which we sometimes hear: God cannot be anointed Christ is God. Therefore, he could not be anointed. Answer: We grant the whole if understood of that nature in which Christ is God, that he cannot be anointed, 1. Because it is impossible for us to add anything of justice, wisdom and power to the Godhead. 2. Because the Holy Spirit, by whom the anointing was effected, is the proper Spirit of Christ, no less, than of the Father. Therefore, just as no one can give thee thy spirit which is in thee, because what thou hast cannot be given to thee; so no one can give the Holy Spirit to God, because he is in him, from him, is his proper Spirit, and is given to others by him.

Objection: But if Christ could not be anointed as to his Divinity, he is then prophet, priest, king and mediator, according to his humanity only; for he is mediator according to that nature only which could be anointed. But it was possible for him to be anointed only as to his humanity. Therefore, he is mediator according to his humanity alone. The minor proposition is proven by the definition of anointing, which is to receive gifts. But he received gifts only as to his human nature. Therefore, it was in respect to this alone that he was anointed. Answer: We deny what is here affirmed, because the definition which is given of anointing is not sufficiently distinct nor full; for anointing does not merely include the reception of the gifts which pertain only to the humanity of Christ, but also an ordination to the office of mediator which has respect to both natures. Therefore, although the humanity of Christ alone could receive the Holy Spirit, yet it does not follow that his Divinity was excluded from this anointing, in as far as it was a designation to the office of mediator. Or we may present the argument clearer by considering it negatively: Christ is not mediator according to the nature in which he is not anointed. He is not anointed as to his Divinity. Therefore he is not mediator in respect to his Godhead. Answer: There are here four terms. In the major, the anointing is taken for both parts thereof, or for the whole anointing—for the designation to the office, and the bestowment of gifts. In the minor, it is considered only in relation to one part of the anointing. Therefore, it follows that Christ was anointed according to each nature, although in a different manner, as has been shown. Hence, Christ is prophet, priest, king and mediator, in respect to each nature, which is confirmed in the word of God by these two fundamental rules:

1. The properties of the one nature of the mediator, are attributed to the whole person in the concrete, according to the communication of properties; but in respect to that nature only to which they are peculiar, as God is angry, suffered, died, viz., according to his humanity. The man Christ is omnipotent, eternal, everywhere, viz., according to his Divinity.

2. The names, also, of the office of mediator, are attributed to the whole person in respect to both natures, yet preserving the properties of each nature, and the differences in the works peculiar to each; because, both the divine and human nature, together with the operations thereof, are necessary to the discharge of the office of mediator. So that each may perform that which is proper to it, in connection with the other.

Irenaeus says, in relation to this subject, that this anointing is to be understood as comprehending the three persons of the Godhead: the Father, as the anointer, the Son, as the anointed, and the Holy Spirit, as the unction, or the anointing.

II. WHAT IS THE PROPHETICAL OFFICE OF CHRIST?

Having considered what we are to understand by the anointing of Christ, we must now speak briefly of the three-fold office, or of the three parts of the office of the mediator unto which Christ was anointed. And in order that we may have a proper understanding of this subject, we must define what the terms prophet, priest, and king signify, which may be gathered from the parts of the office which these persons severally discharged.

The word *prophet* comes from the Greek προφημι, which means to publish things that are to come. In general, a prophet is a person called of God, to declare and explain his will to men concerning things present or future, which otherwise would have remained unknown, inasmuch as the truths which he reveals are of such a nature that men, of themselves, could never have attained a knowledge of them. A prophet is either a minister, or the head and chief of the prophets, which is Christ. Of those prophets which were ministerial, some were of the Old and some of the New Testament. Among the latter there were some that were generally, and others specially, so called.

The prophets of the Old Testament were persons immediately called, and sent of God to his people, that they might reprove their errors and sins, by threatening punishment upon offenders, and inviting men to repentance; that they might declare and expound the true doctrine and worship of God, and preserve it from falsehood and corruption; that they might make known and illustrate the promise of the Messiah—the benefits of his kingdom, and might fore-tell events that were to come, having the gift of miracles, and other sure and divine testimonies so that they could not err in the doctrine which they declared; and at the same time sustaining certain relations to the state, and performing duties of a civil character.

A prophet of the New Testament specially so called, was a person immediately called of God, and furnished with the gift of prophecy for the purpose of fore-seeing, and fore-telling things to come; such were Paul, Peter, Agabus, etc. Whoever has the gift of understanding, explaining, and applying the holy Scriptures to the edification of the church, and individuals, is a prophet, generally, so called. It is in this sense the term is used in 1 Corinthians 14:3–5, 29.

Christ is the greatest and chief prophet, and was immediately ordained of God, and sent by him from the very commencement of the church in Paradise, for the purpose of revealing the will of God to the human race; instituting the ministry of the word and the sacraments, and at length manifesting himself in the flesh, and proving by his divine teaching and works that he is the eternal and con-substantial Son of the Father, the author of the doctrine of the gospel, giving through it the Holy Spirit, kindling faith in the hearts of men, sending apostles, and collecting to himself a church from the human family in which he may be obeyed, invoked and worshipped.

The prophetical office of Christ is, therefore, 1. To reveal God and his whole will to angels and men, which could only be made known through the Son, and by a special revelation. "He who is in the bosom of the Father, he hath declared him" (John 1:18). "I speak to the world those things which I have heard of my Father" (John 8:26). It was also the office of Christ to proclaim the law, and to keep it free from the errors and corruptions of men. 2. To institute and preserve the ministry of the gospel; to raise up and send forth prophets, apostles, teachers, and other ministers of the church; to confer on them the gift of prophecy, and furnish them with the gifts necessary to their calling. "And he gave some apostles, and some prophets, and some evangelists," etc. (Eph. 4:11). "Therefore said the wisdom of God, I will send them prophets, and apostles," etc. (Luke 11:49). "For I will give you a mouth, and wisdom which all your adversaries shall not be able to gainsay, nor resist" (Luke 21:15). "The Spirit of Christ spoke through the prophets" (1 Peter 1:11). 3. It pertains to the prophetical office of Christ that he should be efficacious through his ministry, in the hearts of those that hear, to teach them internally by his Spirit, to illuminate their minds, and move their hearts to faith and obedience by the gospel. "He shall baptize you with the Holy Ghost, and with fire" (Matt. 3:11). "Then opened he their understandings, that they might understand the scriptures" (Luke 24:45). "Christ gave himself for the church that he might sanctify and cleanse it with the washing of water by the word" (Eph. 5:26). "And they went forth, and preached everywhere, the Lord working with them, and confirming the word with signs following" (Mark 16:20). "The Lord opened the heart of Lydia, that she attended unto the things spoken by Paul" (Acts 16:14). "The Lord gave testimony unto the word of his grace" (Acts 14:3). To sum up the whole in a few words, the prophetical office of Christ consists of three parts: To reveal the will of the Father; to institute a ministry, and to teach internally, or effectually through the ministry. These three things Christ has performed from the very commencement of the church, and will perform even to the end of the world, and that by his authority, power and efficacy. Hence, Christ is called the *Word*, not only in respect to the Father, by whom he was begotten when beholding himself in contemplation, and considering the image of himself, not vanishing away, but subsisting, con-substantial, and co-eternal with the Father himself; but also in respect to us, because he is the person that spake to the fathers, and brought forth the living word, or gospel from the bosom of the Father.

Hence it is apparent from what has now been said, what is the difference between Christ and other prophets, and why he is called the greatest teacher, and prophet, and so the chief of all prophets. 1. Christ is the Son of God, and Lord of all; the other prophets were only men, and servants of Christ. 2. Christ brought forth and uttered the word immediately from the Father to men; other prophets and apostles are called and sent by Christ. 3. The prophetical wisdom of Christ is infinite; for even according to his humanity, he excelled all others in every gift. 4. Christ is the fountain of all truth, and the author of the ministry: other prophets merely proclaim and reveal what they receive from Christ. Hence Christ is said to have spoken through the prophets. Neither does he reveal his doctrine to the prophets alone, but to all the godly. Hence it is said, "of his fullness have we all received," etc. (John 1:16). 5. Christ preaches effectually through his own external ministry, and that of those whom he calls into his service, by virtue of the Holy Spirit operating upon the hearts of men: other prophets are the instruments which Christ employs, and are co-workers together with him. 6. The doctrine of Christ is clearer and more complete than that of Moses and all the other prophets. 7. Christ had authority of himself; others have their authority from Christ. We believe Christ when he speaks on account of himself, but we believe others because Christ speaks in them.

III. WHAT IS THE PRIESTLY OR SACERDOTAL OFFICE OF CHRIST?

A priest in general is a person appointed of God, for the purpose of offering oblations and sacrifices, for interceding and teaching others. We may distinguish between those who serve in the capacity of priests, by speaking of them as typical and real. A typical priest is a person ordained of God to offer typical sacrifices, to make intercessions for himself and others, and to teach the people concerning the will of God, and the Messiah to come. Such were all the priests of the Old Testament, among whom there was one that was the greatest, usually called the High Priest; the others were inferior. It was peculiar to the High Priest, 1. That he alone entered once every year into the sanctuary, or most holy place, and that with blood which he offered for himself, and the people, burning incense and making intercession. 2. He had a more splendid and gorgeous apparel than the others. 3. He was placed over the rest. 4. He offered sacrifice, and made intercession for himself and the people. 5. He was to be consulted in matters or questions that were doubtful, weighty and obscure, and returned to the people the answer which God directed him to give. All the rest were inferior, whose office it was to offer sacrifices, to teach the doctrine of the law, and the promises pertaining to the Messiah, and to intercede for themselves and others. Wherefore, although all the priests of the Old Testament were types of Christ, yet the typical character of the High Priest was the most notable of them all, because in him there were many things that represented Christ, the true and great High Priest of the Church.

Objection: But if prophets and priest both teach, they do not differ from each other. Answer: They did indeed both teach the people, yet they were variously distinguished. Prophets were raised up immediately by God, from any tribe, whilst the priests were mediately ordained from the single tribe of Levi. Prophets taught extraordinarily, whilst the priests had the ordinary ministry. The prophets received their doctrine immediately from God, whilst the priests learned it out of the law. The prophets had divine testimonies so that they could not err; the priests could err in doctrine, and often did err in their instructions, and were reproved by the prophets.

The signified and true priest is Christ, the Son of God, who was immediately ordained by the Father, and anointed by the Holy Ghost to this office, that, having assumed human nature, he might reveal the secret will and counsel of God to us, and offer himself a propitiatory sacrifice for us, interceding in our behalf, and applying his sacrifice unto us, having the promise that he is always certainly heard in behalf of all those for whom he intercedes, and obtains for them the remission of sins; and finally through the ministers of the word and the Holy Spirit, collects, illuminates and sanctifies his church.

There are, therefore, four principal parts of the priestly office of Christ: 1. To teach men, and that in a different manner from all others, who are called to act as priests; for he does not merely speak to the ear by his word, but effectually inclines the heart by his Holy Spirit. 2. To offer himself a sacrifice for the sins of the world. 3. To make continual intercession and prayer for us to the Father, that he may receive us into his favor on account of his intercession and will, and on account of the perpetual efficacy of his sacrifice; and to have the promise of being heard in reference to those things which he asks. 4. To apply his sacrifice unto those for whom he intercedes, which is to receive into favor those that believe, and to bring it to pass that the Father may receive them, and that faith may be wrought in their hearts, by which the merits of Christ may be made over to them, so that they are regenerated by the Holy Spirit unto everlasting life.

From what has now been said we may easily perceive the difference between Christ and other priests. 1. The latter teach only with the external voice; Christ teaches also by the inward and efficacious working of the Holy Spirit. 2. Other priests do not make continual intercession, nor do they always obtain those things for which they pray. 3. They do not apply their own benefits to others. 4. They do not offer themselves a sacrifice for others; all of which things belong to Christ alone.

IV. WHAT IS THE KINGDOM OR REGAL OFFICE OF CHRIST?

A king is a person ordained of God, that he may rule over a certain people, according to just laws, that he may have power to reward the good and punish the evil, and that he may defend his subjects, not having any one superior or above him. The King of kings is Christ, who was immediately ordained of God, that he might govern, by his word and Spirit, the church which he purchased with his own blood, and defend her against all her enemies, whom he will cast into everlasting punishment, whilst he will reward his people with eternal life.

The kingly office of Christ is therefore: 1. To rule the church by his word and Spirit, which he does in such a manner that he does not only show us what he would have accomplished in us, but also so inclines and affects the heart by his Spirit, that we are led to do the same. 2. He preserves and defends us against our enemies, both external and internal, which he does by protecting us by his almighty power, arming us against our foes, that we may by his Spirit, be furnished with every weapon necessary for resisting and overcoming them. 3. To bestow upon his church gifts and glory; and finally, to liberate her from all evils; to control and overcome all his enemies by his power, and at length, having fully subdued them, to cast them into inconceivable misery and wretchedness.

The Second Helvetic Confession (1566)[1]

"Confessio et Expositio Brevis et Simplex Sinceræ Religionis Christianæ, etc.," in Schaff, *The Creeds of Christendom*, 3:237–40, 259–62.

"The Second Helvetic Confession, A.D. 1566," in Schaff, *The Creeds of Christendom*, 3:831–34, 854–58.

The Second Helvetic Confession (1566) began as a personal statement of faith by Heinrich Bullinger (1504–75), written when he expected to die from a severe illness. Bullinger's mastery of patristic and medieval theology prepared him to be one of the leading figures of the Reformation. This confession is a theological treatise building on the First Helvetic Confession; at the same time, it offers a convenient summary of Bullinger's thought expressed more at length in his *Decades* (cf. chap. 3). The Second Helvetic Confession is one of the most widespread Reformed creeds and has been translated into many languages. It served the important role of unifying Reformed churches in Switzerland and abroad. This unifying function appears even more clearly in this confession's serving as the organizing document of the *Harmony of Reformed Confessions*, published in 1581 (Latin) and reworked by Peter Hall in 1844 (English).

We reproduce here the first two chapters of the confession, respectively on Scripture as the Word of God and on its interpretation. Central to Bullinger's thought is the Reformed doctrine of *sola Scriptura*. While he manifests great respect for the church's tradition and the interpretations of the ancient church fathers, he affirms that the interpreter of Scripture is Scripture itself. When the fathers, the ancient councils, or church tradition depart from what Scripture teaches, he declares that they must not be followed, in accordance with his belief that Scripture alone is sufficient for the Christian life.

Supplementary Bibliography (cf. chap. 3): Beeke & Ferguson. *Reformed Confessions*. Pp. x–xi. Cochrane. *Reformed Confessions*. Pp. 220–301. Dennison. *Reformed Confessions* 2:809–81. Richard C. Gamble.

1. The subtitles in the Latin are taken from H. A. Niemeyer, ed., *Collectio Confessionum in Ecclesiis Reformatis Publicatarum* (Lipsiæ: Julii Klinkhardti, 1840), 467–70, 487–90. The translations of these subtitles are added from Cochrane, *Reformed Confessions*, 224–26, 247–51.

"Switzerland: Triumph and Decline." Pp. 63–64 in Reid, ed. *John Calvin: His Influence in the Western World*. Dirk Jellema. "Helvetic Confessions." P. 459 in *NIDCC*. Leith. *Creeds of the Churches*. Pp. 131–92. E. F. Karl Müller. "Helvetic Confessions." *NSHERK* 5:216–17. Schaff. *The Creeds of Christendom* 1:390–420, 3:233–306, 3:831–909. Joachim Staedtke, ed. *Glauben und Bekennen: Vierhundert Jahre Confessio Helvetica Posterior*. Zürich: Zwingli Verlag, 1966.

CONFESSIO ET EXPOSITIO BREVIS ET SIMPLEX SINCERÆ RELIGIONIS CHRISTIANÆ, ETC.

CAP. I: DE SCRIPTURA SANCTA, VERO DEI VERBO [Conf. Aug., Art. V]

1. Scriptura Canonica. Credimus et confitemur, Scripturas Canonicas sanctorum Prophetarum et Apostolorum utriusque Testamenti ipsum verum esse verbum Dei, et auctoritatem sufficientem ex semetipsis, non ex hominibus habere. Nam Deus ipse loquutus est Patribus, Prophetis, et Apostolis, et loquitur adhuc nobis per Scripturas Sanctas.

2. Et in hac Scriptura Sancta habet universalis Christi Ecclesia plenissime exposita, quæcunque pertinent cum ad salvificam fidem, tum ad vitam Deo placentem recte informandam, quo nomine distincte a Deo præceptum est, ne ei *aliquid vel addatur vel detrahatur* (Deut. 4:2; Apoc. 22:18–19).

THE SECOND HELVETIC CONFESSION

CHAPTER I: OF THE HOLY SCRIPTURE BEING THE TRUE WORD OF GOD

1. *Canonical Scripture*. We believe and confess the Canonical Scriptures of the holy prophets and apostles of both Testaments to be the true Word of God, and to have sufficient authority of themselves, not of men. For God himself spake to the fathers, prophets, apostles,[2] and still speaks to us through the Holy Scriptures.

2. And in this Holy Scripture, the universal Church of Christ has all things fully expounded which belong to a saving faith, and also to the framing of a life acceptable to God; and in this respect it is expressly commanded by God that nothing be either added to or taken from the same.[3]

2. Heb. 1:1–2.
3. Deut. 4:2; Rev 22:18–19.

3. Scriptura plene docet omnem pietatem. Sentimus ergo, ex hisce Scripturis petendam esse veram sapientiam et pietatem, ecclesiarum quoque reformationem et gubernationem, omniumque officiorum pietatis institutionem, probationem denique dogmatum reprobationemque aut errorum confutationem omnium, sed et admonitiones omnes juxta illud Apostoli: *Omnis Scriptura divinitus inspirata utilis est ad doctrinam, ad redargutionem*, etc. (2 Tim. 3:16–17), et iterum, *Hæc tibi scribo*, inquit ad Timotheum apostolus (in 1 Tim. 3:15), *ut noris, quomodo oporteat, te versari in domo Dei*, etc.

Scripura verbum Dei est. Et idem ille rursus ad Thess.: Cum (ait) acciperetis sermonem a nobis, accepistis non sermonem hominum, sed sicut erat vere, sermonem Dei, etc. (1 Thess. 2:13). Nam ipse in Evangelio dixit Dominus: *Non vos estis loquentes illi, sed Spiritus Patris mei loquitur in vobis. Ergo, qui vos audit, me audit; qui autem vos spernit, me spernit* (Matt. 10:20; Luc. 10:16; Joh. 13:20).

4. Prædicatio verbi Dei est verbum Dei. Proinde cum hodie hoc Dei verbum per prædicatores legitime vocatos annunciatur in Ecclesia, credimus ipsum Dei verbum annunciari et a fidelibus recipi, neque aliud Dei verbum vel fingendum, vel cœlitus esse exspectandum: atque in præsenti spectandum esse ipsum verbum, quod annunciatur, non annunciantem ministrum, qui, etsi sit malus et peccator, verum tamen et bonum manet nihilominus verbum Dei.

3. *Scripture Teaches Fully All Godliness*. We judge, therefore, that from these Scriptures are to be taken true wisdom and godliness, the reformation and government of churches; as also instruction in all duties of piety; and, to be short, the confirmation of doctrines, and the confutation of all errors, with all exhortations; according to that word of the Apostle, "All scripture given by inspiration of God is profitable for doctrine, for reproof," etc. (2 Tim. 3:16–17). Again, "These things write I to thee," says the Apostle to Timothy, "that thou mayest know how thou oughtest to behave thyself in the house of God," etc. (1 Tim. 3:14–15).

***Scripture Is the Word of God*.** Again, the self-same Apostle to the Thessalonians: "When," says he, "Ye received the word of us, ye received not the word of men, but as it was indeed, the Word of God," etc. (1 Thess. 2:13). For the Lord himself has said in the Gospel, "It is not ye that speak, but the Spirit of my Father speaketh in you"; therefore "he that heareth you, heareth me; and he that despiseth you, despiseth me" (Matt. 10:20; Luke 10:16; John 13:20).

4. *The Preaching of the Word of God Is the Word of God*. Wherefore when this Word of God is now preached in the church by preachers lawfully called, we believe that the very Word of God is preached, and received of the faithful; and that neither any other Word of God is to be feigned, nor to be expected from heaven:[4] and that now the Word itself which is preached is to be regarded, not the minister that preaches; who, although he be evil and a sinner, nevertheless the Word of God abides true and good.

---

4. Cf. Gal 1:8.

5. Neque arbitramur, prædicationem illam externam tanquam inutilem ideo videri, quoniam pendeat institutio veræ religionis ab interna Spiritus illuminatione: propterea, quod scriptum sit: *Non erudiet quis proximum suum. Omnes enim cognoscent me* (Jer. 31:34), et: *Nihil est, qui rigat aut qui plantat, sed qui incrementum dat, Deus* (1 Cor. 3:7). Quamquam enim *nemo veniat ad Christum, nisi trahatur a Patre cœlesti* (Joh. 6:44), ac intus illuminetur per Spiritum, scimus tamen, Deum omnino velle prædicari verbum Dei, etiam foris. Equidem potuisset per Spiritum Sanctum, aut per ministerium angeli absque ministerio S. Petri instituisse Cornelium in Actis Deus, ceterum rejicit hunc nihilominus ad Petrum, de quo angelus loquens: *Hic, inquit, dicet tibi, quid oporteat te facere* (Act. 10:6).

6. Interior illuminatio non tollit externam prædicationem. Qui enim intus illuminat, donato hominibus Spiritu Sancto, idem ille præcipiens dixit ad discipulos suos: *Ite in mundum universum, et prædicate evangelium omni creaturæ* (Marc. 16:15). Unde Paulus Lydiæ apud Philippos purpurariæ prædicavit verbum exterius, interius autem *aperuit mulieri cor Dominus* (Act. 16:14): Idemque Paulus collocata gradatione eleganti (ad. Rom. 10:13–17), tandem infert: *Ergo fides ex auditu est; auditus autem per verbum Dei.*

5. Neither do we think that therefore the outward preaching is to be thought as fruitless because the instruction in true religion depends on the inward illumination of the Spirit, or because it is written "No man shall teach his neighbor; for all men shall know me" (Jer. 31:34),[5] and "He that watereth, or he that planteth, is nothing, but God that giveth the increase" (1 Cor. 3:7). For albeit "No man can come to Christ, unless he be drawn by the Heavenly Father" (John 6:44), and be inwardly lightened by the Holy Spirit, yet we know undoubtedly that it is the will of God that his word should be preached even outwardly. God could indeed, by his Holy Spirit, or by the ministry of an angel, without the ministry of Saint Peter, have taught Cornelius in Acts; but, nevertheless, he refers him to Peter, of whom the angel speaking says, "He shall tell thee what thou oughtest to do."[6]

6. Inward Illumination Does Not Eliminate External Preaching. For he that illuminates inwardly by giving men the Holy Spirit, the self-same, by way of commandment, said unto his disciples, "Go ye into all the world, and preach the Gospel to the every creature" (Mark 16:15).[7] And so Paul preached the Word outwardly to Lydia, a purple-seller among the Philippians; but the Lord inwardly opened the woman's heart (Acts 16:10, 14). And the same Paul, upon an elegant gradation fitly placed in the tenth chapter to the Romans, at last infers, "Therefore faith cometh by hearing and hearing by the Word of God" (Rom. 10:14–17).

5. Heb. 8:11.
6. Acts 10:6.
7. Matt. 28:19–20.

7. Agnoscimus interim, Deum illuminare posse homines etiam sine externo ministerio, quos et quando velit, id quod ejus potentiæ est. Nos autem loquimur de usitata ratione instituendi homines, et præcepto et exemplo tradita nobis a Deo.

7. We know, in the mean time, that God can illuminate whom and when he will, even without the external ministry, which is a thing appertaining to his power; but we speak of the usual way of instructing men, delivered unto us from God, both by commandment and examples.

8. Hæreses. Execramur igitur omnes hæreses Artemonis, Manichæorum, Valentinianiorum, Cerdonis et Marcionitarum, qui negarunt Scripturas a Spiritu Sancto profectas: vel quasdam illarum non receperunt, vel interpolarunt et corruperunt.

8. Heresies. We therefore detest all the heresies of Artemon, the Manichaeans, the Valentinians, of Cerdon, and the Marcionites, who denied that the Scriptures proceeded from the Holy Spirit; or else received not, or interpolated and corrupted, some of them.

9. Apocrypha. Interim nihil dissimulamus, quosdam Veteris Testamenti libros a veteribus nuncupatos esse *apocryphos*, ab aliis *ecclesiasticos*, utpote quos in ecclesiis legi voluerunt quidem, non tamen proferri ad auctoritatem ex his fidei confirmandam. Sicuti et Augustinus in lib. *de civitate Dei* (18.38) commemorat, in libris Regum adduci Prophetarum quorundam nomina et libros, sed addit, hos non esse in canone, ac sufficere ad pietatem eos libros, quos habemus.

9. Apocrypha. And yet we do not deny that certain books of the Old Testament were by the ancient authors called *Apocryphal*, and by others *Ecclesiastical*; to wit, such as they would have to be read in the churches, but not alleged to avouch or confirm the authority of faith by them. As also Augustine, in his *De civitate Dei* 18.28, make mention that "in the books of the Kings, the names and books of certain prophets are reckoned"; but he adds that "they are not in the canon," and that "those books which we have suffice unto godliness."

CAP. II: DE INTERPRETANDIS SCRIPTURIS SANCTIS, ET DE PATRIBUS, CONCILIIS, ET TRADITIONIBUS

CHAPTER II: OF INTERPRETING THE HOLY SCRIPTURES; AND OF FATHERS, COUNCILS, AND TRADITIONS

1. Scripturarum vera interpretatio. Scripturas Sanctas, dixit Apostolus Petrus, *non esse interpretationis privatæ* (2 Pet. 1:20). Proinde non probamus interpretationes quaslibet; unde nec pro vera aut genuina Scripturarum interpretatione agnoscimus eum, quem vocant sensum Romanæ ecclesiæ, quem scilicet simpliciter Romanæ ecclesiæ defensores omnibus obtrudere contendunt recipiendum: sed illam duntaxat Scripturarum interpretationem pro orthodoxa et genuina agnoscimus, quæ ex ipsis est petita Scripturis (ex ingenio utique ejus linguæ, in qua sunt scriptæ, secundum circumstantias item expensæ, et pro ratione locorum vel similium vel dissimilium, plurium[8] quoque et clariorum expositæ), cum regula fidei et caritatis congruit, et ad gloriam Dei hominumque salutem eximie facit.

1. *The True Interpretation of Scripture*. The Apostle Peter has said that "the Holy Scriptures are not of any private interpretation" (2 Peter 1:20). Therefore we do not allow all kinds of exposition. Whereupon we do not acknowledge that which they call the meaning of the Church of Rome for the true and natural interpretation of the Scriptures; which, forsooth, the defenders of the Romish Church do strive to force all men simply to receive; but we acknowledge only that interpretation of Scriptures for orthodox and genuine which, being taken from the Scriptures themselves (that is, from the spirit of that tongue in which they were written, they being also weighed according to the circumstances and expounded according to the proportion of places, either of like or of unlike, also of more and plainer), accords with the rule of faith and charity,[9] and makes notably for God's glory and man's salvation.

2. Sanctorum expositiones. Proinde non aspernamur sanctorum Patrum Græcorum Latinorumque interpretationes, neque reprobamus eorundem disputationes ac tractationes rerum sacrarum cum Scripturis consentientes: a quibus tamen recedimus modeste, quando aliena a Scripturis aut his contraria adferre deprehenduntur. Nec putamus, illis ullam a nobis hac re injuriam irrogari, cum omnes uno ore nolint sua scripta æquari canonicis, sed probare jubeant, quatenus vel consentiant cum illis, vel dissentiant, jubeantque consentientia recipere, recedere vero a dissentientibus.

2. *Interpretations of the Holy Fathers*. Wherefore we do not despise the interpretations of the holy Greek and Latin fathers, nor reject their disputations and treatises as far as they agree with the Scriptures; but we do modestly dissent from them when they are found to set down things differing from, or altogether contrary to, the Scriptures. Neither do we thing that we do them any wrong in this matter; seeing that they all, with one consent, will not have their writings matched with the Canonical Scriptures, but bid us allow of them so far forth as they either agree with them or disagree.

---

8. Kindler and Niemeyer read *plurimum*.
9. Cf. 2 Tim. 1:13.

3. Concilia. Eodem in ordine collocantur etiam conciliorum definitiones vel canones.

4. Quapropter non patimur, nos in controversiis religionis vel fidei causis urgeri nudis Patrum sententiis aut conciliorum determinationibus, multo minus receptis consuetudinibus, aut etiam multitudine idem sentientium, aut longi temporis præscriptione. **Judex quis?** Ergo non alium sustinemus in causa fidei judicem, quam ipsum Deum, per Scripturas Sanctas pronunciatem, quid verum sit, quid falsum, quid sequendum sit, quidve fugiendum. Ita judiciis nonnisi spiritualium hominum, ex verbo Dei petitis, acquiescimus. Jeremias certe cæterique prophetæ sacerdocum concilia, contra legem Dei instituta, damnarunt graviter, ac monuerunt diligenter, ne audiamus Patres, aut insistamus viæ illorum, qui, in suis ambulantes adinventionibus, a lege Dei deflexerunt.

5. Traditiones humanæ. Pariter repudiamus traditiones humanas, quæ, tametsi insigniantur speciosis titulis, quasi divinæ apostolicæque sint, viva voce Apostolorum et ceu per manus virorum Apostolicorum succedentibus Episcopis, ecclesiæ traditæ; compositæ tamen cum Scripturis, ab his discrepant, discrepantiaque illa sua ostendunt, se minime esse Apostolicas. Sicut enim Apostoli inter se diversa non docuerunt, ita et Apostolici non contraria Apostolis ediderunt. Quinimo impium esset adseverare, Apostolos viva voce contraria scriptis suis tradidisse.

3. *Councils*. And in the same order we also place the decrees and canons of councils.

4. Wherefore we suffer not ourselves, in controversies about religion or matters of faith, to be pressed with the bare testimonies of fathers or decrees of councils; much less with received customs, or with the multitude of men being of one judgment, or with prescription of long time. ***Who Is the Judge?*** Therefore, in controversies of religion or matters of faith, we can not admit any other judge than God himself, pronouncing by the Holy Scriptures what is true, what is false, what is to be followed, or what to be avoided. So we do not rest but in the judgment of spiritual men, drawn from the Word of God. Certainly Jeremiah and other prophets did vehemently condemn the assemblies of priests gathered against the law of God; and diligently forewarned us that we should not hear the fathers, or tread in their path who, walking in their own inventions, swerved from the law of God.[10]

5. *Human Traditions*. We do likewise reject human traditions, which, although they be set out with goodly titles, as though they were divine and apostolical, delivered to the Church by the lively voice of the apostles, and, as it were, through the hands of apostolical men, by means of bishops succeeding in their room, yet, being compared with the Scriptures, disagree with them; and that by their disagreement betray themselves in not wise to be apostolical. For as the apostles did not disagree among themselves in doctrine, so the apostles' scholars did not set forth things contrary to the apostles. Nay, it were blasphemous to avouch that the apostles, by a lively voice, delivered things contrary to their writings.

10. Ezek. 20:18.

161

6. Paulus disserte dicit: *Eadem se in omnibus ecclesiis docuisse* (1 Cor. 4:17); et iterum *non alia*, inquit, *scribimus vobis, quam quæ legitis aut etiam agnoscitis* (2 Cor. 1:13). Alibi rursus testatur: *Se et discipulos suos* (i.e., viros Apostolicos), eadem ambulare via et eodem spiritu parit*er facere omnia* (2 Cor. 12:18). Habuereunt quondam et Judæi suas traditiones seniorum, sed refutatæ sunt graviter a Domino, ostendente, quod earum observatio legi Dei officiat, *et his Deus frustra colatur* (Matt. 15:8–9; Marc. 7:6–7).

6. Paul affirms expressly that he taught the same things in all churches (1 Cor. 4:17). And, again, "We," says he, "write none other things unto you than what ye read or acknowledge" (2 Cor. 1:13). Also, in another place, he witnesses that he and his disciples—to wit, apostolic men—walked in the same way, and jointly by the same Spirit did all things (2 Cor. 12:18). The Jews also, in time past, had their traditions of elders; but these traditions were severely confuted by the Lord, showing that the keeping of them hinders God's law, and that God is in vain worshiped of such (Matt. 15:8–9; Mark 7:6–7).

Cap. XII: De Lege Dei

Chapter XII: Of the Law of God

1. Lege Dei exponitur nobis voluntas Dei. Docemus, lege Dei exponi nobis voluntatem Dei, quid a nobis fieri velit aut nolit, quid bonum et justum, quidve malum sit et injustum. Bonam igitur et sanctam confitemur esse legem. **Lex naturæ**. Et hanc quidem alias digito Dei i*nscriptam esse in corda hominum, vocarique legem naturæ* (Rom. 2:15), alias autem **Lex Mosis in duabus tabulis**. digito insculptam esse in tubulas Mosis geminas, et libris Mosis copiosius expositam (Ex. 20; Deut 5). Distinguimus illam, perspicuitatis gratia, in moralem, quæ comprehenditur decalogo vel geminis tabulis, per Mosis libros expositis, in ceremonialem item, quæ de cæremoniis cultuque Dei constituit, et in judicialem quæ versatur circa politica atque œconomica.

1. *The Will of God Is Set Down unto Us in the Law of God*. We teach that the will of God is set down unto us in the law of God; to wit, what he would have us do, or not do, what is good and just, or what is evil and unjust. We therefore confess that, "The law is good and holy"[11] ***The Law of Nature*.**; and that this law is, by the finger of God, either "written in the hearts of men" (Rom. 2:15), and so is called the law of nature, ***The Law of Moses is in Two Tables*.** or engraven in two tables of stone, and more largely expounded in the books of Moses (Ex. 20:1–17).[12] For plainness' sake we divide it into the moral law, which is contained in the commandments, or the two tables expounded in the books of Moses; into the ceremonial, which does appoint ceremonies and the worship of God; and into the judicial law, which is occupied about political and domestic affairs.

---

11. Rom. 7:12.
12. Deut 5:22; 9:10.

2. Plenissima et absolutissima est lex. Credimus, hac Dei lege omnem Dei voluntatem, et omnia præcepat necessaria, ad omnem vitæ partem, plenissime tradi. Alioqui enim non vetuisset Dominus, *huic legi nihil vel addi vel adimi* (Deut. 4:2); non præcepisset, *recta ad hanc incedi, neque in dextram vel sinistram deflexo itinere, declinare* (Isa. 30:21).

3. Cur data sit lex? Docemus, legem hanc non datam esse hominibus, ut ejus justificemur observatione: sed ut ex ejus indicio infirmitatem potius, peccatum atque condemnationem agnoscamus, et de viribus nostris deperantes, convertamur ad Christum in fide. Aperte enim Apostolus: *Lex iram*, ait, *operatur* (Rom. 4:15). *Per legem agnitio peccati* (Rom. 3:20). *Si data fuisset lex, quæ posset justificare, vel vivificare, vere ex lege esset justitia: sed conclusit Scriptura* (legis nimirum) *omnia sub peccatum, ut promissio ex fide Jesu daretur credentibus. Itaque lex pædagogus noster ad Christum fuit, ut ex fide justificaremur* (Gal. 3:21–22, 24).

2. *The Law Is Complete and Perfect*. We believe that the whole will of God, and all necessary precepts, for every part of this life, are fully delivered in this law. For otherwise the Lord would not have forbidden that "any thing should be either added to or taken away from this law" (Deut. 4:2; 12:32); neither would he have commanded us to go straight forward in this, and "not to decline out of the way, either to the right hand or to the left."[13]

3. *Why the Law Was Given*. We teach that this law was not given to men, that we should be justified by keeping it; but that, by the knowledge thereof, we might rather acknowledge our infirmity, sin, and condemnation; and so, despairing of our strength, might turn unto Christ by faith. For the apostle says plainly, "The law worketh wrath" (Rom. 4:15); and "by the law cometh the knowledge of sin" (Rom. 3:20); and, "If there had been a law given which would have justified and given us life, surely righteousness should have been by the law. But the Scripture (to wit, of the law) has concluded all under sin, that the promise by the faith of Jesus Christ should be given to them which believe" (Gal. 3:21–22). "Therefore, the law was our schoolmaster to bring us to Christ, that we might be justified by faith" (Gal. 3:24).

13. Josh. 1:7; Isa. 30:21.

Caro non implet legem. Neque vero potuit aut potest ulla caro legi Dei satisfacere, et hanc adimplere, ob imbecilliatem in carne nostra, ad extremum usque spiritum in nobis hærentem aut remanentem. Rursus enim Apostolus: *Quod lex præstare non poterat*, inquit, *quia imbecillis erat per carnem, hoc Deus, proprio Filio misso sub specie carnis peccato obnoxiæ, præstitit* (Rom. 8:3). *Idcirco Christus est perfectio legis et adimpletio nostra* (Rom. 10:4), qui ut *execrationem legis sustulit, dum factus est pro nobis maledictio, vel execratio* (Gal. 3:13), ita communicat nobis per fidem adimpletionem suam, nobisque ejus imputatur justitia et obedientia.

4. Quatenus lex abrogata. Hactenus itaque abrogata est lex Dei, quatenus nos amplius non damnat, nec iram in nobis operator. Sumus enim sub gratia, et non sub lege. Præterea implevit Christus omnes legis figuras. Unde umbræ cesserunt, corpore adveniente, ut jam in Christo et veritatem habeamus et omnem plenitudinem. Attamen legem non ideo fastidientes rejicimus. Meminimus enim verborum Domini, dicentis: *Non veni legem et prophetas solvere, sed implere* (Matt. 5:17). Scimus, lege nobis tradi formulas virtutum atque vitiorum. Scimus, Scripturam legis, si exponatur per Evangelium, Ecclesiæ esse utilem, et idcirco ejus lectionem non exterminandam esse ex Ecclesiæ. Licet enim velo obtectus fuerit Mosis vultus, Apostolus tamen perhibet, velum per Christum tolli atque aboleri. **Sectæ.** Damnamus omnia, quæ hæretici veteres et neoterici contra legem Dei docuerunt.

The Flesh Can Not Fulfill the Law. For neither could there ever, neither at this day can any flesh satisfy the law of God, and fulfill it, by reason of the weakness in our flesh, which remains and sticks fast in us, even to our last breath. For the apostle says again, "That which the law could not perform, inasmuch as it was weak through the flesh, that did God perform, by sending his own Son in the likeness of sinful flesh" (Rom. 8:3). Therefore, Christ is the perfecting of the law, and our fulfilling of it (Rom. 10:4); who, as he took away the curse of the law, when he was made a curse for us (Gal. 3:13), so does he communicate unto us by faith his fulfilling thereof, and his righteousness and obedience are imputed unto us.

4. *How Far the Law Is Abrogated*. The law of God,[14] therefore, is thus far abrogated; that is, it does not henceforth condemn us, neither work wrath in us; "for we are under grace, and not under the law."[15] Moreover, Christ did fulfill all the figures of the law; wherefore the shadow ceased when the body came, so that, in Christ, we have now all truth and all fullness.[16] Yet we do not therefore disdain or reject the law. We remember the words of the Lord, saying, "I came not to destroy the law and the prophets, but to fulfill them" (Matt. 5:17). We know that in the law[17] are described unto us the kinds of virtues and vices. We know that the Scripture of the law,[18] if it be expounded by the Gospel, is very profitable to the Church, and that therefore the reading of it is not to be banished out of the Church. For although the countenance of Moses was covered with a veil, yet the apostle affirms that "the veil is taken away and abolished by Christ."[19] **The Sects**. We condemn all things which the old or new heretics have taught against the law of God.

14. To wit, the moral law, comprehended in the Ten Commandments.
15. Rom. 6:14.
16. Cf. Col. 2:17; Heb. 10:1, 5.
17. To wit, in the moral law.
18. To wit, the ceremonial law.
19. 2 Cor. 3:14.

CAP. XIII: DE EVANGELIO JESU CHRISTI, DE PROMISSIONIBUS, ITEM SPIRITU ET LITERA

1. Veteres habuerunt promissiones Evangelicas. Evangelium quidem opponitur legi. Nam lex iram operatur, et maledictionem adnunciat; Evangelium vero gratiam et benedictionem prædicat. Sed et Joannes dicit: *Lex per Mosen data est, gratia et veritas per Jesum Christum exorta est* (Joh. 1:17); nihilominus tamen certissimum est, eos, qui ante legem et sub lege fuerunt, non omnino destitutos fuisse Evangelio. Habuerunt enim promissiones evangelicas insignes, quales hæ sunt: *Semen mulieris conculcabit caput serpentis* (Gen. 3:15). *In semine tuo benedicentur omnes gentes* (Gen. 22:18). *Non auferetur sceptrum de Juda, nisi prius venerit Silo* (Gen. 49:10). *Prophetam excitabit Dominus de medio fratrum*, etc. (Deut. 18:18).

CHAPTER XIII: OF THE GOSPEL OF JESUS CHRIST: ALSO OF PROMISES; OF THE SPIRIT AND OF THE LETTER

1. *The Ancients Had Evangelical Promises*. The Gospel, indeed, is opposed to the law: for the law works wrath, and does announce a curse; but the Gospel does preach grace and blessing. John also says, "The law was given by Moses, but grace and truth came by Jesus Christ" (John 1:17). Yet, notwithstanding, it is most certain that they who were before the law, and under the law, were not altogether destitute of the Gospel. For they had notable evangelical promises, such as these: "The seed of the woman shall bruise the serpent's head" (Gen. 3:15). "In thy seed shall all the nations of the earth be blessed" (Gen. 22:18). "The scepter shall not depart from Judah, until he comes" (Gen. 49:10). "The Lord shall raise up a Prophet from among his own brethren," etc. (Deut. 18:15; Acts 3:22).[20]

---

20. Acts 7:37.

2. Promissiones duplices. Et quidem agnoscimus, Patribus duo fuisse promissionum genera, sicuti et nobis, revelata. Aliæ enim erant rerum præsentium vel terrenarum, quales sunt promissiones de terra Canaan, de victoriis, et quales hodie adhuc sunt de pane quotidiano. Aliæ vero erant tunc, et sunt etiam nunc, rerum cœlestium et æternarum, gratiæ videlicet divinæ, remissionis peccatorum, et vitæ æternæ, per fidem in Jesum Christum. **Habuereunt Patres etiam promissiones spirituales non tantum carnales**. Habuerunt autem veteres non tantum externas vel terrenas, sed spirituales etiam cœlestesque promissiones, in Christo. Nam *de salute*, ait Petrus, *exquisiverunt et scrutati sunt prophetæ, qui de ventura in nos gratia vaticinati sunt*, etc. (1 Pet. 1:10). Unde et Paulus Apostolus dixit: *Evangelium Dei ante promissum esse per prophetas Dei, in Scripturis sanctis* (Rom. 1:2). Inde nimirum claret, veteres non prorsus destitutos fuisse omni Evangelio.

2. *The Promises Twofold*. And we do acknowledge that the fathers had two kinds of promises revealed unto them, even as we have. For some of them were of present and transitory things: such as were the promises of land of Canaan, and of victories; and such as are nowadays concerning our daily bread. Other promises there were then, and are now, of heavenly and everlasting things; as of God's favor, remission of sins, and life everlasting, through faith in Jesus Christ. ***The Fathers Had Not Only Carnal but Also Spiritual Promises***. Now, the fathers had not only outward or earthly, but spiritual and heavenly promises in Christ. For the Apostle Peter says that "the prophets, which prophesied of the grace that should come to us, have searched and inquired of this salvation" (1 Peter 1:10). Whereupon the Apostle Paul also says, that "the Gospel of God was promised before by the prophets of God in the Holy Scriptures" (Rom. 1:2).[21] Hereby, then, it appears evidently that the fathers were not altogether destitute of all the Gospel.

21. Col. 1:5.

166

3. Evangelium proprie quid? Et, quamvis ad hunc modum patres nostri in Scripturis prophetarum habuerint Evangelium, per quod salutem in Christo per fidem consecuti sunt, Evangelium tamen proprie illud dicitur lætum et felix nuncium, quod nobis primum per Joannem Baptistam, deinde per ipsum Christum Dominum, postea per Apostolos ejus Apostolorumque successores prædicatum est mundo, Deum jam præstitisse, quod ab exordio mundi promisit, ac misisse, imo donavisse nobis Filium unicum, et in hoc reconciliationem cum Patre, remissionem peccatorum, omnem plenitudinem, et vitam æternam. Historia ergo descripta a quatuor Evangelistis, explicans, quomodo hæc sint facta vel adimpleta a Christo, quæ docuerit et fecerit Christus; et quod in ipso credentes omnem habent plenitudinem, recte nuncupatur Evangelium. Prædicatio item et Scriptura Apostolica, qua nobis exponunt Apostoli, quomodo nobis a Patre datus sit Filius, et in hoc vitæ salutisque omnia, recte dicitur doctrina Evangelica, sic, ut ne hodie quidem, si sincera sit, appellationem tam præclaram amittat.

3. *What Is the Gospel Properly Speaking*? And although, after this manner, our fathers had the Gospel in the writings of the prophets, by which they attained salvation in Christ through faith, yet the Gospel is properly called "glad and happy tidings"; wherein, first by John Baptist, then by Christ the Lord himself, and afterwards by the apostles and their successors, is preached to us in the world, that God has now performed that which he promised from the beginning of the world, and has sent, yea, and even given unto us, his only Son, and, in him, reconciliation with the Father, remission of sins, all fullness, and everlasting life. The history, therefore, set down by the four evangelists, declaring how these things were done or fulfilled in Christ, and what he taught and did, and that they who believe in him have all fullness—this, I say, is truly called the Gospel. The preaching, also, and Scripture of the apostles, in which they expound unto us how the Son was given us of the Father, and, in him, all things pertaining to life and salvation, is truly called the doctrine of the Gospel; so as even at this day it loses not that worthy name, if it be sincere.

4. De spiritu et litera. Illa ipsa Evangelii prædicatio nuncupatur item ab Apostolo spiritus et ministerium spiritus, eo, quod efficax et viva fiat per fidem in auribus, imo cordibus credentium, per Spiritum Sanctum illuminantem. Nam litera, quæ opponitur spiritui, significat quidem omnem rem externam, sed maxime doctrinam legis, sine spiritu et fide in animis, non viva fide credentium, operantem iram, et excitantem peccatum. Quo nomine et ministerium mortis ab Apostolo nuncupatur. Huc enim illud Apostoli pertinet, *Litera occidit, spiritus vivificate* (2 Cor. 3:6). Et pseudoapostoli prædicabant Evangelium, lege admixta, corruptum, quasi Christus sine lege non possit servare. **Sectæ**. Quales fuisse dicuntur Ebionæi, ab Ebione hæretico descendentes, et Nazaræi, qui et Minæi antiquitus vocabantur. Quos omnes nos damnamus, pure prædicantes Evangelium, docentesque per Spiritum [ed. note: Other manuscripts have *Christum*] solum, et non per legem justificari credentes. De qua re mox sequetur sub titulo justificationis copiosior expositio.

5. Evangelii doctrina non est nova, sed vetustissima doctrina. Et quamvis Evangelii doctrina collata cum Pharisæorum doctrina legis, visa sit, cum primum prædicaretur per Christum, nova esse doctrina, quod et Jeremias de Novo Testamento vaticinatus sit, revera tamen illa, non modo vetus erat, et est adhuc (nam nova dicitur et hodie a Papistis, collata cum doctrina jam Papistarum recepta) vetus doctrina, sed omnium in mundo antiquissima.

4. *Of the Spirit and the Letter*. That same preaching of the Gospel is by the apostle termed the Spirit, and "the ministry of the Spirit" (2 Cor. 3:8): because it lives and works through faith in the ears, yea, in the hearts, of the faithful, through the illumination of the Holy Spirit. For the letter, which is opposed unto the Spirit, does signify every outward thing, but more especially the doctrine of the law, which, without the Spirit and faith, works wrath, and stirs up sin in the minds of them that do not truly believe. For which cause it is called by the apostle "the ministry of death" (2 Cor. 3:7); for hitherto pertains that saying of the apostle, "the letter killeth, but the Spirit giveth life" (2 Cor. 3:6). The false apostles preached the Gospel, corrupted by mingling of the law therewith; as though Christ could not save without the law. ***The Sects***. Such, also, were the Ebionites said to be, who came of Ebion the heretic; and the Nazarites, who beforetime were called Mineans. All whom we do condemn, sincerely preaching the word, and teaching that believers are justified through the Spirit (or Christ) only, and not through the law.[22] But of this matter there shall follow a fuller exposition, under the title of justification.

5. *The Doctrine of the Gospel Is Not New, but Most Ancient Doctrine*. And although the doctrine of the Gospel, compared with the Pharisees' doctrine of the law, might seem (when it was first preached by Christ) to be a new doctrine (which thing also Jeremiah prophesied of the New Testament[23]); yet, indeed, it not only was, and as yet (though the papists call it new, in regard of popish doctrine, which has of long time been received), an ancient doctrine, but also the most ancient in the world.

22. Acts 15:1; 20:21; cf. Romans; Galatians.
23. Jer. 31:31–33.

6. Deus enim *ab æterno prædestinavit* mundum servare per Christum, et hanc suam prædestinationem et consilium sempiternum *aperuit mundo per Evangelium* (2 Tim. 1:9–10). Unde claret religionem doctrinamque Evangelicam, inter omnes, quotquot fuerunt unquam, sunt atque erunt, omnium esse antiquissimam. **7.** Unde dicimus, omnes eos errare turpiter, et indigna æterno Dei consilio loqui, qui Evangelicam doctrinam et religionem nuncupant nuper exortam, et vix 30 annorum fidem. In quos competit illud Jesaiæ Prophetæ: *Væ his, qui dicunt, malum esse bonum, et bonum malum, qui ponunt tenebras lucem, et lucem tenebras, amarum dulce, et dulce amarum* (Isa. 5:20).

6. For God from all eternity foreordained to save the world by Christ, and this his predestination and eternal counsel has he opened to the world by the Gospel (2 Tim. 1:9–10). Whereby it is appears that the evangelical doctrine and religion was the most ancient of all that ever were or are; **7.** wherefore we say, that all they [the papists] err foully, and speak things unworthy of the eternal counsel of God, who term the evangelical doctrine and religion a newly concocted faith, scarce thirty years old: to whom that saying of Isaiah does very well agree—"Woe unto them that call evil good, and good evil; that put darkness for light, and light for darkness; that put bitter for sweet, and sweet for bitter" (Isa. 5:20).

The Thirty-nine Articles of Religion of the Church of England (1571)

The Latin text and the 1571 English edition are reproduced from Schaff, *The Creeds of Christendom*, 3:487–92, 497–501, 508–11.

The English text is reproduced from "The Articles of the Church of England," in Hall, *Harmony*, 503, 505, 507–8, 512–14, 517–18.

The Thirty-nine Articles are the main confession of Anglican communions worldwide. In 1563, they were written at the request of Queen Elizabeth I (1533–1603); an authoritative version in English was produced in 1571 from the Latin original. The Thirty-nine Articles are a revision of the Forty-two or Edwardian Articles composed by the Reformer Thomas Cranmer (1489–1556). The Thirty-nine Articles display a moderate Protestant viewpoint: while they show clear Lutheran influences (in particular from the Augsburg Confession), they present Reformed positions at key junctures. This confession has also to be understood in reaction to the Council of Trent. For Presbyterians, this confession is also important because the Westminster Assembly started to revise these articles before deciding to draft a new confession (the Westminster Confession of Faith).

Our selection starts with the Trinity and the incarnation (Articles 1–2). It continues with sections specifically related to Scripture: on its sufficiency, on the limits of the canon (Article 6), on the place of the Old Testament (Article 7), and on the three ecumenical creeds and their relation to the Word (Article 8). Then the articles on predestination and salvation are expressed from a scriptural perspective (Articles 17–18). The next articles deal with the church, its authority, and its relation to the Bible (Articles 20–21, 34). The article on the homilies (35) illumines a subsequent selection, which is a homily on Scripture (cf. chap. 21).

Bibliography: E. J. Bicknell. *A Theological Introduction to the Thirty-nine Articles of the Church of England.* 3d ed. Rev. H. J. Carpenter. New York: Longmans, 1955. Dennison. *Reformed Confessions* 2:753–68. Leith. *Creeds of the Churches.* Pp. 266–81. M. A. Noll. "Thirty-nine Articles, The (1563)." P. 1088 in *EDT*. Schaff. *The Creeds of Christendom* 1:592–654, 3:486–516. Philip Schaff and D. S. Schaff. "Thirty-nine Articles, The." *NSHERK* 11:417–18. Stephen S. Smalley. "Thirty-nine Articles." P. 969 in *NIDCC*.

EDITIO LATINA PRINCEPS, 1563 [1562]

Articuli, de quibus in Synodo Londinensi anno Domini, iuxta ecclesiæ Anglicanæ computationem, M.D.LXII. ad tollendam opinionum dissensionem, et firmandum in uera Religione consensum, inter Archiepiscopos Episcoposque utriusque Prouinciæ, nec non etiam uniuersum Clerum convenit.

ENGLISH EDITION, 1571

Articles whereupon it was agreed by the Archbishoppes and Bishoppes of both prouinces and the whole cleargie, in the Conuocation holden at London in the yere of our Lorde God. 1562. according to the computation of the Churche of Englande, for the auoiding of the diuersities of opinions, and for the stablishyng of consent touching true Religion.

MODERN ENGLISH VERSION

The Articles of the Church of England
Agreed upon by the Archbishops and Bishops of both Provinces, and the whole Clergy, in the Convocation holden at London, in the year 1562, for the avoiding of Diversities of Opinions, and for the establishing Consent touching true Religion.

I. De Fide in Sacrosanctam Trinitatem

Vnvs est viuus et uerus Deus æternus, incorporeus, impartibilis, impassibilis, immensæ potentiæ, sapientiæ ac bonitatis: creator et conseruator omnium tum uisibilium tum inuisibilium. Et in Vnitate huius diuinæ naturæ tres sunt Personæ, eiusdem essentiæ, potentiæ, ac æternitatis, Pater, Filius, et Spiritus sanctus.

I. *Of fayth in the holy Trinitie*

There is but one lyuyng and true God, euerlastyng, without body, partes, or passions, of infinite power, wysdome, and goodnesse, the maker and preseruer of al things both visible and inuisible. And in vnitie of this Godhead there be three persons, of one substaunce, power, and eternitie, the father, the sonne, and the holy ghost.

Article 1: *Of faith in the Holy Trinity*

There is but one living and true God, everlasting, without body, parts, or passions; of infinite power, wisdom, and goodness; the maker and preserver of all things, both visible and invisible. And in unity of this Godhead, there be three persons, of one substance, power, and eternity; the Father, the Son and the Holy Ghost.

II. Verbum Dei uerum hominem esse factum

Filius, qui est uerbum Patris ab æterno à Patre genitus uerus et æternus Deus, ac Patri consubstantialis, in utero Beatæ uirginis ex illius substantia naturam humanam assumpsit: ita ut duæ naturæ, diuina et humana integrè atque perfectè in unitate personæ, fuerint inseparabiliter coniunctæ: ex quibus est vnus CHRISTVS, verus Deus et verus Homo: qui uerè passus est, crucifixus, mortuus, et sepultus, ut Patrem nobis reconciliaret, essetque [hostia] non tantùm pro culpa originis, uerum etiam pro omnibus actualibus hominum peccatis.

II. *Of the worde or sonne of God which was made very man*

The Sonne, which is the worde of the Father, begotten from euerlastyng of the Father, the very and eternall GOD, of one substaunce with the Father, toke man's nature in the wombe of the blessed Virgin, of her substaunce: so that two whole and perfect natures, that is to say, the Godhead and manhood, were ioyned together in one person, neuer to be diuided, whereof is one Christe, very GOD and very man, who truely suffered, was crucified, dead, and buried, to reconcile his father to vs, and to be a sacrifice, not only for originall gylt, but also for *all[1]* actuall sinnes of men.

Article 2: *Of the Word, or Son of God, which was made very Man*

The Son, which is the Word of the Father,[2] begotten from everlasting of the Father, the very and eternal God, of one substance with the Father, took man's nature in the womb of the blessed Virgin, of her substance; so that two whole and perfect natures, that is to say, the Godhead and manhood, were joined together in one person, never to be divided; whereof is one Christ, very God, and very man: who truly suffered, was crucified, dead and buried, to reconcile his Father to us,[3] and to be a sacrifice, not only for original guilt, but also for actual sins of men.

VI. Divinæ Scripturæ doctrina sufficit ad salutem.

Scriptura sacra continet omnia quæ sunt ad salutem necessaria, ita ut quicquid in ea nec legitur, neque inde probari potest, non sit à quoquam exigendum, ut tanquam Articulus fidei credatur, aut ad necessitatem salutis requiri putetur.

VI. *Of the sufficiencie of the Holy Scriptures for saluation*

Holy Scripture conteyneth all things necessarie to saluation: so that whatsoeuer is not read therein, nor may be proued therby, is not to be required of anye man, that it shoulde be beleued as an article of the fayth, or be thought requisite [as] necessarie to saluation.

Article 6: *Of the Sufficiency of the Holy Scriptures for Salvation*

Holy Scripture containeth all things necessary to salvation: so that whatsoever is not read therein, nor may be proved thereby, is not to be required of any man, that it should be believed as an article of faith, or be thought requisite or necessary to salvation.

---

1. The omission of 'all' dates from the year 1630, and the revised text of the Westminster Assembly of Divines, 1647. It appears in the edition of 1628, and is restored in modern English editions. See Charles Hardwick, *History of the Articles of Religion*, rev. ed. (Cambridge, 1859), 279.
2. John 1:1, 14.
3. 2 Cor. 5:19.

Sacræ Scripturæ nomine eos Canonicos libros Veteris ut Novi testamenti intelligimus, de quorum autoritate in Ecclesia nunquam dubitatum est.

In the name of holy Scripture, we do vnderstande those Canonicall bookes of the olde and newe Testament, of whose aucthoritie was neuer any doubt in the Churche.

In the name of the holy Scripture we do understand those Canonical books of the Old and New Testament, of whose authority was never any doubt in the Church.

Catalogus librorum sacræ Canonicæ scripturæ Veteris Testamenti

Of the names and number of the Canonicall Bookes

OF THE NAMES AND NUMBER OF THE CANONICAL BOOKS:

Genesis	Genesis	Genesis
Exodus	Exodus	Exodus
Leuiticus	Leuiticus	Leviticus
Numeri	Numerie	Numbers
Deuteronom.	Deuteronomium	Deuteronomy
Iosue	Iosue	Joshua
Iudicum	Iudges	Judges
Ruth	Ruth	Ruth
2 Regum	The 1. booke of Samuel	The First Book of Samuel
Paralipom. 2	The 2. booke of Samuel	The Second Book of Samuel
2 Samuelis	The 1. booke of Kinges	The First Book of Kings
Esdræ 2	The 2. booke of Kinges	The Second Book of Kings
Hester	The 1. booke of Chroni.	The First Book of Chronicles
Iob	The 2. booke of Chroni.	The Second Book of Chronicles
Psalmi	The 1. booke of Esdras	The First Book of Esdras
Prouerbia	The 2. booke of Esdras	The Second Book of Esdras
Ecclesiastes	The booke of Hester	The Book of Esther
Cantica	The booke of Iob	The Book of Job
Prophetæ maiores	The Psalmes	The Psalms
Prophetæ minores	The Prouerbes	The Proverbs
	Ecclesia, or preacher	Ecclesiastes; or, the Preacher
	Cantica, or songes of Sa.	Cantica; or Songs of Solomon
	4. Prophetes the greater	Four Prophets the Greater
	12. Prophetes the lesse	Twelve Prophets the Less

Alios autem Libros (ut ait Hieronymus) legit quidem Ecclesia ad exempla uitæ et formandos mores, illos tamen ad dogmata confirmanda non adhibet: ut sunt

And the other bookes, (as Hierome sayth) the Churche doth reade for example of lyfe and instruction of manners: but yet doth it not applie them to establishe any doctrene. Such are these followyng.

And the other books (as Hierome saith) the Church doth read for example of life, and instruction of manners; but yet doth it not apply them to establish any doctrine: such are these following:

Tertius et quartus Esdræ
Sapientia
Iesus filius Syrach
Tobias
Iudith.
Libri Machabæorum 2

The 3. booke of Esdras
The 4. booke of Esdras
The booke of Tobias
The booke of Iudith
The rest of the booke of Hester
The booke of Wisdome
Iesus the sonne of Sirach
Baruch, the prophet
Song of the 3 Children
The storie of Susanna
Of Bel and the Dragon
The prayer of Manasses
The 1. booke of Machab.
The 2. booke of Machab.

The Third Book of Esdras
The Fourth Book of Esdras
The Book of Tobias
The Book of Judith
The rest of the Book of Esther
The Book of Wisdom
Jesus, the Son of Sirach
Baruch, the Prophet
The Song of the Three Children
The Story of Susanna
Of Bel and the Dragon
The Prayer of Manasses
The First Book of Maccabees
The Second Book of Maccabees

Noui Testamenti Libros omnes (ut uulgo recepti sunt) recipimus et habemus pro Canonicis.

All the bookes of the newe Testament, as they are commonly receaued, we do receaue and accompt them *for* Canonicall.

All the books of the New Testament, as they are commonly received, we do receive, and account them as Canonical.

VII. De Veteri Testamento

Testamentum vetus Nouo contrarium non est, quandoquidem tam in veteri quàm nouo, per Christum, qui vnicus est mediator Dei et hominum, Deus et Homo, æterna vita humano generi est proposita. Quare malè sentiunt, qui veteres tantùm in promissiones temporarias sperasse confingunt. Quanquam Lex à Deo data per Mosen, quoad Ceremonias et ritus, Christianos non astringat, neque ciuilia eius præcepta in aliqua Republica necessariò recipi debeant: nihilominus tamen ab obedientia mandatorum, quæ Moralia vocantur, nullus quantumius Christianus, est solutus.

VII. *Of the Olde Testament*

The olde Testament is not contrary to the newe, for both in the olde and newe Testament euerlastyng lyfe is offered to mankynde by Christe, who is the onlye mediatour betweene God and man. Wherefore they are not to be hearde whiche faigne that the olde fathers dyd looke only for transitorie promises. Although the lawe geuen from God by Moses, as touchyng ceremonies and rites, do not bynde Christian men, nor the ciuile preceptes thereof, ought of necessitie to be receaued in any common wealth: yet notwithstandyng, no Christian man whatsoeuer, is free from the obedience of the commaundementes, which are called morall.

Article 7: *Of the Old Testament*

The Old Testament is not contrary to the New; for both in the Old and New Testament, everlasting life is offered to mankind by Christ, who is the only Mediator between God and man, being both God and man.[4] Wherefore they are not to be heard, which feign that the old fathers did look only for transitory promises.

Although the law given from God by Moses, as touching ceremonies and rites, do not bind Christian men; nor the civil precepts thereof ought of necessity to be received in any commonwealth; yet, notwithstanding, no Christian man whatsoever is free from the obedience of the commandments which are called moral.[5]

VIII. Symbola tria

Symbola tria, Nicænum, Athanasij, et quod vulgo Apostolicum appellatur, omnino recipienda sunt et credenda. Nam firmissimis Scripturarum testimonijs probari possunt.

VIII. *Of the three Credes*

The *three Credes*, Nicene Crede, *Athanasian Crede*, and that whiche is commonlye called the Apostles' Crede, ought *throughlye* to be receaued and beleued: for they may be proued by moste certayne warrauntes of holye scripture.

Article 8: *Of the Three Creeds*

The Three Creeds, Nicene Creed, Athanasius's Creed, and that which is commonly called the Apostles' Creed, ought thoroughly to be received and believed: for they may be proved by most certain warrants of holy Scripture.[6]

4. John 8:56; Heb. 10:1; 11:6.
5. Rom. 8:1–2; Acts 15:1; 28:29.
6. Acts 4:29–31; 1 Thess. 2:13; 2 Cor. 2:17.

XVII. De Prædestinatione et Electione

Prædestinatio ad uitam, est æternum Dei propositum, quo ante iacta mundi fundamenta, suo consilio, nobis quidem occulto, constanter decreuit, eos quos in Christo elegit ex hominum genere, à maledicto et exitio liberare, atque ut uasa in honorem efficta, per Christum ad æternam salutem adducere: Vnde qui tam præclaro Dei beneficio sunt donati, illi spiritu eius opportuno tempore operante, secundum propositum eius uocantur: uocationi per gratiam parent: iustificantur gratis: adoptantur in filios; vnigeniti Iesu Christi imagini efficiuntur conformes: in bonis operibus sanctè ambulant: et demùm ex Dei misericordia pertingunt ad sempiternam fœlicitatem.

XVII. *Of predestination and election*

Predestination to lyfe, is the euerlastyng purpose of God, whereby (before the foundations of the world were layd) he hath constantly decreed by his councell secrete to vs, to deliuer from curse and damnation, those whom he hath chosen in Christe out of mankynd, and to bryng them by Christe to euerlastyng saluation, as vessels made to honour. Wherefore they which be indued with so excellent a benefite of God, be called accordyng to Gods purpose by his spirite workyng in due season: they through grace obey the callyng: they be iustified freely: they be made sonnes of God by adoption: they be made lyke the image of his onelye begotten sonne Jesus Christe: they walke religiously in good workes, and at length by Gods mercy, they attaine to euerlastyng felicitie.

Article 17: *Of Predestination and Election*

Predestination to life is the everlasting purpose of God, whereby (before the foundations of the world[7] were laid) he hath constantly decreed by his counsel, secret to us, to deliver from curse and damnation those whom he hath chosen in Christ out of mankind, and to bring them by Christ to everlasting salvation, as vessels made to honour.[8] Wherefore, they which be endued with so excellent a benefit of God, be called according to God's purpose by his Spirit working in due season: they through grace obey the calling: they be justified freely: they be made sons of God by adoption:[9] they be made like the image of his only-begotten Son, Jesus Christ: they walk religiously in good works: and at length, by God's mercy, they attain to everlasting felicity.[10]

7. Eph. 1:4.
8. Eph. 1:3–11; Matt. 25:34 [?]; Rom. 9:21–22.
9. Rom. 3:24; 8:15–17.
10. Rom. 8:28–30; Eph. 2:8–10.

Quemadmodum Prædestinationis et Electionis nostræ in Christo pia consideratio, dulcis, suauis et ineffabilis consolationis plena est verè pijs et his qui sentiunt in se uim spiritus CHRISTI, facta carnis et membra quæ adhuc sunt super terram mortificantem, animumque ad cælestia et superna rapientem, tum quia fidem nostram de æterna salute consequenda per Christum plurimum stabilit atque confirmat, tum quia amorem nostrum in Deum uehementer accendit; ita hominibus curiosis, carnalibus, et spiritu Christi destitutis, ob oculos perpetuò versari Prædestinationis Dei sententiam, pernitiosissimum, est præcipitium, unde illos Diabolus protrudit, uel in desperationem, uel in æquè pernitiosam impurissimæ vitæ securitatem.

As the godly consyderation of predestination, and our election in Christe, is full of sweete, pleasaunt, and vnspeakeable comfort to godly persons, and such as feele in themselues the working of the spirite of Christe, mortifying the workes of the fleshe, and their earthlye members, and drawing vp their mynde to hygh and heauenly thinges, as well because it doth greatly establyshe and confirme their fayth of eternal saluation to be enjoyed through Christe, as because it doth feruently kindle their loue towardes God. So, for curious and carnal persons, lacking the spirite of Christe, to haue continually before their eyes the sentence of Gods predestination, is a most daungerous downefall, whereby the deuyll doth thrust them either into desperation, or into rechelesnesse of most vncleane liuing, no lesse perilous then desperation.

As the godly consideration of predestination, and our election in Christ, is full of sweet, pleasant, and unspeakable comfort to godly persons, and such as feel in themselves the working of the Spirit of Christ, mortifying the works of the flesh, and their earthly members, and drawing up their mind to high and heavenly things, as well because it doth greatly establish and confirm their faith of eternal salvation to be enjoyed through Christ, as because it doth fervently kindle their love towards God: so, for curious and carnal persons, lacking the Spirit of Christ, to have continually before their eyes the sentence of God's predestination, is a most dangerous downfall, whereby the devil doth thrust them either into desperation, or into wretchlessness of most unclean living, no less perilous than desperation.

Deinde promissiones diuinas sic amplecti oportet, ut nobis in Sacris literis generaliter propositæ sunt: Et Dei voluntas in nostris actionibus ea sequenda est, quam in uerbo Dei habemus disertè reuelatam.

Furthermore,[11] we must receaue Gods promises in such wyse, as they be generally set foorth to vs in holy scripture: and in our doynges, that wyl of God is to be folowed, which we haue expreslye declared vnto vs in the worde of God.

Furthermore, we must receive God's promises in such wise as they be generally set forth to us in holy Scripture. And in our doings, that will of God is to be followed, which we have expressly declared unto us in the word of God.[12]

11. In the Forty-two Articles of 1553 there is the addition: "Although the decrees of predestination are unknown unto us."
12. John 3:16; 1 Tim. 2:3–4.

XVIII. Tantum in nomine Christi speranda est æterna salus

Svnt illi anathematizandi qui dicere audent, vnumquemque in Lege aut secta quam profitetur, esse seruandum: modo iuxta illam et lumen naturæ accurate vixerit: cùm sacræ literæ tantum Iesu Christi nomen prædicent, in quo saluos fieri homines oporteat.

XVIII. *Of obtaynyng eternall saluation, only by the name of Christe*

They also are to be had accursed, that presume to say, that euery man shal be saued by the lawe or sect which he professeth, so that he be diligent to frame his life accordyng to that lawe, and the light of nature. For holy scripture doth set out vnto vs onely the name of Jesus Christe, whereby men must be saved.

Article 18: *Of obtaining eternal Salvation only by the Name of Christ*

They also are to be had accursed, that presume to say, that every man shall be saved by the law or sect which he professeth, so that he be diligent to frame his life according to that law, and the light of nature. For holy Scripture doth set out unto us only the name of Jesus Christ, whereby men must be saved.[13]

XIX. De Ecclesia

Ecclesia Christi uisibilis est cœtus fidelium, in quo uerbum Dei purum prædicatur, et sacramenta, quoad ea quæ necessario exiguntur, iuxta Christi institutum rectè administrantur.

Sicut errauit ecclesia Hierosolymitana, Alexandrina et Antiochena: ita et errauit Ecclesia Romana, non solùm quoad agenda et ceremoniarum ritus, uerum in hijs etiam quæ credenda sunt.

XIX. *Of the Church*

The visible Church of Christe, is a congregation of faythfull men in the which the pure worde of God is preached, and the Sacramentes be duely ministred, accordyng to Christes ordinaunce in all those thynges that of necessitie are requisite to the same.

As the Church of Hierusalem, Alexandria, and Antioche haue erred: so also the Church of Rome hath erred, not only in their liuing and maner of ceremonies, but also in matters of faith.

Article 19: *Of the Church*[14]

The visible Church of Christ is a congregation of faithful men, in the which the pure word of God is preached, and the sacraments be duly ministered according to Christ's ordinance, in all those things that of necessity are requisite to the same.[15]

As the Church of Jerusalem,[16] Alexandria, and Antioch,[17] have erred, so also the Church of Rome hath erred, not only in their living and manner of ceremonies, but also in matters of faith.

---

13. Acts 4:12.
14. Cf. Judg. 20:2 [LXX]; Joel 2:16 [LXX]; Acts 7:38.
15. Matt. 28:19–20; 2 Tim. 4:2.
16. Acts 15; Gal. 2:1–10.
17. Gal. 2:11–21.

XX. De Ecclesiæ autoritate

Habet Ecclesia Ritus statuendi ius, et in fidei controuersijs autoritatem, quamuis Ecclesiæ non licet quicquam instituere, quod verbo Dei scripto aduersetur, nec unum scripturæ locum sic exponere potest, ut alteri contradicat. Quare licet Ecclesia sit diuinorum librorum testis et conseruatrix, attamen vt aduersus eos nihil decernere, ita præter illos nihil credendum de necessitate salutis debet obtrudere.

XX. *Of the aucthoritie of the Church*

The Church hath power to decree Rites or Ceremonies, and aucthoritie in controuersies of fayth: And yet it is not lawfull for the Church to ordayne any thyng that is contrarie to Gods worde written, neyther may it so expounde one place of scripture, that it be repugnaunt to another. Wherefore, although the Churche be a witnesse and a keper of holy writ: yet, as it ought not to decree any thing agaynst the same, so besides the same, ought it not to enforce any thing to be beleued for necessitie of saluation.

Article 20: *Of the Authority of the Church*

The Church hath power to decree rites or ceremonies, and authority in controversies of faith: and yet it is not lawful for the Church to ordain any thing that is contrary to God's word written, neither may it so expound one place of Scripture, that it be repugnant to another. Wherefore, although the Church be a witness and a keeper of holy writ, yet, as it ought not to decree any thing against the same, so besides the same ought it not to enforce any thing to be believed for necessity of salvation.[18]

XXI. De autoritate Conciliorum Generalium

Generalia Concilia sine iussu et uoluntate principum congregari non possunt, et vbi conuenerint, quia ex hominibus constant, qui non omnes spiritu et uerbis Dei reguntur, et errare possunt, et interdum errarunt, etiam in hijs quæ ad normam pietatis pertinent: ideo quæ ab illis constituuntur, ut ad salutem necessaria, neque robur habent, neque autoritatem, nisi ostendi possint è sacris literis esse desumpta.

XXI. *Of the aucthoritie of generall Counselles*

Generall Counsels may not be gathered together without the commaundement and wyll of princes. And when they be gathered together (forasmuche as they be an assemblie of men, whereof all be not gouerned with the spirite and word of God) they may erre, and sometyme haue erred, euen in thinges parteynyng vnto God. Wherfore, thinges ordayned by them as necessary to saluation, haue neyther strength nor aucthoritie, vnlesse it may be declared that they be taken out of holy Scripture.

Article 21: *Of the Authority of General Councils*

General Councils may not be gathered together without the commandment and will of princes. And when they be gathered together (forasmuch as they be an assembly of men, whereof all be not governed with the Spirit and word of God), they may err, and sometimes have erred, even in things pertaining unto God. Wherefore things ordained by them as necessary to salvation, have neither strength nor authority, unless it may be declared that they be taken out of holy Scripture.

---

18. Rom. 3:2.

XXXIII. [XXXIV.] Traditiones Ecclesiasticæ

Traditiones atque ceremonias easdem, non omnino necessarium est esse ubique aut prorsus consimiles. Nam et uariæ semper fuerunt, et mutari possunt, pro regionum, temporum, et morum diuersitate, modo nihil contra uerbum Dei instituatur.

Traditiones et ceremonias ecclesiasticas quæ cum uerbo Dei non pugnant, et sunt autoritate publica institutæ atque probatæ, quisquis priuato consilio uolens et data opera publicè uiolauerit, is, ut qui peccat in publicum ordinem ecclesiæ, quique lædit autoritatem Magistratus, et qui infirmorum fratrum conscientias uulnerat, publicè, ut cæteri timeant, arguendus est.

XXXIV. *Of the traditions of the Churche*

It is not necessarie that traditions and ceremonies be in al places one, or vtterly like, for at all times they haue ben diuerse, and may be chaunged accordyng to the diuersitie of countreys, times, and mens maners, so that nothing be ordeyned against Gods worde.

Whosoeuer through his priuate iudgement, wyllyngly and purposely doth openly breake the traditions and ceremonies of the Church, which be not repugnaunt to the worde of God, and be ordayned and approued by common aucthoritie, ought to be rebuked openly (that other may feare to do the lyke), as he that offendeth agaynst the Common order of the Churche and hurteth the aucthoritie of the Magistrate, and woundeth the consciences of the weake brethren.

Article 34: *Of the Traditions of the Church*

It is not necessary that traditions and ceremonies be in all places one, and utterly like; for at all times they have been diverse, and may be changed according to the diversity of countries, times, and men's manners, so that nothing be ordained against God's word.

Whosoever, through his private judgment, willingly and purposely doth openly break the traditions and ceremonies of the Church, which be not repugnant to the word of God, and be ordained and approved by common authority, ought to be rebuked openly (that others may fear to do the like), as he that offendeth against the common order of the Church, and hurteth the authority of the magistrate, and woundeth the consciences of weak brethren.

Quælibet ecclesia particularis, siue nationalis autoritatem habet instituendi, mutandi, aut abrogandi ceremonias aut ritus Ecclesiasticos, humana tantum autoritate institutos, modò omnia ædificationem fiant.

Euery particuler or nationall Churche, hath aucthoritie to ordaine, chaunge, and abolishe ceremonies or rites of the Churche ordeyned onlye by mans aucthoritie, so that all thinges be done to edifiyng.

Every particular or national Church hath authority to ordain, change, and abolish ceremonies or rites of the Church, ordained only by man's authority, so that all things be done to edifying.[19]

XXXIV. [XXXV.] Catalogus Homiliarum

XXXV. *Of Homilies*

Article 35: *Of the Homilies*

Tomus secundus Homiliarum, quarum singulos titulos huic Articulo subiunximus, continet piam et salutarem doctrinam, et hijs temporibus necessariam, non minus quàm prior Tomus Homiliarum quæ æditæ sunt tempore Edwardi sexti. Itaque eas in ecclesijs per ministros diligenter et clarè, ut à populo intelligi possint, recitandas, esse iudicamus.

The seconde booke of Homilies, the seuerall titles whereof we haue ioyned vnder this article, doth conteyne a godly and wholesome doctrine, and necessarie for these tymes, as doth the former booke of Homilies, which were set foorth in the time of Edwarde the sixt: and therefore we iudge them to be read in Churches by the Ministers diligently, and distinctly, that they may be vnderstanded by the people.

The second book of Homilies, the several titles whereof we have joined under this article, doth contain a godly and wholesome doctrine, and necessary for these times; as doth the former book of Homilies, which were set forth in the time of Edward the Sixth: and therefore we judge them to be read in churches by the ministers, diligently and distinctly, that they may be understood of the people.

19. Rom. 14:19; 1 Cor. 14:26.

[XXXIV.] *Catalogus Homiliarum*

De recto ecclesiæ usu.
Aduersus Idololatriæ pericula.
De reparandis ac purgandis ecclesijs.
De bonis operibus.
De ieiunio.
In gulæ atque ebrietatis uitia.
In nimis sumptuosos uestium apparatus.
De oratione siue precatione.
De loco et tempore orationi destinatis.
De publicis precibus ac Sacramentis, idiomate uulgari omnibusque noto, habendis.
De sacrosancta uerbi divini autoritate.
De eleemosina.
De Christi natiuitate.
De dominica passione.
De resurrectione Domini.
De digna corporis et sanguinis dominici in cœna Domini participatione.
De donis spiritus sancti.
In diebus, qui uulgo Rogationum dicti sunt, concio.
De matrimonij statu.
De otio seu socordia.
De pœnitentia.

Of the names of the Homilies

1 Of the right vse of the Churche.
2 Agaynst perill of Idolatrie.
3 Of repayring and keping cleane of Churches.
4 Of good workes, first of fastyng.
5 Agaynst gluttony and drunkennesse.
6 Agaynst excesse of apparell.
7 Of prayer.
8 Of the place and time of prayer.
9 That common prayer and Sacramentes ought to be ministred in a knowen tongue.
10 Of the reuerente estimation of Gods worde.
11 Of almes doing.
12 Of the Natiuitie of Christe.
13 Of the passion of Christe.
14 Of the resurrection of Christe.
15 Of the worthie receauing of the Sacrament of the body and blood of Christe.
16 Of the gyftes of the holy ghost.
17 For the Rogation dayes.
18 Of the state of Matrimonie.
19 Of repentaunce.
20 Agaynst Idlenesse.
21 Agaynst rebellion.

OF THE NAMES OF THE HOMILIES:

1. Of the right Use of the Church
2. Against Peril of Idolatry
3. Of repairing and keeping clean of Churches
4. Of Good Works: first, of Fasting
5. Against Gluttony and Drunkenness
6. Against Excess of Apparel
7. Of Prayer
8. Of the Place and Time of Prayer
9. That Common Prayers and Sacraments ought to be ministered in a known Tongue
10. Of the reverend Estimation of God's Word
11. Of Alms-doing
12. Of the Nativity of Christ
13. Of the Passion of Christ
14. Of the Resurrection of Christ
15. Of the worthy Receiving of the Sacrament of the Body and Blood of Christ
16. Of the Gifts of the Holy Ghost
17. For the Rogation Days
18. Of the State of Matrimony
19. Of Repentance
20. Against Idleness
21. Against Rebellion

The Second Scots Confession (1581)

The Latin text is reproduced from "Confessio Fidei Scoticanæ II," in Schaff, *The Creeds of Christendom*, 3:480–85.

The English text is reproduced from "The National Covenant; or, The Confession of Faith," in *The Westminster Confession of Faith* (Glasgow: Free Presbyterian Publications, 1646, 1958), 347–49; reprint of *The Confession of Faith; The Larger and Shorter Catechisms, With the Scripture Proofs at Large: Together with the Sum of Saving Knowledge* (London: T. Nelson & Sons, Paternoster Row, 1857).

The Second Scots Confession (1581), also called King's Confession and Negative Confession, was written by John Craig (1512–1600), about twenty years after the first. It was integrated in the famous document known as the National Covenant (1638). The Second Confession was written to counteract Roman Catholicism in Scotland.

After summarizing the First Confession, it opposes Catholic doctrines. This short confession is characterized by its commitment to the perfection and completeness of Scripture. The church's teaching is grounded in the written Word of God. The Second Confession rejects the authority of the pope and the accuracy of Roman Catholic theology on the ground of the Reformation principle of *sola Scriptura*. The text of the Second Confession as found in the National Covenant is reprinted from a Scottish edition of the Westminster Confession of Faith.

Bibliography: "Craig, John." *NSHERK* 3:293–94. J. D. Douglas. "National Covenant (1638)." P. 620 in *DSCH&T*. W. I. P. Hazlett. "King's Confession." P. 459 in *DSCH&T*. Schaff. *The Creeds of Christendom* 1:685–96, 3:437–85. R. W. Stewart and Thomas Lindsay. "Covenanters." *NSHERK* 3:289–91.

CONFESSIO FIDEI ECCLESIÆ SCOTICANÆ;

LATINE REDDITA

Nos universi et singuli subscribentes profitemur, postquam de religionis controversiis diu multumque apud nos deliberatum esset, cunctis ad lydium veritatis divinæ lapidem accuratius examinatis, in veritatis certa persuasione, per Dei Verbum et Spiritum Sanctum, animos nostros acquiescere: ideoque corde credimus, ore profitemur, consignatis chirographis testamur et constanter asserimus, Deo teste invocato, et universo genere humano in conscientiam appellato, hanc unicam esse fidem et religionem Christianam Deo acceptam, hominique salutarem, quæ nunc ex immensa Dei misericordia per evangelii prædicationem mundo patefacta, a multis ecclesiis gentibusque clarissimis, præsertim ab ecclesia Scoticana, rege nostro serenissimo tribusque regni hujus ordinibus, ut æterna Dei veritas et unicum salutis nostræ fundamentum recepta, credita et propugnata est; explicata etiam uberius, in Fidei confessione, plurimis comitiorum publicorum actis confirmata, regisque serenissimi et universorum hujus regni civium publica multorum jam annorum professione approbata. Cui nos Confessioni cultusque divini formulæ, ut veritati divinæ certissima sacrarum autoritate subnixæ, lubentissimis animis in singulis assentimur.

THE NATIONAL COVENANT;

OR, THE CONFESSION OF FAITH

We all and every one of us under-written, protest, That after long and due examination of our own consciences in matters of true and false religion, we are now thoroughly resolved in the truth by the word and Spirit of God: and therefore we believe with our hearts, confess with our mouths, subscribe with our hands, and constantly affirm, before God and the whole world, that this only is the true Christian faith and religion, pleasing God, and bringing salvation to man, which now is, by the mercy of God, revealed to the world by the preaching of the blessed evangel; and is received, believed, and defended by many and sundry notable kirks and realms, but chiefly by the kirk of Scotland, the King's Majesty, and three estates of this realm, as God's eternal truth, and only ground of our salvation; as more particularly is expressed in the Confession of our Faith, established and publickly confirmed by sundry acts of Parliaments, and now of a long time hath been openly professed by the King's Majesty, and whole body of this realm both in burgh and land. To the which Confession and Form of Religion we willingly agree in our consciences in all points, as unto God's undoubted truth and verity, grounded only upon his written word.

Omniaque ideo contraria de religione dogmata aversamur; præsertim vero papismum universum et singula ejus capita, quemadmodum hodie Dei verbo confutata et ab ecclesia Scoticana damnata sunt. Nominatim detestamur antichristi istius Romani in sacras scripturas, in ecclesias, in magistratum politicum, et in hominum conscientias sacrilege vendicatam autoritatem, nefarias omnes de rebus adiaphoris leges, libertati Christianæ derogantes: impium de sacrarum literarum, de legis, de officii Christi, de beati evangelii imperfectione dogma: perversam de peccato originis, de naturæ nostræ impotentia et in legem divinam contumacia, de justificatione per solam fidem: de imperfecta nostra sanctitate et obedientia legi præstanda; de natura, numero et usu sacramentorum doctrinam: quinque adulterina sacramenta; omnesque ritus, ceremonias falsasque traditiones genuinorum sacramentorum administrationi, citra autoritatem verbi divini, accumulatas: crudelem de infantibus ante baptismum morte præreptis sententiam: districtam et absolutam baptismi necessitatem: blasphemam de transsubstantiatione, et corporali præsentia Christi in cœnæ dominicæ elementis, cujus etiam impii fiant participes, atque orali ejusdem manducatione doctrinam: juramentorum perjuriorumque gratiam faciendi arrogatam potestatem: matrimonii in Verbo Dei interdictis permissionem: crudelitatem erga innocentes matrimonii nexu solutos: diabolicam missam: sacrilegum sacerdotium: abominandum pro vivorum mortuorumque peccatis sacrificium: hominum indigetationem seu canonizationem, angelorum mortuorumque invocationem; crucis, imaginum reliquiarumque venerationem; in creaturarum honorem dicata fana et altaria, dies sacratos, vota nuncupata: purgatorium; pro defunctis deprecationem:

And therefore we abhor and detest all contrary religion and doctrine; but chiefly all kind of Papistry in general and particular heads, even as they are now damned and confuted by the word of God and Kirk of Scotland. But, in special, we detest and refuse the usurped authority of that Roman Antichrist upon the scriptures of God, upon the kirk, the civil magistrate, and consciences of men; all his tyrannous laws made upon indifferent things against our Christian liberty; his erroneous doctrine against the sufficiency of the written word, the perfection of the law, the office of Christ, and his blessed evangel; his corrupted doctrine concerning original sin, our natural inability and rebellion to God's law, our justification by faith only, our imperfect sanctification and obedience to the law; the nature, number, and use of the holy sacraments: his five bastard sacraments; with all his rites, ceremonies, and false doctrine, added to the ministration of the true sacraments without the word of God: his cruel judgment against infants departing without the sacrament; his absolute necessity of baptism; his blasphemous opinion of transubstantiation, or real presence of Christ's body in the elements, and receiving of the same by the wicked, or bodies of men; his dispensations with solemn oaths, perjuries, and degrees of marriage forbidden in the word; his cruelty against the innocent divorced; his devilish mass; his blasphemous priesthood; his profane sacrifice for [the] sins of the dead and the quick; his canonization of men; calling upon angels or saints departed, worshipping of imagery, relicks, and crosses; dedicating of kirks, altars, days; vows to creatures; his purgatory, prayers for the dead; praying or speaking in a strange language, with his processions, and blasphemous litany, and multitude of advocates

ignotæ linguæ in precibus sacrisque usum, sacrilegas supplicationum pompas, blasphemam litaniam: mediatorum turbam, ordinum ecclesiasticorum multiplicem varietatem, auricularem confessionem: incertam et desperationis plenam pœnitentiam, generalem et ancipitem fidem: peccatorum per satisfactiones humanas expiatonem, justificationem ex operibus, opus operatum, operum supererogationem, merita, indulgentias, peregrinationes et stationes, aquam lustralem: campanarum baptizationem, exorcismos; bonas Dei creaturas cruce obsignandi, lustrandi, ungendi, conjurandi et consecrandi superstitionem: politicam ipsius monarchiam, impiam hierarchiam: tria vota solennia, variasque rasuræ sectas: impia et sanguinaria concilii Tridentini decreta, omnesque atrocissimæ istius in Christi ecclesiam conjurationis populares et fautores: denique inanes omnes adversamur allegorias, omnesque ritus et signa, traditiones omnes, præter aut contra autoritatem Verbi Dei ecclesiæ obtrusas, et doctrinæ hujus ecclesiæ veræ reformatæ repugnantes. Cur nos ecclesiæ reformatæ, in doctrinæ capitibus, fide, religione, disciplina, et usu sacramentorum, ut vita illius sub Christo capite membra, libentes nos aggregamus: sancte promittentes magnumque et termendum DOMINI DEI NOSTRI NOMEN jurantes, nos in ecclesiæ hujus doctrina et disciplina constanter perseveraturos, et pro cujusque vocatione ac viribus ad extremum spiritum defensuros; sub pœna omnium in lege maledictionum, æternique cum animæ tum corporis exitii periculo in tremendo illo Dei judicio.

or mediators; his manifold orders, auricular confession; his desperate and uncertain repentance; his general and doubtsome faith; his satisfaction of men for their sins; his justification by works, *opus operatum*, works of supererogation, merits, pardons, peregrinations, and stations; his holy water, baptizing of bells, conjuring of spirits, crossing, sayning, anointing, conjuring, hallowing of God's good creatures, with the superstitious opinion joined therewith; his worldly monarchy, and wicked hierarchy; his three solemn vows, with all his shavelings of sundry sorts; his erroneous and bloody decrees made at Trent, with all the subscribers or [or, and] approvers of that cruel and bloody band conjured against the kirk of God. And finally, we detest all his vain allegories, rites, signs, and traditions brought in the kirk, without or against the word of God, and doctrine of this true reformed kirk; to the which we join ourselves willingly, in doctrine, faith, religion, discipline, and use of the holy sacraments, as lively members of the same in Christ our head: promising and swearing, by the great name of the LORD our GOD, that we shall continue in the obedience of the doctrine and discipline of this Kirk,[1] and shall defend the same, according to our vocation and power, all the days of our lives; under the pains contained in the law, and danger both of body and soul in the day of God's fearful Judgment.

---

1. The Confession which was subscribed at Halyrud-house the 25th of February, 1587–88, by the King, Lennox, Huntly, the Chancellor, and about ninety-five other persons, hath here added, "Agreeing to the word." Sir John Maxwell of Pollock hath the original parchment.

Quumque sciamus non paucos, a Satana et antichristo Romano subornatos, promissionibus, subscriptionibus et juramentis se obstringere, et in usu sacramentorum cum ecclesia orthodoxa ad tempus subdole contra conscientiam communicare; versute constituentes, obtento interim religionis velo, in ecclesia verum Dei cultum adulterare et clanculum ac per cuniculos labefactare; tandem per occasionem apertis inimicitiis oppugnare, vana spe proposita veniæ dandæ a pontifice Romano, cujus rei potestatem contra veritatem divinam sibi arrogat, ipsi perniciosam, ejusque asseclis multo magis exitiosam: Nos igitur ut simulationis erga Deum ejusque ecclesiam et insinceri animi suspicionem omnem amoliamur, CORDIUM OMNIUM INSPECTOREM testamur, huic nostræ confessioni, promissioni, juramento et subscriptioni animos nostros usquequaque respondere: nulloque rerum terrestrium momento, sed indubia et certa notitia. ex amore veritatis divinæ per Spiritum Sanctum in cordibus nostris inscriptæ, ad eam nos inductos esse; ita DEUM propitium habeamus eo die quo cordium omnium arcana palam fient.

And seeing that many are stirred up by Satan, and that Roman Antichrist, to promise, swear, subscribe, and for a time use the holy sacraments in the kirk deceitfully, against their own conscience; minding hereby, first, under the external cloak of religion, to corrupt and subvert secretly God's true religion within the kirk; and afterward, when time may serve, to become open enemies and persecutors of the same, under vain hope of the Pope's dispensation, devised against the word of God, to his greater confusion, and their double condemnation in the day of the Lord Jesus: we therefore, willing to take away all suspicion of hypocrisy, and of such double dealing with God, and his kirk, protest, and call the Searcher of all hearts for witness, that our minds and hearts do fully agree with this our Confession, promise, oath, and subscription: so that we are not moved with any worldly respect, but are persuaded only in our conscience, through the knowledge and love of God's true religion imprinted in our hearts by the Holy Spirit, as we shall answer to him in the day when the secrets of all hearts shall be disclosed.

Cum vero nobis constet, per eximiam Dei gratiam huic regno præfectum esse regem nostrum serenissimum, ad ecclesiam in eo conservandam et justitiam nobis administrandam; cujus incolumitate et bono exemplo, secundum Deum, religionis et ecclesiæ tranquillitas et securitas nitatur: sancte, ex animo, eodem adacti sacramento, eademque pœna proposita pollicemur, et consignatis chirographis promittimus, sacratissimi regis nostri incolumitatem et autoritatem in beato Christi evangelio defendendo, in libertate patriæ asserenda, in justitia administranda, in improbis puniendis, adversus hostes quoscunque internos sive externos, quovis etiam bonorum et vitæ discrimine, nos constanter propugnaturos. Ita DEUM NOSTRUM OPTIMUM MAXIMUM potentem et propitium conservatorem habeamus in mortis articulo, et adventu DOMINI NOSTRI JESU CHRISTI, cui cum Patre et Spiritu Sancto, sit omnis honos et gloria in æternum. Amen.

And because we perceive, that the quietness and stability of our religion and kirk doth depend upon the safety and good behaviour of the King's Majesty, as upon a comfortable instrument of God's mercy granted to this country, for the maintaining of his kirk, and ministration of justice amongst us; we protest and promise [solemnly] with our hearts, under the same oath, hand-writ, and pains, that we shall defend his person and authority with our goods, bodies, and lives, in the defence of Christ, his evangel [or Christ's evangel], liberties of our country, ministration of justice, and punishment of iniquity, against all enemies within this realm or without, as we desire our God to be a strong and merciful defender to us in the day of our death, and coming of our Lord Jesus Christ; to whom, with the Father, and the Holy Spirit, be all honour and glory eternally. *Amen.*

The Irish Articles of Religion (1615)

"The Irish Articles of Religion. A.D. 1615," in Schaff, *The Creeds of Christendom*, 3:526–28.

The Irish Articles were chiefly written by James Ussher (1581–1656), professor of theology in Dublin and later archbishop of Armagh, and were adopted by the Irish Episcopalian Church in 1615. Though eclipsed in Ireland by the Thirty-nine Articles in 1635, the Irish Articles are important in the development of Calvinistic creeds. Indeed, they were composed four years before the Synod of Dort and were the most significant source behind the Westminster Confession of Faith.

In this confession, there are 104 articles divided into nineteen heads. The first head, reproduced here from Schaff's *Creeds of Christendom*, deals with Scripture and the creeds. Our faith is grounded in Scripture (Article 1); the boundaries of the canon are defined (Articles 2–3); the Scriptures are to be read by all and thus translated into common tongues (Article 4); though not equally clear in all its parts, Scripture clearly communicates salvation and contains all that is necessary for salvation (Articles 5–6). Finally, three of the Ecumenical Creeds (the Nicene Creed, the Athanasian Creed, and the Apostles' Creed) are accepted because they can be established on the basis of Scripture (Article 7). A comparison with the Westminster Confession of Faith shows its debt to the Irish Articles.

Bibliography: Crawford Gribben. *The Irish Puritans: James Ussher and the Reformation of the Church*. Auburn, MA: Evangelical Press, 2003. "Irish Articles." *NSHERK* 6:32. D. F. Kelly. "Irish Articles (1615)." Pp. 569–70 in *EDT*. Adam Loughridge. "Irish Articles (1615)." P. 517 in *NIDCC*. Schaff. *The Creeds of Christendom* 1:662–65, 3:526–44. "Ussher, James." *NSHERK* 12:114–15.

ARTICLES OF RELIGION

Agreed upon by the Archbishops and Bishops, and the rest of the Clergy of Ireland, in the Convocation holden at Dublin in the Year of our Lord God 1615, for the Avoiding of Diversities of Opinions, and the Establishing of Consent touching True Religion.

OF THE HOLY SCRIPTURE AND THE THREE CREEDS

1. The ground of our religion and the rule of faith and all saving truth is the Word of God, contained in the holy Scripture.

2. By the name of holy Scripture we understand all the Canonical Books of the Old and New Testament, viz.:

Of the Old Testament

The Five Books of Moses
Joshua
Judges
Ruth
The First and Second of Samuel
The First and Second of Kings
The First and Second of Chronicles
Ezra
Nehemiah
Esther
Job
Psalms
Proverbs
Ecclesiastes
The Song of Solomon
Isaiah
Jeremiah, his Prophecy and Lamentation
Ezekiel
Daniel
The Twelve lesser Prophets

Of the New Testament

The Gospels according to
Matthew,
Mark,
Luke,
John,
The Acts of the Apostles
The Epistle of Saint Paul to the Romans
II. Corinthians
Galatians
Ephesians
Philippians
Colossians
II. Thessalonians
II. Timothy
Titus
Philemon
Hebrews
The Epistle of Saint James
Saint Peter II
Saint John III
Saint Jude
The Revelation of Saint John

All which we acknowledge to be given by the inspiration of God, and in that regard to be of most certain credit and highest authority.

3. The other Books, commonly called *Apocryphal*, did not proceed from such inspiration, and therefore are not of sufficient authority to establish any point of doctrine; but the Church doth read them as Books containing many worthy things for example of life and instruction of manners.

Such are these following:

The Third Book of Esdras
The Fourth Book of Esdras
The Book of Tobias
The Book of Judith
Additions to the Book of Esther
The Book of Wisdom
The Book of Jesus, the Son of Sarah, called Ecclesiasticus
Baruch, with the Epistle of Jeremiah
The Song of the Three Children
Susanna
The Prayer of Manasses
The First Book of Maccabæus
The Second Book of Maccabæus

4. The Scriptures ought to be translated out of the original tongues into all languages for the common use of all men: neither is any person to be discouraged from reading the Bible in such a language as he doth understand, but seriously exhorted to read the same with great humility and reverence, as a special means to bring him to the true knowledge of God and of his own duty.

5. Although there be some hard things in the Scripture (especially such as have proper relation to the times in which they were first uttered, and prophecies of things which were afterwards to be fulfilled), yet all things necessary to be known unto everlasting salvation are clearly delivered therein; and nothing of that kind is spoken under dark mysteries in one place which is not in other places spoken more familiarly and plainly, to the capacity both of learned and unlearned.

6. The holy Scriptures contain all things necessary to salvation, and are able to instruct sufficiently in all points of faith that we are bound to believe, and all good duties that we are bound to practice.

7. All and every the Articles contained in the *Nicene Creed*, the *Creed of Athanasius*, and that which is commonly called the *Apostles' Creed*, ought firmly to be received and believed, for they may be proved by most certain warrant of holy Scripture.

16

The Canons of the Synod of Dort (1618–19)[1]

The Latin text is reproduced from "Canones Synodi Dordrechtanæ," in Schaff, *The Creeds of Christendom*, 3:550–52, 554–57, 561, 563–69, 571–77.

The English version is taken from "Synod of Dort," in Hall, *Harmony*, 541–43, 545–46, 547–49, 551, 552, 556–57, 559, 560, 564–66, 567–68, 569, 570–71.

The Synod of Dort (1618–19) was convened by the States General of the Netherlands; it included delegates from Holland and abroad. Thus it represents a consensus of the international Reformed community. The Canons of the Synod of Dort were written in response to the Five Arminian Articles (1610); consequently, the canons represent the Reformed perspective on only one aspect of theology. The canons must be read alongside the Belgic Confession and the Heidelberg Catechism. Together these three creeds constitute the Three Forms of Unity, still authoritative today for many Reformed churches.

The canons are divided into five heads of doctrine, divided into positive and negative articles. The sections correspond roughly to the five points of Calvinism, known under the acronym *TULIP*: section 1 deals with "total depravity" and "unconditional election"; section 2 explains "limited atonement"; sections 3 and 4 revisit "total depravity" and unfold "irresistible grace"; and section 5 exposits the "perseverance of the saints." The canons do not contain one distinct section on Scripture, but they demonstrate a high view of the Bible, especially as it speaks clearly about theological issues. The selection from the canons below shows that the divines at Dort, while respecting the mystery of God's secret ways, also held to the clarity of Scripture. Their perspective in this respect is important to remember in the midst of controversies and is not unlike Luther's and Calvin's approach. In addition, our selection contains articles on the role of the Word and preaching in the unfolding of the *ordo salutis* (order of salvation). The text reproduced here is from Hall's *Harmony*.

1. Ed. note: The Scripture references within the text are from early versions; the references added in footnotes are taken from later editions. The titles of the articles are not from the original, but are added from the version of the Canadian Reformed Church.

Bibliography: *The Articles of the Synod of Dort*. Trans. Thomas Scott. Introductory essay by Samuel Miller. Philadelphia: Presbyterian Board of Publications, 1841, 1856. Beeke & Ferguson. *Reformed Confessions*. Pp. xi–xii. Peter Y. De Jong, ed. *Crisis in the Reformed Churches: Essays in Commemoration of the Great Synod of Dort, 1618–1619*. Grand Rapids: Reformed Fellowship, 1968. William Robert Godfrey. "Calvin and Calvinism in the Netherlands." Pp. 106–11 in Reid, ed. *John Calvin: His Influence in the Western World*. Idem. "Reformed Thought on the Extent of the Atonement to 1618." *WTJ* 37, 2 (1975): 133–71. Idem. "Tensions within International Calvinism: The Debate on the Atonement at the Synod of Dort, 1618–1619." Ph.D. diss., Stanford University, 1974. I. J. Hesselink. "Dort, Canons Of." P. 83 in *DP&RTA*. Dirk Jellema. "Dort, Synod Of." Pp. 309–10 in *NIDCC*. M. E. Osterhaven. "Dort, Synod Of." Pp. 331–32 in *EDT*. H. C. Rogge. "Dort, Synod Of." *NSHERK* 3:494–95. Schaff. *The Creeds of Christendom* 1:508–23, 3:550–97. Stephen Strehle. "The Extent of the Atonement and the Synod of Dort." *WTJ* 51, 1 (Spring 1989): 1–23.

JUDICIUM

SYNODI NATIONALIS REFORMATARUM ECCLESIARUM BELGICARUM, *Habitæ Dordrechti Anno MDCXVIII. et MDCXIX. Cui plurimi insignes Theologi Reformatarum Ecclesiarum Magnæ Britanniæ, Germaniæ, Galliæ, interfuerunt, de Quinque Doctrinæ Capitibus in Ecclesiis Belgicis Controversis: promulgatum VI. Maii MDCXIX.*

PRÆFATIO

IN NOMINE DOMINI ET SERVATORIS NOSTRI JESU CHRISTI. AMEN.

Inter plurima, quæ Dominus et Servator noster Jesus Christus militanti suæ Ecclesiæ in hac ærumnosa peregrinatione dedit solatia, merito celebratur illud, quod ei ad Patrem suum in cœleste sanctuarium abiturus reliquit: Ego, *inquiens*, sum vobiscum omnibus diebus usque ad consummationem sæculi. *Hujus suavissimæ promissionis veritas elucet in omnium temporum Ecclesia, quæ quum non solum aperta inimicorum violentia, et hæreticorum impietate, sed etiam operta seductorum astutia inde ab initio fuerit oppugnata, sane, si unquam salutari promissæ suæ præsentiæ præsidio eam destituisset Dominus, pridem aut vi tyrannorum fuisset oppressa, aut fraude impostorum in exitium seducta.*

THE JUDGMENT

Of the National Synod of the Reformed Belgic Churches, assembled at Dort, ann. 1618 and 1619 (in which Synod were admitted many Divines of note, being of the Reformed Churches of Great Britain, of the County of Palatine of Rhene, of Hassia, of Helvetia, of the Correspondence of Waterau, of Geneva, of Breme, and of Embden), concerning the Five Articles controverted in the Belgic Churches.

THE PREFACE

In the name of our Lord and Saviour Jesus Christ. Amen.

Amongst the manifold comforts, which our Lord and Saviour Jesus Christ hath imparted to his Church militant in this troublesome pilgrimage, that is deservedly extolled, which he left unto her at his departure to his Father into the heavenly sanctuary, saying, "I am with you always unto the end of the world" (Matt. 28:20). The truth of this comfortable promise is manifested from time to time in all ages of the Church: which having from the beginning been oppugned, not only by the open violence of enemies, and impiety of heretics, but further by the under-hand cunning of seducers; certainly, if at any time the Lord should have left her destitute of the guard of his saving presence, she had now long since been either oppressed by the power of tyrants, or, to her utter overthrow, seduced by the fraud of impostors.

Sed bonus ille Pastor, qui gregem suum, pro quo animam suam posuit, constantissime diligit, persecutorum rabiem tempestive semper, et exserta sæpe dextera, miraculose repressit, et seductorum vias tortuosas, ac consilia fraudulenta detexit atque dissipavit, utroque se in Ecclesia sua præsentissimum esse demonstrans. Hujus rei illustre documentum exstat in historiis piorum imperatorum, regum, et principum, quos Filius Dei in subsidium Ecclesiæ suæ toties excitavit, sancto domus suæ zelo accendit, eorumque opera, non tantum tyrannorum furores compescuit, sed etiam Ecclesiæ cum falsis doctoribus religionem varie adulterantibus conflictanti, sanctarum synodorum remedia procuravit, in quibus fideles Christi servi conjunctis precibus, consiliis, et laboribus pro Ecclesia et veritate Dei fortiter steterunt, Satanæ ministris, licet in angelos lucis se transformantibus, intrepide se opposuerunt, errorum et discordiæ semina sustulerunt, Ecclesiam in religionis puræ concordia conservarunt, et sincerum Dei cultum ad posteritatem illibatum transmiserunt.

But that good Shepherd, who loves his flock to the end, for whom he hath laid down his life,[2] hath always opportunely, and many times miraculously, with an outstretched arm, repressed the rage of persecutors, and discovered the winding by-paths of seducers, and scattered their fraudulent purposes; by each of which he hath evidently shewed himself to be present in his Church. Fair evidence hereof is given in the histories concerning godly emperors, kings, and princes, whom the Son of God hath so often raised up for the safeguard of his Church, and inflamed with a holy zeal of his house; and by their means hath not only curbed the fury of tyrants, but also, in his Church's behalf, when it grappled with false teachers diversely corrupting religion, hath procured the remedy of sacred Synods: wherein the faithful servants of Christ have jointly with their prayers, counsels, and labours, courageously stood for God's Church and his truth, fearlessly opposed the instruments of Satan, howsoever changing themselves into angels of light, rooted up the weeds of errors and dissension, preserved the Church in agreement of the pure religion, and left unto posterity the sincere worship of God uncorrupted.

2. Cf. John 10:11.

196

Simili beneficio fidelis noster Servator Ecclesiæ Belgicæ, annos aliquam multos afflictissimæ, gratiosam suam præsentiam hoc tempore testatus est. Hanc enim Ecclesiam a Romani antichristi tyrannide et horribili papatus idololatria potenti Dei manu vindicatam, in belli diuturni periculis toties miraculose custoditam, et in veræ doctrinæ atque disciplinæ concordia ad Dei sui laudem, admirabile reipub. incrementum, totiusque reformati orbis gaudium efflorescentem, JACOBUS ARMINIUS *ejusque sectatores, nomen Remonstrantium præ se ferentes, variis, tam veteribus, quam novis erroribus, primum tecte, deinde aperte tentarunt, et scandalosis dissensionibus ac schismatibus pertinaciter turbatam, in tantum discrimen adduxerunt, ut florentissimæ Ecclesiæ, nisi Servatoris nostri miseratio opportune intervenisset, horribili dissidiorum et schismatum incendio tandem conflagrassent. Benedictus autem sit in sæcula Dominus, qui postquam ad momentum faciem suam a nobis (qui multis modis iram et indignationem ejus provocaveramus) abscondisset, universo orbi testatum fecit, se fœderis sui non oblivisci, et suspiria suorum non spernere.*

With like favour our faithful Saviour hath given a testimony of his gracious presence at this time to the long distressed Church of the Low Countries. For this Church, being by God's mighty hand set free from the tyranny of the Romish antichrist, and from the fearful idolatry of Popery, so often wonderfully preserved amidst the dangers of a long-continuing war, and flourishing in the concord of true doctrine and discipline, to the praise of her God, the admirable increase of the weal-public, and the joy of all other Reformed Churches; hath first covertly, afterwards openly, with manifold both old and new errors been assaulted by one James Harmans, alias Arminius, and his followers, assuming the title of Remonstrants, and brought into so great hazard through the ceaseless turmoils of scandalous dissentions and schisms, that, had not our Saviour's merciful hand in time been interposed, these flourishing Churches had been utterly consumed with the horrible flames of discord and schism. But blessed for ever be the Lord, who, after he had for awhile hidden his countenance from us (who had many ways provoked his wrath and indignation), hath witnessed to the whole world that he is not forgetful of his covenant, and despiseth not the sighs of his people.[3]

---

3. Cf. Ex. 2:14.

Cum enim vix ulla remedii spes humani-
tus appareret, illustrissimis et præ-
potentibus Belgii fœderati ordinibus
generalibus hanc mentem inspiravit,
ut consilio et directione illustrissimi et
fortissimi principis Arausicani legiti-
mis mediis, quæ ipsorum apostolorum,
et quæ eos secutæ Ecclesiæ Christianæ
exemplis longo temporum decursu sunt
comprobata, et magno cum fructu in
Ecclesia etiam Belgica antehac usur-
pata, sævientibus hisce malis obviam
ire decreverint, synodumque ex omnibus,
quibus præsunt, provinciis, authoritate
sua, Dordrechtum convocarint, expetitis
ad eam et favore serenissimi ac potentis-
simi Magnæ Britanniæ regis JACOBI, et
illustrissimorum principum, comitum,
et rerumpublicarum, impetratis plurimis gravissimis theologis, ut communi
tot Reformatæ Ecclesiæ theologorum
judicio, ista ARMINII ejusque sectatorum
dogmata accurate, et ex solo Dei verbo,
dijudicarentur, vera doctrina stabiliretur,
et falsa rejiceretur, Ecclesiisque Belgicis
concordia, pax et tranquillitas, divina
benedictione, restitueretur. Hoc est illud
Dei beneficium, in quo exultant Ecclesiæ
Belgicæ, et fidelis Servatoris sui miserationes humiliter agnoscunt, ac grate
prædicant.

For when in man's understanding, scarce
any hope of remedy appeared, God did
put into the minds of the most illustrious and mighty the States General of the
United Provinces, by the counsel and
direction of the most renowned and valiant Prince of Orange, to determine to
meet these outrageous mischiefs by such
lawful means as have been long time
approved by the example of the apostles
themselves,[4] and of the Christian Church
following them; and also heretofore with
great benefit used even in the Belgic
Church itself: and by their authority
to call together a Synod out of all the
Provinces subject to their government,
to be assembled at Dort: many most
grave divines being intreated thereto,
and obtained by the favour of the most
high James, King of Great Britain, and
of most illustrious and potent Princes,
Landgraves, and Commonwealths;
that by common judgment of so many
divines of the reformed Churches, those
opinions of Arminius and his followers
might be accurately examined and determined by the rule of God's word only,
the true doctrine established, and the
false rejected, and concord, peace, and
tranquility (by God's blessing) restored
to the Church of the Low Countries. This
is that good gift of God, wherein the Belgic Churches triumph, and both humbly confess, and thankfully profess, the
never-failing mercies of their Saviour.

4. Cf. Acts 15:1–35.

Hæc igitur veneranda Synodus (prævia per summi magistratus authoritatem in omnibus Belgicis Ecclesiis, ad iræ Dei deprecationem et gratiosi auxilii implorationem, precum et jejunii indictione et celebratione) in nomine Domini Dordrechti congregata, divini Numinis et salutis Ecclesiæ accensa amore, et post invocatum Dei nomen, sancto juramento obstricta, se solam Scripturam sacram pro judicii norma habituram, et in caussæ hujus cognitione et judicio, bona integraque conscientia versaturam esse, hoc egit sedulo magnaque patientia, ut præcipuos horum dogmatum patronos, coram se citatos, induceret ad sententiam suam de Quinque notis doctrinæ Capitibus, sententiæque rationes, plenius exponendas. Sed cum Synodi judicium repudiarent, atque ad interrogatoria, eo, quo æquum erat, modo respondere detrectarent, neque Synodi monitiones, nec generosorum atque amplissimorum ordinum generalium Delegatorum mandata, imo ne ipsorum quidem illustrissimorum et præpotentum DD. ordinum generalium imperia, quicquam apud illos proficerent, aliam viam eorundem Dominorum jussu, et ex consuetudine jam olim in synodis antiquis recepta, ingredi coacta fuit; atque ex scriptis, confessionibus, ac declarationibus, partim antea editis, partim etiam huic Synodo exhibitis, examen illorum quinque dogmatum institutum est.

Wherefore (a fast and public prayers being formerly enjoined and performed in all the Belgic Churches by the authority of the chief magistrate, for the deprecations of God's anger, and imploring his gracious aid) this venerable Synod, assembled together at Dort in the name of the Lord, inflamed with the love of God's honour, and of the salvation of his Church; and upon the invocation of God's holy name bound by oath, that they would hold the sacred scripture as the only rule of their verdict, and demean themselves in the hearing and determining of this cause with a good and upright conscience; hath diligently and with great patience laboured herein, to persuade the chief patrons of these assertions, cited to appear before them, more largely to unfold their opinion concerning the five notorious controverted Articles, as also the reasons of such their opinion. But they rejecting the judgment of the Synod, and refusing to answer the interrogatories in such manner as was fitting (whenas neither the admonitions of the Synod, nor instance of the generous and worthy deputies of the States General, nay, nor the commands of the most illustrious and mighty lords, the States General themselves, could prevail any thing at all with them); the Synod, by the commandment of the said lords, the State General, was fain to take another course, heretofore used and received in ancient Synods. And so the search of their tenets concerning the five Articles was undertaken out of their own books, confessions, and declarations, partly heretofore set forth, partly now exhibited to this Synod.

Quod cum jam per singularem Dei gratiam, maxima diligentia, fide, ac conscientia, omnium et singulorum consensu absolutum sit, Synodus hæc ad Dei gloriam, et ut veritatis salutaris integritati, conscientiarum tranquillitati, et paci ac saluti Ecclesiæ Belgicæ consulatur, sequens judicium, quo et vera verboque Dei consentanea de prædictis Quinque Doctrinæ Capitibus sententia exponitur, et falsa verboque Dei dissentanea rejicitur, statuit promulgandum.

With search and examination being now by God's singular mercy dispatched and finished with all diligence, conscience, and faithfulness, and with the joint consent of all and every one; this Synod, for the advancement of God's glory, for the upholding of that truth which leadeth to salvation, and for the maintenance of peace and tranquility, as well in men's consciences, as in the Belgic Churches, determineth to publish this their judgment; wherein the true doctrine agreeable with God's word, touching the five aforesaid heads of doctrine is declared, and the false and disagreeing with God's word is rejected: as followeth.

Sententia, de Divina Prædestinatione, et Annexis ei Capitibus,
Quam Synodus Dordrechtana Verbo Dei consentaneam, atque in Ecclesiis Reformatis hactenus receptam esse, judicat, quibusdam Articulis exposita.

The Doctrine of Predestination, and the Points Thereto Annexed,
Which the Synod of Dort judgeth to be agreeable to God's word, and hitherto to have been received in the Reformed Churches, Laid open in certain Articles.[5]

PRIMUM DOCTRINÆ CAPUT,
DE DIVINA PRÆDESTINATIONE

THE FIRST CHAPTER OR HEAD OF DOCTRINE, NAMELY CONCERNING GOD'S PREDESTINATION

III

Ut autem homines ad fidem adducantur, Deus clementer lætissimi hujus nuntii præcones mittit, ad quos vult, et quando vult, quorum ministerio homines ad resipiscentiam et fidem in Christum crucifixum vocantur. *Quomodo enim credent in eum, de quo non audierint? quomodo autem audient absque prædicante? quomodo prædicabunt, nisi fuerint missi?* Rom. 10:14–15.

Article 3: *The Preaching of the Gospel*

And, that men may be brought unto faith, God in mercy sends the preachers of this most joyful message, to whom he will, and when he will;[6] by whose ministry, men are called unto repentance, and faith in Christ crucified.[7] *How shall they believe in him, of whom they have not heard? and how shall they hear without a preacher? and how shall they preach, except they be sent?* (Rom. 10:14–15).

---

5. Ed. note: The above title is taken slightly modernized from *The Judgement of the Synode Holden at Dort* (London: Iohn Bill, 1619), 1; reprinted in Amsterdam by Theatrum Orbis Terrarum in 1974.
6. Isa. 52:7.
7. 1 Cor. 1:23–24.

VI

Quod autem aliqui in tempore fide a Deo donantur, aliqui non donantur, id ab æterno ipsius decreto provenit; *Omnia enim opera sua novit ab æterno:* Actor. 15:18; Ephes. 1:11; secundum quod decretum electorum corda, quantumvis dura, gratiose emollit, et ad credendum inflectit, non electos autem justo judicio suæ malitiæ et duritiæ relinquit.

Atque hic potissimum sese nobis aperit profunda, misericors pariter et justa hominum æqualiter perditorum discretio; sive decretum illud *electionis* et *reprobationis* in verbo Dei revelatum. Quod ut perversi, impuri, et parum stabiles in suum detorquent exitium, ita sanctis et religiosis animabus ineffabile præstat solatium.

XII

De hac æterna et immutabili sui ad salutem electione, electi suo tempore, variis licet gradibus et dispari mensura, certiores redduntur, non quidem arcana et profunditates Dei curiose scrutando; sed fructus electionis infallibiles, in verbo Dei designatos, nt sunt vera in Christum fides, filialis Dei timor, dolor de peccatis secundum Deum, esuries et sitis justitiæ, etc., in sese cum spirituali gaudio et sancta voluptate observando.

Article 6: *God's Eternal Decree*

But whereas, in process of time, God bestoweth faith on some, and not on others, this proceeds from his eternal decree.[8] *For from the beginning of the world God knoweth all his works* (Acts 15:18; Eph. 1:11). According to which decree, he graciously softens the hearts of the elect, however otherwise hard; and as for those who are not elect, he in just judgment leaveth them to their malice and hardness.[9]

And here especially is discovered unto us the deep, and both merciful and just, difference put between men, equally lost; that is to say, the decree of election and reprobation, revealed in God's word. Which as perverse, impure, and wavering men do wrest unto their own destruction,[10] so it affords unspeakable comfort to godly and religious souls.

Article 12: *The Assurance of Election*

Of this their eternal and immutable election unto salvation, the elect, in their time, although by several degrees, and in different measure, are assured; and that, not by searching curiously into the depths and secrets of God,[11] but by observing in themselves,[12] with spiritual joy and holy pleasure, the infallible fruits of election, marked out unto us in God's word; such as are, a true faith in Christ, a filial fear of God, grief for our sins according to God,[13] hungering and thirsting after righteousness, etc.[14]

---

8. Acts 13:48.
9. 1 Peter 2:8.
10. Cf. 2 Peter 3:16.
11. Deut. 29:29; 2 Peter 1:10 [?]; 1 Cor. 2:10–11.
12. 2 Cor. 13:5.
13. 2 Cor. 7:10.
14. Matt. 5:6.

XIV

Ut autem hæc de divina electione doctrina sapientissimo Dei consilio per prophetas, Christum ipsum, atque Apostolos, sub Veteri æque atque sub Novo Testamento, est prædicata, et sacrarum deinde literarum monumentis commendata: ita et hodie in Ecclesia Dei, cui ea peculiariter est destinata, cum spiritu discretionis, religiose et sancte, suo loco et tempore, missa omni curiosa viarum altissimi scrutatione, est proponenda, idque ad sanctissimi nominis divini gloriam, et vividum populi ipsius solatium.

Article 14: *How Election Is to Be Taught*

And as this doctrine touching God's election was by God's appointment declared by the prophets, Christ himself, and the apostles, as well under the Old Testament as the New, and afterwards commended to the records of holy writ; so at this day in God's Church[15] (for which it is peculiarly ordained) it is be propounded with the spirit of discretion, religiously and holily, in its place and time, without any curious searching into the ways of the Most High, and that to the glory of God's most holy name, and lively comfort of his people.[16]

XV

Cæterum æternam et gratuitam hanc electionis nostri gratiam eo vel maxime illustrat, nobisque commendat Scriptura Sacra, qnod porro testatur non omnes homines esse electos, sed quosdam non electos, sive in æterna Dei electione præteritos, quos scilicet Deus ex liberrimo, justissimo, irreprehensibili, et immutabili beneplacito decrevit in communi miseria, in quam se sua culpa præcipitarunt, relinquere, nec salvifica fide et conversionis gratia donare, sed in viis suis, et sub justo judicio relictos, tandem non tantum propter infidelitatem, sed etiam cætera omnia peccata, ad declarationem justitiæ suæ damnare, et æternum punire. Atque hoc est decretum *reprobationis*, quod Deum neutiquam peccati authorem (quod cogitatu blasphemum est) sed tremendum, irreprehensibilem, et justum judicem ac vindicem constituit.

Article 15: *Reprobation Described*

Moreover, the holy scripture herein chiefly manifests and commends unto us this eternal and free grace of our election, in that it further witnesseth, that not all men are elected, but some not elected, or passed over in God's eternal election:[17] whom doubtless God in his most free, most just, unreproachable and unchangeable good pleasure hath decreed to leave in the common misery (whereinto by their own default they precipitated themselves[18]), and not to bestow saving faith and the grace of conversion upon them; but, leaving them in their own ways, and under just judgment,[19] at last to condemn and everlastingly punish them, not only for their unbelief, but also for their other sins, to the manifestation of his justice. And this is the decree of reprobation, which in no wise makes God the author of sin (a thing blasphemous once to conceive), but a fearful, unreproveable, and just judge and revenger.

15. Acts 20:27; Job 36:23–26.
16. Rom. 11:33–34; 12:3; 1 Cor. 4:6; Heb. 6:17–18.
17. Rom. 9:22.
18. 1 Peter 2:8.
19. Acts 14:16.

XVII

Quandoquidem de voluntate Dei ex verbo ipsius nobis est judicandum, quod testatur liberos fidelium esse sanctos, non quidem natura, sed beneficio fœderis gratuiti, in quo illi cum parentibus comprehenduntur, pii parentes de electione et salute suorum liberorum, quos Deus in infantia ex hac vita evocat, dubitare non debent.

Article 17: *Children of Believers Who Die in Infancy*

Seeing we must judge of God's will by his word, which testifies unto us that the children of the faithful are holy, not in their own nature, but by the benefit of the gracious covenant, wherein they together with their parents are comprised; godly parents ought not to doubt the election and salvation of their children, whom God calls out of this life in their infancy.[20]

REJECTIO ERRORUM,
Quibus Ecclesiæ Belgicæ sunt aliquamdiu perturbatæ.

A REJECTION OF THE ERRORS WHEREWITH THE CHURCHES OF THE LOW COUNTRIES HAVE NOW A LONG TIME BEEN TROUBLED

Exposita doctrina Orthodoxa de Electione et Reprobatione, Synodus rejicit Errores eorum:

The Synod, having delivered the orthodox doctrine concerning Election and Reprobation, rejecteth the errors of those:

I: Qui docent, "Voluntatem Dei de servandis credituris, et in fide fideique obedientia perseveraturis, esse totum et integrum electionis ad salutem decretum; nec quicquam aliud de hoc decreto in verbo Dei esse revelatum." Hi enim simplicioribus imponunt, et Scripturæ sacræ manifeste contradicunt, testanti Deum non tantum servare velle credituros, sed etiam certos quosdam homines ab æterno elegisse, quos præ aliis in tempore fide in Christum et perseverantia donaret; sicut scriptum est, *Manifestum feci nomen tuum hominibus, quos dedisti mihi.* Johan. 17:6. Item, *Crediderunt quotquot ordinati erant ad vitam æternam.* Act. 13:48. Et, *Elegit nos ante jacta mundi fundamenta, ut essemus sancti,* etc. Ephes. 1:4.

Paragraph 1: Who teach, *That the will of God to save such as shall believe, and persevere in faith, and the obedience of faith, is the whole and entire decree of election unto salvation; and that nothing else concerning this decree is revealed in the word of God.* For these teachers deceive the simpler sort, and plainly gainsay the holy scripture, which witnesseth that God not only will save such as shall believe, but also from eternity hath chosen some certain men, upon whom, rather than others, he would bestow faith in Christ, and perseverance: as it is written, *I have declared thy name unto the men which thou gavest me* (John 17:6). In like manner, *As many as were ordained unto eternal life, believed* (Acts 13:48). And, *He hath chosen us before the foundation of the world, that we should be holy, etc.* (Eph. 1:4).

---

20. Gen. 17:7; Isa. 59:21; Acts 2:39; 1 Cor. 7:14.

V: Qui docent, "Electionem singularium personarum ad salutem, incompletam et non peremptoriam, factam esse ex prævisa fide, resipiscentia, sanctitate et pietate inchoata, aut aliquamdiu continuata: completam vero et peremptoriam ex prævisæ fidei, resipiscentiæ, sanctitatis, et pietatis finali perseverantia: et hanc esse gratiosam et evangelicam dignitatem, propter quam qui eligitur dignior sit illo qui non eligitur: ac proinde fidem, fidei obedientiam, sanctitatem, pietatem, et perseverantiam non esse fructus sive effectus electionis immutabilis ad gloriam, sed conditiones, et caussas sine quibus non, in eligendis complete prærequisitas, et prævisas, tanquam præstitas." Id quod toti Scripturæ repugnat, quæ hæc et alia dicta passim auribus et cordibus nostris ingerit: *Electio non est ex operibus, sed ex vocante.* Rom. 9:11. *Credebant quotquot ordinati erant ad vitam æternam.* Act. 13:48. *Elegit nos in semetipso ut sancti essemus.* Ephes. 1:4. *Non vos me elegistis, sed ego elegi vos.* Johan. 15:16. *Si ex gratia, non ex operibus.* Rom. 11:6. *In hoc est charitas, non quod nos dilexerimus Deum, sed quod ipse dilexit nos, et misit Filium suum.* 1 Johan. 4:10.

Paragraph 5: Who teach, *That the incomplete and not peremptory election of singular persons is made by reason of foreseen faith, repentance, sanctity, and godliness begun, and continued for some time; but the complete and peremptory election by reason of the final perseverance of foreseen faith, repentance, sanctity, and godliness: and that this is the gracious, and evangelical worthiness, by which he that is chosen becomes worthier than he that is not chosen: and therefore that faith, the obedience of faith, sanctity, godliness, and perseverance are not the fruits or effects of unchangeable election unto glory, but conditions and causes,* sine quibus non *(that is to say, without which a thing is not brought to pass) before required, and foreseen, as already performed by those who are completely to be chosen.* A thing repugnant to the whole scripture, which everywhere beats into our ears and hearts these and such like sayings: *Election is not of works, but of him that calleth* (Rom. 9:11). *As many as were ordained unto life eternal, believed* (Acts 13:48). *He hath chosen us that we should be holy* (Eph. 1:4). *Ye have not chosen me, but I have chosen you* (John 15:16). *If of grace, not of works* (Rom. 11:6). *Herein is love, not that we loved God, but that he loved us, and sent his Son*, etc. (1 John 4:10).

Secundum Doctrinæ Caput, de Morte Christi, et Hominum per eam Redemptione.

V

Cæterum promissio Evangelii est, ut quisquis credit in Christum crucifixum, non pereat, sed habeat vitam æternam. Quæ promissio omnibus populis et hominibus, ad quos Deus pro suo beneplacito mittit Evangelium, promiscue et indiscriminatim annunciari et proponi debet cum resipiscentiæ et fidei mandato.

Rejectio Errorum

Exposita doctrina orthodoxa, rejicit Synodus errores eorum:

I: Qui docent, "Quod Deus Pater Filium suum in mortem crucis destinaverit, sine certo ac definito consilio quemquam nominatim salvandi, adeo ut impetrationi mortis Christi sua necessitas, utilitas, dignitas sarta tecta, et numeris suis perfecta, completa atque integra constare potuisset, etiamsi impetrata redemptio nulli individuo unquam actu ipso fuisset applicata." Hæc enim assertio in Dei Patris sapientiam meritumque Jesu Christi contumeliosa, et Scripturæ contraria est. Sic enim ait Servator: *Ego animam pono pro ovibus, et agnosco eas.* Johan. 10:15, 27. Et de Servatore Esaias propheta: *Cum posuerit se sacrificium pro reatu, videbit semen, prolongabit dies, et voluntas Jehovæ in manu ejus prosperabitur.* Esai. 53:10. Denique, articulum Fidei, quo Ecclesiam credimus, evertit.

The Second Chapter or Head of Doctrine, Concerning Christ's Death, and the Redemption of Men by It

Article 5: *The Universal Proclamation of the Gospel*

Furthermore it is the promise of the Gospel, that whosoever believes in Christ crucified, should not perish, but have life everlasting;[21] which promise, together with the injunction of repentance and faith,[22] ought promiscuously, and without distinction, to be declared and published to all men and people,[23] to whom God in his good pleasure sends the Gospel.

A Rejection of Errors

The Synod, having delivered the orthodox doctrine, rejecteth the errors of them:

Paragraph 1: Who teach, *That God the Father ordained his Son unto the death of the cross without any certain and determinate counsel of saving any particular man expressly; so that its necessity, profit, and dignity, might have remained whole and sound, and perfect, in every respect complete, and entire, to the impetration of Christ's death, although the obtained redemption had never actually been applied to any particular person.* For this assertion is reproachful unto the wisdom of God the Father, and the merit of Jesus Christ; and contrary to the scripture, where our Saviour Christ saith: *I lay down my life for the sheep, and I know them* (John 10:15, 27). And the Prophet Isaiah speaks thus of our Saviour: *When he shall make his soul an offering for sin, he shall see his seed, and prolong his days, and the will of the Lord shall prosper in his hand* (Isa. 53:10). Lastly, it overthrows the article of faith; namely that, wherein we believe that there is a Church.

21. John 3:16.
22. Acts 2:38; 16:31.
23. 1 Cor. 1:23; Matt. 28:19.

TERTIUM ET QUARTUM DOCTRINÆ CAPUT, DE HOMINIS CORRUPTIONE, ET CONVERSIONE AD DEUM EJUSQUE MODO.

THE THIRD AND FOURTH CHAPTERS, OR DOCTRINAL HEADS, NAMELY, CONCERNING MAN'S CORRUPTION, AND CONVERSION TO GOD, TOGETHER WITH THE MANNER THEREOF

VIII

Quotquot autem per Evangelium vocantur, serio vocantur. Serio enim et verissime ostendit DEUS verbo suo, quid sibi gratum sit, nimirum, ut vocati ad se veniant. Serio etiam omnibus ad se venientibus et credentibus requiem animarum, et vitam æternam promittit.

Article 8: *The Earnest Call by the Gospel*

Now, as many soever as are called by the Gospel, are called seriously.[24] For God by his word doth seriously and most truly declare what is acceptable to him; namely, that those that are called, come unto him:[25] and moreover doth seriously promise to all such as come to him, and believe in him, rest for their souls, and life eternal.[26]

IX

Quod multi per ministerium Evangelii vocati, non veniunt et non convertuntur, hujus culpa non est in Evangelio, nec in Christo per Evangelium oblato, nec in Deo per Evangelium vocante, et dona etiam varia iis conferente, sed in vocatis ipsis, quorum aliqui verbum vitæ non admittunt securi; alii admittunt quidem, sed non in cor immittunt, ideoque post evanidum fidei temporariæ gaudium resiliunt; alii spinis curarum et voluptatibus sæculi semen verbi suffocant, fructusque nullos proferunt; quod Servator noster seminis parabola docet, Matt. 13.

Article 9: *Why Some Who Are Called Do Not Come*

Whereas many, being called by the Gospel, do not come, and are not converted, this default is not in the Gospel, nor in Christ offered by the Gospel, nor in God who calleth them by his Gospel, and moreover bestoweth divers special gifts upon them but in themselves, that are called;[27] of whom some are so careless, that they give no entrance at all to the word of life; others entertain it, but suffer it not to sink into their hearts, and so, having only a fading smack of joy, bred by a temporary faith, afterward become revolters; others choak the seed of the word with the thorns of worldly cares and fleshly pleasures, and so bring forth no fruit at all; as our Saviour teacheth in the parable of the sower (Matt. 13).

24. Isa. 55:1; Matt. 22:4.
25. Rev. 22:17.
26. John 6:37; Matt. 11:28–29
27. Matt. 11:20–24; 22:1–8; 23:37.

XII

Atque hæc est illa tantopere in Scripturis prædicata regeneratio, nova creatio, suscitatio e mortuis, et vivificatio, quam Deus sine nobis, in nobis operatur. Ea autem neutiquam fit per solam forinsecus insonantem doctrinam, moralem suasionem, vel talem operandi rationem, ut post Dei (quoad ipsum) operationem, in hominis potestate maneat regenerari vel non regenerari, converti vel non converti; sed est plane supernaturalis, potentissima simul et suavissima, mirabilis, arcana, et ineffabilis operatio, virtute sua, secundum Scripturam (quæ ab Authore hujus operationis est inspirata) nec creatione, nec mortuorum resuscitatione minor, aut inferior, adeo ut omnes illi, in quorum cordibus admiraudo hoc modo Deus operatur, certo, infallibiliter, et efficaciter regenereutur, et actu credant. Atque tum voluntas jam renovata, non tantum agitur et movetur a Deo, sed a Deo acta, agit et ipsa. Quamobrem etiam homo ipse per gratiam istam acceptam credere et resipiscere recte dicitur.

Article 12: *Regeneration Is the Work of God Alone*

And this is that regeneration, second creation, raising from the dead, and quickening (so often incalculated in the holy scriptures[28]), which God worketh in us, but not with us: and which is not brought to pass by bare instruction sounding to the outward ear, nor by moral inducements, no, nor by any kind of operation so carried on, that, when God hath done his part, it should remain in man's choice to be or not to be regenerate; to be or not to be converted: but in a very supernatural, a most powerful, and withal most sweet, a wonderful, hidden, and unspeakable working, being, the mightiness thereof (according to the scriptures, which are the doubtless word of the very author of this mighty work), not inferior to the creation of the world, or raising of the dead.[29] So that all those, in whose hearts God worketh after this admirable manner, are certainly, infallibly, and effectually regenerated, and actually believe.[30] And then the will, being now renewed, is not only drawn and moved by God, but, God having now set it on going, itself also worketh: whereupon a man is rightly said, by this grace received, himself to repent and believe.

28. John 3:3; 2 Cor. 4:6; 5:17; Eph. 5:14; cf. Eph. 2:5.
29. John 5:25; Rom. 4:17.
30. Phil. 2:13.

XVII

Quemadmodum etiam omnipotens illa Dei operatio, qua vitam hanc nostram naturalem producit et sustentat, non excludit sed requirit usum mediorum, per quæ Deus pro infinita sua sapientia et bonitate virtutem istam suam exercere voluit: ita et hæc prædicta supernaturalis DEI operatio, qua nos regenerat, neutiquam excludit, aut evertit usum Evangelii, quod sapientissimus DEUS in semen regenerationis, et cibum animæ ordinavit. Quare, ut Apostoli, et qui eos secuti sunt doctores, de gratia hac DEI ad ejus gloriam et omnis superbiæ depressionem, pie populum docuerunt, neque tamen interim sanctis Evangelii monitis, sub verbi, sacramentorum, et disciplinæ exercitio eum continere neglexerunt: sic etiamnum, absit, ut docentes aut discentes in Ecclesia DEUM tentare præsumant, ea separando, quæ DEUS pro suo beneplacito voluit esse conjunctissima. Per monita enim confertur gratia, et quo nos officium nostrum facimus promptius, hoc ipso DEI in nobis operantis beneficium solet esse illustrius, rectissimeque ejus opus procedit. Cui soli omnis, et mediorum, et salutaris eorum fructus atque efficaciæ debetur gloria in sæcula. Amen.

Article 17: *The Use of Means*

Moreover, as that powerful operation of God, by which he giveth being to this our natural life, and sustaineth the same, doth not exclude, but require, the use of means, by which it pleaseth God, according to his wisdom and goodness, to employ this his own power:[31] even so the aforesaid supernatural working of God, by which he regenerateth us,[32] doth in no wise exclude or overthrow the employment of the Gospel, which God, in his great wisdom, hath ordained to be the seed of regeneration, and food of the soul.[33] Wherefore, as the Apostles and their successors did piously deliver unto the people the doctrine of this grace of God, for the advancing of his glory, and beating down of all manner of pride; and yet withal neglected not by holy admonitions, taken out of the Gospel, to keep their Christian flocks within the compass of the word, sacraments, and exercise of discipline:[34] so in these days also far be it from either teachers or learners in the Church to presume to tempt God by disjoining those things, which God, according to his good-pleasure, hath appointed to go together inseparably. For by such admonitions grace itself is derived to us;[35] and the more readily we perform our duty, thereby the good gift of God working in us made more sensible unto us, and his work itself best cometh to perfection. To the which God alone is due for evermore all the glory of these means, and of the saving fruit and efficacy of them.[36] Amen.

31. Isa. 55:10–11; 1 Cor. 1:21.
32. James 1:18.
33. 1 Peter 1:23, 25; 2:2.
34. Acts 2:42; 2 Cor. 5:11–21; 2 Tim. 4:2.
35. Rom. 10:14–17.
36. Jude 24–25.

Rejectio Errorum

The Rejection of Errors

Exposita doctrina orthodoxa, Synodus rejicit errores eorum:

The Synod, having laid down the true doctrine, now rejecteth the errors of those:

IV: Qui docent, "Hominem irregenitum non esse proprie nec totaliter in peccatis mortuum, aut omnibus ad bonum spirituale viribus destitutum, sed posse justitiam vel vitam esurire ac sitire, sacrificiumque Spiritus contriti, et contribulati, quod Deo acceptum est, offerre." Adversantur enim hæc apertis Scripturæ testimoniis, Ephes. 2:1, 5: Eratis mortui in offensis et peccatis. Et Gen. 6:5 et 8:21: *Imaginatio cogitationum cordis hominis tantummodo mala est omni die.* Adhæc liberationem ex miseria et vitam esurire ac sitire, Deoque sacrificium Spiritus contriti offerre, regenitorum est, et eorum qui beati dicuntur. Psa. 51:19 et Matt. 5:6.

Paragraph 4: That teach, *That an unregenerate man is not properly nor totally dead in sins, nor destitute of all strength tending to spiritual good; but that he is able to hunger and thirst after righteousness, or everlasting life, and to offer the sacrifice of an humble and contrite heart, even such as is acceptable to God.* For these assertions march against the direct testimonies of scripture: *Ye were dead in trespasses, and sins* (Eph. 2:1, 5). And, *Every imagination of the thoughts of man's heart is only evil continually* (Gen. 6:5; 8:21). Moreover the hungering and thirsting for deliverance out of misery, and for life eternal, as also the offering to God the sacrifice of a broken heart, is proper to the regenerate, and such as are called blessed (Ps. 51:17; Matt. 5:6).

QUINTUM DOCTRINÆ CAPUT, DE PERSEVERANTIA SANCTORUM

THE FIFTH CHAPTER, OR DOCTRINAL HEAD, WHICH IS CONCERNING THE PERSEVERANCE OF THE SAINTS

VII

Article 7: *God Will Again Renew His Elect to Repentance*

Primo enim in istis lapsibus conservat in illis semen illud suum immortale, ex quo regeniti sunt, ne illud pereat aut excutiatur. Deinde per verbum et Spiritum suum, eos certo et efficaciter renovat ad pœnitentiam, ut de admissis peccatis ex animo secundum Denm doleant, remissionem in sanguine Mediatoris, per fidem, contrito corde, expetant, et obtineant, gratiam Dei reconciliati iterum sentiant, miserationes per fidem ejus adorent, ac deinceps salutem suam cum timore et tremore studiosius operentur.

For first of all, in these slips, he preserveth in them that his immortal seed, by which they were once born again, that it die not, nor be lost:[37] afterward, by his word and Spirit, he effectually and certainly reneweth them again unto repentance,[38] so that they do heartily, and according unto God, grieve for their sins committed, and with a contrite heart,[39] by faith in the blood of the Mediator, crave and obtain forgiveness of them, recover the apprehension of the favour of God reconciled unto them, adore his mercies and faithfulness,[40] and from thenceforward more carefully work out their salvation with fear and trembling.[41]

X

Article 10: *The Source of This Assurance*

Ac proinde hæc certitudo non est ex peculiari quadam revelatione præter aut extra verbum facta, sed ex fide promissionum Dei, quas in verbo suo copiosissime in nostrum solatium revelavit: ex testimonio *Spiritus Sancti testantis cum spiritu nostro nos esse Dei filios et hæredes.* Rom. 8:16. Denique ex serio et sancto bonæ conscientiæ et bonorum operum studio. Atque hoc solido obtinendæ victoriæ solatio, et infallibili æternæ gloriæ arrha, si in hoc mundo electi Dei destituerentur, omnium hominum essent miserrimi.

And therefore this certainty is not from any special revelation made beside or without the word, but from faith in God's promises, which he hath most plentifully revealed in his word for our comfort; from the testimony of the Holy Spirit bearing witness with our spirit, that we are the sons of God, and heirs (Rom. 8:16–17);[42] lastly, from a serious and holy care of keeping a good conscience,[43] and endeavour of good works. And if God's chosen should want in this world this solid comfort of obtaining the victory,[44] and this infallible pledge and earnest of eternal glory, they were surely of all men the most miserable.[45]

37. 1 Peter 1:23.
38. 1 John 3:9.
39. 2 Cor. 7:10.
40. Pss. 32:5; 51:19.
41. Phil. 2:12.
42. 1 John 3:1–2.
43. Acts 24:16.
44. Rom. 8:37.
45. 1 Cor. 15:19.

XI

Interim testatur Scriptura fideles in hac vita cum variis carnis dubitationibus conflictari, et in gravi tentatione constitutos hanc fidei plerophoriam, ac perseverantiæ certitudinem, non semper sentire. Verum Deus, Pater omnis consolationis, *supra vires tentari eos non sinit, sed cum tentatione præstat evasionem.* 1 Cor. 10:13. Ac per Spiritum Sanctum perseverantiæ certitudinem in iisdem rursum excitat.

Article 11: *This Assurance Not Always Felt*

Nevertheless, the scriptures witness, that the faithful do wrestle in this life with divers doubts of the flesh, and, being plunged in deep temptations, do not always perceive in themselves this full assurance of faith, and certainty of perseverance: but God, the Father of all consolation,[46] suffers them not to be tempted above that they are able, but with the temptation makes a way to escape (1 Cor 10:13), and by his Holy Spirit revives in them the certainty of perseverance.

XII

Tantum autem abest, ut hæc perseverantiæ certitudo vere fideles superbos, et carnaliter securos reddat, ut e contrario humilitatis, filialis reverentiæ, veræ pietatis, patientiæ in omni lucta, precum ardentium, constantiæ in cruce et veritatis confessione, solidique in Deo gaudii vera sit radix: et consideratio istius beneficii sit stimulus ad serium et continuum gratitudinis et bonorum operum exercitium, ut ex Scripturæ testimoniis et sanctorum exemplis constat.

Article 12: *This Assurance Is an Incentive to Godliness*

Now, so far is assurance of perseverance in the truly faithful from making them proud and carnally secure, that, on the contrary, it is the very root of humility, of filial reverence,[47] of true godliness, of patience in all conflicts, of fervent prayer, of constancy in bearing the cross and confessing God's truth, and, lastly, of solid joy in God:[48] and that moreover the consideration of this benefit becometh a goad, or spur, to incite them to a serious and continual exercise of thankfulness and good works;[49] as appeareth by the testimonies of the scriptures, and examples of the saints.

---

46. 2 Cor. 1:3.
47. Rom. 12:1.
48. Ps. 56:12–13.
49. Ps. 116:12; Titus 2:11–14; 1 John 3:3.

XIV

Quemadmodum autem Deo placuit, opus hoc suum gratiæ per prædicationem Evangelii in nobis inchoare; ita per ejusdem auditum, lectionem, meditationem, adhortationes, minas, promissa, nec non per usum sacramentorum illud conservat, continuat, et perficit.

XV

Hanc de vere credentium ac sanctorum perseverantia, ejusque certitudine, doctrinam, quam Deus ad nominis sui gloriam, et piarum animarum solatium, in verbo suo abundantissime revelavit, cordibusque fidelium imprimit, caro quidem non capit, Satanas odit, mundus ridet, imperiti et hypocritæ in abusum rapiunt, spiritusque erronei oppugnant; sed sponsa Christi ut inæstimabilis pretii thesaurum tenerrime semper dilexit, et constanter propugnavit: quod ut porro faciat procurabit Deus, adversus quem nec consilium valere, nec robur ullum prævalere potest.

Cui soli Deo, Patri, Filio, et Spiritui Sancto sit honor et gloria in sempiternum. Amen.

Article 14: *The Use of Means in Perseverance*

And as it has pleased God to begin this his work of grace in us by the preaching of the Gospel, so by the hearing, reading,[50] meditation, exhortations, threats, and promises of the same,[51] as also by the use of the sacraments,[52] he maintaineth, continueth, and perfecteth his said gracious work.

Article 15: *This Doctrine Is Hated by Satan but Loved by the Church*

This doctrine concerning the perseverance of true believers and saints, and the certainty thereof,[53] (which God, to the glory of his name, and comfort of godly souls, hath most abundantly revealed in his word, and imprinteth in the hearts of the faithful), howsoever flesh and blood apprehends it not, Satan hates it, the world laughs at it, ignorant men and hypocrites abuse it, and erroneous spirits impugn it; yet the spouse of Christ hath always most tenderly loved, and constantly defended it, as a treasure of unvaluable price.[54] Which that she may still do, God will provide and bring to pass: against whom neither can any counsel avail, nor strength prevail.[55]

To which only God, the Father, Son, and Holy Ghost, be honour, and glory, for ever and ever.[56] Amen.

50. Deut. 6:20–25.
51. 2 Tim. 3:16–17.
55. Acts 2:42.
53. Rev. 14:12.
54. Eph. 5:32.
55. Ps. 33:10–11.
56. 1 Peter 5:10–11.

REJECTIO ERRORUM CIRCA DOCTRINAM
de PERSEVERANTIA SANCTORUM

*Exposita doctrina orthodoxa, Synodus
rejicit errores eorum:*

I: Qui docent, "Perseverantiam vere
fidelium non esse effectum electionis,
aut donum Dei morte Christi partum,
sed esse conditionem novi fœderis, ab
homine ante sui electionem ac justificationem" (ut ipsi loquuntur) "perem-
toriam, libera voluntate præstandam."
Nam sacra Scriptura testatur eam ex
electione sequi, et vi mortis, resurrec-
tionis et intercessionis Christi electis
donari. Rom. 11:7: *Electio assecuta est,
reliqui occalluerunt.* Item, Rom. 8:32:
*Qui proprio Filio non pepercit, sed pro
omnibus nobis tradidit ipsum, quomodo
non cum eo nobis omnia donabit? Quis
intentabit crimina adversus electos Dei?
Deus est qui justificat. Quis est qui con-
demnet? Christus in est qui mortuus est,
imo qui etiam resurrexit, qui etiam sedet
ad dexteram Dei, qui etiam intercedit pro
nobis: Quis nos separabit a dilectione
Christi?*

THE REJECTION OF ERRORS TOUCHING
the DOCTRINE OF THE PERSEVERANCE
OF THE SAINTS

*The Synod, having declared the orthodox
doctrine, now proceedeth to disavow the
errors of those:*

Paragraph 1: That teach, *That the perseverance of the faithful is not an effect
of election, or any gift of God purchased
by the death of Christ; but that it is a
condition of the new covenant, which is
to be performed on man's part, by his own
free-will, before his* (as they themselves
speak) *peremptory election and justification.* For the holy scripture witnesseth
that it follows upon election, and is given
to the elect by virtue of Christ's death,
resurrection, and intercession, *But the
election hath obtained it, and the rest
were blinded* (Rom. 11:7). Likewise, *He
that spared not his own Son, but delivered
him up for us all, how shall he not with
him also freely give us all things? Who
shall lay any thing to the charge of God's
elect? It is God that justifieth; who is he
that condemneth? It is Christ Jesus that
died, yea or rather that is risen again,
who is even at the right hand of God,
who also maketh intercession for us. Who
shall separate us from the love of Christ?*
(Rom. 8:32–35).

V: Qui docent, "Nullam certitudinem futuræ perseverantiæ haberi posse in hac vita, absque speciali revelatione." Per hanc enim doctrinam vere fidelium solida consolatio in hac vita tollitur, et pontificiorum dubitatio in Ecclesiam reducitur. Sacra vero Scriptura passim hanc certitudinem, non ex speciali et extraordinaria revelatione, sed ex propriis filiorum Dei signis, et constantissimis Dei promissionibus petit. Imprimis Apostolus Paulus, Rom. 8:39: *Nulla res creata potest nos separare a charitate Dei, quæ est in Christo Jesu, Domino nostro.* Et Johannes, Epist. I. 3:24: *Qui servat mandata ejus, in eo manet, et ille in eo: et per hoc novimus ipsum in nobis manere, ex Spiritu quem dedit nobis.*

Paragraph 5: That teach, *That no certainty of future perseverance can be had in this life, without special revelation.* For by this doctrine the solid comfort of true believers in this life is quite taken away, and the doctrine of doubtfulness (avouched by the Papists) is brought again into the Church. Whereas the holy scripture everywhere draweth this assurance, not from special and extraordinary revelations, but from the proper marks and signs of God's children, and from the unfailable promises made by God himself: especially the Apostle Paul, *No creature is able to separate us from the love of God, which is in Jesus Christ* [or *Christ Jesus our Lord*] (Rom. 8:39). And St. John, *He that keepeth his commandments, dwelleth in him, and he in him: and hereby we know that he abideth in us, even by the Spirit which he hath given us* (1 John 3:24).

Conclusio

Atque hæc est perspicua, simplex, et ingenua Orthodoxæ de Quinque Articulis in Belgio controversis doctrinæ declaratio, et errorum, quibus Ecclesiæ Belgicæ aliquamdiu sunt perturbatæ, rejectio, quam Synodus ex verbo Dei desumptam, et Confessionibus Reformatarum Ecclesiarum consentaneam esse judicat. . . .

The Conclusion

And this is the plain, simple, and natural explication of the orthodox doctrine concerning the five articles controverted in united provinces of the Low Countries; as also the rejection of those errors, wherewith the Churches of the said Netherlands have for a time been much troubled. Which their determination the Synod holdeth to be taken out of the God's word, and agreeable to the Confessions of the Reformed Churches. . . .

Calumniatores deinde ipsos serio monet, viderint quam grave Dei judicium sint subituri, qui contra tot Ecclesias, contra tot Ecclesiarum Confessiones, falsum testimonium dicunt, conscientias infirmorum turbant, multisque vere fidelium societatem suspectam reddere satagunt.

And as for rash and slanderous traducers, the Synod earnestly advertiseth them to look unto it, and consider how heavy an account they are to give unto God, that bear false witness against so many Churches, and so many Church Confessions, trouble the consciences of the weak, and labour to draw the society of true believers into suspicion with many.

Postremo hortatur hæc Synodus omnes in Evangelio Christi symmystas, ut in hujus doctrinæ pertractatione, in scholis atque in ecclesiis, pie et religiose versentur, eam tum lingua, tum calamo, ad Divini nominis gloriam, vitæ sanctitatem, et consternatorum animorum solatium accommodent, cum Scriptura secundum fidei analogiam non solum sentiant, sed etiam loquantur; a phrasibus denique iis omnibus abstineant, quæ præscriptos nobis genuini sanctarum Scripturarum sensus limites excedunt, et protervis sophistis justam ansam præbere possint doctrinam Ecclesiarum Reformatarum sugillandi, aut etiam calumniandi.

Lastly, this Synod exhorteth all their fellow-ministers of the Gospel to have a pious and religious care in the handling of this doctrine, whether in schools or pulpits; and whensoever they undertake it by word or pen, discreetly to accommodate the same to the advancement of God's glory, to the promoting of holiness of life, and to the comforting of afflicted and affrighted souls: to frame, not only their judgment, but also their style of speech, by the square of the scriptures, and suitably to the analogy of faith: lastly, to forbear all such phrases, or manner of speech, as pass the bounds set out unto us of the right meaning of the holy scriptures, and withal give wayward wranglers just occasion of traducing or slandering the doctrine of the Reformed Churches.

Filius Dei Jesus Christus, qui ad dextram Patris sedens dat dona hominibus, sanctificet nos in veritate, eos qui errant adducat ad veritatem, calumniatoribus sanæ doctrinæ ora obstruat, et fidos verbi sui ministros spiritu sapientiæ et discretionis instruat, ut omnia ipsorum eloquia ad gloriam Dei, et ædificationem auditorum, cedant. *Amen.*

The Son of God, Jesus Christ, who, sitting at the right hand of his Father, bestoweth gifts on men, sanctify us in his truth; bring back into the way of truth those that are gone astray; stop the mouths of those that slander sound doctrine; and endue the faithful ministers of his word with the Spirit of wisdom and discretion; that all they utter may tend to the glory of God, and the edification of their hearers! Amen.

Huic capiti eadem quæ prius subscribuntur nomina.

This is our opinion and judgment: in witness whereof we have hereto subscribed.

The Westminster Standards

"The Westminster Confession of Faith. A.D. 1647," in Schaff, *The Creeds of Christendom*, 3:600–606.

The Westminster Assembly (1643–48) was convened for the purpose of uniting the churches in England and Scotland. One of the major documents arising from these efforts was the Westminster Confession of Faith, completed at the end of 1646. Though it had a short life as a creed in England, it was adopted by Presbyterian churches throughout the world, especially in Scotland and America. It is the main confession adopted at Westminster Theological Seminary, Philadelphia. Independent and Baptist also appeal to its authority, modifying it slightly to fit their ecclesiologies.

The great Princeton theologian B. B. Warfield asserts that "in the whole mass of confessional literature" there is "no more nobly conceived or ably wrought-out statement of doctrine than the chapter 'Of the Holy Scripture.'" This chapter, reproduced here from Schaff's *Creeds of Christendom*, constitutes a high point in the definition of the doctrine of Scripture, drawing on such authorities as Calvin and the Irish Articles. The confession starts with the doctrine of Scripture and continues with the doctrine of God. Here are a few highlights from the first chapter. The necessity of Scripture is defined in the context of general revelation; the progression and finality of Scripture are noted (Article 1). The canon of Scripture is defined; further, its authority depends on God, not the church. In this context, other evidences for Scripture are subordinated to the witness of the Holy Spirit (Articles 2–5). The sufficiency of Scripture is asserted as well as the need for the Spirit's illumination. Though some passages are more obscure than others, the message of salvation is clear in Scripture (Articles 6–7). Then the inspiration, transmission, and translation of Scripture are addressed (Article 8). Finally, Scripture is to be interpreted by itself (the analogy of faith) and has one sense; and all things are to be decided by the Spirit speaking in Scripture (Articles 9–10). In this chapter, we see how the best of the Reformed doctrine of Scripture has been expressed in a very balanced way.

Bibliography: Beeke & Ferguson. *Reformed Confessions*. P. xii. John L. Carson and David W. Hall, eds. *To Glorify and Enjoy God: A Commemoration of the 350th Anniversary of the Westminster Assembly*. Carlisle, PA: Banner of Truth, 1994. J. Ligon Duncan III, ed. *The Westminster Confession into the 21st Century: Essays in Remembrance of the 350th Anniversary of the Westminster Assembly*. 3 vols. Fearn, UK: Mentor, 2003–2009. S. B. Ferguson. "Westminster Assembly and Documents." Pp. 862–65 in *DSCH&T*. J. M. Frame. "Westminster Confession of Faith (1647)." Pp. 1168–69 in *EDT*. A. H. Freundt. "Adopting Act (1729)." Pp. 13–14 in *DP&RTA*. J. H. Hall. "Westminster Confession of Faith." P. 276 in *DP&RTA*. A. A. Hodge. *The Confession of Faith*. 1869. Repr., Carlisle, PA: Banner of Truth, 1992. Dirk Jellema. "Westminster Confession." Pp. 1039–40 in *NIDCC*. Leith. *Creeds of the Churches*. Pp. 192–230. John Murray. "The Theology of the Westminster Confession of Faith." Pp. 241–63 in *Collected Writings of John Murray*. Vol. 4, *Studies in Theology*. Carlisle, PA: Banner of Truth, 1982. Schaff. *The Creeds of Christendom* 1:753–82, 3:599–673. Philip Schaff and D. S. Schaff. "Westminster Standards." *NSHERK* 12:324–28. B. B. Warfield. *The Westminster Assembly and Its Work*. 1932. Repr., Grand Rapids: Baker, 2000.

Confessio Fidei Westmonasteriensis

Cap. I. De Scriptura Sacro-sancta

I. *Quanquam naturæ lumen, operaque Dei cum Creationis tum Providentiæ, bonitatem ejus, sapientiam, potentiamque eo usque manifestant, ut homines vel inde reddantur inexcusabiles: eam tamen Dei, voluntatisque divinæ cognitionem, quæ porro est ad salutem necessaria, nequeunt nobis ingenerare. Quocirca Domino complacitum est, variis quidem modis vicibusque Ecclesiæ suæ semetipsum revelare, suamque hanc voluntatem patefacere; sed et eandem omnem postea literis consignare, quo et veritati suæ tam conservandæ quam propagandæ melius consuleret, nec Ecclesia sua contra carnis corruptelam, contra malitiam mundi Satanæque, præsidio foret ac solatio destituta. Unde factum est, ut, postquam pristini illi modi, quibus olim populo suo Deus voluntatem suam revelabat, jam desiverint, Scriptura Sacra sit maxime necessaria.*

The Westminster Confession of Faith

Chapter I: *Of the Holy Scripture*

1. Although the light of nature, and the works of creation and providence, do so far manifest the goodness, wisdom, and power of God, as to leave men inexcusable (Rom. 2:14–15; 1:19–20; Ps. 19:1–3; Rom. 1:32; 2:1); yet they are not sufficient to give that knowledge of God, and of his will, which is necessary unto salvation (1 Cor. 1:21; 2:13–14); therefore it pleased the Lord, at sundry times, and in divers manners, to reveal himself, and to declare that his will unto his Church (Heb. 1:1); and afterwards, for the better preserving and propagating of the truth, and for the more sure establishment and comfort of the Church against the corruption of the flesh, and the malice of Satan and of the world, to commit the same wholly unto writing (Prov. 22:19–21; Luke 1:3–4; Rom. 15:4; Matt. 4:4, 7, 10; Isa. 8:19–20); which maketh the holy Scripture to be most necessary (2 Tim. 3:15; 2 Peter 1:19); those former ways of God's revealing his will unto his people being now ceased (Heb. 1:1–2).

II. *Sacræ Scripturæ nomine, seu Verbi Dei scripti continentur hodie omnes illi libri tam Veteris quam Novi Instrumenti,*[1] *nempe quorum inferius subsequuntur nomina.*

2. Under the name of holy Scripture, or the Word of God written, are now contained all the Books of the Old and New Testament, which are these:

Veteris Testamenti:

Of the Old Testament:

Genesis	Genesis
Exodus	Exodus
Leviticus	Leviticus
Numeri	Numbers
Deuteronomium	Deuteronomy
Josua	Joshua
Judices	Judges
Ruth	Ruth
Samuelis 1	I Samuel
Samuelis 2	II Samuel
Regum 1	I Kings
Regum 2	II Kings
Chronicorum 1	I Chronicles
Chronicorum 2	II Chronicles
Ezra	Ezra
Nehemias	Nehemiah
Esther	Esther
Job	Job
Psalmi	Psalms
Proverbia	Proverbs
Ecclesiastes	Ecclesiastes
Canticum Canticorum	The Song of Songs
Isaias	Isaiah
Jeremias	Jeremiah
Lamentationes	Lamentations
Ezechiel	Ezekiel
Daniel	Daniel
Hosea	Hosea
Joel	Joel
Amos	Amos
Obadias	Obadiah
Jonas	Jonah
Micheas	Micah
Nahum	Nahum
Habucuc	Habakkuk
Zephanias	Zephaniah
Haggæus	Haggai
Zacharias	Zechariah
Malachias	Malachi

1. [So the Cambridge editions of 1656 and 1659. The Edinburgh edition reads *Testamenti*.]

Novi autem:	*Of the New Testament*:
Evangelium secundum	The Gospels according to
Matthæum,	Matthew
Marcum,	Mark
Lucam,	Luke
Johannem.	John
Acta apostolorum	The Acts of the Apostles
Pauli epistolæ ad	Paul's Epistles to the
Romanos	Romans
Corinthios I, II	Corinthians I
Galatas	Corinthians II
Ephesios	Galatians
Philippenses	Ephesians
Collossenses	Philippians
Thessalonicens I, II	Colossians
Timotheum I, II	Thessalonians I
Titum	Thessalonians II
Philemonem	to Timothy I
Epist. ad Hebræos	to Timothy II
Jacobi Epistola	to Titus
Petri Epist. I, II	to Philemon
Johan. Epist. I, II, III	The Epistle to the Hebrews
Judæ Epistola	The Epistle of James
Apocalypsis	The First and Second Epistles of Peter
	The First, Second, and Third Epistles of John
	The Epistle of Jude
	The Revelation of John

Qui omnes divina inspiratione dati sunt in Fidei vitæque regulam.

All which are given by inspiration of God, to be the rule of faith and life (Luke 16:29, 31; Eph. 2:20; Rev. 22:18–19; 2 Tim. 3:16).

III. *Libri Apocryphi, vulgo dicti, quum non fuerint divinitus inspirati, Canonem Scripturæ nullatenus constituunt; proinde-que nullam aliam authoritatem obtinere debent in Ecclesia Dei, nec aliter quam alia humana scripta, sunt aut approbandi aut adhibendi.*

3. The Books commonly called Apocrypha, not being of divine inspiration, are no part of the Canon of Scripture; and therefore are of no authority in the Church of God, nor to be any otherwise approved, or made use of, than other human writings (Luke 24:27, 44; Rom. 3:2; 2 Peter 1:21).

IV. *Authoritas Scripturæ sacræ propter quam ei debetur fides et observantia, non ab ullius aut hominis aut Ecclesiæ pendet testimonio, sed a solo ejus authore Deo, qui est ipsa veritas: eoque est a nobis recipienda, quoniam est Verbum Dei.*

4. The authority of the holy Scripture, for which it ought to be believed and obeyed, dependeth not upon the testimony of any man or church, but wholly upon God (who is truth itself), the Author thereof; and therefore it is to be received, because it is the Word of God (2 Peter 1:19, 21; 2 Tim. 3:16; 1 John 5:9; 1 Thess. 2:13).

V. *Testimonium Ecclesiæ efficere quidem potest ut de Scriptura sacra quam honorifice sentiamus; materies insuper ejus cœlestis, doctrinæ vis et efficacia, styli majestas, partium omnium consensus, totiusque scopus (ut Deo nempe omnis gloria tribuatur), plena denique quam exhibet unicæ ad salutem viæ com-monstratio; præter alias ejus virtutes incomparabiles, et perfectionem summam, argumenta sunt quibus abunde se Verbum Dei et luculenter probat; nihilominus tamen plena persuasio et certitudo de ejus tam infallibili veritate, quam authoritate divina non aliunde nascitur quam ab interna operatione Spiritus Sancti, per verbum et cum verbo ipso in cordibus nostris testificantis.*

5. We may be moved and induced by the testimony of the Church to an high and reverent esteem of [2] the holy Scripture (1 Tim. 3:15); and the heavenliness of the matter, the efficacy of the doctrine, the majesty of the style, the consent of all the parts, the scope of the whole (which is to give all glory to God), the full discovery it makes of the only way of man's salvation, the many other incomparable excellencies, and the entire perfection thereof, are arguments whereby it doth abundantly evidence itself to be the Word of God; yet, not withstanding, our full persuasion and assurance of the infallible truth, and divine authority thereof, is from the inward work of the Holy Spirit, bearing witness by and with the Word in our hearts (1 John 2:20, 27; John 16:13–14; 1 Cor. 2:10–12; Isa. 59:21).

2. American editions, *for.*

VI. *Consilium Dei universum de omnibus quæ ad suam ipsius gloriam, quæque ad hominum salutem, fidem, vitamque sunt necessaria, aut expresse in Scriptura continetur, aut consequentia bona et necessaria derivari potest a Scriptura; cui nihil deinceps addendum est, seu novis a spiritu revelationibus, sive traditionibus hominum. Internam nihilominus illuminationem Spiritus Dei ad salutarem eorum perceptionem, quæ in Verbo Dei revelantur, agnoscimus esse necessariam: quin etiam nonnullas esse circumstantias cultum Dei spectantes et Ecclesiæ regimen, iis cum humanis actionibus et societatibus communes, quæ naturali lumine ac prudentia Christiana secundum generales verbi regulas (perpetuo quidem illas observandas) sunt regulandæ.*

6. The whole counsel of God, concerning all things necessary for his own glory, man's salvation, faith, and life, is either expressly set down in Scripture, or by good and necessary consequence may be deduced from Scripture: unto which nothing at any time is to be added, whether by new revelations of the Spirit, or traditions of men (2 Tim. 3:15–17; Gal. 1:8–9; 2 Thess. 2:2). Nevertheless, we acknowledge the inward illumination of the Spirit of God to be necessary for the saving understanding of such things as are revealed in the Word (John 6:45; 1 Cor. 2:9–10, 12); and that there are some circumstances concerning the worship of God, and government of the Church, common to human actions and societies, which are to be ordered by the light of nature and Christian prudence, according to the general rules of the Word, which are always to be observed (1 Cor. 11:13–14; 14:26, 40).

VII. *Quæ in Scriptura continentur non sunt omnia æque aut in se perspicua, aut omnibus hominibus evidentia: ea tamen omnia quæ ad salutem necessaria sunt cognitu, creditu, observatu, adeo perspicue, alicubi saltem in Scriptura, proponuntur et explicantur, ut eorum non docti solum, verum indocti etiam ordinariorum debito usu mediorum, sufficientem assequi possint intelligentiam.*

7. All things in Scripture are not alike plain in themselves, nor alike clear unto all (2 Peter 3:16); yet those things which are necessary to be known, believed, and observed, for salvation, are so clearly propounded and opened in some place of Scripture or other, that not only the learned, but the unlearned, in a due use of the ordinary means, may attain unto a sufficient understanding of them (Ps. 119:105, 130).

VIII. *Instrumentum Vetus Hebræa lingua (antiqua Dei populo nempe vernacula) Novum autem Græca (ut quæ apud Gentes maxime omnium tunc temporis, quum scriberetur illud, obtinuerat), immediate a Deo inspirata, ejusque cura et Providentia singulari per omnia huc usque secula pura et intaminata custodita, ea propter sunt authentica. Adeo sane ut ad illa ultimo in omnibus de religione controversiis Ecclesia debeat appellare. Quoniam autem Originales istæ linguæ non sunt toti Dei populo intellectæ (Quorum tamen et jus est ut scripturas habeant, et interest plurimum, quique eas in timore Dei legere jubentur et perscrutari) proinde sunt in vulgarem cujusque Gentis, ad quam pervenerint linguam transferendæ, ut omnes, verbo Dei opulenter in ipsis habitante, Deum grato acceptoque modo colant, et per patientiam ac consolationem Scripturarum spem habeant.*

8. The Old Testament in Hebrew (which was the native language of the people of God of old), and the New Testament in Greek (which at the time of the writing of it was most generally known to the nations), being immediately inspired by God, and by his singular care and providence kept pure in all ages, are therefore authentical (Matt. 5:18); so as in all controversies of religion the Church is finally to appeal unto them (Isa. 8:20; Acts 15:15; John 5:39, 46). But because these original tongues are not known to all the people of God who have right unto, and interest in the Scriptures, and are commanded, in the fear of God, to read and search them (John 5:39), therefore they are to be translated into the vulgar language of every nation unto which they come (1 Cor. 14:6, 9, 11–12, 24, 27–28), that the Word of God dwelling plentifully in all, they may worship him in an acceptable manner (Col. 3:16), and, through patience and comfort of the Scriptures, may have hope (Rom. 15:4).

IX. *Infallibilis Scripturam interpretandi regula est Scriptura ipsa. Quoties igitur cunque oritur quæstio de vero plenoque Scripturæ cujusvis sensu (unicus ille est non multiplex), ex aliis locis, qui apertius loquuntur, est indagandus et cognoscendus.*

9. The infallible rule of interpretation of Scripture is the Scripture itself; and therefore, when there is a question about the true and full sense of any Scripture (which is not manifold, but one), it must[3] be searched and known by other places that speak more clearly (2 Peter 1:20–21; Acts 15:15–16[4]).

X. *Supremus judex, a quo omnes de religione controversiæ sunt determinandæ, omnia Conciliorum decreta, opiniones Scriptorum Veterum, doctrinæ denique hominum, et privati quicunque Spiritus sunt examinandi, cujusque sententia tenemur acquiescere, nullus alius esse potest, præter Spiritum Sanctum in Scriptura pronunciantem.*

10. The Supreme Judge, by which all controversies of religion are to be determined, and all decrees of councils, opinions of ancient writers, doctrines of men, and private spirits, are to be examined, and in whose sentence we are to rest, can be no other but the Holy Spirit speaking in the Scripture (Matt. 22:29, 31; Eph. 2:20; Acts 28:25).

---

3. American editions, *may.*
4. American editions, John 5:46.

THE WESTMINSTER LARGER CATECHISM (1648)

The Latin text is reproduced from H. A. Niemeyer, ed., *Collectionis Confessionum in Ecclesiis Reformatis Publicatarum Appendix, Qua Continentur Puritanorum Libri Symbolici* (Lipsiæ: Iulii Klinkhardti, 1840), 47, 50, 54, 65–67, 70–71, 85–87, 93.

The English text is taken from "The Larger Catechism," in *The Westminster Confession of Faith* (Glasgow: Free Presbyterian Publications, 1646, 1958), 129–31, 139, 148–49, 178, 180–81, 182–83, 191–96, 246–53, 271–72; reprint of *The Confession of Faith; The Larger and Shorter Catechisms, With the Scripture Proofs at Large: Together with the Sum of Saving Knowledge* (London: T. Nelson and Sons, Paternoster Row, 1857).

After completing the Westminster Confession of Faith, the assembly decided to write two catechisms. The Larger Catechism was completed in 1648. As a more expanded version (196 questions) it serves the purpose of assisting ministers in their task of instructing the faithful and nourishing the more mature Christians. It has a theological outlook similar to that of the confession and also serves as one of the standards of many Presbyterian churches.

The truths about God's Word are scattered throughout the catechisms. The opening questions depict its character and how it is the foundation of our faith and lives (Questions 1–5). Christ acts as Prophet through his Spirit and Word (Question 43). The rules for interpreting the Decalogue and the exposition of the second commandment illustrate the authority of Scripture and the interpretative approach found in the catechism (Questions 99, 108–9). Like the Canons of Dort, the catechism deals with preaching and the Word (Questions 154–60). Finally, Scripture is also the guideline for our prayers (Questions 186–87). Thus, in the Larger Catechism, the same truths about Scripture are presented from a different angle.

Supplementary Bibliography (cf. chap. 17): Beeke & Ferguson. *Reformed Confessions*. P. xiii. J. M. Frame. "Westminster Catechisms." P. 1168 in *EDT*. Schaff. *The Creeds of Christendom* 2:783–87. Chad B. Van Dixhoorn. "The Making of the Westminster Larger Catechism." *Reformation & Revival* 10, 1 (Spring 2001): 97–113.

Catechismus Maior

Quaestio: Quinam est hominis finis summus ac praecipuus?

Responsio: Finis hominis summus ac praecipuus est deum glorificare, eodemque perfecte frui in aeternum.

Q: Unde constat esse deum?

R: Ipsissimum in homine naturae lumen, operaque Dei esse Deum luculenter manifestant: solum autem ipsius verbum Spiritusque eum hominibus revelant sufficienter ac efficaciter ad salutem.

Q: Quid est verbum Dei?

R: Scripturae sacrae Veteris ac Novi Testamenti sunt verbum Dei, unica illa fidei ac obedientiae regula.

Q: Quibus modis mediisque constat Scripturas esse verbum Dei?

R: Scripturae se ostendunt esse verbum Dei, maiestate sua et puritate, partium omnium consensu, totiusque scopo, ut Deo nempe omnis gloria tribuatur; lumine suo et vi mirabili cum convincendi tum convertendi peccatores, fideles autem consolandi ac aedificandi ad salutem: eas autem esse ipsissimum Dei verbum, solus Dei Spiritus in Scripturis et cum Scripturis testimonium praebens in corde hominis plene illi potest persuadere.

The Larger Catechism

Question 1: *What is the chief and highest end of man?*

Answer: Man's chief and highest end is to glorify God (Rom. 11:36; 1 Cor. 10:31), and fully to enjoy him for ever (Ps. 73:24–28; John 17:21–23).

Q. 2: *How doth it appear that there is God?*

A: The very light of nature in man, and the works of God, declare plainly that there is a God (Rom. 1:19–20; Ps. 19:1–3; Acts 17:28); but his word and Spirit only do sufficiently and effectually reveal him unto men for their salvation (1 Cor. 2:9–10; 2 Tim. 3:15–17; Isa. 49:21).

Q. 3: *What is the word of God?*

A: The holy scriptures of the Old and New Testament are the word of God (2 Tim. 3:16; 2 Peter 1:19–21), the only rule of faith and obedience (Eph. 2:20; Rev. 22:18–19; Isa. 8:20; Luke 16:29, 31; Gal. 1:8–9; 2 Tim. 3:15–16).

Q. 4: *How doth it appear that the scriptures are the word of God?*

A: The scriptures manifest themselves to be the word of God, by their majesty (Hos. 8:12; 1 Cor. 2:6–7, 13; Ps. 119:18, 129) and purity (Pss. 12:6; 119:140); by the consent of all the parts (Acts 10:43; 26:22), and the scope of the whole, which is to give all glory to God (Rom. 3:19, 27); by their light and power to convince and convert sinners, to comfort and build up believers unto salvation (Acts 18:28; Heb. 4:12; James 1:18; Ps. 19:7–9; Rom. 15:4; Acts 20:32): but the Spirit of God bearing witness by and with the scriptures in the heart of man, is alone able fully to persuade it that they are the very word of God (John 16:13–14; 1 John 2:20, 27; John 20:31).

Q: *Quid est quod praecipue docent Scripturae?*

Q. 5: *What do the scriptures principally teach?*

R: *Duo imprimis sunt quae Scripturae docent, quid homo de Deo credere debeat, quidque officii ab homine Deus exigat.*

A: The scriptures principally teach what man is to believe concerning God, and what duty God requires of man (2 Tim. 1:13).

Q: *Quid est peccatum?*

Q. 24: *What is sin?*

R: *Peccatum est defectus quilibet conformitatis cum lege Divina, vel transgression cuiusvis Divnae legis, quae data est in regulam creaturae rationali.*

A: Sin is any want of conformity unto, or transgression of, any law of God, given as a rule to the reasonable creature (1 John 3:4; Gal. 3:10, 12).

Q: *Quibus modis exequitur Christus munus Propheticum?*

Q. 43: *How doth Christ execute the office of a prophet?*

R: *Christus exequitur Prophetae munus, Ecclesiae suae, in unoquoque seculo integram Dei voluntatem, de omnibus quae illorum aedificationem spectant et salutem revelando, per verbum quidem suum spiritumque, variis tamen administrandi modis.*

A: Christ executeth the office of a prophet, in his revealing to the church (John 1:18), in all ages, by his Spirit and word (1 Peter 1:10–12), in divers ways of administration (Heb. 1:1–2), the whole will of God (John 15:15), in all things concerning their edification and salvation (Acts 20:32; Eph. 4:11–13; John 20:31).

Q: *Quid homini primum tanquam obedientiae suae regulam revelavit Deus?*

Q. 92: *What did God at first reveal unto man as the rule of his obedience?*

R: *Obedientiae regula Adamo in statu innocentiae, totique in eo humano generi revelata, praeter mandatum speciale de non comedendo fructu arboris scientiae boni malique, erat lex moralis.*

A: The rule of obedience revealed to Adam in the estate of innocence, and to all mankind in him, besides a special command not to eat of the fruit of the tree of the knowledge of good and evil, was the moral law (Gen. 1:26–27; Rom. 2:14–15; 10:5; Gen. 2:17).

Q: *Quis usus legis moralis regenitis specialis?*

Q. 97: *What special use is there of the moral law to the regenerate?*

R: *Quamvis qui regenerantur et in Christum credunt, a lege morali, quatenus erat foedus operum, liberentur, adeo ut inde nec iustificentur, nec condemnentur; nihilominus praeter eius generales usus cum universo humano genere iis communes, est iis porro speciali modo utilis, nempe ut inde intelligere possint quantum Christo debeant, qui eorum loco eorumque bono eam praestitit, eiusque maledictionem subiit; utque adeo inde ad maiorem gratitudinem provocentur, eandemque manifestandam maiori cura semetipsos legi tanquam obedientiae suae normae conformando.*

A: Although they that are regenerate, and believe in Christ, be delivered from the moral law as a covenant of works (Rom. 6:14; 7:4, 6; Gal. 4:4–5), so as thereby they are neither justified (Rom. 3:20) nor condemned (Gal. 5:23; Rom. 8:1); yet, besides the general uses thereof common to them with all men, it is of special use, to shew them how much they are bound to Christ for his fulfilling it, and enduring the curse thereof in their stead, and for their good (Rom. 7:24–25; Gal. 3:13–14; Rom. 8:3–4); and thereby to provoke them to more thankfulness (Luke 1:68–69, 74–75; Col. 1:12–14), and to express the same in their greater care to conform themselves thereunto as the rule of their obedience (Rom. 7:22; 12:2; Titus 2:11–14).

Q: *Ut Decalogus recte intelligatur, quaenam regulae sunt observandae?*

Q. 99: *What rules are to be observed for the right understanding of the ten commandments?*

R: *Ut Decalogus recte intelligatur, isthaec regulae sunt observandae.*

A: For the right understanding of the ten commandments, these rules are to be observed:

1) *Lex est perfecta, unumquemque obligans ad accuratam totius hominis cum iustitia eiusdem congruentiam, ad obedientiam integram et perpetuam, adeo quidem ut summam exigat cuiusque officii perfectionem, gradum vero peccati minimum quemque prohibeat.*

1. That the law is perfect, and bindeth every one to full conformity in the whole man unto the righteousness thereof, and unto entire obedience for ever; so as to require the utmost perfection of every duty, and to forbid the least degree of every sin (Ps. 19:7; James 2:10; Matt. 5:21–22).

2) *Lex est spiritualis, adeoque non minus intellectum, voluntatem, affectiones, ceterasque omnes animae potentias pertingit, quam verba, opera, gestusque externos.*

2. That it is spiritual, and so reacheth the understanding, will, affections, and all other powers of the soul; as well as words, works, and gestures (Rom. 7:14; Deut. 6:5; cf. Matt. 22:37–39; 5:21–22, 27–28, 33–34, 37–39, 43–44).

3) *Res una eademque, respectu alio atque alio, in pluribus mandatis aut praecipitur aut prohibetur.*

3. That one and the same thing, in divers respects, is required or forbidden in several commandments (Col. 3:5; Amos 8:5; Prov. 1:19; 1 Tim. 6:10).

4) *Quemadmodum ubi officium praecipitur, peccatum ei contrarium prohibetur; ubicunque vero prohibetur peccatum quodvis, ibi etiam praecipitur officium eidem contrarium: ad eundem modum ubi promissum subiungitur, includitur ei contraria comminatio; ubi vero interminatio subnectitur, contrarium ibi promissum subintelligitur.*

4. That as, where a duty is commanded, the contrary sin is forbidden (Isa. 53:13; Deut. 6:13; Matt. 4:9–10; 15:4–6); and, where a sin is forbidden, the contrary duty is commanded (Matt. 5:21, 25; Eph. 4:28): so, where a promise is annexed, the contrary threatening is included (Ex. 20:12; Prov. 30:17); and, where a threatening is annexed, the contrary promise is included (Jer. 18:7–8; Ex. 20:7; cf. Pss. 15:1, 4–5; 24:4–5).

5) *Quod Deus prohibet id nullo tempore faciendum est, quod vero praecipit semper quidem tamquam officium nobis incumbit; at unumquodque officium particulare omni tempore praestare non tenemur.*

5. That what God forbids, is at no time to be done (Job 13:7–8; Rom. 3:8; Job 36:21; Heb. 11:25); what he commands, is always our duty (Deut. 4:8–9); and yet every particular duty is not to be done at all times (Matt. 12:7).

6) *Sub uno seu peccato sive officio eiusdem generis omnia aut prohibentur, aut praecipiuntur, una cum omnibus eorum causis, mediis, occasionibus, ut etiam quaecunque eorum vel speciem habent, cum omnibus eorundem irritamentis.*

6. That under one sin or duty, all of the same kind are forbidden or commanded; together with all the causes, means, occasions, and appearances thereof, and provocations thereunto (Matt. 5:21–22, 27–28; 15:4–6; Heb. 10:24–25; 1 Thess. 5:22; Jude 23; Gal. 5:26; Col. 3:21).

7) *Quicquid nobis ipsis aut prohibetur aut praecipitur, illud conari tenemur, pro eo statu in quo sumus constituti, ut etiam ab aliis pro illorum statu ac officio aut declinetur aut praestetur.*

7. That what is forbidden or commanded to ourselves, we are bound, according to our places, to endeavour that it may be avoided or performed by others, according to the duty of their places (Ex. 20:10; Lev. 19:17; Gen. 18:19; Josh. 24:15; Deut. 6:6–7).

8) *Quicquid aliis praecipitur, in eo pro ratione status vocationisque nostrae adiutores iis esse debemus; summe autem cavere ne cum aliis in iis quae ipsis prohibentur simus participes.*

8. That in what is commanded to others, we are bound, according to our places and callings, to be helpful to them (2 Cor. 1:24); and to take heed of partaking with others in what is forbidden them (1 Tim. 5:22; Eph. 5:11).

Q: *Quaenam sunt officia quae in secundo praecepto imperantur?*

R: *Officia quae in secundo praecepto imperantur sunt cultum religiosum ac instituta quae Deus in verbo suo instituit recipere, observare, pura ac integra conservare. Cuiusmodi sunt preces et gratiarum actio in nomine Christi; verbi lectio, praedicatio ac auditio; Sacramentorum administratio et receptio; Ecclesiae regimen ac disciplina; ministrorum ordo ac stipendia; ieiunia religiosa; iurare per nomen Dei, eique vota nuncupare; prout etiam eultus omnis falsi improbatio, detestatio, ac impugnatio; eiusque simul et monumentorum omnium idololatriae, pro ea quam uniuscuiusque status ac vocatio dederit facultate, extirpatio.*

Q. 108: *What are the duties required in the second commandment?*

A: The duties required in the second commandment are, the receiving, observing, and keeping pure and entire, all such religious worship and ordinances as God hath instituted in his word (Deut. 32:46–47; Matt. 28:20; Acts 2:42; 1 Tim. 6:13–14); particularly prayer and thanksgiving in the name of Christ (Phil. 4:6; Eph. 5:20); the reading, preaching, and hearing of the word (Deut. 17:18–19; Acts 15:21; 2 Tim. 4:2; James 1:21–22; Acts 10:33); the administration and receiving of the sacraments (Matt. 28:19; 1 Cor. 11:23–30); church government and discipline (Matt. 18:15–17; 16:19; 1 Cor. 5; 12:28); the ministry and maintainance thereof (Eph. 4:11–12; 1 Tim. 5:17–18; 1 Cor. 9:7–15); religious fasting (Joel 2:12–13; 1 Cor. 7:5); swearing by the name of God (Deut. 6:13), and vowing unto him (Isa. 19:21; Ps. 76:11): as also the disapproving, detesting, opposing, all false worship (Acts 17:16–17; Ps. 16:4); and, according to each one's place and calling, removing it, and all monuments of idolatry (Deut. 7:5; Isa. 30:22).

Q: *Quaenam peccata in secundo mandato prohibentur?*

R: *Peccata in secundo mandato prohibita sunt, cultus cuiusvis religiosi a Deo ipso non instituti excogitatio omnis, per consilia promotio, iniunctio, exercitium, ac approbatio qualiscunque; religionis falsae toleratio; fictio cuiuslibet quod Deum repraesentet, aut tres personas, vel earum quamlibet, seu interne id in animo et mente nostra fiat, sive externe per modum imaginis cuiusvis aut similitudinis creaturae cuiuscunque; omnis eiusdem cultus, aut in eo vel per illud Dei; cuiusvis quod ficta numina repraesentet fabricatio, omnisque eorum cultus, omniaque quae ad ea spectant officia, commenta quaeque superstitiosa, cultum Divinum corrumpentia, eidem addentia vel detrahentia, seu a nobismet ipsis inventa ac suscepta fuerint, sive traditione ab aliis recepta, nomine licet ac titulo antiquitatis, consuetudinis, devotionis, bonae intentionis aut alio praetextu quoviscunque; simonia; sacrilegium; omnis denique cultus ac officiorum divinorum quae Deus instituit, neglectus, contemptus, impeditio, aut impugnatio.*

Q. 109: *What are the sins forbidden in the second commandment?*

A: The sins forbidden in the second commandment are, all devising (Num. 15:39), counseling (Deut. 13:6–8), commanding (Hos. 5:11; Mic. 6:16), using (1 Kings 11:33; 12:33), and any wise approving, any religious worship not instituted by God himself (Deut. 12:30–32); tolerating a false religion (Deut. 13:6–12; Zech. 13:2–3; Rev. 2:2, 14–15, 20; 17:12, 16–17);[5] the making any representation of God, of all or of any of the three persons, either inwardly in our mind, or outwardly in any kind of image or likeness of any creature whatsoever (Deut. 4:15–19; Acts 17:29; Rom. 1:21–23, 25); all worshipping of it (Dan. 3:18; Gal. 4:8), or God in it or by it (Ex. 32:5); the making of any representation of feigned deities (Ex. 32:8), and all worship of them, or service belonging to them (1 Kings 18:26, 28; Isa. 65:11); all superstitious devices (Acts 17:22; Col. 2:21–23), corrupting the worship of God (Mal. 1:7–8, 14), adding to it, or taking from it (Deut. 4:2), whether invented and taken up of ourselves (Ps. 106:39), or received by tradition from others (Matt. 15:9), though under the title of antiquity (1 Peter 1:18), custom (Jer. 44:17), devotion (Isa. 65:3–5; Gal. 1:13–14), good intent, or any other pretence whatsoever (1 Sam. 13:11–12; 15:21); simony (Acts 8:18); sacrilege (Rom. 2:22; Mal. 3:8); all neglect (Ex. 4:24–26), contempt (Matt. 22:5; Mal. 1:7, 13), hindering (Matt. 23:13), and opposing the worship and ordinances which God hath appointed (Acts 13:44–45; 1 Thess. 2:15–16).

5. Ed. note: This phrase is omitted in American editions of the Larger Catechism.

Q: *Quaenam sunt externa illa media quibus Christus nobis mediationis suae communicat beneficia?*

Q. 154: *What are the outward means whereby Christ communicates to us the benefits of his mediation?*

R: *Media externa ac ordinaria quibus Christus communicat Ecclesiae suae mediationis suae beneficia sunt instituta eius omnia; imprimis autem verbum, sacramenta et oratio, quae quidem omnia electis fiunt ad salutem efficacia.*

A: The outward and ordinary means whereby Christ communicates to his church the benefits of his mediation, are all his ordinances; especially the word, sacraments, and prayer; all which are made effectual to the elect for their salvation (Matt. 28:19–20; Acts 2:42, 46–47).

Q: *Quomodo fit verbum efficax ad salutem?*

Q. 155: *How is the word made effectual to salvation?*

R: *Spiritus Dei lectionem verbi, praecipue vero praedicationem reddit medium efficax illuminandi, convincendi, humiliandique peccatores, eosque amoliendi ab omni confidentia sui, ad Christum autem pertrahendi, ac ad imaginem eius conformandi, eiusque eos voluntati subiugandi, quin etiam confirmandi eos adversus tentationes omnes corruptionesque, aedificandi in gratia, eorumque corda in sanctitate ac solatio per fidem ad salutem stabiliendi.*

A: The Spirit of God maketh the reading, but especially the preaching of the word, effectual means of enlightening (Neh. 8:8; Acts 26:18; Ps. 19:8), convincing, and humbling sinners (1 Cor. 14:24–25; 2 Chron. 34:18–19, 26–28); of driving them out of themselves, and drawing them unto Christ (Acts 2:37, 41; 8:27–39); of conforming them to his image (2 Cor. 3:18), and subduing them to his will (2 Cor. 10:4–5; Rom 6:17); of strengthening them against temptations and corruptions (Matt. 4:4, 7, 10; Eph. 6:16–17; Ps. 19:11; 1 Cor. 10:11); of building them up in grace (Acts 20:32; 2 Tim. 3:15–17), and establishing their hearts in holiness and comfort through faith unto salvation (Rom. 16:25; 1 Thess. 3:2, 10–11, 13; Rom. 15:4; 10:13–17; 1:16).

Q: *Estne igitur verbum Dei ab omnibus legendum?*

Q. 156: *Is the word of God to be read by all?*

R: *Quamvis omnibus non sit permissum, ut verbum Dei publice legant coram toto coetu, nullum tamen est genus hominum quod seorsim, ac in familiis suis illud legere non tenetur, in quem finem scripturae sacrae sunt ex originalibus in vulgares linguas transferendae.*

A: Although all are not to be permitted to read the word publickly to the congregation (Deut. 31:9, 11–13; Neh. 8:2–3; 9:3–5), yet all sorts of people are bound to read it apart by themselves (Deut. 17:19; Rev. 1:3; John 5:39; Isa. 34:16), and with their families (Deut. 6:6–9; Gen. 18:17, 19; Ps. 78:5–7): to which end, the holy scriptures are to be translated out of the original into vulgar languages (1 Cor. 14:6, 9, 11–12, 15–16, 24, 27–28).

Q: *Qui legendum est verbum Dei?*

Q. 157: *How is the word of God to be read?*

R: *Scripturae sacrae legendae sunt cum summa illarum veneratione, ac reverentia; cum persuasione firma, esse illas ipsissimum verbum Dei, eumque solum efficere posse ut illas intelligamus; cum desiderio voluntatem Divinam in iis revelatam cognoscendi, credendi, eique obtemperandi; cum diligentia, ac earum materiae scopoque attentione, cum meditatione, applicatione, abnegatione nostri, ac oratione.*

A. The holy scriptures are to be read with an high and reverent esteem of them (Ps. 19:10; Neh. 8:3–10; Ex. 24:7; 2 Chron. 34:27; Isa. 66:2); with a firm persuasion that they are the very word of God (2 Peter 1:19–21), and that he only can enable us to understand them (Luke 24:45; 2 Cor. 3:13–16); with desire to know, believe, and obey the will of God revealed in them (Deut. 17:10, 20); with diligence (Acts 17:11), and attention to the matter and scope of them (Acts 8:30, 34; Luke 10:26–28); with meditation (Pss. 1:2; 119:97), application (2 Chron. 34:21), self-denial (Prov. 3:5; Deut. 33:3), and prayer (Prov. 2:1–6; Ps. 119:18; Neh. 7:6, 8).

Q: *A quibus praedicari debet verbum Dei?*

Q. 158: *By whom is the word of God to be preached?*

R: *Verbum Dei ab iis solis praedicari debet, qui donis sufficienter instructi sunt, atque insuper debite ad id officii approbati vocatique.*

A: The word of God is to be preached only by such as are sufficiently gifted (1 Tim. 3:2, 6; Eph. 4:8–11; Hos. 4:6; Mal. 2:7; 2 Cor. 3:6), and also duly approved and called to that office (Jer. 14:15; Rom. 10:15; Heb. 5:4; 1 Cor. 12:28–29; 1 Tim. 3:10; 4:14; 5:22).

Q: *Quomodo praedicare debent verbum Dei qui sunt ad illud muneris vocati ac designati?*

R: *Qui vocati sunt ad laborandum in verbi ministerio, praedicare debent doctrinam sanam, diligenter, tempestive, intempestive; simpliciter, non in allicientibus humanae sapientiae verbis, verum in demonstratione Spiritus, et potentia; fideliter, totum Dei consilium manifestando; prudenter, variae auditorum necessitati et captui semet accommodando; fervide e flagrante Dei animarumque populi eius amore, sincere, in Dei gloriam, populique conversionem, aedificationem, ac salutem collimando.*

Q: *Quid exigitur a praedicationem verbi audientibus?*

R: *Ab iis qui praedicationem verbi audiunt id exigitur, ut ei cum omni diligentia, praeparatione, ac oratione attendant; ut quicquid audierint, per scripturas examinent; ut fide, amore, lenitate, ac promptitudine animi veritatem excipiant tanquam verbum Dei; de eo meditentur, sermonesque conferant; in cordibus suis abdant; eiusque fructus in vita sua edant.*

Q. 159: *How is the word of God to be preached by those that are called thereunto?*

A: They that are called to labour in the ministry of the word, are to preach sound doctrine (Titus 2:1, 8), diligently (Acts 18:25), in season and out of season (2 Tim. 4:2); plainly (1 Cor. 14:19), not in the enticing words of man's wisdom, but in demonstration of the Spirit, and of power (1 Cor. 2:4); faithfully (Jer. 23:28; 1 Cor. 4:1–2), making known the whole counsel of God (Acts 20:27); wisely (Col. 1:28; 2 Tim. 2:15), applying themselves to the necessities and capacities of the hearers (1 Cor. 3:2; Heb. 5:12–14; Luke 12:42); zealously (Acts 18:25), with fervent love to God (2 Cor. 5:13–14; Phil 1:15–17) and the souls of his people (Col. 4:12; 2 Cor. 12:15); sincerely (2 Cor. 2:17; 4:2), aiming at his glory (1 Thess. 2:4–6; John 7:18), and their conversion (1 Cor. 9:19–22), edification (2 Cor. 12:19; Eph. 4:12), and salvation (1 Tim. 4:16; Acts 26:16–18).

Q 160: *What is required of those that hear the word preached?*

A: It is required of those that hear the word preached, that they attend upon it with diligence (Prov. 8:34), preparation (1 Peter 2:1–2; Luke 8:18), and prayer (Ps. 119:18; Eph. 6:18–19); examine what they hear by the scriptures (Acts 17:11); receive the truth with faith (Heb. 4:2), love (2 Thess. 2:10), meekness (James 1:21), and readiness of mind (Acts 17:11), as the word of God (1 Thess. 2:13); meditate (Luke 9:44; Heb. 2:1), and confer of it (Luke 24:14; Deut. 6:6–7); hide it in their hearts (Prov. 2:1; Ps. 119:11), and bring forth the fruit of it in their lives (Luke 8:15; James 1:25).

232

Q: *Quam nobis praescripsit Deus regulam, qua in orationis officio dirigamur?*

R: *Totum Dei verbum utile nobis esse potest in officio orationis dirigendis, specialis vero directionis norma est illa orationis formula quam Servator nostra Christus docuit disciputolos suos, oratio Dominica vulgo dicta.*

Q: *Quomodo est oratio Dominica adhibenda?*

R: *Oratio Dominica non solum directioni inservit et exemplari, secundum quod aliae preces concipiendae sunt; verum etiam tanquam oratio potest usurpari, modo illud fiat cum intellectu, fide, reverentia, reliquisque gratiis ad orationis officium rite praestandum necessariis.*

Q. 186: *What rule hath God given for our direction in the duty of prayer?*

A: The whole word of God is of use to direct us in the duty of prayer (1 John 5:14); but the special rule of direction is that form of prayer which our Saviour Christ taught his disciples, commonly called The Lord's prayer (Matt. 6:9–13; Luke 11:2–4).

Q. 187: *How is the Lord's prayer to be used?*

A: The Lord's prayer is not only for direction, as a pattern, according to which we are to make other prayers; but may also be used as a prayer, so that it be done with understanding, faith, reverence, and other graces necessary to the right performance of the duty of prayer (Matt. 6:9; Luke 11:2).

THE WESTMINSTER SHORTER CATECHISM (1647)

"The Westminster Shorter Catechism. A.D. 1647," in Schaff, *The Creeds of Christendom*, 3:676, 681, 686–87, 688–89, 695–96, 698. [We have added the biblical proof texts.]

According to plan, the Westminster Assembly also completed the Shorter Catechism in 1647. It is shorter and more concise (only 107 questions); therefore, it is better adapted for basic instructional needs and memorization. As are the other two documents produced by the Westminster Assembly, it is part of the standards of many churches; but it is more widely known, used, and memorized.

Just as in the Larger Catechism, so in the Shorter the doctrine of Scripture is scattered throughout. The Shorter Catechism contains teaching presented in an abridged and vivid fashion. Scripture is the rule of faith and life (Questions 1–3). Christ is our Prophet through the Bible (Question 24). Scripture regulates worship and the Sabbath (Questions 49–52 on the second commandment, and Question 58). Questions 88–90 deal with the Word read and preached and Question 99 with the rule of prayer. Here again the Word is seen as a rule of faith and life with practical ramifications in the life of believers and the church.

Supplementary Bibliography (cf. chap. 17): Beeke & Ferguson. *Reformed Confessions*. Pp. xii–xiii. Schaff. *The Creeds of Christendom* 3:676–704.

CATECHISMUS WESTMONASTERIENSIS MINOR	THE WESTMINSTER SHORTER CATECHISM
Quæstio. Quis hominis finis est præcipuus?	Question 1: *What is the chief end of man?*
Responsio. Præcipuus hominis finis est, Deum glorificare, eodemque frui in æternum.	Answer: Man's chief end is to glorify God (1 Cor. 10:31; Rom. 11:36), and to enjoy him forever (Ps. 73:24–28).
Quæs. Quam nobis regulam dedit Deus, qua nos ad ejus glorificationem ac fruitionem dirigamur?	Q. 2: *What rule hath God given to direct us how we may glorify and enjoy him?*
Resp. Verbum Dei (quod Scripturis Veteris ac Novi instrumenti comprehenditur) est unica regula, qua nos ad ejus glorificationem ac fruitionem dirigamur.	A: The Word of God, which is contained in the Scriptures of the Old and New Testaments[6] (2 Tim. 3:16; Eph. 2:20), is the only rule to direct us how we may glorify and enjoy him (1 John 1:3–4).

6. The London edition of 1658, Dunlop's Collection of 1719, and other editions read *Testament.*

Quæs. *Quid est quod Scripturæ præcipue docent?*

Q. 3: *What do the Scriptures principally teach?*

Resp. *Duo imprimis sunt quæ Scripturæ docent, quid homini de Deo sit credendum, quidque officii exigat ab homine Deus.*

A: The Scriptures principally teach what man is to believe concerning God, and what duty God requires of man (2 Tim. 1:13; 3:16).

Quæs. *Quomodo Prophetæ munere defungitur Christus?*

Q. 24: *How doth Christ execute the office of a Prophet?*

Resp. *Christus defungitur Prophetæ munere, voluntatem Dei in salutem nostram nobis per verbum suum spiritumque revelando.*

A: Christ executeth the office of a Prophet, in revealing to us, by his Word and Spirit, the will of God for our salvation (John 1:18; 1 Peter 1:10–12; John 15:15; 20:31).

Quæs. *Quid autem officii ac observatiæ ab homine exposcit Deus?*

Q. 39: *What is the duty which God requireth of man?*

Resp. *Officium quod ab homine Deus exposcit, est obedientia voluntati ejus revelatæ exhibenda.*

A: The duty which God requireth of man is obedience to his revealed will (Mic. 6:8; 1 Sam. 15:22).

Quæs. *Quid homini primum revelavit Deus, quod foret ipsi obedientiæ regula?*

Q. 40: *What did God at first reveal to man for the rule of his obedience?*

Resp. *Obedientiæ regula, quam Deus homini primum revelavit, erat Lex moralis.*

A: The rule which God at first revealed to man, for his obedience, was the moral law (Rom. 2:14–15; 10:5).

Quæs. *Quodnam est præceptum secundum?*

Q. 49: *Which is the second commandment?*

Resp. *Secundum præceptum est* [Non facies tibi imaginem quamvis sculptilem, aut similitudinem rei cujusvis quæ est in cœlis superne, aut inferius in terris, aut in aquis infra terram; non incuravabis te iis, nec eis servies: siquidem ego Dominus Deus tuus Deus sum Zelotypus, visitans iniquitates partum in filios ad tertiam usque quartamque progeniem osorum mei, exhibens vero misericordiam ad millenas usque diligentium me, ac mandata mea observantium].

A: The second commandment is, *Thou shalt not make unto thee any graven image, or any likeness of any thing that is in heaven above, or that is in the earth beneath, or that is in the water under the earth; thou shalt not bow down thyself to them, nor serve them; for I the Lord thy God am a jealous God, visiting the iniquity of the fathers upon the children unto the third and fourth generation of them that hate me; and showing mercy unto thousands of them that love me and keep my commandments* (Ex. 20:4–6).

Quæs. *Quid exigitur in secundo præcepto?*

Q. 50: *What is required in the second commandment?*

Resp. *Præceptum secundum exigit, ut cultus omnes ac instituta religionis quæcunque Deus in verbo suo constituit, excipiamus, observemus, pura denique ac integra custodiamus.*

A: The second commandment requireth the receiving, observing, and keeping pure and entire, all such religious worship and ordinances as God hath appointed in his Word (Deut. 32:46; Matt. 28:20; Acts 2:42).

Quæs. *Quid est quod in secundo præcepto prohibetur?*

Q. 51: *What is forbidden in the second commandment?*

Resp. *Secundum præceptum interdicit nobis cultu Dei per simulacra, aut alia ratione quaviscunque quam in verbo suo Deus præscripsit.*

A: The second commandment forbiddeth the worshiping of God by images (Deut. 4:15–19; Ex. 32:5, 8), or any other way not appointed in his Word (Deut. 12:31–32).

Quæs. *Quænam sunt rationes præcepto secundo annexæ?*

Q. 52: *What are the reasons annexed to the second commandment?*

Resp. *Rationes secundo præcepto annexæ sunt, supremum Dei in nos dominum, illius jus in nobis peculiare, zelusque quo suum ipsius cultum prosequitur.*

A: The reasons annexed to the second commandment are, God's sovereignty over us (Ps. 95:2–3, 6), his propriety in us (Ps. 45:11), and the zeal[7] he hath to his own worship (Ex. 34:13–14).

Quæs. *Quid a nobis exigit mandatum quartum?*

Q. 58: *What is required in the fourth commandment?*

Resp. *Quartum mandatum a nobis exigit, ut statum illud tempus quod in verbo suo designavit Deus, sanctum ei observemus; integrum nempe Diem e septenis unum in sanctum illi sabbatum celebrandum.*

A: The fourth commandment requireth the keeping holy to God such set times as he hath appointed in his Word; expressly one whole day in seven, to be a holy Sabbath to himself[8] (Deut. 5:12–14).

7. London edition of 1658 reads *property,* and *his* zeal.
8. London edition of 1658: *unto the Lord.*

Quæs. Quænam sunt externa media quibus Christus nobis communicat redemptionis suæ beneficia?

Q. 88: *What are the outward and ordinary[9] means whereby Christ communicateth to us the benefits of redemption?*

Resp. Media externa ac ordinaria quibus Christus nobis communicat redemptionis suæ beneficia sunt ejus instituta, verbum præsertim, sacramenta, et oratio; quæ quidem omnia electis redduntur efficacia ad salutem.

A: The outward and ordinary means whereby Christ communicateth to us the benefits of redemption, are his ordinances, especially the word, sacraments, and prayer; all which are made effectual to the elect for salvation (Matt. 28:19–20; Acts 2:42, 46–47).

Quæs. Qua ratione fit verbum efficax ad salutem?

Q. 89: *How is the word made effectual to salvation?*

Resp. Spiritus Dei lectionem verbi præcipue vero prædicationem ejus reddit medium efficax convincendi, convertendique peccatores, eosdemque in sanctimonia et consolatione ædificandi per fidem ad salutem.

A: The Spirit of God maketh the reading, but especially the preaching of the word, an effectual means of convincing and converting sinners, and of building them up in holiness and comfort through faith unto salvation (Neh. 8:8; 1 Cor. 14:24–25; Acts 26:18; Ps. 19:8; Acts 20:32; Rom. 15:4; 2 Tim. 3:15–17; Rom. 10:13–17; 1:16).

Quæs. Quomodo legi debet ac audiri verbum, ut evadat efficax ad salutem?

Q. 90: *How is the Word to be read and heard, that is may become effectual to salvation?*

Resp. Quo verbum evadat efficax ad salutem, debemus ei cum præparatione, ac oratione diligenter attendere; idemque fide excipere ac amore, in animis nostris recondere, ac in vita notra exprimere.

A: That the Word may become effectual to salvation, we must attend thereunto with diligence (Prov. 8:34), preparation (1 Peter 2:1–2), and prayer (Ps. 119:18); receive it with faith and love (Heb. 4:2; 2 Thess. 2:10), lay it up in our hearts (Ps. 119:11), and practice it in our lives (Luke 8:15; James 1:25).

Quæs. Quam nobis regulum præscripsit Deus precibus nostris dirigendis?

Q. 99: *What rule hath God given for our direction in prayer?*

Resp. Totum Dei verbum utile est nobis in oratione dirigendis; specialis vero directionis norma est illa orationis formula quam discipulos suos edocuit Christus, oratio domica quæ vulgo dicitur.

A: The whole Word of God is of use to direct us in prayer (1 John 5:14), but the special rule of direction is that form of prayer which Christ taught his disciples, commonly called, *The Lord's Prayer* (Matt 6:9–13; Luke 11:2–4).

---

9. Ed. note: *And ordinary* is omitted in earlier editions.

The Confession of the Waldenses (1655)

"The Confession of the Waldenses. A.D. 1655," in Schaff, *The Creeds of Christendom*, 3:757–61.

The Waldensians have a long history. This movement of reform started in the Middle Ages in Italy and France. At the time of the Protestant Reformation, this group grew closer to the Reformed position, especially the Reformation in Geneva. The articles that we are reproducing here are from a later period when the Waldensians of the Piedmont were under heavy persecution by Catholics. John Milton's famous sonnet in their defense starts like this:

> Avenge, O Lord, thy slaughter'd saints, whose bones
> Lie scatter'd on the Alpine mountains cold;
> Ev'n them who kept thy truth so pure of old . . . .

The truth expressed in the Confession of the Waldensians echoes the French Confession of Faith. The Confession of the Waldensians was probably written by one of their leaders, John Leger, in 1655.

We reproduce here the Preface and the first ten articles from Schaff's *Creeds of Christendom*. The confession starts with God and his revelation in nature and Scripture (Articles 1–2). It defines the canon of Scripture and grounds its authority, truth, and divinity in the witness of the Holy Spirit (Articles 3–4). Articles 5–10 on creation, providence, and the fall of mankind provide further context to understand the doctrine of Scripture. Thus from the earliest to this latest Reformed confession there is a consistent witness to the authority and divine character of God's Word.

Bibliography: Alberto Clot. "Waldenses." *NSHERK* 12:241–55. Paul T. Fuhrmann. *An Introduction to the Great Creeds of the Church*. Philadelphia: Westminster Press, 1960. Pp. 69–81. R. Kissack. "Waldenses." Pp. 1025–26 in *NIDCC*. C. T. Marshall. "Waldenses." Pp. 1150–51 in *EDT*. Schaff. *The Creeds of Christendom* 1:565–75, 3:757–70.

BRIÈVE CONFESSION DE FOY DES ÉGLISES
REFORMÉES DE PIÉMONT

Publiée avec leur Manifeste à l'occasion
des effroyables massacres de l'an 1655

*Parce que nous avons apris que nos Adver-
saires ne se contentans pas de nous avoir
persecutés, et dépoüillés de tous nos biens,
pour nous rendre tant plus odieus, vont
encore semans beaucoup de faus bruits,
qui tendent non seulement à fletrir nos
personnes, mais sur tout à noircir par des
infames calomnies la sainte et salutaire
Doctrine, dont nous faisons profession,
nous sommes obligés, pour desabuser
l'esprit de ceux qui pourroient avoir esté
preoccupés de ces sinistres impressions,
de faire une briéve Declaration de nôtre
Foy, comme nous l'avons fait par le passé
et conformement à la Parole de Dieu, afin
que tout le monde voye la fausseté de ces
Calomnies, et le tort qu'on a de nous haïr,
et de nous persecuter pour une Doctrine
si innocente.*

Nous Croyons:

I. *Qu'il y a un seul Dieu, qui est une essence
spirituelle, eternelle, infinie, tout sage, tout
misericordieuse, et tout juste; en un mot
tout parfaite; et qu'il y a trois Personnes en
cette seule et simple essence, le Pere, le Fils,
et le S. Esprit.*

II. *Que ce Dieu s'est manifesté aux hommes
par ses œuvres, tant de la Creation, que de
la Providence, et par sa Parole, revelée au
commencement par Oracles en diverses
sortes, puis redigée par écrit és Livres qu'on
appelle l'Escriture Sainte.*

A BRIEF CONFESSION OF FAITH OF THE
REFORMED CHURCHES OF PIEDMONT

Published with their Manifesto on the
occasion of the frightful massacres of
the year 1655

Having understood that our adversaries not contented to have most cruelly
persecuted us, and robbed us of all our
good and estates, have yet an intention to
render us odious to the world by spreading abroad many false reports, and so not
only to defame our persons, but likewise
to asperse with most shameful calumnies
that holy and wholesome doctrine which
we profess, we feel obliged, for the better
information of those whose minds may
perhaps be preoccupied by sinister opinions, to make a short declaration of our
faith, such as we have heretofore professed
as conformable to the Word of God; and
so every one may see the falsity of those
their calumnies, and also how unjustly we
are hated and persecuted for a doctrine
so innocent.

We believe,

I. That there is one only God, who is a
spiritual essence, eternal, infinite, all-wise,
all-merciful, and all-just, in one word, all-
perfect; and that there are three persons
in that one only and simple essence: the
Father, Son, and Holy Spirit.

II. That this God has manifested himself
to men by his works of Creation and Providence, as also by his Word revealed unto
us, first by oracles in divers manners, and
afterwards by those written books which
are called the Holy Scripture.

III. *Qu'il faut recevoir, comme nous reçevons cette Sainte Ecriture pour Divine, et Canonique, c'est-à-dire pour regle de nôtre Foy, et de nôtre vie, et qu'elle est contenüe pleinement és Livres de l'Ancien et du Nouveau Testament: que dans l'Ancien Testament doivent estre compris seulement les Livres que Dieu a commis à l'Église Judaïque, et qu'elle a toûjours approuvé ou reconnü pour Divins, à sçavoir les cinq Livres de Moise, Josuê, les Juges, Ruth, le 1 et 2 de Samuel, le 1 et 2 des Rois, le 1 et 2 des Chroniques ou Paralipomenon, le 1 d'Esdras, Nehemie, Esther, Job, les Pseaumes, les Proverbes de Salomon, l'Ecclesiaste, le Cantique des Cantiques, les 4 grands Prophetes et les 12 petits: et dans le Nouveau les 4 Evangiles, les Actes des Apôtres, les Epîtres de S. Paul, une aux Romains, deux aux Corinthiens, une aux Galates, une aux Ephesiens, une aux Philippiens, une aux Colossiens [deux aux Thessaloniciens, deux à Timothée, une à Tite, une à Philémon],[1] l'Epître aux Hébreux, une de S. Jacques, deux de S. Pierre, trois de S. Jean, une de S. Jude, et l'Apocalypse.*

IV. *Que nous reconnoissons la Divinité de ces Livres Sacrés, non seulement par le témoignage de l'Église, mais principalement par l'eternelle et indubitable verité de la Doctrine qui y est contenüe, par l'excellence, sublimité, et majesté du tout Divine qui y paroît, et par l'opération du S. Esprit, qui nous fait recevoir avec deferance le témoignage que l'Église nous en rend, qui ouvre nos yeux pour découvrir les rayons de la lumiere celeste qui éclattent en l'Ecriture, et rectifie nôtre goût pour discerner cette viande par la saveur Divine qu'elle a.*

III. That we ought to receive this Holy Scripture (as we do) for divine and canonical, that is to say, for the constant rule of our faith and life: as also that the same is fully contained in the Old and New Testament; and that by the Old Testament we must understand only such books as God did intrust the Jewish Church with, and which that Church has always approved and acknowledged to be from God: namely, the five books of Moses, Joshua, the Judges, Ruth, 1 and 2 of Samuel, 1 and 2 of the Kings, 1 and 2 of the Chronicles, one of Ezra, Nehemiah, Esther, Job, the Psalms, the Proverbs of Solomon, Ecclesiastes, the Song of Songs, the four great and the twelve minor Prophets: and the New Testament containing the four gospels, the Acts of the Apostles, the Epistles of St. Paul—1 to the Romans, 2 to the Corinthians, 1 to the Galatians, 1 to the Ephesians, 1 to the Philippians, 1 to the Colossians [2 to the Thessalonians, 2 to Timothy, 1 to Titus, 1 to Philemon],[1] and the Epistle to the Hebrews; 1 of Saint James, 2 of Saint Peter, 3 of Saint John, 1 of Saint Jude, and the Revelation.

IV. We acknowledge the divinity of these sacred books, not only from the testimony of the Church, but more especially because of the eternal and indubitable truth of the doctrine therein contained, and of that most divine excellency, sublimity, and majesty which appears therein; and because of the operation of the Holy Spirit, who causes us to receive with reverence the testimony of the Church in that point, who opens our eyes to discover the beams of that celestial light which shines in the Scripture, and corrects our taste to discern the divine savor of that spiritual food.

---

1. Omitted by Leger and Hahn, no doubt inadvertently.

V. *Que Dieu a fait toutes choses de rien, par sa volonté toute libre, et par la puissance infinie de sa Parole.*

V. That God made all things of nothing by his own free will, and by the infinite power of his Word.

VI. *Qu'il les conduit et gouverne toutes par sa Providence, ordonnant et adressant tout se qui arrive au monde, sans qu'il soit pourtant ni autheur, ni cause du mal que les créatures font, ou que la coulpe luy en puisse, ou doive en aucune façon estre imputée.*

VI. That he governs and rules all by his providence, ordaining and appointing whatsoever happens in this world, without being the author or cause of any evil committed by the creatures, so that the guilt thereof neither can nor ought to be in any way imputed unto him.

VII. *Que les Anges ayant esté creés purs et saints, il y en a qui sont tombés dans une corruption et perdition irreparable, mais que les autres ont persevheré par un effet de la bonté Divine, qui les a soûtenus et confirmés.*

VII. That the angels were all in the beginning created pure and holy, but that some of them have fallen into irreparable corruption and perdition; and that the rest have persevered in their first purity by an effect of divine goodness, which has upheld and confirmed them.

VIII. *Que l'homme qui avoit esté creé pur et saint, à l'Image de Dieu, s'est privé par sa faute de cét estat bienheureux, donnant ses assentimens aux discours captieus du Diable.*

VIII. That man, who was created pure and holy, after the image of God, deprived himself through his own fault of that happy condition by giving credit to the deceitful words of the devil.

IX. *Que l'homme a perdu par sa transgression, la justice et la sainteté qu'il avoit receüe, encourant avec l'indignation de Dieu, la mort et la captivité, sous la puissance de celuy qui a l'empire de la mort, assavoir le Diable, à ce point que son franc arbitre est devenu serf et éclave du peché, tellement que de nature tous les hommes, et Juifs et gentils, sont Enfans d'Ire, tous morts en leurs fautes et pechés, et par conséquant incapables d'avoir aucun bon movement pour le salut, ni même former aucune bonne pensée sans la grace; toutes leurs imaginations et pensées n'estant que mal en tout tems.*

IX. That man by his transgression lost that righteousness and holiness which he had received, and thus incurring the wrath of God, became subject to death and bondage, under the dominion of him who has the power of death, that is, the devil; insomuch that our free will has become a servant and a slave to sin: and thus all men, both Jews and Gentiles, are by nature children of wrath, being all dead in their trespasses and sins, and consequently incapable of the least good motion to any thing which concerns their salvation: yea, incapable of one good thought without God's grace, all their imaginations being wholly evil, and that continually.

X. *Que toute la posterité d'Adam, est coûpable en luy de sa desobeïssance, infectée de sa corruption, et tombée dans la même calamité jusques aus petits Enfans dés le ventre de leur Mere, d'où vient le nom de Peché orginel.*

X. That all the posterity of Adam is guilty in him of his disobedience, infected by his corruption, and fallen into the same calamity with him, even the very infants from their mothers' womb, whence is derived the name of original sin.

Part Three

EARLY REFORMED INTERPRETATION

THE INTERPRETATION OF SCRIPTURE is closely related to the doctrine of Scripture. In the first part, the focus was on the definition of the nature of Scripture; and while in the second part the confessions touched on the topic of interpretation, in this third part the selections illustrate how a Reformed interpretation derived from its doctrine of Scripture looks. This part begins with two theologians from Switzerland (Heinrich Bullinger and John Calvin), continues with two from the British Isles (Thomas Cranmer and John Knox), and ends up in the New World with Jonathan Edwards.

The first two documents are early Reformed treatises on biblical interpretation. Both of them have been integrated into larger works to present the biblical message: Bullinger's treatise was appended to his commentary on New Testament Epistles, and Calvin's essay served as an introduction to the New Testament in Olivétan's French Bible. Both works also share a common theological and hermeneutical outlook on the Bible. Bullinger's work is one of the earliest syntheses of covenant theology; he sees Scripture as the unfolding of the covenant of God with Abraham, thus reading the Old and New Testaments in a unified way. Likewise, Calvin in his writing conceives the Bible as a revelation of God in a redemptive history that culminates in the manifestation of Christ as the end of the law.

Cranmer's homily belongs to a series of twelve sermons intended for the strengthening and reforming of the church in England. This sermon emphasizes the authority and sufficiency of Scripture and encourages parishioners in their reading of the Bible. Thus, like the previous two selections, it served as a general introduction to biblical interpretation for Christians in the church. Next, selections from the Scots Confession and the First Book of Discipline convey aspects of biblical interpretation in Scotland. The articles of the Scots Confession display a redemptive-historical integration of doctrines from the promise of Genesis 3:15 to an exposition of Christology and ecclesiology. The Ninth Head of the First Book of Discipline illustrates how the Bible was used and revered in the life of the church in Scotland, providing instruction on Bible translation, Bible reading in the home, preaching, and biblical interpretation.

While Edwards's doctrine of Scripture will be considered in the following part, the sermon given here illustrates his approach to biblical interpretation. This sermon was delivered at the occasion of the installation of one of his friends as a pastor; here Edwards not only expounds the covenantal marriage relationship between God and his people starting from a passage of Isaiah, but also applies this redemptive-historical theme to the relations between pastors and their flocks. Thus in one sense Edwards continues in the tradition of interpretation of Bullinger and Calvin.

These texts demonstrate that the Reformed doctrine is not abstract, that it furnishes an overall hermeneutic scheme for the reading of Scripture, and that it has practical implications for the life of the church. These selections also show the close connection between the doctrine of inspiration and hermeneutics. This concern will resurface later in the anthology and is important in the history of Westminster Seminary, as the title of the volume *Inerrancy and Hermeneutic*, edited by Harvie Conn, testifies.

Of the One & Eternal Testament or Covenant of God: A Brief Exposition

HENRY BULLINGER

Henry Bullinger, "Of the One & Eternal Testament or Covenant of God: A Brief Exposition (1534)," in Peter A. Lillback, "The Binding of God: Calvin's Role in the Development of Covenant Theology" (Ph.D. diss., Westminster Theological Seminary, 1985), 499–527.[1]

Heinrich Bullinger made significant contributions to covenant theology. *Of the One & Eternal Testament or Covenant of God*, or *De Testamento*, written in 1534, is a theological treatise rather than a confession (Second Helvetic Confession, chap. 12) or a sermon (*Decades*, chap. 3). In 1549, this treatise was appended to Bullinger's commentary on the New Testament Epistles. Thus it is clearly an important witness to early Reformed interpretation. *De testamento* is Latin for "of the covenant," and Bullinger's is the first monograph written on covenant theology, reflecting a foundational Reformed method of interpreting Scripture. Bullinger developed insights from his predecessor Zwingli.

Bullinger explains that all parts of the Scriptures are an unfolding of the covenant with Abraham (Gen. 17). The covenant is God's plan of redemption as it unfolds in history. It establishes the continuity of the old covenant with the new covenant, which is centered in Christ. This unity of the Bible is due to God's one and eternal covenant of grace that is found only in Christ and revealed only in the Scriptures. We reproduce

---

1. The original translation by Peter A. Lillback was made from Heinrich Bullinger, *In omnes apostolicas epistolas, divi videlicet Pauli XIIII. et VII. Canonicas, Commentarii* (Zurich: Christopher Froshauer, 1549), 2:154–70; for the revision of the translation, the following two other editions have been consulted: Heinrich Bullinger, *De testamento seu foedere dei unico et aeterno Heinrychi Bullingeri brevis expositio* (Zurich: Christopher Froshauer, 1534), and *In omnes apostolicas epistolas, divi videlicet Pauli XIIII. et VII. Canonicas, Commentarii* (Zurich: Christopher Froshauer, 1537), 2:154–70. The page numbers of the 1534 edition are indicated in square brackets in the text.

here the first English translation of this document. Subsequently, McCoy and Baker produced their own translation of the text.

Supplementary Bibliography (cf. chap. 3): Peter A. Lillback. *The Binding of God: Calvin's Role in the Development of Covenant Theology.* Text and Studies in Reformation and Post-Reformation Theology. Grand Rapids: Baker Academic, 2001. Charles S. McCoy and J. Wayne Baker. *Fountainhead of Federalism: Heinrich Bullinger and the Covenantal Tradition.* With a translation of *De testamento seu foedere Dei unico et aeterno* (1534) by Heinrich Bullinger. Louisville, KY: Westminster/John Knox Press, 1991.

Jesus

This is my beloved son in whom my soul is appeased, listen to him (Matt. 15:5).[2]

1534

[2a] I am going to discuss in this short compendium, the one and eternal testament or covenant of God. In this study, the prophets inspired by the divine Spirit will be explained first, and then those who were appointed by the Son of God to add canonical books will be explained also. From the very start, I implore the Spirit of Christ Jesus to fill me, so that I may be able to examine clearly, briefly, soberly, and according to the analogy of faith, a difficult matter that is as necessary as it is useful.

I. Nomenclature of the Covenant

First, however, we must consider the term "covenant" so that its meaning will be established, [2b] since its usage is varied in the Holy Testaments. The intended result is that both brilliant light and greater certainty may be added to the whole debate.

Thus the Hebrew term *Berith* which the *Septuagint* constantly translates with the Greek term *Diatheke*, in Latin, is really a last will and testament. Several times it signifies an inheritance which occurs by a testament. For the Greek verb *Diatithemai* means "to testify," (*testari*) and the Greek expression *to Diathekas Poieo* means "something one gives to heirs by a testament." And in Latin, to compose a testament means "to testify a last will." In fact, some want the word "Testament" to mean a testimony of our will. Ulpianus, the lawyer, defined it as a lawful statement of our will, rather than what one desires to be done after his death. Both Gellius and after him Lorenzo Valla rejected the etymology of the jurists. [3a] Hence, they deny that the word "testament" is a compound word, that is, a witness (*testari*) of one's mind (*mentum*). Rather, they contend that it is a simple extension of meaning from the act of giving witness. A parallel to this can be observed in the Latin term *sacellum*, meaning a "chapel." Instead of being a compound word formed from *sacro*[3] and *cella*,[4] it is a diminutive

2. This quotation is found only in the 1534 edition.
3. The Latin term for "holy."
4. The Latin term for a "store-room," and in a temple "the shrine of a god's image."

246

form of the word "sacro" (holy), that is, a little holy place or a "chapel." Further since the Latin phrase "to compose a testament" is derived from "*testor*" meaning "to declare," a "testator" or "one who declares" is one who composes a testament. Now this is the meaning of its usage by Christ in Matthew 26, as well as by Paul in Galatians 3 and in chapter 9 of the Epistle to the Hebrews. This sense of the term is greatly used too by those experienced in the law. On the other hand, the Greek verb *Diatithemai* in the place of *Suntithemai* means "to covenant" (*paciscor*) and "to bargain" (*stipulo*). Whence *Diatheke* in the singular number signifies a covenant (*Pactum*), an agreement (*Conventum*), and a promise (*Pollicitationem*), which in Greek is *epaggelia*. And in Latin, the word "*testor*" meaning "I witness" is derived from "*teste*" [3b] meaning "a witness." This is because properly, a "testimony" (*testimonium*) is to speak and to affirm something by swearing with an oath. Thus "Testament" is used several times in the Scriptures for a "promise." Yet it is not used only in this way, but also in the sense of something established by swearing with an oath. So Zachariah in Luke 1:72–73 says, "That He was mindful of His holy testament, because He swore an oath to the fathers which is about to be given to us." And Peter says in Acts 3:25, "You are the sons of the prophets and of the testament which God testified to our Fathers." Likewise, *Diatheke* or *Diathekai* in the plural number also signifies a covenant (*Pactum*) and a compact (*Foedus*), which most closely corresponds to the Hebrew word *Berith* (a covenant) because it is derived from *Barat* which means "to agree upon" or "to enter into a covenant." Moses uses the word in this sense in Genesis 15 and 17. We too will use the word in this way in the present exposition.

[4a] II. The Reason For and the Manner of Making a Covenant

Moreover, the Latin grammarians suppose the word "covenant" (*foedus*) to be derived from the word "foul" (*foedus*). This is because in covenants (*foedere*), a pig is struck in a horrible fashion (*foede*), that is, it is cruelly slain. Especially, of course, a covenant only exists between enemies if it separates them from war. Nevertheless, it may be used for acts of friendship and union (*conjunctionis*). In such cases, however, it refers to those which come together solemnly and with certain ceremonies, then conditions. For formerly in the making of covenants, there were certain ceremonies, and certain written conditions, or if you prefer, an appeal to headings, by whose conditions a covenant would form an alliance, as long as it was binding. When one assents to allies by expressed word and ceremony, he establishes a covenant. Afterwards, documents are immediately written. The reason for the written document of every covenant is so that they might be transmitted to posterity and understood by them. And indeed, in Testaments also [4b] there is by no means a dissimilar reason, since first, heirs are written, then the inheritance is delineated, likewise who may divide up the inheritance. And indeed, all of these are entrusted and sealed to documents lest in any way there be fraud. In the meantime, the testament is not valid provided that the death of the testator does not intervene. But to what purpose is this for our discussion? Namely, it was God Himself who deigned to name this mystery of divine union (*unitatis*) and partnership (*societatis*) with a human title. The Same also conformed to human foolishness on account of the weakness (*imbecillitas*) of our nature in the striking of the covenant or the arranging of the testament. Thus I will appear to be advancing most appropriately if I discuss the one and eternal testament of God proceeding in this order and by means of the conditions of the covenant.

[5a] III. The Public Record (*Instrumentum*) of the Covenant

Now God in human foolishness made a covenant with us. The following words of Moses will bear witness to this, which are selected from Genesis 17 for this significance. "Now when Abram was 99 years old, the Lord appeared to him, and said to him, 'I am God the All-mighty or All-sufficient. Walk before me and be innocent (*integer*). And I will make my covenant between me and you and between your seed after you in their generations for an eternal covenant, in order that I may be your God and the God of your seed after you. And I will give to you and to your seed after you all of the land of Canaan as an eternal possession, and I will be their God. And indeed, you will keep my covenant, you and your seed in their generations. This is my covenant [5b] between me and you and your seed after you. Circumcise among you all males. Moreover, the male whose foreskin is not circumcised, that soul will be blotted out from his people: because he makes my covenant void.'" These are the words of the covenant, not given verbatim, but as a collected and inclusive summary. If you examine them carefully, you will see that God checked human foolishness in every way. First, there is set forth those who will agree, namely, God and the seed of Abraham. Then, to which conditions they will agree to, certainly at least to these: the fact that God wills to be the God of Abraham's seed, and the fact that the seed of Abraham is bound to walk innocently before God. Likewise one sees here that the covenant between the same parties is to be struck perpetually. And then, everything is established by a certain bloody ceremony. [6a] There is no need for me to mention the documents, since in place of the documents are the words of Moses which I have just reviewed. Or, if you prefer, the documents are, on a larger scale, the whole of canonical Scripture. Nothing therefore, now prohibits me from speaking concerning each heading (or seal, *sigillatim*).

IV. God Enters into Covenant with the Seed of Abraham

It is indeed a proof of the unspeakable divine mercy and grace, that the very divinity, I say, the very eternal God, the most distinguished offers the covenant itself. Man brings nothing to it by merit. It is rather a pure and native impulse of kindness. Nor do I understand human nature either to be able to grasp this fullness of mystery or to be able to convey it by adequate praise. Indeed, what in the world has been done or heard, I say, that is greater than this, how the eternal power and majesty, I say, the immortal [6b] omniscient and omnipotent God, the founder of the universe, in whom everything continues, from whom everything is, and by whom all things are preserved, joined himself to sin and to miserable corrupt mortals by covenant? This undoubtedly is the origin and foremost head of our religion, namely, that it is only from the kindness and mercy of God that we are saved. This undoubtedly is that which the prophet of the Lord commended in sacred hymn by the famous proclamation to the whole world, singing, "The Lord is compassionate and gracious, slow to wrath, and abounding in mercy. He will not always strive with us, nor will He keep His anger forever. He does not deal with us according to our sins, and he does not reward us according to our iniquities. As far as the height of heaven is above [7a] the earth, so is His mercy to those who fear Him. Just as the distance from the east to the west, so far He removes our transgressions from us. Just as a father has compassion for his sons, so the Lord has compassion on those who fear Him. Indeed, He Himself knows our frame, and that we are dust, etc." (Ps. 103:8–14). So, I say, we owe to divine mercy and goodness whatever we are, and whatever things which are created and ornamented by us for our use and pleasure. Indeed, God formed all things on account of man. Yes indeed, and by far greater mercy He displayed His own proofs in Himself to men. Thus the ones who were faithless and fallen, He immediately lifted up and commanded them to hope (Gen. 3:8–21). And when all the descendants and posterity of Adam had fully deserved by abominable crimes to be destroyed completely, [7b] He exercised His justice by pouring out the flood upon the earth, and He displayed most abundant mercy to Noah and his sons (Gen. 8). And what now has established more clearly the same mercy than the eternal covenant with Abraham and his posterity, a covenant before the eyes of all mortals? Now this I am able to say of God and His goodness, which Sallust said of the one from Carthage, "It is better to be silent than to say a little" (*The War with Jugurtha* 19.2 [Loeb, 175]). Now with all these things, I want this said, that God is the greatest and best, who established the covenant with Abraham and his seed. Now we will speak of the seed of Abraham.

V. Who Are the Seed of Abraham?

Now to put it simply, someone has not covenanted, unless he walks the royal way. But they who consider the conditions of the covenant exactly, neglect the true grace and [8a] promise of God, when they exclude the infants of the covenant. They do so, because children not only do not observe, but do not even understand the heads of the covenant. And consequently, those who observe such a sacrament, ceremony or sign of the covenant[5] reckon those in the covenant, who in reality ought to be excluded. On the other hand, if one distinguishes the two, and there is not only the condition of the covenant but also the promise or mercy of God respecting of age and of reason, then while seizing the ones who believe among the Jews and Gentiles to be that seed of Abraham with whom the Lord entered into covenant, still, the true seed, that is the infants of those in the covenant are by no means to be excluded. Moreover, they who reason in this way fail to see the case of the person who is to be excluded who approaches the conditions of the covenant by the use of reason. Just so, we see children [8b] of parents to be children, indeed, heirs also, even if they in their early years do not know themselves to be either children or heirs of parents. However, they are rejected when the one who comes to the use of reason disregards the command of parents. Then indeed, it becomes evident that those are not sons or heirs, rather it is common to call them degraded good-for-nothing individuals. No less than the parents themselves who are cheated of their prerogative of birth throw away the sons of the family. For nothing separates the one who has violated the laws of duty (*pietatis*) toward parents from a servant. In fact, this is worse than a servant, from him who owes even more to parents by the very law of nature. Hence truly, this is explicated for us by the prophets and apostles in the disputation concerning the seed of Abraham. To be sure, because not all who are born of Abraham are the seed of Abraham. Rather, he who is the son of promise, [9a] that is, of faith, whether it may be Jew or Gentile. Indeed, up to the present time, the Jews have been neglecting the ground conditions of the covenant. In the mean time, they themselves have in fact boasted, nevertheless, to be the people of God by depending on circumcision, and because they have been begotten by Abraham as parent. This Christ truly not only persists in denying, and attacks with the apostles, but also, there is complete agreement among the prophets.

---

5. I.e., infant baptism.

Those of the Old Testament Too Were a Spiritual People and Had Spiritual Promises

We speak now because of those who imagine that the first mention of the spiritual seed of Abraham was made in the New Testament. The case of Jeremiah 4 may be compared, for example, where the prophet discusses the true circumcision, with the second chapter of Paul to the Romans. What Isaiah, Jeremiah, Ezekiel and the rest of the prophets have written in general on the fidelity of the race of Abraham may be compared among themselves, with [9b] that which Christ teaches in John chapter 8, and with what Paul argued in the epistles of Romans and Galatians. And clearly, it will be manifest that it is the same Spirit, who taught by the prophets and apostles equally before and after the birth of Christ concerning the true seed of Abraham. Consequently, what now is said in Scripture against the carnal seed and for the spiritual seed is said against those, who have defiled their birth and circumcision, or, if you will, while trusting in flesh and initiation, and boasting in external things, they in fact have neglected the piety of the soul.

Nevertheless, such as these do not exclude children born of believing parents, who are of God by the grace and the call of the One who promises.

The Children of the Faithful, the Seed of Abraham

For in this passage, God promises by grace and says, "I will be your God and the God of your seed [10a] after you." And even clearer, "This is my covenant between Me and you, and your seed after you. Circumcise every male among you." Again, lest someone assert that this was said to the men of the Old Testament but not likewise to those of the New, let him hear Paul speaking to the Galatians, "However many are of Christ, are the seed of Abraham" (Gal. 3:29). Likewise, "Those who are heirs are the seed of Abraham" (Gal. 3:29). Again, "Those who are holy, are the seed of Abraham."[6] If you join these together—the children are Christ's, they are heirs, they are holy—it follows automatically that the children are the seed of Abraham and in the covenant. To this, indeed, the words of Christ pertain, "Permit the little children to come unto me, of such indeed is the kingdom of heaven" (Luke 18:16). And that passage of Paul, "the unbelieving wife is sanctified by the believing husband. Otherwise, your children [10b] are unclean, now, however, they are holy" (1 Cor. 7:14). Certainly, this is so by the grace and mercy of the Lord. To this, of course, it is objected: Therefore while the parent is unfaithful, the child who has been brought forth from him is excluded from the covenant. And what they mean by "unfaithful" here is the one who profanes the name of the Lord by an impure life because he confesses otherwise with his mouth. But these do not consider the fact that at the very same time a parent is inscribed with the people of God, and that the guilt of the parents does not overflow into the sons. The Lord has indicated this many times in Ezekiel 18. The sons of Israel are called the circumcised and the people of God even though they had been born of evil parents, those whom the Lord had cast down in the desert on account of their impious murmuring. Indeed, He said, "Your little children and sons who today are ignorant of good and [11a] evil, I will separate. These very ones will enter, and to these I will give the land, and they will possess it" (Deut. 1:39). Likewise, the apostle in 1 Corinthians 7 shows sufficiently, how the Lord is gracious to the children who are born of only one parent who confesses the name of the Lord. Nor is it likely that the most merciful God is made less merciful and less favorable to our children after sending the Savior, than He was toward those children, whom He had chosen as His own before

---

6. This can only be taken as an inference from the text rather than a quotation, since the term "holy" is not used by Paul in Galatians.

sending Christ. And it is established sufficiently that their children, even those born of evil parents were circumcised and inscribed among the people of God. And so, we have no doubts concerning the children of Christians, rather, we freely advise baptism to the ones having a baby in the church of the faithful. [11b] More on this will be said below. So far as what is disputed by these remarks, I think it is evident who are the seed of Abraham, and that this is that very seed to whom the inheritance is owed.

VI. The Conditions of the Covenant

Now we descend to the conditions of the covenant. Indeed, those who are connected by covenants are connected by certain precepts (*praescriptionibus*), in order that each may know his particular office, that is, what this one is responsible for to the other, and what in turn the other may expect from the first. Thus God, who in this covenant holds that chief place, first sets forth and produces His nature, such as He wills to manifest Himself to us. And then, He adds what in turn He demands from us, and what we agree to do.

The Promises of God and What He Himself Offers by the Covenant

And so with eloquent words and with great weight He pronounces, "I am God [12a] All-sufficient, full, and the horn of plenty," that is, that power and that good, which alone is able to be enough for man, Who provides all things for all, needing nothing at all. Eternally by means of Himself, He lives, moves and performs. Indeed, all of this, at the same time, the Hebrew word *El-Shaddai* signifies and comprehends in itself. By this name, the Lord shadowed forth concisely, wonderfully and fruitfully, His unity, omnipotence, goodness and all His virtues. Moreover, since very great brevity can produce a great deal of obscurity, He thereupon goes on to explain, "And I will establish My covenant between Me and you and between your seed after you, so that I may be your God and the God of your seed after you." For it is not enough to have believed that God is, or even that He is All-sufficient, except further, [12b] you believe that the omnipotent God, the Creator of all things is your God, yes, the Rewarder of all who seek Him (Heb. 11:6). Now in order that He may plainly demonstrate what it is to be the All-sufficient God, the God of the faithful and the Rewarder of the ones who fear Him, as from living examples, He adds to the subordinate covenanters (*suppactis*), "And I will give to you and to your seed after you all the land of Canaan as an eternal possession, and I will be their God."

The Promises Made to the Ancients Were Not Altogether Carnal

Although these promises concerning the land of Canaan are to be fulfilled materially: for the Lord shows His goodness in things also which pertain to the experience of life, yet the heavenly life is seen to be set forth by many names concerning the eternal inheritance. In the first place, in fact, Paul writes to the Hebrews in these words, "With faith, [13a]Abraham, Isaac and Jacob died although they did not receive the promises, and from a distance they saw them and they believed and they were saved, and they confessed themselves to be strangers and foreigners in the land. For they who say these things, declare themselves to be seeking a home land. Indeed, if those were mindful of where they originated from, they had ample opportunity to return. Now, however, they desire a better land, that is a heavenly land" (Heb. 11:13–16). Consequently, the Lord indeed named the land of Canaan, but in this He bestows the rest—He understood spiritual and greater benefits. Moreover, He willed to declare to him what His nature is, or rather, what He meant when He said, "I will be your God." The remainder provides promises also in explanation of this: "I will bless you and I will magnify [13b] your name, and you will be blessed, and I will bless the one who blesses you, and I will curse the one who curses you, and in you the families of the whole earth will be blessed" (Gen. 12:2–3). Likewise, "Do not fear Abraham, I am your shield and your exceeding great reward" (Gen. 15:1). Again, "I will multiply you according to the stars of heaven, and I will make you the father of many nations" (Gen. 15:5; 17:5). Now by all of these, we can determine what it means for that greatest God, to be our God, to be all sufficient, to be a confederate (*confoederatum*) with us, and that those promises and conditions of sacrifice are not only material, but spiritual also. In fact, in the beginning, the very Lord Jesus, according to the apostle's exposition to the Galatians, is promised to Abraham (Gal. 3:16). In Him is the fullness of all: righteousness, sanctification, [14a] life, redemption and salvation (1 Cor. 1:30). From His fullness, we all receive, grace upon grace (John 1:16), because it pleased the Father that all fullness dwell in Him, and by the blood of His cross to pacify all things which are in heaven and earth (Col. 1:19–20). Now it is by that One that the very inheritance is bequeathed to the ones who believe in this one and eternal testament of God. The summary of this testament (if someone asks for its recapitulation) is this: The God of heaven, both that greatest power and majesty, by which are all things, in whom all things consist and move, willed to be the God of Abraham and his seed. That is, He offers the benefit of Himself to them, inasmuch as He is sufficient for all of these things which are necessary for man, so that now He promises to them all strength and power, [14b] to be their shield, abundance, Preserver. He is the one who is about to strengthen the otherwise weak race of men in soul and body, and by the Lord Christ He is about to liberate from sin and eternal death, and to give eternal life. So much, then, concerning the office and function of God in this covenant, who opened to us all the heavenly treasures, and invited every kind of men to blessing under the figure of the land of Canaan and the blessing of the seed, as He is the horn of plenty (Isa. 55:1–13). Now we may hear what that One demands and expects from us.

VII. The Offices of Man and What Is Fitting to the Same

"You truly," He says, "will keep My covenant, you and your seed in their generations. Walk before Me and be innocent." These, I say, are our duties, these are to be observed by us. "You," He says, "will keep my covenant," [15a] that is, "you will have Me before all as your one and only sufficiency in all things, You will adhere to Me with one whole heart." Indeed, Moses also set this forth in Deuteronomy 13:4, saying, "Follow the Lord your God, fear Him, and keep His commands, and hear His voice. You will serve Him, and you will adhere to Him." What follows next in the very words of the covenant? "Walk before Me"— by these words as nothing is more brief, so nothing can be said more evidently, except that "to walk" can be translated from the Hebrew idiom, into what we express in our idiom as, "Schick dich wol und raecht zewandlen und zelaeben."[7] Moreover, He said, "Before Me," before Him, because it is to "My will and pleasure." The sense therefore is, "Establish your life [15b] throughout to my will." Moreover, what that will of God is, and in what manner we can walk before God, again by clear words He explains, "And be innocent." Now this is the steadfastness and purity of faith, further the innocence and purity of life, that is, the integrity and straight way by which the saints walk before God. And indeed, Moses says in

---

7. This translates into English as "Conform yourself to walk and to live well and right."

Deuteronomy 10:12, "And now Israel, what does the Lord your God ask of you, except that you fear the Lord your God, and walk in His ways, and love Him, and serve the Lord your God with all your heart, and with all your soul?" And Micah 6:8 says, "I have shown you, oh man, what is good, and what the Lord requires from you: certainly, to do justice, and to love mercy, and to walk carefully with your God." [16a] However, what work of many? Our part is to adhere constantly by faith to the one God, seeing that He is the one and only author of all good, and to walk to please Him by an innocent life. For the one who has neglected these things, and to whom these things become strange gods, and who is impiously or foully evil, and has worshipped God with more ceremonies and external things than true sacredness will be excluded, disinherited and rejected from the covenant.

VIII. All Scripture Is Referred to the Covenant as Its Target

Further, in these most brief heads of the covenant, the whole sum of piety consists. In fact, no other teaching of the saints of all ages through the whole Scriptures exists than what is included in these heads of the covenant, except that by the succession of times each one is explained more extensively [16b] and more clearly. Indeed, whatever is said in Holy Scripture of the unity, power, majesty, goodness, and glory of God is included in this one word of the covenant, "I am God All-sufficient." Truly, whatever promises are written of material benefits, of glory, the kingdom, victories, the wealth and necessities of life, are included by this one word of the covenant, "I will give to you and your seed the land of Canaan, and I will be their God." Likewise, what is taught more abundantly after several ages of Christ the Lord as in figure so in truth, concerning His justice, of the sanctification and redemption of the faithful, of the sacrifice, priesthood, and satisfaction of Christ, of the kingdom and eternal life, likewise of the calling of all the Gentiles, [17a] of spiritual blessings, of the abrogation of the law, of the glory of the church collected out of Gentiles and Jews, all of these are foretold in this one promise, "And all nations will be blessed in you, and you will be the father of many nations: whence your name will no longer be Abram, but you will be called Abraham" (Gen. 12:3 with 17:5). Again, what is advanced of faith in God, of the vanity of idols, of the worship of the one God, and of the invocation and worship of the one God, likewise of true laws, of judgment, equity and the cultivated graces, by various laws, by several messages of the prophets, and by the epistles of the apostles, and finally by the gospel narratives, in these most few words all of these are enveloped, "Moreover, you will keep my covenant, walk before Me, and be perfect (*perfectus*) or innocent (*integer*)."

[17b] IX. A Collation of All of Scripture to the Heads of the Covenant

And if it is agreeable, the Law, the prophets, and the very words of the apostles may be joined to these heads of the covenant, and marking all of them by this as being related to this target. **The Law.** For the law (that we may speak of this first) in the Lord's own witness, is taught partly love of God, partly love of neighbor. This very thing is taught by the heads of the covenant. In fact, the very Decalogue is seen to be a certain condition of the covenant, just as a paraphrase. For while this said concisely, "I am the Lord All-sufficient," it is presented in the Decalogue more fully, by this manner of expression, "I am the Lord your God who brought you out of the land of Egypt." Again, what is declared most concisely by the words of the testament, "You will keep my covenant walk before me, and be [18a] perfect."

The same indeed is expressed in the Decalogue by a certain enumeration, "You will have no other gods before Me. You will not make for yourselves images. You will not take the name of your God in vain. You will keep the Sabbath holy. Honor your parents. You shall not kill. You shall not commit adultery, etc., and if there are any others of this sort which describe and establish true integrity. We will speak a little later concerning the ceremonies, when we discuss the doctrine of the Old and New Testament.

Civil or Judicial (Laws)

The judicial or civil laws which instruct concerning the conservation of peace and public tranquillity, of the punishing of the guilty, of the waging of war and the driving back of enemies, of the defense of freedom, of the oppressed, of widows, of orphans, of the fatherland, of the justice and equity of the laws, or purchasing, [18b] loans, possessions, inheritance, and that sort of other legal titles, are they not included in the condition of the covenant and the very utterance which prescribes integrity and commands that we walk before God? Now if to someone this view of ours is seen to be appropriate, firm or clear, that that estimation of Abraham may be considered, who called the father of believers by the apostle (Rom. 4:11), certainly persisted faithfully in the covenant of God and walked before him in integrity. Moreover, because the law pertains to judicial, civil, or external matters, such as certain reasons for the punishing of the guilty, in the making of covenants, in waging war, in possessions, and the conserving of public peace, as a consequence, the law is seen to be nothing other than what was referring to the integrity of the soul, the sincerity of faith, both the love [19a] of virtue and of neighbor. Indeed, which observances Moses himself taught after many years from the dictation by God to the Jewish people (so far as it pertains to the very substance and the main point of the matter). Indeed, those are also the duties of piety, or the necessities of the most holy church, is so far as without them the church cannot appropriately exist, and may never be lacking them without risk. Since according to the word of the Lord, tares always have been in the field of the Lord and yet will not always be (Matt. 13:24–30). Indeed, when the Lord did not want the tares then to be uprooted completely, with their destruction He was concerned of the danger to the wheat, that is, of the good and Holy Church. Indeed, He said, "Let both grow, lest while you rather up the tares, you uproot the wheat with them at the same time." Who doubts that the same thing rightly [19b] also can be imputed to the sickle of justice, where their very great quantity and immaturity and field tend to the subversion of the Church? Thus, the saints consist not only of spirit but also of body. And as long as they have dealings in this world, they do not altogether lay aside human form and are not wholly turned into spirit. Rather, they are compelled to deal out laws concerning external things in their dealings with people, and in the use of the things which pertain to their lives. And for that reason, they need magistrates and the works of civil law with many titles. So all the more, it is seen what insanity drives those who exclude the magistrate from the church of God, as if the church does not require his labors, or that his functions are of such a nature that his labors cannot and ought not to be counted among the saints and the spiritual people of God. [20a] In the meantime, these actions of Abraham which are in truth judicial, are praised by the Holy Spirit of God among the first and most excellent works. And further, this same one is in the true church of Christians inasmuch as he is called by the apostle the father of all believers. And before the law, he is called the friend of God that he might hold the first place, who nevertheless exercised judicial acts.

The Prophets

Next we shall move on from the law to the prophets. These composed both history and messages, which they connected with both public proclamation and sermons and homilies. By historical examples, they present nothing else than illustrations of this covenant, just as Moses also did in his history. There it is seen how God stood by the covenants, that He was God of the seed of Abraham, [20b] that is, the All-sufficient Defender and Savior, and the sum of happiness. Likewise, it is seen how He led Israel into the land of Canaan. There He raised them into the most majestic kingdom; again, how He ruined the enemies of the seed of Abraham by a mighty hand, and mercifully preserved His own. Finally, one sees how the saints walked before Him in integrity, that is, how on the one hand they adhered by a true faith, and on the other hand, how they worshipped by the holiness of their lives. Further, one reads how others of impiety neglected this covenant and paid the penalty. Accordingly, the prophets' histories of this covenant are just as living paradigms. Indeed, in their messages, they treat of nothing other than these very heads of the covenant, teaching what is the nature of God, how He is good, how He is just, powerful, [21a] true, kind, merciful, and how He is to be served in truth, faith, righteousness and love. Likewise, they also severely accuse crimes, that are the result of neglecting the leading parts of the covenant: idolatry, apostasy and infidelity; then, murder, oppression of the poor, usury, injustice, rape, extravagance, adultery, and the rest of this kind of shameful crimes. They exhort repentance; they display the rewards and benefits of God. Again, they discuss most lucidly the seed of Abraham, Christ and His benefits, the kingdom and its whole mystery, the calling of the Gentiles, and the glory of the Church. Therefore, not as something extraordinary, not as a prophecy, they are seen rather to have put together the history of the things of the past.

[21b] X. Christ, the Seal and Living Confirmation of the Covenant

What I am about to say of Christ the Lord is not the entire doctrine. Rather, it is that very point worthy of admiration due to His incarnation, namely, the eternal covenant of God with the race of men, that covenant which He set forth and confirmed in an astonishing and living way. Indeed, when the true God assumed true humanity, immediately it[8] was not treated with more words and arguments, rather, by this thing itself, that greatest mystery is attested to the whole world—that God admitted man into covenant and partnership. Further, He bound man to Himself by an indissovable connection by the highest miracle of love, to be our God. Thus undoubtedly with Isaiah we too believe the name given to Christ: He is called Immanuel, just as if someone might say, "God with us" (Isa. 7:14.). Thus the Gospels [22a] review these innumerable miracles and great benefits of Christ with so many examples. By these indeed, Isaiah declared God to be kind, and therefore the Horn of Plenty, the Father, and *Shaddai* to the human race. To this name also the very death and resurrection of Christ are referred. They[9] are indeed most certain testimonies of the divine mercy, justice, and restitution of life. By Christ, God Himself established and expounded for us all of Himself, before our eyes; blessing us and accepting us as cleansed by Christ, into partnership and the eternal kingdom. All of which John's Gospel says embraced by the few but heavenly words, "In the beginning was the word, and the Word became flesh, and dwelt among us,

8. I.e., the covenant.
9. I.e., the words that compose the name Immanuel.

and we have seen His glory; glory, I say, which was proper for the only-begotten [22b] from the Father, full of grace and truth. Indeed of His fullness, we have received grace for grace. Because the law was given by Moses, grace and truth have appeared by Jesus Christ" (John 1:1, 14, 16–17). You hear this highest truth, that mystery that God has become a man, that is, He has become entirely of us, He Himself dwells among us (2 Cor. 6:16). You hear that He has begun to shine His power and glory to the world, not for any other plan than that He may draw us to Himself by most beautiful benefits in His love, who is the fullness of our God *Shaddai*. For Paul also says, "In Christ dwells all the fullness of God bodily, and you are in Him complete and perfect" (Col. 2:9–10.) In this way, therefore, the Lord Jesus Himself confirmed and displayed the first part of the covenant. The very incarnation [23a] shows that God is God—*Shaddai*, the blessing and eternal happiness of the seed of Abraham.

Now, the second part, as we said above, explains what sort of people we agree to be. The Lord no less diligently and evidently has established the same for us before our eyes in Christ. He has ordained in the conditions of the covenant, "Walk before Me and be perfect." Therefore, Christ the Lord coming into this world, having entered life in the flesh and the way of God, leaves for us an example which we may follow. Indeed, in Christ, the Gospels have described a life more diligent than this, as in a mirror by which we see what is to be followed and to be avoided, what pleases God, and what displeases Him. To this, indeed, those [23b] statements of the Lord pertain, which are found in John's Gospel: "I am the light of the world, he who follows Me shall not walk in darkness, but shall have the light of life" (John 8:12). Likewise, "I have given you an example, that just as I have done, so also you are to do" (John 13:15). To this also pertains that statement which is in John's first epistle: "The one who says he abides in Christ, ought also himself to walk just as that one walked" (1 John 2:6). This is of the life and living example of Christ. Now what pertains to His doctrine, I will not treat with any length. Who indeed does not know that He teaches partly faith in God, partly love to neighbor? The first exhibits the former part of the covenant, the second the latter part. Indeed, faith believes God to be the highest good, justice, and benefit among men. Truly, love [24a] itself is the fount of all innocence and integrity.

XI. The Apostles

We come to the apostles of Christ who are the heralds of the Lord. They themselves are also in entire agreement, since they teach what is the nature of God. They teach that He alone is good, just, saving and *Shaddai*, that He gave to us this blessed promised seed of Abraham, that in this one blessing there is salvation, life, and redemption. Likewise, they tell who are the heirs of this testament, who is the offspring of Abraham, since they seem to have taken the exposition of this covenant out of the promise to Abraham. Is this not what the apostle Paul ever testifies, that he has not invented any sort of new doctrine, but rather teaches the whole of Christianity out of the authority of the Old Scriptures? Indeed, in the first chapter of Romans, the apostle says that he was created [24b] and "separated for the preaching of the gospel of God, which He had fore-promised by His prophets in Holy Scripture" (Rom. 1:1–2). Likewise, before King Agrippa and Festus the Prefect of the Jews, Paul pleading his cause, openly testified that he taught nothing else than what the prophets had predicted was going to be (Acts 26:22). Accordingly, since the apostles acknowledge the prophets as teachers and masters of the true faith, and certainly this establishes them to be interpreters of that eternal and one testament, who does not see that all of the Sacred Scriptures are to be referred to the testament or the covenant as its most certain target?

XII. The Great Unity of the Covenant

Now out of these things, there follows what is third in order, namely, that this testament or covenant is both one and perpetual. Indeed, with plain words, the Lord Himself says in the remaining [25a] words of the covenant, "And I will make My covenant between Me and you and between your seed after you in their generations as an eternal covenant, that I may be your God and the God of your seed after you." Up to this point, we have established nothing with respect to the covenant as it deals with true religion, which the ancestors had not heard, as far as the matter pertains to the substance. Abraham certainly was justified exactly by faith, before circumcision and the law without ceremonies (Rom. 4:1–13). He saw the day of the Lord Jesus and rejoiced (John 8:56). He expected an eternal fatherland, having despised this earthly land, and so sought an eternal land, not just material things and earthly land (Heb. 11:14–16). By the apostles of Christ, in fact, by Christ the Lord Himself, he is displayed for us everywhere to be imitated in faith and innocence (Luke 19:9) [25b] Further, no comparison or equation can be between things which differ in nature. Therefore, unless the faith and innocence of Abraham were true and Christian faith and piety, the Lord wrongly displayed that which is to be imitated (Isa. 51:1–2; John 8:39–40; Heb. 11:8–19). Therefore, there is the testament and one church of all the saints before and after Christ, one way to heaven, likewise, one unchanging religion of all the saints (Pss. 15; 29 [14; 28 Vulgate]).[10] And indeed, several testimonies of this matter I may bring, unless the matter drawn thus far convinces even my opponents by its perspicuity and simplicity. But if someone is influenced by the force of many testimonies, he may hear the Lord Himself in the Matthean declaration, "A multitude from the east and west will come and will lie down [26a] with Abraham, Isaac and Jacob. Truly, the sons of the kingdom will be cast out into extreme darkness, there will be weeping and gnashing of teeth" (Matt. 8:11–12). Likewise, according to the clear words of John's gospel concerning the gathering of the church of the Gentiles, "And other sheep I have, which are not of this sheepfold, those also I must bring and they will hear my voice, and there will be one sheepfold and one pastor" (John 10:16). To this also, several very clear parables from the gospels are pertinent, especially that which is of the wedding, and that one which deals with the vineyard (Matt. 20:10–16; 21:33–41; 22:1–14). In these indeed, the ones invited and the farmers are changed, with the same wedding and the same vineyard always remaining. To these, the parable composed by the apostle of the olive tree and the branches is not dissimilar. Indeed, the same olive tree always remains the same tree, but to the broken off [26b] natural branches are brought the little forks, twigs of the wild olive (Rom. 11:17–24). Likewise, the eloquent words to the Corinthians, "I do not want you," he says, "to be ignorant brethren, that all our fathers ate the same spiritual food, and all drank the same spiritual drink. They drank, indeed, of the spiritual Rock which followed them. And truly, the Rock was Christ" (1 Cor. 10:1–4). But if someone sees our view growing out of these passages from Paul to be a novel proof, let him know that Dr. Aurelius Augustine

---

10. While the 1549 refers to Ps. 24 (Ps. 23 in the Vulgate), the 1534 and 1537 editions refer to Ps. 29 (Ps. 28 in the vulgate). This alternate reading fits more the context.

on this very passage of Paul to the Corinthians concluded the same as this. His words are found in his work on John, section 45, in this brief statement:

> The just who preceded the advent of our Lord Jesus Christ, who was to come humbly in the flesh, were indeed believers in him who was about to come, even as we believe [27a] in him who has come. The times are varied, but not the faith. Indeed, they are in different times, but we see that both entered by one door of faith, that is Christ. We believe our Lord Jesus Christ, born of the Virgin, to have come in the flesh, to have suffered, to have been resurrected, and to have ascended, to be fulfilled, just as you hear the words in the past tense. And those fathers who believed in the coming Virgin-birth, the coming passion, the coming resurrection, in the coming ascent into the heavens are in the society of this faith with us. Those indeed the apostle displayed when he says, 'Moreover, having the same spirit of faith, just as it is written, "I believe, therefore have I spoken," and we believe, therefore we also speak.' (2 Cor. 4:13). The prophet [27b] said, 'I have believed, therefore have I spoken.' The apostle says, 'And we believe, therefore we speak.' Further, in order that you may know the fact that the FAITH IS ONE, hear the phrase, 'Having the same spirit of faith and we believe.' So also in another place, 'Indeed I do not want you, I say, to be ignorant brothers.' And what follows. (*Tractates on the Gospel of John* 45.9 [PL 35:1722–23; NPNF1, 7:252])

The passage intended is, of course, Paul's words in 1 Corinthians 10. Elsewhere in John, He again writes and speaks of the church saying,

> Which brought forth Abel, Enoch, Noah, and Abraham, the same brought forth Moses and the prophets in the later times before the Lord's advent: and which also brought forth the apostles and our martyrs and all good Christians. Indeed, She brought forth all, whose births occurred in different times, but they are contained in the society of one people. [28a] And, the citizens of this commonwealth of pilgrims have experienced hardship and certain ones of them now experience, and continually unto the end others will experience, etc. (Augustine, *Baptism* 1.16.25 [PL 43:123; NPNF1, 4:422])

Truly, out of all this, I consider it to be evident that there is only one church, one testament of the ancients and of us.

XIII. From Where the Names of the Old & New Testaments Arise

Nevertheless, many arguments may be discovered in the Sacred Scriptures, which seem at the very first glance to distinguish far and wide from each other two testaments, two spirits, and two peoples. An example of such is what we read in Jeremiah, "Behold days are coming says the Lord, and I will strike with the house of Israel and Judah a new testament, not like the testament which I made with their fathers, etc." (Jer. 31:31–32). Likewise with Ezekiel, "I will give to you a new heart and [28b] I will put a new Spirit in your midst" (Ezek. 36:26). Likewise in Galatians 4:24, "These are two testaments." It is appropriate that I now explain from where these terms arise, and in what sense they are spoken. Consequently, at first, it is certain that the nomenclature of the Spirit and people of the Old and New Testaments does not spring from the very substance of the covenant. Rather, they arise from certain acquired and accidental things, which were added in the intervals of time. First this, then that, to those things which argue for the diversity of the nation of the Jews. They do not arise as perpetual and particularly necessary for salvation, but as mutable and for the time, and for the reason of persons and situations, without which the covenant itself would continue.

Ceremonies

Some examples of this sort are the ceremonies, the very Aaronic priesthood, likewise the laws prescribing sacrifices, [29a] purifications, and the manner of sacrifice; likewise, the selection of foods, what kind of tabernacle ought to be built and innumerable other examples of this sort. Indeed, the ancient saints such as Enoch, Noah, Abraham, Isaac, Jacob, Joseph lacked these things, who nevertheless at great cost were pleasing to God by faith, and without these they attained salvation. Whence Paul also in Galatians says,

> The promises are spoken to Abraham and his seed; and he does not say to seeds as of many, but as of one, and that seed is Christ. Moreover, I say, this testament before established by God in Christ, the law, which began 430 years later, cannot make void, so that it may abrogate the promise. (Gal. 3:16–17)

Therefore the ancients are saved by the benefit of the covenant, not by law or ceremonies. [29b] For as Abraham believed Him who said, "In you all nations will be blessed" (Gen. 22:18), so Abraham's fathers believed in the preceding times Him who said, "The seed of the woman will crush the head of the serpent" (Gen. 3:15). Indeed, this which he made with Abraham is not the first of all covenants. Rather, the first is what he made with Adam. Whence with clear words in the covenant that followed he may say, "I will erect" or "I will confirm" or "I will establish my covenant with you," that is "I will ever keep firmly the beginning of the covenant." Indeed, it is often renewed. This is because of definite causes, as with Noah after the flood, now with Abraham, afterwards with Moses. Nevertheless, it is one and the same covenant which is confirmed and established with all of these.[11] "Why then," you ask, "did God institute without counsel and a definite reason a law that is useless?"

The Institution of the Law

May it not be. Rather, while the souls of Abraham's seed, that is the Jews, having been corrupted by the long cohabitation in Egypt, so that they were nearly ignorant of the ancestral religion and nearly of the covenant itself, and in time they deserted more and more to Egyptian idolatry and every scheme of Gentile worship, then it was pleasing to the wise and merciful Lord to come up and aid the collapsed covenant with certain props. First, therefore, [30a] He re-established the very heads of the ancient covenant, but He explained it more fully, and He wrote in tables of stone with His own finger. Moreover, in these things there is no mention thus far of ceremonies. Indeed, it is enough that the written rule was for the faithful. Truly, while they continued to be unbelieving and unfaithful, the burden of the ceremonies was imposed by the arms of pity, which the ancients never had. Both to this end and by this counsel, He established the imposition out of an urgent cause, that they not institute the worship of a foreign god. Therefore, He established a special thing, and by this He declared Himself to be pleased for the time of correction, which He was passing over without the true Spirit and without the true completed faith and thus without Christ, so

---

11. The passage from "Indeed, this which he made with Abraham" to this point is not found in 1534 but is found in both 1537 and 1549.

that He might establish the testament even with that plan (Ps. 50:8–11).[12] Further, by this He might cover the mystery of Christ even as by figures, and there might be certain sacraments and visible words.[13] Nor indeed was this explanation born recently to our school of thought. Rather, it was derived from the holy oracles brought to light in the faith of the ancients and the fathers. [30b] Indeed, Tertullian in the *Second Book Against Marcion* says,

> The burdens of the sacrifices too, and the scrupulous troubles of the rituals and oblations no one may censure as if God desired such things especially for Himself, who nevertheless manifestly exclaims, "What to Me are the multitude of your sacrifices? and who desired them from your hands?" (Isa. 1:11–12). But one may perceive that diligence of God by which He willed to bind together a people prone toward idolatry and such transgression of their religious duties, by which things, the superstition of the age was being set in motion. This He did in order that He might divert them from such superstition, commanding these things to be done as if He desired such for Himself, lest the people fail in their duty by imitations. But also, He continually distinguished all encompassing care in the very intercourse of life and the dealings of man with men in the home and in the market places and for even [31a] small vessels, in order that by this legal discipline occurring everywhere, no one might depart for a moment from the respect due to God. (Tertullian, *Against Marcion* 2.18–19 [CCL 1:496; ANF 3:311–12])

Thus Tertullian. Therefore, what pertains to the Decalogue, and the civil law too, nothing arises from the diversity in the testament and people of God. Indeed, everywhere the love of God and neighbor, faith and love maintain their power. It is out of the minds of men and from the acquired things of the testament that the diversities appear. The testament which is with all the pious is one. It is only because of certain acquired things and human superstitions it began to be spoken of as "old" and "new," material and spiritual. And the Old indeed is so called (since reason asks for relationships) on account of the New following, which, promises the remission of sins and further performs such by Christ, [31b] and teaches both faith and love. By which things, it cannot at all be called new, since it teaches nothing novel. For in fact, this has what we have received from the old tradition (1 John 2:7). Therefore, it is designated as the "New" because all the ceremonies were fulfilled by Christ, whom alone it proclaims, as far as they were figures and shadows of eternal things. To that extent, they have gone out of use. Further, that ancient religion which was displayed in those golden times, flourished, was renewed, and so was re-established and completed and completed by Christ more fully and more clearly, as by a new unconcealed light in the world. Indeed, it abounds with a new people, the Gentiles, of course. Paul also spoke on this matter in Hebrews 8 and Ephesians 2. [32a] By the same rule and plan, Scripture spoke of a carnal people, indeed, not those who persist in the testament of God by a true faith, but who were putting their trust to a greater extent in material things rather than in the real and spiritual heads of the testament or promise of God. This testimony of Paul I call to my aid, which was mentioned before: "For these are two testaments" (Gal. 4:24), he reasons, "Tell me you who want to be under law, do you not hear the Law itself? Indeed, it is written that Abraham had two sons, one of a female slave and the other of a free woman" (Gal. 4:21–22). Hence, we conclude that

---

12. The 1534 and 1537 editions have the reference to Ps. 50 (Ps. 49 in the Vulgate); the 1549 edition refers to Ps. 95 (Ps. 94 in the Vulgate).

13. The phrase "and there might be certain sacraments and visible words" is not found in the 1534 edition, but appears in both the 1537 and 1549 editions.

the carnal people are those who want to be under the law. Therefore, not all of Abraham's seed is continually under the law and carnal. In fact, it is called carnal, because it adheres to the laws without knowledge and the Spirit, and by those externals it is confident to be able to save itself. [32b] Indeed, they have the ceremonial features of His Spirit, which to a greater extent Paul explained in detail in the epistle to the Hebrews. And by this spirit and despised or misunderstood judgment of the ceremonies, they abused the law. Further, it is true that the sons of Abraham are free and trust in the promises of God. Therefore, antiquity also had the spiritual Israel. Indeed, they judge wrongly who value the whole from the part, as they are accustomed who mark—not without injury to the saints of God—all the fathers preceding the advent of the Lord with the name of the carnal Israel. In so doing they do not set straight by the use of synecdoche—a common figure in Scripture—how this knotty point is to be burst open. Moreover, lest those complain to themselves about this interpretation by figures, even though we have established sufficiently the superiority of our view, [33a] nevertheless, I will fully provide for them three of the greatest and powerful testimonies in religion. Each of these testimonies claim that Israel was a spiritual people, and further that the prophets taught the same concerning the laws which the apostles taught. First, therefore, in Jeremiah 7:21, 23, he wrote in these words,

> Thus says the Lord of Hosts, the God of Israel, "Bring your sacrifices of victims and give out your flesh. Because I did not speak with your fathers and they were not commanded in the day when I led them out of the land of Egypt concerning the word of sacrifices and victims, rather by this word they were commanded saying, 'Hear my voice and I will be your God, and you will be to Me a people, so that it may be well with you.'"

Now by these words it is clear what was [33b] the doctrine of the prophets and of the laws, likewise what is the summary of all the commands of God, I say, the very summary of the covenant, obedience or faith itself, by which also it is established that the saints are not to be pronounced good by laws. Indeed, the Lord commanded them, but at a distance for another plan, certainly that He might come up to aid the collapsed covenant, and that He might remove all from idolatry and fasten them to Himself by faith: not that he might justify the laborers by these, but so that he might foreshadow by these the coming justice of Christ. Because they are unwilling to understand, they are accused most severely by this place from the prophet. Therefore, the Lord pronounced good the Spirit not the carnal in the Israelites. Therefore, before the birth of Christ, He had a spiritual people out of the Israelites, since to such an extent He did not approve of the carnal things. [34a] Stephen, too, the most holy martyr of Christ, according to Luke in Acts 7, with almost unending examples of the ancients proved the fact that faith in God was acceptable to God before the law, in the law, and after the law, not the ceremonies. Further, he showed that the saints, that is, the patriarchs and the prophets, I say, all the just before the birth of Christ, worshipped God in faith and purity of life not by external things. Behold, you have an entirely spiritual and pledged people. Does not the apostle Paul also claim nearly the same with the ancients in the eleventh chapter of Hebrews, by examples drawn from the fathers from the beginning of the world to the very time of Christ? And so when they have these, who is the one who does not see the names of "old" and "new" both of the people and especially of the testaments [34b] are not able to tear apart the very testament and the very church of the ancients and of us? The Spirit too is the same in both, but due to the carnality and transgressions of those whom the scourges drove in confusion into Babylon, He Himself said He was about to give a new Spirit, by which He meant nevertheless both the abundant riches and gifts of grace He was about to impart to the faithful by Christ. Truly, (of this matter) we have argued something in our commentaries on the Epistle of Peter. Up to this point, I wanted to indicate the unity of the testament and to declare the causes as to why the terms "New" and "Old" began to be used.

XIV. The Things in Which We Excel the Ancients

Now in order that I may not conceal anything in this matter, I will briefly [35a] show how the church of Christians, which was constituted after the birth of Christ excels the ancients. First, in comparison to those who lived their lives under the law, we are happier, because we are relieved from all the burden of ceremonies. We have touched upon the earlier and original instruction of the ancient fathers, which was shining, of course, with faith and obedience without ceremonies, when we spoke of the heads of the covenant. Again, because we rejoice in the clear truth with the shadows scattered by the radiance of the gospel and the figures fulfilled. Thereupon, in truth, because all the fathers died before the advent of Christ, our church is pronounced superior, that is, because we confess that Christ has come, that He has brought the Spirit most abundantly. Likewise, now His glory has spread throughout the whole earth and most completely has been consummated, whom those thus believed was to come, and expected with the greatest [35b] desire. For this reason Simeon, that elderly man himself, cried with the greatest happiness, recounting, "Now, oh Lord, send away your servant in peace according to your Word, because my eyes have seen your salvation, which you have prepared before the face of all people, a light for the revelation of the nations and the glory of your people Israel" (Luke 2:29–32).

XV. The Fifth Chapter of Matthew

Of course, others pointing to Matthew 5 object to our view. They do not see that the Lord Jesus' refined and divine oration does not attack either Moses or the prophets, as if they either supposed or taught differently from Christian doctrine, rather than that he willed to correct the errors of the common people and to teach the true nature of the law. Indeed, He had destroyed every injustice of the time and the ignorance and avarice of the Pharisees. Whence, protesting with ordered words [36a] before He began the exposition of the law, He says, "Except your righteousness exceed that of the scribes and Pharisees, you will not be able to enter the kingdom of heaven" (Matt. 5:20). Therefore, Christ attacked the Pharisees, not the very spirit of the law and of the prophets. He said a little before, "I have not come to loosen (*solvere*) the law, but to fulfill (*adimplere*)" (Matt. 5:17). Moreover, He taught by this sermon that the law is the will of God, which is altogether most elegant, holy, pure, and spiritual; which also regulates the mind and will of man. This is true even to the extent that it prohibits coveting. Since this is not something that man is able to perform, due of course to his most corrupted flesh, who does not see that the plan of the whole sermon considers, what the law may effect in order that it may lead us into a knowledge of ourselves, so that [36b] we might flee from ourselves by utter denial of everything into the mercy of God? In the mean time, however, we regulate both our every plan and especially our actions toward this eternal, highest, and purest will, that is, the law of God; not in the ordinary way, but with the highest and most exact devotion. This and this alone is to walk carefully with God in holiness, who is holy and indeed desires that we be holy (Mic. 6:8, Lev. 16).[14]

XVI. Paul in 2 Corinthians 3

While hallucinating in an error equal to this, they do not see that Paul in 2 Corinthians 3 is disputing against the false prophets, by forcing laws upon the Church of Christ (as may be gathered from the rest of the epistles). For against their superstition and impiety he declared the glory of the gospel, which is more illustrious than the laws. Nor indeed does he speak in this text of the place of the whole law, but [37a] here he only discusses what is done away. In the meantime, he does not command all of the law and prophets to refer to the letter, but also, he does not name just any spirit, as is their inclination, rather, the very Lord Jesus who is the perfection of the law to justification to all who believe (Rom. 10:4).

XVII. How do the Ebionites Mix Together the Law with the Gospel?

Further, they pile up false accusations against us, accusing us of the Ebionite heresy. Indeed, of the Ebionites, Eusebius in book III, chapter 27 of his *Ecclesiastical History* writes in this way:

> They also regard the observance of the law to be kept, nor do they judge only faith in Christ to be sufficient for salvation (indeed, I say, these mingle law with the gospel). Therefore, they keep the fleshly observance of the law. Moreover, all the epistles of the apostle they at the same time reject and call them the very apostasy from the law. (Eusebius, *Ecclesiastical History* 3.27 [Loeb, 1:260–63; NPNF2, 1:159])

[37b] Nor do Irenaeus, Tertullian and Augustine report any differently from this. Truly, there is no one now who may be ignorant of how far different this doctrine of ours concerning the one and eternal testament and of the abrogation of the law is from their blasphemies.

XVIII. The Deuteronomy 5 Passage

However, we may devote some attention to the words of the Lord which are read in this sense from Moses in Deuteronomy 5:2–3: "The Lord our God made with us a covenant in Horeb: not with our fathers did the Lord enter into this pact, but with us who are alive in the present time." Therefore Augustine in his book of questions, on Deuteronomy 5, question 9, explains this text by synecdoche. He understands these fathers to be those whom the blows of God destroyed in the wilderness. [38a] For, he says,

> Those who did not enter into the land of promise, did not pertain to this testament; rather, their sons, those, I say, how ever many were not twenty years and up when God was speaking of the mountain so that then they were able to be counted. Nevertheless, they were able to be nineteen years old and under all the way to the age of children, by which manner those might

14. Bullinger's text has Leviticus 16, but he may have had in mind Leviticus 11:44, since that is the passage that uses the precise words of his quote. Nevertheless, Leviticus 16 is appropriate since that spells out the Day of Atonement, which is a clear picture of God's demand for holiness.

be able to see and to hear and to retain memories of what was done and said. (Augustine, *Quaestiones in Heptateuchum* 7.5.9 [CSEL 28, 2:374–75])

And John Oecolampadius explains in his unpublished commentary on Jeremiah, this point in keeping with this method.

With God, that eternal covenant is one, which is arranged by a diverse variety of times. And in the more inner things of man, too, it was and remained always one; not only is it so in eternal [38b] predestination.[15] Nevertheless, what so ever sort of diversity of the covenant that there is, ought to be heard in the words that the Lord agreed to with Abraham: nothing else than obedience is stipulated from him. Now, under Moses a great abundance was added. These were not a mark to be reckoned to one, but clearly to the whole multitude. Thereupon, many are fortified by the surrounding laws, all of which are to be referred to those ten word of the table of the covenant, etc.

XIX. The Promise of the Land of Canaan

Now what is objected concerning the land of Canaan, or wars and victories, of the glory and happiness of the Jews, which hardly fit with the ignominy of Christians, for which nothing awaits except the cross and exile, inasmuch as Scripture says of these, "All who will live piously in Christ will endure persecutions" (2 Tim. 3:12), is easily cleared up. Indeed, no one denies that the promise of the land [39a] of Canaan in context was restricted. And truly no one in turn is able to deny the same or to affirm without doubt that a similar promise was made equally with all the Gentiles. In fact, Abraham himself, to whom the promise of the Canaan land fell, did not even obtain a foot-step (as Stephen says, Acts 7:5). In the meantime, he acquired great wealth, just as his posterity—Isaac, Jacob, and Joseph—did. Although these certainly did not even occupy the promised land, nevertheless, they were especially distinguished by riches. This was done, I believe, by the Lord in example to all the Gentiles, by which they learned for themselves too that they would lack nothing, if they feared God after the manner of the fathers. And many promises of this sort are met with here and there (Ps. 37:1–40; Matt. 6:25–34; Acts 14:17; 17:26–28; Heb. 13:5–6). [39b] Moreover, because they pertain to the happiness of the fathers, it is certain these are not used with complete chance on this earth. Indeed, by the cross and by many tribulations, they entered into the kingdom of God.

The Cross, Peace and Victory of the Saints

For who does not know how much of weariness Abraham consumed in his long wanderings (which I will not relate)? The patriarch Jacob never more made prosperous use of any good fortune, than they had not been disturbed by the most weighty and various dangers. Of Moses, Joshua, Samuel, David and the remainder of these most distinguished men, there is no need for me to recount much. For, what individual would be sufficient for the enumerating of their hardships, and damaging toils undertaken for the Lord, when, indeed, the Holy Scriptures themselves scarcely relate those things with many books? What about the fact that [40a] the faithful Jewish people endured no fewer persecutions on account of

---

15. This is the only place where Bullinger mentions predestination in this treatise; and that in a citation from Oecolampadius.

piety and faith, sometimes from their own faithless kings, sometimes in truth from foreign tyranny, than the very Church of Christ from the blasphemous and impious Caesars? For as the latter has her Neros, Domitians, Maxentiuses, Julians, Decians, Severuses, Valerians, and Diocletians: so the ancient church had their Pharaohs, Ahabs, Joashes, Manassehs, Jehoiachims, Zedekiahs, Nebuchadnezzars, and Antiochuses. In fact, the Christian martyrs had the priests and prophets of the church's ancient times as examples. For thus the Lord said in Matthew, "Blessed are they who endure persecution for righteousness' sake, because theirs is the kingdom [40b] of heaven. Blessed are you when men have reproached you on account of me. Rejoice and exult, because your reward is great in heaven. For indeed, the prophets were persecuted before you" (Matt. 5:10–12; 23:29–36). Further, it is not doubtful that many thousands of saints have always lived dutifully (*pie*) in Christ, who nevertheless with the name of faith were never driven into exile, or sentenced with capital punishment. Paul, therefore, pronounced that thought, "All who will live piously in Christ will suffer persecution," not as a common law, but as a consolation for the afflicted (2 Tim. 3:12. See Augustine, *Against Two Letters of Gaudentius*, book 2, chapter 13 [CSEL 53:272–74]). Too, there are various kinds of persecution, so that he who is cast into prison or hung from a tree is not the only one who sustains persecution. Rather, he too who [41a] is exercised by various adversities and trials. This is what in general often happens at another time with the enjoyment of the peace and security of piety. For the apostle Paul also was most frequently safe from the unfaithfulness and fury of the persecutors, but he also felt the most heavy anxiety of soul, even though revived in respect to the brethren. For the soul of the Christian indeed is affected by that harm which belongs to another (Rom. 12:15; Heb. 13:3). Whence the Apostle said, "Who is weakened, and I am not weakened? Who is offended, and I am not disturbed?" (2 Cor. 11:29). To this, can be added what the most holy prophet Isaiah describes in those chapters in which the church is to be gathered out of every land in the earth, in which he also mentions the coming kings (Isa. 49:1–7; Pss. 2:1–12; 48:1–14). He did not teach wholly and always that the church had to be exposed by killings, so that what is to be in this whole world is a lack of peace, happiness and victory. And, Dr. Aurelius [41b] Augustine in book V of *The City of God* (CSEL 40, 1:260–66; NPNF2, 2:104–7) in the final chapters (chs. 24–26) brought out that the kingdom of Christians is to be sought by victories, and with wonderful happiness and excellent delight and usefulness. Again, in the twenty-second book *Against Faustus the Manichean* in chapters 64–80 (CSEL 25:659–83; NPNF2, 4:296–305), he frequently debates the subject of war and the law of war, which our discussion will not consider at any length. For by all of these things, we desired to explain what are the conditions of the covenant, that that covenant is one and eternal, and why the terms "new" and "old" are employed. Now we will subjoin a few words concerning the ceremonies and sacraments of the new covenant.

XX. Of Circumcision, the Sacrament of the Covenant

Those who will strike a covenant, will take either a ram heifer, or a she-goat, and will cut them in two parts, thereupon in truth they will cross through the middle of the parts, [42a] adjuring if they stand by the contract so God Himself may divide and entirely destroy them. Evidence of this rite may be seen in Genesis 15:9–18 and Jeremiah 34:15, 17–20. Referring to this method, therefore, God consecrates this covenant by blood, and with plain words He adds an explanation, saying, "And the foreskinned male, the flesh of whose foreskin has not been circumcised, that soul will be blotted out from his people." That this is understood not only of a little cut-off skin, but rather of the whole covenant, because he who will neglect this covenant is to be destroyed by an eternal curse. For this follows logically from the cause which is given us. "Because he has voided or broken My covenant." Moreover, he who has thus broken the covenant through contempt for the instruction of God, neglects the sacrament of God as useless, or else while [42b] he does not neglect it, yet in having received the symbol of the covenant, the covenant itself appears with faithlessness and impurity.

Infants Dying without the Sign of the Covenant

Whence we gather that infants born among the faithful, moreover who die before they began to live or before they were able to be enrolled among the people of God by the holy sign of the covenant, cannot be condemned by any defense from this text. For it speaks of adults and of despisers of the covenant. This is what the very words sufficiently demonstrate which are spoken in this manner, "And the foreskinned male in whose flesh the foreskin has not been circumcised, that soul will be exterminated from his people, etc." Such infants, moreover, we believe to be saved by the mercy and grace of God. This is something to which those who judge them according to such a ministry of the church, do not agree with. [43a] And in circumcision, He held another mystery. For Paul says, "A testament is ratified in death, since it is never in force while the testator lives" (Heb. 9:17). Moreover, God is the testator. Therefore, God had to die. But although He is immutable and immortal, He assumed the seed of Abraham. And in assumed flesh, He suffered and poured out His blood. So that if I may speak in this way, in this manner, He ratified the testament. Moreover, as He taught this mystery to the fathers in figure, He desired the seed of Abraham itself to be circumcised, signifying that the true seed of Abraham, Christ the Lord by His death and blood would confirm that covenant.

Concerning the grace of the matter, the Lord Jesus Himself in Matthew, speaking of the sacrament of the New Covenant, says, "This is My blood, [43b] which is of the New Testament, which is poured out for many for the remission of sins" (Matt. 26:28). Indeed, this old sacrament had to be changed and the new ordained. For after the death of Christ, everything was confirmed. Certainly, those signs which were prefiguring His future death had to be changed. Indeed, in their place had to be substituted what is complete in significance, or what signifies a most perfect justification. This is what we attribute to baptism and the Eucharist in a mystery. For these symbols in the establishment by God of the New Testament with the people now began to be confirmations of the covenant and divine grace by Christ. Further, having to cut the foreskin signified the circumcision of the heart, and the necessity to serve God [44a] in the obedience of faith (Deut. 10:16; Jer. 4:4). Therefore, to those whom it was given by circumcision to these first it was offered by the grace and covenant of God, by the ministry and instruction of God. Indeed, He does not scorn to be the God of the little ones, who likewise first offered Himself out of mere grace, and said, "I will be your God." Then by the same grace God bound the ones who had been consecrated to himself with circumcision, commanding that they cleave to Himself by faith and innocence. From these things, indeed, it appears that the whole of the covenant is contained in the sacrament of the covenant, just as with our sacraments in baptism and the Eucharist is contained the whole reckoning of the covenant. Truly to speak of these things fully at the present would take us a long way from our purpose. It was already enough to have emphasized that God in establishing the sacrament of the covenant willed to have regard [44b] for the interests of the things of mortals, which consist not only of soul but body too. Thus, not infrequently, visible things and signs are introduced into the consideration of the invisible. Therefore, God gave the sacraments (*sacramenta*), which is the term the ancients used to call them, because they are visible signs of an invisible grace.[16] Moreover, he gave to the Old Testament people, circumcision and the Passover, and, to us who are His people after the suffering of Christ, baptism and the Eucharist. Otherwise, what is in these visible and invisible things; what is their power and efficacy, is left for another discussion.

XXI. The Documents of the Testament Are Written

What is last in testaments and covenants, moreover, is the composition of written records or if you will, documents comprehending and transmitting to posterity every reason and testimony of the transaction. And these indeed [45a] are strengthened by the name of covenant or testament. For we call the written documents of the testament or covenant the very covenant or the testament itself. Although, in reality, they are not the testament or covenant. Rather, they are an exact exposition and testimony of the conducted matters and conditions. The Lord did not bother to have any documents written with the ancient fathers, for they were carrying the covenant written in their hearts by the finger of God. Nevertheless, He gave to posterity the whole engraved in stone documents through Moses, because they had waited for the true religion from the fathers almost as if received by hand. The stone documents, He also called the tables of the covenant and the testament. Certainly with the understanding and by the scheme which we here have explained now and again. Further, that something may not be able to be missed by anyone, [45b] Moses says this very thing. (**The Ancients wrote in bronze documents which they wanted for a long and uninterrupted time.**) Thereupon, the prophets, and then the apostles of Christ the Lord wrote uncorrupted and just books concerning this matter, which have earned a title with all and for all ages, from this very thing as they treat of the Old and New Testament. Certainly, because these teach most copiously, how that covenant with Abraham began; how it was presented to the ancient people, and how it led them to life under the hope of Christ's coming through various plans, figures, and ways in religion. These in truth teach how the covenant itself was renewed and was dedicated by a new method by Christ, how every type by Him is fulfilled, and of course, from the multitude of the Gentiles a new people [46a] was called in the unity of faith and established in the true religion, and was led into eternal life by Christ. And these are those books of truth and righteousness, by whose rule, all the learned and holy men of all the ages have perpetually believed the life and faith of the worshippers of the true God to be able to be truly established. For Isaiah cries, "If they have spoken to you, consult the mediums, the diviners, the fortune-tellers and the enchanters. Does not every tribe consult its gods; even the living from the dead? Therefore, to the law and to the testimony with great haste" (Isa. 8:19–20). Further, Christ the Lord says, "They have Moses and the prophets, let them hear them. And if they do not hear them, nor would they believe if someone were resurrected from the dead" (Luke 16:29, 31). Besides, if some legal controversy arises concerning the inheritance between heirs, immediately [46b] they consult the documents. Thus they have faith in these witnesses, so that they treat everything according to the rule of the documents.

---

16. The Latin term *sacramentum* means a "mystery."

Whence, if some dispute arises in the matter of religion concerning the true and false worship of God, we consult the documents of the covenant, and both books of the testament. In these, we may believe. According to them, we may establish everything. For two great luminaries of our religion, David (Ps. 19:7–11) and Paul (2 Tim. 3:16–17), abundantly testify that all piety and righteousness are completely included in these.

XXII. Epilogue—Of the Antiquity of the Christian Religion

Those are, most illustrious readers, what I desired to communicate to you concerning the one and eternal testament or covenant which pertains to God. Truly, those things which belong to this covenant—its conditions, its sacraments, and the documents to which it is entrusted—have been gathered together by the grace given to me by the Lord. [47a] Partly, so that I might serve, in this thing, everyone with us by our brotherly complaints to the ones who loudly and with depravity demand this exposition. Partly, in truth, so that I might indicate in passing the clarity, simplicity, and antiquity of Scripture and our religion, which is badly spoken of today, as if it were heretical. Indeed, it is more ancient than the idolatrous religion of the Gentiles or the worship of images, and indeed more ancient than the others the great men of fame may compute. For those who were from the times of Jupiter, or a little before, believed that the temple and the worship of the gods had been recently established. Moreover, the statements of Herodotus in the second book of his *Histories* (2.37–76 [Loeb, 1:319–63]), and by Strabo in the seventeenth book of *Geography* (17.1–2 [Loeb, 8:2–153]) are seen to be more likely. These, [47b] of course, claimed that the Egyptians were both the first worshippers and authors of the gods, from whom the rest of the nations received the practice of idolatry. Indeed, to the ones who carefully compute the times, it is clear that the worship of Jupiter is several centuries younger than the Mosaic worship. And Moses testifies that not only the Jewish nation saturated with idolatry in Egypt to have erected in the desert to God an image of Apis (the ox-god) after the example of the Egyptians, but also in the times of the Patriarchs the practice of idolatry flourished. Of course, the Jewish religion is also ancient. This I understand to be what is confined by circumcision and the laws, inasmuch as what began partly with the times of Abraham and partly with the times of Moses. Still, Christianity is much older than these. For Abraham was pronounced justified in the sacred books earlier than (he was) circumcised. [48a] Older, than this too, are Noah, Enoch, Seth, Abel and Adam who truly pleased God by faith without circumcision. Moreover, it is now disgusting to examine the Turkish and papist religions under the pretext of the antiquity of religions. For not before many centuries had passed almost to the 630th year after Christ's birth, did the former blaspheme the truth, having sprung up by Mohammed, who is at the same time the most corrupt and most impious author. The latter, on the other hand being almost no older, obscured the simple, pure, and true prophetic and apostolic tradition which had been established by Christ. Here, I say nothing of this faith as the complex of the twelve articles which are confessed by the mouth among us; I am speaking both of the papist dogma and rituals, on which things they lean as if they were the most certain, the oldest, and [48b] infallible things. In this class are the Mass, images, monasticism, and many other things which the primitive saints and Church of God were ignorant of. For Albert the Great—the commander-in-chief of the scholastic theologians—designates the Roman Pontiff Gregory the First, who lived around A.D. 600, as the originator of the Mass. The same Gregory testifies in a certain letter to Serenum the bishop of Marseilles, antiquity allowed (I use his words), that in the places for the veneration of the saints the ancients were to be depicted according to the custom of history. But I do not know how that one might have understood antiquity, because I know Lactantius of Firmianus, a contemporary of Constantine the Great, said with clear words, "There is no doubt, but that where there is no religion,

[49a] the worship of images is everywhere."[17] The opinion of Saint Cyprian, the head priest of Epiphany Salamis, is in no way unlike this statement, from which messenger Jerome has openly pronounced, that images of men are to be placed in the Church of Christ, against the authority of Scripture, and against our religion. And Jerome, according to the authors Eutropius and Prosper of Aquitaine, died in A.D. 422. Therefore, to what extent was Gregory able to produce antiquity for the defense of pictures in the temple? On the contrary, even if he might produce the oldest, nevertheless the prophet of the Lord speaking with irony says of images, "May not those teach you?" (Hab. 2:19). For truly indeed Gregory himself in that same letter of his attacked the worship of images, which nevertheless the popes not only have admitted, but [49b] indeed have taught. And Benedict, the abbot of Casino, whom every mouth of the monastics call father, flourished only a little before the time of Gregory, perhaps by 60 years if Bede's supposition is true concerning the reckoning of the times. For Paul and Anthony, of whom Jerome makes mention, defended nothing of monasticism in the papacy. For in truth, if you compare these times with the ancients, you may discover absolutely that the papist religion is a novelty; compared with the ancestors, it is down to nothing in antiquity. Now although those prefer this religion to all others and compose much concerning its antiquity and certainty, we glory far more justly of the antiquity of our faith. This is because it is older than both the religions of the Gentiles and the Jews. It has endured from the beginning of the world [50a] to this very day, undoubtedly, a total of 5508 years. For 1534 years are computed from the birth of Christ to this day, and from the beginning of the world to the birth of the Lord, 3974 years. In the *Chronicles*, Eusebius gathers 5199. If to these are added 1534, you have 6733 years from the beginning of the world. We, however, have preferred to follow the Holy Bible rather than the commentaries of the Greeks.[18] For indeed, we have proved that the faith of Abraham, of Adam, and of Christ were the same. But Eusebius also asserts the same as us in the first book, chapter one of *Ecclesiastical History* (1.4 [Loeb, 1:38–45; NPNF2, 1:87–88]), whose words it will not be bothersome to add, yet not all of them. The passage [lit. the place] is fairly long, but for many reasons it is worthy to be read carefully.

The Christian or Evangelical Faith, The Most Ancient of All

He says,

All those who are enlisted in the order of generation from Abraham upwards right on toward the first man, although not by name, yet in reality and religion (were) truly Christians. Since indeed the name of Christian reveals this: someone who believes in Christ keeps his [50b] doctrine, faith, devotion, and righteousness; (and) eagerly clings to divine wisdom; and also seeks all that is conducive to virtue. If, I say, these (realities) are revealed by the expression of the name of Christian, and mark him out as an adherent of true religion; we now acknowledge that those holy men, about whom we have spoken earlier, were also Christians. And indeed neither was there corporal circumcision for them, nor the keeping [*observatio*] of the Sabbath (just as there is not even for us). Neither did they have any religious scruple about observance (*observatione*) concerning foods, or the rest (of the observances) which were transmitted through Moses to posterity to be kept (*observanda*) more figuratively and mystically. Since,

---

17. The original contains the following marginal reference, "This letter exists in Tom V, fol. 73."

18. The translation follows here the 1537 and 1549 editions. In the original 1534 edition, Bullinger followed Eusebius computation; the passage can be translated as follows: "It has endured from the beginning of the world to this very day, undoubtedly, a total of 6733 years. For 1534 years are computed from the birth of Christ to this day, and from the beginning of the world to the birth of the Lord, 5199 years."

therefore, without all these practices (*observationibus*) those men, whom we mentioned earlier, were devout [or religious]; moreover (since) they have followed the faith of Christ, whom we [51a] now follow, who has shown himself many times to them and taught thoroughly or warned about the things which relate to faith and piety, (which) we have proved in the preceding (points); how will one doubt that the origin of this people has begun and has been derived from these times? Finally, this religion was to such an extent sent beforehand to and formed beforehand in those, that they were not even held strangers to the name itself (which certainly seems to be [lit. to make] the only difference); indeed already then they were not only shown to be Christians, but they were also called Christs by divine eloquence (cf. Ps. 105:15).

And after certain other arguments, he infers,

Therefore, the religion of Christians is neither new nor foreign, [51b] nor (was it) rising of late. But if it is right freely to point out what is true, (it was) the first (religion) of all and started at the same time as the origin of the universe itself; it received immediately from the beginning appearance and form by the same Christ (as) God, doctor, and maker.

I have retold thus far the words of Saint Eusebius. Now, therefore, I pray, whom does it cause annoyance or who is sorry for even the most difficult labors taken up for the testament of God? [This is even more so] when it is known that all the saints of God have honored God in this (testament) from the beginning of the universe itself; yes indeed, they have laid up their lives for this (testament) itself. Whom, in truth, has he not most strongly (vehemently) encouraged, though (they are) now sweating in the midst of labors? Indeed that eternal God has obligated himself to us with an oath, which he has most solemnly preserved, that eternal testament with all [52a] the saints from the beginning. Certainly, the saints have often been hurled into dangers, religion itself has often been threatened with ruin, (and) more frequently (than not) it appeared defeated and suppressed. Yes to be sure God himself was more frequently imagined to have abandoned his own people. But at the right time, rising up adequately, he has always defended true religion, (while) the wicked are defeated and overthrown. This same (God) is immutable and eternal. This same (God), therefore, even today will not wander away from those who themselves are bound to him in the eternal testament, however insane the universe would be. To (God) himself (be) glory.

Psalm 25:10

All the paths of the Lord are grace [or love] and trustworthiness [or faith] to those who keep his testament and covenant.

1534[19]

19. This is the original publication date of this treatise. As indicated earlier it was republished later in slightly modified forms.

Christic the End of the Law[1]

JOHN CALVIN

John Calvin, "Christ the End of the Law," in *The Practical Calvinist: An Introduction to the Presbyterian & Reformed Heritage. In Honor of Dr. D. Clair Davis*, ed. Peter A. Lillback (Fearn, UK: Christian Focus/Mentor, 2002), 97–113.

This selection from John Calvin, *Christ the End of the Law*, was written in 1535 as an introduction to the New Testament in the French Bible translated by Pierre Robert (1506–38), known as Olivétan. This short writing was republished in many Bibles in both French and English. Thus, like the previous selection, it is a significant example of early Reformed hermeneutics. This early writing by Calvin, written just a year later than Bullinger's *De Testamento*, manifests a similar method of interpreting the Scriptures. Like Bullinger, Calvin was committed to the unity of Scripture. The Reformed tradition, indebted to Calvin's theology, expounds the knowledge of God. Thus this piece shows that the knowledge of God emerges from a covenant theology understood by a redemptive-historical hermeneutic rooted in the Scriptures themselves. In Calvin's perspective, the central theme of Scripture from Genesis to Revelation is the unified and progressive revelation of God's promise to redeem a people for

1. The following new translation is based on the first and only known English translation of Calvin's *Preface to the Geneva Bible of 1550* by Thomas Weedon, Esq., published in 1848 by Henry George Collins (London). This present translation corrects, emends, and supplements Weedon's work, and provides a literal reflection of Calvin's French, with periodic reference to the Latin for clarification of textual variants. Because of certain appreciable gaps in Weedon's translation, several sections of this preface are now provided in English for the very first time. The footnotes serve as a critical apparatus for referencing the original French and Latin in the *CO*, and for referencing Weedon's editorial comments and English phrases that derive from undisclosed sources. In *CO* 9:791–822, the French title of this work is "A Tous Amateurs de Iesus Christ et de son Evangile, Salut," translated "To Those Who Love Jesus Christ and His Gospel, Greetings." The title as written here is an abbreviation of that written in the Bibles and New Testaments printed in Geneva and elsewhere, where the preface is reproduced. This title was "Epistre aux fideles monstrant comment (que) Christ est la fin de la Loy," translated "Letter to the Faithful Showing That Christ Is the End of the Law."

himself, culminating in Christ the end of the law (Rom. 10:4). The present text is a corrected and revised version of Thomas Weedon's translation from the French text by Flavien Pardigon and David B. Garner.

Supplementary Bibliography (cf. chap. 4): Irena Backus and Claire Chimelli, eds. *La Vraie piété: Divers traités de Jean Calvin et Confession de foi de Guillaume Farel*. Geneva: Labor et Fides, 1986. Ford Lewis Battles, ed. "John Calvin's Latin Preface to Olivétan's French Bible (1535)." Pp. 373–77 in John Calvin. *Institutes of the Christian Religion 1536 Edition*. Grand Rapids: Eerdmans, 1975. John Calvin. *Christ the End of the Law, Being the Preface to the Geneva Bible of 1550*. Trans. Thomas Weedon. London: Henry George Collins, 1848. Robert D. Linder. "Olivetan (c. 1506–1538)." Pp. 729–30 in *NIDCC*. Olivier Millet, ed. *Jean Calvin: Oeuvres choisies*. Paris: Gallimard, 1995.

God the Creator, very perfect and excellent Maker of all things, made man—in whom one can contemplate a special excellence—as a masterpiece, even more than his other creatures, in which he had already shown Himself more than admirable. For He formed him in His own likeness and image, so much so that the light of His glory shone brightly in him. Now, that which would have enabled man to remain in that condition in which he had been established was that he would always lower himself in humility before the majesty of God, magnifying it with thanksgiving, and that he should not seek his glory in himself; but, seeing that all things come from above, he would also always look above, to thank for them the one and only God, to whom belongs the praise for them.

But the wretched being, wishing to be something in himself, soon began to forget and fail to recognize the source[2] of his good, and by outrageous ingratitude undertook to elevate himself, and to puff himself up against his Maker and Author of all his graces. For this cause he stumbled into ruin; he lost all the dignity and excellence of his first creation; he was despoiled and stripped of all his glory; he was alienated of the gifts which had been placed in him—in order to confound him in his pride, and make him learn by force[3] that which he did not want to understand of his good will; namely, that he was only vanity, and that he never was anything else, except as much as the Lord of power assisted him.[4]

Hence God also began to hate him,[5] and, as he well merited, to disavow him as His work; seeing that His image and likeness was effaced from him, and that the gifts of His goodness were no longer in it. And, as He had set and ordained him in order to please and delight Himself in him, like a father in his well-beloved child; so, on the contrary, He held him in disdain and abomination, so much that all which had pleased Him before, now displeased Him; that which used to delight Him, angered Him; that which He used to contemplate with benign and parental regards, He now took to detest and to behold with regret. In short, the

---

2. In *CO* 9:791, the text reads in French, "dont." In 1562 and in following editions, this word reads, "d'où," meaning "from where." For English clarity, we have translated the French "d'où" as "source."

3. In all editions prior to 1543, "by force" is missing.

4. Thomas Weedon's translation includes the concluding phrase, "and supported him in the state to which He had created him." This phrase is not contained in any French editions known to the present translators.

5. Weedon adds in brackets, "except those whom He from that time made partakers of his mercy." This phrase is not contained in any French editions known to the present translators.

whole man with all his belongings, his deeds, his thoughts, his words, and his life, totally displeased God, as if he was His special and adversarial enemy, even to the point of saying that He repented that He had made him. After having been cast down into such confusion, he has been fruitful in his cursed seed to beget a race similar to him, that is to say vicious, perverse, corrupt, void and deprived of any good, rich and abounding in evil.

Nevertheless, the Lord of mercy (who not only loves, but Himself is love and charity), wishing still, of His infinite goodness, to love that which is no longer worthy of His love, did not at all waste, doom and sink men into the abyss as their iniquity required; but[6] has sustained and supported them in tenderness and in patience, giving them time and leisure to return to Him, and to come back to the obedience from which they had diverted. And though He hid and kept silent (as if He wanted to hide Himself from them), letting them follow the desires and wishes of their concupiscence, without law, without government, without any correction of His Word, nevertheless, He sent them enough warnings which were meant to incite them to seek, to grope for, and to find Him in order to know Him and to honor Him as is fitting.

For He has raised everywhere, in every place, and in every thing, His ensigns and armorial standards, even under blazons of such clear intelligence, that there is none who can claim ignorance of not knowing such a sovereign Lord, who has so widely exalted His magnificence, when He has written and almost engraved in all parts of the world, in the heavens and in the earth, the glory of His power, goodness, wisdom, and eternity. Therefore, Saint Paul has truly said that the Lord did not leave Himself without witnesses, even towards those to whom He has not sent any knowledge of His Word. Seeing that all creatures from the firmament down to the center of the earth, could be witnesses and messengers of His glory to all men, in order to draw them to seek Him and, after finding Him, to do Him service and homage, according to the dignity of a Lord so good, so powerful, so wise and eternal, and they even help, each in its place, in that pursuit. For the singing young birds sing for God, the beasts clamor for Him, the elements of nature dread His might; the mountains echo Him; the rivers and fountains make eyes at Him; the herbs and flowers laugh before Him. However, it is truly not necessary to seek Him afar, seeing that everyone can find Him in himself, inasmuch as we are all upheld and preserved by His sustaining power dwelling in us.

Nevertheless, to manifest even more largely His goodness and infinite clemency among men, He did not rest satisfied with instructing them all by such teachings as those we have already set forth, but He made His voice heard in a special manner to a certain people, which, of His good will and free grace, He had elected and chosen from among all the nations of the earth. It was the children of Israel, to whom He clearly showed by His Word who He is, and by His marvelous works declared what He can do. For He brought them out from subjection to Pharaoh King of Egypt (under which they were detained and oppressed) to emancipate them and set them at liberty. He accompanied them night and day in their flight, being, as it were, a fugitive in the midst of them. He fed them in the desert; He made them possessors of the promised territory; He gave victories and triumphs into their hands. And, as if He were nothing to the other nations, He expressly wanted to be called "God of Israel," and this one nation to be called His people, under the agreement that they would never

---

6. Weedon inserts, "in order to preserve the Human Race, as much to draw out from it His elect as to render other men more inexcusable." This phrase is not contained in any French editions known to the present translators.

recognize any other lord nor receive any other god. And this covenant was confirmed and ratified by the testament and witness which He gave them as a surety.

Nevertheless, men, exhibiting all their cursed origin, and showing themselves true heirs of the iniquity of their father Adam, were not at all aroused by such remonstrances, and would not listen to the doctrine by which God warned them. The creatures on which is written the glory and magnificence of God were of no avail to the Gentiles to have them glorify Him of whom they testified. The law and the prophecies had no authority over the Jews to conduct them into the right way. All were blind to the light, deaf to the admonitions, and hardened against the commandments.

It is very true that the Gentiles, astonished and convinced by so many benefits which they beheld around them, were constrained to know the secret Benefactor, from whom so much goodness proceeded. But, instead of giving to the true God the glory which is due Him, they forged for themselves a god after their own desire, and according to that which their mad fancy, in its vanity and lie, imagined. And not one god only, but as many as their rash presumptuousness could pretend and found, so that there was neither people nor region which did not make to itself new gods, as seemed good to it. From there did idolatry—the treacherous madam—take its dominion, who has caused men to turn away from God, and to distract themselves with a host of travesties, to which they themselves gave form, name and being.

Touching the Jews, although they had received and accepted the messages and summons which the Lord was sending them by His servants, yet, they immediately broke faith with Him, lightly turned away from Him, violated and despised His law, which they hated. They walked in the law with regret; they alienated themselves from His house, and dissolutely ran after the other gods, committing idolatry after the manner of the Gentiles against His will.

Wherefore, in order to bring men to God, as well Jews as Gentiles, it was necessary that a new covenant would be made: certain, assured, and inviolable. And to establish and confirm it, there was need of a mediator, who would interpose and intercede with the two parties in order to reconcile them, without whom, man remains always under the wrath and indignation of God, and has no means of relieving himself from the curse, misery, and confusion into which he has stumbled. It was our Lord and Savior Jesus Christ, true and only eternal Son of God, who was to be sent and given to men on the part of the Father, to be the Restorer of the world, otherwise dispersed, destroyed, and laid waste, in whom from the beginning of the world was always the hope of recovering the loss made in Adam. For even to Adam, immediately after his ruin, to console and comfort him, was given the promise that by the seed of the woman the head of the serpent would be crushed, which meant that by Jesus Christ born of a virgin, the power of Satan would be beaten down and destroyed.

Since then, this same promise was more amply renewed to Abraham, when God told him that by his seed, all the nations of the earth will be blessed, as from his seed would come forth, according to the flesh, Jesus Christ, by whose blessing all men (of whatever region they might be), will be sanctified. And again, it was continued to Isaac, in the same form and in the same words. And afterwards, many times proclaimed, repeated, and confirmed by the testimony of divers prophets, even to showing fully, for greater confidence, of whom He would be born, at what time, in what place, what afflictions and death He should suffer, the glory in which He should resurrect, what would His reign be, and to what salvation He would conduct His people.

It was first predicted to us in Isaiah how He would be born of a virgin, saying, "The virgin will be with child and will give birth to a son, and will call him Immanuel" (Isa. 7:14 NIV). In Moses the time is set forth to us when the good Jacob said, "The scepter shall not depart from Judah, Nor the ruler's staff from between his feet, Until Shiloh comes, and to him *shall be* the obedience of the peoples" (Gen. 49:10 NASB), which was verified at the time when Jesus Christ came into the world. For the Romans, after having divested the Jews of all government and control, had about thirty-seven years before appointed Herod as king over them, a king who was a stranger, his father Antipater being an Idumaean and his mother from Arabia. It had at times happened that the Jews had been without kings, but they had never been seen like then—without counselors, governors, or magistrates. And another description of it is given in Daniel, by the computation of the seventy weeks. The place of His birth was clearly pointed out to us by Micah, saying, "But you, Bethlehem Ephrathah, though you are small among the clans of Judah, out of you will come for me one who will be ruler over Israel, whose origins are from of old, from ancient times" (Mic. 5:2 NIV). As to the afflictions which He had to bear for our deliverance, and the death which He had to suffer for our redemption, Isaiah and Zechariah have spoken of them amply and with certainty. The glory of His resurrection, the quality of His reign, and the grace of salvation which He should bring to His people have been richly treated by Isaiah, Jeremiah, and Zechariah.

In such promises, announced and testified by these holy persons filled with the Spirit of God, the children and elect of God have rested in peace and comforted themselves, and in them have nourished, sustained, and strengthened their hope, waiting for the Lord to will to exhibit what He had promised them, among whom many kings and prophets strongly desired to see their accomplishment. Yet, nevertheless, they did not fail to apprehend in their hearts and minds by faith that which they could not see with their eyes. And in order to strengthen them even more in all ways in the long wait for this great Messiah, God gave them as a pledge His written law, in which were comprised many ceremonies, purifications and sacrifices, which things were only figures and shadows of the great good things to come by Christ, who alone is the body and truth of them. For the Law could not bring anyone to perfection; in that way it only pointed out and, like a schoolmaster, directed and conducted to Christ, who was (as Saint Paul says) its end and fulfillment.

In like manner, at many times and in different seasons He has sent them some kings, princes and captains to deliver them from the power of their enemies, to govern them in good peace, to recover them their losses, to make their kingdom flourish, and by great feats[7] to make them renowned among all the other people, in order to give them some taste of the great marvels which they will receive from that great Messiah, to whom will be deployed all the might and power of the kingdom of God.

But when the fullness of time had come and the period preordained by God had expired, this much promised and much awaited great Messiah came, perfecting and accomplishing all that was necessary for our redemption and salvation. He was given not only to the Israelites, but also to all men, from all peoples, and regions, in order that by Him human nature would be reconciled to God.[8] *This reconciliation is fully contained and plainly demonstrated in the following book, which we have translated as faithfully as possible according to*

---

7. According to *CO* 9:801, in the Bible of Olivetan, the French word "prouesses" (feats, prowesses) incorrectly reads "promesses." The editors of the *CO* note that all other editions that they have read correct this mistake.

8. The first two sentences of this paragraph are not included in Weedon's translation.

the truth and properties of the Greek language. The production of this translation is intended to enable all French-speaking Christians to hear and acknowledge the law they must keep and the faith they must follow.[9] And this book is called the New Testament in regard to the Old, which, inasmuch as it was to be reduced and reported to the other, being in itself weak and imperfect, and thereupon has been abolished and abrogated. But this Testament is the new and eternal one which will never grow old or fail, because Jesus Christ has been its Mediator, who ratified and confirmed it by His death, in which He accomplished full and complete remission of all transgressions which remained under the first Testament.[10]

The Scripture also calls it Gospel, that is to say, good news and joyful, inasmuch as in it is declared that Christ, the only natural and eternal Son of the living God, was made man to make us children of God His Father by adoption. And thus he is our only Savior, in whom lays entirely our redemption, peace, justice, sanctification, salvation, and life; who died for our sins, resurrected for our justification, who ascended into heaven to make for us an entry there, to take possession for us and in our name, and to remain forever before His Father as our perpetual Advocate and Priest; who sits at His right hand as King, constituted Lord and Master over all, in order to restore all things in heaven and in the earth; that which all the angels, patriarchs, prophets, apostles would never have been able nor have known how to do, for unto that they were not ordained by God.

And, as the Messiah had been so often promised in the Old Testament by many witnesses of the Prophets, so Jesus Christ has by certain and indubitable witnesses been declared to be Him without equal, who was to come and who was awaited. For the Lord God by His voice and His Spirit, by His angels, prophets, and apostles, even by all His creatures, has rendered us so sufficiently certain of it, that no one can contradict it without resisting and rebelling against His power. First, God Eternal by His voice itself (which is without any doubt irrevocable truth), has testified of it to us saying, "This is my Son, whom I love; with him I am well pleased. Listen to him!" (Matt. 17:5 NIV). The Holy Spirit is a great witness of it to us in our hearts, as Saint John says. The Angel Gabriel sent to the virgin Mary told her, "You will be with child and give birth to a son, and you are to give him the name Jesus. He will be great and will be called the Son of the Most High. The Lord God will give him the throne of his father David, and he will reign over the house of Jacob forever; his kingdom will never end" (Luke 1:31–33 NIV). The same message in substance was delivered to Joseph, and also afterwards to the shepherds, to whom it was said that the Savior was born, who is Christ the Lord. And this message was not only brought by an angel, but it was approved

9. In lieu of the italicized passage in the text, we read in the Treatise of 1543 and in all the editions of the Bible that reproduce it, the following sentences: "To declare which, the Lord Jesus, who was the foundation and the substance of it, [after that He had executed His function among the Jews,] ordained His Apostles, to whom He has given charge and commandment to publish His grace through all the world. Now, the Apostles, in order well and completely to fulfill their duty, not only took labor and diligence to execute their embassy by oral preaching, but, after the example of Moses and the Prophets, to leave the eternal memory of their teaching, reduced it to writing; in which they first recited the history of that which our Lord Jesus did and suffered for our salvation; then, afterwards, showed the value of it all, and what benefit we receive from it, and in what way we must take it. All this collection is called the New Testament." The bracketed phrase is included in Weedon's translation, but is not contained in any French editions known to the present translators. *Editor's Note*: This substitution may suggest that Calvin had written the 1535 edition, and allowed the translator of the New Testament, Olivetan, to add his words as translator. Later, when Calvin's name is directly linked to this work, the language of the translator is removed, suggesting all was now his direct words.

10. Weedon adds, "inasmuch as He brought them back to that which ought to be exhibited and performed under the New." This phrase is not contained in any French editions known to the present translators.

by a great multitude of angels, who all together rendered glory to the Lord, and announced peace on earth. Simeon the Just, in prophetic spirit, confessed Him aloud, and taking the little child between his arms, he said: "Sovereign Lord, as you have promised, you now dismiss your servant in peace. For my eyes have seen your salvation, which you have prepared in the sight of all people" (Luke 2:29–31 NIV). John the Baptist also spoke of Him as was suitable, when, seeing Him coming at the river Jordan, he said, "Look, the Lamb of God, who takes away the sin of the world!" (John 1:29 NIV). Peter and all the apostles confessed, bore witness, and preached, all things that concerned salvation and were predicted by the prophets, to be done in Christ the true Son of God. And those, whom the Lord had ordained to be witnesses up to our age, have amply demonstrated it by their writings, as the readers can sufficiently perceive.

All these testimonies unite so well in one, and agree together in such a manner, that by such an agreement it is easy to understand that it is very certain truth. For there could not be in lies such an agreement. Nevertheless, not only the Father, the Son, the Holy Spirit, the angels, the prophets and the apostles bear witness of Jesus Christ, but even His marvelous works demonstrate His very excellent power. The sick, lame, blind, deaf, mute, paralytic, leprous, lunatics, demoniacs, nay, even the dead by Him resurrected, bore the ensigns of it. In His power He resurrected Himself, and in His name He remitted sins. And therefore, it was not without cause that He said that the works which His Father had given Him to do were sufficiently good witnesses to Him. Moreover, even the wicked and the enemies of His glory were constrained by the force of truth, to confess and to acknowledge something of it, like Caiaphas, Pilate and his wife. I do not want to bring forward the testimonies of the devils and foul spirits, seeing that Jesus Christ rejected them.

In sum, all the elements and all the created things have given glory to Jesus Christ. At His command the winds ceased, the troubled sea became calm, the fish brought the didrachma in his belly, the rocks (to bear witness to Him) were crushed, the veil of the temple rent itself down the middle, the sun darkened, the tombs opened themselves, and many bodies resurrected. There was nothing, either in heaven or in earth, which did not testify that Jesus Christ is its God, Lord, and Master, and the great Ambassador of the Father sent here below to effect the salvation of humankind. All these things are announced, demonstrated, written and signed to us in that Testament, by which Jesus Christ makes us His heirs to the kingdom of God His Father, and declares to us His will (as a testator does to his heirs) for it to be executed.

Now we are all called to this heritage without exception of persons: male or female, small or great, servant or lord, master or disciple, clergy or laity, Hebrew or Greek, French or Latin. No one is rejected from it, whoever by sure faith will receive that which is sent to him, will embrace that which is presented to him, in short, who will acknowledge Jesus Christ as He is given of the Father.

And yet shall we, who bear the name of Christians, let that Testament be robbed from us, hidden and corrupted? That which so justly belongs to us, without which we cannot pretend any right to the kingdom of God, without which we are ignorant of the great goods and promises which Jesus Christ has given us, the glory and beatitude which He has prepared for us? We know not what God has commanded or forbidden, we cannot discern good from evil, light from darkness, the commandments of God from the constitutions of men. Without the Gospel we are useless and vain; without the Gospel we are not Christians; without the

Gospel, all wealth is poverty, wisdom is folly before God, strength is weakness, all human justice is damned of God. But by the knowledge of the Gospel we are made children of God, brothers of Jesus Christ, fellows with the saints, citizens of the kingdom of heaven, heirs of God with Jesus Christ, by whom the poor are made rich, the feeble powerful, the fools wise, the sinners justified, the afflicted consoled, the doubters certain, the slaves free.

The Gospel is word of life and of truth. It is the power of God unto the salvation of all believers, and the key of the knowledge of God which opens the door of the kingdom of heaven to the faithful, unbinding them from their sins, and shuts it against the unbelieving, binding them in their sins. Blessed are all those who hear it and keep it, for thereby they show that they are children of God. Wretched are those who will not hear nor follow it, for they are children of the devil.

O Christians, hear and learn this, for indeed the ignorant will perish with his ignorance, and the blind following the other blind will fall with him into the pit. The one and only way unto life and salvation is the faith and certainty in the promises of God, which cannot be had without the Gospel, by the hearing and understanding of which living faith is given, with certain hope and perfect charity in God, and ardent love toward one's neighbor. Where then is your hope if you despise and disdain to hear, to see, to read, and to hold fast this holy Gospel? Those who have their affections stuck in this world pursue by every means what they think belongs to their felicity, without sparing their labor, or body, or life, or renown. And all these things are done to serve this wretched body, of which life is so vain, miserable, and uncertain. When it is a question of the life immortal and incorruptible, of the beatitude eternal and inestimable, of all the treasures of paradise, shall we not constrain ourselves to pursue them? Those who apply themselves to the mechanical arts (however base and vile those may be) undergo much trouble and labor to learn and know them, and those who wish to be reputed the most virtuous torment their spirits night and day to understand something of the human sciences, which are but wind and smoke. How much more ought we to employ ourselves, and to strive in the study of that heavenly wisdom which passes the whole world and penetrates even to the mysteries of God, which He has been pleased to reveal by His holy Word.

What then will be able to estrange and alienate us from this holy Gospel? Will it be insults, curses, opprobriums, privations of worldly honor? But we know well that Jesus Christ passed through such a road, which we must follow if we want to be His disciples, and which is not in refusing to suffer contempt, be mocked, abased and rejected before men, in order to be honored, prized, glorified and exalted at the judgment of God. Will it be banishment, proscriptions, deprivations of goods and wealth? But we know well when we will be banished from one country, that the earth is the Lord's. And when we will be cast out from all the earth, that we will nevertheless not be out of His kingdom; that when we will be plundered and made poor, we have a Father sufficiently rich to nourish us, and even that Jesus Christ made Himself poor, so that we would follow Him in poverty. Will it be afflictions, prisons, tortures, torments? But we know by the example of Jesus Christ that it is the way to reach glory. Finally, shall it be death? But she does not take away from us the life to be desired.

In short, if we have Christ with us, we will find nothing so cursed that it will not be made blessed by Him; nothing so execrable that will not be sanctified; nothing so bad that will not turn into good for us. Let us not be discouraged when we will see all the worldly mights and powers against us. For the promise cannot fail us, that the Lord, from on high, will laugh at all the assemblings and efforts of men who would want to gather themselves together against Him. Let us not be disconsolate (as if all hope was lost) when we see the true servants of God dying and perishing before our eyes. For it was truly said by Tertullian, and has always been proven and will be until the consummation of the age, that the blood of the martyrs is the seed of the Church.[11]

And we even have a better and firmer consolation: it is to turn our eyes away from this world, and to forsake all that we can see before us, awaiting in patience the great judgment of God, by which, in a moment, all that men have ever plotted against Him will be beaten down, annihilated, and overturned. That will be when the reign of God, which we now see in hope, will be manifested, and when Jesus Christ will appear in His majesty with the angels. Then, both the good and the bad must be present before the judgment seat of that great King. Those who will have remained firm in that Testament, and will have followed and kept the will of that good Father, will be on the right hand, as true children, and will receive the blessing, which is the end of their faith, the eternal salvation. And inasmuch as they were not ashamed to avow and confess Jesus Christ, at the time when he was despised and suffered contempt before men, so they will be partakers of His glory, crowned with Him eternally. But the perverse, rebellious, and reprobate, who will have suffered contempt and rejected that holy Gospel, and likewise those who, to entertain their honors, riches and high estates, were unwilling to humble and lower themselves with Jesus Christ, and for fear of men will have forsaken the fear of God, as they were bastards and disobedient to this Father, will be on the left hand. They will be cast into cursing, and as wages for their faithlessness will receive eternal death.

Now, since you have heard that the Gospel presents to you Jesus Christ, in whom all the promises and graces of God are accomplished, and declares to you that He was sent from the Father, came down on earth, conversed with men, perfected all that was of our salvation, as it had been predicted in the law and the prophets, it ought to be very certain and manifest to you that the treasures of paradise are open, the riches of God deployed, and the eternal life revealed to you in it. For this is eternal life, to know the one and only true God, and Him whom He sent, Jesus Christ, whom He has constituted the beginning, the middle, and the end of our salvation. This One is Isaac the well-beloved Son of the Father, who was offered in sacrifice, and yet did not succumb to the power of death. This is the vigilant Shepherd Jacob, taking such great care of the sheep He has charge over. This is the good and pitiable Brother Joseph, who in His glory was not ashamed to recognize His brothers, however contemptible and abject as they were. This is the great Priest and Bishop Melchizedek, having made eternal sacrifice once for all. This is the sovereign Lawgiver Moses, writing His law on the tables of our hearts by His Spirit. This is the faithful Captain and Guide Joshua to conduct us to the promised land. This is the noble and victorious King David, subduing under His hand every rebellious power. This is the magnificent and triumphant King Solomon, governing His kingdom in peace and prosperity. This is the strong and mighty Samson, who, by His death, overwhelmed all His enemies.

And even any good that could be thought or desired is found in this Jesus Christ alone. For He humbled Himself to exalt us; He made Himself a slave to set us free; He became poor to enrich us; He was sold to redeem us, captive to deliver us, condemned to absolve us; He was

---

11. This expression of Tertullian's is actually not a direct quotation, but rather summarizes an idea from his *Apology*. However, the concept is frequently repeatedly by the church fathers.

made malediction for our benediction, oblation of sins for our justice; He was disfigured to re-figure us; He died for our life, in such manner that by Him harshness is softened, wrath appeased, darkness enlightened, iniquity justified, weakness is made strength, affliction is consoled, sin is impeached, despite is despised, dread is emboldened, debt is acquitted, labor is lightened, sorrow turned into joy, misfortune into fortune, difficulty is made easy, disorder made ordered, division united, ignominy is ennobled, rebellion subjected, threat is threatened, ambushes are driven out, assaults assailed, striving is overpowered, combat is combated, war is warred, vengeance is avenged, torment tormented, damnation damned, abyss is thrown into the abyss, hell is helled, death is dead, mortality immortality. In short, mercy has swallowed up all misery, and goodness all wretchedness. For all those things which used to be the arms of the devil to combat us and the sting of death to pierce us, are turned for us into an exercise of which we can profit, so that we can boast with the apostle, saying, "O death,[12] where is your victory? O death, where is your sting?" (1 Cor. 15:55 NASB). From there it comes, that by such a Spirit of Christ promised to His elect, we no longer live, but Christ in us, and we are in spirit seated among the heavenlies, as the world is no longer world to us, though we have our conversation in it, but being content in all, either in countries, places, conditions, clothes, meats, and other like things. And we are comforted in tribulation, joyful in sorrow, glorious in vituperation, abounding in poverty, warmed in nakedness, patient in evil, living in death.

This[13] is in sum what we should seek in the whole Scripture: it is to know well Jesus Christ and the infinite riches which are comprised in Him, and are, by Him, offered to us from God His Father. For when the law and the prophets are carefully searched, there is not to be found in them one word which does not reduce and lead us to Him. And in fact, since all the treasures of wisdom and intelligence are hid in Him, there is no question of having any other end or object, if we wish not, as of deliberate intention, to turn ourselves away from the light of truth, in order to lose our way into the darkness of lies. For this reason does Saint Paul rightly say in another passage that he resolved to know nothing except Jesus Christ and Him crucified. For though the flesh has the opinion that that knowledge is something vulgar and contemptible, the acquiring of it is sufficient to occupy our whole life. And we will not have wasted our time, when we will have employed all our study and applied all our understanding, to profit of it. What more could we ask, for the spiritual doctrine of our souls, than to know God, in order to be transformed into Him, and to have His glorious image imprinted in us, in order to be partakers of His justice, heirs of His kingdom, and to possess it fully to the end? Now it is thus, that from the beginning He gave Himself, and now even more clearly gives Himself to be contemplated in the face of His Christ. It is therefore not lawful that we turn ourselves away and wander here and there, however little it may be. But our understanding must be altogether stopped at this point, to learn in the Scripture to know only Jesus Christ, in order to be conducted by Him straight to the Father, who contains in Himself all perfection.

Behold, *I say again, here*[14] *is contained* all the wisdom that men can understand, and must learn in this life, to which neither angel, nor man, nor dead, nor alive, can add or take

---

12. Calvin in *CO* 9:813 reads "hell" (French, *enfer*) for the first occurrence of "death."

13. This paragraph is not found in the Bible of 1535, but is found for the first time in the Treatise of 1543, and has continued in the different Genevan editions of the New Testament.

14. I.e., in the Scriptures.

anything. For this reason it is the goal where we must stop and limit our understanding, without mixing anything of our own, not receiving any doctrine which is added thereto. For whoever dares undertake to teach one syllable beyond, or above that which is there taught to us, must be cursed before God and His Church.[15]

And you Christian kings, princes and lords, who are ordained by God to punish the wicked, and entertain the good in peace according to the Word of God, it is your responsibility to have that holy doctrine so useful and necessary published, taught, and heard by all your countries, regions, and lordships, in order that God be magnified by you, and His Gospel will be exalted. Do so as legitimately it falls to all kings and kingdoms in all humility to obey and to serve His glory. *Remember[16] that the sovereign Empire, above all kingdoms, principalities and lordships, has been given by the Father to the Lord Jesus, in order that He be feared, dreaded, honored and obeyed everywhere by both great and small. Remember all that was predicted by the prophets—that all kings of the earth will pay Him homage as their Superior and will adore Him as their Savior and their God—must be verified in you. Do not think of it as an infringement to be subjects of such a great Lord, because it is the greatest honor for you to desire to be acknowledged and held as officers and lieutenants of God. By His lordship your majesty and highness is in no way lessened; your honor can exist only as Jesus Christ, in whom God wants to be exalted and glorified, dominates over you. And in fact, it is only reasonable for you to give Him such preeminence, since your power is founded on no one but Him alone. Otherwise, what kind of ungratefulness would it be to want to deny the rights to the one who constituted, maintains, and preserves you in the position of power you occupy? Furthermore, it is imperative for you to know that no better nor firmer foundation exists to maintain your lordships in prosperity, than to have Him for Head and Master, and to govern your peoples under His hand. And also that without Him, not only can your lordships not be permanent or of long duration, but they are cursed of God and will thereby fall into confusion and ruin. Whereas, God has put the sword in your hand to govern your subject in His Name and in His authority; whereas, He granted you the honor to give you His Name and His title;[17] and whereas, He has sanctified your estate above others, in order for His glory and majesty to shine in it, let each one with regard to Him employ himself to magnify and exalt the One who is His true glorious Image, in which He fully presents Himself Now, to do so, it is not enough solely to confess Jesus Christ and to profess to be His. Rather to bear this title truly and actually, one must yield to His holy Gospel and receive it in perfect obedience and humility—which is indeed everyone's office. But it is especially your responsibility that the Gospel would have an audience, and for it to be published in your countries, so that it would be heard by all who are committed in your charge, that they would recognize you as servants and ministers of this great King, in order to serve and honor Him, obeying you under His hand and leadership.*

That is what the Lord requires of you when, by His prophet, He calls you tutors of His Church. For this tutelage or protection does not lay in increasing riches, privileges and honors to the clergy—of which it thereby prides and elevates itself, lives pompously and a

---

15. Several Genevan editions of the New Testament conclude the preface here. This is true also for the Latin text which is complete only in the edition of Lausanne and Hanau.

16. The following italicized text is missing in the 1535 edition. It is found in the Treatise of 1543, and the New Testament editions that reproduced it in its entirety. However, it is not retained in the Latin version.

17. I.e., Lord, King, Ruler, etc.

fully dissolute life, against the order of its estate. Even less does it lay in maintaining the clergy in its pride and its disorderly pomps. On the contrary, this tutelage lays in providing for the doctrine of truth and purity of the Gospel to remain complete, the holy Scriptures to be faithfully preached and read, God to be honored according to the rule of Scripture, the Church to be well ordered, and all that contravenes either to God's honor or to the orderliness of the Church, to be corrected and thrown down, so that the reign of Jesus Christ would flourish in the power of His Word.

O, all of you who are called bishops and pastors of the poor people, see that the sheep of Jesus Christ are not deprived of their proper pasture. Ensure that it not be prohibited nor forbidden that every Christian might read, consider, and hear this holy Gospel freely in his own language, since God wants it, Jesus Christ commands it, and to accomplish this has sent his apostles and servants in the whole world, giving them the grace to speak all tongues, so that they would preach in all languages to all creatures. He has made them debtors to the Greeks and the barbarians, to the wise and to the simple, so that none would be excluded from their teaching. Certainly, if you are truly vicars, successors, and imitators of them, your office is to emulate them, watching the flock, and seeking all possible means for everyone to be instructed in the faith of Jesus Christ by the pure Word of God. Otherwise, the sentence is already pronounced and registered: God will demand their souls from your hands.

May the Lord of lights will to teach the ignorant, strengthen the weak, illumine the blind with His holy and salutary Gospel by His Holy Spirit, and cause His truth to reign over all peoples and nations, so that the whole world would know only one God and only one Savior, Jesus Christ, one faith, and one Gospel. Amen.

The Edwardian Homilies (1547)

The Reformation in England had a window of opportunity during the short reign of Edward VI (1537–53). Though conceived during the reign of Henry VIII (1491–1547), the First Book of Homilies (1547) was published under Edward VI, hence the name Edwardian Homilies. As an aid to the practical application of the Reformation principles on the local church level, this series of twelve sermons, or homilies, was prepared under the leadership of Thomas Cranmer (1489–1556) for use by ministers in their parishes. The Thirty-nine Articles (see chap. 13) mention this book of homilies together with a Second Book of Homilies (1562), and recommend their use. The main themes of these were salvation, justification, and works.

The homily "A Fruitful Exhortation to the Reading and Knowledge of Holy Scripture," most likely composed by Cranmer himself, emphasizes the authority and sufficiency of Scripture, calling the reader to action. According to the doctrine of Scripture set forth in this sermon, the common faithful in England ought to be people who constantly and regularly read the Word of God. The homily reproduces accents found in Cranmer's preface to the Great Bible (1540). Consequently, like Bullinger's and Calvin's previous selections, the Exhortation offers a glimpse into standard Reformed interpretation, this time in an English dress. The text of this homily is from a nineteenth-century reprint; it is also found in Leith, *Creeds of the Churches*.[1]

Bibliography: Peter Newman Brooks. "12. The Theology of Thomas Cranmer." Pp. 150–60 in *The Cambridge Companion to Reformation Theology*. "Cranmer, Thomas." *NSHERK* 3:295–96. Leith. *Creeds of the Churches*. Pp. 230–66. P. C.-H. Lim. "Cranmer, Thomas (1489–1556)." Pp. 164–66 in *BDE*. Diarmaid MacCulloch. *Thomas Cranmer: A Life*. New Haven, CT: Yale University Press, 1996.

1. See also Ronald B. Bond, ed., *Certain Sermons or Homilies (1547): and, A Homily against Disobedience and Wilful Rebellion (1570)* (Toronto: University of Toronto Press, 1987).

A Fruitful Exhortation to the Reading and Knowledge of Holy Scripture

Certain Sermons or Homilies, Appointed to Be Read in Churches in the Time of the Late Queen Elizabeth of Famous Memory (Oxford: At the University Press, 1840), 1–8.

The praise of holy scripture. Unto a Christian man there can be nothing either more necessary or profitable, than the knowledge of holy scripture, forasmuch as in it is contained God's true word, setting forth his glory, and also man's duty. **The perfection of holy scripture**. And there is no truth nor doctrine necessary for our justification and everlasting salvation, but that is, or may be drawn out of that fountain and well of truth. **The knowledge of holy scripture is necessary**. Therefore as many as be desirous to enter into the right and perfect way unto God, must apply their minds to know holy scripture; without the which, they can neither sufficiently know God and his will, neither their office and duty. **To whom the knowledge of holy scripture is sweet and pleasant**. And as drink is pleasant to them that be dry, and meat to them that be hungry; so is the reading, hearing, searching, and studying of holy scripture, to them that be desirous to know God, or themselves, and to do his will. **Who be enemies to holy scripture**. And their stomachs only do loathe and abhor the heavenly knowledge and food of God's word, that be so drowned in worldly vanities, that they neither savour[2] God, nor any godliness: for that is the cause why they desire such vanities, rather than the true knowledge of God. **An apt similitude, declaring of whom the scripture is abhorred**. As they that are sick of an ague, whatsoever they eat and drink, though it be never so pleasant, yet it is as bitter to them as wormwood; not for the bitterness of the meat, but for the corrupt and bitter humour that is in their own tongue and mouth: even so is the sweetness of God's word bitter, not of itself, but only unto them that have their minds corrupted with long custom of sin and love of this world. **An exhortation unto the diligent reading and searching of the holy scripture**. Therefore forsaking the corrupt judgment of fleshly[3] men, which care not but for their carcase; let us reverently hear and read holy scriptures, which is the food of the soul (Matt. 4:4; John 4:14). Let us diligently search for the well of life in the books of the New and Old Testament, and not run to the stinking puddles of men's traditions, devised by men's imagination, for our justification and salvation. **The holy scripture is a sufficient doctrine for our salvation**. For in holy scripture is fully contained what we ought to do, and what to eschew, what to believe, what to love, and what to look for at God's hands at length. In these books we shall find the Father from whom, the Son by whom, and the Holy Ghost in whom, all things have their being and keeping up;[4] and these three persons to be but one God, and one substance. **What things we may learn in the holy scripture**. In these books we may learn to know ourselves, how vile and miserable we be, and also to know God, how good he is of himself, and how he maketh us and

2. Or *favour*.
3. Or *carnal*.
4. Or *conservation*.

all creatures partakers of his goodness. We may learn also in these books to know God's will and pleasure, as much as, for this present time, is convenient for us to know. And, as the great clerk and godly preacher, Saint John Chrysostom saith, whatsoever is required to salvation of man, is fully contained in the scripture of God. He that is ignorant may there learn and have knowledge. He that is hard-hearted, and an obstinate sinner, shall there find everlasting[5] torments, prepared of God's justice, to make him afraid, and to mollify or soften him. He that is oppressed with misery in this world shall there find relief in the promises of everlasting[6] life, to his great consolation and comfort. He that is wounded by the Devil unto death shall find there medicine whereby he may be restored again unto health; if it shall require to teach any truth, or reprove false doctrine, to rebuke any vice, to commend any virtue, to give good counsel, to comfort or to exhort, or to do any other thing requisite for our salvation, all those things, saith Saint Chrysostom, we may learn plentifully of the scripture. There is, saith Fulgentius, abundantly enough, both for men to eat, and children to suck. There is whatsoever is meet[7] for all ages, and for all degrees and sorts of men. **Holy scripture ministereth sufficient doctrine for all degrees and ages**. These books therefore ought to be much in our hands, in our eyes, in our ears, in our mouths, but most of all in our hearts. For the scripture of God is the heavenly meat of our souls (Matt. 4:4; Luke 4:4); the hearing and keeping of it maketh us blessed, sanctifieth us, and maketh us holy (John 17:17); it turneth[8] our souls, it is a light lantern to our feet (Ps. 119:105); it is a sure, steadfast, and everlasting[9] instrument of salvation; it giveth wisdom to the humble and lowly hearts; it comforteth, maketh glad, cheereth, and cherisheth our conscience: **What commodities and profits the knowledge of holy scripture bringeth**. it is a more excellent jewel or treasure than any gold or precious stone; it is more sweet than honey or honey-comb (Ps. 19:10); it is called the *best part*, which Mary did choose (Luke 10:42), for it hath in it everlasting comfort. The words of holy scripture be called words of *everlasting life* (John 6:47): for they be God's instrument, ordained for the same purpose. They have power to turn[10] through God's promise, and they be effectual through God's assistance, and (being received in a faithful heart) they have ever an heavenly spiritual working in them (Col. 1:6): they are lively, quick, and mighty in operation, and *sharper than any two-edged sword, and entereth through, even unto the dividing asunder of the soul and the spirit, of the joints and the marrow* (Heb. 4:12). Christ calleth him a wise builder, that buildeth upon his word, upon his sure and substantial foundation (Matt. 7:24). By this word of God we shall be judged: for *the word that I speak*, saith Christ, *is it, that shall judge in the last day* (John 12:48). He that keepeth the word of Christ, is promised the love and favour of God, and that he shall be the dwelling-place[11] or temple of the blessed Trinity (John 14:23). This word whosoever is diligent to read, and in his heart to print that he readeth, the great affection to the transitory things of this world shall be minished in him, and the great desire of heavenly things (that be therein promised of

---

5. Or *eternal*.
6. Or *eternal*.
7. Or *convenient*.
8. Or *converteth*.
9. Or *a constant and a perpetual*.
10. Or *convert*.
11. Or *mansion-place*.

God) shall increase in him. And there is nothing that so much strengtheneth[12] our faith and trust in God, that so much keepeth up[13] innocency and pureness of the heart, and also of outward godly life and conversation, as continual reading and recording[14] of God's word. For that thing, which (by continual[15] use of reading of holy scripture, and diligent searching of the same) is deeply imprinted and graven in the heart, at length turneth almost into nature. And moreover, the effect and virtue of God's word is to illuminate the ignorant, and to give more light unto them that faithfully and diligently read it, to comfort their hearts, and to encourage them to perform that, which of God is commanded. It teacheth patience in all adversity, in prosperity humbleness; what honour is due unto God, what mercy and charity to our neighbour (1 Kings 14:5–16; 2 Chron. 20:9; 1 Cor. 15:9). It giveth good counsel in all doubtful things. It sheweth of whom we shall look for aid and help in all perils, and that God is the only giver of victory in all battles and temptations of our enemies, bodily and ghostly (1 John 5:4). **Who profit most in reading God's word**. And in reading of God's word, he most profiteth not always that is most ready in turning of the book, or in saying of it without the book; but he that is most turned into it, that is most inspired with the Holy Ghost, most in his heart and life altered and changed[16] into that thing which he readeth; he that is daily less and less proud, less wrathful, less covetous, and less desirous of worldly and vain pleasures; he that daily (forsaking his old vicious life) increaseth in virtue more and more. And, to be short, there is nothing that more maintaineth godliness of the mind, and driveth away[17] ungodliness, than doth the continual reading or hearing of God's word, if it be joined with a godly mind, and a good affection to know and follow God's will. For without a single eye, pure intent, and good mind, nothing is allowed for good before God (Isa. 5:24; Matt. 22:12; 1 Cor. 14:37). **What discommodities the ignorance of God's word bringeth**. And, on the other side, nothing more darkeneth[18] Christ and the glory of God, nor bringeth in[19] more blindness and all kinds of vices, than doth the ignorance of God's word.

The Second Part of the Sermon of the Knowledge of Holy Scripture

In the first part of this sermon,[20] which exhorteth to the knowledge of holy scripture, was declared wherefore the knowledge of the same is necessary and profitable to all men, and that by the true knowledge and understanding of scripture, the most necessary points of our duty towards God and our neighbours are also known. Now as concerning the same matter you shall hear what followeth. If we profess Christ, why be we not ashamed to be ignorant in his doctrine? seeing that every man is ashamed to be ignorant in that learning which he professeth. That man is ashamed to be called a philosopher which readeth not the books of philosophy, and to be called a lawyer, an astronomer, or a physician, that is ignorant

12. Or *establisheth*.
13. Or *conserveth*.
14. Or *meditation*.
15. Or *perpetual*.
16. Or *transformed*.
17. Or *expelleth*.
18. Or *obscureth*.
19. Or *induceth*.
20. Or *homily*.

in the books of law, astronomy, and physic. How can any man then say that he professeth Christ and his religion, if he will not apply himself (as far forth as he can or may conveniently) to read and hear, and so to know the books of Christ's gospel and doctrine? **God's word excelleth all sciences**. Although other sciences be good, and to be learned, yet no man can deny but this is the chief, and passeth all other incomparably. What excuse shall we therefore make, at the last day before Christ, that delight to read or hear men's fantasies and inventions, more than his most holy Gospel? and will find no time to do that which chiefly, above all things, we should do, and will rather read other things than that, for the which we ought rather to leave reading of all other things. Let us therefore apply ourselves, as far forth as we can have time and leisure, to know God's word, by diligent hearing and reading thereof, as many as profess God, and have faith and trust in him. **Vain excuses dissuading from the knowledge of God's word**. But they that have no good affection to God's word (to colour this their fault) allege commonly two vain and feigned excuses. **The first**. Some go about to excuse them by their own frailness and fearfulness, saying, that they dare not read holy scripture, lest through their ignorance they should fall into any error. **The second**. Other pretend that the difficulty to understand it and the hardness thereof is so great, that it is meet to be read only of clerks and learned men. As touching the first: Ignorance of God's word is the cause of all error, as Christ himself affirmed to the Sadducees, saying, that *they erred, because they knew not the scripture* (Matt. 22:29). How should they then eschew error, that will be still ignorant? And how should they come out of ignorance, that will not read nor hear that thing which should give them knowledge? He that now hath most knowledge, was at the first ignorant; yet he forbare not to read, for fear he should fall into error: but he diligently read, lest he should remain in ignorance, and through ignorance in error. And if you will not know the truth of God (a thing most necessary for you) lest you fall into error; by the same reason you may then lie still, and never go, lest, if you go, you fall into the mire; nor eat any good meat, lest you take a surfeit; nor sow your corn, nor labour in your occupation, nor use your merchandise, for fear you lose your seed, your labour, your stock, and so by that reason it should be best for you to live idly, and never to take in hand to do any manner of good thing, lest peradventure some evil thing may chance thereof. And if you be afraid to fall into error by reading of holy scripture, I shall shew you how you may read it without danger of error. **How most commodiously and without all peril the holy scripture is to be read**. Read it humbly with a meek and lowly heart, to the intent you may glorify God, and not yourself, with the knowledge of it: and read it not without daily praying to God, that he would direct your reading to good effect; and take upon you to expound it no further than you can plainly understand it. For, as Saint Augustine saith, the knowledge of holy scripture is a great, large, and a high place[21]; but the door is very low, so that the high and arrogant man cannot run in; but he must stoop low, and humble himself, that shall enter into it. Presumption and arrogancy is the mother of all error; and humility needeth to fear no error. For humility will only search to know the truth; it will search, and will bring together one place with another, and where it cannot find out the meaning,[22] it will pray, it will ask[23] of other that know, and will not presumptuously and rashly define any thing which it knoweth not. Therefore the humble man may search any truth boldly in the

21. Or *palace*.
22. Or *find the sense*.
23. Or *enquire*.

scripture, without any danger of error. And if he be ignorant, he ought the more to read and to search holy scripture, to bring him out of ignorance. I say not nay, but a man may prosper with only hearing; but he may much more prosper with both hearing and reading. This have I said as touching the fear to read, through ignorance of the person. **Scripture in some places is easy, and in some places hard to be understood**. And concerning the hardness[24] of scripture; he that is so weak that he is not able to brook strong meat, yet he may suck the sweet and tender milk, and defer the rest until he wax stronger, and come to more knowledge. For God receiveth the learned and unlearned, and casteth away none, but is indifferent unto all. And the scripture is full, as well of low valleys, plain ways, and easy for every man to use and to walk in; as also of high hills and mountains, which few men can climb[25] unto. **God leaveth no man untaught, that hath good will to know his word**. And whosoever giveth his mind to holy scriptures with diligent study and burning[26] desire, it cannot be, saith Saint Chrysostom, that he should be left without help.[27] For either God Almighty will send him some godly doctor to teach[28] him, as he did to instruct Eunuchus, a nobleman of Ethiope, and treasurer unto queen Candace, who having affection[29] to read the scripture (although he understood it not), yet for the desire that he had unto God's word, God sent his apostle Philip to declare unto him the true sense of the scripture that he read;[30] or else, if we lack a learned man to instruct and teach us, yet God himself from above will give light unto our minds, and teach us those things which are necessary for us, and wherein we be ignorant. **How the knowledge of the scripture may be attained unto**. And in another place Chrysostom saith, that man's human and worldly wisdom or science needeth not to the understanding of scripture, but the revelation of the Holy Ghost, who inspireth the true meaning[31] unto them, that with humility and diligence do search therefore. *He that asketh shall have, and he that seeketh shall find, and he that knocketh shall have the door open* (Matt. 7:7–8). **A good rule for the understanding of scripture**. If we read once, twice, or thrice, and understand not, let us not cease so, but still continue reading, praying, asking of other, and so by still knocking, at the last the door shall be opened; as Saint Augustine saith, Although many things in the scripture be spoken in obscure mysteries, yet there is nothing spoken under dark mysteries in one place, but the selfsame thing in other places is spoken more familiarly and plainly, to the capacity both of learned and unlearned. **No man is excepted from the knowledge of God's will**. And those things in the scripture that be plain to understand, and necessary for salvation, every man's duty is to learn them, to print them in memory, and effectually to exercise them. And as for the dark[32] mysteries, to be contented to be ignorant in them, until such time as it shall please God to open those things unto him. In the mean season, if he lack either aptness or opportunity, God will not impute it to his folly: but yet it behoveth not, that such as be apt should set aside reading, because some other be unapt to read; nevertheless, for the hardness[33] of such places, the reading of the

24. Or *difficulty*.
25. Or *ascend*.
26. Or *fervent*.
27. Or *destitute of help*.
28. Or *instruct*.
29. Or *a great affection*.
30. Cf. Acts 8:26–40.
31. Or *sense*.
32. Or *obscure*.
33. Or *difficulty*.

whole ought not to be set apart. **What persons would have ignorance to continue**. And briefly to conclude, as Saint Augustine saith, by the scripture all men be amended, weak men be strengthened, and strong men be comforted. So that surely none be enemies to the reading of God's word, but such as either be so ignorant, that they know not how wholesome a thing it is; or else be so sick, that they hate the most comfortable medicine that should heal them; or so ungodly, that they would wish the people still to continue in blindness and ignorance of God.

    The holy scripture is one of God's chief benefits. Thus we have briefly touched some part of the commodities of God's holy word, which is one of God's chief and principal benefits, given and declared to mankind here in earth. Let us thank God heartily for this his great and special gift, beneficial favour, and fatherly providence; let us be glad to receive[34] this precious gift of our heavenly father; let us hear, read, and know these holy rules, injunctions, and statutes of our Christian religion, and upon that we have made profession to God at our baptism; **The right reading, use, and fruitful studying in holy scripture**. let us with fear and reverence lay up, in the chest of our hearts, these necessary and fruitful lessons (Ps. 56:4); let us night and day muse, and have meditation and contemplation in them (Ps. 1:2); let us ruminate, and, as it were, chew the cud, that we may have the sweet juice, spiritual effect, marrow, honey, kernel, taste, comfort, and consolation of them; let us stay, quiet, and certify our consciences, with the most infallible certainty, truth, and perpetual assurance of them: let us pray to God (the only author of these heavenly studies[35]) that we may speak, think, believe, live, and depart hence, according to the wholesome doctrine and verities of them. And, by that means, in this world we shall have God's defence,[36] favour, and grace, with the unspeakable solace of peace, and quietness of conscience; and after this miserable life we shall enjoy the endless bliss and glory of heaven: which he grant us all, that died for us all, Jesus Christ, to whom, with the Father and the Holy Ghost, be all honour and glory, both now and everlastingly. Amen.

34. Or *revive*.
35. Or *meditations*.
36. Or *protection*.

John Knox and the Church in Scotland

In this section on the Scottish church, we provide excerpts of the Scots Confession and the First Book of Discipline. The confession was introduced earlier in relation to the doctrine of Scripture; here we cite several articles that illustrate the interpretation of the Bible in Scotland. The confession reveals a redemptive-historical approach to Scripture combined with a concern to integrate doctrines systematically. It reflects in part the theological influence of Calvin. The selection below starting with the promise to Adam (Gen. 3:15) deals with both Christology and the church.

The First Book of Discipline shows how the Bible was to be used in the church. This document was prepared by the same group of men (cf. chap. 9) who worked on the confession and was completed at the end of 1560. This selection of the discipline deals with such topics as the translation of the Bible, the religious instruction in the home, and the preaching and the interpretation of Scripture in the church. We print here the preface and part of the "Ninth Head, Concerning the Policy of the Church" from Knox's *History of the Reformation in Scotland.* We have slightly modernized the spelling. A modernized edition of this book edited by James K. Cameron was published in 1972.

Supplementary Bibliography (cf. chap. 9): James K. Cameron, ed. *The First Book of Discipline.* Edinburgh: St. Andrew Press, 1972. J. D. Douglas. "Calvinism's Contribution to Scotland." Pp. 220–23 in Reid, ed. *John Calvin: His Influence in the Western World.* H. Griffith. "Knox, John." Pp. 614–15 in *EDT.* J. Kirk. "First Book of Discipline (1560)." Pp. 321–22 in *DSCH&T.* R. G. Kyle. "Knox, John (c. 1514–72)." Pp. 465–66 in *DSCH&T.* W. Lee, rev. Henry Cowan. "Knox, John." *NSHERK* 6:362–65.

THE SCOTS CONFESSION

The Latin text is a reproduction of "Confessio Fidei Scoticana I," in Schaff, *The Creeds of Christendom,* 3:441–50, 458–59.

The English text is a reproduction of "IV. From the Confession of Scotland (Article 4–11, 16)," in Hall, *Harmony,* 83–84, 98–101, 224–26.

CONFESSIO FIDEI SCOTICANA I

ART. IV: DE REVELATIONE PROMISSORUM

Constanter enim credimus, quod post formidabilem illam atque horrendam hominis ab obedientia Dei defectionem, rursus Deus Adamum *requisierit, vocaverit nominatim, accusaverit, convicerit: denique promissione illa gaudii plena eum sic consolans promisit,* Futurum ut semen mulieris caput serpentis contereret, *hoc est, universa diaboli opera destrueret ac everteret. Hæc promissio, ut aliis atque aliis temporibus sæpe repetita fuit, ac dilucidius explicata, ita cum summa lætitia recepta, et constanter credita est ab omnibus fidelibus, ab* Adamo *ad* Noam, *a* Noa *ad* Abrahamum, *ab* Abrahamo *ad* Davidem, *ac reliquis deinceps patribus, qui vixerunt sub lege fideles usque ad incarnationem* Christi. *Hi inquam omnes jucundissimos* Jesu Christi *dies viderunt, et gavisi sunt.*

THE SCOTS CONFESSION OF FAITH

Article 4: *Of the Revelation of the Promise*

For this we constantly believe, that God, after the fearful and horrible defection of man from his obedience, did seek Adam again, call upon him, rebuke his sin, convict him of the same, and, in the end made unto him a most joyful promise; to wit, that the seed of the woman should break down the serpent's head (Gen. 3:9, 15), that is, he should destroy the works of the devil: which promise, as it was repeated, and made more clear from time to time, so was it embraced with joy, and most constantly received of all the faithful from Adam to Noah, from Noah to Abraham, from Abraham to David, and so forth to the incarnation of Christ Jesus; all (we mean the faithful fathers under the law) did see the joyful day of Christ Jesus, and did rejoice (Gen. 12:3; 15:5–6; Isa. 7:14; 8:10).[1]

---

1. Gen. 4:7; 2 Sam. 7:14; Isa. 9:6; Hag. 2:7, 9; John 8:56.

ART. V: DE PERPETUA SUCCESIONE,
INCREMENTO ET CONSERVATIONE
ECCLESIÆ

Article 5: *Of the Continuance, Increase, and Preservation of the Church*

Illud quoque constanter persuasum habemus, quod Deus cunctis deinceps ætatibus, ab Adamo *ad* Jesu Christi *adventum in carnem, ecclesiam suam conservaverit, erudierit, multiplicaverit, honore affecerit, decoraverit, et a morte ad vitam evocaverit. Evocavit enim* Abrahamum *e patria, ac majorum suorum sedibus: eum erudiit, semen ejus multiplicavit, multiplicatum mirabiliter conservavit; mirabilius etiam e servitute ac tyrannide* Pharaonis *exemit. His* (posteros Abrahami *intelligimus*) *leges suas, instituta, et ceremonias dedit. Hos ad possidendam terram* Canaan *introduxit. His judices, his* Saulem, *his* Davidem *regem dedit: cui promisit e fructu lumborum ejus futurum, qui perpetuo super regium ejus thronum sederet. Ad hanc ipsam gentem diversis subinde temporibus misit prophetas, qui eam in viam Dei sui reducerent: a qua sæpe ad idolorum cultus deflexerant. Et quanquam ob protervum justitiæ contemptum sæpe eos potestati inimicorum permiserat* (quemadmodum antea per *Mosen* comminatus erat) *adeo ut sancta civitas eversa fuerit, templum incensum, ac universa eorum regio per spatium septuaginta annorum in vastam redacta solitudinem: nihilominus misericordia adductus, eos* Hierosolymam *reduxit; ac civitate instaurata, templo restituto, juxta promissionem eis factam, adversus omnes artes atque oppugnationes Satanæ adventum ibi* Messiæ *expectaverunt.*

We most constantly believe that God preserved, instructed, multiplied, honoured, decored, and from death called to life his Church in all ages, from Adam[2] till the coming of Christ in the flesh (Ezek. 16:6–14). For Abraham he called from his father's country; him he instructed, his seed he multiplied (Gen. 12:1–3); the same he marvelously preserved, and more marvelously delivered from the bondage and tyranny of Pharaoh (Ex. 1–2; 13): to them he gave his laws, constitutions, and ceremonies (Ex. 20:1–21); them he possessed in the land of Canaan (Josh. 1:3);[3] to them, after Judges,[4] and after Saul,[5] he gave David to be King (1 Sam. 16:13); to whom he made promise, that of the fruit of his loins should One sit for ever upon his regal seat.[6] To this same people, from time to time, he sent Prophets, to reduce them to the right way of their God (2 Kings 17:13); from the which oftentimes they declined by idolatry (2 Kings 17:14–15). And albeit that for the stubborn contempt of justice, he was compelled to give them into the hands of their enemies (2 Kings 24:3–4); as before was threatened by the mouth of Moses (Deut. 28:36, 48), insomuch that the holy city was destroyed, the temple burned with fire (2 Kings 25), and the whole land left desolate the space of seventy years;[7] yet of mercy did he reduce them again to Jerusalem, where the city and temple were reedified, and they against all temptations and assaults of Satan, did abide till the Messias came, according to the promise (Jer. 39:8–14; Ezra 1; Hag. 1:14; 2:7–9; Zech. 3:1–2, 8).[8]

2. Gen. 5:1–2.
3. Josh. 23:4.
4. Judg. 1; 1 Sam. 1:23 [?].
5. 1 Sam. 10.
6. 2 Sam. 7:12.
7. Dan. 9:2; Jer. 25:11–12; 29:10.
8. Jer. 30.

ART. VI: DE INCARNATIONE JESU CHRISTI

Cum plenitudo temporis venisset, Deus Filium suum, æternam suam sapientiam, et gloriæ suæ substantiam misit in hunc mundum. Isque Filius, co-operante Spiritu Sancto, humanam assumpsit naturam ex feminæ, ejusdemque virginis, substantia. Atque ita editum est justum illud semen Davidis, *Angelus ille magni consilii. Idem verus fuit* Christus *in lege promissus; quem nos agnoscimus et confitemur* Emmanuel, *verum Deum, verum hominem, unamque, quæ ex duabus perfectis naturis constet, personam.*

Hac itaque nostra confessione damnamus perniciosam et pestilentem Arii, Marchionis, Eutychis, Nestorii, *et aliorum id genus hominum, hæresim, qui aut ceternitatem divinitatis ejus negant, aut humance naturæ veritatem; aut utramque in eo naturam confundunt, aut separant.*

ART. VII: CUR OPORTEAT MEDIATOREM ET PACIFICATOREM VERUM ESSE DEUM ET VERUM HOMINEM

Agnoscimus item et fatemur, hanc maxime admirabilem divinitatis cum humanitate conjunctionem, ab æterno et immutabili Dei decreto profectam: unde omnis nostra salus emanat ac pendet.

Article 6: *Of the Incarnation of Christ Jesus*

When the fullness of time came, God sent his Son (Gal. 4:4), his eternal wisdom, the substance of his own glory, into this world, who took the nature of manhood, of the substance of a woman, to wit, of a virgin, and that by the operation of the Holy Ghost (Luke 1–2):[9] and so was born, the just seed of David,[10] the Angel of the great council of God,[11] the very Messiah promised; whom we acknowledge and confess Emmanuel (Isa. 7:14),[12] very God and very Man, two perfect natures united and joined in one person.[13]

By which our confession, we condemn the damnable and pestilent heresies of Arius, Marcion, Eutiches, Nestorius, and such others, as either did deny the eternity of his Godhead, or the verity of his human nature, or confounded them, or yet divided them.

Article 7: *Why it behoved the Mediator to be very God and very Man*

We acknowledge and confess, that this most wondrous conjunction betwixt the Godhead and the manhood in Christ Jesus, did proceed from the eternal and immutable decree of God, whence also our salvation springeth and dependeth.[14]

9. Matt. 1:18; 2:1.
10. Rom. 1:3.
11. Isa. 9:6 LXX.
12. Matt. 1:23.
13. John 1:45; 1 Tim. 2:5.
14. Eph. 1:3–6.

ART. VIII: DE ELECTIONE

Idem enim sempiternus Deus, ac Pater, qui ex mera sua gratia nos in Christo Jesu *Filio suo elegit, antequam mundi jacta essent fundamenta, eum nobis caput, fratrem, pastorem, ac magnum animorum nostrorum pontificem designavit. Sed quia tam aversa, atque inimica peccatis nostris erat Dei justitia, ut nulla per se caro ad Deum pervenire posset, Deum Filium oportuit ad nos descendere, et corpus e nostro corpore, carnem e carne, os ex ossibus assumere, atque ita idoneum mediatorem et pacificatorem inter Deum et hominem fieri; qui potestatem daret iis qui in eum crederent, ut filii Dei fierent, quemadmodum ipse testificatur,* Vado ad Patrem meum, et Patrem vestrum, Deum meum, et Deum vestrum: *ac per hanc sanctissimam fraternitatem, quicquid in* Adamo *amiseramus, iterum nobis est restitutum; ideoque Deum patrem nostrum appellare non dubitamus, non tam quod ab eo creati sumus id enim nobis cum reprobis est commune, quam quod indulserit, ut unicus ejus Filius frater nobis fieret; idque nobis gratificatus est, ut hunc unum interpretem et pacificatorem, ut est superius memoratum, agnosceremus et amplecteremur. Præterea necesse erat, ut qui verus Messias et redemptor esset futurus, idem verus homo et verus esset Deus: quippe*

Article 8: *Of Election*

For that same eternal God and Father, who of mere grace elected us in Christ Jesus his Son, before the foundation of the world was laid (Eph. 1:4),[15] appointed him to be our head,[16] our brother (Heb. 2:7–8, 11–12), our Pastor, and great Bishop of souls (John 10).[17] But because that the enmity betwixt the justice of God and our sins was such, that no flesh by itself could, or might, have attained unto God:[18] it behoved that the Son of God should descend unto us, and take himself a body of our body, flesh of our flesh, and bone of our bones, and so become the perfect Mediator betwixt God and man;[19] giving power to so many as believe in him, to be the sons of God (John 1:12); as himself doth witness, "I pass up to my Father, and unto your God" (John 20:17). By which most holy fraternity, whatsoever we have lost in Adam, is restored to us again.[20] And for this cause are we not afraid to call God our Father,[21] not so much because he hath created us (which we have common with the reprobate),[22] as for that he hath given to us his only Son to be our brother,[23] and given unto us grace to acknowledge and embrace him for our Mediator, as before is said. It behoved further the Messiah and Redeemer to be very God, and very man; because he was to bear the punishment

---

15. John 1; Matt. 25:34.
16. Eph. 1:22–23.
17. Heb. 13:20; 1 Peter 2:25; 5:4.
18. Pss. 130:3; 143:2.
19. 1 Tim. 2:5.
20. Rom. 5:17–19.
21. Rom. 8:15; Gal. 4:5–6.
22. Acts 17:26.
23. Heb. 2:11–12.

qui pœnas esset pensurus, quas nostro delicto commeriti eramus; et ante tribunal patris sese repræsentaturus esset, ut in pœna luenda pro nostro delicto et inobedientia, nostram sustineret personam, ac morte sua mortis autorem superaret. Et quia nec sola divinitas pati, nec sola humanitas vincere mortem poterat, utramque in unam coaptavit personam: ut alterius infirmitas morti, quam commerueramus esset obnoxia; alterius, id est divinitatis, invicta et immensa vis, de morte triumpharet, nobisque vitam, libertatem, ac perpetuam pareret victoriam. Atque sic confitemur, maximeque indubitanter credimus.

due for our transgressions, and to present himself in the presence of his Father's judgment, as in our person, to suffer for our transgression and disobedience (Isa. 53:5, 8),[24] by death to overcome him that was author of death.[25] But because only Godhead could not suffer death,[26] neither yet could the only manhood overcome the same, he joined both together in one person, that the imbecility of the one should suffer, and be subject to death (which we had deserved), and the infinite and invincible power of the other, to wit, of the Godhead, should triumph and purchase to us life, liberty, and perpetual victory.[27] And so we confess, and most undoubtedly believe.

24. 1 Peter 3:18.
25. Heb. 2:14.
26. Acts 2:24.
27. 1 John 1:2; Acts 20:28; 1 Tim. 3:16; John 3:16.

ART. IX: DE MORTE PASSIONE,
ET SEPULTURA CHRISTI

Item asseveramus, et pro certo persuasum habemus quod Dominus noster Jesus Christus *Patri sese victimam ultro pro nobis obtulerit: quod a peccatoribus contumeliis sit vexatus, quod pro nostris peccatis vulnera passus, quod cum purus et innocens Dei agnus esset, ad tribunal terreni judicis fuerit damnatus, ut nos ante tribunal Dei nostri absolveremur: quod non modo mortem incruce atrocem, et Dei ore execratam subierit; sed, quam peccatores meruerant, iram patris ad tempus tulerit. Nihilo tamen minus asseveramus, quod in medio etiam dolore et cruciatu, quos animo pariter et corpore pertulit (ut peccata hominum plene lueret), semper unice charus et benedictus patri filius esse perseveravit, Deinde fatemur atque etiam affirmamus, nullum post illud pro peccato restare sacrificium. Si qui autem contra affirment, nihil dubitamus eos blasphemos adversus* Christi *mortem, et æternam ejus purgationem, ac satisfactionem, per quam sua morte patrem nobis placavit, asserere.*

Article 9: *Of Christ's Death, Passion, and Burial*

That our Lord Jesus offered himself a voluntary sacrifice unto his Father for us (Heb. 10:4–12),[28] that he suffered contradiction of sinners, that he was wounded and plagued for our transgressions (Isa. 53:5),[29] that he, being the clean innocent Lamb of God,[30] was condemned in the presence of an earthly judge,[31] that we should be absolved before the tribunal-seat of our God;[32] that he suffered not only the cruel death of the cross (which was accursed by the sentence of God [Deut. 21:23; Gal. 3:13]), but also that he suffered for a season the wrath of his Father,[33] which sinners had deserved. But yet we avow that he remained the only well-beloved and blessed Son of the Father, even in the midst of his anguish and torment, which he suffered in body and soul, to make the full satisfaction for the sins of the people.[34] After the which we confess and avow, that there remaineth no other sacrifice for sin (Heb. 10:14);[35] which if any affirm, we nothing doubt to avow, that they are blasphemous against Christ's death, and the everlasting purgation and satisfaction purchased to us by the same.

28. Isa. 53:10, 12; Heb. 7:27; 9:26.
29. Heb. 12:3.
30. John 1:29.
31. Matt. 27:11, 26; Mark 15; Luke 23.
32. Rom. 14:10; 2 Cor. 5:10.
33. Matt. 26:38–39.
34. 2 Cor. 5:21.
35. Heb. 9:12, 28.

ART. X: De Resurrectione

Pro certo etiam credimus, quod quatenus fieri non poterat, ut mortis dolores perpetuam haberent potestatem adversus autorem vitæ, Dominus Jesus, *qui cruci affixus, mortuus et sepultus fuerat, quique ad inferos descenderat, iterum surrexit, ut nos justificaret: et autore mortis (cui æque ac morti eramus obnoxii) devicto, vitam nobis restituit. Scimus etiam resurrectionem ejus fuisse confirmatam acerbissimorum ipsius inimicorum testimoniis; item resurrectione mortuorum, qui apertis sepulchris revixerunt, ac in urbe* Hierosolyma *compluribus se videndos exhiberunt: Confirmata est etiam testimoniis angelorum, item apostolorum, qui eum viderunt et contrectarunt; aliorum item complurium, qui post resurrectionem, consuetudine ejus usi familiariter, cum eo ederunt et biberunt.*

Article 10: *Of His Resurrection*

We undoubtedly believe that, insomuch as it was impossible that the dolours of death should retain in bondage the Author of life (Acts 2:24; 3:15), that our Lord Jesus, crucified, dead, and buried, who descended into hell, did rise again for our justification (Rom. 6:5, 9),[36] and, destroying of him who was the author of death, brought life again to us that were subject to death, and to the bondage of the same.[37] We know that his resurrection was confirmed by the testimony of his very enemies (Matt. 28:4), by the resurrection of the dead, whose sepulchers did open, and they did arise, and appeared to many, within the city of Jerusalem (Matt. 27:52–53; 28:11–15). It was also confirmed by the testimony of his angels (Matt. 28:5–6), and by the senses and judgments of his apostles and others, who had conversation, and did eat and drink with him after his resurrection (John 20:27; 21:7, 12–13).[38]

36. Rom. 4:25.
37. Heb. 2:14–15.
38. Luke 24:41–43.

Art. XI: De Ascensione

Neque dubitamus quin idem corpus, quod ex virgine natum, cruci affixum, mortuum, et resuscitatum fuerat, in cœlum ascenderit, ut omnia impleret nostro nomine, et ad nostri consolationem accepit omnium potestatem in cœlo et in terra; et regno suscepto sedet ad dextram patris, patronus et unicus intercessor pro nobis. Atque hanc gloriam, honorem et prærogativam ille unus e fratribus tenebit, donec ponat inimicos suos scabellum pedum suorum. Ibique credimus usque ad ultimum judicium, futurum; ad quod exercendum, credimus constanter eundem Dominum nostrum Jesum Christum *visibilem, et qualis erat cum ascenderat, venturum: ac tum omnia instauratum et redintegratum iri, usque adeo, ut qui tolerarant [passi sunt] vim, contumelias, injurias, justitiæ ergo [propter justitiam], beatæ illius quæ ab initio promissa est immortalitatis fient heredes. Contra protervi, inobedientes, crudeles, violenti, impuri, idololatræ, ac cætera impiorum genera conjicientur in carcerem tenebrarum exteriorum, ubi nec vermis eorum morietur, nec ignis extinguetur: cujus judicii exercendi dies, ejusque memoria non solum nobis pro fræno est ad voluptates carnis coercendas, sed inestimabilis etiam animi confirmatio, quæ nos ita corroboret, ut neque minis principum terrenorum, neque mortis hujus momentaneæ admoto metu, nec præsentia ulla periculi commoveamur, ut beatam illam dirimamus societatem quæ*

Article 11: *Of His Ascension*

We nothing doubt but the self-same body, which was born of the virgin, was crucified, dead, and buried; that it did rise again, and ascend into the heavens, for the accomplishment of all things (Acts 1:9);[39] where, in our names, and for our comfort, he hath received all power in heaven and earth (Matt. 28:18); where he sitteth at the right hand of the Father, crowned in his kingdom, Advocate, and only Mediator for us (1 John 2:1; 1 Tim. 2:5). Which glory, honour, and prerogative he alone amongst the brethren shall possess, till that all his enemies be made his footstool (Ps. 110:1).[40] As that we undoubtedly believe there shall be a final judgment, to the execution whereof we certainly believe that the same our Lord Jesus shall visibly return, even as he was seen to ascend (Acts 1:11; John 19:37).[41] And then we firmly believe, that the time of refreshing and restitution of all things shall come (Acts 3:20–21): insomuch that those that from the beginning have suffered violence, injury, and wrong, for righteousness' sake, shall inherit that blessed immortality, promised from the beginning:[42] but contrariwise, the stubborn, inobedient, cruel oppressors, filthy persons, idolaters, and all sorts of unfaithful, shall be cast into the dungeon of utter darkness, where their worm shall not die, neither yet the fire shall be extinguished (Rev. 20:15; Isa. 66:24).[43] The remembrance of which day, and of the judgment to be executed

---

39. Luke 24:51.
40. Matt. 22:44; Luke 20:42–43.
41. 2 Thess. 1:7–10.
42. Matt. 25:34; 2 Thess. 1:4.
43. Rev. 21:27; Matt. 25:41; Mark 11:44, 46, 48; Matt. 22:13.
44. Isa. 1:4.

nobis, utpote membris, conflata est cum capite nostro, et unico intercessore Jesu Christo. Quem nos profitemur et asseveramus esse Messiam in lege promissum, unicum ecclesiæ suæ caput, justum nostrum legislatorem, unicum nobis summum pontificem, patronum, et pacificatorem. Ejus hos honores, atque hæc munera si quis hominum aut angelorum arroganter et superbe sibi attribuat, eum nos aspernamur, et detestamur velut blasphemum adversus supremum nostrum rectorem Jesum Christum.

in the same, is not only to us a bridle, whereby our carnal lusts are refrained,[44] but also such inestimable comfort, that neither may the threatening of worldly princes, neither yet the fear of temporal death and present danger, move us to renounce and forsake the blessed society which we the members have with our head and only Mediator Christ Jesus.[45] Whom we confess and avow to be the Messiah promised (Isa. 7:14), the only head of his Church (Col. 1:18),[46] our just Law-giver,[47] our only High Priest (Heb. 6:20; 9:11, 15; 10:21), Advocate, and Mediator.[48] In which honours and office if man or angel presume to intrude themselves, we utterly detest and abhor them, as blasphemous to our Sovereign and Supreme Governor, Christ Jesus.

45. 2 Peter 3:11; 2 Cor. 5:9–11; Luke 21:27–28; John 14:1.
46. Eph. 1:22.
47. Jas. 4:12.
48. 1 John 2:1; 1 Tim. 2:5.

ART. XVI: DE ECCLESIA

Quemadmodum credimus in unum Deum, Patrem, Filium, et Spiritum Sanctum; ita firmissime tenemus, quod ab usque rerum initio fuerit, nunc extet, ac futura sit usque ad mundi finem una ecclesia, id est, unus cœtus et multitudo hominum a Deo electorum, qui recte ac pie Deum venerantur et amplectuntur per veram fidem in Jesum Christum, *qui solus est caput ejus ecclesiæ, quæ et ipsa corpus est et sponsa* Christi. *Eademque est catholica, hoc est, universalis; quia omnium ætatum, nationum, gentium et linguarum electos continet, sive illi* Judæi *sint, seu gentes; iisque communio est et societas cum Deo Patre, cumque ejus Filio* Jesu Christo *per sanctificationem Sancti Spiritus: atque ideo non hominum prophanorum vocatur communio, sed sanctorum, qui etiam* Hierosolymæ *cœlestis sunt cives, fruunturque bonis maxime inæstimabilibus, nempe uno Deo, uno Domino nostro* Jesu, *una fide, et uno baptismo. Extra hanc ecclesiam nulla est vita, nulla æterna fœlicitas; idcirco plane ex diametro abhorremus ab eorum blasphemiis, qui asserunt, cujusvis sectæ, aut religionis professores fore salvos, modo vitæ suæ actiones ad justitiæ et æquitatis normam conformaverint: nam uti absque* Jesu Christo *nulla est vita, nulla salus; ita salutis ejus nemo erit particeps, nisi quem Pater dederit Filio suo* Jesu Christo, *quique ad eum dum tempus habet, adveniet, ejus doctrinam profitebitur, et in eum credet;*

Article 16: *Of the Church*

As we believe in one God, Father, Son, and Holy Ghost; so do we most constantly believe that from the beginning there hath been, and now is, and to the end of the world shall be, one Church: that is to say, a company and multitude of men chosen of God, who rightly worship and embrace him by true faith in Christ Jesus (Matt. 28:19–20; Eph. 1:4, 22);[49] who is the only Head of the same Church; which also is the body and spouse of Christ Jesus. Which Church is Catholic, that is, universal; because it containeth the elect of all ages, of all realms, nations, and tongues, be they of the Jews, or be they of the Gentiles, who have communion and society with God the Father, and with his Son Christ Jesus, through the sanctification of his Holy Spirit (Col. 1:18; Eph. 5:23–32; Rev. 7:9); and therefore it is called the Communion, not of profane persons, but of Saints; who, as citizens of the Heavenly Jerusalem (Eph. 2:19), have the fruition of the most inestimable benefits, to wit, of one God, one Lord Jesus, one faith, and one baptism:[50] out of the which Church, there is neither life nor eternal felicity. And therefore we utterly abhor the blasphemy of those that affirm, that men which live according to equity and justice, shall be saved, what religion soever they have professed. For as without Christ Jesus there is neither life nor salvation,[51] so shall there none be participant

---

49. Matt. 3:9.
50. Eph. 4:4–6.
51. John 3:36.

cum adultis autem parentibus, pueros etiam comprehendi intelligo. Hæc ecclesia invisibilis est, uni Deo cognita, qui solus novit quos elegerit. Hæc æque continet electos, qui jam decesserunt, quos vulgo ecclesiam triumphantem *appellant, ac eos qui nunc vivunt, et adversus peccatum et* Satanam *præliantur eosque qui post nos futuri sunt.*

thereof, but such as the Father hath given unto his Son Christ Jesus, and those that in time come unto him, avow his doctrine, and believe in him (John 5:22, 24; 6:37, 39, 65):[52] (we comprehend the children with the faithful parents).[53] This Church is invisible, known only to God, who alone knoweth whom he hath chosen,[54] and comprehendeth as well (as is said) the elect that be departed, commonly called the Church Triumphant, as those that yet live and fight against sin and Satan, and shall live hereafter.[55]

THE FIRST BOOK OF DISCIPLINE

"The Preface to the Buke of Discipline" and "The Nnyt Heade, Concernyng the Polecie of the Churche," in *The Works of John Knox*, ed. David Laing, vol. 2, *The History of the Reformation in Scotland* (Edinburgh: The Wodrow Society, 1848), 183–84, 240–45. The English has been modernized here.

The Preface to the Book of Discipline

To the Great Council of Scotland now admitted to [the] Regiment, by the Providence of God, and by the common consent of the Estates thereof, your Honors humble Servitors and Ministers of Christ Jesus with the same, wish Grace, Mercy and Peace from God the Father of our Lord Jesus Christ, with the perpetual increase of the Holy Spirit.

From your Honors we received a charge, dated at Edinburgh, the 29th of April, in the year of God 1560, requiring and commanding us, in the name of the Eternal God, as we will answer in his presence, to commit to writing, and in a Book to deliver unto your Wisdoms our judgments touching the Reformation of Religion, which heretofore in this Realm (as in others) has been utterly corrupted. Upon the receipt whereof (so many of us as were in this Town) did convene, and in unity of mind do offer unto your

52. John 17:6.
53. Acts 2:39.
54. 2 Tim. 2:19; John 13:18.
55. Eph. 1:10; Col. 1:20; Heb. 12:4.

Wisdoms these Heads subsequent for common order and uniformity to be observed in this Realm, concerning Doctrine, administration of Sacraments, [election of Ministers, Provision for their sustentation], Ecclesiastical Discipline, and Policy of the Kirk [or Church]; Most humbly requiring your Honors, that as you look for participation with Christ Jesus, that neither you admit any thing which God's plain word shall not approve, neither yet that you shall reject such ordinances as equity, justice, and God's word do specify; For as we will not bind your Wisdoms to our judgments, farther than we be able to prove the same by God's plain Scriptures; so must we most humbly crave of you, even as you will answer in God's presence (before whom both you and we must appear to render accounts of all our facts) that you repudiate nothing for pleasure nor [or pleasure and] affection of men, which you be not able to improve by God's written and revealed Word.

The Ninth Head, Concerning the Policy of the Church[56]

POLICY we call an exercise of the Church[57] in such things as may bring the rude and ignorant to knowledge, or else inflame the learned to greater fervency, or to retain the Church in good order. And thereof there be two sorts: the one utterly necessary; as that the word be truly preached, the sacraments rightly administered, common prayers publicly made; that the children and rude persons be instructed in the chief points of religion, and that offenses be corrected and punished; these things, we say, be so necessary, that without the same there is no face of a visible Kirk. The other is profitable, but not of mere necessity; as, that Psalms should be sung; that certain places of the Scriptures should be read when there is no sermon; that this day or that day, few or many in the week, the church should assemble. Of these and such others we cannot see how a certain order can be established. For in some churches the Psalms may be conveniently sung; in others, perchance, they cannot. Some churches may convene every day; some thrice or twice in the week; some perchance but once. In these and such like must every particular Church, by their own consent, appoint their own Policy.

In great Towns we think expedient that every day there be either Sermon, or else Common Prayers, with some exercise of reading the Scriptures. What day the public Sermon is, we can neither require or [or *nor*] greatly approve that the Common Prayers be publicly used, lest that we shall either foster the people in superstition, who come to the Prayers as they come to the Mass; or else give them occasion to think that those be no prayers which are made before and after Sermon[s].

In every notable Town, we require that one day beside the Sunday, be appointed to the Sermon and Prayers; which, during the time of Sermon, must be kept free from all exercise of labor, as well of the master as of the servants. In smaller towns, as we have said, the common consent of the Church must put order. But the Sunday must straightly be kept, both before and after noon, in all towns. Before noon, must the word be preached and sacraments administered, as also Marriage solemnized, if occasion offer: After noon must the young children be publicly examined in their Catechism

56. In the 1722 edition, Chapter 9.
57. In the 1621 edition, "Policy we call an exercise of the Kirk."

in audience of the people, in doing whereof the Minister must take great diligence, as well to cause the people to understand the questions proponed, as [the] answers, and the doctrine that may be collected thereof.

The order[58] and how much is appointed for every Sunday, is already distinguished in our *Book of Common Order*;[59] which Catechism is the most perfect that ever yet was used in the Church. At after noon also may Baptism be administered, when occasion is offered of great travel before noon. It is also to be observed, that prayers be used at after noon upon the Sunday, where there is neither preaching nor catechism.

It appertains to the Policy of the Church to appoint the times when the Sacraments shall be administered. Baptism may be administered whensoever the word is preached; but we think it more expedient, that it be administered upon (the) Sunday, or upon the day of prayers, only after the sermon; partly to remove this gross error by the which many [are] deceived, think[60] that children be damned if they die without Baptism; and partly to make the people assist the administration of that sacrament with greater reverence than they do.[61] For we do see the people begin already to wax weary be reason of the frequent repetition of those promises.

Four times in the year we think sufficient to the administration of the Lord's Table, which we desire to be distinguished, that the superstition of times may be avoided so far as may be. Your Honors are not ignorant how superstitiously the people run to that action at Pasch [Easter], even as [if] the time gave virtue to the Sacrament; and how the rest of the whole year they are careless and negligent, as [if] that it appertains not unto them but at that time only. We think therefore most expedient, that the first Sunday of March be appointed for one [time]; the first Sunday of June for another; the first Sunday of September for the third; and the first Sunday of December for the fourth. We do not deny but that any several church(es), for reasonable causes, may change the time, and may minister more often; but we study to suppress[62] superstition.

All Ministers must be admonished to be more careful to instruct the ignorant than ready to satisfy[63] their appetite, and more sharp in examination than indulgent, in admitting to that great Mystery[64] such as be ignorant of the use and virtue of the same: and therefore we think that the administration of the Table ought never to be without that examination pass before, especially of those whose knowledge is suspect. We think that none are apt to be admitted to that Mystery who cannot formally say the Lord's Prayer, the Articles of the Belief, and declare the sum of the Law.[65]

58. The editor in 1722 has given this sentence as follows: "The Order to be kept in teaching the Catechism, and how much of it is appointed for every Sunday, is already distinguished in the Catechism printed with the Book of our Common Order."

59. Or, *Order of Geneva*. It was so named from having been compiled for the use of the English congregation at Geneva, while Knox was minister there. It bears this title: *The Forme of Prayers and Ministration of the Sacraments, etc., used in the English Churche at Geneva, etc.* From Knox's share in this *Book of Common Order*, it will be included in a subsequent volume of his Works. Having been subsequently approved and received by the Church of Scotland, the Geneva edition of 1558 was reprinted at Edinburgh in 1562; and it continued with occasional alterations, to be prefixed to most editions of the old metrical version of the Psalms, printed in this country. The translation of Calvin's *Catechism*, first reprinted at Edinburgh in 1564, was also usually adjoined to the volume.

60. In the 1621 edition, "many are deceived, thinking."

61. In the 1621 edition, "to make the people have greater reverence to the administration of the Sacraments then they have."

62. In the 1621 edition, "minister more often, but we study to repress."

63. In the 1621 edition, "to serve."

64. In the 1621 edition, "their great mysteries."

Further, we think it a thing most expedient and necessary, that every Church have a Bible in English, and that the people be commanded to convene to hear the plain reading or interpretation of the Scriptures, as the Church shall appoint; that by frequent reading this gross ignorance, which in the cursed Papistry has overflowed all, may partly be removed. We think it most expedient that the Scriptures be read in order, that is, that some one book of the Old and the New Testament be begun and orderly read to the end. And the same we judge of preaching, where the Minister for [the] most part remains in one place: For this skipping and divagation from place to place of the Scripture, be it in reading, or be it in preaching, we judge not so profitable to edify the Church, as the continual following of a text.

Every Master of household must be commanded either to instruct, or else cause [to] be instructed, his children, servants, and family, in the principles of the Christian religion; without the knowledge whereof ought none to be admitted to the Table of the Lord Jesus: for such as be so dull and so ignorant, that they can neither try themselves, neither yet know the dignity and mystery of that action, cannot eat and drink of that Table worthily. And therefore of necessity we judge (it), that every year at least, public examination be had by the Ministers and Elders of the knowledge of every person within the Church; to wit, that every master and mistress of household come themselves and their family so many as are come to maturity, before the Ministers and Elders, to give confession of their faith, and to answer to such chief points of Religion as the Ministers shall demand. Such as be ignorant in the Articles of their Faith;[66] understand not, nor cannot rehearse the Commandments of God; know not how to pray; neither wherein their righteousness consists, ought not to be admitted to the Lord's Table. And if they stubbornly continue,[67] and suffer their children and servants to continue in willful ignorance, the discipline of the Church must proceed against them unto excommunication; and than must the matter be referred to the Civil Magistrate. For seeing that the just lives by his own faith, and that Christ Jesus justifies by knowledge of himself, insufferable we judge it that men shall be permitted to live and continue in ignorance as members of the Church of God.[68]

Moreover, men, women, and children would be exhorted to exercise themselves in the Psalms, that when the Church convenes, and does sing, they may be the more able together with common heart and voice to praise God.

In private houses we think it expedient, that the most grave and discrete person use the Common Prayers at morn and at night, for the comfort and instruction of others. For seeing that we behold and see the hand of God now presently striking us with diverse plagues, we think it a contempt of his judgments, or a provocation of his anger more to be kindled against us, if we be not moved to repentance of our former unthankfulness, and to earnest invocation of His name, whose only power may, and great mercy will, if we unfeignedly convert unto him, remove from us these terrible plagues which now for our iniquities hang over our heads. "Convert us, O Lord, and we shall be converted."

65. The Editor, in 1722, supplies, at the end of this paragraph: "And understands not the use and virtue of this holy Sacrament."

66. Nearly two lines in this place are omitted in the 1621 and 1722 editions.

67. In the 1621 edition, "stubbornly contemn."

68. In the 1621 edition, "to live as members of the Kirk, and yet to continue in ignorance."

FOR PREACHING,[69] AND INTERPRETING OF SCRIPTURES, etc.

To the end that the Church of God may have a trial of men's knowledge, judgments, graces, and utterances; and also, that such as somewhat have profited in God's word, may from time to time grow to more full perfection to serve the Church, as necessity shall require: it is most expedient that in every Town, where Schools and repair [gathering] of learned Men are, that there be one certain day every week appointed [to] that Exercise, which Saint Paul calls prophesying; the order whereof is expressed by him in these words: "Let two or three prophets speak; and let the rest judge: But if anything be revealed to him that sits by, let the former keep silence: [For] ye may, one by one, all prophecy, that all may learn, and all may receive consolation. And the spirits (that is, the judgments) of the prophets, are subject to the prophets." Of which words of the Apostle, it is evident that in Corinth, when the Church did assemble[70] for that purpose, some place of Scripture was read; upon the which, first one gave his judgment to the instruction and consolation of the auditors; after whom did another either confirm what the former had said, or did add what he had omitted, or did gently correct or explain more properly where the whole verity [truth] was not revealed to the former. And in case some things were hid from the one and from the other, liberty was given to the third to speak his judgment for edification of the Church. Above the which number of three (as appears) they passed not, for avoiding of confusion.

These Exercises, we say, are things most necessary for the Church of God this day in Scotland; for thereby (as said is) shall the Church have judgment and knowledge of the graces, gifts, and utterances of every man within their own body; the simple, and such as have somewhat profited, shall be encouraged daily to study and proceed in knowledge; the Church shall be edified; for this Exercise must be patent to such as list to hear and learn, and every man shall have liberty to utter and declare his mind and knowledge to the comfort and edification of the Church.

But lest that of a profitable Exercise might arise[71] debate and strife, curious, peregrine and unprofitable questions are to be avoided. All interpretation disagreeing from the principles of our faith, repugning [repugnant] to charity, or that stands in plain contradiction to any other manifest place of Scripture, is to be rejected. The Interpreter in that exercise, may not take to himself the liberty of a public Preacher, yea, although he be a Minister appointed; but he must bind himself to his text, that he enter not by digression in explaining common places. He may use no invective in that exercise unless it be with sobriety in confuting heresies. In exhortations or admonitions he must be short, that the time may be spent in opening of the mind of the Holy Ghost in that place; in following the fyle[72] and dependence of the text, and in observing such notes as may instruct and edify the auditor. For avoiding of contention, neither may the interpreter, neither yet any of the assembly, move any question in open audience, whereto himself is not content[73] to give resolution without reasoning with another; but every man ought to speak his own judgment to the edification of the Church.

---

69. In the 1722 edition, Chapter 12 and the title is, as in the 1621 edition, "For Prophesying, or Interpreting of the Scriptures."

70. In the 1621 edition, "that is the Kirk of Corinth, when they did assemble."

71. In the 1621 edition, "least of this profitable exercise there arise."

72. In the 1621 edition, "the sequel."

73. In the 1621 edition, "not able."

If any be noted with curiosity, or bringing in any strange doctrine, he must be admonished by the Moderator(s), the Ministers and Elders, immediately after that the interpretation is ended.

The whole members,[74] and number of them that are of the Assembly, ought to convene together, where examination should be had, how the persons that did interpret did handle and convey the matter; they themselves being removed till every man have given his censure; after the which, the person(s) being called, the faults (if any notable be found) are noted, and the person gently admonished. In that last Assembly all questions and doubts, if any arise, should be resolved without contention.

The Ministers of the Parish churches to Landwart, adjacent to every chief town, and the Readers, if they have any gift of interpretation, within six miles must assist and concur to those that prophecy within the towns; to the end that they themselves may either learn, or else others may learn by them. And moreover, men in whom are [or *is*] supposed any gifts [or *gift*] to be, which might edify the Church if they were well applied, must be charged by the Ministers and Elders to join themselves with that session and company of Interpreters, to the end that the Church may judge whether they be able to serve to God's glory, and to the profit of the Church in the vocation of Ministers or not. And if any be found disobedient, and not willing to communicate the gifts and spiritual graces[75] of God with their brethren, after sufficient admonition, discipline must proceed against them; provided that the Civil Magistrate concur with the judgment and election of the Church. For no man may be permitted to leave[76] as best pleases him within the Church of God; but every man must be constrained, by fraternal admonition and correction, to bestow his labors, when of the Church they are required, to the edification of others.

What day in the week is most convenient for that exercise, and what books of the Scriptures shall be most profitable to be read, we refer to the judgment of every particular Church, we mean, to the wisdom of the Ministers and Elders.

74. In the 1621 edition, "The whole Ministers"; the 1722 edition, after these words, adds, "with a number."
75. In the 1621 edition, "and special graces."
76. In the 1621 edition, "to live."

23

The Church's Marriage to
Her Sons, and to Her God

JONATHAN EDWARDS

Jonathan Edwards, "Sermon II. The Church's Marriage to Her Sons, and to Her God (Isaiah 62:4–5)," in *The Works of Jonathan Edwards* (Carlisle, PA: Banner of Truth, 1974), 2:17–26; first published in 1834.

Jonathan Edwards (1703–58) was a great theologian and pastor in eighteenth-century America. While best remembered as the intellectual leader of the Great Awakening, Edwards also produced many philosophical and theological works. Thus he provides a model of integration of "heart" and "mind." At the same time, these works uncover that Edwards was a keen biblical theologian, whose exegesis of Scripture drove and shaped his thought. This is evident in his great *A History of the Work of Redemption* (1774); it can also be seen in the sermon below.

For all his intellectual achievement, Edwards was first and foremost a preacher. "The Church's Marriage to Her Sons, and to Her God" exemplifies his skills both as a preacher and as a biblical theologian. This sermon was preached at the installation of Samuel Buell, an effective evangelist, on September 19, 1746, as pastor of the church and congregation at East Hampton on Long Island. It shows, therefore, not only Edwards's interpretative approach, but also his vision of the centrality of the Word for the pastoral ministry. Taking Isaiah as a starting point, Edwards navigates through Scripture to illustrate the covenantal marriage relationship between God and his people, and in accordance with the occasion he presents the role of pastors in this scheme. In a subsequent section, we include two briefer selections by Edwards that show more of his philosophical side as he defends the necessity of Scripture. All excerpts from Edwards are taken from the Banner of Truth reprint of his works.

Bibliography: R. W. Caldwell III and D. A. Sweeney. "Edwards, Jonathan (1703–1758)." Pp. 201–5 in *BDE*. Conrad Cherry. *The Theology of Jonathan Edwards: A Reappraisal*. Gloucester, MA: Peter Smith, 1974.

John E. Colwell. "Edwards, Jonathan (1703-58)." Pp. 174-75 in *DHT*. J. H. Edwards. "Edwards, Jonathan (1703-1758)." Pp. 90-91 in *DP&RTA*. Jonathan Edwards. "The Church's Marriage to Her Sons, and to Her God." Pp. 164-95 in Wilson H. Kimnach, ed. *Sermons and Discourses: 1743-1758*. Vol. 25. New Haven, CT: Yale University Press, 2006. Idem. *A History of the Work of Redemption*. 1774. Repr., Carlisle, PA: Banner of Truth, 2003. J. H. Gerstner. "Edwards, Jonathan (1703-58)." Pp. 220-21 in *NDT*. Paul Helm. "Edwards, Jonathan (1703-1758)." P. 334 in *NIDCC*. Stephen R. Holmes. "*Religious Affections* by Jonathan Edwards (1703-1758)." Pp. 285-97 in *The Devoted Life*. George M. Marsden. *Jonathan Edwards: A Life*. New Haven, CT: Yale University Press, 2003. M. A. Noll. "Edwards, Jonathan (1703-1758)." Pp. 343-46 in *EDT*. Edwards A. Park and F. H. Foster. "Edwards, Jonathan (The Elder)." *NSHERK* 4:81-82.

Thy land shall be married. For as a young man marrieth a virgin, so shall thy sons marry thee: and as the bridegroom rejoiceth over the bride, so shall thy God rejoice over thee. (Isaiah 62:4–5)

In the midst of many blessed promises that God makes to his church—in this and the preceding and following chapters—of advancement to a state of great peace, comfort, honour, and joy, after long-continued affliction, we have the sum of all contained in these two verses. In the 4th verse God says to his church, "Thou shalt no more be termed, Forsaken; neither shall thy land any more be termed Desolate: but thou shalt be called Hephzi-bah, and thy land, Beulah: for the Lord delighteth in thee, and thy land shall be married." When it is said, "Thy land shall be married," we are to understand, "the body of thy people, thy whole race"; the land—by a metonymy, very usual in Scripture—being put for the people that inhabit the land.—The 5th verse explains how this should be accomplished in two things, viz., *in being married to her sons, and married to her God.*

1. It is promised that she should be *married to her sons*, or that her sons should marry her? "For as a young man marrieth a virgin, so shall thy sons marry thee." Or, as the words might have been more literally translated from the original: "As a young man is married to a virgin, so shall thy sons be married to thee." Some by this understand a promise, that the posterity of the captivated Jews should return again from Babylon to the land of Canaan, and should be, as it were, married or wedded to their own land; i.e., They should be re-united to their own land, and should have great comfort and joy in it, as a young man in a virgin that he marries. But when it is said, "So shall thy sons marry thee." God does not direct his speech to the land itself, but to the church whose land it was; the pronoun *thee* being applied to the same mystical person in this former part of the verse, as in the words immediately following in the latter part of the same sentence, "And as the bridegroom rejoiceth over the bride, so shall thy God rejoice over thee." It is the church, and not the hills and valleys of the land of Canaan, that is God's bride, or the Lamb's wife. It is also manifest, that when God says, "So shall thy sons marry thee," he continues to speak to her to whom he had spoken in the three preceding verses; but there it is not the land of Canaan, but the church, that he speaks to when he says, "The Gentiles shall see thy righteousness, and all kings thy glory: and thou shalt be called by a new name, which the mouth of the Lord shall name. Thou shalt also be a crown of glory in the hand

of the Lord, and a royal diadem in the hand of thy God. Thou shalt no more be termed Forsaken," etc. And to represent the land itself as a bride, and the subject of espousals and marriage, would be a figure of speech very unnatural, and not known in Scripture; but for the church of God to be thus represented is very usual from the beginning to the end of the Bible. And then it is manifest that the return of the Jews to the land of Canaan from the Babylonish captivity, is not the event mainly intended by the prophecy of which these words are a part. That was not the time fulfilled in the 2nd verse of this chapter, "And the Gentiles shall see thy righteousness, and all kings thy glory: and thou shalt be called by a new name, which the mouth of the Lord shall name." That was not the time spoken of in the preceding chapters, with which this chapter is one continued prophecy. That was not the time spoken of in the last words of the foregoing chapter, when the Lord would cause righteousness and praise to spring forth before all nations: nor was it the time spoken of in the 5th, 6th, and 9th verses of that chapter, when "strangers should stand and feed the flocks of God's people, and the sons of the alien should be their ploughmen, and vine-dressers; but they should be named the priests of the Lord, and men should call them the ministers of God; when they should eat the riches of the Gentiles, and in their glory boast themselves, and their seed should be known among the Gentiles, and their offspring among the people; and all that should see them should acknowledge them, that they are the seed which the Lord hath blessed." Nor was that the time spoken of in the chapter preceding that "when the abundance of the sea should be converted unto the church; when the isles should wait for God, and the ships of Tarshish to bring her sons from far, and their silver and gold with them; when the forces of the Gentiles and their kings should be brought; when the church should suck the milk of the Gentiles, and suck the breast of kings; and when that nation and kingdom that would not serve her should perish and be utterly wasted: and when the sun should be no more her light by day, neither for brightness should the moon give light unto her, but the Lord should be unto her an everlasting light, and her God her glory and her sun should no more go down, nor her moon withdraw itself, because the Lord should be her everlasting light, and the days of her mourning should be ended." These things manifestly have respect to the christian church in her most perfect and glorious slate on earth in the last ages of the world; when the church should be so far from being confined to the land of Canaan, that she should fill the whole earth, and all lands should be alike holy.

These words in the text, "As a young man marrieth a virgin, so shall thy sons marry thee," I choose rather, with others, to understand as expressive of the church's union with her faithful pastors, and the great benefits she should receive from them. God's ministers, though they are set to be the instructors, guides, and fathers of God's people, yet are also the sons of the church, "I raised up of your sons for prophets, and of your young men for Nazarites" (Amos 2:11). Such as these, when faithful, are those precious sons of Zion comparable to fine gold spoken of, "Her Nazarites were purer than snow, they were whiter than milk" (Lam. 4:2, 7). And as he that marries a young virgin becomes the guide of her youth; so these sons of Zion are represented as taking her by the hand as her guide, "There is none to guide her among all the sons whom she hath brought forth; neither is there any that taketh her by the hand of all the sons that she hath brought up" (Isa. 51:18). That by these sons of the church is meant ministers of the gospel, is confirmed by the next verse to the text, "I have set watchmen upon thy walls, O Jerusalem."

That the sons of the church should be married to her as a young man to a virgin, is a mystery not unlike many others held forth in the word of God, concerning the relation between Christ and his people, and their relation to him and to one another. Christ is David's Lord and yet his Son, and both the Root and Offspring of David. Christ is a Son born and a Child given, and yet the everlasting Father. The church is Christ's mother (Song 3:11 and 8:1), and yet his spouse, his sister, and his child. Believers are Christ's mother, and yet his sister and brother. Ministers are the sons of the church, and yet are her fathers. The apostle speaks of himself, as the father of the members of the church of Corinth, and also the mother of the Galatians, travailing in birth with them (Gal. 4:19).

2. The second and chief fulfilment of the promise consists in the church being married to Christ: "And as the bridegroom rejoiceth over the bride, so shall thy God rejoice over thee." Not that we are to understand that the church has many husbands, or that Christ is one husband, and ministers are other husbands strictly speaking. For though ministers are here spoken of as being married to the church, yet it is not as his competitors, or as standing in a conjugal relation to his bride in any wise parallel with his. For the church properly has but one husband; she is not an adulteress, but a virgin, who is devoted wholly to the Lamb, and who follows him whithersoever he goes. But ministers espouse the church entirely as Christ's ambassadors, as representing him and standing in his stead, being sent forth by him to be married to her in his name, that by this means she may be married to him. As when a prince marries a foreign lady by proxy, the prince's ambassador marries her, but not in his own name, but in the name of his master, that he may be the instrument of bringing her into a true conjugal relation to him. This is agreeable to what the apostle says, "I am jealous over you with a godly jealousy; for I have espoused you to one husband, that I may present you as a chaste virgin to Christ" (2 Cor. 11:2). Here the apostle represents himself as being, as it were, the husband of the church of Corinth; for it is the husband that is jealous when the wife commits adultery; and yet he speaks of himself as having espoused them, not in his own name, but in that name of Christ, and for him, and him only, and as his ambassador, sent forth to bring them home a chaste virgin to him. Ministers are in the text represented as married to the church in the same sense that elsewhere they are represented as fathers of the church. The church has but one father, even God, and ministers are fathers as his ambassadors; so the church has but one shepherd, "There shall be one fold and one shepherd" (John 10:16); but yet ministers, as Christ's ambassadors, are often called the church's shepherds or pastors. The church has but one Saviour; but yet ministers, as his ambassadors and instruments, are called her saviours; "In doing this thou shalt both save thyself and them that hear thee" (1 Tim. 4:16). "And saviours shall come upon mount Zion" (Obad. 21). The church has but one Priest; but yet in Isaiah 46:21 speaking of the ministers of the Gentile nations, it is said, "I will take of them for priests and Levites." The church has but one Judge, for the Father hath committed all judgment to the Son; yet Christ tells his apostles, that they shall sit on twelve thrones, judging the twelve tribes of Israel.

When the text speaks first of ministers marrying the church, and then of Christ's rejoicing over her as the bridegroom rejoiceth over the bride; the former is manifestly spoken of as being in order to the latter; even in order to the joy and happiness that the church shall have in her true bridegroom. The preaching of the gospel is in this context spoken of three times

310

successively, as the great means of bringing about the prosperity and joy of the church; once, in the first verse, "For Zion's sake will I not hold my peace, and for Jerusalem's sake I will not rest, until the righteousness thereof go forth as brightness, and the salvation thereof as a lamp that burneth"; and then in the text; and lastly in the two following verses, "I have set watchmen upon thy walls, O Jerusalem, which shall never hold their peace day nor night. Ye that make mention of the Lord, keep not silence; and give him no rest, till he establish, and till he make Jerusalem a praise in the earth."

The text thus opened affords these two propositions proper for our consideration on the solemn occasion of this day.

I. The uniting of faithful ministers with Christ's people in the ministerial office, when done in a due manner, is like a young man's marrying a virgin.

II. This union of ministers with the people of Christ is in order to their being brought to the blessedness of a more glorious union, in which Christ shall rejoice over them, as the bridegroom rejoiceth over the bride.

I. PROPOSITION. The uniting of a faithful minister with Christ's people in the ministerial office, when done in a due manner, is like a young man's marrying a virgin.

I say, the uniting of a faithful minister with Christ's people, and in a due manner: for we must suppose that the promise God makes to the church in the text, relates to such ministers, and such a manner of union with the church; because this is promised to the church as a part of her latter-day glory, and as a benefit that should be granted her by God, as the fruit of his great love to her, and an instance of her great spiritual prosperity and happiness in her purest and most excellent state on earth. But it would be no such instance of God's great favour and the church's happiness, to have unfaithful ministers entering into office in an undue and improper manner. They are evidently faithful ministers that are spoken of in the next verse, where the same are doubtless spoken of as in the text; "I have set watchmen on thy walls, O Jerusalem, which shall never hold their peace day nor night." And they are those that shall be introduced into the ministry at a time of its extraordinary purity, order, and beauty, wherein (as is said in the first, second, and third verses) her "righteousness should go forth as brightness, and the Gentiles should see her righteousness, and all kings her glory, and she should be a crown of glory in the hand of the Lord, and a royal diadem in the hand of her God."

When I speak of the uniting of a faithful minister with Christ's people in a due manner, I do not mean a due manner only with regard to external order; but its being truly done in a holy manner, with sincere upright aims and intentions, with a right disposition, and proper frames of mind in those that are concerned; and particularly in the minister that takes office, and God's people to whom he is united, each exercising in this affair a proper regard to God and one another.—Such an uniting of a faithful minister with the people of God in the ministerial office, is in some respects like a young man marrying a virgin.

1. When a duly qualified person is properly invested with the ministerial character, and does in a due manner take upon him the sacred work and office of a minister of the gospel, he does, in some sense, espouse the church of Christ in general. For though he do not properly stand in a pastoral relation to the whole church of Christ through the earth, and is far from becoming an universal pastor; yet thenceforward he has a different concern with

the church of Christ in general, and its interests and welfare, than other persons have that are laymen, and should be regarded otherwise by all the members of the christian church. Wherever he is providentially called to preach the word of God, or minister in holy things, he ought to be received as a minister of Christ, and the messenger of the Lord of hosts to them. And every one that takes on him this office as he ought to do, espouses the church of Christ, as he espouses the interest of the church in a manner that is peculiar. He is under obligations, as a minister of the christian church, beyond other men, to love the church, as Christ her true bridegroom hath loved her, and to prefer Jerusalem above his chief joy, and to imitate Christ, the great shepherd and bishop of souls and husband of the church, in his care and tender concern for her welfare, and earnest and constant labours to promote it, as he has opportunity. And as he, in taking office, devotes himself to the service of Christ in his church; so he gives himself to the church, to be hers, in that love, tender care, constant endeavour, and earnest labour for her provision, comfort, and welfare, that is proper to his office, as a minister of Providence, as long as he lives; as a young man gives himself to a virgin when he marries her. And the church of Christ in general, as constituted of true saints through the world (though they do not deliver up themselves to any one particular minister as universal pastor, yet), cleave to and embrace the ministry of the church with endeared affection, high honour, and esteem, for Christ's sake. They joyfully commit and subject themselves to them; they resolve to honour and help them, to be guided by them and obey them so long as in the world; as the bride doth in marriage deliver up herself to her husband. And the ministry in general, or the whole number of faithful ministers, being all united in the same work as fellow-labourers, and conspiring to the same design as fellow-helpers, to the grace of God, may be considered as one mystical person, that espouses the church as a young man espouses a virgin: as the many elders of the church of Ephesus are represented as one mystical person, and all called the angel of the church of Ephesus (Rev. 2:1): and as the faithful ministers of Christ in general, all over the world, seem to be represented as one mystical person, and called an angel, "And I saw another angel fly in the midst of heaven, having the everlasting gospel to preach unto them that dwell upon the earth, and to every nation, and kindred, and tongue, and people" (Rev. 14:6).—But,

2. More especially is the uniting of a faithful minister with a particular christian people, as their pastor, when done in a due manner, like a young man marrying a virgin.—It is so with respect to the union itself, the concomitants of the union, and the fruits of it.

(1) The *union itself* is in several respects like that which is between a young man and a virgin whom he marries.

It is so with respect to mutual regard and affection. A faithful minister, that is in a christian manner united to a christian people as their pastor, has his heart united to them in the most ardent and tender affection. And they, on the other hand, have their hearts united to him, esteeming him very highly in love for his work's sake, and receiving him with honour and reverence, and willingly subjecting themselves to him, and committing themselves to his care, as being, under Christ, their head and guide.

And such a pastor and people are like a young man and virgin united in marriage, with respect to the purity of their regard one to another. The young man gives himself to his bride in purity, as undebauched by meretricious embraces; and she also presents herself to him a chaste virgin. So in such an union of a minister and people as we are speaking of, the parties united are pure and holy in their affection and regard one to another. The

312

minister's heart is united to the people, not for filthy lucre, or any worldly advantage, but with a pure benevolence to them, and desire of their spiritual welfare and prosperity, and complacence in them as the children of God and followers of Christ Jesus. And, on the other hand, they love and honour him with a holy affection and esteem; and not merely as having their admiration raised, and their carnal affection moved, by having their curiosity, and other fleshly principles, gratified by a florid eloquence, and the excellency of speech and man's wisdom; but receiving him as the messenger of the Lord of hosts, coming to them on a divine and infinitely important errand, and with those holy qualifications that resemble the virtues of the Lamb of God.

And as the bridegroom and bride give themselves to each other in covenant; so it is in that union we are speaking of between a faithful pastor and a christian people. The minister, by solemn vows, devotes himself to the people, to improve his time and strength, and spend and be spent for them, so long as God in his providence shall continue the union; and they, on the other hand, in a holy covenant commit the care of their souls, and subject themselves, to him.

(2) The union between a faithful minister and a christian people, is like that between a young man and virgin in their marriage, with respect to the *concomitants* of it.

When such a minister and such a people are thus united, it is attended with great joy. The minister joyfully devoting himself to the service of his Lord in the work of the ministry, as a work that he delights in; and also joyfully uniting himself to the society of the saints that he is set over, as having complacence in them, for his dear Lord's sake, whose people they are; and willingly and joyfully, on Christ's call, undertaking the labours and difficulties of the service of their souls. And they, on the other hand; joyfully receiving him as a precious gift of their ascended Redeemer. Thus a faithful minister and a christian people are each other's joy, "That I may come unto you with joy by the will of God, and may with you be refreshed" (Rom. 15:32). "As you have acknowledged us in part, that we are your rejoicing, even as ye are ours" (2 Cor. 1:14).

Another concomitant of this union, wherein it resembles that which becomes a young man and virgin united in marriage, is mutual helpfulness, and a constant care and endeavour to promote each other's good and comfort. The minister earnestly and continually seeks the profit and comfort of the souls of his people, and to guard and defend them from every thing that might annoy them, and studies and labours to promote their spiritual peace and prosperity. They, on the other hand, make it their constant care to promote his comfort, to make the burden of his difficult work easy, to avoid those things that might add to the difficulty of it, and that might justly be grievous to his heart. They do what in them lies to encourage his heart, and strengthen his hands in his work; and are ready to say to him, when called to exert himself in the more difficult parts of his work, as the people of old to Ezra the priest, when they saw him bowed down under the burden of a difficult affair, "Arise, for this matter belongeth to thee: we also will be with thee: be of good courage, and do it" (Ezra 10:4). They spare no pains nor cost to make their pastor's outward circumstances easy and comfortable, and free from pinching necessities and distracting cares, and to put him under the best advantages to follow his great work fully and successfully.

Such a pastor and people, as it is between a couple happily united in a conjugal relation, have a mutual sympathy with each other, a fellow-feeling of each other's burdens and calamities, and a communion in each other's prosperity and joy. When the people suffer in their spiritual interests, the pastor suffers: he is afflicted when he sees their souls in trouble and darkness; he feels their wounds; and he looks on their prosperity and comfort as his own. "Who is weak, and I am not weak? who is offended, and I burn not?" (2 Cor. 11:29.). "We were comforted in your comfort" (2 Cor. 7:13). And, on the other hand, the people feel their pastor's burdens, and rejoice in his prosperity and consolations (see Phil. 4:14 and 2 Cor. 2:3).

(3) This union is like that which is between a young man and a virgin in its *fruits*.

One fruit of it is mutual benefit: they become meet helps one for another. The people receive great benefit by the minister, as he is their teacher to communicate spiritual instructions and counsels to them, and is set to watch over them to defend them from those enemies and calamities they are liable to; and so is, under Christ, to be both their guide and guard, as the husband is of the wife. And as the husband provides the wife with food and clothing; so the pastor, as Christ's steward, makes provision for his people, and brings forth out of his treasure things new and old, gives every one his portion of meat in due season, and is made the instrument of spiritually clothing and adorning their souls. And, on the other hand, the minister receives benefit from the people, as they minister greatly to his spiritual good by that holy converse to which their union to him as his flock leads them. The conjugal relation leads the persons united therein to the most intimate acquaintance and conversation with each other; so the union there is between a faithful pastor and a christian people, leads them to intimate conversation about things of a spiritual nature. It leads the people most freely and fully to open the case of their souls to the pastor, and leads him to deal most freely, closely, and thoroughly with them in things pertaining thereto. And this conversation not only tends to *their* benefit, but also greatly to *his*. And the pastor receives benefit from the people outwardly, as they take care of and order his outward accommodations for his support and comfort, and do as it were spread and serve his table for him.

Another fruit of this union, wherein it resembles the conjugal, is a spiritual offspring. There is wont to arise from the union of such a pastor and people a spiritual race of children. These new-born children of God are in the Scripture represented both as the children of ministers, as those who have begotten them through the gospel, and also as the children of the church, who is represented as their mother that hath brought them forth, and at whose breasts they are nourished; as in Isaiah 54:1 and 66:11; Galatians 4:26; 1 Peter 2:2; and many other places.

Having thus briefly shown how the uniting of faithful ministers with Christ's people in the ministerial office, when done in a due manner, is like a young man marrying a virgin, I proceed now to the

II. PROPOSITION. Viz., that this union of ministers with the people of Christ, is in order to their being brought to the blessedness of a more glorious union, in which Christ shall rejoice over them as the bridegroom rejoiceth over the bride.

1. The saints are, and shall be, the subjects of this blessedness. Of all the various kinds of union of sensible and temporal things that are used in Scripture to represent the relation there is between Christ and his church; that which is between bridegroom and bride, or husband and wife, is much the most frequently made use of both in the Old and New Testament. The Holy Ghost seems to take a peculiar delight in this, as a similitude fit to represent the strict, intimate, and blessed union that is between Christ and his saints. The apostle intimates, that one end why God appointed marriage, and established so near a relation as that between husband and wife, was, that it might be a type of the union that is between

Christ and his church; in Ephesians 5:30–32. "For we are members of his body, of his flesh, and of his bones. For this cause shall a man leave his father and mother, and shall be joined to his wife; and they two shall be one flesh."—*For this cause*, i.e., because we are members of Christ's body, of his flesh, and of his bones, God appointed that man and wife should be so joined together as to be one flesh, to represent this high and blessed union between Christ and his church. The apostle explains himself in the next words, "This is a great mystery, but I speak concerning Christ and the church." This institution of marriage, making the man and his wife one flesh, is a great mystery; i.e., there is a great and glorious mystery hid in the design of it: and the apostle tells us what that glorious mystery is, "I speak concerning Christ and the church"; as much as to say, the mystery I speak of, is that blessed union that is between Christ and his church, which I spoke of before.

This is a blessed union indeed; of which that between a faithful minister and a christian people is but a shadow. Ministers are not the proper husbands of the church, though their union to God's people, as Christ's ambassadors, in several respects resembles the conjugal relation: but Christ is the true husband of the church, to whom the souls of the saints are espoused indeed, and to whom they are united as his flesh and his bones, yea and one spirit; to whom they have given themselves in an everlasting covenant, and whom alone they cleave to, love, honour, obey, and trust in, as their spiritual husband, whom alone they reserve themselves for as chaste virgins, and whom they follow whithersoever he goeth. There are many ministers in the church of Christ, and there may be several pastors of one particular church: but the church has but one husband, all others are rejected and despised in comparison of him; he is among the sons as the apple-tree among the trees of the wood; they all are barren and worthless, he only is the fruitful tree; and therefore, leaving all others, the church betakes herself to him alone, and sits under his shadow with great delight, and his fruit is sweet to her taste; she takes up her full and entire rest in him, desiring no other.—The relation between a minister and people shall be dissolved, and may be dissolved before death; but the union between Christ and his church shall never be dissolved, neither before death nor by death, but shall endure through all eternity: "The mountains shall depart, and the hills be removed; but Christ's conjugal love and kindness shall not depart from his church; neither shall the covenant of his peace, the marriage-covenant, be removed" (Isa. 54:1).—The union between a faithful minister and a christian people is but a partial resemblance even of the marriage union, it is like marriage only in some particulars: but with respect to the union between Christ and his church, marriage is but a partial resemblance, yea, a faint shadow. Every thing desirable and excellent in the union between an earthly bridegroom and bride, is to be found in the union between Christ and his church; and that in an infinitely greater perfection and more glorious manner.—There is infinitely more to be found in it than ever was found between the happiest couple in a conjugal relation; or could be found if the bride and bridegroom had not only the innocence of Adam and Eve, but the perfection of angels.

Christ and his saints, standing in such a relation as this one to another, the saints must needs be unspeakably happy. Their mutual joy in each other is answerable to the nearness of their relation and strictness of their union. Christ rejoices over the church as the bridegroom rejoices over the bride, and she rejoices in him as the bride rejoices in the bridegroom. My text has respect to the mutual joy that Christ and his church should have in each other: for though the joy of Christ over his church only is mentioned, yet it is evident that this is here spoken of and promised as the great happiness of the church, and therefore supposes her joy in him.

The mutual joy of Christ and his church is like that of bridegroom and bride, in that they rejoice in each other, as those whom they have chosen above others, for their nearest, most intimate, and everlasting friends and companions. The church is Christ's chosen, "I have chosen thee, and not cast thee away" (Isa. 41:9). "I have chosen thee in the furnace of affliction" (ch. 48:10). How often are God's saints called his elect or chosen ones! He has chosen them, not to be mere servants, but friends; "I call you not servants;—but I have called you friends" (John 15:15). And though Christ be the Lord of glory, infinitely above men and angels, yet he has chosen the elect to be his companions; and has taken upon him their nature; and so in some respect, as it were, levelled himself with them, that he might be their brother and companion. Christ, as well as David, calls the saints his brethren and companions, "For my brethren and companions' sake I will now say, Peace be within thee" (Ps. 122:8). So in the book of Canticles, he calls his church his sister and spouse. Christ hath loved and chosen his church as his peculiar friend, above others; "The Lord hath chosen Jacob unto himself, and Israel for his peculiar treasure" (Ps. 135:4). As the bridegroom chooses the bride for his peculiar friend, above all others in the world; so Christ has chosen his church for a peculiar nearness to him, as his flesh and his bone, and the high honour and dignity of espousals above all others, rather than the fallen angels, yea, rather than the elect angels. For verily in this respect, "he taketh not hold of angels, but he taketh hold of the seed of Abraham"; as the words are in the original (Heb. 2:16). He has chosen his church above the rest of mankind, above all the heathen nations, and those that are without the visible church, and above all other professing Christians; "My dove, my undefiled is but one; she is the only one of her mother, she is the choice one of her that bare her" (Song 6:9). Thus Christ rejoices over his church, as obtaining in her that which he has chosen above all the rest of the creation, and as sweetly resting in his choice; "The Lord hath chosen Zion: he hath desired it . . . This is my rest for ever" (Ps. 132:13–14).

On the other hand, the church chooses Christ above all others: he is in her eyes the chief among ten thousands, fairer than the sons of men: she rejects the suit of all his rivals, for his sake: her heart relinquishes the whole world: he is her pearl of great price, for which she parts with all; and rejoices in him, as the choice and rest of her soul.

Christ and his church, like the bridegroom and bride, rejoice in each other, as having a special propriety in each other. All things are Christ's; but he has a special propriety in his church. There is nothing in heaven or earth, among all the creatures, that is his, in that high and excellent manner that the church is his: they are often called his portion and inheritance; they are said to be "the first-fruits to God and the Lamb" (Rev. 14:4). As of old, the first fruit was that part of the harvest that belonged to God, and was to he offered to him; so the saints are the first-fruits of God's creatures, being that part which is in a peculiar manner Christ's portion, above all the rest of the creation, "Of his own will begat he us by the word of truth, that we should be a kind of first-fruits of his creatures" (James 1:18). And Christ rejoices in his church, as in that which is peculiarly his, "I will rejoice in Jerusalem, and joy in my people" (Isa. 65:19). The church has also a peculiar propriety in Christ: though other things are hers, yet nothing is hers in that manner that her spiritual bridegroom is hers. Great and glorious as he is, yet he, with all his dignity and glory, is wholly given to her, to be fully possessed and enjoyed by her, to the utmost degree that she is capable of: therefore we have her so often saying in the language of exultation and triumph, "My beloved is mine, and I am his" (Song 2:16; 6:3; and 7:10).

Christ and his church, like the bridegroom and bride, rejoice in each other, as those that are the objects of each other's most tender and ardent love. The love of Christ to his church is altogether unparalleled: the height and depth and length and breadth of it pass knowledge: for he loved the church, and gave himself for it; and his love to her proved stronger than death. And on the other hand, she loves him with a supreme affection; nothing stands in competition with him in her heart: she loves him with all her heart. Her whole soul is offered up to him in the flame of love. And Christ rejoices, and has sweet rest and delight in his love to the church; "The Lord thy God in the midst of thee is mighty; he will save, he will rejoice over thee with joy; he will rest in his love, he will joy over thee with singing" (Zeph. 3:17). So the church, in the exercises of her love to Christ, rejoices with unspeakable joy; "Jesus Christ: whom having not seen, ye love; in whom, though now ye see him not, yet believing, ye rejoice with joy unspeakable, and full of glory" (1 Peter 1:7–8).

Christ and his church rejoice in each other's beauty. The church rejoices in Christ's divine beauty and glory. She, as it were, sweetly solaces herself in the light of the glory of the Sun of righteousness; and the saints say one to another, as in Isaiah 2:5, "O house of Jacob, come ye, let us walk in the light of the Lord." The perfections and virtues of Christ are as a perfumed ointment to the church, that make his very name to be to her as ointment poured forth; "Because of the savour of thy good ointments thy name is as ointment poured forth, therefore do the virgins love thee" (Song 1:3). And Christ delights and rejoices in the beauty of the church, the beauty which he hath put upon her: her christian graces are ointments of great price in his sight (1 Peter 3:4). And he is spoken of as greatly desiring her beauty (Ps. 45:11). Yea, he himself speaks of his heart as ravished with her beauty, "Thou hast ravished my heart, my sister, my spouse; thou hast ravished my heart with one of thine eyes, with one chain of thy neck" (Song 4:9).

Christ and his church, as the bridegroom and bride, rejoice in each other's love. Wine is spoken of as that which maketh glad man's heart (Ps. 104:15): but the church of Christ is spoken of as rejoicing in the love of Christ, as that which is more pleasant and refreshing than wine, "The king hath brought me into his chambers: we will be glad and rejoice in thee, we will remember thy love more than wine" (Song 1:4). So on the other hand, Christ speaks of the church's love as far better to him than wine, "How fair is thy love, my sister, my spouse! how much better is thy love than wine!" (Song 4:10).

Christ and his church rejoice in communion with each other, as in being united in their happiness, and having fellowship and a joint participation in each other's good: as the bridegroom and bride rejoice together at the wedding-feast, and as thenceforward they are joint partakers of each other's comforts and joys: "If any man hear my voice, and open the door, I will come in to him, and sup with him, and he with me" (Rev. 3:20). The church has fellowship with Christ in his own happiness, and his divine entertainments; his joy is fulfilled in her (John 15:11 and 17:13). She sees light in his light; and she is made to drink at the river of his own pleasures (Ps. 36:8–9). And Christ brings her to eat and drink at his own table, to take her fill of his own entertainments; "Eat, O friends, drink, yea, drink abundantly, O beloved" (Song 5:1). And he, on the other hand, has fellowship with her; he feasts with her; her joys are his; and he rejoices in that entertainment that she provides for him. So Christ is said to feed among the lilies (Song 2:16), and she speaks of all manner of pleasant fruits, new and old, which she had laid up (ch. 7:13), and says to him, "Let my beloved come into his garden, and eat his pleasant fruits" (ch. 4:16); and he makes answer in the next verse, "I am come into my garden, my sister, my spouse; I have gathered my myrrh with my spice, I have eaten my honey-comb with my honey, I have drunk my wine with my milk."

And lastly, Christ and his church, as the bridegroom and bride, rejoice in conversing with each other. The words of Christ by which he converses with his church, are most sweet to her; and therefore she says of him, "His mouth is most sweet" (Song 5:16). And on the other hand, he says of her, "Let me hear thy voice: for sweet is thy voice" (ch. 2:14). And, "Thy lips, O my spouse, drop as the honey-comb: honey and milk are under thy tongue" (ch. 4:11).

Christ rejoices over his saints as the bridegroom over the bride at all times: but there are some seasons wherein he doth so more especially. Such a season is the time of the soul's conversion; when the good shepherd finds his lost sheep, then he brings it home rejoicing, and calls together his friends and neighbours, saying, Rejoice with me. The day of a sinner's conversion is the day of Christ's espousals; and so is eminently the day of his rejoicing; "Go forth, O ye daughters of Zion, and behold king Solomon with the crown wherewith his mother crowned him in the day of his espousals, and in the day of the gladness of his heart" (Song 3:11). And it is oftentimes remarkably the day of the saints' rejoicing in Christ; for then God turns again the captivity of his elect people, and, as it were, fills their mouth with laughter, and their tongue with singing; as in Psalm 126 at the beginning. We read of the jailer, that when he was converted, "he rejoiced, believing in God, with all his house" (Acts 16:34).—There are other seasons of special communion of the saints with Christ, wherein Christ doth in a special manner rejoice over his saints, and as their bridegroom brings them into his chambers, that they also may be glad and rejoice in him (Song 1:4).

But this mutual rejoicing of Christ and his saints will be in its perfection, at the time of the saints' glorification with Christ in heaven; for that is the proper time of the saints' entering in with the bridegroom into the marriage (Matt. 25:10). The saints' conversion is rather like the betrothing of the intended bride to the bridegroom before they come together; but at the time of the saints' glorification that shall be fulfilled in Psalm 45:15, "With gladness and rejoicing shall they be brought; they shall enter into the king's palace." That is the time when those whom Christ loved, and for whom he gave himself—that he might sanctify and cleanse them, as with the washing of water by the word—shall be presented to him in glory, not having spot or wrinkle, or any such thing. Then the church shall be brought to the full enjoyment of her bridegroom, having all tears wiped away from her eyes; and there shall be no more distance or absence. She shall then be brought to the entertainments of an eternal wedding-feast, and to dwell for ever with her bridegroom; yea, to dwell eternally in his embraces. Then Christ will give her his loves; and she shall drink her fill, yea, she shall swim in the ocean of his love.

And as there are various seasons wherein Christ and particular saints do more especially rejoice in each other; so there are also certain seasons wherein Christ doth more especially rejoice over his church collectively taken. Such a season is a time of remarkable outpouring of the Spirit of God: it is a time of the espousals of many souls to Christ; and so of the joy of espousals. It is a time wherein Christ is wont more especially to visit his saints with his loving-kindness, and to bring them near to himself, and especially to refresh their hearts with divine communications: on which account, it becomes a time of great joy to the church of Christ. So when the Spirit of God was so wonderfully poured out on the city of Samaria, with the preaching of Philip, we read that "there was great joy in that city" (Acts 8:8). And the time of that wonderful effusion of the Spirit at Jerusalem, begun at the feast of Pentecost, was a time of holy feasting and rejoicing, and a kind of a wedding-day to the church of Christ; wherein "they continuing daily, with one accord, in the temple, and breaking bread from house to house, did eat their meat with gladness, and singleness of heart" (Acts 2:46).

But more especially is the time of that great outpouring of the Spirit of God in the latter days, so often foretold in the Scriptures, represented as the marriage of the Lamb, and the rejoicing of Christ and his church in each other, as the bridegroom and the bride. This is the time prophesied of in our text and context; and foretold in Isaiah 65:19, "I will rejoice in Jerusalem, and joy in my people; and the voice of weeping shall no more be heard in her, nor the voice of crying." This is the time spoken of where the apostle John tells us, he "heard as it were the voice of a great multitude, and as the voice of many waters, and as the voice of mighty thunderings, saying, Alleluia: for the Lord God omnipotent reigneth. Let us be glad and rejoice, and give honour to him: for the marriage of the Lamb is come, and his wife hath made herself ready." And adds, "To her was granted, that she should be arrayed in fine linen, clean and white: for the fine linen is the righteousness of saints. And he saith unto me, Write, Blessed are they which are called unto the marriage-supper of the Lamb" (Rev. 19:6–9).

But above all, the time of Christ's last coming, is that of the consummation of the church's marriage with the Lamb, and of the complete and most perfect joy of the wedding. In that resurrection-morning, when the Sun of righteousness shall appear in our heavens, shining in all his brightness and glory, he will come forth as a bridegroom; he shall come in the glory of his Father, with all his holy angels. And at that glorious appearing of the great God, and our Saviour Jesus Christ, shall the whole elect church, complete as to every individual member, and each member with the whole man, both body and soul, and both in perfect glory, ascend up to meet the Lord in the air, to be thenceforth for ever with the Lord. That will be indeed a joyful meeting of this glorious bridegroom and bride. Then the bridegroom will appear in all his glory without any veil; and then the saints shall shine forth as the sun in the kingdom of their Father, and at the right hand of their Redeemer; and then the church will appear as the bride, the Lamb's wife. It is the state of the church after the resurrection, that is spoken of, "And I John saw the holy city, new Jerusalem, coming down from God out of heaven, prepared as a bride adorned for her husband" (Rev. 21:2). And, "Come hither, I will show thee the bride, the Lamb's wife" (v. 9). Then will come the time, when Christ will sweetly invite his spouse to enter in with him into the palace of his glory, which he had been preparing for her from the foundation of the world, and shall, as it were, take her by the hand, and lead her in with him: and this glorious bridegroom and bride shall, with all their shining ornaments, ascend up together into the heaven of heavens; the whole multitude of glorious angels waiting upon them: and this son and daughter of God shall, in their united glory and joy, present themselves together before the Father; when Christ shall say, "Here am I, and the children which thou hast given me." And they both shall in that relation and union, together receive the Father's blessing; and shall thenceforward rejoice together, in consummate, uninterrupted, immutable, and everlasting glory, in the love and embraces of each other, and joint enjoyment of the love of the Father.

2. That forementioned union of faithful ministers with the people of Christ, is in order to this blessedness.

1. It is only with reference to Christ, as the true bridegroom of his church, that there is any union between a faithful minister and a christian people, that is like that of a bridegroom and bride.

As I observed before, a faithful minister espouses a christian people, not in his own name, but as Christ's ambassador: he espouses them, that therein they may be espoused to Christ. He loves her with a tender conjugal affection, as she is the spouse of Christ, and as he, as the minister of Christ, has his heart under the influence of the Spirit of Christ; as Abraham's faithful servant, that was sent to fetch a wife for his master's son, was captivated with Rebekah's beauty and virtue; but not with reference to an union with himself, but with his master Isaac. It was for his sake he loved her, and it was for him that he desired her. He set his heart upon her, that she might be Isaac's wife; and it was for this that he greatly rejoiced over her, for this he wooed her, and for this he obtained her, and she was for a season, in a sense, united to him; but it was as a fellow-traveller, that by him she might be brought to Isaac in the land of Canaan. For this he adorned her with ornaments of gold; it was to prepare her for Isaac's embraces. All that tender care which a faithful minister takes of his people as a kind of spiritual husband—to provide for them, to lead, and feed, and comfort them—is not as to his own bride, but his master's.

And on the other hand, the people receive him, unite themselves to him in covenant, honour him, subject themselves to him, and obey him, only for Christ's sake, and as one that represents him, and acts in his name towards them. All this love, and honour, and submission, is ultimately referred to Christ. Thus the apostle says, "Ye received me as an angel, or messenger of God, even as Christ Jesus" (Gal. 4:14). And the children that are brought forth in consequence of the union of the pastor and people, are not properly the minister's children, but the children of Christ; they are not born of man, but of God.

2. The things that appertain to that fore-mentioned union of a faithful minister and christian people, are the principal appointed means of bringing the church to that blessedness that has been spoken of. Abraham's servant, and the part he acted as Isaac's agent towards Rebekah, were the principal means of his being brought to enjoy the benefits of her conjugal relation to Isaac. Ministers are sent to woo the souls of men for Christ, "We are then ambassadors for Christ, as though God did beseech you by us: we pray you in Christ's stead, be ye reconciled to God" (2 Cor. 5:20). We read in Matthew 22 of a certain king, that made a marriage for his son, and sent forth his servants to invite and bring in the guests: these servants are ministers. The labours of faithful ministers are the principal means God is wont to make use of for the conversion of the children of the church, and so of their espousals unto Christ. I have espoused you to one husband, says the apostle (2 Cor. 11:2). The preaching of the gospel by faithful ministers, is the principal means that God uses for exhibiting Christ, his love and benefits to his elect people, and the chief means of their being sanctified, and so fitted to enjoy their spiritual bridegroom. Christ loved the church, and gave himself for it, that he might sanctify and cleanse it, as by the washing of water by the word (i.e., by the preaching of the gospel), and so might present it to himself, a glorious church. The labours of faithful ministers are ordinarily the principal means of the joy of the saints in Christ Jesus, in their fellowship with their spiritual bridegroom in this world; "We are helpers of your joy" (2 Cor. 1:24). They are God's instruments for bringing

up the church, as it were, from her childhood, till she is fit for her marriage with the Lord of glory; as Mordecai brought up Hadassah, or Esther, whereby she was fitted to be queen in Ahasuerus's court. God purifies the church under their hand, as Esther (to fit her for her marriage with the king) was committed to the custody of Hegai the keeper of the women, to be purified six months with oil of myrrh, and six months with sweet odours. They are made the instruments of clothing the church in her wedding-garments, that fine linen, clean and white, and adorning her for her husband; as Abraham's servant adorned Rebekah with golden ear-rings and bracelets. Faithful ministers are made the instruments of leading the people of God in the way to heaven, conducting them to the glorious presence of the bridegroom, to the consummate joys of her marriage with the Lamb; as Abraham's servant conducted Rebekah from Padan-aram to Canaan, and presented her to Isaac, and delivered her into his embraces. For it is the office of ministers, not only to espouse the church to her husband, but to present her a chaste virgin to Christ.

I would now conclude this discourse with some exhortations, agreeable to what has been said. And,

1. The exhortation may be to all that are called to the work of the gospel-ministry.—Let us who are honoured by the glorious bridegroom of the church, to be employed as his ministers, to so high a purpose, as has been represented, he engaged and induced by what has been observed, to faithfulness in our great work; that we may be and act towards Christ's people that are committed to our care, as those that are united to them in holy espousals, for Christ's sake, and in order to their being brought to the unspeakable blessedness of that more glorious union with the Lamb of God, in which he shall rejoice over them, as the bridegroom rejoiceth over the bride. Let us see to it that our hearts are united to them, as a young man to a virgin that he marries, in the most ardent and tender affection; and that our regard to them be pure and uncorrupt, that it may be a regard to them, and not to what they have, or any worldly advantages we hope to gain of them. And let us behave ourselves as those that are devoted to their good; being willing to spend and be spent for them; joyfully undertaking and enduring the labour and self-denial that is requisite in order to a thorough fulfilling the ministry that we have received. Let us continually and earnestly endeavour to promote the prosperity and salvation of the souls committed to our care, looking on their calamities and their prosperity as our own; feeling their spiritual wounds and griefs, and refreshed with their consolations; and spending our whole lives in diligent care and endeavour to provide for, nourish, and instruct our people, as the intended spouse of Christ, yet in her minority, that we may form her mind and behaviour, and bring her up for him, and that we may cleanse her, as with the washing of water by the word, and purify her as with sweet odours, and clothed in such raiment as may become Christ's bride. Let us aim that when the appointed wedding-day comes, we may have done our work as Christ's messengers; and may then be ready to present Christ's spouse to him, a chaste virgin, properly educated and formed, and suitably adorned for her marriage with the Lamb; that he may then present her to himself, a glorious church, not having spot or wrinkle, or any such thing, and may receive her into his eternal embraces, in perfect purity, beauty, and glory.

Here I would mention three or four things tending to excite us to this fidelity.

1. We ought to consider how much Christ has done to obtain that joy, wherein he rejoices over his church, as the bridegroom rejoiceth over the bride.

The creation of the world seems to have been especially for this end, that the eternal Son of God might obtain a spouse towards whom he might fully exercise the infinite benevolence of his nature, and to whom he might, as it were, open and pour forth all that immense fountain of condescension, love, and grace that was in his heart, and that in this way God might be glorified. Doubtless the work of creation is subordinate to the work of redemption: the creation of the new heavens and new earth, is represented as so much more excellent than the old, that, in comparison, it is not worthy to be mentioned, or come into mind.

Christ has done greater things than to create the world, in order to obtain his bride and the joy of his espousals with her: for he became man for this end; which was a greater thing than his creating the world. For the Creator to *make* the creature was a great thing; but for him to *become* a creature was a greater thing. And he did a much greater thing still to obtain this joy; in that for this he laid down his life, and suffered even the death of the cross: for this he poured out his soul unto death; and he that is the Lord of the universe, God over all, blessed for evermore, offered up himself a sacrifice, in both body and soul, in the flames of divine wrath. Christ obtains his elect spouse by conquest: for she was a captive in the hands of dreadful enemies; and her Redeemer came into the world to conquer these enemies, and rescue her out of their hands, that she might be his bride. And he came and encountered these enemies in the greatest battle that ever was beheld by men or angels: he fought with principalities and powers; he fought alone with the powers of darkness, and all the armies of hell; yea, he conflicted with the infinitely more dreadful wrath of God, and overcame in this great battle; and thus he obtained his spouse. Let us consider at how great a price Christ purchased this spouse: he did not redeem her with corruptible things, as silver and gold, but with his own precious blood; yea, he gave himself for her. When he offered up himself to God in those extreme labours and sufferings, this was the joy that was set before him, that made him cheerfully to endure the cross, and despise the pain and shame in comparison of this joy; even that rejoicing over his church, as the bridegroom rejoiceth over the bride that the Father had promised him, and that he expected when he should present her to himself in perfect beauty and blessedness.

The prospect of this was what supported him in the midst of the dismal prospect of his sufferings, at which his soul was troubled; "Now is my soul troubled; and what shall I say? Father, save me from this hour: but for this cause came I unto this hour" (John 12:27). These words show the conflict and distress of Christ's holy soul in the view of his approaching sufferings. But in the midst of his trouble, he was refreshed with the joyful prospect of the success of those sufferings, in bringing home his elect church to himself, signified by a voice from heaven, and promised by the Father: on which he says, in the language of triumph, "Now is the judgment of this world: now shall the prince of this world be cast out. And I, if I be lifted up, will draw all men unto me" (vv. 31–32).

And ministers of the gospel are appointed to be the instruments of bringing this to pass; the instruments of bringing home his elect spouse to him, and her becoming his bride; and the instruments of her sanctifying and cleansing by the word, that she might be meet to be presented to him on the future glorious wedding-day. How great a motive then is here to induce us who are called to be these instruments, to be faithful in our work, and most willingly labour and suffer, that Christ may see of the travail of his soul and be satisfied! Shall Christ do such great things, and go through such great labours and sufferings to obtain this joy, and then honour us sinful worms, so as to employ us as his ministers and instruments to bring this joy to pass; and shall we be loth to labour, and backward to deny ourselves for this end?

2. Let us consider how much the manner in which Christ employs us in this great business has to engage us to a faithful performance of it. We are sent forth as his servants; but it is as highly dignified servants, as stewards of his household, as Abraham's servant; and as his ambassadors, to stand in his stead, and in his name, and represent his person in so great an affair as that of his espousals with the eternally beloved of his soul. Christ employs us not as mere servants, but as friends of the bridegroom; agreeable to the style in which John the Baptist speaks of himself (John 3:29); in which he probably alludes to an ancient custom among the Jews at their nuptial solemnities, at which one of the guests that was most honoured and next in dignity to the bridegroom, was styled *the friend of the bridegroom.*

There is not an angel in heaven, of how high an order soever, but what looks on himself honoured by the Son of God and Lord of glory, in being employed by him as his minister in the high affair of his espousals with his blessed bride. But such honour has Christ put upon us, that his spouse should in some sort be ours; that we should marry, as a young man marries a virgin, the same mystical person that he himself will rejoice over as the bridegroom rejoiceth over the bride; that we should be his ministers to treat and transact for him with his dear spouse, that he might obtain this joy: and, in our treaty with her, to be married to her in his name, and sustain an image of his own endearing relation to her; and that she should receive us, in some sort, as himself, and her heart be united to us in esteem, honour, and affection, as those that represent him; and that Christ's and the church's children should be ours, and that the fruit of the travail of Christ's soul should be also the fruit of the travail of our souls; as the apostle speaks of himself as travailing in birth with his hearers (Gal. 4:19). The reason why Christ puts such honour on faithful ministers, even above the angels themselves, is because they are of his beloved church, they are select members of his dear spouse, and Christ esteems nothing too much, no honour too great, for her. Therefore Jesus Christ, the King of angels and men, does as it were cause it to be proclaimed concerning faithful ministers, as Ahasuerus did concerning him that brought up Esther, his beloved queen; "Thus shall it be done to the man that the king delights to honour."

And seeing Christ hath so honoured us, that our relation to his people resembles his, surely our affection to them should imitate his, in seeking their salvation, spiritual peace, and happiness. Our tender care, labours, self-denial, and readiness to suffer for their happiness, should imitate what hath appeared in him, who hath purchased them with his own blood.

3. Let it be considered, that if we faithfully acquit ourselves in our office, in the manner that hath been represented, we shall surely hereafter be partakers of the joy, when the bridegroom and bride shall rejoice in each other in perfect and eternal glory.

God once gave forth a particular command, with special solemnity, that it should be written for the notice of all professing Christians through all ages, that they are happy and blessed indeed, who are called to the marriage-supper of the Lamb; "And he saith unto me, Write, blessed are they which are called unto the marriage-supper of the Lamb. And he saith unto me, These are the true sayings of God" (Rev. 19:9). But if we are faithful in our work, we shall surely be the subjects of that blessedness; we shall be partakers of the joy of the bridegroom and bride, not merely as friends and neighbours that are invited to be occasional guests, but as members of the one and the other. We shall be partakers with the church, the blessed bride, in her joy in the bridegroom, not only as friends and ministers to the church,

323

but as members of principal dignity; as the eye, the ear, the hand, are principal members of the body. Faithful ministers in the church will hereafter be a part of the church that shall receive distinguished glory at the resurrection of the just, which, above all other times, may be looked on as the church's wedding-day; "Many of them that sleep in the dust of the earth shall awake, some to everlasting life. And they that be wise shall shine as the brightness of the firmament, and they that turn many to righteousness, as the stars for ever and ever" (Dan. 12:2–3). They are elders who are represented as that part of the church triumphant that sit next to the throne of God, "And round about the throne were four-and-twenty seats: and upon the seats I saw four-and-twenty elders sitting, clothed in white raiment; and they had on their heads crowns of gold" (Rev. 4:4).

And we shall also be partakers of the joy of the bridegroom in his rejoicing over his bride. We, as the special friends of the bridegroom, shall stand by, and hear him express his joy on that day, and rejoice greatly because of the bridegroom's voice; as John the Baptist said of himself, "He that hath the bride, is the bridegroom: but the friend of the bridegroom, which standeth and heareth him, rejoiceth greatly because of the bride-groom's voice" (John 3:29). Christ, in reward for our faithful service, in winning and espousing his bride to him, and bringing her up from her minority, and adorning her for him, will then call us to partake with him in the joy of his marriage. And she that will then be his joy, shall also be our crown of rejoicing; "What is our hope, or joy, or crown of rejoicing? Are not ye in the presence of our Lord Jesus Christ at his coming?" (1 Thess. 2:19). What a joyful meeting had Christ and his disciples together, when the disciples returned to their Master, after the faithful and successful performance of their appointed service, when Christ sent them forth to preach the gospel; "And the seventy returned with joy, saying, Lord, even the devils are subject unto us through thy name" (Luke 10:17). Here we see how they rejoice: the next words show how Christ also rejoiced on that occasion: "And he said unto them, I beheld Satan as lightning fall from heaven" (v. 18). And in the next verse but two, we are told, that "in that hour Jesus rejoiced in spirit, and said, I thank thee, O Father, Lord of heaven and earth, that thou hast hid these things from the wise and prudent, and hast revealed them unto babes." So if we faithfully acquit ourselves, we shall another day return to him with joy; and we shall rejoice with him and he with us.—Then will be the day when Christ, who hath sown in tears and in blood, and we who have reaped the fruits of his labours and sufferings, shall rejoice together, agreeable to John 4:35–37. And that will be a happy meeting indeed, when Christ and his lovely and blessed bride, and faithful ministers who have been the instruments of wooing and winning her heart to him, and adorning her for him, and presenting her to him, shall all rejoice together.

4. Further to stir us up to faithfulness in the great business that is appointed us, in order to the mutual joy of this bridegroom and bride, let us consider what reason we have to hope that the time is approaching when this joy shall be to a glorious degree fulfilled on earth, far beyond whatever yet has been; I mean the time of the church's latter-day glory. This is what the words of our text have a more direct respect to; and this is what is prophesied of in Hosea 2:19–20, "And I will betroth thee unto me for ever, yea, I will betroth thee unto me in righteousness, and in judgment, and in loving-kindness, and in mercies. I will even betroth thee unto me in faithfulness, and thou shalt know the Lord." And this is what is especially intended by the marriage of the Lamb in Revelation 19.

We are sure this day will come: and we have many reasons to think that it is approaching; from the fulfilment of almost every thing that the prophecies speak of as preceding it, and their having been fulfilled now a long time; and from the general earnest expectations of the church of God, and the best of her ministers and members, and the late extraordinary things that have appeared in the church of God, and appertaining to the state of religion, and the present aspects of divine Providence, which the time will not allow me largely to insist upon.

As the happiness of that day will have a great resemblance of the glory and joy of the eternal wedding-day of the church after the resurrection of the just; so will the privileges of faithful ministers at that time much resemble those they shall enjoy with the bridegroom and bride, as to honour and happiness, in eternal glory. This is the time especially intended in the text, wherein it is said, "as a young man marrieth a virgin, so shall thy sons marry thee." And it is after in the prophecies spoken of as a great part of the glory of that time, that then the church should be so well supplied with faithful ministers. So in the next verse to the text, "I have set watchmen on thy walls, O Jerusalem, that shall never hold their peace, day nor night." So, "Thy teachers shall not be removed into a corner any more, but thine eyes shall see thy teachers: and thine ears shall hear a word behind thee, saying, This is the way, walk ye in it, when ye turn to the right hand, and when ye turn to the left" (Isa. 30:20–21). "And I will give you pastors according to mine heart, which shall feed you with knowledge and understanding" (Jer. 3:15). And, "And I will set up shepherds over them, which shall feed them" (ch. 23:4). And the great privilege and joy of faithful ministers at that day is foretold in Isaiah 52:8, "Thy watchmen shall lift up the voice, with the voice together shall they sing: for they shall see eye to eye, when the Lord shall bring again Zion."

And as that day must needs be approaching, and we ourselves have lately seen some things which we have reason to hope are forerunners of it; certainly it should strongly excite us to endeavour to be such pastors as God has promised to bless his church with at that time; that if any of us should live to see the dawning of that glorious day, we might share in the blessedness of it, and then be called, as the friends of the bridegroom, to the marriage-supper of the Lamb, and partake of that joy in which heaven and earth, angels and saints, and Christ and his church, shall be united at that time.

But here I would apply the exhortation in a few words to that minister of Christ, who above all others is concerned in the solemnity of this day, who is now to be united to and set over this people as their pastor.

You have now heard, Reverend Sir, the great importance and high ends of the office of an evangelical pastor, and the glorious privileges of such as are faithful in this office, imperfectly represented. May God grant that your union with this people, this day, as their pastor, may be such, that God's people here may have the great promise God makes to his church in the text, now fulfilled unto them. May you now, as one of the precious sons of Zion, take this part of Christ's church by the hand, in the name of your great Master the glorious bridegroom, with a. heart devoted unto him with true adoration and supreme affection, and for his sake knit to this people, in a spiritual and pure love, and as it were a conjugal tenderness; ardently desiring that great happiness for them, which you have now heard Christ has chosen his church unto, and has shed his blood to obtain for her; being yourself ready to spend and be spent for them; remembering the great errand on which Christ sends you to them, viz., to woo and win their hearts, and espouse their souls to him, and to bring up his elect spouse, and to fit and adorn her for his embraces; that you may in due time present her a chaste virgin to him, for him to rejoice over, as the bridegroom rejoiceth over the bride. How honourable is this business that Christ employs you in and how joyfully should you perform it! When Abraham's faithful servant was sent to take a wife for his master's son, how engaged was he in the business; and how joyful was he when he succeeded! With what joy did he bow his head and worship, and bless the Lord God of his master, for his mercy and his truth in making his way prosperous! And what a joyful meeting may we conclude he had with Isaac, when he met him in the field, by the well of Laharoi, and there presented his beauteous Rebekah to him, and told him all things that he had done! But this was but a shadow of that joy that you shall have, if you imitate his fidelity, in the day when you shall meet your glorious Master, and present Christ's church in this place, as a chaste and beautiful virgin unto him.

We trust, dear Sir, that you will esteem it a most blessed employment, to spend your time and skill in adorning Christ's bride for her marriage with the Lamb, and that it is work which you will do with delight; and that you will take heed that the ornaments you put upon her are of the right sort, what shall be indeed beautiful and precious in the eyes of the bridegroom, that she may be all glorious within, and her clothing of wrought gold; that on the wedding-day she may stand on the king's right hand in gold of Ophir.

The joyful day is coming, when the spouse of Christ shall be led to the King in raiment of needle-work; and angels and faithful ministers will be the servants that shall lead her in. And you, Sir, if you are faithful in the charge now to be committed to you, shall be joined with glorious angels in that honourable and joyful service; but with this difference, that you shall have the higher privilege. Angels and faithful ministers shall be together in bringing in Christ's bride into his palace, and presenting her to him. But faithful ministers shall have a much higher participation of the joy of that occasion. They shall have a greater and more immediate participation with the bride in her joy; for they shall not only be ministers to the church as the angels are, but parts of the church, principal members of the bride. And as such, at the same time that angels do the part of ministering spirits to the bride, when they conduct her to the bridegroom, they shall also do the part of ministering spirits to faithful ministers. And they shall also have a higher participation with the bridegroom than the angels, in his rejoicing at that time; for they shall be nearer to him than they. They are also his members, and are honoured as the principal instruments of espousing the saints to him, and fitting them for his enjoyment; and therefore they will be more the crown of rejoicing of faithful ministers, than of the angels of heaven.

So great, dear Sir, is the honour and joy that is set before you, to engage you to faithfulness in your pastoral care of this people; so glorious the prize that Christ has set up to engage you to run the race that is set before you.

I would now conclude with a few words to the people of this congregation, whose souls are now to be committed to the care of that minister of Christ, whom they have chosen as their pastor.

Let me take occasion, dear brethren, from what has been said, to exhort you—not forgetting the respect, honour, and reverence, that will ever be due from you to your former pastor, who has served you so long in that work, but by reason of age and growing infirmities, and the prospect of his place being so happily supplied by a successor, has seen meet to relinquish the burden of the pastoral charge over you—to perform the duties that belong to you, in your part of that relation and union now to be established between you and your elect pastor. Receive him as the messenger of the Lord of hosts, one that in his office represents the glorious bridegroom of the church; love and honour him, and willingly submit yourselves to him, as a virgin when married to a husband. Surely the feet of that messenger should be beautiful, that comes to you on such a blessed errand as that which you have heard, to espouse you to the eternal Son of God, and to fit you for and lead you to him as your bridegroom. Your chosen pastor comes to you on this errand, and he comes in the name of the bridegroom, so empowered by him, and representing him, that in receiving him, you will receive Christ, and in rejecting him, you will reject Christ.

Be exhorted to treat your pastor as the beautiful and virtuous Rebekah treated Abraham's servant. She most charitably and hospitably entertained him, provided lodging and food for him and his company, and took care that he should be comfortably entertained and supplied in all respects, while he continued in his embassy; and that was the note or mark of distinction which God himself gave him, by which he should know the true spouse of Isaac from all others of the daughters of the city. Therefore in this respect approve yourselves as the true spouse of Christ, by giving kind entertainment to your minister that comes to espouse you to the antetype of Isaac. Provide for his outward subsistence and comfort, with the like cheerfulness that Rebekah did for Abraham's servant. You have an account of her alacrity and liberality in supplying him, in Gen. 24:18, etc. Say, as her brother did, "Come in, thou blessed of the Lord" (v. 31).

Thus you should entertain your pastor. But this is not that wherein your duty towards him chiefly lies: the main thing is to comply with him in his great errand, and to yield to the suit that he makes to you in the name of Christ, to be his bride. In this you should be like Rebekah: she was, from what she heard of Isaac, and God's covenant with him, and blessing upon him, from the mouth of Abraham's servant, willing for ever to forsake her own country, and her father's house, to go into a country she had never seen, to be Isaac's wife, whom also she never saw. After she had heard what the servant had to say, and her old friends had a mind she should put off the affair for the present—but it was insisted on that she should go immediately—and she was asked "whether she would go with this man," she said, "I will go": and she left her kindred, and followed the man through all that long journey, till he had brought her unto Isaac, and they three had that joyful meeting in Canaan. If you will this day receive your pastor in that union that is now to be established between him and you, it will be a joyful day in this place, and the joy will be like the joy of espousals, as when a young man marries a virgin; and it will not only be a joyful day in East-Hampton, but it will doubtless be a joyful day in heaven, on your account. And your joy will be a faint resemblance, and a forerunner of that future joy, when Christ shall rejoice over you as the bridegroom rejoiceth over the bride, in heavenly glory.

And if your pastor be faithful in his office, and you hearken and yield to him in that great errand on which Christ sends him to you, the time will come, wherein you and your pastor will be each other's crown of rejoicing, and wherein Christ and he and you shall all meet together at the glorious marriage of the Lamb, and shall rejoice in and over one another, with perfect, uninterrupted, never ending, and never fading joy.

Part Four

The Doctrine of Scripture in Reformed Orthodoxy

ACCORDING TO THE RECENT reinterpretation of scholasticism, Reformed orthodoxy is not a radical break away from the theology of the Reformers, but rather a more elaborate and methodologically sophisticated approach to theology. Moreover, this development emerged in the context of challenges from various sides, especially within the academy. Of course, Reformed orthodox theologians continued to respond to Roman Catholicism marked by the Council of Trent and its subsequent apologists. Further, theologians such as John Owen also had to deal with the denial of the sufficiency of Scripture by Quakers, with their notion of inward light. Finally, the greatest challenge was the rise of the Enlightenment and its impact on the church. In its wake, reason was given more authority than Scripture. Francis Turretin and Jonathan Edwards especially had to combat this new threat to the sufficiency and authority of Scripture.

The first two texts are by prominent English Puritan theologians. The first, by William Ames, is from his famous *Marrow of Theology*. In it, he discusses traditional topics about Scripture, such as its divine origin, the preservation of the originals of Scripture, and the canon; yet he situates his discussion of Scripture between sections on "Extraordinary Ministers" and "Ordinary Ministers and Their Office in Preaching," thereby connecting the doctrine of Scripture with his practical and pastoral concerns. The second, by Owen, is a treatise that was originally extracted from his sermons, where he establishes his view of Scripture on the self-witness of the Bible and develops the hotly debated issue of the preservation of Scripture. Both theologians not only are concerned about the Bible in the church, but share with other scholastic theologians an interest in academic theology. Their formulations of the doctrine of Scripture also contribute to a fuller understanding of the background of the Westminster Confession of Faith.

The next two documents are noteworthy witnesses to Reformed orthodoxy on the European Continent. Francis Turretin's work is the classical textbook of the seventeenth century. Despite its length and sophistication, Turretin destined it not primarily for informing scholars, but for instructing and edifying purposes. He therefore continues the Reformed emphasis on Bible reading in the church (cf., e.g., the previous part) and covers all the important topics concerning Scripture, including its inspiration, its attributes, the canon, and its reading and interpretation. In contrast to Catholic views, he argues that the canon is not established by the church, that the Hebrew Old Testament is the inspired text, and that Scripture has a single meaning. The Helvetic Consensus Formula, the last Reformed confession of the post-Reformation era, addresses similar concerns. Besides dealing with the atonement and limited atonement, this document defines the canon and inspiration, and asserts the verbal inspiration of the Hebrew Old Testament up to the very vowels. This text aims to preserve God's sovereignty in salvation and in the inspiration of the Bible.

The two excerpts from Jonathan Edwards defend the sufficiency of the Bible against the challenges of the Enlightenment. Though he uses philosophical language, these texts display a clear Christian outlook on contemporary issues. In the first text, a sermon on Psalm 94:8–11, he argues for the necessity of revelation because of "man's natural blindness." In the second text, a theological essay, "Observations on the Scriptures;—Their Authority—And Necessity," he defends the self-authentication of Scripture and its authority in view of the history of philosophy. This essay is helpful in the consideration of the questions of extracanonical backgrounds to the Bible and the relation of theology to philosophy.

The selections in this part are important not only for subsequent Reformed theology in general, but also for American Reformed theology, especially for Old Princeton and Westminster. In other words, Reformed orthodoxy is a key period for the development of Reformed theology, and its literature is a significant contribution to the appreciation of other texts in this anthology. To illustrate, Ames's book was used as a textbook at Harvard College, and the work by Turretin was widely used in America, especially at Old Princeton. Further, the Helvetic Consensus Formula played a significant role at Old Princeton. Also, both Owen and Edwards are still studied at Westminster Seminary. Though contemporary Reformed theologians will not agree with every detail of the Reformed orthodox doctrine of inspiration (e.g., its view of vowel points), its formulation remains influential and a powerful defense of the divine character of Scripture.

24

William Ames's *The Marrow of Sacred Divinity*

William Ames, "Chapter XXXIIII: Of the Holy Scripture," in *The Marrow of Sacred Divinity, Drawne Out of the Holy Scriptures, and the Interpreters thereof, and Brought into Method* (London: Printed by Edward Griffin for Iohn Rothwell at the Sun in Pauls-Church-yard, 1643), 148–53.

William Ames (1576–1633) was educated at Cambridge University and taught there until he was dismissed because of his Puritan views. He then moved to the Netherlands, where he taught theology at Franeker University. He also served as a theological adviser in the Synod of Dort. Under the influence of the Huguenot Peter Ramus (1515–72) and the Puritan William Perkins (1558–1602), he stressed both doctrine and obedience. His work *De Conscientia* (1530) well illustrates this practical concern. Practice, however, for him was rooted in a theology of covenant that he helped to develop.

Ames had planned to immigrate to America, but death prevented him. His theology, however, rooted itself in the New World, primarily through the work we are considering, *The Marrow of Theology* (1627). This work was influential among English Puritans, but most importantly, before the introduction of Francis Turretin's (1623–87) work, it was the textbook of choice among New England Puritans. Characteristically, Ames's work is divided into two parts: "Faith in God" and "Observance." In a unique manner, Ames discusses the doctrine of Scripture toward the end of the theological first part between sections on "Extraordinary Ministers" and "Ordinary Ministers and Their Office in Preaching." This perhaps reflects the Puritan emphasis on practice and preaching. Ames stresses such topics as the divine origin of Scripture, the preservation of the originals, and the canon of Scripture, therefore providing another possible background for the Westminster Standards. We reproduce here the section "Of the Holy Scripture" from an early English translation from the Latin original (1643) with slightly modernized spelling. A modern translation of the work (1968) by John Dykstra Eusden is also available.

Bibliography: William Ames. *The Marrow of Theology.* Ed. and trans. John Dykstra Eusden. Boston: Pilgrim, 1968. Repr., Grand Rapids: Baker, 1997. Joel R. Beeke and Jan van Vliet. "*The Marrow of Theology* by

William Ames (1576–1633)." Pp. 52–65 in *The Devoted Life*. I. Breward. "Puritan Theology." Pp. 550–53 in *NDT*. G. S. R. Cox. "Ames, William (1576–1633)." P. 36 in *NIDCC*. Andrew T. B. McGowan. "Ames, William (1576–1633)." Pp. 11–12 in *DHT*. E. F. Karl Müller. "Ames, William." *NSHERK* 1:154. K. L. Sprunger. "Ames, William (1576–1633)." P. 40 in *EDT*. C. R. Trueman. "Ames, William (1576–1633)." Pp. 12–14 in *BDE*.

Of the Holy Scripture

1. Extraordinary Ministers were raised up by God, to instruct the Church not only by lively voice, but also by Divine writings, that there might be a perpetual use, and fruit of their Ministry in the Church; even when such Ministers were taken away.

2. For they only could commit the rule of faith and manners[1] to writing, who by reason of the immediate and infallible direction which they had from God, were in that business free from all error.

3. They received a command of writing from God, partly externally, both generally when they were commanded to teach, and especially sometimes, when they were commanded to write: "Write ye the Song" (Deut. 31:19); "Write those things which thou hast seen" (Rev. 1:19); and partly by the inward instinct of the Spirit: "For prophecy came not in old time by the will of man, but holy men spake as they were moved by the Holy Spirit" (2 Peter 1:21); "All Scripture is inspired by God" (2 Tim. 2:16.).

4. They wrote also by the inspiration and guidance of the Holy Spirit, so that the men themselves were as it were instruments of the Spirit. In the place before: "Behold I put my words in thy mouth" (Jer. 1:9); "Well indeed spake the Holy Spirit by Isaiah the Prophet" (Acts 28:25).

5. But Divine inspiration was present with those writers with some variety, for some things to be written were before altogether unknown to the writer, as does sufficiently appear in the History of the Creation past, and in foretelling of things to come: but some things were before known to the writer, as appears in the History of Christ, written by the Apostles: and some of these they knew by a natural knowledge, and some by a supernatural: In those things that were hidden and unknown, Divine inspiration did perform all by itself: in those things which were known, or the knowledge whereof might be obtained by ordinary means, there was also added a religious study, God so assisting them, that in writing they might not err.

6. In all those things which were made known by supernatural inspiration, whether they were matters of right, or fact, he did inspire not only the things themselves, but did dictate and suggest all the words in which they should be written: which notwithstanding was done with that sweet tempering, that every writer, might use those manners of speaking which did most agree to his person and condition.

7. Hence the Scripture is often attributed to the Holy Spirit as to the author, making no mention of the Scribes. "Whereof the Holy Ghost also is a witness to us" (Heb. 10:15).

8. Hence also, although in the inscriptions of the Holy Books it is for the most part declared by whose labor they were written, yet there is sometimes deep silence of this matter, and that without any detriment of such books, or lessening their authority.

---

1. I.e., "practice."

9. Neither yet doth it suffice to make a part of holy writ, if a book be written by some extraordinary servant of God, and upon certain direction of the Spirit: unless it be also publicly given to the Church by divine authority, and sanctified to be a Canon or rule of the same.

10. The thing itself which they committed to writing, as touching the sum and chief end of the matter, is nothing else, than that revealed will of God, which is the rule of Faith and manners.

11. Hence all those things which in the first disputation were spoken of the doctrine of life revealed from God, do properly agree to the Holy Scripture. For the Scripture is nothing else than that doctrine, with the manner of writing joined to it, which manner was not to be handled there, but in this place.

12. Hence the Scripture in respect of the thing and subject meaning, that is, as it was the doctrine revealed from God, it was before the Church: but in respect of the manner in which it is properly called Scripture, it is after the first Church.

13. It is called the Holy Scripture, and by κατ' ἐξοχήν [eminently] the Scripture, and the writers themselves are called holy, partly in respect of the subject, and object matter, which is so called, the true and saving will of GOD, and partly in respect of that direction whereby it was committed to writing (Rom. 1:2; Eph. 3:5; 2 Peter 1:21; 2:22; 3:2; Rev. 18:20).

14. But although divers parts of the Scripture were written, upon some special occasion, and were directed to some certain men, or assemblies: yet in God's intention, they do as well pertain to the instructing of all the faithful through all ages, as if they had been especially directed to them: whence, the exhortation of *Solomon*, which is used in the Proverbs, is said to be spoken to the *Hebrews*, who lived in the Apostles' time, as to children (Heb. 12); and Paul is said to have written to all the faithful in that he wrote to the *Romans* (2 Peter 3:15); that which was said to *Joshua* is said to be spoken to all the faithful (Heb. 13:5).

15. All things which are necessary to salvation are contained in the Scriptures, and also all those things which are necessarily required to the instruction and edification of the Church. "The Holy Scriptures can make thee wise unto salvation, that the man of God might be perfect, perfectly furnished to every good work" (2 Tim. 3:15–17).

16. Hence the Scripture is not a partial, but a perfect rule of Faith, and manners: neither is here anything that is constantly and everywhere necessary to be observed in the Church of God, which depends either upon any tradition, or upon any authority whatsoever and is not contained in the Scriptures.

17. Yet all things were not together and at once committed to writing, because the state of the Church and the wisdom of God did otherwise require: but from the first writing, those things were successively committed to writing which were necessary in those ages.

18. Neither did the Articles of Faith therefore increase according to succession of times, in respect of the essence, but only in respect of the explication.

19. As touching the manner of delivery the Scripture does not explain the will of God by universal, and scientific rules, but by narrations, examples, precepts, exhortations, admonitions, and promises: because that manner does make most for the common use of all kind of men, and also most to affect the will, and stir up godly motions, which is the chief scope of Divinity [or, goal of theology].

20. Also the will of God is revealed in that manner in the Scriptures, that although, the things themselves are for the most part hard to be conceived, yet the manner of delivering and explaining them, especially in those things which are necessary, is clear and perspicuous.

21. Hence the Scriptures need not especially in necessaries [or, in essentials], any such explication whereby light may be brought to it from something else: but they give light to themselves, which is diligently to be drawn out by men, and to be communicated to others according to their calling.

22. Hence also there is only one sense of one place of Scripture: because otherwise the sense of the Scripture should be not only unclear and uncertain, but none at all: for that which does not signify one thing, signifies certainly nothing.

23. For the determining of controversies in Divinity, there is no visible power as it were kingly or praetorian, appointed in the Church: but there is laid a duty on men to inquire; there is bestowed a gift of discerning, both publicly and privately: and there is commanded a desire to further the knowledge and practice of the known truth, according to their calling, unto which also is joined a promise of direction, and blessing from God.

24. But because the Scriptures were given for the use and edification of the Church, therefore they were written in those tongues, which were most commonly vulgar [or, current] in the Church at that time when they were written.

25. Hence all those books which were written before the coming of Christ were written in *Hebrew*: for to the *Jews* "were committed the *Oracles* of God" (Rom. 3:2; 9:4). And upon like reason they that were written afterward were delivered in the *Greek* tongue, because that tongue was most common in those parts where the Church did first flourish.

26. Hence there is some knowledge at least of these tongues necessary to the exact understanding of the Scriptures: for the Scriptures are understood by the same means that other human writings are, many by the skill, and use of *Logic, Rhetoric, Grammar*, and those tongues in which they are expressed: except in this, that there is a singular light of the Spirit always to be sought for by the godly in the Scriptures.

27. Yet the Scripture is not so tied to those first tongues, but that it may and ought also to be translated into other tongues, for the common use of the Church.

28. But among interpreters, neither, those seventy, who turned it into *Greek*, nor *Jerome*, nor any such like did perform the office of a Prophet, so that he should be free from errors in interpreting.

29. Hence no persons are absolutely authentic, but so far forth only as they do express the fountains, by which also they are to be tried.

30. Neither is there any authority in Earth whereby any version may be made simply authentic.

31. Hence the providence of GOD in preserving the Fountains, has been always famous, and to be adored, not only that they did not wholly perish, but also that they should not be maimed by the loss of any book, or deformed by any grievous fault, when in the meanwhile there is no one of the ancient versions that remains whole.

32. Nevertheless, from those human versions there may be all those things perceived which are absolutely necessary, if so be they agree with the fountains in the essential parts, as all those versions that are received in the Churches are wont [or, accustomed] to do, although they differ, and are defective in the smaller things not a few.

334

33. Neither therefore must we always rest in any version that is received: but we must most religiously provide, that the most pure and faultless interpretation be put upon the Church.

34. Of all those books, being delivered from God, and placed, as it were in the Chest of the Church, there is made up a perfect Canon of Faith and manners, whence also they have the name of Canonical Scripture.

35. The Prophets made the Canon of the Old Testament, and Christ himself approved it by his Testimony. The Canon of the New Testament together with the Old, the Apostle *John* approved and sealed up being furnished with Divine authority. "For I do witness together to every one that hears the words of the prophesy of this book: if any shall add to these, God shall lay upon him the plagues written in this book: and if any shall take away any thing from the books of his [or this] prophecy, God shall take away this part out of the book of life" (Rev. 22:18–19).

36. Those books which commonly we call apocryphal, do not pertain to the divine Canon, neither were they rightly enough joined by men of old to the canonical books, as a certain secondary Canon: for first in some of them there are manifest fables told and affirmed for true Histories, as of` *Tobiah [Tobit], Judith, Susanna, Bel,* the *Dragon,* and such like. Secondly, because they contradict both the sacred Scripture and themselves. Oftentimes, thirdly, they were not written in *Hebrew,* nor delivered to the *Jewish* Church, or received by it, to which notwithstanding God committed all his Oracles before the coming of Christ (Rom. 9:4). Fourthly, they were not approved by Christ, because they were not among those books which he set forth when he commanded his to search the Scriptures. Fifthly, they were never received either by the Apostles or the first Christian Church as a part of the Divine Canon.

The Divine Original of the Scripture

JOHN OWEN

John Owen, *Of the Divine Original, Authority, Self-Evidencing Light, and Power of the Scriptures*, in *The Works of John Owen*, ed. William H. Goold (1850–53; repr., London: Banner of Truth, 1968), 16:297–306.

John Owen (1616–83) is another important Puritan theologian. He was a pastor, a counselor to Oliver Cromwell (1599–1658), and a leader of the Congregationalist movement in England. He has produced a great theological corpus. Among his most significant contributions are his defense of the doctrine of limited atonement in *The Death of Death in the Death of Christ* (1647) and his work on the Holy Spirit, *A Discourse concerning the Holy Spirit* (1674). In light of the depth of his theological insight, the relative neglect of his theology is surprising. His theology, however, has left a significant mark on the theological tradition of Westminster Theological Seminary, Philadelphia.

It is therefore fitting to include an excerpt from his writings in this anthology. *Of the Divine Original, Authority, Self-Evidencing Light, and Power of the Scriptures* was first published in 1659. This material was originally preached by Owen. At the time, several influences were at work to undermine the authority of God's Word: notably, the notion of inward light of the Quakers and contemporary biblical scholarship. In the first chapter of this treatise, reproduced in this anthology, Owen demonstrates that the doctrine of Scripture must be established by Scripture itself. The doctrine of preservation, though nuanced by most modern Reformed theologians, is another important facet of Owen's argument. Both aspects were already prominent in the Westminster Confession of Faith (1.4, 8). For this anthology, we use the text from the Banner of Truth edition of Owen's *Works*.

Bibliography: Sinclair Ferguson. *John Owen on the Christian Life*. Carlisle, PA: Banner of Truth, 1987. Stanley N. Gundry. "John Owen on Authority and Scripture." Pp. 189–221 in *Inerrancy and the Church*. Kelly M.

Kapic. *"Communion with God* by John Owen (1616–1683)." Pp. 167–82 in *The Devoted Life.* "Owen, John." *NSHERK* 8:292–93. Alan Spence. "Owen, John (1616–83)." Pp. 412–14 in *DHT.* Peter Toon. "Owen, John (1616–1683)." P. 738 in *NIDCC.* Idem. "Owen, John (1616–1683)." P. 811 in *EDT.* Carl R. Trueman. *The Claims of Truth: John Owen's Trinitarian Theology.* Carlisle, UK: Paternoster, 1998. Idem. "Owen, John (1616–1683)." Pp. 494–97 in *BDE.*

Chapter I

The divine original of the Scripture the sole foundation of its authority—The original of the Old Testament—The peculiar manner of the revelation of the word—The written word, as written, preserved by the providence of God—Cappellus' opinion about various lections considered— The Scripture not ἰδίας ἐπιλύσεως—The true meaning of that expression—Entirely from God, to the least tittle—Of the Scriptures of the New Testament, and their peculiar prerogative.

That the whole authority of the Scripture in itself depends solely on its divine original, is confessed by all who acknowledge its authority. The evincing and declaration of that authority being the thing at present aimed at, the discovery of its divine spring and rise is, in the first place, necessarily to be premised thereunto. That foundation being once laid, we shall be able to educe our following reasons and arguments, wherein we aim more at weight than number, from their own proper principles.

As to the original of the Scripture of the Old Testament, it is said, God SPAKE, πάλαι ἐν τοῖς προφήταις, "of old, or formerly, in the prophets" (Heb. 1:1). From the days of Moses the lawgiver, and downwards, unto the consignation and bounding of the canon delivered to the Judaical Church, in the days of Ezra and his companions, אַנְשֵׁי כְּנֶסֶת הַגְּדֹלָה, the "men of the great congregation"—so God spake. This being done only among the Jews, they, as his church, ἐπιστεύθησαν τὰ λόγια τοῦ θεοῦ, were "intrusted with the oracles of God" (Rom. 3:2; 9:4). God spake, ἐν τοῖς προφήταις ["in the prophets"]; ἐν for διά, *in* for *by* (Chrysostom, Theophylact): διὰ τῶν προφητῶν, "by the prophets" as Luke 1:70, διὰ στόματος τῶν ἁγίων προφητῶν, "by the mouth of the holy prophets." But there seems to be somewhat further intended in this expression.

In the exposition, or giving out the eternal counsel of the mind and will of God unto men, there is considerable [*to be considered*]: 1. His speaking *unto* the prophets; and, 2. His speaking *by* them unto us. In this expression, it seems to be בַּת קוֹל, or *filia vocis* ["the daughter of the voice"]— that voice from heaven that came to the prophets— which is understood. So God spake in the prophets; and in reference thereunto there is propriety in that expression, ἐν τοῖς προφήταις—"in the prophets." Thus the Psalms are many of them said to be, *To this* or that man. מִכְתָּם לְדָוִד, "A golden psalm to David"—that is, from the Lord; and from thence their tongue was as the "pen of a writer" (Ps. 45:1). So God spake *in* them, before he spake *by* them.

The various ways of special revelation, by dreams, visions, audible voices, inspirations, with that peculiar one of the lawgiver under the Old Testament called פָּנִים אֶל־פָּנִים, "face to face" (Ex. 33:11; Deut. 34:10) and פֶּה אֶל־פֶּה ["mouth to mouth"] (Num. 12:8), with that which is compared with it and exalted above it (Heb. 1:1–3) in the New, by the Son, viz., ἐκ κόλπου τοῦ πατρός, "from the bosom of the Father" (John 1:17–18), are not of my present consideration—all of them belonging to the *manner* of the thing inquired after, not the thing itself.

By the assertion, then, laid down, of God "speaking in the prophets of old," from the beginning to the end of that long tract of time (consisting of one thousand years) wherein he gave out the writings of the Old Testament, two things are ascertained unto us, which are the foundation of our present discourse.

1. That the laws they made known, the doctrines they delivered, the instructions they gave, the stories they recorded, the promises of Christ, the prophecies of gospel times they gave out and revealed, were not their own, not conceived in their minds, not formed by their reasonings, not retained in their memories from what they heard, not by any means beforehand comprehended by them (1 Peter 1:10–11), but were all of them immediately from God—there being only a passive concurrence of their rational faculties in their reception, without any such active obedience as by any law they might be obliged unto. Hence,

2. God was so with them, and by the Holy Ghost so spake in them—as to their receiving of the Word from him, and their delivering of it unto others by speaking or writing—as that they were not themselves enabled, by any habitual light, knowledge, or conviction of truth, to declare his mind and will, but only acted as they were immediately moved by him. Their tongue in what they said, or their hand in what they wrote, was עֵט סוֹפֵר ["the stylus of a scribe"], no more at their own disposal than the pen is in the hand of an expert writer.

Hence, as far as their own personal concernments, as saints and believers, did lie in them, they are said ἐρευνᾶν, "to make a diligent inquiry into, and investigation of," the things which ἐδήλου τὸ ἐν αὐτοῖς Πνεῦμα Χριστοῦ, the "Spirit of Christ that spake in themselves did signify" (1 Peter 1:10–11). Without this, though their visions were express, so that in them their eyes were said to be open (Num. 24:3–4), yet they understood them not. Therefore, also, they studied the writings and prophecies of one another (Dan. 9:2). Thus they attained a saving, useful, habitual knowledge of the truths delivered by themselves and others, by the illumination of the Holy Ghost, through the study of the Word, even as we (Ps. 119:104). But as to the receiving of the Word from God, as God spake in them, they obtained nothing by study or meditation, by inquiry or reading (Amos 7:15). Whether we consider the *matter* or manner of what they received and delivered, or their receiving and delivering of it, they were but as an instrument of music, giving a sound according to the hand, intention, and skill of him that strikes it.

This is variously expressed. Generally, it is said דְּבַר הָיָה "the word was" to this or that prophet, which we have rendered "the word came" unto them. Ezekiel 1:3: הָיֹה הָיָה דְבַר, it "came expressly," "essendo fuit"—it had a subsistence given unto it, or an effectual in-being, by the Spirit's entering into him (v. 14). Now, this coming of the word unto them had oftentimes such a greatness and expression of the majesty of God upon it, as filled them with dread and reverence of him (Hab. 3:16), and also greatly affected even their outward man (Dan. 8:27). But this dread and terror (which Satan strove to imitate

338

in his filthy tripods, and ἐγγαστρίμυθοι ["conceived tales," lit. "myths in the womb"]) was peculiar to the Old Testament, and belonged to the pedagogy thereof (Heb. 12:18–21). The Spirit, in the declaration of the New Testament, gave out his mind and will in a way of more liberty and glory (2 Cor. 3). The expressness and immediacy of revelation was the same; but the manner of it related more to that glorious liberty in fellowship and communion with the Father, whereunto believers had then an access provided them by Jesus Christ (Heb. 9:8; 10:19–20; 12:22–24). So our Savior tells his apostles, Οὐχ ὑμεῖς ἐστε οἱ λαλοῦντες, "You are not the speakers" of what you deliver, as other men are, the figment and imagination of whose hearts are the fountain of all that they speak; and he adds this reason, Τὸ γὰρ Πνεῦμα τοῦ πατρὸς τὸ λαλοῦν ἐν ὑμῖν, "The Spirit of the Father *is* that which speaketh in you" (Matt. 10:20). Thus, the word that came unto them was a book which they took *in* and gave *out* without any alteration of one tittle or syllable (Ezek. 2:8–10; 3:3; Rev. 10:9–11).

Moreover, when the word was thus come to the prophets, and God had spoken in them, it was not in their power to conceal it, the hand of the Lord being strong upon them. They were not now only, on a general account, to utter the truth they were made acquainted withal, and to speak the things they had heard and seen (which was their common preaching work) according to the analogy of what they had received (Acts 4:20), but, also, the very individual words that they had received were to be declared. When the word was come to them, it was as a fire within them, that must be delivered, or it would consume them (Ps. 39:3; Jer. 20:9; Amos 3:8; 7:15–16). So Jonah found his attempt to hide the word that he had received to be altogether vain.

Now, because these things are of great importance, and the foundation of all that ensue— viz., the discovery that the Word is come forth unto us from God, without the least mixture or intervenience of any medium obnoxious to fallibility (as is the wisdom, truth, integrity, knowledge, and memory, of the best of all men)—I shall further consider it from one full and eminent declaration thereof, given unto us. The words of the Holy Ghost are, Τοῦτο πρῶτον γινώσκοντες, ὅτι πᾶσα πτοφητεία γραφῆς, ἰδίας ἐπιλύσεως οὐ γίνεται· οὐ γὰρ θελήματι ἀνθρώπου ἠνέχθη ποτὲ προφητεία, ἀλλ' ὑπὸ Πνεύματος ἁγίου φερόμενοι ἐλάλησαν οἱ ἅγιοι Θεοῦ ἄνθρωποι—"Knowing this first, that no prophecy of Scripture is of any private interpretation; for the prophecy came not in old time by the will of man, but holy men of God spake as they were moved by the Holy Ghost" (2 Peter 1:20–21).

That which he speaks of is προφετεία γραφῆς, the "prophecy of Scripture," or written prophecy.

There were then traditions among the Jews to whom Peter wrote, exalting themselves into competition with the written Word, and which not long after got the title of an oral law, pretending to have its original from God. These the apostle tacitly condemns; and also shows under what formality he considered that which (v. 19) he termed λόγος προφητικός, the "word of prophecy," viz., as *written*. The written Word, as such, is that whereof he speaks. Above fifty times is ἡ γραφή ["the writing"] or αἱ γραφαί ["the writings"], in the New Testament, put absolutely for the Word of God. And מִכְתָּב ["writing"] is so used in the Old for the word of prophecy (2 Chron. 21:12). It is the ἡ γραφή that is θεόπνευστος ["inspired by God"], "the writing, or word written, is by inspiration from God" (2 Tim. 3:16). Not only the doctrine in it, but the γραφή ["writing"] itself, or the "doctrine as written," is so from him.

Hence, the providence of God hath manifested itself no less concerned in the preservation of the writings than of the doctrine contained in them; the writing itself being the product of his own eternal counsel for the preservation of the doctrine, after a sufficient discovery of the insufficiency of all other means for that end and purpose. And hence the malice of Satan hath raged no less against the book than against the truth contained in it. The dealings of Antiochus under the Old Testament, and of sundry persecuting emperors under the New, evince no less. And it was no less crime of old to be *traditor libri* ["a traitor of the book"] than to be *abnegator fidei* ["a denier of the faith"]. The reproach of *chartacea scripta* ["scribal paper"], and *membranae* ["parchment"] (Coster, *Enchiridion*, ch. 1), reflects on its author.[1] It is true, we have not the Αὐτόγραφα ["autographs" or "originals"] of Moses and the prophets, of the apostles and evangelists; but the ἀπόγραφα ["apographa"] or "copies" which we have contain every *iota* that was in them.

There is no doubt but that in the copies we now enjoy of the Old Testament there are some diverse readings, or various lections. The קְרִי וּכְתִיב ["What is read and what is written"],[2] the תִּקּוּן סוֹפְתִים,[3] the עִטּוּר סוֹפְתִים,[4] (for the סְבִירִין [*Sebirin*, "suggestions"] are of another nature)—the various lections of Ben Asher, or Rabbi Aaron the son of Rabbi Moses of the tribe of Asher, and Ben Naphtali, or Rabbi Moses the son of David of the tribe of Naphtali—the lections also of the eastern and western Jews, which we have collected at the end of the great Bible with the Masora—evince it. But yet we affirm, that the whole Word of God, in every letter and tittle, as given from him by inspiration, is preserved without corruption. Where there is any variety it is always in things of less, indeed of no, importance.[5] God by his providence preserving the whole entire, suffered this lesser variety to fall out, in or among the copies we have, for the quickening and exercising of our diligence in our search into his Word.

It was an unhappy attempt (which must afterward be spoken unto) that a learned man[6] hath of late put himself upon, viz., to prove variations in all the present Ἀπόγραφα ["apographa" or "copies"] of the Old Testament in the Hebrew tongue from the copies used of old, merely upon *uncertain conjectures* and the credit of *corrupt translations*. Whether that plea of his be more unreasonable in itself and devoid of any real ground of truth, or injurious to the love and care of God over his Word and church, I know not; sure I am, it is both in a high degree. The translation especially insisted on by him is that of the LXX. That this translation—either from the mistakes of its first authors (if it be theirs whose name and number it beam) or the carelessness, or ignorance, or worse, of its transcribers—is corrupted and gone off from the original in a thousand places twice told, is acknowledged by all who know aught of these things. Strange that so corrupt a stream should be judged a fit means to cleanse the fountain; that such a Lesbian rule should be thought a fit measure to correct the

---

1. *Hebraea volumina nec in una dictione corrupta invenies* ["In the Hebrew book you will not come upon one corrupt saying"]. Sant. Pag. ἰῶτα ἕν ἢ μία κεραία οὐ μὴ παρέλθῃ ["One iota, one tittle, will not pass"] (Matt. 5:18).

2. Reading, in the margin, and writing, in the line.

3. *Correctio scribarum* ["correction of the scribes"], or the amendment of some small *apiculi* ["abrupt endings"] in eighteen places.

4. *Ablatio scribarum* ["omission of the scribes"], or a note of the redundancy of י in five places (Vid. Raymund., Pugio Fid. Petrus Galat., bk. 1, ch. 8).

5. *Hebraei V. T. Codices per universum terrarum orbem, per Europam, Asiam, et Africam, ubique sibi sunt similes, eodémque modo ab omnibus scribuntur et leguntur; si forte exiguas quasdam apiculorum quorundam differentias exipias, quae ipsae tamen nullam varietatem efficient* (Johannes Buxtorf, Vin. Ver. Heb. 2, ch. 14).

6. Louis Cappellus, in his *Critica Sacra*.

original by; and yet on the account hereof, with some others not one whit better (or scarce so good) we have one thousand eight hundred and twenty-six various lections exhibited unto us, with frequent insinuations of an infinite number more yet to be collected. It were desirable that men would be content to show their learning, reading, and diligence, about things where there is less danger in adventures.

Nor is the relief Cappellus provides against the charge of bringing things to an uncertainty in the Scripture (which he found himself obnoxious unto) less pernicious than the opinion he seeks to palliate thereby; although it be since taken up and approved by others.[7] "The saving doctrine of the Scripture," he tells us, "as to the matter and substance of it, in all things of moment, is preserved in the copies of the original and translations that do remain."[8]

It is indeed a great relief against the inconvenience of corrupt translations, to consider that although some of them be bad enough, yet, if all the errors and mistakes that are to be found in all the rest should be added to the worst of all, every necessary, saving, fundamental truth, would be found sufficiently testified unto therein. But to depress the sacred truth of the originals into such a condition as wherein it should stand in need of this apology, and that without any color or pretense from discrepancies in the copies themselves that are extant, or any tolerable evidence that there ever were any other in the least differing from these extant in the world, will at length be found a work unbecoming a Christian, Protestant divine. Besides the injury done hereby to the providence of God towards his church, and care of his Word, it will not be found so easy a matter, upon a supposition of such corruption in the originals as is pleaded for, to evince unquestionably that the whole saving doctrine itself, at first given out from God, continues entire and incorrupt. The nature of this doctrine is such, that there is no other principle or means of its discovery, no other rule or measure of judging and determining any thing about or concerning it, but only the writing from whence it is taken; it being wholly of divine revelation, and that revelation being expressed only in that writing. Upon any corruption, then, supposed therein, there is no means of rectifying it. It were an easy thing to correct a mistake or corruption in the transcription of any problem or demonstration of Euclid, or any other ancient mathematician, from the consideration of the things themselves about which they treat being always the same, and in their own nature equally exposed to the knowledge and understanding of men in all ages. In things of pure revelation—whose knowledge depends solely on their revelation—it is not so. Nor is it enough to satisfy us, that the doctrines mentioned are preserved entire; every tittle and ἰῶτα ["iota"] in the Word of God must come under our care and consideration, as being, as such, from God. But of these things we shall treat afterward at large. Return we now to the apostle.

This προφητεία γραφῆς, this written prophecy, this λόγος προφητικός ["prophetic word"], saith he, ἰδίας ἐπιλύσεως οὐ γίνεται—"is not of any private interpretation." Some think that ἐπιλύσεως ["interpretation"] is put for ἐπηλύσεως ["occurrence, impulse"] or ἐπελεύσεως, which according to Hesychius, denotes afflation, inspiration, conception within: so Calvin. In this sense, the importance of the words is the same with what I

7. Proleg. ad Biblia Polyglotta.
8. *Satis ergo est quod eadem salutaris doctrina quae fuit à Mose, prophetis, apostolis, et evangelistis in suis* αὐτογράφοις *primum literis consignata, eadem omnino partier in textibus Graeco et Hebraeo, et in translationibus cum veteribus, tum recentibus, clarè certò et suffienter inveniatur. Pariter illae omnes unà cum textibus Graeco et Hebraeo sunt et dici possunt authenticae, sacrae, divinae,* Θεόπνευστοι*—respectu materiae, etc. Sunt in Scripturis multa alia non usque adeo scitu necessaria, etc.* (Cappellus, *Critica Sacra*, bk. 6, ch. 5, § 10–11).

have already mentioned, viz., that the prophets had not their private conceptions, or self-fancied enthusiasms, of the things they spake. To this interpretation assents Grotius. And ἐπηλύσεως ["occurrence, impulse"] for ἐπιλύσεως ["interpretation"] is reckoned amongst the various lections that are gathered out of him, in the appendix to the Biblia Polyglotta. Thus ἰδίας ἐπιλύσεως οὐ γίνεται ["is not of private interpretation"] is the other side of that usual expression, ἐπῆλθεν ἐπ᾿ ἐμὲ ὁ λόγος ["the word came upon me"], or τὸ πνεῦμα ["the Spirit"]. Camero contends for the retaining of ἐπιλύσεως ["interpretation"]; and justly. We begin a little too late to see whither men's bold conjectures, in correcting the original text of the Scriptures, are like to proceed. Here is no colour for a various lection. One copy, it seems, by Stephen, read διαλύσεως ["loosing up from, ending"], without ground, by an evident error; and such mistakes are not to be allowed the name or place of various readings. But yet, says Camero, ἐπιλύσις ["interpretation"] is such a "resolution" and interpretation as is made by revelation. He adds, that in that sense ἐπιλύειν ["to interpret"] is used by the LXX in the business of Joseph's interpretation of Pharaoh's dream (Gen. 40), which was by revelation. But indeed the word is not used in that chapter. However, he falls in with this sense—as do Calvin and Grotius—that ἰδίας ἐπιλύσεως ["private interpretation"] is not to be referred to our interpretation of the prophets, but to the way and manner of their receiving the counsel and will of God.

And, indeed, ἰδίας ἐπιλύσεως οὐ γίνεται ["is not of private interpretation"]—taking ἐπιλύσις ["interpretation"] for an interpretation of the word of prophecy given out by writing, as our translation bears it—is an expression that can scarcely have any tolerable sense affixed unto it. Γίνεται ["is"], or οὐ γίνεται ["is not"], relates here to προφητεία γραφῆς ["written prophecy"], and denotes the first giving out of the Word, not our after-consideration of its sense and meaning. And without this sense it stands in no coherence with, nor opposition to, the following sentence, which, by its causal connection to this, manifests that it renders a reason of what is hereto affirmed in the first place; and in the latter—turning with the adversative ἀλλά ["but"]—an opposition unto it: Οὐ γὰρ θελήματι ἀνθρώπου ἠνέχθη ποτὲ προφητεία, ἀλλ᾿ ὑπὸ Πνεύματος ἁγίου φερόμενοι ἐλάλησαν ἅγιοι Θεοῦ ἄνθρωποι.—"For prophecy came not at any time by the will of man, but holy men of God spake as they were moved by the Holy Ghost." What reason is in the first part of this verse why the Scripture is not of our private interpretation? or what opposition in the letter to that assertion? Nay, on that supposal, there is no tolerable correspondency of discourse in the whole περιοχή ["passage"]. But take the word to express the coming of the prophecy to the prophets themselves, and the sense is full and clear.

This, then, is the intention of the apostle: The prophecy which we have written—the Scripture—was not an issue of men's fancied enthusiasms, not a product of their own minds and conceptions, not an interpretation of the will of God by the understanding of man—that is, of the prophets themselves. Neither their rational apprehensions, inquiries, conceptions of fancy, or imaginations of their hearts, had any place in this business; no self-afflation, no rational meditation, managed at liberty by the understanding and will of men, had place herein.

Of this saith the apostle, Τοῦτο πρῶτον γινώσκοντες—"Knowing, judging, and determining this in the first place": "this is a principle to be owned and acknowledged by every one that will believe any thing else." Γινώσκω ["to know"] is not only to know, to perceive, to understand; but also to judge, own, and acknowledge. This, then, in our religion, is to be owned, acknowledged, submitted unto, as a principle, without further dispute. To discover the grounds of this submission and acknowledgment is the business of the ensuing discourse.

That this is so indeed, as before asserted, and to give a reason why this is to be received as a principle, he adds (v. 21), Οὐ γὰρ θελήματι ἀνθρώπου ἠνέχθη ποτὲ προφητεία ["For prophecy came not at any time by the will of man"]. That word of prophecy which we have written, is not ἰδίας ἐπιλύσεως—"of private conception"—"for it came not at any time by the will of man." Ἠνέχθη ["It came"], which is the passive conjugation of φέρω ["to carry"] from ἐνέγκω [root for some of the tenses of φέρω], denotes at least to be "brought in"—more than merely it "came"—it was brought unto them by the will of God. The affirmative, as to the will of God, is included in the negative, as to the will of man; or it came as the voice from heaven to our Saviour on the mount (v. 18, where the same word is used). So Ezekiel 1:3, הָיֹה הָיָה דָבָר ["the word came expressly"], "essendo fuit verbum," it was brought into him, as was showed before. Thus God brought the word to them, and spake *in* them, in order of nature, before he spake *by* them. As ἠνέχθη ["it came"], it was brought to them, it was קוֹל יְהֹוָה, "the voice of the Lord" (Gen. 3:8), or בַּת קוֹל ["the daughter of the voice"], as the Jews call it: as spoken by them, or written, it was properly דְבַר־יְהֹוָה, "verbum Dei," "the word of God," which by his immediate voice he signified to the prophets. Thus some of them, in visions, first ate a written book and then prophesied, as was instanced before. And this is the first spring of the Scripture—the beginning of its emanation from the counsel and will of God. By the power of the Holy Ghost it was brought into the organs or instruments that he was pleased to use, for the revelation and declaration of it unto others.

That which remains for the completing of this dispensation of the Word of God unto us is added by the apostle: Ὑπὸ Πνεύματος ἁγίου φερόμενοι ἐλάλησαν ἅγιοι Θεοῦ ἄνθρωποι ["holy men of God spake as they were moved by the Holy Ghost"]. When the word was thus brought to them, it was not left to their understandings, wisdoms, minds, memories, to order, dispose, and give it out; but they were borne, acted, [actuated,] carried out by the Holy Ghost, to speak, deliver, and write all that, and nothing but that—to every tittle—that was so brought to them. They invented not words themselves, suited to the things they had learned, but only expressed the words that they received. Though their mind and understanding were used in the choice of words (whence arise all the differences—that is, in their manner of expression—for they did use דִבְרֵי חֵפֶץ, "words of will," or choice) yet they were so guided, that their words were not their own, but immediately supplied unto them. And so they gave out כָּתוּב יֹשֶׁר, the "writing of uprightness," and דִבְרֵי אֱמֶת, "words of truth" itself (Eccl. 12:10). Not only the *doctrine* they taught was the word of truth—truth itself (John 17:17)—but the *words* whereby they taught it were words of truth from God himself. Thus, allowing the contribution of passive instruments for the reception and representation of words—which answer the mind and tongue of the prophets, in the coming of the voice of God to them—every apex of the written Word is equally divine, and as immediately from God as the voice wherewith, or whereby, he spake to or in the prophets; and is, therefore, accompanied with the same authority in itself, and unto us.

What hath been thus spoken of the scripture of the Old Testament, must be also affirmed of the New, with this addition of advantage and pre-eminence, viz., that ἀρχὴν ἔλαβεν λαλεῖσθαι διὰ τοῦ κυρίου, "it received its beginning of being spoken by the Lord himself" (Heb. 2:3). God spake in these last days, ἐν τῷ Ὑἱῷ, "in the Son" (Heb. 1:2).

Thus God, who himself began the writing of the Word with his own finger (Ex. 31:18)—after he had spoken it (Ex. 20), appointing or approving the writing of the rest that followed (Deut. 31:12; Josh. 23:6; 1 Kings 2:3; 2 Kings 14:6; 17:13; 1 Chron. 22:13; 2 Chron. 25:4; Ezek. 2:8–10; Hab. 2:2; Luke 16:29; John 5:39; 20:31; Acts 17:11)—doth lastly command the close of the immediate revelation of his will to be written in a book; (Rev. 1:11); and so gives out the whole of his mind and counsel unto us in writing, as a merciful and steadfast relief against all that confusion, darkness, and uncertainty, which the vanity, folly, and looseness of the minds of men—drawn out and heightened by the unspeakable alterations that fall out amongst them—would otherwise have certainly run into.

Thus we have laid down the original of the Scriptures from the Scripture itself. And this original is the basis and foundation of all its authority. Thus is it from God—entirely from him. As to the doctrine contained in it, and the words wherein that doctrine is delivered, it is wholly his; what *that* speaks, *he* speaks himself. He speaks in it and by it; and so it is vested with all the moral authority of God over his creatures.

26

Francis Turretin's *Institutes* of *Elenctic Theology*

Francis Turretin, *Institutes of Elenctic Theology*, vol. 1, *First through Tenth Topics*, ed. James T. Dennison Jr., trans. George Musgrave Giger (Phillipsburg, NJ: P&R Publishing, 1992), 55–167.

Francis Turretin (1623–87) served for several years as a professor at the Academy of Geneva. He is best known for his *Institutes of Elenctic Theology*. *Elenctic* in this title means "to refute for the purpose of establishing doctrine." Hence Turretin, in his *Institutes*, seeks to refute common errors and to establish an orthodox Reformed theology (Titus 1:9). The book is written not primarily for scholars, but for those who want to be instructed in the faith. Though Turretin acknowledges reason as a servant, Scripture is the foundation and source of theology. Turretin has been characterized as scholastic, but his scholasticism marks more the method than the content of his theology. Turretin's work is not only a high point in Continental Reformed scholasticism, but also a starting point for much of Reformed theology in America. Indeed, it influenced New England theology, and was used in the nineteenth century at both Union Seminary (Virginia) and Princeton Seminary.

Naturally, Turretin's work belongs to this anthology as we attempt to uncover the roots of Westminster's understanding of Scripture. We reproduce here the second topic of his *Institutes* on the Holy Scriptures. In order to understand his thought rightly, a few words about his pedagogical approach of question and answer are necessary. Characteristically, his "elenctic method" begins with a question; next, he presents arguments both for and against his understanding of Reformed theology; then he attempts to answer his initial question. One will be struck by the amount of exegesis he uses in his answers to his questions concerning Scripture. The primary opponent in this section on Scripture is the Catholic Church ("the papists"). Thus, for example, he affirms that the divine authority of Scripture and the canon does not depend on the church; he defends the preservation and inerrancy of the original text of the Bible (cf. John Owen, chap. 25 above) and asserts that the Scriptures are to be read by all and have a single meaning. This section is also to be understood against the background of a growing rationalism and the challenges of nascent biblical criticism. This latter concern will be the main focus of the next document, the Helvetic Consensus Formula.

345

Bibliography: E. Choisy. "Turrettini." *NSHERK* 12:42–44. Harriet A. Harris. "Turretin, Francis (1623–87)." Pp. 553–54 in *DHT*. Richard A. Muller. "Scholasticism Protestant and Catholic: Francis Turretin on the Object and Principles of Theology." *Church History* 55, 2 (1986): 193–205. T. R. Phillips. "Turretin, Francis (1623–1687)." P. 263 in *DP&RTA*. Francis Turretin. *The Doctrine of Scripture: Locus 2 of the* Institutio theologiae elencticae. Ed. and trans. John W. Beardslee III. Grand Rapids: Baker, 1981. R. J. VanderMolen. "Turretin, Francis (1623–1687)." Pp. 1116–17 in *EDT*.

SECOND TOPIC: THE HOLY SCRIPTURES

First Question: The Word of God

Was a verbal revelation necessary? We affirm.

I. As the word of God is the sole principle of theology, so the question concerning its necessity deservedly comes before all things. Was it necessary for God to reveal himself to us by the word; or was the word of God necessary? For there were formerly (and are even at this day) various persons who believe that there is sufficient assistance in human reason to enable us to live well and happily. Hence they think that any revelation coming from heaven is not only needless, but also ridiculous because it is altogether very likely that nature had a prospective reference to man, no less than to other animals. Therefore they give as their opinion that reason (or the light of nature) is abundantly sufficient for the direction of life and the obtainment of happiness.

II. But the orthodox church has always believed far otherwise, maintaining the revelation of the word of God to man to be absolutely and simply necessary for salvation. It is the "seed" of which we are born again (1 Peter 1:23), the "light" by which we are directed (Ps. 119:105), the "food" upon which we feed (Heb. 5:13–14) and the "foundation" upon which we are built (Eph. 2:20).

THE NECESSITY OF THE WORD IS PROVED BY THE GOODNESS OF GOD

III. (1) The perfect goodness of God (communicative of itself) proves it. For when he had made man for himself (i.e., for a supernatural end and a condition far more happy than this earthly), he was without doubt unwilling that he should be ignorant on this subject and has declared to him by the word, happiness itself and the way to reach it (of which reason was ignorant). (2) The most wretched blindness and corruption of man proves it. Although after sin, man may still have some remaining light to direct him in earthly and worldly things, yet in divine and heavenly things which have a relation to happiness, he is so blind and depraved that he can neither become acquainted with any truth, nor perform any good thing unless God leads the way (1 Cor. 2:14; Eph. 5:8). (3) It is proven by right reason which teaches that God can be savingly known and worshipped only by his light, just as the sun makes itself known to us only by its own light (Ps. 36:9). Neither would impostors (in order to introduce new sacred rites) have feigned conferences with deities or angels (as Numa Pompilius with the nymph Egeria and Muhammad with Gabriel) unless all men were persuaded that the right method of worshipping the deity depended upon a revelation from himself. Hence all nations (even barbarous) agree that it is well for man to seek for some heavenly wisdom in addition to that reason which they call the guide of life. This has given rise to those different religious rites and ceremonies which prevail all over the world. Nor are they to be heard here who maintain that this is only an ingenious contrivance of men to keep the people in duty. For although it is true that cunning men have contrived many things in religion to inspire the common people with reverence and by this to hold their minds more obedient, yet they never could have gained their purpose unless there had already been in the human mind an inborn sense of its own ignorance and helplessness. By reason of this, men suffer themselves to be easily led about by such jugglers and deceivers.

By the twofold appetite of man

IV. The twofold appetite naturally implanted in man proves this: one for truth, the other for immortality; one for knowing the truth, the other for enjoying the highest good that the intellect may be completed by the contemplation of truth and the will by the fruition of good in which a happy life consists. But since these appetites cannot be in vain, a revelation was necessary to show the first truth and the highest good and the way to each (which nature could not do). Finally the glory of God and the salvation of men demanded it because the school of nature was not able either to lead us to a knowledge of the true God and to his lawful worship or to discover the plan of salvation by which men might escape from the misery of sin to a state of perfect happiness growing out of union with God. Therefore the higher school of grace was necessary in which God might teach us by word the true religion, by instructing us in his knowledge and worship and by raising us in communion with himself to the enjoyment of eternal salvation—where neither philosophy, nor reason, could ever rise.

V. Although in the works of creation and providence God had already clearly manifested himself so that the *to gnōston tou Theou* "is manifest in them, and the invisible things of him from the creation of the world are clearly seen" (Rom. 1:19–20), yet after the fall, this real revelation could not be sufficient for salvation, not only as to the subject (because the power of the Spirit did not accompany it by which the blindness and wickedness of man might be corrected), but also with regard to the object (because the mysteries of salvation and the mercy of God in Christ, without which there is no salvation [Acts 4:12], have no place there). God (as an object of knowledge, *to gnōston tou Theou*) indeed presents himself, but not as an object of faith (*to piston*); God the Creator, but not the Redeemer; the power and the Godhead (i.e., the existence of the deity and his infinite power may be derived from the work of creation), but not his saving grace and mercy. Therefore it was necessary that the defect of the former revelation (made useless and insufficient by sin) should be supplied by another more clear (not only as to degree, but also as to species), not only that God should use mute teachers, but that his sacred voice should also not only declare the excellence of his attributes, but open to us also the mystery of his will in order to our salvation.

VI. Although natural revelation may hand over different things concerning God and his attributes, will and works, yet it cannot teach us things sufficient for the saving knowledge

347

of God without a supernatural verbal revelation. Indeed, it shows that God exists (*quod sit Deus*), and of what nature (*qualis*), both in unity of essence and as possessed of different attributes, but does not tell us who he is individually and with regard to the persons. This will (as contained in the law), it imperfectly and obscurely manifests (Rom. 2:14–15), but the mystery of the gospel is entirely concealed. It displays the works of creation and providence (Ps. 19:1–3; Acts 14:15–17; 17:23–28; Rom. 1:19–20), but does not rise up to the works of redemption and grace which can become known to us by the word alone (Rom. 10:17; 16:25–26).

Second Question: The Necessity of Scripture

Was it necessary for the word of God to be committed to writing? We affirm.

I. As in the preceding question we have proved the necessity of the word, so in this we treat of the necessity of the Scriptures (or the written word) against papists. For as they endeavor studiously to weaken the authority of Scripture in order the more easily to establish their unwritten (*agraphous*) traditions and the supreme tribunal of the pope himself; so, for the same reason, they are accustomed in many ways to impair its necessity in order to prove it useful indeed to the church, but not necessary (as Bellarmine shows, VD 4.4, pp. 119–22). Yea Cardinal Hosius does not hesitate blasphemously to say, "Better would it be for the interests of the church had no Scripture ever existed"; and Valentia, "It would be better had it not been written."

STATEMENT OF THE QUESTION

II. As to the state of the question, keep in mind that the word "Scripture" is used in two senses: either materially, with regard to the doctrine delivered; or formally with regard to the writing and mode of delivery. In the former sense (as we said before), we hold it to be necessary simply and absolutely, so that the church can never spare it. But in the latter sense (which we are now discussing), we hold that it is not absolutely necessary with respect to God. For two thousand years before the time of Moses, he instructed his church by the spoken word alone; so he could (if he wished) have taught in the same manner afterwards, but only hypothetically (on account of the divine will) since God has seen fit for weighty reasons to commit his word to writing. Hence the divine ordination being established, it is made necessary to the church, so that it pertains not only to the well-being (*bene esse*) of the church, but also to its very existence (*esse*). Without it the church could not now stand. So God indeed was not bound to the Scriptures, but he has bound us to them.

III. Therefore the question is not whether the writing of the word was absolutely and simply necessary, but relatively and hypothetically; not for every age, but now in this state of things; nor relatively to the power and liberty of God, but to his wisdom and economy as dealing with man. For as in the natural economy parents vary the mode of instruction according to the age of their children (that while infants may be taught at first by spoken word, then by the voice of a master and the reading of books and finally may derive instruction by themselves from books), so the heavenly Father who chasteneth his people as a man chasteneth his son (Deut. 8:5), instructs the church yet in infancy and lisping by the spoken word, the simplest mode of revelation. The church presently growing up and in the beginning of its youth constituted under the law, he teaches it both by spoken word (on account of the remains of its infancy) and by writing (on account of the beginnings of a more robust age in the time of the apostles). At length, as of full age under the gospel, he wishes it to be content with the most perfect mode of revelation (viz., with the light of the written word). So the Scriptures are made necessary not only by the necessity of command, but by the hypothesis of the divine economy which God wished to be various and manifold (*polypoikilon*) according to the different ages of the church (Eph. 3:10).

IV. Hence arose the distinction of the word into unwritten (*agraphon*) and written (*engraphon*), a division not of the genus into species (as the papists maintain, as if the unwritten word were different from the written), but a distinction of the subject into its accidents, because that it was formerly not written and now is written are accidents of the same word. It is therefore called "unwritten" (*agraphon*), not with respect to the present time, but to the past when God saw fit to instruct his church by spoken word alone and not by writing.

V. Although God "at sundry times and in divers manner" (*polymerōs kai polytropōs*) spoke in time past unto the fathers—(Heb. 1:1), now with a clear voice and a discourse delivered (*prophorikō*) in words, then with an internal afflatus (as if by a mental discourse [*endiathetō*], sometimes by sending dreams, at others by exhibiting visions; sometimes by an assumption of the human form, often by the ministry of angels and other symbols of the divine presence)—yet the doctrine was always the same; nor has it been changed by the mode of revelation or delivery, nor by the mutations of time.

THE NECESSITY OF THE SCRIPTURE PROVED

VI. Three things particularly prove the necessity of the Scripture: (1) the preservation of the word; (2) its vindication; (3) its propagation. It was necessary for a written word to be given to the church that the canon of true religious faith might be constant and unmoved; that it might easily be preserved pure and entire against the weakness of memory, the depravity of men and the shortness of life; that it might be more certainly defended from the frauds and corruptions of Satan; that it might more conveniently not only be sent to the absent and widely separated, but also be transmitted to posterity. For by "letters," as Vives well observes, "all the arts are preserved as in a treasury, so that they can never perish, while on the contrary, tradition by the hand is unhappy" (*De disciplinis . . . de Corruptis Artibus* 1 [1636], 5). This is a divine and wonderful advantage of letters, as Quintilian says, "that they guard words and deliver them to readers as a sacred trust" (*Institutio oratoria* 1.7.31 [Loeb, 1:144–45]). Nor for any other reason are the public laws, statutes and edicts of kings and the decrees of the commonality inscribed upon brass or committed to public tablets, except that this is the most sure method of preserving them uncorrupted and of propagating through many ages the remembrance of those things which it is important for the people to know.

SOURCES OF EXPLANATION

VII. Although the church before Moses did not have a written word, it does not follow that it can also do without it now. Then the church was still in its infancy and had not as yet been formed into a body politic, but now it is increased and more populous. Its position in former times was different from what it is now. In those times, the unwritten (*agraphon*) word could be more easily preserved on account of the longevity of the patriarchs, the fewness of the covenanted and the frequency of revelations (although it suffered not a few corruptions). But in other times when the life of man was shortened, and the church was no longer comprehended within one or another family, but increased to a most numerous people and the divine oracles were more sparingly declared, another method of instruction became necessary so that this sacred republic might be governed not only by spoken word, but by written laws.

VIII. Although some particular churches might for a time be without the written word of God (especially when they were first built), yet they could not have been without that which was written (which undoubtedly sounded in their ears by the ministry of man), nor was the church in common then without the Scripture.

IX. The Holy Spirit (the supplier [*epichorēgia*] by whom believers should be God-taught [*theodidaktoi*], Jer. 31:34; John 6:45; 1 John 2:27) does not render the Scripture less necessary. He is not given to us in order to introduce new revelations, but to impress the written word on our hearts; so that here the word must never be separated from the Spirit (Isa. 59:21). The former works objectively, the latter efficiently; the former strikes the ears from without, the latter opens the heart within. The Spirit is the teacher; Scripture is the doctrine which he teaches us. (2) The words of Jer. 31:33–34 and 1 John 2:27 are not to be understood absolutely and simply (as if it was no longer necessary for believers under the New Testament dispensation to use the Scriptures, otherwise there would have been no use in John's writing to them), but relatively because on account of the more copious effusion of the Holy Spirit under the New Testament dispensation they are not to be so laboriously taught as under the Old by rude and imperfect elements. (3) The promise of Jeremiah will be fulfilled completely only in heaven where, on account of the clear vision of God, there will be no more need of the ministry of the Scriptures or of pastors, but each one will see God as he is face to face.

X. It is not true that the church was preserved during the Babylonian captivity without the Scripture. Daniel is said at the end of the seventy years to have understood by the books the number of years (Dan. 9:2), and it is said that Ezra brought the book of the law (Neh. 8:2). The passage in 2(4) Esdras 4:23, being apocryphal, proves nothing. But although Ezra collected the sacred books into one body and even corrected some mistakes made through the negligence of the scribes, it does not follow that the church was entirely destitute of the Scriptures.

XI. Bellarmine falsely affirms that after the time of Moses those of foreign countries who were brought over to the new religion used tradition alone and were without the Scriptures. For proselytes were diligently instructed in the doctrine of Moses and the prophets, as we learn even from the single example of the eunuch of Queen Candace (Acts 8:27–39). Nor were the Scriptures entirely unknown to the Gentiles, especially after they had been translated into Greek in the time of Ptolemy Philadelphus.

XII. Christ is our only teacher (Matt. 23:8) in such a sense as that the ministry of the word is not thereby excluded, but necessarily included because now in it only he addresses us and by it instructs us. Christ is not set in opposition to the Scriptures; rather he is set in opposition to the false teachers of the Pharisees who ambitiously assumed the authority due to Christ alone.

XIII. Although the Scriptures formally are of no personal use to those who cannot read (*analphabētous*), yet materially they serve for their instruction and edification much as the doctrines preached in the church are drawn from this source.

Third Question

Were the sacred Scriptures written only occasionally and without the divine command? We deny against the papists.

STATEMENT OF THE QUESTION

I. This question is agitated between us and the papists. In order to lessen the authority and perfection of the Scripture, they teach not only that it is not so very necessary and that the church could do without it, but also that it was not delivered to the church by the express command of God, but only in peculiar circumstances; that Christ neither commanded the apostles to write nor did the apostles think of writing the gospel with a primary intention, but only with a secondary and occasional intention (Bellarmine, VD 4.3–4, pp. 116–22).

II. The question is not whether the sacred writers were impelled by certain occasions to write. For we do not deny that they often made use of the opportunities offered to commit to writing the mysteries of God. Rather the question is whether they wrote so according to opportunities that they could not also write according to an express divine command. For we think these things should not be opposed to each other, but brought together. They could write both on the presentation of an opportunity and yet by a divine command and by divine inspiration. Yea, they must have written by the divine will because God alone could present such an occasion, for it was neither presented to them without design nor employed of their own accord.

III. A command may be implicit and general or explicit and special. Although all the sacred writers might not have had a special command to write (as many did have, Ex. 17:14; Deut. 31:19; Isa. 8:1; Jer. 36:2; Hab. 2:2; Rev. 1:11), yet they all had a general command. For the command to teach (Matt. 28:19) also includes the command to write, since persons at a distance and posterity can be taught only by writing. Hence preaching is sometimes said to be "in writing," at others "in deed" and again "in word." Further, immediate inspiration and the internal impulse of the Holy Spirit by which the writers were influenced was to them in the place of command. Hence Paul calls the Scriptures God-inspired (*theopneuston*, 2 Tim. 3:16) and Peter says that "prophecy came not in old time by the will of man: but holy men of God spake as they were moved by the Holy Ghost" (*hypo pneumatos hagiou pheromenous*, 2 Peter 1:21). Now it would be absurd (*asystaton*) to say that the apostles wrote as God inspired and moved them and yet that he did not command them. A command is not more efficacious than the inspiration of the things to be written; nor does a faithful ambassador ever depart from his instructions.

IV. Although the apostles do not always make mention of a special command of Christ (which nevertheless they do, as John, Jude and others), they plainly give us to understand this when they: (1) profess to be the universal teachers of all nations; (2) call themselves faithful servants of Christ (and therefore particularly anxious to fulfill his commands); (3) say that they are influenced by the Spirit (2 Peter 1:21). Hence Gregory the Great well remarks, "He himself wrote who dictated these things to be written; he himself wrote who was also the inspirer of the work" ("Preface" to the First Part, *Morals on the Book of Job* [1844], 1:15 [Praef. 1.2, PL 75.517]).

SOURCES OF EXPLANATION

V. Each apostle was not bound to write, although he was bound to preach. For as they committed themselves to divine inspiration in the exercise of preaching, so they were bound to wait for and to follow the same in writing. For the office was equal in those things which were essential to the apostleship that they all might be equally teachers inspired of God (*theopneustoi*), but it was not equal in the exercise of all the particular acts belonging to it. Hence it is not strange that (according to the pleasure of the Holy Spirit) some were employed both in writing and preaching, others only in preaching.

VI. A common book was not composed by all the apostles conjointly, both that they might not seem to have entered into a compact and that it might not appear of greater authority than that which would be written separately by each individual. This seems to have been the reason why Christ abstained from writing—that we might say that here is one who writes his epistle not with ink, but with the Spirit of the living God; not in tables of stone, but in the heart (2 Cor. 3:2). It was sufficient, therefore, for these things to be written by some and approved by the rest. Yea, it adds great weight and authority to the apostolic writings that they wrote in different places, for various reasons and on different occasions, in a different style and method to different persons and yet so consistent with each other.

VII. It was not necessary for the apostles to write a catechism so as to deliver their doctrines professedly. It was enough for them to hand down to us those doctrines in accordance with which all symbolical books and catechisms might be constructed. If they did not formally write a catechism, they did materially leave us either in the gospels or in the epistles those things by which we can be clearly taught the principles of religion (*katēcheisthai*).

VIII. As we ought not to impose a law upon the Holy Spirit and prescribe to him the method of revealing his will, so we ought not to doubt that the method of writing which they followed was the most suitable; not only because the custom of writing by epistles was at that time generally adopted (because this kind of writing was best adapted to disseminate the gospel speedily, which was the principal object of the apostles), but also because this method of writing (simple and popular) suited all (the unlearned as well as the learned) and transmitted a theology not ideal and merely theoretical, but practical and real.

IX. The Apostles' Creed is so called, not efficiently (as delivered by the apostles), but materially (as it was drawn from the doctrines of the apostles and is the marrow and substance of them).

X. They who wrote when an opportunity was offered and by the necessity of it, could nevertheless write by command. Things subordinate are not opposed to each other. The command of Christ was the principal impelling cause and the occasion offered the secondary impelling cause (as it were less principal) which they knew how to use for the glory of God and the edification of men, just as the apostles preached both by command and by occasion.

XI. Although the apostles were bound to write because they were bound to teach, it does not follow that pastors of the present day are equally bound always to write as to teach because they stand in a different relation. Since the apostles were bound to teach all nations, they were ecumenical teachers; not so ordinary pastors who have a particular flock entrusted to them.

Fourth Question: The Authority of the Holy Scriptures

Are the holy Scriptures truly authentic and divine? We affirm.

I. The authority of the Scriptures (which we have just discussed) depends on their origin. Just because they are from God, they must be authentic and divine. Hence arises the question concerning their authority which can be twofold: (1) with atheists and the heathen, who attribute no higher authority to the Scriptures than to any other books; (2) with those Christians who, while acknowledging its authority, nevertheless wish to make it depend (at least as far as we are concerned) upon the testimony of the church. As to the former class, the question is whether the Bible is truly credible of itself (*autopistos*) and divine. But as to the latter, the question is How do we know that it is such; or upon what testimony does the belief in the authenticity (*authentias*) of the Bible mainly rest? Here we take up the first question, not the second.

THE AUTHORITY OF THE SCRIPTURES

II. The first question may seem hardly necessary among Christians who should consider as an incontrovertible truth the fact that the Scriptures are inspired of God (*theopneuston*) as the primary foundation of faith. Yet even among Christians of this age, there are too many atheists and libertines who endeavor in every way to weaken this most sacred truth. Therefore it is of the greatest importance to our salvation that our faith should be in good time fortified against the diabolical cavils of these impious persons.

III. The authority of Scripture (concerning which we here inquire) is nothing else than the right and dignity of the sacred books, on account of which they are most worthy of faith with regard to those things which they propose to be believed and of our obedience in those things which they command us to omit or to do. The divine and infallible truth of these books (which have God for their author) is the foundation because he has the highest right to bind men to faith and duty. But this truth may be either intrinsic or extrinsic. The former is the credibility (*axiopistia*) in itself of the word which is always equal and consistent with itself, whether it has the testimony of men or not. The latter is the estimation or judgment of men in relation to the Scriptures, which is different as the subjects are different.

OF HISTORY AND OF RULE

IV. Again authenticity is either of history or of narrative; or in addition to this of truth and of rule. According to the former, whatever is narrated in Scripture is most true as it narrates either what is good or what is bad, whether it be true or false. But those things are said to have the latter which are so true in themselves that they are given as a rule of faith and practice. All things in Scripture do not have the authenticity of rule (as those things which the wicked and the Devil are reported to have said), but all do have historical authenticity.

STATEMENT OF THE QUESTION

V. The question is not whether the sacred writers (as men simply and in a divided sense) could err (for we readily grant this); or whether as holy men influenced by the Holy Spirit and in a compound sense, they did in fact err (for I think no one of the adversaries, except a downright atheist, would dare to say this). Rather the question is whether in writing they were so acted upon and inspired by the Holy Spirit (both as to the things themselves and as to the words) as to be kept free from all error and that their writings are truly authentic and divine. Our adversaries deny this; we affirm it.

Scripture proves itself

VI. The Bible proves itself divine, not only authoritatively and in the manner of an artless argument or testimony, when it proclaims itself God-inspired (*theopneuston*). Although this may be well used against those Christians who profess to believe it, yet it cannot be employed against others who reject it. The Bible also proves itself divine ratiocinatively by an argument artfully made (*artificiali*) from the marks which God has impressed upon the Scriptures and which furnish indubitable proof of divinity. For as the works of God exhibit visibly to our eyes by certain marks the incomparable excellence of the artificer himself and as the sun makes himself known by his own light, so he wished in the Bible (which is the emanation [*aporroē*] from the Father of lights and the Sun of righteousness) to send forth different rays of divinity by which he might make himself known.

By marks which are either:

VII. But these marks are either external or internal. The former, though not sufficient for a full demonstration of the thing, are of great importance in its confirmation and in the conviction of unbelievers. However, in the latter, the main strength of the argument consists.

External;

VIII. The external are: (1) with regard to the origin (the highest antiquity above all pagan monuments), for "that which is most ancient is most true," as Tertullian says. (2) With regard to the duration; the wonderful preservation (even to this day) of the divine word by his providential care against powerful and hostile enemies who have endeavored by fire and by sword to destroy it, while so many other books, against which nothing of this kind had ever been attempted, have wholly perished. (3) With regard to the instruments and amanuenses; the highest candor and sincerity in the writers, who do not conceal even their own faults (*hēttēmata*), but ingenuously confess them. (4) With regard to the adjuncts; the number, constancy and condition of the martyrs who sealed it with their blood. For since nothing is dearer to man than life, so many thousands of persons of both sexes, of every age and condition, would not (in defense of the Scriptures) so willingly have sought death (even the most cruel), unless thoroughly persuaded of its divinity. Nor would God have employed his omnipotence in working so many and such great miracles both under the law and the gospel, for the purpose of inducing a belief in the divinity of the Bible, if it had been a mere figment of the human brain. The testimony of the adversaries favors our side, as of the heathen concerning Moses, of Josephus and the Talmudists concerning Christ, and of Muhammad himself concerning both testaments (which may be seen in Vives, Plesseus, Grotius and others). Finally, the consent of all people who, although differing in customs (also in opinions about sacred things, worship, language and interest), have nevertheless received this word as a valuable treasury of divine truth and have regarded it as the foundation of religion and the worship of God. It is impossible to believe that God would have suffered so great a multitude of men, earnestly seeking him, to be so long deceived by lying books.

OR INTERNAL.

IX. The internal and the most powerful marks are also numerous. (1) With regard to the matter: the wonderful sublimity of the mysteries (which could have been discovered by no sharp-sightedness of reason) such as the Trinity, incarnation, the satisfaction of Christ, the resurrection of the dead and the like; the holiness and purity of the precepts regulating even the thoughts and the internal affections of the heart and adapted to render man perfect in every kind of virtue and worthy of his maker; the certainty of the prophecies concerning things even the most remote and hidden. For the foreseeing and foretelling of future things (dependent on the will of God alone) is a prerogative of deity alone (Isa. 41:23). (2) With regard to the style: the divine majesty, shining forth no less from the simplicity than the weight of expression and that consummate boldness in commanding all without distinction (*parrēsia*), both the highest and the lowest. (3) With regard to the form: the divine agreement and entire harmony (*panarmonia*) of doctrine, not only between both testaments in the fulfillment of predictions and types, but also between particular books of each testament; so much the more to be wondered at, as their writers both were many in number and wrote at different times and places so that they could not have an understanding among themselves as to what things should be written. (4) With regard to the end: the direction of all things to the glory of God alone and the holiness and salvation of men. (5) With regard to the effects: the light and efficacy of the divine doctrine which is so great that, sharper than any two-edged sword, it pierces to the soul itself, generates faith and piety in the minds of its hearers, as well as invincible firmness in its professors, and always victoriously triumphs over the kingdom of Satan and false religion. These criteria are such as cannot be found in any human writing (which always display proof of human weakness) and prove the Scriptures truly divine especially when, not each by itself, but all collectively (*athroōs*) are considered.

X. We must not suppose these marks shine equally and in the same degree in all the books of the Bible. For as one star differs from another star in light, so in this heaven of Scripture, some books send out brighter and richer rays of light; others far more feeble and fewer in proportion to their being more or less necessary to the church and as containing doctrines of greater or lesser importance. Thus the gospels and Paul's epistles shine with far greater splendor than the book of Ruth or Esther; but yet it is certain that in all are these arguments of truth and majesty, which by themselves prove a book divine and authentic (or at least that nothing can be found in them to make their authenticity [*authentian*] doubtful).

XI. Neither is it necessary that all these marks should occur in every chapter or verse of a canonical book to distinguish it from an apocryphal or in each part of Scripture detached from the whole. It is sufficient for them to be given in the divine writings considered collectively and as a totality.

XII. Although false religions usually claim for their doctrines these criteria, the true religion may appropriate these criteria to herself because the vain and false opinions of men do not weaken the truth of the thing itself. The Turk may most falsely claim divinity for his

Koran and the Jew for his Kabbalah (the contrary of which is evident from the fables and lies with which each of these books is filled). However, this is no reason why the believer should not truly predicate divinity of the sacred Scriptures because everywhere in them he sees the brightest rays of divine truth.

XIII. Although faith may be founded upon the authority of testimony and not upon scientific demonstration, it does not follow that it cannot be assisted by artificial arguments, especially in erecting the principles of faith. For before faith can believe, it must have the divinity of the witness to whom faith is to be given clearly established and certain true marks which are apprehended in it, otherwise it cannot believe. For where suitable reasons of believing anyone are lacking, the testimony of such a witness cannot be worthy of credence (*axiopiston*).

AUTHENTICITY OF THE TESTIMONY OF THE PROPHETS AND APOSTLES WHO WERE NOT DECEIVED

XIV. The testimony of the prophets and apostles is unexceptionable and cannot reasonably be called in question by anyone. For if it were uncertain and fallacious, it would be questionable either because they themselves were deceived or because they deceived others; but neither can be said with truth. They were not deceived and could not be. For if they were deceived, they were deceived either by others or by themselves. The former cannot be said because they were deceived neither by God (who as he can be deceived by no one, so neither does he deceive any man); nor by the angels (who do not deceive); nor by wicked spirits because the whole of this system tends to the overthrow of Satan's kingdom. No more can the latter be said. For if a person is deceived in anything, it arises principally from this: either because he does not see it himself (but receives it upon the testimony of others); or because he has seen it only in passing and cursorily; or because the thing itself is obscure and too difficult to be comprehended by the mind of man; or because the subject is improperly disposed and prevented by some disease from making a proper judgment. But here there was no such thing. For (1) they profess to have received the things which they relate not from an uncertain rumor and from others who had a partial acquaintance with them, but they had the most certain and definite knowledge, perceiving them with their eyes and ears and employing the greatest attention and study to investigate them. (2) Nor do they speak of things remote and distant, but of those which were done in the very places and time in which they wrote. Hence John says, "That which we have heard, which we have seen with our eyes, of the Word of life, declare we unto you" (1 John 1:1). (3) They do not discourse of things obscure and merely speculative (in which the ignorant and illiterate could easily have been deceived, not being able to rise to their sublimity), but of facts cognizable by the senses and before their eyes. For instance, of the resurrection of Christ (with whom they had been familiar before his death) who manifested himself to them after his resurrection, not momentarily, but for a long time; not only once, but often; not before one and then another, but before many of both sexes and all conditions. (4) Finally, it cannot be said that their faculties were impaired or in a diseased state. For besides the fact that they do not show any marks of corrupt imagination and mind (yea, their words and lives manifest wisdom and a well regulated mind), there is this to be said in addition—that not one or another, but many thought and gave utterance to the same thing. Hence it follows that there is no reason for saying that they were deceived.

NOR DID THEY SEEK TO IMPOSE ON OTHERS

XV. As they could not be imposed upon themselves, so neither did they seek to impose on others. For they who deceive and lie have in view some emolument, either that they may obtain glory, or conciliate the favor of men, or procure wealth and advantages. But as we hear their testimony, what desirable thing in life or after death was sought by the men of God? In life, indeed, are all those things by which men are usually deterred from lying—poverty, exile, tortures, the direst punishments—and after death, infamy and eternal suffering. And yet disregarding all these things, they did not hesitate in order to confirm their testimony, to expose themselves willingly to innumerable trials, to endure the vilest reproaches and to suffer the most cruel deaths. Therefore, who can for a moment suppose that they would suffer such things for that which they considered uncertain and false, when even for the most certain and indubitable things scarcely any man can be found who would risk so much as his reputation or property, much less seek death? Indeed, no one can charge them with the guilt of so great a lie who does not at the same time prove them to have been most foolish and wicked. Most foolish because they would then have been willing to lie without any prospect of advantage, with the most certain calamity in view, against the very doctrines of the religion about which they wrote and which so strongly forbids lying. Most wicked because they would have wished to deceive the whole world by lies and to involve it in every evil for no earthly good.

NOR COULD THEY

XVI. Finally, neither could they have imposed on others even if they wished. For they wrote not of things remote and distant (or done in ancient times, or secretly and in some corner as impostors generally do that they may not be convicted of falsehood), but they relate those things which happened in their own day publicly and in the face of the sun (in the very place in which they wrote and indeed in the presence of those to whom they wrote and who might easily have detected fraud and imposture if there had been any). Therefore, if they were not deceived themselves, nor deceived others, their testimony is undoubtedly divine and so all the doctrines depending on and formed upon it are authentic.

XVII. We cannot call in question the fact of the existence of the prophets and apostles and of their having written the books attributed to them without overthrowing the faith of all antiquity and introducing Pyrrhonism. The same doubt might with equal reason be shown over all the writings we possess; but since these books were undoubtedly written by credible authors, what man in his senses would not rather believe that they were written by those whose names they bear (as all Christian churches everywhere have firmly believed, about which no one either of the Jews or of the pagans had the least doubt and which was believed in the most ancient times when they had every opportunity of investigating the truth) than by some other persons?

THE AUTHENTICITY OF THE BOOKS OF MOSES IS SHOWN

XVIII. Whatever is brought forward to weaken faith in the Mosaic history can easily be refuted by a thorough examination. For he who denies that Moses ever lived or that he was the author of the books attributed to him can be convinced without difficulty. For not only Jews and Christians make mention of him, but also many profane writers. Also this was firmly believed by a most numerous nation, nor is there any ground for doubt, unless we wish to destroy entirely belief in all histories and to deny that Plato, Aristotle, Cicero and others ever existed and wrote the books which bear their names (which no one but a fool would say). But this can be said with much less truth of Moses than of the others because no book could have been cast aside by the Jews with greater show of reason. For thus they would have freed themselves from the yoke of a most rigorous law. Yet none was received and preserved by them with greater zeal and eagerness; none ever obtained so suddenly such great authority as to be regarded as a divine law and rule of religion, for no other reason than from a persuasion of the truth contained in it.

XIX. Second, if (finding this position untenable) he flies to another and confesses indeed that Moses existed and wrote these books, but asserts that he was an imposter and a consummate fabler, who imposed upon the Israelites by empty lies and false prodigies in order to bring them into subjection to the law which he proposed (and so to himself), it can with as little difficulty be disproved. For besides the fact that the heathen themselves and the most bitter enemies of Christianity (as Porphyry, bk. 4) give Moses the credit of being a truthful writer, it cannot easily be conceived how the great wisdom and remarkable virtue which shone in the whole life of Moses can be reconciled with so barefaced an imposture; or how he could devise and recommend by fraud and imposture so admirable a law from which all that is good in others has been borrowed and which had for its object the glory of God and the holiness of the people. Again, if he was an impostor, it is wonderful that he adopted a plan directly contrary to his object and by which his deception could easily be discovered. For if the account which he gives of the creation of the world is false, it would have been very easy to convict him of falsehood by the small number of generations which came between Adam and the flood and between the flood and the departure of the people from Egypt; since, in the time of Moses, many persons were still living who had seen Joseph, whose father saw them, who for one hundred years of his life could have been with Methuselah, who saw Adam. Hence without trouble the truth or falsity of the thing could have been ascertained. (3) If Moses was an impostor and wished to deceive the Israelites, he undoubtedly hoped to make them believe his falsehoods and deceptions. But how could he for a moment suppose that he could make them believe so many and so great miracles reported to have been wrought either in Egypt or in the wilderness, if no such things had taken place—especially as he was writing to those who would have been ear-witnesses or eye-witnesses of them? The things of which he wrote are reported to have been done not many ages before, but in their very day; not secretly and in a corner, but openly and publicly before six hundred thousand men (and even before his most bitter enemies) who could have convicted him of falsehood. Could he hope that no one would be found among the people to doubt these things or to inquire of the Egyptians concerning their truth? Is it credible that of so great a number of men whom he constantly and severely upbraids as a rebellious and stubborn nation (yea, whom he several times afflicted with the severest punishments, visiting with sudden death not only hundreds, but also thousands and acting in such a manner as would with reason exasperate them against him), there was no one to bring the charge of fraud and imposture while they so often murmured and rebelled against him? Finally, if he acted as an impostor, he must undoubtedly have proposed to himself some advantage or glory or wealth, either that he might obtain the supreme authority for himself and his posterity, or to secure from men the praise of wisdom and heroic virtue; but how far removed from the desire of gain or of glory Moses was, both the thing itself clearly shows and the sincerity with which he so ingenuously confesses his own sins (and especially his incredulity) abundantly testifies.

XX. But perhaps the Israelites, aware of the falsity of the things which Moses relates, consented to the deception and imposture in order to glorify their nation. But who would believe that the Israelites were so utterly devoid of sense as willingly to consent to so great an imposture by which they were forced to come under the almost unendurable (*abastaktō*) yoke of the strictest law, if they had been altogether certain that this law was a mere fiction of Moses? Or can it be said with any shadow of truth, that of these six hundred thousand all to a man consented to this deception, so that not one was found to oppose it? (2) So far from their gaining glory and praise from other nations, on the contrary, they would thus deservedly bring upon themselves the odium and contempt of all. For who would say that it was a nation's glory to have her murmurings and most heinous sins exposed to the view of men, to be rebuked as stiff-necked (*sklērotrachēloi*) and the most ungrateful of mortals, to have published to the world the severest punishments by which God avenges himself of their stubbornness and rebellion; yea who does not see that these would bring such a nation into everlasting disgrace? In one word, we cannot explain why a people so stiff-necked and devoted to pleasure (*philēdonos*) would so readily and voluntarily submit to the yoke of such a troublesome law and one severely punishing the smallest transgression, unless we believe that they were firmly persuaded of the divine calling of Moses and of the truth of his doctrines.

THE CONVERSION OF THE WORLD PROVES THE DIVINITY OF SCRIPTURE

XXI. The conversion of the world and the success of the gospel is a very clear proof of its divinity. For unless the apostles were men of God and delivered heavenly truth, it cannot be conceived how it happened that their doctrines (destitute of all those helps by which any doctrine of human origin can be recommended and propagated and most obstinately resisted by all those things by which doctrine could be resisted, viz., the authority of magistrates, the customs of the people, the favor of princes, the eloquence of orators, the subtlety of philosophers, accommodation to the morals and dispositions of men promulgated by a few illiterate and weak men, far removed not only from deception, but even from suspicion; endowed with no gifts of eloquence, schooled in no arts of flattery, rejected and despised) by persuasion alone (without any assistance of public authority and favor, without the help of arms, through innumerable trials and deaths often), in the shortest time, in almost every place, were so propagated as to break through all opposition and come forth victorious over the religions which were furnished with all these helps, so that whole nations and even kings themselves, leaving the religion of the country in which they had been born and brought up, without the hope of any advantage (yea, in sure expectation of trials) embraced this which was absurd to reason and disagreeable to the flesh and which seemed to repel rather than allure.

XXII. Certainty can be threefold: (1) mathematical; (2) moral; (3) theological. Mathematical (or metaphysical) is that which belongs to first principles known by nature of themselves and to conclusions demonstrated by principles of this kind (as when the whole is said to be greater than any of its parts and that the same thing cannot both exist and not exist at the same time). (2) Moral certainty accompanies those truths which cannot indeed be demonstrated, but yet persuade by such marks and probable arguments that a sensible man cannot doubt them (as that the *Aeneid* was written by Virgil and the *History of Livy* by Livy). For although the thing does not carry its own evidence with it, yet it has been attended with such a constant testimony that no one, having a knowledge of things and of letters, can doubt it. (3) Theological certainty attends those things, which although they cannot be demonstrated or known of themselves and by nature, are nevertheless founded not only upon probable grounds and moral arguments, but upon truly theological and divine (viz., upon divine revelation). Therefore, this gives them not merely a moral and conjectural certainty, but a truly divine faith. The Scriptures do not possess metaphysical certainty; otherwise the assent which we give to them would bespeak knowledge, not faith. Neither do they possess simply a moral and probable certainty; otherwise our faith would not be more certain than any historical assent given to human writings. But they have a theological and infallible certainty, which cannot possibly deceive the true believer illuminated by the Spirit of God.

SOURCES OF EXPLANATION

XXIII. The prophets did not fall into mistakes in those things which they wrote as inspired men (*theopneustōs*) and as prophets, not even in the smallest particulars; otherwise faith in the whole of Scripture would be rendered doubtful. But they could err in other things as men (just as David erred in his letter concerning the killing of Uriah [which has historical authenticity but not normal]; and Nathan in the directions which he gave to David about building the temple without having consulted God, 2 Sam. 7:3) because the influence of the Holy Spirit was neither universal nor uninterrupted, so that it might not be considered an ordinary excitation or merely an effect of nature (2 Kings 2:17).

XXIV. The apostles were infallible in faith, not in practice; and the Spirit was to lead them into all truth so that they might not err, but not into all holiness that they might not sin because they were like us in all things. The dissimulation and hypocrisy of Peter (Gal. 2:12) was a sin of life, not an error of faith; a lapse in his morality from weakness and the fear of incurring the hatred of the Jews, but not an error of mind from an ignorance of Christian liberty, which he testified sufficiently to have known in his familiar intercourse with the Gentiles before the arrival of the Jews.

XXV. When Paul says, "I speak, not the Lord" (1 Cor. 7:12), he does not deny the inspiration of the Lord (which he claims, 1 Cor. 7:40), but only that this precept or this law was expressly mentioned by the Lord before himself. Thus the meaning is, this controversy concerning willful desertion was not agitated in the time of Christ and there was no occasion for deciding it. Paul (now illuminated by the Spirit) does.

XXVI. Things in the law which seem to be trifling and useless are found (by the pious and devoted) to be of the greatest importance, i.e., to call forth their obedience, to overthrow idolatry, to the formation of their morals and (if they are rightly used) making known the Messiah. The genealogies and other things which seem to be superfluous are the testimonies of the rise, propagation and preservation of the church, and of the fulfillment of the promise concerning the Messiah's being born of the seed of Abraham and David.

XXVII. Hosea is not commanded to take a wife of whoredom, for then the children of such a connection could not be called children of whoredom as they are called in 1:2. But this must be taken allegorically to represent the foul idolatries of Israel.

Fifth Question

Do real contradictions occur in Scripture? Or are there any inexplicable (alyta) passages which cannot be explained and made to harmonize? We deny.

I. Although when the divinity of the Scriptures is proved (as in the preceding question), its infallibility necessarily follows, yet the enemies of true religion and of Scripture in every age flatter themselves that they have found not a few contradictions (*enantiophanē*) in it and boast of their discoveries in order to overthrow its authenticity (*authentian*); as Porphyry, Lucian (of Samosata), Julian the Apostate and others formerly of the Gentiles, and many atheists of the present day who declare that they have met with many contradictions and difficulties (*apora*) in it which cannot in any way be reconciled. Thus there is the necessity of taking up this subject particularly in order that the integrity of the Scriptures may be preserved safe and entire against their wicked darts.

II. We have to deal here not only with declared atheists and Gentiles who do not receive the sacred Scriptures, but also with those who, seeming to receive them, indirectly oppose them. For instance, the Enthusiasts who allege the imperfection of the written word as a pretext for leading men away from it to their hidden word or private revelations; the papists, who while maintaining the divinity of the Scriptures against atheists, do not scruple with arms fitted to themselves to oppose as much as they can its own and so the entire cause of Christianity, and to deliver it up to the enemy by insisting upon the corruption of the original so as to bring authority to their Vulgate version. Lastly, many Libertines who, living in the bosom of the church, are constantly bringing forward these various difficulties (*apora*) and apparent contradictions (*enantiophanē*) in order to weaken the authority of the Scriptures.

III. The learned pursue different methods in answering them. Some think that they can get rid of all difficulties by saying that the sacred writers could slip in memory or err in smaller things; so Socinus, "De sacrae Scripturae auctoritate," *Opera omnia* (1656), 1:265–80; Castellio, *Dialogorum sacrorum* (1651) and others. But instead of being a defense against the atheists, this is a base abandonment of the cause. Others confess that the Hebrew and Greek originals are corrupted in some places by the wickedness of the Jews or of heretics, but that a remedy can easily be found in the Vulgate version and the infallible authority of the church. This opinion is held by many of the papists against whom we will argue when we speak of the purity of the sources. Others again think that a few very slight errors have crept into the Scriptures and even now exist which cannot be corrected by any collation of manuscripts. These are not to be imputed however to the sacred writers themselves, but partly to the injuries of time, partly to the fault of copyists and librarians. Yet on this account, the authenticity (*authentia*) of the Scriptures cannot be weakened because they occur only in things less necessary and important (thus Scaliger, Capellus, Amamus, Vossius and others think). Finally others defend the integrity of the Scriptures and say that these various contradictions are only apparent, not real and true; that certain passages are hard to be understood (*dysnoēta*), but not altogether inexplicable (*alyta*). This is the more common opinion of the orthodox, which we follow as safer and truer.

STATEMENT OF THE QUESTION

IV. The question does not concern the irregular writing of words or the punctuation or the various readings (which all acknowledge do often occur); or whether the copies which we have so agree with the originals as to vary from them not even in a little point or letter. Rather the question is whether they so differ as to make the genuine corrupt and to hinder us from receiving the original text as a rule of faith and practice.

V. The question is not as to the particular corruption of some manuscripts or as to the errors which have crept into the books of particular editions through the negligence of copyists or printers. All acknowledge the existence of many such small corruptions. The question is whether there are universal corruptions and errors so diffused through all the copies (both manuscript and edited) as that they cannot be restored and corrected by any collation of various copies, or of Scripture itself and of parallel passages. Are there real and true, and not merely apparent, contradictions? We deny the former.

That Scripture is not corrupted is proved

VI. The reasons are: (1) The Scriptures are inspired of God (*theopneustos*, 2 Tim. 3:16). The word of God cannot lie (Ps. 19:8–9; Heb. 6:18); cannot pass away and be destroyed (Matt. 5:18); shall endure forever (1 Peter 1:25); and is truth itself (John. 17:17). For how could such things be predicated of it, if it contained dangerous contradictions, and if God suffered either the sacred writers to err and to slip in memory, or incurable blemishes to creep into it?

VII. (2) Unless unimpaired integrity characterize the Scriptures, they could not be regarded as the sole rule of faith and practice, and the door would be thrown wide open to atheists, libertines, enthusiasts and other profane persons like them for destroying its authenticity (*authentian*) and overthrowing the foundation of salvation. For since nothing false can be an object of faith, how could the Scriptures be held as authentic and reckoned divine if liable to contradictions and corruptions? Nor can it be said that these corruptions are only in smaller things which do not affect the foundation of faith. For if once the authenticity (*authentia*) of the Scriptures is taken away (which would result even from the incurable corruption of one passage), how could our faith rest on what remains? And if corruption is admitted in those of lesser importance, why not in others of greater? Who could assure me that no error or blemish had crept into fundamental passages? Or what reply could be given to a subtle atheist or heretic who should pertinaciously assert that this or that passage less in his favor had been corrupted? It will not do to say that divine providence wished to keep it free from serious corruptions, but not from minor. For besides the fact that this is gratuitous, it cannot be held without injury, as if lacking in the necessary things which are required for the full credibility (*autopistian*) of Scripture itself. Nor can we readily believe that God, who dictated and inspired each and every word to these inspired (*theopneustois*) men, would not take care of their entire preservation. If men use the utmost care diligently to preserve their words (especially if they are of any importance, as for example a testament or contract) in order that it may not be corrupted, how much more, must we suppose, would God take care of his word which he intended as a testament and seal of his covenant with us, so that it might not be corrupted; especially when he could easily foresee and prevent such corruptions in order to establish the faith of his church?

VIII. The principal arguments for the integrity of the Scriptures and the purity of the sources are four. (1) The chief of these is the providence of God (who as he wished to provide for our faith by inspiring the sacred writers as to what they should write, and by preserving the Scriptures against the attempts of enemies who have left nothing untried that they might destroy them), so he should keep them pure and uncorrupted in order that our faith might always have a firm foundation. (2) The religion of the Jews who have always been careful even to the point of superstition concerning the faithful keeping of the sacred manuscripts. (3) The diligence of the Masoretes who placed their marks as a hedge around the law that it might not in any way be changed or corrupted. (4) The number and multitude of copies, so that even if some manuscripts could be corrupted, yet all could not.

SOURCES OF EXPLANATION

IX. The contradictions (*antilogia*) found in Scripture are apparent, not real; they are to be understood only with respect to us who cannot comprehend and perceive the agreement everywhere, but not in the thing itself. And if the laws of legitimate contradiction are attended to (that opposites should agree with the same thing [*tō autō*], in the same respect [*kata to auto*], with reference to the same thing [*pros to auto*] and in the same time [*tō autō chronō*]), these various apparent contradictions (*enantiophanē*) in Scripture might be easily reconciled. For the discourse does not concern the same thing, as when James ascribes justification to works, which Paul denies to them. For the former speaks of declarative justification of the effect *a posteriori*, but the latter of justification of the cause, *a priori*. Thus Luke enjoins mercy, "Be ye merciful" (Luke 6:36) which Deuteronomy forbids, "Thou shalt not pity" (Deut. 19:13). The former refers to private persons, the latter to magistrates. Or they are not said in the same respect, as when Matthew denies the presence of Christ in the world, "Me ye have not always" (Matt. 26:11); and yet it is promised, "I am with you alway, even unto the end of the world" (Matt. 28:20). The former is said with regard to his human nature and bodily presence, but the latter with regard to his divine nature and spiritual presence. Or the statements are not made with reference to the same thing, as when something is said absolutely and another comparatively. "Honor thy father" (Ex. 20:12); "if any man hate not his father" (Luke 14:26). The former must be understood absolutely, the latter comparatively for loving less and esteeming less than Christ. Or not in the same time, hence the expression "distinguish times and you will reconcile Scripture." Thus at one time circumcision is extolled as a great privilege of the Jews (Rom. 3:1); at another it is spoken of as a worthless thing (Gal. 5:3). But the former refers to the Old Testament dispensation when it was an ordinary sacrament and a seal of the righteousness of faith, but the latter concerns the time of the gospel after the abrogation of the ceremonial law. At one time the apostles are sent to the Jews alone by a special mission before the passion of Christ and prohibited from going to the Gentiles ("Go not into the way of the Gentiles," Matt. 10:5); at another they are sent to all nations by a general mission after the resurrection (Mark 16:15).

X. Although we give to the Scriptures absolute integrity, we do not therefore think that the copyists and printers were inspired (*theopneustous*), but only that the providence of God watched over the copying of the sacred books, so that although many errors might have crept in, it has not so happened (or they have not so crept into the manuscripts) but that they can be easily corrected by a collation of others (or with the Scriptures themselves). Therefore the foundation of the purity and integrity of the sources is not to be placed in the freedom from fault (*anamartēsia*) of men, but in the providence of God which (however men employed in transcribing the sacred books might possibly mingle various errors) always diligently took care to correct them, or that they might be corrected easily either from a comparison with Scripture itself or from more approved manuscripts. It was not necessary therefore to render all the scribes infallible, but only so to direct them that the true reading may always be found out. This book far surpasses all others in purity.

XI. Although we cannot find out immediately a plain reconciliation and one free from all difficulties between passages of Scripture (which treat either of names or of numerical and chronological subjects), they must not at once be placed among inexplicable things (*alyta*). Or if they are called inexplicable (*alyta*), they will be such only by the inability of the one endeavoring to explain (*tē adynamia tou lyontos*), not in themselves, so that here it will be wiser to acknowledge our own ignorance than to suppose any contradiction. For these histories are not written so in detail as to contain every circumstance. Many things were undoubtedly brought into a narrow compass; other things which did not appear to be so important were omitted. It could also happen that these places had various relations (*scheseis*) well known to the writers, although now unknown to us. Hence Peter Martyr well remarks on 2 Kings 8:17:

> Although there occur obscure places in chronology, we must not, to get over them, say that the sacred text is false. For God, who of his own mercy wished the divine letters to be preserved for us, has given them to us entire and uncorrupted. Wherefore if it ever happens that we cannot explain the number of years, we must confess our ignorance and recollect that the sacred letters speak so concisely that the place where the calculation must be commenced does not readily appear. Therefore the Scriptures remain uncorrupted, which if weakened in one or another place, will also be suspected in others. (Peter Martyr Vermigli, *Melachim id est, Regum libri duo* [1566], 259.).

And:

> It often happens that in this history the number of years assigned to the kings appear to be at variance with each other. But doubts of this kind can be solved in many ways; for sometimes one and the same year is attributed to two persons because it had been completed and perfected by neither. Sometimes sons reigned some years with their parents, and these are assigned now to the reign of the parents and then to that of the children. There occurred also sometimes interregna, and the unoccupied time is attributed now to a former and then to a later king. There were also some years in which rulers were tyrannical and wicked, and therefore these are passed by and not reckoned with the other years of their reigns. (Ibid., 127 on 1 Kings 15:1.)

Of Cainan

XII. The passage in Luke 3:36 concerning the younger Cainan (who is inserted between Arphaxad and Sala contrary to the truth of the Mosaic history, Gen. 11:13) is truly hard to be understood (*dysnoētos*) and has greatly exercised the ingenuity of the learned; yet it should not be considered entirely inexplicable (*alytos*) since various methods of solution can be given. Passing by other opinions, we think that to be the best which makes Cainan surreptitious (*hypobolimaion*) and spurious, having crept in from the version of the Septuagint in which the chronology of Demetrius (according to Eusebius, *Preparation for the Gospel* 9.17.419d [ed. Gifford, 1903], 451) testifies that it existed even before the time of Christ, either from the carelessness of copyists or from a certain pious zeal, that Luke might be consistent with the Septuagint which was then of great authority. This is plainly proved: (1) by the authority of Moses and of the books of Chronicles which, in the genealogical records formed in three places (Gen. 10:24; 11:13; 1 Chron. 1:18), make no mention of him; (2) the Chaldee paraphrases which uniformly omit Cainan in the book of Genesis and Chronicles; (3) Josephus does not mention him, nor Berosus guided by him, nor Africanus whose words Eusebius quotes in his *Chronicorum* (cf. 1.16.13 [PG 19.153–54]); (4) the sacred chronology would thus be disturbed and brought into doubt in the history of Moses, if the years of Cainan are inserted between Arphaxad and Sala. Abraham would not be the tenth from Noah as Moses asserts, but the eleventh. (5) It does not exist in any of the Codices. Our Beza testifies that it is not found in his most ancient manuscript (*Annotationes maiores in Novum . . . testamentum, Pars prior* [1594], 262 on Luke 3:36). Ussher ("De Cainano Arphaxadi filio" in *Chronologia Sacra* 6; cf. *Whole Works* [1847–64], 11:558) asserts that he saw the book of Luke written in Greek-Latin on the most ancient vellum, in characters somewhat large without breathings and accents (which having been brought from Greece to France was laid up in the monastery of St. Irenaeus in the suburbs of Lyons; and being discovered in the year 1562 was afterward carried to England and presented to the University of Cambridge), and in it he could not find Cainan. Scaliger in his prologue to the chronicle of Eusebius ("Prolegomena," *Thesaurus temporum Eusebii . . . chronicorum canonum* [1606/1968], 1:ii) affirms that Cainan is lacking in the most ancient copies of Luke. Whatever the case may be, even if this passage proves to be a mistake, the authenticity (*authentia*) of Luke's gospel cannot be called in question on that account: (a) because the corruption is not universal; (b) this error is of little consequence and a ready means of correcting it is furnished by Moses, so that there was no necessity for that learned man Vossius to throw doubts upon the purity of the Hebrew manuscript in order to establish the authenticity (*authentian*) of the Septuagint.

XIII. If a great variety occurs in the genealogy of Christ (which Matthew and Luke give both as to the persons and their number), it should not seem wonderful. For they are not the same, but different. Matthew gives the genealogy of Joseph, whose family he traces from David through Solomon; but Luke traces the pedigree of Mary upwards through Nathan (another son of David) to the same David. Matthew leaves the pedigree of the spouse to be sought for in the family of the husband according to the Hebrew custom. Luke wished to supply the omission by describing the origin of Mary, so that the genealogy of Christ from both parents might be preserved full and entire, that there might be no ground for the scruples of the weak or the cavils of the enemies of the gospel (and that the former might be made certain and the latter convinced that Christ according to the ancient prophecies was the true and natural son of David, whether a regard should be had to the husband Joseph, into whose family he had passed by the marriage with Mary, or to Mary herself). Especially when we know that virgins (only daughters) who inherited (*epiklērous*) the entire fortunes of their parents (such as was the blessed virgin) were not permitted to marry out of their own tribe and family. But the genealogy is referred by Luke to Joseph and not to Mary because it was not the custom to trace genealogies through the female side (for they were reckoned either in the parents or in the brothers if unmarried or in their husbands if married). Hence the common saying of the Jews: "the family of a mother is no family" (*mshpchth 'm l' mshpchth*).

XIV. Although Jacob is called the father of Joseph by Matthew (but Heli by Luke), there is nevertheless no contradiction because this is to be understood in different respects (*kat' allo kai allo*). First, there is nothing absurd in one son having two fathers considered differently: one natural (who begot the son from himself), the other legal (who adopted the same born from another according to law). Manasseh and Ephraim were the natural sons of Joseph alone, but the legal sons of Jacob by adoption. Obed, the grandfather of David, had one natural father (Boaz), but also a legal father, Mahlon, the former husband of his mother Ruth, to whom Boaz, the second husband, raised up a seed according to law. Thus Jacob was the natural father of Joseph, but Heli (who was the natural father of Mary) can be called the father of Joseph, either the legal (as Africanus thinks) because Heli having died without sons, Jacob married his wife according to the law (Deut. 25:5) and begat from her Joseph, the husband of Mary; or the civil, in relation to the marriage entered into with Mary his daughter by which he became his son-in-law, as Naomi calls her daughters-in-law "her daughters" (Ruth 1:11–12, the common mode of speaking). Or it can be said that not Joseph but Christ is called the son of Heli, as these words *hōs enomizeto hyios Iōsēph* may be included in a parenthesis, the parenthesis not stopping as is commonly supposed, after the word *enomizeto*, in this sense, *ōn* (*hōs enomizeto hyios Iōsēph*) *tou Hēli* (viz., Jesus being [as was supposed the son of Joseph], the son of Heli [i.e., the grandson by his daughter, the virgin Mary]). This transition from grandfathers to grandsons is not unusual especially when the fathers are dead; and on this account the more here because Christ was without father (*apatōr*) as to his human nature.

XV. If it is asked why Matthew 1:8 says that Joram begat Uzziah when it is evident from 2 Kings 8:24 (cf. 1 Chron 3:11–12) that Joram begat Ahaziah, Ahaziah Joash, Joash Amaziah, and so three kings are omitted, and a leap is made from Joram, the great-grandfather, to Uzziah, the great-grandchild's son: we can answer by saying that it is not unusual in Scripture for the descendants of ancestors from the highest antiquity to be called their sons and daughters—as the Jews call themselves the sons of Abraham (John 8:39); Elizabeth is said to be of the daughters of Aaron (Luke 1:5); Christ is called the son of David (Matt. 22:40–46). So it is said that Joram begat Uzziah by a mediate generation, on account of which the grandsons and great-grandsons descending from ancestors are called sons. But why these three kings are omitted and no others is not quite so clear, nor can the reasons given by various persons obtain our assent. It seems more likely that this was done for the sake of the round numbers because Matthew wished to reduce all these generations to fourteen, an abridgment to aid the memory. To obtain this he considered it of little importance to leap over some persons less remarkable, as other historians also have frequently done in giving a summary. But for a peculiar reason these three kings were omitted that the posterity of Ahab even to the third or fourth generation might be distinguished by this mark of the curse (1 Kings 21:22), by erasing the kings who were of the posterity of Ahab, so that they might be regarded as never having lived or reigned. But Joram is not excluded because he did not spring from the cursed blood of Ahab nor his great-grandson Uzziah, although he was descended from Ahab because the divine curse did not usually extend beyond the third or fourth generation.

XVI. If it is asked how Josiah is said to have "begotten Jeconiah" (Matt. 1:11) when (from the books of Kings, 2 Kings 24:6; 1 Chron. 3:15–16) it is evident that Josiah had four sons of different names (*heterōnymous*)—Johanan or Jehoahaz; Jehoiakim or Eliakim; Zedekiah or Mattaniah; and Shallum—but that Jeconiah was the son of Jehoiakim, it can be answered in different ways: either that the text was corupted by librarians and that *Iacheim* should be supplied between Josiah and Jeconiah, Jehoiachim being the son of Josiah and the father of Jeconiah (which is proved by the authority of the ancient manuscript which R. Stephanus and Henry his son used, with whom Stapulensis and Bucer agree); and so the restoration would stand more truly *Iōsias de egennēse ton Iacheim—Iacheim egennēse ton lechonian.* Or that Josiah is called the father of Jeconiah mediately because he was his grandfather, and that Jehoiakim was omitted because, as he was not worthy of sorrow and of a burial with the kings of Judah (Jer. 22:18–19), so he was not worthy of mention in the genealogy of Christ. Or that there were two Jeconiahs and that they are mentioned in Matthew 1:11–12, the first Jehoiakim, the son of Josiah (who is also called Eliakim) and Jeconiah. This should not be wondered at since many of the Jewish kings had two names and even three; as Zedekiah is called also Mattaniah, Uzziah is called Azariah. The other Jeconiah properly (1 Chron. 3:16), or Jehoiakim, the grandson of Josiah mentioned in Matthew 1:12, is plainly distinguished from the former both by the mention of his brothers (whom the latter had not, Jer. 22:18–19) and by the mention of Salathiel born of Jeconiah after the captivity (*meta metoikesian,* Matt. 1:12).

XVII. Although Salathiel is said to have begotten Zerubbabel (Matt. 1:12) and yet is called "the son of Pedaiah" (1 Chron. 3:17–19), there is no contradiction because Salathiel having died without children, Pedaiah his brother could raise up seed for him, and by law as a husband's brother had from his wife Zerubbabel. Hence he is called the son of Pedaiah (1 Chron. 3:19) because he was truly begotten by him; and of Salathiel (Matt. 1:12; Hag. 1:1) because he was raised up to him by his brother; or because Zerubbabel was the successor of Salathiel, Pedaiah having died before Salathiel the father, as he might have been the immediate son of Pedaiah and only the mediate of Salathiel his grandfather.

XVIII. There is no contradiction between 1 Chronicles 3:19, Matthew 1:13 and Luke 3:27 when the sons of Zerubbabel are said in Chronicles to be "Meshullam and Hananiah," but in Matthew "Abiud" and in Luke "Rhesa." This can be easily explained by saying that three different lines of Zerubbabel are meant: one in Chronicles of his oldest son Meshullam and of others whose progeny was distinguished, and from whom the rulers and chiefs were chosen to lead the Jewish nation back from Babylon; the second in Matthew, Abiud, from whom Joseph was descended; the third in Luke, Rhesa, from whom Mary was descended. These two were private men who led an obscure life and therefore seem to have been omitted in the Chronicles. Or we might say with others that there were different Zerubbabels and Salathiels, and so we should not wonder at their posterity being different.

XIX. When it is said Josiah begat Jeconiah *epi tēs metoikesias*, these words are not to be translated literally (i.e., "in the carrying away") since it is evident from the particular divine promise that they did not live to see that evil and died some years before the captivity (2 Chron. 34:28; 35:24). But they are to be translated "at" or "about it" (viz., when the captivity threatened). Thus *epi* coincides with *heōs* (until the carrying away) as *meta* coincides with *apo* (Matt. 1:17). Then *epi* will denote the time in which the thing was done; taken however not strictly, but with some latitude (as Mark 2:26; Luke 3:2) being the same as *b* in Hebrew which often signifies "about" or "near" (Gen. 2:2; Ex. 12:15) and must be translated by "at" or "about" (viz., the carrying away being at hand). Or *epi* is not to be referred to the more remote word "begat," but to the nearer "his brethren" (*epi metoikesias* for *ek metoikesias*, by an enallage of the preposition which is very frequent, for *tous ek metoikesias* who were of the carrying away, i.e., "among those who were carried away to Babylon").

XX. Although it is said that Jeconiah begat Salathiel (Matt. 1:12) and that Salathiel was the "son of Neri" (Luke 3:27), there is no contradiction. There were different Salathiels, one the son of Jeconiah (of whom Matthew speaks), the other the son of Neri (of whom Luke speaks); the former of the line of Solomon, the latter of that of Nathan. And since the ancestors of Salathiel even to David with Luke were entirely different from those of Salathiel with Matthew, it is probable that they speak of different persons. Nor is it any objection that both the Salathiel in Matthew and in Luke are said to be the father of Zerubbabel because there might be also two Zerubbabels, as there is a similar repetition of two or more succeeding each other in the same order (Luke 3:24), Matthat and Levi (Luke 3:29; 1 Chron. 6:7–8), and the same thing is repeated concerning their four grandsons (1 Chron. 6:12).

XXI. Concerning *k'ry* (Ps. 22:17), the passage is not inextricable (*alytos*). For even if the common reading is retained, we must not therefore suppose there is a corruption, but only an anomaly of writing, where the aleph is added by epenthesis, as often elsewhere (*r'mh* for *rmh*, "it shall be lifted up"—Zech. 14:10) and waw is changed into yodh (letters which might very easily be mistaken for each other); "they had taken," *ns'v* for *ns'y* (Ezra 10:44). Marinus calls that letter not yodh, but waw diminutive, and thinks it is put to indicate clearly the marks of the nails of Christ (*Arca Noe* [1593], Pars I, p. 332 on *khrh*). Hence in the royal manuscripts it is written with the yodh pointed, as if it was yodh shurek (*k'ry*) instead of waw shurek as in Jeremiah 50:11. (2) It is confirmed by this—that the Masoretes tell us the word *k'ry* with kamets under the kaph occurs only twice in the Bible and then with a different signification. But Isaiah 38:13 (where it occurs once) cannot be rendered otherwise than "as a lion." Therefore it must be explained here with a different sense; and this since the connection (*allēlouchia*) of the words can be no other than that which is commonly given to it (viz., "they have pierced"). (3) In the great Masora a list is given of words in pairs, written alike, but differing in signification, among which is found that which occurs in Isaiah 38 and this. Hence the signification with the psalmist should be different from that with Isaiah. (4) The most ancient versions so render it. The Septuagint has *ōryxan*; so also the Arabic, Syriac and Ethiopic. (5) The scope of the psalm is to treat about the design of Christ's enemies in his crucifixion which is evident from the parting of garments and casting lots upon his vesture. But who can believe that the principal thing (and the most important of all) should be passed over in silence? (6) The connection of the words demands it; for if we read "as a lion," there would be a hiatus and no sense—"my hands and feet as a lion." There must be some word to complete the sentence and that word can be no other than *krv* ("they pierced") to which the prophecy of Zechariah 12:10 has reference: "they shall look upon him whom they have pierced." (7) Even if we should grant that this passage has been tampered with by the Jews, it would not follow that the corruption is universal because the Masoretes testify that they found the word *k'rv* written in the more approved manuscripts (the marginal Masora to Num. 24:9). And Jacob Ben-Haiim, the collector of the work of the Venetian Masoretes, found written in some corrected copies (i.e., occurring in the text *k'rv*, but read [i.e., placed in the margin] *k'ry*). John Isaac, a converted Jew, testifies that in the Psaltery of his grandfather he found the same thing. This is confirmed by Capito (*Institutionum Hebraicarum* 1.7 [1525], 22). We will believe the papists (who say that the Complutensian Bible has it) and Genebrardus (proved by the testimony of many Jews) that it was so read.

XXII. David is said to have bought from Araunah the threshing floor and the oxen for fifty shekels of silver (2 Sam. 24:24). But in 1 Chronicles 21:25 mention is made of six hundred shekels of gold. The reconciliation is easy from the subject of the purchase. He gave fifty shekels for that part of the threshing floor on which at first he built an altar. After he knew from the fire which fell down from heaven that this was the place God had selected for building a house, not content now with that small threshing floor, he bought the whole field and mountain for six hundred shekels.

XXIII. In 2 Samuel 24:13, seven years of famine are mentioned by God to David as a divine punishment. But in 1 Chronicles 21:12, there is mention of only three. But they may very easily be reconciled by saying either that God at first mentioned seven years which afterwards (David manifesting so much feeling) were reduced to three in answer to the prayer of God or of David (as in Gen. 18:24–32, the number of fifty just persons is reduced to ten). Or that in the number seven (mentioned in the book of Samuel) are included the three years of famine which had already passed by, having been sent to avenge the Gibeonites (which is treated of in 2 Sam. 21:1 together with the closing year). But in the book of Chronicles, mention is made only of the three years which were to come (so think Kimchi, Peter Martyr and Junius).

XXIV. Jehoiachin is said to have commenced his reign when he was eighteen years old (2 Kings 24:8). But in 2 Chronicles 36:9, it is said that he was only eight. That is, in this eighth year he began to reign with his father since it was the custom of the kings at that time (i.e., the fathers to associate their sons with them in office, so that the lawful heir to the throne might as early as possible be designated and acknowledged). But in the eighteenth year (at his father's death) his reign commenced. So Wolphius (cf. Peter Martyr, *Melachim . . . Regum Libri duo* [1599], 409), Sanctius and others (following Kimchi) reconcile these passages. Abrabanel wishes the ten days which are added in the book of Chronicles to be taken for ten years (as often elsewhere). He thinks this is very probable for the following reason: otherwise the day in which kings reigned were not usually mentioned, but only the years or months.

XXV. Many think there is an insoluble contradiction between 2 Chronicles 22:2 and 2 Kings 8:26 where Jehoram, the father of Ahaziah is said to have begun his reign in the thirty-second year of his age (2 Chron. 21:5) and to have reigned eight years, so that he died in the fortieth year of his age (v. 20). But Ahaziah is said to have begun to reign in his forty-second year (2 Chron. 22:2), and thus the son is made older than the father by two years. Again he is said to have begun to reign in his twenty-second and not in his forty-second year (2 Kings 8:26). Yet this is not the opinion of all; nor are there wanting various methods of reconciling them. Some (as Junius and Tremellius, following Rabbi Levi ben Gerson) maintain that in the book of Kings the true year of Ahaziah's age (in which he began to reign, and the length of his life) is told. But in Chronicles not the duration of his own life, but of his mother Omri's family (from the time he began to reign even to his death which happened in this very year by a remarkable judgment of God, on account of the memory

369

of this singular miracle or calculation) is given to Ahaziah who in the same year, with the rest of the family of Ahab and Omri, was slain by the sword of Jehu. For Omri reigned six years in Israel (1 Kings 16:23), Ahab his son twenty-two years (1 Kings 16:29); Ahaziah the son of Ahab two years, Joram his son twelve years—added together these amount to forty-two. But in the twelfth year of Joram, king of Israel, Ahaziah, king of Judah, began to reign (2 Kings 8:25). Some of this same opinion think there is a transposition in 2 Chronicles 22:1 and that they should stand thus: "his mother's name also was Athaliah, the daughter of Omri" (i.e., the granddaughter, being the daughter of Ahab, the son of Omri) "who was in her forty-second year when Ahaziah began to reign." But because this transposition appears rather forced and obscure, others think it would be better to refer the forty-two years not to Omri but to Athaliah herself and thus read: "his mother's name was Athaliah (the daughter of Omri) who was forty-two years old." For there was nothing which more closely concerned either Ahaziah or the state of the Jewish kingdom than the rise of the woman Athaliah, born for the destruction not only of her husband and children, but also for the whole kingdom and especially of the royal progeny. Others, to whom this reconciliation also appears rather forced, add another: Joram, the father of Ahaziah, in addition to the years of his reign and life mentioned in Scripture, lived and reigned twenty years more, but he may be said to have reigned only eight years *bhchzqthv* ("in his strength," i.e., well and happily). However from the time that he fell into the hands of the Arabians and was seized with a terrible disease (2 Chron. 21:16–17, 19), he lived for some years which are not reckoned in his reign, but in that of his son Ahaziah in the book of Kings because he lived ingloriously. Hence it is said that he departed without being desired and was not buried in the sepulchers of the kings (2 Chron. 21:20). But Ahaziah (who began to reign with his father in the twenty-second year of his age) after the death of his father in his forty-second year, reigned alone and only one year (2 Chron. 22:2). So Kimchi, Martyr, Vatablus, Lyranus and others explain it, and this is the opinion of Jerome (*Paralipomenon*, PL 28.1451–52). Others maintain that there is a mistake in the book of Chronicles, attributable not to the sacred writers but to copyists, which easily crept in by their carelessness in the abbreviated writing (*brachygraphia*) which often occurs in the recension of numbers, so that *mb* (which means forty-two) is put for *kb* (which denotes twenty-two). But they deny that on this account the passage is inexplicable (*alyton*) because the knot can be easily untied, and the true reading restored from a comparison of the book of Kings, which gives the number answering to the truth of history and of the years of Joram and Ahaziah. And it is evident that the different versions of the book of Chronicles retain the number twenty-two; as the Syriac, Arabic and many Greek manuscripts—the Oxford, Cambridge and Roman.

XXVI. In Exodus 12:40, it is said the sojourning of the children of Israel in Egypt was four hundred and thirty years. Yet in Genesis 15:13, it is foretold that the posterity of Abraham should be afflicted by strangers four hundred years (which is confirmed in Acts 7:6). The answer is easy. Genesis 15 gives the round number instead of the odd, as is often done both by the sacred and by profane writers. Therefore although from the time at which this prophecy was given to Abraham (from which this number was to begin) 430 years ought in fact to roll around; yet only four hundred are mentioned, as a round number and the odd thirty are left out. Because if the Israelites are said to have dwelt in Egypt 430 years (Ex. 12:40), it does not follow that they remained for as many years in Egypt. It is evident that their stay was only 210 years, but the affliction of the Israelites is referred to Egypt because the beginning of it was from Genesis 12:10 and the end; or because it was of longer continuance, more severe, posterior and rendered remarkable by the reign of Joseph, the multiplication of the Hebrews, and their most weighty oppression and stupendous liberation.

XXVII. The servants of Solomon are said to have fetched from Ophir four hundred and twenty talents of gold (1 Kings 9:28). But in 2 Chronicles 8:18, four hundred and fifty are mentioned. They can readily be reconciled if we say that he speaks not of the same but different removals because Solomon sent ships there every three years (1 Kings 10:22); or because the thirty talents were not brought to the king, but appropriated to the fleet.

XXVIII. The prophecy concerning the thirty pieces of silver and the field bought with them is cited from Jeremiah (Matt. 27:9), which is certainly found in Zechariah 11:12. From this some attribute universal falsehood and slips of the memory (*sphalma mnēmonikon*) to Matthew. But the difficulty can be cleared up in various ways. Some are of the opinion that the name Jeremiah (*Ieremiou*) has crept into the text from the ignorance of transcribers (since *zou* may have been written as an abbreviation of *Zachariou*), but that the error is one of small importance (viz., occurring in a proper name the correction of which is easily made from a comparison of the Old and New Testaments). Others (with better reason) maintain that there is here a blending (*synchysin*) of two prophetical passages from which this testimony is drawn, viz., from Jer. 32 and Zech. 11. Cases similar to this occur in: Matt. 21:5 from Isa. 62:11 and Zech. 9:9; Matt. 21:13 from Isa. 56:7 and Jer. 7:11; Acts 1:20 from Pss. 69:25 and 109:8; 1 Peter 2:7–8 from Ps. 118:22 and Isa. 8:14. Nor is it an unusual thing (when the words or testimonies belong to two persons) to omit one and give only the name of the other (as Mark 1:2–3 where the first part is taken from Malachi, the latter from Isaiah, and yet Malachi is omitted and Isaiah alone mentioned). And this can be done with greater propriety when the one who is cited is either more ancient than the other, and the later has drawn many things from him (as is the case here). For Jeremiah was before Zechariah, and Zechariah borrowed many things from him and imitated (as it were) his addresses (as might easily be shown from Zech. 1:14 which is taken from Jer. 18:11 and 35:15; and Zech. 3:8 from Jer. 23:5). Hence the Jews were in the habit of saying, "the spirit of Jeremiah is in Zechariah." To this it can be added that from the tradition of the Rabbi's in the Babylonion Talmud (Baba Bathra, 14, cf. BT 1:70) which Rabbi David Kimchi quotes in his preface to the prophet Jeremiah, Jeremiah stands at the head of the prophets and is therefore named first (Matt. 16:14). Therefore Matthew (citing these words contained in the book of the prophets) could quote them only under his name because he held the first place there. So in Luke 24:44, the book of holy writings (*Hagiographorum*) is mentioned under the name of the Psalms because this is the first of them. Finally, Jeremiah alone might be mentioned here by Matthew because he wished to give an account, not so much of the thirty pieces of silver or of the price for which Christ was bought (about which Zechariah treats), as of the price of the bought field (about which Jeremiah treats). Therefore what is said here of the price is drawn from Zechariah, and what is said of the field from Jeremiah.

XXIX. A difficult and indeed an intricate knot arises from the collation of Genesis 11:26 with Acts 7:4. In untying this, Joseph Scaliger himself gives up in despair (*epechei*) and does not endeavor to explain it ("Animadversiones in Chronologica Eusebi," in *Thesaurus temporum* [1606/1968], 2:17). Jerome (*Liber Hebraicarum quaestionum in Genesim*, PL 23.1006) and Augustine (*City of God* 16.15 [FC 14:516–19]) confess the difficulty to be insoluble. But there are not wanting fit methods of solution to satisfy humbly inquiring minds. The difficulty consists in this: that Moses says that Abram was born in the seventieth year of Terah (Gen. 11:26), and Stephen expressly asserts that Abraham removed from Haran to Canaan after the death of Terah (Acts 7:4). Now it is plain from Genesis 12:4 that Abraham departed from Haran in his seventy-fifth year, and his father Terah lived to the age of two hundred and five years (Gen. 11:32). Now if it is evident that Abraham was born in the seventieth year of Terah's age and went to Haran in the seventy-fifth year of his own age, he would not have departed after the death of his father (as Stephen said) but sixty years before (i.e., in the one hundred and forty-fifth year of Terah's age). Some suppose that there is here a slip of Stephen's memory in the computation of time, but that it does not impair the credibility (*autopiston*) of Luke's history because he was bound to relate faithfully the words of Stephen and was not anxious about correcting his error. But as it is certain that Stephen, being full of the Spirit, was also inspired (*theopneuston*), he cannot be convicted of error without impairing the credibility (*autopistia*) of the word. Others maintain that the birth of Abram must not be assigned exactly to the seventieth year of Terah's age, but to the hundred and thirtieth year; and that the contrary cannot be gathered from what is said in Genesis 11:26 ("Terah lived seventy years, and begat Abraham, Nahor, and Haran") because although he is placed first, this was not done on account of his age but on account of his importance (as in Gen. 5:32 it is said, "Noah in his five hundredth year begat Shem, Ham and Japheth," i.e., began to beget his three sons, the most illustrious of whom was Shem, although born one or two years after Japheth, the elder). So Terah in his seventieth year began to beget his three sons, the most illustrious of whom was Abram. Therefore he is placed first, though not the firstborn. According to this opinion, Abram (born in the hundred and thirtieth year of Terah's age) lived with him partly in Chaldea, partly in Haran for seventy-five years, even until his death; after which (according to the command of God received in Chaldea) he departed with his family from Haran to Canaan. But others (to whom the postponing of the birth of Abraham to Terah's 130th year appears forced because the Bible says nothing about it and the whole genealogy of Abram would thus be rendered uncertain), in the face of Moses' particular care to have it right, solve the difficulty otherwise. They maintain that there were two calls of Abram: the first from Ur of the Chaldees to Haran, his father being alive and in his 145th year, and Abraham in his seventy-fifth (of which Moses speaks, Gen. 11:31; 12:1). But the other (after the death of his father) from Haran to Canaan which appears to be intimated in Gen. 12:4–5. Stephen indeed plainly refers to this when he says, "Abraham called of God came out of the land of the Chaldeans, and dwelt in Haran; and afterwards and from thence, when his father was dead, he removed him into Canaan" (Acts 7:4). Here God is said to have called him twice: first from Ur of the Chaldees to Haran; afterwards from Haran to Canaan. This seems to be a fit and easy solution of the difficulty. Finally, some think there is an error in the enumeration of the years of Terah's age, which did not reach to 205 years but only to 145, as the Samaritan Pentateuch reads. Eusebius (*Chronicorum* 1.16 [PG 19.157–58]) mentions this: *kata to Samarikon Hebraikon Tharra genomenos etōn o genna ton Abraam kai epezēsen etē oe mechris oe etous Abraam*, "When Terah was seventy years old he begat Abraham and lived afterwards seventy-five years, even to the seventy-fifth year of Abraham." They conjecture that the error arose from mistaking the letter mem, which denotes forty, for kaph, which means one hundred, giving rise to a difference of sixty years. But since it is the common opinion of both Jews and Christians that only the Hebrew Pentateuch and not the Samaritan is authentic, no one would be willing to say that the former should be corrected by the latter.

XXX. If it is asked how the passage where seventy Israelites are said to have gone down to Egypt (Gen. 46:27) can be reconciled with Acts 7:14 (where seventy-five are enumerated), different answers can be given. Some think there is no discrepancy because the places are not parallel, viz., that Moses gives the genealogy of Jacob; or only a catalogue of the posterity coming from his own loins and descending into Egypt with him, the wives of his sons being left out. Thus they are said to have been sixty-six (Gen. 46:26). From this number are to be excluded Joseph and his two sons (who did not go with him into Egypt because they were already there), and Er and Onan (who had died in Canaan) and Dinah, his daughter. Added for the whole number of the sons and grandsons of Jacob, these amounted to seventy-one, from which number if you take five, sixty-six will remain. But in v. 27, Moses gives the catalogue of the whole family, both of those who went down with him into Egypt and of those who were already there (i.e., Joseph and his sons) to whom if you add Jacob, the head of the family, you will have the number seventy. Now Stephen wished to show how many Joseph had called down to Egypt and therefore excluded Joseph with his two sons and the two grandsons of Judah, Hezron and Hamul (Gen. 46:12) who were born in Egypt. But he reckons Jacob by himself, distinguishing him from his relatives (*syngeneia*). So there remain eleven brothers (the sons of Jacob) with Dinah, their sister; fifty-two grandsons, to which are added the eleven wives of his sons (who belonged to his kindred, *tēn syngeneian*); thus we will have the number of seventy-five souls. Others maintain that the passage is corrupted, that Stephen did not say, nor Luke write, *pente*, but *pantes*, which word Moses also expresses in Genesis 46:27, "all the souls." Thus the passage should be translated "who all" (i.e., taken together, there were "seventy" souls) or *pantōs* ("altogether"). But from the carelessness of transcribers *pantes* might easily have been written instead of *pantōs* or *pantōs pente*, both by the Septuagint and by Luke and yet the authenticity of Scripture be preserved. From the comparison with other passages and from the analogy of faith, it could easily be emended and the faith of the doctrine and of the history remain no less safe on that account. Again, others suppose that Stephen did not follow the Hebrew text here, but the Septuagint as the more common and everywhere received—this has the number seventy-five—and that he did not think an attention to the number belonged to what he was speaking about and that the Septuagint collected this number from the five sons of Joseph added from 1 Chronicles 7:14–27, whom Moses does not mention and who were born after going down into Egypt (viz., Machir, Gilead, Shuthelah, Toben and Eden). But whether Stephen followed the Septuagint here or the error in the Septuagint and in Acts crept in through the carelessness of transcribers, it is nevertheless certain that the error is not incurable, since it is easily corrected from the Hebrew text. For Scripture ought to be explained by Scripture.

XXXI. Stephen speaks thus of the patriarchs: "And were carried over into Sychem, and laid in the sepulcher that Abraham bought for a sum of money of the sons of Emmor (*tou Sychem*)" (Acts 7:16). But from Genesis 23:9–10, it is plain that Abraham bought the sepulcher from Ephron near the city of Hebron. From Genesis 33:19 (cf. Josh. 24:32), it appears that not Abraham, but Jacob bought the field of the sons of Hamor, not for a sum of money but for an hundred lambs. Hence an inextricable difficulty seems to arise. Yet it can be cleared up easily, if we say that Stephen did not refer to the purchase of Abraham recorded in Genesis 23:9, but to that of Jacob: "And Jacob came safe to the city of Shechem and bought a parcel of a field at the hand of the children of Hamor, Shechem's father, for an hundred lambs" (Gen. 33:19). This is where Joseph is said to have been buried (Josh. 24:32). Nor can it be objected to this that Stephen says Abraham bought the field and not Jacob. Either Abraham may here be the genitive so as to read *ho tou Abraam* (understand *ekgonos*); or Abraham is used patronymically for a descendant of Abraham (i.e., for Jacob, his grandson). Oftentimes the names of the fathers are put to designate their posterity even when there is a reference to individuals; as David is put for Rehoboam, his grandson ("What portion have we in David?" 1 Kings 12:16); and Rehoboam for Abijah (1 Kings 14:6); and David for Christ (Jer. 30:9; Ezek. 34:23) (cf. Virgil, *Aeneid* 4.660–62 [Loeb, 1:440–41], where Aeneas is called "Dardanus" for a descendant of Dardanus). Or with Beza, we must suppose the name Abraham to be a gloss, which having been written by a sciolist in the margin, afterwards crept into the text (*Annotationes maiores in novum . . . Testamentum, Pars prior* [1594], 482 on Acts 7:16). Thus not Abraham, but Jacob is said to have bought this field. Nor can it be objected that the fathers are said to have been carried over into Sychem when only Joseph is said to have been buried there. For Moses mentions Joseph alone because he only was a prophet and foresaw the deliverance and sought by faith that his bones might be carried away to Canaan (Heb. 11:22), for which he also provided by an oath (Gen. 50:25). Hence it became him to record this because in this way the Israelites freed themselves from this sacred charge (Ex. 13:19). Yet Stephen could speak in the plural by an enallage of number or by a synecdoche of the whole (as often occurs in Scripture). In Matthew 26:8, the disciples are said to have "indignation" which must be understood of Judas Iscariot alone (who alone was indignant at the pouring out of the ointment, as John 12:4–6 explains it). In Matthew 27:44, the thieves are said to have cast the same in the teeth of Christ on the cross (which relates to only one of them, according to Luke 23:39). Again, although Moses does not expressly say so, yet it can easily be inferred that the other brothers of Joseph were buried in the same place because the Jews held all the patriarchs in equal regard and reverence. The same cause which moved Joseph to desire this, they all had (viz., faith in the promise of God, possessions in the land and the hope of resurrection). It is proper to bring in here what Jerome relates (*The Pilgrimage of the Holy Paula* [1887], 13; CCL 55.322) that having turned aside to Shechem, she saw there the sepulchers of the twelve patriarchs. This testimony (being that of an eyewitness) is preferable to that of Josephus (*Jewish Antiquities* 2.199 [Loeb, 4:251]) who says that the patriarchs were buried at Hebron. Nor is it any objection that the father of Sychem is not in the text (as in Gen. 33:19), but simply *tou Sychem*. For with propriety, the word "father" can be supplied, as is often the case elsewhere: Luke 24:10, "Mary of James" (i.e., the mother of James); Herodotus, *Kyros ho Kambyseō*, "Cyrus the father of Cambyses" (Herodotus, *Histories* 1.73 [Loeb, 1:88–89]); *Olympias hē Alexandrou*, "Olympia the mother of Alexander" (cf. Herodotus, *Histories* 5.22 [Loeb, 3:22–23]). Finally, it is no objection that Jacob is said to have bought the field for an hundred lambs according to Moses, but with Luke the field is said to have been bought for a sum of money. For the word *ksyth* denotes money as well as a lamb because coins were then stamped with the figure of a lamb; as in ancient times all money bore the figure of animals because before the use of coins merchandise was exchanged for cattle (see Rabbi David Kimchi on the word *ksyth*;

Johannes Buxtorf [the elder], *Lexicon Chaldaicum, Talmudicum, et Rabbinicum* [1640], 2159–60; Bochart, *Hierozoicon* [1663], 437).

XXXII. There is no contradiction between 2 Corinthians 11:4 and Galatians 1:8 because in the latter it is not said that there is "another gospel" really and as to truth than that preached by the apostles; but in the former only by an impossible supposition, not that it is really granted or can be granted, but to take away all excuse from the Corinthians for their readiness to receive false apostles. As if Paul had said, "If it could happen that coming to you, he could bring another Jesus and another gospel more perfectly, you would rightly receive and accept such a teacher and despise us. But since this is altogether impossible (as you yourselves acknowledge and the false apostles do not dare to deny), you have no excuse to offer."

XXXIII. It is said, "There was nothing in the ark save the two tables of stone" (1 Kings 8:9), and in Hebrews 9:4 the apostle says there were other things in the same place when he writes "in it" (that is in the ark of which he had just spoken) "was the golden pot that had manna, and Aaron's rod that budded, and the tables of the covenant." There occurs no contradiction and the difficulty will be at once removed, if we say that *en hē* refers not to the nearest word *kibōton* ("the ark"), but to the more remote, *skēnēn* (v. 3). We know that the relative is sometimes referred not to the nearest antecedent, but to the more remote; or that the preposition *en* does not here mean "in" (as if the manna and the rod of Aaron were in the ark itself), but "with" or "near" and "at"; and so answers to the Hebrew preposition *b*, which does not always imply that one thing is inside of another, but also that which is added to another and adheres to it. The latter sometimes means "with," as "thou shalt talk with (*bm*) them" (Deut. 6:7); "with bullocks" (*bprym*, 1 Sam. 1:24); "in," that is, "with the beasts" (Hos. 4:3); so "with the glory" (*en doxa*, Matt. 16:27); "in the voice, in the trump," for "with" (1 Thess. 4:16); at others it means "at" or "near"; at Gibeon (Josh. 10:10); "in Kirjath-jearim" (Judg. 18:12), i.e., near that place; "those that bought and sold" are said to have been "in the temple," i.e., in its porches (Matt. 21:12); as also Christ is said to have "walked in the temple," i.e., in Solomon's porch (John 10:23); and elsewhere to have suffered "in Jerusalem" (i.e., near it). So it can well be translated "in" or "near" which ark were the urn and the rod to denote not the placing of them in, but near it; or "with which," i.e., to which ark the pot and rod and the tables of the covenant were joined, but in different ways: the tables indeed within, but the pot and rod without or by the side of the ark.

XXXIV. When Christ forbids us to swear *holōs* ("altogether," Matt. 5:34), he does not intend absolutely and simply to condemn oaths which elsewhere are permitted and approved and even commanded by God (Ex. 22:8, 10–11; Lev. 5:4; Num. 5:19–20; Prov. 18:18 [?]; Heb. 6:16). But only particular kinds of oaths are condemned by Christ as rash and unlawful (i.e., those which the Jews were in the habit of using, of which he speaks in the same place, viz., by "heaven, earth, Jerusalem," the head and other such created things). Universal terms are often restricted to a particular class "all that ever came before me are thieves" (John. 10:8), viz., all those not called or sent, or those saying that they, or some other person, were the door of the sheep. And "all things are lawful for me" (1 Cor. 10:23); "I am made all things to all men" (1 Cor. 9:22), viz., in things lawful and indifferent—for evil and wicked things are not lawful to any person or at any time.

XXXV. Saul is said to have reigned forty years (Acts 13:21), but in 1 Samuel 13:1, only two years. The answer is that it is not said in 1 Samuel 13:1 that Saul reigned only two years, but that he had reigned only two years when he chose the three thousand men mentioned in the following verse. When he had reigned two years, he collected together these military men (his two years then being at an end as the Syrian and Arabian versions show).

XXXVI. From what has been said, it is evident that those different apparently contradictory (*enantiophanē*) passages adduced to destroy the authenticity (*authentian*) of the Scriptures and introduced by us as specimens (although difficult and hard to be understood [*dysnoēta*]) are not altogether inexplicable (*alyta*). There are also some others brought forward by papists to prove the corruption of the sources by Jews or heretics, but they will be satisfactorily disposed of when we speak of the authentic edition.

Sixth Question

From what source does the divine authority of the Scriptures become known to us? Does it depend upon the testimony of the church either as to itself or as to us? We deny against the papists.

OCCASION OF THE QUESTION

I. The object of the papists in this and other controversies set forth by them concerning the Scriptures, is obvious, viz., to avoid the tribunal of Scripture (in which they do not find sufficient help for the defense of their errors) and to appeal to the church (i.e., to the pope himself) and thus become judges in their own cause. Hence, as we treated before of the doctrine of Scripture (whether it agreed with itself or not), we must now inquire concerning the Scriptures themselves whether it is proper that religious controversies should be decided by their authority and testimony. For this purpose a sharp discussion has been kept up concerning its origin and necessity, its perfection and perspicuity, the integrity and purity of the canon and especially concerning its authority; if not entirely to destroy it, nevertheless to weaken it greatly. Thus what Irenaeus says concerning the heretics of his day is appropriate to them: "When they are convicted from Scripture, they turn round and accuse the Scripture, as being corrupt, and having no authority" (Irenaeus, *Against Heresies* 3.2 [ANF 1:415; PG 7.846]).

SOME PAPISTS SPEAK HARSHLY; OTHERS MORE CALMLY

II. But we must here observe that some speak roughly, others more calmly on this subject. For some (*gymnē tē kephalē*, without wish of concealment) altogether deny the authenticity (*authentian*) of Scripture in itself without the testimony of the church and think it worthy of no more belief (I shudder to relate) than the Koran, Titus Livy or the fables of Aesop. In a former age those who undertook to dispute with our men concerning the authority of Scripture belched forth these blasphemies. Such are the impious words of Hosius against Brentius ("Confutatio Prolegomenon Brentii," in *Opera* [1583], 1:530). He asserts that it can be said in a pious sense that "the Scriptures have only as much force as the fables of Aesop, if destitute of the authority of the church." Eck says that "the Scriptures are not authentic, except by authority of the church" (*Enchiridion of Commonplaces* 1 [trans. F. L. Battles, 1979], 13, "On the Church and her Authority"). Baile says that "without the authority of the church we should no more believe Matthew than Titus Livy" (cf. André Rivet, *Sommaire de toutes les controverses touchant la religion* [1615], 217). Andradius says, "There is nothing of divinity in the books in which the sacred mysteries are written and that there cannot be found in them anything to bind us to religion and to believe what they contain; but that the power and dignity of the church are so great as that no one without the greatest impiety can resist it" (*Defensio tridentinae fidei catholicae* 3 [1580]). Stapleton says, "The church must be considered in such a light, as that we ought not to believe the testimony in any other way than the apostles believed the testimony of Christ, and that God is not be believed except on account of the church" (*adversus Whittakerum* [1620], bk. 1, ch. 7). But because others saw that this was deservedly censured by our men as impious and blasphemous, they have spoken more cautiously in thus declaring their opinion. They confess the Scriptures absolutely and in themselves to be authentic and divine, as coming from God (the source of all truth), but yet they say that (relatively and as to us) they have not that authority except on account of the testimony of the church, through whose kindness they become known and are received by us as divine. Hence arose the distinction of authority ("as to itself" [absolute] and "as to us" [relative]) which Bellarmine ("De conciliis Auctoritate," 2.12 in *Opera* [1857], 2:61), Stapleton ("De principiis fidei doctrinalibus controversia," Cont. 5.1 in *Opera* [1620], 1:311–12 and "Authoritatis ecclesiasticae," 2.11 in *Opera* [1620], 1:1019–24) and others have advanced.

III. But in whatever manner they explain their opinion (if we properly consider the thing itself), we will find that this distinction has been framed to deceive and to remove the odium attaching to their impious doctrine rather than to unfold the truth of the thing itself. As authority belongs to the genus of things related *ek tōn pros ti*, it should not be considered absolutely but relatively. Therefore Scripture cannot be authentic in itself without being so as to us. For the same arguments which prove it authoritative in itself ought to induce us to assent to its authenticity as to us; but if its authority as to us is suspended upon the church as the formal reason for which I believe the Scriptures to be divine, it follows that its authority as to itself must also be suspended upon the same. Indeed others have more plainly confessed this. That this is really their opinion may be satisfactorily gathered from the other controversies in which they here engage. For how could they deny either its perfection or perspicuity or purity, if they believed it to be authentic in itself.

STATEMENT OF THE QUESTION

IV. To exhibit the state of the question, the question is not whether the Bible is authentic and divine, for this our opponents do not deny or at least wish to appear to believe. Rather, the question is, Whence is it made known to us as such, or by what argument can this inspiration be proved to us? The papists suspend this authority upon the testimony of the church and maintain that the principal motive by which we are induced to believe the authenticity (*authentian*) of the Scriptures is the voice of the church. But although we do not deny that the testimony of the church has its own weight (as will afterwards be seen), yet we maintain that primarily and principally the Bible is believed by us to be divine on account of itself (or the marks impressed upon it), not on account of the church.

V. Second, it is not asked concerning the foundation or efficient cause of the faith by which we believe the divinity of the Scriptures (i.e., whether the Holy Spirit applies it to us or not). For this belongs to another question concerning free will, and our opponents acknowledge it with us (Stapleton, "Triplicatio inchoate . . . adversus Whitakerum," 9 in *Opera* [1620], 1:1166–71; Canus, "De locis theologicis," 2.8 in *Opera* [1605], 41–53). Rather the question concerns the argument or principal motive which the Spirit uses in persuading us of its truth; whether it is the direct argument of the testimony of the church (as the papists say) or the rational, derived from the marks of the Scripture itself (which we hold).

VI. As a threefold cause can be granted for the manifestation of anything (an objective, efficient and instrumental or organic), so a threefold question can arise about the divinity of the Bible: the first, concerning the argument on account of which I believe; the second, concerning the principle or efficient cause from which I am led to believe; the third, concerning the means and instrument through which I believe. And to this triple question a triple reply can be given. For the Bible with its own marks is the argument on account of which I believe. The Holy Spirit is the efficient cause and principle from which I am induced to believe. But the church is the instrument and means through which I believe. Hence if the question is why, or on account of what, do I believe the Bible to be divine, I will answer that I do so on account of the Scripture itself which by its marks proves itself to be such. If it is asked whence or from what I believe, I will answer from the Holy Spirit who produces that belief in me. Finally, if I am asked by what means or instrument I believe it, I will answer through the church which God uses in delivering the Scriptures to me.

VII. Third, the question does not concern the motive or the introductory (*eisagōgikō*) and ministerial (*leitourgikō*) means, whose assistance the Holy Spirit uses in persuading us of the authority of the Scriptures. This we readily concede to the church. Rather the question concerns the principal argument and motive by which we are brought to faith (not human, but divine) which they place in the church. We believe it is not to be found out of Scripture itself.

VIII. Fourth, the question is not whether divine revelation is the formal reason (simply and absolutely) of our faith, for this our opponents acknowledge with us. Rather the question is What is that first and clearest revelation with respect to us which ought to be received through and on account of itself, and not on account of some other better known to us and therefore the most common and the first principle of faith by which all things ought to be proved, but itself by none prior to it whether that revelation is to be looked for in the Scriptures or in the church? We think that revelation to be contained in the Bible itself which is the first and infallible truth and rule of faith. But papists maintain that it must be sought in the voice and testimony of the church. Stapleton says, "Now therefore the voice of the church is the supreme external testimony on earth" ("Auctoritatis ecclesiasticae," 1.8 in *Opera* [1620], 1:893); and "God speaking by the church speaks not otherwise than if he spoke immediately by visions and dreams, or some other supernatural manner of revelation" (ibid., 1.9, p. 902); and "the whole formal reason of our faith is God revealing by the church" (ibid., 1.14.12, p. 926). Gretser says, "the testimony of the church alone is a fit answer to the question, whence do you know that the Scripture is divinely revealed?" (?"Tractatus de Quaestione, Unde scis scripturam cum generatim . . . ," 7 in *Opera Omnia* [1734–41], 8:961–1003). Bellarmine says, "It is true that we do not certainly know what God has revealed except from the testimony of the church" (VD 3.10, response to argument 13, p. 114); and "Catholics believe what they do because God has revealed it, and they believe that God revealed it because they hear the church so speaking and declaring" ("De gratia et libero arbitrio," 6.3 in *Opera* [1858], 4:435–36).

IX. The question then amounts to this—why, or on account of what, do we believe that the Bible is the word of God; or what argument does the Holy Spirit principally use to convince us of the inspiration of the Scriptures? The testimony and voice of the church, or the marks impressed upon Scripture itself? Our opponents assert the former; we the latter.

THE AUTHORITY OF THE SCRIPTURES DOES NOT DEPEND UPON THE TESTIMONY OF THE CHURCH

X. That the authority of the Scriptures either as to itself or as to us does not depend upon the testimony of the church is proved: (1) because the church is built upon the Scripture (Eph. 2:20) and borrows all authority from it. Our opponents cannot deny this since, when we ask them about the church, they quickly fly to the Scriptures to prove it. Therefore the church cannot recommend the authority of Scripture either as to itself or as to us, unless we wish to make the cause depend upon the effect, the principle upon that which derived from it and the foundation upon the edifice. Nor ought the objection to be brought up here (that both may be true) that the church borrows its authority from the Scriptures, and the Scriptures in turn from the church (just as John bore testimony to Christ who also himself gave testimony to John). For it is one thing to give testimony to someone as a minister, as John testified concerning Christ, that through him (*di' autou*), not on account of him (*di' auton*), the Jews might believe (John 1:7). It is quite a different thing to give authority to him as a lord which Christ did to John. (2) The authority of the church would be prior to that of the Scriptures and so would be the first thing to be believed (upon which our faith at first would depend and into which it would finally be resolved), which our opponents, who make the authority of the church depend upon Scripture, would not admit. (3) A manifest circle would be made since the authority of the church is proved from Scripture, and in turn the authority of the Scripture from the church. (4) Our opponents are not yet agreed as to what is meant by the church—whether the modern or the ancient, the collective or the representative, a particular or the universal; or what is the act testifying concerning the authority of Scripture (whether enacted by some judicial sentence or exercised by a continuous and successive tradition). (5) A fallible and human testimony (as that of the church) cannot form the foundation of divine faith. And if God now speaks through the church, does it therefore follow that she is infallible because there is one kind of inspiration which is special and extraordinary (such as made the apostles and prophets infallible [*anamartētous*], and of which Christ speaks properly when he says that the Holy Spirit would lead the apostles into all truth, John 16:13); another common and ordinary which does not make pastors inspired (*theopneustous*).

BUT IS PROVED BY ITSELF

XI. That the Scripture makes itself known to us is proved: (1) by the nature of the Scripture itself. For as a law does not derive its authority from the subordinate judges who interpret it or from the heralds who promulgate it, but from its author alone—as a will obtains its weight not from the notary to whom it is entrusted, but from the purpose of the testator; as a rule has the power of ruling from its own innate perfection, not from the artificer who uses it—so the Scripture which is the law of the supreme lawgiver, the will of our heavenly Father and the inflexible (*aklinēs*) rule of faith, cannot have authority even as to us from the church, but only from itself. (2) By the nature of the highest genera and of first principles; for those things are known by themselves and are not susceptible (*anapodeikta*) of proof which cannot be demonstrated by any other, otherwise the thing would go on to infinity. Hence Basil says "it is necessary that the first principles of every science should be self-evident" (*anankē hekastēs mathēseōs anexetastous einai tas archas, In Psalmum cxv homilia*, PG 30.104–5). Thus Scripture, which is the first principle in the supernatural order, is known by itself and has no need of arguments derived from without to prove and make itself known to us. If God has stamped such marks upon all first principles that they can be known at once by all men, we cannot doubt that he has placed them upon this sacred first principle (in the highest degree necessary to our salvation). (3) By comparison, as objects of the sense presented to faculties well disposed are immediately distinguished and known without any other external argument, on account of a secret adaptation and propensity of the faculty to the object. Light is immediately most certainly known to us by its own brightness; food by its peculiar sweetness; an odor by its peculiar fragrance without any additional testimony. Thus the Scripture, which is set forth to us in respect to the new man and spiritual senses, now under the symbol of a clear light (Ps. 119:105), then of the most sweetest food (Ps. 19:10; Isa. 55:1–2; Heb. 5:14) and again of the sweetest smelling savor (Song 1:3), may easily be distinguished of itself by the senses of the new man as soon as it is presented to them and makes itself known by its own light, sweetness and fragrance (*euōdia*); so that there is no need to seek elsewhere for proof that this is light, food or a sweet smelling savor. (4) By the testimony of our opponents who prove the inspiration of the Scriptures by its own marks; Bellarmine says, "Nothing is better known, nothing more certain than the sacred Scriptures contained in the writings of the prophets and apostles, so that he must be in the highest degree foolish who refuses to believe in them" (VD 1.2, p. 24); see Cano, "De locis theologicis," 2.8 in *Opera* (1605), 41–53; Gregory de Valentia, *Analysis fidei catholicae* 1.15 (1585), 51–53; (Peter) Soto, *Defensio catholicae confessionis* 47 (1557), 56–58.

SOURCES OF EXPLANATION

XII. We do not deny that the church has many functions in relation to the Scriptures. She is: (1) the keeper of the oracles of God to whom they are committed and who preserves the authentic tables of the covenant of grace with the greatest fidelity, like a notary (Rom. 3:2); (2) the guide, to point out the Scriptures and lead us to them (Isa. 30:21); (3) the defender, to vindicate and defend them by separating the genuine books from the spurious, in which sense she may be called the ground (*hedraiōma*) of the truth (1 Tim. 3:15); (4) the herald who sets forth and promulgates them (2 Cor. 5:19; Rom. 10:16); (5) the interpreter inquiring into the unfolding of the true sense. But all these imply a ministerial only and not a magisterial power. Through her indeed, we believe, but not on account of her; as through John the Baptist the faithful believed in Christ, not on account of him (John 1:7); and through the Samaritan woman Christ was known by the Samaritans, not on account of her (John 4:39).

XIII. The resolution of faith objectively considered (as to the things to be believed) is different from its subjective or formal consideration (as to the act of believing). The former is in Scripture and the external testimony of the Holy Spirit expressed in Scripture; the latter in its internal testimony impressed upon the conscience and speaking in the heart. For as two things are necessary to the generating of faith (the presentation of truth in the word and the application of it in the heart), the Holy Spirit operates in both (i.e., in the word and in the heart). Therefore he is said properly to testify in the word objectively after the manner of an argument on account of which we believe. In the heart, he is also said (but with less propriety) to testify efficiently and after the manner of a first principle, by the power of which we believe. In this sense, the Spirit (who is reckoned among the witnesses of the divinity of Christ and of the truth of the gospel) is said to "bear witness that the Spirit is truth" (1 John 5:6), i.e., the Spirit working in the hearts of believers bears witness that the doctrine of the gospel delivered by the Spirit is true and divine.

XIV. Article 4 of the French Confession says, "We know that the books of Scripture are canonical, not so much from the common consent of the church, as from the internal testimony and persuasion of the Holy Spirit" (Cochrane, *Reformed Confessions*, 145). Hence, we must understand by the Holy Spirit, the Spirit's speaking both in the word and in the heart. For the same Spirit who acts objectively in the word by presenting the truth, operates efficiently in the heart also by impressing that truth upon our minds. Thus he is very different from a Spirit of enthusiasm.

XV. The private judgment of the Spirit (which is such subjectively with regard to the subject in which it inheres) is different from that which is such originally because it depends upon man's own will. The former we allow here, but not the latter. For the Spirit that testifies in us concerning the inspiration of the Scriptures is not peculiar to individuals with regard to the principle and origin. Rather he is common to the whole church and so to all believers in whom he works the same faith, although he is such subjectively with regard to each individual because he is given separately to each believer.

XVI. Although the church is more ancient than the Scriptures formally considered (and as to the mode of writing), yet it cannot be called such with respect to the Scriptures materially considered (and as to the substance of doctrine) because the word of God is more ancient than the church itself, being its foundation and seed. The question does not concern the testimony of the ancient church of the patriarchs (which existed before the Scriptures), but of the Christian church, long after them.

XVII. Although believers are persuaded by the testimony of the Holy Spirit of the inspiration of the Scriptures, it does not therefore follow that all who possess the Spirit should agree in receiving equally every book. Since he is not given to all in an equal measure, so neither does he furnish all with an equal knowledge both as to the principle of religion and as to its doctrines, nor move them to assent by an equal power. Hence some Protestants might doubt concerning one or another canonical book because they were not yet sufficiently enlightened by the Holy Spirit.

XVIII. It is not always necessary that a thing should be proved by something else. For there are some things which are self-evident according to the philosophers (as the highest categories of things, and ultimate differences and first principles) which are not susceptible of demonstration, but are evident by their own light and are taken for granted as certain and indubitable. If perchance anyone denies them, he is not to be met with arguments, but should be committed to the custody of his kinsmen (as a madman); or to be visited with punishment, as one (according to Aristotle) either lacking sense or needing punishment. Aristotle says there are certain axioms which do not have an external reason for their truth "which must necessarily be and appear to be such per se" (*ho anankē einai di' auto kai dokein anankē, Posterior analytics* 1.10 [Loeb, 70–71]); i.e., they are not only credible (*autopiston*) of themselves, but cannot be seriously denied by anyone of a sound mind. Therefore since the Bible is the first principle and the primary and infallible truth, is it strange to say that it can be proved by itself? The Bible can prove itself either one part or another when all parts are not equally called into doubt (as when we convince the Jews from the Old Testament); or the whole proving the whole, not by a direct argument of testimony (because it declares itself divine), but by that made artfully (*artificiali*) and ratiocinative (because in it are discovered divine marks which are not found in the writings of men). Nor is this a begging of the question because these criteria are something distinct from the Scriptures; if not materially, yet formally as adjuncts and properties which are demonstrated with regard to the subject. Nor is one thing proved by another equally unknown because they are better known by us; as we properly prove a cause from its effects, a subject by its properties. The argument of the papists that Scripture cannot be proved by itself (because then it would be more known and more unknown than itself) can with much greater force be turned against the church.

XIX. If any deny the inspiration of the Scriptures, it is not because the object in itself is not known or understandable, but because they are destitute of a well-disposed faculty. To them the gospel is hid because Satan has blinded their eyes (2 Cor. 4:4); as some deny God (who is most capable of being known) because they are fools, or do not see the sun because they are blind; as the blind woman in Seneca complained that the sun did not rise. Yet notwithstanding this the sun always sends forth his rays, which are perceived per se by those who have eyes.

XX. It is one thing to discern and to declare the canon of Scripture; quite another to establish the canon itself and to make it authentic. The church cannot do the latter (as this belongs to God alone, the author of Scripture), but it does only the former, which belongs to it ministerially, not magisterially. As the goldsmith who separates the dross from the gold (or who proves it by a touchstone) distinguishes indeed the pure from the adulterated, but does not make it pure (either as to us or as to itself), so the church by its test distinguishes indeed canonical books from those which are not and from apocryphal, but does not make them such. Nor can the judgment of the church give authority to the books which they do not possess of themselves; rather she declares the already existing authority by arguments drawn from the books themselves.

XXI. The knowledge of a thing may be confused or distinct. The church can be known before the Scriptures by a confused knowledge, but a distinct knowledge of the Scriptures ought to precede because the truth of the church can be ascertained only from the Scriptures. The church can be apprehended by us before the Scriptures by a human faith, as an assembly of men using the same sacred things; yet it can be known and believed as an assembly of believers and the communion of saints by a divine faith, only after the marks of the church which Scripture supplies have become known.

XXII. When the apostle says that "faith is by hearing" (Rom. 10:17), he does indeed give us to understand that the ministry of the church ought to come in as the ordinary means of producing faith in adults. He does not teach, however, that the church is clearer and better known than the Scriptures.

XXIII. To inquire concerning the number, the authors, parts and single words of the sacred books is different from inquiring concerning the fundamental doctrines contained in them. The latter knowledge pertains to every believer, but not the former. Nor will his salvation be in jeopardy who cannot tell who wrote the gospel of Matthew, provided he believes the book to be authentic and divine. The knowledge of the primary author of any book is one thing; that of the amanuensis is another. The latter belongs only to an historical faith, but the former to a divine.

XXIV. Since the circle (according to philosophers) is a sophistical argument (by which the same thing is proved by itself) and is occupied about the same kind of cause in a circuit coming back without end into itself, the circle cannot be charged upon us when we prove the Scriptures by the Spirit, and in turn the Spirit from the Scriptures. For here the question is diverse and the means or kind of cause is different. We prove the Scriptures by the Spirit as the efficient cause by which we believe. But we prove the Spirit from the Scriptures as the object and argument on account of which we believe. In the first, the answer is to the question Whence or by what power do you believe the Scriptures to be inspired? (viz., by the Spirit). But in the second, the answer is to the question Why or on account of what do you believe that the Spirit in you is the Holy Spirit? (viz., on account of the marks of the Holy Spirit which are in the Scriptures). But the papists (who charge the circle upon us) evidently run into it themselves in this question, when they prove the Scriptures by the church and the church by the Scriptures; for this is done by the same means and by the same kind of cause. If we ask why or on account of what they believe the Scriptures to be divine, they answer because the church says so. If we ask again, why they believe the church, they reply because the Scriptures ascribe infallibility to her when they call her the pillar and ground of the truth. If we press upon them whence they know this testimony of Scripture to be credible (*autopiston*), they add because the church assures us of it. Thus they are rolled back again to the commencement of the dispute and go on to infinity, never stopping in any first credible thing. Nor is the question here diverse. In both instances, the question concerns the reason and argument on account of which I believe; not the faculty or principle by which I believe.

XXV. The church is called "the pillar and ground of the truth" (*stylos kai hedraiōma tēs alētheias*, 1 Tim. 3:15) not because she supports and gives authority to the truth (since the truth is rather the foundation upon which the church is built, Eph. 2:20), but because it stands before the church as a pillar and makes itself conspicuous to all. Therefore it is called a pillar, not in an architectural sense (as pillars are used for the support of buildings), but in a forensic and political sense (as the edicts of the emperor and the decrees and laws of the magistrates were usually posted against pillars before the court houses and praetoria and before the gates of the basilica so that all might be informed of them, as noted by Pliny, *Natural History* 6.28 and Josephus, *Jewish Antiquities* 1.70–71 [Loeb, 4:32–33]). So the church is the pillar of the truth both by reason of promulgating and making it known (because she is bound to promulgate the law of God, and heavenly truth is attached to it so that it may become known to all) and by reason of guarding it. For she ought not only to set it forth, but also to vindicate and defend it. Therefore she is called not only a pillar (*stulos*), but also a stay (*hedraiōma*) by which the truth when known may be vindicated and preserved pure and entire against all corruptions. But she is not called a foundation (*themelion*), in the sense of giving to the truth itself its own substructure (*hypostasin*) and firmness. (2) Whatever is called the pillar and stay of the truth is not therefore infallible; for so the ancients called those who, either in the splendor of their doctrine or in the holiness of their lives or in unshaken constancy, excelled others and confirmed the doctrines of the gospel and the Christian faith by precept and example; as Eusebius says the believers in Lyons call Attalus the Martyr (*Ecclesiastical History* 5.1 [FC 19:276; Loeb, 1:415]); Basil distinguishes the orthodox bishops who opposed the Arian heresy by this name (*hoi styloi kai to hedraiōma tēs alētheias, Letter*

243 [70] [FC 28:188; PG 32.908]); and Gregory Nazianzus so calls Athanasius. In the same sense, judges in a pure and uncorrupted republic are called the pillars and stays of the laws. (3) This passage teaches the duty of the church, but not its infallible prerogative (i.e., what she is bound to do in the promulgation and defending of the truth against the corruptions of its enemies, but not what she can always do). In Malachi 2:7, the "priest's lips" are said to "keep knowledge" because he is bound to do it (although he does not always do it as v. 8 shows). (4) Whatever is here ascribed to the church belongs to the particular church at Ephesus to which, however, the papists are not willing to give the prerogative of infallibility. Again, it treats of the collective church of believers in which Timothy was to labor and exercise his ministry, not as the church representative of the pastors, much less of the pope (in whom alone they think infallibility [*anamartēsian*] resides). (5) Paul alludes here both to the use of pillars in the temples of the Gentiles (to which were attached either images of the gods or the laws and moral precepts; yea, even oracles, as Pausanius and Athenaeus testify) that he may oppose these pillars of falsehood and error (on which nothing but fictions and the images of false gods were exhibited) to that mystical pillar of truth on which the true image of the invisible God is set forth (Col. 1:15) and the heavenly oracles of God made to appear; and to that remarkable pillar which Solomon caused to be erected in the temple (2 Chron. 6:13; 2 Kings 11:14; 23:3) which kings ascended like a scaffold as often as they either addressed the people or performed any solemn service, and was therefore called by the Jews the "royal pillar." Thus truth sits like a queen upon the church; not that she may derive her authority from it (as Solomon did not get his from that pillar), but that on her, truth may be set forth and preserved.

THE PASSAGE OF AUGUSTINE

XXVI. The passage of Augustine, "I would not believe the gospel if the authority of the church did not move me" (*Against the Epistle of Manichaeus Called Fundamental* 5 [NPNF1, 4:131; PL 42.176]) does not favor the papists. First, Augustine speaks of himself as still a Manichean and not yet a Christian. What he places in the imperfect is equivalent to the preterite pluperfect: "I would believe and it would move" for "I would have believed and it would have moved"—a very common usage with the Africans (as the learned observe); cf. Augustine, "If I would then love that fruit" for "I would have loved" (*Confessions* 2.8 [FC 21:46; PL 32.682]). Second, the authority of which he speaks is not that of right and power (which our opponents here pretend), as if he would have believed because the church so ordered; but that of worth, derived from the great and remarkable proofs of the providence of God (visible in the church) such as miracles, the agreement of people, the succession, etc. (Augustine, *Against the Epistle of Manichaeus Called Fundamental* 4 [NPNF1, 4:130]) which can lead to faith, although unable to produce it primarily. Third, the external motive to faith is here alluded to and not the infallible principle of believing which chapter 4 teaches us is to be sought in the truth alone. For he acknowledges that truth is to be preferred before everything else, if it is so perfectly exhibited as that it cannot be called into question. "Let us follow those who invite us to believe; first, when we are not as yet able to understand, so that being made more able by the faith itself we may deserve to understand what we believe, having not now men, but God himself as the informer and illuminator of our minds within us" (ibid., 14 [NPNF1, 4:136; PL 42.183]). Thus, Peter d'Ailly (*Questiones super libros sententiarum* [1490/1968], Q. 1, in Sec. 1, Art. 3, [pp. 4–10]) understands it; Canus, "De locis theologicis," 2.8 in *Opera* [1605], 41–53; Gerson, Driedo and Durandus refer it to the primitive and apostolic church, not to the present for whose authority it is here contended. See our "Disputatio theologica de scripturae sacrae authoritate" in *Francisci Turrettini Opera* (1848), 4:253–68.

Seventh Question: The Canon

Has any canonical book perished? We deny.

THE WORD "CANON" IS USED WIDELY OR STRICTLY

I. The distinctions of the word "canon" must be premised so that the various questions concerning the canon of Scripture may be more satisfactorily answered. It is used either widely or strictly. In the former sense, it was used by the fathers for the ecclesiastical decrees and constitutions by which the councils and rulers of the churches usually defined the things pertaining to faith, practice and good order (*eutaxian*). Such are the various canons both of the universal church and of the African church; and the collection of canons of Burchard, Ivo, Gratian and the canonical law itself contained in the Code of the Canons, as distinguished from the divine law included in the code of the sacred Scriptures. In the latter sense, it is applied by way of eminence (*kat' exochēn*) to the Scriptures alone because God has given it to us as a rule of faith and practice. In this sense, it is called by Irenaeus "the invariable rule of truth" (*Kanōn tēs alētheias aklinēs, Against Heresies* 1.9.4 [ANF 1:330; PG 7.545]); and by Chrysostom, "the exact scale, standard and rule of all things" (*hapantōn akribēs zygos kai gnōmōn kai kanōn*, Homily 13, *On Second Corinthians* [NPNF1, 12:346; PG 61.496–97]).

THE CANON OF DOCTRINES AND OF BOOKS

II. But as the word of God can be considered in a two-fold aspect (either for the doctrine divinely revealed or for the sacred books in which it is contained), so there can be a two-fold canon: one of the doctrines, embracing all the fundamental doctrines; and the other of the books, containing all the inspired (*theopneustous*) books. The Scriptures are called canonical for a double reason, both with regard to the doctrines (because they are the canon and standard of faith and practice, derived from the Hebrew *qnh*, which signifies a "reed" or surveyor's pen and is so used in Gal. 6:16 and Phil. 3:16) and with respect to the books (because it contains all the canonical books). In this sense, Athanasius (near the beginning of *Synopsis scripturae sacrae* [PG 28.283]), tells us that the books of the Christians are not infinite but finite and comprehended in a "certain canon."

STATEMENT OF THE QUESTION

III. The first question concerns the integrity of the canon, whether any canonical book has perished or whether the collection of Scripture is now destitute of any book which God introduced into the canon. About this both the orthodox and papists are divided into various parties. Most papists contend that many canonical books have been lost in order that thus they may prove the imperfection of Scripture and the necessity of tradition to supply its defects. Some of our men (as Musculus and Whitaker, following Chrysostom) assert the same, but with a twofold difference. First they affirm this only of some books of the Old Testament and not of the New, as the papists. Second they think nothing is taken from the perfection of Scripture by this circumstance (as the papists do) because they do not infer the integrity of the canon from the number of the sacred books (or their quantitative perfection), but from the fullness of the doctrines and the essential perfection of all things necessary to salvation which abundantly exists in those books which still remain. Yet the more common and sounder opinion is that of those who hold that no books truly canonical have perished, and if any have perished, they were not worthy of this character.

That no canonical book has perished is proved by the testimony of Christ

IV. Proof is derived: (1) from the testimony of Christ—"it is easier for heaven and earth to pass, than one tittle of the law to fail" (Luke 16:17; cf. Matt. 5:18). But if not even one tittle (or the smallest letter) could fail, how could several canonical books perish? Although Christ speaks directly of the doctrine of the law and not of its books, yet it can be applied analogically to them, so as to imply their preservation and so much the more. Mention is made not only of the letters and points of which the Scripture is made up, but also that God wished this doctrine to be preserved in the written books. (2) From the declaration of Luke and Paul: neither could Luke have made mention of all the prophets and of all the Scriptures (Luke 24:27), if any portions of them had perished; nor could Paul have asserted that "whatsoever things were written aforetime were written for our learning" (Rom. 15:4), unless they supposed that all the writings of the Old Testament existed.

From the providence of God

V. (3) From the providence of God perpetually keeping watch for the safety of the church (which cannot be conceived to have allowed her to suffer so great a loss). Otherwise what would become of the wisdom and goodness and power of God if he had willed that such a precious treasure should be shown to his church and then taken away; and that the body of Scripture should exist at this day mutilated and defective? (4) From the duty of the church which is religiously to preserve the oracles of God committed to her and to search them diligently. That she has not been careless to her charge is evident even from this—that neither Christ nor his apostles ever charged the Jews with this crime. This sacrilege they (who did not omit lesser things) would not have passed over in silence, if they had been really guilty. Yea, Paul commends this privilege of the Jews because unto them were committed the oracles of God (*logia tou Theou*, Rom. 3:2; 9:4). (5) From the purpose of the Scripture which was committed to writing as a canon of faith and practice even to the consummation of ages which could not be obtained, if (by the loss of some canonical books) a mutilated and defective canon (or rather no canon at all) has been left to the church. (6) From the practice of the Jews; because no more canonical books of the Old Testament were acknowledged by them than by us, nor copied in their Targums, nor translated by the Septuagint.

Sources of explanation

VI. All things which men of God have written are not therefore divine and inspired (*theopneusta*). For they could study and write some things as men with historical care (according to the richness of their knowledge), some things as prophets by divine inspiration (according to the authority of religion). The former can be judged with freedom; the latter ought to be believed necessarily (as Augustine, *City of God* 18.38 [FC 24:145–46] well remarks). As not everything they said was canonical, so neither everything they wrote. If therefore Solomon did write many books of parables and songs (as concerning plants and animals, 1 Kings 4:32–33), it does not follow that they were canonical. They could have been prepared by human diligence to exhibit the extensive knowledge of things with which he was furnished, but not as a proof of divine and supernatural inspiration.

VII. The books which are supposed to be lost were either not sacred and canonical (such as the book of the wars of the Lord [Num. 21:14]; the book of Jasher [Josh. 10:13; 2 Sam. 1:18]; chronicles of the kings of Judah and Israel [1 Kings 14:19–20; 15:7]), containing no religious doctrines, but either political annals in which the achievements of the Israelites were recorded or tables of public acts and political statutes, as is evident from 1 Kings 11:41. Or the books, supposed to be lost, still remain under different appellations; as the books of Nathan and Gad (1 Chron. 29:29); and of Iddo (2 Chron. 9:29); of Shemaiah and Iddo (2 Chron. 12:15). As the Jews teach, and some of the fathers testify, and many papists of reputation confess (as Sixtus Senensis, Paul Burgensis, Ludovicus de Tena, Sanctius and others), these form part of the books of Samuel and of Kings.

VIII. The book of the Lord (which Isaiah 34:16 mentions) is no other than the prophecy he wrote in the name of the Lord. Therefore he calls it the book of Jehovah. The book of the Lamentations of Jeremiah at the death of King Josiah (mentioned in 2 Chron. 35:25) still remains in the Lamentations.

IX. It is not said in Colossians 4:16 that there was any epistle of Paul to the Laodiceans because it speaks of an epistle "from" (*ek Laodikeias*) not "to" (*pros Laodikeian*) Laodicea (which may have been an epistle written from the Laodiceans to Paul). Since there were some things in it profitable for the Colossians to know, Paul wished it to be read by them with his own. Hence it is evident with how little reason Faber Stapulensis wished to force an epistle to the Laodiceans upon the Christian world (which the wiser papists have acknowledged).

X. Jude 14 does not mention the book of Enoch, but only his prophecy. He is said to have prophesied, not to have written. But this book (if it ever existed) was never contained in the canon. This is evident from the silence both of Josephus and of Jerome and from this—that Moses is reckoned as the first canonical writer in Luke 24:27. Indeed it appears from Augustine (*City of God* 15.23 [FC 14:474]) that there existed in his time an apocryphal book falsely ascribed to Enoch as its author, a fragment of which we owe to Joseph Scaliger ("Animadversiones in chronologica Eusebi," in *Thesaurus temporum* [1606/1968], 2:244–45).

XI. If some passages are quoted from the Old Testament by the apostles, not now to be found expressly in any canonical book, it does not therefore follow that any canonical book in which they were contained has been lost. Either they may be found implicitly as to the sense (*kata dianoian*), as when Matthew says concerning Christ, "He shall be called a Nazarene" (2:23), which is taken either from Isaiah 11:1 (according to Jerome) where Christ is called a "root"; or by intention (from Judg. 13:5, where it treats of Samson the type of Christ who it is said shall be a "Nazarite unto God" from the womb). Or in that which is said in 1 Corinthians 5:9 concerning the epistle which Paul had written to them, there is no objection to our considering it as referring to the one he is writing. A little before, he had ordered them to excommunicate the incestuous person, as when this epistle is read (Col. 4:16), viz., the one he was then writing (*hē epistolē*). Or they are merely historical, as what Jude 9 says of the altercation between Satan and Michael about the dead body of Moses, which he could have learned either from tradition (as some hold) or from some ecclesiastical book (not canonical) that is lost.

XII. Although the autographs of the law and of the prophets (kept in the ark) may have been burnt up with it when the city was overthrown and the temple burned in the time of the Babylonian captivity, it does not therefore follow that all the sacred books perished then (which were again restored within forty days by Ezra as by a second Moses) because many copies could have been in the possession of the faithful from which afterwards the worship of God might have been restored (Ezra 6:18; Neh. 8:2). Nor is it very likely that Ezekiel and the pious priests (as also Jeremiah, Gedaliah and Baruch who received permission to remain in Judea) would have been without them, especially when the preservation and reading of the sacred books belonged to them; in Daniel's case this is plain (Dan. 9:2). The passage 2(4) Esdras 4:23 (cf. 14:21), whence its universal destruction is argued, proves nothing (as it is apocryphal to papists themselves) and is refuted by another apocryphal book which is esteemed canonical by papists, which says that the ark in which was deposited the book of the law (Deut. 31:26) was preserved by Jeremiah in a cave of Mt. Nebo (2 Macc. 2:5). The deep silence of Scripture especially refutes this fiction (which would not have passed by so great a loss without mention of public mourning) seeing that it so bitterly weeps over the pollution of the sanctuary, the destruction of Jerusalem, the taking away of the sacred vessels, the overthrow of the temple and other things. Ezra could therefore have labored to collect, yea and even to correct and restore the copies which had been corrupted in the captivity (which he could best do being inspired of God [*theopneustos*]), but there was no necessity for his giving it to the church entirely new.

Eighth Question

Are the books of the Old Testament still a part of the canon of faith and rule of practice in the church of the New Testament? We affirm against the Anabaptists.

STATEMENT OF THE QUESTION

I. This question brings us into collision with the Anabaptists who reject the books of the Old Testament from the canon of faith, as if they had not the least reference to Christians and as if they should not draw from them doctrines of faith and rules of life. The Mennonites in their Confession (Article 11) teach that "all Christians, in matters of faith, ought to have recourse necessarily only to the gospel of Christ" ("Belydenisse naer Godts heylig woort," Article 11 [?1600] in *The Bloody Theater or Martyrs' Mirror* [comp. T. J. van Braght, 1837/1987], 382). This is confirmed in the Colloquy of Frankenthal (*Protocol . . . de Gansche Handelinge des Gesprecks te Franckenthal . . . Gaspar van der Heyden*, Article 1:57 [1571], 73). On the contrary, the orthodox maintain that the Old Testament no less than the New pertains to Christians and that from both, the doctrines of faith and rules of life must be drawn (French Confession, Articles 4–5; First Helvetic Confession, Article 1—cf. Cochrane, *Reformed Confessions*, 145, 100).

II. The question does not concern the Old Testament in relation to the Mosaic economy, for we grant that this was so abrogated by Christ that there is no place for it any longer in the economy of grace. Rather the question concerns the Old Testament as to doctrine, whether there is no further use for it in the New Testament as a rule of faith and practice.

III. The question is not whether Christ reformed the law given in the Old Testament by correcting and perfecting it under the New (for we will treat of this hereafter with the Socinians). The question is whether the Old Testament Scripture pertains to Christians, so that from it no less than from the New Testament the rule of faith and practice ought to be drawn; and that the religion of Christ is contained in Moses and the prophets as well as in the New Testament and can be demonstrated from them. This our adversaries deny; we assert.

IV. Nor is the question about the distinction between the Old and New Testament and the difference in the doctrine which occurs in both. For we do not deny that this is far clearer in the New than in the Old Testament, both on account of the types in which they are enveloped and on account of the predictions and prophecies which are given in it. Rather the question concerns the principle of the Christian religion; whether it is only the books of the New Testament or also those of the Old. We maintain the latter.

Proof that the Old Testament is canonical to Christians

V. The reasons are: (1) because Christ recommends the Old Testament and enjoins upon believers the hearing of Moses and the prophets (Luke 16:29). This was not said to the Jews exclusively because a general precept is here given embracing all who desire to escape eternal punishment. What is here proposed as a precept, Peter recommends to the practice of Christians: "We have also a more sure word of prophecy; whereunto ye do well that ye take heed, as unto a light that shineth in a dark place, until the day dawn, and the day star arise in your hearts" (2 Peter 1:19). It cannot be objected that a limitation is added by Peter, that this applies only until the time of the New Testament when the day should dawn. If it is understood of the New Testament, the use of the word of prophecy is not therefore restricted by this expression until the time of the New Testament because the *to eōs hou* ("even until") is not always so positive of the past as to be exclusive of the future (this is evidenced by many passages: Gen. 28:15; Matt. 28:20; 1 Cor. 15:25). But if it is referred to the day of eternal life (and so the rising of the day star in the firmament of glory, which is truly the day by way of eminence [*kat' exochēn*], which is clearly evident, because he writes to believers who had obtained like precious faith [*isotimon*] and so in their hearts the day of grace, and the day star of the gospel had already risen) then the argument becomes more powerful, viz., take heed unto this word of prophecy until the end of the world, until that happy day arises (which is the true day), since it will be perpetual and never followed by any night.

VI. (2) The New Testament church is built upon the foundation of the prophets and apostles (Eph. 2:20), i.e., upon their doctrines. Nor can the New Testament prophets be meant here as in Ephesians 3:5 and 1 Corinthians 12:28 because he speaks of the perpetual foundation of the universal church. Now the gift of prophecy under the New Testament was temporary, and the order of collation does not of itself imply a priority or posteriority of time or duration; as in Ephesians 4:11, the prophets of the New Testament are placed before the evangelists, and yet they were not in fact prior to them.

VII. (3) "Whatsoever things were written aforetime were written for our learning, that we through patience and comfort of the Scriptures might have hope" (Rom. 15:4). Now although all things in the Scriptures are not equally important as to matter and use, yet all are equally so as to their source and authenticity (*authentias*) and therefore given equally for the good and edification of the church.

VIII. (4) The canon of the Old Testament suffices for faith and practice, and those sacred writings in which Timothy was instructed from his childhood (when the New Testament canon was not complete) could make him wise (*sophisai*) unto salvation (2 Tim. 3:15–16). And if "the man of God" (i.e., the minister of the gospel) may be thoroughly furnished by them unto every good work, much more are they useful and necessary to the faith of a private man and the direction of his life. And Paul does not refer here only to the time preceding the writing of the New Testament because he speaks in general of all Scripture given by inspiration (*theopneustō*) of God (v. 16).

IX. (5) Christ directs the Jews to search the Scriptures (John 5:39) that from them they might have eternal life. This was not said to the Jews indicatively only, but also imperatively. The design of Christ was to lead the Jews to the reading of the Scriptures, as the means of bringing them to a knowledge of himself and as an unexceptionable witness of himself. Even if Christ had spoken indicatively, it would have amounted to the same thing because he approved that practice.

X. (6) The Old Testament contains the same doctrine in substance with the New, both in matters of faith and practice; nor is any other gospel now set forth to us than that which was promised before in the prophetic writings (Rom. 1:2; 16:25–26). Hence Paul, who declared the whole counsel of God concerning salvation to Christians (Acts 20:27), professes to have said no other things than those which the prophets and Moses said (Acts 26:22). And no other law is prescribed for us than that which was formerly introduced by Moses, commanding us to love God and our neighbor (Matt. 22:37, 39).

XI. (7) If the Old Testament is not important for Christians, it could not be unexceptionably proved against the Jews that Jesus Christ of Nazareth is the true Messiah. This can be done only by a collation of Scriptures and a comparison (*synkrisin*) of marks predicted in the Old Testament concerning the Messiah and of their fulfillment in our Jesus under the New. This was often done by Christ and his apostles (Luke 24:27, 44; Acts 10:43; 17:11; 26:22; Rom. 3:21). Without it, the Jews could not be convinced of their error and brought to faith because they acknowledge no other standard.

XII. By the law and the prophets (who should continue until John, Matt. 11:13) are not meant the books of the Old Testament and their continuance, but the economy of the Old Testament compared with that of the New (of which the former was prophetical, the latter evangelical; the one shadowy and typical, promising a Messiah to come, the other clear and open, announcing the Messiah as already come). Christ in comparing these two modes of revelation together said the former by prophecy (*prophēteian*) continued only until John because as the Messiah had come, he should no longer be predicted as about to come, but the other by the gospel (*euangelismon*, which announced the advent of Christ) began from John.

XIII. When the apostles are called "ministers of the spirit and not of the letter" (2 Cor. 3:5–6), by letter we must not understand the books of the Old Testament, as if there would be no further necessity for them (since they elsewhere often make use of them), but the legal economy in contradistinction to the evangelical (which is in many respects better than the former, not only in clearness and extent, but principally in efficacy because it not only orders and commands duty as the law, but also works by the Spirit in writing the law upon the heart).

XIV. It is one thing for an old covenant to become antiquated as to the mode of administration and the accidents or the external observation of appendages to it (which Paul asserts, Heb. 8:13). It is a very different thing for it to become so as to the thing administered and the substance or internal form of the covenant itself (which we deny).

XV. It is one thing to speak of the life of the Old Testament ceremonies or of the law as related to them. It is quite another to speak of the duration, knowledge and contemplation of the books of the law and the prophets. That which has only a shadow of good things to come does not pertain to Christians, who have the express image of the things, as to practice and observation; yet it can pertain to them as to doctrine and knowledge and relation to the image (*tēn eikona*). Yea, from a comparison of the shadow with the real form, the body itself will stand out more distinctly.

XVI. Christ does not dispute against Moses and the real precepts of the law (Matt. 5), but acts rather as the interpreter and vindicator of the law, rejecting the corruptions and glosses which had been foisted onto it by the Jewish teachers and restoring it to its purity and genuine sense. This we will show particularly when we come to the law.

XVII. Although the New Testament is perfect intensively as to the substance of saving doctrine, yet it is not such extensively as to the whole extent of divine revelation. For it speaks only of Christ already come and not of him about to come, which kind of testimony would be most useful to the confirmation of faith. So then the perfection of the books of the New Testament does not exclude the use of those of the Old, both because they testify to their dependence upon the Old Testament and because the reiterated testimony of many witnesses concerning the same thing is stronger with respect to us and greatly confirms (*asphaleian*) our faith.

XVIII. That which was in no way given by Christ, either mediately or immediately, does not pertain to Christians. But the law which was given by Moses was given also by Christ; by Moses as a servant, by Christ as the Lord. Hence this same angel which appeared to Moses in the wilderness (Acts 7:30, 38) and was Jehovah himself (Ex. 3:2), is said to have "spoken to Moses in Mount Sinai" because the Son of God (who is called the angel of the covenant of his presence) was the primary author and promulgator of that law (of which Moses was only the minister). Nor is the difference between the promulgation of the law and the gospel thus taken away because the Son of God operated in the law mediately only and as without a body (*asarkos*), but he is called the primary author of the gospel, immediately as incarnate (*ensarkos*, Heb. 2:3).

XIX. Christ is called the "end of the law" (Rom. 10:4) both because he was the mark at which the whole law aimed and because he was its perfection (*teleiōsis*) and fulfillment, not by abrogating every use of it, but by fulfilling its predictions and obeying it both in himself (by acting and suffering) and in his people (by writing it on their hearts). Hence he says, "I am not come to destroy the law, but to fulfil it" (Matt. 5:17).

XX. Servants must not be listened to when their master is present, if they testify either without his permission or against him. But they can and ought to be heard, if with his consent they testify of him. This Moses and the prophets have done (John 5:46; Acts 10:43) no less than the apostles. Christ (Luke 16:29) expressly commands us to hear Moses and the prophets. This is not going back from Christ to Moses but proceeding from Moses (who is a schoolmaster to lead us to Christ, Gal. 3:24) to Christ.

XXI. The beginning of John's preaching is well called the "beginning of the gospel" (Mark 1:1) as to the fulfillment and in relation to Christ as already set forth; not as to the promise and in relation to Christ about to be set forth, which properly had place under the Old Testament (Rom. 1:2; Gal. 3:8; Isa. 52:7; 61:1).

Ninth Question: The Apocryphal Books

Ought Tobit, Judith, Wisdom, Ecclesiasticus, the first two books of the Maccabees, Baruch, the additions to Esther and Daniel to be numbered among the canonical books? We deny against the papists.

WHY CALLED APOCRYPHAL

I. The Apocryphal books are so called not because the authors are unknown (for there are some canonical books whose authors are unknown and some apocryphal books whose authors are known); not because they could be read only in private and not in public (for some of them may be read even in public), but either because they were removed from the crypt (*apo tēs kryptēs*) (that sacred place in which the holy writings were laid up) as Epiphanius and Augustine think; or because their authority was hidden and suspected, and consequently their use also was secret since the church did not apply to them to confirm the authority of ecclesiastical doctrines (as Jerome says, 'Praefatio in libros Salomonis' from "Hieronymi Prologus Galeatus" in *Biblia Sacra Vulgata Editionis Sixti V . . . et Clementis VIII* [1865], lii); or, what is more probable, because they are of an uncertain and obscure origin (as Augustine says, *City of God* 15.23 [FC 14:474]).

STATEMENT OF THE QUESTION

II. The question is not about the books of the Old and New Testament which we hold as canonical, for the papists agree with us as to these; nor about all the apocryphal books, for there are some rejected by the papists as well as by us (as the 3rd and 4th of Esdras, 3rd and 4th of Maccabees, the Prayer of Manasses, etc.). The question is only about Tobit, Judith, Baruch, Wisdom, Ecclesiasticus, 1 and 2 Maccabees, the additions to Esther and Daniel, which the papists consider canonical and we exclude from the canon—not because they do not contain many true and good things, but because they do not bear the marks of canonical books.

WHY THE APOCRYPHAL BOOKS ARE EXCLUDED FROM THE CANON

III. The reasons are various. (1) The Jewish church, to which the oracles of God were committed (Rom. 3:2), never considered them as canonical, but held the same canon with us (as is admitted by Josephus, *Against Apion* 1.39–41 [Loeb, 1:178–79], Becanus, *Manuale controversiarum* 1.1 [1750], 11–12) and Stapelton, "De principiis fidei doctrinalibus controversia," Cont. 5.7 in *Opera* [1620], 1:322–23). This they could not have done without the most grievous sin (and it was never charged upon them either by Christ or his apostles) if these books no less than the others had been committed to them. Nor should the canon of the Jews be distinguished here from that of Christians because Christians neither can nor ought to receive other books of the Old Testament as canonical than those which they received from the Jews, their book-servants "who carry the books of us students" (as Augustine calls them, "On Psalm 40 [41]" [NPNF1, 8:132; PL 36.463]). (2) They are never quoted as canonical by Christ and the apostles like the others. And Christ, by dividing all the books of the Old Testament into three classes (the law, the Psalms and the prophets, Luke 24:44), clearly approves of the canon of the Jews and excludes from it those books which are not embraced in these classes. (3) The Christian church for four hundred years recognized with us the same and no other canonical books. This appears from the *Canons of the Synod of Laodicea* 59 (NPNF2, 14:158); Melito, bishop of Sardis, who lived 116 years A.D. (according to Eusebius, *Ecclesiastical History* 4.26 [FC 19:262–63; Loeb 1:387]); from Epiphanius ("De Epicureis," *Panarion* [PG 41.206–23]); Jerome ("Hieronymi Prologus Galeatus," in *Biblia Sacra Vulgatae Editionis Sixti V . . . et Clementis VIII* [1865], xliii–lv); Athanasius (*Synopsis scripturae sacrae* [PG 28.283–94]). (4) The authors were neither prophets and inspired men, since they wrote after Malachi (the last of the prophets); nor were their books written in the Hebrew language (as those of the Old Testament), but in Greek. Hence Josephus (in the passage referred to above) acknowledges that those things which were written by his people after the time of Artaxerxes were not equally credible and authoritative with those which preceded "on account of there not being an indisputable succession of prophets" (*dia to mē genesthai tēn tōn prophētōn akribē diadochēn, Against Apion* 1.41 [Loeb, 1:178–79]).

IV. The style and matter of the books proclaim them to be human, not divine. It requires little acuteness to discover that they are the product of human labor, although some are more excellent than others. For besides the fact that the style does not savor of the majesty and simplicity of the divine style and is redolent with the faults and weaknesses of human genius (in the vanity, flattery, curiosity, mistaken zeal and ill-timed affectation of learning and eloquence, which are often met with), there are so many things in them not only foolish and absurd, but even false, superstitious and contradictory, as to show clearly that they are not divine but human writings. We will give a few specimens of the many errors. Tobias makes the angel tell a falsehood. He says that he is Azariah, the son of Ananias (Tob. 5:12) and that he is Raphael, the angel of the Lord (Tob. 12:15). The angel gives a magical direction for driving away the devil by the smoke of a fish's liver (Tob. 6:6), against that of Christ (Matt. 17:21). He arrogates to himself the oblation of prayers (Tob. 12:12), which belongs to the work of Christ alone. The book of Judith celebrates the deed of Simeon (Jth. 9:2), which Jacob cursed (Gen. 49:5–7); praises the deceits and lies of Judith (Jth. 11), which are not very consistent with piety. Worse still, she even seeks the blessing of God upon them (Jth. 9:13). No mention is made of the city Bethulia in the Scriptures; nor does any trace of the deliverance mentioned there occur in Josephus or Philo, who wrote on Jewish subjects. The author of Wisdom falsely asserts that he was king in Israel (Wisd. of Sol. 9:7–8) that he might be taken for Solomon. Yet he alludes to the athletic contests which in the time of Solomon had not been established among the Greeks (Wisd. of Sol. 4:2). Further, he introduces the Pythagorean metempsychosis (*metempsychōsin*, Wisd. of Sol. 8:19–20) and gives a false account of the origin of idolatry (Wisd. of Sol. 14:15–16). The Son of Sirach (Sir. 46:20) attributes to Samuel what was done by the evil spirit raised by wicked devices (1 Sam. 28:11), falsely speaks of Elijah's bodily return (Sir. 48:10), and excuses his oversights in the prologue.

V. There are so many contradictions and absurdities in the additions to Esther and Daniel that Sixtus Senensis unhesitatingly rejects them. Baruch says that in the fifth year after the destruction of Jerusalem, he read his book to Jeconiah and to all the people of Babylon; but Jeconiah was in prison and Baruch had been taken away to Egypt after the death of Gedaliah (Jer. 43:7). He mentions an altar of the Lord (Bar. 1:10) when there was none, the temple being destroyed. The books of the Maccabees often contradict each other (compare 1 Macc. 1:16 with 9:5, 28 and ch. 10). The suicide (*autocheiria*) of Razis is praised (2 Macc. 14:42). Will-worship (*ethelothrēskeia*) is commended (2 Macc. 12:42) in Judas's offering a sacrifice for the dead contrary to the law. The author apologizes for his youth and infirmity and complains of the painful labor of abridging the five books of Jason, the Cyrenian (2 Macc. 2:23–24; 15:39). If you wish any more specimens from these books, consult Rainold, Chamier, Molinaeus, Spanheim and others who have pursued this line of argument with fullness and strength.

Sources of explanation

VI. The canon of faith differs from the canon of ecclesiastical reading. We do not speak here of the canon in the latter sense, for it is true that these apocryphal books were sometimes read even publicly in the church. But they were read "for the edification of the people" only, not "for establishing the authority of the doctrines" as Jerome says, *Praefatio . . . in libros Salomonis* (NPNF2, 6:492; PL 28.1308). Likewise the legends containing the sufferings of the martyrs (which were so called from being read) were publicly read in the church, although they were not considered canonical. But we speak here of the canon of faith.

VII. The word "canon" is used by the fathers in two senses; either widely or strictly. In the first sense, it embraces not only the canon of faith, but also the canon of ecclesiastical reading. In this way, we must understand the Third Council of Carthage, Canon 47 (Friedrich Lauchert, *Die Kanones der Wichtigsten Alkirchlichen Concilien* [Frankfurt am Main: Minerva, 1896/1961], 173) when it calls these canonical books (if indeed this canon has not been foisted in [*pareisaktos*] because it mentions Pope Boniface who was not at that time pope; hence Surius, the Monk [*Concilia omnia* (1567), 1:508] attributes this canon to the Seventh Council of Carthage, not the Third) not strictly and properly of the canon of faith, but widely, of the canon of reading. The synod expressly says that the sufferings of the martyrs should also be read and so we must understand Augustine when he terms them "canonical." For he makes two orders of canonicals: the first of those which are received by all the churches and were never called in question; the second of those which are admitted only by some and were usually read from the pulpit. He holds that the latter are not to be valued as rightly as the former and have far less authority (Augustine, *Reply to Faustus the Manichaean* 11.5 [NPNF1, 4:180]). But the Apocrypha are spurious, false and worthless writings—the fables of the Scriptures (Augustine, *City of God* 15.23 [FC 14:474]). However the word "canon" is taken strictly for that which has a divine and infallible authority in proving the doctrines of faith. Jerome takes the word in this sense when he excludes those books from the canon. Thus Augustine attached a wider signification to the word "canon" than Jerome, who again takes the word "apocryphal" in a wider sense than Augustine, not only for books evidently false and fabulous, but also for those which (although they might be read in the church) should not be used to prove the doctrines of faith. Thus the seemingly contradictory expressions of these fathers may easily be reconciled. Thus Cajetan near the end explains them: "The words of councils as well as of teachers being brought to the test of Jerome, it will appear that these books are not canonical (i.e., regulars to establish matters of faith), although they may be called canonical (i.e., regulars for the edification of believers), since they were received into the Biblical canon for this purpose" ("In librum Hester commentarii," in *Quotquot in sacra scripturae* [1639], 2:400). Dionysius Carthusianus agrees with him (Prooemium in "Tobiam," in *Opera Omnia* [1898], 5:83–84).

VIII. The papists make a useless distinction between the canon of the Jews and that of Christians. For although our canon taken generally for all the books of the Old and New Testament (in which it adequately consists) is not equally admitted by the Jews, who reject the New Testament; yet if it is taken partially with reference to the Old Testament (in which sense we speak of it here), it is true that our canon does not differ from that of the Jews because they receive into the canon no other books than we do.

IX. When the fathers sometimes mention Deuterocanonical books, they do not mean such as are truly and in the same sense canonical as to faith, but only those which may be placed in the canon of reading on account of their usefulness for piety and edification.

X. The citation of any passage does not of itself prove a book to be canonical, for then Aratus, Menander and Epimenides (quoted by Paul in Acts 17:28; 1 Cor. 15:33; Titus 1:12) would be canonical. (2) The same passages which our adversaries bring forward as quotations from the Apocrypha are found in the canonical books, and the apostles would rather quote from these than from the former.

XI. If they are connected with canonical books, it does not follow that they are of equal authority, but only that they are useful in the formation of manners and a knowledge of history, not for establishing faith.

XII. Although some of the Apocryphal books are better and more correct than the others and contain various useful moral directions (as the book of Wisdom and the Son of Sirach), yet because they contain many other false and absurd things, they are deservedly excluded from the canon of faith.

XIII. Although some have questioned the authenticity of a few books of the New Testament (i.e., the epistle of James, 2 Peter, 2 and 3 John and Revelation, which afterwards were received by the church as canonical), it does not follow that the same can be done with the Apocryphal books because the relation of the books of the Old and New Testaments to this subject are not the same. For the books of the Old Testament were given to the Christian church, not at intervals of time and by parts, but she received at one and the same time from the Jews all the books belonging to her written in one codex after they had been stamped with an indubitable authority, confirmed by Christ and his apostles. But the books of the New Testament were published separately, in different times and places and gradually collected into one corpus. Hence it happened that some of the later books (which came to some of the churches more slowly, especially in remote places) were held in doubt by some until gradually their authenticity was made known to them. (2) Although in certain churches some of the epistles and Revelation were rejected, yet those who received them were always far more numerous than those who rejected them. Yet there was no dispute about the Apocryphal books because they were always rejected by the Jewish church.

Tenth Question: The Purity of the Sources

Have the original texts of the Old and New Testaments come down to us pure and uncorrupted? We affirm against the papists.

I. This question lies between us and the papists who speak against the purity of the sources for the purpose of establishing more easily the authority of their Vulgate version and leading us away to the tribunal of the church.

II. By the original texts, we do not mean the autographs written by the hand of Moses, of the prophets and of the apostles, which certainly do not now exist. We mean their apographs which are so called because they set forth to us the word of God in the very words of those who wrote under the immediate inspiration of the Holy Spirit.

III. The question is not Are the sources so pure that no fault has crept into the many sacred manuscripts, either through the waste of time, the carelessness of copyists or the malice of the Jews or of heretics? For this is acknowledged on both sides and the various readings which Beza and Robert Stephanus have carefully observed in the Greek (and the Jews in the Hebrew) clearly prove it. Rather the question is have the original texts (or the Hebrew and Greek manuscripts) been so corrupted either by copyists through carelessness (or by the Jews and heretics through malice) that they can no longer be regarded as the judge of controversies and the rule to which all the versions must be applied? The papists affirm, we deny it.

IV. However all the papists do not agree. There are some whom they call "Hebraizers" who have recognized the purity of the sources and openly defended it (as Sixtus Senensis, *Bibliotheca sancta* 8 [1575], 2:314–19; Bannes, *Scholastica commentaria in . . . Summae Theologicae* [1585], I, Q. 1, Art. 8, 1:69–70, 72; Andradius, *Defensio Tridentinae fidei catholicae* 4 [1580], 574–709; Driedo, "De ecclesiasticis scripturis et dogmatibus," 2 in *Opera* [1572], 1:23–62; Arias Montanus, "Praefatio," *Biblia sacra Hebraice, Chaldaice, Graece et Latine* [1572], vol. 1; Joannes Isaacus, *Defensio veritatis Hebraicae sacrarum . . . adversus . . . Lindani* [1559]; Bonfrerius, *Pentateuchus Moysis commentario . . . totius Scripturae* 12.5 [1625], 43; Simeon de Muis, "Epistola," *Assertio veritatis Hebraicae adversus exercitationes . . . Ioannis Morini* [1631] and many more). Others, on the contrary, vehemently urge the corruption of the sources: as Stapleton, Lindanus, Cano, Cotton, Morinus, Perronius, Gordon, etc. Others, unwilling to assert that the sources are corrupt, take a middle ground and hold that it is not a consequence of that purity and integrity that all things in the versions ought to be tested and amended by them. This is the opinion of Bellarmine (VD 2.2, pp. 62–65) who on this subject as on others is not at all consistent with himself.

THE PROVIDENCE OF GOD PROVES THAT THE SOURCES HAVE NOT BEEN CORRUPTED

V. The following arguments prove that the sources have not been corrupted. (1) The providence of God which could not permit books which it willed to be written by inspiration (*theopneustois*) for the salvation of men (and to continue unto the end of the world that they might draw from them waters of salvation) to become so corrupted as to render them unfit for this purpose. And since new revelations are not to be expected (after God has recorded in the Scriptures his entire will concerning the doctrine of salvation), what can be more derogatory to God (who has promised his constant presence with the church) than to assert that he has permitted the books containing this doctrine to become so corrupt that they cannot serve as a canon of faith? (2) The fidelity of the Christian church and unceasing labor in preserving the manuscripts; for since Christians have always labored with great zeal to keep this sacred deposit uncorrupted, it is not credible that they would either corrupt it themselves or suffer it to be corrupted by others. (3) The religion of the Jews who have bestowed upon the sacred manuscripts great care and labor amounting even to superstition. Hence Josephus says that after the lapse of ages no one has dared either to add to or take away from or alter the peculiar books of the Jews in any respect and that they think it an honor to die for the Scriptures (*Against Apion* 1.42 [Loeb, 1:180–81]). Philo, in his book on the departure of the Israelites from Egypt (cited by Eusebius, *Preparation for the Gospel* 8.6.357c [ed. Gifford, 1903], 1:387) goes further, asserting that "even up to his time, through a space of more than two thousand years, not so much as a word had been changed in the law of the Hebrews and that any Jew would rather die a hundred times, than suffer the law to be altered in the least." They carry their ridiculous superstition concerning the sacred manuscript to such a length that if a corrected book of the law fell on the ground, they proclaimed a fast and expressed their fears that the whole universe would return to its original chaos, so far were they from corrupting the manuscripts. (4) The carefulness of the Masoretes not only about verses and words, but also about single letters (which, together with all the variations of punctuation and writing, they not only counted, but also wrote down, so that no ground or even suspicion of corruption could arise). Arias Montanus employs this argument in the "Praefatio" to his *Biblia sacra Hebraice, Chaldaice, Graece et Latine* (1572), vol. 1. (5) The multitude of copies; for as the manuscripts were scattered far and wide, how could they all be corrupted either by the carelessness of librarians or the wickedness of enemies? Augustine says, "No prudent man can believe that the Jews however perverse and wicked could do it, in copies so numerous and so far and widely diffused" (*City of God* 15.13 [FC 14:440; PL 41.452]). Vives said this ought to be the reply to those "who argue that the Hebrew manuscripts of the Old Testament and the Greek of the New have been so falsified and corrupted as to make it impossible to draw the truth from these sources" (*Saint Augustine, of the Citie of God with . . . comments of . . . Vives* [1620], 519).

VI. (6) If the sources had been corrupted, it must have been done before Christ or after, neither of which is true. Not before because Christ would not have passed it over in silence (for he does censure the various departures in doctrine), nor could he bear to use corrupted books. Did he disregard the salvation of his people so far that he would neither himself, nor through his apostles, admonish us even by a word that the books of Moses and the prophets had been tampered with; while in the meantime he convicts the Jews from these very books (but to what purpose, if they had been corrupted and falsified?) and invites and urges his disciples to their perusal and search? Not afterward, both because the copies circulated among Christians would have rendered such attempts futile, and because no trace of any such corruption appears. For if this had been the case, why do we find the passages which Christ and the apostles quoted from Moses and the prophets just the same now as then and in no way corrupted? Why do Origen and Jerome, eminent scholars, so explicitly absolve the Jews from this crime? Therefore if no corruption took place either before or after the time of Christ, it never did (which argument Bellarmine follows, VD 2.2, pp. 62–65).

VII. (7) The Jews neither would nor could corrupt the sources. An examination of passages of Scripture proves that they were unwilling (besides their religion of which we have spoken). If they had wished to corrupt anything, they would by all means have tampered with the prophecies which speak of Christ and confirm the faith of Christians. For who can believe that they (if, as is supposed, actuated by hatred towards the Christians) would have falsified those passages from which they could derive no advantage against Christians and left untouched those upon which (as immovable) Christians build the foundation of evangelical truth? The matter stands thus: whatever passages are said to have been corrupted by the Jews, oppose Christians little or not at all; and the most important prophecies concerning Christ remain complete and are much more clear and emphatic (*emphatikōtera*) in the Hebrew than in the versions (as Jerome, *Letter 32* [74], "Ad Marcellam" [NPNF2, 6:45–46], Johannes Isaacus, *Defensio veritatis Hebraicae sacrarum . . . adversus . . . Lindani* 2 [1559], 61–122 and Andradius, *Defensio tridentinae fidei Catholicae* 2 [1580], 167–460 observe). That they could not do it, even if they had strongly desired, not only the multitude of copies proves, but also the watchfulness of the Christians whose copies not all the Jews together could corrupt. The provident wisdom of God (which will not suffer one jot or tittle to pass from the law till all be fulfilled, Matt. 5:18) has much less permitted the body of heavenly doctrine to be weakened by the Jews and so great a treasure to be taken away. He rather wished, as Bellarmine well remarks, "for this very purpose to scatter the Jews over the whole world and the books of the law and the prophets to be carried about that our enemies might afford a testimony to the truth of Christianity" (VD 2.2, arg. 5, p. 63). Hence Augustine calls the Jews "a book-case nation, carrying as porters the law and the prophets as slaves usually carry manuscripts, that they by carrying may be deficient and these by reading may be proficient; for the Jews serve us as book-slaves and amanuenses, carrying the books for us the students" (cf. *Reply to Faustus the Manichaean* 12.23 [NPNF1, 4:191; PL 42.266]; *Psalm 57* [56].7 [9] [NPNF1, 8:227; PL 36.666]; *Psalm 41* [40].13 [14] [NPNF1, 8:132; PL 36.463]); "in heart enemies, in books witnesses" as he elsewhere expresses it (*On Faith in Things Unseen* 6.9 [FC 4:467; PL 40.179]).

SOURCES OF EXPLANATION

VIII. Although various corruptions might have crept into the Hebrew manuscripts through the carelessness of transcribers and the waste of time, they do not cease to be a canon of faith and practice. For besides being in things of small importance and not pertaining to faith and practice (as Bellarmine himself confesses and which, moreover, he holds do not affect the integrity of the Scriptures, VD 2.2, pp. 62–65), they are not universal in all the manuscripts; or they are not such as cannot easily be corrected from a collation of the Scriptures and the various manuscripts.

IX. The hatred of the Jews towards the Christians could indeed be the remote cause of the corruption of the sources, but this could be hindered by another superior cause (viz., by the providence of God which had the same prospective reference to the Christians concerning the sure rule of faith as to the Jews, that the gospel might be built up on an unmistakable basis). This could not have been, if he had suffered the sources to be corrupted.

X. The variance of the Septuagint from the original text does not imply that the text is corrupt, but rather the version is at fault. Jerome even in his time acknowledged this: 'Praefatio . . . in Pentateuchum Moysi,' from "Hieronymi Prologus Galeatus" in *Biblia Sacra Vulgatae Editionis Sixit V . . . et Clementis VIII* (1865), xlviii; 'Praefatio . . . in librum Paralipomenon Praefatio,' from "Hieronymi Prologus Galeatus" in *Biblia Sacra Vulgatae Editionis Sixti V . . . et Clementis VIII* (1865), xlix; and *Letter 106*, "Ad Suniam et Fretellam" (PL 22.838). Bellarmine says that the Septuagint was so corrupted and falsified as to seem an entirely different thing, so that now it is not safe to correct the Hebrew or the Latin texts from the Greek manuscripts (VD 2.6, pp. 68–71).

XI. So far are the *keri* and *kethib* (which amount to 848 in number) from corrupting the text that they rather show the various readings of copies by which all corruptions of later hands are excluded. The same may be said of the *chasir* and *jother*, which mark grammatical defects or redundancies. From this is manifest the superstitious desire of the Masoretes to preserve the text, not to corrupt it even in the smallest degree.

XII. The *tikkun sopherim* (or corrections of the scribes) which are only eighteen, do not imply that there were corruptions in the text. Otherwise Christ (if they had been made before his time) or the orthodox fathers (if after his time) would not have passed them by without censure. Nor are they necessary corrections (as the reader can see), but rather choice readings. They are not so much changes of the sense as of words, made either by men of the great synagogue (of whom Ezra, inspired of God [*theopneustos*] was the chief, who after the return from the Babylonian captivity entirely restored the copies of the sacred books which had been scattered or corrupted and arranged them in their present order); or by the authors themselves (who after the manner of rhetoricians made corrections in the text). But that they are not all necessary, the thing itself proves because the sense is complete, the words in the text being retained; see Glassius, *Philologia sacra* (1713), 1, "Tractatus 1: De integritate and puritate Hebraei V. Test.," 1–174.

XIII. The similarity of certain letters might indeed have been the occasion of the introduction of errors into the various manuscripts through the negligence of transcribers, but they could not have been so universal as not to be detected by others; especially after the work of the Masoretes, who numbered not only the words, but even the letters as often as they occur in the text.

XIV. So far is the work of the Masoretes from being a proof of the corruption of the sources that, on the contrary, it was intended to guard against errors, so that not even one small point could afterwards be altered or destroyed.

XV. Although the apostle renders by *phthongon* (Rom. 10:18) what is expressed by *qvm* (Ps. 19:4 [5]), it does not follow that the Hebrew text is incorrect and that *qvm* ("their line") is put instead of *qvlm* ("their voice" or "sound"). For *qv* signifies not only an extended or perpendicular line, but also a written line or letter by which boys are taught their elements.

In Isaiah 28:10, this word is used to designate the untaught infancy of the people of Israel where the prophet says this people must be taught "precept upon precept, and line upon line" like children. So the psalmist says, "day teaches day and night unto night showeth knowledge" (Ps. 19:2). Now *phthongos* not unfitly answers to this word, as it is not only taken for the sound but also for the writing of a letter, just as we speak of a written diphthong and vowel. Further, Paul does not quote this passage as a proof, but only allusively and by anagoge accommodates it to the preaching of the gospel by the apostles, having regard to the sense rather than to the words.

XVI. The corrupting of words is different from misinterpretation. The Jews have misinterpreted Isaiah 9:6 (5), so as to make the words *vykr' shmv* ("and he shall call his name") refer to the father who calls, not to Christ who is called. But they have not altered the words, for whether taken passively or actively it comes to the same thing. According to the Hebrew idiom, the future active without a subject often has a passive signification; as Ribera, *In librum duodecim prophetarum commentarii* (1611), 303 (on Mic. 2, par. 17). Thus verbs of the third person taken impersonally can be translated now actively and then passively. Therefore the Hebrew lection ("and he shall call his name") must not be altered, but must be explained by supplying the subject; not God the Father (according to the Jews), but everyone (viz., of believers) shall call his (i.e., Christ's) name; and for the sake of clearness it must be taken passively, "his name shall be called." Thus also in Jeremiah 23:6, there is a difference in the interpretation. Not in the words which are properly given, either in the singular ("he shall call him"), the nominative preceding Israel and Judah (as the Septuagint has it); or in the plural ("they shall call") as Pagninus, Vatablus and Arias Montanus translate it following the Chaldee, Syriac, Arabic and Vulgate versions. Jerome retains both readings ("he" and "they shall call") (*Commentariorum in Jeremiam* [PL 24.820] on Jer. 23:6). Nor would any of the ancients say that this was corrupted.

XVII. In Genesis 49:10, the three targums of Onkelos, of Jerusalem, and of Jonathan and Kimchi understand *shylh* of the Messiah. It is evident that the Jews have not corrupted this passage to prove that the Messiah had not yet come. Besides, the name *shylh* which is attributed to the Messiah in the Talmud (BT [1935], "Sanhedrin," 2:667) is no less opposed to the Jews and indicative of Christ than the word *shylh* ("sent"), which they maintain as the true reading, whether it is derived from *shyl*, which means "a son"; or from *shlh* which means "peaceful"; or as the Septuagint has it (and more appropriately for *'shr lv, hō apokeitai*, "to whom the kingdom belongs") as we find a similar phrase in Ezekiel 21:27.

XVIII. Zechariah 9:9 has not been tampered with, when it is predicted of the Messiah that he shall be a king, just and *nvsh'*. This word may be taken either passively (to denote that he was to be saved from death, as the apostle says in Heb. 5:7); or that he was to save himself (as in Isa. 63:5); or as a deponent, it may be used actively, many instances of which are met with in Hebrew; as *nshb'* ("he swore"), *nsl* ("he despoiled"). Thus it will be a participle signifying the same as *mvshy'* ("liberator," "savior").

XIX. Although the sojourning of the children of Israel in Egypt (Ex. 12:40) is said to have been 430 years (which cannot be understood of the time spent in Egypt alone, which was only 215 years; but concerning the time spent both in the land of Canaan and in Egypt, as the Samaritan and Greek parallel texts explain it), the Hebrew manuscripts ought not to be pronounced corrupt for the following reason. It is introduced by way of synecdoche (mentioning only Egypt) because it was the most remarkable exile of the Israelites, the denomination being made from the letter.

XX. There are no verses omitted in Psalm 14 (15), for those quoted in Romans 3:11–18 are not taken from this by the apostle, but collected from many Psalms (as from Pss. 5:9; 10 [11]:7; 36:1; 140:3; and Isa. 59:7–8, which Jerome mentions "Preface" in Book 16, *Commentariorum in Isaiam* [PL 24.547]).

XXI. There is no corruption in the Greek text of 1 Corinthians 15:47, but only in the Vulgate. The latter omits the word *Kyrios* (which here refers to Christ to make it evident that the Lord is Jehovah, not a mere man). Thus the antithesis of the first and second Adam becomes much stronger: "the first man is of the earth, earthy; the second man is the Lord from heaven."

XXII. Although the doxology (*doxologia*) which appears at the end of the Lord's Prayer (Matt. 6:13), is not found in Luke 11, nor in the various copies, it does not follow that the passage is corrupt because our Lord may have twice proposed the same form of prayer: first in the private instruction of his disciples without it and then to a promiscuous crowd where he added it. Nor is it unusual for one evangelist to omit what another has mentioned, since they did not think it necessary to record absolutely everything; as for instance Matthew 6:33 has "seek the kingdom of God and his righteousness," but Luke 12:31 simply "seek the kingdom of God." We must not therefore erase, but supply from Matthew what Luke has omitted, since both were inspired (*theopneustos*), especially as the full form exists in all the Greek copies of Matthew, according to Erasmus and Beza.

XXIII. Although in some manuscripts, we read *kairō douleuontes* ("serving time," Rom. 12:11), it does not appear in all. Indeed Franciscus Lucas says that he saw six manuscripts in which the word *Kyriō* occurs. Beza asserts that it is so in all the most approved manuscripts (*Annotationes maiores in Novum . . . Testamentum: Pars Altera* [1594], 133 on Rom. 12:11) and Dominic de Soto observes that this is the universal reading both in the Greek and Latin.

XXIV. It is true that all the Greek copies differ from the Latin on 1 John 4:3, for where the Greek have "every spirit that confesseth not that Jesus Christ is come in the flesh," the Latin read "every spirit that denies Jesus." Yet it does not follow that the sources are corrupt because the Greek reading is both more majestic and far stronger against the Nestorians and Eutychians.

XXV. A corruption differs from a variant reading. We acknowledge that many variant readings occur both in the Old and New Testaments arising from a comparison of different manuscripts, but we deny corruption (at least corruption that is universal).

XXVI. It is one thing to speak of the attempts of heretics to corrupt some manuscripts (which we readily allow). They gave rise to the complaints of the fathers; as concerning Marcion (Irenaeus, *Against Heresies* 1.27 [ANF 1:352]); and Origen on Romans 16:13 (*Commentariorum . . . ad Romanos* [PG 14.1271]); and Theodoret of Cyrrhus concerning Tatian (*Haereticarum fabularum compendium* [PG 83.370–71]). It is quite a different thing to speak of their success or of entire universal corruption. This we deny, both on account of the providence of God, who would not permit them to carry out their intention, and on account of the diligence of the orthodox fathers, who having in their possession various manuscripts preserved them free from corruptions.

Eleventh Question: The Authentic Version

Are the Hebrew version of the Old Testament and the Greek of the New the only authentic versions? We affirm against the papists.

I. Of the versions of the Scriptures; some are *prōtotypoi* or *archetypoi* ("original" and "primary") which the authors themselves used. Others are *ektypoi* (or "secondary"), namely versions flowing from them into other languages. All admit that the Hebrew of the Old and the Greek of the New Testament are the original and primitive. But we and the papists dispute whether each is authentic, of itself deserving faith and authority and the standard to which all the versions are to be applied.

THE OPINION OF THE PAPISTS

II. Some of the papists may be more favorable to the sources, asserting their purity (as we have already seen), ascribing authenticity to them as a consequence of purity and maintaining that all the versions and even the Vulgate ought to be referred to and can be corrected by them: as Sixtus Senensis (*Bibliotheca sancta* 8, haer. 2 [1575], 2:314–19); Driedo ("De ecclesiasticis scripturis et dogmatibus," 2 in *Opera* [1572], 1:23–62); Andradius (*Defensio tridentinae fidei Catholicae* 2 [1580], 167–460) and others. Yet many are more hostile to them, holding that there is no certainty in the Hebrew text, that we should not refer to the sources in controversies of faith, nor correct the Vulgate version by them: as Stapleton ("De principiis fidei doctrinalibus controversia," Cont. 5, Q. 3, Art. 1 in *Opera* [1620], 1:771–74); Cano ("De locis theologicis," 2.11 and 2.13 in *Opera* [1605], 65–85, 90–100); Lindanus and others who argue for the corruption of the sources. This opinion arose from a decree of the Council of Trent Session 4, which says that "the Latin Vulgate should be held as authentic in the public reading, disputations, preaching, and expositions, so that no one should dare to reject it under any pretext" (Schroeder, *Council of Trent*, 18, 297). A number of the papists (ashamed of this decree) endeavor to attach a different meaning to it, as if the Council had decreed nothing against the authenticity of the originals, nor preferred the Vulgate to the sources, but only chose one of the Latin versions then circulating as better than the rest (Bellarmine, VD 2.10, pp. 75–77). This is also the opinion of Andradius, Salmeron, Serarius and others. But Bannes properly exclaims against this as a distortion of the synodical decree and the very words of the decree plainly show it. For if it ought to be considered authentic, so that no one should dare to reject it under any pretext, is it not put on an equality with the sources themselves; yea, even exalted above them? And even if it varies from the sources, it is not to be corrected by them, but they rather corrected by it. Hence Mariana complains that after this promulgation of the Council of Trent, "the Greek and Hebrew fell at one blow" (*de V.V.*, 99). Our opinion is that the Hebrew of the Old and the Greek of the New Testament have always been and still are the only authentic versions by which all controversies of faith and religion (and all versions) ought to be approved and tested.

WHAT IS AN AUTHENTIC WRITING?

III. An authentic writing is one in which all things are abundantly sufficient to inspire confidence; one to which the fullest credit is due in its own kind; one of which we can be entirely sure that it has proceeded from the author whose name it bears; one in which everything is written just as he himself wished. However, a writing can be authentic in two ways: either primarily and originally or secondarily and derivatively. That writing is primarily authentic which is *autopiston* ("of self-inspiring confidence") and to which credit is and ought to be given on its own account. In this manner, the originals of royal edicts, magistrates' decrees, wills, contracts and the autographs of authors are authentic. The secondarily authentic writings are all the copies accurately and faithfully taken from the originals by suitable men; such as the scriveners appointed for that purpose by public authority (for the edicts of kings and other public documents) and any honest and careful scribes and copiers (for books and other writings). The autographs of Moses, the prophets and apostles are alone authentic in the first sense. In the latter sense, the faithful and accurate copies of them are also authentic.

IV. Again, the authority of an authentic writing is twofold: the one is founded upon the things themselves of which it treats and has relation to the men to whom the writing is directed; the other is occupied with the treatise itself and the writing and refers to the copies and translations made from it. Over all these this law obtains—that they ought to be referred to the authentic writing and if they vary from it, to be corrected and emended. The former authority may be either greater or lesser according to the authority of him from whom the writing comes and in proportion to the power which he has over the persons to whom he directs his writing. But in the sacred Scriptures this authority is the very highest, such as can be in no other writing, since we are bound straightway to believe God for that supreme power which he has over men as over all other things, and for that highest truth and wisdom distinguishing him, and to obey in all things which his most sacred word (contained in the authentic Scripture) enjoins for belief or practice. But the latter consists in this, that the autographs and also the accurate and faithful copies may be the standard of all other copies of the same writing and of its translations. If anything is found in them different from the authentic writings, either autographs or apographs, it is unworthy of the name authentic and should be discarded as spurious and adulterated, the discordance itself being a sufficient reason for its rejection. Of the former authority we spoke in Question Four, "On the Divinity of the Scriptures." We will now treat of the other which occurs in the authentic version.

V. Finally, authenticity may be regarded in two ways: either materially as to the things announced or formally as to the words and mode of annunciation. We do not speak here of authenticity in the former sense for we do not deny this to versions when they agree with the sources, but only in the latter which belongs to the sources alone.

The Hebrew of the Old and the Greek of the New Testament are the only authentic editions

VI. The reasons are: (1) because the sources alone are inspired of God both as to the things and words (2 Tim. 3:16); hence they alone can be authentic. For whatever the men of God wrote, they wrote under the influence of the Holy Spirit (2 Peter 1:21), who, to keep them from error, dictated not only the matter but also the words, which cannot be said of any version. (2) They are the standard and rule to which all the versions should be applied, just as the copy (*ektypon*) should answer to the pattern (*archetypon*) and the stream be distinguished from its source. Here pertains the canon of Gratian, "As the faith of the old books must be tested by the Hebrew volumes, so the truth of the new needs the Greek writing for its rule" ("Decreti, Pt. I," Dist. 9.6 in *Corpus Iuris Canonici* [ed. A. Friedberg, 1955], 1:17). Jerome is full on this subject that he may defend the authority of the Hebrew text as the fountain to which all the streams of the versions ought to be traced and by it corrected (*Letter 26 [102]*, "Ad Marcellam" [PL 22.430–31]; *Letter 72*, "Ad Vitalem" [PL 22.673–76]; *Letter 106*, "Ad Suniam et Fretellam" [PL 22.837–67]). (3) These editions were authentic from the very first and were always considered to be so by the Jewish and Christian church many centuries after Christ. Nor can any reason be given why they should now cease to be authentic. As to the argument from corruption (besides taking for granted the thing to be proved), it has been already answered by us.

VII. (4) If the Hebrew edition of the Old Testament and the Greek edition of the New Testament are not authentic (*authentias*), there would be no authentic version, since none besides this has a divine testimony of its own authenticity. Thus there would be no authentic word of God in the church, no end of contentions because there would be no sure rule of faith and practice in which we might have full confidence. And the Scriptures, like a wax nose or the Lesbian rule, could be turned at pleasure any way. (5) Our opponents acknowledge that in certain cases it is right to have recourse to the sources. Bellarmine asserts: (a) "when in the Latin manuscripts there appears an error of the copyists; (b) when they have various readings and there is an uncertainty as to the true one; (c) when there is any ambiguity in the words or things; (d) when the force (*energeia*) and meaning of the words are not fully expressed" (VD 2.11, p. 78). Now this could not be done if the sources were not authentic. Arias Montanus shows by various considerations that the errors of the versions could not be corrected except upon the truth of the primitive language ("Praefatio," *Biblia sacra Hebraice, Chaldaice, Graece et Latine* [1572], vol. 1). Vives thinks that the sources ought surely and unquestionably to be appealed to (*Saint Augustine, of the Citie of God . . . with . . . comments of Lodovicus Vives* 14.8 [1620], 480). Salmeron, Bonfrerius, Masius, Muis, Jansen, with their disciples and others, are of the same opinion.

Sources of explanation

VIII. The various readings which occur do not destroy the authenticity of the Scriptures because they may be easily distinguished and determined, partly by the connection of the passage and partly by a collation with better manuscripts. Some are of such a kind that although diverse, they may nevertheless belong to the same text.

IX. Although various contentions may spring from the Hebrew and Greek sources, yet it does not follow that they cannot be authentic. If that were the case there would be no authentic edition at all for us to consult, since every language will supply sufficient material of controversy to the contentious. Then again this is not the fault of the sources, but of those who abuse them, either by not understanding or by twisting the words to suit their own purposes and pertinaciously adhering to them.

X. There is no truth in the assertion that the Hebrew edition of the Old Testament and the Greek edition of the New Testament are said to be mutilated; nor can the arguments used by our opponents prove it. Not the history of the adulteress (John 8:1–11), for although it is lacking in the Syriac version, it is found in all the Greek manuscripts. Not 1 John 5:7, for although some formerly called it into question and heretics now do, yet all the Greek copies have it, as Sixtus Senensis acknowledges: "they have been the words of never-doubted truth, and contained in all the Greek copies from the very times of the apostles" (*Bibliotheca sancta* [1575], 2:298). Not Mark 16 which may have been wanting in several copies in the time of Jerome (as he asserts); but now it occurs in all, even in the Syriac version, and is clearly necessary to complete the history of the resurrection of Christ.

XI. In order to weaken the authenticity (*authentian*) of the Hebrew edition, our opponents have recourse to the "newness of the points" (in vain, as if the punctuation was only a human invention devised by the Masoretes and therefore founded upon human authority, not upon divine and infallible authority; and that it can be changed at pleasure without risk and so always leave the meaning of a passage uncertain and doubtful). Several answers may be given to this. (1) Bellarmine agrees with us here "the errors arising from the points do not interfere with truth because they have come from without and do not change the text" (VD 2.2, p. 65). (2) On this hypothesis, not only does the certainty of the original text fall, but also that of the Vulgate which was taken from that source (unless it can be proved that the first author of that version—whether he was Jerome or some other one—received a revelation of necessary words directly from the Spirit which, were this not the case, it would be certain he had received from the tradition of the Jews; if this were uncertain, the whole authority of the sacred text would totter).

XII. (3) Even if the points were lately added (as they maintain who trace their origin to the Masoretes of Tiberias), it would not follow that the punctuation was a merely human invention, depending solely upon human will (which, if established, would greatly weaken the authenticity of the Hebrew manuscript; because the points, at least according to those who hold this opinion, are not supposed to have been made at the pleasure of the Rabbis, but according to the analogy of Scripture, the genius of the sacred language and the sense established by usage among the Jews). For although (according to this latter hypothesis) the points may not have been from the beginning as to form, still it cannot be denied that they were always as to sound and value or power. Otherwise since vowels are the souls of consonants, a doubtful sense (and in fact no sense at all) would constantly arise from the words, unless they were coeval with the consonants. Prideaux well observes, "No one will deny that the points and accents have been from the first as to sound and value, but only as to the marks and characters" (Lectio 12, "De punctorum Hebraicorum origine," in *Viginti-duae lectiones* [1648], 195, 197). And a little afterwards, "the vowels were coeval with the consonants as to sound and subjective power, although the marks and signs might not then have been known" (ibid., 197). Indeed it can scarcely be doubted that the vowels were represented, if not by their present form, yet by some marks in place of points (viz., by the letters '*vy*, as some think) which moreover are called *matres lectionis*, so that the certain and constant sense of the Holy Spirit might be gathered (otherwise it would depend upon mere tradition, and the regulations and memory of men might easily be forgotten and corrupted). This is the opinion of the very learned Walton: "By the use, and according to tradition, by the aid of the three letters '*vy*, called *matres lectionis*, and standing in the place of vowels before the invention of points, the true reading and pronunciation has been preserved" ("De Textuum originariorum integritate et auctoritate," [Prolegomena, 7] in *Biblia sacra polyglotta* [1657], 1:44).

XIII. (4) The adversaries take for granted the very thing to be proved—that the points are a human and recent invention, the contrary of which the Jews with great unanimity thus far (except one Eli, a Levite, who lived a hundred years ago) have asserted. In their footsteps follow many celebrated men, grammarians as well as theologians, Protestants and papists: Junius, Illyricus, Reuchlin, Munster, Cevalerius, Pagninus, M. Marinus, Polanus, Diodati, Broughton, Muis, Taylor, Bootius, Lightfoot, the great majority of modern theologians, and the Buxtorfs, who here say everything before them—the father in his *Tiberias, sive commentarius Masorethicus triplex* (1665), and the son in that very weighty work (*Anticritica: seu vindiciae veritatis Hebraicae* [1653]) in which he opposed the *Arcanii punctationis L. Cappelli vindiciae adversus Joh. Buxtorfii* (in Louis Cappel's *Commentarii et notae criticae in Vetus Testamentum* [1689], 795–979). Nor would it be difficult to establish this opinion by various arguments, if appropriate here. But as this question seems rather to be grammatical than theological, we are unwilling to bring it into our field. Suffer us briefly to say that we have always thought the truer and safer way to keep the authenticity (*authentian*) of the original text safe and sound against the cavils of all profane persons and heretics whatever and to put the principle of faith upon a sure and immovable basis, is that which holds the points to be of divine origin, whether they are referred to Moses or to Ezra (the head of the great Synagogue). Therefore, the adversaries err who wish to impugn the authority of the Hebrew manuscript from the newness of the points.

Twelfth Question

Is the present Hebrew text in things as well as words so authentic and inspired (theopneustos) in such a sense that all the extant versions are to be referred to it as a rule and, wherever they vary, to be corrected by it? Or may we desert the reading it supplies, if judged less appropriate, and correct it either by comparison of ancient translators, or by suitable (stochastikē) judgment and conjecture, and follow another more suitable reading? We affirm the former and deny the latter.

I. As the authority (*authentia*) of the sacred text is the primary foundation of faith, nothing ought to be held as more important than to preserve it unimpaired against the attacks of those who endeavor either to take it entirely away or in any manner to weaken it. For this purpose, the preceding controversy against the papists was taken up. The present question has the same object. In it we will examine the opinion of the celebrated Louis Cappel who, as in his *Arcanum punctationis*, undertook most strenuously to defend the newness of the points as a recent invention of the Masoretes and therefore originating in human diligence and labor. Thus in his *Critica sacra* he strives earnestly to prove that we are not so bound to the present Hebrew text but that we may often lawfully depart from it whenever we can get another better and more suitable reading, either from a comparison of ancient interpreters or by the exercise of right reason or by proper judgment and conjecture (which he fully discusses in *Critica sacra* 6.4–5 [1650], 391–408). In taking up this subject, we do not wish to detract from the reputation of a man deserving well otherwise of the church of God, but only to confirm the opinion thus far constantly held in the church concerning the unimpaired authority (*authentia*) of the sacred text, against those who do not hesitate at this time to adopt these peculiar opinions (*kyrias doxas*) and new hypotheses, or speak of them as trivial and of very little or of no importance to faith.

II. His opinion comes to this: (1) Because the points are a human invention, they can (when necessity calls for it) be altered, and others substituted in their place when the sense which they give is either false or absurd. (2) Not only are we at liberty to change the reading as to the points, but as to the writing itself; still the freedom is greater concerning the former than concerning the latter because the Masoretes (to whom we ought to be bound) often made the former at their pleasure and by the exercise of private judgment. (3) If it can be shown from a collation of ancient interpreters (whether Greek, Chaldee or Latin) that the sense of the versions is either equally good and appropriate or truer and more suitable than that of our Hebrew copy, it will be lawful to change the present reading and to substitute another in its place. (4) This can be done not only from a comparison of interpreters, but also, if we can discover an error in the present reading and a worthless or an absurd and false sense, and can (either by right reason and by the natural faculty of reason or by conjecture) find a plainer and more suitable sense (though a different reading), then in such cases it will be lawful to discard the present reading and to prefer the other. That such is his opinion appears from many passages and particularly from this: "From these it follows that if any reading differing from the present Hebrew text, as to the consonants or letters, and so also as to the words and whole periods, gives a better sense, it is more genuine, true and suitable, wherever it may be found, whether with the LXX, or the Chaldee paraphrases, with Aquila, Symmachus, Theodotion or Jerome (the author of the Vulgate version) and therefore should be followed and embraced rather than that of the Masoretes" (*Critica sacra* 6.5.9 [1650], 402). This he often confirms elsewhere.

III. In order to strengthen this opinion, he brings forward another hypothesis; viz., that the Hebrew manuscripts (which the Septuagint and other interpreters used) differed from that now in use (which he calls contemptuously the Masoretic and Jewish manuscript), and that the discrepancies of the ancient versions from the present Hebrew copy are so many various readings of the Hebrew text (with the exception perhaps of those which have arisen from the blunders of interpreters who either did not get the signification of the Hebrew words or did not pay sufficient attention to them). Hence he denies that our Hebrew Bible constitutes the sole source, asserting that it should be regarded as only one copy and that the true and genuine original authoritative text must be gathered and formed from a collation of all the ancient versions. Thus he distinguishes between the "Hebrew Codex in itself and the present Masoretic Codex." The former exists in all the copies which we now have, whether among the Jews or among Christians. The former is to be collected from a comparison of the present text with the ancient versions, which in certain cases he not only puts on an equality with, but also plainly prefers to the present Codex, since he holds that the sense which they give should be followed as truer and more proper than another which the present Codex gives (as we have seen above). "As much regard should be paid to the Septuagint as to the present Codex, not only when the former gives a better sense but also when it gives a sense just as good and appropriate because the Septuagint is more ancient, and in an equality of reading and sense, the authority of the more ancient prevails" (*De Critica . . . epistola apologetica in qua Arnoldi Bootii* [1651]). And a little afterwards: "The authority of the Septuagint is above that of the present standard, not only in those places where its reading gives a better sense, but also where it gives one as good and appropriate, and that because it is the more ancient. The same can and ought to be said of all the codices of the ancient interpreters."

IV. Far different however is the opinion held in common by our churches; viz., that no other codex should be held as authentic than the present Hebrew one, to which as to a touchstone, all the ancient and modern versions should be referred and if they differ from it be corrected by it, and not it to be amended by them. But although they think the various codices can and ought to be compared with each other that the various readings, arising from the carelessness of transcribers may be discerned; and the errors in whatever codex they occur may be corrected; and do not hesitate to say that no little help in acquiring the true sense comes from a collation of the ancient versions; yet they do deny that they can ever be made equal to, much less be preferred to the original text, so as to make it lawful to adhere to the sense which they give and which may seem to us more appropriate and to reject another which flows from a reading of the present text.

V. That this has ever been the opinion of all Protestants is perfectly clear. The controversy carried on previously with the papists about the authentic edition sufficiently confirms it. The illustrious author in question cannot deny it, for in the beginning of his *Critica sacra*, he says, "The first and most ancient Protestants have said that all things should be examined and corrected by the Hebrew text, which they call the purest source" (1.1 [1650], 3–4). Sixtinus Amama in his celebrated work *Anti-barbarus biblicus* (1656) confirms this after proposing his own opinion on the subject. "We conclude," says he, "that all the versions without exception, ancient as well as modem, should be tested by it" (viz., the Hebrew text); "that it is even now the standard, canon and rule of all versions" (1.3, p. 33); and "that therefore no version whatever can be put on an equality with the Hebrew text much less be preferred to it. Thus all Protestants think concerning all versions, whether ancient or modern" (1.4, p. 35).

STATEMENT OF THE QUESTION

VI. From this the state of the question may easily be inferred. The question is not whether it is lawful to compare the versions with each other and with the original in ascertaining the true sense. Rather the question is whether it is lawful to make equal or prefer to it a reading which arises from them (and seems more appropriate) by substituting it in place of a present reading (in our judgment giving no sense or an absurd and false one). The question is not whether there are not various discrepancies between the present text and the ancient versions; but whether these discrepancies are to be considered as so many various readings of the Hebrew Codex, so that the authentic readings can be no other than that which arises from the collation of the present text and the ancient versions. Lastly, the question is not whether in the examination and collation of codices (both manuscript and printed) we can use our own judgment and the reasoning faculty to distinguish the more approved and to decide which reading is better and more suitable; but whether it is lawful to make critical conjectures about the sacred text (just as in profane authority) by changing letters and points and even whole words, when the sense arising from the present reading does not seem to us appropriate. This the learned man maintains; we deny.

VII. The reasons are: (1) On this hypothesis it follows that there is no authentic text in which we can repose with entire confidence. It would either be the present Hebrew Codex (but according to this opinion this holds the place only of one copy and that reading therefore can be considered as the authentic Hebrew source where there is no dissent among interpreters from the present codex, as the learned man says, *Apol. cont. Boot*, 17) or it would be other codices which the ancient interpreters used. But besides taking for granted that they were different from the present codex (which is his capital error [*prōton pseudos*] as will be proved afterwards), although this is conceded to him, yet they cannot now inspire confidence because they are lacking and no longer exist anywhere except in this version itself (which, since it is human and fallible, cannot become an authentic codex). Finally, who can assure us that the seventy faithfully followed their Hebrew text and that the Greek text (which we now read) is the very same with that which the seventy wrote?

VIII. (2) If all the discrepancies of the ancient versions from the present text were so many various readings of the Hebrew manuscripts different from ours and which the interpreters used, why is there no mention made of such manuscripts by the ancients and no trace of them among the Hebrews (who for many ages have been so careful in observing and collecting even the smallest variations, as the discrepant readings of Ben Ascher and Ben Naphtali, of the orientals and occidentals show)? For who can suppose that these variations of less importance should have remained and that those which were noticed by the ancient interpreters should so utterly perish as to leave no trace behind? For as there were many copies, it is surprising that not one has come down to our time. (a) It is assumed that there are no causes of these discrepancies besides the diversity of manuscripts while there are many others more certain; just as in the present versions, it would be wrong to infer that the interpreters used different manuscripts because innumerable differences of translation occur, when no other except the present copy remains from which they were made. Who does not know that they might more often have attended to the sense rather than to the words, as Jerome frequently says of the seventy? Again, sometimes a discrepancy may have been caused by their ignorance or negligence because they did not notice particularly the words, so that they could often make mistakes in similar letters and words even without a different manuscript. Jerome more than once charges them with this. (b) They might also have used too much liberty in boldly translating in the face of their copy because they did not clearly perceive the sense and connection of the Hebrew text and preferred to follow with a slight change the sense which they thought flowed from it more naturally. (c) The various ancient versions are evidently not such as they are when first issued, but have been greatly corrupted and altered. This is especially true of the Septuagint and Vulgate. (d) Many corruptions may have crept in through the carelessness or ignorance of transcribers. Therefore they have not arisen from a variety of manuscripts.

IX. (3) Thus the ancient versions would be put on an equality with the original text. For if in all the discrepancies, the ancient interpreters are to be tested by the text no more than this by them, but both to be subjected to the common canon of a more suitable sense, so that a better sense shall decide the true reading (whether it occurs in the Hebrew text or in any of the interpreters), the Hebrew text would have no higher authority than the ancient interpreters except that which would arise from a fitter sense. Indeed it would often be thrown below the translations when its reading would be rejected for others.

X. (4) If we are not bound to the present reading of the Hebrew text and the true reading is to be derived partly from a collation of ancient versions, partly from our own judgment and conjectural (*stochastikē*) faculty (so that there shall be no other canon of authoritative reading than that which seems to us to be the fitter sense), the establishment of the authoritative reading will be the work of the human will and reason, not of the Holy Spirit. Human reason will be placed in the citadel and be held as the rule and principle of faith with the Socinians.

XI. (5) If it is lawful to make conjectures on the sacred text, even when the Hebrew codices agree with the versions (as the learned man [Cappel] says, *Critica sacra* 6.8.17 [1650], 424), there could no longer be any certainty of the authenticity (*authentias*) of it, but all would be rendered doubtful and unsettled and the sacred text would be subjected to the will of each conjecturer. Whether this is not to divest it of all authority anyone can readily tell. Nor can it be replied that conjectures are not to be admitted unless they are founded upon and demonstrated by sure reasons and arguments, when the received reading gives a sense either false and absurd or doubtful and disconnected. For everyone will think that he can give reasons for his conjectures and will tax with falsity and absurdity the reading which he endeavors to overthrow. Now who could be the judge whether these conjectures are made rightly and truly? And without a judge, perpetual controversies and disputes would arise between interpreters, each one fighting for his own interpretation and not allowing others to be preferred to his. Nor (if conjectures can have place in the examination of various manuscripts in order to determine the better and more suitable reading) are others therefore to be allowed, founded upon private judgment and not upon the authority of any approved manuscript, not only entirely worthless in themselves, but highly dangerous and destructive to the Scriptures from the great and bold presumption of the human intellect. Neither ought the example of profane authors to be cited here who can freely and without danger be criticized. As if sacred and profane criticism hold an equal rank, and as if there is not the greatest difference between human writings (liable to error) and the divine (God-inspired, *theopneuston*) whose majesty should be sacred, which were received with so great reverence, have been preserved with so much care and approved by so general a consent as to deserve the title of authoritative truth. But what will become of this sacred book, if everyone is allowed to wield a censorious pen and play the critic over it, just as over any profane book?

XII. (6) If no preference is given to the present Hebrew copy over the ancient interpreters, no greater regard paid to it than to them and even the reading of these often preferred when they seem to give a better sense, then Protestants have thus far been contending with the papists on false grounds. For they have asserted the authority of the present Hebrew text above the versions whether ancient or modern. Nor can we any longer press against them that all the versions (and especially the Vulgate) should be examined and corrected by it, if so many versions are not only made equal to it, but also preferred to it.

Sources of explanations

XIII. A different reading is one thing; a different interpretation another. Interpreters may have given various interpretations, but it does not follow that these have arisen from the different readings of various manuscripts, but from the other causes mentioned.

XIV. It is not necessary that the scribes should have been unerring (*anamartētoi*), if we do not suppose there were many Hebrew codices. It is enough that providence has so watched over the integrity of the authoritative codex that although they might have brought into the sacred text many errors either through carelessness or ignorance, yet they have not done so (or not in all the copies), nor in such a way as that they cannot be corrected and restored by a collation of the various manuscripts and of Scripture itself.

XV. Although we may rightly say that the Scripture would be rendered uncertain by the different various readings of various interpreters elicited only from conjecture, it does not follow from this that they are made uncertain by the different interpretations because they have given different translations of one and the same text. For thus indeed the sense is rendered doubtful and uncertain, but not the reading of the words and phrases. It is most difficult with so many various and uncertain readings and conjectures to maintain the certainty of the Scriptures because here is introduced the twofold uncertainty of the reading and the sense. In one case, a sure standard is established to which the discordant interpreters may be referred, but in the other there is no sure foundation and all things are made to depend upon the will and decision of the human mind.

XVI. Although we are bound to the present codex, it is not necessary for it to represent to us the autograph (*autographon*) of Moses and the prophets without even the smallest difference. For in order to preserve a copy exactly conformed to the original, it is sufficient for the same words to occur in each, without which the sense could not exist; and with the words the letters also, without which the words could not exist or be written (although some discrepancies might occur in other minutiae).

XVII. Although this learned man often declares that all the versions ought to be judged and corrected by the Hebrew text and that this is to be preferred to any version whatever, he cannot therefore be freed from the charge (which rests upon him) of putting the ancient versions on an equality with the original text and even of preferring them. For by the Hebrew text he does not mean the present original text which is used by all (both Jews and Christians), but the Hebrew text in general, which he wishes to derive both from the present codex and from the ancient codices which he supposes the ancient interpreters used and (as we said before) rests upon no solid foundation. And all the theologians who thus far have in any way argued concerning the Hebrew text and its authenticity have meant no other than the common and now received text.

XVIII. From what has been said, it appears how dangerous the hypotheses of this learned man are and with how much reason our friends have resisted the publication of this work, lest the cause of God might suffer injury and encouragement be given (although undoubtedly against his will) to the adversaries of the authenticity (*authentian*) of the sacred text.

XIX. Whoever desires to learn more on this subject should consult the *Anticritica: seu vindiciae veritatis Hebraicae* (1653) of the celebrated Buxtorf (which he opposes to the *Critica sacra*) in which he has accurately and most satisfactorily set forth this whole argument. The testimonies of other great men might also be adduced to show how highly displeased they are with his opinion and work. For instance James Ussher, Archbishop of Armagh, who says it contains "a most dangerous error" to be met at once before it has time to spread (Letter 288, "To Dr. Arnold Boate," in his *Whole Works* [1847–64], 16:187). And of the same Arnold Bootius in his epistle (cf. Letters 286, 291, 299, "Boate to the Archbishop of Armagh," *Whole Works* [1847–64], 16:182, 193–97, 234–36) to that venerable bishop and in his *Vindiciis*, in which he styles this work a "most pernicious writing in which there is nothing (*ouden*) sound (*hygies*)" (*Vindiciae seu apodixis apologetica pro Hebraica veritate* 6 [1653], 51). He calls it "an unhappy critique, setting forth an opinion entirely false and highly injurious to the sacred word of God" (ibid., 57). "Its author is the most hostile enemy to the Hebrew verity, depriving it of all certainty and authority" (ibid., 1). Thus many others who loudly complained of it. But as sufficient for the present, we give the testimony of Andrew Rivet, a great man and highly distinguished throughout France and Belgium, who after reading the *Arcanii punctationis* of this learned author, seemed to be drawn over to his opinion, but having read the answer of the celebrated Buxtorf speaks far otherwise in a letter to Buxtorf dated 1645 (which the latter gives in his *Anticritica: seu vindiciae veritatis Hebraicae: adversus Ludovici Cappelli Criticam* [1653]): "As to Capellus, our distinguished friend will send to you his diatribe against you, which I have not yet seen, but know is exposed for sale at Amsterdam where it was published. It will give you an opportunity of examining more closely into other things which he mediates against the sacred text, resting upon dangerous reasoning under the appearance of candor and truth. In these I see that he has imposed upon learned and strong men, but not sufficiently informed on such subjects, some of whom extol his critique not only as an elaborate but also as a highly necessary work. Our colleagues here, thoroughly versed in these subjects, have thought differently and were opposed to our setting it up with their type" (pp. 345–46). In another letter by the same from Breda (dated 1648): "I am firmly convinced that you, influenced by a true zeal for the authenticity (*authentia*) of the divine word, have entirely overthrown the foundation of that pestiferous and profane critique which this man produced and gave as a help to our enemies, when rejected by the orthodox. If he had gained his end, the whole of the Old Testament would resemble the shoe of Theramenis fitting either foot" (ibid., 346). And again: "God will prevent this audacity from going further. I congratulate you heartily that he has raised you up as the pious defender not only of the private cause of your blessed (*tou makaritou*) father, but also of the public possession of the whole true church. May God bless you for your exertions and long spare your life for future labors benefitting us" (ibid.). This judgment many followed, who although at first disposed to favor the new hypotheses, yet when they had more closely examined them and read the writings of Buxtorf and others against them, were not ashamed to alter their former opinion and yield to a better.

Thirteenth Question: Versions

Are versions necessary, and what ought to be their use and authority in the church?

I. This question has two parts. The first relates to the necessity of versions; the second to their authority. As to the former, although the wiser papists recognize their utility and necessity and have themselves made many in various languages, still not a few (taking the opposite ground) condemn them as hurtful and dangerous as Arboreus who says, "the translation of the Scriptures into the vernacular tongue is one source of heresies" (*Primus tomus theosophiae* 8.11 [1540], 247). Asoto, Harding, Baile and many of the Society of Loyola (*Jesuits*) agree with him and censure the pious and holy desire of translating the Scriptures as "a curious invention (*heurēma*) of heretics banished from orthodox religion, and therefore useless to the church, and impiously and iniquitously devised for the purpose of spreading heresy." Against these the orthodox maintain not only the utility, but also the necessity of versions and prove it by many arguments.

VERNACULAR VERSIONS ARE NECESSARY

II. (1) The reading and contemplation of the Scriptures is enjoined upon men of all languages, therefore the translation of it into the native tongues is necessary. Since men speak different languages and are not all familiar with those two in which it was first written, it cannot be understood by them unless translated; it comes as the same thing to say nothing at all and to say what nobody can understand. But here it happens by the wonderful grace of God that the division of tongues (which formerly was the sign of a curse) becomes now the proof of a heavenly blessing. What was introduced to destroy Babel is now used to build up the mystical Zion.

III. (2) The gospel is preached in all languages; therefore it can and ought to be translated into them. The consequence holds good from the preached to the written word because there is the same reason for both and the same arguments (which induced the apostles to preach in the native tongue) prove the necessity of versions. Now although the apostles wrote in only one language, it does not follow that the Scriptures should not be translated into others because there is a different rule as to the sources and versions. The sources ought to be written in only one language and moreover the apostles (as the universal teachers of the church) were bound to write in no other than the universal and most common tongue (which Greek was at that time) just as the Old Testament (intended for the Jews) was written in the Hebrew tongue, their vernacular. But, where the Greek language is not used, there is a need of versions for the spread of the gospel.

IV. (3) Vernacular versions are necessary on account of the constant practice of the church, according to which it is certain that both the oriental and western churches had their versions and performed their worship in the vernacular tongue, as their liturgies evince. Why should the same not be done now when there is the same necessity and reason for instructing the people? Thus since there were two remarkable dispersions of Israel (one among the Chaldeans, the other among the Greeks), and the people of God by using their peculiar idioms almost entirely forgot the Hebrew language, the Targums or Chaldean paraphrases and Greek versions were made for the benefit of the more ignorant classes. There were many Targums. First comes the Chaldean paraphrase of Jonathan ben Uzziel, the disciple of Hillel, the fellow-disciple of Simeon who was born forty years before Christ. When he saw the pure Hebrew language falling into disuse by degrees and employed only by the learned, he made the Chaldean version from this great treasure; we have a version of the earlier and later prophets by him. Onkelos, who flourished after Christ and was contemporary (*synchronos*) with Gamaliel, added to this a translation of the Pentateuch. A paraphrase of the Hagiographa is also extant by an unknown author. There are also extant Syriac, Arabic, Persian and Ethiopic versions, but little used and known. There is a Syriac translation of the New Testament (which is the most ancient) and is attributed by some to the church of Antioch.

V. The numerous Greek versions of the Old Testament follow these. The most celebrated is the Septuagint made about three hundred years before Christ under Ptolemy Philadelphus. The second is that of Aquila of Pontus, under the emperor Hadrian about A.D. 137. Being first a Greek in religion, afterwards a Christian, then being excommunicated from the church for his attachment to the study of astrology, he went over to the Jews and (actuated by hatred of the Christians) translated the Old Testament in order to corrupt the prophecies concerning Christ. Third, that of Theodotion, who lived under Commodus (A.D. 184), born in Pontus, a Marcionite in religion, and afterwards turning Jew made a new version in which he followed the Septuagint for the most part. Fourth, that of Symmachus, under Antoninus and Aurelius (about A.D. 197), who from a Samaritan turned

413

Jew and translated the Old Testament in order to confute the Samaritans. There were also two others of uncertain authors: from Jericho, found in a cask in that city, under Caracalla (A.D. 220); the other, the Nicopolitan, found near Nicopolis in the reign of Alexander Severus (A.D. 230). Out of all these versions Origen made up his Tetrapla, his Hexapla and his Octapla. The Tetrapla contained in distinct columns the four Greek versions of the Septuagint, Aquila, Symmachus and Theodotion. In the Hexapla, he added two Hebrew editions: one in Hebrew, the other in Greek letters. In the Octapla were inserted the two other anonymous Greek versions, those of Jericho and Nicopolis which some call the seventh edition. The eighth was that of Lucian the Martyr who emended the preceding ones and was favored highly by the Constantinopolitans. The ninth was that of Hesychius which the Egyptians and Alexandrians embraced. The tenth was one which the ancients said was translated from the Latin of Jerome into Greek.

VI. Various ancient Latin versions were also made principally from the Greek versions. The most common was the Italian according to Augustine (*On Christian Teaching* 2.15 [FC 2:79; PL 34.46]). Two others were made by Jerome: one from the Septuagint; the other (which he carefully corrected from the Hebrew and Greek text) is supposed to be the present Vulgate, but in process of time became greatly corrupted. Many learned men—Lorenzo Valla, Faber Stapulensis, Cajetan, Arias Montanus and others—have pointed out the corrections. Other more modern versions (some in Latin, some in other languages), we need not notice here because they are well known. Hence it is evident that it has been the perpetual practice of the church to use versions.

SOURCES OF SOLUTION

VII. The title on the cross was written in only three languages, not that these three might be set apart for a sacred use, but because they were then the most known and so the best adapted to spread the fame of Christ throughout the whole world (the design of God in that title).

VIII. The unity of the church (Eph. 4:3) does not depend upon the unity of language, but upon the unity of doctrine. The first councils were brought together lawfully and advantageously held, notwithstanding the diversity of tongues.

IX. The dignity of Scripture arises rather from the sense than from the words and if these three languages appear to increase the dignity, it is accidentally from the superstition of the unlettered multitude, not per se.

X. We do not deny that these three languages (after they have ceased to be vernacular) should be retained more often in the assemblies of the learned, that by them and according to them ecclesiastical business may be transacted and controversies settled. But where the faith and devotion of each one is concerned and in order that he may understand what he is doing, they do not have an equal propriety among the people and in public worship.

XI. Although we do not deny that the Hebrew language was in different ways corrupted among the common people by their intercourse with foreigners in the captivity and that many Chaldean and Syriac words crept into it, yet it does not follow from this either that the text was in any way changed or that it was not understood by the people upon whom it was inculcated. For Zechariah, Haggai and Malachi wrote in the pure Hebrew, which they would not have done if the people could not have understood it. Again, we gather from

Nehemiah 8:8 that Ezra read the book of the law before the whole multitude (to which they listened attentively, which they could not have done if they had not understood it). And if Ezra with the Levites is said to have caused them to understand what was read, this must be referred to an explanation of the sense and of the things themselves rather than as a translation of the words.

XII. Although the versions are not authentic formally and as to the mode of enunciation, yet they ought nevertheless to be used in the church because if they are accurate and agree with the sources, they are always authentic materially and as to the things expressed.

THE AUTHORITY OF VERSIONS

XIII. Hence we gather what the authority of the versions is. Although their utility is great for the instruction of believers, yet no version either can or ought to be put on an equality with the original, much less be preferred to it. (1) For no version has anything important which the Hebrew or Greek source does not have more fully, since in the sources not only the matter and sentences, but even the very words were directly dictated by the Holy Spirit. (2) It is one thing to be an interpreter, quite another to be a prophet, as Jerome says (*Praefatio in Pentateuchum* [PL 28.182]). The prophet as God-inspired (*theopneustos*) cannot err, but the interpreter as a man lacks no human quality since he is always liable to err. (3) All versions are the streams; the original text is the fountain whence they flow. The latter is the rule, the former the thing ruled, having only human authority.

XIV. Nevertheless all authority must not be denied to versions. Here we must carefully distinguish a twofold divine authority: one of things, the other of words. The former relates to the substance of doctrine which constitutes the internal form of the Scriptures. The latter relates to the accident of writing, the external and accidental form. The source has both, being God-inspired (theopneustos) both as to the words and things; but versions have only the first, being expressed in human and not in divine words.

XV. Hence it follows that the versions as such are not authentic and canonical in themselves (because made by human labor and talent). Therefore, under this relation (*schesei*), they may be exposed to errors and admit of corrections, but nevertheless are authentic as to the doctrine they contain (which is divine and infallible). Thus they do not, as such, formally support divine faith as to the words, but materially as to the substance of doctrine expressed in them.

XVI. There is one perfection of thing and truth to which nothing can be added and from which nothing can be taken away; another perfection of the version itself. The former is a strictly divine work and is absolutely and in every way self-credible (*autopiston*). Such perfection is in the word carried over into the versions. The latter is a human work and therefore liable to error and correction—to which indeed authority can belong, but only human (according to the fidelity and conformity with the original text), not divine.

XVII. The certainty of the conformity of the versions with the original is twofold: the one merely grammatical and of human knowledge apprehending the conformity of the words in the versions with the original (this belongs to the learned, who know the languages); the other spiritual and of divine faith, relating to the agreement of things and doctrines (belonging to each believer according to the measure of the gift of Christ, as he himself says, "My sheep hear my voice," John 10:27; and Paul, "he that is spiritual discerneth all things,"

1 Cor. 2:15). Although a private person may be ignorant of the languages, he does not cease to gather the fidelity of a version as to the things themselves from the analogy of faith and the connection of the doctrines: "If any man will do his will, he shall know of the doctrine, whether it be of God, or whether I speak of myself" (John 7:17).

XVIII. Conformity to the original is different from equality. Any version (provided it is faithful) is indeed conformable to the original because the same doctrine as to substance is set forth there. But it is not on that account equal to it because it is only a human and not a divine method of setting it forth.

XIX. Although any version made by fallible men cannot be considered divine and infallible with respect to the terms, yet it can well be considered such with respect to the things, since it faithfully expresses the divine truth of the sources even as the word which the minister of the gospel preaches does not cease to be divine and infallible and to establish our faith, although it may be expressed by him in human words. Thus faith depends not on the authority of the interpreter or minister, but is built upon the truth and authenticity (*authentia*) of the things contained in the versions.

XX. If a version could contain the pure word of God in divine words, no correction could take place. For the sources neither can nor ought to be corrected because they are God-inspired (*theopneustoi*) in things as well as in words. But because it sets forth to us in human words the word of God, it follows that it can admit of correction, not with regard to the doctrine itself (which still remains the same), but with regard to the terms which especially in difficult and obscure passages can be differently rendered by different persons according to the measure of the gift of Christ.

Fourteenth Question: The Septuagint

Is the Septuagint version of the Old Testament authentic? We deny.

I. Among the Greek versions of the Old Testament, that of the seventy interpreters deservedly holds the first place with us. It was so highly valued by the Jews and Christians in the east and west that by the former it was used publicly in the synagogues and by the latter it alone (or versions made from it) was used in their churches. From this version all the translations into other languages (which were anciently approved by the Christian church) were executed (with the exception of the Syriac): as the Arabic, Armenian, Ethiopic, Illyric, Gothic and the Latin version in use before the time of Jerome. To this day the Greek and most other oriental churches recognize it alone.

STATEMENT OF THE QUESTION

II. The question does not concern the time or the manner in which this version was executed, whether it was made under the auspices and at the expense of Ptolemy Philadelphus; or by the Jews for their own convenience (as Scaliger, *Epistolae* 11 [14] [1627], 100–101); or the seventy interpreters who being shut up in separate cells accomplished the whole work in seventy-two days and indeed with the most exact agreement (although each of them understood and performed the whole work separately from the rest); and other things of the same kind which are related of these interpreters both by Aristeas (who has given a prolix account of the circumstances) and by Josephus and the Christians (who, because they used this version, gave a ready ear to these narratives, eagerly taking hold of whatever would establish its authority). These matters are purely historical and therefore do not belong to our design. However, if we were called upon to express an opinion, we would give our cordial assent to that of those learned men who consider all these things as worthy of little credit. Even in his time, Jerome began to exhibit and attack the genuineness of the narratives, and this has been done more clearly and strongly by more modern writers (Vives, *Saint Augustine, of the Citie of God . . . with . . . comments of Lodovicus Vives* 18.42 [1620], 687–88; Scaliger in *Thesaurus temporum Eusebii* [1606]; Drusius, Casaubon, Wouverus, Ussher, Rivet, Heinsius and others). But we speak here only of its authority (i.e., whether such an authority is to be given to it as to make it to be reckoned God-inspired [*theopneustos*] and authentic).

III. Although the papists do not all speak alike, yet most of them agree that this version was divinely inspired and therefore properly obtains divine authority; and that the translators are to be considered not as interpreters but as prophets, who, that they might not err, had the help of the Holy Spirit in a special way, as Bellarmine says (VD 2.6, pp. 68–71). Baile, Stapleton, P. Carthusia (*de Translat. Bibli.* c. iv.5) and Johannes D'Espeires ("Tractatus 2: De Versione Septuaginta Interpretum," Disp. I, Dubium 10, *Auctoritas scripturae sacrae Hebraice, Graeca et Latine* [1651], 183–86) all agree with him, and so especially does John Morinus, who tries hard to establish the authenticity (*authentian*) of this version (*Exercitationis ecclesiasticae et Biblicae* 7.4 [1669]). Among our scholars, that most learned man Isaac Vossius tries to uphold the same idea by a number of arguments in a special treatise (cf. *De Septuaginta interpretibus* [1661–63]).

IV. Although we do not deny that it is of great authority in the church, yet we regard this authority as human, not divine, since what was done by the translators was by human effort only, not by prophets and men who were God-breathed (*theopneustois*) by the direct inspiration of the Holy Spirit.

V. Therefore it is not to be asked whether it should have any authority in the church. We concede that it is of great weight and rightly to be preferred to other translations. (1) It is the oldest of all, made two thousand years ago and so to be honored for its hoary hair. (2) It was read both in public and in private by the Jews wherever they were dispersed. (3) The apostles and evangelists used it in quoting many Old Testament passages and consecrated it, so to speak, by their writings. (4) The apostles gave it to the church when through it they conquered the world for Christ. Thus the Gentile church was born, raised and nourished by it. (5) The Greek and Latin churches held it as the authorized version for six hundred years. (6) The fathers and ancient ecclesiastical writers explained it by commentaries, set it forth to the people in homilies and by it strangled rising heresies. In their councils, they drew canons from it for the regulation of faith and practice. Rather the question is whether it has such an authority as that it ought to be regarded as authentic and equal to the sources. Our adversaries maintain this; we deny it.

The version of the LXX is not authentic

VI. The reasons are: (1) It was executed by human study and labor not divinely inspired (*theopneustois*) men. Its authors were interpreters, not prophets (who ceased after Malachi, called by the Jews the seal of the prophets). It is evident also from this as Aristeas says, "the interpreters conferred with each other, disputing and comparing notes on everything, until at length they could all agree" (*Letter of Aristeas* 302 [trans. H. St. J. Thackeray, 1904], 52).

417

Now if they consulted together, they did not prophesy. For the sacred writers never consulted with each other discussing everything which they might write. But as taught by the Holy Spirit, they committed all things to writing without any disputation or delay. (2) If they wrote under the influence of the Holy Spirit, such a number would have been superfluous (one being sufficient). There would have been no need for men of great learning, skilled in the Hebrew and Greek, if it had been executed without human study and aid. (3) In many instances, it varies from the sources in words and things and has various false interpretations (*parermēneias*) and discrepancies, as has been shown by the handlers of this argument. Hence Morinus was forced at least to confess, "No more authority is to be ascribed to this version than to those made by human industry" (*Exercitationis ecclesiasticae et Biblicae* 7.4 [1669]). (4) It is not considered pure now, but greatly corrupted and interpolated. We have only its ruins and wreck (*leipsana*), so that it can hardly be called *the* version of the Septuagint (like the ship Argo which was so often repaired as to be neither the same nor yet another). Jerome frequently alludes to this (*Letter 112* [89], "Ad Augustinum" [PL 22.928–29]; 'Praefatio . . . in librum Paralipomenon Praefatio,' from "Hieronymi Prologus Galeatus" in *Biblia Sacra Vulgatae Editionis Sixti V . . . et Clementis VIII* [1865], xlix and '. . . in Esdram et Nehemiam Praefatio,' from ibid., 1). Thus it is usually maintained by the learned that it is from the *koinē* version which may be called *loukianis*, as Jerome testifies (*Letter 106* [135], "Ad Suniam et Fretallam" [PL 22.838]).

SOURCES OF THE SOLUTION

VII. The apostles used this version not because they believed it to be authentic and divine, but because it was then the most used and most universally received and because (where a regard for the sense and truth was preserved) they were unwilling either rashly to dispute or to create a doubt in the minds of the more weak, but by a holy prudence left unchanged what when changed would give offense, especially when it would answer their purpose. However, they did this in such a manner that sometimes when it seemed necessary, when the version of the Septuagint seemed to be not only unsuitable but untrue, they preferred the source (as Jerome says, *Jerome's Apology . . . Against the Books of Rufinus* 2.34 [NPNF2, 3:517]). This can easily be gathered from a comparison of Matthew 2:15 with Hosea 11:1; John 19:37 with Zechariah 12:10; Jeremiah 31:15 with Matthew 2:18; Isaiah 25:8 with 1 Corinthians 15:54.

VIII. The quotations in the New Testament from the Septuagint are not authentic *per se* (or because they were translated by the seventy from Hebrew into Greek), but *per accidens* inasmuch as they were drawn into the sacred context by the evangelists under the influence of the Holy Spirit.

IX. If some of the fathers extol this version and assert its authenticity (as we cannot deny was done by Irenaeus, Clement of Alexandria, Augustine and others), they did so more from feeling than knowledge, being almost entirely unacquainted with the Hebrew language. Nor are we bound to adopt their opinion since they, as well as the seventy, were liable to human errors and passions. But Origen and Jerome, the most learned of them, held an entirely different opinion, teaching that they were interpreters, not inspired.

X. Although the church used this version for many years, we must not infer that she held it to be authentic and divine, but only that she held it in great estimation. Ordinary use could not have interfered with the liberty of access to the source as often as might be necessary.

XI. The great discrepancies in chronology between the Hebrew text and the version of the Septuagint (the Hebrew manuscripts making only 1656 years from the creation to the deluge, while the Septuagint makes 2242) does not prove that the version is authentic, but rather that it is corrupt. The consent of the Hebrew codices favors the Hebrew calculation (there being no variation in them on this subject); (2) so too the agreement (*symphōnia*) of all the ancient versions: the Chaldean, the Syriac, the Samaritan, the Arabian and the Latin, which vary from the Septuagint here and follow the Hebrew; (3) also the manifest error of the Greek version in extending the life of Methuselah at least fourteen years beyond the flood (if not twenty) and yet does not say that he was in the ark. For if Methuselah begat Lamech in the 165th year of his age (as the admirable notes in Walton's edition of the Greek version say, *Biblia sacra polyglotta* [1657], 1:20 on Gen. 5:25), Methuselah ought to have lived so many years after the flood. And if some Greek copies have in this instance followed the Hebrew (as Vossius says of the African and Alexandrine Codices), these few (which were no doubt corrected from the Hebrew) ought not to be opposed to the numberless copies which the church and the fathers followed in which this computation does exist.

XII. The arguments for the Greek computation are easily answered. First, as to the years of puberty—these were referred by the Greeks to the two hundredth year (a greater proportion to the whole life), by the Hebrews to the one hundredth year. Since Walton himself (although holding Vossius' opinion) acknowledges the weakness of this argument and says "they are foolish conjectures, unworthy of a man of sound mind" ("De Versionibus Graecis," [Prolegomena 9] in *Biblia sacra polyglotta* [1657], 1:68); and it is also assumed that the years of puberty (or the power of generation [*paidogonian*]) necessarily follow the quadruple or quintuple proportion of the whole life (since they ought to answer to the vigor of the body), it is absurd that in those first ages in which their bodies were very vigorous, puberty should be put off to the two hundredth year. It is clearly evident that in the cases mentioned by Moses, the proportion of puberty to life was not observed: Noah begat in his five hundredth year; Mahalalel in his sixty-fifth; Lamech in his 102nd; Cainan in his seventieth; Enoch in his sixty-fifth. The powers of generation of the postdiluvian patriarchs (although their lives were much shorter) are made almost equal to those of the former by the Greeks and are referred for the most part to the 130th year.

XIII. Second, what they adduce to prove the authenticity (*authentian*) of the Greek text (because no such corruption could happen by chance, which nevertheless has happened, nor by design because no good reason can be given for doing so) are still stronger proofs of the integrity of the Hebrew Codex—to which (other things being equal) the prerogative is not usually denied. Now although this corruption did not exist in the original version, could it not arise from the carelessness or oversight of transcribers (*ablepsia*)? Again, a sufficient and plausible pretext is that in the matter of time they wished to gratify the Egyptians (because the Hebrew text is much more opposed to the antiquity of Egypt than the Greek). For although Walton rejects this reason, yet Vossius considers it of great importance and on this very account prefers the Greek to the Hebrew because that agrees more with the antiquity of the Egyptians than this. By the addition of these 1600 years, the dynasties of the Egyptians might easily be included within the limits of the creation. Scaliger and Gerard Vossius propose a plan in which this can be done, if we admit the additions of the Greek with the Hebrew.

XIV. No importance can be given to the Greek computation from the fact of the Greek church and most of her writers following that computation instead of the Hebrew because this might have arisen from error or from an ignorance of the Hebrew language, inducing them to follow the most universally received version.

XV. The anachronism (*anachronismos*) in the Septuagint in the calculation of the life of the postdiluvian patriarchs (where they extend the number of years above 1700 to the birth of Abraham—the Hebrew making only 292 years—because they add at least one hundred years to the life of each of the patriarchs who lived between the flood and the time of Abraham) cannot favor the authenticity of that version. It demonstrates a glaring error from whatever source it may have arisen. The attempts which Vossius and Walton make to confirm this are not strong enough to weaken the authenticity (*authentian*) of the sacred text (as Robert Baillie, *Operis historici et chronologici* 1.4 [1668], 20–41 powerfully demonstrates at length).

Fifteenth Question: The Vulgate

Is the Vulgate authentic? We deny against the papists.

I. The question does not refer to the utility of the Vulgate and its frequent correspondence with the truth (which no one denies); nor to its antiquity and long use in the church (which also is granted by all). The question is whether its authenticity is of such a nature that it can be made equal to the original and be preferred to all other versions. This we deny and the papists assert, in accordance with the Council of Trent, Session 4, Decree 1: "Whoever will not receive as sacred and canonical these entire books with all their parts, as they have been usually read in the Catholic church, and are contained in the Old Vulgate edition, let him be accursed" (Schroeder, *Council of Trent*, 18). And again: "In addition the same Synod considering that it would be of no little benefit to the church, if it should point out which of all the Latin Editions is to be considered as authentic, determines and declares, that this old and Vulgate edition itself, which has been used for so long a time in the church, should be esteemed authentic in the public reading of the Scriptures, in disputations, in preaching, and in expounding, and that no one should dare to reject it under any pretext whatever" (ibid.).

II. True, there are varying opinions among the papists as to the sense of this decree. Some maintain that no comparison is made between that version and the source, but only with other Latin versions then in use; as Bellarmine, Serarius, Salmeron, Mariana and many others who think that it can even be corrected and emended from the sources. Others maintain that it is absolutely declared to be authentic (so that there is no better) and is to be preferred to all editions in whatever language and, even by it the original codices (as corrupt) must be emended; as Cano, Valentia, Gordon, Gretser, Suarez and others. But whoever attentively considers the words of the decree will easily perceive that it leans to the latter opinion. For if it can be rejected "under no pretext whatever" then not "under the pretext of the Hebrew codex" (which Hart openly maintained in his colloquy with Rainolds; cf. *Summe of the conference between John Rainolds and John Hart* [1584]). Hence Cardinal Ximenes, in the preface to the Complutensian Bible, declares that "he placed the Latin between the Hebrew and the Greek as the two thieves on this side and on that, but Jesus in the middle—that is the Roman or the Latin Church" ("Prologus ad lectorem," *Biblia Polyglotta* [1514–17], vol. 1, leaf 2v). Nor does Mariana receive the support of his companions when (in his book on the Vulgate) he says that it is of no less authority than the sources when it agrees with them and must be pardoned when it differs. Therefore the *Index Expurg.* erased these words *"ubi cum fontibus convenit."* Ludovicus de Tena, confronting Mariana, says, "If the Vulgate is authentic only when it agrees with the sources and faulty when it differs from them, then it is not absolutely authentic and the Tridentine decree gives it no greater certainty as to us than it had before. Even before the decree it was considered authentic under that condition (viz., of agreement with the sources). Therefore if the Council of Trent did so decree, the question still remains unsettled" (*Isagoge in totam sacram scripturam* 1, diff. 6.3 [1620], 31).

THE VULGATE IS NOT AUTHENTIC

III. Although we respect the Vulgate as an ancient version, we deny its authenticity. (1) It was elaborated by human skill and has no God-inspired (*theopneuston*) author which the authentic edition demands. For whether its author was Jerome (as the papists hold) or some other one before his time (who combined the Italian version and the Vulgate so-called) or Sixtus V and Clement VIII (who in many particulars corrected the old one which was used in the church) no one of them was inspired (*theopneustos*).

IV. (2) It was not authentic either before the decree of the Council or after. Not before because it contained many errors, which were freely pointed out by the papists (Nicholas of Lyra, Paul Burgensis, Driedo, Jerome of Oleastro, Cajetan and others—especially by Isidorus Clarius, who says that he observed eighty thousand errors in the Latin Vulgate). Sixtus of Siena says, "We are free to acknowledge that we have corrected many errors from Jerome in the old translation, and so in this our new edition have discovered some blemishes, solecisms, barbarisms, and many improper and ungrammatical translations; obscure and ambiguous interpretations, some things added others omitted; some transposed and corrupted by the fault of the writers, which Pagninus, Oleastrius, Vatablus, Cajetanus have noticed in their interpretations and expositions" (*Bibliotheca sancta* 8 [1575], 2:365). Surely if Pope Leo X had esteemed it authentic before, he would not have authorized Pagninus of Lucca to make a new version because he saw that the celebrated version of Jerome had been grossly corrupted and injured by the carelessness of men and the waste of time (as Sixtus of Siena relates, ibid., 4, p. 265). Nor could it be called authentic after the Council (of Trent) because a council could not make that authentic which was not so before. For as it cannot make our uncanonical book canonical, but only declare it such, so neither can it make a version authentic (since this belongs to God alone who can confer divine authority on whatever writing he pleases). But a council can only declare that the version is faithful and consistent with its source; or, if faults have crept in, to correct them; also to make its use obligatory upon the church.

V. (3) It varies from the sources in many places. Clement VIII grants this concerning the Sixtine edition, emending it although it had been pronounced authentic by the Council and corrected by Sixtus. Two years afterwards, he reviewed it, restored some things which had been expunged by Sixtus and changed and corrected many things. This is evident from a comparison of the examples in the *Bellum Papale* (1678) of Thomas James where (besides innumerable varieties) he brings forward two thousand readings which (confirmed by the apostolic authority of Sixtus against the truth of the Hebrew and Greek) Clement corrected by the same authority and called back to the sources ("Praefatio ad lectorem,"

Biblia Sacra Vulgatae Editionis Sixti V Pontificis . . . et Clementis VIII [1865], xli). These cannot be considered errors of the press, for who can believe that thousands of errors could have crept from the press into that edition upon which Sixtus bestowed so much labor? The preface to the Clementine edition (which Clement pronounced authentic after the Sixtine) shows that it also contains many errors.

> Therefore receive, Christian reader, with the approval of the same pontiff, a Vulgate edition of the Holy Scriptures corrected with whatever care could be given; although it is difficult to call it final in every part, on account of human weakness, yet it cannot be doubted to be more corrected and purer than all the others which have been published up to now. ("Praefatio ad lectorem," *Biblia sacra . . . Vulgatam Clementiam* [1965], xi.)

For if it is difficult to say that it is entirely free from all faults and only purer than those which have preceded it, therefore it does not deny that afterwards more correct ones could be produced, nor can it be what the Council called "fully corrected" (*emendatissima*) (Schroeder, *Council of Trent*, 19). But in what follows this very thing will be more evident when it is expressly said, "in the ancient Vulgate version of the Bible a certain force seems to have altered that which was relinquished by deliberate exchange." Bellarmine, who was among the correctors, does not conceal this: "You see, the Vulgate Bible was not completely corrected by us; for good reason we left much undone which seemed to call for correction" (cf. "In Christo Patri Iacobo Blasaeo . . . Franciscus Lucas," in *Biblia sacra Vulgata* [1624], vol. 2, near the end of the volume).

VI. (4) Formerly many papists (Erasmus, Valla, Pagninus, Cajetan, Oleaster, Forerius, Sixtus of Siena) acknowledge that the Vulgate was filled with mistakes, and many celebrated interpreters of the present day (Salmero, Bonfrerius, Serarius, Masius, Muis and others) agree with them and therefore leave it for the sources.

VII. (5) There are many passages which, being falsely rendered, give occasion or support to the most dangerous errors. *Ipsa* ("she") shall bruise (Gen. 3:15) is referred to the virgin; whereas in Hebrew we read *hv'* (*ipsum*, i.e., "the seed"). *Erat enim Sacerdos* ("he was a priest," Gen. 14:18) for *et erat* ("and he was"). *Invocatur nomen meum super eos* ("let my name be invoked over them," Gen. 48:16) for *vocetur in iis nomen meum* ("let my name be named among them"). *Adorate scabellum pedum ejus* ("worship his footstool," Ps. 99:5) instead of *ad scabellum* ("at his footstool"), if the ark is meant; or *in scabello* (i.e., in the temple) which is his footstool. *Omnia in futurum servantur incerta* ("All things in the future are kept uncertain," Eccl. 9:2) instead of *omnia sunt ante eos* ("all things are alike to all"). *Suggeret vobis omnia, quaecunque dixero vobis* ("suggest to you all that I shall say to you," John 14:26) to favor unwritten (*agraphous*) apostolic traditions; but the Greek is very different, *panta ha eipon hymin* (*omnia quae dixi vobis*, "all that I said to you"). *Adoravit fastigium virgae* ("he worshipped the top of his staff," Heb. 11:21) contrary to the intention of Paul (*prosekynēse epi to akron, adoravit super summitatem baculi*, "he worshipped upon the top of his staff"), i.e., as Beza translates it for *baculo innixus* ("leaning on his staff," *Annotationes maiores in Novum . . . Testament: Pars Altera* [1594], 537 on Heb. 11:21). *Talibus hostiis promeretur Deus* ("with such sacrifices God's favor is merited," Heb. 13:16) instead of *delectatur* ("God is delighted"). *Non ego, sed gratia Dei mecum* ("Not I, but the grace of God with me," 1 Cor. 15:10) for *quae mecum est* ("which is with me"). Other passages may be adduced in which there are errors of omission and of addition; as *Si autem gratia, iam non ex operibus, alioquin gratia iam non est gratia* ("And if by grace, then is it no more of works: otherwise grace is no more grace," Rom. 11:6), a whole clause is lacking after this which is contained in the Greek, "but if it be of works, then it is no more grace; otherwise work is no more work." The words *In propatulo* ("in the open") are omitted three times in Matthew 6:4–6, 18. These words are lacking in Matthew 15:8: "This people draweth nigh to me with their mouth." In Matthew 20:22, these are missing: "and to be baptized with the baptism that I am baptized with?" In 1 Corinthians 6:20, after *in corpore vestro* these are missing: *et in spiritu quae sunt Dei* ("and in your Spirit, which are God's"). The following are errors of addition: Luke 10:1 makes "seventy-two others" which in Greek is *heterous hebdomēkonta* ("seventy others"); Acts 9:29, *loquebatur quoque gentibus, et disputabat cum Graecis* ("he was speaking also with the Gentiles, and disputing with the Greeks"), instead of *loquebatur et disceptabat adversus Graecos* ("he was speaking and disputing against the Greeks"); Romans 4:2, *ex operibus Legis* ("by the works of the Law"), the Greek warants only *operibus* ("by works"). Many similar examples will occur to the reader. See further Whitaker, Chamier, Amamus, James and others of our men who have pointed out the errors of this version.

VIII. (6) Whatever that version may be, which they maintain is partly composed from the ancient version called the Italic (Augustine, *On Christian Teaching* 2.15 [FC 2:79; PL 34.46]) and the Vulgate (Jerome, *Commentariorum in Isaiam prophetam* 13.49 [PL 24.463–74]), partly from the new one of Jerome, it cannot be authentic. For neither was the Vulgate divinely inspired (*theopneustos*) (otherwise it would not have been lawful for Jerome to correct and interpolate it), nor can the new be considered such according to Jerome's own confession.

IX. (7) The decree of the Council of Trent canonized an edition which at the time had no existence and appeared forty-six years afterwards. The decree was made in 1546. In 1590, the work was finished and published by Sixtus V; two years after that it was published by Clement VIII. Now how could a council approve and declare authentic an edition which it had not examined and in fact had not yet been made?

Sources of explanation

X. Although the Hebrews and Greeks may have their own authentic texts, it does not follow that the Latins ought also to have one because the cases are not parallel. For it is evident that the Hebrew text of the Old and the Greek of the New Testament proceeded from prophets and apostles really inspired by the Holy Spirit, yet no one will venture to affirm that the authors and promoters of the Vulgate version were equally inspired (*theopneustous*).

XI. The long use of a version connected with reason can give authority to it, but not authenticity (so that it would be improper under any pretext to depart from it). For such authenticity depends not upon long use, but upon divine inspiration. Again, the use of this version has prevailed in the Latin church alone, not in the Greek and Eastern church.

XII. The true and proper cause of an authentic edition is not the testimony of the fathers, the practice of the church or confirmation by a council. For even according to Bellarmine the church does not make books authentic, but only declares them to be such (VD 1.10, pp. 40–42). Therefore the church cannot declare a version to be authentic which is not so in itself.

XIII. There is no necessity for the common people (who are ignorant of the Hebrew and Greek) to hold the Vulgate as authentic in order to know whether they are reading the Scriptures or not. They can apprehend the truth of Scripture no less from the vernacular versions, which they read and understand, than from the Vulgate, which they do not understand.

Sixteenth Question: The Perfection of the Scriptures

Do the Scriptures so perfectly contain all things necessary to salvation that there is no need of unwritten (agraphois) traditions after it? We affirm against the papists.

I. In order to shun more easily the tribunal of the Scriptures which they know to be opposed to them, the papists endeavor not only to overthrow their authenticity (*authentian*) and integrity, but also to impeach their perfection and perspicuity. Hence arises this question concerning the perfection of the Scriptures between us.

II. On the state of the question consider: (1) that the question is not whether the Scriptures contain all those things which were said or done by Christ and the saints or have any connection whatever with religion. We acknowledge that many things were done by Christ which are not recorded (John 20:30); also that many things occurred as appendices and supports of religion which are not particularly mentioned in the Scriptures and were left to the prudence of the rulers of the church who (according to the direction of Paul, 1 Cor. 14:40) should see that all things be done decently in the church. The question relates only to things necessary to salvation—whether they belong to faith or to practice; whether all these things are so contained in the Scriptures that they can be a total and adequate rule of faith and practice (which we maintain and our opponents deny).

III. The question is not whether all those things are taught in Scripture word for word (*autolexei*), or immediately and expressly. We acknowledge that many things are to be deduced by legitimate inference and to be considered as the word of God. But the question is whether they are so contained in Scripture, be they expressly in it or derivable from it by legitimate inference, that there is no need of another and an unwritten (*agraphō*) rule of faith from which to derive matters of religion and salvation.

IV. The question does not concern the intensive or qualitative perfection relating to the accurate truth of doctrines and precepts and the most perfect method of delivering them. Rather the question concerns the extensive and quantitative perfection relating to all things necessary to faith and practice. The former occurs in every part of Scripture; the latter in the whole body.

V. The question is not whether the perfection of Scripture has always been the same as to degree (for we acknowledge that revelation increased according to the different ages of the church, not as to the substance of the things to be believed, which has always been the same, but as to the clearer manifestation and application of them). The question is whether it is now so complete as to be an adequate rule of faith and practice without the help of any traditions.

VI. The question is not whether there was never an occasion in the church for unwritten (*agraphois*) traditions (for we acknowledge that God sometimes taught the church by unwritten [*agraphō*] words before the time of Moses). Rather the question is whether when the canon of Scripture has been once closed, there is any place for unwritten (*agraphoi*) traditions worthy of as much reverence as the Scriptures (which the papists hold and we deny).

VII. The question is not whether all traditions are to be entirely rejected (for we grant that there may be some use for historical traditions, concerning facts and ritual traditions, concerning rites and ceremonies of free observation). But we here speak only of doctrinal and moral traditions relating to faith and practice, the use of which beside the Scriptures we disapprove.

VIII. The question is not whether the divine and apostolic traditions (i.e., all the doctrines taught by Christ or his apostles) are to be received (for all readily grant this). The question is whether there are any such traditions beside the Scriptures. Therefore until our adversaries prove conclusively that their unwritten (*agraphous*) traditions have indeed flowed from Christ and his apostles (which they never can do), we discard them as human.

IX. The question then amounts to this—whether the Scripture perfectly contains all things (not absolutely), but necessary to salvation; not expressly and in so many words, but equivalently and by legitimate inference, as to leave no place for any unwritten (*agraphon*) word containing doctrinal or moral traditions. Is the Scripture a complete and adequate rule of faith and practice or only a partial and inadequate rule? We maintain the former; the papists the latter, holding that "unwritten traditions pertaining to faith and practice are to be received with the same regard and reverence as the Scriptures," Session 4 (Schroeder, *Council of Trent*, 17–20; Bellarmine, VD 4.2–3, pp. 115–19).

X. The Jews preceded the papists in the reception of traditions, dividing the law into the written and oral. Moses, having received the law on Mt. Sinai, delivered it to Joshua, he to the seventy elders, they to the prophets, they again to the great synagogue and so on until at last it was committed to writing in the Talmud. Hence various *deuterōseis* ("traditions") prevailed among them as calling forth rebukes from Christ—an artifice of Satan to draw the Jews more easily from the written law by this law. By the same device, he has caused the papists to contrive a twofold word of God: one written, the other not written, as if Christ and his apostles taught many things by the spoken word which they did not commit to writing. Hence arose unwritten traditions (so-called *agraphoi*), not because they never have been written, but because (according to Bellarmine) they were not written by the original author or because they are not found written in any apostolic book.

XI. In order to clear themselves of the charge of attributing insufficiency to the Scriptures in this way, some of them distinguish between an explicit and an implicit sufficiency (as Stapleton and Serarius) or mediate and an immediate (as Perronius). And they confess that the Scripture is not indeed sufficient immediately and explicitly, but yet that it can be called so mediately and implicitly because it refers to the church and to tradition what is not contained in itself.

XII. On the other hand, we give to the Scriptures such a sufficiency and perfection as is immediate and explicit. There is no need to have recourse to any tradition independent of them.

THE PERFECTION OF THE SCRIPTURE IS PROVED BY 2 TIMOTHY 3:15–16

XIII. (1) Paul says *pasan graphēn* is *theopneuston* "and is profitable for doctrine, for reproof, for correction, for instruction in righteousness that the man of God may be perfect, thoroughly furnished unto all good works" (2 Tim. 3:15–17). Here many arguments for the perfection of the Scripture are latent. First, the Holy Scriptures "are able to make us wise [*sophisai*] unto salvation" (2 Tim. 3:15). For what do we desire more than to be made partakers of salvation? Second, it is useful for all theoretical and practical purposes, for teaching the faith and forming the manners. Third, it can make the man or minister of God perfect in every good work, and what is sufficient for the shepherd must also be so for the sheep.

XIV. To no purpose do the papists object, first, that it is called useful. Everything useful is not sufficient. Water is useful to life, air to health, yet they are not sufficient. For what is useful not to some things only, but universally to all (by a complete and adequate, not a partial and incomplete utility) must necessarily be sufficient. Now Scripture is here pronounced such when it is said to be able to make a man wise (*sophisai*) unto salvation, and to be useful for the indoctrination (*didaskalian*) of the true and refutation (*elenchon*) of the false, for the correction (*epanorthōsin*) of evil and the instruction (*paideian*) of good, since nothing more is required for perfection. Nor do those comparisons apply here because it is one thing to speak of utility, referred only to a remote and accidental end, such as exists in the air to health and in water to nutrition, for the utility would mean only a help, not a sufficiency; quite another thing to speak of utility as referred to a proper, immediate and natural end; for then it necessarily draws sufficiency along with it, as when fire is said to be useful for the production of warmth. Now it is plain that the Scriptures are said to be useful in this latter sense. Second, it refers only to the Scriptures of the Old Testament. Therefore, if they alone are said to be sufficient for all things, the New Testament would be proved superfluous; or if the New could be added to the Old Testament, there would be no objection to our adding now another to the New. For Paul speaks of all Scripture existing at that time, and we know that not only the Old Testament, but also many parts of the New had then been written. (2) If the Old Testament was sufficient, then so much the more the Old and New together. (3) The sufficiency of the Old Testament for its time does not prove the superfluousness of the New, for as the age of the church varies, the grade of revelation also varies; not that it becomes more perfect as to the substance of doctrines, but only as to the circumstances and their clearer manifestation. (4) If the New Testament was added to the Old, it does not follow that another can be added to the New because now the canon of Scripture is perfect in every way, not only as to the substance of matters of faith, but also as to the mode and degree of revelation which we can have in this life. Third, he does not say *holēn* ("the whole"), but *pasan graphēn* ("all Scripture"). For if the syncetegorema is pressed, that perfection must belong to each part of the Scriptures (which is absurd). For the word *pasa* here is not distributive for particular parts or verses of Scripture, but collective for the whole (as it often means, Matt. 2:3; 27:45; Acts 2:36; Luke 21:32; Acts 20:27). Thus it is understood by Cornelius a Lapide, Estius and the Catechism of the Council of Trent.

XV. (2) God expressly forbids us to add anything unto or to diminish from his word: "Ye shall not add unto the word which I command you, neither shall ye diminish aught from it" (Deut. 4:2); "but though we, or an angel from heaven, preach any other gospel unto you than that ye have received, let him be accursed" (Gal. 1:8); "If any man shall add unto these things, God shall add unto him the plagues that are written in this book: and if any man shall take away anything, God shall take away his part out of the book of life" (Rev. 22:18–19). It cannot be said that he means only the law delivered by spoken voice by Moses (which was fuller than the written) because the written (*engraphon*) and unwritten (*agraphon*) word of Moses differed not in reality, but only in mode. Nor did he teach by spoken voice anything else than what he wrote. Hence he was ordered to write the whole (not a mutilated) law for the perpetual use of the church; and as a faithful servant he did so (Ex. 24:4; Deut. 31:9, 11, 19). So everywhere by "the law" is meant the book of the law (Deut. 28:58; Josh. 1:7); or that it means only the integrity of obedience because integrity of obedience relates to the integrity of the law, which is such that it is wrong to add anything to it; or that it means corrupting and not perfecting additions because no tradition can make that perfect which is already so; nor is corruption and opposition so much condemned as simple addition and opposition. Hence, Paul does not so much say against, but above (*supra*) or beyond (*praeter*); *par' ho* (*evangelizatum est*) as the Vulgate has it (Gal. 1:8). Theophylact properly observes: "He did not say, if they preach anything contrary to, but even if they preach the smallest thing beyond what we have preached" (*ouk eipen hoti ean enantia katangellousi, alla kan mikron ti euangelizontai par' ho euangelisametha, Epistolae . . . ad Galatas expositio* [PG 124.960] on Gal. 1:8). Every addition in matters of faith is a corruption (because added to the foundation which must be the only one) and anything added overthrows it, just as a circle is destroyed if you make the slightest addition, and a weight to be just must not be tampered with. Nor were the prophets and apostles therefore wrong in adding so much to the Mosaic canon. For the ages of the church must be considered in accordance with which revelation ought to increase, not as to the substance of doctrines, but as to the mode and circumstances. On the contrary, Paul (who says that he declared unto believers all the counsel of God, Acts 20:20, 27) nevertheless protests that he had spoken no other things than those which the prophets and Moses spoke (Acts 26:22). Finally, many of the popish additions are not only beyond, but even contrary to it. As to John, he did not mean only to forbid the interpolation of his own prophecy, but as the last of the sacred writers, he closes the whole canon of the Scriptures with his apocalypse and seals it with those last terrible words. Besides the argument in equals always holds good and what is said of this book must apply to the others also.

XVI. (3) The law of God is said to be "perfect, converting the soul and making wise the simple" (Ps. 19:7). Now the conversion and restoration of the soul cannot take place unless all things necessary to salvation are known. Nor can it be said that this refers only to the intensive perfection (as to quality) because the law is immaculate and free from fault as to single parts, and not to the extensive perfection as to quantity and amplitude. For both the primary signification of the word *thmym* denotes such a perfection as needs nothing more; and the very nature of the thing demands it because it speaks of a perfection which can convert the soul and give wisdom to the simple (which would be impossible without a full sufficiency).

FROM THE END OF THE SCRIPTURES

XVII. (4) The design of the Scriptures demand such a perfection for they were given that we might have salvation and life from them (John 20:31; 1 John 5:13; Rom 15:4), but how could that end be answered unless they were perfect and contained all things necessary to salvation? They were designed to be the canon and rule of faith. Now a rule which is not entire and adequate is for that very reason no rule at all because a rule is such a measure as cannot be added to, nor diminished—an inviolable law (*nomos aparabatos*) (as Phavorinus says, "an infallible measure, admitting of no addition or diminution," *kai metron adiapseuston, pasan prosthesin kai aphairesin mēdamōs epidechomenon—Dictionarium Varini Phavorini* [1538], 986 [*kanon*] and 1313 [*nomos*]). They are designed to be the testament of Christ. Now if no one would dare to add anything (*epidiatassesthai*) to a man's testament (Gal. 3:15), how much less to the divine, in which the lawful heir may no less safely than firmly believe the whole will of the testator to be contained? Finally, they were intended to be the contract of the covenant between God and us. Now who would say that either more or different things than those which we now find written were either promised by God or required from us?

XVIII. (5) All doctrinal traditions besides the Scriptures are rejected (Isa. 29:13). "In vain they do worship me, teaching the doctrines and commandments of men" (Matt. 15:4, 9). Nor can it be replied that the Pharisaical traditions are rejected, not the apostolic. All doctrines taught by men and not contained in the Scriptures are rejected and the assumption is gratuitous that there are any apostolic traditions out of the Scriptures. Believers are called to the law and the testimony (Isa. 8:20) and destruction is denounced against those who do not speak according to it. Nor can traditions be meant by the testimony because God everywhere rejects them. Either the law itself (often called "the testimony") is meant as a testimony of God exegetically or the writings of the prophets which were added to the law. Paul forbids us "to be wise above that which is written" (*par' ho gegraptai*, 1 Cor. 4:6), not only as to morals (to be wise in his own eyes, as Solomon has it, Prov. 3:7), but also as to doctrine—to be puffed up with a vain presumption of knowledge inducing him to propose in the church strange doctrines beyond the Scriptures, as the false apostles among the Corinthians did.

BECAUSE NO SATISFACTORY REASONS CAN BE GIVEN FOR TRADITIONS

XIX. (6) No fit reason can be given why God should wish one part of his word to be written and the other to be delivered by spoken voice. And he would have strangely consulted the interests of his church, if he had entrusted a necessary part of doctrine to the uncertain tradition of men, since every tradition must necessarily be corrupted by the lapse of time. Besides there is no rule for the distinguishing of traditions which does not bring us back to the testimony and authority of the church, and this very authority is most strongly controverted. Therefore, since their origin is doubtful, their authority uncertain, the sense often perplexed and ambiguous and the test of them impossible, everyone must see that they are deservedly rejected by us that we may adhere to the Scriptures alone as the most perfect rule of faith and practice.

FROM THE FATHERS

XX. (7) The fathers most decidedly agree with us here. Tertullian: "I adore the fullness of the Scriptures" (*Treatise against Hermogenes* 22.3 [ACW 24:57; PL 2.218]). And again: "Hermogenes may teach that it is written, or if it is not written let him fear that woe to those who add anything" (ibid.). And elsewhere: "We have no need of curiosity after Christ, nor of inquisition, after the gospel. When we believe, we first believe this, that there is nothing beyond which we ought to believe" (*Prescription against Heretics*

7 [ANF 3:246; PL 2.20–21]). Jerome says, "That which does not have authority from the Scriptures, we can as easily despise as approve" (*Commentariorum in evangelium Matthaei* [PL 26.180] on Matt. 23:35–36). Augustine says, "In the things openly declared in the Scriptures, we can find whatever is necessary for faith and practice" (*On Christian Doctrine* 2.9 [FC 2:72; PL 34.42]). Basil says, "It is a proof of unbelief and a sign of pride either to weaken any of those things which are written or to introduce what is not written" (cf. *Concerning Faith* [FC 9:58–59; PG 31.678–79]). Irenaeus says, "We knew not the provision for our salvation through others than those through whom the gospel came to us, which indeed they preached, but afterwards through the will of God delivered to us in the Scriptures, to be the pillar and foundation of our faith" (*Against Heresies* 3.1 [ANF 1:414; PG 7.844]).

SOURCES OF EXPLANATION

XXI. Although all things are not written severally (*kata meros*) as to words and deeds (since there is neither a number nor science of singulars, of which John 20:30 treats), yet they are written as to form (*kat' eidos*), as to the substance of necessary doctrine. Hence we grant that many sayings and doings of Christ and his apostles are not contained in the Scriptures, but deny that any such were different as to substance from those which are recorded there.

XXII. What the papists maintain should be received besides the Scriptures either exist in them really—as the Trinity (as to the thing itself), infant baptism (which Bellarmine proves from Scripture ["De Sacramento Baptismi," 8 in *Opera* (1858), 3:171–74]), baptism not necessary to be repeated, the number of the sacraments (at least those enumerated in Scripture), the admission of females to the Eucharist (Acts 2:42; 1 Cor. 11:5, cf. v. 28), the change of the Sabbath to the Lord's day (Rev. 1:10; 1 Cor. 16:2; Col. 2:16–17); or they are not doctrines necessary to salvation—as the perpetual virginity of Mary even post partum and the obligation to keep the Passover on the Lord's day; or they are false and counterfeit—as the local descent of Christ to hell, purgatory, the Mass, the return of Enoch and Elijah, etc.

XXIII. The trust committed to Timothy (1 Tim. 6:20) refers not to some doctrine delivered by the spoken voice and not written, but either to the form of sounder words (mentioned in 2 Tim. 1:13), instead of the profane novelties and oppositions of science falsely so called (*pseudōnymou gnōseōs*), or to the talents committed to his charge. These have nothing in common with the farrago of unwritten traditions.

XXIV. The many things which the disciples of Christ could not bear (John 16:12) do not imply the insufficiency of the Scriptures or the necessity of traditions. For they were not new doctrines differing in substance from the former (John 14:26), but the same as about to be more fully declared and more strongly impressed by the Spirit. And afterwards, being instructed fully by the effusion of the Spirit, they committed them to writing.

XXV. Second Thessalonians 2:15 does not sanction unwritten (*agraphous*) traditions, but designates the twofold method of delivering the same doctrine by the voice and by writing. The disjunctive particle *eite*, which can also be considered copulative (as in Rom. 12:8; 1 Cor. 15:11; Col. 1:20), marks a diversity not of the thing, but of the mode, which might be one or the other, especially in those primitive days when the canon of the New Testament Scriptures was not yet completed. Again, although all things were not contained in the epistle to the Thessalonians, it does not follow that they were not to be found elsewhere in the Scriptures.

XXVI. Tradition is sometimes taken to mean any doctrine handed down to us whether in writing or by the voice; and again for a doctrine handed down by the voice alone and not written. The question does not concern tradition in the former sense (for then all the doctrines contained in the Scriptures might be called traditions, as Paul calls the institution of the Lord's Supper, 1 Cor. 11:23), but concerning an unwritten doctrine.

XXVII. A false distinction is made by Perronius between mediate and immediate sufficiency, so that the Scriptures may be called sufficient not in the second but in the first sense because they refer us to the church to supply their defects. This would imply a true insufficiency in the Scriptures, for by appealing to the church as having that sufficiency, it would declare its own insufficiency. (2) Then the law might be called perfect for salvation because it refers us to Christ in whom is salvation. (3) The Scriptures do not refer us to the church that she may propose new doctrines, but explain and apply the truths already contained in them. Nor ought the reply to be made here that we hold mediate sufficiency when we maintain that the Scriptures (if not expressly, at least by consequence) contain all things necessary to salvation. When the Scriptures teach anything by consequence, they do not refer us to another for instruction, but give forth from themselves what was virtually latent. Nor can the simile adduced by Perronius of credential letters (*literarum credentiae*, which are called sufficient although they do not contain all the instructions given to the ambassador) apply here. The Scriptures are not only a credential letter, but also the edict of a king, containing so fully all the things to be believed and done that nothing can be added to or taken from them.

XXVIII. The perfection of Scripture asserted by us does not exclude either the ecclesiastical ministry (established by God for the setting forth and application of the word) or the internal power of the Holy Spirit necessary for conversion. It only excludes the necessity of another rule for external direction added to the Scriptures to make them perfect. A rule is not therefore imperfect because it requires the hand of the architect for its application.

XXIX. Some doctrines are positive and affirmative, stating positively what we must believe; others are negative, teaching what we must reject. The question here does not concern the sufficiency of Scripture as to negative articles, as if it ought to contain a rejection of all the errors and heresies which either have arisen or will hereafter arise. For as the right is an index of itself and of the wrong, errors are at once refuted by the laying down of the truth. The question concerns affirmative articles particularly, the very food of the soul.

XXX. Tradition is used either formally for the act of handing down or materially for the thing handed down. Here we do not speak of tradition in the first sense (admitting it, since we possess the Scriptures by it), but in the second, which we deny.

XXXI. The Old Testament Scripture was perfect essentially and absolutely for it contains sufficiently as to that time the substance of doctrine necessary to salvation; although accidentally and comparatively, with respect to the New Testament Scripture, imperfect as to the mode of manifestation, although with respect to the Jewish church it was the age of manhood (Gal. 4:1–4).

XXXII. Jesus, the son of Mary, is the true Messiah; or the Son of God come in the flesh. This is not a new article of faith, but an unfolding and application of what preceded—teaching *in hypothesi* what had already been delivered concerning the Messiah *in thesi* in the Old Testament. Thus when Christ added a facsimile to the original handwriting, a fulfillment to the prediction and a body to the shadow, he did not propose a new doctrine, but only exposed and illustrated an old one.

XXXIII. The tradition of the Scriptures does not sanction other traditions besides. The question properly is not of principles (*principiis*), but of things principiated (*principiatis*): whether, granting the Scriptures, there is need of any oral traditions to supply their defects in things necessary to salvation. Finally, we acknowledge that tradition is formal and active because the oracles of God were committed to the church as their keeper and proclaimer. But the tradition is not material and passive, implying some doctrine delivered in addition to the Scriptures (which we deny). So we have the Scriptures through tradition not as the source of belief, but only as the means and instrument through which they have come down to us.

XXXIV. The Scriptures are said to be perfect not always adequately to the object, as if it fully explained all the mysteries it records. For there are many things in themselves adequately inexplicable (as God, the Trinity, etc.), but adequately to the end because it so states them that they may be apprehended by us sufficiently for salvation.

XXXV. When we say that the Scriptures are perfect inasmuch as being a rule, we understand this as to the whole of Scripture collectively and not distributively (viz., as to its particular parts, as in a material rule, not everything belonging to it is a rule).

XXXVI. Although the fathers often appealed to the traditions, it does not therefore follow that they recognized the oral (*agraphous*) traditions of the papists, for they speak diversely of them. Sometimes tradition is used by them for the "act of tradition" by which the sacred books were preserved by the church in an uninterrupted series of time (also a perpetual succession) and delivered to posterity. This is formal tradition and in this sense Origen says "they learned by tradition that the four gospels were unquestioned in the church universal." Second, it is often taken for the written doctrine which, being at first oral, was afterward committed to writing. Thus Cyprian says, "Sacred tradition will preserve whatever is taught in the gospels or is found in the epistles of the apostles or in the Acts" (*Epistle 74 [73]*, "To Pompey" [ANF 5:387; PL 3.1175–76]). Third, it is taken for a doctrine which does not exist in the Scriptures in so many words, but may be deduced thence by just and necessary consequence; in opposition to those who bound themselves to the express word of the Scriptures and would not admit the word *homoousion* because it did not occur verbatim there. Thus Basil denies that the profession of faith which we make in the Father, Son and Holy Spirit can be found in the Scriptures (meaning the Apostles' Creed, whose articles nevertheless are contained in the Scriptures as to sense) (*On the Spirit* [NPNF2, 8:41, 43]). Fourth, it is taken for the doctrine of rites and ceremonies called "ritual tradition." Fifth, it is taken for the harmony of the old teachers of the church in the exposition of any passage of Scripture which, received from their ancestors, they retained out of a modest regard for antiquity because it agreed with the Scriptures. This may be called "tradition of sense" or exegetical tradition (of which Irenaeus speaks, *Against Heresies* 3.3, [ANF 1:415–16], and Tertullian often as well, *Prescription against Heretics* [ANF 3:243–65]). Sixth, they used the word tradition *ad hominem* in disputing with heretics who appealed to them not because all they approved of could not be found equally as well in the Scriptures, but because the heretics with whom they disputed did not admit the Scriptures; as Irenaeus says, "When they perceived that they were confused by the Scriptures, they turned around to accuse them" (*Against Heresies*, 3.2 [ANF 1:415; PG 8.846]). They dispute therefore at an advantage (*ek periontos*) from the consent of tradition with the Scriptures, just as we now do from the fathers against the papists, but not because they acknowledged any doctrinal tradition besides the Scriptures. As Jerome testifies, "The sword of God smites whatever they draw and forges from a pretended apostolic tradition, without the authority and testimony of the Scriptures" (*Commentarii in prophetas: Aggaeum 1:11* [CCL 76A.725]).

Seventeenth Question: The Perspicuity of the Scriptures

Are the Scriptures so perspicuous in things necessary to salvation that they can be understood by believers without the external help of oral (agraphou) tradition or ecclesiastical authority? We affirm against the papists.

I. The papists, not satisfied with their endeavors to prove the Scriptures insufficient in order to bring in the necessity of tradition, began to question their perspicuity (as if the sense could by no one be ascertained with certainty without the judgment of the church) in order to have a pretext for keeping the people from their perusal. Having concealed the candle under a bushel, they reign in darkness more easily.

STATEMENT OF THE QUESTION

II. As to the state of the question, observe: (1) The question does not concern the perspicuity or the obscurity of the subject or of persons. For we do not deny that the Scriptures are obscure to unbelievers and the unrenewed, to whom Paul says his gospel is hid (2 Cor. 4:3). Also we hold that the Spirit of illumination is necessary to make them intelligible to believers. Rather the question concerns the obscurity or perspicuity of the object or of the Scriptures (i.e., whether they are so obscure that the believer cannot apprehend them for salvation without the authority and judgment of the church—which we deny).

III. The question does not concern the obscurity of the things or mysteries recorded in the Scriptures. We agree that there are many mysteries contained there, so sublime as to transcend the highest flight of our minds and can thus far be called obscure in themselves. Rather the question concerns the obscurity of the mode in which these most abstruse things are delivered and which we maintain are so wonderfully accommodated (*synkatabasei*) by the Lord that the believer (who has the eyes of his mind opened) by attentively reading may understand these mysteries sufficiently for salvation.

IV. The question is not whether the Holy Scriptures are perspicuous in all their parts so as to need no interpreter nor exposition of doubtful passages (which Bellarmine falsely and slanderously charges upon us, stating the question thus: "Are the Scriptures of themselves as perfectly plain and intelligible as to need no interpretation?"—VD 3.1, p. 96). For we unhesitatingly confess that the Scriptures have their *adyta* ("heights") and *bathē* ("depths") which we cannot enter or sound and which God so ordered on purpose to excite the study of believers and increase their diligence; to humble the pride of man and to remove from them the contempt which might arise from too great plainness. Rather the question concerns only things necessary for salvation, and indeed as to them, only so far as they are necessary to be known and cannot be unknown without criminality. For instance, the mystery of the Trinity is plainly delivered as to the fact (*to hoti*) which is necessary, but not as to the how (*to pōs*), which we are not permitted to know (nor is that essential to salvation). For as in nature so also in the Scriptures, it pleased God to present everywhere and make easy of comprehension all necessary things; but those less necessary are so closely concealed as to require great exertion to extricate them. Thus besides bread and sustenance, she has her luxuries, gems and gold deep under the surface and obtainable only by indefatigable labor; and as heaven is sprinkled with greater and lesser stars, so the Scriptures are not everywhere equally resplendent, but are distinguished by clearer and obscurer places, as by stars of a greater or lesser magnitude.

V. The question is not whether things essential to salvation are everywhere in the Scriptures perspicuously revealed. We acknowledge that there are some things hard to be understood (*dysnoēta*) and intended by God to exercise our attention and mental powers. The question is whether things essential to salvation are anywhere revealed, at least so that the believer can by close meditation ascertain their truth (because nothing can be drawn out of the more obscure passages which may not be found elsewhere in the plainest terms). As Augustine remarks: "Admirable and healthily the Spirit has so arranged the Scriptures that by the plainer passages he might meet our desires and by the obscurer remove our contempt" (*On Christian Teaching* 2.6 [FC 2:66; PL 34.39]); and, "We feed in the open places, we are exercised by the obscure; there hunger is driven away, here contempt" (*Sermon 71*, "De verbis Domini," 7.11 [PL 38.450]).

VI. The question does not concern the perspicuity which does not exclude the means necessary for interpretation (i.e., the internal light of the Spirit, attention of mind, the voice and ministry of the church, sermons and commentaries, prayer and watchfulness). For we hold these means not only to be useful, but also necessary ordinarily. We only wish to proscribe the darkness which would prevent the people from reading the Scriptures as hurtful and perilous and compel them to have recourse to tradition when they might rest in the Scriptures alone.

VII. The question then comes to this—whether the Scriptures are so plain in things essential to salvation (not as to the things delivered, but as to the mode of delivery; not as to the subject, but the object) that without the external aid of tradition or the infallible judgment of the church, they may be read and understood profitably by believers. The papists deny this; we affirm it.

THE PERSPICUITY OF THE SCRIPTURES IS PROVED FROM PSALMS 19:8; 119:105; 2 PETER 1:19

VIII. The perspicuity of the Scriptures may be urged: (1) from those parts of them which proclaim this clearness—"the commandment of the Lord is pure, enlightening the eyes" (Ps. 19:8); "thy word is a lamp unto my feet" (Ps. 119:105); "a light shining in a dark place" (2 Peter 1:19); "the law is light" (Prov. 6:23). Nor is Bellarmine's first objection of any force, that only the precepts of the law are meant and not the whole of Scripture. For the word "law" frequently means the whole word of God, and the effects (consolation and renewal) teach that it ought so to be understood. The interlinear gloss of Lyranus and Arias Montanus agree with us. Peter unquestionably calls the whole word of God a light. Bellarmine's other objection is as untenable—that although it may refer to the whole of Scripture, it must be understood in no other sense than that it illuminates the intellect. The Scriptures are said to be luminous not only because they illuminate the intellect, but because they are in themselves luminous and naturally adapted to illuminate those who look upon them with the eyes of faith. Thus they are luminous formally and effectively because like the sun they emit rays and impress themselves upon the eyes of the beholder. Finally, nothing could be more silly. For it is the same as saying that the Scriptures do not illuminate unless they illuminate, for as they illuminate so are they understood.

IX. Deuteronomy 30:11 (where the word is said to be not hidden nor far off from us) refers to the easiness not only of fulfilling, but also of understanding its mandates without which they could not be fulfilled. Nor must this be understood only of the law of Moses, but of the word of God in general. Hence Paul applies it to the word of faith (Rom. 10:8), which cannot be fulfilled by works, but must be believed by faith.

X. The gospel is said to be hidden to unbelievers alone (2 Cor. 4:3) and therefore is plain to believers, not only as preached but also as written. This follows because the apostles wrote the same things they had preached and because the clearness of the gospel is here opposed to the obscurity of the Old Testament (in the reading of which the Jews were occupied and of which Paul treats in 2 Cor. 3:14).

XI. The perspicuity of the Scriptures is further proved: (1) by their efficient cause (viz., God, the Father of men, who cannot be said either to be unwilling or unable to speak plainly without impugning his perfect goodness and wisdom); (2) their design (to be a canon and rule of faith and practice, which they could not be unless they were perspicuous); (3) the matter (viz., the law and the gospel, which anyone can easily apprehend); (4) the form (because they are to us in place of a testament, contract of a covenant or edict of a king, which ought to be perspicuous and not obscure).

XII. The fathers frequently acknowledge it, although they do not deny that the Scriptures have their depths (*bathē*), which ought to excite the study of believers. Chrysostom says, "The Scriptures are so proportioned that even the most ignorant can understand them if they only read them studiously" (*Concionis VII de Lazaro* 3 [PG 48.994]); and "All necessary things are plain and straight and clear" (*In secundam ad Thessalonicensis* [PG 62.485]). Augustine says, "In the clear declarations of Scripture are to be found all things pertaining to faith and practice" (*On Christian Doctrine* 2.9 [FC 2:72; PL 34.42]). Irenaeus says, "The prophetic and evangelic Scriptures are plain and unambiguous" (*Against Heresies* 2.27 [ANF 1:398; PG 7.803]). Gregory says, "The Scriptures have, in public, nourishment for children, as they serve in secret to strike the loftiest minds with wonder; indeed they are like a full and deep river in which the lamb may walk and the elephant swim" ("Preface," *Morals on the Book of Job* [1844], 1:9; PL 75.515).

SOURCES OF EXPLANATION

XIII. The ignorance and blindness of man are not to be compounded with the obscurity of the Scriptures. The former is often pressed upon the Scriptures, but it is not so, nor can the latter be legitimately inferred from the former no more than that the sun is obscure because it cannot be seen by a blind man. Hence if David and other believers desire their eyes to be opened that they may see wonderful things out of the law, it does not therefore prove the obscurity of the Scriptures, but only the ignorance of men. The question here is not Do men need the light of the Holy Spirit in order to understand the Scriptures? (which we willingly grant); but Are the Scriptures obscure to a believing and illuminated man?

Again, illumination may be either theoretical or practical, in its first stage or in its increase. David does not properly seek the former, but the latter.

XIV. When Christ is said to have opened the minds of his disciples that they might understand the Scriptures (Luke 24:45), this does indeed mean that man cannot himself without the aid of grace understand the Scriptures. But this does not thence prove their obscurity, nor can the darkness in the minds of the disciples be imputed to the Scriptures.

XV. It is one thing for *dysnoēta* ("things hard to be understood") to be in the Scriptures, another for *anoēta* ("unintelligible"), which cannot be understood however diligently one studies. Peter says the former (2 Peter 3:16), not the latter. It is one thing to say that there are "some things hard to be understood" (*dysnoēta tina*), which we concede; another that all are so (*dysnoēta panta*), which we deny. It is one thing for them to be hard to be understood (*dysnoēta*) in Paul's manner of delivering the epistles, which we deny; another in the things delivered, which Peter intimates. The relative (*hois*) cannot be referred to the word *epistolai*, as Gagnae (cf. *Biblia magna commentariorum literalum* [1643], 5:1067 on 2 Peter 3:15) and Lorinus confess, but to the things of which he treats. It is one thing to be hard to be understood (*dysnoēta*) by the unlearned and unstable, who by their unbelief and wickedness wrest them to their own destruction (which we hold with Peter); another that they are hard to be understood (*dysnoēta*) by believers who humbly seek the aid of the Holy Spirit in searching them.

XVI. From the obscurity of some parts of the Scriptures (viz., of the ancient prophecies and oracles), the consequence does not hold good as to the obscurity of the whole. Either those prophecies are not of things essential to salvation or whatever is obscure in them is elsewhere made clear. Thus, the "book shut and sealed" (mentioned in Dan. 12:4 and Rev. 5:1), teaches indeed that prophecies are obscure before their fulfillment, but does not prove the whole of Scripture to be so obscure that they cannot be understood by believers in things necessary to salvation.

XVII. Although our knowledge through the Scriptures may be obscure when compared with the knowledge in glory (where we will no longer know through a glass and darkly, but shall see God face to face, 1 Cor. 13:12), it does not follow that it is absolutely and in itself obscure with respect to our present life. It is sufficiently clear for us here, since through it with open face we behold as in a glass the glory of the Lord (2 Cor. 3:18). (2) Paul speaks of the enigmatical knowledge common to all travellers here, himself not excepted. "Now," says he, "we see in a mirror." But were the Scriptures obscure to Paul? The passage, then denotes only the imperfection of our knowledge in this life and the difference between the revelation of grace and glory, but not the obscurity of the Scriptures.

XVIII. Although the Scriptures must be searched (John 5:39), it does not follow that they are everywhere obscure even in things essential to salvation. First because we do not say that they are perspicuous to everyone, but only to the attentive mind and diligent seeker. Moreover there is need of scrutiny because they are perspicuous to the one who searches, for the most evident things will be obscure to the cursory and careless reader. Second we do not deny that the Scriptures have their heights (*adyta*) and depths (*bathē*) of mysteries to be fathomed only by the most laborious study and persevering efforts. But then there are many other things (and these essential) which readily strike the eyes of believers.

XIX. Although the apostles could not fully understand the resurrection and ascension of Christ (John 16:18), it does not follow that the Scriptures were to them obscure. For each one had a knowledge sufficient for his state and the doctrines then revealed. A full revelation of these was to be expected after the resurrection.

XX. The knowledge of the Scriptures may be either literal and theoretical (by which the words are understood as to the letter and grammatically) or spiritual and practical (by which they are apprehended as true by faith). There are many things in the Scriptures theoretically perspicuous even to the natural man. The wicked may dispute most ingeniously of the principal articles of faith, but the practical knowledge is peculiar to believers alone (1 Cor. 2:14–15; 2 Cor. 4:3).

XXI. The reasons for the obscurity of the Scriptures from the mode of delivery adduced by the papists cannot prove them to be so obscure in the essentials of salvation that they cannot be a perfect rule of faith and practice and the necessity of having recourse to the infallible authority of the church and its pretended tribunal for their explanation. For besides the fact that we are never commanded to do so, they are not such as cannot be ascertained by proper study; or the things contained in those passages are either not essential to salvation or they are elsewhere clearly explained.

XXII. It is one thing to speak of the absolute obscurity of the Scriptures in relation to all the ages and states of the church; another to speak of their comparative obscurity in relation to a particular state. We confess that the Old Testament Scriptures are obscure compared with the New Testament, and the state and age of the Christian church; but this does not destroy their perspicuity in themselves and sufficiently in relation to the state of the Old Testament church to which they were given.

Eighteenth Question: The Reading of the Scriptures

Can the Scriptures be profitably read by any believer, and ought he to read them without permission? We affirm against the papists.

Opinion of the papists on the reading of the Scriptures

I. The opinion of the papists can be best collected from Rule IV, "Rules Concerning Prohibited Books" published under the sanction of the Council of Trent, which reads thus: "Since experience has proved that on account of the rashness of men more hurt than profit has arisen from permitting the Bible in the vulgar tongue, they interdict the Bible with all its parts, whether printed or in manuscript, in whatever vulgar tongue it exists" (cf. Schroeder, *Council of Trent*, 274–75). But as this appeared rather too harsh, Pius IV appeared willing to modify it when he left the concession of the reading of the Bible to the "judgment of the ordinary pastor" or "bishop" ("to those who, they knew, would not receive hurt but an increase of faith and piety from such a perusal"). But the following observation of Clement VIII on Rule IV shows that this hope was evidently illusory, since he denies that any such power of granting permission "can be afforded *de novo* to bishops or others which had up to this time been denied by the command of the inquisition" (which practice was to be adhered to). Thus by taking away with one hand what they seemed to give with the other, they show their real object to be to hide this light under a bushel and to snatch the Scriptures from the hands of the people lest their errors should be discovered. Yet it must be confessed that to some of the papists who thought the reading of them should be allowed to believers, this seemed a cruel tyranny. But these are few in comparison with those who advocate its prohibition. Their opinion is received as common to the whole church because founded on a law sanctioned by the authority of a council and a pope. The Council itself proclaimed "his authority to be supreme in the church universal" (Session XIV, Schroeder, *Council of Trent*, 96) expressly commissioned to "ascertain and to publish those things which pertained to the censure of books" (continuation of Session XXV, Schroeder, *Council of Trent*, 255). Therefore, this can be considered in no other light than a universal law of the Roman Church until it shall be expressly repealed, no matter what they may say to the contrary. But we, on the other hand, maintain not only that every believer may freely read the Scriptures, but also ought to without waiting for permission from a bishop or priest.

STATEMENT OF THE QUESTION

II. The question is not whether the reading of the Scriptures is absolutely and simply necessary to all. For both infants are saved without it and many unlettered (*analphabētoi*) persons among adults, who never read it. The question is whether it is so lawful for everyone that no one (although ignorant and unlearned) should be prohibited from reading them.

III. The question is not whether some discretion may and ought not to be used in reading the books of Scripture according to capacity (as formerly the young were not allowed to read some of the scriptural books because deficient in judgment on account of age). This is not so much an interdiction as a method of instruction and can fitly conduce to their greater improvement and edification. The question is whether the reading should be forbidden to anyone (which we deny).

THE READING OF THE SCRIPTURES PROVED

IV. The reasons are: (1) the command of God which applies to all and each one (Deut. 6:6–8; 31:11–12; Ps. 1:2; Col. 3:16; John 5:39; Josh. 1:8; 2 Peter 1:19; Rev. 1:3). (2) The design of the Scriptures, for they were given for the profit and salvation of all and to supply all with arms against our spiritual enemies (2 Tim 3:16; Rom. 15:4; Eph. 6:17). (3) The Scriptures are the Testament of our heavenly father, and should a child be forbidden to read the will of his father? (4) The uniform practice of the church, Jewish and Christian (Deut. 17:18–19; Acts 8:27; 17:11; 2 Peter 1:19; 2 Tim. 3:15–16). Nor are the ancient fathers ever so unanimously zealous as in recommending and inculcating upon all the reading of the Scriptures (cf. Chrysostom frequently in Sermon 6, *Sermones IX in Genesim* [PL 54.608]; "Homily 1," *In Matthaeum* [NPNF1, 10:1–8] and *Concionis VII de Lazaro* 3 [PG 48.995], where he often repeats that ignorance of the Scriptures is the cause of all evils; Augustine, *Confessions* 6.5 [FC 21:135–37]; Sermon 35, *De Tempore* [PL 38.213–14]; Basil, "Homily 10," *On Psalm 1* 1 [FC 46:151–52]; Cyprian, actually Novatian, "The Spectacles" [FC 67:124–25]; Origen, Sermon 9, *In Leviticum* [PG 12.508–25] and Sermon 12, *On Exodus* [FC 71:367–74]; Jerome, Letter 107, "To Laeta" [NPNF2, 6:189–95, esp. 193]).

SOURCES OF EXPLANATIONS

V. That which of itself and properly brings more injury and loss than advantage should not be permitted. But this does not hold good of that which is such only accidentally (i.e., from the fault of men). If men abuse the Scriptures, this does not happen per se, but accidentally from the perversity of those who wrongfully wrest them to their own destruction. Otherwise (if on account of the abuse the use should be prohibited), the Scriptures ought to be taken away not only from the laity, but also from the teachers who abuse them far more. For heresies usually arise not from the common people and the unlearned, but from ecclesiastics.

VI. If errors can arise from the Scriptures improperly understood, so far from keeping them from their perusal, this ought the rather to excite them to searching. Thus, properly understanding them, they may be able to confute such errors.

VII. The liberty of reading the Scriptures does not take away either oral instruction or pastoral direction or other helps necessary to understanding. It only opposes the tyranny of those who do not wish the darkness of their errors to be dissipated by the light of the divine word.

VIII. When Christ forbids giving what is holy to dogs and casting pearls before swine (Matt. 7:6), he does not mean to deny believers the right of reading and using the Scriptures (nor could the sons of God be denominated dogs and swine). He only means that the symbols of divine grace should not be communicated to the impure and every sinner; or that the loftiest mysteries of faith should be rashly obtruded upon unbelievers or upon those who by a desperate obstinacy resist the manifested truth. Rather the symbols of divine grace should be used for the instruction of those who come with a humble and docile spirit.

IX. Is it not sufficient that the reading of the Scriptures is allowed by the papists to some? For that ought not to be granted to some as a privilege which is enjoined upon all as a duty.

Nineteenth Question: The Sense of the Scriptures

Whether the Scriptures have a fourfold sense: literal, allegorical, anagogical and tropological. We deny against the papists.

THE OPINION OF THE PAPISTS ON THE SENSE OF THE SCRIPTURES

I. The papists, in order to force upon us another visible judge of controversies (viz., the church and the pope) besides the Scriptures and the Holy Spirit speaking in them, attribute a manifold sense to them and hence infer that they are doubtful and ambiguous. Therefore they distinguish between the literal and the mystical sense and divide this last into three parts: allegorical, tropological, anagogical. Allegorical, when the sacred history is transferred to things of faith, as what is said of the two covenants or of Sarah and Hagar (Gal. 4:24); anagogical, when the words of Scripture are applied to the things of a future age, as what is said of the rest (Heb. 4:3); tropological, when transferred to morals. All are expressed in the familiar distich:

Litera gesta docet, quid credas allegoria,
Moralis quid agas, quo tendas anagogia.

("The letter teaches facts; what you believe is allegory; The moral is what you do; where you're bound is anagogy"—Nicholas of Lyra, "Prologus in additiones" in *Postilla super totam Bibliam* [1492/1971], vol. 1, B vii [3]).

AND OF THE ORTHODOX

II. We thus think that only one true and genuine sense belongs to the Scriptures. That sense may be twofold: either simple or compound. Simple and historical is that which contains the declaration of one thing without any other signification; as the precepts, the doctrines and the histories. And this again is twofold, either proper and grammatical or figurative and tropical; proper, arising from the proper words; tropical, from figurative words. The composite or mixed sense is in prophecies as types, part of which is in the type, part in the antitype. This does not establish two senses, but two parts of one and the same sense intended by the Holy Spirit, who with the letter considers the mystery, as in that prophecy, "ye shall not break a bone thereof" (Ex. 12:46). The full sense is not obtained unless the truth of the type or paschal lamb is joined with the truth of the antitype or Christ (cf. John 19:36).

STATEMENT OF THE QUESTION

III. The literal sense is not so much that which is derived from proper words and not figurative, as it may be distinguished from the figurative (and is sometimes so used by the fathers); but that which is intended by the Holy Spirit and is expressed in words either proper or figurative. Thus Thomas defines the literal sense as "that which the Holy Spirit or the author intends" (*Summa Theologica*, vol. 1, Q. 1, Art. 10 [New York: Benzinger, 1947], 7); Salmeron says, "that which the Holy Spirit, the author of the Scriptures, wished primarily to signify through words, whether according to the proper inherent grammatical signification, or by tropes and translations" (*Commentarii in evangelicam historiam* [1602–04], vol. 1, Prolegomenon 7, p. 73). The thing said (*to rhēton*) is not therefore always to be sought in proper words, but also in figurative (as we truly retain the thing said [*to rhēton*] in the sacraments because we retain the sense intended by the Holy Spirit). Such also is the sense of the parables employed by our Lord in which we must always keep in mind his intention. Nor is that only to be considered the literal sense, which signifies the thing brought into comparison, but also denotes the application. Hence there is always only one sense and that literal by which (through such a comparison) any truth is set forth.

IV. That the Scriptures have only one sense is evident: (1) from the unity of truth—because truth is only one and simple and therefore cannot admit many senses without becoming uncertain and ambiguous; (2) from the unity of form—because there is only one essential form of any one thing (now the sense is the form of the Scriptures); (3) from the perspicuity of the Scriptures, which cannot allow various foreign and diverse senses.

V. The question is not whether there is only one conception in the sense of the Scriptures, for we grant that often there are many conceptions of one and the same sense (but subordinate and answering to each other especially in the composite sense which embraces type and antitype). The question is whether there may be many diverse and non-subordinated senses of the same passage (which is the opinion of Azorius, *Institutiones morales* [1613], Pt. I, 8.2, pp. 507–9; Thomas, *Summa Theologica*, vol. 1, Q. 1, Art. 1, p. 7; Lyranus, Gretser, Becanus, Salmeron, Driedo, Bellarmine and others).

SOURCES OF EXPLANATION

VI. Distinguish the sense of the Scriptures from their application—the sense is only one, whether simple (in the histories, precepts and prophecies openly proposed) or composite (in the typical); whether proper (enunciated in proper words) or figurative (in figurative words). But the application can be diverse, both for instruction (*didaskalian*), reproof (*elenchon*), correction (*epanorthōsin*), etc., which are the theoretical and practical uses of the Scriptures.

Thus allegory, anagogy and tropology are not so much diverse senses as applications of one literal sense. Allegory and anagogy refer to instruction (*didaskalian*), but tropology to correction (*epanorthōsin*).

VII. Allegory is either innate (or inferred, or intended by the Holy Spirit) or invented by men. In the latter sense, it does not enter into the sense of the Scriptures, but is a consequence drawn from the study of man by manner of application. But the former is contained in the compound sense as a part of it because it cannot be doubted that it was intended by the Spirit and thus from his mind. Hence what is said of the two wives of Abraham is applied to the two covenants (Gal. 4:21–29); what is said of the rest is applied to the heavenly rest (Heb. 4:3–11). So when we proceed from the sign to the thing signified, we do not introduce a new sense, but educe what was implied in the sign so as to have the full and complete sense intended by the Spirit.

VIII. Although the intellect of God is infinite, able to embrace many infirmities at the same time, it does not follow that the sense of the Scriptures is manifold. From the intellect to the words of God, the consequence does not hold good, nor is the signification of expressions to be measured by the copiousness of the speaker (who is infinite here), but by his certain and determinate intention accommodated to the capacities of men to whom he speaks. When God understands, he understands himself as he is infinite and so he understands himself infinitely. But when he speaks, he speaks not to himself, but to us (i.e., in accommodation to our capacity which is finite and cannot take in many senses).

IX. The book written within and on the back side, within and without (Ezek. 2:10; Rev. 5:1), does not mean a twofold sense of one and the same Scripture, but the multitude of things written everywhere—there of the plagues to be inflicted on the Jews, but here of the decrees of God.

X. The difficulty of passages does not imply a manifold intention of God, but some ambiguity in the words or weakness of our intellect. Although words can have various significations *in thesi* ("in the abstract"), yet on the hypothesis of this or that passage, they are referred to only one of these significations by the Holy Spirit. These significations are to be ascertained by a consideration of the context and analogy of faith.

XI. The literal sense is sometimes taken more widely for the whole compass of the sense intended by the Holy Spirit (whether in the type or antitype) and so also contains within it the mystical sense. The literal sense is sometimes taken more strictly for that which the words immediately and proximately afford and so is distinguished from the mystical (which is signified not so much by the words as by the things which the words signify), which arises only mediately from the intention of the speaker.

XII. Although we hold to a composite sense, yet we do not take away the unity of truth and the certainty of the Scriptures which we charge upon the papists. For the truth set forth in these prophecies embraces many relations (*scheseis*), all intended by the Spirit.

XIII. As the Scriptures are most copious containing more things than words, so it is not absurd to say that the Holy Spirit wished to connote to us by one and the same word many things at the same time. Yet these things are mutually subordinate so that the one may be the sign and figure of the other, or have some mutual connection and dependence. Thus the promise of seed given to Abraham referred both to Isaac as the type and to Christ as the antitype (Gal. 3:16). The prophecy about the bones of the lamb not to be broken (Ex. 12:46) belonged both to the Paschal lamb in a figure and to Christ in a mystery (John 19:36). The promise given to David, "I will be his father" (2 Sam. 7:14) applied both to Solomon and to Christ (Heb. 1:5). The prediction concerning the Holy One not seeing corruption (Ps. 16:10) is applied both to David imperfectly and to Christ perfectly (Acts 2:29–30). Such are the numberless scriptural passages which contain various relations (*scheseis*), all of which ought to be taken together in order to gather the full sense. Nor was their fulfillment once and at the same time, but successively and by degrees. Hence the ancient predictions generally had three relations (*scheseis*): to the state of the law in the Jewish church; to the state of grace in the Christian church; and to the state of glory in heaven. Thus the prophecy about the people walking in darkness and beholding a great light (Isa. 9:1–2) has three degrees of fulfillment: (1) in the Babylonian restoration; (2) in the preaching of the gospel (Matt. 4:14–16); and (3) in the last resurrection in which those who sit in the valley of the shadow of death shall see the great light of God's glory. The same remark applies to the prophecy about the dry bones (Ezek. 37:1–14), which was fulfilled when the people went forth from the most mournful Babylonian captivity as from a sepulcher (Ezek. 37:12); it is fulfilled every day in the spiritual resurrection (Eph. 5:14); and will be perfectly fulfilled in the final resurrection (John 5:25).

XIV. The various passages adduced by the papists to prove a multiple sense (Hosea 11:1 with Matt. 2:15; Ps. 2:7 with Acts 13:33; 2 Sam. 7:14 with Heb. 1:5 and 5:5) show indeed that there may be a sense composed from the type and antitype and fulfilled in various degrees—first in the type and second in the antitype. But this does not prove a manifold sense generically diverse.

XV. The mystical sense is either sacred, proposed through the writers by the Holy Spirit and therefore grounded in the Scriptures themselves (as the passages of John 3:14 about the brazen serpent; of Paul about the baptism of the cloud and sea, and the spiritual food and drink of the Israelites, 1 Cor. 10:1–4, and about the allegory of the two wives of Abraham, Gal. 4:22; about the ark and baptism, 1 Peter 3:21); or it is ecclesiastical—used by ecclesiastical writers either for the sake of illustration or for pleasure. Philo first tried this in two books of allegories, and some of the fathers followed—especially Origen who employed this kind of interpretation more than the others and often ran into extravagance. Hence he was not undeservedly rebuked by Jerome, "Origen thinks the acuteness of his genius is a sacrament of the church" (*ep. ad Avitum et Amabilem*, cf. *Commentariorum in Isaiam*, PL 24.154). This latter sense, although suitable for illustration, has no power to prove because it is a human, not a divine interpretation. It probably may recommend, but cannot persuade. But the former has the power of proving doctrines of faith, as it has the Holy Spirit for its author and so is according to his intention. Therefore the common expression—symbolical theology is not demonstrative (*argumentativum*)—has force only in human allegories and parables, not in divine.

XVI. The mystical sense is not found in every part of Scripture, but can be lawfully admitted only where the Holy Spirit gives opportunity and foundation for it. Here we must carefully guard against carrying it beyond the intention of the Spirit and thus failing to preserve its true design.

XVII. As in every passage of Scripture, there is some literal sense (whether proper or figurative), so there is only one sense of the letter of each passage (whether simple as in the histories or compound as in the types). However the application may be different according to the various theoretical or practical uses.

XVIII. To ascertain the true sense of the Scriptures, interpretation is needed. This is true not only of the words which are contained in the versions, but also of the things (called "prophecy" by Paul [Rom. 12:6] and *epilysis* by Peter [2 Peter 1:20]). It is not to be sought by each man's private judgment (which is the *idia epilysis* condemned by Peter), but is to be gathered from the Scriptures themselves as their own best and surest interpreter (Neh. 8:8; Acts 17:11). But for this, after fervent prayer to God, there is need of an inspection of the sources, the knowledge of languages, the distinction between proper and figurative words, attention to the scope and circumstances, collation of passages, connection of what precedes and follows, removal of prejudices and conformity of the interpretation to the analogy of faith. All of this can be referred to these three means: analysis (*analysin*), comparison (*synkrisin*) and analogy (*analogian*). Analysis is threefold: grammatical, which inquires into proper expressions; rhetorical, which inquires into the figurative; and logical, which observes the scope and circumstances and attends to the connection (*allēlouchian*) of words. Comparison (*synkrisis*) compares passages of Scripture with each other (Acts 9:22)—the more obscure with the plainer, similar and parallel with similar, dissimilar with dissimilar. The analogy of faith (Rom. 12:6) signifies not only the measure of faith granted to each believer, but also the constant harmony and agreement of all heads of faith exhibited in the clearer expressions of Scripture (to which all expositions ought to be conformed) that nothing may be determined at variance with the articles of faith or the precepts of the Decalogue.

XIX. We must not rashly and unnecessarily depart from the proper literal sense, unless it really clashes with the articles of faith and the precepts of love and the passage (on this account or from other parallel passages) is clearly seen to be figurative. Now this is the surest criterion (*kritērion*) of a figurative locution: (1) if the words taken strictly give either no sense or an absurd and impossible sense (as when Christ is called the gate of the sheep [John 10:7] and the true vine [John 15:1]); (2) if they are repugnant to the analogy of faith and at variance with any received doctrine, either theoretical or practical. For as the Spirit is always undoubtedly self-consistent, we cannot consider that to be his sense which is opposed to other truths delivered by him. Hence we infer that the words of the Eucharist are to be understood tropically (figuratively) because the strict sense contradicts the various articles of faith concerning the truth of the body of Christ, his ascension to heaven and return to judgment. The words of Hosea 1:2 are not to be explained strictly, but symbolically and allegorically because it commands a crime forbidden by the law. The golden rule also belongs here. "If it is a preceptive locution either forbidding a crime or an evil deed, or commanding a useful or benevolent deed, it is not figurative; but if it seems to command the former or forbid the latter, it is figurative" (Augustine, *On Christian Teaching* 3.16 [FC 2:136; PL 34.74]). The reason is it is proper for God to command what is good because he is good and to prohibit most severely what is evil because he is holy, however often he may permit it to be done.

XX. In addition to this rule of faith, the other means which the papists bring in (as the practice of the church, the consent of the fathers, the decrees of councils), besides being all referable to the will of one pope, are uncertain and (resting upon no solid foundation) are impossible and contradictory. They impede the mind with innumerable difficulties rather than assist it, as we will show hereafter.

Twentieth Question: The Supreme Judge of Controversies and Interpreter of the Scriptures

Whether the Scriptures (or God speaking in them) are the supreme and infallible judge of controversies and the interpreter of the Scriptures. Or whether the church or the Roman pontiff is. We affirm the former and deny the latter against the papists.

I. This is a primary question and almost the only one on account of which all the other controversies about the Scriptures were started. From no other cause is either the authority of the Scriptures called in question by the papists or their integrity and purity attacked or their perspicuity and perfection argued against, than to prove that the Scriptures cannot be the judge of controversies and the necessity of having recourse to the tribunal of the church.

STATEMENT OF THE QUESTION

II. On the state of the question keep in mind: (1) that the question does not concern any kind of judgment (i.e., whether any judgment belongs to the church and its officers in controversies of faith). The orthodox refute the charge made against them by their practice. Rather the question concerns only the supreme and infallible judgment by which everything must necessarily stand or fall—whether this belongs to the Scriptures themselves (as we hold) or to some man or assembly composed of men (as the papists maintain).

III. The threefold judge must be accurately distinguished here. First is the supreme and autocratic (*autokratorikos*), which judges by legislative and absolute authority after the manner of the highest prince, which enacts laws and from which there is no appeal. Second is the subordinate (*hypēretikos*) or ministerial, which interprets the laws after the manner of a public minister. Third is an idiomatic (*idiōtikos*) or private, which both from the laws and from their interpretation judges in the way of private discretion. The first gives a judgment of final and absolute decision. The second gives a judgment of public determination, but subordinate and in accordance with the laws. The third gives a judgment of private discretion without any public authority. Here we dispute not about the ministerial and private judgment, but the supreme and infallible.

IV. The question is not whether the Scriptures are the rule and standard of controversies. This the papists do not object to, at least they appear to be willing to hold it, although what they give with one hand they take away with the other, arguing their obscurity and imperfection. But the question is whether the Scriptures are a total and full rule, not a partial and imperfect rule. For they want it to be only a partial rule, and indeed so it is explained according to the mind of the Roman Catholic church.

V. The opinion of the papists comes to this. (1) They distinguish between the rule and the judge (who ought to bring judgment from the Scriptures). They acknowledge the Scriptures indeed to be a rule, but partial and inadequate to which unwritten (*agraphos*) tradition must be added. The Scripture is not sufficient for settling controversies unless there comes in the sentence of some visible and infallible judge clearly to pronounce which party has the better cause. For otherwise there would be no end of contentions. Now such a judge can be found nowhere else than in the church where they erect four tribunals from which there is no appeal: (1) the church; (2) the councils; (3) the fathers; (4) the pope. But when the votes are properly counted, the pope remains *solus* (alone), to whom they are accustomed to ascribing that supreme and infallible judgment.

VI. That such is their opinion this passage from Andradius (who was in the Council of Trent) proves: "This high authority of interpreting the Scriptures we grant not to individual bishops, but to the Roman pontiff alone, who is the head of the church, or to all the chief officers collected together by his command" (*Defensio tridentinae fidei Catholicae*, bk. 2). "That judge cannot be the Scriptures, but the ecclesiastical prince; either alone or with the counsel and consent of the fellow bishops" (Bellarmine, VD 3.9, p. 110). "The Roman pontiff is the one in whom this authority, which the church has of judging concerning all controversies of faith, resides" (Gregory of Valentia, *Analysis fidei Catholicae* 7 [1585], 216). Still this is not the opinion of all. For although they who exalt the pope above the council ascribe this authority of a judge to him, yet they think differently who hold the council to be above the pope finally. Others, to reconcile these two opinions, think the pope (in the council) or the council (approved by the pope) is that infallible judge.

VII. Now although we do not deny that the church is a ministerial and secondary judge, able to decide controversies of faith according to the word of God (although as to internal conviction [*plērophorian*] we hold that the Holy Spirit, as the principle, must persuade us of the true interpretation of the Scriptures), yet we deny that as to the external demonstration of the object any infallible and supreme judge is to be sought besides the Scriptures. Much less is the pope to be admitted to perform this office. For we think that the Scriptures alone (or God speaking by them) are sufficient for that.

THE SCRIPTURES ALONE ARE THE SUPREME JUDGE OF CONTROVERSY

VIII. The reasons are: (1) God in the Old and New Testaments absolutely and unconditionally sends us to this judge—"and thou shalt do according to the law which they shall teach thee" (Deut. 17:10); "to the law and the testimony, etc." (Isa. 8:20); "They have Moses and the prophets; let them hear them" (Luke 16:29). Christ does not say they have the priests and scribes (who cannot err), but they have Moses and the prophets (viz., in their writings), implying that they are abundantly sufficient for full instruction and that their authority must be acquiesced in. Nor is the meaning of Christ different in Matthew 19:28 where he promises that after his departure the apostles "should sit upon twelve thrones judging the twelve tribes of Israel." This must be referred to the judicial power they would obtain in the church through the word. Thus, "ye do err," said Christ to the Sadducees, "not knowing the Scriptures" (Matt. 22:29). And elsewhere he enjoins upon the Jews the searching of the Scriptures (John 5:39).

FROM THE PRACTICE OF CHRIST AND THE APOSTLES

IX. (2) The practice of Christ and his apostles confirms this for in controversies of faith they appeal to the Scriptures (Matt. 4:4, 6–7; 22:29; John 5:39; 10:34–35; Acts 17:2, 11; 18:28; 26:22) and profess to know nothing besides Moses and the prophets (Luke 24:44; Acts 26:22). Peter compares the word to a heavenly vision, as a more sure word (*logon bebaioteron*), whereunto we do well to take heed (2 Peter 1:19), nothing at all being said about his own privilege or of papal infallibility. The Bereans are commended (Acts 17:11) for comparing what they heard with the rule of the Scriptures, not consulting any oracle of infallibility. On the contrary, the Pharisees and Sadducees are condemned because they departed from them (Matt. 15:3; 22:29).

FROM THE NATURE OF AN INFALLIBLE JUDGE

X. (3) A supreme and infallible judge is one who never errs in judgment, nor is he able to err; is uninfluenced by prejudice and from whom is no appeal. Now these requisites can be found in neither the church, nor councils, nor pope, for they can both err and often have erred most egregiously, and they are the guilty party. They are accused of being falsifiers and corruptors of the Scriptures and from them appeals are often made to the Scriptures (1 John 4:1; Isa. 8:20; John 5:39; Acts 17:11). But God speaking in the Scriptures claims these as his own prerogatives alone, as incapable of error in judgment, being truth itself, uninfluenced by partiality, being no respecter of persons (*aprosōpolēptēs*); nor can any appeal be made from him because he has no superior.

BECAUSE EVERY MAN IS LIABLE TO ERROR AND GOD ALONE IS INFALLIBLE

XI. (4) Man cannot be the infallible interpreter of the Scriptures and judge of controversies because he is liable to error. Our faith cannot be placed in him, but upon God alone from whom depends the sense and meaning of the Scriptures and who is the best interpreter of his own words. As the only teacher, he can best explain the meaning of the law (Matt. 23:8, 10); our lawgiver who is able to save and to destroy (James 4:12). If the rulers of the church are influenced by the Holy Spirit, they do not cease to be men and therefore fallible. For their inspiration is only ordinary and common, not extraordinary and special (conferring the gift of infallibility which the apostles and prophets had).

BECAUSE THE SCRIPTURES RECOGNIZE NONE EXCEPT GOD

XII. (5) If there were such a judge as the papists maintain: (a) it is a wonder that the Lord never mentions this interpreter who is so essential; (b) that Paul in his epistles (and especially in that to the Romans) does not inform them even by a single word of so great a privilege; (c) that Peter in his catholic epistles did not arrogate this as about to be transmitted to his successors, much less exercise it; (d) that the popes were neither able nor willing by that infallible authority to settle the various most important controversies which the Romish church cherished in her own bosom (i.e., between the Thomists and Scotists, the Dominicans and Jesuits, the Jesuits and Jansenists, etc.). For why did they not at once repress those contentions by their infallibility and untie the tangled knots? If they could not, what becomes of their infallibility? If they could, why did they not save the church from such scandals?

BECAUSE THE CHURCH CANNOT BE A JUDGE IN HER OWN CAUSE

XIII. (6) The church cannot be regarded as the judge of controversies because she would be a judge in her own cause and the rule of herself. For the chief controversy is about the power and infallibility of the church, when the very question is whether the church is the judge, or whether the church can err. Shall the same church sit as judge, and must we believe her just because she says so? Must she be supported in denying the Holy Scriptures to be the judge (which all acknowledge to be the infallible word of God); in wishing the church or the pope to sit as judge in her own cause and to be the infallible judge of her own infallibility (concerning which there is the greatest doubt) and which is most evidently not only liable to err, but has often erred? For the papists themselves are forced to confess that not a few popes were heretics or wicked men and devoted to magical arts (Adrian VI, *in 4 Sent.*).

FROM THE FATHERS

XIV. (7) The ancients here agree with us. Constantine (after stating what he thought was clearly taught concerning God in the gospels, the apostolical and prophetical books) adds, "therefore laying aside warring strife, we may obtain a solution of difficulties from the words of inspiration" (*tēn polemopoion oun apelasantes erin, ek tōn theopneustōn logōn labōmen tōn zētoumenōn tēn lysin*, to the Nicene fathers according to Theodoret, *Ecclesiastical History* 1.6 [NPNF2, 3:44; PG 82.920]). Optatus writes, "You say it is lawful, we say it is not lawful; between your permission and our prohibition the minds of the people fluctuate and waver. No one believes you, no one believes us, a judge must be sought from heaven, on earth we can get no decision; but why should we knock at the door of heaven when we have the Testament here in the gospel?" (*De schismate Donatistarum: Adversus Parmenianum* 5.3 [PL 11.1048–49]). Augustine says, "We are brethren, why should we contend? Our father did not die intestate; he made a will . . . open it, let us read, why should we wrangle?" (*Psalm 21* [ACW 29:224; PL 36.180]). And: "This controversy requires a judge. Christ shall judge; the apostle with him shall judge" (*On Marriage and Concupiscence* 2.33 [NPNF1, 5:306; PL 44.470]). Lactantius says, "God speaks in the divine writings as the supreme judge of all things, to whom it belongs not to argue, but to pronounce" (*Divine Institutes* 3.1 [FC 49:166; PL 6.350]). Gregory of Nyssa writes, "The inspired writing is a safe criterion of every doctrine" (*kritērion asphalēs epi pantos dogmatos hē theopneustos graphē*, *Against Eunomius* 1.22 [NPNF2, 5:62; PG 45.341]); cf. Cyprian, *Letter* 63, "To Caecilius," (ACW 46:98); Chrysostom, "Homily 23 on the Acts of the Apostles" (NPNF1, 11:148–55); Augustine, *On Baptism, Against the Donatists* 2.6 (NPNF1, 4:428).

XV. As a prince must interpret his own law, so also God must be the interpreter of his own Scriptures—the law of faith and practice. And the privilege allowed to other authors of interpreting their own words ought not to be refused to God speaking in the Scriptures.

SOURCES OF EXPLANATION

XVI. When we say that the Scriptures are the judge of controversies, we mean it in no other sense than that they are the source of divine right, and the most absolute rule of faith by which all controversies of faith can and should be certainly and perspicuously settled—even as in a republic, the foundations of decisions and of judgments are drawn from the law. So a judge may be taken widely and by metonymy of the adjunct for a normal and not a personal judge. Hence he must not be confounded with the subordinate judge who decides controversies according to the rule of the law and applies the authority of the law to things taken singly (*ta kath' hekasta*). This accords with the Philosopher's rule, "The law must govern all, but the magistrates and the state must decide as to individuals" (*dei ton nomon archein pantōn, tōn de kath' hekasta tas archas kai tēn politeian krinein*, Aristotle, *Politics* 4.4.33–34 [Loeb, 21:304–5]).

XVII. It is not always necessary to make a distinction between the judge and the law. The Philosopher confesses that in prescribing universal rights the law has the relation of a judge; but in the particular application (in things taken singly, *en tois kath' hekasta*) the interpreter of the law performs the office of judge, but a ministerial and subordinate one

(Aristotle, *Politics* 3.6 [Loeb, 21:219–31]). In this sense, we do not deny that the church is the judge, but still always bound by the Scriptures. As in a republic, the decision of a magistrate is so far valid as it is grounded on the law and agrees with it. Otherwise, if at variance with it, it is invalid and appeal may be made from it. Thus in the church the judgment of pastors can be admitted only so far as it agrees with the Scriptures.

XVIII. Although the Scriptures cannot hear the arguments of the contending parties (nor always so give its decision as to acquit by name this one and condemn that one), it does not follow that they are not the supreme judge and perfect rule. For these are not necessary to the supreme but to the ministerial judge, who is bound to give his decision according to the law and must examine witnesses and arguments and inspect the laws because he acts *de facto* not *de jure*. But the supreme judge is he who (aside from every controversy) ordains as to universal rectitude what must be done and avoided and whose prescriptions subaltern judges are bound to observe. Nor do we ever read in the laws the express condemnation of this or that person, Titus or Maevius. Thus it is here, as the cause is of faith *de jure* and not *de facto*, since the question is what must be believed or disbelieved (which the law and the judge can decide without hearing the parties).

XIX. It is not necessary for the supreme judge speaking in the Scriptures to declare a new word to us every day on account of new heresies springing up. For he (who knew all that would happen) so pronounced his truth in the word that faithful ministers may recognize universal truth by it and so refute all errors. Hence from the Scriptures, the fathers most triumphantly refuted the heresies of Pelagius, Arius, Macedonius and others, although nothing is said expressly about them.

XX. It is not necessary that there should be another visible, infallible judge than the Scriptures for settling all controversies. (1) An end of controversies is not to be expected in this life—"for there must be also heresies among you, that they which are approved may be made manifest among you" (1 Cor. 11:19). Even in the time of the apostles, various heresies crept in which were not entirely removed. (2) It is one thing to convince an adversary *de facto* and to stop his mouth so that he cannot answer anything; another to convince him *de jure* so that he may have what will be sufficient to convince him, if he is not obstinate. Although the Scripture does not always do the former on account of the perversity of men, yet it always does the latter, which is sufficient. (3) As in a well-administered republic it is sufficient if there are good laws by which things taken singly (*ta kath' hekasta*) can be decided by subordinate judges, so in the church it is enough if there is an infallible written word whence individual pastors may draw a rule of judgment in particular controversies. (4) A visible judge among the papists has not hindered the rise of innumerable controversies, which he has not yet settled by his infallible authority.

XXI. The Scriptures may have various and ambiguous senses, not from the nature of the thing affirmed or the intention of the affirmer, but from the unskillfulness or obstinacy of the distorter. Therefore this ambiguity and obscurity (if such there is) does not take away their authority, but shows the necessity of the Spirit of illumination and of the minister to explain them.

XXII. Although there may be a dispute about the true interpretation of a passage of Scripture, it is not necessary that there should be any visible, infallible judge besides the Scriptures. They interpret themselves. Man must not be regarded as the author of the interpretation he gives in accordance with them because nothing of his own is mixed with it. He adds nothing to them, but only elicits and educes from the Scriptures what already was contained there, even as one who legitimately deduces a conclusion from premises does not form it at pleasure, but elicits it from the established premises and as latent in them.

XXIII. In the dispute concerning the judge of controversies, we do not properly treat of the principles (i.e., of the questions which relate to the Scriptures), which are here taken for granted to be the principles, not proved to be so. Rather we treat of things principiated (i.e., of the doctrines contained in the Scriptures), which (granting the authority of the Scriptures) we think can be sufficiently ascertained from the Scriptures themselves. We do not deny that the Scriptures prove themselves (as was before demonstrated) not only authoritatively and by way of testimony, but also logically and by way of argument.

XXIV. The Scriptures can be called mute and speechless in reference to judgment, no more than the church in her councils and the fathers in their writings, who nevertheless, the papists maintain, can both speak and judge. If a father speaks in his will and a king in his edicts and letters, why may we not say that our heavenly Father speaks with the clearest voice to us in each Testament and the King of kings in his divine oracles? Nor can there be a doubt on this point, since the Scriptures (or the Holy Spirit in them) are so often said to speak to, accuse and judge men. The law is said to speak to those who are under the law (Rom. 3:19). "They have Moses and the prophets," said Abraham to the man who fared sumptuously (Luke 16:29), not indeed alive and seeing, but neither mute nor speechless; yea even speaking and hearing. So Isaiah is said to "cry out" (Rom. 9:27). Moses accuses the Jews (John 5:45). The law judges (John 7:51). "He that receiveth not my words, hath one that judgeth him (*echei ton krinonta*): the word that I have spoken, the same shall judge him in the last day" (John 12:48). In the same sense, the word of God is said to be *kritikos*—"a judge of the thoughts" (Heb. 4:12).

XXV. An earthly judge in the external court ought to be furnished with compulsory power, but the spiritual judge in the court of conscience holds a different relation. The kingdom of God is not to be advanced by bodily compulsion, but by the spiritual demonstration of the truth (1 Cor. 2:4). Again, although physical compulsion has no place here, even a spiritual and internal compulsion is not desirable, both with respect to believers (whom God, speaking in the Scriptures, gently and sweetly draws and moves to obedience, John 6:44; 2 Cor. 10:4) and with respect to the wicked and unbelieving whose consciences he vexes and torments.

XXVI. The example of Moses and Aaron cannot be applied to establish a supreme and infallible judge besides the Scriptures. For each was a ministerial not autocratic (*autokratorikos*) judge; one extraordinary, the other ordinary. They decided controversies not by their own authority, but according to the law and commands of God: Moses, as a mediator, by appealing to God (Ex. 18:19), but Aaron by answering from the law and according to it—"according to the sentence of the law which they shall teach thee, thou shalt do" (Deut. 17:11). Otherwise, if they spoke contrary to the law, they were not to be heard. (2) The matter here treated of is not as to controversies of faith, but of rites—the judging between blood and blood, leprosy and leprosy. (3) It treats not only of the high priest, but of the whole Levitical priesthood whose decision is binding when done in accordance with the prescriptions of the law. Otherwise, if absolutely binding, Jeremiah (Jer. 26:12–13), Christ (John 9) and the apostles (Acts 3; 13), who departed from it, committed a capital crime. (4) From the high priest the consequence does not hold good to the pope because in the New Testament there is no high priest except Christ, of whom Aaron was a type.

XXVII. The "one shepherd" (Eccl. 12:11) does not mean the typical priest of the Old Testament, but Jesus Christ, the true priest of the New, who is that good shepherd of his people (Ezek. 34:23; John 10:11). From him all the words of wisdom came because men of God spoke as they were moved by the Holy Ghost (2 Peter 1:21), as the papists themselves (Tirinus, Menochius, Cornelius a Lapide) explain it.

XXVIII. In Haggai 2:11 and Malachi 2:7, not any one priest, but indefinitely priests are commanded to be interrogated and, being interrogated, to answer according to the law. Nor does this prove their infallibility, but their duty. Malachi 2:8 nevertheless intimates they did not always do this since it adds, "but ye are departed out of the way."

XXIX. The "seat of Moses" (Matt. 23:2) is not the succession in the place and office of Moses or the external court of a supreme judge to whom the authority in question belongs (for the seat of Moses was not in existence nor was any such privilege attached to it); rather it is the promulgation of the true doctrine delivered by Moses (as the ordinary gloss on Deut. 17 has it, "The seat of Moses is wherever his doctrine is"), and the chair of Peter is wherever his doctrine is heard. So those who have been teachers of the law delivered by Moses are considered to have taught in Moses' seat, as Hilary observes (*Commentarius in Matthaeum* 24.1 [PL 9.1048]). Therefore the Pharisees teaching in Moses' seat were to be heard as far as they faithfully proposed to the people his doctrine, without any admixture of their own.

XXX. Although Christ sends us to the voice of the church (which if anyone will not hear, he is to be regarded as a heathen man and a publican, Matt. 18:17), yet he does not constitute it the infallible judge in matters of faith. (1) For he does not speak of controversies of faith, but of private offenses and fraternal admonition which (if unsuccessful in private) must be referred to the public censure of the church. Not one infallible prelate is to denounce this to all churches, but individual pastors to their own flock. (2) He alludes here to a custom of the Jewish system which excommunicated the contumacious. This applies no more to the Romish church than to every particular church within proper limits. (3) If the argument is drawn from similarity, the church is commanded to be heard as long as she hears Christ and speaks his words; otherwise, if she recedes from Christ and speaks in opposition to him, she is to be anathematized (Gal. 1:8).

XXXI. The councils sometimes asked from absent popes, not confirmative authority, but fraternal assent. Otherwise they could not claim for themselves the right of deposing them, of examining and abrogating their acts (which they did). The fathers and particular churches could in more difficult ecclesiastical affairs consult them, not as infallible judges (to whose decrees they were bound to submit their consciences), but as honorary and prudent arbiters who (before they were poisoned by the breath of pride, superstition and tyranny) were held in great esteem among the churches on account of the dignity (*prōteia*) of the city.

XXXII. Although in the external court of the church every private person is bound to submit to synodical decisions (unless he wants to be excommunicated), and such judgment ought to flourish for the preservation of order, peace and orthodoxy, and the suppression of heretical attempts; it does not follow that the judgment is supreme and infallible. For an appeal may always be made from it to the internal forum of conscience, nor does it bind anyone in this court further than he is persuaded of its agreement with the Scriptures.

XXXIII. Although we allow to individual believers the judgment of private discretion (because "he that is spiritual judgeth all things" [1 Cor. 2:15], and the apostle commands us to "prove all things" [1 Thess. 5:21]), we do not therefore assert in opposition to Peter (2 Peter 1:20) that the Scriptures are of private interpretation (*idia epilysis*). For *epilysis* here does not mean the interpretation of the Scriptures so much as the origin of the prophetic oracles. They may be said to have been written, not by each one's own private impulse and instinct (which is said of those who run although not sent by God, Jer. 23:21), but by the dictation of the Holy Spirit who moved them. Thus *epilysis* here does not pertain to the office of an interpreter, hearer or reader of the Scriptures, but to the power or impulse of prophesying; or to that notion by which the prophet was impelled to speak and to write. This is favored by a comparison with the preceding and following verses in which the question is not Who has the right of interpreting the prophecies? but By whose impulse and influence did the prophets write, and in what regard ought we to hold the prophecies; what reverence is due to them, and why is faith to be placed in them as the unquestionable oracles of God (viz., because they did not flow from man's own impulse and will as if they were a human invention or man's device, but from the impulse and influence of the Holy Spirit by whom holy men of God were moved)? In this sense, *epilysis* will signify the mission of the men of God to prophesy, by which God opened for them as it were the barriers to running (in allusion to the ancient racers who, as soon as the bars at the starting point were removed, rushed forward). But if the word is here taken to mean interpretation (as is done by many from the force of the word *epilysis*, which signifies to expound and explain, Mark 4:34; Acts 19:39), prophecy will be denied to be of private interpretation (*idias epilyseōs*) (which is such as to principle and origin, i.e., from one's own mind, but not as to subject). So that private interpretation here is not opposed to the common or public, but to the adventitious gift of the Holy Spirit.

XXXIV. From this judgment of private discretion attributed to each believer, they are wrong who infer that human reason is the judge of controversies and interpreter of the Scriptures (which the Socinians maintain and has already been refuted by us, Topic I, Question 8). Here the believer is not only moved by the light of reason, but more specially by the influence of the Spirit. And although the interpreter may examine the conceived sense of the Scriptures by natural reason, yet he cannot oppose a dictate of reason to the Holy Scriptures or withhold from it faith on account of some preconceived opinion of reason in opposition to it. Human reason (which is deceptive and slippery) is surely more likely to deviate from the truth of a thing than the Scriptures (which are the word of truth and even truth itself). Thus reason here must be brought under subjection to faith (2 Cor. 10:5) not exalted above it.

XXXV. The uncertainty of human judgment does not prove that God speaking in the Scriptures cannot be a fit judge in our cause, since it cannot be known either who has the Holy Spirit or whether he may actually be obtained. In this matter there is no need of knowing immediately and *a priori* who has the Spirit, but only who speaks according to the Scriptures. When this becomes known by a reference to the Scriptures, we can readily judge *a posteriori* who utters the words of the Spirit and speaks from him. Thus the Bereans did not inquire *a priori* whether Paul who preached to them was moved by the Holy Spirit (for this was known to God alone, the searcher of hearts, *kardiognōstē*), but whether Paul spoke according to the Scriptures. Hence from his agreement with them, they inferred that he spoke not from himself, but by the Spirit. We conclude with the golden words of Basil: "Let the divinely inspired Scriptures then judge for us and let the vote of truth be given to those among whom doctrines are found harmonizing with the Scriptures" (*ouk oun hē theopneustos hēmin diaitēsatō graphē, kai par' hois an heurethē ta dogmata synōda tois theiois logois, epi toutois hēxei pantōs hē theia tēs alētheias psēphos, Letter 189*, "To Eustathius the physician" [NPNF2, 8:229; PG 32.688]).

Twenty-first Question: The Authority of the Fathers

Are the writings of the fathers the rule of truth in doctrines of faith and in the interpretation of the Scriptures? We deny against the papists.

I. Although from the preceding question we are already satisfied that the fathers cannot sit as judges in controversies of faith, yet because the papists frequently recur to them and are accustomed to obtrude upon us the consent of the fathers as a rule of truth, we must devote a separate question to this argument which is of the greatest importance in the controversies of the present day.

WHO ARE MEANT BY THE FATHERS

II. By "the fathers" we do not mean with Augustine the apostles as the first founders and patriarchs of the Christian church (*Psalm 45*, NPNF1, 8:153), but (in accordance with the present usage which is sanctioned by the ancients) the teachers of the primitive church who (after the death of the apostles) taught and illustrated the doctrine of salvation, orally and in writing. On account of age, they lived many years before our times; on account of doctrine (for by inculcating it upon their disciples), they begat sons to God in the church.

III. Although some extend their age down to the tenth century, we do not think it ought to be carried down further than the sixth. For it is certain that purity of doctrine and worship became greatly corrupted after the six hundredth year (in which Antichrist raised his head)—error and superstitions increasing by the just judgment of God. In the first century after the death of the apostles, the principal fathers were Ignatius and Polycarp, fragments of whose writings are extant. In the second, Justin Martyr and Irenaeus. In the third, Tertullian, Clement of Alexandria, Origen, Cyprian, Arnobius, Lactantius. In the fourth, Athanasius, Eusebius of Caesarea, Hilary of Poitiers, Basil, Gregory Nazianzus, Ambrose, Jerome, Gregory of Nyssa, Epiphanius, John Chrysostom. In the fifth, Augustine, Cyril of Alexandria, Theodoret, Hilary of Arles, Prosper of Aquitania, Leo I. In the sixth, Fulgentius the African, Gelasius (Cyzicus), Gregory the Great and others.

IV. There are three opinions among the papists as to the authority of the fathers. First, those who put them on an equality with the Scriptures: to which belong those decrees of the Glossator asserting, "the writings of the fathers to be authentic, individually as well as collectively" (Dist. 9). Second (just the opposite), those who hold their writings to be merely human and therefore incapable of being a rule of faith. This was the opinion of Cajetan ("Praefatio," *Commentarii . . . in quinque Mosaicos libros in sacrae scripturae* [1639], vol. 1) and of the wiser papists. Third, those who, holding a middle ground, concede that the authority of individual fathers is human and fallible, but think that the common and universal consent

451

of the fathers in controversies is infallible and divine. This was the opinion of the Council of Trent, affirming that "the traditions of the fathers pertaining both to faith and practice must be received with an equal affection of piety with the Old and New Testaments" (Session 4, Schroeder, *Council of Trent*, 17). And, in the same place, "It prohibits anyone from daring to interpret the Scriptures contrary to that sense which the holy mother church has held, or now holds . . . or even against the unanimous consent of the fathers" (Session 4, Schroeder, *Council of Trent*, 19). Most of the papists—Stapleton, Bellarmine, Canus, Valentia and others—agree with this.

V. The orthodox (although they hold the fathers in great estimation and think them very useful to a knowledge of the history of the ancient church, and our opinion on cardinal doctrines may agree with them) yet deny that their authority, whether as individuals or taken together, can be called authoritative in matters of faith and the interpretation of the Scriptures, so that by their judgment we must stand or fall. Their authority is only ecclesiastical and subordinate to the Scriptures and of no weight except so far as they agree with them.

Statement of the question

VI. The question is not, Are the fathers to be considered witnesses, giving testimony of the consent of the ancient church and the opinion of the church in their own age? Rather, the question is, Are the fathers to be considered as judges, capable of deciding controversies of faith by their infallible authority? The papists maintain the latter; we hold the former. When we dispute at any time from the fathers against our adversaries, we use them only as witnesses, to approve by their vote the truth believed by us and to declare the belief of the church in their time. We do not use them as judges whose opinion is to be acquiesced in absolutely and without examination and as the standard of truth in doctrines of faith or in the interpretation of the Scriptures.

The fathers cannot be judges

VII. The reasons are: (1) the fathers, regarded either separately as individuals or collectively, were not prophets or apostles who, acting through an immediate call and endowed with extraordinary gifts, had the privilege of infallibility; rather they were men fallible and exposed to error, of imperfect knowledge and capable of being influenced by hearty zeal and swayed by their feelings. Nor did that mediate calling with which they were furnished place them beyond the danger of error. Not only could they err, but they often undoubtedly did err on many vital points, whether as individuals or taken together. This might readily be proved, if the papists themselves did not agree with us here; as Bellarmine who confesses that even the most learned fathers seriously erred in many things (VD 3.3, 10, pp. 101–3, 111–14), contradict each other ("De Christo," 2.2 in *Opera Omnia* [1856], 1:201–2) and that they all sometimes are blind (ibid.). Sixtus Senensis confirms this ("Praefatio" to Book 5, *Bibliotheca sancta* [1575], vol. 2; cf. Salmeron, *Commentarii in evangelicam historiam* [1602–04], vol. 13, Part 3, Disputatio 6, pp. 206–9).

VIII. (2) The writings of the fathers have been in various ways corrupted and tampered with: partly through the various spurious writings circulated under the name of the fathers (which yet in the judgment of the learned are an adulterous offspring iniquitously laid at the door of the fathers) or through the artifice of sycophants, or the frauds and impostures of heretics, or the base love-of-gain (*aischrokerdeian*) of printers or booksellers; partly through corruption and falsification creeping into their genuine writings. These have evidently been corrupted in various ways, either by the injury of copyists, or the audacity of the monks, or above all through the villainy of the Jesuits in correcting, expurgating and castrating them. The learned in previous times have complained of this and our own have proved it by innumerable examples (as may be seen in Rivet, "Critici Sacri," in *Opera* [1651], 2:1041–1152 and Daille, *A Treatise on the Right Use of the Fathers* [1856] and others who handle this argument).

IX. (3) The fathers themselves acknowledge that their writings ought not to be authoritative, nor their bare assertion in matters of religion to be absolutely decisive. Augustine says: "I confess to thy love that I have learned to give this reverence and honor to those books of Scripture alone which are now called canonical, as firmly to believe that no one of their authors erred in writing anything . . . but I so read the others, that however excellent in purity of doctrine, I do not therefore take a thing to be true because they thought so; but because they can persuade me, either through those canonical authors, or probable reason, that it does not differ from the truth. Nor do I think that you, my brother, are of a different opinion. I say further, I do not suppose that you wish your books to be read as if they were the writings of the prophets or apostles, which beyond a doubt are free from any error" (*Letter 82*, "To Jerome" [NPNF1, 1:350; PL 33.277]). "We ought not to consider the disputations of any men, though they be catholic and praiseworthy men, as canonical Scriptures, so that we may not, saving the reverence due to those men, disallow or refuse anything in their writings, if perhaps we find that they thought otherwise than the truth is. Such am I in other men's writings, such will I that other men be understanders of my writings" (Augustine, *Letter 148*, "To Fortunatianus" [NPNF1, 1:502; PL 33.628–29]). "We do no injury to Cyprian when we distinguish any writings of his whatsoever from the canonical authority of the holy Scriptures. For not without cause with such healthful diligence the ecclesiastical canon is appointed, to which certain books of the prophets and apostles do pertain, which we dare not judge at all and according to which we may freely judge of other writings either of faithful men or infidels" (Augustine, *Contra Cresconium* 2.31 [PL 43.489–90]). "I am not bound by the authority of this epistle because I do not account the writings of Cyprian as canonical Scriptures, but I consider of them out of the canonical Scriptures and whatsoever in them agreeth with the authority of the Holy Scripture, I receive with his praise; but whatsoever agreeth not, I refuse it with his leave" [ibid., 2.32 (PL 43.490)]. Even more fully and strongly does he confirm the same thing: "There [i.e., in the canonical Scriptures] if anything strikes me as absurd, it is not lawful to say the author of this book held not the truth; but either the Codex is faulty or the interpreter has erred or you do not understand. But in the productions of those who lived afterwards, which are contained in numberless books, but in no way equal to the most sacred excellence of the canonical Scriptures, even in whatever one of these equal truth is found, yet their authority is far unequal" (*Contra Faustum Manichaeum* 11.5 [NPNF1, 4:180; PL 42.249]). In the same strain, Jerome says, "I know that I esteem the apostles differently from certain tractators [handlers]; the former as always speaking the truth, the latter as men sometimes making mistakes" (*Letter 82*, "To Theophilus Bishop of Alexandria" [NPNF2, 6:173; PL 22.740]). "Origen should be read occasionally, as Tertullian, Novatus and Arnobius, and some ecclesiastical writers, so that we may extract what is good from them and shun the opposite, according to the apostle's direction, prove all things, hold fast that which is good" (Jerome, *Letter 62* [76],

"Ad Tranquillanum" [NPNF2, 6:133; PL 22.606]). Jerome frequently inculcates this and with great freedom repeatedly censors the sentiments and expositions of his predecessors. Indeed he speaks of their writings thus: "If any one will speak better or even more truly, let us acquiesce freely in the better" (*commenta. in Haba. et Zach.*, t. 5). Likewise Ambrose testifies, "I am unwilling that you should believe me. Let the Scriptures be recited. I do not speak from myself because in the beginning was the word, but I hear. I do not attach, but I read" (*The Sacrament of the Incarnation of Our Lord* 3 [FC 44:224; PL 16.857]). Also Cyril, "Do not attend to my fluent comments for possibly you may be deceived; but unless you receive the testimony of the prophets to each particular, you must not believe my words" (*Catechetical Lectures* [NPNF2, 7:73; PG 33.730]).

X. (4) Papists themselves reject the authority of the fathers (when opposed to them) and freely recede from them—so much is their recognition of them as judges in matters of faith worth. More passages to prove this could be adduced than those already referred to in Bellarmine, Sixtus Senensis and Salmeron. Speaking of his commentaries on the Scriptures, Cajetan says,

> If at any time a new sense agreeing with the text occurs, and not contrary either to the Scriptures or to the doctrine of the church, although perhaps it differs from that which is given by the whole current of the holy doctors, I wish the readers not too hastily to reject it, but rather to censure charitably. Let them remember to give every man his due. There are none but the authors of the holy Scriptures alone to whom we attribute such authority, as that we ought to believe whatsoever they have written.

"But as for others," says Augustine, "of however great sanctity and learning they may have been, I so read them that I do not believe what they have written merely because they have written it" (*Letter 82*, "To Jerome" [FC 12:392; PL 33.277]). Melchior Cano after having said from Augustine that only the holy Scriptures are exempt from all error, further adds, "But there is no man, however holy or learned, who is not sometimes deceived, who does not sometimes dote or sometimes slip" ("De Locis theolgicis," 7.3, num. 3 in *Opera* [1605], 353). And afterwards, "We should therefore read the ancient fathers with all due reverence; yet, as they were but men, with discrimination and judgment" (ibid.). "To follow the ancients in all things, and to tread everywhere in their steps as little children do in play, is nothing else but to disparage our own parts and to confess ourselves to have neither judgment nor skill enough for searching into the truth. No, let us follow them as guides, but not as masters" (ibid., num. 10, p. 359). In his comments on the gospels, Maldonatus often says, "So almost all the fathers explain it, with whom indeed I cannot agree" (*Commentary on the Holy Gospels: Matthew* [1888], 2:34, 136, 179–80 on Matt. 16:18; 19:11; 20:22). Petavius says, "The fathers were men. They had their failings and we ought not maliciously to search after their errors that we may lay them open to the world; but that we may take the liberty to note them whenever they come in our way, to the end that none be deceived by them; and that we ought no more to maintain or defend their errors than we ought to imitate their vices, if at least they had any" ("Animadversiones in Epiphanium cum appendice gemina," in *Opera* [1682], 2:205, 244, 285). Baronius frequently blames and refutes the fathers most freely whenever they happen to hold a different opinion from his own. If then our adversaries are discovered to so recklessly despise and trample under foot even the approved fathers whenever they do not agree with them, with what face can they insist upon their being heard as judges in our controversies?

SOURCES OF EXPLANATION

XI. What all the doctors deliver by unanimous consent according to the word of God, the universal church can and ought to believe. But if they do not speak out of the word, but rather against it, so far is the church from being bound to receive it that she is rather bound to anathematize them (Gal. 1:8).

XII. Although the fathers who were nearest to the age of the apostles were necessarily the purest, it does not follow that their writings can be considered as a rule of truth with the apostolic writings. The gift of infallibility was the peculiar distinction (*axiōma*) of the apostleship and cannot belong to their successors who were not furnished with the same gifts.

XIII. The unity of the church may be properly preserved by the unity of faith delivered in the Scriptures, not by the consent of the fathers (which is difficult and almost impossible to ascertain).

XIV. The obedience due to rulers (Heb. 13:17) is not blind and brute, so that we should yield ourselves to everything they say or write. Rather it should be rational, listening to them speaking and delivering the oracles of God which they have received from Christ (Matt. 28:20; 1 Cor. 11:23).

XV. Although we are unwilling to acknowledge the fathers as judges in matters of faith, we do not therefore mean that their authority is null. For they can be of great use (if not to the formation of faith, at least to its illustration and confirmation) to obtain testimony concerning the faith of the ancient church and to convince us that the papists rather boast of the consent of the fathers than follow it. Further that the doctrines which the papists obtrude upon us from tradition contrary to the Scriptures were unheard of in the first centuries.

XVI. In vain do the papists allege the consent of the fathers for the judgment of controversies and the interpretation of Scripture. (1) Even if it could be ascertained, it would make only a human and probable argument (such as might be obtained from the responses of prudent men), but not a necessary and absolute one (*anypeuthynon*), for even the fathers themselves submitted to the judgment of the Scriptures. (2) If not impossible, it is at least most difficult to get such a consent. Nor is that way (so lengthy and intricate and involved in such a labyrinth of volumes) fitted for terminating controversies especially since it is almost impossible to know what the ancients thought about our controversies. This follows: (a) because we have very few writings of the ancient fathers (especially of the first, second and third centuries, which nevertheless are those we are most especially to regard as nearest to the age of the apostles). For those writings of the first three centuries which are extant for the most part treat of subjects widely remote from our controversies and refer to them only in passing and in relation to some other thing. And this follows (b) because the fathers often differ one from another and are not always consistent with themselves in the same matters of faith. They often change their opinions, advancing in the knowledge of the truth with age and, when old, retracting the opinions they held in their youth.

XVII. We do not despise and treat the fathers injuriously when we deny to them that supreme power of judging. Indeed we must take care not to rob them of their just praise, but much more not to defer to them too much (there is more danger of the latter than of the former). Yea, if they could come forth from their graves, they could not endure the attribution of such authority to them and would sharply rebuke us in the words of the apostles to the Lycaonians (who would needs render them divine honor)—"we also are men of like passions [*homoiopatheis*] with you" (Acts 14:14–15). They frequently declare that they wrote not to give authoritative rules, but to be useful. Thus they should be read not with a necessity of believing, but with the liberty of judging. They also openly acknowledge that their works are in no way to be placed on an equality with the authority of the most holy Scriptures, (as Augustine says, *Contra Faustum Manichaeum* 11.5 [NPNF1, 4:180] and *Contra Cresconium* 2.31 [PL 43.489–90]).

XVIII. Therefore we gather that the fathers neither can nor ought to be regarded as judges in our controversies, but as witnesses who (by their wonderful consent) give testimony to the truth of Christianity and prove (by their silence or even by weighty reasons) the falsity of the doctrines introduced by the papists beyond and contrary to the Scriptures. Their writings must be respectfully received and may be read with profit. Yet at the same time they cannot have any other than our ecclesiastical and human authority (i.e., subordinate and dependent on the Scriptures).

The Helvetic Consensus Formula (1675)

The Latin original is reproduced from "Formula Consensus Helvetica," in *Collectio Confessionum in Ecclesiis Reformatis Publicatarum*, ed. H. A. Niemeyer (Lipsiae: Iulii Klinkhardti, 1840), 729–39.

The English translation is taken from "Formula Consensus Helvetica," in Archibald Alexander Hodge, *Outlines of Theology* (New York: Armstrong and Son, 1897), 656–63; reprinted in Leith, *Creeds of the Churches*, 309–23.

The Helvetic Consensus Formula was written in 1675 by theologians in the Swiss Reformed Church, including Francis Turretin. The main purpose of the confession was to address the theology of the School of Saumur, commonly known as Amyraldianism, from its chief proponent, Moise Amyraut (1596–1664). Amyraldianism, also known as "four-point Calvinism," modifies the doctrine of limited atonement. In addition, professors at Saumur developed other ideas that many believed compromised Reformed theology. For instance, Louis Cappel (1585–1658) denied the verbal inspiration of the Hebrew Old Testament, yet he rightly argued that the vowel points were not part of the original Hebrew text. Also, Josué de la Place (Placaeus, 1596–1655) advocated mediate or consequent imputation. Given that these ideas grew in popularity throughout Switzerland and in the Academy of Geneva more particularly, the Helvetic Consensus Formula, the last Reformed confession, was written to supplement and clarify earlier confessions. For a short time it had an authoritative status in the Swiss Reformed churches, but it was soon set aside. Its legacy, however, continues to live on, especially in America.

One of the chief heirs of Turretin and the Helvetic Consensus Formula in America was Princeton Theological Seminary. It is therefore not surprising that Archibald Alexander Hodge (1823–86) appended a translation of this document to his *Outlines of Theology* (1878). As already hinted at, while this confession chiefly addresses the issues of inspiration, limited atonement, and imputation, it does so by adopting the framework of covenant theology. Of particular concern to us is the doctrine of Scripture; this confession is a milestone in the definition of verbal inspiration. The first three articles of a total of twenty-six deal with this question. This confession begins with a definition of the canon and continues with a defense of the verbal inspiration of the Hebrew Old Testament up to the very vowels. While nowadays most do not agree with this last point, this was a common view at the time, yet the intent to defend the integrity of the Hebrew text remains valid. The consensus continues with a discussion of other contentious issues and concludes (Article 26) with a support for the Second Helvetic Confession and the Synod of Dort together with an affirmation of the ultimate authority of the Word of God. According to D. Clair Davis, the concern for the divine origin of faith and of Scripture in the consensus reemerges in the Princeton tradition.

Bibliography: D. Clair Davis. "Princeton and Inerrancy: The Nineteenth-Century Philosophical Background of Contemporary Concerns." Pp. 359–78 in *Inerrancy and the Church*. Emil Egli. "Helvetic Consensus." *NSHERK* 5:217–18. Richard C. Gamble. "Switzerland: Triumph and Decline." Pp. 69–70 in Reid, ed. *John Calvin: His Influence in the Western World*. James I. Good. *History of the Swiss Reformed Church Since the Reformation*. Philadelphia: Publication and Sunday School Board of the Reformed Church in the United States, 1913. Pp. 133–97. Martin I. Klauber. "The Helvetic Consensus Formula (1675): An Introduction and Translation." *Trinity Journal* 11 NS, 1 (Spring 1990): 103–23. Idem. "Jean-Alphonse Turrettin and the Abrogation of the Formula Consensus in Geneva." *WTJ* 53, 2 (Fall 1991): 325–38. Leith. *Creeds of the Churches*. Pp. 308–23. Richard A. Müller. "Reformed Confessions and Catechisms." Pp. 466–85, esp. 482–85, in *DHT*. Schaff. *The Creeds of Christendom* 1:477–89.

FORMULA CONSENSUS

Ecclesiarum Helveticarum
Reformatarum,
Circa
Doctrinam de Gratia
Universali et Connexa,
Aliaque Nonnulla Capita.

FORMULA CONSENSUS HELVETICA

Composed at Zurich, A.D. 1675, by John Henry Heidegger, of Zurich, assisted by Francis Turretin, of Geneva, and Luke Gernler, of Basle, and designed to condemn and exclude that modified form of Calvinism, which, in the seventeenth century, emanated from the theological school at Saumur, represented by Amyrault, Placaeus, and Daille; entitled "Form of Agreement of the Helvetic Reformed Churches Respecting the Doctrine of Universal Grace, the Doctrines Connected Therewith, and Some Other Points."

Canones

I. Deus T. O. M. verbum suum, quod est *potentia ad salutem omni credenti* (Rom. 1:16), non tantum per Mosen, Prophetas et Apostolos scripto mandari curavit, sed etiam pro eo scripto paterne vigilavit hactenus et excubavit, ne Sathanae astu, vel fraude ulla humana vitiari posset. Proinde merito singulari eins gratiae et bonitati Ecclesia acceptum refert, quod habet, habebitque ad finem mundi *sermonem propheticum firmissimum* (2 Petr. 3:19), nec non ἱερὰ γράμματα, *sacras literas* (2 Tim. 3:15), ex quibus, pereunte coelo et terra, *ne apex quidem vel iota unicum peribit* (Matt. 5:18).

Canons

I. God, the Supreme Judge, not only took care to have His word, which is the "power of God unto salvation to every one that believeth" (Rom. 1:16), committed to writing by Moses, the Prophets, and the Apostles, but has also watched and cherished it with paternal care ever since it was written up to the present time, so that it could not be corrupted by craft of Satan or fraud of man. Therefore the Church justly ascribes it to His singular grace and goodness that she has, and will have to the end of the world, a "sure word of prophecy" and "Holy Scriptures" (2 Tim. 3:15), from which, though heaven and earth perish, "one jot or one tittle shall in no wise pass" (Matt. 5:18).

II. In specie autem Hebraicus Veteris Teslamenti Codex, quem ex traditione Ecclesiae Iudaicae, cui olim *Oracula Dei commissa sunt* (Rom. 3:2), accepimus hodieque retinemus, tum quoad consonas, tum quoad vocalia, sive puncta ipsa, sive punctorum saltem potestatem, et tum quoad res, tum quoad verba θεόπνευστος, ut fidei et vitae nostrae, una cum Codice Novi Testamenti sit Canon unicus et illibatus, ad cuius normam, ceu Lydium lapidem, universae, quae extant, Versiones, sive orientales, sive occidentales exigendae, et sicubi deflectunt, revocandae sunt.

III. Eorum proinde sententiam probare neutiquam possumus, qui lectionem, quam Hebraicus Codex exhibet, humano tantum arbitrio constitutam esse definiunt, quique lectionem Hebraicam, quam minus commodam iudicant, configere, camque ex LXX. seniorum aliorumque versionibus Graecis, Codice Samaritano, Targumim Chaldaicis, vel aliunde etiam, imo quandoque ex sola ratione emendare religioni neutiquam ducunt, neque adeo aliam lectionem authenticam, quam quae ex collatis inter se editionibus, ipsiusque etiam Hebraici codicis, quem variis modis corruptum esse dictitant, adhibita circa lectiones variantes humani iudicii κρίσει erui possit, agnoscunt: Tandemque praeter editionem Hebraeam hodiernam, alios esse codices Hebraeos in veterum Interpretum deflectentibus ab Hebraeo nostro contextu versionibus, quae etiamnum variantium olim codicum Hebraeorum indicia sint, decernunt: Atque ita fidei nostrae principium, eiusque authoritatem sacrosanctam anceps in discrimen adducunt.

II. But, in particular, the Hebrew Original of the Old Testament, which we have received and to this day do retain as handed down by the Jewish Church, unto whom formerly "were committed the oracles of God" (Rom. 3:2), is, not only in its consonants, but in its vowels—either the vowel points themselves, or at least the power of the points—not only in its matter, but in its words, inspired of God, thus forming, together with the Original of the New Testament, the sole and complete rule of our faith and life; and to its standard, as to a Lydian stone, all extant versions, oriental and occidental, ought to be applied, and wherever they differ, be conformed.

III. Therefore we can by no means approve the opinion of those who declare that the *text* which the Hebrew Original exhibits was determined by man's will alone, and do not scruple at all to remodel a Hebrew reading which they consider unsuitable, and amend it from the Greek Versions of the LXX and others, the Samaritan Pentateuch, the Chaldee Targums, or even from other sources, yea, sometimes from their own reason alone; and furthermore, they do not acknowledge any other reading to be genuine except that which can be educed by the critical power of the human judgment from the collation of editions with each other and with the various readings of the Hebrew Original itself—which, they maintain, has been corrupted in various ways; and finally, they affirm that besides the Hebrew edition of the present time, there are in the Versions of the ancient interpreters which differ from our Hebrew context other Hebrew Originals, since these Versions are also indicative of ancient Hebrew Originals differing from each other. Thus they bring the foundation of our faith and its inviolable authority into perilous hazard.

IV. Deus ante iacta mundi fundamenta in Christo Iesu, Domino nostro, fecit πρόθεσιν αἰώνιον *propositum seculorum* (Eph. 3:11), in quo ex mero voluntatis suae beneplacito, sine ulla meriti operum vel fidei praevisione, ad laudem gloriosae gratiae suae elegit certum ac definitum hominum in eadem corruptionis massa, et communi sanguine iacentium, adeoque peccate corruptorum numemerum, in tempore per Christum Sponsorem et Mediatorem unicum ad salutem perducendum, eiusdemque merite, Spiritus S. regenerantis potentissima virtute, efficaciter vocandum, regenerandum, et fide ac resipiscentia donandum. Atque ita quidem Deus gloriam suam illustrare constituit, ut decreverit, primo quidem hominem integrum creare, tum eiusdem lapsum permittere, ac demum ex lapsis quorundam misereri, adeoque eosdem eligere, alios vero in corrupta massa relinquere, aeternoque tandem exitio devovere.

V. In gratioso autem illo Electionis divinae decreto ipse quoque Christus includitur, non ut causa meritoria, vel fundamentum ipsam electionem praecedens, sed ut ipse quoque ἐκλεκτός *electus* (1 Petr. 2:4, 6) ante iacta mundi fundamenta praecognitus, adeoque primarium eius exequendae electus mediator, et primogenitus frater noster, cuius pretioso merito, ad conferendam nobis, salva iustitia sua, salutem, uti voluit. Scriptura enim sacra non tantum testatur electionem factam esse *secundum merum beneplacitum consilii et voluntatis divinae* (Matt. 11:26; Eph. 1:5, 9); sed etiam destinationem et dationem Christi, Mediatoris nostri, ab enixo Dei Patris erga *mundum* electorum *amore* arcessit.

IV. Before the foundation of the world God purposed in Christ Jesus, our Lord, an eternal purpose (Eph. 3:11), in which, from the mere good pleasure of His own will, without any prevision of the merit of works or of faith, unto the praise of His glorious grace, out of the human race lying in the same mass of corruption and of common blood, and, therefore, corrupted by sin, *He elected a certain and definite number* to be led, in time, unto salvation by Christ, their Surety and sole Mediator, and on account of His merit, by the mighty power of the regenerating Holy Spirit, to be effectually called, regenerated, and gifted with faith and repentance. So, indeed, God, determining to illustrate His glory, decreed to create man perfect, in the first place, then, permit him to fall, and at length pity some of the fallen, and therefore elect those, but leave the rest in the corrupt mass, and finally give them over to eternal destruction.

V. In that gracious decree of Divine Election, moreover, Christ himself is also included, not as the meritorious cause, or foundation anterior to Election itself, but as being Himself also elect (1 Peter 2:4, 6), foreknown before the foundation of the world, and accordingly, as the first requisite of the execution of the decree of Election, chosen Mediator, and our first born Brother, whose precious merit God determined to use for the purpose of conferring, without detriment to His own justice, salvation upon us. For the Holy Scriptures not only declare that Election was made according to the mere good pleasure of the Divine counsel and will (Eph. 1:5, 9; Matt. 11:26), but also make the appointment and giving of Christ, our Mediator, to proceed from the *strenuous love* of God the Father toward the world of the elect.

VI. Quamobrem neque eorum suffragamur sententiae, qui docent, Deum φιλανθρωπίᾳ, seu praecipuo quodam generis humani lapsi amore motum Electioni praevio, voluntate quadam conditionata, velleitate, misericordia prima, uti vocant, desiderio inefficaci omnium et singulorum, conditionate saltem, si videlicet credant, salutem intendisse: omnibus et singulis lapsis Christum Mediatorem destinasse; ac demum quosdam consideratos, non simpliciter ut peccatores in Adamo primo, sed ut redemptos in Adamo secundo elegisse, hoc est, salutare fidei donum in tempore gratiose concedendum iis destinasse; atque unico hocce actu Electionem proprie dictam absolvi. Haec enim, et si quae alia hisce affinia sunt ab ὑποτυπώσει sanorum de Electione divina sermonum non mediocriter deflectunt. Scriptura quippe propositum Dei, miserendi videlicet hominum, non ad omnes et singulos, sed ad solos electos restringit; exclusis nominatim reprobis; veluti *Esavo*, quem Deus aeterno odio prosecutus est (Rom. 9:11). Testantur eaedem sacrae literae, consilium et voluntatem Dei non nutare, sed *stare immobiliter, et Deum in coelis, quaecunque vult, facere* (Ies. 47:10; Ps. 115:3). Quippe Deus procul abest ab omni imperfectione humana, qualis in affectibus et desideriis inefficacibus, temeritate, poenitentia et consilii mutatione gliscit. Destinatio quoque Mediatoris Christi aeque ac salus eorum, qui ipsi ut peculium et haereditas ἀναφαίρετος dati sunt, ab una eademque Electione arcessitur, non ei ut fundamentum substernitur.

VI. Wherefore we can not give suffrage to the opinion of those who teach: (1) that God, moved by philanthropy, or a sort of special love for the fallen human race, to *previous election*, did, in a kind of conditioned willing—willingness—first moving of pity, as they call it—inefficacious desire—purpose the salvation of all and each, at least, conditionally, i.e., if they would believe; (2) that He appointed Christ Mediator for all and each of the fallen; and (3) that, at length, certain ones whom He regarded, not simply as sinners in the first Adam, but as redeemed in the second Adam, He *elected*, i.e., He determined to graciously bestow on these, in time, the saving gift of faith; and in this sole act Election properly so called is complete. For these and all other kindred teachings are in no wise insignificant deviations from the form of sound words respecting Divine Election; because the Scriptures do not extend unto all and each God's purpose of showing mercy to man, but restrict it to the elect alone, the reprobate being excluded, even by name, as Esau, whom God hated with an eternal hatred (Rom. 9:10–13). The same Holy Scriptures testify that the counsel and the will of God change not, but stand immovable, and God in the heavens *doeth* whatsoever he will (Ps. 115:3; Isa. 46:10); for God is infinitely removed from all that human imperfection which characterizes inefficacious affections and desires, rashness, repentance, and change of purpose. The appointment, also, of Christ, as Mediator, equally with the salvation of those who were given to Him for a possession and an inheritance that can not be taken away, proceeds from one and the same Election, and does not underly Election as its foundation.

VII. Sicut *ab aeterno Deo nota fuerunt omnia opera eius* (Act. 15:18): ita in tempore pro infinita potentia, sapientia et bonitate sua hominem, operum suorum gloriam et coronidem ad imaginem suam, adeoque rectum, sapientem et iustum condidit; conditum foederi operum subiecit, et in eo suam ei communionem, amicitiam et vitam, siquidem ad nutum eius se obedientem gereret, liberaliter promisit.

VIII. Porro promissio illa foederi operum annexa, fuit non terrestris tantum vitae et felicitatis continuatio, sed inprimis vitae aeternae et coelestis, in coelo videlicet, siquidem perfectae obedientiae stadium decurrisset, per ineffabile gaudium in communione Dei tum corpore tum anima transigendae possessio. Id ipsum enim non *Arbor* duntaxat *vitae* Adamo praefiguravit, sed etiam legis potentia, quae a Christo in locum nostrum succedente completa, non aliam quam coelestem vitam in Christo, δικαίωμα τοῦ νόμου implente, nobis addicit, nec non opposita comminatio *mortis*, non temporalis duntaxat sed etiam aeternae, manifeste arguit.

IX. Quamobrem illorum sententiae nulli astipulamur, qui Adamo, siquidem Deo obediret, coelestis beatitudinis praemium propositum esse negant; neque aliam foederis operum promissionem quam vitae perpetuae et affluentis omni bonorum genere, quae tum in animum tum in corpus hominis in statu integrae naturae constituti competere possunt, eiusque in Paradiso terrestri fruendae agnoscunt. Hoc enim et sano sensui verbi divini repugnat, et potentiam legis per se consideratae enervat.

VII. As all His works were known unto God from eternity (Acts 15:18), so in time, according to His infinite power, wisdom, and goodness, He made man, the glory and end of His works, in His own image, and, therefore, upright, wise, and just. Him, thus constituted, He put under the Covenant of Works, and in this Covenant freely promised him communion with God, favor, and life, if indeed he acted in obedience to His will.

VIII. Moreover that promise annexed to the Covenant of Works was not a continuation only of earthly life and happiness, but the possession especially of life eternal and celestial, a life, namely, of both body and soul in heaven—if indeed man ran the course of perfect obedience—with unspeakable joy in communion with God. For not only did the Tree of Life prefigure this very thing unto Adam, but the power of the law, which, being fulfilled by Christ, who went under it in our stead, awards to us no other than celestial life in Christ who kept the righteousness of the law (Rom. 2:26), manifestly proves the same, as also the opposite threatening of death both temporal and eternal.

IX. Wherefore we can not assent to the opinion of those who deny that a reward of *heavenly* bliss was proffered to Adam on condition of obedience to God, and do not admit that the promise of the Covenant of Works was any thing more than a promise of perpetual life abounding in every kind of good that can be suited to the body and soul of man in a state of *perfect* nature, and the enjoyment thereof in an *earthly* Paradise. For this also is contrary to the sound sense of the Divine Word, and weakens the power (*potestas* or *potentia*) of the law in itself considered.

X. Sicut autem Deus foedus operum cum Adamo inivit non tantum pro ipso, sed etiam in ipso, ut capite et stirpe, cum toto genere humano, vi benedictionis naturae ex ipso nasciturae, et eandem integritatem, siquidem in ea perstitisset, haereditaturo: ita Adamus tristi prolapsu, non sibi duntaxat sed toti etiam humano generi, *ex sanguinibus et voluntate carnis* proventuro peccavit, et bona in foedere promissa perdidit. Censemus igitur, peccatum Adami omnibus eius posteris, iudicio Dei arcano et iusto, imputari. Testatur quippe Apostolus *in Adamo omnes peccasse: Unius hominis inobedientia peccateres multos constitui*; et *in eodem omnes mori* (Rom. 5:12, 19; 1 Cor. 15:21–22). Neque vero ratio apparet, quemadmodum haereditaria corruptio, tanquam mors spiritualis, in universum genus humanum iusto Dei iudicio cadere possit, nisi eiusdem generis humani delictum aliquod, mortis illius reatum inducens, praecesserit. Cum Deus iustissimus totius terrae iudex nonnisi sontem puniat.

X. As, however, God entered into the Covenant of Works not only with Adam for himself, but also, in him as the head and root (*stirps*), with the whole human race, who would, by virtue of the blessing of the nature derived from him, inherit also the same perfection, provided he continued therein; so Adam by his mournful fall, not only for himself, but also for the whole human race that would be born of bloods and the will of the flesh, sinned and lost the benefits promised in the Covenant. We hold, therefore, that the sin of Adam is imputed by the mysterious and just judgment of God to all his posterity. For the Apostle testifies that *in Adam all sinned, by one man's disobedience many were made sinners* (Rom. 5:12, 19), and *in Adam all die* (1 Cor. 15:21–22). But there appears no way in which hereditary corruption could fall, as a spiritual death, upon the whole human race by the just judgment of God, unless some sin (*delictum*) of that race preceded, incurring (*inducens*) the penalty (*reatum*, guilt) of that death. For God, the supremely just Judge of all the earth, punishes none but the guilty.

XI. Duplici igitur nomine post peccatum homo natura, indeque ab ortu suo, antequam ullum actuale peccatum in se admittat, irae ac maledictioni divinae obnoxius est; primum quidem ob παράπτωμα et inobedientiam, quam in Adami lumbis commisit: deinde ob consequentem in ipso conceptu haereditariam corruptionem insitam, qua tota eius natura depravata et spiritualiter mortua est, adeo quidem, ut recte peccatum originale statuatur duplex, imputatum videlicet, et haereditarium inhaerens.

XI. For a double reason, therefore, man, because of sin (*post peccatum*) is by nature, and hence from his birth, before committing any actual sin, exposed to God's wrath and curse; first, on account of the transgression and disobedience which he committed in the loins of Adam; and, secondly, on account of the consequent hereditary corruption implanted in his very conception, whereby his whole nature is depraved and spiritually dead; so that original sin may rightly be regarded as twofold, viz., *imputed sin* and *inherent hereditary sin*.

XII. Non possumus proin, salva coelesti veritate, assensum praebere iis, qui Adamum posteros suos ex instituto Dei repraesentasse ac proinde eius peccatum posteris eius ἀμέσως imputari negant, et sub imputationis mediatae et consequentis nomine, non imputationem duntaxat primi peccati tollunt, sed haereditariae etiam corruptionis assertionem gravi periculo obiiciunt.

XIII. Sicut Christus ab aeterno electus est ut Caput, Princeps et Haeres omnium eorum, qui in tempore per gratiam eius salvantur: ita etiam in tempore Novi Foederis Sponsor factus est pro iis solis, qui per aeternam electionem dati ipsi sunt ut populus peculii, semen et haereditas eius. Pro solis quippe electis ex decretorio Patris consilio propriaque intentione diram mortem oppetiit, solos illos in sinum paternae gratiae restituit, solos Deo Patri offenso reconciliavit et a maledictione legis liberavit. Iesus enim noster *salvat populum suum a peccatis* (Matt. 1:21), qui *animam suam redemptionis pretium dedit pro multis ovibus* (Matt. 20:24, 28; coll. Ioan. 10:15) suis, *ad vocem eius attonitis* (Ioan. 10:27–28), pro quibus solis etiam, tanquam divinitus vocatus Sacerdos, postposito *mundo*, intercedit (Ioan. 17:9; Ies. 66:22). Christo proin moriente soli Electi, qui in tempore *nova creatura* fiunt, proque quibus moriens ipse, tanquam piacularis victima, substitutus est *una mortui* et *a peccato iustificati* censentur (2 Cor. 5:17): atque ita voluntas Christi morientis cum consilio Patris, non alios ipsi quam Electos redimendos

XII. Accordingly we can not, without harm to Divine truth, give assent to those who deny that Adam represented his posterity by appointment of God, and that his sin is imputed, therefore, *immediately* to his posterity; and under the term *imputation mediate and consequent* not only destroy the imputation of the first sin, but also expose the doctrine (*assertio*) of hereditary corruption to great danger.

XIII. As Christ was from eternity elected the Head, Prince, and Lord (*Haeres*) of all who, in time, are saved by His grace, so also, in time, He was made Surety of the New Covenant only for those who, by the eternal Election, were given to Him as His own people (*populus peculii*), His seed and inheritance. For according to the determinate counsel of the Father and His own intention, He encountered dreadful death instead of the elect alone, restored only these into the bosom of the Father's grace, and these only he reconciled to God, the offended Father, and delivered from the curse of the law. For our Jesus saves *His people* from their sins (Matt. 1:21), who gave His life a ransom for *many sheep* (Matt. 20:28; John 10:15), His own, who hear His voice (John 10:27–28), and for these only He also intercedes, as a divinely appointed Priest, and not for the world (John 17:9). Accordingly in the death of Christ, only the elect, who in time are made new creatures (2 Cor. 5:17), and for whom Christ in His death was substituted as an expiatory sacrifice, are regarded as having died with Him and as being justified from sin; and thus, with the counsel

dantis, nec non operatione Spiritus saneti non alios quam Electos sanctificantis, et ad vivam spem aeternae vitae obsignantis παναρμονικῶς ita convenit et amice conspirat, ut Patris eligentis, Filii redimentis, et Spiritus S. sanctificantis aequalis περιφορία pateat.

of the Father who gave to Christ none but the elect to be redeemed, and also with the working of the Holy Spirit, who sanctifies and seals unto a living hope of eternal life none but the elect, the will of Christ who died so agrees and amicably conspires in perfect harmony, that the sphere of the Father's election (*Patris eligentis*), the Son's redemption (*Filii redimentis*), and the Spirit's sanctification (*Spiritus S. sanctificantis*) is one and the same (*aequalis pateat*).

XIV. Atque id ipsum amplius etiam inde colliquescit, quod Christus iisdem, pro quibus mortuus est, uti salutem, ita etiam media ad salutem, spiritum inprimis regenerantem et coeleste fidei donum, et meruit et actu confert. Testatur quippe Scriptura, Christum Dominum venisse *ad salvandum perditas oves domus Israelis* (Matt. 15:24), *mittere et eundem Spiritum sanctum*, tanquam suum, regenerationis fontem (Ioan. 16:7–8): interque promissiones meliores Novi Foederis, quarum is factus Mediator et Sponsor est, hanc eminere, quod *legem suam*, fidei videlicet, *cordibus suorum inscripturus sit* (Heb. 8:10): Venire ad Christum, per fidem videlicet, quicquid Pater ipsi dedit: Denique nos esse *electos in Christo, ut simus sancti et inculpati, adeoque filii per ipsum* (Eph. 1:4–5). Ut vero simus sancti et filii Dei, non aliunde quam a fide et spiritu regenerationis proficiscitur.

XIV. This very thing further appears in this also, that Christ merited for those in whose stead He died the *means of salvation*, especially the regenerating Spirit and the heavenly gift of faith, as well as salvation itself, and actually confers these upon them. For the Scriptures testify that Christ, the Lord, came *to save the lost sheep of the house of Israel* (Matt. 15:24), and sends the same Holy Spirit, the fount of regeneration, as His own (John 16:7–8); that among the better promises of the New Covenant of which He was made Mediator and Surety this one is pre-eminent, *that He will write His law*, i.e., the law of faith, *in the hearts of his people* (Heb. 8:10); that *whatsoever the Father has given to Christ will come to Him*, by faith, surely; and finally, that we are *chosen in Christ to be holy and without blame*, and, moreover, *children by Him* (Eph. 1:4–5); but our being holy and children of God proceeds only from faith and the Spirit of regeneration.

XV. Ita autem Christus vice Electorum obedientia mortis suae Deo Patri satisfecit, ut in censum tamen vicariae iustitiae et obedientiae illius, universa eius, quam per totius vitae suae curriculum legi, tanquam, *servus* ille *iustus*, sive agendo sive patiendo praestitit, obedientia vocari debeat. Nihil enim aliud fuit Christi vita, teste quidem Apostolo (Phil. 2:8 sqq.), quam perpetua quidem exinanitio, submissio et humiliatio gradatim ad extremum usque terminum, mortem videlicet crucis procedens; rotundo asserit ore Spiritus Dei Christum sanctissima vita legi et iustitiae divinae pro nobis satisfecisse, et pretium illud, quo empti sumus Deo, non in passionibus duntaxat, sed tota eius vita legi conformata collocat. Morti autem vel sanguini Christi Redemptionem nostram vendicat haud alio sensu, quam quia is per passiones consummatus est. Atque ita quidem ab extremo illo terminante et nobilissimo actu, sine quo salus nostra constare non potuisset, quique omnium virtutum speculum fuit lucidissimum, denominationem facit, ut tamen a morte vitam anteactam neutiquam secludat.

XV. But *by the obedience of his death* Christ instead of the elect so satisfied God the Father, that in the estimate, nevertheless, of His vicarious righteousness and of that obedience, all of that which He rendered to the law, as its just servant, during the whole course of His life, whether by doing or by suffering, ought to be called obedience. For Christ's life, according to the Apostle's testimony (Phil. 2:7–8), was nothing but a continuous emptying of self, submission and humiliation, descending step by step to the very lowest extreme, even the death of the Cross; and the Spirit of God plainly declares that Christ in our stead satisfied the law and Divine justice by His most holy life, and makes that ransom with which God has redeemed us to consist not in His sufferings only, but in His whole life conformed to the law. The Spirit, however, ascribes our redemption to the death, or the blood, of Christ, in no other sense than that it was consummated by sufferings; and from that last terminating and grandest act derives a name (*denominationem facit*) indeed, but in such a way as by no means to separate the life preceding from His death.

XVI. Haec omnia cum ita se omnino habeant, haud sane probare possumus oppositam doctrinam illorum, qui statuunt, Christum propria intentione et coasilio tum suo, tum Patris ipsum mittentis, mortuum esse pro omnibus et singulis, addita conditione impossibili, si videlicet credant; omnibus impetrasse, quae non omnibus tamen applicetur, salutem, morte sua nemini proprie et actu salutem ac fidem meruisse, sed iustitiae duntaxat divinae obstaculum removisse, et Patri potestatem acquisivisse novum foedus gratiae ineundi cum universis hominibus; denique qui iustitiam Christi activam et passivam ita partiuntur, ut asserant, acti vam eum sibi pro sua vindicare, passivam vero demum Electis donare et imputare. Haec omnia, et si quae his similia sunt apertis Scripturis et gloriae Christi, qui fidei et salutis nostrae ἀρχηγὸς καὶ τελειωτὴς est, repugnant, crucem eius evacuant, et per speciem augendi meriti eius, reapse illud imminuunt.

XVI. Since all these things are entirely so, surely we can not approve the contrary doctrine of those who affirm that of His own intention, by His own counsel and that of the Father who sent Him, Christ died for all and each upon the impossible condition, provided they believe; that He obtained for all a salvation, which, nevertheless, is not applied to all, and by His death merited salvation and faith for no one individually and certainly (*proprie et actu*), but only removed the obstacle of Divine justice, and acquired for the Father the liberty of entering into a new covenant of grace with all men; and finally, they so separate the active and passive righteousness of Christ, as to assert that He claims His *active* righteousness for himself as His own, but gives and imputes only His *passive* righteousness to the elect. All these opinions, and all that are like these, are contrary to the plain Scriptures and the glory of Christ, who is *Author and Finisher* of our faith and salvation; they make His cross of none effect, and under the appearance of augmenting His merit, they really diminish it.

XVII. Vocatio ad salutem καιροῖς ἰδίοις, *propriis temporibus* (1 Tim. 2:6), attemperata est. Secundum voluntatem quippe Dei modo restrictior, modo latior et communior, nunquam tamen absolute universalis fuit. Etenim quidem sub Veteri Testamento *annuntiavit Deus Verbum suum Iacobo, statuta sua et iudicia Israëli, non sic fecit ulli genti* (Ps. 147:19–20). In Novo Testamento Deus pace facta in sanguine Christi, et rupto intergerino pariete, praeconii Evangelici et vocationis externae pomoeria hactenus dilatavit, ut *nulla amplius* διαστολὴ, *distinctio sit inter Iudaeos et gentes, sed Deus iam est Dominus omnium, dives erga omnes ipsum invocantes* (Rom. 10:12–13). Neque tamen sic vel absolute universalis est. Testatur enim Christus *multos esse vocatos* (Matt. 20:14), non omnes. Cumque Paulus et Timotheus Bithyniam versus Evangelii ibidem praedicandi causa contenderent, *non sivit eos Spiritus Iesu* (Act. 16:7). Fueruntque, et sunt hodieque, experientia teste, innumerae myriades hominum, quibus Christus ne fando quidem unquam auditus est.

XVII. The call unto salvation was suited to its *due time* (1 Tim. 2:6); since by God's will it was at one time more restricted, at another, more extended and general, but never absolutely universal. For, indeed, in the Old Testament God *showed His word unto Jacob, His statutes and His judgments unto Israel; He dealt not so with any nation* (Ps. 147:19–20). In the New Testament, peace being made in the blood of Christ and the inner wall of partition broken down, God so extended the limits (*pomoeria*) of Gospel preaching and the external call, that there is no longer any *difference between the Jew and the Greek; for the same Lord over all is rich unto all that call upon Him* (Rom. 10:12). But not even thus is the call universal; for Christ testifies that *many are called* (Matt. 20:16), not all; and when Paul and Timothy essayed to go into Bithynia to preach the Gospel, *the Spirit suffered them not* (Acts 16:7); and there have been and there are today, as experience testifies, innumerable myriads of men to whom Christ is not known even by rumor.

XVIII. Interim Deus etiam illis, quos per verbum ad salutem vocare dedignatus est, *se intestatum reliquit neutiquam* (Act. 14:17). *Dedit* quippe *illis spectacula coeli et siderum* (Deut. 4:19). Et *quod de Deo*, ex naturae videlicet et providentiae operibus, cognosci potest, id ipsum, longanimitatem suam testaturus, illis revelavit (Rom. 1:19). Neque tamen statuendum est, naturae illa et providentiae divinae opera per se sufficientia et vocationis externae vicem fungentia organa fuisse, quibus mysterium beneplaciti seu misericordiae Dei in Christo illis innotesceret. Ilico enim Apostolus addit: *Invisibilia eius e creatione mundi rebus factis anidmadversa conspici, aeternam videlicet eius divinitatem et potentiam* (Rom. 1:20), non arcanum beneplacitum in Christo; neque etiam hunc in finem, nt inde mysterium salutis per Christum perdiscerent, sed ut sint ἀναπολόγητοι, *inexcusabiles*, quia videlicet ne residua quidem illa notitia recte usi sunt, sed cognoscentes Deum, non tamen ut Deum glorificarint neque ei gratias egerint. Quamobrem etiam Christus Deum Patrem suum glorificat, quod *haec absconderit a sapientibus et intelligentibus, ac revelaverit infantibus* (Matt. 11:25). Et Apostolus insuper docet: *Mysterium voluntatis Dei notificari nobis secundum beneplacitum eius quod proposuit in Christo* (Eph. 1:9).

XVIII. Meanwhile God *left not himself without witness* (Acts 14:17) unto those whom He refused to call by His Word unto salvation. For He divided unto them the spectacle of the heavens and the stars (Deut. 4:19), and *that which may be known of God*, even from the works of nature and Providence, *He hath showed unto them* (Rom. 1:19), for the purpose of attesting His long suffering. Yet it is not to be affirmed that the works of nature and Divine Providence were means (*organa*), sufficient of themselves and fulfilling the function of the external call, whereby He would reveal unto them the mystery of the good pleasure or mercy of God in Christ. For the Apostle immediately adds (Rom. 1:20), "The invisible things of Him from the creation are clearly seen, being understood by the things that are made, even *His eternal power and Godhead*"; not His hidden good pleasure in Christ, and not even to the end that thence they might learn the mystery of salvation through Christ, but that they might be *without excuse*, because they did not use aright the knowledge that was left them, but *when they knew God, they glorified Him not as God, neither were thankful*. Wherefore also Christ glorifies God, His Father, because *He had hidden these things from the wise and the prudent, and revealed them unto babes* (Matt. 11:25); and the Apostle teaches, moreover, that God has made known unto us the mystery of His will according to His good pleasure which He hath purposed in Himself (*in Christo*) (Eph. 1:9).

XIX. Ipsa quoque vocation externa, quae per praeconium Evangelicum fit, etiam vocantis Dei respectu, seria et sincera est. Verbo enim suo serio et verissime pandit, haud equidem, quae arcana sit sua circa singulorum salutem vel exitium intentio, sed quid nostri sit officii, et quid officium illud facientes vel omittentes maneat. Scilicet haec Dei vocantis voluntas est, ut vocati ad se veniant, tantam salutem non negligant; atque ita venientibus ad se per fidem serio quoque vitam aeternam promittit. *Fidelis* enim *est*, uti loquitur Apostolus, *sermo, si nos commortui sumus, et convivemus: si patimur, etiam conregnabimus: si negabimus, etiam nos negabit: si infideles sumus, ille fidelis manet, negare se ipse non potest* (2 Tim. 2:12–13). Neque voluntas illa respectu eorum, qui vocationi non parent, inefficax est, quia semper Deus id, quod volens intendit, assequitur, demonstrationem videlicet officii, et secutam hinc vel salutem Electorum officium facientium, vel ἀναπολογησίαν reliquorum, officium praescriptum negligentium. Spiritualis certe homo conceptum Dei internum, fidei analogum cum verbo Dei externo prolato, vel scripto, nullo negotio conciliat. Et quia porro Deus probat omnem veritatem, quae ex consilio eius fluit, idcirco recte dicitur etiam voluntas ipsius esse *ut omnis, qui videt Filium et credit in ipsum, habeat vitam aeternam* (Ioan. 6:40). Quanquam hi *Omnes* sunt *Electi* soli, neque Deus ullum universale consilium inivit sine determinatione personarum, Christusque adeo non pro singulis, sed pro solis Electis sibi datis mortuus est: tamen hoc utique universaliter verum esse vult, quod ex speciali et definito eius consilio consequitur. Quod vero voluntate Dei in vocatione

XIX. Likewise the external call itself, which is made by the preaching of the Gospel, is on the part of God also, who calls, earnest and sincere. For in His Word He unfolds earnestly and most truly, not, indeed, His secret intention respecting the salvation or destruction of each individual, but what belongs to our duty, and what remains for us if we do or neglect this duty. Clearly it is the will of God who calls, that they who are called come to Him and not neglect so great salvation, and so He promises eternal life also in good earnest, to those who come to Him by faith; for, as the Apostle declares, "it is a faithful saying: For if we be dead with Him, we shall also live with Him; if we suffer, we shall also reign with Him; if we deny Him, He also will deny us; if we believe not, yet He abideth faithful; He can not deny Himself." Nor in regard to those who do not obey the call is this will inefficacious; for God always attains that which He intends in His will (*quod volens intendit*), even the demonstration of duty, and following this, either the salvation of the elect who do their duty, or the inexcusableness of the rest who neglect the duty set before them. Surely the spiritual man in no way secures (*conciliat*) the internal purpose of God to produce faith (*conceptum Dei internum, fidei analogum*) along with the externally proffered, or written Word of God. Moreover, because God approved every verity which flows from His counsel, therefore it is rightly said to be His will, that *all who see the Son and believe on Him may have everlasting life* (John 6:40). Although these "all" are the elect alone, and God formed no plan of universal salvation without any selection of persons, and Christ therefore died not for

externa universaliter ita proposita soli electi credunt, reprobi vero indurantur, id a sola gratia Dei discriminante criminante proficiscitur; Electio per eandem gratiam credentibus, reprobis vero nativa malitia sua in peccato manentibus, et secundum duritiem suam et cor poenitere nescium iram sibi in diem irae et revelationis iusti iudicii Dei thesaurizantibus.

every one but for the elect only who were given to Him; yet He intends this in any case to be universally true, which follows from His special and definite purpose. But that, by God's will, the elect alone believe in the external call thus universally proffered, while the reprobate are hardened, proceeds solely from the discriminating grace of God: election by the same grace to them that believe; but their own native wickedness to the reprobate who remain in sin, and after their hardness and impenitent heart treasure up unto themselves wrath against the day of wrath, and revelation of the righteous judgment of God (Rom. 2:5).

XX. Falli proin nulli dubitamus illos, qui vocationem ad salutem non sola Evangelii praedicatione, sed naturae etiam ac Providentiae operibus, citra ullum exterius praeconium expediri sentiunt, adduntque, vocationem ad salutem adeo esse ἀδιόριστον et universalem, ut nemo sit mortalium, quin *obiective* saltem, uti loquuntur, sufficienter, sive *mediate*, eo videlicet, quod Deus Naturae lumine recte utenti gratiae lumen superadditurus sit, sive *immediate*, ad Christum et salutem vocetur; denique sine asserta absoluta universalitate gratiae, vocationem externam seriam et veram dici, vel ἁπλότητα et εἰλικρίνειαν Dei vocantis defendi posse, inficias eunt. Haec enim et S. Scripturae et experientiae omnium temporum adversantur, et Naturam cum Gratia, τὸ γνωστὸν τοῦ Θεοῦ cum σοφίᾳ τῇ ἐν μυστηρίῳ, denique lumen rationis cum lumine divinae revelationis manifeste confundunt.

XX. Accordingly we have no doubt that they err who hold that the call unto salvation is disclosed not by the preaching of the Gospel solely, but even by the works of nature and Providence without any further proclamation; adding, that the call unto salvation is so indefinite and universal that there is no mortal who is not, at least objectively, as they say, sufficiently called either *mediately*, namely, in that God will further bestow the light of grace on him who rightly uses the light of nature, or *immediately*, unto Christ and salvation; and finally denying that the external call can be said to be serious and true, or the candor and sincerity of God be defended, without asserting the absolute universality of grace. For such doctrines are contrary to the Holy Scriptures and the experience of all ages, and manifestly confound nature with grace, that which may be known of God with His hidden wisdom, the light of reason, in fine, with the light of Divine Revelation.

XXI. Qui per Evangelii praeconium ad salutem vocantur, credere non possunt, neque vocantem sequi, nisi ex spirituali morte, ea ipsa potentia, qua Deus ex tenebris lucem explendescere iussit, resuscitentur et Deus Spiritus sui flexanima gratia cordibus illorum *illucescat*, ad φωτισμὸν seu *radiationem cognitionis gloriae Dei in facie Iesu Christi* (2 Cor. 4:6). *Animalis* quippe *homo non recipit eu, quae sunt Spiritus Dei: stultitia ei est, neque potest cognoscere, quia spiritualiter iudicantur* (1 Cor. 2:14). Eamque impotentiam penitissimam tot testimoniis, tot emblematibus Scriptura passim convincit, ut vix alia in re sit locupletior. Moralis quidem ea impotentia dici possit, quatenus scilicet circa subiectum et obiectum morale versatur: Naturalis tamen esse simul et dici debet, quatenus homo φύσει, *natura*, adeoque nascendi lege, inde ab ortu est *filius irae* (Eph. 2:2), illamque ita congenitam habet, ut eam haud aliter, quam per omnipotentem et vorticordiam Spiritus Sancti gratiam, excutere possit.

XXI. They who are called unto salvation through the preaching of the Gospel can neither believe nor obey the call, unless they are raised up out of spiritual death by that very power whereby God commanded the light to shine out of darkness, and God shines into their hearts with the soul-swaying grace of His Spirit, to give *the light of the knowledge of the glory of God in the face of Jesus Christ* (2 Cor. 4:6). *For the natural man receiveth not the things of the Spirit of God; for they are foolishness unto him: neither can he know them, because they are spiritually discerned* (1 Cor. 2:14); and this utter inability the Scripture demonstrates by so many direct testimonies and under so many emblems that scarcely in any other point is it surer (*locupletior*). This inability *may*, indeed, be called *moral* even in so far as it pertains to a moral subject or object; but it *ought* at the same time to be also called *natural*, inasmuch as man by nature, and so by the law of his formation in the womb, and hence from his birth, is *the child of disobedience* (Eph. 2:2); and has that inability so innate (*congenitam*) that it can be shaken off in no way except by the omnipotent heart-turning grace of the Holy Spirit.

XXII. Censemus igitur, minus caste, neque sine periculo loqui illos, qui impotentiam illam credendi *moralem* vocant, ac *naturalem* dici non sustinent, adduntque, hominem, quocunque in statu constituatur, posse credere si velit, et fidem, quacunque demum ratione, esse ἐκ τῶν ἐφ' ἡμῖν; quam tamen Apostolus consignatissimis verbis *Dei donum* (Eph. 2:8) nuncupat.

XXII. We hold therefore that they speak with too little accuracy and not without danger, who call this inability to believe *moral* inability, and do not hold it to be *natural*, adding that man in whatever condition he may be placed is able to believe if he will, and that faith in some way or other, indeed, is self-originated; and yet the Apostle most distinctly calls it the gift of God (Eph. 2:8).

XXIII. Duae sunt viae et modi, quibus Deus δικαιοκριτὴς iustificationem promisit, vel per opera seu facta propria in Lege, vel per obedientiam seu iustitiam alienam Christi, videlicet Sponsoris, quae ex gratia imputatur credenti in Evangelio. Ille modus est iustificandi hominem integrum: hic vero iustificandi hominem peccatorem et corruptum. Iuxta duplicem huncce iustificationis modum duplex etiam foedus Scriptura constituit, operum videlicet, cum Adamo primo et singulis eius posteris in ipso initum, at per peccatum irritum factum: et gratiae, cum solis Electis in Christo, Adamo secundo percussum, quod aeternum est, nullique ἀφανισμῷ, sicuti prius illud, obnoxium.

XXIV. Caeterum posterius illud Foedus Gratiae pro diversitate temporum diversas etiam oeconomias recipit. Apostolus enim indigitans τὴν οἰκονομίαν τοῦ πληρώματος τῶν καιρῶν, *administrationem implementi temporum* (Eph. 1:10), adeoque gubernationem temporis ultimi, perspicue significat, aliam fuisse oeconomiam et gubernationem temporibus τὴν προθεσμίαν seu statutum tempus praecedentibus. In utraque tamen gratiosi Foederis oeconomia non aliter electi salvati sunt, quam per *Angelum faciei* (Ies. 63:9), *Agnum illum inde a iactis mundi fundamentis mactatum* (Apoc. 13:8), Christum Iesum, notitiam servi illius iusti, et fidem in ipsum, nec non Patrem et Spiritum eius. Christus enim heri et hodie et in secula idem est (Heb. 13:8). Et per gratiam eius credimus nos servari eundem in modum, quo salvati sunt et illi, Patres videlicet: manentque immotae in utroque

XXIII. There are two ways in which God, the just Judge, has promised justification: either by one's own works or deeds in the law; or by the obedience or righteousness of another, even of Christ our Surety, imputed by grace to him that believes in the Gospel. The former is the method of justifying man perfect; but the latter, of justifying man a sinner and corrupt. In accordance with these two ways of justification the Scripture establishes two covenants: the Covenant of Works, entered into with Adam and with each one of his descendants in him, but made void by sin; and the Covenant of Grace, made with only the elect in Christ, the second Adam, eternal, and liable to no abrogation, as the former.

XXIV. But this later Covenant of Grace according to the diversity of times had also different dispensations. For when the Apostle speaks of the dispensation of the fullness of times, i.e., the administration of the last time, he very clearly indicates that there had been another dispensation and administration for the times which the προθεσμίαν (Gal. 4:2), or appointed time. Yet in each dispensation of the Covenant of Grace the elect have not been saved in any other way than by the *Angel of his presence* (Isa. 63:9), *the Lamb slain from the foundation of the world* (Rev. 13:8), Christ Jesus, through the knowledge of that just Servant and faith in Him and in the Father and His Spirit. For Christ is *the same yesterday, to-day, and forever* (Heb. 13:8); and by His grace we believe that we are saved (*servari*) in the same manner as the Fathers also were saved (*salvati sunt*) and in both

Testamento regulae: *Beati, qui illi* (Filio) *confidunt* (Ps. 2:12): *Qui credit in ipsum, non iudicatur; qui vero non credit, iam condemnatus est* (Ioan. 3:18): *Creditis in Deum,* Patrem videlicet, *credite etiam in me* (Ioan. 14:1). Quod si autem sancti Patres in Christum tanquam *Goël* suum crediderunt, consequitur, ut etiam in Spiritum S. crediderint, absque quo *nemo Iesum Dominum nuncupare potest.* Et vero tot sunt fidei illius Patrum eiusdemque necessitatis in utroque Foedere clarissimae ἀποδείξεις, ut neminem nisi volentem et lubentem latere possint. Tametsi vero illa salutaris Christi et sacro-sanctae Triadis notitia, pro oeconomia temporis illius, non ex sola promissione, sed ex umbris etiam, figuris et aenigmatibus operosius quam nunc in Novo Testamento facto opus est, hauriri et erui debuit: vera tamen, et pro divinae revelationis modulo ad procarandam electis, aspirante Dei gratia, salutem conscientiaeque consolationem sufficiens fuit.

XXV. Improbamus igitur eorum doctrinam, qui tria nobis Foedera, tota natura et medulla disparata, *Naturale* videlicet, *Legale* et *Evangelium* cudunt, atque in iisdem explicandis, eorumque differentiis assignandis adeo quidem intricate versantur, ut solidae veritatis et pietatis nucleum non parum involvant sive affligant: quique de notitiae Christi et fidei in eundem eiusque satisfactionem totamque sacro-sanctam τριάδα necessitate sub Vet. Testamenti oeconomia, aequo quam par est, laxius, neque sine periculo Θεολογεῖν nulli dubitant.

Testaments these statutes remain immutable: *Blessed are all they that put their trust in Him,* the Son (Ps. 2:12); *He that believeth in Him is not condemned, but he that believeth not is condemned already* (John 3:18); *Ye believe in God,* even the Father, *believe also in me* (John 14:1). But if, moreover, the sainted Fathers believed in Christ as their Goël, it follows that they also believed in the Holy Spirit, without whom no one can call Jesus Lord. Truly so many are the clearest exhibitions of this faith of the Fathers and of the necessity thereof in either Covenant, that they can not escape any one unless he wills it. But though this saving knowledge of Christ and the Holy Trinity was necessarily derived, according to the dispensation of that time, both from the promise and from shadows and figures and enigmas, with greater difficulty (*operosius*) than now in the New Testament; yet it was a true knowledge, and, in proportion to the measure of Divine Revelation, was sufficient to procure for the elect, by help of God's grace, salvation and peace of conscience.

XXV. We disapprove therefore of the doctrine of those who fabricate for us three Covenants, the Natural, the Legal, and the Gospel Covenant, different in their whole nature and pith; and in explaining these and assigning their differences, so intricately entangle themselves that they obscure not a little, or even impair, the nucleus of solid truth and piety; nor do they hesitate at all, with regard to the necessity, under the Old Testament dispensation, of knowledge of Christ and faith in Him and His satisfaction and in the whole sacred Trinity, to theologize much too loosely and not without danger.

XXVI. Denique et nobis, quibus in praesentiarum in Ecclesia, quae Domus Dei est, dispensatio credita est et universis Naziraeis nostris, iisque, qui, Deo volente et moderante, in curas quandoque nostras succedent, ad praevertendas tristes dissidiorum, quibus Ecclesia Dei passim diris modis infestatur, faces, hanc serio legem dictam esse volumus,

ut in hac mundi faece, fideli monitore gentium Apostolo, *depositum* fideliter custodiamus omnes, βεβή-λους κενοφωνίας seu *profanas vocum inanitates* devitemus (1 Tim. 6:20), et cognitionis illius, quae est secundum pietatem, εἰλικρίνειαν et simplicitatem religiose custodiamus, charitatis et fidei minime fucatae καλὴν ξυνωρίδα, bigam pulcherrimam, retineamus constanter.

XXVI. Finally, both unto us, to whom in the Church, which is God's house, has been entrusted the dispensation for the present, and unto all our Nazarenes, and unto those who under the will and direction of God will at any time succeed us in our charge, in order to prevent the fearful enkindling of dissensions with which the Church of God in different places is disturbed (*infestatur*) in terrible ways, *we earnestly wish* (*volumus*, will) *this to be a law*:

That in this corruption of the world, with the Apostle of the Gentiles as our faithful monitor, *we all keep faithfully that which is committed to our trust, avoiding profane and vain babblings* (1 Tim. 6:20); and religiously guard the purity and simplicity of that knowledge which is according to piety, constantly clinging to that beautiful pair, Charity and Faith, unstained.

Neve adeo quisquam animum inducat, sive publice sive privatim proponere dubium vel novum aliquod dogma fidei, in Ecclesiis nostris hactenus inauditum, *Verbo Dei, Confessioni nostrae Helveticae, libris nostris symbolicis, et Synodi Dordracenae Canonibus* repugnans, et in publica ἐπισυναγωγῇ fratrum ex Dei verbo non evictum atque sancitum:

Ut necessitatem inprimis sanctificationis diei Dominicae non tantum ex Dei verbo sincere tradamus, sed graviter etiam inculcemus, eiusque observationem instantissime urgeamus. Tandem, ut Canonem heic consignatorum ex Dei indubitato verbo repetitam veritatem in Ecclesiis iuxta atque Scholis, quoties occasio postulaverit, unanimiter fideliterque retineamus, doceamus, asseramus.

Ipse vero Deus pacis in veritate sanctificet nos totos, et integer noster Spiritus et anima et corpus ἀμέμπτως in adventum Domini nostri Iesu Christi servetur! Cui unâ cum Patre et Spiritu S. aeternus sit honor, laus et gloria. Amen!

Moreover, in order that no one may be induced to propose either publicly or privately some doubtful or new dogma of faith hitherto unheard of in our churches, and contrary to God's Word, to our Helvetic Confession, our Symbolical Books, and to the Canons of the Synod of Dort, and not proved and sanctioned in a public assembly of brothers according to the Word of God, let it also be a law:

That we not only hand down sincerely in accordance with the Divine Word, the especial necessity of the sanctification of the Lord's Day, but also impressively inculcate it and importunately urge its observation; and, in fine, that in our churches and schools, as often as occasion demands, we unanimously and faithfully hold, teach, and assert the truth of the Canons herein recorded, truth deduced from the indubitable Word of God.

The very God of peace in truth sanctify us wholly, and preserve our whole spirit and soul and body blameless unto the coming of our Lord Jesus Christ! to whom, with the Father and the Holy Spirit be eternal honor, praise and glory. AMEN!

Jonathan Edwards

Jonathan Edwards, "Man's Natural Blindness in the Things of Religion (Psalm 94:8–11)"; "Chap. VI. Observations on the Scriptures;—Their Authority—And Necessity," in *The Works of Jonathan Edwards*, ed. Edward Hickman (Carlisle, PA: Banner of Truth, 1974), 2:253–54, 474–79.

Edwards has already been introduced for his interpretative approach to Scripture (cf. chap. 23). In these next two selections, Edwards deals with the necessity of Scripture in the context of the rising rationalism of his time. Some are critical of Edwards's use of philosophy in his theology, but here he argues for the insufficiency of human reason and the absolute necessity of God's inspired revelation in Holy Scripture. Even as Edwards was very much attuned to the Enlightenment spirit of his time, he offered a definitely Christian response.

The first text is an extract from "Man's Natural Blindness in the Things of Religion," a sermon on Psalm 94:8–11. Edwards argues here that in spite of a remnant of light in nature, mankind is blind to divine realities—hence the necessity of special revelation, Scripture. The second text, "Observations on the Scriptures;—Their Authority—And Necessity," is an essay on the same subject. There he argues for the self-authenticating character of Scripture and its necessity against current deist philosophies. He begins with more traditional topics such as the authority of the Bible and the canon. He then continues with a powerful argument for the necessity of the Bible by stating that pagan religions and philosophies are bankrupt without special revelation. This argument would provide a helpful theological corrective to current discussions about extracanonical backgrounds to the Bible (cf. chap. 59). Both texts are reproduced from the Banner of Truth edition.

Supplementary Bibliography (cf. chap. 23): John H. Gerstner. *Jonathan Edwards: A Mini-Theology*. Wheaton, IL: Tyndale House, 1987. Idem. "Jonathan Edwards and the Bible." Pp. 257–78 in *Inerrancy and the Church*. Scott Oliphint. "Jonathan Edwards: Reformed Apologist." *WTJ* 57, 1 (Spring 1995): 165–86.

Man's Natural Blindness in the Things of Religion (Psalm 94:8–11)

Section IV. Practical inferences and application of the subject

Having shown how the truth of the doctrine is evident, both by what appears in men's *open profession*, and by those things which are *found* by inward experience, and are *manifest* by what is visible in men's *practice*; I proceed to improve the subject.

I. By this we may see how manifest are the *ruins* of the *fall* of man. It is observable in all the kinds of God's creatures that we behold, that they have those properties and qualities, which are every way proportioned to their end; so that they need no more, they stand in need of no greater degree of perfection, in order well to answer the special use for which they seem to be designed. The brute creatures, birds, beasts, fishes, and insects, though there be innumerable kinds of them, yet all seem to have such a degree of perception and perfection given them, as best suits their place in the creation, their manner of living, and the ends for which they were made. There is no defect visible in them; they are perfect in their kind; there seems to be nothing wanting, in order to their filling up their allotted place in the world. And there can be no reasonable doubt but that it was so at first with mankind. It is not reasonable to suppose, that God would make many thousands of kinds of creatures in this lower world, and one kind the highest of them all, to be the head of the rest; and that all the rest should be complete in their kinds, every way endowed with such qualifications as are proportioned to their use and end: and only this most noble creature of all, left exceeding imperfect, notoriously destitute of what he principally stands in need of to answer the end of his being. The principal faculty by which God has distinguished this noble creature from the rest, is his understanding: but would God so distinguish man in his creation from other creatures, and then seal up that understanding with such an extreme blindness, as to render it useless, as to the principal ends of it; and wholly to disenable him from answering the ends of an intelligent creature, and to make his understanding rather a misery than a blessing to him; and rendering him much more mischievous than useful? Therefore, if the Scripture had not told us so, yet we might safely conclude, that mankind are not now, as they were made at first; but that they are in a *fallen* state and condition.

II. From what has been said, plainly appears the *necessity* of divine *revelation*. The deists deny the Scripture to be the word of God, and hold that there is no *revealed religion*; that God has given mankind no other rule but his own reason; who is sufficient, without any word or revelation from heaven, to give man a right understanding of divine things, and of his duty. But how is it proved in fact? How much trial has there been, whether man's reason, without a revelation, would be sufficient or not! The whole world, excepting one nation, had the trial till the coming of Christ. And was not this long enough for trial, whether man's reason alone was sufficient to instruct him? Those nations, who all that time lay in such gross darkness, and in such a deplorable helpless condition, had the same natural reason that the deists have. And during this time, there was not only one man, or a succession of single persons, that had the trial, whether their own reason would be sufficient to lead them to the knowledge of the truth; but all nations, who all had the same human faculties that we have. If human reason is really sufficient, and there be no need of any thing else, why has it never proved so? Why has it never happened, that so much as one nation, or one city or town, or one assembly of men, have been brought to tolerable notions of divine things, unless it be by the revelation contained in the Scriptures? If it were only one nation that had remained in such darkness, the trial might not be thought so great; because one particular people might be under some disadvantages, which were peculiar. But thus it has been with *all nations*, except those which have been favoured with the Scriptures, and in *all ages*. Where is any people, who to this day have ever delivered themselves by their own reason, or have been delivered without light fetched from the Scriptures, or by means of the gospel of Jesus Christ?

If human reason is sufficient without the Scripture, is it not strange that, in these latter ages—since navigation has been so improved, and America and many other parts of the world have been discovered, which were before unknown—no one nation has any where been found already enlightened, and possessed of true notions about the Divine Being and his perfections, by virtue of that human reason they have been possessed of so many thousand years? The many poor, barbarous nations here, in America, had the faculty of *reason* to do what they pleased with, *before* the Europeans came hither, and brought over the light of the gospel. If human reason alone was sufficient, it is strange, that no one people were found, in any corner of the land, who were helped by it, in the chief concern of man.

There has been a great trial, as to what men's reason can do without divine help, in those endless disputes that have been maintained. If human reason alone could help mankind, it might be expected that these disputes would have helped them, and have put an end to men's darkness. The heathen philosophers had many hundreds of years to try their skill in this way: but all without effect. That divine revelation, which the church of God has been possessed of, has been in the world "as a light shining in a dark place."[1] It is the only remedy which God has provided for the miserable, brutish blindness of mankind, a remedy without which this fallen world would have sunk down for ever in brutal barbarism without any remedy. It is the only means that the true God has made successful in his providence, to give the nations of the world the knowledge of himself; and to bring them off from the worship of false gods.

If human reason be the *only* proper means, the means that God has designed for enlightening mankind, is it not very strange, that it has not been sufficient, nor has answered this end in any one instance? All the right *speculative* knowledge of the true God, which the deists themselves have, has been derived from divine revelation. How vain is it to dispute against fact, and the experience of so many thousand years! and to pretend that human reason is sufficient without divine revelation, when so many thousand years' experience, among so many hundreds of nations, of different tempers, circumstances, and interests, has proved the contrary! One would think all should acknowledge, that so long a time is sufficient for a trial; especially considering the miseries that the poor nations of the world have been under all this while, for want of light: the innumerable *temporal* calamities and miseries—such as sacrificing children, and many other cruelties to others, and even to themselves—besides that *eternal* perdition, which we may reasonably suppose to be the consequence of such darkness.

1. 2 Peter 1:19.

III. This doctrine should make us sensible, how great a *mercy* it is to mankind, that God has sent his own Son into the world, to be the *light* of the world.—The subject shows what great need we stand in of some *teacher* to be sent from God. And even some of the wiser men among the *heathen* saw the *need* of this. They saw that they disputed and jangled among themselves without coming to a satisfying discovery of the truth; and hence they saw, and spoke of, the need there was of a teacher sent from *heaven*. And it is a wonderful instance of *divine mercy* that God has so beheld us in our low estate, as to provide such a glorious remedy. He has not merely sent some *created angel* to instruct us, but his own Son, who is in the bosom of the Father, and of the same nature and essence with him; and therefore infinitely better acquainted with him, and more sufficient to teach a blind world. He has sent him to be the light of the world, as he says of himself, "I am come a light into the world."[2] When he came, he brought glorious light. It was like the day-spring from on high, visiting a dark world, as Zacharias observes. After Christ came, then the glorious gospel began to spread abroad, delivering those "that had sitten in darkness, and in the region of the shadow of death."[3]

What reason have we to rejoice, and praise God, that he has made such excellent provision for us; and has set so glorious a sun in our firmament, such a "Sun of righteousness," after we had extinguished the light which at first enlightened us; and had, as it were, brought the world into that state, in which it was when "without form, and void, and darkness was on the face of it."[4]—The glory of that light which God has sent into the world, is fully answerable to the grossness of that darkness which filled it. For Christ who came to enlighten us, is truth and light itself, and the fountain of all light. "He is *the light*, and in him is no darkness at all."[5]

IV. Hence we may learn, what must be the thing which will bring to pass those glorious days of light, which are spoken of in God's word.—Though mankind be fallen into such darkness, and the world be mostly in the kingdom of darkness; yet the Scripture often speaks of a *glorious day*, wherein light shall fill the earth. "For behold the darkness shall cover the earth, and gross darkness the people; but the Lord shall arise upon thee, and his glory shall be seen upon thee. And the Gentiles shall come to thy light, and kings to the brightness of thy rising."[6] "And he will destroy in this mountain, the face of the covering cast over all people, and the veil that is spread over all nations."[7] "The knowledge of God shall fill the earth, as the waters cover the sea."[8]

By what we have heard, we may on good grounds conclude, that whenever this is accomplished, it will not be effected by human learning, or by the skill or wisdom of great men. What has been before observed of this learned age, is a presumptive evidence of it; wherein spiritual darkness increases with the increase of learning. God will again make foolish the wisdom of this world; and will, as it were, say in his providence, "Where is the wise? Where is the scribe? Where is the disputer of this world?" [cf. 1 Cor. 1:20].

When this shall be accomplished, it will be by *a remarkable pouring out of God's own Spirit, with the plain preaching of the gospel of his Son*; the preaching of the spiritual,

2. John 12:46.
3. Luke 1:77–79.
4. See Jeremiah 4:22–23.
5. 1 John 1:5.
6. Isaiah 9:2–3.
7. Isaiah 25:7.
8. Isaiah 11:9.

mysterious doctrines of Christ crucified, which to the learned men of this world are foolishness; those doctrines, which are the *stumbling-block of this learned age*. "Not by might, nor by power, but by my Spirit, saith the Lord of hosts" [cf. Zech. 4:6]. It will not be by the enticing words of man's wisdom; but by the demonstration of the Spirit, and of power. Not by the wisdom of this world, nor by the princes of this world, that come to nought: but by the gospel, that contains the wisdom of God in a mystery, even the hidden wisdom, which none of the princes of this world, who have nothing to enlighten them but their own learning, know any thing of.

The Spirit of God, who searches all things, even the deep things of God, must reveal it. For let natural men be never so worldly wise and learned, they receive not the things of the Spirit: they are foolishness to them; nor can they know them, because they are spiritually discerned. This great effect, when it is accomplished, will be a glorious effect indeed: and it will be accomplished in such a manner, as most remarkably to show it to be the work of God, and his only. It will be a more glorious work of God than that which we read of in the beginning of Genesis. "And the earth was without form and void, and darkness was upon the face of the deep. And the Spirit of God moved upon the face of the waters: and God said, Let there be light, and there was light."[9]

V. Hence we may learn the misery of all such persons, as are under the power of that darkness which naturally possesses their hearts. There are two degrees of this misery.

1. That of which all who are in a natural condition are the subjects. The doctrine shows, that all such as are in a natural condition, are in a miserable condition: for they are in an extremely dark and blind condition. It is uncomfortable living in darkness. What a sorrowful state would we all be in, if the sun should no more rise upon us, and the moon were to withdraw her shining, and the stars to be put out, and we were to spend the rest of our time in darkness! The world would soon perish in such darkness. It was a great plague in Egypt, when they had a total darkness for three days. They who are deprived of sight, are deprived of the most noble of the senses; they have no benefit of external light, one of the most excellent and needful of all the things which God has made in the visible creation. But they who are without spiritual sight and light, are destitute of that which is far more excellent and necessary.

That natural men are not *sensible* of their blindness, and the misery they are under by reason of it, is no argument that they are not miserable. For it is very much the nature of this calamity to be hid from itself, or from those who are under it. Fools are not sensible of their folly. Solomon says, "The fool is wiser in his own conceit, than seven men that can render a reason."[10] The most barbarous and brutish heathens are not sensible of their own darkness; are not sensible but that they enjoy as great light, and have as good understanding of things, as the most enlightened nations in the world.

2. Another degree of this misery, is of those who are judicially given up of God, to the blindness of their own minds. The Scripture teaches us that there are some such. "What then; Israel hath not obtained that which he seeketh for, but the election hath obtained it, and the rest were blinded."[11] "But their minds were blinded; for until this day remaineth the same veil untaken away."[12] "And he said, Go and tell this people,

9. Genesis 1:2–3.
10. Proverbs 26:16.
11. Romans 11:7.
12. 2 Corinthians 3:14.

Hear ye indeed, and understand not; and see ye indeed, and perceive not. Make the heart of this people fat, and their ears heavy, and shut their eyes; lest they see with their eyes, and hear with their ears, and understand with their hearts, and convert and be healed."[13] This judgment, when inflicted, is commonly for the contempt and abuse of light which has been offered, for the commission of presumptuous sins, and for being obstinate in sin, and resisting the Holy Ghost, and many gracious calls and counsels, warnings and reproofs.

Who the particular persons are, that are thus judicially given up of God to the blindness of their minds, is not known to men. But we have no reason to suppose that there are not multitudes of them; and most in places of the greatest light. There is no manner of reason to suppose, that this judgment, which is spoken of in Scripture, is in a great measure *peculiar* to those old times. As there were many who fell under it in the times of the prophets of old, and of Christ and his apostles; so doubtless there are now also. And though the persons are not known, yet doubtless there may be more reason to fear it concerning some than others. All who are under the power of the blindness of their own minds, are miserable; but such as are given up to this blindness, are especially miserable; for they are reserved, and sealed over to the blackness of darkness for ever.

OBSERVATIONS ON THE SCRIPTURES;— THEIR AUTHORITY—AND NECESSITY

§1. SOME may ask, why the Scripture expresses things so unintelligibly? It tells us of Christ's living in us, of our being united to him, of being the same spirit, and uses many other such like expressions. Why doth it not call directly by their intelligible names, those things that lie hid under these expressions? I answer, Then we should have a hundred pages to express what is implied in these words, "ye are the temple of the Holy Ghost"; neither would it after all be understood by the one fourth part of mankind. Whereas, as it is expressed, it serves as well to practice, if we will believe what God says, that, some way or other, we are inhabited by the Holy Ghost as a temple, and therefore we ought to keep ourselves holy and pure. And we are united to Christ as much as members are to the head; and therefore ought to rejoice, seeing we know that this union proceeds from his love to us; and that the effects of it are joy, happiness, spiritual and eternal life, etc. By such similitudes, a vast volume is represented to our minds in three words; and things that we are not able to behold directly, are presented before us in lively pictures.

§2. There is a strange and unaccountable kind of enchantment, if I may so speak, in scripture history, which although it is destitute of all rhetorical ornaments, makes it vastly more pleasant, agreeable, easy, and natural than any other history whatever. It shines bright with the amiable simplicity of truth. There is something in the relation, that, at the same time, very much pleases and engages the reader, and evidences the truth of the fact. It is

13. Isaiah 6:6, 10.

impossible to tell fully what I mean, to any that have not taken notice of it before. One reason doubtless is this: The Scripture sets forth things just as they happened, with the minute circumstances of time, place, situation, gesture, habit, etc. in such a natural method, that we seem to be actually present; and we insensibly fancy, not that we are readers, but spectators, yea, actors in the business. These little circumstances wonderfully help to brighten the ideas of the more principal parts of the history. And, although the Scripture goes beyond other histories, in mentioning such circumstances; yet no circumstances are mentioned, but those that wonderfully brighten the whole. So the story is told very fully, and without in the least crowding things together, before one has fully taken up what was last related; and yet told in much less room than any one else could tell it. Notwithstanding the minute circumstances mentioned, which other historians leave out, it leads along our ideas so naturally and easily, that they seem to go neither too fast nor too slow. One seems to know as exactly how it is from the relation, as if he saw it. The mind is so led on, that sometimes we seem to have a full, large, and particular history of a long time: so that if we should shut the book immediately, without taking particular notice, we should not suppose the story had been told in half so little room; and yet a long train of ideas is communicated. The story is so narrated, that our mind, although some facts are not mentioned, yet naturally traces the whole transaction. And although it be thus skilfully contrived, yet things are told in such a simple, plain manner, that the least child can understand them. This is a perfection in the sacred writers, which no other authors can equal.

§3. It is an argument with me, that the world is not yet very near its end, that the church has made no greater progress in understanding the mysteries of the Scriptures. The Scriptures, in all their parts, were made for the use of the church here on earth; and it seems reasonable to suppose that God will, by degrees, unveil their meaning to his church. It was made mysterious, in many places having great difficulties, that his people might have exercise for their pious wisdom and study, and that his church might make progress in the understanding of it, as the philosophical world makes progress in the understanding of the book of nature, and in unfolding its mysteries. A divine wisdom appears in ordering it thus. How much better is it to have divine truth and light break forth in this way, than it would have been, to have had it shine at once to every one, without any labour or industry of the understanding? It would be less delightful, and less prized and admired, and would have had vastly less influence on men's hearts, and would have been less to the glory of God.

§4. It seems to be evident, that the church is not as yet arrived to that perfection in understanding the Scripture, which we can imagine is the highest that God ever intended the church should come to. There are a multitude of things in the Old Testament, which the church then did not understand, but were reserved to be unfolded in the christian church, such as most of their types, and shadows, and prophecies, which make up the greatest part of the Old Testament. So I believe there are now many truths that remain to be discovered by the church, in the glorious times that are approaching.

§5. Another thing from which we may draw the same conclusion, is, that it is the manner of God, to keep his church on earth in hope of a still more glorious state: and so their prayers are enlivened, when they pray that the interest of religion may be promoted, and God's kingdom may come. God kept the church, under the Old Testament, in hope of the times of the Messiah. The disciples of Christ were kept in hope of the conversion of the Roman empire, which was effected about three hundred years after. But it seems to me, not likely, that the church, from that time, should have no more to hope for from God's word, no higher advancement, till the consummation of all things. Indeed, there will be a great but short apostasy, a little before the end of the world; but then, it is probable, the thing that the church will hope and long for, will be Christ's last coming, to advance his church to its highest and its everlasting glory; for that will then appear to be the only remedy: for the church will expect no more from the clear light and truth which will have been so gloriously displayed already, under the millennium. Another end of thus keeping his church in hope is, to quicken and enliven their endeavours to propagate religion, and to advance the kingdom of Jesus. It is a great encouragement to such endeavours, to think, that such times are coming, wherein Christianity shall prevail over all enemies. And it would be a great discouragement to the labours of nations, or pious magistrates and divines, to endeavour to advance Christ's kingdom, if they understood that it was not to be advanced. And indeed, the keeping alive such hopes in the church, has a tendency to enliven all piety and religion in the general, amongst God's people.

§6. When we inquire, whether or no we have scripture grounds for any doctrine, the question is, Whether or no the Scripture exhibits it any way to the eye of the mind, or to the eye of reason? We have no grounds to assert, that it was God's intent, by the Scripture, *in so many terms,* to declare every doctrine that he would have us believe. There are many things the Scripture may suppose that we know already. And if what the Scripture says, together with what is plain to reason, leads to believe any doctrine, we are to look upon ourselves as taught that doctrine by the Scripture. God may reveal things in Scripture, which way he pleases. If, by what he there reveals, the thing is any way clearly discovered to the understanding, or eye of the mind, it is our duty to receive it as his revelation.

§7. The greatest part of Christians were very early agreed what books were canonical, and to be looked upon as the rule of their faith. It is impossible, in the nature of things, but some churches must receive the books long after others, as they lay at a greater distance from the places where they were written, or had less convenience of communication with them. Besides, as Christianity, for a long time, laboured under the disadvantages of continual persecution, no general councils could be convened, and so there could be no public notification of universal agreement in this matter. But notwithstanding all these things, it is yet discoverable, that, as soon as can be supposed, after the writing the books, the Christians, in all countries, remarkably agreed in receiving them as canonical.

§8. Several of the first writers of Christianity, have left us, in their works, *catalogues* of the sacred books of the New Testament, which, though made in countries at a vast distance from each other, do very little differ. Great were the pains and care of those early Christians, to be well assured what were the genuine writings of the apostles, and to distinguish them from all pretended revelations of designing men, and the forgeries they published under sacred titles. Thus, when a presbyter of Asia had published a spurious piece, under the name of Paul, he was immediately convicted, and notice of the forgery was soon conveyed to Carthage and the churches of Africa.

§9. Hence it follows, that the primitive Christians are proper judges to determine what book is canonical, and what not. For nothing can be more absurd than to suppose, in those early ages, an agreement so universal, without good and solid foundation: or, in other words, it is next to impossible, either that so great a number of men should agree in a cheat, or be imposed upon by a cheat. But there are some particular circumstances that make the inference more clear as to the christian books, than others; such as, the prodigious esteem the books at first were received with; the constant use that was made of them in their religious assemblies; the translations made of them very early into other languages, etc.[14]

§10. The omission of a book in some one or two particular catalogues, cannot, with any reason, be urged against its canonical authority, if it be found in all, or most of the others, and any good reason can be assigned for the omission, where it occurs. Thus, for instance, the Revelation is omitted, either perhaps because it was not known to the author, or its credit was not sufficiently established in the country where he lived; or perhaps, which may be as probable as the other, because it being so full of mysteries, few or none were judged proper or able to read it to any purpose. This was certainly the case in England: this book being, for this reason, omitted in the public calendar for reading the Scriptures, though it be received into the canon. If, therefore, these, or any such good reasons, can be assigned for the omission of a book in a particular catalogue, it will be very unfair to infer that such book is apocryphal, especially when it is to be found in many or most other catalogues.

§11. The catalogues drawn up by Athanasius, bishop of Alexandria (A.D. 315), by Epiphanius, bishop of Salamis (A.D. 370), by Jerome, of Dalmatia (A.D. 382), by Ruffin, presbyter of Aquilegium (A.D. 390), by Augustine, bishop of Hippo (A.D. 394), by forty-four bishops, assembled in the third council of Carthage (A.D. 416), were perfectly the same with ours now received.[15]

§12. It is exceedingly natural to suppose, that these two things together, would soon lead the apostles to write some history of the acts, and doctrine, and sufferings of Christ, their great Lord, and the head of the christian church; viz., *first*, Their unavoidable experience of the need of such a thing; and, *secondly*, The example of the penmen of the Old Testament, in writing the history of Abraham, Moses, David, Solomon, and others, whose persons and actions they esteemed of vastly less importance than those of the Son of God, who was greater than Jonas, or David, or Solomon, or Moses, or Abraham.

§13. It is a great argument, that there were some genuine gospels, or authentic histories of Christ's life and death, that the christian church had under the name of gospels, that there were such a multitude of forged fabulous accounts, or histories, of Christ, all under the same name of gospels. These fictions are evidently counterfeits or imitations of something that was looked on by all as true and undoubted. And, that there should be such a multitude of counterfeits and imitations of these gospels, shows not only that there were genuine gospels, but also shows the great value and importance of these genuine gospels, and the high repute they had in the christian churches.—Mr. Jones mentions the following spurious gospels, now not extant, mentioned by the writers of the primitive church: By the writers of the second century, the gospel of Judas Iscariot; the gospel of Truth; the gospel of the Egyptians; the gospel of Valentinus; the gospel of Marcion. By writers of the third century, the gospel of the Twelve Apostles; the gospel of Basilides; the gospel of Thomas; the gospel of Matthias. By writers of the fourth century, the gospel of Scythianus; the gospel of Bartholomew; the gospel of Apelles; the gospel of Lucianus; the gospel of Hesychius; the gospel of Perfection; the gospel of Eve; the gospel of Philip; the gospel of the Ebionites; the gospel of Jude; the gospel of the Encratites; the gospel of Cerinthus; the gospel of Merinthus; the gospel of Thaddeus; the gospel of Barnabas; the

14. See Jones's *Canon of the New Testament*, part 1, ch. 5.
15. See Jones's *Canon of the New Testament*, part 1, ch. 8.

gospel of Andrew. And some he mentions besides, that are now extant; as, the gospel of our Saviour's infancy; the gospel of Nicodemus.

§14. Public societies cannot be maintained without trials and witnesses: and if witnesses are not firmly persuaded, that he who holds the supreme power over them, is omniscient, just, and powerful, and will revenge falsehood, there will be no dependence on their oaths, or most solemn declarations.—God therefore must be the supreme magistrate; society depends absolutely on him; and all kingdoms and communities are but provinces of his universal kingdom, who is King of kings, Lord of lords, and Judge of judges.—Thus, as mankind cannot subsist out of society, nor society itself subsist without religion; I mean, without faith in the infinite power, wisdom, and justice of God, and a judgment to come; religion cannot be a falsehood. It is not credible, that all the happiness of mankind, the whole civil world, and peace, safety, justice, and truth itself, should have nothing to stand on but a lie: it is not to be supposed that God would give the world no other foundation. So that religion is absolutely necessary, and must have some sure foundation. But there can be no good, sure foundation of religion, without mankind having a right idea of God, and some sure and clear knowledge of him, and of our dependence on him. Lord Shaftesbury himself owns, that wrong ideas of God will hurt society as much, if not more, than ignorance of him can do.

§15. Now, the question is, "Whether nature and reason alone can give us a right idea of God, and are sufficient to establish among mankind a clear and sure knowledge of his nature, and the relation we stand in to him, and his concern with us? It may well be questioned, whether any man hath this from the mere light of nature. Nothing can seem more strange, than that the wisest and most sagacious of all men, I mean the philosophers, should have searched with all imaginable candour and anxiety for this, and searched in vain, if the light of nature alone is sufficient to give it to, and establish it among, mankind in general."—There never was a man known or heard of, who had an idea of God, without being taught it.—Whole sects of philosophers denied the very being of God; and some have died martyrs to Atheism, as, *Vaninus, Jordanus, Bruno, Cosimir, Liszinsai, and Mahomet Effendi.*—A man, confined to a dungeon all his days, and deprived of all conversation with mankind, probably would not so much as once consider who made him, or whether he was made or not, nor entertain the least notion of God. There are many instances of people born absolutely deaf and blind, who never showed the least sense of religion or knowledge of God.

§16. It is one thing, to work out a demonstration of a point, when once it is proposed; and another, to strike upon the point itself. I cannot tell whether any man would have considered the works of creation as effects, if he had never been told they had a cause. We know very well, that, even after the being of such a cause was much talked of in the world, and believed by the generality of mankind; yet many and great philosophers held the world to be eternal; and others ascribed, what we call the works of creation, to an eternal series of causes. If the most sagacious of the philosophers were capable of doing this, after hearing so much of a first cause and a creation, what would they have done, and what would the gross of mankind, who are inattentive and ignorant, have thought of the matter, if nothing had been taught concerning God and the origin of things; but every single man left solely to such intimation as his own senses and reason could have given him? We find, the earlier ages of the world did not trouble themselves about the question, whether the being of God could be proved by reason; but either never inquired into the matter, or took their opinions, upon that head, merely from tradition. But, allowing that every man is able to demonstrate to himself, that the world, and all things contained therein, are effects, and had a beginning, which I take to be a most absurd supposition, and look upon it to be almost impossible for unassisted reason to go so far; yet, if effects are to be ascribed to similar causes, and a good and wise effect must suppose a good and wise cause, by the same way of reasoning, all the evil and irregularity in the world must be attributed to an evil and unwise cause. So that either the first cause must be both good and evil, wise and foolish, or else there must be two first causes, an evil and irrational, as well as a good and wise principle. Thus, man left to himself, would be apt to reason, "If the cause and the effects are similar and conformable, matter must have a material cause; there being nothing more impossible for us to conceive, than how matter should be produced by spirit, or any thing else but matter." The best reasoner in the world, endeavouring to find out the causes of things, by the things themselves, might be led into the grossest errors and contradictions, and find himself, at the end, in extreme want of an instructor.

§17. In all countries we are acquainted with, knowledge bears an exact proportion to instruction. Why does the learned and well educated reason better than the mere citizen? why the citizen better than the boor? why the English boor better than the Spanish? why the Spanish better than the Moorish? why the Moorish better than the Negro? and why he better than the Hottentot [a member of people of southern Africa]? If, then, reason is found to go hand in hand, and step by step, with education; what would be the consequence, if there were no education? There is no fallacy more gross, than to imagine reason, utterly untaught and undisciplined, capable of the same attainments in knowledge, as reason well refined and instructed: or to suppose, that reason can as easily find in itself principles to argue from, as draw the consequences, when once they are found; I mean, especially in respect to objects not perceivable by our senses. In ordinary articles of knowledge, our senses and experience furnish reason with ideas and principles to work on: continual conferences and debates give it exercise in such matters; and that improves its vigour and activity. But, in respect to God, it can have no right idea nor axiom to set out with, till he is pleased to reveal it.

§18. What instance can be mentioned, from any history, of any one nation under the sun, that emerged from atheism or idolatry, into the knowledge or adoration of the one true God, without the assistance of revelation? The Americans, the Africans, the Tartars, and the ingenious Chinese, have had time enough, one would think, to find out the true and right idea of God; and yet, after above five thousand years' improvements, and the full exercise of reason, they have, at this day, got no further in their progress towards the true religion, than to the worship of stocks and stones and devils. How many thousand years must be allowed to these nations, to reason themselves into the true religion? What the light of nature and reason could do to investigate the knowledge of God, is best seen by what they have already done. We cannot argue more convincingly on any foundation, than that of known and incontestable facts.

§19. Le Compte and Duhald assure us, the Chinese, after offering largely to their gods, and being disappointed of their assistance, sometimes sue them for damages, and obtain decrees against them from the Mandarin. This ingenious people, when their houses are on fire, to the imminent peril of their wooden gods, hold them to the flames, in hopes of extinguishing them by it. The Tyrians were a wise people; and therefore, when Alexander laid siege to their city, they chained Apollo to Hercules, to prevent his giving them the slip.

§20. Revenge and self-murder were not only tolerated, but esteemed heroic, by the best of the heathen. I know not, in all profane history, six more illustrious characters, than those of Lycurgus, Timoleon, Cicero, Cato Uticensis, Brutus, and Germanicus. The first encouraged tricking and stealing, by an express law. The second, upon principle, murdered his own brother. Cicero, with all his fine talk about religion and virtue, had very little of either; as may appear by what he says (I think it is in a letter to Atticus) on the death of his daughter Tullia, "I hate the very gods, who hitherto have been so profuse in their favours to me"; and by deserting his friends and his country, and turning a servile flatterer to Cæsar. Brutus concludes all his mighty heroism with this exclamation: "Virtue, I have pursued thee in vain, and found thee to be but an empty name"; and then kills himself. Cato's virtue was not strong enough to hinder his turning a public robber and oppressor (witness his Cyprian expedition); nor to bear up against the calamities of life: and so he stabbed himself, and ran away, like a coward, from his country and the world. Germanicus, who exceeded all men in his natural sweetness of temper, at the approach of death, called his friends about him, and spent his last moments in pressing them to take revenge of Piso and Plancina, for poisoning or bewitching him; in directing them how this might be best done; and in receiving their oaths for the performance of his request. His sense of religion he thus expressed on that occasion: "Had I died by the decree of fate, I should have had just cause of resentment against the gods, for hurrying me away from my parents, my wife and my children, in the flower of my youth, by an untimely death."

§21. Socrates, Plato, and Cicero, who were more inclined to the belief of a future existence, than the other philosophers, plead for it with arguments of no force: speak of it with the utmost uncertainty; and therefore, are afraid to found their system of duty and virtue on the expectation of it. Their notions of morality were of a piece with their religion, and had little else for a foundation than vain-glory. Tully, in his treatise of Friendship, says, that virtue proposes glory as its end, and hath no other reward. Accordingly, he maintains, that wars undertaken for glory, are not unlawful, provided they are carried on without the usual cruelty. Diogenes, and the sect of the Cynics, held, that parents have a right to sacrifice and eat their children; and that there is nothing shameful in committing the grossest acts of lewdness publicly, and before the faces of mankind. The virtuous sentiments discovered by the philosophers on some occasions, will neither palliate these execrable principles, nor suffer us to think those who could abet them, fit instructors for mankind. Zeno, Cleombrotus, and Menippus, committed murder on themselves: the last, because he had lost a considerable sum of money, which, as he was an usurer, went a little too near his heart. That I do not charge the philosophers with worse principles and practices, than they themselves maintain, and their own pagan historians ascribe to them, any one may satisfy himself, who will consult Diogenes, Laertius, Sextus Empiricus, Lucian, Plutarch, and the works of Plato, Aristotle, and Cicero.

§22. Thus, it is plain, whether we consider what the human understanding could do, or what it actually did, that it could not have attained to a sufficient knowledge of God, without revelation; so that the demonstration brought in favour of some religion, ends in a demonstration of the revealed. When we attentively consider the nature of man, we find it necessary he should have some religion. When we consider the nature of God, we must conclude he never would have made a falsehood necessary to the happiness of his rational creatures; and that therefore there must be a true religion. And when we consider, that, by our natural faculties, it is extremely difficult to arrive at a right idea of God, till he reveals it to us; that all the Gentile world hath run into the grossest theological errors, and, in consequence of these, into the most enormous customs and crimes; and that no legislator ever founded his scheme of civil government on any supposed religious dictates of nature, but always on some real or pretended revelations: we cannot help ascribing all the true religion in the world to divine instruction; and all the frightful variety of religious errors to human invention, and to that dark and degenerate nature, by the imaginary light of which, deists suppose the right idea of God may be easily and universally discovered.

§23. Socrates, who never travelled out of Greece, had nothing to erect a scheme of religion or morality on, but the scattered fragments of truth, handed down from time immemorial among his countrymen, or imported by Pythagoras, Thales, and others, who had been in Egypt and the East. These he picked out from a huge heap of absurdities and errors, under which they were buried; and, by the help of a most prodigious capacity, laying them together, comparing them with the nature of things, and drawing consequences from them, he found reason to question the soundness of the Grecian theology and morality. But this is all the length he seems to have gone. He reasoned extremely well against the prevailing errors of his time; but was able to form no system of religion or morality. This was a work above the strength of his nature, and the lights he enjoyed. He taught his disciples to worship the gods, and to ground the distinction between right and wrong on the laws of their country; in the latter of which he followed the saying of his master Archelaus, who taught, that what is just or dishonest, is defined by law, not by nature.

§24. The notions of Plato concerning the divine nature, were infinitely more sublime and nearer the truth, than those of his master Socrates. He did not content himself merely with removing errors: he ventured on a system; and maintained, that virtue is a science, and that God is the object and source of duty; that there is but one God, the fountain of all being, and superior to all essence; that he hath a Son, called The World; that there is a judgment to come by which the just who have suffered in this life, shall be recompensed in the other, and the wicked punished eternally; that God is omnipresent; and consequently, that the wicked, if he were to dive into the deepest caverns of the earth, or should get wings, and fly into the heavens, would not be able to escape from him; that man is formed in the image of God; and that, in order to establish laws and government, relations made by true traditions and ancient oracles are to be consulted. These points, so much insisted on by Plato, are far from being the growth of Greece, or his own invention, but derived from Eastern traditions, which we know he travelled for, at least as far as Egypt. He was wiser than his teacher (who was a much greater man), because his lights were better: but, as they were not sufficient, he ran into great errors, speaking plainly as if he believed in a plurality of gods; making goods, women, and children, common, etc.

§25. The natural faculties of men, in all nations, are alike; and did nature itself furnish all men with the means and materials of knowledge, philosophy need never turn traveller, either in order to her own improvement, or to the communication of her lights to the world. How came it to pass that Scythia did not produce so many, so great philosophers, as Greece? I think it very evident, that the great difference between these countries as to learning and instruction, arose from this: the latter had the benefit of commerce with the Phœnicians, from whence they came by the knowledge of letters, and probably of navigation; and with the Egyptians, from whom they learned the greater part of their theology, policy, arts, and sciences. Such advantages the Scythians wanted; and therefore, although their natural talents were as good as those of the Grecians, they were not able to make any improvements in philosophy. Why are the Asiatic Scythians at this day as ignorant as ever, while the European Scythians are little inferior to the other nations of Europe in arts and politeness? And how does it come to pass, that we, at this day, take upon us to approve the philosophy of Socrates and Plato, rather than that of Epicurus and Aristippus? The Grecians were divided in this matter; some followed the notions of the former, and others those of the latter. Why did not reason put the matter out of question in those times, or at least immediately after? The infinite contradictions and uncertainties among the ancient philosophers produced the sects of the sceptics. In respect to religion, Socrates and Plato either were, or pretended to be, sceptics, beating down the absurd notions of others, but seldom building up any thing of their own; or, when they did, building on mere conjectures, or arguments suspected by themselves.

§26. If it be said, the finding out of truth by the light of nature, is a work of time; time hath taught the Tartars, Africans, and Americans, little or nothing of true theology or morality, even yet. Time of itself can search nothing. It was the christian religion that opened the eyes of the polite nations of Europe, and even of the deists of this age, wherein their eyes are still open, and they have any true principles by which they are able to examine the philosophy of the ancients, and, by comparing their several opinions one with another, and with the truths derived from the christian revelation, to decide in favour of some against the rest.

§27. As to the doctrine of THE IMMORTALITY OF THE SOUL; it is certain nothing can be more agreeable to reason, when once the doctrine is proposed and thoroughly canvassed; while, at the same time, there is no one probable opinion in the world which mankind, left entirely to themselves, would have been more unlikely to have started. Who, if he was not assured of it by good authority, would ever take it into his head to imagine, that man, who dies, and rots, and vanishes for ever, like all other animals, still exists? It is well, if this, when proposed, can be believed; but, to strike out the thought itself, is somewhat, I am afraid, too high and difficult for the capacity of men. The only natural argument of any weight, for the immortality of the soul, takes its rise from this observation, that justice is not extended to the good, nor executed upon the bad, man in this life; and that, as the Governor of the world is just, man must live hereafter to be judged. But as this only argument that can be drawn from mere reason, in order either to lead us to a discovery of our own immortality, or to support the opinion of it when once started, is founded entirely on the knowledge of God and his attributes; and as we have already seen, that such knowledge is almost unattainable by the present light of nature, the argument itself, which, before the fall, could not possibly have been thought of, is, since the fall, clogged with all the difficulties mere reason labours under, in finding out a right idea of God. And besides, this argument in itself is utterly inconclusive, on the principles of the deists of our age and nation; because they insist that virtue fully rewards, and vice fully punishes itself. It is no wonder that many heathen nations believed a future state, as they received it by tradition from their ancestors.—But yet, there is this evidence that mankind had not this doctrine merely from the easy and plain dictates of reason and nature, that many did not believe it.

§28. Socrates, in the Phaedon of Plato, says, most men were of opinion, that the soul, upon its separation from the body, is dissipated and reduced to nothing. And Tully, in his first Tusculan question, says, Pherecydes Syrus, preceptor to Pythagoras, was the first person known to the learned world, who taught the immortality of the soul. The other arguments brought by Plato and Cicero for the immortality of the soul, besides that already mentioned, are very inconclusive. They themselves thought so. The former, in his Phædon, makes Socrates speak with some doubt concerning his own arguments, and introduces Simias saying to Socrates, after having listened to his principal reasonings, "We ought to lay hold of the strongest arguments for this doctrine, that either we ourselves, or others, can suggest to us. If both ways prove ineffectual, we must however put up with the best proofs we can get, till some *promise* or *revelation* shall clear up the point to us."—One of Plato's arguments for the immortality of the soul, is this: "Every cause produces an effect contrary to itself; and that, therefore, as life produces death, so death shall produce life." Cicero, to prove that the soul will exist after it is separated from the body, endeavours to prove that it existed before it was joined to it; and to that end he insists, "that what we call aptness in children to learn, is nothing more than memory." Another argument of Plato is this: "That alone which moves itself, inasmuch as it is never deserted by itself, never ceases to move: but the mind moves itself, and borrows not its motion from any thing else, and therefore must move, and consequently exist, for ever."

The wisdom of Socrates and Plato united, produce such arguments for a most favourite opinion, as they themselves are dissatisfied with, and therefore call for more than human help.

§29. Cicero being so fond of this opinion, that, as he says, he would rather err with Plato in holding it, than think rightly with those who deny it, poorly echoes the arguments of Plato; adds little to them himself; and, at the conclusion, in a manner giving up the point, with all the arguments brought to support it, endeavours to comfort himself and others against the approach of death, by proving death to be no evil, even supposing the soul to perish with the body. And this great philosopher, with all his knowledge, gives but one lot to the good and evil in another life. It was his opinion, *If the soul is immortal, it must be happy: if it perishes with the body, it cannot be miserable.* This consolation he administers alike to all men, without making any distinction, and consequently leaves moral obligation on a mere temporal footing, which, in effect, is not a whit better than downright atheism. But in his dream of Scipio, when he does not reason nor seem to inculcate any particular doctrine, he indeed introduces the elder Scipio telling the younger, by way of dream, that those who served their country, and cultivated justice and the other virtues, should go to heaven after death: but that the souls of those that had violated the laws of the gods and men, should, after leaving their bodies, be tossed about on the earth, and not return to heaven for many ages. Now, if a person of Cicero's abilities and learning could, from the light of nature, work out no better scheme than this, which renders futurity almost useless to moral obligation, how much farther from truth and reason must we suppose the bulk of mankind to stray, if each ignorant person is to be left entirely to his own thoughts and discoveries, in respect to the future rewards of virtue, and punishments of vice?

§30. Thus, upon considering the extent and strength of human faculties, we have found them at present utterly incapable of attaining to any competent notion of a divine law, if left wholly to themselves. This is vastly confirmed by experience; from which it appears, that mankind, instead of being able, through a long series of ages, by the mere light of nature, to find out a right idea of God and his laws; on the contrary—after having, without doubt, been well acquainted at first with both—gradually, and at length almost universally, lost sight of both; insomuch, that idolatry as bad as atheism, and wickedness worse than brutality, were established for religion and law in all countries. The philosophers who lived in the most knowing countries, and sought for religion and moral truth, but sought in vain, as the wisest of them confess, render this argument still more cogent and conclusive.

§31. As the apostle Paul observes in the first chapter of his epistle to the Romans, men did not like to retain God in their knowledge; and, professing themselves to be wise, they became fools, and changed the glory of the incorruptible God into an image like to corruptible man, and to birds, and four-footed beasts, and creeping things. Thus were their foolish hearts darkened; upon which God gave them over to a reprobate mind, and gave them up to uncleanness, to sins of all kinds, even such as were utterly against nature. Saint Chrysostom, in his descant [comment] on this passage, says, "The Gentiles fell into a kind of madness, insomuch, that having deprived themselves of the light, and involved their minds in the darkness of their own thoughts, their attempt to travel towards heaven ended in a miserable shipwreck, as his must do, who, in a dark night, undertakes a voyage by sea." Being guided by conceit, and too great an attachment to sensible things, they entered upon a wrong way; so that, still the longer they travelled, the farther they wandered from the knowledge of the true God, and right religion. The doctrine of St. Paul, concerning the blindness into which the Gentiles fell, is so confirmed by the state of religion in Africa, America, and even China, where, to this day, no advances towards the true religion have been made, that we can no longer be at a loss to judge of the insufficiency of unassisted reason, to dissipate the prejudices of the heathen world, and open their eyes to religious truths.

§32. The starting of a proposition is one thing, and the proof of it quite another. Every science has its proofs in the nature of things. Yet all sciences require to be taught; and those require it most, the first principles of which lie a little out of the reach of ordinary capacities. The first principles of religion, being of a high and spiritual nature, are harder to be found out than those of any other science; because the minds of men are gross and earthly, used to objects of sense; and all their depraved appetites and corrupt dispositions, which are by nature opposite to the true religion, help to increase the natural weakness of their reason, and clip the wings of their contemplation, when they endeavour, by their own strength, to soar towards God and heavenly things. No man in his, nor hardly in any other time, knew better how to catch at the evidence of divine truths discovered in the works of creation, nor had better opportunities, than Plato. Yet, with all the help he derived from foreign and domestic instruction, he finds himself on every occasion at a loss. When he speaks of God and divine matters, he relies on oracles, traditions, and revelations; and having got a little taste of this kind of instruction, is every now and then confessing his want of more, and wishing for it with the greatest anxiety. And, not thinking the traditions which he was acquainted with sufficient, he talks of a future instructor to be sent from God, to teach the world a more perfect knowledge of religious duties. "The truth is" (says he, speaking in his first book *De Legibus*, concerning future rewards and punishments), "to determine or establish any thing certain about these matters, in the midst of so many doubts and disputations, is the work of God only." In his Phædon, one of the speakers says to Socrates concerning the *immortality of the soul*, "I am of the same opinion with you, that in this life, it is either absolutely impossible, or extremely difficult, to arrive at a clear knowledge in this matter." In the apology he wrote for Socrates, he puts these words into his mouth, on the subject of reformation of manners: "You may pass the remainder of your days in sleep, or despair of finding out a sufficient expedient for this purpose, if

God; in his providence, doth not send you some other instructor." And in his Epinomis he says, "Let no man take upon him to teach, if God do not lead the way."

§33. In the book *De Mundo*, ascribed to Aristotle, we have a remarkable passage to this effect: "It is an old tradition, almost universally received, that all things proceeded from God, and subsist through him; and that no nature is self-sufficient, or independent of God's protection and assistance." In his Metaphysics, he ascribes the belief of the gods, and of this, that the Deity compasses and comprehends all nature, to a traditionary habit of speaking, handed down from the first men to after-ages. Cicero, in his treatise concerning the nature of the gods, introduces Cotta blaming those who endeavoured, by argumentation, to prove there are gods, and affirming that this only served to make the point doubtful, which, by the instructions and traditions of their forefathers, had been sufficiently made known to them, and established. Plutarch, speaking of the worship paid to a certain ideal divinity, which his friend had called in question, says, "It is enough to believe pursuant to the faith of our ancestors, and the instructions communicated to us in the country where we were born and bred; than which, we can neither find out, nor apply, any argument more to be depended on."

§34. It will be further useful to observe, that the thoughts of men, with regard to any internal law, will be always mainly influenced by their sentiments concerning the *chief good*. Whatsoever power or force may do in respect to the outward actions of a man, nothing can oblige him to think or act, as often as he is at liberty, against what he takes to be his chief good or interest. No law, nor system of laws, can possibly answer the end and purpose of a law, till the grand question, what is the chief happiness and end of man, be determined, and so cleared up, that every man may be fully satisfied about it. Before our Saviour's time, the world was infinitely divided on this important head. The philosophers were miserably bewildered in all their researches after the chief good. Each sect, each subdivision of a sect, had a chief good of its own, and rejected all the rest. They advanced, as Varro tells us, no fewer than 288 opinions in relation to this matter; which shows, by a strong experiment, that the light of nature was altogether unable to settle the difficulty. Every man, if left to the particular bias of his own nature, chooses out a chief good for himself, and lays the stress of all his thoughts and actions on it. Now, if the supposed chief good of any man should lead him, as it often does, to violate the laws of society, to hurt others, and act against the general good of mankind, he will be very unfit for society; and consequently, as he cannot subsist out of it, an enemy to himself.

§35. If Christianity came too late into the world, what is called natural religion came full as late; and there are no footsteps of natural religion, in any sense of the words, to be found at this day, but where Christianity hath been planted. In every place else, religion hath no conformity with reason or truth. So far is the light of nature from lending sufficient assistance. It is strange, that the natural light should be so clear, and yet the natural darkness so great, that in all unassisted countries the most monstrous forms of religion, derogatory to God, and prejudicial to man, should be contrived by some, and swallowed by the rest, with a most voracious credulity. I could wish most heartily, that all nations were Christians; yet, since it is otherwise, we derive this advantage from it, that we have a standing and contemporary demonstration of that which nature, left to herself, can do. Had all the world been Christians for some ages past, our present libertines would insist that Christianity had done no service to mankind; that nature could have sufficiently directed herself; and that all the stories told, either in sacred or profane history, of the idolatry and horrible forms of religion in ancient times, were forged by christian priests, to make the world think revelation necessary, and natural reason incapable of dictating true and right notions of religion. But, as the case stands at present, we have such proofs of the insufficiency of unassisted reason in this behalf, as all the subtlety of libertines is unable to evade.

§36. All that the Grecians, Romans, and present Chinese, know of true religion, they were taught traditionally. As to their corrupt notions and idolatries, they were of their own invention. The Grecians, who were by far the most knowing people of the three, were as gross idolaters as the rest, till Plato's time. He travelled into the East, and ran higher towards truth in his sentiments of religion, than others; but still worshipped the gods of his country, and durst [or, dared] not speak out all he knew. However, he formed a great school, and, both through his writings and scholars, instructed his countrymen in a kind of religious philosophy, that tended much more directly and strongly to reformation of manners, than either the dictates of their own reason, or of their other philosophers. All the philosophy of the Gentile nations, excepting that of Socrates and Plato, was derived from the source of self-sufficiency. Only these two acknowledge the blindness of human nature, and the necessity of a divine instructor. No other heathen philosopher founded his morality on any sense of religion, or ever dreamt of an inability in man to render himself happy.[16]

16. From §14—§36, is chiefly out of *Deism Revealed*, second edition.

Part Five

THE DOCTRINE OF SCRIPTURE IN THE SCOTTISH AND DUTCH LEGACY

SCOTLAND AND THE NETHERLANDS were two countries where Reformed theological reflections were very fruitful. In Scotland John Witherspoon, who immigrated to the United States, and William Cunningham both challenged contemporary philosophies and reaffirmed the system of doctrine of the Westminster Standards. In the Netherlands, both Abraham Kuyper and Herman Bavinck had to contend with theological liberalism and the effects of the Enlightenment in European society. These two Dutch theologians did much to further a neo-Calvinistic theology at home and abroad. Louis Berkhof promoted and popularized the insights of these Dutch thinkers in the landscape of Reformed Christianity in America.

The texts by Witherspoon and Cunningham offer two complementary voices from the cradle of Presbyterianism in Scotland. On the one hand, Witherspoon is primarily known for his integration of Common Sense philosophy into the task of theology. Consequently, his treatment of the doctrine of Scripture is marked by an insistence on the evidences supporting the divine character of Scripture. In this presentation, however, he also considers the witness of the Scripture itself, defends a high view of the Bible, and develops his theology within the framework of covenant theology. On the other hand, Cunningham is closer to the formulations of John Calvin, the Westminster Confession of Faith, and the Calvinism of Westminster. Indeed, the lectures offered here are almost a commentary on the Westminster Confession. While also presenting evidences, Cunningham stresses the internal witness of the Holy Spirit. He can thus effectively counteract rationalism and maintain the divine supernatural character of Scripture.

The next two selections include an article by Richard B. Gaffin Jr. on Kuyper and two chapters from Bavinck's magnum opus, *Reformed Dogmatics*. In his article, Gaffin corrects the interpretation of Jack Rogers and Donald McKim by arguing that Kuyper had a high view of Scripture close to that of Calvin and Old Princeton. Gaffin's nuanced historical analysis has wide implication for the history of the doctrine of Scripture in Reformed thought. In his *Reformed Dogmatics*, Bavinck shows himself not only a disciple of Calvin, but also an astute student of the history of doctrine and contemporary debates. In the first chapter, he develops his view of inspiration (theopneustia), first by considering the biblical witness, then by considering competing views in the history of the church, and finally by defining an "organic" view, which includes the divine and human sides of the Bible. In the second chapter, he asserts the perfection of Scripture by discussing the four classical attributes of authority, necessity, clarity or perspicuity, and sufficiency.

Louis Berkhof in his *Systematic Theology* offers a helpful synthesis of the Reformed doctrine of Scripture. Given his Dutch background and his early teaching responsibilities in biblical theology before turning to systematic theology, he was uniquely situated to tackle such issues. The text reprinted here shows continuity with early Reformed orthodox works, especially with his Dutch counterparts. Though Berkhof was more a transmitter than an innovator, one noteworthy feature of his work is his interaction with the emerging neoorthodoxy of Karl Barth and Emil Brunner. His discussion includes considerations of general and special revelation, the inspiration of Scripture, and the witness of the Holy Spirit.

These five authors played significant roles in the theological trajectory of Old Princeton and Westminster. Both schools were influenced by both Scottish and Dutch Reformed theologies (though the Dutch influence was perhaps greater at Westminster than at Princeton). Witherspoon as president of the College of New Jersey had a direct influence on Princeton Seminary, and Cunningham through personal ties had an impact on Old Princeton. Moreover, Kuyper and Bavinck had some personal contact with Princeton theologians, and their views on Scripture had much in common with their counterparts in America. At Westminster, the views of Kuyper impacted the apologetic method of Cornelius Van Til, and Bavinck's theological work is greatly respected. Finally, if Berkhof's theological approach differs slightly from the theology developed by those at Westminster, his high view of Scripture has much in common with them.

The Truth of the Christian Religion in Particular

JOHN WITHERSPOON

John Witherspoon, "Lecture IV: The Truth of the Christian Religion in Particular," in *The Works of the Rev. John Witherspoon, Volume Seven Containing Lectures on Divinity, Letters on Education and Marriage Plus Other Items of Interest* (Harrisonburg, VA: Sprinkle Publications, 2001), 37–44; reprinted from the second edition published in Philadelphia by William W. Woodward in 1802.

John Witherspoon (1723–94) is best remembered for his tenure as president of the College of New Jersey (now Princeton University) and his influence on the shaping of American independence. He was the only clergyman to sign the Declaration of Independence. Ordained in his native Church of Scotland, he continued to preach and teach regularly once in the United States. He also encouraged the adoption of the Westminster Standards at the first General Assembly of the Presbyterian Church in America in Philadelphia (1789).

The selection presented here is Witherspoon's defense of Scripture against the modern philosophical challenges of his day. This is the fourth lecture of a series of lectures on divinity (theology). In this lecture he strives to establish the superiority of Christianity and the greatness of Scripture. On the one hand, he offers a rational argument for Christianity and the Word of God; on the other, he also uses biblical support for his position. It represents an early expression of Old Princeton's doctrine of Scripture with roots that go back to Scottish Presbyterian theology. Note the different emphasis in Witherspoon's theological method than in Calvin, in the Westminster Standards, and in the later Westminster tradition. At the same time, Witherspoon's arguments and evidences still have a place in our theological endeavor. Also, observe his very high view of Scripture. Charles S. McCoy and J. Wayne Baker place Witherspoon in the long line of covenant theologians starting with Bullinger (see chap. 19 above). Thus, Witherspoon's approach builds on covenant thought, not only on Common Sense Realism philosophy. We print the selection from the Sprinkle edition of Witherspoon's works.

Bibliography: Varnum Lansing Collins. *President Witherspoon: A Biography.* Princeton, NJ: Princeton University Press, 1925. D. F. Kelly. "Witherspoon, John (1723–94)." P. 880 in *DSCH&T*. S. T. Logan. "Witherspoon, John (1723–1794)." P. 279 in *DP&RTA*. Jeffry H. Morrison. *John Witherspoon and the Founding of the American Republic.* Notre Dame, IN: University of Notre Dame Press, 2005. Martha Lou Lemmon Stohlman. *John Witherspoon: Parson, Politician, Patriot.* Philadelphia: Westminster Press, 1976. "Witherspoon, John." *NSHERK* 12:395–96.

Having endeavored to establish the truth of revelation in general, we come to the truth of the Christian religion in particular. The proofs of this are so many, and laid down so differently, according as the adversaries of the truth have shifted their ground, that it is impossible to enumerate them, and indeed not easy to class them. There is one introductory way of reasoning, which may be called comparative to reflect on the infinite difference between the Christian, and all other pretended revelations. If the necessity of revelation has been properly and fully established, then comparisons between the several pretences to it seem to be just, and even conclusive. Now, I think it does not admit of hesitation that with respect to purity, consistency, sublimity, dignity and every excellence, which a manifestation of the true God must be supposed to have, the Christian religion is superior to every other. The heathen superstitions have not now so much as an advocate. Infidels do not now plead for Jupiter, Juno, Mars and Apollo, but for the sufficiency of human reason; and indeed, an age or two after the publication of the gospel that whole corrupt system which had been supported so long by ignorance and credulity fell to the ground.

Passing from this detached and preliminary consideration, the proofs of the Christian religion are very commonly divided into evidence *internal* and *external*. By the first of these we are to understand the excellence of the doctrine, as agreeable to the dictates of reason and conscience, and having a tendency to produce the happiest effects. Under this head also comes the character of the founder of the Christian faith, and every thing connected with this or the former particular. By the external evidence we are to understand the miracles wrought in attestation of the truth of the doctrine; the nature and subject of these miracles, the credibility of the witness, and every thing necessary to support this testimony. It is difficult, however, to collect the evidence under those heads without often intermixing the one with the other. I have therefore thought the evidences of the truth of the Christian religion might be as well divided in a different way. First, into two heads under the following titles: 1. Collateral, and 2. Direct and positive proof. And again to divide the collateral into two parts, and take the one of them before and the other after the direct evidence, under the titles of *presumptive* and *consequential*.

I. Let us consider the presumptive evidences of the truth of the Christian religion or those circumstances that recommend it to our esteem and love, and are of the nature of strong probabilities in its favor. These we may, for order sake, divide into such as relate, 1. To the doctrine taught. 2. The person who is the author and subject of it. 3. The circumstances attending its publication, and other probabilities.

1. The doctrine taught. When this is considered in the way of an argument, for its actual truth it rests upon this principle, that every doctrine that comes from God must be excellent; that therefore, if the doctrine did not appear of itself to be excellent it would be rejected without further examination, because not worthy of God; and on the contrary, that if it appears excellent, amiable, useful, it is some presumption that the claim of a divine original is just. It is a just reflection on Christ's doctrine, "Never man spake like this man" (John 7:46), as well as the following, "No man can do these miracles that thou doest, except God be with him" (John 3:2). Under this great head of excellence or a doctrine worthy of God may be considered separately, [1] its Sublimity, [2] Purity, [3] Efficacy, [4] Plainness, and [5] Consistency.

[1] Sublimity. The doctrines contained in Scripture concerning God, his works and creatures, and his relation to them, is what must necessarily have the approbation of unprejudiced reason, and indeed is the most noble that can be conceived. His spiritual nature infinitely removed from inactive matter, incapable of grossness, of sensual indulgence. The unity of God, so contrary to the prevailing sentiments under heathenish darkness, yet how manifestly rational. Strange indeed that the whole world should have been in a mistake on this subject, and the Jews, a despised nation, in an obscure corner in Palestine, only should have discovered and embraced it. The immensity of God filling heaven and earth with his presence. His omnipotence in creating all things by his word. His holiness, justice, goodness and truth; to these we may add the constant influence of his providence, and the Lord of nature, the witness, and the judge of all. Very beautifully the prophet says, "Are there any among the vanities of the Gentiles that can cause rain" (Jer. 14:22); so the apostle Paul, "Nevertheless he left not himself without a witness" (Acts 14:17). The moral government of God, as taught in Scripture, is exceedingly rational and satisfying, representing his great patience, and longsuffering to be followed by a time of holy and righteous retribution. The mixture of good and evil, that is plainly to be observed, is by this means clearly explained, and fully accounted for. On the sublimity of the Scripture doctrines some are fond of dwelling upon the majesty of God, and sublimity of the Scriptures in sentiment and language, as well as matter. Upon this part of the subject, things have been said, and the controversy taken up on different footings. We have one adversary to religion, Lord Shaftsbury,[1] who has been at much pains to vilify the Scriptures on the subject of style and composition, and to pretend that if it were the work of inspired writers it would be evidently in its manner, superior to every human production. In answer to this pretense there was a book written Blackwall's *Sacred Classics*,[2] comparing the Scriptures with the ancient writers, and showing that there is not any blemish in writing to be found in the Scriptures, but may be justified by similar expressions in the most approved classics, and that there is no beauty in the classic authors in which they are not outdone by the sacred penmen. This book I think is well

1. Anthony Ashley Cooper the 3rd Earl of Shaftsbury (1671–1713) had his early studies in part directed by John Locke. Shaftsbury wrote such literature as, *Characteristics of Men, Manners, Opinions, Times and the Inquiry concerning Virtue or Merit* as well as many other pieces. HRR [Pastor H. Rondel Rumburg, the editor of the Sprinkle edition]

2. Anthony Blackwall (1674–1730) of Emanuel College, Cambridge was Lecturer of All-Hallows in Derby. His primary work was *The Sacred Classics Defended and Illustrated; or An Essay humbly offered towards proving the purity, propriety, and true eloquence of the Writers of the New Testament* (London: C. Rivington, 1725). HRR

worth reading by every scholar or divine. Dr. Warburton[3] has been pleased to condemn this way of justifying the Scriptures, and even to affirm that taste is a thing so local and variable that it was a thing impossible to have any book designed for all mankind to answer such an idea, as Lord Shaftsbury seems to have formed; nay, he seems to deny that there is any such thing in nature as a permanent standard of taste, and propriety in writing; but there is one manner for the Oriental, and another for the Western writers, and that such have their excellencies, and no comparison can take place between them. I would not choose to join wholly with either of these. It is I think plain that it was not the design of the Scriptures to be a standard for eloquence, nor does it appear any way connected with the end of revealing divine truth; on the contrary, it seems to be the purpose of God to bring us from glorying in human excellence. On the other hand, as I am persuaded, there is a permanent standard of propriety and taste, so I am fully convinced there are many examples of sublimity and majesty in the Scriptures, superior to any uninspired writings whatsoever.

[2] The next thing to be observed of the doctrine is its purity; that is to say, having an evident tendency to promote holiness in all who believe and embrace it. That this is the design and tendency of the Christian doctrine is very plain. It is its express purpose to set sin and immorality in the most odious light, and not barely to recommend, but to show the absolute necessity of holiness in all manner of conversation. It is pretended by some infidel writers that gravity and apparent sanctity is the essence of impostors, and that all impostors do deliver a system of good morals. But there is not only one excellence in the Christian morals, but a manifest superiority in them, to those which are derived from any other source, and that in three respects: 1. That they are free from mixture, not only many things good, but nothing of a contrary kind. 2. That there are precepts in the Christian morality, and those of the most excellent kind, very little if any thing resembling, which is to be found in uninspired moralists. The love of God, humility of mind, the forgiveness of injuries, and the love of our enemies. The love of God may be inferred consequentially from many of the heathen writers; but it is no where stated with that propriety and fullness as the first obligation on the creature, as it is in the sacred Scriptures. "Humility of mind" as represented in the gospel is wholly peculiar to it. It is observed by some that there is no word, neither in the Greek nor Latin languages to signify it. *Humilitas*[4] in Latin from whence the English is derived has a different meaning, and signifies *low* and *base*. *Mansuetudo animi*[5] in Latin and Πραότης[6] (Praotes) in Greek are the nearest to it, but are far from being that; even the forgiveness of injuries and the love of our enemies are rather contrary to the heathen virtue; and modern infidels have expressly pretended that the Christian religion by

---

3. William Warburton (1698–1779) was born in Newark, England. He was an English prelate, theological controversialist and critic. He became bishop of Gloucester in 1759. At first he was a critic of Alexander Pope, but then became an intimate friend of the same. He penned many volumes and among those were *Miscellaneous Translations, in Prose and Verse, from Roman Poets, Orators, and Historians, Critical and Philosophical Enquiry into the Causes of Prodigies and Miracles, as related by Historians, The Alliance between Church and State, The Divine Legation of Moses Demonstrated, on the Principles of a Religious Deist, from the Omission of the Doctrine of a Future State of Rewards and Punishments in the Jewish Dispensation, View of Bolingbroke's Posthumous Writings, Doctrine of Grace*, etc. He even edited Shakespeare's plays. Warburton was noted for answering his critics via the printed page. HRR

4. *Humilitas* is nearness to the ground, lowness or shallowness.

5. *Mansuetudo* is tameness, mildness, or gentleness. *Animus* is the spiritual or rational principle of life in man as opposed to the body and the principle of physical life. Also, *animus* refers to the soul as the seat of feeling, to character, to the seat of the will and to the seat of thought, intellect or mind.

6. Πραότης is mildness, meekness, or gentleness.

its precepts of humility and meekness, and passive submission to injury has banished that heroism and magnanimity which gives such an air of dignity to the histories of Greece and Rome. 3. The third particular in which the Christian morals exceed all others is the excellence of the principle from which they ought to flow. The law of God is not contracted into governing the outward conduct, but reaches to the very heart, and requires further that our obedience should flow, not principally from a regard to our own happiness, far less to our own honor, but from a principle of subjection in the creature to the Creator, and a single eye to the glory of God.

[3] The excellence of the Scripture doctrine appears from its *efficacy*. By this I mean the power it has over the mind, and its actual influence in producing that holiness it recommends; there are several things that deserve consideration on the efficacy of the Scripture doctrine. 1. It contains the greatest and most powerful motives to duty, and the fittest to work on our hopes and fears. These I confess are much the same in general that always have been proposed as inducements to a moral conduct yet they are opened with a fullness and force in the Scripture no where else to be found. Eternity there makes a very awful appearance. Particularly with respect to the gospel, and the New Testament discoveries; we are told that life and immortality are brought to light by it. 2. It carries the greatest authority with it; the principles of duty are more clearly and fully enforced by the proper authority than any where else; the right of God from creation to the obedience and submission of his creatures, his additional title from continual beneficence, to which ought to be added by Christians the right acquired by redemption; to all which is further to be added the divine nature itself as our pattern. 3. The effectual assistance provided in the Scripture doctrine to deliver us from the bondage of corruption, and bring us to the glorious liberty of the children of God; this is of more consequence than is commonly apprehended, despair of success breaks the powers of the mind, and takes away at once the will to attempt and the power to perform, whereas effectual aid has just the opposite effect. The doctrine of the Holy Spirit taking it singly in this view is most happily calculated to animate men to diligence, and inspire them with courage and resolution, and seems generally to show the efficacy of the Christian doctrine.

[4] Another excellence of the Christian doctrine is plainness; it is level to all capacities, well fitted for all ranks, rich and poor, wise and unwise. It is given as one of the marks of the Messiah's coming, and is one of the glories of the gospel that it is preached to the poor. Religion was plainly designed for all mankind, their interest in it is the same; therefore, it must be plain and simple; whatever is otherwise, whatever system is built upon abstract reasoning and is evidently above the comprehension of the vulgar is for that very reason unfit for their service, and carries a mark of falsehood upon itself. There is even something more in the simplicity of the gospel than barely the plainness of its truths and duties. It is from first to last founded upon facts still plainer, a great part of the inspired writings is history; the Old Testament is founded upon the fall of man, and is filled up with the history of Providence or God's conduct to his chosen people, and the New Testament contains the birth, life and death, the resurrection and ascension of Christ. So material a part of the doctrine do these things comprise that the character of the apostles is just that of being witnesses of Christ's resurrection.

[5] The last excellence to be taken notice of in the Christian doctrine is its consistency. This consistency may be viewed to advantage in two different lights; *first*, its consistency

with itself. It is remarkable that the Christian revelation is not a single system that was or might be supposed to be, the occasional production of one man. It extends from the creation downwards, to the present moment or rather taking in the prophecies to the last day and consummation of all things. It consists of several different revelations, and particularly, two grand different dispensations of providence and grace. The one of these is perfectly consistent with, and suited to the other. It is not easy to suppose an impostor either willing to perform or able to execute any thing of that kind. But when we consider the creation, and the fall of the Old Testament dispensation, and the prophets of the different and distant ages conspiring to forward one great design, and the appearance of the long promised Saviour at the fullness of time so exactly corresponding to it, it takes away the possibility of a concert, and therefore the suspicions of an impostor. It is also consistent with the actual state of the world in which we find two things very remarkable. 1. A great depravity and wickedness. Men may speak and write, what they please, upon the beauty, excellence and dignity of human nature, taking their ideas from the dictates of conscience, as to what we ought to be. But it is beyond all controversy, that if we take mankind from the faithful records of history and examine what they have been, we shall have no great reason to admire the beauty of the picture. What is the fame of the greatest heroes of antiquity? Is it not that either of conquerors or lawgivers? Conquerors give clear testimony to the wickedness of man by filling the earth with blood, and showing us what havoc has been made in all ages of man by man. And what is it that lawgivers have done, but distinguished themselves by the best means of repelling violence and restraining the ungoverned lusts and appetites of men. Now the Christian religion is the only one that gives a clear and consistent account of human depravity, and traces it to its very original source. This consistency of the doctrines of religion, with the actual state of the world, and present condition of the nature of man, is very convincing in the way of collateral or presumptive proof. 2. The other particular, remarkable in the state of the world, is the universal prevalence of the offering of sacrifices, a thing found among all nations, and which continued till the coming of Christ. These sacrifices were a confession of guilt, for they were always considered as an expiation. But besides this, it does not appear how they could have occurred, even in that view, unless they had been at first a matter of revelation, and handed down to mankind by tradition, and carried with them in their dispersion over the whole world. It does not appear how any body could have imagined that taking away the life of a beast should be any atonement for the sin of a man; much less does it appear how every body should have agreed in imagining that same thing. But if you take it in conjunction with the truths of the gospel, its agreement appears manifest, and its universal prevalence is easily accounted for. These sacrifices were instituted and ordained of God, as typical of the great propitiatory sacrifice, to be offered in the fullness of time by Christ upon the cross.

William Cunningham's
Theological Lectures

William Cunningham, *Theological Lectures on Subjects Connected with Natural Theology, Evidences of Christianity, the Canon and Inspiration of Scripture* (New York: Robert Carter and Brothers, 1878), 269–330.

William Cunningham (1805–61) was a Scottish minister and theologian. After several years in parish ministry, he was appointed in 1843 as a professor at New College, Edinburgh. Later he became its principal. There he first taught theology, and then church history. He is best known for his *Historical Theology* (1862), his lectures on church history, published only after his death. He was highly involved in the controversy that arose within the Church of Scotland that gave birth to the formation of the Free Church of Scotland. As a theologian, he greatly valued the inheritance of Francis Turretin. And as a person, he had close ties with Charles Hodge (1797–1878).

The selection presented here comes from lectures that were first given at New College; these were also published posthumously as *Theological Lectures on Subjects Connected with Natural Theology, Evidences of Christianity, the Canon and Inspiration of Scripture* (1878). In large part, these lectures are an exposition of the first chapter of the Westminster Confession of Faith (cf. chap. 17), which addresses the doctrine of Scripture. Like Witherspoon, Cunningham discusses the evidences of Scripture. Yet he puts a welcome stress on the internal witness of the Holy Spirit in his exposition of the confession; this emphasis harks back to Calvin. Thus he can effectively counteract rationalism and maintain the divine supernatural character of Scripture.

Bibliography: Joel R. Beeke. "William Cunningham." Pp. 209–26 in Michael Bauman and Martin I. Klauber, eds. *Historians of the Christian Tradition: Their Methodology and Influence on Western Thought*. Nashville: Broadman & Holman, 1995. "Cunningham, William." *NSHERK* 3:321–22. Alexander (Sandy) Finlayson. *Unity and Diversity: The Founders of the Free Church of Scotland*. Fearn, UK: Christian Focus, 2010. Pp. 83–107. D. Macleod. "Cunningham, William (1805–61)." Pp. 229–31 in *DSCH&T*. Robert Rainy and James Mackenzie. *Life of William Cunningham, D.D.: Principal and Professor of Theology and Church History, New College, Edinburgh*. London: Nelson, 1871.

LECTURE XXI: DIVINE ORIGIN AND AUTHORITY OF THE BOOKS OF SCRIPTURE—EXTERNAL EVIDENCE

In directing your attention to the evidences of Christianity we have generally spoken of the leading proposition to be established, as this, that Christ and his apostles were divinely commissioned teachers, authorised by God to make known his will to men. And it is evident that practically there is no ground for distinguishing between Christ and his apostles, so far as the authoritative communication of God's will to men is concerned, because we have just the very same evidence that Christ authorised the apostles to speak in his name, and required our submission to them in communicating instruction about religious matters, as we have that He himself was sent and commissioned by God, and claimed on that ground our reverence and obedience. It is right and necessary that we should ever cherish a deep sense of the vast, the immeasurable superiority of Jesus Christ above all beings, human or superhuman, whom God has ever employed to make known his will to men, above prophets and apostles, above Moses, and above angels, "for he hath been *made* as much better than the angels, as he hath by inheritance obtained a more excellent name than they"—i.e., he is just as much superior to the angels in official station as he is in the intrinsic dignity of his nature, as being the Son of God, of the same substance with the Father, and equal in power and glory [cf. Heb. 1:4]. But in so far as concerns the truth and certainty of a revelation from God—and with this alone we have at present to do—the dignity of the messenger through whom the revelation is made is of no great practical importance; and if it be indeed true, as can be easily proved from Scripture, that Christ has referred us to his apostles for fuller information as to the will of God, and has thereby in this respect virtually identified himself with them, then we are just as clearly and as certainly bound to receive as coming from God, and of course as entitled to our implicit submission, what they have revealed to us, as what he himself has made known.

Another general consideration to be kept in view is this, that when the great leading facts recorded in the New Testament, by which more directly the truth of Christ's divine commission is established, such as the miracles which Christ wrought, and his resurrection from the dead, are admitted as having been proved by satisfactory evidence, there can be no reason whatever why any other events recorded in the New Testament, even the most extraordinary and miraculous, should be denied or doubted, since they are all clearly connected together as parts of one complete and consistent narrative, and since they all rest upon substantially the same evidence. When convinced that Jesus was a teacher sent from God, we can have no doubt or hesitation about the apostles also working miracles, about the Holy Ghost descending upon them, about their speaking with other tongues as the Spirit gave them utterance, about Paul's miraculous conversion and call to the apostleship, and about his being as fully authorised and qualified to reveal the will of God as those who had personally associated with Jesus during his life on earth.

In investigating the external evidences of the truth of Christianity, we consider the books of the New Testament merely as a collection of historical documents, containing at once the declarations of the parties, and the testimonies of the original witnesses, that we may judge whether the facts there recorded are true, and whether these facts establish the claims which they put forth. When we consider the internal evidences, we contemplate the books of the New Testament as containing a correct representation of the general system of doctrine and duty taught by Christ and his apostles, with the view of ascertaining whether in this system of doctrine and duty itself we can discover any indication that it was not devised or invented by men, and that it proceeded from God. To shew that we are warranted in regarding the books of the New Testament as containing a correct account of the general system of doctrine and duty taught by Christ and his apostles, nothing more is necessary than to prove—first, that they were written by the apostles; and second, that they have been transmitted to us without any such alteration as to affect their substantial integrity; and this is done by the same evidence by which we prove their genuineness, by the quotations of them in a succession of subsequent authors, and by the substantial identity of all the MSS. and ancient versions of those books.

In virtue of the proof that has been adduced of the divine commission of Christ and his apostles, we are bound to receive as infallibly true whatever they have made known to us as the revealed will of God; to believe all the doctrines which they have delivered to us, and to submit implicitly to all the precepts which they have enjoined. They who heard them were called upon, on the ground of the proof adduced of their divine commission, to receive all their instructions as coming from God; and we, having conclusive proof of the divinity of their mission, are bound to be prepared to give their communications the same reception, and to proceed to investigate what means we have of ascertaining what God has revealed to us through them, and what is the will of God thus communicated to us. We have, in the books of the New Testament, a record of the instructions which they delivered, and everything which they taught concerning doctrine or duty we are bound to receive as the word of God, as binding upon us by his supreme authority. God revealed it to them; he has given us abundant proof that he has done so; he has taken care to transmit to us authentic information concerning what they declared; and our duty now is to receive with implicit submission whatever can be proved to have proceeded from them. When our attention is directed to the way and the means by which this revelation has been conveyed to us, the source from which we obtain a knowledge of it, a very important question occurs, viz., Whether we are to regard and receive it as the word of God, not merely the substance of the information concerning doctrine and duty communicated by Christ and his apostles, and conveyed to us in the books of the New Testament, but the whole books themselves which compose that volume. That the books of the Old and New Testament not only contain and convey to us a revelation of God's will, but that they are themselves the Word of God, stamped throughout with divine authority, because produced through divine agency, has been the general opinion of almost all who have been convinced of the truth and divine origin of the Christian revelation; and to the grounds of this persuasion, the arguments by which it can be fully established, we are now called upon to advert. This question, as we have repeatedly had occasion to explain, is different from that which we have already discussed, and requires, in order to its decision, the introduction of some additional considerations, or rather a further extension and application of the points that have already been proved. If God were pleased to make a revelation of his will to men, it is indeed in the highest degree probable that he would take care that the revelation should be committed to writing, and transmitted in integrity, and not left to the uncertainties and contingencies of oral tradition; and if so, he would no doubt secure that it should be correctly committed to writing for preservation and transmission, as well as that it should be correctly promulgated at first by those whom he might employ as his instruments in making it known to men; but we could not assert with perfect confidence, and upon abstract grounds, *à priori*, that the writings in which this revelation might be preserved, and by which it might be transmitted, would contain nothing else but the revelation of God's will, and would be in all their parts traceable to his agency; in other words, to apply this principle to the matter in hand, it would not at once follow, as a matter of course, that because the New Testament contained or embodied the revelation which God made to man through Christ and his apostles, and afforded us sufficient materials for ascertaining correctly what the substance of that revelation was, therefore all the books which compose the New Testament were themselves stamped throughout with divine authority, as being produced as we have them by God's agency. And consequently the question remains, Can it be proved that these books, as they stand, and not merely the substance of the doctrines they contain, are the word of God, stamped with divine authority? And if so, how can this be established?

As, in considering this question, we must include not merely the books of the New Testament, but the whole Bible, we must first briefly advert to the grounds upon which we believe in the divine origin of the Mosaic economy, and the divine mission of the prophets whose predictions form so large a portion of the Old Testament. And the first question here, as in the case of the truth of Christianity, is not about the divine authority of the books which compose the Old Testament, but about the truth of the divine mission of Moses, and the reality of the divine inspiration of the succession of prophets in the subsequent periods of the Jewish history. We do not mean to discuss the subject at any length, but merely to advert to its general nature and place in connection with the other departments of the evidence of the truth of our religion.

The genuineness and general authenticity of the books of the Old Testament may be established independently of the explicit and conclusive testimony borne to them by Christ and his apostles, upon grounds similar to those by which we establish the genuineness and general authenticity of those of the New. And to the truth and reality of those miraculous events by which Moses professed to establish his divine commission, we have the attestation of the Jewish nation in submitting to his authority, and receiving his laws and institutions, upon the ground of the evidence afforded by these miracles that they came from God—an attestation which may be said to have been repeated by every successive generation of Jews from the time of Moses down to the present day. Thus the divine commission of Moses is established; and that there was in the Jewish nation a succession of prophets who received direct communications from God is established by the predictions which it can be proved they delivered, and which were remarkably fulfilled in the history of the Jews, and of the other nations with which they were more or less nearly connected. Thus the divine commission of Moses and the prophets may be established even independently of the attestation given to it by Christ and his apostles. It is not necessary, however, to have recourse to such a line of argument upon this topic; for having once established the divine mission of Christ and his apostles, and being on this ground warranted and bound to believe whatever they have declared, we have of course, in their frequent and unequivocal attestations to the divine mission of Moses and the prophets, abundant reason to believe that God at sundry times and in divers manners revealed his will to men by their instrumentality. The attestation of Christ

508

and his apostles to the divine mission of Moses and the prophets we shall have occasion to explain more fully afterwards when we come to consider the inspiration and canonicity of the Bible, for it proves not only that God commissioned Moses and the prophets to reveal his will to men, but also moreover that the books of the Old Testament were given by divine inspiration, and are possessed of divine authority. It is enough at present to advert generally to the way and manner in which it may be proved that, as God made known his will to men by Christ and his apostles, he did so also by Moses and the prophets. In turning from the proof of the general truth of Christianity, or of the proposition that Christ and his apostles were commissioned by God to reveal his will to men, to the consideration of the origin and character of the books in which this revelation is conveyed to us, we have to distinguish between the divine origin and authority of these books, and their inspiration by the Holy Ghost. It is indeed true that the inspiration of the books of Scripture is often, perhaps generally, used in so wide a sense as to comprehend the whole subject of God's connection with the composition of the books, or the whole of his agency in the production of them, as distinguished from his connection with the substance of the revelation they contain; and there is certainly no impropriety in such a use or application of the word. But we think it may conduce to a more distinct exposition of the whole subject, and a better classification of the proofs, if we advert in the first place to the divine origin and authority of the books of Scripture in general, or to the evidence we have of the general position, that God's agency and authority were interposed in the production of the books themselves, and not merely in communicating the substance of the revelation they contain; so that the books themselves as they stand, and not merely the general system of doctrine and duty which they unfold, may be fairly and truly called the word of God; and then, after establishing this, proceed to consider, under the head of *inspiration*, the less essential though still important question as to the way and manner in which the agency of God was interposed in the production of these books, or what is usually discussed under the head of the nature and extent of inspiration; and this will be naturally followed by the consideration of the subject of the canon, or the investigation of the questions connected with the determination of what the books *are* to which this divine authority and inspiration are to be ascribed. These explanations will, I trust, enable you to understand distinctly the connection and conditions of the argument, and to see *where we are* and *what we mean* when we proceed to advert to the way and manner of proving the divine authority of the books which compose the New Testament.

The divine authority of the books of the New Testament may be proved, like the divine origin of Christianity, by evidence external, internal, and experimental; and these divisions of the evidence are analogous in their general nature and character in both cases. The external evidence is that derived from what we know concerning the authors, and the facts connected with the composition of the books; the internal from the character and contents of the books themselves; and the experimental from the effects which these books have produced, and are still producing.

The distinction that has been sometimes made between the evidence derived from places without the Bible, and that derived from places within the Bible (Chalmers, 2:8)[1] is just as useless here as we shewed it to you to be under the former head, and serves only to introduce confusion. There is a clear distinction between the evidence derived from what we can know

---

1. *The Works of Thomas Chalmers*, vol. 4, *On the Miraculous and Internal Evidences of the Christian Revelation, and the Authority of Its Record* (New York: Robert Carter, 1840), 8.

concerning the men by whom, and the circumstances in which, the books were composed, and that derived from the actual contents or substance of the books themselves; but under the former of these heads, which constitutes the external evidence of the divine authority of the books, we must of necessity include all that we know certainly concerning the history of the authors and the composition of the books, *whether derived from the statements of the books themselves, or from any other authentic source whatever.* Having proved the divine commission of Christ and his apostles, we are now to regard them, not merely as honest men and credible narrators of history, but as infallible authorities in all the statements they make concerning religious subjects, and to believe implicitly whatever information they may convey to us concerning the books of Scripture, or any other topic whatever in regard to which they advance a claim to our submission.

In considering the external evidence of the divine authority of the books of the New Testament, one of the first and most obvious considerations that occurs to us is, that those books were chiefly composed by the apostles themselves, by the very men who were employed by God to reveal to us the system of doctrine and duty which is unfolded in these books. They are not accounts of what was said and done by Christ and his apostles, preserved and transmitted to us by other parties. They are the accounts of the life and discourses of Christ, and of the labours and instructions of the apostles, recorded and transmitted to us by the apostles themselves. The authors of these books were the only men whom God employed to reveal his will, and whom for that purpose he furnished with abundant communications of his Spirit. When *these* men explained the system of Christianity to the people whom they orally addressed, or when they defended their cause and their persons before judicial tribunals, we know that they enjoyed the special presence and assistance of God, the guidance and direction of the Holy Ghost; and we cannot suppose that they were left destitute of the same guidance and direction when they sat down to commit to writing, for the permanent instruction of mankind, the history of the life and discourses of their Master, or when they addressed letters of advice and direction to the churches which had been formed through the success of their oral instructions. It is by the Gospels and the Epistles which they wrote, and by them alone, that the Christian revelation has been transmitted to subsequent ages; and if they had the constant presence and guidance of the Holy Ghost in their personal ministry in proclaiming the truth, in defending themselves against adversaries, and in establishing and organising churches, there can be no reason to doubt, and there is the strongest reason on this ground alone to believe, that they had the same guidance and direction in their writings; and that as God was the author of the revelation which they communicated, so he is to be regarded as the author and source of those writings which were directed to no other object than just to unfold that revelation, and to afford instructions as to the way and manner in which it is to be applied and brought into operation in order that it may produce its intended effects. This point might be illustrated at length, but it is unnecessary. The argument is clear and satisfactory. What such men as the apostles were—men who were endowed with the power of working miracles and of predicting future events—men who were commissioned by God to make known his will, and who in all their official labours were under the immediate guidance and direction of the Holy Ghost—wrote, and wrote in such circumstances and for such purposes, must have been written under the guidance and direction of the Spirit of Truth, and is therefore stamped throughout with divine authority; and accordingly almost all who have professed to believe in the truth of the Christian religion have admitted the divine authority of the books which compose the New Testament, though differing in some questions concerning the nature and extent of inspiration; except Socinians and German rationalists, who have manifestly been influenced by a desire and determination to maintain the supremacy of their own reason, to emancipate themselves from the control of the sacred Scriptures, and to retain the liberty of judging according to their own discretion as to what in the Bible comes from God, and was intended to be of permanent use and obligation, and what, though found in the Scriptures, is possessed of no such binding authority. This is the principal argument under the head of external evidence for the divine authority of the books which compose the New Testament; and it is sufficient of itself to establish it.

The external evidence however comprehends every argument derived, not only from what we know concerning the authors of these books, but also concerning the circumstances and the objects of their composition; and any information we may possess concerning these points, although derived from the statements of the books themselves, comes properly under the head of external evidence, because it applies to the historical matter of fact, as to the source from which these books really proceeded, and forms no part of the indications of a divine origin which the books themselves as such contain. We have not a great deal of direct and explicit information concerning these points in the books of the New Testament itself; still there are statements which afford decided confirmations of the evidence of its divine origin and authority. The statement, for instance, with which Luke commences his Gospel, viz., "It seemed good to me also, having had perfect understanding of all things from the very first, to write unto thee in order, most excellent Theophilus, that thou mightest know the certainty of those things, wherein thou hast been instructed," seems fairly to imply that whatever authority might attach to any information which Luke in his Gospel has communicated to us, attaches equally to the whole of it, i.e., to the writing or book as such. John tells us (John 20:31) that his Gospel was written "that men might believe that Jesus is the Christ the Son of God, and that believing they might have life through his name," a statement which thoroughly identifies the object of his writing, and of course of the whole of what is contained in his Gospel, with that of his preaching; and thus affords at least the strongest presumption that in writing his Gospel he had the same divine guidance and direction as in executing his apostolic commission of proclaiming orally God's will to men. We find the apostles, in their epistles to the churches, claiming for their writings the same divine origin, the same supernatural and infallible authority, as they claimed for their oral instructions, though this is not frequently and formally insisted upon, because the truth of it was really too evident to require proof. It was enough that these writings came from the inspired apostles who were commissioned by God to make known his will, and who had fully established by miracles, which Paul calls the signs of an apostle, their divine commission. Paul may be regarded as plainly enough claiming for his epistles a divine origin and infallible authority, when he commenced them, as he usually did, by assuming the designation of an apostle, and referring to his warrant and authority for assuming that designation, and executing the functions of that office, "Paul, a servant of Jesus Christ, called to be an apostle, separated unto the gospel of God" (Rom. 1:1). His apostolic authority being thus set forth in the commencement of his epistles as the ground or basis of the divine authority of what he was about to write, we have just the same reason for receiving as coming from God, and as stamped with *his* authority whatever we find in these epistles, as his hearers had for receiving as divinely inspired, in virtue of Christ's promises and the Spirit's communications, whatever he delivered to them in his oral instructions. His authority and commission being thus set forth in the commencement of his epistles to the churches as the basis of their obligation to receive them as coming from God, it was not necessary thereafter in the course of the epistles to insist upon this, to say anything more about the true source from which they proceeded, or the authority with which they were invested. The allusions therefore to this matter are only incidental, but quite sufficient to afford decided proofs of the divine authority of the apostolic writings. We may refer to some of these: "If any man think himself to be a prophet, or spiritual (i.e., if any man lay claim to peculiar spiritual gifts, or to supernatural divine communications), let him acknowledge that the things that I *write* unto you are the commandments of the Lord" (1 Cor. 14:37–38); "Let such an one think that such as we are in word by letters, such also are we indeed when we are present," (2 Cor. 10:11), where he manifestly claims the same authority and reverence for his letters as for his oral instructions. And again: "If any man obey not our word by this epistle, note that man, and have no company with him" (2 Thess. 3:14).

We have not in the New Testament any direct and formal declaration as to the divine origin and authority of the books of the New Testament as a whole; and this was not to be expected in the circumstances, when the different books of which it is composed had not been collected into a volume. But we have, both from our Lord and his apostles, the fullest and most explicit attestations to the divine origin and authority of the Old Testament as then and always received by the Jews. We have this attestation embodied both in general declarations and in many specific statements, conclusively establishing, by whatever authority attaches to any declaration of Christ and his apostles, not only that Moses was a divine messenger employed by God to reveal his will, and that the prophets spoke as they were moved by the Holy Ghost, but also moreover that the books which compose the Old Testament were to be traced to God as their author, and were stamped throughout with his divine and infallible authority. Some of these attestations given by Christ and his apostles to the Old Testament it will be necessary for us to examine more carefully; but as we are persuaded that they establish, not only the divine commission of Moses and the prophets, not only the divine authority of the books of the Old Testament in a general sense, which is the point we are at present considering, but also their plenary and verbal inspiration, we shall defer the consideration of them till we come to the investigation of that question. Before leaving this subject of the information to be gathered from the New Testament concerning the divine origin of the books which compose it as a matter of historical fact, it is proper to advert to the attestation given by the Apostle Peter to the divine origin and authority of the epistles of Paul, and we introduce it here, after rather than before the reference to the attestation given by our Lord and his apostles to the divine origin and authority of the Old Testament, because part of the force of Peter's attestation to the authority of Paul's epistles lies in his putting them on the same level in point of authority with the Scriptures of the Old Testament. It is found in 2 Peter 3:15–16: "Even as our beloved brother Paul, according to the wisdom given unto him, hath written unto you; as also in all his epistles, speaking in them of these things, in which are some things hard to be understood, which they that are unlearned and unstable wrest, as they do also the other scriptures, unto their own destruction."

We have said that the external evidence for the divine authority of the books of the New Testament is based upon the information we possess concerning the authors of these books, and the circumstances connected with their origin and composition considered as matters of historical fact, whether derived from the books themselves, or from any other authentic source; and we have information of an authentic kind from other sources which goes to confirm our conviction of their origin and authority.

We have several statements contained in the writings of the Fathers, the truth of which there is no reason to doubt, which may be reckoned as equally credible with any other historical testimony to a matter of fact, and which go to prove that the apostles regarded, and that their followers received their writings as invested with the same divine and infallible authority as their oral instructions. Irenaeus (*Against Heresies* 3.1.1 [ANF 1:414]) tells us that what the apostles first preached, they afterwards wrote in the Scriptures. Eusebius tells us (*Ecclesiastical History* 3.24.5–7 [Loeb 1:250–51]) that Matthew having first preached to the Hebrews, i.e., the Jews, and being about to go to other nations, wrote his Gospel, supplying by writing the want of his presence and oral instructions. Eusebius further informs us that the Apostle John examined and sanctioned the Gospels of Matthew, Mark, and Luke, and wrote his own chiefly to supply some important additional materials which they had not been led to record. And indeed we have the unanimous testimony of the primitive church, from the apostles downwards, to the divine origin of the books of the New Testament. If you have examined with care and attention, as you ought to have done, the testimonies of the early Christian writers, by which we commonly establish the genuineness and authenticity of the books of the New Testament, you must have seen that many of them declare the conviction of their authors that those books came from God, and were given by divine inspiration. And this may be regarded, not merely as the statement of an opinion which the primitive church entertained upon grounds of the validity of which she was satisfied, but as practically and substantially an attestation to a matter of fact, namely this, that the apostles who were the authors of those books, gave them forth to the churches and to their followers as having been composed in the execution of their apostolic commission, under the guidance and direction of the Holy Ghost, and as therefore possessed of divine and infallible authority. And this consideration is sufficient, were there no other, to warrant the declaration contained in the first chapter of our Confession of Faith, viz., "We may be moved and induced by the testimony of the church to an high and reverend[2] esteem of the Holy Scripture," inasmuch as in various ways the testimony of the church, or the reception these books have met with ever since they were first promulgated, does tend greatly, upon the most rational grounds, and without giving to the church's testimony more weight than that to which upon scriptural and Protestant principles it is reasonably entitled, to confirm our conviction that these books were given by inspiration of God, and are able to make us wise unto salvation.

---

2. That is, "reverent."—ED.

LECTURE XXII: INTERNAL EVIDENCE, IN COMMENTARY UPON CONFESSION, CHAPTER 1, SECTION 5

We have given a brief sketch of the external evidence of the divine origin and authority of the sacred scriptures, the divine origin and authority of the books which compose the Bible, as distinguished, on the one hand, from the divine origin of the substance and leading features of the revelation which they contain and convey; and, on the other, from the question of the way and manner in which divine agency was exerted in producing them, or the nature and extent of inspiration. We shewed you that, from what we know as matter of undoubted historical fact concerning the authors of the books of the New Testament, and of the circumstances in which, and the objects for which, they were composed, the conclusion is certain and irresistible, that the apostles, in their writings as well as in their oral instructions, were guided and directed by the Holy Ghost, and that therefore their writings *are* the word of God, possessed of divine and infallible authority; while the attestation of Christ and his apostles, viewing them as divinely accredited messengers, establishes beyond doubt the divine origin and authority of the books which compose the Old Testament. The internal evidence for the divine origin and authority of the books of Scripture is that which is derived from an examination of the character and contents of the books themselves; and in explaining briefly the general nature and bearing of the arguments classed under this head, and derived from this source, we cannot do better than follow the guidance of that section in the first chapter of our Confession of Faith, to which in last lecture we had occasion to refer. It stands thus:

> We may be moved and induced by the testimony of the Church to an high and reverend esteem of the Holy Scripture; and the heavenliness of the matter, the efficacy of the doctrine, the majesty of the style, the consent of all the parts, the scope of the whole (which is to give all glory to God), the full discovery it makes of the only way of man's salvation, the many other incomparable excellencies, and the entire perfection thereof, are arguments whereby it doth abundantly evidence itself to be the Word of God. (WCF 1.5)

The first thing mentioned here, viz., "the testimony of the church," belongs to the head of the external evidence, and as such was adverted to in last lecture. The rest belong chiefly to the internal, though some of them might also, with equal propriety, be classed under the head of the experimental evidence. We shall briefly explain each of them singly, and then advert to the general conclusion that all these things "are arguments whereby the Scripture doth abundantly evidence itself to be the Word of God."

The first is, "the heavenliness of the matter." The matter of the Scriptures, or the various subjects there treated of, have all a reference, more or less direct, to things celestial and divine. They are connected throughout with God, the unseen world, and the eternal destinies of man. No merely human or temporal object, seems to be aimed at or attended to. Everything is connected, more or less directly and palpably, with Him whose throne is in the heavens; with the celestial origin and dignity of his intelligent creatures; with their relations to heaven; and with the end and the means of restoring to heaven those who had forfeited their birthright. Everything connected with this world is represented in the aspect in which it is seen from heaven, and in the light of a higher world. There is nothing that is of the earth earthy. All breathes of heaven, and tends to lead the thoughts and desires to things unseen and eternal. The guilt and depravity of men are indeed set forth in glowing colours, and exhibited in fearful specimens of what man is and has done. But it is held forth as rebellion against the God of heaven. It is represented in the light in which it usually appears, not so much to men themselves as to the purer inhabitants of a higher and a holier region; and it is unfolded for the purpose of shewing men what they have lost, and what difficulties stand in the way of their restoration to heaven and happiness, and in order to lead them to turn their thoughts to that state where there is no more sin and no more sorrow. The Bible indeed shews that God has been pleased to make revelations of his will, conveying regulations about temporal and earthly things, especially in connection with that remarkable people whom he selected to put his name in them. And many of these regulations, though in some respects intended to serve temporary purposes, and not now fitted to effect all the same ends as they once did for a season, are recorded in the same Scriptures, and form a part of the word of God. But even these things were all written for our instruction, on whom the ends of the world have come; they were all fitted and intended to have some reference to the heavenly as well as the earthly Canaan; and they are still found, under the guidance of God's Spirit, to minister instruction that is profitable for guiding and directing men in their journey to the Jerusalem that is above. Such books, containing such matter, and so free from everything that indicates an earthly origin, must have come from God.

The second consideration is "the efficacy of the doctrine." This topic may be regarded as belonging partly to the head of the experimental evidence; for the efficacy of the doctrine comes out most fully and most palpably when exhibited in its actual effects upon men individually and collectively, upon their understandings, motives, character, and conduct; and can be fully understood and appreciated only by those who have experienced it. Still something of the efficacy of the doctrines by which the Scriptures are pervaded, or of their fitness to effect and impress the minds and characters of men in a degree immeasurably superior to any other doctrines or truths that ever have been set before them, may be discerned even by those who have not yet submitted their hearts and lives to its influence, so as to afford even to them some rational ground for the conviction that it came from God, and that the books which it pervades must be traced to his agency. The whole of the doctrines by which the sacred Scriptures are pervaded concerning God, his character, government, and ways; concerning man, his condition, danger, capacities, duties, and prospects; concerning the way of salvation through Christ in all its branches and arrangements; and concerning the everlasting destinies of the human race, is manifestly fitted, in its own nature, when viewed in connection with the actual constitution of man, to exert the most potent influence upon the character and conduct of men. So that men to whom it has been made known, but whose character has not been changed by it, and who are not under its influence increasing in righteousness and holiness, may be fairly said to have never yet believed it. We know indeed that men will never experience its efficacy except through the operation of the Holy Ghost; but this as a matter of fact is traceable solely to the ungodliness and depravity that has been superinduced upon human nature by the fall, and the fact does not affect the question of the fitness and tendency of the doctrines themselves in their own nature to produce the most powerful and the most salutary effects upon the minds and hearts of men, so as to make them suitable instruments of a divine agency, and to afford plain indications that they came from Him who knows the heart of man, and turneth it whithersoever he will; who is the author and the guardian of all holiness throughout the universe. This is the light in which the efficacy of the doctrine may be presented to men who have not themselves submitted to its influence; but when we further attend to the voice of experience as exhibited in the case of those who have been born again of this word, and are now taking it as a light to their feet, we find that not they only, but any to whom their experience and spiritual history may be made known, have good ground to believe that the efficacy of the doctrine is often manifested, not merely in the great leading truths which compose the Christian system, as ascertained from various portions of the Bible, but in single particular statements of Scripture brought home with power to the understanding and the heart, and producing deep and striking impressions of divine things, calling forth conviction of sin, leading men to turn from it unto God, filling them with love to God and Christ, animating them with zeal and ardour, and filling them with strong consolation and good hope through grace; thus plainly pointing, not merely to the general truths or doctrines taught in the Bible, but to its precise and particular statements, as having come from God, and as still employed by him for accomplishing his gracious and saving purposes.

We need not dwell upon the next particular mentioned as an argument for the divine authority of the Scriptures, viz., "the majesty of the style," as it could be illustrated only by producing examples of sublimity, dignity, beauty, and authority in extracts from the Bible, which you can easily find for yourselves, and as, when such specimens are produced, the argument founded upon them just consists of an appeal to the ordinary sentiments and feelings of mankind, and to the impressions which they receive. It ought to be remarked, however, that there are some general characters or qualities attaching more or less to the whole Bible which may be comprehended under the general head of style, or the principles which have regulated or determined the way and manner in which it has been composed, that may be fairly regarded as affording no inconsiderable evidence that it proceeded from one source, and that this source was at least superhuman.

The next argument is "the consent of all the parts," and this, when rightly estimated and fully drawn out, affords a very strong proof of the divine origin and authority of the Bible. The Bible, it is to be remembered, consists of a great number of distinct books, produced by a great variety of authors, who lived in different ages, extending over a period of about 1600 years, i.e., from Moses to John, and placed in a very great variety of external circumstances, but all of them treating more or less of subjects which were in some respects identical. Yet in all these different books, and among all these different authors, we find the most perfect harmony in all the views they entertained, in all the truths they promulgated, in the motives by which they were animated, in the objects they aimed at, and in the kind of means they employed for attaining their ends. And we find pervading the whole of those books, from first to last, not merely a perfect harmony of doctrine, sentiment, and object, but we can trace plainly one great scheme, one grand comprehensive economy, originating in one cause, directed to one object, partially and gradually developed, and at length fully unfolded and consummated. The authors of the different books of Scripture take naturally and obviously the position and aspect of men who were raised up and guided by a superior power, employed as his instruments for effecting his purposes, accomplishing for the time just the object which he had in view, their personal labours and their written productions being designed by him to serve purposes of which they themselves were not fully aware, but which we now see to have been closely and intimately connected with the attainment of one great object, with the completion of one great and glorious scheme. This consent of all the parts, this wonderful harmony that pervades the whole of the sacred Scriptures, may be fairly regarded as a proof that one agency was concerned in the production of them all, and that that was the agency of Him who seeth the end in the beginning, with whom one day is as a thousand years, and a thousand years as one day. The unity, the harmony which we find, as a matter of fact, to pervade the whole Bible from beginning to end, could not have existed—must be regarded as an impossibility—had the books which compose it been the productions of unassisted men, had not the composition of them been superintended, directed, and controlled by one comprehensive mind; in short, had not God's agency been so interposed in the production and composition of them as to make them really the word of God.

Contradictions and inconsistencies have indeed been alleged to exist in the sacred Scriptures, and these have been often adduced and urged, not only by infidels, but even by men who, while professing to believe in the truth of the Christian revelation, have refused to admit the divine origin and authority of the books which compose the Bible. Most of these alleged contradictions and inconsistencies originate in ignorance, carelessness, and prejudice on the part of those who adduce them, and admit of being easily explained or reconciled. If there are any that do not very readily admit of a precise and specific solution individually, there are general considerations, applicable more or less to all ancient books, which afford a sufficient answer to any objections that might be founded on circumstances of this sort. Besides, the alleged inconsistencies and contradictions, especially those of them about which there is any real difficulty in giving a specific solution, respect only very insignificant matters, such as names and numbers, and therefore, even if they did affect the question of the plenary verbal inspiration of the Scriptures, a point to be afterwards considered, cannot affect that great truth which the consent of all the parts, the unity and harmony pervading all the books of Scripture, notwithstanding their having been composed by so many different men in different ages and circumstances, establishes, viz., that they were all composed under the superintendence and direction of one comprehensive mind; in other words, that God's agency was so exerted in the production of them, that they are all his word, possessed of divine authority.

The next topic is "the scope of the whole, which is to give all glory to God." The great truth taught in Scripture that God does everything for his own glory, for the manifestation of his own perfections, can be easily shewn to be in entire conformity with the dictates of right reason; and indeed when men have been led to form any right conceptions of the being whom we designate as God, a being infinitely glorious and excellent, independent, self-existent, self-sufficient, the creator, proprietor, and governor of all things, they are naturally and irresistibly led to deduce from this idea the conclusion that such a being could not be moved or induced to act by a regard to anything *out of himself,* or irrespective of himself. In all his works of creation and providence there is a supreme regard to his own glory, the manifestation of his own perfections. If the Bible be his word, proceeding from him, and stamped with his authority, we might expect it to possess the same character, and to be directed to the same end. And so it is. "The scope of the whole is to give all glory to

God." The whole of the sacred Scriptures is manifestly directed to the object of making God known as he is; of unfolding his character, plans, and government; of leading men to entertain the most exalted conceptions of his excellencies, of the worship and homage that are due to him, of their entire dependence on him, of their unworthiness of all his mercies, and of their obligations to shew forth his praise.

These are objects which men, such as they have usually exhibited themselves in their actions and in their writings, would not have aimed at at all, or in any eminent degree, and which even the best and holiest men whom the world has seen, made so by the power and grace of God himself, would not have prosecuted so singly, so supremely, and so unceasingly as we find is done by the authors of the books of Scripture, unless God himself had animated and directed them. To give all glory to God would not have been so thoroughly and so exclusively the scope of the Bible unless the Bible had been God's own work, unless its various parts had been produced under the immediate superintendence and direction of Him who made all things for himself, and who will not give his glory to another.

The last argument under this head for the divine origin and authority of the Bible is "the full discovery it makes of the only way of man's salvation." It is true, not only that the Bible makes a full discovery of the only way of man's salvation, and that no other book, except among those which are professedly taken from the Bible, does or even professes to do so, but moreover that the great object of the whole Bible is more or less directly to open up and unfold the scheme of salvation, and that every part of the Bible bears more or less upon this object, and is fitted to contribute to this end. This scheme could not have been invented or devised by men. We can see in it plain traces of the wisdom of God, of its adaptation to man's condition, constitution, necessities, and aspirations; and when we find that the Bible is devoted to the development of it, and that the whole of it bears more or less directly upon the great object of unfolding and applying it, of shewing men that they need it, and of directing them as to the way in which they may obtain the benefit of it, we have the strongest ground to believe that the book itself, or rather the collection of books that form the sacred Scriptures, came from Him who alone could devise, execute, and reveal such a scheme.

The Confession adds, "the many other incomparable excellencies, and the entire perfection thereof." These things have been illustrated by many writers, and will be seen and felt by all who set themselves to study the Scriptures in a right frame of spirit, and under the guidance of the Holy Ghost, given in answer to prayer. And the excellencies of the sacred Scriptures, the indications of its self-evidencing power, you should all make it your desire and your object, while you study the Bible, to perceive and appreciate.

These are the chief topics which may be said to constitute the internal evidence for the divine origin and authority of the sacred Scriptures, or to afford some proof of the general position that God's agency was exerted, not only in the communication of the substance of the revelation, but in the production of the books. All these various considerations bear upon the proof of the general truth of the Mosaic and Christian revelations. Some of them bear perhaps more precisely and directly upon that question than upon the divine origin and authority of all the books of which the Bible is composed; and some of them do not admit of being brought out in all their strength for the conviction of infidels and gainsayers, but can be fully estimated and appreciated only by those whose eyes have been opened by the Spirit to see the wondrous things contained in God's law, who have received the truth in the love of it, and submitted their hearts to its influence. But they all involve considerations which do bear more or less clearly and directly upon the divine origin and authority of the Bible, as distinguished from the divine origin and authority of the Mosaic and Christian revelations in general. And they all admit of being made more or less intelligible even to unbelievers, and may be presented in such aspects as should in right reason contribute, upon perfectly rational grounds, to produce the conviction and the admission that the books which compose the Bible were not the work of unassisted men, and that the agency of God was exerted in the production of them, so that the sacred Scriptures may be called the word of God, and should be received and submitted to as stamped with his authority. They are all found in the Bible itself; they may be seen and discerned there by any who will examine it aright, with a real desire to know whether it be indeed the word of God; and hence the truth and justness of the statement in the Confession, that all these things " are arguments whereby the Holy Scripture doth abundantly evidence itself to be the word of God," qualities or properties found in it, upon due examination, which afford reasonable and conclusive grounds for the conviction that, to use the well-known and often quoted words of Locke, "it has God for its author, and truth without any mixture of error for its matter, as well as salvation for its end." The remaining portion of this section of the Confession of Faith,—which is in these words, and contains a great and important truth, viz., "yet notwithstandings our full persuasion and assurance of the infallible truth and divine authority thereof is from the inward work of the Holy Spirit, bearing witness by and with the word in our hearts,"—will be afterwards explained and illustrated.

It cannot be said with truth that every portion of the Bible contains equally clear and palpable internal marks of its divine original. It cannot be doubted that some portions of the Bible contain clearer and plainer traces of God's presence and agency in the production of them than others, the word of God being analogous in this respect to his works of creation and providence. Neither are we prepared to say of every particular book in the Bible, taken singly and separately, that it contains internal proofs of its divine origin and authority, such as could be brought out under any of the general heads to which we have now adverted under the department of the internal evidence, and exhibited plainly and palpably for the conviction of gainsayers. We are disposed to concur in a statement made by Richard Baxter, whose views generally upon the subject of the evidences we formerly had occasion specially to commend to you, and which is quoted with approbation by Dr. Chalmers in a portion of our text-book, which we will by-and-by have occasion to consider:

> For my part, I confess, I could never boast of any such testimony or light of the Spirit (nor reason neither) which, without human testimony, would have made me believe that the book of Canticles is canonical, and written by Solomon, and the book of Wisdom apocryphal, and written by Philo, etc. Nor would I have known all, or any historical books, such as Joshua, Judges, Ruth, Samuel, Kings, Chronicles, Ezra, Nehemiah, etc., to be written by divine inspiration, but by tradition . . . (2:405–6)[3]

But whatever may be the extent to which, from internal evidence alone, we can establish against gainsayers the divine origin and authority of all the different books or portions of Scripture,

---

3. Ed. note: *The Works of Thomas Chalmers*, vol. 4, *On the Miraculous and Internal Evidences of the Christian Revelation, and the Authority of Its Records* (New York: Robert Carter, 1840), 405–6. The original citation by Baxter can be found in *Practical Works of Richard Baxter* (London: Paternoster, 1837), 3:79.

certain it is, from the experience of all in every age, who have made the attempt, that the more men study the Bible with diligence and humility, and with prayer for the divine blessing and guidance, the more clearly will they see through it all the traces of God's presence and agency, the more fully will they experience its self-evidencing power, and the more thoroughly will they be persuaded by what they see and feel, as well as by submission to the authority of God clearly revealing this truth by his apostle, that it is all given by inspiration of God, and is profitable for doctrine, for reproof, for correction, and instruction in righteousness. Believers are liable to be assailed by temptations to error as well as to sin, and they are not always exempted from occasional temptations even to the fatal error of infidelity. And they are commonly enabled to resist these temptations, and to hold fast their profession, through the Spirit opening up to them more fully, and impressing upon them more deeply, what they may have previously seen of the self-evidencing power of the Bible, and what they may have formerly noticed of the efficacy of its doctrines and statements upon themselves, in changing their natures, in enlightening their understandings, in sanctifying their hearts, and in regulating their conduct. Thus they are persuaded that the Bible could not possibly have been a cunningly devised fable, that it must have come from God, and that it is only by cleaving to it as a light unto their feet, and a lamp unto their path, that they can be guided in the way everlasting.

We must remind you, however, that the evidence for the divine origin and authority of the Bible, like that for the truth of the Christian revelation in general, is cumulative in its character, derived from a variety of sources which ought all to be carefully examined, consisting of a variety of branches which ought to be all surveyed, and that all the different proofs, external and internal, which have been brought forward upon this subject, and which really possess any argumentative weight, ought to be viewed in their connection with each other, and in their united bearing upon the conclusion to be established. It is deserving of notice that that portion of the sacred Scriptures which might probably be regarded as having less self-evidencing power, less internal evidence in its own character and contents of its divine origin and authority, has the clearest and most explicit external testimony. There are many portions of the Old Testament which have just as clear internal evidence of their divine original as the books of the New; but this could not be said of the whole of it, of all the books of which it is composed. But then we have the clear and explicit testimony of our Lord and his apostles, assumed of course to have been already proved to be divinely commissioned teachers authorised to reveal God's will, that the Old Testament is the word of God, and is stamped throughout with divine authority. And this testimony is so clear and explicit, it is given so fully and unequivocally, both in general declarations and in specific statements, which imply or assume it, that there is no possibility of evading it except by adopting the principle of the infidel rationalists of Germany, that on this, and on many other occasions, Christ and his apostles stated or admitted, not what they themselves believed, or wished others to believe, but merely what was in accordance with and accommodated to the superstitious and erroneous notions that then generally prevailed among the Jews. And men who take this ground are of course to be regarded and treated as infidels, with whom, when we are called upon to have any discussion with them, we must go back to the first principles of the whole subject of the evidences, and whom we must, in the first place, endeavour to convince by appropriate arguments that Jesus of Nazareth was a man approved of God, by miracles and wonders and signs which God did by him; and that to the apostles whom he sent forth God bore witness with signs and wonders, and divers miracles, and gifts of the Holy Ghost, according to his own will (Acts 2:22; Heb. 2:4).

LECTURE XXIII: DIFFERENT DOCTRINES AS TO THE DIVINE ORIGIN OF THE SCRIPTURES, OR THE AMOUNT OF DIVINE AGENCY IN THE PRODUCTION OF THEM—PRINCIPAL AUTHORS

In introducing the subject of the divine origin and authority of the sacred Scriptures, we explained to you that by these words we meant to describe in general the truth that God's agency was exerted in the production of the books which compose the Bible, and not merely in communicating the substance of the revelations which are there contained; reserving the more detailed and exact investigation of the question as to the way and manner in which God's agency was exerted in the production of these books to be prosecuted under the head of the nature and extent of inspiration. It must be admitted that, as thus explained, the doctrine of the divine origin and authority of the Bible is somewhat vague and indefinite in its import. A very considerable number of writers, who differ in opinion to no small extent from each other, must be all in this sense regarded as holding the divine origin and authority of the Bible. We do not well see, however, how this vagueness and generality can be avoided. There is a clear line of distinction between those who merely admit the divine origin and authority of the Mosaic and Christian revelations, and those who, in addition to this, maintain that God was concerned in, and in some way directed and superintended, the production of the books which compose the Bible. And again, there is a clear line of distinction between those who rest satisfied with the general doctrine of the divine origin and authority of the books, though differing materially among themselves as to the character and extent of God's agency in the matter, and as to the perfection of the writings which resulted from it, and those who hold fully and precisely the great truth of the plenary and verbal inspiration of the whole Scriptures. These are the only very clear and palpable lines of division upon this subject which can be distinctly laid down and described. But as the intermediate class, who hold in a general sense the divine origin and authority of the Bible, without admitting its plenary verbal inspiration, is composed of men whose views differ materially from each other, it may be proper, before proceeding further, to advert somewhat to these differences, and the grounds on which they rest. The view commonly held by Socinians upon this subject, and indeed by Latitudinarian divines in general, by those who have been characterised by their lax and erroneous views of the great doctrines of the gospel, is this, that though Moses and Christ were commissioned by God to make known his will to men, and though we have in the Bible, and God intended that we should have, sufficient materials for ascertaining the substance of the information which he communicated to men through their instrumentality, yet that the books themselves, which compose the Bible, were the productions of men who enjoyed no peculiar divine assistance or direction, and who, though they were honest and faithful narrators, and have given us accounts which may in the main be received as true and correct, yet were liable to err, and did err, and are not therefore to be implicitly followed. This is the common Socinian or Unitarian view; and this is what is meant when it is said, and said truly, that Socinians deny altogether the inspiration of the Scriptures. Upon this theory the Scriptures are really deprived of the character commonly ascribed to them, not only of being a revelation from God, but even of being fully adapted to convey to us an authentic representation of the revelations he has given to men. We have strong grounds to believe that if God was pleased to communicate to men a revelation intended for the permanent benefit of the human race, he would make provision for securing that it should be correctly embodied and transmitted among men; and yet, according to this view, which denies in any sense the inspiration of the Scriptures, no effectual provision has been made for securing this end. This however, so far from being a defect in the estimation of Socinians, is just what recommends the notion to their favour and adoption, as it leaves them at liberty to exercise their own reason at discretion upon the statements of Scripture, and practically to believe as much or as little of it as they think proper, a liberty in which they have always shewn that they are very ready to indulge. This view is of course rejected by all who hold *in any sense* the divine origin and authority of the Bible. They, upon the grounds of which a sketch has been given in the last two lectures, maintain that God not only communicated his will to men, but made effectual provision for securing that his revelation should be correctly embodied in the Bible, and that he so guided and superintended the production of the books of Scripture as that they are His word, stamped with his authority.

Under this general position, however, there is, as we have said, some diversity of sentiment even among those who stop short of the truth of the plenary and verbal inspiration of the whole Scriptures. Some, while they cannot be said to deny inspiration altogether, and while they admit that God's immediate agency was concerned in the production of the books of Scripture, seem anxious to have as little of inspiration or of divine agency in the matter as possible, and are disposed to maintain what is really little better than the Socinian view, viz., that inspiration or divine agency applies only to those parts of the Bible in which something is communicated that could not, without immediate revelation, have been known by men at all, or which contain predictions of future events; and that in the composition of the other portions of Scripture the authors were left to the exercise of their own unaided faculties, and the use and improvement of their ordinary and natural sources of information about the subjects of which they wrote. A notion of this sort prevails extensively among those German writers who are not thorough neologians, and have not gone so far as to deny altogether an immediate supernatural revelation; and some such notion seems to have been entertained by many of those defenders of revelation in our own country, whose defective and unsound views and principles I formerly had occasion to advert to; while an impression of a similar kind, though not so distinctly stated or avowed, prevails, we fear, to some extent among the irreligious portion of professedly Christian society. The general principle upon which the advocates of this view proceed is this, that we must not admit of any divine agency, of any immediate and supernatural interposition of God in effecting or producing anything which could possibly have been effected without it, and they then quietly set up human reason, i.e., themselves, or their own notions, as competent and adequate judges of whether or not, in a particular case, any immediate divine interposition was necessary. With these principles they come to examine the Bible, take the different books of which it is composed, and the different subjects of which it treats, and set themselves to consider in regard to each book, and each subject, or class of subjects, whether mere men, unaided by any special divine assistance, could not possibly have given us such information as is there presented to us; and whenever there is any plausible ground for the allegation that men might possibly have communicated to us the information conveyed, they forthwith conclude that no divine inspiration was granted, that no special divine agency was exerted in guiding and directing them. On these grounds some defenders of revelation have denied anything like divine inspiration and authority to the historical books of Scripture, because, as they allege, the information they contain might have been acquired by men in the ordinary use of their faculties, and in the unaided improvement of the opportunities they enjoyed, and might, without any special divine assistance, have been transmitted to us with all necessary accuracy. On the same ground they are disposed to exclude from any valid claim to inspiration, or to a divine origin and authority, those portions of Scripture which contain plain precepts of morality, or maxims for the wise and prudent regulation of conduct—as, for example, the books of Proverbs and Ecclesiastes. Some writers of this class are even disposed to exclude also the devotional parts of Scripture, as containing in their estimation nothing but what pious and holy men might have spoken and written under the ordinary influences of the Spirit, in expressing their emotions and desires, and describing their spiritual experience. The whole of this general reasoning is unsound, and the application made of it is unwarranted and presumptuous. We are not warranted in laying down the position that God never interposes extraordinarily, never deviates from the ordinary course of nature, never gives special and supernatural communications, when, so far as we can see, the object which he is *supposed* to have had in view, might have been effected without any such interposition. We know too little of the general principles by which God's conduct is or may be regulated to warrant us in laying down any such position. We know little or nothing, except in so far as God may be pleased to inform us, as to what his whole object was in any particular case, and as to what means were necessary in order to effect that object.

It is conceded by those with whom we are now arguing that God intended to embody in writing, and to convey to us through means of the books of Scripture, an authentic and well accredited revelation of his will; and it is surely very evident that we are not warranted in asserting that he would have accomplished this object, or at least that he would have accomplished it so thoroughly and satisfactorily, as for anything we know he might have desired and intended to do, by superintending and directing the men who were employed for this purpose in some part of their works, and leaving them to their own unaided faculties in the rest, or by putting into our hands a book, some part of which he had himself superintended or dictated, and other parts of which men were left to compose without any such divine assistance. A book which is partly the work of God and partly the work of unaided man is at least a very different book from one which has been wholly prepared under the direction of God. The one, it is manifest, might be fitted to serve purposes and to effect results to which the other would be incompetent. Would not every man who was at all anxious to know fully and certainly God's will conveyed to him by writing, earnestly desire to have it in a book which was really and entirely the word of God, in place of being left to the uncertainty of picking out from the mass of the contents of the book, without any certain test or criterion to guide him, what was God's, and therefore to be implicitly received, and what was man's, and might therefore be disregarded or criticised? And if the one of these would be a far greater boon than the other, and manifestly much better fitted to serve the purpose of being an authentic and satisfactory conveyance of a divine revelation, what certain ground can we have *a priori* for the assertion that God has *not* bestowed it upon us? There are many things which, though not coming under the head of matters of pure revelation—i.e., things such that men could have known nothing about them unless God had supernaturally revealed them, and predictions of future events, which it much concerns us to know, and to know accurately, and from which, in point of fact, believing them to be given by inspiration of God, his people do derive important spiritual advantages, and which the authors of the books of Scripture could not have correctly recorded and transmitted to us unless under the guidance and direction of God. What reliance, for instance, could be placed upon an account of the creation of the world, and the important transactions connected with the origin of our race, by a man who lived 2500 years after they had taken place, unless God had directed him? How would men unaided have produced a history of God's mighty deeds, and of his wonderful works, representing God as he ought to be represented, and as he might wish to make himself known to us in the history of providence, and in regard even to the life, actions, and especially the discourses of our Saviour? How could even his apostles, who had seen and heard them, have given a correct and authentic account of them such as we could rely on, unless they had the guidance of the Holy Spirit, according to their Master's promise, to bring things to their remembrance, and to guide them into all truth? Upon such grounds as these, which might be easily drawn out and illustrated, we prove that the allegation of there being no necessity for such divine guidance throughout as is contended for, and no essential benefit, even were we warranted to make our own views upon these points the ground of our judgment, as we are not, is utterly unfounded, and that we can discern plain traces of God's wisdom and goodness in guiding and superintending, even in matters of which they might have had *some* knowledge without revelation and inspiration, the authors of those books from which men in all subsequent ages were to derive the knowledge of himself, and of the way of salvation. But we must remind you that these considerations afford only an answer to an objection of opponents based upon the alleged non-necessity of any further interposition of divine agency in the production of the books of Scripture than what they admit, and that the proper direct proof of the interposition of divine agency to a much larger extent in this matter is to be found in those arguments which we formerly adverted to under the heads of the external and internal evidences of the divine origin and authority of the Bible. These arguments, derived from the explicit declarations of our Lord and his apostles regarding the Old Testament, from the commission and gifts of the authors of the books of the New Testament, and the circumstances in which, and the objects for which, they were written, and, from the evidences of God's presence and agency which pervade the Bible itself, prove, if they prove anything, that God's agency was so exerted in the production of the Bible, as a whole, that it may be fairly and truly called His word, as coming from him, and stamped throughout with his authority.

Some of those who profess to hold the divine origin and authority of the Bible go farther than those we have just described, and say that everything in the Bible which respects matters of religion and morality is to be regarded as coming from God, written under his guidance and direction, while they are disposed to think that in other matters, not affecting, as they imagine, religion and morality, the writers were left to the exercise of their own faculties, without any special or supernatural divine assistance. This mode of stating the doctrine may be so explained as to be practically as loose and unsatisfactory as the former, although it must be admitted that many authors who have adopted this mode of stating the subject, seem to have intended to allow a larger measure of divine agency in the production of the books of

Scripture than those formerly referred to. The same considerations in substance apply to this view of the subject as to the former. This limitation of God's agency in the production of the books of Scripture has no firm foundation to rest upon. It is but an unwarranted and arbitrary supposition, resting only upon certain ill-founded and presumptuous notions of what was necessary, in order to make a full and perfect revelation of God's will, of what God might have been expected to communicate to men supernaturally, and of what men might have produced without any special assistance from him. It assumes, moreover, that there are things in the Bible which can scarcely be supposed to have come from God, as being unworthy of him and beneath his regard; and more especially as having no connection with religion and morality, and being in no degree fitted to promote or increase our knowledge of God, of his plans and his providence, of the way of salvation, of the worship and homage which are due to him, and of the path of duty.

Many men who are for restricting the agency of God in the production of the Scriptures to what they call matters of religion and morality, would probably shrink from laying down distinctly the positions which have now been stated. But it is quite plain that their theory implies or assumes them, and therefore they should be compelled to take the responsibility of openly asserting and maintaining them. And in discussing these positions we need not be afraid to meet them, for we can easily shew, not only that no proof can be adduced in support of them, though that is enough, but that they can be proved to be unfounded and untrue, inconsistent with right views of what we actually find in the Bible, and with what we learn from Scripture itself concerning the books both of the Old and the New Testaments. If we were to indulge in any *a priori* reasonings upon such a subject, though this is a very unsafe and uncertain ground to occupy, we would be inclined to say that the wisdom and goodness of God would lead him to provide that the book, in the production of which he was immediately and supernaturally concerned, and which was designed by him to be the permanent and the only channel through which his revelation of himself was to be conveyed to the human race,—and all this is admitted by those with whom we are at present contending,—should be all produced under his own immediate superintendence, that it should contain nothing which did not bear more or less directly upon the great object for which a revelation was given, i.e., upon matters of religion and morality, and that men would not be left to decide by their own feeble reason as to what things in the book came from God, and were therefore to be applied for increasing their knowledge and guiding them in the path of duty, and what came from men, and were fitted to serve no such end.

There is still a third and higher view upon this subject, held by some who maintain the divine origin and authority of the Bible, but who do not go the whole length of holding its plenary and verbal inspiration. Their view may be stated in this way, that God superintended and directed by his special and immediate agency the whole of what we find recorded in the Bible as to its matter or substance, but not as to the words in which it is set forth. They admit indeed that there are some portions of the Scriptures where the words as well as the matter must have been communicated by divine inspiration. They think, however, that this was not always necessary, and was not always granted; but that in regard to many things contained in the Scriptures the authors were left to select the words in the exercise of their own natural faculties. They have devised accordingly a variety of modes or degrees of inspiration, called commonly by the names of the inspiration of *elevation*, the inspiration of *superintendence* or *direction*, and the inspiration of *suggestion*; or by some such names of similar import.

They think that one kind or degree of inspiration might be necessary for the production of one part of the Bible, that a higher degree might be necessary for producing another portion of it, while a lower might be sufficient for a third; and they are very careful and anxious to admit no higher kind or degree of inspiration in any part of the Bible than they are pleased in their wisdom to think absolutely necessary. The distinction between an inspiration of the matter and an inspiration of the words has no foundation in any of the statements of Scripture. The different kinds and degrees of inspiration which have been laid down and described are mere devices of human wisdom, to which God has given no countenance. The basis and foundation on which they principally rest is just the same as that of the other defective and erroneous views upon this subject to which we have already adverted, viz., an *a priori* resolution to admit no more of divine agency in the matter than is absolutely necessary, combined with certain unwarranted notions as to what kind and degree of divine agency or of inspiration may be necessary for producing the intended result; although at the same time it is but right to mention that they usually profess and attempt to shew that a distinction between the inspiration of the matter and of the words, and the supposition of different kinds and degrees of inspiration are, if not supported by the explicit statements of Scripture, yet suggested and sanctioned by the actual phenomena which the Scripture presents, and afford materials for solving some difficulties connected with the subject of God's agency and man's agency in the production of the books of Scripture, which they think cannot otherwise be easily disposed of. We have now conducted you to the borders of what we believe to be the truth upon this subject, the doctrine of the plenary and verbal inspiration of the Scriptures, and this, upon grounds formerly explained, we mean to treat distinctly and separately under the head of inspiration, as distinguished from the more indefinite and general subject of the divine origin and authority of the Bible.

The observations which have been made in this lecture upon the different views entertained by men who profess to believe in some sense in the divine origin and authority of the Scriptures have been laid before you, not so much because of their intrinsic importance, and not with the view of fully discussing them, but rather for the purpose (which I desire habitually to aim at) of aiding you in your own study of the subject by the perusal of works in which these topics are handled; and you may perhaps find them useful to assist you in understanding, estimating, and appreciating the works you may have occasion to peruse upon this subject. We formerly had occasion to warn you against the loose and erroneous views of the inspiration of the Scriptures which are to be found in many able and standard works upon the evidences, and the same warning must be extended to many valuable works upon the divine origin and authority of the Bible, as distinguished from the truth of the Christian revelation, and to many which profess to discuss the subject of inspiration. You will find that not a few works which profess to treat of the subject of inspiration, and to maintain the divine origin and authority of the Bible, support one or other of the different modifications of sentiment which have been explained in the preceding part of this lecture, that few of them comparatively maintain the plenary verbal inspiration of the Scriptures, while many of them argue against it. They are valuable and useful in their own place, and for their own proper object, just as those works are which establish the external miraculous and historical evidence for the truth of Christianity. But they are not in general satisfactory discussions of the inspiration of Scripture, though they sometimes profess to establish its inspiration; and it is right therefore that you should be warned against their defects and errors upon this important subject. You will find in many of them good and important matter in proof of the divine origin and authority of the Scriptures, in the sense, or rather in some one or other of the senses, in which we have just explained this subject, and *that* you may use and improve for its proper purpose without being led astray by their defective and erroneous views upon the subject of inspiration.

With these observations I would now briefly advert to some of the principal works which have been written upon the subject of the divine origin and authority of the Bible, and which embody some discussion of the nature and extent of God's agency in the production of it, as distinguished from the general truth of Christianity. In the year 1690 there was published in this country a work, entitled *Five Letters concerning the Inspiration of the Holy Scriptures, translated out of the French* [London]. These letters were taken from two works published anonymously, but written by the celebrated Le Clerc, and entitled *Sentiments of some Divines of Holland on Father Simon's Critical History of the Old Testament; and Defence of these Sentiments.*[4] Le Clerc was a man of very loose latitudinarian views upon all theological subjects, and by the boldness and presumption of his speculations contributed, along with Spinoza and the English deists, to lay the foundations of German neology. These letters excited a good deal of notice, and occasioned some controversy. The views which they advocated were just in substance those which we have described in the first part of this lecture, as differing very little from the Socinian view which denies inspiration altogether. The letters are characterised by considerable ingenuity; and, in order to vindicate himself from the charge of being an infidel, Le Clerc has introduced what must be admitted to be a good statement of the substance of the evidence for the general truth of the Christian revelation, as distinguished from the inspiration and divine authority of the Bible. The chief authors whom Le Clerc quotes in support of his views are Erasmus, Grotius, and Episcopius; and though it cannot be proved that they went so far as he did, yet they certainly gave too much countenance to his theory. A reply to Le Clerc was published by Lowth, the author of a well-known and in many respects valuable commentary upon the prophets, and father of the still more celebrated Bishop Lowth. It is entitled *A Vindication of the Divine Authority and Inspiration of the Writings of the Old and New Testament;*[5] and while it contains some good and useful things in answer to the lower views of Le Clerc, it advocates the theory that the inspiration of the sacred writers was confined to matters of religion and morality, and that in other matters they were left to themselves, and sometimes fell into mistakes. Another reply was made to Le Clerc by Lamotte, which I have not seen, but which is said to be a better and abler book than Lowth's. Several other works were published soon after, which, though not intended merely as answers to Le Clerc, opposed his principles, and advocated much sounder though still somewhat defective views of the inspiration and divine authority of the Scriptures. The principal of these were Bishop Williams' *Boyle Lectures*, and two works upon the subject of inspiration by eminent dissenting ministers, Dr. Edmund Calamy and Mr. Benjamin Bennet. These are all valuable works, and contain much important matter. Their authors carry their views of the nature and extent of inspiration much farther than

4. Jean Le Clerc, *Sentimens de quelques théologiens de Hollande sur l'Histoire critique du Vieux Testament, composé par le P. Richard Simon de l'Oratoire. Où en remarquant les fautes de cet Auteur, on donne divers principes utiles pour l'intelligence de l'Ecriture Sainte* (Amsterdam: Henri Desbordes, 1685); and Jean Le Clerc, *Défense des sentimens de quelques théologiens de Hollande sur l'Histoire critique du Vieux Testament: Contre la réponse du prieur de Bolleville* (Amsterdam: Henry Desbordes, 1686).

5. William Lowth, *A Vindication of the Divine Authority and Inspiration of the Writings of the Old and New Testament* (Oxford: At the Theater, 1692).

Lowth, and approach much nearer the truth. None of them formally discusses the question of the verbal inspiration of the Scriptures. They rather leave it out, or pass it, intimating however their opinion that it is not necessary to take up that position, while yet they sometimes make statements so full and sound that consistency would seem to require of them that the verbal inspiration of Scripture should be admitted. The fullest and best of these works is Calamy's, entitled *The Inspiration of the Holy Writings of the Old and New Testament considered and improved*, published in 1710;[6] and his views are, upon the whole, so sound that there is little or nothing to object to, except that he has not asserted and defended the plenary verbal inspiration.

The next two works of any considerable importance that treat of this subject are to be found in well-known commentaries upon the New Testament, viz., Whitby's general "Preface" to his *Paraphrase and Commentary upon the New Testament*,[7] and Doddridge's *Dissertation on the Inspiration of the New Testament*,[8] subjoined to the historical books, in his *Family Expositor*. Both of these works contain able and satisfactory defences of the divine authority, and, in a certain sense, inspiration of the New Testament; but they both deny, and argue against, its plenary verbal inspiration, and they both vindicate those different kinds and degrees of inspiration which the wisdom of man has invented and set forth as sufficient for the production of some parts of the Bible, and as superseding the necessity of ascribing it all to God and the agency of his Spirit.

The only other work to which I think it necessary at present to refer is the late Dr. Dick's *Essay on The Inspiration of the Holy Scriptures*.[9] It is a highly respectable work, and contains much sound and judicious matter; but you will be certainly disappointed if you expect to find in it, what its title seems to promise, a discussion of the subject of inspiration. It is substantially a book upon the evidences of Christianity, including in a general sense the divine origin of the Scriptures, without any investigation of the higher and more specific questions usually comprehended under the head of inspiration. The arguments for the general truth of Christianity and for the divine authority of the Scriptures are mixed up together in a way that is somewhat confused and perplexing; and on the subject of the verbal inspiration of the Scriptures, it gives a somewhat uncertain sound, though the author seems, upon the whole, to be rather unfavourable to what we believe to be the true principle upon that point.

The works which have been mentioned treat rather of the divine origin and authority of the Bible than of its inspiration in its stricter and higher sense. Those which treat more fully and formally of the nature and extent of inspiration will be mentioned when we come to discuss that subject. Before proceeding however to treat of the subject of inspiration in its higher and more restricted sense, we must complete the subject of the evidences by some examination of the subject of the agency and witness of the Spirit in convincing men that the Holy Scripture is the word of God, in illustration of the doctrine which we quoted in last lecture from the fifth section of the first chapter of the Confession of Faith, in opposition to those who deny that any divine testimony is necessary, and to the Papists, who substitute the testimony of the church for the witness of the Holy Ghost.

---

6. Edmund Calamy, *The Inspiration of the Holy Writings of the Old and New Testament Considered and Improved* (London: T. Parkhurst, 1710).

7. Daniel Whitby, *A Paraphrase and Commentary on the New Testament: In Two Volumes* (London: J. Brotherton, 1744).

8. Philip Doddridge, *Dissertation on the Inspiration of the New Testament* (London: T. Longman, 1793).

9. John Dick, *An Essay on the Inspiration of the Holy Scriptures* (Glasgow: Steven & Frazer, 1813).

LECTURE XXIV: DIFFICULTIES IN GENERAL—RATIONAL AND SPIRITUAL EVIDENCE— TESTIMONY OF THE SPIRIT—ROMISH SCEPTICISM

The evidence, external and internal, by which we prove the truth of Christianity and the divine origin and authority of the Bible, is in right reason quite sufficient to establish them. They can be proved conclusively upon grounds and principles which assume nothing that men in the sound exercise of their faculties could deny or disprove. As a mere question of argument upon rational principles, the proof is complete; so that wherever we meet with men who deny the truth of Christianity and the divine origin of the Bible, whatever may be their character, and whatever grounds they may take up, we can rationally establish them upon evidence which they cannot answer, and to which in right reason they ought to yield. Objections and difficulties indeed of various degrees of strength or plausibility have been adduced against all the different departments of the Christian evidence, but most of these have been directly and conclusively answered. And if there are any which do not admit of being fully and directly answered, they are such as respect not the evidence but the contents of revelation, and therefore general answers, derived from the unanswerableness of the proper evidence, from the exalted character of the subject, the ignorance of man, and the weakness of human reason, are, upon sound and generally recognised principles, sufficient to dispose of them. They are mere difficulties, and are neither refutations of the positive proofs, nor proofs of a negative, upon the great general question. It is utterly inconsistent with the principles recognised and acted upon in regard to every other branch of knowledge, that mere difficulties, even though they were much more numerous and formidable than any which attach to the evidence for the truth of Christianity and the Bible, should prevent the submission of the understanding to proof which cannot be overturned, even though it only preponderated over what could be adduced upon the other side. The difficulties which attach more or less to all truths not comprehended within the limits of the exact sciences, and which ingenuity may invest with some plausibility, are virtually tests of men's character, i.e., of their honest love of truth, of their being more ready to seek truth and to follow rational evidence wherever it may lead them, than to indulge any selfish feeling, or to pursue any personal objects of their own. This principle applies more fully to the investigation of the truth of Christianity and the Bible than to any other subject whatever, just because the admission or denial of it bears much more directly and extensively upon character and motive than any other. But the principle holds more or less in the investigation of all moral questions. The difficulties and objections that may be adduced, although of no real or rational weight in opposition to the proofs on the other side, afford a sort of plausible excuse for men taking either side they like, and thus contribute to make their decision the result, not so much of an impartial investigation of the evidence, as of some other collateral motives or objects that may have influenced them. This is virtually the principle that is involved in our Saviour's remarkable declaration to Thomas, "Thomas, because thou hast seen me thou hast believed; blessed are they that have not seen, and yet have believed" (John 20:29). Thomas had previously sufficient and conclusive evidence that Christ had risen from the dead, in the testimony of

529

his fellow-apostles assuring him that they had "seen the Lord." On this ground he ought to have believed it; and it was neither a virtuous nor a rational state of mind which led him to declare that he would not believe unless he were permitted to put his finger into the print of the nails, and to thrust his hand into Christ's side. His Master was pleased to grant him the evidence he demanded, although it was unnecessary in sound reason, and although he had no right to it. But he at the same time gently reproached Thomas for his unreasonable conduct, and intimated plainly that to have believed in the reality of his resurrection upon evidence inferior to that which he had just enjoyed, but yet quite sufficient in itself, would have indicated at once a more rational use of his faculties, and a sounder and more creditable state of heart. There is nothing in our Saviour's declaration which encourages or demands credulity in regard to his claims. It assumes indeed that Thomas had had, and that others would have, sufficient evidence of his resurrection from the dead, without having the evidence of their senses in support of it; and it implies that those who believed in such circumstances would act a more rational and becoming part than he, whose unwillingness to believe, in whatever precise cause it may have originated, had been overcome only by evidence which no unwillingness to believe, and no strength of motive drawing him in an opposite direction could, according to the ordinary principles of man's constitution, have enabled him to resist. This is substantially what is involved in our Saviour's declaration, and it can be proved to be entirely accordant with the dictates of sound philosophy, and the voice of universal experience.

We do not require indeed to have recourse to any such general considerations in actually dealing with unbelievers. Our business in dealing with them is to set before them the proof, the sufficient and satisfactory proof, which should lead those who have not seen to believe that Christ rose from the dead, and to answer their objections against its sufficiency and conclusiveness. But it is satisfactory to ourselves to be able to explain, in accordance with the recognised principles of human nature and the ordinary experience of mankind, how it is that, without being able to answer our arguments, men still continue to reject our conclusions. Grotius had certainly nothing fanatical about him; and yet he has distinctly laid down this principle of the actual strength of evidence for the truth of Christianity, viewed as a mere question of argumentation, and of the plausibility of some of the difficulties that may be adduced against it, operating as a test of character; that is, as putting to the test whether or not men are really influenced by an honest desire of ascertaining and following the truth. In the conclusion of his second book, *De Veritate*, in answer to the allegation that Christianity, if true, should have been more conclusively established by evidence, he makes the following statement upon this subject:

> Voluit autem Deus id, quod credi à nobis vellet . . . non ita evidenter patere, ut quæ sensu aut demonstratione percipiuntur; sed quantum satis esset ad fidem faciendam, remque persuadendam homini non pertinaci; ut ita sermo Evangelii tanquam lapis esset Lydius, ad quem ingenia sanabilia explorarentur. Nam cum ea, quæ diximus, argumenta tam multos probos, eosdemque sapientes in assensum traxerint; hoc ipso liquet, apud cæteros incredulitatis causam non in probationis penuria esse positam, sed in eo, quod nolint verum videri id quod affectibus suis adversatur.[10]

---

10. Hugo Grotius, *De veritate religionis christianae,* ed. Joannes Clericus (Amstelaedami: Apud Franciscum vander Plaats, 1709), 143–44; Hugo Grotius, *The Truth of Christian Religion: In Six Books,* trans. Symon Patrick (London: J. L. for

As we are called upon to be ever ready to give a reason of the hope that is in us, it is our duty to be able to give some explanation of the grounds on which we believe in the truth of Christianity and in the divine origin of the Bible. And it is incumbent upon us to be able to establish them, both for the conviction of gainsayers and the confirmation of believers. All argumentation must be deduced, in some sense, *ex concessis* [by way of concession], from principles conceded or admitted by those with whom we argue, however far back it may sometimes be necessary to go in order to find them; and when we are seeking to explain the grounds by which the truth of Christianity and the divine origin of the Bible may be established for the satisfaction of our own minds, the confirmation of our own faith, or for the confirmation of believers who may have been assaulted with temptations to infidelity, there are considerations which may be adduced, and which may possess real argumentative weight, which would have no force with an unbeliever, just because not based upon principles which he admitted, or could in the first instance, and without some intermediate stages in the argument, and in its impression upon his mind, be required in strict logic to admit. These branches of argument, however, by which we ourselves might be satisfied of the divine origin and authority of the Bible, but which did not admit of being brought to bear upon unbelievers, so as in strict logic to compel their assent, are derived exclusively from two sources—first, from the self-evidencing power of the Bible, or those marks and traces of divine origin and authority which are impressed upon the Bible itself, and which are opened up to the mind in the course of a devout and prayerful study of it; and second, from those effects which the doctrines of Christianity and the statements of the Bible have produced upon our minds and hearts, our character and conduct, in changing our natures, and in leading us to live to God's glory and service. Now, these things apply only to those who have not merely been persuaded that the Bible is the word of God, but who have come into contact with the revelation itself, and submitted their understandings and hearts to its influence, who have been born again of the word of God through the belief of the truth. And this we know, in point of fact, is never done except through the operation and under the influence of God's Spirit. And hence some have distinguished these two departments of evidence, viz., that by which unbelievers may be and should be convinced, and that by which, though it does not admit of the same direct bearing upon unbelievers, may be applied in confirming our own faith, by the names of the *rational* and the *spiritual* evidences. The nomenclature is not very correct, and it is fitted to convey erroneous impressions, and this in two ways:—

1. It seems to imply that the spiritual evidence is not rational; whereas, though seen and felt only by those who have been brought by the operation of the Spirit under the influence of the regenerating and sanctifying force of the truth, and therefore not admitting of being brought to bear fully upon those who have not been the subjects of this operation, it is to those who have it a perfectly rational ground of belief, with which their understandings may be and should be fully satisfied. It is not a fanatical delusion, a vague and mystical

---

Luke Meredith, 1694), 77–78: "And indeed it is the pleasure of *Almighty* God, that those things which he would have us to *believe* . . . should not so evidently *appear,* as those things which are apprehended by *sense* and plain *demonstration,* but only be so far forth *revealed* as may beget *faith,* and a persuasion thereof in the hearts and minds of such as are not *obstinate:* That so the word of the *Gospel* may be as a *touchstone,* whereby Men's dispositions may be tried whether they be curable or not. For seeing these *arguments,* whereof we have spoken, have induced so many honest, godly, and wise Men to approve of this *Religion,* it is thereby plain enough that the fault of other Men's *infidelity* is not for want of sufficient *testimony,* but because they would not have *that* to be had and embraced for *truth,* which is contrary to their affections and desires."

impression, but an argument which can be fully vindicated in accordance with the principles of man's constitution. That some of the materials upon which it rests are derived from our own individual consciousness, and therefore cannot be fully established to the satisfaction of others, who are not bound to believe our testimony upon this point, does not affect its proper intrinsic validity to those who, by their own consciousness, are possessed of these materials. To say that men's consciousness of what they have been enabled mentally to discern and experience may deceive them is true, but not to the purpose; for this is nothing more than may be said of all the powers and capacities by which men acquire knowledge and form judgments. All men's faculties may sometimes deceive them; but this is never regarded—except by mere sceptics, who are beyond the reach of argument—as any reason for denying the possibility of acquiring certain knowledge, or for calling upon men to place no reliance upon the ordinary operations of their faculties.

2. This distinction between the rational and the spiritual evidences may seem to imply a notion which is in some respects the reverse of that which we have just exposed, but which is equally erroneous, viz., that the Spirit does not employ what is comprehended under the head of the rational evidence in producing faith in the divine origin and authority of the Scriptures. Whatever is in right reason a proof of the divine origin and authority of the Scriptures, whatever upon the principles of sound logic possesses real argumentative weight to establish the conclusion, may be employed by the Spirit for producing that faith which is his gift; that is, may be employed by the Spirit for deepening and confirming those convictions which in its own nature, and in virtue of its argumentative weight, it is fitted to produce. For it may be laid down as a general principle that there is no truth connected with religion which the Holy Spirit may not, and does not, as he sees meet, impress upon men's minds; and there is no sound argument that really goes to establish or confirm the truth, which he may not employ for producing conviction. What then has sometimes been called the spiritual evidence is also rational, though it may not be directly available for convincing unbelievers; and what has been called rational is spiritual, at least in this sense, that it may be and has been employed by the Spirit for producing conviction.

The proper deduction to be noticed and preserved upon this subject are these two—First, that the one department of evidence is fitted to convince unbelievers, resting upon principles which they cannot dispute without overturning the certainty of all human knowledge, and conducting by a process of argument which they cannot at any point answer, or overturn, or evade, to the conclusion that Christ was a teacher sent from God, and that the Scriptures came from God; and that the other is directly fitted only to confirm the faith of those whose eyes have already been opened to behold the wondrous things contained in God's law, and who have been born again of the word of God through the belief of the truth. The second distinction is this, that the evidence of the one class may be understood and perceived, and that the conclusion to which it leads may be admitted, without men having enjoyed the Spirit's teaching, or having become the subjects of his operations; while the materials on which the other is based partly are not seen, and partly do not exist, until the Spirit of God has been sent forth into men's hearts, and has produced there some of his leading peculiar results. Whatever difficulty there may be in explaining, or even in describing, the character and conduct of men who profess to be convinced of the truth of Christianity and the divine origin and authority of the Bible, but who yet have never examined the Christian revelation with attention and seriousness, and are manifestly not affected in their character and conduct by the contents of that revelation, we are not entitled to deny that such men, if they have examined the evidences, if they profess themselves convinced of their sufficiency, and are able and willing to give a satisfactory explanation of the grounds of their convictions, and to defend them against the objections of adversaries—are in some sense honestly persuaded of the truth of the revelation, though it may be abundantly evident that their conduct is marked by great inconsistency, and that they have never enjoyed the teaching of the Spirit. They have examined the question of the truth of Christianity just as they would have examined a question in any other department of knowledge, and perhaps just in some measure *because* of their entire carelessness and indifference about the contents of the revelation, and their utter want of any sense of the obligation which an admission of its truth imposes, have come to the conclusion that there is sufficient ground to believe in its divine original. There is sufficient evidence to convince unbelievers of this as a mere question of argument; and it is quite possible that men in the fair use of their faculties, without any special divine assistance, and without any operation of the divine Spirit, may come to this conclusion, and assert and maintain it. They have the whole of the external evidence to deal with. It is perfectly comprehensible by them. It may be understood by them in all its branches; and its force and conclusiveness, as a mere piece of argumentation, may be seen and apprehended. A portion of what is usually comprehended under the head of the internal evidence is also fully subject to their cognizance, and may be apprehended and appreciated by them; we mean everything about the general character and the particular features of the Christian revelation and the sacred Scriptures, which goes directly to establish this proposition, that they could not have been invented and devised by men, especially by men so circumstanced as those from whom the Christian revelation, and the books which contain it, proceeded. This is a proposition which, from its very nature, comes within the cognizance of man's ordinary faculties and capacities of judging; and materials sufficient to establish it may be pointed out in the Christian revelation, and in the New Testament, the perception and appreciation of which do not necessarily require or imply that thorough, intimate, efficacious knowledge of divine truth which proceeds only from the Spirit of God. If we take the word *experimental* in the wide sense which it may not unwarrantably bear, and in which we formerly explained it, as comprehending every argument for the truth of Christianity derived from the reception it has met with, and the effects it has produced upon men collectively and individually, then there is something too under this head, as well as under that of the internal evidence, which may be addressed to unbelievers, which can be logically commended to their understandings, and which may and should operate rationally in leading them to the conviction that Christianity and the Bible came from God, without any special operations of the Holy Spirit, or without requiring the admission or application of any of those materials which his agency alone can provide; especially the arguments derived from the propagation of Christianity, and the general effects which Christianity and the Bible have actually produced upon the state of the world wherever they have been known and received. Thus the whole of the external and a portion of the internal and experimental evidence for the truth of Christianity and the divine origin of the Bible may be addressed to unbelievers; may be established to their satisfaction as a mere question of argument; may, upon the principles of sound reasoning and strict logic, be commended to their understandings, and may produce such a conviction in their minds as in consistency and common sense should lead them to a diligent, serious, and prayerful study of the Bible.

And all this class of arguments, sometimes, as we have said, called the rational evidence, may be used by believers, and may be employed by the Spirit, for confirming them in their most holy faith; while they enjoy also, for their confirmation and encouragement, and to aid them in resisting any temptations to infidelity with which they may be assailed, other arguments coming under the head of the internal and experimental evidence, the materials of which exist partly in the revelation itself and the sacred books which contain it, and partly in their own hearts, but for which, both in their existence and in their application and effect, they are wholly indebted to, and dependent upon, the agency of the Holy Spirit.

It is right that we should understand and appreciate the entire sufficiency and conclusiveness of the evidence by which, upon rational principles, requiring no spiritual discernment, no supernatural opening of the eyes, no radical change of men's moral principles, no immediate agency of the Spirit of God, we can bring home to unbelievers, as a mere question of argument, the truth of the proposition that Christianity and the Bible came from God; by which we can logically compel them to admit this, or to stand self-condemned by their manifest refusal to give their fair rational weight to arguments which they cannot answer, and to follow out principles which they cannot deny without overturning the certainty of all human knowledge, and by which, in regard to other departments of knowledge, they themselves are guided. It is thus that we stop the mouths of gainsayers, and establish against every opponent, and upon rational principles, the thoroughly rational character of our belief in the divine origin of Christianity and the Bible, and can bring home to all with whom we may come into contact, whatever ground they may choose to assume in this matter—unless indeed they take refuge in absolute scepticism, and deny that men can know anything—an obligation to admit the truth of the Christian revelation, and a consequent obligation to receive and submit to it as coming from God.

The other departments of proof, which cannot be brought to bear directly upon unbelievers, as not being based upon principles which, while unbelievers, and as such, they can be logically required to admit, but which are well fitted to confirm the faith of those who have submitted to the truth and have been brought under the agency of the Spirit, are the self-evidencing power of the Bible, coming under the head of the internal evidence, and the effects which Christianity and the Bible have produced upon their own heart and character, coming under the head of the experimental evidence, and constituting indeed what is usually known under that name. Before proceeding to advert more particularly to the agency of the Spirit in this matter, it is proper to mention that, though arguments of this sort do not possess probative power to unbelievers who openly deny the divine origin of Christianity and the Bible, so that they can be compelled, as a matter of argumentation, to admit their soundness, and to submit to their force, or at least to be silent, yet it is most commonly by considerations derived from these sources that unbelievers are in fact converted. Few men who have been led openly to deny the truth of Christianity, and to contend against the force of the arguments by which it is usually commended to the understandings of infidels, have been persuaded of the truth of Christianity and the divine origin of the Bible, by those arguments by which they ought, in right reason and in sound logic, to have been convinced of this. When such persons have been converted, it has been most commonly through the preaching of the gospel, that is, the exposition of the substance and leading features of the Christian revelation, or the reading of the Scriptures, even when previously they did not believe the gospel or the Bible to have come from God. And of course their conversion must have been effected by the Spirit's enabling them to see something of the self-evidencing power of the gospel and the Bible, and satisfying them of their divine origin by the impressions and changes which he himself produced by their instrumentality upon their hearts. When such results take place, then men will soon indeed see the futility of the objections which they may have been accustomed to adduce against the arguments with which they were formerly plied, and be convinced that these arguments are, upon rational grounds, conclusive and unanswerable. But they will soon also see that considerations, which at one time they thought unworthy of serious examination, and fit only to be treated with ridicule, are possessed of a weight and influence well fitted to secure to them at once respect and success. The practical inference to be deduced from this fact—for it is a fact, established by abundant experience—is, that even in dealing with open deniers of the truth of Christianity and the Bible, we should not omit, as means that may be useful, the preaching of the gospel and the reading of the Bible, if they can be prevailed upon to listen.

In that part of the fifth section of the first chapter of the Confession of Faith, which I formerly explained and illustrated, several considerations on which I briefly commented (and which rank partly under the external, though chiefly under the internal evidence), are declared to be "arguments whereby the Holy Scripture doth abundantly evidence itself to be the word of God"; and then the Confession goes on to say, "Yet notwithstanding, our full persuasion and assurance of the infallible truth and divine authority thereof is from the inward work of the Holy Spirit, bearing witness by and with the word in our hearts." The particulars specified in the preceding part of the section, and described as being "arguments whereby the Holy Scripture doth abundantly evidence itself to be the word of God," are all, as I formerly explained to you, such as may be in some measure understood and apprehended even by men who have not been brought under the power of the truth or the influence of the Spirit. Even to these then there are considerations to be found in and to be derived from the Scripture itself, whereby it may be abundantly evidenced to be the word of God. This implies that there are materials for bringing home to them, even without the agency of the Spirit, a conviction to which they ought to yield, and which ought to produce some practical results. And the substance of what is set forth in the clause we are now considering is this, that there is a firmer conviction, a more thorough persuasion of the truth and divine authority of the Scriptures than any which mere arguments as such can produce; that this is to be ascribed to the agency of the Spirit; and that the Spirit produces it in men's hearts through the instrumentality of the word itself. This is a doctrine which can be learned only from the Scriptures, and can be proved only by arguments taken from that source. Its truth can be fully established from the statements of the Bible. But I refer to it at present chiefly for the purpose of giving you a brief statement of some discussions that have taken place with respect to the witness or testimony of the Spirit in connection with the establishment of the divine authority of the Scriptures, and the grounds of our certain persuasion or assured conviction that they are the word of God. The discussions which have taken place upon this subject are of a somewhat intricate and subtle description, and have not always been conducted with sufficient care and perspicuity, even by those whose views were in the main correct. This subject entered largely into the discussions which took place between the Protestants and the Church of Rome at the era of the Reformation; and in some of its aspects it has been discussed also between orthodox and evangelical Protestants and some of the Latitudinarian, or, as they commonly call themselves, rational defenders of Christianity. It has always been one leading artifice of the Church of Rome in controversy, and one by which she has succeeded in deluding and deceiving many, to represent any other system but her own as attended with great doubts and uncertainties, as affording no firm and stable basis on which man's faith and hope may rest; that thus she may shut them up into the authority of an infallible church, which is alleged to enjoy the certain presence and the unerring guidance of the Holy Spirit. The leading questions which she has started with this view, and which she has laboured to involve in as much darkness and obscurity as she could, are these three—1. How can men know with certainty that the Scriptures are the word of God? 2. How can men know with certainty what is the meaning of the statements of Scripture, or be assured that the meaning which they may attach to them is correct? 3. How can men attain to any comfortable assurance that they individually are in a safe state, and may look forward with confidence to heaven as their rest?

The Church of Rome has laboured hard to prove that none of these questions can be satisfactorily answered; that nothing like certainty or assurance can be attained in regard to any of the subjects to which they refer, except by admitting the infallibility of the church and submitting to her guidance. And in discussing these various points, and endeavouring to establish a ground of certainty in regard to them, the Reformers, and indeed evangelical Protestants in general, have given much prominence to the witness or testimony of the Holy Spirit. In regard to the last of these questions, respecting the assurance of personal salvation, it does not come at all within the class of subjects that for the present must occupy our attention. We would only remark in passing, since we have been led to mention it, that it was in consequence of the labours of Romish writers to shew that there could be no certain ground for personal assurance of salvation except in the authority of the church; that there was inserted in what is commonly called *The National Covenant of Scotland* [1638][11] a condemnation of what is described as "the general and doubtsome faith of the Romish Church"; and that the authors of the Westminster Confession, after asserting that believers may in this life be certainly assured that they are in the state of grace, added, "This certainty is not a bare conjectural and probable persuasion founded upon a fallible hope, but an infallible assurance of faith" (WCF 18.2). We may also observe that it was the anxiety of the Reformers to establish a firm ground of personal assurance in opposition to the labours of Papists to overturn every other ground except that miserable one which they hold out to their deluded votaries, and which has sunk millions to hell with a lie in their right hand, that led some of them to fall into the error of representing assurance as of the essence, and to include it in their formal definition of saving faith; an error which has been carefully corrected in the Westminster Confession.

The second of these questions, about the grounds of the certainty of our knowledge of the true meaning of Scripture, we shall have occasion to advert to in a subsequent part of the course, when we have to explain the general principles bearing upon the ascertaining and establishing of the true import of the word of God. It is with the first of these questions only that we have at present to do. But the further prosecution of this subject must be deferred till next lecture.

11. Ed. note: See Part II, chap. 14 above.

LECTURE XXV: TESTIMONY OF THE SPIRIT, FOLLOWING THE CONFESSION OF FAITH

The general subject which I brought under your notice in last lecture, and mean to prosecute in this, is usually discussed by the older divines under the head of the authority of the Holy Scripture, and may be said to comprehend a discussion of the causes, grounds, and reasons of our faith, or firm and assured persuasion of the divine origin and authority of the Bible. The authority of the Scripture is its right to command, to exercise sovereign control, to be received and employed as the supreme and ultimate standard of our opinions and actions. If it has any such right or authority, this must come from God, who alone is Lord of the conscience; and hence the Confession of Faith says, in the fourth section of the first chapter, the one just preceding that to which I have already adverted, and mean again to advert to more fully, "The authority of Holy Scripture, for which it ought to be believed and obeyed, depends not upon the testimony of any man or church, but wholly upon God (who is truth itself), the author thereof, and therefore it is to be received because it is the word of God." This seems a very evident, almost a self-evident principle; and yet, like almost all the other statements in the Confession, it is a deliverance upon a point of controversy, a denial of an error that has been broached. The error that is here denied is one that was maintained by some of the bolder and less scrupulous Papists, who, in their anxiety to depress the Scriptures and to magnify the church, asserted that their authority depended upon, or was derived from, the testimony of the church; or, in other words, that the formal ground or reason why we are bound to submit to the authority of the Scriptures, was, not because God was their author, and has given them to us, requiring us by his own authority to believe and obey them, but merely because the church has propounded them to us as authoritative. It was against this error that the declaration just quoted from the Confession was directed. Some, however, of the abler and more cautious Papists saw that this was a principle too offensive and too evidently erroneous to be maintained with plausibility or success, and invented a distinction between the authority of the Scripture, absolutely and relatively, its authority in itself, and its authority in reference to us—*in se* and *quoad nos*—admitting, in accordance with the principle laid down in the Confession, that its authority, absolutely and in itself, depends only on God its author, i.e., is based upon its being God's word, they still maintain that its authority relatively to us depends upon the testimony of the church proclaiming it to be the word of God and authoritative. By this they mean in substance, not that Scripture derives its authority or its binding and obliging powers from the church, but that the testimony of the church is not merely a part of the proof or evidence by which the Scripture may be shewn to be the word of God, but is the basis and foundation of the whole proof, and affords thereby certain arguments by which men can be thoroughly persuaded that the Scripture is of divine origin, and is therefore possessed of infallible authority. In opposition to this doctrine, the Confession lays down the principle which I quoted in last lecture, viz., "yet notwithstanding, our full persuasion and assurance of the infallible truth and divine authority thereof is from the inward work of the Holy Spirit bearing witness by and with the word in our hearts" (WCF 1.5). A statement which may be regarded as embodying these

537

propositions—first, that men, without believing in the infallibility of any man or church, may attain to a full persuasion and assurance of the infallible truth and divine authority of the Holy Scripture—in other words, to a firm and assured faith or conviction that it is the word of God; and second, that this is to be produced by the inward work of the Holy Spirit bearing witness by and with the word in our hearts. When the Papists put the question, as they often do, "How do you know with certainty that the Scripture is the word of God?" their object, as I explained in the end of my last lecture, is to involve the proof of this truth, which they profess to hold as well as we, in as much doubt or uncertainty as possible, in order to shut up men to the testimony of an infallible church as the only sure and certain evidence in support of it. When Protestants have answered this question by referring to the various branches of evidence by which we can and do prove against unbelievers, first, the general truth of the Christian revelation; and then second, the divine origin and authority of the books of Scripture, some Popish writers have grasped at the opportunity thus afforded them of taking up the infidel cause, and have exerted their ingenuity in labouring to shew that these proofs, even as against infidels, are attended with great and almost inextricable difficulties, and that they cannot form the basis or ground of any firm or certain persuasion. And indeed it is very manifest that many Popish writers have been willing enough to help to make men infidels, if they could only withdraw them from the ranks of Protestantism. They have given abundant evidence that they were ready to contribute to overturn the foundations of all faith and all religion, in the hope of catching some of those who might thus be thrown loose; a fact which tends, along with others of a similar kind, to prove that Satan, though he is no doubt well aware that Papacy is his masterpiece, from the singular skill with which it is fitted to secure and retain a powerful ascendancy over the minds of multitudes, does not care much whether men become Papists or infidels.

Other Popish writers, however, having more regard to decency, and admitting that the controversy between them and Protestants upon this point does not turn upon the question whether the Scriptures are the word of God, and can be satisfactorily proved to be so against those who deny it—as the more respectable Popish writers, when dealing with infidels, establish the divine origin and authority of the Bible, very much in the same way as Protestants do—but upon this question whether or not Protestants denying the infallibility of the church, can have any certain and assured ground for the persuasion they entertain that the Scriptures are the word of God, meet the adduction of the ordinary arguments by which this is proved against infidels, by a statement to this effect, that these arguments, though sufficient to stop the mouths of gainsayers, cannot be the ground of a firm and certain persuasion, since they are based only upon the testimony of man, and upon these general rational arguments or motives of credibility which may apply to other subjects of historical investigation, and cannot lay a basis for that firm and unwavering persuasion which faith implies, and which alone can be satisfactory as the ground of procedure in religious matters. The schoolmen were accustomed to make a distinction between what they called human or acquired faith based upon human testimony, and divine or infused faith based upon divine testimony. The Papists applied this distinction to the matter in hand, and asserted that the ordinary rational arguments by which the Scriptures might be proved as against infidels, resolved ultimately into human testimony, and therefore could not be the basis of a divine faith or a full persuasion and assurance; and that the divine testimony which alone could be the basis of a divine faith, and alone therefore could afford a full security and a satisfactory ground for reliance in the conviction that the Scriptures are the word of God, is to be found only in the testimony of the church, which, being infallibly guided by the Holy Spirit, thus brings a divine testimony to bear upon the conclusive settlement of the question, and the thorough establishment of men's convictions. Now, in dealing with this objection of the Papists, the Reformers generally conceded to them, that a divine as distinguished from a human faith was necessary, in order that God's revelation might produce all its proper intended effects, and that men might derive from it all the benefits which it was intended to convey or confer, and moreover, that this divine faith must rest upon a divine testimony; but they contended—first, that the testimony of the church was not a divine testimony, since its claim to infallibility, or to the constant guidance of the Holy Spirit in preserving it from all error, not only could not be established, but could be proved to be utterly unfounded; and second, that believers, though denying the infallibility of the church, had a divine testimony to the infallible truth and authority of the Holy Scripture, in the testimony or witness of the Spirit.

In regard to the first of these topics, the alleged infallibility of the church, we shall have occasion to advert to it when we come to consider its bearing upon the interpretation of Scripture, or the discovery of its true and certain meaning. It is with the second topic we have at present to do. Our faith in the Christian revelation itself, or in the truth of the contents of the Scriptures, may be said in a sense to rest upon a divine testimony, inasmuch as we believe and submit to it only because we are persuaded that it came from God. But the question we are at present considering respects a different point, viz., whether or not, and if so, how, we have or may have a divine testimony *as the basis of a divine faith that it did come from God, that it is his word.* There is some difficulty in forming a clear and definite conception of some of the views that have been propounded in regard to the distinction between a divine and a human faith, as founded respectively upon a divine and a human testimony. Owen and Halyburton have both laboured this distinction in their books upon the reason of faith, but do not, so far as I can see, give any very clear or satisfactory explanation of it, though these works certainly contain a great deal of valuable and excellent matter.[12] What is necessary practically, and without entering into useless speculations upon this subject, is, that men have such a conviction of the divine origin and authority of the sacred Scriptures, resting upon grounds of the validity of which they are satisfied, as frees them from all doubt and anxiety, as is sufficient to preserve them from danger of falling into infidelity; and especially, and above all, as leads them to study aright the Scripture itself, the word of God, and to submit implicitly to its guidance. That no man has ever had such a faith or conviction of the divine origin and authority of the Bible produced in his mind by the means of what are sometimes called the rational evidences by which this can be established against infidels, as in point of fact led him to such a study of the word that he was thereby made wise unto salvation, we know no grounds whatever for asserting. There is nothing either in the constitution of man, or in any information which God has given us, as to his own ordinary procedure in conferring upon men knowledge and salvation, which precludes the possibility of such a result. It is true that when such a man has been brought

---

12. Ed. note: John Owen, *The Reason of Faith* (London, 1677) in William H. Goold, ed. *The Works of John Owen,* vol. 4 (London: Banner of Truth, 1967), 3–115. Thomas Halyburton, *An Essay, Concerning the Nature of Faith: Or, the Ground upon which Faith Assents to the Scriptures* (Albany, NY: H. C. Southwick, 1812). Another work is closely related, Thomas Halyburton, *Faith and Revelation,* Introduction by Joel R. Beeke (Aberdeen: James Begg Society, 2003).

under the influence of the truth itself, he will, under the guidance of the same Spirit who opened his eyes to behold God's glory and to see Christ, discern both in the self-evidencing power of the Bible, and in the effects which its statements have produced upon himself, new and stronger proofs than ever he had before of its divine origin; and if he thought previously that upon the ground of the rational evidences he was secure against the danger of falling into infidelity, he will feel now more clearly and decidedly that it is in a manner impossible, after what he has seen and experienced, that he should ever come to deny or even to doubt that the Bible is the word of God. All this is true; it is realised in the experience of believers, and in these circumstances, they do or may possess a full persuasion and assurance, such as is quite sufficient to fill them with peace and joy, that in walking by the Bible they are following a safe and sure guide which will conduct them at length to heaven and happiness. A fuller persuasion, however, a higher and more perfect assurance of the divine origin and authority of the Bible, does not seem to be what is intended by the distinction between a human and divine faith, by many authors who have treated of this subject. They treat it as a difference in kind, and not in degree; though it is to be observed that the Confession of Faith does not specify anything as to its nature, properly so called, as distinguished from its cause and source, except that it is a full persuasion and assurance. The ascription indeed of this full persuasion and assurance to the inward work of the Holy Spirit implies that the faith or conviction produced by the mere influence of the rational arguments, which may be made good, according to the ordinary principles of men's constitution and the ordinary rules of reasoning, as against unbelievers, does not possess such strength and certainty as to be entitled to be described by these terms. And this is in entire accordance at once with sound philosophy and ordinary experience. Philosophers are accustomed to speak of probable as distinguished from demonstrative evidence, and indeed to divide all evidence into the two branches of probable and demonstrative, not intending to convey the idea that probable evidence does not sufficiently prove a proposition, and impose upon men a valid obligation to believe and act upon it, but merely that, from the nature of the subjects with which it is conversant, it does not produce the same kind or degree of certainty as that which is called demonstrative does. Demonstrative evidence applies only to necessary truth, as it is called, to abstract ideas or conceptions; and it is only of these subjects that demonstration, strictly so called, is predicated. Contingent truths can have only what is called moral or probable evidence, which may indeed lead men firmly to believe, and impose upon them an imperative obligation to act, but which does not carry with it the same clear and commanding certainty as demonstrative evidence.

Now, the divine origin and authority of the Bible, viewed as a subject to be investigated by men in the ordinary use of their faculties, is a contingent, not a necessary truth. It resolves ultimately into a question of fact—the question, viz., Whether or not God did supernaturally guide and direct the authors of the books of Scripture in composing them, so that they are his word. The fact is established, not, like the truths of the demonstrative sciences, by a mere examination and comparison of abstract ideas, but by the exercise of our ordinary faculties upon a variety of materials derived from all the ordinary sources of human knowledge, especially the evidence of sense and the evidence of human testimony. The divine origin and authority of the Scriptures would therefore be said to rest upon probable evidence, not that the evidence is not sufficient to prove it, and to impose upon men without any special divine interposition an obligation to receive and act upon it as a truth or reality, but merely that it is not fitted of itself to produce that peculiarly full persuasion and commanding assurance which is the result of demonstration. And experience very plainly indicates that when men have only that faith and conviction of the divine origin and authority of the Bible which is just the result of the ordinary exercise of our faculties upon the rational arguments by which, as a matter of fact it is established, their persuasion of its infallible truth and divine authority does not usually seem to be very powerful and efficacious, or to produce the practical results which, in right reason, might be expected from it. Now, the Holy Spirit may, and does, seal this evidence and the truth which it establishes upon men's understandings and hearts, so as to give them a fuller persuasion and assurance of the truth than they would otherwise possess or attain to; and in doing so there is no reason in the nature of the case, as we formerly remarked, why he should not employ, for producing a full persuasion and assurance, any consideration that is really in itself, and on rational grounds, a proof or evidence of the truth which he is ready to seal and impress. This is true; and it is important that we should ever remember that, whatever difficulties may attach to the more minute and precise explanation of this subject, this at least is true and certain, that the operation of the Holy Spirit is necessary to produce a full persuasion and assurance of the infallible and divine authority of the Scripture, and that therefore, in dwelling upon the proof or evidence by which it may be established in argument, either for the conviction of others or for our own confirmation, we should ever cherish a deep sense of our dependence upon his agency, and earnestly seek to enjoy his presence and blessing. But this general truth is not the whole of what was maintained by the Reformers when they conceded the necessity of a divine testimony to the divine origin and authority of the Scriptures, and asserted that believers had this, though they denied the infallibility of the church; nor does it come up to the full import of what is laid down in the declaration of the Confession, to which we have adverted.

The Confession says that "our full persuasion and assurance of the infallible truth and divine authority of the Holy Scripture, and our thorough and efficacious conviction that it is the word of God, is from the inward work of the Holy Spirit bearing witness by and with the word of God in our hearts" (WCF 1.5), which implies, not only that men have not a full persuasion and assurance that the Scripture is the word of God until they become the subjects of the inward work of the Spirit, but also moreover that they have not this full persuasion and assurance until, in this inward work, he bear witness by and with the word itself. This operation of the Spirit is here called his inward work, to distinguish it from what has been called his outward work, or the gifts of the Holy Spirit, the miracles wrought by the apostles under his agency, which also afford an evidence of the divine authority of the Scriptures, though some intermediate processes of argument are necessary before, from that outward work of the Spirit, the conclusion is reached. It is an inward work of his in our hearts, and it is described as his bearing witness. To bear witness in Scripture does not always or necessarily mean to declare directly, or assert in express words, but is sometimes used in a wider and more general sense—in that, viz., of producing or furnishing materials or proofs from which, when rightly used and applied, the conclusion follows, or may be deduced. "But I have greater witness (μαρτυρίαν μείζονα) than that of John; for the works which the Father hath given me to finish, the same works that I do, bear witness of me (μαρτυρεῖ περὶ ἐμοῦ) that the Father hath sent me" (John 5:36). "And God, which knoweth the hearts, bare them witness (ἐμαρτύρησεν αὐτοῖς), giving them the Holy Ghost, even as he did unto us" (Acts

15:8). "God also bearing them witness (συνεπιμαρτυροῦντος) with signs and wonders, and with divers miracles and gifts of the Holy Ghost, according to his will" (Heb. 2:4). All then that is necessarily implied in the position that the Spirit bears witness in our hearts to the divine origin and authority of the Scriptures is, that he is the author or efficient cause of this conviction, and that he produces it by supplying us with the necessary means or materials of effecting it, and directing us in the application of them, so that thus the conviction is firmly and thoroughly established. This is all that the word necessarily implies, and there is no reason whatever why, in these passages of Scripture which speak of the Spirit testifying or bearing witness, or in this passage of the Confession, we should understand it in any other sense; and especially there is no reason why we should regard it as implying that by a distinct intimation or explicit assertion he directly or immediately tells or assures any believer that the Scriptures are the word of God.

The Confession however further specifies the means or materials which the Spirit employs in producing this full persuasion and assurance—it is "by and with the word." There can be no doubt that by these expressions "by and with the word " are meant two different classes of materials or proofs which the Spirit employs in his work of persuading and assuring men of the divine origin and authority of the Bible. When he is said to bear witness *by* the word, the word is viewed objectively, as something out of believers and apart from them, which they contemplate and examine, and in which, when they contemplate and examine it, they are enabled by the Spirit to see plain marks or proofs that it came from God, and is stamped with his authority. In short, this was intended to indicate the internal light of the Bible, including its self-evidencing power, all those things in it, and about it, which, when men's eyes are opened by the Spirit to behold them, do irresistibly lead them to God as its author. It may include the whole of the internal evidence of the divine origin of the Scriptures, everything in the Bible itself which, independently of anything we know concerning the human authors and the actual composition of it, as a matter of fact affords proof of its having come from God, and even those branches of the internal evidences which are in some measure capable of being apprehended and discerned by men who have not yet received the Spirit. For, as the leading object of this whole declaration is just to assert that a full persuasion and assurance of the divine origin and authority of the Scripture is not attained until men have become the subjects of an inward work of the Spirit, there is nothing in the construction of the sentence which necessarily or even fairly implies that those things mentioned in the preceding part of it, and there declared to be arguments whereby the Holy Scripture doth abundantly evidence itself to be the word of God, viz., "the heavenliness of the matter, the efficacy of the doctrine, the majesty of the style, the consent of all the parts, the scope of the whole, which is to give all glory to God, and the full discovery it makes of the only way of man's salvation," though capable of being apprehended in some measure, as we shewed you, by natural men who have not the Spirit, yet being in the word, should be excluded from the materials employed by the Spirit when he bears witness by the word in men's hearts, and thereby produces a full assurance of the divine authority of the Scriptures. It is probable however, though the words do not necessarily imply this, and we are therefore not shut up to this meaning, that the inward work of the Spirit, bearing witness by the word, was intended to refer chiefly to these proofs or marks of the divine origin of the Bible which are to be found indeed in itself, viewed objectively, but which are yet not seen or discerned at all until men have the Spirit working in them, and opening their eyes. And this bearing witness *with* the word in our hearts, as distinguished from his bearing witness *by* the word, is intended to indicate the effects or results produced by the Spirit with the word, i.e., acting in conjunction with it upon men's hearts and characters, usually comprehended under the head of the experimental evidence. The word—i.e., the doctrines and statements of Scripture—produces in a certain sense these changes or results; and the Spirit produces them, acting along with the word, or using it as his instrument, he alone being their efficient cause; and by producing these effects or changes upon men by the instrumentality of the word, and thereby affording abundant proof or materials for the conclusion that it came from God, he bears witness with the word in our hearts to the infallible truth and divine authority of the Holy Scriptures, and produces a full persuasion and assurance of this. In illustration of this assertion of the necessity of this inward work of the Spirit, bearing witness by and with the word in our hearts, I refer you to a passage in Owen's *Reason of Faith* (3:330–38). Indeed, I may remark that Owen's two works on the self-evidencing power of the Bible and on the reason of faith are in reality, though not so intended a very full commentary upon these two sections of the Confession which we have been considering—the fourth and fifth of the first chapter.[13] There can be no doubt that the views which he has there unfolded were very much in their whole scope and substance the same as those entertained by the venerable authors of our Confession upon this subject, though in the detailed elucidation of his sentiments Owen has fallen into some obscurities, and perhaps into some errors and excesses to which the more careful and compendious statement of general principles in the Confession does not afford any countenance. The quotation is a long one, much longer than any which I have ever before had occasion to submit to you; but it is very excellent in itself, and it is a much more valuable and authoritative commentary upon this important declaration of the Confession than any I could either discover or produce.

---

13. Ed. note: John Owen. *Of the Divine Original, Authority, Self-Evidencing Light, and Power of the Scriptures* (Oxford: Henry Hall, 1659) in William H. Goold, ed. *The Works of John Owen* (London: Banner of Truth, 1968), 16:297–307; cf. part IV, chap. 25 above; and John Owen, *The Reason of Faith* (1677).

31

Richard B. Gaffin Jr. on Old Amsterdam (Abraham Kuyper)

Richard B. Gaffin Jr., "Old Amsterdam and Inerrancy," *WTJ* 44, 2 (Fall 1982): 253–89; reprinted in *God's Word in Servant-Form: Abraham Kuyper and Herman Bavinck on the Doctrine of Scripture* (Jackson, MS: Reformed Academic Press, 2008), 7–46.

Abraham Kuyper (1837–1920) was a great churchman, a Calvinist theologian, and a statesman in the Netherlands. After embracing theological liberalism in his studies at Leiden, he returned to a robust Reformed theology during his first pastorate. His accomplishments are too numerous to be listed. Among them, he founded the Free University of Amsterdam (1880) and became the Dutch prime minister from 1901 to 1905. In America, he is probably best known for his *Lectures on Calvinism*, delivered at Princeton University in 1898. In the history of Westminster Theological Seminary, Kuyper's notion of antithesis was influential on Cornelius Van Til's development of his presuppositional apologetic.

The selection presented here was originally published as "Old Amsterdam and Inerrancy?" in the *WTJ* in 1982 and 1983. Fittingly, Richard Gaffin wrote this piece of scholarship to clarify Old Amsterdam's view of Scripture for the hundredth anniversary of the birth of J. Gresham Machen on July 28, 1981. Jack Rogers and Donald McKim, in their award-winning book, *The Authority and Interpretation of the Bible* (1979), had contended that Kuyper and Herman Bavinck (1854–1921) rejected the concept of inerrancy held by scholasticism and B. B. Warfield (1851–1921) and developed a view of Scripture closer to Calvin and neoorthodoxy. Warfield had already stated about Kuyper that "planting himself once for all squarely on the infallible Word and the Reformed Confessions, he consecrated all his great and varied powers to purifying the camp and compacting the forces of positive truth." In his study, Gaffin ably corrects the Rogers/McKim thesis concerning these two Dutch scholars and thus shows their great affinity to the Old Princeton/Westminster trajectory. We reproduce here the first part of the argument on Abraham Kuyper's doctrine of Scripture. The second part, not printed here, addresses the Dutch theologian Herman Bavinck. This article was recently published with slight modification by Reformed Academic Press under the title *God's Word in Servant-Form*.

Bibliography: J. D. Bratt. "Kuyper, Abraham (1837–1920)." P. 140 in *DP&RTA*. Idem. "Kuyper, Abraham (1837–1920)." Pp. 351–54 in *BDE*. W. Robert Godfrey. "Calvin and Calvinism in the Netherlands." Pp. 117–19 in Reid, ed. *John Calvin: His Influence in the Western World*. I. Hexham. "Kuyper, Abraham (1837–1920)." P. 616 in *EDT*. Idem. "Kuyper, Abraham (1837–1920)." Pp. 374–75 in *NDT*. Dirk Jellema. "Kuyper, Abraham (1837–1920)." Pp. 573–75 in *NIDCC*. "Kuyper, Abraham." *NSHERK* 6:390. McKendree R. Langley. "Emancipation and Apologetics: The Formation of Abraham Kuyper's Anti-Revolutionary Party in the Netherlands, 1872–1880." Ph.D. diss., Westminster Theological Seminary, 1995. Witsius H. de Savornin Lohman. "Dr. Abraham Kuyper." *The Presbyterian and Reformed Review* 36 (October 1898): 561–609. Benjamin B. Warfield. "Introductory Note." Pp. xi–xix in Abraham Kuyper. *Encyclopedia of Sacred Theology: Its Principles*. New York: Scribner, 1898.

Kuyper's views on Scripture are found primarily in three places, in *Principles of Sacred Theology*,[1] a translation of a part of the first and the entire second volume of his three-volume work on theological encyclopedia; in *The Work of the Holy Spirit*,[2] reflecting in tone its origin as a series of popularly written articles; and in the *Dictaten dogmatiek*,[3] student notes of his class lectures published with Kuyper's permission.

A passage from *Principles of Sacred Theology*, cited with a slight ellipsis by Rogers and McKim,[4] makes a useful point of departure for examining Kuyper's views (479):

> As the Logos has not appeared *in the form of glory* but in the form of a servant, joining Himself to the reality of our nature, as this had come to be through the results of sin, so also, for the revelation of His Logos, God the Lord accepts our consciousness, our human life *as it is*. The drama He enacts is a tragedy, quickening a higher tendency in the midst of our human misery. The forms, or types, are marred by want and sin. The shadows remain humanly imperfect, far beneath their ideal content. The spoken words, however much aglow with the Holy Ghost, remain bound to the limitations of our language, disturbed as it is by anomalies. As a product of writing, the Holy Scripture, too, bears on its forehead the mark of the form of a servant.

Two conceptions obviously control here: (1) the *analogy* or definite parallel that exists between the incarnation of the Logos and the revelation, including inscripturation, of the Logos, and, consequently, because of this parallel, (2) the *servant-form* of all revelation, including Scripture.

1. (trans. J. DeVries; Grand Rapids: Eerdmans, 1954, reprint of 1898 ed.; the Dutch original appeared in 1894); hereafter, *Principles*. For this and the other translations cited I have occasionally taken the liberty, usually without noting it, of making slight changes when this seemed warranted by the original. Unless otherwise indicated, the italics are Kuyper's.

2. (trans. H. DeVries; Grand Rapids: Eerdmans, 1979, reprint of 1900 ed.; Dutch original in three volumes, 1888, 1889); hereafter, *Holy Spirit*.

3. Vol. 2: *Locus de Sacra Scriptura, creatione, creaturis* (Grand Rapids: J. B. Hulst, n.d.); hereafter, *Dictaten* with the part (1 or 2) and page of the locus on Scripture.

4. Jack Rogers and Donald McKim, *The Authority and Interpretation of the Bible: A Historical Approach* (San Francisco: Harper & Row, 1979), 391; hereafter, *Authority*.

Similar statements in the preceding context illumine these points. Just prior, in protesting "against the effort to interpret Holy Scripture as a transcendent phenomenon standing outside of our human reality," Kuyper writes (478):

> Here, also, the parallel maintains itself between the incarnate and the written Logos. As in the Mediator the Divine nature weds itself to the human, and appears before us in *its* form and figure, so also the Divine factor of the Holy Scripture clothes itself in the garment of our form of thought, and holds itself to our human reality.

And a little earlier (476–77):

> If man is created after the Image of God, and thus disposed to communion with the Eternal, then this *Word of God* also must be able to be grasped by man; and even after his fall into sin,[5] this Word of God must go out to him, though now in a way suited to his condition. This takes place now, since man has received *being* and *consciousness*, in two ways. In the way of the *esse* by the incarnation of the Logos, and in the way of consciousness as this selfsame Logos becomes embodied in the Scripture. Both are the "uttered" Word (*logos proforikos*); but in the one case it is the Word "become flesh," in the other "written," and these two cover each other. Christ is the whole Scripture, and Scripture brings the esse of the Christ to our consciousness.[6]

Kuyper's basic orientation, then, is that because of the results of sin and the need for redemption, there is a necessary, intrinsic parallel between the incarnation and inscripturation of the Logos, which further necessitates for each the form of a servant.[7] The Word of God does not remain aloofly transcendent, apart from our being and consciousness, but enters fully into human life as it is. In the case of Scripture, as well as the entire process of revelatory events and words it inscripturates, this servant-form embraces human realities that "are marred by want and sin," that "remain humanly imperfect, far beneath their ideal content," and involves subjection to "the limitation of our language, disturbed as it is by anomalies."

How are we to evaluate this way of speaking and, in general, Kuyper's notion of the servant-form of Scripture?[8] Do they not rather clearly express an idea of divine accommodation that, for instance, is far removed from, even at odds with, the orientation of the old Princeton theologians and their allegedly "scholastic" concern with inerrancy?[9]

---

5. This reference to sin and the fall clearly indicates that Kuyper has redemptive or "special" revelation in view in these passages.

6. Kuyper goes on here to caution against restricting the Logos, now embodied for us in Scripture, to words. The impact of the Logos on man's consciousness also takes place both by (common and extraordinary) events and by types and shadows. Only when these three—words, signs, and shadows—are seen in their organic relation is the Word of God viewed in its unity and richness. This threefold distinction, by the way, clarifies the paralleling in the first passage cited above, of "drama," "types" ("shadows"), and "spoken words."

7. That this necessity is not absolute or abstractly considered, demanded, say, by the distance between God's eternity and man's finitude, is clear from the statement that immediately precedes the first of the passages quoted above (479): "If, now, in order to be the bearer of the Divine factor, that human form or that human reality were carried up to its *telos*, no contradiction would be born from this in the appearance; but this is not so." The necessity in view stems from the free, condescending love of God, intent on restoring the entirely "natural," created fellowship subsequently ruptured and rendered "unnatural" by human sin.

8. Cf. the discussion of G. C. Berkouwer, *Holy Scripture* (trans. and ed. J. Rogers; Grand Rapids: Eerdmans, 1975), 195–212; esp. on Kuyper and Bavinck, 199–201.

9. So, Rogers and McKim, *Authority*, 390–91, cf. 399.

1. A general guideline for understanding Kuyper, in the light of the way the parallel between incarnation and inscripturation is drawn in the first passage cited above, would appear to be that the servant-form of Scripture corresponds to the servant-form of Christ in "joining Himself to the reality of our nature, as this had come to be through the results of sin," yet, as he makes unmistakably clear elsewhere (e.g., 537–39 and esp. 454–60), without this joining resulting in sin or error in Christ himself. Apparently for Kuyper, what is true in this respect for Christ is also true for Scripture. The discussion that follows will disclose whether or not this in fact is his view.

2. All of the passages so far considered occur within a section whose theme is the unity and multiplicity of Scripture (473–81). Significantly, Kuyper begins with a strong emphasis on *unity*. In the language of older theology, it is nothing less than the *essentia* of Scripture, that is, what makes it Scripture. Affirming the unity of the Bible is "not only right but of *highest* right for faith" (473). In fact, were it not for "such terrible abuse," unity might be the solely sufficient concern for faith. However, since this conception so readily disposes to fragmenting the statements of Scripture into a collection of isolated divine sayings, thus destroying the organic character of revelation, the church has the task of maintaining an appreciation of the multiformity of Scripture. Multiplicity must be emphasized, "not from the desire to exalt the human factor, but to keep the gold vein of the Divine factor pure" (474). Always, however, the unity of Scripture, not its multiformity, must be taken as the starting-point if one is to arrive at its unity. "He who, in the case of the Scripture, thus begins with the multiplicity of the human factor, and tries in this way to reach out after its unity will never find it, simply because he began with its denial in principle" (474).[10]

Kuyper expands on the notion of unity by taking up the old Reformed dogmatic conception of a *predestined Bible*. This has in view "the preconceived *form* [*forma praeconcepta*] of the Holy Scripture" (474, italics added), a form given it already from eternity in the counsel of God. The actual composition of Scripture during the course of history involves the activity of a number of persons, "without the knowledge of a higher purpose" and often without an awareness of the others involved. Without "premeditation" or "agreement," "without ever having seen the whole," they nonetheless contributed to a "structure," according to a plan "hidden, back of human consciousness, in the consciousness of God" (475). "The *conception*, therefore, has not gone out of men, but out of God" (475). All told, then, this conception, the design of Scripture, is such "that in every document and by every writer in the course of the ages there should be contributed that very thing, of such a *content* and in such a *form*, as had been aimed at and willed by God" (475). As a predestined unity, Scripture, considered not only in terms of its content but also its *form*, is "one mighty 'it is written,'" "one coherent utterance" (476).

Plainly, then, Kuyper can hardly be made an advocate for the view that has its focus "on the divine content of Scripture, not on its human form," that finds authority "in the saving

---

10. Toward the close of the section Kuyper comments (480): "And however much it is your duty to study that *multiplicity* and *particularity* in the Scripture (both materially and formally), yet from that multiplicity you must ever come back to the view of the *unity of the conception*, if there is, indeed, to be such a thing for you as a Holy Scripture." It is worth noting, and pondering, that this balanced, yet forthright point of departure in the unity of Scripture, *formal* as well as material as we shall presently see, clearly conflicts with the summarizing remark made by Berkouwer at the close of his study on Scripture, that "the true and only way to obedience" is the "roundabout way" from the message of Scripture, in its mode of multiple human witness, to its unique divine authority (*Holy Scripture*, 366).

content, not the supernatural form of Scripture."[11] Such a view involves a disjunction between content and form, a polarity consisting of concern with the former and depreciation of the latter, a disjunction that is entirely foreign to Kuyper's notion of a predestined Bible, of the preconceived *form* of Scripture.

Kuyper's intention is seen further in his recourse to the old dogmatic distinction between the primary and secondary authors of Scripture. The combination of their authorial activities serves to clarify the relationship between the divine and human factors, paralleled in the incarnation (478). Kuyper even writes (480):

> So far, therefore, as the representation of the secondary authors (*auctores secundarii*) as amanuenses of the Holy Spirit, or also as an instrument played upon by the Holy Ghost, exclusively tended to point to that unity of conception, there is nothing to be said against it. In that sense, one can even say that the Holy Scripture has been given us from heaven.

From the activity of God, the primary author, derives the unity of Scripture, *formal* as well as material. And, "From this unity of conception flows the Divine authority, to which the child of God gives himself captive" (478).

Ultimately this unity resists rationalization. The relation of divine and human factors in Scripture, the conjoint activity of primary and secondary authors, constituting the unity of Scripture, is an incomprehensible reality. "How this unity hides in that wondrous book remains a mystery which refuses all explanation" (478). But it is important to recognize that Kuyper carefully circumscribes this mystery. It is the mystery of the divine *form* (and message) given in, with, inseparable from, and *as* the human form (and content) of Scripture, *not* the mystery of the presence, dialectically, of divine message in human form. Nothing less than the proper conception of the authority of the Bible is at stake for him here.

3. Kuyper's discussion of the unity-multiplicity question provides clear indications of the historical perspective he had on his own work, particularly how he saw himself in relation to the Reformation and post-Reformation orthodoxy. As we have already seen, he takes over from seventeenth-century Reformed dogmatics, sympathetically and with a sense of continuity, the notions of a predestined Bible and the preconceived form of Scripture, as well as the distinction between the primary and secondary authors.

Most instructive, however, is what he has to say in the closing paragraph of the section (480–81). He begins with the statement, already noted above, that the representation of the secondary authors as amanuenses or instruments used by the Holy Spirit is valid for pointing up the unity of Scripture. This is counterbalanced with the observation that if for the sake of unity one ignores the multiformity of Scripture and the "organic way" it came into existence, "then nothing remains but a mechanical lifelessness, which destroys the vital, organic unity." But, Kuyper adds immediately, "This was certainly not intended by our older theologians." He points out that they were capable of careful, detailed historical work concerning various questions of introduction and the differing tendencies of the parts of Scripture. "But yet it can hardly be denied that they had established themselves too firmly in the idea of a logical theory of inspiration, to allow the organism of the Scripture to fully assert itself." And then he closes by noting that careful, thorough attention to the

---

11. Rogers and McKim, *Authority*, 391, 399; cf. Jack Rogers, "A Third Alternative," in *Scripture, Tradition, and Interpretation*, ed. W. W. Gasque and W. S. LaSor (Grand Rapids: Eerdmans, 1978), 78, 83.

diversity and multiformity of Scripture is obligatory to prevent misunderstanding, "just because we *join ourselves as closely as possible* to the historic Theology of the Reformation" (italics added).

Here, very plainly, post-Reformation orthodoxy is seen as part of the "historic Theology of the Reformation," a theology with which Kuyper wishes to identify. As he shows here, he recognizes and is capable of criticizing perceived weaknesses in this theology, particularly in certain of its seventeenth-century developments. But it is equally plain that the view, widely advocated today, by Rogers and McKim among others, that post-Reformation Protestant orthodoxy is the beginning of a decisive departure and eventual decline from the theology of the Reformers which only in this century, largely through the theological renewal generated by Karl Barth, has begun to have a significant reversal, is a church-historical scenario that Kuyper would find totally foreign. In fact, as we shall see more clearly later, it is close to the position of the so-called Ethical theologians, with whom Kuyper was drawn into ongoing conflict, sometimes sharp, over the course of his life.

Nor, as seems rather plainly indicated, does Kuyper view the "mechanical" view of inspiration, at least in its best exponents, and his own "organic" view as polar opposites, representing decisively different, mutually incompatible approaches to Scripture. Instead, he sees a common (church) tradition, a basic continuity between them, with the latter serving to correct the undeniable weaknesses and errors of the former.

4. The results of this initial probe of Kuyper's views on Scripture can be further substantiated and tested, first by looking elsewhere throughout his work on theological encyclopedia.

The fundamental parallel between incarnation and inscripturation (inspiration) finds expression repeatedly.[12] Perhaps most arresting is a passage from the (untranslated) third volume where, in discussing "sacred philology," Kuyper criticizes the seventeenth-century conception of revelation and inspiration as "too mechanical."[13]

> The ray of the divine light, so one imagined, penetrated to our lost race, unbroken and without becoming colored. For that reason every product of revelation had to exhibit for every eye the mark of divine perfection, with reference not only to its content but also to its form. It was not noticed that this entire representation was in conflict with the canon for all revelation, which is given in the incarnation as the center of all revelation. Naturally, if all revelation, including its mode of manifestation [verschijningsform], had come to us in divine perfection, then Christ too ought to have appeared in a state of glory. Now that, on the contrary, he manifested himself in the form of a servant, and appeared in a state of humiliation, it was hereby settled that the ray of the divine light *truly* broke into the atmosphere of our sinful-creaturely life, and for that reason what is *imperfect* and *inadequate* [het *onvolkomene* en *gebrekkige*] in our broken existence had to cling to the manifestation mode [verschijningsform] of revelation.[14]

Here we have a statement of the intrinsic, necessary nature of the tie between incarnation and inscripturation, perhaps, as forceful as any in Kuyper. The incarnation, "as the center

12. E.g., "It is the one *Logos* which in Christ by incarnation, and in the Scripture by inscripturation goes out to humanity at large" (*Principles*, 401); "From this special principium in God the saving power is extended centrally to our race, both by the ways of being and of thought, by incarnation and inspiration" (425); cf. 460.

13. *Encyclopaedie der Heilige Godgeleerdheid*, 3rd ed., 3 vols. (Kampen: J. H. Kok, 1908–9), 3.78–79.

14. Berkouwer, in discussing this passage, changes the sense of "het onvolkomene en gebrekkige" by paraphrasing with "het zondige en gebrekkige" (*De heilige Schrift*, 2 vols. [Kampen: J. H. Kok, 1966–67], 2.153). The English translation only widens this distance from Kuyper's original with "that which is sinful and fallible" (*Holy Scripture*, 220).

of all revelation," is "the canon for all revelation." Further, the *direction* of thought is plain: from the incarnation to inscripturation. Because Christ appeared, not in a state of glory, but in a state of humiliation and the form of servant, this must also be true for all revelation,[15] including Scripture. When Kuyper speaks of the ray of revelation being truly refracted by "our sinful-creaturely life" and of "what is imperfect and inadequate" about our existence having to attach to its manifestation, this is so, "truly," this "has to be," because of what is antecedently the case for Christ. The human form of Scripture has its specific, "humiliated" character, not because it exemplifies what is generically and inherently human,[16] but because of the specific character of the human nature of Christ, prior to his glorification. Accordingly, the categories of sin and error, if they apply to Scripture, must do so in the same sense they would, if applicable, to Christ in his state of humiliation. That this captures Kuyper's intention seems difficult to evade, although his statements in this connection still require further reflection, to which we will return below.

5. Highly instructive for Kuyper's overall outlook on Scripture, especially the relation between its form and content, is the way he handles the perennially debated question of the use of the Old Testament in the New Testament (*Principles*, 447–53).

The immediate context is the section on the testimony of the apostles to the inspiration of the Old Testament. His third and last major point is the apostolic conviction that the Old Testament is "the predestined transcript of God's counsel, of which the instrumental author has, often unconsciously, produced the record, and which, as being of a higher origin, has divine authority" (446). Not only do we find that "there is no hesitancy in announcing God the Holy Spirit as the subject speaking in the Old Testament" (447), but the stringing together of quotations from different books (e.g., Acts 1:20; Rom. 15:9–12; 1 Tim. 5:18) "shows equally clearly, that in the estimation of the apostles the human authors fall entirely in the background" (447–48).

"Such quoting," Kuyper continues, "is only conceivable and warranted by the supposition that all these sayings, however truly they have come to us by several writers, are actually from one and the same author." The illustration he uses is the way we might quote from the different works of the same author. That this in fact is the apostolic supposition is seen from their repeated discovery, in the historical parts as well as in doctrinal and moral statements, that "the words of the Old Testament often contain more than the writers themselves understood" (448). This *sensus plenior* "could not have been the intention of the instrumental authors." Rather, "this intention is thought of as in the 'mind of the first author'" (448). The spiritual and typical significance seen in the crossing of the Red Sea and the wilderness events, in 1 Corinthians 10:1–18 for instance, "*could not* have been intended by the writer of the narrative. That meaning was beyond him, and directed itself from the mind of the primary author to us."

Among the different objections frequently raised against the apostles' use of the Old Testament, Kuyper finds that one in fact sheds important light on this usage. That is the objection that frequently their quotations are not a literal translation, and they follow the Septuagint even when it is incorrect. If we assume that they wrote on their own initiative, without assistance, then we are bound to conclude that "this mode of procedure was faulty and rested upon mistake, either voluntary or involuntary, but in no case pardonable" (450).

---

15. Plainly Kuyper has in view here all revelation since the fall; see above, n. 5.

16. See the qualification already considered above in n. 7.

The issue takes on an entirely new light, however, when we acknowledge an inspiration for the New Testament writers analogous to that of the Old Testament writers they quoted. Then the situation is one where the one and same author is quoting himself and so entitled to a measure of freedom, "bound to the actual content only, and not to the form of what he wrote, except in the face of a third party" (450). Kuyper continues:

> If, therefore, it is the same Holy Spirit who spoke through the prophets and inspired the apostles, it is the same primary author who, by the apostles, *quotes himself*, and is therefore entirely justified in repeating his original meaning in application to the case for which the quotation is made, in a somewhat modified form, agreeably to the current translation.

And (450–51),

> in the apostolic circle the primary author quotes from his own words agreeably to the accepted translated text. No one else could do this but the *author himself*, since he is both authorized and competent to guard against false interpretations of his original meaning.

In discussing the citation of Psalm 40:6 in Hebrews 10:5, he goes to some lengths to show that the faulty Septuagint translation as used in Hebrews nonetheless "can be taken as being equal in sense and thought to the original" Hebrew. Of this way of handling the Old Testament he then observes emphatically, "This would have been indeed unlawful in common quotation by *another*, but offers not the least difficulty since the primary author of Psalm 40 and Hebrews 10 is *one and the same*" (452).

In making this sort of emphasis, Kuyper does not intend to eliminate or suppress the full, spontaneous activity of the various New Testament writers. In contrast to ourselves,[17] the "apostolic circle" knew itself to be involved in the reality of inspiration, which had resumed after Pentecost and which gave it an "organic" rather than "mechanical" contact with existing Scripture. Both the accent and balance Kuyper wishes to maintain come out in his concluding sentence (452–53), "And it is in this way that subjectively, from the side of the apostles, their liberty in the use of Scripture is explained, as we explained it objectively from the identity of the author in the quotation and in what was quoted."

The issue here is not the validity at every point of Kuyper's position on the use of the Old Testament in the New. What is plain, however, is that for him this distinctive complex of usage and citation is not simply the peripheral, historically conditioned, human form that contains a (separable) divine message. Rather, it is, and in terms of the fundamental issue of authorship we may say *primarily*, a matter of the *divine form* (historically mediated, to be sure, through the human authors) integral to the divine meaning and message.

6. A similar emphasis is even stronger in what Kuyper has to say about prophecy as a form of inspiration (527ff.). He distinguishes it from other forms in that "in general it exhibits a conscious dualism of subject, whereby the subject of the prophet has merely an instrumental significance, while the higher subject speaks the word" (527). The "other, higher subject" sometimes breaks through in the Psalms and Wisdom

---

17. Instructive for Kuyper's views on inspiration and Scripture as a whole is the observation he makes here (452), "It presented itself differently to them than to us. For us this inspiration belongs to the past; it is an ended matter; we ourselves stand outside of it."

literature, but not in a pronouncedly dualistic, even antithetic way as in prophecy[18]. For prophecy, "duality of subject is the starting-point for the understanding of its working, and is present where it is not expressly announced" (528). The "fundamental type" is given in Deuteronomy 18:18, "I will put my words in his mouth, and he will tell them everything I command them." This is to be understood quite literally of the originating activity of God, the higher subject, upon the prophet, for no matter how it is viewed, "the chief distinction in prophecy is always that the subject of the prophet merely serves as instrument" (529).

All this may seem to have an almost crassly mechanical ring to it. But Kuyper does not mean to overlook or deny the distinctive personal role of each of the prophets, nor to suggest that "the character or disposition of this instrumental subject was a matter of indifference." The personality of each gives to his prophecy a tone that distinguishes it from the others; these differences must be fully appreciated. Still, while "without reservation we must recognize the personal stamp, including style and word-choice, which a prophet puts upon his prophecy, it may never be inferred that the source of prophecy (*fons prophetiae*) is to be sought in him, and that the primordial (*primoprimi*) issues of thought should not come from the consciousness of God." Prior experience, education, knowledge and assessment of contemporary events must all be recognized as functioning in prophecy. Yet it "remains fact, that so far as the ego of the prophet was active in this it did not go to work from its own spontaneity, but was passively directed by another subject, in whose service it was employed" (530).

Prophecy, in a word, is "epical," by which Kuyper means to signalize "the dualistic character of prophecy, coupled with the suppression of the human subject" (532), "the passivity of the prophet" (533). Evidently, the schema *divine message/human form* is not only inappropriate to, but flatly contradicts Kuyper's understanding of prophecy. For him, the form as well as the content of prophecy originates with the higher, divine subject.

7. Two statements, each important in its own right as a substantial expression of Kuyper's views on Scripture, serve to tie together our discussion to this point, especially of his use of the form-content distinction in relation to its inspiration and authority. The first is his definition of "graphic" inspiration, the inspiration of Scripture, in distinction from the other forms of inspiration in the revelation process lying in back of inscripturation (545):

> By graphic inspiration we understand that guidance given by the Spirit of God to the minds of the writers, compilers and editors of the Holy Scriptures, by which these sacred writings have assumed such a form as was, in the counsel of salvation, predestined by God among the means of grace for His Church.

And in the clearest, most unmistakable terms, particularly because he also includes both (1) the distinction between center and periphery in Scripture and (2) a reference to its authority, is what he writes about the effect of the internal witness of the Holy Spirit (560–61):

> Gradually, however, an evermore vitally organic relation begins to reveal itself between the centrum of the Scripture and its periphery, between its fundamental and its derivative thoughts,

---

18. Employing a German distinction, Kuyper even says of the Psalms and Wisdom literature, in distinction from prophecy, that "there is 'Konsonanz' of subjects, never 'Dissonanz'" (528).

and between its utterances and the facts it communicates. That authority which at first addressed us from that centrum only, now begins to appear to us from what has proceeded from that centrum. We feel ourselves more and more captivated by a power, whose centrum cannot be accepted without demanding and then compelling all unobservedly an ever more general consent for its entire appearance, and all its utterances. Thus it ends by impressing us as *Scripture*, by exercising moral compulsion and spiritual power over us as *Holy Bible*. And in the end the connection between its form and content appears so inseparable, that even the exceptional parts of its form appeal to us, and, in form and content both, the Scripture comes to stand before us as an authority.

Kuyper can hardly be made a sympathizer, much less spokesman, for the view that the authority and inspiration of Scripture lie in its content in distinction from its form, and that the internal testimony of the Spirit is to its message, but not its form. In fact, his position is in emphatic opposition to such views.

8. The points so far under discussion, in Kuyper's work on theological encyclopedia, may now be considered somewhat more briefly in his other writings. The treatment of Scripture in the *Dictaten dogmatiek* (see above, n. 3) is presented, along the lines of traditional Reformed dogmatics, under the five main headings of the essence and four attributes of Scripture (necessity, authority, perspicuity, sufficiency). By far the lengthiest is the head on authority, under which inspiration is discussed extensively, with substantial overlaps with the discussion in *Principles of Sacred Theology*.

In this larger context the summary paragraphs given at the beginning of the section under the title, "The speaker in H. Scripture is God himself," are worth quoting in their entirety because they express so clearly and forcefully the inherent bond, the intrinsic nature of the parallel, between incarnation and inscripturation, and in so doing illumine in a fundamental way much of what we have been considering (1.75):

This authority derives from the fact that the speaker in the Holy Scripture is not a creature but God himself. That speech in Scripture to his church could come to pass by God immediately, i.e., without instruments (*sine instrumento*). This could happen not only because of his omnipotence but also in view of the *luchoth*.[19] But this has not been the way of the Lord: As in the work of redemption he does not continue to confront us transcendently as God, but immanently in Jesus Christ has united the divine and human natures in such a way that the divine life has appeared in a man, so also the Lord God has given us H. Scripture not transcendently but immanently, because he has so intimately united the divine factor with the human factor that the divine word has come to us, always from a human pen, mostly from a human mind, and not seldom from a human heart.

In the union of both these factors now lies the mystery of Holy Scripture. Parallel with the mystery of the incarnation runs the mystery of inscripturation. In both cases the Word of God comes to us, in the manger as Emmanuel in the world where we live, in H. Scripture as Emmanuel in the world of our thoughts and ideas. Both revelations of the Word belong together, just as our living and the consciousness of that living belong together. Thus both mysteries must either be rejected together or confessed together and, if confessed, then on the same ground.

19. The allusion here is apparently to the stone tablets on which God wrote the Ten Commandments, without human mediation of any sort.

Earlier in discussing the necessity of the form in which Scripture comes to us, he writes (1.59, 63):

> In Christ and in Holy Scripture we have to do with related mysteries. In the case of Christ there is a union of divine and human factors. The same is true of Scripture; here, too, there is a primary author and a secondary author. To maintain properly the relationship between these two factors is the great work of dogmatics. . . . Everything depends here on the right insight that the Word has become flesh in Christ and is stereotyped in Scripture.[20] Thus Scripture must be a *graphē theanthrōpeia* [theanthropic writing], truly human and truly divine.

The basic thrust of these passages is plain. Scripture, like Christ,[21] is both truly human and truly divine. Yet in the case of Scripture, as for Christ, these two factors are not equally ultimate. The priority and originating initiative belong to the divine, not the human. Specifically, the Word, in his antecedent identity as the Word, became flesh, and God is the primary author of the Bible, in distinction from the secondary human authors. This specifies the "related mysteries" of Christ and the Bible.

As in *Principles of Sacred Theology*, the intrinsic parallel between incarnation and inscripturation, in fact, this "theanthropic" constitution of Scripture, shapes Kuyper's view of the relationship between the form and content of Scripture. Because Scripture comes in a human form it comes "with all that pertains to human inadequacy" (1.64). Yet this is not a disadvantage to be lamented but entirely necessary, otherwise Scripture could not be believed. "Where God appears on Sinai, everything shrinks back, but where the Christ child lies in the manger, the human heart becomes happy."

Again we encounter the notion of a predestined Bible, not in the general sense true of any book, but in the "concrete sense that the plan of Scripture, comprising the whole and the parts, existed with God before Scripture existed, and that it was the Lord God himself who has realized Scripture according to that design and plan" (1.92). The apostles themselves believed in a predestined Bible and saw inspiration as extending to the individual words and letters (2.177). The scriptural attire (het Schriftgewaad) of the Word is woven by God according to the pattern that he has drawn up for it (1.86). Graphic inspiration in the narrower sense is the operation of the Holy Spirit in the various human authors, "whereby they wrote in just the way and at such a time and in such a form as was necessary for the delivery of that part of Scripture for which each was responsible, finished and adapted to the canonical linking together of all the parts, to that one harmonious whole which the Lord God had foreseen and foreordained for Holy Scripture." This graphic inspiration concerns "the production of the autograph in the form intended by God, at the moment it enters the canon" (2.127).

The form of Scripture, then, is from God, just as much as the content. The "theanthropic mystery" of Scripture is not to be explained by assigning the "truly divine" to the content, the "truly human" to the form. The one distinction cuts across the other: the form of Scrip-

---

20. "The Logos is incarnated in Christ, but is likewise engraved in Scripture" (*Dictaten* 1.72; see also 71).

21. It hardly needs to be stated that this strongly accented parallelism and stress on the "theanthropic" character of Scripture do not involve Kuyper even remotely in some form of bibliolatry nor in obscuring or denying the personal nature of the union between divine and human in the incarnation, in distinction from Scripture. Noteworthy in this connection is the fact that Berkouwer, in marked distinction from Kuyper (and Bavinck), depreciates and largely questions the validity and usefulness of the analogy between incarnation and inscripturation, primarily because the "personal union" essential to the former is not present in the latter (*Holy Scripture*, 198–205).

ture, as well as its content, is both truly divine and truly human, with God as the primary author. Kuyper's overall intention is plain when he can even write: "Therefore it is clear that Scripture is a totality coming to us from heaven" (1.93); "If God himself had come and had dictated the Bible to stenographers, it would not look differently than it now does" (1.77); and, "On the other hand, if I say, 'Holy Scripture is God's Word,' then I mean that God was the stenographer, that God provided the résumé, that God is the historian, the announcer, the informant who is answerable for those documents" (2.133).[22]

On the key question of the relation between the form of Scripture and its authority Kuyper expresses himself emphatically and unmistakably. In its proper and original purport this authority does not concern the form, but the content of Scripture as it commands obedience. "But," Kuyper immediately adds, "in order to be able to exercise absolute authority in the material sense, H. Scripture must equally well be able to assert its claim to absolute authority in the formal sense. Abandoning this formal authority actually removes the absolute character of the material authority as well" (1.65). Elsewhere he offers the assessment that in fact, "Holy Scripture has retained its divine authority only in those circles where at the same time its formal infallibility is confessed" (2.128). The formal and material authority (and infallibility) of Scripture stand or fall together. The *testimonium Spiritus Sancti* concerns not only the conversion of the life and consciousness of the believer, but also the conversion of his understanding. Only with the latter is that testimony complete (2.201):

> Then he starts to read Scripture with hunger, with reverence and receptivity. The conversion of his consciousness bore a synthetic character; now his experiences become analytic. Now he feels how because of one letter, one form, victory falls to Satan or eludes him. He discovers that form and content are inseparably connected. Not only is he concerned with firm spiritual content, but the form in which the content is, must be crystallized for him, otherwise he has no stability in his understanding.

9. Discussion of Scripture in *The Work of the Holy Spirit* occurs primarily in three places in volume 1 (56–78, 146–57, and 164–78). Prominent in this discussion, developed in a more popular vein, are the emphases already noted in the other works.

While the analogy between incarnation and inscripturation is apparently not stated explicitly, the overall trend of the discussion is to make clear the correlation between the revelation-historical process out of which Scripture comes and the history of redemption leading up to and consummated in Christ. Also, a glance at the table of contents for this volume will discover how the chapters on Scripture cluster, on either side, around the chapters on the incarnation and mediatorial office of Christ and the outpouring of the Spirit.

The very first words on Scripture, with their figurative stress on God as primary author, set the tone for the entire discussion (56):

> Among the mighty, majestic works of art produced by the Holy Spirit the marvelous Sacred Scripture stands first. It may seem incredible that the printed pages of a book should excel the spiritual work in human hearts, yet we assign to the Sacred Scripture the most conspicuous place without hesitation.

---

22. These statements have nothing at all to do, at least in Kuyper's mind, with a mechanical or dictation view of inspiration; see, e.g., his rejection of such a viewpoint, in discussing the necessity of the form in which Scripture comes to us, under the subheading: "Why has the Bible not simply descended from heaven?" (1.63–64; cf. 2.160–61).

And again (60): "That the Bible is the unparalleled product of the Chief Artist, the Holy Spirit; that He gave it to the Church and that in the Church He uses it as His instrument, cannot be overemphasized."

This point of departure in the Holy Spirit as the great artist-author of Scripture involves a unique control of the human authors so comprehensive that it even extends to their word choice. Whether or not Moses and others were aware of being inspired is immaterial. In any case (77):

> the Holy Spirit directed them, brought to their knowledge what they were to know, sharpened their judgments in the choice of documents and records, so that they should decide aright, and gave them a superior maturity of mind that enabled them always to choose exactly the right word.[23] . . . But whether He dictates directly, as in the Revelation of St. John, or governs indirectly, as with historians and evangelists, the result is the same: the product is such in form and content as the Holy Spirit designed, an infallible document for the Church of God.

Ultimately, the Holy Spirit is accountable not only for the saving content of Scripture but also for its form. His truthfulness is at stake in the one no less than in the other.

Even though Paul, for instance, had no awareness that his letters would subsequently have a place in Scripture (171),

> surely the Holy Spirit did. As by education the Lord frequently prepares a maiden for her still unknown, future husband, so did the Holy Spirit prepare Paul, John, and Peter for their work. He directed their lives, circumstances, and conditions; He caused such thoughts, meditations, and even words to arise in their hearts as the writing of the New Testament Scripture required. And while they were writing these portions of the Holy Scripture, that one day would be the treasure of the universal Church in all ages, a fact not understood by them, but by the Holy Spirit, He so directed their thoughts as to guard them against mistakes and lead them into all truth. He foreknew what the complete New Testament Scripture ought to be, and what parts would belong to it. As an architect, by his workers, prepares the various parts of the building, afterward to fit them in their places, so did the Holy Spirit by different workers prepare the different parts of the New Testament, which afterward He united in a whole.

Clearly, Kuyper is saying that the *formal* responsibility of the Holy Spirit for Scripture is total, extending from the individual words to the canonical whole.

Furthermore, the *authority* of Scripture is inseparable from this formal accountability. The two stand or fall together (172, translator's italics):

> Believing in the authority of the New Testament, we must acknowledge the authority of the four evangelists to be perfectly equal. As to the *contents*, Matthew's gospel may surpass that of Luke, and John's may excel the gospel of Mark; but their authority is equally unquestionable. The Epistle to the Romans has higher value than that to Philemon; but their authority is entirely the same. As to their *persons*, John stood above Mark, and Paul above Jude; but since we depend not upon the authority of their persons, but only upon that of the Holy Spirit, these personal differences are of no account.

---

23. "het volkomen juiste woord" (*Het Werk van het Heiligen Geest*, 3 vols. [Amsterdam: J. A. Wormser, 1888–89], 1.101). The translation omits "exactly."

It would be easy enough to read this passage, especially in isolation, as betraying the abiding influence of a mechanical view of inspiration and a lingering tendency toward a "leveling" treatment of Scripture, as if any statement or portion has the same function or value as the rest. But that is plainly not Kuyper's intention. He recognizes a spectrum of differences in significance and value for the life of the church, so far as the content of Scripture and the personalities of the human authors are concerned. But the authority of Scripture is neither determined nor differentiated by these material differences. Certainly biblical authority is inseparable from these differences, but they do not give rise to different degrees of authority within Scripture. Rather, the authority of Scripture is rooted in the "formal" reality of that originating activity of the Holy Spirit by which he is ultimately responsible for Scripture in all its parts and as a whole. Because of that originating activity the authority of each portion of Scripture in relation to all the others is "perfectly equal," "equally unquestionable," and "entirely the same."

10. We are now in a position to address directly Kuyper's views on the presence of error in Scripture. An important overall perspective, a perspective revealing the essentially religious nature of this issue for him, as well as his sense of basic continuity with classical Reformed orthodoxy, emerges in the *Dictaten* at the very beginning of his lengthy treatment of the authority of Scripture (1.66). We do *not* begin this chapter, Kuyper says, with the question, Is Scripture infallible? For "If Satan has brought us to the point where we are arguing about the infallibility of Scripture, then we are already out from under the authority of Scripture." Pushing infallibility into the limelight is intellectualism, and that began with the rationalists. The older Reformed theology, in contrast, dealt not with the Bible's infallibility, but with its authority and necessity (in which infallibility was accepted, without hesitation, as implied).

Still, in view of rationalistic preoccupations and denials, repeatedly Kuyper asserts the infallibility (onfeilbaarheid, infallibilitas) and errorlessness (feiloosheid) of Scripture, and he does so without qualification. The infallibility of Scripture is absolute, and the entire Scripture is infallible. There cannot be different degrees of inspiration, "because it is infallible. The idea of infallibility, like every negative idea, is absolute. There can be degrees of certainty, but more or less infallible is an absurdity" (*Dictaten* 2.30). Where historical books have passed through a process of editing before their reception into the canon, the editors, no less than the original author, worked under inspiration so that their redaction, as guaranteed by the Holy Spirit, is "absolutely infallible" (2.77). The authority of Scripture is such "that, without a trace of doubt or hesitation, we should acknowledge the entire Holy Scripture . . . as infallible in what it communicates to us" (1.66). The revelation that comes through the apostles is "made known not in a fallible human manner, but under the infallible authority of the divine Inspirer, the Holy Spirit" (*Heiligen Geist* 1.220; cf. *Holy Spirit*, 166).

The errorlessness of Scripture is a divine, not a human errorlessness (*Dictaten* 1.86, 91–92).[24] Strictly speaking, errorlessness and infallibility are not synonymous. The fact that something is without errors does not settle that it belongs to Scripture and is thus infallible. There are, for instance, sermons without error, "but these are entirely different from inspiration (*toto caelo ab Inspiratione distincta*). For whether these are without error, we decide; but if Scripture is infallible, then it decides for us that there are no errors in it, even though we might also think that to be the case" (*Dictaten* 1.89). Inspired Scripture expresses its content

---

24. The significance of this distinction will occupy us below.

"in a divinely errorless fashion" ("goddelijk feilloos," 1.86). Accordingly, one can no more separate Scripture's material authority from its formal authority than a tree from its bark (1.70), or ink from a blotter (1.73). The *form* of Scripture is "infallibilis" (1.73). Moreover, to acknowledge this is critically important, for "Scripture retains its divine authority only in those circles where at the same time its formal infallibility is confessed" (2.128).

11. Does Kuyper, like Berkouwer,[25] hold, as Rogers and McKim maintain,[26] that biblical infallibility excludes error only in the sense of deception and the intent to deceive, but not deny the presence of other kinds of mistakes and incorrectness?

One passage in the *Dictaten* (1.40–41), where the necessity of Scripture is under discussion, would seem to answer this question decisively. An inscripturated revelation is necessary, for one reason, because oral tradition becomes corrupted. This corruption is inevitable, among other factors, because of falsehood (de Leugen). Falsehood is essentially a malfunction of memory. In all its forms it is a result of sin and includes not only willful suppression but also weakness of memory, forgetfulness as well as falsification. "An uncertain memory is just as much falsehood as intentional falsification." At the end of the passage, he summarizes, "Thus these three: forgetting, lying and unintentional falsifying corrupt all oral tradition." Accordingly, Scripture is necessary and as such is free from *all* error, unintentional mistakes as well as deception.

Subsequently, in discussing the authority of Scripture (2.183), these remarks are recalled and the point is made that regeneration does not eliminate the necessity of Scripture because even after regeneration "the danger of forgetting, error and lying, and the limitation of human nature" remain. Plainly, Scripture is seen to be free from this danger and limitation.

In the summary paragraph at the beginning of the section on the inspiration of Scripture (2.128), we find the flat assertion that, among other purposes, graphic inspiration aims at "the removal and prevention of every error which threatened to creep into any writing through inadvertence and malicious intent." The scope of the error excluded by this generalization is comprehensive, and certainly broader than the intention to deceive.

Kuyper's conception of biblical infallibility is given a particularly sharp profile where he distinguishes it from the views of the Ethical theologians.[27] He has a special concern to make this difference plain. According to Kuyper's representation (*Holy Spirit*, 153), the latter held that inspiration is an unusually high degree of that spiritual sensitivity and enlightenment given to all believers by regeneration. This extraordinary illumination, however, does not remove the possibility of error, and in fact Scripture, while substantially true and reliable, does contain peripheral errors and mistakes. Kuyper calls this a "seductive representation," one against which "the conscience of believers will always protest," because "all such beautifully sounding theories strip the apostolic word of its certainty" ("zekerheid," rendered "infallibility" in the translation).

Kuyper's counterposition (*Dictaten* 2.109–112) is that revelation is an intellectual conception, while regeneration is moral. Certainly the intellectual and the ethical are related; there is an ethical side to inspiration. But the distinction between inspiration and regenera-

25. Holy Scripture, 181–83.

26. *Authority*, 393; cf. 431; see also Jack Rogers, "The Church Doctrine of Biblical Authority," in *Biblical Authority*, ed. J. Rogers (Waco: Word Books, 1977), 44; "Third Alternative," 80–81, 83.

27. Principally D. Chantepie de la Saussaye (1818–74) and J. H. Gunning, Jr. (1829–1905), leading representatives of one of the most influential theological trends in the Netherlands Reformed Church throughout this period.

tion (illumination) must not be blurred. The latter is not the sufficient cause of the former. Otherwise moral and intellectual (in)fallibility would be equivalent. The facts of the matter, however, are that "in a spiritual sense the apostles were in all respects fallible men just like us, but in an intellectual sense they claim infallibility." Similarly, in distinction from the spiritual character of the other forms of inspiration in the actual revelation process, graphic inspiration "is directed, not toward spiritual content, but toward the priority of intellectual action" (2.128). Biblical infallibility, including the kind of error excluded by it, is first of all an *intellectual*, not an ethical, conception.

Elsewhere (2.32–34), in combating the Ethical viewpoint, Kuyper distinguishes the ethical and intellectual sides of inspiration and explores the latter by raising the question of the cause of human error. By considering the case of Adam before the fall, he concludes that all error, not just willful lying, is the result of sin. "Our conclusion is therefore: a lack of a sense of truth, forgetfulness and mistakes are consequences of sin. They did not exist in Adam before the fall, and they will not recur in heaven after death." Accordingly, the infallibility secured by inspiration excludes "the result of sin like forgetting, making mistakes, etc."

What was promised to the apostles, when they functioned as witnesses of Jesus, was "absolute infallibility," which excluded "the possibility of their falling into mistakes or untruths" (*Holy Spirit*, 173).

Against this background it is not surprising to find, among other comments made in passing, that one may not say that something has not happened, when Scripture says it has, because "whoever denies anything in Scripture makes God a liar" (*Dictaten* 1.78). Graphic inspiration functions, among its other provisions, to keep the writers of the New Testament epistles from making any mistakes (2.138; *Holy Spirit*, 177). The kind of truth/error at stake in Scripture is seen in the observation that the creation narrative in Genesis "recorded many centuries ago what so far no man could know of himself, and what at the present time is only partly revealed by the study of geology" (*Holy Spirit*, 77). Plainly, for Kuyper religious truth, specifically the truthfulness of the Bible, and scientific truth are not discontinuous or unrelated, but on the same continuum of truth.

We should not be surprised, then, to find Kuyper closing the lengthy chapter on the authority of Scripture by refuting various post-Enlightenment rationalistic claims of contradiction and error in Scripture (*Dictaten* 2.210ff). Not only does he attend to such "theological" issues like the reconciliation of Paul and James on justification, but he also concerns himself with solutions to alleged discrepancies in numbers and other historical details, like those between Stephen's speech in Acts 7 and Genesis, or between Kings and Chronicles (215–16). Such efforts at harmonization are certainly not prominent in Kuyper's view as a whole. But they are not foreign to it either.

In the sense, as we have seen, of the exclusion of all error the closing sentence to the discussion of apostolic inspiration in *The Work of the Holy Spirit* serves as a fair summary of Kuyper's views on the presence of error in Scripture (p. 157; italics in the Dutch original, 1.208): "And yet in both prophet and apostle inspiration is the wholly extraordinary operation of the Holy Spirit whereby, in a manner for us incomprehensible and to them not always conscious, they were kept from the *possibility* of error."

12. We are now in a position to take up what in more recent discussions appears to be the most frequently quoted passage from Kuyper on Scripture, I sometimes get the impression, almost the only passage quoted. It reads as follows (*Principles*, 550):

When in the four Gospels Jesus, on the same occasion, is made to say words that are different in form of expression, it is impossible that He should have used these four forms at once. The Holy Spirit, however, merely intends to make an impression upon the Church that wholly corresponds to what Jesus said.

Rogers and McKim, for one, cite this passage to show Kuyper's support of their view that the authority of Scripture is located in its divine content in distinction from its human form.[28] Specifically, they believe it evidences Kuyper's (and Bavinck's) openness, so very different from the negative, rejecting attitude of the Princeton theology, to the issues raised by biblical criticism. The differences between the four Gospels belong to the human form of Scripture. As such they are subject to critical scrutiny and evaluation, because they are neither constitutive of nor essential to the divine, saving message of Scripture.

In evaluating these statements the context may not be ignored. The larger chapter division deals with the inspiration of Scripture specifically, or, as Kuyper prefers to call it, graphic inspiration. And the paragraph where this passage occurs begins by recalling that our warrant for accepting this graphic inspiration rests on the self-witness of Scripture. Scripture itself does not provide us with a theory of graphic inspiration, but the nature of the authority that Christ and the apostles attribute to Scripture allows no other conclusion. To say that all Scripture is inspired is not to speak about the personal inspiration of the human authors but about what they wrote. Certainly they remained writers in the truest sense, compiling and examining material, arranging and composing, but "in all these functions the Holy Spirit worked so effectively upon the action of their human minds, that thereby their product obtained divine authority."

This last generalization prompts Kuyper to qualify. The fact that everything the biblical writers wrote has divine authority does not mean everything they wrote has a "divine character." For instance, when the writer recounts what Shimei said (2 Sam. 16:5–8), this does not make his demonic language divine, but certifies that Shimei spoke these evil words.[29]

What graphic inspiration effects, then, is divinely authoritative certification. Concerning this certification Kuyper immediately adds the qualification that it happens "always impressionistically," in the New Testament as well as the Old Testament. Then follow the statements about the four Gospels quoted above. The paragraph goes on to close with the observation that the Old Testament, too, because it has been composed "under one continuous authority," justifies citation with an "it is written," as was done by Jesus, even where it is modified "in nature and character according to the claims of the content."

The point of the passage in question, then, is that the differences between the four Gospels (along with the New Testament use of the Old) exemplify the "impressionistic" character of the biblical records. How, more exactly, does Kuyper understand this impressionistic quality, particularly with reference to the related issues of error in Scripture and the form of Scripture?

(1) On the page immediately preceding the one where this passage is found (*Principles*, 549), attention is directed specifically to the historical books of the Bible and the kind of

28. *Authority*, 390; see also Rogers, "Church Doctrine," 42; "Third Alternative," 76. Berkouwer, *Holy Scripture*, 250–51, takes a similar view.

29. Cf. *Dictaten* 2.130ff. where, in defending the view that the entire Bible is God's word, Kuyper distinguishes between the *lalia* and *graphe* of God; the former, part of which is recorded in Scripture, consists only of revelations (words) from God, while the latter consists in the *lalia* (words) of men and of Satan, as well as of God.

historiography associated with graphic inspiration. Concerning the activity of the human writers the sum of the matter is that "the Holy Spirit worked effectively as a leading, directing and determining power; but their subjectivity was not lost." The presence of the writers' subjectivity is seen in the fact that frequently, for instance in the four Gospels, there is more than one account of the same set of events. These are not merely repetitions. They arise because no single writer could take in the full impact of these mighty events and because the perceptions of one writer necessarily differ from those of another. This is how biblical history lives on. "It gives no notarial acts, but reproduces what has been received in the consciousness, and does this not with that precision of outline which belongs to architecture, but with the impressionistic certainty of life."

This passage makes it reasonably plain that the term "impressionistic" functions as a positive description of biblical narrative in contrast to what it is not. The biblical records are impressionistic; that is, they are not marked by notarial precision or blueprint, architectural exactness. At the same time this impressionistic quality does not detract from their certainty. This certainty, it should be noted, attaches to them fully as historical records, not merely to their saving message in distinction from their narrative form.

This understanding of "impressionistic" is echoed at a number of places elsewhere in Kuyper's writings. One of the chapters in *The Work of the Holy Spirit* (174–78) is given over entirely to stressing the non-notarial character of the New Testament and biblical infallibility. The same point comes out repeatedly in the *Dictaten*. At 2.130–31 he observes that in Scripture for the most part we do not have the word of God exactly as it was spoken. "Whoever in reading Scripture thinks that everything was spoken precisely as it stands in the text, is totally mistaken." Again, he points to the differences between the four Gospels and the New Testament use of the Old Testament as sufficient to show that as a rule the *lalia* of God has not come to us "in its original form."

In typical fashion Kuyper illustrates his point by recalling an aspect of contemporary European parliamentary practice. Both the French and English parliaments keep two kinds of records, one a verbatim account of what a speaker says (a "procès-verbal"), the other a brief résumé or summary account (a "procès-analytique"). As a rule, in Scripture the lalia of God is reported "en procès-analytique," not "en procès-verbal."

It would be a mistake, Kuyper continues, to suppose that the verbatim report is better or more desirable. In some instances, the reverse may well be the case. The critical, in fact the only issue in this respect is whether the speaker makes himself answerable for the record, whether verbatim or summary. Here Kuyper's commitment to the Holy Spirit as the primary author of Scripture in the formal sense comes through unmistakably. The Spirit, as *auctor primarius*, ultimately answers for the biblical records. Therefore, when, for instance, the New Testament quotes the Old in variant forms, the same thought is expressed "in an epexegetically more precise fashion," and we gain more than if the Holy Spirit had simply repeated verbatim. Similarly, in the four Gospels, taken together, the Spirit, as "a stenographer," gives us Jesus' words with a fullness that any one of them could not possibly express. Not only do we not lose by the fourfold form, we gain a "fuller, more mature" perception.

In a similar vein (*Dictaten* 2.141), we ought not to think that the speeches in Job are given precisely as Bildad spoke them. Rather they provide a "romantic representation" or "free rendering" of what was said. But because this happens "under guarantee of the Holy

Spirit," they express what was said "not only not inaccurately, but more accurately and, besides that, more elegantly."

Two factors, then, serve to define Kuyper's biblical impressionism. On the one hand, the biblical narratives do not record the past with stenographic preciseness or photographic exactness.[30] Yet as historical records they are completely accurate and do not at all mislead. The latter point, held without any apparent tension with the former, needs to be appreciated. Nowhere is it more forcefully expressed than in a passage discussing the inspiration of the writing prophets as historians (*Dictaten* 2.76):

> The distinguishing mark of inspiration, however, above everything else is that it guarantees absolute accuracy [absolute juistheid]. The singular character of the writers of the Old and New Testaments lies in the fact that the stamp of truth and certainty is impressed upon their writings. The Holy Spirit so leads their spirits that in them the results of sin are cut off and prevented. This distinguishing mark is not relative, but absolute.

Biblical narrative is absolutely accurate, without being notarially exact. This is the basic thrust of Kuyper's position.

Accordingly, when Kuyper speaks of the possibility of "innocent inaccuracies" in historical records (*Principles*, 457), this expression ought not simply to be lifted out of context and enlisted without further qualification against efforts at harmonization, as Berkouwer does.[31] If we are not to distort Kuyper's meaning, we must not fail to note the specific terms of the contrast that serves to define these "innocent inaccuracies." They "so far from doing harm, rather bring to light the free expression of life above notarial affectation."[32]

A passage like this does point up a consideration important for a discriminating, overall understanding of Kuyper's position, namely his variable usage of terminology for correctness, accuracy, and the like. He uses it either affirmatively, in an impressionistic sense, or pejoratively, in a notarial sense. Only due attention to the context in each instance will be able to decide which sense is intended.

(2) Perhaps the deepest perspective on the sense of the quotation under examination in this section is provided by reflecting further on the distinction, already noted (see above, n. 24), between divine and human errorlessness (feilloosheid). Kuyper develops this distinction in the *Dictaten* (1.86, 91–92), in his initial treatment of the inspiration of Scripture under the head of the authority of Scripture.

What is the difference, Kuyper asks (91), between "divinely errorless" and "humanly errorless"? The latter is bound up with human limitation and so is limited to a particular form, namely meticulous, notarial agreement; it is mechanical, like a photograph. Human errorlessness, however, is always fallible, for no photograph reproduces its subject in truth, even if it reproduces every hair in detail.

Divine errorlessness, in contrast, is like the work of a painter. He is not concerned to number hairs on his subject's head, but to capture an image from the different positions of the subject and to paint that. This picture is not as notarially exact as a mute photographic portrait, but is really much more accurate.

---

30. Note also *Encyclopaedie* 3.68, 73, where he observes that "mechanical, notarial preciseness" is foreign to the whole of revelation.

31. *Holy Scripture,* 245.

32. "De vrije levensuiting boven de gemaniereerdheid van het notarieele" (*Encyclopaedie* 2.411).

In summary, divine errorlessness, like art, gives the essence without error, but without maintaining precisely the same form. Human errorlessness, like photography, gives the form in notarial fashion, but can provide no guarantee for the essence.

The errorlessness of Scripture, then, is divine, not human. Here, as elsewhere, Kuyper illustrates this by the two specific cases of the New Testament quotations of the Old Testament and the differences between the four Gospels. Human errorlessness would require a notarial extract, of the Old Testament passage in the one instance, of the words of Jesus in the other. Divine errorlessness is what we in fact find in Scripture: citation of the Old Testament that is free in its form yet faithful to the thought of the passage quoted, reproduction of the essence of Jesus' words that is completely without error, yet not always in the same form in which they were spoken. The formal variations in these and other instances are not an argument against but *for* the (formal) inspiration of Scripture. God is an artist, not a photographer.

It bears emphasizing, as Kuyper notes in this context, that the Bible's divine errorlessness ultimately roots in its divine authorship, *formally considered*. If I transmit an authoritative message from someone else, then I must do so literally and may not change the wording. But if I convey my own message, then I am free to vary the wording, provided I don't alter the substance. In the case of Scripture, if it were only a matter of human witness, even divinely authorized witness, to a message from God, then the writers would have been bound to convey that message verbatim. But since ultimately it is the Holy Spirit who everywhere speaks in Scripture, formally and materially, *he* is free to make the variations we observe, without any detriment to its divine errorlessness.

Elsewhere Kuyper repeatedly draws a direct, material connection between the pervasively non-notarial character of Scripture and its unique divine origin. By means of free quotations, in graphic inspiration the Holy Spirit maintains himself as the author of underlying material inspiration (*Dictaten* 2.142; cf. 173–79). An abstract, rational proof of graphic inspiration is not possible, because such proof works with a conception of precision that does not lend itself to the revelation of a divine dynamic in human language (2.145). In fact, the Holy Spirit, who alone is able to convince us of graphic inspiration, enables us to perceive that the many incongruities in Scripture could not be left standing in a human author but are in fact a mark of its divinity (2.145).

There are two sorts of precision (2.147–48), mechanical and organic. A mechanically molded statue or piece of artillery precisely resembles from every angle all others cast from the same mold. Among ice floes or winter flowers, however, there are great dissimilarities. The edges of a piece of wood fashioned by an artisan are completely smooth and even; the bark of a tree is quite coarse. "And yet, if someone asks, where is the greatest precision, in the mechanical or the organic, everyone feels that it is not in the mechanical but in the organic that there is the greater precision and most perfect beauty." In the realm of truth, then, the question of the sort of precision or accuracy has to be raised. If mechanical, then we must have a notarial record. But if organic, then it must be judged by its own standard. The classic, rational apologetic for graphic inspiration is not only inappropriate but also counterproductive, because it places the demands of mechanical preciseness on Scripture, which by its nature demands organic precision. Scripture is forced into a mold that is not suited to its organic character.

Later on in the same section (2.154–55), Kuyper observes that the full, multifaceted character of Scripture cannot be exhausted by the finite grasp of our logical, mathematical thinking. One result is that according to intellectual demands and on the flat terrain of logic, everything in Scripture is not in harmony. But certainly that harmony is there, and we see it when, in faith, we view it "from the standpoint of the Holy Spirit."

We may now try to focus our conclusions about the key quotation under examination in this section. Rogers and McKim turn that quotation on its head, giving it a sense almost diametrically opposite to what Kuyper intended. This is not putting it too strongly. For them, the impressionistic, non-notarial quality of biblical narrative is a function of its human form in distinction from its divine message and can be subjected, without concern, to the canons of biblical criticism. For Kuyper, this impressionism is a sure sign of the Bible's *more* than purely human origin. It highlights the unique divine inspiration of the *form*, as well as the message, of Scripture. It, too, gives us "the standpoint of the Holy Spirit." It hardly needs to be pointed out that to misunderstand Kuyper here decisively skews his doctrine of Scripture as a whole.

One other point not yet touched above should be mentioned here. Rogers and McKim introduce this quotation in a short section with the heading, "Salvation Not Science" (*Authority*, 390). According to them Kuyper and Bavinck held that Scripture does not intend to give us "technically correct scientific information." That is true. But at the same time what Kuyper would also want to point out is that in its own fashion—undeniably impressionistic, not notarially precise, not scientifically exact—Scripture gives information that is directly relevant to science. For instance, the creation narrative records "what at the present time is only partly revealed by the study of geology" (*Holy Spirit*, 77). Rogers and McKim seem unaware of this side of the picture. "Salvation not science" is a false dichotomy for Kuyper. Entirely alien to him is the post-Kantian, dimensional understanding of truth with which they are apparently operating.

13. What, at last, is the relationship between Kuyper's accent on its impressionistic character as a distinguishing mark of the Bible's unique divine origin and errorlessness, and his stress, taken as our point of departure for examining his views, on the servant-form of Scripture? Are these two emphases compatible? Where else, if not in this scientifically inexact, notarially imprecise impressionism, would we find evidence of that servant-form which involves Scripture fully in the limitations of human language and the brokenness of our existence, marred by want and sin?

In fact, the solution does not lie in isolating the two—impressionism and servant-form—from each other, as if each represents a sector of concern independent of the other. And apparently for Kuyper the harmony between the two lies in the analogy between incarnation and inscripturation (discussed above in sections 4 and 8). The same phenomenon—nonscientific, inexact narration of events and notarially imprecise recording of speech material—is to be seen both "from above" and "from below." The same *formal* phenomenon is at once both truly divine and truly human. This impressionism is evidence of the genuinely human side of the Scriptures, but not only that. Even more it shows their unique divine origin. The mystery of inspiration involves the reality of this impressionism as it derives from both God and man, but originally from God. Both the Holy Spirit and the human authors are accountable for it, but the Spirit ultimately. Adapting the language of 1 Thessalonians 2:13, Kuyper's view is that the word of Scripture we receive, in its evident, genuine humanness and subjection to the limitations of our language, we receive ultimately, not as the word of men, but as it actually (ἀληθῶς) is, formally as well as materially, the word of God.

The incarnational analogy is obviously foundational to Kuyper's views on Scripture. Its legitimacy is for the most part assumed rather than argued by him. Nor does he discuss its limitations. Still it would plainly be wrong to conclude that he saw an exact symmetry extending to every point, so that the relationship between divine and human in the Bible would, say, form a hypostatic union or be properly circumscribed by the formulations of Chalcedon. Yet for him Scripture's "theanthropic" constitution, formal as well as material, is such that it brings him to hold, in view of his conviction that all error, unintentional as well as intentional, is the result of sin (see above, section 11), that the analogue to the sinlessness of Christ is the errorlessness of the Bible.[33]

On *Dictaten* 1.64 Kuyper uses an illustration that gives the gist of much that we have already seen. In affirming the human form of Scripture and the limitations that consequently cling to it, at the same time he emphatically rejects the further conclusion, drawn by the Ethical theologians, that the Bible contains falsehood. A clerk in an office, he says, is not fired because of the ink spots on his hands but only if he falsifies the books. For Kuyper, the biblical records are kept in ink and by those with ink spots on their hands, but the records themselves are in perfect order.

14. Along the way we have noted something of the way in which Kuyper sees himself in relation to post-Reformation orthodoxy.[34] We come back to that briefly here as well as to the related matter of his attitude toward the biblical criticism of his day.

As we have seen, Kuyper recognizes and criticizes weaknesses in the classical orthodox doctrine of Scripture, particularly what he perceives to be its overly logicizing and ahistorical tendencies. To cite a couple of other examples, he notes how late orthodoxy undercut the internal testimony of the Holy Spirit by trying to develop a system of outward proofs for the divine character of Scripture, able to convince by reason without the enlightening of the Spirit (*Principles*, 558). And he sharply criticizes the misuse of Scripture in preaching and the life of the church to which, in the eighteenth century, the *loca probantia* method of dogmatics eventually led (*Encyclopaedie* 3.173–74). Still, in all he displays a sense of basic, even cordial continuity with Protestant orthodoxy. For instance, the *loca probantia* approach still has its inalienable right if only due attention is given to the context and the place of the text in the history of revelation.

Perhaps the most instructive outlook on Kuyper's stance as a whole is provided by his rectoral address at the founding of the Free University of Amsterdam in 1881 and the controversy this address provoked. The title itself is highly indicative, "Present Day Biblical Criticism in Its Questionable Tendency for the Church of the Living God."[35]

This address is fairly seen as undertaking to vindicate the founding of the Free University and to chart its direction. Its thrust is that contemporary biblical criticism (1) has destroyed theology, replacing it with the science of religion, (2) has robbed the church of the Bible by denying its inspiration and substituting philosophical hypotheses, and so (3) threatens the church with the loss of its freedom in Christ.

The measure of this address is unmistakable in the sharply negative responses it elicited.[36] For instance, J. J. Van Oosterzee charged it with fueling dissension by attacking the good

---

33. On this point Kuyper, among others, would appear to be guilty of what Berkouwer considers an unwarranted extension of the analogy (*Holy Scripture*, 202), although he regularly appeals to Kuyper in support of his own views.

34. See above, section 3.

35. *De hedendaagsche Schriftcritiek in hare bedenkelijke strekking voor de Gemeente des levenden Gods* (Amsterdam: J. H. Kruyt, 1881).

36. This reaction, some of it strident, is sampled by J. C. Rullmann, *Kuyper-Bibliografie*, 3 vols. (Kampen: J. H. Kok, 1923–40), 2.55–61. Rullmann also sketches the background of the address and briefly summarizes it (47–54).

right of biblical criticism on the basis of a mechanical view of inspiration, and suggested that it would have been better for Kuyper to have given a penitential address on "Present Day Church Conflict in Its Questionable Tendency for the Coming of the Kingdom of God." Similarly, another respondent entitled his remarks, "Dr. A. Kuyper's View of Scripture in Its Questionable Tendency for the Church of the Living God."

In a series of periodical articles Kuyper responded particularly to the criticisms of Van Oosterzee. He forcefully denied not only that he held a mechanical view of inspiration but also, highly enlightening for our purposes, that this was ever the view of the older Reformed dogmaticians. Since the time of Herder, Kuyper observes, the opposition between "puppets" and "genuine human personalities," along with the charge that confessional orthodoxy reduced the biblical writers to the former, has been a constant thread ("a fixed runner," "een vaste looper"), picked up by succeeding theological schools. It is not surprising, then, to find Van Oosterzee attempting to make use of "this rusty old runner."

Kuyper dismisses it once for all by appealing back, not to the Reformation, but to the theology of the seventeenth century, in which, as Van Oosterzee would have it, "the light of the Reformation had again been extinguished by scholasticism." Specifically, he cites the *Leiden Synopsis* and notes there (Disputation 3, ch. 7, p. 24, ed. 1632) a clear recognition of the full involvement of the human writers with their various capacities and abilities. "With this clear testimony out of the Egyptian darkness of seventeenth-century scholasticism," Kuyper adds with an edge of sarcasm, "this idle talk is refuted once for all, and from now on the Scholtens and Van Oosterzees can spare themselves the trouble of pointing out differences in style, patterns of thinking, circumstances, character formation, etc." (Rullman, 57). All these human factors are not the discovery of recent biblical studies but have long since been recognized within the Reformed tradition. Kuyper continues:

> No, truly, you esteemed professors of Leiden, Groningen, and Utrecht, you do not really need to imagine that either for the Reformed fathers of an earlier day or for *their legitimate offspring* [italics added] in our time, the human factor in the origin of Scripture has not existed because only the divine factor offers them absolute certainty.

The Reformed tradition is not, nor has it ever been, in any doubt about the *vox humana* of Scripture. "But," Kuyper concludes with an expression of his ultimate concern (Rullman, 58),

> since for the church of Christ the issue is not first of all an *artistic* outlook but is first of all the *gravity of life*, the propitiation of our sins, the salvation of *souls*, stability in the midst of doubt, therefore and therefore alone are we put off, grieved and troubled by your endless enthusiasm over all those human particularities, and for us that holy, that divine factor, which governs the entire Scripture as Scripture, has a much greater and much higher fascination.

Plainly Kuyper's basic affinities are with Reformed orthodoxy. He, along with the emerging Free University, is its "legitimate offspring," particularly in what pertains to the doctrine of Scripture. At the same time, while entirely congenial with the careful, methodical study of the Bible as a collection of historical documents, his antipathy toward contemporary biblical criticism in its deepest intention is unrelenting.

This profile is borne out elsewhere throughout his writings. To take just a handful of examples, in the course of discussing the testimony of Jesus to the graphic inspiration of the Old Testament, he affirms that the basic thrust of this testimony has been captured by "the so-called 'mechanical inspiration.'" In going on to reply to attacks on the latter, he comments parenthetically, "It is called mechanical in order to use a pejorative [lelijk] word; Satan slanders not only persons but the truth itself" (*Dictaten* 2.160). Again (*Dictaten* 2.132), it is hardly a telling argument against the old orthodox view that the entire Bible is God's word, to appeal to the fact that Scripture contains words of Satan. "As if Voetius, in fact even the simplest farmer from Gelderland, didn't know that!" Those who argue in this way only show that they are unfamiliar with "our old theological works."

In the *Dictaten* the lengthy chapter on the authority of Scripture closes with a section concerning various kinds of opposition to its authority (2.202ff). Such opposition ought not to be dealt with incidentally or from purely apologetic concerns, but in a systematic fashion, showing how reason has been made into a false source (*principium*) of knowledge. In fact, in its various turns since the Enlightenment historical criticism as a whole has been controlled by worldly reason (*logos kosmikos*) in rebellion against the holy reason (*logos hagios*) embodied in Scripture (210ff.). Psychologically, the source of "this sinful inclination" is a "false thirst for freedom" which seeks autonomy above Scripture (1.39). To be specific, the school of Wellhausen, Robertson Smith and the Ethical theologians, among others, are not able to affirm in any meaningful sense that the Bible is God's word (1.71–72).

The balance of Kuyper's position is summed up at the close of a brief discussion on the necessity of Scripture (*Holy Spirit*, 64):

> Not as though critical and historical examination were prohibited. Such endeavor for the glory of God is highly commendable. But as the physiologist's search for the genesis of human life becomes sinful if immodest or dangerous to unborn life, so does every criticism of Holy Scripture become sinful and culpable if irreverent or seeking to destroy the life of God's Word in the consciousness of the church.

"Sinful and culpable" criticism? There can be little question that Kuyper has in view primarily most of the biblical criticism of his day.

All told, seen in historical perspective, I cannot escape the noteworthy conclusion that the views on the relation between Reformation and post-Reformation orthodoxy and on contemporary biblical criticism which Rogers and McKim attribute to Kuyper, are almost exactly those of the Ethical theologians, views which in fact he regularly and implacably opposed throughout the course of his life.

15. *Summary and Conclusions*. At the outset six questions were put to the views of Kuyper and Bavinck. Answers to them for Kuyper can now be briefly summarized.

(1) While ahistorical, rationalistic tendencies may be present in post-Reformation orthodoxy, there is a deep, inner continuity between it and Kuyper, as well as the Reformation itself. In particular, it fairly represents the same historic church doctrine of Scripture that he is seeking to uphold in his own day.

(2) The internal testimony of the Holy Spirit is absolutely indispensable to recognizing the divine origin and authority of Scripture. There is no place for a system of external proofs for inspiration, directed to unaided reason.

(3) The form and the content of Scripture are both truly divine and truly human and, as such, are indivisible. The form of Scripture is predestined; as its primary author, the Holy Spirit is ultimately accountable for its form as well as its content. It is wrong to assign its form to the human side, its content or central message to the divine side of Scripture, as if the form/content distinction parallels the human/divine distinction.

(4) The incarnation gives rise to inscripturation, and the latter is intrinsic to the former; the one could not exist without the other. The mystery of Scripture is its unique theanthropic character, without, however, involving any sort of hypostatic union between divine and human elements. Scripture has its servant-form only because Christ was incarnated not in a glorified state but in a state of humiliation. The analogue to the sinlessness of Christ is that Scripture is without error.

(5) Careful, methodical study is demanded in view of the historical origin and human authorship of the biblical documents. But contemporary biblical criticism is for the most part premised on rational autonomy and, whether or not intentionally, undermines the claims and authority of Scripture.

(6) The Bible is without errors, absolutely, not only in its content but also in its form, not only in the sense of deception but also to the exclusion of unintentional mistakes, faulty judgments, lapses of memory and the like.[37] For Scripture to contain errors would mean that God is guilty of error. The truth of Scripture, appropriate to its unique divine authorship, is impressionistic, not notarially precise or scientifically exact. Repeatedly Kuyper speaks of the errorlessness (feilloosheid) of Scripture. While he apparently never uses the closest Dutch equivalent for the term inerrancy (foutloosheid), there is no reason to suppose that he would object to it or find it inappropriate, provided it is understood in an impressionistic, nontechnical sense.

---

37. Kuyper, for one, then, is chargeable with the "serious formalization of the concept of erring" opposed by Berkouwer (*Holy Scripture,* 181–82).

32

Herman Bavinck's *Reformed Dogmatics*, Volume 1, *Prolegomena*

Herman Bavinck, *Reformed Dogmatics*, vol. 1, *Prolegomena*, ed. John Bolt, trans. John Vriend (Grand Rapids: Baker Academic, 2003), 387–494.

Herman Bavinck (1854–1921) was a leading Dutch Reformed theologian in the modern age. He studied at the University of Leiden and the Theological Seminary at Kampen. After a short pastorate, Bavinck taught systematic theology, first at Kampen (1882–1902) and then at the Free University of Amsterdam (1902–20), where he succeeded Abraham Kuyper. Bavinck's greatest theological achievement is his four-volume *Reformed Dogmatics*, now available in English. It is from this translation that the two chapters below are reprinted. A summary of his work was translated in 1956 as *Our Reasonable Faith* (originally entitled *Magnalia Dei*). His Stone Lectures at Princeton Theological Seminary in 1908–9 were published as *The Philosophy of Revelation*. Both texts touch on the topics of revelation and Scripture and thus offer supplementary insights into Bavinck's views, which were welcomed at Princeton; and Louis Berkhof, for one, was greatly influenced by Bavinck's theology in his own theological endeavors. Bavinck's contribution is greatly appreciated at Westminster, as the articles by Cornelius Van Til and Richard B. Gaffin Jr. indicate.

Bavinck's theological approach is characterized by a return to the Reformed theology of John Calvin, a biblical approach, a deep consciousness of historical theology, and a thorough interaction with contemporary views. In the first chapter, he deals with the inspiration of Scripture; the original title, more literally translated as "The Theopneustia of Scripture," harks back to the classic text on inspiration in 2 Timothy 3:16. Here Bavinck begins by considering the Old Testament and New Testament foundations of the doctrine of inspiration, thus appealing to the idea of the self-witness of Scripture. Then he surveys the history of the doctrine in the church and defines his views in the context of Roman Catholicism and the crisis brought on theology by the Enlightenment. At the end of this chapter, he puts forward an "organic" view of biblical inspiration, which is distinct from both a "mechanical" view and a "dynamic" view.

In so doing, Bavinck takes into account both the human side of Scripture and its full divine character. While Scripture's focus is on salvation in Christ, it has implications for science and society.

In the next chapter, Bavinck defines the four classical attributes of Scripture in the theological context of his time: authority, necessity, clarity or perspicuity, and sufficiency. Bavinck expounds these attributes vis-à-vis Roman Catholicism (from Trent to Vatican I), illuminism (starting with the Anabaptists), and modern rationalism. While not denying some role of tradition, the history of interpretation, and the Spirit (illumination), Bavinck in his balanced exposition asserts in no uncertain terms the perfection of Scripture and its self-authenticating character. Thereby he stands in clear continuity with the teaching of the Reformation and post-Reformation orthodoxy. Later in the anthology, we will see how Van Til creatively applies these same attributes to general revelation.

Note on the translation: The editors of the English translation have added "subdivisions and headings." Further, "all Bavinck's original footnotes have been retained and brought up to contemporary bibliographic standards" and "additional notes added by the editor are clearly marked" (p. 21). In addition, "subparagraph numbers" from the original are placed in square brackets to ease reference to the Dutch text (p. 22). The original Dutch edition also included short bibliographies at the beginning of most chapters; we have included these in this selection. Some of the footnotes are also slightly modified to fit the bibliographic style of the anthology.

Bibliography: "Bavinck, Herman." *NSHERK* 2:14–15. J. Bolt. "Bavinck, Herman (1854–1921)." Pp. 37–39 in *BDE*. Eric. D. Bristley. *Guide to the Writings of Herman Bavinck. With an Essay by John Bolt.* Grand Rapids: Reformation Heritage Books, 2008. Richard B. Gaffin Jr. "Old Amsterdam and Inerrancy?" *WTJ* 45, 1 (Spring 1983): 219–72. Repr. pp. 47–103 in *God's Word in Servant-Form: Abraham Kuyper and Herman Bavinck on the Doctrine of Scripture.* Introduction by Peter A. Lillback. Jackson, MS: Reformed Academic Press, 2008. Ron Gleason. *Herman Bavinck: Pastor, Churchman, Statesman, and Theologian.* Phillipsburg, NJ: P&R Publishing, 2010. I. J. Hesselink. "Bavinck, Herman, Influence Of." Pp. 27–28 in *DP&RTA*. Jack B. Rogers & Donald K. McKim. *The Authority and Interpretation of the Bible: An Historical Approach.* San Francisco: Harper & Row, 1979. Pp. 388–93. K. Runia. "Bavinck, Herman (1854–1821)." P. 81 in *NDT*. Henk van den Belt. *The Authority of Scripture in Reformed Theology: Truth and Trust.* Leiden: Brill, 2008. Pp. 229–99. John Van Engen. "Bavinck, Herman (1854–1921)." P. 129 in *EDT*. Cornelius Van Til. "Bavinck the Theologian: A Review Article." *WTJ* 24, 1 (November 1961): 48–64. Repr. in *Bavinck the Theologian*. Philadelphia: Westminster Theological Seminary, 1961. Geerhardus Vos. Review of *Gereformeerde Dogmatiek, Vol. One,* by H. Bavinck. In *The Presbyterian Reformed Review* 7 (1896): 356–63. Repr. in *Redemptive History and Biblical Interpretation: The Shorter Writings of Geerhardus Vos.* Ed. Richard B. Gaffin Jr. Phillipsburg, NJ: Presbyterian and Reformed, 1980. Pp. 475–84. H. M. Vroom. "Scripture Read and Interpreted: The Development of the Doctrine of Scripture and Hermeneutics in Gereformeerde Theology in the Netherlands." *CTJ* 28 (1993): 352–71.

CHAPTER 13: THE INSPIRATION OF SCRIPTURE

E. König, *Der Offenbarungsbegriff des Alten Testamentes,* 2 vols. (Leipzig: J. C. Hinrichs, 1882); K. Walz, *Die Lehre der Kirche von der H. Schrift nach der Schrift selbst geprüft* (Leiden: E. J. Brill, 1884); Joh. Delitzsch, *De inspiratione Scripturae Sacrae quid statuerint Patres Apostolici et Apologetae secundi saeculi* (Leipzig: A. Lorentz Bibliopolam, 1872); P. Dausch, *Die Schriftinspiration: Eine biblisch-geschichliche Studie* (Freiburg im Breisgau: Herder, 1891); K. Holzhey, *Die Inspiration der Heiligen Schrift in der Anschauung des Mittelalters* (München: J. J. Lentner, 1895); C. Pesch, *De Inspiratione Sacrae Scripturae* (Freiburg in Breisgau: Herder, 1906), 11–375; F. Kropatschek, *Das Schriftprinzip der lutherischen Kirche, Geschichtliche und dogmatische Untersuchungen,* vol. 1, *Die Vorgeschichte. Das Erbe des Mittelalters* (Leipzig: A. Deischert, 1903); R. Bellarmine, *Disputationum De controversiis,* vol. 1, *De Verbo Dei in 4 books;* J. B. Franzelin, *Tractatus de divina Traditione et Scriptura,* 3rd ed. (Romae: Typeographia Polyglotta, 1882), C. Pesch, *De Inspiratione Sacrae Scripturae,* 379–637; J. Gehard, *Loci Theologici,* ed. E. Preuss, 9 vols. (Berlin: G. Schlawitz, 1863–75), loc. 1, *De Sacra Scriptura;* J. A. Quenstedt, *Theologia Didacto-polemica sive Systema Theologicum* (1685), 1, chs. 3–4; J. Calvin, *Institutes of the Christian Religion* (1559), 1.6ff.; B. de Moor, *Commentarius Perpetuus in Joh. Marckii Compendium Theologiae Christianae Didactico-elencticum* (Leiden: J. Hasebroek, 1761), 1:114–446; Mart. Vitringa, *Doctrina Christianae Religionis* (Leiden: Joannes Le Mair, 1761), 1:36–123; F. Schleiermacher, *The Christian Faith,* ed. H. R. MacIntosh and J. S. Steward (Edinburgh: T. & T. Clark, 1928), §128ff.; R. Rothe, *Zur Dogmatik* (Gotha: F. A. Perthes, 1862), 121ff.; F. A. Philippi, *Kirchliche Glaubenslehre,* 3rd ed. (Gütersloh: Bertelsmann, 1902), 1:125ff.; A. Kuyper, *Encyclopaedie der Heilige Godgeheerdherd,* 2nd ed. (Kampen: J. H. Kok, 1902), 2:347ff., 429ff.

The Witness of the Old Testament

[106] For the doctrine of inspiration, the Old Testament supplies the following important components.

a. At a certain time in their life, the prophets knew they were being called by the Lord (Ex. 3; 1 Sam. 3; Jer. 1; Ezek. 1–3; Amos 3:7–8; 7:15). In many cases the call ran counter to their own wishes and desire (Ex. 3; Jer. 20:7; Amos 3:8), but YHWH was too strong for them. In Israel there was a general conviction that the prophets were emissaries of God (Jer. 26:5; 27:15), raised up and sent by him (Jer. 29:15; Deut. 18:15; Num. 11:29; 2 Chron. 36:15), his servants (2 Kings 17:23; 21:10; 24:2; Ezra 9:11; Ps. 105:15; etc.), standing before his face (1 Kings 17:1; 2 Kings 3:14; 5:16).

b. They are aware that YHWH has spoken to them and that they have received a revelation from him. He tells them what to say (Ex. 4:12; Deut. 18:18), puts the words in their mouth (Num. 22:38; 23:5; Deut. 18:18), speaks to them (Hos. 1:2; Hab. 2:1; Zech. 1:9, 13; 2:2, 8; 4:1, 4, 13–14; 5:5, 10; 6:4; Num. 12:2, 8; 2 Sam. 23:2; 1 Kings 22:28). A much used formula is: "thus says the Lord," or "the word of the Lord came to me," or word, oracle, נְאֻם (pass. part.), the "utterance" of YHWH. The whole OT Scripture is full of this expression, time after time introducing prophetic discourse. Repeatedly YHWH is even introduced in the first person as the one speaking (Josh. 24:2; Isa. 1:1–2; 8:1, 11; Jer. 1:2, 4, 11; 2:1; 7:1; Ezek. 1:3; 2:1; Hos. 1:1; Joel 1:1; Amos 2:1; etc). Actually it is YHWH speaking through the prophets (2 Sam. 23:1–2), who speaks through their mouth (Ex. 4:12, 15; Num. 23:5) and ministry (Hag. 1:1; 2 Kings 17:13). Their entire message is covered by YHWH's authority.

c. In the prophets this consciousness is so clear and firm that they even tell us the place where and the time when YHWH spoke to them and distinguish the times when he did and when he did not speak to them (Isa. 16:13–14; Jer. 3:6; 13:3; 26:1; 27:1; 28:1; 33:1; 34:1; 35:1; 36:1; 49:34; Ezek. 3:16; 8:1; 12:8; Hag. 1:1; Zech. 1:1; etc.). Moreover, that consciousness is so sharply objective that they clearly distinguish themselves from YHWH; he speaks to them (Isa. 8:1; 51:16; 59:21; Jer. 1:9; 3:6; 5:14; Ezek. 3:26; etc.); they listen with their ears and see with their eyes (Isa. 5:9; 6:8; 21:3, 10; 22:14; 28:22; Jer. 23:18; 49:14; Ezek. 2:8; 3:10, 17; 33:7; 40:4; 44:5; Hab. 3:2, 16; 2 Sam. 7:27; Job 33:16; 36:10), and ingest the words of YHWH (Jer. 15:16; Ezek. 3:1–3).

d. The prophets therefore make a sharp distinction between what God has revealed to them and what arises from within their own heart (Num. 16:28; 24:13; 1 Kings 12:33; Neh. 6:8; Ps. 41:6–7). Their complaint against the false prophets is precisely that they speak from within their own heart (Ezek. 13:2–3, 17; Jer. 14:14; 23:16, 26; Isa. 59:13), without being sent (Jer. 14:14; 29:9; Ezek. 13:6). They are, therefore, false prophets (Jer. 23:32; Isa. 9:15; Jer. 14:14; 20:6; 23:21–22, 26, 31, 36; 27:14; Ezek. 13:6–7; Mic. 2:11; Zeph. 3:4; Zech. 10:2) and fortune-tellers, diviners (Isa. 3:2; Mic. 3:5–6; Zech. 10:2; Jer. 27:9; 29:8; Ezek. 13:9, 23; 21:23, 29; Isa. 44:25).

e. Finally, the prophets are conscious, when speaking or writing, of proclaiming not their own word but the word of the Lord. Indeed, the word was not revealed to them for themselves but for others. They were not at liberty to hide it. They had to speak (Jer. 20:7, 9; Ex. 3–4; Ezek. 3; Amos 3:8; Jonah 1:2) and therefore do not speak to win human favor or out of calculation (Isa. 56:10; Mic. 3:5, 11). Precisely for that reason they are prophets, speakers in YHWH's name and of his word. Therefore, they know that they have to give—no more, no less than—what they have received (Deut. 4:2; 12:32; Jer. 1:7, 17; 26:2; 42:4; Ezek. 3:10).

The writing of the prophets may and must be derived from a similar impulse. The literal texts where a command to write is given are few in number (Ex. 17:14; 24:3–4; 34:27; Num. 33:2; Deut. 4:2; 12:32; 31:19; Isa. 8:1; 30:8; Jer. 25:13; 30:2; 36:2, 24, 27–32; Ezek. 24:2; Dan. 12:4; Hab. 2:2) and apply to only a small part of OT Scripture. The act of recording prophecies in writing, though a later one, is still a necessary stage in the history of prophetism. Surely, many prophecies were never uttered orally but were meant to be read and pondered. The majority have been carefully, even artfully, crafted and show by their very form that they were intended to be written. Behind the inscripturation of these oracles was the idea that Israel could no longer be saved by deeds, that now and in distant generations the service of YHWH had to find acceptance by word and reasoned persuasion.[1] Prophets began to write because they wished to address people other than those who could hear them.

f. There is a difference between the received word and the spoken or written word. It would not have been humiliating for the prophets had they recorded the received word as literally as possible. But even in the moment of divine inspiration, revelation continued, modifying and completing the earlier revelation, and hence the latter was reproduced freely. The prophets therefore demanded the same authority for their written word as for

1. A. Kuenen, *The Prophets and Prophecy in Israel,* trans. Adam Milroy (London: Longmans, Green, 1877; repr., Amsterdam: Philo, 1969) (ed. note: pagination in the Dutch edition, *De Profeten,* 1:74; 2:345–46).

the spoken word. This even applies to the prophet's discourses in between the actual words of YHWH (e.g., in Isa. 6; 10:24–12:6; 31:1–3; 32) or the prophet's elaboration of a word from YHWH (52:7–12; 63:15–64:12). The passage of a statement from YHWH to a statement of the prophet is frequently so abrupt and the two are so closely intertwined (cf. Jer. 13:18–19) that no separation is possible. They have the same authority (Jer. 36:10–11; 25:3). In 34:16 Isaiah calls [the volume of] his own recorded prophecies the Book of YHWH.

g. The prophets did not infer their revelation from the law. Although the scope of the Torah cannot be determined from their writings, prophecy does presuppose a Torah. All the prophets stand on the foundation of a body of law and put themselves along with their opponents on a common basis. They all assume a covenant made by God with Israel, a gracious election of Israel (Hos. 1:1–3; 6:7; 8:3; Jer. 11:6–7; 14:21; 22:9; 31:31–32; Ezek. 16:8–9; Isa. 54:10; 56:4, 6; 59:21). The prophets were not the founders of a new religion, a religion of ethical monotheism. YHWH's relation to Israel was never like that of Chemosh to Moab. The prophets never mention such opposition between their religion and that of the people. They recognize that throughout almost all the centuries of their existence the people committed idolatry; but they always and unanimously view it as unfaithfulness and apostasy on the assumption that the people knew better. With the people they fasten themselves onto the same revelation and the same history. They speak from the conviction that they and the people have in common the same service of God, that YHWH elected and called them to his service. From this conviction they draw their strength and therefore test the people by the legally-existing relation between them and YHWH (Hos. 12:14; Mic. 6:4, 8; Isa. 63:11; Jer. 7:25; etc.).[2]

The torah does not just refer to a divine instruction in general but is often also the name of an already-existing objective revelation of YHWH (Isa. 2:3; Mic. 4:2; Amos 2:4; Hos. 8:1; 4:6; Jer. 18:18; Ezek. 7:26; Zeph. 3:4). God's covenant with Israel, on the foundation of which the prophets stand with all the people, naturally also contains an assortment of statutes and ordinances, and the prophets therefore repeatedly speak of commandments (Isa. 48:18), statutes (Isa. 24:5; Jer. 44:10, 23; Ezek. 5:6–7; 11:12, 20; 18:9, 17; 20:11–12; 36:27; 37:24; Amos 2:4; Zech. 1:6; Mal. 3:7; 4:4), and ordinances (Ezek. 5:7; 11:12; etc.). This torah must have contained the teaching of the oneness of YHWH, his creation and government over all things, the prohibition of idolatry, and other religious and moral commandments, as well as a range of ceremonial (sabbath, sacrifice, purity, etc.) and historical (creation, exodus from Egypt, covenant-making) components. About the scope of the torah before prophetism there may be disagreement, but the relation between the law and the prophets cannot be reversed without violating the whole history of Israel and the essence of prophetism. The prophet in Israel was as it were "the living voice of the law" and "the mediator of its fulfillment" (Staudenmaier). The most negative criticism still finds itself compelled to accept as historical the personality of Moses and his monotheism, the sojourn in Egypt, the exodus, the conquest of Canaan, etc., although, given their critique of the Pentateuch, all ground for that acceptance is lacking.

h. It is a priori likely that in the case of a people long familiar with the art of writing, the law had already long existed in written form as well. This fact seems to be made explicit

---

2. Eduard König, *Die Hauptprobleme der altisraelitischen Religionsgeschichte* (Leipzig: J. C. Hinrichs, 1884), 15ff., 38ff.

in Hosea 8:12.[3] This torah had authority in Israel from the beginning. We hear nothing about doubt or opposition. Moses' place among the prophets was unique (Ex. 33:11; Num. 12:6–8; Deut. 18:18; Pss. 103:7; 106:23; Isa. 63:11; Jer. 15:1; etc.). His relation to YHWH was special: the Lord spoke to him as a friend. He was the mediator of the Old Testament. The law everywhere ascribes to itself a divine origin. It is YHWH who by Moses gave the torah to Israel. Not only the ten words (Ex. 20) and the book of the covenant (Ex. 21–23) but all other laws as well are derived from God's speaking to Moses. Over and over, in the laws of the Pentateuch, we encounter the formula: "The Lord said," or "the Lord spoke to Moses." Almost every chapter begins with it (Ex. 25:1; 30:11, 17, 22; 31:1; 32:7, 33; Lev. 1:1; 4:1; 6:1, 8, 19, 24; Num. 1:1; 2:1; 3:44; 4:1; etc.). And Deuteronomy gives nothing but what Moses spoke to the children of Israel (Deut. 1:6; 2:1–2, 17; 3:2; 5:2; 6:1; etc.).

i. All the historical books of the OT were written by the prophets and in a prophetic spirit (1 Chron. 29:29; 2 Chron. 9:29; 20:34; etc.). In their speeches and writings the prophets not only refer repeatedly to Israel's history, but they are also the people who preserved, edited, and handed it down. But their purpose is by no means to furnish us with an accurate, connected story of the fortunes of the Israelitish people, as other historiographers aim to do. Also in the historical books of the OT, the prophets base themselves on the torah and from its viewpoint regard and describe the history of Israel (Judg. 2:6–3:6; 2 Kings 17:7–23, 34–41). The historical books are commentary on the facts of God's covenant with Israel. They are not history in our sense of the word but prophecy; they are meant to be judged by another standard than the history books of other peoples. It is not their aim that we should acquire accurate knowledge of Israel's history but that *in* the history of Israel we should gain understanding of the revelation of God, his thought and his counsel. The prophets, both when they look back upon history and when they look forward into the future, are always messengers of the word of YHWH.

j. Finally, as it pertains to the strictly poetic books that have been included in the canon, they, like the other OT writings, bear a religious-ethical character. They presuppose the revelation of God as their objective basis and display the detailed development and application of that revelation in the various states and relations of human life. Ecclesiastes sketches the vanity of the world without, and in opposition to, the fear of the Lord. Job is preoccupied with the problem of the justice of God vis-à-vis the sufferings of the pious. Proverbs depicts to us true wisdom in its application to the many aspects of human life. The Song of Solomon celebrates the intimacy and power of love. And, in the mirror of the experiences of God's devout people, the Psalms display the manifold grace of God. Both lyrical and didactic poetry in Israel are deployed in the service of divine revelation. David, the sweet psalmist of Israel, spoke by the Spirit of the Lord, whose word was on his tongue (2 Sam. 23:1–3).

k. As the various writings of the OT originated and became known, they were also recognized as authoritative. The laws of YHWH were deposited in the sanctuary (Ex. 25:22; 38:21; 40:20; Deut. 31:9, 26; Josh. 24:25–26; 1 Sam. 10:25). The poetic products were preserved (Deut. 31:19; Josh. 10:13; 2 Sam. 1:18); at an early stage the Psalms were collected for use in the cult (Ps. 72:20); the men of Hezekiah made a second collection of the Proverbs (Prov. 25:1). The prophecies were widely read: Ezekiel knows Isaiah and Jeremiah; later prophets based themselves on earlier ones. Daniel (9:2) is already familiar with a collection of pro-

---

3. C. J. Bredenkamp, *Gesetz und Propheten: Ein Beitrag zur alttestamentlichen Kritik* (Erlangen: Deichert, 1881), 21ff.; Eduard König, *Der Offenbarungsbegriff des Alten Testamentes* (Leipzig: J. C. Hinrichs, 1882), 2:333.

phetic writings including Jeremiah. In the postexilic community the authority of the law and the prophets is certain and fixed, as is clear from Ezra, Haggai, and Zechariah. Jesus Sirach has a very high view of the law and the prophets (15:1–8; 24:23; 39:1–2; 44–49). In the preface his grandson mentions the three parts in which Scripture is divided. The LXX contains several apocryphal writings, but these themselves witness to the authority of the canonical books (1 Macc. 2:50; 2 Macc. 6:23; Wisdom 11:1; 18:4; Baruch 2:28; Tob. 1:6; 14:7; Sir. 1:5 [marg.]; 17:12; 24:23; 39:1; 46:15; etc.). Philo cites only the canonical books. The fourth book of Ezra ([= 2 Esdras] 14:18–47) knows of the division into 24 books. Josephus counts 22 books divided into three parts. In the opinion of all concerned, the OT canon of Philo and Josephus was identical with ours.[4]

The Witness of the New Testament

[107] For Jesus and the apostles, as for their contemporaries, this canon had divine authority. This is clearly evident from the following facts:

a. The formula with which the OT is cited in the NT varies, but it always shows that to the writers of the NT the OT is of divine origin and bears divine authority. Jesus sometimes cites a verse from the OT by the name of the author, e.g., Moses (Matt. 8:4; 19:8; Mark 7:10; John 5:45; 7:22), Isaiah (Matt. 15:7; Mark 7:6); David (Matt. 22:43, 45), and Daniel (Matt. 24:15), but he also frequently uses the formula "it is written" (Matt. 4:4ff.; 11:10; Luke 10:26; John 6:45; 8:47) or "Scripture says" (Matt. 21:42; Luke 4:21; John 7:38; 10:35) or the name of the primary author, i.e., God or the Holy Spirit (Matt. 15:4; 22:43; Mark 12:26, 36). The evangelists often use the expression "that which was spoken of by the prophet" (cf. Matt. 1:22; 2:15, 17, 23; 3:3; etc.) or "by the Lord" or "by the Holy Spirit" (Matt. 1:22; 2:15; Luke 1:70; Acts 1:16; 3:18; 4:25; 28:25). John usually cites material by the name of the secondary author (1:23, 45; 12:38). Paul always speaks of Scripture (Rom. 4:3; 9:17; 10:11; 11:2; Gal. 4:30; 1 Tim. 5:18; etc.), which is sometimes even portrayed as entirely personal (Gal. 3:8, 22; 4:30; Rom. 9:17). The Letter to the Hebrews most often mentions God or the Holy Spirit as the primary author (1:5–6; 3:7; 4:3, 5; 5:6–7; 7:21; 8:5, 8; 10:16, 30; 12:26; 13:5). This manner of citation clearly and distinctly teaches us that to Jesus and the apostles the Scripture of the old covenant, though composed of various parts and traceable to different authors, actually formed one organic whole whose author was God himself.

b. Several times Jesus and the apostles also definitely affirmed and taught the divine authority of OT Scripture (Matt. 5:17; Luke 16:17, 29; John 10:35; Rom. 15:4; 1 Peter 1:10–12; 2 Peter 1:19, 21; 2 Tim. 3:16). Scripture is a unified whole, which can neither be broken up and destroyed as a totality or in its parts. In the last-cited text [2 Tim. 3:16], the translation "every scripture inspired by God is also profitable" suffers from the fact that after ὠφελιμος the predicate ἐστιν would have had to be present. The translation "every scripture (in general) is inspired by God and profitable" is self-evidently excluded. What remains, therefore, is a choice between only two translations: "all Scripture" or "every Scripture," included, that is, in the sacred writings (v. 15), "is inspired by God" (cf. "whatever was written in former days," Rom. 15:4). Materially this does not yield any difference and, in light of verses like

---

4. G. Wildeboer, *Het ontstaan van den kanon des Oude Verbond* (Groningen: Wolters, 1891), 126ff., 134; in English: *The Origin of the Canon of the Old Testament,* trans. Benjamin Wisner Bacon (London: Luzac, 1895); H. L. Strack, "Kanon des Alten Testaments," *PRE*[3] 9:741–68; Gustav Hölscher, *Kanonisch und Apokryph: Ein Kapitel aus der Geschichte des alt-testamentlichen Kanons* (Leipzig: A. Deichert, 1905).

Matthew 2:3; Acts 2:36; 2 Corinthians 12:12; Ephesians 1:8; 2:21; 3:15; Colossians 4:12; 1 Peter 1:15; James 1:2, πας can apparently also mean "all."

c. Jesus and the apostles never take a critical position toward the content of the OT but accept it totally and without reservation. They unconditionally accept the Scripture of the OT as true and divine in all its parts, not only in its religious-ethical pronouncements or in the passages in which God himself speaks, but also in its historical components. Jesus, for example, attributes Isaiah 6 to Isaiah (Matt. 13:14), Psalm 110 to David (Matt. 22:43), the prophecy cited in Matthew 24:15 to Daniel, and the law to Moses (John 5:46). The historical narratives of the OT are repeatedly cited and unconditionally believed, including the creation of human beings (Matt. 19:4–5), Abel's murder (Matt. 23:35), the flood (Matt. 24:37–39), the history of the patriarchs (Matt. 22:32; John 8:56), the destruction of Sodom (Matt. 11:23; Luke 17:28–33), the burning bush (Luke 20:37), the serpent in the wilderness (John 3:14), the manna (John 6:32), the histories of Elijah and Naaman (Luke 4:25–27), Jonah (Matt. 12:39–41), etc.

d. Dogmatically, to Jesus and the apostles the OT is the foundation of doctrine, the source of solutions, the end of all argument. The OT is fulfilled in the New. Events are frequently presented as though everything happened for the purpose of fulfilling Scripture, "all this took place to fulfill what was said" (Matt. 1:22 [and passim]; Mark 14:49; 15:28; Luke 4:21; 24:44; John 13:18; 17:12; 19:24, 36; Acts 1:16; James 2:23; etc.). That fulfillment is noted even in minor details (Matt. 21:16; Luke 4:21; 22:37; John 15:25; 17:12; 19:28; etc.); everything that happened to Jesus was described in advance in the OT (Luke 18:31–33). Over and over Jesus and the apostles justify their conduct and prove their teaching by an appeal to the OT (Matt. 12:3; 22:32; John 10:34; Rom. 4; Gal. 3; 1 Cor. 15; etc.). And, to their mind, this divine authority of Scripture is extended so far that a single word, even an iota or a dot, is covered by it (Matt. 5:18; 22:45; Luke 16:17; John 10:35; Gal. 3:16).

e. Notwithstanding all this, the OT is consistently quoted in the NT in the Greek translation of the LXX. The writers of the NT, writing in Greek and for Greek readers, commonly used the translation that was known and accessible to them. The citations can be divided, in terms of their relation to the Hebrew text and Greek translation, into three groups. In some texts there is deviation from the LXX and agreement with the Hebrew text (e.g., Matt. 2:15, 18; 8:17; 12:18–21; 27:46; John 19:37; Rom. 10:15–16; 11:9; 1 Cor. 3:19; 15:54). Conversely, in other texts there is agreement with the LXX and deviation from the Hebrew (e.g., Matt. 15:8–9; Acts 7:14; 15:16–17; Eph. 4:8; Heb. 10:5; 11:21; 12:6). In a third group of citations there is more or less significant deviation both from the LXX and Hebrew text (e.g., Matt. 2:6; 3:3; 26:31; John 12:15; 13:18; Rom. 10:6–9; 1 Cor. 2:9). Furthermore, it is noteworthy that some books of the OT, viz., Ezra, Nehemiah, Obadiah, Zephaniah, Esther, Ecclesiastes, and Song of Solomon, are never cited in the NT. Also, although no apocryphal books are cited, in 2 Timothy 3:8, Hebrews 11:34–35, Jude 9–10, 14–15 names and facts are mentioned that do not occur in the OT. Finally, on a few occasions even Greek classics are referred to (Acts 17:18; 1 Cor. 15:33; Titus 1:12).

f. Finally, as for the material use of the OT in the NT, there is great diversity in that as well. Sometimes the citations serve as proof and confirmation of a given truth (e.g., Matt. 4:4, 7, 10; 9:13; 19:5; 22:32; John 10:34; Acts 15:16; 23:5; Rom. 1:17; 3:10–11; 4:3, 7; 9:7, 12–13, 15, 17; 10:5; Gal. 3:10; 4:30; 1 Cor. 9:9; 10:26; 2 Cor. 6:17). Very often the OT is cited to prove that it *had to* be fulfilled and was fulfilled in the NT, either in a literal sense (Matt. 1:23; 3:3;

4:15–16; 8:17; 12:18; 13:14–15; 21:42; 27:46; Mark 15:28; Luke 4:17–18; John 12:38; Acts 2:17; 3:22; 7:37; 8:32; etc.) or typologically (Matt. 11:14; 12:39–40; 17:11; Luke 1:17; John 3:14; 19:36; 1 Cor. 5:7; 10:4; 2 Cor. 6:16; Gal. 3:13; 4:21; Heb. 2:6–8; 7:1–10; etc.). Citations from the OT repeatedly serve simply to clarify, inform, admonish, console, etc. (e.g., Luke 2:23; John 7:38; Acts 7:3, 42; Rom. 8:36; 1 Cor. 2:16; 10:7; 2 Cor. 4:13; 8:15; 13:1; Heb. 12:5; 13:15; 1 Peter 1:16, 24–25; 2:9). In that connection we are often surprised by the meaning that the NT authors find in the text of the OT (esp. in Matt. 2:15, 18, 23; 21:5; 22:32; 26:31; 27:9–10, 35; John 19:37; Acts 1:20; 2:31; 1 Cor. 9:9; Gal. 3:16; 4:22–23; Eph. 4:8–9; Heb. 2:6–8; 10:5). In the case of Jesus and the apostles, this exegesis of the OT in the NT assumes the understanding that a word or sentence can have a much deeper meaning and a much farther reaching thrust than the original author suspected or put into it. This is often the case in classical authors as well. No one will think that Goethe, in writing down his classical poetry, consciously had before his mind the things that are now found in it. "Surely that person has not gotten far in poetry / In whose verses there is nothing more than what he had [consciously] written into them."[5] In Scripture this is even much more strongly the case since, in the conviction of Jesus and the apostles, it has the Holy Spirit as its primary author and bears a teleological character. Not only in the few verses cited above but in its entire view and interpretation of the OT, the NT is undergirded by the thought that the Israelitish dispensation has its fulfillment in the Christian. The whole economy of the old covenant, with all its statutes and ordinances and throughout its history, points forward to the dispensation of the new covenant. Not Talmudism but Christianity is the rightful heir of the treasures of salvation promised to Abraham and his seed.[6]

5. Cf. Robert Hamerling, "Epilog an die Kritiker," *Hamerlings Werke in vier Bänden* (Leipzig: M. Hesse, 1900), 1:142ff. For the meaning of Scripture, see J. J. P. Valeton, "Eenige Opmerkingen over Hermeneutiek met het Oog op de Schriften des Ouden Verbonds," *Theologische Studiën* 3 (1887): 509–25; Franz Theremin, *Die Beredsamkeit eine Tugend* (Berlin: Duncker und Humblot, 1837), 236; in English: *Eloquence a Virtue; or, Outlines of a Systematic Rhetoric,* trans. William G. T. Shedd (Boston: Draper and Halliday, 1867).

6. For the literature about the Old Testament in the New Testament, see Glassius, *Philologia Sacra,* 6th ed. (1691); Surenhuis, "Biblos Katallagés," in *Quo sec. vet. theol. hebr. formulas allegandi et modes interpretandi conciliantur loca V.T. in N.T. allegata* (Amsterdam, 1713); Immanuel Hoffmann, *Demostratio evangelica per ipsum scripturarum concensum in oraculis ex Vet. testamento in novo allegatis declarata,* 3 vols. (Tübingen: Georgii Henrici Reisil, 1773–81); Thomas Randolph, *The Prophecies and Other Texts Cited in the New Testament Compared with the Hebrew Original and with the Septuagint Version* (Oxford: Printed for J. and J. Fletcher, 1782); Henry Owen, *The Modes of Quotation Used by the Evangelical Writers Explained and Vindicated* (London: J. Nichols, 1789); Thomas H. Home, *An Introduction to the Critical Study and Knowledge of the Holy Scriptures* (London: Printed for T. Cadell, 1821), 2:356–463; C. Sepp, *De Leer des Nieuwe Testament over de Heilige Schrift des Oude Verbond* (Te Amsterdam: J. C. Sepp & Zoon, 1849); August Tholuck, *Das Alte Testament im Neuen Testament,* 6th ed. (Gotha: F. A. Perthes, 1877); Richard Rothe, *Zur Dogmatik* (Gotha: F. A. Perthes, 1863), 184ff.; J. C. K. Hofmann, *Weissagung und Erfüllung im alte und neuen Testamente* (Nördlingen: C. H. Beck, 1841); Erich Haupt, *Die alttestamentlichen Citate in den vier Evangelien* (Colberg: Carl Jancke; London: Williams & Norgate, 1871); E. Kautzsch, *De Veteris Testamenti locis a Paulo Apostolo allegatis* (Leipzig: Metzger & Wittig, 1869); Eduard Böhl, *Forschungen nach einer Volksbibel zur Zeit Jesu* (Wien: Wilhelm Braumüller, 1873); idem, *Die alttestamentlichen Citate im Neuen Testament* (Wien: Wilhelm Braumüller, 1878); K. Walz, *Die Lehre der Kirche von der Schrift nach der Schrift selbst geprüft* (Leiden: E. J. Brill, 1884); Kuenen, *De Profeten,* 2:199ff. (English: *The Prophets and Prophecy*); William Caven, "The Testimony of Jesus to the Old Testament," *Presbyterian and Reformed Review* 3 (July 1892): 401–20; August Clemen, *Der Gebrauch des Alten Testamentes in den neutestamentlichen Schriften* (Gütersloh: C. Bertelsmann, 1895); A. Kuyper, *Encyclopaedie der Heilige Godgeleerdheid* (Kampen: J. H. Kok, 1894), 2:378ff.; in English: *Principles of Sacred Theology,* trans. J. Hendrik De Vries (1898; reprinted, Grand Rapids: Eerdmans, 1968), 428ff.; Hans Vollmer, *Die alttestamentlichen Citate bei Paulus textkritisch und biblisch-theologisch gewürdigt* (Freiburg im Breisgau: J. C. B. Mohr [Paul Siebeck], 1895); J. J. P. Valeton, *Christus en het Oude Testament* (Nijmegen: Ten Hoet, 1895); J. Meinhold, *Jesus und das Alte Testament* (Freiburg im Breisgau and Leipzig: Mohr [Siebeck], 1896); Martin Kähler, *Jesus und das Alte Testament* (Leipzig: A. Deichert, 1896); Wilhelm Volck, *Christi und der Apostel Stellung zum Alten Testament* (Leipzig: A. Deichert [Georg Böhme], 1900); Theodor Walker, *Jesus*

[108] In the writings of the apostles, we find the following data for the inspiration of the NT:

a. Throughout the NT Jesus' witness is considered divine, true, infallible. He is the Logos who makes known the Father (John 1:18; 17:6), the faithful and true witness (Rev. 1:5; 3:14; cf. Isa. 55:4), the Amen in whom all the promises of God are "yes" and "amen" (Rev. 3:14; 2 Cor. 1:20). There was no guile (δόλος) on his lips (1 Peter 2:22). He is the apostle and high priest of our confession (Heb. 3:1; 1 Tim. 6:13). He does not speak ἐκ τῶν ἰδίων, like Satan who is a liar (John 8:44), but God speaks through him (Heb. 1:2). Jesus was sent by God (John 8:42) and bears witness only to what he has seen and heard (John 3:32). He speaks the words of God (John 3:34; 17:8) and only bears witness to the truth (5:33; 18:37). For that reason his witness is true (John 8:14; 14:6), confirmed by the witness of God himself (5:32, 37; 8:18).

Not only is Jesus holy and without sin in an ethical sense (John 8:46) but also intellectually he is without error, lies, or deception. It is absolutely true that Jesus was not active in the field of science in a restricted sense. He came to earth to make known the Father and to accomplish his work. The inspiration of Scripture on which Jesus makes pronouncements is not a scientific problem but a religious truth. If he erred in this respect, he was wrong at a point that is most closely tied in with the religious life and can no longer be recognized as our highest prophet in religion and theology either. The doctrine of the divine authority of Holy Scripture constitutes an important component in the words of God that Jesus preached. In the case of Jesus, however, this infallibility was not an extraordinary supernatural gift—no gift of grace or passing act—but *habitus*, nature. If Jesus had written anything, he would not have needed special assistance from the Holy Spirit to do it. He did not need inspiration as an extraordinary gift inasmuch as he did "not receive the Spirit by measure" (cf. John 3:34), was himself the Logos (John 1:1), and the fullness of God dwelt in him bodily (Col. 1:19; 2:9).

b. Jesus has not left to us anything in writing, however, and he himself is gone away. He therefore had to ensure that his true witness was passed on pure and unalloyed to humankind. To that end he chose the apostles. The apostolate is an extraordinary office and an utterly unique ministry in Jesus' church. The apostles were specifically given him by the Father (John 17:6), chosen by himself (John 6:70; 13:18; 15:16, 19), and in various ways prepared and equipped by him for their future task. That task was to serve publicly as Jesus' *witnesses* after his departure (Luke 24:48; John 15:27). They had been the ear- and eyewitnesses of Jesus' words and works. They had seen the Word of life with their eyes and touched him with their hands (1 John 1:1) and were now called to bring this witness concerning Jesus to Israel and to the whole world (Matt. 28:19; John 15:27; 17:20; Acts 1:8). But all human beings are false, and God alone is true (Rom. 3:4). Even the apostles were unfit for the task of witnessing and, accordingly, were not the actual witnesses. Jesus only employs them as his instruments. The actual witness who is faithful and true as he himself is, is the Holy Spirit. He is the Spirit of truth and will bear witness to Jesus (John 15:26); the apostles can only serve as witnesses after and through him (John 15:27). That Spirit, accordingly, is uniquely promised and granted to the apostles (Matt. 10:20; John 14:26; 15:26; 16:7; 20:22). Especially John 14:26 teaches this: he "will bring to your remembrance all that I have said to you." He will take the disciples into his service *with* their personalities and gifts, their memory and judgment (etc.). He will not add to the revelation anything that is materially

und das Alte Testament in ihrer gegenseitigen Bezeugung (Gütersloh: C. Bertelsmann, 1899); W. Dittmar, *Vetus Testamentum in Novo: die alttestamentlichen Parallelen des Neuen Testaments im Wortlaut der Urtexte und der Septuaginta* (Göttingen: Vandenhoeck & Ruprecht, 1899–1903); Erich Klosterman, *Jesu Stellung zum Alte Testament* (Kiel: Robert Cordes, 1904).

new, that was not already present in Christ's person, word, and work, for he takes everything from Christ and only to that extent brings everything to the apostles' remembrance, thus guiding them into all truth (John 14:26; 16:13–14). And this witness of the Holy Spirit by the mouth of the apostles is the glorification of Jesus (John 16:14), just as Jesus' witness was a glorification of the Father (17:4).

c. After the day of Pentecost, equipped with that Spirit in a special sense (John 20:22; Acts 1:8; Eph. 3:5), the apostles now also openly act as witnesses (Acts 1:8, 21–22; 2:14, 32; 3:15; 4:8, 20, 33; 5:32; 10:39, 41; 13:31). The significance of the apostolate lies in bearing witness to what they have seen and heard. To that end they have been called and equipped. From this task they derive their authority. In the face of opposition and challenge, they appeal to this. God, in turn, seals this witness by signs and wonders and spiritual blessing (Matt. 10:1, 8; Mark 16:15–16; Acts 2:43; 3:2ff.; 5:12, 16; 6:8; 8:6–7; 10:44; 11:21; 14:3; 15:8; etc.). From the beginning and in their own right the apostles are the leaders of the Jerusalem church, exercise supervision over the believers in Samaria (Acts 8:14), visit the churches (Acts 9:32; 11:22), make decisions in the Holy Spirit (Acts 15:22, 28), and enjoy generally recognized authority. They speak and act in virtue of the authority of Christ. And although Jesus nowhere left an express command also to record his words and deeds (only in Revelation is there a repeated command to write, 1:11, 19, etc.), the apostles in their writing speak with the same authority, writing being a special form of witness. Also in writing they are witnesses of Christ (Luke 1:2; John 1:14; 19:35; 20:31; 21:24; 1 John 1:1–4; 1 Peter 1:12; 5:1; 2 Peter 1:16; Heb. 2:3; Rev. 1:3; 22:18–19). Their witness is faithful and true (John 19:35; 3 John 12).

d. Among the apostles, Paul again stands by himself. He sees himself called to defend his apostolate against the Judaizers (Gal. 1–2; 1 Cor. 1:10–4:21; 2 Cor. 10:13). Over against this opposition he maintains that he was set apart before he was born (Gal. 1:15), called to be an apostle by Jesus himself (Gal. 1:1), had personally seen Jesus himself (1 Cor. 9:1; 15:8), was granted revelations and visions (2 Cor. 12; Acts 26:16), had received his gospel from Jesus himself (Gal. 1:12; 1 Tim. 1:12; Eph. 3:2–8), and hence is as much an independent and trustworthy witness as the other apostles, especially among the Gentiles (Acts 26:16). Also, his apostolate was confirmed by miracles and signs (1 Cor. 12:10, 28; Rom. 12:4–8; 15:18–19; 2 Cor. 11:23–24; Gal. 3:5; Heb. 2:4) and by spiritual blessings (1 Cor. 15:10; 2 Cor. 11:5; etc.). He is therefore convinced that there is no other gospel than the one he preaches (Gal. 1:7), that he is trustworthy (1 Cor. 7:25), that he has the Spirit of God (1 Cor. 7:40), that Christ speaks through him (2 Cor. 13:3; 1 Cor. 2:10, 16; 2 Cor. 2:17; 5:20), that he preaches the word of God (2 Cor. 2:17; 1 Thess. 2:13), right down to the phraseology and words (1 Cor. 2:4, 10–13), not only when he speaks but also when he writes (1 Thess. 5:27; Col. 4:16; 2 Thess. 2:15; 3:14). Like the other apostles, Paul repeatedly acts with full apostolic power (1 Cor. 5; 2 Cor. 2:9), and issues binding commands (1 Cor. 7:40; 1 Thess. 4:2, 11; 2 Thess. 3:6–14). And though he occasionally appeals to the judgment of the church (1 Cor. 10:15), it is not to subject his statement to their approval or disapproval but, on the contrary, to be vindicated by the conscience and judgment of the church, which, after all, also has the Spirit of God and the anointing of the Holy Spirit (1 John 2:20). Paul is so far from making himself dependent on the judgment of the church that he says (1 Cor. 14:37) that if anyone thinks he is a prophet or spiritual, this will come out in the acknowledgment that what Paul is writing is a command of the Lord.

e. From the very beginning these apostolic writings had authority in the churches where they were known. They were soon circulated and as a result gained ever more extensive authority (Acts 15:22–23; Col. 4:16). The Synoptic Gospels show so much kinship between them that the one must have been known either totally or in part to the others. Jude was known to Peter, and 2 Peter 3:16 already implies familiarity with many letters of Paul and puts them on the same level with the other Scriptures. Gradually translations of NT writings appeared for the purpose of being read in the church. These translations must already have existed in the first half of the second century.[7] A dogmatic use was already made of them by Athenagoras who proves his argumentation by reference to 1 Corinthians 15:33 and 2 Corinthians 5:10. Theophilus also cites texts from Paul with the formula "he teaches," "the word of God orders."[8] Irenaeus, Tertullian and others, the Peshitta and the fragment of Muratori, all establish beyond doubt that in the second half of the second century most NT writings had canonical authority and enjoyed equal status with the books of the Old Testament. Differences continued to exist about some books: James, Jude, 2 Peter, 2 and 3 John, but in the third century the objections against these disputed works (ἀντιλεγομενα) increasingly diminished. And the Synod of Laodicea (366), Hippo Regius (393) and Carthage (397) were able to include them and to close the canon.

These decisions of the church were not self-willed, authoritarian acts but merely the codification and registration of the precedents that had long been operating in the churches with respect to these writings. The canon was not formed by any decree of councils: "The Canon has not been produced, as some say, by a single act of human beings, but little by little by God, the director of minds and times."[9] In the important debate between Harnack and Zahn about the history of the NT canon, Harnack undoubtedly too onesidedly emphasized the terms "divinity," "infallibility," "inspiration," and "canon," i.e., the formal establishment of the dogma of NT Scripture. Long before this occurred, in the second half of the second century the NT writings had achieved generally recognized authority as a result of the authority of the apostles and public reading in the churches. Zahn very correctly called attention to this internal process.[10]

f. The principles that both under the Old and the New Testament guided the church in this recognition of the canonicity of the OT and NT writings cannot be determined with certainty. Apostolic origin cannot have been the deciding factor, for Mark, Luke, and the Letter to the Hebrews were also included. Neither is the recognition of canonicity grounded in the fact that no other writings concerning Christ existed, for Luke 1:1 makes mention of many others and, according to Irenaeus,[11] there was this "immense mass of apocryphal and spurious writings." Nor can the principle of canon formation lie in size or importance, for 2 and 3 John are very small; or in the authors' familiarity with the apostles, for the Letters of Clement and Barnabas were not included; or in originality, for Matthew, Mark, and Luke, the Letters to the Ephesians and Colossians, Jude, and

7. Papias, according to Eusebius, *Ecclesiastical History* 3.39; Justin Martyr, *Apology* 1.66–67.

8. Athenagoras, *Resurrection of the Flesh,* ch. 16; Theophilus, *To Autolychus* 3.4.

9. Ed. note: Bavinck's note reads simply "Loescher cited in *PRE²* 7:424." The reference is to Valentin Loescher, *De Causa Linguae Ebraeae* (1706) and appears in the article "Kanon des alten Testaments," by Herman L. Strack, *PRE²* 7:412–51.

10. On this debate, cf. W. Koeppel, "Die Zahn-Harnacksche Streit über die Geschichte des neutestamentlichen Kanons," *Theologische Studien und Kritiken* 64 (1891): 102–57; F. Barth, "Die Streit zwischen Zahn und Harnack über der Ursprung des N. T. Kanons," *Neue Jahrbuch für deutsche Theologie* (1893): 56–80.

11. Irenaeus, *Against Heresies* 1.20.

2 Peter are interdependent. All that can be said is that the recognition of these writings in the churches occurred automatically, without any formal agreement. With only a few exceptions, the OT and NT writings were immediately, from the time of their origin and in toto, accepted without doubt or protest as holy, divine writings. The place and time at which they were first recognized as authoritative cannot be indicated. The canonicity of the Bible books is rooted in their existence. They have authority of themselves, by their own right, because they exist. It is the Spirit of the Lord who guided the authors in writing them and the church in acknowledging them.[12]

The outcome of this investigation into the doctrine of Scripture concerning itself can be summed up by saying that it considers itself, and makes itself known as, the Word of God. The expression "word of God" or "word of the Lord" has various meanings in Scripture. Often it denotes the power of God by which he creates and upholds all things (Gen. 1:3; Pss. 33:6; 147:17–18; 148:8; Rom. 4:17; Heb. 1:3; 11:3). The term further describes the special revelation by which God makes something known to the prophets. In the OT the expression occurs in this sense on almost every page; over and over we read: "the word of the Lord came." In the NT we find it in this sense only in John 10:35; now the word does not "come" anymore; it does not come now and then from above and without to the prophets but has come in Christ and remains. The "word of God" further denotes the content of revelation. In that use the reference is to a word or words of God, alongside of ordinances, laws, commandments, statutes, which have been given to Israel (Ex. 9:20–21; Judg. 3:20; Pss. 33:4; 119:9, 16–17, etc.; Isa. 40:8; Rom. 3:2; etc.). In the NT it is the name for the gospel, which has been disclosed by God in Christ and proclaimed by the apostles (Luke 5:1; John 3:34; 5:24; 6:63; 17:8, 14, 17; Acts 8:25; 13:7; 1 Thess. 2:13; etc.). It is not unlikely that the term "word of God" is sometimes used in Scripture also to designate the written law, hence a part of Scripture (Ps. 119:105). In the NT such a use cannot be shown to exist. Also in Hebrews 4:12 the "word of God" is not identical with Scripture. Nevertheless the NT in fact regards the books of the OT as nothing other than "the word of God." God, or the Holy Spirit is the primary author who spoke in Scripture through (διά w. gen.) the prophets (Acts 1:16; 28:25). In that case Scripture is so called both on account of its origin and on account of its content. The formal and the material meaning of the expression are most intimately bound up with each other in Scripture.

Finally the designation "word of God" is used for Christ himself. He is the Logos in an utterly unique sense: Revealer and revelation at the same time. All the revelations and words of God, in nature and history, in creation and re-creation, both in the Old and the New Testament, have their ground, unity, and center in him. He is the sun; the individual words of God are his rays. The word of God in nature, in Israel, in the NT, in Scripture may never even for a moment be separated and abstracted from him. God's revelation exists only because he is the Logos. He is the first principle of cognition, in a general sense of all knowledge, in a special sense, as the Logos incarnate, of all knowledge of God, of religion, and theology (Matt. 11:27).

12. A. von Harnack, *History of Dogma* 2:38ff.; Wildeboer, *Het Ontstaan van de Kanon des Oude Verbond,* 107ff.; Eduard Reuss, *Die Geschichte der heiligen Schriften, Neuen Testaments* (Braunschweig: C.A. Schwetschke, 1874), §298f.; William Lee, *The Inspiration of Holy Scripture,* 3rd ed. (Dublin: Hodges, Smith and Co., 1864), 43; Theodor Zahn, "Kanon des Neue Testament," *PRE*[3] 9:768–96; idem, *Grundriss der Geschichte des neutestamentlichen Kanons* (Leipzig: Deichert, 1901).

The Testimony of the Church

[109] From the beginning Holy Scripture was recognized as the Word of God by all Christian churches. There is no dogma about which there is more unity than that of Holy Scripture. The genesis of that belief can no longer be traced; it exists as far back in history as we can go. In the OT, from the most ancient times on, the authority of YHWH's commandments and statutes, i.e., of the torah and of the prophets, is established. In Israel, Moses and the prophets have always been men of divine authority, and their writings were immediately recognized as authoritative. In this connection the Torah [the Pentateuch] is primary. In later times the Jews identified it with divine wisdom and called it the "image of God," "the daughter of God," "the all-sufficient revelation meant for all peoples," "the highest good," "the way to life." If Israel had not sinned, it would have been sufficient. But the prophetic writings were added for the purpose of explaining it. All those writings are divine and holy, the standard of doctrine and life, and have an unbounded content. Nothing in it is superfluous; everything has meaning—every letter, every sign, right down to the very form and shape of the word—for everything comes from God. According to Philo and Josephus, when inspiration struck, the prophets were in a state of ecstasy and unconsciousness, which these authors compared to pagan divination and also occasionally extended to people other than the prophets. But for all that, the divine authority of Holy Scripture was unshakably firm in their thinking. Factually, however, that authority was undermined by the gradually emerging doctrine of tradition. Scripture as such was again judged insufficient after all and was augmented by an oral tradition. This oral tradition too [so it was believed] came from God and was passed on to the scribes by Moses, Aaron, the elders, the prophets, and the men of the great synagogue. It was finally laid down in the Mishna and Gemara, which, as the subordinate norm, was added to the primary norm and harmonized with Scripture with the aid, especially, of thirteen hermeneutical rules.[13]

The Early Church

Although the Christian church, with Jesus and the apostles, rejected the entire Jewish tradition, it did from the beginning recognize the divine authority of OT Scripture.[14] The church was never without a Bible. It immediately accepted the OT, with its divine authority, from the hands of the apostles. From the beginning, the Christian faith included belief in the divine authority of the OT. Clement of Rome taught the inspiration of the OT with utter clarity.[15] He calls the OT writings "the oracles of God" (1 Cor. 53), "the Holy Scriptures which are true and inspired by the Holy Spirit" (ch. 45), cites texts from the OT with the formula: "the Holy Spirit says" (ch. 13) and says of the prophets ("the ministers of God's grace preached . . . with the help of the Holy Spirit" (ch. 8). Extending inspiration also to the apostles, he says that they went forth to preach "with full assurance of the Holy Spirit" (ch. 42) and that Paul had written to the Corinthians "under inspiration of

13. Leopold Zunz, *Die gottesdienstlichen Vorträge der Juden* (Berlin: A. Asher, 1832), 37ff.; F. W. Weber, *System der altsynagogalen palästinischen Theologie* (Leipzig: Dörffling & Franke, 1880), 14ff., 78ff.; Emil Schürer, *Geschichte des juden Volkes*, 3rd ed., 2:305ff.; in English: *A History of the Jewish People in the Time of Jesus Christ* (1890; repr., Peabody, MA: Hendrickson, 1994), 3:306ff.

14. A. von Harnack, *History of Dogma* 1:41ff., 175ff., 287ff.; idem, *The Mission and Expansion of Christianity in the First Three Centuries,* trans. James Moffatt (New York: Harper & Brothers, 1961), 242.

15. The numbered references that follow in the text are to the chapters in Clement's *First Epistle to the Corinthians.*

the Spirit" (ch. 47). For the rest, the Apostolic Fathers furnish little material on the dogma of Scripture. Though there is agreement on inspiration as such, there is some disagreement on its scope and boundaries. Little is said about the NT Scriptures; and apocryphal writings are sometimes cited as though they were canonical. The apologists of the second century compare the authors of Scripture to a cither, lyre, or flute that the divine musician employed as his instrument.[16] The doctrine of the apostles is on the same level as that of the prophets. As Abraham did, so we also have believed "the voice of God which was spoken again through the apostles of Christ and had been declared through the prophets."[17] The gospels share in the same inspiration as the prophets "because all of them as Spirit-bearers have spoken by the one Spirit of God."[18] In Irenaeus there is already present a full recognition of the inspiration of both Testaments: "The Scriptures are perfect for they have been spoken by God and his Spirit." They have a single author and a single purpose.[19] The church fathers further cite the Holy Scriptures as "divine writing," "the Lord's writings," "God-breathed writings," "heavenly literature," "divine voices," "a holy library," "the handwriting of God." The authors are called "ministers of the grace of God," "organs of the divine voice," "the mouth of God," "Spirit-bearers," "Christ-bearers," "inspirited ones," "those borne by God," "those flooded by," or "full of, the divine Spirit," etc.

The event of inspiration is thus presented as an act of driving or leading but especially as an act of dictation by the Holy Spirit. The writers [of Scripture] are not authors but only scribes. God is the author of Holy Scripture and its [human] writers were simply the hands of the Holy Spirit. The Scripture is "a letter of an omnipotent God to his creature."[20] There is nothing in Scripture that is indifferent and superfluous, but everything is full of divine wisdom; "for nothing is without meaning or without the seal that belongs to God."[21] Origen in particular beat this drum and stated that not a jot or tittle was in vain in Scripture, that there was nothing in Scripture "which did not come down from the fullness of the divine majesty." Similarly Jerome said: "Each and every speech, all syllables, marks and periods in the divine scriptures are full of meanings and breathe heavenly sacraments." Hence Holy Scripture was without any defect or error, even in chronological, historical matters.[22] What the apostles have written must be accepted as though Christ himself had written it, for they were his hands, as it were. Augustine, in his letter to Jerome, writes that he firmly believed that none of the canonical writers "erred in anything they wrote." Hence when there is mistake, "one is not allowed to say: the author of this book did not hold to the truth but either the copy of a book is faulty, or the interpreter erred, or you do not understand it."[23] At the same time, over against Montanism, the self-consciousness of the writers in the event of inspiration was stressed as strongly as possible. Irenaeus, Origen, Eusebius, Augustine, Jerome, et al. fully recognized the presence of prior investigation, differences in intellectual development, the use of sources and of memory, differences in

16. Justin Martyr, *Discourse to the Greeks,* ch. 8; Athenagoras, *Embassy for the Christians,* ch. 7.

17. Justin Martyr, *Dialogue with Trypho* 119.

18. Theophilus, *To Autolychus* 3.12.

19. Irenaeus, *Against Heresies* 2.28; 4.9.

20. Cf. Irenaeus, Augustine, Isidore, etc. in P. Dausch, *Die Schriftinspiration: Eine biblisch-geschichtliche Studie* (Freiburg im Breisgau: Herder, 1891), 87.

21. Irenaeus, *Against Heresies* 4.21.3.

22. Theophilus, *To Autolychus* 21; Irenaeus, *Against Heresies* 3.5.

23. Augustine, *Against Faustus* 11.5.

language and style. Some even assumed a difference in the manner of inspiration between Old and New Testament times, or even a difference in the degree of inspiration depending on the moral state of the author.[24] But nothing of all this detracted from [their] belief in the divine origin and authority of Holy Scripture. This conviction was universally accepted. This is even more powerfully evident from the practical use of Scripture in preaching, in argumentation, in the exegetical treatment of Scripture, etc. than from isolated statements these men made. In this first period the church was preoccupied more with the establishment of the canon than with the concept of inspiration but understood by canonical writings the "divine scriptures" and ascribed authority to them alone.[25]

The Medieval Church

The theology of the Middle Ages did not go beyond the church fathers nor further develop the doctrine of inspiration. John of Damascus mentions Scripture only in passing and says that the law and the prophets, evangelists and apostles, pastors and teachers spoke by the Holy Spirit and therefore Scripture is "God-breathed."[26] Erigena states that one must follow the authority of Holy Scripture in all parts, for "true authority does not only not resist right reason" but "all authority which is not approved by right reason is seen to be unsound."[27] Thomas does not treat the doctrine of Holy Scripture any more than Lombard but in his doctrine of prophecy offers his thoughts on inspiration.[28] Prophecy is definitely a gift of the intellect and consists, first, in inspiration, i.e., an "elevation of the mind toward the perception of divine things," which occurs "by a movement of the Holy Spirit." Second, it occurs in revelation, by which divine things can be known, darkness and ignorance are removed, and the prophecy itself is completed. Prophecy further consists in prophetic light by which divine things become visible, as natural things do by the natural light of reason. But that revelation varies; sometimes it occurs by the mediation of the senses, sometimes by the power of the imagination, sometimes also in a purely spiritual manner as in the case of Solomon and the apostles. Prophecy "by intellective vision," speaking generally, is superior to that which occurs "by the vision of the imagination." However, if "intellective light" does not reveal supernatural things but also makes known to us and enables us to discern naturally knowable things in a divine manner, then such an "intellective prophecy" is inferior to the "imaginative vision," which reveals supernatural truth. The writers of hagiographa often wrote about matters that are knowable by nature, speaking in that case "not as if from the person of God but from their own person with the help of divine light." Hence Thomas recognizes various modes and degrees of inspiration. He also writes that the apostles received

---

24. Novatian, *On the Trinity* 4; Origen, *Against Celsus* 7.4.

25. H. Denzinger, *Enchiridion symbolorum et definitionum* (Wirceburgi: Sumptibus Stahelianis, 1865), n. 49, 125; K. R. Hagenbach, *Lehrbuch der Dogmengeschichte*, 3 vols. in 2 (Leipzig: Weidmann, 1840–41), I, §31ff.; English translation: *A Textbook of the History of Doctrines*, trans. C. W. Buch and rev. Henry B. Smith, 2 vols. (New York: Sheldon, 1867); A. Zöllig, *Die inspirationslehre des Origenes* (Freiburg im Breisgau and St. Louis, MO: Herder, 1902); A. G. Rudelbach, *Zeitschrift für die gesammte lutherische Theologie und Kirche* 1 (1840); W. Rohnert, *Die Inspiration der Heiligen Schrift und ihre Bestreiter* (Leipzig: Georg Böhme [E. Ungleich], 1889), 85ff.; Wilhelm Kölling, *Die Lehre von der Theopneustie* (Breslau: C. Dülfer, 1891), 84ff.; Cramer, *Godgeleerde Bijdrage*, 4:49–121; W. Sanday, *Inspiration: Eight Lectures on the Early History and Origin of the Doctrine of Biblical Inspiration; being the Bampton lectures for 1893* (London and New York: Longmans, Green, and Co., 1893).

26. John of Damascus, *The Orthodox Faith* 4.17.

27. J. S. Erigena, *The Division of Nature* 1.66ff.

28. Thomas Aquinas, *Summa Theologica*, II, 2, qu. 171ff.

the gift of languages in order to be able to preach the gospel to all nations, "but so far as it concerns the things which are added by human art and ornate and elegant speech the apostle was instructed in his own language, not in foreign languages"; similarly, the apostles were sufficiently equipped for their office with knowledge but did not know everything there is to be known, e.g., arithmetic, etc. But no error or untruth can occur in Scripture.[29]

Scripture is most extensively treated by Bonaventure in the prologue to his *Breviloquium.* Holy Scripture, he writes, originates, not in human research, but in divine revelation from the Father, through the Son, in the Holy Spirit. No one can know it apart from faith, for Christ is its content. It is the heart of God, the mouth of God (the Father), the tongue of God (the Son), the pen of God (the Holy Spirit). Worthy of consideration are four aspects of Scripture: (1) its *breadth*: it contains many parts, Old and New Testament, and various kinds of books, legal, historical, and prophetic, etc.; (2) its *length*: it describes all times and periods from the beginning of the world to the day of judgment in three phases, under the law of nature, the written law, and the law of grace, or in seven specific periods; (3) its *height*: it describes the different hierarchies, the ecclesiastical, angelical, and divine; (4) its *depth*: it has several figurative meanings. Although Holy Scripture employs various ways of speaking, it is always genuine. There is no falsehood in it. For the all-perfect author, the Holy Spirit, could inspire nothing untrue, trivial, or degraded. Reading and studying Scripture is therefore an urgent necessity; and to this end Bonaventure wrote his precious *Breviloquium.*

While Duns Scotus, in the prologue to his *Sententiae*, does advance various grounds on which belief in Holy Scripture rests (such as prophecy, the internal harmony, the authenticity, the miracles, etc.), he does not deal with the doctrine of Scripture. Elsewhere, too, we find little material for the dogma of Scripture in scholasticism. No need was felt for a special treatment of the locus of sacred Scripture, because its authority was well-established and uncontested. Yet, continued research always finds more than was expected at the outset. Kropatscheck, in his opus,[30] first treats the practical use of Scripture in the Middle Ages and then proceeds to examine the doctrine of Scripture in various theologians such as Grosseste, Occam, Biel, etc. The most remarkable and extensive treatment of the doctrine of Scripture comes from Wycliffe, a most rigorous proponent of the sole and divine authority of Holy Scripture, who says that it is God's holy Word, never lies, has Christ as its content, and is given to all Christians to read and to explore.[31] The so-called formal principle of the Reformation was not first articulated by Luther and Zwingli but existed long before them, both in theory and in practice. At least formally, Scripture enjoyed undisputed sway in the Middle Ages. It was symbolically represented as the water of life, glorified in panegyrics, venerated and adored like the image of Christ, copied, illustrated, bound, and displayed in the most luxurious manner. It occupied a place of honor at the councils, was preserved as a relic, worn around the neck as an amulet, buried along with the dead, and used as basis for taking an oath. It was also read, studied, explained, and translated—much more than Protestants later thought.[32] Opposition to Scripture simply did not exist. Even Abelard does

---

29. Ibid., I, qu. 32, art. 4; II, 2 qu. 110, art. 4 ad. 3.

30. Friedrich Kropatscheck, *Das Schriftprinzip der lutherischen Kirche* (Leipzig: A. Deichert, 1904).

31. John Wiclif, *De Veritate Sacrae Scripturae*, critical edition of Rud Buddensieg, 3 vols. (Leipzig: Dieterich, 1904).

32. F. Vigouroux, *Les Livres Saints et la critique rationaliste* (Paris: A. Roger et F. Chernoviz, 1890), 1:226ff.; J. Janssen, *Geschichte des deutschen Volkes seit dem Ausgang des Mittelalters* (Freiburg im Breisgau: Herder, 1881), 1:48ff.; Kropatscheck, *Das Schriftprinzip*; G. Rietschel, "Bibellesen und Bibelverbot," *PRE*[3] 2:700–713; Franz Falk, *Die Bibel am Ausgange des Mittelalters* (Köln: J. P. Bachem, 1905).

not say that the prophets and apostles erred in writing, only that they sometimes erred as persons.[33] In this connection Abelard appealed to Gregory, who also acknowledged that point in the case of Peter. Sometimes, so he argued, they were deprived of the "grace of prophecy" that they might remain humble and acknowledge that they received and possessed the Spirit of God ("who can neither lie nor deceive") only as gift. Neither is Agobard of Lyon an opponent of inspiration. He only advocated, against Fredegis of Tours, a more organic view, which offers a better explanation of the Bible's language, style, grammatical irregularities, etc.[34] Ecclesiastically, the inspiration and authority of Holy Scripture was repeatedly declared and acknowledged.[35]

Tridentine Roman Catholicism

[110] The Council of Trent, in its Fourth Session, declared that the truth is "contained in the written books and in the unwritten traditions which, received by the apostles from the mouth of Christ himself, or from the Apostles themselves, the Holy Ghost dictating. [They] have come down to us, transmitted as it were from hand to hand. Following, then, the example of the Fathers, [the church] receives and venerates with a feeling of piety, and reverence all the books both of the Old and New Testaments, since one God is the author of both. The traditions [are also accepted] whether they relate to faith or to morals, as having been dictated either orally by Christ or by the Holy Ghost." While inspiration is here extended to the tradition, still it is clearly attributed to Holy Scripture as well. Among Roman Catholic theologians, however, there soon arose disagreement about the nature and scope of inspiration. Both the expression "the author of both [Testaments]," and the word "dictated" were variously interpreted.

In general, the theologians of the sixteenth century were still committed to the more rigorous outlook of the church fathers and scholastics. They were mostly adherents of Augustine in the doctrine of grace, Jansenists, Augustinians, and Dominicans. The most prominent members of this "school" are Melchior Canus, Bannez, Baius and Jansen, Billuart, Rabaudy, Fernandez, but also a number of Jesuits, like Testatus, Costerus, Turrianus, Salmeron, Gregory de Valencia, *et al.* All these men maintained that the Spirit of God exerted a positive influence upon the authors, an influence that extended even to the individual words. But soon there arose a less rigorous school of thought among the Jesuits. In 1586 Lessius and Hamelius started giving lectures at the Jesuit college in Louvain and there defended (*inter alia*) the propositions (1) "that in order for something to be Holy Scripture it is not necessary that its individual words be inspired by the Holy Spirit; (2) nor is it necessary that individual truths and sentences be immediately inspired by the Holy Spirit himself as author; (3) that some book, on the level, say, of 2 Maccabees, though written by human effort without the assistance of the Holy Spirit, yields Holy Scripture if the Holy Spirit later testifies that there is nothing false in it." Verbal inspiration is rejected here; the immediate inspiration of many things—historical times with which the authors were familiar—deemed unnecessary; and for some books a later inspiration (called a "subsequent or a posteriori approbation of the

---

33. P. Abelard, *Sic et Non,* ed. E. L. T. Henke and G. S. Lindenkohl (Marburgi Cattorum: Sumtibus et typis Librariae academ. Elwertianae, 1851), 10–11.

34. W. Münscher, *Dr. Wilhelm Münschers Lehrbuch der christlichen Dogmengeschichte,* ed. D. von Coelln, 3rd ed. (Cassel: J. C. Krieger, 1832–38), 2:1.105; P. A. Klap, "Agobard van Lyon," *Theologische Tijdschrift* 29 (March 1895): 146ff.

35. Heinrich J. D. Denzinger, *Enchiridion symbolorum definitionum et declarationum de rebus fidei et morum* (Wirceburgi: Sumptibus Stahelianis, 1865), n. 296, 386, 367, 600.

Holy Spirit" by Bonfrère) was considered sufficient. The faculties of Louvain and Douai condemned the propositions, but others disapproved of this censorship, and the pope took no decision. The first two propositions were widely accepted, but the third occasioned a difference of opinion on inspiration, which persisted among Catholic theologians even into recent times.

It was the infallible doctrine of the church that God was the primary author of Scripture, and this doctrine was therefore binding upon all and beyond all doubt. But there remained room nevertheless for the question of what kind of activity on the part of God was needed for him to be the author of a Bible book and to confer divine authority on it. In general, the answer was still that the divine activity had to be present and in fact was present in inspiration, but the nature of inspiration itself was in turn very differently interpreted. Some believed it always included revelation, not only of what was unknown to the authors but also of what was known to them. Others were of the opinion that in the latter case inspiration did not have to include revelation but needed only to consist of a divine impulse and divine guidance in writing the book. Still others leaned toward the idea that a negative kind of assistance, one that kept the authors from error, was sufficient, or that in any case a special and positive guidance in the process of writing was limited to matters of faith and conduct. Thus Bonfrère, in his *Praeloquia in Scripturam Sacram* (ch. 8), distinguished three ways in which the Holy Spirit could guide the authors of Bible books: antecedently, concomitantly, and subsequently. The first was real, concrete inspiration and occurred primarily in prophecy when it concerned matters that the authors could not know of themselves. The second consisted in a negative form of assistance, which protected the authors from error and was mainly given in the process of recording history that the authors could know as a result of their investigation. The third, consisting in subsequent approbation of a book by the Holy Spirit, could in the abstract be sufficient as well for the purpose of conferring divine authority on a given book, but Bonfrère said that this was a matter of judgment, not of fact. In fact, according to him, not a single book in Scripture had been made a canonical book solely by a subsequent approbation of God. This theory of inspiration, though in principle it should not be condemned, could therefore in practice be applied, as Mariana said, only to a few sayings of profane authors that were cited in Holy Scripture and so acquired divine authority, such as Acts 17:28 and Titus 1:12. Only a few theologians, such as Daniel Haneberg,[36] went further and asserted that there was also a group of books in the Bible that had secured canonical authority solely by a subsequent approbation.

Much more prevalent, however, was the view that the guidance of the Spirit—at least where it concerned matters that the authors could know of themselves by their own investigation—consisted solely in a passive or negative assistance that preserved the authors from error. This was the view of inspiration held (*inter alis*) by Philipp Neri Chrismann in his *Regula fidei catholicae* (1854) and Richard Simon in his *Histoire critique du Vieux Testament* (1689). A modification of this view was introduced by Holden, a doctor of the Sorbonne, who in his *Divinae fidei analysis* (1770), assumed a real inspiration in the case of truths of faith and morality but with respect to the remaining content of Scripture taught only the kind of assistance that every believer enjoys. Inspiration was thereby limited to the religious-ethical part of Holy Scripture and a greater or lesser degree of fallibility was allowed for the rest

---

36. In his *Versuch einer Geschichte der biblischen Offenbarung als Einleitung in's alte und neue Testament* (Regensburg: G. Joseph Manz, 1850).

of its content. This had earlier already been Erasmus's view and in the nineteenth century found acceptance with a variety of Roman Catholic theologians. Under Schleiermacher's influence, the representatives of the Catholic school of Tübingen, Drey, Kuhn, and Schanz related inspiration to the organism of Scripture and taught, accordingly, that it extended to the different parts of Scripture in varying degrees.[37] Although inspiration was therefore a property of Holy Scripture as a whole, it is linked with infallibility only in the parts that contain truths of faith and morality. In the case of other, incidental, and secondary matters, one may admit that Scripture contains smaller or greater errors. Also later, even after the Vatican Council [I], we encounter this view in the works of various Roman Catholic theologians, among them Bartolo, Cardinal Newman, Abbé Le Noir, Fr. Lenormant, the archbishop of Hulst, de Broglie, Langen, Rohling.

Modern Roman Catholicism

Still, this view of inspiration is far from being the generally accepted one. After the Reformation and even today, the majority of Roman Catholic theologians walk a middle course. On the one hand, they reject the broad kind of inspiration that is assumed to have consisted only in negative assistance or subsequent approbation, for in that case all the decisions of councils, all truth wherever it occurs, could be called inspired. On the other hand, they also reject strict verbal, textual, and "punctual" inspiration according to which not only all matters but even all individual words, consonants, and vowels were dictated and inspired, believing that many matters and words were known to the authors and therefore did not have to be inspired. The differences in language and style, the use of sources, etc. also proves this verbal and literal inspiration is incorrect. Sufficient, therefore, is a "real inspiration," which sometimes consists in specific revelation and sometimes solely in assistance. We find this theory in Bellarmine, C. a Lapide, the Wirceburg theology, Marchini, and numerous theologians in recent times.[38]

It seems also that Vatican Council [I] and the papal pronouncements have taken decisions that favor this trend. Although Vatican Council [I] did not advance any specific theory, it did single out for condemnation the theory of subsequent inspiration and of mere assistance and, after repeating the decree of the Council of Trent, declared that the church regards the books of Holy Scripture "holy and canonical not because they

---

37. J. S. von Drey, *Die Apologetik als wissenschaftliche Nachweisung der Göttlichkeit des Christenthums in seiner Erscheinung* (Mainz: Florian Kupferberg: 1838), 1:204ff.; J. von Kuhn, *Einleitung in die Katholische Dogmatik* (Tubingen: Laupp and Siebeck, 1859), 9ff.; Paul Schanz, *Apologie des Christenthums* (Freiburg im Breisgau: Herder, 1895), 2:318ff.; in English: *A Christian Apology,* 2nd ed., 3 vols., trans. Michael F. Glancey and Victor J. Schobel (Dublin: M. H. Gill; New York: F. Pustet, 1897–1902).

38. J. B. Franzelin, *Tractatus de divina traditione et scriptura,* 3rd ed. (Romae: Typeographia Polyglotta, 1882); G. Perrone, *Praelectiones theologicae* (Lovanii: Vanlinthout et Vandenzande, 1843), 9:66ff.; Joseph Kleutgen, *Die Theologie der Vorzeit* (Münster: Theissing, 1867), 1:50ff.; Franz L. B. Liebermann, *Institutiones theologicae* (Moguntiae: Sumptibus Francisci Kirchhemii, 1857), 1:385; Heinrich Denzinger, *Vier Bücher von der religiösen Erkenntniss* (Würzburg: Verlag der Stahel'schen Buch-und-Kunst-handlung, 1857), 2:108; M. J. Scheeben, *Handbuch der katholischen Dogmatik* (Freiburg im Breisgau: Herder, 1873), 1:109ff.; in English selected translations, see *A Manual of Catholic Theology Based on Scheeben's Dogmatik,* 2nd ed., trans. and ed. Joseph Wilhelm and Thomas B. Scannell, 2 vols. (London: Kegan Paul, Trench, Trübner; New York: Catholic Publication Society, 1899–1901); J. B. Heinrich, *Dogmatische Theologie,* 2nd ed. (Mainz: F. Kirchheim, 1881), 1:709ff.; Franz Schmid, *De inspirationis bibliorum vi et ratione* (Brixinae: Typis et sumptibus bibliopolei Wegeriani, 1885); G. J. Crets, *De divina bibliorum inspiratione* (Lovanii: Excudebant Vanlinthout Fratres, 1886); C. Pesch, *De inspiratione sacrae scripturae* (Friburgi Brisgoviae: Herder, 1906), 402ff.; G. M. Jansen, *Praelectiones Theologiae Fundamentalis* (Utrecht, 1875), 1:767ff.; Paulus Mannens, *Theologiae Dogmaticae Institutiones* (Roermond: J. J. Romen, 1901), 1:190ff.

were composed by human industry alone and later approved by [the church's] authority; nor because they contain revelation without error; but because, written under the inspiration of the Holy Spirit, they have God as their author; and because they have been entrusted as such to the Church." In chapter 2.4 the Council once more calls the books of Holy Scripture "divinely inspired," and in chapter 3, "On Faith," declares that "the divine and catholic faith believes all those matters that are contained in the word of God, whether in Scripture or tradition." This decree is perfectly clear in that it views inspiration as a positive activity of God, on the one hand, and on the other regards the infallibility of Scripture as a consequence of that inspiration. Leo XIII adopted the same position in his encyclical *On the Study of Holy Scripture,* November 18, 1893; in his letter of September 8, 1899, to the French clergy; and in his letter of November 25, 1899, to the Order of the Friars Minor (Franciscan). In the encyclical, inspiration is defined as follows:

> For, by supernatural power, He [the Holy Spirit] so moved and impelled them [the sacred authors] to write—He was so present to them—that the things which He ordered, and those only, they, first, rightly understood, then willed faithfully to write down, and finally expressed in apt words and with infallible truth. Otherwise, it could not be said that He was the Author of the entire Scripture.[39]

Among Roman Catholic theologians, however, all these pronouncements are far from having brought unity in their views on inspiration. They have admittedly had indirect influence. Whereas in the past the proponents of a looser view were inclined to restrict inspiration to the religious-ethical content of Scripture, and in other matters to grant its fallibility, they now look for the solution to the difficulties in another direction. For them the dogma of inspiration, they say, is certain: all of Scripture is inspired and therefore infallible in its entirety and in all of its parts. Thus the difference is not about the dogma itself, they claim, but about that which flows from it for the criticism and exegesis of Scripture. When some theologians deduce from this dogma that Scripture is absolutely infallible in all the matters it contains, this is just as one-sided as the position of others who assume the presence of errors and mistakes in Scripture. Scripture is most certainly true but true in the sense in which Scripture itself intends to be and not in the sense we with our exact natural and historical science would impose on it. Hence before everything else, as we consider every narrative and report in Scripture, we are obligated to examine what the author, and what God through the author, intended to say by it. In general we can already say at this point—and in the abstract this is conceded by everyone—that the Bible is not a handbook for geology, physics, astronomy, geography, or history. That does not mean that Scripture does not contain various statements about them, but in each case we have to examine what the author intended to say by it, whether he really wanted to give us information pertaining to those sciences or whether he included and recorded these statements for another purpose. If in a handbook on logic a sentence is quoted (say: "Gaius is a criminal"), it is not the purpose of the author to communicate a historical fact but only to make known the logical content of that sentence. This is frequently the case in Scripture also. Psalm 14 contains the words "there is no God"; this is not the opinion of the author, however, but a

---

39. Claudia Carlen, ed., *The Papal Encyclicals,* 1878–1903 (Wilmington, NC: McGrath, 1981).

pronouncement cited by him to convey to us the sentiments of a godless person. Paul often uses *ad hominem* arguments, but this is not to give us a lesson in logic, nor to bind us to his argumentation but only to the matter he wants to prove.

This truth must now be expanded and applied to the whole of Scripture. Readers must distinguish between absolute and relative (or economic) truth, between formal and material errors, between what the authors say and what they mean by it, between strictly (natural), scientific or historical truth and literary or poetic truth in general, between the manner in which we write history and the way the ancient Semites did it. If we carefully keep this distinction in mind [so it is said] and apply it in our criticism and exegesis of Scripture, it may very well happen that many parts of Scripture, which up until now we had viewed as history, prove upon study not to be history in our sense at all and were not so intended by the author, hence by the Holy Spirit, either. Materially, therefore, these parts may be fables, myths, sagas, legends, allegories, or poetic representations, which the author, under the guidance of the Holy Spirit, took from other sources or from popular oral traditions, not to tell us that everything literally happened in this way, but to teach us some religious or moral truth by such an illustration. This is, so they argue, probably the case with the creation story, with the story of Adam and Eve in paradise, with many narratives in the first eleven chapters of Genesis and in patriarchal history, etc. Even the authenticity of the books of the Bible may be freely examined. Even if the Pentateuch is not from Moses, and many Psalms attributed to David are not from David, and the second part of Isaiah is from another author than the first part, this does not detract from the divine inspiration and authority of Scripture. The inspiration is certain, but the authenticity is an open question. As a divine book the Bible is above all criticism, but as a human book it may, like all literature, be examined by historicalcritical methods and standards. Roman Catholic theologians were mistaken, it is now said, when some time earlier, under the influence of the strict verbal inspiration theory of Protestants, they turned against their fellow Roman Catholic Richard Simon [1638–1712]. Protestants have no choice but to hold a strict theory of inspiration, for if it should collapse, everything else would collapse for them as well. But Roman Catholics can in all sorts of ways accommodate present-day modern scholarship, inasmuch as for them the dogma remains firm on the basis of the church's authority.[40]

This trend of "concessionism," as it is called in France, has pitched the Roman Catholic doctrine of Scripture into a serious crisis, the further course and outcome of which deserves to be followed with interest. Although many people contradict and oppose it,[41] its influence

40. Marie-Joseph Lagrange, articles in *Revue biblique,* 1896 and 1897 (ed. note: the following pages in *Revue biblique* 5 [1896] contain items written by Lagrange: 5, 78, 127, 199, 281, 381, 440, 452, 485, 618, 644); idem, *La méthode historique surtout à propos de l'Ancien Testament* (Paris: Lecoffre, 1903); F. Prat, "Le nom divin est-il intensif en hébreu?" *Revue biblique* 10 (1901): 497ff.; idem, *La Bible et l'histoire* (Paris: Librairie Bloud et Cie, 1905); A. F. Loisy, *Etudes bibliques* (Paris: A. Picard, 1901); A. Houtin, *La question biblique chez les catholiques de France au XIXe siècle* (Paris: A. Picard, 1902); F. von Hummelauer, *Exegetisches zur Inspirationsfrage* (Freiburg im Breisgau and St. Louis, MO: Herder, 1904); A. Poels, *Katholiek* (December 1898); Rieber, *Der moderne Kampf um die Bibel* (1905); N. Peters, *Die grundsätzliche Stellung der katholische Kirche zur Bibelforschung* (Paderborn: F. Schöningh, 1905); H. Höpfl, *Die höhere Bibelkritik,* 2nd ed. (Paderborn: Ferdinand Schöningh, 1905); C. Holzhey, *Schöpfung, Bibel und Inspiration* (Mergentheim: Carl Ohlinger, 1902). In addition also see the works of Cornely, Knabenhauer, Zapetal, Engelkemper, Schell, Zanecchia, etc.

41. A. J. Delattre, *Autour de la question biblique* (Liége: H. Dessain, 1904); L. Fonck, *Der Kampf um die Wahrheit der h. Schrift seit 25 Jahren* (Innsbrück: F. Rauch, 1905); G. Pletl, *Wie steht's mit de menschliche Autorität der heilige Schrift* (Fulda, 1905); Pesch, *De Inspiratione Sacrae Scripturae,* 511–52; idem, "Zur Inspirationslehre," *Stimmen aus Maria Laach* (January–March 1906); R. Peeters, "Onze heilige boeken," *De Katholiek* (March–April 1906); L. Billot, *De Inspiratione sacrae Scripturae* (Rome: ex Typographia Polyglotta S. C. de Propaganda Fide, 1903).

is spreading, not only in exegetical circles but in the circles of historians and dogmaticians as well, and not just among Jesuits but also among members of other orders. In the case of some scholars, it is also clearly linked with the movement of Americanism or Reform Catholicism. In January 1902, Leo XIII appointed an international commission of fourteen members whose mandate was to study all the Scripture-related issues. Pius X, in his letter of March 27, 1906, insisted on the study of Scripture, calling for scholars not to deviate from the teaching of the church but nevertheless take serious account of recent scholarship. But only the future can tell whether this whole development will end in a papal decision.

The Rise of Critical Protestantism

[111] The Reformers accepted Scripture and its God-breathed and Godbreathing character as it had been handed down to them by the church. Luther now and then, from his soteriological position, expressed an unfavorable opinion about some books of the Bible (Esther, Ezra, Nehemiah, James, Jude, Revelation) and admitted some minor discrepancies, but on the other hand he clung to the inspiration of Scripture in the strictest sense, even extending it to the very letters.[42] Although the Lutheran confessions have no separate article on Scripture, its divine origin and authority is everywhere assumed.[43] The Lutheran dogmaticians, Melanchthon in his preface to his *Loci,* Chemnitz, Gerhard, etc., all have the same view. Quenstedt and Calovius were not the first to use such language, but Gerhard already calls the authors the "amanuenses of God," the "hands of Christ," and the "notaries public" and "stenographers of the Holy Spirit."[44] Later theologians only further developed and applied this notion.[45] Among Reformed scholars we encounter the same doctrine of Scripture. Zwingli frequently gives priority to the internal over the external word, points out historical and chronological inaccuracies, and sometimes extends inspiration also to

42. K. G. Bretschneider, *Luther an Unsere Zeit* (Erfurt: G. A. Keysers, 1817); D. Schenkel, *Das Wesen des Protestantismus* (Schaffhausen: Brodtmann, 1846–51), 2:56ff.; J. Köstlin, *The Theology of Luther,* trans. Charles E. Hay (Philadelphia: Lutheran Publication Society, 1897), 2:521ff.; W. Rohnert, *Was lehrt Luther von der inspiration der Heiligen Schrift* (Leipzig: Ungleich, 1890); Fr. Pieper, "Luther's Doctrine of Inspiration," *Presbyterian and Reformed Review* 4 (April 1893): 249–66; Thimm, "Luther's Lehre von dem Heilige Schrift," *Neue kirchliche Zeitschrift* 7 (1896): 644–75; Undritz, "Die Entwicklung des Schriftprinzips bei Luther in den Anfangjahren der Reformatie," *Neue kirchliche Zeitschrift* 8 (1897): 521–42; J. Kunze, *Glaugensregel, Heilige Schrift, und Taufbekenntnis* (Leipzig: Dörffling & Franke, 1899), 496–529; Johannes Preuss, *Die Entwicklung des Schriftprinzips bei Luther bis zur Leipziger Disputation* (Leipzig: Chr. Herm, Tauchnitz, 1901); K. Thieme, *Luthers testament wider Rom in seinen schmalkaldischen Artikeln* (Leipzig: A. Deichert [Georg Böhme], 1900); Otto Scheel, *Luthers Stellung zur heiligen Schrift* (Tübingen: J. C. B. Mohr [Paul Siebeck], 1902); J. C. S. Locher, *De leer van Luther over Gods woord* (Amsterdam: Scheffer, 1903).

43. *Augsburg Confession,* preface 8, art. 7; *Smalcald Articles,* II, art. 2, 15; *Formula of Concord,* I, Epit. de comp. regula atque norma, 1; cf. Nösgen, "Die Lehre der Lutherischen Symbole von der heilige Schrift," *Neue kirchliche Zeitschrift* 6 (1895): 887–921.

44. I. Gerhard, *Loci Theologici,* 1, ch. 2, §18.

45. Heinrich Heppe, *Dogmatik des deutschen Protestantismus im sechzehnten Jahrhundert* (Gotha: F. A. Perthes, 1857), 1:207–57; K. A. von Hase, *Hutterus redivivus: Oder, Dogmatik der Evangelisch-Lutherischen Kirche* (Leipzig: Breitkopf und Härtel, 1883), §38ff.; H. F. F. Schmid, *Die Dogmatik der evangelisch-lutherischen Kirche* (Erlangen: C. Heyder, 1843), ch. 4.; in English: *The Doctrinal Theology of the Evangelical Lutheran Church,* trans. and rev. Henry E. Jacobs and Charles E. Hay, 5th ed. (Philadelphia: United Lutheran Publication House, 1899); W. Rohnert, *Die Inspiration der heiligen Schrift und ihre Bestreiter* (Leipzig: Georg Böhme [E. Ungleich], 1889), 169ff.; Wilhelm Kölling *Die Lehre von der Theopneustie* (Breslau: C. Dülfer, 1891), 212ff.

pagan authors.[46] But Calvin regards Scripture in the full and literal sense as the Word of God.[47] While he does not recognize the Letter to the Hebrews as Pauline, he does consider it canonical, and he assumes the presence of error in Matthew 22:9 and 23:25 but not in the autographa.[48] The Reformed confessions almost all have an article on Scripture and clearly express its divine authority;[49] and all the Reformed theologians without exception take the same position.[50] Occasionally one can discern a feeble attempt at developing a more organic view of Scripture. Inspiration did not always consist in [new] revelation but, when it concerned familiar matters, it consisted in assistance and direction. The authors were not always passive but also at times active. They used their own intellect, memory, judgment, and style but always in such a way that they were guided and kept from error by the Holy Spirit.[51] Also in that way there was not the least tendency to detract from the divinity and infallibility of Scripture. The writers were not authors but scribes, amanuenses, notaries, the hands and pens of God. Inspiration was not negative but always positive, an "impulse to write" and "the suggestion of matters and words." It not only communicated unfamiliar but also familiar matters and words, for certainly the writers had to know them precisely thus and precisely so, not only materially but also formally, not only humanly but also divinely.[52] Inspiration extended to all chronological, historical, and geographic matters, indeed to the words, even the vowels and the diacritical marks.[53] Barbarisms and solecisms were not accepted in Holy Scripture. Differences in style were explained in terms of the will of the Holy Spirit, who wanted to write now in one way and now in another.[54] Materially, as it concerns letters, syllables, and words, Scripture is "considered from the human perspective" but formally as it pertains to the inspired sense, since it is the mind, the counsel, the wisdom of God, "this is a poor perspective from which to view it."[55] In 1714, according to Tholuck,[56] Nitzsche in Gotha wrote a dissertation on the question of whether Holy Scripture itself was God.

46. Eduard Zeller, *Das theologische System Zwinglis* (Tübingen: L. F. Fues, 1853), 137ff.; C. Sigwart, *Ulrich Zwingli* (Stuttgart and Hamburg: Rudolf Besser, 1855), 45ff.

47. J. Calvin, *Institutes* 1.7–8; *Commentary,* on 2 Timothy 3:16 and 2 Peter 1:20.

48. Cramer, "De Schrift beschouwing van Calvijn [and Other Older Reformed Writers]," *De Heraut* 26 (Juni 1878)–33 (Juli 1878); H. C. G. Moore, "Calvin's Doctrine of Holy Scripture," *Presbyterian and Reformed Review* 4 (January 1893): 49–77.

49. First Helvetic Confession, 1–3; Second Helvetic Confession, 1, 2, 13, 18; Gallican Confession, 5; Belgic Confession, 3; Thirty-Nine Articles, 6; Scots Confession, 18, etc.

50. Z. Ursinus, *Volumen Tractationum Theologicarum* (1584), 1–33; J. Zanchi, *Operum Theologicorum,* VIII, col. 319–451; F. Junius, *Theses Theologicae,* ch. 2; Polanus, *Syntagma Theologiae Christianae,* 1:15; *Synopsis Purioris Theologiae,* disp. 2; G. Voetius, *Selectae disputationes theologicae,* 1:30ff.; Cramer, "De Roomsch-Katholieke en oudprotestanse Schriftbeschouwing," *De Heraut* 26ff (Juni 1878); H. Heppe, *Die Dogmatik der evangelisch-reformirten Kirche* (Elberfeld: R. L. Friedrich, 1861), 9ff.

51. *Synopsis Purioris theologiae,* 3:7; A. Rivetus, *Isagoge, seu introductio generalis ad Scripturam Sacram* (1627), ch. 2; J. H. Heidegger, *Corpus Theologiae,* loc. 2, §§33–34.

52. Schmid, *Dogmatik der evangelische-lutherische Kirche,* 23–24; in English: *Doctrinal Theology of the Evangelical Churches;* G. Voetius, *Selectae disputationes theologicae,* 1:30.

53. J. Buxtorf, *Tractatus de punctorum origine, antiquitate et auctoritate* (1648); idem, *Anticritica* (1653); Alsted, *Praecognitio Theologiae,* 276; Polanus, *Syntagma Theologiae Christianae,* 1:75; G. Voetius, *Selectae disputationes theologicae,* 1:34; *Consensus Helvetica,* art. 2.

54. J. Quenstedt and Hollaz, according to W. Rohnert, *Die Inspiration der Heiligen Schrift?* (Leipzig: Ungleich, 1890), 205, 208; G. B. Winer, *Grammatik des neutestamentlichen Sprachidioms,* 6th ed. (Leipzig: F. C. W. Vogel, 1855), 11ff.; G. Voetius, *Selectae disputationes theologicae,* 1:34; Gomarus, *Opera omnia theologica,* 601.

55. D. Hollaz, *Examen Theologicum Acroamaticum* (Rastock and Leipzig: Russworm, 1750), 992.

56. A. Tholuck, *Vermischte Schriften grösstentheils apologetischen Inhalts* (Hamburg: F. Perthes, 1862), 2:86.

But when the theory of inspiration had drawn its most extreme conclusions, just as it did in the case of the Jews and the Muslims, opposition arose on every side. Even in earlier times there was no lack of criticism vis-à-vis Scripture. Jehoiakim had burned the scroll of Baruch (Jer. 36). Apion summed up all the accusations made by Gentiles against the Jews with reference to circumcision, the prohibition against eating pork, the exodus from Egypt, the sojourn in the wilderness, etc.[57] Gnostics, Manichees, and related medieval sects tore the New Testament apart from the Old and ascribed the Old to a lower deity, a demiurge. Especially Marcion in his *Antitheses*, and his disciples Apelles and Tatian, proceeding from the Pauline opposition of righteousness to grace, law to gospel, works to faith, and flesh to spirit, aimed their attack at the anthropomorphisms, the contradictions, and the immorality of the OT. They asserted that a God who is angry, repents, avenges himself, is jealous, orders theft and lies, descends to earth, issues a strict law, etc., cannot be the true God. They also loved to point to the big difference between Christ, the true Messiah, and the Messiah as the prophets pictured and expected him to be. Marcion rejected all NT writings except those of Luke and Paul and spoiled the latter by abbreviation and interpolation.[58]

Celsus shrewdly continued this battle and sharply criticized the first chapters of Genesis, the creation days, the creation of human beings, the temptation, the fall, the flood, the ark, the building of the tower of Babel, and the destruction of Sodom and Gomorrah. Further, he criticized the books of Jonah, Daniel, the supernatural birth of Jesus, his death, his resurrection, the miracles, and he accused Jesus and the apostles, for lack of a better explanation, of deception. Porphyry made a start with the historical criticism of the Bible books. He opposed the allegorical exegesis of the OT, attributed the Pentateuch to Ezra, considered Daniel a product from the time of Antiochus, and also subjected many narratives in the Gospels to sharp criticism. Later, in his *Speeches against Christians*, Julian [the Apostate] again renewed all these assaults against Scripture. But with that work the criticism of the time ended. Scripture achieved universal and undisputed dominance, and criticism was forgotten. It revived at the time of the Renaissance but was then for a long time held in check by the Reformation and the Roman Catholic Counter-Reformation. Next it surfaced again in rationalism, deism, and French philosophy. First, in the rationalist eighteenth century, it tended to be directed against the content of Scripture. Then, in the historically-minded nineteenth century, it called in question the authenticity of the biblical writings. Porphyry replaced Celsus, Renan followed Voltaire, Paul of Heidelberg made way for Strauss and Baur. But the result consistently remained the same: Scripture is considered a book full of error and lies.

As a result of this criticism, many theologians modified the doctrine of inspiration. First, inspiration was still generally retained as a supernatural operation of the Holy Spirit in the writing process but restricted to the religious-ethical dimension. With respect to chronological, historical, and such matters, it was weakened or denied so that on this level larger or smaller errors could occur. The Word of God was to be distinguished from Holy Scripture, as the Socinians already asserted. The authors of the OT and NT admittedly wrote "under the impulse and dictation of the Holy Spirit," but the OT has merely historical value. Only

---

57. J. G. Muller, ed., *Des Flavius Josephus' Schrift gegen den Apion* (Basel: Barnmaier, 1877).

58. Tertullian, *Against Marcion;* Epiphanius, *Haeresis* 42; Irenaeus, *Against Heresies,* passim; Von Harnack, *History of Dogma,* 1:267ff.; G. Krüger, "Marcion," *PRE*[3] 12:266–77.

doctrine is immediately inspired; in the rest error was easily possible.[59] The Remonstrants took the same position. In their confession they recognized inspiration but conceded that the authors sometimes expressed themselves "less precisely,"[60] or sometimes erred in "circumstantial aspects of the faith,"[61] or—more strongly—neither needed nor received inspiration in producing the historical books.[62] We then find the same theory of inspiration in S. J. Baumgarten, J. G. Töllner, Sember, Michaelis, Reinhard, Vinke, Egeling,[63] and others.

Still, this theory encountered numerous objections. The split between "that which is needed for salvation" and "the incidentally historical" is impossible, since in Scripture doctrine and history are completely intertwined. The distinction fails to do justice to the consciousness of the authors, who certainly did not limit their authority to the religious-ethical dimension but extended it to the whole content of their writings. It is at variance with the way Jesus, the apostles, and the whole Christian church used Scripture. Consequently, this dualistic view made way for another, the dynamic conception of Schleiermacher.[64] Here divine inspiration is transferred from the intellectual to the ethical domain. Inspiration is not primarily a quality or property of Scripture but of the authors. These were born-again holy men; they lived in the proximity of Jesus, underwent his influence, found themselves in the sacred circle of revelation, and were thus renewed also in their thinking and speech. Inspiration is a habitual property of the authors, and their writings share in it, bearing as they do a new and holy character. This inspiration of the authors, therefore, is not essentially different but only different in degree from that of all believers, inasmuch as all believers are led by the Holy Spirit. Nor may it be viewed mechanically, as though it were the experience of the authors only now and then, and then only in connection with some subjects. God's Word is not mechanically contained in Scripture, like a painting in a frame, but penetrates and animates all parts of Scripture, as the soul animates all the organs of the body. Not all parts of Scripture, however, share in this inspiration, this word of God, to the same degree. Rather, the closer a thing is to the center of revelation, the more it breathes the Spirit of God. Scripture, accordingly, is simultaneously a divine and a human book containing the highest truth on the one hand and being at the same time weak, fallible, and imperfect. Scripture is not the revelation itself but only the record of revelation; not the word of God itself but only an account of that word.

While Scripture is in many respects defective, yet it is also an instrument that is sufficient for us to arrive at a fallible knowledge of revelation. Finally it is not Scripture but the person of Christ or revelation in general that is the first principle of theology. This theory of inspiration admits of course of a great many modifications. Divine inspiration can be understood in a more or a less intimate connection with revelation; the operation of the Holy Spirit can be more or less concretely conceived; the possibility of error can be more or less generously conceded. But the fundamental ideas remain the same. Inspiration is in the

59. Otto Fock, *Der Socinianismus* (Kiel: C. Schröder, 1847), 326ff.

60. Episcopius, *Institutiones theologicae,* IV, ch. 4.

61. P. van Limborch, *Theologia Christiana,* I, ch. 4, §10.

62. H. Grotius, *Votum pro pace ecclesiae;* Clericus, according to Cramer, *De Geschiedenis van het Leerstuk der Inspiratie in de laatste Twee Eeuwen* (1887), 24.

63. Cf., e.g., Reinhard, *Grundniss der Dogmatik,* §19; Vinke, *Theologae Christianae Dogmaticae* (1853), 53–57; Egeling, *De Weg der Zaligheid,* 3rd ed., 2:612.

64. F. Schleiermacher, *The Christian Faith,* §128–32.

first place a property of the authors and secondarily of their writings; it is not a momentary act or special gift of the Holy Spirit but a habitual quality. It functions so dynamically that the possibility of error is not excluded in all parts.

This theory has almost completely replaced the old doctrine of inspiration. Only a few theologians are left who have not substantially adopted it. Even men like Franz Delitzsch, A. Köhler, W. Velck, A. J. Baumgartner (*et al.*), who first took the old position, later switched to the critical school of thought and abandoned the infallibility of Scripture. Everywhere, in scientific theology, the inspiration and authority of Scripture is in discussion.[65]

Although in the last several decades a great deal of attention and effort has been devoted to the doctrine of Scripture, no one will claim that a satisfactory solution has been found. While on the one hand the self-testimony of Scripture remains unimpaired, on the other the contemporary investigation of Scripture brings to light phenomena

65. The literature is immense: Rothe, *Zur Dogmatik,* 121ff.; Twesten, *Vorlesungen,* 1:401ff.; Dorner, *Glaubenslehre,* 1:620ff.; in English: *System of Christian Doctrine,* 2:184ff.; Lange, *Dogmatik,* I, §76; A. Tholuk, "Inspiration," *PRE¹* (in the English Schaff-Herzog the article "Inspiration" is co-authored by several scholars); Hermann Cremer, "Inspiration," *PRE³* 183–203; idem, *Glaube, Schrift und heilige Geschichte* (Gütersloh: C. Bertelsmann, 1896); Wilhelm Volck, *Christi und der Apostel Stellung zum Alte Testament* (Leipzig: A. Deichert [Georg Böhme], 1900); J. Chr. K. von Hofmann, *Weissagung und Erfüllung im Alten und Neuen Testamente* (Nördlingen: C. H. Beck, 1841), 1:25ff.; idem, *Der Schriftbeweis,* 2nd ed. (Nördlingen: C. H. Beck, 1857–60), 1:670ff.; 3:98ff.; J. T. Beck, *Vorlesungen über christliche Glaubenslehre,* 2 vols. (Gütersloh: C. Bertelsmann, 1886), 1:424–530; idem, *Einleitung in das System der christlichen Lehre,* 2nd ed. (Stuttgart: J. F. Steinkopf, 1870), §82ff.; F. A. Kahnis, *Die Lutherische Dogmatik* (Leipzig: Dörffling und Francke, 1861–68), 1:254–301; F. H. R. Frank, *System der Christliche Gewissheit* (Erlangen: A. Deichert, 1884), 2:57ff.; idem, *System der Christliche Wahrheit,* 2nd ed. (Erlangen: A. Deichert, 1880), 2:409ff.; W. F. Gess, *Die Inspiration der Helden der Bibel und der Schriften der Bibel* (Basel: Reich, 1892); W. Volck, *Zur Lehre von der Heilige Schrift* (Dorpat: E. J. Karow, 1885); R. Grau, "Über des Grund des Glaubens," *Beweis des Glaubens* 26 (1890): 225ff.; Otto Zöckler, "Zur Inspirationsfrage," *Beweis der Glauben* 28 (1892): 150ff.; Martin Köhler, *Die Wissenschaft der christlichen Lehre* (Erlangen: A. Deichert, 1883), 388ff.; R. B. Kübel, *Über den Unterschied zwischen der positiven und der liberalen Richtung in der modernen Theologie,* 2nd ed. (München: C. H. Beck, 1893), 216ff.; F. Delitzsch, *A New Commentary on Genesis,* trans. Sophia Taylor (Edinburgh: T. & T. Clark, 1899); A. W. Dieckhoff, *Inspiration und Irrthumslosigkeit der heiligen Schrift* (Leipzig: Justus Naumann, 1891); A. Köhler, *Über Berechtigung der Kritik des Alten Testaments* (Erlangen: Deichert, 1895); Bruno Baentsch, *Die moderne Bibel Kritik und die Autorität des Gotteswortes* (Erfurt: H. Güther, 1892); Karl Haug, *Die Autorität der heilige Schrift und die Kritik* (Strassburg: Strabburger Druckerei und Verlagsanstalt, 1891); Eichhorn, *Unsere Stellung zur heilige Schrift* (Stuttgart, 1905); C. Dahle, *Der Ursprung der heilige Schrift aus d. Dän. von H. Hansen* (Leipzig, 1905); August Klostermann, J. Lepsius, D. Haussleiter, K. Müller, D. Lutgert, *Die Bibelfrage in der Gegenwart: Fünf Vorträge* (Berlin: Fr. Zillesen, 1905); L. G. Pareau and H. de Groot, *Lineamenta theologiae Christianae universae: Ut disquisitionis de religione una verissima et praestantissima, sive brevis conspectus dogmatices et apologetices Christianae* (Groningen: C. M. van Bolhuis Hoitsema, 1848), 200ff.; H. de Groot, *De Groninger Godgeleerden* (Groningen: A. L. Scholtens, 1855), 59ff.; H. Bavinck, *De Theologie van Daniel Chantepie de la Saussaye* (Leiden: Donner, 1884); Roozemeyer, in *Stemmen voor Waarheid en Vrede* (July 1891) and (February 1897); Isaäk van Dijk, *Verkeerd bijbelgebruik* (Groningen: Wolters, 1891); François E. Daubanton, *De theopneustie der Heilige Schrift* (Utrecht: Kemink & Zoon, 1892); J. J. Van Oosterzee, *Christian Dogmatics,* trans. J. Watson and M. Evans, 2 vols. (New York: Scribner, Armstrong, 1874), §35ff.; idem, *Theopneustie* (Utrecht: Kemink, 1882); J. I. Doedes, *De leer der zaligheid* (Utrecht: Kemink en Zoon, 1868), §§1–9; idem, *De Nederlandsche Geloofsbelijdenis en de Heidelbergsche Catechismus* (Utrecht: Kemink & Zoon, 1880), 1:11–36; J. J. P. Valeton, *Christus en het Oude Testament* (Nijmegen: Ten Hoet, 1895); H. Zeydner, "De houding des Evangelie dienaars ten opzichte van het Oude Testament," *Theologische Studiën* 14 (1896): 291ff.; Otto Schrieke, *Christus en de Schrift* (Utrecht: C. H. E. Breijer, 1897); A. H. de Hartog, *De historische critiek en het geloof der gemeente* (Groningen: J. B. Wolters, 1905); R. F. Horton, *Inspiration and the Bible,* 8th ed. (London: T. Fisher Unwin, 1906); Matthew Arnold, *Literature and Dogma* (New York: Thomas Nelson, 1873); Charles Gore, *Lux Mundi,* 13th ed. (London: Murray, 1892), 247; F. W. Farrar et al., *Inspiration: A Clerical Symposium,* 2nd ed. (London: J. Nisbet & Co., 1886); W. Gladden, *Who Wrote the Bible?* (Boston: Houghton, Mifflin, 1891); C. A. Briggs, *Inspiration and Inerrancy* (London: J. Clarke, 1891); W. Sanday, *Inspiration: Eight Lectures on the Early History and Origin of the Doctrine of Biblical Inspiration,* 4th ed. (London; New York: Longmans, Green and Co., 1901); J. Clifford, *The Inspiration and Authority of the Bible,* 2nd ed. (London: James Clarke & Co., 1895); Marcus Dods, *The Bible, Its Origin and Nature* (Edinburgh: T. & T. Clark, 1905); A. Sabatier, *Les religions d'authorité et la religion de l'espirit* (Paris: Librairie Fischbacher, 1904), in English: *Religions of Authority and the Religion of the Spirit,* trans. L. S. Houghton (New York: McClure, Phillips, 1904); A. J. Baumgartner, *Traditionalisme et Critique Biblique* (Geneva, 1905); A. Berthoud, *La parole de Dieu* (Lausanne, 1906).

and facts that are hard to reconcile with that self-testimony. One does not do justice to that dilemma by saying that neither the prophets and apostles nor even Christ but only the Jewish tradition has taught the dogma of the inspiration and absolute authority of Scripture. Nor does one resolve the dilemma in all its sharpness by closing one's eyes to the serious objections that careful Bible research derives from the facts it discovers and can advance against the self-testimony of Scripture. This dilemma assumes an even more serious character because throughout all the centuries of its existence and still today in all countries, the church of Christ unconditionally accepts the authority of Scripture and lives by it from day to day. Furthermore, it is clear, on the other hand, that the objections to Scripture definitely do not concern merely a few subordinate points but touch the central truth of Scripture itself. They are not aimed at the periphery but at the center of revelation and are integrally linked with the person of Christ. Others, accordingly, have gone much further and denied all of inspiration as a supernatural and special operation of God's Spirit. To many scholars the Bible has become an accidental collection of human documents, though written by men of a deeply religious temperament and originated among a people who may be called the people of religion par excellence. One can speak of revelation and inspiration only in a metaphorical sense. At best, one can observe a special leading of God's general providence in the origination and collection of those documents. Inspiration differs only in degree from the religious enthusiasm that all devout people share.[66]

To the left of these stand the radicals who have completely finished with Scripture, shed all feelings of reverence toward it, and frequently have nothing left but mockery and contempt for it. In the first centuries Celsus and Lucian were the interpreters of this attitude. Toward the end of the Middle Ages, the blasphemy of "the three impostors" found acceptance. In the eighteenth century this hatred against Christianity was expressed by Voltaire, who from 1760 on had no other name for Christianity (which coincided for him with the Roman Catholic Church) than "the disgrace" ("l'infâme") and from 1764 on usually signed his letters off with the phrase: "Crush the beast!" ("écrasez l'infâme"). In the nineteenth century this apostasy from and hostility toward Christ and his word still gradually increased. Strauss voiced the thoughts of many when, to the question of whether we are still Christians, he gave a negative reply and wanted to replace Christianity with a religion of humanity and morality, for which Lessing's [dramatic poem] Nathan the Wise constituted "the basic holy book."

Still, for the majority of people this goes too far. There is nobody who does not sometimes receive a deep impression of the majesty of Holy Scripture. Even Ernst Haeckel acknowledged that [to him] the Bible was a mixture of some of the worst but also of some of the best components. Modern theologians, for all their criticism, continue to acknowledge the religious value of Holy Scripture, and not only regard it as a source for knowledge of Israel and early Christianity but continue to maintain it as a means for nurturing the religious-

---

66. B. Spinoza, *Tractatus Theologico-Politicus,* ch. 12; J. Wegschneider, *Institutiones Theologiae Christianae Dogmaticae* (Halle: Gebauer, 1819); Strauss, *Die Christliche Glaubenslehre* (Tübingen: C. F. Osiander, 1840), 1:136ff.; Alexander Schweizer, *Die Glaubenslehre der evangelisch-reformirten Kirche* (Zurich: Orell, Füssli, [1847]), 1:43ff.; A. E. Biederman, *Christliche Dogmatik* (Zurich: Orell, Füssli, 1869), §§179–208; O. Pfleiderer, *Grundriss de Christlichen Glaubens- und Sittenlehre* (Berlin: G. Reimer, 1888), §39ff.; R. A. Lipsius, *Lehrbuch der evangelisch-protestantischen Dogmatik* (Braunschweig: C. A. Schwetsche, 1893); J. H. Scholten, *De Leer der Hervormde Kerk,* 2nd ed. (Leiden: P. Engels, 1850), 1:78ff.; S. Hoekstra, *Bronnen en Grondslagen van het Godsdienstelijke Geloof* (Amsterdam: P. N. van Kampen, 1864), 188ff.

ethical life.[67] Among the proponents of a more relaxed view of inspiration, there are a great many people who, though attesting to their agreement with modern criticism, still strive seriously to cause Scripture to be for the church what it was for centuries: the completely reliable Word of God.

Furthermore, Ritschl and his school have contributed to a greater appreciation for Scripture insofar as over against "consciousness-theology" it again powerfully stressed the objective revelation of God in Christ.[68] This comes out clearly, especially in the work of Julius Kaftan. Rejecting the experiential, the speculative, as well as the history-of-religions method, he insisted that dogmatics should again become dogmatics and begin to speak "dogmatically." Straightforwardly he states that authority is indispensable to dogmatics and something totally natural: the "authority principle is the natural first principle of dogmatics." However, dogmatics can only speak in such absolute tones and believe in such an authority principle if it proceeds from belief in a divine revelation and derives its own authority from it. But the latter is inseparable from the former: "the absolute tone goes hand in hand with the authority-principle of divine authority and vice versa." According to the Christian faith, revelation is not first of all to be found in human beings but lies outside them in history. Hence the external historical revelation of God is the cognitive source of the Christian faith and consequently the authority principle, the natural and necessary first principle of dogmatics.[69]

Now Kaftan himself, in various ways, weakens this position, which he so stoutly assumes. He one-sidedly reduces revelation to manifestation, viewing Scripture solely as a record of revelation and denying inspiration, and especially by letting himself be guided in his use of Scripture by the two practical ideas of "the kingdom of God" and of "reconciliation," which he had established in advance as the essential content of the Christian religion. Hence he rejects everything, even in Scripture, that does not agree with those two ideas.[70] In reality, in Kaftan's case, his dogmatics still ends up being under the influence of an a priori neo-Kantian, voluntaristic view of Christianity. He is completely correct, nevertheless, in asserting that the authority of revelation is the indispensable foundation of dogmatics and that Scripture and the confessions are *the* authorities that decide what is Christian and reformational. Just as authority is the condition for all culture,[71] so also in the religious and moral life of humanity it is an essential factor and only comes fully into its own in free and unconditional submission to the supreme, divine authority.[72] It is not surprising, therefore, that the God-breathed character and authority of Scripture not only remains firm in the consciousness of the church but up until most recently still has any number of defenders among scientific theologians as well.[73]

67. S. Hoekstra, *Bronnen en Grondslagen,* 323ff.; Bruining, "De Moderne Richting en de Dogmatiek," *Theologische Tijdschrift* 28 (November 1894): 578ff.

68. A. Ritschl, *Rechtfertigung und Versöhnung,* 4th ed. (Bonn: A. Marcus, 1895–1903), 2:9ff.; W. Herrmann, *Die Bedeutung der Inspirationslehre für die evangelischen Kirche* (Halle: Niemeyer, 1882); J. Kaftan, *Wesen der christlichen Religion* (Basel: Bahnmaier, 1881), 307ff.; C. I. Nitzsch, *System of Christian Doctrine* (Edinburgh: T. &T. Clark), 212–52; E. Haupt, *Die Bedeutung der Heiligen Schrift für den evangelischen Christen* (Bielefeld and Leipzig: Velhagen & Klasing, 1891).

69. J. Kaftan, *Zur Dogmatik* (Tübingen: J. C. B. Mohr [Paul Siebeck], 1904), 21ff., 109ff.

70. J. Kaftan, *Dogmatik* (Freiburg im Breisgau: J. C. B. Mohr, 1897), §§1–5; idem, *Zur Dogmatik,* 47ff., 117ff.

71. Ludwig Stein, *Die soziale Frage im Lichte der Philosophie,* 2d ed. (Stuttgart: F. Enke, 1903), 535.

72. Kaftan, *Zur Dogmatik,* III; cf. L. Ihmels, *Die Bedeutung des Autoritätsglaubens* (Leipzig: Deichert, 1902), 13ff.

73. I. De Costa, *Over de goddelijke Ingeving der Heilige Schrift,* prepared for publication by Rev. Egglestein (Rotterdam: Bredée, 1884); Kuyper, *De Schrift het Woord Gods* (Tiel: H. C. A. Campagne, 1870); idem, *De Hedendaagsche Schriftkritiek* (Amsterdam: J. H. Kruyt, 1881); idem, *Encyclopaedie,* 2:492ff.; J. J. van Toorenenbergen, *Bijdragen tot de verklaring, toetsing,*

The Challenge to Inspiration Doctrine

[112] Holy Scripture nowhere offers a clearly formulated dogma on inspiration but confronts us with the witness of its God-breathed character and in addition furnishes us all the components needed for the construction of the dogma. It contains and teaches the God-breathed character of Scripture in the same sense and in the same way—just as firmly and clearly but just as little formulated in abstract concepts—as the dogma of the Trinity, the incarnation, vicarious atonement, etc. This has repeatedly been denied. Every sectarian and heretical school of thought initially begins with an appeal to Scripture against the confession and would have us believe that its deviation from the doctrine of the church is required by Scripture. But in most cases further investigation leads to the admission that the confession of the church has the witness of Scripture on its side. Modernists today generally concede that Jesus and the apostles accepted OT Scripture as the Word of God.[74] Others like Rothe,[75] though they grant this point with respect to the apostles, believe that church dogmatics cannot appeal to Jesus for its doctrine of inspiration. But Jesus' positive pronouncements about the Old Testament (Matt. 5:18; Luke 16:17; John 10:35) and his citations from and repeated use of OT Scripture leave no doubt whatever that for him, as much as for the apostles, Moses and the prophets were the bearers of divine authority. The contrast that Rothe construes between the teaching of Jesus and that of the apostles does not elevate but in fact undermines the authority of Jesus himself. For we know nothing about Jesus other than what the apostles tell us. Hence those who discredit the apostles and portray them as unreliable witnesses to the truth prevent themselves from finding out what Jesus himself has taught us and immediately also contradict Jesus himself. For he appointed his apostles as totally trustworthy witnesses who by his Spirit would guide them into all truth. Surely this also includes the truth concerning Holy Scripture. In the case of this dogma, as in the case of all other doctrines, the slogan "Back to Christ" is misleading and false if it is opposed to the witness of the apostles.

---

en ontwikkeling van de leer der hervormde kerk (Utrecht: Kemink, 1865), 9ff.; L. Gaussen, *Théopneustie ou, pleine inspiration des Saintes Écritures* (Paris: L.-R. Delay, 1840); idem, *Le canon des Saintes Écritures au double point de vue de la science et de la foi* (Lausanne: George Bridel, 1860); J. H. Merle d'Aubigné, *L'autorité des Écritures inspirées de Dieu* (Toulouse: Librairie protestante, 1850); A. de Gasparin, *Les écoles du doute et l'école de la Foi* (Genève: E. Beroud, 1853); F. A. Philippi, *Kirchliche Glaubenslehre* (Gütersloh: Bertelsmann, 1902), 1:125ff.; F. C. Vilmar, *Dogmatik* (Gütersloh: Bertelsmann, 1874), 1:91ff.; W. Rohnert, *Die Inspiration der heiligen Schrift und ihre Bestreiter* (Leipzig: Georg Böhme [E. Ungleich], 1889); Wilhelm Kölling, *Die Lehre von der Theopneustie* (Breslau: C. Dülfer, 1891); E. Haack, *Die Autorität der Heilige Schrift, ihr Wesen und ihre Begründung* (Schwerin, 1899); W. Walther, *Das Erbe der Reformation im Kampfe der Gegenwart*, vol. 1, *Der Glaube an das Wort Gottes* (Leipzig: A. Deichert, 1903); J. H. Ziese, *Die Inspiration der Heilige Schrift* (Schleswig: I. Johannsens, 1894); K. F. Nösgen, *Die aussagen des Neuen Testaments über den Pentateuch* (Berlin, 1898); F. Bettex, *Die Bibel Gottes wort* (Stuttgart: Steinkopf, 1903); E. Henderson, *Divine Inspiration* (London: Jackson and Walford, 1836); Robert Haldane, *The Verbal Inspiration of the Old and New Testaments* (Edinburgh: T. & T. Clark, 1830); Th. H. Horne, *An Introduction to the Critical Study and Knowledge of the Holy Scriptures*, 2nd ed. (London: Printed for T. Cadell, 1821), vol. 1; Eleazer Lord, *The Plenary Inspiration of the Holy Scriptures* (New York: A. D. F. Randolph, 1858); W. Lee, *The Inspiration of Holy Scripture, Its Nature and Proof*, 3rd ed. (Dublin: Hodges, Smith and Co., 1864); Charles Hodge, *Systematic Theology*, 1:151; W. T. Shedd, *Dogmatic Theology*, 1:61; B. B. Warfield, "The Real Problem of Inspiration," *Presbyterian and Reformed Review* 4 (April 1893): 177–221; idem, "God-Inspired Scripture," *Presbyterian and Reformed Review* 11 (January 1900): 89–130; idem, "The Oracles of God," *Presbyterian and Reformed Review* 11 (April 1900): 217–60; John Urquhart, *The Inspiration and Accuracy of the Holy Scriptures* (London: Marshall Brothers, 1895); W. E. Gladstone, *The Impregnable Rock of Holy Scripture*, 2nd ed. (London: Isbister, 1892).

74. Lipsius, *Dogmatik*, §185; Strauss, *Dogmatik*, 1:79; Otto Pfleiderer, *Der Paulinismus*, 2nd ed. (Leipzig: O. R. Reisland, 1890), 87ff.

75. R. Rothe, *Zur Dogmatik*, 178ff.

There is also another very common contrast, one that is created by those who want to be freed from the witness of Scripture concerning itself. Scripture, so we are told, may teach inspiration here and there, but really to do justice to and fully to understand the teaching of Scripture concerning itself, one must also consult the data that Scripture reveals to us as we investigate its genesis and history, its content and form. Only such a doctrine of inspiration, accordingly, is true and good which is consistent with the phenomena of Scripture and deduced from them. In this connection people very often make it appear as if the opposing party forces its own a priori opinion on Scripture and presses it into the straitjacket of scholasticism. These people use the argument that, over against all those theories and systems, they above all want to let Scripture speak for itself and bear witness of itself. Orthodoxy, they say, above all lacks respect for Scripture. It does violence to the text, to the facts of Scripture.[76]

This idea, when first introduced, sounds attractive and acceptable, but upon further reflection proves untenable. In the first place, it is incorrect to say that the teaching of inspiration, as it is maintained by the Christian church, forms a contrast to what Scripture says about itself. For inspiration is a fact taught by that very Holy Scripture. Jesus and the apostles have given us their witness concerning Scripture. Scripture contains teaching also about itself. Aside from all the dogmatic or scholastic development of this teaching, the question is simply whether or not Scripture deserves credence at the point of this self-testimony. There may be disagreement about whether Scripture teaches this divine inspiration of itself; but if it does, then it must also be believed at this point just as much as in its pronouncements about God, Christ, salvation, etc. The so-called phenomena of Scripture cannot undo this self-testimony of Scripture and may not be summoned against it as a party in the discussion. For those who make their doctrine of Scripture dependent on historical research into its origination and structure have already begun to reject Scripture's self-testimony and therefore no longer believe that Scripture. They think it is better to build up the doctrine of Scripture on the foundation of their own research than by believingly deriving it from Scripture itself. In this way, they substitute their own thoughts for, or elevate them above, those of Scripture.

Furthermore, the witness of Scripture is plain and clear and even recognized as such by its opponents, but the views about the phenomena of Scripture arise from prolonged historical-critical research and change in varying ways depending on the differing positions of the critics. Theologians who want to arrive at a doctrine of Scripture based on such investigations in fact oppose their scientific insight to the teaching of Scripture about itself. But by that method one never really arrives at a doctrine of Scripture. Historical-critical study may yield a clear insight into the origination, history, and structure of Scripture but never leads to a doctrine, a dogma of Holy Scripture. This can, in the nature of the case, be built only on Scripture's own witness concerning itself. No one would dream of calling a history of the origin and components of the Iliad a doctrine. Therefore, it is not just some inspiration theory that [stands or] falls with this method but inspiration itself as a fact and testimony of Scripture. Inspiration in that case—even if the word is still retained—becomes no more than a short summary of what the Bible *is*,[77] or rather of what people *think* the Bible is, and may be diametrically opposed to what the Bible itself says it is, claims to be, and presents itself as being. The method used in that case is at bottom none other than that

---

76. G. Wildeboer, *De Letterkunde des Ouden Verbonds* (Groningen: Wolters, 1893), V.
77. Thus, for example, Horton, *Inspiration and the Bible,* 10.

by which the doctrine of creation, of humanity, of sin, etc. is constructed, not from the witness of Scripture concerning these things, but from one's independent study of those facts. In both cases it is a method of correcting the doctrine of Scripture in light of one's own scientific investigation, making the witness of Scripture dependent on human judgment. The facts and phenomena of Scripture, the results of scientific investigation, may serve to explain and illumine the doctrine of Scripture concerning itself but can never undo the fact of inspiration to which it witnesses. Hence, while on the one side there are those who assert that only such an inspiration is acceptable which agrees with the phenomena of Scripture, on the other side the principle is that the phenomena of Scripture are, not as the critics see them, but as they are in themselves, consistent with its self-witness.

As a rule the term "divine inspiration" serves as a summary of what Scripture teaches concerning itself. The word θεόπνευστος, which in Scripture occurs only in 2 Timothy 3:16, can be taken both actively and passively and can mean both "God-breathing" and "God-breathed." But the latter meaning (contra Cremer's NT Lexicon) undoubtedly deserves preference, for (1) objective verbals compounded with θεός most frequently—though not always—have a passive meaning as in the case of θεογνωστος, θεοδοτος, θεοδιδακτος, θεοκινητος, θεοπεμπτος, etc.; (2) the passive meaning is supported by 2 Peter 1:21, where it is said that holy men spoke "borne by the Holy Spirit" (φερόμενοι); (3) where the word occurs outside the NT it always has a passive meaning; and (4) it is unanimously understood in that sense by all the Greek and Latin church fathers and authors.[78] In the Vulgate it is accordingly translated by "divinitus inspirata" as well.

Originally the word "inspiration" had a much broader meaning. Greeks and Romans attributed to all people who accomplished something great and good a divine afflatus or instinct. "No one ever became a great man without divine inspiration" [Cicero]. "God is within us; we grow warm by him stirring us up" [Ovid]. Now, the inspiration of poets, artists, seers, and others can indeed serve to illumine the inspiration of which Holy Scripture speaks. Almost all great men have stated that their most beautiful ideas arose in their mind suddenly and involuntarily and were a surprise to themselves. One such testimony may suffice here. Goethe once wrote to Ekkermann: "All productivity of the highest sort, every significant perception, discovery, great idea which bears fruit and has consequences is elevated above all earthly power and under no one's control. Human beings have to consider such [things] as unhoped-for gifts from above, as pure offspring of God, which they must receive and honor with joyful thanksgiving. In such cases human beings are to be viewed as vessels found worthy to receive a divine influence."[79] Carlyle for that reason points to heroes and geniuses as the core of the history of humankind. These geniuses, each in his own field, in turn inspired the masses. Luther, Bacon, Napoleon, Hegel, and others have transformed the thinking of millions and changed the human mind. This fact as such teaches us that the action and impact of one mind upon another is a possibility. The manner of it varies when one person speaks to another, such as when an orator electrifies a crowd by his message or a hyp-

---

78. Cf. the thorough argumentation of Prof. B. B. Warfield, "God-Inspired Scripture," *Presbyterian and Reformed Review* 11 (January 1900): 89–130.

79. Other such testimonies by Schopenhauer, Grillparzer, Jean Paul Haydn, can be found in Wynaedts Francken, *Psychologische Omtrekken* (Amsterdam: Scheltema & Holkema, 1900); cf. H. Bavinck, *Bilderdijk als Denker en Dichter* (Kampen: J. H. Kok, 1906), 159.

notizer transfers his ideas to the person being hypnotized, but there is always a process of suggesting thoughts: inspiration in a broad sense.

Now Scripture teaches us that the world is not independent, does not exist and live by itself, but that the Spirit of God is immanent in everything that has been created. The immanence of God is the basis of all inspiration, including divine inspiration (Ps. 104:30; 139:7; Job 33:4). Existence and life is conferred upon every creature from moment to moment by the inspiration of the Spirit. More particularly, that Spirit of the Lord is the principle of all intelligence and wisdom (Job 32:8; Isa. 11:2); all knowledge and skill, all talent and genius proceeds from him. In the church he is the Spirit of rebirth and renewal (Ps. 51:13; Ezek. 36:26–27; John 3:3), the distributor of gifts (1 Cor. 12:4–6). In the prophets he is the Spirit of prediction (Num. 11:25; 24:2–3; Isa. 11:4; 42:1; Mic. 3:8; etc.). So also in the composition of Scripture he is the Spirit of inspiration. This last activity of the Holy Spirit, accordingly, is not an isolated event; it is linked with all his immanent activity in the world and the church. It is the crown and zenith of it all. The inspiration of the authors in writing the books of the Bible is based on all those other activities of the Holy Spirit. It assumes a work of the *Father,* by which the organs of revelation were prepared—long before, from their birth on, indeed even before they were born, in their families of origin, by their environment, upbringing, education, etc.—for the task to which they would later be called with a special vocation (Ex. 3–4; Jer. 1:5; Acts 7:22; Gal. 1:15; etc.). Hence we may not, as modernists do, equate their inspiration with heroic, poetic, or religious inspiration. It is not a work of the general providence of God, not an effect of God's Spirit in the same measure and manner as occurs in the lives of heroes and artists, though it is true that this internal impact of God's Spirit is frequently assumed in the lives of prophets and biblical authors. The Spirit in creation precedes and prepares the way for the Spirit in re-creation. In addition, the actual inspiration [of Scripture] also assumes an antecedent work of the *Son.* The gift of divine inbreathing is granted only within the circle of revelation. Theophany, prophecy, and miracle all precede the actual inspiration. Revelation and inspiration are distinct; the former is rather a work of the Son, the Logos, the latter a work of the Holy Spirit. There is therefore truth in Schleiermacher's idea that the holy authors were subject to the influence of the holy circle in which they lived. Revelation and inspiration have to be distinguished.

If those authors could know or find out the things they had to write from what they had seen or from their personal investigation and consultation of sources, they would not have needed to receive any revelation on those topics. Jesus himself says that his apostles, whose calling was to act in the world as his witnesses, would be reminded by the Holy Spirit of what they themselves had seen and heard (John 14:26). He clearly distinguishes this activity of the Spirit from the activity by which he would reveal to them the things which, though they were included in the appearance of Christ (whence the Holy Spirit would take them), the disciples could not bear to know before the resurrection and ascension of Christ (John 16:12–14). But though there is a clear distinction between revelation and inspiration, this distinction may not be misused to separate inspiration completely from the revelation, to place it outside of the sphere of revelation, and thus in fact totally to deny it.

For, in the first place, while revelation often precedes inspiration, this is not always so. When the Holy Spirit also had the task to make known the things to come, he could collapse this revelation with inspiration. The apostles then received the thoughts of the Holy Spirit as they were writing them down, and inspiration was at the same time revelation. Second, also in matters that the apostles could know from having seen them and from their own inquiries, a special revelation of the Holy Spirit was needed of the kind that Jesus himself describes as a process of learning and remembering things he had said (John 14:26). Third, we need to remember that, while the prophets and apostles could know much of revelation because they had witnessed it, the whole of revelation becomes known to us only from and through their written witness. Hence for the church of all ages, Scripture is *the* revelation, i.e., the only instrument by which the revelation of God in Christ can be known. Accordingly, in inspiration the revelation is concluded, gets its permanent form, and reaches its end point. On the one hand, it is true that "inspiration is not revelation." On the other hand, it is equally true that "all matters inspired are matters revealed."[80] Finally, inspiration usually—but not always—also assumes a work of the Holy Spirit in regeneration, faith, and repentance. Most of the prophets and apostles were holy men, children of God. Hence also this idea of "ethical" theology contains elements of truth.[81] Yet inspiration is not identical with regeneration. Regeneration encompasses the whole person, while inspiration is an operation in the conscious mind. The former sanctifies and renews a person; the latter illumines and instructs the person. The former does not automatically include inspiration, and inspiration is possible without regeneration (Num. 23:5; John 11:51; cf. Num. 22:28; 1 Sam. 19:24; Heb. 6:4). Regeneration is a permanent way of being; inspiration a transient act. Inspiration, accordingly, is closely connected with all the aforementioned activities of God. It may not be isolated from them. It is incorporated in all those influences of God in the created world. But here too we have to oppose the evolutionary theory that the higher can only proceed from the lower by an immanent development. The operations of God's Spirit in nature, in humankind, in the church, in the prophets, and in the biblical authors, though related and analogous, are not identical. There is harmony but no uniformity here.

Differing Views of Inspiration

[113] In what, then, does inspiration consist? Scripture sheds light on that question when it repeatedly states that the Lord speaks through the prophets or through the mouth of the prophets; we read in Scripture "that which was spoken by the Lord through the prophet saying" [cf. Gr. Matt. 1:22]. Of God the preposition ὑπό is used; he is the one speaking, the actual subject. The prophets, however—speaking or writing—are God's instruments; in reference to them the preposition διά with genitive is used, never ὑπό (Matt. 1:22; 2:15, 17, 23; 3:3; 4:14; etc.; Luke 1:70; Acts 1:16; 3:18; 4:25; 28:25). God, or the Holy Spirit, is the actual speaker, the informant, the primary author, and the writers are the instruments by whom God speaks, the secondary authors, the scribes. Additional light is shed by 2 Peter 1:19–21, where the origin of prophecy is not found in the will of humankind but in the impulse of God's Spirit. Being driven (φερεσθαι, cf. Acts 27:15, 17, where the ship is driven by the wind) is essentially distinct from being led (ἀγεσθαι, used of the children of God, Rom. 8:14). The prophets were borne, impelled by the Holy Spirit, and thus spoke. Similarly the preaching of the apostles is called speaking "in the Holy Spirit" (cf. Matt. 10:20; John 14:26; 15:26;

---

80. C. Pesch, *De Inspiratione Sacrae Scripturae,* 414.

81. Ed. note: Bavinck is referring here to a distinct nineteenth-century Dutch Reformed school of theology for whom the living Christ was clearly distinguished from doctrine and propositional truth (see H. Bavinck, *De Theologie van Daniel Chantepie de la Saussaye* [Leiden: Donner, 1885]). The word "ethical," a literal translation of the Dutch "ethische," is misleading. The heart of this theology was not a *moral* Christianity but an *existential,* living faith.

16:7; 1 Cor. 2:10–13, 16; 7:40; 2 Cor. 2:17; 5:20; 13:3). Prophets, and apostles, accordingly, are people "borne by God": it is God who speaks in and through them. The correct view of inspiration apparently depends therefore on putting the primary author and the secondary authors in the right relationship to each other. Pantheism and deism cannot describe that relationship correctly and fail to do justice either (in the case of pantheism) to the activity of human beings or (in the case of deism) to the activity of God. Only the theism of Scripture preserves us from error, both to the right and to the left.

The activity of God in inspiration does not come into its own when it is described as "subsequent approbation," as "mere preservation from error," or even as "dynamic," as the inspiration of persons. It is true that Lessius and Bonfrere did not assert that in fact a given book in Scripture was raised to the rank of an inspired and canonical book by a subsequent divine declaration that there was nothing false in it. However, they did entertain this idea as a possibility, appealing for this position to the citations of profane authors that occur in Scripture (Acts 17:28; Titus 1:12) and that consequently achieved canonical authority. This appeal fails to prove their position, however, because the two cases are not the same. In the biblical references cited, two profane authors are quoted by Paul, confronting us thereby by the fact of a *subsequent approbation on the part of God*. But in the cases assumed by Lessius and Bonfrere such later approbation is missing, unless one wants to find it in the church's formation of the canon. The church, however, did not cause the canon or any single book to be inspired but only recognized and confessed that which had long been established and held authority as an inspired and canonical writing in the church. If the church had raised to the rank of an inspired book any writing that was in fact not inspired, it would have been guilty of deception. Therefore, it is impossible even for God himself, by a simple declaration at a later date, to put a document that had been written without the special leading of the Holy Spirit in a group of writings that had originated with such leading. The Vatican Council [I], session 3, chapter 2, accordingly, rightly rejected Lessius's sentiments and declared that the church does not regard the books of the Bible holy and canonical "because they were composed by human industry alone and later approved by her authority." At the same time and for the same reasons, the council also rejected the sentiments of Chrismann, Jahn, and others, according to which inspiration consists only in "preservation from error." Here too "that which was spoken by God" (ῥηθεν ὑπο θεου) does not fully come into its own. The Christian church, both the Roman Catholic and the Protestant, do not regard the books of the Bible holy and canonical "because they contain revelation without error, but because, written under the inspiration of the Holy Spirit, they have God as their author, and because they have been entrusted as such to the church."

Also opposed to this confession, which is undoubtedly grounded in Scripture, is the view of inspiration according to which it consists only in arousing religious affections in the heart of prophets and apostles, affections that were then expressed in their writings. For this position not only confuses inspiration with regeneration and puts Scripture on a par with devotional literature, but also denies in principle that God revealed himself to human beings by speaking, by thoughts, and by words. All of revelation in Scripture is one continuous proof, however, that God not only speaks to human beings metaphorically, by nature and history, facts and events, but also repeatedly comes down to them to convey his thoughts in human words and language. Divine inspiration is above all God speaking to us by the mouth of prophets and apostles, so that their word is the word of God. What has been written is "that which has been spoken by God"; the Holy Spirit will speak (λαλήσει) whatever he hears and will declare (ἀναγγαλεῖ) the things that are to come (John 16:13). The words of God (λόγια θεοῦ, Acts 7:38; Rom. 3:2; Heb. 5:12; 1 Peter 4:11) are always "oracular utterances, divinely authoritative communications."[82] The word of the apostles is the word of God (1 Thess. 2:13). In 2 Timothy 3:16 Scripture is called "God-breathed," not primarily with a view to its content but in virtue of its origin. It is not "inspirited because and insofar as it inspires" but, conversely, "it breathes God and inspires because it has been inspired by God."[83]

Erring in the other direction are those who favor a *mechanical* inspiration, thereby failing to do justice to the activity of the secondary authors. What we must understand by mechanical inspiration, however, is far from certain. Some writers use this term when they reject all special guidance of the Holy Spirit in the writings of the biblical books. According to them, any kind of miracle, all prophecy, all supernatural influence of God in the world and in human beings is contrary to the nature of things. So no revelation can exist other than that which comes to human beings in the ordinary course of nature and is historically as well as psychologically mediated. The inspiration that the biblical authors enjoyed is then on a par with, or at least only different in degree from, the heroic, poetic, or religious inspiration that other people experienced as well.

After everything we said earlier about revelation, however, it needs no further argument that this view is diametrically opposed to Scripture. Scripture everywhere asserts that God can and actually does reveal himself to human beings, not only by nature and history, by the heart and conscience, but also directly and in the way of extraordinary means. God reveals himself not only *in* human beings but also—by special words and deeds—*to* human beings. Even aside from this, however, on a theistic view it is not at all clear why such a special revelation to humanity is mechanical and in violation of human nature. If it is not mechanical for children to believe their parents and teachers on authority and simply to learn from them, and if it is not unfitting for a hired man to receive orders from his boss—orders he sometimes does not even understand and only has to carry out—then neither is there anything unnatural for human beings to receive a word from God that they have to accept and obey in childlike faith. If someone objects that such a revelation of God, which comes to humanity from without and cannot be inferred and explained from the things that occurred beforehand outside of and within them, always remains outside and above them and cannot be assimilated by them, we have to distinguish two things. To a child who is being brought up; to a student who is being educated; to a scholar, progress and development consists in large part in the reception and acquisition of new knowledge that cannot be derived by reflection and reasoning from what these people knew before. In logic and mathematics this may in the abstract be somewhat possible, but in history and in the natural sciences new knowledge has to be imparted to human beings from without.

At the same time, it is the task of every teacher and every scholar to introduce order into his or her teaching and studies and to proceed step-by-step from one thing to another. Those who neglect the latter cause confusion in people's mind; but those who deny the former—the need for new knowledge—make progress in knowledge impossible. Both of these elements are observed and combined by God in his revelation. By his revelation he

---

82. B. B. Warfield, "The Oracles of God," *Presbyterian and Reformed Review* 11 (April 1900): 217–60.
83. Pesch, *De Inspiratione*, 412.

constantly introduces new knowledge and information; his revelation comes in the shape of a centuries-long history. But in this connection he follows a regular pedagogical order and proceeds from the lower to the higher, from the lesser to the greater. Those in our day who oppose the former—the need for new knowledge—on the ground that human beings cannot assimilate a special revelation, gradually go on to reject all revelation. They relapse into a mechanistic view of nature and lose the right to speak of development and progress in general and specifically in the area of religion. In the end they no longer even have a standard by which to distinguish between the true and the false in what they still consider to be revelation. Those, on the other hand, who neglect the pedagogical order that God follows in his revelation run the danger of adhering to a mechanical view of revelation that is contradicted by Scripture itself.

All this applies to inspiration as well. A mechanical notion of revelation one-sidedly emphasizes the new, the supernatural element that is present in inspiration, and disregards its connection with the old, the natural. This detaches the Bible writers from their personality, as it were, and lifts them out of the history of their time. In the end it allows them to function only as mindless, inanimate instruments in the hand of the Holy Spirit. To what extent theologians in the past held to such a mechanical view cannot be said in a single sweeping statement and would have to be explored separately in each individual case. It is true that the church fathers already started comparing the prophets and apostles, in the process of writing, with a cither, a lyre, a flute, or a pen in the hand of the Holy Spirit. But we dare not draw too many conclusions from these comparisons. In using these similes they only wanted to indicate that the Bible writers were the secondary authors and that God was the primary author. This is evident from the fact that, on the other hand, they firmly and unanimously rejected the error of the Montanists, who claimed that prophecy and inspiration rendered their mouthpieces unconscious, and often clearly recognized the self-activity of the biblical authors as well. Still, from time to time, one encounters expressions and ideas that betray a mechanical view. In general, it can be said without fear of contradiction that insight into the historical and psychological mediation of revelation—now taken in a favorable sense—only came to full clarity in modern times and that the mechanical view of inspiration, to the extent that it existed in the past, has increasingly made way for the organic.

[114] This organic view, far from weakening the doctrine of Scripture at this point, enables it more fully to come into its own. It is Scripture itself that requires us to conceive inspiration—like prophecy—organically, not mechanically. Even what it teaches us in general about the relationship between God and his creature prompts us to suspect that also the leading of God's Spirit in divine inspiration will confirm and strengthen, not destroy, the self-activity of human beings. For in creation God confers on the world a being of its own, which, though not independent, is distinct from his. In the preservation and government of all things, God maintains this distinct existence of his creatures, causes all of them to function in accordance with their own nature, and guarantees to human beings their own personality, rationality, and freedom. God never coerces anyone. He treats human beings, not as blocks of wood, but as intelligent and moral beings. The Logos, in becoming flesh, does not take some unsuspecting person by surprise, but he enters into human nature, prepares and shapes it by the Spirit into his own appropriate medium. In regeneration and conversion he does not suppress and destroy the powers and gifts of human persons but restores and strengthens them by cleansing them from sin. In short, the revelation between God and his

[human] creation, according to Scripture, is not deistic or pantheistic—but theistic, and that is how it will therefore have to be in inspiration as well. Scripture itself teaches this directly and concretely. The Spirit of the Lord entered into the prophets and apostles themselves and so employed and led them that they themselves examined and reflected, spoke and wrote as they did. It is God who speaks through them; at the same time it is they themselves who speak and write. Driven by the Spirit, they themselves yet spoke (ἐλάλησαν, 2 Peter 1:21). In the NT the OT Scriptures are frequently quoted by reference to the primary author (Luke 1:70; Acts 1:16; 3:18; 4:25; 28:25), and always in the Letter to the Hebrews (1:5ff.), but no less often by reference to the secondary authors. This demonstrates that Moses, David, Isaiah, and others, though led by the Spirit, were in fact in the full sense of the word the authors of their books (Matt. 13:14; 22:43; John 1:23, 45; 5:46; 12:38). All the various components that come under consideration in divine inspiration show that the Spirit of the Lord, so far from suppressing the personality of the prophets and apostles, instead heightens the level of their activity. This is evident first of all from the fact that they were set apart, prepared, and equipped from their youth on for the task to which God would later call them (Ex. 3–4; Jer. 1:5; Acts 7:22; Gal. 1:15). Their native disposition and bent, their character and inclination, their intellect and development, their emotions and willpower are not undone by the calling that later comes to them but, as they themselves had been already shaped by the Holy Spirit in advance, so they are now summoned into service and used by that same Spirit. Their whole personality with all of their gifts and powers are made serviceable to the calling to which they are called.

Second, the so-called "impulsion to write" yields a tangible proof of this Spirit-led organic activity of the prophets and apostles, for in only a few texts is there any indication of a direct command to write; and these texts by no means cover the entire content of Scripture. But also the occasions that impelled the prophets and apostles to write belong to the leading of the Spirit; it was precisely through these occasions that he impelled them to write. The prophetic and apostolic calling automatically and naturally included the calling to speak and witness (Ex. 3; Ezek. 3; Amos 3:8; Acts 1:8; etc.) but not that of writing. Indeed, many prophets and apostles did not write. Nor can we infer a special injunction to write from Matthew 28:19. Writing is not mentioned as one of the charismata (1 Cor. 12).[84] But the Holy Spirit guided the history of the church in Israel and in the New Testament in such a way that deeds became words and words were set down in writing. Sellin observes on occasion that while the other prophets addressed the court, the later prophets, beginning with Amos, directed their messages more to the people.[85] To reach the people and to make known to them the thoughts of God, they simply had to utilize the means of writing. Similarly, when the apostles, after having founded the church by their preaching, wanted to impart to it the fullness of the revelation granted them in Christ, the epistolary form naturally presented itself to them as the obvious means to that end. In that respect the task of teaching all the nations, enjoined upon them in Matthew 28:19, gradually also began to take the form of witnessing by means of writing. From this guidance of the church, the calling or impulse to write was born in the life of the prophets and apostles. That activity of writing was the highest, most powerful and most universal witness that could proceed from them. By it the word of God was made permanent and became the possession of the whole human race.

---

84. Bellarmine, *De Verbo Dei*, bk. 4, chs. 3–4.
85. Ernst Sellin, *Beiträge zur Israelitischen und Jüdischen Religionsgeschichte* (Leipzig: A. Deichert, 1896), 1:136n1.

And precisely because the writings of the prophets and apostles did not arise outside of but in history, there is also a branch of theology that explores and makes known all the occasions and circumstances in which the books of the Bible originated. But while "unspiritual" persons stop with these secondary causes, the "spiritual" person [cf. 1 Cor. 2:14–15] goes on to the primary cause and, in the light of Scripture, discovers in all this a special leading of the Holy Spirit.

Third, we observe that the prophets and apostles, as they proceed to write, completely remain themselves. They retain their powers of reflection and deliberation, their emotional states and freedom of the will. Research (Luke 1:1), reflection, and memory (John 14:26), the use of sources, and all the ordinary means that an author employs in the process of writing a book are used. So far from being spurned or excluded by divine inspiration, these means are incorporated into it and made to serve the goal that God has in mind. In several cases the personal experience and life history of the prophets and apostles even yielded the material they needed for their writing. In the Psalms it is the devout singer who alternately laments and shouts aloud in jubilation, sits down in sadness or loudly expresses his joy. In Romans 7 Paul describes his personal life experience; and throughout all of Scripture it is over and over again the persons of the authors themselves whose life and experience, hopes and fears, faith and trust, complaints and wretchedness, are depicted and portrayed. The deep and abundant life experience of the men of God (David, for example) is so shaped and led by the Spirit of the Lord that, incorporated in Scripture, it would serve to instruct later generations, "that by the steadfastness and by the encouragement of the scriptures we might have hope" (Rom. 15:4). It has all been written for our instruction (2 Tim. 3:16). Hence there is room in Scripture for every literary genre, for prose and poetry, ode and hymn, epic and drama, lyrical and didactic poems, psalms and letters, history and prophecy, vision and apocalyptic, parable and fable (Judg. 9:7–8); and every genre retains its own character and must be judged in terms of its own inherent logic.

If, then, the prophets and apostles so witness as they write, they also retain their own character, language, and style. At all times this stylistic variation in the books of the Bible has been recognized, but it has not always been satisfactorily explained. It is not to be explained by saying that the Holy Spirit out of sheer caprice decided to write one way today and another at some other time. Rather, entering these authors, he also entered into their style and language, their character and unique personality, which he himself had already prepared and shaped for this purpose. Integral to this purpose is also that in the OT he chose the Hebrew and in the NT Hellenistic Greek as the vehicle of divine thoughts. This choice was not an arbitrary one either. (Purism, let it be said in passing, in its own awkward way defended an important truth.) Judged by the Greek of Plato and Demosthenes, the NT is full of barbarisms and solecisms; but the marriage between pure Hebrew and pure Attic that resulted in Hellenistic Greek, between the mind of the East and the mind of the West, was the linguistic realization of the divine idea that salvation is from the Jews but intended for all humankind. From a grammatical and linguistic viewpoint, the language of the NT is not the most beautiful, but it is certainly the best suited for the communication of divine thoughts. In this respect, too, the word has become truly and universally human.

In view of all this, the theory of organic inspiration alone does justice to Scripture. In the doctrine of Scripture, it is the working out and application of the central fact of revelation: the incarnation of the Word. The Word (Λόγος) has become flesh (σάρξ), and the word has become Scripture; these two facts do not only run parallel but are most intimately connected. Christ became flesh, a servant, without form or comeliness, the most despised of human beings; he descended to the nethermost parts of the earth and became obedient even to the death of the cross. So also the word, the revelation of God, entered the world of creatureliness, the life and history of humanity, in all the human forms of dream and vision, of investigation and reflection, right down into that which is humanly weak and despised and ignoble. The word became Scripture and as Scripture subjected itself to the fate of all Scripture. All this took place in order that the excellency of the power, also of the power of Scripture, may be God's and not ours. Just as every human thought and action is the fruit of the action of God in whom we live and have our being, and is at the same time the fruit of the activity of human beings, so also Scripture is totally the product of the Spirit of God, who speaks through the prophets and apostles, and at the same time totally the product of the activity of the authors. "Everything is divine and everything is human" (Θεια παντα και ἀνθρωπινα παντα).

Organic Inspiration

[115] This organic view has been repeatedly used, however, to undermine the authorship of the Holy Spirit, the primary author. The incarnation of Christ demands that we trace it down into the depths of its humiliation, in all its weakness and contempt. The recording of the word, of revelation, invites us to recognize that dimension of weakness and lowliness, the servant form, also in Scripture. But just as Christ's human nature, however weak and lowly, remained free from sin, so also Scripture is "conceived without defect or stain"; totally human in all its parts but also divine in all its parts.

Yet, in many different ways, injustice has been done to that divine character of Scripture. The history of inspiration shows us that first, till deep into the seventeenth century, it was progressively expanded even to the vowels and the punctuation (*inspiratio punctualis*) and in the following phase progressively shrunk, from the punctuation to the words (verbal inspiration), from the individual words to the Word, the idea (Word in place of verbal inspiration).[86] Inspiration further shrunk from the word as idea to the subject matter of the word (*inspiratio realis*), then from the subject matter to the religious-ethical content, to that which has been revealed in the true sense, to the Word of God in the strict sense, to the special object of saving faith (*inspiratio fundamentalis, religiosa*), from these matters to the persons (*inspiratio personalis*), and finally from this to the denial of all inspiration as supernatural gift. Now it is a source of joy that even the most negative school of thought still wants to assign to Scripture a place and some value in the religious life and thought of Christianity.

The doctrine of Scripture is not an opinion of this or that school, not the dogma of a particular church or sect, but a fundamental article, an article of faith of the one holy universal Christian church. Its significance for the whole of Christianity is ever better understood; its unbreakable connection with Christian faith and life is ever more clearly recognized. For a certain period the doctrine of Holy Scripture was relegated, in dogmatics, to "the means of grace," but it has again reconquered with honor a place at the entrance of this discipline.[87]

86. Cf. Philippi, *Kirchliche Glaubenslehre*, 3rd ed., 1:252.
87. Nitzsch, *Lehrbuch*, 212.

The entire Roman Catholic Church and the Eastern Orthodox churches are still standing firm in the confession of the divine inspiration of Holy Scripture. Many Protestant churches and schools of theology have up until now resisted every attempt to force them to give up that foundation. The church—by preaching and teaching, by reading and study—continues to live indirectly or directly out of the Scriptures and to feed itself with the Scriptures. Even those who deny Scripture's inspiration in theory often act and speak in practice as though they fully accept it.

According to many people, as it concerns the doctrine of Scripture, orthodoxy is caught up in the dualism of believing and knowing. However, this does not begin to compare with the ambivalent position of mediating theology (*Vermittelungstheologie*), which from university lecterns denies inspiration but actually confesses it from the pulpit.[88] Radicalism is increasingly coming to acknowledge that the inspiration of Scripture is taught by Scripture itself and has to be accepted or rejected along with it. All this shows that life is stronger than theory and that Scripture itself again and again reacts against every naturalistic explanation. Scripture itself claims that it proceeded from the Spirit of God and maintains this claim over against all criticism. Every attempt to divest it of the mysterious character of its origin, content, and power has up until now ended in defeat and in letting Scripture be Scripture. A [doctrine of] inspiration, therefore, is not an explanation of Scripture, nor actually a theory, but it is and ought to be a believing confession of what Scripture witnesses concerning itself, despite the appearance that is against it. Inspiration is a dogma, like the dogma of the Trinity, the incarnation, etc., which Christians accept, not because they understand the truth of it but because God so attests it. It is not a scientific pronouncement but a confession of faith. In the case of inspiration, as in the case of every other dogma, the question is not in the first place how much can I and may I confess without coming into conflict with science, but what is the witness of God and what, accordingly, is the pronouncement of the Christian faith? And then there is only one possible answer: Scripture presents itself as the word of God and in every century the church of God has recognized it as such. Inspiration is based on the authority of Scripture and has received the affirmation of the church of all the ages.

The so-called "personal" and "fundamental" approach to inspiration is in conflict with this dogmatic and religious character of the doctrine of the inspiration of Scripture. It must be granted that there is value also in these views. For it is certainly the inspired persons who were employed by the Holy Spirit, along with all their gifts and powers, and those persons were holy men, men of God, fully equipped for this work. When and as long as we think of this personal inspiration in our doctrine of inspiration, we discover there is even a difference in the measure and extent of it.[89] Just as, in virtue of God's providence, the authors of the books of the Bible were personally distinct from each other, so also the manner in which they were shaped and led by the Holy Spirit differed. There is a distinction here between the prophets and the apostles, and in each category there is diversity among them as well. Among the prophets Moses has primacy: God spoke with him as a friend. In the case of Isaiah, the impulse of the Spirit differs from that in the case of Ezekiel. Jeremiah's prophecies differ in their simplicity and naturalness from those in Zechariah and Daniel. In all the prophets of the OT, the impulse of the Holy Spirit is more or less transcendent; it comes upon them from above and from without, falls upon them, and then ceases. In the

---

88. Cf. G. Hulsman, *Moderne Wetenschap of Bijbelsche traditie?* (Utrecht: Kemink, 1897).
89. A. Kuyper, *Encyclopaedie* 2.425.

case of the apostles, on the other hand, the Holy Spirit dwells immanently in their hearts, leads and impels them, illumines and instructs them. There is therefore a vast amount of difference in the character of personal inspiration and hence also between the different parts of Scripture: not all the books of the Bible are of equal value.

But this difference in personal or so-called prophetic inspiration may not be misused to weaken or limit the so-called "graphic" inspiration, as the proponents of a "personal" and "fundamental" inspiration in fact do. Both of these conceptions, after all, are in conflict with Scripture's self-witness. The "all Scripture" (πᾶσα γραφή) of 2 Timothy 3:16 is decisive here. Even if this expression could not be translated by "all Scripture" or "Scripture as a whole," it certainly does not, as the context shows, refer to some writing in general, which, if it were "God-breathed," would be profitable. Rather, it refers to the "sacred writings" of verse 15 and therefore has in view a certain Scripture, namely that of the Old Testament. Therefore the reference here corresponds in thrust to the phrase "whatever was written" in Romans 15:4. Furthermore, the theory of personal inspiration runs up against the objection(s) that it wipes out the distinction between inspiration and illumination (regeneration), between the intellectual and the ethical life, between the "being borne" of the prophets (2 Peter 1:21) and the "being led" of the children of God (Rom. 8:14), between Holy Scripture and devotional literature. Moreover, along with Roman Catholicism, it turns the relation between Scripture and church into its opposite, robs the church of the certainty it needs, and makes it dependent on science, which has to decide what in Scripture is or is not the word of God.

Many proponents of this theory of inspiration indeed try to escape these objections by appealing to the person of Christ as the source and authority of dogmatics, but this does not benefit them because there is disagreement precisely on the question of who Christ is and what he taught and did. If the apostolic witness concerning Christ is not reliable, no knowledge of Christ is possible. Add to this that if Christ is authoritative he is authoritative also in the teaching concerning Scripture. In that case inspiration has to be accepted above all on his authority. The "personal" theory conflicts with the authority of Christ himself.

The theory of "fundamental" inspiration is distinguished from that of "personal" inspiration by the fact that while it still assumes a special activity of the Spirit in the writing process, it is limited to only certain parts of Scripture. This conception is so deistic and dualistic, however, that it is unacceptable for that reason alone. Furthermore, word and fact, the religious and the historical dimensions, that which was spoken by God and that which was spoken by human beings, is so tightly interwoven and intertwined that separation is impossible. The historical parts in Scripture are also a revelation of God. And, finally, these two theories still do not meet the objections advanced by science against Scripture and its inspiration. For these objections, far from pertaining to a few subordinate points on the periphery of revelation, touch the heart and center of it. The "personal" and "fundamental" theories of inspiration are absolutely not more scientific and rational than the most rigorous theories of verbal inspiration.

The other theories of inspiration ("punctual," "verbal," "real") and also the Word-inspiration of Philippi do not differ all that much from each other. With a more or less mechanical view of divine inspiration, disagreement about its extent can arise easily. Since clear insight into the close connectedness between thoughts (things), words, and letters was lacking, people in the past could often argue over whether inspiration extended only to the first or also to the last.[90] But if divine inspiration is understood more organically, i.e., more historically and psychologically, the importance of these questions vanishes. The activity of the Holy Spirit in the writing process, after all, consisted in the fact that, having prepared the human consciousness of the authors in various ways (by birth, upbringing, natural gifts, research, memory, reflection, experience of life, revelation, etc.), he now, in and through the writing process itself, made *those* thoughts and words, *that* language and style, rise to the surface of that consciousness, which could best interpret the divine ideas for persons of all sorts of rank and class, from every nation and age.

Included in the thoughts are the words; included in the words are the vowels. But from this it does not follow that the vowel signs in our Hebrew manuscripts derive from the authors themselves. Nor does it follow that every word is full of divine wisdom, that every jot and tittle is charged with infinite content. Certainly, everything has its meaning, provided it is seen in its place and in the context in which it occurs. Scripture may not be viewed atomistically as though every word and letter by itself is inspired by God as such and has its own meaning with its own infinite, divine content. This approach leads to the foolish hermeneutical rules of the Jewish scribes and, rather than honoring Scripture, dishonors it.

Inspiration has to be viewed *organically*, so that even the lowliest part has its place and meaning and at the same time is much farther removed from the center than other parts. In the human organism nothing is accidental, neither its length, nor its breadth, nor its color or its tint. This is not, however, to say that everything is equally closely connected with its life center. The head and the heart occupy a much more important place in the body than the hand and the foot, and these again are greatly superior in value to the nails and the hair. In Scripture as well, not everything is equally close to the center. There is a periphery, which moves in a wide path around the center, yet also that periphery belongs to the circle of the divine thoughts. Accordingly, there are no kinds and degrees in "graphic" inspiration. The hair of one's head shares in the same life as the heart and the hand. There is one soul, which is totally present in the whole body and in all of its parts. It is one and the same Spirit from whom, through the consciousness of the authors, the whole of Scripture has come. But there is a difference in the manner in which the same life is present and active in the different parts of the body. There is diversity of gifts, also in Scripture, but it is the same Spirit.

A Defense of Organic Inspiration

[116] Many and very serious objections are raised against this view of the inspiration of Scripture. They derive from the historical criticism that questions the authenticity and credibility of many biblical books. The challenge comes from the mutual contradictions that occur time after time in Scripture; from the manner in which OT texts are cited and interpreted in the NT; and it comes from secular history with which the narratives of Scripture can often not be harmonized. Nature also, which both in its origin and existence contradicts Scripture with its creation and its miracles, raises other issues, as do the areas of religion and morality, which often pass a negative judgment on the faith and life of persons in the Bible. Finally, we encounter objections from the present state of Scripture whose text, according to textual criticism, having been lost with the autographa, is corrupt in the apographa and

---

90. For literature, see C. Vitringa *Doctrina Christianae Religionis,* 1:46; cf. also S. Pesch, *De Inspiratione Sacrae Scripturae,* 439–89.

defective in its translations. It is vain to ignore these objections and to act as if they don't exist. Still, we must first of all call attention to the ethical battle, which at all times has been carried on against Scripture. If Scripture is the word of God, that battle is not accidental but necessary and completely understandable. If Scripture is the account of the revelation of God in Christ, it is bound to arouse the same opposition as Christ himself who came into the world for judgment (κρίσις) and is "set for the fall and rising of many" [Luke 2:34]. He brings separation between light and darkness and reveals the thoughts of many hearts. Similarly Scripture is a living and active word, a "discerner" of the thoughts and intentions of the heart [cf. Heb. 4:12]. It not only *was* inspired but is still "God-breathed" and "God-breathing." Just as there is much that precedes the act of inspiration (all the activity of the Holy Spirit in nature, history, revelation, regeneration), so there is much that follows it as well. Inspiration is not an isolated event. The Holy Spirit does not, after the act of inspiration, withdraw from Holy Scripture and abandon it to its fate but sustains and animates it and in many ways brings its content to humanity, to its heart and conscience. By means of Scripture as the word of God, the Holy Spirit continually wars against the thoughts and intentions of the "unspiritual" person (ψυχικὸς ἀνθρωπος). By itself, therefore, it need not surprise us in the least that Scripture has at all times encountered contradiction and opposition. Christ bore a cross, and the servant [Scripture] is not greater than its master. Scripture is the handmaiden of Christ. It shares in his defamation and arouses the hostility of sinful humanity.

Of course not all opposition to Scripture can be explained in terms of this [spiritual hostility]. Still, the attacks to which Scripture is exposed in this century must not be viewed on their own. They are undoubtedly an integral part of the intellectual trend of this age. It is not for us to judge persons and intentions, but it would be superficial to say that the battle against the Bible in this century stands completely by itself and is controlled by very different and much purer motives than in earlier centuries. It is unlikely that today it is only the head that speaks and that the heart remains completely outside of it. All believers have the experience that in the best moments of their life they are also most firm in their belief in Scripture. The believer's confidence in Christ increases along with their confidence in Scripture and, conversely, ignorance of the Scriptures is automatically and proportionately ignorance of Christ (Jerome). The connection between sin and error often lies hidden deep below the surface of the conscious life. One can almost never demonstrate this link in others, but it is sometimes revealed to our own inner eye [with respect to ourselves]. The battle against the Bible is, in the first place, a revelation of the hostility of the human heart. But that hostility may express itself in various ways. It absolutely does not come to expression only—and perhaps not even most forcefully—in the criticism to which Scripture has been subjected in our time. Scripture as the word of God encounters opposition and unbelief in every "unspiritual" person. In the days of dead orthodoxy, an unbelieving attitude toward Scripture was in principle as powerful as in our historically-oriented and critical century. The forms change, but the essence remains the same. Whether hostility against Scripture is expressed in criticism like that of Celsus and Porphyry or whether it is manifest in a dead faith, that hostility in principle is the same. For not the hearers but the doers of the word [James 1:22] are pronounced blessed. "The servant who knew his master's will but did not make ready or act according to his will will receive a severe beating" [Luke 12:47].

It remains the duty of every person, therefore, first of all to put aside his or her hostility against the word of God and "to take every thought captive to obey Christ" [2 Cor. 10:5]. Scripture itself everywhere presses this demand. Only the pure of heart will see God. Rebirth will see the kingdom of God. Self-denial is the condition for being a disciple of Jesus. The wisdom of the world is folly to God. Over against all human beings, Scripture occupies a position so high that, instead of subjecting itself to their criticism, it judges them in all their thoughts and desires.

And this has been the Christian church's position toward Scripture at all times. According to Chrysostom, humility is the foundation of philosophy. Augustine [once] said: "When a certain rhetorician was asked what was the chief rule in eloquence, he replied, 'Delivery'; what was the second rule, 'Delivery'; what was the third rule, 'Delivery'; so if you ask me concerning the precepts of the Christian religion, first, second, third, and always I would answer, 'Humility.'" Calvin cites this statement with approval.[91] And Pascal cries out to humanity: "Humble yourself, powerless reason! Be silent, stupid nature! . . . Listen to God!"

This has been the attitude of the church toward Scripture down the centuries. And the Christian dogmatician may take no other position. For a dogma is not based on the results of any historical-critical research but only on the witness of God, on the self-testimony of Holy Scripture. A Christian believes, not because everything in life reveals the love of God, but rather despite everything that raises doubt. In Scripture too there is much that raises doubt. All believers know from experience that this is true. Those who engage in biblical criticism frequently talk as if simple church people know nothing about the objections that are advanced against Scripture and are insensitive to the difficulty of continuing to believe in Scripture. But that is a false picture. Certainly, simple Christians do not know all the obstacles that science raises to belief in Scripture. But they do to a greater or lesser degree know the hard struggle fought both in head and heart against Scripture. There is not a single Christian who has not in his or her own way learned to know the antithesis between the "wisdom of the world" and "the foolishness of God." It is one and the same battle, an ever-continuing battle, which has to be waged by all Christians, learned or unlearned, to "take every thought captive to the obedience of Christ" (2 Cor. 10:5).

Here on earth no one ever rises above that battle. Throughout the whole domain of faith, there remain "crosses" (*cruces*) that have to be overcome.[92] There is no faith without struggle. To believe is to struggle, to struggle against the appearance of things. As long as people still believe in anything, their belief is challenged from all directions. No modern believer is spared from this either. Concessions weaken believers but do not liberate them. Thus for those who in childlike faith subject themselves to Scripture, there still remain more than enough objections. These need not be disguised. There are intellectual problems (*cruces*) in Scripture that cannot be ignored and that will probably never be resolved. But these difficulties, which Scripture itself presents against its own inspiration, are in large part not

91. J. Calvin, *Institutes* 2.2.11. Ed. note: According to John T. McNeill, editor of the Battles translation of Calvin's *Institutes* (Library of Christian Classics 20 and 21), the citation from Chrysostom is *De profectu evangelii* 2 (PG 51.312). This reference appears to be in error. PG 51.312 contains a homily on Phil. 1:18, but the reference is more likely to Homily 2 on Philippians 1:8–11, where Chrysostom does relate philosophy to the strength of humility. However this homily is found in PG 62.180 (NPNF1, 13:191). The citation from Augustine, according to McNeill, is *Letters* cxiii, 3, 22 (PL 33.442; cf. FC 18:282). Bavinck also refers to Edwards, *Works* 3:139 without going into further detail.

92. Ed. note: Here and later the author uses the Latin for cross (*crux*) to emphasize difficult problems in the apparent conflict between modern science and the Bible.

recent discoveries of our century. They have been known at all times. Nevertheless, Jesus and the apostles, Athanasius and Augustine, Thomas and Bonaventure, Luther and Calvin, and Christians of all churches have down the centuries confessed and recognized Scripture as the word of God. Those who want to delay belief in Scripture till all the objections have been cleared up and all the contradictions have been resolved will never arrive at faith. "For who hopes for what he sees?" [Rom. 8:24]. Jesus calls blessed those who have not seen and yet believe [John 20:29].

In any case, there are objections and conundrums in every science. Those who do not want to start in faith will never arrive at knowledge. Epistemology, the theory of knowledge, is the first principle of philosophy, but it is riddled with mystery from start to finish. Those who do not want to embark on scientific investigation until they see the road by which we arrive at knowledge fully cleared will never start. Those who do not want to eat before they understand the entire process by which food arrives at their table will starve to death. And those who do not want to believe the Word of God before they see all problems resolved will die of spiritual starvation. "By comprehension we won't make it; therefore lay hold of it uncomprehended" (N. Beets). Nature, history, and every science present as many "cruxes" as Holy Scripture. Nature contains so many enigmas that it can often make us doubt that there exists a wise and just God. There are any number of apparent contradictions on every page of the book of nature. There is an "inexplicable remnant" (Schelling) that defies all explanation. Who, for that reason, abandons belief in the providence of God, which covers all things? Islam, the life and destiny of primitive peoples, are "cruxes" in the history of humankind as big and as difficult as the composition of the Pentateuch and the Synoptic Gospels. Who for that reason questions whether God with his almighty hand also writes the book of nature and history? Of course, here and so also in the case of Scripture, we can throw ourselves into the arms of agnosticism and pessimism. But despair is a death leap also in the area of science. The mysteries of existence do not decrease but instead increase with the adoption of unbelief. And the unease of the heart grows larger.

[117] Nonetheless, the organic view of inspiration does furnish us with many means to meet the objections advanced against it. It implies the idea that the Holy Spirit, in the inscripturation of the word of God, did not spurn anything human to serve as an organ of the divine. The revelation of God is not abstractly supernatural but has entered into the human fabric, into persons and states of beings, into forms and usages, into history and life. It does not fly high above us but descends into our situation; it has become flesh and blood, like us in all things except sin. Divine revelation is now an ineradicable constituent of this cosmos in which we live and, effecting renewal and restoration, continues its operation. The human has become an instrument of the divine; the natural has become a revelation of the supernatural; the visible has become a sign and seal of the invisible. In the process of inspiration, use has been made of all the gifts and forces resident in human nature.

Consequently, and in the first place, the difference in language and style, in character and individuality, that can be discerned in the books of the Bible has become perfectly explicable. In the past, when a deeper understanding was lacking, this difference was explained in terms of the will of the Holy Spirit. Given the organic view, however, this difference is perfectly natural. Similarly, the use of sources, the authors' familiarity with earlier writings, their own inquiries, memory, reflection, and life experience are all included, and not excluded, by the organic view. The Holy Spirit himself prepared his writers in that fashion. He did not suddenly descend on them from above but employed their whole personality as his instrument. Here too the saying "grace does not cancel out nature but perfects it" is applicable. The personality of the authors is not erased but maintained and sanctified. Inspiration, therefore, in no way demands that, literarily or aesthetically, we equate the style of Amos with that of Isaiah or that we deny all barbarisms and solecisms in the language of the NT.

Secondly, the organic view of revelation and inspiration brings with it the notion that ordinary human life and natural life, so far from being excluded, is also made serviceable to the thoughts of God. Scripture is the word of God; it not only contains but *is* the word of God. But the formal and material element in this expression may not be split up. Inspiration alone would not yet make a writing into the word of God in a Scriptural sense. Even if a book on geography, say, was inspired from cover to cover and was literally dictated word-for-word, it would still not be "God-breathed" and "God-breathing" in the sense of 2 Timothy 3:16. Scripture is the word of God because the Holy Spirit testifies in it concerning Christ, because it has the Word-made-flesh as its matter and content. Form and content interpenetrate each other and are inseparable. But in order to paint a full-length portrait of this image of Christ, human sin and satanic lies in all their horror would have to be pictured as well. Shadows are needed in this portrait in order to bring out the light more brilliantly. Sin, also when it occurs in the biblical saints, must be called sin, and error may not be excused even in them. And as the revelation of God in Christ incorporates unrighteousness within itself as antithesis, so also it does not spurn to include elements of human weakness and human nature. Christ counted nothing human as alien to himself; and Scripture does not overlook even the most minor concerns of daily life (2 Tim. 4:13). Christianity is not antithetically opposed to that which is human but is its restoration and renewal.

Thirdly, the intent and purpose of Scripture is integrally given with its content. "Whatever was written in former times was given for our instruction" [Rom. 15:4]. It is "useful for teaching, for reproof, for correction, and for training in righteousness, so that everyone who belongs to God may be proficient, equipped for every good work" (2 Tim. 3:16–17 NRSV). It serves to make us wise unto salvation [2 Tim. 3:15]. Holy Scripture has a purpose that is religious-ethical through and through. It is not designed to be a manual for the various sciences. It is the first foundation (*principium*) only of theology and desires that we will read and study it *theologically*. In all the disciplines that are grouped around Scripture, our aim must be the saving knowledge of God. For *that* purpose Scripture offers us all the data needed. In *that* sense it is completely adequate and complete. But those who would infer from Scripture a history of Israel, a biography of Jesus, a history of Israel's or early-Christian literature, etc. will in each case end up disappointed. They will encounter lacunae that can be filled only with conjectures.

Historical criticism has utterly forgotten this purpose of Scripture. It tries to produce a history of the people, religion, and literature of Israel and a priori confronts Scripture with demands it cannot fulfill. It runs into contradictions that cannot be resolved, endlessly sorts out sources and books, rearranges and reorders them, with only hopeless confusion as the end result. No life of Jesus can be written from the four Gospels, nor can a history of Israel be construed from the OT. That was not what the Holy Spirit had in mind. Inspiration was evidently not a matter of drawing up material with notarial precision. "If indeed in the four gospels words are put in Jesus' mouth with reference to the same occasion but *dis*similar in the form of their expression, Jesus naturally could not have used four different forms; but the Holy Spirit only aimed to bring about for the church an impression which completely corresponds to what came forth from Jesus."[93]

Scripture does not satisfy the demand for exact knowledge in the way we demand it in mathematics, astronomy, chemistry, etc. This is a standard that may not be applied to it. For that reason, moreover, the autographa were lost; for that reason the text—to whatever small degree this is the case—is corrupt; for that reason the church, and truly not just the layman, has the Bible only in defective and fallible translations. These are undeniable facts. And these facts teach us that Scripture has a criterion of its own, requires an interpretation of its own, and has a purpose and intention of its own. That intention is no other than that it should make us "wise unto salvation." The Old Testament, while not a source for the history of Israel's people and religion, is such a source for the history of revelation. The Gospels, while not a source for a life of Jesus, are such a source for a theological (dogmatic) knowledge of his person and work. The Bible is the book for Christian religion and Christian theology. To that end it has been given, and for that purpose it is appropriate. And for that reason it is the word of God given us by the Holy Spirit.

Finally, from this perspective the relation in which Scripture stands to the other sciences becomes clear. Much misuse has been made of Baronius's saying: "Scripture does not tell us how the heavens move but how we move to heaven."[94] Precisely as the book of the knowledge of God, Scripture has much to say also to the other sciences. It is a light on our path and a lamp for our feet, also with respect to science and art. It claims authority in all areas of life. Christ has [been given] all power in heaven and on earth. Objectively, the restriction of inspiration to the religious-ethical part of Scripture is untenable; subjectively the separation between the religious life and the rest of human life cannot be maintained. Inspiration extends to all parts of Scripture, and religion is a matter of the whole person. A great deal of what is related in Scripture is of fundamental significance also for the other sciences. The creation and fall of humankind, the unity of the human race, the flood, the rise of peoples and languages, etc. are facts of the highest significance also for the other sciences. At every moment science and art come into contact with Scripture; the primary principles for all of life are given us in Scripture. This truth may in no way be discounted.

On the other hand, there is also a large truth in the saying of Cardinal Baronius. All those facts in Scripture are not communicated in isolation and for their own sake but with a theological aim, namely, that we should know God unto salvation. Scripture never intentionally concerns itself with science as such. Christ himself, though free from all error and sin, was never, strictly speaking, active in the field of science and art, commerce and industry, law and politics. His was another kind of greatness: the glory of the only begotten of the Father, full of grace and truth. But precisely for that reason he was a source of blessing for science and art, society and state. Jesus is Savior, only that but that totally. He came not only to

---

93. A. Kuyper, *Encyclopaedie* 2.499; cf. also A. W. Dieckhoff, *Die Inspiration und Irrthumslosigkeit der Heilige Schrift* (Leipzig: Justus Naumann, 1891); idem, *Noch einmal über die Inspiration und Irrthumslosigkeit der Heiligen Schrift* (Rostock: Stiller, 1893); Th. Zahn, "Evangelienharmonie," *PRE*³ 5:653–61.

94. Augustine already said, "We do not read in the gospel how our Lord said: 'I will send you the Paraclete who will teach you about the course of the sun and the moon.' For he wanted to make Christians, not mathematicians" (*Acts or Disputation against Fortunatus the Manichaean* 1.10).

restore the religious-ethical life of human beings and to leave all other things untouched as if they were not corrupted by sin and did not need to be restored. Indeed not, for as far as sin extends, so far also the grace of Christ extends.

The same is true for Scripture. It too is religious through and through, the word of God unto salvation, but for that very reason a word for family and society, for science and art. Scripture is a book for the whole of humankind in all its ranks and classes, in all its generations and peoples. But for that very reason too it is not a scientific book in the strict sense. Wisdom, not learning, speaks in it. It does not speak the exact language of science and the academy but the language of observation and daily life. It judges and describes things, not in terms of the results of scientific investigation, but in terms of intuition, the initial lively impression that the phenomena make on people. For that reason it speaks of "land approaching," of the sun "rising" and "standing still," of blood as the "soul" of an animal, of the kidneys as the seat of sensations, of the heart as the source of thoughts, etc. and is not the least bit worried about the scientifically exact language of astronomy, physiology, psychology, etc. It speaks of the earth as the center of God's creation and does not take sides between the Ptolemaic and the Copernican worldview. It does not take a position on Neptunism versus Plutonism, on allopathy versus homeopathy. It is probable that the authors of Scripture knew no more than all their contemporaries about all these sciences, geology, zoology, physiology, medicine, etc. Nor was it necessary. For Holy Scripture uses the language of everyday experience, which is and remains always true. If, instead of this, Scripture had used the language of the academy and spoken with scientific precision, it would have stood in the way of its own authority. If it had decided in favor of the Ptolemaic worldview, it would not have been credible in an age that supported the Copernican system. Nor could it have been a book for life, for humanity. But now it speaks in ordinary human language, language that is intelligible to the most simple person, clear to the learned and unlearned alike. It employs the language of observation, which will always continue to exist alongside that of science and the academy.

In recent times a similar idea has been articulated by many Roman Catholic theologians with respect to the historiography found in Scripture. In order to reconcile the doctrine of divine inspiration with the results of modern Bible criticism, they have made a distinction between absolute and relative truth, between the truth of the thing cited and the truth of the citation, between a story that is true in terms of its content and a story that has simply been taken over for some reason by the biblical authors from other sources or from popular tradition without answering for, or wanting to answer for, the objective truth of its content. According to these theologians, the authors of the biblical books frequently wrote—as they did in speaking about natural phenomena, so also in narrating history—in accord with the subjective appearance of things and not in terms of objective reality.

But, in my judgment, this way of presenting the issue is inadmissible in connection with historiography. For when the prophets and apostles speak in the context of nature about the "sun rising" and the "land approaching," etc., they cannot give us a false impression since they are dealing with phenomena that we still see every day and about which we speak in the same way they do. But if in the area of history they write "in accordance with appearance," that certainly has to mean not in accordance with what happened objectively but in accordance with what many in their day believed subjectively. In that case they give us a false impression and are therefore being compromised in their authority and reliability.

If theologians were to apply this principle consistently, then not only the early chapters of Genesis could be dissolved into myths and legends—as is already happening at the hands of many Roman Catholic theologians today—but the entire history of Israel and original Christianity. If Scripture obviously intends to present a story as historical, the exegete has no right, at the discretion of historical criticism, to turn it into a myth. Yet it is true that the historiography of Holy Scripture has a character of its own. Its purpose is not to tell us precisely all that has happened in times past with the human race and with Israel but to relate to us the history of God's revelation. Scripture only tells us what is associated with that history and aims by it to reveal God to us in his search for and coming to humanity. Sacred history is religious history.

Considered from the viewpoint and by the standards of secular history, Scripture is often incomplete, full of gaps and certainly not written by the rules of contemporary historical criticism. From this it surely does not follow that the historiography of Scripture is untrue and unreliable. Just as a person with common sense can put up a good logical argument without ever having studied logic, so a reporter can very well offer a true account of what has happened without having first studied the rules of historical criticism. If historical criticism should deny this aspect of real life, it degenerates into hypercriticism and destroys the object it is designed to address. But all the historiography in Holy Scripture bears witness to the fact that it follows a direction of its own and aims at a goal of its own. In its determination of time and place, in the order of events, in the grouping of circumstances, it certainly does not give us the degree of exactness we might frequently wish for. The reports about the main events, say, the time of Jesus' birth, the duration of his public activity, the words he spoke at the institution of the Lord's Supper, his resurrection, etc., are far from homogeneous and leave room for a variety of views.

Furthermore, it is perfectly true that there is a distinction between "historical" and "normative" ["descriptive" and "prescriptive"] authority. Not everything that is incorporated and cited in Scripture is for that reason true in terms of content. The "truth of citation" is not identical with the "truth of the thing cited." In Scripture, after all, also the literal words of Satan, the false prophets, and the ungodly are cited. It is evident from the citation that these words have indeed been uttered by these persons, but they do not for that reason contain truth (Gen. 3:1; Ps. 14:1; Jer. 28:2–3). In some cases it is even hard to tell whether or not we are dealing with a citation, whether not just the accuracy of the citation but also its content is covered by the authority of Scripture, whether to a given section of Scripture only a descriptive or also prescriptive authority is due. On these points the dogma of Scripture is far from being fully developed and leaves room for many special studies.

Finally, we must add that, though Scripture is true in everything, this truth is certainly not homogeneous in all its components. Divine inspiration, as we remarked earlier, made all literary genres subservient to its aim. It included prose and poetry, history and prophecy, parable and fable. It is self-evident that the truth in all these scriptural components has a different character in each case. The truth of a parable and fable is different from that of a historical narrative, and the latter again differs from that in wisdom literature, prophecy, and psalmody. Whether the rich man and the poor Lazarus are fictitious characters or historical persons is an open question. Similarly, we can differ about whether and in how far we must regard the book of Job, Ecclesiastes, and the Song of Solomon as history or as historical fiction. This is especially clear in the case of prophecy. The Old Testament prophets picture the future in colors derived from their own environment and thereby in each case confront us with the question of whether what they write is intended realistically or symbolically. Even in the case of historical reports, there is sometimes a distinction between the fact that has occurred and the form in which it is presented. In connection with Genesis 1:3 the Authorized Version [Dutch] comments in the margin that God's speech is his will, his command, his act, and in connection with Genesis 11:5 that this is said of the infinite and all-knowing God in a human way. This last comment, however, really applies to the whole Bible. It always speaks of the highest and holiest things, of eternal and invisible matters, in a human way. Like Christ, it does not consider anything human alien to itself. But for that reason it is a book for humanity and lasts till the end of time. It is old without ever becoming obsolete. It always remains young and fresh; it is the word of life. The word of God endures forever.

CHAPTER 14: ATTRIBUTES OF SCRIPTURE

Attributes in General

R. Bellarmine, *De Verbo Dei*, bk. 4; M. Canus, *Loci Theologici* (1563); J. B. Franzelin, *Tractatus de divina traditione et scriptura*, 3rd ed. (Romae: Typeographia Polyglotta, 1882); J. B. Heinrich, and C. Gutberlet, *Dogmatische Theologie*, 2nd ed. (Mainz: Kirchheim, 1881–1900), 1:699ff.; 2:3ff.; J. Calvin, *Institutes of the Christian Religion* (1559), 1.6–9; 4.10; J. Zanchius, *De sacra scriptura tractatus integer*, in *Operum Theologicorum* (1617), 8:296–452; D. Chamier, *Panstratia Catholicae*, vol. 1, *De canone fidei in 16 books* (1626); W. Ames, *Bellarminus enervatus*, vol. 1, *De Verbo Dei* (Amsterdam, 1630); F. Turretin, *Institutes of Elenctic Theology*, loc II, qu. 16ff.; B. de Moor, *Commentarius Perpetuus in Joh. Marckii Compendium Theologiae Christianae Didactico-elencticum*, 6 vols. (Leiden: J. Hasebroek, 1761–71), 2:332ff.; J. Gerhard, *Loci Theologici*, ed. E. Preuss, 9 vols. (Berlin: G. Schlawitz, 1863–75), loc. 1, chs. 17ff.; J. A. Quenstedt, *Theologia didactico-polemica sive Sytema Theologicum* (1696), 1:86ff.; C. Hodge, *Systematic Theology* (New York: Scribner, 1888), vol. 1, Introduction, chs. 4–6.

[118] The doctrine of the attributes of Scripture has developed completely as a result of the [Reformation's] struggle with Roman Catholicism and Anabaptism. In the confession of the inspiration and authority of Scripture, there was agreement between Rome and the Reformation, but for the rest, as it pertains to the locus of Holy Scripture, there was much disagreement. The way in which Rome had related Scripture and church was fundamentally changed in the Reformation. In the church fathers and the scholastics, Scripture, at least in theory, was on a level far above the church and tradition; it rested in itself, was *trustworthy in and of itself* (αὐτόπιστος), and the primary norm for church and theology. Augustine said "canonical scripture is contained by its own fixed boundaries"[95] and reasons (*Confessions* 6.5; 11.3) as if the truth of Scripture depends only on itself. Bonaventure writes: "For the church

---

95. A. von Harnack, *History of Dogma*, trans. N. Buchanan, J. Miller, E. B. Speirs, and W. McGilchrist and ed. A. B. Bruce (London: Williams & Norgate, 1897), 3:208. Ed. note: The reference is to Augustine's *On Baptism, against the Donatists* 2.3–4.

is founded upon the pronouncements of the Holy Scriptures; if they are deficient, so is the [church's] understanding. . . . For since the church is founded upon Holy Scripture, those who do not know Scripture do not know how to guide the church."[96] Similar statements are cited by Gerhard[97] from the works of Salvian, Biel, Cajetan, Hosius, Valentia, et al. In his *Summa doctrinae christianae* Canisius writes: "Consequently, just as we believe Scripture and attach and attribute great authority [to it], on account of the testimony of the Spirit of God speaking in it, so we also owe loyalty, reverence, and obedience to the church."[98] Also Bellarmine states: "Nothing is more widely known and certain than the Scriptures contained in the prophetic and apostolic writings. Accordingly, anyone who denies that we ought to have faith in them has to be extremely stupid."[99] All of these theologians believed that Scripture could be sufficiently demonstrated to be true from and by [Scripture] itself. It does not depend on the church; on the contrary, the church depends on it. The church with its tradition may be the rule of faith (*regula fidei*); it is not its foundation (*fundamentum fidei*). That distinction belongs to Scripture alone.

In Roman Catholicism, however, the church with its offices and tradition began increasingly to assume an independent position and to acquire authority alongside of Holy Scripture. At first the relation between the two was not precisely defined but soon required further regulation. And when the church continued to increase in power and self-sufficiency, authority was increasingly shifted from Scripture to the church. A series of different moments in history indicate the process by which the church, instead of being subject to Scripture, elevated itself to a place alongside of Scripture and finally to a place above Scripture. The question of which of the two, Scripture or the church, had precedence was first stated clearly and deliberately in the time of the reform councils. Despite the opposition of Gerson, d'Ailly, and especially of Nicolas of Clemange,[100] it was settled in favor of the church. Trent sanctioned this position over against the Reformation. In the struggle against Gallicanism the issue was defined in greater detail and resolved by the Vatican Council (1870) by declaring the church infallible.

The subject of this infallibility, however, was not the listening church, nor the teaching church, nor the bishops gathered collectively in council, but specifically the pope. And the pope was the subject of infallibility, not as a private person, nor as bishop of Rome or patriarch of the West, but as the chief shepherd of the entire church. Granted, he possesses this authority as head of the church and not apart from it; still he possesses it, not through and along with the church, but above and in distinction from it. Even bishops and councils participate in this infallibility, not apart from, but only in union with and submission to the pope. He stands above all and alone makes the church, tradition, councils, and canons infallible. Councils without a pope can err and have erred.[101] The church as a whole, both the teaching and the listening church, is infallible only with and under the Roman pontiff. As a result of this process, the relation between church and Scripture has been reversed. The church, more concretely the pope, has precedence over and stands above Scripture. Where

---

96. Bonaventure, "De Sept. don.," nn. 37–43; cited in the 1881 edition of the *Breviloquium* (Freiburg: Herder, 1881), 370.
97. J. Gerhard, *Loci Theologici*, I, 3 §§45–46.
98. Canisius, *Summa doctrinae Christianae,* "De praeceptis ecclesia," §16.
99. Bellarmine, *De Verbo dei*, bk. 1, ch. 2.
100. Cf. C. Schmidt, "Clémanges," *PRE²* 3:247.
101. Bellarmine, *De Conciliis et Ecclesia*, bk. 2, chs. 10–11.

the pope is, there the church is (*Ubi papa, ibi ecclesia*).[102] The infallibility of the pope renders that of the church, the bishops and councils, as well as that of Scripture, unnecessary.

From this Roman Catholic view of the Scripture-church relation flow all the differences that exist between Rome and the Reformation in the doctrine of Scripture. They concern above all the necessity of Scripture, the Apocrypha of the OT, the Vulgate edition, the proscription of Bible reading, the exposition of Scripture, and tradition. Formally, the reversal in the Scripture-church relation is most clearly demonstrated in the fact that modern Catholic theologians treat the doctrine of the church in the "formal part" of dogmatics. The church belongs to "the first principles of the faith." Like Scripture in the Reformation, so the church, the magisterium, or really the pope, is the formal principle, the foundation of faith, in Roman Catholicism.[103]

Over against this development, the Reformers posited the doctrine of the attributes of Scripture. It bore a polemical character through and through and was consequently fixed, in the main, from the beginning.[104] Gradually it was also included in dogmatics in a more or less systematic and methodical form, not yet in Zwingli, Calvin, Melancthon, et al., to be sure, but certainly already in Musculus, Zanchius, Polanus, Junius, and others[105] and, among the Lutherans, in Gerhard, Quenstedt, Calovius, Hollaz, et al. But they differed among themselves in the manner of treatment. Sometimes a variety of historical and critical matters were discussed. Dogmatics included virtually the whole "Introduction," the theory of "general and special canonics." Also the number and arrangement of the attributes were variously described. The authority, utility, necessity, truth, perspicuity, sufficiency, origin, division, content, apocrypha, council, church, tradition, authentic edition, translations, exposition, the testimony of the Holy Spirit—all this and much more were dealt with in the doctrine of Scripture and its attributes. Gradually the material was more strictly defined. Calovius and Quenstedt distinguished between the primary and secondary attributes. Belonging to the former category were the authority, truth, perfection, perspicuity, the "capacity to interpret its very self," its power to judge, and its efficacy. Counted among the latter were the necessity, the integrity, purity, the authenticity, and "the permission granted to all to read [Scripture]."

Even more simple was the popular order: authority, necessity, perfection or sufficiency, perspicuity, the capacity to interpret its very self, and its efficacy.[106] But even this arrangement can be made more simple. The historical, critical, archeological material, and so forth does not belong in dogmatics but in the bibliological branches of theology. The authenticity, integrity, purity, and so forth, accordingly, cannot be fully treated in dogmatics; there they come up only to the extent that the doctrine of Scripture also provides certain data for its composition. After "inspiration" and "authority," the "truth" [of Scripture] no longer needs separate treatment and would more likely be weakened than strengthened by it. "Efficacy" has its place in the doctrine of the means of grace. Thus only the authority, necessity, suffi-

---

102. G. M. Jansen, *Praelectiones Theologiae Dogmaticae,* 1:506, 511.

103. Ibid., 1:829.

104. H. Heppe, *Dogmatik des deutschen Protestantismus* (Gotha: F. A. Perthes, 1857), 1:207–25.

105. W. Musculus, *Loci communes theologici* (1567), 374ff.; J. Zanchi, "De Sacra Scriptura," *Operum Theologicorum,* 8:319ff.; A. Polanus, *Syntagma Theologiae Christianae,* 17ff.; F. Junius, "Theses Theologicae," *Opuscula Theologiae Selecta,* 1:1594ff.

106. K. A. von Hase, *Hutterus Redivius* (Helsingfors: A. W. Gröndahl, 1846), §43ff.; H. Schmid, *Doctrinal Theology of the Evangelical Churches,* trans. Charles A. Hoy and Henry E. Jacobs (Philadelphia: United Lutheran Publication House, 1899), 27ff.; H. Heppe, *Dogmatik der evangelische reformirten Kirche* (Elberseld: R. L. Friedrich, 1861), 9ff.; Voigt, *Fundamentaldogmatik* (Gotha: F. A. Perthes, 1874), 644ff.; M. Kähler, "Bibel," *PRE*[3] 2:686–91.

ciency, and perspicuity remain. Among these there is still the distinction that the "authority" of Scripture is not coordinate with the other attributes, for it is given with inspiration itself. On the one hand, the necessity, perspicuity, and sufficiency do not all flow from inspiration in the same sense. It is conceivable in fact that an infallible Bible had to be augmented and explained by an infallible tradition. Rome, while recognizing the authority of Scripture, denies its other attributes.

The Authority of Scripture

Rome and the Reformation

[119] The authority of Scripture has always been recognized in the Christian church. Jesus and the apostles believed in the OT as the Word of God and attributed divine authority to it. The Christian church was born and raised under [the influence of] the authority of Scripture. What the apostles wrote must be accepted as though Christ himself had written it, said Augustine.[107] And in Calvin's commentary on 2 Timothy 3:16, he states that we owe Scripture the same reverence we owe to God. Up until the eighteenth century, that authority of Scripture was firmly established in all the churches and among all Christians. On the other hand, between Rome and the Reformation there arose a serious difference about the ground on which this authority is based. The church fathers and the scholastics still frequently taught the self-attested trustworthiness (αὐτοπιστια) of Scripture, but the dynamic drive of the Roman Catholic principle increasingly gave precedence to the church over Scripture. The church, according to what is today the universally accepted Catholic doctrine, is temporally and logically prior to Scripture. It existed prior to Scripture and does not owe its origin, existence, and authority to Scripture but exists in and of itself, i.e., in virtue of Christ or the Holy Spirit who dwells within it. Scripture, on the other hand, proceeded from the church and is now recognized, confirmed, preserved, explained, defended, and so forth by the church. Scripture, accordingly, needs the church, but the reverse is not true. Without the church there is no Scripture, but without Scripture the church still exists. The church joined to an infallible tradition is the original and sufficient means of preserving and communicating revelation. Holy Scripture was added later, is insufficient of itself, but is useful and good as support and confirmation of the tradition. In fact, in the thinking of Rome, Scripture is totally dependent on the church. The authenticity, integrity, inspiration, canonicity, and authority of Scripture are all established as certain by the church.

In this connection, however, Rome does make the distinction that Scripture is totally dependent on the church, not with reference to itself, but with reference to *us*. The church, by its recognition, does not make Scripture inspired, canonical, authentic, and so forth; yet it is the only agency that can infallibly know these attributes of Scripture. Certainly the self-testimony of Scripture does not decide that precisely these books of the Old and New Testament—no other and no fewer—are inspired. Scripture nowhere offers a list of the books that belong to it. The texts that teach the inspiration of Scripture never cover the whole Bible; 2 Timothy 3:16 applies only to the OT. Furthermore, an argument for the inspiration of Scripture that appeals to Scripture itself is unavoidably merely circular. Protestants, accordingly, are divided among themselves about the books that belong to the

107. Augustine, *The Harmony of the Gospels* 1.35.

Bible. Luther's opinion on James differs from that of Calvin, and so forth. The proofs for Scripture derived from the church fathers (etc.) are not sufficiently strong and firm. As "motivations toward belief" (*motiva credibilitatis*) they have great value, yet they offer no more than probability: human and therefore fallible certainty. Only the church furnishes divine, infallible certainty. As Augustine said, "I indeed would not have believed the gospel had not the authority of the Catholic church moved me."[108] Similarly Protestants were able to accept and recognize Scripture as the word of God only because they received it from the hand of the church.[109] The Vatican Council recognized the books of the Old and New Testaments as canonical, "because, written under the inspiration of the Holy Spirit, they have God as their author; and because they have been entrusted as such to the church."[110] Guided by these thoughts, Rome, at the Council of Trent (session 4) and the Vatican council (session 3, ch. 2), established the canon. Following the example of the Septuagint and the practice of the church fathers, it included also the apocryphal books of the OT and in addition declared the Vulgate version to be the authentic text, so that it has final authority both in the church and in theology.

Over against this Roman Catholic doctrine, the Reformation posited the self-attested trust-worthiness (αὐτοπιστια) of Scripture.[111] In this controversy the question was not whether the church had to fulfill a responsibility with respect to Scripture, for on both sides it was agreed that the church is of great significance for the Bible. The church's witness is most important and a motivation toward belief (*motivum credibilitatis*). In its testimonies the church of the early centuries possesses strong support for Scripture. For every person, the church is the guide that leads one to Scripture. In this sense, Augustine's saying is and remains true that he was moved by the church to believe the Scriptures. Protestant theologians[112] have weakened this saying of Augustine by applying it only to the past, to the origin of faith. But Augustine's reasoning in the previously cited text is clear when he confronts his Manichean opponent with a dilemma. Either, he says, you must say to me: believe the Catholics, but they emphatically warn me not[113] to believe you; *or* do not believe the Catholics, but in that case you cannot appeal to the gospel against me either, "because I have believed by the very gospel the Catholics preach."

For Augustine the church is indeed a motive for faith, a motive he here utilizes against the Manicheans. But there is a difference between a motive for believing and the final ground of faith. Elsewhere he himself clears up the way he sees a motive for believing in the church when he says: "Why not rather submit to the authority of the gospel, which is so well founded, so confirmed, so generally acknowledged and admired, and which has an unbroken series of testimonies from the apostles down to our own day."[114] The church with its dignity, power,

---

108. Augustine, *On Two Souls, against the Manichaeans* 5; idem, *Reply to Faustus the Manichaean* 1.28.2, 4, 6.

109. Bellarmine, *De Verbo Dei*, bk. 4, ch. 4; G. Perrone, *Praelectiones Theologicae*, 9:71ff.; J. B. Heinrich and C. Guiberlet, *Dogmatische Theologie*, 2nd ed. (Mainz: Kirchheim, 1881), 1:764; Jansen, *Praelectiones Theologiae*, 1:766ff.

110. *Documents of Vatican Council I, 1869–70*, selected and trans. by John F. Broderick (Collegeville, MN: Liturgical Press, 1971), session 3, ch. 2.

111. J. Calvin, *Institutes* 1.7.3; Ursinus, *Tractationum theologicaruus* (1584), 8ff.; A. Polanus, *Syntagma Theologiae Christianae*, 1:23–30; J. Zanchi, "De Sacra Scriptura," *Operum Theologicorum*, 8:332–53; F. Junius, *Theses Theologicae*, 3–5; *Synopsis Purioris Theologiae*, disp. 2 §29ff.; J. Gerhard, *Loci Theologici*, 1:3.

112. Calvin, *Institutes* 1.7.3; A. Polanus, *Syntagma Theologiae Christianae*, 30; F. Turretin, *Institutes of Elenctic Theology*, II, 6. Ed. note: Bavinck erroneously cites III, 13; J. Gerhard, *Loci Theologici*, 1:3 §51.

113. Ed. note: The Dutch text lacks the negative here, but it seems essential to the argument.

114. Augustine, *Reply to Faustus the Manichaean* 1.32.19; cf. *On the Profit of Believing* 14.

hierarchy, and so forth always made a profound impression on Augustine. It continually moved him toward faith, supported and strengthened him in times of doubt and struggle; it was the church's firm hand that always again guided him to Scripture. But Augustine does not thereby mean to say that the authority of Scripture depends on the church, that the church is the final and most basic ground of his faith. Elsewhere he clearly states that Scripture has authority of itself and must be believed for its own sake.[115]

The Church's Authority

The church has and continues to have a many-sided and profound pedagogical significance for all believers till the day they die. The cloud of witnesses that surrounds us can strengthen and encourage us in our struggle. But this is something very different from saying that the authority of Scripture depends on the church. Even Rome does not yet dare to say this openly. The Vatican Council (1870), after all, recognized the books of the Old and the New Testament as canonical precisely "because, *written under the inspiration of the Holy Spirit, they have God as their author* and as such have been entrusted to the church." And Roman Catholic theologians distinguish between the authority of Scripture with respect to itself (*quoad se*) and with respect to us (*quoad nos*). But this distinction cannot be applied here. For if the church is the final and most basic reason why I believe Scripture, then the church, and not Scripture, is trustworthy in and of itself (αὐτόπιστος). We have to make a choice: either Scripture contains a witness, a teaching about itself, its inspiration and authority, and in that case the church simply accepts and confirms this witness; or Scripture itself does not teach such an inspiration and authority, and in that case the church's dogma about Scripture stands condemned for a Protestant. Roman Catholic theologians, accordingly, face a powerful contradiction. On the one hand, in the doctrine of Scripture they attempt to prove its inspiration and authority from Scripture itself. On the other, having come to the doctrine of the church, they attempt to weaken those proofs and to demonstrate that only the witness of the church offers conclusive certainty.

But if Scripture's authority with respect to itself depends on Scripture, then it is authoritative also for us and the final ground of our faith. The church can only recognize that which is; it cannot create something that is not. The charge that in this way one is guilty of circular reasoning and Scripture is proven by Scripture itself can be thrown back at Rome itself, for it proves the church by means of Scripture and Scripture by means of the church. If in response Rome should say that in the first case it uses Scripture not as the word of God but as a human witness, which is credible and trustworthy, the Protestant theologian can adopt this approach as well: inspiration is first derived from Scripture as reliable witness; with this witness Scripture is then proved to be God's word. Much more important, however, is that in every scientific discipline, hence also in theology, first principles are certain of themselves. The truth of a fundamental principle (*principium*) cannot be proved; it can only be recognized. "A first principle is believed on its own account,

---

115. H. Clausen, *Augustinus sacrae Scripturae interpres* (Hauniae: Schultz, 1827), 125; A. J. Dorner, *Augustinus* (Berlin: W. Hertz, 1873), 237ff.; H. Reuter, *Augustinische Studien* (Gotha: F.A. Perthes, 1887), 348ff.; Schmidt, *Jahrbücher für deutsche Theologie* 6 (1863): 235ff.; Hase, *Protestantische Polemik*, 5th ed. (Leipzig: Breitkopf und Hartel, 1891), 81; A. von Harnack, *History of Dogma*, 5:78–79; A. Kuyper, *Encyclopaedie der Heilige Godgeleerheid* (Amsterdam: J. A. Wormser, 1894), 2:503.

not on account of something else. Fundamental principles cannot have a first principle, neither ought they to be sought."[116]

Scripture itself clearly teaches, accordingly, that not the church but the word of God, written or unwritten, is trustworthy in and of itself (αὐτόπιστος). The church has at all times been bound to the word of God insofar as it existed and in the form in which it existed. Israel received the law on Mount Horeb; Jesus and the apostles submitted to OT Scripture. From the very beginning the Christian church was bound to the spoken and written word of the apostles. The word of God is the foundation of the church (Deut. 4:1; Isa. 8:20; Ezek. 20:19; Luke 16:29; John 5:39; Eph. 2:20; 2 Tim. 3:14; 2 Peter 1:19; etc.). The church can indeed witness to the word, but the word is above the church. It cannot confer on anyone a heart-based belief in the word of God. That is something only the word of God can do by itself and the power of the Holy Spirit (Jer. 23:29; Mark 4:28; Luke 8:11; Rom. 1:16; Heb. 4:12; 1 Peter 1:23). And for that reason alone the church appears to stand on a level below Scripture. Consequently, the church and believers in general can learn to know the inspiration, authority, and canonicity of Scripture from Scripture itself, but they can never announce and determine these attributes on their own authority. The Reformation preferred a measure of uncertainty to a certainty that can be obtained only by an arbitrary decision of the church. For, in fact, Scripture never offers a list of the books it contains. In the most ancient Christian church, and later as well, there was disagreement about some books. Nor does the text of Scripture have the integrity that also Lutheran and Reformed theologians yearned for. The Reformation, nevertheless, maintained the self-attested trustworthiness (αὐτοπιστια) of Scripture over against the claims of Rome, declared the church to be subordinate to the word of God, and so rescued the freedom of Christians.

Descriptive and Prescriptive Authority

[120] In addition to this dispute between Rome and the Reformation about the basis of the authority of Scripture, in the Protestant churches themselves there arose in the seventeenth century a further significant disagreement about the nature of that authority. They were agreed on the premise that Scripture, having God as its author, had divine authority. This authority was further defined by saying that Scripture had to be believed and obeyed by everyone and was the only rule of faith and conduct. This definition, however, automatically led to a distinction between historical (descriptive) and normative (prescriptive) authority. Divine revelation, after all, was given in the form of a history; it has passed through a succession of periods. Far from everything recorded in Scripture has normative authority for our faith and conduct. Much of what was commanded and instituted by God, or prescribed and enjoined by prophets and apostles, no longer applies to us directly and pertained to persons living in an earlier age. The command to Abraham to offer up his son, the command to Israel to kill all the Canaanites, the ceremonial and civil laws in force in the days of the OT, the decrees of the synod of Jerusalem, and many more things, while indeed useful for instruction and correction as history, cannot and may not any longer be obeyed by us. Furthermore, the record of revelation not only includes the good works of the saints but also the evil deeds of the ungodly. Frequently words and actions are recorded in Scripture,

---

116. J. Gerhard, *Loci Theologici,* I, ch. 3; J. Zanchi, *Operum Theologicorum,* 8:339ff.; A. Polanus, *Syntagma Theologiae Christianae,* 1:23ff.; F. Turretin, *Institutes of Elenctic Theology,* II, 6; L. Trelcatius, *Scholastica et methodica locorum communium S. Theologiae Institutio* (1651), 26.

therefore, that, while they are represented as historically true, are not presented as normative. It is far from being the case that these words and actions can be regulatory for our faith and conduct, for in fact they must more often be rejected and censured. Also the sins of the saints, of Abraham, Moses, Job, Jeremiah, Peter, etc., are given as a warning, not as models for our conduct. Finally, with respect to many persons—the patriarchs, Deborah, the judges, the kings, the friends of Job, Hannah, Agur, the mother of Lemuel, the composers of some of the psalms, like the imprecatory psalms (Pss. 73:13–14; 77:7–9; 116:11), and further with respect to Zechariah, Simeon, Mary, Stephen, and others—one may raise the question whether their words are only formally inspired, i.e., as it concerns their being recorded with accuracy, or also materially, as it concerns their content.

Voetius judged that many of these persons, like Job and his friends, cannot be counted as prophets, maintaining this sentiment against Maresius.[117] Granted, this issue had no further consequences but was still in many respects significant. For the first time it clearly brought out that there is a distinction between the word of God in a formal sense and the word of God in a material sense and compelled people to reflect on the relation between them. Now that relation was certainly conceived far too dualistically by the majority of the above-mentioned theologians. The authority of history and the history of a norm cannot be so abstractly separated in Scripture. The formal and the material meaning of the term "word of God" are much too tightly intertwined. Even in the deceptive words of Satan and the evil deeds of the ungodly, God still has something to say to us. Scripture is not only useful for teaching but also for warning and reproof. It teaches and corrects us, both by deterrence and by exhortation, both by shaming and by consoling us. But the above distinction does make clear that Scripture cannot and may not be understood as a fully articulated code of law. Appeal to a text apart from its context is not sufficient for a dogma. The revelation recorded in Scripture is a historical and organic whole. That is how it has to be read and interpreted. A dogma that comes to us with authority and intends to be a rule for our life and conduct must be rooted in and inferred from the entire organism of Scripture. The authority of Scripture is different from the authority of an act of parliament or congress.

Now the nature and basis of the authority of Scripture have been brought up for discussion especially in modern theology. In earlier times the authority of Scripture was based on its inspiration and was implied in it. But when inspiration was abandoned, the authority of Scripture could no longer be maintained. Although this was still attempted in various ways, theologians saw themselves compelled to construe both the grounds and the character of Scripture very differently. The authority of Scripture, to the degree it was still recognized, was based on the premise that it is the authentic record of revelation, expresses the Christian idea in its purest form—just as water is purest at its source. It was based on the conviction that it is the fulfillment of the OT idea of redemption and contains within it, be it germinally, the complete doctrine of the Christian faith and serves as the source of the beginning and ongoing renewal of the Christian spirit in the church. These and similar considerations for

117. G. Voetius, *Selectae disputationes theologicae,* 1:31, 40–44; 5:634–40; S. Maresius, *Theologus paradoxus,* 83–87; J. Maccovius, *Loci Communes Theologici,* 31–32; J. Cloppenberg, *De canone theol. desp.,* 3, op. 2:18–23; H. Witsius, *Miscellanea Sacra,* 1:316–18; B. de Moor, *Commentarius Perpetuus in Joh. Marckii Compendium Theologiae Christianae Didactico-elencticum* (1761), 1:131–34; J. G. Carpzovius, *Critica sacra Veteris Testamenti,* 1:2, §3.

the support of the authority of Scripture can be found in theologians of widely diverging schools.[118]

Nonetheless, all these grounds are not strong enough to support the authority that religion requires. They may be considered useful as motivations toward belief, but as grounds they are untenable. For, in the first place, by the distinction between revelation and its documentation, between the word of God and Scripture, they in fact render the authority of Scripture completely illusory. For if Scripture does not have authority in its entirety but only "the word of God in Scripture," the "religious-ethical dimension," the "revelation," or whatever people want to call it, then people have to decide for themselves what that word of God in Scripture is and do this at their own discretion. The point of gravity is then shifted from the object to the subject. Scripture does not criticize human beings, but they judge Scripture. The authority of Scripture is then dependent on human discretion. It exists only to the degree that people want to acknowledge it and is therefore totally nullified.

Now, even if these grounds could warrant some degree of authority for Scripture, it would still be no other than a purely historical authority. And in religion this is not enough; here a historical, i.e., a human and fallible authority, is not sufficient. Because religion pertains to our salvation and is related to our eternal interests, we can be satisfied with nothing less than divine authority. We must not only know that Scripture is the historical record of our knowledge of Christianity and that it most accurately contains and reproduces the original Christian ideas, but in religion we must know that Scripture is the word and truth of God. Without this certainty there is [for us] no comfort either in life or death. And not only does every Christian need this assurance, but the church itself as institution cannot dispense with this certainty either. For if a minister is not convinced of the divine truth of the word he preaches, his preaching loses all authority, influence, and power. If he is not able to bring a message from God, who then gives him the right to act on behalf of people of like nature with himself? Who gives him the freedom to put himself on a pulpit [a few feet] above them, to speak to them about the highest interests of their soul and life and even to proclaim to them their eternal weal or woe? Who would dare, who would be able to do this, unless he has a word of God to proclaim? Both the Christian faith and Christian preaching require divine authority as their foundation. "Faith will totter if the authority of the divine Scriptures begins to waver."[119]

Moral Authority Only?

It is therefore an error to describe the nature of scriptural authority as "moral." Lessing already began this trend when he said that a thing is not true because it is in the Bible, but it is in the Bible because it is true. Since the time of his audible groaning to be rescued from the authority of the letter and the paper pope, believing on authority has in various ways been made to look absurd. Christian theologians, letting themselves be influenced by this, have

---

118. J. H. Scholten, *Leer der Hervormde Kerk*, 1:78ff.; H. Bavinck, *De theologie van Daniel Chantepie de la Saussaye* (Leiden: Donner, 1884), 53ff.; F. Schleiermacher, *The Christian Faith*, ed. H. R. MacIntosh and J. S. Steward (Edinburgh: T. & T. Clark, 1928), §129ff.; R. Rothe, *Zur Dogmatik* (Gotha: F. A. Perthes, 1863), 166ff.; Lipsius, *Lehrbuch der evangelisch-protestantischen Dogmatik* (Braunschweig: C. A. Schwetschke, 1983), §193ff.; A. E. Biedermann, *Christliche Dogmatik* (Zürich: Orrel, Füssli, 1869); A. Schweizer, *Christliche Glaubenslehre* (Leipzig: S. Hirzel, 1863), 1:178ff.; J. Chr. K. Hofmann, *Weissagung und Erfüllung* (Nördlingen: C. H. Beck, 1841); A. Ritschl, *Rechtfertigung und Versöhnung* (Bonn: A. Marcus, 1882–83), 2:5ff., 9ff.

119. Augustine, *On Christian Doctrine* 1.37.

modified or challenged belief in authority. Doedes, for example, wants nothing to do with believing on authority and confines himself to speaking about moral authority in religion. Saussaye states that there is no other than moral authority and the moral is all the authority there is. There is no intellectual authority; moral authority equals morality, religion itself. People do not believe the truth on authority, but truth has authority, i.e., the right to exact obedience.[120] This way of putting it, however, suffers from conceptual confusion. Certainly, truth has authority; no one denies it. But the question is: what is truth in the area of religion, and where can it be found? To that question there are only two possible answers. Either the apostles, i.e., the Scriptures, tell us what truth is, or, if you will, who Christ is; or this is determined by one's own judgment, by the intellect or by each person's conscience. In the latter case, there is no longer any (scriptural) authority; it is totally subject to the criticism of the subject. In that case, it no longer helps in any way to say with Rothe that the Bible is the perfectly adequate instrument for arriving at a pure knowledge of God's revelation.[121] For any objective criterion by which to judge and to find that revelation in Scripture is lacking.

There is in fact only one ground on which the authority of Scripture can be based, and that is its inspiration. When that goes, also the authority of Scripture is gone and done with. In that case, it is merely a body of human writings, which as such cannot rightfully assert any claim to be a norm for our faith and conduct. And along with Scripture—for the Protestant—all authority in religion collapses. All subsequent attempts to recover some kind of authority—say, in the person of Christ, in the church, in religious experience, in the intellect or conscience—end in disappointment.[122] They only prove that no religion can exist without authority. Religion is essentially different from science. It has a certainty of its own, not one that is based on insight but one that consists in faith and trust. And this religious faith and trust can rest only in God and in his word. In religion a human witness and human trust is insufficient; here we need a witness from God to which we can abandon ourselves in life and in death. "Our heart is restless until it rests in Thee, O Lord!" Accordingly, Harnack is right when he says: "There has never existed a strong religious faith in the world which did not at some decisive point base itself upon an external authority. Only in the abstract discussions of philosophers of religion or in the polemical projects of Protestant theologians was a faith construed which derived its certainty solely from its own inner components."[123] The validity and value of authority in religion is gradually being recognized again.

The Universality of Authority

[121] Though religion can be satisfied only with a divine authority, the nature of that authority still needs to be further examined. Generally speaking, authority is the power of

---

120. Doedes, *Inleiding tot de Leer van God* (Utrecht: Kemink, 1880), 29–40; Saussaye in H. Bavinck, *Theologie van Chantepie de la Saussaye,* 53ff.

121. Rothe, *Zur Dogmatik,* 287.

122. Cf. V. H. Stanton, *The Place of Authority in Matters of Religious Belief* (London: Longmans, 1891); James Martineau, *The Seat of Authority in Religion* (London: Longmans, 1891); C. A. Briggs, *The Authority of Holy Scriptures* (inaugural address), 4th ed. (New York: Scribner, 1892); L. Monod, *Le problème de l'autorité* (Paris: Fischbacher, 1892); E. Doumerge, *L'autorité en matière de foi* (Lausanne: Payot, 1892); E. Ménégoz, *L'autorité de Dieu, réflexions sur l'authorité en matière* (Paris: Fischbacher, 1892). G. Godet, "Vinet et l'autorité en matière de foi," *Revue de théologie et de philosophie* 26, 2 (March 1893): 173–91; A. Sabatier, *Les religions de l'autorité et la religion de l'esprit* (Paris: Fischbacher, 1904); cf. further, P. Lobstein, *Einleitung in die Evangelische Dogmatik* (Freiburg im Breisgau: J. C. B. Mohr, 1897), 94ff.; J. Riemens, *Het Symbol Fideisme* (Rotterdam: Van Sijn & Zoon, 1900), 81ff.

123. A. von Harnack, *History of Dogma,* 5:82; cf. also P. D. Chantepie de la Saussaye, *Zekerheid en Twijfel* (1893), 138ff.

a person who has something to say, the right to have a voice in some matter.[124] Now one can speak of authority only between nonequals: it always expresses a relation between a superior to his inferior. Because there is no equality among human beings but all sorts of distinctions, there can be authority-relations among them. And since that nonequality is so extensive and diverse, authority plays a very large role among people. It is even the foundation of the entire structure of human society. Those who undermine it are engaged in the destruction of society. It is therefore foolish and dangerous to make believing on [the basis of] authority look ridiculous. Augustine already raised the question: "For I ask, if what is not known must not be believed, in what way may children do service to their parents, and love with mutual affection those whom they believe not to be their parents? . . . Many things may be alleged to show that nothing at all of human society remains safe if we shall determine to believe nothing, which we cannot grasp by full apprehension."[125]

We live by authority in every area of life. In the family, in society, and in the state, we are born and nurtured under authority. Parents have authority over their children, teachers over their pupils, the government over its citizens. In each of these cases the authority relation is clear. It gives expression to a power that legally belongs to one person over another. It therefore openly acts by means of commands and laws, demands obedience and submission, and, in case of rebellion, even has the right to employ coercion and to inflict punishment.

But, extending the concept of authority further, we also apply it in science and art. Here, too, there is diversity of gifts, and a relation between "superiors" and "inferiors," between teachers and pupils, arises. There are people who, by their genius and unremitting labor, have achieved mastery in a given field and who can therefore speak with authority in this field. From the discoveries of these masters, those with less mastery, the laypeople, live and learn. Indeed, as a result of the tremendous expansion of knowledge, even the most eminent person can be a master only in a very small area; in all else he or she is a learner and must depend on the research of others. This authority in science and art, however, bears a very different character from that of parents, teachers, and government; it is not juridical in nature but ethical. It cannot and may not use coercion; it does not have the power to punish. However prominent and important these people who act with authority are, their witness counts only to the extent that they can advance grounds for it. Hence their authority finally rests, not in the persons (so that the statement: "he himself said it" would suffice), but in the arguments on which their assertions are based. And since all people have a measure of understanding and judgment, blind faith is impermissible here, and the striving for independent insight, insofar as it is necessary and possible, a duty. Also in the field of history this is the case. In fact, knowledge of history is totally based on authority, on the testimonies of others. These testimonies, however, need not be blindly believed but may and must be rigorously examined so that the historian's own insight comes into its own as much as possible. In short, in the sciences human authority is as strong as its reasons are.

We find this notion of authority, finally, also in religion and theology. Here authority is needed, not less but much more than in the family, society, science, and art. Here it is a necessity of life. Without authority and faith, religion and theology cannot exist for a moment. But the authority in question here bears an utterly unique character. In the very nature of

---

124. Ed. note: Bavinck here adds the etymological information that the Dutch word for authority—*gezag*—originally signified force *(geweld)* or power *(macht)*. He refers the reader to *Woordenboek der Neder-landsche Taal*, s.v. "gezag."

125. Augustine, *On the Profit of Believing* 12.

the case, it has to be a divine authority. And by this fact alone it is different from authority in society and state, science and art. From the latter it differs mainly in that in science and art personal insight *may* judge and decide. But in the case of divine authority, this is out of order. When God has spoken, all doubt has to stop. Divine authority, therefore, cannot be called "moral," at least not in the sense in which we speak when referring to the moral superiority of a person, for religion is not a relation of an inferior to his superior but of a creature to his Creator, of a subject to his Sovereign, of a child to his or her Father. God has the right, when issuing commands to human beings, to demand unconditional obedience. His authority is rooted in his being, not in "reasons." In that respect the authority of God and of his word is like that of the government in the state and of a father in the family. There is nothing humiliating, nor anything that in any way detracts from a person's freedom, in listening to the word of God like a child and in obeying it. Believing God at his word, i.e., on his authority, is in no way inconsistent with human dignity, anymore than that it dishonors a child to rely with unlimited trust on the word of her or his father. So far from gradually outgrowing this authority,[126] Christian believers rather progressively learn to believe God at his word and to renounce all their own wisdom. On earth believers never move beyond the viewpoint of faith and authority. To the degree that they increase in faith, they cling all the more firmly to the authority of God in his word.

On the other hand, there is also a huge difference between the authority of God in religion and that of a father in his family and of a government in the state. A father, if need be, will force his child to conform and by punishing the child make that child submit to his authority; neither does the government bear the sword in vain. Coercion is inseparable from the authority of earthly governments. But God does not coerce people. His revelation is a revelation of grace. And in that revelation he does not come to people with commands and demands, with coercion and punishment, but with an invitation, with the admonition and plea to be reconciled to him. God could act toward people as a sovereign. Someday he will sentence as a judge all those who have disobeyed the gospel of his Son. But in Christ he comes down to us, becomes like us in all things, and deals with us as rational and moral beings in order then, as he encounters hostility and unbelief, to resume his sovereignty, to carry out his counsel, and to prepare glory for himself from every creature. The authority with which God acts in religion, accordingly, is completely in a class of its own. It is not human but divine. It is sovereign but still operates in a moral manner. It does not resort to coercion, yet manages to maintain itself. It is absolute, yet resistible. It invites and pleads yet is invincible.

So also it is with the authority of Scripture. As the word of God it stands on a level high above all human authority in state and society, science and art. Before it, all else must yield. For people must obey God rather than other people. All other [human] authority is restricted to its own circle and applies only to its own area. But the authority of Scripture extends to the whole person and over all humankind. It is above the intellect and the will, the heart and the conscience, and cannot be compared with any other authority. Its authority, being divine, is absolute. It is entitled to be believed and obeyed by everyone at all times. In majesty it far transcends all other powers. But, in order to gain recognition and dominion, it asks for no one's assistance. It does not need the strong arm of the government. It does not

126. Schweizer, *Christliche Glaubenslehre,* 1:186ff.

need the support of the church and does not conscript anyone's sword and inquisition. It does not desire to rule by coercion and violence but seeks free and willing recognition. For that reason it brings about its own recognition by the working of the Holy Spirit. Scripture guards its own authority. In earlier times, therefore, people occasionally also spoke of the "causative authority" (*auctoritas causativa*) by which Scripture "generates and confirms assent to the things to be believed in the human intellect."[127]

The Necessity of Scripture

Against Rome

[122] There is substantial agreement among Christian churches on the authority of Scripture. However, on the three following attributes, there is significant disagreement. Based on the relation it assumes between Scripture and the church, Rome can neither understand nor recognize the necessity of Holy Scripture. In Roman Catholicism the church, living from and by the Holy Spirit, is *trustworthy in and of itself* (αὐτοπιστος), self-sufficient. It possesses the truth, faithfully and purely, and preserves it by means of the infallible teaching office of the pope. Scripture, on the other hand, having proceeded from the church, may be useful and good as norm, but it is not the "first principle" of the truth. It is not necessary for the "being" of the church. The church does not really need Scripture, but Scripture—for its authority, augmentation, exposition, etc.—does need the church. The grounds for this position are derived from the fact that before the time of Moses and the early Christian church the church had no Scripture and that many believers, living under the old and still also under the new covenant, never possessed and read Scripture but lived solely from the tradition.[128]

Against Mysticism

However, not only does Rome oppose the necessity of Holy Scripture, but also many mystical movements have weakened and denied the significance of Scripture for the church and theology. Gnosticism did not just reject the OT but applied the allegorical method to the NT, attempting thereby to harmonize its system with Scripture. Here the perceptible forms and historical facts only have symbolic meaning. Biblical data are the outward shells that are necessary for people on a lower level but that can be omitted for the spiritually enlightened, the πνευματικοι. The Bible is not a source of truth but only the means by which the elite can elevate themselves to the higher level of *gnosis*.[129] In Montanism there appeared a new revelation, which augmented and improved that of the NT. Montanism, especially in its moderate form in Tertullian, on the one hand sought to be nothing new and fully to maintain the authority of Scripture; yet in Montanus it embraced a prophet in whom the Paraclete promised by Jesus, the final and highest revelation, had appeared. In that way Scripture simply had to yield to the new prophecy proclaimed by Montanus.[130]

The church indeed condemned these movements, and the church fathers fought this spiritualism. Augustine, in the prologue to his book on Christian doctrine, wrote against

127. H. Schmid, *Doctrinal Theology,* §8.

128. Bellarmine, *De Verbo Dei,* bk. 4, ch. 4; Heinrich, *Dogmatik,* 1:708ff.; F. B. Liebermann, *Institutiones Theologicae* (1851), 1:449ff.; F. X. Dieringer, *Lehrbuch der Katholischen Dogmatik,* 4th ed. (Mainz: Kirchheim, 1858), 633; C. Gutberlet, *Lehrbuch der Apologetik* (Munster: Theissing'schen, 1894), 3:21; Jansen, *Praelectiones Theologiae,* 1:786.

129. Krüger, "Gnosis," *PRE*³ 6:728–38; A. von Harnack, *History of Dogma,* 2:252–53.

130. Bonwetsch, "Montanismus," *PRE*³ 13:417–26; A. von Harnack, *History of Dogma,* 2:95.

it. Still, Augustine also assumed that the devout, especially monks, are endowed with such a great measure of faith, hope, and love that they could dispense with Scripture for themselves and live in solitude without it.[131] Spiritualism repeatedly reemerged, reacting against the crushing powers of church and tradition. Various sects, the Cathars, Amabric of Bena, Joachim of Floris, the Brothers and Sisters of the Free Spirit, and later the Libertines in Geneva believed that after the era of the Father and the Son that of the Holy Spirit had dawned, an era in which everyone lived by the Spirit and no longer needed the external means of Scripture and church.[132] Mysticism, which flourished during the Middle Ages in France and Germany, sought, by means of ascesis, meditation, and contemplation, to attain a communion with God that could dispense with Scripture. Indeed, Scripture was needed as a ladder to ascend to this high level but became superfluous when union with God, or the vision of God, had been reached.[133] Especially the Anabaptists exalted the internal at the expense of the external Word. As early as 1521, a contrast between Scripture and Spirit was forged, a dichotomy that became a permanent characteristic of Anabaptism.[134] Holy Scripture is not seen as the true word of God but only a witness and a record of it; the true word is that which is spoken in our hearts by the Holy Spirit. The Bible is merely a book containing letters; the Bible is a Babel [of tongues] full of confusion, which cannot generate faith in human hearts. Only the Spirit teaches us the true word. And when the Spirit teaches us, we can do without Scripture as well, since it is a temporary aid and not necessary to the spiritual person.[135] Hans Denck already equated that internal word with natural reason and pointed out numerous contradictions in Scripture. Ludwig Hetzer deemed Scripture totally unnecessary. Knipperdolling demanded at Münster that Holy Scripture be abolished and that people should live by nature and Spirit alone.[136]

Against Rationalism

Mysticism turned into rationalism. Later we see the same phenomenon in the Anabaptist and independentist sects of England at the time of Cromwell, among the Quakers, and in Pietism. The elevation of the internal over the external word always led to the identification of the teaching of the Spirit with the natural light of reason and conscience and thus to complete rejection of revelation and Scripture. No one opposed the necessity of Scripture more fiercely than Lessing in his *Axiomata* against Goeze. He too creates a split between letter and spirit, Bible and religion, theology and religion, the Christian religion and the religion of Jesus, and asserts that the latter did and can exist independently of the former. Religion,

---

131. Augustine, *On Christian Doctrine* 1.39.

132. Zöckler, "Spiritismus," *PRE*³ 18:654–66; J. H. Kurtz, *Lehrbuch der Kirchengeschichte* (Leipzig: Augus Neumanns, 1906), §108, §116; H. Reuter, *Geschichte der religiöser Aufklärung im Mittelalter* (Berlin: W. Hertz, 1875–77), 2:198ff.; Christoph Ulrich Hahn, *Geschichte der Ketzer im Mittelalter* (Stuttgart: J. F. Steinkopf, 1847, 1850), 2:420ff.; 3:72ff.; J. K. L. Giesler, *Kirchengeschichte* (1826), 2.2.437ff.; K. R. Hagenbach, *Kirchengeschichte in Vorlesungen*, 3rd ed. (Leipzig: S. Hirzel, 1886), 2:480ff.

133. A. von Harnack, *History of Dogma*, 6:97–117; Herzog, "Quietismus," *PRE*¹ 12:427ff.

134. C. Sepp, *Kerkhistorische Studiën* (Leiden: E. J. Brill, 1885), 12.

135. A. Hegler, *Geist und Schrift bei Sebastian Franck* (Freiburg im Breisgau: J. C. B. Mohr, 1892); J. H. Maronier, *Het Inwendige Woord* (Amsterdam: T. J. van Holkema, 1890); F. Vigouroux, *Les Livres saints et la critique rationaliste*, 2nd ed. (Paris: A. Roger & F. Chernoviz, 1886), 1:435–53; C. Hodge, *Systematic Theology* (New York: Scribner, 1906), 1:61–104; R. H. Grützmacher, *Wort und Geist* (Leipzig: A. Deichert, 1902); also cf. the articles in *PRE*³ on Denck, Frank, Münzer, David Joris, Münster.

136. D. Thelemann, "Münster (Widertaufer)," *PRE*² 10:362.

after all, existed before there was a Bible. Christianity existed before the evangelists and apostles wrote a word. Thus, the religion they taught can continue to exist even if all their writings were lost. Religion is not true because the evangelists and apostles taught it, but they taught it because it is true. Their writings, accordingly, may and must be interpreted in accordance with the internal truth of religion. An attack on the Bible is not yet an attack on religion. Luther has delivered us from the yoke of tradition; who will now deliver us from the much more intolerable yoke of the letter?

These ideas on the non-necessity of Scripture were, in principle, taken over by Schleiermacher. In his *Christian Faith* he writes that faith in Christ is not based on the authority of Scripture but precedes belief in Scripture and causes us to give special status to Scripture. Among the early Christians, faith in Christ did not arise from Holy Scripture, he says, nor can it arise from it in our case. In both cases faith must have the same ground. Scripture, accordingly, though it is not the source of religion, is its norm. It is the first of a series of Christian writings. It is closest to the source, i.e., the revelation in Christ, and so ran but little risk of absorbing impure constituents. But all these writings of the evangelists and apostles, like all subsequent Christian writings, proceeded from the same Spirit, the "common Spirit" of the Christian church. The church is not built on Scripture; instead, Scripture proceeded from the church.[137] Through Schleiermacher these ideas have become the common property of modern theology. They seem to be so obviously true that no doubt or criticism even arises with respect to them. In virtually all theologians today, one can now find the idea that the church existed before Scripture and can therefore also exist independently of Scripture. The church rests in itself, lives from itself, i.e., from the Spirit, who dwells in it. Holy Scripture, which proceeded from the church at its beginning in the freshness and vitality of its youth, though its norm, is not its source. The source is the personal living Christ who indwells the church. Dogmatics is the description of the life, the explication of religious consciousness, of the church. In that process, as its guideline, dogmatics has Scripture, which interpreted the life of the church first and most clearly. Hence the church is actually the author of the Bible, and the Bible is the reflection of the church.[138]

In Orthodox Protestantism, all these ideas, those of Rome, Anabaptism, mysticism, rationalism, Lessing, Schleiermacher, etc., are mutually and intimately connected. Especially Schleiermacher, by his reversal of the Scripture-church relation, has offered strong support to Rome. All of these groups and persons agree that Scripture is not necessary but at most useful and that the church can also exist from and by itself. The difference is only that, whereas Rome finds the ground and possibility for the continued existence of the Christian religion in the institutional church, i.e., the infallible pope, Schleiermacher and his kind find it in the church as organism, i.e., in the religious community, while mysticism and rationalism find it in religious individuals. All of them explain the continued existence of the church in terms of the leading of the Holy Spirit, the indwelling of Christ, but this has its organ, the pope in the case of Rome, the organism of the church in the case of Schleiermacher, and for Anabaptism, in every believer individually.

---

137. F. Schleiermacher, *Christian Faith,* §128, §129.

138. J. P. Lange, *Philosophische Dogmatik* (Heidelberg: K. Winter, 1849), §77; Rothe, *Zur Dogmatik,* 333ff.; Frank, *System der Christlichen Gewissheit,* 2nd ed. (Erlangen: Deichert, 1884), 2:57ff.; F. A. Philippi, *Kirchliche Glaubenslehre* (Gütersloh: Bertelsmann, 1902), 1:190ff.; Hofstede de Groot, *De Groninger Godgeleerden* (Groningen: A. L. Scholtens, 1855), 71ff., 97ff.; H. Bavinck, *De Theologie van Daniel Chantepie de la Saussaye* (Groningen: A. L. Scholtens, 1855), 49ff.; J. H. Gunning and de la Saussaye Jr., *Het Ethisch Beginsel der Theologie* (Groningen, 1877), 34ff.

It is not hard to see that in this lineup Rome occupies the strongest position. For certainly, there *is* a leading of the Holy Spirit in the church, Christ *did* rise from the dead, *does* live in heaven, and dwells and works in his church on earth. There *is* a mystical union between Christ and his body. The Word alone *is* insufficient: the external principle also requires an internal principle. Protestantism knew all this very well and confessed it heartily. But the question was whether or not the church was bound to the Word, to Scripture, for the *conscious* life of religion. Religion, surely, is not only a matter of the heart, the emotions, the will, but also of the head. God must also be served and loved with the mind. For the *conscious* life, accordingly, the church must have a source from which it draws the truth.

Now Rome, with its infallible pope, can assert that Scripture is not necessary; the infallibility of the church indeed renders Scripture superfluous. But Protestantism has no such infallible organ, neither in the institution, nor in the organism, nor in the individual members of the church. If Protestantism should deny the necessity of Scripture, it would weaken itself, strengthen Rome, and lose the truth, which is an indispensable element of religion. For that reason the Reformation insisted so firmly on the necessity of Holy Scripture. Scripture was the place for the Reformation to stand (δος μοι που στω). It succeeded because, against the authority of church councils and the pope, it could pose the authority of God's Holy Word. One who abandons this position of the Reformation unintentionally works for the upbuilding of Rome. For if not Scripture but the church is necessary to the knowledge of religious truth, then the church becomes the indispensable means of grace. The Word loses its central place and only retains a preparatory or pedagogical role. While Scripture may be useful and good, it is not necessary, neither for the church as a whole, nor for believers individually.

Scripture and the Church

[123] Thus, although against Rome the Reformation found its strength in Scripture and maintained its necessity, yet it did not thereby deny that before Moses the church had long existed without Scripture. It is also true that the church of the NT was founded by the preaching of the apostles and existed for a long time without a NT canon. Furthermore, the church today is still always fed and planted in the non-Christian world by the proclamation of the gospel. The books of the Old and New Testament, further, only originated gradually; before the invention of the art of printing, they were distributed in small numbers. Many believers in earlier and later years died without ever having read and examined Scripture, and even now the religious life seeks to satisfy its needs not just in Scripture but at least as much in a wide assortment of devotional literature. All this can be frankly acknowledged without thereby in any way detracting from the necessity of Scripture. And if it had so pleased God, he could most certainly have kept the church in the truth in some way other than the written word. The necessity of Scripture is not absolute but "based on the premise of the good pleasure of God."

Thus understood, this necessity is beyond all doubt. The word of God has been the seed of the church from the beginning. Certainly before Moses the church existed without Scripture. Yet there was an unwritten (ἄγραφον) word before it was recorded (ἔγγραφον). The church never lived from itself or rested upon itself but always lived by and in the word of God. (Rome, to be sure, does not teach that it lived from itself, but assumes a tradition that infallibly preserves the word of God.) Yet this needs to be asserted over against those who reduce revelation to "life," the infusion of divine powers, the arousal of religious emotions. The church, therefore, may be older than the written word, but it is definitely younger than the spoken word.[139] The common assertion that for a long time the NT church existed without Scripture must be carefully understood as well. It is true that the canon of NT books was not generally recognized until the second half of the second century. But from the beginning the Christian churches had the Old Testament. They were founded by the spoken word of the apostles. At a very early stage many churches came into possession of apostolic writings, which were also shared with other churches, were read publicly in the churches, and were widely distributed. Naturally, as long as the apostles were alive and visited the churches, no distinction was made between their spoken and their written word. Tradition and Scripture were still united. But when the first period was past and the time-distance from the apostles grew greater, their writings became more important, and the necessity of these writings gradually intensified. The necessity of Holy Scripture, in fact, is not a stable but an ever-increasing attribute. Scripture in its totality was not always necessary for the whole church. Scripture came into being and was completed step-by-step. To the extent that revelation progressed, Scripture increased in scope. Whatever part of Scripture existed in a given period was sufficient for that period. Similarly, the revelation that had occurred up until a given time was sufficient for that time. Scripture, like revelation, is an organic whole that has gradually come into being; the mature plant was already enclosed in the seed, the fruit was present in the germ. Revelation and Scripture both kept pace with the state of the church, and vice versa. For that reason one can never draw conclusions for the present based on conditions prevailing in the church in the past. Granted, the church before Moses was without Scripture, and before the completion of revelation the church was never in possession of the whole Bible. But this does not prove anything for the dispensation of the church in which we now live, one in which revelation has ceased and Scripture is complete. For this dispensation Scripture is not only useful and good but also decidedly necessary for the being (*esse*) of the church.

Scripture is the only adequate means of guarding against the corruption of the spoken word and of making it the possession of all human beings. The sound of a voice passes away, but the written letter remains. The brevity of life, the unreliability of memory, the craftiness of the human heart, and a host of other dangers that threaten the purity of transmission all make the inscripturation of the spoken word absolutely necessary if it is to be preserved and propagated. In the case of the revealed word, this applies even to a higher degree. For the gospel is not flattering to human beings; it is directly opposed to their thoughts and wishes, and, as divine truth, gives the lie to their falsehood. Revelation, furthermore, is not intended for one generation and one time only but for all peoples and ages. It must complete its course throughout all humankind and to the end of the ages. There is one truth, and Christianity is the universal religion. How else will this intention of the revealed word be reached except by its being recorded and written? The church cannot perform this ministry of the word. It is nowhere promised infallibility. Always in Scripture the church is referred to the objective word, "to the teaching and to the testimony" [cf. Isa. 8:20]. Actually even Rome does not deny this. The church, i.e., the gathering of believers, is not infallible in the understanding of Rome, neither is the gathering of bishops, but

139. J. Zanchi, *Operum Theologicorum,* 8:343ff.; A. Polanus, *Syntagma Theologiae,* 1:15; *Synopsis Purions Theologiae,* disp. 2; J. Gerhard, *Loci Theologici,* 1:1, §5ff.

only the pope. The declaration of papal infallibility is proof of the Reformation's thesis of the unreliability of tradition, the fallibility of the church, and even of the necessity of Scripture. For this declaration of infallibility implies that the truth of the revealed word is not or can not be preserved by the church as the gathering of believers, inasmuch as the church is still liable to error. The truth of the revealed word can be explained only in the light of the special assistance of the Holy Spirit of which, says Rome, the pope is the beneficiary. Rome and the Reformation agree, accordingly, that the revealed word can be preserved in its purity only by the institution of the apostolate, i.e., by inspiration. And the controversy between them pertains only to whether that apostolate has ceased or is continued in the person of the pope.

On the other hand, the assertion of mediating theology (*Vermittelungstheologie*) that Scripture proceeded from the church and that the church is therefore the actual author of Scripture is completely untenable. One can make this assertion only if one denies the true office of prophets and apostles, equates inspiration with regeneration, and completely divorces Scripture from revelation. According to the teaching of Scripture, however, inspiration is a unique activity of the Holy Spirit, a special gift to prophets and apostles, enabling them to transmit the word of God in pure and unalloyed form to the church of all ages. Scripture, therefore, did not proceed from the church but was given to the church by a special operation of the Holy Spirit in the prophets and apostles. Scripture is part of the revelation that God has given to his people. On this point Rome and the Reformation are agreed. But, against Rome, the Reformation maintains that this special activity of the Holy Spirit has now stopped; in other words, that the apostolate no longer exists and is not continued in the person of the pope. The apostles completely and accurately recorded their witness concerning Christ in the Holy Scriptures. By these Scriptures they have made the revelation of God the possession of humankind.

Scripture is the word of God that has completely entered into the world. It makes that word universal and everlasting, and rescues it from error and lies, from oblivion and transience. To the degree that humankind becomes larger, life becomes shorter, the memory weaker, science more extensive, error more serious, and deception more brazen, the necessity of Holy Scripture increases. Print and the press are gaining in significance in every area of life. The invention of printing was a giant step to heaven and to hell. Scripture also shares in this development. Its necessity becomes ever more clearly evident. It is being distributed and made universally available as never before. As it is translated into hundreds of languages, it comes within the purview of everyone. Increasingly it proves to be the ideal means by which the truth can be brought to the attention of all people. It is true that religious literature remains for many people the primary nourishment for their spiritual life. Still, this proves nothing against the necessity of Holy Scripture. Since directly or indirectly, all Christian truth is drawn from it. The diverted stream also gets its water from the source. It is untenable to say that today we continue to receive Christian truth apart from Holy Scripture. In the first century something like that was possible, but the streams of tradition and Scripture have long since converged, and the former has long been incorporated into the latter. Rome can maintain its position only by its doctrine of the continuation of the apostolate and the infallibility of the pope. But this is impossible for a Protestant. The Christian character of truth can be asserted solely because it is rooted with all its fibers in Holy Scripture.

There is no knowledge of Christ apart from Scripture, no fellowship with him except by fellowship in the word of the apostles.[140]

Beyond Scripture?

[124] Even when the necessity of Scripture is recognized, there can still be disagreement about the duration of that necessity. Even those who believe that Scripture has had its day often readily agree that in its time it was immensely important for the education of individuals and peoples. But in various ways the duration of that necessity has been curtailed. Gnosticism recognized its necessity for the "unspiritual" (ψυχικοι) but denied it for the "spiritual" (πνευματικοι). Mysticism indeed deemed Scripture necessary on the level of thought and meditation, but no longer on the level of the contemplation and vision of God. The rationalism of Lessing and Kant reserved a pedagogical role for revelation, Scripture, and statutory religion in order thus to prepare for the rule of the religion of reason. Hegel similarly judged that in religion the form of visual representation was necessary for the common people but that the philosopher with his conceptual apparatus no longer needed this. And one often hears it said that, while religion is good for the controlling masses, educated and civilized folk are far beyond it.

Now in this depiction of things there is an undeniable and wonderful truth. Revelation, Scripture, the church, the whole Christian religion, indeed bears a provisional, preparatory and pedagogical character. Just as the OT economy of the covenant of grace was left behind, so also this dispensation of the covenant of grace in which we live will one day belong to the past. When Christ has gathered his church and presented it to his Father as a chaste bride, he will deliver the kingdom to God. Moreover, the duality of grace and nature, revelation and reason, authority and freedom, theology and philosophy, cannot last forever. Certainly the supreme goal in religion is that we shall serve God without coercion and fear, motivated only by love, in accordance with our natural inclination. In revelation it is God's own purpose to mold people in whom his image is again fully restored. He gave us not only his Son but also the Holy Spirit in order that the Spirit should regenerate us, write his law in our heart, and equip us for every good work. Regeneration, adoption, sanctification, glorification—are all proofs that God educates his children for freedom, for a ministry of love we will never regret. To that extent the above notions [of mysticism and rationalism] can be considered an anticipation of an ideal that will be realized in the future.

Nevertheless, they indicate a very dangerous line of thought. They all proceed from a confusion between the present dispensation and that of the hereafter. While the New Jerusalem will no longer need a sun or moon, these two heavenly bodies nevertheless remain necessary here on earth. The fact that we will one day walk by sight does not cancel out the necessity of walking by faith in this dispensation. Although the church militant and the church triumphant are fundamentally one, there is nevertheless a difference between them in position and life in the present. The boundary line cannot and may not be erased. We will never achieve a heavenly life while we are here on earth.

---

140. Z. Ursinus, *Tractationum Theologicarum*, 1ff.; J. Zanchius, *Operum Theologicorum*, 8:343ff.; A. Polanus, *Syntagma Theologiae Christianae*, 1:15; *Synopsis Purioris Theologiae*, disp. 2; F. Turretin, *Institutes of Elenctic Theology*, loc. 2, qu. 1–3; H. Heppe, *Dogmatik der evangelischen reformirten Kirche* (Elberseld: R. L. Friedrich, 1861), 25–26.

We walk by faith, not by sight. Now we see in a mirror dimly; in the hereafter, and not before, we will see face to face and will know as we are known. The vision of God has been reserved for heaven. On earth we will never be self-reliant and independent. We remain bound to the cosmos that surrounds us. Authority and its implications can never be surmounted here on earth.

The doctrine of a temporary necessity of Scripture, moreover, creates a huge gap between the "unspiritual" and the "spiritual," between the civilized and the masses, between philosophers and the common people. Yet such a gap is by no means warranted. If religion consisted in knowledge, the erudite would have an advantage over the uneducated. But religiously all people are equal; they have the same needs. In Christ there is no distinction between the Greek and the barbarian. Religion is the same for all people, however much they may differ in class, rank, education, and so forth, for to religion, i.e., before the face of God, all these distinctions of rank and privilege by which people stand out above others are worthless. The division between these two kinds of people, accordingly, is evidence of spiritual pride, which is radically opposed to the essence of the Christian religion, to the humility and lowliness that it requires. In the kingdom of heaven, publicans have precedence over Pharisees and the least over the greatest.

Furthermore, some ground for this division could still be claimed if rationalism were right and revelation consisted in nothing but "the truths of reason." Then these truths, though known provisionally from revelation, could later by reflection be derived from reason itself. But revelation has a totally different content from that of a rational theory. It is history; its content is grace, its center the person of Christ, its purpose the re-creation of humankind. None of this can be discovered by reflection or derived from reason. For human beings to know such a revelation, Scripture remains a necessity at all times. Even a divine revelation to every person individually could not provide what the revelation in Christ now offers through Scripture to all people. The historical character of revelation, the fact and idea of the incarnation, and the organic view of the human race all demand Scripture in which the revelation of God has been laid down for all humankind. Just as one sun illumines the whole earth by its rays, so Christ is the "daybreak" from on high, which appears to those who sit in darkness and the shadow of death [cf. Luke 1:78–79]. So also one Scripture is the light upon everyone's path and the lamp for everyone's feet. It is the word of God to all humankind. History itself bears strong witness to this necessity of Scripture. The most highly spiritual mysticism has over and over turned into the most vulgar rationalism; and "enthusiastic" spiritualism has often ended in the crudest materialism.

Negatively, the necessity of Holy Scripture is as strongly demonstrated from within the schools that oppose it as positively from within the churches that affirm it.

The Clarity of Scripture

[125] Another important attribute that the Reformation ascribed to Scripture in opposition to Rome was perspicuity, or clarity. According to Rome, Scripture is unclear (Ps. 119:34, 68; Luke 24:27; Acts 8:30; 2 Peter 3:16). Also, in the things that pertain to faith and life, it is not so clear that it can dispense with interpretation. It deals, after all, with the deepest mysteries, with God, the Trinity, the incarnation, predestination, and other truths. Even in its moral precepts (e.g., Matt. 5:34, 40; 10:27; Luke 12:33; 14:33), it is often so obscure that

misunderstandings and misconceptions have always abounded in the Christian church. Essential to a correct understanding of Scripture, after all, is a many-sided knowledge of history, geography, chronology, archeology, languages, etc., knowledge that is simply not attainable by laypeople. Protestants themselves, accordingly, write numerous commentaries, and in the case of even the most important texts they differ in the exegesis. Holy Scripture necessarily has to be interpreted. Such interpretation cannot be provided by Scripture itself; Scripture cannot be its own interpreter.

Plato already wrote that the letter is abused and cannot protect itself and therefore needs the help of its father.[141] It is mute and cannot settle disagreements. It is like a law in terms of which the judge issues his verdicts, but it is not simultaneously law *and* judge. The learned Jesuit, Jacob Gretser, a participant in the conference on religion held in Regensburg (1601), made a deep impression when he exclaimed: "We are in the presence of Holy Scripture and the Holy Spirit. Let him pronounce sentence. And if he should say: you, Gretser, are mistaken, your case has collapsed; you, Jacob Heilbrunner, have won; then I will immediately cross over to your seat. Let him come; again, let him come, let him come and condemn me!" Hence there has to be an interpreter and a judge who gives a decision according to Scripture.

In the absence of such a judge [i.e., The Roman Catholic Church], every interpretation becomes completely subjective; everyone judges at his pleasure and considers his own individual opinion infallible. Every heretic (Dutch: *ketter*) has his own favorite text (*letter*).[142] Everyone, as Werenfels's well-known couplet has it, finds precisely his own dogmas in Scripture. [Apart from the Roman Church, so it is claimed] Scripture is at the mercy of all sorts of arbitrariness: individualism, "enthusiasm," rationalism. In the end endless division prevails. Worst of all, in the absence of an infallible interpretation, there is no absolute certainty of faith either. The foundation on which a Christian's hope then rests is pious opinion, scientific insight, but not a divine and infallible witness. It is so far from being the case that a person can shape his own conviction or teaching on the basis of Scripture that even Protestants, actually no less than Roman Catholics, live by tradition and trust in the authority of the church, of synods, fathers, authors, and so forth, to guide them.

But [so Roman Catholics claim], such an infallible divine interpretation of Scripture, however, has been granted by God in his church. Not the dead, uncomprehended, obscure, and bare Bible, but the church, the vital, always present church, which ever renews itself by the power of the Spirit, is the mediatrix of truth and the infallible interpreter of Holy Scripture. Everyone, after all, is the best interpreter of his or her own words. The true interpreter of Scripture, therefore, is the Holy Spirit, its author. And the Spirit possesses his own infallible organ of interpretation, the church; better still, the pope. By tradition, the church is in possession of the truth. It is led by the same Spirit who originated Scripture. The church is akin to Scripture; she alone can understand its meaning. She is the "pillar and bulwark of the truth" (1 Tim. 3:15).

In practice [so it is said] this is how it has always been. Moses, the priests of the OT, Christ, and the apostles explained and decided things on behalf of the church (Ex. 18; Deut. 17:9–10; 2 Chron. 19:9–10; Eccl. 12:12; Hag. 2:2; Mal. 2:7; Matt. 16:19; 18:17; 23:2; Luke 22:32;

141. Plato, *Phaedrus* 274–75.
142. Ed. note: The complete Dutch saying is: "Ieder ketter heeft zijn letter."

John 21:15–16; Acts 15:28; Gal. 2:2; 1 Cor. 12:8–9; 2 Peter 1:19; 1 John 4:1). Popes as well as councils have simply followed their example. For that reason the Council of Trent decided (session 4) that no one may interpret Holy Scripture "contrary to the sense which Holy Mother Church held or holds, since it is her task to judge the true sense and interpretation of Holy Scripture. Similarly, it is not permitted [to interpret Scripture] contrary to the unanimous opinion of the Fathers." Trent thereby restricted exegesis not only negatively—as some Roman Catholics attempted to view the decision—but very definitely also positively. No one may give any exegesis other than that which the church has given through its "fathers," it councils, or its popes.

The "declaration of faith"[143] of Pius IV and the Vatican Council[144] leave no doubt on that score. Not only does this doctrine of the obscurity of Scripture subject scientific exegesis to the authority of the pope; even more dependent and restricted is the layperson. On account of its obscurity, Scripture is not fit reading for laypersons. Without interpretation it is unintelligible to the common people. For that reason Rome increasingly restricted the translation of Scripture into the vernacular and Bible reading by the common people because of the misuse that was made of this privilege in the Middle Ages and later. The reading of Scripture is not allowed to laypeople except by permission of the church authorities. Protestant Bible Societies have been repeatedly condemned by the popes and, in the encyclical dated December 8, 1864, were placed on a par with socialistic and communistic societies.[145] And though Pope Leo XIII in his encyclical *Providentissimus Deus* on the study of Holy Scripture (November 18, 1893) recommended the study of Scripture, this did not apply to laypersons.[146]

The doctrine of the perspicuity of Holy Scripture has frequently been misunderstood and misrepresented, both by Protestants and Catholics. It does not mean that the matters and subjects with which Scripture deals are not mysteries that far exceed the reach of the human intellect. Nor does it assert that Scripture is clear in all its parts, so that no scientific exegesis is needed, or that, also in its doctrine of salvation, Scripture is plain and clear to every person without distinction. It means only that the truth, the knowledge of which is necessary to everyone for salvation, though not spelled out with equal clarity on every page of Scripture, is nevertheless presented throughout all of Scripture in such a simple and intelligible form that a person concerned about the salvation of his or her soul can easily, by personal reading and study, learn to know that truth from Scripture without the assistance and guidance of the church and the priest. The way of salvation, not as it concerns the matter itself but as it concerns the mode of transmission, has been clearly set down there for the reader desirous of salvation. While that reader may not understand the "how" ($\pi\hat{\omega}\varsigma$) of it, the "that" ($\H{o}\tau\iota$) is clear.[147]

143. H. Denzinger, *Sources of Catholic Dogma,* n. 1566.

144. *Vatican Council I,* session 3, ch. 2. Ed. note: see Denzinger, *Enchiridion,* 33rd ed., #3007; also found in Karl Rahner and H. Roos, *The Teaching of the Catholic Church* (Staten Island, NY: Alba House, [1966]), 62.

145. Denzinger, *Sources of Catholic Dogma,* n. 1566.

146. Vincent of Lerins, *Commonitorium,* ch. 3; Bellarmine, *De Verbo Dei,* bk. 3; M. Canus, *Loci Theol.,* 2:6ff.; G. Perrone, *Praelectiones Theologicae,* 9:98ff.; Heinrich, *Dogmatik,* 2nd ed., 764ff.; J. A. Möhler, *Symbolik,* §38ff.; Jansen, *Praelectiones Theologiae,* 1:771ff.; Rietschl, "Bibellesen," *PRE³* 2:700–713; C. Pesch, *Die Inspiratione Sacra Scriptura,* 573ff.

147. U. Zwingli, *De Claritate et certitudine Verbi Dei,* in *Opera,* ed. Schuler and Schulthess (Turici: Officina Schulthessiana, 1842), 1:65ff.; Luther, in J. Köstlin, *Theology of Luther,* trans. Charles E. Hay (Philadelphia: Lutheran Publication Society, 1897), 1:281; J. Zanchi, "De Scriptura Sacra," *Operum Theologicorum,* 8:407ff.; Chamier, *Panstratia Catholica* (1626), loc. I, bk. 1, chs. 13–32; W. Ames, *Bellarminus enervatrus* (Amsterdam, 1630), bk. 1, chs. 4 and 5; F. Turretin, *Institutes of Elenctic*

Thus understood, perspicuity is an attribute Holy Scripture repeatedly predicates of itself. The torah has been given by God to all of Israel, and Moses conveys all the words of the Lord to all the people. The law and the word of the Lord is not far from any of them but a light on their path and a lamp for their feet (Deut. 30:11; Pss. 19:8–9; 119:105, 130; Prov. 6:23). The prophets, whether by speech or in writing, address themselves to all the people (Isa. 1:10–11; 5:3–4; 9:1; 40:1–2; Jer. 2:4; 4:1; 10:1; Ezek. 3:1). Jesus speaks freely and frankly to all the crowds (Matt. 5:1; 13:1–2; 26:55; etc.), and the apostles wrote to all those called to be saints (Rom. 1:7; 1 Cor. 1:2; 2 Cor. 1:1; etc.) and they themselves took responsibility for the circulation of their letters (Col. 4:16). The written word is recommended to the scrutiny of all (John 5:39; Acts 17:11) and is written for the express purpose of communicating faith, endurance, hope, consolation, teaching, etc. (John 20:31; Rom. 15:4; 2 Tim. 3:16; 1 John 1:1–2). There is nowhere any indication of withholding Scripture from laypersons. The believers are themselves of age and able to judge (1 Cor. 2:15; 10:15; 1 John 2:20; 1 Peter 2:9). To them are entrusted the oracles of God (Rom. 3:2).

The church fathers, accordingly, know nothing of the obscurity of Scripture in the later Roman Catholic sense. They do indeed speak often about the depths and mysteries of Holy Scripture,[148] but with equal frequency they praise its clarity and simplicity. Thus Chrysostom, comparing the writings of the prophets and apostles with those of the philosophers, writes: "The prophets and the apostles did the complete opposite; for they established for all the things that are sure and clear, inasmuch as they are the common teachers of the whole world so that each person by himself or herself might be able to understand what was said from the reading alone." And elsewhere he says: "All things are clear and open that are in the divine Scriptures; the necessary things are all plain."[149] Similarly in Augustine we read: "Hardly anything may be found in these obscure places which is not found plainly said elsewhere"; and "Among those things which are said openly in Scripture are to be found all those teachings which involve faith and the mores of living."[150]

Familiar also is the saying of Gregory I, in which he compares Scripture "to a smooth and deep river in which a lamb could walk and an elephant could swim." Even today Roman Catholic theologians still have to admit that much material in Scripture is so plain that not only can the believer understand it, but even the unbeliever, who rejects the plain sense of it, is inexcusable.[151] The church fathers, accordingly, did not dream of forbidding the reading of Scripture to laypeople. On the contrary, over and over they insist on the study of Scripture and tell of the blessing they themselves received from reading it.[152] Gregory I still recommended the reading of Scripture to all laypersons. The restriction of Bible reading did not come up until the twelfth century, when a number of sects began to appeal to Scripture against the church. At that point the idea that the practice of Bible reading by laypersons was the prime source of heresy began to prevail.

Theology, loc. 2, qu. 17; Trigland, *Antapologia,* ch. 3; *Synopsis Purious Theologiae,* disp. 5; J. Gerhard, *Loci Theologici,* loc. 1, chs. 20ff.; S. Glassius, *Philologia Sacra* (1691), 186ff.

148. Cf. places in Bellarmine, *De Verbo Dei,* bk. 3, ch. 1; C. Pesch, *De Inspiratione Sancta Scriptura,* 577.

149. J. Chrysostom, "Homily on Lazarus," homily 3 in 2 Thess.

150. Augustine, *On Christian Doctrine* 2.6 and 9.

151. Heinrich, *Dogmatik,* 2nd ed, 788.

152. F. Vigouroux, *Les livres Saints et la critique rationaliste,* 3rd ed., 1:280ff.

In self-defense Rome then increasingly taught the obscurity of Scripture and tied the reading of it to consent from the church authorities.

[126] Over against Rome, the churches of the Reformation indeed have no more powerful weapon than Scripture. It delivers the deadliest blows to the ecclesiastical tradition and hierarchy. The teaching of the perspicuity of Scripture is one of the strongest bulwarks of the Reformation. It also most certainly brings with it its own serious perils. Protestantism has been hopelessly divided by it, and individualism has developed at the expense of the people's sense of community. The freedom to read and to examine Scripture has been and is being grossly abused by all sorts of groups and schools of thought. On balance, however, the disadvantages do not outweigh the advantages. For the denial of the clarity of Scripture carries with it the subjection of the layperson to the priest, of a person's conscience to the church. The freedom of religion and the human conscience, of the church and theology, stands and falls with the perspicuity of Scripture. It alone is able to maintain the freedom of the Christian; it is the origin and guarantee of religious liberty as well as of our political freedoms.[153]

Even a freedom that cannot be obtained and enjoyed aside from the danger of licentiousness and caprice is still always to be preferred over a tyranny that suppresses liberty. In the creation of humanity, God himself chose this way of freedom, which carried with it the danger and actually the fact of sin as well, in preference to forced subjection. Even now, in ruling the world and governing the church, God still follows this royal road of liberty. It is precisely his honor that through freedom he nevertheless reaches his goal, creating order out of disorder, light from darkness, a cosmos out of chaos. Rome and the Reformation both share the conviction that the Holy Spirit alone is the true interpreter of the word (Matt. 7:15; 16:17; John 6:44; 10:3; 1 Cor. 2:12, 15; 10:15; Phil. 1:10; 3:13; Heb. 5:14; 1 John 4:1). But Rome believes that the Holy Spirit teaches infallibly only through the agency of the pope. The Reformation, however, believes that the Holy Spirit indwells the heart of every believer, that every child of God shares in the anointing of the Holy One. It therefore puts the Bible in the hands of everyone, translates and distributes it, and in church uses no other language than the vernacular.

Rome boasts of its unity, but this unity seems greater than it really is. The split of the Reformation between the Lutheran and the Reformed church has its parallel in the split between the Greek [Orthodox] and the Latin church. In Rome, hidden under the semblance of external unity, there is an almost equally extensive inner dividedness. In Roman Catholic countries the number of unbelievers and indifferent people is not less than in Protestant countries. Rome has no more succeeded in turning the tide of unbelief than the churches of the Reformation have. Even before the Reformation, in Italy for example, unbelief had spread over large areas. The Reformation did not bring it about but rather arrested it and awakened Rome itself into vigilance and resistance. Descartes, the father of rationalism, was Roman Catholic. German rationalists have their counterparts in materialists; Rousseau has his counterpart in Voltaire, Strauss in Renan. Revolution has sunk its deepest roots and borne its most bitter fruits in Roman Catholic countries. It remains to be seen, moreover, whether the number of parties, schools,

---

153. F. Stahl, *Der Protestantismus als Politiek Princip,* 2nd ed. (Berlin: W. Schultz, 1853); D. Chantepie de la Saussaye, *Het Protestantism als Politiek Beginsel* (Rotterdam, 1871); A. Kuyper, "Calvinism: Source and Stronghold of Our Constitutional Liberties," in *Abraham Kuyper: A Centennial Reader,* ed. J. D. Bratt (Grand Rapids: Eerdmans, 1998), 279–322.

and sects that keep surfacing would not be as numerous in Rome as in Protestantism if Rome did not have the power and the courage to suppress every deviant group by means of censorship, excommunication, interdict, and, if need be, even by the sword. It is truly not owing to Rome that so many flourishing Christian churches have appeared alongside of it. Whatever the dark side of the dividedness of Protestantism may be, it does prove that the religious life here is a power that keeps engendering new forms and, for all its diversity, also manifests a deeper unity. In any case, Protestantism with its division is preferable to the frightful superstition in which the people are increasingly becoming entangled in the Greek Orthodox and Roman Catholic Church. Mariolatry, the veneration of relics, image worship, and adoration of the saints increasingly crowd out the worship of the one true God.[154]

On account of this perspicuity, Scripture also possesses the "power of interpreting itself" and is the "supreme judge of all controversies."[155] Scripture interprets itself; the obscure texts are explained by the plain ones, and the fundamental ideas of Scripture as a whole serve to clarify the parts. This was the "interpretation according to the analogy of faith," which was also advocated by the Reformers. They too did not come to Scripture without presuppositions. They adopted the teaching of Scripture, the Apostles' Creed, the decisions of the early councils, virtually without criticism. They were not revolutionary and did not want to begin all over again but only protested against the errors that had crept in. The Reformation was not the liberation of the "natural man" but of the Christian person. From the start, therefore, the Reformers had "an analogy of faith" in which they themselves took position and by which they interpreted Scripture. By that analogy of faith they originally understood the sense derived from the clear texts of Scripture itself, which then was later laid down in the confessions.[156] In connection with that, the church also had a responsibility with respect to the interpretation of Scripture.

In virtue of the power of teaching (*potestas doctrinae*) conferred on it by Christ and the gift of interpretation given to it by the Holy Spirit (1 Cor. 14:3, 29; Rom. 12:6; Eph. 4:11–12), the church has the obligation not only to preserve the Scriptures but also to interpret and defend them, to formulate the truth in its confession, to unmask errors, and to oppose them. Within its own circle and jurisdiction, therefore, the church also is the judge of controversies and has to test all opinions and to judge them in the light of Holy Scripture. It need not, for that purpose, be infallible, for also the judiciary in the state, though bound by the law, is fallible in its pronouncements. The situation in the church is the same. Scripture is the norm, the church the judge. Here too one can appeal to a higher court. Rome, denying this, states that the pronouncements of the church are

---

154. Th. B. Trede, *Das Heidenthum in der Römischen Kirche,* 4 vols. (Gotha: Perthes, 1889–92); T. Kolde, *Die Kirchliche Bruderschaften und das religiose Leben im Moderne Katholismus* (Erlangen: F. Junge, 1895); idem, "Herz-Jesu-Kultus," *PRE³* 7:777; R. Andree, *Votive und Weihegaben des Katholischen Volks in Süddeutschland* (Braunsschweig: F. Vieweg und Sohn, 1904).

155. *Synopsis Purious Theologiae,* disp. 5, §20ff.; A. Polanus, *Syntagma Theologiae Christianae,* bk. 1, ch. 45; F. Turretin, *Institutes of Elenctic Theology,* loc. II, qu. 20; W. Ames, *Bellarminus enervatus,* bk. 1, ch. 5; J. Cloppenburg, "De Canone Theol," disp. 11–15; *Op. Theol.,* 2:64ff.; Moor, *Commentarius in Marckii Compendium,* 1:429ff.; J. Gerhard, *Loci Theologici,* loc. I, chs. 21–22; H. Schmid, *Doctrinal Theology of the Evangelical Churches,* 69ff.

156. G. Voetius, *Selectae disputationes theologicae,* 5:9ff.; Moor, *Commentarius in Marckii Compendium,* 1:436ff; VI, praefatio; F. Turretin, *Institutes of Elenctic Theology,* I, qu. 19; F. Philippi, *Kirchliche Glaubenslehre,* 1:217ff.; O. Zöckler, *Handbuch der theologischen Wissenschaften* (München: C. H. Beck, 1890), 1:663ff.; J. L. S. Lutz, *Biblische Hermeneutik,* 154–76.

supreme and final. From them an appeal to God's judgment is no longer even possible. The Roman Church binds the human conscience.

By contrast, the Reformation asserted that a church, however venerable, can still err. Its interpretation is not "magisterial" but "ministerial." It can bind a person in conscience only to the degree that a person recognizes it as divine and infallible. Whether it indeed agrees with God's Word no earthly power can decide, but it is for everyone to judge solely for himself or herself.[157] The church can then cast someone out as a heretic, but ultimately that person stands or falls before his or her own master [Rom. 14:4]. Even the most simple believer can and may if necessary, Bible in hand, stand up to an entire church, as Luther did to Rome. Only thus the freedom of the Christian, and simultaneously the sovereignty of God, is maintained. There is no higher appeal from Scripture. It is the supreme court of appeal. No power or pronouncement stands above it. It is Scripture, finally, which decides matters in the conscience of everyone personally. And for that reason *it* is the supreme arbiter of controversies.

The Sufficiency of Scripture

[127] Finally, the Reformation also confessed the perfection or sufficiency of Holy Scripture. The Roman Catholic Church believes that in some parts Scripture is incomplete and has to be augmented by tradition. It declared at Trent (session 4) "that it receives and venerates with an equal affection of piety and reverence the said traditions as well as those pertaining to faith and morals as having been dictated either by Christ's own word of mouth or by the Holy Spirit and preserved in the Catholic church by a continuous succession." The Vatican Council (session 3, ch. 2) declared that this supernatural revelation is contained "in written books and in the unwritten traditions that were received from the mouth of Christ Himself by the apostles or from the apostles themselves under the dictation of the Holy Spirit, and that have come down to us, transmitted, as it were, from hand to hand."

The grounds that Rome cites for this doctrine of tradition are various. It is first pointed out that before Moses the church was totally without Scripture and that after that time up until the present many believers lived and died without ever reading or examining Scripture. By far the majority of God's children live by tradition and know little or nothing of Scripture. It would also be strange if in the area of religion and the church this were different from any other area. After all, in law and morals, in art and science, in the family and society, tradition is the bearer and nurturer of human life. Tradition connects us with our ancestors; by it we receive their treasures and again bequeath them to our children. This analogy requires that there should be a tradition also in the church; but here the tradition must be so much more glorious and certain than elsewhere, inasmuch as Christ has given the Holy Spirit to his church and by the Spirit infallibly leads his church into all truth (Matt. 16:18; 28:20; John 14:16). Add to this the many statements of Scripture that recognize the validity and value of tradition (John 16:12; 20:30; 21:25; Acts 1:3; 1 Cor. 11:2, 23; 2 Thess. 2:15; 1 Tim. 6:20; 2 John 12; 3 John 13–14). Both orally and by his Spirit, Jesus taught his disciples many more things, which, though not recorded, were passed down from mouth to mouth. Church

---

157. *Synopsis Purioris Theologiae,* 5:25ff.

fathers, councils, and popes have also from the very beginning recognized such an apostolic tradition.

Actually, the church always lives from and by this vital oral tradition. Scripture by itself is insufficient. Aside from the fact that by far not everything has been recorded, various writings by prophets and apostles have been lost as well. Though the apostles were instructed to witness, they were not told to do this in writing. They resorted to writing only in response to circumstances, "compelled by a kind of necessity." Their writings, accordingly, are mostly occasional writings and fall far short of what is necessary for the teaching and life of the church. For example, we find little or nothing in Scripture about the baptism of women, observance of the Lord's Day, the episcopacy, the seven sacraments, purgatory, the immaculate conception of Mary, the salvation of many Gentiles in the days of the OT, the inspiration and canonicity of several Bible books, and so forth. According to Rome even dogmas like the Trinity, the eternal generation [of the Son], the procession of the Holy Spirit, infant baptism, and so forth cannot be found literally and explicitly in Scripture. In short: while Scripture is useful, tradition is necessary.[158]

The Conflict with Rome

Over against this Roman Catholic doctrine of tradition, the Reformation posited that of the perfection and sufficiency of Holy Scripture. The validity of this polemic against Rome has been highlighted over time by the evolution of the very concept of tradition. The first Christian churches, like the churches in the non-Christian world today, were founded by the preaching of the gospel. The doctrine and practices that they received from the apostles or their associates were for a considerable time passed down from mouth to mouth and from generation to generation. This concept of tradition was clear; it referred to the doctrine and practices that had been received from the apostles and were preserved and reproduced in the churches. But as the distance from the apostolic age became greater, it became progressively more difficult to tell whether a given thing really was of apostolic origin. For that reason the African church protested against the exaggerated value attached in the second half of the second century to this tradition, especially against Gnosticism. Tertullian said: "Our Lord called himself the 'truth,' not 'custom.' "[159] Similarly, Cyprian cited against the tradition (to which the bishop of Rome appealed) the texts Isaiah 29:13; Matthew 15:9; 1 Timothy 6:3–5; and stated: "Custom without truth is the antiquity of error."[160] Christ did not call himself the "custom" but the "truth." The former must yield to the latter.

It therefore became necessary to further define the tradition and to indicate its features. Vincent of Lerin, in his *Commonitory*, chapter 2, defined the criteria of an apostolic tradition by the fact that something "had been believed everywhere, always, and

---

158. Bellarmine, *De Verbo Dei*, bk. 4; M. Canus, *Loci Theol.*, bk. 3; Peronne, *Praelectiones Theologicae*, 9:228ff.; H. Klee, *Katholische Dogmatik*, 1:277; Heinrich, *Dogmatische Theologie*, 2:3ff.; Jansen, *Praelectiones Theologiae*, 1:788ff.; J. A. Möhler, *Symbolik*, §38ff.; J. Kleutgen, *Philosophie der Vorzeit*, 2nd ed. (Münster: Theissing, 1867), 1:72ff.; F. Dieringer, *Lehrbuch der Katholischen Dogmatik*, §126; F. B. Liebermann, *Instutiones Theologicae*, 1:448ff.; C. Pesch, *De Inspiratione Sacra Scripturae*, 578ff. For the Greek Church, cf. F. Kattenbusch, *Confessionskunde* (Freiburg im Breisgau: J. C. B. Mohr, 1892), 1:292.

159. Tertullian, *On the Veiling of Virgins*, ch. 1.

160. Cyprian, *Epistle* 74.

by everyone. And indeed, this is truly and characteristically catholic." First, the mark of tradition was apostolic origin. Now there was added that something may be deemed to be of apostolic origin if it is truly universal, or catholic. Apostolicity can be known from the universality, antiquity, and consensus concerning a doctrine or practice. The Council of Trent, the Vatican Council, and also the theologians adopted these criteria of Vincent. But materially there was divergence; the logical implications did not stop there. It could not be maintained that something was apostolic only if it had really been believed always, everywhere, and by all. Of what doctrine or custom could such absolute catholicity be demonstrated? The three criteria, accordingly, gradually weakened. The church may indeed not pronounce something new to be a dogma and must adhere to the tradition, but the preservation of that tradition must not be understood mechanically as a treasure in a field but organically, the way Mary kept the shepherds' words and pondered them in her heart.[161] A given truth may therefore very well not have been believed in the past, at least not universally; it is nevertheless an infallible apostolic tradition if only it is now believed universally.

These two criteria, antiquity and universality, therefore, are not copulative but distributive marks of the tradition. They do not have to occur together and at the same time since either one of the two is sufficient. Factually antiquity has thereby been sacrificed to universality. But also the latter is again qualified. People raised the question of who or what would be the organ for the preservation and recognition of the tradition. This could not be the church in general. It is true that Möhler still identified the tradition with "the Word which lives perpetually in the hearts of believers,"[162] but this answer was much more a Protestant than a Roman Catholic construal. According to Rome, the task of preserving and defining the teachings of the church could not and should not be laid on the shoulders of the church in general, i.e., on laypeople. In the church one must distinguish between the listening church (*ecclesia audiens*) and the teaching church (*ecclesia docens*). The two indeed belong together and are imperishable, but the former possesses only a passive infallibility, i.e., it is infallible in believing only because and for as long as it remains linked with the teaching church.

But it is questionable whether even the latter is the real organ of doctrinal transmission. Gallicanism, the old Episcopal clergy, and the old Catholics stopped here and attribute infallibility to the body of bishops. But this position is untenable. When are these bishops infallible—outside of or only when gathered in council? If the latter, are they infallible only when they are unanimous or is only the majority infallible? How large must this majority be? Is fifty percent of the votes plus one sufficient? Is the council infallible without or even against the pope or only when in agreement with the pope? All of these questions seriously troubled Gallicanism. The papal system therefore took a further step and ascribed infallibility to the pope. This primacy of the pope is the product of a centuries-long development, the consequence of a trend that was already present in the church from early times. Gradually the pope began to be regarded as the infallible organ of divine truth and therefore also of tradition. Bellarmine [d. 1621] included among the marks of tradition the following rule: "that is to be believed without doubt to have descended from the apostolic tradition which is held to be such by those churches where

---

161. Heinrich, *Dogmatik*, 2:11–12.
162. Möhler, *Symbolik*, 357.

there is an unbroken succession from apostolic times."[163] Now in antiquity, he continues, there were many such churches aside from Rome. Today [1590s?], however, only Rome is left. Therefore "from the testimony of this church alone a sure argument can be derived for the purpose of proving the apostolic traditions."

The church of Rome thus decides what the apostolic tradition is. Later theologians, especially among the Jesuits, have further developed this doctrine. And on July 18, 1870, during the fourth session of the Vatican Council, papal infallibility was publicly proclaimed as dogma. Now it is certainly the case that with respect to this infallibility the pope cannot be viewed in isolation from the church, especially not from the "teaching church." In addition, the symbols, decrees, liturgies, fathers, doctors, and the entire history of the [Catholic] church constitute so many monuments of tradition with which the pope links up and which he has to take into account in establishing a dogma. Still, the tradition is not formally identical with the content of all these monuments. The tradition is infallible; but, in the final analysis, what tradition is is decided by the pope with, without, or, if need be, against the church and the councils. The judgment of whether and in how far something has been believed always, everywhere, and by all cannot be up to the church, neither the listening nor the teaching church, but is naturally and exclusively the responsibility of the infallible pope. For Rome, when the pope proclaims a dogma, it is by that very fact apostolic tradition. The criterion of tradition has therefore been successively found in apostolicity, in episcopal succession, and in papal decision. With that the process has reached its conclusion. The infallible pope is the formal principle of Romanism. When Rome has spoken, the matter is settled (*Roma locuta, res finita*). Where the pope is, there the church is, there the Christian religion is, there the Spirit is (*Ubi Papa, ibi ecclesia, ibi religio Christiana, ibi Spiritua*). One cannot appeal from the pope to a higher authority, not even to God. Through the pope God himself speaks to humanity.[164]

Tradition and Papal Infallibility

[128] This result, the outcome of the course of the development of tradition, demonstrates the falseness of the principle operative in it from the beginning. Papal infallibility can be treated at length only later, in the doctrine of the church. But at this point it is already clear that the sound and true element at stake in the maintenance of tradition in the early centuries has been completely lost. At that time the goal was the preservation of that which, in virtue of apostolic institution, had been believed and was practiced in the churches. It goes without saying that people then attached great importance to the tradition and did not yet understand the indispensability and necessity of the apostolic writings. But the mark of apostolicity, which was then an integral part of the tradition, was bound to disappear when people were further removed from the time of the apostles. The relative independence of tradition alongside of Scripture also disappeared. The streams of Scripture and tradition flowed into a single channel. And soon after the death of the apostles and their contemporaries, it became impossible to prove a thing to be of apostolic

---

163. Bellarmine, *De Verbo Dei*, bk. 4, ch. 9.

164. G. Perrone, *Praelectiones Theologicae*, 1:229; 9:279; Jansen, *Praelectiones Theologiae*, 1:804, 822ff., 829; Heinrich, *Dogmatik*, 1:699 note; 2:157ff.; J. M. de Maistre, *Du Pape, Oeuvres Choisies de Joseph de Maistre* (Paris: Hachette, 1890), 3:71.

origin except by an appeal to the apostolic writings. Apostolic origin cannot be proven of a single dogma the Catholic Church confesses outside of and apart from Scripture. Rome's doctrine of tradition serves only to justify Rome's deviations from Scripture and the apostles. Mariolatry, the seven sacraments, papal infallibility, etc. are the dogmas that cannot survive without tradition. At an evil hour the apostolic tradition was equated with ecclesiastical customs and papal decisions. Tradition, in the case of Rome, says Harnack, is "common superstition, paganism."[165]

Actually, by this doctrine of tradition Scripture is totally robbed of its authority and power. Roman Catholics predicate infallibility of both Scripture and tradition (the pope) but also recognize that there is a big difference between the two. Infallibility in both cases is traced to a special supernatural operation of the Holy Spirit, for Rome understands very well that the infallibility of the tradition cannot be derived from believers as such, from the power and spirit of the Christianity that resides and works in believers. In the church and among believers, after all, many errors occur, errors that often prevail for a long time and lead many people astray. Accordingly, the infallibility of the pope, like that of Scripture, is explained, on the basis of Matthew 16:18; 28:20; John 14:16–17; 15:26; 16:12–13, in terms of a special operation of the Holy Spirit. Yet there is a difference. The activity of the Holy Spirit in the apostles consisted in revelation and inspiration; in the case of the pope it consists in assistance. The Vatican Council (ch. 4) says: "For the Holy Spirit has promised the successors of Peter, not that they may disclose new doctrine by his revelation, but that they may, with his assistance, preserve conscientiously and expound faithfully the revelation transmitted through the Apostles, the deposit of faith."[166]

Scripture, therefore, is the word of God in the true sense, inspired, at least according to many theologians, right down to the individual words. The decrees of councils and popes, on the other hand, are the words of the church, which faithfully reproduce the truth of God. Scripture *is* the word of God; tradition *contains* the word of God. For Rome, Scripture preserves the words of the apostles in their original form; tradition only reproduces the substance of their teaching. The books of the prophets and apostles were often written without investigation, by revelation alone. However, in the case of the divine assistance promised to the church, the persons themselves are always active, investigating, pondering, judging, and deciding. According to Rome, in inspiration the activity of the Spirit was, strictly speaking, supernatural, but in the case of assistance it frequently consists in a complex of providential provisions by which the church is kept from error. Finally, inspiration in Scripture extends to all matters, also those of history, chronology, and so forth; but thanks to the assistance of the Holy Spirit, the pope is infallible only when he speaks *ex cathedra*, i.e., "when in the discharge of his office as shepherd and teacher of all Christians . . . he defines that a doctrine concerning faith and morals must be held by the whole church." In Rome, accordingly, Scripture still has a few prerogatives over tradition.[167]

---

165. Harnack, *History of Dogma,* 3:559 note.
166. *Documents of Vatican Council I, 1869–1870* (Collegeville, MN: Liturgical Press, 1971), session 4.
167. Bellarmine, *De Conciliis et Ecclesia, Controversiis,* bk. 2, ch. 12; Heinrich, *Dogmatik,* 1:699ff.; 2:212ff.; Jansen, *Praelectiones Theologiae,* 1:616; P. Mannens, *Theologiae Dogmaticae Institutiones,* 1:174.

But in fact tradition inflicts great damage on Scripture. In the first place, Trent decrees that Scripture and tradition must be venerated "with an equal affection of piety and reverence." Second, the inspiration of Holy Scripture is conceived by most Catholic theologians as "material" inspiration (*inspiratio realis*): not the individual words, but the subject matter is inspired. Further, in the doctrine of infallibility, form and substance are so tightly bound up with each other that no boundary can be drawn between the two. Also, while the pope is, strictly speaking, infallible only in matters of faith and morals, in order for him to be able to be this he also has to be infallible in his judgment concerning the sources of faith and in interpreting them. This includes the determination of what Scripture and tradition is, what is the authority of the church fathers, of councils, and so forth. It also applies to the assessment of errors and heresies and even basic doctrinal truths (*facta dogmatica*), in the prohibition of books, in matters of discipline, in the endorsement of orders, in the canonization of saints, and so forth.[168] And although in all other things the pope is not, strictly speaking, infallible, his power and authority nevertheless extends over all matters "pertaining to the discipline and governments of the church throughout the world," and this power is "full and supreme" and extends to "all shepherds and all the faithful."[169]

Many Roman Catholics even demand that the pope, in order to exercise this spiritual sovereignty, has to be a secular ruler as well. The claim is, if not directly then indirectly, the Pope has "the supreme power to settle the temporal affairs of all Christians."[170] The power and authority of the pope far exceeds that of Scripture. He is above Scripture, determines its content and meaning, and by his authority establishes the dogmas of the [church's] teaching and conduct. Scripture may be the primary means of proving the harmony of present-day doctrine and tradition with the teaching of the apostles. It may also contain a great deal that would not be well known otherwise and be a divine instruction in the teaching that surpasses all others. Nonetheless, to Rome Scripture is never more than a means that, while useful, is not necessary. The church existed before Scripture, and the church contains the full truth and not just a part, while Scripture contains only a part of the doctrine. Whereas Scripture needs tradition, the confirmation of the pope, tradition does not need Scripture. The tradition is not a supplement to Scripture; Scripture is a supplement to tradition. While Scripture alone is not sufficient, tradition alone is. While Scripture is based on the church, the church is based on itself.[171]

From Tradition to Sufficiency

The development of tradition into papal infallibility and the degradation of Scripture, which necessarily results from it, already implies that the Reformation had good warrant for opposing Rome's tradition. It did not confine itself to attack, however, but over against Rome's doctrine asserted that of the perfection or sufficiency of Scripture.[172] This attribute

---

168. Heinrich, *Dogmatisch Theologie*, 2:536ff.

169. *Documents of Vatican I*, session 4, ch. 3.

170. Bellarmine, "De Romano Pontifice," *Controversiis* I, V; de Maistre, *Du Pape*, 1:2; Jansen, *Praelectiones Theologicae*, 1:651.

171. Heinrich, *Dogmatische Theologie*, 1:702ff.; Mannens, *Theologicae Dogmaticae Institutiones*, 1:171.

172. Luther, in J. Köstlin, *Luther's Theology*, 2:279ff., 501 ff.; J. Gerhard, *Loci Theologici*, loc. 1, 18, 19; Schmid, *Doctrine of Evangelical Churches*, §9; J. Calvin, *Institutes* 4.10; Polanus, *Syntagma Theologiae*, 1:46; J. Zanchi, *Operum Theologicorum*, VIII, col. 369ff.; Ursinus, *Tractationem Theologicarum* (1584), 8ff., 22ff.; Chamier, *Panstratia Catholica*, loc. I, bks. 8 and

of Holy Scripture also must be correctly understood. It does not mean that all that has been said or written by the prophets, by Christ, and the apostles is included in Scripture. Many prophetic and apostolic writings have been lost (Num. 21:14; Josh. 10:13; 1 Kings 4:33; 1 Chron. 29:29; 2 Chron. 9:29; 12:15; 1 Cor. 5:9; Col. 4:16; Phil. 3:1), and Jesus as well as the apostles have spoken many more words and performed many more signs than are recorded (John 20:30; 1 Cor. 11:2, 23; 2 Thess. 2:5, 15; 3:6, 10; 2 John 12; 3 John 14; and so forth). Nor does this attribute imply that Scripture contains all the practices, ceremonies, rules, and regulations that the church needs for its organization but only that it completely contains "the articles of faith" (*articuli fidei*), "the matters necessary to salvation." Neither does this attribute of Scripture mean that these articles of faith are literally and in so many words contained in it. Rather, it only [claims that], either explicitly or implicitly, they are so included that they can be derived from it solely by comparative study and reflection, without the help of another source.

And, finally, this perfection of Holy Scripture must not be interpreted to mean that Scripture was always the same in degree of its perfection (*quoad gradum*) with respect to length. In the different periods of the church, Scripture was unequal in scope right up to its completion, but in every period that word of God, which existed in unwritten or written form, was sufficient for that time. The Reformation also made a distinction between an unwritten and a written word.[173] But Rome assumes their existence side by side, considering them species of a single genus, while the Reformation views this distinction as referring to the same word of God that first existed for a time in unwritten form and was subsequently recorded. The dispute between Rome and the Reformation, accordingly, concerns only the question of whether now, after Scripture has been completed, there still exists another word of God alongside it in unwritten form. In other words, the question is whether the written word of God explicitly or implicitly contains everything we need to know for our salvation and therefore is "the total and sufficient rule of faith and morals" or whether, in addition, we must assume the existence of still another principle of knowledge (*principium cognoscendi*).

Framed in this manner, however, the question hardly allows for a twofold answer. The Roman Catholic Church also acknowledges that Scripture is complete, constitutes an organic whole, and that the canon is closed. However highly it esteemed tradition, in theory it never ventured to put the decisions of the church on a par with Scripture. It still makes a distinction between the word of God and the word of the church. But how, as long as the church still takes the word of God seriously, can it ever teach the insufficiency of Scripture? This never occurred to the church fathers who clearly voice the complete sufficiency of Holy Scripture. Irenaeus says that we know the truth from the apostles, "through whom the gospel came to us which at that time they proclaimed and afterwards by the will of God handed down to us in the Scriptures as the future foundation and pillar

---

9; W. Ames, *Bellarminos enervatus*, bk. 1, ch. 6; H. J. Holtzmann, *Kanon und Tradition* (Ludwigsberg, 1859); E. W. Dieckhoff, *Schrift und Tradition* (Rostock: Stiller, 1870); J. L. Jacobi, *Die Kirchliche Lehre von der Tradition und heiligen Schrift* (Berlin: Luderitz, 1847); P. Tschackert, *Evangelische Polemik gegen die romischen Kirche* (Gotha: F. A. Perthes, 1885); idem, "Tradition," *PRE²* 15:727–32; Hase, *Protestantische Polemik*, 5th ed. (Leipzig: Breitkopf und Hartel, 1891), 77ff.; Harnack, *History of Dogma*, 3:593ff., 623ff.; C. Hodge, *Systematic Theology*, 1:104; Daubanton, *De algenoezaamheid der Heilige Schrift* (Utrecht: Kemink & Zoon, 1882).

173. Belgic Confession, art. 3.

of our faith."[174] Tertullian marvels at the "plenitude" of Scripture and rejects everything that is "extra-Scriptural."[175] Augustine testifies: "Whatever you have heard in it, know that it is good for you; whatever is outside of it, refuse."[176] And numerous others strike the same note.[177]

However, they also most certainly acknowledge the tradition they include in it, an element that undermines their conviction that Scripture is sufficient. This element ends in the later Roman Catholic doctrine of the insufficiency of Holy Scripture and the sufficiency of tradition. Scripture and tradition, in the case of Rome, cannot be maintained side by side; that which is withheld from the one is [bound to be] granted to the other. The tradition can increase only if and to the extent that Scripture decreases. It is very strange, accordingly, that Rome, on the one hand, regards Scripture as completed and considers the canon closed, indeed even recognizes Scripture as the word of God; and, on the other, views Scripture as insufficient and augments it with tradition. Nowadays many Roman Catholic theologians correctly assert that Scripture is—not the necessary but—at most a useful complement of tradition.[178]

A Scriptural View of Tradition

[129] But this theory is diametrically opposed to Scripture itself. At no time is the church in the OT and the NT ever directed to anything other than the always available Word of God, either written or unwritten. By it alone human beings can have a spiritual life. The church finds all it needs in the Scripture available to it at a given time. Subsequent Scriptures presuppose, link up with, and build upon, preceding Scripture. The prophets and psalmists assume the Torah. Isaiah (8:20) calls everyone to the law and to the testimony. The NT considers itself the fulfillment of the OT and refers back to nothing other than the existing Scripture. Even more telling is the fact that all that lies outside of Scripture is as firmly as possible ruled out. Traditions are rejected as the institutions of human beings (Isa. 29:13; Matt. 15:3, 9; 1 Cor. 4:6). The tradition that developed in the days of the OT prompted the Jews to reject the Christ. Over against it Jesus posited his "but I say to you" (Matt. 5:27, 32, 34, 38, 44), and against Pharisees and scribes he again aligned himself with the Law and the Prophets. The apostles appeal only to the OT Scriptures and never refer the churches to anything other than the word of God proclaimed by them. Inasmuch as in the early period tradition sought to be nothing other than the preservation of the things personally taught and instituted by the apostles, it was not yet dangerous. But the Roman Catholic tradition has utterly deteriorated from that level. It cannot be demonstrated that any doctrine or practice is of apostolic origin except insofar as this can be shown from their writings. The Roman Catholic tradition, which gave rise to the mass, to Mariolatry, to papal infallibility, and other Roman distinctives, is nothing but a sanctioning of the actual state of affairs of the Roman Catholic Church, a justification of the superstition that has crept into it.

---

174. Irenaeus, *Against Heresies* 3, preface, ch. 1.
175. Tertullian, *Against Hermogenes*, ch. 22; idem, *On the Body of Christ,* ch. 8.
176. Augustine, *Sermon on Pastorals*, ch. 11.
177. Cf. the references gathered by Chamier, *Panstratia Catholica*, loc. 1, bk. 8, ch. 10.
178. H. Höpfl, *Die Höhere Bibelkritik* (Paderborn: Schöningh, 1902).

Furthermore, the sufficiency of Holy Scripture results from the nature of the NT dispensation. Christ became flesh and completed all his work. He is the last and supreme revelation of God, who declared to us the Father (John 1:18; 17:4, 6). By him God has spoken to us in the last days (Heb. 1:1–2). He is the supreme and only prophet. Even the Vatican Council [I] acknowledges that the divine assistance given to the pope does not consist in revelation and the disclosure of a new doctrine. And Rome still tries as much as possible to urge the necessity of its dogmas, however new they are, from Scripture and to represent them as a development and explication of what is germinally present already in Scripture.[179] But in the process it entangles itself in grave difficulty. For either the dogmas are all in the same sense the explication of elements contained in Scripture (as, e.g., the dogmas of the Trinity and the two natures of Christ), or they are in fact new dogmas, which have no support in Scripture. In the former case tradition is not necessary and Scripture is sufficient, and in the latter case the so-called "divine assistance" to the pope is actually a revelation of new doctrine. The latter may still be denied in theory; in practice it is nevertheless accepted.

Post-Reformation Roman Catholic theologians, accordingly, have as a rule been more generous than their pre-Reformation counterparts in acknowledging that some dogmas are based only on tradition. And so arguments are advanced in support of the tradition today that were not used, at least not in the same sense or to the same degree, in earlier periods. Today the insufficiency of Scripture and the validity of tradition are argued on the grounds that some prophetic and apostolic writings have been lost, that Christ did not teach his apostles everything, and that the apostles recommended many things to the church orally. But the idea that some writings were lost and the issue of whether they were inspired[180] or not[181] are not at all to the point. The question is only whether the present Bible contains everything we need to know for our salvation and not whether it contains everything the prophets and apostles ever wrote and Christ himself said or did. Even if still other prophetic and apostolic writings were found, they could no longer serve as Holy Scripture. The same is true of the instruction given by Jesus and the apostles. They have said and done more than has been written down for our benefit. Though acquaintance with such writings would be historically important, it is religiously unnecessary. For our salvation Scripture is sufficient; we do not need any more documents, even if they came from Jesus himself. That was the teaching of the Reformation. Quantitatively revelation was much richer and more comprehensive than Scripture has preserved for us; but qualitatively and in terms of substance, Holy Scripture is perfectly adequate for our salvation.

Rome, accordingly, can list no other dogmas than those of Mariolatry, the infallibility of the pope, and the like that have developed apart from Scripture out of tradition. All those that pertain to God, humanity, Christ, salvation, and other basic doctrines can also be found in Scripture itself, as Rome admits. Then, what further need of witnesses have we? The Roman Catholic tradition serves only to prove specifically Roman Catholic dogmas, but the Christian dogmas, the truly catholic dogmas, are all, accord-

---

179. P. Lombard, *Sententiae*, III, dist. 25; Thomas Aquinas, *Summa Theologicae*, II, 2 qu. 1, art. 7; qu. 174, art. 6; J. Schwane, *Dogmengeschichte*, 2nd ed. (Freiburg im Breisgau: Herder, 1892), 1:7; Heinrich, *Dogmatische Theologie*, 2:22ff.

180. Bellarmine, *De Verbo Dei*, bk. 4, ch. 4.

181. Augustine, *City of God* 18.38.

ing to Rome itself, grounded in Scripture. This also shows that Scripture is sufficient and that the nature of the NT dispensation logically brings with it and demands this sufficiency of Holy Scripture. Christ has fully—personally and orally, or by his Spirit—revealed everything to the apostles. Upon this word we believe in Christ and have fellowship with God (John 17:20; 1 John 1:3). The Holy Spirit no longer reveals any new doctrines but takes everything from Christ (John 16:14). In Christ God's revelation has been completed. In the same way the message of salvation is completely contained in Scripture. It constitutes a single whole; it itself conveys the impression of an organism that has reached its full growth. It ends where it begins. It is a circle that returns into itself. It begins with the creation of heaven and earth and ends with the recreation of heaven and earth.

The canon of the OT and NT was not closed until all new initiatives of redemptive history were present.[182] In this dispensation the Holy Spirit has no other task than to apply the work of Christ and similarly to explain the word of Christ. To neither does he add anything new. The work of Christ does not need to be supplemented by the good works of believers, and the word of Christ does not need to be supplemented by the tradition of the church. Christ himself does not need to be succeeded and replaced by the pope. The Roman Catholic doctrine of tradition is the denial of the complete incarnation of God in Christ, of the all-sufficiency of his sacrifice, of the completeness of his Word. The history of the Roman Catholic Church shows us the gradual process of how a false principle creeps in. It first subordinates itself to Christ and his Word, then puts itself on a par with him, later elevates itself above him, to end in the complete replacement of Scripture by tradition, of Christ by the pope, of the church community by the church institution. Certainly this process has not yet reached its conclusion. It seems an anomaly that the pope, who gradually assumed a position above Scripture, the church, council, and tradition, is still appointed by fallible people, even though they are cardinals. Who is in a better position than he who is himself infallible to designate his successor? It is therefore very well possible that in the future papal sovereignty will prove to be incompatible with the power of cardinals. In any case Rome has not yet walked the road of the deification of humanity to its conclusion.

Still, for all this, our purpose is not to deny the good and the true component inherent in the theory of tradition. The word *tradition* also has a broader meaning than that which Rome has given it. Rome understands by it a doctrine that has been handed down by the apostles, preserved by the bishops, specifically the pope, and defined and proclaimed by him, a view shown to be untenable. Tradition can also be understood, however, in its reference to the entire scope of religious life, thought, feeling, action, which is found in every religious communion and which comes to expression in a wide assortment of forms, mores, customs, practices, religious language and literature, confessions and liturgies. In this sense there is tradition in every religion. The term can even be further expanded to include all those rich and multifarious bonds that link succeeding generations to preceding ones. In this sense, no family, no generation, no society, no people, no art, and no science can exist without tradition. Tradition is the means by which all the treasures and possessions of our ancestors are transmitted to

---

182. Hofmann, *Weissagung und Erfüllung*, 1:47.

the present and the future. Over against the individualism and atomism of a previous century, de Bonald, Lamennais (et al.) and Bilderdijk (in our own country) have again brilliantly highlighted the significance of community, authority, language, and tradition.

Such a tradition most certainly exists also in religion and in the church. Its very universality demonstrates that we are not dealing here with an accidental phenomenon. We find tradition not only in the Roman Catholic Church but also among Jews, Muslims, Buddhists, and other religions. In the more advanced religions, there is an additional reason for the necessity of tradition. They are all bound to a holy book that originated in a certain period and in that sense becomes ever farther removed from the generation now living. Also the Bible is a book that was written in ancient times and under all sorts of historical circumstances. The various books of the Bible all bear the stamp of the time in which they originated. Hence, however clear the Bible may be in its doctrine of salvation, and however certainly it is and remains the living voice of God, for a correct understanding it still often requires a wide range of historical, archeological, and geographical skills and information. The times have changed, and with the times people, their life, thought, and feelings, have changed. Therefore, a tradition is needed that preserves the connectedness between Scripture and the religious life of our time. Tradition in its proper sense is the interpretation and application of the eternal truth in the vernacular and life of the present generation. Scripture without such a tradition is impossible. Numerous sects in earlier and later times have attempted to live that way. They wanted nothing to do with anything other than the words and letters of Scripture, rejected all dogmatic terminology not used in Scripture, disapproved of all theological training and scholarship, and sometimes got to the point of demanding the literal application of the civil legislation of ancient Israel and the precepts of the Sermon on the Mount. But all these movements thereby doomed themselves to certain destruction or at least to a life that could not flourish. They place themselves outside of society and forego all influence on their people and their age. Scripture does not exist to be memorized and parroted but to enter into the fullness and richness of the entire range of human life, to shape and guide it, and to bring it to independent activity in all areas.

The Reformation, however, adopted another position. It did not reject all tradition as such; it was *reformation,* not *revolution.* It did not attempt to create everything anew from the bottom up, but it did try to cleanse everything from error and abuse according to the rule of God's Word. For that reason it continued to stand on the broad Christian foundation of the Apostles' Creed and the early councils. For that reason it favored a theological science, which thought through the truth of Scripture and interpreted it in the language of the present.

The difference between Rome and the Reformation in their respective views of tradition consists in this: Rome wanted a tradition that ran on an independent parallel track alongside of Scripture, or rather, Scripture alongside of tradition. The Reformation recognizes only a tradition that is founded on and flows from Scripture.[183] To the mind of the Reformation, Scripture was an organic principle from which the entire tradition, living on in preaching, confession, liturgy, worship, theology, devotional literature, etc., arises and is nurtured. It is a pure spring of living water from which all

---

183. Moor, *Commentarius in Marckii Compendium,* 1:351.

the currents and channels of the religious life are fed and maintained. Such a tradition is grounded in Scripture itself. After Jesus completed his work, he sent forth the Holy Spirit who, while adding nothing new to the revelation, still guides the church into the truth (John 16:12–15) until it passes through all its diversity and arrives at the unity of faith and the knowledge of the Son of God (Eph. 3:18–19; 4:13). In this sense there is a good, true, and glorious tradition. It is the method by which the Holy Spirit causes the truth of Scripture to pass into the consciousness and life of the church. Scripture, after all, is only a means, not the goal. The goal is that, instructed by Scripture, the church will freely and independently make known "the wonderful deeds of him who called it out of darkness into his marvelous light" (1 Peter 2:9). The external word is the instrument, the internal word the aim. Scripture will have reached its destination when all have been taught by the Lord and are filled with the Holy Spirit.

33

Louis Berkhof's *Systematic Theology*: The Principia of Dogmatics

Louis Berkhof, *Systematic Theology: New Combined Edition* (Grand Rapids: Eerdmans, 1996), 93–186; reprinted from *Introductory Volume to Systematic Theology* (Grand Rapids: Eerdmans, 1940), 93–186; originally published as *Reformed Dogmatics: Introduction* (Grand Rapids: Eerdmans, 1932), 97–202.

Louis Berkhof (1873–1957) was born in the Netherlands and grew up in the Christian Reformed Church there. In 1882, his family immigrated to Grand Rapids, Michigan. After studies in theology in Grand Rapids and Princeton, and short pastorates, he became a professor at Calvin Theological Seminary in 1906. There he taught successively biblical theology, New Testament, and systematic theology. In 1931, he became the seminary's first president. Though early on Berkhof published on social topics, he is best remembered for his *Systematic Theology*, from which the present selection comes. The great service and strength of Berkhof's work is his transmission and translation of Dutch theology for the American church. In particular, he was greatly influenced by both Kuyper and Bavinck. In addition, he is also indebted to his teacher Geerhardus Vos (1862–1947).

Our selection comes from his introductory volume to theology. Unfortunately, this volume has been for a long time eclipsed by his *Systematic Theology*. But they have been reprinted together, thereby producing a more accurate image of the structure of Berkhof's system of theology. In this system, God's revelation in Scripture is foundational. While Berkhof is primarily a transmitter of Dutch traditions, he did not fail to address the current challenge of neoorthodoxy, in particular that of Karl Barth (1886–1968) and Emil Brunner (1889–1966). In line with his earlier calling in the department of exegesis, Berkhof's treatment of the doctrine of Scripture manifests his desire to have the exegesis of Scripture support the doctrine of Scripture and the theological agenda. After defining systematic theology and surveying its history, he continues by defining the principles of theology: Scripture and God (cf. the beginning of his *Systematic Theology* proper). In our excerpt, after discussing the principles of theology, he deals first with the external principle of knowing, that is, general and special revelation, and the inspiration of Scripture; and second with the internal principle of knowing, that is, faith based on the witness of the Holy Spirit. In relation to the Princeton/Westminster tradition, note the following two points: first, Cornelius Van Til (1895–1987) has a slightly different emphasis on general revelation, regarding its sufficiency (*Christian Apologetics*, 74–76); second, on the question of inspiration, Berkhof shares B. B. Warfield's historic high view of Scripture.

Bibliography: J. D. Bratt. "Berkhof, Louis (1873–1957)." Pp. 32–33 in *DP&RTA*. H. Taylor Coolman. "Berkhof, Louis (1873–1957)." Pp. 45–47 in *BDE*. Sinclair B. Ferguson. "Berkhof, Louis (1873–1957)." Pp. 88–89 in *NDT*. Dirk Jellema. "Berkhof, Louis (1873–1957)." P. 122 in *NIDCC*. F. H. Klooster. "Berkhof, Louis (1873–1957)." Pp. 134–35 in *EDT*. Richard A. Muller. *Dictionary of Latin and Greek Theological Terms*. Grand Rapids: Baker, 1985. Idem. Preface to *Systematic Theology: New Combined Edition* by Louis Berkhof. Grand Rapids: Eerdmans, 1996. Cornelius Van Til. *Christian Apologetics*. Ed. William Edgar. Phillipsburg, NJ: P&R Publishing, 2003. Henry Zwaanstra. "Louis Berkhof." Pp. 153–71 in *Reformed Theology in America*.

I. Principia in General

A. Principia in Non-Theological Sciences

1. DEFINITION OF 'PRINCIPIUM.' In a discussion of principia it is naturally of the greatest importance to know exactly what the term denotes. 'Principium' is a term that is widely used in science and philosophy. It is the Latin rendering of the Greek word *arche*, beginning, a term which Aristotle used to denote the primary source of all being, actuality, or knowledge. The English word 'principle' is derived from it, and corresponds with it in meaning, especially when it denotes a source or cause from which a thing proceeds. The term first principle is an even closer approximation to it. After giving several meanings of the word *arche*, Artistotle says: "What is common to all first principles, is that *they are the primary source from which anything is, becomes, or is known*." Eisler in his *Handwoerterbuch der Philosophie* gives the following definition:

> Prinzip ist also sowohl das, woraus ein Seiendes hervorgegangen ist oder was den Dingen zugrunde liegt (Realprinzip, Seinsprinzip), als das, worauf sich das Denken und Erkennen notwendig stuetzt (Denkprinzip, Erkenntnisprinzip, Idealprinzip formaler und materialer Art), als auch ein oberster Gesichtspunkt, eine Norm des Handelns (praktisches Prinzip).

The statement of Fleming in Krauth-Fleming's *Vocabulary of the Philosophical Sciences* is in perfect agreement with this:

> The word is applied equally to thought and to being; and hence principles have been divided into those of being and those of knowledge, or *principia essendi* and *principia cognoscendi* .... *Principia essendi* may also be *principia cognoscendi* for the fact that things exist is the ground or reason of their being known. But the converse does not hold; for the existence of things is in no way dependent on our knowledge of them.

In ancient philosophy *principia essendi*, and in modern philosophy *principia cognoscendi*, receive the greater amount of attention. There is on the one hand a remarkable similarity between the principia that apply in the non-theological sciences and those that are pertinent to theology; but on the other hand there is also a difference that should not be disregarded. The former bear a natural and therefore general character. They are given with creation itself, are as such adapted to man as man, and have a controlling influence in all non-theological sciences.

2. PRINCIPIA OF THE NON-THEOLOGICAL SCIENCES. These are the following three:

a. *God is the principium essendi*. God is the source and fountain of all our knowledge. He possesses an archetypal knowledge of all created things, embracing all the ideas that are expressed in the works of His creation. This knowledge of God is quite different from that of man. While we derive our knowledge from the objects we perceive, He knows them in virtue of the fact that He has from eternity determined their being and form. While we attain to a scientific insight into things and relations only by a laborious process of discursive thought, He has an immediate knowledge of all things, and knows them not only in their relations but also in their very essence. And even so our knowledge is imperfect, while His knowledge is all-comprehensive and perfect in every way. We are only partly conscious of what we know, while He is always perfectly conscious of all His knowledge. The fulness of the divine knowledge is the inexhaustible source of all our knowledge, and therefore is the *principium essendi* of all scientific knowledge. Naturally, Pantheism with its impersonal and unconscious Absolute cannot admit this, for a God, who has no knowledge Himself, can never be the principle or source of our knowledge. In fact, all absolute Idealism would seem to involve a denial of this principle, since it makes man an autonomous source of knowledge. The origin of knowledge is sought in the subject; the human mind is no more a mere instrument, but is regarded as a real *fons* or source.

b. *The world as God's creation is the principium cognoscendi externum*. Instead of "the world as God's creation" we might also say "God's revelation in nature." Of His archetypal knowledge God has conveyed an ectypal knowledge to man in the works of His hands, a knowledge adapted to the finite human consciousness. This ectypal knowledge is but a faint reproduction of the archetypal knowledge found in God. It is on the one hand real and true knowledge, because it is an imprint, a reproduction, though in temporal and therefore limited forms, of the knowledge of God. On the other hand it is, just because it is ectypal, no complete knowledge, and since sin put its stamp on creation, no perfectly clear nor absolutely true knowledge. God conveyed this knowledge to man by employing the Logos, the Word, as the agent of creation. The idea that finds expression in the world is out of the Logos. Thus the whole world is an embodiment of the thoughts of God or, as Bavinck puts it, "a book in which He has written with large and small letters, and therefore not a writing-book in which we, as the Idealists think, must fill in the words." God's beautiful creation, replete with divine wisdom, is the *principium cognoscendi externum* of all non-theological sciences. It is the external means, by which the knowledge that flows from God is conveyed to man. This view of the matter is, of course absolutely opposed to the principle of Idealism, that the thinking man creates and construes his own world: not only the form of

658

the world of thought (Kant), but also its material and contents (Fichte), and even the world of being (Hegel).[1]

c. *Human reason is the principium cognoscendi internum.* The objective revelation of God would be of no avail, if there were no subjective receptivity for it, a correspondence between subject and object. Dr. Bavinck correctly says: "Science always consists in a logical relation between subject and object." It is only when the subject is adapted to the object that science can result. And God has also provided for this. The same Logos that reveals the wisdom of God in the world is also the true light, "which lighteth every man coming into the world" [cf. John 1:9]. Human reason with its capacity for knowledge is the fruit of the Logos, enables man to discover the divine wisdom in the world round about him, and is therefore the *principium cognoscendi internum* of science. By means of it man appropriates the truth revealed in creation. It is not satisfied with an aphoristic knowledge of details, but seeks to understand the unity of all things. In a world of phenomena which are many and varied, it goes in quest of that which is general, necessary, and eternal—the underlying fundamental idea. It desires to understand the cause, the essential being, and the final purpose of things. And in its intellectual activity the human mind is never purely passive, or even merely receptive, but always more or less active. It brings with it certain general and necessary truths, which are of fundamental significance for science and cannot be derived from experience. This thought is denied by Empiricism in two different ways: (1) by regarding the human spirit as a *tabula rasa* and denying the existence of general and necessary truths; and (2) by emphasizing analytical experience rather than synthetic reason. Dr. Bavinck points out that it ended in Materialism. Says he: "First the thought-content, then the faculty, and finally also the substance of the spirit is derived from the material world."[2]

B. Principia in Religion or Theology

Religion and theology are closely related to each other. They are both effects of the same cause, that is, of the facts respecting God in His relation to the universe. Religion is the effect which these facts produce in the sphere of the individual and collective life of man, while theology is the effect which they produce in the sphere of systematic thought. The principia of the one are also the principia of the other. These principia are not of a natural and general, but of a spiritual and special character. They do not belong to the realm of creation as such, but to the sphere of redemption. Notwithstanding this fact, however, they are also of inestimable value for the Christian pursuit of scientific knowledge in general.

1. GOD IS THE PRINCIPIUM ESSENDI. This is equivalent to saying that all our knowledge of God has its origin in God Himself. God possesses a complete and in every way perfect knowledge of Himself. He knows Himself in the absolute sense of the word, not only as He is related to His creatures, nor merely in His diversified activities and their controlling motives, but also in the unfathomable depths of His essential Being. His self-consciousness is perfect and infinite; there is no sub-conscious life in Him, no subliminal region of unconscious mentality. And of that absolute, perfectly conscious self-knowledge of God, the knowledge which man has of the divine Being is but a faint and creaturely copy or imprint. All human knowledge of God is derived from Him (Matt. 11:27; 1 Cor. 2:10–11). And because there can be no knowledge of God in man apart from self-consciousness in God, Pantheism spells

---

1. Herman Bavinck, *Gereformeerde Dogmatiek* (Kampen: J. H. Kok, 1906), 1:215.
2. Ibid., 221.

death for all theology. It is impossible to deduce a conscious creature from an unconscious God, a creature that knows God from a God that does not know Himself. We can find the principium of our theology only in a personal God, perfect in self-consciousness, as He freely, consciously, and truly reveals Himself.

2. THE PRINCIPIUM COGNOSCENDI EXTERNUM IS GOD'S SPECIAL REVELATION. The knowledge which God desires that we should have of Him is conveyed to us by means of the revelation that is now embraced in Scripture. Originally God revealed Himself in creation, but through the blight of sin that original revelation was obscured. Moreover, it was entirely insufficient in the condition of things that obtained after the fall. Only God's self-revelation in the Bible can now be considered adequate. It only conveys a knowledge of God that is pure, that is, free from error and superstition, and that answers to the spiritual needs of fallen man. Because it has pleased God to embody His special revelation in Scripture for the time being, this, in the words of Bavinck, has the character of a "*causa efficiens instrumentalis* of theology." It is now the *principium unicum*, from which the theologian must derive his theological knowledge. Some are inclined to speak of God's general revelation as a second source; but this is hardly correct in view of the fact that nature can come into consideration here only as interpreted in the light of Scripture. Kuyper warns against speaking of Scripture, or God's special revelation, as the *fons theologiae*, since the word *fons* has a rather definite meaning in scientific study. It denotes in general a certain object of study which is in itself passive, but which embodies certain ideas, and from which man must, by means of scientific study, extract or elicit knowledge. The use of that word in this connection is apt to give the impression that man must place himself above Scripture, in order to discover or elicit from these the knowledge of God, while as a matter of fact this is not the case. God does not leave it to man to discover the knowledge of Him and of divine things, but actively and explicitly conveys this to man by means of His self-revelation. This same idea was later on also stressed by Schaeder and Barth, namely, that in the study of theology God is never the object of some human subject, but is always Himself the subject. We should bear in mind that the word 'principium,' as we use it in theology, has a casual signification, just as the corresponding Hebrew and Greek words do in the Bible, when it speaks of the fear of the Lord as the principle (*reshith*) of wisdom (Ps. 111:10) or knowledge (Prov. 1:7), and of Christ as the principle (*arche*) of creation and of the resurrection (Col. 1:18; Rev. 3:14). By means of His self-revelation God communicates the requisite knowledge of Himself and of divine things to man. Man can know God only because and in so far as God actively reveals Himself. And if we do speak of Scripture as the fountain-head of theology, we shall have to remember that it is a living fountain, from which God causes the streams of knowledge to flow, and that we have but to appropriate these. The same point should be borne in mind, when we follow the common custom in speaking of God's special revelation as the source of theology. Man cannot place himself above his object in theology; he cannot investigate God.

3. THE PRINCIPIUM COGNOSCENDI INTERNUM IS FAITH. As in the non-theological sciences, so also in theology there must be a principium cognoscendi internum that answers to the *principium cognoscendi externum*. Scripture sometimes represents regeneration (1 Cor. 2:14), purity of heart (Matt. 5:8), doing the will of God (John 7:17), and the anointing of the Holy Spirit (1 John 2:20) as such. But it most frequently points to faith as the *principium internum* of the knowledge of God (Rom. 10:17; Gal. 3:3, 5; Heb. 11:1, 3), and this name undoubtedly deserves preference. The self-communication of God aims at conveying the knowledge of

God to man, in order that God may receive honor and glory through man. Therefore it may not terminate outside of man, but must continue right on into the mind and heart of man. By faith man accepts the self-revelation of God as divine truth, by faith he appropriates it in an ever increasing measure, and by faith he responds to it as he subjects his thoughts to the thoughts of God. The *principium internum*, says Bavinck, is sometimes called the *verbum internum* or even the *verbum principale*, because it brings the knowledge of God into man, which is after all the aim of all theology and of the whole self-revelation of God. Barth stresses the fact that it is only by faith that the knowledge of God becomes possible.[3] These three principia, while distinct, yet constitute a unity. The Father communicates Himself to His creatures through the Son as the Logos and in the Holy Spirit.

QUESTIONS FOR FURTHER STUDY: Has the doctrine of the principia always received adequate attention in Reformed theology? What took the place of it under the influence of Rationalism? What was the nature of the so-called 'Prolegomena,' 'Prinzipienlehre,' or 'Fundamentaldogmatik,' which came into vogue under the influence of Schleiermacher? Should theology derive its principia from other sciences or from philosophy? Which are the fundamental objections of modern theology to the doctrine of the principia, as it was stated in the preceding? Does Barth also regard Scripture as the *principium cognoscendi externum* of theology?

REFERENCES: Herman Bavinck, *Gereformeerde Dogmatiek* (Kampen: J. H. Kok, 1906), 1:207–237; Abraham Kuyper, *Encyclopaedie der Heilige Godgeleerdheid* (Amsterdam: J. A. Wormser, 1894), 2:291–346; John L. Girardeau, *Discussions of Theological Questions* (Richmond, VA: Presbyterian Committee of Publication, 1905), 72–272; James Henley Thornwell, *Collected Writings* (Richmond, VA: Presbyterian Committee of Publication, 1871), 1:43–52; Augustus H. Strong, *Systematic Theology* (Philadelphia: American Baptist Publication Society, 1907), 1–15; John Miley, *Systematic Theology* (New York: Eaton & Mains, 1892–94), 7–47; John McPherson, *Christian Dogmatic* (Edinburgh: T. & T. Clark, 1898), 1:18–37.

II. Religion

A brief discussion of religion at this point will have a double advantage. It will enable us to see the rationality of the principia to which attention was called in the preceding, and will prepare us for a more detailed discussion of God's special revelation, the necessary corollary of religion, and the *principium cognoscendi externum* of theology. There is a very close relation between religion and theology. This is evident from the very fact that many regard theology as the science of religion. While this is certainly a mistake, the fact remains that the two are inseparably connected. There is no such thing as theology apart from religion. Religion consists in a real, living, and conscious relationship between a man and his God, determined by the self-revelation of God, and expressing itself in a life of worship, fellowship and service. It presupposes that God exists, that He has revealed Himself, and that He has enabled man to appropriate this revelation. And where man does appropriate the revealed knowledge of God, reflects on it and unifies it, there the structure of theology arises on the basis of God's revelation. We do not proceed on the assumption, so common among modern students of religion, that the essential nature of religion can be determined only in the light of its origin and history, and therefore do not begin this discussion with a historical

3. Karl Barth, *The Doctrine of the Word of God* (New York: T. & T. Clark, 1936), 260–83.

study of the religions of the world. Since our conception of religion is frankly determined by Scripture, it seems more desirable to follow the logical order in its discussion, and to consider first of all the essence of religion.

A. The Essence of Religion

1. THE DERIVATION OF THE WORD 'RELIGION.' The derivation of the word 'religion' is still uncertain, and even if it were certain, would only yield a historical, and not a normative, definition of religion. It would only shed some light on the conception of religion that gave rise to the use of this particular word. Several derivations of it have been suggested in course of time. The earliest of these is that of Cicero, who derived it from *re-legere*, to re-read, to repeat, to observe carefully. In the light of this derivation religion was regarded as a constant and diligent observance of all that pertains to the knowledge of the gods. One of the influential Church Fathers of the fourth century, Lactantius, held that the word was derived from *religare*, to attach, to establish firmly, to bind together, and therefore pointed to religion as the bond between God and man. Gellius suggested the derivation from *relin-quere* in the sense of to separate oneself from someone or something. The word 'religion' would then indicate that which by reason of its holiness is separated from all that is profane. Finally, Leidenroth assumed that it was derived from a supposed root *ligere*, meaning *to see*. Religere would then mean, to look back, and religion, to look back with fear. The derivation of Gellius found no favor whatsoever. That of Lactantius was generally accepted for a long time, but was gradually relinquished when Latin scholars pointed out that it was linguistically impossible to derive 'religion' from 'religare'. Some admit the possibility of the derivation suggested by Leidenroth, but the derivation of Cicero is now preferred by most theologians. Calvin also gave preference to this, though he did not share Cicero's explanation of the term. Says he: "Cicero truly and shrewdly derives the name *religion* from *relego*, and yet the reason which he asigns is forced and far-fetched, namely, that honest worshippers *read and read again*, and ponder what is true. I rather think the name is used in opposition to vagrant license—the greater part of mankind rashly taking up whatever first comes their way, whereas piety, that it may stand with a firm step, confines itself within due bounds."[4]

2. SCRIPTURAL TERMS FOR RELIGION. The Bible contains no definition of religion, nor even a general term descriptive of this phenomenon. It has become customary in Reformed theology to distinguish between objective and subjective religion. The word 'religion' is clearly used in a two-fold sense. When we speak of the Christian religion in distinction from other religions, we mean one thing; and when we say that a man's religion is too intellectual or too emotional, we have something different in mind. In the one case we refer to something that has objective existence outside of man, and in the other, to a subjective phenomenon in the inner life of man, which finds expression in a variety of ways. The term '*religio objectiva*' is used to denote that which determines the nature of man's religion, its regulative norm, namely, the knowledge of God and of man's relation to Him, as this is prescribed by the Word of God. It is sometimes practically equivalent to 'the divine revelation.' And the term '*religio subjectiva*' serves to designate the life that is so regulated or determined by the Word of God, and that expresses itself in worship, fellowship, and service. Now the Bible uses different terms for each of these aspects of religion.

---

4. *Institutes* 1.12.1.

The *religio objectiva* is, as was said, practically identical with God's revelation, and is indicated in the Old Testament by such terms as 'law,' 'commandments,' 'precepts,' 'judgments,' 'ordinances,' and so on. In the New Testament the revelation of God is embodied, not primarily in a set of laws, but in the Person of Christ, in His redemptive work, and in the apostolic *kerugma*, which centers about Christ, and is merely an interpretation of the facts of redemption. Such terms as 'the gospel,' 'the faith,' and 'the kerugma' serve to designate the *religio objectiva*.

The *religio subjectiva* corresponds to the *religio objectiva*, and is described in the Old Testament as "the fear of the Lord," which is repeatedly called "the beginning of wisdom." The term is expressive of the inner disposition of the pious Israelite with reference to the law of God. This fear of God should be distinguished, however, from that anxious solicitude, accompanied with dread, that is so characteristic of heathen religions. The really God-fearing Israelite was not controlled by the distrust, the dread anxiety, and slavish fear, with which the Gentiles thought of their gods. In his case the fear of the Lord was accompanied with other religious dispositions, such as faith, hope, love, trust, taking refuge in, leaning on, and clinging to, God, and therefore was perfectly consistent with joy and peace, childlike confidence and blessedness, in communion with God.

The New Testament rarely employs the terms that are most prominent in classical Greek as designations of religion, such as *deisidaimonia* (fear or reverence for the gods), Acts 25:19, *theosebeia* (reverence towards God), 1 Timothy 2:10, and *eulabeia* (circumspection in religious matters, fear of God, reverence, piety), Hebrews 5:7; 12:28. The only word that occurs with some frequency is *eusebeia* (piety towards God, godliness), which is found fifteen times. These words do not express the characteristic element of New Testament religion. The fear of the Lord is indeed mentioned here as an element in religion (Luke 18:2; Acts 9:31; 2 Cor. 5:11; 7:1), but is far less prominent than in the Old Testament. The usual New Testament term for the *religio subjectiva* in the New Testament is *pistis*, faith. In classical Greek this word is used to denote: (a) a conviction based on the testimony of another; and (b) trust in a person whose testimony is accepted. It does not stand out as a designation of trust in the gods, though it is occasionally so used. And it is exactly this element that is brought to the foreground in the New Testament. To the glorious message of salvation, there is an answering faith on the part of man, a faith consisting in childlike trust in the grace of God, and becoming at the same time a fountain of love to God and of devotion to His service. This faith is not the natural expression of any so-called inborn religious disposition of man, but is the fruit of the supernatural operation of the Holy Spirit. The words *latreia* (Rom. 9:4; 12:1; Heb. 9:1, 6) and *threskeia* (Acts 26:5; Col. 2:18; James 1:27) are used to denote the service of God that springs from the principle of faith.

3. HISTORICAL CONCEPTIONS OF THE ESSENCE OF RELIGION. Religion is one of the most universal phenomena of human life. Man has sometimes been described as "incurably religious." This need not surprise us in view of the fact that man was created in the image of God, and was destined to live in communion with Him. And while it is true that man fell away from God, his fall did not involve a complete loss of the image of God. The Belgic Confession states in Article 14 that man "lost all his excellent gifts which he had received from God, and only retained a few remains thereof, which, however, are sufficient to leave man with excuse." And according to the Canons of Dort III and IV, Article 4: "There remain, however, in man since the fall, the glimmerings of natural light, whereby he retains some

knowledge of God, of natural things, and of the difference between good and evil, and discovers some regard for virtue, good order in society, and for maintaining an orderly deportment." This remaining light, however, does not avail unto salvation, and is even abused by man in natural and civil things. At the same time it does serve to explain the presence of some form of religion even among the lowest and most barbaric tribes of the earth. But however general this phenomenon may be among the nations of the world, this does not mean that there is general agreement as to the essential nature of it. Even the history of the Christian Church reveals considerable difference of opinion on this point. The following are the most important conceptions that come into consideration here:

a. *The conception of the early Church*. The Bible does not furnish us with a definition of religion, nor even with a description of it, though it contains in its entire compass a clear revelation of what God requires of man. There are a few passages, however, which contain some specific indications. Thus Paul says in Romans 12:1: "I beseech you therefore, brethren, by the mercies of God, to present your bodies a living sacrifice, holy, acceptable to God, which is your spiritual (or: reasonable) service (*latreia*)." The Epistle to the Hebrews contains this admonition: "Wherefore receiving a kingdom that cannot be shaken, let us have grace, whereby we may offer service well-pleasing to God with reverence and awe" (Heb. 12:28). In this passage the words *latreio* and *eulabeia* are both used. James adds a specific element in the words: "Pure religion (*threskeia*) and undefiled before our God and Father is this, to visit the fatherless and widows in their affliction, and to keep oneself unspotted from the world" (James 1:27).

In the early Church Christians enjoyed religious experiences and engaged in consecrated service and in reverential worship long before they began to reflect on the exact nature of religion. One of the earliest definitions of it was that of Lactantius in the beginning of the fourth century. He defined religion as *recta verum Deum cognoscendi et colendi ratio* (the right manner of knowing and serving the true God). This definition has always met with considerable favor, and is even now found in some works on dogmatic theology. During the previous century, however, it was criticized as favoring an external conception of religion, in which the heart is not concerned. But this criticism is hardly justified, since the definition does not pretend to specify what is the right manner of knowing and serving God. There is nothing in it to prevent anyone from assuming that the author had in mind a knowledge, which is not only intellectual, but also experiential, and a service which springs from the heart and is truly spiritual. The right manner of knowing and serving God is after all deter-mined by the Word of God, which is not satisfied with a purely intellectual knowledge, nor with a merely external service. It is true, however, that the definition applies to the *religio objectiva*, the religion as prescribed by God in His Word, rather than to the *religio subjectiva*, religion as experienced and practiced by men; and that it does not indicate the connection between the right knowledge and the right service of God.

b. *The conception of the Middle Ages*. It is a well known fact that during the Middle Ages, under the influence of the Church of Rome, religious life was gradually externalized. The one-sided emphasis on the Church as an external organization brought with it a similar emphasis on the performance of external rites and ceremonies, to the neglect of the inner disposition of the heart. And this undue attention to mere ritual punctuality reached its culmination in the scholastic period. Moreover, since the authority of the Church and of tradition gradually surpassed, if it did not supersede, that of Scripture, and the Bible was excluded from the hands of the laity, the element of knowledge was reduced to a minimum in the religious life of the people. The conception of religion, which was then present, finds its best expression in Thomas Aquinas' definition of it as "the virtue by which men render to God the required service and honor." Thus religion takes its place among the human virtues, and is practically identified with the single element of *latreia*. Thomas Aquinas distinguishes between the theological virtues, faith, hope, and charity, which have God for their object, and the moral virtues, justice, fortitude, prudence, and temperance, which find their object in the things that lead us to God. He looks upon religion as a part of the virtue of justice, because in it man renders to God what is His due. While this definition does indeed stress the *religio subjectiva*, it contemplates this one-sidedly as service. Religion is not merely service and worship; it is primarily a disposition of the heart, which expresses itself in service and worship. The definition of Thomas Aquinas is even now found in some Roman Catholic works. Spirago voices the same external conception of religion, when he says: "Religion is not a matter of feeling; it is a matter of the will and of action, and consists in following out the principles that God has laid down."[5]

c. *The conception of the Reformers.* The Reformers broke with the externalism of the Church of Rome in general, and also with its external conception of religion. They could not conceive of religion as being merely one of the moral virtues. In fact they did not regard it as a human virtue at all, but rather as spiritual communion with God, coupled with reverential fear, and expressing itself in grateful worship and loving service. Says Calvin: "Such is pure and genuine religion, namely, confidence in God coupled with serious fear—fear, which both includes in it willing reverence, and brings along with it such legitimate worship as is prescribed by the law." Moreover, he adds: "And it ought to be more carefully considered, that all men promiscuously do homage God, but very few reverence Him. On all hands there is abundance of ostentatious ceremonies, but sincerity of heart is rare."[6]

Since the Reformers regarded religion as a conscious and voluntary spiritual relation to God, which expresses itself in life as a whole but particularly in certain acts of worship, they distinguished between *pietas* as the principle and *cultus* as the action of religion. And even this cultus they regarded as two-fold. They drew a clear line of distinction between a *cultus internus*, which manifests itself primarily in faith, hope and love, and a *cultus externus*, which finds expression in the worship of the Church and in a life of service. Further-more they spoke of a *religio subjectiva* and a *religio objectiva*, and indicated the relation between the two. The *religio subjectiva*, which is primarily a disposition of the heart, disturbed, degenerated, and falsified by sin, but restored by the operation of the Holy Spirit, is determined, directed, and fructified by, and passes into action under the influence of, the *religio objectiva*, consisting in the revealed truth of God, in which God Himself determines the adoration, worship, and service that is acceptable to Him. All will-worship, such as the detailed ritualism of the Roman Catholic Church, and the individualism of the Anabaptists, was regarded a contraband.

The question may be raised at this point, what should be regarded as the really characteristic disposition of the soul in religion. There has been no general agreement on this point. It has been found in piety, fear, reverence, faith, a feeling of dependence, and so on; but these are all emotions or affections which are also felt with reference to man. Otto in

---

5. Francis Spirago, *The Catechism Explained* (New York: Benzinger, 1899), 75.
6. *Institutes* 1.2.3.

his psychological study of religion seems to have hit upon the right idea. He feels that, while Schleiermacher suggested an important idea, when he spoke of "a feeling of dependence," yet this can hardly be regarded as an adequate statement of what is felt in religion. He finds something more, for instance, in the words of Abraham, when he undertakes to plead for the men of Sodom: "Behold now, I have taken upon me to speak unto the Lord, which am but dust and ashes" (Gen. 18:27). Says he:

> There you have a self-confessed "feeling of dependence," which is yet at the same time far more, and something other than, *merely* a feeling of dependence. Desiring to give it a name of its own, I propose to call it "creature-consciousness" or "creature-feeling." It is the emotion of a creature, abased and overwhelmed by its own nothingness in contrast to that which is supreme above all creatures.[7]

The really characteristic thing is this, that in religion the absolute majesty and infinite power of God and the utter insignificance and absolute helplessness of man come into consideration. This does not mean, however, that religion is merely a matter of the emotions, nor that man's absolute subjection to the infinite God is simply a necessity imposed on man. The relation of man to God in religion is a conscious and voluntary one, and instead of enslaving man leads him into the enjoyment of the highest liberty. In religion man knows God on the one hand as a holy Power on which he is absolutely dependent, and on the other hand, as the highest Good, the source of all natural and spiritual blessings. In it he entrusts himself voluntarily to God with all his interests for time and eternity, and thus acknowledges his dependence on Him. And it is exactly by this acknowledgment that the moral life of man gains the highest victory through the grace of God and enters upon the enjoyment of true liberty.

d. *The modern conception of religion.* In more recent times the conception of religion handed down by the Reformers, was changed considerably. The Reformers maintained the right of private judgment, and this soon resulted in a rather considerable number of Churches and Confessions. Consequently a tendency manifested itself in course of time to seek the essence of the *religio objectiva* in that which all Churches had in common. Some found this in the truth as it is expressed in the Apostolic Confession. Quite a different note, however, was sounded by Rationalism, which broke with the Word of God and limited religion in the objective sense to the familiar triad of God, virtue, and immortality. Thus the *religio objectiva* was reduced to a minimum. Kant and Schleiermacher went still farther by transferring the center of gravity from the object to the subject, and divorcing the *religio subjectiva* from the *religio objectiva*. The former regarded religion simply as a form of moral action, in which man recognizes his duties as divine commandments. According to him, says Moore, "morality becomes religion when that which the former shows to be the end of man is conceived also to be the end of the supreme law giver, God."[8] And Schleiermacher considered religion to be merely a condition of devout feeling, a feeling of dependence, a "Hinneigung zum Weltall." In the system of Hegel religion becomes a matter of knowledge. He speaks of it as "the knowledge possessed by the finite mind of its nature as absolute mind"; or, regarded from the divine side, as "the divine Spirit's knowledge of itself through the mediation of the finite spirit." This makes God, not only the object, but also the subject of religion. Thus, in

---

7. Rudolf Otto, *The Idea of the Holy* (New York: Oxford University Press, 1923), 9–10.
8. Edward Caldwell Moore, *History of Christian Thought Since Kant* (New York: Scribner, 1922), 49.

the words of van Oosterzee, religion becomes "a play of God with Himself." Ever since the days of Schleiermacher religion has come to be regarded as something purely subjective, and in modern theology it is generally represented as man's search for God, as if it were possible to discover God apart from divine revelation, and as if God did not first have to find man before men could really find Him. In fact the idea of religion as a conscious and voluntary relation of man to his God, a relation determined by God Himself, was gradually lost. It is now often defined without any reference to God whatsoever, as may be seen from the following examples: Religion is "morality touched with emotion" (Matthew Arnold), "a sum of scruples which impede the free exercise of our faculties" (Reinach), "faith in the conservation of values" (Hoeffding), or "the belief that there is an unseen order and that our supreme good lies in harmoniously adjusting ourselves thereto" (James).

e. *The Barthian conception.* Modern theology turned from the objective to the subjective; it relegated the idea of revelation to the background, and brought the idea of religion prominently to the fore. Moreover, it contemplated religion as something native to man, as the highest achievement of man in the life of the human race, and as a prized possession, on the basis of which man can rise to the heights of God. It saw in religion the manifestation of the divine in man, which makes him continuous with God, enables him to scale the heavens, and makes him entirely fit to dwell in the presence of God. Over against this modern subjectivism, Barth again stresses the objective in religion, and centers attention once more on the divine revelation, on the Word of God. He never wearies of dinning it into the ears of the present generation that there is no way from man to God, not even in religion, but only a way from God to man. He points out that the Bible has nothing commendable to say about the kind of religion of which the Modernists boast, but repeatedly spurns and condemns it. It is like the religion of the Pharisees in the days of Jesus, and of the Judaists in the days of Paul. He even shocked and horrified his modernist contemporaries by stigmatizing this religion as the greatest sin against God. According to him the history of religion, which became so prominent during the last decennia, is really the history of what is untrue in religion. "For," says he, "at the moment when religion becomes conscious of religion, when it becomes psychologically and historically conceivable, it falls away from its inner character, from its truth, to idols. Its truth is its other-worldliness, its refusal of the idea of sacredness, its non historicity."[9] It is his desire to break the strangle-hold which Schleiermacher had for so long a time on modern theology. Says he:

> With all due respect for the genius shown in his work, I can *not* consider Schleiermacher a good teacher in the realm of theology because, so far as I can see, he is disastrously dim sighted in regard to the fact that man as man is not only in *need*, but beyond all hope of saving himself; that the whole of so-called religion, and not least the Christian religion, shares in this need; and that one can *not* speak of God simply by speaking of man in a loud voice.[10]

Barth does not regard religion as a possession of man, something which man has, and which is therefore something historical rather than something that comes to man from above. It is not something by which man can improve himself and thus become fit for heaven, since this loses sight of the qualitative difference between this world and the world to come. It is

9. Karl Barth, *The Word of God and the Word of Man* (New York: T. & T. Clark, 1936), 68.
10. Ibid., 195.

not a historical quantum, on the possession of which man can base his hope for the future, but rather an attitude, a frame of mind, a disposition, into which man is brought when he is confronted with the divine revelation. The truly religious man is the man who despairs of himself and of all that is purely human, the man who cries out with Isaiah, "Woe is me! for I am undone," or with Paul, "Wretched man that I am! who shall deliver me out of the body of this death?" In his *Der Roemerbrief* (2nd ed. [München: Christian Kaiser, 1922], 241) Barth expresses himself as follows:

> It (religion) gives him no solution of his life's problems, but rather makes him an insoluble enigma to himself. It is neither his salvation, nor a discovery of it; it is rather the discovery that he is not saved . . . . It is a misfortune which falls with fatal necessity upon some men, and from them is carried to others. It is the misfortune under the weight of which John the Baptist goes into the wilderness to preach repentance and the judgment to come; under the weight of which such a deeply moving long drawn-out sigh as the second Epistle to the Corinthians was put on paper; under the uncanny weight of which a physiognomy like that of Calvin becomes what it finally was.

While all this is by no means a complete statement of what Barth has to say about religion, it does indicate sufficiently what he regards as the essence of it.[11]

B. The Seat of Religion

A brief consideration of the question as to the real seat of religion in the human soul will undoubtedly promote a proper understanding of its essential nature. The question has been raised in the course of history, whether it has its seat in, and therefore operates through, just one of the faculties of the soul—to speak in the language of the old faculty psychology—or occupies a central place in the life of man and functions through all the powers of the soul. It has been erroneously represented as a function, now of this, and then of that, faculty, while it should undoubtedly be regarded as something in which the soul of man as whole, with all its psychical powers, is operative. Its place in life is fundamental and central, and consequently it affects all the manifestations of life. The following views come into consideration here and call for a brief discussion.

1. IT HAS ITS SEAT IN THE INTELLECT. There is an intellectual conception, which seeks the essence of religion in knowledge, and therefore locates its psychical basis in the intellect. It was especially Hegel that sponsored the intellectual view and brought it to the foreground. According to him the whole life of man is merely a process of thought, and religion is simply a part of the process. In the finite spirit of man the Absolute becomes conscious of itself, and this self-consciousness of the Absolute in the human spirit is religion. According to this view religion is neither feeling nor action—though these are not entirely excluded—but essentially knowledge. At the same time it is not the highest form of knowledge, but a knowledge clothed in symbols, from which only philosophy can extract that which is ideal and permanent. Religion never gets beyond the stage of apprehending reality in concrete and imaginative terms, while philosophy makes the attempt to discover the pure idea that

11. Cf. further his *Der Roemerbrief,* 161–62, 241, 252; his *Die christliche Dogmatik im Entwurf,* Erster Band, *Die Lehre vom Worte Gottes,* 1st ed. (München: Chr. Kaiser, 1927), 305–6; Walter Lowrie, *Our Concern with the Theology of Crisis* (Boston: Meador, 1932), 191–201; R. Birch Hoyle, *The Teaching of Karl Barth* (New York: Scribner, 1930), 115.

lies behind the image. This view is certainly a very serious misconception of the essence of religion, since it reduces this to a sort of imperfect philosophy. This virtually means that one's knowledge determines the measure of one's piety. Certainly, there is also knowledge in religion, but it is knowledge of a specific kind; and the attainment of knowledge does not constitute the real end in religion. Science aims at knowledge, but religion seeks comfort, peace, salvation. Moreover, religious knowledge is not purely intellectual, but above all experiential, a knowledge accompanied with emotions and resulting in action. Religion is not merely a matter of the intellect, but also of the will and of the affections. This consideration should also serve as a warning to all those in the Christian Church who speak and act as if true religion were only a matter of a proper conception of the truth, of sound doctrine and of an orthodox profession of the verities of the Christian religion; and as if Christian experience and the Christian life in all its varied manifestations were matters of comparative insignificance. Cold intellectualism would never have made Christianity the power it proved to be in the world.

2. It Has Its Seat in the Will. Some have simply defined religion as moral action and sought its seat in the will. The way for this view was paved by Pelagianism in its various forms, such as Semi-Pelagianism, Arminianism, Socinianism, Deism, and Rationalism, all of which represent Christianity as a *nova lex*, and stress the fact that faith is a new obedience. Doctrine is made subordinate as a means to a higher end, and that end is practical piety. It was especially Kant that gave prominence to this moralistic type of religion. He stressed the fact that the supernatural is beyond the reach of pure reason, and that the great concepts of God, virtue, and immortality, are but the necessary postulates of the practical reason. In this view faith becomes a knowledge resting on practical grounds, and religion is reduced to moral action determined by the categorical imperative. Moral duties are fundamental in the life of man, and religion begins at the point where man recognizes these duties as divine commands, that is, where he comes to the discovery that God requires those duties of him. Thus the intimate relation between religion and morality is indeed maintained, but the order of the two is reversed. Morality loses its foundation in religion, and in turn itself becomes the foundation of religion. Man becomes morally autonomous, and religion loses its objective character. But a morality that is not rooted in religion cannot itself be religious. Moreover, religion is never mere moral action. There is also knowledge in religion, and a far greater measure of knowledge than that for which the system of Kant made allowance. And in addition to that there is in religion also a self-surrender of man to God, by which he is delivered from guilt and pollution, and becomes a participant in all the blessings of salvation as the reward of the faithful. This moralistic conception of religion has become very popular in the American religious world. This is undoubtedly due in part to the influence of Ritschl, who adopted the fundamental principles of Kant and found many followers in our country, but also in part to the practical temper of the American people and to Pragmatism, in which that temper found philosophical expression. There is a one-sided emphasis on religious action in our country. Many concern themselves very little about religious experience, and even less about religious knowledge. 'Service' is the great watchword of the day, and service only is the mark of true Christianity. There is little concern about the question whether this action springs from true religious principles. It is no wonder that the term 'Activism' is used to characterize American Christianity.

3. IT HAS ITS SEAT IN THE FEELINGS. There have been those who defined religion as feeling, especially in mystical and pietistic circles. Romanticism, which was a reaction of the free emotional life against a rather formal and inflexible classicism, was in no small measure conducive to this view. Schleiermacher was its great apostle. According to him religion is essentially a sense of the infinite, a feeling of dependence, not so much on a personal God as on the universe conceived as a unity. Hence he spoke of religion as a "*Hinneigung zum Weltall.*" In religion man feels himself one with the Absolute. Religion is pure feeling, disconnected from thought on the one hand, and from morality or action on the other. It is, to use the words of Edwards, "a warm, intimate, immediate awareness of the Infinite in the finite, the Eternal in the temporal, a sense of dependence on the Whole."[12] Now it is undoubtedly true that feeling has an important place in religion, but it is a mistake to regard it as the exclusive seat of religion. And it is even more incorrect to regard it as the source of religion, as Schleiermacher does. His conception of religion makes it entirely subjective, a product of human factors, and ignores its relation to absolute truth. In human feeling the great question is, whether a sensation or perception is pleasant or unpleasant, and not whether it is true or false; and yet this is the all-important question in religion. This view of religion is just as one-sided as the other two. True religion is not merely, and is not even fundamentally, a matter of feeling, but also of knowledge, and of volition or moral action. Moreover, this conception easily leads to a confusion of religious and aesthetic feeling, and to an identification of religion and art. And also in connection with this philosophical view it is necessary to remark that it is not a mere abstract theory, but one that reverberates in practical life. Many regard religion purely as a matter of emotional enjoyment, good enough for women, but hardly fit for men. According to them it is something apart from the life of man in general. It really means little or nothing for the serious business of life. It has no controlling influence on the thoughts of man, neither does it determine his action in any way. One can be a Christian with his heart (feeling), and a heathen with his head. He can say, "Lord, Lord" in private or public worship, and at the same time refuse to do the Lord's bidding in daily life. This is not only an un-Scriptural, but also an unpsychological view of religion, and one that has done a great deal of harm to the cause of God in the past.

4. IT HAS ITS SEAT IN THE HEART. The only correct view is that religion has its seat in the heart. Some might be inclined to regard this position as identical with the preceding one, since the word 'heart' may denote the seat of the affections and passions in the life of man, in distinction from the intellect and the will. In that case it is really a designation of the emotional nature, that is, of the feelings. It is used in that sense, when it is said that a man's heart is better than his head. But the word 'heart' is also used in a far more general sense, and may denote even the entire personality of man as capable of being influenced or moved. It is so employed, when it is said that a man loves with all his heart. It is in a somewhat related sense, a sense that is derived from Biblical psychology, that the word is used here. The word is not always used in the same sense even in the Bible, but in some cases has a general, and in others a more specific meaning. And when it is said that religion has its seat in the heart, it is employed in its most general sense. To the question what is meant with the 'heart,' we may answer with Laidlaw that the 'heart' in the language of Biblical psychology means "the focus of the personal and moral life. It never denotes the personal

12. D. Miall Edwards, *The Philosophy of Religion* (New York: George H. Doran, 1924), 140.

subject, always the personal organ. All the soul's motions of life proceed from it, and react upon it."[13] It is the central organ of the soul, and has sometimes been called "the workshop of the soul." Religion is rooted in the image of God in man, and that image is central. It reveals itself in the whole man with all his talents and powers. Consequently, man's relation to God is central and involves the whole man. Man must love God with all his heart, and with all his soul, and with all his mind. He must consecrate himself to his God entirely, body and soul, with all his gifts and talents, and in all relations of life. Thus religion embraces the entire man with all his thoughts and feeling and volitions. It has its seat in the heart, where all the faculties of the human soul are seen in their unity. In view of this fact we can readily understand the Scriptural emphasis on the heart as that which we must give unto the Lord (Deut. 30:6; Prov. 23:26; Jer. 24:7; 29:13). Out of the heart are the issues of life (Prov. 4:23). And in religion the heart takes possession of the intellect (Rom. 10:13–14; Heb. 11:6), of the feelings (Pss. 28:7; 30:12), and of the will (Rom. 2:10, 13; Jas. 1:27; 1 John 1:5–7). The whole man is made subservient to God in every sphere of life. "In de religie," says Dr. J. H. Bavinck, "dalen wij af tot het wezen van den mensch. Daar waar de waarlijk religieuze krachten in den mensch tot ontwaking komen hebben wij het meest met hemzelf te doen. Daar klopt de ziel zelve in, de mensch, in de wereld gevangen, staat op en zegt tot zichzelven: ik zal naar mijnen Vader gaan."[14]

C. The Origin of Religion

Different methods have been applied in the study of the origin of religion. During the last century persistent attempts have been made to explain it as a purely natural phenomenon. This was the inevitable result of the application of the philosophy of evolution. Both the historical and the psychological methods were the fruit of this tendency. It may be said that in these naturalism is largely pitted against supernaturalism. In this chapter little more than a bare indication of these methods can be given.

1. THE HISTORICAL METHOD. The historical method aims at discovering the origin of religion by studying the history of mankind, with special attention to its primitive religions. According to Edwards this method seeks to answer such questions as the following: "How did religion first appear in time and place? In what way did the religious nature of man first express itself? What was the most rudimentary form of religion, from which all other forms may be said to have developed?"[15] But these are questions which no historian can answer with any degree of assurance. He cannot go back far enough in history to observe man *in the process of becoming religious*, for man is already religious at the very dawn of history. Moreover, there are no records of the oldest forms of religion, either in written documents or in trustworthy traditions. And if this is so, then the question naturally arises, How can the historian ever find a satisfactory answer to the questions which present themselves here? Edwards says that "by a sympathetic study of the mind and ways of modern savages and of children, and by constructive imagination on the basis of such study, the anthropologist may rebuild for us the religion of the primitive man. His reconstruction must necessarily

---

13. John Laidlaw, *The Bible Doctrine of Man* (Edinburgh: T. & T. Clark, 1895), 225.

14. J. H. Bavinck, *Inleiding in de Zielkunde* (Kampen: J. H. Kok, 1926), 277. Translation: "In religion we descend to the essential being of man. There where the really religious powers of man are awakened we mostly deal with man himself. The soul itself beats in it; man, captive in the world, arises and says to himself: I shall go to my Father."

15. *The Philosophy of Religion*, 34.

be purely hypothetical."[16] All this means that the historian who would investigate the origin of religion must take his stand on pre-historical ground, and that as a result he can only suggest theories, which may be shrewd guesses but do not carry conviction. Moreover, the advocates of the historical method make a fundamental mistake, when they proceed on the assumption, based on the theory of evolution, that the religious life of the most primitive peoples reflects religion in its earliest and original form. This is, of course, merely a bare assumption rather than an established fact, and does not take into account the possibility that the earliest known forms may be corruptions of a far earlier form. It has long been taken for granted that the original form of religion was polytheistic, but the investigations of Lang, Radin, Schmidt, and others have found traces of the recognition of "high gods," also called "creator gods," among peoples of very low culture, and regard these as evidences of an original monotheism.

We shall mention a few of the theories suggested to explain the origin of religion, not because of their inherent value, but mainly to illustrate the insufficiency of this method. Some anthropologists found the historical explanation of religion in *the cunning of priests or the craft of rules*, who exploited the credulity and the fears of the ignorant masses, in order to gain control over them. This view is so superficial that it finds no support in scientific circles today. Others were of the opinion that the higher forms of religion developed out of *fetish-worship*. But while this may explain the origin of certain forms of religion, it does not explain the origin of religion as such, since this fetish-worship is already religion and therefore itself requires explanation. Moreover, wherever it is in vogue, there are generally also manifest traces of an earlier higher form of religion. The fetishes themselves are frequently mere symbols of religious objects. The theories of Tyler and Spencer are closely related. The former is of the opinion that the conception of a soul or otherself, located somewhere in the body and continuing after death, gradually developed among the earliest men; and that *animism* (from *anima*, soul), as the doctrine of souls, expanded in the course of time into the doctrine of spirits, whether gods or devils, as objects of worship. The theory of Spencer is related to that of Tyler but is more specific. It suggests *ancestorism*, the worship of the souls of departed ancestors, as the most fundamental form of religion. According to him primitive peoples ascribed great influence to the spirits of departed ancestors, and consequently acquired the habit of praying, and of offering sacrifices, to them. But these theories are also unsatisfactory. They fail to explain the very forms they assume, the *worship* of the spirits of the departed, and the universal underlying conviction that these spirits are gods highly exalted above men. Moreover, wherever this spirit-worship is found, there is also a separate and distinct worship of the gods. Durkheim criticized these theories of Tyler and Spencer, and offered instead a sociological theory of the origin of religion. He found the origin of religious belief in the idea of a mysterious impersonal force controlling life, a sense of power derived from the authority of society over the individual. The sense of the power of the social group develops into the consciousness of a mysterious power in the world. The totem is the visible emblem of this power; it is the emblem of the tribe; and in worshipping the totem man worships the tribe. Man's real god is society, and the power which he worships is the power of society. But this theory was also severely criticized by other scientists, and that from various points of view. It is no more satisfactory than the others as an explanation of

16. Ibid., 35.

the origin of religion. The theory of naturism was brought into the limelight especially by Pfleiderer. According to this theory religion was originally merely respect for the great and imposing phenomena of nature, in the presence of which man felt himself weak and helpless. This feeling of respect led to the worship, in some cases of these phenomena themselves, and in others of the invisible power(s) revealing itself in them. But the question naturally arises, How did man ever hit upon the idea of *worshipping* nature? May not this nature-worship, which is undoubtedly prevalent in some tribes, be the result of a decline from a purer stage of religious belief and practice? Like all the preceding hypotheses, this theory also fails to offer any explanation whatsoever of religion on its psychological side. In more recent times it was suggested that the origin of religion is connected with the belief in magic. Some think that the former in some way evolved out of the latter, but Frazer, who is the great authority on this subject, claims that the contribution of magic to religion was negative rather than positive. Man tried magic first, but was disappointed, and the despair of magic gave birth to religion. On the whole the result of this historical investigation is very disappointing *as an explanation of the origin of religion.*

2. The Psychological Method. It was felt in the course of time that the historical method had to be supplemented by the psychological, and this is now regarded as the more important of the two. This method raises the question as to the source of religion in man's spiritual nature, not merely in the beginning, but everywhere and always. Edwards puts the questions thus: What are the constant factors in the inner life of man which, in interplay with the environment, generate the attitude which we call religious? What are the impulses, promptings, motives, felt needs, which lead him to apprehend the supernatural and to adjust his life to it? What is there in his mental make-up that accounts for the fact that wherever man is found he has some form or other of religion?"[17] The psychological method seeks to derive religion from certain factors in man, which are not themselves religious, but which by combination and in cooperation with man's natural environment give rise to religion.

It will hardly do to say, as some have done, that man is religious because he has a *religious instinct*, for this supposed instinct is already religious, and is therefore the very thing to be explained. It is equally unsatisfactory to account for religion, as others have done, by holding that man has a *religious faculty*, for there is no proof for the existence of such a faculty, and if there were, this faculty itself would require explanation. Schleiermacher sought the explanation of religion in feeling, more particularly, in a feeling of dependence, but failed to explain how a mere feeling of dependence passed into a religious attitude. Some suggest that the transition may be found in a feeling of awe, which is akin to fear, in the presence of unknown but mighty powers. But fear is not yet religion and does not necessarily lead to worship. Moreover, religious emotion is far too complex to be explained in such a simple way. It includes not only awe, wonder, and admiration, but also gratitude, love, hope, and joy. Kant and Ritschl find the origin of religion in the desire of man to maintain himself as a free moral being over against the physical world. Man is conscious of the fact that he, as a spiritual being, is of far greater value than the whole natural world, and therefore ought to control this. At the same time he cannot help feeling that, as to the physical side of his being, he is simply a part of nature, and that in striving for ethical and spiritual ends he is repeatedly thwarted by natural conditions. This tension results in an attempt on the

17. Ibid., 34.

part of man to realize his destiny by believing and resting in a higher being that controls the natural order and makes it subservient to spiritual ends. On this view God becomes merely a helper in time of need. But seeking help with a higher being is not yet religious adoration. Moreover, this theory does not explain the origin of such religious phenomena as consciousness of guilt, penitence, desire for redemption, prayer for forgiveness, and so on. Neither does it account for the universality of the felt need of God, despite the fact that discoveries and inventions make it increasingly possible for man to maintain himself over against nature. Evolutionists made the attempt to demonstrate the development of religion out of such characteristics as a sense of dependence, fidelity, attachment, and love, as these are present in the animal world. But this attempted explanation can hardly be called success- ful. The so-called "doctrine" of evolution is still a mere hypothesis, and what is said about the inner "soul" life of the animals is largely conjectural. And the assumptions that seem to be warranted on this point still leave the most important elements of religion unexplained. Modern psychologists differ so greatly in their suggested explanations of the origin of reli- gion that we cannot begin to enumerate them. Nor do we consider it necessary to do this.

The psychological method labors under a difficulty similar to that with which the historical method is burdened. It must take its starting point in a hypothetical man, so undeveloped and barbarian that he has not even a spark of religion in him. Religion must be derived from factors that are not themselves religious. But Dr. Bavinck correctly says that such a man is a pure *Gedankending*, an empty abstraction. In reality such men do not exist. Moreover, this method makes religion dependent on an accidental concourse of circumstances. If the complex in which the explanation of religion is sought had been slightly different, religion would never have originated. This, of course, robs religion of its independent significance, of its universality and necessity, and of its incalculable worth. If it is purely accidental, it lacks the firm foundation on which it ought to rest. But this is not all: religion really becomes an absurdity, when it is explained without assuming the existence of a God. According to the psychological method man creates his own God, and determines how that God must be served. The relation between the *religio objectiva* and the *religio subjectiva* is reversed, and the latter becomes the source of the former. In principle this method conflicts with the essence of religion and virtually destroys the phenomenon which it ought to explain.

3. THE THEOLOGICAL METHOD. Speaking of the origin of religion, Edwards says that there are two views "which were once widely prevalent, but which are now obsolete or obsolescent. The first is the view that traced religion back to a primitive or a special Divine revelation."[18] He rejects this view as being, in its usual forms, too intellectual and mechani- cal, pre-scientific and crudely unpsychological. However, it is the Biblical view of the origin of religion, and is far more satisfying than any of the historical and psychological views that were offered to the world. In distinction from these, it alone contains a real explanation of the universal phenomenon of religion. Both the historical and the psychological method proceed on the assumption that religion, like science and art, must be explained in a purely naturalistic way, though some of their protagonists—Edwards being one of these—feel that it may be necessary in the last analysis to appeal to some sort of revelation. The theological method, on the other hand, maintains that religion can only find its explanation in God. Religion, being communion of the soul with God, naturally implies that God exists, that He

18. Ibid., 30.

has revealed Himself, and that He has so constituted man that the latter can know Him, is conscious of kinship with Him, and is even prompted by nature to seek after Him. While the historical and psychological methods are not even able to explain religion in its most primitive forms, the theological method offers us the key to the explanation, not only of the lowest, but also of the highest there is in religion. And of course a real explanation can be satisfied with nothing less than that. It is the only method that is in harmony with the real nature of religion. Scientists do not start out with a normative view of religion, and then undertake to explain the origin of it. They begin with a study of the phenomena of the religious life, and then adapt their views, their definitions, of religion to their findings. This gives rise to a great number of historical definitions which utterly fail to do justice to that which is essential in religion.

On the basis of God's revelation, the theological method posits the following truths:

a. *The existence of God.* If in religion we are concerned with the most intimate relationship between God and man, then it naturally involves the assumption that God exists. And we frankly proceed on the assumption that there is a personal God. It is true, many consider it unscientific to refer anything back to God. They admit that the Hebrews did this, but find the explanation for that in the fact that these people lived in a pre-scientific age. Consequently their explanations may meet with an indulgent smile, but cannot now be taken seriously. Over against this it may be said, however, that it is a poor science that may not rise above the visible and experimental, and is not permitted to take God into account. And this is doubly true of all scientific attempts to explain the origin of religion without any reference to God, for apart from Him religion is an absurdity. Religion is either an illusion, because God does not exist or cannot be known; or it is founded on reality, but then it presupposes the existence and the revelation of God.

b. *The Divine Revelation.* We also proceed on the assumption that God has revealed Himself. The idea of revelation is, in some form or other, found in all religions, and this proves quite sufficiently that it is a necessary corollary of religion. There is no religion in any real sense of the word apart from a divine revelation. If God had not revealed Himself in nature, in providence, and in experience, there would be no religion among the Gentile nations of the world; and there would be no *true religion* in any part of the world today, if God had not enriched man with His special revelation, enbodied in His divine Word, because it is exactly this revelation, as the *religio objectiva*, which determines the worship and service that is acceptable to Him. The *religio subjectiva* owes its inception, its development, and its proper regulation instrumentally to the *religio objectiva*. Divorced from its objective foundation, religion turns into a will-worship that is purely arbitrary.

c. *Man's creation in the image of God.* A third presupposition is that God so constituted man that he has the capacity to understand and to respond to the objective revelation. Religion is founded in the very nature of man, and was not imposed upon him from without in a somewhat mechanical way. It is a mistake to think that man first existed without religion, and was endowed with this later on as a sort of *superadditum*. The very idea of revelation presupposes the existence of a religious consciousness in man. Created in the image of God, man has a natural capacity for receiving and appreciating the self-communication of God. And in virtue of his original endowment man seeks communion with God, though under the influence of sin he now, as long as he is left to his unaided

675

powers, seeks it in the wrong way. It is only under the influence of God's special revelation and of the illumination of the Holy Spirit, that the sinner can, at least in principle, render to God the service that is due to Him.

This view is not open to the criticism voiced by Edwards in the following words: "In its usual forms the doctrine of revelation has explained the origin of religion in far too intellectual and mechanical a fashion, as if religion began with the impartation to man of a set of ideas, ready-made and finished ideas poured into a mind conceived as a kind of empty vessel. This is a crudely unpsychological view."[19] He speaks of the view that must be traced back to a primitive or special revelation as "obsolete or obsolescent," but admits that the "category of revelation may be ultimately necessary in a statement of the objective ground of the validity of religious beliefs and in order to safeguard the place of the divine initiative in the religious life of man." He insists, however, that it should be the idea of a continuous and progressive revelation. But when he says this he has in mind the kind of revelation which, from another point of view, may also be called human discovery.

QUESTIONS FOR FURTHER STUDY: Does the present emphasis on the immanence of God in any way affect the current conceptions of religion? Can the psychology of religion be of great assistance in the study of the essential nature of religion? How does the philosophy of the psychologists affect their investigations in the field of religion? Is it proper to speak of man as having a religious instinct or a religious faculty? Is it correct to say that affections are more fundamental in religion than either the intellect or the will? Why is it wrong to study merely the lowest forms of the religious life of man, in order to explain the origin of religion? Are there conclusive proofs that the higher forms of religion developed out of the lower? What can be said in favor of the idea that the historical process in religion was one of deterioration rather than of development?

REFERENCES: Herman Bavinck, *Gereformeerde Dogmatiek* (Kampen: J. H. Kok, 1906), 1:207–290; Abraham Kuyper, *Encyclopaedie der Heilige Godgeleedheid* (Amsterdam: J. A. Wormser, 1894), 2:291–369; G. Wisse, *Religie en Christendom* (Dordrecht: Van Brummen, 1925), 25–57; J. H. Bavinck, *Inleiding in de Zielkunde* (Kampen: J. H. Kok, 1926), 265–77; English translation, *An Introduction to the Science of Missions* (Philadelphia: Presbyterian and Reformed, 1960); George Galloway. *The Philosophy of Religion* (New York: Scribner, 1914), 54–187; D. Miall Edwards, *The Philosophy of Religion* (New York: George H. Doran, 1924), 29–178; William Kelley Wright, *A Student's Philosophy of Religion* (New York: Macmillan, 1925); James H. Leuba, *A. Psychological Study of Religion* (New York: Macmillan, 1912); Frank B. Jevons, *Introduction to the Study of Comparative Religion* (New York: Macmillan, 1908); Kirkpatrick, *Religion in Human Affairs*, 1–166; J. S. Lidgett, *The Christian Religion* (London, 1907), 138–224; Francis R. Beattie, *Apologetics* (Richmond, VA: Presbyterian Committee of Publication, 1903), 139–247; Alexander B. Bruce, *Apologetics* (New York: Scribner, 1922), 71–163; Francis L. Patton, *Fundamental Christianity* (New York: Macmillan, 1926), 1–208; James Freeman Clarke, *Ten Great Religions* (1871); Menzies, *History of Religion* (New York, 1895); G. Charles Aalders, *De Heilige Schrift en de Verelijkende Godsdienstwetenschap* (Kampen: J. H. Kok, 1919); Auguste Sabatier, *Outlines of a Philosophy of Religion* (New York: G. H. Doran, 1923), 3–117; William A. Brown, *The Essence of Christianity* (New York: Scribner, 1902); James B. Pratt, *The Religious Consciousness* (New York: Macmillan, 1920); Thomas H. Hughes, *The New Psychology and Religious Experience* (New York: Macmillan, 1908); Edward Caldwell Moore, *The Nature of Religion* (New York: Macmillan, 1936).

19. Ibid., 30–31.

III. The *Principium Cognoscendi Externum* (Revelation)

A. Name and Concept of Revelation

1. CONNECTION BETWEEN RELIGION AND REVELATION. The idea of religion naturally leads on to that of revelation as its necessary corollary. In the study of comparative religion it is recognized ever increasingly that all religion is based on revelation of some kind, and that there is no purely "natural," as distinguished from "revealed," religion. Dr. Orr says: "In a wider respect, there is probably no proposition on which the higher religious philosophy of the past hundred years is more agreed than this—that *all religion originates in revelation*."[20] The study of the *History of Religions* yields abundant evidence of the fact that belief in revelation is quite general among the nations of the world, and that every religion of any importance appeals to some form of revelation. Buddhism has sometimes been regarded as an exception to the rule, but in reality it is no exception, for when it became a religion it regarded Buddha as its god. Not only conservative, but also liberal scholars, grant explicitly that the knowledge of God, and therefore also religion, rests on revelation, though their conception of revelation varies a great deal.[21] To quite an extent the term 'natural theology' has fallen into disuse, and even when it is still used, it is often with the distinct understanding that it should not be regarded as the designation of a theology which is the opposite of 'revealed theology.' W. Fulton finds fault with this old mediaeval distinction, which is still tacitly accepted by J. G. Frazer in his Gifford Lectures, and says: "the knowledge of God derived from the consideration of nature, or from the light of reason, is as much entitled to be called revealed knowledge as the knowledge of God mediated through the Scriptures and the Church."[22] John Caird declares: "There is therefore, we repeat, no such thing as a natural religion or religion of reason distinct from revealed religion."[23] McPherson was perfectly justified in saying: "In the idea and fact of religion, therefore, revelation as the operation of God is the necessary correlate of faith as the spiritual act of man."[24] This could not be otherwise, because religion brings man in contact with an invisible Power, inaccessible to human investigation. If man is ever to know and serve God, the latter must reveal Himself. This is all the more true in view of the fact that in religion man is seeking something which he cannot find in science and art, in commerce and industry, in sensual pleasures and worldly riches, namely, redemption from sin and death, and life in communion with God. He can obtain these blessings only if God reveals Himself in relation to man and points out the way of salvation.

2. THE GENERAL IDEA OF REVELATION. The word 'revelation' is derived from the Latin '*revelatio*,' which denotes an unveiling, a revealing. In its active sense it denotes the act of God by which He communicates to man the truth concerning Himself in relation to His creatures, and conveys to him the knowledge of His will: and in the passive sense it is a designation of the resulting product of this activity of God. It should be observed that in theology it never denotes a mere passive, perhaps unconscious, becoming manifest, but always a conscious, voluntary, and intentional deed of God, by which He reveals or communicates divine truth. The idea of revelation assumes (a) that there is a personal God who actively

---

20. James Orr, *Revelation and Inspiration* (New York: Scribner, 1910), 2.
21. Cf. Herman Bavinck, *Gereformeerde Dogmatiek* (Kampen: J. H. Kok, 1906), 1:291ff.
22. James G. Frazer, *Nature and God*, 18.
23. John Caird, *The Fundamental Ideas of Christianity* (Glasgow: J. MacLehose, 1899), 1:23
24. John McPherson, *Christian Dogmatic* (Edinburgh: T. & T. Clark, 1898), 19.

communicates knowledge; (b) that there are truths, facts, and events which would not be known without divine revelation; and (c) that there are rational beings to whom the revelation is made and who are capable of appropriating it. The words more particularly used in Scripture for revelation are the common words for 'disclose,' 'make known,' or 'reveal,' with a deepened meaning as applied to supernatural communications, or the effect of these. In the Old Testament the outstanding word is '*galah*,' the original meaning of which is 'to be naked.' As applied to revelation, it points to the removal of a covering which obstructs the view. There is no noun derived from this verb, which denotes the concept of revelation. The corresponding New Testament term is '*apokalupto*,' which also signifies the removal of a veil or covering, in order that what is back of it or under it may be seen. The noun '*apokalupsis*' denotes an uncovering, a revelation. Another word that is frequently used is '*phaneroo*' (noun, '*phanerosis*'), to make manifest, to expose to view. The classical passage concerning the revelation of God to man is Hebrews 1:1–2: "God, having of old time spoken unto the fathers in the prophets by divers portions and in divers manners, hath at the end of these days spoken to us in his Son."

3. Historical Conceptions of Revelation. The idea of revelation has had a rather checkered history. There was no general agreement as to just what constituted divine revelation. Baillie distinguishes five periods in the history of human thought on this subject, and a brief characterization of these periods will serve to indicate the conflicting opinions that gained currency in the course of time.

a. *In the earliest times.* Primitive peoples found the final court of appeal in all religious matters in the mass of tribal traditions that were handed down conscientiously from one generation to another. They regarded the knowledge of the gods and of divine things, contained in these traditions, as perfectly reliable, because it had been acquired by the inspired men of the race by divination, that is, by signs provided by the gods in the entrails of animals, the flight and cries of birds, the constellations, and so on. These signs were interpreted by those who were skilled in such matters (artificial divination), or by communications which were directly clear to the mind, and which were made during sleep or in a waking state of ecstacy or frenzy (natural divination). The traditions which originated in this fashion were sometimes embodied in sacred books.

b. *In the philosophy of the Greeks.* The Greeks virtually set aside the idea that the gods revealed themselves to man, and substituted for it the idea that man gradually discovered the gods. They did not deny the reality of divination altogether, but did not consider this sufficient to explain the whole body of religious knowledge. In their opinion the truth about the gods was not suddenly acquired in dreams or visions, but by means of calm and persevering thought. The prevailing opinion was that God and nature were one, and that the study of nature would therefore yield religious knowledge. The philosophy of Socrates and Plato represented, at least to a certain extent a protest against this idea. In a measure they rose above the polytheism of their day.

c. *In the Christian era up to the latter half of the seventeenth century.* Under the influence of the Semitic and the Christian religion a distinction was made between a revelation of God in nature and a special revelation, finally embodied in Scripture. This idea of a twofold revelation prevailed for more than sixteen hundred years without being seriously questioned. The only point in dispute was that of the exact line of demarcation. This was not always stated in the same way. Thomas Aquinas held that natural revelation could lead to the knowledge of God as a unity, and furnished an adequate basis for a scientific theology, but that only special revelation could acquaint man with God as triune and as incarnate in Jesus Christ, and conveyed to man a knowledge of the mysteries of faith.

d. *In the latter half of the seventeenth century and the eighteenth century.* During this period there was a growing tendency to emphasize the revelation of God in nature at the expense of His special revelation in Scripture. The idea, fostered especially by Deism and Rationalism, was that the light of nature is quite sufficient for man, and that the Christian revelation really adds nothing to it, but is merely a "republication" of the truths of nature for the benefit of those who cannot discover or reason out things for themselves. By the "light of nature" they meant "partly certain intuitive or self-evident religious beliefs, and partly certain discursive proofs based on scientific and metaphysical speculation."

e. *Since the beginning of the nineteenth century.* Under the influence of Kant, and especially of Schleiermacher, the difference between the light of nature and the light of God's special revelation was supposedly transcended. They are no more regarded in modern liberal theology as two different avenues to the knowledge of God, but only as two distinct ways of conceiving of the only avenue there is. The doctrine of the immanence of God is beginning to play an important part. Both Kant and Schleiermacher are "convinced that the only argument capable of reaching Deity is one that starts not from external, but from human, nature; and they believe, too, that it is in human nature, and not in its abeyance in trance or dream or frenzy, that God characteristically reveals Himself." They represent neither the doctrine of the light of nature nor that of special revelation in its old form, but resolve both in a higher unity. This new representation is in a measure a return to that of Greek philosophy, and it is especially this view of revelation that is strongly opposed by the Theology of Crisis.

4. THE IDEA OF REVELATION IN MODERN THEOLOGY.

a. *The Deistic conception.* Eighteenth century Deism believed in a personal God and in a general revelation in nature and history, but denied the necessity, the possibility, and the reality of a supernatural revelation. It denied the *necessity* of such a revelation in view of the fact that human reason can discover, in the general revelation of God, all that a special revelation might convey to man. The only conceivable advantage of a special revelation is that it might facilitate the acquirement of the necessary knowledge. Lessing, though not himself a Deist, agreed with them in asserting the all-sufficiency of natural revelation. According to him special revelation offers man nothing "worauf die menschliche Vernunft, sich sellbst ueberlassen, nicht auch kommen wuerde; sondern sie gab und gibt ihm die wichtigsten dieser Dinge nur fruehrer." Deism also considered a supernatural revelation as *impossible*, that is, *metaphysically inconceivable and morally unworthy of God.* Such a revelation would imply that the existing world is defective and, consequently, that the Creator, when He called it into being, was wanting, either in the necessary wisdom to plan a better world, or in the requisite power to create a superior world. The one is just as inconceivable as the other, and both involve an unworthy conception of God. Finally, it also boldly denied the *existence* of any supernatural revelation, since it considered such a revelation as absolutely contrary to the fact that God always works according to the established laws of nature. The world is under the control of an iron-clad system of laws, and therefore necessarily excludes the intrusion of supernatural elements. Prophecy and miracles do not prove the existence of a revelation transcending the bounds of reason, since they admit of a natural explanation. The Deist, then, ruled out the supernatural, and retained only the natural revelation of God, and he was followed in that respect by the philosophy of the Enlightenment. Even Kant did not transcend this view, but argued just as Lessing did before him. His religion was a religion within the bounds of reason.[25]

b. *The modern Idealistic conception.* While Deism placed God at a distance from the world and allowed no point of contact, the idealistic philosophy of the beginning of the previous century stressed the immanence of God in the world, and thereby gave rise to a new conception of revelation. That philosophy was essentially pantheistic and therefore excluded revelation in the sense in which it was always understood by the Church. The fundamental principle of Pantheism is that God and the world are one. God has no independent existence apart from the world; neither does the world exist in distinction from God. A distinction is usually made between the monistic, infinite, and self-sufficient ground of all things, and the temporal, finite, and constantly changing phenomena that necessarily flow from it. These phenomenal forms are only modifications of the unknown something that lies back of them, and that has been variously designated as Brahm (in Indian philosophy), Pure Being (Greeks), Substance (Spinoza), or Pure Thought (Hegel). These are all pure abstractions which, as Bavinck remarks, may mean everything or nothing. Opinions differed as to the way in which the world of phenomena comes forth out of this hidden background. The Indian philosophers spoke of *emanation*, the Greeks, of *manifestation*, Spinoza, of *modification*, and Hegel, of a *process of idealistic evolution*. But this process, of whatever kind it may be, does not, strictly speaking, reveal the Absolute; this remains an unknown quantity. Moreover, on this standpoint one can at best speak of a becoming manifest, and not at all of a conscious, voluntary, and active self-communication. And, finally, this pantheistic view knows no object, to which knowledge could be communicated. Subject and object are one. Moore correctly says that, according to Hegel, "God is revealer, recipient, and revelation all in one."[26]

Through Schleiermacher and his followers the one-sided emphasis of the Idealists on the immanence of God also became popular in theological circles, and was often stressed to the point of Pantheism. The whole of nature was not only regarded as a manifestation of the immanent God, but often identified with Him. The divinity of man was emphasized in view of the fact that the most important revelation of God was found in the inner life of man, in which, according to Hegel, the Infinite comes to self-consciousness. And since Christ was regarded as the purest flower of the human race, the highest revelation of God was also found in Him, primarily in His inner life, but secondarily also in His historical appearance. Thus the continuity of God and man was made emphatic, and the idea of the distance separating the two was minimized and often completely ignored. McGiffert, speaking of the influence of the doctrine of immanence on the idea of revelation, says: "As God is immanent in the life of man divine revelation comes from within, not from without. The religious man looks into his own experience for the disclosure of divine truth, and if he also turns to the pages of a sacred book, it is simply because it is a record of the religious experiences of others who have found God in their own souls and have learned from Him there."[27]

---

25. Cf. Edward Caldwell Moore, *History of Christian Thought Since Kant* (New York: Scribner, 1922), 50.
26. Ibid., 69.
27. Arthur McGiffert, *The Rise of Modern Religious Ideas* (New York: Macmillan, 1919), 204–5.

This Idealism also rules out the supernatural revelation of God. It is true that, while Deism denies the supernatural, Idealism in a formal sense denies the natural, since it regards all thoughts, facts, and events in the natural world as the direct products of the immanent God. All that Deism called natural is denominated supernatural by Idealism. In its estimation the supernatural is, in the last analysis, not distinct from the natural, but finds expression in the common laws of nature and in the ordinary course of events. All the natural is supernatural, and all the supernatural is natural. In view of this fact it is no wonder that present day liberalism sometimes speaks of a "natural supernaturalism" and of a "supernatural naturalism." It might seem therefore that, in this idealistic view, they who contend for a supernatural revelation receive even more than they are asking for; but the gain is merely apparent. It only means that all revelation is regarded as supernatural *in origin*, that is, as coming from God. Hence the question remains, whether there is a revelation of God, which transcends all that man can learn by his natural powers, a revelation, which not only flows from a supernatural source, *but is also mediated and brought to man in a supernatural way*. And at this point Idealism, in spite of all its pretended belief in the supernatural, joins Deism in its denial. Over against it, we must emphasize the fact that there is a revelation of God, *which was mediated and brought to man in a supernatural way*.

There is another point that deserves particular attention here, namely, that concerning the content of the divine revelation. The Church has always regarded the revelation of God as a communication of knowledge to man: knowledge of the nature and of the will of God. But in modern liberal theology, which is dominated by Idealism with its doctrine of the divine immanence, we repeatedly meet with the assertion that revelation is not a communication of divine truth, but assumes the form of experience or of a historical person, namely, Jesus Christ. Sometimes it is said that God reveals Himself in acts rather than in words. This is entirely in line with the common view that Christianity is not a doctrine but a life. G. B. Foster says that the Christian concept of revelation differs from that "of the orthodox ecclesiastical dogmatics. The latter rests on the equivalence of *revelatio specialis* with Sacred Scriptures. In consequence of this, revelation is conceived (a) as communication of doctrine; (b) as internally authoritative and statutory; (c) as miraculous in the sense that main stress is placed on the absence of natural mediations; (d) as historyless."[28] According to Gerald Birney Smith "revelation is more and more being considered as exceptional spiritual insight rather than as a non-human communication of truth."[29] Edwards admits that the category of revelation may be ultimately necessary, but "it must be a revelation of God in terms of the whole life of man and not in terms of mere intellectual knowledge or ideas, conveyed to the mind of man from above."[30] Modesty does not permit the modern liberals to pretend that they are in possession of the truth, and therefore they assume the humble attitude of being seekers after truth. At the same time they have enough confidence in man to think that he can discover the truth, and has even discovered God. And even if they do still believe in divine revelation, they must insist that human discovery goes hand in hand with it.

c. *The conception of the Theology of Crisis.* The Theology of Crisis, represented by such men as Karl Barth, Emil Brunner, E. Thurneysen, F. Gogarten, and A. Bultmann, represents in no small measure a reaction against the modern idealistic view of revelation. Several of

28. George B. Foster, *Christianity in Its Modern Expression* (New York: Macmillan, 1921), 49.
29. Gerald Birney Smith, "Revelation," in *A Dictionary of Religion and Ethics* (New York: Macmillan, 1921), 377.
30. D. Miall Edwards, *The Philosophy of Religion* (New York: George H. Doran, 1924), 31.

its interpreters have already suggested that it might appropriately be called "The Theology of the Word of God." This would be quite in harmony with the title of Barth's Prolegomena, *Die Lehre vom Worte Gottes*.[31] In this theology the "infinite qualitative difference between time and eternity" is stressed, and with it as its necessary corollary the discontinuity between God and man. By taking this position it at once cut the ground from under the modern subjective conception of revelation, in which human discovery plays so great a part. It rebukes the pride of those who imagine that they can build a tower high enough to reach heaven, and places great and repeated emphasis on the fact that there is no way from man to God, but only a way from God to man. God is a hidden God, and man in his spiritual blindness can never find Him. It is a God who finds man and thereby puts him in a crisis. Revelation, according to this theology, has no concrete historical existence, not even in the Bible, and therefore it would not be correct to say, This is the Word of God. It would involve bringing the Word of God down to the level of the historical and relative, and putting it in the power of man to make God an object of study, while, as a matter of fact, God is never object, but always subject. In revelation all the emphasis falls on the free act of God. It is God in the act of speaking, and speaking now to this and then to that man, and bringing the word home to the soul in faith.

The Theology of Crisis speaks of a revelation given once for all. And if the question is raised, when this revelation was given, the answer is, in the incarnation, in which God actually came to man to perform a great all-decisive deed in order to constitute afresh our humanity. However, it is not in the historical life of Jesus that the supreme revelation of God was given, as the modern liberals claim, but only in that which is absolutely new in Him, that in which the eternal comes vertically down from above and penetrates into the horizontal line of history. Camfield says in his Barthian study: "Christ makes the entrance into history of something that is new. In that which makes Him Christ, the revelation of God, he is not continuous with history but discontinuous. In Him, history is lifted out of its temporal sequential setting and set in the light of the divine event of revelation."[32] Brunner speaks in a similar vein: "Jesus Christ means eternity in time, the Absolute within relativity, the fulfilment of time, the beginning of that which is above all temporal change, the *aion mellon*, the coming of the word of God and salvation."[33] The revelation of God came to man therefore in a great central fact rather than in a communication of knowledge. In it God approaches man, not with a teaching that must be believed, but with a challenge that must be met, with a behest or a command that must be obeyed. There is no revelation, even in Christ, however, until there is faith. Faith is not, strictly speaking, to be understood as a spiritual activity of man, by which he accepts the divine revelation, for this would make man subject and put him in possession of the revelation. It is rather the negation of man as subject. It is the creative work of God, and particularly of the Holy Spirit, by which, and by which alone, the revelation finally becomes an accomplished fact. Faith is a miracle, the deed and gift of God; it is revelation on its subjective side. Camfield says: "In faith man becomes the subject of a great aggression upon his life, a great approach of God, which disqualifies his consciousness, his thought-world for purposes of revelation."[34] It is true that Barth

---

31. Karl Barth, *Die Lehre vom Worte Gottes: Prolegomena zur christlichen Dogmatik* (München: Chr. Kaiser, 1927).

32. F. W. Camfield, *Revelation and the Holy Spirit* (New York: Scribner, 1934), 96.

33. Emil Brunner, *The Word and the World* (London: Student Christian Movement, 1931), 36.

34. *Revelation and the Holy Spirit*, 103.

sometimes speaks of faith as the response of man to the divine revelation, but this must be understood in the light of the preceding. He says that it is the Word of God in Christ, the revelation therefore, which itself creates the apprehension of it.

Barth also speaks of the Word of God that came to the prophets and the apostles as the original revelation; and the question naturally arises, how this Word is connected with the revelation in Christ. In his work on *God in Action* Barth represents God as having gone forth as a warrior to meet the hosts of sinful men in a terrible contest, and then says: "This event is God's revelation to man; and whoever fails to understand it in this manner does not know what he is saying when he takes the word 'revelation' on his lips."[35] He points out that the great central revelation came in Jesus Christ, and that the men who bore the brunt of the attack were the men of the first line, that is the prophets and the apostles. To them the revelation of God in Christ came first of all; and since there is no revelation apart from the apprehension of it, the revelation that came to them may be called the original revelation.

They in turn bear witness to the revelation in the Bible, so that the Bible may be called a witness to, or a token of, the divine revelation, and can only in so far be called the Word of God. It is not itself the revelation, for this always comes as an act of God. Says Barth: "Holy Scripture as such is not the revelation. And yet Holy Scripture *is* the revelation, if and in so far as *Jesus Christ* speaks to us through the witness of His prophets and apostles."[36] And again:

> The prophetic apostolic Word is the word, the witness, the proclamation and the preaching of Jesus Christ. The promise given to the Church in this word is the promise of God's mercy—expressed in the person of Him who is true God and true man—which takes to itself us who, because of our enmity towards God, could literally never have helped ourselves.[37]

The word of Scripture may and does become for man the Word of God, the revelation, when it comes to him with the creative force that engenders faith. Barth speaks of the Bible as the second, and of the preaching of the Word, as the third, form of the Word of God. Church proclamation is the gospel of Jesus Christ, *preached with the expectation that it will become for some the Word of God*. It becomes this only in those cases in which it is brought home to the heart in faith, and it is recognized as a divine revelation through the operation of the Holy Spirit—a testimony of the Holy Spirit in each particular case.

The characteristic thing of the revelation of God is not that it communicates truth to man, but that it comes to him as a challenge, as a command, as a behest, which calls for obedience on the part of man, an obedience which is again wrought in faith. It is factual rather than verbal, that is, it comes to man as an act rather than as a word or, to speak in the words of Forsyth, who has been called "a Barthian before Barth," as "a word in the form of an act." Moreover, it is not merely something that took place in the past, but is also something actual and contemporaneous. This is correctly stressed by Walter Lowrie in the following words:

> When we say that revelation is not a question of fact but of actuality, we completely alter the statement of the problem as it was conceived by Protestant as well as by Catholic orthodoxy.

35. Karl Barth, *God in Action* (Edinburgh: T. & T. Clark, 1936), 4.
36. *Revelation*, 67.
37. Karl Barth, *The Doctrine of the Word of God* (New York: Scribner, 1936), 121.

The question now is not first of all whether God *spoke*—some time in the past, more or less remote—and by what criterion we can determine that the record of this speech, a word recorded in Holy Scripture, was really a Word of God. Instead it is a question whether God actually speaks, now, at this moment and to *me*. And whether I hear. For *if* I hear a word addressed to me in God's voice, the question cannot arise *how* I am to recognize it as God's Word. And if I do not thus hear it, I can have no interest in asking such a question. The doctrine of the Reformers that the Word of God authenticates itself, or is authenticated to the individual by the testimony of the Holy Ghost, is much more evidently applicable here than in the connection in which they used it. Regarded as *actual* the Word of God is either heard as the Word of God, or it is not heard at all.[38]

5. The Proper Conception of the Nature of Revelation. The existing variety of opinions respecting the idea of revelation naturally gives rise to the question, how we can arrive at a proper conception of revelation. Is it possible to determine precisely what constitutes a genuine divine revelation, and to define it in a way that will meet with general approval? And if it is possible to arrive at a proper conception of revelation, what method should be pursued in quest of it?

a. *The historical method.* Many are of the opinion that the answer to the question under consideration should be sought by the study of the history of religions. The investigator should approach the study of the subject with an unbiased mind, place himself, as it were, outside of all religions and their supposed revelations, take careful notice of the claims which they present, and then finally draw his conclusions. They regard this as the only scientific way in which the essential elements of a divine revelation can be discovered, and in which a unitary view of revelation can be obtained. But this method is bound to disappoint for various reasons. (1) It is pure self-deception to think that anyone can ever take his stand outside of history, study the various beliefs respecting revelation in the different religions of the world without any presuppositions, and thus reach a purely objective conclusion as to its nature. We are all historically conditioned, and cannot possibly take our stand outside of history. Moreover, we cannot set ourselves aside in our investigations, nor the religious content of our consciousness, and usually reach a conclusion which was in principle determined beforehand. (2) On the supposition that one does succeed in approaching one's subject in an entirely unbiased manner, without any presuppositions on the subject, one, for that very reason, enters upon the study of the subject without a standard by which to determine the genuineness of a revelation. Approaching the matter in such a fashion, it is simply impossible to reach a sound judgment. And if on the other hand one comes to the study with a rather definite standard in mind, one is no more unbiased and is guilty of *petitio principii*, a begging of the question. (3) No science, however, objective, will ever be able to remove the differences of opinion respecting the idea of revelation, and to unify all nations and individuals in the deepest convictions of the heart. Only unity of religion can lead to such a spiritual unity. It cannot be said that the study of the history of religions has led to very gratifying results in this field.

b. *The theological method.* In the study and evaluation of the idea of revelation we must have a standard of judgment. And the all-important question is, Whence shall we derive it? Certainly not from philosophy, for this has no right to determine *a priorily* what constitutes

---

38. Walter Lowrie, *Our Concern with the Theology of Crisis* (Boston: Meador, 1932), 154–55.

genuine revelation. The Christian can derive the real concept of revelation only from what he recognizes as the special revelation of God. This means that we must turn to what we consider to be the divine revelation itself, in order to learn what revelation really is. It will of course be said that in following this method of procedure we are also reasoning in a circle, and we frankly admit this; but it is the same kind of circle as that in which the scientist moves when he turns to the earth, in order to learn what really constitutes it. Edwards feels constrained to resort to the same kind of reasoning, when he seeks to determine the norm of religion in a historical way. Says he:

> In pursuing this inquiry it will be difficult for us to avoid reasoning in a circle—i.e., to avoid using our norm to guide us in our description of the common element as well as using the common element to guide us in our search for the norm . . . . It may be doubted whether in our actual reasoning we ever quite avoid the "circles," except when our reasoning is purely formal, sterile, and pedantic.[39]

The situation is this: If no revelation has ever taken place, all efforts to reflect on the nature of it will be in vain; but if there is a revelation, then this itself must shed light on its essential nature and thus supply us with a standard of judgment. The many so-called revelations constitute no reason why the Christian in his scientific study should set aside his convictions respecting the truth of God's special revelation in Scripture. If it did, then the contention of many in our day that the true, the good, and the beautiful are relative concepts, would also have to constrain us to abandon our convictions concerning the laws of logic, of morals, and of aesthetics. It is perfectly true that people of other religions may argue in the same way, but this makes no essential difference. In the last analysis each one standeth and falleth to his own Lord. It is true that this method does not lead to a unitary view of revelation, but neither does any other method. And it is quite possible that we can do more to heal the existing breach by adhering to our Christian faith also in our scientific study than in any other way. Bavinck says that a science which seeks refuge in indifference does not know what to do with religion and revelation, and finally classes both as superstition.

6. DISTINCTIONS APPLIED TO THE IDEA OF REVELATION. In course of time two different distinctions were applied to the idea of revelation. The earliest of these is that between *natural* and *supernatural* revelation. Later on many abandoned this in favor of the distinction between *general* and *special* revelation. Each one of these modes of distinguishing between different kinds of revelation has its own peculiar fitness and describes a real difference between the two in their essential nature, in their comprehensiveness, and in the purpose which they serve.

a. *Natural and supernatural revelation.* Scripture does not make the distinction between natural and supernatural revelation, though it does afford a basis for it. Neander mistakenly regarded *phaneroun* and *apokaluptein* as being respectively designations of natural and supernatural revelation. In a certain sense it may be said that, according to Scripture, all revelation of God is supernatural, since it comes from God and reveals God, who possesses a life distinct from that of nature. As a rule the Bible does not trace the phenomena of nature to secondary causes, but to their primary cause, which is God or the will of God. The distinction was made rather early in history, however, but was not intended as a des-

---

39. *The Philosophy of Religion*, 136–37.

ignation of a two-fold origin of revelation. It was clearly understood that all revelation of God is supernatural in origin, since it comes from God. It served rather to discriminate between two different modes of revelation. Natural revelation is communicated through the media of natural phenomena, while supernatural revelation implies a divine intervention in the natural course of events; it is supernatural not only in origin, but also in mode. The distinction between natural and supernatural revelation became very prominent in the Middle Ages, and occupied an important place in the discussions of the Scholastics. It was especially the problem of the relation between the two that engaged the attention of several of the most prominent Schoolmen. In their minds the question was really that of the relationship between reason and revelation. Some ascribed the primacy to revelation and expressed their conviction in the words "Credo ut intelligam," while others regarded reason as primary. Toward the end of the scholastic period, however, the distinction took the form of an antithesis, particularly in the teachings of Thomas Aquinas. He considered it necessary to keep the truth of philosophy and the truth of revelation each in its own place, and to handle the problems of philosophy as a philosopher, and those of theology, as a theologian. Of the two methods to be followed the one leads to scientific knowledge, and the other to faith, that is, to an acceptance of the truth, which is not based on intellectual insight. He considered it possible to construct a science on the basis of reason, but not on the basis of faith, though he recognized the possibility of proving some of the propositions of faith or revelation by means of rational argumentation. Revelation, it was thought, added to the knowledge obtained by reason specifically the knowledge of the *mysteria* (Trinity, incarnation, etc.), and these, as resting exclusively on authority, remain a matter of faith. This view led to a dualism, involving an over-valuation of natural, and an under-valuation of supernatural, revelation.

The Reformers retained the distinction, but sought to get away from the dualism of Thomas Aquinas. They denied the possibility of arriving at a strictly scientific knowledge of God from natural revelation, and held that through the entrance of sin into the world God's natural revelation was corrupted and obscured, and man's understanding was so darkened that he was unable to read and interpret correctly God's handwriting in nature. As a result of the fall two things became necessary: (1) that in a supernatural revelation God should re-publish, correct, and interpret the truths which man could originally learn from nature; and (2) that He should so illumine man by the operation of the Holy Spirit as to enable him to see God once more in the works of His hands. Consequently natural theology, which had been emphasized by Scholasticism, lost its independence on the basis of reason, and was incorporated in the Christian system of doctrine. This does not mean, however, that the Churches of the Reformation attached little or no value to natural revelation. Both the Lutherans and the Reformed continued to maintain its great significance. Several Reformed scholars defended it against the Socinians, who regarded all knowledge of God as the fruit of an external communication. It may be said that even the Churches of the Reformation did not entirely escape the dualistic representation of the Scholastics. Reformed scholars have sometimes given the impression—and do this occasionally even now—that there is still a sphere, however small, where human reason reigns supreme and does not need the guidance of faith. Under the influence of the Cartesian philosophy, with its emphasis on reason as the source of all knowledge, some of them published separate works on natural theology. In the eighteenth century English

Deism and German Rationalism gave such prominence to the *theologia naturalis* that the *theologia revelata* was made to appear as altogether superfluous. This culminated in the philosophy of Wolff, who considered it possible to prove everything by a rationalistic procedure and a deductive method, and to present it in a clear way. Kant overthrew this position entirely by pointing out that the supersensual and supernatural lies beyond the reach of human reason. Moreover, the history of the study of religions proved that none of these are based on a purely natural revelation.

b. *General and special revelation.* Alongside of the distinction between natural and supernatural revelation, another distinction arose, namely, that between general and special revelation. The former was considered faulty, since it was found that even heathen religions are based, not exclusively on the revelation of God in nature, but in part also on elements of a supernatural revelation, handed down by tradition and to a great extent perverted. The distinction between general and special revelation runs to a certain degree parallel to the preceding one, though it is not entirely the same. It contemplates the extent and purpose of the revelation rather than its origin and mode. There is, however, a certain overlapping. General revelation rests on the basis of creation, is addressed to all intelligent creatures as such, and is therefore accessible to all men; though as the result of sin they are no more able to read and interpret it aright. Special revelation on the other hand rests on the basis of re-creation, is addressed to men *as sinners* with a view to their redemption, and can be properly understood only by the spiritual man. General revelation is not exclusively natural, but also contains supernatural elements; and special revelation also comprises elements which assume a perfectly natural character. The revelation of the covenant of works before the fall was supernatural and at the same time general. And when the sphere of special revelation was limited to Israel, God repeatedly gave supernatural revelations to non-Israelites, and therefore outside of the sphere of special revelation (Gen. 20:40–41; Judg. 7:13; Dan. 2; 5:5). And on the other hand, when God reveals Himself in the history of Israel, in the providential vicissitudes of that ancient people, and in the ritual worship in tabernacle and temple, He is clothing His special revelation in natural forms. Of course, in so far as these elements are now embodied in the inspired Word of God, they come to us as a part of God's supernatural revelation. In view of the preceding it can hardly be said that natural and general revelation on the one hand, and supernatural and special revelation on the other hand, are in all respects identical. Roman Catholics still give preference to the older distinction, while Reformed theologians prefer the later one, though they do not use it exclusively.

B. General Revelation

General revelation, as we know it, does not come to man in a verbal form. It is a revelation in *res* rather than in *verba*. It consists in those active manifestations to the perception and consciousness of man which come to him in the constitution of the human mind, in the whole framework of nature, and in the course of God's providential government. Divine thoughts are embodied in the phenomena of nature, in the human consciousness, and in the facts of experience or history. As was pointed out in the preceding, this general revelation has sometimes also included elements of supernatural revelation. The existence of such a general revelation was taught in Reformed theology from the very beginning. In Calvin's Institutes we read:

That there exists in the human mind, and indeed by natural instinct, some sense of Deity, we hold to be beyond dispute, since God himself, to prevent any man from pretending ignorance, has endued all men with some idea of his Godhead, the memory of which He constantly renews and occasionally enlarges, that all to a man being aware that there is a God, and that He is their Maker, may be condemned by their own conscience when they neither worship him nor consecrate their lives to his service.[40]

In a following chapter he points out that God has not only been pleased "to deposit in our minds the seed of religion of which we have already spoken, but so to manifest his perfections in the whole structure of the universe, and daily place himself in our view, that we cannot open our eyes without being compelled to behold him."[41] Still farther on he speaks of God's revelation in the providential guidance of the world. At the same time he stresses the fact that man does not derive great benefit from this revelation. Says he: "Bright, however, as is the manifestation which God gives both of himself and his immortal kingdom in the mirror of his works, so great is our stupidity, so dull are we in regard to these bright manifestations, that we derive no benefit from them."[42]

In answer to the question by what means God is known to us, the Belgic Confession says: "We know Him by two means: First by the creation, preservation, and government of the universe; which is before our eyes as a most elegant book, wherein all creatures, great and small, are as so many characters leading us to *see clearly the invisible things of God, even His everlasting power and divinity*, as the apostle Paul says (Rom. 1:20). All which things are sufficient to convince men and leave them without excuse." These words contain a clear recognition of the general revelation of God, as it is taught in Scripture, and a statement of its significance for man.[43] A further recognition of this general revelation is found in Article 14, which speaks of the creation of man in the image of God, of his fall in sin, whereby he lost all his excellent gifts, and of the fact that he "retained only small remains thereof, which, however, are sufficient to leave man without excuse."

Liberal theology greatly over-emphasized the general revelation of God. In distinction from Deism, it found this revelation primarily in man and in his religious experiences, and supremely in the man Christ Jesus, in whom the divine element that is in every man, reached its highest manifestation. The Bible, and particularly the New Testament, was regarded merely as a record of the religious experiences of men who enjoyed special privileges in their close contact with Christ, the source of their deep God-consciousness. In this way it was robbed of its supernatural character and made to differ only in degree from other parts of God's general revelation. The self-disclosure of God in human experience became the all-sufficient revelation of God unto salvation. The immanent God is present in every man and saves all those who heed His promptings.

Over against this view the Theology of Crisis once more places all emphasis on special revelation. In fact, Barth goes to the extreme of denying all natural revelation, whether it be in nature round about us, in the human consciousness, or in the course of historical events. That is, he denies that there is in the work of creation a revelation, from which the natural man can learn to know God, and on the basis of which he can construct a theology, and

40. *Institutes* 1.3.1.
41. *Institutes* 1.5.1.
42. *Institutes* 1.5.2.
43. Article 2.

rejects absolutely the *analogia entis* of the Roman Catholic Church. He is willing to admit that the invisible things of God are visible in the world, but only to seeing eyes, and the natural man is blind. There would be a revelation for him in these things, only if he could see them. But the subjective condition of revelation is utterly wanting in his case. There is no point of contact in him, since the image of God was utterly destroyed by sin. Right here an important difference emerges between Barth and Brunner. The latter does believe in natural revelation, and denies that the image of God was utterly defaced, so that not a trace of it is left. He holds that the image of God was utterly destroyed *materially* but not *formally*, and that there is still an *Anknuepfungspunkt* in the natural man to which revelation can link itself. In this respect he certainly comes closer to the historical position of Reformed theology. Barth takes issue with him on this point in his pamphlet entitled *Nein* [München: Christian Kaiser, 1934].[44]

1. THE VALUE AND SIGNIFICANCE OF GENERAL REVELATION. The fact that after the fall the general revelation of God was superseded by a special revelation, is apt to lead to an under-valuation of the former. But we may not neglect the data of Scripture on this point. The Gospel of John speaks of a light that lighteth every man (John 1:9). Paul says that the invisible things of God "since the creation of the world are clearly seen, being perceived through the things that are made, even His everlasting power and divinity; that they may be without excuse," and speaks of the Gentiles as "knowing God" (Rom. 1:20–21). In the following chapter he says that "they show the work of the law written in their hearts, their consciences bearing witness therewith, and their thoughts one with another accusing or else excusing them (Rom. 2:15). God did not leave Himself without a witness among them (Acts 14:17). There is therefore a general revelation of God, for which the natural man has a certain susceptibility, for it renders him without excuse. And while they who enjoy only this general revelation never live up to the light, and many deliberately go contrary to it, there are also some who do by nature the things of the law. In spite of the fact that God has now revealed Himself in a superior manner, His original revelation remains of great importance.

a. *In connection with the Gentile world.* Though there is no purely natural religion, yet the general revelation of God in nature and history furnishes the firm and lasting foundation for the Gentile religions. It is in virtue of this general revelation that even the Gentiles feel themselves to be the offspring of God (Acts 17:28), that they seek God, if haply they might find Him (Acts 17:27), that they see God's everlasting power and divinity (Rom. 1:19–20), and that they do by nature the things of the law (Rom. 2:14). In spite of that fact, however, Scripture does not regard their religions as true religions, differing from the Christian religion only in degree, as so many students of religion do at the present time, but ascribes them to a wilful perversion of the truth. It passes a severe judgment on them, and describes the condition of the Gentile world, devoid of the light of God's special revelation, as one of darkness (Isa. 9:1–2; 60:2; Luke 1:79; Eph. 4:18), ignorance (Acts 17:30; Rom. 1:18–19; 1 Peter 1:14), folly (1 Cor. 1:18ff.; 2:6; 3:19–20), and of sin and unrighteousness (Rom. 1:24–25; 3:9–10). The heathen gods are no gods, but idols which have no real existence and are really lies and vanity (Isa. 41:29; 42:17; Jer. 2:28; Acts 14:15; 19:26; Gal. 4:8; 1 Cor. 8:4); and the

44. Cf. further on this subject: John McConnachie, *The Significance of Karl Barth* (New York: R. R. Smith, 1931), 142–43; Lowrie, *Our Concern with the Theology of Crisis*, 114, 122–23; Hugh R. Mackintosh, *Types of Modern Theology* (London: Nisbet, 1937), 277–78; John Baillie, *Our Knowledge of God* (London: Oxford University Press, 1943), 18–27; Barth, *Der Roemerbrief*, comments on the first chapter; *The Doctrine of the Word of God*, 147.

heathen religions even give evidence of the operation of demoniacal power (Deut. 32:17; 1 Cor. 10:20–21; Rev. 9:20).

But though Scripture passes a severe judgment on the religions of the Gentiles, and represents them as false religions over against Christianity as the only true religion, it also recognizes true elements in them. There is also among the heathen a revelation of God, an illumination of the Logos, and an operation of the Holy Spirit (Gen. 6:3; Job. 32:8; John 1:9; Rom. 1:18ff.; 2:14–15; Acts 14:16–17; 17:22–30). Nevertheless, it beholds in the Gentile world only a caricature of the living original which is seen in Christianity. What is mere appearance in the former, is real in the latter, and what is sought in the former is found in the latter.

Philosophy has not been satisfied with the explanation which Scripture gives of the religions of the Gentiles, and substituted for it another under the influence of the doctrine of evolution. According to this, mankind gradually developed out of an irreligious condition, through the stages of fetishism, animism, nature-worship, and henotheism, into ethical monotheism. But in recent years some renowned scientists, engaged in archaeological researches, such as Langdon, Marston, and Schmidt, declared themselves in favor of an original Monotheism as the primary form of religion.

b. *In connection with the Christian religion.* General revelation also has a certain value for the Christian religion. Not that it provides us with a *religio naturalis*, which is quite sufficient in itself and therefore renders all supernatural revelation superfluous. Such a natural religion does not exist, and is in fact impossible. Neither can it be said that the Christian derives his knowledge of God first of all from general revelation, and then supplements this with the knowledge of Christ. He derives his theological knowledge of God from special revelation only; this is his *principium unicum*. Yet there is a close relation between the two. Special revelation has incorporated, corrected, and interpreted general revelation. And now the Christian theologian takes his stand on the Word of God, and from that point of vantage also contemplates nature and history. He reads God's general revelation with the eye of faith and in the light of God's Word, and for that very reason is able to see God's hand in nature, and His footsteps in history. He sees God in everything round about him, and is thereby led to a proper appreciation of the world. Moreover, general revelation offers the Christian a basis, on which he can meet and argue with unbelievers. The light of the Logos that lighteth every man is also a bond that unites all men. The whole creation testifies with many voices that man is created in the image of God, and therefore cannot find rest except in God. Finally, it is also due to God's general revelation that His special revelation is not, as it were, suspended in the air, but touches the life of the world at every point. It maintains the connection between nature and grace, between the world and the kingdom of God, between the natural and the moral order, between creation and re-creation.

2. THE INSUFFICIENCY OF GENERAL REVELATION. Pelagians taught the sufficiency of general revelation and of the *religio naturalis* founded on it. They spoke of three different ways of salvation, the very names of which point to *autosoterism*, the doctrine that man saves himself. These three ways were called: (a) the *lex naturae*, (b) the *lex Mosis*, and (c) the *lex Christi*. At the time of the Reformation both the Roman Catholics and the Protestants regarded general revelation as insufficient. But in the eighteenth century Deists and Rationalists again followed the Pelagians in their over-estimation of general revelation. And under the influence of Schleiermacher and of the idealistic philosophy of the nineteenth century, with its one-sided emphasis on the immanence of God, many began to regard the revelation

of God in man as quite sufficient for the spiritual needs of man, and this was tantamount to an admission of the sufficiency of general revelation. Over against this modern tendency it is necessary to stress its insufficiency. There are especially three reasons why it cannot be considered adequate.

a. *It does not acquaint man with the only way of salvation.* By general revelation we receive some knowledge of God, of His power, goodness, and wisdom, but we do not learn to know Christ, the highest revelation of God, in His redemptive work and in His transforming power. And yet an experimental knowledge of Him is the only way of salvation (Matt. 11:27; John 14:6; 17:3; Acts 4:2). Since general revelation knows nothing about grace and forgiveness, it is entirely insufficient for sinners. Moreover, while it teaches certain truths, it changes nothing in the sphere of being. And yet it is absolutely necessary that the sinner should be changed, that a new element should be introduced into history, and that a new process should be set in motion, if the divine purpose is to be realized in the life of mankind.

b. *It does not convey to man any absolutely reliable knowledge of God and spiritual things.* The knowledge of God and of spiritual and eternal things derived from general revelation is altogether too uncertain to form a trustworthy basis, on which to build for eternity; and man cannot afford to pin his hopes for the future on uncertainties. The history of philosophy clearly shows that general revelation is no safe and certain guide. Even the best of philosophers did not escape the power of error. And though some rose to a height of knowledge that compels admiration, they proved quite inadequate to present that knowledge in such a form that it became the common property of the masses. As a rule it was of such a nature that only the limited number of intellectuals could really share it. Paul tells us that the world through its wisdom knew not God.

c. *It does not furnish an adequate basis for religion.* The history of religions proves that not a single nation or tribe has been satisfied with a purely natural religion. Through the devastating influence of sin God's revelation in nature was obscured and corrupted, and man was deprived of the ability to read it aright. This noetic effect of sin remains, and general revelation itself makes no provision for its removal, but leaves the spiritual condition of man as it is. Therefore it cannot serve as a basis for true religion. The socalled natural religion of the Deists and the *Vernunftreligion* of Kant are pure abstractions, which never had any real existence. It has become increasingly evident that such a religion does not, and cannot exist. It is generally admitted at present that all religions are positive and appeal to a greater or less degree to a supposed or real positive revelation.

C. Special Revelation

1. THE SCRIPTURAL IDEA OF REVELATION. Alongside of the general revelation in nature and history, we have a special revelation, which is now embodied in Scripture. The Bible is the book of the *revelatio specialis*, and is in the last analysis the only *principium cognoscendi externum* of theology. It is therefore to this source that we also turn for our knowledge of special revelation. Several words are used in Scripture to express the idea of revelation, such as certain forms of the Hebrew words *galah, ra'ah,* and *yada'*, and the Greek words *epiphanein (epiphaneia), emphanizein, gnorizein, deloun, deiknunai, lalein,* and especially *phaneroun* and *apokaluptein*. These words do not denote a passive becoming manifest, but designate a free, conscious, and deliberate act of God, by which He makes Himself and His will known unto man. Barth stresses the fact that God is absolutely free and sovereign in

revealing Himself to man. Scholten had the mistaken notion that *apokaluptein* refers to subjective internal illumination, and *phaneroun*, to objective manifestation or revelation. The former is also used to denote objective revelation (Luke 17:30; Rom. 1:17–18; 8:18; Eph. 3:5; 2 Thess. 2:3, 6, 8; etc.). Neander was equally mistaken, when he regarded *phaneroun* as a designation of God's general revelation in nature, and *apokaluptein* as a denomination of the special revelation of grace. The former is also used of special revelation (John 17:6; Rom. 16:26; Col. 1:26; 1 Tim. 3:16; 2 Tim. 1:10; etc.), and the latter serves, at least in one passage, to denote general revelation (Rom. 1:18).

It is difficult, if not impossible, to make a distinction between the two that will hold in all cases. Etymologically, *apokaluptein* refers to the removal of a covering by which an object was hidden, and phaneroun, to the manifestation or publication of the matter that was hidden or unknown. *Apokalupsis* removes the instrumental cause of concealment, and *phanerosis* makes the matter itself manifest. This also accounts for the fact that phanerosis is always used of objective, and *apokalupsis* of both subjective and objective, revelation; and that *phanerosis* is repeatedly used to denote either general or special revelation, while *apokalupsis* is, with a single exception, always used of special revelation. There is also a characteristic difference between these two words and the words *gnorizein* and *deloun*. The former stress the fact that matters are brought to light, so that they fall under our observation; and the latter indicate that these matters, by virtue of that revelation, now also become the object of our conscious thought.

2. THE MEANS OF SPECIAL REVELATION. The Christian religion is not only like the heathen religions in its appeal to revelation; even in the means of revelation a certain similarity can be seen. In general these can be reduced to three forms.

a. *Theophanies*. Gentile religions are frequently associated with traditions respecting appearances of the gods. The gods are not considered to be like man and to be living with him on a footing of equality, but are nevertheless represented as coming to man occasionally and bestowing rich blessings upon him. In this respect these religions are somewhat like the Christian religion, which also has, not only a God afar off, but also a God at hand. Scripture teaches us that God dwelt among the cherubim in the days of old (Pss. 80:1; 99:1; etc.). His presence was seen in clouds of fire and smoke (Gen. 15:17; Ex. 3:2; 19:9, 16–17; 33:9; Pss. 78:14; 99:7), in stormy winds (Job 38:1; 40:6; Ps. 18:10–16), and in the gentle zephyr (1 Kings 19:12). These appearances were tokens of God's presence, in which He revealed something of His glory. Among the Old Testament appearances that of "the Angel of the Lord" occupies a special place. This Angel was not a mere symbol, nor a created angel, but a personal revelation, an appearance of God among men. On the one hand He is distinguished from God (Ex. 23:20–23; Isa. 63:8–9), but on the other hand He is also identified with Him (Gen. 16:13; 31:11, 13; 32:28; and other passages). The prevailing opinion is that He was the second Person of the Trinity, an opinion that finds support in Malachi 3:1. Theophany reached its highest point in the incarnation of the Son of God, in Jesus Christ, in whom the fulness of the Godhead dwelt bodily (Col. 1:19; 2:9). Through Him and the Spirit which He sent, God's dwelling among men is now a true spiritual reality. The Church is the temple of the Holy Spirit (1 Cor. 3:16; 6:19; Eph. 2:21). But an even fuller revelation of this will follow, when the new Jerusalem descends out of heaven from God and the tabernacle of God is pitched among men (Rev. 21:2–3).

b. *Communications.* In all religions we meet with the idea that the gods reveal their thoughts and will in some way. The usual representation is that they do this by means of natural phenomena, such as the constellation of the stars, the flight of birds, the intestines of sacrificial animals, and so on. But alongside of this there is another, according to which they do it through the mediation of men in the capacity of soothsayers, visionaries, interpreters of dreams, diviners, consulters with familiar spirits and others claiming special powers. In a parallel line of thought Scripture teaches us that God revealed His thoughts and His will in various ways. Sometimes He spoke with an audible voice and in human language (Gen. 2:16; 3:8–19; 4:6–15; 6:13; 9:1, 8, 12; 32:26; Ex. 19:9–10; Deut. 5:4–5; 1 Sam. 3:4). In other cases He adapted Himself to the use of forms that were rather common among the nations, as the lot and Urim and Thummim.[45] The dream was a very common means of revelation (Num. 12:6; Deut. 13:1–6; 1 Sam. 28:6; Joel 2:28), and was used repeatedly in revelations to non-Israelites (Gen. 20:3–6; 31:24; 40:5; 41:1–7; Judg. 7:13; Dan. 2; 4:4ff; Matt. 2:12). A closely related but higher form of revelation was the vision. It was in this form that the Lord often revealed Himself to the prophets. As a rule they did not receive these visions while they were in a state of ecstasy, in which their own mental life was held in abeyance, but in a state in which their intelligence was fully alert. In some cases the visions seem to have been objective, but in others they were clearly subjective, though not the products of their own minds, but of a supernatural factor. In distinction from the true prophets, the false prophets brought messages out of their own hearts. The following are some of the passages that speak of this form of revelation (Isa. 1:1; 2:1; 6:1; Jer. 1:11; Ezek. 8:2; Dan. 7:2, 7; 8:1–2; Amos 7:1; 8:1; 9:1; Zech. 1:8, 18; 2:1; 3:1). Most generally, however, God revealed Himself to the prophets by some inner communication of the truth, of which the method is not designated. After the prophets received their revelations of God, they in turn communicated them to the people, and habitually designate their message to the people as *debhar Yahweh*, the Word of God. In the New Testament Christ appears as the true, the highest, and, in a sense, the only prophet. As the Logos He is the perfect revelation of God, Himself the source of all prophecy, and as the Mediator He receives the fulness of the Spirit in preparation for His prophetic work (John 3:34). He communicated the Spirit to His disciples, not only as the Spirit of regeneration and sanctification, but also as the Spirit of revelation and illumination (Mark 13:11; Luke 12:12; John 14:17; 15:26; 16:13; 20:22; Acts 6:10; 8:29).

c. *Miracles.* Finally, we also find in all religions a belief in the special intervention of the gods in times of need. The practice of magic is widespread, in which men seek to make the divine power subservient to them by the use of mysterious means, such as sacred words, magic formulas, amulets, and so on. Little understood powers of the human soul were often applied to the performance of so-called miracles. At the present day we often see the operation of these occult powers in spiritualism, theosophy, telepathy, and hypnotism. Scripture clearly testifies to the fact that God also revealed Himself in miracles. That miracles are also regarded in Scripture as means of revelation, is evident from the following passages: Deut. 4:32–35; Ps. 106:8; John 2:11; 5:36; 10:37–38; Acts 4:10. Word-and fact-revelation go hand in hand in the Bible, the former explaining the latter, and the latter giving concrete embodiment to the former. It is especially from this point of view that the miracles of Scripture should be studied. They are designated by various names. Sometimes they are called *niphla'oth*,

---

45. Cf. Article on *Lapidaria*, M. Gaster, "Divination (Jewish)," *Encyclopedia of Religion and Ethics* 4:813.

mophthim, Gr. *terata*, names which point to the unusual in the miracle, that which fills men with amazement. Again, they are called *gebhuroth, ma'asim*, Gr. *dunameis*, to indicate that they are revelations of a special power of God. Finally, they are also designated as *'othoth*, Gr. *semeia*, since they are signs of a special presence of God and often symbolize spiritual truths. The miracles are founded in the creation and preservation of all things, which is a perpetual miracle of God. At the same time they are made subservient to the work of redemption. They serve repeatedly to punish the wicked and to help or deliver the people of God. They confirm the words of prophecy and point to the new order that is being established by God. The miracles of Scripture culminated in the incarnation, which is the greatest and most central miracle of all. Christ Himself is the miracle in the most absolute sense of the word. In Him creation is again brought back to its pristine beauty, for His work results in the *apokatastasis* or restoration of all things (Acts 3:21).

3. THE CONTENTS OF SPECIAL REVELATION. It goes without saying that the knowledge of God forms the content of special revelation. In the nature of the case all revelation of God is self-revelation. God reveals Himself in nature and history, but the study of these is not necessarily theology, since both can be studied simply as they are in themselves, apart from their revelational implications. It is only when they are contemplated in relation to God and considered *sub specie aeternitatis*, that they assume the character of a revelation and enable us to know something of God. God is also the content of special revelation. The difference between general and special revelation does not primarily consist in this that the latter, in distinction from the former, is in all its parts and in every way strictly supernatural, but more particularly in this that it is a revelation of the *gratia specialis*, and therefore gives rise to the Christian religion of redemption. It is a revelation of the way of salvation. While general revelation gives prominence to the *theiotes* (Rom. 1:20), the divine greatness of God, His absolute power and infinite wisdom, special revelation reveals with increasing clearness the triune God in His personal distinctions, and the divine economy of redemption. It reveals a God who is on the one hand holy and righteous, but on the other hand also merciful and gracious. Three points deserve particular attention in connection with special revelation.

a. *It is a historical revelation.* The content of special revelation was gradually unfolded in the course of the centuries. This is clearly demonstrated in the *historia revelationis*, sometimes called Biblical Theology. This study shows that special revelation is controlled by a single thought, namely, that God graciously seeks and restores fallen man to His blessed communion. There is a constant coming of God to man in theophany, prophecy, and miracle, and this coming reaches its highest point in the incarnation of the Son of God, which in turn leads to the indwelling of the Holy Spirit in the Church. The divine *telos*, towards which the whole of revelation moves, is described in Revelation 21:3: "Behold, the tabernacle of God is with men, and He shall dwell with them, and they shall be His peoples, and God Himself shall be with them and be their God."

b. *It is both word and fact-revelation.* The Socinians were undoubtedly wrong in holding that special revelation merely serves the purpose of furnishing man complete information respecting God and the duty of man; but Barth is equally wrong when he speaks as if the revelation of God is factual rather then verbal, and consists in redemptive acts rather than in a communication of knowledge. Special revelation does not consist exclusively in word and doctrine, and does not merely address itself to the intellect. This is more clearly understood at present than it was formerly. The Old Testament revelation is not found in

694

the law and the prophets only, but also in theophany and miracle, and in the whole history of Israel. And in the New Testament Christ is not only prophet, but also priest and king. He is not merely the Word, but also the appearance and servant of God. He is the personal revelation of God's righteousness and holiness on the one hand, and of His mercy and grace on the other. And when the apostles enter the world with their message of redemption, not only their words, but also their charismatic gifts and miracles were revelations of God. The view, once widely held, that revelation consists exclusively in a communication of doctrine, was clearly one sided. At present, however, some go to the other extreme, equally one-sided, that revelation consists only in a communication of power and life. It finds expression in the familiar slogan, that "Christianity is not a doctrine, but a life."

c. *It is a soteriological revelation.* Special revelation is a revelation of salvation, and aims at the redemption of the entire man, both in his being and in his consciousness. This must be maintained over against a false intellectualism, which connects salvation with historical faith, as if the only thing that is necessary is the correction of the error, and the removal of the darkness, of the understanding. But in combatting this view, we should not go to the other extreme. Though God's special revelation is thoroughly soteriological, this does not mean that it consists only in a communication of life. The entire man is corrupted by sin and needs redemption. Sin also includes the lie, the power of error, and the darkness of the understanding, and therefore revelation must also be a communication of truth. Not only grace, but also truth came by Jesus Christ (John 1:17). He is the way, because He is the truth and the life (John 14:6).

4. The Purpose of Special Revelation. In speaking of the purpose of revelation we may distinguish between its final end and its proximate aim. The final end can only be found in God. God reveals Himself, in order to rejoice in the manifestation of His virtues, especially as these shine forth in the work of redemption and in redeemed humanity. The proximate aim of revelation, however, is found in the complete renewal of sinners, in order that they may mirror the virtues and perfections of God. If we bear in mind that revelation aims at the renewal of the entire man, we shall realize that it cannot seek the realization of its aim merely by teaching man and enlightening the understanding (Rationalism), or by prompting man to lead a virtuous life (Moralism), or by awakening the religious emotions of man (Mysticism). The purpose of revelation is far more comprehensive than any one of these, and even more inclusive than all of them taken together. It seeks to deliver from the power of sin, of the devil, and of death, the entire man, body and soul, with all his talents and powers, and to renew him spiritually, morally, and ultimately also physically, to the glory of God; and not only the individual man, but mankind as an organic whole; and mankind not apart from the rest of creation, but in connection with that whole creation, of which it forms an organic part. This purpose also determines the limits of special revelation. The historical process of revelation may be said to reach its end in a measure in Christ. Yet it does not end with the ascension of Christ. This is followed by the outpouring of the Holy Spirit and the special operation of gifts and powers under the guidance of the apostolate. Such a continued revelation was necessary, in order to ensure special revelation a permanent place in the midst of the world, and that not only in Scripture, but also in the life of the Church. But after the revelation in Christ, appropriated and made effective in the Church, has thus been introduced into the world, a new dispensation begins. Then special revelation ceases and no new constitutive elements are added. The work of Christ in furnishing the world

with an objective revelation of God is finished. But the redemption wrought by Christ must still be applied, and this requires a constant operation of the Holy Spirit, always in connection with the objective revelation, for the renewal of man in his being and consciousness. By the Spirit of Christ man is led to accept the truth revealed in Scripture, and becomes a new creature in Christ Jesus, making God's revelation the rule of his life, and thus aiming at the glorification of God. This representation is not in harmony with that of the Theology of Crisis, except in that which is said respecting the purpose of revelation. Says Barth:

> The revelation, Jesus Christ, is the work in which God Himself *restores* the shattered *order* of the relation between Himself and man. We must always apprehend the revelation as this work of restoration, whether we seek to apprehend it relatively to its essence or its tokens. A shattered relation between God and man has to be restored; hence the work of God, if it is not to consist in abandoning man or in annihilating what He has created, must consist in revelation.[46]

Neither Barth nor Brunner believe in a completed, and now objectively existing, revelation. They stress the fact that revelation is simply God speaking, and at the same time, creatively, eliciting from man the desired response. The response is wrought in man by the Holy Spirit through the word of revelation itself. Without it there is no revelation, though there are tokens of it. The word of revelation was addressed to prophets and apostles in the days of old, and is still addressed to men up to the present time, and may in that sense be called continuous, or, perhaps better, frequentative. The revelation is never completed and never becomes an object on which man can lay hold. This refusal to ascribe to the divine revelation an objective character seems to be based fundamentally on an idealistic conception of an object. "An object," says Brunner, "is what I can think myself; a subject is what I cannot think. In my thinking it becomes an object."[47] To regard revelation as an object would seem to put man in control of it. The question may be raised, whether on this view God's revelation is not in the last analysis simply equivalent to the calling of God in Christ Jesus, made effective by the Holy Spirit. If this is really what is meant, it naturally follows that is continues up to the present time.

QUESTIONS FOR FURTHER STUDY: What is the relation between religion and revelation? In how far can we maintain that all religion originates in revelation? Why is it better to speak of general and special, than of natural and supernatural, revelation? Can the *necessary* manifestations of God as the ground of all existing things, or as the indwelling spirit in all creation, properly be called revelation? What is included in what is generally called natural revelation? Is this revelation static or progressive? Is there any such thing as a pure mind, which may serve as an undimmed mirror of natural revelation? How do they who apply the doctrine of evolution to the history of revelation conceive of what we call special revelation? How do the Gentiles testify to the need of special revelation? Does the existence of revelation depend on its subjective apprehension?

REFERENCES: Herman Bavinck, *Gereformeerde Dogmatiek* (Kampen: J. H. Kok, 1906), 1:291–369; Abraham Kuyper, *Encyclopaedie der Heilige Godgeleerdheid* (Amsterdam: J. A. Wormser, 1894), 2:205–41; B. B. Warfield, *Revelation and Inspiration* (New York: Oxford University Press, 1927), 3–49; James Orr,

---

46. *Revelation*, 75.
47. Emil Brunner, *The Word and the World* (London: Student Christian Movement, 1931), 24.

Revelation and Inspiration (New York: Scribner, 1910), 1–154; Charles M. Mead, *Supernatural Revelation* (New York: A. D. F. Randolph, 1889), 1–278; George P. Fisher, *Nature and Method of Revelation* (New York: Scribner, 1890), 1–86; George T. Ladd, *The Doctrine of Sacred Scriptures* (New York: Scribner, 1883), 2:302–451; Henry B. Smith, *Introduction to Christian Theology* (New York: A. C. Armstrong, 1882), 84–187; Heinrich Ewald, *Revelation, Its Nature and Record* (Edinburgh: T. & T. Clark, 1884), 1–299; John J. Given, *Revelation, Inspiration, and the Canon* (Edinburgh: T. & T. Clark, 1881), 9–103; James MacGregor, *The Revelation and the Record* (Edinburgh: T. & T. Clark, 1893); Auguste Sabatier, *Outlines of a Philosophy of Religion* (New York: G. H. Doran, 1902?), 32–66; John Baillie, *The Interpretation of Religion* (New York: Scribner, 1928), 71–76, 449–470; idem, *Our Knowledge of God* (London: Oxford University Press, 1943), 3–43; Edgar P. Dickie, *Revelation and Response* (New York: Scribner, 1938); Edwin Lewis, *A Philosophy of the Christian Revelation* (New York: Harper, 1940); F. W. Camfield, *Revelation and the Holy Spirit* (New York: Scribner, 1934) (Barthian); Karl Barth, *The Doctrine of the Word of God* (New York: Scribner, 1936); Emil Brunner, *The Word and the World* (London: Student Christian Movement, 1931); John Baillie and Hugh Martin, eds., *Revelation* (New York: Faber & Faber, 1937); Etienne Gilson, *Reason and Revelation in the Middle Ages* (New York: Scribner, 1938); *The Word of God and the Reformed Faith* (Grand Rapids: Baker, 1943), 51–79, 102–111.

D. Special Revelation and Scripture

1. Historical Views of the Relation Between the Two

a. *In the patristic period.* The Gnostics and Marcion had erroneous views respecting the Bible, but the early Church Fathers regarded it in all its parts as the revealed Word of God. They frankly spoke of it as inspired, but did not yet have a clear conception of its inspiration. Justin and Athenagoras clearly thought of the writers as passive under the divine influence, and compared them to a lyre in the hands of a player. Clement of Alexandria and Tertullian asserted that both the Old and the New Testament were equally inspired, and as such constituted the infallible Word of God. Eusebius regarded it as presumptious to admit the possibility of error in the sacred books; and Augustine said that the apostles wrote what Christ dictated. Chrysostom called the prophets "the mouth of God," and Gregory the Great spoke of the Holy Spirit as the real author of Scripture. All this goes to show that these Church Fathers regarded the Bible as the Word of God, and therefore identified it with the divine revelation.

b. *During the Middle Ages.* The firm belief in the Bible as the Word of God was not shaken during the Middle Ages. At the same time the thought was developed that there is not only a *written*, but also an *oral*, revelation of God. The idea of an apostolic tradition, handed down from generation to generation, gradually gained currency. This tradition was considered necessary for the establishment of the authority of Scripture, and for the determination of its proper meaning. It was said that without the guidance of tradition Scripture could be made to speak in so many discordant ways that its authority was destroyed altogether. The development of this theory was detrimental to the proper conception of Scripture. It is true, the Bible was still regarded as the infallible Word of God, but its authority and proper meaning was made dependent on tradition, and that means, on the Church. The importance ascribed to so-called apostolic tradition even involved a denial of the absolute necessity, the sufficiency, and the perspicuity of the Bible.

c. *At the time of the Reformation.* The Reformers took position over against the Roman Catholic Church on this point. When they spoke of the Word of God, they had the Bible, and the Bible only, in mind. They rejected the authority of what was called apostolic tradition, and acknowledged the Bible only as the final authority and the absolute norm in all matters of faith and conduct. Instead of admitting its dependence on the testimony of the Church, they boldly declared its *autopistia*. Though they did not yet develop the doctrine of inspiration as fully as it was developed by seventeenth century theologians, it is quite evident from their writings that they regarded the whole Bible as the inspired Word of God in the strictest sense of the word. Though it has often been said by liberal theologians that they drew a distinction between the divine revelation and Scripture, and conceived of the former, not as identical with, but as contained in, the former; and though this view is now echoed by the representatives of the Theology of Crisis in a slightly different way, this contention cannot bear close scrutiny. On the basis of their writings it must be maintained that the Reformers identified the divine revelation and Scripture. It was especially in the seventeenth century that the doctrine of the perfections of Scripture was developed.

d. *In modern theology.* Under the influence of Rationalism strong opposition arose to the strict conception of the Bible as the infallible Word of God. Various philosophical and scientific, critical and historical, studies served to undermine the prevalent belief in the supernatural, and therefore also the doctrine of the divine inspiration of Scripture. The old conception of the Bible as the infallible Word of God was brushed aside as untenable, and several other views of it were suggested as alternatives, but not a single one of them has been able to entrench itself in the hearts and minds of Christian people in general. For a time the idea was rather popular that the Bible is partly human and partly divine, and it became rather popular to say that the divine revelation is *contained* in the Bible, and that parts of the Bible are therefore inspired. But it soon became evident that it was impossible to say where the divine ended and the human began, or what parts of the Bible were, and what parts were not, inspired. Others discarded the idea of inspiration and simply regarded the Bible as the human record of a divine revelation. Idealistic philosophy, with its doctrine of the divine immanence, and the subjectivism of Schleiermacher, led to a new conception of both revelation and inspiration. Inspiration came to be regarded as a special divine illumination, differing only in degree from the spiritual illumination of Christians in general; and revelation, as the resulting heightened insight into the nature of things. This in course of time led on to a certain identification of revelation and human discovery. On this view the Bible becomes a record of rather exceptional human experiences—a record which is purely human. The Theology of Crisis is an attempt to restore the idea of revelation as a supernatural act on the part of God to its rightful place. But it also disowns the doctrine of the infallible inspiration of Scripture, and therefore does not identify the revelation of God and the Bible. The Bible is merely a human witness to the divine revelation, which may, just because it witnesses to the revelation, be called the Word of God in a secondary sense.[48]

2. THE REFORMED CONCEPTION OF THE RELATION BETWEEN THE TWO. According to the great Reformers of the sixteenth century the special revelation of God was given permanent form in Scripture. This idea is not in itself anything out of the ordinary. Among all cultured nations we find magical formulas, liturgical texts, ritual tracts, ceremonial laws, and historical and mythological literature, connected with their religious life. Several religions have holy books, to which divine authority is ascribed, and which serve as rules of doctrine and practice. Every prominent religion possesses a dogma which is expressed in language and

---

48. *The Word of God and the Reformed Faith* (Grand Rapids: Baker, 1943), 51–79; 102–111.

assumes a permanent form in writing. Christianity forms no exception to the rule in that respect. It was of the utmost importance for the special revelation of God that it should be embodied in writing, because it was given in the course of many centuries and comprises deeds and events that are not repeated, but belong to the past, so that the knowledge of them would soon be lost in oblivion, if they were not recorded and thus preserved for posterity. And it was important that this knowledge should not be lost, since the divine revelation contains eternal truths, that are pregnant with meaning for all times, for all peoples, and under all circumstances. Therefore God provided for its inscripturation, so that His revelation now comes to us, not in the form of deeds and events, but as a description of these. In order to guard it against volatilization, corruption and falsification, He gave it permanent form in writing. From this it follows that there is a very close connection between special revelation and Scripture.

It should be pointed out, however, that the word 'revelation' is not always used in the same sense. It may serve to denote the direct, supernatural communications of God to man, which were far more frequent in the old dispensation than in the new, and culminated in the Word made flesh. If the word 'revelation' be understood in that sense, then it cannot be said that special revelation is identical with the Bible, but only that it is contained or recorded in the Bible. Scripture contains a great deal that was not so communicated by God. It should be borne in mind, however, that this does not justify the distinction, sometimes made in modern theology, between the Word of God as divine and its record as human. Neither does it warrant the unqualified statement that the Bible *is not*, but merely *contains* the Word of God. The terms 'Word of God' and 'special revelation' are also used in a sense in which they are identical with 'Scripture.' In most cases revelation or the direct self-communication of God preceded its inscripturation. The prophets usually received their communications some time before they committed them to writing (Jer. 25:13; 30:1–2; 36:2). This is true of the apostles as well. When they received the highest revelation of God in Jesus Christ, they did not at once record it for future generations, but only after the lapse of several years, and even then they did not record everything that was revealed (John 20:30; 21:25). It may be that some things were revealed to them while they were writing. Moreover, in some cases men who received no direct revelations themselves yet recorded them for the future. In view of all this it may be said that there is a sense in which we must distinguish between special revelation and Scripture.

But the term 'revelation' may also be used in a broader sense. It can be applied to that whole complex of redemptive truths and facts, which is recorded in Scripture and has its guarantee as a divine revelation in the fact that the whole of Scripture is infallibly inspired by the Holy Spirit. In that sense the entire Bible from Genesis to Revelation, and it only, is for us God's special revelation. It is only through Scripture that we receive any knowledge of the direct revelations of God in the past. We know absolutely nothing about God's revelations among Israel through the prophets and finally in Christ, except from the Bible. If this is set aside, we abandon the whole of God's special revelation, including that in Christ. It is only through the word of the apostles that we can have communion with Christ. Consequently, it is unthinkable that God gave a special revelation and then took no measures to preserve it inviolate for coming generations. Scripture derives its significance exactly from the fact that it is the book of revelation. By means of Scripture God constantly carries His revelation into the world and makes its content effective in the thought and life of man. It is not merely a narrative of what happened years ago, but the perennial speech of God to man. Revelation lives on in Scripture and brings even now, just as it did when it was given, light, life, and holiness. By means of that revelation God continues to renew sinners in their being and consciousness. Scripture is the Holy Spirit's chief instrument for the extension and guidance of the Church, for the perfecting of the saints, and for the building up of the body of Jesus Christ. It forms a lasting bond of union between heaven and earth, between Christ and His Church, and between God and His people. In it we hear ever anew the voice of God, for it remains the inspired Word of God. And it will not have served its purpose fully until the new creation is completed, when all the children of God will be inspired and will all be fully taught of the Lord.

IV. The Inspiration of Scripture

A. *The Doctrine of Inspiration in History*

Revelation and inspiration stand in the closest possible relation to each other. As far as special revelation is concerned, it may be said that the one is inconceivable without the other. Peter tells us that "no prophecy ever came by the will of man: but men spake from God, being moved by the Holy Spirit" (2 Peter 1:21). The recognition of the Bible as the special revelation of God depends on the conviction that its authors were inspired by the Holy Spirit. But, however closely related the two may be, they should not be identified. Dr. Hodge correctly calls attention to the fact that they differ both as to their object and in their effects.

> The object or design of revelation is the communication of knowledge. The object or design of inspiration is to secure infallibility in teaching . . . . The effect of revelation was to render its recipient wiser. The effect of inspiration was to preserve him from error in teaching.[49]

The doctrine of inspiration was not always held in the same form, and therefore a brief statement of its history would seem to be desirable.

1. BEFORE THE REFORMATION. In a sense it may be said that this doctrine had no history before the Reformation, because it remained essentially the same from the first century down to the sixteenth. Nevertheless it will serve a useful purpose to call specific attention to the fact that throughout all these centuries the Church stood firm in the conviction that the Bible is the inspired, and therefore infallible, Word of God. It is a well known fact that the Jews held the strictest view of inspiration. They regarded first of all the Law as divinely and infallibly inspired, and therefore ascribed to it absolute divine authority, and afterwards ascribed the same inviolable character and authority to the Prophets and the Holy Writings. This view passed right over into the Christian Church. Even liberal scholars, who reject that strict view of inspiration, feel constrained to admit that Jesus and the New Testament writers also held the same view. The early Church Fathers had the same exalted view of the Bible, as appears abundantly from their writings. Sanday admits that from the very first they are found using expressions, which even point to verbal inspiration.[50] Some of their expressions certainly seem to suggest that the writers of the books of the Bible were passive under the influence of the Holy Spirit, and therefore point to a mechanical conception of

---

49. Charles Hodge, *Systematic Theology*, 1:155.
50. William Sanday, *Inspiration* (London: Longmans, Green, 1896), 34.

inspiration. But Dr. Orr calls attention to the fact that the general trend of their teaching shows that it was not their intention to teach a doctrine of inspiration, which involved the suppression of the human consciousness, that Origen contended against such a view, and that Montanism, which held it, was condemned by the Church.[51] Between the time of the early Church Fathers and that of the Reformation the prevailing opinion in the Church did not differ essentially from that previously held. The Scholastics shared the common conviction of the Church, and merely tried to give a more precise definition of some of the details of the doctrine of inspiration. It must be admitted, however, that equal inspiration was ascribed to apostolic tradition, and that in practice this tended to weaken the consciousness of the absolute authority of the written Word of God. Moreover, there were some Mystics, who gloried in a special illumination and in revelations of the divine presence within, and manifested a tendency to undervalue the supernatural inspiration of the writers of the Bible, and to reduce it to the level of that gracious inner teaching which all Christians alike enjoyed. But their subjectivism did not seriously affect the view that was held in the Church at large.

2. AFTER THE REFORMATION. It has become quite the vogue with those who are opposed to what Dr. Warfield calls "the church-doctrine of inspiration," to saddle their own loose views on the great Reformers of the sixteenth century. They find in the works of Luther and Calvin a few expressions which seem to reflect a certain freedom in dealing with canonical questions, and then hastily conclude from this that these great men did not share the current doctrine of inspiration. But why should they rely on mere inferences, when these great Reformers use several expressions and make many plain statements, which are clearly indicative of the fact that they held the strictest view of inspiration, and that this view was not at all, as the opponents claim, an invention of Protestant Scholasticism in the seventeenth century. They even speak of the Holy Spirit as the author of every part of Scripture, and of the human writers as having written what was dictated to them. Such expressions had been common from the earliest times. At the same time it is quite evident from their teachings in general that inspiration, as they conceived of it, did not suppress the individuality and the intellectual activity of the human authors. Seeberg speaks of Calvin as the author of the strict, seventeenth century view of inspiration. The only difference on this point between the Reformers and the following generation of theologians is, that the latter made the subject of inspiration an object of special study and worked it out in details, and that some manifested a tendency to "reduce the inspired man, when under the influence of the Spirit, to the level of an unconscious and unintelligent instrument" (Bannerman). This tendency also found expression in one of the Confessions, namely, the *Formula Consensus Helvetica*, drawn up in 1675 in opposition to the loose views of the school of Saumur. This Confession never found wide acceptance as an ecclesiastical standard.

At a later date, however, when Rationalism made its influence felt, Le Clerc (1657–1736) impugned the strict infallibility of Scripture and asserted the existence of errors in the record, and many of the apologists, who took up the defense, admitted his contentions and felt constrained to have recourse to the theory of an inspiration, differing in degrees in various parts of the Bible, and thus allowing for imperfections and errors in some portions of Scripture. This was a theory that allowed of various modifications. One of these, which enjoyed considerable popularity for a while, was the theory of a *partial* inspiration, that is,

---

51. James Orr, *Revelation and Inspiration* (New York: Scribner, 1910), 207.

an inspiration limited to parts of the Bible, but it soon became evident that it was impossible to reach a unanimous opinion as to the exact extent of inspiration. Since this view will be discussed later on, it is not necessary to enlarge upon it here.

A radically different theory owes its origin especially to Schleiermacher. In distinction from the theory of partial inspiration, which at least ascribed strict inspiration to some parts of Scripture, it altered the character of inspiration altogether by excluding the supernatural element. It held inspiration to be (to express it in the words of Bannerman) "the natural, or at most the gracious, agency of God illuminating the rational or the spiritual consciousness of a man, so that out of the fulness of his own Christian understanding and feelings he may speak or write the product of his own religious life and beliefs."[52] Here inspiration is changed to a divine illumination, differing only in degree from that of Christians in general. The special, supernatural and miraculous operation of the Holy Spirit, is superseded by one of His ordinary operations in the lives of believers. Many of the works on inspiration, written since the days of Schleiermacher are simply variations on this general theme. Some, such as Wegscheider and Parker, went even farther, and spoke of a purely natural operation, common to all men. Such works as those of Lee, Bannerman, McIntosh, Patton, Orr, Warfield, and others naturally form exceptions to the rule. Sad to say, Barth and Brunner also reject the doctrine of the infallible inspiration of Scripture, and regard it as a product of Protestant Scholasticism. Their own views still await clarification.

B. Scriptural Proof for the Inspiration of the Bible

The question arises, whether the record of the divine revelation, as well as the revelation itself, is from God, or whether God, after giving the revelation of redemption, simply left it to man to record this as best he could. Have we in Scripture a merely human or a divinely inspired record? And if God's special revelation was given by inspiration, how far does that inspiration extend? In seeking an answer to these and other similar questions, we turn to Scripture itself. This will not seem strange in view of the fact that for us the Bible is the only *principium cognoscendi externum* of theology. Just as the Bible contains a doctrine of God and man, of Christ and redemption, it also offers us a doctrine concerning itself; and we receive this in faith on the basis of the divine testimony. In saying this, we do not mean to intimate that Scripture contains a clear-cut and well formulated dogma of inspiration, but only that it supplies all the data that are necessary for the construction of such a dogma. We shall consider the Scriptural proof for the inspiration of the authors of Scripture under two headings: (1) proof for their inspiration considered apart from their writing; and (2) proof for their inspiration in writing the books of the Bible.

1. PROOFS FOR THE INSPIRATION OF THE SECONDARY AUTHORS OF SCRIPTURE CONSIDERD APART FROM THEIR WRITING. It may be well to point out first of all that the secondary authors of Scripture were inspired as the organs of divine revelation, even apart from their activity in recording the special revelation of God. Then it will appear that inspiration was deemed necessary for the immediate purpose of revelation. We derive our proof in this respect primarily from prophecy, or what may be called the prophetic inspiration, but also in part from the apostolic inspiration.

52. James Bannerman, *Inspiration of the Scriptures* (Edinburgh: T. & T. Clark, 1865), 142.

a. *Prophetic inspiration.* Several points deserve attention here: (1) *The nature of a prophet.* There are two classical passages in the Bible, which shed light on the Biblical conception of a prophet, namely, Exodus 7:1 and Deuteronomy 18:18. According to these passages a prophet is simply the mouthpiece of God. He receives a message from God, and is in duty bound to transmit it to the people. In his capacity as a prophet of the Lord, he may not bring a message of his own, but only the message which he receives from the Lord. It is not left to his own discretion to determine what he shall say; this is determined for him by his Sender. For the message divinely entrusted to him He may not substitute another. (2) *The consciousness of the prophets.* The prophets of Israel knew that they were called of the Lord at a certain moment, sometimes contrary to their own desire (Ex. 3:1–4:17; 1 Sam. 3; Isa. 6; Jer. 1; Ezek. 1–3). They were conscious of the fact that the Lord had spoken to them, and in some cases even knew that He had put His words into their mouth (Num. 23:5; Deut. 18:18; Jer. 1:9; 5:14). This consciousness was so strong that they even designated the time and place when and where the Lord spoke to them, and distinguished between times in which He did, and times in which He did not, speak to them (Isa. 16:13–14; Jer. 3:6; 13:3; 26:1; 27:1; 33:1; Ezek. 3:16; 8:1; 12:8). Hence they also made a sharp distinction between what the Lord revealed to them and what arose out of the depths of their own hearts (Num. 16:28; 24:13; 1 Kings 12:33; Neh. 6:8). They accused the false prophets of speaking out of their own hearts, without being sent of the Lord (Jer. 14:14; 23:16, 26; 29:9; Ezek. 13:2–3, 6). When they addressed the people, they knew that they were not bringing their own word, but the word of the Lord, and this because the Lord demanded it of them (Jer. 20:7–9; Ezek. 3:4–11; Amos 3:8; Jonah 1:2). (3) *The prophetic formulae.* The prophetic formulae were also very significant in this respect. They were in themselves clear indications of the fact that the prophets were conscious of bringing a message that was inspired by the Lord. There is quite a variety of these formulae, but they all agree in ascribing the initiative to the Lord. The faithful watchmen on the walls of Zion were deeply impressed with the fact that they received the word, with which they came to the people, at the mouth of the Lord. They were ever mindful of the word of the Lord to Ezekiel: "Son of man, I have made thee a watchman unto the house of Israel: therefore hear the word at my mouth, and give them warning from me" (Ezek. 3:17). Moreover, they clearly wanted the people to understand this. Such formulae as the following testify to this: "Thus saith the Lord," "Hear the word of the Lord," "The word that came to . . . from the Lord," "Thus the Lord showed me," "The burden of the word of the Lord." (4) *Failure to understand their own message.* The fact that the prophets sometimes failed to understand the message which they brought to the people, also goes to show that it came to them from without, and did not arise out of their own consciousness. Daniel brought a message which was entrusted to him, but declares that he did not understand it (Dan. 12:8–9). Zechariah saw several visions, which contained messages for the people, but needed the help of an angel to interpret these for him (Zech. 1:9; 2:3; 4:4). And Peter informs us that the prophets, having brought their message respecting the sufferings and the following glory of Christ, often searched into the details of it, in order that they might understand it more clearly (1 Peter 1:10–11).

b. *Apostolic inspiration.* The operation of the Holy Spirit after the day of Pentecost differed from that which the prophets in their official capacity enjoyed. The Holy Spirit came upon the prophets as a supernatural power and worked upon them from without. His action on them was frequently repeated, but was not continuous. The distinction between His activity and the mental activity of the prophets themselves was made to stand out rather clearly. On the day of Pentecost, however, He took up His abode in the hearts of the apostles and began to work upon them from within. Since He made their hearts His permanent abode, His action on them was no more intermittent but continuous, but even in their case the supernatural work of inspiration was limited to those occasions on which they served as organs of revelation. But because of the more inward character of all the Spirit's work, the distinction between His ordinary and His extraordinary work was not so perceptible. The supernatural does not stand out as clearly in the case of the apostles, as it did in the case of the prophets. Notwithstanding this fact, however, the New Testament contains several significant indications of the fact that the apostles were inspired in their positive oral teachings. Christ solemnly promised them the Holy Spirit in their teaching and preaching (Matt. 10:19–20; Mark 13:11; Luke 12:11–12; 21:14–15; John 14:26; 15:26; 16:13). In the Acts of the Apostles we are told repeatedly that they taught "being full of," or "filled with," the Holy Spirit. Moreover, it appears from the Epistles that in teaching the churches they conceived of their word as being in very deed the word of God, and therefore as authoritative (1 Cor. 2:4, 13; 1 Thess. 2:13).

2. PROOFS FOR THE INSPIRATION OF THE SECONDARY AUTHORS IN WRITING THE BOOKS OF THE BIBLE. The guidance of the Holy Spirit was not limited to the spoken word, but also extended to the written word. If God deemed it necessary to guide prophets and apostles in their oral teaching, which was naturally limited to their contemporaries, it would seem to follow as a matter of course that He would consider it far more important to ensure them of divine guidance in committing His revelation to writing for all following generations. It is only in its written form that the Word of God is known in the world, and that His revelation is the continuous speech of God to man. And there are several indications in the New Testament that He did so guide the apostles. These are contained in certain general phenomena, and in some direct assertions.

a. *Certain general phenomena.* (1) *Commands to write the word of the Lord.* Repeatedly the writers of the Old Testament are explicitly commanded to write what the Lord reveals unto them (Ex. 17:14; 34:27; Num. 33:2; Isa. 8:1; 30:8; Jer. 25:13; 30:2; 36:2, 27–32; Ezek. 24:1–2; Dan. 12:4; Hab. 2:2). Some prophecies were evidently not intended to be spoken, but to be written for the careful consideration of the people (Jer. 29; 36:4ff., 27ff.; Ezek. 26–27; 31; 32:39). In such cases the prophetic formulae naturally also refer to the written word. (2) *Suppression of the human factor.* In many of the prophecies the divine factor, as it were, overpowers the human. The prophetic word begins by speaking of God in the third person, and then, without any indication of a transition, continues in the first person. The opening words are words of the prophet, and then all at once, without any preparation of the reader for a change, the human author simply disappears from view, and the divine author speaks apparently without any intermediary (Isa. 10:12; 19:1–2; Hos. 4:1–6; 6:1–4; Mic. 1:3–6; Zech. 9:4–6; 12:8–9). Thus the word of the prophet passes right into that of the Lord without any formal transition. The two are simply fused, and thus prove to be one. Some passages clearly indicate that the word of the Lord and that of the prophet are equally authoritative (Jer. 25:3; 36:10–11). Isaiah even speaks of his own written prophecies as "the book of Jehovah" (Isa. 34:16). (3) *The designation of the Old Testament as he graphe or hai graphai.* In the New Testament we find that the Lord and the apostles, in their appeal to the Old Testament, frequently speak of it as *he graphe* (a term

704

sometimes applied to a single passage of Scripture [Mark 12:10; Luke 4:21; John 19:36]), or as *hai graphai* in view of the fact that it consists of several parts (Luke 24:27; Rom. 1:2). Cf. also *ta hiera grammata* in 2 Timothy 3:15. They evidently regarded this collection as authoritative. An appeal to it was equivalent to "God says," as appears from the fact that the formula *he graphe legein* (the Scripture says) is used interchangeably with others, which clearly indicate that what is quoted is the Word of God, and from cases in which the word quoted is really spoken by God in the Old Testament (Rom. 9:15–17; Gal. 3:8). (4) *Formulae of quotation.* The Lord and His apostles do not always use the same formula in quoting the Old Testament. Sometimes they simply say, "It is written" (Matt. 4:4; John 6:45), or "Scripture says" (Rom. 4:3; Gal. 4:30). In some cases they mention the human author (Matt. 15:7; 24:15), but frequently they name the primary author, that is, God or the Holy Spirit (Matt. 15:4; Heb. 1:5ff.; 3:7). Paul in some cases personifies Scripture, so that it is represented as identical with God (Rom. 9:17; Gal. 3:8, 22; 4:30; cf. also Rom. 4:3; 10:11; 11:2; 1 Tim. 5:18). The writer of the Epistle to the Hebrews usually names the primary author (Heb. 1:5ff.; 3:7; 4:3; 5:6; 7:21; 8:5, 8; 10:15–16).

b. *Direct assertions.* There are several passages in which the divine authority of the Old Testament is clearly asserted, Matt. 5:17; Luke 16:17, 29, 31; John 10:35; Rom. 15:4; 1 Peter 1:10–12; 2 Peter 1:19, 21. This is true especially of the *locus classicus*, 2 Timothy 3:16: "All (every) Scripture is given by inspiration of God, and is profitable for teaching, for reproof, for correction, for instruction which is in righteousness." We read here in the original: *Pasa graphe theopneustos kai ophelimos pros didaskalian*, etc. This passage has been interpreted in various ways, and that not infrequently with the scarcely concealed intention of destroying its evidential value. On the basis of transcriptional evidence some proposed to leave out the word *kai*, but the weight of evidence clearly favors its retention. Because *pasa* stands without the article, some insist on translating *pasa graphe* by "every Scripture"; but such passages as Matt. 2:3; Acts 2:36; Eph. 2:21; 4:16; 1 Peter 1:15, bear evidence of the fact that the word *pas* may mean "all" in the New Testament even when the article is wanting. Materially, it makes very little difference, whether we read "all Scripture," or "every Scripture," since the expression certainly refers back to *ta hiera grammata* in the 15th verse, and this serves to designate the Old Testament writings. There is also a strong tendency (cf. even the American Revised Version) to regard *theopneustos*, not as the predicate, but as a part of the subject, and therefore to read: "All (or, "every") scripture inspired of God is also profitable for teaching," etc. But it would seem that, if it were so intended, the verb *estin* should have been used after *ophelimos*, and there is no good reason why *kai* should have been used before it. There is nothing that compels us to depart from the usual interpretation of the passage. In connection with this statement of Paul, the word of Peter in 2 Peter 1:21 deserves special attention: "For no prophecy ever came by the will of man, but men spake from God being moved by the Holy Spirit." The writers of the New Testament were conscious of the guidance of the Holy Spirit in their writing, and therefore their written productions are authoritative (1 Cor. 7:10; 2 Cor. 13:2–3; Col. 4:16; 1 Thess. 2:13; 2 Thess. 3:14). Peter places the Epistles of Paul on a level with the writings of the Old Testament (2 Peter 3:15–16). And Paul himself says: "If any man thinketh himself to be a prophet, let him take knowledge of the things which I write unto you, that they are the commandments of the Lord" (1 Cor. 14:37).

C. Nature and Extent of Its Inspiration

There has been no general agreement as to the nature and extent of the inspiration of Scripture, and with a view to a proper understanding of these, it may be well to consider the most important views that were held in course of time.

1. THE NATURE OF INSPIRATION. In dealing with the nature of inspiration, we shall consider first of all two erroneous views, which represent opposite extremes, and then state what we consider to be the correct view.

a. *Mechanical inspiration.* There is a rather common misunderstanding, against which we must be on our guard. It is often represented as if verbal inspiration were necessarily mechanical, but this is not the case. The two terms are certainly not synonymous, for they refer to different aspects of the work of inspiration, the one being an indication of the extent, and the other, of the nature of inspiration. And while it is true that mechanical inspiration is from the nature of the case verbal, it is not true that verbal inspiration is necessarily mechanical. It is quite possible to believe that the guidance of the Holy extended to the choice of the words employed, but was not exercised in a mechanical way. According to the mechanical view of inspiration God dictated what the *auctores secundarii* wrote, so that the latter were mere amanuenses, mere channels through which the words of the Holy Spirit flowed. It implies that their own mental life was in a state of repose, and did not in any way contribute to the contents or form of their writings, and that even the style of Scripture is that of the Holy Spirit. This theory has very unfairly and rather persistently been ascribed by its opponents to all those who believe in verbal inspiration, even after these have repeatedly disclaimed that view. It must be admitted that some of the early Church Fathers, the Reformers, and some Lutheran and Reformed theologians of the seventeenth century occasionally used expressions that savoured of such a view; but it should be added that their general teachings clearly show that they did not regard the writers of the Bible as mere passive instruments, but as real authors, whose intellectual powers were alert and operative and who gave expression also to their individuality in their writings. As far as the Reformers are concerned, this appears very clearly from the fact that many of those who do not believe in any real doctrine of inspiration, vie with each other in their attempts to prove that Luther and Calvin did not hold the strict view of inspiration which was current in the seventeenth century. The great historical Confessions, with the exception of the *Formula Consensus Helvetica* (1675) do not express themselves as to the precise nature of the inspiration of Scripture. The one Confession named comes closest to the presentation of a mechanical view of inspiration, but this Confession was recognized only by a few cantons in Switzerland, the land of its birth, and was even there set aside by a following generation. Moreover we should not lose sight of the fact that this Confession represents a reaction against the loose views on inspiration, which were sponsored by Cappelus of the school of Saumur. It may well be doubted, whether there ever has been a considerable number of Reformed theologians who consciously adopted a mechanical view of inspiration. This view is not found in our own *Confessio Belgica*, and is certainly not now the accepted doctrine of Reformed theology. Reformed theologians now generally have an organic conception of inspiration. They do not believe that the *auctores secundarii* of Scripture were mere passive instruments in the hand of God; that they were mere amanuenses who wrote what God dictated; that what they wrote did not in any sense of the word originate in their own consciousness; nor that their style in simply the style of the Holy Spirit. To the contrary, they adopt a view which recognizes them as real authors and does full justice to their personal share in the production of their writings.

b. *Dynamical inspiration.* If we desire on the one hand to avoid the mechanical view of inspiration, we are equally desirous, on the other hand, to steer clear of the so-called dynamical view. The term 'dynamic inspiration' is sometimes used to denote what we would call 'organic inspiration',[53] but is employed here to designate the theory of inspiration that owes its inception to the teachings of Schleiermacher. This theory renounces the idea of a direct operation of the Holy Spirit on the production of the books of the Bible, and substitutes for it a general inspiration of the writers, which really amounts to nothing more than a spiritual illumination, differing only in degree from the spiritual illumination of Christians in general. Strictly speaking, it eliminates the supernatural, transforms the idea of inspiration, and transfers it from the intellectual to the moral sphere. The writers of the New Testament (the Old Testament is not even taken into consideration) were holy men, who moved about in the presence of Jesus and lived in the sphere of revelation, which naturally had a sanctifying influence on their character, thought, and speech. Says Ladd: "The general conception of inspiration is that of a divine influence coming like a breath of wind, or some other fluid, into the soul of man, and producing there a transformation."[54] Bannerman correctly says that in Schleiermacher's theology inspiration is held to be "the natural, or at most the gracious, agency of God illuminating the rational or the spiritual consciousness of a man, so that out of the fulness of his own Christian understanding and feelings he may speak or write the product of his own religious life and beliefs."[55] This view is entirely subjective, makes the Bible a purely human product, and allows for the possibility of errors in the Word of God. Inspiration so conceived was a permanent characteristic of the writers, and in so far naturally also influenced their writings, but was by no means a supernatural operation of the Holy Spirit, which served to qualify the writers for the specific task of committing the divine revelation to writing. It terminated on the writers rather than on their writings. While it naturally influenced their writings, it did not affect them all in the same measure. On the one hand the Bible contains the highest truths, but on the other hand it is still imperfect and fallible. This theory, which is also called the theory of *spiritual insight* or *spiritual intuition*, certainly does not do justice to the Scriptural data on inspiration. It robs the Bible of its supernatural character and destroys its infallibility.

c. *Organic inspiration.* The term 'organic inspiration' is also somewhat ambiguous, because some use it to designate what is usually called 'dynamic inspiration.' The term 'organic' serves to stress the fact that God did not employ the writers of the books of the Bible in a mechanical way, just as a writer wields a pen; did not whisper into their ears the words which He wanted them to write; but acted upon them in an organic way, in harmony with the laws of their own inner being. He used them just as they were, with their character and temperament, their gifts and talents, their education and culture, their vocabulary, diction, and style. He illumined their minds, prompted them to write, repressed the influence of sin on their literary activity, and guided them in an organic way in the choice of their words and in the expression of their thoughts. This view is clearly most in harmony with

53. For instance John L. Girardeau, *Discussions of Theological Questions* (Richmond, VA: Presbyterian Committee of Publication, 1905), 295.

54. George T. Ladd, *The Doctrine of Sacred Scriptures* (New York: Scribner, 1883), 2:468.

55. *Inspiration of the Scriptures*, 142.

the representations of Scripture. It testifies to the fact that the writers of the books of the Bible were not passive but active. In some cases they searched out beforehand the things of which they wrote (Luke 1:1–4). The authors of the books of Samuel, Kings, and Chronicles repeatedly refer to their sources. The messages of the prophets are generally determined by historical circumstances, and the New Testament Epistles also have an occasional character. The psalmists often sing of their own experiences, of sin and forgiveness (Pss. 32 and 51), of surrounding dangers and gracious deliverances (Pss. 48 and 116). Each one of the writers has his own style. Alongside of the sublime poetry and poetical language of poets and prophets, we have the common prose of the historians; alongside of the pure Hebrew of Isaiah, the Aramaic-tinted Hebrew of Daniel; and alongside of the dialectic style of Paul, the simple language of John. The writers put on their literary productions their own personal stamp and the stamp of their times. Thus the Bible itself testifies to the fact that it was not mechanically inspired. The Holy Spirit used the writers as He Himself had formed them for their task, without in any way suppressing their personality. He qualified them and guided them, and thus inspired the books of Scripture organically.

2. THE EXTENT OF INSPIRATION. Different views were held in the course of history, not only respecting the nature of inspiration, but also as to its extent. The three views that come into consideration here especially may be designated as partial inspiration, thought inspiration, and verbal inspiration.

a. *Partial inspiration*. Under the influence of eighteenth century Deism and Rationalism lax views of inspiration were zealously propagated and found ready acceptance in the theological world, and in some cases even met with adherents in the Churches. Le Clerc, who was originally a Reformed theologian, but later on became an Arminian professor at Amsterdam, denied the inspiration of many of the historical portions of Scripture, resolved that of the apostles into a sort of spiritual enlightenment and a strengthening of the faculties of the soul, and limited that of the prophets to the time when they received their revelations. From his time on it became quite common for theologians, who desired to maintain the doctrine of inspiration, at least in some sense of the word, to speak of degrees of inspiration. They distinguished between the doctrinal and the historical portions of Scripture, and regarded the former, containing essential truths, with which the writers were made acquainted by revelation, as plenarily inspired; and the latter, containing non-essential truths, of which the writers had knowledge apart from revelation, as only partially inspired, and as marred by inaccuracies and mistakes. There were also theologians, however, who were even more completely under the influence of Rationalism, and who accepted the idea of a partial inspiration devoid of supernaturalism. According to them the writers of the Bible simply enjoyed a special spiritual enlightenment and guidance, which offered no guarantee against all kinds of historical, chronological, archaeological, and scientific mistakes, but did make the writers reliable witnesses in moral and spiritual matters. Among those who adopt a partial inspiration of Scripture there is no unanimity whatsoever. Some would limit inspiration to doctrinal matters, others to the New Testament, others to the words of Jesus, and still others to the Sermon on the Mount. This shows as clearly as anything can that the theory is purely subjective, and lacks all objective basis. The moment one accepts it in any one of its many forms one has virtually lost one's Bible.

According to the Bible inspiration extends equally to all parts of the Word of God. The Law and the historical books, the Psalms and the Prophets, the Gospels and the Epistles,—

they were all written under the guidance of the Holy Spirit, and are therefore all in the same measure *he graphe*. An appeal to any part of it, is an appeal to the Word of God, and therefore to God Himself. This is indicated in various ways. The Epistles of Paul are placed on a level with the writings of the Old Testament, which are clearly regarded as inspired and authoritative by Jesus and the apostles (2 Peter 3:15–16). It should be noted that the New Testament contains quotations from twenty-five Old Testament books, and among these are several of a historical character, which in the estimation of some are least, if at all, inspired. The Lord Himself and the New Testament writers evidently regarded each one of these books as a part of *he graphe*, and ascribed to them divine authority. Moreover, there are several collective quotations, or catenae of quotations, that is, quotations gathered from several books, which are all advanced as equally authoritative to prove the same point (Rom. 3:10–18; Heb. 1:5–13; 2:12–13). We cannot explain the interpenetration of the divine and the human factors in Scripture, any more than we can explain that of the two natures in Christ. Scripture presents itself to us as an organic whole, consisting of several parts, that are interrelated in various ways, and that find their unity in the central, all-controlling, and progressively unfolding, thought of God reaching out to man, in order to redeem him from sin and to bestow upon him the blessings of eternal salvation. And therefore we should not ask where the divine ends and the human begins, nor where the human ends and the divine begins. We might just as well ask where in man the soul ends and the body begins. No such line of demarcation can be pointed out. Scripture is in its entirety both the Word of God and the word of man.

b. *Thought inspiration.* Some who would defend the doctrine of inspiration against its complete denial, are of the opinion that the advocates of the doctrine should retrench somewhat, and speak of thought—rather than of word—inspiration. The thoughts, they say, were evidently divinely inspired, but the words in which they are clothed were freely chosen by the human authors, and that without any divine guidance. In that way they consider it possible to satisfy the requirements of the Biblical teaching respecting inspiration, and at the same time account for the imperfections and errors that are found in Scripture. But such an inspiration of thoughts without words is an anomaly, and is really inconceivable. Thoughts are formulated and expressed in words. Girardeau correctly remarks: "Accurate thought cannot be disjoined from language. Words are its vehicles both subjectively and objectively. When we think accurately and precisely, we think in words. To give the thought therefore, is to give the words."[56] And Dr. Orr, who would himself rather speak of plenary than of verbal inspiration, admits that the latter name expresses a true and important idea, where it "opposes the theory that revelation and inspiration have regard only to thoughts and ideas, while the language in which these ideas are clothed is left to the unaided faculty of the sacred penman." Moreover, he says: "Thought of necessity takes shape and is expressed in words. If there is inspiration at all, it must penetrate words as well as thought, must mould the expression, and make the language employed the living medium of the idea to be conveyed."[57] As we shall point out in the sequel, Scripture clearly teaches the inspiration of the words of Scripture.

c. *Verbal inspiration.* There are some who believe in the inspiration of every part of the Bible, but would rather not speak of verbal inspiration. because this is apt to suggest the mechanical

---

56. *Discussions of Theological Questions*, 324–25.
57. Orr, *Revelation and Inspiration*, 209.

idea that God dictated what the secondary authors wrote.[58] They would prefer to use the term "plenary inspiration." Others, however, reject the idea of verbal inspiration altogether, because they do not believe in any plenary inspiration. It may be well therefore to call particularly attention to the Scriptural data on this point. (1) *References to verbal communications.* The Pentateuch repeatedly refers to verbal communications of the Lord. The expressions, "The Lord said unto Moses" and "The Lord spoke unto Moses," serve so frequently to introduce a written message, that they almost have the force of a formula (Ex. 3 and 4; 6:1; 7:1; 8:1; 10:1; 12:1; Lev. 1:1; 4:1; 6:1, 24; 7:22, 28; 8:1; 11:1). The Lord certainly did not speak to Moses without words. The word of the Lord repeatedly came to Joshua in the same way (Josh. 1:1; 4:1; 6:2; 8:1). (2) *Prophets are conscious of bringing the very words of the Lord.* The prophets were conscious of the fact that the Lord spoke through them. Isaiah begins his prophecy with the words: "Hear, O heavens, and give ear, O earth, for Jehovah hath spoken" (Isa. 1:2); and he and other prophets constantly use the well known prophetic formulae, "Thus saith the Lord" and, "Hear the word of the Lord." Jeremiah even says: "Then Jehovah put forth His hand, and touched my mouth; and Jehovah said unto me, Behold, I have put my words in thy mouth" (Jer. 1:9). In Ezekiel we read: "Son of man, go, get thee unto the house of Israel, and speak with my words unto them . . . . Son of man, all my words that I shall speak unto thee receive in thy heart, and hear with thine ears. And go, get thee to them of the captivity, unto the children of thy people, and speak unto them, and tell them, Thus saith the Lord Jehovah" (Ezek. 3:4, 10–11). It is not necessary to multiply the examples. (3) *The apostles speak of the words of the Old Testament and of their own words as the words of God.* Paul explicitly says that he gives instruction, not in words of his own choosing, but in Spirit-taught words (1 Cor. 2:13), and claims that Christ is speaking in him (2 Cor. 13:3). And in the Epistle to the Hebrews several words of the Old Testament are quoted, not as words of some human author, but as words of God, or of the Holy Spirit (Heb. 1:5ff.; 2:11–13; 3:7; 4:4–5, 7; 8:8; 10:15–17). (4) *Arguments based on a single word.* There are three cases in which Jesus and Paul base a whole argument on the use of a single word of the Old Testament (John 10:35; Matt. 22:43–45; Gal. 3:16). In doing this they give clear evidence of the fact that they regard the separate words as inspired and infallible, and that the readers share their conviction. If this were not the case, they would not have been able to consider their arguments as conclusive.

D. Attempts to Discredit the Doctrine of Inspiration

Several attempts have been made to discredit or set aside the doctrine of inspiration. Of these the following may be considered as the most important.

1. THEY WHO DEFEND IT ARE REASONING IN A CIRCLE. We are often accused of reasoning in a circle, when we derive our proof for the inspiration of the Bible from Scripture itself. Because the Bible is true, we accept its testimony respecting its inspiration, and because it is inspired, we regard it as true. Apologetically, this argument can be met, and has frequently been answered. It is possible, for the sake of argument, to start out with the assumption that the books of the Bible are purely human productions, which, however, as the productions of eye-and ear-witnesses, which are known as men of high moral standing, can be regarded as entirely trustworthy. Then it can be shown that, according to these books, Christ and the apostles held the strictest view of the inspiration of the Old Testament. From that point

---

58. Cf. ibid.

it is quite possible to reach the conclusion that the Old Testament necessarily required a complement such as is found in the New Testament. And on the basis of this it can be said that therefore the whole Bible must be regarded as an inspired book. By reasoning in that fashion the circle is avoided. This line of argumentation is followed by Bannerman, Patton, Warfield, Van Oosterzee, and others. But it is a question, whether the circle referred to is really as vicious as some would have us believe. Jesus evidently did not think so, when a similar objection was raised against His testimony concerning Himself as the incarnate Word of God (John 8:13–14). In social life people frequently move in the same circle. If they are firmly convinced that a person is thoroughly reliable and trustworthy, they do not hesitate to receive his testimony concerning himself and his actions, when others accuse him of deception and dishonesty. Girardeau pertinently remarks: "Suppose we should use the argument: God declares that He is true; therefore God is true. Here God's truth would be proved by His truth. Would that be a vicious reasoning in a circle? The atheist might say, You assume that there is a God of truth. So we do, and so do all sensible men."[59] Through the testimony of the Holy Spirit in his heart the Christian stands in the unwavering faith that God is true in His revelation, and therefore it is a matter of course that he accepts the testimony of Scripture respecting itself.

2. JESUS DID NOT TEACH THE DOCTRINE OF INSPIRATION. Though modern liberal scholars generally admit that Jesus and the apostles accepted the Old Testament as the inspired Word of God, there are some among them who, in their denial of the doctrine of inspiration, appeal to Jesus as over against the apostles, and especially Paul. The apostles, they say, firmly believed that the writings of the Old Testament were written under inspiration, but Jesus did not share their opinion. And because they regard the testimony of Jesus as decisive, they feel justified in rejecting the doctrine of inspiration. But their fundamental assumption is contrary to the data of Scripture, and apart from these we have no knowledge of what Jesus thought on this subject. They point in quite another direction. The positive statements of Jesus respecting the abiding significance, authority, and inviolability of the Old Testament (Matt. 5:17–18; 24:35; Luke 16:17; John 10:35), His quotations from it as an authoritative source, and His repeated use of it, leave no doubt as to the fact that He, as well as the apostles, recognized the divine authority of the Old Testament. Some who feel constrained to admit the force of the available evidence, but are not willing to draw the inevitable conclusion, seek refuge in the old accommodation theory of Semler. We fully agree with Dr. Burrell, when he says:

> One thing is clear: when Jesus referred to the Scriptures as written by men under the influence of the Spirit, He separated those Scriptures generically from all other "literature" whatsoever. To his mind, the inspiration of these writers was a singular sort of inspiration, which produced a singular book. In his teaching it is represented as the one book having authority.[60]

Moreover, it should be remembered that such a contradistinction between Jesus and the apostles as the opponents assume, in which the attempt is made to play off the former against the latter, is absolutely false, and results in the loss of the Word of God. We know nothing about Jesus save through the testimony of the apostles. He who discredits the apostles bars

---

59. *Discussions of Theological Questions*, 297.
60. David J. Burrell, *The Teaching of Jesus Concerning the Scriptures* (New York: American Tract Society, 1904), 134.

the way for himself and will never be able to discover what Jesus taught. He even contradicts Jesus, who appointed the apostles as faithful witnesses and promised them the Holy Spirit, to guide them in all the truth.

3. THE PHENOMENA OF SCRIPTURE CONTRADICT THE DOCTRINE OF INSPIRATION. Under the influence of historical criticism still another method has been employed to set aside the doctrine of inspiration. They who employ this method are, at least in some cases, willing to admit that the Bible teaches its inspiration, but at the same time maintain that a correct conception of this inspiration can be obtained only by taking account of the peculiar phenomena of Scripture, such as doublets, mistakes, contradictions, misapplied quotations, and so on. Only such a doctrine of inspiration can be regarded as true, which will enable one to account for all these phenomena. The reasoning of those who take this position often sounds very plausible. They do not want a theory of inspiration that is imposed on Scripture from without, but one that is based on an inductive study of the facts. But, however plausible this representation may seem, it does not fit the case. According to it man faces the phenomena of Scripture just as he faces the phenomena of nature and the facts of history, which he must interpret and set forth in their true significance. It loses sight of the fact that the Bible contains a very clear doctrine respecting itself, which man must accept with childlike faith. Even the phenomena of Scripture may not be cited as a witness against this testimony of Scripture. He who does this *eo ipso* rejects the authority of the Bible and virtually adopts a rationalistic standpoint. Instead of humbly accepting the testimony of Scripture, he places himself above it as judge, and opposes to the testimony of Scripture his own scientific insight. History clearly teaches us that the historical-critical method does not lead to a generally accepted and permanent result. The representations vary according to the different standpoint of the critics, and do not lead to a satisfactory doctrine of Scripture. It has already become abundantly evident that this method leads to various views of Scripture, which are absolutely contrary to the teachings of Scripture itself—a veritable babel of confusion. Ladd, whom no one will accuse of being prejudiced in favor of a strict view of inspiration, says that, while the old conception of Scripture as the Word of God was brushed aside as untenable, and several other theories were suggested as alternatives, not a single one succeeded in entrenching itself in the hearts and minds of Christian people in general.[61]

4. THE DOCTRINE OF INSPIRATION APPLIES ONLY TO THE AUTOGRAPHA, AND THEREFORE HAS NO REAL PRACTICAL VALUE. The fact that the doctrine of inspiration, as set forth in the preceding pages, applies only to the autographa (the original writings of the Biblical authors), which are no more in our possession, has led some to the rather hasty conclusion, that the problem of inspiration is of a purely academic character and has no practical bearing whatsoever. How can the inspiration of the originals be of any value for us, they ask, if we have in our possession nothing but defective manuscripts? They often give the impression that this renders the entire contents of Scripture uncertain, and that consequently no one can appeal to it as a divine and authoritative Word. But something may be said in answer to this. We would certainly expect that the Holy Spirit, who so carefully guided the writers of Scripture in the interest of future generations, would also guard and watch over His revelation, in order that it might really serve its purpose. Hence Reformed theologians have always maintained that God's special providence watched over Scripture. Inspiration

61. George T. Ladd, *What Is the Bible?* (New York: Scribner, 1888), 71–75.

naturally called for conservation. And history certainly favors this idea in spite of all the variations that exist.

If we bear in mind that there are more than 4000 Greek MSS. of the New Testament, and in addition to that 6000 MSS. of the Vulgate, and 1000 of other Latin translations, then we understand that it was practically impossible that Scripture should be lost to the world for centuries, just as many of the writings of the Church Fathers were. Then we also understand what Kenyon, an eminent authority on the subject, says:

> The number of manuscripts of the New Testament, of early translations from it, and of quotations from it in the oldest writers of the Church is so large, that it is practically certain that the true reading of every doubtful passage is preserved in some one or other of these ancient authorities. This can be said of no other ancient book in the world.[62]

Textual errors did creep into the text in the course of frequent transcriptions, and the number of the existing variations even sounds very considerable. Nestle speaks of 150,000 in the New Testament, but adds that about nineteen-twentieths of these are devoid of real authority, and that of the remaining 7,500 nineteen-twentieths do not alter the sense of Scripture in any way. Moses Stuart points out that about ninety-five percent of all the existing variations have about as much significance as the question in English orthography, whether the word 'honour' should be spelled with or without the 'u'. According to Nestle there are about 375 variations that bear on the sense of Scripture, and even among these are several of little importance. While admitting the presence of variations, we should bear in mind what Moses Stuart says: "Some change the sense of particular passages or expressions, or omit particular words or phrases; but no one doctrine of religion is changed, not one precept is taken away, not one important fact altered, by the whole of the various readings collectively taken."[63] From the existence of these variations it does not follow that the doctrine of verbal inspiration has no practical value; but only *that we do not know at present in what reading we have the Word of God on those particular points*. The important fact remains, however, that apart from the relatively few and unimportant variations, which are perfectly evident, we are in possession of the verbally inspired Word of God. And therefore it is of great practical importance that we maintain the doctrine of verbal inspiration.

E. Objections to the Doctrine of Inspiration

Several objections have been raised against the doctrine of inspiration, and particularly against the doctrine of verbal inspiration, and it cannot be denied that some of them present real difficulties. It will not do to ignore them, nor to laugh them out of court. They deserve careful consideration and a more detailed discussion than we can devote to them here. We cannot even begin to discuss separate objections here with the necessary care. This must be left to works which deal exclusively with the doctrine of inspiration, such as William Lee, *The Inspiration of the Holy Scripture* [New York: Robert Carter, 1857]; Bannerman, *The Inspiration of the Scriptures*; and Hugh McIntosh, *Is Christ Infallible and the Bible True?* [Edinburgh: T. & T. Clark, 1901]. We can only indicate the general nature of the objections, and give some general suggestions as to the way in which they can be met.

---

62. Frederic G. Kenyon, *Our Bible and the Ancient Manuscripts* (New York: Eyre & Spottiswoode, 1895), 10–11.
63. Quoted by Francis L. Patton, *Inspiration of the Scriptures* (Philadelphia: Presbyterian Board of Publication, 1869), 114.

1. GENERAL NATURE OF THE OBJECTIONS. Some of the objections result from the application of the philosophy of evolution to the origin of the books of the Bible, a scheme which does not fit the facts, and is then made to militate against them. Their force naturally depends entirely on the truth or falsity of that philosophy. Others are derived from the supposed inner discrepancies that are found in Scripture as, for instance, between the numbers in Kings and Chronicles, between the account of Jesus' public ministry in the Synoptics and in the Gospel of John, and between the doctrine of justification in the Epistles of Paul and in the Epistle of James. Still others are drawn from the way in which the Old Testament is quoted in the New. The quotations are not always taken from the Hebrew, but frequently from the Septuagint, and are not always literal. Moreover, the quoted words are often interpreted in a way which does not seem to be justified by the context in which they are found in the Old Testament. There are objections, which result from a comparison of the Biblical narratives with secular history as, for instance, that of the taking of Samaria by Shalmanezer; that of Sennacherib's march against Jerusalem and the slaying of 185,000 Assyrians by an angel of the Lord; that of Esther's elevation to the position of queen; and that of the enrollment mentioned in the second chapter of Luke. Again, it is found that the miracles of Scripture cannot be harmonized with belief in the inflexible laws of nature. The narratives of these miracles are simply declared to be exaggerated, naive representations of historical events which made a deep impression, and after the lapse of years assumed the proportions of miracles in the consciousness of a credulous people. Some objections are the products of the moral judgment passed on Biblical injunctions and practices. Attention is called to the *jus talionis* in the law of Moses, to the polygamy that was prevalent among the Israelites, to the terrible scene of moral corruption in the last chapters of the book of Judges, to David's immorality, to the harem of Solomon, and so on. Finally, texual criticism also gives rise to objections. Scripture in its original text, we are told, is corrupt, and its translations are defective. The MSS. reveal all kinds of variations, which testify to the corruption of the original, and the translations are not always a correct representation of it.

2. GENERAL REMARKS ON THE OBJECTIONS RAISED. First of all the general remark must be made that, though we cannot ignore the objections that are raised but must take account of them, no one has the right to demand of us that we make our belief in the inspiration of Scripture contingent on our ability to remove all objections by solving the problems which they present. The objections raised do not constitute a sufficient reason for setting aside the doctrine of inspiration, which is clearly taught in Scripture. The doctrines of the Trinity, of creation and providence, and of the incarnation, are all burdened with difficulties, but these do not justify anyone in rejecting the clear teachings of Scripture with respect to those truths. Many of the teachings of science are similarly burdened and present problems which cannot be solved at present, but are not therefore necessarily discounted. People confidently speak of atoms and electrons, of genes and chromosomes, though these still present many problems. We should always bear in mind the statement of Dr. Warfield, that it is "a settled logical principle that so long as the proper evidence by which a proposition is established remains unrefuted, all so-called objections brought against it pass out of the category of objections to its truth into the category of difficulties to be adjusted to it."[64]

---

64. B. B. Warfield, *Revelation and Inspiration* (New York: Oxford University Press, 1927), 174.

In connection with the common objections against the doctrine of inspiration the following points should be borne in mind:

a. The present day opposition to Scripture and its inspiration is to a great extent, not merely scientific, but ethical. It clearly reveals the aversion of the natural heart to the supernatural. Opposition is evoked by the very fact that Scripture demands absolute subjection, the subjection of human reason to its authority. This ethical conflict is clearly seen in the opposition to the miracles, the incarnation, the virgin birth, the resurrection of Christ, and other supernatural events.

b. Many of the so-called objections have no factual basis, but are born of faulty assumptions. They often result from the wrong *scientific* attitude, which the opponent assumes to Scripture. If one takes for granted *a priorily* that the contents of Scripture is not the fruit of revelation but of natural evolution, then many facts and events appear to be out of place in the framework in which the Bible places them. Then the laws of Moses become an anomaly at the beginning of Israel's national existence, and the books of Chronicles must be regarded as unhistorical. Then Jesus especially becomes an historical enigma. Again, if it is taken for granted that all the events of history are controlled by an iron-clad system of natural laws, and the supernatural is eliminated, then there is, of course, no place for the miracles of Scripture. And if in the study of the Synoptics a double or triple source theory is taken for granted, *and these sources are made the standard of truth*, a great deal of material will naturally be set aside. But all such objections are the result of false assumptions, and therefore need not be taken seriously.

c. Several of the objections are exaggerated and can easily be reduced. Discrepancies and contradictions are sometimes hastily assumed, which on closer inspection prove to be no discrepancies or contradictions at all. There are so-called doublets in Joshua, Judges, and the books of Samuel, which in fact are merely complementary narratives, introduced in characteristically Hebrew fashion. The Gospel of John has been declared unhistorical, because its representation of the life of Jesus differs from that of the Synoptics; but even these differences can largely be explained in the light of the character and purpose of the different Gospels. A book like that of D. S. Gregory, *Why Four Gospels?* [New York: Funk & Wagnalls, 1876] is very illuminating on this point.

d. There are also a number of objections that would apply on the assumption of a mechanical conception of inspiration, but lose their force entirely if the inspiration of Scripture is organically conceived. Verbal inspiration is sometimes denied, because the writers indicate that their literary work is based on previous investigations, because the individuality of the writers is clearly reflected in their writings, or because there are marked differences of style and language. But it is quite evident that these objections militate only against a mechanical view of inspiration.

e. Finally, objections are frequently derived from the low moral conditions which are reflected in the Bible, especially in its earliest books, and from the imperfections, deceptions, polygamy, and even immorality of some of the chief Bible characters, such as Noah, Abraham, Jacob, Eli, David, and Solomon. But the fact that the Bible gives a faithful picture of the times and the lives of these saints can hardly constitute an objection against its inspiration. The situation would be different, of course, if the Bible approved of such conditions or acts, or even if it condoned them; but as a matter of fact it does quite the contrary.

QUESTIONS FOR FURTHER STUDY: What is plenary, in distinction from verbal, inspiration? Does the fact that the Bible contains truths which transcend reason prove anything as to its inspiration? Is the doctrine of inspiration consistent with the evolutionary view of Scripture? If the Bible is not verbally inspired in all its parts, how can we determine which parts are, and which are not, inspired? What is the difference between prophetic, lyric, chokmatic, and apostolic inspiration? Does the doctrine of inspiration imply that the evangelists always recorded the *ipsissima verba* of Jesus? How does it square with the fact that the human authors of the Bible sometimes derive their material from written sources? Is it possible to deny the doctrine of inspiration and maintain the veracity of Jesus and the apostles? How did the inspiration of the writers of Scripture differ from the ordinary illumination of Christians? How, from the inspiration of the great poets?

REFERENCES: Herman Bavinck, *Gereformeerde Dogmatiek* (Kampen: J. H. Kok, 1906), 1:406–476; Abraham Kuyper, *Encyclopaedie der Heilige Godgeleerdheid*, (Amsterdam: J. A. Wormser, 1894), 2:369–511; idem, *Dictaten Dogmatiek, De Sacra Scriptura* (Kampen: J. H. Kok, 1910), 1:86–100; 2:3:179; idem, *De Hedendaagsche Scriftcritiek* (Amsterdam: Kruyt, 1881); Anthonie G. Honig, *Is de Bijbel op Bovennatuurlijke Wijze Geinspireerd?* (Baarn: Hollandia, 1909); François E. Daubanton, *De Theopneustie der Heilige Schrift* (Utrecht: Kemink & Zoon, 1882); James Bannerman, *Inspiration of the Scriptures* (Edinburgh: T. & T. Clark, 1865); William Lee, *The Inspiration of the Holy Scripture* (New York: Robert Carter, 1857); Hugh McIntosh, *Is Christ Infallible and the Bible True?* (Edinburgh: T. & T. Clark, 1901); Francis L. Patton, *Inspiration of the Scriptures* (Philadelphia: Presbyterian Board of Publication, 1869); James MacGregor, *The Revelation and the Record* (Edinburgh: T. & T. Clark, 1893), 79–117; John J. Given, *Revelation, Inspiration, and the Canon* (Edinburgh: T. & T. Clark, 1881), 104–202; James Orr, *Revelation and Inspiration* (New York: Scribner, 1910), 155–218; George T. Ladd, *The Doctrine of Sacred Scriptures* (New York: Scribner, 1883), 2:452–494; William Sanday, *Inspiration* (London: Longmans, Green, 1896); B. B. Warfield, *Revelation and Inspiration* (New York: Oxford University Press, 1927), 51–456; Jean L. Girardeau, *Discussions of Theological Questions* (Richmond, VA: Presbyterian Committee of Publication, 1905), 273–384; William Cunningham, *Theological Lectures* (New York: Robert Carter, 1878), 343–411; Charles M. Mead, *Supernatural Revelation* (New York: A. D. F. Randolph, 1889), 279–317.

F. The Perfections of Scripture

The Reformation naturally brought the doctrine of Scripture to the foreground. During the Middle Ages the fiction of an apostolic tradition, which was supposed to have come down in oral form from the days of the apostles gradually crystallized and secured a firm hold on the Church. This tradition was placed on a level with the Bible as an authoritative source of theological knowledge, and in practice was often treated as superior to the Bible. It was regarded as the necessary warrant for the authority of the Bible, and as the indispensable guide for the interpretation of Scripture. Moreover, the hierarchical Church of Rome, with its claim to infallibility, placed itself above them both. It posed as the only body which could determine infallibly what was, and what was not, apostolic tradition, and which could give an infallible interpretation of Scripture. Great emphasis was placed on the fact that the Bible owes its origin to the Church, and stands in constant need of the testimony of the Church. The Reformers clearly saw that this position of the Church of Rome was the fruitful source of many errors, and therefore felt that it was incumbent on them to call the people back to the Bible, which had been greatly neglected, and to stress its autopistia. To offset the errors of Rome they deemed it necessary to develop the doctrine of the perfections of Scripture. They themselves did not yet include a systematic presentation of this in their works, but their successors did. It occupies a very important place in the writings of Musculus, Zanchius, Polanus, Junius, and others. We conclude our study of the *principium cognoscendi externum* with a brief discussion of the perfections of Scripture.

1. THE DIVINE AUTHORITY OF SCRIPTURE. The divine authority of Scripture was generally accepted until the chill winds of Rationalism swept over Europe and caused the enthusiasm of faith to go down to the freezing point. This means that in the days of the Reformation the Church of Rome as well as the Churches that parted company with it, ascribed divine authority to Scripture. But in spite of the fact that Roman Catholics and Protestants had the principle of authority in common, they were not altogether agreed as to the nature of this authority. There was a very important difference of opinion with respect to the ground on which it rests. On the part of Rome there was an ever-increasing denial of the *autopistia* of Scripture, that is, of its inherent authority. It maintained that the Church temporarily and logically precedes Scripture, and therefore does not owe its existence to Scripture, but exists in and by itself, that is, through Christ or the indwelling Spirit of God. Scripture rather owes its existence to the Church, and is now further acknowledged, preserved, interpreted, and defended by it. Without the Church there is no Scripture, but without Scripture there is still a Church.

Over against this position of Rome, the Reformers emphasized the *autopistia* of Scripture, the doctrine that Scripture has authority in and of itself as the *inspired* Word of God. They did not hesitate to ascribe great importance to the testimony of the Church to Scripture as a *motivum credibilitatis*, but refused to regard this testimony of the Church as the final ground for the acceptance of Scripture. They firmly maintained the position that the Bible must be believed for its own sake. It is the inspired Word of God and therefore addresses man with divine authority. The Church can and should *acknowledge* the Bible for what it is, but can in no sense of the word *make* it what it is. The Protestant principle is, says Thornwell, "that the truths of the Bible authenticate themselves as divine by their own light."[65]

In Protestant circles, however, a dispute arose in the seventeenth century respecting the authority of Scripture. While Scripture as a whole was recognized as the only and sufficient rule of faith and practice, the question was raised, whether every part of it should be regarded as authoritative. In seeking an answer to this question it became evident that it was necessary to distinguish between the Word of God in a formal and in a material sense, and between an *auctoritas historica* and an *auctoritas normativa*. Scripture has first of all historical authority, that is, it is a true and absolutely reliable record, and as such is entitled to a believing acceptance of all that it contains. But in addition to that it also has normative significance, as a rule of life and conduct, and as such demands absolute subjection on the part of man. And in connection with this the difficult question arose, in how far the normative value that is ascribed to Scripture as a whole also belongs to its separate parts. Do the historical parts of the Bible, do the laws of Moses, and do the words of the speakers that are introduced in Scripture have normative significance for

---

65. James Henley Thornwell, *Collected Writings* (Richmond, VA: Presbyterian Committee of Publication, 1871), 1:49.

us? Happily, we need not grope about entirely in the dark here, for the Bible itself teaches us to make distinctions with respect to this point. It does not demand that we keep every one of the precepts which it contains. It disapproves of some and calls attention to the temporary character of others. Reformed theologians never attempted to lay down hard and fast rules by which we can be governed in this matter. Heppe gives some examples of the manner in which they dealt with the matter.[66] Voetius says that absolute normative significance must be ascribed to the words and works (a) of God, (b) of Christ as God and man, and (c) of the angels. Moreover, he regards those words of the prophets and of the apostles as normative, in which they as public teachers, orally or in writing, edify the Church. He ascribes normative authority to their deeds only when they are approved by Scripture. On the other hand, he does not regard *all* the words of Job as normative, nor the words of the friends of Job. Others explicitly exclude the words of the devils and of wicked persons. Voetius holds that the writings of the Old Testament are just as normative as those of the New Testament.[67] Grosheide calls attention to the fact that absolute normative significance must be ascribed to those statements or commands of God which are clearly intended for all ages, and to all positive statements of an ethical or dogmatical character; but that no such authority can be ascribed to the words of Satan, of wicked persons, or even of the pious, except when they are clearly speaking in the name of God or make statements that are fully in harmony with the moral law; nor to purely historical narratives pertaining to the things of every day life.[68] In general it will not be difficult to determine, whether a certain part of Scripture has normative value for us. Yet there are cases in which the decision is not easy. It is not always possible to say, whether a certain Scriptural precept, which was clearly normative for the original readers, still has normative significance for us. On the whole it is well to bear in mind that the Bible is not exactly a code of laws, and is far more interested in the inculcation of principles than in the regulation of life by specific precepts. Even the laws of Moses and the history of Israel as the Old Testament people of God embody principles of permanent validity. Sometimes we may come to the conclusion that, while certain laws no more apply in the exact form in which they were cast, yet their underlying principle is just as binding today as it ever was. In dubious cases we shall have to be guided to a great extent by the analogy of Scripture and by the moral law.

In modern liberal theology very little remains of the normative significance of the Bible. Schleiermacher denied the normative character of the Old Testament altogether, and regarded only the New Testament as a norm for the Church. And he ascribed this significance to the New Testament, not on account of its supernatural inspiration, for he did not believe in this, but because he saw in it the record of the religious experiences of men, who, as the immediate associates of Jesus, enjoyed a special measure of spiritual illumination. Ritschl did not ascribe normative significance even to the New Testament, but saw in it only a valuable historical record of the beginnings of Christianity, and in no sense of the word a rule of faith. He felt free to reject all those elements which did not harmonize with the postulates of his own system and had no real value for the revelation in Christ as the real founder of the Kingdom of God, nor for the Christian life, as he conceived of it. In general it may be said that these

---

66. Heinrich Heppe, *Dogmatik der evangelich-reformirten Kirche* (Neukirchen: Erziehungsverein, 1935), 22ff.
67. Gisbertus Voetius, *Catechisatie* (Rotterdam: Huge, 1891), 1:71ff.
68. F. W. Grosheide, *Schriftgezag* (Kampen: J. H. Kok, 1918), 28.

two men determined the attitude which modern liberal theology assumes with reference to the Word of God. Strange to say, some present day Dispensationalists, who are strongly opposed to all Liberalism, also maintain that the Old Testament is not normative *for us*. They fully recognize the inspiration of the Old Testament, and consider it to be normative for the Jews, but not for New Testament believers. Cook expresses himself very clearly on this point, when he says that "in all the Old Testament there is not a sentence that applies to the Christian as a Rule of Faith and Practice—not a single command that is binding on him, as there is not a single promise there given him at first hand, except what is included in the broad flow of the plan of Redemption as there taught in symbol and prophecy."[69]

2. THE NECESSITY OF SCRIPTURE. Because the Church of Rome proceeds on the assumption that the Church takes precedence over Scripture, it cannot very well acknowledge the absolute necessity of the latter. The Church, which derives its life from the Holy Spirit, is self-sufficient and therefore *autopistos*. While it does need tradition, it does not really need Scripture, no matter how useful this may be as a norm. The Lord referred those to whom He brought His doctrine, not to a book, but to the living voice of His apostles and of the Church. "He who heareth you," He said to the apostles, "heareth me." Moreover, nearly twenty years elapsed after the ascension of Christ before a single book of the New Testament came into existence, and during all that time an appeal to the New Testament was naturally out of the question. According to Rome it is far more correct to say that the Bible needs the Church than that the Church has need of the Bible. The denial of the necessity of Scripture, however, was not limited to the Church of Rome. Even in the early Church some of the mystical sects, such as the Montanists and the Cathari regarded the Bible as quite superfluous. And in the days of the Reformation the Anabaptists and the Libertines of Geneva were of the same opinion. The Anabaptists especially exalted the inner word at the expense of the external. They did not regard the Bible as the true Word of God, but only as a testimony, a description, a dead and thoroughly impotent letter. In their estimation the real and true Word of God was spoken by the Holy Spirit in the hearts of God's people. Schleiermacher also taught that Scripture was produced by the Church, and is simply the supreme, and therefore also authoritative, expression of its religious life. This may be said to be the prevalent view in modern Liberalism, which draws for its theology far more on the Christian consciousness, informed by the current teachings of science and philosophy, than on the Bible as the Word of God.

When the Reformers defended the necessity of Scripture over against Rome and the Anabaptists, they did not deny that the Church existed before Moses' day, nor that the New Testament Church was in existence long before there was a canon of the New Testament. Neither did they defend the position that Scripture was *absolutely* necessary, in the sense that God could not have made man acquainted with the way of salvation in some other way. They considered Scripture to be necessary in virtue of the good pleasure of God to make the Word the seed of the Church. Even before the time of Moses the unwritten word served that purpose. And the New Testament did not come into existence apart from the spoken word of Jesus and the apostles. As long as these witnesses of the facts of redemption lived, there was little need of a written word, but when they fell away, this changed at once. The historical character of God's revelation, the history of redemption, and the redemptive facts

69. Charles C. Cook, *God's Book Speaking for Itself* (New York: George H. Doran, 1924), 32.

which did not admit of repetition, and were yet of the greatest significance for all coming generations, made it necessary to commit God's special revelation to writing. From that point of view Scripture remains necessary to the very end of time. In this sense of the word Reformed theology has always defended the necessity of Scripture. Even Barth, who does not share the Reformed conception of the Bible as the infallible Word of God, feels constrained to defend its necessity as a witness to the divine revelation.

3. THE PERSPICUITY OF SCRIPTURE. In the estimation of Rome the Bible is obscure, and is badly in need of interpretation even in matters of faith and practice. It contains deep mysteries, such as the doctrine of the Trinity, of the incarnation, and others, and is often so obscure that it is liable to be misunderstood. For that reason an infallible interpretation is needed, and this is supplied by the Church. Peter says distinctly that some parts of the Bible are hard to understand, and the experience of centuries proves conclusively that, without the infallible interpretation of the Church, it is impossible to reach the desired unity in the interpretation of Scripture. Over against this position of the Roman Catholic Church the Reformers stressed the perspicuity of Scripture. They did not intend to deny that there are mysteries in the Bible which transcend human reason, but freely admitted this. Neither did they claim such clarity for Scripture that the interpreter can well dispense with scientific exegesis. As a matter of fact, they engaged in exegetical labors far more than the votaries of Rome. Moreover, they did not even assert that the way of salvation is so clearly revealed in Scripture that every man, whether he be enlightened by the Holy Spirit or not, and whether or not he be deeply interested in the way of salvation, can easily understand it. Their contention was simply that the knowledge necessary unto salvation, though not equally clear on every page of Scripture, is yet conveyed to man throughout the Bible in such a simple and comprehensible form that one who is earnestly seeking salvation can, under the guidance of the Holy Spirit, by reading and studying the Bible, easily obtain for himself the necessary knowledge, and does not need the aid and guidance of the Church and of a separate priesthood. Naturally. they did not mean to minimize the importance of the interpretations of the Church in the preaching of the Word. They pointed out that Scripture itself testifies to its perspicuity, where it is declared to be a lamp unto our feet, and a light unto our path. The prophets and the apostles, and even Jesus Himself, address their messages to all the people, and never treat them as minors who are not able to understand the truth. The people are even declared to be able to judge and to understand (1 Cor. 2:15; 10:15; 1 John 2:20). Because of its perspicuity the Bible can even be said to be self-interpretive. The Reformers had this in mind, when they spoke of an *interpretatio secundum analogiam fidei* or *Scripturae*, and laid down the great principle, *Scriptura Scripturae interpres*. They did not regard the special task of the Church in the interpretation of the Bible as superfluous, but explicitly recognized the duty of the Church in this respect. Hence they spoke of the *potestas doctrinae* of the Church.

4. THE SUFFICIENCY OF SCRIPTURE. Neither Rome nor the Anabaptists regarded the Bible as sufficient. The latter had a low opinion of Scripture, and asserted the absolute necessity of the inner light and of all kinds of special revelations. They attached very little importance to the ministry of the Word. One of their pet slogans was, "The letter killeth, but the Spirit maketh alive" [cf. 2 Cor. 3:6]. From the time of the Middle Ages Rome maintained the absolute necessity of oral tradition as a complement to the written word. This tradition was not always clearly defined. The term originally covered oral teachings and customs of apostolic origin. But in the measure in which the Church moved farther and farther away from the

apostolic age, it became increasingly difficult to determine, whether certain teachings really came down from the apostles. Hence it became necessary to define the characteristics of what might truly be regarded as apostolic tradition. An attempt at this was made in the rule of Vincentius Lerinensis, who declared that to be apostolic which was believed everywhere, always, and by all (*ubique, semper, et ab omnibus, creditum est*). Real apostolic tradition could therefore be recognized by the fact that it was believed everywhere, at all times, and by the whole Church. This definition was adopted by all later Roman Catholic theologians, though in actual practice it was modified. It was very difficult to determine, whether a certain truth was *always* believed, and therefore the question gradually took on the more contemporaneous form, whether such a truth is at any particular time generally believed. The antiquity of the truth was sacrificed to its universality, and the really important question was ignored. It was tantamount to saying that it could not be determined, whether a certain teaching actually came down from the apostles. But even so a formidable difficulty remained. In seeking an answer to the question who was to pass on this question of universality, it was held that the Church in general could not do this, but only the *ecclesia docens*, the bishops in their councils. This is still the position of the Old Catholic Church. But even this position proved untenable. The question arose, When are the bishops infallible in determining the nature of a tradition, always, or only when they are met in council? And if they can give infallible decisions only when they have come together, must their vote be unanimous or is a majority sufficient to lend weight to their decision? And if a majority is sufficient, how great must this be; is a majority of one sufficient? The result of all these deliberations was that the Pope was finally declared infallible in matters of faith and practice, when speaking *ex cathedra*. If the Pope now declares something to be apostolic tradition, that settles the matter, and what is so declared thereby becomes binding on the Church.

Over against the position that Scripture needs some complement, the Reformers asserted the *perfectio* or *sufficientia* of Scripture. This doctrine does not mean that everything that was spoken and written by the prophets, by Christ, and by the apostles, is incorporated in Scripture. The Bible clearly proves that this is not the case (1 Kings 4:33; 1 Cor. 5:9; Col. 4:16; 2 Thess. 2:5). Neither does it mean that all the articles of faith are found in finished form in Scripture. The Bible contains no dogmas; these can be derived from it only by a process of reflection. The Reformers merely intended to deny that there is alongside of Scripture an unwritten Word of God with equal authority and therefore equally binding on the conscience. And in taking that position they took their stand on Scriptural ground. In Scripture each succeeding book connects up with the preceding (except in contemporary narratives), and is based on it. The Psalms and the Prophets presuppose the Law and appeal to it, and to it only. The New Testament comes to us as the fulfilment of the Old and refers back to nothing else. Oral traditions current in the time of Jesus are rejected as human inventions (Matt. 5:21–48; 15:4, 9; 1 Cor. 4:6). Christ is presented to us as the acme of the divine revelation, the highest and the last (Matt. 11:27; John 1:18; 17:4, 6; Heb. 1:1). For the knowledge of the way of salvation we are referred to Scripture only, to the word of Christ, and of the apostles (John 17:20; 1 John 1:3). The Reformers did recognize a Christian tradition, but only a Christian tradition based on, and derived from, Scripture, and not one that equalled or even surpassed it in authority.

QUESTIONS FOR FURTHER STUDY: How do Roman Catholics defend the authority of tradition alongside of that of Scripture? Why do they attach so much importance to apostolic tradition? Is it right to limit the normative authority of Scripture to those parts which teach the doctrine of salvation? Has Scripture any authority in matters of science and art? Does the Bible in any way testify to its necessity? How does modern liberal theology judge of this? Do not the many contradictory interpretations of Scripture disprove its perspicuity? How do the oral law of the Jews and the oral tradition of the Roman Catholics compare? Is the appeal of the Mystics to 2 Corinthians 3:6 to disprove the sufficiency of Scripture, tenable?

REFERENCES: Herman Bavinck, *Gereformeerde Dogmatiek* (Kampen: J. H. Kok, 1906), 1:476–527; Abraham Kuyper, *Dictaten Dogmatiek, De Sacra Scriptura* (Kampen: J. H. Kok, 1910), 2:190–241; George T. Ladd, *The Doctrine of Sacred Scripture* (New York: Scribner, 1883), 2:514–610; William Cunningham, *Theological Lectures* (New York: Robert Carter, 1878), 459–516; David S. Schaff, *Our Fathers' Faith and Ours* (New York: Putnam, 1928), 147–70; W. Wilmers, *Handbook of the Christian Religion* (1891; repr., New York: Benzinger, 1921), 120–51; Heinrich Heppe, *Die Dogmatik der evangelisch-reformirten Kirche* (Neukirchen: Erziehungsverein, 1935), 9–31; idem, *Dogmatik des deutschen Protestantismus im sechzehnten Jahrhundert* (Gotha: F. A. Perthes, 1857), 1:211–57; Charles M. Mead, *Supernatural Revelation* (New York: A. D. F. Randolph, 1889), 318–355; Heinrich Schmid, *Doctrinal Theology of the Evangelical Lutheran Church* (Philadelphia: Lutheran Publication Society, 1899), 61–101; Henricus E. Gravemeijer, *Leesboek over de Gereformeerde Geloofsleer* (Utrecht: H. Ten Hoove, 1894), 1:244–267; John Burgess, *The Protestant Faith* (Sydney: Angus & Robertson, 1928), 59–94.

V. The Principium Cognoscendi Internum

The knowledge of God presupposes, not only that God has revealed Himself, but also that man is capable, either constitutionally or by virtue of a gracious work of renewal, of receiving and appropriating this revelation. If man did not have that ability, the divine revelation, while existing objectively. would forever remain foreign to him and exercise no influence on his life. All knowledge, and consequently also all science, requires a certain correspondence between subject and object. This means that alongside of the *principium cognoscendi externum* there must also be a *principium cognoscendi internum*, a principium in man which enables him to discern and to appropriate God's special revelation. Naturally, the absolute Idealist would not subscribe to this position, for according to him knowledge not only calls for a *correspondence* between subject and object, but for the *identity* of the two. Even the Theology of Crisis feels constrained to put the matter in a different form. It recognizes no objectively existing revelation; nor does it believe in a point of contact in the life of man for special revelation. Revelation simply is not revelation until it is brought home to the heart of man in faith. But this faith is not a permanent receptivity in man for an objectively existing revelation, but is given in and with the revelation itself whenever God reveals Himself. This means that on this point the distinction between the subjective and the objective is really cancelled. Reformed theology, however, recognizes the existence of a *principium cognoscendi internum*, and the question naturally arises, What is the nature of this principium? In the course of history several answers have been given to that question. The organ by which man judges and appropriates the revelation of God was sought successively: (A) in the human understanding, (B) in speculative reason, (C) in devout feeling, and (D) in the moral consciousness. We shall consider these successively.

A. The Human Understanding

Some sought the *principium cognoscendi internum* in the human understanding in general, as distinguished from what is more specifically called the speculative reason. It was their persistent attempt to establish the truth on *historico-apologetical* grounds.

1. HISTORICAL STATEMENT OF THIS POSITION.

a. *Up to the time of the Reformation*. In view of the fact that the revelation of God in Christ does not minister to the pride of man but rather humbles him, it naturally met with a great deal of opposition and was repeatedly in need of defense. This was necessary even in the apostolic age, so that the Bible itself contains apologetical elements. In the second century the Apologetes defended the truth of Christianity over against Jews and Gentiles, and gave an account of the grounds on which it rests. They did not take their starting point in doubt or in any so-called neutrality, but in an unwavering faith and called attention to the superior excellency of Christianity, to the redemptive message of special revelation, to the antiquity and unity, the simplicity and sublimity, the fulness and many-sidedness of Scripture, to prophecies and miracles, and to the testimony of the Church and the blessings of the gospel. These arguments were repeated in the writings of the anti-Gnostic fathers and in later theology, though they were sometimes treated in other connections and did not always assume the same character.

Scholasticism also took its starting point in faith, but by its attempt to change religious truths into concepts of reason effected a separation of natural and supernatural truths that was detrimental to both. According to them the former could be proved by reason, but the latter could only be accepted on authority. In the former scientific certainty was possible, but in the latter it was not possible to rise above the level of faith. The order which they usually followed, though with several variations, was the following: first they sought to demonstrate by rational argumentation the truths of natural revelation; then they proved in a similar way the possibility, necessity, and reality of special revelation; and finally they urged reason, on the mere ground of the existence of a special revelation, to accept its contents blindly in faith. The motives that were adduced for belief in a special revelation were generally called *motiva credibilitatis*. The argument that Scripture as a divine revelation rests on the testimony of the Church was developed by the Roman Catholics especially after the Reformation. All such arguments, however, though they may demonstrate the reasonableness of accepting Scripture as the Word of God, can only produce a *fides humana* and never a *fides divina*. Even among the Roman Catholics some are willing to admit this, though on the whole they have a high opinion of Apologetics. The general Roman Catholic representation as to the way in which man arrives at the knowledge of God's revelation is the following: (1) Supernatural revelation rises on the basis of natural revelation, and can only be appropriated successively by degrees. (2) By various proofs man in his natural state is first led to the natural theology, which constitutes the preamble of faith. At this point even science is possible, since the proofs are demonstrative. Ordinarily we cannot yet speak of faith at this stage. (3) He who has reached this point is now, through the motives of credibility, of which the Church is the most important, put in a position to see and admit the trustworthiness of God's revelation and the reasonableness of faith. (4) After man has thus been led to the fides humana (human faith) he is raised by an infused grace to the supernatural order and prepares himself by good works for the vision of God.

b. *After the Reformation.* The Protestants took a different position, but did not always consistently maintain it. The Reformers did not take their starting point in human reason, but in the Christian faith, and stressed the fact that this faith rests only on divine authority and is wrought by the Holy Spirit. Protestant theologians did not always remain true to this principle, but frequently returned to the doctrine of a natural theology, and to the historical proofs for the truth of revelation. Under the influence of Cartesius, who took his starting point in doubt, Rationalism gradually found its way into the Churches, and the historico-apologetical method came into vogue. It clearly came to the foreground in Supranaturalism. In the application of this method the purpose was to prove that God has revealed Himself in a supernatural way rather than to exhibit the reasonableness of revelation. And in order to prove this, attention was called to the miracles of Scripture, to the fulfilment of prophecies, often of a very special character, to the striking correspondence of the various parts of Scripture, to the moral influence of the gospel, and so on. The purpose was to lead men to faith by such intellectual considerations. It cannot be denied that some who followed this method did it with the best intentions. Some of their works are even now mentioned with honor in Christian Apologetics, though the method now followed and the arguments adduced are quite different. Yet this method was bound to lead to Rationalism. Even Butler could pen a sentence like the following: "For though natural religion is the foundation and principal part of Christianity, it is not in any sense the whole of it."[70] Reason is accorded the right to examine and explain the credentials of revelation, and is thus placed above Scripture. For that reason this method stands condemned from a theological point of view. Moreover, its untenableness clearly appeared from the history of Supranaturalism itself, and from the sharp criticism of Rousseau and Lessing, of Kant and Schleiermacher. For a long time even Reformed authors continued to speak of natural theology as *fundamental* theology, but in many Reformed circles it is entirely discredited at present.

2. EVALUATION OF THIS POSITION. As intimated in the preceding, the historico-apologetical method does not meet with approval from a theological point of view, because it underrates both religious truth and faith. Religious truth is not like some theorem of science, and faith is not purely intellectual insight into some result of scientific investigation. Baillie calls attention to the fact that this whole method of reasoning is called in question today.[71] It also does scant justice to the Christian religion. The Word of God presupposes the darkness and error of the natural man, and would therefore contradict itself, if it submitted itself to the judgment of that man. It would thereby acknowledge one as judge whom it had first disqualified. Finally, this method does not lead to the desired result. In the beginning of the previous century miracles and prophecies could serve as proofs, but in the present day they themselves require proof.

This does not mean, however, that Apologetics is devoid of all real value. It may undoubtedly serve a useful purpose in some respects, but cannot, without forfeiting its theological character, precede faith nor prove the truth of revelation *a priorily*. It presupposes in its votaries a believing acceptance of the truth. A threefold value may be ascribed to it: (a) It compels theology to give an account of its contents and of the grounds on which it rests, and thus promotes theological self-consciousness. (b) It makes the Christian conscious of the fact that he need not feel embarrassed in the presence of the enemy, but finds support

70. Joseph Butler, *The Analogy of Religion*, Part II, Ch. 1.
71. John Baillie, *Our Knowledge of God* (London: Oxford University Press, 1943), 129.

in nature and history, in science and art, and in the heart and conscience of every man. (c) Though it cannot of itself bring any man to the acknowledgment of the truth by compelling proofs, it may, like the ministry of the Word, give him a profound impression of the truth, which he cannot easily shake off.

In actual practice, however, Apologetics has often moved in the wrong direction. (a) It has divorced itself from faith, assuming a place outside of, above, and preceding theology, and has thereby laid claim to an authority to which it is not entitled. (b) It has separated faith and knowledge in such a way as to cause religious truth to rest wholly or in part on purely intellectual grounds, something that is entirely contrary to the nature of that truth. (c) The result was that it cherished exaggerated expectations with reference to its scientific labors, as if it could change the heart through the intellect, and by means of sound reasoning could cultivate piety.

B. Speculative Reason

The position of those who regarded speculative reason as the organ by which to discern, and judge, and appropriate religious truth, did not differ essentially from those who ascribed these functions to the human understanding in general. The one as well as the other made human reason the arbiter of the truth as well as its appropriating organ. Both belong to that broader category generally known as Rationalism. And one of the fundamental assumptions of Rationalism, says Paterson is, "that the mind has been restricted to the use of its natural powers in the discovery and appropriation of religious and moral truth. The notion is rejected that at any stage of the process the mind has been aided by an immediate action upon it of the Divine Spirit, as the result of which it is enabled to take possession of truth that would otherwise lie beyond its ken and grasp."[72] At the same time they who exalted speculative reason to the place of honor presented a system that was far more profound and comprehensive than that of vulgar Rationalism, that is, the Rationalism of the Wolffian type. They made speculative reason not only the norm and the necessary faculty for the reception of the truth, but even regarded it as the source of the truth, and by so doing broke the more effectively with the idea of a special divine revelation.

1. HISTORICAL STATEMENT OF THIS POSITION. The vulgar Rationalism of the eighteenth century, represented by Deism and the Wolffian school of philosophy, finally yielded to the critical onslaughts of Rousseau and Lessing, of Kant and Schleiermacher. The superficial structure which it reared was swept from its foundation. With Kant and Schleiermacher the autonomy of the subject began. At first the reaction went so far as to discount the objective world. According to Kant man cannot know *noumena* or the essence of things, but knows merely phenomena, and even these only in the forms which the thinking subject imposes on them. The subject thus produces the form of the phenomenal world. Fichte went a step farther and denied the existence of an objective world, in distinction from the subject. In his opinion the world of external things exists only in the one universal mind and is the product of this mind. At first Schleiermacher also assumed this standpoint. In course of time it was felt, however, that there must be something that has objective reality and therefore normative value. That consideration led to the so-called restauration, in which the attempt was made to get back to the objective, while retaining the same subjective starting point. Hegel was the

---

72. William P. Paterson, *The Rule of Faith* (London: Hodder & Stoughton, 1912), 113.

great representative of this tendency. He raised the subjective, ethical Idealism of Fichte to an objective, logical Idealism, and substituted for the idea of being that of becoming. In his system of thought the whole world became a process, a development of the logical idea, in which all being is simply represented as thought. In that evolution religion also has its place. It, too, is pure thought or knowledge, namely, the knowledge which the Absolute has of itself in forms of the imagination. It is clothed in forms and symbols, or pictorial representations, of which only speculative reason can fathom the deep significance. According to Hegel it is the task of philosophy to rid the dogmas of religion of their historical forms, which are after all mere husks, and to discover and elucidate the idea, which is the precious hidden kernel. Thus the great truths of Christianity, such as the doctrine of the Trinity, of the incarnation, of the atonement, and others, not only became objects of philosophical speculation, but in their essential nature and ideal form really became the fruits of this speculation. Apart from Scripture and every other authority, these truths were represented as *necessary thoughts of reason*, and were therefore shown to be highly reasonable. The real proof for the truths of religion was found in the fact that they presented themselves to the mind as *necessary thoughts*. This was in harmony with the fundamental principle of Hegel: "All that is rational is real." Whatever one thought *with logical necessity* and proved to be a coherent part of the whole system of truth, was regarded as true. Logical necessity of thought or coherence was thus made the standard of truth in matters of religion. This method was applied in theology by Daub, Marheineke, Strauss, Vatke, Weisse, Biedermann, and others, though not always to the same degree, nor with the same result. It also found some favor among the followers of Schleiermacher, the father of modern theology, who shared the subjective starting point of Hegel, though he took position in the affections rather than in reason.

2. EVALUATION OF THIS POSITION. They who regard speculative reason as the criterion of religious truth are wedded to the speculative method in appropriating and judging this truth. This method undoubtedly has an advantage over the historico-apologetical method. Supranaturalism pretended to be able to demonstrate the dogmas of religion so clearly as to silence all objections. It made a determined effort to give a definite and clear representation of the truth, so that the reasonableness of it could at once be seen. But its sharp distinctions led to an intellectualism in which truth was divorced from life. The speculative method broke with this demand for *clearness*, and recognized the deep sense of the dogmata, and the mysterious elements in religion. Moreover, it emphasized the fact that religion occupies a unique place in human life, and therefore demands a corresponding organ in human nature. Hegel found this in speculative reason, and Schleiermacher, in the feelings. Both were mistaken, but nevertheless called attention to an important matter, when they stressed the necessity of a proper organ for religion, a matter that is of the greatest importance for the study of theology, and is therefore entitled to grateful recognition.

But the speculative method did not stop at the thought that thinking and being necessarily correspond to each other; it proceeded to the identification of the two. This is the fundamental error of speculative philosophy. The great question is, Do we think a thing because it exists, or does it exist because we necessarily think it. Speculative philosophy claims the latter, but without any warrant. At this point Hegel took an impossible leap. The existence of a thing does not follow from the fact that we think it, for existence is not an emanation of thought, but rests on an act of power. It is true that God thought things eternally, but He brought the things which existed *ideally* into *real* existence only by a creative act. We can only reflect on what God thought long before and has creatively brought to our consciousness in the existing world of reality. If we reject all that comes to us from without, we retain only a vague principle without any content, from which nothing can be derived. Notwithstanding its high pretensions and its, ostensibly, good intentions, the speculative method did not succeed in changing the despised doctrines of the Christian religion into a philosophical system of universal truth, quite acceptable to the world. The word of the cross remained foolishness to them that perish. It broke away from the objective basis of God's revelation, and therefore could not succeed in constructing a real system of theology.

C. Devout Feeling or Religious Intuition

A third position with respect to the *principium cognoscendi internum* of theology, is that of those who find the organ by which religious truth is acquired and discerned in devout feeling or religious intuition. Schleiermacher is generally recognized as the father of this view. This conception of the internal or subjective principle of knowledge in theology has this in common with that of Hegel, that it does not involve any preliminary assumption as to the derivation of the subject-matter from revelation. But in distinction from those who championed the speculative method and virtually changed theology into philosophy, the advocates of this method are inclined to banish all philosophy from theology. They are like the speculative philosophers and theologians, however, in their failure to distinguish between the norm or criterion and the source of religious truth. Since they recognize their own subjective feelings as the source of this truth, the question for them is not so much a question of the appropriation, as of the appraisal, of religious truth or, to express it in a different way, a question of recognizing it *as religious truth*. Their special characteristic is that they seek religious certitude in a religious-empirical way. Devout feeling is the criterion of religious truth, and the test applied to it is the test of experience.

1. HISTORICAL STATEMENT OF THE POSITION. When both of the preceding methods led to no result, many theologians took refuge in religious experience and sought support in it for the certainty and truth of Christianity. It is particularly in the application of this method that the influence of Schleiermacher is felt. He and his followers had the laudable desire to restore theology to honor again, and they attempted to accomplish this by taking position in the believing consciousness. In answer to the question, What prompts us to accept the truths of Christianity? the advocates of this method do not appeal to historical or rational proofs, nor to the authority of Scripture or of the Church, but to the experience of salvation in the heart of the sinner. Schleiermacher wants the theologian to start with the data given in the confession of a particular Church, and by these data he means, not so much the doctrines that are formulated in the Creeds, as the living and effectual beliefs, which are voiced in the preaching and teaching of the Church. Then these doctrines or beliefs must be traced to their original source, which is not found in Scripture, but in the devout feeling which results from the relation of the soul to Jesus Christ. And, finally, they must be reproduced in a systematized form in the light of the fact that they are the reflex of distinctly pious feelings. This means that the doctrines are derived from pious or religious feelings, and also find in these the ground of their certitude. It is only in the light of such feelings that their truly religious character stands out.

Frank, one of the outstanding theologians of the Erlangen school of theology, is also one of the most representative advocates of this theory. His system already marks a real advance upon that of Schleiermacher, since he does not start from a general state of feeling, but from the specific experience of regeneration. In his work on *The System of the Christian Certainty* he seeks the answer to this question: What leads man to depend on the objective factors of salvation, such as God, Christ, Scripture, and others, and to accept Scripture as the Word of God? And his answer is that this is not due to historical or rational proofs, nor to the authority of Scripture, of the Church, or of tradition, but only to the experience of regeneration. The Christian certainty of which he speaks is not the assurance of salvation, but the assurance respecting the reality of the truth. Christian certitude, in the sense of certainty respecting the truth, finds its basis, according to Frank, in the Christian life, that is, in the believer's moral and spiritual experience. The Christian knows that a mighty change has taken place in his life, and from this experience of regeneration he infers the whole content of Christian truth. This truth arranges itself in three groups around the experience of regeneration. (a) There are truths which are immediately involved in that experience, such as the reality of sin, of judgment, and of future perfection (immanent and central truths). (b) Then there are truths which must be assumed, in order to explain the new condition, such as the reality of a personal God, the existence of God as triune, and the redemption wrought by the God-man (transcendent truths). (c) Finally, these lead right on to the means by which the preceding agents work, such as the Church, the Word of God, the sacraments, miracles, revelation, and inspiration (transeunt truths). This answer of Frank undoubtedly contains an important truth, since regeneration is indeed necessary, in order to see the Kingdom of God. But the manner in which he elaborates his thought is very dubious, and this is probably the necessary result of his subjective standpoint. He does not consistently work out a single thought, but constantly confuses the manner in which religious truths are derived, and the manner in which certainty respecting these is obtained. Since his work is entitled The System of the Christian Certainty, it raises the expectation that the author simply desires to show how the believer reaches Christian certitude. But in that case he should have limited himself to the task of elucidating the origin and nature of Christian certainty, and should not in addition have discussed the contents of the religious consciousness. Then he would not have given us a system of the objects to which this certainty pertains; and yet this is exactly what he does, when he derives all religious truths from the experience of regeneration.

2. EVALUATION OF THIS POSITION. There are many objections to this starting point and method. (a) Regeneration and all other experiences of the Christian are always connected with the objective factors of the Church, the Scriptures, and so on, while Frank divorces the two. (b) In his second work, *The System of the Christian Truth* [*Sytem der christlichen Wahreit* (1878)], he himself gives precedence to these objective factors, and thus recognizes their priority. For that very reason he should have maintained this order throughout his system. (c) The method in which he derives the objective dogmata from the certainty of the Christian, is one that does not fit in theology. It is borrowed from speculative philosophy, which derives religious truth from the necessity of logical coherence. (d) This method goes contrary to all religious experience. No Christian ever obtained certainty respecting objective truths in the manner described by Frank. Scarcely anyone has adopted his method. And even among those who have adopted it in a modified form there is a difference of opinion as to the significance of experience for the *principia* of theology. The application of this method carries with it a threefold danger. (a) It easily leads into the danger of forming a

wrong conception of religious experience, and of expecting from it what it cannot yield. While it is possible to experience certain emotions, such as those of penitence, fear, hope, and so on, it is not possible to experience historical facts. (b) It really makes it impossible for uneducated Christians to obtain knowledge and certainty respecting the historical facts of Christianity, since these can only be deduced from experience by an elaborate process of reasoning. (c) It is apt to rob historical Christianity ever increasingly of its real significance. Experience is loaded down with a burden which it cannot bear. The truth of Christianity cannot rest on it as a final ground. And the consciousness of this may easily lead to a reduction of the burden by divorcing the contents of faith from all historical facts and limiting it to religious and ethical experiences.

D. The Moral Consciousness

Finally, there is still another view of the norm of religious truth, and of the manner in which we come to recognize and acknowledge it as such, a view that is somewhat akin to the preceding, but which, in distinction from the preceding, with its emotional appeal, stresses the ethical element in religion. It is a view that finds its roots in the moralism of Kant, and that became popular in theology through the influence of the Neo-Kantianism of Ritschl and his followers. It makes the moral consciousness the real judge of religious truth. The real emphasis in this view is not on emotional experience, but on ethical self-maintenance. The great and determinative question is, whether a certain truth satisfies the moral requirements of the heart or the conscience, and thus answers to a real practical need. Hence the method applied by its advocates is called *ethical-psychological* or *ethical-practical*.

1. HISTORICAL STATEMENT OF THE POSITION. If the immediately preceding method connects up with Schleiermacher, this method finds its main support in Kant. For its adherents Christianity in general is not so much a doctrine that must be demonstrated and accepted as true, nor a historical fact that calls for proof, but a religious and ethical power that addresses itself to the heart and the conscience of man. According to them Christianity cannot be made acceptable to all men without distinction, but only to those who have a proper moral disposition, a feeling of dissatisfaction, a sense of the good, a desire for redemption, and so on. When Christianity comes in contact with such men, it commends itself to their hearts and consciences as divine truth without any reasoning or further proof. It satisfies their religious needs, answers to their higher aspirations, reconciles them with themselves, brings them peace, comfort, and salvation, and thus proves itself to be the consolation and the wisdom of God.

This kind of argumentation did not begin with Kant. Tertullian already appealed to the testimony which the soul involuntarily gives to Christ. The Apologetes pointed out that the heathen religions of their day were not able to satisfy the religious needs of man, nor to foster a truly ethical life. Duns Scotus called attention to the moral influence of God's revelation and to its sufficiency in enabling man to reach his destiny. Both Roman Catholic and Protestant theologians sought to prove the truth of the Christian religion by pointing to its operation and influence on the intellectual, moral, social, and political life of individuals and nations. Pascal and Vinet especially brought this method to honor, but did not yet place it in opposition to historical argumentation. The former even admitted the great value of historical proofs, though he did not assign to them their usual place; and the latter did not despise them, though he regarded them as inferior to the moral and religious proof. In later years this method was adopted by Astie, Pressencé, Secretan, de la Saussaye, and others, who generally neglected and sometimes even disdained historical proofs.

However, the influence of Kant was of great significance for this method. According to him the theoretical reason necessarily yields three ideas, namely, those of God, freedom, and immortality. These three are therefore general. It does not assure us, however, that there are corresponding realities, nor enlighten us as to the nature of these realities. The corresponding realities are demanded, however, by the practical reason with its categorical imperative. This clearly testifies to the existence of a moral order, and demands that this order shall finally triumph over the natural order. This being so, it naturally follows that man must be free, that there must be a future life in which the moral will be really triumphant, and that there must be a highest Judge to punish vice and reward virtue. Only that view of the world is true that answers to our inner life and satisfies our moral needs.

When the insufficiency of the speculative method appeared, there was a tendency to go back to Kant. In theology Kantianism was reintroduced especially by Ritschl and Lipsius, though these men differed from Kant in several particulars. It is especially in the school of Ritschl that the ethicopsychological method is brought into prominence. This school regards Christianity as a historical phenomenon, but especially as a religious and ethical power of the greatest significance for the heart and conscience of man. Ritschl finds in religion especially two elements: on the one hand that of dependence on God, and on the other, that of spiritual freedom or supremacy over nature, which, in the estimation of Ritschl, is its main element. The Christian religion gives answer to the question, how man as a free moral being, who is yet hemmed in by nature and in many ways dependent on it, can maintain his freedom and rise superior to nature. And the answer is that man can gain the mastery over nature through communion with God in Christ and by making God's end his own, that is, by seeking the Kingdom of God in a life for God, motivated by love. In this practical power of Christianity Ritschl finds the real proof for the truth of the revelation of God in Christ and of the Christian religion. It is not a theoretical, but a practical proof. Like Schleiermacher, he too would banish all metaphysics from theology. In science theoretical proofs apply, but in religion only judgments of value. As a matter of fact, however, neither one of the two succeeded in excluding philosophy. Moreover, Kaftan, one of the most prominent and one of the ablest followers of Ritschl, stressed the fact that judgments of value cannot be divorced from theoretical judgments of being.

2. EVALUATION OF THIS POSITION. This and the immediately preceding method undoubtedly deserve to be preferred above the historical and speculative methods. The method now under consideration does not regard religion merely as a doctrine to be proved, nor as a condition of the subject to be analyzed intellectually, as the first two methods do respectively. It looks upon the Christian religion as a historical, objective power that answers to the moral needs of man, and finds in this its proof and justification. Nevertheless, there are serious objections to this method. (a) Though a religion that does not satisfy the religious and ethical life, that offers no comfort in sorrow and death, and does not give strength unto the battles of life, is not worthy of the name of religion; yet the fact that the Christian religion does do this, is no absolute proof of its truth, since there are other religions which also give a certain degree of satisfaction in this respect. (b) It is dangerous to make the truth of Christianity dependent on judgments of value. There would be no great objection, if it were only intended to stress the fact that a dogma must always have religious and ethical value,

or that intellectual reasoning can never give us perfect certainty respecting religious truths, while this can be obtained by experiencing the religious values expressed by the dogmas. In that case the subjective evaluation would presuppose the objective reality of the religious truths and would only serve as a means to obtain certainty respecting that reality. Then the value of a thing would not be represented as the ground of its existence, but would simply enable us to acknowledge it subjectively. In the system of Ritschl it is quite different, however, since the judgments of value are divorced from all metaphysics. (c) Moreover, in this way we can never reach objectivity. The needs that find satisfaction in the Christian faith are virtually created by that same faith through the work of the ministry. Hence the question arises, whether those needs are real in the life of man, or have merely been awakened artificially and are therefore purely imaginary. In other words, the question of the truth of the Christian religion remains.

QUESTIONS FOR FURTHER STUDY: What is the difference between a *fides humana* and a *fides divina*? Can we be satisfied with historical certainty in theology? How can the transition from the historico-apologetical, to the speculative, method be explained? Is subjectivism, which makes the human reason or human experience the source of Christian truth, compatible with absolute certainty? Can absolute Idealism ever lead to a satisfying Christian certitude? Is the test of experience and the pragmatic test ever applied to the truth in Scripture? What makes these tests so popular in the present day? What more objective test does Troeltsch recommend? How should we judge of the psychological approach to religion, as exhibited in Horton's A Psychological Approach to Theology? Does the position taken by Baillie in his *Our Knowledge of God* differ materially from that of Schleiermacher?

REFERENCES: Herman Bavinck, *Gereformeerde Dogmatiek* (Kampen: J. H. Kok, 1906), 1:528–602; John Miley, *Systematic Theology* (New York: Eaton & Mains, 1892), 1:34–47; Douglas C. Macintosh, *Theology as an Empirical Science* (New York: Macmillan, 1919), 7–26; Isaac A. Dorner, *A System of Christian Doctrine* (Edinburgh: T. & T. Clark, 1880), 1:58–168; Jean L. Girardeau, *Discussions of Theological Questions* (Richmond, VA: Presbyterian Committee of Publication, 1905), 73–125; William P. Paterson, *The Rule of Faith* (London: Hodder & Stoughton, 1912), 92–173; Julius Kaftan, *The Truth of the Christian Religion* (Edinburgh: T. & T. Clark, 1894), 1:230–316; Franz H. R. Frank, *The System of the Christian Certainty* (Edinburgh: T. & T. Clark, 1886); John Baillie, *The Interpretation of Religion* (New York: Scribner, 1928), 174–339; Andrew D. Heffern, *Apology and Polemic in the New Testament* (New York: Macmillan, 1922); R. M. Wenley, *Contemporary Theology and Theism* (New York: Scribner, 1897), 11–124; Erich Schaeder, *Theozentrische Theologie*, vols. 1 and 2 (Leipzig: A. Deichert, 1925, 1928), 1–55; Walter M. Horton, *A Psychological Approach to Theology* (New York: Harper, 1931); John Baillie, *Our Knowledge of God* (London: Oxford University Press, 1943); Edgar P. Dickie, *Revelation and Response* (New York: Scribner, 1938); Hugh R. Mackintosh, *Types of Modern Theology* (London: Nisbet, 1937).

E. Faith, the Proper Principium Internum

Under the influence of Schleiermacher most theologians have come to the conclusion that religion is a unique phenomenon in human life, and can only be understood in a manner corresponding to its nature. By assuming this position theology takes its starting point in the subject, but should not, simply for that reason, be accused of subjectivism. No science has another starting point, since the objective world exists for us only as it is reflected in our consciousness. There must always be a *principium internum* that answers to the *principium externum*. Moreover, Christian theology from the very beginning took its starting point in the believing subject, was born of faith, and was guided and controlled by the rule: *per fidem ad intellectum*. And this is also entirely in harmony with Scripture, which speaks not only of a revelation of God outside of us, but also of an inner illumination of the Holy Spirit. If the accusation of subjectivism could be lodged against this starting point with any degree of justice, it could also be urged against all science, against theology as a whole, and even against Scripture itself. Such an accusation is warranted only, however, when the subjective condition absolutely necessary for the knowledge of a thing is made the source of that knowledge. An organ by which we take cognizance of the objective world round about us, is not the source from which that world proceeds.

1. THE NAME OF THE PRINCIPIUM COGNOSCENDI INTERNUM. The *principium internum* is usually called *faith* in Scripture. Other terms are also used, such as *regeneration* (John 3:3; 1 Cor. 2:12, 14), *purity of heart* (Matt. 5:8), *love to the will of God* (John 7:17), and *the Spirit of God* (1 Cor. 2:13). For several reasons, however, the term *faith* deserves preference. (a) It is the term that stands out prominently in Scripture. (b) It directs attention at once to the conscious life, and thus involves a recognition of the fact that all the knowledge of man is mediated by his consciousness. And (c) it indicates better than any other name the close connection between religious knowledge and all other knowledge of man. In general it may be said that we obtain knowledge in no other way in religion than we do in the other sciences. We should remember that faith is not a new organ of science. Men sometimes speak of believing and knowing as opposites, but in such cases they use the word 'believe' in the weak sense of having an opinion for which the proper evidence is lacking. The word 'faith' has a far more profound meaning, however. It is frequently used to denote *the positive knowledge that does not rest on external evidence nor on logical demonstration, but on an immediate and direct insight*. In that sense it can ever be said to be fundamental to all the sciences. Intuitive knowledge and immediate insight occupy an important place in human life. There is not a single field of endeavor, nor a single phase of life in which we can get along without it.

2. DISTINCTIVE NATURE OF THE KNOWLEDGE OF FAITH. The correspondence between general and religious knowledge should not cause us to lose sight of the existing difference. There is a very important difference between faith in the sense of immediate certainty and faith in the religious sense. In the Christian religion faith has a unique significance, as the following points will show. (a) In the New Testament it denotes a religious relation of man to God, and includes not only a *certain* knowledge, that is, an assured knowledge, but also a heartful trust in God, a complete surrender to Him, and a personal appropriation of the promises of the gospel. (b) While the faith we exercise in connection with the external world, for instance with respect to the reliability of our senses, the pertinency of the laws of thought, and so on, rests on our own inner observation, Christian faith is directed to that which is invisible and cannot be observed (Heb. 11:1). (c) Faith in the religious sense is distinguished from that in the sense of immediate certainty in this that it rests on the insight of others rather than on our own. We are made acquainted with the grace of God in Jesus Christ through the testimony of prophets and apostles. (d) Finally, Christian faith differs from faith as immediate certainty also in the fact that it does not arise spontaneously in human nature. While it is perfectly human, and may even be called the restoration of human

nature, it grates on the pride of the natural man and arouses hostility in his heart. God is not only its object, but also its author. Barth and Brunner go so far as to call God, rather than man, the subject of faith. While they also speak of it as man's response to the divine revelation, they really regard it as that in which God completes His revelation. The revelation itself gives birth to the response. As long as it does not do this, there is no revelation.

According to Scripture this faith carries its own certainty with it. It does this, not because it is so firm and certain in itself, but because it rests on the testimony and the promises of God. It makes the invisible blessings of salvation just as certain for man, yea even more certain, than his own insight or any scientific proof can ever make anything. Scripture represents certainty as one of the characteristics of faith. Alongside of the certainty of science we have, therefore, the certainty of faith, practically demonstrated in the believing Church, in its martyrs and steadfast confessors, and theoretically professed and developed in Christian theology. It is a certainty that is unwavering and indestructible. But this faith does not necessarily involve the truth of that which is believed. There is a great difference between subjective certainty and objective truth. In this respect everything depends on the grounds on which faith rests.

F. The Ground of Faith

By faith we accept the testimony of God as it is contained in Scripture. But now the question arises, How do we know that that testimony is true, and therefore perfectly reliable? What is the ground on which our faith in the Word of God rests? Or, perhaps better still, By what means is the conviction respecting the truth of the special revelation of God wrought in our hearts? In answer to these questions Reformed theologians point to the testimony of the Holy Spirit. It is this subject that calls for a brief discussion in this concluding chapter.

1. THE DOCTRINE OF THE TESTIMONIUM SPIRITUS SANCTI IN THE CHURCH. It was admitted from the earliest Christian centuries on that none of the intellectual or historical proofs adduced for the truth of the Christian religion provide an adequate assurance. While they may lead to a *fides humana*, divine grace is necessary to engender faith in the heart. Augustine was the first one of the Church Fathers who clearly saw and taught the absolute necessity of inward grace for the acceptance of Scripture as the Word of God. It is true that he also attached great value to the testimony of the Church as a *motivum credibilitatis*, but he did not regard this as the last and deepest ground of faith. Theoretically, even the Church of Rome held that only the Holy Spirit can give one absolute certainty respecting the truth of revelation, but in practice there was a tendency to replace the testimony of the Holy Spirit by the testimony of the Church.

The Reformers consciously and deliberately placed testimony of the Holy Spirit in the foreground. They derived their certainty respecting the truth of the divine revelation from the work of the Spirit of God in the hearts of believers. They took position against the Church of Rome with its undue emphasis on the testimony of the Church, and also against the Anabaptists and other Mystics, who revealed a tendency to divorce the testimony of the Holy Spirit from the external testimony contained in Scripture. Calvin was the first one to give a detailed exposition of the doctrine of the testimony of the Holy Spirit.[73] Since his day this doctrine is quite generally accepted by both Lutheran and Reformed theologians.

---

73. *Institutes* 1.7.

Of late, however, it has suffered eclipse. This is due in part to the fact that many confuse the testimony of the Holy Spirit with the argument from experience, which is so popular in many circles today, and in part, to the mystical conception which some have of the testimony of the Holy Spirit, in connection with the widespread aversion to the supernatural. It is not unnecessary therefore to indicate precisely what is meant with the testimony of the Holy Spirit.

We should bear in mind, that the particular work of the Holy Spirit described by that name does not stand by itself, but is connected with the whole work of the Holy Spirit in the application of the redemption wrought in Christ. The Spirit renews the sinner, not only in his being, but also in his consciousness. He removes the spiritual darkness of the understanding and illumines the heart, so that the glory of God in Christ is clearly seen. It is only in virtue of the special operation of the Holy Spirit that man confesses Jesus Christ as Lord (1 Cor. 12:3). The work of the Holy Spirit enables him to accept the revelation of God in Christ, to appropriate the blessings of salvation, and to attain to the assurance of faith. And the testimony of the Holy Spirit is merely a special aspect of His more general work in the sphere of redemption. For that reason the two should never be dissociated.

2. MISTAKEN NOTIONS OF THE TESTIMONIUM SPIRITUS SANCTI. There are especially two views of the testimony of the Holy Spirit against which we must be on our guard.

a. *That it brings a new revelation*. The Mystics conceived of it as an inner revelation to the effect that the Bible is the Word of God. This was evidently the conception which Strauss had of it, for he maintained that, when Protestants accepted the doctrine of the *testimonium Spiritus Sancti*, they virtually adopted the principle of Mysticism. He interpreted it as the communication of a new truth, namely, *that the Bible is really the Word of God*. If this interpretation were correct, his assertion would be justified, for then the Christian would indeed be receiving a new revelation through the testimony of the Holy Spirit, just as the prophets did in the days of old. This revelation would then, of course, call for a new attestation, and so on *ad infinitum*. Such a conception of the testimony of the Holy Spirit makes our belief in Scripture as the Word of God dependent on this new revelation, and naturally involves a denial of its *autopistia*. The older Protestant theologians never had such a conception of the testimony of the Holy Spirit. They all stressed the *autopistia* of Scripture and were strongly opposed to the mysticism of the Anabaptists. Even the somewhat related representation, that we must conceive of the testimony of the Holy Spirit as an influence producing in believers a blind or unfounded conviction that the Bible is the Word of God, proved unacceptable to them. Faith is a conviction founded on a testimony, which in the absence of proper evidence does not make its appearance.

b. *That it is identical with the argument from experience*. The testimony of the Holy Spirit should not be confused, as is often done, with the testimony of experience. The Holy Spirit does indeed work in believers the experience of salvation in Christ, which cannot be explained apart from Scripture, but is wrought through the instrumentality of the Word, and therefore implicitly testifies to the fact that the Bible is of divine origin. This is an inference, in which we conclude, from an experience which we regard as divine, that the Bible, through which the experience is wrought in us, is the inspired Word of God. This argument has been elaborated, though not in the same form, by such theologians as Frank, Koestlin, Ihmels, Stearns, and many others. In itself it is perfectly legitimate and is not devoid of evidential value, but it is something quite different from the testimony of the

Holy Spirit. They who identify the two do not distinguish properly between the efficient cause of faith and the motives for faith. The testimony of experience may certainly be a motive for faith, but just as certainly cannot be the origin of it, since it already presupposes faith. The testimony of the Holy Spirit, on the other hand, is the *causa efficiens* of faith. Without it all the motives for faith would have no convincing power. Moreover, the testimony of experience respecting Scripture is no objective testimony of God, but simply the testimony of our own heart respecting the Scriptures. Finally, it has the character of a mere inference, or may even be said to involve more than one inference, since it concludes from a certain experience to Scripture as its origin, and from the fact that this experience is wrought through to the instrumentality of the revealed Word to the fact that this revelation is indeed the Word of God. It does not, therefore, have the character of an immediate testimony of the Holy Spirit. And because the testimony of experience is entirely subjective, the faith that is founded on it rests, in the last analysis, on the inner experience of the soul rather than on the objective testimony of God in His Word, which is after all the ground of all Christian certitude.

3. CORRECT VIEW OF THE TESTIMONIUM SPIRITUS SANCTI. Calvin absolutely rejects the idea that the authority of Scripture rests on the testimony of the Church, as well as some other erroneous views. He finally says: "Let it therefore be held as fixed, that those who are inwardly taught by the Holy Spirit acquiesce implicitly in Scripture; that Scripture, carrying its own evidence along with it, deigns not to submit to proofs and arguments, but owes the full conviction with which we ought to receive it to the testimony of the Spirit. Enlightened by Him, we no longer believe, either on our own judgment or that of others, that the Scriptures are from God; but, in a way superior to human judgment, feel perfectly assured—as much so as if we beheld the divine image visibly impressed on it—that it came to us, by the instrumentality of men, from the very mouth of God."[74] The Testimony of the Holy Spirit is simply the work of the Holy Spirit in the heart of the sinner, by which he removes the blindness of sin, so that the erstwhile blind man, who had no eyes for the sublime character of the Word of God, now clearly sees and appreciates the marks of its divine nature, and receives immediate certainty respecting the divine origin of Scripture. Just as one who has an eye for the beauties of architecture, in gazing up into the dome of the Saint Peter's Church at Rome, at once recognizes it as the production of a great artist, so the believer in the study of Scripture discovers in it at once the earmarks of the divine. The redeemed soul beholds God as the author of Scripture and rests on its testimony with childlike faith, with a *fides divina*. It is exactly the characteristic mark of such faith that it rests on a testimony of God, while a *fides humana* merely rests on a human testimony or on rational arguments. Of course, rational arguments may be adduced for the divine origin of Scripture, but these are powerless to convince the unrenewed man. The Christian believes the Bible to be the very Word of God in the last analysis on the testimony which God Himself gives respecting this matter in His Word, and recognizes that Word as divine by means of the testimony of God in his heart. The testimony of the Holy Spirit is therefore, strictly speaking, not so much the final ground of faith, but rather the means of faith. The final ground of faith is Scripture only, or better still, the authority of God which is impressed upon the believer in the testimony of Scripture. The ground of faith is identical with its contents, and cannot

---

74. *Institutes* 1.7.5.

be separated from it. But the testimony of the Holy Spirit is the moving cause of faith. We believe Scripture, not because of, but through the testimony of the Holy Spirit.

QUESTIONS FOR FURTHER STUDY: In how many different senses is the word 'faith' used? How do faith and knowledge compare in the estimation of Locke, and in that of Kant? What do the Ritschlians mean when they speak of "faith-knowledge"? Is faith a matter of the intellect, of the will, of the emotions, or of all three combined? How does Calvin work out the doctrine of the testimony of the Holy Spirit? What is the difference between the *testimonium Spiritus Sancti generale* and *speciale*? Does the testimony of the Holy Spirit apply to the different parts of the Bible separately?

REFERENCES: Herman Bavinck, *Gereformeerde Dogmatiek* (Kampen: J. H. Kok, 1906), 1:603–670; Abraham Kuyper, *Encyclopaedie. der Heilige Godgeleerdheid* (Amsterdam: J. A. Wormser, 1894), 2:501–511; Charles Hodge, *Systematic Theology* 2:69–86; G. Wisse, *Geloof en Wetenschap* (Kampen: J. H. Bos, 1908), 41–212; Randolph S. Foster, *Studies in Theology, Prolegomena* (Cincinnati: Granston & Stowe, 1891), 74–246; Francis J. Hall, *Dogmatic Theology*, vol. 1, *Introduction to Dogmatic Theology* (New York: Longmans, Green, 1907), 84–141; Franz H. R. Frank, *The System of Christian Certainty* (Edinburgh: T. & T. Clark, 1886); Lewis F. Stearns, *The Evidence of Christian Experience* (New York: Scribner, 1890); Ludwig Ihmels, *Centralfragen der Dogmatik in der Gegenwart* (Leipzig: A. Deichert, 1921), 1–21, 134–65; Julius Kaftan, *The Truth of the Christian Religion*, vol. 2 (Edinburgh: T. & T. Clark, 1894); Valentin Hepp, *Testimonium Spiritus Sancti, Generale* (Kampen: J. H. Kok, 1914); C. Wistar Hodge, "The Witness of the Holy Spirit to the Bible," *Princeton Theological Review* 11, 1 (1913): 41–84.

Part Six

Other Nineteenth-Century European Contributions

FROM NINETEENTH-CENTURY EUROPE emerged some able Reformed defenders of Scripture. Most of them had to struggle individually against the appeal of rationalism. Louis Gaussen fought against the Protestant establishment in Geneva to maintain a confessional stance. Both Adolphe Monod and Ernst Wilhelm Hengstenberg had to overcome periods of doubt before becoming valiant defenders of historic Christianity. Charles Spurgeon, too, combatted the liberal tendencies of his peers.

Gaussen is best known for his book *Theopneustia*. The text reproduced in the anthology is a "Catechical Sketch" on the doctrine of inspiration. In the form of questions and answers he deals with the crucial points of the debates with both rationalism and Roman Catholic views. This work displays a scholarly approach and a nuanced affirmation of inspiration, showing that Gaussen stands in line with the Second Helvetic Confession and the Helvetic Consensus Formula. The meditations by Monod from his classic *Farewell* offer practical and focused reflections on Scripture. The results of his lifelong preoccupation with the subject, they offer mature statements in compact form. In them he develops the analogy between Christ and the Scripture while maintaining a very high view of the divine and supernatural character of the Bible. Hengstenberg was a prolific Old Testament exegete who taught at the University of Berlin while at the same time defending conservative views and opposing Enlightenment rationalism. In the selection, an appendix to his *Christology of the Old Testament*, he defends the supernatural nature of Old Testament prophecies. He elaborates this important topic partly in response to Friedrich Schleiermacher's view of Scripture and prophecy. Spurgeon is best known as a Baptist preacher with affinities with the Puritans and Princeton's Calvinism. In his sermon on biblical interpretation, he puts forward a reading of the Old Testament that centers on the gospel and Christ. Spurgeon also highly commended the work of his contemporary Gaussen.

Just as influences besides the Westminster Standards and the Three Forms of Unity are discernible at Westminster, so other strands of Calvinism than those of the Scots and the Dutch are present. The four theologians in this part belong to these broader influences. Gaussen's defense was appreciated by Edward J. Young. After his arrival at

Princeton, B. B. Warfield referred to Monod's views favorably. Further, both Warfield and Young had the highest respect for Hengstenberg as an exegete. Hengstenberg had a great influence on Old Princeton (starting with Hodge) and Westminster. Finally, while Spurgeon's interpretational stance might benefit from the sophistication and restraint of Westminster hermeneutics, his Christ-centered and vivid preaching are respectively reflected in the preaching of Edmund P. Clowney and Jay Adams.

34

Louis Gaussen's *Theopneustia*

BRIEF DIDACTIC ABSTRACT OF THE
DOCTRINE OF THE DIVINE INSPIRATION

Louis Gaussen, *Theopneustia: The Plenary Inspiration of the Holy Scriptures*, trans. David D. Scott (Chicago: The Bible Institute Colportage Association, 1915), 106–39.

François Samuel Louis Gaussen (1790–1863) was a Swiss Reformed pastor and theologian from Geneva. Converted under the influence of the Scot Robert Haldane, he became involved in the fight for orthodoxy and helped to found an independent seminary in Geneva (1834). He also supported the publication of the Second Helvetic Confession. Old Princeton Seminary valued his work on the inspiration of Scripture, and E. J. Young (1907–1968) counts him among the great defenders of the doctrine of inspiration. Gaussen's work also stands in line with the Helvetic Consensus Formula. Gaussen's endeavor, while sharply criticized by some, was welcomed by many evangelicals. It should be noted, however, that his argument is more subtle and scholarly than his critics would acknowledge. Further, as is evident from Gaussen's itinerary, his theological position has to be understood within a Reformed confessional framework.

The selection of Gaussen is taken from his famous *Theopneustia: The Plenary Inspiration of the Holy Scriptures* (1840), already translated into English in 1841. The section we reproduce, "Catechetical Sketch of the Main Points of the Doctrine," is an elegant summary of the argument and furnishes, almost in the form of a creed, a popular defense in the face of the challenges of the time. While, like the Princetonians, Gaussen defends the verbal inspiration of the originals, he does not adopt a dictation view of inspiration that negates the individual character of individual biblical writers (cf. Questions XXIII–XXVI). This point has often been misunderstood. The sophistication of his argument is noteworthy. Our text is taken from a 1915 edition of this work translated by David D. Scott.

739

Bibliography: E. Barde. "Gaussen, François Samuel Robert Louis." *NSHERK* 4:437–38. William Edgar. *La carte protestante: Les réformés francophones et l'essor de la modernité (1815–1848)*. Histoire et Société 34. Geneva: Labor et Fides, 1997. Pp. 165–76. Robert P. Evans. "Gaussen, François Samuel Louis (1790–1863)." P. 402 in *NIDCC*. Kenneth J. Stewart. "A Bombshell of a Book: Gaussen's *Theopneustia* and Its Influence on Subsequent Evangelical Theology." *Evangelical Quarterly* 75, 3 (2003): 215–37. Idem. *Restoring the Reformation: British Evangelicalism and the Francophone 'Réveil' 1816–1849*. Studies in Evangelical History and Thought. Milton Keynes, UK: Paternoster, 2006. Pp. 212–21. John D. Woodbridge and Randall H. Balmer. "The Princetonians and Biblical Authority." Pp. 251–79 in *Scripture and Truth*.

The turning-point of the battle between those who hold "the faith once delivered to the saints," and their opponents, lies in the true and real inspiration of the Holy Scriptures. This is the Thermopylæ of Christendom. If we have in the Word of God no infallible standard of truth, we are at sea without a compass, and no danger from rough weather without can be equal to this loss within. "If the foundations be removed, what can the righteous do?" and this is a foundation loss of the worst kind.

In this work the author proves himself a master of holy argument. Gaussen charms us as he proclaims the Divine veracity of Scripture. His testimony is clear as a bell.

—CHARLES H. SPURGEON

It has been our desire that this work should not bear so strictly theological a character, as that Christian women, or other persons not conversant with certain studies, and not acquainted with the sacred languages, should be deterred from the perusal of it. Nevertheless, we should be wanting to part of our object if the doctrine were not, on some points, stated with more precision. We have to request, therefore, that in order to avoid being led off, under another form, into an excessive length of development, we may be allowed to exhibit it here in a more didactic shape, and to sum it up in a short catechetical sketch. We will do little more than indicate the proper place of the points already treated; and will enter somewhat at large into the consideration of those only that have not yet been mentioned.

Section I: Catechetical Sketch of the Main Points of the Doctrine

I. What, then, are we to understand by divine inspiration?

Divine inspiration[1] is the mysterious power put forth by the Spirit of God on the authors of holy writ, to make them write it, to guide them even in the employment of the words they use, and thus to preserve them from all error?

II. What are we told of the spiritual power put forth on the men of God while they were writing their sacred books?

We are told that they were *led* or *moved* (φερόμενοι) "not by the will of man, but by the Holy Ghost; so that they set forth the things of God, not in words which man's wisdom

---

1. Ed. note: Lit. "theopneustia," the word has been translated by alternate expressions throughout.

teacheth, but which the Holy Ghost teacheth."[2] "God," says the apostle, "spake BY THE
PROPHETS at sundry times, and in divers manners (πολυμερῶς καὶ πολυτρόπως)";[3] sometimes enabling them to understand what he made them say; sometimes without doing so;
sometimes by dreams[4] and by visions which he afterwards made them relate; sometimes
by giving them words internally (λόγῳ ἐνδιαθέτῳ), which he caused them immediately to
utter; sometimes by words transmitted to them externally (λόγῳ προφόρικῳ), which he
caused them to repeat.[5]

III. But what passed in their hearts and minds while they were writing?
This we cannot tell. It is a fact which, subject besides to great varieties, could not be for
us an object either of scientific inquiry or of faith.

IV. Have not modern authors, however, who have written on this subject, often distinguished in the Scriptures three or four degrees of inspiration (*superintendence, elevation,
direction, suggestion*)?
This is but idle conjecture; and the supposition, besides, is in contradiction with the Word
of God, which knows but one kind of inspiration. Here, there is none true but suggestion.

V. Do we not see, however, that the men of God were profoundly acquainted, and often
even profoundly affected, with the sacred things which they taught, with the future things
which they predicted, with the past things which they related?
No doubt they might be so—nay, in most instances they were so—but they might not have
been so; this happened in different measures, of which the degree remains to us unknown,
and the knowledge of which is not required of us.

VI. What then must we think of those definitions of divine inspiration, in which
Scripture seems to be represented as the altogether human expression of a revelation
altogether divine;—what, for example, must we think of that of Baumgarten, who says,
that "inspiration is but the means by which revelation, at first immediate, became
mediate, and took the form of a book (*medium quo revelatio immediata, mediata facta,
inque libros relata est*)"?[6]
These definitions are not exact, and may give rise to false notions of inspiration. I say
they are not exact. They contradict facts. Immediate revelation does not necessarily precede
inspiration; and when it precedes it, it is not its measure. The empty air prophesied;[7] a hand
coming forth from a wall wrote the words of God;[8] a dumb animal reproved the madness of
a prophet.[9] Balaam prophesied without any desire to do so; and the believers of Corinth did
so without even knowing the meaning of the words put by the Holy Ghost on their lips.[10]

2. 2 Peter 1:21; 1 Cor. 2:13.
3. Heb. 1:1.
4. Num. 12:6; Job 33:15; Dan. 1:17; 2:6; 7:1; Gen. 20:6; 31:10; 1 Kings 3:5; Matt. 1:20; 2:12, 22; Acts 2:17.
5. Num. 20:6; 24:4; Job 7:14; Gen. 20:3; Ps. 139:19; Matt. 17:9; Acts 2:17; 9:10–12; 10:3, 17, 19; 11:5; 12:9; 16:9–10; 2 Cor. 12:1–2.
6. Jacobus Baumgarten, *De discrimine revelationis et inspirationis* (Hilliger, 1745).
7. Gen. 3:14, etc.; 4:6; Ex. 3:6, etc.; 19:3, etc.; Deut. 4:12; Matt. 3:17; 17:5.
8. Dan. 5:5.
9. 2 Peter 2:16.
10. 1 Cor. 14.

I would next observe, that these definitions produce or conceal false notions of inspiration. In fact, they assume its being nothing more than the natural expression of a supernatural revelation; and that the men of God had merely of themselves, and in a human way, to put down in their books what the Holy Ghost made them see in a divine way, in their understandings. But inspiration is more than this. Scripture is not the mind of God elaborated by the understanding of man, to be promulgated in the words of man; it is at once the mind of God and the word of God.

VII. The Holy Ghost having in all ages illuminated God's elect, and having moreover distributed miraculous powers among them in ancient times, in which of these two orders of spiritual gifts ought we to rank inspiration?

We must rank it among the extraordinary and wholly miraculous gifts. The Holy Ghost in all ages enlightens the elect by his powerful inward virtue; he testifies to them of Christ;[11] gives them the unction of the Holy One; teaches them all things, and convinces them of all truth.[12] But, besides these *ordinary* gifts of illumination and faith, the same Spirit shed *extraordinary* ones on the men who were commissioned to promulgate and to write the oracles of God. Divine inspiration was one of those gifts.

VIII. Is the difference, then, between illumination and inspiration a difference of kind or only of degree?

It is a difference of kind, and not of degree only.

IX. Nevertheless, did not the apostles, besides *inspiration*, receive from the Holy Ghost *illumination* in extraordinary measure, and in its most eminent degree?

In its most eminent degree, is what none can affirm; in an extraordinary degree, is what none can contradict.

The apostle Paul, for example, did not receive the gospel from any man, but by a revelation from Jesus Christ.[13]

He wrote "ALL HIS EPISTLES," Saint Peter tells us,[14] not only in words taught by the Holy Ghost,[15] as had been the OTHER SCRIPTURES (of the Old Testament), but according to a wisdom which had been given to him.[16] He had the knowledge of the mystery of Christ.[17] Jesus Christ had promised to give his disciples not only "a mouth, but wisdom to testify of him."[18] David, when he seemed to speak only of himself in the Psalms, KNEW that it was of the Messiah that his words were to be understood: "Being a prophet, and knowing that of the fruit of his loins, according to the flesh, God would raise up Christ to sit on his throne."[19]

X. Why, then, should we not say that divine inspiration is but illumination in its most exalted and abundant measure?

11. John 15:26.
12. 1 John 2:20–27; John 4:16–26; 7:38–39.
13. Gal. 1:12, 16; 1 Cor. 15:3.
14. 2 Peter 3:15–16.
15. 1 Cor. 2:13.
16. 2 Peter 3:15–16.
17. Eph. 3:3.
18. Luke 21:15.
19. Acts 2:30.

We must beware of saying so; for thus we should have but a narrow, confused, contingent, and constantly fluctuating idea of inspiration. In fact:

1. God, who often conjoined those two gifts in one man, often also saw fit to disjoin them, in order that he might give us to understand that they essentially differ, the one from the other, and that, when united, they are independent. Every true Christian has the Holy Ghost,[20] but every Christian is not inspired, and such an one who utters the words of God, may not have received either life-giving affections or life-giving light.

2. It may be demonstrated by a great many examples, that the one of these gifts was not the measure of the other; and that the divine inspiration of the prophets did not observe the ratio of their knowledge, any more than that of their holiness.

3. Far, indeed, from the one of those gifts being the measure of the other, one may even say that divine inspiration appeared all the more strikingly the more that the illumination of the sacred writer remained in arrear of his illumination. When you behold the very prophets, who were most enlightened by God's Spirit, bending over their own pages after having written them, and endeavouring to comprehend the meaning which the Spirit in them had caused them to express, it should become manifest to you that their divine inspiration was independent of their illumination.

4. Even supposing the prophet's illumination raised to its utmost pitch, still it did not reach the altitude of the divine idea, and there might be much more meaning in the word dictated to them than the prophet was yet cognizant of. David, doubtless, in hymning his psalms, knew[21] that they referred to "Him who was to be born of his loins, to sit upon his throne for ever." Most of the prophets, like Abraham their father, saw the day of Christ, and when they saw it, were glad;[22] they searched what the Spirit of Christ, which was in them, did signify, when it testified beforehand of the sufferings of the Messiah, and the glory that should follow.[23] Yet notwithstanding all this, our Lord attests to us that the simplest Christian, the least (in knowledge) in the kingdom of God, knows more on that subject than the greatest of the prophets.[24]

5. These gifts differ from each other in essential characters, which we will presently describe.

6. Finally, it is always the inspiration of the book that is presented to us as an object of faith, never the inward state of him that writes it. His knowledge or ignorance nowise affects the confidence I owe to his words; and my soul ought ever to look not so much to the lights of his understanding as to the God of all holiness, who speaks to me by his mouth. The Saviour desired, it is true, that most of those who related his history should also have been witnesses of what they related. This was, no doubt, in order that the world might listen to them with the greater confidence, and might not start reasonable doubts as to the truth of their narratives. But the Church, in her faith, looks much higher than this: to her the intelligence of the writers is imperfectly known, and a matter of comparative indifference—what she does know is their inspiration. It is never in the breast of the prophet that she goes to look for its source; it is in that of her God. "Christ speaks in me," says Saint Paul, "and God

---

20. 1 John 2:20–27; Jer. 31:34; John 6:45.

21. Acts 2:30.

22. John 8:56.

23. 1 Peter 1:11.

24. Matt. 11:11. John-David Michaelis, *Introduction au Nouveau Testament*, 4ème edition, tome 1er, French translation (Geneva: J. J. Paschoud, 1822), 116–29. (That author thinks, that in this passage *the least* means *the least prophet*.)

hath spoken to our fathers in the prophets."[25] "Why look ye so earnestly on us," say to her all the sacred writers, "as though by our own power or holiness we had done this work?"[26] Look upwards.

XI. If there exist, then, between these two spiritual graces of illumination and inspiration a specific difference, in what must we say that it consists?

Though you should find it impossible to say what that difference is, you would not the less be obliged by the preceding reasons to declare that it does exist. In order to be able fully to reply to this question, it were necessary that you should know the nature and the mode of both these gifts; whereas the Holy Ghost has never explained to us, either how he infuses God's thoughts into the understanding of a believer, or how he puts God's words into the mouth of a prophet. Nevertheless, we can here point out two essential characters by which these two operations of the Holy Ghost have always shown themselves to be distinct: the one of these characters relates to their duration, the other to their measure.

In point of duration, illumination is continuous, whereas inspiration is intermittent. In point of measure, illumination admits of degrees, whereas inspiration does not admit of them.

XII. What are we to understand by saying that illumination is continuous, and inspiration intermittent?

The illumination of a believer by the Holy Ghost is a permanent work. Having commenced for him on the day of his new birth, it goes on increasing, and attends him with its rays to the termination of his course. That light, no doubt, is but too much obscured by his acts of faithlessness and negligence, but never more will it leave him altogether. "His path," says the wise man, "is like the shining light, shining more and more unto the perfect day."[27] "When it pleased God, who separated me from my mother's womb, to reveal his Son in me,"[28] he preserves to the end the knowledge of the mystery of Jesus Christ, and can at all times set forth its truths and its glories. As it was not flesh and blood that had revealed these things to him, but the Father,[29] that unction which he received from the Holy One[30] abides in him, says Saint John, and he needs not that any man teach him; but as the same anointing teacheth him of all things, and is truth, so, even as he hath been taught by it, he will remain in it. Illumination, therefore, abideth on the faithful; but it is not so with miraculous gifts, nor with the divine inspiration, which is one of those gifts.[31]

As for miraculous gifts, they were always intermittent with the men of God, if we except the only man who "received not the Spirit by measure."[32] The apostle Paul, for example, who at one time restored Eutychus to life, and by whom God wrought such special miracles[33] (so as that it sufficed that handkerchiefs and aprons should touch his body and be laid upon

25. 2 Cor. 13:3; Heb. 1:1 (ἐν).
26. Acts 3:12.
27. Prov. 4:18.
28. Gal. 1:15.
29. Matt. 16:17.
30. 1 John 2:20, 27.
31. 1 Cor. 14:1; Acts 19:6.
32. John 3:34.
33. Acts 19:11–12.

the sick, in order to cures being effected); at other times could not relieve either his colleague Trophimus or his beloved Epaphroditus, or his son Timothy.[34] It is the same with inspiration, which is only the most excellent of miraculous gifts. In the Lord's prophets, it was exerted only by intervals. The prophets, and even the apostles, who (as we shall show) were prophets, and more than prophets,[35] did not prophesy as often as they pleased. Inspiration was sent to them by intervals; it came upon them according as the Holy Ghost saw fit to give it to them (καθὼς τὸ Πνεῦμα ἐδίδου αὐτοῖς ἀποφθέγγεσθαι);[36] for "never did prophecy come by the will of man," says Saint Peter;[37] "but holy men of God spake as they were moved by the Holy Ghost." God spake in the prophets (ἐν τοῖς προφήταις), says Saint Paul, when he wished to do so, at sundry times (πολυμερῶς), as well as in divers manners (πολυτρόπως). On such a day, and at such a time, it is often written, "the word of Jehovah was upon such a man (ויהי דבריהוה אלי)." "In the tenth year, on the twelfth day of the tenth month, the word of Jehovah came to me," said the prophet.[38] "In the fifteenth year of the reign of Tiberius . . . the word of the Lord came unto John, the son of Zacharias (ἐγένετο ῥῆμα Θεοῦ ἐπὶ 'Ιωάννην)";[39] "and on the eighth day . . . Zacharias, his father, was filled with the Holy Ghost, and prophesied, saying."[40]

So then we ought not to imagine that the divine infallibility of the language of the prophets (and even of the apostles), lasted longer than the times in which they were engaged in their miraculous task, and in which the Spirit caused them to speak. Without divine inspiration, they were in most instances enlightened, sanctified, and preserved by God, as holy and faithful men in our own days may still be; but then they no more spoke as moved by the Holy Ghost—"their language might still be worthy of the most respectful attention; but it was a holy man that spoke; it was no longer God: they again became fallible."

XIII. Can any examples be adduced of this fallibility being attached to their language, when unaccompanied with Divine inspiration?

A multitude of instances occur. Men are often, after having been for a time the mouth of the Lord, seen to become false prophets, and mendaciously to pretend to utter the words of Jehovah, after the Spirit had ceased to speak in them; "although the Lord sent them not, neither commanded them, neither spake unto them." "They speak a vision of their own heart, not out of the mouth of the Lord."[41]

But without referring to those wicked men, or to the profane Saul, or to Balaam, who were for some time numbered among the prophets, shall it be thought that all the words of king David were infallible during the course of that long year which he passed in adultery? Yet "these," saith the Scripture, "be the last words of David, the sweet psalmist of Israel: THE SPIRIT OF THE LORD SPAKE BY ME, AND HIS WORD WAS IN MY TONGUE."[42] Shall it be thought that all the words of the prophet Solomon still continued infallible, when he fell into idolatry

34. 2 Tim. 4:20; Phil. 2:27; 1 Tim. 5:23.
35. Eph. 3:4–5; 4:11; Rom. 16:25–27.
36. Acts 2:4.
37. 2 Peter 1:21.
38. Ezek. 29:1, and elsewhere.
39. Luke 3:1–2.
40. Luke 1:59, 67, 41–42.
41. Jer. 14:14; 23:11, 16; Ezek. 13:2–3.
42. 2 Sam. 23:1–2.

in his old age, and the salvation of his soul became a problem for the Church of God? And to come down to Christ's *holy apostles and prophets* (Eph. 3:5), shall it be thought that all the words of Paul himself were infallible, and that he still could say that "Christ spoke by him"[43] when there was a sharp contention (παροξυσμὸς) betwixt him and Barnabas;[44] or when, in the midst of the council, under a mistaken impression with regard to the person of the High Priest, he "spoke evil of the Ruler of his people," and cried, "God shall strike thee, thou whited wall"; or further (since there may remain some doubt as to the character of this reprimand), shall it be thought that all the words of the apostle Saint Peter were infallible, when, at Antioch, he showed himself "so much to be blamed" (κατεγνωσμένος); when he feared those that came from Saint James; when he dissembled; and when he forced the apostle Saint Paul "to withstand him to his face before them all, because he walked not uprightly according to the truth of the gospel (οὐκ ἦν ὀρθοποδήσας)?"[45]

XIV. What, then, are we to conclude from this first difference which we have recognised as existing between illumination and inspiration, with respect to the duration of those gifts?

We must conclude from it,

1. That these two operations of the Holy Ghost differ in their essence, and not in their degree only.

2. That the infallibility of the sacred writers depended not on their illumination (which, although raised to an extraordinary measure in the case of some of them, they nevertheless enjoyed in common with all the saints), but solely on their divine inspiration.

3. That divinely-inspired words, having been miraculous, are also all of them the words of God.

4. That as our faith in every part of the Bible rests no longer on the illumination of the writers, but on the inspiration of their writings, it may dispense henceforth with the perplexing study of their internal state, of the degree in which they were enlightened, or of that of their holiness; but must stay itself in all things on God, in nothing on man.

XV. If such have been the difference between illumination and inspiration in the prophets and the apostles, as respects the *duration* of those gifts, what has it been as respects their *measure*?

Illumination is susceptible of degrees; inspiration does not admit of them. A prophet is more or less enlightened by God; but what he says is not more or less inspired. It is so, or it is not so; it is from God, or it is not from God; here there is neither measure nor degree, neither increase nor diminution. David was enlightened by God; John Baptist more than David; a simple Christian possibly more than John Baptist; an apostle was more enlightened than that Christian, and Jesus Christ more than that apostle. But the inspired word of David, what do I say? the inspired word of Balaam himself is that of God, as was that of John Baptist, as was that of Saint Paul, as was that of Jesus Christ! IT IS THE WORD OF GOD. The most enlightened of the saints cannot speak by inspiration, whilst the most wicked, the most ignorant, and the most impure of men, may speak not of his own will (ἀφ᾽ ἑαυτοῦ οὐκ εἰπεῖν), but by inspiration (ἀλλὰ προφητεῦσαι).[46]

43. 2 Cor 13:3.
44. Acts 15:39.
45. See Gal. 2:11, 14.
46. John 11:51.

In a man who is truly regenerated, there is always the divine spirit and the human spirit, which operate at once—the one enlightening, the other darkening; and the illumination will be so much the greater, the more that of the divine Spirit surpasses that of the human spirit. In the prophets, and, above all, in the apostles, these two elements also are to be found. But, thanks be to God, our faith in the words of Scripture nowise depends on the unknown issue of that combat which was waged between the Spirit and the flesh in the soul of the sacred writers. Our faith goes directly to the heart of God.

XVI. Can much harm result from the doctrine according to which the language of inspiration would be no more than the human expression of a superhuman revelation, and, so to speak, of a natural reflection of a supernatural illumination?

One or other of two evils will always result from it; either the oracles of God will be brought down to the level of the words of the saints, or these last will be raised to the level of the Scriptures.

This is a deplorable consequence, the alternative involved in which has been reproduced in all ages. It became unavoidable.

All truly regenerated men being enlightened by the Holy Ghost, it would follow, according to this doctrine, that they would all possess, though in different degrees, the element of inspiration; so that, according to the arbitrary idea which you would form to yourselves of their spiritual condition, you would be led inevitably sometimes to assimilate the sacred writers to them, sometimes to raise them to the rank of writers inspired from above.

XVII. Might religious societies be mentioned in which the former of these two evils is realized; I mean to say, where people have been led, by this path, to lower the Scriptures to the level of the sayings of saints?

All the systems of the Protestant doctors who assume that there is some mixture of error in the Holy Scriptures, are based on this doctrine; from Semler and Ammon to Eichhorn, Paulus, Gabler, Schuster, and Restig; from M. de Wette to the more respectable systems of Michaelis, Rosenmüller, Scaliger, Capellus, John Le Clerc, or of Vossius. According to these theories, the divine light with which the intellects of the sacred writers was enlightened, might suffer some partial eclipses, through the inevitable effect of their natural infirmities, of a defect of memory, of innocent ignorance, of popular prejudice; so that traces of these have remained in their writings, and so that we can perceive in these where their shadows have fallen.

XVIII. Might religious societies be mentioned also, where the latter of these evils has been consummated; I mean to say, where, in consequence of having been willing to confound inspiration with illumination, saints and doctors have been elevated to the rank of divinely inspired men?

Of these, two in particular may be mentioned, the Jews and the Latins.

XIX. What have the Jews done?

They have considered the rabbins of the successive ages of the Dispersion as endowed with an infallibility which put them on a level with (if not above) Moses and the prophets. They have, to be sure, attributed a kind of divine inspiration to holy Scripture; but they have prohibited the explanation of its oracles otherwise than according to their traditions. They have called the immense body of those commandments of men the oral law (תורה שבעל פה), the *Doctrine*, or the *Talmud* (תלמוד), distinguishing it into the *Mishna*, or Second Law (משנה), and *Gémara, complement* or *perfection* (גמרא). They have said that it passed from God to Moses, from Moses to Joshua, from Joshua to the prophets, from the prophets to Esdras, from Esdras to the doctors of the great synagogue, and from them to the rabbins Antigone, Soccho, Shemaia, Hillel, Schammai, until at last Juda the saint deposited it in the *traditions* or *repetitions* of the law (משניות, δευτερώσεις), which afterwards, with their commentary or complement (the *gémara*), formed, first, the Talmud of *Jerusalem*, and afterwards that of *Babylon*.

"One of the greatest obstacles that we have to encounter in dealing with the Jews," says the missionary MacCaul, "is their invincible prejudice in favour of their traditions and of their commentaries, so that we cannot prevail on them to buy our Bibles without notes or commentaries."[47]

"The law they say is salt; the mishna, pepper; the talmuds, aromatics:" "the Scripture is water; the mishna, wine; the gémara, spiced wine." "My son," says rabbi Isaac, "learn to pay more attention to the words of the scribes than to the words of the law." "Turn away your children" (said rabbi Eleazar, on his deathbed, to his scholars, who asked him the way of life), "turn away your children from the study of the Bible, and place them at the feet of the wise." "Learn, my son," says the rabbi Jacob, "that the words of the scribes are more agreeable than those of the prophets!"[48]

XX. And what has been the result of these monstrous principles?

It is, that by this means millions and millions of immortal souls, although wandering upon the earth, although weary and heavy laden, although every where despised and persecuted, have contrived to carry the book of the Old Testament, intact and complete, among all the nations of the whole world, without ceasing to read it in Hebrew every Sabbath, in thousands of synagogues, for the last eighteen hundred years, ... without, notwithstanding all this, recognising there that Jewish Messiah whom we all adore, and the knowledge of whom would be at this day their deliverance, as it behoves one day to be their happiness and their glory!

"Full well," said Jesus to them, "full well ye reject the commandment of God, that ye may keep your own tradition."[49]

XXI. And what have the Latins done?

They have considered the fathers, the popes, and the councils of the successive ages of the Roman Church, as endowed with an infallibility which puts them on a level with Jesus, the prophets, and the apostles, if not above them. They have differed greatly, it is true, from each other on the doctrine of the inspiration of the Scriptures; and the faculties of Douay

---

47. Letter from Warsaw, 22nd March 1827.

48. In the Talmud of Jerusalem—*Encyclopédie méthodique* (Paris: Panckoucke, 1788), 3:231, at the word *Juif*.

49. Mark 7:9, see also 13 and Matt. 15:3–9. The mischief of those traditions begins at last to reveal itself to the Jews of our days: "The time is come," says the Israelite doctor Creissenach (*Entwickelungs Geschichte des Mosaischen Ritual Gesetzes*, Pref.), "the time is come when the Talmud will precipitate the Jewish religion into the most profound and humiliating downfall, if all the popular teachers of the Jews do not loudly declare that its statutes are of human origin, and may be changed."

and Louvain, for example, have vigorously opposed[50] the opinion of the Jesuits, who would see nothing in the operation of the Holy Ghost but a direction preserving the sacred writers from error; but all have forbidden the explanation of the Scriptures otherwise than by their traditions.[51] They have thought themselves entitled to say, in all their councils, as did the apostles and prophets at Jerusalem, "It hath seemed good to the Holy Ghost and to us" (Acts 15:28). They have declared that it appertained to them to pronounce upon the true meaning of holy Scripture. They have called the immense body of those commandments of men, the *oral law*, the *unwritten traditions*, the *unwritten law*. They have said that they have been transmitted by God, and dictated by the mouth of Jesus Christ, or of the Holy Ghost, by a continual succession.

"Seeing," says the Council of Trent, "that the saving truth and discipline of manners are contained in the written books and the unwritten traditions, which, having been received by the apostles from the mouth of Jesus Christ, or from the inspiration of the Holy Ghost, by succession of time are come down to us, following the example of the apostolic fathers, the Council receives with the same affection and reverence (*pari pietatis affectu ac reverentia*), and honours all the books of the Old and New Testament (seeing that God is their author), and *together with them* the TRADITIONS relating to faith as well as manners, as having been dictated by the mouth of Jesus Christ or of the Holy Ghost, and preserved in the Catholic Church by continual succession."[52] "If any one receive not the whole of the said books, with all their parts, as holy and canonical as they have been wont to be read in the Catholic Church, and in the old vulgate translation" (that of Jerome,[53] which, especially in Job and the Psalms, is crammed with very numerous, very serious, and very evident errors, and has even been corrected abundantly since by other popes),[54] "or knowingly despises the said traditions, let him be accursed!"

They have thus put the bulls of the bishops of Rome, and the decrees of their synods, above the Scriptures. "Holy Scripture," say they, "does not contain all that is necessary for salvation, and is not sufficient."[55] "It is obscure."[56] "It does not belong to the people to read Holy Scripture."[57] "We must receive with obedience of faith many things that are not contained in Scripture."[58] "We must serve God according to the tradition of the ancients."[59]

The bull *Exsurge* of Leo X[60] places in the number of Luther's heresies his having said, "That it is not in the power of the Church, or of the Pope, to establish articles of faith."

---

50. Censure of 1588.

51. *Council of Trent*, Session 4, Decree 2, 8th April 1546 (Schroeder, *Council of Trent*, 18–19).—Robert Bellarmine, "De Ecclesia," 3.14; 4.3, 5–8 in *De controversiis christianae fidei adversus haereticos*, vol 2.—Pierre Coton, *Institution Catholique* (1612), 2.24, 34–35.—Jacques du Perron, *Refutation de l'écrit de maistre Daniel Tilenus* (1602).

52. *Council of Trent*, Session 4, Decree 1 [Schroeder, *Council of Trent*, 17].

53. It was in vain that the Abbot Isidore Clarius represented at the Council that there was temerity in ascribing inspiration to a writer who himself assures us that he had none (Father Paul [Fra Paolo Sarpi], *History of the Council of Trent* [London: Mearne, 1676], 148).

54. See Thomas James, *Bellum Papale sive Concordia Discors Sexti V. et Clementis VIII.*

55. Bellarmine, "De verbo Dei," Book 4 in *De controversiis christianae fidei adversus haereticos*, vol 1.

56. Idem, Book 3.—Pierre Charron, *Les trois véritez.*—Coton, *Institution Catholique*, 2.19.—Bayle, *Traité.*

57. Bellarmine, "De verbo Dei," 2.19.

58. Bellarmine, "De verbo Dei," 4.3, and du Perron, *Refutation de l'écrit de maistre Daniel Tilenus.*—Coton, *Institution Catholique*, 2.24.

59. Bellarmine, "De verbo Dei," 4.5.—Coton, *Institution Catholique*, 2.34–35. *Council of Trent*, Session 4.

60. 1520, Concil., Harduini, 9:1893.

The bull *Unigenitus*[61] condemns to perpetuity, as being respectively false, captious, scandalous, pernicious, rash, suspected of heresy, savouring of heresy, heretical, impious, blasphemous, etc., the following propositions:—"It is profitable at all times, in all places, and for all sorts of persons, to study the Scriptures, and to become acquainted with their spirit, piety, and mysteries" (on 1 Cor. 16:5).[62] "The reading of Holy Scripture in the hands of a man of business, and a financier, shows that it is intended for every body" (on Acts 8:28).[63] "The holy obscurity of the Word of God is no ground for the laity's being dispensed from reading it" (on Acts 8:30–31). "The Lord's day ought to be sanctified by the reading of books of piety, and especially of the Scriptures. They are the milk which God himself, who knows our hearts, has supplied for them. It is dangerous to desire being weaned from it" (Acts 15:29). — "It is a mistake to imagine that the knowledge of the mysteries of religion ought not to be communicated to that sex (women) by the reading of the holy books, after this example of confidence with which Jesus Christ manifests himself to this woman (the Samaritan)." "It is not from the simplicity of women, but from the proud learning of men, that abuse of the Scriptures has arisen, and heresies have been generated" (on John 4:26). — "It amounts to shutting the mouth of Christ to Christians, and to wresting from their hands the holy book, or to keep it shut to them by depriving them of the means of hearing it" (1 Thess. 5:2). — "To interdict Christians from reading it, is to interdict children from the use of light, and to subject them to a kind of excommunication" (on Luke 11:33).[64]

Still more lately, in 1824, the encyclical epistle of Pope Leo XII mournfully complains of the Bible Societies, "which," it says, "violate the traditions of the fathers (!!!) and the Council of Trent, by circulating the Scriptures in the vernacular tongues of all nations."[65] "In order to avert this pest," he says, "our predecessors have published several constitutions . . . tending to show how pernicious for the faith and for morals this perfidious institution (the Bible Society) is! (ut ostendatur quantopere fidei et moribus vaferrimum hocce inventum noxium sit!)"

XXII. And what has been the result of these monstrous principles?

It is this, that millions and millions of immortal souls in France, in Spain, in Italy, in Germany, and in America, and even in the Indies, although they carry every where intact and complete the New Testament, although they have not ceased to read it in Latin, every Lord's day, in thousands and thousands of churches, for twelve hundred years, ... have been turned away from the fountains of life, have, like the Jews, "paid more attention to the words of the scribes than to those of the law"; have diverted their children, according to the counsel of Eleazer, "from the study of the Bible, to place them at the feet of the wise." They have found, like rabbi Jacob, "the words of the scribes more agreeable than those of the prophets." It is thus that they have contrived, for twelve centuries, to

61. Clement XI of 8th September 1713.
62. Proposition 79.
63. Proposition 80.
64. Propositions 82–85.
65. "*Non vos latet, venerandi fratres, societatem quamdam, dictam vulgo* BIBLICAM, *per totum orbem audacter vagari quæ spretis S. S. Patrum traditionibus (!!!) et contra notissimum Tridentini Concilii decretum, in id collatis viribus ac modis omnibus intendit, ut in vulgares linguas nationum omnium sacra vertantur vel potius pervertantur Biblia.*"

maintain doctrines the most contrary to the Word of God,[66] on the worship of images;[67] on the exaltation of the priests; on their forced celibacy; on their auricular confession; on the absolution which they dare to give; on the magical power which they attribute even to the most impure among them, of creating his God with three Latin words, *opere operato*; on an ecclesiastical priesthood, of which Scripture has never said a word; on prayers to the dead; on the spiritual pre-eminence of the city which the Scripture has called Babylon; on the use of an unknown tongue in worship; on the celestial empire of the blessed but humble woman to whom Jesus himself said, "Woman, what have I to do with thee?" on the mass; on the taking away of the cup; on the interdiction of the Scriptures to the people; on indulgences; on purgatory; on the universal episcopate of an Italian priest; on the interdiction of meals; so that just as people annul the sole priesthood of the Son of man by establishing other priesthoods by thousands, just as they annul his divinity by acknowledging thousands of demigods or dead men, present in all places, hearing throughout the whole earth the most secret prayers of human beings, protecting cities and kingdoms, working miracles in favour of their worshippers; . . . just so, also, they annul the inspiration of Scripture, by acknowledging by thousands other writings which share in its divine authority, and which surpass and swallow up its eternal infallibility!

It was in opposition to the very similar tenets maintained by the heretics of his time, that Saint Irenaeus said, "For when convicted by the Scriptures, they turn about and accuse the Scriptures themselves, as if they were imperfect, and wanting in authority, and uncertain, and as if one could not find the truth in them, if ignorant of tradition; for that was given, not in writing, but by the living voice."[68]

"Full well," says Jesus to them too, "ye reject the commandments of God, that ye may keep your own traditions! *Bene irritum facitis præceptum Dei, ut traditionem vestram servetis!*" (Mark 7:9).

XXIII. Without pretending anyhow to explain how the Holy Ghost could dictate the thoughts and the words of the Scriptures (for the knowledge of this mystery is neither given to us, nor asked of us), what is it that one can perceive in this divine action?

Why, two things; first, an *impulsion*, that is, an action on the *will* of the men of God, in order to make them speak and write; and, secondly, a *suggestion*, that is to say, an action on their understandings and on their organs, in order to their producing, first, *within them* more or less exalted notions of the truth they were about to utter; and, then, *without them* such human expressions as were most divinely suitable to the eternal thought of the Holy Ghost.

XXIV. Meanwhile, must it be admitted that the sacred writers were no more than merely the pens, hands, and secretaries of the Holy Ghost?

They were, no doubt, hands, secretaries, and pens; but they were, in almost every case, and in very different degrees, living pens, intelligent hands, secretaries docile, affected by what they wrote, and sanctified.

---

66. Ex. 20:4–5.

67. Quisquis elanguerit erga venerabilium imaginum adorationem (προσκύνησιν), hunc anathemizat sancta nostra et universalis synodus! (was written to the Emperor, in the name of the whole Second Council of Nice). (Concil., 7:585).

68. *Adversus haereses* [*Against Heresies*], 3.2: "Cum enim ex Scripturis arguuntur, in accusationem convertuntur ipsarum Scripturarum, quasi non rectè habeant, neque sint ex auctoritate, et quia variè sunt dictæ, et quia non possit ex his inveniri veritas ab his qui nesciant traditionem Non enim per litteras traditam illam, sed per vivam vocem."

XXV. Was not the Word of God, however, often written as suggested by the occasion?

Yes, no doubt; and the occasion was prepared by God, just as the writer was. "The Holy Ghost," says Claude, "employed the pen of the evangelists . . . and of the prophets. He supplied them with the occasions on which they wrote; he gave them the wish and the strength to do so; the matter, form, order, economy, expressions, are from his immediate inspiration and direction."[69]

XXVI. But do we not clearly recognise, in the greater part of the sacred books, the individual character of the person who writes?

Far from disowning this, we, on the contrary, admire its being so. The individual character which comes from God, and not from sin and the fall, was prepared and sanctified by God for the work to which it had been destined by God.

XXVII. Ought we, then, to think that all has been equally inspired of God, in each of the books of Holy Scripture?

Scripture, in speaking of what it is, does not admit any distinction. All these sacred books, without exception, are the word of the Lord. ALL SCRIPTURE, says Saint Paul (πᾶσα γραφὴ), IS INSPIRED BY GOD.

This declaration, as we have already said, is susceptible of two constructions, according as we place the verb, not expressed but understood, before or after the Greek word which we here translate *inspired by God*;—both these constructions invincibly establish, that in the apostle's idea, all without exception, in each and all of the books of the Scriptures, is dictated by the Spirit of God. In fact, in both the apostle equally attests that these HOLY LETTERS (τὰ ἱερὰ γράμματα), of which he had been speaking to Timothy, are all *divinely inspired Scriptures.*

Now, we know that in the days of Jesus Christ, the whole Church meant one SOLE AND THE SAME COLLECTION OF BOOKS by *the Scripture*, the *Holy Scripture*, or *the Scriptures*, or *the Law and the Prophets*, or *the Holy Letters* (γραφὴ,[70] or ἡ γραφὴ ἁγία,[71] or αἱ γραφαὶ,[72] or ὁ νόμος καὶ οἱ προφήται,[73] or τὰ ἱερὰ γράματτα[74]). These were the twenty-two sacred books which the Jews held from their prophets, and on which they were all perfectly agreed.[75]

This entire and perfect divine inspiration of all the Scriptures of the Jews was so fully, in the days of Jesus Christ, the doctrine of the whole of that ancient people of God (as it was that of Jesus Christ, of Timothy, and of Saint Paul), that we find the following testimony to it in the works of the Jewish general Josephus (who had reached his thirtieth year[76] at the time when the Apostle Paul wrote his Second Epistle to Timothy). "Never" (says he, in speaking of "the twenty-two books"[77] of the Old Testament, which he calls τὰ ἰδία

---

69. Jean Claude, *Œuvres Posthumes* (Amsterdam: Pierre Savouret, 1688), 4:228.

70. 2 Peter 1:20; John 10:35; 17:12; 19:37.

71. Rom. 1:2.

72. John 5:39; Matt. 21:42; 26:54; Rom. 15:4; 1 Cor. 15:3.

73. Acts 24:14; Luke 16:16, 29, 31; Matt. 5:17–18; John 10:34.

74. 2 Tim. 3:15.

75. See Krebs and Læsner, on 2 Tim. 3:15.

76. He was born in the year 37. See his Life, ed. Aureliæ Allobr., 999.

77. *Against Apion* 1.8.38, 42 (δύο μόνα πρὸς τοῖς εἴκοσι βιβλία). Our Bibles reckon thirty-nine books in the Old Testament; but Josephus and the ancient Jews, by making one book each of the two books of Samuel, of Kings, and of Chronicles, by throwing together Ruth and Judges, Esdras and Nehemiah, Jeremiah and Lamentations, and finally, Hosea

γράμματα, as Saint Paul calls them here τὰ ἱερὰ γράμματα, "never, although many ages have elapsed, has any one dared either to TAKE AWAY, or to ADD, or to TRANSPOSE in these any thing whatever;[78] for it is with all the Jews, as it were an inborn conviction (ΠΑΣΙ δὲ δύμφυτόν ἐστιν), from their very earliest infancy,[79] to call them GOD'S TEACHINGS, to abide in them, and, if necessary, to die joyfully in maintaining them."[80]

"They are given to us" (he says further) "by the inspiration that comes from God (κατὰ τὴν ἐπίπνοιαν τὴν ἀπὸ τοῦ Θεοῦ); but as for the other books, composed since the times of Artaxerxes, they are not thought worthy of a like faith."[81]

These passages from Josephus are not quoted here as an authority for our faith, but as an historical testimony, showing the sense in which the apostle Saint Paul spoke, and attesting to us that, in mentioning the holy letters (τὰ ἱερὰ γράμματα), and in saying that they are all divinely inspired Scriptures, he meant to declare to us that, in his eyes, there was nothing in the sacred books which was not dictated by God.

Now, since the books of the New Testament are ἱερὰ γράμματα, *Holy Scriptures, the Scriptures, the Holy Letters*, as well as those of the Old; since the apostles have put their writings, and since Saint Peter, for example, has put ALL THE LETTERS OF PAUL (πάσας τὰς ἐπιστολὰς) in the same rank with the REST OF THE SCRIPTURES (ὡς καὶ τὰς λοιπὰς ΓΡΑΦΑΣ) [cf. 2 Peter 3:16], hence we ought to conclude that all is inspired by God in all the books of the Old and New Testament.

XXVIII. But if all the sacred books (τὰ ἱερὰ γράμματα) are divinely inspired, how can we discover that such and such a book is a sacred book, and that such another is not one?

This, in a great measure, is a purely historical question.

XXIX. Yet, have not the Reformed Churches maintained that it was by the Holy Ghost that they recognised the divinity of the sacred books; and, for example, has not the Confession of Faith of the Churches of France said in its 4th article, that "we know these books to be canonical, and a very certain rule of our faith, not so much by the common accord and agreement of the Church, as by the testimony and the persuasion of the Holy Ghost, which enables us to discern between them and the other ecclesiastical books"?

This maxim is perfectly true, if you apply it to the sacred books as a whole. In that sense the Bible is evidently an αὐτόπιστος book, which needs *itself only* in order to be believed. To the man, whoever he be, that studies it "with sincerity and as before God,"[82] it presents itself evidently, and of itself, as a miraculous book; it reveals all that is hidden in men's consciences; it discerns the thoughts and affections of the heart. It has foretold the future; it has changed the face of the world; it has converted souls; it has created the Church. Thus it produces in men's hearts "an inward testimony and conviction of the Holy Ghost," which attests its inimitable divinity, independently of any testimony of men. But we do not think that our Churches ever ventured to affirm that one might be content to abide by this mark

and the eleven minor prophets that follow respectively, into one book, reduced our modern calculation of their sacred books by seventeen units.

78. Οὔτε ΠΡΟΣΘΕΙΝΑΙ τις οὐδὲν οὔτε ΑΦΕΛΕΙΝ αὐτῶν, οὔτε ΜΕΤΑΘΕΙΝΑΙ τετόλμηκεν.
79. Εὐθὺς ἐκ τῆς πρωτῆς γενέσεως ὀνομάζειν αὐτὰ ΘΕΟΥ ΔΟΓΜΑΤΑ (according to others: *from the first generation*).
80. Ὑπὲρ αὐτῶν εἰ δέοι θνήσκειν ἡδέως.
81. Πίστεως δὲ οὐχ' ὁμοίας ἠξίωται.
82. 2 Cor. 2:17.

for discerning such or such a book, or such or such a chapter, or such or such a verse of the Word of God, and for ascertaining its celestial origin. They think that for this detail one must look, as they did, "to the common accord and agreement of the Church." We ought to admit as divine the entire code of the Scriptures, before each of its parts has enabled us to prove by itself that it is of God. It does not belong to us to judge this book; it is this book which will judge us.

XXX. Nevertheless, has not Luther,[83] starting from a principle laid down by Saint Paul[84] and by Saint John,[85] said, that "the touchstone by which one might recognise certain scriptures as divine, is this: Do they preach Christ or do they not preach him?"[86] And among the moderns, has not Dr. Twesten also said, "that the different parts of the Scriptures are more or less inspired, according as they are more or less *preaching*; and that inspiration does not extend to words and historical matters beyond what has a relation to the Christian conscience, beyond what proceeds from Christ, or serves to show us Christ"?[87]

Christ is, no doubt, the way, the truth, and the life; the spirit of prophecy, no doubt, is the testimony of Jesus;[88] but this touchstone might in our hands prove fallacious: 1st, Because many writings speak admirably of Christ without being inspired; 2nd, Although all that is to be found in the inspired Scriptures relates to Jesus Christ, possibly we might fail to perceive this divine character at a first glance; and 3rd, In fine, because we ought to BELIEVING BEFORE SEEING it, that "all Scripture is profitable for doctrine, for reproof, for correction, and for instruction in righteousness: that the man of God may be perfect, throughly furnished unto all good works."[89]

XXXI. What reasons have we, then, for recognising as sacred each of the books which, at the present day, form for us the collection of the Scriptures?

For the Old Testament we have the testimony of the Jewish Church; and for the New Testament the testimony of the Catholic Church.

XXXII. What must here be understood by the testimony of the Jewish Church?

We must understand by it the common opinion of all the Jews, Egyptian and Syrian, Asiatic and European, Sadducean and Pharisees,[90] ancient and modern, good and bad.

XXXIII. What reason have we to hold for divine, the books of the Old Testament which the Church of the Jews has given us as such?

83. In his preface to the Epistles of James and Jude.
84. 1 Cor. 3:9–10.
85. 1 John 4:2.
86. "Ob sie Christum treiben, oder nicht."
87. August Twesten, *Vorlesungen über die Dogmatik der evangelisch-lutherischen Kirche* (Hamburg: F. Perthes, 1829), 1:421–29.
88. John 14:6; Rev. 19:10.
89. 2 Tim. 3:16–17.
90. See Josephus, *Against Apion* 1.8 — Philo in Eichorn. — Josephus in Nov. Repert., p. 239. — De Ægypticis Judæis; cf. Johann Gottfried Eichorn, *Einleitung in das Alte Testament*, ch. 1, pp. 73, 89, 91, 113–14, 116. — De Sadducaeis, § 35, p. 95. — And Semler (*Apparatus ad liberalem, V. T. interpretatiom*, 11.) — Eichorn, *Allgemeine Bibliothek der biblischen Litteratur*, 4:275–76.

It is written, "that unto them were committed the oracles of God";[91] which means, that God in his wisdom chose them for being, under the Almighty government of his providence, sure depositories of his written word. Jesus Christ received their sacred code, and we accept of it as he did.

XXXIV. Shall our faith then depend upon the Jews?

The Jews often fell into idolatry; they denied the faith; they slew their prophets; they crucified the King of kings; since that they have hardened their hearts for near two thousand years; they have filled up the measure of their sins, and wrath "is come upon them to the uttermost."[92] Nevertheless, to them were committed the oracles of God. And albeit that these oracles condemn them, albeit that the veil remains on their hearts when they read the Old Testament;[93] albeit they have for ages despised the Word of God, and worshipped their Talmud; they HAVE NOT BEEN ABLE not to give us the *book of the Scriptures* intact and complete; and the historian Josephus might still say of them what he wrote eighteen hundred years ago: "After the lapse of so many centuries (τοσούτου γὰρ αἰῶνος ἤδη ταρῳχηκότος), no one among the Jews has dared to ADD or to TAKE AWAY, or to transpose any thing in the sacred Scriptures."[94]

XXXV. What, then, have been the warranty, the cause, and the means of this fidelity on the part of the Jews?

We shall reply to this question in but a very few words. Its warranty is to be found in the promises of God; its cause in the providence of God; and its means in the concurrence of the five following circumstances:

1. The religion of the Jews, which has carried their respect for the very letter of Scriptures even to a superstitious length.

2. The indefatigable labours of the Masorethes, who so carefully guarded its purity, even to the slightest accents.

3. The rivalry of the Judaical sects, none of which would have sanctioned any want of faithfulness on the part of the others.

4. The extraordinary dispersion of that people in all countries long before the ruin of Jerusalem; for "of old time," says Saint James, "Moses hath in every (pagan) city them that preach him, being read in the synagogues every Sabbath-day."[95]

5. Finally, the innumerable copies of the sacred book diffused among all nations.

XXXVI. And with respect to the New Testament, what are we now to understand by the testimony of the Catholic Church?

By this we are to understand the universal agreement of the ancient and modern Churches, Asiatic and European, good and bad, which call on the name of Jesus Christ; that is to say, not only the faithful sects of the blessed Reformation, but the Greek sect, the Arminian sects, the Syrian sect, the Roman sect, and perhaps we might add the Unitarian sects.[96]

91. Rom. 3:2.
92. 1 Thess. 2:16.
93. 2 Cor. 3:15.
94. See this quotation at question 27.
95. Acts 15:21. Josephus often attests the same fact.
96. Following the example of the Scripture, we believe we may employ the word *church* as denoting, sometimes all that are enclosed in the nets of the Gospel, sometimes only all that in these is pure and living. And as for the word *sect* (αἵρε-

XXXVII. Should our faith then be founded on the Catholic Church?

All Churches have erred, or might have erred. Many have denied the faith, persecuted Jesus Christ in his members, denied his divinity, made his cross of none effect, restored the worship of statues and graven images, exalted the priests, shed the blood of the saints, interdicted the use of the Scriptures to the people, committed to the flames those of the faithful who desired to read them in the vernacular tongue, have set up in the temple of God him who sits there as a God, have trampled upon the Scriptures, worshipped traditions, warred against God, and cast down the truth. Nevertheless, the new oracles of God have been committed to them, as those of the Old Testament were to the Jews. And albeit these oracles condemn them; albeit for ages they have despised the Scriptures and almost adored their traditions; they have NOT BEEN ABLE not to give us the Book of the Scriptures of the New Testament intact and complete; and one may say of them, as Josephus said of Jews, "After the lapse of so many ages, never has any one in the Churches dared either to add or take away any thing in the Holy Scriptures." They have been compelled, *in spite of themselves*, to transmit them to us in their integrity.

XXXVIII. Nevertheless has there not been in Christendom one powerful sect, which for three hundred years has introduced into the canon of the Scriptures the Apocryphal Books, disavowed as they have been by the Jews[97] (as even Pope Saint Gregory himself attests),[98] and rejected by the fathers of the ancient Church[99] (as Saint Jerome attests)?

This, it is true, is what was done for the Latin sect by the fifty-three persons who composed, on the 8th of April 1546, the famous Council of Trent, and who pretended to be the representatives of the CHURCH UNIVERSAL OF JESUS CHRIST.[100] But they could do it for the Old Testament only, which was entrusted to the Jews and not to the Christians. Neither that Council, nor any even of the most corrupt and idolatrous Churches, *have been able* to add a single Apocryphal Book to the New Testament. God has not permitted this, however mischievous may have been their intentions. It is thus that the Jews have been able to reject the New Testament, which was not committed to them; while they HAVE NEVER BEEN ABLE to introduce a single book of man into the Old Testament. God has never permitted them to do so; and, in particular, they have always excluded from it those which the fifty-three ecclesiastics of Trent were daring enough to cause to be inserted in it, in the name of the universal Church.

XXXIX. And what have been the warranty, the cause, and the means of that fidelity, which the universal Church has shown in transmitting to us the oracles of God in the New Testament?

οις, Acts 24:14; 26:5; 28:22), following the apostle's example, we employ it here neither in a good sense nor in a bad sense.

97. Josephus, *Against Apion* 1.8 (38); Eusebius, *Ecclesiastical History* 3.10.1 [Loeb, 1:227].

98. *Exposition of the Book of Job [Moralia]*. See Father Paul's *History of the Council of Trent*, 2:143.

99. Origen (Eusebius, *Ecclesiastical History* 6.25.1 [Loeb, 2:73]). — Saint Athanasius (Pascal Epistle) — Saint Hilary (Prologue to *Exposition of the Psalms* [Paris, 1693], 9). — Saint Epiphanius (Lardner, 4:312.) — Saint Gregory Nazianzen (*Carmina* 33, Op. 2:98).

100. Jerome, In præf. ad *libr. Regum; sive Prologo-galeato* (see Lardner 5:16–22). — "Judith, et Tobiæ et Macchabæorum libros legit quidem Ecclesia: sed eas inter canonicas Scripturas non recipit" (Jerome, Præfat. in *Libros Salom-Epist.* 115). — See also Rufinus, *Commentarius in symbolum apostolorum* (Paris, 1602), 9:186. — "Some thought it strange that five cardinals and forty-eight bishops should so easily define the most principal and important points of religion, never decided before, giving canonical authority to books held for uncertain and apocryphal," etc.—Father Paul's *History of the Council of Trent*, 2:153. Most were Italians.

To this question we shall reply but in a very few words.

The warranty has lain in the promises of God; the cause in the providence of God; and the means principally in the concurrence of the following circumstances:—

1. The religion of the ancient Christians, and their extraordinary respect for the sacred texts; a respect shown on all occasions in their churches,[101] in their councils,[102] in their oaths,[103] and even in their domestic customs.[104]

2. The pains taken by learned men in different ages to preserve the purity of the sacred text.

3. The many quotations made from Scripture by the fathers of the Church.

4. The mutual jealousy of the sects into which the Christian Church has been subdivided.

5. The versions made from the first ages in many ancient tongues.

6. The number and abundant dissemination of manuscripts of the New Testament.

7. The dispersion of the new people of God as far as the extremities of Asia, and to the farthest limits of the west.

XL. Does it then result from these facts that the authority of the Scriptures is founded for us, as Bellarmine[105] has said, on that of the Church?

The doctors of Rome, it is true, have gone so far as to say, that without the testimony of the Church the Scripture has no more authority than Livy, the Alcoran, or Æsop's fables;[106] and Bellarmine, horrified no doubt at such impious opinions, would fain distinguish the authority of the Church *in itself,* and *with respect to us* (quoad se, et quoad nos). In this last sense, he says, the Scripture has no authority except by the testimony of the Church. Our answer will be very simple.

Every manifestation having three causes, an objective cause, a subjective cause, and an instrumental cause, one may say also that the knowledge that we receive of the authority of the Scriptures has, first of all, for its *objective cause,* the Holy Bible itself, which proves its divinity by its own beauty, and by its own doings; in the second place, for *subjective* or efficient cause, the Holy Ghost,[107] who confirms and seals to our souls the testimony of God; and in fine, in the third place, for *instrumental cause,* the Church, not the Roman, not the Greek, more ancient than the Roman, not even the Syriac, more ancient than either, but the Universal Church.

The pious Saint Augustine expresses this triple cause, in his book *Against the Letter of the Manichaean,* called *Fundamenti* [5.6; NPNF1 4:131]. In speaking of the time at which he was still a Manichean, he says:[108] "I should not have believed in the gospel had I not been

---

101. Plotius contra Manich., t. i.; apud Wolf. anecd., pp. 32ff. — I. Ciampini Rom. vetera monum., 1, pp. 126ff. All the Christian congregations in the East, even the poorest, kept a collection of the sacred books in their oratories. See Scholz, Proleg.

102. Cyril of Alexandria in *Apol. ad Theodos.*, imp. — *Act. Concil.*, ed. Mansi, 6:579; 7:6; 9:187; 12:1009, 1052, al. Prohibition, under pain of excommunication, against selling the sacred book to druggists, or other merchants, who don't buy them to read (6th Council, in Trullo, Can. 68).

103. Corb. byz., 1, p. 422, al.

104. See Saint Jerome, preface on Job. — Saint Chrysostom, Homily 19, *De Statuis.* Women, says he, are wont to suspend copies of the Gospels from their children's necks. See the 68th canon of the 6th Council in Trullo.

105. "De Conciliis," 2.12 in *De controversies christianae fidei adversus haereticos,* vol. 2.

106. Hosius, "Confutatio prolegomenon Brentii" (1583), bk. 3. — Eckius, de auth. Ecclesiæ. — Bayli Tractat. 1, Catech., 9. 12. — Diego Andradius, *Defensio Conc. Tridentinae fidei Catholicae* (1580), bk. 3. — Stapleton, *Triplication inchoata adversus . . . Whitakerum,* 1:17.

107. Isa. 54:13; 59:21.

108. Evangelio non crederem (according to the African usage for *credidissem*, as *Confessions,* 2.8 [Loeb, 1:90]: *Si tunc amarem,* for *amavissem*) nisi me Ecclesiæ commoveret (commovisset) authoritas (ch. 5). (This, besides, is very classical

drawn to it by the authority of the Church"; but he takes care to add: "Let us follow those who invite us first to believe, when we are not yet in a state to see: in order that, being rendered more capable (*valentiores*) by faith itself, we may deserve to comprehend what we believe. Then it will no more be men, it will be God himself within us, who will confirm our souls and illuminate them."

In this affair, then, the Church is a servant and not a mistress; a depositary and not a judge. She exercises the office of a minister, not of a magistrate, *ministerium non magisterium*.[109] She delivers a testimony, not a judicial sentence. She discerns the canon of the Scriptures, she does not make it; she has recognised their authenticity, she has not given it. And as the men of Sichem believed in Jesus Christ by means of the impure but penitent woman who called them to him, we say to the Church: "Now we believe, not because of thy saying; for we have heard him ourselves, and know that this is indeed the Christ, the Saviour of the world."[110] We have believed, then, *per eam*, not *propter eam*, through her means, not on her account. We found her on her knees; she showed us her Master; we recognised him, and we knelt down along with her. Were I to mingle in the rear of an imperial army, and should I ask those around me to show me their prince, they would do with respect to him, for me, what the Church has done with regard to the Scriptures. They would not call their regiment the *œcumenical army*; above all, they would not say that the emperor has no authority but what is derived from its testimony, whether as it respected itself or with respect to us; whether *quoad se* or *quoad nos* (to use Bellarmine's language). The authority of the Scriptures is not founded, then, on the authority of the Church: it is the Church that is founded on the authority of the Scriptures.

XLI. If the authenticity of the Scriptures is proved in a great measure by history, how is their inspiration established?

Solely by the Scriptures.

XLII. But is such an argument rational? Does it not involve a begging of the question, and the proving of inspiration by inspiration?

There would be a begging of the question here, if, in order to prove that the Scriptures are inspired, we should invoke their testimony while assuming them to be inspired. But we are far from adopting this process. First of all, the Bible is viewed solely in the light of an historical document, deserving our respect from its authenticity, and by means of which one may know the doctrine of Jesus Christ, nearly as one would learn that of Socrates from the books of Plato, or that of Leibnitz from the writings of Wolff. Now this document declares to us, in all its pages, that the whole system of the religion which it teaches, is founded on the grand fact of a miraculous intervention of God in the revelation of its history and its doctrines.

The learned Michaelis, who held such loose principles on inspiration, himself declares that the inspiration of the apostolic writings necessarily results from their authenticity.

Latin: *Non ego hoc ferrem*, says Horace, for *tulissem*, [*Odes*, 3.14; Loeb, 180]). "Eos sequamur qui nos invitant prius credere, quum nondum valemus intueri, ut ipsâ fide valentiores facti, quod credimus intelligere mereamur, non jam hominibus, sed ipso Deo intrinsecus mentem nostram firmante et illuminante" (c. 14). Opera August., Paris, Mabillon, t. viii.

109. Turrettini, *Institutio Theologiae elencticae*, Book I, Second Topic, Question 6, 20.

110. John 4:42.

There is no other alternative, says he; if what they relate is true, they are inspired; if they were not inspired, they would not be sincere; but they are sincere, therefore they are inspired.

There is nothing in such reasoning that can be thought like a begging of the question.

XLIII. If it be by the Bible itself that we establish the dogma of a certain inspiration in the sacred books, by what can it be proved that that inspiration is universal, and that it extends to the minutest details of the instructions they convey?

If it be the Scriptures that tell us of their divine inspiration, it is they too that will be able to inform us in what divine inspiration consisted. In order to our admitting their inspiration on their own sole testimony, it should have sufficed for us to be assured that they were authentic; but, in order to our admitting their plenary inspiration, we shall have something more; for we shall then be able to invoke their testimony as writings already admitted to be divine. It will no longer be authentic books only that say to us, I am inspired; but books, both authentic and inspired, will say to us, I am so altogether. The Scriptures are *inspired*, we affirm, because, being authentic and true, they say of themselves that they are inspired; but the Scriptures are *plenarily inspired*, we also add, because, being inspired, they say that they are so entirely, and without any exception.

Here, then, there is neither more nor less than a doctrine which the Bible will teach us, as it teaches us all the rest. And just as we believe, because it tells us so, that Jesus Christ is God, and that he became man; so also we believe that the Holy Ghost is God, and that he dictated the whole of the Scriptures.

35

Adolphe Monod's *Farewell to His Friends and the Church*

Adolphe Monod, *Living in the Hope of Glory*, ed. and trans. Constance K. Walker (Phillipsburg, NJ: P&R Publishing, 2002), 3–8, 70–73, 139–44, 26–35.

Adolphe Monod (1802–56) was one of the greatest French preachers. His vocation, however, started in a somber way. After his studies in Geneva, under the sway of rationalism, the student and then young pastor went through a great crisis of faith. Only slowly, under the patient guidance of Thomas Erskine (1788–1870), was he brought back to an orthodox and living faith. Monod gained great distinction as an evangelist. He also served as professor in the Reformed seminary at Montauban. At the end of his life, he ministered as the pastor of the famous Oratoire Church in Paris. Then he went through a prolonged sickness, being bedridden for several months. During this time, friends regularly gathered around him and he preached what would become a spiritual classic, his *Farewell to His Friends and the Church* (1856). Monod's sermons were widely circulated and translated into English. Further, he had ties with those at Princeton Seminary. They valued his contribution as a preacher, and he wrote a preface to the French translation of Charles Hodge's commentary on Romans.

We reprint here extracts from Monod's classic work *Farewell*. These short meditations are the fruit of his lifelong ministry and reflections. In particular, the subject of the inspiration of Scripture always preoccupied him. He wrote a thesis on the subject (1824), and his discourse *L'inspiration prouvée par ses oeuvres* given in Paris in 1852 was published posthumously in 1864. The topics taken from his *Farewell* range from the perfection of Scripture, to practical advice on reading and studying Scripture, to the nature of Scripture. Of special interest is that his doctrine of Scripture was honed in the furnace of rationalism. As Warfield did later, Monod built on the analogy between Scripture and the two natures of Christ, between the inscripturated Word and the incarnate Word. Though this analogy has often been challenged, Monod carefully places this definition in the context of the supernatural understanding of the revelation of God in Scripture. We reprint this selection from the translation published by P&R Publishing in 2002.

Bibliography: David Bundy. "Monod, Adolphe." Pp. 783–84 in Donald M. Lewis, ed., *The Blackwell Dictionary of Evangelical Biography, 1730–1860*, vol. 2 (Cambridge, MA: Blackwell, 1995). Boris Decorvet and Emile G. Léonard. "Esquisse Biographique." Pp. 9–63 in Adolphe Monod. *Les adieux*. Vevey (Suisse): Groupes Missionaires, 1956. Robert P. Evans. "Monod, Adolphe (1802–56)." P. 672 in *NIDCC*. Hughes Oliphant Old. *The Reading and Preaching of the Scriptures in the Worship of the Christian Church*. Vol. 6, *The Modern Age*. Grand Rapids: Eerdmans, 2007. Pp. 18–31. James L. Osen. *Prophet and Peacemaker: The Life of Adolphe Monod*. Lanham, MD: University Press of America, 1984. C. Pfender. "Monod, Adolphe (Louis Frédéric Théodore)." *NSHERK* 7:472–73.

Measureless Word, Measureless God
(Everything in Scripture Is Ideal)

(October 14, 1855)

My dear friends, beloved brothers and sisters, I am so happy and grateful to be able to receive with you the body and blood of our Savior—that flesh which is "real food" and that blood which is "real drink" (see John 6:55) for those who receive them in faith by the Holy Spirit.

There is one characteristic of Scripture that would, by itself, be sufficient to identify it as the Word of God: everything in it is ideal. There is nothing in Scripture but the absolute and the perfect. It never dreams of calling us to a certain measure of holiness by a certain measure of faith. All measure is contrary to the instinct of the Bible because it is contrary to God.

The ideal of Scripture is not at all like that of poets, who take the things of this world in order to raise them to the third heaven. Scripture does just the opposite. In it the visible things are only types of the invisible, which alone are real, and it considers all things from God's point of view. This statement struck me this morning as I was reflecting before the Lord on what I could say to you about communion and about the cross of Jesus Christ, in which alone we find remission of sins.

Everywhere Scripture presents us with ideal *sin*. There is not one of us who has any idea of the horror and crime of sin before God. We have always lived in an atmosphere so saturated with sin, on this earth that drinks iniquity like water and eats it like bread, that we no longer know how to discern the sin that engulfs us from every side.

Here, in a few words, is my experience. We find in the Bible this statement, "At one time we too were foolish, disobedient, deceived and enslaved by all kinds of passions and pleasures. We lived in malice and envy, being hated and hating one another" (Titus 3:3). For a long time it was impossible for me to agree with that statement, which seemed to me to be clearly marked by exaggeration. I confess that even after God, in his grace, had turned my heart to him on the day that he had set from time eternal, I was for a long while still unable to accept it completely. What is more, I confess that ever since, and even today, I cannot comprehend it in its fullness. Yet I am convinced that it is perfectly true and that if I have not really grasped it in my experience, the fault is entirely mine.

It is just here that I have understood the necessity of a witness existing before, outside of, and above us. I accept that statement from Titus 3:3 as coming from God because I find it in his Word, and I beseech him to finish revealing its meaning to me by his Spirit. By God's grace I have come—not year by year, things don't go that fast, but from one interval of several years to another—to see this doctrine more clearly and to sense its truth more forcefully in my heart. I am convinced that when the veil of this flesh has fallen, I will recognize that this is the most faithful painting and the portrait with the greatest likeness that was ever drawn of my heart—and by this I mean my natural heart.

Let us ask God to reveal to us our sinful state, yet without pressing too hard, because he knows full well that if he made us grow in that knowledge faster than in the knowledge of his mercy, we would fall into despair.

But *pardon* is also depicted to us everywhere in Scripture as ideal. If only part of our sins were pardoned; if out of a thousand sins or a million sins (if our sins could be counted) only one were left that was not deal with, then that pardon would be useless to us. But our pardon is complete.

The passage that was cited a moment ago (2 Cor. 5:21) is one of my favorites.[1] Jesus Christ did not simply make atonement for some sins, he made atonement for *sin* itself. He was not considered to be a sinner, he was made to be *sin*; and, mystery of mysteries, the full curse of God was gathered together on that innocent, holy head. Likewise, we are not simply made righteous in him, we are made to be *righteousness* itself, in such a way that when God looks at us in Jesus Christ he sees us as his own beloved Son and finds in us everything that could attract his gaze and kindness.

We who believe have been given by God to Jesus Christ as the recompense of his sacrifice. He can no more break his word to us than to Jesus Christ, and all of his perfection is so thoroughly committed in this relationship that this gift of his infinite mercy becomes like a right due to us by virtue of our perfect righteousness in Jesus Christ.

Even the terms used in Scripture to show us the nature of sin before God also show us how he has blotted out our sins. He has "put all my sins behind [his] back" (Isa. 38:17) as if he were afraid of seeing them again; he "will hurl all our iniquities into the depths of the sea" (Mic. 7:19); he has "swept away [our] offenses like a cloud, [our] sins like the morning mist" (Isa. 44:22). Here we see what it is for God to forget sin. The Lord is shown to us as making an effort to forget, or rather not to forget but to eradicate.

Finally, Scripture is ideal in what it says to us about *sanctification*. We have no idea what Scripture demands of us and the degree of holiness to which we can and must attain. What fullness there is in this verse: "May God himself, the God of peace, sanctify you through and through. May your whole spirit, soul and body be kept blameless at the coming of our Lord Jesus Christ" (1 Thess. 5:23). And in order to prove to us that this is not simply a wish, the apostle immediately adds, "The one who calls you is faithful and he will do it" (1 Thess. 5:24). It is no more possible for him to refuse us this grace than it is for us to conceive of him breaking his word.

And how can we arrive at this holiness? Consider the holy men the Bible gives us as examples. How were they great? It was not by their enlightenment or by their natural gifts but by their faith. Look at Saint James (James 5:16). In order to show us the power of faith

---

1. "For our sake he made him to be sin who knew no sin, so that in him we might become the righteousness of God" (ESV).

and of prayer, he takes perhaps the most miraculous man in the Bible in the most miraculous of his miracles. He gives us the boldness of that prayer by Elijah as something completely natural and offers him as an example to the smallest, to the most humble, in order to show us what the fervent prayer (literally, the "energetic" prayer) of a righteous man can do.

If we were able, each one of us, beginning today, to sense in our heart the enormity of sin, the fullness of our pardon, and the power of the holiness to which we must attain, what a change in our life, what a healthy influence for the church itself!

PRAYER

Oh, God! You who know all of the evil and suffering that sin has brought on our poor earth and on this poor humanity, you who see all that is being suffered at this very moment and that we could not stand to look at, we lift up to you all those who are afflicted so that you might pour out on them the treasures of your grace and consolation. We cannot name them all to you, but you yourself know their names.

We lift up to you the victims of war—so many families deep in mourning and so many others who live in continual anxiety. We lift up to you those who are oppressed and perse-cuted for righteousness' sake. We lift up to you the slaves; think of these thousands, these millions of slaves oppressed by men who profess your name, by servants of Christ who are not servants. We lift up to you the poor—ah, the poor!—the sick, the sick who are poor.

We lift up to you all those who know you, that you would sustain them and pour out on them your peace and your comfort. And as for those who don't know you, we commend them to your grace so that you might reveal yourself to them, because if they do not possess you, their only other alternative is despair.

As for me who suffers a little, I confess Christ and his peace. I thank you for the joy that you have poured into my soul. You will call us, perhaps, to be separated for a little while, but what is that? We know that by your grace we will all one day be reunited close to you.

SCRIPTURE'S REWARDS
(READING THE BIBLE)

(November 11, 1855)

It is my custom on these occasions to address a few words of Christian exhortation to the few friends who are kind enough to gather around me. Today my state of suffering forbids me that consolation, so I must content myself with giving you an example from Christian experience that will be able to lead you into healthy reflection on the value of the Word of God. I take this example, it in all simplicity, from what happened to me this past week.

During one of those nights in which I suffered much and slept little, toward morning, at around 4:30 a.m., I had settled myself in my bed with the hope of getting a little rest. Then I invited the person keeping watch over me—one of those fine young men who have the goodness to devote part of their strength to me[2]—to read me a chapter from God's Word. He offered to read the eighth chapter of the Epistle to the Romans. I accepted while asking him to go back to the sixth and even the fifth chapters so as to follow the development of the ideas.

After we read chapters 5, 6, 7, and 8 in order, my attention, my interest, and my admiration had been so stirred by the heavenly language of Saint Paul—or rather of the Holy Spirit speaking through Saint Paul—that I no longer dreamed of sleep. So we read the ninth chapter and the following ones, right to the end, always with the same sustained interest. Finally, we read the first four chapters in order to have left nothing out and to have read the entire epistle.

The reading had taken about two hours, and I no longed dreamed of anything except hearing the Word of God and profiting from it. The Lord in his goodness had provided for the rest that I had been missing.

I don't know how to communicate to you how much I was struck in that reading of the entire Epistle to the Romans with that mark of divinity, of truth, of holiness, of love, and of power that is imprinted on every page and on every word. We sensed, my young friend and I, without at first communicating our thoughts, that we were listening to a voice from heaven. We sensed that, independent of all those testimonies that witness to the inspiration and divine authority of Scripture, it provides a completely sufficient testimony to itself, just as Jesus Christ did to himself through his works.

We also sensed how useful it is to read Scriptures as a whole and how much one loses in taking only portions, fragments, detached verses. A book is understood only when, from time to time, it is read as a whole. This led us to understand that one needs to make two studies of the Word of God: a comprehensive one to produce in us the very blessed impression that we had just received, and a detailed one to let each verse and each word be taken into account.

But our principal impression was one of humiliation. We said to one another, "What! We have such a treasure as this near us, and we fail to draw on it!" We had just spent two hours in heaven. We found ourselves transported not only into the midst of the best among men—those instruments who were inspired and favored by the Holy Spirit—but also into the midst of the elect angels and into the company of Jesus Christ.

We have resolved, while relying on the only one who can guard his children's resolutions, to give ourselves over with renewed zeal to study Scripture, sacrificing, if need be, a myriad of other readings that are instructive and useful but that cannot compare with the Word of God. We have resolved to live with that Word as we desire to live with God himself, because the reading of that Word inspired by God's Spirit is like a conversation with God.

I commend to you, my dear friends, the Word of God as something for constant, in-depth study and meditation. It will lift us up above everything else. It will, through Jesus Christ,

---

2. This small group of young friends, almost all of whom were medical students, watched over Adolphe Monod each night for over six months, easing his long hours of sleeplessness and suffering through their devotion and affectionate care. (Footnote taken from *Les Adieux* [Vevey, Suisse: Editions des Groupes Missionaires, 1956].)

be the strength of our lives, the joy of our hearts, and our powerful consolation in life and in death. I ask it for you as for myself. Amen!

FEEDING ON GOD'S WORD
(A DYING MAN'S REGRETS:
2. THE STUDY OF GOD'S WORD)

(January 20, 1856)

My dear friends, last Sunday under the theme *A Dying Man's Regrets* I began to explain the new perspective that one who is dying receives about the many things he would now like to have done differently and that he would like to do differently if he were called back from his half-open tomb. One of the most important of these is our study of God's Word. Ah, certainly in such a case one says to himself, "I should have acted differently with regard to the Word of God. I should have studied it more deeply and possessed it more fully so as to practice it better while communicating it more effectively to others!" Let us stop for a few brief moments on this healthy thought so that we may humble those for whom the end of time is coming and enlighten those to whom more time is given but who don't know for how long.

What is Holy Scripture? Never will men be able to explain how it was formed or, in particular, how God's Spirit and man's spirit are combined there to make it a divine word, as high as the heavens, and yet, at the same time, a human word very close to us. This is no less difficult to explain than how in Jesus Christ the divine and human natures are united. This comparison does not come from me but from Scripture, which calls itself the written Word and Jesus Christ the living Word.

No matter how it was formed, Holy Scripture is heaven spoken on earth. It is the maxims of the kingdom of heaven that are communicated to men in a human language. It is as if the invisible kingdom had descended into their midst and been placed before their eyes. There is no other book, even among the best, that communicates the mysteries of the kingdom of heaven to us as this one does. They are all mixed with human error; only Scripture is exempt from it. It is God's book filled with God's truth. In it we hear God speaking through the Holy Spirit; we see God, man, the present, the future, time, and eternity described such as they are.

If someone has thus taken account of what Scripture is, it will not be hard for him to confess the use to which he should put it. We would interrogate Scripture just as we would like to interrogate an angel from heaven sent expressly by God at this very moment in order to instruct us. Or, what is even better, we should interrogate it as we would interrogate our Lord Jesus Christ if we had him near to us right now and could speak to him and hear him. In effect, we really do speak to him and hear him when we read Holy Scripture, and as it reveals him to us, it reveals everything else to us through his Spirit and on his behalf.

Oh, how can we surround this book with enough attention and respect? No doubt Scripture is not the truth that saves us, but it is the road to that truth. It is not salvation, but it is the book that reveals our salvation, a salvation we would never be able to know without it. Through Scripture and in proportion to our growth in understanding it, we will also become better acquainted with Jesus, the Savior of our souls.

No Christian will argue the truth of these principles, and yet those who study Scripture in depth are rare indeed! Most read them superficially and content themselves with a few great general truths when they could be probing ever deeper and becoming aware (as much as they can) of all that is there, as it is written: "The secret things belong to the LORD our God, but the things revealed belong to us and to our children forever" (Deut. 29:29). Why is there this singular contradiction within ourselves? It is because of the difficulties that such a reading presents.

We must agree that when one begins to read Scripture in depth, he finds many difficulties and obscurities. Since it takes a lot of work to dissipate them and since man's spirit is naturally lazy and lax, little by little he loses courage and contends himself with reading and rereading Scripture always at the same level. This study scarcely penetrates below the surface and teaches nothing new. Rather, by always recapturing the same things, it even sometimes inspires in us a sort of weariness, as if the Word of God were not interesting, as if we were not able ever and always to instruct us, as if it were not as inexhaustible as God himself!

Nevertheless, let us guard ourselves against thinking that these difficulties are insurmountable. No, my friends, but it takes effort, and here, as in prayer and in all other aspects of the Christian life, God desires that man might be a co-laborer with him. Knowledge of the Bible, the flavor of the Bible, is the fruit and the reward of this humble and sincere and persevering effort.

Ah, that each one might return to his Bible with a new zeal! Take book after book, seeking to gain from reading it not simply general feelings of obvious piety but a thorough and growing acquaintance with the kingdom of heaven. Study a book until you have understood it as well as you can. Then go on to a second, then to a third, and so on. You will find that on a second and third reading many of the seemingly insurmountable difficulties will disappear, and even when some remain, you will nevertheless gain the fruit of your labor before God.

Do not exempt from this study even the most difficult books, the prophets, the minor prophets, which many Christians leave aside as unintelligible. If you want to make the effort to study them, you will see a multitude of very interesting things there. Besides, there are by God's grace good books and commentaries on certain parts of Scripture that can serve as a key for the others. In availing ourselves of these good books, we probe ever deeper in the knowledge of God's Word. Then we can apply ourselves more particularly to those parts of Scripture that address themselves more specifically to Christians, but, I repeat, without neglecting any of them.

The fruit and the reward of those who are faithful and persevering will be to understand the Word of God, to love it, to penetrate ever further into it, and to find the time ever too short to know it well. I knew a man who spent seven hours each day studying the Bible and who found ever-increasing delights through that study.

If someone, in faith, using the resources God has placed at his disposal and counting on God to guide him, acted on these thoughts that I can only indicate briefly at this time, he would find as yet unsuspected treasures in God's Word. Thus it would become for him just as firm a support as it was for Jesus tempted in the wilderness. It would become for him what it was for all the saints of the New Testament and the Old Testament (with the portions of Scripture that existed before them); what it was for David and for Daniel, what it was for Saint Paul, what it was for all the saints of God.

May God grant each of us this grace! And may he for whom it is no more difficult to bless in a short time than in a long one, nor to bless one with little strength than one with much, be pleased to make these words of mine so penetrate into your hearts that they will work a transformation in your study of the Bible, a transformation for which you will bless God through all eternity! Amen.

THE TWO VOICES OF SCRIPTURE (SCRIPTURE)

(February 24, 1856)

My dear friends in Christ who give me such a great a token of your love, those of you who have been present at several of these gatherings know that the thing that I enjoy most when I address these few words to you is to recount the memories of a Christian who believes himself ready to appear before God. I then like to sum up in God's presence and communicate to you the main results of this man's studies of the Word of God and also the convictions in which he desires to finish living and dying. Having in this way shown the results at which I have arrived concerning sin and the person of the Lord Jesus Christ, I come today to speak for a few moments about his Word.

I declare, as though before the judgment seat of Jesus Christ, where I expect soon to appear, my unshakable conviction that when Scripture speaks, it is God who speaks. All my research and my studies, whether of Scripture or church history or my own heart, and all of the discussions that have been raised in these last years on the inspiration and divine authority of God's Word have only strengthened me in this conviction. Throughout my three-phase ministry (three periods of about ten years each, at Lyon, Montauban, and Paris), by pathways that God's wisdom has made somewhat diverse, I have become increasingly convinced that when Scriptures speaks, God speaks. When Scripture proclaims God's will or the way of salvation or the great doctrines of sin and grace, and of the Father, Son, and Holy Spirit, what it tells us is no less true and no less certain than if heaven were opened above us at this very moment and the voice of God resounded, as it once did at Sinai, saying these same things to us.

There are no bounds to the trust and submission that we owe the Scriptures, any more than there are limits to the truth and the faithfulness of God. Thus, when the day arrives that I enter into the invisible world (a day of which only God knows the number and that I long for as for a deliverance without ever daring to hasten it), I do not expect to find things any different from the way in which the Word of God has represented them to me here. Of course there will be the enormous difference in the condition and state of the soul before and after death, in time and in eternity, but, fundamentally, the voice that I will hear then, that will be clothed with full power to judge, that will rule over all creatures—that voice will be the same one that I listen to today on earth. Thus I will say,

"That is just what God was saying to me, and how I thank him today that I did not wait until I had seen before believing!"

I have this confidence because Scripture is the divine expression of the truths and maxims that form the very foundation of the invisible and eternal realm. It is like a letter that God has written from the invisible world to his children detained in the visible one, so that henceforth through faith in God they might learn the true nature of things and that, as a result, they might act to bring about the salvation of their souls. Those who believe God will save their souls, but how could those who don't believe God ever save them?

Scripture is thus the Word of God in the highest sense of that expression, but also in the simplest and most familiar sense. It is the only sure rule of faith and life, a rule to which all others must be submitted. All the meetings in the world, all the committees, conferences, prayers, and common quests[3] have no value at all unless each is submitted and subordinated to the sovereign, infallible, unchangeable authority of God's Word.

The testimony that I bear to Scripture is not just the testimony that is given to it by Moses or David or Saint Paul or Saint John or Augustine or Chrysostom. It is not just the testimony of all the saints of all ages. It is the testimony that is given to it by God himself and by Jesus Christ, who gives to the Word of God the same glory that he receives from it.

Experience and observation, which we are permitted to invoke provided that we do so with humble diffidence, come mercifully to confirm all these testimonies. For never has it been granted to any man or any group of men to compose a book, even a very short book, that equals Holy Scripture and that could produce the same effects of comfort, sanctification, and conversion. Never *will* it be granted to any man or group of men unless the Holy Spirit guides them in the same special way that he guided the apostles and prophets.

It is not a question of personal holiness, for the holiness we have just recognized in Scripture is no less present in the words of Saint Paul than in the words of Jesus Christ. Rather it is a question of divine direction. That direction is even more apparent when one considers that this book was written in a completely historical order and that, in spite of being spread out over nearly two thousand years, it still has a coherent and consistent doctrine on each point.

The Bible is a book apart, which no other ever has or ever could equal. It reigns alone over all the systems, all the uncertainties, and all the questions that concern or upset mankind.

But (and here I enter into a new train of thought), no sooner have I, for my part, sanctioned the name Word of God, which the Bible has received from God himself and from Jesus Christ, than in looking closely at this book I find it full of man. It contains so many marks of humanity. At first I might even feel a certain fear, as if I had gone too far before in the testimony that I gave it. In effect, I recognize in the writers of this book a marked individuality of style and character. If, by some impossibility, some lost book were to be discovered today that, through some error, had not previously been included in the canon, there is no one who is at all versed in the Holy Scriptures who would not be able to say instantly whether it was by Jeremiah or Isaiah; whether it was by Peter, John, or Paul. That is how different these writers were and how clearly each one left the mark of his individual character on all that he wrote.

I also find many things in this book that its writers could have said without the special help of the Spirit of God (for example, 2 Tim. 4:13), and since God does not perform any

---

3. Or, "searching the Scriptures." The meaning of this phrase is unclear. Perhaps it refers to times when believers gather together to seek God's will through prayer.

useless miracles, we see there the spirit of the man, which has its own part in the composition of the Word of God.

There is more. I find touches in Scripture that remind us of human infirmity, as when Saint Paul tries to recollect, without daring to trust his memory, how many people he baptized at Corinth. But he doesn't become preoccupied with the question, "for Christ did not send me to baptize, but to preach the gospel" (1 Cor. 1:14–17). It was clearly part of God's plan that on each page of this book that we call the Word of God we should also recognize a word of man.

But if someone who has not reflected on this question can experience a kind of fear, he will not be long in reassuring himself and in seeing, on the contrary, a measure of blessing, light, and spirituality in the human side of the composition of Scripture. In the last analysis, how could it have been avoided? It could have been avoided only if Scripture had been dictated word for word, without any influence from personal character or historical events.

Let us take an extreme example, which I cite with the deepest respect. When God places words of reproof against an unfaithful prophet in the mouth of a dumb animal, it is very clear that his word acts without an intermediary endowed with a will of its own.[4] The *inspiration* (for it surely is one) is that much more visible in this case when the instrument is completely passive. But what in this inspiration of a being deprived of reason can compare with the inspiration of an apostle, infused as it is with his experience and personal feelings? A similar consideration of all the intermediate levels of activity or passivity of the instrument would reveal that, to the extent that the inspiration becomes more personal, it gains interest without losing any of its authority.

Also, how much more beautiful, how much more touching Scripture is in the way it was given! It was given by God in the course of history through men whose spirits were led by the Spirit of God; men like us who were able to say, "I believed, therefore I spoke" (Ps. 116:10 NKJV). It was given through men of whom it can be said, for example, "Elijah was a man just like us. He prayed earnestly that it would not rain, and it did not rain on the land for three and a half years" (James 5:17).

The Word of God was given in history to men like us. It was not brought by superior, invisible beings but by men weak like ourselves and saved like ourselves; by men who were the first to believe and who could say, "I have believed what I exhort you to believe." Because of this, it has a life, a freshness, a power that can touch our hearts all the more deeply. A familiarity and something like a secret friendship forms between those hearts and that Word, so that the most solemn of books is, at the same time, the dearest and most tender. In all this, there is a deep understanding of the human heart and one of the most intimate beauties of the Word of God.

Though it was composed by simple men who did not cease, in writing it, to fight against sin and to depend personally on the faith they announced, the Bible is no less the Word of God. Rather it is all the more divine for being more human. That is to say that one is more aware of the power and the presence of God's Spirit and of his influence on our souls when, in writing the Bible, God uses those instruments in whom only his Spirit could cause such supernatural light and power to operate, turning them into vessels destined to carry the truth to the very ends of the earth. That is how Holy Scripture gains access to the deepest

---

4. See the story of Balaam in Numbers 22–24, especially Numbers 22:15–35.

recesses of our hearts. That is how it teaches us on God's part while, at the same time, it teaches us through men. It joins together simultaneously all the elements capable of touching, of enlightening, of converting to God, of sustaining in the shadows of this age, and of accomplishing all in all.

There is, my friends (and this is my last thought), a contrast, or rather a comparison that, for the Christian, can clarify everything and confirm what I have just said. It is the view that we had last Sunday[5] and that is given to us throughout Scripture of Jesus Christ uniting in himself the divine nature and human nature in such marvelous way that we cannot give an account of it, and yet it is the very foundation and the comfort of our faith.

Last Sunday we began by considering Jesus Christ in his human perfection, after which we contemplated him in his divinity. Suppose that we had reversed that order. Suppose that we had spoken first of the divine nature of Jesus Christ and of our obligation to worship him as God, and that we had then gone on to make for the first time the observation that Jesus Christ is a man, able to suffer and die. I do not know what other fear could have slipped itself into our soul as easily as the fear that we had attributed too much divinity to him.

But, as we saw in that same Sunday teaching, Scripture shows us everywhere that perfect divinity is united in him with perfect humanity and that each increases the value of the other without in any way compromising its reality. It even reveals that Jesus is all the more man for being more God and that he is all the more God for being more man. In which moments is Jesus Christ most human? Is it not in the temptation in the desert, in the anguish of Gethsemane, and in the fearful agony of the cross? And are these not also the moments when he is most God? He gains victory over the tempter, overcomes pain, and triumphs over the cross by the power of the Spirit of God that dwells in him, for the Spirit does not dwell in him with measure as he does in us, but without measure, as in the only Son of the Father.

It is the same with the Word of God. It is God's Word, true and eternal, and, at the same time, it is man's word where one senses the gleam of the human spirit and the beat of the human heart. It is precisely in the moments where one best senses (in a Saint Paul or a Saint John, for example) the fight of faith and the persevering struggle against sin that one also senses best how divine is the light diffused into their souls. This light was given first of all that they might battle on their own behalf and then that they might, with divine virtue, diffuse it out into the whole world. That is why we can say that the Word is all the more divine for being more human.

How wonderful this comparison between Jesus Christ and Holy Scripture appears to me! Moreover, you may be sure that it is not a comparison that I dreamed up in my head but one that is furnished to me by God's Word. For someone who knows that it "cannot be broken" (John 10:35), it is enough to recall a most astonishing thing: Scripture sometimes gives the same name to Jesus Christ and to Holy Scripture. It calls them both *Word of God*. One of these words, Jesus Christ, is the living Word of God, the personal manifestation of his invisible perfections in the bosom of humanity. The other, Scripture, is the written Word of God, the verbal manifestation, given through language, of these same invisible perfections.

These two are inseparable for us. Jesus Christ is revealed to us only through Scripture, and Scripture is given to us only in order to reveal Jesus Christ. Thus Scripture is the written Word of God just as Jesus Christ is the living Word of God. Those who rely on the human

5. The previous meditation was on the person of Jesus Christ.

characteristics of Scripture to belittle its divinity use the same sort of reasoning as those who rely on the human personality of Jesus Christ in order to deny him the title of God. They fail to understand that human nature and divine nature are united in the person of Jesus Christ just as the human word and the divine word are united in the Scriptures. It is no more astonishing that Scripture, though the Word of God, should at the same time bear so many marks of humanity than that Jesus Christ, though God, should be man.

As to the way that the two natures fuse together in the one case and the two voices in the other, it is the very essence of faith's object on this point. It is a deep mystery, but, as Saint Paul tells us, "the mystery of godliness" (1 Tim. 3:16). It is a mystery that fills our soul with joy and hope.

Yes, Scripture is the unique path by which we can arrive at knowing Jesus Christ without risk of error, just as Jesus Christ is the unique path by which we can arrive at the Father. Yes, if you want to save your souls, you must believe in the Word of God; you must submit to the Word of God. You must not search inside yourself for anything—whether it is under the name of reason or intelligence or feeling or conscience or some other lovely thing—that dominates or judges or controls the Word of God. It is not a matter of controlling it but of being controlled by it. The greatest of all God's servants are those who bow before that Word. Saint Paul, David, Luther, Calvin were jealous to humble themselves in the dust before it, and if possible they would have gone still lower.

May it reign alone, this Word of my Savior God to which I am so delighted to be able to give this testimony again "before I depart and am no more" (Ps. 39:13). I give this testimony while waiting for the banner of eternal life (which we here on earth know how to open only half way) to be unfurled for us in the pure and serene light from above!

Importance of the Messianic Prophecies

ERNST WILHELM HENGSTENBERG

Ernst Wilhelm Hengstenberg, "Appendix I. Importance of the Messianic Prophecies," in *Christology of the Old Testament: And a Commentary on the Messianic Predictions* (Edinburgh: T&T Clark, 1878), 4:229–40.

Ernst Wilhelm Hengstenberg (1802–69) was an influential conservative biblical scholar and professor. Warfield describes him as "one of the most searching expounders of the Scriptures that God has as yet given His church." He was also involved in theological controversies. In the context of rationalism, he was converted to confessional Christianity. He founded and edited for many years the journal *Evangelishe Kirchenzeitung*, which sought to combat rationalism. In spite of his conservative views, he maintained a professorship in biblical exegesis at the University of Berlin. Besides his polemical writings, he wrote many biblical commentaries, many of which were translated into English. Charles Hodge (1797–1878) studied with him and was greatly influenced by him. Hengstenberg was influential not only on Old Princeton, but also on Westminster, in particular on Edward J. Young (1907–68). One of Hengstenberg's significant works is his four-volume *Christology of the Old Testament* (1835–39).

The selection reprinted here is an appendix to this last-mentioned work entitled "Importance of the Messianic Prophecies." This text illustrates his approach to Scripture and touches on an important aspect of the Bible. In this short essay, Hengstenberg discusses first the importance of messianic prophecies in the Old Testament as preparation for the coming of Christ. Then he argues for the continuing significance of these prophecies for the church, which was a burning question as rationalism downgraded their significance. In particular, Hengstenberg responds to the challenges raised by Friedrich Schleiermacher. This piece of work offers an able defense of the historic supernatural view of Scripture, prevalent from the Old Testament to the time of Christ and his apostles, and down through the ages in the church (Hengstenberg calls on the testimony of Blaise Pascal to exemplify the church's view). This article also illustrates

Hengstenberg's approach to the Old Testament, which was greatly influential in the Old Princeton/Westminster tradition of interpretation. We reproduce here this essay as found in the 1878 T&T Clark translation of this seminal work.

Bibliography: Annette G. Aubert. "A Transatlantic Study: Charles Hodge and Emanuel V. Gerhart on Theological Method and the Doctrine of the Atonement, with Special Consideration Given to the Influence of Nineteenth-Century German Theology." Ph.D. diss., Westminster Theological Seminary, 2010. Johannes Bachmann. *Ernst Wilhelm Hengstenberg: Sein Leben und Wirken.* 3 vols. Gütersloh: C. Bertelsmann, 1876–92. Idem. "Hengstenberg, Ernst Wilhelm." *NSHERK* 5:224–25. D. Clair Davis. "The Hermeneutics of E. W. Hengstenberg: Edifying Value as Exegetical Standard." Dr. Theol. diss., University of Göttingen, 1960. Wayne Detzler. "Hengstenberg, Ernst Wilhelm (1802–1869)." Pp. 459–60 in *NIDCC*. M. Elliott. "Hengstenberg, Ernst Wilhelm (1802–1869)." Pp. 517–20 in *DMBI* (2007). John Rogerson. *Old Testament Criticism in the Nineteenth Century: England and Germany.* Philadelphia: Fortress, 1984, 1985. Philip Schaff. *Germany; Its Universities, Theology, and Religion.* Philadelphia: Lindsay and Blakiston, 1857. Pp. 300–319. Esp. pp. 135–36. Benjamin Breckinridge Warfield. "The Divine Messiah in the Old Testament." Pp. 3–49 in *Christology and Criticism.* 1932. Repr., Grand Rapids: Baker, 2000. Edward J. Young. *An Introduction to the Old Testament.* Grand Rapids: Eerdmans, 1949, 1964.

The term Messianic is derived from Psalm 2:2 and Daniel 9:25–26, where the Redeemer is called משיח, "anointed one." In the symbolical phraseology of the Scriptures, anointing represents the communication of the gifts of the Holy Spirit. The kings of Israel, especially, were called anointed men, because they received a peculiarly abundant measure of the Spirit for their exalted office, whenever they opened their hearts to the grace of God. In Psalms 84:9 and 132:10, 17, David is called the anointed of the Lord, with reference to the occurrence recorded in 1 Samuel 16:13–14, where the figure is embodied in a symbolical action; and the whole family of David is similarly described in Psalms 18:5; 89:38, 51; Habakkuk 3:13; and Lamentations 4:20. In the highest sense, however, this term was applied to him in whom the family of David reached its culminating point, and who received the Holy Spirit without measure (John 3:34; compare Isa. 9:1).

When we observe that the Messianic announcements, which are peculiar to Israel alone, have their origin in the primeval age; that for many successive centuries they continue to reappear again and again; that they do not occur merely incidentally, and in an isolated form in the midst of other prophecies, but constitute the very centre and soul of all prophecy; that they stand out in great prominence even in the Psalms, in which utterance is given to the living faith of the people of God, under the quickening influence of the law and the prophets—we cannot for a moment doubt that to the people of the ancient covenant the anticipation of a Messiah must have been one of all-absorbing importance.

1. The members of the ancient covenant were in imminent danger of looking merely at the present, and indulging, in consequence, a spirit of narrow-minded exclusiveness, which could not fail to lead to the most disastrous results. It led them, on the one hand, to form low and unworthy conceptions of God, and to detract from either his love or his power (for if the God of Israel were to be regarded as nothing more than this, he would cease to be God

altogether); and, on the other, to form extremely pernicious ideas of their own merits, since it was very natural that, supposing the pre-eminence of Israel above the heathen nations to be permanent in its character, they should trace it to a certain innate superiority, which rendered them more worthy than any other to be the recipients of the grace of God. It was of the utmost importance, therefore, for the maintenance of a living faith in Israel, that its view should be directed beyond the preparatory institutions to the ultimate issue, in order that the means should be fully recognised as means and nothing more. Hence, even before the establishment of the Old Testament economy, it was distinctly announced, and after its establishment the fact was again impressed upon the minds of the people, that the peculiar relation in which God stood to Israel was merely a temporary one; that the day would come when the Redeemer and King of the whole world would appear; and that, until the time of his appearance, the form assumed by the kingdom of God was merely provisional. The necessity for this announcement is especially obvious when we observe how, notwithstanding these lucid prophecies, the greater portion of the Jews were blinded by a carnal mind, and were the victims of the most disastrous exclusiveness.

2. The announcement of the Messiah was one of the means employed to maintain the fidelity of the nation towards the Lord in the midst of troublous circumstances. Proclaimed by the different messengers sent by God with the confidence produced by the Holy Ghost, depicted in the most glowing colours, and brought, as it were, from the future into the present, the Messiah became more and more the banner around which all the downcast, the spiritually downcast of Judah and the dispersed of Israel, collected together. Thus, for example, in Isaiah 7:14, the image of Immanuel is placed before the eyes of the nation, which is in despair on account of Aram and Ephraim. And thus also do Jeremiah (in ch. 23:5–6) and Ezekiel (in ch. 34:23) comfort those who are terrified at the aspect of the imperial power, by directing their minds to the coming Redeemer. And if it not infrequently happens that the prophets administer consolation by pointing to joyous events of an inferior kind in the immediate future, they almost always come back to this as the most important, the condition of all the rest, the centre of all the hopes of salvation. For example, when the existence of the nation is threatened by Assyria, Isaiah first of all predicts the overthrow of Assyria in chapter 10:5–34, and then in chapter 11 points to the complete salvation to be effected in Christ for the people of God, which constitutes the pledge of every inferior communication of blessing. This design of the Messianic prophecies had respect to the entire nation, and was partially secured even when they were falsely interpreted in consequence of a misapprehension of their figurative disguise. For that portion of the nation whose Messianic expectations were for the most part sinfully carnal was thereby preserved from outward apostasy; and even this was of consequence, since the maintenance of the outward form of the kingdom of God was the primary condition of the coming of Christ, and, in addition to this, the kernel was protected by the shell.

3. The glaring contrast between the idea of the nation of God and the form which it actually assumed during the whole of the Old Testament period, would inevitably have given rise to erroneous opinions as to the former if the fact had not been forcibly impressed upon the minds of the people, by the constantly repeated announcement of the Messiah, that the contrast was only a transient one. In the outward condition of the nation, this contrast was especially apparent. The nation of God, which, from the very fact that it was such, was necessarily called to universal dominion, was for many a long and anxious century kept in

subjection by the powers of the world. The "kingdom of priests" groaned in utter prostration under the oppression of the heathen. Such a state of things would have been intolerable if hope had not furnished a counterpoise. From this point of view, for example, Isaiah predicts, in chapter 2:2–4, that the kingdom of God, which is now despised, will be exalted in the days of the Messiah above all the kingdoms of the world, and will become an object of desire even to the proud heathen themselves. From the same point of view, Daniel also announces, in chapters 2 and 7, that the kingdom of Christ will follow the four kingdoms of the world, and bring in the world-wide dominion of the people of God. Haggai, again, in chapter 2:1–9, points to the completion of the kingdom of God in Christ as a solace to the people, who have just been awakened to a consciousness of the glaring contrast between the idea and the reality, by the comparative insignificance of the new temple. When Amos has foretold (in chs. 9, 11, and 12) the passing away of every kind of glory from Israel and Judah, he passes at once to an announcement of the restoration of the tabernacle of David and the extension of the kingdom of God far beyond the limits of the heathen. The hope that the time would arrive when the actual condition of the nation of God would be brought into harmony with its primary idea, could never have taken root, unless in the reference to the person of a mediator, at once human and divine, there had been given a pledge of the reality of such a hope, which could not have been realized in any other way—unless, in fact, this exalted person had been placed before the eyes of the people in as distinct a form as possible, and the *Logos* had, as it were, become a partaker of flesh and blood in this prophetic announcement, even before the period of his incarnation.

At the same time, there was no less ground for anxiety on account of the contrast between the true idea of the nation of God and its visible realization in a *moral* point of view. Under the Old Testament, the nation of God was still, to a great extent, destitute of the gifts which are its essential characteristics, and by which it is distinguished from the world. The righteous and the wicked were also mixed up together, and in most ages the latter had the upper hand. But if this contrast were regarded as permanent, as surely as the commandment, "Be ye holy, for I am holy," involved a promise, so surely would the contrast give rise to errors respecting the kingdom of God. In allusion to this, Joel announces that in the times of the Messiah the Lord will pour out his Spirit upon all flesh; Jeremiah speaks of the new covenant, which will be attended by more abundant provisions of transforming grace; and Ezekiel declares that in future the Lord will take away the heart of stone, and give in its place a heart of flesh. But these hopes would never have acquired their proper consistency if there had not been set before the mind, in the personal appearance of the Redeemer, a new and hitherto unheard of union between heaven and earth, and between God and man. In this alone could a reasonable basis for such hopes be found. But along with the inwardly-transforming power, an outwardly-sifting and judicial process must take place, even to remove the existing contrast so far as morality was concerned. It is from this point of view that we are to understand such announcements as that of the Messianic judgment in Zechariah 5 and 11, and that of the destruction of the city and temple in Daniel 9: "Thy people all righteous"; this is a necessary postulate of the kingdom of God, which is sure to be realized in due time, though possibly not till the development is complete. The wheat must eventually be separated from the chaff, and the latter burned up with unquenchable fire.

4. The announcement of a Messiah contained within itself the strongest motives of an ethical description. As the Messianic era was represented as the consummation alike of

blessing and of punishment, the contemplation would inevitably act in the case of the righteous as a powerful impulse to steadfastness, and in that of the wicked as an impulse to conversion. We may learn from Micah 2:12–13; 4:1–8; Isaiah 40:3–5; and Malachi 4:1–6 (3:19–24 MT), in what manner the prophets availed themselves of this announcement as a motive to repentance.

5. Even under the Old Testament, the gospel, which proclaims the forgiveness of sins through the mercy of God, existed side by side with the law. How greatly then must it have facilitated the acceptance of mercy in the case of those in whom the object of the law had been secured, to have the condition of salvation, the coming of him who was to bear their sins as he has borne our own, placed before their minds in such prophecies as that contained in the 53rd chapter of Isaiah! That the prophecy did answer its end in this respect is evident, to take a single example, from John the Baptist, who bore witness, on the simple ground of Isaiah 53, to "the Lamb of God that taketh away the sin of the world." According to Luke 1:77, forgiveness of sins was the centre of all the hopes of salvation indulged by the more earnest minds.

6. But the principal design of the Messianic prophecies was to prepare in such a way for the coming of Christ, that, when he should come, he might at once be recognised from a comparison of prophecy with its fulfilment, And the very fact that, notwithstanding this preparation, the greater portion of the people failed to recognise him, is in itself a proof of its necessity. As it was, the only persons who did not receive him were such as had lost their capacity for an impartial examination of prophecy and history through their ungodliness of mind. But if there had been no signs at all, the recognition would have been rendered infinitely difficult even to the *upright in heart*. The importance of the Messianic prophecies from this point of view is attested by New Testament authorities. When John the Baptist says, in John 1:20, "I am not the Christ," he points to Jesus as the Christ. As Bengel says, "By thus limiting his speech . . . (I) . . . he gives a handle to the thought which suggests itself, that the Christ is not far off."[1] He speaks of Him with evident allusion to the prophecies of the Old Testament, as "he, who, coming after him, was before him" (vv. 27, 30), and with a reference to Isaiah 53 as "the Lamb of God." Andrew, his disciple, on the strength of what he has heard from him, says to his brother Simon in verse 41, "we have found the Messiah." It is true that Christ himself teaches that the first prerequisite to a recognition of himself is a certain state of mind, which creates a susceptibility for the outward proofs of his divine mission (John 7:17), and traces the unbelief of the Jews to the fact, that this is not their state of mind (John 5:39–47).[2] He represents himself as the promised Messiah, in John 4:25–26; Matthew 26:63–64; and 11:3–6. In Luke 24:25–26, he reproves the apostles as being "fools and slow of heart," because they do not discern the harmony between prophecy and its fulfilment, which is so conspicuous in his history. In Luke 24:45, he is said to "open their understanding" that they may understand "the prophecies relating to his person," and in this way to strengthen their faith. He sets forth these prophecies in various ways, describing their great importance as the force by which history is determined, in such words as these, "thus it is written," and "thus it *must* be"; Luke 24:26, 46, and Matthew 26:54. The importance which he attached to the agreement between prophecy and its fulfilment, as forming

---

1. See Bengel on John 1:20; John Albert Bengel, *New Testament Word Studies,* trans. Charlton T. Lewis and Marvin R. Vincent, vol. 1 (1864; repr., Grand Rapids: Kregel, 1971). Translated from *Gnomon Novi Testamenti* (1742).

2. See E. W. Hengstenberg, *Christology of the Old Testament* (Edinburgh: T. & T. Clark, 1878), 1:99.

part of his credentials, is apparent from the fact that, on the occasion of his last entry into Jerusalem, he arranged all the incidents in such a way as to ensure an exact correspondence to the statements of prophecy (Matt. 21:1 and John 12:12–16).[3] The first of the evangelists brings forward proofs at the very outset that Jesus is the Christ, the Messiah promised in the Old Testament. This was the problem that had first of all to be solved. That Jesus was the Christ, was one of the leading topics in the preaching of the apostles (Acts 3:18; 10:43; 1 Cor. 15:3–4; 2 Cor. 1:20). In Acts 26:22, Paul claims to obtain a hearing for his preaching of the gospel, on the ground that he says nothing but what Moses and the prophets have already foretold; and in verse 27 he expressly asserts that whoever believes the prophets must of necessity believe in Christ as well.

There can be no doubt, therefore, as to the great importance of the Messianic prophecies, so far as the people of the Old Testament were concerned. But the question still remains whether they are of the same importance to the Christian Church. To this question an affirmative reply has been constantly and decidedly given. A passage written by the excellent Pascal may serve to exhibit the attitude which the Church has assumed towards these prophecies. In his *Pensées* (Art. 10, "Preuves de Jésus-Christ par les Prophéties"), he says,

> La plus grande des preuves de Jésus-Christ ce sont les prophéties. C'est aussi à quoi Dieu a le plus pourvu; car l'événement qui les a remplies est un miracle subsistant depuis la naissance de l'Église jusqu'à la fin. Aussi Dieu a suscité des prophètes durant seize cents ans; et pendant quatre cents ans après, il a dispersé toutes ces prophéties avec tous les Juifs, qui les portaient, dans tous les lieux du monde. . . . Quand un seul homme aurait fait un livre des prédictions de Jésus-Christ, pour le temps et pour la manière, et que Jésus-Christ serait venu conformément à ces prophéties, ce serait une force infinie. Mais il y a bien plus ici. C'est une suite d'hommes . . . qui, constamment et sans variation, viennent l'un ensuite de l'autre, prédire ce même avènement. C'est un peuple entier, qui l'annonce.[4]

But, following the example of the rationalists, Schleiermacher in particular has broken away from this common conviction of the whole Christian Church.[5]

---

3. According to Franz Delitzsch (*Die biblisch-prophetische Theologie* [Leipzig: Gebauer, 1845], 170), the connection between the two is the opposite of this. He appropriates the words of Augustine, "Christ did not act thus because the prophet had foretold it; but the prophet made the announcement because this was the way in which Christ would act." That this statement of Augustine's, however, is not applicable to the form, but only to the *essence*, that is, to the fundamental idea contained in the prophecy and expressed in the word עֲנִי, is evident from this, that there were circumstances connected with the affair which were unimportant in themselves, and derived their importance solely from their connection with the prophecy, such, for example, as the fact of the she-ass being taken as well as the foal. If the attention to individual traits, such, for example, as the riding upon an ass, is to be rejected without hesitation as a reprehensible attempt to "idealize," what are we to do with such passages as Isaiah 50:6, "and my cheeks to them that plucked off the hair," of which no historical fulfilment can be pointed out?

4. "The most weighty proofs of Jesus are the prophecies. It is for them that God made most provision, for the event which fulfilled them is a miracle, continuing from the birth of the Church to the end. Thus God raised up prophets for 1,600 years and for 400 years afterwards dispersed all the prophecies with all the Jews, who carried them into every corner of the world."

"If a single man had written a book foretelling the time and manner of Jesus's coming and Jesus had come in conformity with these prophecies, this would carry infinite weight.

But there is much more here. There is a succession of men . . . coming consistently and invariably one after the other, to foretell the same coming; there is an entire people proclaiming it." Blaise Pascal, *Pensées*, trans. A. J. Krailsheimer (New York: Penguin Books, 1966), 130, 129.

5. *Glaubenslehre [Der christliche Glaube]* (Berlin: G. Reimer, 1821), 1:116 (§ 14); "Zweites Sendschreiben an Lücke," *Theologische Studien und Kritiken* 2, 3 (1829): 497.

The question of primary importance here is whether there are really any Messianic prophecies in the Old Testament. Schleiermacher answers this in the negative. He found nothing but indefinite presentiments, utterances of a subjective consciousness of the need of redemption, "a yearning of human nature for Christianity," such as may be proved to have existed in heathenism as well. In making such an assertion, he placed himself in decided antagonism to the authority of Christ and his apostles. For it is evident, not only from the passages just quoted, but from many others which have been referred to in the course of this work, that they did acknowledge the existence of actual prophecies in the Scriptures. And the fallacy of the assertion is quite as apparent, if we examine the prophecies themselves. We have brought forward proofs that the Scriptures contain a long series of genuine prophecies. Compare, for example, what has already been observed in Hengstenberg, *Christology of the OT*, 3:267 with reference to Zechariah's description of the future. Compare also Daniel 9, where the anointing of Christ with the Holy Ghost, his death, the forgiveness of sins to be secured by him, and the judgment to be executed on Jerusalem by a foreign prince, are announced. The nation from which the Redeemer is to arise is foretold in the Old Testament, and even the tribe (Gen. 49 and other passages), the family (first of all in 2 Sam. 7), the place (Mic. 5), and the *time of his birth*, viz. during the period of the political existence of Judah (see Hengstenberg, *Christology of the OT*, 1:62), previous to the destruction of the second temple (Haggai), in the time of the fourth monarchy (Dan. 2:7), and in the seventieth week (Dan. 9). The prophets point out clearly and distinctly the *condition* of both the family and nation at the time of the coming of Christ, and fully agree in predicting that before that event all the glory of Israel will pass away (Hengstenberg, *Christology of the OT*, 1:516), the tabernacle of David fall into ruins (Amos 9:11), and the line of David sink into the obscurity of private life (Hengstenberg, *Christology of the OT*, 2:110). The prophets foretell that with Christ's coming a new spiritual and vital principle will begin to work in the human race (Joel 3; Jer. 31:31–40; Ezek. 11:19), and history has confirmed the announcement. "All nations," says Pascal, "were sunk in infidelity and concupiscence; but the whole earth now burned with charity, princes forsook their glory, and girls endured martyrdom. Whence came this power? The Messiah had arrived." The prophets also place in connection with the coming of Christ a severe judgment upon Judah, and its expulsion from the Lord's own land (e.g., Zech. 5 and 11; Mal. 3). The fulfilment is before our eyes, as well as that of the prophecies which announce the spread of the kingdom of God among the heathen in the days of the Messiah, such, for example, as Ezekiel 17:22–24, and Malachi 1:11, "from the rising of the sun unto the going down of the same, my name shall be great among the Gentiles."

Again, the assertion that an agreement between the prophecies and the actual result in matters of detail is of no importance whatever, is no more reconcilable with the authority of Christ and the apostles than the denial of the existence of genuine prophecies. For if this be the case, why is the harmony between prophecy and fulfilment expressly pointed out in connection with the most remarkable circumstances of the life of Christ? Why did Christ explain to his apostles, after his resurrection, the passages in all the Scriptures relating to his sufferings and glory? Why did he add, after saying to his disciples "all ye shall be offended because of me this night"; "for it is written, I will smite the shepherd, and the sheep of the flock shall be scattered abroad?" (Matt. 26:31.) Why did he say to the disciples (v. 54), "how then shall the Scriptures be fulfilled?" and to the crowd (v. 56) "all this was done that the Scriptures of the prophets might be fulfilled?" He that is of the truth will listen in this matter to the voice of him who has said, "I am the truth." If Schleiermacher's views were correct, how could it be recorded of the people at Berea as a thing deserving praise, that they carefully compared the gospel statements with the Scriptures of the Old Testament, "searching the Scriptures daily, whether those things were so." Philip would rather be deserving of blame for founding his address to the treasurer of Queen Candace upon Isaiah 53. If it was a matter of importance to that age that the perfect agreement between prophecy and fulfilment should be clearly demonstrated, it is of no less importance now. This is obvious from the fact that the apostles themselves do not attach importance to it solely when they have to do with Jews, but also when writing and preaching to the Gentiles. In the present day, not merely the great mass of the Jews, but also a great portion of those who are living in outward fellowship with the Christian Church, are in just the same condition as the Jews of the time of Christ. They have no true knowledge of Christ, but have yet to learn to know him. It is true that this knowledge can no more be obtained by them from the Messianic prophecies *alone* than by the Jews of that day. On the contrary, external evidence of the truth of Christianity, whatever its objective validity may be, can never accomplish anything without the existence of the only state of mind that can create a susceptibility for the impression, which evidence of this description is fitted to produce. But where this state of mind does exist, a perception of the harmony between prophecy and fulfilment may produce the most beneficial results. There is the less room to deny this on account of the clear testimony of history itself. Conscientious converts from Judaism are hardly ever to be met with, whose convictions are not to a great extent attributable to this.[6] And even in the case of many who had fallen victims to rationalistic unbelief, such prophecies as Isaiah 53 have frequently afforded important aid in leading them back to the way of salvation. But the importance of the Messianic prophecies is not restricted to the first stages of Christian experience; it continues even in the case of such as are further advanced. For, on the one hand, there are none whose faith is so strong that they can afford to despise one of the means of fortifying it, which have been provided by God himself; and the more firmly a Christian holds by the *historical* Christ, and breaks away from the nebulous image of an ideal Saviour, who, if he want no credentials, can afford neither strength nor consolation, the greater is the improbability of his ever doing this. On the other hand, advanced Christians feel more and more the need of comprehending the divine institutions of salvation as a connected whole, and tracing the whole plan devised by the wisdom of God. This is a delightful study, full of incitement to seek the knowledge and love of God. In this nothing can be regarded as trivial, since even the smallest line acquires importance from its connection with the whole. There is nothing isolated; action and reaction are visible everywhere, and whilst light is thrown by the fulfilment upon the preparatory stages, the latter throw light upon the fulfilment in return.[7]

Another objection adduced by Schleiermacher against the Messianic prophecies is this, that we cannot desire to base our firm faith in Christianity upon our much weaker faith in

---

6. Thus, for example, the unbelief of Augusti gave way when he was engaged in writing a work upon Isaiah, and came to the 53rd chapter. See the account of the life and conversion of F. A. Augusti, formerly a Jewish Rabbi, but afterwards for fifty-three years a teacher of Christianity; E. F. A. Augusti, *Nachricht vom Leben, Schicksal und Bekehrung F. A. Augusti* (Gotha: Reyher, 1783). Other examples are to be met with in Hausmeister's *Lebens und Bekehrungsgeschichten Jüdischer Proselyten* (Basel, 1835).

7. "Est etiam pars verbi divini prophetica suavissimum studii perpetui exercitium, ubi incrementum successive capimus, quod fastidium detergit, sed finem nunquam reperimus, gaudemus tamen alimento spirituali, fidem, spem et caritatem roborante et excitante."

Judaism. But Steudel has justly replied to this, that we do not attribute the force of proof to the prophecies themselves, but to the harmony between the prophecies and their fulfilment. And Karl Heinrich Sack has pointed out the unscriptural character of the contrast which is thus drawn between Judaism and Christianity, by showing that prophecy forms no part of Judaism as dissociated with Christianity, but according to the New Testament view, the prophets are organs of the Holy Ghost, of the Spirit of Christ, who thus manifested himself to the Church of God through their instrumentality before his actual appearance in the flesh (1 Peter 1:11).[8]

The really classical passage of the New Testament by which this thoroughly abnormal and unchristian theory of Schleiermacher is completely refuted, is contained in 2 Peter 1:19–21, a passage the depth of which is a sufficient proof of its apostolical origin. "We have," says the apostle, "a more sure word of prophecy, whereunto ye do well that ye take heed, as unto a light that shineth in a dark place, until the day dawn and the day-star arise in your hearts; knowing this first, that no prophecy of the Scripture is of any private interpretation, for the prophecy came not in old time by the will of man, but holy men of God spoke as they were moved by the Holy Ghost." The Messianic prophecies (that the "word of prophecy" relates especially to these, is evident from the connection with what precedes) are of *even greater importance* to Christians than to Jews. The word of prophecy is to them a *surer* word, since they can compare the predictions with the fulfilment. The apostle's preaching of Christ did not rest upon arbitrary speculations, but according to verse 16, upon the fact that the apostles were "eye-witnesses of his majesty." From these historical facts the word of prophecy acquired still greater firmness and importance. For this reason it is doubly advantageous to Christians to pay attention to those things from which Schleiermacher attempted with all his might to draw away the Church of Christ. The apostle does not say "ye did well," but "ye do well." It is not Jews but Christians whom he praises for giving heed to the word of prophecy, and that not merely as the foundation of faith, but also as the means of strengthening their belief. It could only lead to confusion[9] to connect ἕως οὗ, etc., with προσέχοντες, instead of φαίνοντι (compare Matt. 11:13). In this case the present would be unsuitable. The apostle is writing to those who already are, not to those who are to become, Christians, "to them that have obtained like precious faith with us" (v. 1). Hence he does not say how long they are to be attentive, but how long the light has shined. The period when the light first shone in the dark place (a light which could only be kindled by the inspiration of God) was the coming of Christ in the flesh, when the day-star immediately rose in the *hearts*. It is to those on whom the day has dawned that the light shining in a dark place first gives a really brilliant light. (Bengel: "By the greater light the lesser is both acknowledged to be less, and is strengthened."[10]) The importance of Messianic prophecy depends upon the relation between the preparatory or preliminary stages and the thing itself, and this relation cannot be properly discerned till the fulfilment has taken place.— "Knowing this first" (= "First of all" [1 Tim. 2:1]), he who is ignorant of this is blind as to the whole affair, a blindness which is far more culpable since the day has dawned. What the apostle here represents as the *first* step, namely, the inspiration of God, without which it would be impossible to speak of a light shining in a dark place, is the very thing which Schleiermacher denies. For prophecy

---

8. Karl Heinrich Sack, *Christliche Apologetik* (Hamburg: Friedrich Perthes, 1841), 258.

9. See, on the other hand, Knapp, *Opusc.,* 16.

10. See Bengel on 2 Peter 1:19; Bengel, *New Word Studies,* 2:767.

he substitutes a merely subjective presentiment; and in his estimation the "prophecy of the Scripture" is throughout ἰδίας ἐπιλύσεως. It is evident from the passages in Philo, which may be found quoted in Wetstein and Knapp (e.g., προφήτης ἴδιον οὐδὲν αποφθέγγεται, ἀλλότρια δέ πάντα ὑπηχοῦντος ἑτέρου ["a prophet utters nothing of his own, but everything foreign is spoken by another"]),[11] and also from the entire context, that it is not to the interpretation of the prophets by others that the apostle here refers. The explanation is given afterwards: in prophecy throughout we have not a mere production of "Judaism," or certain disclosures made by the prophets on their own authority. The prophecies of the Bible do not belong to the sphere of personal conjecture, like those of heathenism; and the prophets of the Scriptures are not, like the false prophets referred to in Jeremiah, to whom Schleiermacher's theology would compare them, "prophets of their own heart."

11. Philo, *Who Is the Heir?* 259 (Loeb 4:416–17); cf. also, Philo, *On the Life of Moses* 1:281, 286 (Loeb 6:420–25); cf. Jacobus Wettstein, *Novum Testamentum Graecum* (repr., Graz: Akademischen Druck- und Verlagsanstalt, 1962), 2:703.

How to Read the Bible

C H A R L E S   H .   S P U R G E O N

Charles H. Spurgeon, "How to Read the Bible (Matthew xii. 3–7)," in *The Metropolitan Tabernacle Pulpit: Sermons Preached and Revised by C. H. Spurgeon during the Year 1879*, vol. 25, no. 1503 (1879; repr., Pasadena, TX: Pilgrim, 1972), 625–36. Online: http://www.bible-researcher.com/spurgeon2.html, last accessed May 27, 2008 (11 pp.).

Charles Haddon Spurgeon (1834–92) was a very influential Baptist preacher. Not only was he a successful pastor, most famously preaching in the Metropolitan Tabernacle from 1861 on, but he was also involved in charitable works. He founded a college for pastors, and was a prolific writer. He engaged in various polemics, from debates with Anglicans over baptism to a defense of orthodoxy within his own Baptist denomination. He was greatly impacted by the theology of the Puritans and appreciated the theological emphasis of Princeton Seminary. A contemporary of Archibald Alexander Hodge (1823–86) and Benjamin Breckinridge Warfield (1851–1921), he corresponded with them. Spurgeon's forte was as a preacher; his gifts as a communicator were appreciated within the Westminster community in a study by Jay Adams.

In this anthology we reproduce one of his sermons: "How to Read the Bible" (1879). This sermon on the interpretation of Scripture shows, like the work by Monod, a practical and pastoral concern. His exegetical approach is centered on the gospel and Christ. He illustrates this by saying that as from any village in England there is a way to London, so from anyplace in Scripture there is a way to Christ. This Christocentric reading will be found again in the biblical theology at Westminster, in particular in the work of Edmund Clowney (cf. chap. 48).

Bibliography: Jay E. Adams. *Sense Appeal in the Sermons of Charles Haddon Spurgeon*. Nutley, NJ: Presbyterian and Reformed, 1976. J. Armstrong. "Spurgeon, Charles Haddon (1834–1892)." Pp. 624–27 in *BDE*. R. Brown. "Spurgeon, Charles Haddon (1834–1892)." P. 658 in *NDT*. Arnold Dallimore. *Spurgeon: A New*

Biography. Carlisle, PA: Banner of Truth, 1985. J. E. Johnson. "Spurgeon, Charles Haddon (1834–1892)." P. 1051 in *EDT*. Iain H. Murray. *The Forgotten Spurgeon*. 2nd ed. Carlisle, PA: Banner of Truth, 1966, 1973. J. G. G. Norman. "Spurgeon, Charles Haddon (1834–1892)." P. 928 in *NIDCC*. Hughes Oliphant Old. *The Reading and Preaching of the Scriptures in the Worship of the Christian Church*. Vol. 6, *The Modern Age*. Grand Rapids: Eerdmans, 2007. Pp. 422–43. Charles H. Spurgeon. "How to Read the Bible (I Timothy iv. 13)." Pp. 421–33 in *The Metropolitan Tabernacle Pulpit: Sermons Preached and Revised by C. H. Spurgeon during the Year 1866*. Vol. 58, no. 1503. 1912. Repr., Pasadena, TX: Pilgrim, 1979. "Spurgeon, Charles Haddon." *NSHERK* 11:57–58.

"Have ye not read? . . . . . Have ye not read? . . . . . If ye had known what this meaneth?" (Matt. 12:3–7)

The scribes and Pharisees were great readers of the law. They studied the sacred books continually, poring over each word and letter. They made notes of very little importance, but still very curious notes—as to which was the middle verse of the entire Old Testament, which verse was halfway to the middle, and how many times such a word occurred, and even how many times a letter occurred, and the size of the letter, and its peculiar position. They have left us a mass of wonderful notes upon the mere words of Holy Scripture. They might have done the same thing upon another book for that matter, and the information would have been about as important as the facts which they have so industriously collected concerning the letter of the Old Testament. They were, however, intense readers of the law. They picked a quarrel with the Saviour upon a matter touching this law, for they carried it at their fingers' ends, and were ready to use it as a bird of prey does its talons to tear and rend. Our Lord's disciples had plucked some ears of corn, and rubbed them between their hands. According to Pharisaic interpretation, to rub an ear of corn is a kind of threshing, and, as it is very wrong to thresh on the Sabbath day, therefore it must be very wrong to rub out an ear or two of wheat when you are hungry on the Sabbath morning. That was their argument, and they came to the Saviour with it, and with their version of the Sabbath law. The Saviour generally carried the war into the enemy's camp, and he did so on this occasion. He met them on their own ground, and he said to them, "Have ye not read?"—a cutting question to the scribes and Pharisees, though there is nothing apparently sharp about it. It was a very fair and proper question to put to them; but only think of putting it *to them*. "Have ye not read?" "Read!" they could have said, "Why, we have read the book through very many times. We are always reading it. No passage escapes our critical eyes." Yet our Lord proceeds to put the question a second time—"Have ye not read?" as if they had not read after all, though they were the greatest readers of the law then living. He insinuates that they have not read at all; and then he gives them, incidentally, the reason why he had asked them whether they had read. He says, "If ye had known what this meaneth," as much as to say, "Ye have not read, because ye have not understood." Your eyes have gone over the words, and you have counted the letters, and you have marked the position of each verse and word, and you have said learned things about all the books, and yet you are not even readers of the sacred volume, for you have not acquired the true art of reading; you do not understand, and therefore you do not truly read it. You are mere skimmers and glancers at the Word: you have not read it, for you do not understand it.

I. That is the subject of our present discourse, or, at least, the first point of it, that IN ORDER TO THE TRUE READING OF THE SCRIPTURES, THERE MUST BE AN UNDERSTANDING OF THEM.

I scarcely need to preface these remarks by saying that we must read the Scriptures. You know how necessary it is that we should be fed upon the truth of Holy Scripture. Need I suggest the question as to whether you do read your Bibles or not? I am afraid that this is a magazine-reading age—a newspaper-reading age—a periodical-reading age, but not so much a Bible-reading age as it ought to be. In the old Puritan times men used to have a scant supply of other literature, but they found a library enough in the one Book, the Bible. And how they did read the Bible! How little of Scripture there is in modern sermons compared with the sermons of those masters of theology, the Puritan divines! Almost every sentence of theirs seems to cast side lights upon a text of Scripture; not only the one they are preaching about, but many others as well are set in a new light as the discourse proceeds. They introduce blended lights from other passages which are parallel or semi-parallel thereunto, and thus they educate their readers to compare spiritual things with spiritual. I would to God that we ministers kept more closely to the grand old book. We should be instructive preachers if we did so, even if we were ignorant of "modern thought," and were not "abreast of the times." I warrant you we should be leagues ahead of our times if we kept closely to the word of God. As for you, my brothers and sisters, who have not to preach, the best food for you is the word of God itself. Sermons and books are well enough, but streams that run for a long distance above ground gradually gather for themselves somewhat of the soil through which they flow, and they lose the cool freshness with which they started from the spring head. Truth is sweetest where it breaks from the smitten Rock, for at its first gush it has lost none of its heavenliness and vitality. It is always best to drink at the well and not from the tank. You shall find that reading the word of God for yourselves, reading *it* rather than notes upon it, is the surest way of growing in grace. Drink of the unadulterated milk of the word of God, and not of the skim milk, or the milk and water of man's word.

But, now, beloved, our point is that much apparent Bible reading is not Bible reading at all. The verses pass under the eye, and the sentences glide over the mind, but there is no true reading. An old preacher used to say, the Word has mighty free course among many nowadays, for it goes in at one of their ears and out at the other; so it seems to be with some readers—they can read a very great deal, because they do not read anything. The eye glances but the mind never rests. The soul does not light upon the truth and stay there. It flits over the landscape as a bird might do, but it builds no nest therein, and finds no rest for the sole of its foot. Such reading is not reading. Understanding the meaning is the essence of true reading. Reading has a kernel to it, and the mere shell is little worth. In prayer there is such a thing as praying in prayer—a praying that is in the bowels of the prayer. So in praise there is a praising in song, an inward fire of intense devotion which is the life of the hallelujah. It is so in fasting: there is a fasting which is not fasting, and there is an inward fasting, a fasting of the soul, which is the soul of fasting. It is even so with the reading of the Scriptures. There is an interior reading, a kernel reading—a true and living reading of the Word. This is the soul of reading; and, if it be not there, the reading is a mechanical exercise, and profits nothing. Now, beloved, unless we understand what we read we have not read it; the heart of the reading is absent. We commonly condemn the Romanists for keeping the daily service in the Latin tongue; yet it might as well be in the Latin language as in any other tongue if it be not understood by the people. Some comfort themselves with the idea that they have done a good action when they have read a chapter, into the meaning of which they have not entered at all; but does not nature herself reject this as a mere superstition? If you had turned the book upside down, and spent the same times in looking at the characters in that direction, you would have gained as much good from it as you will in reading it in the regular way without understanding it. If you had a New Testament in Greek it would be very Greek to some of you, but it would do you as much good to look at *that* as it does to look at the English New Testament unless you read with understanding heart. It is not the letter which saves the soul; the letter killeth in many senses, and never can it give life. If you harp on the letter alone you may be tempted to use it as a weapon against the truth, as the Pharisees did of old, and your knowledge of the letter may breed pride in you to your destruction. It is the spirit, the real inner meaning, that is sucked into the soul, by which we are blessed and sanctified. We become saturated with the word of God, like Gideon's fleece, which was wet with the dew of heaven; and this can only come to pass by our receiving it into our minds and hearts, accepting it as God's truth, and so far understanding it as to delight in it. We must understand it, then, or else we have not read it aright.

Certainly, the benefit of reading must come to the soul by the way of the understanding. When the high priest went into the holy place he always lit the golden candlestick before he kindled the incense upon the brazen altar, as if to show that the mind must have illumination before the affections can properly rise towards their divine object. There must be knowledge of God before there can be love to God: there must be a knowledge of divine things, as they are revealed, before there can be an enjoyment of them. We must try to make out, as far as our finite mind can grasp it, what God means by this and what he means by that; otherwise we may kiss the book and have no love to its contents, we may reverence the letter and yet really have no devotion towards the Lord who speaks to us in these words. Beloved, you will never get comfort to your soul out of what you do not understand, nor find guidance for your life out of what you do not comprehend; nor can any practical bearing upon your character come out of that which is not understood by you.

Now, if we are thus to understand what we read or otherwise we read in vain, this shows us that when we come to the study of Holy Scripture *we should try to have our mind well awake to it*. We are not always fit, it seems to me, to read the Bible. At times it were well for us to stop before we open the volume. "Put off thy shoe from thy foot, for the place whereon thou standest is holy ground." You have just come in from careful thought and anxiety about your worldly business, and you cannot immediately take that book and enter into its heavenly mysteries. As you ask a blessing over your meat [food] before you fall to, so it would be a good rule for you to ask a blessing on the word before you partake of its heavenly food. Pray the Lord to strengthen your eyes before you dare to look into the eternal light of Scripture. As the priests washed their feet at the laver before they went to their holy work, so it were well to wash the soul's eyes with which you look upon God's word, to wash even the fingers, if I may so speak—the mental fingers with which you will turn from page to page—that with a holy book you may deal after a holy fashion. Say to your soul—"Come, soul, wake up: thou art not now about to read the newspaper; thou art not now perusing the pages of a human poet to be dazzled by his flashing poetry; thou art coming very near to God, who sits in the Word like a crowned monarch in his halls. Wake up, my glory; wake up, all that is within me. Though just now I may not be praising and glorifying God, I am about to consider that which should lead me so to do, and therefore it is an act of devotion. So be on the stir, my soul: be on the stir, and bow not sleepily before the awful throne of the Eternal." Scripture reading is our spiritual meal time. Sound the gong and call in every faculty to the Lord's own table to feast upon the precious meat which is now to be partaken of; or, rather, ring the church-bell as for worship, for the studying of the Holy Scripture ought to be as solemn a deed as when we lift the psalm upon the Sabbath day in the courts of the Lord's house.

If these things be so, you will see at once, dear friends, that, if you are to understand what you read, *you will need to meditate upon it*. Some passages of Scripture lie clear before us—blessed shallows in which the lambs may wade; but there are deeps in which our mind might rather drown herself than swim with pleasure, if she came there without caution. There are texts of Scripture which are made and constructed on purpose to make us think. By this means, among others, our heavenly Father would educate us for heaven—by making us think our way into divine mysteries. Hence he puts the word in a somewhat involved form to compel us to meditate upon it before we reach the sweetness of it. He might, you know, have explained it to us so that we might catch the thought in a minute, but he does not please to do so in every case. Many of the veils which are cast over Scripture are not meant to hide the meaning from the diligent but to compel the mind to be active, for oftentimes the diligence of the heart in seeking to know the divine mind does the heart more good than the knowledge itself. Meditation and careful thought exercise us and strengthen the soul for the reception of the yet more lofty truths. I have heard that the mothers in the Balearic Isles, in the old times, who wanted to bring their boys up to be good slingers, would put their dinners up above them where they could not get at them until they threw a stone and fetched them down: our Lord wishes us to be good slingers, and he puts up some precious truth in a lofty place where we cannot get it down except by slinging at it; and, at last, we hit the mark and find food for our souls. Then have we the double benefit of learning the art of meditation and partaking of the sweet truth which it has brought within our reach. We must meditate, brothers. These grapes will yield no wine till we tread upon them. These olives must be put under the wheel, and pressed again and again, that the oil may flow therefrom. In a dish of nuts, you may know which nut has been eaten, because there is a little hole which the insect has punctured through the shell—just a little hole, and then inside there is the living thing eating up the kernel. Well, it is a grand thing to bore through the shell of the letter, and then to live inside feeding upon the kernel. I would wish to be such a little worm as that, living within and upon the word of God, having bored my way through the shell, and having reached the innermost mystery of the blessed gospel. The word of God is always most precious to the man who most lives upon it. As I sat last year under a wide-spreading beech, I was pleased to mark with prying curiosity the singular habits of that most wonderful of trees, which seems to have an intelligence about it which other trees have not. I wondered and admired the beech, but I thought to myself, I do not think half as much of this beech tree as yonder squirrel does. I see him leap from bough to bough, and I feel sure that he dearly values the old beech tree, because he has his home somewhere inside it in a hollow place, these branches are his shelter, and those beech-nuts are his food. He lives upon the tree. It is his world, his playground, his granary, his home; indeed, it is everything to him, and it is not so to me, for I find my rest and food elsewhere. With God's word it is well for us to be like squirrels, living in it and living on it. Let us exercise our minds by leaping from bough to bough of it, find our rest and food in it, and make it our all in all. We shall be the people that get the profit out of it if we make it to be our food, our medicine, our treasury, our armoury, our rest, our delight. May the Holy Ghost lead us to do this and make the Word thus precious to our souls.

Beloved, I would next remind you that for this end *we shall be compelled to pray.* It is a grand thing to be driven to think, it is a grander thing to be driven to pray through having been made to think. Am I not addressing some of you who do not read the word of God, and am I not speaking to many more who do read it, but do not read it with the strong resolve that they will understand it? I know it must be so. Do you wish to begin to be true readers? Will you henceforth labour to understand? Then you must get to your knees. You must cry to God for direction. Who understands a book best? The author of it. If I want to ascertain the real meaning of a rather twisted sentence, and the author lives near me, and I can call upon him, I shall ring at his door and say, "Would you kindly tell me what you mean by that sentence? I have no doubt whatever that it is very dear, but I am such a simpleton, that I cannot make it out. I have not the knowledge and grasp of the subject which you possess, and therefore your allusions and descriptions are beyond my range of knowledge. It is quite within your range, and commonplace to you, but it is very difficult to me. Would you kindly explain your meaning to me?" A good man would be glad to be thus treated, and would think it no trouble to unravel his meaning to a candid enquirer. Thus I should be sure to get the correct meaning, for I should be going to the fountain head when I consulted the author himself. So, beloved, the Holy Spirit is with us, and when we take his book and begin to read, and want to know what it means, we must ask the Holy Spirit to reveal the meaning. He will not work a miracle, but he will elevate our minds, and he will suggest to us thoughts which will lead us on by their natural relation, the one to the other, till at last we come to the pith and marrow of his divine instruction. Seek then very earnestly the guidance of the Holy Spirit, for if the very soul of reading be the understanding of what we read, then we must in prayer call upon the Holy Ghost to unlock the secret mysteries of the inspired word.

If we thus ask the guidance and teaching of the Holy Spirit, it will follow, dear friends, that *we shall be ready to use all means and helps towards the understanding of the Scriptures.* When Philip asked the Ethiopian eunuch whether he understood the prophecy of Isaiah he replied, "How can I, unless some man should guide me?" Then Philip went up and opened to him the word of the Lord. Some, under the pretense of being taught of the Spirit of God refuse to be instructed by books or by living men. This is no honouring of the Spirit of God; it is a disrespect to him, for if he gives to some of his servants more light than to others— and it is clear he does—then they are bound to give that light to others, and to use it for the good of the church. But if the other part of the church refuse to receive that light, to what end did the Spirit of God give it? This would imply that there is a mistake somewhere in the economy of gifts and graces, which is managed by the Holy Spirit. It cannot be so. The Lord Jesus Christ pleases to give more knowledge of his word and more insight into it to some of his servants than to others, and it is ours joyfully to accept the knowledge which he gives in such ways as he chooses to give it. It would be most wicked of us to say, "We will not have the heavenly treasure which exists in earthen vessels. If God will give us the heavenly treasure out of his own hand, but not through the earthen vessel, we will have it; but we think we are too wise, too heavenly minded, too spiritual altogether to care for jewels when they are placed in earthen pots. We will not hear anybody, and we will not read anything except *the book* itself, neither will we accept any light, except that which comes in through a crack in our own roof. We will not see by another man's candle, we would sooner remain in the dark." Brethren, do not let us fall into such folly. Let the light come from God, and though a child shall bring it, we will joyfully accept it. If any one of his servants, whether Paul or Apollos or Cephas, shall have received light from him, behold, "all are yours, and ye are Christ's, and Christ is God's," and therefore accept of the light which God has kindled, and ask for grace that you may turn that light upon the word so that when you read it you may understand it.

I do not wish to say much more about this, but I should like to push it home upon some of you. You have Bibles at home, I know; you would not like to be without Bibles, you would think you were heathens if you had no Bibles. You have them very neatly bound, and they are very fine looking volumes: not much thumbed, not much worn, and not likely to be so, for they only come out on Sundays for an airing, and they lie in lavender with the clean pocket-handkerchiefs all the rest of the week. You do not read the word, you do not search it, and how can you expect to get the divine blessing? If the heavenly gold is not worth digging for you are not likely to discover it. Often and often have I told you that the searching of the Scriptures is not the way of salvation. The Lord hath said, "Believe in the Lord Jesus Christ, and thou shalt be saved." But, still, the reading of the word often leads, like the hearing of it, to faith, and faith bringeth salvation; for faith cometh by hearing, and reading is a sort of hearing. While you are seeking to know what the gospel is, it may please God to bless your souls. But what poor reading some of you give to your Bibles. I do not want to say anything which is too severe because it is not strictly true—let your own consciences speak, but still, I make bold to enquire, Do not many of you read the Bible in a very hurried way—just a little bit, and off you go? Do you not soon forget what you have read, and lose what little effect it seemed to have? How few of you are resolved to get at its soul, its juice, its life, its essence, and to drink in its meaning. Well, if you do not do that, I tell you again your reading is miserable reading, dead reading, unprofitable reading; it is not reading at all, the name would be misapplied. May the blessed Spirit give you repentance touching this thing.

II. But now, secondly, and very briefly, let us notice that IN READING WE OUGHT TO SEEK OUT THE SPIRITUAL TEACHING OF THE WORD. I think that is in my text, because our Lord says, "Have ye not read?" Then, again, "Have ye not read?" and then he says, "If ye had known what this meaneth"—and the meaning is something very spiritual. The text he quoted was, "I will have mercy, and not sacrifice"—a text out of the prophet Hosea. Now, the scribes and Pharisees were all for the letter—the sacrifice, the killing of the bullock, and so on. They overlooked the spiritual meaning of the passage, "I will have mercy, and not sacrifice"—namely, that God prefers that we should care for our fellow-creatures rather than that we should observe any ceremonial of his law, so as to cause hunger or thirst and thereby death, to any of the creatures that his hands have made. They ought to have passed beyond the outward into the spiritual, and all our readings ought to do the same.

Notice, that this should be the case when we read *the historical passages*. "Have ye not read what David did, when he was an hungered, and they that were with him; how he entered into the house of God, and did eat the shew-bread, which was not lawful for him to eat, neither for them which were with him, but only for the priests?" This was a piece of history, and they ought so to have read it as to have found spiritual instruction in it. I have heard very stupid people say, "Well, I do not care to read the historical parts of Scripture."

Beloved friends, you do not know what you are talking about when you say so. I say to you now by experience that I have sometimes found even a greater depth of spirituality in the histories than I have in the Psalms. You will say, "How is that?" I assert that when you reach the inner and spiritual meaning of a history you are often surprised at the wondrous clearness—the realistic force—with which the teaching comes home to your soul. Some of the most marvelous mysteries of revelation are better understood by being set before our eyes in the histories than they are by the verbal declaration of them. When we have the statement to explain the illustration, the illustration expands and vivifies the statement. For instance, when our Lord himself would explain to us what faith was, he sent us to the history of the brazen serpent; and who that has ever read the story of the brazen serpent has not felt that he has had a better idea of faith through the picture of the dying snake-bitten persons looking to the serpent of brass and living, than from any description which even Paul has given us, wondrously as he defines and describes. Never, I pray you, depreciate the historical portions of God's word, but when you cannot get good out of them, say, "That is my foolish head and my slow heart. O Lord, be pleased to clear my brain and cleanse my soul." When he answers that prayer you will feel that every portion of God's word is given by inspiration, and is and must be profitable to you. Cry, "Open thou mine eyes, that I may behold wondrous things out of thy law."

Just the same thing is true with regard to all *the ceremonial precepts*, because the Saviour goes on to say, "Have ye not read in the law, how that on the Sabbath days the priests in the temple profane the Sabbath, and are blameless?" There is not a single precept in the old law but has an inner sense and meaning; therefore do not turn away from Leviticus, or say, "I cannot read these chapters in the books of Exodus and Numbers. They are all about the tribes and their standards, the stations in the wilderness and the halts of the march, the tabernacle and furniture, or about golden knops and bowls, and boards, and sockets, and precious stones, and blue and scarlet and fine linen." No, but look for the inner meaning. Make thorough search; for as in a king's treasure that which is the most closely locked up and the hardest to come at is the choicest jewel of the treasure, so is it with the Holy Scriptures. Did you ever go to the British Museum Library? There are many books of reference there which the reader is allowed to take down when he pleases. There are other books for which he must write a ticket, and he cannot get them without the ticket; but they have certain choice books which you will not see without a special order, and then there is an unlocking of doors, and an opening of cases, and there is a watcher with you while you make your inspection. You are scarcely allowed to put your eye on the manuscript, for fear you should blot a letter out by glancing at it; it is such a precious treasure; there is not another copy of it in all the world, and so you cannot get at it easily. Just so, there are choice and precious doctrines of God's word which are locked up in such cases as Leviticus or Solomon's Song, and you cannot get at them without a deal of unlocking of doors; and the Holy Spirit himself must be with you, or else you will never come at the priceless treasure. The higher truths are as choicely hidden away as the precious regalia of princes; therefore *search* as well as read. Do not be satisfied with a ceremonial precept till you reach its spiritual meaning, for that is true reading. You have not read till you understand the spirit of the matter.

It is just the same with *the doctrinal statements* of God's word. I have sorrowfully observed some persons who are very orthodox, and who can repeat their creed very glibly, and yet the principal use that they make of their orthodoxy is to sit and watch the preacher with the view of framing a charge against him. He has uttered a single sentence which is judged to be half a hair's breadth below the standard! "That man is not sound. He said some good things, but he is rotten at the core, I am certain. He used an expression which was not eighteen ounces to the pound." Sixteen ounces to the pound are not enough for these dear brethren of whom I speak, they must have something more and over and above the shekel of the sanctuary. Their knowledge is used as a microscope to magnify trifling differences. I hesitate not to say that I have come across persons who

"Could a hair divide,
Betwixt the west and north-west side,"

in matters of divinity, but who know nothing about the things of God in their real meaning. They have never drank them into their souls, but only sucked them up into their mouths to spit them out on others. The doctrine of election is one thing, but to know that God has predestinated you, and to have the fruit of it in the good works to which you are ordained, is quite another thing. To talk about the love of Christ, to talk about the heaven that is provided for his people, and such things—all this is very well; but this may be done without any personal acquaintance with them. Therefore, beloved, never be satisfied with a sound creed, but desire to have it graven on the tablets of your heart. The doctrines of grace are good, but the grace of the doctrines is better still. See that you have it, and be not content with the idea that you are instructed until you so understand the doctrine that you have felt its spiritual power.

This makes us feel that, in order to come to this, we shall need to feel Jesus present with us whenever we read the word. Mark that fifth verse, which I would now bring before you as part of my text which I have hitherto left out. "Have ye not read in the law, how on the Sabbath days the priests in the temple profane the Sabbath, and are blameless? But I say unto you, That in this place is one greater than the temple." Ay, they thought much about the letter of the word, but they did not know that *he* was there who is the Sabbath's Master—man's Lord and the Sabbath's Lord, and Lord of everything. Oh, when you have got hold of a creed, or of an ordinance, or anything that is outward in the letter, pray the Lord to make you feel that there is something greater than the printed book, and something better than the mere shell of the creed. There is one person greater than they all, and to him we should cry that he may be ever with us. O living Christ, make this a living word to me. Thy word is life, but not without the Holy Spirit. I may know this book of thine from beginning to end, and repeat it all from Genesis to Revelation, and yet it may be a dead book, and I may be a dead soul. But, Lord, be present here; then will I look up from the book to the Lord; from the precept to him who fulfilled it; from the law to him who honoured it; from the threatening to him who has borne it for me, and from the promise to him in whom it is "Yea and amen." Ah, then we shall read the book so differently. He is here with me in this chamber of mine: I must not trifle. He leans over me, he puts his finger along the lines, I can see his pierced hand: I will read it as in his presence. I will read it, knowing that he is the substance of it, that he is the proof of this book as well as the writer of it; the sum of this Scripture as well as the author of it. That is the way for true students to become wise! You will get at the soul of Scripture when you can keep Jesus with you while you are reading. Did you never hear a sermon as to which you felt that if Jesus had come into that pulpit while the man was making his oration, he would have said, "Go down, go down; what business have you here? I sent you to preach about me, and you preach about a dozen other things. Go home and learn of me, and then come and talk." That sermon which does not lead to Christ, or of which Jesus Christ is not the top and the bottom, is a sort of sermon that will make the devils in hell to laugh, but might make the angels of God to weep, if they were capable of such emotion. You remember the story I told you of the Welshman who heard a young man preach a very fine sermon—a grand sermon, a highfaluting, spread-eagle sermon; and when he had done, he asked the Welshman what he thought of it. The man replied that he did not think anything of it. "And why not?" "Because there was no Jesus Christ in it." "Well," said he, "but my text did not seem to run that way." "Never mind," said the Welshman, "your sermon ought to run that way." "I do not see that, however," said the young man. "No," said the other, "you do not see how to preach yet. This is the way to preach. From every little village in England—it does not matter where it is—there is sure to be a road to London. Though there may not be a road to certain other places, there is certain to be a road to London. Now, from every text in the Bible there is a road to Jesus Christ, and the way to preach is just to say, 'How can I get from this text to Jesus Christ?' and then go preaching all the way along it." "Well, but," said the young man, "suppose I find a text that has not got a road to Jesus Christ." "I have preached for forty years," said the old man, "and I have never found such a Scripture, but if I ever do find one I will go over hedge and ditch but what I will get to him, for I will never finish without bringing in my Master." Perhaps you will think that I have gone a little over hedge and ditch tonight, but I am persuaded that I have not, for the sixth verse comes in here, and brings our Lord in most sweetly, setting him in the very forefront of you Bible readers, so that you must not think of reading without feeling that he is there who is Lord and Master of everything that you are reading, and who shall make these things precious to you if you realize him in them. If you do not find Jesus in the Scriptures they will be of small service to you, for what did our Lord himself say? "Ye search the Scriptures, for in them ye think ye have eternal life, but *ye will not come unto me* that ye might have life"; and therefore your searching comes to nothing; you find no life, and remain dead in your sins. May it not be so with us?

III. Lastly, SUCH A READING OF SCRIPTURE, as implies the understanding of and the entrance into its spiritual meaning, and the discovery of the divine Person who is the spiritual meaning, IS PROFITABLE, for here our Lord says, "If ye had known what this meaneth, I will have mercy, and not sacrifice, ye would not have condemned the guiltless." It will save us from making a great many mistakes if we get to understand the word of God, and among other good things we shall not condemn the guiltless.

I have no time to enlarge upon these benefits, but I will just say, putting all together, that the diligent reading of the word of God with the strong resolve to get at its meaning often begets spiritual life. We are begotten by the word of God: it is the instrumental means of regeneration. Therefore love your Bibles. Keep close to your Bibles. You seeking sinners, you who are seeking the Lord, your first business is to believe in the Lord Jesus Christ; but while you are yet in darkness and in gloom, oh love your Bibles and search them! Take them to bed with you, and when you wake up in the morning, if it is too early to go downstairs and disturb the house, get half-an-hour of reading upstairs. Say, "Lord, guide me to that text which shall bless me. Help me to understand how I, a poor sinner, can be reconciled to thee." I recollect how, when I was seeking the Lord, I went to my Bible and to Baxter's

Call to the Unconverted, and to Alleine's *Alarm*, and Doddridge's *Rise and Progress*,[1] for I said in myself, "I am afraid that I shall be lost but I will know the reason why. I am afraid I never shall find Christ but it shall not be for want of looking for him." That fear used to haunt me, but I said, "I will find him if he is to be found. I will read. I will think." There was never a soul that did sincerely seek for Jesus in the word but by-and-by he stumbled on the precious truth that Christ was near at hand and did not want any looking for; that he was really there, only they, poor blind creatures, were in such a maze that they could not just then see him. Oh, cling you to Scripture. Scripture is not Christ, but it is the silken clue which will lead you to him. Follow its leadings faithfully.

When you have received regeneration and a new life, keep on reading, because it will comfort you. You will see more of what the Lord has done for you. You will learn that you are redeemed, adopted, saved, sanctified. Half the errors in the world spring from people not reading their Bibles. Would anybody think that the Lord would leave any one of his dear children to perish, if he read such a text as this: "I give unto my sheep eternal life, and they shall never perish, neither shall any pluck them out of my hand"? When I read that, I am sure of the final perseverance of the saints. Read, then, the word and it will be much for your comfort.

It will be for your nourishment, too. It is your food as well as your life. Search it and you will grow strong in the Lord and in the power of his might.

It will be for your guidance also. I am sure those go rightest who keep closest to the book. Oftentimes when you do not know what to do, you will see a text leaping up out of the book, and saying, "Follow me." I have seen a promise sometimes blaze out before my eyes, just as when an illuminated device flames forth upon a public building. One touch of flame and a sentence or a design flashes out in gas. I have seen a text of Scripture flame forth in that way to my soul; I have known that it was God's word to me, and I have gone on my way rejoicing.

And, oh, you will get a thousand helps out of that wondrous book if you do but read it; for, understanding the words more, you will prize it more, and, as you get older, the book will grow with your growth, and turn out to be a greybeard's manual of devotion just as it was aforetime a child's sweet story book. Yes, it will always be a new book—just as new a Bible as it was printed yesterday, and nobody had ever seen a word of it till now; and yet it will be a deal more precious for all the memories which cluster round it. As we turn over its pages how sweetly do we recollect passages in our history which will never be forgotten to all eternity, but will stand for ever intertwined with gracious promises. Beloved, the Lord teach us to read his book of life which he has opened before us here below, so that we may read our titles clear in that other book of love which we have not seen as yet, but which will be opened at the last great day. The Lord be with you, and bless you.

PORTION OF SCRIPTURE READ BEFORE SERMON—PSALM 119:97–112.

---

1. Richard Baxter, *A Call to the Unconverted to Turn and Live* (1657; repr., Grand Rapids: Zondervan, 1953); Joseph Alleine, *An Alarm to the Unconverted* (1671; repr., Evansville, IN: Sovereign Grace Publishers, 1959); Philip Doddridge, *The Rise and Progress of Religion in the Soul: Illustrated in a Course of Serious and Practical Addresses Suited to Persons of Every Character and Circumstance: With a Devout Meditation and Prayer Added to Each Chapter* (Greenville, SC: Greenville Presbyterian Theological Seminary, 1991).

Part Seven

THE DOCTRINE OF SCRIPTURE IN THE THEOLOGY OF OLD PRINCETON

AFTER HAVING CONSIDERED the Scottish and the Dutch background of Westminster and other European influences on it, we take into consideration the more immediate context of Westminster Theological Seminary in its parent institution, Princeton Theological Seminary. Westminster Theological Seminary was founded by J. Gresham Machen, then professor at Princeton Seminary, upon the reorganization of that seminary in 1929. As a result, there is great continuity between the Reformed tradition at Old Princeton and Westminster.

The first text, by Charles Hodge, includes pages from his *Systematic Theology*, the main theological work at Old Princeton. This work updates post-Reformation theology (that of Francis Turretin and the Westminster Confession of Faith) to meet the challenges of the nineteenth century. Hodge does this by using his skills as an exegete and integrating his knowledge of the latest developments of current Continental scientific and modern theology (Friedrich Schleiermacher and his heirs). In this selection, Hodge does more than define inspiration and revelation; he also confutes competing views and is concerned about the reading and interpretation of the Bible in the church. He thus rejoins the pastoral concern of previous generations of Reformed divines. The chapters by Archibald Alexander Hodge, the son of Charles Hodge, could have well served as an introduction to Old Princeton's view of Scripture; chronologically, however, they fall after the *Systematic Theology* of Hodge the elder. The younger Hodge was a great popularizer of theology. Characteristic of his treatment of the doctrine of Scripture is his integration of Reformed confessions and his interaction with the then recent First Vatican Council (1869–70). B. B. Warfield, who wrote a famous article on inspiration with A. A. Hodge, brings his great scholarly and exegetical acumen to bear on the topic of inspiration. The article "The Real Problem of Inspiration" is one of many essays by Warfield that deal with this topic. There he identifies the real problem in that Scripture itself enunciates the doctrine of verbal inspiration. Therefore, to deny verbal inspiration is to set oneself at odds with the teaching of the Bible. In this article, he also examines opposing views and discusses how to integrate the phenomena of Scripture that appear at times to cause difficulty (the question of harmonization is discussed in this regard). Moisés Silva, formerly professor of New Testament at Westminster, characterizes the faculty of Old Princeton as the "best exponents" of inerrancy, defining this biblical doctrine as they do within a confessional framework and with the help of rigorous scholarship. He then goes on to relate their views to those of the founders of Westminster and discusses challenging issues such as eschatology, the interpretation of the early chapters of Genesis, and harmonization.

Theologians at Princeton Seminary helped to define the doctrine of inspiration in the best way possible, not only for Reformed Christians, but also for evangelicals in the twentieth century and beyond. The texts by these three prominent theologians of Old Princeton and the analysis of Silva on their contribution clarify their views and help us to move forward. Old Princeton both upheld a high view of God's inerrant Word and conveyed nuanced formulations and great respect for scholarly debates. In these regards, this tradition has much in common with the best of Dutch Reformed theology represented by Abraham Kuyper and Herman Bavinck (Bavinck refers favorably several times to Warfield's studies).

Charles Hodge's *Systematic Theology*

THE PROTESTANT RULE OF FAITH

Charles Hodge, "Chapter VI. The Protestant Rule of Faith," in *Systematic Theology* (Peabody, MA: Hendrickson, 1999), 1:151–88; reprinted from Grand Rapids: Eerdmans, 1952; first published: New York: Scribner, 1871.

The leading nineteenth-century American theologian Charles Hodge (1797–1878) was raised in the congregation of Second Presbyterian Church of Philadelphia under the ministry of Ashbel Green. Hodge studied at the College of New Jersey and then Princeton Theological Seminary. He began his teaching career in 1822, teaching the Greek and Hebrew courses at Princeton Seminary; later he also taught biblical studies. From 1826 to 1828, he went to France and Germany to study under the greatest scholars of his time. There, he came under the influence of Friedrich August Treu Tholuck (1799–1877) and Ernst Wilhelm Hengstenberg (1802–69). Along with Francis Turretin and the Westminster Standards, these European influences were significant in Hodge's theology. In 1840, Hodge began to teach didactic theology. Hodge taught over three thousand pastors at Princeton, was the founder and editor of the Journal of Princeton Seminary, and had a great influence in the Presbyterian church. On the literary side, besides his *Systematic Theology*, he published major exegetical commentaries on Romans, 1 and 2 Corinthians, and Ephesians. He wrote numerous articles in the *Journal* on a variety of topics. He penned books of popular piety such as *The Way of Life* (1841).

The selection is from his *Systematic Theology*, which to this day remains a classic Reformed text and is known for its thorough treatment of theological topics. This work replaced Turretin as a textbook in the curriculum at Princeton Seminary and is still used at Westminster Seminary. Hodge here helpfully distinguishes and defines revelation and inspiration and addresses contemporary challenges to the Reformed doctrine of Scripture that arose during his tenure at Princeton Seminary. After defining his topic in depth, he provides arguments and discusses competing views, especially those of Schleiermacher. But he also contends that all Christians ought to read the Bible and suggests guidelines for its interpretation. Hodge's work can be understood as an update of Turretin's approach in the context of the nineteenth century: The main dialogue partner is not Roman Catholicism anymore, but rather the new scientific development within the academia. Hodge's treatment also provides the backdrop for later trends at Princeton and Westminster.

Bibliography: Annette G. Aubert. "A Transatlantic Study: Charles Hodge and Emanuel V. Gerhart on Theological Method and the Doctrine of the Atonement, with Special Consideration Given to the Influence of Nineteenth-Century German Theology." Ph.D. diss., Westminster Theological Seminary, 2010. Paul C. Gutjahr. *Charles Hodge: Guardian of American Orthodoxy.* New York: Oxford University Press, 2011. A. A. Hodge. *Life of Charles Hodge.* 1880. Repr., Carlisle, PA: Banner of Truth, 2010. Mark A. Noll. "Hodge, Charles (1797–1878)." Pp. 513–14 in *EDT.* Idem. "Hodge, Charles (1797–1878)." Pp. 312–13 in *NDT.* Francis L. Patton. "Hodge, Charles." *NSHERK* 5:305–6. J. W. Stewart. "Hodge, Charles (1797–1878)." Pp. 122–23 in *DP&RTA.* John W. Stewart and James H. Moorhead, eds. *Charles Hodge Revisited: A Critical Appraisal of His Life and Work.* Grand Rapids: Eerdmans, 2002. P. J. Wallace. "Hodge, Charles (1797–1878)." Pp. 303–7 in *BDE.* David F. Wells. "Charles Hodge." Pp. 36–59 in *Reformed Theology in America.*

§1. Statement of the Doctrine

All Protestants agree in teaching that "the word of God, as contained in the Scriptures of the Old and New Testaments, is the only infallible rule of faith and practice."

In the Smalcald Articles, the Lutheran Church says: "Ex patrum—verbis et factis non sunt exstruendi articuli fidei—Regulam autem aliam habemus, ut videlicet verbum Dei condat articulos fidei et praeterea nemo, ne Angelus quidem."[1] In the Formula of Concord, it is said: "Credimus, confitemur et docemus, unicam regulam et normam secundum quam omnia dogmata omnesque Doctores aestimari et judicari oporteat, nullam omnino aliam esse, quam Prophetica et Apostolica scripta cum Veteris, tum Novi Testamenti."[2]

The symbols of the Reformed churches teach the same doctrine. The Second Helvetic Confession says: "In Scriptura Sancta habet universalis Christi Ecclesia plenissime exposita, quæcunque pertinent cum ad salvificam fidem, tum ad vitam Deo placentem."[3] "Non alium . . . in causa fidei judicem, quam ipsum Deum per Scripturas sacras pronuntiantem, quid verum sit, quid falsum, quid sequendum sit quidve fugiendum."[4] The French Confession

---

1. Part II.2.15 (Karl August von Hase, *Libri symbolici ecclesiae evanglicae sive Concordia* [Lipsiae: Klinkhardti, 1837], 308). "It will not do to make articles of faith out of the holy Fathers' words or works. . . . This means that [latin: We have another rule, namely that] the Word of God shall establish articles of faith and no one else, not even an angel" (Tappert, 295).

2. Part I.1 (Hase, *Libri symbolici*, 570). "We believe, teach, and confess that the prophetic and apostolic writings of the Old and New Testaments are the only rule and norm according to which all doctrines and teachers alike must be appraised and judged" (Tappert, 464).

3. Chapter I (Hermann Niemeyer, *Collectio confessionum in ecclesiis reformatis publicarum* [Lipsiae: Klinkhardti, 1840], 467). "And in this Holy Scripture, the universal Church of Christ has all things fully expounded which belong to a saving faith, and also to the framing of a life acceptable to God" (Schaff, 3:831).

4. Chapter II (Niemeyer, *Collectio confessionum,* 469). "Therefore, in controversies of religion or matters of faith, we can not admit any other judge than God himself, pronouncing by the Holy Scriptures what is true, what is false, what is to be followed, or what is to be avoided" (Schaff, 3:834).

of Faith: "Cumque haec (SS.) sit omnis veritatis summa, complectens quicquid ad cultum Dei et salutem nostram requiritur, neque hominibus neque ipsis etiam Angelis fas esse dicimus, quicquam ei verbo adiicere vel detrahere, vel quicquam prorsus in eo immutare."[5] In the Thirty-Nine Articles of the Church of England, it is said: "Holy Scripture containeth all things necessary to salvation: so that whatsoever is not read therein, nor may be proved thereby, is not to be required of any man, that it should be believed as an article of faith, or be thought requisite or necessary to salvation."[6] The Westminster Confession teaches: "Under the name of Holy Scripture, or the Word of God written, are now contained all the books of the Old and New Testament, which are these: . . . . All which are given by inspiration of God, to be the rule of faith and life."[7] "The whole counsel of God concerning all things necessary for his own glory, man's salvation, faith, and life, is either expressly set down in Scripture, or by good and necessary consequence may be deduced from Scripture; unto which nothing at any time is to be added whether by new revelations of the Spirit or traditions of men."[8] "All things in Scripture are not alike plain in themselves, nor alike clear unto all; yet those things which are necessary to be known, believed, and observed, for salvation, are so clearly propounded and opened in some place of Scripture or other, that not only the learned, but the unlearned, in a due use of the ordinary means, may attain unto a sufficient understanding of them."[9]

From these statements it appears that Protestants hold, (1) That the Scriptures of the Old and New Testaments are the Word of God, written under the inspiration of the Holy Spirit, and are therefore infallible, and of divine authority in all things pertaining to faith and practice, and consequently free from all error whether of doctrine, fact, or precept. (2) That they contain all the extant supernatural revelations of God designed to be a rule of faith and practice to his Church. (3) That they are sufficiently perspicuous to be understood by the people, in the use of ordinary means and by the aid of the Holy Spirit, in all things necessary to faith or practice, without the need of any infallible interpreter.

The Canon

Before entering on the consideration of these points, it is necessary to answer the question, What books are entitled to a place in the canon, or rule of faith and practice? Romanists answer this question by saying, that all those which the Church has decided to be divine in their origin, and none others, are to be thus received. Protestants answer it by saying, so far as the Old Testament is concerned, that those books, and those only, which Christ and his Apostles recognized as the written Word of God, are entitled to be regarded as canonical. This recognition was afforded in a twofold manner: First, many of the books of the Old Testament are quoted as the Word of God, as being given by the Spirit; or the Spirit is said to have uttered what is therein recorded. Secondly, Christ and his Apostles refer to the sacred writings of the Jews—the volume which they regarded as divine—as being what it claimed to be, the Word of God. When we refer to the Bible as of divine authority, we refer to it as

---

5. Article V (Niemeyer, *Collectio confessionum*, 330). "And inasmuch as it [the Word] is the rule of all truth, containing all that is necessary for the service of God and for our salvation, it is not lawful for men, nor even for angels, to add to it, to take away from it, or to change it" (Schaff, 3:362).

6. Article 6.

7. WCF 1.2.

8. WCF 1.6.

9. WCF 1.7.

a volume and recognize all the writings which it contains as given by the inspiration of the Spirit. In like manner when Christ or his Apostles quote the "Scriptures," or the "law and the prophets," and speak of the volume then so called, they give their sanction to the divine authority of all the books which that volume contained. All, therefore, that is necessary to determine for Christians the canon of the Old Testament, is to ascertain what books were included in the "Scriptures" recognized by the Jews of that period. This is a point about which there is no reasonable doubt. The Jewish canon of the Old Testament included all the books and no others, which Protestants now recognize as constituting the Old Testament Scriptures. On this ground Protestants reject the so-called apocryphal books. They were not written in Hebrew and were not included in the canon of the Jews. They were, therefore, not recognized by Christ as the Word of God. This reason is of itself sufficient. It is however confirmed by considerations drawn from the character of the books themselves. They abound in errors, and in statements contrary to those found in the undoubtedly canonical books.

The principle on which the canon of the New Testament is determined is equally simple. Those books, and those only which can be proved to have been written by the Apostles, or to have received their sanction, are to be recognized as of divine authority. The reason of this rule is obvious. The Apostles were the duly authenticated messengers of Christ, of whom He said, "He that heareth you, heareth me."

§2. The Scriptures are Infallible, i.e., Given by Inspiration of God

The infallibility and divine authority of the Scriptures are due to the fact that they are the word of God; and they are the word of God because they were given by the inspiration of the Holy Ghost.

A. The Nature of Inspiration: Definition

The nature of inspiration is to be learnt from the Scriptures; from their didactic statements, and from their phenomena. There are certain general facts or principles which underlie the Bible, which are assumed in all its teachings, and which therefore must be assumed in its interpretation. We must, for example, assume, (1) That God is not the unconscious ground of all things; nor an unintelligent force; nor a name for the moral order of the universe; nor mere causality; but a Spirit—a self-conscious, intelligent, voluntary agent, possessing all the attributes of our spirits without limitation, and to an infinite degree. (2) That He is the creator of the world, and extra-mundane, existing before, and independently of it; not its soul, life, or animating principle; but its maker, preserver, and ruler. (3) That as a spirit He is everywhere present, and everywhere active, preserving and governing all his creatures and all their actions. (4) That while both in the external world and in the world of mind He generally acts according to fixed laws and through secondary causes, He is free to act, and often does act immediately, or without the intervention of such causes, as in creation, regeneration, and miracles. (5) That the Bible contains a divine, or supernatural revelation. The present question is not, Whether the Bible is what it claims to be; but, What does it teach as to the nature and effects of the influence under which it was written?

On this subject the common doctrine of the Church is, and ever has been, that inspiration was an influence of the Holy Spirit on the minds of certain select men, which rendered them the organs of God for the infallible communication of his mind and will. They were in such a sense the organs of God, that what they said God said.

B. Inspiration Supernatural

This definition includes several distinct points. First. Inspiration is a supernatural influence. It is thus distinguished, on the one hand, from the providential agency of God, which is everywhere and always in operation; and on the other hand, from the gracious operations of the Spirit on the hearts of his people. According to the Scriptures, and the common views of men, a marked distinction is to be made between those effects which are due to the efficiency of God operating regularly through second causes, and those which are produced by his immediate efficiency without the intervention of such causes. The one class of effects is natural; the other, supernatural. Inspiration belongs to the latter class. It is not a natural effect due to the inward state of its subject, or to the influence of external circumstances.

No less obvious is the distinction which the Bible makes between the gracious operations of the Spirit and those by which extraordinary gifts are bestowed upon particular persons. Inspiration, therefore, is not to be confounded with spiritual illumination. They differ, first, as to their subjects. The subjects of inspiration are a few selected persons; the subjects of spiritual illumination are all true believers. And, secondly, they differ as to their design. The design of the former is to render certain men infallible as teachers; the design of the latter is to render men holy; and of course they differ as to their effects. Inspiration in itself has no sanctifying influence. Balaam was inspired. Saul was among the prophets. Caiaphas uttered a prediction which "he spake not of himself" (John 11:51). In the last day many will be able to say to Christ, "Lord, Lord, have we not prophesied in thy name? and in thy name have cast out devils? and in thy name done many wonderful works?" To whom he will say: "I never knew you; depart from me, ye that work iniquity" (Matt. 7:22–23).

C. Distinction between Revelation and Inspiration

Second. The above definition assumes a difference between revelation and inspiration. They differ, first, as to their object. The object of revelation is the communication of knowledge. The object or design of inspiration is to secure infallibility in teaching. Consequently they differ, secondly, in their effects. The effect of revelation was to render its recipient wiser. The effect of inspiration was to preserve him from error in teaching. These two gifts were often enjoyed by the same person at the same time. That is, the Spirit often imparted knowledge, and controlled in its communication orally or in writing to others. This was no doubt the case with the Psalmists, and often with the Prophets and Apostles. Often, however, the revelations were made at one time, and were subsequently, under the guidance of the Spirit, committed to writing. Thus the Apostle Paul tells us that he received his knowledge of the gospel not from man, but by revelation from Jesus Christ; and this knowledge he communicated from time to time in his discourses and epistles. In many cases these gifts were separated. Many of the sacred writers, although inspired, received no revelations. This was probably the fact with the authors of the historical books of the Old Testament. The evangelist Luke does not refer his knowledge of the events which he records to revelation, but says he derived it from those "which from the beginning were eyewitnesses, and ministers of the Word" (Luke 1:2). It is immaterial to us where Moses obtained his knowledge of the events recorded in the book of Genesis; whether from early documents, from tradition, or from direct revelation. No more causes are to be assumed for any effect than are necessary. If the sacred writers had sufficient sources of knowledge in themselves, or in those about them, there is no need to assume any direct revelation. It is enough for us that they were rendered infallible as teachers. This distinction between revelation and inspiration is commonly made by systematic writers. Thus Quenstedt (1685) says:

> Distingue inter revelationem et inspirationem. Revelatio vi vocis est manifestatio rerum igno-tarum et occultarum, et potest fieri multis et diversis modis. . . . . Inspiratio . . . . est interna conceptum suggestio, seu infusio, sive res conceptæ jam ante Scriptori fuerint cognitæ, sive occultæ. Illa potuit tempore antecedere scriptionem, hæc cum scriptione semper fuit conjuncta et in ipsam scriptionem influebat.[10]

Often, however, the distinction in question is overlooked. In popular language, inspiration is made to include both the supernatural communication of truth to the mind, and a supernatural control in making known that truth to others. The two gifts, however, differ in their nature, and should therefore be distinguished. Confounding them has sometimes led to serious error. When no revelation was necessary, no inspiration is admitted. Thus Grotius says:

> Vere dixi non omnes libros qui sunt in Hebræo Canone dictatos a Spiritu Sancto. Scriptos esse cum pio animi motu, non nego; et hoc est quod judicavit Synagoga magna, cujus judicio in hac re stant Hebræi. Sed a Spiritu Sancto dictari historias nihil fuit opus: satis fuit scriptorem memoria valere circa res spectatas, aut diligentia in describendis Veterum commentariis.[11]

It is an illogical conclusion, however, to infer that because a historian did not need to have the facts dictated to him, that therefore he needed no control to preserve him from error.

D. Inspired Men the Organs of God.

A third point included in the Church doctrine of inspiration is, that the sacred writers were the organs of God, so that what they taught, God taught. It is to be remembered, however, that when God uses any of his creatures as his instruments, He uses them according to their nature. He uses angels as angels, men as men, the elements as elements. Men are intelligent voluntary agents; and as such were made the organs of God. The sacred writers were not made unconscious or irrational. The spirits of the prophets were subject to the prophets (1 Cor. 14:32). They were not like calculating machines which grind out logarithms with infallible correctness. The ancients, indeed, were accustomed to say, as some theologians have also said, that the sacred writers were as pens in the hand of the Spirit; or as harps, from which He drew what sounds He pleased. These representations were, however, intended simply to illustrate one point, namely, that the words uttered or recorded by inspired men were the words of God. The Church has never held what has been stigmatized as the mechanical theory of inspiration. The sacred writers were not machines. Their self-consciousness was not suspended; nor were their intellectual powers superseded. Holy men spake as they were

10. Johann Andreas Quenstedt, *Theologia didactico-polemica* (Wittenberg: Schumacher, 1685), 68a; Part I; Chapter 4; Section 2; Question 3; ἔχθεσις; 3.
11. "Votum pro Pace Ecclesiastica contra Examen Adreae Riveti." Hugo Grotius, *Opera* (London, 1679), 3:672.

moved by the Holy Ghost. It was men, not machines; not unconscious instruments, but living, thinking, willing minds, whom the Spirit used as his organs. Moreover, as inspiration did not involve the suspension or suppression of the human faculties, so neither did it interfere with the free exercise of the distinctive mental characteristics of the individual. If a Hebrew was inspired, he spake Hebrew; if a Greek, he spake Greek; if an educated man, he spoke as a man of culture; if uneducated, he spoke as such a man is wont to speak. If his mind was logical, he reasoned, as Paul did; if emotional and contemplative, he wrote as John wrote. All this is involved in the fact that God uses his instruments according to their nature. The sacred writers impressed their peculiarities on their several productions as plainly as though they were the subjects of no extraordinary influence. This is one of the phenomena of the Bible patent to the most cursory reader. It lies in the very nature of inspiration that God spake in the language of men; that He uses men as his organs, each according to his peculiar gifts and endowments. When He ordains praise out of the mouth of babes, they must speak as babes, or the whole power and beauty of the tribute will be lost. There is no reason to believe that the operation of the Spirit in inspiration revealed itself any more in the consciousness of the sacred writers, than his operations in sanctification reveal themselves in the consciousness of the Christian. As the believer seems to himself to act, and in fact does act out of his own nature; so the inspired penmen wrote out of the fulness of their own thoughts and feelings, and employed the language and modes of expression which to them were the most natural and appropriate. Nevertheless, and none the less, they spoke as they were moved by the Holy Ghost, and their words were his words.

E. Proof of the Doctrine

That this is the Scriptural view of inspiration; that inspired men were the organs of God in such a sense that their words are to be received not as the words of men, but as they are in truth, as the words of God (1 Thess. 2:13), is proved:

1. From the signification and usage of the word. It is, of course, admitted that words are to be understood in their historical sense. If it can be shown what idea the men living in the apostolic age attached to the word θεόπνευστος [*theopneustos*] and its equivalents, that is the idea which the Apostles intended to express by them. All nations have entertained the belief not only that God has access to the human mind and can control its operations, but that He at times did take such possession of particular persons as to make them the organs of his communications. Such persons were called by the Greeks θεοφόροι (those who bore a God within them); or, ἔνθεος (those in whom a God dwelt). In the Septuagint the word πνευματοφόρος is used in the same sense. In Josephus, the idea is expressed by the phrase "τῷ θείῳ πνεύματι κεκινήμενος";[12] to which the words of Peter (2 Peter 1:21) exactly answer, ὑπὸ πνεύματος φερόμενοι; and what is written by men under this influence of the Spirit is called γραφὴ θεόπνευστος (2 Tim. 3:16). Gregory of Nyssa, having quoted the words of our Lord in Matthew 22:43, "How then doth David in Spirit call him Lord," adds, οὐκοῦν τῇ δυνάμει τοῦ Πνεύματος οἱ θεοφορούμενοι τῶν ἁγίων ἐμπνέονται, καὶ διὰ τοῦτο πᾶσα γραφὴ θεόπνευστος λέγεται, διὰ τὸ τῆς θείας ἐμπνεύσεως εἶναι διδασκαλίαν, that is, "Hence those of the saints who by the power of the Spirit are full of God are inspired, and therefore all Scripture is called θεόπνευστος, because the instruction is by divine inspira-

---

12. "Moved [or overruled, νενικημένος] by the divine Spirit," *Jewish Antiquities* 4.118 (6, 5) [Loeb 4:532–33].

tion" (*Against Eunomius* 7.1 [NPNF2, 5:192–93])[13] The idea of inspiration is therefore fixed. It is not to be arbitrarily determined. We must not interpret the word or the fact, according to our theories of the relation of God to the world, but according to the usage of antiquity, sacred and profane, and according to the doctrine which the sacred writers and the men of their generation are known to have entertained on the subject. According to all antiquity, an inspired man was one who was the organ of God in what he said, so that his words were the words of the god of which he was the organ. When, therefore, the sacred writers use the same words and forms of expression which the ancients used to convey that idea, they must in all honesty be assumed to mean the same thing.

Argument from the Meaning of the Word Prophet

2. That this is the Scriptural idea of inspiration is further proved from the meaning of the word prophet. The sacred writers divide the Scriptures into the "law and the prophets." As the law was written by Moses, and as Moses was the greatest of the prophets, it follows that all the Old Testament was written by prophets. If, therefore, we can determine the Scriptural idea of a prophet, we shall thereby determine the character of their writings and the authority due to them. A prophet, then, in the Scriptural sense of the term, is a spokesman, one who speaks for another, in his name, and by his authority; so that it is not the spokesman but the person for whom he acts, who is responsible for the truth of what is said. In Exodus 7:1, it is said, "See, I have made thee a god to Pharaoh; and Aaron thy brother shall be thy prophet," i.e., thy spokesman. This is explained by what is said in Exodus 4:14–16, "Is not Aaron the Levite thy brother? I know that he can speak well. . . . . Thou shalt speak unto him, and put words into his mouth; and I will be with thy mouth, and with his mouth, and will teach you what ye shall do. And he shall be thy spokesman unto the people; and he shall be, even he shall be, to thee instead of a mouth, and thou shalt be to him instead of God" (see Jer. 36:17–18). This determines definitely, what a prophet is. He is the mouth of God; one through whom God speaks to the people; so that what the prophet says God says. So when a prophet was consecrated, it was said, "Behold, I have put my words in thy mouth" (Jer. 1:9; Isa. 51:16). That this is the Scriptural idea of a prophet is moreover evident from the formulas, constantly recurring, which relate to his duties and mission. He was the messenger of God; he spoke in the name of God; the words, "Thus saith the Lord," were continually in his mouth. "The word of the Lord" is said to have come to this prophet and on that; "the Spirit came upon," "the power," or "hand" of God was upon him; all implying that the prophet was the organ of God, that what he said, he said in God's name and by his authority. It is true, therefore, as Philo says, "For a prophet utters nothing of his own, but everything he utters belongs to another and is prompted by another [προφήτης γὰρ ἴδιον οὐδὲν ἀποφθέγγεται ἀλλότρια δὲ πάντα ὑπηχοῦντος ἑτέρου]" (*Who Is the Heir?* 259 [Loeb 4:416–17]).[14]

This is precisely what the Apostle Peter teaches when he says (2 Peter 1:20–21), "No prophecy of the Scripture is of any private interpretation. For the prophecy came not in old time by the will of man: but holy men spake as they were moved (φερόμενοι, *borne along* as a ship by the wind) by the Holy Ghost." Prophecy, i.e., what a prophet said, was not human,

---

13. "*Contra Eunomium Oratio,*" in *Opera omnia* (Paris, 1615), 2:187.
14. *Opera omnia: Graece et Latine*, ed. August Friedrich Pfeiffer (Erlangen: Walther, 1788), 4:116.

but divine. It was not the prophet's own interpretation of the mind and will of God. He spoke as the organ of the Holy Ghost.

What the Prophets said God said

3. It is another decisive proof that the sacred writers were the organs of God in the sense above stated, that whatever they said the Spirit is declared to have said. Christ himself said that David by the Spirit called the Messiah Lord (Matt. 22:43). David in the 95th Psalm said, "To-day if ye will hear his voice, harden not your heart"; but the Apostle (Heb. 3:7), says that these were the words of the Holy Ghost. Again, in chapter 10:15, the same Apostle says, "Whereof the Holy Ghost also is a witness to us: for after that he had said before, This is the covenant that I will make with them after those days, saith the Lord." Thus quoting the language of Jeremiah 31:33, as the language of the Holy Ghost. In Acts 4:25, the assembled Apostles said, "with one accord," "Lord thou art God. . . . . Who by the mouth of thy servant David hast said, Why did the heathen rage?" In Acts 28:25, Paul said to the Jews, "Well spake the Holy Ghost by Esaias the prophet unto our fathers." It is in this way that Christ and his Apostles constantly refer to the Scriptures, showing beyond doubt that they believed and taught, that what the sacred writers said the Holy Ghost said.

Inspiration of the New Testament Writers

This proof bears specially, it is true, only on the writings of the Old Testament. But no Christian puts the inspiration of the Old Testament above that of the New. The tendency, and we may even say the evidence, is directly the other way. If the Scriptures of the old economy were given by inspiration of God, much more were those writings which were penned under the dispensation of the Spirit. Besides, the inspiration of the Apostles is proved, (1) From the fact that Christ promised them the Holy Spirit, who should bring all things to their remembrance, and render them infallible in teaching. It is not you, He said, that speak, but the Spirit of my Father speaketh in you. He that heareth you heareth me. He forbade them to enter upon their office as teachers until they were endued with power from on high. (2) This promise was fulfilled on the day of Pentecost, when the Spirit descended upon the Apostles as a mighty rushing wind, and they were filled with the Holy Ghost, and began to speak as the Spirit gave them utterance (*dabat eloqui*, as the Vulgate more literally renders the words). From this moment they were new men, with new views, with new spirit, and with new power and authority. The change was sudden. It was not a development. It was something altogether supernatural; as when God said, Let there be light, and there was light. Nothing can be more unreasonable than to ascribe this sudden transformation of the Apostles from narrow-minded, bigoted Jews, into enlightened, large-minded, catholic Christians, to mere natural causes. Their Jewish prejudices had resisted all the instructions and influence of Christ for three years, but gave way in a moment when the Spirit came upon them from on high. (3) After the day of Pentecost the Apostles claimed to be the infallible organs of God in all their teachings. They required men to receive what they taught not as the word of man but as the word of God (1 Thess. 2:13); they declared, as Paul does (1 Cor. 14:37), that the things which they wrote were the commandments of the Lord. They made the salvation of men to depend on faith in the doctrines which they taught. Paul pronounces anathema even an angel from heaven who should preach any other gospel than that which he had taught (Gal. 1:8). John says that whoever did not receive the testimony which he bore concerning Christ, made God a liar, because John's testimony was God's testimony (1 John 5:10). "He that knoweth God, heareth us; he that is not of God, heareth not us" (4:6). This assertion of infallibility, this claim for the divine authority of their teaching, is characteristic of the whole Bible. The sacred writers all, and everywhere, disclaim personal authority; they never rest the obligation to faith in their teachings, on their own knowledge or wisdom; they never rest it on the truth of what they taught as manifest to reason or as capable of being proved by argument. They speak as messengers, as witnesses, as organs. They declare that what they said God said, and, therefore, on his authority it was to be received and obeyed.

The Testimony of Paul

The Corinthians objected to Paul's preaching that he did not attempt any rational or philosophical proof of the doctrines which he propounded; that his language and whole manner of discourse were not in accordance with rhetorical rules. He answers these objections, first, by saying that the doctrines which he taught were not the truths of reason, were not derived from the wisdom of men, but were matters of divine revelation; that he simply taught what God declared to be true; and secondly, that as to the manner of presenting these truths, he was the mere organ of the Spirit of God. In 1 Corinthians 2:7–13, he sets forth this whole subject in the clearest and most concise manner. The things which he taught, which he calls "the wisdom of God," "the things of the Spirit," i.e., the gospel, the system of doctrine taught in the Bible, he says, had never entered into the mind of man. God had revealed those truths by his Spirit; for the Spirit is the only competent source of such knowledge. "For what man knoweth the things of a man, save the spirit of man which is in him? even so, the things of God knoweth no man, but the Spirit of God." So much for the source of knowledge, and the ground on which the doctrines he taught were to be received. As to the second objection, which concerned his language and mode of presentation, he says, These things of the Spirit, thus revealed, we teach "not in the words which man's wisdom teacheth; but which the Holy Ghost teacheth," πνευματικοῖς πνευματικὰ συγκρίνοντες, *combining spiritual with spiritual*, i.e., clothing the truths of the Spirit in the words of the Spirit. There is neither in the Bible nor in the writings of men, a simpler or clearer statement of the doctrines of revelation and inspiration. Revelation is the act of communicating divine knowledge by the Spirit to the mind. Inspiration is the act of the same Spirit, controlling those who make the truth known to others. The thoughts, the truths made known, and the words in which they are recorded, are declared to be equally from the Spirit. This, from first to last, has been the doctrine of the Church, not-withstanding the endless diversity of speculations in which theologians have indulged on the subject. This then is the ground on which the sacred writers rested their claims. They were the mere organs of God. They were his messengers. Those who heard them, heard God; and those who refused to hear them, refused to hear God (Matt. 10:40; John 13:20).

4. This claim to infallibility on the part of the Apostles was duly authenticated, not only by the nature of the truths which they communicated, and by the power which those truths have ever exerted over the minds and hearts of men, but also by the inward witness of the Spirit of which Saint John speaks, when he says, "He that believeth on the Son of God hath the witness in himself" (1 John 5:10); "an unction from the Holy One" (1 John 2:20). It was confirmed also by miraculous gifts. As soon as the Apostles were endued with power from on high, they spake in "other tongues"; they healed the sick, restored the lame and the blind.

"God also," as the Apostle says, "bearing them witness, both with signs, and wonders, and with divers miracles, and gifts of the Holy Ghost, according to his own will" (Heb. 2:4). And Paul tells the Corinthians that the signs of an Apostle had been wrought among them "in all patience, in signs, and wonders, and mighty deeds" (2 Cor. 12:12). The mere working of miracles was not an evidence of a divine commission as a teacher. But when a man claims to be the organ of God, when he says that God speaks through him, then his working of miracles is the testimony of God to the validity of his claims. And such testimony God gave to the infallibility of the Apostles.

The above considerations are sufficient to show, that according to the Scriptures, inspired men were the organs, or mouth of God, in the sense that what they said and taught has the sanction and authority of God.

F. Inspiration extends equally to all Parts of Scripture

This is the fourth element of the Church doctrine on this subject. It means, first, that all the books of Scripture are equally inspired. All alike are infallible in what they teach. And secondly, that inspiration extends to all the contents of these several books. It is not confined to moral and religious truths, but extends to the statements of facts, whether scientific, historical, or geographical. It is not confined to those facts the importance of which is obvious, or which are involved in matters of doctrine. It extends to everything which any sacred writer asserts to be true.

This is proved, (1) Because it is involved in, or follows as a necessary consequence from, the proposition that the sacred writers were the organs of God. If what they assert, God asserts, which, as has been shown, is the Scriptural idea of inspiration, their assertions must be free from error. (2) Because our Lord expressly says, "The Scripture cannot be broken" (John 10:35), i.e., it cannot err. (3) Because Christ and his Apostles refer to all parts of the Scriptures, or to the whole volume, as the word of God. They make no distinction as to the authority of the Law, the Prophets, or the Hagiographa. They quote the Pentateuch, the historical books, the Psalms, and the Prophets, as all and equally the word of God. (4) Because Christ and the writers of the New Testament refer to all classes of facts recorded in the Old Testament as infallibly true. Not only doctrinal facts, such as those of the creation and probation of man; his apostasy; the covenant with Abraham; the giving the law upon Mount Sinai; not only great historical facts, as the deluge, the deliverance of the people out of Egypt, the passage of the Red Sea, and the like; but incidental circumstances, or facts of apparently minor importance, as *e.g.* that Satan tempted our first parents in the form of a serpent; that Moses lifted up a serpent in the wilderness; that Elijah healed Naaman, the Syrian, and was sent to the widow in Sarepta; that David ate the shew-bread in the temple; and even that great stumbling-block, that Jonah was three days in the whale's belly, are all referred to by our Lord and his Apostles with the sublime simplicity and confidence with which they are received by little children. (5) It lies in the very idea of the Bible, that God chose some men to write history; some to indite psalms; some to unfold the future; some to teach doctrines. All were equally his organs, and each was infallible in his own sphere. As the principle of vegetable life pervades the whole plant, the root, stem, and flower; as the life of the body belongs as much to the feet as to the head, so the Spirit of God pervades the whole Scripture, and is not more in one part than in another. Some members of the body are more important than others; and some books of the Bible could be far better spared than others. There may be as great a difference between Saint John's Gospel and the Book of Chronicles as between a man's brain and his hair; nevertheless the life of the body is as truly in the hair as in the brain.

G. The Inspiration of the Scriptures extends to the Words

1. This again is included in the infallibility which our Lord ascribes to the Scriptures. A mere human report or record of a divine revelation must of necessity be not only fallible, but more or less erroneous.

2. The thoughts are in the words. The two are inseparable. If the words, priest, sacrifice, ransom, expiation, propitiation, purification by blood, and the like, have no divine authority, then the doctrine which they embody has no such authority.

3. Christ and his Apostles argue from the very words of Scripture. Our Lord says that David by the Spirit called the Messiah Lord, i.e., David used that word. It was in the use of a particular word, that Christ said (John 10:35), that the Scriptures cannot be broken. "If he call them gods unto whom the word of God came, and the Scripture cannot be broken," etc. The use of that word, therefore, according to Christ's view of the Scripture, was determined by the Spirit of God. Paul, in Gal. 3:16, lays stress on the fact, that in the promise made to Abraham, a word used is singular and not plural, "seed," "as of one," and not "seeds as of many." Constantly it is the very words of Scripture which are quoted as of divine authority.

4. The very form in which the doctrine of inspiration is taught in the Bible, assumes that the organs of God in the communication of his will were controlled by Him in the words which they used. "I have put my words in thy mouth" (Jer. 1:9). "It is not ye that speak, but the Spirit of your Father which speaketh in you" (Matt. 10:20). They spake "as the Spirit gave them utterance" (Acts 2:4). "Holy men of God spake as they were moved by the Holy Ghost" (2 Peter 1:21). All these, and similar modes of expression with which the Scriptures abound, imply that the words uttered were the words of God. This, moreover, is the very idea of inspiration as understood by the ancient world. The words of the oracle were assumed to be the words of the divinity, and not those selected by the organ of communication. And this, too, as has been shown, was the idea attached to the gift of prophecy. The words of the prophet were the words of God, or he could not be God's spokesman and mouth. It has also been shown that in the most formally didactic passage in the whole Bible on this subject (1 Cor. 2:10–13), the Apostle expressly asserts that the truths revealed by the Spirit, he communicated in words taught by the Spirit.

Plenary Inspiration

The view presented above is known as the doctrine of plenary inspiration. Plenary is opposed to partial. The Church doctrine denies that inspiration is confined to parts of the Bible; and affirms that it applies to all the books of the sacred canon. It denies that the sacred writers were merely partially inspired; it asserts that they were fully inspired as to all that they teach, whether of doctrine or fact. This of course does not imply that the sacred writers were infallible except for the special purpose for which they were employed. They were not imbued with plenary knowledge. As to all matters of science, philosophy, and history, they stood on the same level with their contemporaries. They were infallible only as teachers, and when acting as the spokesmen of God. Their inspiration no more made them astronomers than it made them agriculturists. Isaiah was infallible in his predictions, although he shared with his countrymen the views then prevalent as to the mechanism of the universe. Paul could not err in anything he taught, although he could not recollect how many persons he had baptized in Corinth. The sacred writers also, doubtless, differed as to insight into the truths which they taught. The Apostle Peter intimates that the prophets searched diligently into the meaning of their own predictions. When David said God had put "all things" under the feet of man, he probably little thought that "all things" meant the whole universe (Heb. 2:8). And Moses, when he recorded the promise that childless Abraham was to be the father "of many nations," little thought that it meant the whole world (Rom. 4:13). Nor does the Scriptural doctrine on this subject imply that the sacred writers were free from errors in conduct. Their infallibility did not arise from their holiness, nor did inspiration render them holy. Balaam was inspired, and Saul was among the prophets. David committed many crimes, although inspired to write psalms. Peter erred in conduct at Antioch; but this does not prove that he erred in teaching. The influence which preserved him from mistakes in teaching was not designed to preserve him from mistakes in conduct.

H. General Considerations in Support of the Doctrine

On this point little need be said. If the questions, What is the Scriptural doctrine concerning inspiration? and, What is the true doctrine? be considered different, then after showing what the Scriptures teach on the subject, it would be necessary to prove that what they teach is true. This, however, is not the position of the Christian theologian. It is his business to set forth what the Bible teaches. If the sacred writers assert that they are the organs of God; that what they taught He taught through them; that they spoke as they were moved by the Holy Ghost, so that what they said the Holy Spirit said, then, if we believe their divine mission, we must believe what they teach as to the nature of the influence under which they spoke and wrote. This is the reason why in the earlier period of the Church there was no separate discussion of the doctrine of inspiration. That was regarded as involved in the divine origin of the Scriptures. If they are a revelation from God, they must be received and obeyed; but they cannot be thus received without attributing to them divine authority, and they cannot have such authority without being infallible in all they teach.

The organic unity of the Scriptures proves them to be the product of one mind. They are not only so united that we cannot believe one part without believing the whole; we cannot believe the New Testament without believing the Old; we cannot believe the Prophets without believing the Law; we cannot believe Christ without believing his Apostles; but besides all this they present the regular development, carried on through centuries and millenniums, of the great original promise, "The seed of the woman shall bruise the serpent's head." This development was conducted by some forty independent writers, many of whom understood very little of the plan they were unfolding, but each contributed his part to the progress and completion of the whole.

If the Bible be the work of one mind, that mind must be the mind of God. He only knows the end from the beginning. He only could know what the Bible reveals. No one, says the Apostle, knows the things of God but the Spirit of God. He only could reveal the nature, the thoughts, and purposes of God. He only could tell whether sin can be pardoned. No one knows the Son but the Father. The revelation of the person and work of Christ is as clearly the work of God as are the heavens in all their majesty and glory.

Besides, we have the witness in ourselves. We find that the truths revealed in the Bible have the same adaptation to our souls that the atmosphere has to our bodies. The body cannot live without air, which it receives and appropriates instinctively, with full confidence in its adaptation to the end designed. In like manner the soul receives and appropriates the truths of Scripture as the atmosphere in which alone it can breathe and live. Thus in receiving the Bible as true, we necessarily receive it as divine. In believing it as a supernatural revelation, we believe its plenary inspiration.

This doctrine involves nothing out of analogy with the ordinary operations of God. We believe that He is everywhere present in the material world, and controls the operations of natural causes. We know that He causes the grass to grow, and gives rain and fruitful seasons. We believe that He exercises a like control over the minds of men, turning them as the rivers of water are turned. All religion, natural and revealed, is founded on the assumption of this providential government of God. Besides this, we believe in the gracious operations of his Spirit, by which He works in the hearts of his people to will and to do; we believe that faith, repentance, and holy living are due to the ever-present influence of the Holy Spirit. If, then, this wonder-working God everywhere operates in nature and in grace, why should it be deemed incredible that holy men should speak as they were moved by the Holy Ghost, so that they should say just what He would have them say, so that their words should be his words.

After all Christ is the great object of the Christian's faith. We believe him and we believe everything else on his authority. He hands us the Old Testament and tells us that it is the Word of God; that its authors spoke by the Spirit; that the Scriptures cannot be broken. And we believe on his testimony. His testimony to his Apostles is no less explicit, although given in a different way. He promised to give them a mouth and a wisdom which their adversaries could not gainsay or resist. He told them to take no thought what they should say, "For the Holy Ghost shall teach you in the same hour what ye ought to say" (Luke 12:12). "It is not ye that speak but the Spirit of your Father which speaketh in you." He said to them "he that receiveth you receiveth me"; and He prayed for those who should believe on Him through their word. We believe the Scriptures, therefore, because Christ declares them to be the Word of God. Heaven and earth may pass away, but his word cannot pass away.

I. Objections

A large class of the objections to the doctrine of inspiration, which for many minds are the most effective, arise from the rejection of one or other of the presumptions specified on a preceding page. If a man denies the existence of a personal, extramundane God, he must deny the doctrine of inspiration, but it is not necessary in order to prove that doctrine that we should first prove the being of God. If he denies that God exerts any direct efficiency in the government of the world, and holds that everything is the product of fixed laws, he cannot believe what the Scriptures teach of inspiration. If the supernatural be impossible, inspiration is impossible. It will be found that most of the objections, especially those of recent date, are founded on unscriptural views of the relation of God to the world, or on the peculiar philosophical views of the objectors as to the nature of man or of his free agency.

A still larger class of objections is founded on misconceptions of the doctrine. Such objections are answered by the correct statement of what the Church believes on the subject. Even a man so distinguished for knowledge and ability as Coleridge, speaks with contempt of what he regards as the common theory of inspiration, when he utterly misunderstands the real doctrine which he opposes. He says:

> All the miracles which the legends of monk or rabbi contain, can scarcely be put in competition, on the score of complication, inexplicableness, the absence of all intelligible use or purpose, and of circuitous self-frustration, with those that must be assumed by the maintainers of this doctrine, in order to give effect to the series of miracles by which all the nominal composers of the Hebrew nation before the time of Ezra, of whom there are any remains, were successively transformed into *automaton* compositors, etc.[15]

But if the Church doctrine of inspiration no more assumes that the sacred writers "were transformed into automaton compositors," than that every believer is thus transformed in whom God "works to will and to do," then all such objections amount to nothing. If God, without interfering with a man's free agency, can make it infallibly certain that he will repent and believe, He can render it certain that he will not err in teaching. It is in vain to profess to hold the common doctrine of Theism, and yet assert that God cannot control rational creatures without turning them into machines.

Discrepancies and Errors

But although the theologian may rightfully dismiss all objections founded on the denial of the common principles of natural and revealed religion, there are others which cannot be thus summarily disposed of. The most obvious of these is, that the sacred writers contradict each other, and that they teach error. It is, of course, useless to contend that the sacred writers were infallible, if in point of fact they err. Our views of inspiration must be determined by the phenomena of the Bible as well as from its didactic statements. If in fact the sacred writers retain each his own style and mode of thought, then we must renounce any theory which assumes that inspiration obliterates or suppresses all individual peculiarities. If the Scriptures abound in contradictions and errors, then it is vain to contend that they were written under an influence which precludes all error. The question, therefore, is a question of fact. Do the sacred writers contradict each other? Do the Scriptures teach what from any source can be proved not to be true? The question is not whether the views of the sacred writers were incorrect, but whether they taught error? For example, it is not the question Whether they thought that the earth is the centre of our system? but, Did they teach that it is?

The objection under consideration, namely, that the Bible contains errors, divides itself into two. The first, that the sacred writers contradict themselves, or one the other. The second, that the Bible teaches what is inconsistent with the facts of history or science.

As to the former of these objections, it would require, not a volume, but volumes to discuss all the cases of alleged discrepancies. All that can be expected here is a few general remarks: (1) These apparent discrepancies, although numerous, are for the most part trivial; relating in most cases to numbers or dates. (2) The great majority of them are only apparent, and yield to careful examination. (3) Many of them may fairly be ascribed to errors of transcribers. (4) The marvel and the miracle is that there are so few of any real importance. Considering that the different books of the Bible were written not only by different authors, but by men of all degrees of culture, living in the course of fifteen hundred or two thousand years, it

---

15. Samuel Taylor Coleridge, "Confessions of an Inquiring Spirit," Letter 6, *Works* (New York: Harpers, 1853), 5:612.

is altogether unaccountable that they should agree perfectly, on any other hypothesis than that the writers were under the guidance of the Spirit of God. In this respect, as in all others, the Bible stands alone. It is enough to impress any mind with awe, when it contemplates the Sacred Scriptures filled with the highest truths, speaking with authority in the name of God, and so miraculously free from the soiling touch of human fingers. The errors in matters of fact which skeptics search out bear no proportion to the whole. No sane man would deny that the Parthenon was built of marble, even if here and there a speck of sandstone should be detected in its structure. Not less unreasonable is it to deny the inspiration of such a book as the Bible, because one sacred writer says that on a given occasion twenty-four thousand, and another says that twenty-three thousand, men were slain. Surely a Christian may be allowed to tread such objections under his feet.

Admitting that the Scriptures do contain, in a few instances, discrepancies which with our present means of knowledge, we are unable satisfactorily to explain, they furnish no rational ground for denying their infallibility. "The Scripture cannot be broken" (John 10:35). This is the whole doctrine of plenary inspiration, taught by the lips of Christ himself. The universe teems with evidences of design, so manifold, so diverse, so wonderful, as to overwhelm the mind with the conviction that it has had an intelligent author. Yet here and there isolated cases of monstrosity appear. It is irrational, because we cannot account for such cases, to deny that the universe is the product of intelligence. So the Christian need not renounce his faith in the plenary inspiration of the Bible, although there may be some things about it in its present state which he cannot account for.

Historical and Scientific Objections

The second great objection to the plenary inspiration of the Scripture is that it teaches what is inconsistent with historical and scientific truth.

Here again it is to be remarked, (1) That we must distinguish between what the sacred writers themselves thought or believed, and what they teach. They may have believed that the sun moves round the earth, but they do not so teach. (2) The language of the Bible is the language of common life; and the language of common life is founded on apparent, and not upon scientific truth. It would be ridiculous to refuse to speak of the sun rising and setting, because we know that it is not a satellite of our planet. (3) There is a great distinction between theories and facts. Theories are of men. Facts are of God. The Bible often contradicts the former, never the latter. (4) There is also a distinction to be made between the Bible and our interpretation. The latter may come into competition with settled facts; and then it must yield. Science has in many things taught the Church how to understand the Scriptures. The Bible was for ages understood and explained according to the Ptolemaic system of the universe; it is now explained without doing the least violence to its language, according to the Copernican system. Christians have commonly believed that the earth has existed only a few thousands of years. If geologists finally prove that it has existed for myriads of ages, it will be found that the first chapter of Genesis is in full accord with the facts, and that the last results of science are embodied on the first page of the Bible. It may cost the Church a severe struggle to give up one interpretation and adopt another, as it did in the seventeenth century, but no real evil need be apprehended. The Bible has stood, and still stands in the presence of the whole scientific world with its claims unshaken. Men hostile or indifferent to its truths may, on insufficient grounds, or because of their personal opinions, reject its authority; but, even in the judgment of the greatest authorities in science, its teachings cannot fairly be impeached.

It is impossible duly to estimate the importance of this subject. If the Bible be the word of God, all the great questions which for ages have agitated the minds of men are settled with infallible certainty. Human reason has never been able to answer to its own satisfaction, or to the assurance of others, the vital questions, What is God? What is man? What lies beyond the grave? If there be a future state of being, what is it? and How may future blessedness be secured? Without the Bible, we are, on all these subjects, in utter darkness. How endless and unsatisfying have been the answers to the greatest of all questions, What is God? The whole Eastern world answers by saying, "That He is the unconscious ground of being." The Greeks gave the same answer for philosophers, and made all nature God for the people. The moderns have reached no higher doctrine. Fichte says the subjective Ego is God. According to Schelling, God is the eternal movement of the universe, subject becoming object, object becoming subject, the infinite becoming finite, and the finite infinite. Hegel says, Thought is God. Cousin combines all the German answers to form his own. Coleridge refers us to Schelling for an answer to the question, What is God? Carlyle makes force God. A Christian child says: "God is a Spirit, infinite, eternal, and unchangeable in his being, wisdom, power, holiness, justice, goodness, and truth." Men and angels veil their faces in the presence of that answer. It is the highest, greatest, and most fruitful truth ever embodied in human language. Without the Bible, we are without God and without hope. The present is a burden, and the future a dread.

§3. Adverse Theories

Although substantial unanimity as to the doctrine of inspiration has prevailed among the great historical Churches of Christendom, yet there has been no little diversity of opinion among theologians and philosophical writers. The theories are too numerous to be examined in detail. They may, perhaps, be advantageously referred to the following classes.

A. Naturalistic Doctrine

There is a large class of writers who deny any supernatural agency in the affairs of men. This general class includes writers who differ essentially in their views.

First, there are those who, although Theists, hold the mechanical theory of the universe. That is, they hold that God having created the world, including all that it contains, organic and inorganic, rational and irrational, and having endowed matter with its properties and minds with their attributes, leaves it to itself. Just as a ship, when launched and equipped, is left to the winds and to its crew. This theory precludes the possibility not only of all miracles, prophecy, and supernatural revelation, but even of all providential government, whether general or special. Those who adopt this view of the relation of God to the world, must regard the Bible from beginning to end as a purely human production. They may rank it as the highest, or as among the lowest of the literary works of men; there is no possibility of its being inspired in any authorized sense of that word.

Secondly, there are those who do not so entirely banish God from his works. They admit that He is everywhere present, and everywhere active; that his providential efficiency and control are exercised in the occurrence of all events. But they maintain that He always acts

811

according to fixed laws; and always in connection and cooperation with second causes. According to this theory, also, all miracles and all prophecy, properly speaking, are excluded. A revelation is admitted, or at least, is possible. But it is merely providential. It consists in such an ordering of circumstances, and such a combination of influences as to secure the elevation of certain men to a higher level of religious knowledge than that attained by others. They may also, in a sense, be said to be inspired in so far as that inward, subjective state is purer, and more devout, as well as more intelligent than that of ordinary men. There is no specific difference, however, according to this theory, between inspired and uninspired men. It is only a matter of degrees. One is more and another less purified and enlightened. This theory also makes the Bible a purely human production. It confines revelation to the sphere of human knowledge. No possible degree of culture or development can get anything more than human out of man. According to the Scriptures, and to the faith of the Church, the Bible is a revelation of the things of God; of his thoughts and purposes. But who knoweth the things of God, asks the Apostle, but the Spirit of God? The things which the Bible purports to make known, are precisely those things which lie beyond the ken of the human mind. This theory, therefore, for bread gives us a stone; for the thoughts of God, the thoughts of man.

Schleiermacher's Theory

Thirdly, there is a theory far more pretentious and philosophical, and which of late years has widely prevailed, which in reality differs very little from the preceding. It agrees with it in the main point in that it denies anything supernatural in the origin or composition of the Bible. Schleiermacher, the author of this theory, was addicted to a philosophy which precluded all intervention of the immediate efficiency of God in the world. He admits, however, of two exceptions: the creation of man, and the constitution of the person of Christ. There was a supernatural intervention in the origin of our race, and in the manifestation of Christ. All else in the history of the world is natural. Of course there is nothing supernatural in the Bible; nothing in the Old Testament which the Adamic nature was not adequate to produce; and nothing in the New Testament, which Christianity, the life of the Church, a life common to all believers, is not sufficient to account for.

Religion consists in feeling, and specifically in a feeling of absolute dependence (or an absolute feeling of dependence), i.e., the consciousness that the finite is nothing in the presence of the Infinite—the individual in the presence of the universal. This consciousness involves the unity of the one and all, of God and man. "This system," says Dr. Ullmann, one of its more moderate and effective advocates, "is not absolutely new. We find it in another form in ancient Mysticism, especially in the German Mystics of the Middle Ages. With them, too, the ground and central point of Christianity is the oneness of Deity and humanity effected through the incarnation of God, and deification of man."[16]

Christianity, therefore, is not a system of doctrine; it is not, subjectively considered, a form of knowledge. It is a life. It is the life of Christ. Ullmann again says explicitly: "The life of Christ *is* Christianity."[17] God in becoming man did not take upon himself, "a true body and *a* reasonable soul," but generic humanity; i.e., humanity as a generic life. The effect of

---

16. C. Ullmann, "Ueber den unterscheidenden Character des Christenthums, mit Beziehung auf neuere Auggassungseweisen," *Theologische Studien und Kritiken* 18, 1 (1845): 59; translated in Dr. John W. Nevin, *The Mystical Presence* (Philadelphia: Lippincott, 1846), 42.

17. Ullmann, ibid.

the incarnation was to unite the human and divine as one life. And this life passes over to the Church precisely as the life of Adam passed over to his descendants, by a process of natural development. And this life is Christianity. Participation of this divine-human life makes a man a Christian.

The Christian revelation consists in the providential dispensations connected with the appearance of Christ on the earth. The effect of these dispensations and events was the elevation of the religious consciousness of the men of that generation, and specially of those who came most directly under the influence of Christ. This subjective state, this excitement and elevation of their religious life, gave them intuitions of religious truths, "eternal verities." These intuitions were by the logical understanding clothed in the form of doctrines. This, however, was a gradual process as it was effected only by the Church-life, i.e., by the working of the new divine-human life in the body of believers.[18] Mr. Morell in expounding this theory, says: "The essential germ of the religious life is concentrated in the absolute feeling of dependence—a feeling which implies nothing abject, but, on the contrary, a high and hallowed sense of our being inseparably related to Deity."[19] On the preceding page he had said, "Let the subject become as nothing—not, indeed, from its intrinsic insignificance or incapacity of moral action, but by virtue of the infinity of the object to which it stands consciously opposed; and the feeling of dependence must become *absolute*; for all finite power is as nothing in relation to the Infinite."

Christianity, as just stated, is the life of Christ, his human life, which is also divine, and is communicated to us as the life of Adam was communicated to his descendants. Morell, rather more in accordance with English modes of thought, says, "Christianity, like every other religion, consists essentially in a state of man's inner consciousness, which develops itself into a system of thought and activity only in a community of awakened minds; and it was inevitable, therefore, that such a state of consciousness should require time, and intercourse, and mutual sympathy, before it could become moulded into a decided and distinctive form."[20] He represents the Apostles as often meeting together and deliberating on essential points, correcting each other's views; and, after years of such fellowship, Christianity was at last brought into form.

Revelation is declared to be a communication of truth to our intuitional consciousness. The outward world is a revelation to our sense-intuitions; beauty is a revelation to our esthetic intuitions; and "eternal verities," when intuitively perceived, are said to be revealed; and this intuition is brought about by whatever purifies and exalts our religious feelings. "Revelation," says Morell, "is a process of the intuitional consciousness, gazing upon eternal verities; while theology is the reflection of the understanding upon those vital intuitions, so as to reduce them to a logical and scientific expression."[21]

Inspiration is the inward state of mind which enables us to apprehend the truth. "Revelation and inspiration," says Morell,

18. The English reader may find this theory set forth, in John Daniel Morell's *Philosophy of Religion* (London: Longman, Brown, Green, and Longmans, 1849); in Archdeacon Wilberforce's work on the Incarnation; in Frederick D. Maurice's *Theological Essays* (Cambridge: Macmillan, 1853); in Dr. John W. Nevin, *Mystical Presence* and in the pages of *The Mercersburg Quarterly Review*, a journal specially devoted to the defence of Schleiermacher's doctrines and of those of the same general character.
19. Morell, *Philosophy of Religion*, 77.
20. Ibid., 104.
21. Ibid., 141.

indicate one united process, the result of which upon the human mind is, to produce a state of spiritual intuition, whose phenomena are so extraordinary, that we at once separate the agency by which they are produced from any of the ordinary principles of human development. And yet this agency is applied in perfect consistency with the laws and natural operations of our spiritual nature. Inspiration does not imply anything generically new in the actual processes of the human mind; it does not involve any form of intelligence essentially different from what we already possess; it indicates rather the elevation of the religious consciousness, and with it, of course, the power of spiritual vision, to a degree of intensity peculiar to the individuals thus highly favoured of God.[22]

The only difference, therefore, between the Apostles and ordinary Christians is as to their relative holiness.

According to this theory there is no specific difference between genius and inspiration. The difference is simply in the objects apprehended and the causes of the inward excitement to which the apprehension is due. "Genius," says Morell, "consists in the possession of a remarkable power of intuition with reference to some particular object, a power which arises from the inward nature of a man being brought into unusual harmony with that object in its reality and its operations."[23] This is precisely his account of inspiration. "Let," he says, "there be a due purification of the moral nature—a perfect harmony of the spiritual being with the mind of God—a removal of all inward disturbances from the heart, and what is to prevent or disturb this immediate intuition of divine things."[24]

This theory of inspiration, while retaining its essential elements, is variously modified. With those who believe with Schleiermacher, that man "is the form in which God comes to conscious existence on our earth," it has one form. With Realists who define man to be "the manifestation of generic humanity in connection with a given corporeal organization"; and who believe that it was generic humanity which Christ took and united in one life with his divine nature, which life is communicated to the Church as his body, and thereby to all its members; it takes a somewhat different form. With those again who do not adopt either of these anthropological theories, but take the common view as to the constitution of man; it takes still a different, and in some respects, a lower, form. In all, however, inspiration is the intuition of divine truths due to the excitement of the religious nature, whatever that nature may be.

Objections to Schleiermacher's Theory

To this theory in all its forms it may be objected:

1. That it proceeds upon a wrong view of religion in general and of Christianity in particular. It assumes that religion is a feeling, a life. It denies that it is a form of knowledge, or involves the reception of any particular system of doctrine. In the subjective sense of the word, all religions (i.e., all religious doctrines) are true, as Twesten says,[25] but all are not

---

22. Ibid., 151.
23. Ibid., 184.
24. Ibid., 186.
25. August Twesten, *Vorlesungen über die Dogmatik der Evangelisch-Lutherischen Kirche* (Hamburg: Friedrich Perthes, 1838), 1:2. "Das Verhältniss des Erkennen zur Religion." Karl von Hase's *Dogmatik*, "Jede Religion als Ergebniss einer Volksbildung ist angemesen oder subj. wahr; wahr an sich ist die, welche der vollendeten Ausbildung der Menschheit entspricht." See also his *Hutterus Redivivus, oder Dogmatik der Evangelisch-Lutherischen Kirche* (Leipzig: Johann Friedrich Leich, 1833), 7.

equally pure, or equally adequate expressions of the inward religious principle. According to the Scriptures, however, and the common conviction of Christians, religion (subjectively considered) is the reception of certain doctrines as true, and a state of heart and course of action in accordance with those doctrines. The Apostles propounded a certain system of doctrines; they pronounced those to be Christians who received those doctrines so as to determine their character and life. They pronounced those who rejected those doctrines, who refused to receive their testimony, as antichristian; as having no part or lot with the people of God. Christ's command was to teach; to convert the world by teaching. On this principle the Apostles acted and the Church has ever acted from that day to this. Those who deny Theism as a doctrine, are atheists. Those who reject Christianity as a system of doctrine, are unbelievers. They are not Christians. The Bible everywhere assumes that without truth there can be no holiness; that all conscious exercises of spiritual life are in view of truth objectively revealed in the Scriptures. And hence the importance everywhere attributed to knowledge, to truth, to sound doctrine, in the Word of God.

2. This theory is inconsistent with the Scriptural doctrine of revelation. According to the Bible, God presents truth objectively to the mind, whether by audible words, by visions, or by the immediate operations of his Spirit. According to this theory, revelation is merely the providential ordering of circumstances which awaken and exalt the religious feelings, and which thus enable the mind intuitively to apprehend the things of God.

3. It avowedly confines these intuitions, and of course revealed truth, to what are called "eternal verities." But the great body of truths revealed in Scripture are not "eternal verities." The fall of man; that all men are sinners; that the Redeemer from sin was to be of the seed of Abraham, and of the house of David; that He was to be born of a virgin, to be a man of sorrows; that He was crucified and buried; that He rose again the third day; that He ascended to heaven; that He is to come again without sin to salvation, although truths on which our salvation depends, are not intuitive truths; they are not truths which any exaltation of the religious consciousness would enable any man to discover of himself.

4. According to this theory the Bible has no normal authority as a rule of faith. It contains no doctrines revealed by God, and to be received as true on his testimony. It contains only the thoughts of holy men; the forms in which their understandings, without supernatural aid, clothed the "intuitions" due to their religious feelings. "The Bible," says Morell,

> cannot in strict accuracy of language be termed a revelation, since a revelation always implies an actual process of intelligence in a living mind; but it contains the records in which those minds who enjoyed the preliminary training or the first brighter revelation of Christianity, have described the scenes which awakened their own religious nature to new life, and the high ideas and aspirations to which that new life gave origin.[26]

The Old Testament is the product of "the religious consciousness" of men who lived under a rude state of culture; and is of no authority for us. The New Testament is the product of "the religious consciousness" of men who had experienced the sanctifying influence of Christ's presence among them. But those men were Jews, they had Jewish modes of thinking. They were familiar with the services of the old dispensation; were accustomed to think of God as approachable only through a priesthood; as demanding expiation for sin, and regeneration

26. *Philosophy of Religion*, 143.

of heart; and promising certain rewards and forms of blessedness in a future state of existence. It was natural for them, therefore, to clothe their "intuitions" in these Jewish modes of thought. We, in this nineteenth century, may clothe ours in very different forms, i.e., in very different doctrines, and yet "the eternal verities" be the same.

Different men carry this theory to very different lengths. Some have such an inward experience that they can find no form for expressing what they feel, so suitable as that given in the Bible, and therefore they believe all its great doctrines. But the ground of their faith is purely subjective. It is not the testimony of God given in his Word, but their own experience. They take what suits that, and reject the rest. Others with less Christian experience, or with no experience distinctively Christian, reject all the distinctive doctrines of Christianity, and adopt a form of religious philosophy which they are willing to call Christianity.

5. That this theory is antiscriptural has already been said. The Bible makes revelation as therein contained to be the communication of doctrines to the understanding by the Spirit of God. It makes those truths or doctrines the immediate source of all right feeling. The feelings come from spiritual apprehension of the truth, and not the knowledge of truth from the feelings. Knowledge is necessary to all conscious holy exercises. Hence the Bible makes truth of the greatest importance. It pronounces those blessed who receive the doctrines which it teaches, and those accursed who reject them. It makes the salvation of men to depend upon their faith. This theory makes the creed of a man or of a people of comparatively little consequence.

In the Church, therefore, Christianity has always been regarded as a system of doctrine. Those who believe these doctrines are Christians; those who reject them, are, in the judgment of the Church, infidels or heretics. If our faith be formal or speculative, so is our Christianity; if it be spiritual and living, so is our religion. But no mistake can be greater than to divorce religion from truth, and make Christianity a spirit or life distinct from the doctrines which the Scriptures present as the objects of faith.

B. Gracious Inspiration

This theory belongs to the category of natural or supernatural, according to the meaning assigned to those terms. By natural effects are commonly understood those brought about by natural causes under the providential control of God. Then the effects produced by the gracious operations of the Spirit, such as repentance, faith, love, and all other fruits of the Spirit, are supernatural. And consequently the theory which refers inspiration to the gracious influence of the Spirit, belongs to the class of the supernatural. But this word is often used in a more limited sense, to designate events which are produced by the immediate agency or volition of God without the intervention of any second cause. In this limited sense, creation, miracles, immediate revelation, regeneration (in the limited sense of that word), are supernatural. As the sanctification of men is carried on by the Spirit by the use of the means of grace, it is not a supernatural work, in the restricted sense of the term.

There are many theologians who do not adopt either of the philosophical theories of the nature of man and of his relation to God, above mentioned; and who receive the Scriptural doctrine as held by the Church universal, that the Holy Spirit renews, sanctifies, illuminates, guides, and teaches all the people of God; and yet who regard inspiration to be one of the ordinary fruits of the Spirit. Inspired and uninspired men are not distinguished by any specific difference. The sacred writers were merely holy men under the guidance of the ordinary influence of the Spirit. Some of those who adopt this theory extend it to revelation as well as to inspiration. Others admit a strictly supernatural revelation, but deny that the sacred writers in communicating the truths revealed were under any influence not common to ordinary believers. And as to those parts of the Bible (as the Hagiographa and Gospels), which contain no special revelations, they are to be regarded as the devotional writings or historical narratives of devout but fallible men. Thus Coleridge, who refers inspiration to that "grace and communion with the Spirit which the Church, under all circumstances, and every regenerate member of the Church, is permitted to hope and instructed to pray for"; makes an exception in favour of "the law and the prophets, no jot or tittle of which can pass unfulfilled."[27] The remainder of the Bible, he holds, was written under the impulse and guidance of the gracious influence of the Spirit given to all Christian men. And his friends and followers, Dr. Arnold, Archdeacon Hare, and specially Maurice, ignore this distinction and refer the whole Bible "to an inspiration the same as what every believer enjoys."[28] Thus Maurice says, "We must forego the demand which we make on the conscience of young men, when we compel them to declare that they regard the inspiration of the Bible as generically unlike that which God bestows on His children in this day."[29]

Objections to the Doctrine that Inspiration is common to all Believers

That this theory is anti-scriptural is obvious. 1. Because the Bible makes a marked distinction between those whom God chose to be his messengers, his prophets, his spokesmen, and other men. This theory ignores that distinction, so far as the people of God is concerned.

2. It is inconsistent with the authority claimed by these special messengers of God. They spoke in his name. God spoke through them. They said, "Thus saith the Lord," in a sense and way in which no ordinary believer dare use those words. It is inconsistent with the authority not only claimed by the sacred writers, but attributed to them by our Lord himself. He declared that the Scripture could not be broken; that it was infallible in all its teachings. The Apostles declare those anathema who did not receive their doctrines. This claim to divine authority in teaching was confirmed by God himself in signs, and wonders, and divers miracles, and gifts of the Holy Ghost.

3. It is inconsistent with the whole nature of the Bible, which is and professes to be a revelation of truths not only undiscoverable by human reason, but which no amount of holiness could enable the mind of man to perceive. This is true not only of the strictly prophetic revelations relating to the future, but also of all things concerning the mind and will of God. The doctrines of the Bible are called μυστήρια, *things concealed*, unknown and unknowable, except as revealed to the holy Apostles and prophets by the Spirit (Eph. 3:5).

4. It is inconsistent with the faith of the Church universal, which has always made the broadest distinction between the writings of the inspired men and those of ordinary believers. Even Romanists, with all their reverence for the fathers, never presumed to place their writings on a level with the Scriptures. They do not attribute to them any authority but as witnesses of what the Apostles taught. If the Bible has no more authority than is due to the writings of pious men, then our faith is vain and we are yet in our sins. We have no sure foundation for our hopes of salvation.

---

27. "Confessions of an Inquiring Spirit," Letter 7, *Works*, 5:619.
28. See James Bannerman, *Inspiration of the Scriptures* (Edinburgh: T. & T. Clark, 1865), 145, 232.
29. *Theological Essays*, 339.

C. *Partial Inspiration*

Under this head are included several different doctrines.

1. Many hold that only some parts of Scripture are inspired, i.e., that the writers of some books were supernaturally guided by the Spirit, and the writers of others were not. This, as mentioned above, was the doctrine of Coleridge, who admitted the inspiration of the Law and the Prophets, but denied that of the rest of the Bible. Others admit the New Testament to be inspired to an extent to which the Old was not. Others again hold the discourses of Christ to be infallible, but no other part of the sacred volume.

2. Others limit the inspiration of the sacred writers to their doctrinal teaching. The great object of their commission was to give a faithful record of the revealed will and purpose of God, to be a rule of faith and practice to the Church. In this they were under an influence which rendered them infallible as religious and moral teachers. But beyond these limits they were as liable to error as other men. That there should be scientific, historical, geographical mistakes; errors in the citation of passages, or in other unessential matters; or discrepancies as to matters of fact between the sacred writers, leaves their inspiration as religious teachers untouched.

3. Another form of the doctrine of partial, as opposed to plenary inspiration, limits it to the thoughts, as distinguished from the words of Scripture. Verbal inspiration is denied. It is assumed that the sacred writers selected the words they used without any guidance of the Spirit, to prevent their adopting improper or inadequate terms in which to express their thoughts.

4. A fourth form of the doctrine of partial inspiration was early introduced and has been widely adopted. Maimonides, the greatest of the Jewish doctors since the time of Christ, taught as early as the twelfth century that the sacred writers of the Old Testament enjoyed different degrees of divine guidance. He placed the inspiration of the Law much above that of the Prophets; and that of the Prophets higher than that of the Hagiographa. This idea of different degrees of inspiration was adopted by many theologians, and in England for a long time it was the common mode of representation. The idea was that the writers of Kings and Chronicles needed less, and that they received less of the divine assistance than Isaiah or Saint John.[30]

In attempting to prove the doctrine of plenary inspiration the arguments which bear against all these forms of partial inspiration were given or suggested. The question is not an open one. It is not what theory is in itself most reasonable or plausible, but simply, What does the Bible teach on the subject? If our Lord and his Apostles declare the Old Testament to be the Word of God; that its authors spake as they were moved by the Holy Ghost; that what they said, the Spirit said; if they refer to the facts and to the very words of Scripture as of divine authority; and if the same infallible divine guidance was promised to the writers of the New Testament, and claimed by themselves; and if their claim was authenticated by God himself; then there is no room for, as there is no need of, these theories of partial inspiration. The whole Bible was written under such

---

30. This view of different degrees of inspiration was adopted by William Lowth, *Vindication of the Divine Authority and Inspiration of the Old and New Testament* (1692). Daniel Whitby, in "The General Preface" to his *A Paraphrase and Commentary on the New Testament* (1700). Philip Doddridge, *Dissertation on the Inspiration of the New Testament* (1793). George Hill, *Lectures on Divinity* (1833). John Dick, *Essay on the Inspiration of the Holy Scriptures* (1803). Daniel Wilson, *Evidences of Christianity* (1829). Ebenezer Henderson, *Divine Inspiration* (1836).

an influence as preserved its human authors from all error, and makes it for the Church the infallible rule of faith and practice.

§4. The Completeness of the Scriptures

By the completeness of the Scriptures is meant that they contain all the extant revelations of God designed to be a rule of faith and practice to the Church. It is not denied that God reveals himself, even his eternal power and Godhead, by his works, and has done so from the beginning of the world. But all the truths thus revealed are clearly made known in his written Word. Nor is it denied that there may have been, and probably were, books written by inspired men, which are no longer in existence. Much less is it denied that Christ and his Apostles delivered many discourses which were not recorded, and which, could they now be known and authenticated, would be of equal authority with the books now regarded as canonical. All that Protestants insist upon is, that the Bible contains all the extant revelations of God, which He designed to be the rule of faith and practice for his Church; so that nothing can rightfully be imposed on the consciences of men as truth or duty which is not taught directly or by necessary implication in the Holy Scriptures. This excludes all unwritten traditions, not only; but also all decrees of the visible Church; all resolutions of conventions, or other public bodies, declaring this or that to be right or wrong, true or false. The people of God are bound by nothing but the Word of God. On this subject little need be said. The completeness of Scripture, as a rule of faith, is a corollary of the Protestant doctrine concerning tradition. If that be true, the former must also be true. This Romanists do not deny. They make the Rule of Faith to consist of the written and unwritten word of God, i.e., of Scripture and tradition. If it be proved that tradition is untrustworthy, human, and fallible, then the Scriptures by common consent stand alone in their authority. As the authority of tradition has already been discussed, further discussion of the completeness of the Scriptures becomes unnecessary.

It is well, however, to bear in mind the importance of this doctrine. It is not by Romanists only that it is denied, practically at least, if not theoretically. Nothing is more common among Protestants, especially in our day, than the attempt to coerce the conscience of men by public opinion; to make the opinions of men on questions of morals a rule of duty for the people, and even for the Church. If we would stand fast in the liberty wherewith Christ has made us free, we must adhere to the principle that in matters of religion and morals the Scriptures alone have authority to bind the conscience.

§5. Perspicuity of the Scriptures. The Right of Private Judgment

The Bible is a plain book. It is intelligible by the people. And they have the right, and are bound to read and interpret it for themselves; so that their faith may rest on the testimony of the Scriptures, and not on that of the Church. Such is the doctrine of Protestants on this subject.

It is not denied that the Scriptures contain many things hard to be understood; that they require diligent study; that all men need the guidance of the Holy Spirit in order to right knowledge and true faith. But it is maintained that in all things necessary to salvation they are sufficiently plain to be understood even by the unlearned.

It is not denied that the people, learned and unlearned, in order to the proper under-standing of the Scriptures, should not only compare Scripture with Scripture, and avail themselves of all the means in their power to aid them in their search after the truth, but they should also pay the greatest deference to the faith of the Church. If the Scriptures be a plain book, and the Spirit performs the functions of a teacher to all the children of God, it follows inevitably that they must agree in all essential matters in their interpretation of the Bible. And from that fact it follows that for an individual Christian to dissent from the faith of the universal Church (i.e., the body of true believers), is tantamount to dissenting from the Scriptures themselves.

What Protestants deny on this subject is, that Christ has appointed any officer, or class of officers, in his Church to whose interpretation of the Scriptures the people are bound to submit as of final authority. What they affirm is that He has made it obligatory upon every man to search the Scriptures for himself, and determine on his own discretion what they require him to believe and to do.

The arguments in support of the former of these positions have already been presented in the discussion concerning the infallibility of the Church. The most obvious reasons in support of the right of private judgment are:

1. That the obligations to faith and obedience are personal. Every man is responsible for his religious faith and his moral conduct. He cannot transfer that responsibility to others; nor can others assume it in his stead. He must answer for himself; and if he must answer for himself, he must judge for himself. It will not avail him in the day of judgment to say that his parents or his Church taught him wrong. He should have listened to God, and obeyed Him rather than men.

2. The Scriptures are everywhere addressed to the people, and not to the officers of the Church either exclusively, or specially. The prophets were sent to the people, and constantly said, "Hear, O Israel," "Hearken, O ye people." Thus, also, the discourses of Christ were addressed to the people, and the people heard him gladly. All the Epistles of the New Testament are addressed to the congregation, to the "called of Jesus Christ"; "to the beloved of God"; to those "called to be saints"; "to the sanctified in Christ Jesus"; "to all who call on the name of Jesus Christ our Lord"; "to the saints which are in (Ephesus), and to the faithful in Jesus Christ"; or "to the saints and faithful brethren which are in (Colosse)"; and so in every instance. It is the people who are addressed. To them are directed these profound discussions of Christian doctrine, and these comprehensive expositions of Christian duty. They are everywhere assumed to be competent to understand what is written, and are everywhere required to believe and obey what thus came from the inspired messengers of Christ. They were not referred to any other authority from which they were to learn the true import of these inspired instructions. It is, therefore, not only to deprive the people of a divine right, to forbid the people to read and interpret the Scriptures for themselves; but it is also to interpose between them and God, and to prevent their hearing his voice, that they may listen to the words of men.

The People commanded to search the Scriptures

3. The Scriptures are not only addressed to the people, but the people were called upon to study them, and to teach them unto their children. It was one of the most frequently recurring injunctions to parents under the old dispensation, to teach the Law unto their children, that they again might teach it unto theirs. The "holy oracles" were committed to the people, to

be taught by the people; and taught immediately out of the Scriptures, that the truth might be retained in its purity. Thus our Lord commanded the people to search the Scriptures, saying, "They are they which testify of me" (John 5:39). He assumed that they were able to understand what the Old Testament said of the Messiah, although its teachings had been misunderstood by the scribes and elders, and by the whole Sanhedrim. Paul rejoiced that Timothy had from his youth known the Holy Scriptures, which were able to make him wise unto salvation. He said to the Galatians, "Though we, or an angel from heaven . . . if any *man* preach any other gospel unto you than that ye have received, let him be accursed" (Gal. 1:8–9). This implies two things, first, that the Galatian Christians, the people, had a right to sit in judgment on the teaching of an Apostle, or of an angel from heaven; and secondly, that they had an infallible rule by which that judgment was to be determined, namely, a previous authenticated revelation of God. If, then, the Bible recognizes the right of the people to judge of the teaching of Apostles and angels, they are not to be denied the right of judging of the doctrines of bishops and priests. The principle laid down by the Apostle is precisely that long before given by Moses (Deut. 13:1–3), who tells the people that if a prophet should arise, although he worked wonders, they were not to believe or obey him, if he taught them anything contrary to the Word of God. This again assumes that the people had the ability and the right to judge, and that they had an infallible rule of judgment. It implies, moreover, that their salvation depended upon their judging rightly. For if they allowed these false teachers, robed in sacred vestments, and surrounded by the insignia of authority, to lead them from the truth, they would inevitably perish.

4. It need hardly be remarked that this right of private judgment is the great safeguard of civil and religious liberty. If the Bible be admitted to be the infallible rule of faith and practice in accordance with which men are bound on the peril of their souls, to frame their creed and conduct; and if there be a set of men who have the exclusive right of interpreting the Scripture, and who are authorized to impose their interpretations on the people as of divine authority, then they may impose on them what conditions of salvation they see fit. And the men who have the salvation of the people in their hands are their absolute masters. Both reason and experience fully sustain the dictum of Chillingworth, when he says,

> He that would usurp an absolute lordship and tyranny over any people, need not put himself to the trouble and difficulty of abrogating and disannulling the laws, made to maintain the common liberty; for he may frustrate their intent, and compass his own design as well, if he can get the power and authority to interpret them as he pleases, and add to them what he pleases, and to have his interpretations and additions stand for laws; if he can rule his people by his laws, and his laws by his lawyers.[31]

This is precisely what the Church of Rome has done, and thereby established a tyranny for which there is no parallel in the history of the world. What renders this tyranny the more intolerable, is, that, so far as the mass of the people is concerned, it resolves itself into the authority of the parish priest. He is the arbiter of the faith and morals of his people. No man can believe unless the ground of faith is present to his mind. If the people are to believe that the Scriptures teach certain doctrines, then they must have the evidence that such doctrines are really taught in the Bible. If that evidence be that the Church so interprets the sacred

---

31. William Chillingworth, *Works* (Philadelphia: Herman Hooker, for Robert Davis, 1848), 105.

writings, then the people must know what is the Church, i.e., which of the bodies claiming to be the Church, is entitled to be so regarded. How are the people, the uneducated masses, to determine that question? The priest tells them. If they receive his testimony on that point, then how can they tell how the Church interprets the Scriptures? Here again they must take the word of the priest. Thus the authority of the Church as an interpreter, which appears so imposing, resolves itself into the testimony of the priest, who is often wicked, and still oftener ignorant. This cannot be the foundation of the faith of God's elect. That foundation is the testimony of God himself speaking his word, and authenticated as divine by the testimony of the Spirit with and by the truth in the heart of the believer.

§6. Rules of Interpretation

If every man has the right, and is bound to read the Scriptures, and to judge for himself what they teach, he must have certain rules to guide him in the exercise of this privilege and duty. These rules are not arbitrary. They are not imposed by human authority. They have no binding force which does not flow from their own intrinsic truth and propriety. They are few and simple.

1. The words of Scripture are to be taken in their plain historical sense. That is, they must be taken in the sense attached to them in the age and by the people to whom they were addressed. This only assumes that the sacred writers were honest, and meant to be understood.

2. If the Scriptures be what they claim to be, the word of God, they are the work of one mind, and that mind divine. From this it follows that Scripture cannot contradict Scripture. God cannot teach in one place anything which is inconsistent with what He teaches in another. Hence Scripture must explain Scripture. If a passage admits of different interpretations, that only can be the true one which agrees with what the Bible teaches elsewhere on the same subject. If the Scriptures teach that the Son is the same in substance and equal in power and glory with the Father, then when the Son says, "The Father is greater than I," the superiority must be understood in a manner consistent with this equality. It must refer either to subordination as to the mode of subsistence and operation, or it must be official. A king's son may say, "My father is greater than I," although personally his father's equal. This rule of interpretation is sometimes called the analogy of Scripture, and sometimes the analogy of faith. There is no material difference in the meaning of the two expressions.

3. The Scriptures are to be interpreted under the guidance of the Holy Spirit, which guidance is to be humbly and earnestly sought. The ground of this rule is twofold: First, the Spirit is promised as a guide and teacher. He was to come to lead the people of God into the knowledge of the truth. And secondly, the Scriptures teach, that "the natural man receiveth not the things of the Spirit of God: for they are foolishness unto him; neither can he know them, because they are spiritually discerned" (1 Cor. 2:14). The unrenewed mind is naturally blind to spiritual truth. His heart is in opposition to the things of God. Congeniality of mind is necessary to the proper apprehension of divine things. As only those who have a moral nature can discern moral truth, so those only who are spiritually minded can truly receive the things of the Spirit.

The fact that all the true people of God in every age and in every part of the Church, in the exercise of their private judgment, in accordance with the simple rules above stated, agree as to the meaning of Scripture in all things necessary either in faith or practice, is a decisive proof of the perspicuity of the Bible, and of the safety of allowing the people the enjoyment of the divine right of private judgment.

39

Archibald Alexander Hodge's
Outlines of Theology

Archibald Alexander Hodge, *Outlines of Theology: For Students & Laymen*, rev. ed. (London: Thomas Nelson, Paternoster Row, 1879), 65–93; reprinted by Grand Rapids: Eerdmans, 1949; and Carlisle, PA: Banner of Truth, 1972.

Archibald Alexander Hodge (1823–86) was the son of Princeton Seminary professor Charles Hodge. He graduated from the College of New Jersey in 1841 and Princeton Seminary in 1846. In 1847 he was ordained by the New Brunswick Presbytery as a missionary to India. After three years he returned to the United States because of ill health and pastored several churches before becoming professor of didactic theology at Western Theological Seminary, Allegheny, Pennsylvania (now merged into Pittsburgh Theological Seminary), in 1864. In 1877 he joined his father, Charles Hodge, as professor at Princeton Seminary. Hodge the younger wrote several books: among others, a biography, *The Life of Charles Hodge* (1880), and a commentary on the Westminster Confession, *The Confession of Faith* (1869, 1885). He is known for several influential articles or monographs, on the *Ordo Salutis* (1878), *The Atonement* (1867), and most notably with Warfield on *Inspiration* (1881). His posthumous *Popular Lectures on Theological Themes* (1887) presents a broad vision of Calvinism.

His writings were not as thorough as those of his father, yet his pastoral experience coupled with strong academic competence resulted in a highly accessible summary of the Old Princeton Presbyterian doctrine. Our selection from his *Outlines of Theology* supplies a very readable account of the doctrine of Scripture of the Princeton school. For chronological reasons, we place this selection after that of Charles Hodge, but it could also be read as an introduction to Princeton's doctrine of Scripture, given its popular style and the great influence A. A. Hodge had in the definition of this essential doctrine. Here we reproduce two chapters. One deals with the definition of inspiration; this chapter ends with statements from confessions of the church that A. A. Hodge seems to have been fond of. The other treats the interpretation and the function of Scripture in the church. Notable is its particular focus on Roman Catholicism in response to the First Vatican Council (1869–70).

Bibliography: W. A. Hoffecker. "Hodge, Archibald Alexander (1823–1886)." P. 513 in *EDT*. Idem. "Hodge, A(rchibald) A(lexander) (1823–1886)." Pp. 121–22 in *DP&RTA*. Francis L. Patton. "Archibald Alexander Hodge: A Memorial Discourse." Pp. ix–xli in A. A. Hodge. *Evangelical Theology: A Course of Popular Lectures*. 1890. Repr., Carlisle, PA: Banner of Truth, 1976. Idem. "Hodge, Archibald Alexander." *NSHERK* 5:303–4. C. A. Salmond. *Princetonia: Charles and A. A. Hodge*. New York: Scribner & Welford, 1888. P. J. Wallace. "Hodge, Archibald Alexander (1823–1886)." Pp. 302–3 in *BDE*.

CHAPTER IV: THE INSPIRATION OF THE BIBLE

Necessary Presuppositions

1. What are the necessary presuppositions, as to principles, and matters of fact, which must be admitted before the possibility of inspiration, or the inspiration of any particular book can be affirmed?

1st. The existence of a personal God, possessing the attributes of power, intelligence, and moral excellence in absolute perfection.

2d. That in his relation to the universe he is at once immanent and transcendant. Above all, and freely acting upon all from without. Within all, and acting through the whole and every part from within, in the exercise of all his perfections, and according to the laws and modes of action he has established for his creatures, sustaining and governing them, and all their actions.

3d. His moral government over mankind and other intelligent creatures, whereby he governs them by truth and motives addressed to their reason and will, rewards and punishes them according to their moral characters and actions, and benevolently educates them for their high destiny in his communion and service.

4th. The fact that mankind, instead of advancing along a line of natural development from a lower to a higher moral condition, have fallen from their original state and relation, and are now lost in a condition involving corruption and guilt, and incapable of recovery without supernatural intervention.

5th. The historical integrity of the Christian Scriptures, their veracity as history, and the genuineness and authenticity of the several books.

6th. The truth of Christianity in the sense in which it is set forth in the sacred record.

All of these necessary presuppositions, the truth of which is involved in the doctrine that the Scriptures are inspired, fall under one of two classes:

(1) Those which rest upon intuition and the moral and spiritual evidences of divine truth, such as the being and attributes of God, and his relations to world and to mankind, such as the testimony of conscience and the moral consciousness of men as sinners justly condemned, and impotent.

(2) Those which rest upon matters of fact, depending upon historical and critical evidence as to the true origin and contents of the sacred books.

If any of these principles or facts are doubted, the evidence substantiating them should be sought in their appropriate sources, e.g., the department of Apologetics—the Theistic argument and Natural Theology, the evidences of Christianity, the Historic Origin of the Scriptures, the Canon, and Criticism and Exegesis of the Sacred Text.

Statement of the Church Doctrine of Inspiration

2. *In what sense and to what extent has the Church universally held the Bible to be inspired?*

That the sacred writers were so influenced by the Holy Spirit that their writings are as a whole and in every part God's word to us—an authoritative revelation to us from God, indorsed by him, and sent to us as a rule of faith and practice, the original autographs of which are absolutely infallible when interpreted in the sense intended, and hence are clothed with absolute divine authority.

3. *What is meant by "plenary inspiration"?*

A divine influence full and sufficient to secure its end. The end in this case secured is the perfect infallibility of the Scriptures in every part, as a record of fact and doctrine both in thought and verbal expression. So that although they come to us through the instrumentality of the minds, hearts, imaginations, consciences, and wills of men, they are nevertheless in the strictest sense the word of God.

4. *What is meant by the phrase "verbal inspiration," and how can it be proved that the words of the Bible were inspired?*

It is meant that the divine influence, of whatever kind it may have been, which accompanied the sacred writers in what they wrote, extends to their expression of their thoughts in language, as well as to the thoughts themselves. The effect being that in the original autograph copies the language expresses the thought God intended to convey with infallible accuracy, so that the words as well as the thoughts are God's revelation to us.

That this influence did extend to the words appears—1st, from the very design of inspiration, which is, not to secure the infallible correctness of the opinions of the inspired men themselves (Paul and Peter differed, Gal. 2:11, and sometimes the prophet knew not what he wrote), but to secure an infallible record of the truth. But a record consists of language.

2d. Men think in words, and the more definitely they think the more are their thoughts immediately associated with an exactly appropriate verbal expression. Infallibility of thought can not be secured or preserved independently of an infallible verbal rendering.

3d. The Scriptures affirm this fact (1 Cor. 2:13; 1 Thess. 2:13).

4th. The New Testament writers, while quoting from the Old Testament for purposes of argument, often base their argument upon the very words used, thus ascribing authority to the word as well as the thought (Matt. 22:32 and Ex. 3:6, 16; Matt. 22:45 and Ps. 110:1; Gal. 3:16 and Gen. 17:7).

5. By what means does the Church hold that God has effected the result above defined?

The Church doctrine recognizes the fact that every part of Scripture is at once a product of God's and of man's agency. The human writers have produced each his part in the free and natural exercise of his personal faculties under his historical conditions. God has also so acted concurrently in and through them that the whole organism of Scripture and every part thereof is his word to us, infallibly true in the sense intended and absolutely authoritative.

God's agency includes the three following elements:

1st. His PROVIDENTIAL agency in producing the Scriptures. The whole course of redemption, of which revelation and inspiration are special functions, was a special providence directing the evolution of a specially providential history. Here the natural and the supernatural continually interpenetrate. But, as is of necessity the case, the natural was always the rule and the supernatural the exception; yet as little subject to accident, and as much the subject of rational design as the natural itself. Thus God providentially produced the very man for the precise occasion, with the faculties, qualities, education, and gracious experience needed for the production of the intended writing. Moses, David, Isaiah, Paul, or John, genius and character, nature and grace, peasant, philosopher, or prince, the man, and with him each subtle personal accident, was providentially prepared at the proper moment as the necessary instrumental precondition of the work to be done.

2d. REVELATION of truth not otherwise attainable. Whenever the writer was not possessed, or could not naturally become possessed, of the knowledge God intended to communicate, it was supernaturally revealed to him by vision or language. This revelation was supernatural, objective to the recipient, and assured to him to be truth of divine origin by appropriate evidence. This direct revelation applies to a large element of the sacred Scriptures, such as prophecies of future events, the peculiar doctrines of Christianity, the promises and threatenings of God's word, etc., but it applies by no means to all the contents of Scripture.

3d. INSPIRATION. The writers were the subjects of a plenary divine influence, called inspiration, which acted upon and through their natural faculties in all they wrote, directing them in the choice of subject and the whole course of thought and verbal expression, so as while not interfering with the natural exercise of their faculties, they freely and spontaneously produce the very writing which God designed, and which thus possesses the attributes of infallibility and authority as above defined.

This inspiration differs, therefore, from revelation—(1) In that it was a constant experience of the sacred writers in all they wrote, and it affects the equal infallibility of all the elements of the writings they produced. While, as before said, revelation was supernaturally vouchsafed only when it was needed. (2) In that revelation communicated objectively to the mind of the writer truth otherwise unknown. While Inspiration was a divine influence flowing into the sacred writer subjectively, communicating nothing, but guiding their faculties in their natural exercise to the producing an infallible record of the matters of history, doctrine, prophecy, etc., which God designed to send through them to his Church.

It differs from spiritual illumination, in that spiritual illumination is an essential element in the sanctifying work of the Holy Spirit common to all true Christians. It never leads to the knowledge of new truth, but only to the personal discernment of the spiritual beauty and power of truth already revealed in the Scriptures.

Inspiration is a special influence of the Holy Spirit peculiar to the prophets and apostles, and attending them only in the exercise of their functions as accredited teachers. Most of them were the subjects both of inspiration and spiritual illumination. Some, as Balaam, being unregenerate were inspired, though destitute of spiritual illumination.

The Proof of the Church Doctrine of Inspiration

6. *From what sources of evidence is the question as to the nature and extent of the Inspiration of the Scriptures to be determined?*

1st. From the statements of the Scriptures themselves.
2d. From the phenomena of Scripture when critically examined.

The Statements of the Scriptures as to the Nature of Their Own Inspiration

7. *How can the propriety of proving the Inspiration of the Scriptures from their own assertions be vindicated?*

We do not reason in a circle when we rest the truth of the inspiration of the Scriptures on their own assertions. We come to this question already believing in their credibility as histories, and in that of their writers as witnesses of facts, and in the truth of Christianity and in the divinity of Christ. Whatever Christ affirms of the Old Testament, and whatever he promises to the Apostles, and whatever they assert as to the divine influence acting in and through themselves, or as to the infallibility and authority of their writings, must be true. Especially as all their claims were indorsed by God working with them by signs and wonders and gifts of the Holy Ghost. It is evident that if their claims to Inspiration and to the infallibility and authority of their writings are denied, they are consequently charged with fanatical presumption and gross misrepresentation, and the validity of their testimony on all points is denied. When plenary inspiration is denied all Christian faith is undermined.

8. *How may the Inspiration of the apostles be fairly inferred from the fact that they wrought miracles?*

A miracle is a divine sign (σημεῖον) accrediting the person to whom the power is delegated as a divinely commissioned agent (Matt. 16:1, 4; Acts 14:3; Heb. 2:4). This divine testimony not only encourages, but absolutely renders belief obligatory. Where the sign is God commands us to believe. But he could not unconditionally command us to believe any other than unmixed truth infallibly conveyed.

9. *How may it be shown that the gift of Inspiration was promised to the apostles?*

Matt. 10:19; Luke 12:12; John 14:26; 15:26–27; 16:13; Matt. 28:19–20; John 13:20.

10. *In what several ways did they claim to have possession of the Spirit?*

They claimed:
1st. To have the Spirit in fulfilment of the promise of Christ (Acts 2:33; 4:8; 13:2–4; 15:28; 21:11; 1 Thess. 1:5).
2d. To speak as the prophets of God (1 Cor. 4:1; 9:17; 2 Cor. 5:19; 1 Thess. 4:8).
3d. To speak with plenary authority (1 Cor. 2:13; 1 Thess. 2:13; 1 John 4:6; Gal. 1:8–9; 2 Cor. 13:2–4). They class their writings on a level with the Old Testament Scriptures (2 Peter 3:16; 1 Thess. 5:27; Col. 4:16; Rev. 2:7).—Dr. Hodge.

11. *How was their claim confirmed?*

1st. By their holy, simple, temperate, yet heroic lives.
2d. By the holiness of the doctrine they taught, and its spiritual power, as attested by its effect upon communities and individuals.
3d. By the miracles they wrought (Heb. 2:4; Acts 14:3; Mark 16:20).
4th. All these testimonies are accredited to us not only by their own writings, but also by the uniform testimony of the early Christians, their contemporaries, and their immediate successors.

12. *Show that the writers of the Old Testament claim to be inspired.*

1st. Moses claimed that he wrote a part at least of the Pentateuch by divine command (Deut. 31:19–22; 34:10; Num. 16:28–29). David claimed it (2 Sam. 23:2).
2d. As a characteristic fact, the Old Testament writers speak not in their own name, but preface their messages with, "Thus saith the Lord," "The mouth of the Lord hath spoken it," etc. (Jer. 9:12; 13:13; 30:4; Isa. 8:1; 33:10; Mic. 4:4; Amos 3:1; Deut.18:21–22; 1 Kings 21:28; 1 Chron. 17:3).—Dr. Hodge.

13. *How was their claim confirmed?*

1st. Their claim was confirmed to their cotemporaries by the miracles they wrought, by the fulfilment of many of their predictions (Num. 16:28–29), by the holiness of their lives, the moral and spiritual perfection of their doctrine, and the practical adaptation of the religious system they revealed to the urgent wants of men.
2d. Their claim is confirmed to us principally—(1) By the remarkable fulfillment, in far subsequent ages, of many of their prophesies. (2) By the evident relation of the symbolical religion which they promulgated to the facts and doctrines of Christianity, proving a divine preadjustment of the type to the antitype. (3) By the indorsement of Christ and his apostles.

14. *What are the formulas by which quotations from the Old Testament are introduced into the New, and how do these forms of expression prove the inspiration of the ancient Scriptures?*

"The Holy Ghost saith" (Heb. 3:7). "The Holy Ghost this signifying" (Heb. 9:8). "God saith" (Acts 2:17 and Isa. 44:3; 1 Cor. 9:9–10 and Deut. 25:4). "The Scriptures saith" (Rom.

4:3; Gal. 4:30). "It is written" (Luke 18:31; 21:22; John 2:17; 20:31). "The Lord by the mouth of his servant David says" (Acts 4:25 and Ps. 2:1–2). "The Lord limiteth in David a certain day, saying" (Heb. 4:7; Ps. 95:7). "David in spirit says" (Matt. 22:43 and Ps. 110:1).

Thus these Old Testament writings are what God saith, what God saith by David, etc., and are quoted as the authoritative basis for conclusive argumentation; therefore they must have been inspired.

15. How may the Inspiration of the Old Testament writers be proved by the express declarations of the New Testament?

Luke 1:70; Heb. 1:1; 2 Tim. 3:16; 1 Peter 1:10–12; 2 Peter 1:21.

16. What is the argument on this subject drawn from the manner in which Christ and his apostles argue from the Old Testament as of final authority?

Christ constantly quotes the Old Testament (Matt. 21:13; 22:43). He declares that it can not be falsified (John 7:23; 10:35); that the whole law *must* be fulfilled (Matt. 5:18); and all things also foretold concerning himself "in Moses, the prophets, and the Psalms" (Luke 24:44). The apostles habitually quote the Old Testament in the same manner, "That it might be fulfilled which was written," is with them a characteristic formula (Matt. 1:22; 2:15, 17, 23; John 12:38; 15:25; etc.). They all appeal to the words of Scripture as of final authority. This certainly proves infallibility.

The Phenomena of Scripture Considered as Evidence of the Nature and Extent of Its Inspiration

17. What evidence do the Phenomena of the Scriptures afford as to nature and extent of the human causes conspiring to produce them?

Every part of Scripture alike bears evidence of a human origin. The writers of all the books were men, and the process of composition through which they originated was characteristically human. The personal characteristics of thought and feeling of these writers have acted spontaneously in their literary activity, and have given character to their writings in a manner precisely similar to the effect of character upon writing in the case of other men. They wrote from human impulses, on special occasions, with definite design. Each views his subject from an individual standpoint. They gather their material from all sources—personal experience and observation, ancient documents, and contemporary testimony. They arrange their material with reference to their special purpose, and draw inferences from principles and facts according to the more or less logical habits of their own minds. Their emotions and imaginations are spontaneously exercised, and flow as co-factors with their reasoning into their compositions. The limitations of their personal knowledge and general mental condition, and the defects of their habits of thought and style, are as obvious in their writings as any other personal characteristics. They use the language and idiom proper to their nation and class. They adopt the *usus loquendi* ["way of speaking"] of terms current among their people, without committing themselves to the philosophical ideas in which the usage originated. Their mental habits and methods were those of their nation and generation. They were for the most part Orientals, and hence their writings abound with metaphor and symbol; and although always reliable in statement as far as required for their purpose, they never aimed at the definiteness of enumeration, or chronological or circumstantial narration, which characterizes the statistics of modern western nations. Like all purely literary men of every age, they describe the order and the facts of nature according to their appearances, and not as related to their abstract law or cause.

Some of these facts have, by many careless thinkers, been supposed to be inconsistent with the asserted fact of divine guidance. But it is evident, upon reflection, that if God is to reveal himself at all, it must be under all the limits of human modes of thought and speech. And if he inspires human agents to communicate his revelation in writing, he must use them in a manner consistent with their nature as rational and spontaneous agents. And it is evident that all the distinctions between the different degrees of perfection in human knowledge, and elegance in human dialect and style, are nothing when viewed in the light of the common relations of man to God. He obviously could as well reveal himself through a peasant as through a philosopher; and all the better when the personal characteristics of the peasant were providentially and graciously preadjusted to the special end designed.

18. *What evidence do the Phenomena of the Scriptures afford as to the nature and extent of the divine agency exercised in their production?*

1st. Every part of Scripture affords moral and spiritual evidence of its divine origin. This is, of course, more conspicuous in some portions than in others. There are transcendant truths revealed, a perfect morality, an unveiling of the absolute perfections of the Godhead, a foresight of future events, a heartsearching and rein-trying knowledge of the secrets of the human soul, a light informing the reason and an authority binding the conscience, a practical grasp of all the springs of human experience and life, all of which can only have originated in a divine source. These are characteristics of a large portion of the Scriptures, and of the Scriptures alone in all literature, and together with the accompanying witness of the Holy Ghost, these are practically the evidences upon which the faith of a majority of believers rests.

2d. But another characteristic of the Scriptures, taken in connection with the foregoing, proves incontestibly their divine origin as a whole and in every part. The sacred Scriptures are an organism, that is an whole composed of many parts, the parts all differing in matter, form, and structure from each other, like the several members of the human body, yet each adjusted to each other and to the whole, through the most intricate and delicate correlations mediating a common end. Scripture is the record and interpretation of redemption. Redemption is a work which God has prepared and wrought out by many actions in succession through an historical process occupying centuries. A supernatural providence has flowed forward evolving a system of divine interventions, accompanied and interpreted by a supernaturally informed and guided order of prophets. Each writer has his own special and temporary occasion, theme, and audience. And yet each contributed to build up the common organism, as the providential history has advanced, each special writing beyond its temporary purpose taking its permanent place as a member of the whole, the gospel fulfilling the law, antitype has answered to type and fulfilment to prophecy, history has been interpreted by doctrine, and doctrine has given law to duty and to life. The more minutely the contents of each book are studied in the light of its special purpose, the more wonderfully various and exact will its articulations in the general system and ordered structure of the whole be discovered to be. This is the highest conceivable evidence of design, which in the present case is the proof of a divine supernatural influence comprehending the whole, and reaching to every part, through sixteen centuries, sixty-six distinct writings, and about forty co-operating human agents. Thus the divine agency in the genesis of every part of Scripture is as clearly and certainly determined as it is in the older genesis of the heavens and the earth.

19. *What is the objection to this doctrine drawn from the free manner in which the New Testament writers quote those of the Old Testament, and the answer to that objection?*

In a majority of instances the New Testament writers quote those of the Old Testament with perfect verbal accuracy. Sometimes they quote the Septuagint version, when it conforms to the Hebrew; at others they substitute a new version; and at other times again they adhere to the Septuagint, when it differs from the Hebrew. In a number of instances, which however are comparatively few, their quotations from the Old Testament are made very freely, and in apparent accommodation of the literal sense.

Rationalistic interpreters have argued from this last class of quotations that it is impossible that both the Old Testament writer quoted from, and the New Testament writer quoting, could have been the subjects of plenary inspiration, because, say they, if the *ipsissima verba* ["the very words"] were infallible in the first instance, an infallible writer would have transferred them unchanged. But surely if a human author may quote himself freely, changing the expression, and giving a new turn to his thought in order to adapt it the more perspicuously to his present purpose, the Holy Spirit may take the same liberty with his own. The same Spirit that rendered the Old Testament writers infallible in writing only pure truth, in the very form that suited his purpose then, has rendered the New Testament writers infallible in so using the old materials, that while they elicit a new sense, they teach only the truth, the very truth moreover contemplated in the mind of God from the beginning, and they teach it with divine authority (see Patrick Fairbairn, *Hermeneutical Manual, or, Introduction to the Exegetical Study of the Scriptures of the New Testament* [Edinburgh: T. & T. Clark, 1858], 3:357–460). Each instance of such quotation should be examined in detail. as Dr. Fairbairn has done.

20. *What objection to the doctrine of Plenary Inspiration is drawn from the alleged fact that "Discrepancies" exist in the Scriptural Text? and how is this objection to be answered?*

It is objected that the sacred text contains numerous statements which are inconsistent with other statements made in some part of Scripture itself, or with some certainly ascertained facts of history or of science.

It is obvious that such a state of facts, even if it could be proved to exist, would not, in opposition to the abundant positive evidence above adduced, avail to disprove the claim that the Scriptures are to some extent and in some degree the product of divine inspiration. The force of the objection would depend essentially upon the number and character of the instances of discrepancy actually proved to exist, and would bear not upon the fact of Inspiration, but upon its nature and degree and extent.

The fact of the actual existence of any such "discrepancies," it is evident, can be determined only by the careful examination of each alleged case separately. This examination belongs to the departments of Biblical Criticism and Exegesis. The following considerations, however, are evidently well-grounded, and sufficient to allay all apprehension on the subject.

1st. The Church has never held the verbal infallibility of our translations, nor the perfect accuracy of the copies of the original Hebrew and Greek Scriptures now possessed by us. These copies confessedly contain many "discrepancies" resulting from frequent transcription. It is, nevertheless, the unanimous testimony of Christian scholars, that while these variations embarrass the interpretation of many details, they neither involve the loss nor abate the evidence of a single essential fact or doctrine of Christianity. And it is moreover reassuring to know that believing criticism, by the discovery and collation of more ancient and accurate copies, is constantly advancing the Church to the possession of a more perfect text of the original Scriptures than she has enjoyed since the apostolic age.

2d. The Church has asserted absolute infallibility only of the original autograph copies of the Scriptures as they came from the hands of their inspired writers. And even of these she has not asserted infinite knowledge, but only absolute infallibility in stating the matters designed to be asserted. A "discrepancy," therefore, in the sense in which the new critics affirm and the Church denies its existence, is a form of statement existing in the original text of the Hebrew and Greek Scriptures evidently designed to assert as true that which is in plain irreconcilable contradiction to other statements existing in some other portions of the same original text of Scripture, or to some other certainly ascertained element of human knowledge. A "discrepancy" fulfilling in every particular this definition must be proved to exist, or the Church's doctrine of plenary verbal inspiration remains unaffected.

3d. It is beyond question, that, in the light of all that the Scriptures themselves assert or disclose as to the nature and the extent of the divine influence controlling their genesis, and as to their authority over man's conscience and life as the voice of God, the existence of any such "discrepancies" as above defined is a violent improbability. Those who assert the existence of one or more of them must bring them out, and prove to the community of competent judges, that all the elements of the above definition meet in each alleged instance, not probably merely, but beyond the possibility of doubt. The *onus probandi* ["burden of proof"] rests exclusively on them.

4th. But observe that this is for them a very difficult task to perform, one in any instance indeed hardly possible. For to make good their point against the vast presumptions opposed to it, they must prove over and over again in the case of each alleged discrepancy each of the following points: (1) That the alleged discrepant statement certainly occurred in the veritable autograph copy of the inspired writing containing it. (2) That their interpretation of the statement, which occasions the discrepancy, is the only possible one, the one it was certainly intended to bear. The difficulty of this will be apprehended when we estimate the inherent obscurity of ancient narratives, unchronological, and fragmentary, with a background and surroundings of almost unrelieved darkness. This condition of things which so often puzzles the interpreter, and prevents the apologist from proving the harmony of the narrative, with equal force baffles all the ingenious efforts of the rationalistic critic to demonstrate the "discrepancy." Yet this he must do, or the presumption will remain that it does not exist. (3) He must also prove that the facts of science or of history, or the Scriptural statements, with which the statement in question is asserted to be inconsistent, are real facts or real parts of the autograph text of canonical Scripture, and that the sense in which they are found to be inconsistent with the statement in question is the only sense they can rationally bear. (4) When the reality of the opposing facts or statements is determined, and their true interpretation is ascertained, then it must, in conclusion, be shown not only that they appear inconsistent, nor merely that their reconciliation is impossible in our present state of knowledge, but that they are in themselves essentially incapable of being reconciled.

5th. Finally it is sufficient for the present purpose, to point to the fact that no single case of "discrepancy," as above defined, has been so proved to exist as to secure the recognition of the community of believing scholars. Difficulties in interpretation and apparently irreconcilable statements exist, but no "discrepancy" has been proved. Advancing knowledge removes some difficulties and discovers others. It is in the highest degree probable that perfect knowledge would remove all.

21. *Explain the meaning of such passages as* 1 Corinthians 7:6, 12, 40, Romans 3:5 and 6:19, and Galatians 3:15, *and show their perfect consistency with the fact of the plenary inspiration of the whole Bible.*

"I speak as a man," is a phrase occurring frequently, and its sense is determined by the context. In Romans 3:5, it signifies that Paul was, for argument's sake, using the language common to men; it was the Jews' opinion, not his own. In Romans 6:19, it signifies "in a manner adapted to human comprehension," and in Galatians 3:15, it signifies "I use an illustration drawn from human affairs," etc.

"I speak this by permission, not of commandment" (1 Cor. 7:6), refers to verse 2. Marriage was always permitted, but under certain circumstances inexpedient.

"And unto the married I command, *yet* not I but the Lord." "But to the rest speak I, not the Lord" (1 Cor. 7:10 and 12). Reference is here made to what the "Lord," that is Christ, taught in person while on earth. The distinction is made between what Christ taught while on earth, and what Paul teaches. As Paul puts his word here on an equal basis of authority with Christ's word, it of course implies that Paul claims an inspiration which makes his word equal to that of Christ in infallibility and authority.

"And I think also that I have the Spirit of God" (1 Cor. 7:40). "*I think* (δοκῶ) *I have*, is only, agreeably to Greek usage, an urbane way of saying, *I have* (cf. Gal. 2:6, 1 Cor. 12:22). Paul was in no doubt of his being an organ of the Holy Ghost." Charles Hodge, *Commentary on First Corinthians* [1857].[1]

Defective Statement of the Doctrine

22. *State what is meant by theological writers by the inspiration "of superintendence," "of elevation," "of direction," and "of suggestion."*

Certain writers on this subject, confounding the distinction between inspiration and revelation, and using the former term to express the whole divine influence of which the

1. Cf. Charles Hodge, *A Commentary on 1 & 2 Corinthians* (Carlisle, PA: Banner of Truth, 1974), 134.

sacred writers were the subjects, first, in knowing the truth, second, in writing it, necessarily distinguish between different degrees of inspiration in order to accommodate their theory to the facts of the case. Because, *first,* some of the contents of Scripture evidently might be known without supernatural aid, while much more as evidently could not; *second,* the different writers exercised their natural faculties, and carried their individual peculiarities of thought, feeling, and manner into their writings.

By the "inspiration of superintendence," these writers meant precisely what we have above given as the definition of inspiration. By the "inspiration of elevation," they meant that divine influence which exalted their natural faculties to a degree of energy otherwise unattainable.

By the "inspiration of direction," they meant that divine influence which guided the writers in the selection and disposition of their material.

By the "inspiration of suggestion," they meant that divine influence which directly suggested to their minds new, and otherwise unattainable truth.

23. *What objections may be fairly made to these distinctions?*

1st. These distinctions spring from a prior failure to distinguish between revelation the frequent, and inspiration the constant, phenomenon presented by Scripture; the one furnishing the material when not otherwise attainable, the other guiding the writer at every point, (1) in securing the infallible truth of all he writes; and (2) in the selection and distribution of his material.

2d. It is injurious to distinguish between different degrees of inspiration, as if the several portions of the Scriptures were in different degrees God's word, while in truth the whole is equally and absolutely so.

False Doctrines of Inspiration

24. *What Principles necessarily lead to the denial of any supernatural Inspiration?*

All philosophical principles or tendencies of thought which exclude the distinction between the natural and the supernatural necessarily lead to the denial of Inspiration in the sense affirmed by the Church. These are, for example, all Pantheistic, Materialistic, and Naturalistic principles, and of course Rationalistic principles in all their forms.

25. *In what several forms has the doctrine of a Partial Inspiration of the Scriptures been held?*

1st. It has been maintained that certain books were the subjects of plenary inspiration, while others were produced with only a natural providential and gracious assistance of God. S. T. Coleridge admittted the plenary inspiration of "the law and the prophets, no jot or tittle of which can pass unfulfilled," while he denied it of the rest of the canon.[2]

2d. Many have admitted that the moral and spiritual elements of the Scriptures, and their doctrines as far as these relate to the nature and purposes of God not otherwise ascertainable, are products of inspiration, but deny it of the historical and biographical elements, and of all its allusions to scientific facts or laws.

---

2. Samuel Taylor Coleridge, "Confession of an Inquiring Spirit," Letter 7, *Works,* 5:619.

3d. Others admit that the inspiration of the writers controlled their thoughts, but deny that it extended to its verbal expression.

In one, or in all of these senses, different men have held that the Scriptures are only "partially" inspired. All such deny that they "ARE the word of God" as affirmed by the Scriptures themselves and by all the historical Churches, and admit merely that they "*contain* the word of God."

26. *State the doctrine of Gracious Inspiration.*

Coleridge, in his "Confessions of an Inquiring Spirit," Letter 7, holds that the Scriptures, except the Law and the Prophets, were produced by their writers assisted by "the highest degree of that grace and communion with the Spirit which the Church under all circumstances, and every regenerate member of the Church of Christ, is permitted to hope and instructed to pray for."[3] This is the doctrine of Maurice (Frederick Maurice, *Theological Essays* [Cambridge: Macmillan, 1853], 339) and virtually that of Morell (John Daniel Morell, *Philosophy of Religion* [London: Longman, Brown, Green, and Longmans, 1849], 186) and of the Quakers. These admit an objective supernatural revelation, and that this is contained in the Scriptures, which are highly useful, and in such a sense an authoritative standard of faith and practice; that no pretended revelation which is inconsistent with Scripture can be true, and that they are a judge in all controversies between Christians. Nevertheless they hold that the Scriptures are only "a secondary rule, subordinate to the Spirit from whom they have all their excellency," which Spirit illumes every man in the world, and reveals to him either with, or without the Scriptures, if they are unknown, all the knowledge of God and of his will which are necessary for his salvation and guidance, on condition of his rendering a constant obedience to that light as thus graciously communicated to him and to all men. Barclay's *Apology*, "Theses Theologicae," Propositions 1, 2, and 3.[4]

Authoritative Statements

ROMAN CATHOLIC: *Canons and Decrees of Council of Trent*, Session 4 [Schroeder, 17], "Which gospel . . . our Lord Jesus Christ, the Son of God, first promulgated with his own mouth, and then commanded to be preached by his apostles to every creature, . . . and seeing clearly that this truth and discipline are contained in the written books, and the unwritten tradition, which received by the apostles from the mouth of Christ himself, or from the apostles themselves, the Holy Ghost dictating, have come down even unto us, transmitted as it were from hand to hand: [the Synod] following the example of the orthodox Fathers, receives and venerates with an equal affection of piety and reverence, all the books both of the Old and of the New Testament—seeing God is the author of both—as also the said traditions, as well those appertaining to faith as to morals, as having been dictated, either by Christ's own word of mouth, or by the Holy Ghost, and preserved in the Catholic Church by a continuous succession."

Dogmatic Decrees of the Vatican Council, 1870, Session 1, Ch. 2, "Further this supernatural revelation, according to the universal belief of the Church, declared by the sacred Synod of Trent, is contained in the written books and unwritten traditions which have come down to us, having been received by the apostles from the mouth of Christ himself, or from the apostles

---

3. Ibid.
4. Robert Barclay, *Apology for the True Christian Divinity* (1678; repr. Philadelphia: Friends' Book-store, 1800), 13–15.

themselves, by the dictation of the Holy Spirit, have been transmitted as it were from hand to hand. And these books of the Old and New Testament are to be received as sacred and canonical, in their integrity, with all their parts, as they are enumerated in the decree of the said Council, and are contained in the ancient Edition of the Vulgate. These the Church holds to be sacred and canonical, not because having been carefully composed by mere human industry, they were afterwards approved by her authority, nor merely because they contain revelation with no admixture of error; but because, having been written by the inspiration of the Holy Ghost, they have God for their author, and have been delivered as such to the Church herself."[5]

LUTHERAN: *Formula of Concord*, "Epitome" 1. "We believe, confess, and teach that the only rule and norm, according to which all dogmas and all doctors ought to be esteemed and judged, is no other whatever than the prophetic and apostolic writings of the Old and New Testament, as it is written (Ps. 119:105 and Gal. 1:8)."

REFORMED: *Second Helvetic Confession*, Ch. 1, "Concerning Holy Scripture," "We believe and confess, that the canonical Scriptures of the holy prophets and apostles of each Testament are the true word of God, and that they possess sufficient authority from themselves alone and not from man. For God himself spoke to the fathers, to the prophets, and to the apostles, and continues to speak to us through the Holy Scriptures."

The Belgic Confession, Article 3, "We confess that this word of God was not sent nor delivered by the will of man, but that *holy men of God spake as they were moved by the Holy Ghost*, as the apostle Peter saith. And that afterwards God, from a special care which he has for us and our salvation, commanded his servants, the prophets and apostles, to commit his revealed word to writing, and he himself wrote with his own finger the two tables of the law. Therefore we call such writings holy and divine Scriptures."

Westminster Confession of Faith 1.1, 4, "Therefore it pleased the Lord, at sundry times and in divers manners, to reveal himself and to declare his will unto his Church; and afterwards, for the better preserving and propagating of the truth, and for the more sure establishment and comfort of the Church against the Corruption of the flesh and the malice of Satan and of the world, to commit the same wholly unto writing." "The authority of the Holy Scripture, for which it ought to be believed and obeyed, dependeth not upon the testimony of any man or church, but wholly upon God (who is truth itself) the Author thereof; and therefore it is to be received because it is the word of God."

CHAPTER V: THE RULE OF FAITH AND PRACTICE

THE SCRIPTURES OF THE OLD AND NEW TESTAMENTS, HAVING BEEN GIVEN BY INSPIRATION OF GOD, ARE THE ALL-SUFFICIENT AND ONLY RULE OF FAITH AND PRACTICE, AND JUDGE OF CONTROVERSIES.

(This chapter is compiled from Dr. Hodge's unpublished "Lectures on the Church.")

5. Cf. Schaff, *The Creeds of Christendom*, 2:241–42: Session III, April 24, 1870, Chapter II.

1. *What is meant by saying that the Scriptures are the only infallible rule of faith and practice?*

Whatever God teaches or commands is of sovereign authority. Whatever conveys to us an infallible knowledge of his teachings and commands is an infallible rule. The Scriptures of the Old and New Testaments are the only organs through which, during the present dispensation, God conveys to us a knowledge of his will about what we are to believe concerning himself, and what duties he requires of us.

2. *What does the Romish Church declare to be the infallible rule of faith and practice?*

The Romish theory is that the complete rule of faith and practice consists of Scripture and tradition, or the oral teaching of Christ and his apostles, handed down through the Church. Tradition they hold to be necessary, 1st, to teach additional truth not contained in the Scriptures; and, 2d, to interpret Scripture. The Church being the divinely constituted depository and judge of both Scripture and tradition (*Canons and Decrees of Council of Trent*, Session 4, and Peter Dens, *Theologia moralis et dogmatica* [Dublin: Richardi Coyne, 1832], 2:126–29, N. 80 and 81).

3. *By what arguments do they seek to establish the authority of tradition? By what criterion do they distinguish true traditions from false, and on what grounds do they base the authority of the traditions they receive?*

1st. Their arguments in behalf of tradition are—(1) Scripture authorizes it (2 Thess. 2:15; 3:6). (2) The early fathers asserted its authority and founded their faith largely upon it. (3) The oral teaching of Christ and his apostles, when clearly ascertained, is intrinsically of equal authority with their writings. The Scriptures themselves are handed down to us by the evidence of tradition, and the stream can not rise higher than its source. (4) The necessity of the case. (a) Scripture is obscure, needs tradition as its interpreter. (b) Scripture is incomplete as a rule of faith and practice; since there are many doctrines and institutions, universally recognized, which are founded only upon tradition as a supplement to Scripture. (5) Analogy. Every state recognizes both written and unwritten, common and statute law.

2d. The criterion by which they distinguish between true and false traditions is Catholic consent. The Anglican ritualists confine the application of the rule to the first three or four centuries. The Romanists recognize that as an authoritative consent which is constitutionally expressed by the bishops in general council, or by the Pope ex-cathedra, in any age of the church whatever.

3d. They defend the traditions which they hold to be true. (1) On the ground of historical testimony, tracing them up to the apostles as their source. (2) The authority of the Church expressed by Catholic consent.

4. *By what arguments may the invalidity of all ecclesiastical tradition, as a part of our rule of faith and practice, be shown?*

1st. The Scriptures do *not*, as claimed, ascribe authority to oral tradition. Tradition, as intended by Paul in the passage cited (2 Thess. 2:15 and 3:6), signifies all his instructions, oral and written, communicated *to those very people themselves*, not handed down. On the other hand, Christ rebuked this doctrine of the Romanists in their predecessors, the Pharisees (Matt. 15:3, 6; Mark 7:7).

2d. It is improbable *à priori* that God would supplement Scripture with tradition as part of our rule of faith. (1) Because Scripture, as will be shown below (questions 7–14), is certain, definite, complete, and perspicuous. (2) Because tradition, from its very nature, is indeterminate, and liable to become adulterated with every form of error. Besides, as will be shown below (question 20), the authority of Scripture does not rest ultimately upon tradition.

3d. The whole ground upon which Romanists base the authority of their traditions (viz., history and church authority) is invalid. (1) History utterly fails them. For more than three hundred years after the apostles they have very little, and that contradictory, evidence for any one of their traditions. They are thus forced to the absurd assumption that what was taught in the fourth century was therefore taught in the third, and therefore in the first. (2) The church is not infallible, as will be shown below (question 18).

4th. Their practice is inconsistent with their own principles. Many of the earliest and best attested traditions they do not receive. Many of their pretended traditions are recent inventions unknown to the ancients.

5th. Many of their traditions, such as relate to the priesthood, the sacrifice of the mass, etc., are plainly in direct opposition to Scripture. Yet the infallible church affirms the infallibility of Scripture. A house divided against itself can not stand.

5. *What is necessary to constitute a sole and infallible rule of faith?*

Plenary inspiration, completeness, perspicuity, and accessibility.

6. *What arguments do the Scriptures themselves afford in favor of the doctrine that they are the only infallible rule of faith?*

1st. The Scriptures always speak in the name of God, and command faith and obedience.

2d. Christ and his apostles always refer to the written Scriptures, then existing, as authority, and *to no other rule of faith whatsoever* (Luke 16:29; 10:26; John 5:39; Rom. 4:3; 2 Tim. 3:15).

3d. The Bereans are commended for bringing all questions, even apostolic teaching, to this test (Acts 17:11; see also Isa. 8:16).

4th. Christ rebukes the Pharisees for adding to and perverting the Scriptures (Matt. 15:7–9; Mark 7:5–8; see also Rev. 22:18–19, and Deut. 4:2; 12:32; Josh. 1:7).

7. *In what sense is the completeness of Scripture as a rule of faith asserted?*

It is not meant that the Scriptures contain every revelation which God has ever made to man, but that their contents are the only supernatural revelation that God does now make to man, and that this revelation is abundantly sufficient for man's guidance in all questions of faith, practice, and modes of worship, and excludes the necessity and the right of any human inventions.

8. How may this completeness be proved from the design of Scripture?

The Scriptures profess to lead us to God. Whatever is necessary to that end they must teach us. If any supplementary rule, as tradition, is necessary to that end, they must refer us to it. "Incompleteness here would be falsehood." But while one sacred writer constantly refers us to the writings of another, not one of them ever intimates to us either the necessity or the existence of any other rule (John 20:31; 2 Tim. 3:15–17).

9. By what other arguments may this principle be proved?

As the Scriptures profess to be a rule complete for its end, so they have always been practically found to be such by the true spiritual people of God in all ages. They teach a complete and harmonious system of doctrine. They furnish all necessary principles for the government of the private lives of Christians, in every relation, for the public worship of God, and for the administration of the affairs of his kingdom; and they repel all pretended traditions and priestly innovations.

10. In what sense do Protestants affirm and Romanists deny the perspicuity of Scripture?

Protestants do not affirm that the doctrines revealed in the Scriptures are level to man's powers of understanding. Many of them are confessedly beyond all understanding. Nor do they affirm that every part of Scripture can be certainly and perspicuously expounded, many of the prophesies being perfectly enigmatical until explained by the event. But they do affirm that every essential article of faith and rule of practice is clearly revealed in Scripture, or may certainly be deduced therefrom. This much the least instructed Christian may learn at once; while, on the other hand, it is true, that with the advance of historical and critical knowledge, and by means of controversies, the Christian church is constantly making progress in the accurate interpretation of Scripture, and in the comprehension in its integrity of the system therein taught.

Protestants affirm and Romanists deny that private and unlearned Christians may safely be allowed to interpret Scripture for themselves.

11. How can the perspicuity of Scripture be proved from the fact that it is a law and a message?

We saw (question 8) that Scripture is either complete or false, from its own professed design. We now prove its perspicuity upon the same principle. It professes to be (1) a law to be obeyed; (2) a revelation of truth to be believed, to be received by us in both aspects upon the penalty of eternal death. To suppose it not to be perspicuous, relatively to its design of commanding and teaching, is to charge God with dealing with us in a spirit at once disingenuous and cruel.

12. In what passages is their perspicuity asserted?

Pss. 19:7–8; 119:105, 130; 2 Cor. 3:14; 2 Peter 1:18–19; Hab. 2:2; 2 Tim. 3:15, 17.

13. *By what other arguments may this point be established?*

1st. The Scriptures are addressed immediately, either to all men promiscuously, or else to the whole body of believers as such (Deut. 6:4–9; Luke 1:3; Rom. 1:7; 1 Cor. 1:2; 2 Cor. 1:1; 4:2; Gal. 1:2; Eph. 1:1; Phil. 1:1; Col. 1:2; James 1:1; 1 Peter 1:1; 2 Peter 1:1; 1 John 2:12, 14; Jude 1; Rev. 1:3–4; 2:7). The only exceptions are the epistles to Timothy and Titus.

2d. All Christians promiscuously are commanded to search the Scriptures (2 Tim. 3:15, 17; Acts 17:11; John 5:39).

3d. Universal experience. We have the same evidence of the light-giving power of Scripture that we have of the same property in the sun. The argument to the contrary is an insult to the understanding of the whole world of Bible readers.

4th. The essential unity in faith and practice, in spite of all circumstantial differences, of all Christian communities of every age and nation, who draw their religion directly from the open Scriptures.

14. *What was the third quality required to constitute the Scriptures the sufficient rule of faith and practice?*

Accessibility. It is self-evident that this is the pre-eminent characteristic of the Scriptures, in contrast to tradition, which is in the custody of a corporation of priests, and to every other pretended rule whatsoever. The agency of the church in this matter is simply to give all currency to the word of God.

15. *What is meant by saying that the Scriptures are the judge as well as the rule in questions of faith?*

"A rule is a standard of judgment; a judge is the expounder and applier of that rule to the decision of particular cases." The Protestant doctrine is:

1st. That the Scriptures are the only infallible rule of faith and practice.

2d. (1) Negatively. That there is no body of men who are either qualified, or authorized, to interpret the Scriptures, or to apply their principles to the decision of particular questions, in a *sense binding upon the faith of their fellow Christians.* (2) Positively. That Scripture is the only infallible voice in the church, and is to be interpreted, in its own light, and with the gracious help of the Holy Ghost, who is promised to every Christian (1 John 2:20–27), by each individual for himself, with the assistance, though not by the authority, of his fellow Christians. Creeds and confessions, as to form, bind only those who voluntarily profess them, and as to matter, they bind only so far as they affirm truly what the Bible teaches, and because the Bible does so teach.

16. *What is the Romish doctrine as to the authority of the church as the infallible interpreter of the rule of faith and the authoritative judge of all controversies?*

The Romish doctrine is that the church is absolutely infallible in all matters of Christian faith and practice, and the divinely authorized depository and interpreter of the rule of faith. Her office is not to convey new revelations from God to man, yet her inspiration renders her infallible in disseminating and interpreting the original revelation communicated through the apostles.

The church, therefore, authoritatively determines—1st. What is Scripture? 2d. What is genuine tradition? 3d. What is the true sense of Scripture and tradition, and what is the true application of that perfect rule to every particular question of belief or practice.

This authority vests in the pope, when acting in his official capacity, and in the bishops as a body; as when assembled in general council, or when giving universal consent to a decree of pope or council (*Canons and Decrees of Council of Trent*, Session 4; Dens, *Theologia*, 2:126–29, 133–36, 154–62, N. 80, 81, 84, 93, 94, 95, 96. Bellarmine, Book 3, de eccles., ch. 14, and Book 2, de council., ch. 2).[6]

17. *By what arguments do they seek to establish this authority?*

1st. The promises of Christ, given, as they claim, to the apostles, and to their official successor, securing their infallibility, and consequent authority (Matt. 16:18; 18:18–20; Luke 24:47–49; John 16:13; 20:23).

2d. The commission given to the church as the teacher of the world (Matt. 28:19–20; Luke 10:16; etc).

3d. The church is declared to be "the pillar and ground of the truth" (1 Tim. 3:15), and it is affirmed that "the gates of hell shall never prevail against her" (Matt. 16:18).

4th. To the church is granted power to bind and loose, and he that will not hear the church is to be treated as a heathen (Matt. 16:19; 18:15–18).

5th. The church is commanded to discriminate between truth and error, and must consequently be qualified and authorized to do so (2 Thess. 3:6; Rom. 16:17; 2 John 10).

6th. From the necessity of the case, men need and crave an ever-living, visible, and cotemporaneous infallible Interpreter and Judge.

7th. From universal analogy every community among men has the living judge as well as the written law, and the one would be of no value without the other.

8th. This power is necessary to secure unity and universality, which all acknowledge to be essential attributes of the true church.

18. *By what arguments may this claim of the Romish church be shown to be utterly baseless?*

1st. A claim vesting in mortal men a power so momentous can be established only by the most clear and certain evidence, and the failure to produce such converts the claim into a treason at once against God and the human race.

2d. Her evidence fails, because the promises of Christ to preserve his church from extinction and from error do none of them go the length of pledging infallibility. The utmost promised is, that the true people of God shall never perish entirely from the earth, or be left to apostatize from the essentials of the faith.

---

6. Robert Bellarmine, *De Controversiis Christianae Fidei Adversus Haereticis,* vol. 2 (Rome: Giunchi & Menicanti, 1836), 123–25: Book III: De Ecclesia Militante Tote Orbe Diffusa, Chapter XIV: Ecclesium non posse errare; 44–47: Book II: De Conciliorum Auctoritate, Chapter II: Concilia generalia a Ponitifice confirmata, errare non posse; ex Scripturis demonstratur.

3d. Her evidence fails, because these promises of Christ were addressed not to the officers of the church as such, but to the body of true believers. Compare John 20:23 with Luke 24:33, 47–49 and 1 John 2:20, 27.

4th. Her evidence fails, because the church to which the precious promises of the Scriptures are pledged is not an external, visible society, the authority of which is vested in the hands of a perpetual line of apostles. For—(1) the word church (ἐκκλησία) is a collective term, embracing the effectually called (κλητοὶ) or regenerated (Rom. 1:7; 8:28; 1 Cor. 1:2; Jude 1; Rev. 17:14; also Rom. 9:24; 1 Cor. 7:18–24; Gal. 1:15; 2 Tim. 1:9; Heb. 9:15; 1 Peter 2:9; 5:10; Eph. 1:18; 2 Peter 1:10). (2) The attributes ascribed to the church prove it to consist alone of the true, spiritual people of God as such (Eph. 5:27; 1 Peter 3:5; John 10:27; Col. 1:18, 24). (3) The epistles are addressed to the church, and in their salutations explain that phrase as equivalent to "the called," "the saints," "all true worshippers of God"; witness the salutations of 1st and 2d Corinthians, Ephesians, Colossians, 1st and 2d Peter and Jude. The same attributes are ascribed to the members of the true church as such throughout the body of the Epistles (1 Cor. 1:30; 3:16; 6:11, 19; Eph. 2:3–8, 19–22; 1 Thess. 5:4–5; 2 Thess. 2:13; Col. 1:21; 2:10; 1 Peter 2:9).

5th. The inspired apostles have had no successors. (1) There is no evidence that they had such in the New Testament. (2) While provision was made for the regular perpetuation of the offices of presbyter and deacon (1 Tim. 3:1–13), there are no directions given for the perpetuation of the apostolate. (3) There is perfect silence concerning the continued existence of any apostles in the church in the writings of the early centuries. Both the name and the thing ceased. (4) No one ever claiming to be one of their successors have possessed the "signs of an apostle" (2 Cor. 12:12; 1 Cor. 9:1; Gal. 1:1, 12; Acts 1:21–22).

6th. This claim, as it rests upon the authority of the Pope, is utterly unscriptural, because the Pope is not known to Scripture. As it rests upon the authority of the whole body of the bishops, expressed in their general consent, it is unscriptural for the reasons above shown, and it is, moreover, impracticable, since their universal judgment never has been and never can be impartially collected and pronounced.

7th. There can be no infallibility where there is not self-consistency. But as a matter of fact the Papal church has not been self-consistent in her teaching. (1) She has taught different doctrines in different sections and ages. (2) She affirms the infallibility of the holy Scriptures, and at the same time teaches a system plainly and radically inconsistent with their manifest sense; witness the doctrines of the priesthood, the mass, penance, of works, and of Mary worship. Therefore the Church of Rome hides the Scriptures from the people.

8th. If this Romish system be true then genuine spiritual religion ought to flourish in her communion, and all the rest of the world ought to be a moral desert. The facts are notoriously the reverse. If, therefore, we admit that the Romish system is true, we subvert one of the principal evidences of Christianity itself, viz., the self-evidencing light and practical power of true religion, and the witness of the Holy Ghost.

19. By what direct arguments may the doctrine that the Scriptures are the final judge of controversies be established?

That all Christians are to study the Scriptures for themselves, and that in all questions as to God's revealed will the appeal is to the Scriptures alone, is proved by the following facts:
1st. Scripture is perspicuous, see above, questions 11–13.

2d. Scripture is addressed to all Christians as such, see above, question 13.

3d. All Christians are commanded to search the Scriptures, and by them to judge all doctrines and all professed teachers (John 5:39; Acts 17:11; Gal. 1:8; 2 Cor. 4:2; 1 Thess. 5:21; 1 John 4:1–2).

4th. The promise of the Holy Spirit, the author and interpreter of Scripture, is to all Christians as such (Compare John 20:23 with Luke 24:47–49; 1 John 2:20, 27; Rom. 8:9; 1 Cor. 3:16–17).

5th. Religion is essentially a personal matter. Each Christian must know and believe the truth explicitly for himself, on the direct ground of its own moral and spiritual evidence, and not on the mere ground of blind authority. Otherwise faith could not be a moral act, nor could it "purify the heart." Faith derives its sanctifying power from the truth which it immediately apprehends on its own experimental evidence (John 17:17, 19; James 1:18; 1 Peter 1:22).

20. *What is the objection which the Romanists make to this doctrine, on the ground that the church is our only authority for believing that the Scriptures are the word of God?*

Their objection is, that as we receive the Scriptures as the word of God only on the authoritative testimony of the church, our faith in the Scriptures is only another form of our faith in the church, and the authority of the church, being the foundation of that of Scripture, must of course be held paramount.

This is absurd, for two reasons:

1st. The assumed fact is false. The evidence upon which we receive Scripture as the word of God is not the authority of the church, but—(1) God did speak by the apostles and prophets, as is evident (a) from the nature of their doctrine, (b) from their miracles, (c) their prophecies, (d) our personal experience and observation of the power of the truth. (2) These very writings which we possess were written by the apostles, etc., as is evident, (a) from internal evidence, (b) from historical testimony rendered by all competent cotemporaneous witnesses in the church or out of it.

2d. Even if the fact assumed was true, viz., that we know the Scriptures to be from God, on the authority of the church's testimony alone, the conclusion they seek to deduce from it would be absurd. The witness who proves the identity or primogeniture of a prince does not thereby acquire a right to govern the kingdom, or even to interpret the will of the prince.

21. *How is the argument for the necessity of a visible judge, derived from the diversities of sects and doctrines among Protestants, to be answered?*

1st. We do not pretend that the private judgment of Protestants is infallible, but only that when exercised in an humble, believing spirit, it always leads to a competent knowledge of essential truth.

2d. The term Protestant is simply negative, and is assumed by many infidels who protest as much against the Scriptures as they do against Rome. But Bible Protestants, among all their circumstantial differences, are, to a wonderful degree, agreed upon the essentials of faith and practice. Witness their hymns and devotional literature.

3d. The diversity that does actually exist arises from failure in applying faithfully the Protestant principles for which we contend. Men do not simply and without prejudice take their creed from the Bible.

4th. The Catholic church, in her last and most authoritative utterance through the Council of Trent, has proved herself a most indefinite judge. Her doctrinal decisions need an infallible interpreter infinitely more than the Scriptures.

22. *How may it be shown that the Romanist theory, as well as the Protestant, necessarily throws upon the people the obligation of private judgment?*

Is there a God? Has he revealed himself? Has he established a church? Is that church an infallible teacher? Is private judgment a blind leader? Which of all pretended churches is the true one? Every one of these questions evidently must be settled in the private judgment of the inquirer, before he can, rationally or irrationally, give up his private judgment to the direction of the self-asserting church. Thus of necessity Romanists appeal to the Scriptures to prove that the Scriptures can not be understood, and address arguments to the private judgment of men to prove that private judgment is incompetent; thus basing an argument upon that which it is the object of the argument to prove is baseless.

23. *How may it be proved that the people are far more competent to discover what the Bible teaches than to decide, by the marks insisted upon by the Romanists, which is the true church?*

The Romanists, of necessity, set forth certain marks by which the true church is to be discriminated from all counterfeits. These are (1) Unity (through subjection to one visible head, the Pope); (2) Holiness; (3) Catholicity; (4) Apostolicity (involving an uninterrupted succession from the apostles of canonically ordained bishops)—*Catechism of Council of Trent*, Part 1, Ch. 10.[7] Now, the comprehension and intelligent application of these marks involve a great amount of learning and intelligent capacity upon the part of the inquirer. He might as easily prove himself to be descended from Noah by an unbroken series of legitimate marriages, as establish the right of Rome to the last mark. Yet he can not rationally give up the right of studying the Bible for himself until that point is made clear.

Surely the Scriptures, with their self-evidencing spiritual power, make less exhaustive demands upon the resources of private judgment.

ROMAN CATHOLIC DOCTRINE AS TO THE PRIVATE INTERPRETATION OF SCRIPTURE, AND AS TO TRADITION, AND AS TO THE INFALLIBILITY OF THE POPE

1st. AS TO THE INTERPRETATION OF SCRIPTURE.—*Canons and Decrees of Council of Trent*, Session 4: "Moreover the same sacred and holy Synod . . . ordains and declares, that the said old and vulgate edition, which, by the lengthened usage of so many ages, has been

7. *The Catechism of the Council of Trent*, trans. J. Donovan (Baltimore: Fielding Lucas Jr., 1830), 74–78: Part I, Article IX.

approved of in the Church, be, in public lectures, disputations, sermons, and expositions, held as authentic; and that no one is to dare or presume to reject it under any pretext whatever.

"Furthermore, in order to restrain petulant spirits, it decrees that no one, relying on his own skill, shall, in matters of faith and of morals pertaining to the edification of Christian doctrine, wresting the sacred Scripture to his own senses, presume to interpret the said sacred Scripture contrary to that sense which holy mother Church—whose it is to judge of the true sense and interpretation of the Holy Scriptures—hath held and doth hold; or even contrary to the unanimous consent of the Fathers; even though such interpretations were never (intended) to be at any time published."[8]

Dogmatic Decrees of the Vatican Council, ch. 2: "And as the things which the holy Synod of Trent decreed for the good of souls concerning the interpretation of Divine Scripture, in order to curb rebellious spirits, have been wrongly explained by some, we, renewing the said decree, declare this to be their sense, that, in matters of faith and morals, appertaining to the building up of Christian doctrine, that is to be held as the true sense of Holy Scripture which our holy mother Church hath held and holds, to whom it belongs to judge of the true sense of the Holy Scripture; and therefore that it is permitted to no one to interpret the sacred Scripture contrary to this sense, nor, likewise contrary to the unanimous consent of the Fathers."[9]

2d. AS TO TRADITION.—"Professio Fidei Tridentinæ" (A.D. 1564), ii and iii: "I most steadfastly admit and embrace apostolic and ecclesiastic traditions, and all other observances and constitutions of the same Church. I also admit the Holy Scriptures, according to that sense which our holy mother Church has held and does hold, to which it belongs to judge of the true sense and interpretation of the Scriptures; neither will I ever take and interpret them otherwise than according to the unanimous consent of the Fathers."[10]

Council of Trent, Session 4: "And seeing clearly that this truth and discipline are contained in the written books, and the unwritten traditions which, received by the apostles from the mouth of Christ himself, or from the apostles themselves the Holy Ghost dictating, have come down even unto us transmitted as it were from hand to hand."[11]

3d. AS TO THE ABSOLUTE AUTHORITY OF THE POPE.—*Dogmatic Decisions of the Vatican Council*, ch. 3: "Hence we teach and declare that by the appointment of our Lord . . the power of jurisdiction of the Roman Pontiff is immediate, to which all, of whatever rite and dignity, both pastors and faithful, both individually and collectively, are bound, by their duty of hierarchical subordination and true obedience, to submit not only in matters which belong to faith and morals, but also in those that appertain to the discipline and government of the Church throughout the world. . . We further teach and declare that he is the supreme judge of the faithful, and that in all causes, the decision of which belongs to the Church, recourse may be had to his tribunal, and that none may reopen the judgment of the Apostolic See, than whose authority there is no greater, nor can any lawfully review his judgment. Wherefore they err from the right course who assert that it is lawful to appeal from the judgments of the Roman Pontiff to an œcumenical council, as to an authority higher than that of the Roman Pontiff."[12]

---

8. Cf. Schroeder, *Council of Trent*, 18–19.
9. Cf. Schaff, *The Creed of Christendom*, 2:242.
10. Cf. Schaff, *Creeds of Christendom*, 2:207
11. Cf. Schroeder, *Council of Trent*, 17.
12. Cf. Schaff, *Creeds of Christendom*, 2:262–63, 265.

4th. Concerning the Absolute Infallibility of the Pope as the Teacher of the Universal Church.—*Dogmatic Decrees of the Vatican Council*, ch. 4: "Therefore faithfully adhering to the tradition received from the beginning of the Christian faith, for the glory of God our Saviour, the exaltation of the Catholic religion, and the salvation of Christian people, the sacred Council approving, we teach and define that it is a dogma divinely revealed: That the Roman Pontiff when he speaks *ex cathedra*, that is, when in discharge of the office of pastor and doctor of all Christians, by virtue of his supreme Apostolic authority, he defines a doctrine regarding faith or morals to be held by the universal Church, by the divine assistance promised to him in blessed Peter, is possessed of the infallibility with which the divine Redeemer willed that his Church should be endowed for defining doctrine according to faith and morals; and that therefore such definitions of the Roman Pontiff are irreformable of themselves, and not from the consent of the Church. But if any one—which may God avert—presume to contradict this our definition: let him be anathema."[13]

Cardinal Manning in his *Vatican Council* says, "In this definition there are six points to be noted:

"1. First, it defines the meaning of the well-known phrase, *loquens ex cathedra*; that is, speaking from the Seat, or place, or with the authority of the supreme teacher of all Christians, and binding the assent of the Universal Church.

"2. Secondly, the subject matter of the infallible teaching, namely, the doctrine of faith and morals.

"3. Thirdly, the efficient cause of infallibility, that is, the divine assistance promised to Peter, and in Peter to his successors.

"4. Fourthly, the act to which this divine assistance is attached, the defining of doctrines of faith and morals.

"5. Fifthly, the extension of this infallible authority to the limits of the doctrinal office of the Church.

"6. Lastly, the dogmatic value of the definitions *ex cathedra*, namely that they are in themselves irreformable, because in themselves infallible, and not because the Church, or any part or member of the Church, should assent to them."[14]

Dogmatic Decrees of Vatican Council, ch. 4: "For the Holy Spirit was not promised to the successors of Peter, that by his revelation they might make known new doctrine; but that by his assistance they might inviolably keep and faithfully expound the revelation or deposit of faith delivered through the Apostles."[15]

---

13. Cf. Schaff, *Creeds of Christendom*, 2:270–72.

14. Henry Edward Manning, *The Vatican Council and Its Definitions: A Pastoral Letter to the Clergy*, Second Edition (New York: D. & J. Sadlier, 1871), 63.

15. Schaff, *Creeds of Christendom*, 2:269.

The Real Problem of Inspiration

BENJAMIN BRECKINRIDGE WARFIELD

Benjamin Breckinridge Warfield, "The Real Problem of Inspiration," in *Revelation and Inspiration* (Grand Rapids: Baker, 2000), 169–226; reprint of Oxford University Press, 1932; this article was originally printed in *The Presbyterian and Reformed Review* 4 (1893): 177–221; also published as *The Inspiration and Authority of the Bible*, ed. Samuel G. Craig, introduction by Cornelius Van Til (Philadelphia: Presbyterian and Reformed, 1948), 169–226.

Benjamin Breckinridge Warfield (1851–1921) is a great American theologian and biblical exegete. From near Lexington, Kentucky, Warfield studied at both the College of New Jersey and Princeton Seminary, where he studied under Charles Hodge. Originally interested in science, he later felt a call to the ministry while studying in Europe (1876–77). After a brief time in the pastorate, he taught New Testament at Western Seminary (1878–87) and then succeeded A. A. Hodge as professor of systematic theology at Princeton in 1887. He combined great exegetical skills, a thorough knowledge of European scholarship, and a deep commitment to the Westminster Standards. Warfield, in contrast to Charles Hodge, did not write a systematic theology and had a limited engagement in the life of the church. He directed his scholarly attention to several fields of study. In accordance with his earlier teaching post, he thoroughly studied New Testament criticism (see his *An Introduction to the Textual Criticism of the New Testament* [1899]) and the issue of the canon of the New Testament. He also contributed to the history of theology, in particular to the study of Augustine, Calvin, and the Westminster Standards. He made a special contribution to Christology. He also attempted to harmonize Darwinism with his Reformed understanding of providence. Most of his findings were published in articles collected and republished posthumously in multivolume sets.

This selection, "The Real Problem of Inspiration," comes from his work *The Inspiration and Authority of the Bible*. It originally appeared in *The Presbyterian and Reformed*

Review in 1893. Warfield wrote it when biblical higher criticism was starting to impact the American church. Thus, Warfield spoke of "the present problem of inspiration." In a later section, Peter Lillback will address an analogous current "hermeneutical crisis" (cf. chap. 60). Warfield begins by reiterating the classical position of the church that under "the Spirit's superintendence" the words of the Bible are inspired (verbal inspiration) and without error (inerrancy). He then distinguishes between the Bible's teaching about itself from historic evidences (the phenomena of Scripture). The real problem is that denying the doctrine of inspiration amounts to rejecting the Bible as a reliable guide to establish doctrine. Thus it leaves us with the authority of reason alone. Warfield continues by rebutting four common ways of undermining the historic biblical notion of inspiration. He also makes the important clarification that "the plenary inspiration of Scripture," like other doctrines, is grounded on the biblical witness. Hence, though important, it is not to be absolutized. Finally, he concludes by suggesting how to relate it to the sometimes difficult "phenomena" of the Bible. First, phenomena ought to be viewed from the right perspective. Moreover, harmonization should not be forced, but faith always relies on the trustworthiness and harmony of the Bible. Warfield clearly presents important avenues of thought that are still central to the Westminster understanding of inspiration.

Bibliography: J. H. Gerstner. "Warfield's Case for Biblical Inerrancy." Pp. 115–42 in *God's Inerrant Word*. Ed. J. Warwick Montgomery. Minneapolis: Bethany Fellowship, 1974. B. J. Gundlach. "Warfield, Benjamin Breckinridge." Pp. 698–701 in *BDE*. W. Andrew Hoffecker. "Benjamin B. Warfield." Pp. 60–86 in *Reformed Theology in America*. Idem. "Warfield, Benjamin Breckinridge (1851–1921)." Pp. 272–73 in *DP&RTA*. Gary L. W. Johnson, ed. *B. B. Warfield: Essays on His Life and Thought*. Phillipsburg, NJ: P&R Publishing, 2007. Henry Krabbendam. "B. B. Warfield versus G. C. Berkouwer on Scripture." Pp. 413–46 in Norman L. Geisler, ed. *Inerrancy*. Grand Rapids: Zondervan, 1980. Mark A. Noll. "Warfield, Benjamin Breckinridge (1851–1921)." P. 1156 in *EDT*. Idem. "Warfield, Benjamin Breckinridge (1851–1921)." Pp. 716–18 in *NDT*. Jack B. Rogers. "Van Til and Warfield on Scripture in the Westminster Confession. Response by C. Van Til." Pp. 154–71 in E. R. Geehan, ed. *Jerusalem and Athens: Critical Discussions on the Theology and Apologetics of Cornelius Van Til*. Nutley, NJ: Presbyterian and Reformed, 1971. T. F. Torrance. Review of Warfield, *Inspiration and Authority of the Bible*. *Scottish Journal of Theology* 7 (1954): 104–8. Cornelius Van Til. Introduction to *The Inspiration and Authority of the Bible*, by Benjamin Breckinridge Warfield. Philadelphia: Presbyterian and Reformed, 1948. "Warfield, Benjamin Breckinridge." *NSHERK* 12:273. Ethelbert D. Warfield. "Biographical Sketch of Benjamin Breckinridge Warfield." Pp. vi–ix in Benjamin Breckinridge Warfield. *Revelation and Inspiration*. New York: Oxford University Press, 1927. Michael D. Williams. "The Church, a Pillar of Truth: B. B. Warfield's Church Doctrine of Inspiration." Pp. 23–47 in David B. Garner, ed. *Did God Really Say? Affirming the Truthfulness and Trustworthiness of Scripture*. Phillipsburg, NJ: P&R Publishing, 2012. Fred G. Zaspel. *The Theology of B. B. Warfield: A Systematic Summary*. Foreword by Sinclair B. Ferguson. Wheaton, IL: Crossway, 2010.

A great deal is being said of late of "the present problem of inspiration," with a general implication that the Christian doctrine of the plenary inspiration of the Scriptures has been brought into straits by modern investigation, and needs now to adapt itself to certain assured but damaging results of the scientific study of the Bible. Thus, because of an assured "present distress," Canon Cheyne, in a paper read at the English Church Congress of 1888, commended a most revolutionary book of Mr. R. F. Horton's, called *Inspiration and the Bible*,[1] which explains away inspiration properly so called altogether, as the best book he could think of on the subject. And Mr. Charles Gore defends the concessive method of treating the subject of inspiration adopted in *Lux Mundi*, by the plea that the purpose of the writers of that volume, "was 'to succour a distressed faith'; by endeavoring to bring the Christian creed into its right relation to the modern growth of knowledge, scientific, historical, critical."[2] On our side of the water, Dr. Washington Gladden has published a volume which begins by presenting certain "new" views of the structure of the books of the Bible as established facts, and proceeds to the conclusion that: "Evidently neither the theory of verbal inspiration nor the theory of plenary inspiration can be made to fit the facts which a careful study of the writings themselves brings before us. These writings are not inspired in the sense which we have commonly given to that word." According he recommends that under the pressure of these new views we admit not only that the Bible is not "infallible," but that its laws are "inadequate" and "morally defective," and its untrustworthiness as a religious teacher is so great that it gives us in places "blurred and distorted ideas about God and His truth."[3] And Prof. Joseph H. Thayer has published a lecture which represents as necessitated by the facts as now known, such a change of attitude towards the Bible as will reject the whole Reformed doctrine of the Scriptures in favor of a more "Catholic" view which will look upon some of the history recorded in the Bible as only "fairly trustworthy," and will expect no intelligent reader to consider the exegesis of the New Testament writers satisfactory.[4] A radical change in our conception of the Scriptures as the inspired Word of God is thus pressed upon us as now necessary by a considerable number of writers, representing quite a variety of schools of Christian thought.

Nevertheless the situation is not one which can be fairly described as putting the old doctrine of inspiration in jeopardy. The exact state of the case is rather this: that a special school of Old Testament criticism, which has, for some years, been gaining somewhat widespread acceptance of its results, has begun to proclaim that these results having been accepted, a "changed view of the Bible" follows which implies a reconstructed doctrine of inspiration, and, indeed, also a whole new theology. That this changed view of the Bible involves losses is frankly admitted. The nature of these losses is stated by Dr. Sanday in a very interesting little book[5] with an evident effort to avoid as far as possible "making sad the heart of the righteous whom the Lord hath not made sad," as consisting chiefly in making "the intellectual side of the connection between Christian belief and Christian practice a matter of greater difficulty that it has hitherto seemed to be," in rendering it "less easy to find proof texts for this or that," and in making the use of the Bible so much

1. Robert F. Horton, M.A., Late Fellow of New College, Oxford, *Inspiration and the Bible: An Inquiry*, Fourth Edition (London: T. Fisher Unwin, 1889).

2. *Lux Mundi*, Tenth Edition (London: John Murray, 1890), xi.

3. Washington Gladden, *Who Wrote the Bible? A Book for the People* (Boston: Houghton, Mifflin, 1891), 61 (cf. 57, 92–100), 21, 25, 154 (cf. 105, 166, 37, etc.).

4. Joseph Henry Thayer, Professor in Harvard University, *The Change of Attitude Towards the Bible: A Lecture Given under the Auspices of the Boston Board of the American Institutes of Sacred Literature, February 17, 1891* (Boston: Houghton, Mifflin, 1891), 9, 10, 22, 52, 65.

5. William Sanday, *The Oracles of God* (New York: Longmans, 1891), 5, 45, 76.

less simple and less definite in its details that "less educated Christians will perhaps pay more deference to the opinion of the more educated, and to the advancing consciousness of the Church at large." If this means all that it seems to mean, its proclamation of an indefinite Gospel eked out by an appeal to the Church and a scholastic hierarchy, involves a much greater loss than Dr. Sanday appears to think—a loss not merely of the Protestant doctrine of the perspicuity of the Scriptures, but with it of all that that doctrine is meant to express and safeguard—the loss of the Bible itself to the plain Christian man for all practical uses, and the delivery of his conscience over to the tender mercies of his human instructors, whether ecclesiastical or scholastic. Dr. Briggs is more blunt and more explicit in his description of the changes which he thinks have been wrought. "I will tell you what criticism has destroyed," he says in an article published a couple of years ago. "It has destroyed many false theories about the Bible; it has destroyed the theory of inerrancy; it has destroyed the false doctrine that makes the inspiration depend upon its attachment to a holy man."[6] And he goes on to remark further "that Biblical criticism is at the bottom" of the "reconstruction that is going on throughout the Church"—"the demand for revision of creeds and change in methods of worship and Christian work." It is clear enough, then, that a problem has been raised with reference to inspiration by this type of criticism. But this is not equivalent to saying that the established doctrine of inspiration has been put in jeopardy. For there is criticism and criticism. And though it may not be unnatural for these scholars themselves to confound the claims of criticism with the validity of their own critical methods and the soundness of their own critical conclusions, the Christian world can scarcely be expected to acquiesce in the identification. It has all along been pointing out that they were traveling on the wrong road; and now when their conclusions clash with well-established facts, we simply note that the wrong road has not unnaturally led them to the wrong goal. In a word, it is not the established doctrine of inspiration that is brought into distress by the conflict, but the school of Old Testament criticism which is at present fashionable. It is now admitted that the inevitable issue of this type of criticism comes into collision with the established fact of the plenary inspiration of the Bible and the well-grounded Reformed doctrine of Holy Scripture based on this fact.[7] The cry is therefore, and somewhat impatiently, raised that this fact and this doctrine must "get out of the way," and permit criticism to rush on to its bitter goal. But facts are somewhat stubborn things, and are sometimes found to prove rather the test of theories which seek to make them their sport.

Nevertheless, though the strain of the present problem should thus be thrown upon the shoulders to which it belongs, it is important to keep ourselves reminded that the doctrine of inspiration which has become established in the Church, is open to all legitimate criti-

6. The article appeared in *The Christian Union*, but we quote it from *Public Opinion*, 10, 24 (March 25, 1891): 576.

7. This remark, of course, does not imply that there are none who assert that the results of this type of criticism leave "inspiration" untouched. Dr. S. R. Driver does not stand alone when he says, in the Preface to his *Introduction to the Literature of the Old Testament* (1891): "Criticism in the hands of Christian scholars does not banish or destroy the inspiration of the Old Testament; it *presupposes* it" (p. xxii). But Prof. Driver would be the last to maintain that the "inspiration" which criticism leaves to the Old Testament is what the Church has understood by the plenary inspiration of the Bible. Accordingly, Prof. James Robertson speaks directly to the point when he remarks in the Preface to the First Edition of his *Early Religion of Israel* (New York: E. R. Herrick, 1892), xiii, that "such scholars would do an invaluable service to the Church, at the present time, if they would explain what they mean by inspiration in this connection." The efforts to do this, on our side of the water, are not reassuring. On the relation of the new views to inspiration see the lucid statement by Dr. Edwin Cone Bissell in "The Pentateuchal Analysis and Inspiration," *The Hartford Seminary Record* 2, 1 (October 1891): 5–20.

cism, and is to continue to be held only as, and so far as, it is ever anew critically tested and approved. And in view of the large bodies of real knowledge concerning the Bible which the labors of a generation of diligent critical study have accumulated, and of the difficulty which is always experienced in the assimilation of new knowledge and its correlation with previously ascertained truth, it is becoming to take this occasion to remind ourselves of the foundation on which this doctrine rests, with a view to inquiring whether it is really endangered by any assured results of recent Biblical study. For such an investigation we must start, of course, from a clear conception of what the Church doctrine of inspiration is, and of the basis on which it is held to be the truth of God. Only thus can we be in a position to judge how it can be affected on critical grounds, and whether modern Biblical criticism has reached any assured results which must or may "destroy" it.

The Church, then, has held from the beginning that the Bible is the Word of God in such a sense that its words, though written by men and bearing indelibly impressed upon them the marks of their human origin, were written, nevertheless, under such an influence of the Holy Ghost as to be also the words of God, the adequate expression of His mind and will. It has always recognized that this conception of co-authorship implies that the Spirit's superintendence extends to the choice of the words by the human authors (verbal inspiration[8]), and preserves its product from everything inconsistent with a divine authorship—thus securing, among other things, that entire truthfulness which is everywhere presupposed in and asserted for Scripture by the Biblical writers (inerrancy). Whatever minor variations may now and again have entered into the mode of statement, this has always been the core of the Church doctrine of inspiration. And along with many other modes of commending and defending it, the primary ground on which it has been held by the Church as the true doctrine is that it is the doctrine of the Biblical writers themselves, and has therefore the whole mass of evidence for it which goes to show that the Biblical writers are trustworthy as doctrinal guides. It is the testimony of the Bible itself to its own origin and character as the Oracles of the Most High, that has led the Church to her acceptance of it as such, and to her dependence on it not only for her doctrine of Scripture, but for the whole body of her doctrinal teaching, which is looked upon by her as divine because drawn from this divinely given fountain of truth.

Now if this doctrine is to be assailed on critical grounds, it is very clear that, first of all, criticism must be required to proceed against the evidence on which it is based. This evidence, it is obvious, is twofold. First, there is the exegetical evidence that the doctrine held and taught by the Church is the doctrine held and taught by the Biblical writers themselves. And secondly, there is the whole mass of evidence—internal and external, objective and subjective, historical and philosophical, human and divine—which goes to show that the Biblical writers are trustworthy as doctrinal guides. If they are trustworthy teachers of doctrine and if they held and taught this doctrine, then this doctrine is true, and is to be accepted and acted upon as true by us all. In that case, any objections brought against the doctrine from other spheres of inquiry are inoperative; it being a settled logical principle that so long as the proper evidence by which a proposition is established remains unrefuted, all so-called objections brought against it pass out of the category of objections to its truth

---

8. It ought to be unnecessary to protest again against the habit of representing the advocates of "verbal inspiration" as teaching that the mode of inspiration was by dictation. The matter is fully explained in the paper: Profs. A. A. Hodge and B. B. Warfield, *Inspiration* (Philadelphia: Presbyterian Board of Publication, 1881), 19–23.

into the category of difficulties to be adjusted to it. If criticism is to assail this doctrine, therefore, it must proceed against and fairly overcome one or the other element of its proper proof. It must either show that this doctrine is not the doctrine of the Biblical writers, or else it must show that the Biblical writers are not trustworthy as doctrinal guides. If a fair criticism evinces that this is not the doctrine of the Biblical writers, then of course it has "destroyed" the doctrine which is confessedly based on that supposition. Failing in this, however, it can "destroy" the doctrine, strictly speaking, only by undermining its foundation in our confidence in the trustworthiness of the Scripture as a witness to doctrine. The possibility of this latter alternative must, no doubt, be firmly faced in our investigation of the phenomena of the Bible; but the weight of the evidence, be it small or great, for the general trustworthiness of the Bible as a source of doctrine, throws itself, in the form of a presumption, against the reality of any phenomena alleged to be discovered which make against its testimony. No doubt this presumption may be overcome by clear demonstration. But clear demonstration is requisite. For, certainly, if it is critically established that what is sometimes called, not without a touch of scorn, "the traditional doctrine," is just the Bible's own doctrine of inspiration, the real conflict is no longer with "the traditional theory of inspiration," but with the credibility of the Bible. The really decisive question among Christian scholars (among whom alone, it would seem, could a question of inspiration be profitably discussed), is thus seen to be, "What does an exact and scientific exegesis determine to be the Biblical doctrine of inspiration?"

The Biblical Doctrine of Inspiration Clear

The reply to this question is, however, scarcely open to doubt. The stricter and the more scientific the examination is made, the more certain does it become that the authors of the New Testament held a doctrine of inspiration quite as high as the Church doctrine. This may be said, indeed, to be generally admitted by untrammeled critics, whether of positive or of negative tendencies. Thus, for instance—to confine our examples to a few of those who are not able personally to accept the doctrine of the New Testament writers—Archdeacon Farrar is able to admit that Paul "shared, doubtless, in the views of the later Jewish schools—the Tanaim and Amoraim—on the nature of inspiration. These views . . . made the words of Scripture coextensive and identical with the words of God."[9] So also Otto Pfleiderer allows that Paul "fully shared the assumption of his opponents, the irrefragable authority of the letter as the immediately revealed Word of God."[10] Similarly, Tholuck recognizes that the application of the Old Testament made by the author of the Epistle to the Hebrews, "rests on the strictest view of inspiration, since passages where God is not the speaker are cited as words of God or of the Holy Ghost (Heb. 1:6–8; 4:4, 7; 7:21; 3:7; 10:15)."[11] This fact is worked out also with convincing clearness by the writer of an odd and sufficiently free Scotch book published a few years ago, who formulates his conclusion in the words: "There is no doubt that the author of Hebrews, in common with the other New Testament writers, regards the whole Old Testament as having been dictated by the Holy Ghost, or, as we should say, plenarily, and, as it were, mechanically inspired."[12] And more recently still Prof. Stapfer,

9. F. W. Farrar, *The Life and Work of Paul* (New York: E. P. Dutton, 1880), 1:49.
10. Otto Pfleiderer, *Paulinism*, trans. Eward Peters (London: Williams & Norgate, 1877), 1:88.
11. August Tholuck, "The Citations of the Old Testament in the New," *Bibliotheca Sacra* 11 (July 1854): 612.
12. James Stuart, *Principles of Christianity* (London: Williams & Norgate, 1888), 346.

of Paris,[13] though himself denying the reality not only of an infallibility for the Bible, but also of any inspiration for it at all, declaring that "the doctrine of an Inspiration distinct from Revelation and legitimating it, is an error"—yet cannot deny that Paul held a different doctrine—a doctrine which made the Old Testament to him the divine Word and the term, "It is written," equivalent to "God says."[14]

A detailed statement of the evidence is scarcely needed to support a position allowed by such general consent. But it will not be improper to adjoin a brief outline of the grounds on which the general consent rests. In the circumstances, however, we may venture to dispense with an argument drawn up from our own point of view,[15] and content ourselves with an extract from the brief statement of the grounds of his decision given by another of those critical scholars who do not believe the doctrine of plenary inspiration, but yet find themselves constrained to allow that it is the doctrine of the New Testament writers. Richard Rothe seeks, wrongly, to separate Christ's doctrine of the Old Testament from that of the apostles; our Lord obviously spoke of the Scriptures of His people out of the same fundamental conception of their nature and divinity as His apostles. But he more satisfactorily outlines the doctrine of the apostles as follows:

> We find in the New Testament authors the same theoretical view of the Old Testament and the same practice as to its use, as among the Jews of the time in general, although at the same time in the handling of the same conceptions and principles on both sides, the whole difference between the new Christian spirit and that of contemporary Judaism appears in sharp distinctness. Our authors look upon the words of the Old Testament as *immediate* words of God, and adduce them expressly as such, even those of them which are not at all related as direct sayings of God. They see nothing at all in the sacred volume which is simply the word of its human author and not at the same time the very Word of God Himself. In all that stands 'written' God Himself speaks to them, and so entirely are they habituated to think only of this that they receive the sacred Word written itself, as such, as God's Word, and hear God speaking in it *immediately*, without any thought of the human persons who appear in it as speaking and acting. The *historical* conception of their Bible is altogether foreign to them. Therefore they cite the abstract ἡ γραφή or αἱ γραφαί or γραφαὶ ἅγιαι (Rom. 1:2), or again τὰ ἱερὰ γράμματα (2 Tim. 3:15), without naming any special author, as self-evidently God's Word, e.g., John 7:38; 10:35; 19:36–37; 20:9; Acts 1:16; James 2:8; Rom. 9:17; Gal. 3:8, 22; 4:30; 1 Peter 2:6; 2 Peter 1:20; etc.; and introduce Old Testament citations with the formulas, now that God (Matt. 1:22; 2:15; Acts 4:25; 13:34; Rom. 1:2), now that the Holy Spirit (Acts 1:16; 28:25; Heb. 3:7; 9:8; 10:15; cf. also Acts 4:25; 1 Peter 1:11; 2 Peter 2:20) so speaks or has spoken. The Epistle to the Hebrews unhesitatingly adduces with a ὁ θεὸς λέγει and the like, even passages in which God is spoken of expressly in the third person (1:6–8 *seq.*; 4:4, 7; 7:21; 10:30), and even (1:10) cites a passage in which in the Old Testament text God Himself (according to the view of the author it is, however, the Son of God) is addressed, as a word spoken by God. In 2 Timothy 3:16

13. "Séance de Rentrée des Cours de la Faculté de Théologie Protestante de Paris, le Mardi 3 Novembre, 1891." *Leçon d'Ouverture de M. le Professeur Edmond Stapfer* (Paris: Fischbacher, 1891), 26, 42.

14. Compare also Abraham Kuenen, *The Prophets and Prophecy in Israel* (London: Longmans, Green and co., 1877), 449; Edward Reuss, *History of Christian Theology in the Apostolic Age*, (London: Hodder & Stoughton, 1872), 1:352–54; Eduard Riehm, *Der Lehrbegriff des Hebräerbriefes* (Basel: Balmer & Riehm, 1867), 1:173, 177, etc.

15. Those who wish to see a very conclusive and thorough statement of Paul's doctrine of inspiration should consult Dr. George T. Purves's paper on "St. Paul and Inspiration," published in *The Presbyterian and Reformed Review* 13 (January 1893): 1–24. For our Lord's doctrine, see Dr. William Caven's paper on "The Testimony of Christ to the Old Testament," *The Presbyterian and Reformed Review* 11 (July 1892): 401–20.

the ἱερὰ γράμματα (verse 15) are expressly called θεόπνευστα, however the sentence may be construed or expounded; and however little a special theory of the inspiration of the Bible can be drawn from an expression of such breadth of meaning, nevertheless this *datum* avails to prove that the author shared in general the view of his Jewish contemporaries as to the peculiar character of the Old Testament books, and it is of especial importance inasmuch as it attributes the inspiration, without the least ambiguity, directly to the writings themselves, and not merely to their authors, the prophets. No doubt, in the teaching of the apostles the conception of prophetic inspiration to which it causally attributes the Old Testament, has not yet the sharp exactness of our ecclesiastical dogmatic conception; but it stands, nevertheless, in a very express analogy with it. . . . Moreover, it must be allowed that the apostolical writers, although they nowhere say it expressly, refer the prophetic inspiration also to the *actus scribendi* of the Biblical authors. The whole style and method of their treatment of the Old Testament text manifestly presupposes in them this view of this matter, which was at the time the usual one in the Jewish schools. With Paul particularly this is wholly incontrovertibly the case. For only on that view could he, in such passages as Romans 4:23–24; 15:4; 1 Corinthians 9:10; 10:11—in which he distinguishes between the occurrence of the Old Testament facts and the recording of them—maintain of the latter that it was done with express teleological reference to the needs of the New Testament believers, at least so far as the selection of the matter to be described is concerned; and only on that view could he argue on the details of the letter of the Old Testament Scriptures, as he does in Galatians 3:15–16. We can, moreover, trace the continuance of this view in the oldest post-apostolical Church. . . . So far as the Old Testament is concerned, our ecclesiastical-dogmatic doctrine of inspiration can, therefore, in very fact, appeal to the authority, not indeed of the Redeemer Himself—for He stands in an entirely neutral attitude towards it—but no doubt of the apostles.[16]

A keen controversialist like Rothe does not fail, of course—as the reader has no doubt observed—to accompany his exposition of the apostolic doctrine with many turns of expression designed to lessen its authority in the eyes of the reader, and to prepare the way for his own refusal to be bound by it; but neither does he fail to make it clear that this doctrine, although it is unacceptable to him, is the apostles' doctrine. The apostles' *doctrine*, let it be observed that we say. For even so bald a statement as Rothe's will suffice to uncover the fallacy of the assertion, which is so often made, that the doctrine of verbal inspiration is based on a few isolated statements of Scripture to the neglect, if not to the outrage, of its phenomena—a form of remark into which even so sober a writer as Dr. W. G. Blaikie has lately permitted himself to fall.[17] Nothing, obviously, could be more opposite to the fact. The doctrine of verbal inspiration is based on the broad foundation of the carefully ascertained *doctrine* of the Scripture writers on the subject. It is a product of Biblical Theology. And if men will really ask, not, "What do the creeds teach? What do the theologians say? What is the authority of the Church? but, What does the Bible itself teach us?" and "fencing off from the Scriptures all the speculations, all the dogmatic elaborations, all the doctrinal adaptations that have been made in the history of doctrine in the Church," "limit themselves strictly to the theology of the Bible itself"—according to the excellent programme outlined by Dr. Briggs[18]—it is to the

16. Richard Rothe, *Zur Dogmatik*, 2nd ed. (Gotha: F. A. Perthes, 1869), 177–81.
17. William G. Blaikie, *Letter to the Rev. Andrew A. Bonar, D.D.: On a Manifesto Issued by Him on the Dods and Bruce Cases* (Edinburgh: Macniven & Wallace, 1890).
18. Charles A. Briggs, "The Edward Robinson Chair of Biblical Theology in the Union Theological Seminary," *The Authority of Holy Scripture: An Inaugural Address* (New York: Scribner, 1891), 5–6.

doctrine of verbal inspiration, as we have seen, that they must come. It is not Biblical criticism that has "destroyed" verbal inspiration, but Dr. Briggs' scholastic theories that have drawn him away in this matter from the pure deliverances of Biblical Theology.[19]

Much more, of course, does such a statement as even Rothe's uncover the even deeper error of the assertion latterly becoming much too common, that, the doctrine of verbal inspiration, as a recent writer puts it, "is based wholly upon an *a priori* assumption of what inspiration *must be*, and not upon the Bible as it actually exists."[20] It is based wholly upon an exegetical fact. It is based on the exegetical fact that our Lord and His apostles held this doctrine of Scripture, and everywhere deal with the Scriptures of the Old Testament in accordance with it, as the very Word of God, even in their narrative parts. This is a commonplace of exegetical science, the common possession of the critical schools of the left and of the right, a prominent and unmistakable deliverance of Biblical Theology. And on the establishment of it as such, the real issue is brought out plainly and stringently. If criticism has made such discoveries as to necessitate the abandonment of the doctrine of plenary inspiration, it is not enough to say that we are compelled to abandon only a "particular theory of inspiration," though that is true enough. We must go on to say that that "particular theory of inspiration" is the theory of the apostles and of the Lord, and that in abandoning *it* we are abandoning *them* as our doctrinal teachers and guides, as our "exegetes," in the deep and rich sense of that word which Dr. Vincent vindicates for it.[21] This real issue is to be kept clearly before us, and faced courageously. Nothing is gained by closing our eyes to the seriousness of the problem which we are confronting. Stated plainly it is just this: Are the New Testament writers trustworthy guides in doctrine? Or are we at liberty to reject their authority, and frame contrary doctrines for ourselves? If the latter pathway be taken, certainly the doctrine of plenary inspiration is not the only doctrine that is "destroyed," and the labor of revising our creeds may as well be saved and the shorter process adopted of simply throwing them away. No wonder we are told that the same advance in knowledge which requires a changed view of the Bible necessitates also a whole new theology. If the New Testament writers are not trustworthy as teachers of doctrine and we have to go elsewhere for the source and norm of truth as to God and duty and immortality, it will not be strange if a very different system of doctrine from that delivered by the Scriptures and docilely received from them by the Church, results.

And now, having uncovered the precise issue which is involved in the real problem of inspiration, let us look at it at various angles and thus emphasize in turn two or three of the more important results that spring from it.

I. Modifications of the Biblical Doctrine Undermine the Authority of the Scriptures

First, we emphasize the fact that, this being the real state of the case, we cannot modify the doctrine of plenary inspiration in any of its essential elements without undermining our confidence in the authority of the apostles as teachers of doctrine.

19. The substance of some of the preceding paragraphs was printed in *The Homiletical Review* 21 (May 1891): 410–16, under the title of "The Present Problem of Inspiration."

20. "Exegesis." An address delivered at the Opening of the Autumn Term of Union Theological Seminary, September 24, 1891. Marvin R. Vincent, D.D., *Exegesis* (New York: Scribner, 1891), 40.

21. *Exegesis*, 5–12.

Logically, this is an immediate corollary of the proposition already made good. Historically, it is attested by the driftage of every school of thought which has sought to find a ground of faith in any lower than the Church's doctrine of a plenarily inspired Bible. The authority which cannot assure of a hard fact is soon not trusted for a hard doctrine. Sooner or later, in greater or less degree, the authority of the Bible in doctrine and life is replaced by or subordinated to that of reason, or of the feelings, or of the "Christian consciousness"— the "conscious experience by the individual of the Christian faith"—or of that corporate Christian consciousness which so easily hardens into simple ecclesiastical domination. What we are to accept as the truth of God is a comparatively easy question, if we can open our Bibles with the confident belief that what we read there is commended to us by a fully credible "Thus saith the Lord." But in proportion as we allow this or that element in it not to be safeguarded to us by this divine guarantee, do we begin to doubt the trustworthiness of more and more of the message delivered, and to seek other grounds of confidence than the simple "It is written" which sufficed for the needs of our Lord and His apostles. We have seen Dr. Sanday pointing to "the advancing consciousness of the Church at large," along with the consensus of scholars, as the ground of acceptance of doctrines as true, which will be more and more turned to when men can no longer approach the Bible so simply as heretofore. This is the natural direction in which to look, for men trained to lay that great stress on institutional Christianity which leads Mr. Gore to describe the present situation as one in which "it is becoming more and more difficult to believe in the Bible without believing in the Church."[22] Accordingly Dr. Sterrett also harmonizes his Hegelianism and Churchliness in finding the ground of Christian certitude in the "communal Christian consciousness," which is defined as the Church, as "objective, authoritative reason for every Christian," to which he must subordinate his individual reason.[23] Men of more individualistic training fall back rather on personal reason or the individual "Christian consciousness"; but all alike retire the Bible as a source of doctrine behind some other safeguard of truth.

It may not be without interest or value to subject the various pathways which men tread in seeking to justify a lower view of Scripture than that held and taught by the New Testament writers, to a somewhat close scrutiny, with a view to observing how necessarily they logically involve a gradual undermining of the trustworthiness of those writers as teachers of doctrine. From the purely formal point of view proper to our present purpose, four types of procedure may be recognized.

CHRIST VERSUS THE APOSTLES

1. There is first, that, of which Richard Rothe is an example, which proceeds by attempting to establish a distinction between the teaching of Christ and the teaching of His apostles, and refusing the latter in favor of the former.

As we have already remarked, this distinction cannot be made good. Rothe's attempt to establish it proceeds on the twofold ground, on the one hand, of an asserted absence from our Lord's dealings with the Scriptures of those extreme facts of usage of it as the Word of God, and of those extreme statements concerning its divine character, on the ground of

---

22. Charles Gore, ed. *Lux Mundi*, American Edition (New York: John W. Lovell, 1890), 283.
23. J. MacBride Sterrett, D.D., Professor in Seabury Divinity School, *Reason and Authority in Religion* (New York: T. Whittaker, 1891), 176.

which in the apostles' dealing with it we must recognize their high doctrine of Scripture; and on the other hand, of an asserted presence in Christ's remarks concerning Scripture of hints that He did not share the conception of Scripture belonging to contemporary Judaism, which conception we know to have been the same high doctrine that was held by the apostles. He infers, therefore, that the apostles, in this matter, represent only the current Jewish thought in which they were bred, while Christ's divine originality breaks away from this and commends to us a new and more liberal way.

But in order to make out the first member of the twofold ground on which he bases this conclusion, Rothe has to proceed by explaining away, by means of artificial exegetical expedients, a number of facts of usage and deliverances as to Scripture, in which our Lord's dealings with Scripture culminate, and which are altogether similar in character and force to those on the basis of which he infers the apostles' high doctrine. These are such passages as the quotation in Matthew 19:4–5, of Adam's words as God's Word, which Lechler appeals to as decisive just as Rothe appeals to similar passages in the epistles—but which Rothe sets aside in a footnote simply with the remark that it is not decisive here; the assertion in John 10:35, that the "Scripture cannot be broken," which he sets aside as probably not a statement of Christ's own opinion but an *argumentum ad hominem*, and as in any case not available here, since it does not explicitly assert that the authority it ascribes to Scripture is due "to its origination by inspiration"—but which, as Dr. Robert Watts has shown anew,[24] is conclusive for our Saviour's view of the entire infallibility of the whole Old Testament; the assertion in Matthew 5:18 (and in Luke 16:17) that not "one jot or one tittle (ἰῶτα ἓν ἢ μία κεραία) shall pass away from the law till all be fulfilled," which he sets aside with the remark that it is not the law-codex, but the law itself, that is here spoken of, forgetful of the fact that it is the law itself *as written* that the Lord has in mind, in which form alone, moreover, do "yodhs and horns" belong to it; the assertion in Matthew 22:43, that it was "in the Spirit" that David called the Messiah, "Lord," in the one hundred and tenth Psalm which he sets aside with the remark that this does prove that Jesus looked upon David as a prophet, but not necessarily that he considered the one hundred and tenth Psalm inspired, as indeed he does not say γράφει but καλεῖ—forgetful again that it is to the written David alone that Christ makes His appeal and on the very language written in the Psalm that He founds His argument.

No less, in order to make out the second member of the ground on which he bases his conclusion, does Rothe need to press passages which have as their whole intent and effect to rebuke the scribes for failure to understand and properly to use Scripture, into indications of rejection on Christ's part of the authority of the Scriptures to which both He and the scribes appealed. Lest it should be thought incredible that such a conclusion should be drawn from such premises, we transcribe Rothe's whole statement.

24. Robert Watts, D.D., *Faith and Inspiration*, The Carey Lectures for 1884 (London: Hodder & Stoughton, 1885), 139. "The sole question is: What, according to the language employed by Him, was His estimate of the Old Testament Scripture? It will be observed that He does not single out the passage on which He bases His argument, and testify of it that it is unbreakable, making its infallibility depend on His authority. Stated formally, His argument is as follows: Major—The Scripture cannot be broken. Minor—'I said ye are God's,' is written in your law, which is Scripture. Conclusion—'I said ye are God's' cannot be broken. . . . He argues the infallibility of the clause on which He founds His argument from the infallibility of the record in which it occurs. According to His infallible estimate, it was sufficient proof of the infallibility of any sentence or phrase of a clause, to show that it constituted a portion of what the Jews called 'the Scripture' (ἡ γραφή)."

On the other hand, we conclude with great probability that the Redeemer did *not* share the conception of His Israelitish contemporaries as to the inspiration of their Bible, as stated above, from the fact that He repeatedly expresses his dissatisfaction with the manner usual among them of looking upon and using the sacred books. He tells the scribes to their face that they do not understand the Scriptures (Matt. 22:29; Mark 12:24), and that it is delusion for them to think to possess eternal life in *them*, therefore in a *book* (John 5:39), even as He also (in the same place) seems to speak disapprovingly of their searching of the Scriptures, because it proceeds from such a perverted point of view.[25]

Thus Jesus' *appeal* to the Scriptures as testifying to Him, and His rebuke to the Jews for not following them while professing to honor them, are made to do duty as a proof that He did not ascribe plenary authority to them.[26]

Furthermore, Rothe's whole treatment of the matter omits altogether to make account of the great decisive consideration of the general tone and manner of Christ's allusions and appeal to the Scriptures, which only culminate in such passages as he has attempted to explain away, and which not only are inconsistent with any other than the same high view of their authority, trustworthiness and inspiration, as that which Rothe infers from similar phenomena to have been the conception of the apostles, but also are necessarily founded on it as its natural expression. The distinction attempted to be drawn between Christ's doctrine of Holy Scripture and that of His apostles is certainly inconsistent with the facts.

But we are more concerned at present to point out that the attempt to draw this distinction must result in undermining utterly all confidence in the New Testament writers as teachers of doctrine. So far as the apostles are concerned, indeed, it would be more correct to say that it is the outgrowth and manifestation of an already present distrust of them as teachers of doctrine. Its very principle is appeal from apostolic teaching to that of Christ, on the ground that the former is not authoritative. How far this rejection of apostolic authority goes is evidenced by the mode of treatment vouchsafed to it. Immediately on drawing out the apostles' doctrine of inspiration, Rothe asks, "But now what dogmatic value has this fact?" And on the ground that "by their fruits ye shall know them," he proceeds to declare that the apostles' doctrine of Scripture led them into such a general use and mode of interpretation of Scripture as Rothe deems wholly unendurable.[27] It is not, then, merely the teaching of the apostles as to what the Scriptures are, but their teaching as to what those Scriptures teach, in which Rothe finds them untrustworthy. It would be impossible but that the canker should eat still more deeply.

Nor is it possible to prevent it from spreading to the undermining of the trustworthiness of even the Lord's teaching itself, for the magnifying of which the distinction purports to be drawn. The artificial manner in which the testimony of the Lord to the authority of the Scriptures is explained away in the attempt to establish the distinction, might be pleaded indeed as an indication that trust in it was not very deeply rooted. And there are other

---

25. Rothe, *Zur Dogmatik*, 177.

26. Compare Heinrich A. W. Meyer on John 5:38–40, *Critical and Exegetical Commentary on the New Testament: Part II. The Gospel of John*, E. T. (Edinburgh: T. & T. Clark, 1879), 1:262, note: "Even Rothe . . . takes δοκεῖτε in the sense of a *delusion*, namely, that they possessed eternal *life* in a *book*. Such explanations are opposed to the high veneration manifested by Jesus towards the Holy Scriptures, especially apparent in John."

27. *Zur Dogmatik*, 181–82.

indications that had the Lord been explained to be of the apostles' mind as to Scripture, a way would have been found to free us from the duty of following His teaching.[28] For even *His* exegesis is declared not to be authoritative, seeing that "exegesis is essentially a scientific function, and conditioned on the existence of scientific means, which in relation to the Old Testament were completely at the command of Jesus as little as of His contemporaries"; and the principle of partial limitation at least to the outlook of His day which is involved in such a statement is fully accepted by Rothe.[29] All this may, however, be thought more or less personal to Rothe's own mental attitude, whereas the ultimate undermining of our Lord's authority as teacher of doctrine, as well as that of His apostles, is logically essential to the position assumed.

This may be made plain at once by the very obvious remark that we have no Christ except the one whom the apostles have given to us. Jesus Himself left no treatises on doctrine. He left no written dialogues. We are dependent on the apostles for our whole knowledge of Him, and of what He taught. The portraiture of Jesus which has glorified the world's literature as well as blessed all ages and races with the revelation of a God-man come down from heaven to save the world, is limned by his followers' pencils alone. The record of that teaching which fell from His lips as living water, which if a man drink of he shall never thirst again, is a record by his followers' pens alone. They have painted for us, of course, the Jesus that they knew, and as they knew Him. They have recorded for us the teachings that they heard, and as they heard them. Whatever untrustworthiness attaches to them as deliverers of doctrine, must in some measure shake also our confidence in their report of what their Master was and taught.

But the logic cuts even deeper. For not only have we no Christ but Him whom we receive at the apostles' hands, but this Christ is committed to the trustworthiness of the apostles as teachers. His credit is involved in their credit. He represents His words on earth as but the foundation of one great temple of doctrine, the edifice of which was to be built up by Him through their mouths, as they spoke moved by His Spirit; and thus He makes Himself an accomplice before the fact in all they taught. In proportion as they are discredited as doctrinal guides, in that proportion He is discredited with them. By the promise of the Spirit, He has forever bound His trustworthiness with indissoluble bands to the trustworthiness of His accredited agents in founding His Church, and especially by that great promise recorded for us in John 16:12–15:

> I have yet many things to say unto you, but ye cannot bear them now. Howbeit when he, the Spirit of truth, is come, he will guide you into all truth; for he shall not speak of himself; but whatsoever he shall hear, that shall he speak: and he will show you things to come. He shall glorify me: for he shall receive of mine, and shall show it unto you. All things that the Father hath are mine: therefore said I, that he shall take of mine and shall show it unto you.

28. Ibid., 174–75.

29. Even on an extreme Kenotic view, it is, however, not so certain that *error* should be attributed to the God-man. Prof. Augustin Gretillat, of Neuchâtel, a Kenotist of the type of Gess and his own colleague Godet, is able to teach that "by reason of the relation which unites the intelligence with the will," our Lord must needs be free not only from sin, but also from all error (*Exposé de théologie systématique* [Paris: Fishbacher, 1899], 4:288). Tholuck occupied a position similar to Rothe's; yet he reminds us that: "Proofs might be brought to show that, even in questions pertaining to learned exegesis"— which are such as our Lord needed to *learn* as a man—"such as those concerning the historical connection of a passage, the author and age of a book, an original spiritual discernment without the culture of the schools may often divine the truth" (Tholuck, "Citations of the Old Testament in the New," 615).

Says Dr. C. W. Hodge:

> It is impossible to conceive how the authority of the Master could be conveyed to the teaching of the disciples more emphatically than is here done by Christ. He identifies His teaching and the teaching of the Spirit as parts of one whole; His teaching is carrying out My teaching, it is calling to remembrance what I have told you; it is completing what I have begun. And to make the unity emphatic, He explains why He had reserved so much of His own teaching, and committed the work of revelation to the Spirit. He, in His incarnation and life, comprised all saving truth. He was the revealer of God and the truth and the life. But while some things He had taught while yet with them, He had many things to say which must be postponed because they could not yet bear them. . . . If Christ has referred us to the apostles as teachers of the truths which He would have us know, certainly this primary truth of the authority of the Scriptures themselves can be no exception. All questions as to the extent of this inspiration, as to its exclusive authority, as to whether it extends to words as well as doctrines, as to whether it is infallible or inerrant, or not, are simply questions to be referred to the Word itself.[30]

In such circumstances the attempt to discriminate against the teaching of the apostles in favor of that of Christ, is to contradict the express teaching of Christ Himself, and thus to undermine our confidence in it. We cannot both believe Him and not believe Him. The cry, "Back to Christ!" away from all the imaginations of men's hearts and the cobweb theories which they have spun, must be ever the cry of every Christian heart. But the cry, "Back to Christ!" away from the teachings of His apostles, whose teachings He Himself represents as His own, only delivered by His Spirit through their mouths, is an invitation to desert Christ Himself. It is an invitation to draw back from the Christ of the Bible to some Christ of our own fancy, from the only real to some imaginary Christ. It is to undermine the credit of the whole historical revelation in and through the Christ of God, and to cast us for the ascertainment and authentication of truth on the native powers of our own minds.

ACCOMMODATION OR IGNORANCE?

2. Another method is that of those who seek to preserve themselves from the necessity of accepting the doctrine of inspiration held by the writers of the New Testament, by representing it as merely a matter of accommodation to the prejudices of the Jews, naturally if not necessarily adopted by the first preachers of the Gospel in their efforts to commend to their contemporaries their new teaching as to the way of life.

This position is quite baldly stated by a recent Scotch writer, to whose book, written with a frank boldness, a force and a logical acumen which are far above the common, too little heed has been paid as an indication of the drift of the times.[31] Says Mr. James Stuart:

> The apostles had not merely to reveal the Gospel scheme of salvation to their own and all subsequent ages, but they had to present it in such a form, and support it by such arguments, as should commend it to their more immediate hearers and readers. Notwithstanding its essentially universal character, the Gospel, as it appears in the New Testament, is couched in a particular form, suited to the special circumstances of a particular age and nation. Before

---

30. Sermon on "The Promise of the Spirit," in *Princeton Sermons*, by the Faculty of the Seminary (New York: Fleming H. Revell, 1893), 33. The whole of this noble sermon should be read.

31. James Stuart, M.A., *The Principles of Christianity*, 67–69.

the Gospel could reach the hearts of those to whom it was first addressed, prejudices had to be overcome, prepossessions had to be counted on and dealt with. The apostles, in fact, had just to take the men of their time as they found them, adapting their teaching accordingly. Not only so, but there is evidence that the apostles were themselves, to a very great extent, men of their own time, sharing many of the common opinions and even the common prejudices, so that, in arguing *ex concessis*, they were arguing upon grounds that would appear to themselves just and tenable. Now one of the things universally conceded in apostolic times was the inspiration and authority of the Old Testament; another was the legitimacy of certain modes of interpreting and applying the Old Testament. The later Jews, as is well known, cherished a superstitious reverence and attached an overwhelming importance to the letter of the Old Testament, which they regarded as the "Word of God" in the fullest and most absolute sense that can possibly be put upon such an expression. The doctors taught and the people believed that the sacred writings were not only inspired, but inspired to the utmost possible or conceivable extent. In the composition of Scripture, the human author was nowhere, and the inspiring Spirit everywhere; not the thoughts alone, but the very words of Scripture were the Word of God, which He communicated by the mouth of the human author, who merely discharged the duty of spokesman and amanuensis, so that what the Scripture contains is the Word of God in as complete and full a sense as if it had been dictated by the lips of God to the human authors, and recorded with something approaching to perfect accuracy. . . . Such being the prevalent view of the inspiration and authority of the Old Testament writings, what could be more natural than that the apostles should make use of these writings to enforce and commend their own ideas? And if the Old Testament were to be used for such a purpose at all, evidently it must be used according to the accepted methods; for to have followed any other—assuming the possibility of such a thing—would have defeated the object aimed at, which was to accommodate the Gospel to established prejudices.

Now, here too, the first remark which needs to be made is that the assertion of "accommodation" on the part of the New Testament writers cannot be made good. To prove "accommodation," two things need to be shown: first, that the apostles did not share these views, and, secondly, that they nevertheless accommodated their teaching to them. "Accommodation" properly so called cannot take place when the views in question are the proper views of the persons themselves. But even in the above extract Mr. Stuart is led to allow that the apostles shared the current Jewish view of the Scriptures, and at a later point he demonstrates this in an argument of singular lucidity, although in its course he exaggerates the character of their views in his effort to fix a stigma of mechanicalness on them.[32] With what propriety, then, can he speak of "accommodation" in the case? The fact is that the theory of "accommodation" is presented by Mr. Stuart only to enable him the more easily to refuse to be bound by the apostolic teaching in this matter, and as such it has served him as a stepping stone by which he has attained to an even more drastic principle, on which he practically acts: that whenever the apostles can be shown to agree with their contemporaries, their teaching may be neglected. In such cases, he conceives of the New Testament writers "being inspired and guided by current opinion,"[33] and reasons thus:

Now it is unquestionable that the New Testament writers in so regarding the Old Testament were not enunciating a new theory of inspiration or interpretation, they were simply adopting

32. Ibid., 345–51.
33. Ibid., 213.

and following out the current theory. . . . In matters of this kind . . . the New Testament writers were completely dominated by the spirit of the age, so that their testimony on the question of Scripture inspiration possesses no independent value.[34]

If these popular notions were infallibly correct before they were taken up and embodied in the New Testament writings, they are infallibly correct still; if they were incorrect before they were taken up and embodied in the New Testament writings, they are incorrect still.[35]

This is certainly most remarkable argumentation, and the principle asserted is probably one of the most singular to which thinking men ever committed themselves, viz., that a body of religious teachers, claiming authority for themselves as such, are trustworthy *only* when they teach *novelties*. It is the apotheosis of the old Athenian and new modern spirit, which has leisure and heart "for nothing else but either to tell or hear some new thing." Nevertheless, it is a principle far from uncommon among those who are seeking justification for themselves in refusing the leadership of the New Testament writers in the matter of the authority and inspiration of the Scriptures. And, of late, it is, of course, taking upon itself in certain quarters a new form, the form imposed by the new view of the origin of Christian thought in Hellenic sources, which has been given such vogue by Dr. Harnack and rendered popular in English-speaking lands by the writings of the late Dr. Hatch. For example, we find it expressed in this form in the recent valuable studies on the First Epistle of Clement of Rome, by Lic. Wrede.[36] Clement's views of the Old Testament Scriptures are recognized as of the highest order; he looks upon them as a marvelous and infallible book whose very letters are sacred, as a veritable oracle, the most precious possession of the Church. These high views were shared by the whole Church of his day, and, indeed, of the previous age: "The view which Clement has of the Old Testament, and the use which he makes of it, show in themselves no essential peculiarities in comparison with the most nearly related Christian writings, especially the Pauline epistles, the Epistle to the Hebrews and the Epistle of Barnabas." And yet, according to Wrede, this view rests on "the Hellenistic conception of inspiration, according to which the individual writers were passive instruments of God."[37] Whether, however, the contemporary influence is thought to be Jewish or Greek, it is obvious that the appeal to it in such matters has, as its only intention, to free us from the duty of following the apostles and can have as its only effect to undermine their authority. We may no doubt suppose at the beginning that we seek only to separate the kernel from the husk; but a principle which makes husk of all that can be shown to have anything in common with what was believed by any body of contemporaries, Hebrew or Greek, is so very drastic that it will leave nothing which we can surely trust. On this principle the Golden Rule itself is not authoritative, because something like it may be found in Jewish tradition and among the heathen sages. It certainly will not serve to make novelty the test of authority.

From the ethical point of view, however, this theory is preferable to that of "accommodation," and it is probable that part, at least, of the impulse which led Mr. Stuart to substitute it for the theory of "accommodation," with which he began, arose from a

---

34. Ibid., 348–50.

35. Ibid., 70. The immediate reference of these last words is to matters of criticism and exegesis; but according to the contextual connection they would also be used of matters of inspiration.

36. Lic. Theol. William Wrede, Privatdocent der Theologie in Göttingen. *Untersuchungen zum ersten Klemensbriefe* (Göttingen: Vanderhoeck & Ruprecht, 1891), 60, 75–80.

37. Compare the review of Wrede by Prof. H. M. Scott, in *The Presbyterian and Reformed Review* 4 (January 1893): 163.

more or less clear perception of the moral implications of the theory of "accommodation." Under the impulse of that theory he had been led to speak of the procedure of the apostles in such language as this: "The sole principle that regulates all their appeals to the Old Testament, is that of obtaining, at whatever cost, support for their own favorite ideas."[38] Is it any wonder that the reaction took place and an attempt was made to shift the burden from the *veracity* to the *knowledge* of the New Testament writers?[39] In Mr. Stuart's case we see very clearly, then, the effect of a doctrine of "accommodation" on the credit of the New Testament writers. His whole book is written in order to assign reason why he will not yield authority to these writers in their doctrine of a sacrificial atonement. This was due to their Jewish type of thought. But when the doctrine of accommodation is tried as a ground for the rejection of their authority, it is found to cut too deeply even for Mr. Stuart. He wishes to be rid of the authority of the New Testament writers, not to impeach their veracity; and so he discards it in favor of the less plausible, indeed, but also less deeply cutting canon, that the apostles are not to be followed when they agree with contemporary thought, because in these elements they are obviously speaking out of their own consciousness, as the products of their day, and not as proclaimers of the *new* revelation in Christ. Their inspiration, in a word, "was not *plenary* or *universal*— extending, that is, to all matters whatever which they speak about—but *partial* or *special*, being limited to securing the accurate communication of that plan of salvation which they had so profoundly experienced, and which they were commissioned to proclaim."[40] In all else "the New Testament writers are simply on a level with their contemporaries." It may not be uninstructive to note that under such a formula Mr. Stuart not only rejects the teachings of these writers as to the nature and extent of inspiration, but also their teaching as to the sacrificial nature of the very plan of salvation which they were especially commissioned to proclaim. But what it is our business at present to point out is that the doctrine of accommodation is so obviously a blow at not only the trustworthiness, but the very veracity of the New Testament authors, that Mr. Stuart, even after asserting it, is led to permit it to fall into neglect.

And must it not be so? It may be easy indeed to confuse it with that progressive method of teaching which every wise teacher uses, and which our Lord also employed (John 16:12–15); it may be easy to represent it as nothing more than that harmless wisdom which the apostle proclaimed as the principle of his life, as he went about the world becoming all things to all men. But how different it is from either! It is one thing to adapt the teaching of truth to the stage of receptivity of the learner; it is another thing to adopt the errors of the time as the very matter to be taught. It is one thing to refrain from unnecessarily arousing the prejudices of the learner, that more ready entrance may be found for the truth; it is another thing to adopt those prejudices as our own, and to inculcate them as the very truths of God. It was one thing for Paul to become "all things to all men" that he might gain them to the truth; it was another for Peter to dissemble at Antioch, and so confirm men in their error. The accommodation attributed to the New Testament writers is a method by which they did and do not undeceive but deceive; not a method by which they teach the truth more winningly and to more; but a method by which they may be held to have taught along with the truth

38. Stuart, *The Principles of Christianity*, 66.
39. Ibid., 353.
40. Ibid., 258.

also error. The very object of attributing it to them is to enable us to separate their teaching into two parts—the true and the false; and to justify us in refusing a part while accepting a part at their hands. At the best it must so undermine the trustworthiness of the apostles as deliverers of doctrine as to subject their whole teaching to our judgment for the separation of the true from the false; at the worst, it must destroy their trustworthiness by destroying our confidence in their veracity. Mr. Stuart chose the better path; but he did so, as all who follow him must, by deserting the principle of accommodation, which leads itself along the worse road. With it as a starting point we must impeach the New Testament writers as lacking either knowledge or veracity.

TEACHING VERSUS OPINION

3. A third type of procedure, in defense of refusal to be bound by the doctrine of the New Testament writers as to inspiration, proceeds by drawing a distinction between the belief and the teaching of these writers; and affirming that, although it is true that they did believe and hold a high doctrine of inspiration, yet they do not explicitly teach it, and that we are bound, not by their opinions, but only by their explicit teaching.

This appears to be the conception which underlies the treatment of the matter by Archdeacon (then Canon) Farrar, in his *Life and Work of St. Paul*. Speaking of Paul's attitude towards Scripture, Dr. Farrar says:

> He shared, doubtless, in the views of the later Jewish schools—the Tanaim and Amoraim—on the nature of inspiration. These views, which we find also in Philo, made the words of Scripture coextensive and identical with the words of God, and in the clumsy and feeble hands of the more fanatical Talmudists often attached to the dead letter an importance which stifled or destroyed the living sense. But as this extreme and mechanical literalism—this claim to absolute infallibility even in accidental details and passing allusions—this superstitious adoration of the letters and vocables of Scripture, as though they were the articulate vocables and immediate autograph of God—finds no encouragement in any part of Scripture, and very distinct discouragement in more than one of the utterances of Christ, so there is not a single passage in which any approach to it is dogmatically stated in the writings of St. Paul.[41]

This passage lacks somewhat more in point of clearness than it does in point of rhetorical fire. But three things seem to be sufficiently plain: (1) That Dr. Farrar thinks that Paul shared the views of the Tanaim, the Amoraim and Philo as to the nature of inspiration. (2) That he admits that these views claimed for Scripture "absolute infallibility even in accidental details and passing allusions." (3) That nevertheless he does not feel bound to accept this doctrine at Paul's hands, because, though Paul held it, he is thought not to have "dogmatically stated" it.

Now, the distinction which is here drawn seems, in general, a reasonable one. No one is likely to assert infallibility for the apostles in aught else than in their official teaching. And whatever they may be shown to have held apart from their official teaching, may readily be looked upon with only that respect which we certainly must accord to the opinions of men of such exceptional intellectual and spiritual insight. But it is more difficult to follow Dr. Farrar when it is asked whether this distinction can be established in the present matter. It does not seem to be true that there are no didactic statements as to inspiration in Paul's

41. Farrar, *Life and Work of St. Paul*, 1:49

864

letters, or in the rest of the New Testament, such as implicate and carry into the sphere of matters taught, the whole doctrine that underlies their treatment of Scripture. The assertion in the term "theopneustic" in such a passage as 2 Timothy 3:16, for example, cannot be avoided by any construction of the passage; and the doctrine taught in the assertion must be understood to be the doctrine which that term connoted to Paul who uses it, not some other doctrine read into it by us.

It is further necessary to inquire what sources we have in a case like that of Paul, to inform us as to what his opinions were, apart from and outside of his teachings. It might conceivably have happened that some of his contemporaries should have recorded for us some account of opinions held by him to which he has given no expression in his epistles; or some account of actions performed by him involving the manifestation of judgment—somewhat similar, say, to Paul's own account of Peter's conduct in Antioch (Gal. 2:11–14). A presumption may be held to lie also that he shared the ordinary opinions of his day in certain matters lying outside the scope of his teachings, as, for example, with reference to the form of the earth, or its relation to the sun; and it is not inconceivable that the form of his language, when incidentally adverting to such matters, might occasionally play into the hands of such a presumption. But it is neither on the ground of such a presumption, nor on the ground of such external testimony, that Dr. Farrar ascribes to him views as to inspiration similar to those of his Jewish contemporaries. It is distinctly on the ground of what he finds on a study of the body of official teaching which Paul has left to us. Dr. Farrar discovers that these views as to the nature of Scripture so underlie, are so assumed in, are so implied by, are so interwoven with Paul's official teaching that he is unwillingly driven to perceive that they were Paul's opinions. With what color of reason then can they be separated from his teaching?

There is raised here, moreover, a very important and far-reaching question, which few will be able to decide in Dr. Farrar's sense. What is taught in the New Testament? And what is the mode of its teaching? If we are to fall in with Dr. Farrar and say that nothing is taught except what is "dogmatically stated" in formal didactic form, the occasional character of the New Testament epistles would become a source of grave loss to us, instead of, as it otherwise is, a source of immense gain; the parabolic clothing of much of Christ's teaching would become a device to withhold from us all instruction on the matters of which the parables treat; and all that is most fundamental in religious truth, which, as a rule, is rather assumed everywhere in Scripture as a basis for particular applications than formally stated, would be removed out of the sphere of Biblical doctrine. Such a rule, in a word, would operate to turn the whole of Biblical teaching on its head, and to reduce it from a body of principles inculcated by means of examples into a mere congeries of instances hung in the air. The whole advance in the attitude of Dogmatics towards the Scriptures which has been made by modern scholarship is, moreover, endangered by this position. It was the fault of the older dogmatists to depend too much on isolated proof-texts for the framing and defense of doctrine. Dr. Farrar would have us return to this method. The alternative, commended justly to us by the whole body of modern scholarship, is, as Schleiermacher puts it, to seek "a form of Scripture proof on a larger scale than can be got from single texts," to build our systematic theology, in a word, on the basis, not of the occasional dogmatic statements of Scripture alone, taken separately and, as it were, in shreds, but on the basis of the theologies of the Scripture—to reproduce first the theological thought of each writer or group of writers and then to combine these several theologies (each according to its due historical place) into the one consistent system, consentaneous parts of which they are found to be.[42] In rejecting this method, Dr. Farrar discredits the whole science of Biblical Theology. From its standpoint it is incredible that one should attribute less importance and authoritativeness to the fundamental conceptions that underlie, color and give form to all of Paul's teaching than to the chance didactic statements he may have been led to make by this or that circumstance at the call of which his letters happened to be written. This certainly would be tithing mint and anise and cummin and omitting the weightier matters of the law.

That this mode of presenting the matter must lead, no less than the others which have already come under review, to undermining the authority of the New Testament writers as deliverers of doctrine, must already be obvious. It begins by discrediting them as leaders in doctrinal thought and substituting for this a sporadic authority in explicit dogmatic statements. In Dr. Farrar's own hands it proceeds by quite undermining our confidence in the apostles as teachers, through an accusation lodged against them, not only of holding wrong views in doctrine, but even of cherishing as fundamental conceptions theological fancies which are in their very essence superstitious and idolatrous, and in their inevitable outcome ruinous to faith and honor. For Dr. Farrar does not mince matters when he expresses his opinion of that doctrine of inspiration—in its nature and its proper effects—which Philo held and the Jewish Rabbis and in which Paul, according to his expressed conviction, shared. "To say that every word and sentence and letter of Scripture is divine and supernatural, is a mechanical and useless shibboleth, nay, more, a human idol, and (constructively, at least) a dreadful blasphemy." It is a superstitious—he tells us that he had almost said fetish-worshiping—dogma, and "not only unintelligible, but profoundly dangerous." It "has in many ages filled the world with misery and ruin," and "has done more than any other dogma to corrupt the whole of exegesis with dishonest casuistry, and to shake to its centre the religious faith of thousands, alike of the most ignorant and of the most cultivated, in many centuries, and most of all in our own."[43] Yet these are the views which Dr. Farrar is forced to allow that Paul shared! For Philo "held the most rigid views of inspiration"; than him indeed "Aqiba himself used no stronger language on the subject"[44]—Aqiba, "the greatest of the Tanaites";[45] and it was the views of the Tanaim, Amoraim and Philo, which Dr. Farrar tells us the apostle shared. How after this Dr. Farrar continues to look upon even the "dogmatic statements" of Paul as authoritative, it is hard to see. By construction he was a fetish worshiper and placed Scripture upon an idol's pedestal. The doctrines which he held and which underlie his teaching were unintelligible, useless, idolatrous, blasphemous and profoundly dangerous, and actually have shaken to its centre the religious faith of thousands. On such a tree what other than evil fruits could grow?

No doubt something of this may be attributed to the exaggeration characteristic of Dr. Farrar's language and thought. Obviously Paul's view of inspiration was not altogether identical with that of contemporary Judaism; it differed from it somewhat in the same way that his use of Scripture differed from that of the Rabbis of his day. But it is one with Philo's and Aqiba's on the point which with Dr. Farrar is decisive: alike with them he looked upon Scripture

---

42. The present writer has tried to state the true relations of Systematic and Biblical theology in a discussion of *The Idea of Systematic Theology Considered as a Science* (Inaugural Address) (New York: A. D. F. Randolph, 1888), 22–28. He ventures to refer the reader to it.

43. Rev. Archdeacon Farrar and others, *Inspiration: A Clerical Symposium*, 2nd ed. (London: James Nisbet, 1888), 219, 241.

44. F. W. Farrar, D.D., *History of Interpretation*, Bampton Lectures (London: Macmillan, 1880), 147.

45. Ibid., 71.

as "absolutely infallible, even in accidental details and passing allusions," as the very Word of God, His "Oracles," to use his own high phrase, and therefore Dr. Farrar treats the two views as essentially one. But the situation is only modified, not relieved, by the recognition of this fact.

In any event the pathway on which we enter when we begin to distinguish between the didactic statements and the fundamental conceptions of a body of incidental teaching, with a view to accepting the former and rejecting the latter, cannot but lead to a general undermining of the authority of the whole. Only if we could believe in a quite mechanical and magical process of inspiration (from believing in which Dr. Farrar is no doubt very far) by which the subject's "dogmatical statements" were kept entirely separate from and unaffected by his fundamental conceptions, could such an attitude be logically possible. In that case we should have to view these "dogmatical statements" as not Paul's at all, standing, as they do *ex hypothesi*, wholly disconnected with his own fundamental thought, but as spoken through him by an overmastering spiritual influence; as a phenomenon, in a word, similar to the oracles of heathen shrines, and without analogy in Scripture except perhaps in such cases as that of Balaam. In proportion as we draw back from so magical a conception of the mode of inspiration, in that proportion our refusal of authority to the fundamental conceptions of the New Testament writers must invade also their "dogmatical statements." We must logically, in a word, ascribe like authority to the whole body of their teaching, in its foundation and superstructure alike, or we must withhold it in equal measure from all; or, if we withhold it from one and not the other, the discrimination would most naturally be made against the superstructure rather than against the foundation.

Facts versus Doctrine

4. Finally, an effort may be made to justify our holding a lower doctrine of inspiration than that held by the writers of the New Testament, by appealing to the so-called phenomena of the Scriptures and opposing these to the doctrine of the Scriptures, with the expectation, apparently, of justifying a modification of the doctrine taught by the Scriptures by the facts embedded in the Scriptures.

The essential principle of this method of procedure is shared by very many who could scarcely be said to belong to the class who are here more specifically in mind, inasmuch as they do not begin by explicitly recognizing the doctrine of inspiration held by the New Testament writers to be that high doctrine which the Church and the best scientific exegesis agree in understanding them to teach.[46] Every attempt to determine or modify the Biblical

46. On the contrary these writers usually minimize the Biblical definition of inspiration. Thus Dr. Marvin R. Vincent, who is immediately to be quoted ("The Septuagint as Related to New Testament Inspiration," *Magazine of Christian Literature* [April 1892]: 15), tells us "Scripture does not define the nature and extent of its own inspiration. The oft-quoted passage, 2 Timothy 3:16, really gives us no light on that point. . . . The passage does indeed point out certain *effects* which attend the use of inspired writings. . . . But after all, we are no nearer than ever to an answer to the question, What *is* inspiration? . . . So that we must fall back on the facts, on the phenomena of the Bible as we have it." But the deck is not cleared by such remarks; after all, Paul does assert *something* by calling the Scriptures Theopneustic, and what the thing is that he asserts in the use of this predicate, is not discoverable from an examination into what the Scriptures *are*, but only by an examination into what Paul *means*; but what Paul *understands* by theopneustic, Dr. Vincent makes no effort to investigate. This whole procedure is typical. Thus, for example, the Rev. J. Paterson Smyth, in his recent book, *How God Inspired the Bible* (New York: James Pott, 1892), 64, proceeds in an exactly similar manner. "Our theory of inspiration must be learned from the facts presented in the Bible, and in order to be correct it must be consistent with all these facts. . . . I want to find out what I can about inspiration. God has nowhere revealed to me exactly what it is. He has told me it is a divine influence, an

doctrine of inspiration by an appeal to the actual characteristics of the Bible must indeed proceed on an identical principle. It finds, perhaps, as plausible a form of assertion possible to it in the declaration of Dr. Marvin R. Vincent that "our only safe principle is that *inspiration is consistent with the phenomena of Scripture*"[47]—to which one of skeptical turn might respond that whether *the inspiration claimed by Scripture* is consistent with the phenomena of Scripture after all requires some proof, while one of a more believing frame might respond that it is a safer principle that the phenomena of Scripture are consistent with its inspiration. Its crudest expression may be seen in such a book as Mr. Horton's *Inspiration and the Bible*, which we have already had occasion to mention. Mr. Horton chooses to retain the term, "inspiration," as representing "the *common sense* of Christians of all ages and in all places" as to the nature of their Scriptures,[48] but asserts that this term is to be understood to mean just what the Bible is—that is to say, whatever any given writer chooses to think the Bible to be. When Paul affirms in 2 Timothy 3:16 that every Scripture is "inspired by God," therefore, we are not to enter into a philological and exegetical investigation to discover what Paul meant to affirm by the use of this word, but simply to say that Paul must have meant to affirm the Bible to be what we find it to be. Surely no way could be invented which would more easily enable us to substitute our thought for the apostles' thought, and to proclaim our crudities under the sanction of their great names. Operating by it, Mr. Horton is enabled to assert that the Bible is "inspired," and yet to teach that God's hand has entered it only in a providential way, by His dealings through long ages with a people who gradually wrought out a history, conceived hopes, and brought all through natural means to an expression in a faulty and often self-contradictory record, which we call inspired only "because by reading it and studying it we can find our way to God, we can find what is His will for us and how we can carry out that will."[49] The most naïve expression of the principle in question may be found in such a statement as the following, from the pen of Dr. W. G. Blaikie: "In our mode of dealing with this question the main difference between us is, that you lay your stress on certain general considerations, and on certain specific statements of Scripture. We, on the other hand, while accepting the specific statements, lay great stress also on the

in-breathing of the Holy Ghost on the spirit of the ancient writers. But I cannot tell how much that means or what effects I should expect from it. I have, therefore, no way of finding out except by examining the phenomena presented by the Bible itself." This method amounts simply to discarding the guidance of the doctrine of Scripture in favor of our own doctrine founded on our examination of the nature of Scripture. Mr. Smyth cannot close his eyes to certain outstanding facts on the surface of Scripture, indicatory of the doctrine as to Scripture held by the Biblical writers (pp. 36 and 106), though he makes no effort to collect and estimate all such phenomena. And when he realizes that some may be affected even by his meagre statement of them so far as to say that "the strong expressions just here quoted from some of the Bible writers, and even from our Lord Himself, convince me that the theory of verbal inspiration is most probably true," he has only such an answer as the following: "Well, reader, you will find a good many thoughtful people disagreeing with you. Why? Because, while fully receiving these arguments as a proof of God's inspiration of the Bible, they have looked a little further than the surface to judge how much God's inspiration implies, and they cannot believe from their examination of Scripture that it implies what is known as verbal inspiration" (p. 109). Mr. Smyth means by "verbal inspiration "the theory of mechanical dictation. But putting that aside as a man of straw, what it is difficult for us to understand is how "thoughtful people" can frame a theory of inspiration after only such shallow investigation of the Scriptural doctrine of inspiration, and how "thoughtful people" can assign their inability to believe a doctrine, an inability based on their own conception of what Scripture is, as any proof that that doctrine is not taught by the "strong expressions" of the Bible writers and the Lord Himself. Is it any more rationalistic to correct the Scriptural doctrine of the origin of the universe from our investigations of the nature of things, than it is to correct the Scriptural doctrine of inspiration from our investigations of the nature of Scripture?

47. Vincent, "The Septuagint as Related to New Testament Inspiration," 15.
48. Horton, *Inspiration and the Bible*, 5.
49. Ibid., 240.

structure of Scripture as we find it, on certain phenomena which lie on the surface, and on the inextricable difficulties which are involved in carrying out your view in detail."[50] This statement justly called out the rebuke of Dr. Robert Watts, that "while the principle of your theory is a mere inference from apparent discrepancies not as yet explained, the principle of the theory you oppose is the formally expressed utterances of prophets and apostles, and of Christ Himself."[51]

Under whatever safeguards, indeed, it may be attempted, and with whatever caution it may be prosecuted, the effort to modify the teaching of Scripture as to its own inspiration by an appeal to the observed characteristics of Scripture, is an attempt not to obtain a clearer knowledge of what the Scriptures teach, but to *correct* that teaching. And to *correct* the teaching of Scripture is to proclaim Scripture untrustworthy as a witness to doctrine. The procedure in question is precisely similar to saying that the Bible's doctrine of creation is to be derived not alone from the teachings of the Bible as to creation, but from the facts obtained through a scientific study of creation; that the Bible's doctrine as to man is to be found not in the Bible's deliverances on the subject, but "while accepting these, we lay great stress also on the *structure* of man as we find him, and on the inextricable difficulties which are involved in carrying out the Bible's teaching in detail"; that the Bible's doctrine of justification is to be obtained by retaining the term as commended by the common sense of the Christian world and understanding by it just what we find justification to be in actual life. It is precisely similar to saying that Mr. Darwin's doctrine of natural selection is to be determined not solely by what Mr. Darwin says concerning it, but equally by what we, in our own independent study of nature, find to be true as to natural selection. A historian of thought who proceeded on such a principle would scarcely receive the commendation of students of history, however much his writings might serve certain party ends. Who does not see that underlying this whole method of procedure—in its best and in its worst estate alike—there is apparent an unwillingness to commit ourselves without reserve to the *teaching* of the Bible, either because that teaching is distrusted or already disbelieved; and that it is a grave logical error to suppose that the teaching of the Bible as to inspiration can be corrected in this way any otherwise than by showing it not to be in accordance with the facts? The proposed method, therefore, does not conduct us to a somewhat modified doctrine of inspiration, but to a disproof of inspiration; by correcting the doctrine delivered by the Biblical writers, it discredits those writers as teachers of doctrine.

Let it not be said that in speaking thus we are refusing the inductive method of establishing doctrine. We follow the inductive method. When we approach the Scriptures to ascertain their doctrine of inspiration, we proceed by collecting the whole body of relevant facts. Every claim they make to inspiration is a relevant fact; every statement they make concerning inspiration is a relevant fact; every allusion they make to the subject is a relevant fact; every fact indicative of the attitude they hold towards Scripture is a relevant fact. But the characteristics of their own writings are not facts relevant to the determination of *their doctrine.* Nor let it be said that we are desirous of determining the true, as distinguished from the Scriptural, doctrine of inspiration otherwise than inductively. We are averse, however, to supposing that in such an inquiry the relevant "phenomena" of Scripture are not

---

50. William G. Blaikie, D.D., LL.D., *Letter to the Rev. Andrew A. Bonar, D.D.*, 2nd ed., 5.

51. Robert Watts, D.D., LL.D., *A Letter to the Rev. Prof. William G. Blaikie, D.D., LL.D.* (Edinburgh: R. W. Hunter, 1890), 30.

first of all and before all the claims of Scripture and second only to them its use of previous Scripture. And we are averse to excluding these primary "phenomena" and building our doctrine solely or mainly upon the characteristics and structure of Scripture, especially as determined by some special school of modern research by critical methods certainly not infallible and to the best of our own judgment not even reasonable. And we are certainly averse to supposing that this induction, if it reaches results not absolutely consentaneous with the teachings of Scripture itself, has done anything other than discredit those teachings, or that in discrediting them, it has escaped discrediting the doctrinal authority of Scripture.

Nor again is it to be thought that we refuse to use the actual characteristics of Scripture as an aid in, and a check upon, our exegesis of Scripture, as we seek to discover its doctrine of inspiration. We do not simply admit, on the contrary, we affirm that in every sphere the observed fact may throw a broad and most helpful light upon the written text. It is so in the narrative of creation in the first chapter of Genesis; which is only beginning to be adequately understood as science is making her first steps in reading the records of God's creative hand in the structure of the world itself. It is preëminently so in the written prophecies, the dark sayings of which are not seldom first illuminated by the light cast back upon them by their fulfillment. As Scripture interprets Scripture, and fulfillment interprets prediction, so may fact interpret assertion. And this is as true as regards the Scriptural assertion of the fact of inspiration as elsewhere. No careful student of the Bible doctrine of inspiration will neglect anxiously to try his conclusions as to the teachings of Scripture by the observed character-istics and "structure" of Scripture, and in trying he may and no doubt will find occasion to modify his conclusions as at first apprehended. But it is one thing to correct our exegetical processes and so modify our exegetical conclusions in the new light obtained by a study of the facts, and quite another to modify, by the facts of the structure of Scripture, the Scrip-tural teaching itself, as exegetically ascertained; and it is to this latter that we should be led by making the facts of structure and the facts embedded in Scripture co-factors of the same rank in the so-called inductive ascertainment of the doctrine of inspiration. Direct exege-sis after all has its rights: we may seek aid from every quarter in our efforts to perform its processes with precision and obtain its results with purity; but we cannot allow it results to be "modified" by extraneous considerations. Let us by all means be careful in determining the doctrine of Scripture, but let us also be fully honest in determining it; and if we count it a crime to permit our ascertainment of the facts recorded in Scripture to be unduly swayed by our conception of the doctrine taught in Scripture, let us count it equally a crime to permit our ascertainment of its doctrine to be unduly swayed or colored by our conception of the nature of the facts of its structure or of the facts embedded in its record. We cannot, therefore, appeal from the doctrine of Scripture as exegetically established to the facts of the structure of Scripture or the facts embedded in Scripture, in the hope of modifying the doctrine. If the teaching and the facts of Scripture are in harmony the appeal is useless. If they are in disharmony, we cannot follow both—we must choose one and reject the other. And the attempt to make the facts of Scripture co-factors of equal rank with the teaching of Scripture is ascertaining the true doctrine of inspiration, is really an attempt to modify the doctrine taught by Scripture by an appeal to the facts, while concealing from ourselves the fact that we have modified it, and in modifying corrected it, and, of course, in correcting it, discredited Scripture as a teacher of doctrine.

Probably these four types of procedure will include most of the methods by which men are to-day seeking to free themselves from the necessity of following the Scriptural doctrine of inspiration, while yet looking to Scripture as the source of doctrine. Is it not plain that on every one of them the outcome must be to discredit Scripture as a doctrinal guide? The human mind is very subtle, but with all its subtlety it will hardly be able to find a way to refuse to follow Scripture in one of the doctrines it teaches without undermining its authority as a teacher of doctrine.

II. Immense Weight of Evidence for the Biblical Doctrine

It is only to turn another face of the proposition with which we are dealing towards us, to emphasize next the important fact, that, the state of the case being such as we have found it, the evidence for the truth of the doctrine of the plenary inspiration of Scripture is just the whole body of evidence which goes to show that the apostles are trustworthy teachers of doctrine.

Language is sometimes made use of which would seem to imply that the amount or weight of the evidence offered for the truth of the doctrine that the Scriptures are the Word of God in such a sense that their words deliver the truth of God without error, is small. It is on the contrary just the whole body of evidence which goes to prove the writers of the New Testament to be trustworthy as deliverers of doctrine. It is just the same evidence in amount and weight which is adduced in favor of any other Biblical doctrine. It is the same weight and amount of evidence precisely which is adducible for the truth of the doctrines of the Incarnation, of the Trinity, of the Divinity of Christ, of Justification by Faith, of Regeneration by the Holy Spirit, of the Resurrection of the Body, of Life Everlasting. It is, of course, not absurdly intended that every Biblical doctrine is taught in the Scriptures with equal clearness, with equal explicitness, with equal frequency. Some doctrines are stated with an explicit precision that leaves little to systematic theology in its efforts to define the truth on all sides, except to repeat the words which the Biblical writers have used to teach it—as for example the doctrine of Justification by Faith. Others are not formulated in Scripture at all, but are taught only in their elements, which the systematician must collect and combine and so arrive finally at the doctrine—as for example the doctrine of the Trinity. Some are adverted to so frequently as to form the whole warp and woof of Scripture—as for example the doctrine of redemption in the blood of Christ. Others are barely alluded to here and there, in connections where the stress is really on other matters—as for example the doctrine of the fall of the angels. But however explicitly or incidentally, however frequently or rarely, however emphatically or allusively, they may be taught, when exegesis has once done its work and shown that they are taught by the Biblical writers, all these doctrines stand as supported by the same weight and amount of evidence—the evidence of the trustworthiness of the Biblical writers as teachers of doctrine. We cannot say that we will believe these writers when they assert a doctrine a hundred times and we will not believe them if they assert it only ten times or only once; that we will believe them in the doctrines they make the main subjects of discourse, but not in those which they advert to incidentally; that we will believe them in those that they teach as conclusions of formal arguments, but not in those which they use as premises wherewith to reach those conclusions; that we will believe them in those they explicitly formulate and dogmatically teach, but not in those which they teach only in their separate parts and elements. The question is not *how* they teach a

871

doctrine, but *do* they teach it; and when that question is once settled affirmatively, the weight of evidence that commends this doctrine to us as true is the same in every case; and that is the whole body of evidence which goes to show that the Biblical writers are trustworthy as teachers of doctrine. The Biblical doctrine of inspiration, therefore, has in its favor just this whole weight and amount of evidence. It follows on the one hand that it cannot rationally be rejected save on the ground of evidence which will outweigh the whole body of evidence which goes to authenticate the Biblical writers as trustworthy witnesses to and teachers of doctrine. And it follows, on the other hand, that if the Biblical doctrine of inspiration is rejected, our freedom from its trammels is bought logically at the somewhat serious cost of discrediting the evidence which goes to show that the Biblical writers are trustworthy as teachers of doctrine. In this sense, the fortunes of distinctive Christianity are bound up with those of the Biblical doctrine of inspiration.

Let it not be said that thus we found the whole Christian system upon the doctrine of plenary inspiration. We found the whole Christian system on the doctrine of plenary inspiration as little as we found it upon the doctrine of angelic existences. Were there no such thing as inspiration, Christianity would be true, and all its essential doctrines would be credibly witnessed to us in the generally trustworthy reports of the teaching of our Lord and of His authoritative agents in founding the Church, preserved in the writings of the apostles and their first followers, and in the historical witness of the living Church. Inspiration is not the most fundamental of Christian doctrines, nor even the first thing we prove about the Scriptures. It is the last and crowning fact as to the Scriptures. These we first prove authentic, historically credible, generally trustworthy, before we prove them inspired. And the proof of their authenticity, credibility, general trustworthiness would give us a firm basis for Christianity prior to any knowledge on our part of their inspiration, and apart indeed from the existence of inspiration. The present writer, in order to prevent all misunderstanding, desires to repeat here what he has said on every proper occasion—that he is far from contending that without inspiration there could be no Christianity. "Without any inspiration," he added, when making this affirmation on his induction into the work of teaching the Bible[52]—"without any inspiration we could have had Christianity; yea, and men could still have heard the truth and through it been awakened, and justified, and sanctified, and glorified. The verities of our faith would remain historically proven to us—so bountiful has God been in His fostering care—even had we no Bible; and through those verities, salvation." We are in entire harmony in this matter with what we conceive to be the very true statement recently made by Dr. George P. Fisher, that "if the authors of the Bible were credible reporters of revelations of God, whether in the form of historical transactions of which they were witnesses, or of divine mysteries that were unveiled to their minds, their testimony would be entitled to belief, even if they were shut up to their unaided faculties in communicating what they had thus received."[53] We are in entire sympathy in this matter, therefore, with the protest which Dr. Marcus Dods raised in his famous address at the

52. *Discourses Occasioned by the Inauguration of Benj. B. Warfield, D.D., to the Chair of New Testament Exegesis and Literature in the Western Theological Seminary, April 25th, 1880* (Pittsburgh: Nevin Brothers, 1880), 46. Cf. A. A. Hodge and B. B. Warfield, *Inspiration*, 7–8 (also in *The Presbyterian Review* 2, 6 [April 1881]: 226–27). Also, Francis L. Patton, D.D., *The Inspiration of the Scriptures* (Philadelphia: Presbyterian Board of Publication, 1869), 22–23, 54.

53. George P. Fisher, "Biblical Criticism and the Authority of the Scriptures," *The Congregationalist* (Nov. 3, 1892); *The Magazine of Christian Literature* (Dec. 1892): 236, first column. This whole column should be read; its statement and illustration are alike admirable.

meeting of the Alliance of the Reformed Churches at London, against representing that "the infallibility of the Bible is the ground of the whole Christian faith."[54] We judge with him that it is very important indeed that such a misapprehension, if it is anywhere current, should be corrected. What we are at present arguing is something entirely different from such an overstrained view of the importance of inspiration to the very existence of Christian faith, and something which has no connection with it. We do not think that the doctrine of plenary inspiration is the ground of Christian faith, but if it was held and taught by the New Testament writers, we think it an element in the Christian faith; a very important and valuable element;[55] an element that appeals to our acceptance on precisely the same ground as every other element of the faith, viz., on the ground of our recognition of the writers of the New Testament as trustworthy witnesses to doctrine; an element of the Christian faith, therefore, which cannot be rejected without logically undermining our trust in all the other elements of distinctive Christianity by undermining the evidence on which this trust rests. We must indeed prove the authenticity, credibility and general trustworthiness of the New Testament writings before we prove their inspiration; and even were they not inspired this proof would remain valid and we should give them accordant trust. But just because this proof is valid, we must trust these writings in their witness to their inspiration, if they give such witness; and if we refuse to trust them here, we have in principle refused them trust everywhere. In such circumstances their inspiration is bound up inseparably with their trustworthiness, and therefore with all else that we receive on trust from them.

On the other hand, we need to remind ourselves that to say that the amount and weight of the evidence of the truth of the Biblical doctrine of inspiration is measured by the amount and weight of the evidence for the general credibility and trustworthiness of the New Testament writers as witnesses to doctrine, is an understatement rather than an overstatement of the matter. For if we trust them at all we will trust them in the account they give of the person and in the report they give of the teaching of Christ; whereupon, as they report Him as teaching the same doctrine of Scripture that they teach, we are brought face to face with divine testimony to this doctrine of inspiration. The argument, then, takes the form given it by Bishop Wordsworth: "The New Testament canonizes the Old; the INCARNATE WORD sets His seal on the WRITTEN WORD. The Incarnate Word is God; therefore, the inspiration of the Old Testament is authenticated by God Himself."[56] And, again, the general trustworthiness of the writers of the New Testament gives us the right and imposes on us the

54. This address, "How Far Is the Church Responsible for Present Scepticism?," may be most conveniently consulted in *The Expositor* 8 (October 1888): 301–2. In expressing our concurrence with portions of this address and of Dr. Fisher's papers just quoted, we are not to be understood, of course, as concurring with their whole contents.

55. How important and valuable this element of the Christian faith is, it is not the purpose of this paper to point out. Let it suffice here to say briefly that it is (1) the element which gives detailed certitude to the delivery of doctrine in the New Testament, and (2) the element by which the individual Christian is brought into immediate relation to God in the revelation of truth through the prophets and apostles. The importance of these factors in the Christian life could not be overstated. The importance of the recognition of plenary inspiration to the preservation of sound doctrine is negatively illustrated by the progress of Rationalism, as thus outlined briefly by Dr. Charles Hodge (*Systematic Theology*, 3:195): "Those who admitted the divine origin of the Scriptures got rid of its distinctive doctrines by the adoption of a low theory of inspiration and by the application of arbitrary principles of interpretation. Inspiration was in the first instance confined to the religious teachings of the Bible, then to the ideas or truths, but not to the form in which they were presented, nor to the arguments by which they were supported. . . . In this way a wet sponge was passed over all the doctrines of redemption and their outlines obliterated." It looks as if the Church were extremely slow in reading the most obvious lessons of history.

56. Christopher Wordsworth, *On the Inspiration of the Holy Scripture; or, On the Canon of the Old and New Testament, and on the Apocrypha*, American Edition (Philadelphia: Herman Hooker, 1854), 51.

duty of accepting their witness to the relation the Holy Ghost bears to their teaching, as, for example, when Paul tells us that the things which they uttered they uttered "not in words taught by human wisdom, but in those taught by the Spirit; joining Spirit-given things with Spirit-given things" (1 Cor. 2:13), and Peter asserts that the Gospel was preached by them "in the Holy Spirit" (1 Peter 1:12); and this relation asserted to exist between the Holy Ghost and their teaching, whether oral or written (1 Cor. 14:37; 2 Thess. 2:15; 3:6–14), gives the sanction of the Holy Ghost to their doctrine of Holy Scripture, whatever that is found to be. So that, even though we begin on the lowest ground, we may find ourselves compelled to say, as Bishop Wilberforce found himself compelled to say: "In brief, my belief is this: The whole Bible comes to us as 'the Word of God' under the sanction of God, the Holy Ghost."[57] The weight of the testimony to the Biblical doctrine of inspiration, in a word, is no less than the weight to be attached to the testimony of God—God the Son and God the Spirit.

But our present purpose is not to draw out the full value of the testimony, but simply to emphasize the fact that on the emergence of the exegetical fact that the Scriptures of the New Testament teach this doctrine, the amount and weight of evidence for its truth must be allowed to be the whole amount and weight of the evidence that the writers of the New Testament are trustworthy as teachers of doctrine. It is not on some shadowy and doubtful evidence that the doctrine is based—not on an *a priori* conception of what inspiration ought to be, not on a "tradition" of doctrine in the Church, though all the *a priori* considerations and the whole tradition of doctrine in the Church are also thrown in the scale for and not in that against this doctrine; but first on the confidence which we have in the writers of the New Testament as doctrinal guides, and ultimately on whatever evidence of whatever kind and force exists to justify that confidence. In this sense, we repeat, the cause of distinctive Christianity is bound up with the cause of the Biblical doctrine of inspiration. We accept Christianity in all its distinctive doctrines on no other ground than the credibility and trustworthiness of the Bible as a guide to truth; and on this same ground we must equally accept its doctrine of inspiration. "If we may not accept its account of itself," asks Dr. Purves, pointedly, "why should we care to ascertain its account of other things?"[58]

III. Immense Presumption Against Alleged Facts Contradictory of the Biblical Doctrine

We are again making no new affirmation but only looking from a slightly different angle upon the same proposition with which we have been dealing from the first, when we emphasize next the fact, that the state of the case being as we have found it, we approach the study of the so-called "phenomena" of the Scriptures with a very strong presumption that these Scriptures contain no errors, and that any "phenomena" apparently inconsistent with their inerrancy are so in appearance only: a presumption the measure of which is just the whole amount and weight of evidence that the New Testament writers are trustworthy as teachers of doctrine.

It seems to be often tacitly assumed that the Biblical doctrine of inspiration cannot be confidently ascertained until all the facts concerning the contents and structure and char-

---

57. A. R. Ashwell and Reginald G. Wilberforce, *Life of the Right Reverend Samuel Wilberforce, D.D.* (New York: E. P. Dutton, 1883), 398.

58. Purves, "St. Paul and Inspiration," 21.

acteristics of Scripture are fully determined and allowed for. This is obviously fallacious. What Paul, for example, believed as to the nature of Scripture is obviously an easily separable question from what the nature of Scripture really is. On the other hand, the assumption that we cannot confidently accept the Biblical doctrine of inspiration as true until criticism and exegesis have said their last word upon the structure, the text, and the characteristics of Scripture, even to the most minute fact, is more plausible. But it is far from obviously true. Something depends upon our estimate of the force of the mass of evidence which goes to show the trustworthiness of the apostles as teachers of truth, and of the clearness with which they announce their teaching as to inspiration. It is conceivable, for example, that the force of the evidence of their trustworthiness may be so great that we should be fully justified in yielding implicit confidence to their teaching, even though many and serious difficulties should stand in the way of accepting it. This, indeed, is exactly what we do in our ordinary use of Scripture as a source of doctrine. Who doubts that the doctrines of the Trinity and of the Incarnation present difficulties to rational construction? Who doubts that the doctrines of native demerit and total depravity, inability and eternal punishment raise objections in the natural heart? We accept these doctrines and others which ought to be much harder to credit, such as the Biblical teaching that God so loved sinful man as to give His only-begotten Son to die for him, not because their acceptance is not attended with difficulties, but because our confidence in the New Testament as a doctrinal guide is so grounded in unassailable and compelling evidence, that we believe its teachings despite the difficulties which they raise. We do not and we cannot wait until all these difficulties are fully explained before we yield to the teaching of the New Testament the fullest confidence of our minds and hearts. How then can it be true that we are to wait until all difficulties are removed before we can accept with confidence the Biblical doctrine of inspiration? In relation to this doctrine alone, are we to assume the position that we will not yield faith in response to due and compelling evidence of the trustworthiness of the teacher, until all difficulties are explained to our satisfaction—that we must fully understand and comprehend before we will believe? Or is the point this—that we can suppose ourselves possibly mistaken in everything else except our determination of the characteristics and structure of Scripture and the facts stated therein? Surely if we do not need to wait until we understand how God can be both one and three, how Christ can be both human and divine, how man can be both unable and responsible, how an act can be both free and certain, how man can be both a sinner and righteous in God's sight, before we accept, on the authority of the teaching of Scripture, the doctrines of the Trinity, of the Incarnation, of man's state as a sinner, of God's eternal predestination of the acts of free agents, and of acceptance on the ground of Christ's righteousness, because of the weight of the evidence which goes to prove that Scripture trustworthy as a teacher of divine truth; we may on the same compelling evidence accept, in full confidence, the teaching of the same Scripture as to the nature of its own inspiration, prior to a full understanding of how all the phenomena of Scripture are to be adjusted to it.

No doubt it is perfectly true and is to be kept in mind that the claim of a writing to be infallible may be mistaken or false. Such a claim has been put forth in behalf of and by other writings besides the Bible, and has been found utterly inconsistent with the observed characteristics of those writings. An *a priori* possibility may be asserted to exist in the case of the Bible, that a comparison of its phenomena with its doctrine may bring out a glaring inconsistency. The test of the truth of the claims of the Bible to be inspired of God through comparison with its contents, characteristics and phenomena, the Bible cannot expect to escape; and the lovers of the Bible will be the last to deny the validity of it. By all means let the doctrine of the Bible be tested by the facts and let the test be made all the more, not the less, stringent and penetrating because of the great issues that hang upon it. If the facts are inconsistent with the doctrine, let us all know it, and know it so clearly that the matter is put beyond doubt. But let us not conceal from ourselves the greatness of the issues involved in the test, lest we approach the test in too light a spirit, and make shipwreck of faith in the trustworthiness of the apostles as teachers of doctrine, with the easy indifference of a man who corrects the incidental errors of a piece of gossip. Nor is this appeal to the seriousness of the issues involved in any sense an appeal to deal deceitfully with the facts concerning or stated in the Bible, through fear of disturbing our confidence in a comfortable doctrine of its infallibility. It is simply an appeal to common sense. If you are told that a malicious lie has been uttered by some unknown person you may easily yield the report a languid provisional assent; such things are not impossible, unfortunately in this sinful world not unexampled. But if it is told you of your loved and trusted friend, you will probably demand the most stringent proof at the point of your walking stick. So far as this, Robert Browning has missed neither nature nor right reason, when he makes his Ferishtah point out how much more evidence we require in proof of a fact which brings us loss than what is sufficient to command.

> "The easy acquiescence of mankind
> In matters nowise worth dispute."

If it is right to test most carefully the claim of every settled and accepted faith by every fact asserted in rebuttal of it, it must be equally right, nay incumbent, to scrutinize most closely the evidence for an asserted fact, which, if genuine, wounds in its vitals some important interest. If it would be a crime to refuse to consider most carefully and candidly any phenomena of Scripture asserted to be inconsistent with its inerrancy, it would be equally a crime to accept the asserted reality of phenomena of Scripture, which, if real, strike at the trustworthiness of the apostolic witness to doctrine, on any evidence of less than demonstrative weight.

But we approach the consideration of these phenomena alleged to be inconsistent with the Biblical doctrine of inspiration not only thus with what may be called, though in a high sense, a sentimental presumption against their reality. The presumption is an eminently rational one, and is capable of somewhat exact estimation. We do not adopt the doctrine of the plenary inspiration of Scripture on sentimental grounds, nor even, as we have already had occasion to remark on *a priori* or general grounds of whatever kind. We adopt it specifically because it is taught us as truth by Christ and His apostles, in the Scriptural record of their teaching, and the evidence for its truth is, therefore, as we have also already pointed out, precisely that evidence, in weight and amount, which vindicates for us the trustworthiness of Christ and His apostles as teachers of doctrine. Of course, this evidence is not in the strict logical sense "demonstrative"; it is "probable" evidence. It therefore leaves open the metaphysical possibility of its being mistaken. But it may be contended that it is about as great in amount and weight as "probable" evidence can be made, and that the strength of conviction which it is adapted to produce may be and should be practically equal to that produced by demonstration itself. But whatever weight it has, and whatever strength of conviction it is adapted to produce, it is with this weight of evidence behind us and with this strength of conviction as to the unreality of any alleged phenomena contradictory of the Biblical doctrine of inspiration, that we approach the study of the characteristics, the structure, and the detailed statements of the Bible. Their study is not to be neglected; we have not attained through "probable" evidence apodeictic certainty of the Bible's infallibility. But neither is the reality of the alleged phenomena inconsistent with the Bible's doctrine, to be allowed without sufficient evidence. Their reality cannot be logically or rationally recognized unless the evidence for it be greater in amount and weight than the whole mass of evidence for the trustworthiness of the Biblical writers as teachers of doctrine.

It is not to be thought that this amounts to a recommendation of strained exegesis in order to rid the Bible of phenomena adverse to the truth of the Biblical doctrine of inspiration. It amounts to a recommendation of great care in the exegetical determination of these alleged phenomena; it amounts to a recommendation to allow that our exegesis determining these phenomena is not infallible. But it is far from recommending either strained or artificial exegesis of any kind. We are not bound to harmonize the alleged phenomena with the Bible doctrine; and if we cannot harmonize them save by strained or artificial exegesis they would be better left unharmonized. We are not bound, however, on the other hand, to believe that they are unharmonizable, because we cannot harmonize them save by strained exegesis. Our individual fertility in exegetical expedients, our individual insight into exegetical truth, our individual capacity of understanding are not the measure of truth. If we cannot harmonize without straining, let us leave unharmonized. It is not necessary for us to see the harmony that it should exist or even be recognized by us as existing. But it is necessary for us to believe the harmony to be possible and real, provided that we are not prepared to say that we clearly see that on any conceivable hypothesis (conceivable to us or conceivable to any other intelligent beings) the harmony is impossible—if the trustworthiness of the Biblical writers who teach us the doctrine of plenary inspiration is really safeguarded to us on evidence which we cannot disbelieve. In that case every unharmonized passage remains a case of difficult harmony and does not pass into the category of objections to plenary inspiration. It can pass into the category of objections only if we are prepared to affirm that we clearly see that it is, on any conceivable hypothesis of its meaning, clearly inconsistent with the Biblical doctrine of inspiration. In that case we would no doubt need to give up the Biblical doctrine of inspiration; but with it we must also give up our confidence in the Biblical writers as teachers of doctrine. And if we cannot reasonably give up this latter, neither can we reasonably allow that the phenomena apparently inconsistent with the former are real, or really inconsistent with it. And this is but to say that we approach the study of these phenomena with a presumption against their being such as will disprove the Biblical doctrine of inspiration—or, we may add (for this is but the same thing in different words), correct or modify the Biblical doctrine of inspiration—which is measured precisely by the amount and weight of the evidence which goes to show that the Bible is a trustworthy guide to doctrine.

The importance of emphasizing these, as it would seem, very obvious principles, does not arise out of need for a very great presumption in order to overcome the difficulties arising from the "phenomena" of Scripture, as over against its doctrine of inspiration. Such difficulties are not specially numerous or intractable. Dr. Charles Hodge justly characterizes those that have been adduced by disbelievers in the plenary inspiration of the Scriptures, as "for the most part trivial," "only apparent," and marvelously few "of any real importance." They bear, he adds, about the same relation to the whole that a speck of sandstone detected here and there in the marble of the Parthenon would bear to that building.[59] They do not for the most part require explaining away, but only to be fairly understood in order to void them. They constitute no real strain upon faith, but when approached in a candid spirit one is left continually marveling at the excessive fewness of those which do not, like ghosts, melt away from vision as soon as faced. Moreover, as every student of the history of exegesis and criticism knows, they are a progressively vanishing quantity. Those which seemed most obvious and intractable a generation or two ago, remain today as only too readily forgotten warnings against the ineradicable and inordinate dogmatism of the opponents of the inerrancy of the Bible, who over-ride continually every canon of historical and critical caution in their eager violence against the doctrine that they assail. What scorn they expressed of "apologists" who doubted whether Luke was certainly in error in assigning a "proconsul" to Cyprus, whether he was in error in making Lysanias a contemporary tetrarch with the Herodian rulers, and the like. How easily that scorn is forgotten as the progress of discovery has one by one vindicated the assertions of the Biblical historians. The matter has come to such a pass, indeed, in the progress of discovery, that there is a sense in which it may be said that the doctrine of the inerrancy of the Bible can now be based, with considerable confidence, on its observed "phenomena." What marvelous accuracy is characteristic of its historians! Dr. Fisher, in a paper already referred to, invites his readers to read Archibald Forbes' article in the *Nineteenth Century* (March 1892), on "Napoleon the Third at Sedan," that they may gain some idea of how the truth of history as to the salient facts may be preserved amid "hopeless and bewildering discrepancies in regard to details," in the reports of the most trustworthy eye-witnesses. The article is instructive in this regard. And it is instructive in another regard also. What a contrast exists between this mass of "hopeless and bewildering discrepancies in regard to details," among the accounts of a single important transaction, written by careful and watchful eye-witnesses, who were on the ground for the precise purpose of gathering the facts for report, and who were seeking to give an exact and honest account of the events which they witnessed, and the marvelous accuracy of the Biblical writers! If these "hopeless and bewildering discrepancies" are consistent with the honesty and truthfulness and general trustworthiness of the uninspired writers, may it not be argued that the so much greater accuracy attained by the Biblical writers when describing not one event but the history of ages—and a history filled with pitfalls for the unwary—has something more than honesty and truthfulness behind it, and warrants the attribution to them of something more than general trustworthiness? And, if in the midst of this marvel of general accuracy there remain here and there a few difficulties as yet not fully explained in harmony with it, or if in the course of the historical vindication of it in general a rare difficulty (as in the case of some of the statements of Daniel) seems to increase in sharpness, are we to throw ourselves with desperate persistency into these "last ditches" and strive by our increased insistence upon the impregnability of *them* to conceal from men

---

59. *Systematic Theology*, 1:169–70: We have purposely adduced this passage here to enable us to protest against the misuse of it, which, in the exigencies of the present controversy, has been made, as if Dr. Hodge was in this passage admitting the reality of the alleged errors. The passage occurs in the reply to objections to the doctrine, not in the development of the doctrine itself, and is of the nature of an *argumentum ad hominem*. How far Dr. Hodge was from admitting the reality of error in the original Biblical text may be estimated from the frequency with which he asserts its freedom from error in the immediately preceding context—152, 155, 163 (no less than three times on this page), 165–66, 169 (no less than five times).

that the main army has been beaten from the field? Is it not more reasonable to suppose that these difficulties, too, will receive their explanation with advancing knowledge? And is it not the height of the unreasonable to treat them like the Sibylline books as of ever-increasing importance in proportion to their decreasing number? The importance of keeping in mind that there is a presumption against the reality of these "inconsistent phenomena," and that the presumption is of a weight measurable only by the weight of evidence which vindicates the general trustworthiness of the Bible as a teacher of doctrine, does not arise from the need of so great a presumption in order to overcome the weight of the alleged opposing facts. Those facts are not specially numerous, important or intractable, and they are, in the progress of research, a vanishing quantity.

The importance of keeping in mind the principle in question arises rather from the importance of preserving a correct logical method. There are two ways of approaching the study of the inspiration of the Bible. One proceeds by obtaining first the doctrine of inspiration taught by the Bible as applicable to itself, and then testing this doctrine by the facts as to the Bible as ascertained by Biblical criticism and exegesis. This is good logical procedure; and in the presence of a vast mass of evidence for the general trustworthiness of the Biblical writings as witnesses of doctrine, and for the appointment of their writers as teachers of divine truth to men, and for the presence of the Holy Spirit with and in them aiding them in their teaching (in whatever degree and with whatever effect)—it would seem to be the only logical and proper mode of approaching the question. The other method proceeds by seeking the doctrine of inspiration in the first instance through a comprehensive induction from the facts as to the structure and contents of the Bible, as ascertained by critical and exegetical processes, treating all these facts as co-factors of the same rank for the induction. If in this process the facts of structure and the facts embedded in the record of Scripture—which are called, one-sidedly indeed but commonly, by the class of writers who adopt this procedure, "the phenomena" of Scripture—alone are considered, it would be difficult to arrive at a precise doctrine of inspiration, at the best: though, as we have already pointed out, a degree and kind of accuracy might be vindicated for the Scriptures which might lead us to suspect and to formulate as the best account of it, some divine assistance to the writers' memory, mental processes and expression. If the Biblical facts and teaching are taken as co-factors in the induction, the procedure (as we have already pointed out) is liable to the danger of modifying the teaching by the facts without clear recognition of what is being done; the result of which would be the loss from observation of one main fact of errancy, viz., the inaccuracy of the teaching of the Scriptures as to their own inspiration. This would vitiate the whole result: and this vitiation of the result can be avoided only by ascertaining separately the teaching of Scripture as to its own inspiration, and by accounting the results of this ascertainment one of the facts of the induction. Then we are in a position to judge by the comparison of this fact with the other facts, whether this fact of teaching is in accord or in disaccord with those facts of performance. If it is in disaccord, then of course this disaccord is the main factor in the case: the writers are convicted of false teaching. If it is in accord, then, if the teaching is not proved by the accord, it is at least left credible, and may be believed with whatever confidence may be justified by the evidence which goes to show that these writers are trustworthy as deliverers of doctrine. And if nice and difficult questions arise in the comparison of the fact of teaching with the facts of performance, it is inevitable that the relative weight of the evidence for the trustworthiness of the two sets of facts should be the deciding factor in determining the truth. This is as much as to say that the asserted facts as to performance must give way before the fact as to teaching, unless the evidence on which they are based as facts outweighs the evidence on which the teaching may be accredited as true. But this correction of the second method of procedure, by which alone it can be made logical in form or valid in result, amounts to nothing less than setting it aside altogether and reverting to the first method, according to which the teaching of Scripture is first to be determined, and then this teaching to be tested by the facts of performance.

The importance of proceeding according to the true logical method may be illustrated by the observation that the conclusions actually arrived at by students of the subject seem practically to depend on the logical method adopted. In fact, the difference here seems mainly a difference in point of view. If we start from the Scripture doctrine of inspiration, we approach the phenomena with the question whether they will negative this doctrine, and we find none able to stand against it, commended to us as true, as it is, by the vast mass of evidence available to prove the trustworthiness of the Scriptural writers as teachers of doctrine. But if we start simply with a collection of the phenomena, classifying and reasoning from them, whether alone or in conjunction with the Scriptural statements, it may easily happen with us, as it happened with certain of old, that meeting with some things hard to be understood, we may be ignorant and unstable enough to wrest them to our own intellectual destruction, and so approach the Biblical doctrine of inspiration set upon explaining it away. The value of having the Scripture doctrine as a clue in our hands, is thus fairly illustrated by the ineradicable inability of the whole negative school to distinguish between *difficulties* and *proved errors*. If then we ask what we are to do with the numerous phenomena of Scripture inconsistent with verbal inspiration, which, so it is alleged, "criticism" has brought to light, we must reply: Challenge them in the name of the New Testament doctrine, and ask for their credentials. They have no credentials that can stand before that challenge. No single error has as yet been demonstrated to occur in the Scriptures as given by God to His Church. And every critical student knows, as already pointed out, that the progress of investigation has been a continuous process of removing difficulties, until scarcely a shred of the old list of "Biblical Errors" remains to hide the nakedness of this moribund contention. To say that we do not wish to make claims "for which we have only this to urge, that they cannot be absolutely disproved," is not to the point; what is to the point is to say, that we cannot set aside the presumption arising from the general trustworthiness of Scripture, that its doctrine of inspiration is true, by any array of contradictory facts, each one of which is fairly disputable. We must have indisputable errors—which are not forthcoming.

The real problem brought before the Churches by the present debate ought now to be sufficiently plain. In its deepest essence it is whether we can still trust the Bible as a guide in doctrine, as a teacher of truth. It is not simply whether we can explain away the Biblical doctrine of inspiration so as to allow us to take a different view from what has been common of the structure and characteristics of the Bible. Nor, on the other hand, is it simply whether we may easily explain the facts, established as facts, embedded in Scripture, consistently with the teaching of Scripture as to the nature, extent and effects of inspiration. It is specifically whether the results proclaimed by a special school of Biblical criticism—which are of such a character, as is now admitted by all, as to necessitate, if adopted, a new view of the Bible and of its inspiration—rest on a basis of evidence strong enough to meet and overcome the weight of evidence, whatever that may be in kind and amount, which goes to show that the Biblical writers are trustworthy as teachers of doctrine. If we answer this question in the affirmative, then no doubt we shall have not only a new view of the Bible and of its inspiration but also a whole new theology, because we must seek a new basis for doctrine. But if we answer it in the negative, we may possess our souls in patience and be assured that the Scriptures are as trustworthy witnesses to truth when they declare a doctrine of Inspiration as when they declare a doctrine of Incarnation or of Redemption, even though in the one case as in the other difficulties may remain, the full explanation of which is not yet clear to us. The real question, in a word, is not a new question but the perennial old question, whether the basis of our doctrine is to be what the Bible teaches, or what men teach. And this is a question which is to be settled on the old method, viz., on our estimate of the weight and value of the evidence which places the Bible in our hands as a teacher of doctrine.

Old Princeton, Westminster, and Inerrancy[1]

M O I S É S   S I L V A

Moisés Silva, "Old Princeton, Westminster, and Inerrancy," *WTJ* 50, 1 (Spring 1988): 65–80; reprinted in *Inerrancy and Hermeneutic*, 67–80.

Moisés Silva taught New Testament at Westminster Theological Seminary from 1981 to 1996 (for more details on Silva, see chap. 50 below). The selection presented here originally appeared in the *WTJ* in 1988. It is a revised version of Silva's inaugural lecture as professor of New Testament delivered on February 19, 1985. This essay is also reprinted in *Inerrancy and Hermeneutic*. Here Silva explores what it means to hold to the doctrine of inerrancy as "has been understood by its best exponents." In particular he examines the famous article by A. A. Hodge and B. B. Warfield on inspiration. Silva shows how this view of Scripture was foundational to the founding of Westminster Theological Seminary in the context of rigorous scholarship and a confessional framework. In these parameters, he shows how a certain diversity of views can coexist. In particular, Silva's study addresses challenging issues such as eschatology, the interpretation of Genesis 1–3, and harmonization (cf. Raymond B. Dillard, chap. 58 below). This address offers helpful insight from within the Princeton/Westminster perspective of biblical scholarship.

Bibliography: D. Clair Davis. "Princeton and Inerrancy: The Nineteenth-Century Philosophical Background of Contemporary Concerns." Pp. 359–78 in *Inerrancy and the Church*. A. A. Hodge and B. B. Warfield. "Inspiration." *Presbyterian Review* 2, 6 (April 1881): 225–60. Repr., *Inspiration*. Introduction by Roger R. Nicole. Grand Rapids: Baker, 1979. Mark A. Noll, ed. *The Princeton Defense of Plenary Verbal Inspiration.* New York: Garland, 1988. John D. Woodbridge and Randall H. Balmer. "The Princetonians and Biblical Authority: An Assessment of the Ernest Sandeen Proposal." Pp. 251–79, 396–410 in *Scripture and Truth*.

1. Revised version of an address delivered by the author on the occasion of his inauguration as Professor of New Testament at Westminster Theological Seminary on February 19, 1985.

Warm devotion to the Reformed faith. Noble aggressiveness in the defense of historical orthodoxy. Emphasis on the exegesis of the original languages of Scripture. Commitment to the blending of piety and intellect. Willingness to engage opposing viewpoints with scholarly courtesy and integrity. These and other qualities combined to give Princeton Theological Seminary, from its inception through the 1920s, a powerful distinctiveness in the ecclesiastical and academic worlds. It was this distinctiveness that the founders of Westminster Theological Seminary sought to preserve when the new institution was established in 1929.

We would betray the genius of this tradition if we were to identify any one issue as all-important or determinative. And yet, given the historical contexts that brought Princeton into new prominence in the late nineteenth century and that brought Westminster into existence half-a-century ago, one must fully acknowledge the unique role played by the doctrine of inerrancy as that doctrine has been understood by its best exponents, notably B. B. Warfield. It may be an exaggeration, but only a mild one, to say that the infallibility of Scripture, with its implications, has provided Westminster's *raison d'être*. Indeed, as far as the present faculty is concerned, we would sooner pack up our books than abandon our conviction that the Scriptures are truly God's very breath.

What I would like to stress in this chapter, however, is the definition of inerrancy implied by the words in the previous paragraph: *as that doctrine has been understood by its best exponents*. The contemporary debate regarding inerrancy appears hopelessly vitiated by the failure—in both conservative and non-conservative camps—to mark how carefully nuanced were Warfield's formulations. The heat generated by today's controversies has not always been accompanied by the expected light, and for every truly helpful statement one will easily encounter ten that blur the issues. The unfortunate result is that large numbers of writers and students assume, quite incorrectly, that their ideas about inerrancy correspond with the classic conception.

One effective way to demonstrate this point would be to conduct a survey that asked people to identify selected quotations. Take the following statement on biblical inspiration:

> It is not merely in the matter of verbal expression or literary composition that the personal idiosyncracies of each author are freely manifested . . . , but the very substance of what they write is evidently for the most part the product of their own mental and spiritual activities. . . . [Each author of Scripture] gave evidence of his own special limitations of knowledge and mental power, and of his personal defects as well as of his powers.

Here is another one:

> [The Scriptures] are written in human languages, whose words, inflections, constructions and idioms bear everywhere indelible traces of error. The record itself furnishes evidence that the writers were in large measure dependent for their knowledge upon sources and methods in themselves fallible, and that their personal knowledge and judgments were in many matters hesitating and defective, or even wrong.

Where do these remarks come from? A nineteenth-century liberal like Briggs? Some recent radical theologian like Bultmann? Those words, it turns out, come from what is widely regarded as the classic formulation of biblical inerrancy by the two great Princeton theologians A. A. Hodge and B. B. Warfield.[2] Most evangelicals, I am sure, would be quite surprised to hear this. Some of them might even decide that Warfield didn't really believe the Bible after all. The situation is even worse among nonevangelical writers, very few of whom would be able to understand that the quotations above are indeed consistent with a belief in inerrancy.

This widespread ignorance works to the detriment of the doctrine. For example, when modern conservative scholars seek to nuance the discussion, they are more often than not accused of putting the doctrine to death through a thousand qualifications. Indeed, these scholars are perceived as back-pedaling on their commitment to inerrancy and redefining its boundaries more or less after the fact—as though they were making up the rules as they go along. Sadly, that assessment is accurate enough in certain cases, and one can fully understand (and even share) the concern expressed in some quarters.

The passages quoted above, however, should make it plain that, in its original form, the Princetonian doctrine was carefully qualified, and that contemporary scholars who do the same are not necessarily undermining inerrancy but possibly preserving it. The common conception of Warfield is that he came up with a "deductive" approach to inspiration which did not take into account the phenomena of Scripture. Such an approach would in any case have been unlikely when one considers Warfield's expertise in the fine points of textual criticism and exegesis,[3] and our two quotations leave no doubt that the common view is a grotesque misconception. Similarly, it makes little sense to accuse modern evangelical scholars of (a) being insensitive to the text if they happen to believe in inerrancy, or (b) being untrue to inerrancy if they take fully into account the human qualities of Scripture.

Before proceeding any further, however, it is crucial to point out that the two passages quoted above cannot be taken, by themselves, as an adequate representation of the Hodge/Warfield view. The whole thesis of their famous work is that the Bible, whose primary author is God, teaches no errors. That thesis is the broad context necessary to understand their qualifications. One can easily imagine how some contemporaries who wish to preserve their identity as evangelicals while abandoning the doctrine of inerrancy might gleefully inscribe those two quotations on their personal banners and announce to the world their solidarity with Warfield.

But that is hardly fair to the Old Princeton theology. Indeed, it would constitute one more example of the kind of shoddy use of sources that got us into our present confusion to begin with. Writers (liberals and conservatives) who like to quote Warfield's strongest expressions of inerrancy without paying attention to the nuances that accompany them are

2. A. A. Hodge and B. B. Warfield, *Inspiration* (1881; repr., Grand Rapids: Baker, 1979), 12–13, 28. Interestingly, the second quotation was attacked at the time of publication as reflecting a lowered view of inspiration. Cf. Warfield's responses, included as Appendices 1 and 2 in *Inspiration,* 73–82.

3. Warfield became a member of the Society of Biblical Literature and Exegesis as early as 1882 and contributed a number of technical articles to *Journal of Biblical Literature* and other periodicals. One interesting example is "Notes on the *Didache*," *Journal of Biblical Literature* 5 (June 1886): 86–98. For other material, cf. John E. Meeter and Roger Nicole, *A Bibliography of Benjamin Breckinridge Warfield, 1851–1921* (n.p.: Presbyterian and Reformed, 1974).

no worse than individuals who look for the qualifications alone and ignore the very thesis that is being qualified.

Without seeking to exegete those two quotations, we should at least identify the basic qualification that the authors have in view, namely, the need to distinguish between official teaching and personal opinion. Elsewhere Warfield stated that such a distinction

> seems, in general, a reasonable one. No one is likely to assert infallibility for the apostles in aught else than in their official teaching. And whatever they may be shown to have held apart from their official teaching, may readily be looked upon with only that respect which we certainly must accord to the opinions of men of such exceptional intellectual and spiritual insight.
>
> A presumption may be held to lie also that [Paul] shared the ordinary opinions of his day in certain matters lying outside the scope of his teachings, as, for example, with reference to the form of the earth, or its relation to the sun; and it is not inconceivable that the form of his language, when incidentally adverting to such matters, might occasionally play into the hands of such a presumption.[4]

Warfield did not mean, of course, that every chapter of the Bible may well contain erroneous personal opinions and that we are left to our subjective judgment regarding the authoritative character of each proposition. Such an interpretation of Warfield's words would be a complete travesty. What he surely had in view was the occasional occurrence of certain forms of expression, such as conventional phrases, that *reflect* commonly held views regarding history, nature, etc.

Inspiration does not convey omniscience, and since the personal limitations of any one biblical writer are not all miraculously suspended by virtue of his being inspired, we may expect to see here and there some evidences that he was indeed a limited human being. The marvel of inspiration resides precisely in this fact, that the divine origin of Scripture insures the preservation of both the divine truth being communicated and the unique personality of each writer. The Holy Spirit, in other words, prevents the authors from teaching falsehood or error without overriding their personal traits.

Warfield's distinction between the "official teaching" of Paul and on the other hand those "matters lying outside the scope of his teachings" is exceedingly important for our concerns. In effect, it forces us to consider the thorny issue of authorial purpose or intention.[5] And this issue in turn reminds us of the crucial role that exegesis must play in our discussion. Not everything found in the Scriptures is actually affirmed or taught by the biblical authors (e.g., "There is no God," Ps. 14:1). The text must therefore be studied so that we can determine what it teaches. Such is the task in view when we say that we must identify the author's intent. To put it simply, we must figure out what the writer wishes to communicate. Unfortunately, the words *intention* and *purpose* have become veritable shibboleths in the

---

4. B. B. Warfield, *The Inspiration and Authority of the Bible* (Philadelphia: Presbyterian and Reformed, 1948), 196–97. The passage comes from an article, "The Real Problem of Inspiration," originally published in the *Presbyterian and Reformed Review* 4 (1893): 177–221.

5. One issue that cannot detain us here, however, is the distinction among such factors as divine meaning, author's meaning, audience meaning, and so on. I must assume that the readers of this article recognize the primary importance of ascertaining the original historical meaning of a document (whatever credence they may or may not give to the possibility of additional meanings intended by God or read into the text by later readers).

contemporary debate. Some writers, in fact, argue that the appeal to intention undermines biblical authority.[6]

Their concern is understandable, since these terms are a little vague. A theologian, for instance, may have in mind the broad purpose of Scripture and argue that, while the Bible could be full of errors, yet it is infallible in its explicit teachings about salvation. Again, another writer may suggest that the intention of the biblical author is a psychological element behind the text and to be distinguished from the text—a position reminiscent of the old argument that it is the thoughts, not the words, of Scripture that are inspired and infallible. These and comparable formulations are indeed destructive of biblical authority and must be rejected.[7]

It would be a grave mistake, however, if we allowed these abuses to force us into the indefensible position of denying the crucial exegetical role played by an author's intention, for this is the fundamental element of the principle of *sensus literalis*. Grammatico-historical exegesis is simply the attempt to figure out what the biblical writer, under divine guidance, was saying. The basic question is then, What did the author mean? The only evidence we have to answer that question is the text itself. In other words, we dare not speak about the Bible's infallibility in such a way that it legitimizes random and arbitrary interpretations of the text.

Our best theologians made it clear all along that inerrancy was being claimed for the Bible on the assumption that the Bible would be interpreted responsibly, and such a proper interpretation consists in determining what the original author meant, what he intended. As Hodge and Warfield stated it: the Bible gives us "a correct statement of facts or principles intended to be affirmed. . . . Every statement accurately corresponds to truth just as far forth as affirmed."[8]

It may be useful to illustrate our problem by referring to 1 Corinthians 10:8, where Paul makes mention of 23,000 Israelites who died because of their immorality, in apparent conflict with Numbers 25:9, where the number given is 24,000. Notice the following attempt to solve the problem:

It is not unheard of, *when there is no intention* of making an exact count of individuals, to give an approximate number. . . . Moses gives the upper limits, Paul the lower.

6. Nelson Kloosterman, for example, speaks pejoratively of those who "hold to a Bible whose authority is limited by the human author's intentions, intentions which can presumably be exposed and defended by a certain kind of theological scholarship" ("Why You Need Mid-America Theological Seminary," *The Outlook* 31, 12 [December 1981]: 3). Similarly, Harold Lindsell, in *The Battle for the Bible* (Grand Rapids: Zondervan, 1976), makes the same point repeatedly. Even Lindsell, of course, finds it necessary to appeal to the concept of intention, as in his discussion of the parable of the mustard seed: "The *American Commentary* says of this passage that it was popular language, and it was the intention of the speaker to communicate the fact that the mustard seed was 'the smallest that his hearers were accustomed to sow.' And indeed this may well be the case. In that event there was no error" (p. 169).

7. Norman L. Geisler has rightly attempted to discredit these approaches in "The Relation of Purpose and Meaning in Interpreting Scripture," *Grace Theological Journal* 5 (1984): 229–45. Unfortunately, Geisler draws too sharp a distinction between meaning and purpose. Determining the purpose of a text is one of the elements necessary to identify the context of the document. On p. 231 Geisler attacks interpreters of Genesis 1–2 who believe that those chapters intend merely to draw men to worship God. Geisler seems unaware that his own understanding of those chapters (with which I concur) also assumes a certain purpose, namely, the intent to state certain historical facts. Cf. these comments by Hodge and Warfield: "No objection [to inspiration] is valid . . . which overlooks the prime question: What was the professed or implied purpose of the writer in making this statement? . . . Exegesis must be historical as well as grammatical, and must always seek the meaning *intended*, not any meaning that can be tortured out of a passage" (*Inspiration*, 42 and 43; italics in the original).

8. Hodge and Warfield, *Inspiration*, 28–29. It is very important to note that Warfield emphasized this particular qualification when he responded to criticisms of the article (cf. pp. 79–80).

The next quotation, though longer, seems to make the same point:

> Neither of the writers *intended to state* the exact number, this being of no consequence to their object. . . . It was not at all necessary, in order to maintain their character as men of veracity, that they should, when writing *for such a purpose*, mention the exact number. The particularity and length of the [exact] expression would have been inconvenient, and might have made a less desirable impression of the evil of sin, and the justice of God, than expressing it more briefly in a round number; as we often say, with a view merely to make a strong impression, that in such a battle ten thousand, or fifty thousand, or half a million were slain, no one supposing that we mean to state the number with arithmetical exactness, as *our object does not require this.* And who can doubt, that the divine Spirit might lead the sacred penman to make use of this principle of rhetoric, and to speak of those who were slain, according to the common practice in such a case, in round numbers?

Here is another author that takes a similar approach:

> Are there errors in the Bible? Certainly not, so long as we are talking in terms *of the purpose of its authors* and the acceptable standards of precision of that day. . . . *For the purpose* that Paul had in mind [the variation] made no difference. His concern was to warn against immorality, not to give a flawless performance in statistics.

All three of these writers seem concerned to deny that the apostle is guilty of an error, yet none of them attempts some artificial harmonization (for example, the view that Paul is speaking about those who fell "in one day," while Numbers includes the additional 1,000 who died later). Moreover, all three of them assume that inerrancy does not necessarily demand mathematical exactness. Finally, all of them appeal to Paul's intention or purpose to use a round number. I am unable to see any substantive difference among these three explanations.

The three authors quoted above happen to be John Calvin, the nineteenth-century American theologian Leonard Wood (one of the most forceful defenders of biblical inerrancy prior to B. B. Warfield), and our contemporary Robert H. Mounce.[9] My reason for bringing these three quotations together is to point out that Harold Lindsell quotes the third of those statements as evidence that Mounce does not believe in inerrancy, yet a few pages later he presents the quote from Calvin as giving an acceptable treatment of the problem![10] It may be that the tone of Mounce's brief article (it sounds as though the author is apologizing for the evangelical view) led Lindsell to believe that Mounce had indeed rejected the doctrine of inerrancy. It is impossible, however, to prove that point from the quotation above—or, for that matter, from the other statements by Mounce to which Lindsell refers.

In any case, we can see clearly how easy it is to misconstrue qualifying statements, even when the qualification in view is very much a part of the evangelical tradition. In short, the appeal to the author's intent, if properly understood, is an integral element in the classical affirmations of biblical inerrancy. And the reason is, if I may repeat myself, that we cannot

---

9. John Calvin, *The First Epistle of Paul the Apostle to the Corinthians* (Grand Rapids: Eerdmans, 1961), 208–9; Leonard Wood, *The Works of Leonard Wood, D.D.* (Boston: Congregational Board of Publications, 1854), 1.173; R. H. Mounce, "Clues to Understanding Biblical Accuracy," *Eternity* 17, 6 (June, 1966): 18. (The italics are mine, except for the phrase *such a purpose* in the second quotation.) In connection with Wood, note the very helpful discussion of pre-Warfield inerrantists by Randall H. Balmer, "The Princetonians and Scripture: A Reconsideration," *WTJ* 44 (1982): 352–65.

10. Lindsell, *Battle*, 168.

claim to know what the Scripture infallibly teaches unless we have done our exegetical homework.

Our discussion so far has made it apparent that one can hardly speak of inerrancy without getting involved in hermeneutics. And yet, an exceedingly important caveat is necessary here, for while the two concepts are closely related or even inseparable, they are also distinct. For inerrancy to function properly in our use of Scripture, an adequate hermeneutics is a prerequisite. But that is a far cry from suggesting that the doctrine of inerrancy automatically provides us with the correct hermeneutics, except in the rather general sense that it precludes any interpretation that makes out God to lie or to err.

A few examples will clarify the issue. As recently as two decades ago it was not unusual to come across devout Christians who were persuaded that, when interpreting prophecy, a premillennialist eschatology was the only approach consistent with the doctrine of infallibility. For many of these brethren—of whom a few remain, I am sure—a so-called literal interpretation of prophetic passages was taken as evidence, maybe even as the most important piece of evidence, that an individual believed the Bible; and it was taken for granted that amillennialists, therefore, were "liberals." But such an equation is baseless, since the doctrine of inerrancy does not determine that any one prophecy (or set of prophecies) must be interpreted "literally." That can only be determined by an exegesis of the passage(s) in question.

Let's take a more disturbing example: the historicity of Genesis 1–3. All inerrantists, so far as I know, believe in the factual character of that material. This state of affairs creates a certain presumption that inerrancy *by itself* demands such an interpretation. But the presumption is false; indeed, it is an equivocation. The doctrine of biblical infallibility no more requires that narratives be interpreted "literally" than it requires that prophetic passages be interpreted "literally." That decision must be arrived at by textual evidence and exegetical argument.

Now I happen to believe that the essential historicity of Genesis 1–3 is a fundamental article of Christian orthodoxy. It would surely require hermeneutical prestidigitation to argue that the original writer meant those chapters to be taken as "less historical" than the later patriarchal narratives (and could the original audience have discovered any such distinction between the early and the later chapters of the book?). For that reason and others, such as Paul's argumentation in Romans 5 and 1 Corinthians 15, I would want to argue very strongly that the proper interpretation of the Genesis material is one that does justice to its historical claim.

And yet I would want to argue just as strongly that such an interpretation is independent of my commitment to inerrancy. These are two distinct questions. Of course, once we have established exegetically that the first three chapters of Genesis teach historical facts, then our belief in infallibility requires us to accept those chapters as factual. But infallibility, apart from exegesis, does not by itself determine historicity. Otherwise we would be obligated to accept as historical Nathan's story in 2 Samuel 12:1–4 or even the parable of the trees in Judges 9:7–15.

I have deliberately chosen my two examples from polar opposites. Relatively few evangelicals would argue that inerrancy entails premillennialism, but many seem ready to argue that it does require a historical interpretation of Genesis 1–3. Between these two extremes are countless interpretations that have traditionally been held by conservatives and that are viewed as necessary consequences of accepting biblical infallibility. It may therefore prove worthwhile pointing out that the Princeton/Westminster tradition, though it has stood forcefully and unequivocally for biblical inerrancy, has never degenerated into the practice of assuming, apart from exegetical demonstration, that this doctrine requires the adoption of particular interpretations.

My first example comes from the area of the relationship between the Bible and science. Students familiar with Warfield's writings are well aware of his positive attitude toward modern scientific theories regarding origins. Though it is a little difficult to determine specifically Warfield's position, it appears that his view came relatively close to what we call theistic evolution (without compromising, to be sure, the direct creation of man).[11]

J. Gresham Machen, in sharp contrast to the fundamentalism of his day, refused to become involved in the evolution controversy.[12] More recently, Meredith G. Kline proposed an interpretation of Genesis 1 that parted company with traditional views. Kline's colleague on the Westminster faculty, E. J. Young, took issue with that interpretation, but at no point in his argument did he accuse Kline of abandoning the doctrine of infallibility. Nor did Young simply assume that such a doctrine entailed the traditional view of Genesis but rather sought to refute Kline through careful exegetical argumentation.[13]

A second example has to do with higher criticism. This is one area, it must be admitted, where a belief in inerrancy appears to have a direct bearing on interpretation. If the author of a New Testament epistle, for example, claims to be the apostle Paul, we would be questioning the moral integrity of the author if we were to argue that the letter was not in fact written by Paul. Yet this set of questions too has to be decided on exegetical grounds, and not on the assumption that inerrancy entails a traditional view of authorship, date, etc.

It is no secret that E. J. Young, who was uncompromisingly conservative on virtually every higher-critical issue, came to the conclusion that the Book of Ecclesiastes was not composed by Solomon, even though that appears to be the claim of the book itself.[14] Professor Young was among the most conservative in the long line of biblical scholars in Old Princeton and Westminster. It is doubly significant, therefore, that he did not apparently see a necessary connection between a belief in inerrancy and the traditional view of Solomonic authorship for Ecclesiastes.

A third and particularly instructive example is the way different writers approach the difficult problem of Gospel harmonization. Take the story of the rich young ruler. According to Mark 10:17–18 and Luke 18:18–19 this ruler addressed Jesus as "Good Teacher" and asked what he could do to inherit eternal life; Jesus replied, "Why do you call me good?" In Matthew 19:16–17, however, the word "good" is transferred to the man's actual question ("Teacher, what good thing shall I do . . .?") and so Jesus' rebuke takes a different form: "Why do you ask me about the good?" Our first quotation seeks to solve the problem by incorporating both versions into one account:

11. Cf. Mark A. Noll, *The Princeton Theology, 1812–1921: Scripture, Science and Theological Method from Archibald Alexander to Benjamin Breckinridge Warfield* (Grand Rapids: Baker, 1983), 289, 293–94.

12. See Ned B. Stonehouse, *J. Gresham Machen: A Biographical Memoir* (Grand Rapids: Eerdmans, 1954), 401–2.

13. E. J. Young, *Studies in Genesis One* (Philadelphia: Presbyterian and Reformed, 1964), 58–64.

14. E. J. Young, *An Introduction to the Old Testament* (Grand Rapids: Eerdmans, 1949), 340. The revised 1964 edition omits the strongest paragraph, but it is clear that his position had not changed in spite of the fact that not a few feathers had been ruffled by it.

In all probability, the full question was, "Good teacher, what good thing shall I do that I may possess eternal life?" To this the complete answer of the Lord may have been, "Why callest thou Me good and why askest thou Me concerning that which is good?" . . . No one of the evangelists, however, has seen fit to give the complete question or the complete answer.

The second quotation reflects quite a different approach:

One must allow for the possibility that Matthew in his formulation of 19:16–17 has *not only been selective* as regards subject matter but also that he used some freedom in the precise language which he employed. The singular use of the adjective "good" might then be a particularly clear example of his use of that freedom. . . . One tendency [in the history of the harmonization of the Gospels] that is both conservative and simple, has been to join divergent features and to seek to weave them together into a harmonious whole. Where, however, the divergent elements are exceedingly difficult to combine in that way, it is insisted that the narratives must be regarded as reporting different events or different sayings. . . . there is, in my judgment, a sounder attitude to most problems of harmonization than that which was characterized above as conservative and simple.

Neither of these writers is against harmonization in principle, but they differ rather substantively in what they consider necessary to defend the integrity of the narrative. One could certainly argue that the second writer is directly reacting against the viewpoint espoused by the first. Remarkably, these two passages were written by contemporaries on the Westminster faculty. The first one comes from E. J. Young's famous work on inerrancy, published in the late 1950s, while the second statement was written just a few years later by Ned B. Stonehouse.[15] One is intrigued by the question whether Stonehouse remembered Young's discussion; if so, was he deliberately distancing himself from that approach? In any case, the differences are most instructive.

What shall we infer from these examples?[16] Should evangelical scholars be insulated from criticism if they appear to be bucking historic Christian tenets without clear biblical support? So far from it, that the Princeton/Westminster tradition has consistently deepened the evangelical conception of biblical authority within the framework of Reformed orthodoxy. No doubt, some may wish to appeal to the disagreements described above and argue that, therefore, "anything goes"—that the increasingly positive attitude toward higher criticism by a number of contemporary evangelical scholars is quite consistent with the doctrine of inerrancy. Such a move would hardly be honest, however, especially when one considers that the Princetonian formulations of inerrancy were meant precisely to counteract the growing popularity of nineteenth-century critical theories. What then can we learn from the history we have briefly surveyed?

15. E. J. Young, *Thy Word Is Truth: Some Thoughts on the Biblical Doctrine of Inspiration* (Grand Rapids: Eerdmans, 1957), 131; Ned B. Stonehouse, *Origins of the Synoptic Gospels: Some Basic Questions* (Grand Rapids: Eerdmans, 1963), 108–9, my emphasis. Warfield's own approach, which seems close to Young's, may be found in *The Person and Work of Christ* (Philadelphia: Presbyterian and Reformed, 1950), 160: "It lies in the nature of the case that the two accounts of a conversation which agree as to the substance of what was said, but differ slightly in the details reported, are reporting different fragments of the conversation, selected according to the judgment of each writer as the best vehicles of its substance."

16. Other intriguing examples of diversity could be mentioned. Particularly important (because of its relation to the field of ethics) is the case of Paul Woolley, professor of church history, who took a rather "liberal" position on a wide variety of social and political issues. On many questions of this sort Professor Woolley stood alone or nearly alone within the Westminster faculty, but to the best of my knowledge his devotion and commitment to biblical authority was never called into question.

The hermeneutical flexibility that has characterized our tradition would probably come as a surprise to many observers who view Westminster as excessively rigid. Ironically, our confessional documents, the Westminster Confession and Catechisms, are far more extensive and detailed than those found in most evangelical institutions. Our theological parameters are indeed very clearly defined, and yet those parameters themselves have made possible a diversity of viewpoints that would not have been tolerated in some other institutions.

It can even be argued, I think, that there is a direct connection between such a diversity and the fact that the Princeton/Westminster tradition has provided consistent leadership to the evangelical world in the area of biblical authority. Why is this so? The doctrine of infallibility assures us that we can have total confidence in God's revelation to us. It does not mean, however, that we may have total confidence in our particular interpretations of the Bible.

For many believers, unfortunately, assurance that the Bible is true appears to be inseparable from assurance about traditional interpretive positions, so that if we question the latter we seem to be doubting the former. George E. Ladd is absolutely right when he states:

> "Thus saith the Lord" means that God has spoken His sure, infallible Word. A corollary of this in the minds of many Christians is that we must have absolute, infallible answers to every question raised in the historical study of the Bible....
>
> This conclusion, as logical and persuasive as it may seem, does not square with the facts of God's Word; ... the authority of the Word of God is not dependent upon infallible certainty in all matters of history and criticism.[17]

I do not know to what extent Ladd agrees or disagrees with Warfield's position, but this quotation is perfectly consistent with it; more to the point, Ladd's qualification belongs to the very essence of the classical doctrine of inerrancy. Yet—inexplicably—Lindsell quotes those words as evidence that Ladd has abandoned biblical infallibility.[18]

Uncertainty is not a pleasant thing, and our instinct to avoid it can lead us into trouble. Concerned not to leave the door open to excesses, we are tempted to raise artificial barriers. But this medicine can be worse than the disease. I mention these things because there is a strong current of opinion in evangelical circles that says we need to tie inerrancy down to certain hermeneutical boundary lines. But to speak in this way is once again to increase the conceptual confusion. It is of course true that a commitment to inerrancy entails that we will believe such interpretations as are clearly demonstrable from the scriptural text, but inerrancy does not automatically settle interpretive debates, such as the mode of baptism, the doctrine of unconditional election, the practice of charismatic gifts, and so on.

Many evangelicals have awakened to the fact that belief in inerrancy does not insure acceptance of traditional positions, and several recent writers have emphasized the wide and significant disagreements that exist within the evangelical community. Some infer, not surprisingly, that the doctrine of inerrancy is of little value for Christian living and should therefore be given up. Conservatives then tend to overreact and argue that we need to define inerrancy in such a way as to guarantee that evangelicals will agree on important issues.[19]

---

17. George E. Ladd, *The New Testament and Criticism* (Grand Rapids: Eerdmans, 1967), 16–17.

18. Lindsell, *Battle*, 114. In fairness to Lindsell, I should point out that Ladd's language (in the larger section from which the quotation is taken) does not seem designed to inspire confidence in biblical infallibility.

19. I have treated this matter more extensively in *Has the Church Misread the Bible? The History of Interpretation in the Light of Current Issues* (Grand Rapids: Zondervan, 1987).

Nothing could be more wrongheaded. Forced hermeneutical unanimity is meaningless; worse, it would be destructive of biblical authority. To say that the doctrine of inerrancy demands acceptance of a particular interpretation is to raise human opinion to the level of divine infallibility; in such a case, said interpretation cannot be questioned and need not be defended. On the other hand, to acknowledge a measure of interpretive ambiguity, rattling though that may be, indicates our conviction that the Bible, and the Bible alone, is inerrant. To be sure, the Christian church may and must condemn hermeneutical approaches as well as specific interpretations that contradict the teaching of Scripture. But the point is this: the church cannot simply appeal to the infallibility of the Bible. The church is obligated to show persuasively that these interpretations are wrong. In short, we must exegete that infallible Bible and demonstrate that we have understood its teachings.

Perhaps it is now clear why, in my opinion, the hermeneutical flexibility that has found expression on the faculties of Old Princeton and Westminster has actually contributed to (instead of undermining) the influence these institutions have exerted with regard to the doctrine of biblical authority. Precisely because they accepted the reality of hermeneutical uncertainty, they worked especially hard to remove that uncertainty through careful exegesis.

It is no accident that Old Princeton and Westminster have been so obnoxious in requiring students to learn Greek and Hebrew. It was not some methodological misconception that led John Murray to teach courses in systematic theology that looked more like courses in exegesis. It was no blunder that made a Warfield or a Machen or a Stonehouse pay an enormous amount of attention to the work of liberal and radical scholars. These and other "oddities" are direct consequences of a commitment not to leave any stones unturned to find out what the Bible really says. Our whole ministry is, in its own way, a response to our Lord's penetrating criticism, "You err because you do not know the Scriptures." With Warfield we devote ourselves to the task of knowing the unerring Scriptures so that we will not err.

Part Eight

THE THEOLOGY OF SCRIPTURE OF THE FOUNDING FATHERS OF WESTMINSTER

THE FOUR THEOLOGIANS considered in this part exemplify well the transition from Princeton Theological Seminary to the beginnings of Westminster Theological Seminary. J. Gresham Machen and Robert Dick Wilson had long careers of teaching at Princeton Seminary before starting their endeavors at Westminster. Both were established biblical exegetes in the fields of New Testament and Old Testament, respectively. Their two younger colleagues Cornelius Van Til and John Murray had both studied at Princeton Seminary and taught there for a short time before joining the faculty at Westminster. While Van Til brought to bear his Dutch background in theology and apologetics, Murray carried with him the Presbyterian theology of his native Scotland. These last two had long and influential careers at Westminster.

Machen's text was originally one of the radio addresses he gave near the end of his earthly pilgrimage. In these addresses he communicated to large audiences the heritage of Old Princeton Calvinism in clear terms. This selection may be his final words on the doctrine of Scripture, which was foundational for the vision of Westminster. His colleague Wilson was an acknowledged philologist, Old Testament scholar, and defender of the faith. The two articles by him typify the early efforts at defending the truth of Scripture at Westminster. The first speaks directly about the study of the Bible at the seminary. The second is a response to various challenges in the field of Oriental studies and summarizes his thoughts on the topic, on which he has written larger monographs. The short tributes that follow, the first of which was written by his colleague Oswald T. Allis, encapsulate Wilson's contributions both to the academy and to the church.

Van Til distinguished himself in the field of apologetics, to which he contributed his own unique presuppositionalist method. In this essay he relates in a creative way the doctrine of Scripture to that of general revelation. Then he applies his Christian perspective to an analysis of theology and philosophy from Thomas Aquinas to Karl Barth. This text therefore illustrates his theological approach and his apologetic concern. Murray labored in the field of systematic theology. In the first essay, he discusses the crucial question of the "Attestation of Scripture." In contrast to neoorthodox theology, he insists on both the objective witness of Scripture about itself and the witness of the Holy Spirit. Murray's definition of the doctrine of Scripture also enables him to articulate the relation between the divine character of the Bible and its human authors. The other articles taken from his *Collected Writings* are shorter essays or addresses to popular audiences. These deal successively with the following topics: first, the infallibility of Scripture based on the Bible's self-witness; second, the finality and sufficiency of Scripture and therefore its authority for doctrine and life in the church; third, biblical theology, where he finds that the unifying theme of both Testaments is the covenant of grace fulfilled in Christ; fourth and finally, the importance of the Westminster Confession of Faith as a subordinate standard and especially in relation to the doctrine of Scripture defined in the first chapter of the confession.

In these pages we discover a clear commitment by the early founders of Westminster to the study and defense of the Bible. A concern for a scholarly approach and a nuanced acknowledgment of the doctrine of Scripture shine through. Further, typical Reformed themes are present, such as the self-witness of Scripture, the role of the Spirit, the relationship between the divine and human side of Scripture, and the affirmation of both special and general revelation.

J. Gresham Machen's Last Words on the Word of God

THE LIVING AND TRUE GOD

J. Gresham Machen, "1: The Living and True God," in *The Christian View of Man* (Carlisle, PA: Banner of Truth, 1965), 13–23; reprinted from *The Christian View of Man* (Grand Rapids: Eerdmans, 1947), 1–14; originally published as *The Christian View of Man* (New York: Macmillan, 1937).

J. Gresham Machen (1881–1937) was educated in the classics at Johns Hopkins University. After graduating as the valedictorian at Johns Hopkins, Machen entered Princeton Theological Seminary, and then spent a year in Germany studying under the leading liberal theologians of his day. This time in Germany caused Machen to question his faith and his own view of Scripture. Machen resolved his internal struggle and became a leading defender of the trustworthiness of Scripture. He was teaching New Testament at Princeton Seminary from 1906 until the reorganization of the seminary in 1929. After that, under his leadership, Westminster Theological Seminary was established in 1929 with the Pauline motto: "the whole counsel of God (ΠΑΣΑ Η ΒΟΥΛΗ ΤΟΥ ΘΕΟΥ)" (Acts 20:27). He was also instrumental in the creation of the church that would become the Orthodox Presbyterian Church in 1936.

Machen distinguished himself as a New Testament scholar, in particular with *The Origin of Paul's Religion* (1921) and *The Virgin Birth of Christ* (1930). He was a defender of historic Christianity, especially seen in his *Christianity and Liberalism* (1923). There he defines in bold contrast the difference between liberalism and the true Christian faith. In the selection here, we encounter him in a different mode. "The Living and True God" was one of the several radio addresses he gave shortly before his death. He communicates the heritage of Old Princeton Calvinism in clear terms to twentieth-century audiences. Thus, this section may be his final words on the doctrine of Scripture.

Bibliography: D. G. Hart. *Defending the Faith: J. Gresham Machen and the Crisis of Conservative Protestantism in Modern America*. Baltimore: Johns Hopkins University Press, 1994. Idem. "Machen, J(ohn) Gresham (1881–1937)." Pp. 145–46 in *DP&RTA*. D. F. Kelly. "Machen, John Gresham." Pp. 673–74 in *EDT*. P. C. Kerneny. "Machen, John Gresham (1881–1937)." Pp. 389–93 in *BDE*. Stephen J. Nichols. *J. Gresham Machen: A Guided Tour of His Life and Thought*. Phillipsburg, NJ: P&R Publishing, 2004. Mark A. Noll. "Machen, John Gresham (1881–1937)." Pp. 407–8 in *NDT*. W. Stanford Reid. "J. Gresham Machen." Pp. 102–18 in *Reformed Theology in America*. Ned B. Stonehouse. *J. Gresham Machen: A Biographical Memoir*. Grand Rapids: Eerdmans, 1954. Barry Waugh, ed. *Letters from the Front: J. Gresham Machen's Correspondence from World War I*. Phillipsburg, NJ: P&R Publishing, 2012.

As we begin to consider the Christian view of man, with the decrees of God which underlie man's existence, we certainly find ourselves in the midst of a troubled world. We are living certainly today in a time of rapid changes. Less than twenty years after a war that was supposed to have been fought to make the world safe for democracy, democracy almost everywhere is lying prostrate, and liberty is rapidly being destroyed. Who would have thought, twenty years ago, that within so short a period of time all freedom of speech and of the press would have been destroyed in large sections of western Europe? Who would have thought that Europe would sink back so soon into a worse than medieval darkness?

America has been no exception to this decadence. Liberty is being threatened, and there is coming up before us in the near future the spectre of the hopeless treadmill of a collectivistic state.

Certainly when we take the world as a whole, we are obliged to see that the foundations of liberty and honesty are being destroyed, and the slow achievements of centuries are being thrown recklessly away.

In such a time of kaleidoscopic changes, is there anything that remains unchanged? When so many things have proved to be untrustworthy, is there anything that we can trust?

One point, at least, is clear—we cannot trust the Church. The visible Church, the Church as it now actually exists upon this earth, has fallen too often into error and sin.

No, we cannot appeal from the world to the Church.

Well, then, is there anything at all to which we can appeal? Is there anything at all that remains constant when so many things change?

I have a very definite answer to give to that question. It is contained in a verse taken from the prophecy of Isaiah: "The grass withereth, the flower fadeth: but the word of our God shall stand forever" [Isa. 40:8]. There are many things that change, but there is one thing that does not change. It is the Word of the living and true God. The world is in decadence, the visible Church is to a considerable extent apostate; but when God speaks we can trust Him, and His Word stands forever sure.

Where has God spoken? Where shall we find that Word of God? I tried to give the answer in the first part of this series of talks, which has appeared under the title of *The Christian*

Faith in the Modern World.[1] We can find the Word of God in the Bible. We do not say merely that the Bible contains the Word of God; we say that the Bible is the Word of God. In a time of turmoil and distress, and in the perplexity and weakness of our own lives, we can turn with perfect confidence to that blessed Book.

When we say that the Bible is the Word of God, we mean something very definite indeed. We mean that the Bible is true. We mean that the writers of the Bible, in addition to all their providential qualifications for their task, received an immediate and supernatural guidance and impulsion of the Spirit of God which kept them from the errors that are found in other books, and made the resulting book, the Bible, to be completely true in what it says regarding matters of fact, and completely authoritative in its commands. That is the great doctrine of the full or plenary inspiration of Holy Scripture.

That doctrine does not, as is so often charged, do violence to the individuality of the Biblical writers; and it does not mean that they became mere automata without knowledge of what they were doing. But it does mean that the work of the Holy Spirit in inspiration was a supernatural work. It was not a mere work of God's providence; it was not a mere employment by God of the resources of the universe that He had made: but it was a gracious interposition into the course of nature by the immediate power of God.

That doctrine means that the Bible is God's book, not man's book. Other books give advice that is good and advice that is bad; this book gives only advice that is good, or rather it issues commands that come with the full authority of the sovereign God.

It is upon that high view of the Bible that the present series of talks is based. I am going to seek to explore the Bible with you in order to see what God, and not merely man, has said.

In that presentation of what God has told us in the Bible I hope indeed not to be without sympathy for the man who does not believe as I believe; I hope not to be without sympathy for the man who has doubts. I hope to be able to show such a man as I go along that some of the objections to the teaching of the Bible which are current among men today are based upon misunderstanding of what the Bible means or upon a failure to consider important confirmatory evidence of the Bible's truth. But all that should not obscure what I am trying to do. I am not trying to present to you things that I have discovered for myself, and I am not trying to help you to discover things for yourselves; but I am asking you to listen with me to what God has told us in His Word.

In the series of which the present series is the continuation, I made a beginning of talking to you about what God has told us in His Word.

The revelation of God which is contained in the Bible, we observed, is not the only revelation that God has given. God has revealed Himself through the universe that He has made. "The heavens declare the glory of God, and the firmament sheweth his handywork" [Ps. 91:1]. He has also revealed Himself through His voice within us, the voice of conscience. "When the Gentiles that have not the law do by nature the things contained in the law, these, having not the law, are a law unto themselves" [Rom. 2:14]. The Bible puts the stamp of its approval upon what may be called "natural religion."

But the revelation of God through nature is not the only revelation that God has given. In addition to it He has given a revelation that is called "supernatural" because it is above nature.

Such supernatural revelation was needed for two reasons.

---

1. Cf. J. Gresham Machen, *The Christian Faith in the Modern World* (New York: Macmillan, 1936), 1–102.

In the first place, the revelation of God through nature had become hidden from men's eyes through sin. The wonders of God's world ought to have made men worship and glorify the Creator, but their foolish heart was darkened. The voice of conscience ought to have told plainly what is right and what is wrong, but men's conscience had become seared as with a hot iron. So a new and plain confirmation of what nature and conscience said was needed by sinful man.

In the second place—and this is even more important to observe—man as sinner needed to have revealed to Him about God certain things of which nature and conscience provided no slightest hint. He needed to have revealed to him the grace of God. He was not only blinded by sin, but he was lost in sin. He was under its guilt and curse. He was under its power. He needed to be told the way in which God had saved him. Nature said nothing whatever about that. Knowledge of that could come to sinful man only in a way which was in the strictest sense supernatural.

How wonderfully rich is that supernatural revelation as it is found in the Bible! How far it transcends the revelation of God through nature! The whole doctrine of the Trinity, the whole appearance and work of the Lord Jesus Christ, the entire application of the work of Christ to the believer through the Holy Spirit, the whole glorious promise of a world to come—these things are not told us through nature; they are told us in the Bible and in the Bible alone. They are told us by a revelation that is not natural but supernatural.

In the previous series, I made a beginning of talking to you about that revelation. I talked to you about the great Biblical doctrine of the Triune God. There is but one God, but God is in three persons—Father, Son and Holy Ghost.

At the heart of that establishment in the Bible of the doctrine of the Trinity, we saw, is the teaching of the Bible regarding the deity of Jesus Christ.

Some nineteen hundred years ago, there lived in Palestine a certain person, Jesus.

There are two opinions about Him.

Some regard Him simply as a great religious genius, the founder of one of the world's great religions, a man who kept His own person out of His gospel, did not ask that men should have any particular opinion about Him but simply proclaimed to them the Father God, asked not that men should have faith in Him but only that they should have faith in God like the faith which He had in God. According to those who hold that view Jesus was simply a teacher and example, the pathfinder for mankind on the way to God. That view is the view of unbelievers.

But there is another view of Jesus. According to that other view, the person known to history as Jesus of Nazareth existed from all eternity. He was infinite—eternal and unchangeable God. It was through Him that this vast universe was made. He came into this world by His own voluntary act. He took upon Himself our nature, being born as a man in order that He might redeem His people on the cross. When He was on earth, He offered Himself to men as the object of their faith, not asking them merely to have faith in God like the faith which He had in God, but asking them to have faith in Him. Upon faith in Him he made salvation to depend. He died on the cross as a sacrifice to satisfy divine justice and reconcile us to God. He rose from the dead. He is God and man in two distinct natures and one person forever. He will come again and we shall see Him. He will come again and we shall see Him with our very eyes. This view of Jesus is the view of Christians.

We saw that that Christian view of Jesus is the view that is taught in the Bible, and that it is the view that Jesus taught regarding Himself.

Did Jesus really present Himself when He was on earth merely as an example for men's faith? Did He say merely: "Have faith in God like the faith which I have in God"? Was He indifferent to what men thought of Him?

These questions are easy to answer if we take the Bible record of Jesus as a whole. The Jesus who is presented in the Bible as a whole clearly offered Himself to men as the object of their faith, and made faith in Him essential to the attaining of eternal life.

But unbelievers will not accept the Bible record of Jesus as a whole. Very well, then, I will say to an unbelieving friend: "Here is a New Testament. Take it and choose any passage in it that you will in order to prove that your view of Jesus is right. You do not like my passages. Well, let us see what your passages say."

We observed in our last series of talks that there is one passage which an unbeliever is more likely to choose when so challenged than any other. It is the passage called the Sermon on the Mount. There, it is said by unbelievers, we have a non-theological Jesus, a Jesus who issued lofty commands and supposed that those commands could be obeyed no matter what men thought of Him. We are constantly told that. Theology, we are told, is not the important thing, even the theology that deals with Jesus Christ. If, we are told, men would just get up and do what Jesus says in the Sermon on the Mount, that would be far better than coming to any particular opinion about Him or about the meaning of His death.

"Well," I will just say to such an unbelieving friend, "let us just take that passage which you have chosen, let us just take that Sermon on the Mount, to see whether it really bears out your view of Jesus, whether it really presents to us a Jesus who was merely a teacher and example and did not ask men to have any particularly high view of Him."

We did that in our last series. We took the Sermon on the Mount to examine it in that way. And what did we find? Did we find a Jesus who kept His own person out of His gospel and did not care what men thought of Him?

Most emphatically we did not. Instead, we found in the Sermon on the Mount a Jesus who in the most amazing way dispensed the rewards in the Kingdom of God, a Jesus who placed His commands fully on an equality with the commands of God in the Old Testament Scriptures, a Jesus who did not say as the prophets said, "Thus saith the Lord," but who said, "*I say to you*" [Matt. 5:17], a Jesus who pronounced blessedness upon the men who stood in a certain relation to Him—"Blessed are ye when men shall revile you and persecute you and say all manner of evil against you falsely *for my sake*" [Matt. 5:11]—a Jesus who claimed that He would one day sit on the judgment seat of God and determine the final destinies of men, sending some into everlasting punishment and others into eternal life.

No, we cannot in the Sermon on the Mount find any escape from the Christ of the rest of the New Testament. We cannot find in that passage—favorite passage of unbelievers though it be—any merely human Jesus who was indifferent to what men thought of Him and merely asked them to take Him as their example and to follow His leading on the pathway to God. We find in that passage as in every other passage one Christ and one Christ only—the Christ who was truly man and truly God.

If, moreover, we did find in the New Testament the Christ that some men are seeking, a mere leader and example, a mere explorer of the pathway which leads men to God, what possible good could such a Christ be to our souls? What possible good could a mere example and guide be to those who, like us, are dead in trespasses and sins and are under the just wrath and curse of God?

I remember that several years ago I addressed a meeting here in Philadelphia that was devoted to a consideration of the topic "The Responsibility of the Church in Our New Age." One of the speakers, who was not a Christian—I mean not even a professing Christian at all—had some very kind things to say about Jesus. But the climax of his address came when he quoted Jesus' words from the Old Testament regarding love of God and of one's neighbor: "Thou shalt love the Lord thy God with all thy heart, and with all thy soul, and with all thy mind, and thou shalt love thy neighbor as thyself."

"Is that not dogma enough for anybody?" said the speaker.

Well, of course, it is not dogma at all, or doctrine, but a command. But was the speaker right in holding that it is large enough for anybody; and if he was right in holding that it is large enough for anybody, why do we Christians insist on adding to it extensive doctrines including the doctrine of the deity of Christ? Why do we not just content ourselves with saying, "Thou shalt love the Lord thy God, and thou shalt love thy neighbor as thyself"? Is that not indeed large enough for anybody?

What is the answer from the Christian point of view? The answer from the Christian point of view is very simple. Yes, certainly that great double command of Jesus, "Thou shalt love the Lord thy God with all thy heart, and with all thy soul, and with all thy mind, and thou shalt love thy neighbor as thyself" is plenty large enough for anybody. Ah, but do you not see, my friends, it is far too large. There is the whole trouble. That is the whole reason why we are Christians. That stupendous command of Jesus is too large; it is so large that we have not succeeded in keeping it. If we had loved God and our neighbor, in the high sense in which Jesus meant that command, all would have been well with us; we should then have needed nothing more; we should not have needed any doctrine of the Cross of Christ because we should not have needed any cross of Christ; we should not have needed any doctrine of the person of Christ—God and man in two distinct natures and one person forever—because there would have been no necessity for Christ to become man at all. We should have been righteous, and should have needed no Saviour.

But as it is we are sinners. That is the reason why we need more than a teacher and example and lawgiver; that is the reason why we need what unbelievers despise as being merely doctrine and we prefer to call the gospel; that is why we cling with all our souls to the great Bible doctrines of the person and work of Jesus Christ.

Suppose I had listened to Jesus merely as a great example and lawgiver. Suppose I had heard Him say, "Thou shalt love the Lord thy God and thy neighbor as thyself"; suppose I had heard Him say, in the Sermon on the Mount, "Blessed are the pure in heart; for they shall see God." What should I say to Him then? Should I say: "I thank you, Jesus; that is all I needed to know; I am so glad to know that if I love God and my neighbour and am pure in heart all will be well and I shall enter the Kingdom of God."

Well, my friends, I do not know what you would say. But I know that I could say nothing of the kind. I could only say, after listening to those commands of Jesus: "Alas, I am undone; I have not loved God and my neighbor; I am not pure in heart; I am a sinner; Jesus, have you anything, despite your high commands, to say to me?"

When I come thus to Jesus as a sinner, confessing that I have not obeyed His commands, confessing that I have nothing to offer to Him, but am utterly unworthy and utterly helpless,

900

has He anything to say to me? Does He say merely: "You have heard my high commands; that is all that I have to say; that is all the gospel that I have to give you; that is all the doctrine you can have."

No, thank God, that is not all that He has to give me—that cold comfort of a command that I have not kept and cannot keep. He gives me something more than that. He gives me Himself. He offers Himself to me in the Bible as my Saviour who died for me on the Cross and who now lives as the one whom I can trust. He offers Himself to me in the great doctrines of His person and His work. If He were some other, He could not save me and I could not trust Him to save me. But because He is very God, He could save me and did save me and I have been united to Him by the Holy Spirit through faith.

Do you not see, my friends? That is the reason why the Christian clings to the doctrine of the deity of Christ. He does not approach it as a cold academic matter, but he comes to it as a drowning man lays hold of a plank that may save him from the abyss. No lesser Christ could save us; this Christ alone could save us from eternal death.

It is in that way that we are going to approach the things that we hope to deal with in the talks that follow. The doctrine presented in the Bible is not to us just a matter of curious interest; it is not a thing to be relegated to schools or classrooms. It is a matter of tragic import; it is a matter of life or death. Here we stand on the brink of eternity. We are sinners. We deserve God's wrath and curse. There is hope for us only in what God has told us in His Word. Let us listen to it while there is time.

Robert Dick Wilson

Robert Dick Wilson (1856–1930) was one of the founding professors of Westminster Theological Seminary. He was educated at the College of New Jersey (now Princeton University), Western Theological Seminary, and the University of Berlin. Before coming to Westminster, Wilson served as professor of Old Testament at Princeton Theological Seminary. His commitment to Reformed orthodoxy led him to join J. Gresham Machen at Westminster. Wilson was a master of many ancient languages, and he put his linguistic genius to good use by thoroughly studying the translations of the Old Testament in light of the Hebrew original. Through this method he sought to defend the authority and infallibility of Scripture against the rising tide of critical scholarship. His scholarship still deserves careful attention, given the importance of Holy Scripture and the deadly influence of higher criticism on the vitality of the church worldwide. Wilson's work regained new life through the revision of his *A Scientific Investigation of the Old Testament* by Edward J. Young in 1957.

Late in life Wilson embarked on the adventure of Westminster, but he had only about a year of service in this new institution. His colleague at Princeton and then at Westminster Oswald T. Allis evaluates Wilson's contribution to his field of study. Next, three other tributes look at the influence of Wilson on the life of the church. Given Wilson's importance in the founding of Westminster, we provide several short texts that offer a window into his life and work. The first two articles are penned by him. First, "The Study and Defense of the Bible in Westminster Seminary" (1930) is an early witness to Westminster's mission and goal to defend the authority of the Bible. This article appears in *Christianity Today*, published back then by Presbyterian and Reformed. Second, in "Groundless Attacks in the Field of Oriental Scholarship," Wilson uses his scholarship in the field of Old Testament and philology to defend the truth of the Bible. The last two articles pay tribute to the contributions of this pioneer at Westminster Seminary.

Bibliography: D. G. Hart. "Allis, O(swald) T(hompson) (1880–1973)." P. 17 in *DP&RTA*. Idem. "Wilson, Robert Dick (1856–1930)." P. 278 in *DP&RTA*. Walter C. Kaiser Jr. "Robert Dick Wilson." Pp. 73–81 in *Bible Interpreters of the 20th Century*. John H. Skilton. "Oswald T. Allis." Pp. 123–30 in *Bible Interpreters of the 20th Century*. Marion Ann Taylor. *The Old Testament in the Old Princeton School (1812–1929)*. San Francisco: Mellen Research University Press, 1992. Pp. 267–72. Robert Dick Wilson. *A Scientific Investigation of the Old Testament*. Rev. Edward J. Young. Chicago: Moody Bible Institute, 1959. Repr., Birmingham, AL: Solid Ground Christian Books, 2007. John J. Yeo. *Plundering the Egyptians: The Old Testament and Historical Criticism at Westminster Seminary (1929–1998)*. Lanham, MD: University Press of America, 2010. Pp. 7–92.

THE STUDY AND DEFENSE OF THE BIBLE IN WESTMINSTER SEMINARY

By Robert Dick Wilson, Ph.D., D.D., LL.D. Professor of Semitic Philology and Old Testament Criticism, Westminster Theological Seminary, Philadelphia.

Robert Dick Wilson, "The Study and Defense of the Bible in Westminster Seminary." *Christianity Today* 1, 2 (Mid-June 1930): 5–6.

(Dr. Wilson is by common consent the leading scholar in the world holding to the historic position of the Christian Church concerning the Old Testament. Recently Professor R. H. Charles and Dr. H. H. Rowley, famed British critics, have attempted to answer Dr. Wilson's criticism of the late Dr. S. R. Driver with reference to the significance of the Aramaisms of Daniel, as has likewise Professor W. Baumgarten of Marburg, Germany. It is safe to say that no Old Testament scholar in the world is today commanding such attention as is Dr. Wilson.)

Westminster Seminary has been founded by men who believe that the Westminster Confession is a correct synopsis of the Word of God, the Scriptures of the Old and New Testaments, which we hold is the only infallible rule of faith and practice, teaching us what we are to believe concerning God and what duty God requires of man. This God whom we worship is a Spirit, infinite, eternal, and unchangeable, in His being, wisdom, power, holiness, justice, goodness, and truth.

The Boaz and Jachin of the temple of our faith are: Our God is the God of the Word; and, The Word of God is true. In short, our motto is: The God of the Word and the Word of God.

We professors are set to do our level best by tongue and pen to remove the doubts from the minds of the doubting Thomases in the seminary and in the Church, and to produce such faith in God and in His Word among all who hear or read our words that they will go and preach the gospel and teach Christ's commandments to every creature. Now, fifty years ago, most of the men who came to the seminaries believed with all their heart in the God of the Bible and in the Word of God. Today, alas, many of them come filled with doubts as the sparks fly upward. They know little about the Bible but are bristling with objections to it like a porcupine with spines. And yet many of them have never learned that there are certain rules that govern thinking, commonly embraced under the head of logic, such as: that the validity of a conclusion depends upon that of the major and minor premises; that a statement as to fact is never self-evident but always is true only as the evidence is in its favor; that a definition is correct only when based upon a complete induction of the facts entering into and bearing upon it; and, especially, the introduction of the fourth term, that "nigger in the woodpile." They have never learned that it does not prove that a thing is not true that you cannot prove that it is; nor, that an event is not impossible simply because you cannot see how it could have occurred.

Now, in the fifty years since I began to teach, I have learned that if they give me a student who wants to believe in God and his Word, his objections and doubts as to both will be dissipated by showing him the fallacies and absurdities that underlie the objections and doubts which he has had; and, on the other hand, his faith will be awakened and strengthened by presenting the evidence in favor of it and the reasonableness of it in the light of the divine revelation presented in the Scriptures.

This then, as I understand it, is the great work that is incumbent upon us at Westminster Seminary. We are defenders of the Christian faith: negatively, by the removal of doubts and objections; positively, by the increasing of it through showing the reasonableness of it, and more specifically, by presenting its content and its claims,—the subjective and objective evidence for it.

For example, to illustrate from my own department which is that of Old Testament criticism: I have made it an invariable habit never to accept an objection to a statement of the Old Testament without subjecting it to a most thorough investigation, linguistically and factually. If I find that the objector bases his objection upon a general theoretical consideration such as the denial of miracles or of predictive prophecy, I just smile at the objector and turn him over to the department of Theism to learn who and what the God of the Bible is. "He that sitteth in the heavens shall laugh" at them, and I for one laugh with Him. But if a man believes in the probability or certainty of miraculous events wherein God is working but is precluded from faith in the claims of the Bible to be a divine revelation by doubts arising from objections to its trustworthiness based upon alleged historical, scientific, or philological evidence, then I consider it to be my duty to do my best to show that this alleged evidence is irrelevant, inconclusive, and false.

At last, then, behold the professor and his boys sitting down together and taking up with avidity the investigation of the writings of the old Hebrew prophets. Where shall we begin? Why begin, of course, with a careful reading of the books to see what they contain and what they claim to be. Read them all through once at least. Do they claim to contain a revelation from God and to have been written under his supervision? They do. Then here we have a new and marvelous thing among the literary productions of the world. No class work of the college curriculum, no Homer, no Vergil, no work of Goethe or Schiller, no Dante or Victor Hugo, makes claims like these of Moses and David and Isaiah, that God speaks through them; nor grips like them at the very vitals of our intellect and imagination. Here are works which treat of God the author of all beings, the Alpha and the Omega of the ages. He lifts the veil that hid His face and the brightness of His glory and the revelation of His will from Sakya Mouni and Confucius and Plato, and speaks apparently face to face with His chosen ones as a man speaketh with his friends. Can these wonders of love be true? Come, let us see. A revelation, we must admit, is what we must expect from the Creator who made us what we are, and who is represented by the prophets as being what they portray in their writings.

But could these works have been put into writing as early as Abraham and Moses? Why, certainly, they could and must have been. For writing was practiced in Egypt and Babylonia long before their time. Can they have been written in Hebrew? Yes. For we have documentary evidence in both Egyptian and Cuneiform that Hebrew was known in Syria and Palestine and Egypt as early as the times of Abraham. And was this Hebrew written in Palestine down to the time that the last book of the Old Testament was written? Yes. For we have Ecclesiasticus in Hebrew from the second century B.C., and the Zadokite Fragment and the Pirke Aboth from about the time of Christ. And the forms of literature from the earliest book of the Old Testament down to the latest—unless we except the somewhat peculiar style of the prophetic rhapsodies (?)—are found in the literature of Egypt and Assyria and Babylon.

But, admitting that these works could have been written, could they have been handed down? Why, certainly. We have a part of the Egyptian Book of the Dead in manuscripts from the twelfth, the eighteenth, the twenty-second, and the thirtieth dynasties. The three last are not copies from the first, but all are from an earlier and complete original. Some lines of these manuscripts are exactly alike although the earliest and the latest are separated by two thousand years at least. And, further, Assurbanipal has left us thousands of tablets which were copied by his scribes from other tablets going back to the time of Abraham. So the works of Abraham and Moses could have been handed down to the time of Ezra and to that of the translation of the Seventy.

But have we any evidence that the text not merely could be but that it has been handed down from the original writers to our own time? Yes. Here again God has not left us without sufficient witnesses. More than a thousand manuscripts of the Old Testament, in whole or in part, now exist in the libraries of the world, from 250 to 400 of every book. From these we learn that the variations of one manuscript from the others are unimportant, mostly affecting neither the form or the sense of the common text. The notes of the old scribes, which were affixed to the Hebrew text about 500 A.D., corroborate the care and accuracy with which the manuscripts were copied. And, finally, a large number of versions from the third century B.C. down to the present time show that the same original text lay back of all of them. The New Testament and the Targums also show that their writers had substantially the same text of the Old Testament that we now possess.

But can we go back of the time of Christ and of the Septuagint? Yes. We can even do that. For scores of proper names in the Old Testament are to be found also in the contemporary documents of the Egyptians, Assyrians, Babylonians, and Persians, carrying us back to the times of Shishak and Solomon and even to that preceding the Exodus. Shishak, Tiglath-Pileser III, Sennacherib, and Cyrus also mention events, more or less at length, which correspond to events recorded in the Scriptures. And the very ruins of Palestine are now giving their testimony to the general accuracy of the Old Testament history.

And lastly, the languages in which the books of the Old Testament are written, are now rising up from the sleep of millenniums to testify to the trustworthiness of the documents which were written in them. For more than a century the objectors to the veracity of the Old Testament Scriptures have been appealing to the evidence of the languages in which the books are written to prove that they are not historical. And many Christians, even professors in our seminaries, and almost the whole Protestant church at home and abroad, have accepted these dicta of the critics instead of the Bible; so the whole church has been shaking in its shoes. The Pentateuch, Daniel, in short the whole Bible has been reconstructed and largely rewritten, and largely on the basis of the forms and the meanings of words found in the documents.

Now it is my claim that the *prima facie* evidence of the languages of the books themselves is in the light of our present knowledge correct. First, because the critics themselves assume that text to be correct whenever it suits them. Secondly, because an examination of the proper names of kings and countries shows that the present text of the Scriptures spells these names exactly as they are spelled in the contemporary documents of the kings of Egypt, Assyria, Babylon and Persia. And, thirdly, because a scientific examination of all the foreign words to be found in the Old Testament shows that the foreign words occur just where we would expect to find them *if the documents in which they occur were written near the time when the events mentioned in the documents are said in the documents themselves to have occurred.* Thus, in the records of Abraham and his predecessors, we find the foreign words embedded in the documents to be Sumerian and Babylonian, the languages of Ur of the Chaldees; in the history of Joseph and Moses we find Egyptian words; in the records from the times of Nebuchadnezzar and Darius we find Persian words. As you determine the age of the rocks by the foreign substances embedded in them, so you can determine the age of the documents by the foreign words embedded in them. And my contention is that these foreign words demonstrate that the history of God's chosen people follows the chronological lines laid down in Chronicles and Ezra-Nehemiah. No scientific philologist will deny the facts in evidence. They are to be found in every Hebrew Bible. They can be investigated and tested scientifically by all who have sufficient knowledge or who trust the most modern of scientific grammars and dictionaries. It is scientific work. Its statements can be tested just like the rocks in mineralogy.

And so, strong in an enlightened faith, we lead our students on to defy the allegations of the objectors to the infallible rule of Holy Scripture. We thoroughly believe that the Scriptures are right and the objectors wrong. We fervently hope that Westminster Seminary may be a place where an intelligent defense of the fundamentals of the Christian religion (which is grounded upon a belief in the historical character of the divine records) may be taught to the future Ministers of the church, It is our firm belief that a revival of the old-time religion for which we hope and pray, will only come when faith in the trustworthiness of the simple record shall have been restored. We can not expect an educated people to believe a book which they think to be untrustworthy. Let us waken up. Let us begin our scientific defense of the historical character of the Scriptures by gathering together a library of books containing all the published documents from Egypt, Assyria, Babylon, and elsewhere that contain any evidence whatsoever bearing upon the Bible and its times. These books are what we now need most. For without them we cannot thoroughly investigate the objections of the critics of our times. And then let us secure young men of faith who love the Lord, and train them till they are able to use all the evidence of all the documents, so that the doubts of God's people, and especially of Christ's Ministers, may be removed and their faith confirmed.

But enough for the present. We defenders of the faith—professors and students in Westminster Seminary, Ministers and laymen who are supporting us—are in this fight for God's Word to a finish. We want to confound infidelity by laying the foundation of belief on a scientific basis of fact and knowledge. This basis lies in books and documents. We must have them or we are bound in the long run to fail. We cannot make bricks without straw. Who will supply the straw? We depend on believing laymen to supply what will enable us to train and strengthen the faith of God's Ministers in this world-wide war for God and the Word. Let us all do our best for Him who loved us and gave Himself for us.

GROUNDLESS ATTACKS IN THE FIELD OF ORIENTAL SCHOLARSHIP

Robert Dick Wilson

Robert Dick Wilson, "Groundless Attacks in the Field of Oriental Scholarship," *The Bible Student and Teacher* 1, 6 (June 1904): 356–60.

As the time allotted to me is limited, I shall speak merely upon the groundlessness of certain of the attacks made upon the Scriptures in the region of paleography and philology.

But before plunging into my subject let me state that in my opinion the only way in which the conservative party can maintain its position in the field of Biblical criticism is by showing that the premises of the radical critics are false; by showing, through a more thorough investigation of the facts, that the foundations upon which the magnificent structures of the radical critics rest are indeed groundless, unscientific and illogical, unproven and often incapable of proof.

The Attack in the Field of Palaeography

I. I remark that many of the premises of the radical critics are fallacious, because of assumptions based upon an unjustifiable use of the vowel letters and signs.

It is a point admitted by writers of all schools, that the vowel points of the Massoretic text were not fixed till some centuries after Christ. A study of the variants of the Hebrew MSS. will show further that there is scarcely an internal vowel letter that has been invariably written either fully or defectively. The omission of all internal vowel letters (as well as word signs) is shown conclusively, also, on the inscriptions of the ancient Phenicians, Aramaeans, Moabites and Hebrews. Now, in view of these facts, what do you think of arguments like the following?

Wellhausen says (on page 389 of his History of Israel), that

Za-kar; "male" is in earlier times **Za-kur**; for this is the writing of Ex. 23:17; 34:23; Deut. 16:16; 20:13; and if it is right in these passages, as we can not doubt it is, it must be introduced in Ex. 34:19; Deut. 15:19; 1 Kings 11:15ff., as well. In the priestly code, Za-khar occurs with great frequency and elsewhere only in the later literature, Deut. 4:16; Isa. 66:7; Judg. 21:11–12; etc."

You all see, that if the vowels did not exist in the original text, that the documents of the original text can not be distinguished by the vowels of that text.

2. The second paleographical assumption arises from wilful changes made in the consonantal text.

By wilful changes, I mean those for which there is no evidence in MSS., or versions, or palæography, or the monuments. The worst sinners in this respect are Professors Klostermann, of Kiel, and Cheyne, of Oxford.

In his latest work, *Critica Biblica*,[1] just coming out, Prof. Cheyne attempts to reconstruct the text of the Old Testament on a theory so incredible, so entirely without any foundation

---

1. Thomas K. Cheyne, *Critica Biblica* (New York: Macmillan, 1903–1904).

in facts, historical and textual, that it seems to me, to surpass all the groundless theories that have before been proposed.

Did you ever hear of the **Jerahmeelites**? They are mentioned once in the Bible and their progenitor **Jerahmeel** once also. Now could you believe it possible, that a professor in Oxford would attempt to string the whole text of the Prophets and Histories of the Old Testament upon the thread of this word, which he has inserted times almost innumerable in the four parts of his work already published?

One can not but wonder, whether Professor Cheyne ever expected anybody to accept as fact these fanciful reconstructions of his. I can perceive how the radical critics might in despair give up all attempts to reconstruct the original text of the Scriptures; but I can not understand why they do not, one and all, perceive that any attempt to reconstruct the text out of their own heads, is doomed to failure. One Oxford Professor tried to reconstruct the original Hebrew text of Ecclesiasticus, by re-translating it from the Greek and Syrian versions. When the original Hebrew text was found, his text agreed with the original in only three places out of 100!

Would you like to have a sample of Professor Cheyne's method? On page 135, he asserts that "corruptions based on transpositions are common"; and hence he changes the word **tomekh** into **maakhath**. But notice: (1) That there is no MS. nor version, that supports this change; and (2) that such transpositions can not, comparatively speaking, be called **common**. For the past fifteen years I have been making a collection of such transpositions for which there is authority in the MSS., parallel passages, versions, or critical editions (including large parts of the Polychrome Bible), and so far my list counts sixty-four examples in all. When you consider that these examples are collected from the whole Bible, and that the consonant letters in the Bible number about 1,200,000, you will perceive that these changes number about one in 18,000 from all sources whatsoever. But (3), even if the instances of simple transposition were much more numerous, what Professor Cheyne claims in the case before us, is not a simple transposition of two letters; but the 1st is made the 4th, the 3rd the 1st, the 4th the 3rd, and the 2nd is changed from one letter to another, which it resembles in no Semitic alphabet as yet discovered!

3. The third palæographical assumption arises from ignorance of the Hebrew, or from a misunderstanding of some version of it.

Some critics are always on the lookout for variants. When they do not see the connection in meaning between the Hebrew word and its version, they jump at the conclusion that there has either been a change in the original or that the translators have misunderstood their text.

An example of what I mean is to be found in 1 Samuel 13:6, when the Book renders the Hebrew word by a word meaning "grave." **Ewald**, the great critic of the middle of the last century, asserted that the Hebrew word here used did not mean "grave," but "tower"; and, hence, many critics rejected the Hebrew text, because, they said, people do not hide in **towers**, and generally adopted the Greek version as giving the true meaning. Klostermann proceeds to reconstruct the Hebrew text by changing the present Hebrew word to another one which means "sepulchres." Now the fallacy here lies in assuming a variation where there is none. The Greek is right in having the word for "grave." The Hebrew word found in the text also means "grave." If you would look in the Arabic dictionary you would find the exact philological equivalent of the Hebrew used ordinarily in the sense of "grave." The variation is the figment of the critic's imagination. And the persistence in claiming that there is a variation is one evidence among many that there is a **traditional** interpretation among the radical as well as among the conservative critics.

4. But the most groundless of all of the assumptions of the radical critics with regard to the text of the Old Testament Scriptures is that the text, as it emerged into historic times, had already been so changed from its original form as to be utterly unrecognizable by its own composers.

Yet what convincing evidence is there to prove that such radical changes were ever made in the original text of the Old Testament? None whatsoever, except an analogy derived from the Egyptian and Babylonian liturgies and legends. No trace of any such radical changes can be found in the parallel portions of the Old Testament, nor in any statements of the Scriptures, nor in any tradition of the Jews. On the contrary, so far back as we can go with MSS. and versions (i.e., to 200 B.C.), the evidence is overwhelming and convincing, that in general no changes, even in sporadic cases of consonantal letters, have been made in the text of the Old Testament; except such as might occur in the copying or translating of any document, especially one of a long past age. The Egyptian papyri, recently discovered and published, some of them more than 2,000 years old, show that some of the fragments of the Classics differ by not a single letter from the texts of the ordinary text-books now used in the preparatory schools. No evidence has yet been found in support of a tendency theory on the part of either copyists, or translators, of the Old Testament, except, perhaps, in the case of two or three books of the LXX, and in a few changes in the Targums. Such tendency theories are another creature of the critics' imagination. The only tendency theory that the authors of the Old Testament Scriptures recognize is that which tends from the Paradise of the fall to the Cross of Calvary, and from the Cross of Calvary to the Paradise of the redeemed.

The Attack in the Field of Philology

In the second place, the groundlessness of the radical attack may be shown in the field of philology.

I. The first of the many false assumptions are those made as to the meaning, the origin, and the use of words.

Time forbids that I should mention more than one or two examples of these kinds of assumptions. Their wide-reaching character can be judged, however, from one as well as from many examples. Let us take the Aramaic word for **King** as an example of a false assumption based on the meaning of a word. Belshazzar, as you know, is said in the Aramaic portion of Daniel to have been king of Babylon. Now, inasmuch as the monuments do not state that Belshazzar was ever king in the sense that Nebuchadnezzar and Nabonaid were; it has been assumed that he could have been king in no sense at all.

To harmonize the monuments with Daniel, it is only necessary to remember that the Aramaic word **mal-kah**, "king," is equivalent to two, or more, words found in the Assyrio-Babylonian or Hebrew. In the Aramaic, the word **mal-kah**, "king," is used, not merely of the emperor of the Greeks, and of the shah-in-shah, the king of kings, the king of Persia; but also of the mayor of a city or of a village, or of the chief of a tribe. Belshazzar may have been king of the city of Babylon, while his father was king of the land.

The second word which I shall mention illustrates the fallacies based upon false assumptions as to the origin and use of words. I shall take the familiar New Testament word **korban**, "a gift." Wellhausen asserts that this word is a late importation into the Hebrew from the

Aramaic; that it occurs nowhere in the Pentateuch, except in the Priestly Code; and that its presence there is an evidence of the late date of that work.

Now, inasmuch as both the root and the derivative are found in Arabic and Assyrio-Babylonian, as well as in Hebrew and Aramaic, is it not most probable that both root and derivative were used by the primitive Semites; and, hence, that in their use there is no indication of derivation, or date? Wellhausen, at least, gives no evidence except his mere assertion that the Hebrews derived the word from the Aramaeans.

2. The second philological assumption is that the date of books can be determined from the use of sporadic forms and of once-written words, to many of which the indefinite term "Aramaism" is applied.

But notice, first, that as to the relations existing in early times between the Hebrews and the Aramaean peoples, aside from the statements of the Scriptures, we know absolutely nothing. So far as Aramaisms are concerned, there are no conclusive grounds for asserting that a book like Ecclesiastes must have been written in the age of the Maccabees rather than in that of Solomon. A large proportion of the words which even conservative critics supposed a few years ago to be Aramaisms, can now be shown not to be necessarily such at all. In Keil's "Introduction to Ecclesiastes," about half of the most important words, which he classes as Aramaisms, are found in Arabic and Assyrian as well.[2] The presumption is that they are all from primitive Semite roots and that they might have occurred in any book which was written at any time in the history of the Hebrews, or of any other Semitic people.

3. The third philological assumption lies in the contention that the employment of certain words rather than others implies a difference of author, or date, rather than a difference of idea to be expressed, or a different way of expressing the ideas.

This assumption lies at the basis of the divisive hypothesis of the Pentateuch. Without going into a discussion of the words for God, about which there is so much that is disputable, let us take the word "subdue" [Note, **qa-vash**] as an example of the fallacy that diction alone is an indication of a separate document, or a different author. This word is said to be indicative of P. If this were so, if a characteristic of P lies in the word here used, we should expect to find J or E using some other word to express the idea "subdue." As a matter of fact, however, we find no word for "subdue" in either J or E. J, to be sure, uses twice a verb "to bow down." [Note, **ka-ra'**], which in the causative means "to subdue." A third word, the causative of the word "to humble" [Note, **ka-na'**], is used once in P and once in D. The two other words used in Hebrew to denote the idea of subduing [Note, **da-var** and **ra-dad**], do not occur in the Pentateuch. It will thus be seen, that of the five Hebrew words meaning "subdue," P employs two (of which D once uses one); but J and E never use any one of the five. Any difference, therefore, between P and JE is one of idea and not of words to express the idea. Nor could anyone maintain, that either the word or the idea may have been unknown to the writers of J or E. The Hebrew word for "subdue" found in Genesis 1. is found, also, in Assyrio-Babylonian, Aramaic and Arabic. Hence, it may be assumed, in the absence of all evidence to the contrary, to have belonged to the primitive Semitic language; and, if it belonged to the primitive language, there is no reason why it may not have been used at any time in the history of any one of its descendants. That the idea expressed by the word "subdue" may have been unknown to the authors of J or E, is a supposition which, in view

2. Cf. Friedrich Karl Keil and Franz Delitzsch, *Commentary on the Song of Songs and Ecclesiastes,* trans. M. G. Easton (Grand Rapids: Eerdmans, 1950), 190–96.

of the endless subjugations of nature and man revealed by the monuments and languages of ancient nations, is too preposterous for sober discussion.

In the second place, a difference of words, involved in the same general idea, does not necessarily imply a different author, nor a separate document; but may rather imply a fine discrimination of synonyms, or a slightly different way of expressing the same idea. Take, for example, the words for "likeness," "form," etc. P alone used the words "image" (shadow) and "likeness" [Note, **tselem** and **d'mooth**]; but only in Genesis 1 and 5. P and D both use "pattern" (form or build [Note, **tav-neeth**], D and E use the word for "form." [Note, **t'moo-nah** a word of unknown origin and doubtful meaning.] Now, if a difference of words to express the same general idea implies a difference of authorship or document; we would here have three Ps and two Ds, and the assumption would be that no author can ever use a synonym. But, if they express simply a different shade of meaning under the same general idea, their use is no indication of separate documents or different authors. Whichever horn of the dilemma the critic takes, he stands to fall.

4. The fourth and last philological assumption that I shall mention is that made by Frederich Delitzsch and others when they assert, without any sufficient evidence from the vocabulary, that the Hebrews derived their religious ideas from the Babylonians.

Two years ago, I made an exhaustive comparative study of the vocabularies of the four great Semitic languages, especially of the words found in Hebrew and Babylonian, with the following result: I found that while there were many words common to all the Semitic languages; that these words were most common in the lower spheres of life; and that, as you rise from the physical and phenomenal to the mental and religious spheres, the similarities of the vocabularies become less and less; until when you come to the highest sphere of all (the doctrines of God, sin, grace, pardon, salvation, faith, the Messiah, and the kingdom of God), the vocabularies have become largely distinct, and the ideas in great measure dissimilar.

To those who would magnify the influence of the ancient Babylonian upon the ideas of the Israelites, let me emphasize the fact, that the stories of the creation and the flood, the belief in the existence of angels, the observance of a Sabbath, and the use of sacrifices and of the name Jehovah (one or all of which are certainly found in the monuments to have prevailed in the age of Abraham), do not invalidate the Scriptures, but rather confirm them. The remarkable thing is, that we find such close resemblances of names and institutions in Genesis and so few in Exodus and Leviticus. While on this part of my subject and in conclusion, I can not refrain from calling the attention of this audience to the long line of opposition between the religions and the policy of the Hebrews and Babylonians, which extends from the time when Abraham was called out of Ur of the Chaldees to leave his country and his kindred, until, in the Apocalypse and the later Jewish literature, Babylon became the height and front of the offending against the kingdom of the God of Israel. All through that extended and extensive literature of the ancient Hebrews, all through those long annals of the Assyrians and Babylonians, wherever the Hebrews and the Assyrio-Babylonians were brought into contact, it was by way of opposition. The only exceptions were in the cases of some weakling, Jehovah-distrusting kings. But with these exceptions, prophets and kings and poets emphasize and reiterate the antagonism, essential and eternal, existing between the worship of Jehovah and the worship of the idols of Babylon. And when the children of Israel had been carried away to the rich plains of Babylon, so beautiful, so vast, was it as a Greek patriot to the Athens of his dreams, or a Scotsman to his "ain countrie?" Not thus.

911

But they wept when they remembered Zion: "How shall we sing the Lord's songs in a strange land?" Not thus does the Catholic pilgrim sing when he treads the streets of papal Rome and stands in awe beneath the dome of Saint Peter's. Not thus does the Arab Hadji pray when he bows within the sacred precincts of the Kaaba. But thus has every Jew through-out the ages felt, the record of whose thoughts and feelings has been preserved to us; and thus does every child of Abraham according to the promise feel—that not to Babylon, the golden city, the mother of science and art and commerce, and of idolatry and harlotries and sorceries, do we look for the springs of our religion and the hope of our salvation,—but to Jerusalem the Golden, the city of the great King.

ROBERT DICK WILSON—DEFENDER OF GOD'S WORD

By Oswald T. Allis, Ph.D., D.D.
Professor of Old Testament in Westminster Theological Seminary

Oswald T. Allis, "Robert Dick Wilson—Defender of God's Word," *Christianity Today* 1, 7 (Mid-November 1930): 4–6.

On October 1st the Opening Exercises of the second year of Westminster Theological Seminary were held in Witherspoon Hall, Philadelphia. On this occasion Dr. Wilson, as senior professor, addressed a few words of greeting to the new students. It was his last public appearance. Two weeks later his body was laid to rest in the beautiful cemetery of the Western Pennsylvania county-seat, Indiana, where he was born nearly seventy-five years ago. It was peculiarly fitting that his last words should be spoken as a teacher to students. For it was just fifty years since, as an instructor in Old Testament at Western Theological Seminary, Pittsburgh, he entered upon the work of theological education to which he devoted half a century of fruitful service. Teachers are legion: great teachers are few. A great teacher must be a man and a lover of men: an ardent lover of knowledge, tireless in seeking it, skilful in imparting it: a passionate lover of truth and zealous in proclaiming it. It was because he was all of these that Dr. Wilson endeared himself to so great a number of students and Bible-lovers scattered all over the world who today mourn the loss of a friend, a teacher, a scholar and a great defender of the Word of God.

It is as a teacher that Dr. Wilson's students will most often think of him. He loved to teach and teaching never became a routine with him. His methods never became stereotyped, his material never became stale. His students appreciated the enthusiasm with which he threw himself into teaching. Whether the subject was the Hebrew alphabet or the refutation of some dangerous and subtle theory of the "higher critics," Dr. Wilson was all aglow with enthusiasm. For a number of years at Princeton he gave the new students a lecture on the importance of Hebrew. He called it his "Cui Bono?" (i.e., "What's the Use [of Hebrew]?") lecture. And it became an institution; upper classmen who had heard the lecture once or twice already would come to hear Dr. Wilson enlarge upon a theme so dear to his heart.

As a teacher Dr. Wilson impressed his students most of all with his thorough mastery of his subject. He did not entrench himself behind the professor's desk, read lectures written years before and discourage student-questions as an impertinence. He would leave his desk and walk the floor, emphasizing with voice and gesture the point that he was driving home. A question or objection from the class would often lead to a digression in which he would pour out a wealth of information quite overwhelming to the inquirer or confounding to the caviller. This readiness on Dr. Wilson's part was due primarily to his great learning, but fully as much to the remarkably retentive memory that made it possible for him to draw at will and without consulting lecture-notes or card-index on the rich treasures of accumulated information which were his. Yet he was careful not to trust too much to memory and especially in quoting the views of an opponent he endeavored to be scrupulously fair and to have the evidence before him in black and white. With all his learning, he never felt that he was doing full justice to his classes unless he made special preparation, often a great deal of preparation, to meet them. His Hebrew class, of course, he could have conducted in his sleep!

Dr. Wilson was a very conscientious teacher. The students might feel entitled to an occasional "cut." But he set them a fine example of fidelity to duty. And sometimes when one of them had allowed himself a little unauthorized holiday the cordiality with which Dr. Wilson welcomed him back and the solicitude with which he inquired after his health and general welfare, served to convince the returning prodigal that his absence had been noted. Dr. Wilson knew all his students and made them feel his interest in them. His home was always open to them and he often visited them in their rooms. He was never happier than when he had a group of them around him for informal talk. He looked upon them as his "boys" and when his only son died nearly twenty years ago, soon after graduating from Princeton University, this bond became even closer and more intimate and his boys took the place of the son that he had lost.

With all his brilliancy and fire Dr. Wilson was remarkably patient as a teacher. Many great scholars find it difficult to get down to the level of their students. Others less gifted become impatient with what they think the pupil's slowness because they have themselves traversed the ground so often that they have forgotten the difficulties which beset their path when first they travelled over it. Dr. Wilson was not concerned to dazzle his students, to impress them with the greatness of his erudition. His aim was rather to teach them the subjects and convince them of the truths which he deemed of prime importance for them. It was this which made him so successful as teacher and as lecturer.

Especially characteristic of Dr. Wilson as a teacher was his geniality and the pleasant humor which showed itself in his classroom. He did not stand on his dignity, yet the students were few who took unwarranted liberties with him. I remember his telling of an experience of some forty years ago. There was a student in his class who thought himself wiser than the youthful teacher and assumed an unbecoming attitude. The teacher ignored it for several days. Then without warning he called on this student to recite, quizzed him for nearly an hour, and so completely exposed his unpreparedness that there was nothing left for self-sufficient ignorance to build upon. But it was rare that Dr. Wilson found it necessary to exert his authority. The boys respected him and loved him and that was enough. One afternoon at Princeton before the Hebrew recitation a student introduced a member of the canine species into the classroom. Dr. Wilson apparently took no notice. He merely went to the blackboard, wrote the word "dog" in Hebrew letters, remarked to the class, "Gentlemen, *dog*, is *fish* in Hebrew," and started the class as if nothing had happened. But in the next written recitation the Hebrew word "dog" was included. He frequently spiced his lectures with joke or anecdote. He held this to be sound psychology. But it was more than pedagogical expedient; it was as natural and spontaneous as the breath he drew.

One cannot speak of Dr. Wilson the teacher, without speaking also of Dr. Wilson the scholar. As already intimated, it was because of his great learning, expert and highly specialized, yet also unusually broad and comprehensive, that Dr. Wilson was so influential as a teacher. His students realized that he knew whereof he spake. As a boy his special interest had been in history. After graduating from Princeton University with the Class of 1876 and studying and teaching at Western Theological Seminary he spent two years in special language study at the University of Berlin, then perhaps the greatest centre of Semitic studies in the world. In 1883 he returned to Western Seminary as Instructor and soon was made Professor of Old Testament. While there he devoted much of the spare time allowed by a heavy schedule of teaching to the study of language. For some years he endeavored to add one new language each year to the list of those which he already had at his command. In 1891 he published his *Manual* and *Grammar* of Elementary Syriac, following the inductive method which President Harper of Chicago University had applied so successfully to the study of Hebrew.[3] While at Princeton he prepared a *Hebrew Grammar* and a *Syntax*.[4] But despite his rare linguistic talent Dr. Wilson's interest was never exclusively or even primarily linguistic. Languages were to him a means, not an end. They were the means of studying at first hand all those records of the past which could throw any light upon the Old Testament, which he was privileged to teach and to defend.

The death, in 1900, of Dr. William Henry Green of Princeton Seminary came as a great loss not only to that institution but to the Church at large. Dr. Green had been the great Presbyterian protagonist of the Biblical and historical view of the Old Testament Scriptures against the so-called Higher Criticism. It was a high tribute to Dr. Wilson's ability and reputation that he was called to Princeton to occupy the William Henry Green Chair of Semitic Philology and Old Testament Criticism. He accepted the call; and he proceeded with all fidelity to carry on the great work of his famous predecessor. It was no easy task that was thus laid upon him. From the first chapter of Genesis to the last chapter of Malachi the Old Testament Scriptures were under fire. This had been true in Dr. Green's day. But the task was made increasingly difficult by the fact that these unscriptural views were becoming increasingly popular and even being regarded in many circles as "assured results," established facts no longer open to discussion. Furthermore the new light which the archaeologist was constantly providing, as, for example, the Code of Hammurabi and the Elephantine Papyri, while throwing welcome light upon the history of the past laid an increasing burden upon the scholar who would master the records of that past in order to use them in the defense of the Scriptures. The interest which Dr. Wilson took in every new discovery and the care with which he canvassed it for any light upon the Scriptures appears on almost every page of his writings.

3. Robert Dick Wilson, *Introductory Syriac Method and Manual* (New York: Scribner, 1891) and *Elements of Syriac Grammar by an Inductive Method* (New York: Scribner, 1891).

4. Robert Dick Wilson, *A Hebrew Grammar for Beginners* (Leipzig: Drugulin, 1908) and *Notes on Hebrew Syntax* (1892).

The method used by Dr. Wilson in defending the Scriptures and confounding the critics is so characteristic that it must be stated briefly. Everyone at all familiar with the "Higher Critics" is at times appalled with the multitude of arguments and assertions put forward by them in support of their "reconstruction" of the Bible. There are two ways in which the defender of the Scriptures can proceed: he may approach the subject along general and at times theoretical lines setting forth the objections to the theory as a whole, or he may concern himself with specific points and definite charges. Dr. Wilson did not neglect the former, but he much preferred the latter of these methods. When he went to Princeton, the best and clearest statement in English of the higher critical position was Canon Driver's *Introduction to the Literature of the Old Testament.* Here was an authoritative presentation of the views of leading critics. Dr. Wilson proceeded to test the stability of this imposing structure as a prospector might bore for oil. He would take an assertion here, a denial there, and subject them to an intense and searching scrutiny. He did not care how much labor this might involve. It might take months of study to settle a single important point. It might require twenty, fifty, a hundred pages of carefully collected facts and ordered argument to disprove a sentence or a paragraph of higher critical assertion. That did not matter. What did matter, what Dr. Wilson was supremely concerned to do was to show by example after example, test-case after test-case, that wherever they could be tested by the facts the allegations brought by the critics against the Bible were wrong and the Bible was right.

In his *Studies in the Book of Daniel* (1917) Dr. Wilson has given a number of examples of his method. In discussing "Darius the Mede," for example, he first quotes the "objections" to the correctness of the Biblical statements in the exact form in which they are given by three leading critics. This occupies the greater part of a page. He then analyzes the assertions of these critics into *nine* distinct "assumptions" which he states briefly. He then proceeds to examine each one of these assumptions in detail. The complete answer covers more than one hundred pages of the *Studies*, and is a masterpiece of penetrating scrutiny and careful reasoning.

Dr. Wilson is most widely known through the little brochure entitled *Is the Higher Criticism Scholarly?* (Philadelphia: Sunday School Times Company, 1922). Here he brought together and stated in popular form the results of many of his most fruitful investigations. He regarded the accuracy with which the names of foreign kings are written in the Hebrew Scriptures "a Biblical phenomenon unequalled in the history of literature." This booklet has surpassed many a "best seller" in America and Great Britain and has been translated into several foreign languages. It would be hard to estimate the service it has rendered in confirming the faith of thousands in the trustworthiness of the Bible. But only one familiar with Dr. Wilson's weighty articles published mainly in *The Princeton Theological Review* will appreciate the long years of arduous and indefatigable labor which were needed before he was ready to write this little book. In 1926 he published another popular work, *A Scientific Investigation of the Old Testament* (Philadelphia: Sunday School Times Company, 1926), in which he dealt with the text, grammar, vocabulary, history and religion of the Old Testament.

Since it is the studied policy of the "critics" to ignore as "unscholarly" and "unscientific" everyone who has the temerity to question their "assured results," it is a matter of interest that an English scholar, Mr. H. H. Rowley, has recently attempted (*The Aramaic of the Old Testament* [London: Oxford University Press, 1929]) to answer the "strictures" pronounced seventeen years ago by Dr. Wilson on the claim of Dr. Driver and other critics that the characteristics of the Aramaic in which part of the Book of Daniel is written support the view that it is of late date and unhistorical. The author describes his book as "long overdue"; and it is to be regretted that it did not appear several years ago. But it is fortunate that it came to Dr. Wilson's hands in time for him to devote part of the last summer of his life to examining it. His reply was nearly ready when he died; and it will probably appear in *The Evangelical Quarterly* (Edinburgh) in the not far distant future.

As a result of his vigorous defense of the Old Testament in his classroom, on the lecture platform and through the printed page, Dr. Wilson came to be very widely recognized as the foremost living defender of the Old Testament. In consequence of this, he was much in demand as a lecturer at home and abroad. His most notable lecture trip was to the Far East in 1923 when he lectured in Japan, Korea and China. On this trip he did much to confirm the faith of missionaries and native Christians in the Sacred Oracles, but he was distressed by the inroads which modernism was making in the Far East. His unwillingness to ignore this issue brought him into difficulties with missionary leaders in the Church at home. But it was impossible for him to ignore on the mission field what he had been for years opposing and combating in the home land.

Although not himself a graduate of Princeton Seminary Dr. Wilson became so thoroughly representative of that institution that his stalwart defense of the Scriptures led many to suppose that Princeton, as in the days of Dr. Green, stood four square for the *defense* of the faith once delivered to the saints. Consequently, it cast the shadow of tragedy over Dr. Wilson's latter days to know that while he was fighting the battle of the Old Princeton against the liberal hosts without the gate, there was a conflict within the walls of which many had no knowledge, and the meaning of which many would not see. It is not necessary to retell the story. It is well known to readers of *Christianity Today*. Princeton was first "investigated," then "reorganized."

Dr. Wilson might, indeed, have remained at Princeton. He was already past the age for retirement. He might have continued teaching for a year or so and then have retired to spend his old age in literary work, with a pension sufficient for his needs and one of the greatest theological libraries in America ready to his hand. The inducements and allurements he saw clearly. Who could see them better? He knew quite well that he would be misunderstood, that many would regard him a fool. But he believed that to remain would be to countenance and tacitly approve a reorganization which he held to be destructive of the Princeton which he loved and where he had labored for nearly thirty years. So in his seventy-fourth year and with the infirmities of age upon him he left the scene of his best labors and most abundant successes and went forth to begin again and to begin at the beginning, to lay the foundation of a new institution, which should, God willing, ever stand for that brave and uncompromising defense of the Bible as the Word of God to which he had devoted his life. It was the crowning act of a great defender of the faith. And it was one which Dr. Wilson never regretted. He loved Westminster Seminary and saw in the good hand of God upon her the evidence that his work of faith and labor of love had not been in vain.

In estimating the enduring value of the service which Dr. Wilson has rendered to the Church, it is important to remember that his first interest, his prime concern, was not books, but men. He liked to remember that as a young man he had served for a short time as an evangelist. The evangelistic note was present in all his work. He was an ambassador and advocate. He aimed not only to refute error but to establish truth and win men for Him who is the Truth. Consequently the greatest monument to Dr. Wilson is in the multitude of men and women, boys and girls, whose faith in the Bible he has strengthened or renewed. They are a mighty host who rise up today to call him blessed.

But while all this is true and should never be forgotten the amazing thing is that Dr. Wilson was also so preeminent for his great learning and for his many contributions to a true and sound Biblical scholarship. Living in an age over-proud of its "science" Dr. Wilson matched a devout and believing scholarship with the best which "science" and "criticism" could put forward and proved again and again that the foundation of God *standeth sure*. We who are still in the thick of the battle may find it hard to estimate rightly the strength of the adversary or the nearness and greatness of the victory which God is preparing for His people. But when the smoke has cleared away and the noise of combat has changed to the triumph song, the name of this Christian warrior will receive the honor it deserves. He fought a good fight, he finished his course, he kept the faith.

TRIBUTES TO DR. WILSON

"Tributes to Dr. Wilson," *Christianity Today* 1, 8 (Mid-December 1930): 3, 8–9.

We should like to call our readers' attention to several tributes to the late Dr. ROBERT DICK WILSON which appear on other pages of this issue. Many notices of the life and work of Dr. WILSON have been published during the last month in the religious press. We have not space to publish other fine remembrances of this great man of GOD which have come unsolicited to us. All these notices bear witness to the love in which Dr. WILSON was held by so many, and to the secure place he will undoubtedly occupy as one of the great scholars of the Church universal. It was a cause of rejoicing to Dr. WILSON to the end of his days, as it is to so many now, that GOD spared him long enough so that he could make his witness in no uncertain way when the clear call came to establish Westminster Seminary.

THREE TRIBUTES TO DR. WILSON

Among the many tributes to the life and work of the late Dr. Robert Dick Wilson, the three following are typical. Two are selected from Church Bulletins. The first is from the pen of the Rev. H. H. McQuilkin, D.D., minister of the First Presbyterian Church of Orange, N.J. The second is from the bulletin of the Benedict Memorial Presbyterian Church of New Haven, Conn., and was written by the Rev. L. Craig Long, the minister of that Church. The third is from a leaflet recently issued by Westminster Seminary.

"A Wise Masterbuilder"

"Westminster Theological Seminary in Philadelphia has sustained an irreparable loss in the death of this great scholar, inspiring teacher, stalwart defender of the faith. He was master of more than 30 languages and always carried on his investigations in the original tongues—a thing that scholars like even Prof. Driver of Oxford could not do.

"For fifty years he had ferreted out every fact that has any bearing on the Old Testament Scriptures. Toilfully, open-mindedly, eagerly he ransacked the treasures of knowledge. The results of his search brought assurance that the Christian has a sure foundation for his faith in the Sacred Word.

"He taught first in the Western Theological Seminary at Pittsburgh, where the writer was one of his 'boys,' as he always called his former students. Then for thirty years he shed the light of his brilliant attainments on Princeton Theological Seminary. When the control of Princeton was shifted, he, knowing intimately all the inside workings of the matter, was constrained by his conscience and convictions, and at great sacrifice materially, to withdraw and take the lead in founding Westminster. His family testify that his year in the new institution was the happiest of his life. Here as a wise masterbuilder, he laid the foundation of a theological school that is destined to strengthen and enrich the entire Protestant body with its positive, emphatic, triumphant testimony to the faith of the Reformers.

"His name will forever remain entwined with Westminster's. From her portals he went home to God. The splendor of his fame and faith will linger with the faculty and students of Westminster like some superb sunset against the sky, and will surely raise up men and women of faith throughout the Church to aid in maintaining and expanding the work he loved so well."

One Who Fought the Good Fight

"Many hearts have been filled with sorrow during the past week because God has called Home, one of His faithful servants. Those who shall miss him are those who have loved him, and who have looked to him for more than fifty years, as one who has been able to build up intelligent faith in those who studied in his classes, in the accuracy and infallibility of the Old Testament. Dr. Wilson began his theological study more than fifty years ago, and has held professorships in three Seminaries: Western, Princeton, and finally Westminster. As a student, he realized the great need for a type of Biblical scholarship which would be objective and thorough in dealing with facts that could be known only by exhaustive research over the whole range of the ancient languages related to the Bible. He faced the need, and answered the call. In his preparation, he mastered some twenty-six languages; to these he added many others in his later study. Babylonian, Ethiopic, Phoenician, all the Aramaic dialects, and Egyptian, Coptic, Persian, and Armenian, Arabic, Syriac and Hebrew, were just some of those which he learned in order that he might read for his own study the original manuscripts, versions and copies, from which our translations have come. When asked, on one occasion by Mr. Philip E. Howard, Publisher of the Sunday School Times,—'Professor, what do you try to do for your students?' He instantly replied, 'I try to give them such an intelligent faith in the Old Testament Scriptures that they will never doubt them as long as they live. I try to give them evidence. I try to show them that there is a reasonable ground for belief in the history of the Old Testament. Whenever there is sufficient documentary evidence to make an investigation, the statements of the Bible, in the original texts, have stood the test.' The writer of this brief tribute is but one of thousands of Ministers who owes much to Dr. Wilson for the part that he had in the establishment of his faith in the Bible. One of his greatest contributions was made, when after Princeton Seminary had been reorganized by the General Assembly, he became an inspiration and a leader, with Dr. Machen and Dr. Allis, in the establishment of Westminster Theological Seminary. The Hymn printed on the front-page of this Bulletin ('When I survey the wondrous Cross'), is one which holds great meaning for many who have known and loved him. It was sung on two occasions as a favorite. The one time was on the first commencement day of the New Seminary, when thirteen young men were receiving their diplomas. It was after Dr. Wilson, a veteran soldier of the cross, had given final charge to these, his last students, that the hymn was sung. In closing he said, 'Fight the good fight of faith' . . . 'Until we meet at Jesus feet' . . . A summer past, the second year of the Seminary opened, Dr. Wilson met one class, and then 'went Home.' Not much wonder that many who attended his final service in Westminster on Tuesday, October fourteenth, had a new meaning placed upon the old hymn 'When I survey the wondrous Cross,' when it was again sung that day by the Seminary quartet. Only a man like Dr. Wilson could so perfectly prove by example that the words of this hymn were the feelings of his heart. A few of us who knew him intimately, and who received new Christian courage at each hand-clasp, shall miss his living faith, as we thank God that He spared him for such a long life of service for Presbyterianism. Let us pray that his students and followers may follow in his footsteps of faith, singing, with sincere meaning the words—'When I survey the wondrous Cross.'"

The Power of a Noble Example

On Saturday, October 11, 1930, the Rev. Robert Dick Wilson, Ph.D., D.D., LL.D., Professor of Semitic Philology and Old Testament Criticism in Westminster Theological Seminary, entered into his heavenly reward.

Dr. Wilson was a notable scholar. Where others were content to take the results of philological investigation at second hand, he had recourse to the sources. His linguistic attainments were broad and deep.

He was at home not only in Hebrew and Aramaic, and of course in Latin, Greek and modern languages, but also in Babylonian, Arabic, Syriac, and other tongues. His knowledge of the Old Testament was profound.

He devoted all of this vast learning to the defence of Holy Scripture. He believed with all his mind and heart that the Bible is true, and he supported his belief with a wealth of scientific material which even his opponents could not neglect. Only a short time before his death he was engaged in an answer to a notable monograph, published at Oxford, which had recently devoted itself to a consideration of his views.

He was greatly beloved as a teacher and as a friend. With the simplicity of a true scholar, he was always ready to cast reserve aside and receive his students into his heart. He called them his "boys," and they responded with affection as well as with respect.

But great as were Dr. Wilson's achievements throughout a long and fruitful life, his greatest achievement was his last. It was the achievement by which, putting selfish considerations and unworthy compromise of principle aside, he left his home at Princeton and entered the Faculty of a new institution devoted unreservedly to the Word of God.

Many arguments might have been adduced to lead Dr. Wilson to remain at Princeton Seminary after the reorganization of that institution in 1929. He was at that time in his seventy-fourth year. An honorable and advantageous retirement awaited him whenever he desired. He had a good salary and a comfortable home. He had the friends that he had made at Princeton during a residence there of nearly thirty years. Might he not retain these advantages without being unfaithful to the cause to which he had devoted his life? Would not the new Board of Princeton Seminary keep in the background, for a time at least, the real character of the revolution that had been wrought? Would not the doctrinal change be gradual only, as at so many other institutions, formerly evangelical, which have conformed to the drift of the times? Could he not, meanwhile, serve God by teaching the truth in his own class-room, no matter what the rest of the institution did? Could he not round out his life in peace? Could he not leave to younger men the battle for the Faith?

Those considerations and many like them were no doubt presented to Dr. Wilson in very persuasive form. But he would have none of them. His Christian conscience, trained by a lifetime of devotion to God's Word, cut through such arguments with the keenness of a Damascus blade. He penetrated to the real essence of the question. He saw that for him to remain at Princeton would be to commend as trustworthy what he knew to be untrustworthy, that it would be to lead Christ's little ones astray. He knew that a man cannot have God's richest blessing, even in teaching the truth, when the opportunity to teach the truth is gained by compromise of principle. He saw clearly that it was not a time for him to think of his own ease or comfort, but to bear testimony to the Saviour who had bought him with His own precious blood.

He did bear that testimony. He left his home at Princeton, and all the emoluments and honors that awaited him there. He cast in his lot with a new institution that had not a dollar of endowment and was dependent for the support of its professors upon nothing but faith in God.

Dr. Wilson was supremely happy in that decision. He never regretted it for a moment. He entered joyfully into the life of the new seminary, and God richly blessed him there. Then, having rounded out more than the allotted period of three-score years and ten, a Christian soldier without tarnish of compromise upon his shield, he entered into the joy of his Lord.

His example is a precious possession for those whom he has left behind. He is, indeed, no longer with us in bodily presence. His great learning is with us only in his writings and in the knowledge of the Bible that he has imparted to his host of students throughout the world. But the power of his example will not be lost. Westminster Seminary, by God's grace, will ever be true to the Lord Jesus, as this beloved teacher was true. Trustees, Faculty and students will be moved always to sacrifice themselves for an institution to which Dr. Wilson gave so much.

His example will touch also the hearts of those throughout the Church who love the gospel that he loved, and who know that that gospel cannot well be preached unless there be a school of the prophets to train men to preach it in all its purity and all its power. The Seminary that was so dear to Dr. Wilson's heart, and in whose founding he had so large a share, will not, we think, be allowed to call now in vain; but gifts will pour in from those who, like Dr. Wilson, have hearts full of gratitude to Him who loved us and gave Himself for us.

Nature and Scripture

CORNELIUS VAN TIL

Cornelius Van Til, "Nature and Scripture," in *The Infallible Word*, ed. Paul Woolley, 3rd rev. printing (Philadelphia: Presbyterian and Reformed, 1967), 263–301; reprinted from Philadelphia: Presbyterian Guardian, 1946.

Cornelius Van Til (1895–1987), pastor, professor, and presuppositionalist apologist, was born in the Netherlands and immigrated to the United States early in 1905. After studying in Grand Rapids at Calvin College and Seminary, he pursued studies at Princeton Theological Seminary and completed a Ph.D. in philosophy at Princeton University. After one year of teaching apologetics at Princeton Seminary, he joined J. Gresham Machen at Westminster Seminary in 1929, where he taught until 1975. During his tenure at Westminster, Van Til was also involved in the life of the Orthodox Presbyterian Church. His presuppositional apologetics, which combines elements of Dutch Calvinism (in the line of Kuyper and Bavinck) and of Old Princeton (in particular Warfield and Vos), is one of the hallmarks of Westminster Seminary's theology.

Several of Van Til's works develop the topics of revelation and inspiration. For example, in the second chapter of his *Christian Apologetics* (a basic summary of his approach), Van Til elaborates the topic of general revelation in a manner similar to that in the selection below. In *An Introduction to Systematic Theology* (a companion to his class on the introduction to theology), Van Til expounds both the question of revelation and that of Scripture. Further, in the second chapter of *A Christian Theory of Knowledge*, "The Holy Scriptures," he affirms the self-sufficient and self-attesting character of the Bible. Finally, Van Til's expanded introduction to B. B. Warfield's *The Inspiration of the Bible* is valuable in its own right (cf. chap. 40 above).

The present selection, "Nature and Scripture," taken from the Westminster symposium on Scripture, *The Infallible Word* (1946), elaborates the relationship between special and general revelation in important ways. Greg Bahnsen describes it as a "crucial article" and considers the way in which Van Til draws a "parallel between the attributes of Scripture—necessity, authority, sufficiency, perspicuity—and the corresponding attributes of natural revelation": "brilliant." After applying these four traditional attributes of Scripture to natural revelation (cf. chap. 32 above on Bavinck), Van Til considers and evaluates alternative views of natural theology from Thomas Aquinas to Karl Barth, including major philosophers. Thus this article, in addition to shedding indirect light on Van Til's doctrine of Scripture, gives a sampling of Van Til's skills as a theologian and apologist. Along these lines, John Frame describes the second half of the essay as "his most concise survey and critique of the history of secular philosophy, Scholasticism, and modern theology."

Bibliography: Greg L. Bahnsen. *Van Til's Apologetic: Readings and Analysis*. Phillipsburg, NJ: P&R Publishing, 1998. Esp. pp. 177–219. H. M. Conn. "Van Til, Cornelius (1895–1987)." P. 267 in *DP&RTA*. John M. Frame. *Cornelius Van Til: An Analysis of His Thought*. Phillipsburg, NJ: P&R Publishing, 1995. E. R. Geehan, ed. *Jerusalem and Athens: Critical Discussions on the Theology and Apologetics of Cornelius Van Til*. Nutley, NJ: Presbyterian and Reformed, 1971. Idem. "Van Til, Cornelius (1895–1987)." Pp. 682–84 in *BDE*. D. F. Kelly. "Van Til, Cornelius (1895–1987)." Pp. 704–5 in *NDT*. David E. Kucharsky. "At the Beginning, God: An Interview with Cornelius Van Til." *Christianity Today* 22, 6 (December 30, 1977): 18–22. John R. Muether. *Cornelius Van Til: Reformed Apologist and Churchman*. Phillipsburg, NJ: P&R Publishing, 2008. Wesley A. Roberts. "Cornelius Van Til." Pp. 119–32 in *Reformed Theology in America*. Lane G. Tipton. "The Triune Personal God: Trinitarian Theology in the Thought of Cornelius Van Til." Ph.D. diss., Westminster Theological Seminary, 2004. Cornelius Van Til. *Christian Apologetics*. 2nd ed. Ed. William Edgar. Phillipsburg, NJ: P&R Publishing, 1976, 2003. Idem. *An Introduction to Systematic Theology*. 2nd ed. Ed. William Edgar. Phillipsburg, NJ: P&R Publishing, 1974, 2007. William White Jr. *Van Til: Defender of the Faith*. Nashville: Thomas Nelson, 1979.

We have been dealing, in this book, with the doctrine of Scripture. But Scripture claims to come to sinners. And sinners are such as have, through the fall of Adam, become "wholly defiled in all the faculties and parts of soul and body." Man made himself "incapable of life" by his disobedience to God's original revelation of himself in paradise. It is in order, then, that a discussion of the doctrine of Scripture should include an investigation of God's revelation in nature. Moreover, Scripture does not claim to speak to man, even as fallen, in any other way than in conjunction with nature. It is therefore of the utmost importance that the two forms of revelation—revelation through nature and revelation in Scripture—be set in careful relationship to one another. Do the two forms of God's revelation to sinners cover two distinct interests or dimensions of human life? Do they speak with different degrees of authority? Just what, we are bound to ask, is the relation between them?

It is well known that Reformed theology has a distinctive doctrine of Scripture. It is our purpose in this chapter to show that for this reason it has an equally distinctive doctrine of natural revelation. To accomplish this purpose we shall limit ourselves largely to the Westminster Standards. Dividing our discussion into two main parts, we shall set forth positively the doctrine of natural theology that is found in these standards and then contrast this natural theology with another natural theology, the natural theology that has its origin in Greek thought.

I. The Natural Theology of the Confession

The distinctive character of the natural theology of the Westminster Confession may be most clearly brought to view if we show how intimately it is interwoven with the Confession's doctrine of Scripture. And this may perhaps be most easily accomplished if it is noted that, just as the Confession's doctrine of Scripture may be set forth under definite notions of its necessity, its authority, its sufficiency and its perspicuity, so the Confession's doctrine of revelation in nature may be set forth under corresponding notions of necessity, authority, sufficiency and perspicuity.

A few general remarks must therefore first be made with respect to the concepts of necessity, authority, sufficiency and perspicuity as these pertain to the Confession's doctrine of Scripture.

According to the Confession, Scripture speaks to sinners in terms of a covenant. It tells us that man was originally placed on earth under the terms of the covenant of works. It informs us further that man broke this covenant of works and that God was pleased to make a second covenant with men that they might be saved. Thus Scripture may be said to be the written expression of God's covenantal relationship with man.

The four characteristics of Scripture enumerated above may now be regarded in relation to this general covenant concept. The necessity of Scripture lies in the fact that man has broken the covenant of works. He therefore needs the grace of God. There is no speech or knowledge of grace in nature. God has accordingly condescended to reveal it in Scripture.

The revelation of grace can be seen for what it is only if it be seen in its own light. The light of grace outshines in its brilliance the light of nature as the sun outshines the moon. The kind of God that speaks in Scripture can speak only on his own authority. So the authority of Scripture is as basic as its necessity.

To this necessity and authority there must be added the sufficiency or finality of Scripture. When the sun of grace has arisen on the horizon of the sinner, the "light of nature" shines only by reflected light. Even when there are some "circumstances concerning the worship of God, the government of the church, common to human actions and societies, which are to be ordered by the light of nature and Christian prudence," they are to be so ordered "according to the general rules of the word, which are always to be observed." The light of Scripture is that superior light which lightens every other light. It is also the final light. God's covenant of grace is his final covenant with man. Its terms must be once for all and finally recorded "against the corruption of the flesh, and the malice of Satan and of the world."

To the necessity, authority and sufficiency of Scripture must finally be added its perspicuity. The distribution of God's grace depends in the last analysis upon his sovereign will, but it is mediated always through fully responsible image-bearers of God. God's being is wholly clear to himself and his revelation of himself to sinners is therefore also inherently clear. Not only the learned but also the unlearned "in a due use of the ordinary means" may "attain unto a sufficient understanding" of God's covenant of grace as revealed in Scripture.

With this general view of Scripture in mind, we turn to the question of God's revelation of himself in nature. The first point that calls for reflection here is the fact that it is, according to Scripture itself, the same God who reveals himself in nature and in grace. The God who reveals himself in nature may therefore be described as "infinite in being, glory, blessedness, and perfection, all-sufficient, eternal, unchangeable, incomprehensible, every where present, almighty, knowing all things, most wise, most holy, most just, most merciful and gracious, long-suffering, and abundant in goodness and truth."[1] It is, to be sure, from Scripture rather than from nature that this description of God is drawn. Yet it is the same God, to the extent that he is revealed at all, that is revealed in nature.

Contemplation of this fact seems at once to plunge us into great difficulty. Are we not told that nature reveals nothing of the grace of God? Does not the Confession insist that men cannot be saved except through the knowledge of God, "be they ever so diligent to frame their lives according to the light of nature; and the law of that religion they do profess"?[2] Saving grace is not manifest in nature; yet it is the God of saving grace who manifests himself by means of nature. How can these two be harmonized?

The answer to this problem must be found in the fact that God is "eternal, incomprehensible, most free, most absolute." Any revelation that God gives of himself is therefore absolutely voluntary. Herein precisely lies the union of the various forms of God's revelation with one another. God's revelation in nature, together with God's revelation in Scripture, form God's one grand scheme of covenant revelation of himself to man. The two forms of revelation must therefore be seen as presupposing and supplementing one another. They are aspects of one general philosophy of history.

1. The Philosophy of History

The philosophy of history that speaks to us from the various chapters of the Confession may be sketched with a few bold strokes. We are told that man could never have had any fruition of God through the revelation that came to him in nature as operating by itself. There was superadded to God's revelation in nature another revelation, a supernaturally communicated positive revelation. Natural revelation, we are virtually told, was from the outset incorporated into the idea of a covenant relationship of God with man. Thus every dimension of created existence, even the lowest, was enveloped in a form of exhaustively personal relationship between God and man. The "ateleological" no less than the "teleological," the "mechanical" no less than the "spiritual," was covenantal in character.

Being from the outset covenantal in character, the natural revelation of God to man was meant to serve as the playground for the process of differentiation that was to take place in the course of time. The covenant made with Adam was conditional. There would be *additional* revelation of God in nature after the action of man with respect to the tree of the knowledge of good and evil. This additional revelation would be different from that which had preceded it. And the difference would depend definitely upon a self-conscious covenant act of man with respect to the positively communicated prohibition. We know something of the nature of this new and different revelation of God in nature consequent upon the covenant-breaking act of man. "For the wrath of God is revealed from heaven against all ungodliness and unrighteousness of man" (Rom. 1:18).

Thus God's covenant wrath is revealed in nature after the one all-decisive act of disobedience on the part of the first covenant head. But, together with God's wrath, his grace is also manifest. When the wrath of God made manifest in nature would destroy all men, God makes covenant with Noah that day and night, winter and summer, should continue to the end of time (Gen. 9:11). The rainbow, a natural phenomenon, is but an outstanding

1. The Larger Catechism, Q. 7.
2. The Confession of Faith, Chapter X.

illustration of this fact. But all this is in itself incomplete. The covenant with Noah is but a limiting notion in relation to the covenant of saving grace. Through the new and better covenant, man will have true fruition of God. And this fact itself is to be mediated through nature. The prophets, and especially the great Prophet, foretell the future course of nature. The priests of God, and most of all the great High Priest of God, hear the answers to their prayers by means of nature. The kings under God, and most of all the great King of Israel, make nature serve the purposes of redemption. The forces of nature are always at the beck and call of the power of differentiation that works toward redemption and reprobation. It is this idea of a supernatural-natural revelation that comes to such eloquent expression in the Old Testament, and particularly in the Psalms.

Here then is the picture of a well-integrated and unified philosophy of history in which revelation in nature and revelation in Scripture are mutually meaningless without one another and mutually fruitful when taken together.

To bring out the unity and therewith the meaning of this total picture more clearly, we turn now to note the necessity, the authority, the sufficiency and the perspicuity of natural revelation, as these correspond to the necessity, the authority, the sufficiency and the perspicuity of Scripture.

2. The Necessity of Natural Revelation

Speaking first of the necessity of natural revelation we must recall that man was made a covenant personality. Scripture became necessary because of the covenant disobedience of Adam in paradise. This covenant disobedience took place in relation to the supernatural positive revelation that God had given with respect to the tree of the knowledge of good and evil. God chose one tree from among many and "arbitrarily" told man not to eat of it. It is in this connection that we must speak of the necessity of natural revelation. If the tree of the knowledge of good and evil had been naturally different from other trees it could not have served its unique purpose. That the commandment might appear as purely "arbitrary" the specially chosen tree had to be naturally like other trees. For the supernatural to appear as supernatural the natural had to appear as really natural. The supernatural could not be recognized for what it was unless the natural were also recognized for what it was. There had to be regularity if there was to be a genuine exception.

A further point needs to be noted. God did not give his prohibition so that man might be obedient merely with respect to the tree of the knowledge of good and evil, and that merely at one particular moment of time. He gave the prohibition so that man might learn to be self-consciously obedient in all that he did with respect to all things and throughout all time. Man was meant to glorify God in the "lower" as much as in the "higher" dimensions of life. Man's act with respect to the tree of the knowledge of good and evil was to be but an example to himself of what he should or should not do with respect to all other trees. But for an example to be really an example it must be exceptional. And for the exceptional to be the exceptional there is required that which is regular. Thus we come again to the notion of the necessity of natural revelation as the presupposition of the process of differentiation that history was meant to be.

So far we have spoken of the necessity of natural revelation as it existed before the fall. Carrying on this idea, it follows that we may also speak of the necessity of natural revelation after the fall. Here too the natural or regular has to appear as the presupposition of the exceptional. But the exceptional has now become redemptive. The natural must therefore appear as in need of redemption. After the fall it is not sufficient that the natural should appear as merely regular. The natural must now appear as under the curse of God. God's covenant wrath rests securely and comprehensively upon man and upon all that man has mismanaged. Before the fall the natural as being the merely regular was the presupposition of the supernatural as being pre-redemptively covenantal; after the fall the natural as under the covenant wrath of God is the presupposition of the supernatural as redemptively covenantal. Grace can be recognized as grace only in contrast with God's curse on nature.

Then too the idea of the supernatural as "example" is again in order here. Grace speaks to man of victory over sin. But the victory this time is to come through the obedience of the second Adam. The regeneration of all things must now be a gift before it can become a task. The natural must therefore by contrast reveal an unalleviated picture of folly and ruin. Nor would the Confession permit us to tone down the rigid character of the absolute contrast between the grace and the curse of God through the idea of "common grace." Common grace is subservient to special or saving grace. As such it helps to bring out the very contrast between this saving grace and the curse of God. When men dream dreams of a paradise regained by means of common grace, they only manifest the "strong delusion" that falls as punishment of God upon those that abuse his natural revelation. Thus the natural as the regular appears as all the more in need of the gift of the grace of God.

Yet the gift is in order to the task. The example is also meant to be a sample. Christ walks indeed a cosmic road. Far as the curse is found, so far his grace is given. The Biblical miracles of healing point to the regeneration of all things. The healed souls of men require and will eventually receive healed bodies and a healed environment. Thus there is unity of concept for those who live by the Scriptural promise of comprehensive, though not universal, redemption. While they actually expect Christ to return visibly on the clouds of heaven, they thank God for every sunny day. They even thank God for his restraining and supporting general grace by means of which the unbeliever helps to display the majesty and power of God. To the believer the natural or regular with all its complexity always appears as the playground for the process of differentiation which leads ever onward to the fullness of the glory of God.

3. The Authority of Natural Revelation

So far we have found that the Confession's conception of the necessity of Scripture requires a corresponding conception of the necessity of revelation in nature. It is not surprising, then, that the Confession's notion of the authority of Scripture requires a corresponding notion of the authority of revelation in nature. Here too it is well that we begin by studying the situation as it obtained before the entrance of sin.

In paradise, God communicated directly and positively with man in regard to the tree of life. This revelation was authoritative. Its whole content was that of a command requiring implicit obedience. This supernatural revelation was something exceptional. To be recognized for what it was in its exceptionality, a contrast was required between it and God's regular way of communication with man. Ordinarily man had to use his God-given powers of investigation to discover the workings of the processes of nature. Again, the voice of authority as it came to man in this exceptional manner was to be but illustrative of the fact that, in and through the things of nature, there spoke the self-same voice of God's command. Man was given permission by means of the direct voice of authority to control and subdue the powers of nature. As a hunter bears upon his back in clearly visible manner the number of his hunting license, so Adam bore indelibly upon his mind the divine right of dealing with nature. And the divine right was at the same time the divine obligation. The mark of God's ownership was from the beginning writ large upon all the facts of the universe. Man was to cultivate the garden of the Lord and gladly pay tribute to the Lord of the manor.

Man's scientific procedure was accordingly to be marked by the attitude of obedience to God. He was to realize that he would find death in nature everywhere if he manipulated it otherwise than as being the direct bearer of the behests of God. The rational creature of God must naturally live by authority in all the activities of his personality. All these activities are inherently covenantal activities either of obedience or of disobedience. Man was created as an analogue of God; his thinking, his willing and his doing is therefore properly conceived as at every point analogical to the thinking, willing and doing of God. It is only after refusing to be analogous to God that man can think of setting a contrast between the attitude of reason to one type of revelation and the attitude of faith to another type of revelation.

By the idea of revelation, then, we are to mean not merely what comes to man through the facts surrounding him in his environment, but also that which comes to him by means of his own constitution as a covenant personality. The revelation that comes to man by way of his own rational and moral nature is no less objective to him than that which comes to him through the voice of trees and animals. Man's own psychological activity is no less revelational than the laws of physics about him. All created reality is inherently revelational of the nature and will of God. Even man's ethical reaction to God's revelation is still revelational. And as revelational of God, it is authoritative. The meaning of the Confession's doctrine of the authority of Scripture does not become clear to us till we see it against the background of the original and basically authoritative character of God's revelation in nature. Scripture speaks authoritatively to such as must naturally live by authority. God speaks with authority wherever and whenever he speaks.

At this point a word may be said about the revelation of God through conscience and its relation to Scripture. Conscience is man's consciousness speaking on matters of directly moral import. Every act of man's consciousness is moral in the most comprehensive sense of that term. Yet there is a difference between questions of right and wrong in a restricted sense and general questions of interpretation. Now if man's whole consciousness was originally created perfect, and as such authoritatively expressive of the will of God that same consciousness is still revelational and authoritative after the entrance of sin to the extent that its voice is still the voice of God. The sinner's efforts, so far as they are done self-consciously from his point of view, seek to destroy or bury the voice of God that comes to him through nature, which includes his own consciousness. But this effort cannot be wholly successful at any point in history. The most depraved of men cannot wholly escape the voice of God. Their greatest wickedness is meaningless except upon the assumption that they have sinned against the authority of God. Thoughts and deeds of utmost perversity are themselves revelational, revelational, that is, in their very abnormality. The natural man accuses or else excuses himself only because his own utterly depraved consciousness continues to point back to the original state of affairs. The prodigal son can never forget the father's voice. It is the albatross forever about his neck.

927

4. The Sufficiency of Natural Revelation

Proceeding now to speak of the sufficiency of natural revelation as corresponding to the sufficiency of Scripture, we recall that revelation in nature was never meant to function by itself. It was from the beginning insufficient without its supernatural concomitant. It was inherently a limiting notion. It was but the presupposition of historical action on the part of man as covenant personality with respect to supernaturally conveyed communication. But for that specific purpose it was wholly sufficient. It was *historically* sufficient.

After the fall of man natural revelation is still historically sufficient. It is sufficient for such as have in Adam brought the curse of God upon nature. It is sufficient to render them without excuse. Those who are in prison and cannot clearly see the light of the sun receive their due inasmuch as they have first abused that light. If nature groans in pain and travail because of man's abuse of it, this very fact—that is, the very curse of God on nature—should be instrumental anew in making men accuse of excuse themselves. Nature as it were years to be released from its imprisonment in order once more to be united to her Lord in fruitful union. When nature is abused by man it cries out to her creator for vengeance and through it for redemption.

It was in the mother promise that God gave the answer to nature's cry (Gen. 3:15). In this promise there was a two-fold aspect. There was first the aspect of vengeance. He that should come was to bruise the head of the serpent, the one that led man in setting up nature as independent of the supernatural revelation of God. Thus nature was once more to be given the opportunity of serving as the proper field of exercise for the direct supernatural communication of God to man. But this time this service came at a more advanced point in history. Nature was now the bearer of God's curse as well as of his general mercy. The "good," that is, the believers, are, generally, hedged about by God. Yet they must not expect that always and in every respect this will the case. They must learn to say with Job, be it after much trial, "Though he slay me, yet will I trust in him" (Job 13:15). The "evil," that is, the unbelievers, will generally be rewarded with the natural consequences of their deeds. But this too is not always and without qualification the case. The wicked sometimes prosper. Nature only shows tendencies. And tendencies point forward to the time when tendencies shall have become the rules without exception. The tendency itself is meaningless without the certainty of the climax. The present regularity of nature is therefore once again to be looked upon as a limiting notion. At every stage in history God's revelation in nature is sufficient for the purpose it was meant to serve, that of being the playground for the process of differentiation between those who would and those who would not serve God.

5. The Perspicuity of Natural Revelation

Finally we turn to the perspicuity of nature which corresponds to the perspicuity of Scripture. We have stressed the fact that God's revelation in nature was from the outset of history meant to be taken conjointly with God's supernatural communication. This might seem to indicate that natural revelation is not inherently perspicuous. Then too it has been pointed out that back of both kinds of revelation is the incomprehensible God. And this fact again might, on first glance, seem to militate strongly against the claim that nature clearly reveals God. Yet these very facts themselves are the best guarantee of the genuine perspicuity of natural revelation. The perspicuity of God's revelation in nature depends for its very meaning upon the fact that it is an aspect of the total and totally voluntary revelation of a

God who is self-contained. God's incomprehensibility to man is due to the fact that he is exhaustively comprehensible to himself. God is light and in him is no darkness at all. As such he cannot deny himself. This God naturally has an all-comprehensive plan for the created universe. He has planned all the relationships between all the aspects of created being. He has planned the end from the beginning. All created reality therefore actually displays this plan. It is, in consequence, inherently rational.

It is quite true, of course, that created man is unable to penetrate to the very bottom of this inherently clear revelation. But this does not mean that on this account the revelation of God is not clear, even for him. Created man may see clearly what is revealed clearly even if he cannot see exhaustively. Man does not need to know exhaustively in order to know truly and certainly. When on the created level of existence man thinks God's thoughts after him, that is, when man thinks in self-conscious submission to the voluntary revelation of the self-sufficient God, he has therewith the only possible ground of certainty for his knowledge. When man thinks thus he thinks as a covenant creature should wish to think. That is to say, man normally thinks in analogical fashion. He realizes that God's thoughts are self-contained. He knows that his own interpretation of nature must therefore be a re-interpretation of what is already fully interpreted by God.

The concept of analogical thinking is of especial significance here. Soon we shall meet a notion of analogy that is based upon the very denial of the concept of the incomprehensible God. It is therefore of the utmost import that the Confession's concept of analogical thinking be seen to be the direct implication of its doctrine of God.

One further point must here be noted. We have seen that since the fall of man God's curse rests upon nature. This has brought great complexity into the picture. All this, however, in no wise detracts from the historical and objective perspicuity of nature. Nature can and does reveal nothing but the one comprehensive plan of God. The psalmist does not say that the heavens possibly or probably declare the glory of God. Nor does the apostle assert that the wrath of God is probably revealed from heaven against all ungodliness and unrighteousness of men. Scripture takes the clarity of God's revelation for granted at every stage of human history. Even when man, as it were, takes out his own eyes, this act itself turns revelational in his wicked hands, testifying to him that his sin is a sin against the light that lighteth every man coming into the world. Even to the very bottom of the most complex historical situations, involving sin and all its consequences, God's revelation shines with unmistakable clarity. "If I make my bed in hell, behold thou art there" (Ps. 138:8). Creatures have no private chambers.

Both the perspicuity of Scripture and the perspicuity of natural revelation, then, may be said to have their foundation in the doctrine of the God who "hideth himself," whose thoughts are higher than man's thoughts and whose ways are higher than man's ways. There is no discrepancy between the idea of mystery and that of perspicuity with respect either to revelation in Scripture or to revelation in nature. On the contrary the two ideas are involved in one another. The central unifying concept of the entire Confession is the doctrine of God and his one unified comprehensive plan for the world. The contention consequently is that at no point is there any excuse for man's not seeing all things as happening according to this plan.

In considering man's acceptance of natural revelation, we again take our clue from the Confession and what it says about the acceptance of Scripture. Its teaching on man's acceptance of Scriptural revelation is in accord with its teachings on the necessity, authority,

929

sufficiency and perspicuity of Scripture. The Scriptures as the finished product of God's supernatural and saving revelation to man have their own evidence in themselves. The God who speaks in Scripture cannot refer to anything that is not already authoritatively revelational of himself for the evidence of his own existence. There is no thing that does not exist by his creation. All things take their meaning from him. Every witness to him is a "prejudiced" witness. For any fact to be a fact at all, it must be a revelational fact.

It is accordingly no easier for sinners to accept God's revelation in nature than to accept God's revelation in Scripture. They are no more ready of themselves to do the one than to do the other. From the point of view of the sinner, theism is as objectionable as is Christianity. Theism that is worthy of the name is Christian theism. Christ said that no man can come to the Father but by him. No one can become a theist unless he becomes a Christian. Any God that is not the Father of our Lord Jesus Christ is not God but an idol.

It is therefore the Holy Spirit bearing witness by and with the Word in our hearts that alone effects the required Copernican revolution and makes us both Christians and theists. Before the fall, man also needed the witness of the Holy Spirit: Even then the third person of the Holy Trinity was operative in and through the naturally revelational consciousness of man so that it might react fittingly and properly to the works of God's creation. But then that operation was so natural that man himself needed not at all or scarcely to be aware of its existence. When man fell, he denied the naturally revelatory character of every fact including that of his own consciousness. He assumed that he was autonomous; he assumed that his consciousness was not revelational of God but only of himself. He assumed himself to be non-created. He assumed that the work of interpretation, as by the force of his natural powers he was engaged in it, was an original instead of a derivative procedure. He would not think God's thoughts after him; he would instead think only his own original thoughts.

Now if anything is obvious from Scripture it is that man is not regarded as properly a judge of God's revelation to him. Man is said or assumed from the first page to the last to be a creature of God. God's consciousness is therefore taken to be naturally original as man's is naturally derivative. Man's natural attitude in all self-conscious activities was therefore meant to be that of obedience. It is to this deeper depth, deeper than the sinner's consciousness can every reach by itself, that Scripture appeals when it says: "Come let us reason together." It appeals to covenant-breakers and argues with them about the unreason-ableness of covenant-breaking. And it is only when the Holy Spirit gives man a new heart that he will accept the evidence of Scripture about itself and about nature for what it really is The Holy Spirit's regenerating power enables man to place all things in true perspective.

Man the sinner, as Calvin puts it, through the testimony of the Spirit receives a new power of sight by which he can appreciate the new light that has been given in Scripture. The new light and the new power of sight imply one another. The one is fruitless for salvation without the other. It is by grace, then, by the gift of the Holy Spirit alone, that sinners are able to observe the fact that all nature, including even their own negative attitude toward God, is revelational of God, the God of Scripture. The wrath of God is revealed, Paul says, on all those who keep down the truth. Man's sinful nature has become his second nature. This sinful nature of man must now be included in nature as a whole. And through it God is revealed. He is revealed as the just one, as the one who hates iniquity and punishes it. Yet he must also be seen as the one who does *not yet* punish to the full degree of their ill desert the wicked deeds of sinful men.

All this is simply to say that one must be a believing Christian to study nature in the proper frame of mind and with proper procedure. It is only the Christian consciousness that is ready and willing to regard all nature, including man's own interpretative reactions, as revelational of God. But this very fact requires that the Christian consciousness make a sharp distinction between what is revelational in this broad and basic sense and what is revelational in the restricted sense. When man had not sinned, he was naturally anxious constantly to seek contact with the supernatural positive revelation of God. But it is quite a different matter when we think of the redeemed sinner. He is restored to the right relationship. But he is restored in principle only. There is a drag upon him. His "old man" wants him to interpret nature apart from the supernatural revelation in which he operates. The only safeguard he has against this historical drag is to test his interpretations constantly by the principles of the written Word. And if theology succeeds in bringing forth ever more clearly the depth of the riches of the Biblical revelation of God in Scripture, the Christian philosopher or scientist will be glad to make use of this clearer and fuller interpretation in order that his own interpretation of nature may be all the fuller and clearer too, and thus more truly revelational of God. No subordination of philosophy or science to theology is intended here. The theologian is simply a specialist in the field of Biblical interpretation taken in the more restricted sense. The philosopher is directly subject to the Bible and must in the last analysis rest upon his own interpretation of the Word. But he may accept the help of those who are more constantly and more exclusively engaged in Biblical study than he himself can be.

II. The Natural Theology of Greek Origin

With these main features of the idea of a natural revelation that is consistent with the concept of Biblical revelation as set forth in the Confession before us, we must look by way of contrast at another view of natural theology. This other view is characterized by the fact that it allows no place for analogical reasoning in the sense that we have described it. Instead of boldly offering the idea of the self-contained God as the presupposition of the intelligent interpretation of nature, it starts with the idea of the self-contained character of nature and then argues to a god who must at best be finite in character. Instead of starting with the wholly revelational character of the created universe, including the mind of man, this natural theology starts with the non-revelational character of the universe and ends with making it revelational of the mind of would-be autonomous man.

This sort of natural theology has had its origin in Greek speculation, and more particularly in the systems of Plato and Aristotle. With no lack of appreciation for the genius of these great Greek thinkers it must yet be maintained that they, will all men, inherited the sinfulness of Adam and, accordingly, had their reasons for not wishing to hear the voice of God. With all men they assume that nature is self-sufficient and has its principles of interpretation within itself.

The pre-Socratics make a common monistic assumption to the effect that all things are at bottom one. They allow for no basic distinction between divine being and human being. With Heraclitus this assumption works itself out into the idea that all is flux. With Parmenides this same tendency works itself out into the idea that all is changeless. In both cases God is nature and nature is God.

The natural theologies of Plato and Aristotle are best viewed against this background. Neither of these men forsook the monistic assumption of their predecessors.

931

1. The Natural Theology of Plato

As for Plato this may be observed first from the hard and fast distinction that he makes between the world of being that is wholly known and the world of non-being that is wholly unknown. For Plato any being that is really to exist must be eternal and changeless. Similarly any knowledge that really can be called knowledge must be changeless comprehensive knowledge. It is in terms of these principles that Plato would explain the world phenomena. This world is intermediate between the world of pure being that is wholly known and the world of pure non-being that is wholly unknown. The being that we see constitutes a sort of tension between pure being and pure non-being. So also the learning process constitutes a sort of tension between pure omniscience and pure ignorance.

Plato's view of the relation of sensation and conceptual thought corresponds to this basic division between the worlds of pure being and pure non-being. The senses are said to deceive us. It is only by means of the intellect as inherently divine that man can know true being. The real philosopher bewails his contact with the world of non-being. He knows he has fallen from his heavenly home. He knows that is real only to the extent that he is divine. He seeks to draw away from all contact with non-being. He seeks for identification with the "wholly Other," which, for the moment, he can speak of only in negative terms. When Socrates speaks of the Good he can only say what it is not. The Ideal Table is never seen on land or sea. Piety must be defined as beyond anything that gods or men may say about it. True definition needs for its criterion an all-inclusive, supra-divine as well as supra-human, principle of continuity. Ultimate rationality is as much above God as above man.

The result is that for Plato, too, nature is revelational. But it is revelational as much of man as of God. To the extent that either of them is real, and known as real, he is wholly identical with the rational principle that is above both. On the other hand, as real and known in the rational principle, both are face to face with the world of non-being. And this world of non-being is as ultimate as the world of pure being. So God and man are wholly unknown to themselves. Thus both God and man are both wholly known and wholly unknown to themselves. Reality as known to man is a cross between abstract timeless formal logic and equally abstract chance. Yet in it all the ideal pure rationality as pure being dominates the scene.

It requires no argument to prove that on a Platonic basis there can be neither natural nor supernatural revelation such as the Confession holds before us. Natural revelation would be nothing more than man's own rational efforts to impose abstract rational unity upon the world of non-being. Supernatural revelation would be nothing more than that same task to the extent that it has not yet been finished or to the extent that it can never be finished. Those who undertake to defend Platonism as a fit foundation for Christianity are engaged in a futile and worse than futile enterprise.

2. The Natural Theology of Aristotle

As over against Plato, Aristotle contends that we must not look for rationality as a principle wholly beyond the things we see. Universals are to be found within particulars. All our troubles come from looking for the one apart from the other. We must, to be sure, think of pure form at the one end and of pure matter at the other end of our experience. But whatever we actually know consists of pure form and pure matter in correlativity with one another. Whenever we would speak of Socrates, we must not look for some exhaustive description of him by means of reference to an Idea that is "wholly beyond." Socrates is numerically distinct from Callias because of pure potentiality or matter. Rational explanation must be satisfied with classification. The definition of Socrates is fully expressed in terms of the lowest species. Socrates as a numerical individual is but an instance of a class. Socrates may weigh two hundred pounds and Callias may weigh one hundred pounds. When I meet Socrates downtown he may knock me down; when I meet Callias there I may knock him down. But all this is "accidental." None of the perceptual characteristics of Socrates, not even his snub-nosedness, belong to the Socrates that I define. By means of the primacy of my intellect I know Socrates as he is, forever the same, no matter what may "accidently" happen to him. And what is true of Socrates is true of all other things.

Aristotle's philosophy, then, as over against that of Plato, stresses the correlativity of abstract rationality and pure Chance. Aristotle takes Plato's worlds of pure being and pure non-being and insists that they shall recognize a need of one another. Neither Plato nor Aristotle speaks of limiting concepts in the sense that modern philosophers use this term. Yet both Plato and Aristotle in effect use such limiting concepts and Aristotle more so than Plato. That is to say, the notion of God as transcendent is ever more clearly seen to be inconsistent with the accepted principle of interpretation.

It follows that the God of Aristotle is very difficult to handle. If he exists as a numerical unit, he exists as such because he is utterly potential or non-rational. For all individuation is by means of pure potentiality. Hence, if God exists, he exists or may exist in indefinite numbers. As Gilson says, Aristotle never escaped from simple polytheism.[3] On the other hand, Aristotle's God is the very opposite of pure potentiality or pure materiality. He must have none of the limitations that spring from pure potentiality. He must therefore not be a numerical individual. He must be the highest genius. And as such he must be utterly devoid of content. He is to be described in wholly negative terms. He is not this and he is not that. When we speak of him in positive terms, we know that we speak metaphorically. God did not really create the world. He does not really control the world. He does not even really know the world.

What then of God's revelation to man? The answer is plain. If he exists as a numerical individual, he must be revealed to himself by means of a principle beyond himself. He cannot reveal himself without utterly losing his individuality. But if he so reveals himself, if he is identified with abstract rationality, he needs once more to hide himself in pure existential particularity. If he does not so hide himself, he is revealed to no one, not even to himself. Such is the fruit of Aristotle's potential identification of the human intellect with the divine. Aristotle's natural theology is but the precursor of modern phenomenalism. And the polytheism of post-Kantian anti-intellectualism is but the great-grandchild of the polytheism of Aristotle's intellectualism.

3. The Natural Theology of Thomas Aquinas

It appears then that the natural theology of Aristotle is, if possible, still more hostile to the natural theology of the Confession than the natural theology of Plato could be. Yet the Roman Catholic Church has undertaken the task of harmonizing Aristotle's philosophic method with the Christian notion of God. Rome has sought to do so by means of its doctrine

---

3. Etienne Gilson, *The Spirit of Medieval Philosophy*, trans. A. H. C. Downes (New York: Scribner, 1936).

of analogy of being (*analogia entis*). Thomas Aquinas thinks it is possible to show that the mysteries of the Christian faith are not out of accord with the proper conclusions of reason. And by reason he means the form-matter scheme of Aristotle as we have spoken of it. These mysteries, he contends, may be above but cannot be said to be against reason.

Reasoning, according to Thomas, must be neither wholly univocal nor wholly equivocal; it must be analogical.[4] If with Aristotle he warns us against the definition-mongers, with Aristotle he also warns us against those who are no better than a plant.

First then, as over against those who reason univocally, Thomas insists that when we speak of God's essence our principal method must be that of "remotion," that is, of negation. "For the divine essence by its immensity surpasses every form to which our intellect reaches; and thus we cannot apprehend it by knowing what it is."[5] Form without the idea of pure potentiality is empty. For all positive knowledge we require the idea of pure contingency. Nature requires that there be luck or chance. Nature includes the wholly non-rational as well as the wholly rational. If it were not for pure contingency we should be driven with Parmenides to define being in such a way as to make it virtually identical with non-being. We should be going 'round in circles of pure analysis.

Then as over against those who would reason equivocally, Thomas argues that, though we need the idea of pure contingency, we never meet it in actual experience. Generation, corruption and change must be kept within rational control. Our irrationalism must not go so deep as to endanger our rationalism. "For it is clear that primary matter is not subject to generation and corruption, as Aristotle proves."[6] The matter that we meet is not pure matter; it is "proper matter" that adjusts itself quite readily to reasonable ends. Potentiality and actuality belong to the same genus. The soul is not destroyed by the action of a contrary, "for nothing is contrary thereto, since by the possible intellect it is cognizant and receptive of all contraries."[7] Determinate predication presupposes the idea of a principle of continuity that is as extensive as potentiality itself. If we do not hold to this we have, Aristotle would say, given up rational inquiry itself; we are then no better than a plant.

In the system of Thomas, then, true knowledge demands that we hold pure univocation and pure equivocation in perfect balance with one another. Rationality must never be permitted to go off by itself and contingency must never be permitted to go off by itself. The result is a sort of pre-Kantian phenomenalism. "Now being is not becoming to form alone, nor to matter alone, but to the composite: for matter is merely in potentiality, while form is *whereby* a thing is, since it is act. Hence, it follows that the composite, properly speaking, is."[8]

Thus the very notion of being is virtually reduced to that which is known *to us*. Thomas presents us with a sort of pre-Kantian deduction of the categories. There is to be no awareness of awareness with the idea of pure potentiality.[9] On the other hand, the possibility of reaching at all requires a validity that is objective at least *for us*. The harmony is found in the

4. By "univocal Thomas means reasoning based on the idea of a complete identification of man with God while by "equivocal" reasoning he means reasoning based on the idea of the complete separation of man from God.

5. Saint Thomas Aquinas, *The Summa Contra Gentiles,* Literally Translated by the English Dominican Fathers From the Latest Leonine Edition (London: Burns Oates & Washbourne, 1924), 1:33.

6. Ibid., 2:229.

7. Ibid., 2:222.

8. Ibid., 2:98.

9. Ibid., 3:105ff.

idea of *act*. *"The intellect in act and the intelligible in act are one*, just as *the sense in act and the sensible in act."*[10] Erich Przywara contends that by the *analogia entis* concept Rome is in the fortunate position of standing with one foot in, and with one foot outside, the tangle of problems that confronts the natural reason of man.[11] Our reply will be that the Thomistic procedure has but prepared the way for the modern forms of pure immanentism. Thomas is not able to escape the dilemma that faced Aristotle. His God too exists and is unknown, or is known but does not exist. Thomas accords existence to God by means of pure potentiality, and knowability by abstract rationality. The result is that God is virtually identified with nature as phenomenal reality to man.

The sharp distinction Thomas makes between the truths of reason and the mysteries of the faith may, at first sight, seem to militate against this conclusion. The two acts of believing and reasoning are said to be diverse. In consequence the objects to which these acts are directed are also said to be diverse. Reason deals with universals that appear in the particulars of sense; faith deals with the wholly unconditioned above sense. Only that which is exhaustively conceptualized is really known and only that which is wholly unknown can be the object of faith. It might seem that the two could never meet. But the Aristotelian form-matter scheme is made for just such emergencies. Harmony is effected by a sort of pre-Kantian limiting concept. In the hereafter, by the "light of glory," we shall see the essence of God. If in this life we are the most miserable of men because faith and reason stand in contradiction to one another, in the hereafter potentiality will be actuality. We posit the idea of an intellect that is comprehensive enough to describe all particulars and a will controlling enough to make all facts fits the requirements of such an intellect. Thus all becoming will have become being; luck and chance themselves will be subject unto us. But then thunder breaks forth in heaven. Lest we should be swallowed up of God, lest the definition-mongers should have their way after all, Thomas once more brings in pure contingency. The light or the vision of God, he says, must still be distinguished from conceptual knowledge. The vision of God must be a sort of global insight, a sort of representative *Wesensschau*, by which we see intuitively the first principles of demonstration. If these first principles of demonstration. If these first principles were themselves demonstrable, we should after all be going 'round in circles with Plato. Thus though the numerical infinite remains wholly unknowable, the infinite of global vision is wholly known.

It is by means of these principles, all summed up in the one idea of analogy as a cross between pure univocation and pure equivocation, that Thomas makes reasonable to the natural reason such mysteries of the faith as the trinity, the incarnation, the church and the sacraments. The living voice of the church is required inasmuch as all revelation of God to man is subject to historical relativity and psychological subjectivity. The necessity, the authority, the sufficiency and the perspicuity of both the revelation of God in nature and the revelation of God in Scripture are subordinate to this living voice, the voice of Aristotle speaking through the Pope. Herein lies the guarantee of certainty for the faithful. But lest these faithful should be compelled to go around in circles of pure analysis, this certainty is always counterbalanced by pure contingency. The certainties of the church, such as the sacraments, have an ideal operational efficiency on their account. Yet all differentiation has its source in pure potentiality. The gifts of God are ideally efficient. The grace of God

10. Ibid., 2:149.
11. Erich Przywara, *Polarity*, trans. A. E. Bouquet (Oxford: Oxford University Press, 1935).

is irresistible. All men, inclusive of Esau, may therefore be saved. Yet all men may fall from grace. Thus univocity and equivocity always maintain their balance.

4. The Natural Theology of the Pre-Kantian Modern Philosophy

The two types of natural theology, with their utterly diverse concepts of analogy, the one represented by the Confession and the other represented by Thomas Aquinas now stand before us. In modern times there has been a fearful conflict between these two. Only a few words can now be said about this modern war.

It has been suggested that the natural theology of Thomas Aquinas, conceived after the form-matter scheme of Aristotle, was but the forerunner of modern phenomenalism. The basic differentiation of Romanism is abstract impersonal form or logic and abstract or ultimate potentiality kept in correlativity with one another. The same may be said for modern phenomenalism. It is this modern phenomenalism that must now briefly engage our attention.

Only a brief remark can be allowed for the period preceding Kant. In this period there is, first, the line of rationalism coming to its climax in Leibniz and there is, second, the line of empiricism coming to a head in Hume.

The period as a whole may be said to one of transition. It is the period when men begin to realize that their immanentistic principle of interpretation should lead them to deny the unconditioned altogether, while yet they are not fully prepared to do so. Their reasoning is to all intents and purposes anti-metaphysical in the post-Kantian sense of the term, while yet they bring God as somehow self-existent into the picture all the time. Men were beginning to feel that it was time for an open declaration of independence from God while yet they dared not quite accept the consequence of such a step. It was not till Kant that modern philosophy became self-consciously anti-metaphysical.

The rationalistic view, exhibited at its highest and best by Leibniz, represents the idea of univocal reasoning in its first modern garb. By means of refined mathematical technique, Leibniz hopes to reach that for which the ancients strove in vain, namely, individuation by complete description. God stands for the idea of pure mathematics by means of which all reality may be described as seen at a glance. All historical facts are essentially reducible to the timeless equations of mathematical formulae. Such is the nature and consequence of his ontological proof for the existence of God. There could be no revelation of God to man on such a basis. How could God tell man anything that he was not able eventually to discover by means of the differential calculus? God becomes wholly revealed to man, but with the result that he is no longer God.

In opposition to the position of Leibniz, the rationalist, stands that of Hume, the skeptic. Concepts, he argued, are but faint replicas of sensations, and the laws of association by which we relate these concepts are psychological rather than logical in character. As Leibniz sought to be wholly univocal, so Hume sought to be wholly equivocal in his reasoning. As in the philosophy of Leibniz God lost his individuality in order to become wholly known, so in the philosophy of Hume God maintained his individuality but remained wholly unknown.

To be sure, neither Leibniz nor Hume was able to carry his position to its logical conclusion. Leibniz paid tribute to brute fact as Hume paid tribute to abstract logic. Leibniz maintained the necessity of finite facts and therefore of evil, lest his universal should be reduced to the blank identity of Parmenides, lest he should have all knowledge of a being that is interchangeable with non-being. Hume, on his part, virtually makes universal negative propositions covering all objective possibility. To make sure that no God such as is found in the Confession, a God who controls all things by the counsel of his will, would speak to him, Hume had virtually to assert that such a God cannot possibly exist and that there cannot at any point in the past of future be any evidence of the existence of such a God. So Leibniz the rationalist, was an irrationalist and Hume, the irrationalist, was a rationalist. It is impossible to be the one without also being the other.

5. *The Natural Theology of Pre-Kantian Apologists*

It was Kant who told the world this fact in unmistakable terms. Before examining his phenomenology it is well that a word be said here as to what Christian apologists were doing during the period of rationalism and empiricism. The answer is that by and large Protestant apologists followed closely after the pattern set by Thomas Aquinas. With Thomas they walked the *via media* between abstract univocal and abstract equivocal reasoning.

Two outstanding instances may be mentioned in substantiation of this claim. Bishop Butler's *Analogy* is plainly patterned after the *analogia entis* concept already analyzed. And Paley in his *Natural Theology* follows in the footsteps of Butler. Both Butler and Paley depend for their positive argument upon pure univocism and for their negative argument upon pure equivocism. For both, God is known to man to the extent that with man he is subject to a specific unity and God is above man to the extent that he is wholly unknown.

By a "reasonable use of reason," that is, by a carefully balanced mixture of univocism and equivocism, Butler contends, it may be shown that Christianity is both like and unlike the "course and constitution of nature." The atonement of Christ is like that which we daily see, namely, the innocent suffering for the guilty. Yet the atonement is also wholly other than anything that appears in nature.[12] According to Paley God's providence is fully patent in the world, patent even in spite of poisonous reptiles and fleas. This is a happy world after all. Yet the God whose providence is so plain cannot be known except by way of negation. " 'Eternity' is a negative idea, clothed with a positive name ... 'Self-existence' is another negative idea, namely, the negation of a preceding cause, as a progenitor, a maker, an author, a creator."[13]

In the view of what has been said it is not surprising that the supernatural theology of both Butler and Paley has basic similarities to that of Aquinas. Butler and Paley hold to an abstract Arminian sort of theology which, like the theology of Rome, deals with abstract possibilities and classes rather than with individuals. For Butler and for Paley, as for Thomas Aquinas, the objective atonement is an abstract form that is somehow present in and yet meaningless without the initiative taken by utterly independent individuals. Whatever there is of true Christianity in Rome, or in such positions as those of Butler and Paley, is there in spite of, rather than because of, the Aristotelian form-matter scheme that controls the formation of their natural theologies. A true Biblical or covenant theology could not be based upon such foundations as Butler and Paley laid.

6. *The Natural Theology of Kant*

The field has now been narrowed down considerably. The natural theology of the Confession, derived as it was largely from the theology of Calvin, stands over against the natural

12. *The Works of Joseph Butler,* ed. The Right Hon. W. E. Gladstone (Oxford: Clarendon Press, 1896), 1:272.
13. William Paley, *Natural Theology and Horae Paulinae* (New York: American Tract Society, 1850), 289.

theology as it has come from Aristotle through Rome into much of Protestant, even ortho-dox Protestant, thought. These two types of natural theology are striving for the mastery in our day.

The Aristotelian form of natural theology has, moreover, been greatly strengthened in our times by the critical philosophy of Kant. Indeed it may be asserted that the typical form of that natural theology which we have found to be inconsistent with the Confession is identi-cal with some form of critical phenomenalism. The main concepts of this phenomenalism must therefore be analyzed.

Kant's great contribution to philosophy consisted in stressing the activity of the experienc-ing subject. It is this point to which the idea of a Copernican revolution is usually applied. Kant argued that since it is the thinking subject that itself contributes the categories of uni-versality and necessity, we must not think of these as covering any reality that exists or may exist wholly independent of the human mind. By using the law of non-contradiction we may and must indeed determine what is possible, but the possibility that we thus determine is subjective rather than objective. It is a possibility *for us*. To save rationality, Kant argues, we must shorten the battle-line and reduce its claims even in its own domain. Hereafter reason must claim to legislate only in that area that can always be checked by experience and even in this area it must ever be ready to receive the wholly new. The validity of universals is to be taken as frankly due to a motion and a vote it is conventional and nothing more. Thus the univocation of Leibniz is to be saved by casting it into the sea of equivocation stirred up by Hume.

Again stressing the original activity of the thinking subject, Kant argued that it is impos-sible ever to find the entirely single thing of Hume. Like a sausage-grinder, the mind of man forms things into molds as it receives them. We never see either pork or beef; we see only sausages that, according to the butcher's word, contain both. Thus we always make facts as much as we find them. The only facts we know are instances of laws.

Kant's argument against the rationalists was like the argument of Aristotle against the "definition monger" who wanted to know all things. His argument against Hume was like Aristotle's arguments against Protagoras, the skeptic, who went on speaking even when his principle allowed him to say nothing determinate. Science, Kant argued, does not need and could not exist with such objective universality as Leibniz desired, but it does need and actually has the subjective validity that the autonomous man supplies in the very act of interpretation. Kant argues, as it were, that Aristotle was right in seeking for universals in the particulars rather than above them, but that he did not have the courage of his convic-tions and did not go far enough. Science requires us to have done once and for all with all antecedent being, with all metaphysics except that which is immanentistic. Hereafter the notions of being, cause and purpose must stand for orderings we ourselves have made; they must never stand for anything that exists beyond the reach of our experience. Any God who wants to make himself known, it is now more clear than ever before, will have to do so by identifying himself exhaustively with his revelation. And any God who is so revealed, it is now more clear than ever before, will then have to be wholly hidden in pure possibility. Neither Plato nor Aristotle were entitled, by the methods of reasoning they employed, to reach the Unconditioned. The Unconditioned cannot be rationally related to man.

There is no doubt but that Kant was right in this claim. Plato and Aristotle no less than Kant assumed the autonomy of man. On such a basis man may reason univocally and reach a God who is virtually an extension of himself or he may reason equivocally and reach a God who has no contact with him at all. Nor will adding two zeros produce more than zero. The addition of pure pantheism to pure deism will not bring forth theism. It was Kant's great service to the Christian church to teach us this. No theistic proof, either of the *a priori* or of the *a posteriori* sort, based on Platonic Aristotelian assumptions could do anything but disprove the God of the Confession.

But if Kant has done so great a service, his service has of course been wholly negative. Orthodox apologists have all too often overlooked this fact. Did not Kant make room for faith? Did he not challenge the pride of the rationalist in its denial of a God whose thoughts are higher than man's thoughts? Is not the scientist who today works on the basis of his principles a very humble sort of person, satisfied with the single dimension of the phenomenal, leaving the whole realm of the noumenal to the ministers of religion? And does not Scripture ascribe to reason the power and right to interpret at least an area of reality, restricted though it be, in its own right? Surely the God of Scripture does not mean to dictate to the man who merely describes the facts as he sees them in the laboratory.

In all this there is profound confusion. Nor is this to be blamed primarily on Kant. Kant knew well enough what sort of Christianity is involved in the natural theology of his *Critique of Pure Reason*. His own statement of it is unmistakable and frank. To him the only Christianity that accords with the principles of his thought is a Christianity that is reduced from its historic uniqueness to a universal religion of reason. And modernist theologians working with his principles today make similar reductions of historic Christianity. We can but admire their consistency. The very idea of Kant's Copernican revolution was that the autonomous mind itself must assume the responsibility for making all factual differentiation and logical validation. To such a mind the God of Christianity cannot speak. Such a mind will hear no voice but its own. It is itself the light that lighteth every man that comes into the world. It is itself the sun; how can it receive light from without? If Plato and Aristotle virtually identified the mind of man with that of God, Kant virtually identified the mind of God with that of man. Such a mind describes all facts as it sees them, but it sees them invariably through colored lenses. The miracles of Scripture are always reduced to instances of laws and laws themselves are reduced to conventional and purely contingent regularities. Prophetic prediction that has come true is always reduced to pure coincidence in a world of chance. Conventional law and brute fact are the stock and trade of the Kantian philosopher and scientist. His phenomenal world is built up of these.

7. The Natural Theology of Post-Kantian Phenomenalism

Working out the consequences of the Kantian position, Heinrich Rickert has stressed the fact that modern science has virtually abolished the distinction between the description and the explanation of facts. The facts which the scientist thinks he merely describes are such as have already been explained by his philosophical *confrères*.[14] Philosophers have so thoroughly canvassed the field of possibility that the scientist will never meet any facts that will not inevitably turn out to be instances of conventional, wholly man-made laws.

---

14. Heinrich Rickert, *Die Grenzen der naturwissenschaflichen Begriffsbildung,* 5th ed. (Tübingen: J. C. B. Mohr [Paul Siebeck], 1929).

Modern phenomenalism then, it must be stressed, is comprehensive in its sweep. It is a philosophy covering the whole reality. It may be anti-metaphysical, but this is only to say that it is against such metaphysics of transcendence as the Confession presents. Modern phenomenalism cannot by its principle admit of any of the facts and doctrines of historic Christian theism.

Dialectical theology has, to be sure, made the attempt to combine the main *Critique* of Kant and the *Institutes* of Calvin. But the magnitude of its undertaking is itself the best instance in proof that such a thing cannot logically be done. Barth and Brunner have satisfied the requirements of Kant's criticism, but in so doing they have at same time denied the God of Calvin.

Largely influenced by the phenomenalism or existentialism of such men as Kierkegaard and Heidegger, Barth and Brunner have been consistently anti-metaphysical in the Kantian sense of the term. That is to say, they have insisted that God is wholly unknown as a numerical individual and that he is wholly identical with his revelation as a specific unity. In other words, the God of the Confession is for Barth and Brunner nothing but an idol. The God of the Confession claims to have revealed himself directly in nature and in Scripture. And all direct revelation, Barth and Brunner continually reassert, is paganism. Barth and Brunner are as certain as was Kant that the Unconditional cannot make himself known as such in the phenomenal world. They could not maintain such a position except upon the assumption of the idea of the autonomous man which legislates, at least negatively, for the whole field of possibility.

Dialectical theology then fits in well with the natural theology of the Aristotle-Thomas Aquinas-Kant tradition. In fact, it may be said to be nothing more than a natural theology cut after this pattern. It is as hostile to the natural as to the special revelation concepts of the Confession. And the same must also be said with respect to such modified forms of dialecticism as are offered by Reinhold Niebuhr, Richard Kroner, Paul Tillich, Nels Ferré and John Mackay.

Certain lines have now been drawn in the modern chaos. The modern chaos is not so chaotic as it may at first sight appear. There are at bottom only two positions. There is the position of the Confession. This position consists of a natural theology that serves as the proper foundation for the full theology of grace that is found in the Reformed Confessions alone. It consists of a natural theology whose fundamental meaning and significance is found in the very fact of its being the field of exercise for the historical differentiation of which the Reformed theology of grace is but the narrative. There is, on the other hand, the position of Plato, Aristotle, Thomas Aquinas and Kant. It consists of a natural theology that must, according to the force of its interpretative principle, reduce the historic process of differentiation, as told in the Confession, to dialectical movements of a reason that is sufficient to itself.

Between these two there is and can be no peace. And the natural theology of the Confession, though unpopular now both within and beyond the church, cannot but be victorious at last. For all its vaunted defense of reason, the natural theology of Aristotle and his modern followers destroys reason. The autonomous man cannot forever flee back and forth between the arid mountains of timeless logic and the shoreless ocean of pure potentiality. He must at last be brought to bay. He cannot forever be permitted to speak of nothing that reveals itself exhaustively into nothing and yet pretend to convey meaning in his speech. The autonomous man has denied the existence of a rationality higher than itself that has legislated for all reality. Yet it also allows for pure potentiality that is beyond all rational power. It has undertaken to do, or rather claims already to have done, what it also says is inherently impossible of accomplishment. On the other hand, the natural theology of the Confession, with its rejection of autonomous reason, has restored reason to its rightful place and validated its rightful claims. In recognizing the Sovereign God of grace, the God who is infinite, eternal and unchangeable in his being, wisdom, power, goodness, justice and truth, as its chief and ultimate principle of interpretation, the natural theology of the Confession has saved rationality itself. Without the self-contained God of the Confession, there would be no order in nature and no employment for reason.

45

John Murray

John Murray (1898–1975), after studying and teaching at Princeton Seminary, joined Machen in his endeavor to establish Westminster Theological Seminary in 1930. Professor Murray represents part of the Scottish influence at Westminster, which is significant in the seminary's history. Following this tradition, he displays both a deep piety and a commitment to the theology of the Westminster Confession of Faith. In addition, as a disciple of both Warfield and Vos, Murray exhibits a theology characterized by careful exegesis and a sensitivity to biblical theology. Though Murray did not write a systematic theology, he left us some significant works. He wrote a commentary on Romans for the New International Commentary on the New Testament, a biblical ethics in *Principles of Conduct* (1957), and a significant monograph on the atonement, *The Imputation of Adam's Sin* (1959). Murray was also a careful student of historical theology. For this volume, his *Calvin on Scripture and Divine Sovereignty* (1960) is of special relevance. The following excerpts on the doctrine of Scripture are from the symposium *The Infallible Word* and his *Collected Writings* (vol. 1).

Murray's "The Attestation of Scripture" begins the important collection of essays by Westminster professors. In the tradition of Calvin and the Westminster Standards, Murray argues both for the objective self-attestation of Scripture and for the subjective witness of the Holy Spirit. In other words, the doctrine of Scripture, like any other doctrine, has to be defined by the Bible itself, thus being rooted in biblical exegesis. Yet this formulation is confirmed by the Holy Spirit. In this Murray agrees with Gaussen and Warfield. Further, this balanced understanding stands in contrast to the neoorthodox view about Scripture. This theological framework is crucial for providing an accurate definition of the doctrine of Scripture. In particular it helps the student of Scripture to understand, as the Reformed theological tradition maintains, that the Bible is the Word of God, yet simultaneously that it was written through human instrumentality. Murray explains how these two truths interconnect.

The other articles in this selection are from volume 1 of his *Collected Writings* and are either shorter articles or addresses given to a more popular audience. Both display clarity and depth of insights. In "The Infallibility of Scripture," an address given to students, Murray explains what is meant by the infallibility of Scripture. This doctrine cannot be proved but is based on the witness of Scripture to its own nature. The affirmation of this doctrine has broad implication for the practice of theology and for our salvation.

In "The Finality and Sufficiency of Scripture," Murray explains that Scripture is not only infallible, but also final, complete, and sufficient for the Christian life. Thus it is the authoritative judge of doctrine and life in the church. His study harks back to the Westminster Confession of Faith's teaching on Scripture. Murray demonstrates the importance of understanding the contours of redemptive history when interpreting Scripture. With the close of the apostolic age, Murray argues, the Scriptures are complete and sufficient for life and godliness.

In the address "The Unity of the Old and New Testaments," Murray offers his thoughts on biblical theology. While Christ's coming was a turning point in human history, it can be understood only as the fulfillment of Old Testament expectations. Murray was an advocate of a covenantal hermeneutic that affirms the continuity between the old covenant and the new covenant, in the one covenant of grace in Christ. Without this covenantal understanding of Scripture, there is no clear explanation for why the Old Testament is still relevant for the Christian today. The abiding relevance of the old covenant is evident, however, when one realizes that the new covenant is the fulfillment of the old, and that the new covenant in Christ is the antitype of the Old Testament types and shadows. The unity of the Bible in Christ and his redemptive work has vast implications for biblical interpretation.

In "The Importance and Relevance of the Westminster Confession," while Murray affirms the rich value of the theological inheritance transmitted in this confession, he also acknowledges the subordinate authority of this standard in relation to the infallible Scriptures. This creed is crucial to Murray: historic Scottish Presbyterianism and Westminster Calvinism are almost synonymous. In this selection, he explains why the Westminster Confession is important not only in Murray's day, but also for the twenty-first century. For him no other confession, Reformed or otherwise, can rival the Westminster Confession of Faith. Even as he surveys various doctrines, especially important is the confession's first chapter on the doctrine of Scripture.

Bibliography: Edmund P. Clowney. "Professor John Murray at Westminster Theological Seminary." Pp. 27–40 in David VanDrunen, ed. *The Pattern of Sound Doctrine: Systematic Theology at the Westminster Seminaries. Essays in Honor of Robert B. Strimple.* Phillipsburg, NJ: P&R Publishing, 2004. S. B. Ferguson. "Murray, John (1898–1975)." Pp. 447–48 in *NDT.* Idem. "Murray, John (1898–1975)." P. 612 in *DSCH&T.* Idem. "Murray, John (1898–1975)." Pp. 463–65 in *BDE.* R. B. Gaffin Jr. "Murray, John (1898–1975)." P. 166 in *DP&RTA.* Jeong Koo Jeon. *Covenant Theology: John Murray's and Meredith G. Kline's Response to the Historical Development of Federal Theology in Reformed Thought.* Lanham, MD: University Press of America, 1999. Pp. 103–90. Iain H. Murray. "Life of John Murray." Pp. 1–158 in *Collected Writings of John Murray.* Vol. 3. Carlisle, PA: Banner of Truth, 1982.

The Attestation of Scripture

John Murray, "The Attestation of Scripture," in *The Infallible Word*, ed. Paul Woolley, 1–54; 3rd rev. printing (Philadelphia: Presbyterian and Reformed, 1967), 1–54; reprinted from Philadelphia: The Presbyterian Guardian, 1946.

I. The Objective Witness

Christians of varied and diverse theological standpoints aver that the Bible is the Word of God, that it is inspired by the Holy Spirit and that it occupies a unique place as the norm of Christian faith and life. But such general confessions do not of themselves settle for us the view entertained with respect to the origin, authority, and character of Holy Scripture. A passing acquaintance with the literature on this subject will show that such propositions are made to do service for wholly diverse views of the nature of Scripture. It becomes incumbent upon us, therefore, to define and examine the statement that the Bible is the Word of God.

Diversity of viewpoint with respect to this proposition has generally, if not always, taken its starting-point from the recognition that the Bible has come to us through human instrumentality. Every book of the Bible has had its human author. The Bible did not come to us directly from heaven; in its totality and in all its parts it has come to us through human agency. Since this is the case, every serious student of the Bible has to take cognizance of the human factor in the preparation, composition, and completion of what we know as the canon of Holy Writ.

If, then, human instruments have performed a function in producing the Bible, does it not necessarily follow that the marks of human fallibility and error must be imprinted on the Bible? Since the fall of our first parents, no perfect human being has walked upon this earth. It is true there was one, indeed human, who was holy, harmless, undefiled, and separate from sinners. But he was more than human; he was the eternal Son of God manifest in the flesh. If he had written the Bible, then the question with which we are now faced would not need to be asked. In any case, there would be at hand a very ready answer to the question. The infallibility of Christ's human nature would provide us with a simple answer to the urgent and difficult question: How can the Bible be the Word of God and at the same time the work of man? The resolution of the apparent antinomy would be provided by the fact that the person who wrote it was himself perfect God and perfect man.

The Lord Jesus Christ, however, did not write the Bible nor any part of it. When he left this world and went to the Father, he left no books that were the product of his pen. So in every case the Bible and all the Bible was written by those who were mere men and therefore by men who, without exception, were themselves imperfect and fallible.

This plain and undisputed fact has led many students of the Bible to the conclusion that the Bible cannot be in itself the infallible and inerrant Word of God. Putting the matter very bluntly, they have said that God had to use the material he had at his disposal and, since the material he had was fallible men, he was under the necessity of giving us his Word in a form that is marred by the defects arising from human fallibility. In the words of Dr. J. Monro Gibson:

It is important at the outset to remember that the most consummate artist is limited by the nature of his material. He may have thoughts and inspirations far above and beyond what he can express in black-and-white or in colours, in marble or in bronze, in speech or in song; but however perfect his idea may be, it must, in finding expression, share the imperfections of the forms in which he works. If this very obvious fact had only been kept in mind, most of the difficulties which beset the subject of inspiration need never have arisen.[1]

And then Dr. Gibson proceeds to enumerate some of the limitations with which God had to deal, the limitations of human agency, human language and literary forms.

It is by plausible argument of this sort that students of the Bible have too rashly come to the conclusion that the human factor or, as we should prefer to call it, human instrumentality settles this question and that the Bible, though God's Word, must at the same time be errant and fallible, at least in scientific and historical detail, simply because it came to us through the ministry of men. Dr. Gibson is very jealous that we should follow the facts and let the Bible speak for itself rather than approach the Bible with a preconceived notion of divine infallibility. It is, however, just because we are jealous that the Bible should speak for itself that we must not take it for granted that human authorship necessitates errancy and fallibility.

The fact of human authorship does indeed seem to provide a very easy argument for the errancy and fallibility of Scripture. Or, to state the matter less invidiously, human authorship seems to provide a very easy and necessary explanation of what are alleged to be the facts of errancy and fallibility. We must accept the facts, it is said, rather than hide behind the theory of inerrancy.[2]

Those who thus contend should, however, be aware of the implications of their position. If human fallibility precludes an infallible Scripture, then by resistless logic it must be maintained that we cannot have any Scripture that is infallible and inerrant. All of Scripture comes to us through human instrumentality. If such instrumentality involves fallibility, then such fallibility must attach to the whole of Scripture. For by what warrant can an immunity from error be maintained in the matter of "spiritual content" and not in the matter of historical or scientific fact? Is human fallibility suspended when "spiritual truth" is asserted but not suspended in other less important matters?[3]

---

1. John Monro Gibson, *The Inspiration and Authority of Holy Scripture* (New York: F. H. Revell, n.d.), 146; cf. Emil Brunner, *Revelation and Reason*, trans. Olive Wyon (Philadelphia: Westminster Press, 1946), 128–29.

2. It must be emphasized that the proponents of Biblical inerrancy do not ignore "facts" nor do they fail to take these into account in their construction of inspiration. "It must be emphatically stated that the doctrine of biblical inerrancy . . . is not based on the assumption that the criterion of meticulous precision in every detail of record or history is the indispensable canon of biblical infallibility. To erect such a canon is utterly artificial and arbitrary and is not one by which the inerrancy of Scripture is to be judged. It is easy for the opponents of inerrancy to set up such artificial criteria and then expose the Bible as full of errors. . . . Every one should recognize that in accord with accepted forms of speech and custom a statement can be perfectly authentic and yet not pedantically precise. Scripture does not make itself absurd by furnishing us with pedantry" (*Calvin on Scripture and Divine Sovereignty*, by the present writer [Grand Rapids: Baker, 1960], 30; cf. Ned B. Stonehouse, *Origins of the Synoptic Gospels* [Grand Rapids: Eerdmans, 1963], 109–10).

3. The phrase "spiritual truth" is used here by way of accommodation to the views of those who in the discussion of this question stress the distinction between the outward form of the Bible and the religious content of which the Bible is the vehicle. Cf., e.g., William Sanday, *The Oracles of God* (London: Longmans, Green, 1891), 29–30; Richard H. Malden, *The Inspiration of the Bible* (London: Oxford University Press, 1935), 5–6. Karl Barth is consistent in this respect. Fallibility, he claims, applies to the religious and theological as well as to the historical and scientific. Referring to the witnesses to revelation "as fallible, erring men like ourselves" he says: "We can read and try to assess their word as a purely human word. It can be subjected to all kinds of immanent criticism, not only in respect of its philosophical, historical and ethical

Furthermore, if infallibility can attach to the "spiritual truth" enunciated by the Biblical writers, then it is obvious that some extraordinary divine influence must have intervened and become operative so as to prevent human fallibility from leaving its mark upon the truth expressed. If divine influence could thus intrude itself at certain points, why should not this same preserving power exercise itself at every point in the writing of Scripture? Again, surely human fallibility is just as liable to be at work in connection with the enunciation of transcendent truth as it is when it deals with the details of historical occurrence.

It is surely obvious that the appeal to human fallibility in the interest of supporting, or at least defending, Biblical fallibility is glaringly inconsequent, if it is maintained that God has at any point given us through human agency an infallible and inerrant Word. Either *a priori* argument from human fallibility has to be abandoned or the position must be taken that human fallibility has left its mark upon all of Scripture and no part of it can be called the infallible Word of God, not even John 3:16. We cannot too strenuously press the opponents of Biblical inerrancy to the implications of their position. Human fallibility cannot with any consistency be pleaded as an argument for the fallibility of Scripture unless the position is taken that we do not have in the Scriptures content of any kind that is not marred by the frailty of human nature.

This plea for consistency does not mean however, that Biblical infallibility is thereby proven. While it is necessary to remove any *a priori* argument, drawn from human fallibility, that would do prejudice to the evidence, the doctrine of Biblical inerrancy must rest upon the proper evidence. In this case, as in all other doctrine, the evidence is the witness of Scripture itself. Does the Scripture claim inerrancy for itself and, if so, must this claim be accepted?

It must be freely admitted that there are difficulties connected with the doctrine of Biblical infallibility. There appear to be discrepancies and contradictions in the Bible. Naturally we cannot be expected to believe what we perceive to involve a contradiction. Furthermore, disingenuous and artificial attempts at harmony are to be avoided, for they do not advance the cause of truth and of faith. The conscientious student has, therefore, great difficulty sometimes in resolving problems raised by apparent contradictions. It is true that many such resolve themselves when careful study is applied to them, and oftentimes the resolution of the difficulty in the light of the various factors involved becomes the occasion for the discovery of a harmony and fullness of meaning that otherwise would not have been recognized by us. But some difficulties, perhaps many, remain unresolved. The earnest student has no adequate answer and he may frankly confess that he is not able to explain an apparent discrepancy in the teaching of Scripture.

It might seem that this confession of his own inability to resolve seeming discrepancy is not compatible with faith in Scripture as infallible. This is, however, at the best, very superficial judgment. There is no doctrine of our Christian faith that does not confront us with unresolved difficulties here in this world, and the difficulties become all the greater just as we get nearer to the center. It is in connection with the most transcendent mysteries of our faith that the difficulties multiply. The person who thinks he has resolved all the difficulties surrounding our established faith in the Trinity has probably no true faith in the Triune God. The person who encounters no unresolved mystery in the incarnation of the Son of

---

content, but even of its religious and theological" (*Church Dogmatics*, English translation, vol. I, 2 [Edinburgh: T. & T. Clark, 1956], 507; cf. also, 509). Barth can do this, compatibly with his position, because he does not equate Scripture with the revelatory Word; Scripture only witnesses to revelation.

God and in his death on Calvary's tree has not yet learned the meaning of 1 Timothy 3:16. Yet these unanswered questions are not incompatible with unshaken faith in the Triune God and in Jesus Christ, the incarnate Son. The questions are often perplexing. But they are more often the questions of adoring wonder rather than the questions of painful perplexity.

So there should be no surprise if faith in God's inerrant Word should be quite consonant with unresolved questions and difficulties with regard to the content of this faith.

The defense of the foregoing position that faith is not inconsistent with unresolved questions is far more crucial in this debate than might at first appear. It lies very close to the vital question of what is the proper ground of faith in the Bible as the Word of God. The ground of faith emphatically is not our ability to demonstrate all the teaching of the Bible to be self-consistent and true. This is just saying that rational demonstration is not the ground of faith. The demand that apparent contradictions in the Bible should have to be removed before we accord it our credit as God's infallible Word rests, therefore, upon a wholly mistaken notion of the only proper ground of faith in the Bible. It is indeed true that we should not close our minds and researches to the ever-progressing resolution of difficulties under the illumination of the Spirit of truth, but those whose approach to faith is that of resolution of all difficulty have deserted the very nature of faith and of its ground.

The nature of faith is acceptance on the basis of testimony, and the ground of faith is therefore testimony or evidence. In this matter it is the evidence God has provided, and God provides the evidence in his Word, the Bible. This means simply that the basis of faith in the Bible is the witness the Bible itself bears to the fact that it is God's Word, and our faith that it is infallible must rest upon no other basis than the witness the Bible bears to this fact. If the Bible does not witness to its own infallibility, then we have no right to believe that it is infallible. If it does bear witness to its infallibility then our faith in it must rest upon that witness, however much difficulty may be entertained with this belief. If this position with respect to the ground of faith in Scripture is abandoned, then appeal to the Bible for the ground of faith in any other doctrine must also be abandoned. The doctrine of Scripture must be elicited from the Scripture just as any other doctrine should be.[4] If the doctrine of Scripture is denied its right to appeal to Scripture for its support, then what right does any other doctrine have to make this appeal? Faith in the Trinity does not have to wait for the resolution of all difficulties that the teaching of Scripture presents to us on this question; it does not have to wait for the resolution of all apparent contradictions in the teaching of Scripture on the Trinity. So neither does faith in Scripture as the inerrant Word of God have to wait for the resolution of all difficulties in the matter of inerrancy.

The real question then becomes: What is the witness of Scripture with reference to its own character? It is important to appreciate the precise scope of this question; it is to elicit from the Scripture the evidence it contains bearing upon its origin, character, and authority. This approach is very different from the approach that too many claim to be the only scientific and inductive approach. It is often said that we must not go to the Bible with an *a priori* theory of its infallibility but we must go to the Bible with an open mind and find out what the facts are and frame our theory from the facts rather than impose our theory upon the facts. There is an element of truth in this contention. It is fully granted that we

---

4. Sanday states this principle well enough when he says that "we may lay it down as a fundamental principle that a true conception of what the Bible is must be obtained from the Bible itself" (*The Oracles of God*, 47). But he does not apply this principle consistently.

should never approach Scripture with an *a priori* theory of its character and impose that theory upon the evidence. We just as vigorously repudiate any such method as do others, and we have to impute to many liberal and radical students the very fault which they are too ready to impute to the orthodox believer. But while the *a priori* method of approach must on all accounts be condemned, it does not follow that the proper approach is that of the alleged inductive and scientific method. We do not elicit the doctrine of Scripture from an inductive study of what we suppose determines its character. We derive our doctrine of Scripture from what the Scripture *teaches* with respect to its own character—in a word, from the testimony it bears to itself.

This procedure does not by any means imply that the believer in Biblical infallibility can afford to be indifferent to the difficulties that may arise in connection with apparent discrepancies nor to the attacks made upon infallibility from various sides on the basis of what are alleged to be disharmonies and contradictions. The believer cannot at any time afford to be obscurantist; and orthodox scholarship must set right criticism over against wrong criticism. The motto of faith must be: "prove all things, hold fast that which is good." The believer must always be ready to give a reason for the faith that is in him. But he must also remember that the character and content of his faith in Scripture as the Word of God must be dictated by the divine witness bearing directly upon that precise question. What then is the testimony of the Scripture regarding itself? For to this question we must now address ourselves.

First of all, there is the negative evidence. The Scripture does not adversely criticize itself. One part of Scripture does not expose another part as erroneous. It goes without saying that, if Scripture itself witnessed to the errancy and fallibility of another part, then such witness would be a finality, and belief in the inerrancy of Scripture would have to be abandoned. But it is a signal fact that one Scripture does not predicate error of another. It is true that the Scripture contains the record of much sin and error in the history of men, of Satan and of demons.[5] The Bible, of course, is to a large extent historical in character and, since history is strewn with sin, the Bible could not fail to record the dark and dismal story. Indeed, the frankness and candor of the Bible in this regard is one of its most striking features. The openness with which it exposes even the sins of the saints is one of the most signal marks of its authenticity. But the condemnation of the sin and error the Bible records is not witness to its own fallibility. It is rather an integral part of the witness to its own credibility and, so far from constituting any evidence against itself as inerrant Scripture, it thereby contributes evidence that is most germane to the establishment of its infallibility.

It is also true that the Bible fully recognizes the temporary and provisional character of many of the regulations and ordinances which it represents as imposed by divine authority. The most relevant case in point here is the temporary character of many of the regulations of the Mosaic law. That the observance of these preparatory and temporary precepts, rites and ceremonies has been discontinued with the advent and establishment of the Christian economy is the express teaching of the New Testament. But in such teaching there is no

---

5. The statement in Genesis 3:4: "Ye shall not surely die" is not the word of God but of the tempter. But the *information* given us respecting the lie of the tempter is the Word of God and is brim full of revelatory significance. It is that of which our Lord's word is the commentary, "He was a liar from the beginning" (John 8:44). It is this obvious distinction that is applicable to all falsehoods of which Scripture informs us and exemplifies how Scripture is not merely a record but is itself revelatory, not even simply a record of revelation but is itself revelation.

reflection whatsoever on the divinely authoritative character of such provisions under that economy in which they were operative and, far more, no reflection upon the infallibility of that Old Testament Scripture which embodies the revelation to us of that divine institution. For example, when Paul in the epistle to the Galatians writes, "Behold, I Paul say unto you, that if ye be circumcised, Christ shall profit you nothing" (Gal. 5:2), he in no way casts any aspersion on the truth of those Old Testament books which inform us of the institution of circumcision and of its divinely authorized practice among the people of God from Abraham onwards. In fact, the same Paul lends the strongest corroboration to the truth of the Old Testament in this regard when he says elsewhere with reference to Abraham, "And he received the sign of circumcision, a seal of the righteousness of the faith which he had yet being uncircumcised" (Rom. 4:11).

Our thesis at this point will, of course, be challenged. It will be said that abundant evidence can be produced to show that Scripture does expose as erroneous the distinct representations of other parts of Scripture. To put the opposing argument otherwise, it is said that one part of Scripture says one thing and another part of Scripture dealing with the same situation says something else. For example, the Pentateuch represents the Levitical laws with respect to sacrifice as ordained by divine revelation and authority after the children of Israel came out of Egypt and while they were sojourning in the wilderness. It cannot be questioned that this is the story of the Pentateuch. But the prophet Jeremiah writes as the word of the Lord, "For I spake not unto your fathers, nor commanded them in the day that I brought them out of the land of Egypt, concerning burnt offerings or sacrifices: but this thing commanded I them, saying, Obey my voice, and I will be your God, and ye shall be my people: and walk ye in all the ways that I have commanded you, that it may be well unto you" (Jer. 7:22–23).

It must be replied that the argument based on this antithesis in the prophecy of Jeremiah fails to appreciate one of the basic principles of Biblical interpretation, namely, that a relative contrast is often expressed in absolute terms. What is being protested in Jeremiah 7:22–23 is the externalism and formalism of Israel. Mere ritual, even when the ritual is of divine institution, is religiously worthless, indeed is hypocrisy, if the real religious import of that ritual is not understood and particularly when the moral requirements of God's law are trampled under foot. Ceremonial ritual without ethical integrity and particularly without regard to spiritual attachment and obedience to the Lord God is mockery. And it is just of this formalism and hypocrisy that Isaiah writes, "Your new moons and your appointed feasts my soul hateth: they are a trouble unto me; I am weary to bear them" (Isa. 1:14).

The objection arising from such passages, however, confuses the precise question of our present thesis. Such passages as these, however great may appear to be the discrepancy in the witness of Scripture, do not fall into the category with which we are now dealing. For they are not, even on the most radical interpretation of the discrepancy, exposures of error on the part of one writer of Scripture of statements made by another writer. Jeremiah in other words does not quote the Pentateuch and then say that the statement concerned is an error and must therefore be corrected. While Jeremiah 7:22–23 constitutes an apparent discrepancy in the testimony of Scripture, Jeremiah does not quote another writer and overtly or impliedly say that this writer was in error. It is in that particular question we are now interested.

The passages in what is generally called the Sermon on the Mount, where Jesus appears to set up an antithesis between his own teaching and the regulatory statutes of the Pentateuch, might plausibly be appealed to in this connection as instituting criticism of some of the Mosaic ordinances. Even though Jesus did not write Scripture, yet the finality of his teaching would make an appeal to his authority quite relevant to the present phase of our discussion. If it could be demonstrated that these passages in Matthew do involve criticism of the Mosaic regulations which Jesus quotes, then the divine character of the Pentateuch would in these particulars be impugned.

It must be recognized at the outset that, even if Jesus could be shown to appeal to his own authority as setting aside the Mosaic provisions concerned, this does not establish the errancy of these provisions nor overthrow the fact of their divine authority and sanction under the Mosaic dispensation. We have already shown that the abrogation of the temporary legislation of the Pentateuch does not in the least impugn its authenticity, infallibility, or divine character and authority. So Jesus might well have abrogated the observance of certain Mosaic ordinances and yet not in the least reflected upon their divine origin and character nor upon their divine authority during the period of their application and operation.[6] Surely nothing more than this could with any reason be elicited from these passages in Matthew and it is obvious that such does not provide us with any evidence that Jesus taught the errancy or fallibility of the five books of Moses.

We must, however, insist that it is not at all apparent that the notion of abrogation is the key to the interpretation of these antitheses. It should be remembered that the preface to this whole section in Jesus' teaching is in these words:

> Think not that I am come to destroy the law, or the prophets: I am not come to destroy, but to fulfill. For verily I say unto you, Till heaven and earth pass, one jot or one tittle shall in no wise pass from the law, till all be fulfilled. Whosoever therefore shall break one of these least commandments, and shall teach men so, he shall be called the least in the kingdom of heaven: but whosoever shall do and teach them, the same shall be called great in the kingdom of heaven. (Matt. 5:17–20)

A careful reading of this passage will show that any reflection upon the character of the law and the prophets or any insinuation of their errancy is entirely out of the question. As we shall see later, the import of such references to the law and the prophets is to the opposite effect. But, with more precise reference to our present discussion of the idea of abrogation, it would seem very strange indeed that Jesus would have made such an unequivocal appeal to the inviolability of every jot and tittle of the law and to the sanctions attending the breach of one of these least commandments as well as to the divine blessing accruing to the observance of them, and then have proceeded forthwith to teach the abrogation of these very commandments. There would be contradiction in any such view of the sequence and in such an interpretation of the import of the antitheses. We must therefore turn in some other direction for the meaning of Jesus' teaching in these verses. Dr. Stonehouse has admirably shown that

> Understood as illustrations of Jesus' fulfillment of the law, the antitheses then provide no support of the thesis that they involve an abrogation of the objective authority of the law. In

6. The word "abrogated" is used in this sentence with reference merely to the discontinuance of *observance* and should not be understood to conflict with what will be later maintained respecting the permanent validity and meaning of the law.

the single instance where an enactment through Moses is set aside as provisional, namely, in the instance of the provision for a bill of divorcement, Jesus appeals decisively to the teaching of the law which is not circumscribed by reference to a temporary state of affairs. In the five other cases the design of Jesus is to show that current interpretations are inadequate as abiding by the externals or are in error as to the actual requirements of the law.[7]

These antitheses then constitute no evidence that Jesus taught or even insinuated that any part of the Pentateuch or of the Old Testament was in error and therefore calculated to misinform us as to fact or doctrine.

We must now turn, in the second place, to the positive evidence the Scripture contains with respect to the character of Scripture. However significant and important the absence of evidence calculated to deny the inerrancy of Scripture may be, it is upon positive evidence that the doctrine of Biblical infallibility must rest.

In the Old Testament we find a great deal of evidence that bears directly upon the divine character and authority of what is written. Much that is written by the prophets, for example, is, by introductory statements such as "Thus saith the Lord," asserted to be divine in origin, content and authority. In the most express way the divine seal is attached to what is written. Obviously, if error could be discovered in or predicated of any of the passages bearing this seal, then there are only two alternatives. The claim to be the Word of the Lord must be rejected or fallibility must be predicated of the divine utterance. From the latter every Christian must recoil. The former must reject the testimony of Scripture with respect to the character of its own content. If that is done then our argument is at an end. The premise of our whole thesis, indeed our thesis itself, is that the doctrine of Scripture must be based upon the witness of Scripture just as any other doctrine in the whole realm of Christian confession. So the adoption of this alternative means the abandonment of the witness of Scripture as the basis of Christian doctrine. If the witness of Scripture is not accepted as the ground of the doctrine of Scripture, if it is not reliable in this department of doctrine, then by what right can its witness be pleaded as the authority in any department of truth?

Again, in the Old Testament the way in which the later books of the Old Testament appeal to the laws enunciated in the Pentateuch presupposes the divine authority and sanction of these laws. For example, there is the indictment which the last of the Old Testament prophets, Malachi, brings against his people.

> Ye said also, Behold what a weariness is it! and ye have snuffed at it, saith the Lord of hosts; and ye brought that which was torn, and the lame, and the sick; thus ye brought an offering: should I accept this of your hand? saith the Lord. But cursed be the deceiver, which hath in his flock a male, and voweth, and sacrificeth unto the Lord a corrupt thing: for I am a great King, saith the Lord of hosts, and my name is dreadful among the heathen. (Mal. 1:13–14)

> Even from the days of your fathers ye are gone away from my ordinances, and have not kept them. Return unto me, and I will return unto you, saith the Lord of hosts. But ye said, Wherein shall we return? Will a man rob God? Yet ye have robbed me. But ye say, wherein have we robbed thee? In tithes and offerings. (Mal. 2:7–8)

---

7. Ned B. Stonehouse, *The Witness of Matthew and Mark to Christ* (Philadelphia: The Presbyterian Guardian, 1944), 209; cf. by the present writer, *Principles of Conduct* (Grand Rapids: Eerdmans, 1957), 149–80.

Such accusations are meaningless on any other assumption than that of the divine authority and obligation of the Levitical law (cf. Mal. 2:4–8). And the endorsement of Moses is put beyond all question when at the end of his prophecy Malachi writes, "Remember ye the law of Moses my servant, which I commanded unto him in Horeb for all Israel, with the statutes and judgments" (Mal. 4:4). It is surely of the greatest weight that the long line of Old Testament prophetic witness should come to its close with so insistent an appeal for devotion to the law of Moses, the Lord's servant, and that the intertestamentary period should be bridged, as it were, by the retrospective and the prospective, the appeal to Moses, on the one hand, and the promise of the resumption of the prophetic voice in him than whom there should not have arisen a greater, namely, John the Baptist, on the other (cf. ch. 4:5).

It is not, however, in the Old Testament that the most cogent evidence of a positive character, relative to this question, appears. For we do not have in the Old Testament any reference on the part of its writers to that collection of canonical writings in its entirety. In the nature of the case this could not reasonably be expected. Consequently we should not expect in the Old Testament any express predication or witness with respect to the whole collection of Old Testament books looked at in their unity as a fixed canon of sacred writings. In the New Testament the perspective is quite different. When the New Testament era opens to our view, the Old Testament books comprise a fixed collection of sacred writings. They exist before the speakers and writers of the New Testament period as a distinct corpus of authoritative writings viewed not only in their diversity but also and very distinctly in their unity as the canon of faith. Consequently, we find in the New Testament the most express and distinct estimate of the character of this body of writings viewed in their sum and unity as an entity capable of such characterization. It is such witness that is most directly pertinent to the present subject. What is the witness of the New Testament to the character of the Old Testament?

When we say the witness of the New Testament we mean, of course, the authoritative speakers and writers of the New Testament. First and foremost among such authoritative witnesses is our Lord himself. His word is a finality; on any other supposition the whole superstructure of Christian faith must totter and crumble. What then is our Lord's testimony with respect to the Old Testament?

We have had occasion to quote and discuss the passage in Matthew 5:17–19 in another context. It is relevant to our present purpose in that it provides us with one of the most striking testimonies to the estimate of the Old Testament entertained by Jesus. It is highly probable that, when Jesus says "the law or the prophets," he denotes by these two designations the whole of the Old Testament, the law denoting what we know as the Pentateuch and the prophets the rest of the Old Testament. It is possible that by the prophets he means the specifically prophetic books of the Old Testament, and by the law he may have had in mind the law of Moses in the more specific sense of the legislative economy embodied in the Pentateuch. If lie is using these terms in the more specific sense it would be wholly arbitrary, indeed casuistic and contrary to all of the evidence, to suppose that there is the least hint in such a specific use of the terms "law" and "prophets" that other parts of the Old Testament are in a different category in respect of authority. In this passage, then, Jesus gives us his estimate of at least a very large part of the Old Testament and his conception of the relation that it sustained to his messianic work. He came not to destroy the law or the prophets; he came to fulfill.

The word "destroy" (καταλύω) is peculiarly significant. It means to abrogate, to demolish, to disintegrate, to annul or, as J. A. Alexander points out, "the destruction of a whole by the complete separation of its parts, as when a house is taken down by being taken to pieces."[8] His emphatic denial of any such purpose in reference to either the law or the prophets means that the discharge of his messianic mission leaves the law and the prophets intact. He utters, however, not only this emphatic denial but also adds the positive purpose of his coming—he came to fulfill, to complete. And so his work with reference to both law and prophets is completory, not destructive. He who can speak in the immediately succeeding context with such solemn asseveration and imperious authority brings all that is involved in such asseveration and authority to bear upon the confirmation of the abiding validity, stability, and authority of both law and prophets. And not only so, but he also grounds his own mission and task upon such permanent validity, and defines his work in terms of fulfillment of all that the law and the prophets provided.

In verse 18 Jesus proceeds to apply the general statement of verse 17 to the minutiae of the law. It is this application of the general assertion to the minutest details that is particularly pertinent to our present topic. General statements may sometimes not cover, or provide for, certain exceptions in detail. But here Jesus precludes any possibility of discrepancy between the general and the particular. He is saying in effect, "This proposition that I came not to destroy but to fulfill applies not simply in general terms but also to the minutest particulars." And not simply is this the case; the connection expressed by the conjunction is also that the general statement of verse 17 is grounded in the fact that not one jot or tittle, not the minutest detail, will pass from the law till all be fulfilled. To enforce and seal the veracity of this, Jesus uses the formula that combines asseveration and authority, "Verily I say unto you."

The "jot" is the smallest letter of the Hebrew alphabet and the "tittle" is the minute horn or projection that distinguishes consonants of similar form from one another. It would be impossible to think of any expression that would bespeak the thought of the meticulous more adequately than precisely this one used here by our Lord. In respect of the meticulous, our English expression "one letter or syllable" is scarcely equivalent. Could anything establish more conclusively the meticulous accuracy, validity, and truth of the law than the language to which Jesus here attaches his own unique formula of asseveration? Many professing Christians recoil from the doctrine of verbal inspiration, the doctrine which means simply that the inspiration of Scripture extends to the very words as well as to the thoughts. It is difficult to understand why those who assent to inspiration should stumble at *verbal* inspiration. For words are the media of thought and, so far as Scripture is concerned, the written words are the only media of communication. If the thoughts are inspired, the words must be also. But whatever the case may be in the sphere of logic, the antipathy to verbal inspiration has little in common with the very obvious import of Jesus' representation in this passage. The indissolubility of the law extends to its every jot and tittle. Such indissolubility could not be predicated of it if it were in any detail fallible, for if fallible it would some day come to nought. And this is just saying that in every detail the law was in his esteem infallible and therefore indissoluble. It is indeed strange prejudice that professes adherence to the

8. Joseph Addison Alexander, *The Gospel according to Matthew Explained* (London: James Nisbet, 1884), 126.

infallibility of Christ and yet rejects the clear implications of his teaching. Nothing could be plainer than this, that in the smallest details he regards the law as incapable of being made void and that in the smallest details it is taken up by him and finds, in his fulfillment of it, its permanent embodiment and validity. By the most stringent necessity there is but one conclusion, namely, that the law is infallible and inerrant.[9]

In our discussion of Matthew 5:17–19, we left open the possibility that Jesus was using the terms "law" and "prophets" in a more restricted and specific sense. It is far from being certain that this interpretation of the scope of his words is justifiable. It is far more reasonable to believe that he had the whole Old Testament in mind. But we must not prejudice the argument by insisting upon this, for the argument we are now pursuing does not rest upon it. The witness of our Lord to the character of the Old Testament is so copious that what is not supplied by one passage is supplied by another. If the books other than those of Moses and the prophets are not expressly alluded to in Matthew 5:17–19 they certainly are in other places. One of the most striking of these is John 10:33–36, and to this part of his witness we may now turn.[10]

The occasion for his speaking these words was that created by the reaction of the Jews to his claim, "I and the Father are one." The Jews rightly interpreted this claim as meaning that Jesus placed himself on an equality with God. This they regarded as blasphemy and they took up stones to stone him. Jesus' claim was, of course, a stupendous one and there are only two alternatives. Either his claim was true or he did utter blasphemy. Here Jesus did not simply claim to be the Messiah; he claimed to be equal with the Father. The charge brought by the Jews was not a whit too severe if their conception of Jesus were correct. Quite logically on their own presuppositions their charge struck at the center of Jesus' claim and therefore at the basis of his mission and work. The charge denied his deity and his veracity. If validated, it would have exposed Jesus' claim as the most iniquitous imposture.

It was a charge with such implications that Jesus had to answer. If ever the resources of effective rebuttal needed to be drawn upon, it was at such a juncture. How did he meet the charge? "Jesus answered them, Is it not written in your law, I said ye are gods? If he called them gods unto whom the word of God came, and the scripture cannot be broken, say ye of him whom the Father sanctified and sent into the world, Thou blasphemest, because I said I am the Son of God." As we read this reply, we are amazed at what appears to be the facility and composure with which it is given as well as at what appears to be its restraint.

9. Dewey M. Beegle evades the force of Matthew 5:17–18 by appeal to what he alleges to be the contrast in Paul's teaching between the letter of the law and its spirit (*The Inspiration of Scripture* [Philadelphia: Westminster Press, 1963], 75–76). If anything should point to the fallacy of this interpretation of both Paul and Jesus, it is Matthew 5:17–18. In 2 Corinthians 3:6, to which Beegle appeals, the contrast between the letter and the Spirit is the contrast between the law in its condemning and death-inflicting power and the life-giving efficacy of the Holy Spirit. To find in this passage or others the outworn popular notion of a contrast between the letter and the spirit of the law is to abandon exegesis; it is alien to Paul's thought and misses completely the contrasts of the passage. Cf. J. Gresham Machen, *What Is Faith?* (Grand Rapids: Eerdmans, 1946), 186–92.

It should also be remembered that when speaking of verbal or jot and tittle inspiration, we are never thinking of words, or letters, or tittles in themselves or in abstraction. This would not be verbal inspiration, for the simple reason that no such words (or letters or tittles) occur in Scripture. They are always words in relationship, in clauses, sentences, paragraphs, books, and, in fact, relationship to the whole of Scripture. Their significance resides in this relationship and only in that relationship are they inspired. It is easy to show how far-reaching the change of a letter or tittle could be. It is to this Matthew 5:17–18 bears witness.

10. It is not within the scope of this study to discuss the critical questions raised with respect to John's Gospel and other New Testament writings.

Indeed, on superficial reading it might appear to be weak and ineffective. But the facility, composure, and restraint, which we believe are real, as well as the apparent weakness, which is not real, all converge to demonstrate the significance for our present purpose of his appeal to Scripture. He staked his argument for the rebuttal of the most serious allegation that could be brought against him upon a brief statement drawn from Psalm 82:6. It is this appeal to Scripture that is the pivot of his whole defense. This cannot be explained on any other basis than that he considered the Scriptures as the unassailable instrument of defense. For "the scripture cannot be broken."

Just as eloquent of Jesus' use of Scripture is, what appears to us, the obscurity of the passage to which he appeals. It would seem to have no direct bearing upon the question at issue. Yet Jesus uses this apparently obscure and less important passage as his argument to answer an attack that was aimed at the center of his person and teaching and work. And furthermore, this passage is drawn from that part of the Old Testament that possibly, so far as our argument is concerned, did not come within his purview in Matthew 5:17. Does this not show that his attitude to every jot and tittle of the Psalms was identical with that to every jot and tittle of the law? Upon any other supposition his appeal to a brief and relatively obscure statement of the book of Psalms would be quite forceless and inconclusive.

Finally, the force of the brief parenthetical clause, "the scripture cannot be broken," has to be noted. It might be plausibly argued that Jesus in his reply to the Jews was simply taking advantage of an *ad hominem* argument. In the question "Is it not written in your law?" Jesus is meeting his adversaries on their own assumptions. And so, it might be said, no argument bearing upon Jesus' own view of Scripture could be based on this passage. But Jesus' remark, "the scripture cannot be broken," silences any such contention. In this remark Jesus expresses not simply the attitude of the Jews to Scripture but his own view of the inviolability of Scripture. He appeals to Scripture because it is really and intrinsically a finality. And when he says the Scripture cannot be broken, he is surely using the word "Scripture" in its most comprehensive denotation as including all that the Jews of the day recognized as Scripture, to wit, all the canonical books of the Old Testament. It is of the Old Testament without any reservation or exception that he says, it "cannot be broken." Here then there can be no question as to how much of the Old Testament came within the purview or scope of his assertion. He affirms the unbreakableness of the Scripture in its entirety and leaves no room for any such supposition as that of degrees of inspiration and fallibility. Scripture is inviolable. Nothing less than this is the testimony of our Lord. And the crucial nature of such witness is driven home by the fact that it is in answer to the most serious of charges and in the defense of his most stupendous claim that he bears this testimony.

In passages such as those with which we have just dealt, our Lord's view of Scripture comes to explicit expression and exposition. It is not, however, in a few passages that his viewpoint is attested. There is a mass of evidence that corroborates the express teaching of the more explicit passages. Indeed, corroboration is too weak a word to do justice to the import of the mass of evidence bearing upon the question. Rather should we say that the teaching of our Lord is so steeped in the appeal to Scripture, so steeped in the use of the formula, "it is written," so pervaded by the recognition that what Scripture says God says, so characterized by the acceptance of the finality of the word of Scripture, that the doctrine of Scripture clearly enunciated in some passages is the necessary presupposition of the correlative evidence. The inescapable fact is that the mass of direct and indirect statement leads to one conclusion that, for our Lord, the Scripture, just because it was *Scripture*, just because it fell within the denotation of the formula, "it is written," was a finality. His attitude is one of meticulous acceptance and reverence. The only explanation of such an attitude is that what Scripture said, God said, that the Scripture was God's Word, that it was God's Word because it was Scripture and that it was or became Scripture because it was God's Word. That he distinguished between the Word of God borne to us by Scripture and the written Word itself would be an imposition upon Jesus' own teaching wholly alien to the identifications Jesus makes and to the reverence for the letter of Scripture so pervasive in all of his witness.

To institute a contrast between the teaching of our Lord and of his apostles on the question of Scripture would, of course, disrupt the harmony of the New Testament witness. The establishment of such disharmony would admittedly be a serious matter and it would have far-reaching consequences for the whole construction of Christian truth. Regarding the respective views of Scripture, discrepancy between Jesus and the writers of the New Testament could be sought in either of two directions. It could be sought in the direction of trying to find a more liberal view of Scripture reflected in the writers, or at least in some of the writers, of the New Testament, or it might be sought in the direction of showing that in the writings of the New Testament there is a petrifying and mechanizing process at work so that the more organic and elastic view of Jesus is transformed and brought into accord with the allegedly more scholastic and legalistic bias of later developments. We already found what our Lord's teaching was. We found it to be nothing less than that of the infallible character and authority of the Old Testament. A higher view of plenary or verbal inspiration we could not expect to find. If discrepancy between Jesus and the writers of the New Testament is to be sought it would not be reasonable, in view of the evidence, to seek it in the greater liberalism of Jesus. When we turn in the other direction, do we find any relaxation of the rigidity of Jesus' teaching in those who were his appointed witnesses?

Any adequate examination of this question would lead us far beyond our space in this volume. But is it not of the greatest pertinence that the books of the New Testament show that same characteristic which is so patent in the teaching of Christ, namely, appeal to what had been written? It is singular that the New Testament, not only in the reporting of Jesus' teaching but also as a whole, should as it were rest its case so frequently upon the adduction of Scripture proof and should authenticate the history of the Old Testament by such copious reference to it. Its witness in general is to the same effect as is summed up in the words of Paul, "For whatsoever things were written aforetime were written for our learning, that we through patience and comfort of the scriptures might have hope" (Rom. 15:4), an appraisal of the whole of the Old Testament that is preceded by a thoroughly typical appeal to the Old Testament as testifying beforehand to the example of Christ that he pleased not himself and as therefore not only witnessing to the fact that Christ pleased not himself but as also supporting the exhortation, "Let every one of us please his neighbour for his good to edification" (Rom. 15:2). It is precisely in such estimation of the Scriptures and in such allusion to them, as not only prophetic of what took place in the fullness of time but also as having direct bearing upon the most practical and abiding of Christian duties, that the New Testament abounds. And this is just saying that the Old Testament is not simply true as history, prophecy, and law but that it is also of abiding validity, application, and authority.

But, just as we found in the case of our Lord that the high view of the inspiration of Scripture not only underlies the formulae and allusions in which his teaching abounds but also comes to explicit expression in specific passages, so is it in the case of the other authoritative New Testament witnesses. The doctrine of Scripture becomes in some passages the subject of express teaching. Perhaps most notable among these is 2 Timothy 3:16, "All scripture is given by inspiration of God."[11]

In the preceding context of this passage, Paul refers to the "holy writings" which Timothy knew from a child. These "holy writings" can be none other than the sacred Scriptures of the Old Testament. It is with these Scriptures in mind that Paul says, "All scripture is God-breathed." The word that Paul uses predicates of all Scripture or of every Scripture a certain quality. More particularly, the predicate reflects upon its origin; it is the product of God's creative breath. The terseness of Paul's affirmation here must not be allowed to obscure its significance. It is that Scripture, the denotation of which is placed beyond all doubt by the context, is God's mouth, God's breath, and therefore God's oracle. Paul makes no qualifications and no reservations. Every Scripture is God-breathed and therefore, so far as divine origin and resultant character are concerned, there is no discrimination. And in respect of the benefit accruing to men, all of Scripture is, for the reason that it is God-inspired, also profitable for doctrine, for reproof, for correction, for instruction in righteousness, that the man of God may be perfect, thoroughly furnished unto every good work.

Paul was, of course, well aware that God used human instruments in giving us these Scriptures. In his epistles he makes repeated allusion to the human authors of the sacred books. But the recognition of human instrumentality did not in the least inhibit Paul from making the stupendous affirmation that all Scripture is God-breathed, which means that Scripture is of divine origin and authorship and therefore of divine character and authority.

The predication which Paul here makes is nothing less than the high doctrine of plenary inspiration. For Paul is not here speaking of an inbreathing on the part of God into the writers of holy Scripture nor even into holy Scripture itself. The term Paul uses represents the concept of "breathing out" rather than that of "breathing in" and is far removed from the notion that a human product or witness is so interpenetrated with divine truth or influence that it becomes the Word of God. The whole emphasis is upon the fact that all Scripture proceeds from God and is therefore invested with a divinity that makes it as authoritative and efficient as a word oracularly spoken by God directly to us.

In 2 Timothy 3:16 Paul says nothing with respect to the human authors of Scripture nor with respect to the way in which God wrought upon the human authors so as to provide us with God-breathed Scripture. The apostle Peter, however, though not by any means furnishing us with a full definition of the mode of inspiration, does go farther than does Paul in 2 Timothy 3:16 in stating the relation that obtained between the Holy Spirit and the inspired human witnesses. "No prophecy of scripture," he writes, "is of private interpretation. For not by the will of man was prophecy brought aforetime, but as borne by the Holy Spirit men spake from God" (2 Peter 1:20–21). That Peter's statement here bears upon the agency of the Holy Spirit in the giving of Scripture is obvious from the phrase, "prophecy of scripture."

Peter's teaching in this passage is both negative and positive. Negatively, he denies that the prophecy of Scripture owes its origin to human initiative, volition, or determination. It is not the product of individual reflection or imagination. Positively, human instrumentality

11. See, for an examination of the meaning of θεόπνευστος, B. B. Warfield, *Revelation and Inspiration* (New York: Oxford University Press, 1927), 229–80, *The Inspiration and Authority of the Bible* (Philadelphia: Presbyterian and Reformed, 1948), 245–96, and for an exegesis of 2 Timothy 3:16, these same, respectively, 79–81 and 133–35.

is asserted. "Men spake from God." False inferences that might be drawn from the absolute terms of the preceding negations are obviated by the recognition of human agency. But while men spake, they spake from God, and it is this datum that harmonizes the fact of human agency with the negations of private interpretation and the will of man. They spake from God because they were borne along or borne up by the Holy Spirit.[12] Here there is plainly the conjunction of human and divine agency. But the divine character of the prophecy is insured by the peculiar character of the Spirit's agency. He took up the human agents in such a way that they spoke God's Word, not their own.

In this context it is the stability of the prophetic Word that is being emphasized. The ground upon which this stability rests is that it came from God, that the Holy Spirit was not only operative in the writers of Scripture but carried them to his destination and that this prophetic Word is not a momentary utterance or passing oracular deliverance but the Word of God that has received through Scripture permanent embodiment and authentication.

Summing up the witness of the New Testament, we find that human authorship or instrumentality is fully recognized and yet human agency is not conceived of as in any way impairing the divine origin, character, truth, and authority of Scripture. It is divine in its origin because it is the product of God's creative breath and because it was as borne by the Holy Spirit that men spoke from God. For these reasons it bears an oracular character that accords it an authority as real and divine as if we heard the voice of God speaking from heaven. This oracular character is a permanent feature and so Scripture has an abiding stability and application—it is unbreakable and indissoluble.

The witness with which we have so far dealt confines itself to the express testimony of the New Testament with reference to the Old. What then of the evidence on which may be founded a similar judgment with respect to the character of the New Testament? It must be acknowledged that the great mass of the evidence we possess bearing upon the inspiration of Scripture is the witness of the New Testament with reference to the Old. We do not have from the New Testament writers or authoritative witnesses the same abundance of testimony to the inspiration of the New Testament. That this should be the state of the case should not surprise us. When the New Testament witnesses spoke or wrote there was no finished New Testament canon to which they could refer as a unified and completed corpus of writings. Particularly is this true of our Lord himself. None of the books of the New Testament was written when he spoke upon earth. Witness to the character of the New Testament as a whole such as we find in the New Testament with reference to the Old would have been impossible for any writer of the New Testament except the last and only then as an appendix to his own last canonical writing. This type of witness it would be unreasonable for us to demand as the necessary seal upon the divine character and authority of the entire New Testament.

While we do not have the same mass of testimony to the inspiration of the New Testament as to the Old, and while the circumstances were such that we could not expect the same kind of inclusive characterization, it does not follow that we have no evidence upon which to maintain the divine origin and character of the New Testament. We have sufficient evidence, and to such we now turn our attention.

The organic unity of both Testaments is the presupposition of the appeal to the authority of the Old Testament and of allusion to it in which the New Testament abounds. This fact

---

12. Cf. B. B. Warfield, *op. cit.*, respectively, 82–83 and 135–36.

of organic unity bears very directly upon the question of the inspiration of the New Testament. For if, as we have found, the authoritative witness of the New Testament bears out the unbreakable and inerrant character of the Old, how could that which forms an organic unit with the Old be of an entirely different character as regards the nature of its inspiration? When the implications of organic unity are fully appreciated, it becomes impossible to believe that the divinity of the New Testament can be on a lower plane than that of the Old. Surely then, if the Old Testament, according to the testimony that in this matter has the greatest relevance or authority, is inerrant, the New Testament must also be.

This argument from organic unity has peculiar force when we properly understand the implications of progressive revelation. The New Testament stands to the Old in the relation of consummation to preparation; it embodies a fuller and more glorious disclosure of God's character and will. This is signalized by the fact that in these last days God hath spoken unto us by his Son who is the brightness of his glory and the express image of his being (Heb. 1:1–3). In Paul's language the glory of the New Testament is the glory that excels (2 Cor. 3:10–11). The New Testament Scripture enshrines and conveys to us the content of that new and better covenant, established upon better promises. Is it at all consonant with the completory nature of the New Testament, with the more excellent glory inherent in the New Testament and with the finality attaching to the revelation of God's own Son to suppose that the Scripture of such an economy should be lacking in that inerrancy which the authoritative witnesses—our Lord and his apostles—predicate of the Old Testament? It would be contrary to all sound analogy and reason to entertain such a supposition.[13]

The cogency of this argument is made all the more apparent when we bear in mind the meaning of Pentecost. The Old Testament was God-breathed, possessing unshakable stability and permanent validity, because it was as borne by the Holy Spirit men spoke from God. Yet so much more abundant were the operations of the Spirit introduced by Pentecost that it can be described in terms of "giving" and "sending forth" the Holy Spirit. Are we to believe that this greater fulness and abundance of the Spirit's operation gave us a Scripture less reliable and less inerrant than the Scripture that the Spirit gave before the abundant effusion of Pentecost took place? Are we to believe that the Scripture that is the only abiding witness to and embodiment of the full and abundant administration of the Spirit is a Scripture less characterized by the activity of the Spirit that imparted divinity and authority to the Old Testament? To ask these questions is to show that once the witness of the New Testament to the inspiration and inerrancy of the Old is accepted, once the relations which the two Testaments sustain to one another are understood and appreciated, the infallible character of the Old Testament furnishes us with the most cogent considerations in support of a similar judgment with respect to the character of the New Testament.

We must not think, however, that these considerations constitute the whole basis of faith in the New Testament as inerrant Scripture. For the New Testament is not without direct witness to its own character. It is true that we do not have the mass of testimony that we have in connection with the Old Testament. But, in a manner analogous to the witness the Old Testament bears to its own divinity, the New Testament not only bears the unmistakable marks of its divine origin but also bears direct witness to its own divine character and authority.

---

13. Cf. Louis Gaussen, *Theopneustia* (Cincinnati: George S. Blanchard, 1859), 74–75.

If the New Testament is the Word of God with all the fulness of meaning that the authoritative witnesses of the New Testament ascribe to the Old, it must be by reason of that same plenary inspiration of the Holy Spirit operative in the writing of the Old Testament. The promises that Christ gave to his disciples with respect to the Holy Spirit have, therefore, the closest bearing upon this question. When Jesus sent out his disciples to preach the kingdom of God he said to them, "But when they deliver you up, take no thought how or what ye shall speak, for it shall be given you in that hour what ye shall speak. For it is not ye that speak but the Spirit of your Father that speaketh in you" (Matt. 10:19–20; cf. Mark 13:11; Luke 12:12; 21:14–15). Such a promise assures to the disciples that in the "passing exigencies" and "to subserve interests of the narrowest range"[14] there would be afforded to them an inspiration of the Holy Spirit that would make their spoken words not simply their words but the words of the Holy Spirit. This same promise of the Spirit is given greatly increased scope and application when on the eve of his crucifixion Jesus said, "It is expedient for you that I go away. For if I go not away, the Comforter will not come unto you, but if I depart I will send him unto you. . . . He will guide you into all the truth" (John 16:7, 13). After his resurrection Jesus performed what must be construed as the act of official impartation of the Holy Spirit when he breathed on his disciples and said, "Receive ye the Holy Ghost" (John 20:22). And before his ascension he assured them, "Ye shall receive power after that the Holy Spirit is come upon you, and ye shall be my witnesses both in Jerusalem and in all Judea and in Samaria and unto the uttermost part of the earth" (Acts 1:8). The work and functions of the disciples are therefore to be discharged, in accordance with the promise and commission of Christ, by the direction and inspiration of the Holy Spirit. It is no wonder then that we find in the writings of the New Testament a note of authority, of certainty and of finality that it would be presumptuous for men to arrogate to themselves, a note of authority that is consistent with truth and sobriety only if the writers were the agents of divine authority and the subjects of inspiration by the Holy Spirit. Relevant to the question of inspiration, this note of authority is one of the most significant features of the New Testament.

The passage in 1 Corinthians 7:10–12 is sometimes understood as if Paul were instituting a contrast between the authoritative teaching of Christ and his own unauthoritative judgment on questions bearing upon marriage and separation—"But to the married I give charge, not I but the Lord. . . . But to the rest I say, not the Lord." A careful reading of the whole passage will, however, show that the contrast is not between the inspired teaching of Christ and the uninspired teaching of the apostle but rather between the teaching of the apostle that could appeal to the express utterances of Christ in the days of his flesh, on the one hand, and the teaching of the apostle that went beyond the cases dealt with by Christ, on the other. There is no distinction as regards the binding character of the teaching in these respective cases. The language and terms the apostle uses in the second case are just as emphatic and mandatory as in the first case. And this passage, so far from diminishing the character of apostolic authority, only enhances our estimate of that authority. If Paul can be as mandatory in his terms when he is dealing with questions on which, by his own admission, he cannot appeal for support to the express teaching of Christ, does not this fact serve to impress upon us how profound was Paul's consciousness that he was writing by divine authority, when his own teaching was as mandatory in its terms as was his reiteration

14. Gaussen, *Theopneustia*, 77.

of the teaching of the Lord himself? Nothing else than the consciousness of enunciating divinely authoritative law would warrant the terseness and decisiveness of the statement by which he prevents all gainsaying, "And so ordain I in all the churches" (1 Cor. 7:17).

That Paul regards his written word as invested with divine sanction and authority is placed beyond all question in this same epistle (1 Cor. 14:37–38). In the context he is dealing specifically with the question of the place of women in the public assemblies of worship. He enjoins silence upon women in the church by appeal to the universal custom of the churches of Christ and by appeal to the law of the Old Testament. It is then that he makes appeal to the divine content of his prescriptions. "If any man thinketh himself to be a prophet or spiritual, let him acknowledge that the things I write unto you are the commandment of the Lord. And if any man be ignorant, let him be ignorant." Paul here makes the most direct claim to be writing the divine Word and coordinates this appeal to divine authority with appeal to the already existing Scripture of the Old Testament.

In the earlier part of this epistle Paul informs us, in fashion thoroughly consonant with the uniform teaching of Scripture as to what constitutes the word of man the Word of God, that the Holy Spirit is the source of all the wisdom taught by the apostles. "God hath revealed them unto us through the Spirit. For the Spirit searcheth all things, yea, the deep things of God" (1 Cor. 2:10). And not only does Paul appeal here to the Holy Spirit as the source of the wisdom conveyed through his message but also to the Spirit as the source of the very media of expression. For Paul continues, "which things also we speak, not in the words which man's wisdom teacheth, but which the Spirit teacheth, combining spiritual things with spiritual" (1 Cor. 2:13).[15] Spirit-taught things and Spirit-taught words! Nothing else provides us with an explanation of apostolic authority.

Much else that supports and corroborates the foregoing position could be elicited from the witness of the New Testament. But in the brief limits of the space available enough has been given to indicate that the same plenary inspiration which the New Testament uniformly predicates of the Old is the kind of inspiration that renders the New Testament itself the Word of God.

Frequently the doctrine of verbal inspiration is dismissed with supercilious scorn as but a remnant of that mediaeval or post-Reformation scholasticism that has tended to petrify Christianity.[16] Such contempt usually accompanies the claim that open-minded scientific research has made adherence to Biblical inerrancy inconsistent with well-informed honesty and therefore untenable. This boast of scientific honesty is plausible, so much so that it is often

---

15. It is possible that συγκρίνοντες could be rendered "interpreting." But, in that event, the immediately preceding context would indicate that the rendering of the clause would be: "interpreting spiritual things by spiritual words." This would have the same effect for the question being discussed as the rendering given above. The rendering that has been proposed: "interpreting spiritual things to spiritual men" is quite unnatural and cannot compete with the other renderings. The clause in question surely stands in apposition to what precedes: "which things also we speak, not in words taught of human wisdom, but in words taught of the Spirit." The thought is the combination of *the things* of the Spirit and *words* taught of the Spirit. The well-established meaning of συγκρίνω, namely, "combine," together with the thought of the preceding context and the syntax of the whole sentence point clearly to the translation: "combining spiritual things with spiritual words."

16. Verbal inspiration is not to be equated with a theory of mechanical dictation. The classic exponents of the doctrine of verbal inspiration have not attempted to define the mode of inspiration. It is true that the term "dictation" sometimes occurs, but its use was not intended to specify the mode of inspiration as that of dictation. Full allowance is made for the manifold activities and processes by which the books of Scripture were brought into being and full recognition given to the diversity characterizing those who were the instruments in the production of Scripture. Cf. B. B. Warfield, *op. cit.*, respectively, 99–106 and 153–60; *Calvin and Calvinism* (New York: Oxford University Press, 1931), 62–68.

the password to respect in the arena of theological debate. The plea of the present contribution has been, however, that the summary dismissal of Biblical infallibility is lamentably unscientific in its treatment of the very data that bear directly on the question at issue and that such dismissal has failed to reckon with the issues at stake in the rejection of what is established by straightforward scientific exegesis of the witness of Scripture to its own character. If the testimony of Scripture on the doctrine of Scripture is not authentic and trustworthy, then the finality of Scripture is irretrievably undermined. The question at stake is the place of Scripture as the canon of faith. And we must not think that the finality of Christ remains unimpaired even if the finality of Scripture is sacrificed. The rejection of the inerrancy of Scripture means the rejection of Christ's own witness to Scripture. Finally and most pointedly, then, the integrity of our Lord's witness is the crucial issue in this battle of the faith.

II. The Internal Testimony

The thesis maintained above in our examination of the objective witness is that Scripture is authoritative by reason of the character it possesses as the infallible Word of God and that this divine quality belongs to Scripture because it is the product of God's creative breath through the mode of plenary inspiration by the Holy Spirit. The rejection of such a position has appeared to many to involve no impairment of the divine authority of the Bible because, even though the infallibility of Scripture has to be abandoned, there still remains the ever abiding and active witness of the Holy Spirit, and so infallible authority is fully conserved in the internal testimony of the Holy Spirit. Scripture is authoritative, it is said, because it is borne home to the man of faith by the internal testimony of the Spirit.

That there is such an activity of the Holy Spirit as the internal testimony is beyond dispute, and that there is no true faith in Scripture as the Word of God apart from such inward testimony is likewise fully granted. It might seem, therefore, that it belongs to the situation in which we are placed, relative to the Holy Spirit, to say that the divine authority that confronts us is not that emanating from a past and finished activity of the Spirit but rather the influence of the Spirit which is now operative with reference to and in us. Does not the positing of divine authority in an activity of the Spirit that to us is impersonal and external, as well as far distant and now inactive, do prejudice to the real meaning of that directly personal and presently operative address of the Holy Spirit to us and in us?

This question is that which defines what is the most important cleavage within Protestantism today. It is the cleavage between what is called Barthianism and the historic Protestant position. The Barthian view is that Scripture is authoritative because it witnesses to the Word of God; it is the vessel or vehicle of the Word of God to us. In that respect Scripture is said to be unique and in that sense it is called the Word of God. But what makes Scripture really authoritative, on this view, is the ever-recurring act of God, the divine decision, whereby, through the mediacy of Scripture, the witness of Scripture to the Word of God is borne home to us with ruling and compelling power. The Scripture is not authoritative antecedently and objectively. It is only authoritative as here and now, to this man and to no other, in a concrete crisis and confrontation, God reveals himself through the medium of Scripture. Only as there is the ever-recurring human crisis and divine decision does the Bible become the Word of God.

It is apparent, therefore, that for the Barthian the authority-imparting factor is not Scripture as an existing corpus of truth given by God to man by a process of revelation and inspiration in past history, not the divine quality and character which Scripture inherently possesses, but something else that must be distinguished from any past action and from any resident quality. The issue must not be obscured. Barth does not hold and cannot hold that Scripture possesses binding and ruling authority by reason of what it is objectively, inherently and qualitatively.

An objection to this way of stating the matter is easily anticipated. It is that this sharp antithesis is indefensible. For, after all, it will be said, Scripture is unique. It is the Word of God because it bears witness to God's Word. It occupies a unique category because there was something unique and distinctive about that past activity by which it came to be. It differs radically from other books written at the time of its production and also from all other books. It can, therefore, have no authority in abstraction from that quality that belongs to it as the human witness to the revelation given by God in the past. So, it may be argued, the factor arising from past events and activities enters into the whole complex of factors that combine and converge to invest Scripture with that unique character which makes it the fit medium for the ever-recurring act of divine revelation. It is not then an *either or* but a *both and*.

The objection is appreciated and welcomed. But it does not eliminate the issue. After making allowance for all that is argued in support of the objection, there still remains the fact that, on Barthian presuppositions, it is not the divine quality inherent in Scripture nor the divine activity by which that quality has been imparted to it that makes Scripture authoritative. That past activity and the resultant quality may constitute the prerequisites for the authority by which it becomes ever and anon invested, but they do not constitute that authority. It is rather the ever-recurring act of God that is the authority-constituting fact. This ever-recurring activity of God may be conceived of as the internal testimony of the Spirit and so it is this testimony that constitutes Scripture authoritative.[17]

It is sometimes supposed that this construction of the authority of Scripture represents the classic Protestant or indeed Reformed position. Even the Westminster Confession has been appealed to as enunciating this position when it says that "our full persuasion and assurance of the infallible truth and divine authority thereof, is from the inward work of the Holy Spirit bearing witness by and with the Word in our hearts" (WCF 1.5). A little examination of Chapter 1 of the Confession will expose the fallacy of this appeal. Indeed, the Westminster Confession was framed with a logic and comprehension exactly adapted not only to obviate but also to meet this construction. Section 5, from which the above quotation was given, does not deal with the nature or ground of the authority of Scripture. The preceding section deals with that logically prior question. It states clearly that the authority of Scripture resides in the fact that it is the Word of God. "The authority of the Holy Scripture, for which it ought to be believed and obeyed, dependeth not upon the testimony of any man, or Church; but wholly upon God (who is truth itself) the author thereof: and therefore it is to be received because it is the Word of God." In one word, Scripture is authoritative because God is its author and he is its author because, as is stated in Section 2, it was given by inspiration of God. Nothing could be plainer than this: that the Confession represents the authority of Scripture as resting not upon the internal testimony of the Holy Spirit but upon the inspiration of the Spirit, a finished activity by which, it is clearly stated, the sixty-six books enumerated were produced and in virtue of which they are the Word of God written.

---

17. Cf. Karl Barth, *Church Dogmatics*, vol. I, 1, English translation (Edinburgh: T. & T. Clark, 1936), 207ff.

It is, however, by "the inward work of the Holy Spirit bearing witness by and with the Word in our hearts" that we become convinced of that authority. The authority of Scripture is an objective and permanent fact residing in the quality of inspiration; the conviction on our part has to wait for that inward testimony by which the antecedent facts of divinity and authority are borne in upon our minds and consciences. It is to confuse the most important and eloquent of distinctions to represent the former as consisting in the latter. The Confession has left no room for doubt as to what its position is, and in formulating the matter with such clarity it has expressed the classic Reformed conception.

What then is the nature of this internal testimony and what is the Scriptural basis upon which the doctrine rests?

If, as has been shown in the earlier part of this discussion, Scripture is divine in its origin, character, and authority, it must bear the marks or evidences of that divinity. If the heavens declare the glory of God and therefore bear witness to their divine Creator, the Scripture as God's handiwork must also bear the imprints of his authorship. This is just saying that Scripture evidences itself to be the Word of God; its divinity is self-evidencing and self-authenticating. The ground of faith in Scripture as the Word of God is therefore the evidence it inherently contains of its divine authorship and quality. External evidence, witness to its divinity derived from other sources extraneous to itself, may corroborate and confirm the witness it inherently contains, but such external evidence cannot be in the category of evidence sufficient to ground and constrain faith. If the faith is faith in the Bible as God's Word, obviously the evidence upon which such faith rests must itself have the quality of divinity. For only evidence with the quality of divinity would be sufficient to ground a faith in divinity. Faith in Scripture as God's Word, then, rests upon the perfections inherent in Scripture and is elicited by the perception of these perfections. These perfections constitute its incomparable excellence and such excellence when apprehended constrains the overwhelming conviction that is the only appropriate kind of response.

If Scripture thus manifests itself to be divine, why is not faith the result in the case of every one confronted with it? The answer is that not all men have the requisite perceptive faculty. Evidence is one thing, the ability to perceive and understand is another. "The natural man receiveth not the things of the Spirit of God: for they are foolishness unto him: neither can he know them, because they are spiritually discerned" (1 Cor. 2:14). It is here that the necessity for the internal testimony of the Spirit enters. The darkness and depravity of man's mind by reason of sin make man blind to the divine excellence of Scripture. And the effect of sin is not only that it blinds the mind of man and makes it impervious to the evidence but also that it renders the heart of man utterly hostile to the evidence. The carnal mind is enmity against God and therefore resists every claim of the divine perfection. If the appropriate response of faith is to be yielded to the divine excellence inherent in Scripture, nothing less than radical regeneration by the Holy Spirit can produce the requisite susceptibility. "Except a man be born again, he cannot see the kingdom of God" (John 3:3). "The natural man receiveth not the things of the Spirit of God" (1 Cor. 2:14). It is here that the internal testimony of the Spirit enters and it is in the inward work of the Holy Spirit upon the heart and mind of man that the internal testimony consists. The witness of Scripture to the depravity of man's mind and to the reality, nature, and effect of the inward work of the Holy Spirit is the basis upon which the doctrine of the internal testimony rests.

When Paul institutes the contrast between the natural man and the spiritual and says with respect to the latter, "But he that is spiritual judgeth all things, yet he himself is judged of no one" (1 Cor. 2:15), he means that the "spiritual" person is the person endowed with and indwelt by the Holy Spirit. It is only such an one who has the faculty to discern the things revealed by the Spirit. By way of contrast with the natural man he receives, knows, and discerns the truth.

Earlier in this same chapter Paul tells us in terms that even more pointedly deal with our present subject that the faith of the Corinthians in the gospel was induced by the demonstration of the Spirit and of power. "And my speech and my preaching was not in persuasive words of wisdom, but in demonstration of the Spirit and of power, in order that your faith might not be in the wisdom of men but in the power of God" (1 Cor. 2:4–5). No doubt Paul here is reflecting upon the manner of his preaching. It was not with the embellishments of human oratory that he preached the gospel but with that demonstration or manifestation that is produced by the Spirit and power of God. He is saying, in effect, that the Spirit of God so wrought in him and in his preaching that the response on the part of the Corinthians was the solid faith which rests upon the power of God and not that evanescent faith which depends upon the appeal of rhetorical art and worldly wisdom. It is in the demonstration of which the Holy Spirit is the author that the faith of the Corinthians finds its source. It is, indeed, faith terminating upon the Word of God preached by Paul. But it is faith produced by the accompanying demonstration of the Spirit and manifestation of divine power.

In the first epistle to the Thessalonians Paul again refers to the power and confidence with which he and his colleagues preached the gospel at Thessalonica. "For our gospel came not unto you in word only, but also in power and in the Holy Spirit and much assurance" (1 Thess. 1:5). In this text the reference to power and assurance appears to apply to the power and confidence with which Paul and Silvanus and Timothy proclaimed the Word rather than to the conviction with which it was received by the Thessalonians. The gospel came in the Holy Spirit and therefore with power and assurance. But we must not dissociate the reception of the Word on the part of the Thessalonians from this power and confidence wrought by the Spirit. For Paul proceeds, "And ye became imitators of us and of the Lord, having received the word in much affliction with joy of the Holy Spirit" (v. 6). The resulting faith on the part of the Thessalonians must be regarded as proceeding from this activity of the Holy Spirit in virtue of which the gospel was proclaimed "in power and in the Holy Spirit and much assurance." That the Thessalonians became imitators of the Lord and received the Word with joy is due to the fact that the gospel came not in word only, and it came not in word only because it came in the power of the Holy Spirit. Their faith therefore finds its source in this demonstration of the Spirit, just as the joy with which they received the Word is the joy wrought by the Spirit.

When the Apostle John writes, "And ye have an anointing from the Holy One and ye know all things. I have not written to you because ye do not know the truth, but because ye know it, and that no lie is of the truth" (1 John 2:20–21; cf. v. 27), he is surely alluding to that same indwelling of the Spirit with which Paul deals in 1 Corinthians 2:15. This anointing is an abiding possession and invests believers with discernment of the truth and steadfastness in it.

Summing up the conclusions drawn from these few relevant passages, we may say that the reception of the truth of God in intelligent, discriminating, joyful, and abiding faith is the effect of divine demonstration and power through the efficiency of the Holy Spirit, and that this faith consists in the confident assurance that, though the Word of God is brought through the instrumentality of men, it is not the word of man but in very truth the Word of God. We again see how even in connection with the internal testimony of the Spirit the ministry of men in no way militates against the reception of their message as the Word of God.

This witness of the Holy Spirit has been called the internal testimony of the Spirit. The question arises, why is the inward work of the Spirit called *testimony*? There does not appear, indeed, to be any compelling reason why it should be thus called. There is, however, an appropriateness in the word. The faith induced by this work of the Spirit rests upon the testimony the Scripture inherently contains of its divine origin and character. It is the function of the Holy Spirit to open the minds of men to perceive that testimony and cause the Word of God to be borne home to the mind of man with ruling power and conviction. Thereby the Holy Spirit may be said to bear perpetual witness to the divine character of that which is his own handiwork.

The internal testimony of the Spirit has frequently been construed as consisting in illumination or in regeneration on its noetic side. It is illumination because it consists in the opening of our minds to behold the excellence that inheres in Scripture as the Word of God. It is regeneration in its noetic expression because it is regeneration manifesting itself in our understanding in the response of the renewed mind to the evidence Scripture contains of its divine character. Anything less than illumination, in the sense defined above, the internal testimony cannot be.

The question may properly be raised, however, whether or not the notion of illumination is fully adequate as an interpretation of the nature of this testimony. On the view that it consists merely in illumination, the testimony, most strictly considered, resides entirely in the Scripture itself and not at all in the ever-present activity of the Spirit. And the question is, may we not properly regard the present work of the Spirit as not only imparting to us an understanding to perceive the evidence inhering in the Scripture but also as imparting what is of the nature of positive testimony? If we answer in the affirmative, then we should have to say that the power and demonstration with which the Holy Spirit accompanies the Word and by which it is carried home to our hearts and minds with irresistible conviction is the ever-continuing positive testimony of the Spirit. In other words, the seal of the Spirit belongs to the category of testimony strictly considered. If this construction should be placed upon the power and seal of the Spirit, there is a very obvious reason why this doctrine should be called, not only appropriately but necessarily, the internal testimony of the Spirit.

The most relevant passages (1 Cor. 2:4–5; 1 Thess. 1:5–6) speak of this witness of the Spirit as demonstration (ἀπόδειξις) and power (δύναμις) and as such is supplementary to the word of the gospel itself. These terms, especially the term "demonstration," convey the notion of proof, of attestation, of confirmation. Since this activity of the Spirit is not inherent in the Word (cf. 1 Thess. 1:5) and produces the full assurance of faith (cf. also 1 Thess. 2:13), it must be construed as additional attestation, as a sealing witness of the Holy Spirit by which there is induced in us the irresistible conviction of the truth conveyed. This means that the work of the Spirit concerned is itself positive testimony collateral and correlative with the evidence which the Scripture contains of its divine origin and authority. This collateral witness coalesces with and confirms the witness resident in Scripture. It must never be identified or confused with the witness borne by our consciousness. It is witness *to* our consciousness and is wholly the work of the Spirit.

Whether we view the internal testimony as merely illumination or as illumination plus a positive supplementation construed as testimony in the stricter sense of the word, there is one principle which it is necessary to stress, namely, that the internal testimony does not convey to us new truth content. The whole truth content that comes within the scope of the internal testimony is contained in the Scripture. This testimony terminates upon the end of constraining belief in the divine character and authority of the Word of God and upon that end alone. It gives no ground whatsoever for new revelations of the Spirit.

When Paul writes to the Thessalonians, "Our gospel came not unto you in word only, but also in power and in the Holy Spirit and much assurance," he is surely making a distinction between the actual content of the gospel and the attendant power with which it was conveyed to them and in virtue of which it was carried home with conviction to the hearts of the Thessalonians. In like manner in 1 Corinthians 2:4–5 the content of Paul's word and preaching will surely have to be distinguished from the demonstration of the Spirit and of power by which Paul's message was effectual in the begetting of faith in the Corinthian believers. And we are likewise justified in recognizing a distinction between the truth which John says his readers already knew and the abiding anointing of the Spirit which provided them with the proper knowledge and discernment to the end of bringing to clearer consciousness and consistent application the truth which they had already received (1 John 2:20–27). In each case the illumining and sealing function of the Spirit has respect to truth which has been received from another source than that of his confirming and sealing operations.

The internal testimony of the Spirit is the necessary complement to the witness Scripture inherently bears to its plenary inspiration. The two pillars of true faith in Scripture as God's Word are the objective witness and the internal testimony. The objective witness furnishes us with a conception of Scripture that provides the proper basis for the ever-active sealing operation of the Spirit of truth. The internal testimony insures that this objective witness elicits the proper response in the human consciousness. The sealing function of the Spirit finds its complete explanation and validation in the pervasive witness that Scripture bears to its own divine origin and authority. And the witness to plenary inspiration receives its constant confirmation in the inward work of the Holy Spirit bearing witness by and with the Word in the hearts of believers.

COLLECTED WRITINGS OF JOHN MURRAY

John Murray, *Collected Writings of John Murray*, vol. 1, *The Claims of Truth* (Carlisle, PA: Banner of Truth, 1976), 9–26, 316–22.

The Infallibility of Scripture[18]

Scripture as the Word of God has many attributes. But no one of these is more precious to the believer than infallibility. This attribute assures him of its stability and it imparts to him that certitude by which alone he can be steadfast in the faith once for all delivered to the saints. The doctrine of infallibility rests upon proper grounds and only as we examine these grounds can we properly understand its meaning and assess its significance.

18. An address given to students belonging to The Inter-Varsity Fellowship (now Universities and Colleges Christian Fellowship), probably circa 1960.

The Warrant

When we say that Scripture is infallible, on what ground or by what authority do we make this confession? When we ask the question, we should realize how momentous is the confession. In this world in which sin and misery abound, in which error is rampant, in which it is so difficult to discover the truth about any complex situation, that there should be an entity in the form of a collection of documents of which we predicate infallibility is a fact with staggering implications. And so, when we ask the question of warrant, we are asking a question of the greatest moment. The authority must be as ultimate as the proposition is stupendous.

We say Scripture is infallible not because we can prove it to be infallible. The impossibility of proof lies on the face of Scripture. For example, how could we prove that the first chapter of Genesis is substantially true, not to speak of its being infallible? This chapter deals with the origin of created realities, and what collateral or independent evidence do we possess regarding the action by which created entities began to be? We must not depreciate science. But science has to deal with existing realities, not with that which was antecedent to created existence. Or again, if we think of the third chapter of Genesis, who can prove that the events there recorded are true, or that it provides us with an infallible account of what is alleged to have occurred?

It is, of course, necessary to take account of what is our province and duty. It is our obligation to defend Scripture against allegations of error and contradiction. We can often show from the data of Scripture that the Scripture is consistent with itself. And we can also show that its representations are not contradicted by data derived from other authentic sources of information. Oftentimes, though we may not be able to demonstrate the harmony of Scripture, we are able to show that there is no necessary contradiction. There is ample place and scope for this type of defence in order to meet on the basis of all the data provided for us the charges which doubt and unbelief bring against Scripture.

But the main point of interest now is that when we thus defend the Scripture we do not thereby prove its infallibility. We are indeed vindicating the authenticity of Scripture, authenticity without which it would be futile to maintain its infallibility. But we do not thereby prove its infallibility. For one thing there are areas of Scripture, and these the most important, in connection with which we are not able to engage even in the aforementioned type of defence or vindication. How could we prove that when Christ died upon the cross he expiated the sins of a countless number of lost men? How are we to prove that Christ after his ascension entered into the holy places at the right hand of the Majesty in the heavens? It can be demonstrated that the Scripture so teaches but not that these things are true.

Thus, on the question of warrant for the proposition that Scripture is infallible, what are we to say? The only ground is the witness of Scripture to itself, to its own origin, character, and authority.

This may seem an illegitimate way of supporting the proposition at issue. Are we not begging the question? We are seeking for the ground of the proposition that Scripture is infallible. And then we say: we believe this because the Scripture says so, which, in turn, assumes that we are to accept the verdict of Scripture. If we accept this verdict, we imply that its verdict is true, and not only so, but *infallibly true* if the verdict is to support the declaration that Scripture is infallible. This is the situation and we must frankly confess it to be so. It can be no otherwise in the situation that belongs to us in God's providential grace.

The Uniqueness of Scripture

Let us try to assess the situation in which we are placed. Apart from the Scriptures and the knowledge derived from them, we today would be in complete darkness respecting the content of our Christian faith. We must not deceive ourselves as to the darkness and confusion that would be ours if there were no Bible. We depend upon the message of Scripture for every tenet of our faith, for every ray of redemptive light that illumines our minds, and for every ray of hope against the issues of time and eternity. Christianity for us today without the Bible is something inconceivable.

We are not presuming to limit God. He could have brought the revelation of his redemptive will by other means than that of Scripture. But the issue now is not what God could have done if he had so pleased. The issue is what he has done. It is the *de facto* situation of God's providential ordering. And the upshot is that Scripture occupies an absolutely unique position. The case is not simply that Scripture is indispensable. Much else besides Scripture is indispensable in our actual situation. There is the witness of the church, there is the Christian tradition, and there is the mass of Christian literature. The fact is that Scripture as an entity, as a phenomenon, if you will, is absolutely unique. We are deceiving ourselves and refusing to face reality if we think that we can maintain even the most attenuated Christian belief or hope without presupposing and acknowledging that absolute uniqueness belonging to Scripture as a collection of written documents. It is this absolute uniqueness that must be taken into account when we speak of accepting its verdict.

It may be objected: does not the foregoing position impinge upon what is central in our faith? Is not Christ, the Son of God incarnate, crucified, risen, exalted, and coming again the Christian faith? Might it not even be objected that this emphasis gives to Scripture the place of God?

Of course, the Scripture is not God and to give Scripture the place of God would be idolatry. Of course, Christ is Christianity and saving relation to him as Lord and Saviour is the only hope of lost men.

But the absolute uniqueness of Scripture is not impaired. Scripture is unique, not because it takes the place of God, nor the place of Christ, but because of its relationship to God, to Christ, and to the Holy Spirit. It is unique because it is the only way whereby we come into relationship to God in the redemptive revelation of his grace, and the only way whereby Christ in the uniqueness that belongs to him as the Son of God incarnate, as the crucified, risen, and ascended Redeemer, comes within the orbit of our knowledge, faith, experience, and hope. We have no encounter with God, with Christ, and with the Holy Spirit in terms of saving and redeeming grace apart from Scripture. It is the only revelation to *us* of God's redemptive will. That is its uniqueness.

Here then is the conclusion proceeding from its uniqueness, its incomparable singularity in the situation that is ours in God's providence. If we do not accept its verdict respecting its own character or quality, we have no warrant to accept its verdict respecting anything else. If its witness respecting itself is not authentic, then by what warrant may we accept its witness on other matters? By reason of what Scripture is and means in the whole compass of Christian faith and hope we are shut up to what Scripture teaches respecting its origin, character, and authority.

The Witness of Scripture

What is this witness? Certain passages are of particular relevance. Paul says, "All scripture is God-breathed" (2 Tim. 3:16), and Peter, "For prophecy was not brought of old time by the will of man, but as borne by the Holy Spirit men spoke from God" (2 Peter 1:21). In both passages it is the divine authorship and the character resulting therefrom that are emphasized. Scripture is in view in both passages. Even in 2 Peter 1:21 this is apparent from the preceding verse which defines "prophecy" as "prophecy of scripture," or, as we might say, inscripturated prophecy. These two texts have closer relationship to one another than we might be disposed to think. For in the usage of Scripture the Word of God, the breath of God, and the Spirit of God are closely related. And when Paul says "all scripture is God-breathed," he is saying nothing less than that all Scripture is God's speech, God's voice invested with all the authority and power belonging to his utterance. Peter explains how what is given through the agency of men can be God's speech—"as borne by the Holy Spirit men spoke from God."

We think also of the words of our Lord: "Till heaven and earth pass one jot or one tittle shall in no wise pass from the law, till all be fulfilled" (Matt. 5:18); "the scripture cannot be broken" (John 10:35). In both passages it is the inviolability of Scripture that is asserted.

There are not only these express passages. There is a mass of witness derived from appeal to Scripture in ways that imply its finality, its divine authority, and its equivalence to God's word or speech. For our Lord, "Scripture says" is equivalent to "God says." And Paul, when referring to the body of Scripture committed to Israel, can speak of it as "the oracles of God" (Rom. 3:2).

Here then we have the verdict of Scripture. To avow any lower estimate is to impugn the witness of our Lord himself and that is to assail the dependability and veracity of him who is the truth (John 14:6). And it is also to impugn the reliability of the Holy Spirit who is also the truth as well as the Spirit of truth (1 John 5:6; John 16:13). If we reject the witness of both to the character of that upon which we must rely for our knowledge of the whole content of faith and hope, then we have no foundation of veracity on which to rest. It was the foundation of all faith, confidence, and certitude that the apostle appealed to when he said, "Let God be true, but every man a liar" (Rom. 3:4). It is significant that he forthwith corroborated this truth by appeal to Scripture.

The Context of This Witness

The doctrine of the infallibility of Scripture is derived from the witness of Scripture. It is equally necessary to bear in mind that this witness is to be understood in the context of Scripture as a whole. Any doctrine severed from the total structure of revelation is out of focus. It is necessary to insist on this for two reasons.

First, it is possible to give formal confession to the infallibility of Scripture and yet belie this confession in dealing with it. The dogma of infallibility implies that Scripture is itself the revelatory Word of God, that it is the living and authoritative voice or speech of God. Unless we are arrested by that Word and summoned by it into his presence, unless we bow in reverence before that Word and accord to it the finality that belongs to it as God's oracular utterance, then our confession is only formal.

Second, unless we assess infallibility in the light of the data with which Scripture provides us, we shall be liable to judge infallibility by criteria to which Scripture does not conform. This is one of the most effective ways of undermining biblical infallibility.

The inspiration of Scripture involves verbal inspiration. If it did not carry with it the inspiration of the words, it would not be inspiration at all. Words are the media of communication. It is nothing less than verbal inspiration that Paul affirms when he says in 1 Corinthians 2:13, "combining spiritual things with spiritual." He is speaking of truths taught by the Spirit, as the preceding clauses indicate. But when we say "words" we mean words in relationship, in grammatical and syntactical relationship, first of all, then in the broader contextual relationship, and last of all in relation to the whole content and structure of revelation as deposited in Scripture. They are words with the meaning which Scripture, interpreted in the light of Scripture, determines. They are Spirit-inspired words in the sense in which they were intended by the Holy Spirit. This is to say that the sense and intent of Scripture is Scripture and not the meaning we may arbitrarily impose upon it.

When the Scripture uses anthropomorphic terms with reference to God and his actions, we must interpret accordingly and not predicate of God the limitations which belong to us men. When Scripture conveys truth to us by the mode of apocalyptic vision, we cannot find the truth signified in the details of the vision literalised. If Scripture uses the language of common usage and experience or observation, we are not to accuse it of error because it does not use the language of a particular science, language which few could understand and which becomes obsolete with the passing phases of scientific advancement. The Scripture does not make itself ridiculous by conforming to what pedants might require.

There are numerous considerations that must be taken into account derived from the study of Scripture data. And it is a capital mistake to think that the criteria of infallibility are those that must conform to our preconceived notions or to our arbitrarily adopted norms.

Conclusion

The doctrine of infallibility is not peripheral. What is at stake is the character of the witness which the Scripture provides for the whole compass of our faith. It is concerned with the nature of the only revelation which we possess respecting God's will for our salvation, the only revelation by which we are brought into saving encounter with him who is God manifest in the flesh, the only revelation by which we may be introduced into that fellowship which is eternal life, and the only revelation by which we may be guided in that pilgrimage to the city which hath the foundations, whose builder and maker is God. In a word the interests involved are those of faith, love, and hope.

The Finality and Sufficiency of Scripture

In the Westminster Confession of Faith the finality of Scripture is expressed in these terms: "The Old Testament in Hebrew . . . and the New Testament in Greek . . . , being immediately inspired by God, and by his singular care and providence kept pure in all ages, are therefore authentical; so as, in all controversies of religion, the church is finally to appeal unto them" (WCF 1.8). "The supreme Judge, by which all controversies of religion are to be determined, and all decrees of councils, opinions of ancient writers, doctrines of men, and private spirits, are to be examined and in whose sentence we are to rest, can be no other but the Holy Spirit speaking in the Scripture" (WCF 1.10). This statement of the case is oriented admittedly to the refutation of Rome's appeal to tradition and the voice of the church on the one hand, and to the fanatical claim to special revelation by means of mystical inner light on the other. These divergent positions are still with us and the finality of Scripture as conceived of and formulated by the Westminster Assembly more than three centuries ago is still relevant and worthy of careful examination.

There is one clause in this formulation sometimes misunderstood and mis-applied. It is the clause "the Holy Spirit speaking in the Scripture." This does not refer to the internal testimony of "the Holy Spirit bearing witness by and with the Word in our hearts." With this the Confession had dealt in section 5, which is concerned with the agency by which "our full persuasion and assurance of the infallible truth and divine authority," of Scripture are induced. But in section 10 the Confession is dealing with the Scripture as canon, and uses the expression "the Holy Spirit speaking in the Scripture" to remind us that Scripture is not a dead word but the living and abiding speech of the Holy Spirit. The Reformers needed to emphasize this quality of Scripture in order to offset the plea of Rome that a living voice is necessary for the faith and guidance of the Church and also to meet the same argument of enthusiasts for the inner voice of the Spirit in the believer. The Confession had earlier in section 6 enunciated the sufficiency of Scripture. In section x it is the correlative quality, the finality, that is reflected on, but formulated with a finesse of expression that is of relevance for us today in a context that the divines of the Assembly could not have anticipated.

As we read a great deal of the theological output of the present day, the output that claims the greatest amount of attention, we find that one of its most striking features is the well-nigh total absence of any attempt to expound or be regulated in thought by the Scripture itself. This is because the regulative principle of the Reformation, especially of its Reformed exponents, has been abandoned, and with it, by necessity, the finality of Scripture. No one has been given more attention in the last two years than John A. T. Robinson, Bishop of Woolwich, and perhaps no one has been given as much. We are shocked, no doubt, when we read *Honest to God* [Philadelphia: Westminster Press, 1963] and *The New Reformation?* [Philadelphia: Westminster Press, 1965], and we wonder how far removed from the whole biblical framework of thought and feeling a bishop of the Church of England can be. While we may be in sympathy with Dr. Robinson in his devastating criticism, for example, of the colossus of organizational structure found in so many denominations and particularly in his own, while we must agree that the professing church has failed to meet the situation of a secularized generation, and while we may admire his courage in exposing the sterility of a church that has lived on its fat and the fat is running out, yet we cannot but be appalled by the complete disparity between the basic patterns of his thought and those that Scripture would dictate and create. All of this lies on the face of the books I have mentioned.

But perhaps we should not be surprised. Our surprise arises, I fear, from our failure to assess the significance of what has been going on for a hundred years or more within the Protestant camp. We are suddenly awakened by the outspokenness of John Woolwich. But all of this and more is implicit in seeds sown long before we were born, when the axe was laid at the root of the tree in the denial of the veracity of Scripture. Incipient denials may take decades to work out their consequences and bear their bitterest fruit. But the fruit is now being borne, and we can see it not only in the realm of doctrine and faith but in the staggering proportions of moral disintegration.

When we speak of the sufficiency and finality of Scripture, we must, first of all, assess what Scripture is. There is no validity in the claim to finality unless the high estimate involved in finality is grounded in our conception of what Scripture is. It is here that we must appreciate the significance of inscripturation. For when we speak of Scripture we refer to what is written and, therefore, to inscripturated word as distinguished from word communicated by other means. The finality of Scripture has for us a distinctive import because of the place we occupy in the history of God's unfolding redemptive will. There is a term that is much in use, *Heilsgeschichte*, salvation history. I want to make use of that concept in its true and proper application. It is all-important in our theme.

There were periods in the history of God's redemptive revelation when the finality of Scripture had no meaning. There was no inscripturated revelatory Word. God's mind and will were communicated and transmitted by other methods. Even when revelation began to be committed to writing and was therefore to some extent inscripturated, there were centuries of redemptive history in which the finality of Scripture did not have for the church the precise import it has for us today. Undoubtedly there was a finality to what had been written. This is evident in the finality which our Lord himself attached to what was written. "It is written" and "Thus saith the Scripture" were for him the formulae of irrefutable appeal. And yet his own teaching was, in terms of his own claims, invested with a finality. "Heaven and earth shall pass away, but my words shall not pass away." And beyond what he had taught them he gave to his disciples the assurance that, when the Holy Spirit as the Spirit of truth would come, he would guide them into all truth, and that it was, therefore, expedient that he himself should depart in order that he might send the Spirit unto them for this purpose.

It is apparent that revelation was not complete even with the advent of the Lord of glory himself. And so when he ascended on high there was not to extant Scripture the finality of which we speak now, the reason being that the revelatory process was still in operation. Unless we believe that revelation is still in process as it was in the days of the prophets, in the days of our Lord, and in the days of the apostles subsequent to our Lord's ascension, then Scripture occupies for us an exclusive place and performs an exclusive function as the only extant mode of revelation. It is granted by those with whom we are particularly concerned in this address that Scripture does not continue to be written, that it is a closed canon. Once this is admitted, then we must entertain, what our opponents are not willing to grant, namely, that conception of Scripture taught and pre-supposed by our Lord and his apostles, and insist that it is this conception that must be applied to the whole canon of Scripture. Since we no longer have prophets, since we do not have our Lord with us as he was with the disciples, and since we do not have new organs of revelation as in apostolic times, Scripture in its total extent, according to the conception entertained by our Lord and his apostles, is the only revelation of the mind and will of God available to us. This is what the finality of Scripture means for us; it is the only extant revelatory Word of God.

There is a position pleaded with a good deal of plausibility and with vehement insistence, that this view of Scripture incarcerates and petrifies the Word of God, particularly that it deprives revelation of its personal character and thus of the personal encounter which revelation involves. The argument is that Christ is the incarnate Word, that he is the revelation of God, and that he is the centrum of Scripture itself. Scripture is the medium of encounter with him, and only in him is God manifest. All that is claimed for the centrality of Christ we not only admit but unreservedly proclaim. But with all this emphasis, and even more respecting the uniqueness of Christ in the history of revelation and redemption, can we fail to discern the place of Scripture in the revelation that Christ is, and in the encounter with him? It is only in and through Scripture that we have any knowledge of or contact with him who is the image of the invisible God. As in the days of his flesh the disciples had no understanding of Jesus, or faith in him apart from his spoken word, so we are wholly dependent upon their witness, witness indeed anticipated and foreshadowed in the Old Testament, but embodied and inscripturated in the New. Without Scripture we are excluded completely from the knowledge, faith, and fellowship of him who is the effulgence of the Father's glory and the transcript of his being, as destitute of the Word of life as the disciples would have been if Jesus had not disclosed himself through his spoken word; and not only from the knowledge, faith and fellowship of the Son, but also from the knowledge and fellowship of the Father and the Spirit.

Our dependence upon Scripture is total. Without it we are bereft of revelatory Word from God, from the counsel of God "respecting all things necessary for his own glory, man's salvation, faith and life" (WCF 1.6). Thus when the church or any of its spokesmen fails to accord to Scripture this eminence, and fails to make it the only rule of faith and life, then the kind of affront offered to Father, Son and Holy Spirit is that of substituting the wisdom of man for the wisdom of God, and human invention for divine institution. As we read the literature that claims the admiration of so many, we discern the tragedy of Satanic deception that can be indicted as no less than apostasy from the simplicity that is unto Christ. And this is apparent not only in the overt divergences from and denials of the witness of Scripture, but also in the confused conglomeration of ideas and proposals, confused and self-contradictory to some extent because of the attempt to fuse a modicum of Christian tradition with what is derived from the fountains of unbelief.

The finality of Scripture, if it has any meaning, demands that those who profess commitment to Christ and the church in its collective capacity, direct all thought, activity, and objective by this Word as the revelation to us of God's mind and will.

There is no gainsaying the fact that the situation in which we are placed today is one of peculiar gravity. There is, as the spokesmen of heterodoxy are constantly reminding us, the intense secularism of the man of today. To this mentality the supernaturalness of the gospel and of the revelation that embodies the gospel is wholly irrelevant. The leading writers of the Protestant fold are doing us the service of dinning this into our ears, and we may not close our ears to the thunder. They have, to a large extent, analysed this modern framework of thought and attitude in a way that we must reckon with in our witness to the gospel. It is, however, as we are confronted with this mentality that we must appreciate with renewed confidence the implications of the finality of Scripture and the correlative doctrine of its sufficiency. It is the challenge of the secularized mind, the technologically conditioned mind, and the supposed irrelevance to this outlook of the gospel as historically understood, that have constrained the leading exponents of today's Protestantism to reconstruct the gospel so that it will be relevant. This is the capital sin of our generation. Taking their starting point from the modern man's mentality they have revised the gospel to meet the dilemma in which the church has found itself in the face of wholesale indifference and hostility. But the question for us is: how are we, holding to the sufficiency and finality of Scripture, going to meet the secularism, or whatever else the attitude may be, of this modern man?

Here, I believe, we have too often made the mistake of not taking seriously the doctrine we profess. If Scripture is the inscripturated revelation of the gospel and of God's mind and will, if it is the only revelation of this character that we possess, then it is this revelation in all its fulness, richness, wisdom, and power that must be applied to man in whatever religious, moral, mental situation he is to be found. It is because we have not esteemed and prized the perfection of Scripture and its finality, that we have resorted to other techniques, expedients, and methods of dealing with the dilemma that confronts us all if we are alive to the needs of this hour. Some of us may have relied upon our heritage, our tradition, and may have been content with the reiteration of certain traditional formulae prescribed for us by our forefathers in a noble tradition, and with the reproduction of patterns eminently appropriate and fruitful in past generations. I do not say but signal blessing from God attends such a ministry. God blesses inadequate witness in the sovereignty of his grace. Some, on the other hand, may be so enamoured of modernity, that without abandoning a basically sound proclamation of the gospel, they have nonetheless been to such an extent influenced by the flabbiness of present-day thinking that witness to the whole counsel of God has suffered at the points of both breadth and depth. Again, I do not say that God does not bless such witness though it be impoverished and to some extent compromising. But what I do say, and with all due emphasis, is that both are failing to bring to faithful expression the finality and suffi-ciency of Scripture. Let us learn from our tradition, let us prize our heritage, let us enter into other men's labours; but let us also know that it is not the tradition of the past, not a precious heritage, and not the labours of the fathers, that are to serve this generation and this hour, but the Word of the living and abiding God deposited for us in Holy Scripture, and this Word as ministered by the church. And we must bring forth from its inexhaustible treasures, in exposition, proclamation, and application—application to every sphere of life—what is the wisdom and power of God for man in this age in all the particularity of his need, as for man in every age. There will then be commanding relevance, for it will be the message from God in the unction and power of the Spirit, not derived *from* the modern mentality, but declared *to* the modern mentality in all the desperateness of its anxiety and misery.

Likewise, let us not refuse any of the parcels of enlightenment on many aspects of truth which even this confused generation may bring us. But let us beware of the controlling framework of modern thinking lest its patterns and presuppositions become our own, and then, before we know it, we are carried away by a current of thought and attitude that makes the sufficiency and finality of Scripture not only extraneous but alien to our way of thinking. Sadly enough this is what has taken place so often, and there comes to be no basic affinity between the faith entertained and proclaimed, on the one hand, and that which the implications of the sufficiency and finality of Scripture demand and constrain, on the other.

Let us reassess the significance of *Scripture* as the Word of God and let us come to a deeper appreciation of the deposit of revelation God in his grace and wisdom has given unto us as the living Word of God, sharper than any two-edged sword, and let us know and experience its power in its sufficiency for every exigency of our individual and collec-tive need, until the day dawn and the day-star arise in our hearts. "All scripture is given by inspiration of God and is profitable for doctrine, for reproof, for correction, for the instruction which is in righteousness, that the man of God may be perfect, thoroughly furnished unto every good work" (2 Tim. 3:16).

The Unity of the Old and New Testaments[19]

There are certain texts that are familiar or at least ought to be. They teach us the place in history occupied by the New Testament or, more precisely, the new covenant economy (Gal. 4:4; Heb. 9:26; 1 Cor. 10:11). The New Testament era is "the fulness of the time," "the consummation of the ages," "the ends of the ages," the consummating era of this world's history. Correlative with this characterization is "the last days" (Acts 2:17; Heb. 1:2; 1 John 2:18). These began with the coming of Christ: So the world period is the last days.

This implies ages of this world's history that were not the last days; they were prior, preparatory, anticipatory. The last days are characterized by two comings, notable, unprecedented, indeed astounding—the coming into the world of the Son of God and the Spirit of God. In order to accentuate the marvel of these comings we must say that God came into the world, first in the person of the Son and then in the person of the Holy Spirit. They came by radically different modes and for different functions. But both are spoken of as comings and they are both epochal events. These comings not only introduce and characterize the last days; they create or constitute them.

Nothing in the history of the world could be comparably significant, and that is why the era is invested with such momentous finality so as to be the fulness of the time, the consummation of the ages.

These comings are not to be conceived of as continuous with and an extension of creation, as if the revelation given in creation required these comings in order to perfect it and put the cope stone upon it. They are both related to and the provisions of grace for the exigencies created by sin. In a word, they are redemptive, reparatory, restorative in character. The revelation involved is always redemptively conditioned, redemptively revelatory and revelationally redemptive.

In the nature of the case the Old Testament pointed forward; the New realized and fulfilled. But in a true sense, as will be shown later, the realities which give character and such momentous significance to the New Testament are those that give meaning to the Old Testament. In this sense the Old Testament revelation is derived from and based upon realities that transpired in the New, realities summed up in the coming of the Son and of the Holy Spirit. The New embodies the archetypal, heavenly, transcendent realities that validate and explain the Old Testament revelation and the corresponding acts of redemptive grace. This can also be stated in reverse.

With this perspective in view we see the unity. And nothing demonstrates the unity more than to observe how the pivotal events connected with the coming of the Son and of the Spirit are anticipated and disclosed in the Old Testament.

The great miracle of history is the coming of the Son of God. He came by becoming man, by taking human nature into union with his divine person. The result was that *he* was both God and man, God in uncurtailed Godhood, in the fulness of divine being and attributes, and man in the integrity of human nature with all its sinless infirmities and limitations, uniting in one person infinitude and finitude, the uncreated and the created. This is the great mystery of history. And since Christianity is the central and commanding fact of history, it is the mystery of Christianity, "the mystery of godliness" (1 Tim. 3:16). So unique is this fact that we might well think that disclosure would have to wait for the fulfilment. But

19. From the author's notes of an address given to the Christian Union of the University of Dundee, 1970.

astounding is the fact that the Old Testament furnishes the elements, and we read: "Unto us a child is born, unto us a son is given" (Isa. 9:6). Again: "There shall come a shoot out of the stock of Jesse" (Isa. 11:1).

Observe the precision. When the Son of God came into the world, it was not as Adam without genealogy. He was made of a woman and of a particular line—"made of the seed of David" (Rom. 1:3). Hence Isaiah writes "a child is born," "a shoot out of the stock of Jesse." In his incarnation there is genetic continuity with the human race.

Yet, though made of the woman and of the seed of David, he did not come by ordinary generation. He was begotten by the Holy Spirit (Matt. 1:20–21; Luke 1:26–35). The Old Testament announces this (Isa. 7:14). And so Matthew: "And so all this was done that it might be fulfilled which was spoken of the Lord by the prophet, saying, Behold a virgin shall be with child, and shall bring forth a son" (1:22–23).

When the Son of God came, the first signal event in his introduction to Israel was his baptism by John. There are two outstanding features as a result—the witness of the Father and enduement with the Holy Spirit. "This is my beloved Son, in whom I am well pleased" (Matt. 3:17). And Jesus "saw the Spirit of God descending like a dove, and lighting upon him" (Matt. 3:16). Both have their counterpart in the Old Testament (Ps. 2:7; Isa. 42:1; 11:2; 61:1).

When we take account of Jesus' character, he was meek and lowly in heart. Probably this prompted John the Baptist's question (Matt. 11:3) and Jesus' reply is corroborative (11:4–6). The prophets did not fail to disclose this (Isa. 42:1–7; Ps. 72:2–4).

But we must hasten to the climactic events of Jesus' commission—death upon the cross and resurrection. No passage in Scripture is more replete with delineation than Isaiah 52:13–53:12. Note the personage, the Lord's action, the Servant's action, the spectacle, the reason, the triumphal sequel.

With reference to the cross there is the relation to the powers of darkness (John 12:31; Col. 2:15; Heb. 2:14; 1 John 3:8). The first promise is in these terms (Gen. 3:15).

The resurrection of Christ is clearly a theme of the Old Testament (Pss. 16:10–11; 68:18).

The events of New Testament realization, as noted, afford validity and meaning to the Old Testament. They not only validate and explain; they are the ground and warrant for the revelatory and redemptive events of the Old Testament period. This can be seen in the first redemptive promise (Gen. 3:15). We have a particularly striking illustration in Matthew 2:15: "Out of Egypt have I called my son." In Hosea 11:1 (cf. Num. 24:8) this refers to the emancipation of Israel from Egypt. But in Matthew 2:15 it is applied to Christ and it is easy to allege that this is an example of unwarranted application of Old Testament passages to New Testament events particularly characteristic of Matthew. But it is Matthew, as other New Testament writers, who has the perspective of organic relationship and dependence. The deliverance of Israel from Egypt found its validation, basis, and reason in what was fulfilled in Christ. So the calling of Christ out of Egypt has the primacy as archetype, though not historical priority. In other words, the type is derived from the archetype or antitype. Hence not only the propriety but necessity of finding in Hosea 11:1 the archetype that gave warrant to the redemption of Israel from Egypt.

In this perspective, therefore, we must view both Testaments. The unity is one of organic interdependence and derivation. The Old Testament has no meaning except as it is related to the realities that give character to and create the New Testament era as the fulness of time, the consummation of the ages.

The Importance and Relevance of the Westminster Confession

The Westminster Assembly was called by ordinance of both Houses of Parliament and met for the first time on July 1, 1643. Nearly all the sessions were held in the Jerusalem Chamber in Westminster Abbey.

The first work which the Assembly undertook was the revision of the Thirty-Nine Articles of the Church of England. On October 12, 1643, when the Assembly was engaged in the revision of the sixteenth Article, there came an order from both Houses of Parliament to treat of such discipline and government as would be most agreeable to God's Word, and most apt to procure and preserve the peace of the Church at home and nearer agreement with the Church of Scotland and other Reformed Churches abroad, and also to treat of a directory for worship. It was in pursuance of this order that the Assembly prepared what are known as "The Form of Presbyterial Church Government" and "The Directory for the Public Worship of God."

On August 20, 1644, a committee was appointed by the Assembly to prepare matter for a Confession of Faith. A great deal of the attention of the Assembly was devoted to this Confession during the years 1645 and 1646. It was not until December 4, 1646, that the text of the Confession was completed and presented to both Houses of Parliament as the 'humble advice' of the divines. This did not, however, include the proof texts. These were not presented to the Houses until April 29, 1647.

The amount of work and time expended on the Confession of Faith will stagger us in these days of haste and alleged activism. But the influence exerted all over the world by the Confession can only be understood in the light of the diligent care and prayerful devotion exercised in its composition.

The Westminster Confession is the last of the great Reformation creeds. We should expect, therefore, that it would exhibit distinctive features. The Westminster Assembly had the advantage of more than a century of Protestant creedal formulation. Reformed theology had by the 1640s attained to a maturity that could not be expected a hundred or even seventy-five years earlier. Controversies had developed in the interval between the death of Calvin, for example, and the Westminster Assembly, that compelled theologians to give to Reformed doctrine fuller and more precise definition. In many circles today there is the tendency to depreciate, if not deplore, the finesse of theological definition which the Confession exemplifies. This is an attitude to be deprecated. A growing faith grounded in the perfection and finality of Scripture requires increasing particularity and cannot consist with the generalities that make room for error. No creed of the Christian Church is comparable to that of Westminster in respect of the skill with which the fruits of fifteen centuries of Christian thought have been preserved, and at the same time examined anew and clarified in the light of that fuller understanding of God's Word which the Holy Spirit has imparted.

The Westminster Confession was the work of devoted men and the fruit of painstaking, consecrated labour. But it was still the work of fallible men. For that reason it must not be esteemed as sacrosanct and placed in the same category as the Bible. The latter is the only infallible rule of faith and life. The framers of the Confession were careful to remind us of this. "All synods or councils, since the Apostles' times, whether general or particular, may err; and many have erred. Therefore they are not to be made the rule of faith, or practice; but to be used as a help in both" (WCF 31.4). It is not superfluous to take note of this reminder. We are still under the necessity of avoiding the Romish error. One of the most eloquent statements of the Confession is that of 1.6: "The whole counsel of God concerning all things necessary for his own glory, man's salvation, faith and life, is either expressly set down in Scripture, or by good and necessary consequence may be deduced from Scripture: unto which nothing at any time is to be added, whether by new revelations of the Spirit, or traditions of men."

In the category to which the Confession belongs, it has no peer. No chapter in the Confession evinces this assessment more than that which the framers chose for good and obvious reasons to place at the beginning—"Of the Holy Scripture." In the whole field of formulation respecting the doctrine of Scripture nothing is comparable to that which we find in these ten sections. With the most recent deviations from biblical doctrine in mind, it is as if this chapter had been drawn up but yesterday in order to controvert them. Section i, for example, is so carefully constructed that, if chronology were forgotten, we might think that what is being guarded is the doctrine that Scripture itself is the revelatory Word of God in opposition to the present-day dialectical theology which regards it as merely the witness to revelation. When the Confession says, "Therefore it pleased the Lord . . . to commit the same wholly unto writing." what is in view as committed wholly to writing is *God's self-revelation* and *the declaration of his will unto his church*. And so in the next section we find that Holy Scripture is stated to be synonymous with, or defined in terms of "the Word of God written."

Again, the distinction drawn so clearly between the ground upon which the *authority* of Scripture rests (section 4) and the way by which this authority is attested to us (section 5) is one exactly framed to meet a current error. Those influenced by this error who aver that the Confession teaches that the authority of Scripture is derived from the "inward work of the Holy Spirit bearing witness by and with the Word in our hearts" (section 5) have failed to pay attention to what is elementary in the sequence of these two sections. The authority rests upon the fact that God is the author of Scripture; it is *our* full persuasion and assurance that is derived from the internal testimony of the Spirit. The Confession could not have been more explicit in setting forth this distinction. Thereby it has given direction for all proper thinking on the question of authority.

One of the most controversial chapters in the Confession is the third, "Of God's Eternal Decree." The development of this chapter and the finesse of formulation are masterful. There are three subjects dealt with, the decree of God in its cosmic dimensions, the decree of God as it respects men and angels, and the decree of God as it respects men. In connection with the first, the all-inclusiveness of the decree, embracing sin itself, is asserted, but with equal emphasis also that "God is not the author of sin, nor is violence offered to the will of the creatures" (section 1). In connection with angels and men, the statement most offensive to critics is that some are "foreordained to everlasting death" (section 3). What is too frequently overlooked is that this statement, as it has respect to men, is explicated more fully in section 7. Here the doctrine, often called that of reprobation, is analyzed as to its elements in a way unsurpassed in the whole compass of theological literature. Nowhere else in so few words is this delicate topic handled with such meticulous care and discrimination. The concluding section (8) places the "high mystery of predestination" in proper perspective in relation to human responsibility and the comfort to be derived from it for all those who sincerely obey the gospel. Sovereign election of grace is not alien to the gospel. It is a tenet of the gospel, and the fount from which the gospel flows, as well as the guarantee that the gospel will not fail of its purpose.

All true theology is realistic; it takes the data of revelation and the facts of life seriously. At no point does a theology governed by sentiment rather than by facts quibble with the teaching of Scripture more than on the subject of sin. The Confession is not afraid to enunciate the doctrine of total depravity, and thus it says unequivocally that by original corruption "we are utterly indisposed, disabled, and made opposite to all good, and wholly inclined to all evil" (WCF 6.4). Less than this is not a true transcript of the biblical teaching that there is none that doeth good, no, not even one, that the imagination of the thought of man's heart is only evil continually, and that the carnal mind is enmity against God. The severity of the Scripture's indictment, reflected in the Confessional teaching, is complemental to the radical concept of grace which the Confession entertains. However necessary it is to be true to the data of Scripture and the facts of life on the doctrine of depravity, this would only seal despair, were it not that grace is as thorough as sin is total. Herein lies the grandeur of sovereign grace. "Those of mankind that are predestinated unto life, God, before the foundation of the world was laid, according to His eternal and immutable purpose, and the secret counsel and good pleasure of His will, hath chosen, in Christ, unto everlasting glory, out of his mere free grace and love" (WCF 3.5).

It is this theme of sovereign grace and love that the Confession pursues and unfolds in its various aspects. One of the most remarkable chapters for fulness of doctrine and condensation of expression is "Of Christ the Mediator" (WCF 8). The whole doctrine of the person of Christ, of his finished work and continued ministry is set forth. If we are thinking of Chalcedon and the doctrine then formulated, nothing is more adequate or succinct than "that two whole, perfect, and distinct natures, the Godhead and the manhood, were inseparably joined together in one person, without conversion, composition, or confusion" (WCF 8.2). If we are thinking of the atonement in both its nature and design, what in so few words could be more inclusive than: "The Lord Jesus, by his perfect obedience, and sacrifice of himself, which he, through the eternal Spirit, once offered up unto God, hath fully satisfied the justice of his Father; and purchased, not only reconciliation, but an everlasting inheritance in the kingdom of heaven, for all those whom the Father hath given unto him"? (WCF 8.5).

When the Confession deals with the application of redemption, it is noteworthy how the various topics are arranged. It sets forth first the phases which are the actions of God—Calling, Justification, Adoption, Sanctification (WCF 10–13)—and then those which are concerned with human response—Faith, Repentance, Good Works, Perseverance, Assurance of Grace (WCF 14–23). Undoubtedly, the consideration that salvation is of the Lord and that all saving response in men is the fruit of God's grace dictated this order. It is consonant with the pervasive emphasis upon the sovereignty of grace.

That the application should be regarded as having its inception in effectual calling should not be overlooked. This is where Scripture places it, and it is rightly conceived of as an efficacious translation out of a state of sin and death into one of grace and salvation by Jesus Christ. Calling is not to be defined in terms of human response. The latter is the *answer* to the call. This perspective in the Confession needs to be appreciated—effectual calling is an act of God and of God alone. There is, however, one shortcoming in the definition the Confession provides. Calling is specifically the action of God the Father and this accent does not appear in the Confession.

In the two Catechisms produced by the Westminster Assembly, it is striking to observe how large a proportion is devoted to the exposition of the ten commandments. This shows how jealous the divines were in the matter of the Christian life. A similar proportion is not devoted to the law of God in the Confession. But the emphasis is proportionate to what a Confession should incorporate. It is well to note what is said about good works (WCF 16), the law of God (WCF 19), Christian liberty (WCF 20), the Sabbath day (WCF 21), marriage and divorce (WCF 24). Grace has often been turned into license. No creed guards against this distortion more than the Confession of the Westminster Assembly. Grace pure and sovereign is the theme throughout. But grace is unto holiness, and it confirms and enhances human responsibility. "The moral law doth for ever bind all, as well justified persons as others, to the obedience thereof. . . . Neither doth Christ, in the gospel, any way dissolve, but much strengthen this obligation" (WCF 19.5).

In days of increasing encroachment upon the liberties which are God-given, the charter of liberty needs again to be resounded: "God alone is Lord of the conscience, and hath left it free from the doctrines and commandments of men which are, in any thing, contrary to his Word, or beside it, in matters of faith or worship" (WCF 20.2). And when the church thinks that the modes of worship are a matter of human discretion, we need to be recalled to the regulative principle that "the acceptable way of worshipping the true God is instituted by himself, and so limited by his own revealed will, that he may not be worshipped according to the imaginations and devices of men, or the suggestions of Satan, under any visible representation, or any other way not prescribed in the holy Scripture" (WCF 21.1). Or, when the sacred ties of matrimony are lightly regarded and even desecrated, what could be more relevant than the principles and restrictions enunciated in chapter 24?

The flabby sentimentality so widespread is not hospitable to the rigour and vigour of a document like the Confession. Its system of truth and way of life do not comport with current patterns of thought and behaviour. This is the reason for the collapse of the religious and moral standards which our Christian faith represents. It is folly to think that we can retain or reclaim Christian culture on any lower level than that which the Westminster Assembly defined. Christian thought may never be stagnant. When it ceases to be progressive, it declines. But we do not make progress by discarding our heritage. We build upon it or, more accurately, we grow from it.

Oftentimes it is pleaded that the Christian message must be adapted to the modern man. It is true that the message must be proclaimed to modern man, and to modern man in the context in which he lives and in language he can understand. But it is much more true and important to plead that modern man must be adapted to the gospel. It is not true that the doctrine of the Confession is irrelevant to the modern man. It is indeed meaningless to him until he listens to it. But when a man today becomes earnest about the Christian faith, when he gives heed to Scripture as the Word of God, when he faces up to the challenge of unbelieving ways of thought and life and demands the answer which Christianity provides, he cannot rest with anything less than the consistency and vigour which the Confession exemplifies. Unbelief is potent and subtle, and the believer requires the truth of God in its fullest expression if he is to be furnished to faithful witness and confession.

Part Nine
The Birth of Biblical Theology

The discipline of biblical theology within Reformed circles can be traced back to the Old Princeton theologian Geerhardus Vos, and it is central, along with the apologetic of Cornelius Van Til, to the theological makeup of Westminster. After offering Vos's foundational definition of the discipline, we turn to its application by Ned B. Stonehouse to the Gospels and by Edmund P. Clowney to preaching. The last three authors tackle specific ramifications of the use of biblical theology in the study of the Bible.

Vos's two texts clarify the nature and task of biblical theology. The first is his inaugural address as professor of biblical theology at Princeton Seminary, in which he communicates that the redemptive plan of God culminating in the work of Christ provides the unifying framework for the understanding of the Bible. Unlike other biblical theologians of his time, Vos maintained a high view of Scripture and a commitment to historic confessional Christianity. The second text is a selection from the introduction to his *Biblical Theology*, which is the fruit of his teaching on this topic. Characteristically, the work deals with both Testaments, and again he views Scripture as the unfolding of the plan of redemption. He relates the discipline of biblical theology to other theological disciplines and lays out the practical implications of biblical theology. Stonehouse, a founding father of Westminster and a disciple of Vos, developed as a New Testament scholar a particular expertise in the study of the Synoptic Gospels. The chapter reproduced here deals with the witness of Christ to the Old Testament. Stonehouse shows how Jesus self-consciously fulfilled the predictions of the Old Testament. The argument of this text has implication for both the authority of the Old Testament and that of Christ. Clowney, professor of practical theology at Westminster as well as its first president, had a keen interest in biblical theology. Of particular concern to him was the integration of this discipline to preaching in the churches. In this article, a redemptive-historical reading of the Old Testament enables him to sustain a Christological understanding while avoiding the twin danger of "Moralism" and "Allegory." This text expresses a passion for preaching centered on Christ and for expounding the Old Testament.

The two texts by Vern S. Poythress apply his knowledge of philosophical hermeneutics to the interpretation of the Bible. In the first essay, he discusses a redemptive-historical understanding of the dual authorship of the Bible (divine and human), in which God is sovereign over the production of Scripture. Given the supernatural origin of the Bible, the meaning of a passage goes at times beyond the intention of its human author. In the second text, taken from *God-Centered Biblical Interpretation*, he discusses the purpose of the Bible. His hermeneutical approach is characterized by both a Trinitarian outlook and a perspective that builds on Van Til and stays in line with John Frame. Moisés Silva's two chapters, from his book *Has the Church Misread the Bible?*, offer a bridge between biblical theology and the history of interpretation. These texts tackle the following questions from a historical and theological perspective: the relationship between the divine and human aspects of the Bible, the clarity of Scripture in relation to difficult passages, and the Reformed views of tradition and allegory. Finally, Richard B. Gaffin Jr. examines the contribution of the new hermeneutic to the study of the New Testament. He evaluates this movement in theology brought about by both neoorthodox theology and philosophical reflections on interpretation by applying the insights of biblical theology to meet these new challenges; in particular, he expresses that we live in the same redemptive epoch as the writers of the New Testament.

This part describes how biblical theology developed among Reformed theologians with the groundbreaking work of Vos that was carried on at Westminster Seminary. These texts not only offer illustrations of biblical-theological studies, but also provide ways to apply the relatively recent theological discipline to other aspects of the theological curriculum. Finally, because the doctrine of Scripture is intimately bound to its interpretation, these selections further illumine Westminster's views on Scripture, especially by clarifying the nature of its central message.

46

Geerhardus Vos

The Dutch-born theologian and exegete Geerhardus Vos (1862–1949) moved to the United States in his youth. He studied at what would become Calvin Seminary and at Princeton Seminary. He continued postgraduate studies in Berlin and Strasbourg. In Strasbourg he earned a Ph.D. in Oriental languages in 1886. After teaching systematic theology at Calvin Seminary for a short while, he moved to Princeton to occupy the newly formed chair of biblical theology at the seminary in 1893. Within the Reformed community, Vos was a pioneer in his study of the progressive character of biblical theology. Unlike the proponents of biblical theology at the time, however, Vos maintained a high view of Scripture and a commitment to orthodox Reformed theology. Biblical theology in the tradition of Vos, together with Van Til's presuppositional apologetics, is one of the hallmarks of the Westminster tradition. Among Vos's works on biblical theology of both the Old and New Testaments, two deserve special mention: *The Teaching of Jesus concerning the Kingdom of God and the Church* (1903) and *The Pauline Eschatology* (1930). Regarding the former, Stonehouse thought that every minister should read it once a year. The latter is a seminal work for the study of Paul's theology.

"The Idea of Biblical Theology as a Science and as a Theological Discipline" (1894) is Vos's inaugural address to the chair of biblical theology at Princeton Theological Seminary. This programmatic piece of work in the field of Reformed biblical theology was reprinted in the collection of Vos's shorter writings. When modern biblical scholars were denying the integrity of the Scriptures, Vos established himself as the father of orthodox biblical theology. He stressed here the unity of Scripture as the progressive revelation of God. By *progressive* Vos means that God revealed more and more of his plan of redemption in history until that plan reached its climax in the person and work of Christ. Vos's great contribution is explaining how all of Scripture is ultimately a coherent whole. He offers helpful definitions and clarifications of what biblical theology is and its relationship to the other theological disciplines. In particular, systematic theology and biblical theology complement each other.

The next selection is from *Biblical Theology: Old and New Testaments*. This book originated as class material given at Princeton Seminary and was edited by Vos's son Johannes G. Vos. This book covers the whole span of the "History of Special Revelation" (another expression for *biblical theology*) and illustrates well the outworking of Vos's program outlined in his inaugural address. The introduction to his *Biblical Theology*, entitled "The Nature and Method of Biblical Theology," is reprinted here. There Vos advanced the Reformed tradition's understanding of Scripture by explaining how Scripture is organic like a budding flower. By *organic* he meant that there is an inherent unity of meaning in the text throughout its development even as there is an inner unity between the otherwise dissimilar appearances of a seed, a tree, and its fruit. God's plan of redemption becomes clearer as history progresses. The present selection provides a more in-depth explanation and definition of biblical theology and its relations to other theological disciplines. It also touches on its method and practical application. Vos's approach affirms the inspiration of Scripture and the supernatural character of revelation. His commitment to the truth of the Bible is expressed, for instance, in his "Christian Faith and the Truthfulness of Bible History" (1906; see *Shorter Writings*, 458–71).

Bibliography: James T. Dennison Jr. "Geerhardus Vos." Pp. 82–92 in *Bible Interpreters of the 20th Century*. Sinclair B. Ferguson. Introduction to *Grace and Glory: Sermons Preached in the Chapel of Princeton Theological Seminary*, by Geerhardus Vos. Carlisle, PA: Banner of Truth, 1994. Pp. vii–xii. R. B. Gaffin Jr. Introduction to *Redemptive History and Biblical Interpretation: The Shorter Writings of Geerhardus Vos*. Phillipsburg, NJ: Presbyterian and Reformed, 1980. Pp. ix–xxiii. Idem. "Vos, Geerhardus (1862–1949)." P. 269 in *DP&RTA*. Idem. "Vos, Geerhardus (1862–1847)." P. 713 in *NDT*. Anthony A. Hoekema. *The Bible and the Future*. Grand Rapids: Eerdmans, 1979. Pp. 298–301. Richard Lints. "Two Theologies or One? Warfield and Vos on the Nature of Theology." *WTJ* 54, 2 (Fall 1992): 235–53. John Sandys-Wunsch and Laurence Eldredge. "J. P. Gabler and the Distinction between Biblical and Dogmatic Theology: Translation, Commentary, and Discussion of His Originality." *Scottish Journal of Theology* 33, 2 (1980): 133–58. Marion Ann Taylor. *The Old Testament in the Old Princeton School (1812–1929)*. San Francisco: Mellen Research University Press, 1992. Pp. 261–67. Peter J. Wallace. "The Foundations of Reformed Biblical Theology: The Development of Old Testament Theology at Old Princeton, 1812–1932." *WTJ* 59, 1 (Spring 1997): 41–69.

THE IDEA OF BIBLICAL THEOLOGY AS A SCIENCE AND AS A THEOLOGICAL DISCIPLINE[1]

Geerhardus Vos, "The Idea of Biblical Theology as a Science and as a Theological Discipline," in *Redemptive History and Biblical Interpretation: The Shosrter Writings of Geerhardus Vos*, ed. Richard B. Gaffin Jr. (Phillipsburg, NJ: Presbyterian and Reformed, 1980), 3–24.

Mr. President and Gentlemen of the board of directors:

It is with no little hesitation that I enter upon the work to which you have called me and to-day more formally introduced me. In reaching the conclusion that it was my duty to accept the call with which you had honored me, I was keenly alive to the incongruity of

---

1. Inaugural address as professor of biblical theology in Princeton Theological Seminary, delivered in the First Presbyterian Church of Princeton on May 8, 1894. Originally published by Anson D. F. Randolph & Co. (New York, 1894), 40 pp.

my name being associated in the remotest manner with the names of those illustrious men through whom God has glorified Himself in this institution. Some of those at whose feet I used to sit while a student here, are fallen asleep; a smaller number remain until now. The memory of the former as well as the presence of the latter make me realize my weakness even more profoundly than the inherent difficulty of the duties I shall have to discharge. While, however, on the one hand, there is something in these associations that might well fill me with misgivings at this moment, I shall not endeavor to conceal that on the other hand they are to me a source of inspiration. In view of my own insufficiency I rejoice all the more in having behind and around me this cloud of witnesses. I am thoroughly convinced that in no other place or environment could the sacred influences of the past be brought to bear upon me with a purer and mightier impulse to strengthen and inspire me than here. The pledge to which I have just subscribed is itself a symbol of this continuity between the past and the future; and I feel that it will act upon me, not merely by outward restraint, but with an inwardly constraining power, being a privilege as well as an obligation.

Although not a new study, yet Biblical Theology is a new chair, in this Seminary; and this fact has determined the choice of the subject on which I purpose to address you. Under ordinary circumstances, the treatment of some special subject of investigation would have been more appropriate, and perhaps more interesting to you, than a discussion of general principles. But Biblical Theology being a recent arrival in the Seminary curriculum and having been entrusted to my special care and keeping, I consider it my duty to introduce to you this branch of theological science, and to describe, in general terms at least, its nature and the manner in which I hope to teach it.

This is all the more necessary because of the wide divergence of opinion in various quarters concerning the standing of this newest accession to the circle of sacred studies. Some have lauded her to the skies as the ideal of scientific theology, in such extravagant terms as to reflect seriously upon the character of her sisters of greater age and longer standing. Others look upon the new-comer with suspicion, or even openly dispute her right to a place in the theological family. We certainly owe it to her and to ourselves to form a well-grounded and intelligent judgment on this question. I hope that what I shall say will in some degree shed light on the points at issue, and enable you to judge impartially and in accordance with the facts of the case.

The Idea of Biblical Theology as a Science and as a Theological Discipline

Every discussion of what is to be understood by Biblical Theology ought to proceed from a clear understanding of what Theology is in general. Etymology, in many cases a safer guide than *a priori* constructions, tells us that Theology is *knowledge concerning God*, and this primitive definition is fully supported by encyclopedic principles. Only when making Theology knowledge concerning God do we have the right to call it a separate science. Sciences are not formed at haphazard, but according to an objective principle of division. As in general science is bound by its object and must let itself be shaped by reality; so likewise the classification of sciences, the relation of the various members in the body of universal knowledge, has to follow the great lines by which God has mapped out the immense field of the universe. The title of a certain amount of knowledge to be called a separate science depends on its reference to such a separate and specific object as is marked off by these God-drawn lines of distinction. We speak of a science of Biology, because God has made the phenomena of life distinct from those of inorganic being. Now, from this point of view we must say that no science has a clearer title to separate existence than Theology. Between God as the Creator and all other things as created the distinction is absolute. There is not another such gulf within the universe. God, as distinct from the creature, is the only legitimate object of Theology.

It will be seen, however, on a moment's reflection, that Theology is not merely distinguished from the other sciences by its object, but that it also sustains an altogether unique relation to this object, for which no strict analogy can be found elsewhere. In all the other sciences man is the one who of himself takes the first step in approaching the objective world, in subjecting it to his scrutiny, in compelling it to submit to his experiments—in a word, man is the one who proceeds actively to make nature reveal her facts and her laws. In Theology this relation between the subject and object is reversed. Here it is God who takes the first step to approach man for the purpose of disclosing His nature, nay, who creates man in order that He many have a finite mind able to receive the knowledge of His infinite perfections. In Theology the object, far from being passive, by the act of creation first posits the subject over against itself, and then as the living God proceeds to impart to this subject that to which of itself it would have no access. For "the things of God none knoweth, save the Spirit of God" [1 Cor. 2:11]. Strictly speaking, therefore, we should say that not God in and for Himself, but God in so far as He has revealed Himself, is the object of Theology.

Though applying to Theology in the abstract and under all circumstances, this unique character has been emphasized by the entrance of sin into the human race. In his sinful condition, while retaining some knowledge of God, man for all pure and adequate information in divine things is absolutely dependent on that new self-disclosure of God which we call supernatural revelation. By the new birth and the illumination of the mind darkened through sin, a new subject is created. By the objective self-manifestation of God as the Redeemer, a new order of things is called into being. And by the depositing of the truth concerning this new order of things in the Holy Scriptures, the human mind is enabled to obtain that new knowledge which is but the reflection in the regenerate consciousness of an objective world of divine acts and words.

This being so, it follows immediately that the beginning of our Theology consists in the appropriation of that supernatural process by which God has made Himself the object of our knowledge. We are not left to our own choice here, as to where we shall begin our theological study. The very nature of Theology requires us to begin with those branches which relate to the revelation-basis of our science. Our attitude from the outset must be a dependent and receptive one. To let the image of God's self-revelation in the Scriptures mirror itself as fully and clearly as possible in his mind, is the first and most important duty of every theologian. And it is in accordance with this principle that, in the development of scientific theology through the ages, a group of studies have gradually been separated from the rest and begun to form a smaller organism among themselves, inasmuch as the receptive attitude of the theological consciousness toward the source of revelation was the common idea underlying and controlling them. This group is usually designated by the name Exegetical Theology. Its formation was not a matter of mere accident, nor the result of definite agreement among theologians; the immanent law of development of the science, as rooted in its origin, has brought it about in a natural manner.

In classifications of this kind general terms are apt to acquire more or less indefinite meanings. They tend to become formulas used for the purpose of indicating that certain studies belong together from a practical point of view or according to a methodological principle. In many cases it would be fanciful to seek any other than a practical justification for grouping certain branches together. So it is clear on the surface that much is subsumed under the department of Exegetical Theology, which bears only a very remote and indirect relation to its central idea. There are subservient and preparatory studies lying in the periphery and but loosely connected with the organic center. Nevertheless, if Exegetical Theology is to be more than a conglomerate of heterogeneous studies, having no other than a practical unity, we must expect that at its highest point of development it will appear to embody one of the necessary forms of the essential idea of all Theology, and will unfold itself as *knowledge concerning God* in the strict sense of the term. The science in which this actually happens will be the heart of the organism of Exegetical Theology.

Exegetical Theology deals with God under the aspect of Revealer of Himself and Author of the Scriptures. It is naturally divided into two parts, of which the one treats of the formation of the Scriptures, the other of the actual revelation of God lying back of this process. We further observe that the formation of the Scriptures serves no other purpose than to perpetuate and transmit the record of God's self-disclosure to the human race as a whole. Compared with revelation proper, the formation of the Scriptures appears as a means to an end. Bibliology with all its adjuncts, therefore, is not the center of Exegetical Theology, but is logically subordinated to the other division, which treats of revelation proper. Or, formulating it from the human point of view, all our investigations as to the origin of the Scriptures, their collection into a Canon, their original text, as well as the exegetical researches by which the contents of the Biblical writings are inductively ascertained, ultimately serve the one purpose of teaching us what God has revealed concerning Himself. None of these studies find their aim in themselves, but all have their value determined and their place assigned by the one central study to which they are leading up and in which they find their culminating point. This central study that gives most adequate and natural expression to the idea of Exegetical Theology is Biblical Theology.

In general, then, Biblical Theology is that part of Exegetical Theology which deals with the revelation of God. It makes use of all the results that have been obtained by all the preceding studies in this department. Still, we must endeavor to determine more precisely in what sense this general definition is to be understood. For it might be said of Systematic Theology, nay of the whole of Theology, with equal truth, that it deals with supernatural revelation. The specific character of Biblical Theology lies in this, that it discusses both the form and contents of revelation from the point of view of the revealing activity of God Himself. In other words, it deals with revelation in the active sense, as an act of God, and tries to understand and trace and describe this act, so far as this is possible to man and does not elude our finite observation. In Biblical Theology both the form and contents of revelation are considered as parts and products of a divine work. In Systematic Theology these same contents of revelation appear, but not under the aspect of the stages of a divine work; rather as the material for a human work of classifying and systematizing according to logical principles. Biblical Theology applies no other method of grouping and arranging these contents than is given in the divine economy of revelation itself.

From this it follows that, in order to obtain a more definite conception of Biblical Theology, we must try to gather the general features of God's revealing work. Here, as in other cases, the organism of a science can be conceived and described only by anticipating its results. The following statements, accordingly, are not to be considered in the light of an *a priori* construction, but simply formulate what the study of Biblical Theology itself has taught us.

The first feature characteristic of supernatural revelation is *its historical progress*. God has not communicated to us the knowledge of the truth as it appears in the calm light of eternity to His own timeless vision. He has not given it in the form of abstract propositions logically correlated and systematized. The simple fact that it is the task of Systematic Theology to reproduce revealed truth in such form, shows that it does not possess this form from the beginning. The self-revelation of God is a work covering ages, proceeding in a sequence of revealing words and acts, appearing in a long perspective of time. The truth comes in the form of growing truth, not truth at rest. No doubt the explanation of this fact is partly to be sought in the finiteness of the human understanding. Even that part of the knowledge of God which has been revealed to us is so overwhelmingly great and so far transcends our human capacities, is such a flood of light, that it had, as it were, gradually to be let in upon us, ray after ray, and not the full radiancy at once. By imparting the elements of the knowledge of Himself in a divinely arranged sequence God has pointed out to us the way in which we might gradually grasp and truly know Him. This becomes still more evident, if we remember that this revelation is intended for all ages and nations and classes and conditions of men, and therefore must adapt itself to the most various characters and temperaments by which it is to be assimilated.

We feel, however, that this explanation, however plausible in itself, is but a partial one, and can never completely satisfy. The deeper ground for the historic character of revelation cannot lie in the limitations of the human subject, but must be sought in the nature of revelation itself. Revelation is not an isolated act of God, existing without connection with all the other divine acts of supernatural character. It constitutes a part of that great process of the new creation through which the present universe as an organic whole shall be redeemed from the consequences of sin and restored to its ideal state, which it had originally in the intention of God. Now, this new creation, in the objective, universal sense, is not something completed by a single act all at once, but is a history with its own law of organic development. It could not be otherwise, inasmuch as at every point it proceeds on the basis of and in contact with the natural development of this world and of the human race, and, the latter being in the form of history, the former must necessarily assume that form likewise. It is simply owing to our habit of unduly separating revelation from this comprehensive background of the total redeeming work of God, that we fail to appreciate its historic, progressive nature. We conceive of it as a series of communications of abstract truth forming a body by itself, and are at a loss to see why this truth should be parcelled out to man little by little and not given in its completeness at once. As soon as we realize that revelation is at almost every point interwoven with and conditioned by the redeeming activity of God in its wider sense, and together with the latter connected with the natural development of the present world, its historic character becomes perfectly intelligible and ceases to cause surprise.

In this great redeeming process two stages are to be distinguished. First come those acts of God which have a universal and objective significance, being aimed at the production of an organic center for the new order of things. After this had been accomplished, there follows a second stage during which this objective redemption is subjectively applied to individuals. In both the stages the supernatural element is present, though in the former, owing to its objective character, it appears more distinctly than in the latter. The whole series of redeeming acts, culminating in the incarnation and atoning work of the Mediator and the pouring out of the Holy Spirit, bears the signature of the miraculous on its very face. But the supernatural, though not objectively controllable, is none the less present during the later stage in each case where an individual soul is regenerated. Revelation as such, however, is not co-extensive with this whole process in both its stages. Its history is limited to the former half, that is, it accompanies in its progress the gradual unfolding of the central and objective salvation of God, and no sooner is the latter accomplished than revelation also has run its course and its voice ceases to speak. The reason for this is obvious. The revelation of God being not subjective and individual in its nature, but objective and addressed to the human race as a whole, it is but natural that this revelation should be embedded in the channels of the great objective history of redemption and extend no further than this. In point of fact, we see that, when the *finished* salvation worked out among Israel is stripped of its particularistic form to extend to all nations, at the same moment the *completed* oracles of God are given to the human race as a whole to be henceforth subjectively studied and appropriated. It is as unreasonable to expect revelations after the close of the Apostolic age as it would be to think that the great saving facts of that period can be indefinitely increased and repeated.

Even this, however, is not sufficient to show the historic character of revelation in its full extent. Up to this point we have only seen how the disclosure of truth in general follows the course of the history of redemption. We now must add that in not a few cases revelation is *identified* with history. Besides making use of words, God has also employed acts to reveal great principles of truth. It is not so much the prophetic visions or miracles in the narrower sense that we think of in this connection. We refer more specially to those great, supernatural, history-making acts of which we have examples in the redemption of the covenant-people from Egypt, or in the crucifixion and resurrection of Christ. In these cases the history itself forms a part of revelation. There is a self-disclosure of God in such acts. They would speak even if left to speak for themselves. Forming part of history, these revealing acts necessarily assume historical relations among themselves, and succeed one another according to a well-defined principle of historical sequence. Furthermore, we observe that this system of revelation-acts is not interpolated into the larger system of biblical history after a fanciful and mechanical fashion. The relation between the two systems is vital and organic. These miraculous interferences of God to which we ascribe a revealing character, furnish the great joints and ligaments by which the whole framework of sacred history is held together, and its entire structure determined. God's saving deeds mark the critical epochs of history, and as such, have continued to shape its course for centuries after their occurrence.

Of course we should never forget that, wherever revelation and the redemptive acts of God coincide, the latter frequently have an ulterior purpose extending beyond the sphere of revelation. The crucifixion and resurrection of Christ were acts not exclusively intended to reveal something to man, but primarily intended to serve some definite purpose in reference to God. In so far as they satisfied the divine justice it would be inaccurate to view them under the aspect of revelation primarily or exclusively. Nevertheless, the revealing element is essential even in their case, the two ends of satisfaction and of revelation being combined into one. And in the second place, we must remember that the revealing acts of God never appear separated from His verbal communications of truth. Word and act always accompany each other, and in their interdependence strikingly illustrate our former statement, to the effect that revelation is organically connected with the introduction of a new order of things into this sinful world. Revelation is the light of this new world which God has called into being. The light needs the reality and the reality needs the light to produce the vision of the beautiful creation of His grace. To apply the Kantian phraseology to a higher subject, without God's acts the words would be empty, without His words the acts would be blind.

A second ground for the historic character of revelation may be found in its eminently practical aspect. The knowledge of God communicated by it is nowhere for a purely intellectual purpose. From beginning to end it is a knowledge intended to enter into the actual life of man, to be worked out by him in all its practical bearings. The Shemitic, and in particular the Biblical, conception of knowledge is distinguished from the Greek, more intellectualistic idea, by the prominence of this practical element. To know, in the Shemitic sense, is to have the consciousness of the reality and the properties of something interwoven with one's life through the closest intercourse and communion attainable. Now in this manner God has interwoven the supernaturally communicated knowledge of Himself with the historic life of the chosen race, so as to secure for it a practical form from the beginning. Revelation is connected throughout with the fate of Israel. Its disclosures arise from the necessities of that nation, and are adjusted to its capacities. It is such a living historical thing that it has shaped the very life of this nation into the midst of which it descended. The importance of this aspect of revelation has found its clearest expression in the idea of the covenant as the form of God's progressive self-communication to Israel. God has not revealed Himself in a school, but in the covenant; and the covenant as a communion of life is all-comprehensive, embracing all the conditions and interests of those contracting it. There is a knowledge and an imparting of knowledge here, but in a most practical way and not merely by theoretical instruction.

If in the foregoing we have correctly described the most general character of revelation, we may enlarge our definition of Biblical Theology by saying that it is that part of Exegetical Theology which deals with the revelation of God in its historic continuity. We must now advance beyond this and inquire more particularly in what specific type of history God has chosen to embody His revelation. The idea of historic development is not sufficiently definite of itself to explain the manner in which divine truth has been progressively revealed. It is not until we ascribe to this progress an organic character that the full significance of the historic principle springs into view.

The truth of revelation, if it is to retain its divine and absolute character at all, must be perfect from the beginning. Biblical Theology deals with it as a product of a supernatural divine activity, and is therefore bound by its own principle to maintain the perfection of revealed truth in all its stages. When, nevertheless, Biblical Theology also undertakes to show how the truth has been gradually set forth in greater fullness and clearness, these two facts can be reconciled in no other way than by assuming that the advance in revelation resembles the organic process, through which out of the perfect germ the perfect plant and flower and fruit are successively produced.

Although the knowledge of God has received material increase through the ages, this increase nowhere shows the features of external accretion, but throughout appears as an internal expansion, an organic unfolding from within. The elements of truth, far from being mechanically added one to the other in lifeless succession, are seen to grow out of each other, each richer and fuller disclosure of the knowledge of God having been prepared for by what preceded, and being in its turn preparatory for what follows. That this is actually so, follows from the soteriological purpose which revelation in the first instance is intended to serve. At all times, from the very first to the last, revealed truth has been kept in close contact with the wants and emergencies of the living generation. And these human needs, notwithstanding all variations of outward circumstance, being essentially the same in all periods, it follows that the heart of divine truth, that by which men live, must have been present from the outset, and that each subsequent increase consisted in the unfolding of what was germinally contained in the beginning of revelation. The Gospel of Paradise is such a germ in which the Gospel of Paul is potentially present; and the Gospel of Abraham, of Moses, of David, of Isaiah and Jeremiah, are all expansions of this original message of salvation, each pointing forward to the next stage of growth, and bringing the Gospel idea one step nearer to its full realization. In this Gospel of Paradise we already discern the essential features of a covenant-relation, though the formal notion of a covenant does not attach to it. And in the covenant-promises given to Abraham these very features reappear, assume greater distinctness, and are seen to grow together, to crystallize as it were, into the formal covenant. From this time onward the expansive character of the covenant-idea shows itself. The covenant of Abraham contains the promise of the Sinaitic covenant; the latter again, from its very nature, gives rise to prophecy; and prophecy guards the covenant of Sinai from assuming a fixed, unalterable form, the prophetic word being a creative word under the influence of which the spiritual, universal germs of the covenant are quickened and a new, higher order of things is organically developed from the Mosaic theocracy, that new covenant of which Jeremiah spoke, and which our Saviour brought to light by the shedding of His blood. So dispensation grows out of dispensation, and the newest is but the fully expanded flower of the oldest.

The same principle may also be established more objectively, if we consider the specific manner in which God realizes the renewal of this sinful kosmos in accordance with His original purpose. The renewal is not brought about by mechanically changing one part after the other. God's method is much rather that of creating within the organism of the present world the center of the world of redemption, and then organically building up the new order of things around this center. Hence from the beginning all redeeming acts of God aim at the creation and introduction of this new organic principle, which is none other than Christ. All Old Testament redemption is but the saving activity of God working toward the realization of this goal, the great supernatural prelude to the Incarnation and the Atonement. And Christ having appeared as the head of the new humanity and having accomplished His atoning work, the further renewal of the kosmos is effected through an organic extension of His power in ever widening circles. In this sense the Apostle speaks of the fashioning anew of the body of our humiliation, that it may be conformed to the body of the glory of Christ, saying that this will happen "according to the working whereby He is able to subject even all things unto Himself" (Phil. 3:21). If, then, this supernatural process of transformation proceeds on organic principles, and if, as we have shown, revelation is but the light accompanying it in its course, the reflection of its divine realities in the sphere of knowledge, we cannot escape from the conclusion that revelation itself must exhibit a similar organic progress. In point of fact, we find that the actual working of Old Testament redemption toward the coming of Christ in the flesh, and the advance of revealed knowledge concerning Christ, keep equal pace everywhere. The various stages in the gradual concentration of Messianic prophecy, as when the human nature of our Saviour is successively designated as the seed of the woman, the seed of Abraham, the seed of Judah, the seed of David, His figure assuming more distinct features at each narrowing of the circle—what are they but disclosures of the divine counsel corresponding in each case to new realities and new conditions created by His redeeming power? And as in the history of redemption there are critical stages in which the great acts of God as it were accumulate, so we find that at such junctures the process of revelation is correspondingly accelerated, and that a few years show, perhaps, more rapid growth and greater expansion than centuries that lie between. For, although the development of the root may be slow and the stem and leaves may grow almost imperceptibly, there comes a time when the bud emerges in a day and the flower expands in an hour to our wondering sight.[2] Such epochs of quickened revelation were the times of Abraham, of Moses, of David, and especially the days of the Son of Man.

This progress, moreover, increases in rapidity the nearer revelation approaches to its final goal. What rich developments, what wealth of blossoming and fruitage are compressed within the narrow limits of that period—no more than one lifetime—that is covered by the New Testament! In this, indeed, we have the most striking proof of the organic nature of the progress of revelation. Every organic development serves to embody an idea; and as soon as this idea has found full and adequate expression, the organism receives the stamp of perfection and develops no further. Because the New Testament times brought the final realization of the divine counsel of redemption as to its objective and central facts, therefore New Testament revelation brought the full-grown Word of God, in which the new-born world, which is complete in Christ, mirrors itself. In this final stage of revelation the deepest depths of eternity are opened up to the eye of Apostle and Seer. Hence, the frequent recurrence of the expression, "before the foundation of the world." We feel at every point that the last veil is drawn aside and that we stand face to face with the disclosure of the great mystery which was hidden in the divine purpose through the ages. All salvation, all truth in regard to man, has its eternal foundation in the triune God Himself. It is this triune God who here reveals Himself as the everlasting reality, from whom all truth proceeds, whom all truth reflects, be it the little streamlet of Paradise or the broad river of the New Testament losing itself again in the ocean of eternity. After this nothing higher can come. All the separate lines along which through the ages revelation was carried, have converged and met at a single point. The seed of the woman and the Angel of Jehovah are become one in the Incarnate Word. And as Christ is glorified once for all, so from the crowning glory and perfection of His revelation in the New Testament nothing can be taken away; nor can anything be added thereunto.

There is one more feature of the organic character of revelation which I must briefly allude to. Historic progress is not the only means used by God to disclose the full contents of His eternal Word. Side by side with it we witness a striking multiformity of teaching employed

---

2. Cf. Thomas Dehany Bernard, *The Progress of Doctrine in the New Testament* (London: Macmillan, 1866), 44.

for the same purpose. All along the historic stem of revelation, branches are seen to shoot forth, frequently more than one at a time, each of which helps to realize the complete idea of the truth for its own part and after its own peculiar manner. The legal, the prophetic, the poetic elements in the Old Testament are clearly-distinct types of revelation, and in the New Testament we have something corresponding to these in the Gospels, the Epistles, the Apocalypse. Further, within the limits of these great divisions there are numerous minor variations, closely associated with the peculiarities of individual character. Isaiah and Jeremiah are distinct, and so are John and Paul. And this differentiation rather increases than decreases with the progress of sacred history. It is greater in the New Testament than in the Old. The laying of the historic basis for Israel's covenant-life has been recorded by one author, Moses; the historic basis of the New Testament dispensation we know from the fourfold version of the Gospels. The remainder of the New Testament writings are in the form of letters, in which naturally the personal element predominates. The more fully the light shone upon the realization of the whole counsel of God and disclosed its wide extent, the more necessary it became to expound it in all its bearings, to view it at different angles, thus to bring out what Paul calls the *much-variegated*, the manifold, wisdom of God. For, God having chosen to reveal the truth through human instruments, it follows that these instruments must be both numerous and of varied adaptation to the common end. Individual coloring, therefore, and a peculiar manner of representation are not only not detrimental to a full statement of the truth, but directly subservient to it. God's method of revelation includes the very shaping and chiselling of individualities for His own objective ends. To put it concretely: we must not conceive of it as if God found Paul "ready-made," as it were, and in using Paul as an organ of revelation, had to put up with the fact that the dialectic mind of Paul reflected the truth in a dialectic, dogmatic form to the detriment of the truth. The facts are these: the truth having inherently, besides other aspects, a dialectic and dogmatic side, and God intending to give this side full expression, chose Paul from the womb, molded his character, and gave him such a training that the truth revealed through him necessarily bore the dogmatic and dialectic impress of His mind. The divine objectivity and the human individuality here do not collide, nor exclude each other, because the man Paul, with his whole character, his gifts, and his training, is subsumed under the divine plan. The human is but the glass through which the divine light is reflected, and all the sides and angles into which the glass has been cut serve no other purpose than to distribute to us the truth in all the riches of its prismatic colors.

In some cases growth in the organism of revelation is closely dependent on this variety in the type of teaching. There are instances in which two or more forms of the one truth have been brought to light simultaneously, each of which exercised a deepening and enlarging influence upon the others. The Gospel of John contains revelations contemporaneous with those of the Synoptists, so that chronologically we can distribute its material over the pages of Matthew, Mark, and Luke. Nevertheless, taken as a whole and in its unity, the Gospel of John represents a fuller and wider self-revelation of Christ than the Synoptists; and not only so, but it also represents a type of revelation which presupposes the facts and teachings of the other Gospels, and is, in point of order, subsequent to them. The same thing might be said of Isaiah in its relation to Micah. So the variety itself contributes to the progress of revelation. Even in these cases of contemporaneous development along distinct lines and in independent directions, there is a mysterious force at work, which makes "the several parts grow out of and into each other with mutual support, so that the whole body is fitly joined together and compacted by that which every joint supplies, according to the effectual working in the measure of every part."

We may now perhaps attempt to frame a complete definition of our science. The preceding remarks have shown that the divine work of revelation did not proceed contrary to all law, but after a well-defined organic principle. Wherever there is a group of facts sufficiently distinct from their environment, and determined by some law of orderly sequence, we are justified in making these facts the object of scientific discussion. Far from there being in the conception of Biblical Theology anything at variance with the idea of Theology as based on the revealed knowledge of God, we have found that the latter even directly postulates the former. Biblical Theology, rightly defined, is nothing else than *the exhibition of the organic progress of supernatural revelation in its historic continuity and multiformity.*

It must be admitted, however, that not everything passing under the name of Biblical Theology satisfies the requirements of this definition. From the end of the preceding century, when our science first appears as distinct from Dogmatic Theology, until now, she has stood under the spell of un-Biblical principles. Her very birth took place under an evil star. It was the spirit of Rationalism which first led to distinguishing in the contents of the Scriptures between what was purely human, individual, local, temporal—in a word, conditioned by the subjectivity of the writers—and what was eternally valid, divine truth. The latter, of course, was identified with the teachings of the shallow Rationalism of that period. Thus, Biblical Theology, which can only rest on the basis of revelation, began with a denial of this basis; and a science, whose task it is to set forth the historic principles of revelation, was trained up in a school notorious for its lack of historic sense. For to this type of Rationalism history, as such, is the realm of the contingent, the relative, the arbitrary, whilst only the deliverances of pure reason possess the predicate of absoluteness and universal validity. In this Biblical Theology of Rationalism, therefore, the historical principle merely served to eliminate or neutralize the revelation-principle. And since that time all the philosophical tendencies that have influenced Theology in general have also left their impress upon Biblical Theology in particular. It is not necessary for our present purpose to trace the various lines and currents of this complicated history; the less so since there can be no doubt but that they are rapidly merging into the great stream of Evolutionistic Philosophy, which, whatever truth there may be in its application to certain groups of phenomena, yet, as a general theory of the universe, is the most direct antithesis to the fundamental principles of revelation and Christianity.

That the influence of this philosophy, as it expresses and in turn molds the spirit of the age, is perceptible in the field of Theology everywhere, no careful observer of recent events will deny. But Biblical Theology is, perhaps, more than any other branch of theological study affected by it, because its principle of historic progress in revelation seems to present certain analogies with the evolutionary scheme, and to offer exceptional opportunities for applying the latter, without departing too far from the real contents of Scripture. This analogy, of course, is merely formal, and from a material point of view there is a world-wide difference between that philosophy of history which the Bible itself outlines, and which alone Biblical Theology, if it wishes to remain Biblical, has a right to adopt, and, on the other hand, the so-called facts of the Bible pressed into the evolutionary formulas. It is especially in two respects that the principles of this philosophy have worked a radical departure from the right treatment of our science as it is prescribed by both the supernatural character of

Christianity and the nature of Theology. In the first place, evolution is bent upon showing that the process of development is everywhere from the lower and imperfect to the higher and relatively more perfect forms, from impure beginnings through a gradual purification to some ideal end. So in regard to the knowledge of God, whose growth we observe in the Biblical writings, evolution cannot rest until it shall have traced its gradual advance from sensual, physical conceptions to ethical and spiritual ideas, from Animism and Polytheism to Monolatry and Monotheism. But this of necessity rules out the revelation-factor from Biblical Theology. Revelation as an act of God, theistically conceived of, can in no wise be associated with anything imperfect or impure or below the standard of absolute truth. However much Christian people may blind themselves to the fact, the outcome will show, as it does already show, that the principles of supernatural redemption and natural evolution are mutually exclusive. Hence, even now, those who accept the evolutionary construction of Biblical history, either openly and without reserve renounce the idea of supernatural revelation, or strip it of its objectivity so as to make it less antagonistic to that of natural development. In the same degree, however, that the latter is done, revelation loses its distinctively theistic character and begins to assume more and more the features of a Pantheistic process, that is, it ceases to be revelation in the commonly accepted sense of the term.

In the second place, the philosophy of evolution has corrupted Theology by introducing its leaven of metaphysical Agnosticism. Inasmuch as only the phenomenal world can become an object of knowledge to us and not the mysterious reality hidden behind the phenomena, and inasmuch as Theology in the old, traditional sense pretended to deal with such metaphysical realities as God and heaven and immortality, it follows that Theology must either be entirely abolished, or must submit to such a reconstruction as will enable her to retain a place among the phenomenalistic sciences. The former would be the more consistent and scientific, but the latter is usually preferred; because it is difficult at one stroke to set aside a thing so firmly rooted in the past. Theology, therefore, is now defined as *the science of religion*, and that, too, in the sense chiefly of a phenomenology of religion, in which by far the greater part of the investigation is devoted to the superficial external side of religion and the heart of the matter receives scant treatment. Applied to Biblical Theology, this principle involves that no longer the historic progress of the supernatural revelation of God, but *the development of the religion* recorded in the Biblical writings, shall become the object of our science. Theology having become the science of religion, Biblical Theology must needs become the history of one, be it the greatest, of all religions, the history of the religion of Israel and of primitive Christianity.

How far this evil has penetrated may be inferred from the fact that there is scarcely a book on Biblical Theology in existence in which this conception of the object of our science is not met with, and in which it does not very largely determine the point of view. It has even vitiated so excellent a work in many respects as Oehler's Old Testament Theology.[3] Of course, there are many degrees in the thoroughness with which this subjectivizing principle is carried through and applied. Between those who are just beginning to descend the ladder and those who have reached its lowest step, there is a very appreciable difference.

First, there are those who think that, though God has supernaturally revealed Himself in words and acts, nevertheless this revelation pure and simple, cannot be for us an object of

---

3. Cf. Gustav Friedrich Oehler, *Theology of the Old Testament* (New York: Funk & Wagnalls, 1883).

scientific discussion, except in so far as it has blended with and produced its effect upon the religious consciousness of the people to whom it was given; and that, consequently, we must posit as the object of Biblical Theology the religion of the Bible, and can hope at the utmost to reason back from this religion as the result, to revelation as the cause that has produced it. To this we would answer, that there is no reason to make Biblical Theology, so conceived, a separate science. The investigation of the religion of Israel as a subjective phenomenon, together with the objective factors called in to explain it, belongs nowhere else than in the department of Biblical History. Furthermore, we believe that the Bible itself has recorded for us the interaction of the objective and the subjective factors in sacred history in such a manner that their joint product is nowhere made the central thought of its teaching, but much rather we are invited everywhere to fix our gaze on the objective self-revelation of God, and only in the second place to observe the subjective reflex of this divine activity in the religious consciousness of the people.

Others are more reserved in their recognition of the supernatural. They would confine the revelation of God to acts, and derive all the doctrinal contents of the Bible from the source of human reflection upon these divine acts. In this manner a compromise is obtained, whereby both the objectivity of revelation and the subjective development of Biblical teaching can be affirmed. This view is unsatisfactory, because it loses sight of the analogy between divine revelation and the ordinary way in which man communicates his thoughts. To man, made in the image of God, speech is the highest instrument of revealing Himself, and it would be strange if God in His self-disclosure entirely dispensed with the use of this instrument. Nor does this view leave any place for prophecy. The prophetic word is frequently a divine word preceding the divine act. Although, as we have seen, the progress of revelation is clearly conditioned by the actual realization of God's plan of redemption, yet this by no means implies that the saving deeds of God always necessarily go before, and the revelations which cast light on them always follow. In many cases the revealing word comes as an anticipation of the approaching events, as a flash of lightning preceding the thunder of God's judgments. As Amos strikingly expresses it: "Surely the Lord God will do nothing, but He revealeth His secret unto His servants the prophets" (Amos 3:7).

The supernatural factor, however, is reduced to still smaller proportions and entirely deprived of its objectivity by a third group of writers on Biblical Theology. According to these, supernatural revelation does not involve the communication of divine thoughts to man in any direct manner either by words or by actions. Revelation consists in this, that the divine Spirit, by an unconscious process, stirs the depths of man's heart so as to cause the springing up therein afterward of certain religious thoughts and feelings, which are as truly human as they are a revelation of God, and are, therefore, only relatively true. It is owing to the influence of the Ritschlian or Neo-Kantian school of Theology that this view has gained new prevalence of late. The people of Israel are held to have possessed a creative religious genius, just as the Greek nation was endowed with a creative genius in the sphere of art. And, although the productions of this genius are ascribed to the impulse of the divine Spirit, yet this Spirit and His working are represented in such a manner that their distinction from the natural processes of the human mind becomes a mere assumption, exercising no influence whatever on the interpretation of the phenomenal side of Israel's religion. Writers of this class deal as freely with the facts and teachings of the Bible as the most extreme anti-supernaturalists. But with their evolutionistic treatment of the phenomena they combine the hypothesis of this mystical influence of the Spirit, which they are pleased to call revelation. It is needless to say that revelation of this kind must remain forever inaccessible to objective proof or verification. Whatever can pretend to be scientific in this theory lacks all rapport with the idea of the Supernatural, and whatever there lingers in it of diluted Supernaturalism lacks all scientific character.

I have endeavored to sketch with a few strokes those principles and tendencies by which the study of Biblical Theology is almost exclusively controlled at the present time, because they seem to me to indicate the points which ought to receive special emphasis in the construction of our science on a truly Scriptural and theological basis. The first of these is *the objective character of revelation*. Biblical Theology must insist upon claiming for its object not the thoughts and reflections and speculations of man, but the oracles of God. Whosoever weakens or subjectivizes this fundamental idea of revelation, strikes a blow at the very heart of Theology and Supernatural Christianity, nay, of Theism itself. Every type of Biblical Theology bent upon ignoring or minimizing this supreme, central idea, is a most dangerous product. It is an indisputable fact that all modern views of revelation which are deficient in recognizing its objective character, fit far better into a pantheistic than into a theistic theory of the universe. If God be the unconscious background of the world, it is altogether natural that His truth and light should in a mysterious manner loom up from the unexplorable regions that underlie human consciousness, that in His very act of revealing Himself He should be conditioned and entangled and obstructed by man. If, on the other hand, God be conscious and personal, the inference is that in His self-disclosure He will assert and maintain His personality, so as to place His divine thoughts before us with the stamp of divinity upon them, in a truly objective manner. By making revelation, both as to its form and contents, a special object of study, Biblical Theology may be expected to contribute something toward upholding this important conception in its true objectivity, toward more sharply defining it and guarding it from confusion with all heterogeneous ideas.

The second point to be emphasized in our treatment of Biblical Theology is that the historical character of the truth is not in any way antithetical to, but throughout subordinated to, its revealed character. Scriptural truth is not absolute, notwithstanding its historic setting; but the historic setting has been employed by God for the very purpose of revealing the truth, the whole truth, and nothing but the truth. It is not the duty of Biblical Theology to seek first the historic features of the Scriptural ideas, and to think that the absolute character of the truth as revealed of God is something secondary to be added thereunto. The reality of revelation should be the supreme factor by which the historic factor is kept under control. With the greatest variety of historical aspects, there can, nevertheless, be no inconsistencies or contradictions in the Word of God. The student of Biblical Theology is not to hunt for little systems in the Bible that shall be mutually exclusive, or to boast of his skill in detecting such as a mark of high scholarship. What has been remarked above, in regard to the place of individuality in the plan of revelation, may be applied with equal justice to the historic phases through which the progressive delivery of the truth has passed. God has done for the historic unfolding of His word as a whole what He has done for the reproduction of its specific types and aspects through the forming and training of individuals. As He knew Jeremiah and Paul from the womb, so He knew Israel and prepared Israel for its task. The history of this nation is not a common history; it is *sacred* history in the highest sense of having been specially designed by God to become the human receptacle for the truth from above.

In the third place, Biblical Theology should plant itself squarely upon the truthfulness of the Scriptures as a whole. Revelation proper announces and records the saving deeds of God, but a mere announcement and record is not sufficient to furnish a complete history of redemption, to produce a living image of the new order of things as it is gradually called into existence. No true history can be made by a mere chronicling of events. Only by placing the bare record of the facts in the light of the principles which shape them, and the inner nexus which holds them together, is the work of the chronicler transformed into history. For this reason God has not given us His own interpretation of the great realities of redemption in the form of a chronicle, but in the form of the historical organism of the inspired Scriptures. The direct revelations of God form by far the smaller part of the contents of the Bible. These are but the scattered diamonds woven into the garment of the truth. This garment itself is identical with the Scriptural contents as a whole. And as a whole it has been prepared by the hand of God. The Bible contains, besides the simple record of direct revelations, the further interpretation of these immediate disclosures of God by inspired prophets and apostles. Above all, it contains, if I may so call it, a divine philosophy of the history of redemption and of revelation in general outlines. And whosoever is convinced in his heart of the inspiration of the Holy Scriptures and reads his Bible as the Word of God, cannot, as a student of Biblical Theology, allow himself to reject this divine philosophy and substitute for it another of his own making. Our Theology will be Biblical in the full sense, only when it not merely derives its material from the Bible, but also accepts at the hands of the Bible the order in which this material is to be grouped and located. I for one am not ashamed to say that the teachings of Paul concerning the historic organism of the Old Testament economy possess for me greater authority than the reconstructions of the same by modern scholars, however great their learning and critical acumen.

Finally, in designating our science as *Biblical Theology*, we should not fail to enter a protest against the wrong inferences that may be easily drawn from the use of this name. The name retains somewhat of the flavor of the Rationalism which first adopted it. It almost unavoidably creates an impression as if in the Bible we had the beginning of the process that later gave us the works of Origen, Augustine, Thomas Aquinas, Luther, and Calvin. Hence some do not hesitate to define Biblical Theology as the History of Dogmatics for Biblical times. To us this sounds as strange and illogical as if one should compare the stars of the firmament and their history with the work and history of astronomy. As the heavens contain the material for astronomy and the crust of the earth for geology, so the mighty creation of the Word of God furnishes the material for Theology in this scientific sense, but *is* no Theology. It is something infinitely higher than Theology, a world of spiritual realities, into which all true theologians are led by the Spirit of the living God. Only if we take the term Theology in its more primitive and simple meaning, as the practical, historic knowledge of God imparted by revelation and deposited in the Bible, can we justify the use of the now commonly accepted name of our science. As for the scientific elaboration of this God-given material, this must be held to lie beyond the Biblical period. It could only spring up after revelation and the formation of the Scriptures had been completed. The utmost that can be conceded would be that in the Apostolic teaching of the New Testament the first signs of the beginning of this process are discernible. But even that which the Apostles teach is in no sense primarily to be viewed under the aspect of Theology. It is the inspired Word of God before all other things. No theologian would dare say of his work what Paul said to the

Galatians: "But though we or an angel from heaven preach unto you any gospel other than that which we preached unto you, let him be anathema" (Gal. 1:8).[4]

In the foregoing I have endeavored to describe to you the nature and functions of Biblical Theology as a member in the organism of our scientific knowledge of God. I have not forgotten, however, that you have called me to teach this science for the eminently practical purpose of training young men for the ministry of the Gospel. Consequently, I shall not have acquitted myself of my task on this occasion unless you will permit me to point out briefly what are the advantages to be expected from the pursuit of this study in a more practical way.

First of all, Biblical Theology exhibits to the student of the Word the organic structure of the truth therein contained, and its organic growth as the result of revelation. It shows to him that in the Bible there is an organization finer, more complicated, more exquisite than even the texture of muscles and nerves and brain in the human body; that its various parts are interwoven and correlated in the most subtle manner, each sensitive to the impressions received from all the others, perfect in itself, and yet dependent upon the rest, while in them and through them all throbs as a unifying principle the Spirit of God's living truth. If anything, then, this is adapted to convince the student that what the Bible places before him is not the chance product of the several human minds that have been engaged in its composition, but the workmanship of none other than God Himself. The organic structure of the truth and the organic development of revelation as portrayed in the Bible bear exactly the same relation to Supernaturalism that the argument from design in nature bears to Theism. Both arguments proceed on precisely analogous lines. If the history of revelation actually is the organic history, full of evidences of design, which the Bible makes it out to be, then it must have been shaped in an altogether unique fashion by the revealing activity of God.

In the second place, Biblical Theology is suited to furnish a most effective antidote to the destructive critical views now prevailing. These modern theories, however much may be asserted to the contrary, *disorganize* the Scriptures. Their chief danger lies, not in affirmations concerning matters of minor importance, concerning errors in historical details, but in the most radical claims upsetting the inner organization of the whole body of truth. We have seen that the course of revelation is most closely identified with the history described in the Bible. Of this history of the Bible, this framework on which the whole structure of revelation rests, the newest criticism asserts that it is falsified and unhistorical for the greater part. All the historical writings of the Old Testament in their present state are tendency-writings. Even where they embody older and more reliable documents, the Deuteronomic and Levitical paste, applied to them in and after the exile, has obliterated the historic reality. Now, if it were known among believing Christians to what an extent these theories disorganize the Bible, their chief spell would be broken; and many would repudiate with horror what they now tolerate or view with indifference. There is no other way of showing this than by placing over against the critical theories the organic history of revelation, as the Bible itself constructs it. As soon as this is done, everybody will be able to see at a glance that the two are mutually subversive. This very thing Biblical Theology endeavors to do. It thus meets the critical assaults, not in a negative way by defending point after point of the

---

4. In view of the Rationalistic associations connected with the name Biblical Theology, and in view of its being actually used for the propagation of erroneous views, the name History of Revelation would perhaps be better adapted to express the true nature of our science. This name has been lately adopted by Karl Friedrich Nösgen in his *Geschichte der Neutestamentlichen Offenbarung*, 2 vols. (München: C. H. Beck, 1891, 1893).

citadel, whereby no total effect is produced and the critics are always permitted to reply that they attack merely the outworks, not the central position of the faith; but in the most positive manner, by setting forth what the principle of revelation involves according to the Bible, and how one part of it stands or falls together with all the others. The student of Biblical Theology has the satisfaction of knowing that his treatment of Biblical matters is not prescribed for him exclusively by the tactics of his enemies, and that, while most effectually defending the truth, he at the same time is building the temple of divine knowledge on the positive foundation of the faith.

In the third place, I should mention as a desirable fruit of the study of Biblical Theology, the new life and freshness which it gives to the old truth, showing it in all its historic vividness and reality with the dew of the morning of revelation upon its opening leaves. It is certainly not without significance that God has embodied the contents of revelation, not in a dogmatic system, but in a book of history, the parallel to which in dramatic interest and simple eloquence is nowhere to be found. It is this that makes the Scriptures speak and appeal to and touch the hearts and lead the minds of men captive to the truth everywhere. No one will be able to handle the Word of God more effactually than he to whom the treasure-chambers of its historic meaning have been opened up. It is this that brings the divine truth so near to us, makes it as it were bone of our bone and flesh of our flesh, that humanizes it in the same sense that the highest revelation in Christ was rendered most human by the incarnation. To this historical character of revelation we owe the fullness and variety which enable the Scriptures to mete out new treasures to all ages without becoming exhausted or even fully explored. A Biblical Theology imbued with the devout spirit of humble faith in the revealed Word of God, will enrich the student with all this wealth of living truth, making him in the highest sense a householder, bringing forth out of his treasures things new and old.

Fourthly, Biblical Theology is of the greatest importance and value for the study of Systematic Theology. It were useless to deny that it has been often cultivated in a spirit more or less hostile to the work in which Systematic Theology is engaged. The very name *Biblical* Theology is frequently vaunted so as to imply a protest against the alleged un-Biblical character of Dogmatics. I desire to state most emphatically here, that there is nothing in the nature and aims of Biblical Theology to justify such an implication. For anything pretending to supplant Dogmatics there is no place in the circle of Christian Theology. All attempts to show that the doctrines developed and formulated by the Church have no real foundation in the Bible, stand themselves without the pale of Theology, inasmuch as they imply that Christianity is a purely natural phenomenon, and that the Church has now for nineteen centuries been chasing her own shadow. Dogmatic Theology is, when rightly cultivated, as truly a Biblical and as truly an inductive science as its younger sister. And the latter needs a constructive principle for arranging her facts as well as the former. The only difference is, that in the one case this constructive principle is systematic and logical, whereas in the other case it is purely historical. In other words, Systematic Theology endeavors to construct a circle, Biblical Theology seeks to reproduce a line. I do not mean by the use of this figure, that within Biblical Theology there is no grouping of facts at all. The line of which I speak does not represent a monotonous recital of revelation, and does not resemble a string, even though it be conceived of as a string of pearls. The line of revelation is like the stem of those trees that grow in rings. Each successive ring has grown out of the preceding one. But out of the sap and vigor that is in this stem there springs a crown with branches and leaves and flowers and fruit. Such is the true relation between Biblical and Systematic Theology. Dogmatics is the crown which grows out of all the work that Biblical Theology can accomplish. And taught in this spirit of Christian willingness to serve, our science cannot fail to benefit Systematic Theology in more than one respect. It will proclaim the fact, too often forgotten and denied in our days, that true religion cannot dispense with a solid basis of objective knowledge of the truth. There is no better means of silencing the supercilious cant that right believing is of small importance in the matter of religion, than by showing what infinite care our Father in heaven has taken to reveal unto us, in the utmost perfection, the *knowledge* of what He is and does for our salvation. Biblical Theology will also demonstrate that the fundamental doctrines of our faith do not rest, as many would fain believe, on an arbitrary exposition of some isolated proof-texts. It will not so much prove these doctrines, as it will do what is far better than proof—make them grow out organically before our eyes from the stem of revelation. Finally, it will contribute to keep Systematic Theology in living contact with that soil of divine realities from which it must draw all its strength and power to develop beyond what it has already attained.

Let us not forget, however, that as of all theology, so of Biblical Theology, the highest aim cannot lie in man, or in anything that serves the creature. Its most excellent practical use is surely this, that it grants us a new vision of the glory of Him who has made all things to the praise of His own wonderful name. As the Uncreated, the Unchangeable, Eternal God, He lives above the sphere of history. He is the Being and never the Becoming One. And, no doubt, when once this veil of time shall be drawn aside, when we shall see face to face, then also the necessity for viewing His knowledge in the glass of history will cease. But since on our behalf and for our salvation He has condescended to work and speak in the form of time, and thus to make His works and His speech partake of that peculiar glory that attaches to all organic growth, let us also seek to know Him as the One *that is, that was, and that is to come*, in order that no note may be lacking in that psalm of praise to be sung by the Church into which all our Theology must issue.

The Nature and Method of Biblical Theology
from his *Biblical Theology*

Geerhardus Vos, "One: Introduction: The Nature and Method of Biblical Theology," in *Biblical Theology: Old and New Testaments* (Carlisle, PA: Banner of Truth, 1975), 3–18; reprinted from Grand Rapids: Eerdmans, 1948.

The best approach towards understanding the nature of Biblical Theology and the place belonging to it in the circle of theological disciplines lies through a definition of Theology in general. According to its etymology, Theology is *the science concerning God*. Other definitions either are misleading, or, when closely examined, are found to lead to the same result. As a frequent instance, the definition of Theology as "the science of religion" may be examined. If in this definition "religion" be understood subjectively, as meaning the sum-total of religious phenomena or experiences in man, then it is already included in that part of the science of anthropology which deals with the psychical life of man. It deals with man, not with God. If, on the other hand, religion be understood objectively, as the religion which is normal and of obligation for man because prescribed by God, then the further question must arise, why God demands precisely this and no other religion; and the answer to this can be found only in the nature and will of God; therefore ultimately, in thus dealing with religion, we shall find ourselves dealing with God.

From the definition of Theology as the science concerning God follows the necessity of its being based on revelation. In scientifically dealing with impersonal objects we ourselves take the first step; they are passive, we are active; we handle them, examine them, experiment with them. But in regard to a spiritual, personal being this is different. Only in so far as such a being chooses to open up itself can we come to know it. All spiritual life is by its very nature a hidden life, a life shut up in itself. Such a life we can know only through revelation. If this be true as between man and man, how much more must it be so as between God and man. The principle involved has been strikingly formulated by Paul: "For who among men knoweth the things of a man, save the spirit of the man which is in him? even so the things of God none knoweth, save the Spirit of God" (1 Cor. 2:11). The inward hidden content of God's mind can become the possession of man only through a voluntary disclosure on God's part. God must come to us before we can go to Him. But God is not a personal spiritual being *in general*. He is a Being infinitely exalted above our highest conception. Suppose it were possible for one human spirit to penetrate directly into another human spirit: it would still be impossible for the spirit of man to penetrate into the Spirit of God. This emphasizes the necessity of God's opening up to us the mystery of His nature before we can acquire any knowledge concerning Him. Indeed, we can go one step farther still. In all scientific study we exist alongside of the objects which we investigate. But in Theology the relation is reversed. Originally God alone existed. He was known to Himself alone, and had first to call into being a creature before any extraneous knowledge with regard to Him became possible. Creation therefore was the first step in the production of extra-divine knowledge.

Still a further reason for the necessity of revelation preceding all satisfactory acquaintance with God is drawn from the abnormal state in which man exists through sin. Sin has deranged the original relation between God and man. It has produced a separation where previously perfect communion prevailed. From the nature of the case every step towards rectifying this abnormality must spring from God's sovereign initiative. This particular aspect, therefore, of the indispensableness of revelation stands or falls with the recognition of the fact of sin.

Division of Theology into Four Great Departments

The usual treatment of Theology distinguishes four departments, which are named Exegetical Theology, Historical Theology, Systematic Theology and Practical Theology. The point to be observed for our present purpose is the position given Exegetical Theology as the first among these four. This precedence is due to the instinctive recognition that at the beginning of all Theology lies a passive, receptive attitude on the part of the one who engages in its study. The assumption of such an attitude is characteristic of all truly exegetical pursuit. It is eminently a process in which God speaks and man listens. Exegetical Theology, however, should not be regarded as confined to Exegesis. The former is a larger whole of which the latter is indeed an important part, but after all only a part. Exegetical Theology in the wider sense comprises the following disciplines:

(*a*) the study of the actual content of Holy Scripture;

(*b*) the inquiry into the origin of the several Biblical writings, including the identity of the writers, the time and occasion of composition, dependence on possible sources, etc. This is called *Introduction*, and may be regarded as a further carrying out of the process of Exegesis proper;

(*c*) the putting of the question of how these several writings came to be collected into the unity of a Bible or book; this part of the process bears the technical name of *Canonics;*

(*d*) the study of the actual self-disclosures of God in time and space which lie back of even the first committal to writing of any Biblical document, and which for a long time continued to run alongside of the inscripturation of revealed material; this last-named procedure is called the study of *Biblical Theology.*

The order in which the four steps are here named is, of course, the order in which they present themselves successively to the investigating mind of man. When looking at the process from the point of view of the divine activity the order requires to be reversed, the sequence here being

(*a*) the divine self-revelation;

(*b*) the committal to writing of the revelation-product;

(*c*) the gathering of the several writings thus produced into the unity of a collection;

(*d*) the production and guidance of the study of the content of the Biblical writings.

Definition of Biblical Theology

Biblical Theology is that branch of Exegetical Theology which deals with the process of the self-revelation of God deposited in the Bible.

In the above definition the term "revelation" is taken as a noun of action. Biblical Theology deals with revelation as a divine activity, not as the finished product of that activity. Its nature and method of procedure will therefore naturally have to keep in close touch with, and so far as possible reproduce, the features of the divine work itself. The main features of the latter are the following:

[1] *The historic progressiveness of the revelation-process*

It has not completed itself in one exhaustive act, but unfolded itself in a long series of successive acts. In the abstract, it might conceivably have been otherwise. But as a matter of fact this could not be, because revelation does not stand alone by itself, but is (so far as Special Revelation is concerned) inseparably attached to another activity of God, which we call *Redemption.* Now redemption could not be otherwise than historically successive, because it addresses itself to the generations of mankind coming into existence in the course of history. Revelation is the interpretation of redemption; it must, therefore, unfold itself in instalments as redemption does. And yet it is also obvious that the two processes are not entirely co-extensive, for revelation comes to a close at a point where redemption still continues. In order to understand this, we must take into account an important distinction within the sphere of redemption itself. Redemption is partly objective and central, partly subjective and individual. By the former we designate those redeeming acts of God, which take place on behalf of, but outside of, the human person. By the latter we designate those acts of God which enter into the human subject. We call the objective acts central, because, happening in the centre of the circle of redemption, they concern all alike, and are not in need of, or capable of, repetition. Such objective-central acts are the incarnation, the atonement, the resurrection of Christ. The acts in the subjective sphere are called individual, because they are repeated in each individual separately. Such subjective-individual acts are regeneration, justification, conversion, sanctification, glorification. Now revelation accompanies the process of objective-central redemption only, and this explains why redemption extends further than revelation. To insist upon its accompanying subjective-individual redemption would imply that it dealt with questions of private, personal concern, instead of with the common concerns of the world of redemption collectively. Still this does not mean that the believer cannot, for his subjective experience, receive enlightenment from the source of revelation in the Bible, for we must remember that continually, alongside the objective process, there was going on the work of subjective application, and that much of this is reflected in the Scriptures. Subjective-individual redemption did not first begin when objective-central redemption ceased; it existed alongside of it from the beginning.

There lies only one epoch in the future when we may expect objective-central redemption to be resumed, viz., at the Second Coming of Christ. At that time there will take place great redemptive acts concerning the world and the people of God collectively. These will add to the volume of truth which we now possess.

[2] *The actual embodiment of revelation in history*

The process of revelation is not only concomitant with history, but it becomes incarnate in history. The facts of history themselves acquire a revealing significance. The crucifixion and resurrection of Christ are examples of this. We must place act-revelation by the side of word-revelation. This applies, of course, to the great outstanding acts of redemption. In such cases redemption and revelation coincide. Two points, however, should be remembered in this connection: first, that these two-sided acts did not take place primarily for the purpose of revelation; their revelatory character is secondary; primarily they possess a purpose that transcends revelation, having a God-ward reference in their effect, and only in dependence on this a man-ward reference for instruction. In the second place, such act-revelations are never entirely left to speak for themselves; they are preceded and followed by word-revelation. The usual order is: first word, then the fact, then again the interpretative word. The Old Testament brings the predictive preparatory word, the Gospels record the redemptive-revelatory fact, the Epistles supply the subsequent, final interpretation.

[3] *The organic nature of the historic process observable in revelation*

Every increase is progressive, but not every progressive increase bears an organic character. The organic nature of the progression of revelation explains several things. It is sometimes contended that the assumption of progress in revelation excludes its absolute perfection at all stages. This would actually be so if the progress were non-organic. The organic progress is from seed-form to the attainment of full growth; yet we do not say that in the qualitative sense the seed is less perfect than the tree. The feature in question explains further how the soteric sufficiency of the truth could belong to it in its first state of emergence: in the seed-form the minimum of indispensable knowledge was already present. Again, it explains how revelation could be so closely determined in its onward movement by the onward movement of redemption. The latter being organically progressive, the former had to partake of the same nature. Where redemption takes slow steps, or becomes quiescent, revelation proceeds accordingly. But redemption, as is well known, is eminently organic in its progress. It does not proceed with uniform motion, but rather is "epochal" in its onward stride. We can observe that where great epoch-making redemptive acts accumulate, there the movement of revelation is correspondingly accelerated and its volume increased. Still further, from the organic character of revelation we can explain its increasing multiformity, the latter being everywhere a symptom of the development of organic life. There is more of this multiformity observable in the New Testament than in the Old, more in the period of the prophets than in the time of Moses.

Some remarks are in place here in regard to a current misconstruction of this last-mentioned feature. It is urged that the discovery of so considerable an amount of variableness and differentiation in the Bible must be fatal to the belief in its absoluteness and infallibility. If Paul has one point of view and Peter another, then each can be at best only approximately correct. This would actually follow, if the truth did not carry in itself a multiformity of aspects. But infallibility is not inseparable from dull uniformity. The truth is inherently rich and complex, because God is so Himself. The whole contention ultimately rests on a wrong view of God's nature and His relation to the world, a view at bottom Deistical. It conceives of God as standing outside of His own creation and therefore having to put up for the instrumentation of His revealing speech with such imperfect forms and organs as it offers Him. The didactic, dialectic mentality of Paul would thus become a hindrance for the ideal communication of the message, no less than the simple, practical, untutored mind of Peter. From the standpoint of Theism the matter shapes itself quite differently. The truth having inherently many sides, and God having access to and control of all intended organs of revelation, shaped each one of these for the precise purpose to be served. The Gospel having a precise, doctrinal structure, the doctrinally-gifted Paul was the fit organ for expressing this, because his gifts had been conferred and cultivated in advance with a view to it.

[4] *The fourth aspect of revelation determinative of the study of Biblical Theology consists in its practical adaptability*

God's self-revelation to us was not made for a primarily intellectual purpose. It is not to be overlooked, of course, that the truly pious mind may through an intellectual contemplation of the divine perfections glorify God. This would be just as truly religious as the intensest occupation of the will in the service of God. But it would not be the full-orbed religion at which, as a whole, revelation aims. It is true, the Gospel teaches that to know God is life eternal. But the concept of "knowledge" here is not to be understood in its Hellenic sense, but in the Semitic sense. According to the former, "to know" means to mirror the reality of a thing in one's consciousness. The Semitic and Biblical idea is to have the reality of something practically interwoven with the inner experience of life. Hence "to know" can stand in the Biblical idiom for "to love," "to single out in love." Because God desires to be *known* after this fashion, He has caused His revelation to take place in the milieu of the historical life of a people. The circle of revelation is not a school, but a "covenant." To speak of revelation as an "education" of humanity is a rationalistic and utterly un-scriptural way of speaking. All that God disclosed of Himself has come in response to the practical religious needs of His people as these emerged in the course of history.

The Various Things Successively Designated by the Name of Biblical Theology

The name was first used to designate a collection of proof-texts employed in the study of Systematic Theology. Next it was appropriated by the Pietists to voice their protest against a hyperscholastic method in the treatment of Dogmatics. Of course, neither of these two usages gave rise to a new distinct theological discipline. This did not happen until a new principle of treatment, marking it off from the disciplines already existing, was introduced. The first to do this was J. P. Gabler in his treatise *De justo discrimine theologiae biblicae et dogmaticae* (1787) [*On the Proper Distinction between Biblical and Dogmatic Theology*]. Gabler correctly perceived that the specific difference of Biblical Theology lies in its historical principle of treatment. Unfortunately both the impulse of the perception and the manner of its application were influenced by the Rationalism of the school to which he belonged. The chief characteristic of this school was its disrespect for history and tradition and the corresponding worship of Reason as the sole and sufficient source of religious knowledge. A distinction was drawn between (*a*) past beliefs and usages recorded in the Bible as a matter of history and (*b*) what proved demonstrable by Reason. The former was *a priori* rejected as unauthoritative, while the latter was received as truth—not, however, because found in the Bible, but because in agreement with the deliverances of Reason. If the question was put, what use could then possibly be served by its presentation in the Bible, the answer was given that at an earlier stage of development men were not yet sufficiently acquainted with Reason to base on it their religious convictions and practice, and consequently God accommodated Himself to the ancient method of basing belief on external authority, a method now superseded.

It is important to observe that this so-called *Rationalismus Vulgaris* ["common rationalism"] was not (and, so far as it still survives, is not) a purely philosophical or epistemological principle, but has a specifically religious coloring. Rationalism has so long and so violently attacked religion that it cannot seem amiss to turn the tables and for a moment criticize rationalism from the view-point of religion. The main point to notice is its undue self-assertiveness over against God in the sphere of truth and belief. This is a defect in religious endowment. Reception of truth on the authority of God is an eminently religious act. Belief in the inspiration of Scripture can be appraised as an act of worship under given circumstances. This explains why rationalism has by preference asserted itself in the field of religion even more than in that of pure philosophy. This is because in religion the sinful mind of man comes most directly face to face with the claims of an independent,[5] superior authority. Closely looked at, its protest against tradition is a protest against God as the source of tradition, and its whole mode of treatment of Biblical Theology aims not at honoring history as the form of tradition, but at discrediting history and tradition. Further, rationalism is defective, ethically considered, in that it shows a tendency towards glorification of its own present (that

---

5. Ed. note: The original American edition read "heteronomous" instead of "independent."

is, at bottom, *of itself*) over against the future no less than the past. It reveals a strong sense of having arrived at the acme of development. The glamour of unsurpassability in which rationalism usually sees itself is not calculated to make it expect much from God in the future. In this attitude, the religious fault of self-sufficiency stands out even more pronouncedly than in the attitude towards the past.

It was formerly considered a merit to have stressed the importance of tracing the truth historically, but when this was done with a lack of fundamental piety it lost the right of calling itself theology. The rationalistic brand of Biblical Theology, at the same time that it stresses the historical, declares its product religiously worthless.

To define the issue between ourselves and this type of treatment sharply, we should remember, that it is not a question of the apprehensive function of the reason in regard to religious truth. Man is psychically so constructed that nothing can enter into his knowledge except through the gateway of the reason. This is so true, that it applies equally to the content of Special Revelation as to the ingress of truth from any other source. Nor is it a question about the legitimate functioning of the reason in supplying the mind of man with the content of natural revelation. Still further, reason has its proper place in the thinking through and systematizing of the content of Special Revelation. But the recognition of all this is not identical with nor characteristic of what we technically call rationalism. The diagnosis of the latter lies in the atmosphere of irreligion and practical disdain of God which it carries with itself wherever appearing. The main fault to be found with people of this kind is that to the pious mind their whole outlook towards God and His world appears uncongenial because lacking in the most primary sense the sensorium of religion.

Ever since its birth in this rationalistic environment Biblical Theology has been strongly affected, not only in the way in which philosophical currents have touched Theology in general, but in a special manner to which its nature especially lays it open. This is shown in the extent to which, at the present time, the treatment of Biblical Theology is influenced by the philosophy of evolution. This influence is discernible in two directions. In the first place, the qualitative advancement found by the hypothesis of evolution in the world-process is extended to the emergence of religious truth. It becomes an advance, not only from the lower to the higher, but from the barbarous and primitive to the refined and civilized, from the false to the true, from the evil to the good. Religion, it is held, began with animism; next came polytheism, then monolatry, then monotheism. Such a view, of course, excludes revelation in every legitimate sense of the word. Making all things relative, it leaves no room for the absoluteness of the divine factor.

In the second place, the philosophy of evolution belongs to the family of positivism. It teaches that nothing can be known but phenomena, only the impressionistic side of the world, not the interior objective reality, the so-called "things in themselves." Such things as God, the soul, immortality, a future life, etc., cannot enter into human knowledge, which in fact is no knowledge in the old solid sense. Consequently all these objective verities come to be regarded as lying beyond the province of Theology. If the name *Theology* is still retained, it is as a misnomer for a classification and discussion of religious phenomena. The question is no longer as to what is true, but simply as to what has been believed and practised in the past. Alongside of this general camouflage of the science of religion under the name of Theology, and inseparable from it, runs the turning inside out of Biblical Theology in particular. This becomes the phenomenology of the religion recorded in the literature of the Bible.

Guiding Principles

Over against these perversive influences it is of importance clearly to lay down the principles by which we propose to be guided in our treatment of the matter. These are:
(*a*) the recognition of the infallible character of revelation as essential to every legitimate theological use made of this term. This is of the essence of Theism. If God be personal and conscious, then the inference is inevitable that in every mode of self-disclosure He will make a faultless expression of His nature and purpose. He will communicate His thought to the world with the stamp of divinity on it. If this were otherwise, then the reason would have to be sought in His being in some way tied up in the limitations and relativities of the world, the medium of expression obstructing His intercourse with the world. Obviously the background of such a view is not Theism but pantheism.
(*b*) Biblical Theology must likewise recognize the objectivity of the groundwork of revelation. This means that real communications came from God to man *ab extra* ["from outside"]. It is unfair to pass this off with a contemptuous reference to the "dictation" view. There is nothing undignified in dictation, certainly not as between God and man. Besides, it is unscientific, for the statements of the recipients of revelation show that such a process not seldom took place.

Our position, however, does not imply that all revelation came after this objective fashion. There is an ingredient which may properly be called "subjective revelation." By this is meant the inward activity of the Spirit upon the depths of human sub-consciousness causing certain God-intended thoughts to well up therefrom. The Psalms offer examples of this kind of revelation, and it also occurs in the Psalmodic pieces found here and there in the prophets. Although brought up through a subjective channel, we none the less must claim for it absolute divine authority; otherwise it could not properly be called revelation. In this subjective form revelation and inspiration coalesce. We must, however, be on our guard against the modern tendency to reduce all revelation in the Scriptures to this category of the *ab intra* ["from inside"]. That is usually intended to deprive revelation of its infallibility. A favorite form is to confine revelation proper to the bare acts of self-disclosure performed by God, and then to derive the entire thought-content of the Bible from human reflection upon these acts. Such a theory, as a rule, is made a cover for involving the whole teaching of the Bible in the relativity of purely human reflection, whose divine provenience cannot any longer be verified, because there is nothing objective left to verify it by.

The belief in the joint-occurrence of objective and subjective revelation is not a narrow or antiquated position; it is in reality the only broad-minded view, since it is willing to take into account all the facts. The offence at "dictation" frequently proceeds from an underestimate of God and an over-estimate of man. If God condescends to give us a revelation, it is for Him and not for us *a priori* to determine what forms it will assume. What we owe to the dignity of God is that we shall receive His speech at full divine value.
(*c*) Biblical Theology is deeply concerned with the question of inspiration. All depends here on what we posit as the object with which our science deals. If its object consist in the beliefs and practices of men in the past, then obviously it is of no importance whether

the subject matter be considered as true in any other or higher sense than that of a reliable record of things once upon a time prevailing, no matter whether inherently true or not. A Biblical Theology thus conceived ought to classify itself with Historical Theology, not with Exegetical Theology. It professes to be a History of Doctrine for Biblical times. It treats Isaiah as it would treat Augustine, the sole question being what was believed, not whether it was true or not. Our conception of the discipline, on the other hand, considers its subject matter from the point of view of revelation from God. Hence the factor of inspiration needs to be reckoned with as one of the elements rendering the things studied "truth" guaranteed to us as such by the authority of God.

Nor should it be objected that in this way we can postulate inspiration for so much in the Bible only as pertains to the special occasions when God engaged in the act of revelation, so that as Biblical theologians we could profess indifference at least to the doctrine of "plenary inspiration." The conception of partial inspiration is a modern figment having no support in what the Bible teaches about its own make-up. Whenever the New Testament speaks about the inspiration of the Old, it is always in the most absolute, comprehensive terms. Consulting the consciousness of the Scriptures themselves in this matter, we soon learn that it is either "plenary inspiration" or nothing at all. Further, we have found that revelation is by no means confined to isolated verbal disclosures, but embraces facts. These facts moreover are not of a subordinate character: they constitute the central joints and ligaments of the entire body of redemptive revelation. From them the whole receives its significance and coloring. Unless, therefore, the historicity of these facts is vouched for, and that in a more reliable sense than can be done by mere historical research, together with the facts the teaching content will become subject to a degree of uncertainty rendering the revelation value of the whole doubtful. The trustworthiness of the revelations proper entirely depends on that of the historical setting in which they appear.

Again it should be remembered that the Bible gives us in certain cases a philosophy of its own organism. Paul, for instance, has his views in regard to the revelation structure of the Old Testament. Here the question of full inspiration, extending also to the historical teaching of Paul, becomes of decisive importance. If we believe that Paul was inspired in these matters, then it ought greatly to facilitate our task in producing the revelation structure of the Old Testament. It were superfluous labour to construct a separate view of our own. Where that is attempted, as it is by a certain school of Old Testament criticism, the method does not rest on an innocent view about the negligibility of the factor of inspiration, but on the outright denial of it.

Objections to the Name "Biblical Theology"

We shall now consider the objections that have been made to the name *Biblical Theology*.
(a) The name is too wide, for, aside from General Revelation, all Theology is supposed to rest on the Bible. It suggests a droll degree of presumption to preempt this predicate "Biblical" for a single discipline.
(b) If it be answered that "Biblical" need not be understood of an exceptional claim to Biblical provenience, but only concerns a peculiar method employed, viz., that of reproducing the truth in its original Biblical form without subsequent transformation, then our reply must be that, on the one hand, this of necessity would seem to cast a reflection on other theological disciplines, as though they were guilty of manipulating the truth,

and that, on the other hand, Biblical Theology claims too much for itself in professing freedom from transforming treatment of the Scriptural material. The fact is that Biblical Theology just as much as Systematic Theology makes the material undergo a transformation. The sole difference is in the principle on which the transformation is conducted. In the case of Biblical Theology this is historical, in the case of Systematic Theology it is of a logical nature. Each of these two is necessary, and there is no occasion for a sense of superiority in either.

(c) The name is incongruous because ill-adjusted to the rest of our theological nomenclature. If we first distinguish the four main branches of theology by prefixing to the noun "Theology" an adjective ending in "-al," and then proceed to name a subdivision of one of these four on the same principle, calling it Biblical Theology, this must create confusion, because it suggests five instead of four main departments, and represents as a coordination what in reality is a subordination.

For all these reasons the name "History of Special Revelation" is greatly to be preferred. It expresses with precision and in an uninvidious manner what our science aims to be. It is difficult, however, to change a name which has the sanction of usage.

The Relation of Biblical Theology to Other Disciplines

We must now consider the relation of Biblical Theology to other disciplines of the theological family.

(a) Its relation to Sacred (Biblical) History. This is very close. Nor can it fail to be so, since both disciplines include in their consideration material which they have in common with each other. In Sacred History redemption occupies a prominent place, and to deal with redemption without drawing in revelation is not feasible, for, as shown above, certain acts are both redemptive and revelatory at the same time. But the same is true *vice versa*. Revelation is so interwoven with redemption that, unless allowed to consider the latter, it would be suspended in the air. In both cases, therefore, the one must trespass upon the other. Still logically, although not practically, we are able to draw a distinction as follows: in reclaiming the world from its state of sin God has to act along two lines of procedure, corresponding to the two spheres in which the destructive influence of sin asserts itself. These two spheres are the spheres of being and of knowing. To set the world right in the former, the procedure of redemption is employed; to set it right in the sphere of knowing, the procedure of revelation is used. The one yields Biblical History, the other Biblical Theology.

(b) Its relation to Biblical Introduction. As a rule Introduction has to precede. Much depends in certain cases on the date of Biblical documents and the circumstances of their composition for determining the place of the truth conveyed by them in the scheme of revelation. The chronology fixed by Introduction is in such cases regulative for the chronology of Biblical Theology. This, however, does not mean that the tracing of the gradual disclosure of truth cannot reach behind the dating of a document. The Pentateuch records retrospectively what unfolding of revelation there was from the beginning, but it also contains much that belongs to the chapter of revelation to and through Moses. These two elements should be clearly distinguished. So much for the cases where Biblical Theology depends on the antecedent work of Introduction. Occasionally, however, the order between the two is reversed. Where no sufficient external evidence exists for dating a document, Biblical Theology may be able

1012

to render assistance through pointing out at which time the revelation content of such a writing would best fit in with the progress of revelation.

(c) Its relation to Systematic Theology. There is no difference in that one would be more closely bound to the Scriptures than the other. In this they are wholly alike. Nor does the difference lie in this, that the one transforms the Biblical material, whereas the other would leave it unmodified. Both equally make the truth deposited in the Bible undergo a transformation: but the difference arises from the fact that the principles by which the transformation is effected differ. In Biblical Theology the principle is one of historical, in Systematic Theology it is one of logical construction. Biblical Theology draws a *line* of development. Systematic Theology draws a *circle*. Still, it should be remembered that on the line of historical progress there is at several points already a beginning of correlation among elements of truth in which the beginnings of the systematizing process can be discerned.

The Method of Biblical Theology

The method of Biblical Theology is in the main determined by the principle of historic progression. Hence the division of the course of revelation into certain periods. Whatever may be the modern tendency towards eliminating the principle of periodicity from historical science, it remains certain that God in the unfolding of revelation has regularly employed this principle. From this it follows that the periods should not be determined at random, or according to subjective preference, but in strict agreement with the lines of cleavage drawn by revelation itself. The Bible is, as it were, conscious of its own organism; it feels, what we cannot always say of ourselves, its own anatomy. The principle of successive *Berith*-makings (Covenant-makings), as marking the introduction of new periods, plays a large role in this, and should be carefully heeded. Alongside of this periodicity principle, the grouping and correlation of the several elements of truth within the limits of each period has to be attended to. Here again we should not proceed with arbitrary subjectivism. Our dogmatic constructions of truth based on the finished product of revelation, must not be imported into the minds of the original recipients of revelation. The endeavor should be to enter into their outlook and get the perspective of the elements of the truth as presented to them. There is a point in which the historic advance and the concentric grouping of truth are closely connected. Not seldom progress is brought about by some element of truth, which formerly stood in the periphery, taking its place in the centre. The main problem will be how to do justice to the individual peculiarities of the agents in revelation. These individual traits subserve the historical plan. Some propose that we discuss each book separately. But this leads to unnecessary repetition, because there is so much that all have in common. A better plan is to apply the collective treatment in the earlier stages of revelation, where the truth is not as yet much differentiated, and then to individualize in the later periods where greater diversity is reached.

Practical Uses of the Study of Biblical Theology

It remains to say something about the practical uses of the study of Biblical Theology. These may be enumerated as follows:

(a) It exhibits the organic growth of the truths of Special Revelation. By doing this it enables one properly to distribute the emphasis among the several aspects of teaching and preaching. A leaf is not of the same importance as a twig, nor a twig as a branch, nor a branch as the trunk of the tree. Further, through exhibiting the organic structure of revelation, Biblical Theology furnishes a special argument from design for the reality of Supernaturalism. (*b*) It supplies us with a useful antidote against the teachings of rationalistic criticism. This it does in the following way: The Bible exhibits an organism of its own. This organism, inborn in the Bible itself, the critical hypothesis destroys, and that not only on our view, but as freely acknowledged by the critics themselves, on the ground of its being an artificial organism in later times foisted upon the Bible, and for which a newly discovered better organism should be substituted. Now by making ourselves in the study of Biblical Theology thoroughly conversant with the Biblical consciousness of its own revelation structure, we shall be able to perceive how radically criticism destroys this, and that, so far from being a mere question of dates and composition of books, it involves a choice between two widely divergent, nay, antagonistic conceptions of the Scriptures and of religion. To have correctly diagnosed criticism in its true purpose is to possess the best prophylaxis against it.

(*c*) Biblical Theology imparts new life and freshness to the truth by showing it to us in its original historic setting. The Bible is not a dogmatic handbook but a historical book full of dramatic interest. Familiarity with the history of revelation will enable us to utilize all this dramatic interest.

(*d*) Biblical Theology can counteract the anti-doctrinal tendency of the present time. Too much stress proportionately is being laid on the voluntary and emotional sides of religion. Biblical Theology bears witness to the indispensability of the doctrinal groundwork of our religious fabric. It shows what great care God has taken to supply His people with a new world of ideas. In view of this it becomes impious to declare belief to be of subordinate importance.

(*e*) Biblical Theology relieves to some extent the unfortunate situation that even the fundamental doctrines of the faith should seem to depend mainly on the testimony of isolated proof-texts. There exists a higher ground on which conflicting religious views can measure themselves as to their Scriptural legitimacy. In the long run that system will hold the field which can be proven to have grown organically from the main stem of revelation, and to be interwoven with the very fiber of Biblical religion.

(*f*) The highest practical usefulness of the study of Biblical Theology is one belonging to it altogether apart from its usefulness for the student. Like unto all theology it finds its supreme end in the glory of God. This end it attains through giving us a new view of God as displaying a particular aspect of His nature in connection with His historical approach to and intercourse with man. The beautiful statement of Thomas Aquinas is here in point: (*Theologia*) *a Deo docetur, Deum docet, ad Deum ducit* [(Theology) (which) is taught by God, teaches God, leads to God].

The Authority of the Old Testament and the Authority of Christ

NED B. STONEHOUSE

Ned B. Stonehouse, "Chapter VII: The Authority of the Old Testament and the Authority of Christ," in *The Witness of the Synoptic Gospels to Christ* (Grand Rapids: Baker, 1979), 188–225; reprint from *The Witness of Matthew and Mark to Christ* (Philadelphia: Presbyterian Guardian, 1944).

Ned Bernard Stonehouse (1902–62) was one of the founding faculty members of Westminster Theological Seminary. He was educated at Princeton Seminary and received his Ph.D. from the University of Amsterdam. He taught New Testament for over thirty years. He was also involved in the life of the Orthodox Presbyterian Church. Stonehouse worked within Westminster Seminary's characteristic biblical-theological tradition of Geerhardus Vos. Stonehouse was the founder and editor of the New International Commentary on the New Testament. He was widely respected as a New Testament scholar; in particular, he contributed significantly to the study of the distinct emphasis of each Synoptic Gospel.

The selection below illustrates his approach to the Gospels. In this chapter, originally published in his *The Witness of Matthew and Mark to Christ* (1944), Stonehouse develops the Old Testament predictions of the coming of Christ and the authority of the Son of God, who self-consciously fulfills the Old Testament's predictions. Thus he develops crucial concerns of biblical theology: the authority of the Old Testament together with the authority of Christ himself the Messiah. In these matters Stonehouse stands close to his mentor, Vos, to whom he refers many times.

Bibliography: Richard B. Gaffin. "Stonehouse, Ned Bernard (1902–1962)." Pp. 253–54 in *DP&RTA*. William L. Lane. Foreword to *Origins of the Synoptic Gospels: Some Basic Questions*, by Ned B. Stonehouse.

Grand Rapids: Baker, 1979. Pp. v–vii. Dan G. McCartney. "Ned Bernard Stonehouse." Pp. 154–64 in *Bible Interpreters of the 20th Century*. Mark A. Noll. *Between Faith and Criticism: Evangelicals, Scholarship, and the Bible in America*. 1986. Repr., Vancouver: Regent College, 1998. Pp. 107–9. Moisés Silva. "Ned B. Stonehouse and Redaction Criticism." *WTJ* 40, 1 (Fall 1977): 77–88; 40, 2 (Spring 1978): 281–303. Paul Woolley. "Stonehouse, Ned Bernard (1902–1962)." P. 933 in *NIDCC*.

SYNOPSIS

I. *Jesus and the Old Testament*

A. Matthew's appeal to prophecy: establishes the divine character of the history of Christ; involves a philosophy of the history of revelation; the question whether this philosophy coincides with that of Jesus depends on the historicity of the messianic consciousness and of Jesus' use of the Old Testament to interpret this consciousness.

B. The pervasive evidence in Matthew of Jesus' affirmation of the Scriptures of the Old Testament: (1) Jesus' appeal to the Old Testament in controversy; (2) Matthew 5:17–19 implies validity of the Old Testament, but also the dawn of a new era of divine action and speech; (3) The antitheses in Matthew 5 stress the absoluteness of Jesus' authority, but not at the expense of the authority of the Old Testament:

a. Shown especially in teaching concerning anger, fleshly desire, and hate, where Jesus affirms the law but also utters a polemic against an externalistic interpretation of the law, but

b. Also true of the other antitheses, as shown particularly by the teaching concerning divorce, in which Jesus demands that a legal provision directed to a particular occasion be seen in the perspective of the basic teaching of the law.

II. *The Authority of the Son of God*

A. The authority with which Jesus speaks alongside of the Old Testament is grounded in his personal qualification as Son of God: the fundamental character of Matthew 11:27, intimating that the Son is both subject and object of sovereign divine disclosure; Matthew 14:33 and 16:16 as two extraordinary instances of apprehension of the divine revelation concerning Jesus; the latter, recording Peter's confession, expresses an estimate of Jesus implicit in Mark's account; Matthew 16:17 does not imply that a new epochal disclosure was made at this juncture, nor does it intimate that Peter experiences a completely new subjective apprehension, but contrasts the apprehension of those who had eyes to see with the purely human estimates of others; Matthew 14:33 then is not anachronistic; its harmony with Mark 6:51–52.

B. The question whether Matthew tones down the human side of Christ: the emotional life of Jesus is not completely absent, although not as prominent as in Mark; not the result of theological dogmatizing but to be traced to the personal qualities of the evangelist and especially to his distinctive aim; the latter clearly includes the purpose to set forth the history of Jesus in the perspective of the history of revelation, and this would call for less occupation with the subjective aspects of his life; that Jesus had a truly human life is everywhere presupposed; the Son of David as well as the Son of God.

In pursuance of our effort to discover the distinctiveness of the testimony of Matthew, our attention has been directed to certain features which come to conspicuous disclosure through a comparison of the disposition of this gospel with that of Mark. The occupation with details of the life of Jesus before his public ministry and after the resurrection and the extensive report of the message of Jesus obviously comprise two of these distinguishing features. Yet neither serves effectively to set Matthew off from the other gospels. The former feature he shares with Luke and, in part, with John; the latter likewise is characteristic of Luke and John, and, in any case, in view of the space which Mark devotes to the teaching of Jesus, is of relative importance. There is, however, a third feature of Matthew's narrative which apparently provides a cue for the understanding of this evangelist's individual approach to his subject, namely, that afforded by his interpretation of the history of Christ by reference to Old Testament prophecy. This trait is in truth not completely absent from the other gospels, but it is so prominent in Matthew that few readers can have failed to notice it. Only as he depicts the life and ministry of Jesus as the fulfillment of the revelation of the Old Testament does the evangelist, as it were, write in the first person singular; otherwise his personality remains completely hidden behind the proclamation of the gospel. Accordingly the ultimate question of the authority of Jesus Christ must be approached by way of the consideration of the affirmation of the authority of the Scriptures of the Old Testament.

Matthew's appeal to the Old Testament, we have had occasion to observe in Chapter 5, is displayed prominently in his record of the birth and infancy of Jesus (Matt. 1:22–23; [2:5–6]; 2:15, 17–18, 23). As a matter of fact there are nearly as many appeals to prophetic testimony in this brief section as in the whole of the rest of the gospel, this concentration receiving its most adequate explanation perhaps from the fact that, when Jesus began his public ministry, his own deeds and words served to indicate the divine nature of his person and mission. Nevertheless, the Matthaean portrayal of the public ministry is distinguished from the Marcan record which it parallels by several indications that the ministry of Jesus had followed a divine plan which had been intimated to the prophets long beforehand. The initiation of his work in Galilee and the entrance into Jerusalem just before his death, the two focal points of Jesus' mission, fulfill declarations made through the prophet Isaiah and Zechariah (Matt. 4:14–16; 21:4–5). Specific aspects of the healing and teaching ministry, moreover, are represented as being performed in order to fulfill prophetic testimony. From the Isaianic discourses concerning the Suffering Servant, Matthew derives both the active and passive aspects of the healing ministry of Jesus, both the mercy which he constantly demonstrated toward the afflicted and humble and the quiet reserve which commanded that he should not be made manifest (Matt. 8:17; 12:17–21). A passage from the Psalter is fulfilled in Jesus' parabolic discourses concerning the kingdom of heaven (Matt. 13:35). In the passion narrative of Matthew, as in that of Mark, the fulfillment of the divine will is fully disclosed by Jesus' own references to the Scriptures, but Matthew also observes that certain details of the unfolding of the events, the reward which Judas received for his iniquity and its final disposition, as well as the manner of Jesus' entrance upon the scene of his death, has been intimated in the Scriptures (Matt. 27:9–10; 21:4–5).

An impressive confirmation of the evangelist's faith in the divine character of the Old Testament revelation is provided by these concrete quotations. But his affirmation of the Old Testament is not introduced for its own sake, for it is clearly incidental to an affirmation of the divine character of the history of Christ. The evangelist is not developing an argument for the divinity of the prophetic record by reference to the fulfillment of specific predictions, but, presupposing with his readers the inspiration of the Old Testament, he is concerned to establish or confirm the belief that the history of Jesus, in its origin, purpose, unfolding and consummation, was to be understood as the action of God in fulfilling his own word to the prophets. Here there is involved therefore a philosophy of revelation, an understanding of the history of revelation, which is of the most profound significance for the illumination of the whole of Matthew's gospel.

The interpretation of the history of revelation in terms of prophecy and fulfillment, it may be observed, involves a doctrine of the progressive character of revelation. In recognizing the revelation as progressive, however, we must take note that, while it as such is antithetical to a mechanical conception of revelation, it also must be qualitatively distinguished from an evolutionary interpretation of religion. The disclosures of the divine purpose and action in the history of Christ are not isolated blocks of revelation which are to be joined to blocks which have been previously placed in position, nor are they related to what had come before simply as the full flowering of a bud. Both the divine prophecy and the divine fulfillment require to be comprehended in their distinctiveness and in their unity, neither one being stressed at the expense of the other. There is a unity guaranteed by the single divine actor and expressed in a single message of righteousness and salvation, but there is also a qualitative difference between prophecy and fulfillment which excludes the supposition that the latter follows from the former as a matter of course. In Matthew's appeal to the Old Testament, in other words, there is implicit the doctrine of the covenants, the old and the new, each representing a separate manifestation of the divine action and speech.

Among the questions which have risen in our times with reference to Matthew's use of the Old Testament, none is more pressing than that which raises the issue of the historical validity of his interpretation of the career of Jesus in terms of divine prophecy. Is Matthew himself, or one of the early Christian communities, responsible for this feature as an aspect of the primitive defense of the truth of Christianity? Or does this interpretation of the history of Jesus rest ultimately upon Jesus' own interpretation of the meaning of his life?

The final decision between these two main positions is bound up with the decision reached as to the credibility of the witness of Matthew, and of the other gospels, to the messianic consciousness of Jesus. For, by common consent, the position of Matthew, shared with the other records, is that Jesus was controlled by the conviction that he was the promised Messiah of the Old Testament. While Matthew himself appears to be responsible for the several separate instances of appeal to prophetic testimony which have been mentioned, he clearly was not the originator of the belief that Jesus viewed his own history as the fulfillment of messianic prophecy. To establish that proposition would require nothing less than the demonstration that all of the other records derived their messianic estimate of Jesus from him.

The most explicit evidence of Jesus' messianic self-appraisal is found in the record of the discourses delivered during the last days in Jerusalem. Direct appeal is made to the Old Testament to substantiate the judgment that, though rejected of "the builders," he was made "the head of the corner" in the new structure of God's building (Matt. 21:42–44; Ps.

118:22–23; cf. Mark 12:1–11; Luke 20:17). In a controversy with the Pharisees, wherein indeed he does not make direct claim of messiahship, he proves from an inspired word of David that the Messiah's sovereignty extends even to David himself, and that therefore the title Son of David does not express the full transcendence and authority of the Messiah (Matt. 22:43–46; Ps. 110:1; cf. Mark 12:35–37; Luke 20:41–44). Similarly the divine instrumentality in his death is expressed by use of Zechariah's description of the Shepherd whom the Lord would smite (Matt. 26:31; Zech. 13:7; cf. Mark. 14:27). The frequency of such appeals to Old Testament prophecy in the climactic situations at the end of his career may not, however, be construed as proof that this characteristic emerged as a late development in the process of his self-appraisal. Only slightly less clearly does Jesus reflect upon his person and mission in his employment of Isaianic prophecy to answer the inquiry of the Baptist and in his quotation from Malachi to interpret the preparatory significance of the forerunner (Matt. 11:4–6, 10; Isa. 35:5–6; 61:1; Mal. 3:1; cf. Luke 7:22–23, 27). Moreover, it is now admitted on all sides that the gospels represent Jesus as being completely sure of his mission at least as early as the beginning of his public ministry.

In order to appreciate Jesus' regard for the Old Testament prophetic teaching concerning himself, and on its background to evaluate Matthew's distinctive appeal to prophecy, it is necessary to divest one's self of the notion that the correspondence discovered between isolated utterances of the prophets and isolated details of Jesus' history involves a mechanistic or atomistic understanding of the revelation of Scripture. The isolated utterances are not thought of as so many individual disclosures as to the future, but as integral parts of an organism. As an organism, for all of its diversity and growth, it constitutes in its entirety a revelation of the will of God. Since the Messiah as the Anointed of the Lord is invested with divine authority and appointed to accomplish the divine will, his appearance and activity on the scene of history must at every point give evidence of correspondence and compliance with the revealed will of God. Religion for Jesus was not mysticism; it was rather the conscious response of the individual to the revelation of God in history. The evidences of agreement with the Old Testament supplied by Matthew's comments and by Jesus' quotations alike have meaning only on this high view of the Old Testament.[1]

The evidence that Jesus' appeal to messianic prophecy involved an affirmation of the whole of the revelation of the Old Testament Scriptures, and not merely of a few isolated prophetic utterances, is supplied by Matthew in abundant measure. Critics who are busy with efforts to reconstruct the "historical" life of Jesus commonly seek to dissociate Jesus from the Matthaean portrayal of his attitude toward the Old Testament, but there is little readiness to deny that the Jesus of Matthew's testimony accepted the Old Testament as inspired Scripture. In his replies to Satan's temptations in the wilderness, the decisive word is constantly the authoritative commands of Scripture: it is sufficient to say simply, "It is written" (Matt. 4:4, 6, 10; cf. Luke 4:4, 8, 12). Likewise the final court of appeal in his controversies

---

1. Cf. Geerhardus Vos, *The Teaching of Jesus Concerning the Kingdom of God and the Church* (New York: American Tract Society, 1903), 12–13: "No array of explicit statements in which he acknowledges his acceptance of the Old Testament Scriptures as the word of God can equal in force this implied subordination of himself and of his work to the one great scheme of which the ancient revelation given to Israel formed the preparatory stage. Indeed, in appropriating for himself the function of bringing the kingdom, in laying claim to the Messianic dignity, Jesus seized upon that in the Old Testament which enabled him at one stroke to make its whole historic movement converge in himself. There is in this a unique combination of the most sublime self-consciousness and the most humble submission to the revelation of God in former ages. Jesus knew himself at once as the goal of history and the servant of history."

with the Jewish leaders, Pharisees and Sadducees alike, is the Scriptures. His reply to the Sadduceean attack upon the doctrine of the resurrection took the form of the simple query whether they had not read what God had spoken in Exodus 3:6 (Matt. 22:23–33; cf. Mark. 12:18–27; Luke 20:27–38). While Jesus shared the Sadduceean affirmation of the authority of the Pentateuch, his position had greater formal agreement with that of the Pharisees who accepted the rest of the Old Testament as well. In spite of his agreement with the Pharisees on the extent of the Scriptures, however, he regarded their position as in reality impinging upon the divine authority of the Scriptures. Jesus charged the Pharisees with transgressing and making void the commandment and word of God since they accorded their traditions a place alongside of and in effect above the law of God, thus obscuring the qualitative distinction between the word of God and the commandments of men, and actually abrogating the divine law (Matt. 15:1–9; cf. Mark. 7:1).[2]

And in addition to the impressive weight of the testimony borne by Jesus' use of Scripture, we learn from Matthew of his express didactic teaching of the binding force of the law and the prophets:

> Think not that I came to destroy the law or the prophets; I came not to destroy, but to fulfill. For verily I say unto you, until heaven and earth pass away, one jot or one tittle shall in no wise pass from the law until all things be accomplished. Whosoever therefore shall break one of these least commandments, and shall teach men so, shall be called least in the kingdom of heaven, but whosoever shall do and teach them, he shall be called great in the kingdom of heaven. (Matt. 5:17–19)

The fulfillment and accomplishment of the law and the prophets, as opposed to their destruction and mutilation, which Jesus expresses here as the purpose of his mission, involves inescapably the conviction that the entire Old Testament possesses permanent validity as the Word of God.

To observe that this teaching of Jesus involves his affirmation of the divine character of the Old Testament does not, however, exhaust its implications. The fulfillment of the law, like the fulfillment of the prophets, while presupposing and reaffirming its divine truth

---

2. Cf. also Matthew 19:3–9; 21:42; 22:41–46 for other instances of Jesus' appeal to the Scriptures to silence his opponents.

Matthew 23:2–3, which places the scribes and Pharisees on Moses' seat, and enjoins obedience to their injunctions, apparently contradicts the qualitative distinction between the law of God and the tradition of the elders. "Here," says Streeter, "we have attributed to our Lord an emphatic commandment to obey, not only the Law, but the scribal interpretation of it. That is to say, He is represented as inculcating scrupulous obedience to that very 'tradition of the elders' which He specifically denounces in Mk. vii. 13." Burnett Hillman Streeter, *The Four Gospels: A Study of Origins* (London: Macmillan, 1924), 257. And Streeter adds that the point of view is to be explained as due to the derivation of this discourse in large part from a special source of the evangelist.

In spite of the *prima facie* impression that, in affirming the validity of the Law of Moses, these verses go to the extreme of acknowledging the authority of the teaching of the scribes and Pharisees, this interpretation must be set aside, for it involves a contradiction with the rest of the discourse. In the very next verse (Matt. 23:4) Jesus speaks evidently without approval of their imposition of "heavy burdens" upon men. In Matthew 23:16–22 he condemns them as "blind guides" because of their casuistic deliverances regarding swearing, and in 23:23–24 he condemns them for leaving undone "the weightier matters of the law, justice and mercy and faith." The polemic against the scribes and Pharisees in this chapter is therefore by no means confined to their sins of omission; it also is directed against their traditions. In so far then as Jesus approves their teaching because they "sit on Moses' seat," he cannot be understood as countenancing interpretations of Moses which added to Moses, or in effect set him aside. In the light of the whole discourse therefore, the teaching of Jesus in Matthew 23:2–3 is to the effect that the scribes and Pharisees were to be honored in their affirmation of the law of Moses, but decidedly not to be imitated in their non-observance of it.

and authority, predicates the dawn of a new era. The law and the prophets do not produce their own fulfillment. It is the presence of Christ alone which accomplished this end, and this fact, in the light of Matthew's total witness to Christ, clearly involves new divine action and speech. The fulfillment of the law and the prophets represents not a mere repetition or reiteration of the old revelation, but the announcement of the appearance of the age to which the old revelation looked forward. Accordingly, Matthew's witness to Christ finds its distinctiveness, or at least a highly important aspect of it, in its portrayal of the history of Jesus Christ in the perspective of the history of revelation. And this means far more than that he was the Messiah of the Old Testament Scriptures. The profound affirmation of Matthew is that *the coming of the Messiah of promise signifies the coming of one whose life and teaching were themselves a new epochal revelation that was the consummation of the old.*

That Jesus' fulfillment of the Old Testament law involved far more than an affirmation of the validity of the law appears unmistakably in the illustrations of his interpretation of the law provided by the antitheses of the Sermon on the Mount. The accent on the authoritative new utterances of Christ in truth is so powerful that in certain instances an apparent impingement upon the abiding authority of the law is disclosed. Six times Jesus, completely on his own authority, and without any attempt to vindicate his categorical declarations, seems to set his own pronouncements in antithesis to "that which had been spoken," the latter deliverances consisting of, or at least including, in every instance a quotation from the law of Moses (Matt. 5:21–26, 27–30, 31–32, 33–37, 38–42, 43–48). It was the absoluteness with which Jesus spoke, as possessing authority in his own right, and not deriving the authority of his utterances from Scripture or revered traditions like the scribes, that caused the crowds to express amazement at this teaching (Matt. 7:28). There had appeared on the scene a new self-confident voice, the voice of one who assumed an authority which was in no sense inferior to that of the commandments of God given through Moses.

The sovereignty with which Jesus speaks is so absolute and unequivocal that his fulfillment of the law seems to carry with it the invalidation of the law of Moses. In the light of Jesus' categorical affirmation of the validity of the law and the prophets which immediately precedes the antithesis, and of his decisive use of the authority of the Scriptures in controversy, however, it would be rash to conclude, without the most careful scrutiny of Jesus' words, that he actually meant to abrogate the authority of the law.

In three of the antitheses it is perfectly clear that Jesus' pronouncements presuppose the authority of the Old Testament commands, and that his own teaching represents a proclamation of the full implications of these commandments in opposition to the casuistic and legalistic interpretations of the scribes. What Jesus says about the sins of anger against one's brother, of fleshly desire, and of hate against one's enemies (Matt. 5:21–26, 27–30, 43–47), cannot plausibly be construed as impinging in the least upon the validity of the sixth and seventh commandments of the Decalogue and of the injunction to love one's neighbor. No hint is given of a relaxing of the authority of the law; on the contrary he indicates that the demands of God are more comprehensive and more exacting than men had supposed. Most pointedly his utterances are directed against the current interpretations of the law. It is perhaps in the sixth of the antitheses that this implication appears most clearly:

> Ye have heard that it was said, Thou shalt love thy neighbor, and thou shalt hate thine enemy. But I say unto you, Love your enemies, and pray for those who persecute you. (Matt. 5:43–44)

Only the words, "Thou shalt love thy neighbor," comprise a divine injunction (Lev. 19:18); the conclusion, "Thou shalt hate thine enemy," is an inference which could be drawn only on the basis of an externalistic and atomistic approach to the law of God.[3]

That the approach of Jesus to the Scriptures was far from being externalistic and atomistic is confirmed at many points. Not all of the commands stood on the same level as isolated precepts, but all were unified and controlled by the commandments to love God himself with heart, soul, mind and strength, and one's neighbor as one's self (Matt. 22:37–39; cf. Mark. 12:29–31; Luke 10:27–37). Similarly he comprehends the demands of the law and the prophets under the injunction, "All things therefore whatsoever ye would that men should do unto you, even so do ye also to them" (Matt. 7:12). The same repudiation of a shallow externalism appears in Jesus' teaching concerning the fourth command. Without implying for a moment that the command was no longer valid, he condemns the application of the Pharisees on the ground that they failed to comprehend it in the light of the preeminent requirement of mercy (Matt. 12:7; cf. 9:13; 23:23–24).[4]

It follows from these observations that the formulae employed to introduce the first member of the several antitheses, whether in the form, "Ye have heard that it was said unto them of old time" (Matt. 5:21, 33),[5] or, "Ye have heard that it was said" (Matt. 5:27, 38, 43), or simply, "It was said" (Matt. 5:31), are not intended to correspond to "It is written," which Jesus often employs in appealing to the final authority of Scripture. In every other instance where the form "it was said," or its equivalent, is used in connection with a passage of Scripture, it is specifically stated that the speaker is the Lord himself or one of his prophets (cf., e.g., Matt. 1:22; 2:17; 22:31; 24:15). Here, on the contrary, the non-designation of the speaker and the ostensible reference to instruction which had been *heard* by the people from their teachers rather than read directly from the Scriptures, taken in connection with the polemic which Jesus is directing against the Pharisees in his teaching concerning righteousness (cf., e.g., Matt. 5:20), indicates that the quotations of Scripture are introduced as illustrations of scribal interpretations rather than as Jesus' own evaluations of the meaning of the commandments.

With respect to the other three antitheses, which concern divorce, oaths and *ius talionis*, there appears at first blush to be an abrogation on Jesus' part of that which had been written in the law of Moses. He seems to set aside Mosaic provisions which allowed for separation from a wife, for swearing and for retribution, and to have substituted for them absolute prohibitions. Since these utterances are commonly regarded as evidences of a radical break

3. According to Billerbeck, Str-B 1:353, the injunction, "Thou shalt hate thine enemy," cannot be traced to any particular source, and he conjectures that it probably was a popular maxim of the day. In reviewing the rabbinic teaching, pp. 364–68, he indicates that in general hate was condemned, but in certain instances it was permitted and in others even commanded.

4. Cf. Vos, *The Teaching of Jesus Concerning the Kingdom of God and the Church*, 109: "He once more made the voice of the Law the voice of the living God, who is present in every commandment, so absolute in his demands, so personally interested in man's conduct, so all-observant, that the thought of yielding to him less than the whole inner life, the heart, the soul, the mind, the strength, can no longer be tolerated. Thus quickened by the spirit of God's personality, the law becomes in our Lord's hands a living organism, in which soul and body, spirit and letter, the greater and smaller commandments are to be distinguished, and which admits of being reduced to great comprehensive principles in whose light the weight and purport of all single precepts are to be intelligently appreciated."

5. The AV renders τοῖς ἀρχαίοις "by them of old time," and this construction finds some modern support, e.g., by Frederik Willem Grosheide, *Het Heilig Evangelie Volgens Mattheus*, Kommentaar op het Nieuwe Testament (Kampen: J. H. Kok, 1954), 79, 87. The contrast is then between "the ancients" and Jesus (ἐγώ). In support of the position that the dative is an indirect object, in contrast to ὑμῖν, see the comments of Alexander, Zahn (221n90), McNeile, Klostermann. This view is grammatically easier and is intrinsically strong, whether "the ancients" are understood as the men of Moses' time or more broadly as referring to earlier generations.

with the objective authority of the law, and as requiring that Matthew 5:17–19 be interpreted either as allowing for such a relaxation of the law, or as originating from Matthew rather than from Christ (involving then the presence in the early church of a legalism from which Christ himself was free), it is obligatory to consider these passages with care. In our judgment, no escape from the plain implications of Matthew 5:17–19 is possible by way of exegesis. The explicit and emphatic affirmation of the authority of the law and the prophets excludes the interpretation of "fulfillment" and "accomplishment" as euphemisms for "relaxation" or "invalidation" or "spiritualization." The real issue is therefore whether Matthew introduces a contradiction into the record of Jesus' teaching by making him affirm most emphatically the validity of the law and then equally emphatically its annulment.[6]

Does Jesus' teaching on divorce involve a weakening of the authority of the law of Moses? Several considerations bear upon the determination of the answer to this question. So far as the quotation from Deuteronomy 24:1 is concerned, it may not be overlooked that it is not introduced into the discussion by Jesus, introduced, that is, only in order to contradict it, but as a passage which the Pharisees were wont to cite in order to substantiate a lax attitude towards divorce. This appears not only from the repetition of the formula, "It was said," which in this context points to Pharisaic interpretations, but also from the contexts in which the reference appears here and in Matthew 19:3–11 (cf. Mark 10:2–12). In the latter context the passage is explicitly quoted by the Pharisees in order to ground a liberal policy, and in Matthew 5:32 the implication of Jesus' words is to the same effect. The meaning of Matthew 5:31 is therefore somewhat as follows: "Ye have heard of the appeal of Jewish teachers to Deuteronomy 24:1 in the interest of substantiating a policy which permits husbands, freely at their own pleasure, to divorce their wives simply by providing them with a duly attested document of the transaction."

The Deuteronomic passage definitely implies then a reckoning with the practice of divorce when the husband found "something unseemly" in his wife, and makes provision for the issuance of a certification of the divorce. There was a dispute among the rabbis as to what might be included under "something unseemly," the school of Shammai maintaining that it referred to something distinctly shameful while the school of Hillel allowed that it might even include the provocation caused by the burning of his food.[7] It is clear then that the passage was appealed to currently to substantiate a much more liberal attitude toward

---

6. For the position that understands Matthew 5:17–19 as implying a Judaistic legalism, see Rudolf Bultmann, *Jesus* (Berlin: Deutsche Bibliothek, 1926), 60–61 (English translation, *Jesus and the Word* [New York: Scribner, 1934], 62–63); *Die Geschichte der synoptischen Tradition* (Göttingen: Vandenhoeck & Ruprecht, 1931), 146–47. Dibelius similarly speaks of legalistic and secular influences: Martin Dibelius, *The Message of Jesus Christ* (New York: Scribner, 1939), 160–61; cf. *Jesus* (Berlin: W. de Gruyter, 1939), 100. See also Streeter, *The Four Gospels*, 256–57. The merit of this position is that it plainly recognizes that these verses imply the objective validity of the law and the prophets.

As an example of the point of view which seeks to resolve the problem by an exegesis which in effect denies that Jesus meant to affirm the objective authority of the Old Testament, I may cite Theodore H. Robinson's estimate of the meaning of Jesus: "He did not come to destroy, but to fulfil, to make complete, to perfect, to emend, to give the temporary thing, with its numerous occasional details, an eternal validity. The Law had been an interim expedient, the best that could be devised until the fulness of time, for the securing of certain ends. But under the regime of Jesus these ends can be still better secured, and the Law, though superseded as the final authority, will be fulfilled, completed, absorbed into a higher rule of life" (cf. his *The Gospel of Matthew*, The Moffatt New Testament Commentary [London: Hodder & Stoughton, 1928], 35). On our part, of course, we are far from disregarding the progressive character of divine revelation, including especially the radical implications of the new revelation in Christ, but these implications are set forth in the teaching of Jesus with an insistence upon continuity with respect to truth and authority between the revelation of the Old Testament and that of the new dispensation.

7. See Billerbeck, Str-B 1:312–18.

divorce than Jesus was willing to countenance. However, whatever grounds for divorce the Mosaic enactment may have had in view, the thrust of the passage in its original setting is not to establish grounds for divorce, but, presupposing the practice of divorce on various grounds, to provide some protection for the woman from the harshness of her husband. The aim of the legislation is not to condone divorce as such, but to mitigate its evil consequences. Although then the use made of this passage in order to substantiate laxness was illegitimate, the fact remains that the Mosaic provision for the protection of the woman assumes that divorce was permissible. Christ condemns what Moses accepted as part of the *status quo*.

Does it follow, however, that Jesus actually implies that he is setting aside the objective authority of the law of Moses? Before anyone presumes to answer this question in the affirmative, he must take account of certain weighty considerations on the other side. In this very context where Jesus disputes with the Pharisees concerning the legitimacy of divorce, he assumes the validity of the law! For he appeals to the record of the creation and of the creation ordinance of marriage in Genesis to substantiate his teaching that the marriage union is indissoluble (Matt. 19:4–9; Gen. 1:27; 5:2; 2:24). Moreover, in condemning divorce as adultery, he condemns it as a violation of the seventh commandment. If therefore Jesus were setting aside the law he would have to be acknowledged as doing so by way of affirming the binding authority of the same law. There is then no impingement of the authority of the law as such, but there is an insistence that a certain isolated provision be placed in its proper perspective within the context of the entire law. As we have observed above, the affirmation of the authority of law on Jesus' part did not carry with it the implication that its provisions were to be understood mechanically and atomistically. The lesser commands are to be subordinated to the greater commands of the law; the details must be regarded as elements in a comprehensive unity.

The particular place which the Deuteronomic provision occupied within the revelation of the entire law is intimated by Jesus himself in his observations in Matthew (Matt. 19:8–9; cf. Mark. 10:5). He states that the commandment with reference to a bill of divorce was enacted "with regard to the hardness of their heart." It was not a commandment dictated by the nature of God and his righteousness in relation to his creatures, as was true of the creation ordinance of marriage, but by the subjective state of sinful men. The commandment was contingent, not absolute; it was temporary and positive rather than permanent as an expression of God's moral will.[8] This distinction between the permanent and temporary in God's law does qualify one's understanding of it and its application to a concrete situation, but in no wise diminishes the objective authority of the law and the prophets.

Jesus indeed is so far from substituting his own authority for that of the law in his teaching concerning divorce that, as a matter of fact, the sovereignty of his own utterance, introduced by the formula, "But I say unto you," does not receive quite the same accent as in the antitheses previously reviewed. There is not even the semblance of the enunciation of new principles, but rather the authoritative interpretation of the revealed will of God as, from the beginning, involving the inference which he explicitly pronounces,

8. Whether the reference to the hardness of men's hearts as the occasion of the enactment respecting a bill of divorce has in view the harshness of the husband which was to be mitigated, a thought entirely in keeping with the context in Deuteronomy, or envisages the generally low spiritual state of the children of the Exodus, is difficult to decide. In either case the occasion is a concrete historical situation in the life of the theocracy, and the legislation bears more of a civil than a moral character. See Joseph Addison Alexander on Mark 10:5 (cf. *The Gospel according to Mark* [New York: Scribner, 1858], 273, 275).

namely, that "he who divorces his wife, saving for the cause of fornication, maketh her an adulteress" (Matt. 5:32).

We turn now to a consideration of the questions raised by the fourth of the antitheses which concerns the utterance of oaths (Matt. 5:33–37). The teaching of Jesus that the disciples should not swear at all appears to set up an antithesis between his doctrine and the Old Testament provisions with respect to oaths. And the authority with which Jesus speaks on this subject seems to be asserted at the expense of the authority of the Old Testament. If one looks beneath the surface, however, appearance and reality will be seen again not to coincide. The words quoted as spoken to "them of old time" are accurate enough as a summary of Old Testament teaching, although not a precise quotation (Ex. 20:7; Lev. 19:12; Num. 30:2; Deut. 23:21). Evidently, this formulation, considered as a summary of the divine requirements concerning swearing, was represented as implying that if only swearing were not to a false proposition and did not profane the name of God, there was no need to take oaths seriously. Once again a fundamentally false approach to the divine law is in view and is being condemned, an approach which through externalistic and casuistic interpretation of isolated passages resulted in the justification of frivolous oaths, oaths by heaven and earth, by Jerusalem, by one's head, or the like.[9] Jesus condemns such vain efforts to avoid a reckoning with God in all of one's asseverations, whether in the form of oaths or not, by the declaration that they were not to swear at all. Although no qualification of this statement is mentioned, it clearly is qualified by the context so as to demand its confinement to the relationship between brethren. The righteousness of the kingdom, Jesus teaches, involves such a regard for the truth that simple affirmations and denials should suffice. That the declaration of Jesus cannot be meant to apply to oaths as required in civil relationships, for example, is confirmed by the fact that Jesus himself, when adjured by the high priest to say whether he was the Christ, the Son of God, gave his assent (Matt. 26:63). To discover in Jesus' teaching in Matthew 5:34–37 an absolute prohibition of oaths under all circumstances, and to conclude that Jesus took issue with the requirements of the Mosaic law concerning false or profane swearing, is to apply to these words the same externalistic approach which Jesus condemned in the Pharisees. The fulfillment of the law in this instance likewise, therefore, does not relax the authority of the law but sets forth its radical and ultimate meaning. It remains significant, nevertheless, that it is Jesus who, setting aside current misinterpretation, pronounces with sovereign self-assurance what God truly requires.

Brief consideration must also be given to the fifth antithesis (Matt. 5:38–42). If Jesus' teaching concerning retaliation is viewed in the light of the principles which have emerged from a study of the other antitheses, the harmony of his pronouncement of his own authority with the recognition of the objective authority of the Old Testament cannot be denied. Jesus' quotation of *ius talionis*, as recorded in Exodus 21:24 and other passages, was evidently not intended to express his own judgment as to what the Old Testament taught on the subject of personal rights, but as a recollection of the teaching which had been appealed to in order to justify personal revenge. The purpose of Jesus is not to annul the law of retribution as applying to civil life, but to set forth the ethical principles which are demanded by the righteousness of God and which must come to expression in the kingdom of God. Hence

---

9. Cf. Matthew 5:34–36; 23:16–22. See Billerbeck, Str-B 1:332–36, for illustrations from rabbinic teaching.

he teaches in characteristically paradoxical and figurative form that, rather than resort to vindictiveness, one should readily allow one's self to suffer loss.[10]

Understood as illustrations of Jesus' fulfillment of the law, the antitheses then provide no support of the thesis that they involve an abrogation of the objective authority of the law. In the single instance where an enactment through Moses is set aside as provisional, namely, in the instance of the provision for a bill of divorcement, Jesus appeals decisively to the teaching of the law which is not circumscribed by reference to a temporary state of affairs. In the five other cases the design of Jesus is to show that current interpretations are inadequate as abiding by the externals or are in error as to the actual requirements of the law. As we have intimated, however, the significance of the utterances of Jesus in these contexts is by no means exhausted in the evidence they provide of his affirmation of the binding force of the revelation of the old covenant. For alongside of the affirmations of the law there is found constantly an emphatic note of authority, independent of the authority of the law itself, which fulfills it by declaring the radical demands of the righteousness of God. Ultimately, the thought of two independent authorities, both coming with absolute binding force, is to be sure intolerable and inconceivable. And it was such for Jesus. The only absolute authority which he recognized was the authority of the living God. But standing where he did, and conscious of his messianic authority, he called attention inevitably to the structure of the history of revelation, and, without setting aside the old covenant, proclaimed the arrival of a new authority which had to be obeyed because it, too, was divine.

The independent authority of Christ, so conspicuously displayed on the background of the maintenance of the authority of the Old Testament Scriptures, finds further emphasis in Matthew in the frequency of the use of the first person singular of the verb "to say." This form occurs far more often in Matthew than in the other gospels in the record of Jesus' utterances: some fifty-five times as compared with some forty-three in Luke, thirty-four in John, and only eighteen in Mark. Although the emphatic personal pronoun of the first person is found outside of the antitheses in only a single saying (Matt. 16:18), "I say" often gains solemnity from the conjunction of "verily." Of the fifty-five instances mentioned above, Matthew reports thirty-one in the form, "Verily, I say unto you." Even John has only twenty-six cases of "Verily, verily, I say unto you," while Mark contains only thirteen and Luke six passages like Matthew's, although in four other cases the latter uses other similar expressions (Luke 4:25; 9:27; 12:44; 21:3). Matthew's distinctive use of this solemn expression is concentrated in the five long sections of discourse material. Of the eighteen times that it is used in these discourses, only one or two can be paralleled from the other gospels, while some six of the other thirteen instances in Matthew find parallels in Mark or Luke or both.

In a pervasive fashion, therefore, Matthew presents Christ as constituting a new authority alongside that of the Old Testament. While he affirms the revelation of the law and the

---

10. Cf. Matthew 5:29–30. See Alexander, *The Gospel according to Matthew* (New York: Scribner, 1873), 141–43, and Herman N. Ridderbos, *De Strekking der Bergrede naar Mattheus* (Kampen: J. H. Kok, 1936), Paragraph 36, pp. 167–74. It is interesting that Solomon Zeitlin, *Who Crucified Jesus?* (New York: Harper & Brothers, 1942), 119–121, while admitting that the Pharisees set aside the lex talionis by a legal fiction, holds that Jesus affirmed the validity of this law. The difference between Jesus and the Pharisees on this point, he says, was that instead of following the pharisaic process of "interpretation," Jesus "appealed to the conscience of the plaintiff not to demand an eye for an eye and not to resist evil by repaying evil" (p. 121). Actually Jesus went far beyond appealing to men not to use their rights, for the heart of his instruction is that personal vindictiveness is to be condemned as contrary to God's will. See the writer's discussion in Ned B. Stonehouse, "Who Crucified Jesus?" *WTJ* 5, 2 (May 1943): 137–65, esp. 156–60. The quotation from *Who Crucified Jesus?* is by permission of the publishers, Harper & Brothers.

prophets, and is even subservient to it, yet paradoxically his own authority is not derived from the revelation that had gone before, and even completes and transcends it. As not derived from the Old Testament or from any other extraneous source, his authority is seen to inhere in his own person, that is, in his sheer right, simply because of who and what he is, to speak as he spoke. Consequently, one may not isolate his teaching from his person. The former cannot be affirmed without the latter. Consequently, not his words only but his person and life also come as a new revelation. The revelatory meaning of Jesus himself, implying that to fail to comprehend him as constituting a divine disclosure is to fail utterly to understand him at all, is taught in all the gospels, but it is preëminently the testimony of Matthew. It is Matthew who is chiefly concerned to show the place of the history of Christ and of his disclosures within the whole structure of God's word to men. In a word this is done by demonstrating that Jesus came for the very purpose of fulfilling the law and the prophets.

That the authority with which Jesus spoke was bound up with his estimate of his own person needs now to be set forth in some detail. An important part of the evidence for this proposition is implicit in the exalted titles which Jesus used in speaking of himself and which were employed by others in addressing him. As the Son of Man, for example, he claimed to possess authority of a most exalted and comprehensive kind. Reserving the discussion of the use of that title for the following chapter, where it may more appropriately be considered in connection with the study of the message of the coming of the kingdom, we shall here limit ourselves chiefly to the revelatory significance associated with the use of the name Son of God.

In Mark, too, Christ is conspicuously disclosed as the Son of God, whose words and deeds are clothed with divine authority, and who may with all propriety be regarded as the object of worship. In view of the sheer transcendence and supernaturalness of the person of Christ in Mark, we are not much impressed with many attempts to cite Matthew as the representative of a higher Christology. It is true indeed that Matthew records the use of the name Son of God at a number of points where Mark is silent as, for example, in Matthew 14:33 and 16:16. Moreover, he alone reports the discourse after the resurrection in which "the Son" is spoken of as a person in the divine trinity (Matt. 28:19). And like Luke, in characterizing the Son's exclusive knowledge of the Father (Matt. 11:27; Luke 10:22), he implies the equality of the Son and the Father. While then Matthew's witness of Christ contains several highly significant instances of the name Son of God which are lacking in Mark, these data, in our judgment, serve not so much to display a Christological emphasis as to confirm the observation that Matthew is chiefly occupied with the exhibition of the place held by Jesus Christ, the Son of God, in the history of divine revelation.

The conjunction of divine sonship and divine revelation is most perspicuous in Matthew 11:25–27:

> At that season Jesus answered and said, I thank thee, O Father, Lord of heaven and earth, that thou didst hide these things from the wise and understanding, and didst reveal them unto babes; yea, Father, for thus it was well-pleasing in thy sight. All things have been delivered unto me of my Father, and no one knoweth the Son save the Father; neither doth any know the Father save the Son, and he to whomsoever the Son willeth to reveal him.

Here Jesus claims such an exclusive knowledge of the Father, and a consequent exclusive right to reveal the Father (both corresponding with the Father's exclusive knowledge and revelation of the Son), that nothing less than an absolutely unique self-consciousness, on an equality with that of the Father, is involved. To summarize Zahn's comment on this passage, the Son is not only the organ of revelation but is himself a mystery to be revealed; the knowledge of the Father and the knowledge of the Son are two sides of the same mystery, which is now revealed, and so the Father and the Son in fellowship with one another are both subject and object of revelation.[11] What Jesus is speaking about is no mere mystical perception of God, for even if a mystic would dare to claim to know God as God knows him, he would not so easily forget his devotion to the mystic ideal as to conceive of his mission in terms of revelation to others.[12] What is strikingly distinctive in this passage, as compared with Mark's total witness, is not the estimate of the person of Christ but the specific place given to his revelatory character as both subject and object of sovereign divine disclosure. After his resurrection the same Christ speaks of the new commission which has been given unto him who is the transcendent Son, the establishment of the fellowship of those who in all the world acknowledged him and obeyed his commands, and his perpetual activity on their behalf (Matt. 28:18–20), but even during his ministry on earth he possessed, in virtue of his sonship, an exclusive knowledge of the Father, and a commission to make him known to whomsoever he would. Here then is to be found the explanation of the amazing words, heard so often throughout the gospel: "I say unto you." Matthew 11:27 accordingly does not introduce a foreign note into the gospel. It cannot be set aside as a "Johannine logion." Rather it makes explicit what is expressed or is implicit at many points in the total witness of Matthew to Jesus. It brings the whole of Christ's ministry under the head of revelation. Jesus, who reveals the Father, himself becomes known through the Father's disclosure of the Son. Since the Father's revelation of the Son is inextricably bound up with the Son's revelation of the Father, since, that is to say, one cannot know God as the Father of Christ without knowing Christ as the Son of the Father, ultimately the two mysteries coincide and the action of revelation is conceived of as a single action. This action of the Father in

11. Theodor Zahn, *Das Evangelium des Matthäus* (Leipzig: Deichert, 1903), 442, See also the discussion of this passage by Geerhardus Vos, *The Self-Disclosure of Jesus* (New York: George H. Doran, 1926), 142–60. On the textual questions, see also John Martin Creed, *Luke* (London: Macmillan, 1930), 149–50. The absence of the "Father . . . Son" clause in a single Latin ms. of Luke, the variations between the present and past tenses of the verb "know" in certain patristic quotations, and instances of the inversion of the clauses in a few testimonies, plainly provide an altogether inadequate basis for the transformation of this passage into a declaration of ethico-religious sonship or mystical human experience. One particular point may be noticed here. Justin, the earliest father to quote the passage, in one instance (*Dialogue with Trypho* 100.1) uses the present form γινώσκει, but in two other passages (*Apology* 63.3, 13) the aorist ἔγνω. However, it is illuminating that in the latter passages, in both cases, the saying of Jesus is immediately preceded by quotations of Isaiah 1:3 which twice in the LXX uses ἔγνω with reference to the knowledge of God. The reversal of the clauses may be simple inadvertence, but may be due here, as in other patristic quotations, to the fact that the subject in the foreground of thought is the knowledge of God rather than specifically the knowledge of the Son.

12. The attempt of Eduard Norden, *Agnostos Theos* (Leipzig: Teubner, 1913), 277–308, followed closely by Martin Dibelius, *From Tradition to Gospel,* trans. Bertram Lee Woolf (London: Ivor Nicholson and Watson, 1934), 279–83, to interpret the saying as expressing oriental mysticism, cannot be regarded as successful, nor are the supposed parallels from Hellenistic mysticism really pertinent. It is also significant that both writers adopt some modification of the text. Norden, for example, even on his assumption that the verb "know" was originally an aorist, is far from doing justice to the implications of the passage when he interprets it as meaning that "Das Erkennen Gottes von seiten des Menschen setzt also voraus, dass der Mensch seinerseits von Gott zuvor erkannt wurde [Thus the knowledge of God from man's side presupposes that man on his part be known by God beforehand]" (p. 287)! On the basis of the patristic citations which reverse the clauses of Matthew 11:27, Dibelius (280n2) is ready to conclude that "The theme is thus the knowledge of the Father, and that may be the original because Jesus the revealer from whom men should learn is not really the unknown"! To assume that Jesus is not really the unknown is to beg the question at issue. It appears that the high Christology of the passage can be eradicated on through radical excisions from the text.

fellowship with the Son is carried out in the historical life of Christ, and hence that life is both history and revelation, in short a revelation in history. Nevertheless, the revelation is apprehended only by "babes" according to the Father's good-pleasure (Matt. 11:25; cf. v. 27).

Matthew 14:33 and 16:16 accordingly are two extraordinary instances of apprehension on the part of the disciples of the revelation which the Father has chosen to make concerning the Son, and wherein the Father is himself necessarily made known. The latter passage, relating the confession voiced by Peter in Caesarea Philippi, is highly meaningful for the understanding of Matthew for at least two outstanding reasons. The first reason is that Matthew reports the confession in the form, "Thou art the Christ, the Son of the living God," whereas Mark merely has, "Thou art the Christ." In Mark Peter might seem to recognize merely the messiahship of Jesus whereas Matthew reports the acknowledgment of his divine nature. Yet, as our study of Mark has shown, in the context of that gospel as a whole, and in the light of the previous disclosures of his divine messiahship, Mark must be understood as implying as much as Matthew records. It is inconceivable that he means to imply that Peter acknowledged Jesus as Messiah in some inferior and inadequate sense. Rather the Messiah, who is about to go to the cross, is acknowledged at his true worth, only Peter finds it intolerable that the one whose proper dignity and glory he has just confessed should insist upon the necessity of his passion and death (Mark 8:29–33). While then there is no basis for the judgment that Matthew and Mark contain two diverse evaluations of Jesus, the form of the confession as reported by Matthew serves to underscore the implication of this episode that Peter expresses an acknowledgment of Jesus which corresponds with his own self-estimate.

The second reason why Matthew's report of Peter's confession is noteworthy is that he alone records the declaration of Jesus that Peter's apprehension of the true nature of Christ was the result of the revelation of the Father (Matt. 16:17). In discussing the Marcan portrayal of the events connected with Caesarea Philippi the position was taken that the epochal character of this episode is not to be construed as constituted by a fresh disclosure of the Messiahship of Jesus. None is recorded or implied. What is new is the instruction concerning the passion of Christ which Jesus prepared for by eliciting an open avowal of his messianic dignity.[13] It is necessary to insist here that the situation is not otherwise in Matthew, in spite of the conspicuous reference to the divine revelation. If Matthew 16:17 is viewed in the perspective which Matthew 11:27 provides, as well as in the light of the entire previous record of the activity of Christ, it will appear that no new objective revelation of the moment can be in mind. Rather, the entire history of Christ has been in the nature of a divine revelation which the disciples, with greater or lesser clarity, and with admixture of doubt and bewilderment, have come to comprehend. In Peter's confession we are invited to observe then, not a new objective revelation, but genuine subjective apprehension. And even this apprehension is not clearly intimated to be a completely new apprehension. The fundamental contrast of the narrative is not between the disciples' previous lack of apprehension and their suddenly bestowed understanding, but between the inadequate and erroneous estimates of men, who held that he was at best one of the prophets, and the evaluation of his disciples who belonged to the inner circle and who had eyes to see and ears to hear. (Matt. 16:13–20; cf. Matt. 13:11–17).[14]

---

13. See Ned B. Stonehouse, *The Witness of Matthew and Mark to Christ* (Philadelphia: The Presbyterian Guardian, 1944), 66–69.

14. It is not overlooked in the discussion above that the verb "reveal" as used in Matthew 11:25, 27 and 16:17 evidently includes the idea of the subjective perception of what is objectively disclosed. But this would not warrant the inference that the disclosure which comes through Jesus and of which he is the object is conceived of by Matthew as wholly subjective. His historical life, including his deeds and his words, are viewed as an objectively valid disclosure of the divine will, and men are

From this perspective no difficulty is presented by the acknowledgment of Jesus as God's Son which appears in Matthew 14:33. If the confession of Peter in Matthew 16:16 represented a turning-point in the attitude of the disciples, grounded in a completely new revelation of the person of Jesus to them, the acknowledgment of Jesus' sonship which Matthew records in the narrative of the walking upon the sea might appear to introduce confusion and inconsistency into Matthew's delineation of the historical developments. Since, however, the whole of the ministry of Jesus is viewed as constituting a divine revelation, the apprehension of the revelation expressed in the words, "Of a truth thou art God's Son," does not imply that Matthew is reading back into an earlier stage of the disciples' experience an estimate of Christ's person which actually emerged at a later juncture. In fact, the confession in Matthew 14:33 is fully as intelligible as that in Matthew 16:16 since in the context the response is called forth by the miraculous action of Jesus in walking upon the water, rescuing Peter from the deep, and apparently also quieting the wind, besides Jesus' words of challenge to faith and of rebuke for doubt (Matt. 14:24–32).

Although then the acknowledgment of Jesus as God's Son in Matthew 14:33 is completely consistent with the implications of Matthew 16:16, there emerges an acute problem of a different sort when this passage is compared with the same story as recorded in Mark. Even if neither evangelist is controlled by a concept of development which would exclude such apprehension at this stage of the ministry, the two narratives seem to leave two mutually exclusive impressions:

And they that were in the boat worshipped him, saying, Of a truth thou art God's Son. (Matt. 14:33)

And they were exceedingly astonished in themselves; for they understood not concerning the loaves, but their heart was hardened. (Mark 6:51b–52)

The claim has been frequently advanced that Matthew has altered Mark in the interest of a more favorable view of the disciples.[15] Appearances to the contrary notwithstanding we believe that the two evangelists intimate essentially the same reaction. The amazement and lack of understanding are not of one piece, as has been pointed out before. The latter is introduced as an explanation of the former, indicating why there had not been an immediate apprehension of Christ as he came walking on the sea. On the background of their first reaction of fright,

---

judged by their response to his historical manifestation. Matthew 13:16–17 happily combine the objective and subjective in characterizing the true followers of Jesus as having the gift of hearing and seeing, that is, of understanding and faith, along with the privilege of beholding and hearing the things which many prophets and righteous men desired to see and hear. The recognition of the essential place given to the divinely granted apprehension of the divine disclosure does not, therefore, require a modification of the conclusions (1) that the confession of Peter is not grounded in a new epochal disclosure of the messiahship at this juncture, and (2) that it is not represented as a sudden new apprehension of Christ on his part.

The fact, moreover, that Matthew, in addition to the disclosure concerning the passion (Matt. 16:21), includes also the highly meaningful declaration concerning the church (Matt. 16:17–18), does not affect the main issue. The point of Jesus' evaluation of Simon is not that it indicates a completely new estimate of Peter's significance, but that it constitutes a divinely authoritative evaluation, occasioned indeed by Peter's divinely granted response as well perhaps as other historical circumstances. Whereas, on the one hand, Peter expresses the divine evaluation of Jesus as the Christ, the Son of the living God, an evaluation completely at variance with ordinary human estimates of Jesus, Jesus, on the other hand, declares the significance which the person known to men as Simon obtains in the establishment of the church. There is then, as the introductory words of Matthew 16:18 confirm, a striking parallelism between the two affirmations, "Thou art the Christ" and "Thou art Peter."

15. Recently, e.g., by Morton Scott Enslin, *Christian Beginnings* (New York: Harper & Brothers, 1938), 395.

their dawning apprehension took the form of amazement. And it must not be overlooked that Mark uses the term "astonishment" to describe a normal attitude of a disciple in the presence of the supernatural working of God's power.[16] Now it is important to observe that only the astonishment expressed in Mark 6:51, and not the lack of understanding in Mark 6:52, is properly parallel to Matthew 14:33, and thus the words which Matthew attributes to the disciples are completely consonant with the astonishment described by Mark. One who is filled with astonishment because of a sudden apprehension of the action of God through Christ might appropriately exclaim: "Of a truth thou art God's Son." Matthew as well as Mark dwells on the original fear of the disciples, but includes in addition a picture of Peter's lack of faith (Matt. 14:26, 28–31). Mark differs therefore only in that he explains their previous lack of apprehension, intimating that it had been due to the consideration that they had been passing through a period during which their hearts had been hardened.

For Matthew then as for Mark Jesus is the Son of God. In keeping with the larger compass of Matthew, and his purpose to set forth the revelatory and eschatological significance of Christ on the background of the disclosures of the law and the prophets, however, some matters that are merely intimated in Mark come to sharper and fuller expression in Matthew. Before leaving the subject of Matthew's delineation of Jesus as the Son of God, nevertheless, some consideration must be given to the charge that Matthew demonstrates its secondary and inferior character by its omission of details that reflect the human nature of Christ's life.[17] On the whole, in truth, it may be admitted that Matthew devotes little space to the portrayal of the emotional life of our Lord, and it is profitable to consider the reason for this lack. First, however, we do well to observe that such elements are not completely lacking. If Matthew may be charged with dehumanizing Jesus because the reference to the compassion of Christ in Mark 1:41 is not paralleled in Matthew 8:3, what is to explain his readiness to mention it in the two other instances where Mark reports it, and besides to mention it in Matthew 9:36 and 20:34? We doubt therefore that the lack of emphasis upon such details in the gospel as a whole may be explained as due to theological dogmatizing. If we seek the reason for Matthew's relative silence concerning the subjective side of the life of Jesus in the personal qualities of the evangelist and in his distinctive aims, we shall be on more solid ground. So far as the personality of the evangelist is concerned, we must admit that nothing positive can be affirmed. It may be that this evangelist lacked the capacity for strong emotional reactions which characterized Peter, and which seems to have left its impress upon Mark's gospel. We are on surer ground when we explore the significance of the distinctive aims of Matthew for the understanding of the manner in which the human life of Jesus is intimated in his gospel.

Whereas Mark portrays Christ as the Son of God whose appearance and actions come with startling abruptness, and provoke powerful emotional reactions among those who are confronted with his display of power and authority, Matthew is concerned less with subjective action and interaction than with the external developments. As has been frequently observed, Matthew is much more concise in his record of many incidents of the public ministry.[18] Vivid details found in Mark are often lacking. He often seems content to present to the reader a

---

16. See Stonehouse, *The Witness of Matthew and Mark to Christ*, 71, 106.

17. See ibid, 82–83, and for certain literature bearing on this point 82n21.

18. Cf. e.g., John C. Hawkins, *Horae Synopticae: Contributions to the Study of the Synoptic Problem* (Oxford: Clarendon Press, 1909), 158ff.

summary and contracted narration of what had happened. A partial explanation for such brevity may be the limitation of space dictated by the length of a papyrus roll together with his particular interest to report in considerable detail the teaching of Jesus.[19] In observing the greater conciseness of Matthew, however, care must be taken to avoid the impression that this is due to any lack of interest in the external events themselves. Apart from a positive interest in the historical career of Christ there can be no explanation of the evangelist's extensive report of the life of Christ which preceded the public ministry. In contrast to Mark's almost cryptic narration of the appearance of the Baptist, the coming of Jesus for baptism, and the temptation, Matthew finds room for a record of genealogy, an account of Christ's birth and infancy, as well as for a much more detailed record of the events which introduced the public ministry. As we have seen, however, Matthew does not treat the external course of Christ's life as a biographer. Rather his treatment of the years before the appearance in Galilee is explicable only if there is a perception of his purpose to set forth the meaning of the history of Christ as a part, in truth nothing less than the most significant part, of the history of revelation. His narration of subsequent events likewise discloses this motive, as well through the concentration upon the outward aspects of the divine action as through the specific indications of the fulfillment of divine prophecy.

This central motif of Matthew also illuminates the issue raised by the relative silence concerning the subjective, emotional side of the life of Jesus. Revelation by its very nature represents an action that proceeds from God to man; it is not human experience, nor even merely fellowship with the divine, but an objective disclosure from God to men. Hence the subjective reactions of Christ to human sin and weakness—his anger at their hardness of heart, his wonder at their unbelief, his sighing at their obtuseness—would not require mention as indispensable for the understanding of the place which the history of Christ occupied within the total structure of the history of revelation.

It remains to point out that in Matthew's record of the external events of the life of Christ an important place is given to its truly human character. If Matthew's account were the result of a process of dogmatizing dictated by an increasing reverence for Christ, it would be inexplicable that he preserves so full a record of the birth, temptation, and suffering of Jesus. The virgin birth, for example, while certainly not at variance with the affirmation of the deity of Jesus, does not establish his divine sonship in the highest sense. It presupposes a supernatural act of God in the origin of the human life of Jesus, but it also establishes the truth of his human life. Mark, it will be recalled, does not take time to tell of his birth as a man. Hence, the sinlessness of Jesus, presupposed by the Matthaean account of the baptism, does not introduce a heightening of Jesus' character. What Matthew makes explicit is surely implied in Mark of the one who appears, meteor-like, on the historical scene as the Son of God and the Son of Man.[20] But even the denial of Jesus' subjective need for baptism, as recorded by Matthew, goes hand in hand with the recognition that it was necessary to humble himself in order to fulfill the divine will for his life (Matt. 3:14–15).

Perhaps the most characteristic evidence of Matthew's recognition of the humanity of Jesus is found in the record of the use of the title Son of David. Only in a single context in

---

19. On the length of papyrus rolls, see Frederic G. Kenyon, *Our Bible and the Ancient Manuscripts* (New York: Harper, 1940), 10.

20. For a discussion of the allegation that Mark 10:18 constitutes a confession of sin on the part of Jesus, see the article by B. B. Warfield, "Jesus' Alleged Confession of Sin," *Princeton Theological Review* 12 (April 1914): 177–228, and reprinted in *Christology and Criticism* (New York: Oxford University Press, 1929), 97–145.

Mark and Luke is Jesus acknowledged as the Son of David (Mark 10:47–48; Luke 18:38–39; cf. Matt. 20:30).[21] In Matthew the name appears in several additional instances. He reports two additional cases of its use by those who sought Christ's aid (Matt. 9:27; 15:22) and a somewhat hesitant use by the crowds (Matt. 12:23). Of greater significance perhaps is his report of the employment of this title in the acclamation which Jesus received as he entered Jerusalem, which may be compared with the records of the other synoptists:

> Hosanna to the Son of David! Blessed is he that cometh in the name of the Lord. Hosanna in the highest. (Matt. 21:9, 15)

> Hosanna! Blessed is he that cometh in the name of the Lord. Blessed is the kingdom that cometh, the kingdom of our Father David. Hosanna in the highest. (Mark 11:9–10)

> Blessed is the king that cometh in the name of the Lord; peace in heaven and glory in the highest. (Luke 19:38)

In all three reports there is the same expectation of the messianic kingdom and of the coming king, and Mark as well as Matthew recalls the promise made to David, but only Matthew's quotation centers attention explicitly on Christ as Son of David. Most forcibly of all, however, Matthew's witness to Jesus as the Son of David is exhibited by the conspicuous place accorded this designation at the beginning of the gospel, where both the genealogy and the birth narrative proclaim him as the promised Son of David (Matt. 1:1, 20).

The name Son of David, we freely recognize, is a messianic title, and as such is used to express his royal prerogatives and mission rather than merely the fact of his physical descent from David; nevertheless, the opening sections of Matthew stress the conviction, evidently shared by Jesus' Jewish contemporaries, that Davidic descent was an indispensable qualification of the messianic king. Accordingly, in conspicuous fashion Matthew recognizes the true humanity of Jesus, certainly not less conspicuously than Mark, but he does so in a manner that conforms to his total witness to Christ as the one who fulfills the law and the prophets, and himself establishes, through the divine word and deed, the new order of God's rule. The survey of the use of this name has inevitably taken us beyond the specific theme of this chapter, in which we have been principally concerned with the witness of Matthew to the authority of Jesus Christ, the Son of God, to the testimony which it offers to Jesus as the messianic king who proclaimed and brought to realization the kingdom of God. To the consideration of this theme we shall turn in the following chapter.

---

21. In Matthew 22:41–46 (Mark 12:35–37; Luke 20:41–44) Jesus himself, without specific reference to his own person, demonstrates to the Pharisees on the basis of Psalm 110:1 that the messianic Son of David is David's sovereign Lord. It has often been said that this passage represents a polemic against the Son of David concept on the part of the church which had come to acknowledge Jesus as Lord. Cf. e.g., Wilhelm Bousset, *Kyrios Christos* (Göttingen: Vandenhoeck & Ruprecht, 1913), 5, 51; Bultmann, *Die Geschichte der synoptischen Tradition*, 70, 144–46. This position is strong exegetically in so far as it recognizes the plain implications of transcendent messiahship and even preexistence in Jesus' declaration. It breaks down historically, however, in the face of the pervasive recognition of Jesus as Son of David in the Christian records. Bultmann virtually admits this when he conjectures that the point of view represented by this passage represents, not that of the Christian church as a whole, but only that of a narrow circle.

It may be added that reflection on the Davidic origin of Jesus is prominent in Luke's introductory sections. Cf. Luke 1:27, 32, 69; 2:4, 11; 3:31. In John the only allusion is found in 7:42 where some who doubted Jesus' messiahship offer as their reason the Scriptural attestation of the Christ's Davidic origin in Bethlehem, contradicted as it was supposed by his origin in Galilee.

Preaching Christ from All the Scriptures

EDMUND P. CLOWNEY

Edmund P. Clowney, "Preaching Christ from All the Scriptures," in *The Preacher and Preaching: Reviving the Art in the Twentieth Century*, ed. Samuel T. Logan Jr. (Phillipsburg, NJ: Presbyterian and Reformed, 1986), 163–91.

Edmund P. Clowney (1917–2005) taught practical theology at Westminster Seminary, Philadelphia (1952 onward), and served as the seminary's first president (1966–82). Clowney was educated at Wheaton College, Westminster, and Yale Divinity School. He was ordained in the Orthodox Presbyterian Church. Since 1984 he served in the young Presbyterian Church in America. His leadership at Westminster brought great expansion to the school and added an emphasis on practical theology. He also taught many years at Westminster Seminary California. His teaching focused in particular on the doctrine of the church and preaching. His insights on ecclesiology were brought out in his book *The Church* (1995). His special contribution to preaching was to integrate a Christ-centered biblical theology to preaching. A detailed presentation can be found in his *Preaching and Biblical Theology* (1975). In this endeavor he carried on the legacy of Vos at Westminster and in the church. His insistence on Christ-centered preaching reached far beyond Westminster and continues to influence Reformed and Presbyterian churches.

In "Preaching Christ from All the Scriptures," Clowney shows how all of Scripture points to Christ and how this reality must shape the church's preaching. This text offers a convenient summary of Clowney's approach. There he communicates his passion not only for Christ-centered preaching, but also for preaching the Old Testament. The essay begins with a challenge to preachers in this respect. His method embraces the entirety of Scripture. Further, following his approach, a single passage of the Bible studied together with other Scriptures takes on fresh lights. By a careful consideration of the "History of Revelation," the preacher can also avoid the twin dangers of "Moralism" and "Allegory." This selection is full of illustrations of Christ-centered exegesis. Other helpful works by Clowney include *The Unfolding Mystery: Discovering Christ in the Old Testament* (1988) and *Preaching Christ in All of Scripture* (2003). Another of his essays, "How Christ Interprets the Scripture," offers a similar short introduction to the topic.

Bibliography: Edmund P. Clowney. "How Christ Interprets the Scriptures: Luke 24:26, 27." Pp. 33–53 in *Can We Trust the Bible?* Ed. Earl D. Radmacher. Wheaton, IL: Tyndale House, 1979. Harvie M. Conn, ed. *Practical Theology and the Ministry of the Church, 1952–1984: Essays in Honor of Edmund P. Clowney.* Phillipsburg, NJ: Presbyterian and Reformed, 1990.

May I invite you to inspect your Bible? Flex the binding; look closely at the signs of wear along the page edges. Unless your Bible is quite new or you are an unusual preacher, I will predict that you can find with your thumbnail where the New Testament begins. It is where the shiny gold has worn off the page edges in a decided line. Very likely you can pick out the Psalms or Isaiah by the worn edges, too.

You might make another measurement by looking over your file of sermons. In what proportion have you preached from Old and New Testament texts?

If we are going to carry Bibles and not simply pocket Testaments, we should surely be using the Old Testament more than we do. The missionary Bible of the apostolic church was the Old Testament Scripture. Our Lord in the synagogue of Nazareth (Luke 4), Peter at Pentecost (Acts 2), Paul in the synagogues of Asia Minor and Greece—these all preached the gospel from the Old Testament. During the time in which the apostolic witness to Christ was still being recorded, the Old Testament was the Scripture from which the church preached Christ.

Why do we use the Old Testament so little in our preaching? Some preachers might neglect the Old Testament because they do not preach from biblical texts at all. They prefer to preach, more or less biblically, on topics. Others feel that the Old Testament is too remote from contemporary life. But one great obstacle has been the uneasy feeling that Old Testament texts do not present the gospel with clarity. Christian preachers may well fear preaching synagogue sermons, or becoming legalistic or moralistic in their pulpit ministry.

If we are to preach from the whole Bible, we must be able to see how the whole Bible bears witness to Jesus Christ. The Bible has a key, one that unlocks the use of the Old Testament by the New. That key is presented at the end of the Gospel of Luke (Luke 24:13–27, 44–48). It is found in the teaching of Jesus after His resurrection. When Jesus met the two discouraged disciples returning to Emmaus on Easter morning, He did not end their grief by revealing Himself to them at once. He did not bring recognition by saying "Cleopas!" as He had earlier said "Mary!" (John 20:16). Instead He rebuked them for their foolish sorrow. They could not believe in the resurrection even after hearing the women's report of the empty tomb. Why not? Because they were "slow of heart to believe in all that the prophets have spoken" (Luke 24:25b). They did not recognize that the Christ must suffer these things and enter into glory. Jesus began with the books of Moses, and proceeding through all the prophets He "interpreted to them in all the scriptures the things concerning himself" (v. 27). Their hearts burned within them as they saw how all the Scriptures focused on Christ. Only after that learning experience were their eyes opened to recognize the Lord in the breaking of the bread.

Later, the risen Christ continued His instruction, teaching "that all things must be fulfilled, which are written in the law of Moses, and in the prophets, and in the psalms, concerning me. Then opened he their understanding, that they might understand the scriptures" (Luke 24:44b–45).

What did Jesus teach His disciples during the forty days between His resurrection and ascension? Apparently the coverage was extensive: Moses, the prophets, the psalms—these are the three major divisions of the Hebrew Scriptures. There was progression, too. The phrase "beginning at Moses and all the prophets" and the use of the verb *diermēneuō* indicate reasoned interpretation. Jesus did not present a course in "eisegesis." He interpreted what the Scriptures *do* say and opened His disciples' minds to understand it. Understanding brought conviction, a burning heart. Although Jesus Himself was their teacher, He did not assume that only He could so interpret Scripture. Rather, He blamed them as fools and slow of heart because they had not perceived the plain meaning of the Old Testament. Indeed, so clear is the message of the Scriptures that their misunderstanding must be accounted for by a mental block of some kind, a blindness to the truth expressed.

Do you wish you could have attended Christ's seminar during the forty days? Do you conclude ruefully that you haven't a clue as to what Christ's comprehensive, cogent interpretation of the Old Testament was?

Stop for a moment. Luke puts this spotlight on Old Testament interpretation right in the heart of his two-volume work on what Jesus did *and taught* both before and after His resurrection and ascension (Acts 1:1). Is Luke, then, describing secret teaching in Gnostic style? Does he picture Jesus as giving arcane instruction to a few disciples who are initiates? Of course not! What Jesus explained to the disciples about the Old Testament became the key for their preaching. Luke reports to us how the apostles used their new understanding in preaching Christ from all the Scriptures. Peter's sermon at Pentecost interpreted passages from Joel and from Psalms 16 and 110 (Acts 2:17–21, 25, 28, 34). Later Peter declared in the temple the fulfillment of "the things which God foreshowed by the mouth of all the prophets" (Acts 3:18). He quoted from Deuteronomy and added, "Yea and all the prophets from Samuel . . . as many as have spoken, they also told of these days" (Acts 3:24).

When Stephen made his defense, he surveyed the history of the Old Testament to point to Christ (Acts 7). Philip began with Isaiah 53:7 to preach Jesus to the Ethiopian eunuch (Acts 8:34); Paul traced God's redemption in the Exodus and reviewed the rulers God gave to Israel in order to point to the Messiah, the seed of David (Acts 13:16–41). Like Peter, Paul quoted from the psalms.

In all the preaching recorded in the Book of Acts we find the same themes reappearing. Plainly Luke did not think that we are left in the dark about Jesus' interpretation of the Old Testament. What the Lord taught the disciples, they declared to the church. The whole New Testament interprets the fulfillment of the promises of God. Without the Old Testament the gospel message itself cannot be well understood. Quotations from the Old Testament are spread throughout the New; allusions are even more abundant. Look through a Nestle edition of the Greek Testament: the Old Testament phrases alluded to are in boldface type, and they are sprinkled on almost every page.

With this wealth of interpretive guidance, why should we be so uncertain about our use of the Old Testament? No doubt we have neglected what the Spirit of God has given us. The sweep and boldness of the interpretation in the New Testament has proved too much for us. We have become puzzled. Does the New Testament really interpret the Old, or does it only use the language, filling the old wineskins with new wine? Far from perceiving the principles used in the New Testament to interpret the Old, we often fall short of crediting the interpretations that are given. We would not dare to find Christ in passages where the New Testament does not expressly find Him, and we have difficulty with some of the passages where it does.

If our preaching of the Old Testament is to be renewed, we need that opening of the mind that Christ gave to His disciples; we also need to use the key that He gave for opening the Scriptures: that key is the witness of the Scriptures to Christ.

1. God's Structuring Promise

All the Old Testament Scriptures, not merely the few passages that have been recognized as messianic, point us to Christ. We are all familiar with messianic prophecy in the Old Testament. When Philip ran up to the chariot of the Ethiopian official and heard him reading from Isaiah 53:7, the evangelist began with that passage and preached Jesus (Acts 8:35). We have a good idea as to what Philip might have said. In the same way, we can understand that Psalm 22 is messianic since Jesus uttered its opening cry on the cross. Jesus Himself alluded to Psalm 110, and in its opening invitation to David's Lord to sit at the right hand of God we can recognize a prophecy of Christ's exaltation (Ps. 110:1; Mark 12:36; 14:62).

But what of the structure of the Old Testament as a whole? We may begin by asking, How do we have a written Old Testament? What accounts for this collection of seemingly diverse writings composed over so many centuries?

The Old Testament itself provides a clear answer. Scripture is given by God in the history of His covenant with Israel. Written Scripture appears first in Old Testament history as the text of the covenant treaty that God made with Israel at Sinai. Just as the speaking of the Lord from the mount provides the model of divine revelation, so the writing of the Lord on the tablets of stone provides the model of divine inscripturation. "And he gave unto Moses, when he had made an end of communing with him upon Mount Sinai, the two tables of testimony, tables of stone, written with the finger of God" (Ex. 31:18; cf. 24:12; 32:16).

The stone tablets are called the "tablets of witness" (Ex. 31:18; 40:20); the ark is called the "ark of the witness" (Ex. 25:16, 21–22; 26:33; 39:55). The treaty form of the covenant explains the term "witness" or "testimony." The stipulations and promises of God's covenant with Israel are attested or witnessed by the written record. Duplicate copies are required for the same reason.[1] One copy is God's, the other copy is Israel's. Both are deposited in the ark. The lid of the ark is the mercy seat, the symbol of God's throne in the midst of His people. God's covenant testimony is stored under His throne.

---

1. Meredith Kline, "The Two Tables of the Covenant," *WTJ* 22 (May 1960): 133–46.

If God were to be unfaithful to His covenant promise, the people could appeal to the witness that He Himself had given. If, however, the people were to be unfaithful, God's "testimonies" engraved in stone and written by Moses were in God's keeping as evidence of the terms of His covenant. Throughout the Pentateuch, and particularly in Deuteronomy, it is clear that Israel will break God's covenant and that its sanctions will be applied (e.g., Deut. 30:1–3).

Scripture, then, is presented as God's covenantal witness. What is true of the first written words of God continues to be true of the rest.

For example, the institution of the prophetic office is modeled on Moses' ministry (Deut. 18:18). The prophets are God's mouthpieces, bringing God's Word, just as Aaron was Moses' mouthpiece, bringing his word (Ex. 4:12, 16). Further, the prophets serve to remind the people of God's covenant given through Moses. They reinforce the warnings and the promises. They also underscore the "witness" of God to Israel's unfaithfulness. The prophet Micah proclaims God's covenant controversy with Israel; God bears witness to His faithfulness and to Israel's covenant-breaking (Mic. 6:1–5).

Stern predictions of disaster are the prophesied outcome of Israel's covenant-breaking. Yet the prophets do not end with the doom of divine wrath. They regularly point beyond wrath to mercy. In Deuteronomy 30:1–10 we find an overview of covenantal history. The blessings God has promised will all be fulfilled; Israel will enter the land and drive out their enemies; God will set His name in their midst at the place of His choosing. But Israel will continue to rebel and the curses of the covenant will also be realized. The people will be driven from the land into exile. Then, after the blessings and the curses, God will gather His scattered people and circumcise their hearts to love the Lord with all their heart and soul, that they may live.

This structure shapes the whole of the Old Testament. The promised blessings are realized. Israel enters the land; the enemy nations are subdued under Joshua, the judges, and King David. Every man finds rest under his own vine and fig tree (1 Kings 4:25). Solomon dedicates the temple and praises God for fulfilling all the promises that He made: "Blessed be the Lord, that hath given rest unto his people Israel, according to all he promised; there hath not failed one word of all his good promise, which he promised by Moses his servant" (1 Kings 8:56).

But this glorious pinnacle proves to be the edge of a precipice. Solomon's wisdom becomes folly as he builds idol shrines for his heathen wives. Rehoboam, his son, is more foolish still; the kingdom is divided. The open apostasy of the northern tribes is followed by Judah as well; both go into captivity: Israel to Assyria and Judah to Babylon.

The prophets record this sad history and pronounce their mournful judgments. Yet the master-plan of Deuteronomy 30 holds. The judgment is not total or final, because God is a God of mercy and of unimaginable grace. He will not destroy *all* His people: a *remnant* will be preserved. He will not destroy them *forever*: a glorious future of *renewal* will come. The "latter days," the time *after* both blessing and cursing, will be the time when God will restore the tabernacle of David that is fallen down and establish a new covenant in sovereign grace (Amos 9:11–12; Jer. 31:31–34; 32:36–41).

How can such a glorious finale be written to the history of God's covenant with a rebellious people? Only if God Himself intervenes to be the Savior of His own, not merely from their enemies, but from themselves.

God must come, because the plight of Israel is so hopeless that only God can save. Ezekiel sees a vision of the people in captivity. The prospect is appalling. He is in the midst of a great valley, a valley of the dead. Stretching away from Him in every direction are windrows of bones: not even skeletons, but scattered bones. Only the Spirit of God can give life to these bones and bring resurrection from the grave for this people (Ezek. 37:1–4).

God sees that there is none to deliver His people from their oppressors, and so He will put on the breastplate of His righteousness and the helmet of His salvation. He will come Himself to save them (Isa. 59:15b–21). The priests and leaders of the people are false shepherds who care nothing for the sheep. God Himself will come to be the good Shepherd who delivers His sheep (Ezek. 34:1–16).

On the other hand, God's promises are so great that only God can make good on them. Solomon could indeed praise God for having kept His promises by having given Israel peace in the land of their possession. But out of the sin and rebellion of Israel there emerges another level of divine promises. The mercy that will follow God's wrath will surpass all imagining. God promises not only restoration from captivity, but universal blessing. The curse on nature will be removed as God blesses the field and the forest (Isa. 43:18–21; 65:17). Creation will be transformed: the sun will give greater light, the animal creation will live in peace, and the knowledge of the Lord will cover the earth as the waters cover the sea (Isa. 11:6–9; 60:19–22; 30:23–26). To the restored of Israel there will be added the remnant of the nations (Isa. 49:6; 19:19–25; 66:19–21), and all the earth will flow to the mount of the Lord to praise His Name (Isa. 2:2–4; 25:6–8).

To accomplish such consummation blessings, fulfilling all the promises to Adam, Abraham, Moses, and David, God must redeem His people from their sins. This He will do, for in His coming He will not only subdue all the enemies of the people of God (Mic. 7:14–17); He will also subdue their iniquities underfoot "and thou wilt cast all their sins into the depths of the sea" (Mic. 7:18–20).

What coming of God can accomplish such marvels? It must be a coming in vengeance against the hostile powers: God is the Warrior who fights to deliver the poor and oppressed (Isa. 59:16–17). It must be a coming in mercy to gather and lead the scattered flock: God is the Shepherd who redeems His people as He did in the time of the Exodus when He brought them out of Egypt and led them through the wilderness (Ezek. 34:10–16; Isa. 40:3, 11). It must be a coming in creation as God makes new the very fabric of heaven and earth (Isa. 65:17). God is the Creator Spirit who breathes new life and makes all things new (Ezek. 37:11–14).

But the mystery runs yet deeper, for promise seems set against promise. God's deliverance will be in judgment, in the great day of the Lord. Yet those who cry for that day do not know what they seek (Mal. 3:2; Amos 5:18–20). God will come, but who shall stand when He appears? In mercy God cries, "Ephraim, how shall I give thee up?" (Hos. 11:8), but in justice God pronounces doom on His sinful people. They are no people (*Lo-ammi*), those who can receive no mercy (*Lo-ruhamah*, Hos. 1:9, 6). If fire must renovate the earth to bring in a new order of life, light, and holiness, what can survive the holocaust of final judgment? The burst of glory from the presence of the Lord will consume every fallen sinner.

When that paradox was set before Israel in the desert, God foreshadowed its resolution. God was too holy to dwell in the midst of sinful Israel. He must consume them in a moment (Ex. 33:5). Should He then not dwell in their midst after all? Should He keep His distance and meet with Moses outside the camp (Ex. 33:7–11)? He could go before them in the presence of the angel, drive out their enemies and give them the land without dwelling in their midst (Ex. 33:1–3). Moses rightly saw in that scenario the loss of true salvation: "If thy presence go not with us, carry us not up hence" (Ex. 33:15). Moses prayed the right prayer, "Show me, I pray thee, thy glory" (Ex. 33:18). Communion with the living God is the meaning of salvation.

Salvation is *in* and *of* the Lord; we may possess it only as we have the Lord as our inheritance, and as we become the inheritance of God, and know as we are known (Ex. 34:9). God must come among us, dwell in our midst, and there reveal the light of His glory and the saving power of His holy Name. In symbol God gave that to Moses. He proclaimed His Name to Moses as the God of sovereign grace (Ex. 33:19; 34:6–7). He did not do what He had threatened to do. He did not cancel the building of the tabernacle in the *midst* of the camp in favor of a tent of meeting *outside* the camp. Rather, God did, in a figure, dwell in the midst of Israel. The tabernacle with its furnishings provided both a screen to contain the holy threat of the Lord's presence and a way of approach by which sinners could come before Him through the shedding of blood and the mediation of the priesthood.

The life of Israel was built around that symbol. But what of the reality that was symbolized? The prophet Ezekiel sees a temple that holds the fountain of the water of life, watering a land that becomes a new Eden. Beside the river that flows from the temple, the tree of life again grows, with healing for the nations (Ezek. 47). But what sacrifice shall be offered when God comes? What dwelling will suffice when He comes, not in the symbol of the pillar of cloud, but in the reality of fulfillment?

And what of the fulfillment of God's covenant? If God comes, how can Israel come to meet Him? Who will have clean hands and a pure heart to enter the presence of the Lord (Ps. 24)? God is the Lord of the covenant, but what of the servant of the covenant?

God's justice is clear; His requirements cannot be compromised. It will not do for God to come only as Lord, even as Warrior, Shepherd, and Creator. To bring the salvation He has promised He must fulfill the part of the Servant as well as the part of the Lord of the covenant.

The tabernacle pictured the way of approach through the altar of sacrifice. But the blood of bulls and goats cannot atone for sin. The final and true sacrifice must be not merely the lamb of the flock, but the son of the bosom. The Passover threat against the first-born must be fulfilled against the representative Seed of the promise, the Isaac God has provided. Abraham's beloved son is the promised seed, but not yet the Son of God. The promise is "Jehovah-Jireh": the Lord Himself must provide the Son who is also the Lamb of God that takes away the sin of the world (Gen. 22).

When the prophets promise the coming of God, they are brought to see that God's Anointed must come: if God is the Shepherd, so is the Son of David, God's Prince (Ezek. 34:23). When the Servant of the Lord comes, He will fulfill the role of Israel (Isa. 49:3). He will also gather the lost sheep of Israel, restore the remnant of the people, and be a light to the Gentiles, God's salvation to the end of the earth (Isa. 49:6).

The name of the Messiah will be "Wonderful, Counsellor, the Mighty God, Everlasting Father, Prince of Peace" (Isa. 9:6). The house of David will indeed be as God, for as the mystery unfolds, God Himself comes in the tabernacle of human flesh. The Lord must come; the Servant must come. Jesus Christ comes, who is Lord and Servant: Immanuel, God with us!

The Old Testament, then, in its very structure is formed by God's promise: the promise to Adam and Eve in the garden (Gen. 3:15); the promise to Abraham (Gen. 12:1–3); the promise to Israel (Deut. 30:6); the promise to David (2 Sam. 7:12–16). These are not mere episodes or occasional oracles. They mark the unfolding of God's redemptive plan. The promises of the Seed of the woman and of the Seed of Abraham are given in the Pentateuch; they present both the background and the purpose in the calling of Israel. Without them the perspective of blessing to the nations through Israel might be lost from view. Before the call of Abraham in Genesis 12, Israel is to read the table of the nations in Genesis 10. Israel must perceive its own calling in the light of God's purpose for the nations and of God's promise of the Seed to come.

For that reason the theme of blessing upon the remnant of the nations with the remnant of Israel (e.g., Isa. 19:19–25) is not a new twist added by more cosmopolitan prophets. It is the reaffirmation of God's original calling of His people, and a vision of the new form of the people of God in the wonder of God's own coming.

The focus on Christ in the Old Testament does not spring simply from the fact that Old Testament revelation is given in the framework of a history that does actually lead to Christ. Or, more pointedly, the history that leads to Christ is not a random succession of events. Neither is it simply history under God's providential control, serving His sovereign purpose. It is rather the history of God's own intervention in history, the history of His great work of salvation as He prepares for His own coming in the person of His Son.

The epiphany of the Son of God is not a divine afterthought, an *ad hoc* emergency plan developed to meet the unforeseen disaster of the apostasy of the elect nation. It is not the failure of Israel that necessitates the coming of Christ, as though an obedient people would have made a divine and incarnate Savior unnecessary.

No, the story of the Old Testament is the story of the Lord: what He has done, and what He has purposed to do. The Old Testament does not provide us with biographies or national history. It is the story of God's work, not men's. It speaks of men in the context of God's covenant with them. Since salvation is of the Lord and not of men, the issue is always faith. The heroes of the Old Testament, as the author of Hebrews plainly tells us, are men and women of faith. They trust in God, believe the promises, and look for the city that has foundations, whose builder and maker is God (Heb. 11:10).

2. Typology and Fulfillment

This God-centered and therefore Christ-centered nature of Old Testament revelation provides the ground and rationale of the typological interpretation of the Old Testament in the New. If God had not begun His work of salvation before sending His Son into the world, the Marcionite view of the Old Testament would be correct. We would then have in the religion of Israel only another example of the false religions of the world, and in the Yahweh of the Old Testament a tribal deity whose worship is idolatry. On the other hand, if God's work in the Old Testament is only continued and not transformed in the coming of Christ, then the new is subordinate to the old. Rabbinical interpretation of the Old Testament sought zealously to apply its texts to contemporary life. But they could not conceive of the transformation that Jesus brought, for they did not understand the partial, provisional and temporary character made evident in the old covenant by its anticipation of the power and glory of the new (cf. Matt. 22:29; Jer. 31:31–34; Heb. 1:1–2).

Typology is grounded in God's design. It flows from the continuity and difference in God's saving work. There is continuity, for it is God who begins His work of salvation long before He gives His Son. Yet there is discontinuity, too. Salvation in Christ is not simply an improvement on Old Testament salvation. It is not just the final phase of God's dealings with His people. It is rather the *ground* of Old Testament salvation. God's call to Israel presupposes the sending of Jesus Christ. Salvation in Christ is the only real salvation, the only salvation with ultimate and eternal meaning. Abraham partakes of salvation because, by faith, he saw Christ's day and was glad (John 8:56; cf. Rom. 4:3). To consider the old should in itself force us to see the need for the new; indeed, this is the message of the wisdom literature, as well as of the prophets.

If the real and final salvation is in Christ alone, in what sense can God begin His work of salvation before Christ? Obviously, by anticipating that final work. The anticipation takes place when God brings men into a saving relation with Himself by means of the future work of Christ. God reckons Christ's work as completed because of the certainty of God's own decree. Christ is the Lamb slain from the foundation of the world (Rev. 13:8 NIV; Eph. 1:4).

But God is pleased to bring men into relation with Himself by faith. He wishes them to know that He alone can save them; He requires them to commit themselves to Him in trust. To instruct faith, God provides a model, an analogy of His final and ultimate salvation. That model must show that God alone is the Savior. It must also avoid diverting faith from God Himself to an image separate from God.

The use of models, images, or symbols is part of God's design to anticipate the fullness of meaning that cannot yet be revealed. The blood of bulls and goats cannot make atonement for sin (Heb. 10:4). But the blood of sacrificial animals may convey *signi*ficance. It may serve as a sign, a symbol that points beyond itself to the reality of Christ's atoning sacrifice.

Yet there are limits to the function of symbolism. This is dramatically depicted in the tabernacle. The sanctuary of God in the wilderness pictures His dwelling in the midst of His people. This symbol is developed as a master model, elaborated by rich architectural and ceremonial detail. The very throne of God is symbolized in the "mercy seat" (Ex. 25:17), the golden covering of the ark of the covenant. The cherubim of gold above it represent the heavenly guardians of the throne. But here at the heart of God's model of His dwelling there is that which cannot be modeled. The throne on the ark is empty. No image may stand in the place of God Himself (Deut. 4:15–24). This is not to say that there can be no image of God, for God has made man in His image (Gen. 1:27). Rather, the absence of any image at the center of Israel's worship shows that Israel does not worship a representation of God, but God Himself, the true and living God who has redeemed His people and brought them unto Himself (Ex. 19:3), in order that they might stand before Him (Ex. 19:17; 20:3), and that He might dwell in their midst (Ex. 34:9; cf. 33:3–4, 15).

The mercy seat pictures God's throne as it is reserved for Jesus Christ, "who is the image of the invisible God" (Col. 1:15), "for in him dwelleth all the fullness of the Godhead bodily" (Col. 2:9). The God-man, the incarnate Lord, is not a mere symbol of God's presence, an image to represent Him. He is Himself the Lord, the second person of the Trinity. "He that hath seen me hath seen the Father" (John 14:9).

In the empty place between the cherubim God is present in the darkness, veiled from the sight of Israel, but dwelling in their midst. The golden wings of symbolism surround that which is not symbolical, the real presence of God. The symbol and the reality are closely joined, but are not identical. When Christ came, the reality came; God could be worshiped in the visible manifestation of His presence, "which we have seen with our eyes . . . and our hands handled, concerning the Word of life" (1 John 1:1), for "the Word became flesh and dwelt among us (and we beheld his glory, glory as of the only begotten from the Father), full of grace and truth" (John 1:14).

Because the incarnate Lord is not a symbol of God's presence, but God Himself present with us, all the symbolism of the tabernacle points to Him and is fulfilled in Him. For this reason

Jesus can tell the woman of Samaria, "Woman, believe me, the hour cometh, when neither in this mountain, nor in Jerusalem, shall ye worship the Father. . . . The hour cometh, and now is, when the true worshippers shall worship the Father in spirit and truth" (John 4:21, 23).

The mountain where the Samaritans believed God should be worshipped was Mount Gerizim, the mountain that loomed up beyond Jesus as He talked with the woman. The Samaritans were wrong; as Jesus said, "Salvation is of the Jews" (John 4:22). Jerusalem was the place where God had set His name. But Jesus removes Jerusalem along with Gerizim as the place for worship. How can He declare this? It is not simply on the ground of God's spirituality. Jesus does not contend that God cannot be worshipped in any one place simply because He is a Spirit and therefore cannot be confined to a place. If that were Jesus' point there would be no reason to speak of a coming hour when worship would be no longer at Jerusalem. (God is always a Spirit!) The coming hour is the hour of Jesus' death and resurrection (John 2:4; 17:1; 16:32; cf. 5:25, 28; 11:25). The earthly place of sacrifice must lose its significance when the true and final sacrifice is offered. Jesus has come as the true Temple (John 1:14). He said, "Destroy this temple, and in three days I will raise it up" (John 2:19).

Jesus does not call the woman to "temple-less" worship, but to worship in truth (John 4:24); He is the Truth, the true Temple, and the Spirit in whom worship must be offered is the Spirit that He gives, the water springing up to eternal life (John 4:14). The woman must therefore come to the Father through Jesus—"I that speak unto thee am he!" (John 4:26). In Jesus the Father seeks true worshippers, and finds one in a disgraced Samaritan woman by Jacob's well.

In Jesus, therefore, both the reality and the symbols of God's dwelling in the midst of His people find fulfillment. The key to the New Testament understanding of typology is found in the sense in which fulfillment comes in Jesus Christ. Leonhard Goppelt has pointed out the distinctive meaning that *typos* gains in the New Testament.[2] That meaning is clear in Romans 5:8 where Paul speaks of Adam as a *typos* of Him that was to come. Christ is the Man from heaven (1 Cor. 15:47): not only the head of a new humanity, but the realization of the image of God in man (Heb. 2:6–9). Christ is not simply another Adam in the sense of being *like* Adam; neither is He a second Adam in the sense of beginning again another race, as though there were to be another cycle of history comparable to the one begun in the first Adam. Rather, Christ is Himself the fullness of the image of God; Christ is the *meaning* of created human nature. The completeness, the glory of created human sonship is uniquely manifested in the God-man. What defines the type in New Testament thought is not simply the surpassing glory of the eschatological dimension, not even the transformation by which the patterns of the Old Covenant are renewed. The heart of the understanding of "type" in the New Testament lies in the New Testament doctrine of Christ. Only in Christ as the divine Savior do we find the transcending and transforming fulfillment that creates a whole new dimension. That dimension in the Gospel of John is the "true," not in contrast to the false (although John makes that contrast, too), but in contrast to the shadow, the promise, the anticipation. Jesus is the *true* Vine (John 15:1), the *true* Son of God, the *true* Israel (Isa. 49:3; Rom. 15:8), the *true* Bread from heaven (John 6:32–33). In Him the reality appears, and in Him that reality is given to His people.

The typical function of Old Testament history is not limited, therefore, to a few instances of graphically symbolic events: the exodus from Egypt as God opens a path through the

2. Leonard Goppelt, *Typos: The Typological Interpretation of the Old Testament in the New*, trans. D. H. Madvig (Grand Rapids: Eerdmans, 1982), 199. See also his article "Typos" in Gerhard Kittel, Gerhard Friedrich, eds., *Theological Dictionary of the New Testament*, trans. Geoffrey W. Bromiley (Grand Rapids: Eerdmans, 1972), 8:252ff.

waters of death, or the entrance into the land as God gives to His people their inheritance. Rather, the whole history of redemption before the coming of Christ has a symbolic dimension. God delivers His people, guides them, blesses them, judges them. Yet because God's full and final salvation has not come, His dealings with His people are always anticipatory. The land is not the new creation of God's final promise; victory over the Amalekites or the Canaanites is not victory over Satan and the powers of darkness; the fruit of the vine is not the fruit of the Spirit. Because God binds His people to Himself in living fellowship, their salvation is not *merely* a shadow, an outward husk to be discarded. Abraham by faith knows the Lord and can perceive the reality that lies behind and beyond the promises of temporal blessing. But the faith of the Old Testament saints gives us the key for understanding and interpreting the revealed history of their earthly pilgrimage (Heb. 11:13–16). They did not and could not find rest until the promise was fulfilled, not just in Isaac, but in Christ (Heb. 4:8–9).

The New Testament proclaims the fulfillment of all the typical symbols of the Old Testament in Christ. The fulfillment is greater than the type: a greater than Solomon (Matt. 12:42), than Jonah (Matt. 12:41), than the temple (John 2:19–21) has come. The Son of David is greater than David: David therefore hails his Son as his Lord (Matt. 22:41–46). But, as we have seen, Jesus is not simply greater by a relative degree, but by a transcendent measure. John, the greatest of the prophets, baptized in water, but Jesus baptizes in the Spirit (Matt. 3:11–12). In the Passover symbol, the people choose a lamb of the flock, but Jesus is the Lamb of God that takes away the sin of the world (John 1:29).

We may diagram the rationale of New Testament typology by basing it on the unfolding of redemptive history and its climax in Jesus Christ.

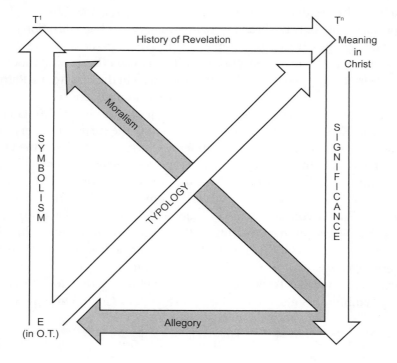

If we represent that history by a horizontal line leading to Christ, we may assume that all the truths of God's revelation are fulfilled in Christ. Truths may be emphasized in one period of redemptive history more than in another, but no truth is eliminated or forgotten. The meaning of any Old Testament symbol is the concept that is symbolized. In the biblical context the concept is affirmed or denied; it is related to other concepts in such a way that some statement is made. A truth is expressed. An Old Testament event, a ceremony, or a prophetic, priestly, or royal action may therefore symbolize, pointing to a revealed truth at a particular point in the history of redemption (truth to the first power: T^1). We may be sure that this truth will be carried forward to Jesus Christ (truth to the "nth" power: T^n). We may therefore connect the event, ceremony, or action directly with that truth as it comes to full expression in Christ. This line is the hypotenuse of the triangle it forms, and it is the line of typology. If the symbolism of an Old Testament incident or person is not perceived, or does not exist, no line of typology can be drawn. Nor can the event be a type in a sense different from its symbolic function in its Old Testament setting.

Since the exodus event, for example, is manifestly symbolic, we discover its typical meaning by perceiving its symbolic meaning in its Old Testament setting. It symbolizes God's deliverance of His people from the power of another lord so that they might be free to worship and serve Him as their only Lord and Master (Ex. 4:22–23). Further, their deliverance is solely the work of God in a situation in which no deliverance is humanly possible. Much more is included in the details of the symbolism, including the ceremonial of the Passover, and the figure of the cloud. But an outstanding feature of the deliverance is that it is not only *from* death, but *through* death. The waters of the Red Sea threaten Israel with death before them just as much as the chariots of Pharaoh threaten with death behind them. Further, the depth of the sea in the Old Testament is the abyss, a synonym for the grave (cf. Jonah 2). It is through the depths that Israel is led to deliverance from the dominion of Pharaoh.

In Luke's account of the transfiguration of Jesus, we learn that Moses talked with Jesus about His "exodus" that He was to accomplish at Jerusalem (Luke 9:31). The truth of deliverance from the power of Satan into the liberty of the sons of God is to find its full accomplishment in Jesus Christ. Christ's miracles are indeed signs, but they differ from the miracles of Moses not only in being miracles of blessing rather than of judgment. They differ also in being signs that point directly to the Lord who performs them, and therefore to the realization of the promises that Moses' deliverance symbolized. Moses confronts Pharaoh, and the signs given to him from the Lord overwhelm the magic of Pharaoh's priests (Ex. 7:12). But Jesus confronts Satan and, having overcome the "strong man," is able to deliver those in captivity to him (Luke 11:19–22; Matt. 12:27–29). He not only casts out demons and delivers those oppressed by Satan; He forgives sins, and brings men and women from the kingdom of darkness into the kingdom of light (Mark 2:5–11; Col. 1:12–13).

In His death and resurrection Jesus accomplishes His "exodus." He passes through the tide of death for us and enables us to sing the song of Moses and of the Lamb in the experience of resurrection joy granted already to those who trust in Him (1 Peter 1:3–5; Rev. 15:3; Ex. 15:2; Ps. 118:14; Isa. 12:1–2).

To preach the exodus event as an example of political liberation obviously does not do justice to the framework of God's covenantal promise by which He delivers Israel. God does not only strike off the yoke so that Israel may go free (Lev. 26:13). He frees Israel from the service of Pharaoh so that Israel may serve Him (Ex. 4:23). He brings Israel out of Egypt and bears them on eagles' wings unto Himself (Ex. 19:4). Yet even awareness of God's calling to Sinai and to Zion does not prepare us to preach the meaning of the exodus. We must perceive the reality of Christ's salvation as it is prefigured in the exodus event. Only in the fulfillment in Christ does the exodus have significance for us.

We must therefore complete the diagram by dropping a line from the *meaning* of the truth as it is accomplished and revealed in Christ, to the *significance* of the truth as it is perceived by us. This means that two other possible lines in the diagram are illegitimate. We certainly should not look back directly from our situation to the exodus in the Old Testament without considering the truth that was symbolized by the exodus. Sometimes this is done by allegorizing. The Old Testament events are made symbols for illustrating any significance that the preacher chooses to find in them. (This misinterpretation is indicated by the bottom, horizontal dotted line in the diagram.) The preacher can then read the account of Moses' sign and hold forth on rods that become snakes to warn against the misuse of authority, or to describe virtues becoming vices. His imagination is free of any constraint of Scripture.

A less blatant failure in scriptural interpretation is moralizing. (This is represented by the diagonal dotted line pointing back to the truth revealed at a particular point in the Old Testament.) The moralizing preacher does not arbitrarily seize on any element in the text that catches his fancy. He does take account of the meaning of the text in its original setting. He interprets for his hearers the significance that this truth has for them in their own lives and experience. But he completely fails to show how this truth comes to its full meaning in Christ, and only in Christ.[3]

The moralistic approach has sometimes been defended as interpretation pure and simple, proclaiming only what the text says and all that the text says, neither more nor less. But to ignore the dimension of promise in the Old Testament is to misinterpret it altogether. It is to forget the message of the primary Author of Scripture, the Holy Spirit. The Spirit of Old Testament Scripture is the Spirit of Christ who inspired the human authors to testify of the sufferings of Christ and the glories that should follow (1 Peter 1:11).[4]

Liberation theology at best offers an example of a moralistic interpretation of the exodus deliverance. It fails to appreciate the significance of the exodus in the history of redemption. Indeed, it dismisses the orthodox interpretation as spiritualizing, as individualistic pietism that does not recognize that politics is God's work in the world. Pietism has been guilty of individualism and of ignoring the corporate view of the people of God that the symbolism of the exodus presents. But pietism nevertheless recognized the gospel and the centrality of Jesus Christ in whom our exodus is accomplished.

3. The Preaching of Christ Recognizes the Significance of the Old Testament

When the Old Testament is interpreted in the light of its own structure of promise and when that promise is seen as fulfilled in Jesus Christ, then the significance of the Old Testament can be preached in theological depth and in practical power. Preaching that does not

---

3. I am grateful to the Rev. Richard Craven, who as a student at Westminster Seminary suggested the lines of "moralism" and "allegory" as part of the diagram.

4. For a further discussion of meaning vs. significance in biblical interpretation, see Hendrik Krabbendam's chapter, "Hermeneutics and Preaching" in *The Preacher and Preaching: Reviving the Art in the Twentieth Century*, ed. Samuel T. Logan Jr. (Phillipsburg, NJ: Presbyterian and Reformed, 1986), 212–45.

center on Christ will always miss the dimension of depth in Old Testament revelation. It is in this dimension that the real significance of that revelation lies.

Without reference to Christ the covenant law of the Old Testament becomes legalism. A preacher may present a series of sermons on the Ten Commandments. Since he appreciates the Reformed creeds, he uses the Larger Catechism of the Westminster Assembly or the Heidelberg Catechism to guide his reflection. He is preaching, let us say, on the seventh commandment. His sermon has two parts: first, what the commandment forbids; second, what the commandment requires. He succeeds in describing a catalogue of vices in which lust finds expression; he also presents the central virtue of chastity that overcomes such sins. The sermon ends in warning, a call to repentance and to amendment of life for those who would be obedient to God's law.

No doubt the preacher will also enforce his warnings by examples from the Bible (David and Bathsheba) and from contemporary life. On the positive side, he may offer suggestions about the benefits of other interests and occupations to reduce the temptations to lust springing from idleness. He may counsel the avoiding of lascivious films and TV movies.

Is this a caricature? Perhaps, to a degree. What biblically grounded preacher would fail to connect the seventh commandment with our Lord's teaching? Certainly he will emphasize Jesus' word that adultery is not only the outward act, but the inward thought. As the commandment is carried forward into the context of Christ's teaching, however, its significance is at once deepened. If the preacher recognizes this, he will be drawn into preaching the heart of the law as Christ presented it. The issue is then not simply the subduing of lust, but the expression of love, the love that fulfills the law. What is that love, according to Jesus? It is the love shown by the Good Samaritan, the love of compassion, of self-denying, spontaneous, sacrificial mercy. That love is modeled on the love of God in Jesus Christ. Love for neighbor flows from love for God, and love for God is our response to His love for us.

Only at the cross do we know the real meaning of love—of God's redeeming love. Only at the cross can our lusts be crucified. Only from the fountain opened at Calvary flows the blood of cleansing and the living water of the Spirit. It is not only true that the law should not be preached without the gospel. More profoundly, the law itself cannot be understood without its fulfillment in the gospel. It is to a redeemed people that God gives His law, and *God's* law, the law that centers on Him, requires more of us than simple justice. It requires us to forgive as we have been forgiven, to love as we have been loved by our gracious Father in heaven.

The preacher must not divorce the catechism's analysis of the commandments from the rest of the catechism. The commandments are there carefully placed in the context of redemption. As preachers we must do the same.

Further, because God gives His commandments to His redeemed people, we must understand their twofold purpose: they reveal His holy nature so that we may know Him, and they shape our lives so that we may reflect His glory. Both sides of God's purpose come to their realization in Christ.

We may ask, Why did God forbid adultery to His covenant people? The answer is not simply that God wished to provide stable family life for the sociological well-being of Israel. There is a deeper reason, one closely related to the very nature of God's saving covenant. God would emphasize and sanctify the reality of a jealous love. The love of the marriage bond, expressed in sexual union, is not to be shared with others who are not joined by that bond. The faithfulness of jealous love in marriage provides Israel with a model for understanding the faithful love that God's people are to show to Him, a response to His jealous, electing love for them. God reveals Himself to Israel as a jealous God: "For thou shalt worship no other god: for the Lord, whose name is Jealous, is a jealous God" (Ex. 34:14).

The constant biblical metaphor that compares idolatry to adultery is grounded in an analogy that God has appointed by His ordering of the marriage relationship. God will be known not only as the Father of Israel His son, but also as the husband and Lord of Israel His bride.

Without the analogy to God's jealousy for Israel's exclusive devotion we might suppose that any sexual liaison would be legitimate that was consummated with love. On the other hand, without the analogy to the jealous love of a husband for his wife, we might imagine that God would approve of acts of religious worship directed toward any deity whatever, since He alone is God and could therefore receive them for Himself.

But the analogy that permeates Scripture teaches us otherwise. God would have us know the intensity of a pure love that is exclusive in character, a commitment of the heart that is profaned if one turns from it to seek a relation of the same intimacy with another. The worship of the idols is not an indirect way of adoring the one true God who has revealed Himself to Israel. It is apostasy, turning away from the Lord; it is spiritual adultery. Solomon joins his heathen wives in worshiping Ashtoreth, the goddess of the Sidonians; Milcom, the "abomination" of the Ammonites; Chemosh, of Moab; and Molech, of Ammon. When he does so he turns his heart away from the Lord (1 Kings 11:1–13; cf. Ex. 34:10–17). No longer does he love the Lord his God with all his heart, soul, and might (Deut. 6:5).

Further, the sacrifices of the Gentiles are not at last offered to merely imaginary, mythical beings. They are offered to demons (1 Cor. 10:20). For that reason Paul says, "Or do we provoke the Lord to jealousy?" (1 Cor. 10:22). God is jealous, zealous for His own holy Name. He cannot tolerate the blasphemy of attributing to the powers of darkness the glory that is due to Him. Of course, what God requires is also that which delivers us from delusion, bondage, and destruction. Yet God must require it not merely for our sake but for His. God must be true to Himself.

The nature of God's jealousy for His Name and for His people is revealed in Jesus Christ. As we learn of the triune nature of God we are able to understand better the meaning of His holy jealousy. Jesus as the Son of God is jealous for the Name and glory of His Father. He drives the hucksters out of the temple: "Take these things hence; make not my Father's house a house of merchandise" (John 2:16). His disciples remembered the Scriptures, "Zeal for thy house shall eat me up" (John 2:17; Ps. 69:9). Jesus is consumed with jealousy for the pure worship of His Father in heaven. His jealousy is more than that of the true servant of God (like Phinehas, Num. 25:10–11). His is the jealousy of the Son for the Name and honor of His Father.

So, too, the Father is jealous for His Son. His voice from heaven acknowledged His beloved Son; He has exalted Him above all creation in heaven and earth and given Him a Name that is above every name, that at the Name of Jesus every knee might bow and every tongue confess that Jesus Christ is Lord (Phil. 2:9–11).

God's commandment forbidding adultery should therefore be understood in its context: the unfolding history of God's redemption. Not just sexual purity, but covenant devotion is the underlying requirement of this commandment. For this reason the apostle Paul, when he describes the jealous love that a man should have for his wife, cannot help continually reflecting on God's jealous love for His people in Jesus Christ (Eph. 5:25–33). The great wonder and mystery for Paul is not the mystery of married love, but the mystery of divine love for which it provides a created analogy. Paul is no longer Saul the legalistic Pharisee whom Jesus met on the road to Damascus. He does not separate the commandments from the Lord who gave them or from His purposes in redemption. Marital faithfulness is the service of the Lord not simply because God has commanded it, but because it manifests love that springs from God's redeeming love. That vision of serving the Lord touches the deepest springs of motivation for the Christian. In loving others we manifest our love for Him who first loved us.

In christological perspective the law is not legalism, nor is covenantal history moralism. As we have seen, the Old Testament does not furnish us with a scrapbook of narratives useful for purposes of illustration. Rather it contains the record of God's ongoing work of redemption in the conflict between the Seed of the woman and the seed of the serpent. We dare not preach David's encounter with Goliath as an example of bravery to be emulated in our conflicts with the "giants" that assault us. Such an approach trivializes the Old Testament revelation. David's calling and enduement as the Lord's anointed has its deep significance in revealing the redemptive work of God. The Lord prepares us to understand something of the significance of Christ's final victory over Satan and the powers of darkness. The salvation wrought by David has typical significance that is not detached from its historical reality, but rather grounded in it.

In one other brief example, the poetry, as much as the law, of the Old Testament is grounded in the history of redemption. Many of the psalms are written in the first person plural. The people of God confess their faith in their Lord, ascribing praise to His Name and seeking deliverance from their enemies. The individual psalmist does not express merely private emotions. In many cases the psalmist is David, crying to God in full awareness that he is the Lord's anointed (2 Sam. 22:51). Even when another inspired individual is the author of a psalm, it is written in the representative capacity of one called to serve the Lord.

The function of the psalms in God's dealings with His people is made clear at the beginning when the song of Moses is given by God's inspiration (Deut. 31:19). The song is not a direct prophecy addressed to Israel; nor does it have the form of covenantal law, like the Ten Commandments. Rather, it has the form of response to God's revelation in praise. Yet it forms part of God's witness to Israel. Memorized and sung as part of Israel's heritage, it will "testify before them as a witness" when they prove unfaithful to the Lord their Rock (Deut. 31:21–22). The later inspired songs of Israel have the same function.

When the Lord's people or the Lord's servants call upon His name, their songs are evidently written for worship and supplication, not for entertainment. As expressions of worship they are stamped by the distinctiveness of God's dealings with Israel, that is, by the history of redemption. The praises of God that describe His attributes do not have the motivation of such hymns among the polytheistic Gentiles. The inspired psalmist does not have the problem of a polytheist. Like a philanderer with many girlfriends the polytheist must convince the god whose favors he seeks that he is the winner among all the gods, at least for the moment.

Rather, the psalms of Israel are characterized by declarative as well as descriptive praise.[5] The Lord is adored for what He has done, as well as for who He is. He is the God of the

5. On this distinction, and the contrast between the Psalms and ancient Near Eastern hymns, see Claus Westermann, *The Praise of God in the Psalms*, trans. Keith Crim (London: Epworth, 1966), 15–51.

exodus (Pss. 80; 81; 114), the God who redeemed Israel and made His covenant with David (Ps. 89). The history of God's salvation forms the basis for confession of sin and for petition for the renewal of God's saving mercies (Pss. 74; 80). The psalms also proclaim the fulfillment of God's promises when the Lord Himself will come again as the Redeemer, Judge, and Deliverer of His people (Ps. 96:10–13). The new song of salvation will be sung in that great day (Pss. 96:1; 98:1; cf. 144:9).[6]

In their theological depth the psalms are songs of God's covenant and of the hope of the covenant. Since God's great work of salvation will be accomplished by the Son of David, the psalms are explicitly messianic. Jesus confronts His enemies with passages from the psalms. They have not understood that David's Son must also be His Lord (Ps. 110:1; Matt. 22:41–46). They do not know that it is the stone rejected by the builders that God has made the head of the corner (Ps. 118:22–23; Matt. 21:42–43).

But it is not only in a few "messianic psalms" that the songs of Israel point to Jesus Christ. Indeed, we may perceive from plainly messianic psalms principles of interpretation that apply to many others.

Psalm 22, for example, is clearly messianic. The opening cry of the psalm is the cry of Christ on the cross, and the details of the sufferer's anguish are remarkably specific in their application to Calvary. The author of Hebrews cites Psalm 22:22 in reference to Christ (Heb. 2:11–12). Not only the cry of abandonment, but also the vow of praise are Christ's own utterances. This is true not only because Jesus in His earthly ministry sang the psalms and in that way made them His own, but also because He fulfilled them. David as a righteous sufferer, persecuted because he was the Lord's anointed, prefigures the truly righteous sufferer, God's own Son and Holy One. Not just the first verse of Psalm 22 is Christ's; the whole psalm is His.

In addition to overtly messianic psalms (such as Ps. 22), there are other categories of psalms that no less unmistakably point to Christ. The "royal psalms," songs of Zion and of Zion's king, are pointedly messianic in the light of New Testament fulfillment. When the king of glory enters Zion, triumphant after subduing all his foes (Ps. 24), the scene that is pictured is fulfilled in Christ's ascension. The Lord who marches through the wilderness and enters into His holy hill, receiving and giving gifts to men (Pss. 68; 18) is the Lord whose way in the wilderness was prepared by John the Baptist (Isa. 40:3; Matt. 3:1–3). He who is the coming Judge (Pss. 96:13; 97:7; cf. Heb. 1:6) is the Savior who leads His people with Him in triumphant procession. His throne is established forever (Pss. 2; 110); He has universal dominion (Pss. 2; 72; 110). The King receives His bride and His household as the crown of blessing (Ps. 45). In Jesus both the psalms that exalt the King of David's line and the Eternal King are joined.

4. Conclusion

Only as we perceive the focus on Christ do we sense the depth of meaning in the Old Testament. It is precisely the discovery of this theological depth that will give our preaching practical power. Some would object to christological preaching of the Old Testament not because they dispute the possibility of making a case for it, but because they think it is just too complicated.

6. Geerhardus Vos, "The Eschatology of the Psalter," reprinted in *The Pauline Eschatology* (Grand Rapids: Eerdmans, 1953), 323–65.

That objection will end the matter if we are unwilling to be workmen in the Word, laboring in the Word and teaching (1 Tim. 5:17). It is much easier to build sermons out of wood, hay, and stubble than to be craftsmen using gold, silver, and precious stones (1 Cor. 3:12–15).

Christological preaching calls for patient comparing of Scripture with Scripture, extensive use of concordances, and a lifetime commitment to Bible study, meditation, and prayer. Christological preaching is not contrived, however; nor are its lines obscure in the Bible. "Salvation is of the Lord" (Jonah 2:9) is the great text of the Bible and reminds us that we must not sacrifice the objective reality of what God does in salvation in order to stress the subjective reality of our knowledge of the Lord and experience of His mercy. If we mistakenly think that focusing on our experience is more practical or reaches men where they live, we will overlook the overwhelming gospel fact that salvation is God's work. We do not kindle faith by describing it but by describing Christ. Paul never tires of speaking of God's work; for him the *indicative* of what God has done always comes before the *imperative* of what we are to do (e.g., Col. 3:1–4).

Preaching Christ from all the Scriptures joins faith to grace. God is the Savior in Christ. The Old Testament believers trusted as they waited for that salvation to come. They are examples to us as *believers*—not apart from the objective facts of God's redemption, but as those who lived by faith.

The obedience of love flows from that faith relation. Like faith, love is kindled not by introspection, but by looking to Jesus, the Author and Finisher of our faith. We love because He first loved us; it is the love of God that is shed abroad in our hearts.

The Scriptures are full of moral instruction and ethical exhortation, but the ground and motivation of all is found in the mercy of Jesus Christ. We are to preach all the riches of Scripture, but unless the center holds all the bits and pieces of our pulpit counseling, of our thundering at social sins, of our positive or negative thinking—all fly off into the Sunday morning air.

Paul was resolved to know nothing at Corinth but Jesus Christ and Him crucified. Let others develop the pulpit fads of the passing seasons. Specialize in preaching Jesus!

Vern S. Poythress

Vern S. Poythress, professor of New Testament interpretation, joined the faculty at Westminster in 1976. He earned a Ph.D. in mathematics from Harvard University in 1970. He then studied at Westminster and continued studies in New Testament at the Universities of Cambridge and Stellenbosch. He combines a wide array of interests: from the integration of faith and science to apologetics, theology, linguistics, and biblical interpretation. His writings on biblical interpretation integrate biblical theology and the presuppositional approach of Van Til, both at the center of Westminster tradition. In *Symphonic Theology: The Validity of Multiple Perspectives in Theology* (1987), Poythress develops his perspectival approach to theology, which is illustrated by his fair evaluation of dispensationalism in *Understanding Dispensationalists* (1987). Further, in the steps of Clowney, he explores Christ in the Old Testament in *The Shadow of Christ in the Law of Moses* (1991) while at the same time evaluating the movement of theonomy. The two selections that follow present his approach to biblical interpretation.

"Divine Meaning of Scripture" was originally published in the *WTJ* in 1986. A shorter version of this essay, under the title "What Does God Say through Human Authors?," can be found in the symposium on Scripture *Inerrancy and Hermeneutic*. Here the original version is reproduced. Poythress discusses the question of the relationship of the divine authorship and the human authorships of Scripture. He approaches the issue from different angles and illustrates his points with examples. The argument presupposes the results of biblical theology and its progressive understanding of the Bible. He also introduces categories of philosophical hermeneutics to clarify the dual authorship of Scripture. A belief in the supernatural origin of the Bible implies that the meaning of Scripture goes beyond the intention of the human authors. Thus, grammatical-historical exegesis is not enough. In this context, Poythress welcomes and evaluates discussions about the *sensus plenior* and canonical interpretation.

Poythress's teaching at Westminster includes core classes in biblical interpretation. *God-Centered Biblical Interpretation* offers the fruit of his reflection on this topic. It teaches a Trinitarian interpretation of Scripture. The selection presented here, "The Purpose of the Bible," asks the question: what is the Bible's purpose? Poythress answers by demonstrating how the Bible reveals three perspectives, a triad, of God's work—control, meaning, and presence. These three are rooted in the person and works of the triune God of the Bible. In this Poythress expresses insights from Van Til and John Frame. Whereas the Bible has several purposes, Poythress also argues with Clowney that Christ is the center of Scripture.

DIVINE MEANING OF SCRIPTURE

Vern Sheridan Poythress, "Divine Meaning of Scripture," *WTJ* 48, 2 (Fall 1986): 241–79.

What is the relation between God and human authors of the Bible? Does God's meaning at every point coincide with the intention of the human author? Can we use the same procedures of interpretation as we would with a noninspired book?

Even if we hold an orthodox, "high" view of inspiration, the answer to these questions is not easy. Many, of course, would deny that God is the author of the Bible in any straightforward way. They argue that the books of the Bible are to be interpreted as so many human writings, subject to the errors, distortions, and moral failures of human beings everywhere else.[1]

If, however, we believe in the testimony of Jesus Christ, the apostles, and the OT, we know that books of the Bible are both God's word and the word of the human authors. The exact historical, psychological, and spiritual processes involved in the production of individual books of the Bible may, of course, have varied from book to book. In many cases we simply do not have much firm information about these processes. In all cases, however, the result was that the literary product (specifically, the autograph) was *both* what God says *and* what the human author says (see, e.g., Deut. 5:22–33; Acts 1:16; 2 Peter 1:21).[2]

Suppose, then, that we confine ourselves to people who hold to this classic doctrine of inspiration. We still do not have agreement about the relation of God's meaning to the meaning of the human author. A recent article by Darrell Bock delineates no less than four

---

1. E.g., James Barr, *The Bible in the Modern World* (London: SCM, 1973); idem, *The Scope and Authority of the Bible* (Philadelphia: Westminster, 1980); idem, *Holy Scripture: Canon, Authority, Criticism* (Philadelphia: Westminster, 1983); may be taken as representative of one form of this view. Barr along with many interpreters in the historical-critical tradition wants to retain a diffuse authority for the Bible. Theologians are still called upon to reflect upon the Bible, and say what they think the implications are for our doctrine. But this is not to say that they treat the Bible as what God says [see chap. 57 below].

A more conservative Barthian view, or a "canonical" approach like that of Brevard Childs (*Introduction to the Old Testament as Scripture* [Philadelphia: Fortress, 1979]), would leave more room for a distinctively "theological" interpretation based on historical-critical interpretation or alongside of it. But such approaches, in my opinion, still compromise divine authorship and authority by allowing errors in the propositional content of Scripture. See, e.g., John M. Frame, "God and Biblical Language: Transcendence and Immanence," in *God's Inerrant Word*, ed. John Warwick Montgomery (Minneapolis: Bethany Fellowship, 1974), 159–77.

2. I am aware that almost any biblical passage one could cite concerning inspiration has been disputed by deniers of inerrancy. Moreover, with few exceptions the direct statements about inspiration refer primarily to the OT (or parts of it) rather than to the NT. Hence some additional arguments are needed. But it is outside the scope of this article to deal with such disputations.

distinct approaches among evangelicals.[3] The specific issue which Bock discusses is the question of NT interpretation of the OT. Does NT use of OT texts sometimes imply that God meant more than what the human author thought of? Walter C. Kaiser Jr., says no, while S. Lewis Johnson, James I. Packer, and Elliott Johnson say yes.[4] Bruce K. Waltke introduces still a third approach emphasizing the canon as the final context for interpretation. A fourth approach, represented by E. Earle Ellis, Richard Longenecker, and Walter Dunnett, emphasizes the close relation between apostolic hermeneutics and Jewish hermeneutics of the first century.[5]

Admittedly the NT use of the OT has some complexities of its own. We cannot here look at all of the ways in which the NT makes use of the OT. Instead, we will concentrate on the problem of dual authorship, a problem touching on our understanding of the entire Bible, rather than on the NT or OT specifically.

1. Divine Meaning and Human Meaning

Disagreements in interpretation arise from differing views of the relation of divine and human authorship. The chief question is this: what is the relationship between what God says to us through the text and what the human author says? Let us consider two simple alternatives. First, we could take the view that the meaning of the divine author has little or nothing to do with the meaning of the human author. For instance, according to an allegorical approach, commonly associated with Origen,[6] whenever the "literal" meaning is unworthy of God, it is to be rejected. And even when the "literal" meaning is unobjectionable, the heart of the matter is often to be found in another level of meaning, a "spiritual" or allegorical meaning. If we were to take such a view, we could argue that the spiritual or allegorical meaning is part of the *divine* meaning in the text. But the human author was not aware of it.

The difficulties with this view are obvious. When we detach the divine meaning from the human author, the text itself no longer exercises effective control over what meanings we derive from it. The decisive factor in what we find God to be saying is derived from our allegorical scheme and our preconceptions about what is "worthy" of God. We can read in what we afterwards read out. God's Lordship over us through his word is in practice denied.

When we see the dangers of this view, we naturally become sympathetic with the opposite alternative. In this case, we say that what God says is simply what the human author says: no more, no less.[7] Sometimes, of course, there may be difficulties in determining what a

3. Darrel L. Bock, "Evangelicals and the Use of the Old Testament in the New," *Bibliotheca sacra* 142 (1985): 209–23.

4. Elliott Johnson, however, wishes to express this "more" as more references ("references plenior"), not more sense ("sensus plenior").

5. Bock, "Evangelicals and the Use of the OT."

6. Frederic W. Farrar, *History of Interpretation* (Grand Rapids: Baker, 1961), 191–98. But see R. P. C. Hanson, *Allegory and Event A Study of the Sources and Significance of Origen's Interpretation of Scripture* (London: SCM, 1959), for a more balanced presentation of Origen. Note also the article by Dan G. McCartney, "Literal and Allegorical Interpretation in Origen's *Against Celsus*," *WTJ* 48, 2 (Fall 1986): 281–301.

7. Walter C. Kaiser Jr. might seem to be a representative of this "singlemeaning" approach, by virtue of his strong statements in favor of the single meaning of biblical texts ("Legitimate Hermeneutics," in *Inerrancy* [ed. Norman L. Geisler; Grand Rapids: Zondervan, 1980], 125, 127; idem, *Toward an Exegetical Theology Biblical Exegesis for Preaching and Teaching* [Grand Rapids: Baker, 1981], 47). But Kaiser's position contains much more besides this. He provides detailed instructions for treating the question of applying the Bible to the present day (pp. 34, 149–63). And he advises us, when interpreting a passage, to take into account "antecedent Scripture": books of the Bible composed before the composition of the pas-

particular human author says at a particular point. Moreover, sometimes what authors say may be not perfectly precise. Sometimes they may choose to be ambiguous or to hint at implications without blurting them out. But the difficulties here are the same difficulties that confront us with all interpretation of human language. Such difficulties have never prevented us from understanding one another sufficiently to carry on. The divine authorship of the Bible does not alter our procedure at all.

I am sympathetic with this view. With some qualifications it can serve us well: much better, certainly, than the procedure of unbridled allegorization. However, there are several nuances and complexities about interpretation that this view does not handle well.

First of all, and perhaps most obviously, this view, at least as described so far, does not tell us enough about how the Bible speaks to our situation and applies to ourselves.[8] Some of the human authors of the Bible were, perhaps, consciously "writing for posterity," but most, at least, were writing primarily to their contemporaries. They did not write with us directly in view. Nor did they foresee all our circumstances and needs. We can still *overhear* what they said to people in their own time, but that is not the same as hearing them speak *to* us. How do we know what they want us to do with their words, if they did not have us in mind?

A popular solution to this difficulty is to invoke E. D. Hirsch's distinction between "meaning" and "significance."[9] "Meaning," in Hirsch's view, is what the human author expressed, including what is expressed tacitly, allusively, or indirectly. It includes what can legitimately be inferred. "Significance" is a relation that we as readers draw between what is said and our own (or others') situation. Interpretation of a biblical passage, narrowly speaking, determines the meaning of the human author. Application involves the exploration of the significance *for us* of that one meaning, and action in accordance with it.

Let us take as an example Malachi 3:8–12. Malachi here instructs his readers that they have robbed God in tithes and offerings, and that they are to bring the tithes to the temple storehouse, as Moses commanded. Both the general principle of not robbing God and the specific application to keep the law of tithes are part of the "meaning." Malachi did not have our modern situations immediately in view. Nevertheless, modern readers are to apply Malachi's meaning to themselves. In a comprehensive way, they are to devote all their lives and substance to the Lord, and specifically they are liberally to give a portion (some would say, at least one tenth) of their gains to the church and Christian causes. These applications are "significances," based on a relation between Malachi's meaning and the modern situation.

So far this is reasonable. But there is a difficulty. "Significance" is here understood as any kind of relation that readers perceive between their own situations and the passage. There are many possible "significances," even for a single reader. There are many possible

---

sage in question (pp. 131–47). This is not *merely* a way of saying that we should understand general historical and literary backgrounds of the passage. We must do that with any kind of text whatsoever. But, in addition, in the case of Scripture we should also devote particular attention to those texts which have the same divine author (pp. 133–34). Finally, Kaiser acknowledges the need for systematic theology, integrating the teaching of the whole Bible (p. 161). This presupposes the value of viewing the whole of Scripture as the product of a single divine author. Hence Kaiser is concerned to protect the value of historical backgrounds and progressive revelation, rather than to deny the value of looking at the whole of the canon at some later stage of synthesis.

8. Kaiser sees the deficiency here and presents a remedy (*Exegetical Theology*, 149–63).

9. Eric D. Hirsch, *Validity in Interpretation* (New Haven/London: Yale University, 1967); idem, *The Aims of Interpretation* (Chicago: University of Chicago, 1976); cf. Emilio Betti, *Die Hermeneutik als allgemeine Methodik der Geisteswissenschaften* (Tübingen: Mohr, 1962); Charles Altieri, *Act & Quality: A Theory of Literary Meaning and Humanistic Understanding* (Amherst: University of Massachusetts, 1981), 97–159; Kaiser, *Exegetical Theology*, 32.

applications. What then distinguishes a good from a bad application of a passage of the Bible? Is it up to the reader's whim? In cases when we read Shakespeare, Camus, or some other human writer, we may derive "lessons" from what we read, and apply things to ourselves. But, as Hirsch and other theorists in his camp assert, it is we as readers who decide how to do this, based on our own framework or values.[10] To be sure, even a human writer may want to challenge our values. But we treat that challenge as simply a challenge from another human being, fallible like ourselves.

In the case of the Bible it is different. Precisely because it has divine authority, and for no other reason, we must allow it to challenge and reform even our most cherished assumptions and values. But how do we do this? We listen to the human author of, say, Malachi. But he speaks to the Jewish audience of his day, not to us. Hypothetically, therefore, modern readers might evade applying Malachi 3:8–12 to themselves by any of several strategies. (1) God's intention is simply Malachi's intention: that Malachi's Jewish readers repent concerning their attitude and practice in tithing. There is no implication for us. (2) God intends us to understand that we ought not to rob God, but this applies simply to our general attitude toward possessions, since there is no longer a temple in the OT sense. (3) God intends us to understand that if we are remiss in our financial obligations in our day, he will send a prophet to let us know about it.

Note that these construals do not dispute the "meaning" of Malachi 3:8–12 in a Hirschian sense. They dispute only the applications ("significances"). There are several possible replies. For one thing, we could argue that the rest of Scripture, and the NT in particular, shows that we are to give proportionally (1 Cor. 16:1–4), and that in various other ways we are to be good stewards of God's gifts. That is not disputed. The question is whether *Malachi* shows us such applications.

Second, we may say that, in the light of the rest of the Bible, we know that God intends us to apply *Malachi* to our proportional giving. But if we say that God intends(!) each valid application of Malachi, then in an ordinary sense each valid application is part of God's meaning (= intention), even if it was not immediately in the view of the human author of Malachi. This seems to break down the idea that there is an *absolute, pure* equation between divine intention and human author's meaning. Divine intention includes more, inasmuch as God is aware of the all the future applications.

Third, we may say that even though the human author did not have all the applications in mind, they are part of his "unconscious intention."[11] That is, the (valid) applications are the "kind of thing he had in mind." Once Malachi saw our circumstances, he would acknowledge the legitimacy of our applications. This is quite reasonable. But there are still some complexities. (1) Some people, with a very narrow conception of "meaning," might object that this breaks down the initial distinction between meaning and significance. I do not think that this is so, but it is sometimes hard to know where the exact line is drawn between "meaning" and "significance." (2) We still need to discuss what guidelines to use in drawing applications. How do we go about determining what Malachi would say were he confronted by a situation very different from any that he confronted in his own lifetime? We have only his text to go by. Or do we have also the rest of the biblical canon, which expresses thoughts consonant with Malachi's? But appealing to the rest of the canon as revealing

10. Hirsch, *Aims*, 95–158.
11. Hirsch, *Validity*, 51–57.

the mind of God takes us beyond the mind of Malachi, unless we say that all this is in his "unconscious intention." (3) Even if Malachi were acquainted with our situation, he would never be as well acquainted with it as God is. Moreover, there is an undeniable difference between God's understanding of the text and Malachi's, since God is conscious of those aspects of Malachi's intention which are unconscious to Malachi himself.

What are we to do with these difficulties? I think it indicates that when we come to the point of application, we must somewhere along the way appeal directly to God's knowledge, authority, and presence. Otherwise, we are simply "overhearing" a human voice from long ago, a voice to which we may respond in whatever way suits our own value system. To be sure, the idea of simply equating divine and human meaning in the Bible is a useful one. It directs us away from the arbitrariness of an allegorical system. But when we use this idea in order simply to stick to human meaning, arbitrariness can still exist in the area of the application. No technical rigidity in our theory of meaning will, by itself, allow us to escape this easily, because there are an indefinite number of applications, and many of them are not *directly* anticipated in the text of Scripture.

I propose, then, to deal with this area of application. I count as "applications" both effects in the cognitive field (e.g., concluding mentally, "I ought to have a practice of giving to my church") and effects in the field of overt action (e.g., putting money in the collection plate). "Application" in this sense *includes* all inferences about the meaning of a biblical text. Such inferences are always applications in the cognitive field. For example, to conclude that Malachi teaches tithing (inference about meaning) is simultaneously to come to *believe* that "Malachi teaches tithing" (a cognitive effect in the reasoner).

With this in mind, the central question confronting us is, "What applications of a biblical passage does God approve?" To answer this, we have to look at some characteristics of communication through language.

2. Interpreting Human Discourse

Let us first consider communication from one human being to another. Person A speaks discourse D to person B. Now, given almost any fixed sequence of words (D), we can plausibly interpret them in several different conflicting ways. We can do this by imagining different contexts in which they are spoken or written. "The door is open" can easily be intended to imply, "Please shut it," or "Get out," or "That is the cause of the draft," or "Someone was careless." Or it may simply convey a bit of information. To understand what another human being A is saying, in the discourse D, is not simply to explore the range of all possible interpretations of a sequence of words. Rather, it is to understand what the *speaker as a person* is saying. We do this using clues given by the situation and by what we know of the person. We must pay attention to the author and to the situation as well as to the exact choice of words.

Moreover, many different things are happening in an act of communication. For one thing, speakers make assertions about the world. They formulate hypotheses, they express assumptions, and otherwise make reference to the world. Let us call this the "referential" aspect of communication. But referring to the world is not all that speakers do. They may also be trying to bring about actions or changes of attitude on the part of their hearers. They are trying to achieve some practical result. Let us call this the "conative" aspect of communication. Next, whether they want to or not, speakers inevitably tell their hearers something about themselves and their own attitudes. Let us call this the "expressive" aspect of communication. In fact, Roman Jakobson, in analyzing communicative acts, defines no less than six planes or aspects of communication.[12] For our purposes, we may restrict ourselves to three prominent aspects: referential, conative, and expressive.

Note that most of the time a speaker is not doing only one of these. In fact, any of the three indirectly implies the others. Facts about the speaker's attitudes (expressive) are also one kind of fact about the world (referential). And facts about the speaker's goals or attempts to change the hearer (conative) are also one kind of fact about the world (referential). Conversely, any of statements about the world (referential) simultaneously give information about what a speaker believes (expressive) and what the speaker wants others to believe (conative).

3. Interpreting Divine Speech

Now consider what is involved in interpreting speech from God to a human being. I have in mind instances such as God's speeches to Abraham (e.g., Gen. 12:1–3; 15:1–21; 17:1–21) and God's pronouncements from Mount Sinai to the people of Israel (Ex. 20:2–17). Of course, these speeches (or-portions or condensations of them) are later on recorded in written form by human authors writing the books of the Bible. But for the moment let us concentrate on the original oral communication. This is useful, because no human being mediates these original acts of communication. In these cases, does interpretation proceed in the same way as with human speech? In a fundamental sense it does. For one thing, the speeches come in a human language (in this case Hebrew). They are sometimes directly compared with speech from one human being to another (Ex. 20:19). The audiences are expected to proceed in a way similar to what they do with speech from a human being. They interpret what God says in terms of the situation in which he speaks (Ex. 20:2; 20:18, 22), and in terms of what they already know about God and his purposes (Ex. 20:2; 20:11). But here lies the decisive difference, of course. The people are listening to *God*. Using the "same" interpretive process that we use with human speech is precisely what causes us to acknowledge the profound difference and uniqueness of divine speech—for God is unique.

Now consider what it means to know that God is speaking. We earlier observed that a discourse detached from any author and any situation could mean any number of things. Moreover, if we attribute a discourse to a different author or a different situation that the real one, we will often find that we interpret the same sequence of words in a different fashion. For example, if we think that the wording of Colossians 1:15 is a writing of Arius, we will interpret it differently than if we think it is a writing of the Apostle Paul.

Likewise, if we think that the wording of God's speech at Mount Sinai is spoken by someone else, or if we have mistaken conceptions about God, this will more or less seriously affect our interpretation of the speech. What is authoritative about God's speech at Mount Sinai? Divine authority does not attach to whatever meaning other people may attach to the words. They may even choose to speak the same sequence of words as in Exodus 20:2–17, yet mean something different. In this sense, we may freely admit that many "meanings" can be attached to these same words. But that is not the issue. Rather, divine authority belongs to what *God* is saying. What is crucial is what *God* means. To

---

12. Roman Jakobson, "Closing Statement: Linguistics and Poetics," *Style in Language*, ed. Thomas A. Sebeok (Cambridge: Massachusetts Institute of Technology, 1960), 350–77. Cf. Vern S. Poythress, "A Framework for Discourse Analysis: The Components of a Discourse, from a Tagmemic Viewpoint," *Semiotica* 38–3/4 (1982): 277–98.

find this out, we must interpret the words in accordance with what we know about God, just as we would take into account what we know of human authors when we interpret what they say.

But, someone may say, this is circular. How can we know God except by what he says and does? And how can we properly understand what he says and does unless we already know him? Well, how do we come to know another human being? In both cases there is a certain "theoretical" circularity. But in fact, it is more like a spiral, because earlier incorrect impressions may be corrected in the process of seeing and hearing more from a person.

In addition, we may say something about the application of God's words. God expects his words to be applied in many situations throughout history. He binds us to obey, not only what he says in the most direct way ("meaning"), but what he implies ("application"). Each valid application is something that God intended from the beginning, and as such has his sanction. Divine authority attaches not only to what he says most directly, but to what he implies. It attaches to the applications.

Of course, we must be careful. We may be wrong when we extend our inferences too far. We must respect the fact that our inferences are not infallible. Where we are not sure, or where good reasons exist on the other side, we must beware of insisting that our interpretation must be obeyed. But if it turns out that we did understand the implications and applications correctly, then we know that those applications also had divine sanction and authority.

This means, then, that we do not need a rigid, precise distinction between meaning and application, in the case of God's speech. To be sure, some things are said directly ("meaning"), and some things are left to be inferred in the light of seeing a relation between what is said and our situation ("significance", "application"). But the distinction, as far as I can see, is a relative one. It is a distinction between what is said *more or less directly*, and between what needs *more or less* reckoning with a larger situation in order to be inferred.

The usual way of distinguishing between meaning and application is to say that meaning has to do with what the text itself says (in itself), whereas application has to do with a *relation* between the text and the reader's situation. But we have already seen that, in general, we cannot properly assess "meaning" even in the narrowest possible sense apart from attention to the author's situation. This situation includes the hearers. *All* assessment of an author's expressed meaning must reckon with the intended hearers and their situation. In the case of divine speech, all future hearers are included, hence all their situations are included. Therefore, focus on what the text says most directly and obviously, and focus on what it is seen to say in the light of relation to a situation, are both a matter of degree.

Next, we may observe that God's speeches include referential, expressive, and conative aspects. God's speeches make assertions about the world and about ethical standards for our lives (the referential aspect). Secondly, we meet *God* when we hear him speaking (the expressive aspect). And thirdly, we are affected and transformed by what we hear (the conative aspect). God's word may empower us to do good, but it may also harden our hearts when we are rebellious.

These three aspects of God's communication are not so many isolated pieces. Rather, they are involved in one another. In fact, each one can serve as a perspective on the whole of God's communication.

First of all, all of God's speech is referential in character. In all of what God says, he is bringing us to *know* him and his world. For knowledge includes not just information (knowing that), but skills in living (knowing how) and personal communion with God (knowing a person).

Second, in all of what God says, we meet him: he "expresses" himself. God is present with his word.

Third, in all of what God says, he affects us ("conatively") for good or ill, for blessing or for cursing (e.g., 2 Cor. 2:15–16).

These three aspects of God's speech are expressions of his knowledge (referential), his presence (expressive), and his active power (conative). These are nothing less than attributes of God. It is no wonder that we find these features in all that God says.

4. Divine Speech as Propositional and Personal

We may already draw some conclusions with respect to modern views of revelation. Neo-orthodoxy and other modernist views of divine revelation typically argue that revelation is personal encounter and therefore not propositional. But these are not exclusive alternatives. Human communication in general is simultaneously both. That is, it simultaneously possesses a referential and an expressive aspect. To be sure, one or other aspect may be more prominent and more utilized at one time, but each tacitly implies the other. Moreover, to know a person always involves knowing true statements about the person, though it means also more than this. If the supposed "encounter" with the divine is indeed "personal," it will inevitably be propositional as well. When I say that communication is "propositional," I do not of course mean that it must be a logical treatise. I mean only that communication conveys information about states of affairs in the world. One may infer from it that certain statements about the world are true.

In our claims about divine speech we do not rely only on general arguments based on the nature of human communication. The reader of Scripture over and over again finds accounts of divine communication that involve both propositional statements and personal presence of God. (Exodus 20 may serve as well as many other examples.)

But there are lessons here also for evangelicals. Evangelicals have sometimes rebounded against modernist views into an opposite extreme. In describing biblical interpretation, they have sometimes minimized the aspect of personal encounter and divine power to transform us. There is no need to do this. The issue with modernism is rather what *sort* of divine encounter and personal transformation we are talking about: is it contentless, or does it accompany what is being said (referentially and propositionally) about the world?

Moreover, there may be a tiny grain of truth in the slanders from modernists about evangelicals "idolizing" the pages of the Bible. We say that divine speech is "propositional." To begin with, we mean only that God makes true statements referring to the world. That is correct. But then, later on, we may come to mean something else. We think that we can isolate that referential and assertive character of what God is saying into gem-like, precise, syllogistic nuggets which can be manipulated and controlled by us, from then on, without further reflection on God's presence and power at work in what we originally heard. The "proposition," now isolated from the presence of God, can become the excuse for evading God and trying to lord it over and rationally master the truth which we have isolated. And then we have become subtly idolatrous, because we aspire to be lords over God's word.

I do not mean to bar us from reasoning from Scripture. We *must* do this in order to struggle responsibly to apply the Bible to ourselves. We must take seriously its implications as well as what is said most directly. What I have in mind is this. Even with the discourses from human beings, it would be unfair not to take into account what we know of their character, their views and their aspirations when we draw out the implications of an individual sentence. A statement with no explicit qualifications, and with no explicit directions as to the way in which we are to draw implications, may nevertheless not be completely universal. It may not have all the implications that we think. A larger knowledge of the author forms one kind of guide to the drawing of implications. At least this much is true with respect to the situation where God is the author.

5. Speech with Two Authors

So far we have discussed speech with a single author. But of course the Bible as we have it is a product of both the divine author and various human authors. How do we deal with this situation?

Well, the Bible makes it very clear that what God says does not cease to be what God says just because a human intermediary is introduced (Deut. 5:22–33). After all, it is God who chose the human intermediary and who fashioned his personality (Ps. 139:13–16). Hence everything that we have said about divine speech, such as God's speeches to Abraham, applies also to God's speeches through human spokesmen. In particular, it applies to all of the Bible, as the written word of God.

Conversely, what human beings say to us does not cease to be what they say when they become spokesmen of God. Hence, it would appear, everything that we have said about human communication applies to all of the Bible, as the writings of men.

But now we have a complex situation. For we have just argued that interpretation of a piece of writing interprets the words in the light of what is known of the author and his situation. If the same words happen to be said by two authors, there are two separate interpretations. The interpretations may have very similar results, or they may not, depending on the differences between the two authors and the way in which those differences mesh with the wording of the text. But, in principle, there may be differences, even if only very subtle differences of nuances.

Hence it would seem to be the case that we have two separate interpretations of any particular biblical text. The first interpretation sees the words entirely in the light of the human author, his characteristics, his knowledge, his social status. The second sees the same words entirely in the light of the divine author, his characteristics, his knowledge, his status. In general, the results of these two interpretations will differ.

But couldn't we still stick to a single interpretation? Couldn't we say that interpretation in the light of the human author is all that we need? Then, after we complete the interpretation, we assert that the product is, pure and simple, what God says.

Well, that still leaves us with the earlier problems about applications. But in addition to this, there are now several further objections. First, the strongest starting point of the "single interpretation" approach is its insistence on the importance of grammatical-historical exegesis. But it has now ended by hedging on one of the principles of grammatical-historical exegesis, namely the principle of taking into account the person of the author. When we come to interpreting the Bible, we must pay attention to who God is.

Secondly, this view seems dangerously akin to the neo-orthodox view that when God speaks, his attributes of majesty are somehow wholly hidden under human words. That is why the neo-orthodox think that they need not reckon with the divine attributes when they subject Scripture to the historical-critical method. As evangelicals, we do not want to use the antisupernaturalist assumptions of historical-critical method. We will not do that when it comes to miracles described in the Bible. But are we going to do it when we deal with the actual reading of the Bible?

Third, we must remember that God's speech involves his presence and power as well as propositional affirmations. At the beginning of interpretation we cannot arbitrarily eliminate the power and presence of God in his word, in order to tack them on only at the end. That automatically distorts what is happening in biblical communication from God. Hence it is asking for skewed results at the end.

Fourth, this procedure virtually demands that, at the first stage, we *not* reckon with the fact that God is who he is in his speaking to us. We must put wholly into the background that he is speaking to us. We must simply and *exclusively* concentrate on the human author. But how can we *not* reckon with all that we know of God as we hear what he says? This seems to be at odds with the innate impulse of biblical piety.

But there may still be a way to save this "single interpretation" approach. Namely, we can claim that God in his freedom decided to "limit" what he said to the human side. Namely, God decided to say simply what we arrive at through the interpretation of biblical passages when treated as though simply human.

This is a valiant effort. It is close to the truth. But, myself, I think that it will not work. First, it is difficult to see how one can justify this from Scripture. Deuteronomy 5:22–33 is a natural passage with which to begin. It describes the nature of God's communication through Moses. Since later Scripture builds on Moses, Deuteronomy 5:22–33 indirectly illuminates the nature of all God's later communication through human beings. Now Deuteronomy 5:22–33 starts first with divine communication. The human instrument is taken up into the divine message, rather than the divine message being "trimmed down" to suit the human instrument. If we were willing to use the analogy with the person and natures of Christ, we could say that Deuteronomy 5:22–33 is analogous to the Chalcedonian view (human nature taken up into the divine person), whereas the "single interpretation" approach is analogous to a kenotic view (divine person "losing" some attributes for the sake of assuming human nature).

Second, I find it psychologically impossible to maintain the experience of God's power and presence on the one hand, and on the other to exclude all reckoning with them when we come to assessing the referential aspect of biblical communication. It is not so easy thus to separate the referential from the expressive and the conative aspects of communication. God speaks to us as whole people. Moreover, if one could separate them, one would have arrived back at an essentially neo-orthodox dichotomy between propositional content and personal encounter.

Third, I think that scholarly hesitation about emphasizing God's role in authorship, though understandable, is groundless. Perhaps some scholars are influenced by the modernist atmosphere. Since modernists disbelieve in divine authorship, naturally their hermeneutical approach will demand its exclusion. We may unknowingly have absorbed some of this atmosphere.

But scholars have another cause for hesitation. Mention of God's role easily leads to dehistoricizing the message of the Bible. Readers reason to themselves that since God wrote the book, and since God is not subject to the limitations of knowledge of any historical period, he can be expected to write to all historical periods equally. Hence the historical circumstances in which the Bible appeared are irrelevant. The Bible is just like a book dropped directly from heaven.

Against this argument we may point to Exodus 20. There God speaks without a human intermediary. But this speech is not simply a speech "for posterity." It is a speech directly to specific people in specific circumstances (Ex. 20:2, 12), people subject to specific temptations (Ex. 20:17). The most important factor leading to a historically rooted message is not the human intermediary (though this further emphasizes it), but the fact that God chooses to speak to people where they are. He can do so fluently because he is competent in Hebrew, Greek, Aramaic, and is master of all the customs of each culture into which he chooses to speak. Over against this, the dehistoricizing approach not only neglects human intermediaries. It unwittingly denies *God's* linguistic and cultural competence!

Hence, I conclude, the confinement to purely human meaning is not correct. But if this is not the answer, what is? If we do not collapse the two interpretations into one, do they simply exist side by side, with no necessary relation to one another? This would result in reproducing the problems of the old allegorical approach.

6. Personal Communion of Authors

The Bible itself shows the way to a more satisfactory resolution of the difficulty. In the Bible itself, the two authors, human and divine, do not simply stand side by side. Rather, each points to the other and affirms the presence and operation of the other.

First, God himself points out the importance of the human authors. For example, when God establishes Moses as the regular channel for conveying his word to the people of Israel, he makes it clear that Moses, not merely God, is to be active in teaching the people (Deut. 5:31; 6:1). Similarly, the commissioning of prophets in the OT often includes a mention of their own active role, not only in speaking God's word to the people, but in actively absorbing it (Ezek. 2:8–3:3; Dan. 10:1–21; Jer. 23:18). This is still more clear in the case of Paul's writings, where his own personality is so actively involved. Now, what happens when we pay careful attention to God as the divine author? We find that we must pay attention to what he says about the role of the human authors. Sometimes he directly affirms the significance of their involvement; sometimes this is only implied. But whichever is the case, it means that God himself requires us to interpret the words of Scripture against the background of what we know about the human author. We cannot simply ignore the human author, when we concentrate on what *God* is saying.

Conversely, the human authors of the Bible indicate that they intend us to interpret their words as not merely words that they speak as ordinary persons. For example, here and there Isaiah says, "Thus says the Lord." What is the effect of such phrases? Would the inhabitants of Jerusalem in Isaiah's time say, "Now we must interpret what our friend Isaiah is saying simply in terms of everything we know about him: his relations with his family, his opinions about agriculture and politics, and so on." Certainly not! When Isaiah says, "Thus says the Lord," it is no doubt still Isaiah who is speaking. But Isaiah himself, by using these words, has told people to create a certain distance between himself, merely viewed as a private individual, and what the Lord has commissioned him to convey. In addition to this, consider what happens when Isaiah makes detailed predictions about the distant future. If the hearers treat him simply as a private human being, they would say, "Well, we know Isaiah, and we know the limits of his knowledge of the future. So, because of what we know about him, it is obvious that he is simply expressing his dreams or making artistically interesting guesses." Again, such a reaction misunderstands Isaiah's claims.

We may try to focus as much as possible on Isaiah as a human author. The more carefully we do our job, the more we will realize that he is not just any human author. He is one through whom God speaks. His own intentions are that we should reckon with this. It is not a denial of human authorship, but an affirmation of it, when we pay attention to God speaking. In particular, in the case of predictions, we pay attention to all that we know of God, God's knowledge of the future, the wisdom of his plan, and the righteousness of his intentions. This is in accord with Isaiah's intention, not contrary to it. In fact, we might say that Isaiah's intention was that we should understand whatever God intended by his words.[13] Hence there *is* a unity of meaning and a unity of application here. We do not have two diverse meanings, Isaiah's and God's, simply placed side by side with no relation to one another.

But the matter is complex. What we have here is a situation of personal communion between God and prophet. Each person affirms the significance of the other's presence for proper interpretation. On the one hand, God has formed the personality of the prophet, has spoken to him in the heavenly counsel (Jer. 23:18), has brought him into inner sympathy with the thrust of his message. What the prophet says using his own particular idiom fits exactly what God decided to say. On the other hand, the prophet affirms that what God is saying is true even where the prophet cannot see all its implications.

This situation therefore leaves open the question of how far a prophet understood God's words at any particular point. The Bible affirms the prophets' inner participation in the message. In addition extraordinary psychological experiences were sometimes involved. Because of this, it would be presumptuous to limit dogmatically a prophet's understanding to what is "ordinarily" possible. On the other hand, it seems to me equally presumptuous to insist that at every point there must be complete understanding on the part of the prophet. Particularly this is so for cases of visionary material (Dan. 7; 10; Zech. 1–6; Rev. 4:1–22:5) or historical records of divine speech (e.g., the Gospel records of Jesus' parables). Why should we have to say, in the face of Dan. 7:16; Zech. 4:4–5; Rev. 7:14, and the like, that the prophets came to understand everything that there was to understand, by the time that they wrote their visions down? Isn't it enough to stick with what is clear? It is clear that the prophet faithfully recorded what he saw and heard. He intended that we should understand from it whatever there is to understand when we treat it as a vision from God. Similarly, there is no need to insist that Luke understood all the ramifications of each of Jesus' parables. He may have, but then again he may not have. The results for our interpretation of the parables in the Gospel of Luke will be the same.

I have spoken primarily about the role of prophets in speaking the word of God. But, of course, prophecy is not the only form in which the Bible is written. The different genres of biblical writings, prophecy, law, history, wisdom, song, each call for different nuances in our approach. The relation between divine and human participation in the writing is not always exactly the same.[14]

13. See, e.g., Ben F. Meyer, *The Aims of Jesus* (London: SCM, 1979), 246: "In prophecy what the symbol intends is identical with what God, for whom the prophet speaks, intends. This may enter the prophet's own horizon only partially and imperfectly."

14. Abraham Kuyper notices some of these differences and argues for a division into the categories of lyric, chokmatic, prophetic, and apostolic inspiration (*Principles of Sacred Theology* [Grand Rapids: Eerdmans, 1968], 520–44, the section on "The Forms of Inspiration").

For instance, consider the case of Mosaic law. The background of the meeting at Mount Sinai forms a framework for Moses's later writings, and leads us to reckon more directly with the divine source of the law. On the other hand, Moses's close communion with God (Num. 12:6–8) hints at his inner understanding of the law.

In the case of prophecy, narrowly speaking, the prophet's pronouncement, "Thus says the Lord," and the predictive elements in his message frequently have the effect of highlighting the distinction between the prophet as mere human being and the prophet as channel for the Lord's message. The prophet himself steps into the background, as it were, in order to put all the emphasis on God's speaking. In visionary experiences this may be all the more the case, inasmuch as it is often not clear how much the prophet understands.

With the psalms and the NT epistles, on the other hand, the human author and his understanding come much more to the front. The Apostle Paul does not continually say, "Thus says the Lord." That is not because he has no divine message. Rather, it is (largely) because he has so thoroughly absorbed the message into his own person. He has "the mind of Christ" (1 Cor. 2:13, 16), as a man indwelt by the Spirit.[15]

Here we confront still another complexity. What is human nature, and what does it mean to analyze a passage as the expression of a human author? If the human author is Paul, that means Paul filled with the Holy Spirit. We are not dealing with "bare" human nature (as if human beings ever existed outside of a relationship to God of one kind or another). We are already dealing with the divine, namely the Holy Spirit. Paul as a human being may not be immediately, analytically self-conscious of all the implications of what he is saying. But people always know more and imply more than what they are perfectly self-conscious of. How far does this "more" extend? We are dealing with a person restored in the image of Christ, filled with the Holy Spirit, having the mind of Christ. There are incalculable depths here. We cannot calculate the limits of the Holy Spirit and the wisdom of Christ. Neither can we perform a perfect analytical separation of our knowledge from our union with Christ through the Holy Spirit.

7. Christological Fulness in Interpretation

The complexities that we meet here are only a shadow of the greatest complexity of all: the speeches of the incarnate Christ. Here God is speaking, not through a mere human being distinct from God, but in his own person. The eternal Word of God, the Second Person of the Trinity, speaks. Hence we must interpret what he says in the light of all that we know of God the author. At the same time a man speaks, Jesus of Nazareth. With respect to his human nature, he has limited knowledge (Luke 2:52). Hence we must interpret what he says in the light of all that we know of Jesus of Nazareth in his humanity.

This is a permanent mystery! Yet we know that we do not have two antithetical interpretations, one for the human nature speaking and one for the divine nature speaking. We know that there is a unity, based on the unity of the one person of Christ. However, it is possible, with respect to his *human nature*, that Jesus Christ is not exhaustively self-conscious of all the ramifications, nuances, and implications of what he says. He nevertheless does

---

15. See Peter R. Jones, "The Apostle Paul: A Second Moses according to II Corinthians 2:14–4:7" (Ph.D. diss., Princeton Theological Seminary, 1973); idem, "The Apostle Paul: Second Moses to the New Covenant Community: A Study in Pauline Apostolic Authority," in *God's Inerrant Word,* ed. John Warwick Montgomery (Minneapolis: Bethany Fellowship, 1974), 219–44.

take responsibility for those ramifications, as does any other human speaker. As the *divine* Son, Jesus Christ does know all things, including all ramifications, applications, etc., of his speech. There is a distinction here, but nevertheless no disharmony.

In addition to this, we may say that Jesus in his human nature was especially endowed with the Spirit to perform his prophetic work, as planned by God the Father (Luke 3:22; 4:18–19). When we interpret his speech, we should take into account that the Holy Spirit speaks through him. Thus, we are saying that we must take into account the ultimately Trinitarian character of revelation, as well as the unique fulness of the Spirit's endowment in Christ's Messianic calling.

In short, when we interpret Christ's speech, we interpret it (as we do all speech) in the light of the author. That is, we interpret it as the speech of the divine Son. But Christ says that the Father speaks through him (John 14:10; 12:48–50). Hence it is the speech of the Father. Since the Holy Spirit comes upon Jesus to equip him for his Messianic work, we also conclude that it is the speech of the Spirit. And of course it is the speech of the man Jesus of Nazareth. Each of these aspects of interpretation is distinct, at least in nuance!

What we meet in Christ is verbal communication undergirded by a communion and fellowship of understanding. In Christ's being there is no pure mathematical identity of divine persons or identity of two natures, but harmony. The result is that there is no pure mathematical identity in the interpretive product. That is, we cannot in a pure way analyze simply what the words mean as (for instance) proceeding from the human nature of Christ, and then say that precisely that, no more, no less, is the exhaustive interpretation of his words.

The case of divine speech through apostles and prophets is, of course, secondary, but none the less analogous. The revelation of Jesus Christ is the pinnacle (Heb. 1:1–3). All other revelations through prophets and apostles are secondary to this supreme revelation. There is ultimately no other way to gain deeper insight into the secondary than through the pinnacle. Hence we cannot expect to collapse the richness of divine presence into a mathematical point, when we are dealing with the words of the Bible.

8. Progressive Understanding

A further complexity arises because the many human authors of the Bible write over a long period of time. None of the human authors except the very last can survey the entire product in order to arrive at an interpretation of the whole.

Once again, we may throw light on the situation by starting with a simpler case. Suppose that we have a single uninspired human author speaking or writing to a single audience over a period of time. Even if we are dealing with only a single long oral discourse, the discourse is spread out in time. Individual statements and individual paragraphs near the beginning of the discourse are understood first, then those near the end. Moreover, an audience is in a better position to draw more inferences from earlier parts of a discourse once they have reached the end. Typically, all the parts of a discourse qualify and color each other. We understand more by reading the whole than we do from reading any one part, or even from all the parts separately. The effect is somewhat like the effect of different parts of an artist's picture. If we just attend to small bits of paint within the picture, one by one, we may miss many implications of the whole. The "meaning" of the picture does not reside merely in a mechanical, mathematical sum of the blobs of paint. Rather, it arises from the joint effect of the individual pieces. Their joint effect arises from the relations between the pieces. Likewise, the import of author's discourse arises partly from the reinforcements, qualifications, tensions, complementations, and other relations between the individual words and sentences, as well as from the effects of each sentence "in itself."

The over-all effect of this is that an audience may understand what the first part of a discourse means, and then have that understanding modified and deepened by the last of the discourse.

Now consider a particular example of two people in communication over a long period of time. Suppose a father teaches his young son to sing "Jesus Loves Me." Later on, he tells the story of the life of Christ from a children's Bible story book. Still later, he explains how the OT sacrificial system depicted aspects of Christ's purpose in dying for us. Finally, the son becomes an adult and does extended Bible study for himself. Suppose then that the son remembers how his father taught him "Jesus Loves Me." He asks, "What was my father saying in telling me the words of the song?" At the time, did I understand what he was saying? The answer may well be yes. The son understood what the father expected that he would have capacity to understand at that point. But the father knew as well that the child's initial understanding was not the end point. The father intended that the earlier words should be recalled later. He intended that the son should understand his father's mind better and better by comparing those earlier words with later words that the father would share.

Now, suppose that there was no misunderstanding, no misjudgement at any point. There is still more than one level of understanding of the father's words. There is what one may understand on the basis of those words more or less by themselves, when not supplemented by further words, and when seen as words adapted to the capacity of the young child. And there is what one may understand on the basis of comparing and relating those words to many later words (and actions) of the father. The first of these understandings is a legitimate one, an understanding not to be underestimated. As long as the child has only those words of the father, and not all the later history, it would be unfair of him to build up an exact, elaborate analysis of all the ramified implications of the statements. But once the father has said a lot more, it throws more light on what the father intended all along that those words should do: they should contribute along with many other words to form and engender an enormously rich understanding of Christ's love, an understanding capable of being evoked and alluded to by the words of the song.

The complexity arises, as before, from the dynamic and relational character of communicative meaning. The understanding we achieve from listening arises not only from individual words or sentences in the discourse but from the complex relations that they have to one another and to the larger situation, including what we know of the author himself. In particular, the song, "Jesus Loves Me," conveys meaning not simply in virtue of the internal arrangement of the words, but also in virtue of the context of who is saying it, what else is being said by way of explanation, and so on. True, there is something like a "common core" of meaning shared by all or nearly all uses of the song. But the implications that we may see around that common core may differ. (Imagine the song being used by a liberal who believes that in fact Jesus is merely human, and therefore still dead. In his mouth, the song is only a metaphorical expression of an ideal of human love.)

9. Progressive Revelation

Now we are ready to raise the crucial question: does something analogous to this happen with God's communication to his people over the period of time from Adam onwards? Is God like a human father speaking to his child?

The basic answer is obviously yes. But, for those who do not think it is so obvious, we can supply reasons.

(1) Israel is called God's son (Ex. 4:22; Deut. 8:5), and Paul explicitly likens the OT period to the time of a child's minority (Gal. 4:3–4). These passages are not directly discussing the question of biblical interpretation, but they are nevertheless suggestive.

(2) From very early in the history of the human race God indicates in his speeches to us that more is to come. History and the promises of God are forward-looking. The story is yet to be completed. It is altogether natural to construe this as implying that earlier promissory statements of God may be more deeply understood once the promises begin to be fulfilled, and especially when they are completely fulfilled. Similar reflections evidently apply even to the hope we now have as Christians (1 Cor. 13:12).

(3) In at least a few cases, within the pages of the OT, we find prophecies whose fulfillments take unexpected form. One of the most striking is Jacob's prophecy about the dispersion of Simeon and Levi (Gen. 49:7b).[16] If we attend *only* to the immediate context (49:7a), we are bound to conclude that God undertakes to disgrace both tribes by giving them no connected spot of settlement. The actual fulfillment is therefore quite surprising in the case of Levi. But it is not out of accord with God's character of turning cursings into blessings. What we know about him includes his right to exceed our expectations. This whole affair is more easily understood when we take into account the fact that Gen. 49:7 is not an isolated word of God, but part of a long history of God's communications, yet to be completed. We are not supposed to make dogmatically precise judgements without hearing the whole.

In short, God's actual ways of bringing fulfillments may vary. Some of them may be straightforward, others may be surprising. This is true just as it is true that an author may continue a discourse in a straightforward way, or in a surprising way that causes us to reassess the exact point of the first part of what he says.

(4) The symbolic aspects of OT institutions proclaim their own inadequacy (Heb. 10:1, 4). They are not only *analogous* to the final revelation of God, but at some points *disanalogous* (Heb. 10:4). Suppose that people stand in the OT situation, trying to understand what is symbolized. They will inevitably continue with *some* questions unanswered until they are able to *relate* what is said and done earlier to what God does at the coming of Christ. Until the point of completion, the interpretation must remain open-ended (but not contentless).

(5) Likewise, the speech of God is not complete until the coming of Christ (Heb. 1:1–3). We must, as it were, hear the end of the discourse before we are in a position to weigh the total context in terms of which we may achieve the most profound understanding of each part of the discourse.

I conclude, then, that any particular passage of the Bible is to be read in three progressively larger contexts, as follows.

16. Oswald T. Allis, *Prophecy and the Church* (Philadelphia: Presbyterian and Reformed, 1945), 30.

(a) Any passage is to be read in the context of the particular book of the Bible in which it appears, and in the context of the human author and historical circumstances of the book. God speaks truly to the people in particular times and circumstances.

(b) Any passage is to be read in the context of the total canon of Scripture available up to that point in time.[17] The people originally addressed by God must take into account that God's speech does not start with them, but presupposes and builds on previous utterances of God.

(c) Any passage is to be read in the context of the entire Bible (the completed canon). God intended from the beginning that his later words should build on and enrich earlier words, so that in some sense the whole of the Bible represents one long, complex process of communication from one author.

For example, Ezekiel 34 is to be understood (a) in terms of the immediate context of the book of Ezekiel and the historical circumstances in which the book first appeared; (b) in terms of its continuation of the word of God recorded in the law of Moses and the preexilic prophets; (c) in terms of what we can understand in the light of the whole completed Bible, including the NT.[18]

In addition to these three analyses of the passage we may, in more fine-grained reflection, distinguish still other possibilities. In principle, we may ask what the passage contributes at any point during the progressive additions to canon through further revelation. For example, Bruce K. Waltke argues that in the case of the Psalms (and presumably many other OT books), it is illuminating to ask about their meaning at the time when the OT canon was complete but before the dawn of the NT era.[19] For simplicity we confine the subsequent discussion to the approaches (a), (b), and (c).

As we have said again and again, what we understand from a passage depends not only on the sequence of words of the passage, but the context in which it occurs. Hence the three readings (a), (b), and (c) can, in principle, lead to three different results. Some people might want to speak of three meanings. Meaning (a) would be the meaning obtained from focusing most on the human author and his circumstances. Meaning (c) would be the meaning obtained from focusing most on the divine author and all that we know about him from the whole of the Bible.

However, for most purposes I myself would prefer to avoid calling these three results three "meanings." To do that suggests that three unrelated and perhaps even contradictory things are being said. But these three approaches are complementary, not contradictory. The difference between these three approaches is quite like the difference between reading one chapter of a book and reading the whole of the book. After taking

17. This point is rightly emphasized by Kaiser, *Exegetical Theology*, 79–83.

18. My approach is virtually identical with that of Bruce K. Waltke, "A Canonical Process Approach to the Psalms," in *Tradition and Testament: Essays in Honor of Charles Lee Feinberg*, ed. John S. Feinberg and Paul D. Feinberg (Chicago: Moody, 1981), 3–18. My arguments rest more on the general features of communication, whereas Waltke's arguments rely more on the concrete texture of OT revelation. Hence the two articles should be seen as complementary. See also William Sanford LaSor, "The *Sensus Plenior* and Biblical Interpretation," in *Scripture, Tradition, and Interpretation*, ed. W. Ward Gasque and William Sanford LaSor (Grand Rapids: Eerdmans, 1978), 260–77; Douglas Moo, "The Problem of *Sensus Plenior*," in *Hermeneutics, Authority, and Canon*, ed. D. A. Carson and John D. Woodbridge (Grand Rapids: Zondervan, 1986).

19. Waltke, "A Canonical Process Approach," 9.

into account the whole book, we understand the one chapter as well as the whole book more deeply. But it does not mean that our understanding of the one chapter by itself was incorrect. Remember again the example of "Jesus Loves Me."

10. Psalm 22:12–18 as an Example

To see how this works, let us consider Psalm 22:12–18. Let us begin with approach (a), focusing on the human author. The passage speaks of the distress of a person who trusts in God (Ps. 22:2–5, 8–10), but is nevertheless abandoned to his enemies. In a series of shifting metaphors the psalmist compares his suffering to being surrounded by bulls (Ps. 22:12–13), to being sick or weak in body through emotional distress (Ps. 22:14–15), to being caught by ravening dogs (22:16), to being treated virtually like a carcass (Ps. 22:17–18).[20] The psalmist's words evidently spring from his own experience of a situation of abandonment.

We encounter a special complexity in the case of psalms. The actual author (David, according to the title of Psalm 22)[21] and the collector or collectors who under inspiration included Psalm 22 in the larger collection both have a role. The psalm receives a new setting when it is included in the Book of Psalms. This provides a new context for interpretation. In my opinion, it means that the collector invites us to see Psalm 22 not simply as the experience of an individual at one time, but a typical or model experience with which the whole congregation of Israel is to identify as they sing and meditate on the psalm.[22] Hence, in the context of the Book of Psalms (the context with divine authority), we compare this psalm of lament and praise (Ps. 22:25–31) with other psalms. We understand that there is a general pattern of suffering, trust, vindication, and praise that is to characterize the people of Israel.

Now we move to approach (b). We consider Psalm 22 in the light of the entire canon of Scripture given up until the time when the Book of Psalms was compiled. But there is some problem with this. The Book of Psalms may have been compiled in stages (e.g., many scholars think that Book 1, Pss. 1–41, may have been gathered into a single collection before some of the other psalms had been written). Whatever the details, we do not know exactly when the compilation of the book took place. Hence we do not know exactly what other canonical books had already been written.

We may still proceed in a general way. We read Psalm 22 in the light of the promise to David (2 Sam. 7:8–16) and its relation to the earlier promises through Abraham and Moses. Then we understand that the people of Israel are represented preeminently by a king in the line of David. The deficiencies and failures of David's immediate descendents also point to the need for a perfect, righteous king who will truly establish David's line forever. OT prophecies make it progressively clear that the hopes centered in David's line will ultimately be fulfilled in a single great descendent, the Branch (Isa. 11:1ff.; Zech. 6:12; Isa. 9:6–7). The experiences of suffering, trust, and vindication expressed in Psalm 22 and other psalms

---

20. See Charles A. Briggs and Emilie G. Briggs, *A Critical and Exegetical Commentary on the Book of Psalms*, International Critical Commentary (Edinburgh: T. & T. Clark, 1906), 1:196–97; A. A. Anderson, *The Book of Psalms*, New Century Bible, 2 vols (London: Oliphants, 1972), 1:190–91; Derek Kidner, *Psalms 1–72* (London: InterVarsity, 1973), 107–8; Joseph A. Alexander, *The Psalms* (1864; repr., Grand Rapids: Zondervan, 1955), 101–3. Commentators have some disagreements over the details of the picture, particularly over the interpretation of verse 16, "they have pierced my hands and feet." But it is clear that in the original context the speech is dominated by metaphorical comparisons between the psalmist's enemies and fierce animals.

21. We need not at this point discuss whether the superscriptions are inspired.

22. See, e.g., Anderson, *Psalms,* 1:30.

we expect to be fulfilled in a climactic way in a messianic figure, the Branch who is kingly Davidic representative of all Israel.[23]

What the messianic mediator will be like becomes progressively revealed in the course of the OT. Yet it is never made very clear just how the experience of the Messiah ties in with Psalm 22 in detail. We know that Psalm 22 is related to the prophetic passages, but just how is not so clear.

Finally, let us proceed to approach (c). Let us consider Psalm 22 in the light of the completed canon. In this light, we know that Christ has come to fulfill all righteousness (Matt. 3:15), to fulfill all God's promises (2 Cor. 1:20; Rom. 15:8; Luke 24:45–48). We know too that Christ used the opening words of Psalm 22 when he was on the cross (Matt. 27:46). This already suggests that he is in a brief way indicating the relevance of the *whole* psalm to himself. If we remain in doubt, other NT passages assure us that that is indeed the case (Matt. 27:35; John 19:24; Heb. 2:12).

We proceed, then, to read through Psalm 22 afresh. We compare it with the accounts of the crucifixion in the NT, and with NT theology explaining the significance of Christ's death. We see that in Psalm 22:12–18 Christ describes his own distress, and in Psalm 22:25–31 he expresses the "fruit of the travail of his soul" (Isa. 53:11), the benefits that will follow. In particular, certain details in the psalm which appeared to be *simply* metaphorical in the original OT context strike home with particular vividness (Ps. 22:16, 18).[24]

11. What Is "in" a Verse

Now let us ask, "What is the *correct* understanding of what God is saying in verses like Psalm 22:1, 16, 18?" Is it the understanding that we gain from approach (a), or the understanding that we gain from approach (c)? The answer, I think, is both. If we simply confine ourselves to approach (a), or even to approach (b), we neglect what can be learned by reading the whole of the Bible as the word of the single divine author. On the other hand, if we simply confine ourselves to approach (c), we neglect the fact that God's revelation was progressive. We need to remember that God was interested in edifying people in OT times. Moreover, what he made clear and what he did not make so clear are both of interest to us, because they show us the ways in which our own understanding agrees with and sometimes exceeds previous understanding, due to the progress in revelation and the progress in the execution of God's redemptive program.

Moreover, certain dangers arise if we simply confine ourselves to approach (a) or to approach (c). If we neglect approach (a), we miss the advantage of having the control of a rigorous attention to the historical particulars associated with each text of the Bible. Then we run the danger that our systematic understanding of the Bible as a whole, or our subjective hunches, will simply dictate what any particular text means.

On the other hand, if we neglect approach (c), we miss the advantage of having the rest of the Bible to control the inferences that we may draw in the direction of applications.

23. See Waltke, "A Canonical Process Approach," 10–14.

24. See Kidner, *Psalms 1–71,* 107: "While verses 14–15, taken alone, could describe merely a desperate illness, the context is of collective animosity and the symptoms could be those of Christ's scourging and crucifixion; in fact verses 16–18 had to wait for that event to unfold their meaning with any clarity." Many commentators in the classical historical-critical tradition, by contrast, refuse in principle to let the NT cast further light on the implications of the verses, because they do not allow the principle of unified divine authorship to exercise an influence on interpretation.

Perhaps we may refuse to apply the text at all, saying to ourselves, "It was just written for those people back there." Or we may apply it woodenly, not reckoning with the way in which it is qualified by the larger purposes of God. We miss the Christocentric character of the Bible, proclaimed in Luke 24:45–48. We refuse to see the particulars in the light of the whole, and so we may repeat an error of the Pharisees, who meticulously attended to detail, but neglected "justice and the love of God" (Luke 11:42).

But how can these approaches be combined? They combine in a way analogous to the way in which a human son combined earlier and later understandings of "Jesus Loves Me." There is a complex interplay.

But I think that we can be more precise. In scholarly research, we may begin with approach (a) as a control. For Psalm 22, we focus narrowly on the original historical context, and what is known within that context. We do grammatical-historical exegesis as the foundation for all later systematizing reflection. We try to avoid simply "reading in" our total knowledge of Scripture, or else we lose the opportunity for the Bible to criticize our views. As a second, later step, we relate Psalm 22 to earlier canonical books and finally to the NT. Whatever we find at this stage must harmonize with the results of approach (a). But we come to "extra" insights and deeper understanding as we relate Psalm 22 to the NT. These extra things are not "in" Psalm 22 in itself. They are not somehow mystically hidden in the psalm, so that someone with some esoteric key to interpretation could have come up with them just by reading the psalm in isolation from the rest of the Bible. Psalm 22 in itself gives us only what we get from approach (a). The extra things arise from the *relations* that Psalm 22 has with earlier canonical books (approach [b]), with the NT, and with the events of Christ's death. These relations, established by God, provide the basis for our proceeding another stage forward in understanding.

Hence, we are not talking about some purely subjective process of letting one's imagination run wild. Nor are we talking about a traditional Roman Catholic view of authority, where church tradition provides extra input with divine authority to enrich biblical understanding.[25] Rather, the "extra" understanding comes from the biblical canon itself, taken as a whole.

But now suppose we consider the case of nonscholars, of ordinary people. Suppose that we are not scholars ourselves, but that we have been Christians for many years. Suppose that through the aid of the Holy Spirit we have been growing spiritually and studying the Bible diligently for the whole time. From our pastors and from other scholarly sources we have gained some knowledge of OT and NT times, but not elaborate knowledge. But we have gained a thorough knowledge of the Bible as a whole. Much of this knowledge might be called unconscious or subconscious knowledge. Especially when it is a matter of large

---

25. My views have certain affinities with the idea of *sensus plenior*. See Raymond E. Brown, "The *Sensus Plenior* of Sacred Scripture" (Ph.D. diss., St. Mary's University, Baltimore, MD, 1955). But Roman Catholic discussions of *sensus plenior* sometimes appear to be interested in including church tradition, not simply the biblical canon, in their reckoning. For instance, Brown mentions that *sensus plenior* may be needed to account for the dogmas of the immaculate conception and the assumption of Mary (ibid., 74; see also Raymond E. Brown, "The *Sensus Plenior* in the Last Ten Years," *Catholic Biblical Quarterly* 25 [1963]: 272). And his full definition of *sensus plenior* seems to leave an opening for the entrance of later church tradition. He speaks of studying biblical texts "in the light of further revelation [later canonical books] or development in the understanding of revelation" (Brown, "The *Sensus Plenior* of Sacred Scripture," 92). The last phrase, "development in the understanding of revelation," might mean only that we should pay attention to the achievements and opinions of previous generations. But that is true of any scholarly investigation of any subject. Hence the phrase seems superfluous unless it implies a greater role for tradition than what Protestants would grant.

themes of the Bible, we might not be able to say clearly what we knew, and exactly what texts of the Bible had given us our knowledge.

When we read Psalm 22, we read it against the background of all that unconscious knowledge of biblical truths. When we see the opening words of Psalm 22:1, we naturally assume that the psalm speaks of Christ's suffering. We read the rest of the psalm as a psalm about Christ. In each verse we see Christ's love, his suffering, his rejection by his enemies.

The results we gain may be very similar to the results gained by the scholar who goes through all the distinct "steps." But the scholar knows that his understanding arises from the relations of Psalm 22 to the rest of the Bible. He self-consciously distinguishes what arises from the psalm viewed more or less in itself, and what arises from other passages of the Bible as they illumine the significance of the psalm. Laypeople may have the same "results," but without being able to say exactly what all the stages were by which they could logically come to those results.

The psychological perception of what is "in" the text of Psalm 22 may also be different. Lay readers are not *consciously* aware of the immense and important role played by our general knowledge of the rest of the Bible. Hence it seems that all the depth of insight that laypeople receive as they read Psalm 22 comes from Psalm 22. It is all "in" the psalm. By contrast, the scholar knows where things come from, and prefers to speak of the depth of insight as arising from the relations between many, many individual texts of the whole Bible, as these are brought into relation to Psalm 22 in a systematizing process.

But now consider once more the central question: what is *God* saying in Psalm 22? Well, he is saying what he said to the original OT readers of the psalm. He speaks the truth to them. Hence, scholars are correct in taking care to distinguish what comes from the psalm itself and what comes from the psalm seen in the light of the whole Bible.

But God also intends that we should read Psalm 22 in the light of the rest of what he says. Scholars are correct in going on to a second stage in which they relate the psalm to the whole Bible. And laypeople are correct when they do the same thing. Of course, we must suppose that the laypeople are sober, godly readers, well versed in the Scripture. Then, as they read Psalm 22, all the depth that they receive is a depth that God intends them to receive. God is saying all that richness to them as they read. But that means that their psychological perception is correct. All that richness is "in" the psalm as a speech that God is speaking to them now.

Hence, I believe that we are confronted with an extremely complex and rich process of communication from God. The scholarly psychological process of making the distinctions is important as a check and refinement of laypeople's understanding. But that lay understanding, at its best, is not to be despised. We are not to be elitists who insist that everyone become a self-conscious scholar in reading the Bible. Laypeople have a correct perception, even psychologically, of what God intends a passage like Psalm 22 to say. God does say more, now, through that passage, than he said to the OT readers. The "more" arises from the stage of fuller revelation, and consequent fuller illumination of the Holy Spirit, in which we live.

All this is true without any need to postulate an extra, "mystical" sense. That is, we do not postulate an extra meaning which requires some esoteric hermeneutical method to uncover. Rather, our understanding is analogous to the way that a son's understanding of "Jesus Loves Me" arises and grows. At the end of a long period of reading and digesting a rich communication, we see each particular part of the communication through eyes of knowledge that have been enlightened by the whole. Through that enlightenment, each part of the whole is rich.

What relation does all this have to the discussions of *sensus plenior*?[26] Raymond E. Brown's dissertation defines *sensus plenior* as follows:

> The *sensus plenior* is that additional, deeper meaning, intended by God but not clearly intended by the human author, which is seen to exist in the words of a biblical text (or group of texts, or even a whole book) when they are studied in the light of further revelation or development in the understanding of revelation.[27]

My distinction between the intention of the human author and divine intention, as well as my discussion of the role of later revelation, shows affinities with this definition. But I am also concerned to distinguish, from a scholarly point of view, between what is "in" the passage and what arises from comparison of the passage with later revelation. This shows affinities with the rejection of *sensus plenior* by John P. Weisengoff.[28] Weisengoff rejects *sensus plenior* precisely in order to protect the idea that the added knowledge comes from the new revelation.[29] In fact, the situation is complex enough to include the major concerns of both points of view.[30]

12. New Testament Interpretation of the Old Testament

Our reflections up to this point also throw light on some of the problems arising from NT interpretation of the OT.[31] I would claim that the NT authors characteristically do *not* aim merely at grammatical-historical exegesis of the OT. If we expect this of them, we expect something too narrow and with too exclusively a scholarly interest. The NT authors are not scholars but church leaders. They are interested in showing how OT passages apply to the church and to the NT situation. Hence, when they discuss an OT text, they consider it in the light of the rest of the OT, in the light of the events of salvation that God has accomplished in Christ, and in the light of the teaching of the Jesus himself during his earthly life. They bring all this knowledge to bear on their situation, in the light of all that they know about that situation. In this process they are not concerned, as scholars would be, to distinguish with nicety all the various sources that contribute to their understanding. Both they and their readers typically presuppose the context of later revelation. Hence, what they say using an OT passage may not always be based on the OT text *alone*, but on relations that the text has with this greater context. There is nothing wrong or odd about this process, any more than there is anything wrong with laypeople who read Psalm 22 in the light of their knowledge of the whole of Scripture.

26. Brown, "The *Sensus Plenior* of Sacred Scripture"; idem, "The History and Development of the Theory of a *Sensus Plenior*," *Catholic Biblical Quarterly* 15 (1953): 141–62; idem, "The *Sensus Plenior* in the Last Ten Years," 262–85; James M. Robinson, "Scripture and Theological Method: A Protestant Study in *Sensus Plenior*," *Catholic Biblical Quarterly* 27 (1965): 6–27; LaSor, "The *Sensus Plenior* and Biblical Interpretation."

27. Brown, "The *Sensus Plenior* of Sacred Scripture," 92.

28. Weisengoff, Review of *Problèmes et méthode d'exégèse théologique* by Cerfaux, Coppens, Gribomont, in *Catholic Biblical Quarterly* 14 (1952): 83–85.

29. Ibid. See the reply in Brown, "The *Sensus Plenior* of Sacred Scripture," 123–26.

30. This synthesis may be anticipated in Waltke, "A Canonical Process Approach," 8–9.

31. Cf. similar concerns in the discussion of *sensus plenior* in Brown, "The *Sensus Plenior* of Sacred Scripture," 68–71; Moo, "The Problem of *Sensus Plenior*."

13. Scholarly Use of Grammatical-Historical Exegesis

In conclusion, let us ask what implications we may draw concerning scholarly grammatical-historical exegesis. By grammatical-historical exegesis I mean an approach like approach (a), which self-consciously focuses on each biblical book as a product of a human author, in a particular historical setting. On the positive side, we have seen that grammatical-historical exegesis has an important illumining role. Several points can be mentioned.

(1) In writing the Bible God spoke to people in human language, in human situations, through human authors. God himself in the Bible indicates that we should pay attention to these human factors in order to understand what he is saying and doing.

(2) On a practical level, grammatical-historical exegesis serves to warn the church against being swallowed up by traditionalism, in which people merely read in the system of understanding which afterwards is read out. It alerts us to nuances in meaning that we otherwise overlook or even misread.

(3) It serves to sensitize us to the genuinely progressive character of revelation. God did not say everything all at once. We understand him better the more we appreciate the wisdom involved in the partial and preliminary character of what came earlier (Heb. 1:1).

On the other hand, grammatical-historical exegesis is not all that there is to responsible biblical interpretation. Again, we can summarize the results in several points.

(1) If grammatical-historical exegesis pretends to pay attention to the human author *alone*, it distorts the nature of the human author's intention. Whether or not they were perfectly self-conscious about it, the human authors intend that their words should be received as words of the Spirit.

(2) God's meets us and speaks to us in power as we read the Bible. God's power and presence must be taken into account from the beginning, just as we take into account all that characterizes a human author of any human text. We cannot, with perfect precision, analytically isolate God's propositional content from his personal communion. To attempt to perform grammatical-historical exegesis by such an isolating procedure is impious.

(3) It is legitimate to explore the relations between what God says in all the parts of the Bible. When we perform such a synthesis, what we conclude may go beyond what we could derive from any one text in isolation. Yet it should not be in tension with the results of a narrow grammatical-historical exegesis. (Of course, sometimes because of the limitations of our knowledge we may find no way to resolve all tensions.)

(4) We are not to despise laypeople's understanding of the Bible. We are not to reject it just because on the surface it appears to "read in" too much. Of course, laypeople may sometimes have overworked imaginations. But sometimes their conclusions may be the result of a synthesis of Bible knowledge due to the work of the Holy Spirit. Scholars cannot reject such a possibility without having achieved a profound synthetic and even practical knowledge of the Bible for themselves.

(5) When later human writers of Scripture interpret earlier parts of Scripture, they typically do so without making fine scholarly distinctions concerning the basis of their knowledge. Hence we ought not to require them to confine themselves to a narrow grammatical-historical exegesis. In many respects their interpretations may be similar to valid uses of Scripture by nonscholars today.

(6) God intends that the Bible's words should be applied in people's lives today. In complex personal, social and political situations, we may not always be sure what the correct

applications are. But applications genuinely in accord with God's word are part of God's intention. Hence, in a broad sense, they are part of what God is saying to us through the Bible as a whole. God continues to speak today. When we read the Bible aware that it is God's word, we understand that he is speaking to us now. We are constrained to obey, to rejoice in him, and to worship.

THE PURPOSE OF THE BIBLE FROM HIS
GOD-CENTERED BIBLICAL INTERPRETATION

Vern S. Poythress, "The Purpose of the Bible," in *God-Centered Biblical Interpretation* (Phillipsburg, NJ: P&R Publishing, 1999), 51–61.

What is the purpose of the Bible? Understanding purpose is crucial to interpretation. People may, if they wish, use Milton's *Paradise Lost* to teach English, to practice counting letters, or to study poetic rhythms. But none of these is the main purpose for which Milton composed the poem. People may miss the main point if they use the poem for other purposes.

Indeed, this is part of the problem with the Bible discussion group that Libbie Liberal organized. The participants play with fascinating ideas that they spin off from their reading of the Bible. But they do not adequately reckon with God's purpose in it. Even in the Bible discussion that Chris Christian organized, people disagree. Peter Pietist thinks that the purpose of the Bible is devotion. Dottie Doctrinalist thinks that its purpose is to teach doctrine. Curt Cultural-Transformationist thinks that it is to set transforming human action in motion. Missy Missiologist thinks that the purpose is to bring the message of God to all cultures.

Let us again listen in on the conversation in Chris Christian's Bible discussion group. We join in the middle of a discussion of biblical purpose.

Oliver Objectivist: *The purpose of any passage in the Bible is exactly the purpose that the human author expressed in the passage.*

Fatima Factualist: *Unless there is explicit indication to the contrary, we should assume that the purpose is to tell what happened or what someone believes.*

Herman Hermeneut: *But can't we see a larger purpose in a whole work, such as in the prophecy of Isaiah? Isaiah has a larger purpose in mind than stating each sentence, one at a time. If he does, doesn't God have a larger purpose in giving us the entire canon of Scripture, a purpose perhaps larger than that of any one book of the Bible?*

Amy Affirmationist: *The Holy Spirit could have different purposes for each person who reads the Bible.*

Many Purposes

According to Scripture, the Bible does have many purposes. It is "useful for teaching, rebuking, correcting and training in righteousness, so that the man of God may be thoroughly equipped for every good work" (2 Tim. 3:16–17). Paul tells Timothy to "preach the Word; be prepared in season and out of season; correct, rebuke and encourage—with great patience and careful instruction" (2 Tim. 4:2). There are many different functions for various parts of the Bible, in teaching and instructing, rebuking and encouraging. At the same time, since God is one, there is naturally a unity of purpose to all his word. All his words manifest his glory (cf. John 17:1). In all his words to us, God enjoins us to "be holy, because I am holy" (1 Peter 1:16; Lev. 19:2; 20:7). Or, as James says, "Do not merely listen to the word, and so deceive yourselves. Do what it says" (James 1:22). All of the Bible leads to Christ (Luke 24:44–49).

We may misconstrue the Bible either by paying attention only to one purpose, or by reducing all the purposes to one, or by artificially isolating the purposes, as if we could adequately accomplish one in isolation from the rest. To avoid the extremes of isolation and reduction, we can once again use the model provided by the Trinity. We have already seen a unity in diversity and a diversity in unity in considering the forms of the word of God. The archetype for unity and diversity is found in God himself. Hence, we may conveniently begin with God's Trinitarian character.

Triune Purpose

In John 17, the Son reflects on his work by speaking of the "word" that the Father has spoken and that he has delivered. He also speaks of mutual indwelling (vv. 21–23) and of manifesting glory (vv. 4–5, 24). He speaks of communicating "the love you have for me" (v. 26), of having made and continuing to "make you known" (v. 26), and of the disciples' work in the world in imitation of his work (v. 18). We have many purposes here. But it is rather easy to see that they are all perspectives or ways of talking about one purpose, a comprehensive purpose involving the entire redemptive plan of the Father. The Son can express that one purpose in more than one way, and can describe it from more than one angle.

The angles of expression reflect in certain ways the distinctions and the unities among the persons of the Trinity. The statements about "work" focus preeminently on the work of the Son on earth. The Son has completed "the work you gave me to do" (v. 4). On the basis of this work, the disciples are sent out to work (v. 18).

The Son uses many expressions in speaking about his work. But since they all point to the same work, even one expression would in principle include the whole. For convenience, and to remind ourselves of the diversity as well as the unity in the work, we may sum up the expressions under three headings, corresponding respectively to the prominence of the Father, the Son, and the Spirit.

First, the Son asks that the Father equip, protect, and sanctify the disciples. The work of God involves action, power, and control from the Father. We may view the entire work from the perspective of *control*. (We associate *control* with the Father.)

Second, the work of God involves giving and receiving the truth, primarily through the Son: "I have made you known to them, and will continue to make you known" (v. 26); "I gave them the words you gave me and they accepted them. They knew with certainty that I came from you (v. 8). Truth is manifested in the Son (cf. John 14:6). We may view God's entire work, then, from the perspective of *meaning*, truth, and knowing. (We associate *meaning* with the Son.)

Third, God is personally present with the disciples through the process of indwelling, mediated by the Holy Spirit (vv. 21–23). Thus, we may view God's entire work from the perspective of personal *presence*. (We associate *presence* with the Spirit.)

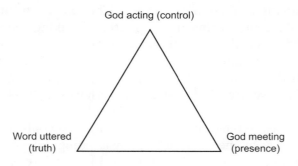

Figure. Triad of purpose

In sum, we have three perspectives: control, meaning, and presence.[32] These are three ways of looking at the work of God in the world. We look at God controlling events; we look at the meaning and the truth that God makes known; we look at God's presence in the world and among his people. Through any one of these, as through a window, we can examine any particular work of God, or all the works comprehensively, just as Jesus did in John 17. Each is then a perspective on the whole.

We may apply this triad of perspectives specifically to God's word. The communication of words is one aspect to which Jesus refers (John 17:8, 14, 17). Since it coheres with the other aspects, we should expect that it manifests them all—and it does. The word of God controls people and events in the world. The word of God expresses and asserts meaningful truth. The word of God makes God himself present with us. God brings himself into contact with those addressed by his word.

Let us confirm these points one at a time. First, the word of God controls the sanctification of the disciples (John 17:17). Similarly, through the name of God (closely related to the word of God), the disciples are "kept" (vv. 11–12). Second, the words that Jesus speaks in John 17 are themselves representative of the "word" about which he speaks; they have infinite meaning. Third, through the words that Jesus speaks, the Father, as well as the Son, is personally present (John 14:9–10). The words "my words remain in you" in John 15:7 are parallel to "I in them" in John 17:23. The author is present in the words that he speaks. As the words remain in the disciples, they bear fruit through union with him.[33] Let us call this triad of terms (*control, meaning*, and *presence*) the triad of purpose, because each term represents one aspect of the way in which God expresses his purposes.

We saw that control, meaning, and presence can, in John 17, be correlated respectively with the Father, the Son, and the Holy Spirit. But the correlation is mysterious. And we must not think that it is the whole story. Because of the coinherence of the persons of the Trinity, they share in acts of control, meaning, and presence. For example, through the presence of the Holy Spirit (John 14:16–17), the Son also will come and be present (v. 18). Both the Father and the Son dwell in the believer (v. 23). Thus, all three persons participate in God's personal presence with believers. Similarly, all three persons exercise control in God's works, and all three express meaning in the word of God. All three persons share in the one purpose of God.

---

32. These three are a slight variation on John Frame's triad of authority, control, and presence (with the order of authority and control reversed). See John Frame, *The Doctrine of the Knowledge of God* (Phillipsburg, NJ: Presbyterian and Reformed, 1987), 15–18, 42–48.

33. For further use of the triad of authority, control, and presence, see ibid.

Remember now the triad of imaging, mentioned earlier, consisting of the originary, manifestational, and concurrent perspectives. How does this earlier triad relate to the present triad of purpose, consisting of control, meaning, and presence? When we compare triads like these, we may expect coinherence without mere mathematical identity. The two triads are not merely two names for exactly the same thing. Rather, the triad of imaging focuses on God's representation of himself, while the triad of purpose focuses on God's carrying out of his purposes. So the two triads speak in two different ways about the unity and diversity in God. Each term in one triad therefore involves features relating to all three terms in the other triad.

For example, God's control involves an originary aspect, consisting in God's attribute of omnipotence. God's control involves a manifestational aspect, consisting of actual acts of control over what he has made. God's control involves a concurrent aspect, in that the acts of control are in harmony with who God is in his omnipotence. Similarly, God's meaning involves originary, manifestational, and concurrent aspects. God's truth as it is eternally known to himself is originary. God's truth as it is made known to us is manifestational. And the harmony between our knowledge and God's originary knowledge is concurrent.

Although all these aspects involve one another, we may also sometimes notice a tantalizing relationship between the two triads. One triad, in some fashion, "mirrors" the second triad. For example, God's meaning exists even before it is manifested, which is closely related to the originary perspective. Thus, in some sense, meaning mirrors the originary perspective. God's control involves his action, which is closely related to his manifestation of himself. Control mirrors manifestation. God is present with us through indwelling, which is the concurrent aspect. Presence mirrors concurrence. (But note that we have reversed the normal order of control and meaning. Such rearrangements of order can occur when we try to compare two triads.)

The triad of control, meaning, and presence exists archetypally in the eternal relations of the persons of the Trinity. It applies ectypally in God's communication to the world and to us. His word to us exhibits control, meaning, and presence. It also applies ectypally when human beings communicate to one another. Each of us exerts control by communicating; we have something that we say (truth, or sometimes error); we say it to someone, drawing ourselves into a personal relationship with someone (presence). Receiving a communication involves responding to this control, hearing what the person says (meaning), and listening to the person as he is present with us in the communication.

How does this triad apply to the Bible? The Bible is the word of God to human beings, and hence it ectypally manifests the same triad. In the Bible we undergo transformation by God's control. We hear truth (the word). We meet God (personal presence). We may thus say that the purposes of the Bible are three: for God to transform people, for him to teach the truth, and for God himself to be present.

But, as we might expect, these three purposes are also one. The triad consisting of control, truth (meaning), and personal presence derives from Trinitarian interrelationships. It is an ectype of the Trinity, which is the archetype. The persons of the Trinity are coinherent, so the three aspects are ectypally coinherent. That is, they mutually involve one another. Meeting God always involves knowing something about him, and thus knowing truth. Knowing truth involves knowing God, who is the truth. Meeting God involves being transformed by his presence. We are overwhelmed and cannot remain the same. Even if we rebel against

God, we do not remain the same, but become more guilty than we were before (cf., e.g., Ex. 7:5, 17; 14:4). If we are transformed, it is only through the power of God working in us (Phil. 2:13; cf. Lam. 3:37–38; Eph. 1:11; Ps. 103:19).[34]

What are the implications for the practical study of the Bible? On the one hand, God has a plurality and richness of purposes for the Bible. We ought not to reduce it all to one monolithic purpose. For example, we ought not to reduce the Bible simply to personal encounter. We are not to be mystics, who try to achieve personal encounter with God without the presence of conceptual truth. Such was the tendency of Pietist in the Bible discussion group. In addition, we do not reduce the Bible to intellectual meaning. We are not to be intellectualists, who try to store up truth without paying attention to meeting God or practical living (doing what it says). Such was the tendency of Doctrinalist. We are not to be pragmatists, who care only for "the bottom line" of visible effects, without attending either to truth or to the God who speaks. Such was the tendency of Cultural-Transformationist.

But in emphasizing the diversity of purposes, we still affirm a unity. Each purpose points to and even encompasses the others. For instance, rightly knowing truth irreducibly involves knowing God, who is the truth (John 14:6). Hence, meaning, properly understood, includes personal presence. Knowing the truth also includes practical effects (2 Cor. 3:18; John 17:3). Hence, meaning includes control. Conversely, response in action, the practical side of obedience, includes cognitive action, that is, knowing truth. Similarly, response is proper only if it is response to the God who comes, response that reaches out in the personal encounter of worship. Thus, the aspect of control encompasses the aspect of personal presence. In a similar way, we can see that each aspect encompasses the other two aspects.[35] The aspects are coinherent.

Now this coinherence has a specific implication. Truth and application are distinguishable, but not isolatable from one another. They are two aspects of a coinherent triad. Truth is the content of Scripture (the meaning aspect), while application is the control of Scripture over our selves, our thoughts, and our behavior (the control aspect). The two coinhere.

God means and intends to communicate certain truths. He also means and intends that the truths be applied. The application is thus an integral aspect of the meaning. Meaning includes application. But, conversely, application includes meaning. Any particular application is an application of something, an application of a truth or truths. It is an application of the meanings of specific words or texts that are being applied. The application illustrates the meaning on which it is based. Moreover, the totality of application includes application in the mental sphere. Applying a verse includes applying it to our beliefs. It includes altering our beliefs so that they agree with what the verse says. That is, it includes attention to the meaning of the verse.

Consider a simple example: "Then in accordance with what is written, they celebrated the Feast of Tabernacles with the required number of burnt offerings prescribed for each day" (Ezra 3:4). "What is written" alludes to Numbers 29:12–38, Leviticus 23:33–43, and other passages in the Law of Moses. An aspect of the meaning of Numbers 29:12–38 is that people should celebrate with certain sacrifices. One implication of that meaning is that the

---

34. One may find many other instances of perspectival relations in Frame, *Doctrine of the Knowledge of God*; Frame, *Perspectives on the Word of God: An Introduction to Christian Ethics* (Phillipsburg, NJ: Presbyterian and Reformed, 1990); and Vern S. Poythress, *Symphonic Theology: The Validity of Multiple Perspectives in Theology* (Grand Rapids: Zondervan, 1987).

35. See Frame, *Doctrine of the Knowledge of God*, 17–18, for the coinherence of the three aspects in a general context.

people of Zerubbabel's time were required to do so. The action in Zerubbabel's time was an application of the text from Moses' time. That application was an implication of the meaning of the earlier text, and as such was an aspect of that meaning. But now there is another way of looking at the matter. One application of Numbers 29 is mental application. People should mentally grasp what God is prescribing. When Zerubbabel and others correctly grasp God's law, they grasp its meaning. Meaning is thus application in the mental sphere. Meaning is an aspect of application.

The same intertwining of meaning and application occurs in the foundational text in John 17. The Father has given his word to Christ, and Christ has given the word to the disciples (v. 14). He gives them the word with the intent that the Father will sanctify them by the truth (v. 17). This sanctifying is an aspect of the intention and the effect of giving the word; it is an aspect of the meaning of the communicative act. Conversely, one aspect of sanctifying is mental sanctifying, which is achieved through understanding the meaning. Thus, meaning is an aspect of the application, that is, the sanctifying. Meaning and application are even more impressively intertwined when we consider them on the level of divine action. The control exercised through the sanctifying work of the Father and the truth expressed through the word of the Son coinhere through the indwelling of the Father and the Son in one comprehensive work.

As we might expect, coinherent unity and diversity exist wherever we look in Scripture, whether our focus is on personal fellowship with God, on truth, or on application. Consider first the matter of personal fellowship with God. There is one God, and hence all Christian fellowship is fellowship with one God. Fellowship rests on the unity of the unchanging character of God. Such is the unity of fellowship. There is also diversity: many people enjoy God's fellowship, at many times, in many stages of growth, as 1 Corinthians 12 reminds us.

Or consider the matter of application. We obviously may find diverse applications to the diverse circumstances in which we live. Yet all the applications have a unified goal: they aim at holiness (Heb. 12:14; 1 Peter 1:15–16). They all aim at glorifying God (1 Cor. 10:31). Or, to express it differently, they aim at being like Christ, at conforming to the image of Christ (Rom. 13:14; 2 Cor. 3:18; 1 Cor. 15:49).

Finally, consider the issue of truth. The Bible contains many distinct truths in the distinct assertions of its distinct verses. But all these cohere in the One who is the Truth (John 14:6).

Christ as the Center of Scripture

It is worthwhile to develop in more detail the Christocentric character of biblical truth. A number of passages of Scripture indicate in more than one way that Christ is at the center of the Bible and the truth. John 14:6, "I am . . . the truth," is only one.

Colossians 2:3 says that "all the treasures of wisdom and knowledge" are hidden in Christ. "All the treasures" obviously includes all the truths of all the verses of Scripture. All of them are hidden in Christ.

John 1:1 and Revelation 19:13 indicate that Jesus Christ is the Word of God. As we have seen above, all particular divine words, from the words of creation onward, are manifestations of this one eternal Word.

Second Corinthians 1:20 says, "No matter how many promises God has made, they are 'Yes' in Christ." The promises of God all find fulfillment in him. Of course, only some parts of the Bible have the explicit form of a promise. But perspectivally speaking, all of the Bible contains a promissory aspect, since God commits himself to his people when he speaks to them.

First Timothy 2:5 and other passages indicate that Christ is the unique, indispensable mediator between God and men, by which we are saved and are able to listen to God without dying. Christ is indispensable for our right reception of Scripture. And since Scripture has the function of bringing salvation, it is fundamentally about Christ. "Preaching must be theological. Salvation is of the Lord, and the message of the gospel is the theocentric message of the unfolding of the plan of God for our salvation in Jesus Christ. He who would preach the Word must preach Christ."[36]

The claims in Luke 24:25–27 and 24:44–49 are particularly important. The disciples on the road to Emmaus felt defeated after Jesus' crucifixion. But Jesus rebuked them (vv. 25–27).

> How foolish you are, and how slow of heart to believe all that the prophets have spoken! Did not the Christ have to suffer these things and then enter his glory? And beginning with Moses and all the Prophets, he explained to them what was said in all the Scriptures concerning himself.

Thus, in this discussion on the road to Emmaus, Christ himself indicates that the Old Testament from beginning to end is about himself.

Sometimes people have thought that Christ is claiming only that a verse here and a verse there speak of the coming Messiah. And it is of course true that some verses speak more directly in this way. But the whole of the Old Testament is about God working out salvation. And salvation is to be found only in Christ. So the whole Old Testament, not just a few isolated verses, speaks of Christ. Luke 24:44–47 makes this claim more explicitly.

> He said to them, "This is what I told you while I was still with you: Everything must be fulfilled that is written about me in the Law of Moses, the Prophets and the Psalms."
> Then he opened their minds so they could understand the Scriptures. He told them, "This is what is written: The Christ will suffer and rise from the dead on the third day, and repentance and forgiveness of sins will be preached in his name to all nations, beginning at Jerusalem."

"The Law of Moses, the Prophets and the Psalms" cover most, if not all, of the Old Testament. The Jews conventionally divided the Old Testament into three parts, the Law of Moses, the Prophets, and the Writings. The Law of Moses consisted of Genesis through Deuteronomy. The Prophets included "the Former Prophets," or the historical writings of Joshua, Judges, 1–2 Samuel, and 1–2 Kings, as well as "the Latter Prophets," Isaiah through Malachi (but Daniel was customarily reckoned with the Writings). The Writings included all the other books, the most prominent of which was the book of Psalms. Since the Writings were a more miscellaneous collection, they did not until later have a standardized name.[37] It appears that at an early period "Psalms" was used as a convenient designation for this third group.[38] Thus, Jesus probably referred to the whole group of Writings, speaking of the Psalms as its most prominent member. But even if he did not— that is, even if he was referring only to the book of Psalms and not to the other books

---

36. Edmund P. Clowney, *Preaching and Biblical Theology* (Grand Rapids: Eerdmans, 1961), 74.

37. See Sirach 1:1; Roger T. Beckwith, *The Old Testament Canon of the New Testament Church and Its Background in Early Judaism* (Grand Rapids: Eerdmans, 1985), especially 110–80.

38. Ibid., 111–17.

included among the Writings—he still encompassed the great bulk of the Old Testament within the sweep of his claims.

Note also that verse 45 says, "He opened their minds so they could understand the Scriptures." Here the entire Scriptures are in view, not just some of them, and certainly not just a few scattered messianic texts. Verses 46–47 indicate in what this understanding consists. "What is written"—the substance of the message of the Scriptures—he explained to be that "the Christ will suffer and rise from the dead on the third day." The whole Old Testament, we conclude, has as its central message the suffering and resurrection of Christ. This conclusion confirms what was said in Luke 24:25–27. The whole Old Testament is about the work of Christ, in that it points forward to this work as what "must be fulfilled" (v. 44).

Few would challenge the idea that Christ is the core of the message of the New Testament writings. But Luke 24 is striking in making an analogous claim about the Old Testament. Christ's work is the core of the purpose and import of the Old Testament as well as the New. But how can that be so, and how do we arrive at such an understanding? We do not want simply to force a Christological message onto a text in an artificial way. That would not be "understanding" the scriptural text in question, but simply imposing a meaning from some other (New Testament) text. But neither do we want to avoid taking up the challenge that Luke 24 offers. The alternative to a Christocentric understanding of the Old Testament is not understanding it rightly—not understanding it as Christ desired.

Understanding the Christocentric character of the Old Testament is not easy. The Scriptures are profound, and we cannot exhaust their implications. A good beginning can be made by studying the quotations and more direct allusions to the Old Testament that are found throughout the New Testament. In those passages Christ himself and his apostles instruct us in the proper understanding of the Old Testament. The book of Hebrews is particularly important because, of all the books in the New Testament, it contains the most lengthy discussion of the fulfillment of the Old Testament.

This matter is so important that is deserves a book-length treatment. Indeed, books have been written on the subject of Christ's fulfillment of the Old Testament.[39] Because of the availability of some of these works, we will go on to consider other topics, rather than expounding the Christological implications of the Old Testament in detail.

---

39. See Clowney, *Preaching and Biblical Theology*; Edmund P. Clowney, *The Unfolding Mystery: Discovering Christ in the Old Testament* (repr., Phillipsburg, NJ: Presbyterian and Reformed, 1991); Vern S. Poythress, *The Shadow of Christ in the Law of Moses* (repr., Phillipsburg, NJ: Presbyterian and Reformed, 1995); Mark R. Strom, *Days Are Coming: Exploring Biblical Patterns* (Sydney: Hodder and Stoughton, 1989). Older works on typology are of considerable value: see Patrick Fairbairn, *The Typology of Scripture* (repr., Grand Rapids: Baker, 1975).

50

Moisés Silva's *Has the Church Misread the Bible?*

Moisés Silva, "2. Obstacles in the Study of the History of Interpretation," and "4. Clear or Obscure?" in *Has the Church Misread the Bible? The History of Interpretation in the Light of Current Issues*, Foundations of Contemporary Interpretations 1 (Grand Rapids: Zondervan, 1987), 27–45, 77–97.

Moisés Silva taught New Testament at Westminster from 1981 to 1996. After studying at Westminster, he obtained a Ph.D. in New Testament studies from the University of Manchester. Before his tenure at Westminster, he taught at Westmont College, and afterward he held the Mary French Rockefeller Distinguished Chair in New Testament at Gordon-Conwell Theological Seminary. Silva is known for his keen abilities in philology. Following the lead of his mentor, James Barr, he published *Biblical Words and Their Meaning: An Introduction to Lexical Semantics* (1983, rev. 1994). Also notable is his commentary on *Philippians* (1992). In addition, he distinguished himself as a student of textual criticism and the Septuagint. His scholarly interests also include the relationship of exegesis to theology.

Silva's book *Has the Church Misread the Bible? The History of Interpretation in the Light of Current Issues* (1987) represents this interest. Here he discusses various crucial issues in biblical interpretation in light of the history of biblical interpretation. He offers a healthy reminder to scholars, but also to Reformed Christians, that there is a long history of interpreting the Bible. This anthology excerpts two chapters (chapters 2 and 4) from his work. In "Obstacles in the Study of the History of Interpretation," he outlines his specific perspective on the history of interpretation and tackles the topic of the relationship between the divine and human aspects of the Bible. The other chapter, "Clear or Obscure," examines in a nuanced way the interpretation of the Reformation, a "hermeneutical revolution" and its focus on the *plain reading of Scripture*. He deals with such topics as the clarity of Scripture, the relationship of interpretation to tradition, and the Reformation's attitude toward allegory. His treatment of "Erasmus Versus Luther" sheds light on the first selection of this anthology. Silva helps to develop a Reformed hermeneutics in continuity with the church throughout the ages.

OBSTACLES IN THE STUDY OF THE HISTORY OF INTERPRETATION

Before we can launch into the various disciplines outlined in the previous chapter, preliminary attention must be given to the historical roots of biblical interpretation. It must be made clear from the outset, however, that I do not intend to provide in this volume a full-blown history of biblical hermeneutics.[1] The usual chronological approach is convenient, and for certain purposes, pedagogically effective. Unfortunately, surveys of this type lead to a somewhat atomistic, item-by-item description that fails to uncover some of the more interesting and suggestive connections.

Moreover, we need to avoid the antiquarian's approach to this history—as though the concerns of ancient and medieval interpreters were oddities to be observed and then set aside. The truth is that no aspect of the current hermeneutical crisis developed spontaneously without any prior connections. The problems *we* face can be dealt with satisfactorily only if we recognize that they are not altogether new, that many of the old controversies (silly though they may look to us) are not substantially different from those that divide contemporary readers of the Bible.

Of particular importance is the popular assumption that the Christian church, through most of its history, has misread the Bible. Did an invalid hermeneutics reign among interpreters while crucial theological issues were being decided? Before we can address this fundamental question, it may be useful to review briefly the common perception of the history of biblical interpretation.

The Usual Conception

A typical survey of the church's interpretation of the Bible might take this form:

The origins of biblical interpretation are to be found within Judaism, which provided the context for different approaches. First, among sectarians, such as the people of the Dead Sea Scrolls, biblical interpretation had a marked eschatological note. Passage after passage in the Old Testament was understood as referring to the end times, which were in the process of being fulfilled in the context of the Qumran community.

Second, among the rabbis, whose approach developed into mainstream Judaism, exegesis consisted of mechanical and artificial rules that paid virtually no attention to the context of the biblical passages. In the more extreme cases, such as the methods of Akiba, an irrational literalism and obsession with trivial details led to wholesale distortions of the Scriptures.

Third, in the Jewish Hellenistic world, particularly Alexandria, Greek allegorical methods used in the interpretation of Homeric legends were applied to the Bible. Best known among

---

1. The most influential work in English has been Frederic W. Farrar, *History of Interpretation* (New York: Dutton, 1886), impressive and learned—but also very misleading, as we shall see. A recent and popular description is Robert M. Grant, *A Short History of the Interpretation of the Bible*, 2nd ed. with additional material by David Tracy (Philadelphia: Fortress, 1984). Most Bible dictionaries contain useful surveys. See especially *The Interpreter's Dictionary of the Bible* 2:718–24 (K. Grobel) and pp. 436–56 in the *Supplementary Volume* (multiauthor). D. P. Fuller, *The International Standard Bible Encyclopedia* (rev. ed.) 2:863–74, emphasizes developments in the twentieth century. A highly regarded survey in the Continent is G. Ebeling, "Hermeneutik," *Die Religion in Geschichte und Gegenwart* 3:242–62.

Jewish allegorizers is Philo, who rejected literalism on the grounds that it led to blasphemous and even immoral interpretations. For him, biblical narratives, if interpreted literally, were at best irrelevant: we must discover the underlying meaning of these passages, which usually corresponds to the best in Greek philosophy.

In contrast to these approaches, the New Testament shows a remarkably balanced method of interpretation. There may be a very few examples of allegorization (perhaps Gal. 4:21–31 and Heb. 7:1–10), but even these passages are rather moderate in comparison with Philo. Again, some rabbinic rules of interpretation seem to be reflected in various New Testament passages, but apostolic exegesis shows considerable respect for the Old Testament context. And while one must recognize that the apostles, like the Qumran community, used an eschatological hermeneutics, their approach was built upon a distinctively christological foundation.

As we move to the postapostolic period, the picture changes dramatically. Since the Qumran community had been destroyed in A.D. 70, its peculiar exegesis was basically unknown in the Christian church. Moreover, rabbinic methods had little impact on the Gentile church, partly because very few Christians were familiar with Hebrew and partly because anti-Jewish feelings prevented any significant communication (there were of course some important exceptions, such as Origen and Jerome, but even they did not adopt rabbinic exegesis).

Allegorical exegesis, however, was something else. Since Philo had written in Greek, his works were accessible to the Gentile church. Moreover, Christians were faced with the need to confront Greek culture, and Philo appeared to provide a way of doing so in an intellectually responsible way. Origen in particular made the allegorical method a central feature of his exegesis and his theology, and his influence was to be felt for many centuries.

To be sure, important Christian leaders such as Tertullian rejected any attempt to mix the gospel with Greek philosophy. And in Antioch an exegetical approach was developed during the fourth century that was self-consciously opposed to Origen and that could be described as "grammatico-historical," if only in a limited way. (Important representatives of this school were John Chrysostom and Theodore of Mopsuestia.) As a whole, however, the allegorical interpretation was adopted by the church and hardly anything of exegetical value was produced during the Middle Ages.

Fortunately, the Reformation came along. Thanks in part to the Renaissance, which resurrected an interest in linguistic and historical investigation, the Reformers attacked the allegorical method as a major source of the many evils that had developed in the church. Many new commentaries, particularly those of John Calvin, inaugurated a new epoch in the interpretation of Scripture.

These advances were to some extent nullified by seventeenth-century orthodox theologians who reintroduced a scholastic mentality, but the eighteenth-century Enlightenment finally brought in a truly scientific approach to the interpretation of the Bible. While some scholars took matters to an extreme and their rationalism was damaging to the Christian faith, by and large the grammatico-historical method of exegesis established itself firmly during the nineteenth century and continues to be used in our day.

So much for the usual description. Depending on the theological stance of the person reporting this history, some aspects and details may differ here and there, particularly in the evaluation of post-Enlightenment scholarship. Generally speaking, however, our brief survey reflects rather accurately the usual understanding of the church's interpretation of the Scriptures. Unfortunately, there are some serious problems with this understanding.

Objections

In the first place, our survey did not go back far enough, since it paid no attention to the earliest stage of biblical interpretation, namely, the Old Testament itself. The books of the Old Testament were written over a very long period of time, and it would be surprising if the later books made no use of the earlier ones. No one has denied that various kinds of references of this sort exist, but only recently have scholars focused on this issue with a view to drawing hermeneutical inferences.[2]

This field of study presents us with a few problems, not the least of which is the uncertainty we face when trying to establish the relative date of some of the documents. In certain cases—particularly the date of the Pentateuch—disagreement among scholars creates a serious obstacle, but we still have a number of clear instances in which later Old Testament writers have used, expanded, or otherwise applied earlier passages.

We might take, for instance, Jacob's prophecy that the scepter would not depart from Judah before *šlh* should come (Gen. 49:10). Is that Hebrew word the proper name *Shiloh*, as some translations have it? Or should we render the clause as the NIV does, "until he comes to whom it belongs"? In favor of the latter option is an apparent reference to this prophecy by Ezekiel, who predicts the removal of the crown from the prince of Israel and adds: "It will not be restored until he comes to whom it rightfully belongs; to him I will give it" (Ezek. 21:27).

One can find many other passages that almost surely depend on earlier material. An especially fruitful example is the way 1–2 Chronicles retells the historical material found in the Books of Samuel and Kings.[3] Even in such clear instances, however, it is seldom easy to identify a particular principle or technique that we can readily apply to our own exegetical efforts. Much work remains to be done in this area.

A second problem with the usual approach to the history of interpretation is the strongly negative note with which the subject is treated. Farrar's famous *History* is little more than a compilation of errors. Already in the preface he warns us about "the apparently negative character of much that is here dwelt upon," and in the first chapter he states his thesis thus:

> The task before us is in some respects a melancholy one. We shall pass in swift review many centuries of exegesis, and shall be compelled to see that they were, in the main, centuries during which the interpretation of Scripture has been dominated by unproven theories, and overladen by untenable results. We shall see that these theories have often been affiliated to each other, and augmented at each stage by the superaddition of fresh theories no less mistaken. Exegesis has often darkened the true meaning of Scripture, not evolved or elucidated it.

Near the end of that first chapter he tells us that "the misinterpretation of Scripture must be reckoned among the gravest calamities of Christendom." Much of the blame goes to the Septuagint, whose "intentional variations may be counted by scores, and their unintentional errors by hundreds; and alike their errors and their variations were in a multitude of instances

2. See esp. Michael A. Fishbane, *Biblical Interpretation in Ancient Israel* (Oxford: Clarendon Press, 1985), for the most thorough treatment of this question. Much briefer but also helpful is James L. Kugel and Rowan A. Greer, *Early Biblical Interpretation,* Library of Early Christianity (Philadelphia: Westminster, 1986), part one.

3. See the study by Raymond B. Dillard, "The Chronicler's Solomon," *WTJ* 43 (1980–81): 289–300.

accepted by Christian interpreters as the infallible word of God."[4] Although Farrar has some complimentary words here and there (particularly with reference to the Antiochenes and the Reformers), one is hard-pressed to find much in that history that would help us in our exegetical work—except possibly to avoid a multitude of errors.

Apart from the general negativism of the standard approaches, it is important to point out the particular areas that come under heavy attack. One of the main objects of derision is rabbinic exegesis. Here is Farrar's opinion of the Talmud:

> But it may be said, without fear of refutation, that, apart from a few moral applications and ritual inferences in matters absolutely unimportant, for every one text on which it throws the smallest glimmer of light, there are hundreds which it inexcusably perverts and misapplies. . . . [Hillel's rule known as Gezerah Shawa] furnished an excuse for masses of the most absurd conclusions. . . . Hillel was personally a noble Rabbi; yet by his seven rules he became the founder of Talmudism, with all its pettiness, its perversion of the letter of the Scripture which it professed to worship, and its ignorance of the spirit, of which no breath seemed to breathe over its valley of dry bones.[5]

Farrar believes that Christian exegesis, fortunately, did not share the particular perversions of the rabbis, but his introduction to patristic interpretation is not encouraging either:

> The history of exegesis thus far has been in great measure a history of aberrations. If we turn to the Fathers with the hope that now at last we shall enter the region of unimpeachable methods and certain applications, we shall be disappointed. . . . [Though admittedly one can find much that is valuable in the Fathers,] their exegesis in the proper sense of the word needs complete revision both in its principles and in its details.[6]

The main culprit behind patristic misinterpretation is of course Origen of Alexandria, who gave respectability to Philo's allegorical method. With regard to Philo's approach, Farrar had already stated: "It must be said quite plainly and without the least circumlocution that it is absolutely baseless. . . . his exegesis is radically false. It darkens what is simple and fails to explain what is obscure." Origen was hardly successful in improving upon Philo. What Origen regarded as exegetical "proofs" were nothing "but the after-thoughts devised in support of an unexamined tradition. They could not have had a particle of validity for any logical or independent mind."[7]

In addition to rabbinic exegesis and the allegorical method, a third object of Farrar's criticism is medieval scholasticism. We should note that, during the past few decades, spe-

4. Farrar, *History*, xi, xviii, 8–9, 39, 122. A similar attitude can be found in Samuel Davidson, *Sacred Hermeneutics: Developed and Applied* (Edinburgh: T. & T. Clark, 1843), esp. 187. Grant, *Short History*, is better, but even he has some unnecessarily harsh remarks about Barnabas, Justin, and Protestant orthodoxy (pp. 41, 45, 97).

5. Ibid., 10, 20, 22; see also 50 and 88.

6. Ibid., 162; on p. 165 he describes their interpretation as consisting of "a chaos" of diverse elements. David C. Steinmetz is probably correct when he views Farrar's book as "a triumph of what the late Sir Herbert Butterfield of Cambridge called 'Whig' historiography. Farrar admires about the past precisely those elements in it most like the present and regards the present, indeed, as the inevitable culmination of all that was best in the past" ("John Calvin on Isaiah 6: A Problem in the History of Exegesis," *Interpretation* 36 [1982]: 169; reprinted in *Calvin in Context* [New York: Oxford University Press, 1995], 95).

7. Ibid., 153, 191. Farrar concludes that the very foundations of Origen's "exegetic system are built upon the sand" (p. 201). Even Saint Augustine, for all his greatness, made little advance in interpretive method. For Farrar, Augustine's exegesis "is marked by the most glaring defects. Almost as many specimens of prolix puerility and arbitrary perversion can be adduced from his pages as from those of his least gifted predecessors" (p. 236).

cialists have developed a much more positive appreciation of the Middle Ages than was the case in Farrar's generation. Nowadays many scholars are ready to argue, for example, that "the medieval hermeneutical tradition . . . can be characterized as an authentic attempt to establish the *sensus literalis* of Scripture as its principal meaning, and to give it a theologically normative role in the formation of Christian theology."[8] In Farrar's opinion, on the other hand, the Schoolmen were "paralysed by vicious methods, traditional errors, and foregone conclusions," while their exegesis was "radically defective—defective in fundamental principles, and rife on every page of it with all sorts of erroneous details."[9]

Behind all of this invective is Farrar's conviction that, first, many of these errors are still to be found "here and there, unexorcised, in modern commentaries," and, second, that the main cause of these old exegetical perversions is the theory of "verbal dictation."[10] Farrar's own view of inspiration, incidentally, helps explain why he does not feel threatened by the miserable failure of the church in interpreting the Bible. In his opinion, inspiration assures only that the message of salvation, broadly understood, is preserved in Scripture: "the Bible is not so much a revelation as the *record* of revelation, and the inmost and most essential truths which it contains have happily been placed above the reach of Exegesis to injure."[11]

Toward a Positive Evaluation

Whatever we may think of Farrar's doctrine of Scripture, it is difficult to accept the thoroughgoing negativism with which he recounts the history of interpretation. After all, the individuals he discusses were believers seeking to make sense of God's Word, with a view to obeying the divine will. Are we to suppose that their efforts were, with the rarest of exceptions, virtually fruitless? Must we really think that, prior to the development of modern exegesis, the church lacked the Spirit's guidance?

Farrar appears to suggest that only two options are available to us: Either we accept modern exegetical methods and reject a good 95 percent of pre-eighteenth-century biblical interpretation, or else we condemn ourselves to adopting countless errors. Perhaps, however, we can be genuinely critical of shortcomings on the part of the Fathers and still learn something more positive than how to avoid their errors. Surely, it is conceivable that their failures may have been counterbalanced by other factors that can help us to formulate a valid hermeneutical approach. David C. Steinmetz comments that the answer to Farrar is not to point out examples of "modern" exegesis in the Middle Ages (or howlers in modern times): "The principal value of precritical exegesis is that it is not modern exegesis; it is alien, strange, sometimes even, from our perspective, comic and fantastical."[12]

8. James Samuel Preus, *From Shadow to Promise: Old Testament Interpretation from Augustine to Young Luther* (Cambridge, MA: Harvard University Press, Belknap, 1969), 3. For a renewed appreciation of medieval exegesis, we are largely indebted to Beryl Smalley's work, particularly *The Study of the Bible in the Middle Ages*, 2nd ed. (Oxford: Blackwell, 1952).
9. Farrar, *History*, 267, 302.
10. Ibid., xii, xx, 190, 283, 430, etc. Farrar shows considerable confusion in dealing with this matter, as can be seen particularly in the footnotes on p. xx. In the first place, he equates "verbal dictation" with the doctrine of infallibility. Moreover, he refers with apparent approval to Tholuck's claim that this view is no earlier than the seventeenth century—even though such a claim blatantly contradicts his repeated attribution of that doctrine to many early historical figures, such as Philo, the rabbis, Athenagoras, Tertullian, and Origen (see pp. 148, 152, 162, 171, 177, 190).
11. Ibid., xiv; cf. also 303.
12. Steinmetz, "John Calvin," 170.

In any case, we can hardly claim to have developed a satisfactory approach *if our exegesis is in essence incompatible with the way God's people have read the Scriptures throughout the centuries.* A genuine effort must be made to view the history of interpretation in a more positive light than is usually done. The reason why this is so necessary is not difficult to understand. Most believers even today lack the specialized skills that characterize modern "scientific" exegesis. Since they therefore read the Scriptures in a "nonscientific" way, they are basically in the same position as earlier Christians who lived in a prescientific period.

Moreover, one may argue that scholarly exegesis, though it rightly uses highly specialized methods, fails to provide proper guidance if it disregards the simple or instinctive response to Scripture on the part of lay readers. It may indeed appear impossible for modern biblical scholarship to discover any relationship between the historical method and the quasi-allegorical approach that is standard fare among lay Christians. The failure to confront this dilemma head-on, however, can only lead to an unbearable divorce between scholarly work and common piety.

There is, in addition to these concerns, a profound intellectual problem with the usual negative analysis. Take the case of Origen. It is agreed on all sides that Origen was one of the brightest luminaries in his day—not only within the Christian community, but even in the context of the whole cultural scene in the third century. How, then, does one account for his constructing a hermeneutical system that draws bitter scorn from moderns?

Origen's allegorical method was not some peripheral concern that we might disregard as an uncharacteristic quirk. Quite the contrary, it belonged at the center of his theological thinking. If, as Farrar claimed, his exegetical proofs had no "particle of validity for any logical or independent mind," are we not compelled to conclude that Origen's mind was neither logical nor independent? And is not that conclusion clear evidence that we have failed to solve, or maybe even to identify, the problem?

If my own experience as a seminarian was at all typical, most students find Origen a difficult, distant, unhelpful personality. One can find many objectionable elements in his writings and few that appear genuinely constructive. The more one reflects on the subsequent history of interpretation, however, the more one becomes aware of the significance of Origen's thought. He anticipated virtually every substantive hermeneutical debate in the history of the church, including some that have persisted to this day. It would no doubt be an exaggeration to say that the history of biblical interpretation consists of a series of footnotes to Origen, but there is enough truth in that remark to make us sit up and take notice. Accordingly, the chapters that follow pay a great deal of attention to Origen's writings. Even if we decide to reject his answers, it is impossible to avoid his questions.

Now what Origen's questions most clearly reveal is that the task of biblical interpretation seems to pull the believer in several different directions. I propose in this volume to study the history of interpretation precisely in that light. My thesis is simply that this history is characterized by the church's appreciation, sometimes implicit rather than consciously formulated, that we face a series of difficult "tensions" in our reading of Scripture:[13]

13. I use quotation marks here to alert the reader to a certain ambiguity in the word *tension*. I am using the term not in any sophisticated fashion but in a simple, popular sense. As we seek to understand the Scriptures, we sometimes feel as

- The Bible is divine, yet it has come to us in human form.
- The commands of God are absolute, yet the historical context of the writings appears to relativize certain elements.
- The divine message must be clear, yet many passages seem ambiguous.
- We are dependent only on the Spirit for instruction, yet scholarship is surely necessary.
- The Scriptures seem to presuppose a literal and historical reading, yet we are also confronted by the figurative and nonhistorical (e.g., the parables).
- Proper interpretation requires the interpreter's personal freedom, yet some degree of external, corporate authority appears imperative.
- The objectivity of the biblical message is essential, yet our presuppositions seem to inject a degree of subjectivity into the interpretive process.

The attempt to hold these seeming polarities in tension is the principle that brings unity to the great diversity of problems surrounding the history of biblical interpretation. It may well be that the one great aim in our own interpretation of Scripture must be that of resisting the temptation to eliminate the tensions, to emphasize certain features of the Bible at the expense of others.

Divine or Human?

The first item listed above—the Bible as both divine and human—constitutes the most basic question of all. Strictly speaking, it is not so much a hermeneutical question as it is one of theology, even though, as we shall see in the course of our discussions, one can hardly divorce doctrine from interpretation. Since the present book is not intended to serve as a text for Christian theology, I consider here only briefly the doctrine of biblical inspiration.[14]

But treat it we must, for the relationship between the divine and human elements of Scripture directly affects how we handle every other item on the list. I do not say, of course, that our view of the character of Scripture automatically determines whether we will, for example, take prophetic passages in a literal or nonliteral way. Nevertheless, it is hardly possible to formulate a coherent set of hermeneutical principles unless one takes fully into account how those principles relate to the essential nature of the documents being interpreted.

Origen's most important theological work, *On First Principles*, consists of four books, the last of which is devoted to principles of biblical interpretation. Not surprisingly, the first chapter of that book deals with inspiration, and Origen intends to establish the divine character of Scripture as the foundation for hermeneutics. Origen develops his argument by appealing to fulfilled prophecy, the success of the apostles, and other types of evidence. As he approaches the end of the chapter, he writes:

Now when we thus briefly demonstrate the divine nature of Jesus and use the words spoken in prophecy about him, we demonstrate at the same time that the writings which prophesy

---

though contradictory responses are expected of us. Besides such feelings, we also may experience intellectual frustration. But the believer knows well that these difficulties arise from our own ignorance and sin.

14. In addition to A. A. Hodge and B. B. Warfield, *Inspiration* (1881; repr., Grand Rapids: Baker, 1979), note the important articles by Warfield brought together in *The Inspiration and Authority of the Bible*, ed. Samuel G. Craig (Philadelphia: Presbyterian and Reformed, 1948), esp. chs. 2–4. One of the most recent and learned discussions, particularly valuable in addressing contemporary objections to Evangelicalism, is Carl F. H. Henry, God, *Revelation, and Authority*, 6 vols. (Waco, TX: Word, 1976–83), esp. vol. 4, ch. 6.

about him are divinely inspired and that the words which announce his sojourning here and his teaching were spoken with all power and authority and that this is the reason why they have prevailed over the elect people taken from among the nations.[15]

Origen also appeals to the reader's subjective response: "And he who approaches the prophetic words with care and attention will feel from his very reading a trace of their divine inspiration and will be convinced by his own feelings that the words which are believed by us to be from God are not the compositions of men." He realizes, of course, that not everyone who reads the Bible acknowledges it as divine, and so in section 7 he draws an analogy based on the failure of many people to detect God's existence through the works of providence:

> But just as providence is not abolished because of our ignorance, at least not for those who have once rightly believed in it, so neither is the divine character of scripture, which extends through all of it, abolished because our weakness cannot discern in every sentence the hidden splendour of its teachings, concealed under a poor and humble style.[16]

The very last clause just quoted, we may note, entails a recognition that there is *more* to be said about Scripture than that it is divine. The human character of Scripture does not concern Origen at this point (in fact, he nowhere deliberately reflects on the implications of that fact with the same thoroughness he displays in treating the Bible's divine character). As a result, he may appear to disregard or even ignore it. We have already seen his comment that the biblical writings "are not the compositions of men." In section 4.2.2 he identifies himself with "those who believe that the sacred books *are not the works of men*, but that they were composed and have come down to us as a result of the inspiration of the Holy Spirit."[17] It would be easy to multiply quotations from Origen's extensive writings that suggest he viewed the Scriptures as exclusively divine.

The very nature of his scholarly labors, however, belies such a conclusion. His concern with textual and philological details makes sense only on the assumption that he recognized the important role played by language and other human factors.[18] Our discussion in subsequent chapters should make clear that Origen's primary concern with what *God* says in Scripture does not necessarily preclude a commitment to find out what its human authors meant.

At any rate, we must acknowledge that heavy emphasis on the divine character of Scripture has characterized most of the history of interpretation. One reason for this emphasis, of course, is simply that some of the human features of the Bible are patent and undeniable: it was written by real-life historical individuals rather than appearing from nowhere, it was written in human languages rather than in some unknown angelic tongue, and so on. In other words, the church has not had to deal with people who deny, at least in any conscious

---

15. Origen, *Origen on First Principles*, trans. G. W. Butterworth (1938; repr., New York: Harper & Row, 1966), 4.1.6, p. 264.

16. Ibid., 4.1.7, pp. 265, 267.

17. Ibid., 4.2.2, p. 272, my emphasis.

18. How this recognition affected Origen's practice of interpretation may be illustrated from the preface to *On First Principles*. Answering an objection based on a passage from *The Teaching of Peter* (a writing that Origen did not accept as inspired, though he granted its inspiration for the sake of the argument), he stated: "And the words must be understood in the sense intended by the author of that writing" (section 8 of the preface, p. 5). We are not concerned here primarily with Origen's critical labors, the best known of which was the Hexapla. It may be worth pointing out, however, that he saw such works, not as ends in themselves, but as the first steps in understanding the divine message.

or explicit form, the fact that there is a human side to the Scriptures, whereas it has had to respond to many who deny their divine origin.

One must admit, however, that in actual practice Origen and most of the interpreters who followed him in the ancient and medieval periods tended to disregard the human (and therefore historical) aspects of the text because of their commitment to its divine character. This tendency led to many interpretive errors, such as the full-scale development of allegorical exegesis, which usually focused on the divine meaning "behind" the human words, a matter that we consider in chapter 3 [cf. Silva, *Has the Church Misread the Bible?* 47–75].

The Renaissance witnessed a renewed interest in the historical character of ancient writings, including the Bible. Its effect on the Reformers, particularly Calvin, was direct. It must not be thought that the Reformers downplayed the divine origin of Scripture; their concern with the "plain" meaning of the Bible (that is, the meaning intended by the *human* author, as that sense can be plainly determined by the literary and historical context) did not entail a change in their view of inspiration. Significantly, Calvin at times so stressed the divine character of Scripture that he, like Origen, appeared to deny its humanity: "not the word of the apostles but of God himself; not a voice born on earth but one descended from heaven."[19] Although the arguments he used to defend the doctrine of inspiration marked a substantive advance over previous discussions, they have much in common with those of Origen. Calvin's commitment to the "paradox" that the Bible is both divine and human is no doubt a major reason why moderns can appeal to some of his statements as evidence that he did not believe in verbal inspiration, while other comments make absolutely no sense unless he did.[20]

Without denying the distinctiveness of the Reformers' contribution, then, we do well to remember their basic sense of continuity with earlier centuries, at least with respect to the divine character of Scripture. The Reformation, of course, also retained the medieval concern for application, though it sought to bind application to the clear meaning of the text.

The rise of the critical method, on the other hand, marked a radical change in the way students of the Bible approached the text. To begin with, there was a tendency to view exegesis as an end in itself. And for the first time in the history of the church, scholars who professed some form of Christian commitment argued that the Bible was to be understood just like any other book. In a sense, of course, the best exegetes had always attempted to interpret the Bible in this way, that is, according to the normal rules of language, paying attention to logic, literary conventions, historical data, and so on.

Now, however, interpreters argued that the Bible must be subjected to the same kind of full-blown *criticism* that one might apply to any human writing, even if the analysis leads to a negative assessment of its value at any point.[21] Proponents of this method did not agree with each other concerning whether the Bible could still be regarded as divine (and if so, in what sense), but they did agree that such a factor could not play a role in its interpretation.

19. John Calvin, *Institutes of the Christian Religion*, ed. John T. McNeill, trans. Ford Lewis Battles, Library of Christian Classics 20 (Philadelphia: Westminster, 1967), 4.11.1, p. 1213. See section 1.6–8 for his defense of inspiration.

20. In my opinion, one can hardly doubt that Calvin's view of the authority of Scripture corresponds in all essential respects to that of Warfield. See John Murray, *Calvin on Scripture and Divine Sovereignty* (Philadelphia: Presbyterian and Reformed, 1960), esp. ch. 1. The apparent inconsistency of expression is more remarkable in Jerome; see Farrar, *History*, 230–31.

21. More accurately, it was claimed that critical exegesis should not consist in value judgments. The eighteenth-century scholar K. A. G. Keil, for example, argued that proper biblical interpretation could not ask whether the text is right or wrong. This restriction, however, meant that one must disregard inspiration (see W. G. Kümmel, *The New Testament: The History of the Investigation of Its Problems* [Nashville: Abingdon, 1972], 108; cf. 110 on L. I. Rückert). In other words, the divine element was excluded, and with it the possibility that the Scriptures were always reliable.

The whole conception of biblical authority, therefore, if not blatantly abandoned, was drastically altered: an individual's reason first had to make a judgment regarding the validity of a biblical statement or injunction before one could believe it.

The development of biblical hermeneutics during the past two centuries cannot possibly be separated from the application of critical tools to the biblical text. This factor raises a series of major problems. In the first place, the interpretation of the Bible now appears to require expertise in a number of highly specialized subdisciplines. Does this qualification put the Scriptures out of the reach of most believers? Can we possibly claim that the Bible is *clear*? (We consider this issue in, "Clear or Obscure," see below.)

Second, we are faced with a new and most difficult dilemma. On the one hand, many of the critical tools used by modern scholarship are patently consistent with a high view of scriptural authority; that is, scholars with strong evangelical convictions can plainly make use of, say, textual criticism without compromising their view of biblical inspiration. On the other hand, most of these tools have taken shape in the context of blatant unbelief. The point here is not merely that some unbelievers have had a hand in their development but that such a development assumed, in the very nature of the case, that the Scriptures must be fallible. Are these tools therefore inherently "tainted," whether we realize it or not, and therefore unusable by anyone committed to the full authority of the Bible? Some conservative Christians would answer this question affirmatively. For that matter, liberal scholars often accuse Evangelicals of inconsistency in holding on to inerrancy while making use of critical tools.

> Troeltsch poured scorn on those of his contemporaries who attacked the historical method as a manifestation of unbelief while employing something like it to vindicate the truth of their own views. The method, he claimed, did not grow from an abstract theory, nor could one ignore the cumulative significance of its extraordinary results. "Whoever lends it a finger must give it a hand." Nor could the critical method be regarded as a neutral thing. It could not be appropriated by the church with only a bit of patchwork here and there on the seamless garment of belief. "Once the historical method is applied to the Biblical science and church history," he wrote, "it is a leaven that alters everything and, finally, bursts apart the entire structure of theological methods employed until the present."[22]

Third, and most directly relevant to our present concerns, it is now claimed that a full acceptance of the critical method, with its assumption of biblical fallibility, is the only approach that does justice to the humanity of Scripture. Ironically, conservatives become the theological felons, charged with a form of *docetism*, an ancient heresy that denied the true humanity of Christ.

The analogy between Scripture and the twofold nature of Christ, though very popular in some circles, suffers from some deep ambiguities.[23] Even if it did not, however, one wonders how the charge of docetism contributes to the discussion, other than by affecting the objectivity of the debate through the "slur" factor. Strangely, I have never heard anyone accused of *Arianism* in his

22. Van Austin Harvey, *The Historian and the Believer: The Morality of Historical Knowledge and Christian Belief* (New York: Macmillan, 1966), 5. From a somewhat different angle, James Barr has been particularly anxious to show that Evangelicals have a very equivocal approach to scholarship. See his *Fundamentalism* (London: SCM, 1977), esp. ch. 5. Barr observes, "The deservedly high reputation of some conservative scholarship rests to a large extent on the degree to which it *fails* to be conservative in the sense that the conservative evangelical public desiderate" (p. 128).

23. For a perceptive discussion, see G. C. Berkouwer, *Holy Scripture*, Studies in Dogmatics (Grand Rapids: Eerdmans, 1975), ch. 7. See also D. A. Carson, "Recent Developments in the Doctrine of Scripture," in *Hermeneutic, Authority, and Canon*, ed. D. A. Carson and John D. Woodbridge (Grand Rapids: Zondervan, 1986), 5–48, esp. his criticism of Bruce Vawter on pp. 26–28.

or her view of Scripture, though it could be argued that, once we abandon the doctrine of infallibility, there is no meaningful way in which we can speak of the divine character of the Bible.

The last point can best be illustrated by referring to a World Council of Churches study report on biblical authority presented in 1971. Heavily influenced by Karl Barth's theology, the members of the committee were reluctant to base the authority of Scripture on the notion of inspiration, and so they pointed rather to "the experience in which the message of the Bible proves itself authoritative." To their credit, they went on to ask the embarrassing question:

> If the assertion that the Bible is inspired is a conclusion drawn from actual encounter with God through the Bible, the question arises as to why this should only be true of the Bible.... Indeed, why should we not also speak of inspiration in the case of today's preaching which can also lead to an encounter with God and thus prove itself inspired in the same way as happens with the Bible?

It would certainly be difficult to think of a more fundamental question than that of the uniqueness of scriptural authority. The fact that this notion had lost all meaning for the committee may be inferred from their remarkable response: "Obviously a clearer explanation is required as to whether and in what sense God has bound Himself through the Spirit to the Bible in its entirety."[24] To paraphrase: We have no idea in what way the Bible is unique.

The position taken in this book is that error is not inherent to humanity—it may be true that to err is human, but it is most certainly untrue that to be human is to err! A human being can (and often does) utter sentences that contain no errors or falsehoods (e.g., "Hitler is dead" or, under the appropriate circumstances, "I saw my mother yesterday"). Accordingly, we do not jeopardize the humanity of Scripture if we say that all it affirms is true. At the same time, we may readily acknowledge that an evangelical view of Scripture has led many to downplay its human character—if not in theory, certainly in the practice of interpretation.

As with Calvin, our attempt to affirm both the divine and human sides of Scripture will almost inevitably lead to statements that appear inconsistent. This problem only reminds us of our finiteness. But the alternative would be to deny one or the other element, which we dare not do.

CLEAR OR OBSCURE?
REFORMATION DOCTRINE AND
THE CONTEMPORARY CHALLENGE

It is no exaggeration to say that the sixteenth-century Reformation was, at bottom, a hermeneutical revolution. Luther's meeting with Cardinal Cajetan at Augsburg in 1518 developed into a discussion of *Unigenitus* (a papal bull published in 1343), which asserted the

---

24. Ellen Flesseman-van Leer, ed., *The Bible: Its Authority and Interpretation in the Ecumenical Movement*, Faith and Order Paper 99 (Geneva: World Council of Churches, 1980), 54–55.

notion of a treasury of merits. In response Luther wrote a statement in which he refused "to discard so many important clear proofs of Scripture on account of a single ambiguous and obscure decretal of a Pope who is a mere human being." Not surprisingly, Cajetan objected that *someone* has to interpret the Bible and that the Pope is supreme in this area. Interpretation, however, had been a crucial element in Luther's "individual struggle for spiritual existence." He therefore unambiguously denied the Pope's supreme authority and proceeded to make his hermeneutical concerns a key element in the religious conflict that followed.[25]

The connection between this chapter and the previous one is very close. The main contribution of the Protestant Reformers to biblical hermeneutics is their insistence on *the plain meaning* of Scripture. Their concern, however, focused specifically on the need to rescue the Bible from the allegorical method. We see this element strikingly expressed in many of Luther's remarks: "The Holy Spirit is the plainest writer and speaker in heaven and earth and therefore His words cannot have more than one, and that the very simplest sense, which we call the literal, ordinary, natural sense."[26] He can refer to allegories as dirt and scum that lead to idle speculations; indeed, for Luther, all heresies arise from neglecting the simple words of Scripture.[27]

As we have already noted, the contrast between the Reformers and the medieval scholastics should not be exaggerated. Not only had medieval scholarship made notable advances in historical and grammatical exegesis; it is also true that the Reformers' disapproval of allegory was not always consistent. Still, it is quite accurate to describe the Reformers as opponents of the allegorical method.

My concern in this chapter, however, is to identify their reason for that opposition. Up to the time of the Reformation, the Bible was perceived by most people as a fundamentally obscure book. The common folk could not be expected to understand it, and so they were discouraged from reading it.[28] Indeed the Bible was not even available in a language they could understand. They were almost completely dependent on the authoritative interpretation of the church.

But suppose the Bible is not to be allegorized. Suppose each passage has, not several meanings, but one, simple, literal meaning. In that case, all Christians may be encouraged to read the Bible. The Scriptures should be translated into the common tongue. Each believer has a right to private interpretation. Luther in particular was very insistent on these points, and he expended tremendous energy on his most enduring work, the translation of the Bible into German.

The very fact that a *translation* was needed, however, raises certain problems for the view that the Scriptures are easily accessible to common Christians. If a Christian is unable to read the Bible in its original languages, then he or she is dependent on knowledgeable individuals to analyze the biblical text, understand its meaning, and express it clearly in the

25. A. Skevington Wood, *Luther's Principles of Biblical Interpretation* (London: Tyndale, 1960), 5–6.

26. *Works of Martin Luther* (Philadelphia: Holman, 1930) 3:350.

27. Frederic W. Farrar, *History of Interpretation* (New York: Dutton, 1886), 327–28.

28. This statement is an overgeneralization and has been disputed, esp. by H. Rost, *Die Bibel im Mittelalter: Beiträge zur Geschichte und Bibliographie der Bibel* (Augsburg: Kommissions-Verlag M. Seitz, 1939). Moreover, Smalley points out that the revival of popular preaching in the twelfth century led to the use of allegory for the specific purpose of instructing the laity (Beryl Smalley, *The Study of the Bible in the Middle Ages*, 2nd ed. [Oxford: Blackwell, 1952], 244). It can hardly be denied, however, that the authorities discouraged private Bible reading and that the problem became worse by the eve of the Reformation.

language of the reader. For this reason and others, many Christians feel that the doctrine of the clarity of Scripture has become more and more difficult to defend.

In the first place, the tremendous advances in specialized knowledge during the past century are sufficient to intimidate even the brashest among us. We could point to numerous interpretations of Scripture that have been proved wrong by recent advances. Does not that fact raise serious questions about the measure of certainty we can claim to have for our present opinions? What is true more generally seems also to be true of the interpretation of Scripture: the more we know, the more conscious we are of our ignorance.

In the second place, to say that the Scriptures are clear seems to fly in the face of the realities of contemporary church life. As pointed out in chapter 1,[29] even those who share significant areas of doctrinal agreement find themselves at odds in the interpretation of important biblical passages—passages dealing with baptism and the Lord's Supper, passages that address the question of violence, and passages that have relevance for serious ethical problems such as war, capital punishment, and abortion. If those who are wholeheartedly devoted to the authority of Scripture cannot agree on such questions, has the doctrine of the clarity of Scripture become meaningless?

In the third place, there appears to be a new sensitivity to the significance of corporate authority in the church. The Reformers' emphasis on the right of private interpretation was often balanced by a recognition that no Christian is an island but is part of the body of Christ. Modern Evangelicalism, however, afraid of the abuse of church authority and influenced by a strong sense of individualism, has not always appreciated the need for Christians to submit their understanding of Scripture to the judgment of the established church.

Yet things seem to be changing. One detects a strong sense of humility among a growing number of believers. Without succumbing to the opposite danger of compromising their convictions, many Christians show a genuine desire to submit to the wisdom and counsel of their elders in the faith. Though this development is a wholesome one, does it not challenge our conviction that the meaning of the Scriptures is plain and readily accessible to the common reader?

Erasmus Versus Luther

These questions are all serious, but they are not really new. Without minimizing the distinctive pressures that characterize modern Christianity, we need to appreciate how much help we can receive from Christians in earlier ages. Already in the fourth century, for example, John Chrysostom had recognized the need for both affirming and qualifying this notion of the clarity of Scripture: in his words, *panta ta anankaia dēla*, "all the things that are necessary are plain."[30] Even Origen, though not so explicitly, was making the same point when he argued that virtually all Christians understand what he believed to be one of the most fundamental doctrines: the spiritual significance of the law.[31]

A qualification of this sort may seem to leave the door open for abuse: could not someone define *necessary* and *fundamental* in such a way that vast portions of the Bible remain inaccessible to believers? Indeed one could, but we need to remember that such abuses are

29. Cf. Silva, "1. Today's Hermeneutical Challenge," in *Has the Church Misread the Bible?* 1–25.
30. See Farrar, *History*, p. 329n. (I have not been able to verify Farrar's vague reference.)
31. Origen, *Origen on First Principles*, trans. G. W. Butterworth (1936; repr., New York: Harper & Row, 1966), 2.7.2, p. 117.

possible whenever we seek to be careful and responsible in our formulation of doctrine. Any attempt we make to avoid simplistic answers by clarifying and qualifying our statements runs the risk of being misunderstood and misapplied. It is important to note, however, that the Reformers themselves—tempted though they must have been to overstate their position in the face of controversy—defined their doctrine of biblical clarity, or perspicuity, by focusing on the foundational truths of Scripture.

Particularly instructive in this regard is Luther, since no one was more forceful in affirming that the meaning of the Bible is plain and accessible to all. Perhaps the most revealing discussion is found in his famous essay *On the Bondage of the Will*, in which he responded to a series of criticisms Erasmus had made some time earlier.[32] Erasmus, in the preface to his work *On the Freedom of the Will*, had objected to Luther's statements on human freedom because this subject, he felt, was a very obscure one:

> For there are some secret places in the Holy Scriptures into which God has not wished us to penetrate more deeply and, if we try to do so, then the deeper we go, the darker and darker it becomes, by which means we are led to acknowledge the unsearchable majesty of the divine wisdom, and the weakness of the human mind.[33]

Echoing Chrysostom's remark about the things that are "necessary," Erasmus argues that just a few things are "needful to know" about the doctrine of free choice and that it is irreverent to "rush into those things which are hidden, not to say superfluous." Then follows an important statement that could be interpreted as an affirmation of the clarity of Scripture on those matters that are truly significant:

> There are some things which God has willed that we should contemplate, as we venerate himself, in mystic silence; and, moreover, there are many passages in the sacred volumes about which many commentators have made guesses, but no one has finally cleared up their obscurity: as the distinction between the divine persons, the conjunction of the divine and human nature in Christ, the unforgivable sin; yet there are other things which God has willed to be *most plainly evident*, and such are the precepts for the good life. This is the Word of God, which is not to be bought in the highest heaven, nor in distant lands overseas, but it is close at hand, in our mouth and in our heart. These truths must be learned by all, but the rest are more properly committed to God, and it is more religious to worship them, being unknown, than to discuss them, being insoluble.[34]

Finally, he argues that certain topics, even if they can be understood, should not be discussed in the presence of the "untutored multitude," who might find them offensive and damaging.

As we might expect, Luther contests Erasmus's claim in the strongest of terms:

> But that in Scripture there are some things abstruse, and everything is not plain—this is an idea put about by the ungodly Sophists, with whose lips you also speak here, Erasmus; but they have never produced, nor can they produce, a single article to prove this mad notion of theirs. Yet with such a phantasmagoria Satan has frightened men away from reading the Sacred Writ,

---

32. See E. G. Rupp et al., eds., *Luther and Erasmus: Free Will and Salvation*, Library of Christian Classics 17 (Philadelphia: Westminster, 1969).

33. Ibid., 38.

34. Ibid., 39–40, my emphasis.

and has made Holy Scripture contemptible, in order to enable the plagues he has bred from philosophy to prevail in the Church.[35]

More important for our present purposes, however, is Luther's recognition that there *are* indeed certain kinds of obscurities in Scripture that require (as his words certainly imply) scholarly research:

> I admit, of course, that there are many texts in the Scriptures that are obscure and abstruse, not because of the majesty of their subject matter, but because of our ignorance of their vocabulary and grammar; but these texts in no way hinder a knowledge of the subject matter of Scripture.

Luther defines "subject matter" as "the supreme mystery brought to light, namely, that Christ the Son of God has been made man, that God is three and one, that Christ has suffered for us and is to reign eternally." Having thus defined the focus of his concern, Luther goes on:

> The subject matter of the Scriptures, therefore, is all quite accessible, even though some texts are still obscure owing to our ignorance of their terms. Truly it is stupid and impious, when we know that the subject matter of Scripture has all been placed in the clearest light, to call it obscure on account of a few obscure words. If the words are obscure in one place, yet they are plain in another; and it is one and the same theme, published quite openly to the whole world, which in the Scriptures is sometimes expressed in plain words, and sometimes *lies as yet hidden* in obscure words.[36]

His conviction that difficult passages are made clear by others (a point that will occupy us again shortly) echoes Augustine's teaching:

> Accordingly the Holy Spirit has, with admirable wisdom and care for our welfare, so arranged the Holy Scriptures as by the plainer passages to satisfy our hunger, and by the more obscure to stimulate our appetite. For almost nothing is dug out of those obscure passages which may not be found set forth in the plainest language elsewhere.[37]

One could argue that Erasmus and Luther were not really at odds on the question of the clarity of Scripture: they both affirmed such a doctrine with regard to its essential message. They did differ, however, on how one defines that message; moreover, the tone and basic thrust in Erasmus's essay naturally lead one to distrust the ability of the common believer to understand the Bible. Luther's most fundamental concerns were diametrically opposed to that tendency.[38]

35. Ibid., 110.

36. Ibid., 110–11 (my emphasis). Cf. Origen's remark: "If some time, as you read the Scripture, you stumble over a thought, good in reality yet a stone of stumbling and a rock of offence, lay the blame on yourself. For you must not give up the hope that this stone of stumbling and this rock of offence do possess meaning" (from Homily 39 on Jeremiah, quoted in R. B. Tollinton, *Selections from the Commentaries and Homilies of Origen* [London: SPCK, 1929], 49–50).

37. Augustine, *On Christian Doctrine* 2.6 (NPNF2, 537). On the notion of Scripture as its own best interpreter, see further below (pp. 103–4).

38. These comments are too simple; I have ignored other complicating factors in the debate that are not directly relevant to our purpose. It should also be noticed that, if Erasmus and Luther did indeed differ in their identification of the essential message of Scripture, that factor itself could be used as an objection against the clarity of Scripture: if the Bible is so clear, why could not Luther and Erasmus agree on its fundamental subject matter? Luther's likely response to this question may be inferred from the subsequent discussion.

The Need for Qualifications

We must remember, however, that Luther did not for a moment deny the limitations of the interpreter's knowledge. For one thing, Christians differ in their level of maturity; indeed, extensive ministry in the church is almost a prerequisite for correct interpretation:

> No-one can understand the Bucolics of Virgil who has not been a herdsman for five years; nor his Georgics unless he has labored for five years in the fields. In order to understand aright the epistles of Cicero a man must have been full twenty years in the public service of a great state. No one need fancy he has tasted Holy Scripture who has not ruled the churches for a hundred years with prophets, like Elijah and Elisha, with John the Baptist, Christ and the apostles.[39]

More to the point, the clarity of Scripture does not at all preclude the need for specialists who seek to bridge the gap that separates us from the languages and cultures of the biblical writers. Luther himself was a man of broad erudition and of fine philological skills. He could argue that "to expound Scripture, to interpret it rightly and to fight against those people who quote wrongly . . . cannot be done without knowledge of the languages."[40] The energies he expended on his translation of the Bible are the clearest testimonial to his conviction that the common folk did, in an important sense, depend on the expertise of scholars.

In any case, it would be a misunderstanding of the Reformers to interpret their emphasis on the perspicuity of Scripture in such a way as to make biblical scholarship unnecessary or unimportant. Developments in the various relevant disciplines during the last century or two heighten our sense of dependence on the careful work of scholars, yet at the same time such developments ought to increase our confidence that the Bible is not a locked mystery box but an accessible book that continues to open up its truths to those willing to search them out.

The essence of the Protestant position is captured well by the Westminster Confession of Faith (1647). The first chapter of that document contains a full statement regarding the character of Scripture, and paragraph 7 addresses directly the doctrine of perspicuity:

> All things in Scripture are not alike plain in themselves, nor alike clear unto all; yet those things which are necessary to be known, believed, and observed for salvation, are so clearly propounded, and opened in some place of Scripture or other, that not only the learned, but the unlearned, in a due use of the ordinary means, may attain unto a sufficient understanding of them.

Here the confession achieves a remarkable balance in its formulation. The emphasis falls heavily on the clarity of the biblical message, but the framers have been careful to qualify the doctrine in several ways: (1) not every part of Scripture is equally clear; (2) the matters in view are those that are necessary for salvation; (3) readers of the Bible must be willing to make use of "ordinary means"—personal study, fellowship with other believers, attention to the preaching of the Word; and (4) the interpreter's understanding will not be complete but will certainly be "sufficient" for the purpose stated.

---

39. Wood, *Luther's Principles*, 16. This quotation comes from a note written by Luther two days before his death; cf. P. Stuhlmacher, *Vom Verstehen des Neuen Testaments: Eine Hermeneutik,* Grundrisse zum Neuen Testament Ergänzungsreihe 6 (Göttingen: Vandenhoeck & Ruprecht, 1979), 98.

40. Wood, *Luther's Principles*, 29. Wood notes Luther's attention to detail: on one occasion Luther and two of his helpers spent four days translating three lines in the Book of Job (ibid.).

One should notice, incidentally, the phrase "nor alike clear unto all." This qualification reminds us of the relative obscurity to be found in the minds of individual readers, a topic that occupies a prominent place in Luther's work. Luther was well aware that to acknowledge incidental obscurities in the text of Scripture did not fully address the problem raised by Erasmus. Accordingly, Luther goes on to deal with an additional factor.

> It is true that for many people much remains abstruse; but this is not due to the obscurity of Scripture, but to the blindness or indolence of those who will not take the trouble to look at the very clearest truth. [Here he quotes 2 Cor. 3:15 and 4:3–4.] . . . Let miserable men, therefore, stop imputing with blasphemous perversity the darkness and obscurity of their hearts to the wholly clear Scriptures of God.

As he comes to the end of this discussion, Luther summarizes his doctrine by pointing out that there are two kinds of clarity and two kinds of obscurity:

> one external and pertaining to the ministry of the Word, the other located in the understanding of the heart. If you speak of the internal clarity, no man perceives one iota of what is in the Scriptures unless he has the Spirit of God. . . . For the Spirit is required for the understanding of Scripture, both as a whole and in any part of it. If, on the other hand, you speak of the external clarity, nothing at all is left obscure or ambiguous, but everything there is in the Scriptures has been brought out by the Word into the most definite light, and published to all the world.[41]

Human Darkness and the Spirit's Light

Luther's emphasis on the darkness of the human heart is nothing new, of course. We saw how significant this principle was in the medieval development of allegorical interpretation. It may be useful, moreover, to remind ourselves of Origen's conception that part of the divine aim was to conceal truth. We should not be too quick to condemn Origen, since he could have easily appealed to several important passages of Scripture in support of his view.

For example, even if we allow for some degree of literary hyperbole in Isaiah 6:9–10, we cannot do justice to that passage unless we recognize that at least one aspect of Isaiah's mission was to darken the hearts of many Israelites.

> Go and tell this people:
> "Be ever hearing, but never understanding;
>   be ever seeing, but never perceiving."
> Make the heart of this people calloused;
>   make their ears dull and
>   close their eyes.
> Otherwise they might see with their eyes,
>   hear with their ears,
>   understand with their hearts,
> and turn and be healed.

41. Rupp, *Luther and Erasmus*, 111–12; cf. Ralph A. Bohlmann, *Principles of Biblical Interpretation in the Lutheran Confessions*, rev. ed. (St. Louis: Concordia, 1983), 53–63.

This passage clearly speaks of divine retribution against those who have set themselves against the God of Israel. The point is developed from a different angle in Isaiah 8:14–15, where the Lord describes himself, not only as a "sanctuary" (to believers), but also as

> a stone that causes men to stumble
> and a rock that makes them fall.
> And for the people of Jerusalem he will be
> a trap and a snare.
> Many of them will stumble;
> they will fall and be broken,
> they will be snared and captured.

These portions of Scripture became very important to the apostles as they sought to understand Israel's rejection of the gospel message. Jesus himself had appealed to Isaiah 6 in connection with his practice of speaking in parables. The relevant passage is Mark 4:10–12, one that itself has become quite a stone of stumbling to modern scholars, who think it is absurd to take Jesus' words in their apparent meaning. After all, parables are intended to illustrate and clarify a message! Why would our Lord say anything that was actually designed to keep people from understanding?[42]

In truth, however, Jesus' message had the same two-edged function as Isaiah's ministry: a blessing to believers and a curse to God's enemies. The elderly Simeon, as he held the baby Jesus in his arms, declared that Jesus was "destined to cause the falling and rising of many in Israel" (Luke 2:34). The apostle Paul described his message as a fragrance of life, the aroma of Christ for salvation, but he acknowledged that, to those who are perishing, it is "the smell of death" (2 Cor. 2:14–16). Not surprisingly, both Paul and Peter quote Isaiah 8:14 as they deal with the difficult problem of seeing many reject the message of the gospel (Rom. 9:32–33; 1 Peter 2:4–8; it should be noted that both of these passages have a very strong predestinarian motif).[43]

It was unfortunate that Origen should make the factor of God's concealing truth so basic in his hermeneutical system, but we dare not forget the principle altogether. Even those who have responded in faith to the divine message continue to be sinners. The corruption of sin will always affect our understanding of Scripture to a greater or lesser extent; part of our responsibility, therefore, is to learn to depend more and more on the illumination of the Holy Spirit.

We need to be careful, of course, not to use this blessing to justify our prejudices and laziness. The guidance of the Spirit does not preclude our making use of "the ordinary means" that the Westminster Confession refers to. Moreover, we need to appreciate that the passages that stress the role of the Spirit in interpreting God's message (one thinks primarily of 1 Cor. 2:6–14) do not focus on difficult exegetical details but precisely on those matters that are needful for salvation. Quite properly, therefore, the Westminster Confession reminds us: "Nevertheless, we acknowledge the inward illumination of the Spirit of God to be necessary *for the saving understanding* of such things as are revealed in the Word" (WCF 1.6; my emphasis).

42. According to C. F. D. Moule, it would be "perversely literalistic" to suggest "that parables are used in order to exclude" (*The Birth of the New Testament*, 3rd rev. ed. [New York: Harper & Row, 1982], 116–17).

43. On the use of "stone" passages in the New Testament, see esp. Barnabas Lindars, *New Testament Apologetic: The Doctrinal Significance of the Old Testament Quotations* (London: SCM, 1961), 169–86.

This factor helps us to deal with a troublesome matter: does it make sense to use commentaries written by unbelieving scholars? Why should we depend on the judgment of those whose hearts have not been enlightened by the ministry of the Spirit? The usual answer is that many of the issues modern commentators deal with do not directly affect Christian doctrine. Such a response, by itself, is not wholly satisfactory, yet there is enough truth in it to serve our present purposes. Even a heart deeply antagonistic to the gospel does not lead a scholar to identify a noun as a verb. Leaning on the expertise of scholars who have specialized interests should be regarded as one more instance of using "ordinary means" in the study of Scripture.

This perspective can help us make sense of a frequently cited verse that is both reassuring and puzzling: "As for you, the anointing you received from him remains in you, and you do not need anyone to teach you" (1 John 2:27). Some Christians tend to absolutize this statement and to resist the notion that scholarly work is helpful and important. They forget, of course, that they cannot even read the Bible without depending on the scholarly work that has made Bible translations possible. *Someone* had to learn Greek and Hebrew; *someone* had to study ancient culture; *someone* had to develop expertise in transferring the message of the original to clear, forceful English—all of which had to happen before modern American believers could claim that they need no one to teach them about the Bible!

The Role of Scholarship

We do indeed need help not at all because the Scriptures are inherently obscure but because we are far removed from the biblical writers in time and culture. Even a document written carefully in clearly formulated English, such as the Declaration of Independence, can *appear* obscure two hundred years later. The very opening phrase, "When in the course of human events," will be partially lost to a modern reader who does not realize that the word *course* carried some strong philosophical nuances in the eighteenth century.[44] What shall we say, then, about a document written not two hundred but two thousand years ago? not in English but in very different languages? not in America but in the Mediterranean world?

The history of biblical interpretation during the past century or two—whatever objectionable features it has had—must be understood primarily as an attempt to bridge this massive linguistic and cultural gap between us and the original text. The development of highly specialized critical tools may appear to create a wall between the simple believer and the Bible, but in effect it facilitates bringing the two together. Not all scholars, of course, view their work in this way—and many who do often fail to meet such a goal. Furthermore, modern critical approaches should not be viewed naively as completely neutral with respect to the question of faith.[45] A believing scholar must bring any hermeneutical approach (even those developed by evangelical scholars!) under the searching light of Scripture itself.

---

44. Gary Wills, *Inventing America: Jefferson's Declaration of Independence* (Garden City, N.Y.: Doubleday, 1978), 93 and ch. 8.

45. Cf. Troeltsch's views mentioned above in "Obstacles in the Study of the History of Interpretation." The most significant contribution to this fundamental question is the controversial thesis of the "twofold division of science," propounded by Abraham Kuyper (*Encyclopedia of Sacred Theology: Its Principles* [New York: Scribner, 1898], 150–82). Though in many respects believing and unbelieving science have the same character, argued Kuyper, they move in different directions because of their different starting points (p. 155). Cornelius Van Til has insisted on the same point in many of his writings;

In spite of such qualifications, we can state unequivocally that modern biblical scholarship has helped to open up the meaning of innumerable passages of Scripture, sometimes in very dramatic ways. The discovery and analysis of the Egyptian papyri, for example, has increased our understanding of New Testament Greek almost beyond reckoning. The development of Old Testament form criticism, though it has spun many questionable and radical theories, has made it possible for us to uncover the significance of various kinds of literary genres within the Hebrew Bible.[46] And so on and on.

We dare not confuse, therefore, the peculiar and often harmful proposals of radical scholars with the actual advances of biblical scholarship as a whole. Someone committed to the authority of Scripture and convinced that those proposals must be rejected can still recognize the enormous contribution of modern scholarship to the understanding of the Bible.[47]

If we think that nowadays we face more exegetical problems than earlier generations did, the reason is precisely that we know more about the Bible and therefore have a greater awareness of our ignorance. Two hundred years ago, Bible readers only thought that they understood many passages that now we have doubts about. Paradoxically, our *subjective sense* of the clarity of Scripture seems diminished at the same time that we have *greater objective evidence* regarding the clear meaning of the Bible. To recognize this fact is to remind ourselves that we cannot confuse what Luther called the external and internal aspects of the doctrine of scriptural perspicuity. We dare not attribute to Scripture the limitations of our minds and hearts.

Even more to the point, however, is our need to appreciate that all of the advances in modern scholarship—and all of the new questions raised by it—do not affect the basic outlines of Christian theology. Many individual scholars, of course, reject the great doctrines of the Reformation on the basis of modern philosophical commitments.[48] But changes in our understanding of individual passages of Scripture do not require or even suggest that we alter the essence of the Christian message.

Referring again to the Westminster Confession of Faith, perhaps the most comprehensive theological statement arising from the Reformation, we may ask: Is there any chapter in that document that needs revision because we now conclude that, say, the Song of Solomon was written, not as an allegory, but as a description of human love? Is there even a paragraph that must now be excised because of advances in textual criticism or philology? The answer is a definitive and unequivocal no.

Neither this document nor any other theological confession is perfect; we must recognize that Christians have grown in their understanding of Scripture and may indeed wish to

---

see *A Christian Theory of Knowledge* (n.p.: Presbyterian and Reformed, 1969), 21–22 and passim. For an attempt to develop the implications of this thesis, see Gary North, ed., *Foundations of Christian Scholarship: Essays in the Van Til Perspective* (Vallecito, CA: Ross House, 1976).

46. In addition to the well-known research of A. Deissmann, J. H. Moulton, and others at the beginning of the century, see the recent work by G. H. R. Horsley, *New Documents Illustrating Early Christianity* (North Ryde, N.S.W.: Macquarie University, 1981–). See also Tremper Longman III, "Form Criticism, Recent Developments in Genre Theory, and the Evangelical," *WTJ* 47 (1985): 46–67.

47. It is ironic that wrong-headed and obnoxious theories very often sensitize responsible scholars to valid questions that would otherwise not have occurred to them. See my article "The Place of Historical Reconstruction in New Testament Criticism," in *Hermeneutics, Authority, and Canon*, ed. Carson and Woodbridge, 122–33.

48. In particular, many scholars have adopted a thoroughgoing naturalism. Useful surveys documenting the development of biblical scholarship during the past two centuries are the essays by W. Neil and A. Richardson in *The Cambridge History of the Bible*, ed. P. R. Ackroyd et al., vol. 3 (Cambridge University Press, 1970), 238–338. For greater detail on the development of British views on Scripture, see the highly regarded work by H. G. Reventlow, *The Authority of the Bible and the Rise of the Modern World* (Philadelphia: Fortress, 1984).

revise certain aspects of any doctrinal statement. But all of the increased knowledge and sophistication of the modern era does not suggest for a moment that previous generations of Christians misunderstood the gospel message.

The Whole Counsel of God

The reason for such stability in the face of dramatic advancement is that the great teachings of Scripture are not dependent on the interpretation of any particular verse in isolation from others. Though Christians sometimes rely heavily on certain proof texts, the church has come to understand the divine message by developing sensitivity to the *consistent* teaching of the Bible *as a whole*.

The believer is thus not at all a slave to scholarly pronouncements. Believers may express puzzlement and even distress upon hearing a new interpretation of some favorite text, but they will usually adjust to it if they can eventually see how it fits their understanding of Scripture as a whole. What they will not tolerate—and rightly so—is an interpretation that obviously conflicts with the consistent tenor of the biblical teaching. In the most fundamental sense, believers need no one to teach them (1 John 2:27), and the most imposing scholarship will not intimidate them.

A most interesting sidelight to this discussion is the fact that even Origen justified his hermeneutical program along lines similar to those we have been considering. At one point, after acknowledging the validity of the literal meaning, he argued that we have the need and responsibility, not merely to grasp the sense of any given passage, but to assimilate the *entire* meaning of Scripture.[49] Origen did not expand on this idea, and perhaps we should not make too much of it, but he apparently maintained a strong sense of the importance of contextual interpretation. Because of the unity of the Bible, the whole of Scripture constitutes the context to any one passage, and Christians who are spiritually mature may be expected to draw all the threads together. We make a serious mistake if we do not see this process as an essential aspect of allegorical interpretation. And what was true of Origen was certainly true of the Fathers in general:

> They knew what was their aim in handling scripture. It was not to produce an entirely consistent system of doctrine which would somehow fit in every little detail of the Bible, nor was it to set up a biblical literalism which would treat the Bible as one treats a railway timetable. It was to discover, and to preach and teach, the burden, the purport, the drift, the central message of the Bible.[50]

A corresponding principle vigorously formulated at the time of the Reformation is that Scripture is its best interpreter. We earlier noticed that Luther appealed to this notion in

---

49. Origen, *On First Principles* 4.3.5, pp. 296–97. Wiles asked, from a somewhat different perspective, what criteria controlled a method as flexible as that of allegory: "An important part of the answer to that question is Origen's conviction that scripture must always be consistent with itself, that the real meaning of every passage will be part of the truth of the one Christian faith" (M. F. Wiles, "Origen as Biblical Scholar," *The Cambridge History of the Bible*, ed. P. R. Ackroyd et al. [Cambridge: Cambridge University Press, 1963], 1:454–89, esp. 1:479–80).

50. Hanson, "Biblical Exegesis," *The Cambridge History of the Bible* 1:412–53, esp. 1:452. On the same issue, see Michael Andrew Fahey, *Cyprian and the Bible: A Study in Third-Century Exegesis*, Beitrag zur Geschichte der biblischen Hermeneutik 9 (Tübingen: J. C. B. Mohr, 1971), 473. The great Charles Spurgeon, in spite of his questionable use of certain texts as the basis for his sermons, was kept from distorting the biblical message through his impressive familiarity with the overall teaching of Scripture.

response to the charge that there are obscurities in the Bible ("If the words are obscure in one place, yet they are plain in another"). As early as the second century, Irenaeus articulated this principle when he argued against certain gnostic views:

> For no question can be solved by means of another which itself waits solution; nor, in the opinion of those possessed of sense, can an ambiguity be explained by means of another ambiguity, or enigmas by means of another greater enigma, but things of such character receive their solution from those which are manifest, and consistent, and clear.[51]

Oddly, Farrar objects to the idea that "Scripture interprets itself, a rule which exegetically considered has no meaning."[52] Quite the opposite, this rule is the most fundamental hermeneutical principle when dealing with any piece of literature; it is, in effect, the principle of contextual interpretation. Anyone who views God as the author of Scripture can hardly afford to ignore it.

Church and Tradition

One final problem requires our attention in this chapter—the question that we raised earlier concerning submissiveness to the teaching of the church. How does the clarity of Scripture relate to this question? Should we depend on the church to teach us about the Scripture?

For that matter, what is the role of tradition? The Protestant Reformation is usually characterized as a massive break with tradition. There is a very important element of truth in that characterization, but here again a crucial caveat is necessary. The Reformers opposed the authority of tradition and of the church, but *only insofar as this authority usurped the authority of Scripture*. They never rejected the value of the church's exegetical tradition when it was used in submission to the Scriptures.

> Luther could not have been the exegete he was without the help of the church's tradition. The tradition gave him a footing on which he could and did move and shift, but which he never lost. But this was so because he believed that under this footing was the foundation of the Scriptures themselves, which he, as an expositor of the Scriptures and also as a son of the church, was to receive gratefully.... Luther knew the difference between gratitude and idolatry in the reception of the church's heritage. In this sense he advanced the audacious claim that by his exposition of the Scriptures he was a most loyal defender of the tradition, and that the idolatrous traditionalism of his opponents could mean the eventual destruction both of Scripture and of tradition.[53]

Consider in this regard John Calvin's development. Calvin had no peer in the sixteenth century as an expositor of Scripture, but he was under no illusion that he could somehow skip a millennium and a half of exegetical tradition and approach the Bible free from the

---

51. Irenaeus, *Against Heresies* 2.10.1 (ANF 1:370); cf. Bertrand de Margerie, *Introduction à l'histoire de l'exégèse* (Paris: Cerf, 1980), 1:70, who also refers to 2.10.2 and 3.27.1 and to Salvator Herrera, *Saint Irénée de Lyon exégète* (Paris: A. Savieta, 1920), 120ff. Origen also held to this principle; see R. P. C. Hanson, *Allegory and Event: A Study of the Sources and Significance of Origen's Interpretation of Scripture* (London: SCM, 1959), 180.

52. Farrar, *History*, 332n1. He does observe, however, that the watchword *analogia fidei* is a wise one insofar as it forbids us "to isolate and distort any one passage into authoritative contradiction to the whole tenor of Scripture" (p. 333). Cf. the positive treatment in Bohlmann, *Principles*, ch. 6.

53. Jaroslav Pelikan, *Luther the Expositor: Introduction to the Reformer's Exegetical Writings*, companion vol. to *Luther's Works* (St. Louis: Concordia, 1959), 88.

influence of the past. The first edition of his *Institutes of the Christian Religion* appeared in 1536, when Calvin was only in his twenties. Enlarged editions appeared in 1539 and 1541 and more significant alterations beginning in 1543, but the work did not reach its final form until 1559. During these two decades Calvin was immersed in biblical exposition and preaching. "As his understanding of the Bible broadened and deepened, so the subject matter of the Bible demanded ever new understanding in its interrelations within itself, in its relations with secular philosophy, in its *interpretation by previous commentators*."[54]

This last point is most important, for Calvin also spent considerable time studying the major theologians of the church. Indeed, beginning with the 1543 edition, there were "vastly increased" references to the Fathers, including Augustine, Ambrose, Cyprian, Theodoret, and others.[55] Calvin's position was well thought out:

> Insofar as possible, we should hold to the work of earlier exegetes. The Reformer saw himself as bound by and indebted to the exegetical tradition of the church, above all the early church, especially Augustine. He was unwilling to give up the consensus of interpretation.[56]

It is clear, then, that the Reformation marked a break with the *abuse* of tradition but not with the tradition itself. This fact tells us a great deal about the Reformers' sense of corporate identity with the Christian church as a whole. It would not have occurred to them to interpret the Scripture as autonomous individuals. On the contrary, they were most forceful in their interpretations when they were convinced that they were giving expression to the truth *given to the church*.

Unfortunately, some would have us believe that the genius of the Reformation was a breaking loose from authority in general and that post-Enlightenment biblical critics, in their radical abandonment of church guidance and scriptural authority, were really giving more consistent expression to the fundamental principle of the Reformation.[57] Disturbing too is the fact that even conservative scholars in our day sometimes give much higher priority to individualism than to corporate responsibility. The idea of pursuing truth "wherever it may lead us" becomes a pious but misconceived motto, for truth rarely if ever manifests itself in isolation.

No doubt there are cases when a scholar hits on an idea whose time has not come, and the fact that the church is not immediately convinced of its validity is no reason to abandon it altogether. On the other hand, new theories and strange interpretations have been suggested by the thousands, most of them never to be propounded again. The humble believer who, innocent of historical and critical methods, cannot see how these interpretations fit in with the church's understanding of the truth may thereby show greater perception of the meaning of Scripture. In a paradoxical way, the clarity of Scripture thus proves triumphant over the misguided attempts of human wisdom, and Jesus' prayer finds a new application: "I praise you, Father, Lord of heaven and earth, because you have hidden these things from the wise and learned, and revealed them to little children. Yes, Father, for this was your good pleasure" (Matt. 11:25–26).

54. T. H. L. Parker, *John Calvin: A Biography* (Philadelphia: Westminster, 1975), 132, my emphasis.
55. Ibid., 106.
56. Hans-Joachim Kraus, "Calvin's Exegetical Principles," *Interpretation* 31 (1977): 11. Note also Peter Stuhlmacher, *Historical Criticism and Theological Interpretation of Scripture: Toward a Hermeneutics of Consent* (Philadelphia: Fortress, 1977), 34–35.
57. Troeltsch's thesis clearly implies this view; note Van Austin Harvey, *The Historian and Believer: The Morality of Historical Knowledge and Christian Belief* (New York: Macmillan, 1966), 3–9.

51

Contemporary Hermeneutics and the Study of the New Testament[1]

RICHARD B. GAFFIN JR.

Richard B. Gaffin Jr., "Contemporary Hermeneutics and the Study of the New Testament," *WTJ* 31, 2 (May 1969): 129–44; reprinted in *Studying the New Testament Today*, ed. John H. Skilton, The New Testament Student 1 (n.p.: Presbyterian and Reformed, 1974), 3–18.

Richard B. Gaffin Jr. taught biblical and systematic theology at Westminster Theological Seminary in Philadelphia for forty years. He studied at Calvin College, Westminster, and Göttingen. Gaffin taught first New Testament and then also systematic theology. He continued the legacy of the Princetonian professor Geerhardus Vos concerning biblical theology, and he also promoted the teaching of Van Til. After contributing to Reformation studies with his *Calvin and the Sabbath* (1962), Gaffin offered a breakthrough in Pauline studies in *The Centrality of the Resurrection* (1978) (or *Resurrection and Redemption: A Study in Paul's Soteriology*). More recently, he has engaged with the challenges of the new perspective on Paul. His book *By Faith, Not by Sight: Paul and the Order of Salvation* (2006) addresses the new perspective and clarifies the application of redemption in Paul, in particular.

In the wake of the theological shift effected by Karl Barth (1886–1968) and twentieth-century reflections on theories of interpretation, a new concern arose in the church for language and interpretation in the movement known as the *new hermeneutic*. Richard Gaffin's article "Contemporary Hermeneutics and the Study of the New Testament" (1968), originally a presentation at Westminster, discusses hermeneutical method as an important matter for discussion and debate within the church.

1. A paper delivered at the conference of the Board of Trustees and the faculty of Westminster Theological Seminary on October 21, 1968.

Gaffin rightly predicted the challenges facing the church in the present day based on the hermeneutical shifts that took place among biblical scholars in the first half of the twentieth century. Tracing the effects of Enlightenment thinking, he explains the impact that some of the resulting "language games" have had on the interpretation of Scripture. Gaffin both uncovers the unchristian presuppositions of this new movement and provides a positive response with the help of reflections on biblical theology. He concludes that since we live in the same redemptive epoch as the New Testament writers, our theology ought to be shaped by redemptive history or biblical theology. This perspective offers an orthodox, but not static, answer to contemporary concerns.

Bibliography: Peter A. Lillback. "The Rev. Dr. Richard B. Gaffin, Jr.: Sancti Libri Theologicus Magnus Westmonasteriensis." *WTJ* 74, 1 (Spring 2012): 1–31. Lane G. Tipton and Jeffrey C. Waddington, eds. *Resurrection and Eschatology: Theology in Service of the Church. Essays in Honor of Richard B. Gaffin Jr.* Phillipsburg, NJ: P&R Publishing, 2008.

The question of hermeneutics (or *how* the Bible is to be interpreted) is at the center of contemporary theological debate. In fact, it does not go too far to say that today all theological discussion is, in one form or another, *hermeneutical* discussion. Particular lines of inquiry are seen to converge in a hermeneutical focus. Specific issues are considered to be reducible to a hermeneutical common denominator. In a word, the *problem*—for it is recognized to be such—the problem of hermeneutics is felt to be *the* theological problem par excellence.

As long as one continues to operate with the conventional understanding of hermeneutics, this all-consuming interest in the subject remains unintelligible or its significance is, at best, only dimly perceived. Traditionally, hermeneutics has been conceived of as a particular theological discipline, closely associated with, yet distinguished from, exegesis, as both have reference to the biblical text. To be more specific, hermeneutics and exegesis are related to each other as theory to practice. Hermeneutics is concerned with enunciating *principles* of interpretation derived, for the most part, from previously established epistemological and philological considerations, principles which, in turn, are to facilitate understanding of the text as they are applied in the concrete act of exegesis. This, for instance, is the conception of hermeneutics developed by Abraham Kuyper in the third volume of his monumental work on theological encyclopedia: hermeneutics is "de logica der exegese."[2]

In marked contrast to this traditional point of view is the new grasp of the proportions and nature of the hermeneutical task which has been emerging since the appearance of Karl Barth's commentary on the book of Romans and which has become increasingly dominant since about 1950. This significant expansion of the hermeneutical horizon is seen most easily in the influential encyclopedia article on "Hermeneutik" by the German church historian, Gerhard Ebeling, which appeared in 1959.[3] An excellent statement of this new orientation has been provided for the English reader by James M. Robinson in his essay, "Hermeneutic

---

2. *Encyclopaedie der Heilige Godgeleerdheid* (Kampen: J. H. Kok, 1909), 3:90.

3. Kurt Galling, ed., *Die Religion in Geschichte und Gegenwart*, 3rd ed. (Tübingen: J. C. B. Mohr, 1959), 3:242–62.

since Barth."[4] Guided by etymological reflection upon the three root meanings of the Greek verb which directly underlies the word "hermeneutics" and its equivalents in other modern European languages, Ebeling maintains that in his interest in explaining the text the exegete must take into consideration as well the hermeneutical significance not only of translation (from the Hebrew or Greek) but especially of the *language itself*. It is this—what Robinson refers to as the "interpretative interrelatedness" of these three aspects: language, translation, and exposition—which is held to have profound implications for the hermeneutical task and to serve as an indication of its true breadth. Hence in an effort to distinguish the more primal, foundational nature of this outlook over against the earlier, more limited conception, the leading movement in current developments refers to itself as the "new hermeneutic" (singular) in distinction from hermeneutics (plural).

It needs especially to be underscored that what is central to this viewpoint is its concern with the phenomenon of language. Nothing is more characteristic of contemporary hermeneutic than its attention to language, be it that of the text *or* the interpreter. In this connection, two emphases of a more formal character stand out: (1) The first of these is the positive and indispensable role of language in understanding. Language is not secondary to meaning. Language is not the surface distortion of a presumably deeper level of meaning. Rather, one must make his point of departure, as Robinson puts it, "the unbroken linguisticality of understanding." (2) A second stress, correlate with the first, is that *all language is itself interpretation*. The significant implication of this point, so far as the text is concerned, is that as it points to the subject matter, the language of the text is not only in need of interpretation but is already itself an initial interpretation of the subject matter. In terms of this combination of factors: the necessary correlation of language and understanding and the hermeneutically problematic character of all language, one can begin to see why the question of hermeneutics has taken on such central importance. Hermeneutics has (of necessity, as we shall see) come more and more to deal with the phenomenon of understanding itself. It has felt compelled to concern itself with the nature of understanding, how understanding is at all possible, and other related and equally crucial questions: what is meaning? what is the nature of language? what is the precise relation between language and meaning? In other words, the hermeneutical vista has been extended to include some of the most basic questions and problems that man raises and tries to answer; and these are being treated as specifically hermeneutical questions and problems. To describe the situation in a way which serves to point up the revolutionary reshaping of theology which is taking place, we may observe that the action confined formerly to the area of prolegomena to systematic theology is now taking place on a broad front which involves equally all of the theological disciplines. In a word, today theology *is* hermeneutic.

This background needs to be kept in view in any approach to the matter of hermeneutics. Such an awareness, moreover, is particularly integral to a consideration of the topic I have been asked to deal with this evening: the question of hermeneutics as it relates to the study of the New Testament. For it is primarily in the area of New Testament studies that the contemporary preoccupation with hermeneutics which dominates all of the theological disciplines has had its origin and continues to receive its stimulus and direction. Hence

4. James M. Robinson and John B. Cobb Jr., eds., *The New Hermeneutic*, New Frontiers in Theology 2 (New York: Harper & Row, 1964), 1–77.

the scope of this paper has been kept broad deliberately. It is intended as an orientation, to provide a necessary first step toward understanding an exceedingly complex state of affairs. First, I shall try to sketch somewhat further but still in necessarily bold strokes the origin and contours of the controlling hermeneutical outlook of our day, and then, with my special interest in the New Testament, to indicate something of the response which appears to be demanded. The discussion which follows may serve to bring out required qualifications and corrections.

Contemporary hermeneutics is intelligible only as it is seen to have its proximate roots in the so-called "Enlightenment." That is, contemporary hermeneutics has its origin in that period (during the latter part of the seventeenth and during the eighteenth century) when the principle of human autonomy—which has always been latent in the heart of man—begins to come to consistent, well-worked-out, one may say, blatant expression. Man's reason is canonized as the final authority. The notion of an external authority of equal magnitude, be it that of Scripture or the church, is emphatically rejected. Coupled with the elimination of what has been referred to as the "God-hypothesis," is an assertion of unbounded confidence in the ability of man to penetrate the mysteries of the cosmic order. History and nature are presumed capable of a completely immanent explanation. The pointed hermeneutical significance of this Enlightenment principle of autonomy may be stated in a single sentence: "Man is his own interpreter."

The consequences of this hermeneutical outlook for the interpretation of the Bible in particular are far-reaching. Several factors need to be noted here, factors which, it should be stressed, are inextricably related: (1) The doctrine of verbal inspiration, the notion of the divinely spirated, God-breathed origin of the biblical text is abandoned along with the broader understanding of the nature of God and his activity of which this doctrine is a part. (2) A distinction begins to be made, an element of discontinuity introduced, between revelation, the Word of God, on the one hand, and the Bible, the words of men, on the other. (3) The methodological inference which is inevitably drawn is that no exceptions are to be granted to the Bible when it is dealt with as a text. It is to be treated like any other document which comes down to us out of the past. Scripture like all things historical has perhaps its relative right but no more than that. The presence of errors is a necessary methodological assumption. To put the matter more formally, the Bible (like any other historical document) is held to be the proper object of that methodology which in the past two hundred years has become more and more clearly defined and universally applied, the so-called "historical-critical" method. According to this method, the task of interpretation consists not only in explaining the text but also in passing judgment on the authenticity of what is reported and the rightness of the views which are expressed. In short, the center of authority passes from the text of Scripture to the interpreter.

The awesome, truly abysmal difficulties of this position were not immediately apparent. One may say that in its initial stages the "Enlightenment" was blinded by what is recognized on all sides today to be an incredibly naive, dogmatic Rationalistic outlook. However, it did not take long for the fundamental problem to surface. Because there are so many facets to this problem, it can be given various formulations. For our purposes it may be put as follows: if all historical phenomena (the biblical text included) are exposed to the corrosive effects of time, the relativity of history; then by what reason, on what basis, do the interpreter and his interpretation escape this same relativizing erosion and decay?

1111

It is not inaccurate to say that this is *the* question which (in one way or another) has moved virtually all theological and philosophical reflection during the past 150 years. To express it again in the plaintive words of Ernst Troeltsch: "Where in life was support to be found, if all of its contents are historically conditioned and therefore fleeting and transitory?"[5] The nineteenth century may be seen as one long, involved but futile attempt to evade the inevitable answer. Idealistic philosophy, in particular, gives special attention to this problem and seeks to secure the autonomous human subject by establishing that personality (or some aspect thereof) is untouched by and therefore impervious to the flow of history. The result, however, was a hopeless historicism which the periodic revival of a rancid rationalism could perhaps temporally suppress but not alleviate.

On the whole, the twentieth century has been somewhat more sober and careful. To be more precise, the movements within the orbit defined by the axis between Barth and Bultmann have shown themselves to be more sober and careful. But this sobriety does not involve in any final sense a repudiation of Enlightenment presuppositions. It by no means includes a rejection of the "historical-critical" method of biblical interpretation. On the contrary, this method is applied with increasing refinement and rigor. It is held to be a common, extra-theological motive. Acceptance of the historical-critical method is made the price of admission to the guild of theologians. It bears repeating here that the principal developments in theology during this century are not an abandonment, only a more subtle recasting, a more shaded reassertion, of the principle of autonomy. Hence the designation of these developments (or segments of them) as a "neo-orthodoxy" is a misnomer whose inappropriateness becomes increasingly apparent.

Contemporary theology does differ from that of the nineteenth century, however, in that it has given up trying to secure man against history. On the contrary, it has come to assert—and to assert emphatically—the historicness (*Geschichtlichkeit*) of human existence. This notion of historicness is a difficult and many-faceted one. It has built into it the basic structural elements of the dominant theological outlook of our day. At this point in our discussion, however, it is sufficient to note in particular that it involves the idea of the radical temporality, the transitoriness, the unmitigated relativity, of man's being.

Such an outlook is not without significant consequences for hermeneutics. The primary hermeneutical implication now is that *both*—the interpreter as well as the text—are caught up and swept along in the relativizing flow of history. No longer is the interpreter held to survey the text in regal objectivity and presuppositionless splendor. Rather he, like the text he seeks to interpret, is limited in his outlook and restricted by his presuppositions, which are bound to give way and be replaced in another time and place. This "preunderstanding" of the interpreter, however, is absolutely essential. No interpretation can take place without it.

Hence that which gives distinguishing character to contemporary hermeneutic is its understanding of interpretation as *dialogical* in nature. Interpretation is dialogue in the most profound and fundamental sense of the word. The hermeneutical situation is understood as the interplay, the conversation, between text and interpreter, each with its definitely restricted perspective, each with its only limited validity. It is this back and forth movement which has given rise to speaking about the "hermeneutical circle." In dealing with the text, the interpreter is not a spectator in the balcony, but an actor on the stage. He too is involved

---

5. "Wo gab es einen Halt im Leben, wenn alle seine Inhalte historisch bedingt und also historisch vergänglich sind?"; quoted by H.-G. Gadamer, "Historismus," in *Religion in Geschichte und Gegenwart*, 3rd ed., 3:370.

in the flow of history. Consequently, not only does he interrogate and interpret the text, but the text addresses, challenges, "interprets" him (the interpreter).

The revelation or, to describe it in more explicitly hermeneutical fashion, the meaning which *occurs* in this moment of interpretative encounter between text and interpreter is the claim upon his person which the interpreter hears, acknowledges, and responds to. This encounter opens up to him the possibility of his existence which is realized in his action; existence is constituted in a free, autonomous expression of love. It is essential to grasp, then, that this claim which the interpreter hears, this staking out of possibility, is not to be explained *horizontally*; that is, it is not to be explained in terms of any causal connection between text and interpreter. To be sure, such a genetic tie exists. It is indispensable; without it interpretation, encounter, could not take place. But the meaning, the revelation, which obtains is not to be defined positively in terms of this bond. Certainly, it is not the case that revelation and meaning have to do with the communication of information or commandments which serve as the basis for my decision or course of action. On the contrary, on this dialectical construction, in which history is seen as open-ended, the temporal process as an indeterminate, indefinitely extended flow, something out of the past (the biblical text included) or a past event as such, that is, in its character as past, has no meaning. Rather the meaning of the text is an *occurrence*, that which *takes place* in the ever-repeated and ever-varying moment of encounter with its interpreter. Strictly speaking, then, the meaning of the text is its *future*. Or, to paraphrase the way in which it has been put by one proponent of this position, "The meaning and power of a text are identical."[6]

It is in the same vein that recently the followers of Bultmann, in particular, have begun to speak of a "language event" in describing what takes place between text and interpreter. For this interaction, this dialogue, is held to be the purest exemplification, the most perfect realization, of the linguisticality or the "speaking" character of human existence, that is, authentic historical existence. In other words, man's *Geschichtlichkeit* is said now to consist precisely in his *Sprachlichkeit*; historicness has its focus in linguisticality.[7] A favorite model used to describe the nature of this speech event, this linguisticality, is the distinction between seeing and hearing. Man in his essence is not one who sees, but one who hears. He is not one whose *concreated* task is to subdue the earth and conquer it. He is not so much one who surveys and makes definitive statements about something or someone. Language can be used in this way (as it is for instance in science), but then it is being employed superficially, inauthentically. Rather man is one who is addressed and hears, who ever speaks to and is spoken to. (Here one comes upon the deeper motive for the current stress on preaching and proclamation.) Correlative to this view of man, history is not seen primarily as an ordered, connected sequence of events. Rather its essence is a dynamic, interpersonal reality, fluid and open in character.

Despite the complex and shaded idiom of much of current absorption with the question of hermeneutics, the motive which drives it is not too difficult to understand. In bringing this sketch to a close, I would underscore that the intensity of this preoccupation reflects

6. Gerhard Ebeling, "Word of God and Hermeneutic," *The New Hermeneutic*, 103: "Word is, taken strictly, happening word. It is not enough to inquire into its intrinsic meaning, but that must be joined up with the question of its future, of what it effects. For ultimately the questions as to the content and the power of words are identical."

7. Ernst Fuchs, "Was ist ein Sprachereignis?," *Zur Frage nach dem historischen Jesus, Gesammelte Aufsätze* 2 (Tübingen: J. C. B. Mohr, 1960), 429: "Deshalb ging ich dazu über, die Geschichtlichkeit der Existenz als Sprachlichkeit der Existenz aufzuweisen und den Text selbst als Helfer für dieses Bemühen in Anspruch zu nehmen."

just how pressing has become the dilemma created by the rejection of the divine origin and authority of the Bible. A crisis in understanding is the price paid for autonomy, for making man the interpreter constitutive for meaning and revelation. Ours is a day when, as never before, man has become a question to himself. Man himself has become hermeneutically problematic, and his entire existence is conceived of as one great interpretative endeavor. In a world in which it is held that the only absolute is uncertainty, he searches for norms. From the aimless roll of time in which he is caught up he tries to wrest meaning. On the ever-drifting sands of historical theology he attempts the impossible task of erecting a coherent statement of faith.

The question inevitably arises concerning the response God's people are to make as they are called to confession in this hermeneutically charged atmosphere. Or to restrict ourselves to but one aspect of this question and give it a somewhat more personal tone: what is the responsibility of the theologian? In dealing with this question here, my interest is not so much in a direct confrontation with contemporary hermeneutics. Rather against the background of the outline just given I shall try to indicate several fundamental perspectives which it appears to me must be maintained. It goes without saying that much which could be said and even needs to be said will remain unsaid.

1) Opposition to the presuppositions of the "Enlightenment" must continue to be sharply focused and unabated. To put it positively, the consideration of most profound, most fundamental hermeneutical significance is very simply this: the Bible is God's word. That this is basic is obvious, but just *how* basic does not always appear to be sufficiently grasped.

The Bible is God's word—one must say that this, strictly speaking, is a pre-hermeneutical or, if you will, a meta-hermeneutical consideration. To be sure, the way in which this truth is brought to expression may be challenged. Whether or not the doctrine of verbal inspiration admits to a more adequate expression always remains an open question. But the conviction which is reflected in this statement: the Bible is God's Word—that conviction which arises directly and immediately out of exposure not only (perhaps not even primarily) to the "All Scripture is God-breathed" of 2 Timothy 3:16, but from exposure to Scripture in all its parts—that conviction may not be called in question or made hermeneutically problematic. Let me be crystal clear concerning the conviction I am talking about here. It is *not* a deeply rooted persuasion about the central message of the Bible; it is *not* a being grasped by the basic theme of Scripture, although this, to be sure, is involved. Rather it is a settled conviction, a firm belief, concerning the text *as text*. The words of the text in all their plurality and literality are the words of God. The book of Romans, these words penned in ink on the papyrus (perhaps by an amanuensis!), just as surely as Paul, indeed more properly, have God as author. Again, it is possible to challenge the propriety of these statements as far as their form is concerned. It is conceivable that they could be improved upon in terms of their intention. It could be said better. However, at the same time it needs to be recognized that in the debate over Scripture there comes a point when, if there is still a tendency to qualify the "is" in the statement "the Bible is God's Word," to introduce an element of discontinuity, no matter how slight, between "God's word" and "Bible," if there is still an inclination to shade the divine authorship of Scripture; then, most probably, the problem is not one of simply hermeneutical proportions, that is, there is not simply need for further clarification. Rather the problem has a pre-hermeneutical, a pre-functional basis. There is need for that pre-hermeneutical clarification known otherwise as the regenerating, convincing, teaching power of the Holy Spirit about which Paul writes in 1 Corinthians 2. Belief in the divine origin of the text, of course, saves no one. But it appears to me increasingly necessary to insist that the conviction that the words of the Bible are the very words of God is an integral and inamissible component of saving faith.

Perhaps there are some even in this group who feel that this puts the matter too strongly. It is certainly true that in all this concentrated speaking about the text one can fall into abstraction. There is danger of losing sight of the fact that Scripture has its place and functions only as the instrument of the resurrected Christ, the life-giving Spirit. Or one can fail to recognize that God's Word is broader than the Bible, that Scripture has its origin within the larger history of God's revealing activity. It strikes me, however, that these are neither the most real nor the most pressing dangers which confront the Reformed world today. At any rate, the recognition that the Bible is God's word is the underlying consideration which directs and regulates that hermeneutical reflection which alone is appropriate to and demanded by the text. Where this direction and control are wanting, in one form or another, perhaps quite subtly, meaning and certainty begin to be sought *in spite of* the text, and a hermeneutical dilemma of crisis proportions, like the one we are witnessing today, will be the eventual and inevitable result.

2) All the hermeneutical consequences which flow from the conviction that the Bible is God's word cannot possibly be enumerated here. Central is recognition of the unity of Scripture as text, "the consent of all the parts," as the Westminster Confession (WCF 1.5) puts it, and hence the hermeneutical principle of the Reformation that Scripture is its own best interpreter. A rather obvious factor—yet one which is all too frequently overlooked, just in a time when it is in need of particular stress—is the basic understanding of the nature of language which is given. On almost all sides in contemporary discussion language is dealt with as if it were a purely human phenomenon. No attitude is more at variance with Scripture, both as a phenomenon and in terms of its teaching. According to the Bible, language is primarily, natively, antecedently divine in character. Speaking is first of all and intrinsically an activity of God. And it is in this light, with this fundamental qualification, that man's linguistic activity is viewed. Man in his linguistic function as in all else he is and does (I would say, man especially and pointedly in his linguistic functions) is understood as the creature who is God's image. In other words, as our being has God's being as exemplar (we exist because he exists), as our knowledge is an analogue of his knowledge (we know because he knows), so our language is derived from his language. We speak because he has spoken and continues to speak.

This is a hermeneutical axiom than which there is none more basic. It provides an indispensable perspective for understanding the "hermeneutical situation" so far as the text of Scripture is concerned. The language or, more pointedly, the interpretation of God is the ground for our language, our interpretation. The former provides both the possibility and the necessity for the latter. Hence in contrast to the currently prevailing notion of dialogue between text and interpreter, one must recognize the essentially *monological* nature of this relationship. To be sure, as Professor Berkouwer is always reminding us,[8] one must not lose sight of the element of correlation and reciprocity. We may even speak of dialogue and relativity. But now we are talking about that dialogue between creator and creature—not

---

8. E.g., recently and with explicit reference to the question of hermeneutics, *De Heilige Schrift* (Kampen: J. H. Kok, 1966), 1:163–67.

an endless back and forth movement, but dialogue which in all its moments has God-given direction and structure and hence in its deepest sense is monologue. We are talking about relativity, not that of a chip tossed about on the formless flow of time, but of a part in an organically unfolding process, in the coherent whole of history. It is not the case that text and interpreter call back and forth to each other interminably, each with impaired validity and as each is caught up in the sweep of an open and indeterminate history. Rather the text is that *historical* instance by which the sovereign Lord of history, the one who knows end from beginning, calls forth the interpretative response of man in the interests of accomplishing his determinate purpose and good pleasure.

3) From what has been said it becomes clear just how wrong and confusing it is, with an eye to the contemporary scene, to speak of *the* hermeneutical problem, as if all without differentiation are entangled in the same dilemma. Those who know the text to be the voice of the great Shepherd need not and cannot assume the burden of hermeneutical difficulties created by those who refuse to listen. For the former the question of hermeneutics has a specific, definitely qualified form, a form which is not self-defeating but life-giving: What is the precise nature of the unity of the Bible? How *does* the Bible interpret itself? Or, in the classic language of the Confession (WCF 1.10), how does the Holy Spirit speak in the Scripture? One must grasp that also, one should say especially, in the area of hermeneutics the antithesis makes itself felt.

Once this basic distinction has been made, however, it is essential to stress that the question of hermeneutics, or better—and here I think we learn from current debate—the question of theological method remains a vital concern to the church. This will probably always be the case, at least until the resurrection transformation of believers becomes open, until faith turns to sight. In bringing this paper to a close, I wish to deal with one point which, it appears to me, deserves special attention in this connection, a point which lies at the heart of a methodologically responsible approach to the New Testament.

In seeking to maintain the settled and abiding character of God's word, particularly over against the activistic thought-currents of our day, it is tempting to conclude that the solution lies in recourse to some form of staticism. In other words, there is danger that, in one way or another, we begin to treat time as an enemy of God's truth and seek to secure ourselves against history. One must certainly share Professor Zuidema's recently expressed pique over the caricature that orthodoxy views the Bible as a book which has been dropped down straight out of heaven.[9] Still, it is difficult to deny that in the orthodox tradition justice has not been done to the historical character of the Bible, either in terms of its origin or its contents. There has been and continues to be a tendency to view Scripture as a quarry of proof texts for the building of a dogmatic edifice, as a collection of moral principles for the construction of a system of ethics. That is to say, there is a tendency to force the Bible into a mold, to impose upon it a unity which, to a greater or lesser degree, is foreign to it.

The Bible *is* "the only infallible rule of faith and practice." Scripture *does* teach "what man is to believe concerning God and what duty God requires of man." But the biblical revelation is and does these things only in its distinguishing character as either description or explanation, that is, interpretation of God's redemptive *activity*. Inscripturated revelation never stands by itself. It is always concerned either explicitly or implicitly with redemptive

9. "Holy Scripture and Its Key," *International Reformed Bulletin* 32–33 (Jan.-Apr. 1968): 49.

accomplishment. God's speech is invariably related to his actions. Redemption is revelation's reason for being. An unbiblical, one could say, quasi-gnostic notion is the inevitable result, when one views revelation of and by itself or as providing timeless truths, self-evident in and of themselves. Precisely in its character as *revelation* the Bible transcends itself. It points beyond itself to the history of redemption which it infallibly attests and expounds. In other words, the specific unity of Scripture is redemptive-historical in character.

Recognition of the orientation of revelatory word to redemptive act or, more broadly, of the history of revelation to the history of redemption has become a theological commonplace. It was introduced into Reformed scholarship primarily and most effectively by Geerhardus Vos and has been taken up by others. It does not appear to me, however, that the *methodological* significance of this correlation has been reflected upon sufficiently. Here I can give only the briefest indication of the lines along which it would seem this reflection should proceed for the study of the New Testament.

A fundamental consideration is that interpretation of the Bible must understand itself as *interpretation of interpretation*. To be sure, in saying this one must not obscure the important differences between our interpretation and the interpretation furnished by the biblical writers. Ours is dependent upon and derived from theirs. Theirs is God-breathed and inerrant; ours is always tentative and in need of correction. *But* these differences are properly understood only as they are seen in the light of a more basic, underlying *continuity*. Both—our interpretation and the interpretation provided by Scripture—are concerned with the same subject matter. Both are oriented to, and derived from, the history of redemption. In a word, they share a common *interpretative* interest.

This point can be made more precise and concrete as far as the writers of the New Testament are concerned. From a redemptive-historical perspective—a perspective which for the believer there is and can be none more basic—the interpreter today is in the *same situation* as was, say, the apostle Paul. Together they look back upon the climactic events of Christ's death, resurrection, and ascension, while together they "wait for his Son from heaven" (1 Thess. 1:10). Both are concerned with explicating the same redemptive-historical tension between "already" and "not yet" in which they are caught up. In dealing with the New Testament, then, we must avoid that distorting outlook which consists, as Vos puts it, in "viewing the new revelation too much by itself, and not sufficiently as introductory and basic to the large period following."[10] Rather we must see, again quoting Vos, that "we ourselves live just as much in the N.T. as did Peter and Paul and John."[11] I would express it somewhat more pointedly by saying that, in terms of those factors which are most basic in defining the task of interpretation, namely, the nature of the subject matter and the position of the interpreter, we must understand that our interpretation today, that is, interpretation in the context of the church, stands closer to the teaching of Paul or the preaching of Peter than the latter stand to the prophecy of Isaiah or the psalms of David.

This outlook has many implications which need to be explored further. I indicate here one which especially interests me. The proper, pointed theological concern of Christ's people is concern with history, the history which has realized their redemption. This concern begins already in the New Testament. More particularly, in a dialectically gifted, synthetically disposed thinker like Paul, the coherent normative statement for which the church strives

10. Geerhardus Vos, *Biblical Theology: Old and New Testaments* (Grand Rapids: Eerdmans, 1948), 325.
11. Ibid., 326.

begins to take shape. This means, then, that over its entire expanse, particularly the areas of soteriology and eschatology, systematic theology must work hand in hand with New Testament biblical theology and be guided by it. More than has been the case heretofore, dogmatics must be controlled by biblical theology, not only in its material but also in the way it structures this material, in the questions it asks, and perhaps even in the methods it employs. Among other things, such control should help to insure that, when drawn, the "good and necessary consequence" of which the Confession speaks (WCF 1.6) is really good and necessary.

In the days in which we find ourselves it is necessary more than ever that every believer have a sense of history—a sense of redemptive history. But it is especially demanded of the minister of the Word in whatever capacity that he understand himself in his labors as one, together with Paul, "upon whom the ends of the ages have come" (1 Cor. 10:11). There is need that in his methods, as in all else, everyone involved in the theological enterprise—not just the New Testament scholar—seek to make good his status, shared with the apostle, as "minister of a new covenant, not of the letter, but of the Spirit" (2 Cor. 3:6). This, it seems to me, was the approach of that prince of Reformed exegetes, Geerhardus Vos. It explains not only why he reaped such a rich harvest from Scripture but also why, in so doing, he was able to undercut heresies and errors so effectively, often before they had even entered the heads of their proponents. On the field of hermeneutical conflict as elsewhere a good offense will prove to be the best defense.

Part Ten

THE AUTHORITY OF THE
OLD TESTAMENT AND NEW TESTAMENT
CANON OF SCRIPTURE

NOT ONLY IS IT ESSENTIAL to define the inspiration of Scripture and to explore the way it ought to be interpreted, but it is also crucial to establish the limit of the canon of Scripture—in other words, to have a list of the books belonging to special revelation. This issue was raised early in the history of the Christian church; later the Reformers challenged both the Catholic Church's list of Old Testament books and her understanding of the basis of their inclusion in the canon (many of the confessions included in this anthology deal with those issues); nowadays, the issue of the canon remains urgent, especially since many want to erode the distinction between New Testament writings and other documents from the first century. On this fundamental issue, we present three contributions by scholars from Westminster Seminary, one on the Old Testament and two on the New Testament.

While E. J. Young's articles and Ned B. Stonehouse's article are taken from the earlier symposium by Westminster professors, *The Infallible Word* (1946), Richard B. Gaffin Jr.'s essay comes from another collection by Westminster professors, *Inerrancy and Hermeneutic* (1988). Like John Murray in the same volume (cf. chap. 45 in this anthology), Young bases his treatment of the authority of the Old Testament on the objective self-witness of the Bible and the inner witness of the Holy Spirit. For him the Old Testament is a collection of authoritative writings with a history paralleling that of God's dealing redemptively with his people Israel. In this he anticipates the more comprehensive study of Meredith G. Kline, *The Structure of Biblical Authority* (1971). His adoption of the threefold Jewish division of the Old Testament reinforces the decision of the Reformation to follow Judaism in defining the limits of the Old Testament canon.

The two articles on the New Testament canon also follow a biblical-theological approach to the question. Stonehouse begins by clarifying what is meant by the authority of the New Testament. It derives its authority not from the church, but from what the New Testament itself (the self-witness of Scripture) asserts about it. His analysis is also sensitive to the different genres of the New Testament. Thus Stonehouse combines in his analysis of the issue the best insights of the Reformation and later Reformed theologians (from Princeton and the Netherlands) with the latest developments in biblical theology. The title of Gaffin's article, "The New Testament as Canon," echoes the title of the work on the canon edited by Ernst Käsemann; in it, Gaffin addresses some of the latest challenges to the New Testament canon—for instance, the idea of a canon within the canon. Following the lead of one of his mentors, Herman Ridderbos, Gaffin integrates the findings of biblical theology with the issues of canonics. Gaffin is also strong on the question of the completeness of the New Testament in light of recent views on the Holy Spirit's work.

The Authority of the Old Testament

Edward J. Young, "The Authority of the Old Testament," in *The Infallible Word*, ed. Paul Woolley, 3rd rev. printing (Philadelphia: Presbyterian and Reformed, 1967), 55–91; reprinted from Philadelphia: Presbyterian Guardian, 1946.

Edward J. Young (1907–68) belongs to the first generation of Westminster professors, though he started to teach in 1936, only one year before Machen's death. He studied at Stanford University and San Francisco Theological Seminary before transferring to Westminster. He did graduate studies at Leipzig with Albrecht Alt and completed his Ph.D. at Dropsie College in 1943. Young was a gifted linguist, and he used his knowledge of many languages to the service of Old Testament scholarship. He was also an ordained minister in the Orthodox Presbyterian Church, and actively contributed to her life. He was a popular speaker and penned several devotional writings. His focus in Old Testament studies was on the Prophets. Notably, he wrote a three-volume commentary on Isaiah, *The Book of Isaiah* (1965, 1969, 1972). His work is marked both by a thorough knowledge of critical scholarship and by a clear stand for and defense of the Bible in its supernatural character. His *An Introduction to the Old Testament* (1949) and *Studies in Genesis One* (1964) well illustrate this point.

Young contributed to the 1946 symposium on Scripture by the Westminster faculty *The Infallible Word*, the volume to which Murray had contributed the opening article (see chap. 45 above). In his piece on the canon of the Old Testament, "The Authority of the Old Testament," Young addresses issues such as Christ's relation to the Old Testament, the canonization of the Old Testament, and critical scholarship. His argument fits nicely with Murray's argument. Young assumes the objective witness of Scripture and the inner witness of the Holy Spirit. He argues that the Old Testament should be viewed as a growing collection of authoritative writings in the community of Israel. This view builds on a redemptive-historical understanding of Scripture and anticipates aspects of the more comprehensive study of Meredith G. Kline, *The Structure of Biblical Authority* (1971). Young also advocates the threefold Jewish division of the Old Testament, which structures his *An Introduction to the Old Testament*.

Bibliography: Richard B. Gaffin Jr. "Young, Edward Joseph (1907–1968)." P. 284 in *DP&RTA*. Allan Harman. "Edward Joseph Young." Pp. 189–201 in *Bible Interpreters of the 20th Century*. Tremper Longman III. "Young, E(dward) J(oseph) (1907–1968)." Pp. 1068–72 in *DMBI* (2007). John J. Yeo. *Plundering the Egyptians: The Old Testament and Historical Criticism at Westminster Seminary (1929–1998)*. Lanham, MD: University Press of America, 2010. Pp. 93–206.

In the versions of the Old Testament commonly in use in Christendom there are thirty-nine books. These same thirty-nine books are also found in the Hebrew Scriptures. By the Jews they have been looked upon as sacred, and by the Christian church they are considered to be the very Word of God.

It is interesting to note that throughout the entire present era, the Christian church has accepted the Scriptures of the Old Testament as the infallible revelation of God. Nor is such an attitude toward them representative merely of a portion of the church; it is, rather, the expression of a conviction which appears to have characterized the church universal.

This conviction was also shared by our Lord himself. Christ regarded the Hebrew Scriptures as divinely revealed and as absolutely authoritative. He appealed to them constantly to support his claims. "Till heaven and earth pass," he said, "one jot or one tittle shall in no wise pass from the law, till all be fulfilled" (Matt. 5:18). Our Lord's earthly life was lived in the very atmosphere of the Old Testament Scriptures, and because he believed them to be God's Word, his church has followed him in this respect.

Was Christ, however, justified in so regarding the Old Testament, and are Christians today justified in sharing his opinion? This question is pertinent, indeed; for now, as probably never before, this traditional attitude is being questioned and doubted and attacked. What grounds has the Christian for his belief that the Old Testament Scriptures are the very Word of God? How may he be sure that these writings are indeed authoritative and reliable? What assurance does he possess that, in the law and the prophets and the writings, God has spoken, and that he, the Christian, may rest upon these promises, convinced that he is heeding, not the word of man, but the word of the living God? These are the questions which will occupy our attention in the present chapter.

A. Christ and the Old Testament

At first sight it might appear that for the devout Christian the answer to the questions which have just been raised is not at all difficult. "Jesus Christ was indeed justified in considering the Old Testament to be the Word of God and therefore I also may so regard it," is no doubt the response which many a true believer in Christ would offer. And his response, we think, would be perfectly correct for, as a matter of fact, Jesus Christ did look upon the Old Testament as inspired Scripture.

So simple a solution to the problem, however, will by no means meet with universal approval. It is necessary to examine more fully, therefore, what is involved in the assertion that Christ considered the Old Testament to be the Word of God. In making such an examination, we shall proceed upon the assumption that the words of Christ as they are presented in the New Testament are fully worthy of trust. This is not the place to discuss certain questions raised by form and source criticism which would appear to impair the New Testament picture of Jesus. The subjective nature of these types of criticism will, as time passes, more and more force itself into the open, and the day will come, we believe, when they will be largely discarded as legitimate methods of studying the Bible. At any rate, we shall regard the witness to our Lord which the New Testament offers as completely authoritative.

It must be apparent to anyone who reads the Gospels carefully that Jesus Christ, in the days of his flesh, looked upon that body of writings which is known as the Old Testament as constituting an organic whole. To him the Scriptures were a harmonious unit which bore a unique message and witness. Nothing could be farther from the truth than to say that he thought of the Scriptures as merely a group of writings which were in conflict among themselves and which bore no particular relationship to one another. This may easily be seen by the consideration of one or two relevant passages.

When, for example, the Jews took up stones to cast at our Lord, believing him to have been guilty of blasphemy, he opposed them by an appeal to the Old Testament (cf. John 10:31–36). In this appeal he quoted Psalm 82:6, and assumed the truth of what was stated in the Psalm by asserting that "the scripture cannot be broken." The force of his argument is very clear, and may be paraphrased as follows: "What is stated in this verse from the Psalms is true because this verse belongs to that body of writings known as Scripture, and the Scripture possesses an authority so absolute in character that *it cannot be broken*." When Christ here employs the word Scripture, he has in mind, therefore, not a particular verse in the Psalms, but rather the entire group of writings of which this one verse is a part.

That Christ regarded the Scriptures as constituting a unit is also seen when, at the time of his betrayal, he acknowledged the need for his arrest and sufferings if the Scriptures were to be fulfilled (cf. Matt. 26:54). Indeed, he was concerned that the Scriptures must be fulfilled. To him it was more important that this should take place than that he should escape from arrest. By his use of the plural, he made it abundantly clear that there existed a plurality of writings, each of which had this in common with the others: that it belonged to the category of Scripture and that, taken as a whole, it had direct reference to the sufferings which he was about to undergo. Thus, by his manner of speech, did he bear witness to the fact that the Old Testament is an organic whole and so, by implication, to the consent and harmony of all its parts.

This testimony of our Lord to the nature of the Old Testament is by no means an isolated phenomenon. Rather, not only is it made expressly clear by certain individual passages,[1] but also it underlies his entire treatment of the Scriptures. In adopting such an attitude Christ placed himself squarely in opposition to those views, so prevalent in our day, which look upon the Old Testament as merely a collection of more or less loosely related, heterogeneous material, a library rather than a Book.

1. Cf. Matthew 21:42; 22:29; Mark 14:49; John 6:45; 15:25.

Not only did Jesus Christ look upon the Old Testament as forming an organic whole but also he believed that both as a unit and in its several parts it was finally and absolutely authoritative. To it appeal might be made as to the ultimate authority. Its voice was final. When the Scriptures spoke, man must obey. From them there was no appeal. When, for example, the Tempter would have the Son of God command the stones to be made bread, he was silenced by the assertion, "It is written." This appeal to the Old Testament ended the matter. That which was written was for Christ the deciding voice.

Not only, however, was such authority attributed to the Scriptures as a unit and to particular verses or utterances, but it was also extended to include individual words and even letters. This is shown by a statement such as the following, "It is easier for heaven and earth to pass, than for one tittle of the law to fail" (Luke 16:17). In some instances Christ based his argument merely upon a word, as for example when, seeking to refute the Jews, he singled out the word "gods" in Psalm 82:6. A careful reading of the Gospels will reveal the fact that the Scriptures of the Old Testament, in all their parts, were believed by Christ to be authoritative.

Is there, however, any dependable method by which one may determine precisely what books Christ regarded as belonging to the category of Scripture? Is it not possible that some books upon which he placed the stamp of his approval have been irretrievably lost, whereas others which would not have been recognized by him are now looked upon as part of the Old Testament?

It may with confidence be said that Christ recognized as canonical the same books as those which comprise the Old Testament as we have it today. Of course, he did not leave a list of these books nor did he expressly quote from each of them. Hence, we must look elsewhere for evidence to support our statement.

From our Lord's references to the Old Testament it is possible to determine the extent of the canon which he recognized. He quoted abundantly, and the nature of his quotation often lends its sanction not only to the book in which the quotation is found, but even to the entire collection itself. The force of this impresses itself upon us more and more as we notice how Christ chose from this and that book statements which would enforce and support his arguments. It appears that his earthly life was steeped in the teaching of the Old Testament. Not only were whole verses frequently upon his lips, but also his own speech was clothed with expressions from the Scriptures.

There is, however, one passage in particular in which he gives a clue as to the extent of the Old Testament of his clay. On the walk to Emmaus, after his resurrection, he said to his companions, "These are the words which I spake unto you, while I was yet with you, that all things must be fulfilled, which were written in the law of Moses, and in the prophets, and in the psalms, concerning me" (Luke 24:44). Here he clearly recognizes that there are three divisions to the Old Testament, and that the things which were written in each of these divisions must be fulfilled. The designation "law of Moses" refers, of course, to the first five books of the Bible; the "prophets" includes the historical books and the works of the great writing prophets. As to the identity of these two divisions there would seem to be little doubt.

What, however, is meant by Christ's use of the word "psalms"? Did he thereby intend to refer to all the books in the third division of the canon, or did he merely have in mind the book of Psalms itself? The latter alternative, we think, is probably correct. Christ singled out the book of Psalms, it would appear, not so much because it was the best known and most influential book of the third division, but rather because in the Psalms there were many predictions about himself. This was the Christological book, *par excellence*, of the third division of the Old Testament canon.

Most of the books of this third division do not contain direct messianic prophecies.[2] Hence, if Christ had used a technical designation to indicate this third division, he would probably have weakened his argument to a certain extent. But by the reference to the Psalms he directs the minds of his hearers immediately to that particular book in which occur the greater number of references to himself.

This does not necessarily mean that he did not make reference to the messianic prophecies which appear, for example, in the book of Daniel. Nor does it mean that the third division of the canon was not yet complete. It would appear, rather, that by his language Christ set the seal of his approval upon the books of the Old Testament which were in use among the Jews of his day, and that this Old Testament consisted of three definite divisions, the Law, the Prophets and a third division which as yet had probably not received any technical designation.[3]

B. The Canonization of the Scriptures

When Christ thus set the seal of his approval upon the Jewish Scriptures of his day, it meant that he considered those Scriptures to be divinely inspired. When, however, did the Jewish people who lived before him so come to regard them? To this question many answers are given, and it is to this question that we must now direct our attention.

By the term canonical writings is meant those writings which constitute the inspired rule of faith and life. Canonical books, in other words, are those books which are regarded as divinely inspired. The criterion of a book's canonicity, therefore, is its inspiration. If a book has been inspired of God, it is canonical, whether accepted by men as such or not. It is God and not man who determines whether a book is to belong to the canon. Therefore, if a certain writing has indeed been the product of divine inspiration, it belongs in the canon from the moment of its composition.

That this is so, appears from the very nature of the case. If man alone were capable in his own strength of identifying accurately the Word of God, then man would be equal in knowledge with God. If God is truly God, the creator of all things and utterly independent of all that he has created, it follows that he alone can identify what he has spoken. He alone can say, "This is my Word, but that has not proceeded from my mouth."

Hence, it will be seen that the word "canon" means far more than merely a list of books. If this low view of the meaning of the word be adopted, we by no means even begin to do justice to the various factors which are involved. The reason why many discussions of the problem of the canon are unsatisfactory is that they proceed upon the assumption that

---

2. The following books are reckoned as belonging to the Writings or *Hagiographa:* the three poetical books, Psalms, Proverbs, Job; the five *Megilloth:* Song of Solomon, Ruth, Lamentations, Ecclesiastes, Esther; and Daniel, Ezra, Nehemiah, 1 and 2 Chronicles. Apparently, however, this classification has not always been held. See Robert Dick Wilson, "The Rule of Faith and Life," *Princeton Theological Review* 26, 3 (July 1928): 423–50; Solomon Zeitlin, *An Historical Study of the Canonization of the Hebrew Scriptures* (Philadelphia: The American Academy for Jewish Research, 1933).

3. There is every reason for believing that the canon of Christ and the canon of the Jews of his day were identical. There is no evidence whatever of any dispute between him and the Jews as to the canonicity of any Old Testament book. What Christ opposed was not the canon which the Pharisees accepted but the oral tradition which would make this canon void. From statements in Josephus and the Talmud, it is possible to learn the extent of the Jewish canon of Christ's day.

the canon is merely a list of books which the Jewish people itself came to regard as divine, and they neglect the theological aspect of the question almost entirely.[4] To the Christian, however, the word "canon" has a far higher connotation; to him it constitutes the inspired rule of faith and practice. The writings of the Bible claim to be the Word of God, and their contents are in entire harmony with this claim. The Christian recognizes the Scriptures as inspired, because they are such, and bear in themselves the evidences of their divinity. Basic, therefore, to any consideration of how man comes to recognize the Bible as God's Word is the fact that it is indeed divine.

It is one of the strengths of the Westminster Confession that it so clearly and forcefully states this fact. All the canonical books of the Old and New Testaments are expressly said to be the Word of God written (WCF 1.2), and to be given by inspiration of God to be the rule of faith and life. Furthermore, the Confession presents several of the reasons why the Bible evidences itself to be the Word of God. It mentions "the heavenliness of the matter, the efficacy of the doctrine, the majesty of the style, the consent of all the parts, the scope of the whole (which is to give all glory to God), the full discovery it makes of the only way of man's salvation, the many other incomparable excellencies, and the entire perfection thereof" (WCF 1.5).

In themselves, however, these arguments do not bring us to full persuasion that the Bible is God's Word, and the reason for this is that the human understanding is darkened by sin. What is needed is an opening of the eyes that man may see what is so clear. This opening of the eyes of the understanding is the work of God's Spirit, as the Confession says, "our full persuasion and assurance of the infallible truth and divine authority thereof, is from the inward work of the Holy Spirit bearing witness by and with the Word in our hearts" (WCF 1.5). What the Confession teaches is the teaching of the Scriptures. For example, Paul writes: "But as it is written, What no eye has seen, nor ear heard, nor the heart of man conceived, what God has prepared for those who love him, God has revealed to us through the Spirit. For the Spirit searches everything, even the depths of God" (1 Cor. 2:9–10; cf. also, Heb. 4:12; 1 Cor. 2:3–5; 1 Thess. 1:5a; 1 John 2:20, 27).

Without attempting to give a full definition of this doctrine of the internal testimony of the Holy Spirit we may say that bearing witness by and with the Word in our hearts the Holy Spirit convinces and persuades us that the Scriptures are the Word of God.

These points will perhaps be more clearly understood if we examine the history of the collection of the Old Testament Scriptures. No complete history of this process has been preserved, but certain important statements are made in the Bible itself, and these statements must be taken into consideration in any discussion of the subject.

The Law of Moses

In the first place, therefore, we turn to the first five books of the Old Testament, which are commonly known as the Pentateuch or the Law of Moses. Traditionally, by both Jews and Christians, Moses has been regarded as the author of these books. We believe that tradition is in this point correct, and that the essential Mosaic authorship of the Pentateuch may be maintained. There may indeed be certain few minor additions, such as the account of Moses' death, which were inserted into the Pentateuch under divine inspiration by a later edition, but this by no means runs counter to the common tradition that Moses is the author of these books.

---

4. This question will be discussed more fully at a later point.

To maintain that Moses was the author of the Pentateuch does not imply that he received by direct divine revelation everything that he wrote. Quite probably large portions of the Law had existed in written form before the time of Moses. If this were so it would account for some of the variations in style and emphasis which are often erroneously attributed to different documents. Moses may very well have pieced together different fragments which had been written long before his time. In a certain sense he may have engaged in the work of compiling. He, however, was responsible for the finished work, and in composing this finished work, the writings which we call the Pentateuch, he labored under the superintendence of the Spirit of God.

When these writings had been completed they were accepted by the devout in Israel as divinely authoritative. Express provision was made for their protection and custody. "And it came to pass, when Moses had made an end of writing the words of this law in a book, until they were finished, that Moses commanded the Levites, who bare the ark of the covenant of Jehovah, saying, Take this book of the law, and put it by the side of the ark of the covenant of Jehovah your God, that it may be there for a witness against thee" (Deut. 31:24–26). The priests were commanded to read the Law to the people, "Thou shalt read this law before all Israel in their hearing" (Deut. 31:11). When Israel would have a king, that king was to possess a copy of the Law (Deut. 17:18–19). Joshua was commanded to guide the people in the light of the Law. "This book of the law shall not depart out of thy mouth, but thou shalt meditate thereon day and night, that thou mayest observe to do according to all that is written therein" (Josh. 1:8).

Throughout the history of Israel, the Law was regarded as divinely authoritative. David charged Solomon to give his obedience thereto. Jeroboam was denounced because of disobedience to God's commands. Some of the kings of Judah are particularly commended because of their adherence to the Law, whereas others are condemned for their lack of such adherence. The very exile itself is considered by the sacred writers to be due to infractions of the statutes and the covenant which God made with Israel's ancestors. And on the return from exile, the Israelites governed themselves in accord with the Law of Moses.

It will be seen then that upon the testimony of the only contemporary writings of ancient Israel, the Law of Moses was regarded from the earliest times as divinely inspired and authoritative. It was final. What it commanded was to be obeyed, and what it prohibited was not to be done. Such is the picture which the Old Testament itself presents, if it be accepted as it stands.

The Prophetical Books

Not only was the Law of Moses regarded as God's Word, but the words and writings of the prophets were also so considered. In Deuteronomy it had been said of the prophets that God would put his "words in his [i.e., the prophet's] mouth, and he shall speak unto them all that I shall command him" (Deut. 18:18). The prophets themselves believed that they spoke in the Name of the Lord and that they declared his very word to men. How frequently do they exclaim, "The word of the Lord came unto me, saying . . . ," "Thus saith the Lord . . . ," "Hear the word of the Lord!" The message which they proclaimed, therefore, was, according to their own testimony, not a message of their own devising, but the actual Word of God.

The prophets demanded that same obedience to their words which was due unto the Law of God. They had no hesitation in candidly telling Israel that her calamities and misfortunes had befallen her, not only because of her disobedience to the Law, but also because she had transgressed their words. And they frankly assert that, unless she gives heed to their message, dire distress and suffering will come upon her. The evidence to support these statements is not isolated. Rather, if one will read the prophetical writings to see what is the testimony of the prophets to their authority, he will note how frequently and consistently they assert that they are declaring the final, absolute Word of Jehovah. (Cf., e.g., Isa. 8:5; 31:4; Jer. 3:6; 13:1; Ezek. 21:1; 25:1; Amos 3:1; 7:1–9; etc.)

If, therefore, we are to accept the testimony of the Bible itself, we see that the words of the prophets were regarded in Israel as authoritative, decisive, and inspired. Consequently, it may easily be understood how these words in their written form would be preserved in the church and regarded as the Word of Jehovah.

It is true that the Old Testament does not relate how the books which are commonly called the Former Prophets (i.e., Joshua, Judges, 1 and 2 Samuel, 1 and 2 Kings) came to be included with the other canonical books. However, the answer to this question, it would appear, is readily at hand. The authors of these books, whoever they may have been, were men who occupied the office of prophet. In ancient Israel this was a special and unique office. The prophet was an Israelite who acted as a mediator between God and man. Just as the priest represented the people before God, so the prophet represented God before the people. In a very special sense, therefore, he was the recipient of revelation. God so implanted his words in the prophet's mouth, that the resultant delivered message was the actual Word of God.

Not all prophets wrote down their messages. As we have seen, Israel did gather and preserve the words of those prophets who committed their messages to writing. But no doubt many messages were delivered which were not recorded. However, when men of the status of prophets wrote an interpretative history of Israel, it may readily be understood why such a history would be accepted by the Israelitish church as the Word of God. For in their interpretation of history, these authors often profess to speak as in the Name of God. These writings, therefore, are historical in character, and profess to trace the hand of God in Israel's history.

Furthermore, despite the assertions of some critics, these writings are in harmony with the written prophecies. Not only are they a perfect complement to those written prophecies, but they are a necessary completion to the history contained in the Law of Moses. Upon the basis of the Law of Moses we should expect such a history of the subsequent developments in Israel. Without this interpretative history, much in the prophets would be obscure. So far as is known, none of these books has ever been disputed as to its canonicity. The former prophets, then, were accepted as part of the Word of God, and therefore as canonical, because they were written by men who held the high office of prophet, and who, as inspired prophets, interpreted Israel's history.

The Writings

How did the third division of the Old Testament, the so-called *Hagiographa*, or Writings, come to be collected and regarded as canonical? There is no direct answer given to this question in the Scriptures. The Bible does not tell us who collected these books nor at what time they were gathered. The books which belong to this third division of the canon were written by men inspired of God who nevertheless did not occupy the office of prophet. Some of the authors, however, such as David and Daniel, did possess the prophetic gift although not occupying the official status of prophet. This accounts for the fact that a book such as Daniel is found not among the Prophets but among the Writings. The official status of Daniel, as a careful study of the Old Testament will reveal, was not that of prophet, but of statesman. Daniel, however, did possess the gift of prophecy.

An objection is often made to this argument. If it is true that the status of the authors of the *Hagiographa* was that of inspired men who did not occupy the prophetic office, then the book of Amos, it is claimed, should be included among the *Hagiographa* and not among the Prophets. Amos, it is asserted, distinctly maintained that he was neither a prophet nor the son of a prophet (Amos 7:14). However, this argument is based upon a fallacious interpretation of the passage to which appeal is made. In this passage Amos is relating his prophetic call. He disclaims that he is earning his livelihood by being a prophet, since he is a shepherd and a plucker of sycamore fruit. However, God called him to be a prophet. "Go, prophesy unto my people Israel," the Lord had said to him. These are the words by which he was inducted into the prophetic office. This objection to our argument, therefore, is without merit.

In the prologue to *Ecclesiasticus* (written about 130 B.C.) mention is made of "the law itself, and the prophecies, and the rest of the books." Here is witness to a third division, namely, "the rest of the books." The language does not tell how many or which books were considered by the author as coming under this category. However, it does imply a fixed group of books, and also implies, we think, that these books had been in existence for some time. The designation here given of the third group is as definite and explicit as are those given to the first two divisions of the canon.

The writer of the prologue also speaks of the "law and the prophets and the others that followed after them" and states that his grandfather, the author of *Ecclesiasticus* (ca. 190 B.C.), gave himself largely to the reading of "the law and the prophets and the other books of the fathers." In the mind of the writer of the prologue, then, there existed three definite divisions to the Old Testament Scriptures.

We need not be alarmed because the author does not use a technical term to designate the third division. As a matter of fact, he is not consistent even in his reference to the second division. He speaks of it now as "the prophecies" (αἱ προφητεῖαι) and now as "the prophets" (τῶν προφητῶν). The technical designation *Writings* was only applied to these books long afterward. The miscellaneous character of their contents would make it difficult to employ an adequately descriptive designation, such as was enjoyed by the Law and the Prophets. Upon the basis of what is stated in the prologue to *Ecclesiasticus*, there does not appear to be warrant for assuming that the third division of the canon was still in process of collection.

In all probability these books were gathered by Ezra and those who immediately followed him. Concerning this period very little is known, but it seems to have been a time when attention was given to the Scriptures, and it may well have been that these sacred books were then collected. Nor does this necessarily mean that some inspired additions were not made to certain books at a later time. Such may very well have been the case.

It need not be maintained that from the beginning there was a recognition of a threefold division of the canon. For this reason, some lists may contain books which from the standpoint herein presented would seem to be in the wrong division of the canon. Nevertheless, this threefold division flows naturally from the position of the writer in the Old Testament economy. When the threefold division as such was first recognized we may not be able to tell. That it is a Scriptural division would seem to admit of no doubt.

To sum up, we may say that the books of the Old Testament, being immediately inspired of God, were recognized as such by his people from the time when they first appeared. That there may have been questions and minor differences of opinion about certain books does not at all detract from this fact.

It is well-known that in the later Jewish schools there were certain disputes as to the canonicity of particular books, notably, Esther and Ecclesiastes. However, it is questionable whether these disputes were really more than academic. It is questionable whether they really represented the attitude of the people to any great extent.

How the books were gathered we are not told. Apparently, no religious council in ancient Israel ever drew up a list of divine books. Rather, in the singular providence of God, his people recognized his Word and honored it from the time of its first appearance. Thus was formed the collection of inspired writings which are known as the canonical books of the Old Testament.

It has sometimes been held that a Jewish Synod was held at Jamnia in Palestine and that this synod made pronouncements concerning the extent of the canon. After Titus and his armies had destroyed Jerusalem in 70 A.D. Rabbi Johanan ben Zakkai settled in Jamnia and carried on his literary activity there. Jamnia did become a center of Biblical study and the canonicity of certain books was discussed, and in particular, it would seem, whether these books should be excluded from the canon. But that there was a Synod which discussed whether certain books were to be included in the Canon is very questionable. Professor H. H. Rowley has written very wisely concerning Jamnia: "It is indeed, doubtful, how far it is correct to speak of the Council of Jamnia. We know of discussions that took place there amongst the Rabbis, but we know of no formal or binding decisions that were made, and it is probable that the discussions were informal, though none the less helping to crystallize and to fix more firmly the Jewish tradition" (*The Growth of the Old Testament* [London: Hutchinson's University Library, 1950], 170).

C. Critical Views of the Canonization of the Scriptures[5]

The view of the collection of the canon of the Old Testament which has just been outlined by no means finds universal acceptance today. However, it would appear to be the view which is most congruous with what is related in the Old Testament as it stands. It would seem too that essentially this position has been traditionally embraced by the Christian church.

At the present time, however, it is not only being set aside but is even strongly attacked in many quarters. In its place, diverse theories are being offered.

The theory of canonization which has been outlined above, it will be remembered, finds that that which determines the canonicity of any book is the book's inspiration. A book which is inspired of God, therefore, is *ipso facto* canonical. Furthermore, the book is canonical whether it is bound up with other canonical books or not. It is God who sets the limits to the canon and not man. Due, however, to God's providential leading and due to the inward testimony of the Holy Spirit in the hearts of his people, the people of God have been enabled

5. Strictly speaking, every careful student of the Old Testament and of the problem of its canonization may be called a critic. However, in common parlance the word "critical" has come to connote an attitude towards the problems of Old Testament study which is generally destructive of and hostile to traditional views. It is in this latter sense that the words "critic" and "critical" are employed in this paper, and this merely to avoid confusion in the mind of the reader who may not be well acquainted with the present state of Old Testament studies.

to recognize his Word. And remarkable, indeed, has been the unanimity of their witness to the identity of the canon.

The theories which are now about to be considered, however, although differing among themselves in many respects, nevertheless have this in common, that they reject inspiration as the determining principle in the formation of the canon. Such rejection, indeed, is not always conscious. Furthermore, there may truly be, among those who advance critical theories of the formation of the canon, some who are firm believers in the supernatural. Nevertheless, it must be confessed that among the advocates of recent critical theories the greater number do reject the working of God in any adequate sense in Israel's history.

The question involved in the formation of the Old Testament canon is basically the question of the supernatural. If one firmly believes in the triune God, he will, if he is consistent, adopt essentially the theory of the canon which has been presented because this theory alone adequately takes into account the working of God in the inspiration of the books of the Old Testament. If, however, one does not accept the orthodox Christian doctrine of God, it follows that, in the very nature of the case, he will be compelled to reject the high view of the formation of the canon for which we have been contending.

Furthermore, the critical views which we are about to consider are for the most part bound up with attitudes toward the authorship, dates and composition of the individual Old Testament books which are considerably out of harmony with the traditional views upon these subjects. This is not the place in which to enter upon any detailed discussion of the merits of these theories. Suffice it to say that the writer believes that these recent positions are for the most part not in accord with the facts.[6]

According to many scholars, the three divisions of the Old Testament are in reality three separate canons. In order, therefore, properly to understand the formation of the canon, as a whole, we must, they say, first discover how each of the three individual canons came into being.

1. The Pentateuch

The Pentateuch, or first five books of the Bible, was, according to many, not written by Moses. Rather, it owes its present form to a process of growth which covered many centuries. In reality, it is not the work of one man at all, but of several men, all unknown, who in many cases lived many centuries apart. It was therefore only when the writings of these different authors were finally edited and combined, to result in approximately the present Pentateuch, that the work was canonized.

When, however, did this canonization take place? For a time it was thought that the final redaction and editing of the Pentateuch was the work of Ezra and his contemporaries. When the Law was read before the assembled multitude in Jerusalem, as is related in Nehemiah 8–10, the Pentateuch was thereby rendered canonical. As a matter of fact, however, there had been, according to many of the supporters of this position, even an earlier canonization. Josiah, the king, it has been claimed, was responsible for the canonization of Deuteronomy.

---

6. For a discussion of the questions of special introduction from a liberal or critical standpoint, the reader is referred to S. R. Driver, *An Introduction to the Literature of the Old Testament* (Edinburgh: T. & T. Clark, 1909); Robert H. Pfeiffer, *Introduction to the Old Testament* (New York: Harper & Brothers, 1941). The question is very capably treated from the standpoint of tradition and consistent Biblical supernaturalism by Oswald T. Allis, *The Five Books of Moses* (Philadelphia: Presbyterian and Reformed, 1943).

But it was at the public reading by Ezra that the entire Law was first publicly recognized as authoritative.

Such is the view of the canonization of the Pentateuch which has more or less consistently held the field among certain critics of the Old Testament for the past half-century. Indeed, as long as the Pentateuch is regarded as consisting of a number of conflicting documents deriving from different ages and composed by unknown authors, so long will this or some similar low view of its canonization be held.

In his scholarly and valuable introduction to the Old Testament, Dr. Robert H. Pfeiffer broke with the traditional critical account of the canonization of the Pentateuch in at least two respects.

In the first place, he refused to admit that Nehemiah 8–10 is an account of the canonization of the Law of Moses, because he believed that the historicity and chronology of the events recorded therein are too doubtful to support such an interpretation. We do not agree with him in his denial of the historicity of the contents of these chapters, but we do agree that they do not present the account of the canonization of the Law. According to Pfeiffer, the Pentateuch was canonized about 400 B.C. and not when Ezra read the Law to the assembled people. Thus, it would appear that Pfeiffer has taken away the one available incident to which appeal might be made for an evidence of canonization.

In the second place, Pfeiffer has stressed the question of the canonization of Deuteronomy, which earlier critics had also noted, and, as a result, has brought into clearer focus certain difficulties which those who reject the clear Biblical witness to itself must face.

In order to understand these difficulties, it will be necessary to examine cursorily Pfeiffer's theory of the canonization of the Pentateuch. Briefly it is as follows. When, in the eighteenth year of Josiah, the book of the Law was found in the temple, it was regarded as the word of Jehovah and its precepts were immediately enforced. Thus the newly-discovered book of the Law was canonized, and this is the first instance of such canonization in human history. This book, so the theory runs, was Deuteronomy.

There were also already in existence other literary works in ancient Israel. About 650 B.C. these were combined and edited to form a great national epic. Thus Israel, according to the theory which we are now considering, came to have her own national history. However, this national history was not regarded as canonical. About 550 B.C., however, the canonical Deuteronomic Code was inserted into the non-canonical national epic. Apparently, therefore, this transaction imparted canonicity to the national epic. Sometime during the fifth century B.C. there was composed the so-called priestly portion of the Pentateuch which deals with laws, genealogies and the origin of sacred institutions. This portion, however, did not obtain canonical standing until it was later inserted in the already existing combined work of Deuteronomy and the national history. Such an insertion probably took place about 400 B.C. and thus, as soon as this final edition of the Pentateuch was issued, it was received as canonical.

Credit is certainly due to the author of this theory because of his endeavor to construct a satisfying account of the canonization of the Pentateuch. It must be obvious, however, to anyone who has examined it that it cannot stand if Moses were actually the author of the Pentateuch. This is not the place to discuss in any great detail the question of the Mosaic authorship of the first five books of the Bible, but it may be noted that there are compelling reasons for believing in such authorship. That Moses was the author has been the traditional viewpoint of the Christian church, and there seems to be sufficient evidence for assuming that Christ himself held this opinion. The tradition which asserts Mosaic authorship is, therefore, extremely well-founded. Furthermore, despite whatever difficulties there may be in believing that Moses composed the Pentateuch, the difficulties in any alternate theory of its composition are far more serious.

Pfeiffer proceeds upon the assumption that the original edition of Deuteronomy was written a few years before 621 B.C., and that Deuteronomy was the book discovered in the temple during the reign of Josiah. However, this position is so weak that it is being abandoned today even by some who do not admit that Moses was the author of Deuteronomy. It becomes more and more apparent, if one carefully studies the statements of the Bible itself regarding the book discovered in the temple, that the volume found was not merely Deuteronomy, but a well-known book of law embracing Deuteronomy and far more. Unless the critics can prove otherwise, and they cannot, we may very naturally assume that this book was the Law of Moses, and essentially our present Pentateuch.

Likewise, there is serious objection to the position that a great national epic was edited about 650 B.C., and there is very strong objection also to asserting that the priestly portion of the Pentateuch was composed some time during the fifth century. However, these questions have been discussed thoroughly many times elsewhere. It is another type of objection which we now wish to bring against Pfeiffer's theory, and against most modern views of the canonization of the Pentateuch.

In the first place, Pfeiffer appears to hold a very low view of the meaning of the word "canonical." Apparently his view is that a work may exist for a century and be regarded as merely a human writing and then suddenly become recognized as canonical. Thus, the national epic, it is said, was edited in 650 B.C., but it was not until the insertion of Deuteronomy about a hundred years later that it was actually considered by the people to be canonical. Thus the one who determines the extent of the canon is not God but man. In reality, this makes the canon to be but a list of books which the Jews regarded as sacred. It rules out of the picture the adequate working of God in the inspiration of the Scriptures and also in the inward testimony of his Spirit in the hearts of his people. It asserts that the Jews were led to consider certain books as divine, not because these books actually were divine, but because of mere external reasons. The theory therefore is fallacious because it is too one-sided; it does not take into account all the facts.

Secondly, this viewpoint assumes that the devout Jews of antiquity would incorporate a book which they regarded as canonical into one which hitherto they had looked upon as non-canonical. It also assumes that they would insert a work which they considered to be of mere human origin (e.g., the priestly legislation) into one which they believed to be divine. These assumptions create a tremendous psychological difficulty. Would devout Jewish editors unite a writing which they knew to be non-canonical with a volume which they looked upon as the Word of God? It is almost inconceivable that they should do so. Before them, according to Pfeiffer's theory, lay Deuteronomy. To them it was the very Word of God, and therefore to be obeyed. Before them also lay another book—their national history, a remarkable and praiseworthy writing, but not divinely inspired. Can we possibly conceive of these pious Jewish editors combining the two and from that time on declaring them both to be the Word of God? No! No matter how helpful the national history would be in meeting Israel's religious needs, devout Israelites would never regard it as inspired in the manner in which this theory assumes.

In the last place, this theory would make the unknown authors of the Pentateuch to be guilty of fraud. Thus, when Josiah read the book of the Law, he believed it to be the work of Moses. In this, however, it appears that he erred, for Moses did not write it at all. Rather, it was written by an unknown priest who had been influenced by the prophetic movement and who sought, by using the authority of the name of Moses, to bring about a reformation in religious life. Whether this priest be called sincere, and inspired by noble religious ideals or not is beside the point. The fact remains that he employed a dishonest means to secure his end. When he perceived that Josiah accepted his writing as Mosaic and as the authoritative Word of God, he should, if he had been an honest man, have told Josiah the truth.

In connection with the production of the priestly portions of the Pentateuch also, we cannot escape the fact that fraud was employed, if Pfeiffer's theory be correct. Whether the men of that day believed that what they were doing was wrong or not, is beside the question. As a matter of fact, what they were doing was very wrong. They were using the name of Moses to gain a hearing for their own ideas. They were not merely writing to entertain; they were writing to convince. And when they saw that their own productions were being regarded as divine and authoritative, they should have done something about it. If they actually thought that God was speaking through them, why did they employ the name of Moses?

Thus, on the basis of Pfeiffer's theory and of the theories of many modern critics, the Jews came to accept as canonical a Pentateuch which was produced in a dishonest method. To deny this fraud or dishonesty by talking about the sincerity of the authors or the nobility of their aims and ideals does not change the picture. All honor to Dr. Pfeiffer, who frankly asserted that three of the most influential writings in the Old Testament were technically fraudulent. Would that more critics were as candid as he!

We feel constrained, therefore, because of the tremendous difficulties which it involves, to reject the theory of the canonization of the Pentateuch which was offered by the distinguished professor at Harvard. In fact, if the first five books of the Bible are not essentially the work of Moses, but are a compilation of documents composed by various unknown authors living at widely separated periods of time, the whole question of the canonicity of these books becomes an insoluble mystery and the fact that the Jews ever regarded them as divine one of the greatest enigmas of all time.

2. The Remaining Books

In the discussion of Pfeiffer's theory of the canonization of the Pentateuch it was noted that, according to this position, a book might exist for many years before it finally came to be credited with canonicity. This implies that the author of the book had not intended his work to be regarded as sacred and divine and lasting. At first the work was not venerated as inspired Scripture, but in the course of time it did come to receive such veneration.

Not only, however, is the assumption that a book was not intended to be regarded as divine evident in the theory which we have just been considering, it is also particularly apparent in connection with many theories as to the canonization of the remaining books of the Old Testament. It is not always explicitly stated but is clearly implied in the writings of many critics. It is indeed a basic weakness in the critical position, because it raises an unanswerable question. If the books of Scripture were not intended to be regarded as inspired and canonical, what was it that led to their being eventually so regarded? What caused a people, which for years had considered these writings to be uninspired, to change its position and to ascribe to them a canonicity which formerly had been denied? Obviously it could not be the inspiration of the books themselves which produced this change. Rather, the change must have been due, in the very nature of the case, to external causes. What, then, were these external causes which induced the Jewish nation to accept just these particular books and no others? That is the question which critics must answer, and that is precisely the question which critics cannot satisfactorily answer. The reason why no satisfactory answer can be given to this question lies in the fact that the critical theories endeavor to discuss the question of canonicity from an historical standpoint alone. They would rule out of the picture the theological question. Does God exist? Did God actually inspire the writers of the individual books of the Old Testament? Does the Holy Spirit by his inward testimony produce within the hearts of his people a conviction that he is the author of the Scriptures? These questions are ignored by the critics or are pushed aside as belonging to the realm of "faith" and not to that of historic fact. And it is precisely because of this unconsciously prejudiced attitude that the critic cannot answer the questions which have just been raised.

Any theory which refuses to deal with the theological questions involved is one which refuses to take all of the facts into consideration. The Old Testament books claim to have been spoken by the Lord. Is that claim correct or is it not? To consider that claim one must ask whether there is a Lord and whether he actually spoke to man? This claim permeates practically the entire Old Testament, and yet the critical theories pay little or no attention to it. Did God actually speak these words? That question the critics would either ignore or else by inference deny. Hence the difficulty in which they find themselves.

Let us make no mistake about it. We can never successfully answer the question as to why the Jewish nation recognized these particular books until we deal with all the facts involved. If these books are indeed the Word of the living and true God, as they claim to be, then we may see that in his good providence his people were led to accept those books of which he was truly the author, and the manner in which they came thus to accept them was in its essence very probably that which has already been outlined. If, however, these books of the Old Testament are actually not the Word of God, or if we refuse to consider the question of their inspiration because that question belongs to the realm of "faith," we shall never satisfactorily ascertain why it was that the Jews came to accept precisely these writings.

However, the critics are ready with their answers to the problem, and to these answers we must now devote some attention. It has been asserted that the canon consisted merely of the national literature of the Hebrews. This collection was made so that the second temple, built after the exile, might possess all the advantages of the earlier temple which had been destroyed. Hence, the national literature of Israel was gathered, and thus there came into being the canon of the Old Testament. This explanation, which comes from the heart of German rationalism, has little to commend it, and it possesses a fatal weakness. The Old Testament itself speaks of early Israelitish books, such as the Book of Jashar. Why were not these works also included within the canon, if this explanation be correct? Also, why were those prophetical books included which denounce Israel so strongly? Why should the people desire to perpetuate writings which condemned them so unsparingly?

It has also been maintained that language was the determining principle in the formation of the canon. Books which were written in Hebrew were included, whereas those which were written in Greek or other languages were excluded. However, this assertion is not in accord with the facts, and consequently has been generally rejected. For in Israel there were books composed in Hebrew which have never been recognized as canonical.

Again it has been held that the books which are in the Old Testament represent the religion of Israel in its greatest purity. This very obviously implies that the Israelites themselves were capable of deciding of which books this was true. The subjective element is surely prominent here. Why also did the Jews include both the prophetical books with their stress upon spiritual religion and books of law with their emphasis upon sacrifice and form? Were not these Israelites as keen in their discernment of "incongruities" as are the modern critics?

Nor can it be successfully maintained that books were accepted only because they agreed with the teaching of the Pentateuch. There is, as a matter of fact, an element of truth in this assertion. The remaining books of the Old Testament do indeed agree with the Law of Moses. They are truly based upon the Pentateuch. However, according to the critics, the Law is in conflict with itself, being composed by different anonymous authors who lived at widely distant periods. It is this supposed internal conflict which might be called one of the chief axioms of modern Old Testament criticism. If, then, the Law really is what the critics claim, how can we possibly account for the acceptance of Amos, Isaiah and Jeremiah, with their condemnation of sacrifice, or of Ezekiel, who is supposed to be so much at variance with the priestly portion of the Pentateuch? This theory implies that the ancient Jews could perceive in the five books of the Law a unity which the modern critic cannot discover. It in reality becomes, therefore, an argument for the unity of the Pentateuch. Why, too, we may ask in passing, if this theory be correct, was a book such as *Jubilees* omitted from the canon?

Again, it has been urged that the intrinsic worth of the books, their moral and spiritual quality, led to their acceptance. If by this is meant their inspiration, we can heartily agree, but if, however, there is intended merely the fact that these books are of a superior moral and spiritual quality, we find ourselves once again floundering in difficulty. Why, for example, all other considerations apart, is Esther then included and *First Maccabees* excluded? Also, we today know very little about the quality of other writings in ancient Israel. May there not have been other books of very high quality which, for one reason or another, have perished? Do we today know enough to assert that these books were chosen merely because of their moral and spiritual quality?

Other answers also have been offered. One scholar has suggested that the collection of the prophetical books was due to a desire to secure a weapon against the Samaritans. Another has intimated that possibly the spread of Hellenic culture as a result of Alexander's victories had given the final impetus to the Jewish community to include the prophetical books in its canon. Again, it has been suggested that the idea of a canon arose only in the Greek period when the Jews were compelled to issue a pronouncement which would distinguish authoritative books from apocryphal and other writings. But, if this were the case, how did the nation come to distinguish between authoritative and apocryphal books? What determining principle brought about the exclusion of *First Maccabees*, for example, and the inclusion of Daniel?

It has also been held that the criterion which guided the Jews in the selection of the books was the desire to give to the post-exilic temple the advantages of the earlier temple, or that it was the criterion of language, or that the chosen books represent the religion of Israel in its purest form. Again, it has been held that these books speak of a covenant between God and man, or they are in agreement with the Pentateuch, or their authors were prophets, or the books taught Christ, or the books were chosen because of their intrinsic worth and merit.

A particular problem faces the critics when they endeavor to account for the inclusion of the historical books among the prophets. According to some, this inclusion was due to the fact that these books contained utterances of old prophets such as Samuel and Nathan, and these utterances gave sanction to the entire historical narrative. However, if this be so, why were not books such as *The Words of Nathan the Prophet* or *The Visions of Jedo the Seer* (see 2 Chronicles 9:29) and similar writings included? Nor is it satisfactory to hold that they were accepted merely because of their prophetic authorship, because other books of prophetic authorship have perished. Likewise, if their canonicity be attributed to their popularity and to their religious and patriotic significance, we would reply that other books may have been just as popular and have also had great religious and patriotic significance. Popularity alone does not insure the permanent survival of a book.

Why too, we may ask, were the individual books of the Writings, or third part of the Old Testament, accepted? It is not sufficient to maintain that in mere survival or popularity lies the explanation. Nor can it consistently be held that anonymity was required. Why were certain other anonymous books, such as the *Wisdom of Solomon*, excluded?

It must be apparent that these explanations do not begin to satisfy the requirements of the case. Consequently some of the more thoughtful critics have sought to discover the answer to the problem not merely in external circumstances, but have thought that the practical religious life of the Jews compelled them at last to accept these books, and that the Jews did as a matter of fact declare them to be canonical because they considered them to be, to a certain extent at least, divine. However, even with this statement of the case, we cannot rest content. For here, also, theological argument is ignored, and there is assumed the position that the Jews themselves, after the books had already been in existence some time, came to recognize them as canonical. It cannot, as a matter of fact, be too strongly insisted that there is no historical evidence whatsoever that the Jews before the time of Christ ever made any official pronouncement as to the identity of the books which they accepted as canonical. And there certainly is no evidence to support the view that there were three canons, that the Pentateuch was first accepted as canonical, then, at a later time, the Prophets and, finally, the Writings.

It is a hopeful sign that this fact is gradually being realized. A German scholar, Hölscher, has admitted that this almost fundamental dogma of the modern critical school must now be abandoned. In this he has been followed in certain recent popular introductions to the Old Testament. Hölscher has thus shown himself to be a pioneer. His own explanation of the formation of the canon, namely, that the spread of apocalyptic books and ideas caused the idea of a canon to arise, is itself untenable. However, a break has at last been made from what has been a most cherished dogma of certain critics.[7]

---

7. Gustav Hölscher, *Kanonisch und Apokryph* (Naumburg: Lippert, 1905). By means of the idea of the canon, thinks Hölscher, the Jews were able to combat the influence of apocalyptic literature. Hence, the rabbis considered as canonical only books which they thought were written between the time of Moses and Ezra, the classical period of divine inspiration. Why, however, did the Jews, since their purpose was to combat apocalyptic, accept writings such as Daniel, which they considered to have been the product of the classic period of inspiration? Would not apocalyptic literature, on Hölscher's view, have been dangerous, no matter when it was produced?

Conclusion

The Old Testament is the Word of the living and true God. It is not merely the national or religious literature of the ancient Hebrews. It is rather the life-giving oracles of God. It speaks of God the Creator, the Almighty One, who by the Word of his power, brought all things into existence. It speaks of man's creation and of man's transgression whereby he was brought into an estate of sin and misery. It speaks of God's promise of deliverance through a Redeemer. It points forward, in its entirety and in its individual parts, to the coming of that one who said, "Search the Scriptures, for in them ye think ye have everlasting life, for they are they which testify of me."

The fact that certain critical scholars choose to refuse to discuss the theological questions involved in the formation of the Old Testament canon need not deter us from so doing. When men endeavor to account for the Old Testament canon upon the basis of historical considerations alone, how unsatisfactory their attempts are! In reality they create more problems than they solve.

The devout Christian need not hesitate boldly to declare his belief in the Old Testament as the inspired Word of God. He need not fear to believe that the authority of these Scriptures resides in the fact that God is their author. True, there is difficulty in adopting this position but, apart from it, the Old Testament must ever remain a mystery. Why it has been preserved we can then never know. One man's suggestion is as good as another's. We are left in the hopeless abyss of agnosticism.

The Authority of the New Testament

NED B. STONEHOUSE

Ned B. Stonehouse, "The Authority of the New Testament," in *The Infallible Word*, ed. Paul Woolley, 3rd rev. printing (Philadelphia: Presbyterian and Reformed, 1967), 92–140; reprinted from Philadelphia: Presbyterian Guardian, 1946.

Stonehouse was already introduced in the section on biblical theology (cf. chap. 47). In addition to his focus on the Synoptic Gospels, Stonehouse wrote his dissertation on Revelation in the early church, published as *The Apocalypse in the Ancient Church* (1929). This research equipped him well to write the article on the canon of the New Testament reproduced here. Like the previous article by Young, this selection comes from the Westminster Seminary faculty symposium *The Infallible Word* (1946). In this selection, "The Authority of the New Testament," Stonehouse blends his New Testament expertise with the best of Reformed traditions from both Princeton and the Netherlands. In drawing our attention to the authority of the New Testament, he explains that not everyone means the same thing when they speak of the authority of the New Testament. Therefore, Stonehouse turns to the Scriptures, in order to present what the New Testament itself means when it claims to be authoritative. Contrary to the scholars of his day who emphasized the role of the church in the formation of the canon, Stonehouse argues that the New Testament itself must be where one discovers what it means for the New Testament to be an authoritative text. Further, Stonehouse presents how the different genres of the New Testament assert their distinctive authority.

When men speak today of the authority of the New Testament, radically variant estimates of this volume may be in view. If one shares the distinctively modern approach of

C. H. Dodd, for example, the New Testament may be judged to possess "the authority of corporate experience."[1] Such an estimate is frankly far from attributing any objective authority to these writings as a corollary of divine origin. On the other hand, there is the historic use of the designation "authority"—historic because given expression in the great creeds of Christendom—which views authority as the equivalent of "canonicity."[2] It is the latter conception of authority which is in view in this discussion, and in the interest of avoiding ambiguity and confusion it must at once be defined and circumscribed as precisely as possible.

To accept the New Testament as canonical is, in a word, to acknowledge the twenty-seven writings in the second part of the Holy Bible as possessing divine authority and as constituting, accordingly, an integral part of the divine rule for faith and life. In attributing divine authority to these writings, the Christian church obviously judges that such authority is to be acknowledged only because these writings are held to possess inherently, that is, by virtue of what they actually are, the right to such a claim. In other words, this authority is conceived of, not as superimposed upon the writings at a time when their true character had become obscured or hidden, but as an authority which the books possessed from the very moment of their origin. There is implicit in the claim of canonicity, therefore, the judgment that divine inspiration has constituted these writings with a quality which sets them apart from all merely human writings. Those who accept this high view of the New Testament, accordingly, do not shrink from identifying it as the Word of God, the infallible and inerrant rule of faith and life.

The canonicity of the New Testament involves more, however, than the divine authority of its constituent parts. The authority of the New Testament attaches not only to the twenty-seven writings *severally* but also to the closed collection considered *as a unit* alongside of the Old Testament. Just as the scriptures of the old covenant form a closed collection, the twenty-seven writings of the new covenant too are received as enjoying a completeness and unity of their own. They are the perfect inscripturated revelation of the new covenant. None is lacking and all belong. There is implicit in this high view of Scripture, therefore, besides the acknowledgment of the authority of the several writings due to their inspiration, the recognition that in the process of their collection into a single volume, to the exclusion of

---

1. *The Authority of the Bible* (London: Nisbet, 1938), 131–90. Dodd also speaks of the authority of the Bible as "the authority of the men of religious genius who speak in it" (pp. xv, 31, 193). His own view is set sharply over against the traditional view which has regarded the Bible as "the supreme doctrinal authority in faith and morals, divine in origin and consequently infallible" (p. 8).

2. The first chapter of the Westminster Confession of Faith would be acknowledged by most historians as presenting the classic Protestant creedal formulation of the doctrine of Scripture. Section 2 lists the sixty-six books of Holy Scripture "or the Word of God written" and refers to them as "given by inspiration of God, to be the rule of faith and life." In Section 3 they are distinguished from the Apocrypha which "not being of divine inspiration, are no part of the canon of Scripture; and therefore are of no authority in the Church of God, nor to be any otherwise approved, or made use of, than other human writings." Section 4 rests the authority of Holy Scripture wholly upon God "the author thereof."

The Council of Trent (Session 4) also affirmed the inspiration and divine authority of the Scriptures, and rested their authority upon divine authorship. However the divine authority of the Scripture is qualified in various respects. Not only are certain traditions preserved in the church accorded a place alongside of the Scriptures, but also the "holy mother church" alone is held to be "the judge of the true sense and interpretation of the holy scriptures." Moreover, in effect the council canonized tradition when it judged that the Vulgate, indeed the Vulgate in current use, was the "authentic" text of Scripture, and "that no one is to dare or to presume to reject it under any pretext whatever." Cf. *Dogmatic Canons and Decrees* (New York: Devin-Adair, 1912), 7–10. Thus the doctrine of the ultimate authority of the living church takes precedence over the authority of Scripture, and a fundamentally different estimate of the place of authority in religion, and of religion itself, comes to expression in Roman Catholicism.

all other writings, there has been a divine control which has governed the formation of the canon.[3] Only thus could the final result, the acknowledgment of the canonicity of the single volume of twenty-seven writings, follow after a period during which the writings came into existence at different times and in different places, and during which they circulated for some time either separately or in smaller groups.

This high view of canonicity must be set over against various current notions which appear to fall short of an adequate estimate of its implications. We regard it as fundamental that canonicity must not be identified merely with sacredness. To evaluate a writing as sacred, even to regard it with "high and reverent esteem,"[4] is not necessarily the same as to acknowledge it as possessing absolute divine authority. A writing might be esteemed reverently because its contents as a whole, or to a considerable extent, were regarded as highly significant for religion, but the essential ingredient of authority as a divine writing might be lacking.

Even the approach of the great Lutheran scholar Zahn suffered from a failure to carry through an unambiguous conception of canonicity. His monumental work has been charged, with a measure of justice, with being a history of the public and private use of writings which came to be accepted as canonical rather than strictly a history of the canon of the New Testament. There is indeed a most intimate connection between the use of Christian writings in public worship and their acceptance as canonical. As the *Muratorian Canon*, for example, shows, decisions as to the right of works to be read in the church, and as to the exclusion of others from that privilege, frequently involved the determination of their divine inspiration and authority. It is held, for example, that the *Shepherd of Hermas* ought to be read privately but, as belonging neither to the prophets nor to the apostles, its public reading to the people in the church is condemned. Nevertheless, the circle of writings regarded as sufficiently edifying to be read, at least occasionally, in the services of the church was evidently somewhat larger than the circle of strictly canonical writings.[5]

Other writers fail to draw a sharp line between the canonicity of Scripture and of its revelatory contents. An example may be found in the recently published work of John Knox on the New Testament canon. He is on solid ground when he defines "Scripture" as "a collection of books which have unique authority and value because they are accepted as standing in a unique relation to what is believed to have been a unique revelation of God."[6] But obviously all depends on how that "unique relation" is conceived. If the books are thought of as the inspired inscripturation of the revelation of God, they will no doubt qualify as canonical. Knox, however, seems to fall definitely short of according to the writings an adequate relationship to the revelation to warrant that conclusion. For he affirms that it is "nearness to the revealing events or personalities" that determines canonicity, such nearness that the collection of books is "as unduplicable as the revelation and tends soon to be thought of as being the revelation itself."[7] But *proximity* to a revelation and the *tendency* to

3. This is not to imply that the idea of a collection, or even of a closed collection, is as fundamental to canonicity as the idea of intrinsic divine authority. As soon as any Christian book was accorded a place of absolute divine authority alongside the Old Testament, there was a concrete expression of the idea of the New Testament canon.
4. WCF 1.5.
5. Eusebius reports, e.g., that *1 Clement* had from the beginning been read in the church at Corinth (*Ecclesiastical History* 4.23.11 [Loeb, 1.383]).
6. *Marcion and the New Testament* (Chicago: University of Chicago Press, 1942), 24–25.
7. Ibid., 25.

become identified with revelation hardly suffice to confer canonicity. The divine authority of inspired Scripture is not adequately grounded in the judgment that it serves in a unique fashion to transmit revelation; its canonicity involves the judgment that it is divinely constituted as Scripture, and thus from the beginning bears the character of divine revelation.

The Issues at Stake

If one concentrates upon the leading issues in dispute among historians of the canon of the New Testament, some progress can perhaps be expected even in a brief discussion of this intricate subject. On certain aspects of the actual course of events, there is a considerable measure of agreement; on other issues the differences are radical and far-reaching.

Few scholars today would maintain that the New Testament stood complete immediately, or almost so, after the last of the twenty-seven writings came into existence. On the understanding that the books possess divine authority because of their origin as inspired scriptures, indeed, the canon was *ideally* complete at that time. The actual collection of the writings into a single volume and their recognition, individually and as a unit, as possessing divine authority alongside of the Old Testament, however, took considerably more than a few years. On this point the expressions of some orthodox scholars seem misleading. Apostolic sanction is regarded as the decisive fact in the history of the New Testament canon, and this is understood as meaning that the apostles imposed the several writings as law upon the churches.[8] In our judgment this view lacks specific confirmation from the available evidence and, moreover, cannot account for the diversity with respect to the limits of the New Testament which prevailed for decades and even for centuries.

If there is today a virtual consensus of belief that the New Testament as a single authoritative volume did not stand ready about the end of the first Christian century, there is likewise a remarkable agreement that only a century later the great centers of the Christian church were in conscious possession of a New Testament. Moreover, although some uncertainty still remains about A.D. 200 as to the right of certain books to a place in the New Testament, and as to the necessity of excluding others from it, there is substantial agreement as to its contents. The New Testament about the year 200 consisted of our four canonical gospels, the Acts, thirteen epistles of Paul, some of the general epistles, and the Revelation of John.[9]

It follows, then, that the most acute differences of judgment among historians relate to developments prior to the close of the second century. The main question in dispute, in other words, is how the church about the end of that century came into possession of the New Testament. The most radical, and apparently also the most influential, position is that of which Harnack was the brilliant exponent. On his understanding of the second century, the New Testament came into being suddenly about A.D. 175, so suddenly, in fact, that its origin may be described as a *creation* of the Old Catholic Church. Harnack does not suppose that it was a creation *ex nihilo*, for he allows, of course, that the individual books came into existence long before and recognizes, moreover, that various powerful historical factors prepared the way for a New Testament canon. He maintains, nevertheless, that largely

8. See, e.g., W. M. McPheeters, "Apostolic Origin or Sanction, the Ultimate Test of Canonicity," and "Objections to Apostolic Authorship of Sanction as the Ultimate Test of Canonicity," *Presbyterian and Reformed Review* 3 (1892): 246–57 and 6 (1895): 26–68 respectively; B. B. Warfield, *Revelation and Inspiration* (New York: Oxford University Press, 1927), 451.

9. Some scholars would contest the right of the Revelation to be included here. On its place in the canon of the New Testament see my *The Apocalypse in the Ancient Church* (Goes, Netherlands: Oosterbaan & Le Cointre, 1929).

through the impulse and example provided by the heretic Marcion the church came to a qualitatively new judgment concerning certain writings that had been in circulation in the church for some time. Farthest removed from Harnack's construction is that of historians like Westcott and Zahn who conceive of the process as far more gradual and continuous than sudden and abrupt. Other scholars, like Jülicher and Lietzmann, occupy a position somewhere between these poles, allowing that the events of the latter half of the second century affected the development in decisive fashion, and yet insisting that considerably prior to A.D. 175 certain churches accepted a New Testament canon both in its fundamental idea and in concrete fact.

The study of the authority of the New Testament raises other issues, however—far more profound and divisive issues than those which concern the outward course of the developments within the early centuries of the history of the Christian church. It appears that one cannot discuss the origin of the New Testament without initiating a broad inquiry as to the Christianity in which it came into being, and no discussion concerning the nature of Christianity in its first stages can escape a decision as to the person and purpose of Jesus Christ. And in turn the decision as to the meaning of Jesus Christ is bound up with the most ultimate questions concerning reality—questions concerning God and man, revelation and religion.

It is our conviction that the idea of canonicity has meaning and validity only if Christian theism, the theism of the Bible, is true. Implicit in the idea of a divinely authoritative Scripture is the thought of God as self-existent and self-sufficient, the creator and ruler of the universe. His works necessarily constitute a disclosure of his mind and purpose. And in order that sinful men, darkened in their understanding and at enmity with God, might receive knowledge of their true condition and of the divine remedy for that condition with a view to their glorification of God, it was necessary that God should reveal himself directly in history by word and deed. That special and direct revelation in history, which found its center and goal in the history of Jesus Christ, possesses an objective, final character, of permanent validity and significance for men. The inscripturation of that revelation through the agency of the Holy Spirit was due precisely to the need that a permanent and trustworthy record should be provided of the fact and the meaning of the divine action in history.

The charge is often made that this view of revelation involves a static conception of God, which does not leave him free to act when and how he pleases. The objection might be valid if God were conceived as being or becoming a part of the historical process. But such is not the case. Because the world and history belong to him and are under his control, he can make himself known directly in history. And to set aside that direct revelation as irrelevant is to declare one's own independence from God. The defense of the divine freedom then turns out to be merely an assertion of the autonomy of the human spirit.

The charge that the divine freedom is impaired by this doctrine of Scripture is seen to be unfounded, moreover, in view of the consideration that only Christian theism maintains a true doctrine of transcendence, and this alone allows for the sovereign action of the living God in contemporaneous history. It is a significant historical phenomenon that John Calvin, who asserted without ambiguity the objective authority of the Scriptures, was "the theologian of the Holy Spirit." A true response to the divine word and deed, made known in his works and in Scripture, is possible, Calvin maintained, only through the inward testimony of the Holy Spirit. This doctrine of the inward witness of the Spirit does not sacrifice the objective authority of the Scriptures, as is often maintained.[10] It does not serve as a means to discover and to distinguish within the Scriptures certain revelatory elements and thus to set aside others as non-revelatory. But it recognizes that man, the sinner, requires a gracious inward action of the divine Spirit in order to receive "the full persuasion and assurance of the infallible truth and divine authority" of Scripture, as he also needs the gracious illumination of the Spirit for its true interpretation. The Reformed doctrine of God is then neither static nor activistic; it neither confines God in his past actions nor restricts his significant acts to the present moment. But God is honored as the God of history and of the present, who "was and is and is to come"; his direct, objective disclosures in history and his regenerating activity in the heart of man are both maintained.

It is patent that there are abroad today many notions of the nature of reality and religion which are in conflict with the doctrine that genuine religion finds its foundation in divinely authoritative Scripture. Such hostility is by no means confined to philosophies which are openly anti-theistic. Idealistic philosophy and Mysticism are no less exclusive of such a view of revelation; in both there is a supreme indifference to the sphere of historical phenomena; neither arrives at a true transcendence doctrine, since the human spirit is virtually deified or absolutized.

Other philosophical and religious viewpoints appear less antithetical to the idea of Scripture. Because it postulates the unique significance of the history of Jesus for religion, modern Liberalism might seem to maintain a point of view akin to that of historic Christianity. Actually the differences are thoroughgoing and radical. The distinction between the noumenal and the phenomenal, which it derives from Kant by way of the Ritschlian theology, does not provide a background for the affirmation of the Christian doctrine of revelation. For there inheres in the Kantian dialectic a fundamental agnosticism concerning ultimate reality in combination with a readiness to accord to purely naturalistic phenomena the evaluation of revelation. Thus the personality and teaching of the man Jesus, as a unique manifestation of the human spirit, is accorded a measure of authority. In the nature of the case, however, the authority attached to Jesus is qualitatively different from the objective, divine authority attributed in the confessions to the Scriptures.

This state of affairs becomes abundantly clear from the writings of Harnack, who has enjoyed a signal influence both through his exposition of Liberalism and his interpretation of the rise of the New Testament. It is altogether consistent that the scholar who declared that "The gospel as Jesus proclaimed it has to do with the Father only, and not with the Son"[11] should also have declared that "The New Testament itself, when compared with what Jesus purposed, said, and was, is already a tradition which overlies and obscures."[12] How uncongenial his conception of religion finds the element of Scriptural authority is also evident in his affirmation that through the formation of the canon the Spirit was chased

---

10. *Institutes* 1.8.12 (cf. 1.7.4–5). Among those who have failed to distinguish clearly between the objective authority of the Bible, and its objective witness to its own divinity, on the one hand, and the inward witness of the Spirit in the heart of the believer, on the other hand, and who thus tend to subjectivize the authority of the Bible, and even to set up the subjective witness of the Spirit as the test of canonicity, are Charles A. Briggs, *Biblical Study* (Edinburgh: T. & T. Clark, 1884), 108–112, 123; *The Bible, the Church and Reason* (New York: Scribner, 1892), 55ff.; Johannes Leipoldt, *Geschichte des neutestamentlichen Kanons*, Teil 2 (Leipzig: Hinrichs, 1908), 144–45; C. H. Dodd, *The Authority of the Bible*, 296–97.

11. *Das Wesen des Christentums* (Leipzig: Hinrichs, 1902), 91; English translation, *What is Christianity?* (London: William & Norgate, 1901), 144.

12. *Die Entstehung des Neuen Testaments* (Leipzig: Hinrichs, 1914), 31; English translation, *The Origin of the New Testament* (London: Williams & Norgate, 1925), 43–44.

away into a book![13] He could hardly have expressed his antipathy to the idea of a direct historical, objectively valid, revelation in more vigorous terms.

It appears to many today that in the Barthian movement one can find the antithesis and antidote to the Liberalism of Harnack. Barthianism proclaims God as "the wholly Other" and polemicizes against the immanentism of modern Protestantism. It insists that theology must be a theology based upon revelation, the theology of the Word of God. It even maintains that the church may not distinguish between the Word of God and the word of men in the Bible; it must recognize that the canon is finished and that the Scripture as it stands is a witness to the divine revelation. Yet, for all of these apparent affirmations of orthodoxy, the Barthian theology of the Word is basically as antithetical to the historic Christian doctrine of the canonicity of Scripture as the Ritschlian. In spite of the polemic of Barth against the immanentism and subjectivism of modern thought, his position sustains a far larger measure of continuity with that thought than it does with traditional orthodoxy. This is due no doubt to the essentially Kantian starting point which it shares with Liberalism. Appearances to the contrary, notwithstanding, Barthianism also is fundamentally agnostic; it maintains that God remains wholly hidden in his revelation. The phenomenal world, the world of history, it is held, cannot be the medium in which revelation finds expression (and it cannot because it is not a world which came into being by divine fiat). Revelation is said to cease to be revelation if it is direct in history and objectively valid for all time; to be revelation it must be a momentary, contemporaneous divine act. The Bible is full of blunders and contradictions. Hence it may not be identified with revelation or the Word of God; it is only a witness to the divine revelation. There is accordingly a polemic here, just as there is in Ritschlianism, against the idea of a direct historical, objectively valid, revelation.[14]

I. The Testimony of Scripture

The attestation of the canonicity of the New Testament, in the nature of the case, cannot be provided by Jesus in the manner that his words offer a ratification of the authority of the Old Testament. The writings themselves came into existence after the ascension of our Lord. And their collection and acknowledgment as canonical were not finally accomplished even at the close of the first Christian century. The attestation of the canonicity of the New Testament, in contradistinction from that of the Old Testament, might seem to have to depend exclusively upon an ecclesiastical affirmation. If this were true, it might appear that the New Testament is at a most serious disadvantage, lacking the high sanction that the Old Testament enjoys. As we hope to show later the attestation of the church, as a matter of fact, is exceedingly consequential. The history of the canon is the history of its recognition on the part of the church as divinely authoritative. Nevertheless, back of the attestation provided by the church, there is a witness of the Scriptures themselves, a witness

---

13. Ibid., 25 (English translation, 36). Cf. Edgar J. Goodspeed, *Formation of the New Testament* (Chicago: University of Chicago Press, 1926), 1: "Christianity began as a religion of the spirit. The primitive believers sought guidance from within, believing that in their own hearts the Spirit of God had taken up its abode, and that it would guide them to the truth. In accepting the authority of a collection of books they sacrificed this early attitude, and seemed to go to the opposite extreme. What occasioned this remarkable change, which concerned something so central in early Christian religious thought?"

14. Cf. Karl Barth, *Die Christliche Dogmatik, Die Lehre vom Wort Gottes* (München: Christian Kaiser, 1927), 38–47, 334–62; *Die Kirchliche Dogmatik, Die Lehre vom Wort Gottes,* Erster Halbband (München: Christian Kaiser, 1932), 101–113, 168–94, 274–75; English translation (Edinburgh: T. & T. Clark, 1936), 111–24, 184–212, 298–99; Zweiter Halbband (München: Christian Kaiser, 1938), 505–598; English translation (Edinburgh: T. & T. Clark, 1956), 457–537.

which, on the church's understanding of the relation of the Lord to the Scriptures, provides the New Testament with an attestation from the Lord himself. The manner in which the Lord provides that attestation to the New Testament is, naturally enough, different from his specific affirmations of the authority of the Old Testament. The only concrete form in which that attestation can come, if it is not to be derived from another objective revelation from the Lord of heaven, must be nothing other than the voice of Scripture itself.

A. *The Testimony of the Old Testament Canon*

A good starting point for our argument may be found in the fact of the Old Testament, or, to state the matter more precisely, in the fact of Christianity's acceptance of the divine authority of the Scriptures of Palestinian Judaism of the time of Christ. The preceding chapters have indicated at sufficient length how unequivocal the evidence of the New Testament writings is for this conclusion concerning the fundamental belief of Christianity. We are aware that various attempts have been made in modern times to distinguish between the church's acknowledgment of the canonicity of the Old Testament and a supposedly freer attitude of Jesus himself. With respect to such constructions, suffice it to say here that they achieve their end only by finding the tradition of the teaching of Jesus at variance with itself, and by attributing to Jesus a view which is flatly contradicted by a considerable body of the tradition of his teaching. A sound historical interpretation of the data leads, in our judgment, to the conclusion that Jesus consistently upheld the objective divine authority of the Old Testament.[15]

Christianity's acceptance of the Old Testament is of the greatest conceivable importance for the understanding of Christianity itself, and in particular for the understanding of its fundamental philosophy of the history of revelation, which is basic to the concept of canonicity. One stands amazed that in so many able discussions of primitive Christianity this fact fails to come to its own rights. We have in view here the efforts to find the genius of the earliest Christianity in a narrowly conceived futurist eschatology, which is held to have controlled the church's perspectives and interests in drastic fashion. In particular the claim is often made that the expectation of a momentary return of Christ so dominated the thoughts of the early Christians that they could have had no interest in provisions for the regulation of its historical life in the world. An answer to this charge that is partial and yet sufficient is that an entirely different view of history is involved in the readiness of the church to yield to the authority of the historical Scriptures of the Old Testament.

Implicit in the church's acknowledgment of the Old Testament, then, was the affirmation of the Christian-theistic view of history with its supernaturalistic conception of redemption and revelation. To put the matter in the most concrete and specific terms, Christianity began as a religion of a divine book, as a religion of authority which definitely acknowledged a book as an objective expression of the divine mind and will. Were it not that so many modern writers have approached the study of the New Testament canon with the assumption that Christianity is basically not a religion of authority but a religion of "the spirit," it would hardly seem necessary to emphasize the point that the idea of an inscripturated canon, far from being uncongenial to Christianity, forms an integral element of the Christian faith

15. Cf. my discussion in *The Witness of Matthew and Mark to Christ* (Philadelphia: The Presbyterian Guardian, 1944), 193–96; cf. above part IX, chapter 47.

from the very beginning of its life. One must fly in the face of solid fact, accordingly, to insist that Christianity is fundamentally the religion of man's free, unfetterable, spirit. For the same reason, only at the sacrifice of historical realism can one maintain that the Christian conception of revelation is of a revelation which is momentary, completely contemporaneous, and activistic rather than one that is historical, and, even when completed in the past, remaining objectively valid in the present.

The significance of Christianity's acknowledgment of the divine authority of the Old Testament extends beyond its validation of the fundamental idea of canonicity of Scripture. The acceptance of the Old Testament not only is eloquent of Christianity's regard for the past; it also bears witness to Christianity's interpretation of itself as the fulfillment of the Old Testament revelation. The Old Testament itself is characterized by an eschatological outlook, that is, it looks beyond itself to a new age which brings consummation and finality. There was a time when the criticism of the Old Testament was so completely under the domination of an evolutionary and unmessianic point of view that no serious place was allowed for eschatology. To some extent at least this fault has been overcome in the approach of scholars like Gressmann. The conclusion is, in our judgment, inescapable that the Old Testament history of revelation looks forward to the establishment of a new covenant, constituted by new divine action and speech, and inaugurated by the appearance in history of one who is described both as the Lord himself and as the Lord's Anointed.[16] But even if there remained doubt as to the true interpretation of the Old Testament itself, it would remain incontrovertible that the Christianity which began with the Old Testament understood it in this messianic sense. And in identifying its own history with the promised messianic age, Christianity inevitably gave expression to its consciousness of constituting the new order which was to be brought into being by new divine action and speech. In short, the acceptance of the Old Testament itself implied that the history of the Christ was regarded as a history of new divine revelation.

If then the Old Testament looked beyond itself to a new era of revelation which was to come, and if Christianity regarded itself as constituting that new era, a sufficient answer is provided to the common allegation that Christianity, having begun with the Old Testament canon, would not have felt the need of a new canon of Scripture. It has been maintained that the Old Testament canon was a formidable obstacle in the path of a new canon.[17] Since the Old Testament was accepted as a closed and complete revelation, and since its prophetic teaching provided an authoritative delineation of the Christ, it is held that some significant new development would have had to be forthcoming before the church could think of evaluating other writings in the same manner as the Old Testament. This position breaks down, we believe, because it does not take into account at all adequately the decisive accent upon new divine revelation with which the new movement began, and which was even bound up with its attitude towards the Old Testament. It may not be overlooked, indeed, that the Old Testament was regarded as complete; and the new canon consequently could never have been conceived of merely as a kind of expansion of the Old Testament. Rather it was a philosophy of the history of revelation finding expression in terms of the old and new covenant and rooted in the Old Testament itself, which is basic to the acknowledgment of the canon of the New Testament.

16. See B. B. Warfield, "The Divine Messiah in the Old Testament," in *Christology and Criticism* (New York: Oxford University Press, 1929), 3–49.

17. Harnack, *Die Entstehung des Neuen Testaments*, 22 (English translation, 31).

B. The Testimony of the New Testament

Our appeal to the fact of the acknowledgment of the Old Testament has proceeded from a distinctly Christian position, not from the Old Testament as an isolated fact, and consequently our previous discussion has already taken us into the territory of the New Testament. It is necessary now, however, to approach our subject more directly from the vantage point of the testimony of the writings of the New Testament.

Most simply and at once most comprehensively stated, we may affirm that there is one authority that speaks forth from the New Testament, namely, the authority of the Lord Jesus. The Lord who ratified the authority of the Old Testament speaks with independent and absolute authority alongside of the Old Testament. In a word, the New Testament attests the binding authority of the ancient Scriptures and of the Lord who spoke "as having authority and not as the scribes."

To a point, modern historians agree with this affirmation; they agree that the Christian authorities were "the Scriptures and the Lord." I say there is an agreement to a point only, because in the last analysis profound Christological differences emerge if one probes beneath the surface. Was the lordship of Jesus, in an absolute sense, an integral aspect of the Christian faith from the beginning? Or did the church first acknowledge him as the divine Lord in a Hellenistic environment? And behind such questions relating to the Christology of the early Christian church there press upon us questions as to the Christology of Jesus himself. Was he a mere man who, at the most, claimed a kind of relative spiritual supremacy? Or was there inherent in his claims nothing short of an asseveration of equality with God? On the decisions reached on these issues hang ultimately the final judgments as to the validity of the New Testament canon. If the sovereignty of Jesus is something less than divine, no matter how little less, it is not enough to ground the affirmation of the absolutely binding authority of the New Testament. Only an absolute Lord may occupy the place of absolute authority for faith and life. Only his word may constitute divine revelation.

The New Testament canon presupposes more, however, than the deity of the person of Jesus. While the acknowledgment of his deity provides an adequate conception of authority, it does not serve to place that authority definitely within the structure of history. Only if that authority is viewed in the perspective of the history of revelation will one be able to define the authority of the Lord in relation to that of the Old Testament. Now this want is fulfilled by the consideration that Jesus, the Lord, is the divine Messiah. As the Messiah he occupies a well-defined place in the history of revelation. Only when he is recognized as the divine Messiah can one understand him as standing in solid continuity with the preparatory revelation and yet bringing it to absolute consummation.

The distinctiveness of the historic Christian view of revelation as the revelation of the divine Messiah may be seen in sharper focus if it is set in contrast to the approach of the heretic Marcion, who has frequently been claimed as the real creator of the New Testament canon. In dependence upon Matthew 11:27 (Luke 10:22), which speaks of the absoluteness of the Son's knowledge of the Father and of the sovereignty of his disclosure of the Father, Marcion grasped the truth of the absoluteness and newness of the Christian revelation. But the God whom Jesus proclaimed he held to be an unknown, stranger God. The Old Testament consequently had to be set aside. Now these radical conclusions were bound up with his failure to understand Jesus in the perspective of history, or, in other words, to recognize him as the Messiah. It is exactly the concept of messiahship which demands both continuity with the old order and its fulfillment. Messiahship is essentially unintelligible apart from the presupposition of the old covenant and it remains unrealized unless it ushers in the new covenant. Hence we see that there emerged in the case of Marcion an essentially new conception of Christian revelation, a conception radically at variance with that which was implicit in the historic acknowledgment of Jesus as the divine Messiah.

If then the messiahship of Jesus, as well as his lordship, is basic to the final decisions as regards canonicity, it will appear that the modern debate concerning the historicity of the messianic consciousness of Jesus is an important aspect of the larger debate as to the essence of Christianity and the character of true religion. If Jesus did not think of himself as the Messiah, or if, in affirming messiahship, he regarded it as merely a formal or peripheral aspect of his consciousness, or even as uncongenial and burdensome, and thus as not definitely determinative of his central thought concerning his life, the follower of Jesus will hardly in any serious fashion interpret that history as constituting divine revelation. If, on the other hand, he regarded himself as the Messiah of the Old Testament (and if he so regarded himself that conviction must have been so overwhelming and so all-controlling that it could not have been merely formal), his history, the history of the divine Messiah, immediately and inevitably stands apart from merely human history. The Liberal holds that "supreme importance" came to be assigned to the history of Jesus, and especially to his death and resurrection, only in the primitive church. But if the messiahship of Jesus is affirmed and taken seriously, Jesus must himself have attached supreme importance to his own history.

The decision on this great question is in brief the decision as to whether the witness of the Gospels to Jesus is true. There is no real debate today as to whether the Gospels actually represent Jesus as living and dying and rising as the Messiah. The ablest interpreters of the Gospels freely acknowledge that they were written from the point of view of such a belief in Jesus. To mention only one conspicuously pertinent fact, he is represented as one who taught that through his death the new covenant was inaugurated (Luke 22:20; cf. Mark. 14:24). The debate is whether we shall accept the evangelical testimony to him or not. Those who have sought to recover an "historical" Jesus—that is, a mere man—behind the figure of the divine Messiah of the New Testament have, we think, not achieved success. No really objective criteria, not excluding the criteria advanced by form-criticism, have been discovered whereby one may remove the supposedly unhistorical accretions of tradition and get back to an original historical stratum of solid fact. The more consistent and thoroughgoing criticism has landed in skepticism.

The divine messiahship of Jesus is then the basic fact behind the formation of the New Testament. But we must freely acknowledge that this fact alone is far from bringing us to the goal of our investigation. The acknowledgment of the presence of the divine Messiah does not carry with it the necessary embodiment of that revelation in a corpus of writings. Jesus left behind no literary productions. The Christian church apparently for a considerable time was content to rely upon *oral* tradition for its knowledge of Jesus. A most crucial phase of our subject is bound up, therefore, with our judgment as to the factors that served to link the historical career of Jesus with the composition of the New Testament documents.

According to the New Testament, it was the apostles who constituted the link between the Lord himself and the Scriptures of the New Testament. The student of the early history of the canon likewise will freely concede that there is a close connection between canonicity and apostolicity. But at once difficult questions emerge when we try to define that connection precisely. With our eye upon the origin of the several writings of the New Testament we may not identify canonicity with apostolic authorship, for then several writings would fail to qualify. Nor can we make real progress by defining apostolicity more broadly, as signifying apostolic sponsorship or apostolic sanction, for, as stated previously, the facts of history do not support such constructions. If then apostolicity will not serve as a touchstone of canonicity, must we infer that apostolicity is inconsequential and irrelevant for our subject? In our judgment the apostles occupied such a unique place in the life of the early church that such an inference must be set aside.

According to the consistent witness of the New Testament, Jesus chose a company of persons who were qualified, both by their personal witness of his life and by their endowment by the Spirit of Christ, to declare authoritatively the Christian message.[18] The tradition which ascribes to the circle of the immediate disciples of Jesus a unique qualification and authority to publish the Christian message has been subjected to severe criticism. Although there may be a readiness on the part of some to acknowledge that there was a small circle of confidants who enjoyed special privileges and for whom Jesus predicted special honors in the kingdom of God, it is widely held that the tradition, in so far as it ascribes to them the right to speak with decisive authority in the church of Christ, reflects a late stage of development in which the apostles had come to be accorded a place of spiritual authority never intended by Jesus. Our answer to this historical skepticism, briefly stated, is that the evangelical delineation of the relation of the apostles to Jesus is as historical as its portrait of Jesus. The conception of the apostolate is really a messianic concept, that is, it has meaning only on the background of Jesus' consciousness of his mission as the Messiah to establish the church.

Now it is clear that Paul, too, claimed the authority of an apostle to declare the Christian gospel. Although he did not accompany Jesus in the days of his flesh, he insisted that, like the others, he was a witness of the resurrection of Jesus and had been otherwise qualified for the apostolic task (1 Cor. 9:1; 15:8–11; 2 Cor. 12:12). He maintained that his authority as an apostle was quite independent of the authority of the other apostles; it was an apostolic authority immediately derived from the Lord (Gal. 1:1, 11, 17; cf. 4:14). He was not one whit behind the chiefest apostles (2 Cor. 11:5; 12:11–12). He implies also that the leaders at Jerusalem recognized the validity of his claims (Gal. 2:8–9). And everywhere his epistles breathe a consciousness of absolute authority to set forth the Lord's mind and will to the churches; he even assumed without argument the right to regulate the exercise of the charismatic gifts of the Christian prophets (1 Cor. 14:29–32, 37).

In connection with this estimate of the place occupied by the apostles in early Christianity, we think it of the greatest importance to underscore the observation that the apostolic authority was never conceived of as an authority independent of, or even on a level with, the authority of the Lord. Modern writers often represent the inclusion of the apostolic writings in the canon, even writings like the epistles of Paul, as involving an unforeseen and indefensible exaltation of the apostles to a place alongside of the Lord. Let us hear Harnack as he approaches the question why the New Testament contains other books beside the Gospels, and appears as a compilation of two divisions ("Evangelium" and "Apostolus"):

18. Cf., e.g., Mark 1:16–20; 3:13–14; 4:10–11; 6:7–13; 9:9; Luke 6:12–16; Acts 1:1–2, 22–26; John 14:26–29; 15:26–27; 16:25–28.

In the New Testament letters which serve momentary and particular needs are set on a level of equal value with the Gospels; what is merely personal with what is of universal import; the Apostles with Christ; their work with His work! In a compilation which is invested with Divine authority we must read: "Drink a little wine for thy stomach's sake," and "my cloak I left at Troas." Side by side with words of Divine mercy and loving kindness in the Gospels we meet with out-breaks of passionate personal strife in the Epistles; side by side with the stories of the Passion and Resurrection, the dry notes of the diary of a missionary journey![19]

Before the New Testament came to be designated with a name that expressed its unity, it appears indeed that for a time it was spoken of as "Gospel and Apostle." The recognition of that division within the New Testament was natural enough. Yet we are convinced that altogether too much has been made of this twofold division in modern discussions, too much because the fact of the recognition of the single divine authority of the collection tends to be obscured. It is far too simple an analysis of the history of the New Testament canon to imply that the fourfold Gospel canon was accepted because of the absolute authority of the Lord whereas the rest of the New Testament was received because the apostles came in the course of events to be accorded a place on a level with the Lord.

The sharp distinction which is drawn between the Gospels and the Epistles breaks down in at least two ways. In the first place, the Gospels no less than the Epistles were directed to specific historical situations. They too, in a sense, are occasional writings. To recognize them as serving the immediate needs of their time, however, is not to infer that they were not of universal import. The universal import of the Epistles ought to be evident from a consideration of their proclamation and application of the gospel. And it is certainly demonstrated from the use which has been made of them in the history of the church.

In the second place, the apostolic authority which speaks forth in the New Testament is never detached from the authority of the Lord. In the Epistles there is consistent recognition that in the church there is only one absolute authority, the authority of the Lord himself. Wherever the apostles speak with authority, they do so as exercising the Lord's authority. Thus, for example, where Paul defends his authority as an apostle, he bases his claim solely and directly upon his commission by the Lord (Gal. 1 and 2); where he assumes the right to regulate the life of the church, he claims for his word the Lord's authority, even when no direct word of the Lord has been handed down (1 Cor. 14:37; cf. 1 Cor. 7:10). Nor may it be overlooked that the Gospels are also apostolic. They were so characterized by the Christian church of the end of the second century, which is regarded by Harnack as the creator of the New Testament.[20] And the Gospels themselves, in so far as they make any explicit claims of authority, appeal to the apostolic testimony which they contain (Luke 1:1–4; John 21:24). In spite of the diversity of the contents of the New Testament, therefore, it does not consist of "two absolutely disparate entities."[21] The only one who speaks in the New Testament with an authority that is underived and self-authenticating is the Lord. Since, however, his message required to be mediated to the church through human

---

19. *Die Entstehung des Neuen Testaments,* 30 (English translation, 42–43). Cf. also Ernest Cadman Colwell, *The Study of the Bible* (Chicago: University of Chicago Press, 1937), 3–4, and Knox, *Marcion and the New Testament,* 29–31. For a discussion of the latter work, see Ned B. Stonehouse, review of *Marcion and the New Testament,* by John Knox, in *WTJ* 6, 1 (May 1943): 86–98 and of this point, 93–94.

20. Cf. Irenaeus, *Against Heresies* 3.1–2; Tertullian, *Against Marcion* 4.2; *Muratorian Canon.*

21. Harnack, *Die Entstehung des Neuen Testaments.*

instrumentalities, it was necessary that those who had been appointed and qualified by the Lord should become his spokesmen.

Although then the revelation of the new covenant is apostolic, without ceasing to be the Word of the Lord, the apostolic origin of that revelation does not as such constitute the twenty-seven writings of the New Testament as divine Scripture. If Mark and Luke, for example, are to be judged canonical, their canonicity cannot be made to rest exclusively upon the consideration that they report apostolic tradition, however important that consideration may be for our estimate of their intrinsic character and historical significance. If the writings of Mark and Luke are to be judged canonical, it must be because these evangelists were controlled by the Spirit of the Lord in such a manner that their writings, and not merely the apostolic message which they set forth, are divine. In other words, it is Mark's inspiration (which, to be sure, is not to be isolated from his historical qualifications), and not Peter's inspiration, which provides the finally indispensable ground for the acceptance of that work as canonical.

We necessarily face, therefore, the question whether the witness of the individual writings themselves is of such a character as to justify the high claims that are made for them when they are received as the divinely inspired and authoritative Scriptures of the New Covenant. Now we have no right to insist, if the high judgment of the church concerning these writings is to be vindicated, that the inherent divine authority of the individual writings will have impressed itself upon them in any stereotyped fashion. In the nature of the case a book of history will not bear upon its surface the evidence of its divine origin in the way that prophetic writings necessarily do. The witness of the individual writings, as in the case of the books of the Old Testament canon, varies with the individual character of the writings.

The Revelation of John, the only prophetical book in the New Testament, bears express marks of its claims to inspiration. That which is written is what the Spirit says to the churches (Rev. 1:10–11; 2:1, 7; etc.). The book may be described as constituting the revelation and witness of Jesus Christ and as the Word of God (Rev. 1:1–2). Consequently, those who hear and keep what is written in it are promised a special blessing, whereas those who presume to add to or to take away from the things that are written come under the divine curse (Rev. 1:3; 22:18–19).[22]

In the case of the epistles the right to be heard and to be obeyed is made to rest on the personal relation which exists between the writers and their readers, the authority expressed or implied being inherent in the recognized qualifications of the authors. Paul, as noted above, everywhere claims to speak with the authority of the Lord. And he consequently attaches the highest significance to his own writings. He is solicitous for their exchange (Col. 4:16) and intimates, therefore, that he considers them of more than momentary worth. Of more importance, we observe that he considers it so important that his earliest (so most scholars judge) epistle be read to the church that he even *adjures* its recipients to see that this is done (1 Thess. 5:27). The extraordinary significance which he attached to obedience to his written word finds striking expression in 2 Thessalonians 3:14: "And if any man obeyeth not our word by this epistle, note that man, that ye have no company with him, to the end that he may be ashamed." It is no wonder then that at an early date

---

22. Hans Windisch, in an article entitled "Der Apokalyptiker Johannes als Begründer des neutestamentlichen Kanons" (*Zeitschrift für die neutestamentliche Wissenschaft* 10 [1909]: 159) maintained that the author of the Revelation shows that he was conscious of creating a canonical book.

the epistles of Paul were collected and received as worthy of a place alongside of the Old Testament (cf. 2 Peter 3:16).

There are other canonical epistles—the Epistle to the Hebrews, James and Jude—which do not claim specific apostolic origin and authority. They nevertheless in their own way assert their authority in the church. James and Jude speak as servants of Jesus Christ. The author of the Epistle to the Hebrews, while distinguishing himself from the apostolic circle, everywhere speaks as qualified to set forth a true and authoritative expression of the preeminent revelation of the new covenant, a revelation "in a Son" and "spoken through the Lord," and "confirmed unto us by those who heard" (Heb. 2:1–4; cf. Heb. 1:1–4; 13:22).

The Gospels assert their authority in still another way. As witnesses to Christ, the evangelists take little or no time to accredit themselves as qualified to publish the gospel with divine authorization. The personality of the evangelists tends to stay so completely in the background that it remains for their messages to authenticate themselves as authoritative proclamations of the gospel. It is true, nevertheless, that the original readers must have known the identity of the writers. Moreover, Luke and John are not, properly speaking, anonymous works. Luke is at pains to set forth at the very beginning his qualifications, method and goal. In particular he informs Theophilus that he is competent to supply a completely trustworthy account of the career of the supernatural figure whom he depicts. He is competent to supply such an account as provided certainty as regards the origins of Christianity. And the evangelist John brings to the attention of his readers the figure of an intimate disciple "whom Jesus loved" evidently in order to exhibit his qualifications to bear witness to Jesus and to supply a written record of that witness (John 13:23–24; 19:26–27, 35; 20:2–10; 21:24; cf. John 18:15; 1:25, 37, 40). Mark, in spite of its anonymity, claims for itself far more than ordinary significance when in the opening verse it designates itself as "gospel," that is, as the glad tidings of salvation which came to be realized in the history of Jesus Christ.[23] Although Matthew does not contain any similar self-characterization, yet it likewise was evidently written to serve the same fundamental purpose as Mark. The Gospels then, explicitly or implicitly, claim to set forth the gospel of Christ. That gospel as the proclamation of the divine action and word in history is essentially revelatory. And since the revelation is historical, the implication is that it must be published authoritatively by those who stood in intimate connection with the events and could declare their meaning.

The self-evaluation of the records, therefore, is not at variance with the claim of canonicity. We must admit, however, that the later formulations with regard to the character of the writings of the New Testament assume characteristically a specific form not explicit in most of the writings. It does not appear that the church everywhere and at once recognized exactly these writings as divine. And only after some time did the church precisely define the relation of these writings individually and as a unit to the Old Testament. We must inquire more particularly, therefore, as to the nature of the process in which these results were achieved.

II. The Attestation of the Church

In this section we propose to limit ourselves to certain leading phases of the early history of the New Testament canon. We have noted above that historians today are sharply

---

23. See *The Witness of Matthew and Mark to Christ*, 7–11.

at variance as to many of the decisive facts and factors of the development in the second century; they differ, for example, on the questions whether the New Testament came into being as late as about A.D. 175, whether Marcion's collection affected the course of events in any decisive fashion, whether Justin Martyr gives evidence of a New Testament. The decision on these and other questions is admittedly difficult. One dares not overlook the fact that the history of the New Testament canon is but a part of the complex history of the Christian church. And our search for positive results is often thwarted by the paucity of extant evidence. Nevertheless, even in a few pages it will be possible to examine some of the most pertinent evidence and to gain certain broad perspectives concerning the development as a whole. In order to achieve this end, however, we shall be compelled to limit our discussion to the testimony provided by a few key figures.

The document known as *1 Clement*, a letter from the church at Rome to the church at Corinth about A.D. 95, provides one of the most important of the early testimonies. The document indeed has serious limitations for our subject. It provides knowledge of developments in only a small segment of the church, not of the church universal. Moreover, it is not a treatise on canonicity; in fact, what it has to tell us on this subject is told in the most incidental fashion. Nevertheless, its positive statements and its silences contribute significantly to our knowledge of the formation of the New Testament.

The attitude of *1 Clement* toward the New Testament writings may be judged on the background of its regard for the Old Testament. It everywhere displays the same high reverence for the Old Testament that is disclosed in the New Testament. There are more than one hundred quotations, and they are frequently introduced with "It is written" or similar formulae. Evidently referring to the Old Testament, the author writes on one occasion: "Ye have studied the sacred scriptures, which are true and given by the Holy Spirit. You know that nothing unjust or counterfeit is written in them" (45:2–3). Now since this epistle never speaks in similar fashion concerning the writings of the New Testament, it would seem to follow that the New Testament canon had not yet emerged as a concrete reality at the end of the first century in Rome. Still this broad conclusion needs to be qualified. In spite of the secure place which the Old Testament enjoyed as authoritative for the church, this document also affirms, alongside the Old Testament, the authority of "the Lord Jesus" (13:1; 46:7–8). There is also the recognition that the authority of the Lord was mediated by the apostolic proclamation of the gospel and as well by the apostolic appointment of ecclesiastical government (42:1–4; 44:1–2). Not only the words of the Lord then, but also the apostolic proclamation of the Lord, was regarded as possessing authority.

But how do the writings of the New Testament stand related to the authoritative apostolic proclamation? *1 Clement* uses several of these writings, but as we have observed above, the mere use of writings does not establish canonicity. And it is a striking fact that the New Testament documents are not formally quoted as Scripture. In fact, with a single exception, they are not referred to specifically at all. It knows of the gospel but never speaks of Gospels. So far as the testimony of this witness goes, therefore, the New Testament writings had not yet come to be characterized in terms identical with those applied to the Old Testament. To acknowledge that the church of about the end of the first century had not yet formulated in explicit terms its doctrine of the canonicity of the New Testament is not to admit, however, that the later evaluation was not already implicit in the earliest characterizations. Alongside of the Old Testament, as we have noted, there was an acceptance of the Christian gospel as authoritative because of its provenience from the apostles, who in turn "received the gospel from the Lord Jesus Christ" (42:1). Now it may be acknowledged that as late as the end of the first Christian century the oral tradition of the apostolic proclamation was a highly significant factor in the life of the church. Nevertheless, the written tradition of that proclamation can hardly have been regarded as being at a disadvantage as over against the oral tradition. The use which *1 Clement* makes of the written documents is sufficient proof of that. And most eloquent of all is the fact that, although this writer makes specific mention of only one apostolic document, he does so in a manner that makes perfectly clear that certain writings were accorded the highest possible degree of authority. For in referring to 1 Corinthians he says, "Take up the epistle of the blessed Paul, the apostle. What did he write unto you at the beginning of his preaching? With true inspiration (ἐπ' ἀληθείας πνευματικῶς) he charged you concerning himself and Cephas and Apollos, because even then you had made yourselves partisans" (47:1–3).[24]

If then *1 Clement* had spoken specifically of other writings which had come down from the apostles, he could hardly have failed to claim for them also the authority of the Lord and of his Spirit. While then we must recognize that the formulation of the church's estimate of the New Testament writings at this time was far from being what it was about one hundred years later, nevertheless the kernel of the matter is already present. In other words, the explicit recognition of the canonicity of the New Testament does not represent a development sharply at variance with what one might have expected about the year 100; rather, the unique estimate of the authority of the apostles was a guarantee that the specific relation of the apostolic proclamation to the Old Testament would come to be formulated along the line of the church's eventual expression.

About twenty years after the transmission of *1 Clement* to Corinth another highly significant witness appeared. Ignatius, bishop of Antioch, passing through Asia Minor on his way to Rome as a condemned man, wrote seven epistles of remarkable originality of thought and expression. If they had been written in the quiet of an episcopal study, they might well have contained many more quotations than they do, and those which appear might have approximated the literalness characteristic of the quotations in *1 Clement*. However, Ignatius was clearly such a vigorous and original personality that we cannot imagine him writing in stereotyped fashion, no matter how academic his surroundings might be. The paucity of specific references to the Old Testament and to apostolic writings is, accordingly, compensated by the freshness of his observations. Ignatius indeed displays a knowledge of many writings of Scripture, and it is meaningful for our understanding of the place which the New Testament writings had come to occupy in the life of the church that, in contrast to the usage of *1 Clement*, his letters display a far greater dependence upon the language of the New Testament than upon that of the Old Testament. But again it is not so much the quotation of, or allusion to, language of Scripture that is significant for the study of canonicity as certain specific reflections upon the history of revelation. Around these passages indeed there has developed a considerable amount of discussion,

24. The observation might be made that, if *1 Clement* bears witness to the inspiration of Paul, he also does so to himself, since he states that he wrote "through the Holy Spirit" (63:2). It is significant, however, that in this immediate context this writer characterizes his writing as an "entreaty" and says "you will give us joy and gladness if you are obedient to the things which we have written." Since, however, this writer merely entreats, there is clearly a qualitative distinction between the inspiration of Paul and his own endowment with the Holy Spirit.

which cannot be weighed here, and we can only indicate our understanding of some of the more perspicuous passages.

On one occasion the comparison between the two dispensations of revelation takes the following form: "But the gospel has somewhat of preëminence, the coming of the Saviour, our Lord Jesus Christ, his passion, and the resurrection. For the beloved prophets had a message pointing to him, but the gospel is the perfection of incorruption" (Ignatius, *To the Philadelphians* 9:2). Here the new revelation in Christ is viewed as the fulfillment of the prophetic disclosures. Its preeminence is recognized. It seems clear that the "gospel," as Ignatius refers to it, is not a document or collection of documents, but the *message* of Christianity (cf. also Polycarp, *To the Philippians* 5:1–2; Ignatius, *To the Smyrnaeans* 5:1; 7:2).

The very considerable accent which Ignatius puts on the New Testament revelation finds interesting expression in another passage which has been much discussed. A slightly paraphrased rendering of the original which seems to us to express most adequately its meaning follows:

> But I beseech you to do nothing in factiousness, but after the teaching of Christ. For I heard some men saying, "If I find it not [the point at issue] in the charters [archives], I do not believe it if it is only in the gospel." And when I said to them, "It is written," they answered me, "That remains to be settled." But to me the charters are Jesus Christ, the inviolable charter is his cross, and death, and resurrection, and the faith which is through him. . . .[25]

The passage clearly implies that certain opponents of Ignatius, apparently of a Judaizing sort, insisted on making the Old Testament Scriptures the touchstone of Christian truth, and Ignatius agrees with them to the extent that he too acknowledges the Old Testament, and on his part he insists that the Christian gospel has received prophetic expression in the ancient scriptures. Nevertheless, he adds that the New Testament revelation does not require the attestation of the Old; it is inherently authoritative. An important and difficult question remains. How did Ignatius conceive of the New Testament revelation? When he refers to the "gospel" in this passage, and particularly when he describes Jesus Christ as constituting "the charters" alongside of the "charters" of the Old Testament, does he have specific Christian writings in mind? So indeed some able interpreters of Ignatius have judged. My own conclusion is that the language does not clearly support that interpretation. Here, as in the other passages cited above, the "gospel" appears to refer to the Christian message, without reflection upon its form, whether oral or written. And though the term "charters" as applied to the Christian gospel strikingly indicates the parity, and more than parity, which Ignatius attributed to the distinctive Christian revelation, it seems to be used with reference to the contents of that revelation rather than to its written formulation.

There are other data in the epistles of Ignatius, however, which illuminate the question of the specific character of that Christian message. The apostles are accorded a place of unique authority and privilege as proclaimers of the gospel; their ordinances possess the same authority as the Lord (*Philadelphians* 5:1–2; *Magnesians* 13:1; *Trallians* 12:2; *Ephesians* 11:2). Ignatius himself speaks with a high measure of authority to the churches to which he

---

25. *Philadelphians* 8:2: The Greek text of the difficult conditional sentence follows: ἐὰν μὴ ἐν τοῖς ἀρχείοις εὕρω ἐν τῷ εὐαγγελίῳ οὐ πιστεύω.

writes, but for all of his claims he is far from associating himself with the apostles. Writing to the Romans, for example, he says, "I do not command you as Peter and Paul; they were apostles, I am a condemned man" (*Romans* 4:3; cf. *Trallians* 3:3). The Christian revelation, according to Ignatius, therefore, decidedly is not a contemporaneous revelation; it is a revelation in the past which found its embodiment in Jesus Christ and found authoritative expression in the deliverances of the apostles. To some extent Ignatius may have depended upon oral transmission of the apostolic tradition, but there can be little question that he relied chiefly upon its written expression. It is generally acknowledged, for example, that he knew and used our canonical Matthew, and though he does not refer specifically to this book or identify it with "the gospel," it must have been to him an expression of the apostolic proclamation of the past which he acknowledged as standing on a level with, and even transcending, the Old Testament Scriptures. So also when he speaks of a collection of epistles of Paul, he evidently regards them as an authoritative expression of the ordinances of the apostles (*Ephesians* 12). The testimony of Ignatius like that of *1 Clement*, accordingly, demonstrates that the collection of New Testament writings, and their acknowledgment as authoritative alongside of the Old Testament, were but the concrete realization in history of principles operative in the first decades of the second century.

Our next witness is a voice from Asia Minor. Papias of Hierapolis was the author of a work entitled *Exposition of Oracles of the Lord* which was published within the second quarter of the second century. To our great loss this work is no longer extant, although fortunately a few fragments have been preserved, chiefly by Eusebius. The Eusebian quotations are so meager and isolated that dogmatism with respect to the views of Papias must be eschewed; at the same time they are so significant, as containing some of the earliest traditions concerning the New Testament, that one may not fairly challenge their right to a preeminent place in modern discussions.

A particular reason for including Papias in this brief survey is that he is often held to demonstrate that as late as a time close to the middle of the second century a Christian churchman could be quite indifferent to the canonicity of the New Testament. Quite recently, for example, John Knox has spoken of "Papias' depreciation of written Gospels and his preference for 'the living voice.' "[26] The passage which has been supposed to ground such conclusions is the final sentence of the Eusebian quotation from the preface of Papias' work, in which he says: "For I did not suppose that the things from books would profit me as much as those from a living and abiding voice." The context indeed indicates the interest of Papias in oral tradition, specifically in the tradition handed down from the earliest disciples of the Lord. We must deny, however, the validity of the inference commonly drawn from Papias' statement. Can one seriously allow that Papias depreciated written gospels when one considers his characterization of the Gospel according to Mark? He represents Mark as an accurate and trustworthy account of the things either said or done by the Lord as they had been proclaimed by the apostle Peter. "Of one thing he took forethought," says Papias, "not to omit anything of the things he had heard or to falsify anything in them" (*Ecclesiastical History* 3.39.15 [Loeb, 1:297]).

Moreover, although this is disputed, we think that Papias is so far from depreciating the gospels that he even characterizes them as being or consisting of "the oracles of the Lord."

26. *Marcion and the New Testament*, 114.

1157

He implies that Mark carried out what Peter had himself failed to do, namely, to make a composition of oracles of the Lord. And speaking of Matthew he also characterizes his work as a composition of "the oracles," thus indicating that he has a written work in mind. If Papias is using the word "oracles" in the title of his work in this same sense, it follows that his aim was to provide *an exposition of the gospels*. The question remains how then he could express a preference for oral tradition as compared with books. It seems commonly to be overlooked that, in the opening sentence of the portion of the preface quoted by Eusebius, Papias sets forth clearly enough the subordinate place to be occupied by oral traditions within the structure of his work, for he says that he will not hesitate "*to append* to the interpretations" the things that had come down to him orally from ancient witnesses. In other words, his exposition or interpretation of the oracles is primary, the recollection of ancient oral tradition is secondary. If then Papias characterizes the gospels as "the oracles of the Lord" in the Marcan passage, and apparently also in the title of his work, we possess a most significant testimony to the reverent regard with which he held the ancient writings. He applies to them a designation which expresses their inspired character; he applies to them the designation which was employed to express the oracular character of the Old Testament.[27]

When we turn from Papias to Justin Martyr we enjoy the great advantage of being able to judge his testimony in the context of writings of considerable length. Justin Martyr wrote in Rome in the sixth decade of the second century, but his earlier contacts with eastern regions of the church make him a witness for a far wider area. The testimony of Justin is most crucial. His testimony and his silences are commonly made the basis for the conclusion that, in the middle of the century, the church had not yet arrived at a New Testament canon. Justin, says Harnack, "is simply crying for a New Testament" but "cannot produce it."[28] It is true, of course, that Justin's writings present an extraordinary witness to the secure place which the Christian church accorded to the canonicity of the Old Testament. Moreover, he makes pervasive use of the Old Testament for apologetic purposes: in his apology to the heathen world employing it to establish the antiquity of Christianity, and in his argument with Trypho, the Jew, as providing a common ground for discussion. Admittedly Justin does not use and characterize the apostolic writings in the same fashion. But the question to be kept before the historian in the evaluation of evidence like that of Justin, in our judgment, is not primarily the question whether New Testament writings are appealed to specifically as "Scripture" but whether they are acknowledged as possessing divine authority alongside of the Old Testament. When the question is put in such terms we are convinced that the answer demanded by the testimony of Justin is different from that often provided.

In the first place, we cannot doubt that Justin fully acknowledged the coming of a new era of revelation which found its origin and authority, as well as its central content, in Jesus Christ. Jesus Christ is the authoritative teacher of the Christians and it is his life, the life of the Son of God, which constitutes the fulfillment of the prophetic revelation. Christ is the "new law and the new covenant" (*Dialogue with Trypho* 11).

In the second place, the new revelation finds expression in Christian documents. It is not confined to the prophetic word of the Old Testament. It is not merely an oral tradition of

27. Cf. esp. Romans 3:2. For the meaning of the term, see the important article of B. B. Warfield, "The Oracles of God," in *Revelation and Inspiration*, 335–91.

28. *Die Entstehung des Neuen Testaments,* 12 (English translation, 16). See also Knox, *Marcion and the New Testament*, 24 and especially note 9.

Christian content. The manner in which Justin speaks of certain Christian documents, and especially of the Gospels, prohibits any other conclusion. In the *Apology*, perhaps because the stress of his argument falls upon the antiquity of Christianity, there are few definite allusions to the Gospels. In the famous passage in which he describes the worship of the Christians, however—a passage, therefore, in which he is more didactic than apologetic—he accords them the highest place alongside of the Old Testament. In the preceding paragraph, where he has been concerned with the Eucharist, he refers its authority to the apostolic record: "For the apostles in the memoirs which were composed by them, which are called gospels, thus delivered unto us what was commanded them" (1.66). The authority of the apostolic record, an authority ultimately derived from the Lord himself, is here clearly recognized. Now the nature of that authority is most precisely set forth in the passage which treats of the service on the Lord's Day:

> And on the day called Sunday there is a gathering together to one place of all those who live in cities or in the country, and the memoirs of the apostles or the writings of the prophets are read, as long as time permits. Then when the reader has ceased the president presents admonition and invitation to the imitation of these good things. (1.67)

Here then is reflected not merely the personal slant of Justin but the common Christian practice in Rome and perhaps also in other parts of the Christian world for which Justin could speak. The authority of the apostolic gospels does not fall short of the authority of the prophetic writings; in fact, he mentions the apostolic writings before the others and intimates that they may be read in place of the Old Testament, and not merely along with the Old Testament. It will not be pertinent to retort that public reading is not decisive evidence of canonicity. Our appeal to this passage is not to the effect that the public lection of apostolic writings is evidence of canonical regard, but rather that Justin clearly did not place the Gospels in a category inferior to the Old Testament. He is not speaking, moreover, of an occasional reading of apostolic writings but of their regular use in the church alongside of the Old Testament.

In the *Dialogue* the references to the Gospels accumulate, perhaps because Trypho was well acquainted with them. And it is highly significant that in a number of cases he employs the formula "It is written," or similar language, in introducing quotations from the Gospels (*Dialogue with Trypho* 49, 103, 105, 107). The question arises, however, whether after all we may allow that Justin regarded the Gospels as Scripture in view of his failure ever to characterize them as inspired by the Holy Spirit. If Justin had spoken of the apostolic writings as inspired, we should indeed have reason to regard such testimony as confirmation of our general conclusion. Still the absence of such language does not establish the contrary. The characteristic difference in the designation of prophetic and apostolic writings may be explained from the different evaluation of their place within the total structure of revelation. The significance of the Old Testament was chiefly due to its prophetic character—it was the product of the Spirit of prophecy. The significance of the apostolic memoirs, on the other hand, was that they constituted the historical fulfillment of prophecy, and they are described as the product of the Lord and of the apostles as his instruments. Although the apostles are not described as inspired, they are acknowledged as the spokesmen of the Lord in the new dispensation as the prophets were of the Spirit in the old (*Dialogue with Trypho* 119; cf. *Apology* 1.33, 49–50, 39).

Accordingly, a New Testament is present both in idea and fact according to Justin's testimony. We miss a well-rounded statement of the canonicity of the New Testament. Its limits are not defined. But inasmuch as Christian writings are accorded a place of absolute authority alongside of the Old Testament the essence of the matter is present.

A further question must be raised, even though no completely satisfactory answer can be provided. That question is whether the New Testament of Justin contains only Gospels. It is remarkable that he refers only to "the memoirs of the apostles," which evidently are Gospels, in speaking of the Christian public service. It is also noteworthy that he nowhere, in spite of his knowledge of Pauline epistles, appeals to Paul as an authority. We can only wish that Justin had commented expressly on his estimate of the epistles in relation to the Gospels. There are real problems which press for solution. Nevertheless, we think the silence of Justin on these matters is not of sufficient weight to require the definite conclusion that only the Gospels were accepted as authoritative. It may not be forgotten that Justin is not concerned to describe the contents of the New Testament. His references are quite incidental, and there is no doubt that his extensive use of the Gospels was dictated by their significance for his apologetic argument. Moreover, his estimate of the apostles as spokesmen of the Lord, which has been noted above, precludes the judgment that he depreciated them. The Gospels too are accepted as apostolic. And it is significant that he acknowledges the Revelation of John as apostolic and as a divine revelation (*Dialogue with Trypho* 81). It appears therefore that his description of the apostolic writings which were read alongside of the Old Testament was not exhaustive.

The scope of this discussion does not permit or require any detailed examination of the documents which tell of the developments near the close of the second century. In the writings of church fathers like Irenaeus, Tertullian and Clement of Alexandria, and in the *Muratorian Canon*, we are on firm ground. The church is in conscious possession of a New Testament. Some writers speak of it precisely as "the New Testament." It is described as Scripture and as inspired by the Holy Spirit. There is clear indication that it includes, besides the Gospels, the Acts, a considerable collection of epistles, and the Revelation.

It seems to us altogether certain that the struggle with Gnosticism, Marcion and Montanism contributed to the clear-cut formulation of the church's doctrine of Scripture. This contribution has commonly been exaggerated but it may not be ignored. The evidence does not warrant the conclusion that the church about the year 175 came to create a New Testament and thus arrived at an essentially new estimate of the apostolic writings. But in the formulation of the canonicity of the New Testament, as in the formulation of doctrine generally, a definite impulse, not to say compulsion, resulted from the claims made by the heretics. Marcion's rejection of the Old Testament and his distinctive treatment of certain apostolic writings required the church to set forth in explicit terms the view of the apostolic writings which accorded with its own fundamental view of the history of revelation. Similarly the Montanist affirmation of contemporaneous revelation, and of its superiority to the apostolic revelation, demanded that the unique authority of the apostolic disclosure should be unequivocally affirmed. Our general conclusion then is not to the effect that the situation as regards the New Testament canon about the year 200 corresponded exactly with that of the year 100. It is, however, a protest against the current view that the formation of the New Testament was a sudden development late in the second century. There is development in the collection and recognition of the New Testament writings as canonical, but in all the history there is a solid continuity which comprehends not only the second century but the first as well.

That whole development was a complex historical process. We cannot fully explain how exactly the twenty-seven writings of the New Testament, to the exclusion of all others, came to be acknowledged as inspired and authoritative. The development as a matter of fact was by no means complete at the end of the second century. Athanasius of Alexandria, writing in A.D. 367, provides the earliest testimony, so far as our present evidence goes, to a list which corresponds exactly with our present list of New Testament writings. However complex the process was, we may observe various historical factors which were operative. And we regard it as unmistakable that the historical factor of most fundamental significance was the conception that the revelation of the new covenant was essentially an historical revelation, a revelation which found its embodiment in the history of Jesus Christ, and which was mediated to the church through the apostles. The inscripturation of that revelation was not confined to the apostles, nor indeed do we possess evidence of a definite apostolic sanction of the new writings, but the essentially apostolic character of the new revelation is everywhere in view.

Although it is highly important that this historical process be studied and analyzed as a part of our effort to comprehend the implications of the church's doctrine of Scripture, we also insist that the comprehension of the whole development depends on a recognition of divine control of history and of the special guidance of the Spirit of God. Just as the Old Testament church was "intrusted with the oracles of God" (Rom. 3:2), the New Testament church was intrusted with the oracles of the Lord. The acknowledgment of the Old Testament as canonical did not await the ratification which the Lord Jesus Christ provided but, as it were, established itself in the organic life of the people of God. Likewise the Spirit who inspired holy men provided that outward control and inward illumination which guaranteed that exactly the divine writings should be brought together and acknowledged at their true worth.[29]

It will hardly be contested that, according to the New Testament, the church was constituted to be the pillar and ground of the truth, and that the Lord Jesus Christ, its establisher and head, sent forth the Spirit to lead it into all truth. The church is not the creator of the truth but serves to support and exhibit the truth. It receives the truth and is assured a recognition and apprehension of the truth.

As a part of its confession of faith in God the church came to declare that the truth of God committed to it finds concrete expression in the Scriptures. Hence, although the church lacks infallibility, its confession with regard to the Scriptures, represents not mere opinion but an evaluation which is valid as derived from, and corresponding with, the testimony of the Scriptures to their own character. The basic fact of canonicity remains, then, the testimony which the Scriptures themselves bear to their own authority. But the historian of the canon must recognize the further fact that that intrinsic authority established itself in the history of the church through the government of its divine head.

---

29. Cf. Frederik Willem Grosheide, *Algemeene Canoniek van het Nieuwe Testament* (Amsterdam: H. A. van Bottenburg, 1935), 122, 132ff., 158, 182–83, 204–5; Abraham Kuyper, *Encyclopaedie der Heilige Godgeleerdheid*, 2nd ed. (Kampen: J. H. Kok, 1908), 2:415; English translation, *Encyclopedia of Sacred Theology* (New York: Scribner, 1898), 461.

This reckoning with the divine rule in the formation of the canon does not represent, we contend, an obscurantist flight from reality. Rather this approach to the history of the canon, like the fundamental idea of canonicity itself, as previously observed, is involved in Christian theism. And Christian theism, far from being a philosophy of last resort, constitutes a foundational and all-embracing philosophy of reality. This point of view stands sharply against any view of reality which finds its beginning and end in man, against those views which find the ultimate standard of judgment in the autonomy of man as an individual as also against those whose appeal to the authority of men in their corporate relationships, including even the supposed final authority of the living church. Man must choose whom he will serve: God or man. To choose a philosophy which makes man ultimate is, in our judgment, to commit intellectual and moral suicide. To acknowledge the final authority of the God of Christian theism, the God of the Bible, is, however, to guarantee intellectual and moral integrity. True religion, as involving a right relationship to the living God, must accept God and him alone as the infallible rule of faith and life. His Word must necessarily bear witness to its intrinsic divine character and must establish its authority in history.

The New Testament as Canon

RICHARD B. GAFFIN JR.

Richard B. Gaffin Jr., "The New Testament as Canon," in *Inerrancy and Hermeneutic*, 165–83.

Chapter 51 above already provides a brief introduction of Richard B. Gaffin Jr. One of the central issues of the doctrine of Scripture is the definition of the canon. Stonehouse had taken up the issue in 1946. A little over forty years later, Gaffin in "The New Testament as Canon" examines the topic afresh. In this present selection, Gaffin considers the historical development and the criteria of canonicity, demonstrating that ultimately God is the Author of the canon. He concludes his article by stating the implications of this commitment. Following Herman Ridderbos, *Redemptive History and the New Testament Scriptures* (1963, 1968), Gaffin integrates in a characteristic way the discipline of canonics together with the discipline of biblical theology. In addition, Gaffin's ideas on the completeness of the New Testament are congruent with views expressed in his book *Perspectives on Pentecost: New Testament Teaching on the Gifts of the Holy Spirit* (1979).

To accept the New Testament as canonical is, in a word, to acknowledge the twenty-seven writings in the second part of the Holy Bible as possessing divine authority and as constituting accordingly, an integral part of the divine rule for faith and life. In attributing divine authority to these writings, the Christian church obviously judges that such authority is to be acknowledged only because these writings are held to possess inherently, that is, by virtue of what they actually are, the right to such a claim.

—NED B. STONEHOUSE, 1946

Applied to the New Testament as the written Word of God, the word *canon* describes it as a collection of documents that, together with the Old Testament, possesses final authority in matters of faith and life.[1] This historic Christian confession is subject to scrutiny from two basic angles—historical and theological: (1) When and how did the church in fact come to accept these twenty-seven books as canon? (2) Was and is the church warranted in regarding them as canon? The second of these questions is the concern of this chapter.

On its theological side, the canon question is, one may say, the crucial question of New Testament Introduction; the answer given to it decisively controls subsequent interpretation, especially in overall understanding of the New Testament. In the study of the Bible, however, historical and theological questions may not be divorced from each other; the answers to the two sorts of questions inevitably condition each other (because of the historical nature of the biblical documents). This is especially so for the issue of the New Testament canon. When theological reflection takes place in isolation from historical investigation, the former becomes abstract and speculative; in concentrating on the theological side of the canon question, we must be careful not to forget or distort the historical picture. It will be useful, then, to preface our discussion by noting, however briefly, the results of historical inquiry concerning the canon.

Contemporary scholarship, for the most part, is agreed that by the end of the second century (ca. A.D. 180) the four Gospels, Acts, the thirteen letters of Paul, 1 Peter, and 1 John were widely accepted throughout the church as canonical, that is, as constituent parts of a "New Testament," on a par in revelatory character and authority with what by that acceptance became its "Old Testament." Among the primary evidence for this consensus are the writings of Irenaeus and the earliest extant list of books, the Muratorian Canon. The canonical status of other documents (some eventually included in the canon, some ultimately rejected) continued to be debated for approximately two centuries until, in the last third of the fourth century, the present twenty-seven-book canon, facilitated by several ecclesiastical decisions, secured its fixed and permanent place in the life of the church—although random, peripheral exceptions continued for a time.

Scholars are also largely agreed on the importance of Marcion and other second-century heretics in forcing the Great Church to give its attention to the canon question. Division of opinion persists, however, over the nature of that influence. Basically the issue is this: Did Marcion create the idea of the New Testament canon, introducing something previously foreign or at least nonexistent in the life of the church? Or did Marcion's canon have a catalytic effect, forcing the mainstream of the church to account more explicitly for what it already possessed (and was already aware of possessing)? Does the New Testament canon antedate the middle of the second century or not?[2]

Noncanonical materials available from before that time are relatively sparse and do not yield a decisive answer to this question. Consequently, scholarly attention has shifted to the New Testament documents themselves in order to clarify the historical picture. With that shift canon has ceased to be purely an issue in New Testament Introduction. Increasingly in this century, especially within the historical-critical tradition, the question of canon has

---

1. See, e.g., WCF 1.2–3.

2. A helpful survey of the history of the recognition, formation, and closing of the canon is provided by A. B. du Toit, "The Canon of the New Testament," in *Guide to the New Testament* (Pretoria: N. G. Kerkboekhandel, 1979), 1:184–257; see also E. F. Harrison, *Introduction to the New Testament* (Grand Rapids: Eerdmans, 1971), 98–134; more briefly, Bruce M. Metzger, "Canon of the New Testament," in *Hastings Dictionary of the Bible*, rev. ed., ed. F. C. Grant and H. H. Rowley (New York: Scribner, 1963), 123–27; most recent is Metzger's magisterial treatment in *The Canon of the New Testament* (Oxford: Clarendon Press, 1987), 39–247; cf. 289–93, 305–15.

become as much an exegetical/hermeneutical as an introductory one. Accordingly, historical and theological considerations patently intertwine. Concern with the New Testament as canon has become inseparable from (and in some cases virtually identical to) concern with the theology/theologies of the New Testament and various efforts to specify its presumably normative center (the "canon within the canon").[3] Invariably, it seems, attention to the canon question brings to light one's own basic presuppositions and theological commitments. That is true as well of the discussion that follows.

The Problem

On the assumption, substantiated below, that inscripturated revelation was given in conjunction with the completion of Christ's work and the founding of the church, the real problem of the New Testament as canon is its completed or closed character. Why does the church accept this concrete collection, just these twenty-seven books and no others? How do we know that there is not some document, now unknown, which may some day be discovered and consequently deserve to be included? Alternatively, how do we know that something has not slipped in which really does not belong?

The status of these questions, it should be noted, differs in important respects from the situation of the Old Testament. The canonical standing of the Old Testament as a whole (see, e.g., Luke 24:44–45) and of most of the individual books is clearly established on the inspired authority of Christ and the New Testament writers and also corroborated in Judaism by the end of the first century A.D. For the New Testament, however, there is no such subsequent inspired, authoritative testimony to its constituent documents and their canonicity.

The questions just raised can take on a pressing, perhaps even distressing, character when we pose them in the light of what we know about the actual course of developments in the early church. As noted above, it was a slow process, covering roughly three hundred years, before the canon accepted in the church was the same as our twenty-seven-book canon. Athanasius's so-called Easter Letter of 367 is apparently the first official, ecclesiastical decision to that effect. And there were significant differences at earlier stages (for example, over Hebrews and Revelation), even among orthodox figures. Why, for instance, did the Shepherd of Hermas, despite initial support, eventually go by the board, while 2 Peter, at first subject to much uncertainty, ultimately find a secure place in the canon?

All told, how do we know that in accepting the present New Testament—and the authority that goes with it—we are not simply following well-intentioned but nonetheless fallible decisions of people like ourselves?

Criteria of Canonicity?

It may seem that the solution to this problem lies in the direction of establishing or distinguishing certain criteria—an index or mark that, by its presence or absence, demonstrates the canonicity or the noncanonical status of a book in question. That, notice carefully, would have to be a criterion in the sense of a *sufficient* as well as necessary condition for canonicity—that is, not simply any characteristic, no matter how essential, but a mark distinguishing each of the documents in the canon and just these documents alone.

---

3. This trend is especially clear in the collection of essays in Ernst Käsemann, ed., *Das Neue Testament als Kanon* (Göttingen: Vandenhoeck & Ruprecht, 1970); cf. H. Y. Gamble, *The New Testament Canon* (Philadelphia: Fortress, 1985), 73–92.

This approach, promising at a first glance, is not viable. History shows that in fact the church has not been able to establish the criterion or set of criteria (*notae canonicitatis*) required. Nor, as I will try to show, can the church ever do so.

The most frequent proposal by far has been *apostolicity*. Certainly, as we will note below, there is a close connection between the apostles and the canon. But the difficulties for apostolic authorship or origin as a criterion are apparent.

Mark, Luke-Acts, Hebrews, Jude, and most likely James do not have apostles for authors. This objection has been countered by expanding the notion of apostolicity to include those who were close to the circle of apostles, so that what they wrote was associated with the authority of a particular apostle. But such an expansion fatally weakens apostolicity as a criterion of canonicity. There were no doubt other materials that would qualify as apostolic in an expanded sense but have not been included in the New Testament (see Luke 1:1). And an apostolic matrix for Hebrews is at best uncertain.

An even greater difficulty is posed by the references to Paul's "previous" letter to the Corinthians (1 Cor. 5:9) and his letter to the church at Laodicea (Col. 4:16). There is perhaps as well an allusion to previous written communication in Philippians 3:1. These documents, though evidently on a par with the canonical letters of Paul in apostolic authority, are not in the New Testament.

Other criteria that have been proposed are antiquity, public lection, and inspiration. *Antiquity*—only the earliest documents have been included in the canon—is really a variation on apostolicity, and it founders on the same difficulties; the "previous" letter of 1 Corinthians 5:9 is earlier, say, than Hebrews. *Public lection*—only those documents first read aloud in public worship are canonical—encounters the obstacle that, at an early point, documents like the Shepherd of Hermas and the Didache were used in public worship, while no evidence exists for such early usage of 2 Peter, 2 and 3 John, or Jude.

Inspiration, though necessary to canonicity, does not coincide with it. Paul's previous letter to the Corinthians and his letter to the Laodiceans carry full apostolic authority and are therefore presumably inspired. Without unduly multiplying nonextant documents, those letters suggest that he, along with at least some of the other apostles, produced a somewhat larger volume of inspired material (exactly how much is difficult to say) than has subsequently been included in the canon. Furthermore, there would be the insuperable difficulty of having to *demonstrate* inspiration for each New Testament document—if it is to serve as a criterion of canonicity.

This classical quest for criteria of canonicity should not be confused with what went on in the early church; the two differ markedly from each other. The former considers the New Testament as a completed entity already accepted by the church; it seeks to account, after the fact, for the inclusion of the twenty-seven books and those alone. In contrast, until late in the fourth century and beyond, the church was still in the process of reaching a consensus concerning which documents belong to the New Testament.

That earlier effort also made use of criteria—notably apostolic authorship and conformity to apostolic teaching (orthodoxy). Yet here, too, the application of criteria (in the strict sense) was defective. Hebrews, for instance, was accepted only when and where the church concluded that Paul was its author. In this case, ultimately, the early church made the right decision for the wrong reason.

Within the so-called historical-critical tradition, to comment briefly, the canon question has been approached along radically different lines. As the work of J. S. Semler (1725–91) already made unmistakably clear,[4] that approach, premised on the assumed rational autonomy of the interpreter/historian, has resulted in rejecting the church's historic conception of the canon (along with its accompanying understanding of biblical inspiration) as an outdated, unenlightened piece of supernaturalism. Operating characteristically with a radicalized version of Luther's criterion *was Christum treibet* ("what urges/promotes/inculcates Christ"), the formal authority of the New Testament documents as a collective entity is rejected, and the search goes on for some element of material authority within them (a "canon within the canon").

Increasingly in this century the impact of activistic, nonverbal conceptions of revelation (e.g., that of Karl Barth) has given rise to views of canonicity in which a normative center is played off in an activistic, more or less dialectical fashion against the competing, even contradictory teaching and theologies allegedly contained in the New Testament as a whole (see, e.g., the views of E. Käsemann: the New Testament itself is an ongoing "battleground" [*Kampfplatz*] for the gospel, wherein Christ and Antichrist, faith and superstition, struggle against each other).[5]

The church, as we have seen, has in fact failed to establish criteria of canonicity. Even more telling, however, is the recognition that, in principle, all attempts to demonstrate such criteria must fail and threaten to undermine the canonicity of Scripture. For example, suppose we take X (say, apostolicity) to be a criterion of canonicity. That would mean entering into a historical investigation to identify and circumscribe X. But such a procedure could only mean subjecting the canon to the relativity of historical study and our fallible human insight. That is, it would destroy the New Testament as canon, as absolute authority.

In the final analysis the attempt to demonstrate criteria (the necessary and sufficient conditions) of canonicity seeks, from a position above the canon, to rationalize or generalize about the canon as a unique, particular historical state of affairs. It relativizes the authority of the canon by attempting to contain it (*kanōn*) within an all-embracing criterion (*kritērion*).

Instead we must recognize that we are shut up to the New Testament canon as a self-establishing, self-validating entity. Canonicity is a unique concept. It neither coincides with what is apostolic nor even with what is inspired. Rather, canonical is what belongs to the New Testament, and what belongs to the New Testament is canonical. (The evident circularity of the last sentence is not unintended!)

God Is Canon

We ought not, then, to try to secure for ourselves an Archimedean point outside or above the New Testament canon. Yet, in another respect, the canon does point back beyond itself—to God, its origin and author. When we think of the idea of canon (supreme authority), we may not think of anything or any other person than God. God is canon; God is supreme authority.

In dealing with the question of the canon and its closing, we must not lose sight of this personal reference in the notion of canon. Otherwise we will fall into some form of viewing history as, at least to some degree, an autonomous, impersonal process. Here (as in all historical studies)[6] we are to think concretely, "personalistically," so that history is recognized for

---

4. J. S. Semler, *Abhandlung von der freien Untersuchung des Kanons . . .* (Halle, 1771–75).

5. Ernst Käsemann, "Zusammenfassung," in *Das Neue Testament als Kanon*, 407–8.

6. See the valuable discussion by Cornelius Van Til, "The Christian Philosophy of History," in *Common Grace and the Gospel* (Philadelphia: Presbyterian and Reformed, 1947), 1–13.

what it is—down to its most minute details the realization of God's eternal, predeterminate counsel and good pleasure.

The collection of New Testament documents is not a historical phenomenon to be explained in terms of purely immanent factors—contingent factors, in turn, without an ultimate explanation. The New Testament is not a collection that "just happened," a kind of brute fact hanging there on the horizon of the past. Rather, it is the historical phenomenon by which God, the sovereign Architect and Lord of history, asserts and maintains himself as canon, that is, by which his supreme authority comes to expression.

With these observations we have arrived at a provisional answer to the question of an opened or closed canon, though that answer needs to be elaborated and further substantiated. How can we avoid confessing that God is the author of the Bible (the New Testament) as a whole, the architect of the collective entity? The only other alternative, on the assumption of inscripturated verbal revelation, is that the Bible (the New Testament) is a human anthology of divinely inspired writings and, if so, is open, in principle, to revision and requires verification. But such a human-anthology view of the canon, as we will presently see, runs counter to the witness of the New Testament documents themselves. In the sense that God is the author of the whole as well as the constituent parts, the New Testament canon is closed or complete.

This conclusion involves an important distinction. The origin of the New Testament canon is not the same as its reception by the church. We must avoid confusing the existence of the canon with its recognition, what is constitutive (God's action) with what is reflexive (the church's action). The activity of the church—statements of church fathers, decrees of councils, and so forth concerning the contents of the New Testament—does not create the canon.

The New Testament Canon and the History of Redemption (Apostolicity and Canonicity)

The viewpoint just expressed is sometimes called the a priori of faith. But that a priori, as so far stated, is not the last word, which would make further discussion of the canon issue unnecessary.[7]

"Faith comes by hearing and hearing by the word of Christ" (Rom. 10:17). Taken in the context of verses 14–16, this statement reminds us that true faith is nothing apart from its content, the content given to it and that it receives. Only this content-full faith provides a biblically warranted a priori.

That involves, among other things, recognizing that the New Testament canon is bound up with the giving of revelation in history. Scripture has not been dropped straight down from heaven, as it were. As much as possible, then, our statements about the canon should be qualified historically. Without, on the one hand, abandoning our a priori or, on the other, trying to make faith (or redemptive history) a criterion of canonicity in a strict sense, we need to reflect further on that faith a priori in the light of Scripture. We will seek to explicate within the circle of faith, without leaving that circle.

7. For the discussion in this section, see esp. Herman Ridderbos, *Redemptive History and the New Testament Scriptures* (Phillipsburg, NJ: Presbyterian and Reformed, 1988), part 1; Ned B. Stonehouse, "The Authority of the New Testament," in *The Infallible Word*, ed. Ned B. Stonehouse and Paul Woolley (Phillipsburg, NJ: Presbyterian and Reformed, 1980), 92–140; du Toit, "Canon of the New Testament," 91–170.

The apostles as representatives of Christ: the christological dimension. The Greek noun *apostolos*, related to the much more common verb *apostellō* (to send, send out), refers in general to a messenger or, more formally, to an envoy or delegate. Traditionally, then, the New Testament apostle has been understood primarily as a religious figure like a missionary, someone sent to communicate the gospel. That understanding no doubt has a large element of truth.

More recently, however, studies in the background of the New Testament have shed new light on the figure of the apostle in the New Testament. In particular, a line has been drawn to the figure of the *šālîah* in intertestamental Judaism. In fact, that relationship and the extent to which the latter influenced the former continue to be debated. But that debate does not have to be settled here for us to recognize that the Jewish institution does at least serve as a backdrop to illumine an important point of New Testament teaching about apostolicity.

In the Judaism contemporary to the writing of the New Testament, the *šālîah* (from *šālîah*, "to send") has a significance that is legal, not religious.[8] The *šālîah* is someone authorized to execute a task in the interests of another person or group. The content of this commission can vary greatly (from economic tasks like carrying out a business deal to social activities like arranging a marriage). The fact of his authorization rather than a particular content distinguishes the *šālîah*. He is an authorized, authoritative representative, akin to someone today who exercises power of attorney. Furthermore, the *šālîah* was identified fully with the one who commissioned him; in some instances he was free to take initiatives in discharging his commission. This full authority, the fulness of empowered representation, is reflected in the Talmudic formula that "a man's *šālîah* is the same as himself."

Something of this background is reflected in the figure of the apostle in the New Testament. In John 13:12–20, the issue of authority is prominent (the point, paradoxically, is the authority to serve others, exemplified in Jesus' washing the disciples' feet). The focus of verse 16 is the derivative nature of the apostles' authority—"no servant is greater than his master, nor is an *apostolos* greater than the one who sent him" (cf. Heb. 3:1–2, where Jesus is "appointed" by God as *apostolos*). Verse 20 not only expresses this point of derivation but accents the identification of the sender and the one sent: "whoever accepts anyone I send accepts me; and whoever accepts me accepts the one who sent me."

At issue, then, is the uniqueness and fulness of apostolic authority. The apostles encountered in the New Testament, with the few exceptions noted in the next paragraph, are "apostles of Christ." As such they are authorized representatives of Christ, deputized personal exemplifications of his authority. Note, for instance, Galatians 4:14, where Paul says of himself as an angel-apostle (cf. 1:1–2:10) that the Galatians received him "as if I were Christ Jesus himself."

A certain elasticity does attach to the New Testament usage of *apostolos*. Second Corinthians 8:23 ("apostles of the churches") and Philippians 2:23 (perhaps, too, Acts 14:4, 14) refer in a looser, most likely temporary, ad hoc sense to messengers or representatives sent by a local church for a specific task. This usage is in distinction from the apostles of Christ in the strict sense, who are "first" in the (one, universal) church (1 Cor. 12:28; cf. Eph. 4:11). In which sense the reference in Romans 16:7 is to be taken is difficult to say.

---

8. See e.g., K. H. Rengstorf, in G. Kittel, ed., *Theological Dictionary of the New Testament,* trans. and ed. G. W. Bromiley (Grand Rapids: Eerdmans, 1964), 1:414–20.

The apostles as foundation of the church: the ecclesiological dimension. The apostle of Christ does not operate on his own. He is not an unusually resourceful, charismatic free-lancer. Rather, he has his apostolic identity and function only as part of a group, a unified structure that the New Testament itself describes with the abstract noun *apostolē* (apostleship, apostolate—Acts 1:25; Rom. 1:5; 1 Cor. 9:2; Gal. 2:8). That function is always in the interests of the church.

This point can be amplified by considering the basic New Testament figure of the church as a house. This is a dynamic-historical figure: the church results from the construction activity of God as architect-builder in the period between the resurrection and return of Christ.

In terms of this house model, the apostles are the foundation of the church structure. Note Matthew 16:18, "You are Peter, and on this rock I will build my church." Peter is the foundation on which Christ, looking to the future beyond his resurrection and ascension, will build the church. This promise is not made to Peter in the abstract but in view of his confession (vv. 16–17) and as he, with that confession, represents the other apostles (the apostolate). The rock foundation of the church is to be confessing Peter as primus inter pares, first among apostolic equals.

See also Ephesians 2:20, "built on the foundation of the apostles and prophets, with Christ Jesus himself as the chief cornerstone." In the immediate context (vv. 19–22), the house model is even more explicit (cf. 1 Peter 2:4–8). Christ is the cornerstone; in the foundation his is the critical place that supports everything. In fact, in view of his unique, once-for-all work of redemption there is "no other foundation" (1 Cor. 3:11 RSV). Yet in some specific respect, still to be determined, the apostles are associated with Christ as the foundation; they, too, are constitutive for the foundation.

The redemptive-historical place and function of the apostolate bears emphasizing. The house building in view in the last half of Ephesians 2 is a comprehensive historical figure (see vv. 11–22). It is a dynamic model, taking in the church in its broadest unity, in every time and place. Accordingly, the foundation of the church-house is temporally qualified. It is a historical category: laying the foundation of a building is a one-time activity; the ensuing construction is on the superstructure, not the constant, repeated re-laying of the foundation. This temporal limitation ties in with the fact, already noted, that the foundation involves the work of Christ in its once-for-all historicity. Hence, we are pointed to the conclusion that in the church the office of apostle is not intended to be perpetual; the apostolate is a temporary institution.

Several other passages reinforce this conclusion. According to Acts 1:21–26, a prerequisite for being an apostle was to have been among Jesus' disciples during the entire period of his earthly ministry (v. 21) and especially to have been an eye and ear witness of the resurrected Christ (v. 22)—a prerequisite that Paul sees as being met, with an exception, in his own case (1 Cor. 9:1; see also 15:7–9). In other words, a historically limiting restriction attaches to who may be an apostle.

In 1 Corinthians 15:7–9, Paul states in effect that he is the last of the apostles (explicitly in 4:9, probably without the inclusion of Apollos): he is "the least of the apostles" (15:9), inasmuch as the resurrected Christ appeared to him "last of all," as one born abnormally (v. 8), after he had already appeared to "all the apostles" (v. 7; see also Gal. 1:17).

In the Pastoral Epistles Paul plainly views Timothy, as much as anyone else, as his personal successor; the task of gospel ministry about to be laid down by him is to be taken up by Timothy and others. Yet Paul never refers to Timothy or Titus as an apostle.

These considerations prompt the observation that in a personal sense the expression "apostolic succession" is a contradiction in terms. The New Testament maintains the once-for-all character of the apostolate. The presence of apostles in the church is foundational, that is, temporary.

Notice, in passing, that Ephesians 2:20 associates prophets with the apostles in the church's foundation, in the historical sense just indicated. That these are New Testament prophets follows (1) from the word order ("the apostles and prophets"—not "the [Old Testament] prophets and [New Testament] apostles"), (2) from 3:5, where "now" refers to "God's holy apostles and prophets," just in contrast to "other [Old Testament] generations," and (3) because they are prophets in the church seen as still in the future in Matthew 16:18.

Consequently, we are drawn to recognize that the New Testament prophets, included with the apostles as part of the foundation of the church, are, like the apostles, a temporary institution in its life. The presence of the prophets is limited, by God's architectural design, to the foundational, apostolic era of the church.

The only way to avoid this conclusion, apparently, is to argue either (1) that the New Testament teaches two kinds of prophecy in the church—foundational, noncontinuing prophecy and prophecy, like that mentioned in 1 Corinthians 12–14 and elsewhere, that continues until Christ's return—or (2) that in Ephesians 2:20 the prophets in view are actually apostles, that is, the apostles as prophets. Both these views, however, especially the second, rest on exegesis that seems unlikely, even forced. The "prophethood" of all believers, a truth taught in Acts 2:17–18, for instance, and recaptured especially by the Reformation, is another matter and is certainly not being denied here; in fact, as we will see, that universal prophetic office rests on the once-for-all, foundational ministry of "the apostles and prophets."

The apostles as witnesses: the revelatory dimension. The single most important function of the apostles is their witness-bearing (*marturia*). The focus of apostolic witness, especially in Acts, is Christ's resurrection (e.g., Acts 1:21; 2:32; 3:15; 10:40–41), not as an isolated event but in the context of his whole work, especially his death (e.g., 2:22–24; 1 Cor. 15:3–4), and as the consummation of redemptive history (e.g., Acts 3:12–26; 13:16–41). The apostles testify to the already-accomplished redemptive basis of the church. That testimony, specifically, makes the apostles the foundation of the church. Their witness is the foundational witness to the foundational work of Christ; to the once-for-all work of Christ is joined a once-for-all witness to that work (Eph. 2:20).

Apostolic witness is normative; the apostles are uniquely authorized and empowered to be witnesses of Christ. This binding, *šālîaḥ* like character of the apostles' witness is seen in the equation of apostolic proclamation with the Word of God. Paul, for instance, says of the Thessalonians that they received his preaching "not as the word of men, but as it actually is, the word of God" (1 Thess. 2:13 NIV). Most likely, 1 Corinthians 11:23 ("For I received from the Lord what I also passed on to you") points to the exalted Lord himself as the author-bearer of apostolic tradition. According to Galatians 1:12, Paul's gospel is revelation received directly from Christ; yet, verse 18 intimates (in context) that revelation is on a par with the tradition he received through contact with the other apostles. Such an equation exists because, ultimately, both come from the exalted Christ (cf. Acts 9:26–27; 1 Cor. 15:1–4).

The promise of the coming of the Spirit as *paraklētos* (Counselor-Advocate, Helper) in John's Gospel (14:16, 26; 15:26–27; 16:7; cf. 16:13–15; Acts 1:8) is not given directly and indiscriminately to all believers. A specific historical qualification attaches to the "you" who are its immediate recipients. The "you" who are to testify are those who have been with Jesus during his earthly ministry "from the beginning," (John 15:27; note similar qualifications of "you" in 14:26; 16:7, 12). These promises are to be understood (at least primarily) in a foundational sense, that is, in terms of apostolic witness-bearing.

Apostolic witness, then, is not merely personal testimony. Instead, it is infallibly authoritative, legally binding deposition, the kind that stands up in a law court. Accordingly, that witness embodies a canonical principle; it provides the matrix for a new canon, the emergence of a new body of revelation to stand alongside the covenantal revelation of the Old Testament.[9]

The apostles and the canon: the canonical dimension. Plainly, as the apostles die and pass out of the picture, the need is for the preservation of apostolic witness in and by the church. In fact, the New Testament itself gives indications of an apostolic concern for such preservation.

Already at the time of the apostles, their witness is called "tradition" (*paradosis*). Its authoritative, binding character is seen in the fact that Paul, for instance, commands his readers to hold firmly to it (1 Cor. 11:2; 2 Thess. 2:15; cf. 3:6). Second Thessalonians 2:15 is especially instructive in referring to those traditions passed on "whether by word of mouth or by letter." Notice that here—shortly after 1 Thessalonians, perhaps the earliest New Testament document—written as well as oral apostolic tradition is already in view as authoritative.

Paul instructs Timothy to guard the *parathēkē* (deposit, what has been entrusted; see 1 Tim. 6:20; 2 Tim. 1:14 (12?); cf. 2:2). Here *parathēkē* is similar in meaning to *paradosis* and has the same authoritative ring: Timothy is to preserve and maintain the authoritative deposit of truth.

The New Testament itself, then, anticipates and initiates a trend; it fixes the coordinates of a trajectory. As the apostles die off and their foundational witness is completed, as their oral witness ceases and living apostolic oversight of that witness comes to an end, written apostolic witness becomes increasingly crucial and focal, until it, exclusively, is the foundational Word of God on which the church is being built.

This trend, as just noted, corresponds to the intention of Paul, for instance. Broadly considered, developments in the church concerning the canon during the second through fourth centuries complement that apostolic intention. Those developments involve the increasing awareness in the postapostolic church of its distance from the apostolic past and so an increasing awareness of the foundational, revelatory nature of inscripturated apostolic witness or tradition (note the sense of distance present already in 1 Clement [ca. A.D. 95] and the letters of Ignatius [ca. 110]).

The complement to the apostolic intention, in other words, is postapostolic recognition of the New Testament canon. Furthermore, that process of recognition—because it answers to an apostolic intention—reflects as well, we may say, the intention of Christ. No one less than the exalted Christ himself is the architect of that process.

9. For a stimulating development of the thesis that the canon is a function of the covenant, see Meredith G. Kline, *The Structure of Biblical Authority* (Grand Rapids: Eerdmans, 1972), 68–75 bear particularly on the New Testament, including the notion of the apostle as covenant witness.

Notice, however, how little this undeniable, substantial connection between the apostles and the canon provides a criterion of canonicity, even in a looser sense. Most of the New Testament documents with non-apostolic authors do display, either on internal grounds or by reliable tradition, a direct tie to one or other of the apostles. But that is not so clearly the case for Jude and not at all for Hebrews. In Hebrews 2:3, the author seems to separate himself from the apostolic circle while emphatically affirming apostolic tradition. Hebrews is the perennial "loose end" of every effort to provide an airtight rationale for the canon in terms of apostolic provenance.

The New Testament canon and the history of revelation: the redemptive-historical dimension. The foundational witness of the apostles to the work of Christ brings to light an important characteristic of all verbal revelation—the correlation between redemptive act and revelatory word; God's Word is given to attest and interpret his saving work. This correlation holds true throughout the entire history of redemption, beginning in the Garden of Eden and reaching its climax in the death, exaltation, and return of Christ. Accordingly, the ongoing history of revelation is a strand within covenant, redemptive history as a whole; the process of verbal revelation conforms to the contours of that larger history.

The history of redemption has an epochal character; it moves forward in decisive steps, not in a uniform or smoothly evolutionary fashion. Consequently, in view of the correlation just noted, high points in redemptive history are accompanied by copious outpourings of verbal revelation. Old-covenant revelation, for instance, tends to cluster around critical junctures like the exodus, key events in the monarchy, the exile, and the return of the remnant.

The negative side of this correlation bears particularly on the issue of the canon and its closing. Times of inactivity in the history of redemption are, correlatively, times of silence in the history of revelation. The rebuilding of the temple and the return of the remnant from exile are the last critical developments before the coming of Christ. After that there is a lull; redemptive history pauses until the final surge forward at Christ's coming. Correspondingly, the ministries of postexilic figures like Haggai, Zechariah, Malachi, Ezra, and Nehemiah and the Old Testament books associated with them focus on those events, and then follows, as intertestamental Judaism in part subsequently recognized, a period of revelatory, prophetic silence, until the time of Christ.

Similarly, after the exaltation of Christ and the founding of the church, there is a pause or delay in the epochal forward movement of redemptive history. Only one event in that history is still future: the return of Christ (with its concomitants). Accordingly, following the contemporaneous outpouring of revelation focused on the first coming of Christ, the history of revelation lapses into silence. Confirming that silence is the disappearance of the apostolate, that prophetic institution established by Christ specifically to provide revelatory attestation and interpretation of the redemption consummated in his person and work.

To say that redemptive history is "on hold" until Christ's return is not to deny the full reality and redemptive significance of what is happening in the church today. Ongoing church history, however, is not an extension of redemption. It is not a prolongation in series with Christ's work but the reflex of that work, the application of its benefits. It is not part of the foundation of the church but the building being erected on the finished, once-for-all redemptive foundation laid by Christ.

As far as the church today is concerned, then, the history of revelation is closed until Christ's return. The expectation of new revelation in whatever form runs counter to the witness of Scripture itself. At issue here is the correlation between redemptive act (in the sense of once-for-all accomplishment) and word revelation; where the former is lacking, there is no place for the latter. The completion or cessation of revelation is a function of the finished work of Christ (see Heb. 1:2, where the work of Christ, along with the corroborating witness of the apostles [or, in 2:3, "those who heard"], is God's final, "last days" revelation-speech).

Recognizing the redemptive-historical character of revelation is crucial to a proper view of the canon. Revelation does not consist of divinely given information and directives *pro me*, just for me. The impact of revelation on the believer ought to be intimate and personal, but it is not individualistic. In its virtually limitless applications to the circumstances of individual believers of whatever time and place, revelation has a corporate, covenantal character; it is for the one people of God as a whole. To the extent we fall into individualistic misunderstandings of revelation, to that extent we will be left with a sense of the insufficiency and incompleteness of the Bible. We will have difficulty in seeing that God's revelation to his people is complete and, so, that the New Testament canon is closed.

The New Testament Canon Is Closed

Relative to its concrete situation as the postapostolic church waiting for Christ's return—and not by some abstract, historically detached notion of closedness—the church can be confident that its New Testament is complete; there is nothing included that should be excluded, nothing missing that should be included. This conclusion can be focused by reflecting on the proverbial question of what ought to be done should an inspired apostolic writing one day be discovered—say, the previous letter mentioned in 1 Corinthians 5:9.

The sheer improbability of that discovery ought to be appreciated. Such an expectation is detached from a recognition of why God has given Scripture to the church in the first place. It is a matter of tradition which he intends for the church to hold fast and preserve. And the church cannot retain what it does not have.

The church would have to be far less fragmented than it has been for the past thousand years for it to recognize and then reach a consensus that such a writing is indeed canonical. Furthermore, such recognition could hardly claim continuity with what took place in the church during the first four centuries, when it was always a matter of deciding about documents that had all along been known, at least to some degree. But now there would be a new document abruptly introduced after nearly two thousand years.

But suppose, after all, that this hypothetical document were discovered and that it could be decided that it ought to be included in the church's Scriptures. That would still not mean that the present canon is or had been open or incomplete. Rather we ought to conclude that the church, by this addition, has been given a new canon. But just this idea of a new canon—an abrupt expansion, after such a long time, of the church's apostolic foundation—is highly speculative and difficult to square with the trajectories of New Testament teaching.

Granting the existence of inscripturated revelation, then, there are three basic positions on the New Testament canon. Two of these involve some form of the inherently self-contradictory notion of an "open" canon. One view is that *the New Testament is a human anthology of divinely inspired writings*. Strictly speaking, this view denies that God is the author of Scripture (as a whole). The collective entity is the product of fallible human beings, not the infallible construct of God; what we have in Scripture ultimately is the "whole counsel of man," not of God.

Inevitably on this view the meaning of the canon is impaired and its authority rendered defective. Each inspired document of Scripture does not have its authority or its overall intelligibility in isolation but in relation to the others, within the context provided by the Bible as a whole. All the documents of Scripture together constitute the frame in terms of which any one is to be understood finally and comprehensively. Consequently, to say that that frame is not divinely fixed, or is humanly fixed, precludes talking about the unity of the Bible. It casts a shadow of uncertainty on every single document and so undercuts the supreme authority of Scripture.

On another view, *the New Testament is, relatively speaking a complete entity shaped by God, but is continually supplemented by additional, new word revelation, by living prophetic voices in the church.* This view involves a dualistic misunderstanding of revelation. In one way or other, a distinction is made between a completed, canonical revelation for the whole church and ongoing private revelations for individual believers or particular groups of believers—between a collective, inscripturated revelation of what is necessary for salvation and revelations that go beyond the Bible and specifically address individual life situations, needs, and concerns.

The problem with this view is that it is in tension—even conflict—with what, as we have already intimated, the Bible itself shows to be the covenantal, redemptive-historical character of all revelation. God does not reveal himself along two tracks, one public and one private.

Certainly we may not dictate to God what he can or cannot do, on occasion, in revealing himself today. We must guard against boxing in the Holy Spirit by our theological constructions. At all times the Spirit is sovereign and free, like the wind, as Jesus says, that "blows wherever it pleases" (John 3:8). In his freedom, however, the Spirit orders his activity, and that order, according to Scripture, does not encourage believers today to seek or otherwise expect forms of extrabiblical revelation.[10]

The third view is that *the New Testament is that complete entity in which, along with the Old Testament, God gives his Word and brings his authority to expression, without restriction, in a definitive and absolute way.* This view, as I have tried to show, is most faithful to the apostolic witness of the New Testament itself. Admittedly, this view does not settle all difficulties. For one, the quantitative question remains: Why, of all the inspired apostolic writings, just these twenty-seven? Why not twenty-eight or twenty-six, or some other number?

To this question we must be content to say that just these twenty-seven books are what God has chosen to preserve, and he has not told us why. It seems difficult to improve on the comment of Calvin: "These [books] which the Lord judged to be necessary for his church have been selected by this providence for everlasting remembrance."[11]

In the matter of the New Testament as canon, too, until Jesus comes "we walk by faith, not by sight" (2 Cor. 5:7 RSV). But that faith, grounded in the apostolic tradition of the New Testament, is neither arbitrary nor blind. It has its reasons, its good reasons; it is in conflict only with the autonomy of reason.

Postscript: The New Testament Canon and Textual Criticism

The questions of canon and of the original text of the New Testament documents are not of the same order. To decide between variant readings is not to be involved, as it were, with the canon issue on its smallest scale.

---

10. See my *Perspectives on Pentecost* (Phillipsburg, NJ: Presbyterian and Reformed, 1986), 93–102, esp. 96–99 and 118–20.

11. John Calvin, *Commentaries on the Epistles of Paul to the Galatians and Ephesians,* trans. W. Pringle (1854; repr., Grand Rapids: Baker, 1979), 249.

The key to the categorical difference between these two concerns—text and canon—lies in the historically progressive and differentiated character of revelation. Inscripturated revelation did not come straight down from heaven into history, already written and all at once. The Bible in this respect differs markedly from the claims made, for instance, for the Book of Mormon (a translation of gold tablets all unearthed at the same time) or for the Koran (dictated to Muhammad in a series of night visions over a relatively short time span). Scripture, instead, originates in history, through the full personal involvement and instrumentality of various human writers, over a long period of time, and with a great variety of literary genres. The Bible is not uniform, a monolithic set of words or sequence of statements. In its unity it is manifold, multiplex (see Eph. 3:10).

The theological importance—even necessity—of this consideration should be appreciated. Its diverse and progressive character is intrinsic to biblical revelation, bound up with the ongoing movement of the history of redemption and the accompanying correlation, already discussed, between revelatory word and redemptive act. To use a figure, inscripturated revelation is not one large gold ingot produced at one point in time but a variety of pure gold nuggets given over an extended period of time.

This figure helps to identify the qualitative rather than the merely quantitative, arithmetic difference between the questions of canon and text. The concern of the former is to identify the collection of gold nuggets—what gold nuggets belong to the collection? The concern of the latter is the transmission of the collection and the removal of the specks of tarnish that have built up on this or that nugget. The difference between the canon question and textual criticism is, in a word, the difference between recognizing the gold and removing the tarnish.

It should not be thought, then, that the logic of an approach to the issue of canon that stresses the a priori of faith, like that adopted above, demands the superiority of either the Received or Majority texts of the Greek New Testament. It is wrong-headed to suppose that, if we admit uncertainty about particular textual variants or recognize that the Majority text is not the best and needs to be corrected, we are then denying God's wise and providential oversight of the transmission of the text and so are pitched into uncertainty about the New Testament canon as a whole.

In this regard, it needs to be remembered that plenary, verbal inspiration (inspiration at the level of words and extending to every word) does not mean that every word in Scripture has the same semantic importance or is equally crucial to its meaning. Nor does verbal inspiration mean that we must have every word of an autograph if we are to understand any word.

The issue of textual criticism needs to be kept in balance. Certainly its principles are not to be canonized and are always open to review and even revision. But as often pointed out, if we adopt any one of the current, mutually conflicting theories of the transmission of the New Testament text and reconstruct, in terms of that particular theory, the best and worst texts, the resulting differences are minimal and do not affect any substantial element of biblical teaching. This observation applies in particular to the differences between the Majority text (or the Received text) and a critically reconstructed text. Giving full, legitimate scope to textual criticism still enables us to continue confessing that God's inscripturated Word, "by His singular care and providence," has been "kept pure in all ages."[12]

12. WCF 1.8.

Part Eleven

CHALLENGES TO THE REFORMED DOCTRINE OF SCRIPTURE

GIVEN THAT CHALLENGES to the Reformed doctrine of Scripture have recently arisen, especially in the field of Old Testament studies, this part features discussions of specific topics relevant for Old Testament studies. The first two authors provide a more systematic outlook on the doctrine of inspiration. John M. Frame considers anew the doctrine of the self-witness of Scripture and moves on to respond to then-current philosophical and theological challenges. Raymond B. Dillard and Bruce K. Waltke both look at a specific challenge to the articulation of the doctrine of Scripture. Finally, Peter A. Lillback offers a more historical angle by examining some of the views of Peter Enns in relation to Westminster Seminary's commitment to the Westminster Standards (cf. chap. 17 above).

Edward J. Young's two chapters from his classic defense of the inspiration of Scripture offer not only a systematic presentation of the topic, but also the perspective of an Old Testament scholar. In the first chapter, he discusses the precise definition of inspiration. While not advocating mechanical inspiration, he asserts that the entirety of the Bible is inspired. He supports his view by a theistic argument close to the apologetic of his colleague Cornelius Van Til: If the Scriptures were to contain errors, then God himself would not be free from error. In the second chapter, he engages the topic of the human authorship of the Bible. He clearly defines his doctrine of Scripture on the basis of the self-witness of Scripture. His views allow for a full account of the human side of the Bible and its richness while preserving the infallible inspiration by the Spirit. Young can do this, in line with B. B. Warfield, because of his conviction that the sovereign God controlled the process of inspiration. Sinclair B. Ferguson expresses similar views in a very clear fashion. In contrast to modern critical scholars, he asserts that the doctrine of Scripture has to be defined by Scripture itself. He surveys the whole Bible to glean what it has to say about its own inspiration, authority, reliability, and necessity. Finally, he invites us to consider with humility the difficulties of the Bible (its phenomena), but to accept by faith and in full confidence its own teaching about itself.

Frame's two essays, originally contributions to *God's Inerrant Word* (1973), move from systematic considerations to responding to philosophical and theological challenges. The first essay advances the definition of the traditional doctrine of the self-witness of Scripture by considering the witness of the entire Bible in the footsteps of Meredith G. Kline. This self-witness is also conceived as an expression of God's lordship that permeates the whole of Scripture. The essay ends with a response to the skepticism of Karl Barth and Emil Brunner about the inspiration of Scripture. The second essay discusses the converging philosophical and theological challenges that question the adequacy of human language to communicate divine revelation. Frame responds on the basis of God's transcendent and immanent character that it is natural to conceive of God's revealing himself through human language.

The next two articles deal with crucial difficulties in the interpretation of the Old Testament. First, Dillard presents the question of harmonization. This is not a new question at Westminster Seminary: Young had perhaps a slightly different take on harmonization, and his colleague Ned B. Stonehouse, in his approach to the Gospels, comes closer to Dillard in his recognition of the uniqueness of each Gospel. Dillard, an expert on 1 and 2 Chronicles, developed his views in the study of the relationship between these two books and other parallel Old Testament narratives. After defining harmonization and discussing its positive and negative uses, he proposes that a consideration of various genres in Scripture and the distinct voices of the human authors enable one to handle harmonization in a more responsible way. In the process, the diversity of divine revelation is better appreciated. Second, by treating the topic of oral tradition, Waltke touches on a subject with wide ramifications in Old Testament studies. Indeed, he intimates that many methodologies used in Old Testament scholarship presuppose the existence of oral tradition. Waltke concludes his survey of various ancient texts by stating that oral tradition is not as prevalent as usually assumed and that greater room should be given to a consideration of written documents and traditions. Besides this specific conclusion, Waltke offers us here a model of responsible and scholarly polemic.

Lillback's essay examines current challenges to the Bible, in particular the debate over Enns's views on inspiration in light of the Westminster Standards, which have subordinate authority under the Word of God at Westminster Seminary. Enns's approach is found to be at odds not only with that of the Old Testament Westminster professor E. J. Young, but also with that of the Reformed theologian G. C. Berkouwer.

This part helps us to make sense of the Westminster controversy by focusing more deeply on Old Testament studies. In these pages we hear the voices of several generations of professors at Westminster. They speak from the perspective of systematic theology, apologetics and philosophy, Old Testament studies, and historical theology. Further, while a variety of scholarly opinions is found, a unified commitment to the inspiration and inerrancy of the Bible emerges as well. This doctrine of Scripture is based on the self-witness of the Bible. Yet the self-witness of the Bible—that is, statements in the Bible about its inspiration and nature—should be distinguished from unresolved difficulties (the phenomena of Scripture), which ought not to overrun the self-witness of Scripture.

55

Edward J. Young's *Thy Word Is Truth*

Edward J. Young, *Thy Word Is Truth: Some Thoughts on the Biblical Doctrine of Inspiration* (Grand Rapids: Eerdmans, 1957, 1963), 38–61, 64–82.

We have already made the acquaintance of E. J. Young in the previous part in our survey of the authority of the Bible. Young's *Thy Word Is Truth: Some Thoughts on the Biblical Doctrine of Inspiration*, published in 1957, is a thorough treatment of the doctrine of inspiration. The longer and more robust subtitle found in earlier editions summarizes Young's point well. It is worth quoting it in full: *Thy Word Is Truth: A Forthright Defense of the Bible as the Infallible and Inerrant Word of God, with Explanations of Apparent Contradictions, Based on the Evidence of the Bible Itself; and a Pointed Refutation of Some Modern Theories That Reject a Verbally Inspired Bible.* When Young alludes to the word of Jesus in John 17:17 KJV, he from the outset appeals to the witness of Jesus about Scripture. Thus, he defends its self-evidencing character. The title of this anthology, *Thy Word Is Still Truth*, wishes to express Westminster's continuity with those who stood for Scripture before the present time. Also see the recent publication of Young's lecture in commemoration of the centennial of his birth, *The God Breathed Scripture* (2007, originally given in 1966).

From Young's classic, *Thy Word Is Truth*, this anthology reproduces chapters 3 and 4. First, in "The Extent of Inspiration," Young addresses questions such as these: What do theologians mean when they say that the Bible is inspired? Does this inspiration reach to the thoughts of the human authors of the Bible? Does this turn the writing of the Bible into some kind of mechanical process? Young argues that if the Scriptures were to contain errors, then God himself would not be free from error, thereby asserting the foundational significance of the doctrine of the inspiration of the Holy Scriptures. This theistic argument is akin to the thought of his colleague Van Til. Young argues that the autographa of the Bible are inerrant and infallible. While we do not have these original copies, God preserved the Scripture, and we have access to the Word of God.

In the next chapter, "The Human Writers of Scripture," Young turns to another set of questions. As we have already observed in this anthology, the relationship of the human authors of Scripture to the divine Author is a challenging topic. Young in this selection argues that scholars must do full justice to what the Bible says about its human authorship. Note again the doctrine of Scripture's self-witness. Rather than being dictated, the Word of God is spoken and written through human instrumentality. Exactly how this happened, Young teaches, is a mystery. Nevertheless, this mystery does not open the door to error in the Scriptures, since the mysterious process of inspiration of the human writers of Scripture was an infallible inspiration by the Spirit. The inspiration of Scripture through human authors presupposes a sovereign God in control of the process. Thus, God is ultimately its Author. Young sets in place a paradigm that includes the human side of Scripture without compromising its divine origin and infallibility.

Supplementary Bibliography (cf. chap. 52): Edward J. Young. *The God Breathed Scripture: The Bauman Memorial Lectures for 1966 Delivered at Grace Theological Seminary and College*. Foreword by R. B. Gaffin Jr. Willow Grove, PA: Committee for the Historian of the Orthodox Presbyterian Church, 2007.

Chapter 2: The Extent of Inspiration

We cannot say of the writings of the Holy Spirit that anything in them is useless or superfluous, even if they seem to some obscure.

—Origen

There is no discord between the Law and the Gospel, but harmony, for they both proceed from the same Author.

—Clement of Alexandria

All Scripture, as it has been given to us by God, will be found to be harmonious.

—Irenaeus

One who desires to be able to identify counterfeit money should make himself thoroughly familiar with the genuine article. If he knows the genuine thoroughly, he will not have much difficulty in detecting the counterfeit. On the other hand, if he knows only what is false, he will have great difficulty in distinguishing genuine from counterfeit. It is for this reason that we intend to spend some time in a study of what we believe to be the true and genuine doctrine of inspiration. If we have a clear picture of what the Bible itself teaches about inspiration, we shall be in a far better position to deal with views and opinions which, although quite prevalent, are nevertheless to be placed in the category of counterfeit.

One reason, it may be observed in passing, why many today are willing to embrace new views of inspiration is possibly to be found in the fact that the Scriptural teaching is not well known. The American Protestant Church of the first half of this century can hardly be characterized as one in which doctrinal preaching and catechetical instruction have held a very large place. As a result the membership of the Protestant Church is quite ignorant of doctrine and even of the simple contents of the Bible. It is an easy prey to whatever happens to come along, and modern theology, because of its usage of orthodox terminology, is readily misunderstood by many. Very few seem able to distinguish between what is Scriptural and what is not.

If the Scriptural doctrine of inspiration were better known, the newer views would have more difficulty lodging themselves in the modern Church. It will be necessary therefore to examine in more detail what the Bible itself teaches concerning inspiration. If what we have been saying in the preceding chapter is true, the great issue before the Church today is whether to listen to the voice of God or of man. That expresses itself, we have seen, in the question whether one may any longer regard the Bible as a trustworthy teacher of doctrine. Throughout the course of Church History the Church has derived her doctrines from the Bible. Is she now, at long last, when so many alternatives and substitutes are being proposed, to reject the testimony which the Bible gives concerning itself? Since the Bible is God's Word, to reject what the Bible has to say about itself is to reject the voice of God Himself. What lies before the Church at the present time is the old issue of supernatural versus man-made religion.

In turning to the Bible to discover what it has to say of itself we learn that the Scriptures are said to be God-breathed; that holy men spake from God as they were borne by the Holy Spirit; and that, in the words of the Lord Himself, the Scripture cannot be broken. Before we devote any attention to alternative views, it is first necessary to examine more closely this teaching of the Bible and to notice certain of its implications.

The passages of Scripture to which we have given consideration teach that the Bible is the Word of God, actually spoken from His mouth. The expression "Word of God" will be more readily understood if we state clearly what a word itself is. A word is simply the vehicle by means of which thought is communicated from one mind to another. And when we then speak of the Word of God, we are employing an expression to designate the means which God uses to convey to us the thoughts of His heart. God has spoken to us in order that we may know what He would have us do: through the medium of words He has revealed His will.

Whatever Word He has uttered, since it has come from His mouth, is true and trustworthy. "The words of the Lord *are* pure words," the Psalmist declares, "*as* silver tried in a furnace of earth, purified seven times."[1] What has been spoken by God, who cannot lie, must be pure and true altogether. Every word which proceedeth from the mouth of the heavenly Father must in the very nature of the case be absolutely free from error. If this is not so, God Himself is not trustworthy.

If, therefore, the Scriptures are the Word of God, breathed out by Him, it follows that they, too, are absolutely true and infallible. The passage in 2 Timothy to which we have already given attention certainly teaches that the Scriptures are the Word of God. Is it, however, an isolated passage? Is there no other line of evidence that we can follow? Does this one verse stand by itself, a lonely signpost pointing to the Divine origin of the Scriptures? Happily, such is not the case. The testimony of the Bible to itself is abundant and compelling.

The word which God in sundry times and in divers manners spake in time past unto the fathers by the prophets was a God-breathed word. It was inspired. Those whom God raised up to declare unto the nation His truth were inspired of Him. "I will place my words in his mouth," said the Lord of Moses, "and he shall speak all that which I command Him." From this passage (Deut. 18:18) we learn in the first place that God did reveal His Word unto the

---

1. Psalm 12:6.

prophets. Now it is very important to understand what is meant by the term "revelation." It is very important and necessary to know what we mean when we say that God revealed His word unto the prophets. Revelation, in the Bibical sense of the term, is the communication of information. When God reveals His Word unto the prophets, for example, He tells them something which beforehand they had not known. The purpose of the Lord in granting revelation is to impart knowledge. It is, of course, true that revelation need not be imparted by means of words. The entire creation, including man himself, is a revelation of the glory and power of God. In accents strong, though not of words, the created universe declares the mighty power and greatness of God the Creator. God has, however, also spoken in words, and the Bible lays great emphasis upon the fact that He has thus spoken.

What kind of a Word, however, did God reveal unto His servants the prophets? When they proclaimed their messages, were they preserved and kept from error so that the spoken word was actually what God had revealed unto them? Were the prophets, in other words, inspired teachers? According to the Bible they were. God placed His Word in their mouths, and consequently what they uttered was precisely what He wished them to utter. Inspiration is designed to secure the accuracy of what is taught and to keep the Lord's spokesman from error in his teaching. We must therefore make a distinction between revelation and inspiration. It is true that the two are very closely related, and it is true that in the broad sense inspiration is a form or mode of revelation. At the same time, it is well to keep in mind the fundamental distinction that, whereas revelation is essentially the communication of knowledge or information, inspiration is designed to secure infallibility in teaching. The prophets were the recipients of revelation. God did, in most loving and wondrous fashion, speak unto them and reveal what they themselves in their own strength and wisdom could never have learned. At the same time, the Word which He gave them was one which He placed in their mouth, one which, coming from Him, was pure and true and trustworthy. He also saw to it that they spoke precisely what He had commanded them. As a consequence they were men who in their public teaching were kept from error. They spoke, not the thoughts of their own hearts, but rather the Word which had been given them of God. They were, in other words, inspired organs to whom Divine revelation had come.

Very helpful for our present purpose is Exodus 7:1–2. "And the Lord said unto Moses, See, I have made thee a god to Pharaoh: and Aaron thy brother shall be thy prophet. Thou shalt speak all that I command thee: and Aaron thy brother shall speak unto Pharaoh, that he send the children of Israel out of his land." According to these words Moses stands in relation to Pharaoh as a god, and Aaron is the prophet. The origin of the message is from God; it is to be a Divine revelation. More than that, however, it is to be an infallible and trustworthy revelation. Aaron is to be the prophet of Moses and he is told the message which he is to declare. In an earlier passage, Exodus 4:15, we read: "And thou shalt speak unto him, and put words in his mouth: and I will be with thy mouth, and with his mouth, and will teach you what ye shall do." Here the idea of the inspiration of the prophet is clearly set forth. The same thought finds expression in Jeremiah 1:9, "Then the Lord put forth his hand, and touched my mouth. And the Lord said unto me, Behold, I have put my words in thy mouth." Jeremiah the prophet is clearly conscious of the fact that he has been inspired of God. The Lord has actually placed the words in his mouth, and he is told to speak "unto them all that I command thee" (v. 17). God sees to it that the prophet utters what has been revealed to him. Jeremiah is not permitted to develop the revealed message and present it in his own words. It does not come to him as a seed thought, to fructify in his own mind. Rather, the actual words which have been revealed are themselves of Divine origin, and it is these Divine words, these and no others, which Jeremiah is to declare.

That this is the case is further seen in the formula which the prophets so often employ, "Thus saith the Lord," a formula which means that the words to follow are the actual words which the Lord Himself has placed in the mouth of the prophet. The hearers are to understand thereby that these words are not the prophet's, a development of the seed thought planted in him by God, but are the identical words which God Himself has revealed. A strong confirmation of this fact has come from archaeology. In the Near East many letters have been unearthed which contain this precise formula, "Thus saith X." The words which follow the formula are then the very words which the composer has uttered. When the prophets give forth their messages, they are calling specific attention, not to themselves and their opinions, but rather to the precise words which the Lord Himself has spoken. Now, if it is true that the words which the prophet proclaims are the precise words which the Lord has revealed, it is evident that the prophet has been inspired of God, and is an inspired organ of revelation.

Strange indeed is the manner in which the prophets of the Old Testament, without any warning, lapse into the first person, as though it were God Himself who was speaking. In that tender parable of the vineyard, for example, Isaiah, who has shown a great devotion to his friend whose vineyard had been so carefully tended, yet which had disappointed its owner by bringing forth wild grapes, abruptly abandons speaking of the owner in the third person and, putting himself in the role of his friends, speaks in the first person, "And now, O inhabitants of Jerusalem, and men of Judah, judge, I pray you, betwixt me and my vineyard."[2] It is God who speaks. It is God who passes judgment upon the men of Judah and tells them what He will do to them because they have destroyed His vineyard. But how dare the prophet speak in such a fashion? What right has he to assume the prerogatives which belong to God alone, and to speak as though he were God? Certainly, no right at all, unless he believed that, in speaking as he did, he was uttering words which God actually placed in his mouth. Nor is Isaiah alone in this procedure. Other prophets did the same thing. So overcome were they by their message that they spoke in the first person. There was, however, no deception. The prophets did not claim to speak in their own right; nor is there any evidence that those who heard them were deceived. What a clear picture of inspired teaching this is! Are we to think for a moment that these words which the prophets proclaimed were mistaken words, tinged with error and faults? Did the prophets garble their messages? Did they somehow obscure the Word which God gave them? Were their messages not trustworthy? Against all such conceptions this fact stands out as a strong protest: though they speak in the first person, these bold men speak for God, and the words which they declare are precisely those which they have received from God Himself.

When we turn to the New Testament we discover the same thing. Those men who were the recipients of God's revelation were men who were taught of the Spirit and so were kept from error in their teaching. Our Lord promised to His Church the gift of the Holy Spirit who would "teach you all things, and bring all things to your remembrance, whatsoever I have said unto you" (John 14:26). The Apostles were not to be left on their own. They would not need to depend upon their own fallible hearts and minds to tell them what to say. Rather,

---

2. Isaiah 5:3.

to them had been promised an infallible Teacher, even God and the Holy Ghost. It was thus that the Apostles themselves understood their own words. How amazing are the words that Paul sends to the Thessalonians, "thank we God without ceasing, because, when ye received the word of God which ye heard of us, ye received *it* not *as* the word of man, but as it is in truth, the word of God, which effectually worketh also in you that believe" (1 Thess. 2:13). What a remarkable verse this is! How mad Paul would have been to speak of his message to the Thessalonians in this way, if he were not uttering the solemn truth! If Paul were speaking the truth, then he was conscious that the Holy Ghost was with him, and that the words which he had so earnestly and sincerely proclaimed were not his own but the very Word of God. If he were not speaking the truth then he was, of course, the worst possible sort of impostor. In Paul's words, however, there rings a depth of earnestness which makes it clear he was no deceiver. He was conscious of setting forth the very truth which God had given him: and this Word, he says, worketh effectually in those that hear and receive it. Can there be any doubt that Paul is here represented as an inspired teacher, one who is setting forth precisely what God has given to him?

If what we have been saying, then, is correct, it follows that those to whom God gave His revelation were men borne of the Holy Spirit, whose messages were infallibly delivered and absolutely free from error, being precisely the words that God Himself wished to have declared. We might therefore assume that since God inspired the organs of revelation when they uttered the spoken Word, He would also have inspired them when they set forth the written Word. However, have we been justified in maintaining that these organs of inspiration were inspired when they proclaimed the spoken Word? It should be clear that the entire argument rests upon the assumption that the written Scriptures are trustworthy and accurate witnesses. If the Bible does not present a true picture of the inspiration of the prophets and apostles, then, of course, the argument is ended. We must, therefore, face squarely the question whether the Scriptures claim inspiration for themselves. In other words, Do they claim to be the Word of God?

The reader who has followed the discussion of the Scripture passages adduced in the previous chapter will have an idea of how we propose to answer this question. We are convinced that the Scriptures do indeed claim to be the Word of God, and since they are from Him and find their origin in Him, are therefore infallible and entirely free from error of any kind. Since their Author is Truth and cannot lie, so His Word, the Sacred Scriptures, is truth and cannot lie. The Biblical evidence to support this thesis is very clear and cogent. We shall not attempt to present all the evidence; rather, we shall content ourselves with some of the main thoughts which Scriptures has to offer upon the question.

When the New Testament mentions the Scriptures, it has in mind, for the most part, the Old Testament and it is most instructive to note the epithets which it applies to these Scriptures. Paul says that they are holy (Rom. 1:2). They are holy for their Author is holy. To Paul there is a depth of meaning in this word "holy" which we in our daily usage often overlook. To Paul these Scriptures are holy because they partake of the character of Him who spoke their very words. In another verse, the Apostle does not hesitate to designate them as the "oracles of God" (Rom. 3:2). An oracle is something that is spoken. The oracles of God, therefore, are those things which God has spoken to us. They are the very words of God. In the epistle to Timothy, Paul gives them a definite religious quality when he speaks of the "sacred" Scriptures.

Not only are such high designations attributed to the Scriptures, but their very words are equated with the words of God. A few examples of this striking occurrence will suffice. In writing to the Romans (9:17) the Apostle quotes from the book of Exodus, "For the scripture saith unto Pharaoh, Even for this same purpose have I raised thee up, that I might shew my power in thee, and that my name might be declared throughout all the earth." In the book of Exodus, however, these words are attributed to God Himself. It is God who utters them through Moses to Pharaoh. According to Paul, therefore, the Scripture is saying the very things that God says. The actual words of the Old Testament are attributed to God Himself.

Very cogent is the reference of Paul in Galatians 3:8, "And the scripture, foreseeing that God would justify the heathen through faith, preached before the gospel unto Abraham, *saying*, In thee shall all nations be blessed." When we turn to Genesis when these words are taken (22:18), we notice that it is God Himself who speaks. What the Scripture declares is attributed to God. Paul here identifies Scripture with God. Scripture foresees that God would justify the heathen by faith and so it speaks. What it speaks is the very Word of God.

A few more references will be in place. In the tender and beautiful prayer of the Apostles, recorded in the fourth chapter of the book of Acts, we read, "Who by the mouth of thy servant David hast said, Why did the heathen rage, and the people imagine vain things?" The quotation is from the second Psalm, the human authorship of which is attributed to David, and it is through the mouth of David that God Himself is said to have spoken. Very similar is the passage in Acts 28:25: "Well spake the Holy Ghost by Esaias the prophet unto our fathers." Paul here has reference to the Old Testament Scriptures, to the sixth chapter of Isaiah. The human author of this book was Isaiah, but it was the Holy Spirit who spoke through him.

It will perhaps be well to bring to a close our brief survey of the Scriptural teaching concerning itself by a reference to the gracious remarks which the Apostle Peter made concerning the epistles of Paul. He speaks of these epistles in the category of "other Scriptures," and that means, of course, that Peter regards them as Scripture. More than that, he makes the bold statement that those who wrest these Scriptures, the epistles of our beloved brother Paul, do so to their own destruction. It is a phrase laden with terrible meaning. How all-important these Scriptures are to Peter! A man who wrests them does so to his own destruction and the eternal loss of his soul. It is impossible to conceive of a higher view of Paul's epistles. Very cogent, we may conclude, and very clear is this witness of the Bible to itself and its Divine infallible character. Modern man may deny its true nature, but it speaks with loud, compelling voice, for it is the infallible Word of the one living and true God.

It is conceivable that at this point an objection may be made. It may be objected that in the few passages adduced above not one word from the Lord Jesus Christ is considered. What view of Scripture, it may be asked did Jesus Christ entertain? The question is perfectly legitimate. Not that the recorded words of Christ are more trustworthy than other passages of Scripture, but what Christ has said concerning the authority of the Bible must itself always be regarded as having the utmost authority. We must always remember, however, that it is possible to know what Christ did and believed, only upon the assumption that the Scripture itself is a trustworthy and accurate witness to what He said and taught. What, then, did the Lord believe concerning the Scriptures?

An answer to this question is found in the quotation to which reference has already been made. "The scriptures cannot be broken," Christ had declared, and we may very well expect that all His utterances about the Bible will be in line with this one great statement. And indeed, this is exactly the case. A brief glance at only a few verses will provide a convincing answer. In referring to the Psalmist, Jesus Christ declared, "How then doth David in spirit call him Lord?" (Matt. 22:43). Very clearly and without any equivocation the Redeemer regards David as having spoken in the Holy Spirit. The passage which He has in mind is Psalm 110 and it is the words from this particular Psalm which the eternal Son of God says have been spoken by David in the Spirit.

Very, interesting and worthy of consideration are the words with which our Redeemer refuted the Tempter. "It is written," He said (and for Christ that was sufficient), "Man shall not live by bread alone, but by every word that proceedeth out of the mouth of God" (Matt. 4:4). How cogent this passage is! The evil one would seek to deflect our Lord from His determined course of saving His own. How can the Tempter be silenced? There is one sure way. It is to quote the Scripture. It is written, and therefore, since it is written, the issue is settled. What the devil has to say is without force, for God has already spoken. "It is written," and that ends the matter.

"Search the scriptures," our Lord commanded upon another occasion (His reference being to the Old Testament), "for in them ye think ye have eternal life: and they are they which testify of me" (John 5:39). In almost the same breath He goes on to say, "For had ye believed Moses, ye would have believed me: for he wrote of me. But if ye believe not his writings, how shall ye believe my words?" (John 5:46–47).

That our Lord believed the Scriptures to be trustworthy and to possess an authority that was absolute is a fact that cannot be gainsaid. It is acknowledged even by some who do not themselves believe in his deity. We may disagree with the Lord on this point but, if the Scriptures have given an accurate picture of Christ, we must acknowledge that He held that the Scriptures were infallible—they could not be broken.

It should be clear to anyone who has carefully read the passages of the Bible which we have adduced that the view of inspiration which the Bible teaches is strongly opposed to the idea that only in parts the Scriptures are infallible and trustworthy. It is not only in specific teachings or in great doctrines that the Scriptures cannot be broken. Rather, in all its parts, in its very entirety, the Bible, if we are to accept its witness to itself, is utterly infallible. It is not only that each book given the name of Scripture is infallible but, more than that, the content of each such book is itself Scripture, the Word of God written and, hence, infallible, free entirely from the errors which adhere to mere human compositions. Not alone to moral and ethical truths, but to all statements of fact does this inspiration extend. That inspiration which the Bible claims for itself is one that is full; it is plenary inspiration. As our Lord said, in giving expression to this very doctrine, "Think not that I am come to destroy the law; or the prophets: I am not come to destroy, but to fulfil. For verily I say unto you, Till heaven and earth pass, one jot or one tittle shall in no wise pass from the law, till all be fulfilled" (Matt. 5:17–18).

If, therefore, the inspiration of the Bible is plenary, it should be evident that it is one which extends to the very words. It is, to state the matter baldly, a verbal inspiration. That such is the case is manifest from the passages which we have already considered. With this representation of the Bible, however, there are many who do not agree. We are living in a day when men depreciate the idea that God has spoken in words. If there is any one point upon which modern thinkers are agreed, it is that they are heartily and cordially opposed to the doctrine of a verbal inspiration. When one picks up a modern book upon the nature of the Bible, he is almost certain to find the author asserting that the time has come for a new doctrine of inspiration and, coupled with this assertion, he will doubtless encounter a rejection of verbal inspiration.

It would, of course, be impossible to divorce the thoughts of the Bible from its words. The thoughts are indeed "God-breathed" thoughts, and to them we are to give our entire soul's obedience. The doctrines and the teachings of the Bible are to be our very rule of life and faith. In what manner, however, has God seen fit to reveal those thoughts to us? To ask the question is to answer it. He has revealed them through the media of words. It is just about impossible for us to conceive of any other satisfactory manner of communicating information. When we wish in adequate fashion to communicate our thoughts we are compelled to employ words; indeed, for this reason has God given us speech. We cannot have the blessed life-giving doctrines of Holy Writ apart from the words in which they are expressed. Our purpose at present, however, is not to defend this doctrine of verbal inspiration. For the present we are merely pointing out that, whether modern man likes the doctrine or no, the Bible teaches it. More than that, despite the dislike of modern man, it is our Lord Jesus Christ Himself who embraced this doctrine. Only one doctrine of inspiration is taught in the Bible, namely, that of a plenary and verbal inspiration to which the modern mind is so hostile.

The reader who has followed the argument to the present point, will, if he has meditated upon those passages of Scripture which have been presented, probably agree that the Bible itself does claim to be the Word of God. He will also agree, if he is consistent, that if the Bible is the Word of God, it must be pure and free from error. Can *Holy* Scripture contain error? Can the "oracles" of God be tinged with falsehood? The question which we are facing is, in reality, whether God Himself is pure and free from error. And if God Himself is truth, no word which has proceeded from His mouth can possibly be anything other than the absolute truth. When therefore the claim is sometimes made that the Bible does not attribute infallibility to itself, or that it does not profess to be free from error, we must insist that this claim disregards both the fact that the Bible is the Word of God and that it also claims to be pure and true.

In 1923 the General Assembly of the Presbyterian Church in the U.S.A. declared among other things the following: "the Holy Spirit did so inspire, guide and move the writers of Holy Scripture as to keep them from error." This declaration on the part of the Assembly, a declaration which is in perfect harmony with the teaching of the Bible itself, was met by strong opposition.

A counterstatement appeared in a document which, because of the city in which it was drawn up, has come to be known as the "Auburn Affirmation." The Affirmation was an attack not only upon the particular declaration just quoted, but also upon several other cardinal doctrines of the Christian faith. With respect to the statement of the Assembly concerning the Scriptures, the Affirmation maintained that "there is no assertion in the Scriptures that their writers were kept 'from error.'" "The doctrine of inerrancy, intended to enhance the authority of the Scriptures, in fact impairs their supreme authority for faith and life, and weakens the testimony of the church to the power of God unto salvation through Jesus Christ." "We hold that the General Assembly of 1923, in asserting that 'the Holy Spirit did so inspire, guide and move the writers of Holy Scripture as to keep them from error,' spoke without warrant of the Scriptures or of the Confession of Faith" (i.e., the Westminster Confession).[3]

Whether the General Assembly spoke without warrant of the Westminster Confession, the reader may judge for himself by consulting the Appendix of this book and reading the Confession. Whether the Assembly spoke without warrant of the Scriptures is likewise a matter that can easily be decided. That the Scriptures claim to be, and that Jesus Christ believed them to be, the infallible revelation of God is a matter beyond dispute. We today may not believe them to be infallible, but it was Jesus Christ who proclaimed of these Holy Scriptures that they cannot be broken. "Heaven and earth shall pass away, but my words shall not pass away." The omniscient Son of the living God would never have placed the imprimatur of His approval upon the erroneous statements of the Auburn Affirmation.

To realize that the Auburn Affirmation cannot be regarded as a serious treatment of the subject, one need but read in the Bible the sad account of the arrest and betrayal of the Lord. And indeed, we have mentioned this Affirmation, not because of any intrinsic merit which it possesses, for it certainly possesses very little, but rather because of the great influence which it has exerted. In the light of what is said about the Scriptures in the Passion narratives, however, the Affirmation's statements sound very hollow and unconvincing.

It was while they were at the table just before the Savior instituted the Last Supper that He, in looking ahead to His death, spoke, "The Son of man indeed goeth, as it is written of him." Seated about Him at this table were the twelve, they who had left all and followed Him. They were His disciples, and yet, one from their midst would now betray Him. He knew that this would be, and He knew which disciple would be the betrayer. He knew, furthermore, that this giving of Himself over to death would be in accordance with what the Scriptures had already said. He would go, and the course of His betrayal would be in accordance with what had already been written. It was a betrayal previously determined. It must be thus, and could not be otherwise. for it had been written. That which had been written must be fulfilled. Scripture not infallible? Scripture not inerrant? Scripture subject to the errors that attend everything human? Modern man with his superficial view of religion may think it so, but on that dark night, when the eternal Son of God faced death for His own, the words loomed large: *as it is written*. It could not be otherwise.

When they had gone out and come to the Mount of Olives, the Lord again spoke, "All ye shall be offended because of me this night: for it is written, I will smite the shepherd, and the sheep shall be scattered" (Mark 14:27). To imagine the tragedy of the scene is almost impossible. On the slope of the Mount, the sky filled with the brightness of the stars—and how brightly they shine in the Palestinian sky!—the Lord is again with the small band of disciples. They were His disciples, but that very night they would flee; they would be offended in Him. Could not such a tragic situation be averted? Could not they show themselves to be stronger men? Could not they abide with him through the hours of His agony? Why must this sad course of events follow? Why? Simply because it had been written in the indefectible Scripture: "for it is written." The matter was determined; Christ could not swerve from His course. The disciples could not do otherwise but what they were about to do. Scripture had spoken. Our Lord must face death without the support of these His fol-

---

3. Cf. "AN AFFIRMATION designed to safeguard the unity and liberty of the Presbyterian Church in the United States of America," Section 2.

lowers. But the Auburn Affirmation would have us believe that the Scriptures are not, and do not claim to be, infallible.

At the time of His arrest the Lord simply said, "I was daily with you in the temple teaching, and ye took me not: but the scriptures must be fulfilled" (Mark 14:49). We may well ask, Why must these Scriptures be fulfilled? The answer is that they are the Word of God. What they utter, according to our Lord, must in the very nature of the case come to fulfillment. There is no possible alternative. How obedient He is to these Scriptures! After rebuking the one that had struck the servant of the high priest, Christ made it abundantly clear that He believed He could then and there have more than twelve legions of angels. What an aid that would have been! With twelve legions of angels the Lord could easily have escaped from the hands of the band of men who had come to arrest Him. Would not that have been the course of wisdom? Yet, He would not take advantage of the opportunity. "But how then shall the scriptures be fulfilled, that thus it must be?" (Matt. 26:54). The Lord is more concerned that the Scriptures be fulfilled than that He escape from the hand of the enemy. These words are strange to one who does not share the Redeemer's high estimate of the Bible. If Christ's utterance does not give evidence that He believed the Scriptures to be infallible, we are at a loss to understand its meaning. "Thus it must be," it cannot conceivably be otherwise. There is no possibility of change. Scripture must be fulfilled.

The evangelist Matthew, in describing the answer which the Lord gave to those who had come out to take Him, simply says, "But all this was done, that the scriptures of the prophets might be fulfilled" (26:56). This is remarkable language. The disgraceful arrest of Him who was "holy, harmless and undefiled" took place in order that the Scriptures of the prophets might be fulfilled. It is well to pause and ponder the thought. Here is the explanation for the whole sad tragedy. Here is the heart of the matter, the reason why that blessed One was betrayed and arrested and condemned to an unjust death. It was done that the Scriptures might be fulfilled, and in fulfilling the Scriptures, the Savior brought life and salvation to all who were given Him by the Father before the foundation of the world. Throughout the sad account of the last days of the Lord, days which lead up to the Cross, there is interwoven that strange note, "the scriptures must be fulfilled." Over Jerusalem there lay a cloud. It was the hour of the powers of darkness. Wicked men lifted their hands against the Son of God. Satan was preparing to bruise the heel of the Seed of the woman, yet Satan was facing his own defeat. "Now is the judgment of this world: now shall the prince of this world be cast out."[4] Now was the Son of God ready to be lifted up and to draw all men unto Him. And the Scriptures were being fulfilled. One who reads the Passion narratives carefully will not be impressed with the assertion that the Scriptures do not claim to be infallible.

The Auburn Affirmation, we may conclude, was no friend to the true Scriptural teaching on inspiration; sometimes, however, even those who do embrace the doctrine from the heart for one reason or another make statements which tend to confuse and to obscure what the Bible makes so plain. In his remarkable work *Fundamental Christianity*, the late Francis L. Patton has some rather unfortunate things to say about inspiration.[5] They are unfortunate because they are out of keeping with the high supernaturalism which characterizes, and which Dr. Patton intended to characterize, his work. It is on the whole a fine book, and the present writer received much encouragement from it when he was a student

---

4. John 12:31.
5. Francis L. Patton, *Fundamental Christianity* (New York: Macmillan, 1926).

in college, troubled by the many charges that were leveled against orthodox Christianity. We can indeed be thankful to God for the much good that is found in this book. "Conceding now the inspiration of the Scripture," writes Dr. Patton, "you cannot on that account assume that it is errorless" (p. 163). It would seem at first blush that the author was in agreement with the Auburn Affirmation. If, however, by the word "inspiration" we are to accept Paul's definition, and Dr. Patton apparently does, it must surely follow that what is "God-breathed" is the very Word of God, and since it is the Word of God, it must, as we have sought to point out, be pure and free from error. If, in making this statement, Dr. Patton had reference to the copies of the Bible which we now possess, one could readily agree that these present copies are not free of error, but it is not perfectly clear that this is what he means. For our part, we regard his discussion of inspiration as unfortunate and as not taking into account the consequences which can be drawn from it.

Dr. Patton further beclouds the issue when he says, "The real question is whether the Bible is true, not whether it is inspired."[6] At first hearing this declaration sounds Scriptural, but it will soon appear that it seeks to make an unwarranted disjunction. What right have we to make a separation between the truth and the inspiration of the Bible? It should be noted that the Bible itself claims to be inspired of God. Is the claim true? If it is true, the Bible is inspired, and so we see that the inspiration of the Bible and its truth go hand in hand. Inspiration, let us never forget, is for the purpose of securing accuracy. Unless we were convinced that the Bible reports accurately, we could not at all be sure of the truthfulness of what it says. "Must a book," asks Dr. Patton, "be inspired in order to be true?"[7] To this we answer, "Of course not." There are countless books which are true and which are not inspired. The question, however, is really beside the point. There are many books that are uninspired and yet are true. These books, however, are not the Bible. They are of human origin and, let us say, eyewitness accounts of an historical happening, and what they relate is in accord with the facts. But these writings are not of Divine origin, nor do they claim to be; they deal with matters susceptible of scientific check which can be correctly reported.

Very different, however, is the case with the Bible. If the Bible is not inspired, it cannot be completely true. It is quite possible, of course, that in an uninspired Bible there may be certain statements that are true. There might be in an uninspired Bible an accurate account of the discovery of the empty tomb. That is, up to a point the account might be accurate. The *meaning* of the Resurrection, however, would not be something that the unaided human mind could of itself discover. For that revelation is needed, and this revelation must be given to man in such a way that it is not garbled. If the Bible is a revelation from God, then that Bible must accurately speak to us, else we cannot be sure of the truthfulness of anything that it says. How are we to determine the truthfulness of what the Bible says about creation, the fall of man, the Trinity, the Person of the Lord, the Atonement, the Resurrection, the future life, the Second Advent? These are not subjects that the mind of man without Divine revelation can discover. How do we know that the Bible speaks the truth on these matters? We know it because the Bible is trustworthy in all that it says. And we believe that the Bible is trustworthy in all that it says for the simple reason that it is the Word of God. To maintain that we may first assume the truthfulness of the Bible, and then turn to the

6. Ibid., 147.
7. Ibid.

question of its inspiration, as Dr. Patton wishes to do, is to deceive ourselves. It is to engage in a method of apologetics which, in effect, has given up the battle at the outset. It is God the Holy Spirit who causes us to see the marks of divinity in Holy Scripture, so that we may receive the Word of God written, as did the Thessalonians the Word of God spoken, "not as the word of men, but as it is in truth, the word of God, which effectually worketh also in you that believe" (1 Thess. 2:13b). When once the Spirit has opened our eyes, we believe the Scriptures to be Divine and we place our confidence in their statements, for the simple reason that those statements are found in the Scriptures.

What, however, shall we say with respect to those copies of the Bible that are now in existence? Is the English Bible from which we read our devotions and which we hear read in the worship service on the Lord's Day an inspired Bible? Are the Hebrew and Greek texts which are now in our possession inspired copies of Holy Scripture? It should be obvious that on the basis of the definition of inspiration which we have been using, such is not the case. If the Scripture is "God-breathed," it naturally follows that only the original is "God-breathed." If holy men of God spoke from God as they were borne by the Holy Spirit, then only what they spoke under the Spirit's bearing is inspired. It would certainly be unwarrantable to maintain that copies of what they spoke were also inspired, since these copies were not made as men were borne of the Spirit. They were therefore not "God-breathed" as was the original. This fact, of course, is not only taught in Scripture, but has also been recognized by the Church. The Nicene Creed, for example, states that the Holy Spirit spake by the prophets. That means that the words which the prophets uttered were Spirit-indicted words. It does not mean that copies of those words were spoken by the Spirit. To come closer to the present day, we may note that the Westminster Confession, which gives such a grand survey of the Scriptural teaching, asserts that the Bible was "immediately inspired of God." This, of course, means that the Bible was inspired "without means"; inspiration is a work of the immediate power of God Himself, and since this is so, it is clear that the Westminster Confession considered as inspired Scripture only those documents which were original.

Nevertheless, despite these testimonies, there have been those who apparently think that the idea that only the original manuscripts of Scripture are inspired is a somewhat recent invention designed to avoid the difficulty caused by the presence of errors in the copies of the Bible which we now possess. In the nature of the case, however, if the Bible is actually "God-breathed," there must have been an original, and that original must have been free from error. Can it conceivably have been otherwise?

Those who oppose the doctrine of inerrancy sometimes assert that God evidently did not regard the preservation of this original as a matter of importance. He apparently was content for us to have imperfect copies of the Scripture. It is, of course, a fact which all admit, that the original copy of the Bible is not preserved. Is the loss, however, a great one? Are the copies of the Bible which are now in our possession so poor that from them we cannot learn the true Word of God? If that were the case, if the Bible that is now before us were so far removed from the original that we could not learn from it the will of God, then the situation would be tragic indeed. Then we could probably say nothing whatever about the original. We might think that it was without error, but we could not know. We would have no trustworthy Bible and we would be left to our own imaginations. Those, for example, who wish to learn something of the death of our Lord from the Talmud will find there only seriously garbled traditions. The truth has been so corrupted that they cannot place their confidence in what the Talmud has to say. So it would be with us if the copies of the Bible which are extant were hopelessly corrupt.

Are these copies, however, hopelessly corrupt? For our part, we are convinced that they are not. We believe that the Bible which we have is accurate and that it is a remarkably close approximation to the original manuscripts.

Suppose that a schoolteacher writes a letter to the President of the United States. To her great joy she receives a personal reply. It is a treasure which she must share with her pupils and so she dictates the letter to them. They are in the early days of their schooling, and spelling is not yet one of their strong points. In his copy of the letter Johnny has misspelled a few words. Mary has forgotten to cross her t's and to dot her i's. Billy has written one or two words twice, and Peter has omitted a word now and then. Nevertheless, despite all these flaws about thirty copies of the President's letter have been made. Unfortunately, the teacher misplaces the original and cannot find it. To her great sorrow it is gone. She does not have the copy which came directly from the President's pen; she must be content with those that the children have made.

Will anyone deny that she has the words of the President? Does she not have his message, in just those words in which he wrote it to her? True enough, there are some minor mistakes in the letters, but the teacher may engage in the science of textual criticism and correct them. She may correct the misspelled words, and she may write in those words which have been omitted and cross out those which are superfluous. Without any serious difficulty she may indeed restore the original.

It should be clear that errors are bound to appear in almost anything that is copied. If the reader will copy out five pages of his English Bible he will doubtless make the discovery, on reading over his work, that he has made some mistakes. This does not mean that there are mistakes in the Bible but merely that there are some mistakes of copying (copyist's errors, as they are called) in what the reader has written out.

Such is the case with the manuscripts of the Bible which are extant. They are remarkably close approximations to the original, and by means of the careful study of textual criticism it is more and more possible to approach that original. An example will make this fact clear. The Hebrew language, in which our present manuscripts of the Old Testament are written, consists solely of consonants, and to these consonants there are added signs to indicate the different vowel sounds. These signs are written both within, above and below the consonant. Hence it will easily be apparent how difficult it is to write with Hebrew characters. Nevertheless, despite this difficulty, the Hebrew manuscripts have been transmitted with remarkable accuracy. There are in Hebrew three basic short vowels, and these three vowels are written with different signs, depending upon the kind of syllable in which they are to appear. They follow the rules with an almost mathematical precision. When Hebrew words are compared for spelling with those of the other Semitic languages, there is quite an uncanny agreement. One cannot but exclaim, after having spent much time in a study of the Hebrew text—and, of course, the same is true of the Greek manuscripts of the New Testament—that these manuscripts have been preserved by the singular care and providence of God.

What is the nature of the difficulties that are found in our extant Biblical manuscripts? Dr. Charles Hodge, that staunch defender of the doctrine of plenary and verbal inspiration, has well remarked:

As to the former of these objections [i.e., that the sacred writers contradict themselves, or one the other], it would require, not a volume, but volumes to discuss all the cases of alleged discrepancies. All that can be expected here is a few general remarks: (1) These apparent discrepancies, although numerous, are for the most part trivial; relating in most cases to numbers or dates. (2) The great majority of them are only apparent, and yield to careful examination. (3) Many of them may fairly be ascribed to errors of transcribers. (4) The marvel and the miracle is that there are so few of any real importance. Considering that the different books of the Bible were written not only by different authors, but by men of all degrees of culture, living in the course of fifteen hundred or two thousand years, it is altogether unaccountable that they should agree perfectly, on any other hypothesis than that the writers were under the guidance of the Spirit of God. In this respect, as in all others, the Bible stands alone. It is enough to impress any mind with awe, when it contemplates the Sacred Scriptures filled with the highest truths, speaking with authority in the name of God, and so miraculously free from the soiling touch of human fingers. The errors in matters of fact which skeptics search out bear no proportion to the whole.[8]

At this point we must inject a note of caution. It is perfectly true, and it would be the part of folly to deny it, that there are things in the Bible which we cannot fully understand. There are difficulties which we cannot completely solve. There are apparent contradictions in the manuscripts which we now possess, and there are men who seem to make it their business to discover such difficulties and then to declare in triumph that the Bible is not free from error. Hence, if at present we mention even one of these difficulties, we shall make it clear that we also recognize their presence. In 1 Kings 15:14, to take but one example, it is said with respect to Asa: "But the high places were not removed." In the parallel passage in 2 Chronicles 14:5, on the other hand, we read: "Also he took away out of all the cities of Judah the high places and the images." Here there seems to be a contradiction. One passage says that the high places were not taken away whereas the other says that they were. What shall we do? Shall we throw overboard the Biblical doctrine of inspiration and join in the popular hue and cry that the Bible contains errors? That is what many are doing, and if we were to follow that procedure, we should be in a large company. We could then get along very well with modern thought. There would be many seeming advantages. Would we, however, be doing the right thing? For our part, we want no such easy and cavalier solution on the problem as that.[9]

The question resolves itself to this. Are we to abandon the Scriptural doctrine of Divine inspiration because of a few difficulties in the way of its acceptance? That would certainly be a foolish thing to do.[10]

In every doctrine of revealed religion, including that of the inspiration of the Bible, there are difficulties, and they exist because we are but finite creatures, unable to plumb the depths of those things which God has revealed. One thing, however, is surely clear; if there are points of obscurity in Christianity, those involved in any proposed substitutes are far greater, even

---

8. Charles Hodge, *Systematic Theology* 1:169–70.

9. We shall have occasion later to discuss the question of the relationship between these two passages (see Young, *Thy Word Is Truth*, 123). For the present we wish to make it clear that there is no real contradiction at all.

10. In the doctrine of the Trinity there are things hard to understand, for we are finite and have limited knowledge and apprehension. Should we therefore reject this blessed teaching of the Scripture? There are likewise perplexing questions which arise in connection with what the Bible says of the Person of our Lord. Shall we for that reason turn our backs on Jesus Christ? How much there is in the Christian view of God that raises problems in our minds? Are we then to disbelieve in Him?

incalculable. In our doctrine of inspiration we are faced with certain perplexities, and they are real. Let us grant that freely. Nevertheless, they seem almost trifling when compared with the tremendous problems which face those who do not accept the Scriptural doctrine. Those who do not receive the Biblical witness to itself must explain the Bible. How did it come to be? Whence came the heavenly doctrine that is found within its pages? What is its origin? These are some of the baffling questions which face those who reject the Scriptural witness to itself. And the sad fact is that most of those who reject its witness do not realize the nature of the problem before them. Modern treatises on inspiration, modern attempts to explain the Bible, despite their constant usage of orthodox terminology, often do not even begin to come to grips with the real matters involved.

There are, then, difficulties in the doctrines which the Scripture teaches. There is this point, however, which must be kept in mind: it is that we are not omniscient, and since we are but creatures, we have no warrant for thinking that we shall ever be omniscient. It should not surprise us, therefore, if there are matters in the Bible which we cannot understand.

As knowledge increases, many things in the Bible which once were considered obscure, have been clarified. A scholar of the last century, Hartmann, thought it questionable whether writing was known in Moses' day. Not until the period of the Judges, he believed, which was some time after Moses, did writing appear among the Hebrews. Consequently, Hartmann denied the Mosaic authorship of the first five books of Scripture, the Pentateuch. On the other hand, Jesus Christ had explicitly asserted that Moses had written of Him. If, however, there was no writing in Moses' day, obviously Moses did not write the Pentateuch, and Christ was plainly mistaken in what He had said.

It is an old objection, and one which even today is sometimes heard in ignorant attacks upon the Bible. However, it has lost its validity, because the discoveries of archaeology have proved beyond any shadow of a doubt that writing was known long before Moses' day. No educated person today would dream of declaring that, since the art of writing would have been unknown to him, Moses could not have written the Pentateuch.

This example is instructive and may serve as a warning. Difficulties in the Bible there are, and many of them we cannot now solve to our complete satisfaction; but that they are actual errors is another matter. There must always be kept in mind the limitations of human knowledge. Much that scholars of a previous day have pronounced to be in error is now acknowledged to be true. The archaeologist's spade has revolutionized many an opinion concerning statements of the Bible and attitudes toward the Bible.

In the nature of the case, then, inspiration extends only to the original manuscripts of Scripture. Since these manuscripts were inspired they were free from error. The originals are lost and we are today in possession only of copies, copies which contain textual errors and difficulties that no serious Christian can afford to ignore. These copies, however, do give the actual Word of God. No point of doctrine has been affected. The doctrine shines before us in all its purity. Why God was not pleased to preserve the original copies of the Bible, we do not know. Perhaps, in His infinite wisdom, He did not wish us to bow down to these manuscripts as unto images. Perhaps their preservation would have directed towards them veneration as relics and would have deflected one's attention from their message. One thing at least is clear. In His mysterious providence, God has preserved His Word. We do not have a Bible which is unreliable and glutted with error, but one that in most wondrous fashion presents the Word of God and the text of the original.

How good God has been to give us such a Bible! Whatever our need, here is the voice of the heavenly Father speaking to us. Nor must we search with great difficulty to discover this heavenly voice. Not merely here and there, not merely in some stray passage which we come upon after reading pages of error do we suddenly arrive at the Word of God. Rather, in its fullness and entirety this Word is before us. How rich and manifold it is! How well adapted to our every want and need! Gentle are its commands; tender its precepts; heavenly its doctrine. It is the Holy Bible, a "lamp unto our feet and a light unto our path."

Chapter 3: The Human Writers of the Scriptures

As light that passes through the colored glass of a cathedral window, we are told, is light from heaven, but is stained by the tints of the glass through which it passes; so any word of God which is passed through the mind and soul of a man must come out discolored by the personality through which it is given, and just to that degree ceases to be the pure word of God. But what if this personality has itself been formed by God into precisely the personality it is, for the express purpose of communicating to the word given through it just the coloring which it gives it? What if the colors of the stained-glass window have been designed by the architect for the express purpose of giving to the light that floods the cathedral precisely the tone and quality it receives from them? What if the word of God that comes to His people is framed by God into the word of God it is, precisely by means of the qualities of the men formed by Him for the purpose, through which it is given?

—BENJAMIN B. WARFIELD

There is one very important factor in the doctrine of inspiration which hitherto has been mentioned only in cursory fashion. That is the human side of the Scriptures. Peter stated expressly that "holy men who were borne along of the Holy Ghost spake" (2 Peter 1:21). We have said little about these holy men whom God used in the composition of the Bible. We have simply sought to make it clear, since they themselves also emphasize this fact, that the Scriptures are from God. It is, we have contended, necessary to recognize the Divine origin of the Bible, and the implications of such recognition.

It is likewise necessary and important to do full justice to what the Bible has to say about its human side. This is today the more important because of the constant misrepresentations of this aspect of the doctrine. We are told, for example, that the human writers were mere pen holders whose hands moved under the direction of the Spirit. The historic doctrine is quite frequently parodied as being "static." The writers wrote as mere automata, so the parody runs, having received what was dictated to them and then placed it in writing. When modern authors proclaim, "We want no mechanical theory of inspiration," they give one the impression that they believe they are refuting an actual error. As a matter of fact, however, the idea of mechanical dictation is nothing more than a straw man. Recent conservative writers on the subject of inspiration have sought to do justice to the human side of Scripture; they have been far from advocating a mechanical dictation theory.

What shall we say about this word dictation in regard to the doctrine of inspiration? It was a word that Calvin, to take one example, did not hesitate to employ. "Whoever, then," he says, "wishes to profit in the Scriptures, let him, first of all, lay down this as a settled point, that the Law and the Prophets are not a doctrine delivered according to the will and pleasure of men, but dictated by the Holy Spirit."[11] In speaking in such a vein, Calvin is simply following the thought of the Bible itself. Paul, in writing to the Corinthians, did not hesitate to say, "Which things also we speak, not in the words which man's wisdom teacheth, but which the Holy Ghost teacheth; comparing spiritual things with spiritual" (1 Cor. 2:13). If we were to attempt to bring out more clearly the precise force of the Apostle's language, we might render, "in *words* taught of the Spirit." Paul is saying as patently as he can that the words which he is employing are those which the Spirit has taught him, and this is precisely what Calvin also maintains.

At the same time, although the term dictation in itself is not objectionable and expresses forcefully the Divine origin of the words of the Bible, it is perhaps unwise to use the word today without some qualification. A new connotation has come upon the term which it obviously did not have in the day of Calvin. When we speak of dictation, there immediately comes to mind the thought of the businessman dictating a letter to his stenographer, or the teacher dictating an exercise to her pupils. In both these instances it does not make too great a difference who takes down the dictation. One stenographer can probably do it as well as another, and if one is not available, another can easily be obtained. Likewise, when the teacher dictates a passage to her class, the important thing is that the pupils take down precisely what has been dictated, and do not add to it or subtract from it. The person of the stenographer or of the pupil is in reality a comparatively negligible factor. Such, however, is not the situation with respect to the human writers of the Bible. True enough, the words which they employed were taught them by the Holy Spirit, but it is not the case that it makes no difference who wrote those words. It is not true that Peter might just as well have written the Pauline epistles as the great Apostle himself. It would serve the interests of clarity, therefore, if, in the discussion of this doctrine, we lay stress upon the fact that although the Bible teaches that its very words are from God, it most emphatically does not teach a mechanical dictation view of inspiration.

Men like Turretin, Calvin and others who have written on this subject have been as eager to do justice to the human side of the Bible as have some of the modern rejectors of the Biblical doctrine. It is a sad thing that scholarly men of our day constantly erect a straw man and seek to attack it instead of coming to grips with the Scriptural teaching itself. Those who believe the Bible and who wish to do justice to its teaching are as concerned as anyone to refute the notion that inspiration was a mechanical kind of dictation, that the human writers were mere automata whose personalities were entirely suspended in the writing of the books of the Bible.

Let us then proceed to notice in more detail the emphasis which the Bible places upon these human writers. "How then," we read, "doth David in spirit call him Lord?" (Matt. 22:43). It is David who calls the Messiah Lord. And there are particular conditions under which he does this. It is while he is in the Spirit that he so speaks. The implication is that there are also times when David is not in the Spirit, when, in other words, he is not inspired. When David spoke of the Messiah as Lord, however, he did so being in the Spirit. David, therefore, is the human author of the utterance; it is his, and it is as a conscious responsible human being that he speaks. At the same time, the conditions under which the Psalmist spoke were not the normal conditions of everyday life; he spoke not as a normal man, but rather under peculiar circumstances; David was in the Spirit.

---

11. Calvin on 2 Timothy 3:16 in *Commentaries on the Epistles to Timothy, Titus, and Philemon,* trans. William Pringle, p. 249.

Of particular interest is the statement, "For David himself said by the Holy Ghost" (Mark 12:36). Very strong is the emphasis that it was the man David who spoke. This emphasis receives additional confirmation and strength from the passage, "And David himself saith in the book of Psalms" (Luke 20:42). Of unusual relevancy is this verse because it attributes the authorship of certain words to the man David. In the place of saying that it was in the Spirit that he spoke, it substitutes the phrase "in the book of Psalms."

In the words addressed to God "who by the mouth of thy servant David hast said, Why did the heathen rage and the people imagine vain things?" a passage from the second Psalm is attributed to David. It is God who uttered these words; they find their origin in Him; they are His; He, and He alone, is their author. Nevertheless, He spoke them by the mouth of His servant David. David spoke, but God spoke through him. Similar is the statement to the effect that the Lord received the name Jesus in fulfillment of the words which were "spoken of the Lord by the prophet" (Matt. 1:22). The tender and mysterious prophecy of the Virgin was of Divine origin, but God spoke it through the mouth of the prophet.

In referring to the passage about the burning bush which He says is in the "book of Moses," Christ quotes, "God spake unto him, saying . . ." (Mark 12:26). The words are regarded by Christ as those which God Himself has spoken, but they are to be found in a book written by the man Moses. In another place, however, no reference is made to the human author other than the question "have ye not read?" which implies that the words uttered by God are nevertheless to be found in a book where they can be read (cf. Matt. 22:32). In a similar type of statement the Apostle Paul makes reference to the Old Testament, "Well spake the Holy Ghost by Esaias the prophet unto our fathers, saying" (Acts 28:25–26a). Paul would here make it clear that the Holy Spirit spoke, yet at the same time it was through the mouth of the individual Isaiah that He gave His utterance. The prophet was the human author of the message, yet the one who was speaking through Isaiah was none other than the Spirit of God Himself.

A careful consideration of the above passages should make it clear that God, in revealing His Word, spoke through the instrumentality of men. In the first place, they were holy men; men who knew and loved their God. This does not mean at all that they were not sinful men; they were sinful, sometimes great sinners. David, for example, had committed sins which few, if any, men would forgive, but David, nevertheless, was one through whom the Spirit spoke. The writers of the Bible were indeed sinners, but they were men who, despite their sins, loved God and were used of Him in the composition of Scripture.

It would be most unjust to the data of Scripture to maintain that God merely looked about to see if here and there He could find a man through whom He might speak to the world. There is nothing in the Bible to support or to sustain this idea; in fact, everything teaches the very opposite. Did it matter, we may ask, through whom the Divine message was spoken? According to the Bible it mattered very greatly. In the first verse of Amos' rugged prophecy we read, "The words of Amos . . . which he saw." Only nine short chapters, yet from them we learn something of the man who wrote them. How different they are from the quiet tenderness of Hosea! How unsuited was Amos to have undergone the sad experiences of a Hosea! At the same time, different as each was from the other, each was clearly conscious of speaking forth the words of God.

The same is true when we turn to the pages of the New Testament. Do not the human writers of the New Testament also differ greatly one from another? It would seem that God had chosen specific men to write specific portions of His Word. And such was indeed the case. Not only, however, did the Lord select certain men to write certain portions of His Word but, more than that, they were used as real men. Their personalities were not held in abeyance; their talents were not obscured; they were not somehow placed in a state of suspended animation. Rather, God used them as they were. All their gifts of training and native talent God called into play.

The matter may be very clearly illustrated by the case of the Apostle Paul. God very obviously did not look about to discover if there were somewhere on the face of the earth a man who might be used in the composition of those writings which we now call the Pauline Epistles. There was only one man that could have written those Epistles, and that man was the Apostle himself. The Apostle, however, required training and preparation before he could commit to writing the glorious epistles which now bear his name. His very birth and upbringing in the city of Tarsus were of importance. The instruction which he received at the feet of Gamaliel and his indoctrination into the tenets of the Pharisees served as a background which stood him in good stead throughout the remainder of his life. Not the least of his talents was his ability to use the Greek language both in speaking and preaching. After his conversion he spent three years in Arabia, years, we may well suppose, in which he engaged in study and meditation.

Did all this, however, occur simply through chance? Not at all; it was God who was at work in the events of Paul's life, shaping him so that he would be precisely the man whom God wanted and whom He needed to write the great epistles. It was a providential preparation; a schooling and training conducted at the hands of God Himself through the ordinary course of His providential working.

Similar was the case with Moses. Here again we note the long years of preparation. In childhood and youth Moses learned of the afflictions of his people in Egypt. He knew well the Egyptian mind, and how to deal with the taskmaster. Then came the period of training in the desert, where, in the stillness of the wasteland, he might mediate and reflect. Thus, through this time, followed by his own participation in the events of the Exodus, Moses came to the place where he was prepared for the task of writing the first five books of the Bible. It is clear that these books represent a unified plan and that they are the work of a great mind. Only a mind such as that of Moses could have composed them. And for this work of writing, Moses, in the providence of God, had been prepared and equipped. How graciously did the Lord deal with His recalcitrant and stubborn servant! How wondrously He led the man on, step by step, until Moses was ready to write.

Very wondrous was God's providential preparation and equipment of those men whom He had appointed to be the human instruments in the writing of the Scripture. Thus He prepared and raised up an Isaiah, a Jeremiah, a John, and a Paul. His work of providence and His special work of inspiration should be regarded as complementing one another. Those through whom the Spirit desired to give the Scriptures were individuals who had been equipped for the task in the providence of God. When, therefore, the Spirit bore a holy man of old (2 Peter 1:21) it was not *any* man who happened to be on the scene, but rather, just *that* holy man whom God, through years of training, had prepared to speak and to write precisely that portion of the Scripture which He desired to have him write.

The question may very well be raised how the Spirit actually controlled the writers of Scripture so that they wrote expressly what He desired and yet at the same time were responsible individuals whose personalities were not stifled. How, for example, could the prophet write, "The words of Amos . . . which he saw?" Does not this verse contain a glaring contradiction? If the words are truly those of Amos, how could they at the same time be those which had found their origin in God? If God was the Author, how could Amos also be regarded as an author?

Legitimate as such questions are, however, they cannot be fully answered. God has not seen fit to reveal to us the mode by which He communicated His Word to His servants, placing that word in their mouths and "carrying" them until the Word was accurately committed to writing. We have come, in other words, into an area of mystery. There is much about this precious Scriptural doctrine which God has not revealed. The Scripture is silent as to the mode which God employed to preserve His Word from error. In this as in so many doctrines of the Bible there is mystery. It is of course, to be expected that such would be the case. We are but men and our understanding is at best limited and finite. We can only know as a created being knows. God, on the other hand, is the One who in His understanding is infinite. We cannot probe into His dealings in such a way as to obtain full and comprehensive knowledge thereof. He is not such a One as can be brought down and placed under the scrutiny of the microscope of the human mind.

In the doctrine of the Trinity likewise there is mystery. He who thinks that he can remove that mystery and fully understand the doctrine deceives no one but himself. This deep truth must be received in faith, and the believing heart rejoices simply because God has revealed this mystery in His Word. How wondrous is this revelation which God has given of Himself! How great, we are compelled to say, is our Holy God! When the mind delights itself in the thought that He is the one living and true God, it finds itself suddenly brought face to face with the fact that He is also Triune. Likewise, when it contemplates the Father, the Son, and the Holy Spirit, it is worshipping Him beside whom there is no other. The One reminds us of the Three, and the Three bring us to the One. Before Him, the one God in three Persons, we bow in adoration. We praise Him, we worship Him, we extol His matchless Name, we meditate upon His infinite attributes and perfections. Never, however, can we remove the mystery that adheres to the revelation which He has given of Himself as Triune.

It is the same with the doctrine of inspiration. When we have set forth all that the Scripture has to say, we can go no further. It may well be that questions arise in our minds, but they are questions which, at present at least, we cannot answer. Our duty is to believe all that God has revealed and to bow in humble acceptance of the truth which He has given. Scripture has spoken; it has permitted us to learn much concerning its inspiration. It has not, however, told us all. We may then freely acknowledge that there are difficulties in the Scriptural position, and also that there are questions which we cannot at present answer. Our portion is to be believers. God has spoken. Let us hear His voice, and beyond that let us not seek to go.

At this point, however, it is necessary to consider in some detail and with some care an objection to the above teaching which is frequently being voiced in our day. When the Word of God came through human personality, it is very often maintained, the Word was obscured to some extent. God was limited in His choice of available instruments through whom His Word might come to us, and therefore He did the best that He could with the personalities and means that were at His disposal. Consequently, the character of the revelation which we have depends not only upon God but also upon the human media through which it came.

Since the Word did come through human agents and instrumentality, it is claimed, there must adhere to it some of the error and imperfection which is found in everything human. It is just like plunging one's arm into muddy water: in withdrawing the arm some of the mud will adhere to it; or it is like rays of sunlight which are less bright when shining through a dirty window than a clear one.

The character of the Divine revelation, therefore, according to this view, depends not only on God, but also on those media through which that revelation came. If those media were fallible, then the revelation itself partook of that fallibility. God Himself was limited by the means at hand. He could communicate Himself and His truth to men only in so far as men themselves were spiritually mature to receive His revelation. Men with spiritual failings could mar and prevent that revelation from coming to mankind.

Those, who insist that the Word of God in coming through human instruments has itself been affected and has acquired imperfections, for the most part believe that they can themselves detect these imperfections. Generally they wish to limit the errors and flaws which have supposedly crept into the Word of God to minor matters of fact or history. Sometimes a comparison is made with the incarnation of the Lord. The Word which became incarnate was subject to all the limitations and hardships of human life, it is sometimes maintained, and likewise the embodiment of the spoken Word of God in the history of a people such as the Hebrews involved all the crudities and the errors that such a people would probably make.

One need not look far today for a statement of this position. It is to be found in much that is written on the subject. Whenever someone writes on the Bible, he seems to feel the necessity of pointing out that it contains errors, and that these errors are a result of the human agents who were employed in the writing down of Scripture. It seems to be taken for granted that error must in the nature of the case be found in whatever is written by human hands.

As we hear this objection to the Scriptural teaching, there are several questions which arise. In the first place, we would ask, What kind of a God is He who cannot reveal to the world a message that is free from error? Surely, He must be limited and restricted indeed! Those of us who from time to time engage in a bit of writing are happy to have a stenographer who types our work accurately. If we discover that the stenographer is constantly making mistakes in her typing, and these mistakes are of so serious a nature that our work is actually obscured and marred thereby, we shall probably change stenographers. God, however, if the position which we are now considering is correct, cannot even do this. God is far more limited than are we mortals. We have the ability of hiring someone who will do our work for us as we desire it done; God, on the other hand, cannot even do that. When God would speak to mankind in writing, He cannot get His message across without having it cluttered up with irritating errors.

It is well to consider this question carefully. God, we are being told, had to use the means at His disposal. Those means were human beings. Therefore, when God revealed His Word, that Word, in passing through the media of human writers, acquired the characteristics of those writers, including their error, their ignorance, their crudities. Well may we exclaim at the poverty and weakness of such a God! If indeed man can thus thwart Him, it is pertinent to ask, Is He really worth knowing after all?

One thing, however, is clear. Such a God, limited as He is by the human agents through whom He gives His Word, is not the God of the Bible. He may very well serve as the god of modern theology, but he is not the Creator of heaven and earth, the one true eternal God. If it were really true—and thank God that it is not—that the Father in heaven were restricted in His power by man and were limited in His ability to reveal His Word, we could then be sure that at the best he was only a finite being like ourselves. He might be more powerful than we, yet, since we can clutter up His revelation with our error, even that assumption is questionable. Since He is limited by His creatures, such a God is no God at all.

Very different is the God of whom Scripture speaks. This God, whom the Christian worships as the Creator, is One who doeth according to His will, "and none can stay his hand, or say unto him, What doest thou?" (Dan. 4:35b). This God, in whom are hid all the treasures of wisdom and knowledge, is One who can take up and bear the writers of Scripture so that what they have written is exactly what He desired to have written. He is One who in His infinite power can use as His agents and instruments fallible human beings, who can bring into His employ all the gifts, talents, and characteristics of those human beings, and yet can cause them to pen His own Word, and keep that Word utterly separate and distinct from their own sinful nature and the consequent imperfections which are the result of that nature.

There is, however, another point which must be raised in this connection. Those who believe that there are errors in the Bible, as we have seen, seek to account for the presence of these supposed errors upon the assumption that their origin is to be attributed to the human writers. Since human authors are fallible, they reason, the Scripture itself must therefore partake of fallibility. If this is actually the case, it follows that not merely part of Scripture partakes of fallibility, but all. Whatever is the Word of God has passed through human instruments. Whatever passes through human instruments, so this argument runs, must therefore partake of fallibility. All Scripture has passed through human instrumentality; consequently, all Scripture has become fallible. There is no escape from this position. It will not do to say that fallibility has attached itself only to statements of historical and geographical fact. To do that would be to be guilty of gross inconsistency. Like a leach that cannot be removed, human fallibility attaches itself to all Scripture without exception. Whatever is the Word of God is also fallible; no part is free from error and imperfection.

It may very well be that this is not what modern writers believe but, be that as it may, it is the logical conclusion of their position, and it is well to note what that conclusion is. God grant that those who are so insistent that humanity must give to the Divine Word the character of fallibility, would realize what is involved in their claim. They have not solved any difficulties; rather they have created incalculably difficult questions and problems.

An example will reveal how dire are the consequences of this position. When we are called to a home where death has come, how inadequate we are. At such a time how trite and unsatisfactory are mere words of ours! How the heart grieves at the thoughtlessness and cruelty of those who have nothing more to offer than mere banality and platitude. Cold and unthinking they are indeed! Can we on the other hand, offer anything of greater comfort? We turn to the pages of the Bible and read, "I am the resurrection, and the life: he that believeth in me, though he were dead, yet shall he live: and whosoever liveth and believeth in me shall never die" (John 11:25–26). "Is that true?" asks the one in sorrow. "Is Jesus really the One who has taken my loved one to be with Him?" "Well," we reply, "we believe that it is true. Of course, this Word of God, like everything else in the Bible is tinged with fallibility. Like the remainder of Scripture it also has imperfection and error."

To speak in that vein would be mockery. It would offer no comfort to the soul who is in sorrow. Yet, how else could one answer? To the one in need there would be nothing better to say, since all Scripture is fallible. We could never be sure as to what it said about God, nor could we, for that matter, have any assurance that its prescriptions for our conduct upon this earth were free from error. Serious and tragic in the extreme are the consequences of adopting this modern error. We can only be thankful that its adherents are themselves inconsistent in their practice. For our part, we want nothing to do with a position which logically can lead to such results. Thank God that when it came through human agents His blessed Word was not coated with fallibility. Those agents did not control or circumscribe Him; they did not affect His Word, but rather, under His sovereign Spirit, were rendered the willing instruments to carry out what He wished accomplished.

Furthermore, if fallible human writers have given to us a Bible that is fallible, how are we ourselves, who most certainly are fallible, to detect in the Bible what is error and what is not? To this the answer is given that with the increase in knowledge, we can easily detect errors which the ancient writers made. They had crude ideas of geography and history, it is said, but we today have much greater knowledge. Where they went astray, we can furnish a check and correct their errors. To speak this way, however, is not to settle the issue at all. What about those parts of the Bible upon which we cannot check? How are we to discern what in those parts is error and what is not? How are we to separate the fallible from the inerrant?

To take an example, the Bible speaks of Palestine and Jerusalem. We may today travel to Palestine and Jerusalem, and thus we have a check. When the Bible mentioned these places, it was telling us the truth; such places do exist. The Bible also mentions certain customs of antiquity. Abraham, for example, took his concubine, Hagar, and from her a son was born. Archaeology has made it perfectly clear that this custom was as a matter of fact practiced in Abraham's day. Well and good, but what about those parts of the Bible upon which we cannot check? How shall we evaluate the God of Scripture? How do we know whether we can separate the wheat from the chaff in the Biblical teaching about God? The answer is that we simply cannot do so. If all Scripture is fallible, then all that Scripture says about God is fallible, and we have no way of detecting what is and what is not in accord with fact. We ourselves are likely to err. How then can we judge the Scripture? Judge the Scripture we cannot; we are left in a hopeless skepticism. It will not do to say that modern knowledge has made it possible to separate the wheat and the chaff in the Bible. It has done nothing of the kind. We are ourselves like the authors of Scripture and the only thing that can help us in an infallible Word from God. Since, however, God cannot give us an infallible Word, there is nothing that we can do. Here is the Bible, shot full of error, and we must make the best of it. Disastrous indeed is this conclusion. Disastrous as it is, however, it is the end at which we are bound to arrive if we adopt the view which we are now seeking to answer.

This brings us to another point which must be raised in opposition to the assertion that human fallibility precludes infallibility in the Scripture. It is that the advocates of this position are for the most part extremely inconsistent. Certain parts of the Bible, they tell us, are pure and true. For example, the injunction to love one's enemies is acceptable to modern theologians. There, certainly, is the Word of God. That we are to obey. In saying this, however, modern theology is in effect admitting the very case which it wishes to deny. In admitting that there is even one bit of Scripture that is the pure and infallible and trustworthy Word of God, the modern theologian is tacitly acknowledging that at least some of the Word of God has come through the medium of fallible human writers without itself becoming fallible. It was protected from error so that we today might regard it as trustworthy. It is the truth free from error; our duty in fact is to love our enemies. If, however, even a portion of the Word may have been transmitted through fallible human channels without error, why may not all have been so transmitted? To acknowledge that some may be preserved from error is to give the case away. If some may thus have been kept from imperfection, without doubt all may likewise have been so kept. Moreover, if it is true that humanity, because it is necessarily fallible, may thwart the revelation of God, so that that revelation comes to us marred, what is to be said about Christ? Jesus Christ was a true man, and if manhood necessarily involves fallibility, Jesus Christ was fallible. If humanity, simply because it is humanity, is characterized by error and imperfection, Jesus Christ is not our Savior.

From these consequences we cannot flee. We are not warranted in making an exception of the Person of our Lord, and if we have once adopted the position that the human necessarily entails imperfection, let us be consistent and admit that Christ also is imperfect. It is a sad conclusion to draw; sad as it is, however, it is one that we must draw if the premise which we have adopted is correct. If our Lord, in His human nature, was necessarily subject to fallibility, then, of course, He was not what He claimed to be; He was subject to sin. There is no escape from this conclusion, none whatever. If Jesus Christ was a sinner (for fallibility is the consequence of sin) we might as well face the fact that He is not, nor could He be, our Savior. As a matter of fact, however, this vicious premise is not correct. The God whom we worship is powerful enough to convey His revelation through human channels and to do so in such a manner that His revelation does not acquire the imperfections that adhere to sinful humanity. In the Person of His Son, He is able to take to Himself a true human nature which is not touched with sin. Although error and imperfection are found in sinful human nature they are not at all necessary characteristics of human nature as such.

Is it not, the charge is sometimes made, an illogical position to adopt, this position which asserts that God can give an infallible revelation through fallible channels? Man is fallible; man is the only instrument available to God through which this revelation can come. Simple logic demands that said revelation must then partake of fallibility. Thus the view for which we are contending is dismissed as "illogical."

But is this view, as a matter of fact, illogical? The charge, grave as it is, is based upon the premise that man is capable of qualifying or affecting the revelation which God gives through him. Is this premise, however, warranted by the facts? Can man, in truth, control God's revelation? Is God the Revealer subject to man? According to the Bible this premise is utterly and completely false. According to the Bible God has created man in His own image. Man therefore is subject to God and dependent upon Him. God, on the other hand, is utterly independent of man, and self-sufficient unto Himself. "For of him, and through him, and to him, are all things" (Rom. 11:36a).

Man is entirely subject to the law of God. As created by God, Adam, although finite, was nevertheless not fallible. Adam, however, sinned, and all mankind sinned in him and fell with him. Man, therefore, is a sinful creature and as a sinner is subject to error. God, since He is the omnipotent Creator, has absolute control over those whom He has created. In His good pleasure, which is a sovereign good pleasure, He may bear the human writers of the Bible, so controlling them, yet preserving intact their personalities, that they can write His revelation exactly as He wishes. If once we think rightly about God, other matters will appear in their proper perspective. Once we realize that God is in control of the situation, it will become clear that the Biblical doctrine of inspiration, mysterious as it may be, is nevertheless not illogical.

Thus we come to that which is basic in modern thought. In all this talk of the Word of God we would ask the question, What is it that modern theologians have in mind when they are speaking of the Word of God? Who is this God in whose Word they are so interested? It is difficult to identify Him. He seems to be a creation in the image of man, and not the Triune God who has spoken in the Bible. The issue involved is in reality that of theism. Who is our God? Are we followers of the King, or have we bowed the knee to Baal? Unless first we become as little children and acknowledge the true God in all our ways, we shall not speak profitably on the subject of that Word which has been breathed forth from His mouth. The modern god, created by man, lives and rules in the City of Destruction. From him and from his reign, however, we have been delivered by the God of Holy Scripture.

It should be clear from the discussion so far that the Bible is not to be regarded as a "joint" product, the combined effort of God and man. Surely the Bible itself does not make such a claim. There were indeed human writers of the Scripture, but they are not to be considered as co-authors with God. It is not that God contributed certain parts of the Scriptures, and men supplemented these, and it most certainly is not the case that men contributed the greater portion of Scripture to have it supplemented by God. Nor did God and man take counsel together as to what should be included in the Scripture. God did not consult man as to what should be written. The Bible is truly the Word of God. He is the final and the ultimate Author; the Bible comes from God. Without Him there could have been no Bible. Without men, however, there could have been a Bible. God could have given us His Word in some other manner than that which He actually did choose. As a matter of fact, He did choose to speak through inspired men but He was not compelled to do so. In no sense was He limited. That he employed human writers was an act of grace, and the heart of faith will ever adore and revere Him that He so honored the human race as to employ lost sinners as writers of His pure and holy Word. While the human authors were true authors, nevertheless they were not the originators of the words and the thoughts that are found in the Bible. They were holy men indeed, but they were holy men who were borne by the Spirit.

Were these human writers infallible, even when they were not borne by the Spirit? Obviously the Bible does not teach that this was so. They were men of their own day. No doubt their own views of astronomy, for example, were not one whit more advanced than those of their contemporaries. On the other hand, when they were the penmen of the Spirit of God, they were expressing the words of God. The thoughts which they were penning had been revealed to them by God; they were placed in their minds by the Spirit Himself. It therefore will not do to assert that they did not have a knowledge of modern astronomy and hence could not have written an account of the creation that was scientifically accurate. If Moses had depended only upon the wisdom of the Egyptians, he would have produced a rather clumsy account of Creation. If he had relied alone upon the thoughts and opinions of his own heart, he would have composed a first chapter of Genesis that for crudity and error might have equaled the writings of Babylonia. Moses, however, in writing the first chapter of Genesis was not drawing upon his own ideas and thoughts. He was giving expression to thoughts which he had learned by revelation of God. He was an inspired penman. What went on in his own mind as he wrote we can never tell, but he acted as a conscious, responsible human being. Without doubt he must have realized that he was writing far more deeply than he himself could fathom. However he composed, however he gathered his material and set it down in writing, whether he wrote and crossed out and polished, we do not know. Nevertheless he worked, and what was finally set down as the completed product was just what the God of Truth desired to have written down; it was the Word of God.

At other times, however, to continue our use of Moses as an illustration, what Moses may have said and done, and what he may have written down, was no more free from error, no more infallible, than any other purely human word or composition. Not at all times was he kept from error, but only when he served as the penman to write down the Divine oracles. The same is true of the other writers of the Bible. Hence, the folly of Reimarus' objection that the moral character of some of the human writers would preclude them from being the recipients of Divine revelation. In giving the Bible to mankind God did not make use of men who were free from sin. David was a sinful man, and yet through him God gave many of the Psalms. Moses was a murderer. Paul persecuted the Church of God. Yet God selected them to be His instruments of inspiration. That they were thus chosen in no sense condones or excuses their sins. If anything, it would seem to heighten their guilt. What they wrote, however, and what they said when they were not borne by the Spirit was not inspired; it was as subject to error as the utterances of anyone else. Only when borne of the Spirit were the authors infallible in what they wrote.

In the book of 2 Samuel there is recorded a letter which David wrote to his general Joab (11:15). When David penned this letter he was doing a despicable thing. It is a tragedy indeed that the man who had composed many of the Psalms should also have stand out against him the words of this letter: "Set ye Uriah in the forefront of the hottest battle, and retire ye from him, that he may be smitten, and die." Those words will ever stand to blacken the record of David. An evil thing indeed was the writing of this letter. Was David inspired when he wrote it? Most obviously he was not. It was something that was composed from his evil heart; this was the stratagem which he devised to cover up his own sin by removing the innocent Uriah from the scene. David did not write this letter under the impulsion of the Spirit of God.

Inspiration naturally extends only to that which the writers produced when they were under the impulsion of God's Spirit. How then, it may be asked, do we find a copy of this letter in the Sacred Scriptures? The answer must be that the writer of the book of Samuel was inspired as he recorded the letter. It was the intention of God to include this letter in the Scripture, and the author of Samuel, being borne of the Spirit, has given an accurate copy thereof. We have, in other words, a correct copy of the words which David wrote. To draw from this the conclusion that the letter had the approval of God upon its contents would be unwarranted indeed. In writing this letter David did an evil thing, and it was the will of God that we today should know of this evil thing; for that reason the letter was included in the Scripture. The writer has given an accurate copy of the letter, for inspiration secures accuracy. Inspiration does not, however, involve Divine approval of the contents of all that is inspired.

We may then say with assurance that the writers of the Bible were inspired only when they were actually engaged in composing the books of Scripture. Apart from that they were men of their times, and erred just as other men err. They were sinful human beings, and inspiration did not by some magical process keep them from error. It was only when the Spirit mysteriously came upon them as they wrote down His Word that they were in His power and so kept from making in their writings errors such as adhere to everything merely human.

Very remarkable is this doctrine of inspiration! It is remarkable above all because it is taught in the Bible itself. The Bible is God's Word, we may say, but the Bible is also the work of men. They were not, however, men who wrote under their own power and under ordinary circumstances. Great indeed was the honor which had been placed upon them. There were times when they were lifted from the ordinary level of human experience. There were times when what they set down in writing was free from error. There were times when they were under the compulsion of the Spirit of God. There were times when these chosen few of the human race were the writers of Scripture.

How Does the Bible Look at Itself?

SINCLAIR B. FERGUSON

Sinclair B. Ferguson, "3. How Does the Bible Look at Itself?" in *Inerrancy and Hermeneutic*, 47–66.

Sinclair Ferguson was professor of systematic theology at Westminster Theological Seminary from 1982 to 1998. He is now distinguished visiting professor of systematic theology. He obtained a Ph.D. in theology at the University of Aberdeen in 1979. His dissertation on John Owen was later published as *John Owen on the Christian Life* (1987). A pastor-scholar, Ferguson was Minister of St. George's Tron in Glasgow (1998–2003) and is now senior pastor of First Presbyterian Church, Columbia, South Carolina (2006–). Ferguson has written numerous devotional books, often translating insights from the Puritans to modern Christians. *The Christian Life: A Doctrinal Introduction* (1981) illustrates this blending of doctrine and piety. Standing on the shoulders of giants in Reformed theology and biblical theology, Ferguson offers us a monograph on an important locus in *The Holy Spirit* (1996) in the series Contours of Christian Theology.

One of the last sources that modern critical scholars consult when formulating a doctrine of Scripture is Scripture. In "How Does the Bible Look at Itself?" Ferguson sets the theological tone for the symposium *Inerrancy and Hermeneutic*, and clearly departs from modern tendencies that fail to consider the Bible's self-witness. Ferguson unfolds his insights from the entire corpus of Scripture to discover what the Bible has to say about itself. He exhibits what the Scriptures teach concerning their own inspiration, authority, reliability, and necessity. Ferguson invites us to consider with humility the difficulties of the Bible (its phenomena), but to accept by faith and in full confidence its own teaching about itself.

If the Bible does not witness to its own infallibility, then we have no right to believe that it is infallible. If it does bear witness to its infallibility then our faith in it must rest upon that witness, however much difficulty may be entertained with this belief. If this position with respect to the ground of faith in Scripture is abandoned, then appeal to the Bible for the ground of faith in any other doctrine must also be abandoned. The doctrine of Scripture must be elicited from the Scripture just as any other doctrine should be. If the doctrine of Scripture is denied its right of appeal to Scripture for support, then what right does any other doctrine have to make this appeal?

—JOHN MURRAY, 1946

In the final Latin edition of his *Institutes* (1559), John Calvin wrote that "Scripture exhibits fully as clear evidence of its own truth as white and black things do of their color, or sweet or bitter things do of their taste. . . . Let this point therefore stand: that those whom the Holy Spirit has inwardly taught truly rest upon Scripture, and that Scripture indeed is self authenticated [*autopiston*]."[1] Few things more characterize the view of Scripture espoused by Calvin's evangelical successors than the assumptions implicit in his words: (1) Scripture bears witness to its own character as God's Word; (2) Scripture is the Word of God written; and (3) Scripture as written bears the marks of its human authors; as God-given, it bears the marks of its divine origin, namely, uncompromised reliability.

This view is based on several biblical passages, notably 2 Timothy 3:16 and 2 Peter 1:19–21, and on a host of ancillary statements scattered throughout both Testaments. But it has never been regarded as the last word on Scripture. Indeed, it is simply the first word, providing a solid foundation for the rigorous discipline of biblical exposition. For such a conviction about Scripture does not answer in an a priori fashion many of the questions we might raise about its teaching. As a biblical doctrine it will influence the interpretation of other passages. But any decision about the "meaning" of a given passage must still be decided on the basis of careful exegetical study. Only when we lapse from such sensitivity to the text does the principle of the self-witness of Scripture become confused with an a priori dogmatism about what certain texts must mean.

Implicit in this whole approach to the doctrine of Scripture lies a presupposition which was, in the past, rarely expounded, largely because it was so universally held to be self-evident. It was assumed that we can in fact speak about "Scripture's view of itself." Today that assumption is contested and therefore needs to be established as legitimate. Since Scripture could not be a finalized entity until the last of its books had been written, is it not anachronistic to speak of "Scripture's view of itself"?

The issue is expressed with characteristically pugilistic vigor by James Barr, when he writes:

According to conservative arguments, it is not only Jesus who made "claims"; the Bible made "claims" about itself. The Book of Daniel "claims" to have been written by a historical Daniel some time in the sixth century B.C.; the Book of Deuteronomy "claims" to have been written by Moses; and more important still, the Bible as a whole "claims" to be divinely inspired. All this is nonsense. There is no "the Bible" that "claims" to be divinely inspired, there is no "it" that has a "view of itself." There is only this or that source, like 2 Timothy or 2 Peter, which makes statements about certain other writings, these rather undefined. There is no such thing

1. John Calvin, *Institutes of the Christian Religion*, ed. John T. McNeill (Philadelphia: Westminster, 1960), 1:76, 80.

as "the Bible's view of itself" from which a fully authoritative answer to these questions can be obtained. This whole side of traditional conservative apologetic, though loudly vociferated, just does not exist; there is case to answer.[2]

Barr's powers of debunking are considerable, and well known. Nor have they been directed exclusively against those he regards as fundamentalists. His critique cannot, therefore, be treated in an off-hand fashion. Indeed, it underlines a hiatus in much conservative writing on the doctrine of Scripture. But is he correct in suggesting that we cannot legitimately speak of "Scripture's view of itself"? If so, he would seem to have destroyed a linchpin in the traditional orthodox view of Scripture and shown that the so-called biblical view is essentially nonbiblical. How can it be claimed that "Scripture teaches X or Y about Scripture" if such reflection does not (and in the very nature of the case, could not) take place in Scripture itself?

This argument has the appearance of devastating power; but in fact it fails to take account of the direction of the evidence Scripture provides. In what follows, our intention is (1) to demonstrate the legitimacy of speaking of "Scripture's view of itself," and (2) to expound briefly what this view entails for the doctrine of Scripture.

Does the Bible Have "A View of Itself"?

Can we really speak about "the Bible's view of itself," or, with Barr, say only that X (a biblical author) said Y about Z (a section of the Christian canon of Scripture)?

Merely to cite 2 Timothy 3:16 to defend the view that Scripture does indeed have a view of itself is an inadequate response. It begs the question, since (1) Paul here refers apparently to the Old Testament (the "holy Scriptures," v. 15), not to the entire Christian canon; (2) evidence must be offered that 2 Timothy 3:16 is itself Scripture, to show that it gives Scripture's view of Scripture; and (3) evidence must be furnished that 2 Timothy 3:16 has the rest of the New Testament canon in view. Only when these conditions are met can this statement justify the claim that it presents Scripture's view of itself.

Is the traditional conservative view of Scripture then justifiable? In the very nature of the case, such justification must rise above the mere citation of proof texts.

If one objects that any sophisticated reasoning or preunderstanding would bar the ordinary Christian from reaching the conviction that Scripture claims to be the Word of God, the answer is at hand. We are ultimately persuaded of the inspiration and authority of Scripture not on the basis of coherent arguments in textbooks of doctrine but through "the inward work of the Holy Spirit, bearing witness by and with the Word in our hearts."[3] It is by reading Scripture under the Spirit's influence, rather than by skill in logic, that trust in God's Word is born.

There is no finer illustration of this principle than J. Gresham Machen's experience when exposed in his earlier years to the cream of German liberal theological teaching. It was his reading of the Gospels themselves that strengthened his faith in biblical inspiration and authority.

The function of our discussion here is not to usurp the ministry of the Holy Spirit but to vindicate the inner consistency of the view that Scripture *does* bear witness to its own

---

2. James Barr, *Fundamentalism* (London: SCM, 1977), 78.
3. WCF 1.5.

character. We seek to show that such a conviction is neither incoherent nor irrelevant because of a category mistake.

What, then, are the propositions involved in saying that Scripture bears witness to its own nature? We may note briefly four of them.

First, there is evidence within the Old Testament of a canonical self-consciousness, a recognition that what is written is given by God to rule and direct his people. That is already indicated by the fact that written documentation accompanies the covenant relationship between God and his people and is intended to rule and direct their lives (see Deut. 5:22, 32; 29:9; 30:9–10, 15–16; 31:24–29; Josh. 1:7–8; 8:34). The rest of the books of the Old Testament are written, in various ways, in exposition of this authoritative, canonical, covenant word. The Old Testament grows from this root. Out of this flows, in part, the Chronicler's covenantal, canonical interpretation of history and the confidence of the prophetic "This is what the Sovereign Lord says." New Scripture is written in the confidence that it is "Scripture" only because of its inherent relationship to what God has already given.[4]

Second, there is, in the New Testament, the clear recognition of the divinely given canon we now know as the Old Testament. The New Testament's use of the word *Scripture* and such expressions as "the law and the prophets," "it is written," "God said," and "Scripture says" abundantly illustrate this fact. Both Jesus and the apostles use Scripture in a normative canonical role. In Jesus' life, Scripture must be fulfilled, simply because it is Scripture. For him, as for the apostles, the appeal to the Old Testament settles all matters, because of its canonical status for God's people. It is "the mouth of God," by whose every word people are to live (Matt. 4:4).

To the authors of the New Testament, the Old Testament is God's Word. But further development of this proposition is required. It must be shown that the New Testament is organically one with the Old, and self-consciously Scripture, to enable us to affirm that this is Scripture's view of Scripture.

Third, there is, in the New Testament, a consciousness among the authors as a whole that the authority of their own writing is on a par with that of the Old Testament and that the content of the revelation given to them is, in some sense, superior to it, not in terms of inspiration, but in the clarity and progress of the revelation recorded (see, e.g., Eph. 3:2–6). This consciousness in the apostolic writings is tantamount to a deliberate addition to the canon in order to bring it to completion in the light of Christ's coming. In this sense, the New Testament as canon is virtually demanded by the coming of Christ. If the older revelation, which was spasmodic and fragmentary (Heb. 1:1), was inscripturated, how much more is inscripturation anticipated of the consummation of revelation?

We find hints of this self-conscious adding to canonical Scripture throughout the New Testament. These are, in the nature of the case, often subtle, but they are almost commonplace. Thus, for example, in keeping with New Testament practice, John's Gospel introduces quotations from the Old Testament with the words, "it is written (6:31; 8:17; 12:14; etc.). It is a phrase which "in the New Testament puts an end to all contradiction."[5] But a similar expression, "these are written," marks the rounding off of John's own work (20:31). In John's Gospel the allusion is unlikely to be accidental. Here, as elsewhere, the verb *graphō* (write)

---

4. For an extended discussion of a similar argument, see Meredith G. Kline, *The Structure of Biblical Authority* (Grand Rapids: Eerdmans, 1972), esp. 21–68.

5. Herman Ridderbos, *Studies in Scripture and Its Authority* (Grand Rapids: Eerdmans, 1978), 21.

seems to retain its quasi-authoritative sense (cf. Pilate's words: "What I have written, I have written" [19:22]).[6]

Hebrews 2:2–3 argues from the lesser authority of the Law, given through the angels, to the greater authority of the gospel, given through the preaching of the apostles. But if the apostles' spoken word was regarded as the Word of God (as they themselves believed it to be [1 Thess. 2:13]), no less will be their written word. No one knows God's thoughts, except God's Spirit. But God's Spirit teaches the apostles to speak the words he teaches (1 Cor. 2:11–13). Those who posses the Spirit therefore recognize the divine canonicity of the apostolic word. Nor is this simply the conclusion of deductive logic. What Paul writes are the Lord's commands, and a mark of a truly spiritual person is that he or she recognizes them as such (1 Cor. 14:37). Disobedience to the teaching given in his letters can lead to excommunication (2 Thess. 3:14). Here Paul aligns his written teaching with the Law of the old covenant; rejection of it as canon for life involves the repudiation of the covenant of which it is the canonical record and then the coming under the divine curse of expulsion from the covenant community. For this reason, apostolic letters are read not only by the church but alongside the sacred writings of the Old Testament, in and to the church (Col. 4:16).

The same inherent canon-consciousness emerges in the opening and closing sections of the Book of Revelation. It is assumed that the book will be read in public to the church (1:3). Both reader and hearer are promised "blessing"—that is, divine, covenantal benediction. In view of this, a similarly covenant-oriented warning closes the book: "I warn everyone who hears the words of the prophecy of this book: If anyone adds anything to them, God will add to him the plagues described in this book. And if anyone takes words away from this book of prophecy, God will take away from him his share in the tree of life and in the holy city, which are described in this book" (22:18–19).

These words are not a naive piece of personal vindictiveness. Rather, they reflect the apex of canon-consciousness in the New Testament. They deliberately echo the warnings of the Old Testament canonical Scripture: "Do not add to what I command you and do not subtract from it, but keep the commands of the LORD your God that I give you" (Deut. 4:2; see also vv. 5, 14, 40; 12:32). Here, the Book of Revelation "claims" the authority which it assumes for the Old Testament itself. This is nothing less than self-conscious canonicity.

Fourth, in the New Testament we also notice that some sources express a sense not only of their own canonical character but of the existence of a class of literature sharing that status. Admittedly this cross-fertilization does little more than surface in the New Testament documents. But the fact that it does surface is adequate justification for believing that it reflects a wider ecclesiastical consciousness that God was giving a new canon of Scripture for the new age of the gospel.

This sense may be the explanation of the otherwise mysterious citing of words in 1 Timothy 5:18 (from both Deut. 25:4 and Luke 10:7) under the common rubric "for the Scripture says." Another interpretation is possible, namely, that the rubric refers only to the first citation, the second being a "free" logion of Jesus. But there is nothing inherently questionable about the first interpretation, and it is in fact the more natural reading of the text. Moreover, given the emergence of the canon of the New Testament and the citation of New Testament documents by the apostolic fathers, it would seem inevitable that already in the

6. G. Kittel, ed., *Theological Dictionary of the New Testament,* trans. and ed. G. W. Bromiley (Grand Rapids: Eerdmans, 1964), 1:747.

first century—and especially by Paul, to whom Luke was such a faithful companion—the Gospel of Luke would be cited as "Scripture."

More certain yet is the well-known statement of 2 Peter 3:16. Paul's "letters contain some things that are hard to understand, which ignorant and unstable people distort, as they do the other Scriptures (*tas loipas graphas*), to their own destruction." Here we find confirmation of the fact that Paul's letters are already regarded as Scripture. To refer to his writings in the same category as "the rest of the Scriptures" assumes their canonicity. Paul's letters, therefore, are placed on a par with the Old Testament. It is possible that Peter has in view in the phrase "the rest of the Scriptures" (2 Peter 3:16) other apostolic writings. We have already noted a sufficiently wide-ranging canon-consciousness in the New Testament documents for that to be possible, perhaps even probable. But in strict logic, this statement enables us to affirm only that Peter regarded Paul's letters as canonical Scripture. More, however, may yet be affirmed.

Why does 2 Peter recognize Paul's letters as Scripture? Materially we may here appeal to the testimony of the Spirit. As in the contemporary church, so in the early church the Holy Spirit bore witness to canonical Scripture. He gave the inner persuasion that it was Sacred Writ. But formally, the answer lies in the recognition of Paul's apostolic office and its significance. Apostleship existed in order to give Scripture to the church.

This is the thrust of several statements of Jesus' farewell discourse in John 13–17. An apostle of Christ is his special representative: "I tell you the truth, whoever accepts anyone I send accepts me; and whoever accepts me accepts the one who sent me" (13:20). "The Holy Spirit, whom the Father will send in my name, will teach you all things and will remind you of everything I have said to you" (14:26). "When the Counselor comes . . . the Spirit of truth . . . he will testify about me. And you also must testify, for you have been with me from the beginning" (15:26–27). "But when he, the Spirit of truth, comes, he will guide you into all truth . . . he will tell you what is yet to come" (16:3).

All this is part of the same strand of teaching which begins in such passages as Luke 10:16 and culminates in the Great Commission in Matthew 28:20. The apostles were to testify to and teach everything that Christ had commanded. They were already prepared to bear their unique witness by their relationship to Jesus and the promise of the Spirit. But implicit in the perspective that their labors will last "to the very end of the age" is the prospect—indeed, the necessity—of the development of a new canonical Scripture flowing from the apostolic circle.

The apostles were called precisely for the purpose of being witnesses of Jesus (note, with the above, Paul's affirmation that he was a witness-apostle to the risen Lord Jesus Christ [1 Cor. 9:1]; see also Acts 1:8, 22; 2:32; 3:15; 5:32; 10:39, 41; 13:31; 22:15; 26:16). They were vehicles of new revelation which was written down (see Eph. 3:2–5) and therefore conscious, to a degree, that they were adding to the already-received canon of Scripture. This is not to insist that every book in the New Testament was written directly by an apostle; but we have no reason to believe that any book emerged from outside the general apostolic circle.

Such is the relationship, therefore, between apostleship and Scripture that the connection (in 2 Peter 3:16) between Paul and the "other Scriptures" (and by parity of reasoning, between the apostles and the "other Scriptures") is not at all surprising. In a sense it might even be anticipated by the sensitive reader of the New Testament.

In what way, then, do these considerations justify our speaking of "Scripture's view of itself"? They indicate a consciousness of canonical status within the books of the Old Testament; they emphasize that this canonicity is confirmed by the documents of the New Testament and that they place themselves in the same category as canonical Scripture. The New Testament, then, views the whole of the Old Testament as Scripture, and in the very act of being given to the church by the apostles seals its own canonicity. We may conclude, then, that inherent in the books of our New Testament, as well as the Old, is the self-consciousness of belonging to a divinely given canon.

Clearly there is nothing simple about this reasoning. But it would be a mistake to think that we could or should have a "simple" explanation. The manner in which God has given Scripture to the church—in space and time, through a variety of human authors—precludes such a simple demonstration of Scripture's self-testimony. Nevertheless, that self-testimony does exist with sufficient clarity for us to speak legitimately of "Scripture's view of itself."

The Bible's View of Itself

Assuming the validity of our earlier considerations, what is "the Bible's view of itself"? Within the scope of this essay, four features of Scripture's self-testimony call for attention: inspiration, authority, reliability, and necessity.

Inspiration

No element is more central to Scripture's testimony to its own nature than the concept of inspiration. Many passages point in this direction, especially Paul's consciously programmatic statement in 2 Timothy 3:16 that "all Scripture is inspired by God" (NASB).

It has long been realized that the term *inspiration* is problematic and, indeed, an inadequate translation of *theopneustos*. "It is very desirable that we should free ourselves at the outset from influences arising from the current employment of the term 'inspiration.' This term is not a biblical term, and its etymological implications are not perfectly accordant with the biblical conception of the modes of the divine operation in giving the Scripture."[7]

At first glance this may appear an inexplicable statement from one of the greatest of all defenders of the inspiration of Scripture. The words "Warfield denies Bible is inspired" would make a startling headline! But this would of course be to misconstrue Warfield (and Paul) completely. What is in view here is that theopneustos refers not to the in-breathing of God (either into the authors or into the text of Scripture) but to the "God-breathed" character of the product of the author's writing. What is stressed is not the manner of Scripture's coming into being but its divine source. Paul's language therefore obviates what many readers of the Bible have found to be a stumbling block: large parts of the Bible do not seem very inspiring, and it is difficult to see how the authors of them were in an "inspired" state of mind when writing them. Paul affirms that the product is God-breathed. But it came into being through a variety of means (careful research and study, ecstatic experience, and even, in the case of some parts, dictation).

Paul's words require future elucidation. Three issues of interpretation arise. First, does the anarthrous *pasa graphē* suggest that Paul means "every Scripture," rather than "all Scripture"? That meaning is possible. But in fact the point is of minimal importance. If every Scripture

---

7. B. B. Warfield, *The Inspiration and Authority of the Bible* (Philadelphia: Presbyterian and Reformed, 1951), 153.

is God-breathed, it follows that all Scripture will also be God-breathed. Either translation underlines the inspiration of the entire Old Testament.

Second, should *theopneustos* be taken in an attributive sense ("all God-breathed Scripture is useful")? If so, it could be taken to limit the extent of inspiration and to imply that some Scripture may not be God-breathed.

In the very nature of the case we cannot demonstrate that every single verse of Scripture is spoken of seriatim as God-breathed. But the fact that all sections of Scripture are cited almost randomly in the New Testament, with equal force, emphasizes how far removed such a distinction was from the minds of the New Testament writers. So widespread are the New Testament's quotations and allusions from the Old Testament that no distinction surfaces between the "God-breathed" and the "manmade." Such a distinction is alien to the evidence of Scripture itself and cannot therefore have been the apostle's meaning.

Third, should *theopneustos* be taken in an active, rather than a passive, sense (God-breathing, rather than breathed out by God)? While *theopneustos* appears only here in the New Testament, the translation "all [every] Scripture is God-breathed" is favored by the testimony of the rest of Scripture. The idea of Scripture as the Word of God, that which is carried forth by the breath or speech of God, is commonplace. The notion of Scripture as "breathing out God" (rather than breathed out by God) is foreign to the statements of Scripture concerning its own nature.

Abundant evidence exists to substantiate this view. Jeremiah's experience may be taken as paradigmatic of biblical writers: "Then the LORD reached out his hand and touched my mouth and said to me, 'Now, I have put my words in your mouth'" (Jer. 1:9; cf. Isa. 6:7). Similarly, David's final oracle (the word itself is significant) assumes what is true of all of "the oracles of God," or "the very words of God" (Acts 7:38; Rom. 3:2; Heb. 5:12; 1 Peter 4:11): "The Spirit of the LORD spoke through me; his word was on my tongue" (2 Sam. 23:2). When Jesus quotes Deuteronomy 8:3 with such manifest approval, he speaks of man's living not by bread alone but by "every word that comes from the mouth of God" (Matt. 4:4). Again, the way in which God's speech and the words of Scripture are virtually synonymous terms in biblical usage underlines the equation of Scripture with what has been breathed out by God. (See Rom. 9:17 and Gal. 3:8, where "Scripture" is really equivalent to "God"; and Matt. 19:4–5 [quoting Gen. 2:24], Heb. 3:7 [Ps. 95:7], and Acts 4:24–25 [Ps. 2:1], where "Scripture says" and "God says" are equivalent expressions.) Such evidence, coupled with Warfield's extensive demonstration that the form *theopneustos* is active rather than passive, leaves the issue beyond doubt.[8]

About this inspiration several features should be noted.

Inspiration is given no final explanation. No doctrine of the exact nature of inspiration is gained from 2 Timothy 3:16. This passage considers, as we have seen, the product of God's powerful working (his "breath"), not the way in which his Spirit has engaged men's lives and minds in order to create the product of Scripture. The nature of inspiration cannot be determined in an a priori fashion from the simple fact of it. Nor, indeed, does 2 Peter 1:21, which speaks of the Holy Spirit's carrying or bearing the biblical authors, shed much light. The mode of inspiration must be discovered exegetically, not dogmatically, in an a posteriori manner, by the examination of the whole of Scripture, with special attention to its reflec-

8. Ibid., 245–96.

tion on the mode of the production of its various parts. This exercise will drive us to the conclusion that we can no more fully explain inspiration than we can explain providence.

In fact, Scripture came into being through a variety of modes. Some passages are the fruit of ecstatic experience; others are the product of historical research and thoughtful interpretation—such as Luke's account of Christ, or the Chronicler's account of the history of Israel from a covenantal perspective. There is poetry, much of which must have been the fruit of hard literary labor (only those who have never written poetry assume it is always the result of immediate "inspiration"); but there is also material which is indeed the immediate fruit of profound experience.

In view of this, two elements characterize the manner of inspiration. The first is God's general providential superintendence of the lives, experiences, and circumstances of the biblical authors. "If God wished to give his people a series of letters like Paul's, he prepared a Paul to write them, and the Paul he brought to the task was a Paul who simultaneously would write just such letters."[9]

But second, Scripture is the result of the activity of divine power, through the Spirit. He works in the lives of the authors specifically in the production of Scripture. He bears them along (2 Peter 1:21) so that the product of their writing is safeguarded as God's own Word. In this sense, God not only governs their lives in equipping them but actually (if mysteriously) teaches them the words they use (see 1 Cor. 2:13).

Inspiration characterizes all Scripture. We have argued above that Paul did not intend to limit the inspiration in Scripture. Even if 2 Timothy 3:16 were translated "All God-breathed Scripture is useful . . . ," the connotation that only parts of Scripture are God-breathed is completely absent. Inspiration extends to every section of Scripture.

This point is well illustrated by a glance through the United Bible Societies' edition of the Greek New Testament (which prints citations and allusions from the Old Testament in bold in the text). The index lists some 300 texts from the Old Testament quoted in the New, and more than 1500 allusions from the Old Testament employed in the New. The random, rather than selective, use of Scripture is manifest. If any part is God-breathed, then the whole is God-breathed.

We must not, however, draw unbiblical deductions from this conclusion. For while there are no degrees of inspiration, there are degrees of revelation. Inspiration is not subject to levels of development, but revelation is—it is progressive and cumulative. It develops through the epochs of redemptive history, reaching several high points before coming to its peak in Jesus Christ. Yet, each stage of revelation, when recorded, is enshrined in an equally inspired Scripture. It is to the embarrassment of those who see different levels of inspiration in the Old Testament that the New Testament writers cite with equanimity the imprecatory psalms (e.g., Pss. 69:25 and 109:8 in Acts 1:20), while they do not directly cite Psalm 23!

The universality of inspiration is epitomized in the notion of verbal inspiration, which affirms that the inspiration of Scripture is not limited to its general teaching or to particular doctrines but extends even to the words. This fact Paul affirms of apostolic teaching in 1 Corinthians 2:13. But such words do not stand in isolation from one another, nor do they possess their God-intended meaning apart from each other.[10] Because words express

---

9. Ibid., 155.

10. See John Murray, "The Attestation of Scripture," in Paul Woolley and Ned B. Stonehouse, eds., *The Infallible Word*, 3rd ed. (Philadelphia: Presbyterian and Reformed, 1967), 23n.9.

meaning, and a particular word may possess different meanings in different contexts, the meaning communicated depends on the significance of all the words used. If Scripture is God-breathed at all, that inspiration must extend to all the words that are employed. For evangelical scholars this teaching is clearly one of the great motives for the pursuit of so-called textual criticism. If inspiration reaches to the words, the identification of what was originally written is a sacred task to be pursued with joy and zeal.

Inspiration does not render redundant the necessity of interpretation. No passage of Scripture discloses its meaning to us apart from actual exegesis. Conviction about the fact of inspiration does not guarantee that we understand even 2 Timothy 3:16 aright or the precise nature of inspiration. Correspondingly, differences of interpretation do not necessarily involve differences in conviction about inspiration.

But if this is so, why is it so important to emphasize Scripture's inspiration? Because our doctrine of inspiration affects our understanding of and response to biblical authority.

Authority

If Scripture made no claim to divine inspiration, it could still possess authority—as the unique (and, to that extent, authoritative) witness of the people of God to the acts of God in history and as the source book of all original Christian tradition. It could even be regarded as possessing supreme authority for the faith and life of the church.

The doctrine of plenary divine inspiration implies that Scripture comes to us as an expression of divine authority. It is the "mouth of God" (Matt. 4:4). What Scripture says, God says. It speaks with his authority. Hence Calvin's famous formulation: "The Scriptures obtain full authority among believers only when men regard them as having sprung from heaven, as if there the living words of God were heard."[11] This authority is already evident within the pages of Scripture itself.

The fact of biblical authority. Nothing is more characteristic of the New Testament's appeal to the Old Testament as Scripture, and therefore characteristic of Scripture as a class, than the expression "it is written." The appeal is not the naive one of "if it is in a book, it must be true." Rather, the phrase means: It is written in the document of divine authority, in the canon of the community of God's people. Since what is written there is divinely inspired, appeal to it settles all discussion.

Such an appeal to Scripture's authority is, it should be stressed, an appeal to Scripture rightly interpreted. Scripture erroneously interpreted is no longer God's Word—as Jesus' confrontation with Satan in the wilderness underlines (Matt. 4:1ff.; John 10:34).[12]

Interestingly, precisely in such contexts Jesus gives expression to the final authority of Scripture in his own life. But perhaps even more striking is his use of Scripture immediately before his arrest and immediately after his resurrection. On both occasions, the one under intense duress, the other as Son of God in the power of the new and resurrected humanity (Rom. 1:4), Jesus appeals to the authority of Scripture (see Matt. 26:24, 31; Luke 24:44, 46).

---

11. Calvin, *Institutes* 1:74.

12. The fact that Christians sometimes make right decisions on the basis of wrong interpretations of Scripture in no way negates this principle. In such circumstances account must be taken of (1) the providential overruling by God of his people's lives (Rom. 8:28), and (2) the fact that such actions may be consistent with Scripture's teaching generally, even when based on a misunderstanding of one part of Scripture. Such a misunderstanding is not necessarily the same as the repudiation of the teaching of Scripture as a whole.

If there was any point in his ministry at which it would have been instinctive or appropriate to refer to his own authority instead of the authority of Scripture, these would have been occasions. But precisely in these circumstances he places enormous stress on Scripture's authority.

This use of Scripture and recognition of its authority by Jesus give special significance to his mandate to the apostles to teach whatever he has commanded them to all the world and to every age (Matt. 28:18–20). At the back of the apostles' incessant appeals to Scripture as divinely authoritative lies what they first learned from Jesus himself. The authority of the Old Testament was given the imprimatur of Jesus the Son of God; the authority of the New Testament is anticipated in the words of the Great Commission. On his authority the apostles are to teach throughout the ages what he has taught them. Enshrined in these words is the concept that such teaching must be preserved in Scripture for the church to come.

The extent of Scripture's authority. Already the complexity of this issue is apparent. Simply put, "The Bible says" ends all questioning—except the great question, "What does the Bible say?"

Scripture is given in the context of ongoing redemptive history, and the authority of its several parts is related to this phenomenon. There is teaching in Scripture which is either further developed or even superseded before the last book of the Bible is written. Thus, to take an obvious example, the dietary laws of the Mosaic legislation and epoch do not carry the final authority for the New Testament Christian that they did for the Old Testament believer (Mark 7:19; Rom. 14:14). All Scripture is authoritative, but its authority is intimately related to its context in the flow of redemptive history.

The authority of God in Scripture is also expressed in an accommodated, phenomenological form, and with specific focus. Not only do the Scriptures actually make us "wise for salvation through faith in Christ Jesus" (2 Tim. 3:15); that is also their specific intention. They may do other things incidentally; they do this task intentionally. Thus Calvin, commenting on the biblical account of creation writes: "He who would learn astronomy [*astrologia*], and other recondite arts, let him go elsewhere."[13] The Bible is not intended to be an authoritative textbook on physics, chemistry, mathematics, or human biology. The word *heart* in Scripture rarely means the organ in the body! Scripture's focus lies elsewhere: it has been given "for teaching, rebuking, correcting and training in righteousness, so that the man of God may be thoroughly equipped for every good work" (2 Tim. 3:16–17).

Is, then, the authority of Scripture limited? The use of the word *limited* here may be misleading, because it masks a false dichotomy. If we say that Scripture's authority is limited, we are in danger of denying its plenary authority as God's Word; if we say that it is not limited, without further explanation of what we mean, we may be in danger of misreading its intentions.

If the Scriptures are God-breathed, they carry God's authority. All they say, on every subject on which they speak, will be authoritative. But they speak on every subject from a particular perspective, not in the intentionally exhaustive fashion of a textbook. That fact does not diminish their authority, nor the universality of their applicability, but provides both with the focus in which it is to be understood and applied.

---

13. John Calvin, *Commentary on Genesis,* trans. and ed. John King (Grand Rapids: Eerdmans, 1948), 1:79.

The Scriptures are like a stone thrown into the water, creating a whole series of concentric circles around the point of entry. Scripture's authority dominates the whole of life, but it does so in different ways through its entry into the human situation. In some areas its authority is immediate and direct, in others it is indirect and mediated. The computer programmer who is a member of God's church sees Scripture as his or her final authority. But that authority functions in different ways. It is not diminished in any sphere. It is one's authority in the fellowship of the church; but one's whole approach to programming will also be dominated and influenced by what God's Word says. But we do not read the Scriptures to learn computer programming, because we realize God has not given them in the form of a textbook for such a purpose. Biblical authority is not compromised one iota by recognizing this principle.

Authority and Sufficiency. Scripture's authority is intimately related to its sufficiency as our guide to the way of salvation (2 Tim. 3:15). This is the meaning of the Reformation watchword *sola Scriptura*, Scripture alone.

Sola Scriptura did not emerge as an issue only with the Reformation.[14] But at the Reformation it stood over against any principle which either added to or usurped the prerogative of God to speak adequately through his Word. In particular, the teaching office of the Roman church was in view. In this context it remains necessary to insist on *sola Scriptura*.

Today it is also necessary to recognize that אר חפּ‬רצס אלס contrasts with much current evangelical teaching. In many of the debates over the question of spiritual gifts, it has not always been realized how central this question is. Involved in the view that such gifts as prophecy and tongues have ceased is the fact that the New Testament regards certain gifts as signs of the apostle and evidence of the apostolic nature of the church (2 Cor. 12:12; Heb. 2:3b–4). But also implied is the conviction that, *as revelatory*, these gifts were exercised prior to the coming into being and universal recognition of the entire New Testament canon. Insofar as prophecy and tongues plus interpretation were regarded as divine revelation, they served an interim function prior to the inscripturating of the apostolic message.

Any contemporary declaration which adds to information given in Scripture and is prefaced by the words "this is what the Lord says," formally implies more than merely illumination. It is a claim to be new divine revelation. This dynamic is not always recognized. In principle, is there any difference between a Protestant claim to give (immediate) revelation in prophecy and interpreted tongues and a Roman Catholic claim to give (carefully thought out) revelation through the teaching office of the church? Rapprochement between Protestant and Roman Catholic "charismatic Christians" suggests that this mindset is often shared quite unconsciously. Debates over the continuation or cessation of certain spiritual gifts will never make headway until it is realized that, to Christians in the Reformed tradition of Calvin, Owen, and Warfield, reservations of the exercise of such gifts are deeply rooted in *sola Scriptura*. To them it is not merely a traditional conviction about the cessation of gifts that is at stake, but 2 Timothy 3:16 itself.

Reliability

The Scriptures, said Jesus almost incidentally, "cannot be broken" (John 10:35). These words appear in the context of a wider ad hominem argument. But this part of his state-

---

14. Heiko Oberman, *The Harvest of Medieval Theology* (Cambridge: Harvard University Press, 1963), 201, 361–63, 388–90.

ment is not itself ad hominem in nature. Jesus is not merely accepting his opponents' point of view for the sake of argument, basing his position on a presupposition shared equally by them—the authority and reliability of the Old Testament. Its authority in this respect, as even Bultmann recognizes, "stands just as fast for him as for the scribes, and he feels himself in opposition to them only in the way he understands and applies the Old Testament."[15]

But what is claimed when Scripture's reliability (inability to be "broken") is thus affirmed? It is not only that Scripture in the form of prophecy must be fulfilled (e.g., Matt. 26:24, 31, 54, 56). It is that God's Word is truth (John 17:17).

What kind of reliability does this teaching imply? Does Scripture function (as neoorthodoxy so frequently suggests) like a scratched record? The lyrics can still be clearly heard, even through the distortions. Is Scripture the fallible word of man, through which can be heard the eternal Word of God, who alone is infallible? More than this is claimed in Scripture. We have seen how Jesus assumes that an incidental statement in the psalms (and by parity of reasoning, the rest of the Scripture) is absolutely reliable and trustworthy. His debate with the Pharisees proceeds on the issue not of Scripture's reliability but of its meaning. This same principle lies behind the conviction that Scripture must be fulfilled—simply because it is Scripture.

The kind of reliability claimed for Scripture, therefore, is an infallible, inerrant reliability, precisely because Scripture is the Word of a God who cannot lie. Dewey Beegle calls this position the "syllogism of inerrancy."[16] If God is infalliable and if Scripture is God's word, then Scripture must also be divinely infallible. Beegle, in keeping with others, questions this "philosophical assumption."[17]

But such language simply clouds the issue; it is pejorative, not descriptive, and uses an honorable adjective in a dishonorable and emotive sense. It does not honestly admit what, for Christians who claim Scripture as God's Word in any sense, would be the alternative position:

God is infallible.

What God says is infallible.

But what God says through men is not and cannot be infallible.

The assumption here is that human fallibility stubbornly resists the infallible purpose of God. But the biblical witness contains no hint of this position. And with good reason, for this alternative syllogism is tantamount to the denial of Scripture's own statements. Applied universally, this logic would repudiate God's sovereign, teleological rule of a fallen universe for his own perfect purpose (cf. Eph. 1:11b).

Having noted this point, however, our doctrine of Scripture's infallibility requires fine tuning. It will immediately be said that already the doctrine is exposed to "the death of a thousand qualifications." But this is to misunderstand. *Infallibility* is not a biblical term. It belongs to the realm of theology as a science and as such requires careful delineation and

15. Rudolf Bultmann, *The Theology of the New Testament* (London: SCM, 1952), 1:16.
16. Dewey Beegle, *Scripture, Tradition, and Infallibility* (Ann Arbor: Pryor Pettengell, 1979), 198.
17. Ibid., 85.

definition. In other sciences such definition or qualification is not a weakness but a matter of accuracy. We do not abandon any other Christian doctrine because it requires precision in its statement and even then retains elements of mystery. One needs to think only of the doctrines of providence or of the two natures of Christ, or the doctrine of the Trinity, to realize how important is the further elucidation, description, and qualification of principal statements. In the same way we need to describe and elucidate our definition of Scripture.

How can we further define Scripture's infallibility? What do we mean when we deduce that, as God's Word, it is free from error? Here, again, only a skeletal answer can be given. Three things should be noted. First, the nature of biblical infallibility cannot be described apart from the actual material of Scripture. As the canon of God's people's lives (not understood in any other category), it lays claim to infallibility. It would therefore be a mistake (made often enough in the past) to discuss whether the Hebrew and Greek of Scripture come to us as examples of perfect grammar. Such a topic is misleading, for grammar is a matter of custom and development, not (normally) a matter of truth and error. In any event, Scripture's infallibility could not be compromised by grammatical infelicities, any more than its meaning is altered by them. The presence of human idiosyncrasy (or eccentricity, for that matter) is not an argument against the infallibility of the product. Thus the young B. B. Warfield wrote:

> No one claims that inspiration secured the use of good Greek in Attic severity of taste, free from the exaggerations and looseness of current speech, but only that it secured the accurate expression of truth, even (if you will) through the medium of the worst Greek a fisherman of Galilee could write and the most startling figures of speech a peasant could invent.[18]

Second, the Bible, which claims such infallibility, speaks phenomenologically, according to the appearance of things, employing accepted customs of speech. In Scripture "the sun rises." That no more commits us to a three-decker view of the universe than does our saying, in the late twentieth century, "the sun rises." The person who regards such language as erroneous is insensitive to the complexity of human language, the spheres in which it is used, and to the subtle nuances of human communication.

For some writers, these elements are what Abraham Kuyper called "innocent inaccuracies."[19] It is not difficult to understand what Kuyper is saying. Indeed, one may appreciate his desire to allow God's Word to stand just as it comes to us. But there is something infelicitous about such a statement in connection with God's Word. It brings Scripture to the wrong bar of judgment altogether. Scripture comes to us in the *koine*, the language of the world of the people. Its statements are to be assessed in that universe of discourse alone.

Third, in the very nature of the case, the Christian cannot prove the infallibility of Scripture. Many biblical statements are not amenable to proof of this kind, or if they were, they are no longer. We cannot prove that "Christ died for our sins according to the Scriptures" (1 Cor. 15:3) is an infallible statement. We do affirm that such a statement is coherent with itself, the rest of Scripture, and the universe in which we live. We subscribe to biblical infallibility not on the grounds of our ability to prove it but because of the persuasiveness of its testimony to be God's own Word.

18. A. A. Hodge and B. B. Warfield, *Inspiration* (Philadelphia: Presbyterian Board of Publication, 1881), 43.
19. Abraham Kuyper, *Principles of Sacred Theology* (Grand Rapids: Eerdmans, 1954), 457.

This position is frequently accused of involving circular reasoning. So be it. We cannot abandon the ultimate authority for our faith when it comes to discussing the nature of that ultimate authority. It should, however, be noted that the argument here is not "Scripture is infallible because it claims to be infallible" (as, for example, Barr suggests).[20] Rather, Scripture testifies to its character as the infallible Word of God. The Christian is persuaded of that testimony (through the ministry of the Spirit); he or she recognizes it to be self-consistent and on that basis confesses it to be true. We know that the Word of God could be nothing less.

Belief in the infallibility of Scripture does not imply that we know how to resolve every prima-facie inconsistency in Scripture. Indeed, we are not under obligation to do this in order to believe in biblical inerrancy, although we will seek to do so for exegetical and apologetic reasons. We believe in the perfect love, righteousness, and sovereignty of God, although we cannot understand their operation in connection with every individual circumstance of life. So too our faith in the inerrancy of Scripture rests on the Bible's own testimony, and in view of the self-consistency of that testimony, we anticipate further resolutions to those passages which as yet we do not fully understand.

We ought not to be driven by the existence of some "problem passages" into abandoning inerrancy, on the grounds that we are unable to prove it in every conceivable instance. It is important to recognize that "there are difficulties in Scripture which are at present insoluble and will probably remain so till the last day."[21] Failure to recognize this limitation has made some grasp at any solution to difficulties, however implausible, or has led others to abandon inerrancy altogether. Nor is it necessary, when a variety of resolutions is open to us, to commit ourselves dogmatically to any of them. One may be correct, or none may be correct. Our conviction of inerrancy does not depend on our possession of final answers to all questions.

Does this mean that the inerrantist ignores the "difficulties" for inerrancy present in Scripture and lives ostrichlike, with head in the sand? On the contrary, in our examination of the text and teaching of the Bible, we find no solid reason to yield up our conviction of Scripture's inerrancy any more than we find reason to yield up our conviction about God's perfect love for us because we cannot harmonize all the ways of the Lord in our own lives.

Necessity

Why, then, is Scripture so necessary? It makes us wise for salvation through faith in Christ Jesus (2 Tim. 3:15). But there is a sense in which the existence of Scripture was not, in terms of strict logic, necessary for salvation. It is Christ and his work, not the Bible and its inspiration, that saves—according to Scripture's testimony.

Here, we return, therefore, to the practical function of Scripture. Consistently the church has recognized that the Bible is a gift of grace to humankind, who otherwise would forget, distort, and even destroy God's revelation of himself in space and history. The purpose of Scripture is to preserve for all people, in all places, the revelatory Word God has spoken. Its function is, in the fullest sense, evangelistic.

The perspicuity of Scripture is best understood within this framework. Scripture must be studied with the best tools at our disposal. Many of these are academic in nature (history, geography, foreign languages, etc.), although not necessarily in use. But this requirement

20. Barr, *Fundamentalism*, 72–73.

21. Auguste Lecerf, *An Introduction to Reformed Dogmatics*, trans. André Schlemmer (London: Lutterworth, 1949), 314.

should not lead us to conclude that a high level of preunderstanding is essential for grasping clearly the message of Scripture. Since Scripture was written for the common people, we should anticipate that its message about the things necessary for salvation is not difficult to understand (in terms of levels of education required): "The unlearned, in a due use of the ordinary means, may attain unto a sufficient understanding of them."[22]

This principle of the perspicuity of Scripture is underlined by Jesus and the apostles. It is a source of disappointment to Jesus that the Scripture is misunderstood so seriously (see, e.g., Luke 24:25—"how foolish you are"!). Scripture's message is clear enough; people's minds are darkened not by below average intelligence but by sin. The function of the testimony of the Holy Spirit is not to introduce perspicuity to Scripture but to bring illumination to our darkened understanding of it. In this process the Lord of the Scriptures rejoices, knowing that God has hidden the mystery of the kingdom from the wise and understanding and revealed it to babes (Matt. 11:25–27).

If we affirm the inspiration, authority, infallibility, and necessity of Scripture, we are by no means suggesting that to hold "Scripture's view of itself" is to have all the answers. We have already indicated that these are the first words, not the last word, about Scripture. We have many questions, even puzzles and unreconciled difficulties remaining, which indicate that the continued disciplined exegesis of Scripture is necessary. We therefore have the greatest of motives to learn how to handle God's Word correctly (2 Tim. 2:15). Such study is based on the recognition of what Scripture is: God's mouth, every word from which sustains us in daily life.

Those who study Scripture in such a humble spirit will find that there is yet more truth to break forth from God's Holy Word. This attitude has never been better expressed than in the words of John Murray:

> There is no doctrine of our Christian faith that does not confront us with unresolved difficulties here in this world, and the difficulties become all the greater just as we get nearer to the center. It is in connection with the most transcendent mysteries of our faith that the difficulties multiply. The person who thinks he has resolved all the mysteries surrounding our established faith in the Trinity has probably no faith in the Triune God. The person who encounters no unresolved mystery in the incarnation of the Son of God and in his death on Calvary's tree has not yet learned the meaning of 1 Timothy 3:16. Yet these unanswered questions are not incompatible with unshaken faith in the Triune God and in Jesus Christ, the incarnate Son. The questions are often perplexing. But they are more often the questions of adoring wonder rather than the questions of painful perplexity.
>
> So there should be no surprise if faith in God's inerrant Word should be quite consonant with unresolved questions and difficulties with regard to the content of this faith.[23]

In such knowledge we rest on the testimony of God's Word to itself.

22. WCF 1.7.
23. Murray, "Attestation of Scripture," 7–8.

57

John M. Frame

A native of the Pittsburgh area, John M. Frame studied at Princeton University, Westminster Theological Seminary, and Yale University, where he studied both theology and philosophy. His areas of expertise are theology, apologetics, and philosophy. From 1968 to 1980 he taught at Westminster Theological Seminary in Philadelphia, first systematic theology and later also apologetics. At the time of the founding of Westminster in California (1980), he moved to help the newly formed seminary, where he taught until 2000. From then until the present, he has been teaching at Reformed Theological Seminary in Orlando, where he holds the J. D. Trimble Chair of Systematic Theology and Philosophy.

The two essays reproduced here were prepared for a conference on the inspiration and authority of Scripture at Ligonier, Pennsylvania, in 1973. The contributions to this conference were then reproduced as *God's Inerrant Word: An International Symposium on the Trustworthiness of Scripture* (1973). The articles by Frame were recently republished among the appendices to his recent volume on Scripture, *The Doctrine of the Word of God* (2010). Other writings of Frame relevant for his views on Scripture are his volume on epistemology, *The Doctrine of the Knowledge of God* (1987), and his short introduction to ethics, *Perspectives on the Word of God: An Introduction to Christian Ethics* (1990). Both these books develop his characteristic perspectivalism, which he shares with Vern S. Poythress (see chap. 49 above).

In the first essay, "Scripture Speaks for Itself," Frame expounds on a traditional aspect of the doctrine of Scripture in Reformed theology, that of the self-witness of Scripture (this theme reoccurs at many points among the texts in this anthology). He develops his biblical argument with the help of the early generation of Westminster professors (especially John Murray and Cornelius Van Til) and the biblical-theological approach of Meredith G. Kline. For Frame, the self-witness is not limited to a few scattered proof texts (cf. Kline's view of the canon and E. J. Young's views in chap. 52 of this anthology); rather, the entire Scripture breathes the authority of God our Lord. This latter aspect anticipates a major theme in Frame's approach, a theology of lordship. Frame's essay also advances the argument by seeking to explain the modern rejection of this self-witness of Scripture, in particular by neoorthodox theologians such as Karl Barth and Emil Brunner. With this emphasis on apologetics, he builds on the work of his teacher Van Til.

The second essay, "God and Biblical Language: Transcendence and Immanence," considers then-current philosophical and theological challenges to the doctrine of Scripture. By focusing on these difficulties, this essay fits well with the other essays in this part, which examine modern objections to inspiration and inerrancy. It also illustrates the more general argument made in the first essay. In this second installment, Frame considers the philosophical and theological arguments to the effect that human language is inadequate to hold divine revelation. These arguments were presented, for instance, by the philosopher Antony Flew and the theologian Karl Barth. Frame replies that the language of Scripture is both "odd" and "ordinary," reflecting the character of God as both transcendent and immanent. Thus, based on Christian presuppositions, the verbal character of Scripture's inspiration holds its ground.

Bibliography: John M. Frame. *The Doctrine of the Knowledge of God*. A Theology of Lordship. Phillipsburg, NJ: Presbyterian and Reformed, 1987. Idem. *The Doctrine of the Word of God*. A Theology of Lordship. Phillipsburg, NJ: P&R Publishing, 2010. John J. Hughes, ed. *Speaking the Truth in Love: The Theology of John M. Frame*. Phillipsburg, NJ: P&R Publishing, 2009.

SCRIPTURE SPEAKS FOR ITSELF

Originally published in John W. Montgomery, ed., *God's Inerrant Word* (Grand Rapids: Bethany Fellowship [a division of Baker Publishing Group], 1974), 178–200; reprinted as Appendix F in John M. Frame, *The Doctrine of the Word of God*, A Theology of Lordship (Phillipsburg, NJ: P&R Publishing, 2010), 440–62.

What does Scripture say about itself? The question is both momentous and commonplace.

It is momentous: the self-witness of Scripture has been for centuries the cornerstone of the orthodox Christian argument for biblical authority. For one thing, there would never be any such argument unless there were reason to believe that Scripture *claimed* authority. If Scripture renounced all claim to authority, or even remained neutral on the subject, there would not be much reason for Christians today to claim authority *for* Scripture. But if Scripture *does* claim authority over us, then we are faced with a momentous challenge indeed! Acceptance or rejection of that claim will influence every aspect of Christian doctrine and life.

Furthermore, the authority of Scripture is a doctrine of the Christian faith—a doctrine like other doctrines—like the deity of Christ, justification by faith, sacrificial atonement. To prove such doctrines, Christians go to Scripture. Where else can we find information on God's redemptive purposes? But what of the doctrine of the authority of Scripture? Must we not, to be consistent, also prove *that* doctrine by Scripture? If so, then the self-witness of Scripture must not only be the *first* consideration in the argument; it must be the final and decisive consideration also.

Now of course someone may object that that claim is not competent to establish itself. If the Bible *claims* to be God's word, that does not prove that it is God's word. That is true in a sense. Many documents claim to be the word of some god or other. The Koran, the Book of Mormon and countless other books have made such claims. In no case does the claim in itself establish the authority of the book. The claim must be compared with the evidence. But the evidence through the presuppositions furnished by, among other things, our religious convictions. A Christian must look at the evidence with Christian assumptions; a rationalist must look at the evidence with rationalistic assumptions. And the Christian finds his most basic assumptions in the Bible!

As I have argued elsewhere,[1] it is impossible to avoid circularity of a sort when one is arguing on behalf of an *ultimate criterion*. One may not argue for one ultimate criterion by appealing to another. And the argument over Scriptural authority is precisely an argument over ultimate criterion!

We must not, of course, simply urge non-Christians to accept the Bible because the Bible says so. Although there is much truth in that simplicity, it can be misleading if stated in that form without further explanation. A non-Christian must start where he is. Perhaps he believes that Scripture is a fairly reliable source, though not infallible. He should then be urged to study Scripture as a historical source for Christian doctrine, as the *original* "source." He will be confronted with the claims of Scripture—about God, about Christ, about man, about itself. He will compare the biblical way of looking at things with his own way. And if God wills, he will see the wisdom in looking at things Scripture's way. But we must not mislead him about the demand of Scripture. He must not be allowed to think that he can become a Christian and go on thinking the same old way. He must be told that Christ demands a *total* repentance—of heart, mind, will, emotions—the whole man. He must learn that Christ demands a change in "ultimate criterion." And thus he must learn that even the evidentiary procedures he uses to establish biblical authority must be reformed by the Bible. He must learn that "evidence" is at bottom an elaboration of God's self-witness; that "proving" God is the same as hearing and obeying him.

So the question[2] of the biblical self-witness is a momentous one indeed. In a sense it is the *only* question. If by "self-witness" we mean, not merely the texts in which the Bible explicitly

---

1. See the next selection in the same chapter of this anthology, "God and Biblical Language."

2. We shall cite some of the most helpful sources, in these questions. The classic nineteenth century work on the subject, still useful, is Louis Gaussen, *The Inspiration of the Holy Scriptures*, trans. D. D. Scott (Chicago: Moody Press, 1949). The most impressive piece of scholarly work in this area to date remains Benjamin Breckinridge Warfield, *The Inspiration and Authority of the Bible*, ed. S. G. Craig (Philadelphia; Presbyterian and Reformed, 1948). In relating the doctrine of inspiration to a comprehensive Christian world and life view, Abraham Kuyper's *Principles of Christian Theology*, trans. J. H. De Vries (Grand Rapids: Eerdmans, 1965) is unsurpassed. Almost the only new things that have been said in the last few years about the doctrine have been said by Meredith G. Kline in his *Structure of Biblical Authority* (Grand Rapids: Eerdmans, 1972). A helpful guide through the issues raised by New Testament biblical scholarship is Herman Ridderbos, *The Authority of the New Testament Scriptures*. ed. J. M. Kik, trans. H. de Jongste (Philadelphia: Presbyterian and Reformed, 1963); The soundest overall guide to the theological controversies (in my opinion) is Cornelius Van Til, *A Christian Theory of Knowledge* (Philadelphia: Presbyterian and Reformed, 1969); cf. his "unpublished" syllabus, "The Doctrine of Scripture" (Ripon, CA: Den Dulk Foundation, 1967). For general summaries of the issues, see: *The Infallible Word*, ed. Ned B. Stonehouse and Paul Woolley, 3rd rev. ed. (Philadelphia: Presbyterian and Reformed, 1967)—the article by John Murray is especially helpful; Carl F. H. Henry, ed., *Revelation and the Bible* (Grand Rapids: Baker, 1958); and, on the more popular level, but most eloquent and cogent, Edward J. Young, *Thy Word Is Truth* (Grand Rapids: Eerdmans, 1957). Other recent works useful to resolving the question of the Bible's self-witness are René Pache, *The Inspiration and Authority of Scripture*, trans. H. Needham (Chicago: Moody Press, 1969); Clark Pinnock, *Biblical Revelation* (Chicago: Moody Press, 1971); and John W. Wenham, *Christ and the Bible* (Chicago: InterVarsity, 1973).

claims authority, but the whole character of the Bible as it confronts us, then the question of biblical authority is purely and simply the question of biblical self-witness.

On the other hand, the question is also commonplace: Simply because it is so important, the question has been discussed over and over again by theologians. Although I feel greatly honored by the invitation to speak and write on such a basic question, I must confess also to a slight feeling of numbness. What can I say that hasn't been said already? What can I say that Giiussen, Warfield, Kuyper, Murray, Young, Van Til, Kline, Ridderbos, Pache, Wenham, Packer, Montgomery, Pinnock and Gerstner haven't said? Even in this collection, some of the other papers will overlap this topic! No doubt, in a collection of papers of this sort, someone ought to summarize the basic material. But I can't help thinking it might be best just to quote snatches from other authors whose scholarship and eloquence is far superior to my own. It *might* be; but I won't follow that course here, because I do have a few reasons for attempting an individual, if not independent, study.

Past orthodox Christian discussions of this matter have, in my opinion, done a very adequate job on the whole. As in all human endeavors, however, there is room for improvement here. The improvements I have in mind are chiefly two:

1. There needs to be a greater emphasis upon the *pervasiveness* throughout Scripture of the biblical self-witness. As we suggested earlier, there is a sense in which *all* of the Bible is self-witness. Whatever the Bible says, in a sense, it says about itself. Even the genealogies of the kings tell us about the content, and therefore the character of Scripture. The *way* in which the Bible speaks of kings and vineyards and wilderness journeys and God and man and Christ—its *manner* is a testimony to its character. More specifically: the overall doctrinal structure of Scripture is an important element of the biblical self-witness. For when the Bible speaks of atonement, reconciliation, justification, glorification, it speaks of these in such a way as to presuppose a crucial role for itself. Or, to look at redemption from a more historical perspective, from the beginning of God's dealings with men God has taught them to give his words a particular role in their lives, a lesson which is taught again and again through the thousands of years of redemptive history. Now when we neglect this emphasis on the pervasiveness of the biblical self-witness, at least two bad things happen: (a) People can get the idea that the concept of biblical authority is based largely on a few texts scattered through the Bible, texts which may not be very important in the overall biblical scheme of things. They might even get the idea that the doctrine of inspiration is based largely upon a *couple* of texts (2 Peter 1:21; 2 Tim. 3:16) which liberal scholars dismiss as being late and legalistic. Thus it may seem as though the doctrine of biblical authority is a rather peripheral doctrine, rather easily dispensable for anyone who has even the slightest inclination to dispense with unpalatable doctrines. (b) People can get the idea that Christ and the Bible are separable, that you can believe in and obey Christ without believing in and obeying the Bible. They may think that Scripture is unimportant to the Christian message of redemption.

2. If, as orthodox people maintain, the biblical self-witness to its authority and infallibility is *obvious, clear*—and certainly if it is "pervasive"!—then we must face more squarely the question of why not-so-orthodox people see the matter differently. At one level, of course, it is legitimate to say that they fail to see the truth because of their unbelief: the god of this world has blinded their minds.[3] Sin is "irrational"—it turns away from the obvious. But

3. 2 Cor. 4:4.

sinners, when they are scholars, at least, generally do things for a *reason*, perverse as that reason may be. And perverse or not, such reasoning is often highly plausible. If orthodox people can identify that reasoning, explain its surface plausibility, and expose its deeper error, then the orthodox view of the biblical self-witness will be stated much more cogently.

In the remaining portion of this essay, I shall present an essentially traditional argument concerning the character of the biblical self-witness; but I shall structure the discussion in such a way as to implement the above two concerns—not comprehensively, to be sure, probably not adequately—but to greater degree than one might expect in a paper of this length.[4] The first section will examine the role of verbal revelation in the biblical understanding of salvation. The second will discuss the relationship of that verbal revelation to Scripture, and the third will analyze what I take to be the most common and plausible objection to the previous line of reasoning.

I. Revealed Words and Salvation

We have suggested that the whole Bible is self-witness; but the Bible is not *only* or *primarily* self-witness. It is first and foremost, not a book about a book, but a book about God, about Christ, about the salvation of man from sin. But that message of salvation includes a message about the Bible. For this salvation requires *verbal revelation*. In saving man, God *speaks* to him.

A. Lord and Servant

God spoke to man even *before* man fell into sin. The first human experience mentioned in Scripture is the hearing of God's word; for immediately after the account of man's creation we read,

> And God blessed them: and God said unto them, "Be fruitful, and multiply, and replenish the earth, and subdue it; and have dominion over the fish of the sea, and over the birds of the heavens, and over every living thing that moveth upon the earth."[5]

It is appropriate that the hearing of these words be presented in Scripture as man's first experience. For this was the experience by which the whole course of man's life was determined. When man heard these words of God, he heard his own *definition*. God was telling man who man was, what his task was. Everything else that man did was to be in obedience to this command. Whether a shepherd, a farmer, a miner, a businessman, a teacher, a homemaker—his main job was to replenish and subdue the earth in obedience to this command. The command covered *all* of life, not just some compartments of it. The command was not to be questioned; it was God's sovereign determination of man's responsibility. The command asserted God's claim to *ultimate* authority; for, paradoxically, while the command declared man to have dominion over the earth, it also declared God's dominion over man! Whatever dominion man enjoys, he receives from God; he enjoys it at God's pleasure; he enjoys it out of obedience to God's command.

---

4. As such, the paper will also *fail* to do justice to *other* legitimate concerns.
5. Gen. 1:28.

Why? Simply because God is God, and man is man. God is Lord; man is servant. God commands; man must obey. To have a Lord is to be under authority. A servant is one responsible to obey the *commands* of another. What kind of lordship would there be without commands? The very idea is absurd. Without commands, no obedience; without obedience, no responsibility; without responsibility, no authority; without authority, no lordship.

Man was created in obedience; he fell through disobedience—disobedience to another command, this time the command concerning the forbidden tree.[6] The simplest biblical definition of sin is "lawlessness"[7]—rejection of, disobedience to God's commands. Therefore just as the word of God defines our status as God's creatures and servants, it also defines our status as *fallen* creatures, as sinners.

Redemption, according to Scripture, involves a re-assertion of God's lordship. The fall, of course, did not annul God's lordship; God's lordship over fallen man is vividly expressed in divine judgment against sin. But if man is to be saved, he must be brought to realize again that God is Lord and demands man's unconditional obedience. When God saved Israel from Egypt, He called himself by the mysterious name Jehovah which, though its exact meaning is uncertain, clearly asserts his claim to unconditional lordship.[8] And throughout the history of redemption, God continually asserted this claim by making *absolute demands* upon his people.

God's demands are absolute in at least three senses: (1) They *cannot be questioned*. The Lord God has the right to demand unwavering, unflinching obedience. God blessed Abraham because he "obeyed my voice, and kept my charge, my commandments, my statutes, and my laws."[9] He did not waver[10] even when God commanded him to sacrifice his son Isaac, the son of the promise.[11] To waver—even in that horrible situation!—would have been sin. (2) God's demand is absolute also in the sense that it *transcends all other loyalties*, all other demands. The Lord God will not tolerate competition; he demands *exclusive* loyalty.[12] The servant must love his Lord with all his heart, soul and strength.[13] One cannot serve two masters.[14] One of the most remarkable proofs of the deity of Christ in the New Testament is that there Jesus Christ demands—and receives—precisely this kind of loyalty from his followers, the same sort of loyalty which Jehovah demanded of Israel.[15] The Lord demands *first* place. (3) God's demand is also absolute in that it *governs all areas of life*. In the Old Testament period, God regulated not only Israel's worship, but also the diet, political life, sex life, economic life, family life, travel, calendar of his people. No area of life was immune to God's involvement. To be sure, the New Testament gives us more freedom on a certain sense: the detailed dietary restrictions, uncleanness rituals, animal sacrifices and other elements of the old order are no longer literally binding. But the New Testament, if anything, is *more* explicit than the Old on the comprehensiveness of God's demand: *Whatsoever* we do, even eating and drinking, must

---

6. Gen. 2:17; 3:6, 11–12.

7. 1 John 3:4.

8. Ex. 3:14; note context. In later years, when this sacred name was considered too sacred to be pronounced, the Jews read the word *Adonai*, Lord, in its place.

9. Gen. 26:5.

10. Rom. 4:20.

11. Gen. 22:18.

12. Ex. 20:3, "Thou shalt have no other gods before me."

13. Deut. 6:4–5; cf. Matt. 22:37–40 and parallels in the other Gospels.

14. Matt. 6:22–24.

15. Matt. 19:16–30; cf. 8:19–22; 10:37; Phil. 3:8.

be done to the glory of God.[16] We must never shut the Lord out of any compartment of our lives; there must be no areas kept to ourselves. God's lordship involves such *absolute demands*.

B. Savior and Sinner

But salvation is more than a reassertion of God's lordship. If God merely reasserted his lordship, we would be without hope, for we have turned against him and deserve death at his hand.[17] If God merely spoke to us absolute demands, we would perish, for we have not obeyed these demands. But our God is not only Lord; he is also *savior*. And he speaks to us not only demands, not only law, but also *gospel*—the good news of Jesus Christ. But we must emphasize that he *speaks* the gospel. The gospel is a *message*, a revelation in words. How can we know that the death of Christ is sufficient to save us from sin? Now human wisdom could have figured that out! Only God can declare sinners to be forgiven; only God has the right to promise salvation to those who believe! The same lord who speaks to demand obedience, also speaks to promise salvation. As Abraham,[18] we are called to believe the gospel simply because it is God's own promise. We know that believers in Christ are saved because Jesus has told us they are.[19] Only the Lord can speak the word of forgiveness, that word which declares sinners to be forgiven, and promises eternal life.

Just as there can be no lordship without an absolute demand, so there is no salvation without a gracious and certain promise. Therefore the whole biblical message presupposes the *necessity of verbal revelation*. Without revealed words, there is neither lordship nor salvation. To "accept Christ as Savior and Lord" is to accept from the heart Christ's demand and promise. Let there be no misunderstanding: you *cannot* "accept Christ" without accepting his words! Christ himself emphasizes this point over and over again.[20] If we set aside the words of Christ in favor of a vague, undefined "personal relationship" to Christ, we simply lose the biblical Christ and substitute a Christ of our own imagination.

And not just any words will do! They must be *God's* words—words of divine, and not merely human authority; words which *cannot* be questioned, transcend all other loyalties, govern all areas of life. They must be words which cannot be contradicted by human philosophies or theologies—or even by the "assured results of modern scholarship"! Without words like *that*, we have no Lord and we have no Savior.

But where can we find words like *that*? No mere philosopher or theologian or scholar speaks such words! Many religions, indeed, claim to have such words; but how are we to judge among these many claims? How do we distinguish the voice of God from the voice of devils and the imaginations of our own hearts?

II. Revealed Words and Scripture

Scripture tells us to go to Scripture! Or, rather, the *God* of Scripture tells us in Scripture to go to Scripture!

16. 1 Cor. 10:31—A New Testament dietary law! Cf. Rom. 14:23; 2 Cor. 10:5; Col. 3:17.
17. Rom. 3:23; 6:23.
18. Rom. 4:19–20.
19. John 5:24.
20. Matt. 7:24–29; Mark 8:38; Luke 9:26; 8:21; John 8:31, 47, 51; 10:27; 12:47–50; 14:15, 21, 23–24; 15:7, 10, 14; 17:6, 8, 17. The relationship between Christ and his words is essentially the same as that between God and his words in the Old Testament.

Of course we must note at the outset that the Bible is not the *only* word that God has spoken. God has spoken words to and by his apostles and prophets that are not recorded in the Bible. He has also spoken, in a sense, to the earth, to the storms, to the winds and waves.[21] And in a mysterious sense, the word of God may also be identified with God Himself[22] and particularly with Jesus Christ.[23] But God does not always tell us what he says to the winds and waves, and he has not always provided us with prophets at a handy distance! Rather, he has directed us to a *book*! That is where we are to go for daily, regular guidance. That is where we may always find the demands of the Lord and the promise of the Savior.

Writing goes back a long way in the history of redemption. The book of Genesis appears to be derived largely from "books of generations."[24] We don't know much about the origin of these books, but it is significant that (1) they include inspired prophecies[25] and (2) they were eventually included among Israel's authoritative writings. From a very early time, God's people began to *record* the history of redemption for their posterity. It was important from the beginning that God's covenants, his demands and his promises be written down lest they be forgotten. The first explicit reference, however, to a divinely authorized book occurs in connection with the war between Israel and Amalek shortly after the Exodus:

> And Joshua discomfited Amalek and his people with the edge of the sword. And the Lord said unto Moses, "Write this for a memorial in a book, and rehearse it in the ears of Joshua: that I will utterly blot out the remembrance of Amalek from under heaven." And Moses built an altar, and called the name of it Jehovah-nissi; and he said, "The Lord hath sworn: the Lord will have war with Amalek from generation to generation."[26]

Not only does the Lord authorize the writing of the book; the content of it is God's own oath, his pledge. It is the word of God, a word of absolute authority and sure promise. Because God has spoken it, it will surely happen.

But an even more important example of divine writing occurs a few chapters later. In Exodus twenty, God speaks the Ten Commandments to the people of Israel. The people are terrified, and they ask Moses to act as mediator between themselves and God. From Exodus 20:22 to 23:33, God presents to Moses further commandments in addition to the ten, which Moses is to convey to the people. In Exodus 24:4, we learn that Moses wrote down all these words and in verse seven read them to the people. The people received these words as the word of God himself—"All that the Lord hath spoken will we do, and be obedient."[27] They accepted these *written* words as words of absolute demand! But something even more remarkable occurs a few verses later. The Lord calls Moses alone to ascend the mountain, "and I will give thee the tables of stone, and the law and the commandment which I have written,

---

21. Pss. 119:90–91; 147:15–18; 148:5–6; Gen. 1:3; Ps. 33:6, 9; cf. Matt. 8:27.

22. John 1:1.

23. John 1:14.

24. Gen. 5:1; cf. 2:4; 6:9; 10:1; 11:10, 27; 25:12, 19; 36:9; 37:2.

25. Gen. 9:25–27. Though Noah is speaking, he is administering covenantal blessing and curse which can only take effect under divine sanction. The fulfillment of these words at a much later period shows that these words were in essence the words of God. Cf. Gen. 25:23; 27:27–29; etc.

26. Ex. 17:13–16. The language here suggests a parallel with the divine "book of life," as though this earthly book were a kind of copy of the divine original.

27. Ex. 24:7.

that thou mayest teach them."[28] Note the pronouns in the first person singular! *God* did the writing! In fact, the implication of the tenses is that God had completed the writing before Moses ascended the mountain. Moses was to go up the mountain to receive a completed, divinely written manuscript! Nor is this the only passage that stresses divine authorship of the law. Elsewhere, too, we learn that the tables were "written with the finger of God";[29] they were "the work of God, and the writing was the writing of God, graven upon the tables."[30]

What was going on here? Why the sustained emphasis upon divine writing? Meredith G. Kline[31] suggests that this emphasis on divine writing arises out of the nature of covenant-making in the ancient near East. When a great king entered a "suzerainty covenant relation" with a lesser king, the great king would produce a *document* setting forth the terms of the covenant. The great king was the author, because he was the lord, the sovereign. He set the terms. The lesser king was to read and obey, for he was the servant, the vassal. The covenant document was the Law; it set forth the commands of the great king, and the servant was bound to obey. To disobey the document was to disobey the great king; to obey it was to obey him. Now in Exodus twenty and succeeding chapters, God is making a kind of "suzerainty treaty" with Israel. As part of the treaty relation, he authors a document which is to serve as the official record of his absolute demand. Without the document there would be no covenant.

Later, more words were added to the document; and we read in Deuteronomy that Moses put all these words in the ark of the covenant, the dwelling place of God, the holiest place in Israel, "that it may be there for a witness against thee."[32] The covenant document is not man's witness concerning God; it is God's witness *against* man. Man may not add to or subtract anything from the document;[33] for the document is God's word, and must not be confused with any mere human authority.

This divine authority takes many forms. In the extra-biblical suzerainty covenants, certain distinct elements have been discovered:[34] the self-identification of the lord (the giving of his name), the "historical prologue" (proclaiming the benevolent acts of the lord to the vassal), the basic demand for exclusive loyalty (called "love"), the detailed demands of the lord, the curses upon the disobedient, the blessings upon the obedient, and finally the details of covenant administration, use of the document, etc. In the law of God, all of these elements are present. God tells who he is,[35] he proclaims his grace through his acts in history,[36] he

---

28. Ex. 24:12.

29. Ex. 31:13.

30. Ex. 32:16; cf. also 34:1; Deut. 4:13; 9:10–11; 10:2–4. In Exodus 34:27–28, Moses, too, is said to have done some writing—probably portions of the law other than the ten commandments. And yet the written work of Moses is no less authoritative than that of the Lord himself—cf. Ex. 34:32. Moses was the mediator of the covenant and as such was a prophet conveying God's word to the people. Cf. Ex. 4:10–17; Deut. 18:15–19. The unique "finger of God" writing therefore is not necessary to the authority of the documents; humanly *written* documents may be equally authoritative, as long as the words are God's. But the "finger of God" picture places awesome *emphasis* upon the authority of the words.

31. Kline, *Structure of Biblical Authority*.

32. Deut. 31:26.

33. Deut. 4:2; 12:32; cf. Prov. 30:6; Rev. 22:18–19. How then, could any additions be made to the document? For some additions clearly were made (Josh. 24:26, etc.). Since no man could add or subtract, the addition of a book to the covenant canon carries with it the claim that the addition has *divine* sanction.

34. Kline, *Structure of Biblical Authority*; we are listing the elements Kline finds in treaties of the second millennium, B.C. He regards the decalogue and the book of Deuteronomy as having this basic structure (thus implying a second millennium date for Deuteronomy!), and he regards the entire Old Testament canon as an outgrowth of these "treaties."

35. Ex. 20:2, "I am the Lord thy God"; cf. 3:14, etc.

36. Ex. 20:2, "Who brought thee out of the land of Egypt, out of the house of bondage."

demands love,[37] he sets forth his detailed demands,[38] he declares the curses and blessings contingent on covenant obedience,[39] and he sets up the machinery for continuing covenant administration, laying particular emphasis on the use of the covenant book.[40] All of these elements of the covenant are authoritative; all are words of God.

Theologians generally oversimplify the concept of biblical authority. To some theologians, it is God's personal self-manifestation (as in the giving of the divine name) which is authoritative. To others, it is the account of historical events. To others, the demand for love is the central thing. To others it is the divine self-commitment to bless. But the covenantal structure of revelation has room for all of these elements, and what's more, places them in proper relation to one another. There is both love and law, both grace and demand, both *kerygma* and *didache*, both personal disclosure (stated in "I-thou" form) and objective declarations of facts, both a concept of history and a concept of inspired words. The covenant document contains authoritative *propositions* about history (the servant has no right to contradict the lord's account of the history of the covenant), authoritative *commands* to be obeyed, authoritative *questions* (demanding the vassal's pledge to covenant allegiance), authoritative *performatives* (God's self-commitment to bless and curse).[41] The propositions are infallible; but infallibility is only part of biblical authority. This authority also includes the authority of non-propositional language as well.

We have seen that the idea of a "canon," an authoritative written word of God, goes back to the very beginning of Israel's history, back to its very creation as a nation. The Scripture is the constitution of Israel, the basis for its existence. The idea of a written word of God did *not* arise in twentieth-century fundamentalism, nor in seventeenth-century orthodoxy, nor in the post-apostolic church, nor in 2 Timothy, nor in post-exilic Judaism. The idea of a written word of God is at the very foundation of biblical faith. Throughout the history of redemption, therefore, God continually calls his people back to the written word. Over and over again he calls them to keep "the commandments of the Lord your God, and his testimonies, and his statutes which he hath commanded thee."[42] These are the words of absolute demand and sure promise, the words of the Lord. These were the words that made the difference between life and death. These were the words which could not be questioned,

37. Ex. 20:3, "Thou shalt have no other gods before me." Cf. Deut. 6:4–5 where the term "love" is actually used to denote this exclusive covenant loyalty. The demand for love follows the account of God's gracious acts in history, and is regarded as the vassal's response of gratitude for the Lord's benevolence. Cf. the New Testament emphasis, "We love, because he first loved us," 1 John 4:19.

38. Ex. 20:12–17. Though the division cannot be sharply made, the first four commandments might be said to represent the fundamental love-requirement, while the last six describe some of its detailed outworkings.

39. Ex. 20:5–6, 12. We have been tracing these covenant elements through the Decalogue, but we could have used many other parts of Scripture as well.

40. This emphasis is not found in the Decalogue, but it is a major emphasis of Deuteronomy (see 31:24–29), which Kline also identifies as a covenant document.

41. Performatives ("I pronounce you man and wife," "You are under arrest," "Cursed be all who do not obey") do not merely state facts, but "perform" various sorts of actions. When spoken by one in authority, they "accomplish" what they set out to do. Performatives of the Lord in Scripture are uniquely authoritative, but their authority is not *adequately* characterized by the term "infallibility." "Infallibility" is important, but it is only *part* of the meaning of biblical authority. "Infallibility" is, not too strong, but too *weak* a term adequately to characterize biblical authority.

42. Deut. 6:17; cf. 4:1–8; 5:29–33; 6:24–25; 7:9–11; 8:11; 10:12–13; 11:1, 13, 18–23, 27–28; 12:1, 28; 13:4. In Deuteronomy, almost every page contains exhortations to obey God's commandments and statutes and ordinances! But not only in Deuteronomy! Cf. Josh. 1:8; 8:25–28; Pss. 1:1–3; 12:6–7; 19:7–11; 33:4, 11; 119:1–176; Isa. 8:16–20; Dan. 9:3ff.; 2 Kings 18:6. Read over these and the many similar passages and let the message sink into your heart! The conclusion concerning the authority of the written word is simply inescapable.

which transcended all other demands, which governed all areas of life. When Israel sinned and returned to the Lord, she returned also to the law of God.[43]

From time to time there were new words of God. Joshua added to the words which Moses had placed in the ark.[44] How could a mere man add to the words of God in view of the command of Deuteronomy 4:2? The only answer can be that Joshua's words were also recognized as God's words. The prophets also came speaking God's words,[45] and some of them were written down.[46]

Thus the "Old Testament" grew. By the time of Jesus there was a well-defined body of writings which was generally recognized as God's word, and which was quoted as supreme authority, as Holy Scripture. Jesus and the apostles did not challenge, but rather accepted this view. Not only did they accept it, but they actively testified to it by word and deed. The role of Scripture in the life of Jesus is really remarkable: although Jesus was and is the Son of God, the second person of the Trinity, during his earthly ministry he subjected himself completely to the Old Testament Scripture. Over and over again, he performed various actions "so that the Scripture might be fulfilled."[47] The whole point of his life—his sacrificial death and resurrection was determined beforehand by Scripture.[48] Jesus' testimony to Scripture, then, is not occasional, but pervasive. His whole life was a witness to biblical authority! But listen particularly to what Christ and the apostles say concerning the Old Testament! Listen to the way in which they cite Scripture, even in the face of Satan, to "clinch" an argument, to silence objections.[49] Listen to the titles by which they describe the Old Testament: "Scripture," "holy Scripture," "law," "prophets," "royal law of liberty. . . . the oracles of God."[50] Listen to the formulae by which they cite Scripture: "It is written"; "it says"; "the Holy Spirit says"; "Scripture says."[51] All of these phrases and titles denoted to the people of Jesus' day something far more than a mere human document. These terms denoted nothing less than inspired, authoritative words of God. As Warfield pointed out, "Scripture says" and "God says" are interchangeable![52]

And consider further the explicit *teaching* of Jesus and the apostles concerning biblical authority:

1. Think not that I am come to destroy the law or the prophets: I came not to destroy, but to fulfill. For truly I say to you, 'till heaven and earth pass away, one jot or one tittle shall in no wise pass away from the law; until all things are accomplished. Whosoever therefore shall break one of the least of these commandments, and shall teach men so, shall be called least

---

43. 2 Kings 23:2–3, 21, 25; Neh. 8. The whole Old Testament history is a history of obedience and disobedience: obedience and disobedience to what? To God's commands; and after Exodus 20, to God's written word! The self-witness of the Old Testament is therefore present on every page. "Pervasive," as we said.

44. Josh. 24:26.

45. Deut. 18:15–19; Isa. 59:21; Jer. 1:6–19; Ezek. 13:2–3, 17. The mark of the prophet was the phrase "Thus saith the Lord," which is found over and over again in the prophetic literature. Many theologians hostile to the orthodox view of biblical authority recognize that the prophets *claimed* an identity between their words and God's. See, e.g., Emil Brunner, *Dogmatics*, vol. 1, *The Christian Doctrine of God*, trans. Olive Wyon (Philadelphia: Westminster Press, 1950), 18, 27, 31–32.

46. Isa. 8:1; 30:3ff.; 34:16ff.; Jer. 25:13; 30:2; 36:1–32; 51:60ff.; Dan. 9:1–2.

47. Matt. 4:14; 5:17; 8:17; 12:17; 13:35; 21:4; 26:54–56; Luke 21:22; 24:44; John 19:28.

48. Luke 24:26: "*Behooved* not." Scripture imposes a *necessity* upon Christ!

49. Matt. 4; 22:29, 33; etc.

50. See Warfield, *The Inspiration and Authority of the Bible,* esp. 229–41, 361–407.

51. Ibid., 229–348.

52. Ibid.

in the kingdom of heaven: but whosoever shall do and teach them, he shall be called great in the kingdom of heaven.[53]

Jots and tittles were among the smallest marks used in the written Hebrew language. Jesus is saying that *everything* in the law and the prophets (equals the Old Testament) carries divine authority. And obedience to that law is the criterion of greatness in the kingdom of heaven.

> 2. Think not that I will accuse you to the Father: there is one that accuses you, even Moses, whom you trust. For if ye believed Moses, ye would believe me; for he wrote of me. But if ye believe not his writings, how shall ye believe my words?[54]

The Jews claimed to believe Moses' writings, but they rejected Christ. Jesus replies that they do not *really* believe Moses; and he urges them to a *greater* trust in the Old Testament. He urges them to believe *all* of the law, and thus come to accept his messiahship. We see here that Jesus did not merely quote Scripture because it was customary among the Jews. Rather, he *criticized* the prevailing custom because it was insufficiently loyal to Scripture. Jesus' view of Scripture was *stronger* than that of the Pharisees and Scribes. Jesus sees Moses justly accusing the Jews because of their unbelief in Scripture. Believing Moses is the prerequisite to believing Christ.

> 3. The Jews answered him, "For a good work we stone thee not, but for blasphemy; even because thou, being a man, makest thyself God." Jesus answered them, "Is it not written in your law, I said, 'Ye are gods'? If he called them gods unto whom the word of God came (and the Scripture cannot be broken), say ye of him whom the Father sanctified and sent into the world, 'Thou blasphemest'; because I said, 'I am the Son of God'?"[55]

A difficult passage, this; but note the parenthesis. Concerning a fairly obscure Psalm, Jesus says that "scripture cannot be broken." It cannot be wrong; it cannot fail; it cannot be rejected as we reject human words.

> 4. For whatsoever things were written aforetime were written for our learning, that through patience and through comfort of the scriptures we might have hope.[56]

Here, the apostle Paul tells us that the Old Testament is relevant, not only for the people of the Old Testament period, but for us as well. It teaches us, gives us patience, comfort, hope. And most remarkably, the *whole* Old Testament is relevant! None of it is dated; none of it is invalidated by more recent thought. Of what human documents may *that* be said?

> 5. And we have the word of prophecy made more sure; whereunto ye do well that ye take heed, as unto a lamp shining in a dark place, until the day dawn, and the day star arise in your hearts:

---

53. Matt. 5:17–19. For detailed exegesis, see John Murray, *Principles of Conduct* (Grand Rapids: Eerdmans, 1957), 149–57. Cf. also his essay, "The Attestation of Scripture," in *The Infallible Word*, 15–17, 20–24.
54. John 5:45–47.
55. John 10:33–36; cf. Warfield, *The Inspiration and Authority of the Bible*, 138–41.
56. Rom. 15:4.

knowing this first, that no prophecy of scripture is of private interpretation. For no prophecy ever came by the will of man: but men spake from God, being moved by the Holy Spirit.[57]

Note the context of this passage: Peter expects to die soon, and he wishes to assure his readers of the truth of the gospel.[58] He knows that false teachers will attack the church, deceiving the flock.[59] He insists that the gospel is not myth or legend, but the account of events which he himself had witnessed.[60] Yet even when the eyewitnesses have left the scene, the believers will still have a source of sure truth. They have the "word of prophecy"—the Old Testament Scriptures—a word which is "more sure."[61] They are to "take heed" to that word, and forsake all conflicting teaching; for the word is light, and all the rest is darkness. Moreover, it did not originate through the human interpretative process; it is not a set of human opinions about God; nor did it originate in any human volition. Rather the Holy Spirit carried the biblical writers along, as they spoke for him! The Holy Spirit determined their course and their destination. The Bible consists of human writings, but its authority is no mere human authority!

> 6. All Scripture is God-breathed and profitable for doctrine, reproof, correction, instruction in righteousness: that the man of God may be complete, furnished completely unto every good work.[62]

Note again the context, for it is similar to that of the last passage. Paul in this chapter paints a gloomy picture of deceivers leading people astray. How shall we know the truth in all this confusion? Paul tells Timothy to hang on to the truth as he learned it from Paul,[63] but also to the "holy scriptures"[64] (which, we note, are available even to us who have not been taught personally by Paul). This Scripture is "inspired of God" as the KJV says, or more literally "God-breathed"—*breathed out by God*. In less picturesque language, we might say simply "spoken by God"; but the more picturesque language also suggests the activity of the Holy Spirit in the process, the words for "spirit" and "breath" being closely related in the original Greek. Scripture is *spoken* by God; it is *his Word*; and as such it is *all* profitable, and it is *all* that we need to be equipped for good works.

Both Old and New Testaments then pervasively claim authority for the Old Testament scriptures. But what about the New Testament scriptures? Can we say that they, also, are the word of God?

We have seen the importance of verbal revelation in both Old and New Testaments. Both Testaments insist over and over again that such words are a necessity of God's plan of

---

57. 2 Peter 1:19–21; cf. Warfield, *The Inspiration and Authority of the Bible*, 135–38.

58. 2 Peter 1:12–15.

59. 2 Peter 2.

60. 2 Peter 1:16–18; in the current theological scene it is worth noting that Peter denies any mythological character to the message. It is not *mythos*.

61. Is the word "more sure" in the sense of being confirmed by eyewitness testimony? Or is it, as Warfield suggests (above reference) "more sure" *than* eyewitness testimony? In either case, the passage places a strong emphasis upon the *certainty* of the word.

62. 2 Tim. 3:16–17. For detailed exegesis, see Warfield, *The Inspiration and Authority of the Bible*, 133–35, and also 245–96 (a comprehensive treatment of the meaning of "God-breathed").

63. 2 Tim. 3:14.

64. 2 Tim. 3:15.

salvation. As we have seen, the concepts of lordship and salvation presuppose the existence of revealed words. And in the New Testament, Jesus Christ is Lord and Savior. It would be surprising indeed if Jehovah, the Lord of the Old Testament people of God, gave a written record of his demand and promise, while Jesus, the Lord incarnate of whom the New Testament speaks, left no such record. Jesus told his disciples over and over again that obedience to *his words* was an absolute necessity for kingdom service and a criterion for true discipleship.[65] We *need* the words of Jesus! But where are they!? If there is no written record, no New Testament "covenant document," then has Jesus simply left us to grope in the dark?

Praise God that He has not! Jesus promised to send the Holy Spirit to lead his disciples into all truth.[66] After the Holy Spirit was poured out on the day of Pentecost, the disciples began to preach with great power and conviction.[67] The pattern remains remarkably consistent throughout the Book of Acts: the disciples are filled with the Spirit, and *then* they speak of Jesus.[68] They do not speak in their own strength. Further, they constantly insist that the source of their message is God, not man.[69] Their words have absolute, not merely relative, authority.[70] And this authority attaches not only to their spoken words, but also to their written words.[71] Peter classes the letters of Paul together with the "other Scriptures"![72] Paul's letters are "Scripture"; and we recall that "Scripture" is "God-breathed"![73]

We conclude, then, that the witness of Scripture to its own authority is *pervasive*: (1) The whole biblical message of salvation presupposes and necessitates the existence of revealed words—words of absolute demand and sure promise; without such words, we have no Lord, no Savior, no hope. (2) Throughout the history of redemption, God directs his people to find these words in written form, in those books which we know as the Old and New Testaments.

III. Revealed Words and Modern Theologians

Our conclusion, however, raises a serious problem. If the witness of Scripture to its own authority is *pervasive*, then why have so many biblical scholars and theologians failed to see it?

---

65. Matt. 7:21–24, 28–29; Mark 8:38; Luke 8:21; 9:26; John 8:47; 10:27; 12:47; 14:15, 21, 23–24; 15:7, 10, 14; 17:6, 8, 17; 18:37; cf. 1 John 2:3–5; 3:22; 5:2–3; 2 John 6; 1 Tim. 6:3; Rev. 12:17; 14:12. Again: look these up, and allow yourself to be impressed by the *pervasiveness* of this emphasis.

66. John 16:13; cf. Acts 1:8.

67. Acts 2

68. Acts 2:4; 4:8, 31; 6:10 (cf. 3 and 5); 7:55; 9:17–20; 13:9–10, 52.

69. 2 Thess. 2:2; Gal. 1:1, 11–12, 16; 2:2; 1 Cor. 2:10–13; 4:1; 7:40; 2 Cor. 4:1–6; 12:1, 7; Eph. 3:3; Rom. 16:25.

70. Rom. 2:16; 1 Thess. 4:2; Jude 17–18; and cf. the passages, listed in the preceding and following notes.

71. Col. 4:16; 1 Thess. 5:27; 2 Thess. 3:14; 1 Cor. 14:37.

72. 2 Peter 3:16. Cf. 1 Tim. 5:18, which appears to couple a quotation from Luke with a quotation from the law of Moses under the heading "Scripture."

73. The question of what books are to be regarded as New Testament Scripture is beyond the scope of this paper, since no actual list can be found as part of the New Testament's self-witness. We may certainly assume, however, on the basis of what has been said, that if revealed words are a *necessary* ingredient of biblical salvation, and if specifically the words of the incarnate Christ and his apostles have such necessity, our sovereign God will "somehow" find a way to enable us to find those words! And surely he has! Although there have been disputes among different churches concerning the *Old Testament* canon, there have never been any church-dividing disputes over the *New Testament* canon! Through history, of course, some New Testament books have been questioned. But once all the facts have gotten before the Christian public, it seems, the questions have always melted away. This is rather amazing, for the Christian church has always been, to its shame, a very contentious body! And yet no serious contentions have ever arisen over the matter of canonicity, a matter which many have found baffling! Try an experiment: read Paul's letter to the Corinthians (canonical), and then read Clement's (non-canonical). *Think* about it; *pray* about it. Is there not an *obvious* difference? Christ's sheep hear his voice!

We are not asking why it is that these theologians fail to *believe* the claim of Scripture. The unbelief of theologians is at bottom rather uninteresting; it is not much different from the unbelief of anyone else. Yet it is surely possible to disbelieve Scripture's claim while at the same time admitting that Scripture makes such a claim. And some liberal theologians have indeed accepted this option: the Bible *claims* inspiration and authority, but modern men cannot accept such a claim.[74] But others have refused to admit even that Scripture makes that claim! Or more often: they have recognized this claim in some parts of Scripture, but they have judged this claim to be inconsistent with other, more important Scriptural teachings, and thus have felt that Scripture "as a whole" opposes the notion of authoritative Scripture in our sense.

Putting the same question differently: is it possible to construct a sound *biblical* argument for biblical *fallibility*? Some theologians, amazingly enough, have said "yes," despite the evidence to the contrary we and others have adduced. Is this simply a wresting of Scripture in the interest of a heresy? Is it at bottom simply another form of modern unbelief (and therefore as "uninteresting" as the unbelief alluded to earlier)? In the final analysis, I would say, the answer is yes. But some analysis, final or not, is called for. The argument must be scrutinized, lest we miss something important in the biblical self-witness.

We are not here going to argue specific points of exegesis. Some thinkers would question our interpretation of Matthew 5:17–19, arguing that in the Sermon on the Mount and elsewhere Jesus makes "critical distinctions" among the Old Testament precepts. Some, too, would question our reading of the phrase "inspired of God" or "God-breathed" in 2 Timothy 3:16. And indeed, some would argue from 2 Peter 1:21 (but in defiance of 2 Tim. 3:16!) that inspiration pertains only to the writers of Scripture and not to the books which they have written. For enlightenment on these controversies, see the references in the footnotes. In general, we may say that even if it is possible to question a few points of our exegesis, the evidence is so *massive* that the general conclusion is still difficult to avoid:

The effort to explain away the Bible's witness to its plenary inspiration reminds one of a man standing safely in his laboratory and elaborately expounding—possibly by the aid of diagrams and mathematical formulae—how every stone in an avalanche has a defined pathway and may easily be dodged by one of some presence of mind. We may fancy such an elaborate trifler's triumph as he would analyze the avalanche into its constituent stones, and demonstrate of stone after stone that its pathway is definite, limited, and may easily be avoided. But avalanches, unfortunately, do not come upon us, stone by stone, one at a time, courteously leaving us opportunity to withdraw from the pathway of each in turn: but all at once, in a roaring mass of destruction. Just so we may explain away a text or two which teach plenary inspiration, to our own closet satisfaction, dealing with them each without reference to the others: but these texts of ours, again, unfortunately do not come upon us in this artificial isolation; neither are they few in number. There are scores, hundreds, of them: and they come bursting upon us in one solid mass. Explain them away? We should have to explain away the whole New Testament. What a pity it is that we cannot see and feel

74. Cf. Warfield, *The Inspiration and Authority of the Bible,* 115, 175–81, 423–24. More recently, F. C. Grant admits that the New Testament writers assume Scripture to be "trustworthy, infallible, and inerrant": *Introduction to New Testament Thought* (Nashville: Abdingdon Press, 1950), 75

the avalanche of texts beneath which we may lie hopelessly buried, as clearly as we may see and feel an avalanche of stones![75]

Not even the cleverest exegete can "explain away" the biblical concepts of lordship and salvation and the necessary connection of these concepts with the revealed words of Scripture! No exegete can explain away *all* the verses which call God's people to obey "the commandments, statutes, testimonies, ordinances" of the Lord; *all* the "it is written" formulae; all of the commands delivered by apostles and prophets in authoritative tone.

Rather than such detailed questions, therefore, we shall confine our attention to broader considerations which have carried considerable weight in contemporary theological discussion. For just as we have argued that the biblical concepts of lordship and salvation require the existence of revealed words, so others have argued that certain basic biblical concepts *exclude the possibility of* such words!

The primary appeal of these theological views is to the divine transcendence; as the following quotes from Karl Barth and Emil Brunner respectively will indicate:

> Again it is quite impossible that there should be a direct identity between the human word of Holy Scripture and the Word of God, and therefore between the creaturely reality in itself and as such and the reality of God the creator.[76]

> It is therefore impossible to equate any human words, any "speech-about-Him" with the divine self-communication.[77]

Such statements have a kind of primitive religious appeal. God alone is God, and nothing else may be "equated with him." To "equate" or "directly identify" something else with God is idolatry. Now surely we must agree that Scripture endorses this sentiment, for Scripture clearly opposes idolatry and exalts God above all other things! And if this is the case, then it seems that Scripture requires us to distinguish sharply between God Himself on the one hand, and language about him on the other; the transcendence of God is surely a central biblical concept! And if transcendence requires us to eliminate all thought of "revealed words," even though other biblical doctrines suggest otherwise, then perhaps we ought to give serious thought to this issue.

However, Barth's concept of "direct identity" is a difficult one, as is Brunner's reference to "equating." What does it mean to assert—or deny—a "direct identity" or "equation" between God and language? Clearly, no one wants to say that "God" and "language about God" are synonymous terms! Nor has anyone in recent memory suggested that we bow down before words and sentences. Even the most orthodox defenders of biblical infallibility maintain that there is *some* distinction to be made between God and language. Further: even the most orthodox agree that the words of Scripture are in some sense creaturely, and thus specifically because of their creatureliness to be distinguished from God. On the other hand, if such words are *God's* words, and not *merely* human, then they are closely related

75. Warfield, *The Inspiration and Authority of the Bible*, 119–20.
76. Karl Barth, *Church Dogmatics*, vol. 1, *The Doctrine of the Word of God*, ed. G. W. Bromiley and T. F. Torrance, trans. G. T. Thomson and Harold Knight (New York: Scribner, 1956), 2:499.
77. Brunner, *The Christian Doctrine of God*, 15.

to him, at least as closely as in words are related to me. If God has spoken them, then their truth is his truth; their authority is his authority; their power is his power. Barth is willing to say that from time to time Scripture *becomes* the word of God; therefore he admits that *some* close relation between God and Scripture is essential. The question then becomes: in what way is God "distinct" from this language, and in what way is he "related" to it? A pious appeal to God's transcendence, eloquent though it may be, does not really answer this sort of question. Both the orthodox and the Barthian would like to avoid being charged with idolatry. But *what kind* of distinction between God and language is required by the divine transcendence?

Barth is most reluctant to give any positive description of this relationship. Commenting upon 2 Timothy 3:16, he says:

> At the centre of the passage a statement is made about the relationship between God and Scripture, which can be understood only as a disposing act and decision of God Himself, which cannot therefore be expanded but to which only a—necessarily brief—reference can be made. At the decisive point all that we have to say about it can consist only in an underlining and delimiting of the inaccessible mystery of the free grace in which the Spirit of God is present and active before and above and in the Bible.[78]

Inspiration, says Barth, is a mystery, because it is an act of God's grace. We cannot define what it is; we can only assert the graciousness of the process. At another point, however, he does venture to describe inspiration, alluding to the term used in 2 Timothy 3:16:

> *Theopneustia* in the bounds of biblical thinking cannot mean anything but the special attitude of obedience in those [biblical writers] who are elected and called to this obviously special service . . . But in nature and bearing their attitude of obedience was of itself—both outwardly and inwardly—only that of true and upright men.[79]

Inspiration is an act of God to create in men a special attitude of human obedience. It does not give them more than ordinary human powers. Therefore,

> The Bible is not a book of oracles; it is not an instrument of direct impartation. It is genuine witness. And how can it be witness of divine revelation, if the actual purpose, act and decision of God in His only-begotten Son, as seen and heard by the prophets and apostles in that Son, is dissolved in the Bible into a sum total of truths abstracted from that decision—and those truths are then propounded to us as truths of faith, salvation and revelation? If it tries to be more than witness, to be direct impartation, will it not keep from us the best, the one real thing, which God intends to tell and give us and which we ourselves need?[80]

The question, of course, is rhetorical. Barth is appealing to something he thinks his reader will concede as obvious. And this much we will concede: that if the Bible tries to be more than it is, if it exceeds its rightful prerogatives and usurps those of God Himself, then it will

---

78. Barth, *The Doctrine of the Word of God*, 2:504.
79. Ibid., 505; in my view and Warfield's, Barth offers here a most inadequate exegesis of the "God-breathed" of 2 Timothy 3:16.
80. Barth, *The Doctrine of the Word of God*, 2:507.

indeed hide from us the real message of God's transcendence. But what *are* the "rightful prerogatives" of Scripture? That must be established before the rhetoric of divine transcendence can have force. The rhetoric of transcendence does not itself determine what those prerogatives are.

It is clear from the last quoted section at least that Barth denies to Scripture one particular prerogative—the prerogative of presenting "truths of revelation in abstraction from" God's saving act in Christ. But what does "in abstraction from" mean in this context? An abstraction is always some sort of distinction or separation, but what kind of distinction or separation? An orthodox theologian will insist that the biblical "truths of revelation" are *not* "in abstraction from" God's act in Christ. On the contrary, we learn about this act, we come to adore this act, because the Bible gives us a true account of it.

I think that in the back of Barth's mind—perhaps in the front of it!—is a concern of many academic people. When we teachers see students cramming for theological exams, stuffing truths into their heads, we sometimes wonder what all of this has to do with the kingdom of God! And the students wonder too! The whole business of "mastering truths" somehow seems "abstract." It almost trivializes the message. Often there is here no real sense of the presence of God, no real spirit of prayer and thankfulness; it seems as if we are taking God's word and making a *game* of it!

Well, theology examinations, theological study can be a spiritual trial! But surely if we lose touch with God in studying His truths, it is our fault, not his for providing the truths! And sometimes, at least, the study of truths can be downright inspiring; sometimes, even in the academy, the law of the Lord purifies the soul! The evil in Barth's mind (as I understand him) is not an evil that can be remedied by eliminating the concept of revealed truth. It would be nice if such personal sinfulness could be eliminated by such a conceptual shift! But the sin of trivializing God's word is one of which we are all guilty—Barthians as much as anyone! We cannot eliminate that in Barth's way, nor ought we to try to construct a doctrine of Scripture that will make such trivialization impossible. That is the wrong way to go about constructing doctrinal formulations. Doctrines must not be arbitrarily constructed to counteract current abuses; they must be constructed on the basis of God's revelation.

"Abstraction," then, can't be avoided by renouncing the idea of revealed truths or revealed words. Nor can it be avoided by renouncing biblical infallibility. And in the absence of any other clearly stated threat to God's transcendence in the doctrine we have advocated, we are compelled to stand our ground. The orthodox view does *not* "abstract revelation from God's act," and it does not compromise the greatness and majesty of God. On the contrary: the true greatness of God, his Lordship and saviorhood as described in Scripture, *requires* the existence of revealed truths. Without such truths, we have no Lord, no Savior, no basis for piety. Without such truths, all that we say, think and do will be hopelessly "abstracted" from the reality of God. Without such truths, we have no hope. A Barthian or liberal or "neo-liberal" theology can provide no such words; it can locate no words of absolute demands and sure promise. Rather such a theology retains the right to judge the truth or falsity of *all* words with no divinely authorized criterion. Such theologies must be decisively rejected by the church of Christ, if she is to have any power, any saving message for our time. When Scripture speaks for itself, it claims to be no less than God's own word, and the claim is pervasive and unavoidable. Insofar as we deny that claim, we deny the Lord.[81] Insofar as we honor that word, we honor Christ.[82]

God and Biblical Language:
Transcendence and Immanence

Originally published in John W. Montgomery, ed., *God's Inerrant Word* (Grand Rapids: Bethany Fellowship [a division of Baker Publishing Group], 1974), 159–77; reprinted as Appendix E in John M. Frame, *The Doctrine of the Word of God*, A Theology of Lordship (Phillipsburg, NJ: P&R Publishing, 2010), 422–38.

One of the most persuasive and frequent contemporary objections to the orthodox view of biblical authority goes like this: the Bible cannot be the word of God because no human language can be the word of God. On this view, not only the Bible, but human language *in general* is an unfit vehicle—unfit to convey infallibly a message from God to man.

This objection takes various forms, three of which I shall discuss:

1. Some linguists and philosophers of language have suggested that language is never completely true—that the undeniable discrepancy which always exists between symbol and reality (the word "desk" is not a desk, for instance) injects falsehood into every utterance. This contention is sometimes buttressed by the further assertion that all language is metaphorical, figurative—and thus can never convey the "literal" truth. There is, however, something odd about any view which attributes falsehood to all language. For one thing, the assertion that "all sentences are false" is self-refuting if taken literally; and if we don't take it literally, what does it mean? Perhaps the real point is that language never conveys the "*whole* truth"—that it never conveys the truth with absolute precision or absolute comprehensiveness. But consider: (a) Some sentences are, in one sense, perfectly precise and comprehensive. Take "Washington is the capital of the United States": could that fact be stated more precisely? more comprehensively? (b) Of course, even the aforementioned sentence is not comprehensive in the sense of "saying everything there is to say" about Washington and the U.S. But no human being ever *tries* to say all that, at least if he has any sense at all! Nor does the Bible claim to say "everything" about God. The claim to infallibility does not entail a claim to comprehensiveness in this sense. And where no claim to comprehensiveness is made, lack of comprehensiveness does not refute infallibility. (c) Nor is imprecision necessarily a fault. "Pittsburgh is about 300 miles from Philadelphia" is imprecise in a sense, but it is a perfectly good sentence and is in no usual sense untrue. An "infallible" book might contain many imprecise-but-true statements of this sort. Granting, then, that there is a sense in which language never conveys the "whole truth," we need not renounce on that account any element of the orthodox view of biblical authority.

81. Mark 8:38.
82. John 8:31, and those passages cited above in our note 65.

More might be said about this first form of the objection we are discussing—its reliance upon the discredited referential theory of meaning, its strangely generalized concept of "metaphor," its dubious presuppositions about the origin and development of language, its ultimate theological roots. These topics, however, have been adequately discussed elsewhere,[83] and my own interests and aptitudes demand that I press on immediately to other aspects of the problem. The following discussion will raise some basic issues which I trust will shed further light on this first area of concern.

2. If the first form of our objection was raised primarily by linguists, philosophers of language and their entourage, the second form (though similarly focused on language) arises out of broader epistemological and metaphysical concerns. In the 1920s and 30s, the philosophy of logical positivism attempted to divide all philosophically important language into three categories: (a) tautologies ("A book is a book," "Either it is raining or it is not raining"), (b) contradictions ("It is raining and it is not raining." "The table is square and it is not square"), and (c) assertions of empirical fact ("There is a bird on the roof," "The President has put price controls on beef"). Tautologies, on this view, were said to be true purely by virtue of the meanings of the terms, and contradictions false on the same account. Empirical assertions could be either true or false, and their truth or falsity was said to be ascertainable by something like the methods of natural science. When someone claims to state a fact, but upon examination it turns out that this "fact" cannot be verified or falsified by such methods, then, said the positivists, this utterance is not a statement of fact at all; it is not an "empirical assertion"; it is neither true nor false. Such an unverifiable utterance may have a use as poetry, expression of feeling or the like, but it does not state any fact about the world; it is (to use the positivists' technical term) "cognitively meaningless," it does not measure up to the "verification criterion of meaning." On such grounds, the positivists dismissed metaphysical statements ("Mind is the absolute coming to self-consciousness") and theological statements ("God is love") as cognitively meaningless. Ethical statements ("Stealing is wrong") also were seen, not as statements of fact, but as expressions of attitude, commands, or some other non-informative type of language.[84]

As a general theory of meaningfulness, logical positivism was too crude to last very long. Disputes quickly arose over what methods of verification were to be tolerated, how conclusive the verification or falsification must be and other matters too technical to discuss here. Many felt that the whole project was to some extent a rationalization of prejudice—not an objective analysis of what constitutes "meaningfulness," but an attempt to get rid of language distasteful to various philosophers by constructing a "principle" arbitrarily designed for that purpose.[85]

No thinker of any consequence today subscribes to the "verification principle" as a general criterion of meaningfulness. One aspect of the positivists I concern, however, is very

83. One helpful discussion of these matters from an orthodox Christian perspective can be found in Gordon H. Clark, *Religion, Reason and Revelation* (Philadelphia: Presbyterian and Reformed, 1961), 111–50.

84. The classical exposition of logical positivism in the English language is A. J. Ayer, *Language, Truth and Logic* (New York: Dover, 1946).

85. One of the sharpest debates was over the status of the verification principle itself. Surely it was not to be regarded as a tautology; but it did not seem to be "verifiable" either in any quasi-scientific sense. Was it then to be dismissed as "cognitively meaningless"? Ayer himself (see previous note) came to the view that the verification principle was a "convention" (see his introduction to the anthology *Logical Positivism* [Glencoe, IL: Free Press, 1959], 15). He maintained that this "convention" had some basis in ordinary usage, but admitted that it went beyond ordinary usage in crucial respects.

much with us. Although we do not buy the whole logical positivist theory, many of us are quite impressed with the basic notion that a *fact ought to make a difference*. This concern is vividly presented in the oft-quoted parable of Antony Flew:

> Once upon a time two explorers came upon a clearing in the jungle. In the clearing were growing many flowers and many weeds. One explorer says, 'Some gardener must tend this plot.' So they pitch their tents and set a watch. No gardener is ever seen. 'But perhaps he is an invisible gardener.' So they set up a barbed-wire fence. They electrify it. They patrol with bloodhounds. (For they remember how H. G. Wells's *The Invisible Man* could be both smelt and touched though he could not be seen.) But no shrieks ever suggest that some intruder has received a shock. No movements of the wire ever betray an invisible climber. The bloodhounds never give cry. Yet still the Believer is not convinced. 'But there is a gardener, invisible, intangible, insensible to electric shocks, a gardener who has no scent and makes no sound, a gardener who comes secretly to look after the garden which he loves.' At last the Sceptic despairs, 'But what remains of your original assertion? Just how does what you call an invisible, intangible, eternally elusive gardener differ from an imaginary gardener or even from no gardener at all?'[86]

If there is *no difference* between "invisible gardener" and "no gardener," then surely the dispute between Believer and Sceptic is not about facts. If there is no difference, then talk of an "invisible gardener" may be a useful way of expressing an attitude toward the world, but it cannot make any empirical assertion about the world. Flew is not asking the Believer to verify his view in some quasi-scientific way (although one suspects that is what would make him most happy); he is simply asking him to state what *difference* his belief makes.

As we might suspect, Flew thinks that much language about God makes "no difference." Believers say that "God is love" even though the world is full of cruelty and hatred. How does such a God differ from a devil, or from no God at all? And if "God is love" makes no difference, how can it be a fact? How can it be, as the positivists liked to say, "cognitively meaningful"?

Flew does not suggest that *all* religious language succumbs to this difficulty, or even that all language about God is in jeopardy. He seems to be thinking mainly of what "often" happens in the thought of "sophisticated religious people."[87] Still, his knife cuts deep. Can any Christian believer offer a straightforward answer to Flew's concluding question, "What would have to occur or to have occurred to constitute for you a disproof of the love of, or of the existence of, God?"[88] Our first impulse is to say with the apostle Paul, "If Christ hath not been raised, then is our preaching vain, and your faith is also vain."[89] The Resurrection shows that God does make a difference! Disprove the Resurrection, and you disprove God. The Resurrection (but of course not only the Resurrection!) demonstrates the great difference between God and no-God. But push the argument back another step: What would have to occur or to have occurred to constitute for you a disproof of the *Resurrection*? Do we have a

---

86. Antony Flew, *et al.*, "Theology and Falsification," *New Essays in Philosophical Theology*, ed. Antony Flew and Alasdair MacIntyre (London: SCM Press, 1955), 96. [Editor's Note: As the title of Antony Flew's 2008 book *There Is a God: How the World's Most Notorious Atheist Changed His Mind* (New York: HarperOne, 2008) suggests, since the publication of his article "Theology and Falsification" in 1955 in *New Essays in Philosophical Theology* (cited here), Flew (d. 2010) changed from championing atheism to advocating deism.]

87. Ibid., 98.

88. Ibid., 99.

89. 1 Cor. 15:14.

clear idea of how the Resurrection may be falsified? Paul appeals to witnesses,[90] but the witnesses are dead. What if a collection of manuscripts were unearthed containing refutations of the Christian message by first century Palestinian Jews? And what if these manuscripts contained elaborate critiques of the Pauline claim in 1 Corinthians 15, critiques backed up with massive documentation, interviews with alleged witnesses, etc. And then: what if the twenty-five most important New Testament scholars claimed on the basis of this discovery that belief in the physical Resurrection of Christ was untenable!? Would that be sufficient to destroy our faith in the Resurrection? It would be hard to imagine any stronger sort of "falsification" for any event of past history. And I don't doubt that many would be swayed by it. But many would not be. I for one would entertain all sorts of questions about the biases of these documents and those of the scholars who interpreted them. I would want to check out the whole question myself before conceding the point of doctrine. And what if I did check it out and found no way of refuting the anti-Resurrection position? Would that constitute a disproof? Not for me, and I think not for very many professing Christians. We all know how abstruse scholarly argument can be; there are so many things that can go wrong! In such a situation, it is not difficult to say "Well, I can't prove the scholars wrong, but they may be wrong nonetheless." And if the love of Christ has become precious to me, and if I have been strongly convinced that the Bible is his word, I am more likely to believe what he says in 1 Corinthians 15 than to believe what a lot of scholars say on the basis of extra-biblical evidence. Could we *ever* be persuaded that the Resurrection was a hoax? Perhaps; but such a change would be more than a change in opinion; it would be a loss of faith. In terms of Scripture, such a change would be a yielding to temptation. For our God calls us to believe his Word even when the evidence appears against it! Sarah shall bear a son, even though she is ninety and her husband is a hundred![91] God is just, even though righteous Job must suffer! The heroes of the faith believed the Word of God *without* the corroboration of other evidence: they walked by faith, not by sight.[92] As long as we remain faithful, God's Word takes precedence over other evidence.

Flew's objection, therefore, is not to be lightly dismissed. There is a sense in which, not only the language of "sophisticated religious people" but even the language of simple Christian believers, fails to measure up to his challenge. God-language *resists* falsification. It is difficult to say what would refute a faith-assertion; for faith requires us to resist all temptation to doubt, within the faith-language, no terms can be specified for renouncing the faith-assertions; for faith *excludes, prohibits*, such renouncement.

Does this, then, mean that the Resurrection "makes no difference"? We hope not! We certainly want to say that it *does* make a difference. Yet we find it difficult to say what would refute our belief in the Resurrection. We find it difficult to conceive of any state of affairs in which we would abandon our belief. We find it difficult to say what the Resurrection rules out. And thus we find it difficult to state *what difference it makes*! Perhaps, then, talk of the Resurrection does not really concern any empirical fact. Perhaps all God-talk is cognitively meaningless. And perhaps, then, God cannot be spoken of at all in human language. And if that is true, all talk of Scripture as the Word of God is clearly nonsense.

90. 1 Cor. 15:5–8.
91. Gen. 17:16–17.
92. Heb. 11. The contrast between faith and sight alludes to 2 Cor. 5:7.

This, then, is the second form of the objection which I stated at the beginning of the paper, the second way in which human language is said to be disqualified as a medium of divine speech. Let us briefly examine the third form of the objection before presenting our response:

3. The third form of our objection is more distinctively theological. Karl Barth, for example, suggests on theological grounds that human language is unfit to convey truth about God:

> The pictures in which we view God, the thoughts in which we think Him, the words with which we can define Him, are in themselves unfitted to this object and thus inappropriate to express and affirm the knowledge of Him.[93]
>
> The Bible, further is not itself and in itself God's past revelation, but by becoming God's Word it attests God's past revelation and is God's past revelation in the form of attestation. . . . Attestation is, therefore, the service of this something else, in which the witness answers for the truth of this something else.[94]

This sort of point, which is very common in twentieth-century theology, is essentially a religious appeal to the divine transcendence. God is the Lord, the creator, the redeemer. To him belong all praise and glory. How can any human language ever be "fitted" to the conveyance of his word? Surely human language, like everything human and finite, can only be a servant, confessing its own *un*fitness, its own *in*adequacy. The Bible cannot *be* revelation; it can only *serve* revelation. To claim anything more for human language, for the Bible, is to dishonor God, to elevate something finite and human to divine status. To claim anything more is to think of revelation "in abstraction from" God himself and from Jesus Christ.[95] It is not just a mistake; it is an impiety.

At the same time, Barth does insist that the words of revelation have an importance:

> Thus God reveals Himself in propositions by means of language, and human language at that, to the effect that from time to time such and such a word, spoken by the prophets and apostles and proclaimed in the Church, becomes His Word. Thus the personality of the Word of God is not to be played off against its verbal character and spirituality.
>
> The personification of the concept of the Word of God . . . does not signify any lessening of its verbal character.[96]

The words are still unfit; they are not themselves revelation; they are not necessarily true themselves, but they witness to the truth of "something else." Nevertheless the words are important, because from time to time God may use them to communicate with man. Even when they are false, they are God's instruments. God uses them, however, not as true propositional representations of his message, but as the instruments for an encounter that no human language is fit to describe.

Barth, therefore, like Flew, argues that God cannot be truly spoken of in human language. Here, it would seem, the resemblance between Barth and Flew ceases; for Barth argues "from above," Flew "from below." Barth argues that God is too great for language; Flew argues that language cannot speak meaningfully of God. But are the two positions really that far

---

93. Karl Barth, *Church Dogmatics*, vol. 2, *The Doctrine of God*, ed. G. W. Bromiley and T. F. Torrance, trans. T. H. L. Parker, W. B. Johnston, H. Knight, and J. L. M. Haire (New York: Scribner, 1957), 1:188.

94. Karl Barth, *Church Dogmatics*, vol. 1, *The Doctrine of the Word of God*, ed. G. W. Bromiley and T. F. Torrance, trans. G. T. Thomson (New York: Scribner, 1936), 1:125.

95. Ibid., 155ff.

96. Ibid., 156–57.

apart? Thomas McPherson suggests that an alliance is possible between the logical positivist philosophers and theologians like Rudolph Otto (McPherson might also have cited Karl Barth in this connection) who stress the transcendence of God over language:

> Perhaps positivistic philosophy has done a service to religion. By showing, in their own way, the absurdity of what theologians try to utter, positivists have helped to suggest that religion belongs to the sphere of the unutterable. And this may be true. And it is what Otto, too, in his way, wanted to point out. Positivists may be the enemies of theology, but the friends of religion.[97]

Enemies of *some* theology!—not of Otto's theology, nor of Barth's, nor of Buber's (to which McPherson refers in a footnote), nor (I would judge) of the broad tradition of dialectical and existential theologies of the twentieth century. In positivism and in these modern theologies, God belongs to the sphere of the unutterable, and human language (when "cognitively meaningful") belongs to the sphere of the humanly verifiable. Let us then consider the Flew problem and the Barth problem as one.

Response

Religious language is "odd" in a great number of ways. Not only does it tend to resist falsification, as Flew has pointed out; it also tends to claim certainty for itself, as opposed to mere possibility or probability.[98] It also tends to be connected with *moral* predicates—as if disbelief in it were a *sin*, rather than a mere mistake.[99] It is frequently spoken with great passion; with Kierkegaard we tend to be suspicious of allegedly religious language which seems detached or uncommitted.

On the other hand, religious language is in some respects very "ordinary," very similar to other language. It is not a technical, academic language like that of physics or philosophy; it is the language of ordinary people. It is not restricted to some limited and distinctive compartment of human life; rather it enters into all human activities and concerns. We pray for the healing of a loved one, for help in a business crisis; we seek to "eat and drink to the glory of God."[100] I We believe that our faith "makes a difference" in the real world, that God can enter into all the affairs of our life and make his presence felt. In this respect, the "action of God in history" is like the action of *anyone* in history. God can change things, can make them different. And what he does does not occur unless he chooses to do it. God makes a difference, and in that sense he is *verifiable*—much as the existence of any person is verifiable (or so, at least, it appears to the simple believer!). Few religious people would claim that their faith is a blind leap in the dark. They have "reasons for faith." These reasons may be the technical theistic arguments of the philosophers, or simply the childlike appeal to experience, "He lives within my heart." One who really

---

97. Thomas McPherson, "Religion as the Inexpressible," *New Essays in Philosophical Theology*, ed. Antony Flew and Alasdair MacIntyre (London: SCM Press, 1955), 140–41. In a footnote, McPherson notes a similar view in Martin Buber's *I and Thou*, 2nd ed. (New York: Scribner, 1958).

98. Note Ludwig Wittgenstein's interesting discussion of this point in *Lectures and Conversations on Aesthetics, Psychology and Religious Belief, Compiled from Notes taken by Yorick Smythies, Rush Rhees and James Taylor*, ed. Cyril Barrett (Oxford: Blackwell, 1966), 53–59. Wittgenstein seems to make the extreme suggestion that religious belief *never* is "probable" in character. Wittgenstein obviously never spent much time around seminary students and academic theologians!

99. Cf. Ibid., 59.

100. 1 Cor. 10:31.

believes (as opposed to one who merely drifts along in a religious tradition) believes for a *reason*, because he thinks God has somehow made his presence felt, because God now *makes a difference*—to him!

Religious language, then, is "odd" and it is "ordinary." If an analysis of religious language is to be adequate, it must take *both* features into account, not just one of them. Flew and Barth do not reflect very much upon the "ordinariness" of religious language. They seem to imply that it is a sort of delusion, for it makes a claim to verifiability which cannot on analysis be sustained, or because it betrays a spirit of human pride, because it brings God down to man's level. For Barth at least, we gather that the "ordinariness" of religious language is a mark of its *humanity*, a mark of its *unfitness* to convey the word of God. There is, however, another interpretation of the data—one which does not write off the "ordinariness" of religious language as a delusion, one which accounts both for the verifiability of religious statements and for their tendency to resist verification, one which illumines the ways in which Scripture itself speaks of God.

Religious language is language of *basic conviction*. It is the language by which we state, invoke, honor, advocate (and otherwise "bring to bear") those things of which we are most certain, those things which are most important to us, those things which we will cling to even though we must lose all else. Not all language of "basic conviction" is religious in the usual sense. Many people who consider themselves irreligious have "basic convictions" of some sort. In fact, it may well be disputed whether anyone can avoid having *some* basic conviction—whether it be a faith in reason, in material success, in a philosophical absolute, or in a god. But all language which *is* religious in the usual sense is language of basic conviction.

Someone may object that for many people their religion is *not* their most basic commitment. A man may mumble through the church liturgy every Sunday while devoting his existence almost exclusively to acquiring political power. For him, surely, the liturgy does *not* express his "basic commitment." True; but that is because there is something wrong! A man like this we call a hypocrite; for the liturgy is *intended* to express basic conviction and our fanatical politician utters the words deceitfully. He does not *really* "believe in God, the father almighty" in the sense of biblical faith, though he says he does. His real faith is in something else. The man is a liar. But his lying use of the language does not change the meaning of it, which is to confess true faith in God.

All of us have basic convictions, unless possibly we are just confused. Positivists do too—and Barthians! And insofar as we try to be consistent, we try to bring all of life and thought into accord with that basic conviction.[101] Nothing inconsistent with that conviction is to be tolerated. An inconsistency of that sort amounts to a divided loyalty, a confusion of

---

101. Some readers may be helped here by the observation that there are many different degrees of "basicness" among our convictions. All of our convictions govern life to some degree. When someone disagrees with one of our opinions, we naturally tend to try to defend it—either to refute our opponent's argument or to show that his position is compatible with ours. The learning process is such that we always try to interpret new knowledge in such a way as to minimize disturbance to past opinions. Some opinions we hold more tenaciously than others. It is fairly easy to convince me that I am wrong about, say, the team batting average of the Pittsburgh Pirates. It is much more difficult to persuade me that the earth is flat! In the first instance, citation of one presumable competent authority is enough. In the second instance, the intrinsic unlikelihood of a flat earth would bring into question the competence of any "presumably competent authority" who held such a position. Nevertheless, if there were a full-scale revolution among scientists over systems of measurement, and cogent reasons could be given for reverting to a flat earth view, I might be persuaded to reconsider. Some convictions, then, we relinquish less easily than others; and the "most basic convictions" (which we focus upon in the text of the article) are relinquished least easily of all. In fact, we *never* relinquish those unless at the same time we change in our basic concept of rationality.

life-direction. Most of us, at least, try to avoid such confusion. The conviction becomes the paradigm of reality, of truth and of right, to which all other examples of reality, truth and right must measure up. As such, it is the cornerstone of our metaphysics, epistemology and ethics. It is not, be it noted, the *only* factor in the development of a system of thought. Two people may have virtually identical "basic commitments" while differing greatly in their systems of thought. The two will both try to develop systems according with their common presupposition, but because of differences in experience, ability, secondary commitments and the like, they may seek such consistency in opposite directions. But though the "basic commitment" is not the *only* factor in the development of thought (and life), it is (by definition) the most important factor.

We have suggested that religious language is a subdivision of "basic-commitment language." The next point is that basic commitment language in general displays the same kinds of "oddness" and "ordinariness" that we have noted in religious language. We state our basic commitments as certainties, not merely as possibilities or probabilities, because our basic commitments are the things of which we are most sure, the paradigms of certainty against which all other certainties are measured. Basic commitments are paradigms, too, of *righteousness*; challenges to those commitments invariably seem to us unjust because such challenges if successful will deny our whole reason for living. And basic-commitment language is (almost tautologically) the language of *commitment*, not of detached objectivity. And to these "oddnesses" we must add the oddness of resistance to falsification.

Take a man whose basic commitment in life is the earning of money. To him, the legitimacy of that goal is a *certainty*, beyond all question. When that goal conflicts with other goals, the basic goal must prevail. Questions and doubts, indeed, may enter his mind; but these questions and doubts are much like religious temptations. Insofar as he takes them seriously, he compromises his commitment; he becomes to that extent double-minded, unstable. He faces then a crisis wherein he is challenged to change his basic commitment. Under such pressure he may do so. But then the new commitment will demand the same kind of loyalty as the old one. Challenges *must* be resisted. Evidence against the legitimacy of the commitment must be somehow either ignored, suppressed, or accounted for in a way that leaves the commitment intact. "Are people starving in India? We must be compassionate, of course; but the best means of helping the poor is by teaching them the virtues of free enterprise and self-help: if everyone were truly dedicated to earning money there would be no poverty. We do them no favor by compromising our commitment"! A rationalization? It might not seem so to one so committed, especially if no other answer to the poverty question lies close at hand.

Let us rephrase Flew's question as it might be addressed to the mammon-worshipper: What would have to occur or to have occurred to constitute for you a disproof of the primacy of money-making? What would have to happen to cause him to abandon his faith? Well, one simply cannot say in advance! Committed as he is, he devoutly hopes that *nothing* will bring about such a change. He not only hopes, he *knows* (or so he thinks)—because he interprets all reality so as to accord with that commitment. Some event, indeed (we can't say what), may cause him to change—if he yields to the temptation of regarding that event from a non-mammon perspective. He changes them because he has already compromised; it is like a change in religious faith.

The basic-commitment language is "odd" indeed; but it is also "ordinary." It is not something strange or esoteric; we use it all the time. It enters into every area of life, simply because it is so basic, so important. It is important because it "makes a difference"—more difference than anything else. Without it nothing would make sense. All of experience, then, "verifies" the validity of the commitment. We can "prove" our commitment true in any number of ways. The evidence is there.

But how can a commitment be verifiable and nonverifiable at the same time? How can it present proof, and at the same time resist falsification by contrary evidence? The resolution of this paradox gets us to the heart of the matter. Think of a philosopher who is committed to establishing all truth by the evidence of his senses. Sense-experience is his criterion of truth. What evidence would disprove that criterion? In one sense none; for if sense-experience is truly his criterion, then all objections to the criterion will have to be verified through sense-experience. They will have to be tested by the criterion they oppose. "Disproof," as with other basic commitments, will come only when there is something like a crisis of faith. At the same time, all evidence *proves* the criterion. The philosopher will argue very learnedly to establish his conviction. He will refute contrary claims, he will produce carefully constructed arguments.

The arguments, of course, will be "circular." Arguments for the sense-criterion must be verified by the sense-criterion itself. The philosopher must argue for sense-experience by appealing to sense-experience. What choice does he have? If he appeals to something else as his final authority, he is simply being inconsistent. But this is the case with any "basic commitment." When we are arguing on behalf of an absolute authority, then our final appeal must be to that authority and no other. A proof of the primacy of reason must appeal to reason; a proof of the necessity of logic must appeal to logic; a proof of the primacy of mammon must itself be part of an attempt to earn more money; and a proof of the existence of God must appeal in the final analysis to God.

Such arguments are circular; but they are also arguments. A "proof" of, say, the primacy of reason, can be highly persuasive and logically sound even though, at one level, circular. The circularity is rarely blatant; it lurks in the background. One never says "Reason is true because reason says it is." One says instead, "Reason is true because one must presuppose it even to deny it." The second argument is just as circular as the first. Both presuppose the validity of reason. But in the second argument the presupposition is implicit rather than explicit. And the second one is highly persuasive! The irrationalist cannot help but note that he is (in many cases) presenting his irrationalism in a highly rational way. He is trying to be more rational than the rationalists—a contradictory way to be! He must decide either to be a more consistent irrationalist (but note the paradox of that!) or to abandon his irrationalism. Of course he might renounce consistency altogether, thus renouncing the presupposition of the argument. But the argument shows him vividly how *hard* it is to live without rationality. The argument is circular, but it draws some important facts to his attention. The argument is persuasive though circular because down deep in our hearts we *know* that we cannot live without reason.[102]

102. *How* do we know? That's hard to say; but we do. Some circular arguments simply are more plausible than others. "Truth is a giant onion, for all true statements are onion shoots in disguise." That argument is best interpreted as a circular one, the conclusion being presupposed in the reason offered. But there is something *absurd* about it. "Reason is necessary,

Some circular arguments are persuasive to us, others not. Those circular arguments which verify the most basic commitments of our lives are by definition the *most* persuasive to us. And because we believe those commitments true, we believe that those arguments ought to be persuasive to others too. A Christian theist, while conceding that the argument for God's existence is circular, nevertheless will claim that the argument is sound and persuasive. For he devoutly believes that his position is true, and he believes that it can be recognized clearly as such. He believes that God made men to think in terms of *this* circularity, rather than in terms of some competing circularity.[103]

Basic-commitment language, therefore, is both "odd" and "ordinary"; it resists falsification, it refuses to be judged by some antithetical commitment; yet it accepts the responsibility to verify itself. It accepts the responsibility of displaying whatever rationality and consistency it may claim.

What is Antony Flew's "basic commitment"? To reason? To "academic integrity" of some sort? To a secular ethic? To religious agnosticism? I don't know, but I would assume that he has one, since he does not seem like the sort of person who accepts values unreflectively. And more can be said: If with the Bible we divide the human race into Christian and non-Christian, those who know God and those who don't, those who love God and those who oppose him, clearly Flew by his writings has identified himself with the God-opposing group. If this self-identification truly represents his heart commitment, then according to Scripture Flew is committed to "hindering the truth" of God, "exchanging the truth of God for a lie."[104] According to Scripture, he is committed at a basic level to opposing, contradicting, resisting the truth of God which in some sense he nevertheless "knows."[105] This commitment too will be unfalsifiable and yet self-verifying, for it is a basic commitment;

---

for one must use reason even in order to deny it." That too, is circular, but it seems much more plausible. A sceptic might say that the second argument seems plausible because it is *our* argument, while the first is not.

"Knowledge" itself is dreadfully hard to define. Logicians, epistemologists and scientists have devoted countless hours to the task of finding criteria for genuine knowledge. Yet knowledge may not be defined as the observance of any such criteria. Knowledge occurred in human life long before there was any science of logic or epistemology or biology, and people still gain knowledge without referring to such disciplines. These disciplines try to conceptualize, define, understand a phenomenon which exists independently of those disciplines. They do not make knowledge possible. And their concepts of knowledge change rather frequently. It would be presumptuous indeed to suppose that these disciplines have succeeded at last in defining everything which constitutes "knowledge." Thus, if the recognition of plausibility in a circular argument does not fit any existing technical criteria of "knowledge," then so much the worse for those criteria.

The fact is that recognition of such plausibility is a type of knowledge which epistemologists are obligated to note and account for. "Basic convictions" cannot be avoided; and such convictions may be proved only through circular argument. Therefore circular argument is unavoidable, at the level of basic conviction. This sort of circularity is not a defect in one system as opposed to others. It is an element of all systems. It is part of the human condition. It is altogether natural, then, that the term "knowledge" be applied to basic convictions, and if no technical account has yet been given of this sort of knowledge, then such an account is overdue.

Within a particular system, the basic convictions are not only truths; they are the most certain of truths, the criteria of other truths. If we deny the term "knowledge" to these greatest of all certainties, then no lesser certainty can be called "knowledge" either. And no epistemologist may adopt a view which, by doing away with all knowledge, does away with his job! Knowledge is not an ideal; it is not something which we strive for and never attain. It is a commonplace of everyday life. It is the job of epistemologists to account for that commonplace, not to define it out of existence. One may not define "knowledge" in such a way as to require us to transcend our humanity in order to know. One must defer to the commonplace. And "knowledge of basic principles" is part of that commonplace.

103. These are the terms in which the matter must be phrased. The controversy is between competing circularities, not between circularity and non-circularity.

104. Rom. 1:18–25

105. Rom. 1:19–21a; note the phrase *gnontes ton theon*, "knowing God."

and for all its irreligiosity it is logically like a religious commitment. Let us illustrate by a parody on Flew's parable:

> Once upon a time two explorers came upon a clearing in the jungle. A man was there, pulling weeds, applying fertilizer, trimming branches. The man turned to the explorers and introduced himself as the royal gardener. One explorer shook his hand and exchanged pleasantries. The other ignored the gardener and turned away: "There can be no gardener in this part of the jungle," he said; "this must be some trick. Someone is trying to discredit our previous findings." They pitch camp. Every day the gardener arrives, tends the plot. Soon the plot is bursting with perfectly arranged blooms. "He's only doing it because we're here—to fool us into thinking this is a royal garden." The gardener takes them to a royal palace, introduces the explorers to a score of officials who verify the gardener's status. Then the sceptic tries a last resort: "Our senses are deceiving us. There is no gardener, no blooms, no palace, no officials. It's still a hoax!" Finally the believer despairs: "But what remains of your original assertion? Just how does this mirage, as you call it, differ from a real gardener?"

A garden indeed! How convenient that we should be talking about gardens—for that is where the Bible's own story begins. Adam and Eve lived in a garden, and they knew the divine Gardener. He talked to them, worked with them, lived with them; until one day Eve—and Adam!—denied that he was there. Irrational it was, for sin is at its root irrational. And Scripture tells us that ever since that day sinners have been guilty of the same irrationality. God is verifiable, knowable, "clearly seen" in his works;[106] but men still—"irrationally" because sinfully—deny him. To the Christian, the denials lapse into cognitive meaninglessness—an attempt to evade God by using atheistic language to describe a patently theistic world.

From a "neutral" point of view, both Flew and the Christian are in the same boat. Both have beliefs which are "odd" and "ordinary"; resistant to falsification, yet verifiable on their own terms. But of course there is no "neutral" point of view. You are either for God or against Him. You must place yourself in one circle or the other. Logically, both systems face the difficulties of circularity. But one is true and the other is false. And if man is made to know such things, then you can tell the difference. You *know* you can!

Our response to Flew, in short, is that (1) He has only told half the story: religious language does resist falsification, as he says; but it also often claims to be verifiable in terms of its own presuppositions. (2) These epistemological peculiarities attach to all "basic-commitment language," not just to religious or Christian language—and thus they attach to unbelieving language as well. Therefore, these considerations may not be urged as a criticism of Christianity. They are simply descriptive of the human epistemological condition. (3) Scripture pictures the *unbeliever* as the truly ridiculous figure, who ignores patent evidence and makes mockery of reason, on whose basis *no* knowledge is possible. To the Christian, the unbelieving circle is, or ought to be, absurd: something like "Truth is a giant onion; therefore truth is a giant onion."

Flew, therefore, does not succeed in showing religious language to be "cognitively meaningless"; and therefore he fails to show that human language cannot speak of God. But what of the third form of our objection? What of Karl Barth? Should we simply leave him behind?

---

106. Rom. 1:20.

Let us go back to the "oddness" and "ordinariness" of religious language, and Christian language in particular. The oddness of Christian language derives from the transcendence of God, and the ordinariness of it derives from God's immanence. Christian language is odd because it is the language of basic commitment; and the transcendence of God's Lordship demands that our commitment be basic. This language is odd because it expresses our most ultimate presuppositions; and these presuppositions are the demands which God makes upon us—nothing less. It is odd because it attempts to convey God's demands—his demands for all of life. It will not be "falsified" by some secular philosophical criterion, because God will not be judged by such a criterion. "Let God be true, though every man a liar."[107] God's own word, the paradigm of all Christian language, is therefore *supremely* odd.

Christian language is "ordinary," verifiable, because God is not only the transcendent Lord; he is also "with us," close to us. These two attributes do not conflict with one another. God is close to us *because* he is Lord. He is Lord, and thus free to make his power felt everywhere we go. He is Lord, and thus able to reveal himself clearly to us, distinguishing himself from all mere creatures. He is Lord, and therefore the most central fact of our experience, the least avoidable, the most verifiable.

And because God's own word is supremely odd, it is supremely ordinary. Because it is supremely authoritative, it is supremely verifiable. Because it furnishes the ultimate presuppositions of thought, it furnishes the ultimate *truths* of thought.

Barth's argument essentially reverses this picture (derived from Scripture) of God's transcendence and immanence. To Barth, God's transcendence implies that he *cannot* be clearly revealed to men, clearly represented by human words and concepts. This view of God's transcendence contradicts the view of God's immanence which we presented. Similarly, Barth has a view of God's immanence which contradicts the view of transcendence which we presented. To Barth, the immanence of God implies that words of merely human authority, words which are fallible, may from time to time "become" the word of God. Thus the only authority we have, in the final analysis, is a fallible one. The only "word of God" we have is a fallible human word. God does not make authoritative demands which require unconditional belief; he does not determine the presuppositions of our thought; he does not resist all falsification—rather he endorses falsehood and sanctifies it.

Well, who is right? Does God's transcendence include or exclude an authoritative verbal revelation of himself to men? Note that this question must be faced squarely. It is not enough to say that revelation must be seen in the context of God's transcendence; for that transcendence has been understood in different ways, and one must therefore defend his particular view of it. One does not get into the heart of the matter by saying that one view sees revelation "in abstraction from" God's lordship; for the two sides do not agree on the nature of this lordship or the relation that revelation is supposed to sustain to that lordship.

Both views claim Scriptural support. Barth can appeal to the basic creator-creature relationship as presented in Scripture: man is a creature; his ultimate trust must rest solely in God. To put ultimate confidence in something finite is idolatry. Human words are finite. Therefore to put ultimate confidence in Scripture is idolatry. And in a fallen world, such confidence is all the more foolish; for human words are sinful as well as finite. Sinful speech can never perfectly honor God. The Gospel precisely requires us to *disown* any claim to per-

107. Rom. 3:4.

fection, to confess the *inadequacy* of all human works, to cast all our hope on the mercy of God. How can we put ultimate trust in human words and in God's mercy at the same time?

Barth's view can be stated very persuasively as long as it focuses on the general facts of creation and redemption. Scripture *does* condemn idolatry; it *does* condemn reliance on merely human means of salvation. But when this view turns specifically to the concept of revelation, its unbiblical character becomes obvious. For Scripture itself never deduces from God's transcendence the inadequacy and fallibility of all verbal revelation. Quite to the contrary: in Scripture, verbal revelation is to be obeyed without question, *because* of the divine transcendence:

> Hear, O Israel: The Lord our God is one Lord: and thou shalt love the Lord thy God with all thy heart, and with all thy soul, and with all thy might. And these words, which I command thee this day, shall be in thy heart; and thou shalt teach them diligently unto thy children, and shalt talk of them when thou sittest in thy house, and when thou walkest by the way, and when thou liest down, and when thou risest up. . . . Ye shall diligently keep the commandments of the Lord your God, and his testimonies, and his statutes, which he hath commanded thee.[108]

One who serves God as Lord will obey his verbal revelation without question. One who loves Christ as Lord will keep his commandments.[109] God's lordship, transcendence, demands unconditional belief in and obedience to the words of revelation; it *never* relativizes or softens the authority of these words. But how can that be? Is Scripture itself guilty of idolizing human words? The answer is simply that Scripture does not regard verbal revelation as merely human words. Verbal revelation, according to Scripture, is the Word of *God*, as well as the word of man. As with the incarnate Christ, verbal revelation has divine qualities as well as human qualities. Most particularly, it is divine as to its *authority*. To obey God's word is to obey *Him*; to disobey God's word is to disobey *Him*. Unconditional obedience to verbal revelation is not idolatry of human words; it is simply a recognition of the divinity of God's own words. It is the deference which we owe to God as our creator and redeemer.

Dishonoring the divine is just as sinful as idolizing the creature. The two are inseparable. To disobey God is to obey something less than God. When we turn from God's words, we idolize human words. If Scripture is right, if verbal revelation does have divine authority, then it is Barth's view which encourages idolatry. For Barth's view would turn us away from proper deference to God's words, and would have us instead make a "basic commitment" to the truth of some other words—our own, perhaps, or those of scientists, or those of theologians.

These considerations do not prove that Scripture is the word of God. They do show, however, that the biblical doctrine of divine transcendence does not compromise the authority of verbal revelation. One may, indeed, prefer Barth's concept of transcendence to the biblical one; but such a view may not be paraded and displayed as the authentic Christian position.

We conclude, then, that the "objection" before us is unsound in all of its three forms. Human language *may* convey the infallible word of God, because God is *Lord*—even of human language!

---

108. Deut. 6:4–7, 17.
109. John 14:15, 21, 23; 15:10. On these matters, cf. my other essay, "Scripture Speaks for Itself" [see the previous selection in this chapter of the anthology].

58

Harmonization: A Help
and a Hindrance

RAYMOND B. DILLARD

Raymond B. Dillard, "9. Harmonization: A Help and a Hindrance," in *Inerrancy and Hermeneutic*, 151–64.

Raymond Dillard was professor of Old Testament at Westminster Theological Seminary from 1971 until his untimely death in 1993. He studied at Westminster Theological Seminary and earned a Ph.D. from Dropsie University. Dillard was an inspiring teacher, eager to disclose how Christ could be seen in the Old Testament. He had a special interest in the study of the Chronicler; his efforts culminated in the writing of a commentary on 2 Chronicles in 1987 for the distinguished series The Word Biblical Commentary. He also cowrote with Tremper Longman III the widely used textbook *An Introduction to the Old Testament* (1994).

In "Harmonization: A Help and a Hindrance," Dillard tackles the complex and controversial question of harmonization; indeed, many difficulties arise when trying to compare parallel passages in the Bible. In the Westminster tradition, Stonehouse had already paved the way to better understand the distinctiveness of each Synoptic Gospel, thus offering a different perspective on harmonization (see the comments of Silva in chap. 41). In Old Testament studies, the issue appears especially in relation to the parallel accounts of 1 Samuel to 2 Kings and 1 and 2 Chronicles. In "Harmonization," Dillard revisits this problem and offers insights from his research and perspective on the Bible as the Word of God. He deals with the apparent contradictions of Scripture, commenting on both the positives and negatives of harmonization, or the attempt to reconcile two apparently contradictory texts. Dillard offers criteria to know when it is appropriate to harmonize texts and when one must avoid doing so. Perhaps his distinct contribution is to pay closer attention to different genres in Scripture and allow the various voices of the human authors of Scripture to be more clearly heard.

Bibliography: M. Patrick Graham, Kenneth G. Hoglund, and Steven L. McKenzie, eds. *The Chronicler as Historian.* Journal for the Study of the Old Testament: Supplement Series 238. Sheffield: Sheffield Academic Press, 1997. "In Memoriam: Raymond Bryan Dillard (1944–93)." *WTJ* 55, 2 (Fall 1993): ii–iii. "Memorials: Raymond Bryan Dillard." *Journal of the Evangelical Theological Society* 37, 1 (March 1994): 155–56. John J. Yeo. *Plundering the Egyptians: The Old Testament and Historical Criticism at Westminster Seminary (1929–1998).* Lanham, MD: University Press of America, 2010. Pp. 207–78.

It may very well be that there are some passages which, save by strained and forced attempts, we cannot harmonize. If such is the case, by all means let us be sufficiently honest and candid to admit that we cannot harmonize the particular passages in question; for to employ strained and forced methods of harmonization is not intellectually honest. If we do employ such methods, we shall only bring upon our heads the deserved charge of intellectual dishonesty. Far better it is to admit our inability than to produce harmonization at the expense of honesty and integrity. Much as we might wish that we could explain all difficulties, we can console ourselves with the thought—and a true thought it is—that those who have rejected the Biblical doctrine of inspiration have far greater problems and difficulties to solve, and that, upon the basis upon which they proceed, these difficulties cannot be solved.

—Edward J. Young, 1957

Much of the debate about the integrity of the Bible has centered on its apparent contradictions and discrepancies in matters of historical detail. The synoptic portions of the Bible (Samuel—Kings and Chronicles; the Gospels) provide the primary exhibits of what are considered factual lapses, though the range of evidence is by no means confined to parallel passages.[1] Harmonization is the effort to provide scenarios by which two apparently contradictory statements or one improbable statement can be considered historically accurate.[2] Where one Gospel puts Jesus' sermon on a mountain (Matt. 5:1) and another on level ground (Luke 6:17), the harmonist replies by suggesting that there was a plateau on the side of the mountain or that Jesus gave the same sermon in different locales; the factuality of both texts is thereby preserved. Such apparent discrepancies are reasonably common in the Bible and characteristically involve numerical contradictions, chronological and geographical dislocations, different quotations of what appear to be the same speech, or similar types of problems. A number of handbooks attempt to provide a catalogue and an answer to many of these problems.[3]

1. For a history of preparing synopses of the parallel portions of the Bible, see Ronald Youngblood, "From Tatian to Swanson, from Calvin to Bendavid: The Harmonization of Biblical History," *Journal of the Evangelical Theological Society* 25 (1982): 415–23.

2. I am defining harmonization primarily in terms of what Craig Blomberg has called "additive harmonization" ("The Legitimacy and Limits of Harmonization," in *Hermeneutics, Authority, and Canon*, ed. D. A. Carson and J. D. Woodbridge [Grand Rapids: Zondervan, 1986], 135–74). The scope of his article is considerably wider than intended here, and the taxonomy of harmonistic solutions he offers is helpful.

3. As examples, see John W. Haley, *An Examination of the Alleged Discrepancies of the Bible* (Boston: Estes and Lauriat, 1881), and Gleason Archer, *An Encyclopedia of Bible Difficulties* (Grand Rapids: Zondervan, 1982).

Is a harmonistic component in exegesis a necessary and inevitable consequence of the doctrine of inerrancy? Or conversely, is rejection of harmonistic exegesis or reluctance to practice it equivalent to a rejection of inerrancy? What role should harmonization play in biblical studies? These are inherently difficult questions, and they are complicated by the considerable theological and emotional investment many have in the answers. Many evangelicals consider answers to questions in this area as somewhat of a theological watershed, a convenient touchstone or shibboleth dividing acceptable and unacceptable views about the Bible. I have a friend who is fond of saying that "for every difficult, complex, hard question there is always a simple, clear, unambiguous, wrong answer." It is tempting to want a quick and easy answer to these questions, but the set of issues involved requires more than a simple slogan. A summary of the assets and liabilities involved in harmonization will hopefully clarify the issues. I will draw primarily from Chronicles for illustrative purposes; it has been the focus of my own work for some time and presents some of the most interesting and difficult material.

Harmonization as a Help—Its Assets

Its Inevitability

The question is not "should we harmonize or not," for harmonization is a virtually universal and inevitable feature of daily life. At home parents confront sharply differing versions of a recent squabble between children, the children often sincerely believing their own accounts and arranging the data to make a particular point, usually their own innocence and the culpability of the other combatant. The parent hears both accounts and tries to create a scenario closer to "reality," that is, closer to what a more detached observer would have reported or what would have been recorded on videotape. A close and trusted friend who is a salesman calls on you at your office and extols the virtue of the equipment he would like to sell, while you are left trying to reconcile his account with the complaints of other friends who use this item regularly in their own offices. Encounters like these are regular features of daily life. You hope that, if a friend hears information that appears to be in tension with something that you have told him, he will at least mentally reconcile the discrepancies or investigate further before accusing you of falsehood or error. One must give the Scriptures the same benefit of doubt. This daily reconciliation of observed discrepancies is part and parcel with harmonization as a component of exegesis. It is an inevitable and natural reaction. One cannot a priori or simplistically repudiate harmonization of biblical data without contradicting what would be a routine and natural response to data in other areas of life. Harmonization in this sense appears to be a universal convention of human reasoning. Scholars writing from within almost any theological or critical stance in theory make allowance for harmonization in exegesis, though in practice factual difficulties are the grist from which scholars compose theories of sources, redaction, and so on, and efforts to harmonize are often dismissed with ridicule. Such facile rejection too often forgets the realities of daily life.

Its Antiquity

Harmonization in biblical studies did not develop de novo among religious conservatives after the Enlightenment as a way of defending their view of Scripture. Quite to the contrary, if harmonization is a routine and universal activity applied to many facets of life, one would expect to find harmonization practiced in antiquity as well. There is ample evidence that this was so.

One could argue that a certain amount of intrabiblical exegesis reflects this effort.[4] In his treatment of Hezekiah, the Chronicler omits the report of Hezekiah's submission to Sennacherib and his despoliation of the temple (2 Kings 18:14–16); it is out of accord with his generally positive portrayal of Hezekiah and does not fit well with the deliverance of Jerusalem as reported in both Kings and Chronicles (2 Kings 19:35–37; 2 Chron. 32:20–23). The Chronicler also eliminates the double appearance of the Rab-shaqeh before the city (2 Kings 18:17–19:9a, 36–37; and 2 Kings 19:9b–35) and integrates these into a single appearance (2 Chron. 32:9–19), perhaps suggesting he recognized the accounts in Kings as parallel texts of the same event.[5] At a larger level, the Book of Kings, which explains the fall of the kingdoms and the end of the temple to an exilic audience (2 Kings 17:7–23; 21:1–15), has been viewed as harmonizing these events with the earlier promises of God to Israel concerning the temple and David's descendants. Kings is a theodicy—it justifies God's actions to human beings; theodicy is by its very nature a sort of harmonization. The ancient scribes also practiced harmonization with some regularity. Many textual variations reflect not copying errors but the efforts of the scribes to reconcile tension in historical details. Consider two examples, 1 Chronicles 29:22 and 2 Chronicles 22:8.[6]

Chronicles contains a quite different account of the transfer of power from David to Solomon than that found in Kings.[7] In First Kings 1, an aged and bedridden David faces a coup supported by members of the royal household, cultic officers, and the military (vv. 7–9); the kingdom is saved for Solomon only by the intervention of Bathsheba and Nathan, just in the nick of time. Solomon's anointing as king was hastily done; David himself could not attend his own son's anointing (vv. 28–40). The picture in Chronicles contrasts sharply (1 Chron. 28–29). David presides over a national assembly (28:1) and specifically names his son Solomon as his successor and charges him with the construction of the temple. Solomon receives the immediate and wholehearted support of all the people (29:21–30), including specifically (v. 24) those who in 1 Kings 1:9 supported Adonijah's attempt to seize power.[8] In the Masoretic text (MT) of 1 Chronicles 29:22, it is reported that Solomon was made king a *second* time. However, the word *second* is not found in LXX(B) or the Peshitta. Since 1 Chronicles does mention that Solomon was made king at an earlier point (23:1), the best explanation of this textual difficulty would be that a scribe inserted the word *second* to harmonize the two references in Chronicles to Solomon's being made king.

In Second Chronicles 22:8, the LXX reports that Jehu found and killed the "brothers of Ahaziah," while the MT reports that he killed "the sons of the brothers of Ahaziah." A

---

4. Michael A. Fishbane (*Biblical Interpretation in Ancient Israel* [Oxford: Clarendon Press, 1985], 221–28) suggests a process of harmonization and correction in Pentateuchal legal materials and other corpora of the Old Testament.

5. This is one of the *cruxes* of modern Old Testament study. A recent article by Dana Fewell ("Sennacherib's Defeat: Words at War in 2 Kings 18:13–19:37," *Journal for the Study of the Old Testament* 34 [1986]: 79–90) provides a fresh approach which views the mutiple accounts in Kings from the vantage of aesthetic or literary criticism; she presents an insightful reading of the pericope that concludes that the text is a cohesive unit.

6. Raymond Dillard, "Reward and Punishment in Chronicles: The Theology of Immediate Retribution," *WTJ* 46 (1984): 164–72; or idem, *Second Chronicles,* Word Biblical Commentary 15 (Waco: Word, 1987), 76–81.

7. Raymond Dillard, "The Chronicler's Solomon," *WTJ* 43 (1980): 289–300; or idem, *Second Chronicles,* chs. 1–7.

8. It should be noted that 1 Kings 1:51 reports that Adonijah acceded to Solomon's rule after his abortive effort; presumably this change of heart included his supporters.

number of explanations for this small variation are possible. Perhaps the most compelling of these is that a scribe inserted the word for "sons" into the MT in order to harmonize this account with his awareness that the "brothers of Ahaziah" had already been killed (21:17; 22:1; cf. 2 Kings 10:13–14).[9]

Examples from the period of the scribes could be multiplied many times. Some of the variations in the textual witnesses to the chronological notes in Kings probably represent harmonistic efforts on the part of the scribes. Their harmonizations were not confined to matters of historical detail. They included, for example, assimilating parallel passages in Jeremiah to one another, leveling differences in legal formulations, and so forth.[10]

Its Contributions

Though it is ordinarily impossible to prove a harmonization right or wrong, in a few instances harmonistic approaches to biblical texts have led to fairly certain results. Nebuchadnezzar, king of Babylon, set siege to Jerusalem in the third year of Jehoiakim, according to Daniel 1:1, though Jeremiah 25:1 equates Jehoiakim's fourth year with Nebuchadnezzar's first. The reference to Nebuchadnezzar as king in Daniel 1:1 is readily explained as a prolepsis: he is given this title in anticipation of his accession. Few would quarrel that this is a satisfactory explanation. However, Edwin Thiele provided an alternate explanation for this and many similar phenomena in Old Testament chronologies.[11] Two distinctions crucial to his approach (the distinction between accession-year reckoning and non-accession-year reckoning and between Nisan or Tishri as the first month of the year) have accounted for many problem passages and apparent discrepancies. Since the great empires around Israel varied in their calendrical and regnal reckoning, there is archaeological data making it reasonable to expect a mix of these systems in biblical chronologies. Though Thiele's system may not ultimately achieve consensus in all its particulars,[12] anyone working in Old Testament chronologies must grapple with his approach. Its explanatory power is sufficiently great that it cannot be simply dismissed as "unconscionably harmonistic."

Its Respect for the Author

Oswald Allis cites with approval the advice of Coleridge that, "when we meet an apparent error in a good author, we are to presume ourselves ignorant of his understanding, until we are certain that we understand his ignorance."[13] In this regard, harmonistic exegesis has much in common with aesthetic or literary-critical approaches to the Bible. Phenomena which in the past were most frequently regarded as evidence of editorial bumbling now find their explanation as features of fairly sophisticated literary devices used by skilful authors. The Chronicler reports the appearance of the glory cloud twice at the dedication of Solomon's temple (2 Chron. 5:13–14 [note the parallel in 1 Kings 8:10–11] and 7:1–3). This fact is ordi-

9. There was no need for the scribal correction; no contradiction exists if the Hebrew word for "brothers" is translated by another legitimate sense, "relatives." The same ambiguity attaches to the Greek term. Cf. the similar issue in 2 Chron. 36:10: Zedekiah was the uncle, rather than the brother, of Jehoiachin.

10. Fishbane, *Biblical Interpretation in Ancient Israel*, 220–21.

11. Edwin Thiele, *The Mysterious Numbers of the Hebrew Kings,* rev. ed. (Grand Rapids: Zondervan, 1983).

12. Raymond Dillard, "The Reign of Asa (2 Chron. 14–16): An Example of the Chronicler's Theological Method," *Journal of the Evangelical Theological Society* 23 (1980): 207–18.

13. O. T. Allis, *The Five Books of Moses* (Nutley, N.J.: Presbyterian and Reformed, 1964), 125.

narily explained as the forgetfulness of some later editor who inserted a second report of the appearance of the cloud at the same place where it is found in the parallel text of Kings. However, a far better explanation regards the double appearance of the glory cloud as one feature of a chiastic device the Chronicler has used to fashion his entire account of Solomon's reign.[14] Similar examples could be multiplied in other contexts or books of the Bible.

Its Theological Warrant

Though all of the above considerations play a role, harmonization draws its principal operating strength from its theological warrant. God is true and cannot lie, and the Scriptures share in this attribute. The incarnational analogy is fundamental: just as the living Word was divine and without error, so also the written Word. More than any other single factor, it is the belief in the divine origin and authority of the Bible that has given harmonization its hold in exegetical method. The work of exegesis is influenced or controlled by an overriding apologetic concern.

Harmonization as a Hindrance—Its Liabilities

Harmonization is used primarily as a tool for solving problems; however, it is not itself free of difficulties.

Its Arbitrariness

Harmonizations are too often offered almost cavalierly. Hackles are raised by what appears to be ad hoc invoking of any set of circumstances that will reconcile passages; to those steeped in higher-critical methods, such special pleading is rejected because it lacks any particular methodological control beyond the need for a quick solution. Nor are harmonizations readily amenable to proof or disproof; they may have varying degrees of probability, some more convincing than others, and some altogether too ingenious to commend the solution they attempt.

Again a few examples might help: (1) the large numbers in Chronicles; (2) places where the numbers in Chronicles differ with those in parallel texts; and (3) 2 Chronicles 2:13–14 and the parallel in 1 Kings 7:13–14. Each of these questions needs more discussion than space allows, but we can at least sketch an outline of the issues.

The large numbers in Chronicles have always been something of a stumbling block, especially the large numbers of troops under the command of the kings of the rather small kingdom of Judah (1 Chron. 12:23–40; 21; 27; 2 Chron. 12:3; 13:3–4, 17; 14:9; 17:12–19; 25:5–6; 26:12–13; 28:6–8); a small kingdom raised armies and inflicted casualties greater than in the mechanized battles of World War II. Almost everyone feels the need to reduce these numbers in some way; articles by J. Barton Payne and John Wenham represent fairly typical efforts to cope with these figures.[15] The Hebrew word *'elep,* "thousand," is also used for a subunit of a tribe, perhaps at the level of a clan or phratry (a group of clans). This use is almost certainly found in Judges 6:15; Numbers 1:16; Micah 5:2; 1 Samuel 10:19–21.

14. Raymond Dillard, "The Literary Structure of the Chronicler's Solomon Narrative," *Journal for the Study of the Old Testament* 30 (1984): 85–93. Cf. the briefer treatment in idem, *Second Chronicles,* chs. 5–7.
15. J. Barton Payne, "The Validity of Numbers in Chronicles," *Bibliotheca Sacra* 136 (1979): 109–28, 206–20; John Wenham, "Large Numbers in the Old Testament," *Tyndale Bulletin* 18 (1967): 19–53.

These tribal units would have consisted of considerably less than a thousand individuals. Furthermore, by changing the vowels on the word *'elef,* one can create the word *'allûf,* "officer, warrior, leader of an *'alef* "; in this latter case the meaning "thousand" is reduced to a single individual. Both of these procedures transform the large troop numbers in Chronicles radically, and this approach is rather widely adopted among evangelicals. When applied to the approximately 360,000 men who attended David's coronation (1 Chron. 12:23–40), this large number would be reduced to a more manageable 2000 (Wenham) or even 400 (Payne), numbers that can more readily be justified rationally. But there is a problem: What has become of "the army of God" (v. 22)? The numbers are reduced, but at the expense of the very point the biblical author is trying to make. It is hard to escape the conclusion that the Chronicler intends to be using plain numbers, not the number of tribal subunits or officers.

A similar issue can be raised in connection with 1 Chronicles 5:18–21. The Trans-Jordanian tribes captured 50,000 camels, 250,000 sheep, 2000 donkeys, and 100,000 captives. One cannot arbitrarily reduce the number of captives by appealing to "thousands" that are really subunits of tribes or individual soldiers in this context, without treating the other numbers similarly. But the other numbers are not amenable to this sort of reduction (sheep are not counted by phratries and are not officers!), suggesting that the Chronicler is using plain numbers. The drive for a solution to the issue of large numbers in Chronicles in these cases is at the expense of the biblical author.

In the second example, Chronicles often reports numbers that differ when compared with those found in Samuel-Kings. Payne provides an exhaustive survey and divides these differences into two basic classes, (1) those where no genuine difference exists, and (2) those where there is a difference. Under (1), Payne explains the apparent discrepancies by suggesting that in fact they report different instances—different items were being enumerated or different measures were being used that actually arrive at the same quantities. For example, where 2 Samuel 24:24 reports that David paid fifty shekels of silver for Araunah's threshing floor and oxen, 1 Chronicles 21:25 says David paid six hundred shekels of gold for "the place." No contradiction exists, since Samuel speaks of a fairly small parcel, while the Chronicler reports the price presumably for the whole area of Mount Moriah.[16] For (2), where a genuine difference between the two texts does exist, Payne appeals to errors in textual transmission primarily based on misread numerical notations using either the Canaanite alphabet, the later Aramaic alphabet, or a numeral system similar to Egyptian hieratic numerals. There is no direct evidence for the use of either of the alphanumeric systems before the Maccabean period, nor is there direct evidence showing the use of a numeral system for writing numbers instead of spelling them out in biblical texts.[17] The harmonistic argument here shares the circularity of many hypotheses: explanatory systems are invoked to explain the discrepancies, and the discrepancies become the warrant for the suggested explanation. Though the suggested explanations may have been a factor in the transmission of the text, one has the feeling that they are invoked somewhat arbitrarily.

16. Payne, "Validity of Numbers in Chronicles," 120. See also Raymond Dillard, "David's Census: Perspectives on 2 Samuel 24 and 1 Chronicles 21," in *Through Christ's Word,* ed. Robert Godfrey and Jesse Boyd III (Phillipsburg, N.J.: Presbyterian and Reformed, 1985), 94–107.

17. H. L. Allrik, "The Lists of Zerubbabel (Nehemiah 7 and Ezra 2) and the Hebrew Numeral Notation," *Bulletin of the American Schools of Oriental Research* 136 (1954): 21–27.

Finally, in 1 Kings 7:13–14, Hiram says that Huram-Abi's mother was from Naphtali, whereas in 2 Chronicles 2:13–14, she was from Dan. I once asked an adult Sunday school class consisting entirely of people without formal theological training if they could reconcile the differences. I received seven different scenarios that could have accounted for the two verses: some suggested that she was really from Dan but lived in Naphtali; others that his mother was born to parents from both tribes so that her own ancestry could be reckoned through either; another suggested that she may have lived in disputed territory contiguous to both tribes and claimed by both; one felt that Hiram of Tyre could have been mistaken in one case, and corrected by the biblical historian in another, and so forth. This was an interesting confirmation for me that harmonization is not hard to do, can always be done, can usually be done in several different ways, and cannot ordinarily be shown right or wrong. Nearly any conceivable scenario could be invoked, and for logicians it looks like unbridled special pleading.

Occasionally harmonization can become so ingenious as to undermine the very biblical authority it seeks to establish. Perhaps the most notorious example involves reconstructing the account of Peter's denial with the result that he denied Jesus six times before the cock crowed twice.[18] The account of the death of Ahaziah is quite different in 2 Kings 9:2–28 and 2 Chronicles 22:8–9. One can concoct an amalgam of the two passages, so that Ahaziah fled from Jehu in Jezreel south to hide in Samaria, where he was found and brought to Jehu, who fatally wounded him near Ibleam. Ahaziah then fled by chariot northwest toward Megiddo, where he died; his body was subsequently taken to Jerusalem for burial. But the uneasy feeling persists that this "solution" is forced and contrived.[19]

Its Adequacy

At first glance the practice of harmonization appears to be a simple and straightforward way to deal with historical difficulties, but in actual application the approach becomes occasionally blurred and problematic. Intrabiblical quotations provide a case in point.

Most evangelicals adhering to the doctrine of inerrancy do not consider variations in reports of speech materials reason for harmonization. One Gospel may say that Jesus asked the rich young ruler, "Why do you ask me about what is good?" (Matt. 19:17), whereas another reports the question to have been, "Why do you call me good?" (Luke 18:19). The soldier at the cross said, "Surely this was a righteous man" (23:47), or "Surely he was the Son of God" (Matt. 27:54). Some may feel that Jesus or the centurion must have said both or that these are two different instances. But for the most part, evangelical theologians have seen variations like these as acceptable paraphrase and find no need to harmonize them.

18. A convenient summary of this suggestion can be found in Harold Lindsell, *The Battle for the Bible* (Grand Rapids: Zondervan, 1976), 174–76.

19. The Chronicler often uses death reports, particularly the honor accorded at death and the place of burial, as indicative of his judgment regarding a king. Cf. the similar issue regarding the death of Josiah (2 Kings 23:29–30; 2 Chron. 35:24). Some interpret the Chronicler's report of the death of Josiah in Jerusalem instead of Megiddo as an effort to ease the tension with the prophecy of Huldah that Josiah would go to his grave in peace (2 Kings 22:20; 2 Chron. 34:28) or as an effort to assign this righteous king death in the city of David instead of in defeat on a battlefield. See the discussions in H. G. M. Williamson, "The Death of Josiah and the Continuing Development of the Deuteronomic History," *Vetus Testamentum* 32, 2 (1982): 242–48; idem, "Reliving the Death of Josiah: A Reply to C. T. Begg," ibid., 37, 1 (1987): 9–15; Christopher T. Begg, "The Death of Josiah in Chronicles: Another View," ibid., 1–8; see also my own *Second Chronicles,* pp. 292–93. A similar issue is raised by the Chronicler's treatment of the last four kings of Judah; see ibid., 294–303.

New Testament citations of the Old Testament often follow the LXX instead of the MT. Hebrews 1:6 cites Deuteronomy 32:43 in a reading that is found in the LXX and a Qumran text, and it is difficult to be sure what the original text of the verse may have been. Some might insist that the New Testament has erroneously cited the Old Testament. Others might be tempted to say that the LXX represents the correct text. However, most evangelical theologians would say that inerrancy cannot be used to make text-critical decisions; the writer of Hebrews simply used the Bible he had before him. Nothing that he said was false, and his citation is no occasion for harmonization. Compare as other examples the citations of the Old Testament in Hebrews 2:6–8, James 4:6, and 1 Peter 4:18.

Galatians 3:17 presents a similar case in its allusion to Exodus 12:40, though the stakes appear to be a bit higher. Compare the text of Exodus 12:40 in the MT, LXX, and Samaritan Pentateuch (SP):

MT: The length of time the children of Israel lived in Egypt was 430 years.

LXX: The length of time the children of Israel lived in Egypt *and Canaan* was 430 years.

SP: The length of time the children of Israel *and their fathers* lived in Egypt *and Canaan* was 430 years.

In Galatians 3:17, Paul appears to be saying that the Law came 430 years after Abraham. Paul may have derived this information from a text of Exodus that agreed with either the LXX or the SP. Even if we were certain that the MT represented the correct text of the verse, one could argue that Paul has not been false. He has simply followed the Bible that he had before him; inerrancy does not require that the text-critical question be decided in favor of the LXX or the SP.[20]

Following in the same vein, one other illustration may heighten the difficulty a bit more. Ever since the Qumran discoveries, it has become clear that the Chronicler was following a version of Samuel that had numerous differences with the MT of that book. The MT and LXX of 2 Samuel 5:21 report that after a battle the Philistines "abandoned their gods there, and David and his men took them." The Lucianic recension of this verse reports that the Philistines left the idols but that David "gave orders to burn them in fire." When the Chronicler reports this incident (1 Chron. 14:12), he says that the Philistines abandoned their gods and that David "gave orders and they burned them in fire." David's actions conform to Deuteronomy 7:25 in the Lucianic edition of Samuel and in the Chronicles MT, but his actions are out of accord with the Law in the Samuel MT and the LXX. Assuming for the sake of the argument that the Samuel MT represents an earlier text,[21] it appears that the Lucianic revision and the Chronicler both worked from a text of Samuel in which a scribe had conformed David's actions to the Law. Once again one could argue that the Chronicler was simply using the Bible he had at hand. However, the historical character of the account

20. There are, of course, other solutions to this difficulty. Some have suggested that, though the text appears to date the Law 430 years after Abraham, Paul in fact had the last time the promise was given in mind, so that the MT is correct, and the time between the last giving of the promise to Jacob and the Law is 430 years.

21. This is by no means to be taken for granted. The quality of the MT in Samuel has long been a matter of debate; the Qumran discoveries in general confirm that there are numerous difficulties in Samuel MT.

has been modified by transmission history.[22] Similar illustrations could be drawn from other passages (e.g., 2 Sam. 8:4 and the parallel in 1 Chron. 18:4; or 2 Sam. 24:16–17 and its parallel in 1 Chron. 21:15–17).

The initial reluctance to harmonize intrabiblical citations when little is at stake leads inevitably to involvement in complicated historical questions. Considerable exegetical, theological, and hermeneutical work is needed to clarify the relationship between such intrabiblical citations and the doctrine of inerrancy.

Its Focus

The goal of harmonistic exegesis is primarily to defend a doctrine of Scripture. That goal is immeasurably important. However, in actual practice, it has occasionally had unfortunate results. Too often, evangelical commentators on the historical books in particular have treated them as books full of problems and have commented on the Old Testament basically with an apologetic purpose in mind. This sort of focus tends to concentrate on minutiae and problem solving, and writers feel they can move on to the next passage once they have rebuffed critical opinion and thereby secured the faith of their readers in the Scriptures.

Though an apologetic component in writing about the Bible is laudable and necessary, the focus of exegesis is less defending a doctrine of Scripture than it is elucidating a text. The focus is on what the author and text say to a particular audience and to us; the text may not directly address the doctrine of Scripture at all.

Often the difficulties that are the grist for harmonization provide keys into the author's larger purpose. A later biblical author may provide an alternate account in order to portray an individual or event in a particular light. Matthew's reporting Jesus' sermon on a mountain may reflect his portraying Jesus as a second Moses, a second lawgiver on a mountain. When the Chronicler records Huram-Abi's ancestry in the tribe of Dan, he is carefully molding Huram-Abi as a kind of second Oholiab;[23] it is just one of a number of differences in his account that perfect a parallel between the building of the temple and Israel's original sanctuary, the tabernacle. The consistency with which the Chronicler portrays divine blessing through God's giving righteous kings large armies speaks to basic themes he wants his reader to understand. Read in this way, these "difficulties" are not so much problems as they are opportunities, open windows to the big picture.[24]

Good biblical study calls for a balance. We may not allow preoccupation with higher criticism and problems to cause us to miss what the biblical writer is trying to say, nor may we neglect attending to the outworking of the doctrine of Scripture in particular

---

22. A typical harmonistic solution would be to suggest overlying the passages, e.g., "David took them up [Samuel MT] and burned them [Chronicles MT]." This solution would not give much weight to the fact that the Chronicler appears to be simply copying his source of Samuel at this point: the Chronicler would have had yet another version of the same event from which he chose this variant detail.

23. Dillard, "Chronicler's Solomon."

24. I have provided some further reflection on methodological questions in the introduction to *Second Chronicles,* xviii–xix. The Chronicler was an individual, interacting with written texts at his disposal. I have described this interaction by saying that he "recasts, shapes, models, enhances, modifies, transforms, edits, rewrites" the material at his disposal. This vocabulary describes the Chronicler's activity and does not of itself prejudge historical questions. It is my own conviction that, understood within the allowable historiographical practices of his own culture and time, the Chronicler is a reliable and trust-worthy historian.

pericopes. We want to know all about the twigs and leaves on the branches, but we cannot afford to miss the forest.

We believe that the Scriptures are all that God wants them to be, without any compromise of his own glory and veracity. But the nature of Scripture is not established alone from the proof texts so often cited in reference to that doctrine, but also from the phenomena we observe there. The doctrine of Scripture, like all other doctrines, must be derived from Scripture itself and not subjected to some other more ultimate standard derived from modern philosophy.

In sum, harmonization as an exegetical method has a long history and has made many important contributions to biblical studies. But it has also been somewhat of a mixed blessing. When too facilely employed, it tends to lack credibility and does not commend the cause (the doctrine of Scripture) it seeks to uphold.

In those instances where no plausible harmonization offers itself, how should the theologian respond? Several avenues are open. E. J. Young's approach was essentially to wait patiently for better evidence and explanations and meanwhile to avoid making forced harmonizations.[25] The history of biblical studies has frequently ratified this approach.

A further avenue for addressing these problems is through genre criticism. After sober study one could conclude that a book of narrative prose in the Old Testament belongs to some other literary genre in which historical canons are suspended or modified. This approach is reflected in affirmation 13 of the Chicago Statement on Biblical Hermeneutics, issued by the International Council on Biblical Inerrancy: "We affirm that awareness of the literary categories, formal and stylistic, of the various parts of Scripture is essential for proper exegesis, and hence we value genre criticism as one of the many disciplines of biblical study."

The importance of genre criticism has long been recognized for books like Song of Songs and Ecclesiastes. One's reading strategy for Song of Songs is determined by whether it is identified as an allegory, a drama, or an anthology of love poems; all three positions and numerous variations have been advocated in the history of interpretation, and all three result in substantially different understandings of the book. Young himself approached the authorship of Ecclesiastes through questions of genre.[26] The writer of Ecclesiastes implies that he is Solomon by claiming to be king in Jerusalem and wiser than all before him—yet the oblique way in which this very claim is made suggests that the author is using pseudonymy, an accepted literary convention of his time, and that the book itself may be dated later in light of additional evidence.[27]

Making a determination of genre is itself problematic. A genre identification may not be sufficiently compelling so as to enable firm conclusions or to commend general adoption. In studying a particular narrative, we are able to make broad generalizations at the outset, while perfecting, modifying, and nuancing this identification through interaction with the phenomena of the text and through comparisons with other biblical literature and the literature of the geographically proximate and contemporary cultures.

Approaching biblical narratives with this tool is rife with difficulties; it has the potential of devouring much of the facticity of biblical historiography. Yet the fact that this method

25. E. J. Young, *Thy Word Is Truth* (Grand Rapids: Eerdmans, 1957), 124–25.

26. E. J. Young, *An Introduction to the Old Testament* (London: Tyndale, 1966), 347–49.

27. See Tremper Longmann III, "Storytellers and Poets in the Bible: Can Literary Artifice Be True?" in *Inerrancy and Hermeneutic*, 137–49.

(along with almost any other) is capable of abuse is not sufficient reason for outright rejection. Rather than dismissal in one broad sweep of the hand, the appeal to genre identifications must be evaluated for the strength of the argument, as with any other aspect of exegesis.

Yet one further note needs to be added. Evangelical theologians must be ever wary of imposing on the Bible hermeneutical or exegetical principles derived from outside it. The Scriptures and the Scriptures alone are the ultimate canon for truth and must not be subjected to some other standard. This position raises a series of interesting and difficult hermeneutical questions. At the very least it requires that we scrutinize the historiosophical principles affecting our reading of the Bible. Should evangelical theology share the premises and canons for truthfulness dictated by the historical-critical method? Engaging the historical-critical method is unavoidable, but part of that engagement must be a transcendental criticism of the very methods and canons with which it operates, rather than adopting them wholesale into Christian theology. This area needs attention but unfortunately would take us far beyond the scope of this chapter.

59

Oral Tradition

BRUCE K. WALTKE

Bruce Waltke, "1. Oral Tradition," in *A Tribute to Gleason Archer*, ed. Walter C. Kaiser Jr. and Ronald F. Youngblood (Chicago: Moody, 1986), 17–34; reprinted in *Inerrancy and Hermeneutic*, 117–35.

Bruce Waltke was a professor of Old Testament at Westminster from 1985 to 1990. His pilgrimage and education is rich and varied. He earned a Th.D. from Dallas Theological Seminary in 1958 and a Ph.D. from Harvard University, dealing with the Samaritan Pentateuch in 1965. After starting his career at Dallas Seminary, he came to teach at Westminster Seminary. This move was partly prompted by a shift in his understanding of the Bible. Later, he pursued his teaching career at Regent College, Reformed Theological Seminary, and Knox Theological Seminary. A very prolific author, he distinguished himself as a commentator. In particular, he commented on Genesis with Cathi J. Fredricks (2001), on Proverbs (2004), and on Micah (2007). Two coauthored volumes stand out as major contributions to the field of biblical studies: with M. O'Connor, *An Introduction to Biblical Hebrew Syntax* (1990), and with Charles Yu, *An Old Testament Theology: An Exegetical, Canonical, and Thematic Approach* (2007).

In "Oral Tradition," also reprinted in *Inerrancy and Hermeneutic*, Waltke explains how oral tradition impacts critical scholarship and an orthodox doctrine of Scripture, and the extent to which oral tradition is accurate and trustworthy. He observes that the assumption of the existence of oral traditions supports much Old Testament scholarship (form criticism, tradition criticism, and canonical criticism). He concludes his survey of oral tradition in the world of the Bible by stating that oral tradition is not as prevalent as usually assumed. Moreover, Waltke claims that written documents and traditions are more likely to stand behind the Old Testament than is usually thought, and that we also have to acknowledge the Old Testament as revelation from God. This essay helps to engage Old Testament scholarship critically and responsively. We reproduce here the article as it appeared in *A Tribute to Gleason Archer* (1986). The later version is slightly updated; in particular it integrates the important work by R. N. Whybray, *The Making of the Pentateuch: A Methodological Study*, Journal for the Study of the Old Testament Supplement Series 53 (Sheffield: University of Sheffield, 1987). The earlier and shorter version of Waltke's article, however, still captures the argument well.

Bibliography: J. I. Packer and Sven K. Soderlund, eds. *The Way of Wisdom: Essays in Honor of Bruce K. Waltke*. Grand Rapids: Zondervan, 2000.

Form criticism, tradition criticism, and canonical criticism are all based on at least two principles: (1) that most of the literature of the Old Testament had a long prehistory before being written down, and (2) that during its oral stage, the "literature" was often transposed into new settings with new meanings. Source critics thing that much of the biblical material was transmitted orally at local sanctuaries by tridents who preserved, reinterpreted, reformulated, and supplemented Israel's diverse traditions and theological heritage.

H. S. Nyberg stated the first conviction in a famous quote:

Transmission in the East is seldom exclusively written; it is chiefly *oral* in character. The living speech from ancient times to the present plays a greater role in the East than the written presentation. Almost every written work in the Orient went through a longer or shorter oral transmission in its earliest history, and also even after it is written down the oral transmission remains the normal form in the preservation and use of the work.[1]

More popularly and less guardedly Gene M. Tucker expressed the concensus of form critics on this point: "All ancient . . . cultures had a body of oral 'literature'—that is, folklore—long before they developed written records and literature."[2]

After tracing the development of scholarly opinion regarding oral tradition from Hermann Gunkel through the views of Scandinavian scholars such as H. S. Nyberg, Ivan Engnell, Harris Birkeland, Sigmund Mowinckel, and Eduard Nielsen,[3] Walter E. Rast expressed the second principle of source critics who attempt to reconstruct the history of a text even in its oral stage: "Such study shows that the messages of the Old Testament texts have experienced development over long period of time. Different generations have taken them up, either in oral or written form, and transposed them into fresh settings and understandings."[4]

These convictions of form critics and their successors profoundly influence the way in which one regards the historical accuracy of the Bible and its meaning. Concerning the former, it stands to reason that if the "literature" in its oral stage was flexible and reworked like putty, it contains only a kernel of historical accuracy. As William F. Albright noted,

1. H. S. Nyberg, *Studien zum Hoseabuche* (Uppsala: Lundequistska, 1935), 7 (translation mine, italics his).
2. Gene M. Tucker, *Form Criticism of the Old Testament* (Philadelphia: Fortress, 1971), 17.
3. For a full survey of the work of Scandinavian scholars, see Douglas A. Knight, *Rediscovering the Traditions of Israel*, Society of Biblical Literature Dissertation Series 9 (Missoula, MT: Scholars Press, 1973).
4. Walter E. Rast, *Tradition History and the Old Testament* (Philadelphia: Fortress, 1972), 18.

In recent decades there has been steady increase of the use of aetiology (the analysis of stories explaining ancient names and practices) to identify legendary accretions in orally transmitted material. The discovery and application of the method of form criticism, especially by H. Gunkel, M. Dibelius, and their followers, have given a great impetus to the utilization of the aetiological method, which has now reached a point where its leading exponents are inclined to deny the historicity of nearly all early stories of both the Old and the New Testaments.[5]

In spite of Albright's caveat that this view has gone too far, it still prevails. Tucker's words are representative:

> Sagas usually tell us more about the life and time of the period in which they were circulated and written down than they do about the events they mean to describe. A careful form critical and traditio-historical analysis . . . can help the historian to distinguish between the old and new and the historically reliable and the unreliable in those sagas.[6]

Also, the notion that Israel's sacred heritage was handed down in a fluid and very complicated prehistory raises a whole complex of problems about authorial meaning. For if tradents reworked and reformulated the "literature" to meet changing needs, it stands to reason that many meanings lie buried within it. The canonical critics view that only the final meaning of a text in the Jewish canon matters relieves this problem to some extent. Nevertheless, one is still left with the uneasy conscience that the text's original meaning(s) to the people of God has/have been deliberately obfuscated by the final redactor.

The common teaching that the literature of the Bible has passed through a long and often complicated oral prehistory must be critically appraised for the sake of both true knowledge and sound doctrine. In this study I aim to debunk both of the principles outlined above. With pleasure I dedicate it to my friend, Gleason L. Archer, who has advanced sound knowledge and doctrine through his many publications and his teaching.[7]

The first and major part of the study attempts to demonstrate that proper evidence (that is, evidence from the ancient Near East) leads to the conviction that the biblical literature had a short oral prehistory and was transmitted conservatively. In the second and much more brief section the goal is to show that even more inferential evidence (that is, evidence from shortly after the time of the Old Testament's completion at about 400 B.C. and/or evidence from neighboring non-Semitic-speaking peoples) does suggest that oral traditions were transmitted in a fluid state. Finally, the question will be addressed as to whether the prepatriarchal narratives in Genesis, which contain stories of happenings before the invention of writing, depend on oral tradition. If it can be established that the oral tradition played a minor role in the transmission of the text and not in the way envisioned by men such as Albrecht Alt and Gerhard von Rad and their schools, this will help both to restore more confidence in the Old Testament's reliability and to clarify its meaning.

---

5. William F. Albright, *From the Stone Age to Christianity*, 2nd ed. (Garden City, N.Y.: Doubleday, 1957), 70.

6. Tucker, *Form Criticism,* 20. For a survey of literature treating the relationship between historicity and oral tradition, see Jan Vansina, *Oral Tradition: A Study in Historical Methodology* (London: Routledge and Kegan Paul, 1965).

7. Ed. note: This personal note found in the earlier version of this essay was dropped when it was reprinted in the volume *Inerrancy and Hermeneutic.*

Oral Tradition in the Ancient Near East

To decide whether the literature of the Old Testament was changed by tradents over a long period of oral transmission, it will be instructive to turn to the cultures of the ancient Near East, which undoubtedly influenced all of the Old Testament's literary genres: to Ebla in northern Syria (ca. 2350 B.C.); then successively to Mesopotamia, whose coherent culture can be traced with confidence for over two millennia until it was dealt what proved to be a fatal blow by Alexander the Great (ca. 330 B.C.); to the Hittites (1450 to 1250 B.C.); to Ugarit (ca. 1400 B.C.); to the Egyptian culture, whose literatures stretch from about 2500 to 500 B.C.; and finally to the Northwest Semites. In this last connection the Hebrews will be considered, including the internal evidence of the Old Testament itself. In this wide-ranging survey a single question is asked: "Did the people under investigation preserve their cultural heritage through an oral tradition subject to alteration or through written texts precisely with a view that its heritage not be corrupted?" If the evidence for the former is negative, there is no reason to accept the first principle, along with the historical exegetical difficulties entailed, on which form, tradition, and canonical critics construct their methods.

EBLA

According to Giovanni Pettinato, the texts unearthed from the royal archives of Ebla include the following types: economic and administrative texts (regarding the various branches of industry, such as metals, wood, and textiles), historical and historical-juridical texts, lexical texts ("scientific" lists of animals in general, fishes and birds in particular; lists of professions and personal names; of objects in stone, metal, and wood; various lexical texts; grammatical texts with verbal paradigms; and finally bilingual vocabularies in Sumerian and Eblaite), and true literary texts (myths, epic tales, hymns to divinities, incantations, rituals, and collections of proverbs).[8] This ancient city, which antedates the Hebrew patriarchs by three to five centuries and Moses by about a millennium, was highly literate and preserved its culture and heritage in writing. So far as they have been translated and published, the Ebla texts make no mention of oral tradition or tradents. But much still remains to be deciphered.

MESOPOTAMIA

In Mesopotamia there is much evidence that the Akkadian culture conservatively transmitted its heritage in writing. By comparing collections of Sumerian proverbs that achieved canonical status among the Akkadians as early as circa 1500 B.C. with later collections dated to the Neo-Babylonian period (ca. 600 B.C.), it can be shown that they were transmitted in writing with relatively little modification.[9]

The great Akkadian creation epic, *Enuma elish*, was probably composed during the time of Hammurabi (ca. 1700 B.C.), and its earliest extant copy, clearly not the original, is dated only a hundred years later.

The lawcodes of Lipit-Ishtar, Eshnunna, Hammurabi, and others antedate Moses by centuries. Moreover, they promised blessing to those who preserved the written laws and threatened judgment against those who altered them. The stele containing Lipit-Ishtar's

---

8. Giovanni Pettinato, *The Archives of Ebla: An Empire Inscribed on Clay* (Garden City, NY: Doubleday, 1981), 42–48.
9. Bruce K. Waltke, "The Book of Proverbs and Ancient Wisdom Literature," *Bibliotheca Sacra* 136 (1979): 221–38.

lawcode reads: "May he who will not commit any evil deed with regard to it, who will not damage my handiwork, who will [not] erase its inscription, who will not write his own name upon it—be presented with life and breath of long days."[10] The epilogue to Hammurabi's code is similar:

> If that man heeded my words which I wrote, on my stela,
> and did not rescind my law,
> has not distorted my words,
> did not alter my statutes,
> may Shamash make that man reign. . . .

> If that man did not heed my words . . .
> and disregarded my curses, . . .
> but has abolished the law which I enacted,
> has distorted my words,
> has altered my statutes, . . .
> may mighty Anum . . .
> deprive him of the glory of sovereignty . . .
> the disappearance of his name and memory from the land.[11]

According to Otto Weber, it was the rule among the Akkadians that only an agreement fixed in writing was juridically valid.[12]

Hymns from the early Sumerian period (ca. 1900 B.C.) are also found in Mesopotamia. What arrests our attention about them here is that, though they were intended to be sung at cultic centers, they were written down. In fact their technical terms, probably related to their liturgical use, have not as yet been deciphered by Sumerologists, even as the same kind of notices in the biblical psalms cannot at present be deciphered by Hebraists.[13]

Letters were read from written texts, as evidenced by letters from Mari. These typically state: "Your tablet which you did send forth, I have heard."[14]

Representing the historical literary genre in Mesopotamia we have the famous Sumerian king lists and the later and equally famous Assyrian annals. Representatives of the religious genre include rituals, incantations, and descriptions of festivals. We may infer that events referred to in this literature that occurred before the invention of writing were transmitted by word of mouth, but we cannot reconstruct its nature. After writing evolved to communicate effectively, there is no indication that a fluid oral transmission alone was the principal means of preserving memory in Mesopotamia. In this literature there is no mention of either tradents or oral tradition. Eduard Nielsen, contending for oral tradition in the Near East, conceded: "The fact that religious and epic texts of major importance in the high cultures of the Ancient Near East were ordinarily put into written form has already been stressed in the case of Egyptian literature. The evidence points in a similar direction in the case of Mesopotamian literature."[15]

10. J. B. Pritchard, ed., *Ancient Near Eastern Texts Relating to the Old Testament*, 3rd ed. (Princeton: Princeton University Press, 1969), 161 (hereafter cited as *ANET*).

11. Ibid., 178–79.

12. Otto Weber, *Die Literatur der Babylonier und Assyrer* (Leipzig: Hinrichs, 1970), 249.

13. Samuel N. Kramer, *The Sumerians* (Chicago: University of Chicago Press, 1963), 207.

14. See *Archives Royales de Mari* (Paris: P. Geuthner, 1941), 1. 6:5, 9:5, and others.

15. Eduard Nielsen, *Oral Tradition: A Modern Problem in Old Testament Introduction* (London: SCM, 1954), 28–29.

What evidence is there for oral tradition after the invention and evolution of writing? The best Nielsen can offer against George Widengren's contention that texts were always written is one example, which may introduce a minor correction. A colophon in a hymn reads: "Written from the scholar's dictation, the old edition I have not seen."[16] In fact, however, Nielsen's one exception actually proves Widengren's rule. Commenting on this text, J. Laessoe observed: "It would seem to appear that oral tradition was only reluctantly relied upon, and in this particular case only because for some reason or other an original written document was not available."[17] The situation reflected by this colophon differs *toto caelo* from that supposed by source critics, who presuppose a long and often complex oral tradition. The scribe is a faithful copyist, not a tradent manipulating his heritage.

There is evidence, however, that redaction of older written sources into later ones did occur. As Donald J. Wiseman pointed out,

> Tigay has shown that redactors completed the remoulding of the earlier Sumerian poems into one "Gilgamesh" tradition (ca. 1800 B.C.) about the same time as the Hittites made a summary of 5 tablets of Gilgamesh into one; and about the same time as the Kassite period of Babylonia (1540–1250) when scribes began copying the Gilgamesh, and other epics, in a traditional way which was to hand them on virtually unchanged for more than a thousand years.[18]

Some texts show that the written tradition was to be accompanied with memorization for oral recital. Nielsen called attention to the following: (1) from the Irra myth: "The scribe who learns this text by heart escapes the enemy"; (2) from Ashurbanipal's prayer to Shamash: "Whosoever shall learn this text [by heart and] glorify the gods"; (3) from tablet 7 of *Enuma elish*: "The sage and the learned shall together ponder [them], father shall tell [of them] to son and teach [them to] him."[19] These texts, however, do not argue for a long and complicated oral prehistory before the material in view was written down. Rather they suggest that oral recitation accompanied the written texts. R. K. Harrison rightly commented:

> Modern scholars have largely misunderstood the purpose and function of oral transmission in the ancient Near East. The firm tradition of the Mosaic period, as well as of ancient peoples other than the Hebrews, was that any events of importance were generally recorded in written form quite soon after they had taken place. . . . The principal purpose of oral transmission was the dissemination of the pertinent information. . . . It is entirely fallacious to assume . . . that an oral form of a narrative was the necessary and normal precursor of the written stage. There can be little doubt that in many cases both oral and written traditions existed side by side for lengthy periods.[20]

Bendt Alster explored the possibility that, because poetic lines turn up in the same form in several Sumerian poems, these may be traditional formulas of an oral tradition.[21] In fact, however, traditional formulas may point to oral composition, not to a long and flexible

---

16. Ibid.

17. Jorgen Laessoe, *Literary and Oral Tradition in Ancient Mesopotamia* (1953), 205.

18. Donald J. Wiseman, "Israel's Literary Neighbours in the 13th Century B.C.," *Journal of Northwest Semitic Languages* 5 (1977): 82.

19. Nielsen, *Oral Tradition*, 19–20.

20. R. K. Harrison, *Introduction to the Old Testament* (Grand Rapids: Eerdmans, 1969), 209–10.

21. Bendt Alster, *Dumuzi's Dream: Aspects of Oral Poetry in a Sumerian Myth* (Copenhagen: Akademisk Forlag, 1972).

oral tradition, and there is no direct evidence about how such texts were composed. Ruth Finnegan argued against any fundamental, qualitative difference between oral and written literature: "We can only discuss a continuum rather than a distinction between oral and written literature."[22]

In sum, from Mesopotamia there is evidence of redaction from earlier written sources into later complexes followed by a conservative transmission of the literary achievement with an accompanying oral recital, but there is no evidence of a flexible oral tradition.

HITTITES

The Hittite literature and history are mostly known from the archives recovered from its capital at Hattusilis (modern Boğaz-köy). These archives yielded texts similar to those encountered elsewhere in the ancient Near East. Its international suzerainty treaties, which are remarkably parallel to the Book of Deuteronomy, according to George Mendenhall,[23] Klaus Baltzer,[24] and Meredith Kline,[25] enjoyed canonical status. A treaty between Suppiluliumas and Mattiwaza contains this provision against change:

> In the Mitanni land (a duplicate) has been deposited before Tessub.... At regular intervals shall they read it in the presence of the king. . . . Whoever will remove this tablet from before Tessub . . . and put in a hidden place, if he breaks it or causes anyone else to change the wording of the tablet—at the conclusion of this treaty we have called the gods to be assembled and the gods of the contracting parties to be present, to listen and to serve as witnesses.[26]

In sum, the Hittites, like the other great peoples of the ancient Near East, committed their important literature to sure writing instead of an oral tradition.

UGARIT

Richard E. Whitaker discovered that 82 percent of the language of the Ugaritic poems is formulaic. This high frequency of formulae and formulaic structures led him to suppose that "we are dealing here with an orally created poetry."[27] But once again it is necessary to note that he is talking about oral composition, not about a long and complicated prehistory before its transposition to writing. The fact is that the peoples of ancient Ugarit wrote down their hymns and myths celebrating their nature deities and recited them at their sanctuaries. Nothing in them suggests that oral recitation existed apart from written texts or that it had priority over the written witnesses to their beliefs. It seems plausible to suppose that these potent, magical words were considered as unalterable and written down either at the time of composition or shortly thereafter.

22. Ruth Finnegan, *Oral Literature in Africa* (Oxford: Clarendon Press, 1970), 61, cited by R. C. Culley, "Oral Tradition and the OT: Some Recent Discussion," *Semeia* 5 (= *Oral Tradition and Old Testament Studies;* 1976). The title of this issue of *Semeia* may cause confusion by confounding oral composition with oral tradition. Evidence for the first is not evidence for the second, as that term has been traditionally understood in Old Testament studies.

23. George E. Mendenhall, *Law and Covenant in Israel and the Ancient Near East* (Pittsburgh: Biblical Colloquium, 1955).

24. Klaus Baltzer, *The Covenant Formulary* (Oxford: Blackwell, 1971).

25. Meredith Kline, *Treaty of the Great King* (Grand Rapids: Eerdmans, 1963).

26. *ANET,* 205.

27. Richard E. Whitaker, "A Formulaic Analysis of Ugaritic Poetry" (Ph.D. diss., Harvard University, 1969), 157.

EGYPT

From Egypt have come numerous texts of many of the literary genres represented in the Bible. These texts demonstrate that Egyptian scribes attempted to preserve their heritage in writing as accurately as possible. Albright wrote:

> The prolonged and intimate study of the many scores of thousands of pertinent documents from the ancient Near East proves that sacred and profane documents were copied with greater care than is true of scribal copying in Graeco-Roman times. Even documents which were never intended to be seen by other human eyes, such as mortuary texts, manuscripts of the Book of the Dead, and magical texts, are copied so that we can nearly always read them without difficulty if the state of preservation permits.[28]

Kenneth A. Kitchen called attention to the colophon of a text dated circa 1400 B.C. in which a scribe boasted: "[This book] is completed from its beginning to its end, having been copied, revised, compared, and verified sign by sign."[29]

Is there any evidence of oral tradition among the Egyptians? Boudoun van de Walle laid an excellent foundation for understanding the development of textual criticism of Egyptian literary works.[30] Askel Volten in his editions of the Teaching of *Any*[31] and *Insinger*[32] laid down the main types of error to be encountered: (1) entirely graphic error, (2) auricular errors, (3) slips of memory, and (4) the usual unintentional slips due to carelessness. Gunter Burkard took issue with Volten's thesis that by far the majority of errors were *Hoerfehler*, "mistakes of hearing," but argued rather that the most common type of mistake, apart from simple carelessness, arose from copying directly from a written text and that the next largest group of errors was caused by writing texts from memory.[33] This procedure led to omission of verses, transpositions of maxims or lines, the substitution of synonyms, and on occasion the intermingling and confusion of maxims or pericopes. Such scribal errors do not provide a foundation for building a theory that the Egyptians transmitted their heritage in a pliable oral tradition. All three scholars describe these changes as errors in *the writing of the texts*, assuming that the scribe intended to preserve and transmit the written heritage in writing and that the material was memorized for personal edification and dissemination. By contrast the hypothetical tradents imagined by modern source critics do not accidentally change the text through faulty memory that accompanies the written tradition but intentionally alter it, sometimes drastically, to keep the traditions contemporary with changing historical conditions.

NORTHWEST SEMITIC

Apart from the Ugaritic texts, treated above, and the Old Testament itself, the literature from the Northwest Semitic cultures is poorly preserved, probably because of the perishable

---

28. Albright, *Stone Age*, 79.

29. Kenneth A. Kitchen, *Ancient Orient and Old Testament* (Chicago: InterVarsity, 1966), 140.

30. Boudon van de Walle, *La transmission des textes littéraires égyptiens* (Brussels: Fondation égyptologique reine Elisabeth, 1948), 12.

31. Aksel P. F. Volten, *Studien zum Weisheitsbuch des Ani* (Copenhagen: Levin and Munksgaard, 1937).

32. Aksel P. F. Volten, *Das demotische Weisheitsbuch: Studien und Bearbeitung,* Analecta Aegyptiaca 1, 2 (Copenhagen: Munksgaard, 1941).

33. Gunter Burkard, *Textkritische Untersuchungen zu ägyptischen Weisheitslehre des alten und mittleren Reiches,* Ägyptologische Abhandlungen 34 (Wiesbaden: Harrassowitz, 1977).

nature of materials other than clay and rock in a hostile climate. What evidence exists suggests widespread literacy in this part of the ancient Near East due to the invention of the alphabet based on the acrophonic principle at circa 1600 B.C. The Proto-Sinaitic inscriptions (ca. 1475 B.C.) represent the written prayers of Semites enslaved by the Egyptians,[34] giving us strong reason to think that Abraham's descendants, though lowly slaves in Egypt, were literate.

The Old Testament witness about the manner of its transmission comports favorably with what has been found elsewhere in the ancient Near East, namely, that its sacred literature was transmitted in writing with oral dissemination. Its authors appeal to literary sources: "The Book of Songs" (3 Kings 8:53 LXX); "The Book of the Upright" (Josh. 10:13); "The Book of the Wars of Yahweh" (Num. 21:14); "The Diaries of the Kings" (Kings and Chronicles). The Hebrew Scriptures represent its laws as having been written down in books at the time of composition (Ex. 24:7; Deut. 31:9; Josh. 24:25–27; 1 Sam. 10:25) that must not be changed (Deut. 4:2; 12:32). The prophets refer to the law as a written document (Hos. 8:12). And to judge from Isaiah 8:16 and Jeremiah 36, the originally oral messages of the prophets were written down shortly after their delivery, exactly in the same way as happened in the case of the Quran (as we shall see shortly).

Even Moses' song was written down at the time of its original recitation (Deut. 31:19, 30). From this evidence may we not assume that the same was true of other songs mentioned in the Hebrew Scriptures (cf. Num. 21:17 and elsewhere)?

By comparing the Ugaritic poetry and the Amarna glosses (ca. 1400 B.C.) as his *terminus a quo* for the earliest forms of Hebrew poetry and Amos and Micah as his *terminus ad quem* for the later standard forms, David A. Robertson concluded (with the qualification that each one contains standard forms) that Exodus 15 is unqualifiedly early and that Deuteronomy 32, Judges 5, 2 Samuel 22 (Ps. 18), Habakkuk 3, and Job are qualifiedly early.[35] Even if they were passed on through the generations by word of mouth, they were not drastically reformulated.

A man must write a bill of divorce (Deut. 24:3); kings had secretaries to assist them in their writing (2 Sam. 8:17). According to Judges 8:14, a young man wrote down for Gideon the names of the seventy-seven officials of Succoth. This text assumes the literacy of Israel's youth.

To be sure, the law was to be memorized and recited orally (Ex. 12:24–26; Deut. 6:6, 20–25; Josh. 1:8; Ps. 1:2), as were the proverbs (e.g., Prov. 22:18) and Israel's sacred history (see Ps. 44:1), but we must not pit this oral activity against a stable written tradition. The evidence from the surrounding countries strongly suggests that the two kinds of tradition complemented one another: the written to preserve Israel's religious treasure, the oral to disseminate it.

By comparing synoptic passages in the Bible, Helmer Ringgren demonstrated that variants crept into the text in the same ways as Volten and van de Walle uncovered in Egypt.[36] But he too speaks of them as "mistakes," assuming that copyists were attempting to preserve the tradition rather than that tradents were at work deliberately reformulating and

---

34. William F. Albright, *The Proto-Sinaitic Inscriptions* (Cambridge: Harvard University Press, 1969).

35. David A. Robertson, *Linguistic Evidence in Dating Early Hebrew Poetry* (Missoula, MT: Society for Biblical Literature, 1972), 154. For the problems involved in dating documents, see Bruce K. Waltke and M. O'Connor, *An Introduction to Biblical Hebrew Syntax* (Winona Lake, IN: Eisenbrauns, 1990), 13–15.

36. Helmer Ringgren, "Oral and Written Transmission in the Old Testament," *Studia Theologica* 3 (1950–51): 34–59.

re-presenting it. In sum, these changes introduced by copyists are both qualitatively and quantitatively different from that supposed by critics who base their theories on a protracted and complicated oral tradition.

Robert C. Culley thought that formulaic language found in the psalms pointed to their origin in a tradition of oral formulaic composition. He wisely left open the question, however, of whether any of the present psalms were originally oral compositions.[37] In any case his study pertains to poetry and to oral composition, not to a pliable oral tradition.

Oral Tradition Outside the Ancient Near East

Obviously analogies from the literature of non-Semitic-speaking peoples and/or from a time later than the composition of the Old Testament do not carry as much weight in deciding the issue addressed as analogies from the ancient Near Eastern literatures or from the Old Testament itself. Nevertheless, a consideration of this data is instructive.

HOMER AND THE CLASSICS

According to Milman Parry, Homer composed poetic epics for easy oral recital in a pre-literature society.[38] Once again, however, it is important to note that the topic here is oral composition in contrast to a complex oral transmission. Furthermore, according to Robert B. Coote, the material in Homer is altogether different in type and extent from that of the Bible,[39] and Parry's evidence for oral composition in Homer is not applicable in the case of the Bible. Coote wrote: "None of the characteristics . . . which make Parry's designation of repeated lines and phrases in Homer as oral formulas by analogy with the Yugoslav oral formula so compelling is to be found in the Hebrew tradition."[40]

Some classicists are inclined to visualize a period of oral transmission in pre-Homeric times.[41] It is beyond my competence to make a judgment here. The fact that pupils were expected to memorize Homer and Virgil in classical antiquity is parallel to the use of oral tradition in the ancient Near East.

THE JEWS AND THE TALMUD

The Mishna and Gemara were both composed and transmitted orally for some period of time. But it may be supposed that these interpretations of the written laws found in the Bible were regarded at first during their oral stage as qualitatively different from the Scriptures themselves. In fact, they were probably put into writing only after they achieved an authoritative status among the Jews.

THE HINDUS AND THE RIG-VEDA

The Rig-Veda is the most striking example of a religious tradition passed on by word of mouth over centuries, from probably before 1200 B.C. to no earlier than about the fifth

---

37. Robert C. Culley, *Oral Formulaic Language in the Biblical Psalms* (Toronto: University of Toronto Press, 1976).

38. Milman Parry, "Studies in the Epic Technique of Oral Verse-Making. I: Homer and Homeric Style," *Harvard Studies in Classical Philology* 41 (1930): 43–147.

39. Robert B. Coote, "The Application of the Oral Theory to Biblical Hebrew Literature," *Semeia* 5 (1976): 52.

40. Ibid., 56–57.

41. Albert B. Lord, *The Singer of Tales* (Cambridge: Harvard University Press, 1960).

century B.C. The oral transmission of the later Vedas and the Brahmanas also embraced centuries. This manner of preserving religious literature in the environs of the Indus River stands in striking contrast to what is known of the civilizations along the Nile and Tigris-Euphrates rivers. But even this more remote evidence does not support the second principle of modern source critics that the text underwent complex reformulations. Projecting back from the modern Hindu practice where thousands of Brahmins still accurately learn the Rig-Veda by heart (153,826 words!)[42] to the earlier centuries, it may be supposed that those reciting this tradition aimed not to change it. And, of course, what is disconcerting about modern source critics is not so much their theory of oral transmission as their presumption that an oral tradition in the case of the Bible entailed a complex development of the literature, calling into question both its historical reliability and the clarity of authorial intention.

THE ARABS AND THE QURAN

Arabic literatures provide us with a much closer analogy to the Hebrew Scriptures. South Arabic inscriptions, which are notoriously difficult to date, do show that even Bedouin were literate. From a much later period Widengren demonstrated that Muhammad not only contributed directly or indirectly to putting the Quran into writing but even made some interpolations into the text.[43] Regarding the role of oral tradition in the composition of the Quran, Widengren wrote: "We are confronted with the fact that in the earliest Islamic period the first generation were the collectors of traditions."[44] The situation in Islam seems very similar to that of Christianity: Within the generation or two that witnessed Jesus Christ, written testimonies about him were made.

Regarding pre-Islamic poetry, Bridget Connelly pointed to an article by James T. Monroe arguing that, on the basis of formulaic expressions, these poems were composed for oral recitation.[45] Once again, oral composition is not directly relevant to the present study. However, Mary C. Bateson's investigation of five pre-Islamic Arabic codes rejected even this possibility.[46]

OLD ICELANDIC AND SERBO-CROATIAN

The best evidence for an oral tradition such as that proposed by modern source critics comes from Indo-European peoples of a much later time, especially from Old Icelandic (ca. A.D. 1300). Here one finds a mighty priesthood trained in the oral transmission of their religious heritage. But the objections to founding a theory on this sort of evidence ought not to require demonstration. In fact, to make an appeal to it appears to be an act of desperation and actually weakens the case. Widengren asked:

42. Max Muller, "Literature Before Letters," in *Last Essays* (1st ser.), 123, 130, cited in Nielsen, *Oral Tradition,* 24.

43. George Widengren, *Literary and Psychological Aspects of the Hebrew Prophets* (Uppsala: Universitets Arsskriff, 1948), 10, 49.

44. George Widengren, "Oral Tradition and Written Literature Among the Hebrews in Light of Arabic Evidence, with Special Regard to Prose Narratives," in *Acta Orientalia* 23 (1959): 201–62.

45. Bridget Connelly, "Oral Poetics: The Arab Case" (paper prepared for the Oral Literature Seminar, Modern Language Association, 1974), cited in Culley, *Oral Formulaic Language,* 6.

46. Mary C. Bateson, *Structural Continuity in Poetry: A Linguisitic Study in Five Pre-Islamic Arabic Odes* (The Hague: Mouton, 1970), cited in Culley, *Oral Formulaic Language,* 6.

Is it not queer to observe that in order to prove the predominant role of oral tradition among such a Semitic people in antiquity as the Hebrews all real evidence from their closely related neighbors, the Arabs, has been left out of consideration . . . whereas evidence from all kinds of Indo-European peoples was adduced, so that even the old Icelanders were called upon to render their service in which case neither the "great interval of time" nor that of space seems to have exercised any discouraging effect?![47]

The field of study of Parry and Albert Lord on a living oral tradition of Yugoslav narrative poetry showed that the poets did not memorize their traditional poems but freshly created them in each performance.[48] But the objections to applying their study to the Bible are obvious. First, the date is not comparable. Coote wrote: "The severest obstacle to the application of the theory to the OT is the lack of verse analogous in type and extent to that of Homer or Yugoslavia."[49] Second, the biblical literature was composed and received as the inspired Word of God, and therefore it would have been treasured as authoritative at the time of composition and less likely to be changed. Finally, the evidence is too far afield in time and culture to be convincing.

Conclusion

Having examined the literatures of the ancient Near East and other literatures as well, no evidence has been found in any Semitic cultures, including Islam, that tradents molded an oral tradition to meet changing situations over the centuries. John van Seters hit the nail on the head when he said, "Gunkel, Alt, von Rad, Noth, Westermann, and others . . . have not made a case for regarding the traditions of Genesis as . . . deriving from an oral base."[50]

The Source of the Patriarchal Narratives

On first reflection it may seem necessary to assume that the stories in Genesis about the patriarchs must have been handed down orally. William Sanford LaSor, David Allan Hubbard, and Frederic W. Bush assume that the patriarchal narratives (that is, family history) were handed down primarily by oral tradition. They see no objection to the hypothesis that the narratives were put into writing in Moses' time.[51] The case for oral tradition becomes most strong, however, for the stories in the first eleven chapters of Genesis, some of which must antedate by centuries the invention of writing. Though admitting that Israel's memory of the patriarchs was handed down by means of an uncertain oral tradition, Gleason Archer nevertheless pointed in the right direction in this statement: "The legacy of faith was handed down through the millennia from Adam to Moses in oral form, for the most part, but the final written form into which Moses cast it must have been especially superintended by the Holy Spirit in order to insure its divine trustworthiness."[52]

47. Widengren, "Oral Tradition," 225.

48. Lord, *Singer of Tales*. For a survey of field studies on oral poetry and oral prose in India, Africa, Mongolia, etc., see Culley, *Oral Formulaic Language*, esp. 2–4, 9–12.

49. Coote, "Application of Oral Theory," 52.

50. John van Seters, *Abraham in History and Tradition* (New Haven, CT: Yale University Press, 1975), 148.

51. William Sanford LaSor, David Allan Hubbard, and Frederic W. Bush, *Old Testament Survey: The Message, Form, and Background of the Old Testament* (Grand Rapids: Eerdmans, 1982), 108–9.

52. Gleason L. Archer Jr., *A Survey of Old Testament Introduction* (Chicago: Moody, 1964), 21n4.

The only reliable information we have about the antediluvian and postdiluvian patriarchs is not from oral tradition but from the written records preserved in the canon. Furthermore, it is gratuitous to assume that the anonymous author of Genesis—and all biblical narrators are anonymous—depended on oral tradition for their information. The truth is, as Robert Alter pointed out so brilliantly, that every biblical narrator is omniscient.[53] They know the thoughts of God in heaven and characterize the earthly subjects not by adjectives, such as the "wily Jacob," but by telling us their most private thoughts and conversations. Such storytellers are not dependent on oral tradition. Did men originally learn either about the creation of the cosmos as recorded in Genesis 1, assigned by literary critics to P, or about the creation of the man out of the earth in Genesis 2, assigned by the same critics to J, from oral tradition? In the final analysis these creation stories derive either from creative imagination or from revelation. The Bible and Spirit affirm that we are dealing not with prose fiction but with true knowledge, and we have no reason to think that it was not revealed to the storyteller himself, who inscripturated it in Holy Writ. The biblical authors are surrogates for God and as such are not dependent on oral tradition. That is not to deny that the successive patriarchs knew God's earlier promises to their fathers, and there is nothing objectionable in thinking that the author of Genesis, who prefers to remain anonymous, used them. It is inapposite, however, to think that he (or any other of the omniscient narrators of the Bible) was dependent on oral tradition. Undoubtedly the successive patriarchs knew antecedent revelation, but we do not know the extent or form of it.

It is difficult to verify or refute the claim that oral tradition lies behind the patriarchal narratives referring to events before the invention of writing. Whatever be the types and extent of sources that our omniscient narrator may have used, and the manner in which he may have used them, the important point is that God's inspired spokesman told the sacred stories in his own way. For this reason there is no reason to doubt their historicity or to be uncertain about his meaning.[54]

53. Robert Alter, *The Art of Biblical Narrative* (New York: Basic Books, 1981), 128.
54. Lest I be misunderstood, let me state that my objection to form criticism pertains not to the objective identification of literary genres and forms—this practice is an indispensable exegetical tool—but to the subjective practice of tracing the history of a tradition.

60

"The Infallible Rule of Interpretation of Scripture": The Hermeneutical Crisis and the Westminster Standards[1]

PETER A. LILLBACK

Peter A. Lillback, "'The Infallible Rule of Interpretation of Scripture': The Hermeneutical Crisis and the Westminster Standards," in *Resurrection and Eschatology: Theology in Service of the Church. Essays in Honor of Richard B. Gaffin Jr.*, ed. Lane G. Tipton and Jeffrey C. Waddington (Phillipsburg, NJ: P&R Publishing, 2008), 283–339.

Peter Lillback is president and professor of historical theology at Westminster Theological Seminary, Philadelphia. He studied at Cedarville College and Dallas Theological Seminary. He completed his Ph.D. in historical theology at Westminster in 1985. His dissertation was published in 2001 as *The Binding of God: Calvin's Role in the Development of Covenant Theology* in the series Texts and Studies in Reformation and Post-Reformation, edited by Richard Muller. He served as the pastor of three churches. His interests range from the history of covenant theology, the interpretation of the Bible, the Huguenots, and the history of the founding of America. Besides several scholarly publications in historical theology, he provides a thorough investigation of George Washington's religious life in *George Washington's Sacred Fire* (2006).

The present selection, "'The Infallible Rule of Interpretation of Scripture': The Hermeneutical Crisis and the Westminster Standards," is taken from a festschrift in

1. It is a privilege to offer this article in honor of Professor Richard B. Gaffin Jr.'s long and illustrious career at Westminster Theological Seminary. In seeking to honor his labors, I have selected themes that have been close to his life's work—the theology of biblical inspiration and the Westminster Standards. Consider, for example, his soon-to-be-republished articles, "Old Amsterdam and Inerrancy?—I," *WTJ* 44, 2 (Fall 1982): 250–89; and "Old Amsterdam and Inerrancy?—II," *WTJ* 45, 2 (Fall 1983): 219–72. They will be published with the new title, *God's Word in Servant Form* (Greenville, SC: Reformed Academic Press, 2008). Consult also his "Biblical Theology and the Westminster Standards" in *The Practical Calvinist* (Fearn, Ross-shire: Mentor/Christian Focus, 2002), 425–42.

honor of Richard B. Gaffin Jr. In this essay Lillback examines current challenges to the Bible, in particular the debate over Peter Enns's views on inspiration in light of the Westminster Standards, which have subordinate authority under the Word of God at Westminster Seminary. Enns's approach is found to be at odds not only with the Westminster Standards, but also with the Old Testament Westminster professor E. J. Young and the Reformed theologian Berkouwer.

A "controversial Bible,"[2] the "Battle for the Bible,"[3] the "Problem of the Old Testament,"[4] and the "messiness of the Old Testament"[5] are a few of the shibboleths revealing the strained relationship between recent biblical studies and the historic evangelical theology of Holy Scripture. Indeed, for some, "reading the Bible has already become a serious theological problem—perhaps even a crisis."[6] Berkouwer explains:

> A crisis has arisen in the hearts and minds of many people concerning this knowledge and certainty. There is a very close connection between this crisis and the development of the so-called historical criticism of Scripture, which drew attention to the nature of these scriptures as *human* writings.[7]

> It was inevitable that this radical question—and many others implied in it—should have a profound effect upon the life of the church, which until then had unquestioningly accepted the trustworthiness of Holy Scripture.[8]

> When the radical critics concluded from the "human character" of Scripture that they had a right to criticize it—and many of them claimed that an honest historical examination left little or nothing of the nimbus of infallibility, supernaturalness, and uniqueness—their opponents were tempted to present the divine character of Scripture in such a manner that the human character could be of little significance.[9]

As we engage the hermeneutical crisis, it behooves us to remember Berkouwer's appeal to the astute observation of Bavinck where he avers that opposition to Scripture can arise from both within as well as from without orthodoxy.

2. G. C. Berkouwer observes that "Holy Scripture has become in Claus Westermann's words, a 'controversial Bible,'" *Holy Scripture*, Studies in Dogmatics (Grand Rapids: Eerdmans, 1975), 9. For cogent critiques of the "controvesial Bible" occasioned by Rogers/McKim thesis, see Gaffin, "Old Amsterdam and Inerrancy?" and John D. Woodbridge, *Biblical Authority: A Critique of the Rogers/McKim Proposal* (Grand Rapids: Zondervan, 1982).

3. Cf. Harold Lindsell, *The Battle for the Bible* (Grand Rapids: Zondervan, 1976). The "battle for the Bible" has focused especially on inerrancy.

4. Peter Enns, *Inspiration and Incarnation: Evangelicals and the Problem of the Old Testament* (Grand Rapids: Baker Academic, 2005), 15–16.

5. Ibid., 108, 110.

6. Ibid., 15.

7. Berkouwer, *Holy Scripture*, 12.

8. Ibid., 13.

9. Ibid., 17.

There are different kinds of opposition to the real authority of Scripture that are not precluded or conquered by any kind of theory. When Bavinck reflects on the attack upon Holy Scripture, he sees this attack first of all as enmity of the human heart, which can manifest itself in various ways: "It is by no means only, and maybe not even most, prominent in the criticism to which Scripture is subjected in our day. Scripture as the Word of God meets with opposition and unbelief from every psychic human being. In the period of dead orthodoxy unbelief in Scripture was in principle just as powerful as in our historico-critical age."[10]

Similarly, the hermeneutical crisis that wrestles with "the real authority of Scripture" can be found not only at the fault line between orthodoxy and secular biblical criticism, but also within the boundaries of those who openly profess a sincere commitment to Scripture as divine self-revelation.

The Hermeneutical Crisis, the Westminster Standards, and Westminster Seminary

In this crisis context, what should we think of the Westminster Confession of Faith, the climactic statement of Reformed theology, as it developed its theology during the period of High Orthodoxy?[11] The confession, having defined the canon of Scripture, says of the canonical books, "All which are given by inspiration of God, to be the rule of faith and life" (WCF 1.2). Can this high and historical view of Scripture, championed by the Westminster Divines[12] as well as by Calvin,[13] Kuyper,[14] the Princetonian forerunners[15] and founders of

10. Ibid., 34–35.

11. Philip Schaff says of the Westminster Assembly and its influence, "Whether we look at the extent or ability of its labors, or its influence upon future generations, it stands first among Protestant councils," *Creeds of Christendom* (Grand Rapids: Baker, 1983), 1:728. Richard A. Muller defines the epoch of 1640–1700 as the period of "High Orthodoxy" for Reformed theology (see *Post-Reformation Reformed Dogmatics*, vol. 1, *Prolegomena to Theology* [Grand Rapids: Baker, 1987], 46). The Westminster Assembly met from 1643 to 1649.

12. Westminster Confession of Faith Chapter 1 is titled "Of the Holy Scripture," and is a classic statement of the Reformed understanding of Scripture. This succinct summary of the doctrine of Scripture touches many themes including Scripture's necessity, the definition of its canon, its divine authority, the divine source of human assurance concerning its infallibility, its sufficiency and perspicuity, the authority of its original languages, its preservation and propriety of its translation, its interpretation, and its finality for controversy.

13. J. I. Packer notes, "It seems obvious from what has been said that Calvin could never have consciously entertained the possibility that human mistakes, whether of reporting or of interpreting facts of any sort whatever, could have entered into the text of Scripture as the human writers gave it. Nor did he," "John Calvin and the Inerrancy of Holy Scripture," in *Inerrancy and the Church*, ed. John D. Hannah (Chicago: Moody, 1984), 178. Summarizing Calvin, John Murray writes, "God speaks in Scripture. In it he opens his sacred mouth." *Calvin on Scripture and Divine Sovereignty* (Philadelphia: Presbyterian & Reformed, 1960), 50.

14. Kuyper's views are well summarized by Gaffin, "Old Amsterdam—I," 272–75.

15. Benjamin B. Warfield, *Revelation and Inspiration* (New York: Oxford University Press, 1927), 74, 173; repr., *The Inspiration and Authority of the Bible* (Philadelphia: Presbyterian and Reformed, 1948), 128, 173; Archibald A. Hodge and Benjamin B. Warfield, *Inspiration* (Grand Rapids: Baker, 1979). Paul D. Feinberg writes in "The Meaning of Inerrancy," "As has already been indicated, for at least a fair number of biblical and theological scholars of former days inspiration was synonymous with inerrancy. To say that the Bible is inspired was to say that it is absolutely accurate or inerrant. Two men among those who held such a view were B. B. Warfield and Charles Hodge." Norman L. Geisler, ed., *Inerrancy* (Grand Rapids: Zondervan, 1980), 287.

Westminster such as Geerhardus Vos,[16] John Murray,[17] Cornelius Van Til,[18] and E. J. Young,[19] remain in force in the face of the hermeneutical crisis confronting the church?

Westminster Seminary Professor E. J. Young believed it could. As a keen advocate of the relevancy of the confession's teaching on Scripture, Young declared:

> We do not believe that the "facts" which the modern "scientific" study of the Bible has brought to light compel us to change or modify or abandon the historic doctrine of inspiration which finds such a classic expression, for example, in the first chapter of the Westminster Confession of Faith.[20]

Similarly, Moisés Silva declares that the confession's teaching on Scripture is intact even in the face of the advance of biblical studies.[21]

Harvie Conn, however, concerned for cultural contextualization in hermeneutics and the hermeneutical spiral,[22] was less sure, at least in terms of the use of the confession. Thus

16. Geerhardus Vos, the founder of Reformed biblical theology, issued a clarion call for inerrancy as a *sine qua non* in the principles of biblical theology. On May 8, 1894, Vos delivered his inaugural address as professor of biblical theology entitled, "The Idea of Biblical Theology as a Science and as a Theological Discipline." (Originally published in 1894 by Anson D. F. Randolph and Company, this essay is now in the public domain.) In this historic address, Vos elucidates the dual nature of Scripture, simultaneously underscoring the primacy of divine authorship and the indispensably human and historical nature of revelation. Vos emphasizes the critical point that the historical character of biblical truth is not in any way antithetical to, but throughout subordinated to, its *revealed* character. The historical setting of Scripture has been employed by God for the very purpose of *revealing absolute* truth. Vos also warns against historicist presuppositions, present in the critical tradition of biblical theology that Vos himself self-consciously opposed, that deny the absolute character of biblical truth as a revelation from the triune God. Vos' warning is perhaps more relevant today than in 1894.

17. John Murray, "The Attestation of Scripture," in *The Infallible Word: A Symposium by the Members of the Faculty of Westminster Theological Seminary*, ed. Ned B. Stonehouse and Paul Woolley (Phillipsburg, NJ: Presbyterian and Reformed, 1978), 6–9.

18. Cornelius Van Til, "Introduction" to Benjamin B. Warfield, in *The Inspiration and Authority of the Bible* (Philadelphia: Presbyterian and Reformed, 1948), 66–68. A change in one's doctrine of Scripture impacts one's theological apologetics, as Van Til notes in the preface to his *An Introduction to Systematic Theology*, ed. William Edgar (Phillipsburg, NJ: P&R Publishing, 2007), 12.

19. Edward J. Young, *Thy Word Is Truth: Some Thoughts on the Biblical Doctrine of Inspiration* (Grand Rapids: Eerdmans, 1957). The front cover of the ninth printing in 1976 declares, "A forthright defense of the Bible as the infallible and inerrant Word of God, with explanations of apparent contradictions, based on the evidence of the Bible itself; and a pointed refutation of some modern theories that reject a verbally inspired Bible." See also Edward J. Young, *The God-Breathed Scripture*, The Bauman Memorial Lectures for 1966 delivered at Grace Theological Seminary and College. Foreword by R. B. Gaffin Jr. (Willow Grove, PA: The Committee for the Historian of the Orthodox Presbyterian Church, 2007).

20. Young, *Thy Word Is Truth*, 17.

21. "Referring again to the Westminster Confession of Faith, perhaps the most comprehensive theological statement arising from the Reformation, we may ask: Is there any chapter in that document that needs revision because we now conclude that, say, the Song of Solomon was written, not as an allegory, but as a description of human love? Is there even a paragraph that must now be excised because of advances in textual criticism or philology? The answer is a *definitive and unequivocal no*." Moisés Silva, *Has the Church Misread the Bible? The History of Interpretation in the Light of Current Issues* (Grand Rapids: Zondervan, 1987), 92 (italics added).

22. Harvie M. Conn ("Normativity, Relevance, and Relativism," in *Inerrancy and Hermeneutic*, 185–209) asks, "Can one believe in the Bible as the only infallible rule of faith and practice and, at the same time, affirm its culturally oriented particularity? . . . Will our current sensitivity to the New Testament as a word addressed to our century relativize our parallel commitment to it as a word addressed also to the first century?"(185). He continues, "Following the lead of Hans-Georg Gadamer, scholars associated with what has been called the New Hermeneutic have described this process of understanding as a hermeneutical circle. But the model has its problems. Evangelicals have feared that to bind text and exegete into a circle is to create a relationship of mutuality where 'what is true for me' becomes the criterion of 'what is true.' Instead, it has become more popular among evangelicals to speak of a hermeneutical spiral. Behind the idea of the spiral is the idea of progress in understanding; it is closer to the biblical image of sanctification, of growth in grace. Within the spiral, two complementary processes are taking place. As our cultural setting is matched with the text and the text with our setting,

Conn specified the dangers of "gnosticizing" culture and "remythologizing" the confession.[23] He expressed his worries over "the evangelical's perception of theology as some sort of comprehensively universal science . . . the Queen of the sciences, the watchdog of the academic world, the ultimate universal Confessional theology." He believed that "our creedal formulations, structured to respond to a sixteenth-century cultural setting and its problems," would "lose their historical character as contextual confessions of faith and become cultural universals, having comprehensive validity in all times and settings." What was the resulting danger in Conn's mind for this view of the Westminster Confession? He explains: "The possibility of new doctrinal developments for the Reformed churches" would be "frozen into a time warp that gnosticizes the particularity of time and culture." The cure for these dangers was the "contextualization" of the creeds and the recognition of "how we have diminished their historical, contextual character."[24]

The Reformed confessions, to be sure, have a historical context. Consequently it can be claimed, as Conn implies, that the Reformed confessions are time bound, because they were primarily aiming at Roman Catholic/anti-Protestant apologetics. Yet it is important also to keep in mind what Turretin[25] recognized: "in every age the enemies of true religion and of Scripture have thought that they had found contradictory passages in Scripture. . . . various

---

the text progressively reshapes the questions we bring to it, and in turn, our questions force us to look at the text in a fresh way" (194). He then adds, "At the same time, our participation in hermeneutics is real also. And as we have noted, that is not a neutral participation without theological, cultural, or psychological presuppositions. We cannot escape the influence of our preunderstandings in looking for meaning and significance. How, then, does my specific sociocultural and psychological background aid or distort my reading of Scripture?" (203). Berkouwer also addresses the "hermeneutical circle" in *Holy Scripture,* "This leads us to what is now commonly called the 'hermeneutical circle.' The term usually describes the relationship of the understanding of the whole of Scripture to its parts and *vice versa.* It is understandable that the circle has also been invoked in opposition to the 'pre-understanding' (i.e., the interpreter is no *tabula rasa*). The idea is that understanding though it focuses on the text, is yet not the sum total of variously understood parts, since the 'pre-understanding' cannot be eliminated. The part which subjectivity plays in the process of understanding must be recognized. In all of this the circle itself is not at stake, inasmuch as it demands attention to the particular involvement of the interpreter, who does not approach the text of Scripture with a clean slate. The critical question in regard to this is whether or not the 'encounter,' the positing of the *a priori* of the text over against all of the interpreter's baggage and presuppositions, is completely recognized. Only then does the circle avoid being a necessarily vicious one. Only when the aim is a correlation between kerygma and existence, in which existence itself, despite every accent on the text, is made the final 'canon' for its understanding, will such a peculiarly vicious circle be created" (119–20).

23. In his inaugural address as professor of missiology at Westminster, Harvey Conn, for example, expresses his concern of a perceived "gnosticizing" of culture that impedes missiological and doctrinal advances: "Related to this struggle is the evangelical's perception of theology as some sort of comprehensively universal science. Theology becomes functionally the Queen of the sciences, the watchdog of the academic world, the ultimate universal. Combined with Western ethnocentrism, it produces the tacit assumption 'that the Christian faith is already fully and properly indigenized in the West.' Our creedal formulations, structured to respond to a sixteenth-century cultural setting and its problems, lose their historical character as contextual confessions of faith and become cultural universals, having comprehensive validity in all times and settings. The possibility of new doctrinal developments for the Reformed churches of Japan or Mexico is frozen into a time warp that Gnosticizes the particularity of time and culture. The Reformation is completed and we in the West wait for the churches of the Third World to accept as their statements of faith those shaped by a Western church three centuries before in a *corpus christianum.* In all this, there is no desire to diminish the place of the creed as the expression of the progressive understanding of truth conveyed by the Holy Spirit. Nor do we want to minimize or question the system of doctrine found in the Reformed creeds of these centuries. Our concern is over how we have diminished their historical, contextual character. The creed as a missionary document framed in the uniqueness of an historical moment has too often been remythologized by white paternalism into a universal essence for all times. Contextualization, as a missionary demand of theologizing, is relegated to the non-Western 'mission field.'" "The Missionary Task of Theology: A Love/Hate Relationship?" *WTJ* 45, 1 (1983): 16–17.

24. Ibid.

25. Critics of inerrancy see philosophical motivations rather than biblical concerns at work in Turretin's development of his doctrine of Scripture. Jack B. Rogers and Donald K. McKim claim, "Falling back on the philosophy of Aristotle and the

libertines, who, although living in the bosom of the church, never stop calling attention to some 'irreconcilable differences' and 'contradictions,' so as to erode the authority of Scripture."[26] This latter group extends far beyond the compass of Roman Catholic theology.

Under Conn's lead, a faculty symposium was published addressing the interplay between inerrancy and hermeneutics,[27] reflecting a breadth of opinions within Westminster's confessional tradition.[28] The essays in general, however, made minimal explicit reference to the confession's implications for the task of hermeneutics.[29]

More recently, Professor Peter Enns, professor of Old Testament and hermeneutics at Westminster Theological Seminary,[30] has published a hermeneutical study that repeatedly calls for a reconsideration of the evangelical doctrine of Scripture.[31] Enns seeks a "Reassessment

---

theological categories of Thomas Aquinas, Turretin produced a scholastic theology that placed great emphasis on precise definition and systematic, scientific statement." *Authority and Interpretation*, 235.

26. Turretin writes (*Institutes*, II.5.1–2), "When the divine quality of Scripture, which was argued in the preceding question, has been accepted, its infallibility follows of necessity. But in every age the enemies of true religion and of Scripture have thought that they had found contradictory passages in Scripture, and have vigorously presented them in order to overthrow its authority; for example, Porphyry, Lucian, and Julian the Apostate among the pagans of antiquity, and today various atheists, who in hostile fashion declare that there are contradictions and irreconcilable differences which cannot be harmonized in any way. Therefore this particular question must be discussed with them, so that the integrity of Scripture may be upheld against their impiety by a completed fabric and covering. Our controversy is not with open atheists and pagans, who do not recognize Holy Scripture, but with others who although they seem to accept it, yet indirectly deny it in this manner; for example, the enthusiasts, who allege the imperfection of the written word in order to attract people to their esoteric word or special revelations . . . and finally, various libertines, who, although living in the bosom of the church, never stop calling attention to some 'irreconcilable differences' and 'contradictions,' so as to erode the authority of Scripture." *The Doctrine of Scripture*, ed. and trans. John W. Beardslee III (Grand Rapids: Baker, 1981), 57–58.

27. Conn's introductory article in *Inerrancy and Hermeneutic*, "A Historical Prologue: Inerrancy, Hermeneutic, and Westminster," surveys the development of the views of Scripture held by Westminster Seminary's faculty. He concludes on page 34, "The chapters in this volume are, as stated in the preface, only bridge building in intention. They attempt to sketch the agenda changes over four decades. They are catch-up exercises for the evangelical, concerned with affirming the reliability of our fundamental commitment to the inerrant Word of God in the face of new questions. The problems shift and move; the Word of our God abides forever."

28. Silva writes, "The hermeneutical flexibility that has characterized our tradition would probably come as a surprise to many observers who view Westminster as excessively rigid. Ironically, our Confessional documents, the Westminster Confession and Catechisms, are far more extensive and detailed than those found in most evangelical institutions. Our theological parameters are indeed very clearly defined, and yet those parameters themselves have made possible a diversity of viewpoints that would not have been tolerated in some other institutions." Moisés Silva, "Old Princeton, Westminster, and Inerrancy," in *Inerrancy and Hermeneutic*, 78.

29. In the fourteen essays presented in *Inerrancy and Hermeneutic* edited by Harvie Conn, there are only eight references to the Westminster Standards. Two are general references to the Westminster Confession. Five are specific citations of the confession, one is a reference to the first question of the Shorter Catechism, and none refers to the Larger Catechism. The five specific citations of the confession are all to the first chapter, namely 1.2–3, 4, 5, 7, 8. The salient point is that there is no citation of 1.9 of the confession, the central text that directly links infallibility and hermeneutics! This relevant passage defines "the only infallible rule of interpretation of Scripture." And specifically, Professor Conn's extensive citations of literature in his two articles in *Inerrancy and Hermeneutic* do not include any citation of the Westminster Standards. Ironically, *Inerrancy and Hermeneutic* references Bultmann eight times.

30. Enns once references Westminster Seminary but does not refer to the Westminster Standards: "Also influential has been my own theological tradition, represented by my colleagues at Westminster Theological Seminary, past and present, and the wider tradition of which that institution is a part. This is not to imply that I speak for that institution or tradition. Nevertheless, I am thankful for being part of such a solidly faithful group, that does not shy away from some difficult yet basic questions and with whom I am able to have frank and open discussions." *Inspiration and Incarnation*, 9.

31. Enns emphasizes this point: "My focus . . . to look at these data [data that biblical scholars work with every day] with a clear view toward discussing their *implications for an evangelical doctrine of Scripture*" (9, emphasis added). He indicates that, "The purpose of this book is to bring *an evangelical doctrine of Scripture* into conversation with the implications generated by some important themes in modern biblical scholarship—particularly Old Testament scholarship—over the past 150 years. To put it this way is to suggest that such a conversation has not taken place, at least not to the degree that it could have" (13, emphasis added). He explains, "In my view, however, what is needed is not simply

of doctrine on the basis of external evidence. . . . My concern is that, at least on a popular level, a defensive approach to the evidence tends to dominate the evangelical conversation."[32]

This appears to be a significant step beyond the perspective of Professor Conn. Conn concluded his essay, ". . . in the face of new questions. The problems shift and move; the Word of our God abides forever."[33] But Professor Enns begins his study by connecting "the problems" directly with the Bible, with the Old Testament, as seen in his provocative title: *Inspiration and Incarnation: Evangelicals and the Problem of the Old Testament.*

For Enns, the external evidence about the Bible that has accumulated since the 1800s requires a new synthesis of doctrine and data. He writes:

> My aim is somewhat more foundational . . . . I want to contribute to a growing opinion that what is needed is to move beyond both sides [i.e., liberal vs. conservative] by thinking of better ways to account for some of the data, while at the same time having a vibrant, positive view of Scripture as God's word. . . . To put it another way, my aim is to allow the collective evidence to affect not just how we understand a biblical passage or story here and there within the parameters of earlier doctrinal formulations. Rather, I want to move beyond that by allowing the evidence to affect how we think about what Scripture as a whole *is*. . . .

---

for evangelicals to work *in* these areas, but to engage the *doctrinal implications* that work in these areas raises. Without wanting to overstate the matter, I know or hear of a fair number of Christians who conclude that the contemporary state of biblical scholarship makes an evangelical faith unviable. These are the primary readers I envision for this book, those who desire to maintain a vibrant and reverent doctrine of Scripture, but who find it difficult to do so because they find familiar and conventional approaches to newer problems to be unhelpful" (13). Elaborating, he says, "On the one hand, I am very eager to affirm that many evangelical instincts are correct and should be maintained, for example, the conviction that the Bible is ultimately from God and that it is God's gift to the church. Any theories concerning Scripture that do not arise from these fundamental instincts are unacceptable. On the other hand, *how the evangelical church fleshes out its doctrine of Scripture* will always have somewhat of a provisional quality to it. This is not to say that each generation must disregard the past and start afresh, formulating ever-new doctrines, bowing to all the latest fads. But it is to say that at such time when new evidence comes to light, or old evidence is seen in a new light, we must be willing to *engage that evidence and adjust our doctrine accordingly*" (13–14, emphasis added). Then he boldly asserts that, "*Reassessment of doctrine on the basis of external evidence,* therefore is nothing new. To state it differently, our topic is the age-old question of the relationship between special revelation (the Bible) and general revelation (creation, i.e., everything else). My concern is that, at least on a popular level, a defensive approach to the evidence tends to dominate the evangelical conversation. . . . The terms are familiar, liberal vs. conservative, modernist vs. fundamentalist, mainline vs. evangelical, progressive vs. traditionalist. . . . My aim is somewhat more foundational . . . I want to contribute to a growing opinion that what is needed is to move beyond both sides by thinking of better ways to account for some of the data, while at the same time having a vibrant, positive view of Scripture as God's word. . . . To put it another way, *my aim is to allow the collective evidence to affect not just how we understand a biblical passage or story here and there within the parameters of earlier doctrinal formulations. Rather, I want to move beyond that by allowing the evidence to affect how we think about what Scripture as a whole is*" (14–15, emphasis added). He then reasons that, "The end result, I truly hope, will be to *provide a theological paradigm* for people who know instinctively that the Bible is God's word, but for whom reading the Bible has already become a serious theological problem—perhaps even a crisis" (15, emphasis added). Fleshing out his argument, he says, "Regardless of how we organize the data, the issue before us is not how we handle this verse or this issue, one at a time. Rather, what needs to happen is that we take a step back from the details and allow these issues to challenge us on a more fundamental level. What is needed is a way of thinking about Scripture where these kinds of issues are addressed from a very different perspective—where these kinds of problems cease being problems. . . . It is not enough simply to say that the Bible is the word of God or that it is inspired or to apply some other label. The issue is how these descriptions of the Bible bear fruit when we touch down in one part of the Bible or another. How does the study of Scripture in the contemporary world affect *how we flesh out descriptions such as 'word of God' or 'inspired'?*" (16–17, emphasis added). The result is that, "The *doctrinal implications* of these discoveries have not yet been fully worked out in evangelical theology" (25, emphasis added). According to Enns, this means that "the *doctrinal implications* of the Bible being so much a part of its ancient contexts are still not being addressed as much as they should" (47, emphasis added).

32. Enns, *Inspiration and Incarnation*, 14.
33. Conn, "A Historical Prologue: Inerrancy, Hermeneutic, and Westminster," 34.

But to those who struggle to synthesize their own doctrinal commitments with what we have learned about the Bible over the past 150 years, these ways of handling the evidence can be both frustrating and even debilitating. . . .

The findings of the past 150 years have made extrabiblical evidence an unavoidable conversation partner. The result is that, as perhaps never before in the history of the church, we can see how truly provisional and incomplete certain dimensions of our understanding of Scripture can be. On the other hand, we are encouraged to encounter the depth and riches of God's revelation and to rely more and more on God's Spirit, who speaks to the church in Scripture.[34]

There is indeed a hermeneutical crisis, one whose magnitude, if we accept Peter Enns's phrase, is monumental in proportion: "perhaps never before in the history of the church."[35] Given that such is the case, even after the hyperbole is taken into account, it seems appropriate to borrow Harvie Conn's language and embellish his desire "to sketch the agenda changes over four decades."[36] To do so, let us contrast two OT faculty members of Westminster, namely, E. J. Young and Peter Enns. By doing so, the changed OT hermeneutical agenda fueling this crisis and impacting the historic confessional view of Scripture and hermeneutic taught at Westminster will thereby come into sharper relief.

Reflecting, then, on the same "data" and "extrabiblical evidence" impacting OT scholars and their doctrine of Scripture referenced by Enns, Young, earlier Westminster professor of OT, wrote:

In the face of this constant demand for a new doctrine of inspiration, what attitude is the Christian man to adopt? . . . Have the findings of "scientific" biblical study actually demonstrated the untenability of the traditional attitude toward inspiration? There are some evangelical Christians who apparently think that such is the case.[37]

When we have once grasped the idea that we must derive our doctrine of inspiration from the Bible, we may begin to understand what the real issue before the Church is. The real issue is

---

34. Enns, *Inspiration and Incarnation*, 14–15, 48, 49, respectively.

35. There is some confusion as to the audience that Enns is addressing: the troubled evangelical or the historic evangelical. D. A. Carson (at the online e-zine *Reformation* 21, May 2006), writes, "Who are the intended readers? The answer to that question, in the case of this book, must be an integral part of the evaluation. Enns himself, it must be recalled, states that his envisaged readers are the 'fair number of Christians who conclude that the contemporary state of biblical scholarship makes an evangelical faith unviable' (13). In other words, granted the historical/literary/archaeological/historical difficulties cast up by 'biblical scholarship,' how can 'evangelical faith'—presumably what evangelical faith says about the Bible—be viable? Taking this at face value, the difficulties should be the 'given' in the minds of the envisaged readers, and the book would then either challenge some of those 'difficulties' in order to maintain evangelicalism's stance on the Bible, or it would accommodate the difficulties and provide a more sophisticated understanding of 'evangelical faith,' or perhaps a revision of it. Yet in the three substantive chapters, most of the space is devoted instead to convincing the reader that the difficulties Enns isolates are real, and must be taken more seriously by evangelicals than is usually the case. In other words, despite his initial claim that he is writing the book to comfort the disturbed, as it were, the actual performance aims to disturb the comfortable. This makes the book rather difficult to evaluate. Moreover, Enns's ambitions are vaulting: the evidence cast up by biblical scholarship, we are told, is of the sort that requires that an 'adjustment' be made in how we think of Scripture, akin to the re-interpretation generated by the Copernican revolution (13). Wow. So are we explaining how evangelical faith accommodates biblical scholarship, or are we asserting that a Copernican revolution must take place within evangelical faith so as to accommodate biblical scholarship?" D. A. Carson, "Three Books on the Bible: A Critical Review" [accessed January 8, 2008]. Online: http://www.reformation21.org/Past_Issues/2006_Issues_1_16_/2006_Issues_1_16_Shelf_Life/May_2006/May_2006/181/vobId__2926/. For this review now in print, see D. A. Carson, *Collected Writings on Scripture*, compiled by Andrew David Naselli (Wheaton, IL: Crossway, 2010), 267.

36. Conn, "A Historical Prologue: Inerrancy, Hermeneutic, and Westminster," 34.

37. E. J. Young, *Thy Word Is Truth*, 16.

not whether we are to substitute one doctrine of inspiration for another. That is at the most a somewhat secondary question. The real issue before the Church today, and for that matter before every individual Christian, is whether the Bible is any longer to be regarded and accepted as a trustworthy teacher of doctrine. In other words, when the Bible testifies as to its own nature, are we to pay heed to what it has to say?[38]

The Bible, therefore, whether we will or not, is constantly being thrust into the forefront of discussion and one can only be amazed, to say nothing of being saddened, at the glibness with which many speak of the old-fashioned view of inspiration as being out of date and not relevant for the present age.[39]

To understand the present demand for a new doctrine of inspiration and a new attitude toward the Bible one must know something about the background and soil from which much of our modern religious life and thought has sprung. . . .[40]

Clearly, the hermeneutical crisis is real and has impacted Westminster Seminary. There are two theologies of Scripture wrestling in the faculty room. The question before us, to use an OT image, is whether the elder theology shall serve the younger. In answering this, the role of the Westminster Standards and the faculty vow to those standards take on high importance.

The Hermeneutical Crisis and the Historic Presbyterian Subscription to the Confession

The importance of the question of the relationship between the confession and biblical studies is especially important in the context of biblically oriented Presbyterian churches in general and Westminster Theological Seminary in particular. This is because subscription to these standards is required. The subscription made by ordained Presbyterian officers in the Orthodox Presbyterian Church (OPC) and in the Presbyterian Church in America (PCA) is well known.[41] Perhaps less well known, the faculty and board of Westminster Theological Seminary make an extensive and even more explicit *ex animo* commitment to the Westminster Standards.[42]

---

38. Ibid., 28.
39. Ibid., 15.
40. Ibid.
41. See, *Book of Church Order*, OPC, 23.8, "(2) Do you sincerely receive and adopt the Confession of Faith and Catechisms of this Church, as containing the system of doctrine taught in the Holy Scriptures?"; *Book of Church Order*, PCA, 21–25, "2. Do you sincerely receive and adopt the *Confession of Faith* and the *Catechisms* of this Church, as containing the system of doctrine taught in the Holy Scriptures; and do you further promise that if at any time you find yourself out of accord with any of the fundamentals of this system of doctrine, you will on your own initiative, make known to your Presbytery the change which has taken place in your views since the assumption of this ordination vow?"
42. Westminster Theological Seminary's constitution prescribes the following pledge for every voting member of the faculty: "I do solemnly declare, in the presence of God, and of the Trustees and Faculty of this Seminary, that (1) I believe the Scriptures of the Old and New Testaments to be the Word of God, the only infallible rule of faith and practice; and (2) I do solemnly and *ex animo* adopt, receive, and subscribe to the Westminster Confession of Faith and Catechisms in the form in which they were adopted by this Seminary in the year of our Lord 1936, as the confession of my faith, or as a summary and just exhibition of that system of doctrine and religious belief, which is contained in Holy Scripture, and therein revealed by God to man for his salvation; and I do solemnly, *ex animo*, profess to receive the fundamental principles of the Presbyterian form of church government, as agreeable

Alongside this confessional subscription, OPC and PCA officers as well as Westminster faculty and trustees have also specifically subscribed to the infallibility of the Scriptures. The language of the seminary's subscription is identical to that of the OPC and nearly so to the PCA. The only difference of the OPC and Westminster subscriptions from that of the PCA is that the PCA's text adds a phrase indicating commitment to the inerrancy of the *autographa*:

> Westminster: I believe the Scriptures of the Old and New Testaments to be the Word of God, the only infallible rule of faith and practice. (See note 43.)

> OPC: Do you believe the Scriptures of the Old and New Testaments to be the Word of God, the only infallible rule of faith and practice? (*Book of Church Order*, OPC, 23.8, [1].)

> PCA: Do you believe the Scriptures of the Old and New Testaments, as originally given, to be the inerrant Word of God, the only infallible rule of faith and practice? (*Book of Church Order*, PCA, 21–5, 1.)

Clearly, the historic Presbyterian commitment to the authority of the Westminster Standards and to the infallibility of the Scriptures has been maintained by Westminster Seminary, the OPC, and the PCA as evidenced by these explicit vows.[43]

---

to the inspired oracles. And I do solemnly promise and engage not to inculcate, teach, or insinuate anything which shall appear to me to contradict or contravene, either directly or impliedly, any element in that system of doctrine, nor to oppose any of the fundamental principles of that form of church government, while I continue a member of the Faculty in this Seminary. I do further solemnly declare that, being convinced of my sin and misery and of my inability to rescue myself from my lost condition, not only have I assented to the truth of the promises of the Gospel, but also I have received and rest upon Christ and His righteousness for pardon of my sin and for my acceptance as righteous in the sight of God and I do further promise that if at any time I find myself out of accord with any of the fundamentals of this system of doctrine, I will on my own initiative, make known to the Faculty of this institution and, where applicable, my judicatory, the change which has taken place in my views since the assumption of the vow."

43. Cf. Peter A. Lillback, "Confessional Subscription among the Sixteenth Century Reformers," in *The Practice of Confessional Subscription*, ed. David W. Hall (Lanham, MD: University Press of America, 1995), 33–66. In regard to the nature of the authority of the Protestant confessions, Schaff writes,

"The value of creeds depends upon the measure of their agreement with the Scriptures. In the best case a human creed is only an approximate and relatively correct exposition of revealed truth, and may be improved by the progressive knowledge of the Church, while the Bible remains perfect and infallible. The Bible is of God; the Confession is man's answer to God's word. The Bible is the *norma normans*; the Confession the *norma normata*. The Bible is the rule of faith (*regula fidei*); the Confession the rule of doctrine (*regula doctrina*). The Bible has, therefore a divine and absolute, the Confession only an ecclesiastical and relative authority. The Bible regulates the general religious belief and practice of the laity as well as the clergy; the symbols regulate the public teaching of the officers of the Church, as Constitutions and Canons regulate the government, Liturgies and Hymn-books the worship of the Church. Any higher view of the authority of symbols is unprotestant and essentially Romanizing. Symbololatry is a species of idolatry, and substitutes the tyranny of a printed book for that of a living pope. It is apt to produce the opposite extreme of a rejection of all creeds, and to promote rationalism and infidelity." *The Creeds of Christendom*, 1:7–8.

But if the Westminster Standards are a norm that is normed by Scripture, to what *extent* can they be considered authoritative? Are they to be subscribed because (*quia*) they are scriptural or are they to be subscribed as far as (*quatenus*) they are scriptural? Klotsche explains,

"To decide this question we must remember that the object of a confession is, not to find out what God teaches, for this we find in the Scriptures, but to show what we believe. A quatenus-subscription is no real confession, but an evasion and leaves it to a person's subjective judgment what to accept and what to reject. The church must ask for a quia-subscription, for she must know where her ministers and teachers stand. A confession of faith is to the church what a constitution is to a society, and no one has a right to enter or remain in any Christian church except as its terms of membership give him that right.

Given the criticisms of the primacy afforded to the Westminster Standards, both from without and from within the Westminster tradition,[44] a significant question arises concerning the Westminster Standards' impact on the interpretation of the "infallible" Scriptures. In light of the hermeneutical crisis, the question to be considered here is: what are the hermeneutical parameters the Westminster Standards establish for the interpreters of Holy Scripture who have subscribed to these standards?

The Regulative Principle of Hermeneutics: The Westminster Standards' Parameters and "Infallible" Hermeneutical Principle

Moisés Silva, writing at the time as a professor of New Testament at Westminster, notes that there are significant theological parameters established by the Westminster Standards that are vital for hermeneutics:

> The hermeneutical flexibility that has characterized our tradition would probably come as a surprise to many observers who view Westminster as excessively rigid. Ironically, our Confessional documents, the Westminster Confession and Catechisms, are far more extensive and detailed than those found in most evangelical institutions. Our theological parameters are indeed very clearly defined, and yet those parameters themselves have made possible a diversity of viewpoints that would not have been tolerated in some other institutions.[45]

Westminster's discussion of the doctrine of Scripture under the lead of Richard B. Gaffin Jr. has identified deeply with the Reformed tradition reflected by Abraham Kuyper

---

"Not only the heretical sects connected with Protestantism but also the liberal theologians of the church have raised an outcry against the authority of symbols as inconsistent with 'the right of private judgment.' They style the church's attitude in respect to symbols 'symbololatry,' worship of symbols, and see in the symbols only a yoke of human authority, a new popery in the form of printed documents. Making all due allowance for the prejudice which many of the opponents of the church's confessions have displayed, and for their ignorance which lies behind most of their comments on the subject, nevertheless, we cannot in the least support such a tirade against the symbols of the church, for the church does not *compel* anyone to accept her doctrines. A candidate for the ministry offers himself to the church for service, and his offer is accepted by the church on the ground that he is one with her in faith. If he cannot subscribe to the confessions of his church, he should not seek her ministerial office; or if, as a minister of the church, he has abandoned the faith of his church, he will, if he is at all sincere, leave that church and join another with which he is one in faith." E. H. Klotsche, *Christian Symbolics or Exposition of the Distinctive Characteristics of the Catholic, Lutheran and Reformed Churches as well as the Modern Denominations and Sects Represented in this Country* (Burlington, IO: The Lutheran Literary Board, 1929), 15–16.

Thus the Protestant confessional tradition simultaneously recognizes the subordinate character of its standards with respect to the Scriptures and the superiority of its standards with respect to the qualifications of its ministers and officers.

44. Harvie M. Conn, as noted above, expresses his concern for a "gnosticizing" of culture as well as a fear of a "remythologized" confession. "The Missionary Task of Theology," 16–17. In this context consider Berkouwer's criticisms of Edmund Clowney's critique of the United Presbyterian Church's proposed confession in *Holy Scripture*, 163–65.

45. Moisés Silva, "Old Princeton," 78. Berkouwer affirms the inescapable connection of theology and hermeneutic, *Holy Scripture,* 106, "The fact that hermeneutics is continually busy with rules for the exposition of Scripture shows a desire to oppose the arbitrariness which, despite the recognition of Scripture as God's Word, neglects its concrete authority. It is impossible for any theological study to bypass these questions. For in every hermeneutical question lies an aspect which is intrinsically tied to the confession of scriptural authority." See also Silva, *Has the Church Misread the Bible?* 38, "The first item listed above—the Bible as both divine and human—constitutes the most basic question of all. Strictly speaking, it is not so much a hermeneutical question as it is one of theology, even though, as we shall see in the course of our discussions, one can hardly divorce doctrine from interpretation."

and Herman Bavinck,[46] and has thereby avoided the conundrums created by the theology of fundamentalism.[47]

Nevertheless, the question before us in Silva's words is whether the "diversity of viewpoints that . . . have been tolerated" and "made possible" at Westminster by these "theological parameters" have begun to erode or even breach the parameters that sheltered and enabled them in the first place?

In this context, it appears significant that Enns's expressed desire is to "move beyond" the "parameters of earlier doctrinal formulations."

> My aim is to allow the collective evidence to affect not just how we understand a biblical passage or story here and there within the parameters of earlier doctrinal formulations. Rather,

46. See for example, "Old Amsterdam—I," where the point emerges that "the biblical records are impressionistic; that is, they are not marked by notarial precision or blue-print, architectural exactness. . . . This understanding of 'impressionistic' is echoed at a number of places elsewhere in Kuyper's writings. . . . 'Whoever in reading Scripture thinks that everything was spoken precisely as it stands in the text, is totally mistaken.' Again, he points to the differences between the four Gospels and the NT use of the OT as sufficient to show that as a rule the *lalia* of God has not come to us 'in its original form.' In typical fashion, Kuyper illustrates his point by recalling an aspect of modern European parliamentary practice. Both the French and English parliaments keep two kinds of records; one is a verbatim account of what a speaker says (a 'procès-verbal'), the other a brief resume or summary account (a 'procès-analytique'). . . . It would be a mistake, Kuyper continues, to suppose that the verbatim report is better or more desirable. . . . In a similar vein, we ought not to think that the speeches in Job are given precisely as Bildad spoke them. Rather they provide a 'romantic representation' or 'free rendering' of what was said. But because this happens 'under guarantee of the Holy Spirit,' they express what was said 'not only not inaccurately [*onjuist*], but more accurately [*juister*] and, besides that, more elegantly.' . . . On the one hand, the biblical narratives do not record the past with stenographic preciseness or photographic exactness. Yet as historical records they are completely accurate and do not at all mislead. . . . 'The distinguishing mark of inspiration, however, above everything else is that it guarantees absolute accuracy [*absolute juistheid*]. The singular character of the writers of the Old and New Testaments lies in the fact that the stamp of truth and certainty is impressed upon their writings. The Holy Spirit so leads their spirit that in them the results of sin are cut off and prevented. This distinguishing mark is not relative, but absolute.' Biblical narrative is absolutely accurate without being notarially exact" (278–79).

47. Cf. Berkouwer, who says in *Holy Scripture*, "It is true that fundamentalists do not deny the human element in Scripture, but they allow their apologetics to be determined by the fear that emphasis on the human witness may threaten and overshadow Scripture's divinity" (22). "Fundamentalists allowed themselves, however, to be guided by the 'wholly divine or wholly human' dilemma, and thus they allowed the camp they opposed to force a problem on them" (24). "Bavinck points to the self-witness of Scripture, which is unalterable, and he acknowledges moreover that the examination of Scripture in recent years comes up with 'phenomena and facts that can hardly be reconciled with this self-witness.' The difference between fundamentalism and Bavinck is not that his confession regarding Scripture is less positive than fundamentalism's, but that he gives much more attention to the manner in which Scripture came to us as *human* witness. Because of the divine nature of Scripture, the human witness does not become less important to Bavinck; rather, it receives special significance. This does not result from a relativizing of Scripture, but from his great respect for the manner of revelation that itself compels us to reflect on the nature of Scripture's authority" (25). "Bavinck did not capitulate in any way to the criticism of Scripture of his day. Instead, he analyzed this criticism and arrived at the conclusion that the critics had totally lost sight of the purpose of Holy Scripture. . . . he calls attention to what the *intent*—the specific and emphatic objective—of Scripture is. The important thing to notice is that Bavinck's rejection of biblical criticism takes the form of a positive contribution to the understanding of the nature of Scripture. It goes without saying that here many new questions could be raised. For example, what exactly is this 'goal' (*scopus*) of Scripture?" (26). But Gaffin rightly points out that Berkouwer is not a completely faithful expositor of Kuyper and Bavinck. In "Old Amsterdam—I," 279–80, he observes, "Accordingly, when Kuyper speaks of the possibility of 'innocent inaccuracies' in historical records (*Principles*, 457), this expression ought not simply to be lifted out of context and enlisted without further qualification against efforts at harmonization, as Berkouwer does. If we are not to distort Kuyper's meaning, we must not fail to note the specific terms of the contrast that serves to define these 'innocent inaccuracies': they 'so far from doing harm, rather bring to light the free expression of life above notarial affectation.'" "Perhaps the deepest perspective on the sense of the quotation under examination in this section is provided by reflecting further on the distinction, already noted, between divine and human errorlessness. . . . What is the difference, Kuyper asks, between 'divinely errorless' and 'humanly errorless'? . . . Divine errorlessness, in contrast, is like the work of a painter. . . . In summary, divine errorlessness, like art, gives the essence without error, but without maintaining precisely the same form. . . . The errorlessness of Scripture, then, is divine, not human."

I want to move beyond that by allowing the evidence to affect how we think about what Scripture as a whole *is*.

The end result, I truly hope, will be to provide a theological paradigm for people who know instinctively that the Bible is God's word, but for whom reading the Bible has already become a serious theological problem—perhaps even a crisis.[48]

What then are the confession's theological parameters and presuppositions concerning Scripture? Are there confessional hermeneutical parameters and principles for interpreting Scripture? Young believed that these existed and identified them when he placed the entire first chapter of the Westminster Confession as an appendix to his defense of inerrancy,[49] while Enns leaves his understanding of what is intended by the "parameters of earlier doctrinal formulations" vague and undefined.[50]

Although not directly addressed in *Inerrancy and Hermeneutic* nor by Enns in *Inspiration and Incarnation*, it is evident that the confession in chapter one, "Of the Holy Scripture," establishes an overarching hermeneutical parameter or hermeneutic principle when it declares:

> The infallible rule of interpretation of Scripture is the Scripture itself: and therefore, when there is a question about the true and full sense of any Scripture (which is not manifold, but one), it must be searched and known by other places that speak more clearly. (WCF 1.9)

Thus the principle of Scripture interpreting Scripture is declared to be of foundational importance. The confession's mandate for this hermeneutical method is patent and principial: it is an "*infallible* rule of interpretation." Further, it is sweeping in its impact since it relates to the "true and full sense of *any* Scripture." In fact, this interpretive method is not optional, but obligatory, since the meaning of any Scripture "*must* be searched and known." The *canonical* self-interpreting character of this scriptural hermeneutic is captured in the words, "by *other*

---

48. Enns, *Inspiration and Incarnation*, 15.

49. Young, *Thy Word Is Truth*, 277–80.

50. The closest statement of theological disclosure that Enns provides is: "Also influential has been my own theological tradition, represented by my colleagues at Westminster Theological Seminary, past and present, and the wider tradition of which that institution is a part. This is not to imply that I speak for that institution or tradition" (*Inspiration and Incarnation,* 9). The lack of theological clarity in Enns's theological position has been expressed by the *OPC Mid-Atlantic Presbytery's Report*: "This general neglect of any detailed interaction with the classical Reformed treatments of Inspiration is notable. He seems to embrace Warfield's concept of concursus but does not tell us how he differs from Warfield. He is able to simultaneously place Warfield and J. Patterson Smyth in his 'Further Reading' section (*Inspiration*, 22) seeming to commend Smyth for 'honesty and spiritual sensitivity.' Yet Warfield was not so favorable to Smyth's work. While reviewing it along with two other works (*Presbyterian and Reformed Review* 5, 1894), Warfield states: 'These are therefore three very instructive little books. They exhibit to us the working of the new leaven in its mildest form; and advertise to us what is the least change in our attitude towards the Bible which will satisfy the most moderate adherents of the new views. As such, they are not reassuring. It becomes evident at once not only that an entire revolution in the doctrine of sacred Scripture incorporated in our creeds, and held indeed by the whole Christian past, will be required of us (which is a comparatively small matter); but also that on the new ground we can no longer occupy the same attitude towards Scripture that our Lord and His apostles occupied. The attempts of these books being taken as samples, it becomes equally evident also that no consistent doctrine of inspiration, conservative of the detailed divine authority of the Scriptures, can be framed on the basis of the new views.'"

If we are to open a new trajectory in our understanding of inspiration, it would at least be helpful to gain some sense of where and why the boundaries suggested by Warfield—or perhaps better yet Bavinck—are not adequate. If Enns is not saying anything that Bavinck has not said, he should acknowledge his debt. If he is saying something new, he should step forward and show the Reformed community—not just broad evangelicals—where they need further reformation.

places that speak more clearly."[51] Finally, all of these words substantiate what is intended by the word *rule*—a *rule* is to be observed. As Larger Catechism question 99 says, "For the right understanding... these rules are to be observed." Hence, the confession's hermeneutical principle is given an importance that cannot be ignored or diminished if the Scripture's authority as the "only infallible rule of faith and practice" is consciously recognized with the seriousness that an *ex animo* subscription requires. This confessional rule for the interpretation of Scripture might well be denominated, *the regulative principle of hermeneutics.*

The historic understanding of this principle of comparing Scripture with Scripture is enunciated by Turretin:

> Comparison matches one passage of Scripture to another (Acts 9:22), by comparing the more obscure with the more understandable, similar or parallel ones with those like them, and the dissimilar with the dissimilar. The analogy of the faith (Rom. 12:6) means not only a measuring standard for the faith, or a measure given to each of the believers, but also the constant harmony or agreement of all the articles of faith in the most glorious words of the revealed Scripture, to which all expositions must conform, lest anything be taught contrary to the articles of faith or the commandments of the Decalogue. (*Institutes*, II.19.18)[52]

Turretin reasons that this method is required since we must recognize that God possesses the authority to interpret His own words.

> Just as a ruler is the interpreter of his own law, so also God is the interpreter of his own Scripture, which is the law of faith and conduct. And the privilege which is proper for other writers that each one is the interpreter of his own words, should not be denied to God when he speaks in Scripture. (*Institutes*, II.20.15)[53]

Westminster NT professor Vern Poythress well illustrates this principle:

> At a fundamental level, there is no such thing as a passage in and of itself. John 2:16 is part of the Bible, and God intends that we read it and understand it in relation to all the other parts of the Bible. When he caused these words to be written in the Gospel of John, he already intended that they should be seen as we are seeing them, namely, in connection with other passages that together unfold the purpose of God.[54]

Moreover, this is the teaching of the confession in 1.5, where it speaks of "the consent of all the parts" that "doth abundantly evidence itself to be the Word of God."

51. Cf. Turretin (*Institutes*, II.17.5): "It is not a question of whether matters necessary for salvation are presented clearly everywhere in Scripture. Indeed we grant that there are many passages that are difficult to understand, by which God wills to exercise our effort and the skill of the scholar. The question is whether these necessary matters are presented somewhere in such a manner that a believer can recognize their truth when he has given them serious consideration, because nothing is learned from the more obscure passages that is not found most plainly taught elsewhere. As Augustine says, 'the Holy Spirit has arranged the Scriptures in such a wonderful and wholesome manner, that hunger is remedied by the plainer passages and pride by the more obscure...,' and, 'We feed on the clear passages, and are disciplined by the obscure; in the one our appetite is overcome, in the other our pride.'" *Doctrine of Scripture*, 187.
52. Ibid., 207.
53. Ibid., 215.
54. Vern S. Poythress, *God-Centered Biblical Interpretation* (Phillipsburg, NJ: P&R Publishing, 1999), 45.

Sola Scriptura: Scripture, Science, and the "Infallible Rule of Interpretation"

In the midst of the hermeneutical crisis, the importance of the reformational principle of *Sacra Scriptura sui ipsius interpres* (Sacred Scripture is its own interpreter) must again be affirmed. For what is at stake is nothing less than the Reformation's commitment to *sola Scriptura*. As Berkouwer explains, the principle of Scripture interpreting Scripture is the logical outgrowth of a full and deep commitment to *sola Scriptura*. Berkouwer, who also is concerned not to miss the human dimension of Scripture, underscores this point.

> Nowhere was the relationship between authority and interpretation so clearly expressed as in the Reformation confession of Scripture, which, based on *sola Scriptura*, offered a perspective on the real relationship between authority and interpretation, and expressed it in its hermeneutical rule: *Sacra Scriptura sui ipsius interpres* (Sacred Scripture is its own interpreter).[55]

The principle might appear to be primarily an apologetic for the Reformation. "Calvin," for example, "spoke of the Holy Spirit as 'a unique self-interpreter,' since he spoke by the prophets."[56] Berkouwer declares, however, that this hermeneutical principle actually emerges from Scripture.

> On hearing this rule, one can react that it is polemically understandable but really not a concrete and fruitful notion for the present interpretation of Scripture. The formula is indeed a polemical focusing of the *sola Scriptura* on interpretation. This already excludes the possibility of speaking of a purely formal rule without diverse perspectives. It contains a concrete rejection of other interpretations which are foreign to the nature of Scripture. By so doing it naturally reminds us of the scriptural message that no prophecy of Scripture is a matter of one's own interpretation (2 Peter 1:20).[57]

And so in the context of the current hermeneutical crisis, what happens to the Reformation's hermeneutical principle flowing from *sola Scriptura* when the issues of modern science[58] or scholarship in their many forms enter this discussion? Berkouwer pointedly asks this question:

> It has been repeatedly pointed out that behind many of the questions presently related to the interpretation of Holy Scripture looms the important presence of science. . . . The way in which this relationship is usually discussed is by maintaining that certain results of science, be it natural science or historical research can provide the "occasion" for understanding various aspects of Scripture in a different way than before. If this is indeed the case, then what is the relationship between such an "occasion" and the authoritative power of "Sacred Scripture is its own interpreter"?[59]

55. Berkouwer, *Holy Scripture*, 127.
56. Ibid., 127–28.
57. Ibid., 127.
58. "Science" in Berkouwer's mind is broader than what is often intended in the American use of the word. Jack B. Rogers, translator of *Holy Scripture*, 133n80, explains, "The word 'science' is used throughout this book in a much broader sense than is usual in the U.S.A. Berkouwer's concept of a science is equivalent to our notion of an academic discipline. Thus, studies done in the humanities and social sciences as well as the natural sciences are included. Theology is also a science, since it proceeds by orderly academic research and reflection."
59. Berkouwer, *Holy Scripture*, 133–34. The Reformed theologians Kuyper and Bavinck also wrestled with the findings of science and their impact on the theology of the inspiration of the Bible. See Gaffin, "Old Amsterdam—I," 281–82: "The classic,

Berkouwer asks, "Does it mean that science has become a fellow interpreter, or is it impossible to state the problem in such a way?"[60] Enns seems to answer affirmatively: "the findings of the past 150 years have made extrabiblical evidence an unavoidable conversation partner."[61] Yet for Berkouwer, if science becomes part of biblical hermeneutics, the principle of *sola Scriptura* is lost. Berkouwer explains:

> It is not true that, as far as the Reformation was concerned, Scripture alone was its own interpreter and that now we see a second interpreter being added. If that were the case, it might be better to recognize that the Reformation scriptural principle now appears insufficient and out of date.[62]

> When, however, the *sui ipsius interpres* receives increasingly concrete attention, it also becomes apparent that science cannot become an "interpreter" alongside Scripture itself. This is one pretension not found in the circles of science itself, except for odd cases of vain scientific idealism which are convinced that the light of Scripture has been permanently extinguished by that of science. Not just to spite science, but rather because of its totally different nature and of the secret of Scripture—the secret of the gospel—we will have to continue on the basis of the "is its own interpreter" and thus continue to honor Scripture as canon.[63]

Indeed, for Berkouwer, the "trustworthiness" of Scripture denies the legitimacy of the "new hermeneutic," which coercively forces concessions on the canonical hermeneutical principle of the Reformation.

> The discussion about Scripture, its God-breathed character and authority, cannot take place via a coerced concession to a new hermeneutical method and the "occasion" of science. It can only take place in the perspective of that trustworthiness of Scripture which enables us to abandon ourselves in complete trust to its authority and to preach its message.[64]

To fail to see the uniqueness of Scripture in this regard has but one end in Berkouwer's mind—being "seized by irresolute doubt."

> Those who, because of the complicated questions of interpretation, the dangers of projection and twisting, of subjectivism and objectivism, want to give up trying to understand Scripture in accordance with its divine intent, have been seized by irresolute doubt. . . . To overcome doubt of this kind, we must not allow any questions of interpretation, including those arising from newly disclosed knowledge, to hinder new essays into scriptural understanding from

---

rational apologetic for graphic inspiration is not only inappropriate but counterproductive, because it places the demands of mechanical preciseness on Scripture, which by its nature demands organic precision; Scripture is forced into a mold which is not suited to its organic character. . . . Kuyper observes that the full, multifaceted character of Scripture cannot be exhausted by the finite grasp of our logical, mathematical thinking. One result is that according to intellectual demands and on the flat terrain of logic, everything in Scripture is not in harmony. But certainly that harmony is there, and we see it when, in faith, we view it 'from the standpoint of the Holy Spirit.' . . . Kuyper and Bavinck held that Scripture does not intend to give us 'technically correct scientific information.' That is right. But at the same time what Kuyper would also want to point out is that in its undeniably impressionistic, not notarially precise, not scientifically exact, fashion, Scripture gives information that is directly relevant to science."

60. Berkouwer, *Holy Scripture*, 133–34.
61. Enns, *Inspiration and Incarnation*, 49.
62. Berkouwer, *Holy Scripture*, 134.
63. Ibid.
64. Ibid., 138

the vantage point of the *sui ipsius interpres*. On these voyages we will be aware that no single postulate that circumvents this dictum can in fact block our way. There is no single technique able to provide the key to the secret of Scripture, not even a perfected hermeneutics.[65]

We can scarcely summarize Berkouwer's point here more cogently than by reaffirming his declaration of the uniqueness of Scripture that he denominates "the secret of Scripture":

> Not just to spite science, but rather because of its totally different nature and of the secret of Scripture—the secret of the gospel—we will have to continue on the basis of the "is its own interpreter" and thus continue to honor Scripture as canon.[66]

Given the infallibility, extensiveness, and mandatory character of the Westminster Confession's hermeneutical rule (WCF 1.9), all other "scientific" considerations for interpreting Scripture must be viewed as having secondary importance. Whether they are historical, archaeological, linguistic, or extra-biblical phenomena, as helpful as they may be to reflect the historical milieu of Scripture and to provide insights into the nature and meaning of biblical language, they must be considered subordinate and not equivalent in interpretive force to the self-interpreting character of Scripture.

Moreover, as Kuyper argued, there are two kinds of science—that which operates within the Christian worldview and that which comports with a naturalistic philosophy.[67] Consequently, the "canon"[68] for biblical hermeneutics as opposed to naturalistic hermeneutics is and must be the canon of Scripture.[69] This alone preserves *"sola Scriptura."* At this point it

65. Ibid., 135.

66. Ibid., 134.

67. Abraham Kuyper explains, "Our proposition that there are two kinds of science is, from the nature of the case, merely the accommodation to a linguistic usage. The two sciences must never be coordinated with each other. In fact, no one can be convinced that there is more than one science, and that which announces itself as science by the side of, or in opposition to, this can never be acknowledged as such in the absolute sense. As soon as the thinker of palingenesis has come to that point in the road where the thinker of naturalism parts company with him, the latter's science is no longer anything to the former but 'science falsely so called.' Similarly the naturalistic thinker is bound to contest the name of science for that which the student of the 'wisdom of God' derives from his premises. That which lies outside of the realm of these different premises is common to both, but that which is governed, directly or indirectly, by these premises comes to stand entirely differently to the one from what it does to the other. Always in this sense, of course, that only one is right and in touch with actual reality, but is unable to convince the other of wrong. It will once be decided, but not until the final consummation of all things." Abraham Kuyper, *Principles of Sacred Theology*, trans. J. Hendrik de Vries (Grand Rapids: Baker, 1980), 176.

68. For a helpful summary of the development of the meanings of "canon," see *Nicene and Post-Nicene Fathers*, vol. 14, *The Seven Ecumenical Councils of the Undivided Church: Their Canons and Dogmatic Decrees, Together with the Canons of All the Local Synods Which Have Received Ecumenical Acceptance*, ed. Henry R. Percival (Peabody, MA: Hendrickson, 1995), 14:9–10.

69. In Reformed theology, the Holy Spirit's ministry was not absent from the creation of the canon of Scripture, cf. Gaffin, "Old Amsterdam—I," 268, where he says, "The apostles themselves believed in a predestined Bible and saw inspiration as extending to the individual words and letters (Kuyper, *Principles of Sacred Theology* 2.177). The scriptural attire (*het Schriftgewaad*) of the Word is woven by God according to the pattern that he has drawn up for it (1.86). Graphic inspiration in the narrower sense is the operation of the Holy Spirit in the various human authors, 'whereby they wrote in just the way and at such a time and in such a form as was necessary for the delivery of that part of Scripture for which each was responsible, finished and adapted to the canonical linking together of all the parts, to that one harmonious whole which the Lord God had foreseen and foreordained for Holy Scripture.' This graphic inspiration concerns 'the production of the autograph in the form intended by God, at the moment it enters the canon' (2.127)." And 270, "The Holy Spirit directed them, brought to their knowledge what they were to know, sharpened their judgments in the choice of documents and records, so that they should decide aright, and gave them a superior maturity of mind that enabled them always to choose exactly the right word. . . . But whether He dictates directly, as in the Revelation of St. John or governs indirectly, as with historians and evangelists, the result is the same: the product is such in the form and content as the Holy Spirit designed,

is interesting, perhaps even ironic, to observe that the "modern" Berkouwer is in sympathy with the "Protestant orthodox" Turretin. The latter writes,

> The purpose of Scripture requires this perfection, for it was given that we might have salvation and life from it (John 20:31; 1 John 5:13; Rom. 15:4). How could this purpose be accomplished, unless Scripture were perfect, containing all that is necessary for salvation? It was given to be canon and rule of faith but a rule which is not full and sufficient is no rule; a rule is a standard from which nothing can be taken and to which nothing can be added, "an inviolable law and infallible measure, allowing no addition or substitution," as Favorinus says. (*Institutes*, II.16.17)[70]

The vows of the OPC, the PCA, and Westminster all reflect Turretin's "canon and rule of faith" and "inviolable law and infallible measure" when they unitedly declare belief in "*the only infallible rule of faith and practice*."[71] Such an "infallible rule" would appear to be "a rule" or "standard from which nothing can be taken and to which nothing can be added."

"A Modern Doctrine of Scripture"? "Provisional Theologizing" and the Confession's "Infallible Rule of Interpretation"

As we turn from this consideration of the Reformers', Turretin's, and Berkouwer's understanding of *sola Scriptura* to the views of Professor Enns, we must engage Professor Enns's emphasis on the humanity of Scripture and his concomitant insistence that the doctrine of Scripture be developed without "blissful isolation" from extrabiblical evidence. Do the archaeological discoveries of scholars require a mere provisional confession of our doctrine of Scripture?

Professor Enns has strongly pressed these issues and has here given his views in unmistakable terms. His "two assumptions," his stated presuppositions, clarify his perspective:

1. I assume that the extrabiblical archeological and textual evidences should play an important role in our understanding of Scripture.... I reject the notion that a modern doctrine of Scripture can be articulated in blissful isolation from the evidence we have.
2. All attempts to articulate the nature of Scripture are open to examination, including my own. I firmly believe . . . that the Spirit of God is fully engaged in such a theological process and at the same time that our attempts to articulate what God's word is have a necessarily provisional dimension. To put it succinctly: The Spirit leads the church to truth—he does not simply drop us down in the middle of it. To say this is not a low view of Scripture or of the role of the Holy Spirit. It is simply to recognize what has been the case throughout the history of the church, that diverse views and changes of opinion over time have been the constant companions of the church and that God has not brought this process to a closure.[72]

Here Enns assumes the view that both Berkouwer and Turretin have just rejected. Thankfully, Enns does not advance in place of the confession's "infallible rule of interpretation"

---

an infallible document for the Church of God" (quoting Kuyper, *The Work of the Holy Spirit*, 77). (Cf. R. Laird Harris, *Inspiration and Canonicity of the Scriptures* [Greenville, SC: A Press, 1995]).

70. Turretin, *Doctrine of Scripture*, 175.
71. See "The Hermeneutical Crisis and the Historic Presbyterian Subscription to the Confession" above.
72. *Inspiration and Incarnation*, 48–49.

the "irresolute doubt" identified by Berkouwer. But he does overtly confess a "provisional" doctrine of Scripture:[73]

> If even God expresses himself in the Bible through particular human circumstances, we must be very ready to see the necessarily culturally limited nature of our own theological expressions today. I am not speaking of cultural relativism, where all truth is up for grabs and the Bible ceases being our standard for faith. I simply mean that all of our theologizing, because we are human beings living in particular historical and cultural moments, will have a temporary and **provisional**—even fallen—dimension to it. In other words, there is no absolute point of reference to which we have access that will allow us to interpret the Bible stripped of our own cultural context.[74]

The theme of the provisional doctrine of Scripture is a repeated element of his study:

> On the one hand, I am very eager to affirm that many evangelical instincts are correct and should be maintained, for example, the conviction that the Bible is ultimately from God and that it is God's gift to the church. Any theories concerning Scripture that do not arise from these fundamental instincts are unacceptable. On the other hand, **how the evangelical church fleshes out its doctrine of Scripture** will always have somewhat of a **provisional** quality to it. This is not to say that each generation must disregard the past and start afresh, formulating ever-new doctrines, bowing to all the latest fads. But it is to say that at such time when new evidence comes to light, or old evidence is seen in a new light, we must be willing to **engage that evidence and adjust our doctrine accordingly**.[75]

> The findings of the past 150 years have made extrabiblical evidence an unavoidable conversation partner. The result is that, as perhaps never before in the history of the church, we can see how truly **provisional** and incomplete certain dimensions of our understanding of Scripture can be. On the other hand, we are encouraged to encounter the depth and riches of God's revelation and to rely more and more on God's Spirit, who speaks to the church in Scripture.[76]

> Perhaps, then, it makes more sense to speak of the incarnational *parallel* between Christ and the Bible. This should lead us to a more willing recognition that the expression of our confession of the Bible as God's word has a **provisional** quality to it. By faith, the church confesses that the Bible *is* God's word. It is up to Christians of each generation, however, to work out what that means and what words work best to describe it.[77]

> It would be very difficult for someone holding to such a view to have a meaningful conversation with linguists and historians of the ancient world. To argue in such hypothetical terms can sometimes become an excuse for maintaining a way of thinking that is otherwise unsupportable. It is just such explanations that some readers might find problematic, for they **seem motivated by a desire to protect one's theology rather than to engage the available evidence**. . . . regardless of when Genesis was written and in what language, it still reflects an ancient Near Eastern worldview that clearly is significantly older.[78]

73. In the following quotations, Professor Enns's use of "provisional" and related concepts is highlighted by bold type.
74. Enns, *Inspiration and Incarnation*, 168–69.
75. Ibid., 13–14.
76. Ibid., 49.
77. Ibid., 168.
78. Ibid., 52.

Because our theologies are necessarily limited and **provisional**, the church today must be open to listening to how other Christians from other cultures read Scripture and live it out in their daily lives. . . . The incarnational analogy helps us to see it differently: diverse expressions of God's one, but multidimensional gospel are precisely what he wanted.[79]

This provisional nature of the churches' confessions results in a process without "clear rules or guidelines to prevent us from taking this process too far." Professor Enns acknowledges that this results in a kind of uncertainty with regard to the Scriptures given the questions that may be raised by evidence yet to be discovered:

There do not seem to be any clear rules or guidelines to prevent us from taking this process too far. But again, this is why the metaphor of journey or pilgrimage is so appealing. The path we walk may contain risks, unexpected bumps, twists, and turns. We do not always know what is coming around the corner—we were not able to anticipate the discovery of ancient Near Eastern creation texts or the Dead Sea Scrolls for example. But yet, we have turned a few important corners over the past several generations. It is always an option, I suppose, to halt the journey and stand still, or perhaps turn around and walk back a few hundred yards, so as to stand at a safe distance from what lies ahead. We should continue the journey, however; not because we are sure of our own footing, but because we have faith in God who placed us on this journey to begin with.[80]

Is Enns really saying by his word "provisional" that *sola Scriptura* and the "infallible rule of interpretation" can no longer be the foundational hermeneutic of the Reformed tradition? If so, the stakes are high indeed. Simply put, the hermeneutical crisis has brought us to a major crossroads of theology.

Young would agree:

The Church is indeed at the crossroads. Shall she listen to God or to man? Will she receive what the Spirit says concerning inspiration, or, turning her back upon Him, will she cleave unto man? This is the choice to be made. Sad is it, however, that many do not realize the necessity for making a choice. Having their vision obscured by the dense fog that modern theology is casting over the way, many do not realize that there is a crossroad. They are not aware that they must decide which road they will follow. Unless something is done, they will travel on, taking the wrong turning, until the road leads them at last into the valley of lost hope and eternal death.[81]

But this is not merely the "traditionalist" view of Young the "conservative." Even Berkouwer the "progressive" agrees:

Those who see the *lamp* of the Word of God on a continuum with the new and increased *light* of science, lit before all the world, inevitably arrive at a dangerous crossroads. They will either follow a course condescending to Scripture and its message, or they will tend to abandon every new question about interpretation because of the danger involved. Both paths must be avoided.[82]

79. Ibid., 169.
80. Ibid., 171.
81. Young, *Thy Word Is Truth*, 35.
82. Berkouwer, *Holy Scripture*, 135.

Yet Enns unflinchingly writes, "In other words, there is no absolute point of reference to which we have access that will allow us to interpret the Bible stripped of our own cultural context."[83] But in saying this, does he not strip the church of *sola Scriptura* and the hermeneutical principle afforded us by the Bible which the confession declares to be the "infallible rule of interpretation"?

The crossroads is now clear.[84] We must either confess an "infallible rule of interpretation" (WCF 1.9) reflecting the hermeneutical rule of *sola Scriptura*, or confess a "provisional" (168) theology subject to the "bumps, twists and turns" (171) of the unanticipated discoveries of "extrabiblical evidence" (48). Moreover, all of this occurs on a "journey or pilgrimage" (171) led by Professor Enns and others who assure us that we walk no "slippery slope" (172) on this "appealing" (171) journey. Nevertheless, we are not "sure of our footing" (171), and "there do not seem to be any clear rules or guidelines to prevent us from taking this process too far" (171). Consequently, all Enns leaves for the church is "faith in God who placed us on this journey" (171). The "infallible rule of interpretation" (WCF 1.9) that emerges from divine "infallible truth" (WCF 1.5) is nowhere to be found since "there is no absolute point of reference to which we have access that will allow us to interpret the Bible" (169).

Consequently, Enns also seems to dismiss or redefine another type of "evidence" that the confession affirms. Referring to Holy Scripture, the confession says that it abundantly provides "**evidence** . . . to be the Word of God: yet notwithstanding, our full persuasion and assurance of the infallible truth and divine authority thereof, is from the inward work of the Holy Spirit bearing witness by and with the Word in our hearts" (WCF 1.5).

To be sure, Enns does not deny "the role of the Holy Spirit" in relationship to human understanding of Scripture.

> I firmly believe . . . that the Spirit of God is fully engaged in such a theological process *and at the same time* that our attempts to articulate what God's word is have a necessarily provisional dimension. To put it succinctly: The Spirit *leads* the church to truth—he does not simply drop us down in the middle of it. To say this is not a low view of Scripture or of the role of the Holy Spirit.[85]

But what Enns affirms here does not appear to cohere with the confession's explanation of the Spirit's intimate "witness **by and with the Word** in our hearts." He confesses that "The Spirit leads the church to truth—he does not simply drop us down in the middle of it." Although he claims that "this is not a low view of Scripture or of the role of the Holy Spirit," this does not appear warranted when it is compared with the affirmations of the confession: "the Word of God . . . full persuasion and assurance . . . infallible truth and divine authority . . . the Holy Spirit bearing witness by and with the Word in our hearts. . . . the Holy Spirit speaking in the Scripture" (WCF 1.5, 10).[86] The confession binds together Word and Spirit far more closely than Enns appears willing to do.

83. Enns, *Inspiration and Incarnation*, 169.

84. The quoted phrases in this paragraph can be found in *Inspiration and Incarnation* on the identified pages.

85. *Inspiration and Incarnation*, 48–49.

86. There is a clear epistemological emphasis in the Westminster Standards. The Westminster Confession of Faith 1.1 states, "Although the light of nature, and the works of creation and providence do so far manifest the goodness, wisdom, and power of God, as to leave men unexcusable; yet are they not sufficient to give that knowledge of God, and of his will, which is necessary unto salvation. Therefore it pleased the Lord, at sundry times, and in divers manners, to reveal himself, and to declare that his will unto his church; and afterwards, for the better preserving and propagating of the truth, and for the more sure establishment and comfort of the church against the corruption of the flesh, and the malice of Satan and of the world,

Indeed, Enns's phrases are a stunning contrast with those in the confession. His phrases are as follows: "the word of God," "not sure of our footing," "provisional," "The Spirit leads the church to truth—he does not simply drop us down in the middle of it," "no absolute point of reference to which we have access that will allow us to interpret the Bible." These statements are difficult to reconcile with the union of Word and Spirit reflected by Larger Catechism question 2: "How does it appear that there is a God? Answer: The very light of nature in man, and the works of God, declare plainly that there is a God; but his Word and Spirit only do sufficiently and effectually reveal him unto men for their salvation." Enns's uncertainty seems inconsistent with the knowledge of God claimed by Larger Catechism question 6, which asks: "What do the Scriptures make known of God? Answer: The Scriptures make known: What God is, the persons in the Godhead, his decrees, and the execution of his decrees."

At the heart of the hermeneutical crisis there is an epistemological crisis[87] that denies to men the certainty of divine knowledge.[88] Thus Helm critiques Enns's theological method,

---

to commit the same wholly unto writing: which maketh the Holy Scripture to be most necessary; those former ways of God's revealing his will unto his people being now ceased." Larger Catechism question 192: "What do we pray for in the third petition? Answer: In the third petition (which is, Thy will be done in earth, as it is in heaven), acknowledging, that by nature we and all men are not only utterly unable and unwilling to know and do the will of God, but prone to rebel against his Word, to repine and murmur against his providence, and wholly inclined to do the will of the flesh, and of the devil: we pray, that God would by his Spirit take away from ourselves and others all blindness, weakness, indisposedness, and perverseness of heart; and by his grace make us able and willing to know, do, and submit to his will in all things, with the like humility, cheerfulness, faithfulness, diligence, zeal, sincerity, and constancy, as the angels do in heaven." Harvie Conn agrees with D. A. Carson in "Normativity, Relevance, and Relativism," 191, in calling attention to the non-neutrality of all interpreters: "In short, we are all biased already in our thinking and knowing, bringing assumptions structured by our cultural perceptions, even by the language symbols we use to interpret reality. 'We are, that is, 'interested' before we begin to read a text and remain active as we read it. We belong, to a great extent through language, to the theological, social, and psychological traditions that have moulded us as subjects and without whose mediation we could understand nothing.' D. A. Carson puts it bluntly: 'No human being living in time and speaking any language can ever be entirely culture-free about anything.' In sum, the idea that the interpreter is a neutral observer of biblical data is a myth. How then do we avoid hermeneutical discoveries based largely on what we have assumed? If what we hear from the text, and how we act upon what we have heard, is so heavily influenced by the baggage we carry with us in the process, how do we avoid the relativism of selective listening and selective obedience?"

87. For a representative study of the deep commitment of the Reformed faith to an epistemology built upon the accessibility by revelation of divine knowledge for the Christian in spite of man's metaphysical agnosticism given the noetic effects of sin and his autonomous rebellion from the Creator, see Cornelius Van Til, *An Introduction to Systematic Theology.*

88. Enns defends God's own lack of divine knowledge, *Inspiration and Incarnation*, 103–7. Although ostensibly distancing himself from the "openness of God" theology (106), he ultimately cannot fully do so because he rejects the confession's "infallible principle" of Scripture interpreting Scripture. He writes, "*In this story*, God did not know until the test was passed" (103). "Any attempt to force the God *of Genesis 6* into a mold cast by certain theological commitments or to reconcile this description to other biblical passages simply amounts to reading past this story" (104). "The Bible really does have authority if we let it speak, and not when we—intentionally or unintentionally—suspend what the Bible says about God in some places while we work out our speculations about what God is 'really' like, perhaps by accenting other portions of the Bible that are more amenable to our thinking" (106). This appears to be a denial of WCF 1.9, "The infallible rule of interpretation of Scripture is the Scripture itself: and therefore, when there is a question about the true and full sense of any Scripture (which is not manifold, but one), it must be searched and known by other places that speak more clearly." Perhaps Enns's insistence on the primacy of the specific narrative over the theological metanarrative of the Scripture's system of doctrine as well as its infallible hermeneutic reflects the hermeneutic of Lyotard, the postmodern whose dictum is "narrative not metanarrative." Jean-François Lyotard has been a leader in postmodern thought, a contemporary form of skeptical philosophy. Postmodernism questions and critiques all claims for certainty. Lyotard dismissed the claim for universal theories of truth, claiming that arguments defending "grand narratives" were no longer credible. Thus Lyotard's opposition to the grand narrative, as well as its inherent authority, led him to defend the idea of the "little narrative," namely the stories of individual human beings, which require no foundational or epistemological defense (cf. his *The Postmodern Condition: A Report on Knowledge,* trans. Geoff Bennington and Brian Massurmi [Minneapolis: University of Minnesota Press, 1984], 60). His summary of postmodernism declares, "I define postmodern as incredulity toward metanarratives. This incredulity is undoubtedly a product of progress in the sciences: . . . To the obsolescence of the metanarrative . . . corresponds, most notably, the crisis of metaphysical philosophy. . . . The narrative function is losing . . . its great goal.

We see now that Enns' problems have little or nothing to do with the discoveries and claims of Old Testament scholarship. Instead, they are due to two basic failures. A failure in theological method, that of starting from difficulties instead of from dogma. And a failure in epistemology, a commitment to the idea of universal cultural bias that makes objectivity and finality about our faith impossible.[89]

When we consider Professor Enns's repeated statements in this regard, it seems as if a believer can trust God, but he may not necessarily be able to trust Scripture:

We are to place our trust in God who gave us Scripture, not in our own conceptions of how Scripture ought to be.[90]

This should lead us to a more willing recognition that the expression of our confession of the Bible as God's word has a provisional quality to it. By faith, the church confesses that the Bible *is* God's word. It is up to Christians of each generation, however, to work out what that means and what words work best to describe it.[91]

The second concerns the Bible's *integrity*, its trustworthiness. It is a common expectation that the Bible be unified in its outlook, be free of diverse views, if we are being asked to trust it as God's word (does not God have just one opinion on things?).[92]

There are many ways of asking these questions, but they all boil down to this: *Is the Bible still the word of God?*[93]

If anything, would we not expect the Bible, which records God's revelation, to "get it right" by *not* allowing authors to be biased like all the other histories of the surrounding cultures, but instead just giving us the objective and neutral facts? No evangelical can consider this issue and not feel the force of this argument. If the Bible does not tell us what actually happened, how can we trust it about anything?[94]

My intention below is to explore how the biblical and extrabiblical evidence can affect these assumptions. If, in full conversation with the biblical and extrabiblical evidence, we can *adjust our expectations* about how the Bible should behave, we can begin to move beyond the impasse of the liberal/conservative debates of the last several generations.[95]

Lacking in Enns is the insistence of Berkouwer on the trustworthiness of Scripture.

It is being dispersed in clouds of narrative language" (p. xxiv). Postmodernism in general claims that a correct description of reality is impossible, reflecting the skepticism of Nietzsche, Wittgenstein, Popper, and Kuhn. The core beliefs of postmodernity include: 1. Truth is limited, approximate, and is constantly evolving; 2. No theory can ever be proved true (a theory can only be shown to be false); 3. No theory can ever explain everything; 4. Thus absolute and certain truth that explains all things is unobtainable.

89. Paul Helm (in the e-zine *Reformation 21*, April 2006), a "Review of *Inspiration and Incarnation* [Accessed January 8, 2008]." Online: http://www.reformation21.org/Reformation_21_Blog/Reformation_21_Blog/58/vobId__2801/.

90. Enns, *Inspiration and Incarnation*, 169.

91. Ibid., 168.

92. Ibid., 16.

93. Ibid., 39.

94. Ibid., 45.

95. Ibid., 48.

The discussion about Scripture, its God-breathed character and authority, cannot take place via a coerced concession to a new hermeneutical method and the "occasion" of science. It can only take place in the perspective of that trustworthiness of Scripture which enables us to abandon ourselves in complete trust to its authority and to preach its message.[96]

At the core of the hermeneutical crisis there is a contrast of great importance. The Westminster Confession presents an "infallible rule of interpretation" while Enns proposes a hermeneutic that embraces a method without "clear rules." When Young and Berkouwer can agree on the gravity of what is at stake in the hermeneutical crisis, should we not heed their warnings before we "blissfully" embrace the "modern doctrine of Scripture"[97] advocated by Professor Enns?

The Starting Point: A Unique or Non-Unique Scripture?

The hermeneutical crisis is born at the intersection of the question concerning the nature of Scripture and the consideration of the starting point for its interpretation. Does one begin the interpretation of Holy Scripture viewing it primarily as divine revelation or instead as a human book?[98]

Bavinck's description of the eternal and yet human relevance of Holy Scripture helps to set the stage for this discussion:

In a human manner it always speaks of the highest and most holy, of the eternal and invisible things. Like Christ, it considers nothing that is human strange. But that is why it is a book for mankind and lasts until the end of the ages. It is old, without ever aging. It always remains young and flourishing; it is the language of life. *Verbum Dei manet in aeternum* [The word of God remains forever].[99]

Should not this high view of Scripture flow from Enns's view of Christ's incarnation? This would seem to be so, particularly when he writes,

The starting point for our discussion is the following: *as Christ is both God and human, so is the Bible.* . . . Jesus is 100 percent God and 100 percent human—at the same time. . . . In the same way that Jesus is—*must be*—both God and human, the Bible is also a divine and human book.[100]

But when Enns moves beyond the starting point for his "discussion" and elaborates his starting point for engaging *Scripture*, it becomes clear that he does not believe that the starting point is the Bible's full divinity or its uniqueness. Instead, his starting point for hermeneutics is the Bible's non-uniqueness given its full humanity:

96. *Holy Scripture*, 138.

97. *Inspiration and Incarnation*, 48.

98. Other important hermeneutical issues raised by Professor Enns cannot be addressed here since they are beyond the purview of this study. For significant discussions of how the NT writers quote the OT, consider the following: Enns, *Inspiration and Incarnation*, 113–65; G. K. Beale, *The Right Doctrine from the Wrong Text? Essays on the Use of the Old Testament in the New* (Grand Rapids: Baker, 1994); Walter C. Kaiser Jr., "Legitimate Hermeneutics," in *Inerrancy*, 117–47; Dan G. McCartney, "The New Testament's Use of the Old Testament," in *Inerrancy and Hermeneutic*, 101–16; Dennis E. Johnson, *Him We Proclaim: Preaching Christ from All the Scriptures* (Phillipsburg, NJ: P&R Publishing, 2007), 137–64; Young, *Thy Word Is Truth*, 143–61.

99. Cited in Berkouwer, *Holy Scripture*, 27.

100. Enns, *Inspiration and Incarnation*, 17.

It is essential to the very nature of revelation that the Bible is not unique to its environment. The human dimension of Scripture is essential to its being Scripture. This, I argue, is the proper starting point for looking at the relationship between the Bible and the issues we will discuss in this book. That the Bible is so easily situated in its ancient context is a source of difficulty for many modern readers.[101]

The "100 percent divine" of Christ's incarnation seems here in the context of the Bible to have little relevance and seems to have been eclipsed by the "100 percent human."

Accordingly, Enns finds the Genesis stories mirrored in the Babylonian texts as evidence of the Bible's humanity and apparent dependence on other human and pre-or non-Hebrew sources.[102] But when Young reviews these Babylonian texts in light of Scripture he instead proclaims the Bible's uniqueness[103] and the divine origin and inerrancy of Scripture.[104] In fact

101. Ibid., 20. Enns repeatedly affirms the non-uniqueness of Scripture. See, for example, 15, 16, 18, 20–21, 31–32, 42–43, 46–47, 168.

102. Enns writes, "In both their oral and written versions, the stories of Genesis seem to be younger than the stories of other ancient Near Eastern cultures. If pressed, one could attempt to mount the argument that the Israelite stories are actually older than all the Ancient Near Eastern stories but were only *recorded* later in Hebrew. Such a theory—for that is what it is, a theory—would need to *assume* that the biblical stories are the pristine originals and that all the other stories are parodies and perversions of the Israelite original, even though the available evidence would be very difficult to square with such a conclusion. But could it have happened this way? Yes, I suppose one could insist on such a thing, but it would be very difficult for someone holding to such a view to have a meaningful conversation with linguists and historians of the ancient world. To argue in such hypothetical terms can sometimes become an excuse for maintaining a way of thinking that is otherwise unsupportable. It is just such explanations that some readers might find problematic, for they seem motivated by a desire to protect one's theology rather than to engage the available evidence. . . . regardless of when Genesis was written and in what language, it still reflects an ancient Near Eastern worldview that clearly is significantly older. It stretches logic and common sense to try to protect the uniqueness of the Genesis accounts by arguing that Mesopotamian peoples, who existed long before Israel came on the scene and who were the dominant cultures of the day, had no creation myths for hundreds of years and simply waited for Israelite slaves to provide the prototype, which they then corrupted." *Inspiration and Incarnation*, 52. In engaging Enns's claims here, one should consider Herman Bavinck's concept of "primitive revelation" or "original revelation" in *The Philosophy of Revelation* (Grand Rapids: Baker, 1979), 171, 188–89, "Both in earlier and later times in the Christian church the truth and wisdom found among the heathen have been generally derived from a primitive revelation, from the continuous illumination by the Logos, from acquaintance with the literature of the Old Testament, or from the operation of God's common grace." "All these fundamentals are given from the beginning in human nature; they are transmitted from generation to generation, and are at the same time grounded in the very nature of man, so that dependence and independence work together here. And they all point back to a divine origin: 'all knowledge is,' at least so far as principles and foundations are concerned, 'of divine origin.' Knowledge in this sense flows from revelation. To this original revelation is joined on that revelation which according to the Old Testament was bestowed upon Israel. The latter is built upon the former and rests upon it, and is at the same time the continuation, the development and completion of it. The distinction between what has come to be called general and special revelation does not begin until the call of Abraham; before that the two intermingle, and so far have become the property of all peoples and nations. Special revelation certainly is set antithetically over against all the corruption which gradually entered into the life of the peoples, but it takes up, confirms, and completes all that had been from the beginning put into human nature by revelation and had been preserved and increased subsequently in the human race."

103. Young explains, "When compared with other literature from the ancient Near East, the Bible stands out like a fair flower in a dreary, barren desert. We read the crude polytheism of the Babylonian documents, and then open the pages of Holy Scripture and learn of Him who is good and true and holy. We read the pseudo-creation accounts of the ancient world and then listen to the majestic account of true creation given in the Bible. We read of the struggles and strivings of men to atone in one way or another for sins. How dark was the light of ancient religion! Then we learn from the Bible that man cannot save himself, but that God has provided the one Lamb that taketh away the sin of the world. How unspeakably grand is the doctrine of salvation by grace! . . . Many and convincing are these evidences whereby the Scriptures reveal their Divine origin. Yet, despite their clarity, not all men are willing to accept these evidences, and the reason for this unwillingness is not far to seek. Is it because there is some defect in the evidences themselves? Are not they of sufficient clarity and cogency to convince all men? The answer is that the evidences are clear enough; indeed so clear are they that he who is not convinced by them has no excuse." *Thy Word Is Truth*, 33.

104. Young writes, "If then we may arrive at the position (and it is the only position at which one may legitimately arrive) that the early chapters of Genesis purport to be history let us next ask the question whether, as a matter of actual fact, they are filled with the errors which inescapably accompany a pre-scientific age. The answer to this question must be in the negative. In their statements these chapters are scientifically accurate. They do not teach anything that is not in accord with the facts. Can anyone point out an actual error, for example, in the first chapter of Genesis? Particularly interesting does this question become when one compares

the uniqueness of Scripture in Young's mind is a foundational perspective that necessarily flows from the doctrine of providence affirmed by the Westminster Confession.[105]

In this context, consider D. A. Carson's critique of what he believes to be the one-sided use of the incarnational analogy in Enns's hermeneutic:

> Using the incarnational analogy, the "human dimension" of the God/man not only places him in the human environment, but leaves him unique in that environment since only he is without sin. And even more strikingly, of course, what makes Jesus most strikingly unique to the human environment is that, without gainsaying his thorough, perfect, humanness for an instant, he is also God, and thus the perfect revealer of God, such that what Jesus says and does, God says and does. But when Enns speaks of "the very nature of the revelation of the Bible" as "not unique in its environment," he looks only at its "human dimension" and integrates nothing of what else must be said if we are to understand what the Bible is in this "human environment."[106]

Moreover, Paul Helm's assessment of Enns's incarnational hermeneutical methodology finds that a non-unique Bible results in a "disturbingly new" approach that moves Enns ever "farther away" from an "orthodox doctrine of Scripture."

> However what is new, disturbingly new, is the claim that Enns makes about this cultural embeddedness. We discover that the Bible itself is far from unique: it's a diverse, culturally-

---

the first chapter of Genesis with the so-called Babylonian account of creation. Are there errors in the Babylonian account? To ask this question is to give the answer. No one would think seriously of defending the Babylonian narrative from the charge of error, for the simple reason that it is so full of it. In the midst of the polytheism and superstition of that ancient world the first chapter of the Bible, on the other hand, stands out like a fair flower in a barren wilderness. The Genesis account differs completely from the cosmogonies of the ancient world. In it there is a robust and vigorous monotheism; the Creator is glorified and His wondrous work in creation exalted. Here God is honored in such a way that the reader may come to marvel at the greatness of Him who by the word of His mouth brought all things into being. Are there errors in the first chapter of the Bible? Let us say without fear of contradiction that no one has been able to demonstrate the presence of error in this majestic opening chapter of Scripture." *Thy Word Is Truth*, 167.

105. Young writes, "There is of course no question but that the events of the Bible are unique events. We may very legitimately speak of the uniqueness of these things which God wrought in history for the salvation of sinners. We are saved from our sins, not by the exploits of Alexander the great, but by the death of Jesus Christ upon the cross. For the believer, the latter event is rich with meaning that is lacking in the former. The Christian is naturally more interested in those events in history by means of which his redemption was obtained. When all this is granted, however, we must insist that the events of Biblical history took place in history. They were, in other words, historical events. As such, they are related to all other events of history. Since the sovereign God in His providence upholds all things, we may be assured that all events of history are related. The matter has been accurately stated—accurately, because it is in agreement with the teaching of the Bible—by the Westminster Confession of Faith: 'God the great Creator of all things doth uphold, direct, dispose, and govern all creatures, actions, and things from the greatest even to the least, by His most wise and holy providence, according to His infallible fore-knowledge, and the free and immutable counsel of His own will, to the praise of the glory of His wisdom, power, justice, goodness and mercy.' All things that occur, according to the Confession's statement are ordained of God. They occur because he has decreed that they should occur. All are parts of His over-all plan. All are parts of His one all-embracing eternal purpose and decree. Inasmuch as this is the case, all events of history in the very nature of the case, are related. With the words of Pascal, we may well agree, 'If the nose of Cleopatra had been shorter, the whole face of the earth would have been changed.' The events of Biblical history are parts of this eternal purpose of God. As such they occur in the realm of history. They cannot be removed or separated from their historical context and background. Our salvation was wrought by the Lord of Glory when He died upon the cross and rose again from the dead. . . . Christianity, therefore, is rooted and grounded in history. At the same time it is true, as we noted above, that there is a uniqueness about biblical history. This uniqueness has been expressed in the words of the Westminster Confession as follows: 'As the providence of God doth, in general reach to all creatures, so, after a most special manner, it taketh care of His Church, and disposeth all things to the good thereof.' Jesus Christ is, without controversy, the center of history. There is a *Before Christ* and an *In the year of our Lord*. The distinction is perfectly legitimate. There is a certain sense in which all things may be said to subserve the purposes of God in salvation." *Thy Word Is Truth*, 254–57. Also compare how differently Young handles the Nuzi tablets, 201ff., from Enns, *Inspiration and Incarnation*, 29–31.

106. Carson (Reformation 21, May 2006); cf. *Collected Writings on Scripture*, 269–70.

biased product, which we can only ever hope to understand provisionally. It'll be best to assess the book by considering a set of answers from Enns to three questions: Is our interpretation of the Bible provisional? Is the Bible unique? And finally, and most importantly, Is the Bible objective? These are among the central questions the author himself raises. My argument in this review is that in his answers to such questions Professor Enns has not gone too far—as he occasionally fears, perhaps—but that he has not gone far enough. The book is troubling not because of the profundity of the treatment but rather because of its superficiality. We shall find that Enns's answers to each of these questions take him farther and farther away from being able to maintain an orthodox doctrine of Scripture.[107]

Whether one agrees or disagrees with Carson's and Helm's critiques of Enns, one thing is clear. The methodology of Enns is to express concern for previous "doctrinal formulations" but not to quote those "formulations" as he develops his own doctrine of Scripture.

A summary of Professor Enns's doctrine of Scripture manifests that he assiduously avoids the traditional theological terminology that hitherto has articulated the evangelical and Reformed doctrine of Scripture. Conspicuous by their absence are: "infallible," "verbally inspired," "verbal plenary inspiration," "God-breathed," and "inerrant." Nevertheless, Professor Enns does employ specific phrases to develop his doctrine of Scripture.

Enns begins[108] by speaking of "a vibrant and reverent doctrine of Scripture" (13) and affirms that "the Bible is ultimately from God and that it is God's gift to the church" (14). Thus he can speak of "a vibrant positive view of Scripture as God's word" (15), and he declares that "the Bible is God's word" (15). However, "It is not enough simply to say that the Bible is the word of God or that it is inspired" (17), because "the Bible is also a divine and human book" (17). Thus Enns asks, "How does Scripture's full humanity and full divinity affect what we should expect from Scripture?" (18). His desire for "a high and healthy view of Scripture as God's word" (46), and for "a sound doctrine of Scripture" (56), leads him to emphasize extrabiblical evidence and incarnation: "A doctrine of Scripture that does not think through this incarnational dimension is inadequate in light of the evidence we have" (67). Hence for Enns's doctrine of Scripture, "the bottom line is this: how we conceive of the normativity or authority of the Old Testament must be in continual conversation with the incarnate dimension of Scripture" (67–68). And this "incarnate dimension" means "our confession of the Bible as God's word has a provisional quality to it" (168).

What then are the consequences of Enns's "provisional" doctrine of God's Word as incarnate Scripture? There seem to be four. First, there is a new definition of the uniqueness of Scripture: "Its uniqueness is seen not in holding human cultures at arm's length, but in the belief that Scripture is the only book in which God speaks incarnately" (168). Second, there is no longer any basis to place our trust in our confession of Scripture: "We are to place our trust in God who gave us Scripture, not in our own conceptions of how Scripture ought to be" (169). Third, the Bible's significance for ethics is significantly redefined: so from now on we are to consider "the Bible not as a timeless rule book or owner's manual for the Christian life—so that we can lift verses here and there and apply them" (169–70). Finally, "It is in the person and work of Christ that Christians seek to read the Old Testament, to search out how it is in Christ that the

107. Helm (*Reformation 21,* April 2006).
108. The quoted phrases in these paragraphs can be found in *Inspiration and Incarnation* on the identified pages.

Old Testament has integrity, how it is worthy of trust, how the parts cohere. . . . A christotelic coherence is not achieved by following a few simple rules of exegesis" (170).

Does this summation of Professor Enns's teaching on Scripture substantiate Helm's claim that Enns's approach moves him away from an orthodox doctrine of Scripture? Perhaps a more specific and precise question is this: Does Professor Enns's doctrine of Scripture reveal that he is departing from the Westminster Standards' teaching on Holy Scripture?

We conclude this study by a comparison of Enns's doctrine of Scripture and hermeneutics as summarized above with the teachings of the Westminster Standards. As we do, the following seven questions will be briefly addressed:

1. Is the confession therefore "inadequate" in that it has not thought "through this incarnation dimension" that incorporates "extrabiblical evidence"?
2. Is the confession's view of biblical "authority in continual conversation with the incarnate dimension of Scripture"?
3. Does the confession argue for the uniqueness of the Scriptures because God therein uniquely speaks "incarnately"?
4. Does the confession view itself as a "provisional" confession and thus not a trustworthy guide for how we understand what "Scripture ought to be"?
5. Does the confession prohibit viewing the Bible as a "timeless rule book . . . for the Christian life"?
6. Does the confession teach that the only dimension of the Scripture's trustworthiness is in its specific focus on Christ, i.e., a "christotelic coherence"?
7. Does the confession reject the idea that there are a few basic rules of exegesis?

If we discover that these elements do not "cohere" with the confession, then we must conclude that Professor Enns's doctrine of Scripture is out of accord with the Westminster Standards.

Inspiration and Incarnation Contra the Westminster Standards

Since Professor Enns has stated, "All attempts to articulate the nature of Scripture are open to examination, including my own,"[109] let us now examine his doctrine of Scripture in light of the confession. To do so, we will assess the principles we have just distilled from his doctrine of Scripture.

1. Is the confession therefore "inadequate" in that it has not thought "through this incarnation dimension" that incorporates "extrabiblical evidence"?

In making this claim, Enns is actually taking a position not contained in the confession, since the Reformed confessions do not use the incarnational analogy to explain the doctrine of Scripture. As Berkouwer declares, "it is useful to remember that the church did not adopt this parallel in its confessions."[110]

As we have seen above, the confession rejects the notion of a required extrabiblical criteria for biblical hermeneutics given its expressed hermeneutical principle of *sola Scriptura* in 1.9. Indeed, it calls this canonical hermeneutic the "infallible rule of interpretation." This

109. Enns, *Inspiration and Incarnation*, 48.
110. Berkouwer, *Holy Scripture*, 199.

of God" is found in Scripture and is understood only by the "inward illumination of the Spirit of God."[117] Hence the idea of an "infallible rule" that flows from these foundational truths of Scripture along with its attendant divine authority does not comport with the vicissitudes and variability implied by Professor Enns's principle of "continual conversation." Hence, this principle of Professor Enns is also incompatible with the Westminster Confession's doctrine of Scripture.

3. Does the confession argue for the uniqueness of the Scriptures because God therein uniquely speaks "incarnately"?

We have already seen that this cannot be viewed as a confessional position, since the Reformed confessions do not utilize the incarnational analogy. However, the literature in this context reveals there is substantial disagreement over the propriety of using the incarnational analogy to present the doctrine of Scripture. Great Reformed theologians take positions both in favor of and in opposition to the analogy's value for developing the doctrine of Scripture.[118]

We must therefore ask how Enns can make this controverted principle the definition of the Bible's uniqueness? It clearly is less convincing when this theological principle is not accepted by many in the Reformed tradition and when it is a theological paradigm that is not employed in any Reformed confession, let alone the Westminster Standards.

If we seek the uniqueness of the Scriptures according to the confession, however, it is clear that the Scriptures are unique because they are divine,[119] even though Scripture is very available to men in human form.[120] Hence the Bible's uniqueness is discovered in what the

---

the consent of all the parts, the scope of the whole (which is, to give all glory to God), the full discovery it makes of the only way of man's salvation, the many other incomparable excellencies, and the entire perfection thereof, are arguments whereby it doth abundantly evidence itself to be the Word of God: yet notwithstanding, our full persuasion and assurance of the infallible truth and divine authority thereof, is from the inward work of the Holy Spirit bearing witness by and with the Word in our hearts."

117. WCF 1.6: "The whole counsel of God concerning all things necessary for his own glory, man's salvation, faith and life, is either expressly set down in Scripture, or by good and necessary consequence may be deduced from Scripture: unto which nothing at any time is to be added, whether by new revelations of the Spirit, or traditions of men. Nevertheless, we acknowledge the inward illumination of the Spirit of God to be necessary for the saving understanding of such things as are revealed in the Word: and that there are some circumstances concerning the worship of God, and government of the church, common to human actions and societies, which are to be ordered by the light of nature, and Christian prudence, according to the general rules of the Word, which are always to be observed."

118. See, for example, Gaffin, "Old Amsterdam"; Silva, *Has the Church Misread the Bible?* 38–45; Berkouwer, *Holy Scripture*, 195–212.

119. Cf. Gaffin, "Old Amsterdam—I," 276: "Rogers and McKim, for one, cite this passage to show Kuyper's support of their view that the authority of Scripture is located in its divine content in distinction from its human form." Yet Gaffin points out (277), "What graphic inspiration effects, then, is divinely authoritative certification. Concerning this certification Kuyper immediately adds the qualification that it happens 'always impressionistically,' in the NT as well as the OT. . . . The point of the passage in question, then, is that the differences between the four Gospels (along with the NT use of the OT) exemplify the 'impressionistic' character of the biblical records. . . . Concerning the activity of the human writers the sum of the matter is that 'the Holy Spirit worked effectively as a leading, directing and determining power; but their subjectivity was not lost.' . . . This is how biblical history lives on. 'It gives no notarial acts, but reproduces what has been received in the consciousness, and does this not with the precision of outline which belongs to architecture, but with the impressionistic certainty of life.'"

120. Compare here, Kuyper's view of the divinity of Scripture cited in Gaffin, "Old Amsterdam—I," 266, "This authority derives from the fact that the speaker in the Holy Scripture is not a creature but God himself. That speech in Scripture to his church could come to pass by God immediately, i.e., without instruments (*sine instrumento*). . . . But this has not been the way of the Lord: As in the work of redemption he does not continue to confront us transcendently

confession calls its "infallibility."[121] This unique reality of the Scriptures has led the church to speak of the Scripture's inerrancy[122] or "errorlessness."[123] This uniqueness or high doctrine of Scripture is also evidenced in the Westminster Standards when it speaks of Scripture as "the Word of God,"[124] and God's "revealed will."[125]

Along with the confession's emphasis on the divine character of Scripture, it also recognizes Scripture's human form. Scripture was originally in Hebrew and Greek, and was committed wholly to writing.[126] Divine revelation has come into human history in various ways which have now ceased with the finality of Scripture.[127] Since divine revelation in Scripture came into human history with specific purposes, some parts of Scripture no longer carry authority, as the abrogation of the laws of Israel attests.[128] All

---

as God, but immanently in Jesus Christ he has united the divine and human natures in such a way that the divine life has appeared in a man, so also the Lord God has given us H. Scripture not transcendently but immanently, because he has so intimately united the divine factor with the human factor that the divine word has come to us, always from a human pen, mostly from a human mind, and not seldom from a human heart. In the union of both these factors now lies the mystery of Holy Scripture. Parallel with the mystery of the incarnation runs the mystery of inscripturation. In both cases the Word of God comes to us, in the manger as Emmanuel in the world where we live, in H. Scripture as Emmanuel in the world of our thoughts and ideas. Both revelations of the word belong together, just as our living and the consciousness of that living belong together. Thus both mysteries must either be rejected together or confessed together and if confessed, then on the same ground."

121. WCF 1.5, 9.

122. Cf., for example, Young, *Thy Word Is Truth*, 113–85.

123. See Young, *Thy Word Is Truth*, 185, where he argues for the need to reserve judgment about errors in the Bible given its divine character. See also Gaffin, "Old Amsterdam—I," 281, "It bears emphasizing, as Kuyper notes in this context, that the Bible's divine errorlessness ultimately roots in its divine authorship, *formally considered*. If I transmit an authoritative message from someone else, then I must do so literally and may not change the wording. . . . But since ultimately it is the Holy Spirit who everywhere speaks in Scripture, formally and materially, *he* is free to make the variations we observe, without any detriment to its divine errorlessness. . . . By means of free quotations, in graphic inspiration the Holy Spirit maintains himself as the author of underlying material inspiration. . . . In fact, the Holy Spirit, who alone is able to convince us of graphic inspiration, enables us to perceive that the many incongruities in Scripture could not be left standing in a human author but are in fact a mark of its divinity. . . . There are two sorts of precision: mechanical and organic. A mechanically molded statue or piece of artillery precisely resembles from every angle all others cast from the same mold; among ice floes or winter flowers, however, there are great dissimilarities. The edges of a piece of wood fashioned by an artisan are completely smooth and even; the bark of a tree is quite coarse. 'And yet, if someone asks, where is the greatest precision, in the mechanical or the organic, everyone feels that it is not in the mechanical but in the organic that there is the greater precision and most perfect beauty.'"

124. Larger Catechism question 3: "What is the Word of God? Answer: The Holy Scriptures of the Old and New Testaments are the Word of God, the only rule of faith and obedience." Larger Catechism question 4: "How does it appear that the Scriptures are the Word of God? Answer: The Scriptures manifest themselves to be the Word of God, by their majesty and purity; by the consent of all the parts, and the scope of the whole, which is to give all glory to God; by their light and power to convince and convert sinners, to comfort and build up believers unto salvation: but the Spirit of God bearing witness by and with the Scriptures in the heart of man, is alone able fully to persuade it that they are the very Word of God."

125. The answer to Shorter Catechism question 39 speaks of "obedience to his revealed will." The answer to Shorter Catechism question 40 states, "The rule which God at first revealed to man for his obedience, was the moral law." Larger Catechism question 11 asks, "How does it appear that the Son and the Holy Ghost are God equal with the Father? Answer: The Scriptures manifest that the Son and the Holy Ghost are God equal with the Father." Larger Catechism question 157 speaks of "the will of God revealed in them."

126. WCF 1.1, 8.

127. WCF 1.1.

128. WCF 19.4. See also John H. Gerstner, Douglas F. Kelly, and Philip Rollinson, *A Guide to the Westminster Confession Faith*, ch. 19, "Concerning the Law of God": "19.4 In addition to these CEREMONIAL LAWS for the church in her former state GOD ALSO GAVE THE ISRAELITES, AS A POLITICAL BODY, VARIOUS JUDICIAL LAWS. These traditional laws EXPIRED when that state of the church changed. While the moral law never changes, other laws not only change but actually EXPIRE. For example, the sixth commandment against killing remains, but the judicial law that *certain violators* of the moral law should be executed has not. Since capital punishment for such a violation as breaking the sabbath is not part of the moral law but only of the judicial, it EXPIRES with the end of the Israelite church-state."

parts of Scripture are not equally plain to all and not all parts are equally clear.[129] It is not exhaustive and so requires human logic, the light of nature, and Christian prudence to interpret and apply.[130] Its written texts have faced the vicissitudes of transmission requiring God's providential care.[131] Engagement with the Scriptures can generate controversies of religion.[132] The Scriptures must be translated.[133] The canon itself has not been easily or fully recognized as seen by a canonical listing that excludes the apocryphal books.[134] The idea of "general equity" in interpreting relevance of the laws of Israel for the NT era also affirms the humanity of Scripture.[135] Because the Bible is a human book, it welcomes human means to interpret its message.[136]

Consequently, Professor Enns's view that the Bible's uniqueness is in its human incarnate form is the opposite emphasis of the confession, which instead highlights its divine character. Hence his view appears to be incompatible with the Westminster Confession's emphasis on the priority of the divine infallibility of Scripture.

4. Does the confession view itself as a "provisional" confession and thus not a trustworthy guide for how we understand what "Scripture ought to be"?

129. WCF 1.7.
130. WCF 1.1, 6.
131. WCF 1.8.
132. WCF 1.10.
133. WCF 1.8.
134. WCF 1.2–3.
135. WCF 19.4. For a consideration of the notions of equity and general equity, see the "Report of the Committee on Women in the Military and in Combat," *Minutes of the Sixty-Seventh General Assembly (July 5–12, 2000) of the Orthodox Presbyterian Church* (Willow Grove, PA: Orthodox Presbyterian Church, 2000), 277–79. Cf. Robert Shaw, *An Exposition of the Westminster Confession of Faith*, "Chapter 19: Of the Law of God" (Fearn, Ross Shire: Christian Focus, 1973), 245: "The *judicial* law respected the Jews in their political capacity, or as a nation, and consisted of those institutions which God prescribed to them for their civil government. This law, as far as the Jewish polity was peculiar, has also been entirely abolished; but as far as it contains any statute founded in the law of nature common to all nations, it is still obligatory." See also George S. Hendry, *The Westminster Confession for Today*, "Chapter 21: Of the Law of God" (Richmond: John Knox, 1960), 177: "While God's law is the fundamental determination of man's being, and is, as such, absolutely and permanently binding upon all men, it involves obligations which are relative to the concrete situations in which it has to be obeyed . . . judicial laws were involved in the fact that Israel was at once a church and a state ('a body politic'), and they were necessary for the regulation of its life in its political aspect; since they were formulated in view of the peculiar historical conditions and geographical circumstances of the life of Israel as a primitive agrarian society, they are no longer obligatory, except in so far as they reflect general principles of equity."
136. Larger Catechism question 157: "How is the Word of God to be read? Answer: The Holy Scriptures are to be read with an high and reverent esteem of them; with a firm persuasion that they are the very Word of God, and that he only can enable us to understand them; with desire to know, believe, and obey the will of God revealed in them; with diligence, and attention to the matter and scope of them; with meditation, application, self-denial, and prayer." Larger Catechism question 159: "How is the Word of God to be preached by those that are called thereunto? Answer: They that are called to labor in the ministry of the Word, are to preach sound doctrine, diligently, in season and out of season; plainly, not in the enticing words of man's wisdom, but in demonstration of the Spirit, and of power; faithfully, making known the whole counsel of God; wisely, applying themselves to the necessities and capacities of the hearers; zealously, with fervent love to God and the souls of his people; sincerely, aiming at his glory, and their conversion, edification, and salvation." Turretin writes (*Institutes*, II.17.6), "It is not a question of a perspicuity that excludes necessary means for interpretation, such as the inner light of the Spirit, the attention of the mind, the voice and ministry of the church, lectures and commentaries, prayers and vigils. We acknowledge such means are not only useful but also normally are necessary, but we want to deny any obscurity that keeps the common people from reading Scripture, as if it were harmful or dangerous, or that leads to a falling back on traditions when one should have taken a stand on Scripture alone." *Doctrine of Scripture*, 187–88.

It is important to recognize here that the confession never calls for acceptance for its own sake.[137] Instead, it points all to Holy Scripture, as when it identifies in 1.9 the "infallible rule of interpretation":

> The infallible rule of interpretation of Scripture is the Scripture itself: and therefore, when there is a question about the true and full sense of any Scripture (which is not manifold, but one), it must be searched and known by other places that speak more clearly.

Since this hermeneutical principle is "infallible"—as "infallible" as "the Word of God . . . the infallible truth" (1.5) from which it is drawn, there is consequently no "provisionality" about what the Word of God is.

The confession, consistent with its claim to present an infallible Scripture that gives to the church an infallible hermeneutical rule, seeks to focus on and exclusively to present the teaching of the Scriptures by its vast, consistent and insistent appeal to the Scriptures.[138] There are many who criticize the confession's alleged "proof text" method. Yet, what the confession seeks to do is to interpret Scripture with Scripture.[139] Hence the confession could best be described as a subordinate standard making a consistent, albeit fallible, attempt to apply an infallible hermeneutical rule derived from an infallible written divine revelation.

The point here is that Professor Enns's principle of provisionality with regard to the Westminster Standards *per se* is not ultimately incompatible with the Westminster Standards' teaching since the standards are in fact subordinate standards. Yet his perspective of provisionality becomes incompatible with the historic Presbyterian vows to Scripture and confession discussed above when it is remembered that the "infallible rule" itself is not provisional. It is instead the mandated method established by the infallible truth of Scripture, which is the Word of God in human form. Hence Professor Enns's principle of provisionality is incompatible with the confession's teaching on the nature of Scripture and in regard to the confession's "infallible rule of interpretation of Scripture."

5. Does the confession prohibit viewing the Bible as a "timeless rule book . . . for the Christian life"?

Contrary to Professor Enns's desire for a doctrine of Scripture that removes the notion of timeless rules for the Christian life, the confession consistently affirms that there are important "rules that are to be observed" by the Christian, whether in interpreting the Scriptures, or observing the Ten Commandments—which are the standards or rules for

---

137. For a discussion of the confession as a subordinate standard to Scripture, see notes 44 and 45 above.

138. The scriptural citations in the Westminster Standards number well over two thousand.

139. Cf. here Berkouwer, *Holy Scripture*, 279–85, concerning "the so-called proof from Scripture," and Young, *Thy Word Is Truth*, 219–21. Young writes, "On all sides one hears it asserted that we must not use the Bible as a book of proof texts. To use the Bible in such a way is, we are told, to betray a profound misunderstanding of its nature. . . . One thing, however, may be said about this practice. It was employed by none other than our Lord Himself" (219). Berkouwer writes, "Many of these 'proofs from Scripture' stem from a deep awareness of the humanity and coherence of Scripture. . . . Clearly there is room for 'therefores' and 'so that's' in conclusions and counter arguments within the realm of the gospel (2 Tim. 3:16). . . . Anselm's question 'Why did God become man?' should not automatically be rejected as rationalism. For we read everywhere of the coherence, centrality and depth of God's actions," 280, 282–83.

the Christian life—or engaging in prayer and worship. The places in the standards where timeless scriptural rules for the Christian life are directly stated are listed below.

Shorter Catechism question 2: The Word of God, which is contained in the Scriptures of the Old and New Testaments, is the only rule to direct us how we may glorify and enjoy Him.

Shorter Catechism question 24: What is sin? Answer: Sin is any want of conformity unto, or transgression of, any law of God, given as a rule to the reasonable creature.

Shorter Catechism question 40: What did God at first reveal to man for the rule of his obedience? A. The rule which God at first revealed to man for his obedience, was the moral law.

Shorter Catechism question 99: What rule hath God given for our direction in prayer? A. The whole Word of God is of use to direct us in prayer; but the special rule of direction is that form of prayer which Christ taught his disciples commonly called *The Lord's Prayer*.

All which [the canonical books] are given by inspiration of God to be the **rule** of faith and life. (WCF 1.2)

According to the general **rules** of the Word, which are always to be observed. (WCF 1.6)

The infallible **rule** of interpretation of Scripture is the Scripture itself. (WCF 1.9)

The Law . . . continued to be a perfect **rule** of righteousness. (WCF 19.2)

The Law . . . a **rule** of life informing them of the will of God, and their duty. (WCF 19.6)

To set down **rules** and directions for the better ordering of the public worship of God. (WCF 31.2)

All synods or councils since the apostles' times, whether general or particular, may err, and many have erred; therefore they are **not** to be made the **rule** of faith or practice, but to be used as a help in both. (WCF 31.3)

Larger Catechism question 3: The Old and New Testament are the Word of God, the only **rule** of faith and obedience.

Larger Catechism question 24: Or transgression of any law of God given as a **rule** to the reasonable creature.

Larger Catechism question 92: The **rule** of obedience revealed to Adam in the estate of innocence, and to all mankind.

Larger Catechism question 97: Their greater care to conform themselves thereunto as the **rule** of their obedience.

Larger Catechism question 186: But the special **rule** of direction is that form of prayer which our Saviour Christ taught his disciples.

Most significantly here, Larger Catechism question 99 must be noted, as this answer teaches, "For the right understanding of the Ten Commandments, **these rules are to be observed**."

Beyond this, the very vows of Westminster, the OPC, and the PCA recognize the "only infallible rule of faith and practice" that everyone taking the vow is to believe and so to obey. Therefore Professor Enns's principle of a Bible without timeless rules for the Christian life is incompatible with the Westminster Confession.

6. Does the confession teach that the only dimension of the Scripture's trustworthiness is in its specific focus on Christ, i.e., a "christotelic coherence"?

Professor Enns writes,

Not only do we no longer share the conventions of the ancient Near Eastern world, but we also live in union with the crucified and risen Christ, in whom all of the Old Testament finds its completion. All this to say that the central function of the Old Testament may not be there to "tell us what to do." It may be more a part of a larger story that God brings to an end many hundreds of years later in Christ.[140]

Clearly the christological focus of the Bible is one of the major theological paradigms advanced by the confession.[141] This can be seen in the history of the covenant of grace outlined by the Westminster Standards in chapters 7 and 8 that reflect the history of salvation in the covenant of grace in Christ.[142] Moreover, the idea of the Bible having a goal or "scope" is also referenced by the confession.[143]

140. Enns, *Inspiration and Incarnation*, 67.

141. There are a number of theological and interpretive paradigms or theological constructs offered by the Westminster catechisms. These include: a decretal theology: Larger Catechism question 6; a theology of union with Christ: Larger Catechism question 79; a covenant theology that focuses on the history of redemption: Shorter Catechism question 59, Larger Catechism questions 33–36, 101, 121; a covenant theology structured on theological covenants: Larger Catechism questions 30–32; a theology of kingdom and eschatology: Shorter Catechism question 102; and a theology of the offices and estates of Christ: Larger Catechism questions 42–45.

142. Turretin, *Doctrine of Scripture*, 204–5 (*Institutes*, II.19.13), reflects an implicit appreciation for christocentric interpretation, or the historical redemptive nature of Scripture when it is interpreted in light of Christ. He says, "Since Scripture, which contains much more than words, is very rich in meaning, it is not absurd to say that the Holy Spirit wanted to give many teachings to us in the same word, but always one subordinated to the other so that one is the sign and figure of the other, or that they have some connection and dependency. Thus the promise given Abraham concerning his descendants refers both to Isaac as type and to Christ as antitype (Gal. 3:16). The oracle forbidding the breaking of the bones of the lamb (Ex. 23:46) refers both to the paschal lamb as a figure and to Christ in mystery (John 19:36). The promise given David, 'I will be a father to him' (2 Sam. 7:14), refers both to Solomon and to Christ (Heb. 1:5). The prediction in Psalm 16:10 that the holy one will not see corruption applies both to David, although incompletely, and to Christ, completely (Acts 2:29–30). There are any number of such texts in Scripture, which have various aspects which must be held together in order to have the full meaning of the oracle, and they are fulfilled not all at once, but in stages over a period of time. Thus many of the ancient oracles had three aspects: for the dispensation of the law in the Jewish church, for the dispensation of grace in the Christian church, and for the dispensation of glory in heaven. Thus Isaiah 9:1, about the people who walked in darkness and saw a great light, has three stages of fulfillment: the liberation from Babylon, the proclamation of the gospel (Matt. 4:14–16), and the final resurrection, through which those who were living in the valley of the shadow of death will see the great light of the glory of God. Likewise in Ezekiel 37, it can be observed concerning the dry bones that the oracle had already been fulfilled when the people went out from their most bitter captivity in Babylon as from the tomb (v. 12), it is being fulfilled today in the spiritual resurrection (Eph. 5:14), and it will be perfectly fulfilled in the final resurrection (John 5:25)."

143. Cf. Berkouwer, *Holy Scripture*, 124–37.

But what does the confession declare the "scope" of Scripture to be? In 1.5 it says, "the scope of the whole (which is to give glory to God)." Larger Catechism question 4 says, "the scope of the whole, which is to give all glory to God." Larger Catechism question 157, discussing how the Word of God is to be read, states "with diligence and attention to the matter and scope of them." What all of this seems to be saying is that the "scope" of the Word of God is God's glory, while the "matter" of the Bible is Christ and His saving work. Thus the Westminster Standards present the doxological purpose of Scripture[144] that fits not only with the famous first question of the Shorter Catechism, but also parallels other passages of the standards that refer to God's glory such as Larger Catechism questions 112, 113, and 190.

If the christotelic principle of Professor Enns is arguing for a christocentricity to Scripture, this is consistent with the Westminster Confession. But this understanding of his term may not be accurate or sufficient. His further explication of christotelic seems to make the Scripture's focus so much on Christ as the ultimate fulfillment of Scripture that the ethical dimension is diminished or removed.[145] In that case, there is a loss of the Shorter Catechism's emphasis on the dual teachings of the Scriptures— "what we are to believe concerning God and what duty God requires of man" (Shorter Catechism question 3).

If this de-emphasis of the Christian duty to obey God's law is an inherent aspect of a christotelic hermeneutic, it would then be inconsistent with the confession. A commitment to christomonism, that is, a scriptural hermeneutic where only Christ is found in Scripture, without the concomitant pursuit of Christ's glory through the new obedience of the believer, is a perspective that is incompatible with the theology and ethic of the confession. The potential for christotelic exegesis to devolve into christomonism seems possible, since it appears to be a group quest for biblical meaning by an exclusive focus on Christ in the Bible. Moreover, there does not appear to be a clear sense of when this goal is achieved, according to Professor Enns.[146]

144. Francis R. Beattie, *The Presbyterian Standards: An Exposition of the Westminster Confession of Faith and Catechisms*, "Chapter 34: Summary and Conclusions" (Richmond: Presbyterian Committee of Publication, 1896), 413: "The inquiry now raised may be considered from a twofold point of view: First, A general view of the principle upon which the entire Standards are constructed may be taken. Here what may be termed the theocentric principle rules. Everything is from God, is subject to God, and is for the glory of God. The absolute sovereignty of God in creation, in providence, and in grace, is the fundamental idea of the Standards. He is sovereign in the sphere of natural or physical government, and in the realm of moral government, as well as in the domain of his spiritual redemptive government. Thus the sovereignty of God, rightly regarded and applied, is the root idea of the generic Calvinism of the Standards, and it supplies their constructive principle. The first question in the Catechisms strikes the key-note, and the entire contents of the Standards are in harmony with this view. God is the ruler of nature, and he is the Lord of the head, the heart, the conscience, and the life of all men. He is also King of kings and Lord of lords, as well as the king and head of his church. The theocentric principle is the constructive principle of the Standards as a whole, and it gives great majesty and remarkable completeness to the doctrines, ethics, and polity which they contain."

145. "Not only do we no longer share the conventions of the ancient Near Eastern world, but we also live in union with the crucified and risen Christ, in whom all of the Old Testament finds its completion. All this to say that the central function of the Old Testament may not be there to 'tell us what to do.' It may be more a part of a larger story that God brings to an end many hundreds of years later in Christ." Enns, *Inspiration and Incarnation*, 67.

146. "I am very intentional here in saying that this is something we *seek* after. A christotelic coherence is not achieved by following a few simple rules of exegesis. It is to be sought after, over a long period of time, in community with other Christians, with humility and patience. Biblical interpretation is . . . a path we walk rather than a fortress we defend." Enns, *Inspiration and Incarnation*, 170.

If a christotelic hermeneutic necessitates a christomonism such as summarized here, then this perspective is incompatible with the Westminster Standards' christocentricity, which is the heart of the confession's teaching on the covenant of grace and which calls for a saving faith in Christ that also seeks to bring glory to God by obedience to his law. The doxological end of the Christian life is simply portrayed by Shorter Catechism questions one and two, which declare,

Q. 1. What is the chief end of man?
A. 1. Man's chief end is to glorify God, and to enjoy him for ever.
Q. 2. What rule hath God given to direct us how we may glorify and enjoy him?
A. 2. The Word of God, which is contained in the Scriptures of the Old and New Testaments, is the only rule to direct us how we may glorify and enjoy him.

7. Does the confession reject the idea that there are a few basic rules of exegesis?

Berkouwer writes,

> The fact that hermeneutics is continually busy with rules for the exposition of Scripture shows a desire to oppose the arbitrariness which, despite the recognition of Scripture as God's Word, neglects its concrete authority. It is impossible for any theological study to bypass these questions. For in every hermeneutical question lies an aspect which is intrinsically tied to the confession of scriptural authority.[147]

It appears, then, that the notion of *rule* is intrinsic not only to the confession, but also to hermeneutics. Thus this proposed principle of Professor Enns seems to be not only anomalous to the confession, but strangely inconsistent with the science of hermeneutics itself. We have already considered the confession's "infallible rule" of hermeneutics above. We have also seen that Westminster, the OPC, and the PCA each affirm a belief in the "only infallible rule of faith and practice."

But finally, there are other significant hermeneutical rules for living the Christian life presented in the standards. Perhaps most directly, let us cite Larger Catechism question 99:

Question 99: For the right understanding of the Ten Commandments, these rules are to be observed:

1. That the law is perfect, and binds everyone to full conformity in the whole man unto the righteousness thereof, and unto entire obedience forever; so as to require the utmost perfection of every duty, and to forbid the least degree of every sin.
2. That it is spiritual, and so reaches the understanding, will, affections, and all other powers of the soul; as well as words, works, and gestures.
3. That one and the same thing, in divers respects, is required or forbidden in several commandments.
4. That as, where a duty is commanded, the contrary sin is forbidden; and, where a sin is forbidden, the contrary duty is commanded: so, where a promise is annexed, the

---

147. Berkouwer, *Holy Scripture*, 106.

contrary threatening is included; and, where a threatening is annexed, the contrary promise is included.

5. That what God forbids, is at no time to be done; what he commands, is always our duty; and yet every particular duty is not to be done at all times.

6. That under one sin or duty, all of the same kind are forbidden or commanded; together with all the causes, means, occasions, and appearances thereof, and provocations thereunto.

7. That what is forbidden or commanded to ourselves, we are bound, according to our places, to endeavor that it may be avoided or performed by others, according to the duty of their places.

8. That in what is commanded to others, we are bound, according to our places and callings, to be helpful to them; and to take heed of partaking with others in what is forbidden them.

These eight rules that "are to be observed" cohere with Shorter Catechism question 2,[148] but also prohibit the development of a christomonism. Thus, they stand as a critique of the potential christomonism in Professor Enns's christotelic hermeneutics, which admits that it has no "clear rules or guidelines to prevent us from taking this process too far."[149]

Given this emphasis on these rules for interpreting the Ten Commandments, as well as the other references to the rules of interpretation considered above, it is clear that Enns's hermeneutic is incompatible with the Westminster Standards.

Conclusion: Crossroads, Slippery Slope, and Watershed

To use Young's and Berkouwer's metaphor, the hermeneutical crisis has brought us to a crossroads. Since Professor Enns's hermeneutical proposals are not compatible with historic Reformed hermeneutics, they lead in a direction that the evangelical and Reformed churches ought not to travel, or if they do, to do so at their own risk. Although Professor Enns denies that he has led the church to a "slippery slope to unbelief,"[150] the crossroads has in fact brought us to a watershed as well.

Francis Schaeffer some years ago wrote about the "watershed" issue of inerrancy.

We must say that if evangelicals are to be evangelicals, we must not compromise our view of Scripture. There is no use in evangelicalism seeming to get larger and larger, if at the same time appreciable parts of evangelicalism are getting soft at that which is the central core—namely, the Scriptures. We must say with sadness that in some places, seminaries, institutions and individuals who are known as evangelical no longer hold to a full view of Scripture. The issue is clear: is the Bible truth and without error wherever it speaks, including where it touches history and the cosmos, or is it only in some sense revelational where it touches religious subjects? That is the issue. The heart of neoorthodox existential

---

148. Shorter Catechism question 2. "What rule hath God given to direct us how we may glorify and enjoy him? Answer: The Word of God, which is contained in the Scriptures of the Old and New Testaments, is the only rule to direct us how we may glorify and enjoy him."

149. Enns, *Inspiration and Incarnation*, 171.

150. Ibid., 172.

theology is that the Bible gives us a quarry out of which to have religious experience, but that the Bible contains mistakes where it touches that which is verifiable—namely, history and science. But unhappily we must say that in some circles this concept now has come into some of that which is called evangelicalism. In short, in these circles the neoorthodox existential theology is being taught under the name of evangelicalism. The issue is whether the Bible gives propositional truth (that is, truth that may be stated in propositions) where it touches history and the cosmos, and this all the way back to pre-Abrahamic history, all the way back to the first eleven chapters of Genesis, or whether instead of that it is only meaningful where it touches that which is considered religious.[151]

The evangelical church stands again at a watershed, but this time it is the precipice of a hermeneutical watershed. Lest we are swept away by the flow of the hermeneutical crisis, we must once again stand fast on the infallible Scriptures and interpret them by the "only infallible rule for the interpretation of Scripture" which "is Scripture itself."

When Schaeffer summoned the church to a recommitment to inerrancy, he quoted a statement attributed to Luther,

> If I profess with the loudest voice and clearest exposition every portion of the truth of God except precisely that little point which the world and the Devil are at that moment attacking, I am not confessing Christ, however boldly I may be professing Christ. Where the battle rages, there the loyalty of the soldier is proved, and to be steady on all the battle front besides, is merely flight and disgrace if he flinches at that point.[152]

In this context of the hermeneutical crisis I would like to appeal to Luther as well. But as I do, I wish to note that there are strong parallels between the Germanic courage of Martin Luther and Peter Enns. Both have been willing to take on their known world about what they believe to be true about the Bible. Both have stood strongly for their views in the face of disagreements by colleagues and criticisms from theological authorities. Both have written down their beliefs and have been unwilling to change. But there is a difference and it is an important one. Luther boldly affirmed his commitment to *sola Scriptura* when he declared at the Diet of Worms, "My conscience is bound by the Word of God. Here I stand, I can do no other." In stark contrast Enns boldly affirms that "our confession of the Bible as God's word has a provisional quality to it"[153] and declares that he is bound by "the trajectory of flexibility set out in Scripture itself."[154]

If Luther's motto—*sola Scriptura*—is now to be replaced, what should take its place? Should the new motto be *Scientia et scriptura*, to reflect the new hermeneutic that calls for the "adjustment" of "the evangelical doctrine of Scripture" in light of "extrabiblical evidence"?

But rather than walk with Enns on his theological "journey" of "bumps, twists and turns," let us instead continue to stand with Luther on God's Word and sing,

---

151. *The Complete Works of Francis A. Schaeffer,* vol. 2, *A Christian View of the Bible As Truth, No Final Conflict* (Wheaton, IL: Crossway, 1982), 121–22.

152. Ibid., 122.

153. Enns, *Inspiration and Incarnation,* 168.

154. Ibid., 170.

That Word above all earthly powers,
No thanks to them, abideth;
The Spirit and the gifts are ours,
Thru him who with us sideth.
Let goods and kindred go,
This mortal life also;
The body they may kill;
God's truth abideth still;
His kingdom is forever.

Only thereby can we truly keep our historic vow to believe the "only infallible rule of faith and practice" and at the same time keep our footing before the crossroads, the watershed, and the slippery slope created by the hermeneutical crisis of our generation.

Part Twelve

THE WESTMINSTER CONTROVERSY

THE TWO DOCUMENTS reproduced here, "Westminster Board Statement" (chap. 61) and "Affirmations and Denials Regarding Recent Issues" (chap. 62), were given by the Board of Trustees of Westminster Theological Seminary in the wake of the Peter Enns controversy. This controversy was ignited by the publication of *Inspiration and Incarnation* (2005) by Peter Enns, then professor of Old Testament at Westminster. His redefinition of inspiration stirred much debate within the Westminster community and the evangelical world at large (for a thorough evaluation of his views, see the article by Lillback in chap. 60 above). The two documents from the board clarify Westminster's current position on the issue and its vision for the future as an institution after the resignation of Professor Enns in 2008.

The "Westminster Board Statement" briefly reasserts Westminster's commitment to serve the church by providing a scholarly training rooted in the infallible Scriptures and consonant to the Westminster Standards. The "Affirmations and Denials" clarifies in more detail Westminster's commitment to the authority of Scripture and to the subordinate standards of the Westminster tradition. In particular, it addresses the issues raised by the Enns controversy. Though it is not an additional authoritative standard of the seminary, this document by its format comes close to the genre of a confession. Like the "Chicago Statement on Biblical Inerrancy," it defines its position both by stating its position positively and by rebutting opposing views.

Bibliography: Susan Bauer. "Messy Revelation." *Books and Culture* 12, 3 (May–June 2006): 8–9. C. K. Beale. "Did Jesus and the Apostles Preach the Right Doctrine from the Wrong Texts? Revisiting the Debate Seventeen Years Later in the Light of Peter Enns' Book, *Inspiration and Incarnation*." *Themelios* 32, 1 (2006):18–43. Idem. *The Erosion of Inerrancy in Evangelicalism: Responding to New Challenges to Biblical Authority.* Wheaton, IL: Crossway, 2008. Idem. "Myth, History, and Inspiration: A Review Article of *Inspiration and Incarnation* by Peter Enns." *Journal of the Evangelical Theological Society* 49, 2 (2006): 287–312. Idem. "A Surrejoinder to Peter Enns on the Use of the Old Testament in the New." *Themelios* 32, 3 (2007): 14–25. Idem. "A Surrejoinder to Peter Enns's Response to G. K. Beale's *JETS* Review Article of His Book, *Inspiration and Incarnation*." *Southern Baptist Journal of Theology* 11, 1 (2007): 16–36. M. Daniel R. Carroll. Review of *Inspiration and Incarnation*, by Peter Enns. In *Denver Journal* 8 (June 1, 2005). No pp. Cited November 22, 2011. Online: http://www.denverseminary.edu/article/inspiration -and-incarnation/. D. A. Carson. "Three More Books on the Bible: A Critical Review." *Trinity Journal* 27 NS (2006): 1–62. Repr., D. A. Carson. *Collected Writings on Scripture*. Comp. Andrew David Naselli.

Wheaton, IL: Crossway, 2010. Pp. 237–301. Leonard J. Coppes. Review of *Inspiration and Incarnation*, by Peter Enns. In *Mid-America Journal of Theology* 17 (2006): 291–300. John D. Currid. "Inspiration and Incarnation and the Problem of the Old Testament." *The Banner of Truth* 521 (February 2007): 22–27. Peter Enns. "Apostolic Hermeneutics and an Evangelical Doctrine of Scripture: Moving beyond the Modern Impasse." *WTJ* 65, 2 (Fall 2003): 263–87. Idem. *Inspiration and Incarnation: Evangelicals and the Problem of the Old Testament*. Grand Rapids: Baker Academic, 2005. Idem. "Interaction with Bruce Waltke." *WTJ* 71, 1 (Spring 2009): 97–114. Idem. "Response to G. K. Beale's Review Article of *Inspiration and Incarnation*." *Journal of the Evangelical Theological Society* 49, 2 (2006): 313–26. Idem. "Response to Professor Greg Beale." *Themelios* 32, 3 (2007): 5–13. Michael Eschelbach. Review of *Inspiration and Incarnation*, by Peter Enns. In *Journal of the Evangelical Theological Society* 48, 4 (December 2005): 811–12. Brenton C. Ferry. Review of *Inspiration and Incarnation*, by Peter Enns. In *New Horizons in the Orthodox Presbyterian Church* (October 2005): 23–24. John M. Frame. Review of *Inspiration and Incarnation*, by Peter Enns. No pp. Cited November 22, 2011. Online: http://www.frame-poythress.org /frame_articles/2008Enns.htm. Repr., "Appendix J: Review of Peter Enns, *Inspiration and Incarnation*." Pp. 499–516 in John M. Frame. *The Doctrine of the Word of God*. A Theology of Lordship. Phillipsburg, NJ: P&R Publishing, 2010. David B. Garner, ed. *Did God Really Say? Affirming the Truthfulness and Trustworthiness of Scripture*. Phillipsburg, NJ: P&R Publishing, 2012. Joel B. Green. Review of *Inspiration and Incarnation*, by Peter Enns. In *Review of Biblical Literature* 9 (2007): 243–44. Paul Helm. Review of *Inspiration and Incarnation*, by Peter Enns. No pp. Online: http://www.reformation21.org/Life/Shelf_Life /Shelf_Life/181?vobId=2938&pm=434. Tremper Longman III. Review of *Inspiration and Incarnation*, by Peter Enns. In *Modern Reformation* 14, 6 (November–December 2005): 33–34. Mark A. Noll. *Jesus Christ and the Life of the Mind*. Grand Rapids: Eerdmans, 2011. Pp. 132–45. Rick Phillips. "Thoughts on the Enns Suspension." No pp. Cited November 28, 2011. Online: http://www.reformation21.org/blog/2008/03 /thoughts_on_the_enns_suspension.php. Vern Sheridan Poythress. *Inerrancy and Worldview: Answering Modern Challenges to the Bible*. Wheaton, IL: Crossway, 2012. Richard Pratt. "A 'Conversation' with Richard Pratt's 'Westminster and Contemporary Reformed Hermeneutics.'" *Reformed Perspective Magazine* 10, 3 (January 2008). No pp. Cited November 29, 2011. Online: http://www.thirdmill.org/magazine/. Sarah Pulliam. "Westminster Theological Suspension." *Christianity Today* (April 2008). No pp. Cited November 22, 2011. Online: http://www.christianity.today.com/ct/2008/aprilweb-only/114-24.0.html. David J. Reimer. Review of *Inspiration and Incarnation*, by Peter Enns. In *Journal for the Study of the Old Testament* 30, 5 (2006): 99. Matthew R. Schlimm. Review of *Incarnation and Inspiration*, by Peter Enns. In *Scottish Journal of Theology* 62, 2 (2009): 240–42. James W. Scott. "The Inspiration and Interpretation of God's Word, with Special Reference to Peter Enns. Part I, Inspiration and Its Implications." *WTJ* 71, 1 (Spring 2009): 129–83. Idem. "The Inspiration and Interpretation of God's Word, with Special Reference to Peter Enns. Part II: The Interpretation of Representative Passages." *WTJ* 71, 2 (Fall 2009): 247–79. Bruce K. Waltke. "Interaction with Peter Enns." *WTJ* 71, 1 (Spring 2009): 115–28. Idem. "Revisiting *Inspiration and Incarnation*." *WTJ* 71, 1 (2009): 83–95.

Statement from the Board of Trustees, Westminster Theological Seminary (September 24, 2008)

ON JULY 23RD, the resignation of Professor Peter Enns was announced. This event was the culmination of intense and lengthy faculty and board discussions and deliberations. Out of a desire to continue the theological transparency that the Seminary evidenced by its release in April of several pertinent theological documents, the Board wishes to state its understanding of the significance of this eventuality.

First, the Board recognizes that theological debate is a necessary part of the pursuit of the meaning and application of God's eternal Word to man's changing world. This is one of the foundational reasons why Westminster has cherished its Biblical and Confessional heritage. The authority of the Scriptures and, subordinate to that authority, the parameters for theological discussions afforded by the Westminster Standards are safeguards to preserve the Church and her leaders from the lure of cultural compromise, the deceptions of autonomous reason, and the fads of theological trends.

Second, Westminster continues to value its legacy of rigorous scholarship that does not, in the words of founding Old Testament Professor Robert Dick Wilson, "shirk the difficult questions." Likewise, the Seminary continues to value its legacy of rigorous scholarship in the service of Biblical orthodoxy for the good of the church. Only in this way can J. Gresham Machen's vision for a Seminary that trains "Specialists in the Bible" be possible.

Third, the theological issues raised, directly or indirectly, in the controversy prompted by Professor Enns's writings need to be briefly addressed. In sum, the Board wishes to reassert that the self-witness of Scripture to its truth as the Word of God requires that its authority, its reliability, its non-mythical character as well as its uniqueness, must be maintained in all discussions and evaluations of extra-Biblical evidence. Moreover, Westminster's apostolic Christ-centered model of interpretation of Scripture must continue to be given pre-eminence in hermeneutical questions whether they emanate from ancient or historical cultural contexts or from newer interpretive paradigms.

Further, when questions of the NT's use of the OT occur it must be remembered that the Scriptures are "the only infallible rule of faith and practice," and that they therefore must be interpreted by the "infallible rule of interpretation of Scripture," which is as our Confession declares, "Scripture itself" (WCF 1.9).

In conformity with the Scriptures and our Confession the Board once again declares that the Scriptures "are given by inspiration of God to be the rule of faith and life" (WCF 1.2); and, that "holy Scripture . . . is to be received, because it is the Word of God" (WCF 1.4).

In sum, the Board wishes to reassure our constituencies and to assert to the watching world that it is still the core commitment of Westminster Theological Seminary to prepare pastors, leaders and scholars for the Church and the Kingdom of Christ. Such specialists in the Bible are discerning believers in Scripture who do not shirk the difficult questions, but who also address such questions from the vantage point of Westminster's historic heartfelt (ex animo) vow to the infallible Word of God.

Affirmations and Denials
Regarding Recent Issues

ADOPTED BY THE BOARD OF TRUSTEES,
WESTMINSTER THEOLOGICAL SEMINARY,
PHILADELPHIA, PENNSYLVANIA
(DECEMBER 3, 2008)

Introduction

Westminster Theological Seminary is a Reformed seminary that is committed to the infallibility of Scripture and has a well-defined doctrinal basis in the subordinate standards of the Westminster tradition. Each voting faculty member and each member of the Board of the Seminary is required to subscribe to the Westminster Standards, that is, the Westminster Confession of Faith (WCF), the Westminster Larger Catechism (WLC), and the Westminster Shorter Catechism (WSC). Each voting faculty member is required to make the following pledge:

> I do solemnly declare, in the presence of God, and of the Trustees and Faculty of this Seminary, that (1) I believe the Scriptures of the Old and New Testaments to be the Word of God, the only infallible rule of faith and practice; and (2) I do solemnly and ex animo adopt, receive, and subscribe to the Westminster Confession of Faith and Catechisms in the form in which they were adopted by this Seminary in the year of our Lord 1936, as the confession of my faith, or as a summary and just exhibition of that system of doctrine and religious belief, which is contained in Holy Scripture, and therein revealed by God to man for his salvation; and I do solemnly, ex animo, profess to receive the fundamental principles of the Presbyterian form of church government, as agreeable to the inspired oracles. And I do solemnly promise and engage not to inculcate, teach, or insinuate anything which shall appear to me to contradict or contravene, either directly or impliedly, any element in that system of doctrine, nor to oppose

any of the fundamental principles of that form of church government, while I continue a member of the Faculty in this Seminary. I do further solemnly declare that, being convinced of my sin and misery and of my inability to rescue myself from my lost condition, not only have I assented to the truth of the promises of the Gospel, but also I have received and rest upon Christ and His righteousness for pardon of my sin and for my acceptance as righteous in the sight of God and I do further promise that if at any time I find myself out of accord with any of the fundamentals of this system of doctrine, I will on my own initiative, make known to the Faculty of this institution and, where applicable, my judicatory, the change which has taken place in my views since the assumption of the vow.

Each member of the Board of Trustees subscribes to a similar pledge:

I hereby solemnly declare in the presence of God and this Board (1) that I believe the Scriptures of the Old and New Testaments to be the Word of God, the only infallible rule of faith and practice, (2) that I sincerely receive and adopt the Confession of Faith and Catechisms of the Presbyterian Church in America in the form which they possessed in 1936, as containing the system of doctrine taught in the Holy Scriptures, (3) that, approving the Charter of Westminster Theological Seminary, I will faithfully endeavor to carry into effect the articles and provisions of said Charter and to promote the great design of the Seminary. I do further solemnly declare that, being convinced of my sin and misery and of my inability to rescue myself from my lost condition not only have I assented to the truth of the promises of the Gospel, but also I have received and rest upon Christ and His righteousness for pardon of my sin and for my acceptance as righteous in the sight of God.

We continue to embrace the Westminster Standards. We remain convinced that they are a sound and valuable confessional basis for the work and instruction in the Seminary.

Theological discussion at Westminster Theological Seminary has revealed several areas where it may be appropriate for the Board of the Seminary to reaffirm our continued commitment to the Westminster Standards and to Presbyterian government, and to restate the nature of our commitment. We see the affirmations and denials below not as an addition to our historic subscription, but as reaffirmations and clarifications of the implications of our continued subscription.

These affirmations and denials are not in any way exhaustive. Rather, they are to be seen as selective, and as addressing only some of the matters implied in confessional subscription. The complete affirmation to which voting faculty members are bound is the faculty pledge, as quoted above and set out in the Constitution of the Seminary.

Affirmations and Denials

I. Confessional Subscription

A. Basic character of subscription

We affirm that the Standards are subordinate standards. Scripture itself, as the primary standard, is the only infallible rule of faith and practice (see the faculty pledge; WCF 1.2; 1.10; WLC 3; WSC 2).

We deny that the primacy of Scripture makes confessional subscription unimportant or dispensable or superfluous (WCF 22).

We affirm that our subscription to the Standards includes a cordial and full affirmation that the Standards are a just exhibition of the system of doctrine and religious belief, which is contained in Holy Scripture (see faculty pledge).

We deny that our subscription merely requires that a faculty member is to be instructed or guided by the Standards.

We affirm that the Westminster Standards are fallible, that is, that it is possible in principle that they may err, and, further, that they are open to revision (WCF 31.4).

We deny that the Westminster Standards are infallible.

B. Progress in understanding Scripture

We affirm that Scripture contains truths not included in the Westminster Standards (WCF 1.6).

We deny that there are truths found in Scripture but not in the Standards that overthrow or undermine any element in the system of doctrine expounded in the Standards.

We affirm that God himself enjoins us to seek an ever deeper and more comprehensive understanding of his word (WLC 157).

We deny that we cannot add to or deepen the understanding of God's word expressed in the Standards.

C. Specific obligations implied by the pledge

We affirm that a person who voluntarily pledges subscription to the Standards is bound to keep his pledge (WCF 22; 31.3).

We deny that the Westminster Standards lack binding force on those who subscribe to them.

We affirm that a voting faculty member is not permitted to teach or insinuate something contrary to any element in the system of doctrine, even if the faculty member judges that what he is going to teach is based on Scripture (Faculty pledge).

We deny that an alleged Scriptural basis for a teaching eliminates the obligation imposed by the faculty pledge.

We affirm that a faculty member may present to the faculty or the Board an idea that might later be judged out of accord with the system of doctrine, in order to have that idea tested and sifted.

We deny that the confidential presentation of ideas to the faculty or Board for the purpose of testing and evaluation is in itself out of accord with the faculty pledge.

We affirm that individual faculty members may take exception to or express a scruple about a particular item or wording within the Standards.

We deny that taking an exception to a particular item necessarily implies introducing a mental reservation into the faculty pledge, or is necessarily inconsistent with the faculty pledge.

D. Judgments about subscription

We affirm that, with regard to any exception or scruple, or any other views of a faculty member, the Board and the faculty have a responsibility, both at the time of initial appointment and at all subsequent times, to make a judgment as to whether such an exception or such a view undermines the intent of the Seminary's subscription pledge.

We deny that Board and faculty judgments about compatibility with the Standards constitute an illegitimate interference with an individual's conscience or an illegitimate abridgment of academic freedom.

We affirm that, in the context of subscription by voting faculty and Board members, the meaning of any particular teaching in the Standards is determined by the Board, by referring to the historical record of orthodox Reformed tradition, and is not determined by the private interpretation of any one individual faculty member.

We deny that an individual faculty member has the right to import a private meaning into the Standards when he subscribes, thereby avoiding the meaning commonly understood in the Reformed tradition.

II. CONFESSION AND MISSION

A. Universality of truth

We affirm that the truths affirmed in the Standards are true for all times, all places, all languages, and all cultures (WCF 1.1, 6, 8).

We deny that the truths affirmed in the Standards are true only for their seventeenth century situation or only for some cultures or circumstances.

We affirm that a person's agreement with the content of the Standards includes agreement with all its affirmations as perennially normative, not merely agreement that they were an appropriate response to the theological, ecclesiastical, and pastoral needs of the seventeenth century.

1326

We deny that a person's agreement with the Standards is adequate if, at any point, it merely means agreeing pragmatically with the way in which the Standards addressed the needs of their situation.

We affirm that the Standards have instructional value for all times and all cultures.

We deny that the Standards have instructional value only in some cultures.

B. The legitimacy of pedagogical adaptation

We affirm that teaching of the Standards in a particular language or culture can and should take into account the existing previous theological understanding and education, crucial theological and pastoral issues in the circumstances, and problems and opportunities arising in the church and in the surrounding culture (WLC 159).

We deny that theological teaching need not attend to such circumstances.

We affirm that theological teaching can legitimately adjust in teaching style, phraseology, selection of content, use of illustrations, and many other ways that prove significant in facilitating the communication and grasp of truth in the target language and culture (WLC 159).

We deny that adjustments in pedagogy and communicative strategy imply compromise of the truths affirmed in the Standards.

III. SCRIPTURE

A. The inspiration of Scripture

We affirm that the Holy Scripture is to be believed and obeyed, because it is the word of God (WCF 1.4; WLC 157, 160).

We deny that the Holy Scripture is to be believed or obeyed merely because it contains the word of God, or merely because it conveys the word of God, or merely because the Holy Spirit uses it to effect a personal encounter with God.

We affirm that what Scripture says, God says (WCF 1.4; 1.10; 14.2).

We deny that what Scripture says is only sometimes or only partly what God says, or that Scripture only becomes what God says in the act of communication to some person.

We affirm that in causing his word to be written down in the Bible, God, the primary author, used human writers, the secondary authors, often employing them in the full range of their personalities and existing gifts and abilities, with the exception that he kept them from error (WCF 1.2, 4 prooftexts).

We deny that God produced the scripture without using human authors.

We affirm that God remains true, good, pure, righteous, all-knowing, and immutable when he delivers Scripture to us, and what Scripture says—both in each detail and as a whole—is always consistent with and manifests his character (WCF 1.4; 2.1).

We deny that the presence of human agents in the writing of Scripture, or any other use of means, or any relation to cultural or historical circumstances in the writing, allow the interpreter to dismiss or cease to reckon with the fact that what God says in Scripture is always consistent with his character.

B. The interpretation of Scripture

We affirm that each verse and passage belongs to a larger context of other Scripture, to which God expects us to attend (WCF 1.2, 1.9; WLC 157).

We deny that any verse or passage can be given its full and proper interpretation by taking it in isolation from the book to which it belongs, or from the Scripture as a whole.

We affirm that we can understand passages of Scripture more deeply when we take into account the historical and cultural circumstances that they addressed (WLC 157).

We deny that historical and cultural circumstances are irrelevant to understanding Scriptural passages.

We affirm that Scripture makes known clearly those things necessary to be believed and observed for salvation, so that even the unlearned may come to sufficient understanding through due use of ordinary means (WCF 1.7).

We deny that extra-biblical knowledge of ancient customs or circumstances is necessary to understand the gospel of salvation in Christ as the central message of Scripture.

C. The pertinence of ancient contexts: Ancient Near Eastern and First Century Mediterranean World

We affirm that God in his wisdom addressed Scripture to his people of long ago in a manner that takes into account their historical setting and their previous knowledge (WCF 7.5; 2.1).

We deny that Scripture fails to take into account the setting of its ancient addressees, or that it fails adequately to address ancient people.

We affirm that what Scripture affirms to its ancient addressees is always true (WCF 2.1).

We deny that limitations in ancient addressees and their setting may ever allow the inclusion of untruths as a part of what Scripture affirms or what it implies.

We affirm that God in producing the canon of Scripture addresses peoples of all subsequent times, places, and cultures (WCF 1.1; 1.8; WLC 155; 156).

We deny that God addresses only the people who lived at the time that a book was written.

We affirm that what the Scripture affirms is to be believed and obeyed by people in all places and cultures (WCF 1.4; 14.2; WLC 156).

We deny that what Scripture affirms lays obligations of belief and obedience only on the original recipients, or only on some cultures.

We affirm that some earlier commands of Scripture have meaning such that their application to our present circumstances must reckon with the changed redemptive-historical conditions in which God addresses us. For example, animals sacrifices that were prescribed in the Old Testament are no longer legitimate now, because Christ has offered the final sacrifice (WCF 19.3–4).

We deny that there are no commands whose application varies with the changing redemptive-historical context.

D. The truthfulness of Scripture

We affirm that the Holy Scripture contains a system of doctrine (Faculty pledge).

We deny that the Holy Scripture lacks doctrinal unity on any point of doctrine, or that it does not always agree with itself.

We affirm that the Holy Scripture is harmonious in all its teaching (WCF 1.9).

We deny that there are real contradictions in Scripture.

We affirm that Scripture is truthful and without error in what it affirms (WCF 1.4; 2.1).

We deny that Scripture affirms anything that is factually erroneous or is incorrect.

We affirm that Scripture can quote from, allude to, or otherwise represent, in a manner distinct from its own affirmations, the fallible speech and thought deriving from fallible, sinful human beings (e.g., "The fool says in his heart, 'There is no God,'" Ps. 14:1).

We deny that Scripture's quotation or representation of fallible thought implies Scripture's own fallibility.

E. The role of the Holy Spirit

We affirm that the work of the Holy Spirit in a person is necessary for that person properly and savingly to understand the Scripture and that full acceptance and a willingness to submit unconditionally to its teaching is essential to such proper understanding (WCF 10.1; 14:2; WLC 104; 155; 157; WSC 89).

We deny that exercise of the rational powers of fallen man is sufficient for a right understanding of Scripture.

We affirm that God's truthfulness and self-consistency belong to what the Scripture says, not merely to what the Holy Spirit may be later alleged to show us through the Scripture (WCF 1.4).

We deny that God's authority belongs only to the Spirit's teaching from the Scripture, rather than to the Scripture itself as well.

IV. SPECIAL AREAS OF INTEREST

A. Special Area: Harmony of Scripture

We affirm that some things in Scripture are difficult to understand, and that we may not always be able easily to explain apparent contradictions (WCF 1.7).

We deny that all parts of Scripture are easy to understand.

We affirm that, through the illumination of the Holy Spirit, we can rightly become convinced from Scripture itself that it is the word of God, even when we do not have an explanation for some of the apparent discrepancies in Scripture (WCF 1.5).

We deny that we must find explanations for each apparent discrepancy before accepting the divine authority of Scripture and submitting to its teaching.

We affirm that each individual passage of Scripture is consistent in its affirmations with every other passage (WCF 1.9).

We deny that passages may contradict one another.

We affirm that when interpreting any passage, the true meaning must be found by comparing the one passage with the rest of Scripture (WCF 1.9).

We deny that it is legitimate to give an interpretation of a passage that is not in harmony with what is affirmed in another passage or passages.

We affirm doctrinal unity and coherence in a given passage between the meaning of God, as its primary author, and the meaning of the human author, however limited may have been the understanding of the latter of what he wrote (WCF 1.4–5).

We deny that in a given passage the intentions of God and the human writer are doctrinally divergent or discordant.

B. Special Area: Implications of Details in Scripture, Including New Testament Use of the Old Testament

We affirm that we must submit to all that Scripture affirms, not merely to its main points (WCF 1.4; WLC 157, 160).

We deny that the divine authority of Scripture belongs only to its main purpose or only to the main points of its various passages.

We affirm that we must submit to the New Testament affirmations concerning the Old Testament, and not merely to the conclusions that the New Testament draws from them.

We deny that it is ever allowable to submit to conclusions but not to other affirmations in the Scripture.

We affirm that the methods and reasoning that Scripture uses in reaching its conclusions are valid.

We deny that any Scripture uses invalid methods or reasoning to draw valid conclusions.

C. Special Area: Old Testament Teaching

We affirm that in the Old Testament God spoke to his people in a way that took into account their lack of detailed knowledge of the coming salvation to be revealed in the New Testament (WCF 7.5).

We deny that there are no differences between the Old and New Testaments.

We affirm that what God said in the Old Testament is always in harmony with later teaching in the New Testament, though it may not always be as full or explicit (WCF 7).

We deny that the New Testament shows any contradiction to what is in the Old Testament.

We affirm that we can sometimes understand passages in the Old Testament more deeply in the light of the later revelation that God has given us in Christ (WCF 7.5).

We deny that we can never have more understanding of an Old Testament passage than what was available to people when it was first given.

We affirm that God's intention with respect to an Old Testament passage is consistent with his later reference to or allusion to that passage in the New Testament (WCF 1.9).

We deny that God's intentions at two different points in time, or in two different texts, are ever in disharmony.

We affirm doctrinal continuity and harmony between the original historical and human meaning of an Old Testament text and the meaning a New Testament writer attributes to that text (WCF 1.5; 1.9).

We deny that there is any doctrinal divergence or disparity between the original historical and human meaning of an Old Testament text and its use in the New Testament.

D. Special Area: Old Testament History

We affirm that Adam and Eve were real flesh-and-blood individual human beings and that their fall into sin was subsequent to their creation as the first human beings (WCF 6.1; 7.2; WLC 17).

We deny that the narrative in Genesis 3 is merely symbolic for what is true of mankind in general.

We affirm that God's acts of creation, as listed in each of the six days of Genesis 1, really happened in space and time (WCF 4.1; WLC 15).

We deny that Genesis 1 merely teaches that God made everything.

We affirm that in Genesis 1 God communicated to ancient people in a manner intelligible to them (WCF 1.7).

We deny that Genesis 1 requires special modern knowledge or scientific knowledge for it to be understood.

We affirm that in the Scripture God does not endorse at any point a faulty worldview or cosmology or a faulty aspect thereof (WCF 1.4; 2.1).

We deny that Scripture at any point affirms a faulty cosmology.

We affirm that Noah, Abraham, Isaac, and Jacob were real people who went through the experiences that Genesis describes them as going through (WCF 1.4; 2.1; 14.2; WLC 160).

We deny that the narratives in Genesis about the patriarchs are merely legendary, or that only some smaller core of events really happened.

Westminster Seminary Distinctives

Westminster Theological Seminary defines its distinctive role most basically by its confessional commitment to the Westminster Standards. But we also value the insights that have grown up at Westminster over the decades as the faculty has continued to reflect on the Bible within the doctrinal framework provided by the Standards. We affirm the value of systematic theology in the tradition of John Murray, of biblical theology in the tradition of

Geerhardus Vos, of presuppositional apologetics in the tradition of Cornelius Van Til, of biblical counseling in the tradition of Jay Adams, and of missiology in the tradition of Harvie Conn. When rightly done, these programs of investigation and practice build on the truths articulated in the Westminster Standards. The Standards guide us in these disciplines by giving them a sound doctrinal basis. The disciplines show the fruit of the truths of Scripture by applying them to new areas of reflection.

We affirm the value of the disciplines of systematic theology, biblical theology, presuppositional apologetics, biblical counseling, and missiology as these have been practiced at Westminster Seminary.

We deny that these disciplines, when rightly understood and practiced, are in tension with our confessional Standards.

We affirm the importance of conducting these disciplines in conformity with the Standards and the faculty pledge.

We deny that these disciplines need freedom to reach conclusions that may prove to be contrary to the Standards.

We affirm that these disciplines can offer fruitful service both for the church and for growth in understanding of the doctrines of the Standards.

We deny that we have nothing to learn from these disciplines that could deepen or improve our understanding of doctrine.

We affirm that biblical theology (attention to the text in its redemptive-historical context) is the indispensable servant of systematic theology—indispensable because it is essential for the sound exegesis on which systematic theology depends, a servant because it contributes to the presentation, under appropriate topics, of the teaching of Scripture as a whole and in its overall unity that systematic theology is concerned to provide for the life of the church and its mission in the world.

We deny that biblical theology and systematic theology, properly understood, are in conflict or are alternative approaches to Scripture independent of each other, or that either is dispensable.

We affirm that the teachings of Scripture concerning God, Christ, man, sin, salvation, and other topics, as those teachings are summarized in systematic theology, offer a sound framework in which to conduct the work of exegesis and biblical theology.

We deny that exegesis or biblical theology can be properly conducted without submission to or in tension with the teaching of Scripture as a whole.

Part Thirteen

CONCLUSION

63

Peter A. Lillback's Introduction to Gaffin's *God's Word in Servant-Form*

Peter A. Lillback, Introduction to *God's Word in Servant-Form: Abraham Kuyper and Herman Bavinck on the Doctrine of Scripture*, by Richard B. Gaffin Jr. (Jackson, MS: Reformed Academic Press, 2008), v–xvi.

Peter Lillback's introduction to Richard Gaffin's *God's Word in Servant-Form* is a fitting conclusion to our anthology in several ways. First, it encapsulates in a few words Westminster's commitment to Scripture. Second, it was published in 2008, arising out of the urgency of the current controversy. Third, this essay is a witness to the continuity of Westminster Seminary's confession to the truth of God's Word. Indeed, Lillback's text introduces the classic study by Gaffin (reproduced in part in chap. 31), which itself was a tribute to Machen. Also, Lillback illustrates his argument with citations and thoughts from theologians in the Westminster tradition.

HISTORIC REFORMED CHRISTIANITY believes that God in His eternal counsel determined that the Scriptures would be written by men. The supernatural agency of the Holy Spirit superintended the human authors, producing a Deposit which is fully inspired. By this divine and human concursus, the authors of Holy Scripture were enabled to write the infallible words of God, even though they continued to use their own vocabulary, experiences, personality and style to compose their contributions to the written Word of God. Expressing this theanthropic nature of Scripture is complex, and requires doxological precision analogous to the Christological formulae at Nicea and Chalcedon.[1] To that end, the Church through the centuries has preserved the divine/human understanding of Scripture, insisting on dual authorship – maintaining the

---

1. It is precisely in this analogy to Christ's incarnation that Karl Barth finds formal scriptural infallibility idolatrous. See Timothy Ward, "The Incarnation and Scripture" in *The Word Became Flesh: Evangelicals and the Incarnation*, ed. David Peterson (Carlisle, Cumbria, UK: Paternoster, 2003), 154–57.

1337

primacy of the Holy Spirit in inscripturation, and simultaneously apprehending the human agency in composing the very Word of God.[2]

The highest view of inspiration has been termed "inerrancy" since it holds that the original texts written under the inspiration of the Holy Spirit were not only true, but free from error in all their teaching. While the term inerrancy is relatively recent,[3] the Church "has always recognized that this conception of co-authorship implies that the Spirit's superintendence extends to the choice of the words by the human authors (verbal inspiration), and preserves its product from everything inconsistent with a divine authorship—thus securing, among other things, that entire truthfulness which is everywhere presupposed in and asserted for Scripture by the Biblical writers (inerrancy)."[4] To be clear, the doctrine of inerrancy flatly rejects dimensionalism—where, for example, redemptive doctrine is infallible but the Bible's teaching on the scientific is subject to human error. Any suggestion, furthermore, of an inerrant divine message expressed by fallible human words is untenable. Because the Author of the meaning of the Bible is also the Sovereign of its milieu, inerrancy permeates the very written words themselves on every topic addressed. While the Bible is not a text book, the Creator and Redeemer has spoken, and because *He* has done so, inerrancy pervades content, intent, and form.

Moreover, contrary to the claim of Jack B. Rogers and Donald K. McKim that inerrancy is a product of Reformed Scholasticism developed in the tradition of the "Aristotelian" Turretin,[5] this view of Scripture can be traced back in unmistakable terms to the Church Fathers,[6] who homogeneously recognized the Bible as the self-authenticating, inscripturated Word of God. More than a millennium before Turretin, the "Platonic" Augustine, who scarcely had an Aristotelian bone in his body, held to inerrancy. Augustine wrote to Jerome, "I have learned to yield this respect and honour only to the canonical books of Scripture: of these alone do I most firmly believe that the authors were completely free from error." What did Augustine

2. This historical perspective finds expression in the WCF 1.5 speaking of "the holy Scripture" describes it as "infallible truth." The same respect for Scripture is again found in WCF 1.9, "The infallible rule of interpretation of Scripture is the Scripture itself." In 1978, fresh expression of the doctrine of inspiration was expressed in "The Chicago Statement on Biblical Inerrancy". A copy of this document can be found in *Inerrancy*, ed. Norman L. Geisler (Grand Rapids: Zondervan, 1980), 493–502.

3. Jack B. Rogers and Donald K. McKim identify the first usage of the English word *inerrant* in seventeenth century astronomy, and link its theological usage to the defense of the Bible against deism by eighteenth century Reformed Protestants. Jack B. Rogers and Donald K. McKim, *The Authority and Interpretation of the Bible: An Historical Approach* (San Francisco: Harper & Row, 1979), 235.

4. Benjamin Breckenridge Warfield, *The Inspiration and Authority of the Bible* (Philadelphia: Presbyterian and Reformed, 1948), 173. Warfield protests the assumption that such a view mandates mechanical dictation. See Archibald A. Hodge and Benjamin B. Warfield, *Inspiration* (Grand Rapids: Baker, 1979).

5. "Falling back on the philosophy of Aristotle and the theological categories of Thomas Aquinas, Turretin produced a scholastic theology that placed great emphasis on precise definition and systematic, scientific statement." Rogers and McKim, *The Authority and Interpretation of the Bible*, 173. These authors further contend that Reformed Scholasticism gave "false importance to a doctrine of inerrancy" (186), and this newly-invented scholastic approach "represented a spirit, a mood, a mind-set quite different from that of Calvin, the Augustinian-humanist Reformer." (185) This doctrine of inerrancy, which they define as a "mechanistic, mathematical model by which the Bible was judged" (235), was not only itself errant, but as developed within Princeton theology, bears the responsibility for "continuing strife on the American religious scene." (247)

6. See John D. Woodbridge, *Biblical Authority: A Critique of the Rogers/McKim Proposal* (Grand Rapids: Zondervan, 1982). Mystified by the Rogers and McKim argument against monumental documented evidence, church historian Woodbridge cites and notes among others, Clement of Rome, Justin Martyr, Irenaeus, Origen, Chrysostom, Augustine as evident proponents of a doctrine fully reflective of inerrancy (31–46). Regarding Origen, Woodbridge concurs with Bruce Vawter, "a good case can be made for Origen the inerrantist." (34) Cf. E. J. Young, *Thy Word Is Truth: Some Thoughts on the Biblical Doctrine of Inspiration* (Grand Rapids: Eerdmans, 1957); Ward, "The Incarnation and Scripture, 152–53.

do with apparent contradictions in the Bible? To this question he replied, "I do not hesitate to suppose that either the ms. is faulty or the translator has not caught the meaning of what was said, or I myself have failed to understand it." Elsewhere Augustine wrote, "It seems to me that the most disastrous consequence must follow upon our believing that anything false is found in the sacred books," for, he adds, "if you once admit into such a high sanctuary of authority one false statement, . . . there will not be left a single statement of those books which, . . . if appearing to anyone difficult in practice or hard to believe, may not by the same fatal rule be explained away."[7] God's Word for Augustine stood or fell on inerrancy.

Bearing the mantra *Sola Scriptura*, and scrupulously and consciously arming themselves with the classic church doctrine of Scripture, the Reformers marched into the theological battlefield. As they saw it, nothing less than the inerrant inscripturated revelation was a worthy weapon. "John Calvin, typical of all the Reformers and their orthodox successors, regarded the Bible in the same way, making even clearer, over against the claims for the authority of church teaching, that it is through the Bible that God's Word is to be heard: 'daily oracles are not sent from heaven, for it pleased the Lord to hallow his truth to everlasting remembrance in the Scriptures alone.'"[8] In his study of Calvin's doctrine of Scripture, John Murray concedes that "there are passages in Calvin that cannot be dismissed with a wave of the hand,"[9] but firmly concludes, "our final observation must be that his jealousy for the original text cannot be dissociated from his estimate of Scripture as the oracles of God, that Scripture has nothing human mixed with it, and that in all its parts it is as if we heard the mouth of God speaking from heaven."[10] To Calvin, the Scripture as the Word of God was by its own self-attestation inerrant,[11] and he fastidiously exegeted even the most troublesome passages from this basic presupposition.

In the face of virulent criticism from modern biblical scholarship, inerrancy was also a pivotal concern of the old Princeton theologians Charles Hodge and B. B. Warfield,[12] so pivotal, in fact, that for these early Presbyterian theologians inspiration and inerrancy were essentially equivalent terms.[13] Not unlike Calvin, these scholars were fully versed in the challenges that various Scriptures presented and were simultaneously diligent to articulate reasoned answers. With scholarly perception, pastoral eloquence, and a consciousness of theological continuity with the Church before and after him, Warfield comments,

> The question is not, whether the doctrine of plenary inspiration has difficulties to face. The question is, whether these difficulties are greater than the difficulty of believing that the whole

7. Augustine, *Letters* LXXXII, 3, XXVIII, 3.

8. Ward, "The Incarnation and Scripture," 153. Cf. Calvin, *Institutes* 1.7.1.

9. John Murray, *Calvin on Scripture and Divine Sovereignty* (Philadelphia: Presbyterian and Reformed, 1960), 12. This article can also be found in John Murray, *Collected Works*, vol. 4, *Studies in Theology* (Carlisle, PA: Banner of Truth, 1982).

10. Murray, *Calvin on Scripture and Divine Sovereignty*, 28. Summarizing Calvin, Murray continues, "God speaks in Scripture. In it he opens his sacred mouth" (50).

11. See J. I. Packer, "John Calvin and the Inerrancy of Holy Scripture" in *Inerrancy and the Church*, ed. John D. Hannah (Chicago: Moody, 1984), 143–88. "It seems obvious from what has been said that Calvin could never have consciously entertained the possibility that human mistakes, where of reporting or of interpreting facts of any sort whatever, could have entered into the text of Scripture as the human writers gave it. Nor did he" (178).

12. See Benjamin Breckinridge Warfield's classic study, *The Inspiration and Authority of the Bible*.

13. "As has already been indicated, for at least a fair number of biblical and theological scholars of former days inspiration was synonymous with inerrancy. To say that the Bible is inspired was to say that it is absolutely accurate or inerrant. Two men among those who held such a view were B. B. Warfield and Charles Hodge." Paul D. Feinberg, "The Meaning of Inerrancy," in *Inerrancy*, ed. Norman L. Geisler (Grand Rapids: Zondervan, 1980), 287.

church of God from the beginning has been deceived in her estimate of the Scriptures committed to her charge—are greater than the difficulty of believing that the whole college of the apostles, yes and Christ himself at their head, were themselves deceived as to the nature of those Scriptures which they gave the church as its precious possession, and have deceived them with twenty Christian centuries, and are likely to deceive twenty more before our boasted advancing light has corrected their error,—are greater than the difficulty of believing that we have no sure foundation for our faith and no certain warrant for our trust in Christ for salvation. We believe this doctrine of the plenary inspiration of the Scriptures primarily because it is the doctrine which Christ and his apostles believed, and which they have taught us. It may sometimes be difficult to take our stand frankly by the side of Christ and his apostles. It will always be found safe.[14]

John Murray, Cornelius Van Til, and Geerhardus Vos, the founding fathers of the theological tradition of Westminster Theological Seminary, each carried on this historic Reformed commitment to inerrancy. Murray, in stride with Warfield, never plays down the difficulties encountered in the text of Scripture by the serious exegete, yet confidently insists upon the doctrine of inerrancy. He comments, "It must be freely admitted that there are difficulties connected with the doctrine of Biblical infallibility. There appear to be discrepancies and contradictions in the Bible. Naturally we cannot be expected to believe what we perceive to involve a contradiction. Furthermore, disingenuous and artificial attempts at harmony are to be avoided, for they do not advance the cause of truth and of faith." There are times, however, even after diligent exegesis, that "some difficulties, perhaps many, remain unresolved. The earnest student has no adequate answer and he may frankly confess that he is not able to explain an apparent discrepancy in the teaching of Scripture." To admit the existence of biblical conundrum though is not worthy cause for abandoning faith, nor rejecting biblical inerrancy. "The ground of faith emphatically is not our ability to demonstrate all the teaching of the Bible to be self-consistent and true. This is just saying that rational demonstration is not the ground of faith. The demand that apparent contradictions in the Bible should have to be removed before we accord it our credit as God's infallible Word rests, therefore, upon a wholly mistaken notion of the only proper ground of faith in the Bible." Why? Because "there is no doctrine of our Christian faith that does not confront us with unresolved difficulties here in this world, and the difficulties become all the greater just as we get nearer to the center. It is in connection with the most transcendent mysteries of our faith that the difficulties multiply." Whether regarding the Trinity, the incarnation, the atonement, *or the inerrancy of Scripture*, unanswered questions are "not incompatible with unshaken faith" and "are more often the questions of adoring rather than the questions of painful perplexity." Ultimately, Murray concludes, "rational demonstration is not the ground of faith." While we must not

close our minds and researches to the ever-progressing resolution of difficulties under the illumination of the Spirit of truth . . . those whose approach to faith is that of resolution of all difficulty have deserted the very nature of faith and its ground. The nature of faith is acceptance on the basis of testimony, and the ground of faith is therefore testimony or evidence. In this matter it is the evidence God has provided, and God provides the evidence in his

14. Benjamin Breckinridge Warfield, *Revelation and Inspiration* (New York: Oxford University Press, 1927), 74.

Word, the Bible. This means simply that the basis of faith in the Bible is the witness the Bible itself bears to the fact that it is God's Word, and our faith that it is infallible must rest upon no other basis than the witness the Bible bears to this fact. If the Bible does not witness to its own infallibility, then we have no right to believe that it is infallible. If it does bear witness to its infallibility then our faith in it must rest upon that witness, however much difficulty may be entertained with this belief.

Murray claims this reliance on God's self-authenticating revelation as absolutely critical for every doctrine of the Bible, and just as "faith in the Trinity does not have to wait for the resolution of all difficulties that the teaching of Scriptures presents . . . so neither does faith in Scripture as the inerrant Word of God have to wait for the resolution of all difficulties in the matter of inerrancy." For Murray, defense of inerrancy derives from appeal to the highest epistemological authority, the Scripture itself.[15]

Murray's colleague Cornelius Van Til, in expressing his commitment to Warfield's conception of inerrancy, linked it with the theology of Calvin rather than simply to the inerrancy of Warfield or the broader evangelicalism of his day. Van Til explains,

> The view of Scripture as so ably presented and defended by Warfield is held by orthodox Protestants alone. And among these orthodox Protestants it is only the followers of Calvin who have a theology that fully fits in with this idea of Scripture. Only a God who controls whatsoever comes to pass can offer to man His interpretation of the course of history in the form of an existential system. An evangelical, that is a virtually Arminian, theology makes concessions to the principle that controls a "theology of experience." In admitting and even maintaining a measure of autonomy for man, such evangelicalism is bound to admit that the non-Christian principles of continuity and of discontinuity have a measure of truth in them. And to the precise extent that evangelicalism makes these concessions in its theology does it weaken its own defense of the infallible Bible. Such evangelicals have done and are doing excellent detail work in the defense of Scripture but they lack the theology that can give coherence to their effort. Therefore they also lack the general apologetic methodology that can make their detail-work stand out in its real challenge against the principle of experience.[16]

In fact, Van Til claims that there are vast implications of inerrancy not just for theology, but for all human endeavor.

> And in all this the theology of Experience is of a piece with modern science and modern philosophy. The prodigal is at the swine-trough but finds that he cannot as a rational creature feed himself with the husks that non-rational creatures eat.
>
> It is this situation that the present volume goes out, beseeching the prodigal to return to the father's house. In the father's house are many mansions. In it alone will the "son" find refuge and food. The presupposition of all intelligible meaning for man in the intellectual, the moral and the aesthetic spheres is the existence of the God of the Bible who, if he speaks at all in grace cannot, without denying himself, but speak in a self-contained infallible fashion. Only in a return to the Bible as infallibly inspired in its autography is there hope for science,

---

15. John Murray, "The Attestation of Scripture," in *The Infallible Word: A Symposium by the Members of the Faculty of Westminster Theological Seminary* (Philadelphia: Presbyterian and Reformed, 1978), 6–9.

16. Cornelius Van Til, "Introduction" to B. B. Warfield's *The Inspiration and Authority of the Bible*, 66–67.

for philosophy and for theology. Without returning to this Bible science and philosophy may flourish with borrowed capital as the prodigal flourished for a while with his father's substance. But the prodigal had no self-sustaining principle. No man has till he accepts the Scripture that Warfield presents.[17]

Geerhardus Vos, the founder of Reformed Biblical Theology, issued a clarion call for inerrancy as a *sine qua non* in the principles of Biblical Theology. On May 8, 1894, Vos delivered his inaugural address as Professor of Biblical Theology, entitled "The Idea of Biblical Theology as a Science and as a Theological Discipline."[18] In this famed address, Vos elucidates the dual nature of Scripture, simultaneously underscoring the primacy of divine Authorship and the indispensably human and historical nature of revelation.

> The historical character of the truth is not in any way antithetical to, but throughout subordinated to, its revealed character. Scriptural truth is not absolute, notwithstanding its historic setting; but the historic setting has been employed by God for the very purpose of revealing the truth, the whole truth, and nothing but the truth. It is not the duty of Biblical Theology to seek first the historic features of the Scriptural ideas, and to think that the absolute character of the truth as revealed of God is something secondary to be added thereunto. The reality of revelation should be the supreme factor by which the historic factor is kept under control. With the greatest variety of historical aspects, there can, nevertheless, be no inconsistencies or contradictions in the Word of God.

The issue of inerrancy inevitably arises whenever the serious task of Biblical Theology is pursued. In fact, Vos himself was developing his nascent science of Reformed Biblical Theology in the milieu of a radical departure from a high view of Scripture among the theologians of his day. In this Princeton address, he offers a number of caveats: an imposition of evolutionary thought on Biblical history,[19] a subjectivizing denial of Scripture's objectivity as the very Word of God,[20] the elevation of and emphasis upon the historical character of Scripture over its revelatory character,[21] the pantheistic spirit that denies revelation by the admission of errors in the Biblical text,[22] and the general

17. Ibid., 67–68.
18. Originally published in 1894 by Anson D. F. Randolph and Company, this essay is reprinted in *Redemptive History and Biblical Interpretation: The Shorter Writings of Geerhardus Vos*, ed. Richard B. Gaffin Jr. (Phillipsburg, NJ: Presbyterian and Reformed, 1980), 3–24; the following citation is on p. 19.
19. The "principle of historic progress in revelation seems to present certain analogies with the evolutionary scheme, and to offer exceptional opportunities for applying the latter, without departing too far from the real contents of Scripture. This analogy, of course, is merely formal, and from a material point of view there is a world-wide difference between that philosophy of history which the Bible itself outlines, and which along Biblical Theology, if it wishes to remain biblical, has a right to adopt, and, on the other hand, the so-called facts of the Bible pressed into the evolutionary formulas" (p. 16).
20. "Biblical Theology must insist upon claiming for its object not the thoughts and reflections and speculations of man, but the oracles of God. Whosoever weakens or subjectivizes this fundamental idea of revelation, strikes a blow at the very heart of Theology and Supernatural Christianity, nay, of Theism itself" (p. 19).
21. "Scriptural truth is not absolute, notwithstanding its historic setting; but the historic setting has been employed by God for the very purpose of revealing the truth, the whole truth, and nothing but the truth. It is not the duty of Biblical Theology to seek first the historic features of the Scriptural ideas, and to think that the absolute character of the truth as revealed of God is something secondary to be added thereunto. The reality of revelation should be the supreme factor by which the historic factor is kept under control. With the greatest variety of historical aspects, there can, nevertheless, be no inconsistencies or contradictions in the Word of God" (p. 19).
22. "Those who accept the evolutionary construction of Biblical history, either openly and without reserve renounce the idea of supernatural revelation, or strip it of its objectivity so as to make it less antagonistic to that of natural develop-

metaphysical agnosticism that comes from evolution postulated as a worldview.[23] The dangers of the zeitgeist of Vos' day had been born under an "evil star" of rationalism.[24] Theologians may not have been faced in his day with a "slippery slope", a phrase often used today, but they had begun to "descend the ladder" leading from a high objective view to a lower subjective view of revelation.[25] The dangers emanating from the Vosian milieu have only intensified in the more than century time lapse since he wrote.[26]

---

ment. In the same degree, however, that the latter is done, revelation loses its distinctively theistic character and begins to assume more and more the features of a Pantheistic process, that is, it ceases to be revelation in the commonly accepted sense of the term" (p. 16).

23. "The philosophy of evolution has corrupted Theology by introducing its leaven of metaphysical Agnosticism" (p. 16).

24. "From the end of the preceding century, when our science first appears as distinct from Dogmatic Theology, until now, she has stood under the spell of un-Biblical principles. Her very birth took place under an evil star. It was the spirit of Rationalism which first led to distinguishing in the contents of the Scriptures between what was purely human, individual, local, temporal—in a word, conditioned by the subjectivity of the writers—and what was eternally valid, divine truth" (p. 15).

25. "How far this evil has penetrated may be inferred from the fact that there is scarcely a book on Biblical Theology in existence in which this conception of the object of our science is not met with, and in which it does not very largely determine the point of view. It has even vitiated so excellent a work in many respects as Oehler's Old Testament Theology. Of course, there are many degrees in the thoroughness with which this subjectivizing principle is carried through and applied. Between those who are just beginning to descend the ladder and those who have reached its lowest step, there is a very appreciable difference" (p. 17).

26. Ed. note: The original essay ended with the following two paragraphs: "It is in this context, then, that I welcome Westminster Seminary's distinguished Professor Richard Gaffin's revision and republication of his classic study, 'Old Amsterdam and Inerrancy?' The central issues concerning Scripture addressed by Professor Gaffin in his first edition of this study published in 1982 and 1983, in the *Westminster Theological Journal*, are still critical in the theological life of the Reformed faith. Indeed, the central Biblical concerns addressed by the Reformed luminaries, Calvin, Turretin, Hodge, Warfield, Kuyper, Bavinck, Murray, Van Til, and Vos must still be confronted by the Reformed Christian theologian in the academy, the seminary and in the church.

Thus with great appreciation to Dr. Gaffin for his careful labor and keen scholarship in updating and preparing his classic study, I heartily commend God's Word In Servant-Form: Abraham Kuyper and Herman Bavinck on the Doctrine of Scripture to students and scholars around the world. A careful perusal of this study will surely further and sustain growth in wisdom and knowledge in one's theological understanding of the inspiration, infallibility and inerrancy of the Holy Scriptures as discovered and developed in the best of classic Reformed theology."

Conclusion and Postscript to Gaffin's
God's Word in Servant-Form

Richard B. Gaffin Jr., *God's Word in Servant-Form: Abraham Kuyper and Herman Bavinck on the Doctrine of Scripture* (Jackson, MS: Reformed Academic Press, 2008), 100–107.

The following pages include Richard Gaffin's concluding remarks from his essay on Herman Bavinck and the postscript he wrote in 2008 for *God's Word in Servant-Form*. Peter Lillback's previous pages introduce this volume, and Gaffin's words appropriately complement and conclude our anthology.

Gaffin's concluding words are beneficial in several ways. First, they contain a summary of Bavinck's views in the context of his discussion of Abraham Kuyper (cf. chaps. 31 and 32 in this anthology, which contain, respectively, Gaffin's article on Kuyper and a selection from Bavinck's *Reformed Dogmatics*). In particular, while Gaffin acknowledges that Bavinck is more aware of the challenges to the Bible than is Kuyper, their positions are in basic agreement. Second, Gaffin's comments suggest a harmony between the Old Princeton/Westminster trajectory and that of Old Amsterdam on the foundational issue of the doctrine of Scripture. Third, Gaffin's synthesis relates his findings in historical theology to the current theological debates with theologians influenced by postmodernism. The text is reproduced with some minor editorial changes (chiefly in the notes) to fit the current format of our anthology.

As we have considered the trials and controversies of the past up to the present in this anthology, may we look ahead with hope and discernment at the inevitable challenges that will surely come.

Summary and Conclusions on Bavinck's View of Scripture

The six questions posed at the beginning of this study (see above, pp. 4–5) and answered for Kuyper (see above, pp. 45–46) may now be answered for Bavinck.[1]

1. Ed. note: The page numbers in this section are from the book version, *God's Word in Servant-Form*. The conclusion to the article on Kuyper can be found above in chap. 31.

(1) A deep continuity and harmony exists between the Reformation and post-Reformation orthodoxy.[2] Especially in its later development, this orthodoxy does display a too mechanical, atomistic approach towards Scripture that needs to be corrected by a more organic outlook. But this deviation, by no means negligible, does not put post-Reformation orthodoxy outside the central church tradition on Scripture.

(2) The internal testimony of the Holy Spirit produces recognition of the inspiration and authority of Scripture. The focus of this testimony is Scripture as such, its form as well as and inseparable from its content. This witness is absolutely indispensable. No amount of proofs appealing to unaided reason can ever replace or supplement it.[3]

(3) The form and the content of Scripture are both fully divine and fully human and, as such, in their organic coherence, indivisible. As the primary author of Scripture, God is ultimately accountable for its form as well as the content. The form, in its genuinely human character, expresses the specifically authorial intention of the Spirit. The form/content distinction does not parallel the human/divine distinction. The form is not the merely human side of Scripture, in distinction from the content or central message as the exclusively divine side.

(4) Inscripturation arises necessarily from the incarnation and would not exist apart from it. This reality determines the origin and composition of Scripture from beginning to end. It specifies more concretely the organic nature of inspiration as a whole. It gives Scripture a unique theanthropic character ("everything divine and everything human"), without, however, involving some sort of hypostatic union between divine and human elements. Scripture has its distinctive servant-form, not because of its "humanity," generally considered, but because Christ was incarnated, not in a state of glory but of humiliation. The correlate to the sinlessness of Christ is that Scripture is without error.

(5) Disciplined, scholarly study of Scripture is necessary, especially in order to reach a better understanding of its organic, incarnate origin and composition. But the crucial issue raised by contemporary biblical criticism is primarily ethical. Much of this criticism is heart-directed rebellion against the authority of Scripture as God's word.

(6) The Bible is without error. Since all error, unintentional mistakes as well as deception, results from sin, it would be misleading at best to speak of errors in Scripture, either in form or content, in any sense. To find error in Scripture would be to fault its primary author and

2. In the opinion of the neo-orthodox theologian Th. L. Haitjema, "Nevertheless Bavinck endeavored to give an optimistic assessment of the theological outlook of the seventeenth century as a further development of the Reformation era" (quoted by Jan Veenhof, *Revelatie en inspiratie* [Amsterdam: Buijten & Schipperheijn, 1968], 502); cf. R. H. Bremmer (*Herman Bavinck als dogmaticus* [Kampen: J. H. Kok, 1961], 314): Bavinck's *Dogmatiek* "was a self-conscious attempt to arrive at a renewal of historic Reformed theology and dogmatics, which in the course of the eighteenth [*sic;* "seventeenth" is almost certainly intended] century ended in Reformed scholasticism, and for which figures like Heidegger and Francis Turretin may be called the last representatives."

3. The question needs to be asked here how much this view of Bavinck (and Kuyper) really differs from that of Warfield and the other Princeton theologians. There may be differences, particularly concerning the way reason functions in relation to the internal testimony. It seems to me, however, that much of the discussion on this point does not take into consideration, for example, Warfield's sustained positive, even enthusiastic exposition of Calvin's development of the doctrine of the internal testimony ("Calvin's Doctrine of the Knowledge of God," *Calvin and Calvinism* [New York: Oxford University Press, 1931] 70–130, esp. 70–116). Certainly the treatment of Jack Rogers and Donald McKim [*The Authority and Interpretation of the Bible: A Historical Approach* (San Francisco: Harper & Row, 1979), 333–34] cannot be considered adequate. At any rate, among his contemporaries Warfield sees William Cunningham, Charles Hodge, Kuyper, and Bavinck (and himself tacitly) as "true successors of Calvin" in this doctrine (125). Cf. John Woodbridge, *Biblical Authority: A Critique of the Rogers/McKim Proposal* (Grand Rapids: Zondervan, 1982), 137–38.

undermine his authority. The truth of Scripture is not notarially precise or scientifically exact. Ultimately this nontechnical, impressionistic quality is appropriate to and explained by its unique divine authorship and specific, incarnate character, not the involvement and limitations of the human authors. Unlike Kuyper, Bavinck does not speak of the errorlessness of Scripture. In the material we have examined he does not even use the word infallibility.[4] But every consideration leads us to suppose that he would not object nor find it inappropriate to speak of the inerrancy of Scripture, provided that, like Kuyper, we understand that in an impressionistic, nontechnical sense.

When we compare the positions of Kuyper and Bavinck over the range of our examination certain differences appear. Leaving to the side interesting variations in style, disposition of material and the development of basic concepts, most striking perhaps is the fact, already noted, that, in contrast to Bavinck, Kuyper stresses the infallibility and errorlessness of Scripture. Bavinck's reserve in this regard, however, is not a sign of uncertainty or indifference. As we have seen, with him, too, the concern to maintain that Scripture is without error is present.

Also, there is truth in the observation of Berkouwer mentioned above (see above, note 62)[5]: Bavinck, unlike Kuyper, seems to sense the storms of the future over the doctrine of Scripture. With reference to the attacks of biblical criticism, Bavinck is not any less confident than Kuyper, but, we may say, Kuyper is more triumphant. Bavinck's comments about the (probably) unsolvable difficulties that Scripture itself presents to its inspiration, and his eloquent statements concerning the nature of faith, including faith in Scripture, as a constant struggle against the appearance of things (441–42) sound a note which is not present in Kuyper.[6]

But certainly far more important, and obvious, than the differences is the deep, pervasive, and cordial agreement between them on Scripture. Together they maintain and defend what they are convinced is the central church doctrine, in continuity especially with the Reformers and post-Reformation orthodoxy.

Their perception of this central church tradition, however, differs from that of Rogers and McKim. It is so different, in fact, that Kuyper and Bavinck can be fitted into the latter perception only by turning their position on its head and making them into representatives of viewpoints they consistently opposed, as, we have seen, Rogers and McKim do. This cannot help but prompt us to ask questions like the following. Where, if not in Kuyper and Bavinck, do we find the central church doctrine of Scripture as Rogers and McKim construe it? Have they perhaps not also misunderstood and misrepresented the views of Warfield and the Old Princeton theologians at decisive points? Can all modern and contemporary concern for biblical inerrancy be fairly dismissed as a late innovation of those dominated,

4. But note elsewhere, for example, "The Future of Calvinism," *Presbyterian and Reformed Review* 5 (1894): 17, where he rejects the view that "the Holy Scriptures are not the infallible Word of God, but contain the Word of God; and side by side with its divine elements, the Bible has also its human and fallible elements."

5. Ed. note: Note 62 on page 49 gives the following references: G. C. Berkouwer, *A Half Century of Theology*, trans. and ed. Lewis B. Smedes (Grand Rapids: Eerdmans, 1977), 11–16; similarly, Veenhof, *Revelatie,* 133 and the opinions of K. J. Popma and others cited there in note 120.

6. The page number references here and below are from Herman Bavinck, *Gereformeerde Dogmatiek,* 4 vols. (Kampen: J. H. Kok, 1895–1901; 2nd revised and enlarged ed., 1906–11). The second edition (volume 1, 1906) has been reprinted unaltered several times, except for different pagination beginning with the fourth edition (1928). References here are to the sixth edition of 1976. The sections dealing directly with Scripture are on pp. 348–465.

wittingly or not, by an Aristotelian mindset or Common Sense Realism? But these, and others, are questions for another study.[7]

Postscript

One feature of Bavinck's *Dogmatics*, particularly noteworthy for this study, is the lengthy survey of the history and literature of dogmatics/systematic theology he provides in volume one (116–204). Strikingly for this study, the entire survey closes with an overview of Reformed and Presbyterian theology in North America to the present (200–204). Particularly instructive and significant for our concerns are his very last words (204):

> Thus the Reformed church and theology in America are in a serious crisis. The doctrines of the infallibility of Holy Scripture, of the trinity, of the fall and inability of man, of particular atonement, of election and reprobation, of eternal punishment are secretly denied or even openly rejected. The future for Calvinism there is not rosy.[8]

This pessimism is expressed largely with reference to recent developments in Presbyterianism, and Charles Augustus Briggs and his "heterodoxy" are mentioned particularly (203). But Bavinck knows of an exception, if only one, to this otherwise bleak picture, "a glorious exception" (204) in fact. That is Princeton Seminary with its "excellent set of professors" (Warfield, for one, is mentioned by name) and the *Princeton Theological Review* that maintains "the Reformed position with honor."

One should value the concern of Rogers and McKim to maintain an evangelical doctrine of Scripture. One should also recognize their desire to lead the church in that direction by clarifying its past. But perhaps by now the reader can recognize, even though I have focused on only a small segment of their work, why I cannot consider them reliable guides. Perhaps, too, as this study was originally written in memory of the 100th anniversary of the birth of J. Gresham Machen, readers can understand why I do not view what transpired around him with the formation of Westminster Seminary as "the scholastic separation from Princeton Seminary" or "scholastic protest and withdrawal" (*Authority*, 362, 367).

I recognize how useless, even counterproductive, it can be to keep on fighting battles that are already over. But in this case the issues are still too critical, still too relevant to be set aside, as the work of Rogers and McKim in its own way evidences. The spirit that forced the reorganization of Princeton Seminary and the departure of Machen was not the spirit of the central church tradition on Scripture, in opposition to recent scholastic innovations and deviations. It was a decidedly different, alien spirit. It was, as Bavinck says, "the modern spirit" (204). It was a spirit, exemplified, for instance, in Briggs, itself decidedly opposed to the spirit of the central church doctrine, to the spirit of Augustine, Luther and Calvin, of the Westminster Divines, of Hodge and Warfield, of Kuyper and Bavinck. Or that, at least, is how Bavinck, along with Kuyper, Hodge, and Warfield, would have understood it.

By now my deep sympathy for the views of Kuyper and Bavinck is as apparent as my conviction that they offer much on Scripture that we need to hear today. But that is really beside the main point of this study. Nor am I wanting to suggest that they have spoken

---

7. See esp. Woodbridge's critique (*Biblical Authority*).

8. See the sobering and thought-provoking comments on this passage by C. Trimp, "De tragedie van de brede weg" ["The Tragedy of the Broad Way"], *Betwist Schriftgezag* (Groningen: De Vuurbaak, 1970), 179–91.

the last word on the doctrine of Scripture or that their position is without its difficulties and unresolved questions. My primary concern, rather, has been historical, for accurate representation of their views. Rogers and McKim themselves tell us, "Significant questions remain to be discussed regarding the role of the Bible in churches today. But we must first set the historical record straight" (*Authority*, xxiii). This is undoubtedly right and so all the more regrettable and itself a source of no little confusion is the failure of their own work to measure up at crucial points to its subtitle, "A Historical Approach."

Presently, as the perennial "Battle for the Bible" continues unabated in the opening decade of the twenty-first century, differences over Scripture, its authority and interpretation, continue to polarize within the evangelical community, especially as a result of recent developments styled "post-conservative evangelical."[9] On many issues there are no quick and easy answers. But one thing is certain. We will only be able to move out of this present impasse and achieve solid growth in the doctrine of Scripture when we share at least a common mind-set concerning the past and what in fact the central church doctrine is. To the extent that the historical record is not set straight but remains uncertain or misrepresented, evangelical and Reformed theology today, not only in this country but elsewhere, lacks direction, and its future, in Bavinck's words, is "not rosy"— a not exactly optimistic but necessary note on which to end this study.

---

9. I have in mind, to cite only one example, the overall view of the Bible, no more hospitable to the central church doctrine of Kuyper and Bavinck, it seems to me, than that of Rogers and McKim, that informs the work of J. R. Franke; see his *The Character of Theology: An Introduction to Its Nature, Task, and Purpose* (Grand Rapids: Baker Academic, 2005), identified on its front cover as "A Postconservative Evangelical Approach"; see also J. R. Franke, "Reforming Theology: Toward a Postmodern Reformed Dogmatics," *WTJ* 65, 1 (2003): 1–26; R. B. Gaffin Jr., "Response to John Franke," *WTJ* 65, 2 (2003): 327–30; J. R. Franke, "Postmodern and Reformed? A Response to Professors Trueman and Gaffin," *WTJ* 65, 2 (2003): 331–43, esp. 340–43.

List of Contributors

Allis, Oswald T.—VIII.43

Ames, William—IV.24

Bavinck, Herman—V.32

Berkhof, Louis—V.33

Bullinger, Henry—I.3, II.7, 12, III.19

Calvin, John—I.4, II.8, III.20

Clowney, Edmund P.—IX.48

Craig, John—II.14

Cranmer, Thomas—II.13, III.21

Cunningham, William—V.30

de Brès, Guido—II.10

de Chandieu, Antoine—II.8

Dillard, Raymond B.—XI.58

Edwards, Jonathan—III.23, IV.28

Ferguson, Sinclair B.—XI.56

Frame, John M.—XI.57

Gaffin, Richard B., Jr.—V.31, IX.51, X.54, XIII.64

Gaussen, Louis—VI.34

Haller, Berthold—II.6

Hengstenberg, Ernst Wilhelm—VI.36

Hodge, Archibald Alexander—VII.39

Hodge, Charles—VII.38

Knox, John—II.9, III.22

Kolb, Francis—II.6

Leger, John—II.18

Lillback, Peter A.—III.19, XI.60, XIII.63

Long, L. Craig—VIII.43

Luther, Martin—I.1

Machen, J. Gresham—VIII.42

McQuilkin, H. H.—VIII.43

Monod, Adolphe—VI.35

Murray, John—VIII.45

Olevianus, Caspar—II.11

Owen, John—IV.25

Poythress, Vern Sheridan—IX.49

Silva, Moisés—VII.41, IX.50

Spurgeon, Charles H.—VI.37

Stonehouse, Ned B.—IX.47, X.53

Turretin, Francis—IV.26–27

Ursinus, Zacharias—II.11

Ussher, James—II.15

Van Til, Cornelius—VIII.44

Vos, Geerhardus—IX.46

Waltke, Bruce K.—XI.59

Warfield, Benjamin Breckinridge—VII.40

Wilson, Robert Dick—VIII.43

Witherspoon, John—V.29

Young, Edward J.—X.52, XI.55

Zwingli, Ulrich—I.2, II.5–6

Index of Scripture and Deuterocanonical Books

1373

Index of Themes and Names